Editor H. J. de Blij

Oxford University Press
Editorial/Research Ben Keene
Gazetteer Design Nora Wertz

Published by Oxford University Press, Inc.
198 Madison Avenue
New York, NY, 10016
http://www.oup.com/us/atlas

Cartography by Philip's

Philip's, a division of Octopus Publishing Group Ltd
2–4 Heron Quays
London E14 4JP, UK
http://www.philips-maps.co.uk

Library of Congress Cataloging-in-Publication Data

Atlas of North America.
p. cm.
Includes bibliographical references and index.
ISBN 0-19-516993-X
1. North America--Maps. I. Oxford University Press.
G1105.A8 2004
912.7--dc22

2004045005

ISBN 0–19–516993–X

Printed in Spain

References and Acknowledgements
The publishers wish to thank various government agencies and others for providing many of the figures used in this atlas. While every effort has been made to secure permission, we apologize if in any case we have failed to trace the copyright holder.

North American Geography

- p. 11 Adapted from *Modern Physical Geography*, 2nd ed., Thompson & Turk, Saunders, 1997.
- p. 12–13 After Orme, *The Physical Geography of North America*, Oxford, 2002.
- p. 17 (top) Adapted from "Groundwater Resources" Map Supplement © 1993, National Geographic Society.
- p. 21 Adapted from *North American Terrestrial Vegetation*, 2nd ed., Barbour & Billings, Cambridge, 1999.
- p. 22 After J. L. Hough, *Geology of the Great Lakes*, University of Illinois, 1958.
- p. 23 After Orme, *The Physical Geography of North America*, Oxford, 2002.
- p. 24 From H. Driver et al, *Indiana University Publications in Anthropology and Linguistics*, 1953.
- p. 25 After Greenberg and the 1998 Britannica Book of the Year.
- p. 26 Adapted from *World Atlas of the Past, The Age of Discovery*, volume 3, Haywood, Oxford, 2000.
- p. 35 Adapted from *La Agricultura en Mexico*, Hurtada & Calderon, UNAM, 2003.
- p. 45 After Gaustad and Barlow, *New Historical Atlas of Religion in America*, Oxford, 2001.
- p. 47 Adapted from "Federal Lands" Map Supplement © 1996 National Geographic Society.

Gazetteers
The "At a Glance" sections of the atlas were compiled from data collected by the U.S. Census Bureau, Statistics Canada, and the Instituto Nacional de Estadistica Geografica e Informatica (INEGI). All rights reserved. This information is published with the permission of the aforementioned agencies.

All photographs that appear in the Gazetteers are part of the Photodisc image collection copyright Getty Images, Inc. 2004.

Satellite Imagery
pp. 8, 50–51, 170–171, 208–209
Courtesy of NPA Group, Edenbridge, Kent, UK (www.satmaps.com)

City Maps
The following city maps utilize base data supplied courtesy of MapQuest.com, Inc. (© MapQuest):
United States Baltimore, Charlotte, Cincinnati, Cleveland, Dallas–Fort Worth, Denver, Detroit, Houston, Indianapolis, Las Vegas, Memphis, Milwaukee, Minneapolis–St. Paul, New Orleans, Norfolk, Orlando, Philadelphia, Phoenix, Pittsburgh, Portland, St. Louis, Salt Lake City, San Antonio, San Diego, Seattle,Tampa & St. Petersburg;
Canada Ottawa, Vancouver;
Mexico Guadalajara, Monterrey.

FOREWORD

This is an appropriate time for the publication of an atlas of North America. More than 30 years have passed since Oxford University Press published the Second Edition of its *Regional Economic Atlas of the United States and Canada*, and during this period momentous changes have transformed this geographic realm. These changes necessitated an extension of coverage from the United States and Canada (the regional limits of the 1975 atlas) to include Mexico, so that the present atlas incorporates the three largest countries on the continent. Mexico has been profoundly affected by its participation in the North American Free Trade Association (NAFTA); the United States is strongly influenced by immigration from Mexico. The forces of regional integration are at work from Yukon to Yucatán.

In this context, this atlas is therefore more than an atlas of North America: it is an atlas of North America augmented by cartographic representation of the dominant country of Middle America. The geographic terms "Anglo America" (for Canada and the United States) and "Latin America" (for everything to the south) are no longer appropriate in this multicultural hemisphere. But the Americas extend virtually from pole to pole, and geographic variation, physical as well as cultural, marks the transition. Regionally, Canada and the United States comprise North America; Mexico, the Central American republics and the Caribbean constitute Middle America; and Brazil and its neighbors comprise South America. North America and North American influences, however, do not stop abruptly at the Rio Grande any more than Middle American influences stop at the California border or the Straits of Florida. Hence Mexico's inclusion in this atlas.

The *Atlas of North America* consists of several parts. An opening section presents useful regional economic and other data and a series of spectacular satellite images of the landmass. This is followed by a thematic section that highlights numerous aspects of the physical, cultural, economic and political geography of North America, supported by detailed text and captions. The focus then shifts to each of the three country components: the United States, Canada, and Mexico. Each section presents, in order, state or provincial maps, city maps, descriptive text, and statistical data. A substantial number of the maps are newly drawn, and additional cartography has been derived from Philip's published stock. The cartographer in charge was David Gaylard.

For assistance in the preparation of the layout and content of the atlas I am grateful to Peter O. Muller, Professor of Geography at the University of Miami, who served as Chair of a Board of Advisors whose members were Adrián Guillermo Aguilar, Professor and Director of the Institute of Geography at the Universidad Nacional Autonoma de Mexico, Patricia Gober, Professor of Geography and Co-Director of the Decision Center for a Desert City at Arizona State University, Richard E. Groop, Professor and Chair of the Department of Geography at Michigan State University, Glen M. MacDonald, Professor and Chair of the Department of Geography at the University of California, Los Angeles, Ian MacLachlan, Associate Professor of Geography at the University of Lethbridge, Canada, and Barney Warf, Professor and Chair of the Department of Geography at Florida State University. All of us appreciate the sterling work done throughout this project by Ben Keene, Trade Reference Editor at Oxford University Press.

H. J. de Blij, Ph.D., Editor
Distinguished Professor of Geography
Michigan State University

CONTENTS

North American Statistics 6–7

NORTH AMERICAN GEOGRAPHY

North America: Satellite image 8

North America: Political 9

Physical Geography and Geology 10–11

Tectonic Provinces and Physiography 12–13

Energy and Minerals 14–15

Surface Water and Drainage 16–17

Climate and Weather 18–19

Soil and Vegetation 20–21

Pleistocene Land Cover and Glaciation 22–23

Indigenous Peoples 24–25

Early Settlement and Expansion 26–27

Population and Social Diversity 28–29

Immigration and Population Change 30–31

Urbanization 32–33

Land Use and Agriculture 34–35

United States: Manufacturing Industries 36–37

United States: Service Industries 38–39

Trade and Telecommunications 40–41

Highways and Railroads 42–43

Languages and Religions 44–45

National Parks and Federal Lands 46–47

Maritime Zones and Claims 48

UNITED STATES

Map symbols 49

United States: Satellite image 50–51

United States 52–53
1:9 600 000

Eastern United States 54–55
1:4 800 000

Middle United States 56–57
1:4 800 000

Western United States 58–59
1:4 800 000

Alabama 60
1:2 000 000

Alaska 61
1:8 000 000

Arizona 62
1:2 000 000

Arkansas 63
1:2 000 000

California 64–65
1:2 000 000

Colorado 66
1:2 000 000

Florida 67
1:2 000 000

Georgia 68
1:2 000 000

Hawai‘i 69
1:2 000 000

Idaho 70
1:2 000 000

Illinois 71
1:2 000 000

Indiana 72
1:2 000 000

Iowa 73
1:2 000 000

Kansas 74
1:2 000 000

Louisiana 75
1:2 000 000

Maine 76
1:2 000 000

Maryland, Delaware and District of Columbia 77
1:1 000 000

Massachusetts, Connecticut and Rhode Island 78
1:1 000 000

Michigan 79
1:2 000 000

Minnesota 80
1:2 000 000

Mississippi 81
1:2 000 000

Missouri 82
1:2 000 000

Montana 83
1:3 000 000

Nebraska 84
1:2 000 000

Nevada 85
1:2 000 000

New Hampshire and Vermont 86
1:1 000 000

New Jersey 87
1:1 000 000

New Mexico 88
1:2 100 000

New York 89
1:2 000 000

North Carolina and South Carolina 90
1:2 400 000

North Dakota and South Dakota 91
1:2 400 000

Ohio 92
1:2 000 000

Oklahoma 93
1:2 000 000

Oregon 94
1:2 000 000

Pennsylvania 95
1:2 000 000

Tennessee and Kentucky 96–97
1:2 000 000

Texas 98–99
1:2 400 000

Utah 100
1:2 000 000

Washington 101
1:2 000 000

West Virginia and Virginia 102
1:2 000 000

Wisconsin 103
1:2 000 000

Wyoming 104
1:2 000 000

Puerto Rico and the U.S. Pacific Territories 105

U.S. Outlying Areas
1:76 000 000

Puerto Rico and the Virgin Islands
1:1 375 000

Northern Marianas
1:16 000 000

Guam
1:800 000

Saipan and Tinian (Northern Marianas)
1:800 000

Samoan Islands
1:20 000 000

Tutuila (American Samoa)
1:800 000

Manua Islands (American Samoa)
1:800 000

UNITED STATES CITY MAPS

Atlanta 106
Baltimore 107
Boston 106
Charlotte 107
Chicago 108
Cincinnati 107
Cleveland 107
Dallas–Fort Worth 109
Denver 109
Detroit 109
Houston 110
Indianapolis 110
Las Vegas 110
Los Angeles 110–111
Memphis 112
Miami–Fort Lauderdale 112
Milwaukee 112
Minneapolis–St. Paul 113
New Orleans 113
New York 114–115
Norfolk 115
Orlando 115
Philadelphia 116
Phoenix 116
Pittsburgh 116
Portland 116
St. Louis 117
Salt Lake City 117
San Antonio 117
San Diego 117
San Francisco 118
Seattle 118
Tampa and St. Petersburg 119
Washington 119

UNITED STATES GAZETTEER 120–168

CANADA

Map Symbols 169

Canada: Satellite image 170–171

Atlantic Provinces 172–173
1:2 000 000

Newfoundland 174
1:2 000 000

Northern Québec and Labrador 175
1:5 600 000

Southern Québec 176–177
1:2 000 000

Southern Ontario 178–179
1:2 000 000

Central Ontario – Lake Superior 180–181
1:2 000 000

Southern Manitoba and Saskatchewan 182–183
1:2 000 000

Southern Alberta 184–185
1:2 000 000

Southern British Columbia 186–187
1:2 000 000

Northwest Canada 188–189
1:6 400 000

Nunavut 190–191
1:6 400 000

CANADA CITY MAPS

Montréal 192
Ottawa 192
Toronto 193
Vancouver 193

CANADA GAZETTEER 194–206

MEXICO

Map symbols 207

Mexico: Satellite image 208–209

Baja California 210–211
1:2 000 000

Sonora and Chihuahua 212–213
1:2 000 000

Coahuila, Nuevo León, Tamaulipas and San Luis Potosí 214–215
1:2 000 000

Nayarit, Sinaloa, Durango, Zacatecas and Aguascalientes 216–217
1:2 000 000

Central Mexico 218–219
1:2 000 000

Veracruz, Puebla and Oaxaca 220–221
1:2 000 000

Tabasco and Chiapas 222
1:2 000 000

Yucatán, Quintana Roo and Campeche 223
1:2 000 000

MEXICO CITY MAPS

Guadalajara 224
Mexico City 224–225
Monterrey 224

MEXICO GAZETTEER 226–238

INDEX TO MAPS

239–320

NORTH AMERICAN STATISTICS

UNITED STATES

State	Area (sq. km)	Area (sq. miles)	Population	Capital
Alabama	131,426	50,744	4,500,752	Birmingham
Alaska	1,481,353	571,951	648,818	Juneau
Arizona	294,313	113,635	5,580,811	Phoenix
Arkansas	134,856	52,068	2,725,714	Little Rock
California	403,934	155,959	35,484,453	Sacramento
Colorado	268,630	103,718	4,550,688	Denver
Connecticut	12,549	4,845	3,483,372	Hartford
Delaware	5,061	1,954	817,491	Dover
Florida	139,671	53,927	17,019,068	Tallahassee
Georgia	149,977	57,906	8,684,715	Atlanta
Hawai'i	16,636	6,423	1,257,608	Honolulu
Idaho	214,315	82,747	1,366,332	Boise
Illinois	143,963	55,584	12,653,544	Springfield
Indiana	92,896	35,867	6,195,643	Indianapolis
Iowa	144,701	55,869	2,944,062	Des Moines
Kansas	211,901	81,815	2,723,507	Topeka
Kentucky	102,896	39,728	4,117,827	Frankfort
Louisiana	112,826	43,562	4,496,334	Baton Rouge
Maine	79,933	30,862	1,305,728	Augusta
Maryland	25,315	9,774	5,508,909	Annapolis
Massachusetts	20,306	7,840	6,433,422	Boston
Michigan	147,122	56,804	10,079,985	Lansing
Minnesota	206,190	79,610	5,059,375	St. Paul
Mississippi	121,489	46,907	2,881,281	Jackson
Missouri	178,415	68,886	5,704,484	Jefferson City
Montana	376,980	145,552	917,621	Helena
Nebraska	199,098	76,872	1,739,291	Lincoln
Nevada	284,449	109,826	2,241,154	Carson City
New Hampshire	23,227	8,968	1,287,687	Concord
New Jersey	19,210	7,417	8,638,396	Trenton
New Mexico	314,312	121,356	1,874,614	Sante Fe
New York	122,284	47,214	19,190,115	Albany
North Carolina	126,161	48,711	8,407,248	Raleigh
North Dakota	178,648	68,976	633,837	Bismarck
Ohio	106,055	40,948	11,435,798	Columbus
Oklahoma	177,848	68,667	3,511,532	Oklahoma City
Oregon	248,632	95,997	3,559,596	Salem
Pennsylvania	116,076	44,817	12,365,455	Harrisburg
Rhode Island	2,707	1,045	1,076,164	Providence
South Carolina	77,982	30,109	4,147,152	Columbia
South Dakota	196,542	75,885	764,309	Pierre
Tennessee	106,752	41,217	5,841,748	Nashville
Texas	678,054	261,797	22,118,509	Austin
Utah	212,753	82,144	2,351,467	Salt Lake City
Vermont	23,958	9,250	619,107	Montpelier
Virginia	102,548	39,594	7,386,330	Richmond
Washington	172,349	66,544	6,131,445	Olympia
West Virginia	62,362	24,078	1,810,354	Charleston
Wisconsin	140,663	54,310	5,472,299	Madison
Wyoming	251,489	97,100	501,242	Cheyenne

CANADA

Province	Area (sq. km)	Area (sq. miles)	Population	Capital
Alberta	642,317	248,000	2,974,810	Edmonton
British Columbia	925,186	357,216	3,907,735	Victoria
Manitoba	553,556	213,729	1,119,585	Winnipeg
New Brunswick	71,450	27,587	729,500	Fredericton
Newfoundland and Labrador	373,872	144,353	512,930	St. Johns
Northwest Territories	1,183,085	456,792	37,360	Yellowknife
Nova Scotia	53,338	20,594	908,005	Halifax
Nunavut	1,936,113	747,537	26,745	Iqaluit
Ontario	917,741	354,342	11,410,045	Toronto
Prince Edward Island	5,660	2,185	135,290	Charlottetown
Québec	1,365,128	527,079	7,237,480	Québec
Saskatchewan	591,670	228,445	978,935	Regina
Yukon Territory	474,391	183,163	28,675	Whitehorse

MEXICO

State	Area (sq. km)	Area (sq. miles)	Population	Capital
Aguascalientes	5,471	2,112	944,285	Aguascalientes
Baja California	69,921	26,997	2,487,367	Mexicali
Baja California Sur	73,475	28,369	424,041	La Paz
Campeche	50,812	19,619	690,689	Campeche
Chiapas	74,211	28,653	3,920,892	Tuxtla Gutiérrez
Chihuahua	244,938	94,571	3,052,907	Chihuahua
Coahuila	149,982	57,908	2,298,070	Saltillo
Colima	5,191	2,004	542,627	Colima
Distrito Federal	1,479	571	8,605,239	Mexico City
Durango	123,181	47,560	1,448,661	Durango
Guanajuato	30,491	11,773	4,663,032	Guanajuato
Guerrero	64,281	24,819	3,079,649	Chilpancingo
Hidalgo	20,813	8,036	2,235,591	Pachuca
Jalisco	80,386	31,037	6,332,002	Guadalajara
México	21,355	8,245	13,096,686	Toluca
Michoacán	59,928	23,138	3,985,667	Morelia
Morelos	4,950	1,911	1,555,296	Cuernavaca
Nayarit	26,979	10,417	920,185	Tepic
Nuevo León	64,924	25,067	3,834,141	Monterrey
Oaxaca	93,952	36,275	3,438,765	Oaxaca
Puebla	33,902	13,090	5,076,686	Puebla
Querétaro	11,449	4,420	1,404,306	Querétaro
Quintana Roo	50,212	19,387	874,963	Chetumal
San Luis Potosí	63,068	24,351	2,299,360	San Luis Potosí
Sinaloa	58,238	22,486	2,536,844	Culiacán
Sonora	182,052	70,290	2,216,969	Hermosillo
Tabasco	25,267	9,756	1,891,829	Villahermosa
Tamaulipas	79,384	30,650	2,753,222	Ciudad Victoria
Tlaxcala	4,016	1,551	962,646	Tlaxcala
Veracruz	71,699	27,683	6,908,975	Jalapa Enríquez
Yucatán	38,402	14,827	1,658,210	Mérida
Zacatecas	73,252	28,283	1,353,610	Zacatecas

LARGEST CITIES

CITIES OF THE UNITED STATES

Metropolitan area	Population
New York-Northern New Jersey-Long Island (NY-NJ-PA)	18,323,002
Los Angeles-Long Beach-Santa Ana (CA)	12,365,627
Chicago-Naperville-Joliet (IL-IN-WI)	9,098,316
Philadelphia-Camden-Wilmington (PA-NJ-DE)	5,687,147
Dallas-Fort Worth-Arlington (TX)	5,161,544
Miami-Fort Lauderdale-Miami Beach (FL)	5,007,564
Washington-Arlington-Alexandria (DC-VA-MD)	4,796,183
Houston-Baytown-Sugar Land (TX)	4,715,407
Detroit-Warren-Livonia (MI)	4,452,557
Boston-Cambridge-Quincy (MA-NH)	4,391,344
Atlanta-Sandy Springs-Marietta (GA)	4,247,981
San Francisco-Oakland-Fremont (CA)	4,123,740
Riverside-San Bernardino-Ontario (CA)	3,254,821
Phoenix-Mesa-Scottsdale (AZ)	3,251,876
Seattle-Tacoma-Bellevue (WA)	3,043,878
Minneapolis-St. Paul-Bloomington (MN-WI)	2,968,806
San Diego-Carlsbad-San Marcos (CA)	2,813,833
St. Louis (MO-IL)	2,698,687
Baltimore-Towson (MD)	2,552,994
Pittsburgh (PA)	2,431,087
Tampa-St. Petersburg-Clearwater (FL)	2,395,997
Denver-Aurora (CO)	2,179,240
Cleveland-Elyria-Mentor (OH)	2,148,143
Cincinnati-Middletown (OH-KY-IN)	2,009,632
Portland-Vancouver-Beaverton (OR-WA)	1,927,881

CITIES OF CANADA

Metropolitan area	Population
Toronto (Ontario)	5,101,600
Montréal (Québec)	3,574,500
Vancouver (British Columbia)	2,134,300
Ottawa-Gatineau (Ontario-Québec)	1,132,200
Calgary (Alberta)	1,016,600
Edmonton (Alberta)	990,500
Québec (Québec)	705,900
Hamilton (Ontario)	702,900
Winnipeg (Manitoba)	698,200
London (Ontario)	457,200
Kitchener (Ontario)	444,100
St. Catharines-Niagara (Ontario)	393,600
Halifax (Nova Scotia)	377,900
Windsor (Ontario)	329,000
Victoria (British Columbia)	326,700

CITIES OF MEXICO

Metropolitan area	Population
Cuidad de México (Distrito Federal)	17,806,527
Guadalajara (Jalisco)	3,677,531
Monterrey (Nuevo León)	3,243,466
Puebla (Puebla)	2,220,236
Tijuana (Baja California)	1,274,240
León (Guanajuato)	1,235,081
Ciudad Juárez (Chihuahua)	1,187,275
Toluca (México)	1,151,651
Torreón (Coahuila)	1,007,291
San Luis Potosí (San Luis Potosí)	850,828
Mérida (Yucatán)	842,188
Querétaro (Querétaro)	787,341
Aguascalientes (Aguascalientes)	707,516
Cuernavaca (Morelos)	705,405
Chihuahua (Chihuahua)	677,117

The city population figures are taken from the most recent census or estimate available and represent the urban agglomeration.

HIGHEST MOUNTAINS

Name	meters	feet	Country
Mt. McKinley (Denali)	6,194	20,322	U.S.
Mt. Logan	5,959	19,551	Canada
Pico de Orizaba (Citlaltepetl)	5,610	18,406	Mexico
Mt. St Elias	5,489	18,009	U.S./Canada
Popocatépetl	5,452	17,887	Mexico
Mt. Foraker	5,304	17,402	U.S.
Iztaccíhuatl	5,230	17,159	Mexico
Mt. Lucania	5,226	17,146	Canada
Mt. King	5,173	16,972	Canada
Mt. Steele	5,073	16,644	Canada
Mt. Bona	5,005	16,421	U.S.
Mt. Blackburn	4,996	16,391	U.S.
Mt. Sanford	4,949	16,237	U.S.
Mt. Wood	4,842	15,886	Canada
Mt. Vancouver	4,785	15,699	Canada

LONGEST RIVERS

Name	km	miles	Feeds into
Mississippi-Missouri	6,020	3,740	Gulf of Mexico
Mackenzie	4,240	2,630	Arctic Ocean
Mississippi	3,780	2,350	Gulf of Mexico
Missouri	3,780	2,350	Mississippi
Yukon	3,185	1,980	Pacific Ocean
Rio Grande	3,030	1,880	Gulf of Mexico
Arkansas	2,340	1,450	Mississippi
Colorado	2,330	1,445	Pacific Ocean
Red	2,040	1,270	Mississippi
Columbia	1,950	1,210	Pacific Ocean
Saskatchewan	1,940	1,205	Lake Winnipeg
Snake	1,674	1,040	Columbia
Platte	1,594	990	Missouri
Ohio	1,579	981	Mississippi
Pecos	1,491	926	Rio Grande

LARGEST ISLANDS

Name	sq. km	sq. miles	Country
Baffin	508,000	196,100	Canada
Victoria	212,200	81,900	Canada
Ellesmere	212,000	81,800	Canada
Newfoundland	108,860	42,031	Canada
Banks	70,028	27,038	Canada
Devon	55,247	21,331	Canada
Axel Heiberg	43,178	16,671	Canada
Melville	42,149	16,274	Canada
Southampton	41,214	15,913	Canada
Prince of Wales	33,339	12,872	Canada
Vancouver	31,285	12,079	Canada
Somerset	24,786	9,570	Canada
Bathurst	16,042	6,194	Canada
Prince Patrick	15,848	6,119	Canada
King William	13,111	5,062	Canada

LARGEST LAKES

Name	sq. km	sq. miles	Country
Lake Superior	82,350	31,800	Canada/U.S.
Lake Huron	59,600	23,010	Canada/U.S.
Lake Michigan	58,000	22,400	U.S.
Great Bear Lake	31,800	12,280	Canada
Great Slave Lake	28,500	11,000	Canada
Lake Erie	25,700	9,900	Canada/U.S.
Lake Winnipeg	24,400	9,400	Canada
Lake Ontario	19,500	7,500	Canada/U.S.
Lake Athabasca	7,920	3,058	Canada
Lake Reindeer	6,330	2,444	Canada
Lake Winnipegosis	5,403	2,086	Canada
Lake Nettilling	5,051	1,950	Canada
Lake Nipigon	4,843	1,870	Canada
Lake Manitoba	4,706	1,817	Canada
Great Salt Lake	4,662	1,800	U.S.

RECORDS

Highest Temperature	°C	°F	Date
Death Valley, California	56.7	134	10 July 1913
Lowest Temperature	**°C**	**°F**	**Date**
Snag, Yukon Territory	–63	–81.4	3 February 1947
Highest Annual Rainfall	**cm**	**inches**	**Date**
Henderson Lake, British Columbia	650.2	256	1990
Lowest Annual Rainfall	**cm**	**inches**	**Date**
Batagues, Mexico	3	1.2	1990
Largest Volcanic Eruption	**VEI***	**Ash Dispersal**	**Date**
Katmai, Alaska	6	120,000 sq. km (46,000 sq. mi)	1912

Deadliest Volcanic Eruption	VEI*	Deaths	Date
El Chichón, Mexico	5	2,000	1982
Largest Earthquake	**Magnitude**	**Deaths**	**Date**
Prince William Sound, Alaska	9.2	125	28 March 1964
Most Snowfall (single season)	**cm**	**inches**	**Date**
Mt Baker Ski Area, Washington	2,895.6	1,140	July 1998 – June 1999
Highest Wind Speed	**km/h**	**mph**	**Date**
Mt Washington, New Hampshire	372	231	12 April 1934
Largest Hailstone	**Diameter**	**Circumference**	**Date**
Aurora, Nebraska	17.8 cm (7 inches)	47.6 cm (18.75 inches)	22 June 2003

**Volcanic Explosivity Index*

UNESCO WORLD HERITAGE SITES

UNITED STATES (date of inscription)

- Mesa Verde (1978)
- Yellowstone (1978)
- Grand Canyon National Park (1979)
- Everglades National Park (1979)
- Kluane/Wrangell-St. Elias/Glacier Bay/Tatshenshini-Alsek (1979,1992, 1994)
- Independence Hall (1979)
- Redwood National Park (1980)
- Olympic National Park (1981)
- Mammoth Cave National Park (1981)
- Cahokia Mounds State Historic Site (1981)
- Great Smoky Mountains National Park (1983)
- Yosemite National Park (1984)
- Statue of Liberty (1984)
- Monticello and the University of Virginia in Charlottesville (1987)
- Hawai'i Volcanoes National Park (1987)
- Chaco Culture National Historical Park (1987)
- Pueblo de Taos (1992)
- Carlsbad Caverns National Park (1995)
- Waterton Glacier International Peace Park (1995)

CANADA (date of inscription)

- Nahanni National Park (1978)
- L'Anse aux Meadows National Historic Site (1978)
- Dinosaur Provincial Park (1979)
- Kluane/Wrangell-St. Elias/Glacier Bay/Tatshenshini-Alsek (1979,1992,1994)
- Head-Smashed-In Buffalo Jump (1981)
- SGaang Gwaii (Anthony Island) (1981)
- Wood Buffalo National Park (1983)
- Canadian Rocky Mountain Parks (1984, 1990)
- Historic District of Québec (1985)
- Gros Morne National Park (1987)
- Waterton Glacier International Peace Park (1995)
- Old Town Lunenburg (1995)
- Miguasha National Park (1999)

MEXICO (date of inscription)

- Historic Center of Mexico City Xochimilco (1987)
- Historic Center of Puebla (1987)
- Pre-Hispanic City of National Park of Palenque (1987)
- Historic Center of Oaxaca and Archeological Site of Monte Albán (1987)
- Sian Ka'an (1987)
- Pre-Hispanic City of Teotihuacan (1987)
- Pre-Hispanic City of Chichén Itzá (1988)
- Historic Town of Guanajuato and Adjacent Mines (1988)
- Historic Center of Morelia (1991)
- El Tajin, Pre-Hispanic City (1992)
- Whale Sanctuary of El Vizcaino (1993)
- Historic Center of Zacatecas (1993)
- Rock Paintings of the Sierra de San Francisco (1993)
- Earliest 16th-Century Monasteries on the Slopes of Popocatépetl (1994)
- Historic Monuments Zone of Querétaro (1996)
- Pre-Hispanic Town of Uxmal (1996)
- Hospicio Cabañas (1997)
- Historic Monuments Zone of Tlacotalpan (1998)
- Archeological Zone of Paquimé (1998)
- Archeological Zone of Xochicalco (1999)
- Historic Fortified Town of Campeche (1999)
- Ancient Maya City of Calakmul (2002)
- Franciscan Missions in the Sierra Gorda of Querétaro (2003)
- Luis Barragán House and Studio (2004)

NORTH AMERICAN GEOGRAPHY

ARCTIC OCEAN
RUSSIA
GREENLAND (KALAALLIT NUNAAT) (Denmark)
ICELAND
Reykjavík
Denmark Strait
Beaufort Sea
Queen Elizabeth Is.
Ellesmere I.
Baffin Bay
Baffin Island
Victoria I.
Davis Strait
Nuuk
Cape Farewell
Bering Strait
Bering Sea
St. Lawrence I.
Arctic Circle
Yukon
ALASKA (U.S.A.)
Porcupine
Anchorage
Kodiak I.
Gulf of Alaska
YUKON TERRITORY
NORTHWEST TERRITORIES
Mackenzie
Great Bear L.
Back
NUNAVUT
Hudson Strait
Liard
Great Slave L.
Dubawnt
Hudson Bay
NEWFOUNDLAND & LABRADOR
CANADA
BRITISH COLUMBIA
Skeena
Peace
L. Athabasca
Athabasca
Churchill
Nelson
ALBERTA
Edmonton
MANITOBA
St John's
St.-Pierre et Miquelon (Fr.)
Eastmain
QUÉBEC
St. Lawrence
PRINCE EDWARD I.
NEW BRUNSWICK
NOVA SCOTIA
Halifax
Fraser
SASKATCHEWAN
L. Winnipeg
Saskatchewan
Calgary
Regina
ONTARIO
Québec
Victoria
Vancouver
Seattle
WASHINGTON
Spokane
Tacoma
Winnipeg
Missouri
L. Superior
MAINE
C. Sable
Montréal
Portland
Ottawa
VT
NH
Portland
Columbia
MONTANA
NORTH DAKOTA
MINNESOTA
L. Huron
Toronto
L. Ontario
MA
Boston
Providence
RI
OREGON
IDAHO
Boise
Snake
Minneapolis
St Paul
WISCONSIN
L. Michigan
Buffalo
NEW YORK
CT
Hartford
NEW YORK
PHILADELPHIA
SOUTH DAKOTA
MICHIGAN
Detroit
Madison
Erie
Cleveland
PA
NJ
WYOMING
Milwaukee
CHICAGO
Toledo
Pittsburgh
DE
MD
SAN FRANCISCO
Sacramento
San Jose
Fresno
NEBRASKA
IOWA
Platte
OHIO
Baltimore
UNITED STATES
Omaha
ILLINOIS
INDIANA
Columbus
Washington DC
Richmond
Norfolk
NEVADA
Salt Lake City
UTAH
Indianapolis
Cincinnati
WV
VIRGINIA
CALIFORNIA
Denver
COLORADO
Kansas City
KANSAS
Missouri
St. Louis
MISSOURI
Ohio
Louisville
KENTUCKY
Bermuda (U.K.)
Las Vegas
Nashville
NORTH CAROLINA
Raleigh
Charlotte
NORTH ATLANTIC OCEAN
PACIFIC OCEAN
LOS ANGELES
Arkansas
TENNESSEE
Tennessee
Memphis
SOUTH CAROLINA
Colorado
ARIZONA
Albuquerque
Oklahoma City
OKLAHOMA
ARKANSAS
Atlanta
Charleston
San Diego
Phoenix
NEW MEXICO
Little Rock
Birmingham
GEORGIA
Tijuana
Mexicali
Tucson
Fort Worth
Dallas
MISSISSIPPI
Mississippi
Jackson
ALABAMA
Montgomery
Jacksonville
BAJA CALIFORNIA
El Paso
TEXAS
Guadalupe (Mex.)
SONORA
Ciudad Juárez
Rio Grande
Rio Bravo
Austin
Baton Rouge
LOUISIANA
New Orleans
FLORIDA
Orlando
Hermosillo
San Antonio
Houston
Tampa
Miami
Tropic of Cancer
BAHAMAS
MEXICO
CHIHUAHUA
COAHUILA
Florida Str.
Turks & Caicos Islands (U.K.)
BAJA CALIFORNIA SUR
SINALOA
NL
Monterrey
Gulf of Mexico
DURANGO
Culiacán
ZACATECAS
TAMAULIPAS
Havana
CUBA
Tampico
SL
San Luis Potosí
DOMINICAN REP.
San Juan
HAITI
Port-au-Prince
Santo Domingo
PUERTO RICO (U.S.A.)
NAYARIT
YUCATÁN
Mérida
AG
GJ
QA
Cayman Is. (U.K.)
JAMAICA
León
Guadalajara
JALISCO
HG
CAMPECHE
QUINTANA ROO
Revilla Gigedo Is. (Mex.)
COLIMA
MICHOACÁN
MÉXICO
TL
DF
MR
PA
Puebla
Veracruz
VZ
TA
Caribbean Sea
BELIZE
GUERRERO
Acapulco
OAXACA
CHIAPAS
GUATEMALA
HONDURAS
Caracas
Maracaibo
Guatemala
San Salvador
EL SALVADOR
NICARAGUA
Lake Nicaragua
Barranquilla
VENEZUELA
COSTA RICA
PANAMA
Medellín
Bogotá
COLOMBIA
Equator
ABBREVIATIONS
UNITED STATES
CT CONNECTICUT
DC DISTRICT OF COLUMBIA
DE DELAWARE
MD MARYLAND
MA MASSACHUSETTS
NH NEW HAMPSHIRE
NJ NEW JERSEY
PA PENNSYLVANIA
RI RHODE ISLAND
VT VERMONT
WV WEST VIRGINIA
MEXICO
AG AGUASCALIENTES
DF DISTRITO FEDERAL
GJ GUANAJUATO
HG HIDALGO
MR MORELOS
NL NUEVO LEÓN
PA PUEBLA
QA QUERETARO
SL SAN LUIS POTOSÍ
TA TABASCO
TL TLAXCALA
VZ VERACRUZ
CAPITAL CITIES
MÉXICO
Washington D.C.
Ottawa
Projection: Bonne
COPYRIGHT PHILIP'S
130
120
110
100
90
80
70
10
20
30
40
50
60

Physical Geography and Geology

PHYSICAL GEOGRAPHY

The physical geography of North America displays much diversity and strong regional contrasts. Relief in the eastern part of the continent is generally low, notably on the coastal plain from the Yucatán Peninsula to Cape Cod, where a wide continental shelf adjoins the coast. High mountains from Alaska to Mexico dominate western landscapes, where coastal scenery is often spectacular and earthquakes and volcanic activity mark a geologically fast-changing landscape. The Great Lakes embody the east; the Rocky Mountains crown the west.

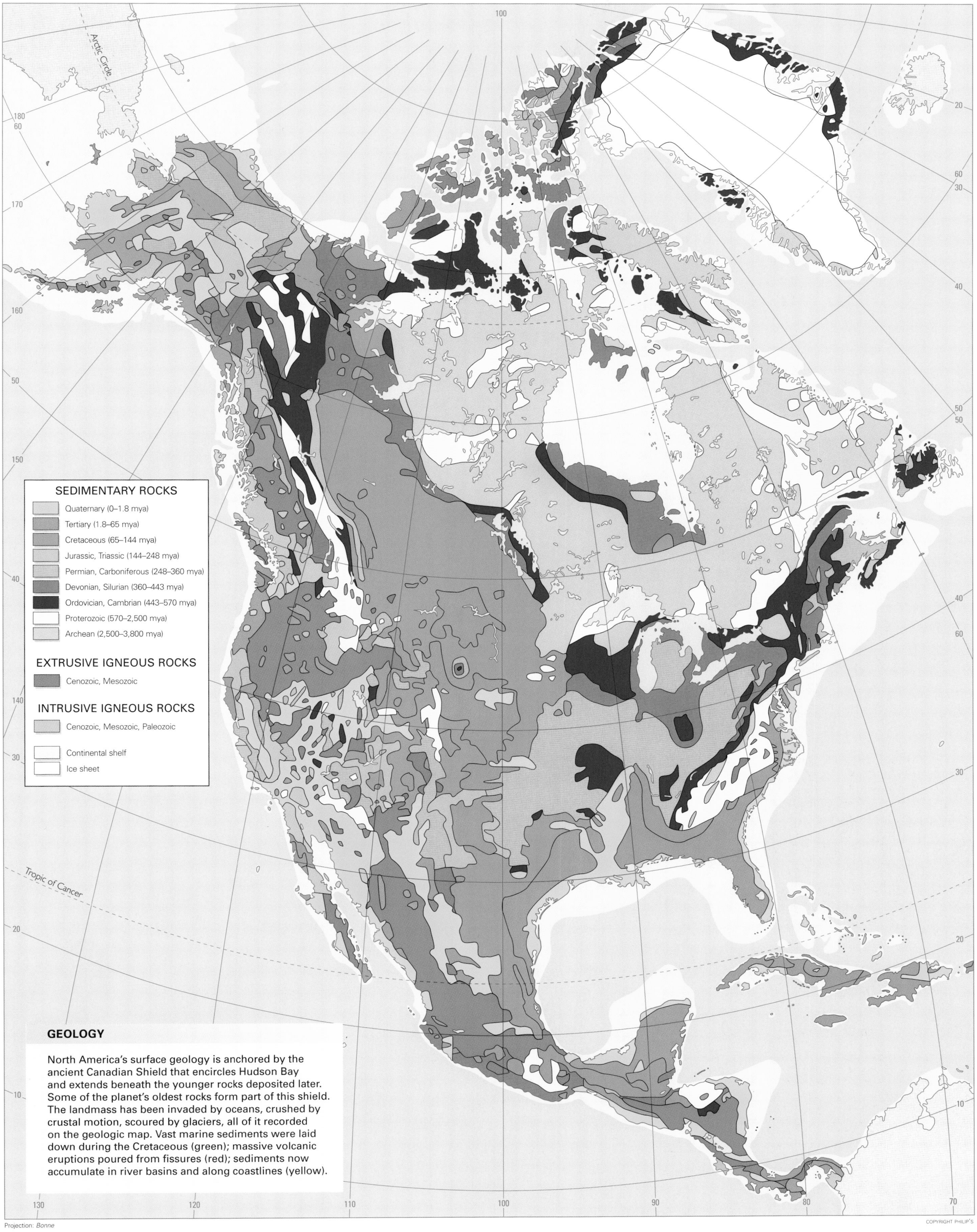

GEOLOGY

North America's surface geology is anchored by the ancient Canadian Shield that encircles Hudson Bay and extends beneath the younger rocks deposited later. Some of the planet's oldest rocks form part of this shield. The landmass has been invaded by oceans, crushed by crustal motion, scoured by glaciers, all of it recorded on the geologic map. Vast marine sediments were laid down during the Cretaceous (green); massive volcanic eruptions poured from fissures (red); sediments now accumulate in river basins and along coastlines (yellow).

Projection: *Bonne*

Tectonic Provinces and Physiography

WORLD TECTONIC PLATES – THE PACIFIC 'RING OF FIRE'

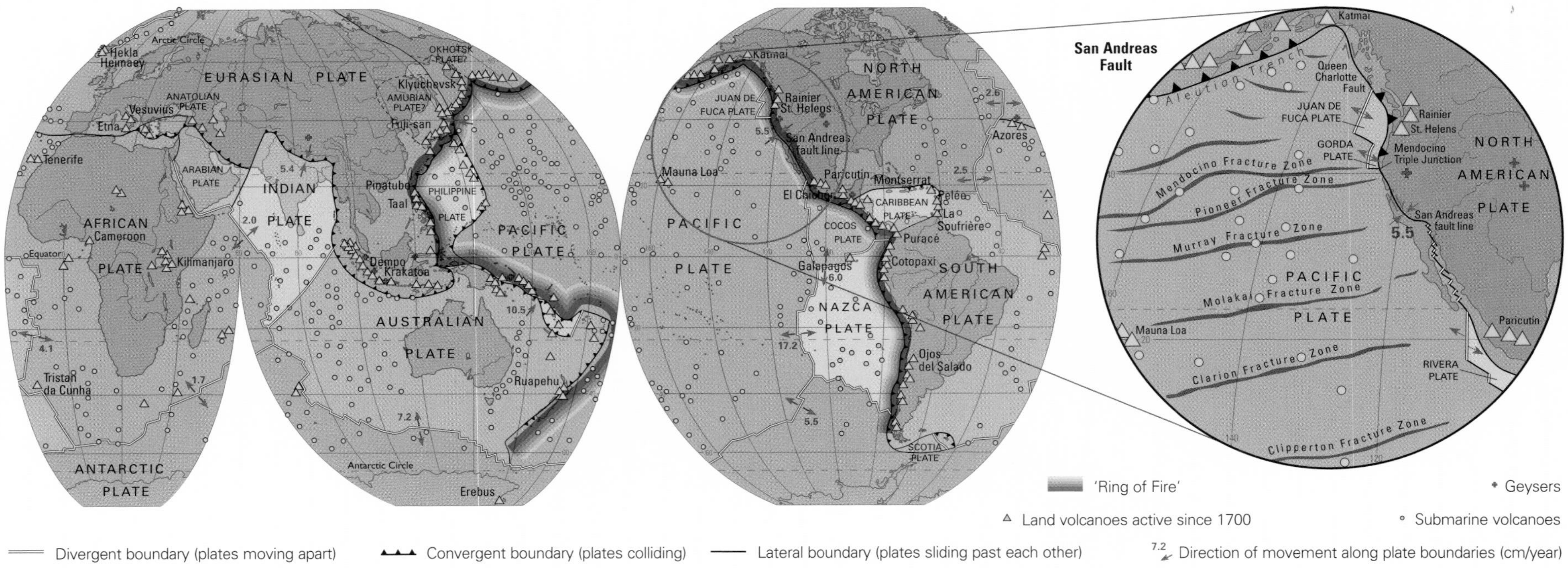

TECTONIC PROVINCES

The familiar outline of North America shown on atlas maps marks the current interface between land and surface water, but a substantial part of the landmass lies submerged during the current glacier-melting warm period. As this map indicates, approximately one-quarter of the continent lies under water today.

The ancient, crystalline core or *shield* of North America, shown in yellow on the adjacent map, extends far beyond its exposed, glacially-scoured limits. Younger sediments of the Interior Plains, creating the Great Plains and the Central Lowlands, and including glacial deposits laid down during the Pleistocene, cover much of it. The recent, Cenozoic sediments of the Coastal Plain facing the Atlantic Ocean and the Gulf of Mexico also form the ocean floor to the continental slope.

As the map of World Tectonic Plates (above) shows, the North American landmass rests on the North American tectonic plate, one of eight major, slow-moving lithospheric plates forming most of the Earth's crust (the remainder is made up by numerous smaller plates such as the Juan de Fuca and Gorda Plates off Washington and Oregon).

The eastern boundary of the North American tectonic plate is marked by the divergent Mid-Atlantic Ridge, where new rock emerges molten from below and where the North American and Eurasian/African plates are pulling apart.

On its western margin, the North American plate is converging with the Pacific Plate in a process called *subduction* where the continental plate overrides the heavier oceanic plate and pushes it downward, resulting in the mountainous, earthquake-prone and volcano-studded landscapes that extend from Alaska to Central America. The San Andreas Fault is a manifestation of this gigantic collision.

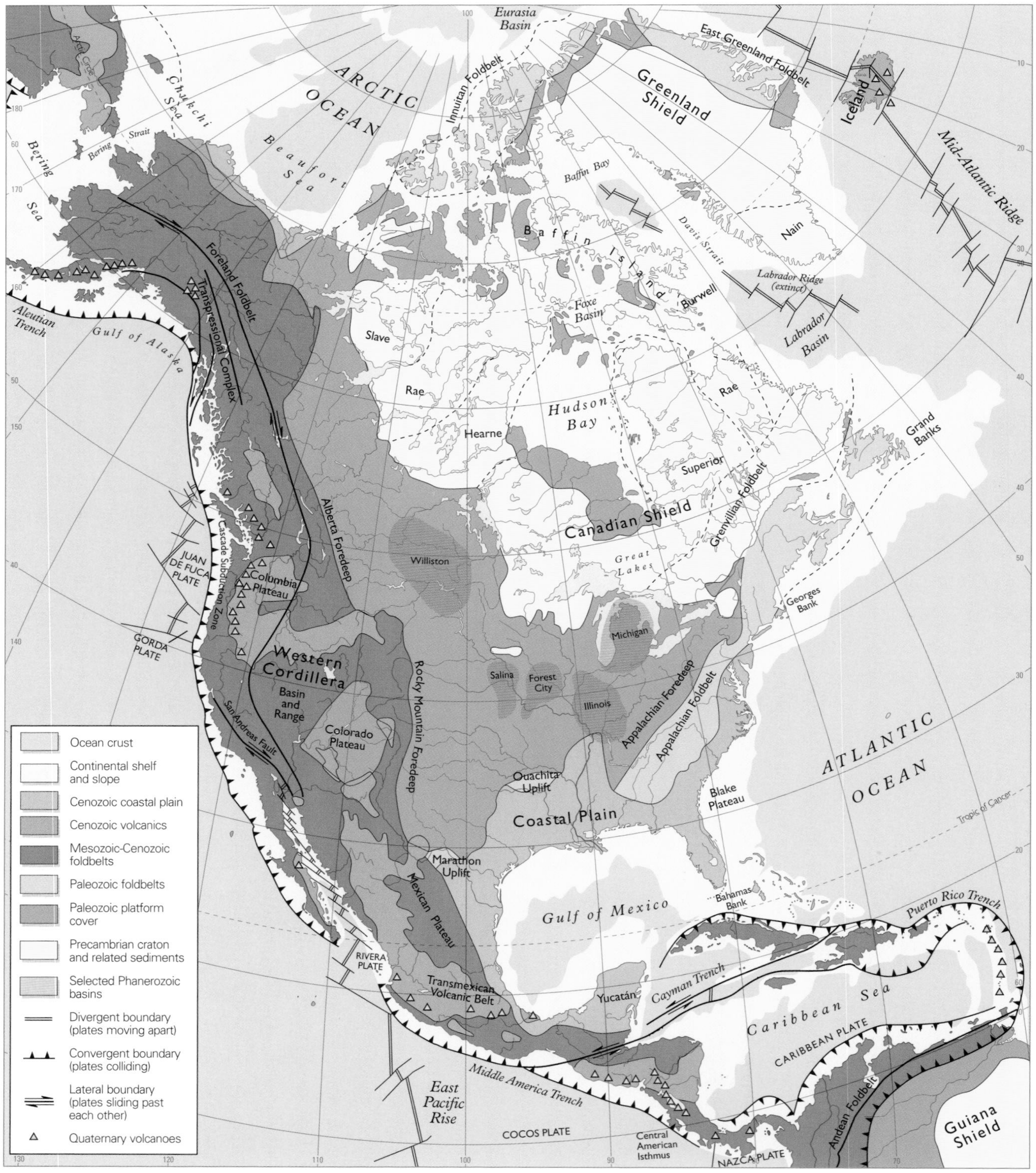

PHYSIOGRAPHIC REGIONS

Geographers divide North America into first-order terrestrial-environmental units called *physiographic realms* (for example the Interior Plains on this map); these in turn fragment into physiographic *regions* or *provinces* such as, in the case of the Interior Plains, the Great Plains and the Central Lowlands. Rock type, relief, slope, climate, soil, and vegetation are among the criteria used to derive this map, which delimits such familiar regions as the Rocky Mountains, Coastal Plain, and Colorado Plateau.

Energy and Minerals

OIL AND GAS

All three countries possess significant oil and natural gas reserves. Both Canada and Mexico export oil and gas to the United States, the world's largest consumer of energy resources. Canada's largest concentration of reserves lies along the eastern flank of the Rocky Mountains; Mexico's oilfields cluster along the southern shores of the Gulf of Mexico; United States reserves are widely dispersed and include those along Alaska's north coast. A vast system of pipelines carries oil and gas from producing zones to consumers.

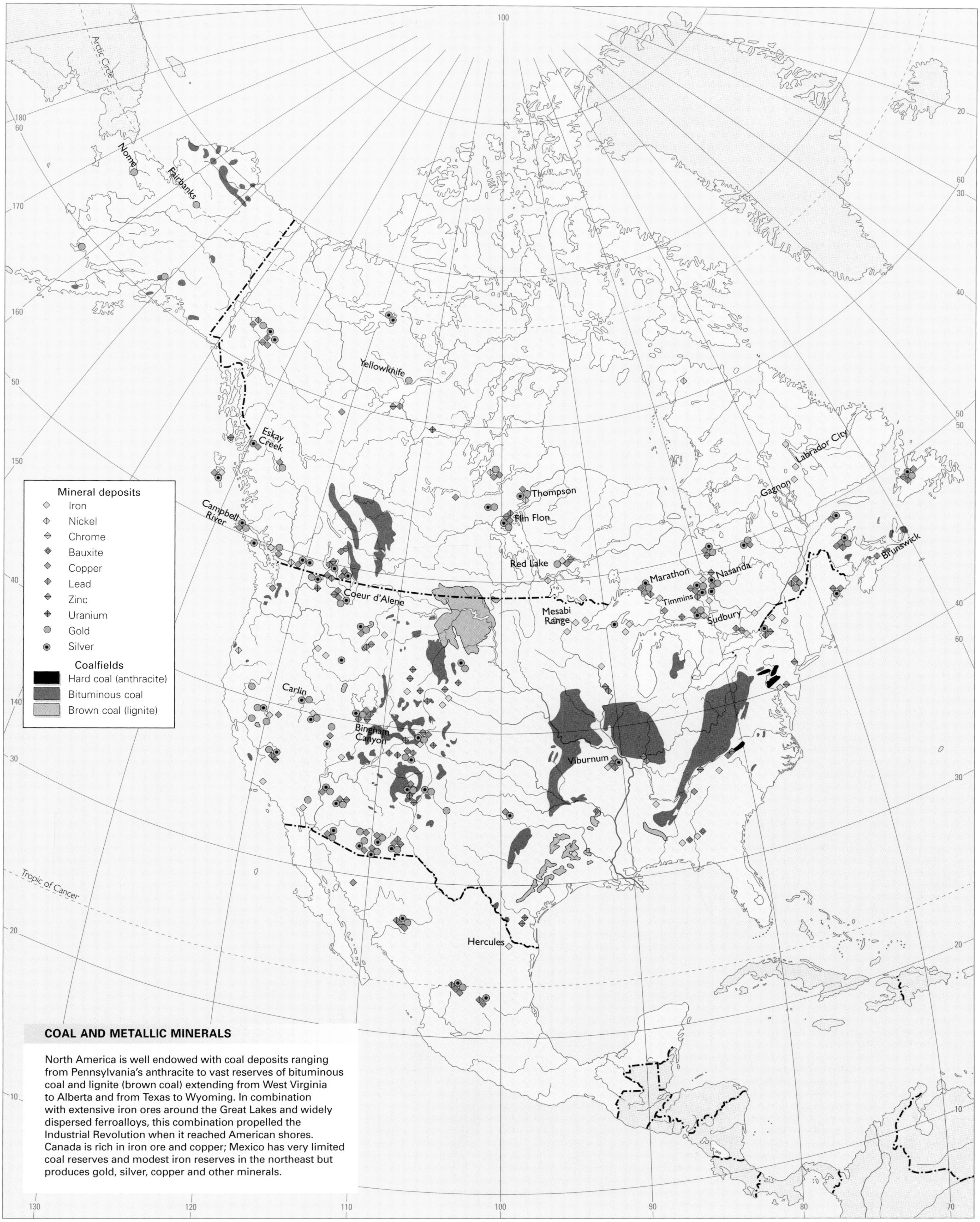

COAL AND METALLIC MINERALS

North America is well endowed with coal deposits ranging from Pennsylvania's anthracite to vast reserves of bituminous coal and lignite (brown coal) extending from West Virginia to Alberta and from Texas to Wyoming. In combination with extensive iron ores around the Great Lakes and widely dispersed ferroalloys, this combination propelled the Industrial Revolution when it reached American shores. Canada is rich in iron ore and copper; Mexico has very limited coal reserves and modest iron reserves in the northeast but produces gold, silver, copper and other minerals.

Surface Water and Drainage

SURFACE WATER AND DRAINAGE

Cyclonic weather systems in the Westerlies Wind Belt, high-mountain ice and snow melting in spring and summer, hurricanes and other seasonal storms fill lakes and streams from Alaska to the Yucatán. In general, the western half of the continent is drier than the eastern, but Rocky Mountain snowmelts sustain rivers that support major cities even in the driest parts of the U.S. Southwest. The Mississippi–Missouri–Ohio drainage system, the continent's largest, empties into the Gulf of Mexico and forms one of the planet's great deltas.

GROUNDWATER

Rivers contain but a small fraction (0.03 percent) of all the planet's freshwater. Ten times as much is held in lakes, but by far the greatest proportion (about 75 percent) is locked in glaciers. Most of what remains is hidden beneath the ground as groundwater and comes to the surface by natural processes in springs or by artificial means through wells.

Rainwater or meltwater percolating downward under the influence of gravity saturates the pores between grains in sedimentary rock, creating subsurface reservoirs or aquifers that vary widely in extent and volume. Permanent aquifers are replenished by nature, but they are subject to overuse and depletion.

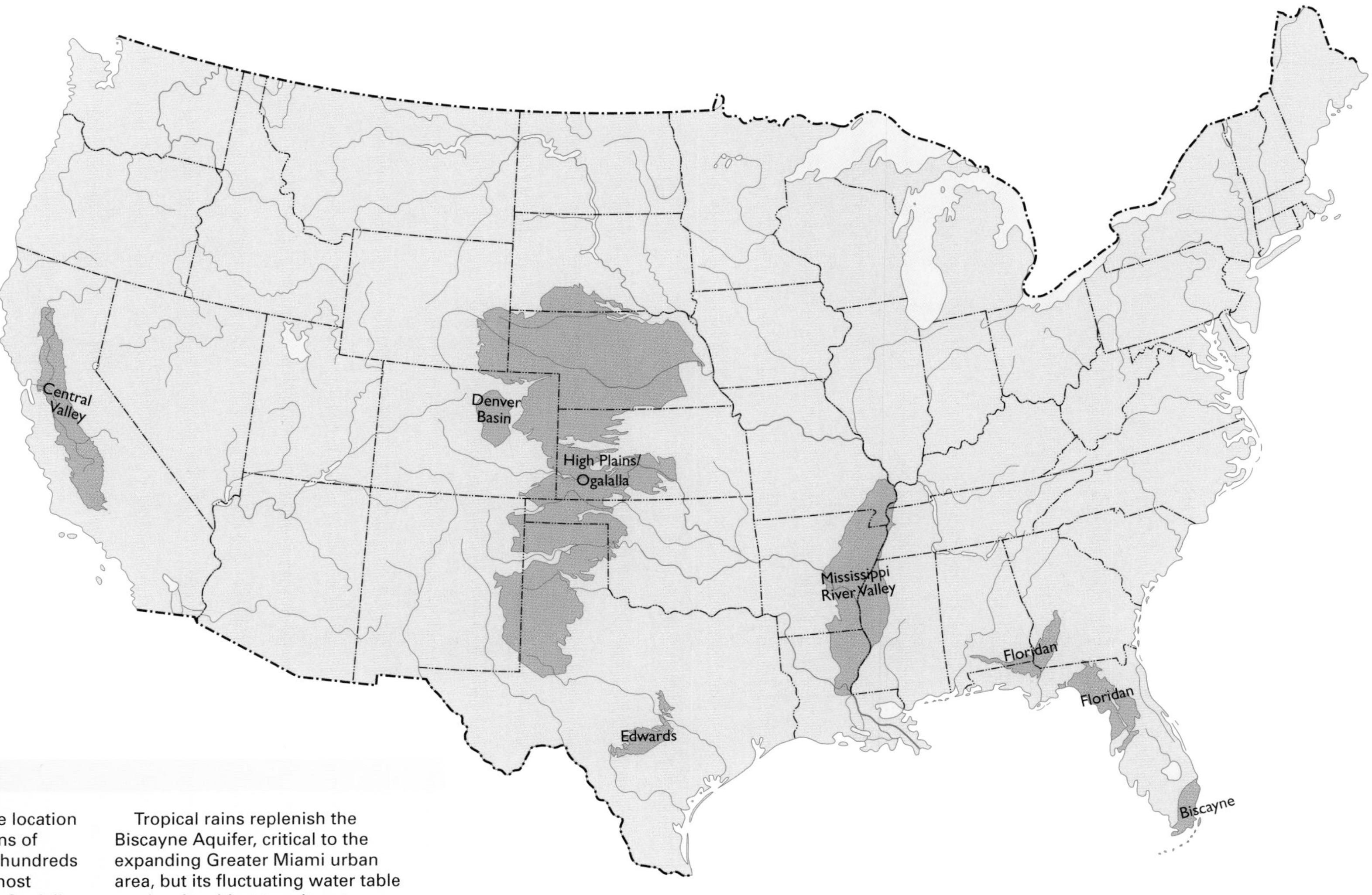

AQUIFERS

The map above shows the location and subsurface dimensions of some of North America's hundreds of aquifers. Largest and most famous is the High Plains-Ogalalla Aquifer extending from North Dakota to Texas beneath the U.S. Great Plains, which has supported irrigated agriculture for many decades but is being exhausted by ever-increasing demand and ever-more efficient pumps.

Tropical rains replenish the Biscayne Aquifer, critical to the expanding Greater Miami urban area, but its fluctuating water table renders it subject to salt-water invasion. The Mississippi River Valley Aquifer fills the basin of that great river and farmers as well as urbanites rely on California's Central Valley Aquifer, sustained by meltwaters from neighboring mountains.

WATER SUPPLY AND SUBSIDENCE IN MEXICO CITY

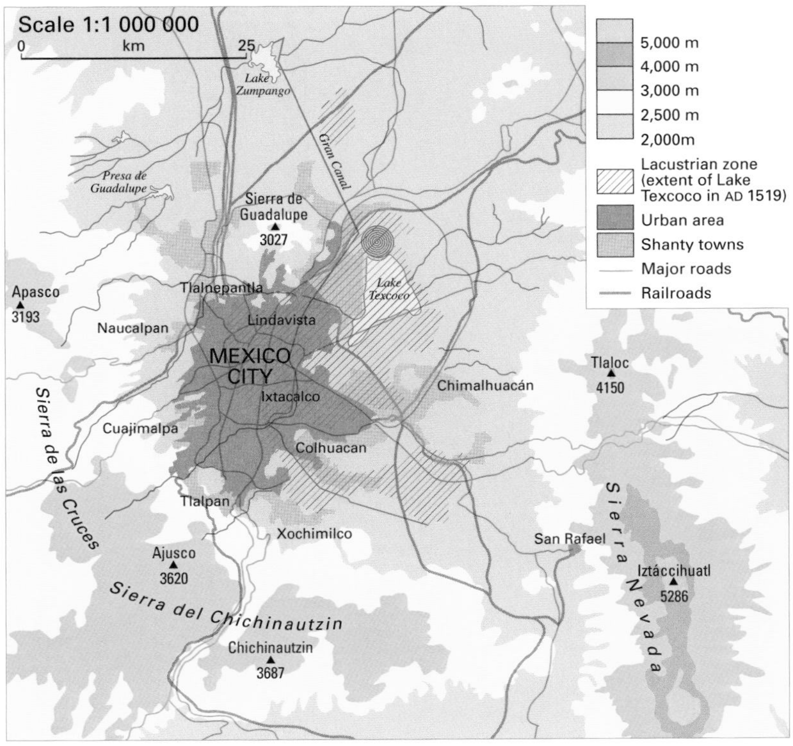

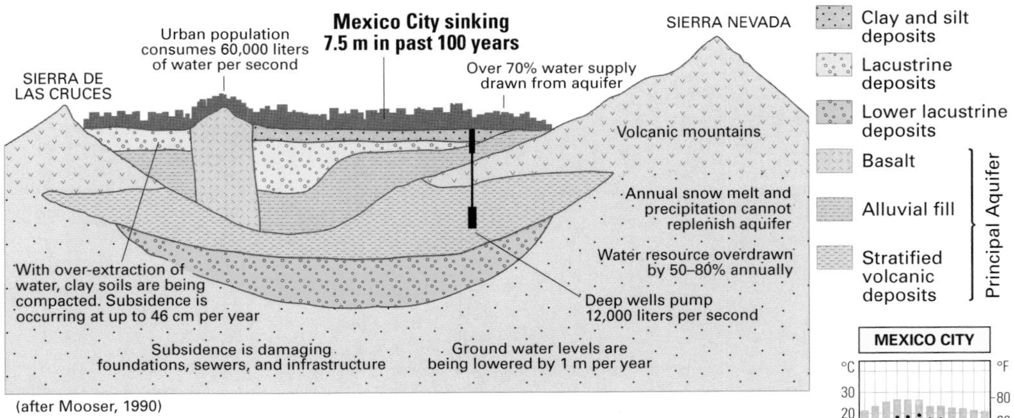

(after Mooser, 1990)

- Mexico City, situated at 2,200 m above sea level with an urban area of 3,800 sq km and a population estimated at more than 25 million, has a limited water supply.
- As the population expands and the demand for water increases, the aquifer under the city is being exploited.
- With over-extraction of water from the aquifer, the water table is being lowered, subsidence is occurring, and the city of Mexico is sinking.
- High summer rainfall and inadequate sewerage/drainage systems make Mexico City prone to flooding. Effluent leaks into the soil and groundwater, and gradually the aquifer is becoming contaminated.
- Gran Canal was built in 1900 to extract waste from the city by gravity. With subsidence, the canal now runs uphill and requires pumping stations to keep the sewerage flowing.

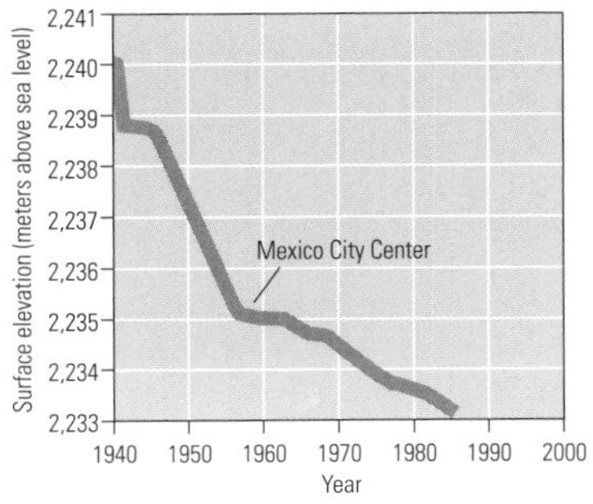

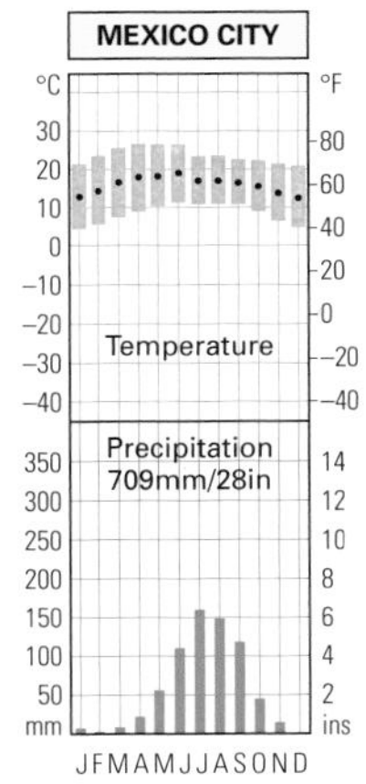

Climate and Weather

ATLANTIC HURRICANES

TORNADO ZONES

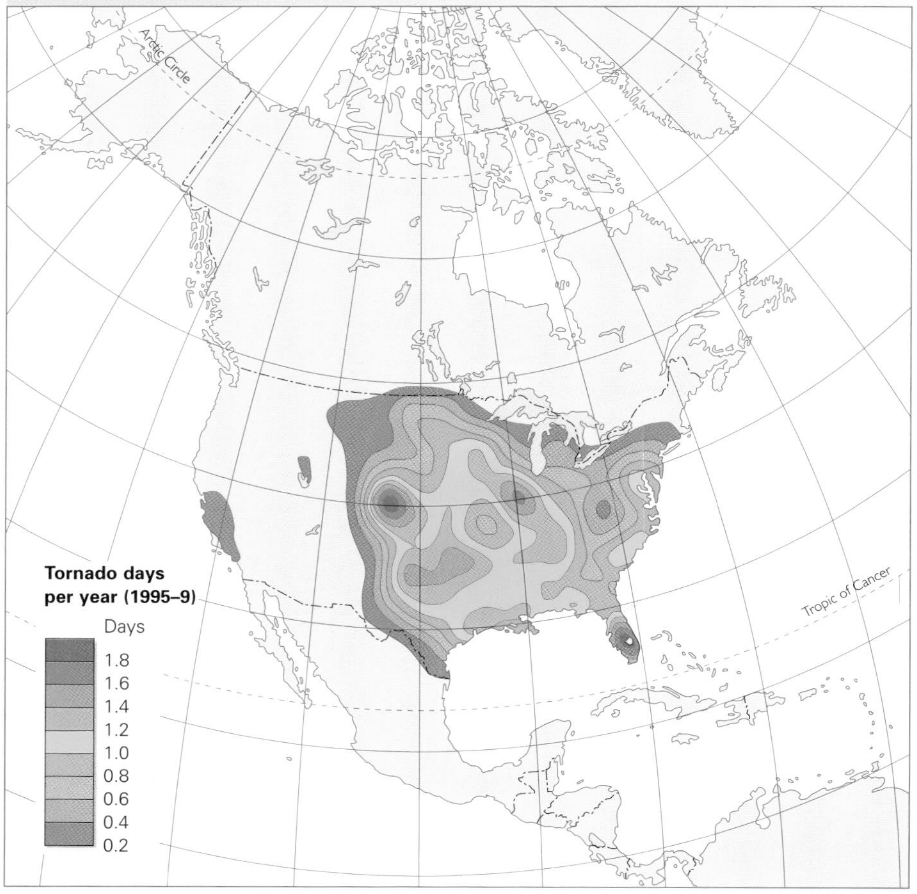

THE 10 COSTLIEST U.S. HURRICANES

Rank	Hurricane	Year	Damage (US$ million)
1	Andrew (SE FL, SE LA)	1992	34,955
2	Charley (FL)	2004	15,000
3	Hugo (SC)	1989	9,740
4	Agnes (FL, NE USA)	1972	8,602
5	Betsy (SE FL, SE LA)	1965	8,517
6	Camille (MS, SE LA, VA)	1969	6,992
7	Diane (NE USA)	1955	5,541
8	Frederic (AL, MS)	1979	4,965
9	Floyd (NC & NE USA)	1999	4,667
10	Unnamed (NEW ENGLAND)	1938	4,749

Hurricanes in the Atlantic zone tend to track westward in the low-latitude Trade Wind Belt and then recurve northward and eventually northeastward as they come under the influence of the westerly winds of the middle latitudes. This map underscores the vulnerability of the U.S. southeast coast to hurricane impacts, as well as the Caribbean region and the entire rim of the Gulf of Mexico. Although some storm systems survive as far north as Newfoundland, they tend to weaken (and wind speeds decline) as they reach cooler environs.

MONTHLY TORNADO OCCURRENCES

Three-year average, 2001–3

January	4	July	94
February	16	August	78
March	41	September	73
April	127	October	87
May	222	November	105
June	133	December	61
		Total	**1,039**

The "Tri-State Tornado" on March 18, 1925 – early in the season – swept across Missouri, Illinois, and Indiana and killed 689 persons in 45 minutes.

No landmass on Earth suffers as severely from tornado impacts as does North America, where topography and weather systems combine to create the conditions favorable to tornado development. Clashing airmasses and heat-generated, violent thunderstorms produce twisting funnel clouds 330–1,650 ft (100–500 meters) in diameter around pressure centers that may be 100–200 millibars below the surrounding air. This triggers winds of 100–300 mph (150–450 kph) with devastating effect on the surface they traverse.

AIR MASSES AND WEATHER MAKERS

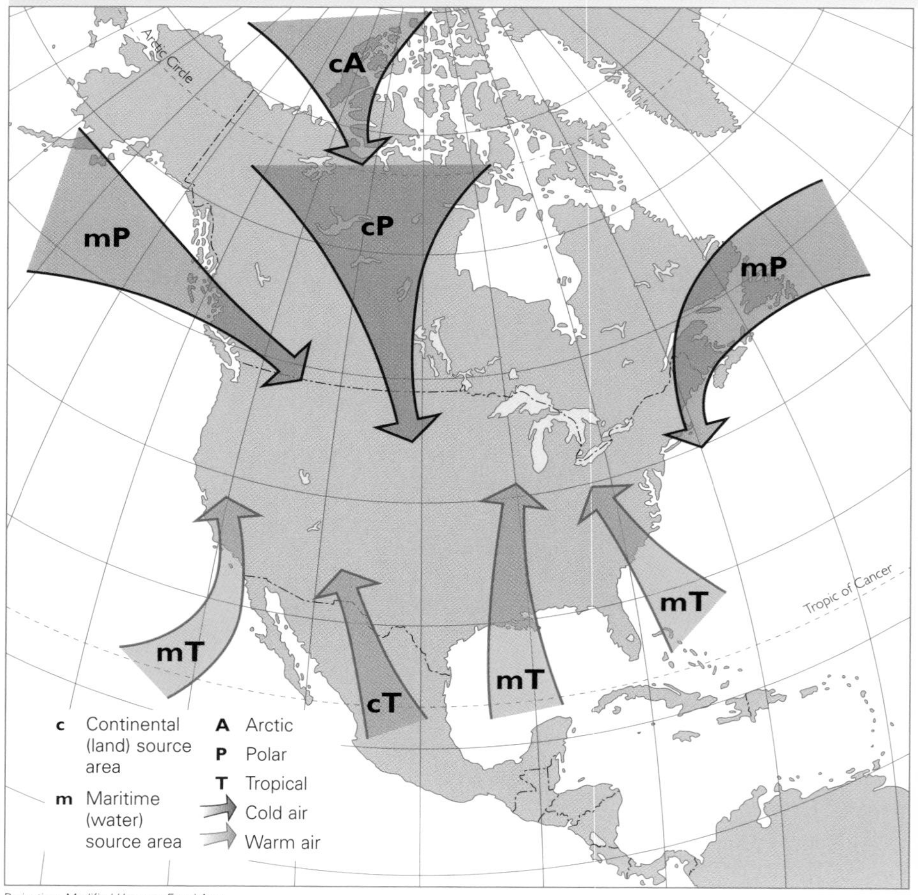

Projection: *Modified Hammer Equal Area*

Weather conditions in all parts of the world result from a combination of factors among which the properties of air masses are critical. When large parcels of air (1,500 km across or more) remain relatively stationary for several days over cold, warm, moist, or dry surface environments, they take on the characteristics of these surfaces. Then, when they are steered away from their source regions by the general atmospheric circulation, they carry those conditions to other locales, where they form powerful weather makers. In this way, dry arctic cold penetrates the heart of North America in winter, warm tropical air reaches Canada during the summer, and rain from moist Pacific air drenches the slopes of British Columbia, Washington, and Oregon.

The key properties of air masses are signaled by a two-letter acronym that reflects their continental (c) or their maritime (m) sources and, in the case of North America, their Arctic (A), polar (P), or tropical (T) origins. For example, "cT" air, dry and hot, originates in northern Mexico and is drawn into the U.S. Southwest, and "mP" air, comparatively moist but cold, flows from beyond the Labrador Sea into the northeastern corner of the continent.

When air masses move, they bring the weather conditions of their source areas to distant regions, so that frigid arctic conditions may prevail for several successive winter days in the U.S. Midwest while oppressive, humid summer heat can blanket Canada north of the Great Lakes in summer.

When air masses with strongly contrasting properties collide, their frontal contact can generate strong storms punctuated by dangerous tornadoes. In North America, this hazard is amplified by the continent's topography: nothing interferes with the movement of air masses between the Rocky Mountains to the west and the Appalachians to the east, creating an unmatched arena of air-mass collision and associated storms whose cumulative cost, in lives and damage, is incalculable.

The maps and charts on page 19 display the contrasting continental January and July temperatures and climographs for selected stations across the realm. The annual precipitation map (bottom left) reveals the rain-shadow effect of the western mountains, where orographic rainfall drenches western slopes, and arid conditions on the mountains' lee side.

The map of climatic regions (bottom right) summarizes the prevailing conditions into ten regional categories. Deserts and highlands prevail in the west, humid and warm-summer conditions in the southeast, and cold-winter conditions from the U.S. Midwest northward. Polar environments in the far north, a dry-summer Mediterranean regime along the west coast, and equatorial conditions in eastern Mexico complete this variable regional picture. In the United States, only the tip of Florida is truly tropical.

JANUARY TEMPERATURE

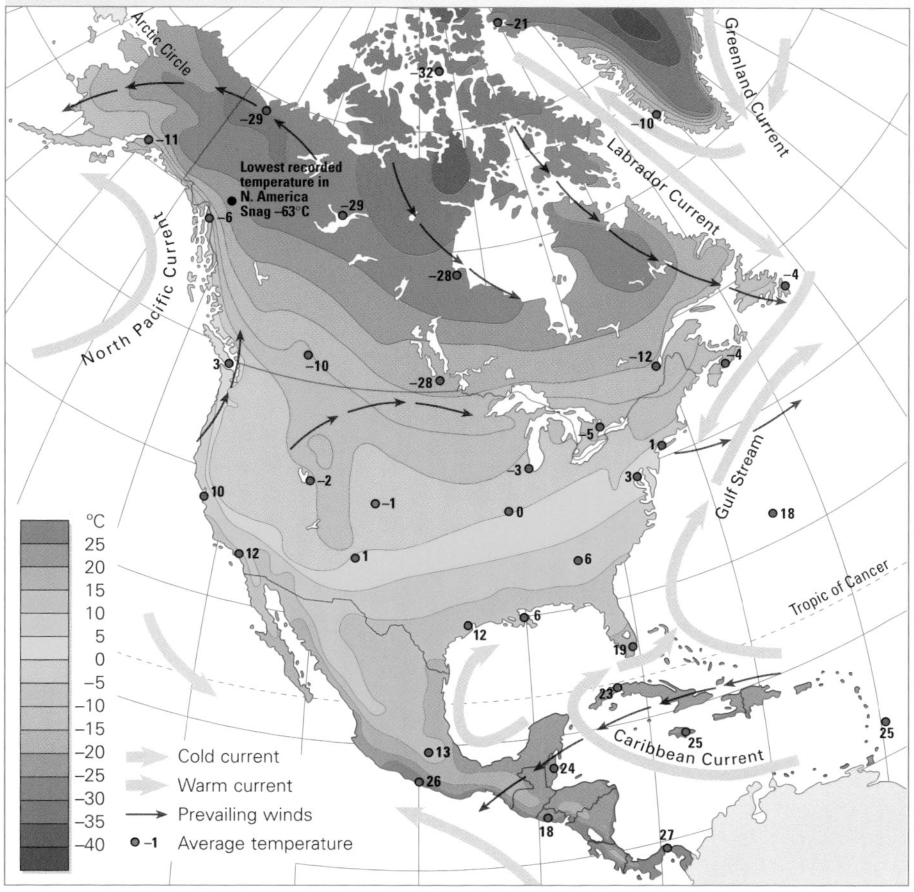

JULY TEMPERATURE

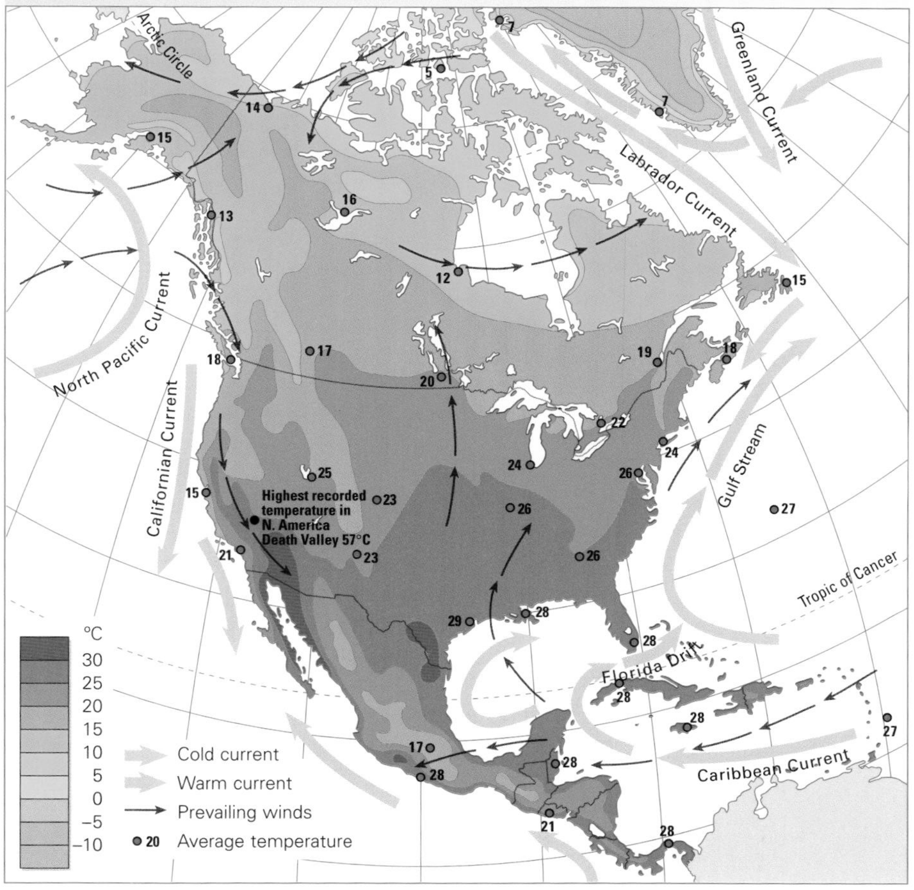

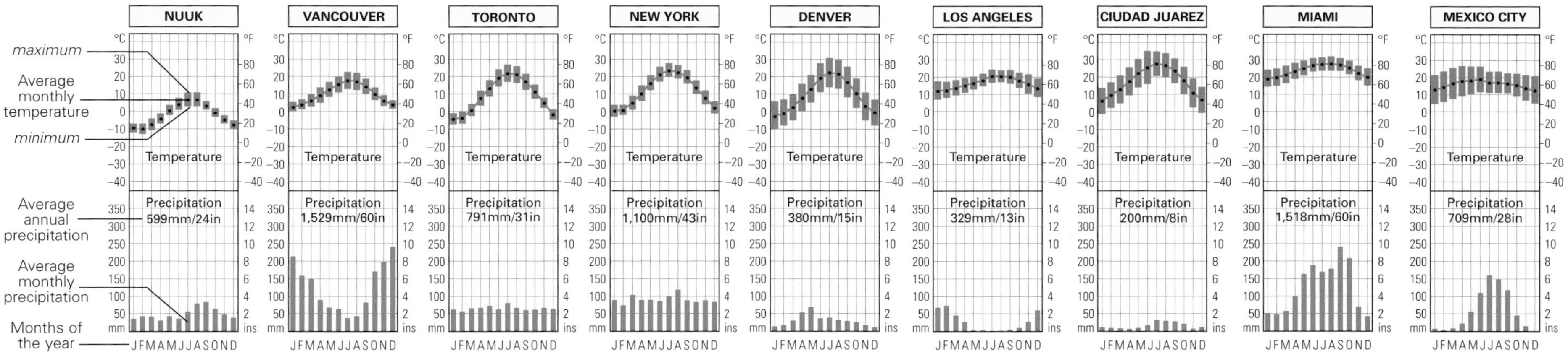

ANNUAL PRECIPITATION

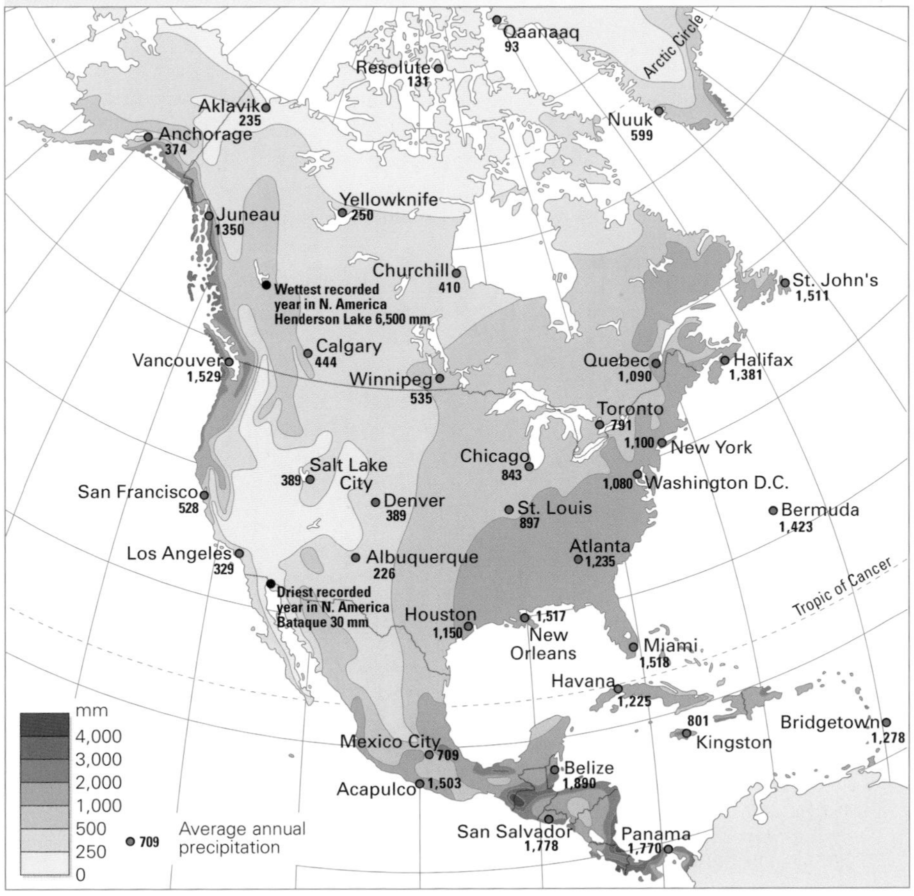

Projection: *Modified Hammer Equal Area*

CLIMATE REGIONS (after Köppen-Geiger)

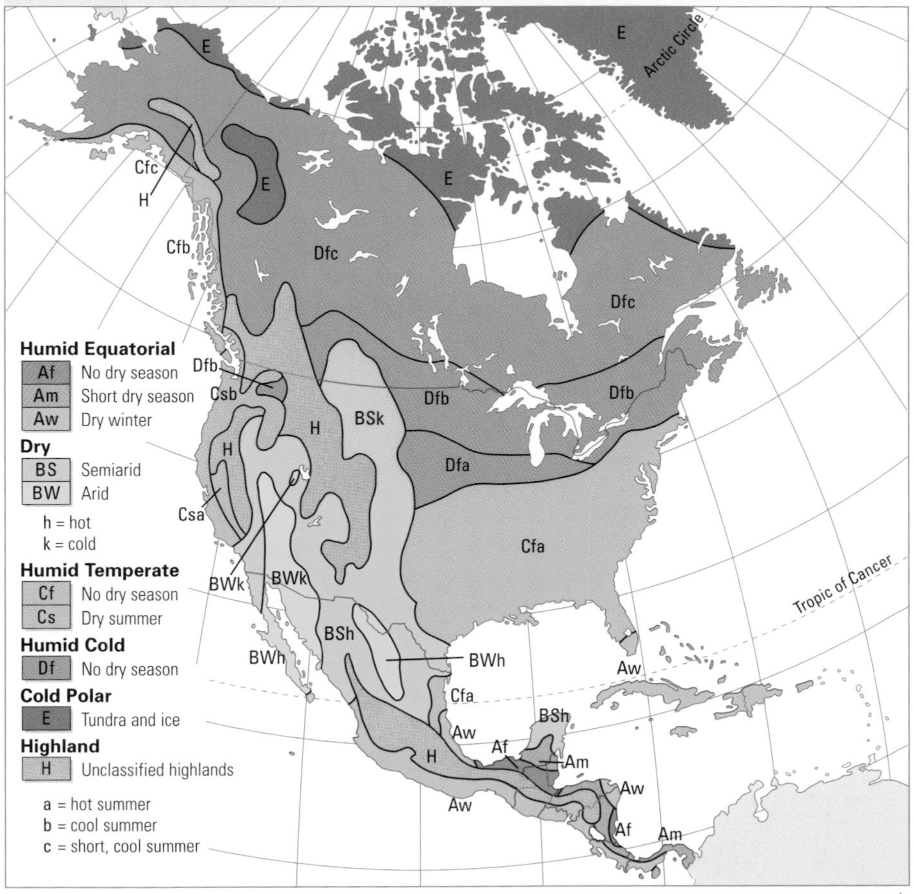

Soil and Vegetation

SOIL REGIONS

It is useful to compare this map of North America's soils with the map of regional climates, page 19. Although various factors (geology, terrain, moisture) complicate the pattern, older, fertile ultisols dominate in the southeastern United States, grain-crop supporting mollisols extend from southern Canada to northern Mexico, pine-forest sustaining spodosols lie in a zone across Canada south of the frigid gelisols of Alaska and Nunavut, and dry-climate aridisols prevail in the U.S. Southwest and parts of northern Mexico.

VEGETATION REGIONS OF NORTH AMERICA

Generalizing vegetation spatially is problematic, and botanists and geographers have devised several schemes to represent the broadest assemblages of plants in North America. The map on this page, therefore, is only one such approximation. It is based on the notion of the *biome*, the broadest justifiable assemblage of plants (and animals) that forms an ecological unit of subcontinental dimensions.

The lines on the map, however, do not represent clear breaks on the ground. They reflect broad transition zones. The taiga (northern coniferous forest) that extends from Newfoundland across Canada to Alaska thins out as it yields southward to the mixed deciduous forests of the U.S. Midwest and Northeast and to the grasslands of the central plains. To the north the taiga becomes patchy, its trees stunted as it surrenders to the Arctic tundra.

In the south, Mexico's tropical forests flank Pacific and Gulf shores to a latitude close to the Tropic of Cancer, but toward the interior, rising elevation influences the pattern and temperate coniferous forests dominate. Deserts and highland biomes dominate northern Mexico, although the grasslands of the interior plains reach across the U.S. border in the northwest.

In the eastern United States, the mixed temperate deciduous forests of the coastal plain yield to the oak-pine forests of the Appalachians; in the west, the forests and alpine assemblages of the Rocky Mountains separate the grasses of the interior Great Plains from the diverse biomes fronting the Pacific Ocean.

The Pacific Coastal-Cascadian forests extend from Alaska to northern California, where the distinctive Mediterranean biome (grasslands, chaparral, and woodlands) prevails. Toward the interior the forests of the Sierra Nevada flank this biome, and to the south the Mojave and Sonoran Deserts dominate.

The biome mapped as the Central Prairies and Plains can be subdivided on the basis of the height of its grasses. In general, tall-grass prairie prevails in the east of this region, and short-grass prairie in the drier west.

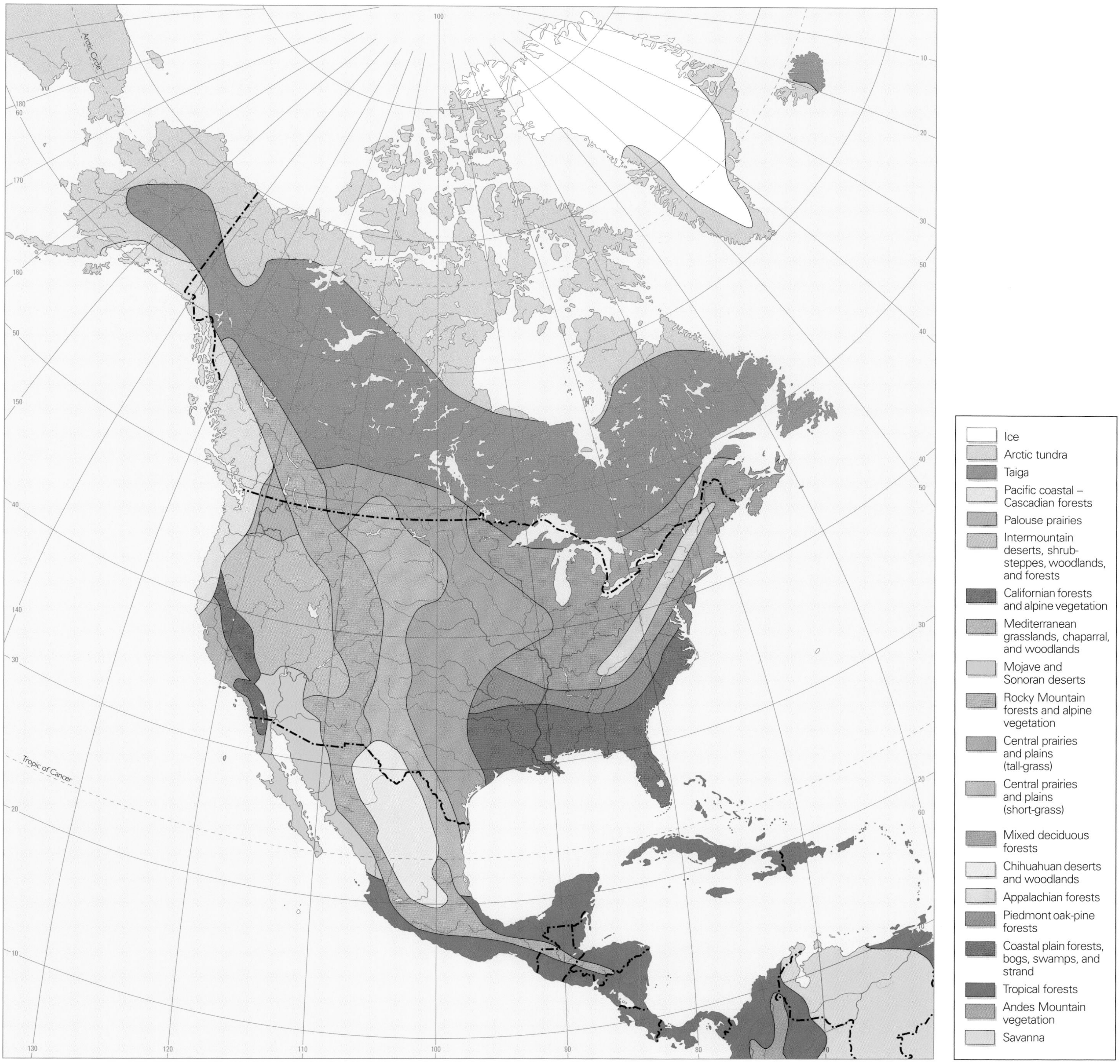

Pleistocene Land Cover and Glaciation

PLEISTOCENE LAND COVER

Planet Earth has been subject to the vagaries of rapidly changing environmental conditions throughout its 4,650-million-year existence. Long periods of global warmth, ample moisture, luxuriant vegetation, and exuberant animal life were abrogated by sudden declines in temperature, spreading droughts, and floral and faunal dislocation accompanied by mass extinctions. When an ice age commences, glacial ice forms over ever-larger areas in high latitudes, permanent ice develops on high mountains in all latitudes, oceans cool, sea level drops, and precipitation declines in many parts of the world. The process can be quite sudden, forcing plant life to shift to lower latitudes and lesser altitudes and animals to move to new ranges and niches.

Ice ages last for tens of millions of years, but they are not uniformly or continuously frigid. Extremely cold periods or glaciations, when ice advances from polar zones and mountaintops, are interrupted by warmer interglacials, when the ice recedes and life spreads poleward again. Glaciations tend to be much longer than full-scale interglacials, but the short warm spells occur even during glacial times.

The Earth is experiencing an ice age today, the Late Cenozoic Ice Age. The Antarctic ice sheet began to form about 35 million years ago (mya); high-elevation glaciers appeared some 23 mya, North Polar ice became permanent around 12 mya, and global cooling continued until, 1.8 mya, the Pleistocene epoch brought the conditions that prevail today.

The Pleistocene has been marked by a series of lengthy glaciations, each lasting over 100,000 years and marked by comparatively brief mild spells, separated by interglacials lasting 10,000 years or longer. The previous interglacial, the Eemian, ended about 120,000 years ago and produced temperatures even warmer

GREAT LAKES FORMATION

The continental glaciers that advanced and receded several times during the Pleistocene epoch repeatedly transformed the landscape of the northern and central parts of North America. Eroding as they went, they picked up vast amounts of bedrock, crushed it into particles ranging from boulders to silt, and carried it hundreds of kilometers from its source. In the process, the sediment-laden ice moved into pre-existing stream valleys, widening and deepening them. Eventually the melting and receding glaciers dropped their sedimentary loads, burying the bedrock below and leaving ridges called *terminal moraines* where their forward motion stopped.

When such moraines lay astride glacier-enlarged valleys and basins, the dammed-up meltwater formed lakes among which the five North American Great Lakes are the most extensive. The maps below show the approximate position of the ice at two stages during the recession, approximately 13,000 and 10,000 years ago. As the ice receded, the water bodies expanded, and for a time ancient Lake Algonquin encompassed present-day Lake Michigan as well as a vast Lake Huron. Ancient Lake Iroquois, the future Lake Ontario, drained via the Hudson River into the Atlantic.

Just after the ice had melted away completely, in the early Holocene, ancient Lake Nipissing drained via the Ottawa River into the St. Lawrence River. The Great Lakes will continue to change in response to human activity, crustal rebound following the disappearance of the ice, and climate variation.

Glacial retreat (Woodfordian substage)

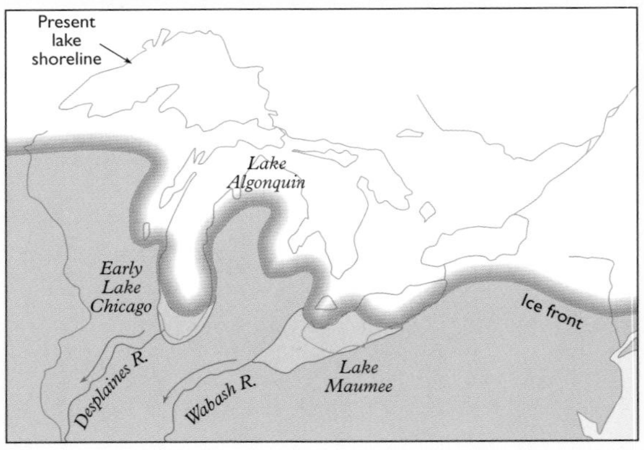

Glacial retreat (Post-Valderan)

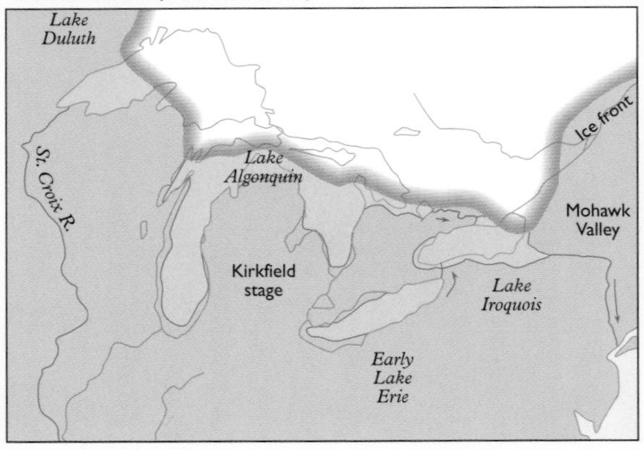

Post-Glacial Great Lakes

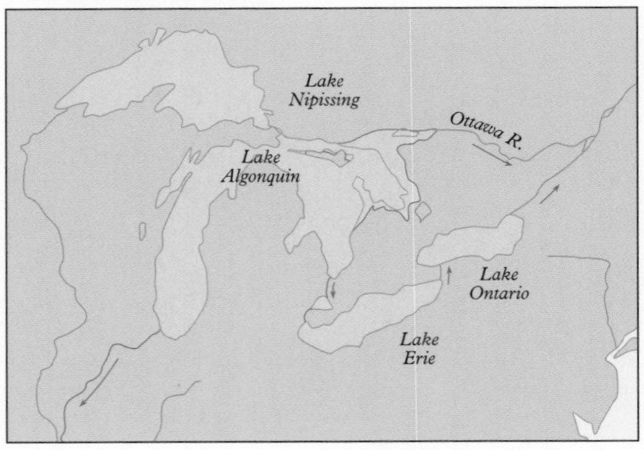

than those of today. The Eemian interglacial was followed by the Wisconsinan glaciation, when great ice sheets covered the Midwest and pushed as far south as the Ohio River valley. About 18,000 years ago, global warming began to melt the Wisconsinan's glaciers, and after a brief return to frigid temperatures the current interglacial – the Holocene – began approximately 10,000 years ago.

What was North America like when the Pleistocene ice sheets spread over the northern one-third of the continent? Reconstructing Pleistocene-glacial environments is a complicated process, and the map on this page is but an approximation of what may have happened (*see right*). In the low-relief east, a zone of tundra vegetation adjoined the ice. To the west, in the mountains and along the cold Pacific shores, desert, semidesert, and steppe prevailed because glaciation causes aridity as well as frigidity. The spruce forests of present-day Canada migrated south to the Appalachians (today's Blue Ridge forests are remnants of that shift) and into the Mississippi Valley, thinning out westward and yielding to arid steppe in the southern Great Plains. Deciduous forests stood in Florida and along the Gulf coast to the west. Pine forests covered the Southwest and parts of present-day Mexico; savanna vegetation extended from the Yucatán Peninsula to Costa Rica. The only area of tropical forest to survive on the landmass was in Panama.

This process has occurred numerous times during the Pleistocene's 1.8 million years, and it is likely to take place again. But the end of the Holocene will be sharply different from the end of the Eemian interglacial, when the Earth had a minuscule human population and North America had none at all. Today the planet has 6.4 billion inhabitants and North America's three most populous countries count 430 million, their activities affecting atmosphere and oceans and playing a role in modifying climate. Imagine the dislocation even a partial return to the conditions reflected by the map at right would cause!

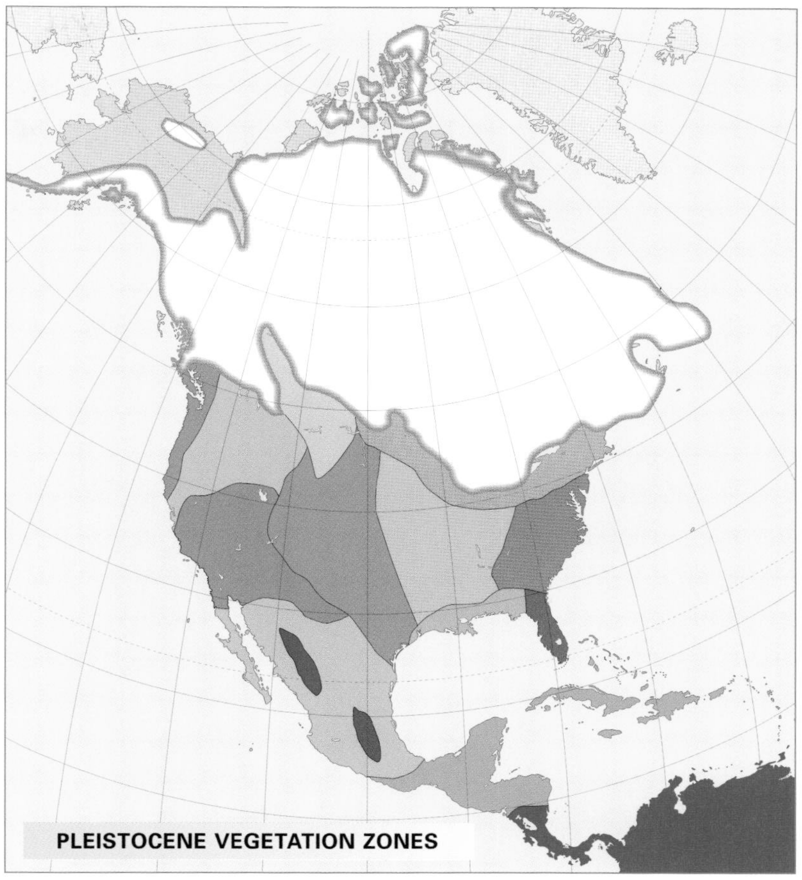

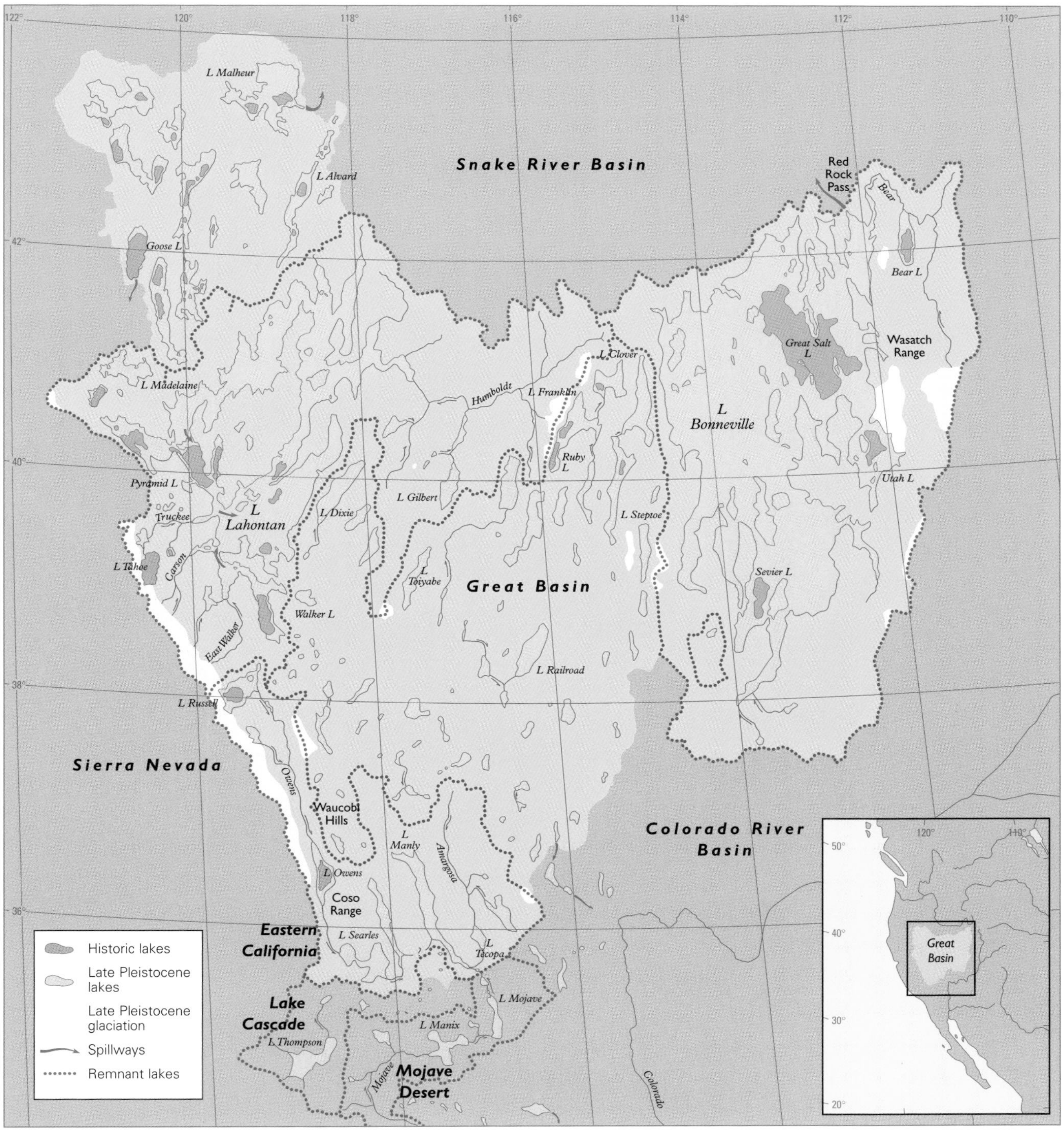

THE PLUVIAL LAKES

The continental glaciers, as the map on this page shows, never reached Utah, Nevada, Oregon, or California. But even there the glacial episodes had far-reaching effects. As the climate map on page 19 shows, much of the U.S. Southwest and Far West is arid today. But during the glaciations, precipitation in these areas was substantial, and more than 100 lakes, known as pluvial lakes, formed as a result.

The remnant of the largest of these, Lake Bonneville, still survives as the Great Salt Lake in Utah. Glacial Lake Bonneville at one stage was approximately as large as Lake Michigan is today. It reached a maximum depth of 300 meters and overflowed northward through Idaho into the Snake River and hence into the Columbia River and the Pacific Ocean.

Climate change during and following deglaciation desiccated the area, however, lake levels dropped, and the salinity of the water increased as rainfall declined. The dimensions of former Lake Bonneville, and the other pluvial lakes of the region, can be deduced from the shoreline terraces they left behind, visible on the slopes of the mountains that encircled them. Today, water remains in only a few basins of the once-plentiful pluvial lakes.

Indigenous Peoples

INDIGENOUS DOMAINS

Anthropologists, historical geographers and others have attempted to reconstruct the Pre-columbian map of North America on the basis of archeological, linguistic, environmental, subsistence, and other evidence. This map, modified from a version published by the National Geographic Society, represents one of the earliest attempts to delineate indigenous North America. Lifeways formed the dominant criterion for this framework: older versions of this map refer to Subarctic caribou hunters, Northeast corn farmers, Northwest salmon fishers, Southwest desert foragers. But such generalizations conceal the diversity and adaptations of life in native North America.

Projection: *Bonne*

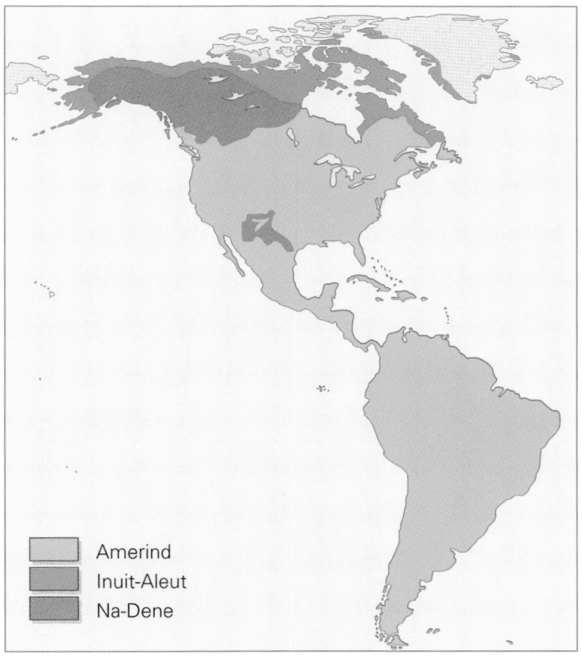

ETHNOLINGUISTIC REGIONS

The American linguist Joseph Greenberg has proposed that North America's indigenous languages represent three major language families, each corresponding to a major wave of migration into North America from East Asia. The oldest, largest, and most widely dispersed family is the Amerind, which spread from the shores of Hudson Bay to the coasts of Tierra del Fuego. The next oldest, second-largest, but much less widely dispersed family is the Na-Dene, whose languages are spoken by the First Nations of northwest Canada and part of Alaska, and by the Apache and Navajo. Last to bring their languages to North America were the Inuit-Aleut, still concentrated today along Arctic and near-Arctic shores.

LAND AND PEOPLE

The maps above and below display the distribution of native populations in Canada and the United States respectively. The aboriginal rights of Canada's widely dispersed First Nations and Inuit peoples are protected by the federal government, which has recently moved to endorse limited tribal self-government in northern British Columbia and has made territorial concessions in the far north. In the U.S., the relentless westward push of white settlement devastated indigenous society, eventually leaving what remained of the country's Native American nations with about 4 percent of U.S. territory in the form of mostly impoverished reservations, concentrated in the southwest and scattered across the north.

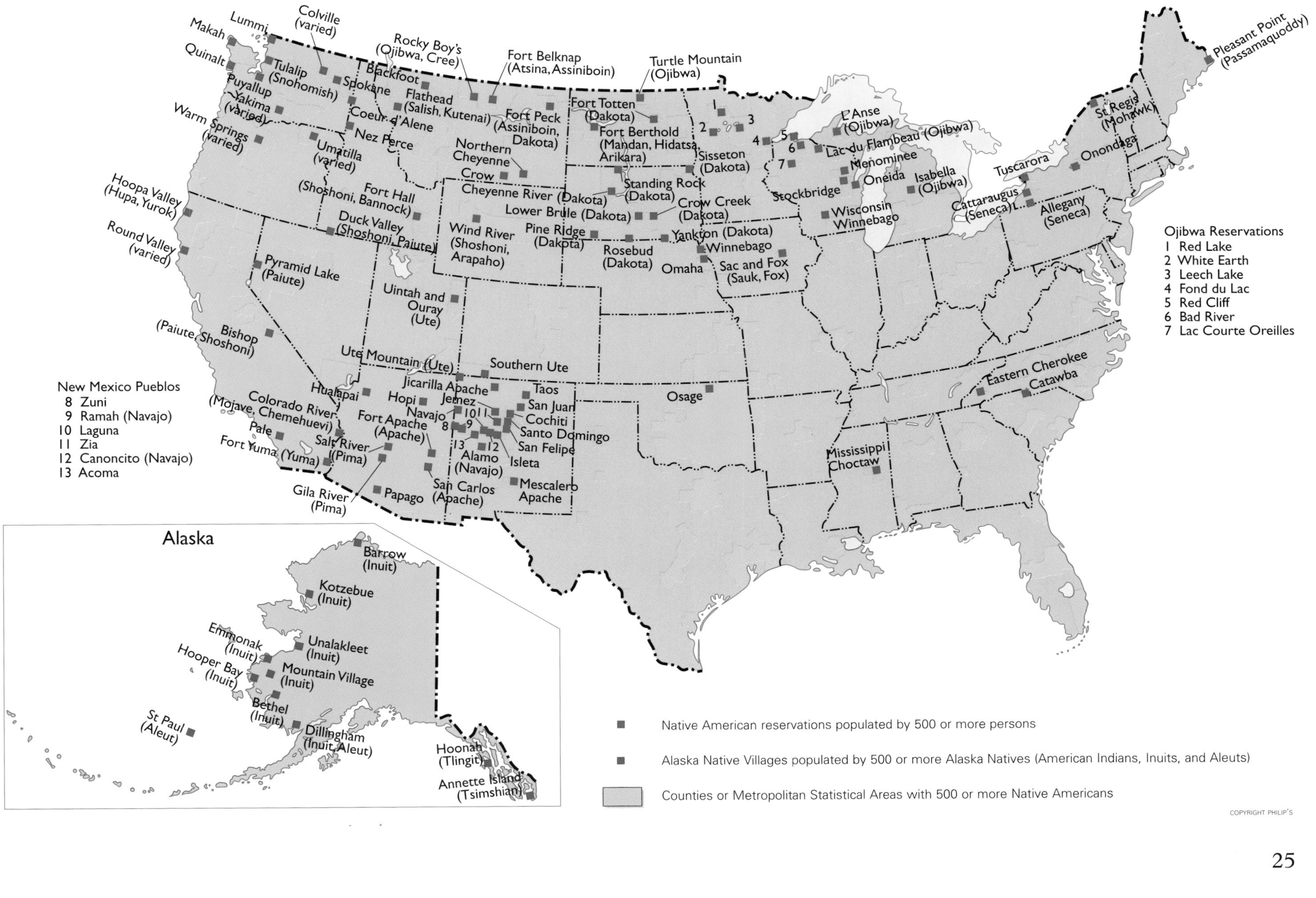

Early Settlement and Expansion

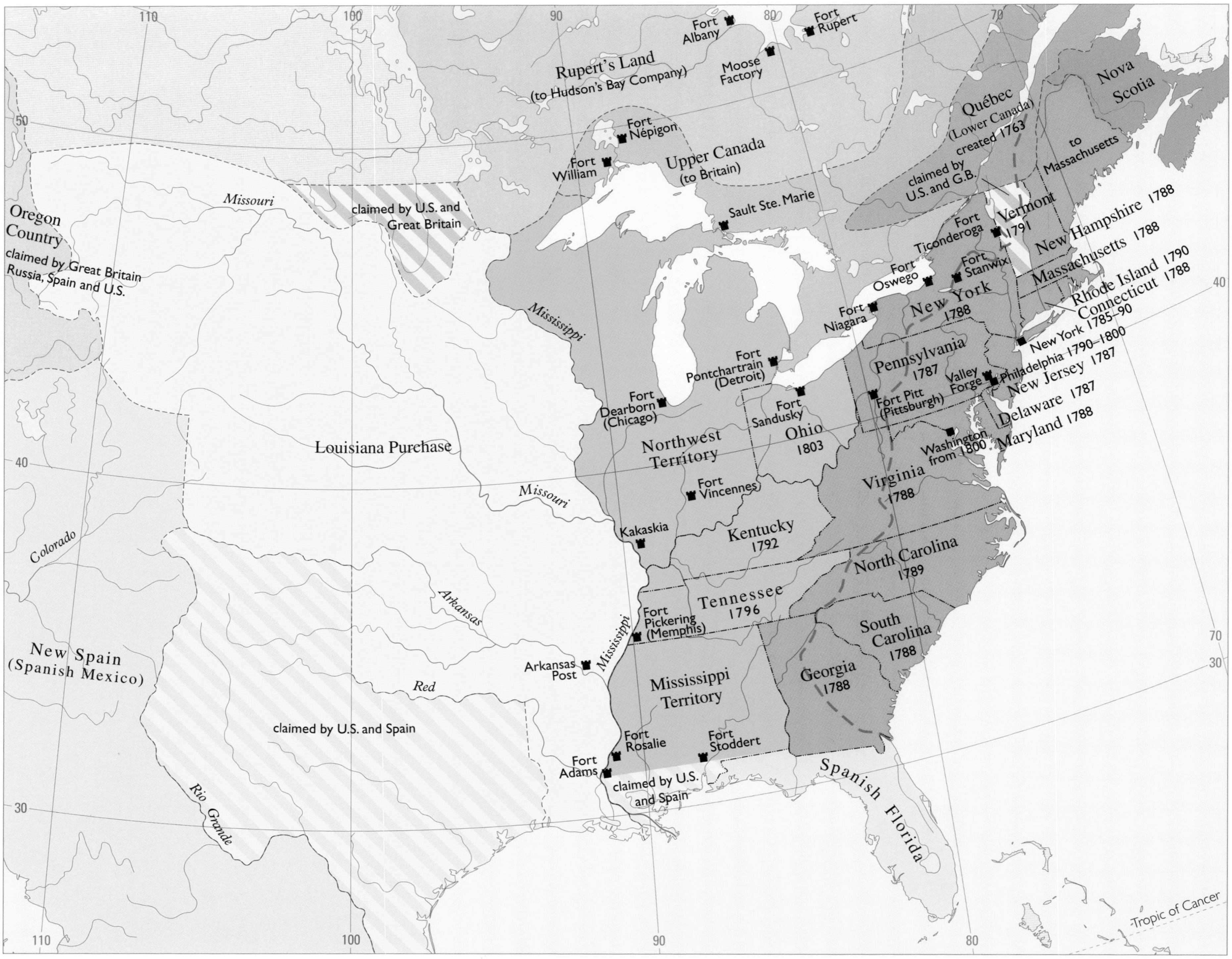

EARLY SETTLEMENT AND EXPANSION

European settlement and land alienation uprooted Native American peoples and drove them westward even as Europeans fought among themselves for political primacy. The French acquired a vast sphere of influence from Québec to Louisiana; the major British holding consisted of 13 colonies along the east coast extending from Maine to Georgia, and New Spain extended Spanish sway from Mexico into California and beyond. In the 13 colonies, anti-British resentment rose over the imposition of taxes and restrictions on overseas trade, as well as Britain's delimitation of the so-called Proclamation Line, which prohibited white settlement west of the Appalachians.

France's defeat in 1763 allowed the British to organize Canada, but the colonies rebelled and proclaimed independence in 1776. Expansion westward resumed, and in 1803 Napoleon, needing money to finance his European war effort, sold Louisiana to the young republic. The stage was set for the Union's final push to the Pacific and the ouster of the Spanish from "New Spain."

EXPANSION OF CANADA

- Rupert's Land (Hudson's Bay Company)
- Québec (created 1763)
- Nova Scotia
- Upper and Lower Canada (Britain)

EXPANSION OF THE UNITED STATES

- Thirteen Colonies
- 1783 Settlement and Native American cessions
- Louisiana Purchase, 1803
- New Spain/East Florida
- Oregon Country
- Forts and trading posts
- Proclamation Line, 1763

MEXICO 1814

- Mexican Provinces
- Greater Mexico
- United States
- Approximate limit of provinces

LATER NATIONAL CONSOLIDATION

Major reorganization and politico-geographical adjustment of the three countries continued into the 20th century. In Canada, Newfoundland did not join the Commonwealth until 1949 and Nunavut was established in 1999. Alaska, purchased by the United States in 1867, did not attain statehood until 1959. Following the loss of its vast northern frontier, Mexico reorganized in the aftermath of the revolution that brought independence from Spain and later on the basis of its 1917 Constitution.

Population and Social Diversity

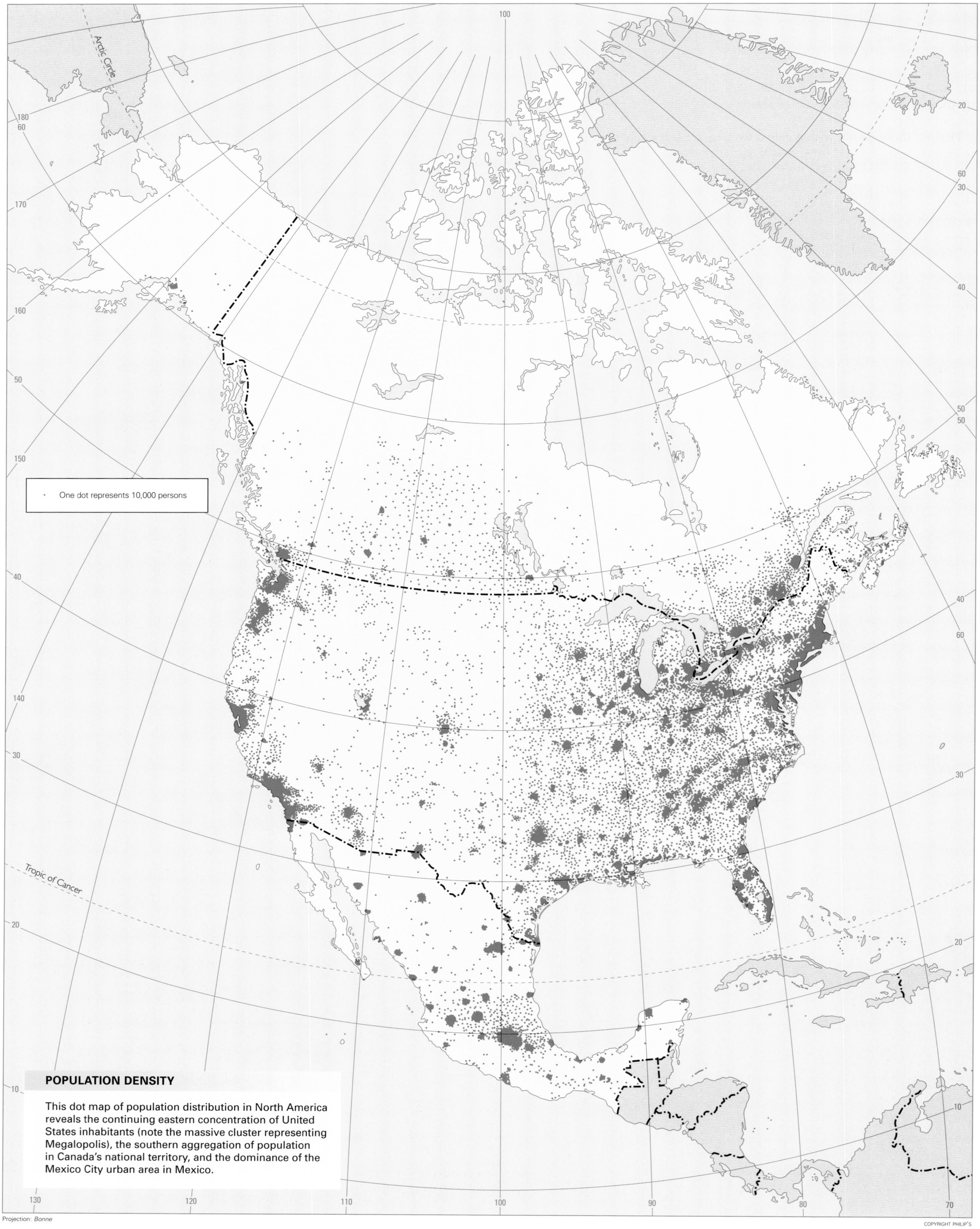

POPULATION DENSITY

This dot map of population distribution in North America reveals the continuing eastern concentration of United States inhabitants (note the massive cluster representing Megalopolis), the southern aggregation of population in Canada's national territory, and the dominance of the Mexico City urban area in Mexico.

WOMEN IN THE U.S.

American women made remarkable progress during the 20th century but face daunting challenges in the quest for genuine equality of opportunity. They achieved breakthroughs in occupations such as law and medicine that were once the exclusive domain of men, and several female superstars now lead "Fortune 500" corporations.

Despite these highly visible gains, women are less likely than men to hold a bachelor's degree and more likely to live in households below the poverty level. Most are concentrated in low-wage, female-dominated occupations such as secretary, waitress, teacher, and childcare provider. Women in North America continue to constitute comparatively small minorities on university faculties and in professional associations, and they are far from achieving parity in local or national political arenas.

NORTH AMERICA: LIFE EXPECTANCY

North American women live longer and healthier lives than they did 100 years ago. At the dawn of the 20th century, the life expectancy of the typical Mexican woman was little more than 30 years, while the average Canadian and U.S. woman lived only into her late forties.

Major causes of death were influenza, typhoid, tuberculosis, cholera, and, of course, childbirth. Year-to-year fluctuations were high, as in the conspicuous trough in 1918 (see center graph at right), marking a major influenza outbreak.

Advances in sanitation as well as medical care, immunization against infectious diseases, and higher standards of living brought consistency to the annual regime and extended life expectancy to today's 82 years in Canada, 80 in the U.S., and 78 in Mexico.

The gender gap – women's advantage over men in life expectancy – has grown from around 2 years in 1900 to between 5 and 6 years today.

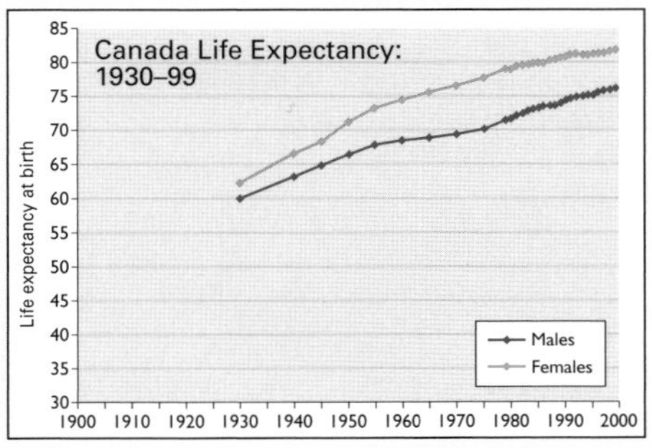

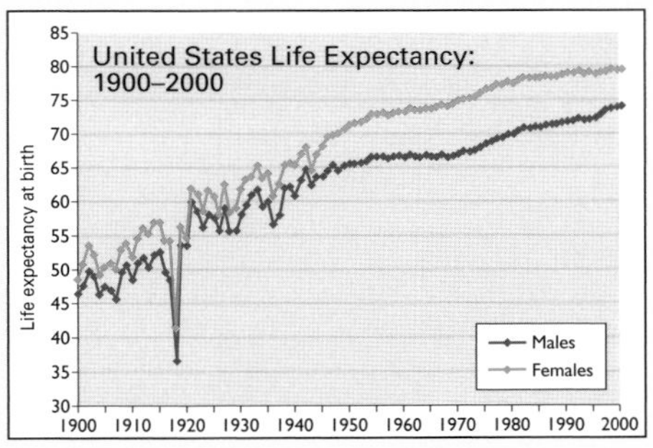

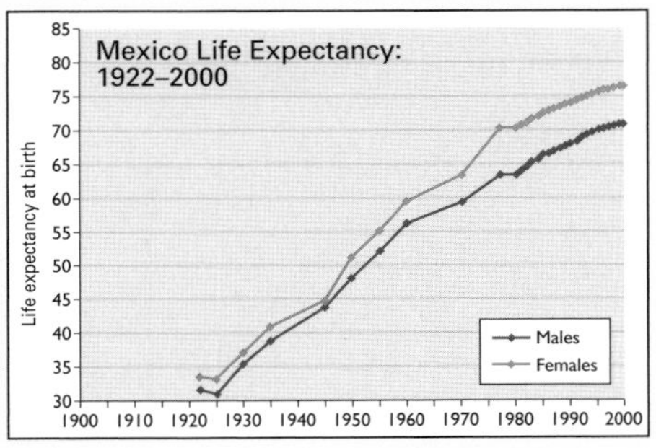

NORTH AMERICA: FERTILITY RATE AND LABOR FORCE

The rising status of women is linked to better control of reproduction and greater economic autonomy. As Mexico modernized and urbanized, its total fertility rate – the number of children that a typical woman has as she passes through her reproductive years – plummeted from almost 7 in 1970 to around 2.5 today. With fewer children, women are far more likely to work outside the home. Mexican women now comprise one-third of the nation's workforce. Female labor force participation in the U.S. rose from just 25 percent immediately after World War II to almost 60 percent today as society's views of acceptable roles for women changed.

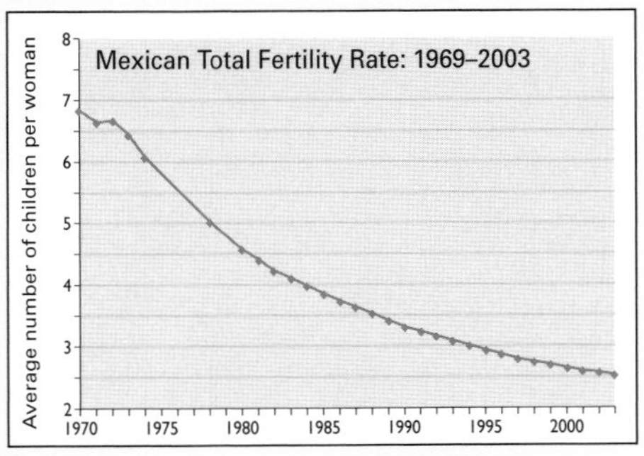

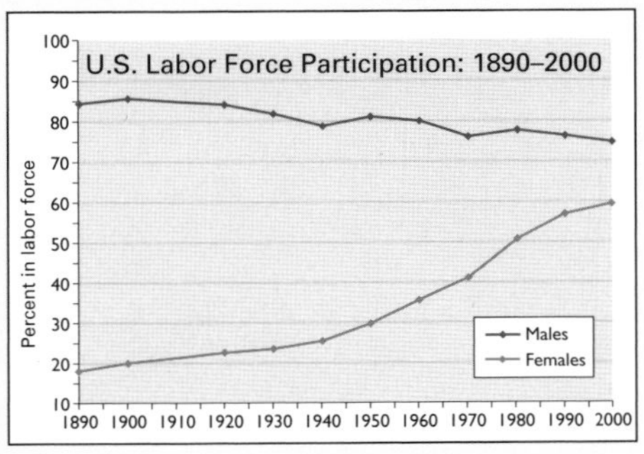

WOMEN IN NORTH AMERICA

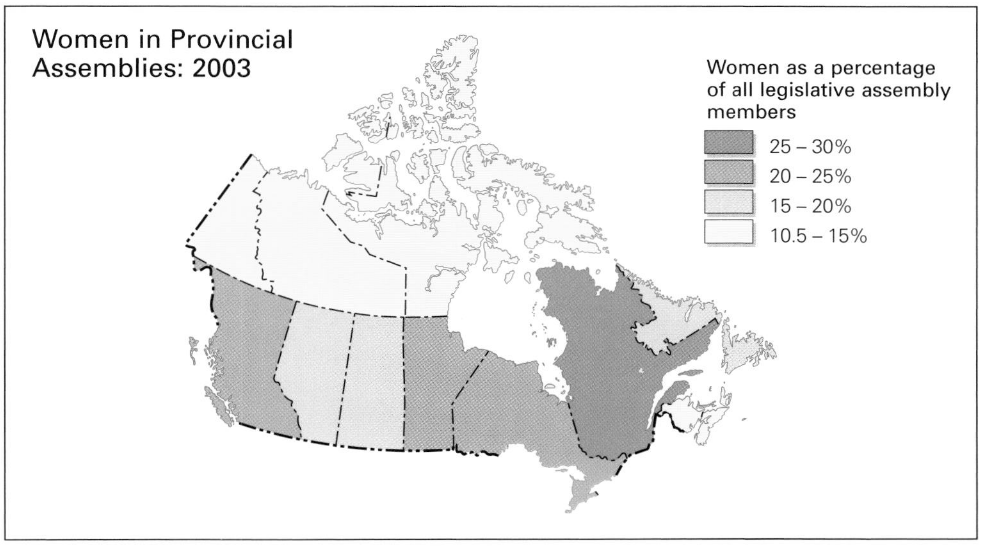

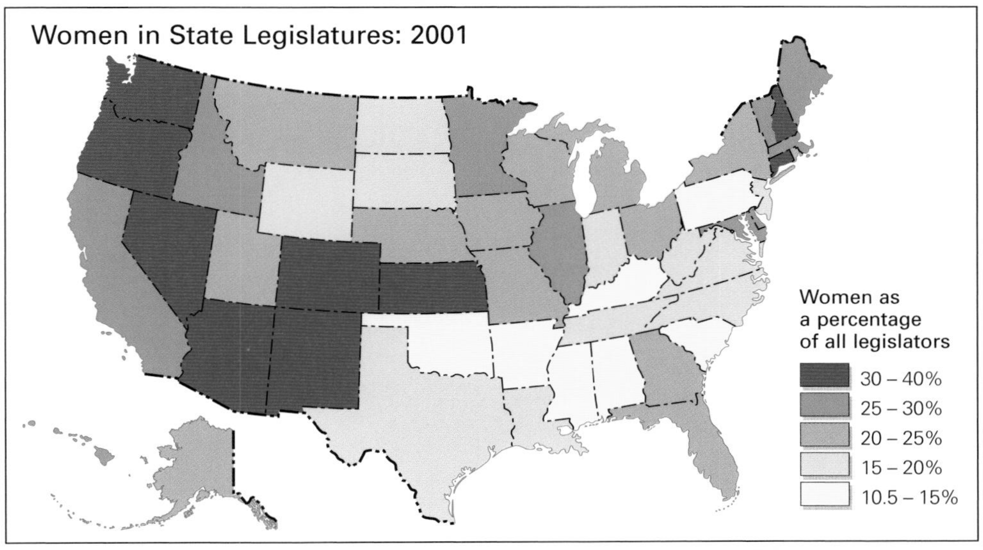

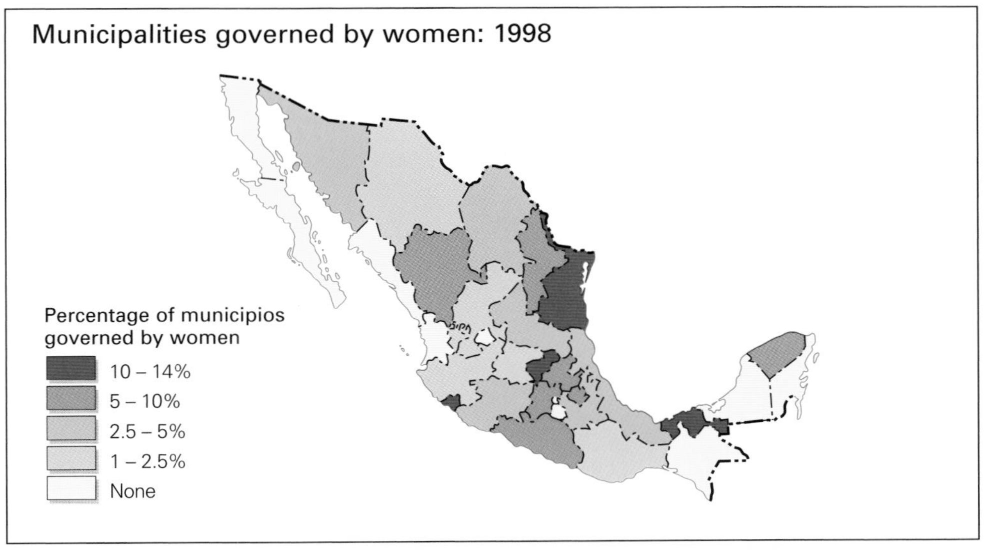

Canada did not enfranchise women until 1918, the United States in 1920, and Mexico in 1953, so that male domination of political institutions and networks, well established and deeply entrenched, will take some considerable time to overcome.

However, sweeping political and social change has opened the political process to the women of North America. Women represent a majority of the electorate, and they are choosing in increasing numbers to orchestrate political events, run campaigns, join movements, and seek elective office.

The year 1992 was dubbed "The Year of the Woman" in the U.S., as a record number of women were elected to Congress. Today, there are 62 women in the U.S. House of Representatives and 14 in the Senate. The Canadian House of Commons has 63 women, and there are 35 in the Senate. Women who achieve national office often cut their teeth by holding office at the regional level.

In the U.S., women have the greatest success in being elected to state legislatures in New England and the West, while in Canada the women of Québec occupy proportionately more legislative positions than those in the Yukon, Northwest Territories, or Nunavut.

During the past 15 years, Mexico's political process has been opened to groups, including women, who previously had little say in policy-making and the electoral process. Women are especially influential at the local or *municipio* level where their involvement in government is tied to meeting daily needs or by crises in the neighborhood or local community.

Immigration and Population Change

IMMIGRATION

International migration – people moving across national borders – is on the rise due to the globalization of the world economy, growing inequalities between the rich and the poor, continuing demographic pressure in high-growth countries, and widespread civil war and ethnic strife. North America figures prominently in the global migration system because it includes major origin and destination regions for international movements. Mexico sends between 200,000 and 300,000 documented migrants to the United States each year. The U.S. and Canada, which together account for just 5 percent of the world's population, are destinations for one-half of the world's immigrants.

Global migrants do not move randomly around the world but in well-defined streams that connect particular origins and destinations. Immigrants rely on friends and relatives from their native countries for information about potential destinations and help in finding jobs and places to live. Living together in an ethnic enclave allows immigrants to speak a familiar language, enjoy native foods, join social clubs, and find work in immigrant-owned businesses. Low-skilled migrants are especially dependent upon family members to provide help in finding work and establishing a new life, and are therefore very likely to concentrate near already established immigrants.

Streams of international migrants to the U.S. and Canada are strongly focused on large gateway cities and metropolitan regions. Almost 95 percent of new immigrants to the United States settle initially in one of the nation's metropolitan regions. Cities and suburbs of Southern California and the New York City area capture nearly one-quarter of new arrivals, followed by the Miami, Chicago, and Washington, DC areas. The tendency for immigrants to concentrate in large urban regions is even more prevalent in Canada as one-half of all international migrants settle in the Toronto area, 14 percent in the vicinity of Montreal, and 13 percent in Vancouver. The channelized nature of international migration streams accounts for the fact that different source areas contribute migrants to cities across the continent, creating unique blends of culture, religion, language, architecture, and cuisine.

Annual Immigration to the U.S. and Canada: 1820–2002

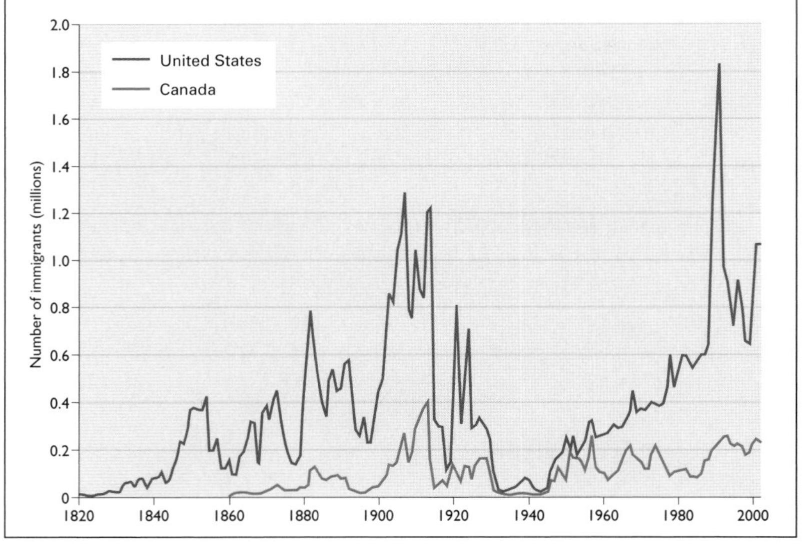

There is precedent for the current influx of immigrants to North America from across the world. Large numbers of Europeans entered the U.S. and Canada during the late-19th and early 20th centuries. Immigration was severely restricted by government policy after World War I, and during the Great Depression of the 1930s few Europeans wanted to immigrate.

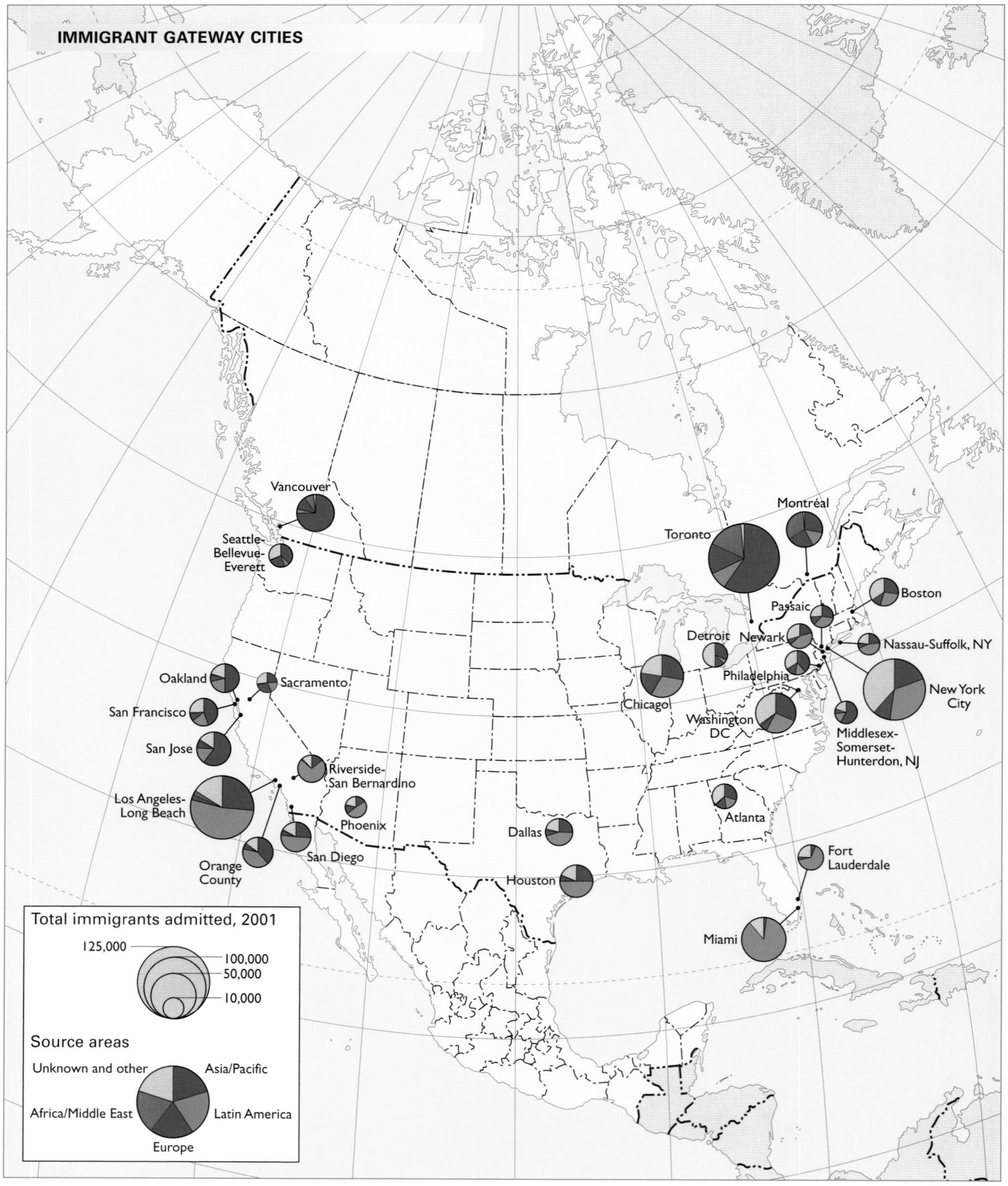

MEXICO POPULATION

Mexican migration to the United States began in earnest with the recruitment of rural workers for farm work to replace American men drafted into World Wars I and II. Migration continued as employers came to depend upon cheap Mexican labor and Mexicans came to depend upon income earned in the U.S. Liberalization of U.S. immigration policy in the mid 1960s accelerated northward migration. Americans are now moving southward, albeit in much smaller numbers, as retirees settle in amenity-rich communities along the Pacific coast and the Lake Chapala Riviera located in the state of Jalisco.

Mexican-origin population in the U.S.: 1900–2002

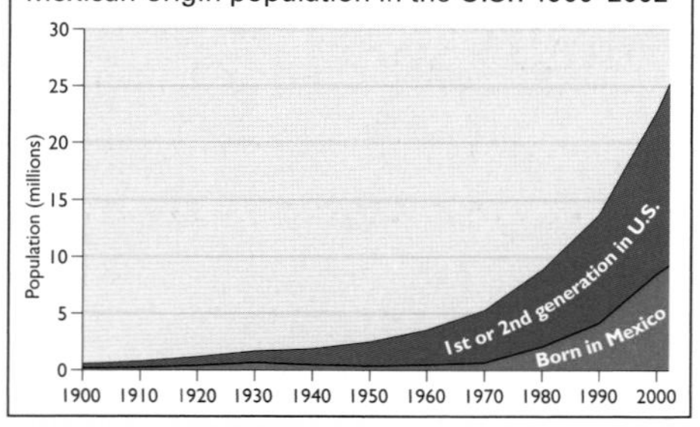

Foreign-born population in Mexico: 2000

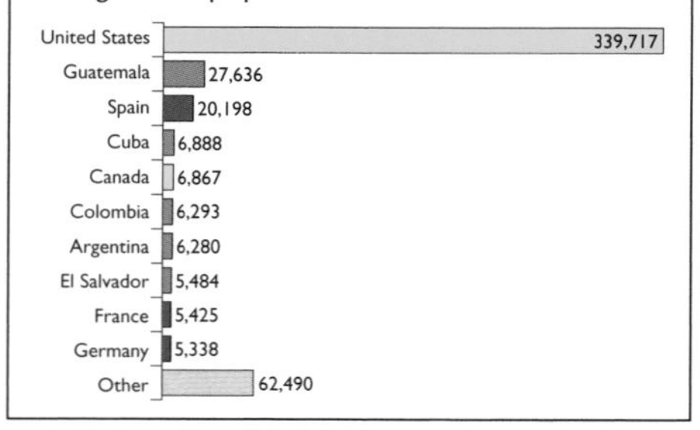

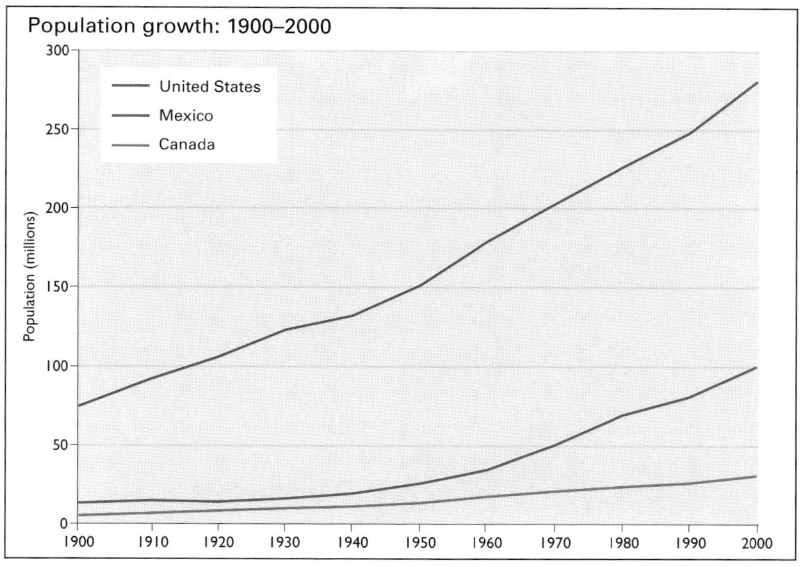

Just a century ago, the combined population of the United States, Mexico, and Canada was about 100 million. Today that total exceeds 425 million. The U.S. population approaches 300 million; Mexico's tops 100 million, and Canada has more than 30 million inhabitants. Population projections suggest that, by 2025, the U.S. population will near 350 million, Mexico's will surpass 130 million, and Canada's will reach 36 million.

POPULATION CHANGE

The populations of the three largest North American countries continue to grow, albeit at different rates and for different reasons. In 2004, Mexico's annual rate of natural increase was by far the highest, 2.1 percent, substantially higher than the world average (1.2 percent). This demographic picture is reflected by the country's age-distribution pyramid (*below*), with the numbers of youngsters in the population far exceeding those in the older categories. At present, Mexico's population is doubling in only 33 years. Canada, by contrast, is growing at a rate of only 0.4 percent, with a doubling time of 175 years.

As the population pyramids of Canada and the United States indicate, older people make up a far larger percentage of the population than is the case in Mexico. The U.S. and Canadian pyramids also evince the longer life expectancy of women in these maturing populations.

While Mexico's rate of natural increase fairly accurately reflects the overall growth rate of the population, the United States and to a lesser degree Canada are growing faster than the figures suggest because of immigration. In the case of the United States, documented and undocumented immigration combined may be boosting the overall growth rate to above 1.0 percent.

Long-term population gains and losses in North America result from economic, environmental, and social conditions. Hardships in the heartland, the Canadian Maritimes, the U.S. Northeast, and rural Mexico are driving people to the cities. The southward and westward "sunbelt" migration continues. And Nevada is gaining so fast because life in California, for many, is not what it used to be.

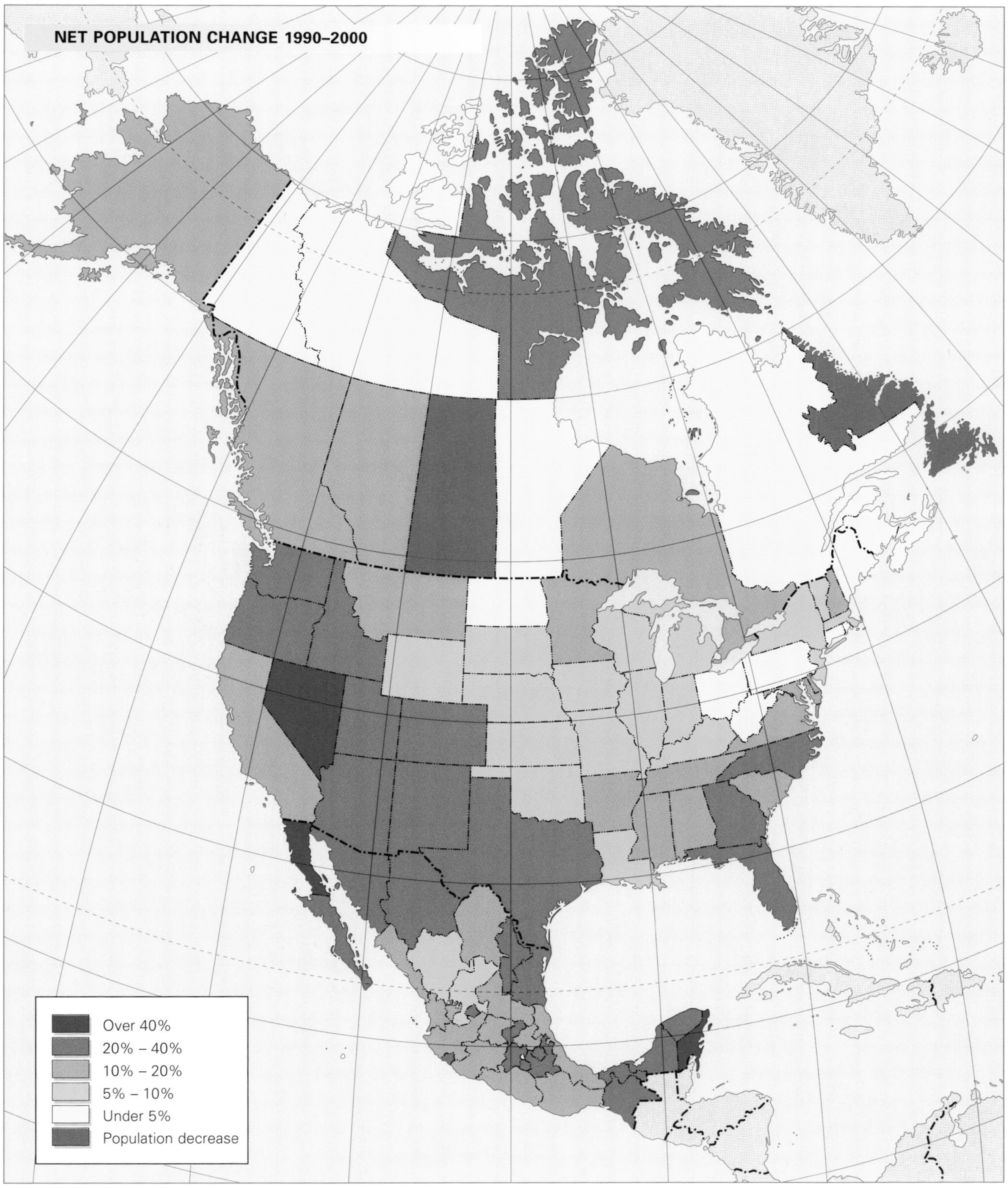

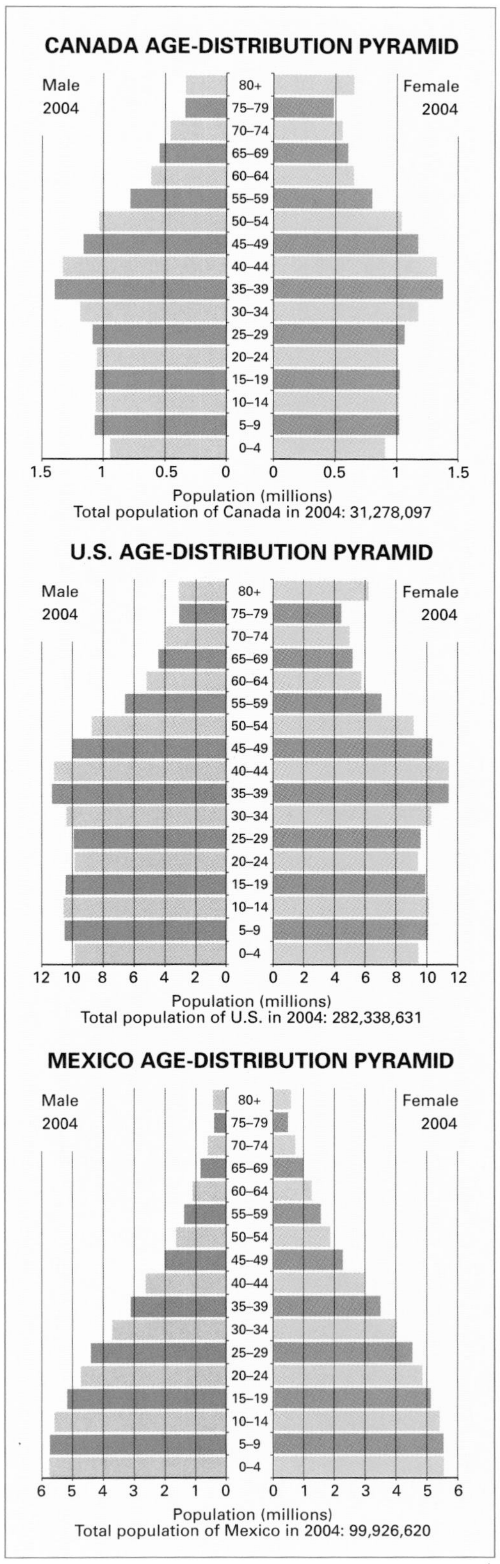

URBANIZATION

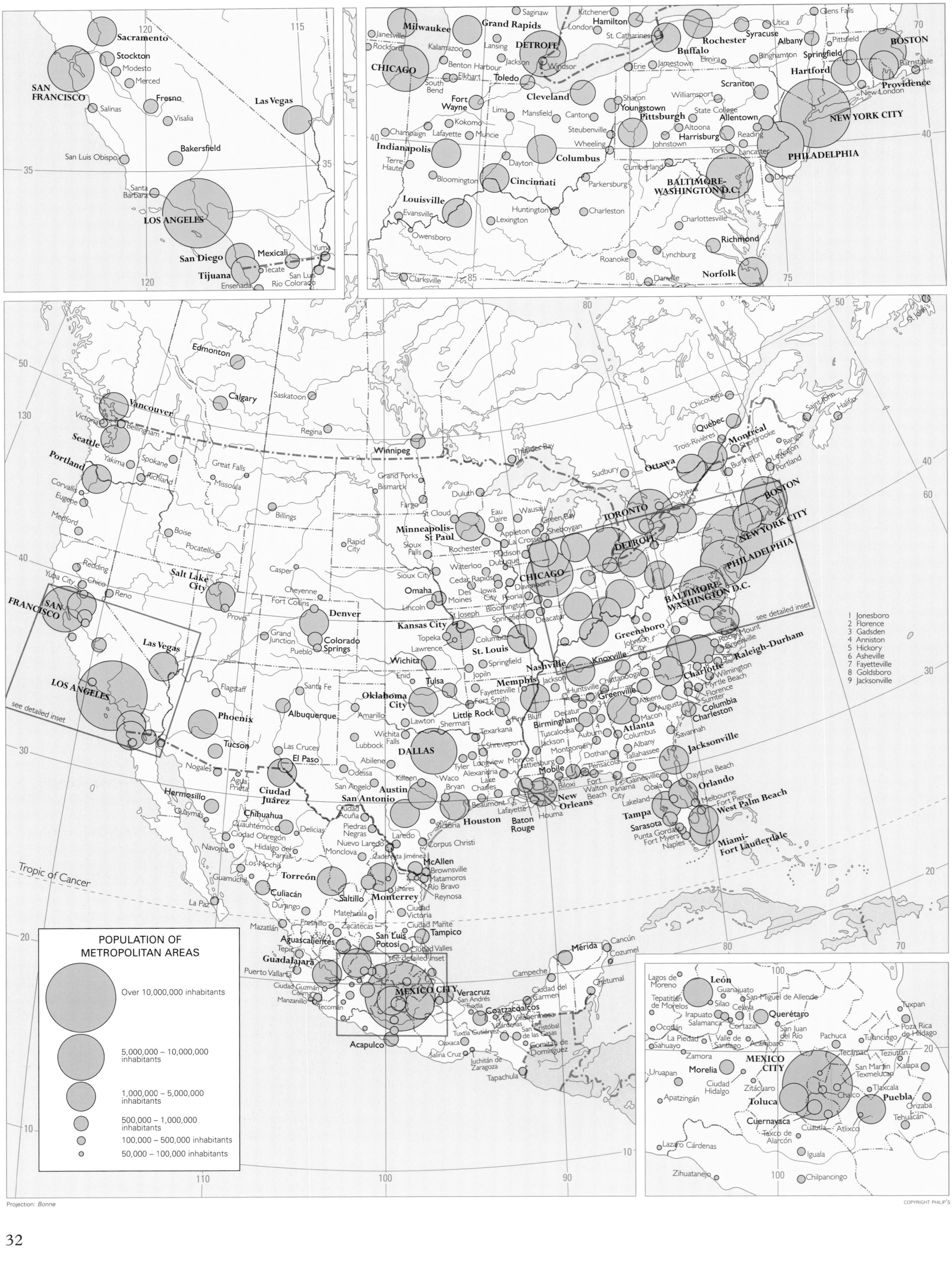

Projection: *Bonne*

MEGALOPOLIS

The United States is an urbanized society: more than 75 percent of its inhabitants live in cities and towns, and migration to the metropolitan areas continues. These two maps illustrate the consequences. On the Atlantic seaboard, metropolitan areas have grown so large that they have coalesced, creating a nearly continuous urbanized area from Boston, Massachusetts in the north to Richmond and Norfolk, Virginia in the south. The famed geographer Jean Gottmann was the first to call this vast built-up corridor *megalopolis*, and later the prefix *Bosnywash* was attached to it for Boston-New York-Washington, three of the region's largest urban complexes.

The megalopolis phenomenon is not unique to the northeastern United States, nor to North America: other highly urbanized regions of the world are experiencing the same process, including Western Europe, Japan, and Pacific-Rim China. In North America, megalopolitan development is taking place in the Midwest from Chicago to Pittsburgh, in Canada along "Main Street" from Windsor to Québec, in California from San Francisco to San Diego, in the Northwest from Vancouver to Portland anchored by Seattle, in Florida from Miami to Orlando, and in Mexico around the capital, Mexico City, which now lies at the heart of a fast-growing megalopolis.

In addition, secondary megalopolitan coalescence is taking place in such areas as the Colorado Piedmont. This map illustrates the progress of the urbanizing Rocky Mountain front around Denver and several smaller nearby cities and towns over the past half-century. Already, Boulder is part of the Denver metropolitan area, and Denver expands southward even as Colorado Springs grows northward.

BOSNYWASH MEGALOPOLIS

1 : 3 800 000

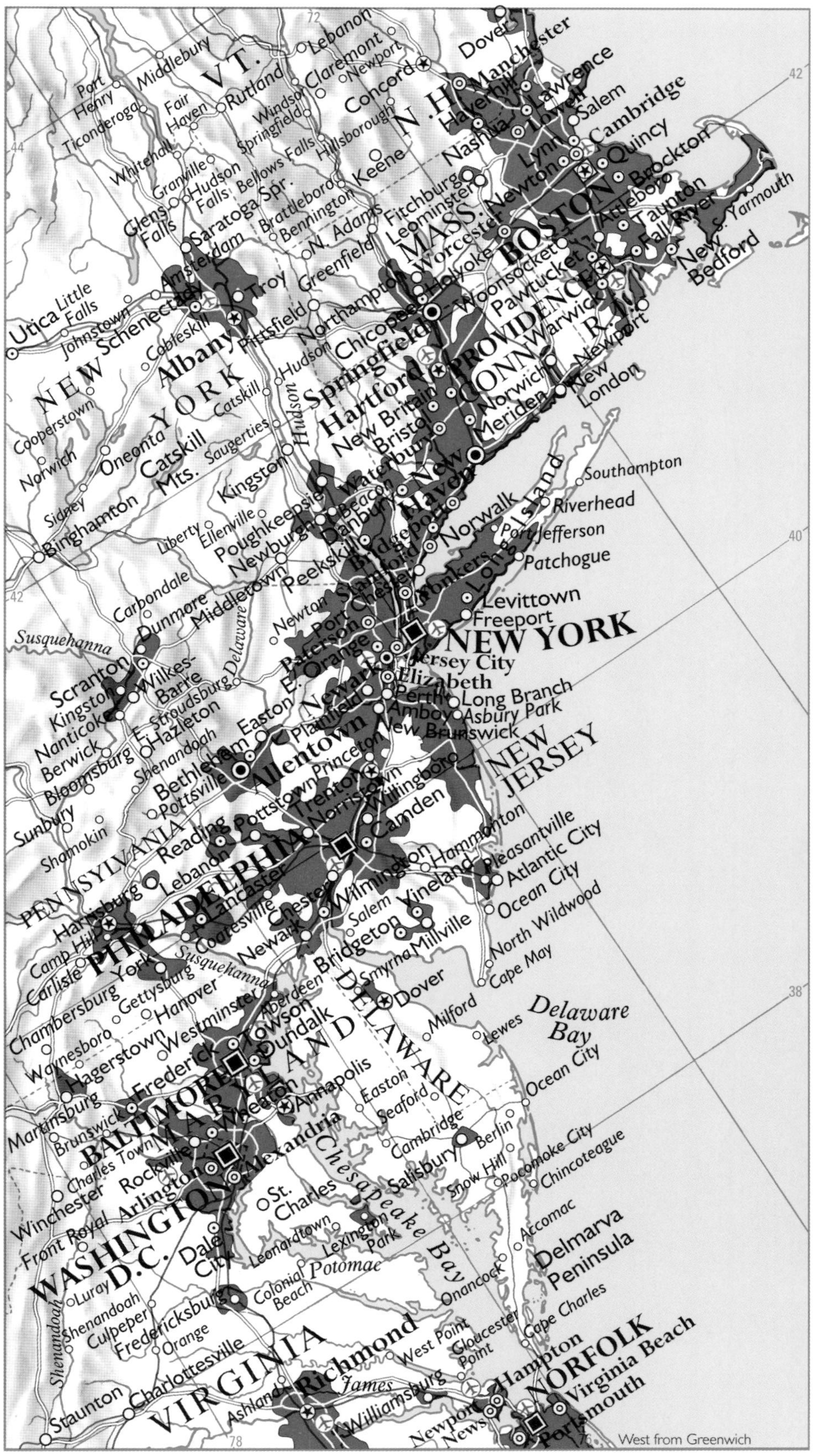

INCIPIENT COLORADO MEGALOPOLIS

1 : 1 333 333

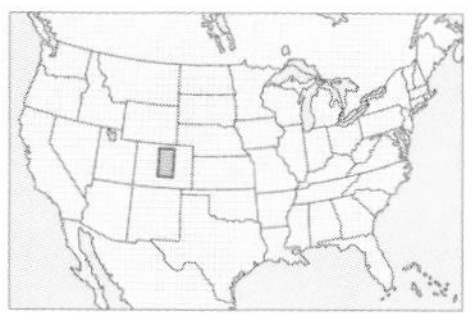

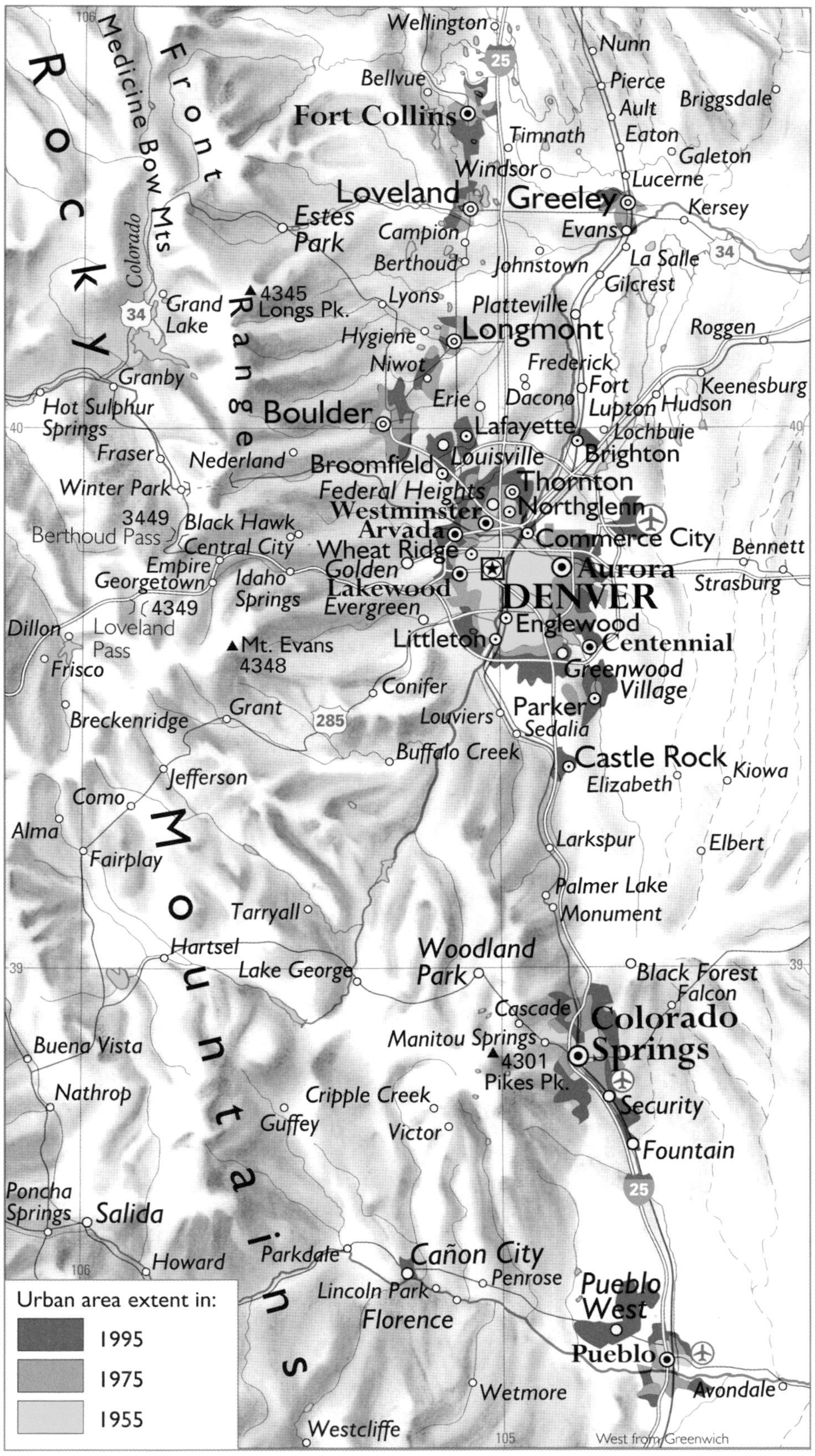

Land Use and Agriculture

LAND USE

Land use in North America shows the most productive arable land, much of it derived from tills deposited during the most recent glaciation, in the U.S. Midwest and Great Plains and extending into Canada. Mixed farmland and pasture lies interspersed with this agricultural heartland. Forests extend from Alaska to Québec, in the higher elevations of the east from Newfoundland to the Appalachians, on large areas of the coastal plain, and in eastern as well as western Mexico. Dry areas of the U.S. West and northern Mexico include some low-productivity pastures.

Total cattle production (2003), North America: 140,250,000 head

CATTLE

◀ The largest herds of beef cattle in the United States and Canada are on the pastures of the Great Plains from Texas to Alberta east of the Rocky Mountains; dairy cattle are raised near Canada's eastern cities, in Wisconsin and in the U.S. East from Virginia and Kentucky to Florida. Mexico's large herds are concentrated in four areas.

CORN

▶ The U.S. Corn Belt is still clearly delimited on this map, but the primacy of corn in this area is declining as soybean production increases. Mexico's comparatively small production comes from states in the center and south of the country, and almost all of Canada's corn is grown in southern Ontario and Québec.

Total corn production (2003), North America: 257,000,000 tons

Total hogs production (2003), North America: 92,250,000 head

HOGS

◀ Factory-farm hog raising marks the large principal production zone in the U.S. Midwest, but North Carolina has become a major producer. Mexico's main production areas are along the northwest and southeast coasts and west of the capital. Canada's production is scattered.

SOYBEANS

▶ Almost all soybean production in North America comes from a U.S. area larger than the Corn Belt and extending from the Canadian border to southern Louisiana. Soybean production has increased significantly over the past two decades.

Total soybeans production (2003), North America: 77,250,000 tons

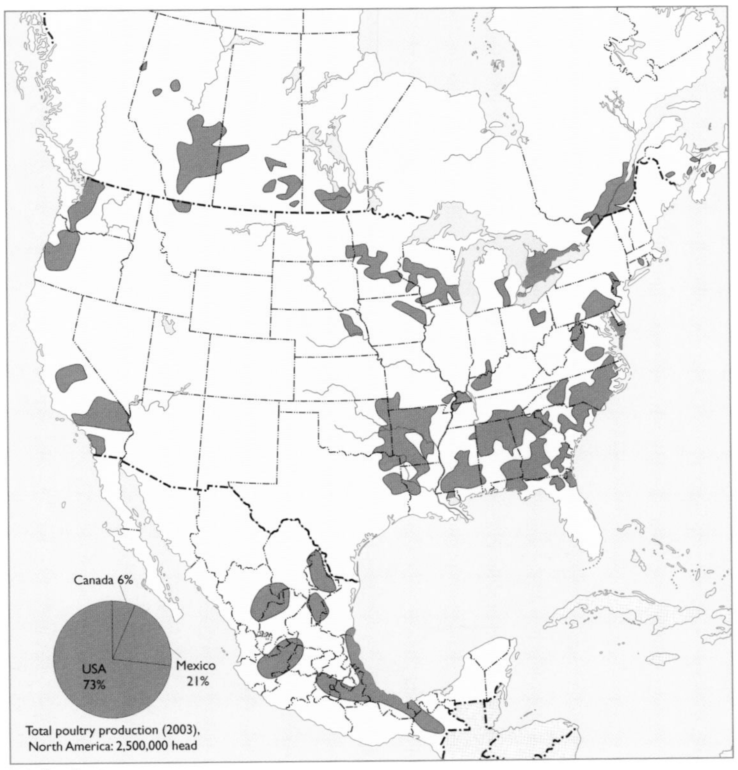

Total poultry production (2003), North America: 2,500,000 head

POULTRY

◀ North Americans have a huge appetite for poultry, supporting a large fast-food industry in which chicken is a staple. Production in all three countries is scattered widely though U.S. production is concentrated in a zone from southern Pennsylvania to eastern Texas.

WHEAT

▶ The U.S. and Canada are two of the world's largest wheat producers. The spring wheat belt extends from Canada to Montana and the Dakotas; the winter wheat belt centers on Kansas. Mexico's relatively small production comes from Michoacan and coastal Sonora and Sinaloa.

Total wheat production (2003), North America: 63,500,000 tons

Projection: *Bonne*

United States: Manufacturing Industries

THE CHANGING MAP OF INDUSTRY

The geography of North America's industrial production has long been dominated by a "Manufacturing Belt" whose durability was ensured by proximity to industrial resources, including iron and coal, and by its easy access to the continent's largest and richest market. But today the distribution of North American industry is changing as interregional transport methods and costs modulate, market proximity matters less, energy derives increasingly from oil and gas, high-technology manufacturing depends less on low-skill labor, and foreign competition forces business decisions that close plants and relocate production facilities. In the process, venerable operations such as the steel industry suffer from obsolescence and contraction. Parts of the old Manufacturing Belt became a Rust Belt.

But, as this series of maps focusing on the United States experience illustrate, a new industrial era has dawned, sometimes referred to as the "Post-industrial Revolution." High-technology, white-collar, office-based activities lead this postindustrial economy, whose geographic imprint is dispersed, not clustered as was the case in the days when heavy manufacturing anchored the industrial map. Climatic amenities have also played a role, and the Sunbelt continues to attract industrial growth.

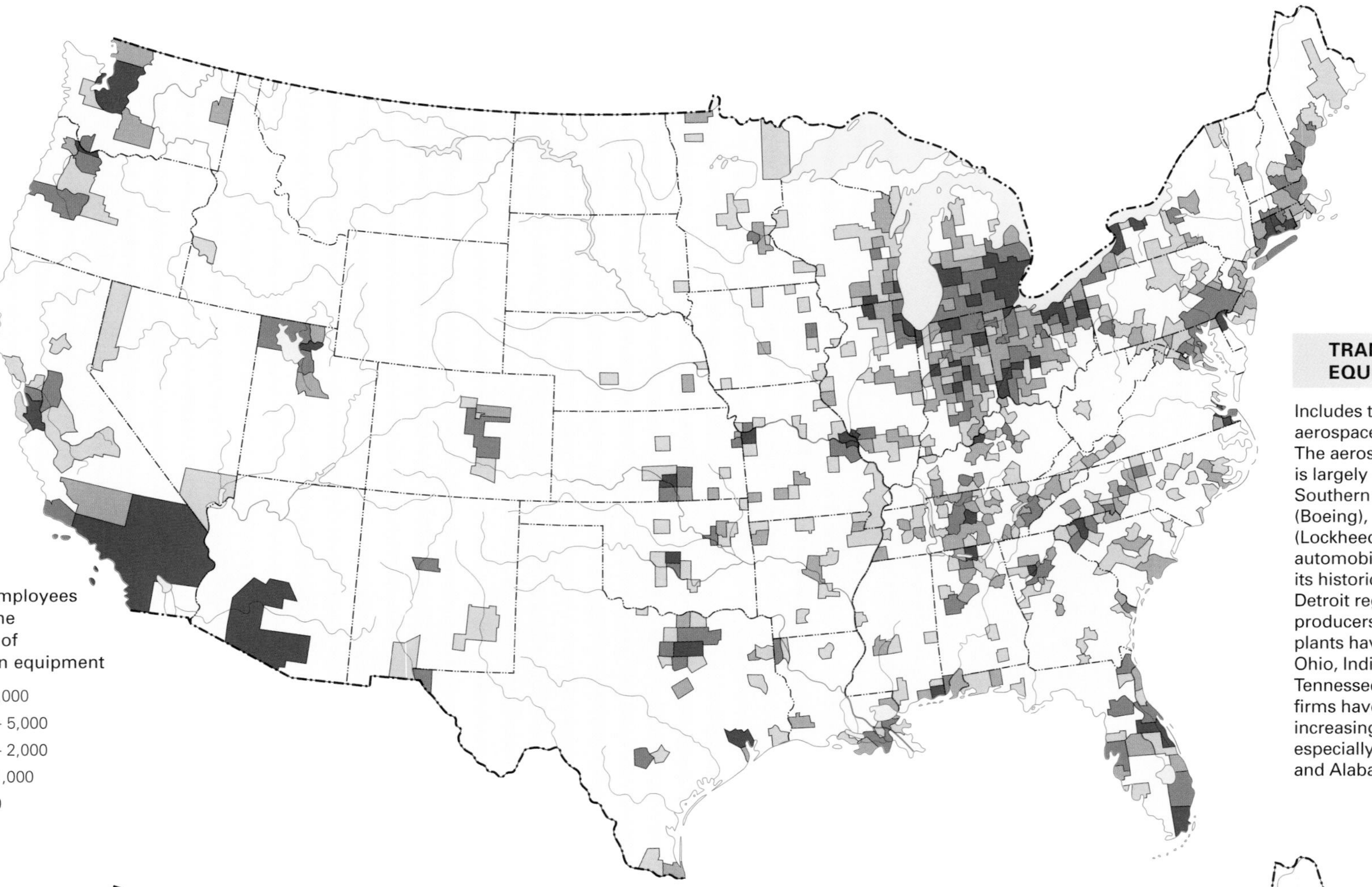

Number of employees engaged in the manufacture of transportation equipment

- Over 5,000
- 2,000 – 5,000
- 1,000 – 2,000
- 500 – 1,000
- 0 – 500

TRANSPORTATION EQUIPMENT

Includes two vital sectors, aerospace and automobiles. The aerospace industry is largely concentrated in Southern California, Seattle (Boeing), and Missouri (Lockheed-Martin). The automobile industry retains its historical focus in the Detroit region, although parts producers and assembly plants have diffused into Ohio, Indiana, Kentucky, and Tennessee. Foreign-owned firms have become increasingly important, especially in South Carolina and Alabama.

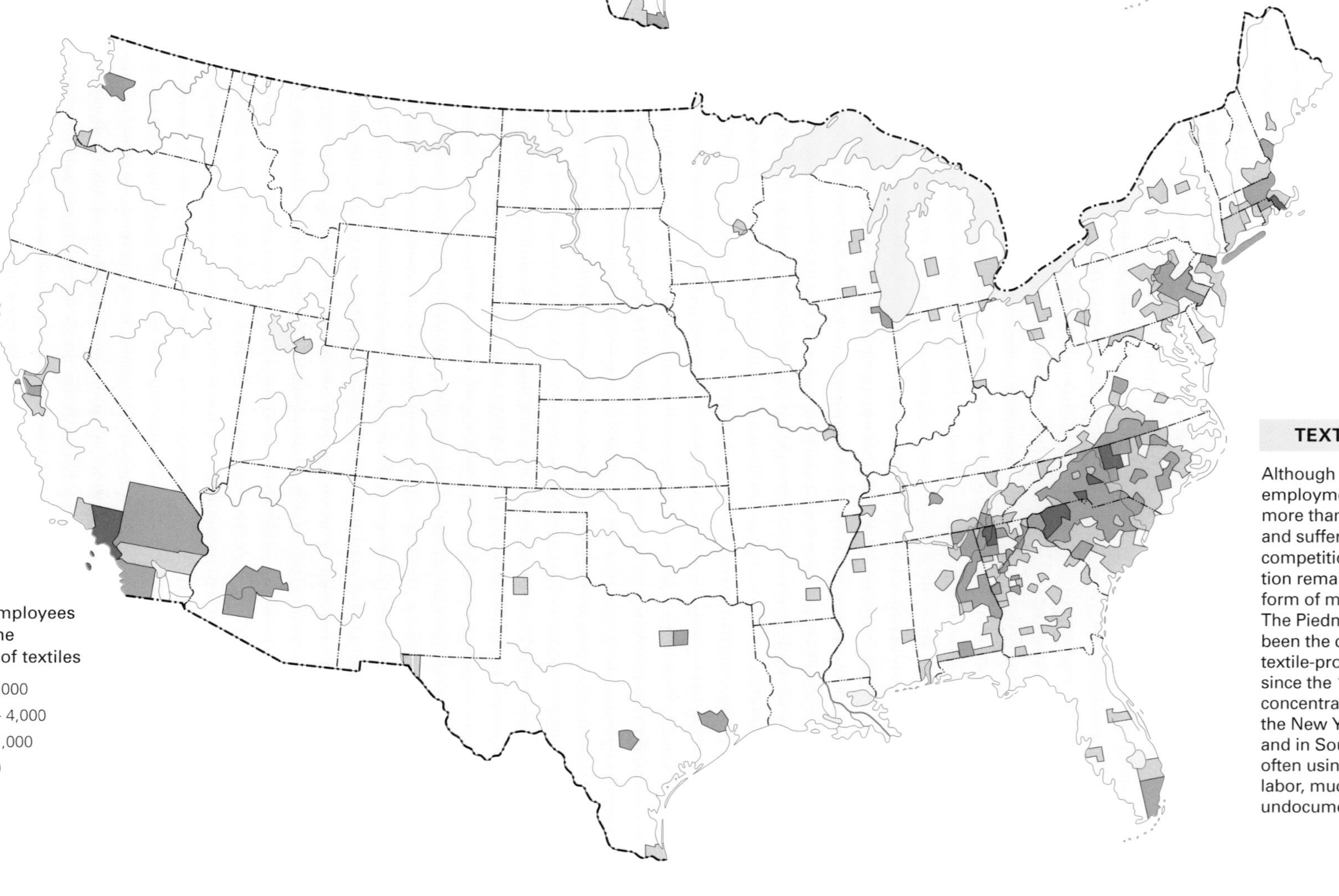

Number of employees engaged in the manufacture of textiles

- Over 4,000
- 1,000 – 4,000
- 350 – 1,000
- 0 – 350

TEXTILES

Although it has experienced employment decline for more than four decades and suffers from foreign competition, textile production remains an important form of manufacturing. The Piedmont South has been the country's major textile-producing region since the 1920s. Secondary concentrations remain in the New York-Northeast area and in Southern California, often using immigrant labor, much of which is undocumented.

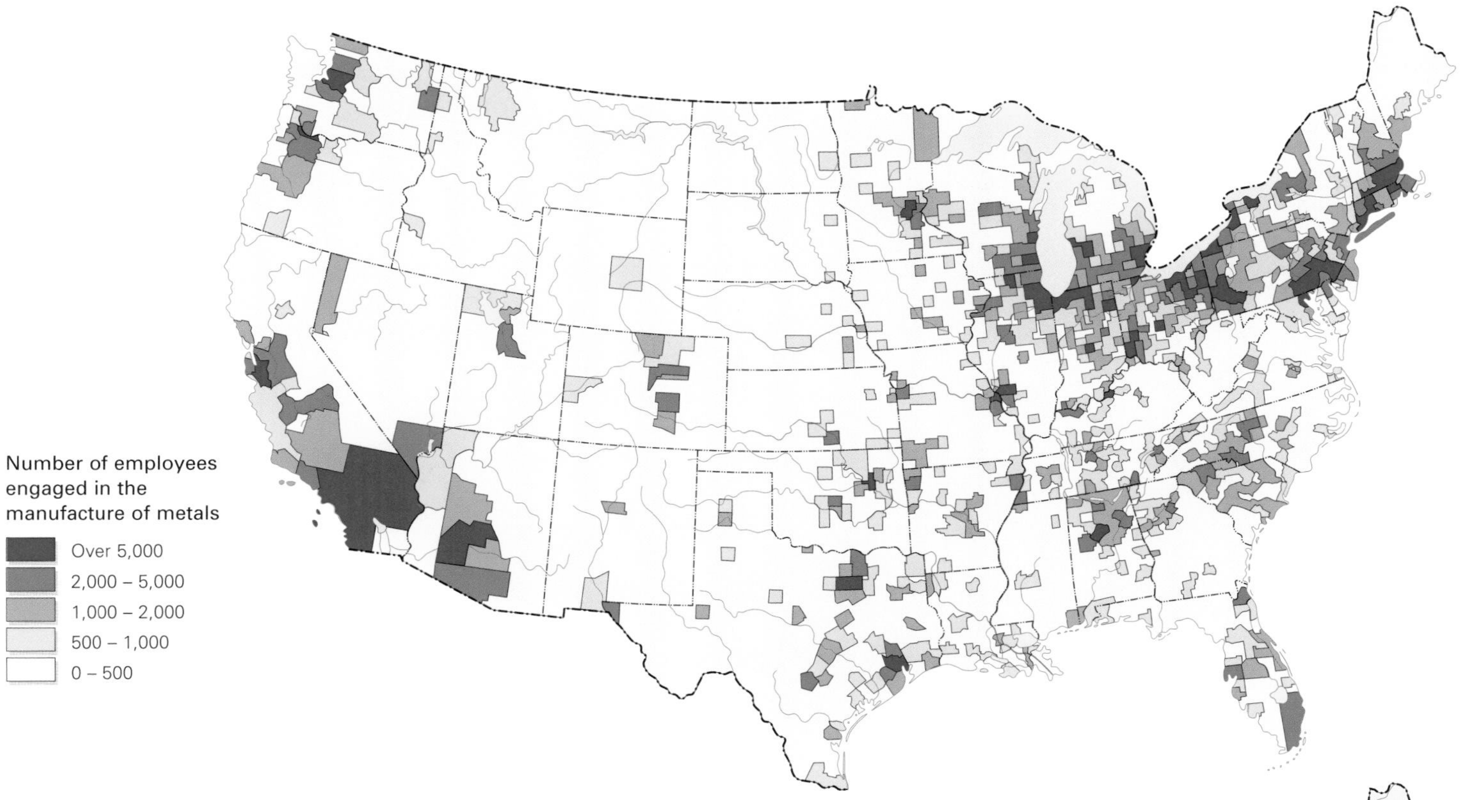

METALS

The metallurgical industries, including iron and steel, copper and nickel, are vital to numerous manufactured products including machine tools, construction equipment, aircraft, automobiles, household appliances, and many other domestic goods. The three largest concentrations of this sector are the Chicago-Gary (Indiana) metropolitan region, Eastern and Western Pennsylvania, and Southern California, but these industries are locally dispersed.

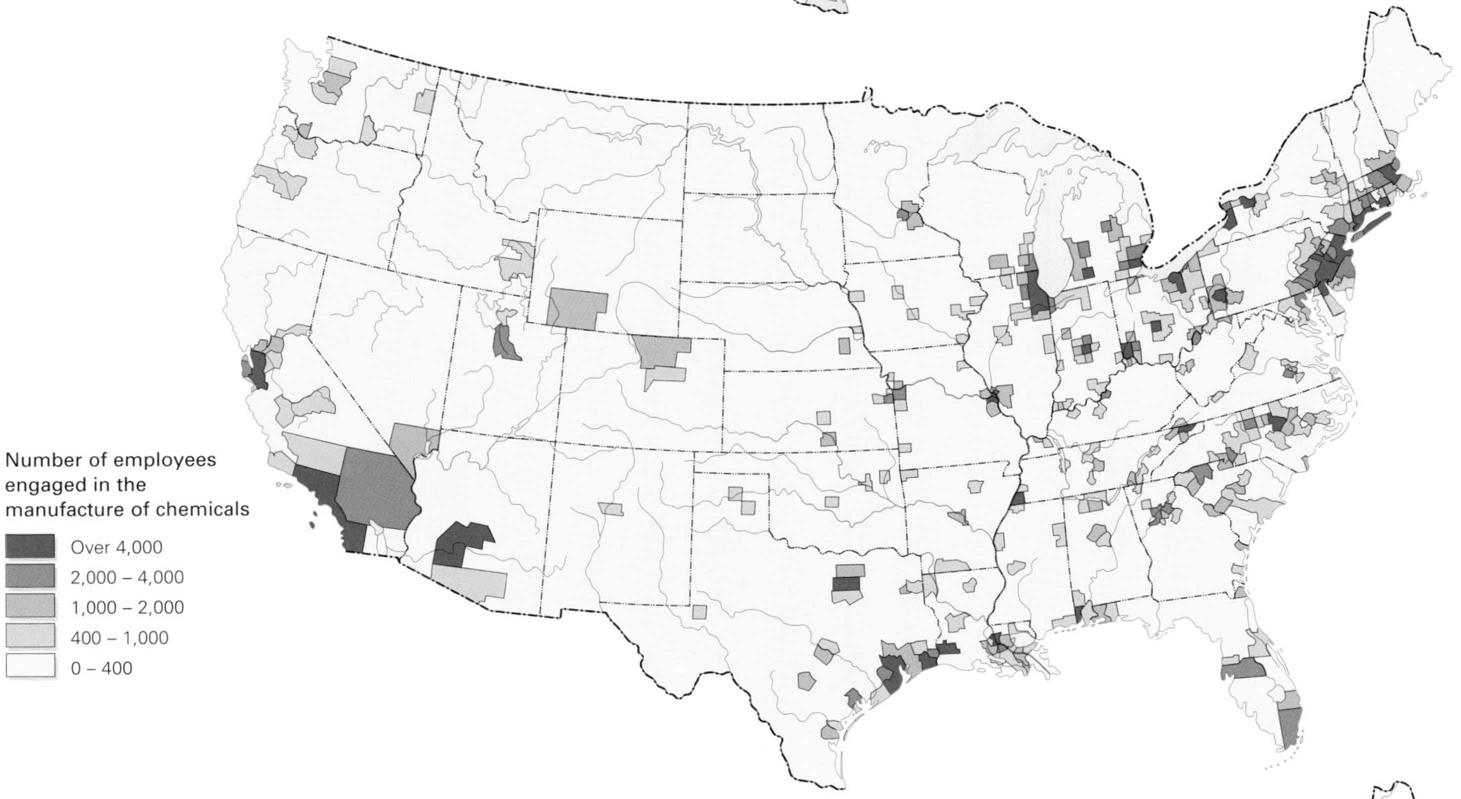

CHEMICALS

The chemical industry is closely associated with petrochemicals and related products, which explains its concentration in four regions of the country: the Texas Gulf Coast centered on Houston, the New York-New Jersey area, the Chicago-Gary area, and Southern California. The industry is widely dispersed, with additional employment concentrations in central Megalopolis, Ohio, and Michigan.

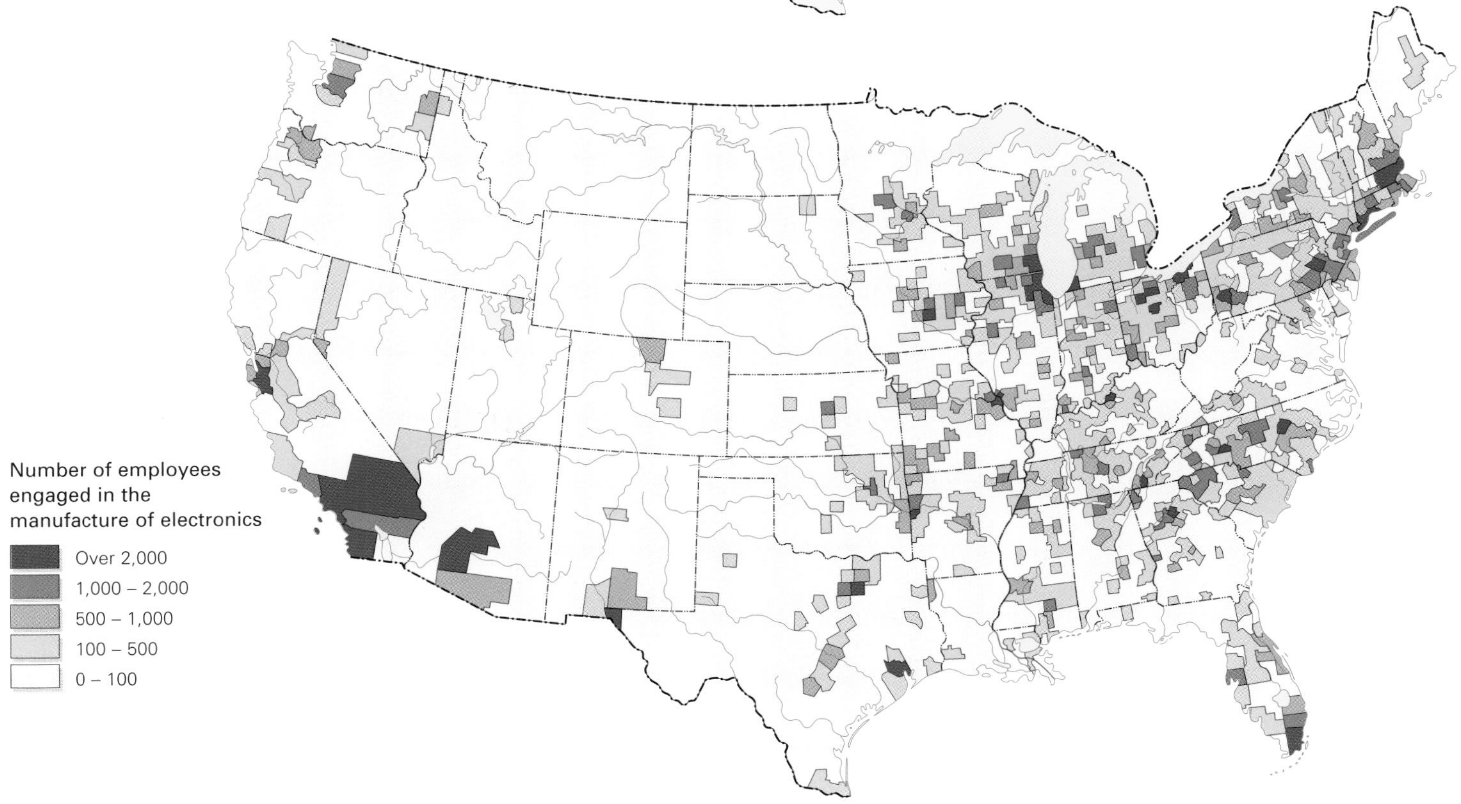

ELECTRONICS

The electronics industry includes diverse functions demanding various labor skills ranging from the assembly of radios and televisions to the design of new computers. This map reveals the concentration of firms in a few major regions including metropolitan Boston, Chicagoland, North Carolina's Research Triangle, Northern California's Silicon Valley, central Arizona, and Southern California, where electronics firms are oriented toward the aerospace industry.

UNITED STATES: SERVICE INDUSTRIES

SERVICE INDUSTRIES

Economic activity is often grouped into four categories, of which the primary (extractive) and secondary (manufacturing) have been mapped in earlier parts of this thematic section.

The tertiary and quaternary activities form the subject of pages 38 and 39. These are the hallmark activities of the postindustrial era: the service industries, representing a large array of functions ranging from retailing and finance to education and administration, and the information industries, which collect, process, manipulate, and disseminate knowledge.

Over the past 200 years, each of these activities has successively dominated U.S. and Canadian economic geography. Agriculture and mining, then manufacturing, then services, and now the quaternary (information) industries, still rising, have been the leading employers of North American labor.

Today in the United States, 2 percent of workers are in agriculture, 15 percent in manufacturing, 18 percent in services, and 65 percent in information industries. The maps on these pages illustrate the spatial aspects of contemporary tertiary and quaternary industries.

FINANCIAL

Commercial and investment banks, savings and loan organizations, insurance, and real estate comprise this sector. Commercial banks, many of them small, are now widely dispersed across the country. The New York area remains the center of this industry, although the Los Angeles area is becoming increasingly important. Deregulation of the industry has boosted other centers, notably Charlotte, NC, and Miami, FL.

LEGAL SERVICES

Organizations such as law firms and other law-related organizations employ large numbers of workers in the United States. Large law firms, often global corporations, tend to be based in major urban areas, although most other firms today are quite widely dispersed. The main concentrations remain in the metropolitan regions of New York, Washington, DC, Chicago, and Los Angeles.

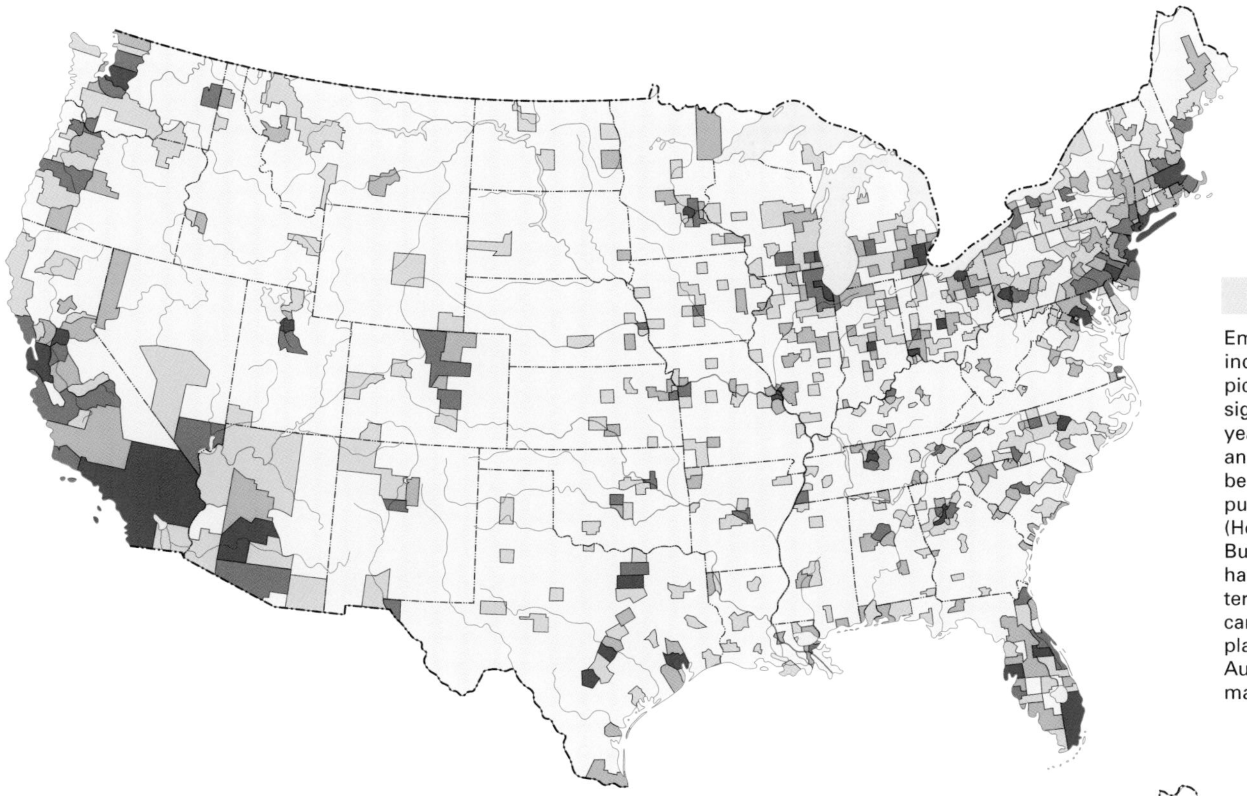

Number of employees engaged in publishing and motion pictures

- Over 4,000
- 1,500 – 4,000
- 500 – 1,500
- 200 – 500
- 0 – 200

PUBLISHING

Employment in the publishing industries (including motion pictures) has changed significantly over the past 25 years. New York (Manhattan) and San Francisco used to be the undisputed leaders in publishing, and Los Angeles (Hollywood) in motion pictures. But major publishing houses have abandoned their long-term metropolitan bases and can now be found in such places as Orlando, FL, and Austin, TX, while movie-making, too, has dispersed.

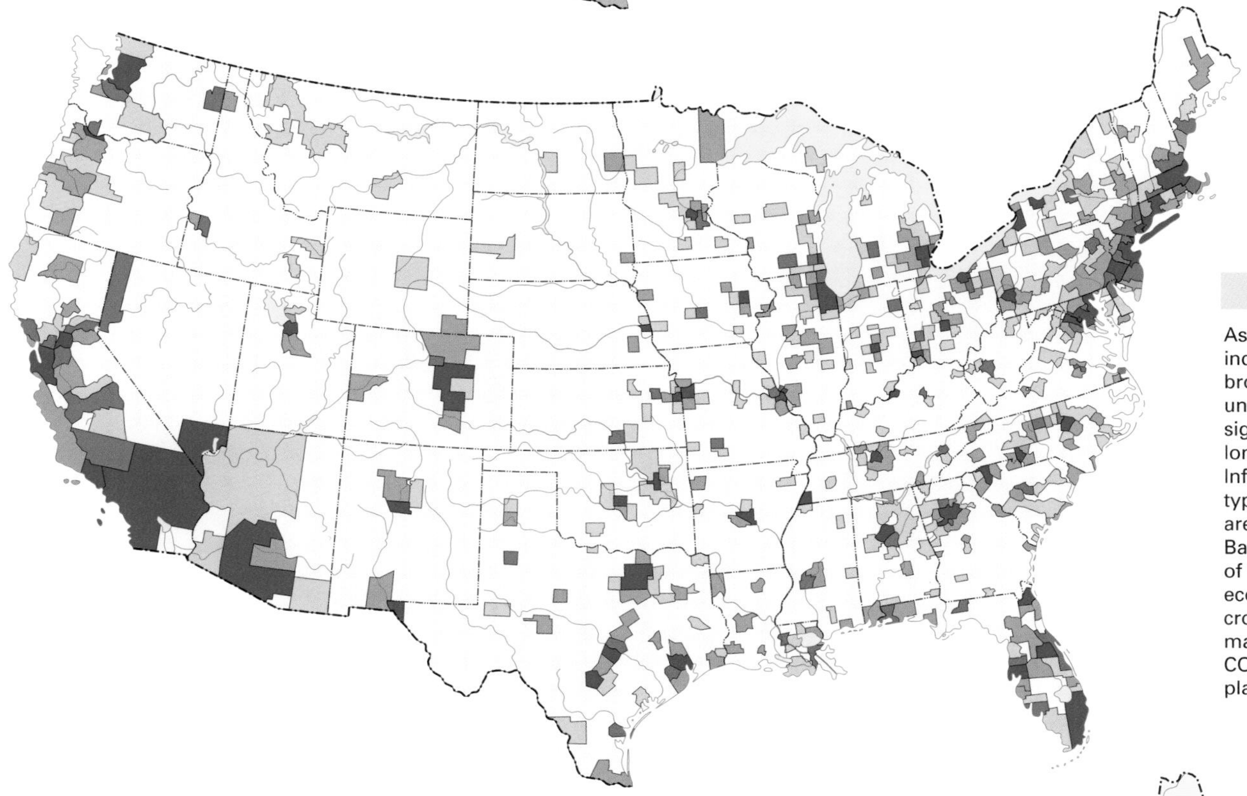

Number of employees engaged in broadcasting and telecommunications

- Over 4,000
- 2,000 – 4,000
- 700 – 2,000
- 300 – 700
- 0 – 300

MEDIA

As the map suggests, this industry, representing broadcasting and telecommunications, has also seen significant dispersal from long-term metropolitan bases. Information-intensive industries typically locate in large urban areas such as San Francisco's Bay Area and the megalopolis of the Eastern seaboard, but economic attractions of less crowded, smaller towns have made such places as Boulder, CO, and Columbus, OH, major players in this field.

Corporations

The circle size shows the number of employees working at the corporate headquarters of publicly quoted companies situated within the top 50 metropolitan areas

- Over 100
- 50 – 100
- 25 – 50
- 10 – 25
- 1 – 10

CORPORATIONS

Corporate headquarters, the decision-making centers of large, often global firms, play vital roles in administration and management, finance, research and development, marketing, labor negotiations, and legal mediation. Typically such institutions locate in large metropolitan areas, benefiting from the agglomeration of available services there. But the long-term leader, New York City, has lost much of its primacy as corporate headquarters have moved to other cities in the nation's urban system.

Trade and Telecommunications

IMPORTS AND EXPORTS

Proximity remains a powerful factor in trade relationships among countries, as these diagrams representing imports and exports of the three major countries of North America suggest. For all three countries, immediate neighbors are the leading sources of imports as well as the top destinations for exports. This is especially true of Canada and Mexico: for both, the U.S. is by far the leading trade partner. Even for the United States, Canada and Mexico rank first and second in terms of exports; Canada still outranks China in terms of imports, with Mexico a close third.

NAFTA (North American Free Trade Agreement), of course, played a major role in strengthening these relationships, and as the pie charts show, transport equipment and machinery form the largest trade category. Among exports-producing states of the U.S., California and Texas lead, followed by three Midwestern states (automobiles), New York State, and Washington State (aircraft).

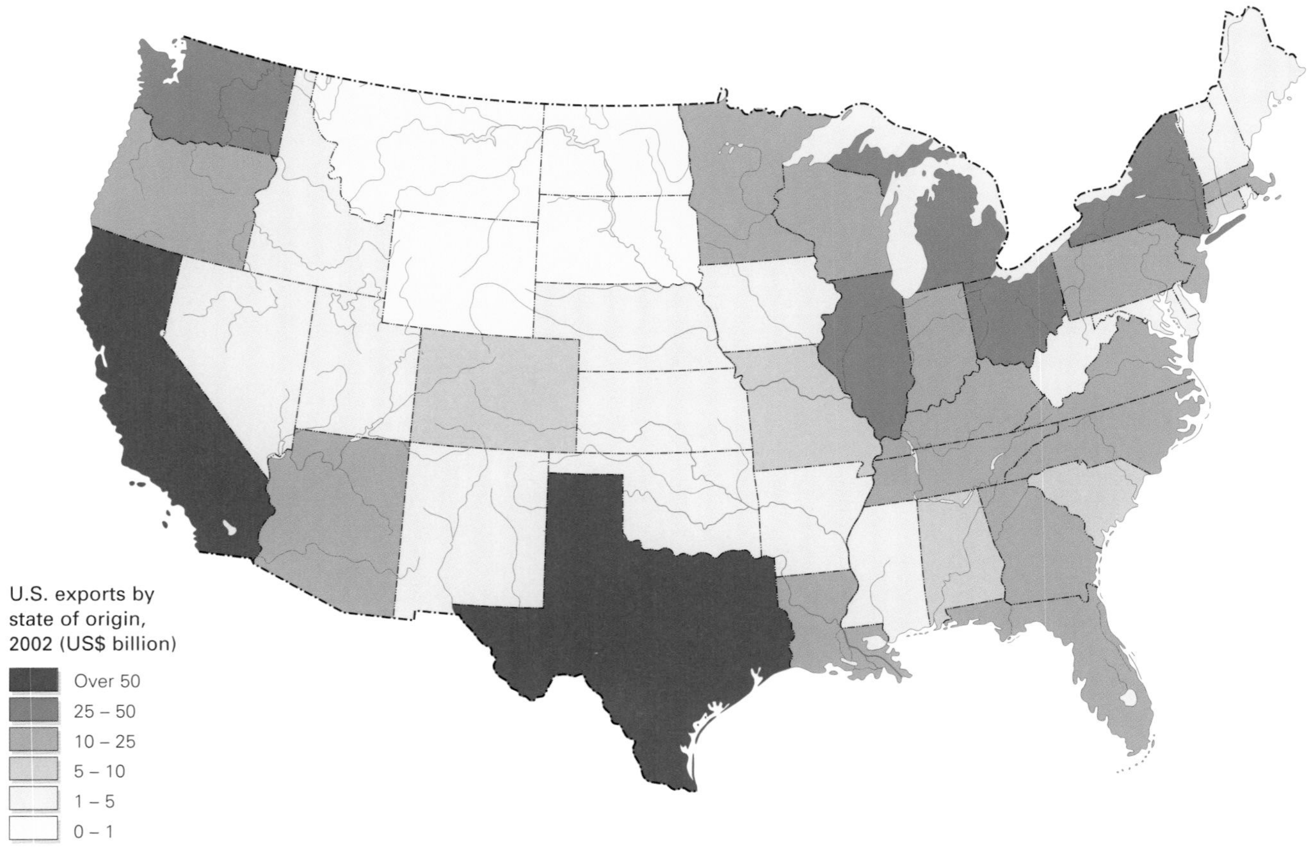

IMPORTS – CANADA

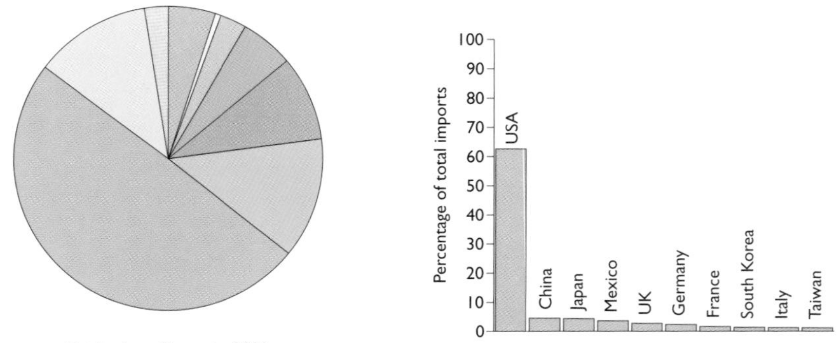

Total value of imports, 2001:
US$ 221.3 billion

Proportion of total imports derived from top ten partners (%)

EXPORTS – CANADA

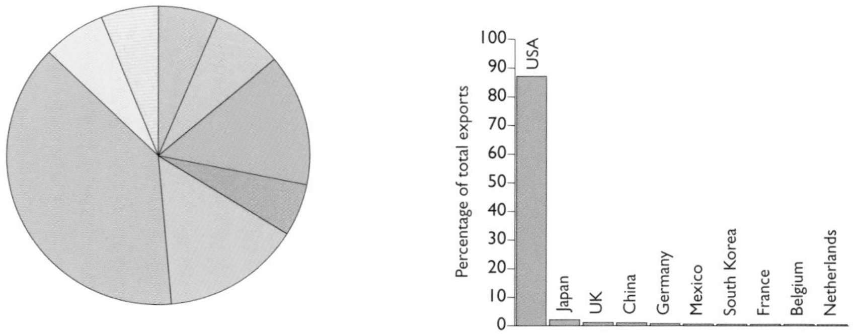

Total value of exports, 2001:
US$ 256.8 billion

Proportion of total exports sent to top ten partners (%)

IMPORTS – UNITED STATES

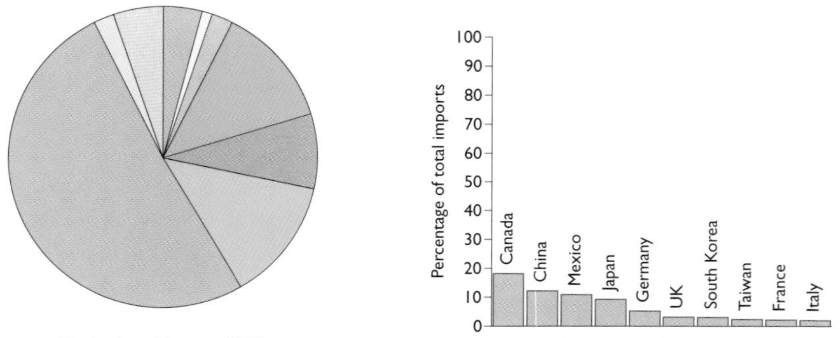

Total value of imports, 2001:
US$ 992.7 billion

Proportion of total imports derived from top ten partners (%)

EXPORTS – UNITED STATES

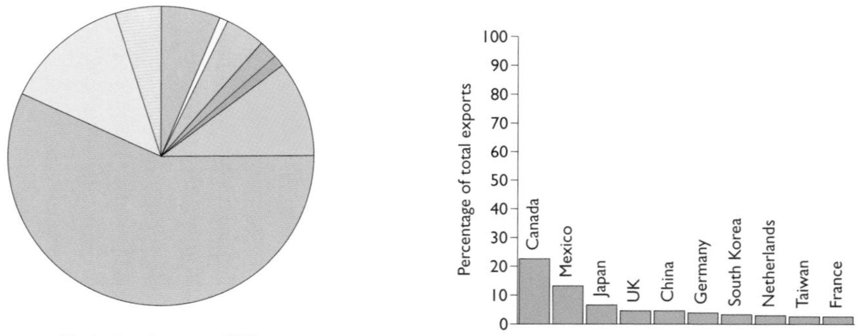

Total value of exports, 2001:
US$ 657.7 billion

Proportion of total exports sent to top ten partners (%)

IMPORTS – MEXICO

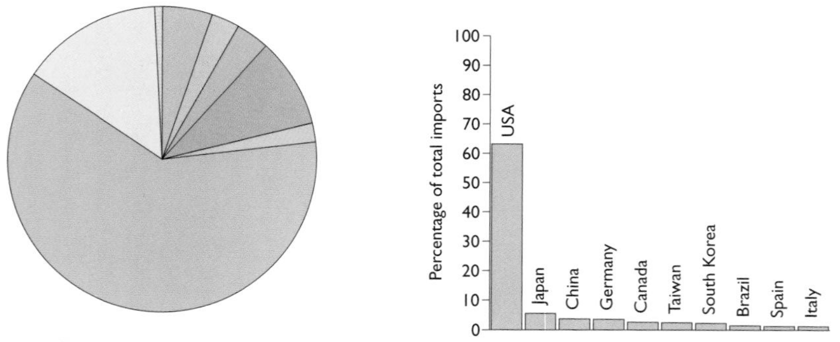

Total value of imports, 2001:
US$ 160.9 billion

Proportion of total imports derived from top ten partners (%)

EXPORTS – MEXICO

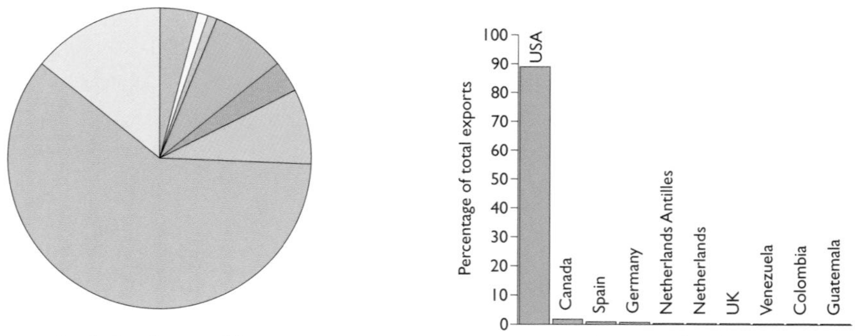

Total value of exports, 2001:
US$ 158.5 billion

Proportion of total exports sent to top ten partners (%)

KEY TO PIE CHARTS: Food · Beverages · Crude materials · Mineral fuels · Chemicals · Manufactured goods · Machinery and transport equipment · Miscellaneous manufactures · Other commodities and transactions

Internet backbone cities

The circle size shows the amount of backbone capacity connected to each city

4,000 megabits per second
1,000 megabits per second
250 megabits per second

City pairs connected by more than 270 mbps backbone capacity

Over 450 megabits per second
270–450 megabits per second

INTERNET CITIES

The geography of the Internet is forged in part by the network of powerful fiber optic cables that transmit large quantities of data. The development of this backbone system is the result of several decades of public policy and corporate activity. Today in the U.S., Internet backbone lines connect large metropolitan areas where numerous information-industry firms are concentrated.

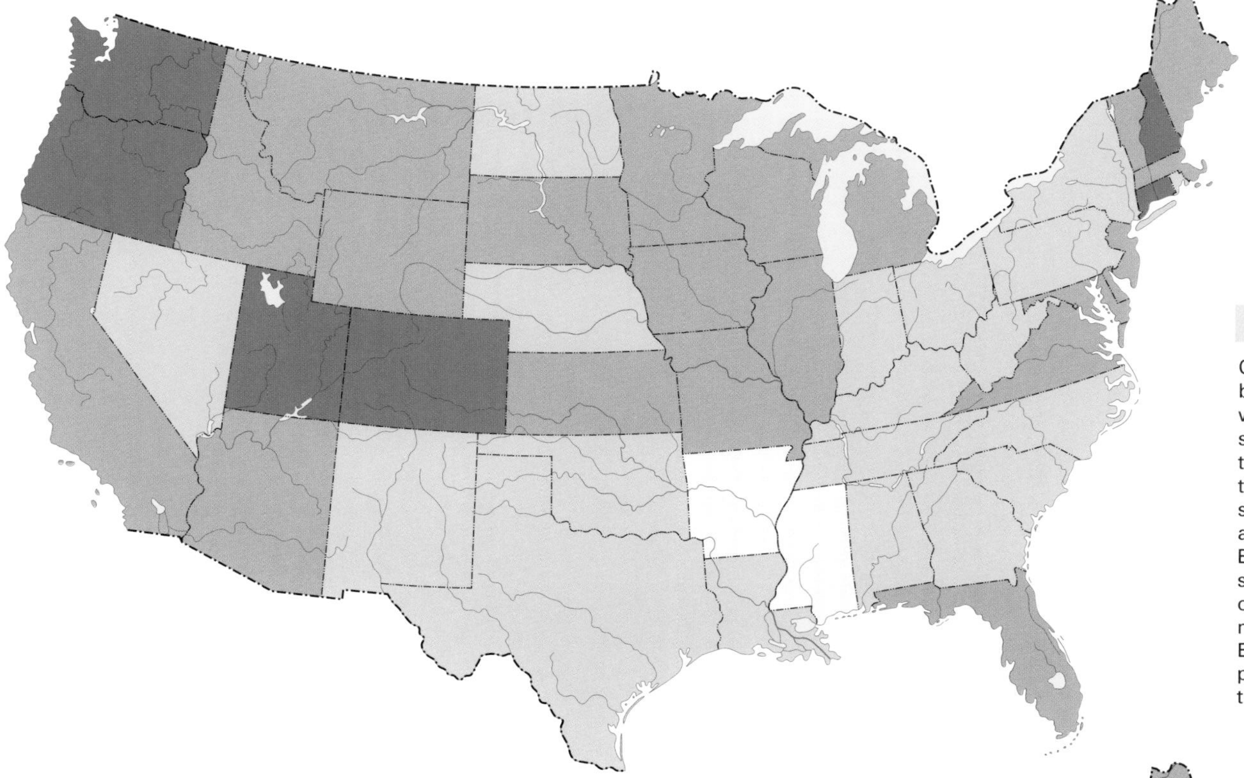

Percentage of adult population with access to a computer

- Over 50%
- 40 – 50%
- 30 – 40%
- 0 – 30%

COMPUTERS

Computer access, as measured by the percentage of homes with computer equipment, is still far lower, overall, than is the case with telephones or televisions. This map, which shows higher degrees of access in the Northeast, East, Midwest, and West, should be read with caution: one university-dominated metropolis such as Denver-Boulder (Colorado) in small-population states can bias the pattern.

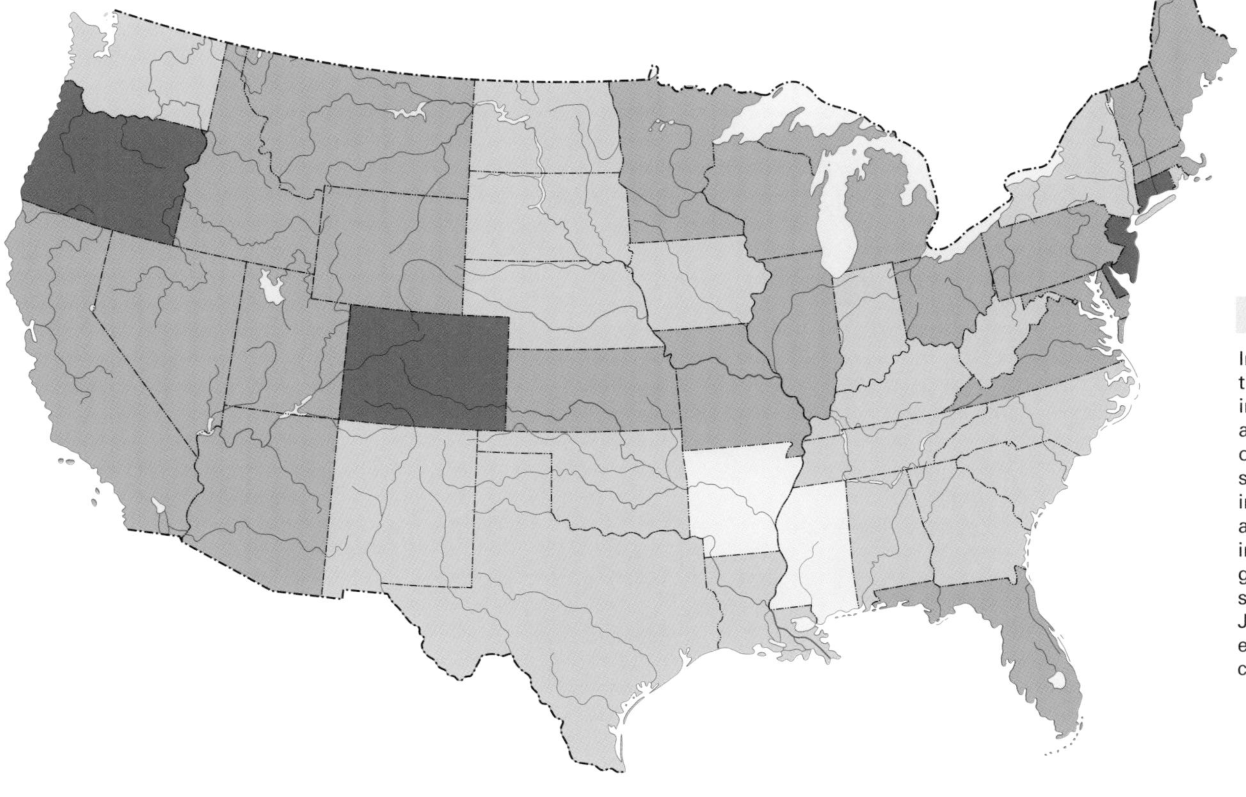

Percentage of adult population with access to the Internet

- Over 50%
- 40 – 50%
- 30 – 40%
- 0 – 30%

INTERNET

In a digital age, access to the Internet has important implications for professional and personal well-being. Rates of access reflect a variety of socio-demographic variables, including income, education, and employment in service industries. In the U.S., generally prosperous states such as Connecticut, New Jersey, Oregon, and Colorado exhibit the highest levels of connectivity.

Highways and Railroads

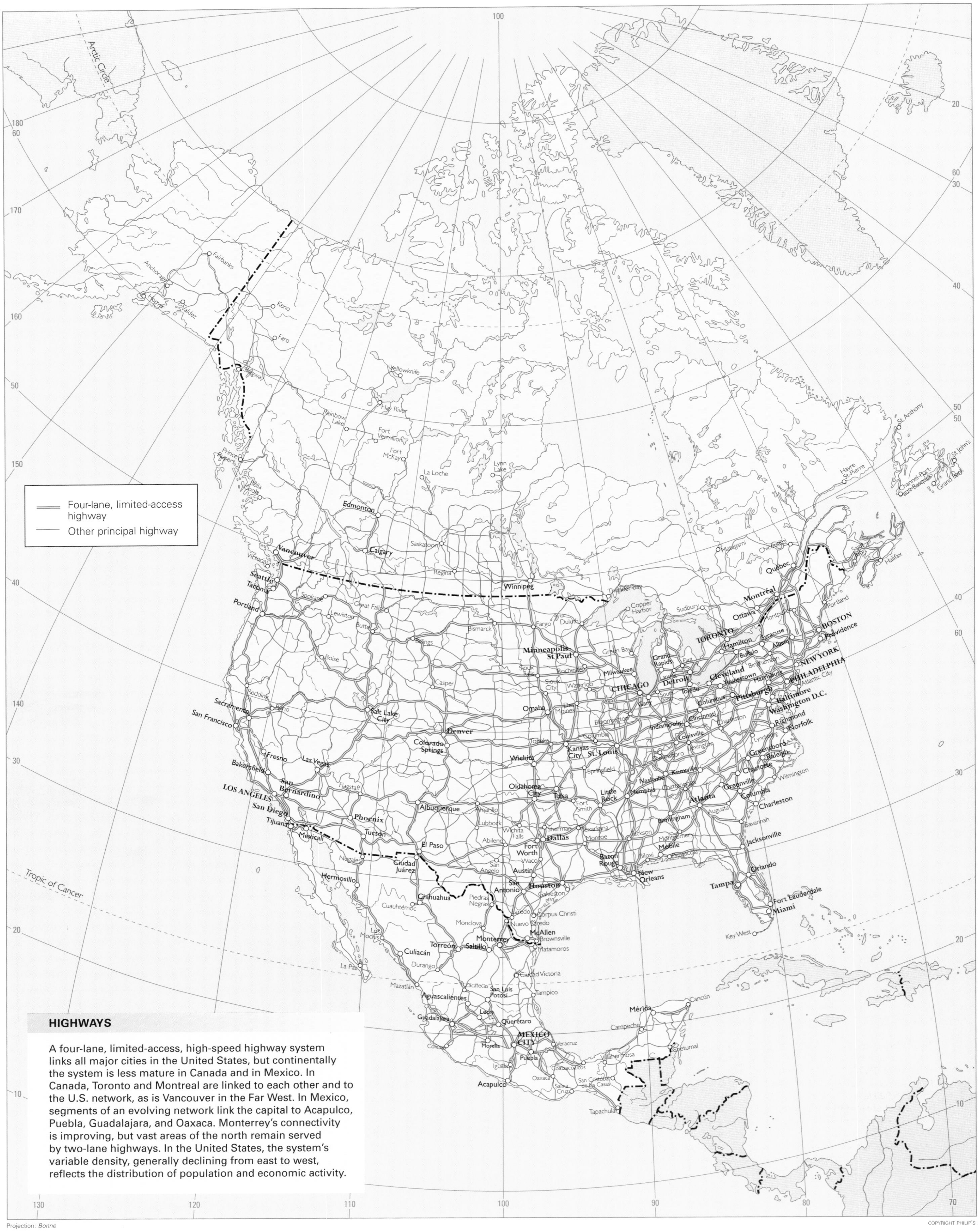

HIGHWAYS

A four-lane, limited-access, high-speed highway system links all major cities in the United States, but continentally the system is less mature in Canada and in Mexico. In Canada, Toronto and Montreal are linked to each other and to the U.S. network, as is Vancouver in the Far West. In Mexico, segments of an evolving network link the capital to Acapulco, Puebla, Guadalajara, and Oaxaca. Monterrey's connectivity is improving, but vast areas of the north remain served by two-lane highways. In the United States, the system's variable density, generally declining from east to west, reflects the distribution of population and economic activity.

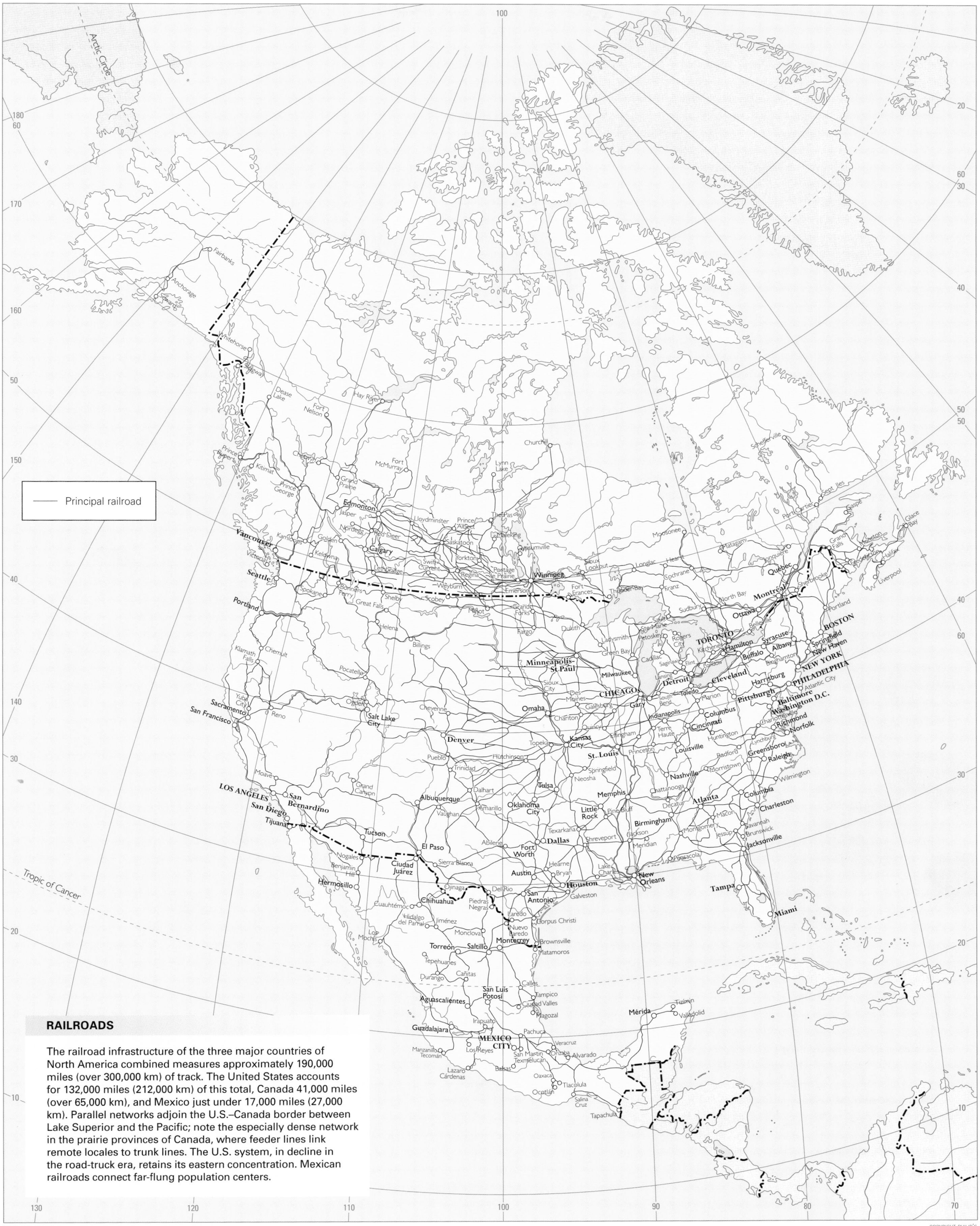

RAILROADS

The railroad infrastructure of the three major countries of North America combined measures approximately 190,000 miles (over 300,000 km) of track. The United States accounts for 132,000 miles (212,000 km) of this total, Canada 41,000 miles (over 65,000 km), and Mexico just under 17,000 miles (27,000 km). Parallel networks adjoin the U.S.–Canada border between Lake Superior and the Pacific; note the especially dense network in the prairie provinces of Canada, where feeder lines link remote locales to trunk lines. The U.S. system, in decline in the road-truck era, retains its eastern concentration. Mexican railroads connect far-flung population centers.

Projection: *Bonne*

Languages and Religions

CANADIAN LANGUAGES

Canada is officially a bilingual country, with nearly 60% English speakers and 23% French (17% speak another language as their mother tongue). The spatial clustering of more than 90 percent of Canada's Francophones in the province of Québec accentuates this social division, but the French linguistic region does not coincide with Québec's borders: numerous Anglophone communities lie within Québec along the Ontario and U.S. borders as well as in Montréal. Conversely, a significant Francophone minority exists in New Brunswick, and in smaller communities in every other province.

Percentage of the Canadian population in 1996 whose mother tongue was French

- 90 – 100%
- 60 – 90%
- 20 – 60%
- 5 – 20%
- 2.5 – 5%
- 0 – 2.5%

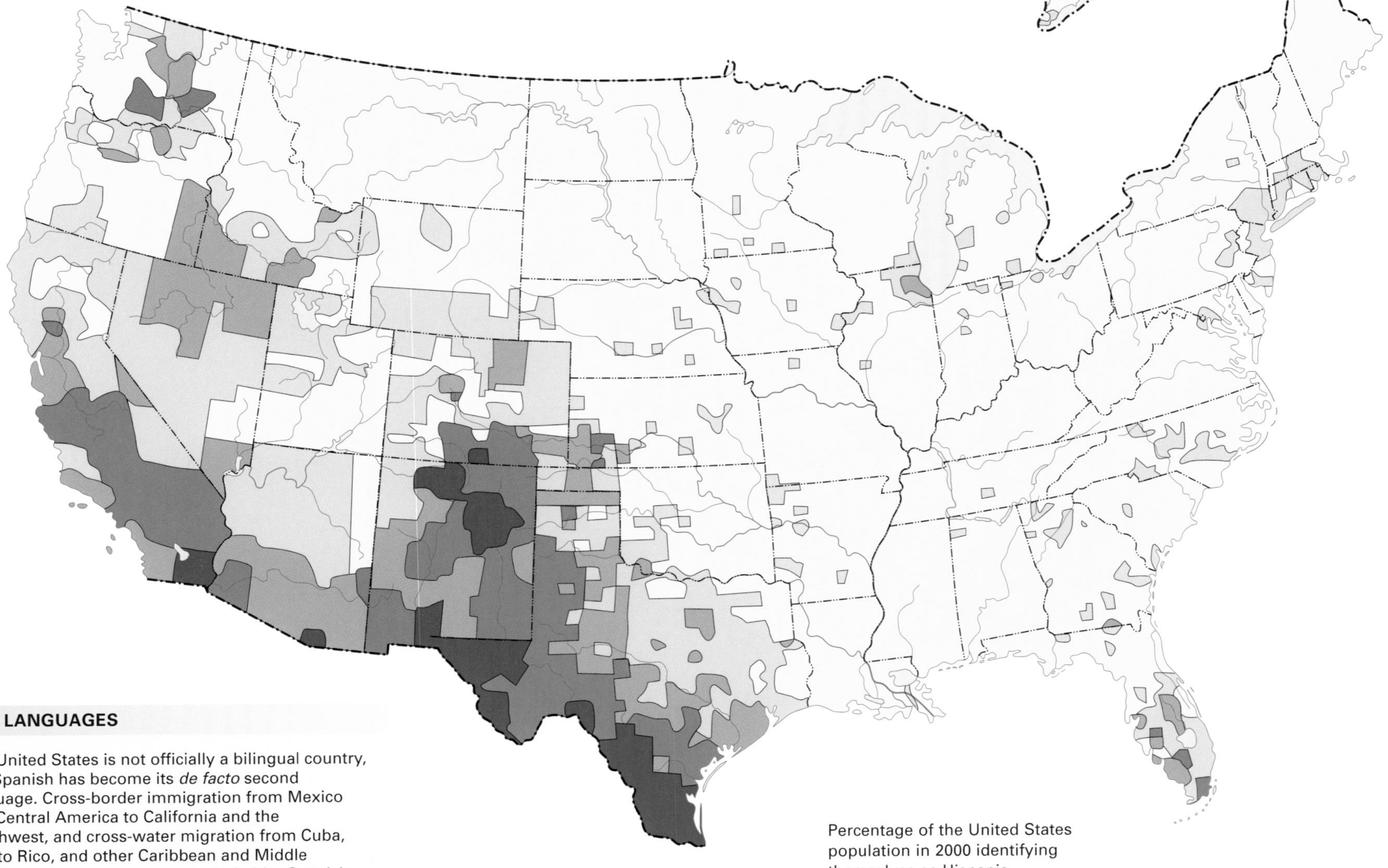

U.S. LANGUAGES

The United States is not officially a bilingual country, but Spanish has become its *de facto* second language. Cross-border immigration from Mexico and Central America to California and the Southwest, and cross-water migration from Cuba, Puerto Rico, and other Caribbean and Middle American sources, have augmented older Spanish-speaking communities and created a new version of the "melting pot." Large urban Hispanic communities beyond Florida and the Southwest (notably in the New York and Chicago areas) are serving as springboards for wider dispersal hinted at by scattered counties from Alabama to Minnesota.

Percentage of the United States population in 2000 identifying themselves as Hispanic

- 61.1 – 100%
- 34.7 – 61.1%
- 17.4 – 34.7%
- 6 – 17.4%
- 0 – 6%

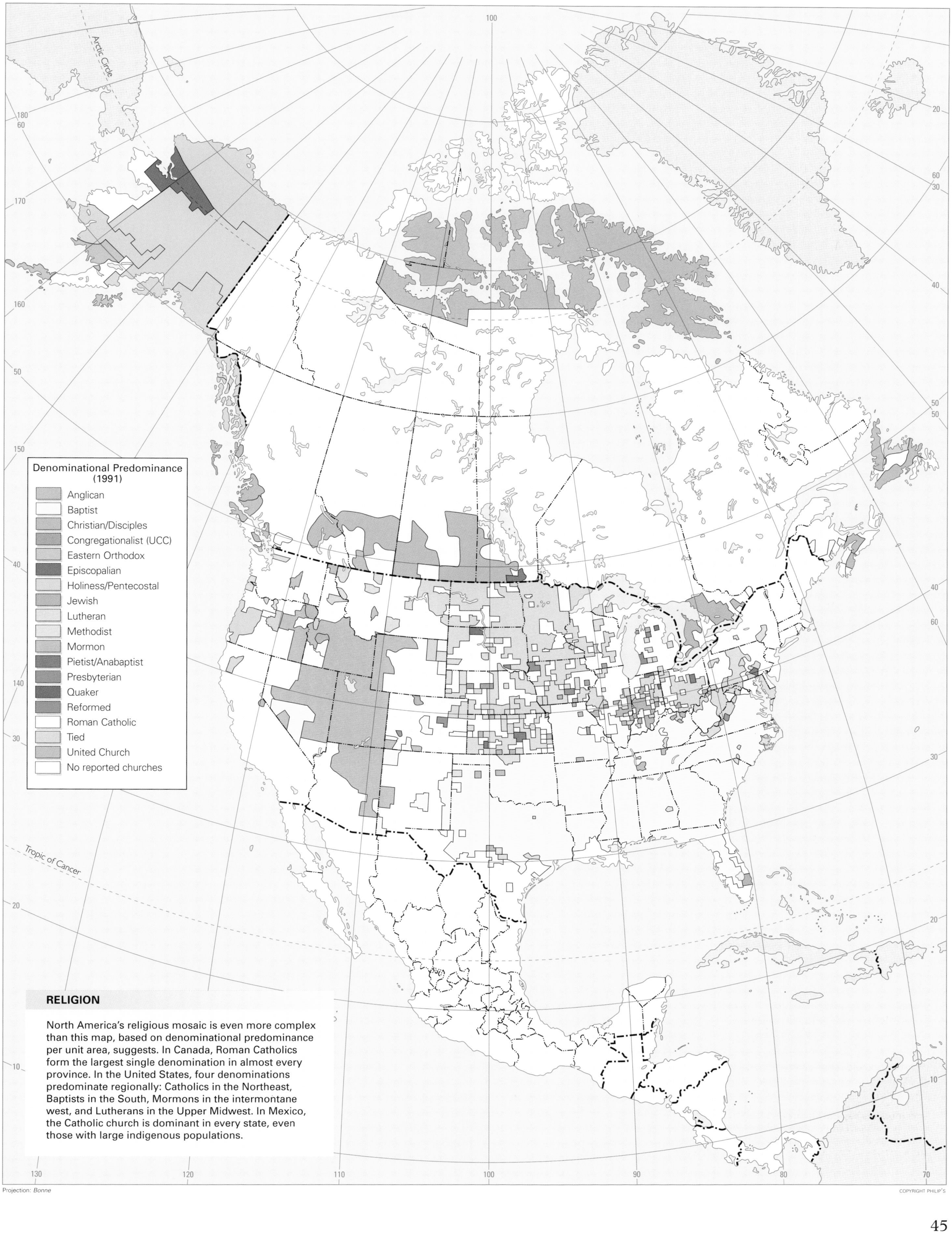

RELIGION

North America's religious mosaic is even more complex than this map, based on denominational predominance per unit area, suggests. In Canada, Roman Catholics form the largest single denomination in almost every province. In the United States, four denominations predominate regionally: Catholics in the Northeast, Baptists in the South, Mormons in the intermontane west, and Lutherans in the Upper Midwest. In Mexico, the Catholic church is dominant in every state, even those with large indigenous populations.

National Parks and Federal Lands

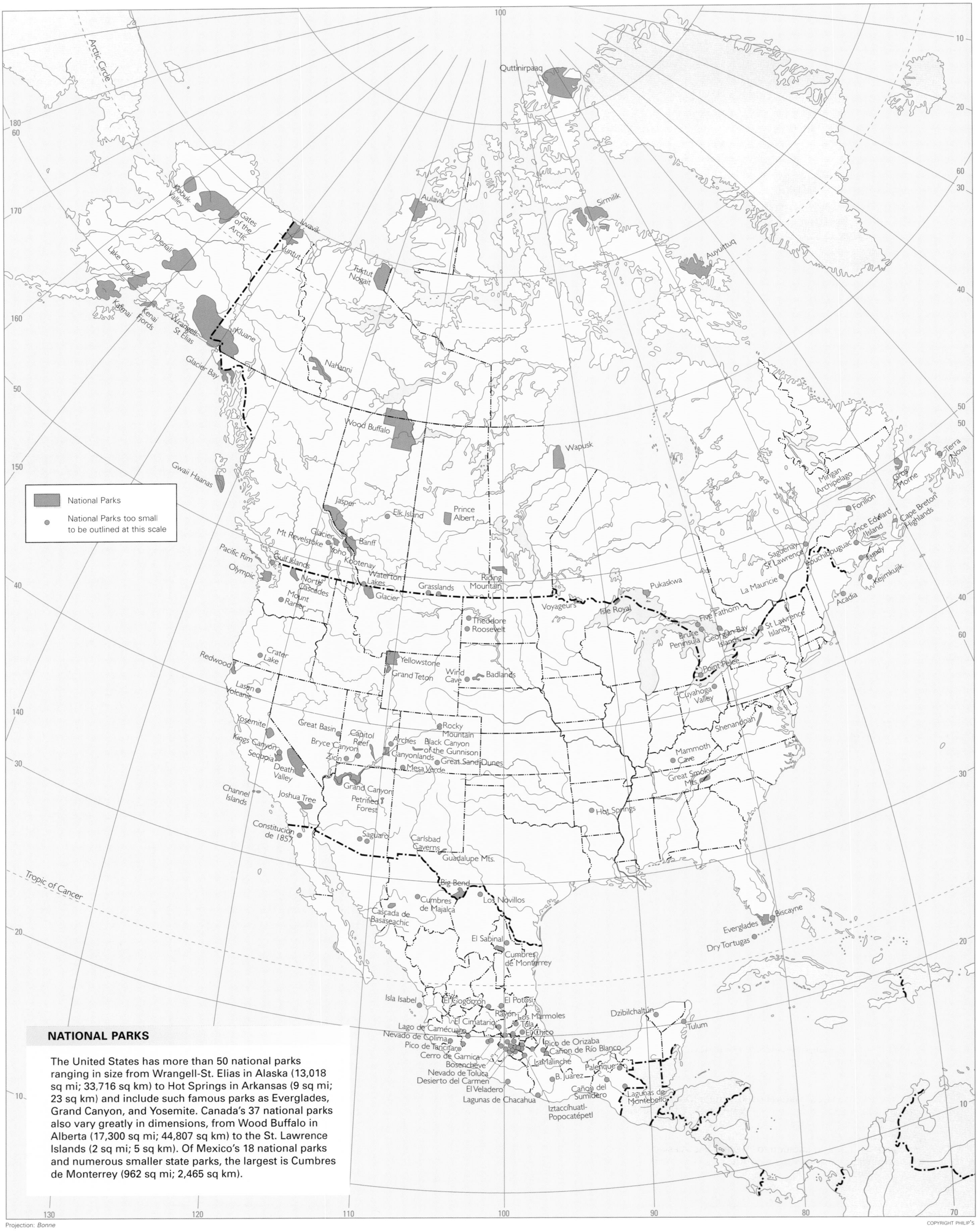

NATIONAL PARKS

The United States has more than 50 national parks ranging in size from Wrangell-St. Elias in Alaska (13,018 sq mi; 33,716 sq km) to Hot Springs in Arkansas (9 sq mi; 23 sq km) and include such famous parks as Everglades, Grand Canyon, and Yosemite. Canada's 37 national parks also vary greatly in dimensions, from Wood Buffalo in Alberta (17,300 sq mi; 44,807 sq km) to the St. Lawrence Islands (2 sq mi; 5 sq km). Of Mexico's 18 national parks and numerous smaller state parks, the largest is Cumbres de Monterrey (962 sq mi; 2,465 sq km).

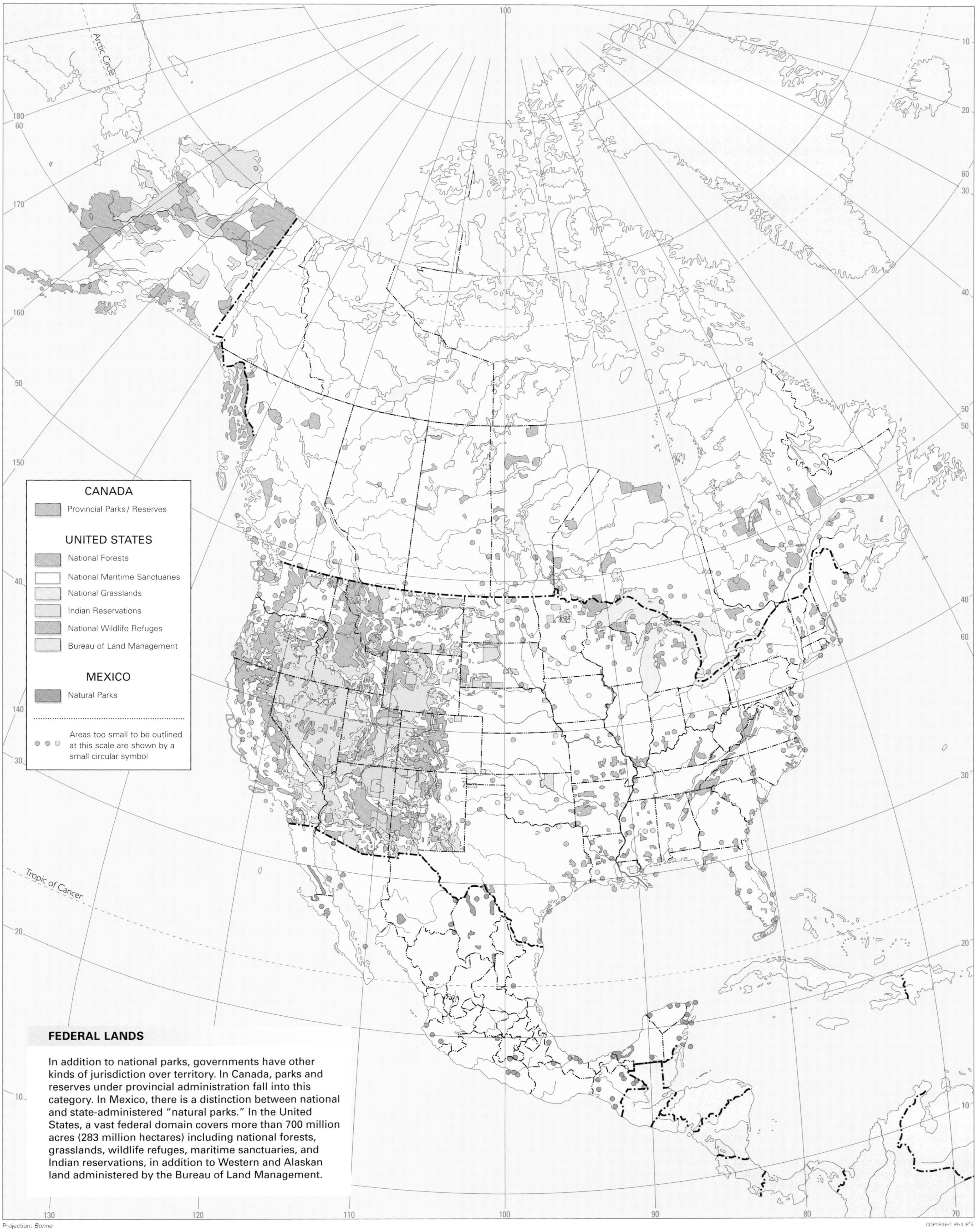

FEDERAL LANDS

In addition to national parks, governments have other kinds of jurisdiction over territory. In Canada, parks and reserves under provincial administration fall into this category. In Mexico, there is a distinction between national and state-administered "natural parks." In the United States, a vast federal domain covers more than 700 million acres (283 million hectares) including national forests, grasslands, wildlife refuges, maritime sanctuaries, and Indian reservations, in addition to Western and Alaskan land administered by the Bureau of Land Management.

Maritime Zones and Claims

MARITIME ZONES

Claims to resources in and beneath the sea, coupled with concerns over ocean pollution and national security, have led to the extension of national jurisdiction over adjacent waters and the *subsoil* below. This is an ongoing process that started centuries ago when European coastal countries heavily dependent on fishing closed off bays and estuaries to fishing boats from other countries, leading to the notion of the *territorial sea*, a continuous offshore zone where a coastal state claimed all the rights it had on its territory.

In the 17th and 18th centuries, such territorial seas were 3, 4 or at most 6 nautical miles wide (1 nautical mile = 1.15 statute miles or 1.85 km). Beyond lay the *high seas*, free and open to all.

During the 19th century, European states were more concerned with consolidating their colonial empires than expanding their maritime claims, but the 20th century was the scene of a "scramble for the oceans," and not just the oceans but also the subsoil and its resources. After the United States laid claim to the continental shelf down to a depth of 100 fathoms (600 feet), unleashing the scramble, the United Nations convened a series of conferences to control the contest, which had cold-war overtones.

These conferences produced a convention, still not signed by the United States by 2004, that awarded all states sovereign rights over a 12-mile territorial sea and an *Exclusive Economic Zone* (EEZ) extending to 200 miles offshore, within which states have rights to resources but also conservation responsibilities.

MARITIME CLAIMS

Canada, the United States, and Mexico all have lengthy coastlines on open waters, and the three large nations of North America benefited greatly from the United Nations Convention on the Law of the Sea (UNCLOS) that awarded coastal states a 200-mile EEZ.

The map above shows the approximate maritime areas under each state's jurisdiction. Because islands have their own EEZs, offshore possessions effectively extend EEZs seaward, as is the case off the west coast of mainland Mexico. On its east coast, Mexico's EEZ is hemmed in by Cuba and Guatemala, but Mexico has a large share of the resources of the Gulf of Mexico.

The United States has a full-width EEZ from north Florida northward to the Canadian border, an equally wide EEZ in the west, and a vast maritime sphere off Alaska and the Aleutian Islands. The U.S. EEZ meets that of Russia in the Bering Strait.

Canada's western EEZ is confined to a section off British Columbia between the southern end of the Alaska Peninsula and the Juan de Fuca Strait, but its eastern and northern EEZ encompasses a vast maritime area from Nova Scotia to the border with Alaska.

In recent years, the United Nations has begun to authorize states to extend their claims to the continental shelves beyond the 200-mile limit if they can prove that these extensions are "natural prolongations" of their landmasses.

As our map shows, the United States and Canada would be leading beneficiaries of this new provision. In the case of Canada, it would help mitigate a problem created by the delimitation of the 200-mile EEZ off its east coast (map at right). The shallow Grand Bank is bisected by the EEZ boundary, leaving the "Nose" and "Tail" of the Bank outside its jurisdiction, creating disputes with foreign countries over fishing activities and causing management problems.

The push for maritime claims is not over yet, but the international order achieved by the United Nations has controlled the process, has established strict rules for claimants and has saved what remains of the high seas from unrestricted invasion.

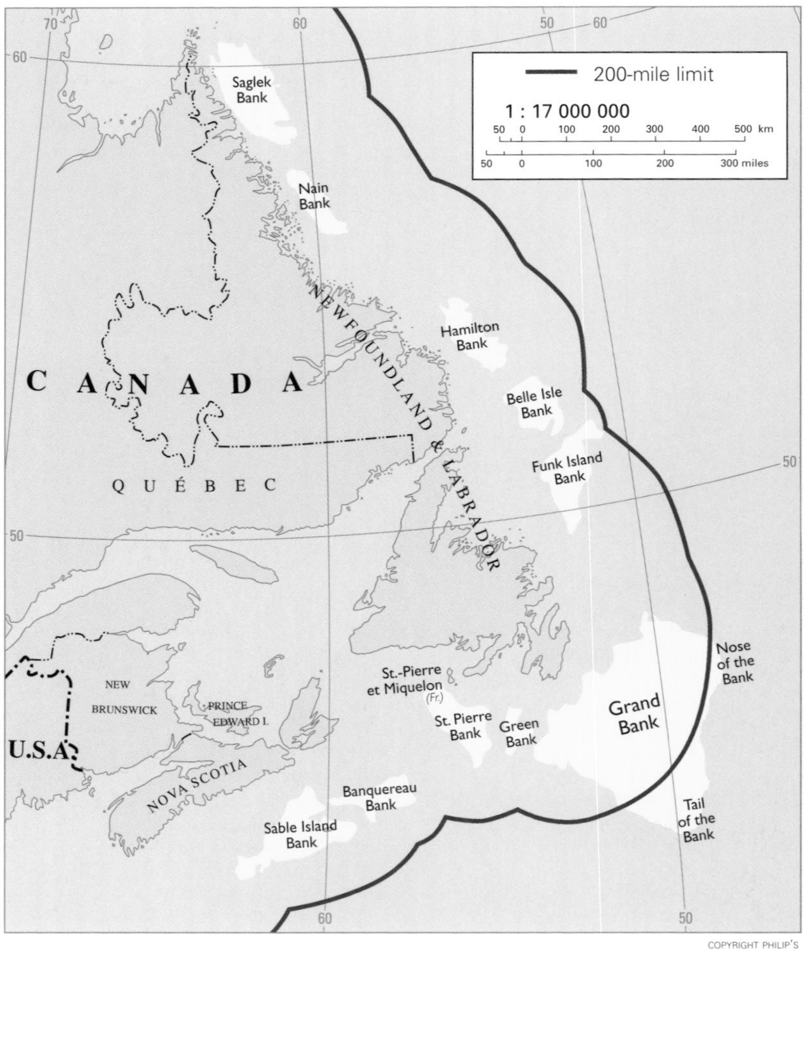

UNITED STATES

STATE MAPS

Settlements
(number of inhabitants)

NEW YORK	Over 5,000,000
SEATTLE	2,000,000 – 5,000,000
SACRAMENTO	1,000,000 – 2,000,000
Albuquerque	500,000 – 1,000,000
Omaha	250,000 – 500,000
Abilene	100,000 – 250,000
Charleston	50,000 – 100,000
Sandusky	20,000 – 50,000
Twentynine Palms	10,000 – 20,000
Pecos	5,000 – 10,000
Deadwood	Less than 5,000
	Extent of urban areas (over 1,000,000 inhabitants)

Population figures for settlements are from the U.S. Census 2000 Summary file. Population figures for settlements with over 500,000 inhabitants are for urban areas.

Administration

	International boundaries
	State boundaries
	County boundaries (parishes in Louisiana and census areas in Alaska)
CALHOUN	County names
NAVAJO IND. RES.	Indian reservations
MESA VERDE NAT. PARK	National parks *
NANTAHALA NAT. FOREST	National forests and grasslands
FORT A.P. HILL	Military and federal reserves
WASHINGTON D.C.	National capital
PHOENIX	State capitals with over 1,000,000 inhabitants
Dover	State capitals with less than 1,000,000 inhabitants
JOHN F. KENNEDY SPACE CENTER	Selected points of interest

** Includes national monuments, national preserves, national recreation areas, national scenic areas, national memorials, national historic sites, national seashores, national wildlife refuges, and selected state parks.*

Communications

	Limited-access highways
	Limited-access highways under construction
	Other highways
70	Interstate route numbers
40	U.S. route numbers
13	State route numbers
	Principal railroads (Amtrak)
	Other railroads
	Railroad tunnels
JFK	Principal airports (with location identifiers)
	Other airports
	Transportation canals and aqueducts

CITY MAPS

	Free limited-access highways (with interchange)
	Toll limited-access highways
	Tunnels
	Primary divided highways
	Primary undivided highways
	Secondary divided highways
	Secondary undivided highways
	Other roads
70	Interstate route numbers
40	U.S. route numbers
13	State route numbers
	Railroads
Union Terminal	Principal railroad stations
	Principal airports
	Other airports
	City centers
	City center map coverage
	Urban areas
Lynn Clifton Swampscott	Suburbs (size of type indicates relative populations)
	Woodlands and parks
Zoo	Points of interest

CITY CENTER MAPS

	Free limited-access highways
	Toll limited-access highways
	Through routes
	Secondary routes
	Divided highways
	Other roads
	Tunnels
	Railroads
	Railroad stations
S M	Subway stations
	Urban areas
BEACON HILL	Suburbs
	Woodlands and parks
	Public buildings
	Churches
	Cathedrals
Museum	Points of interest

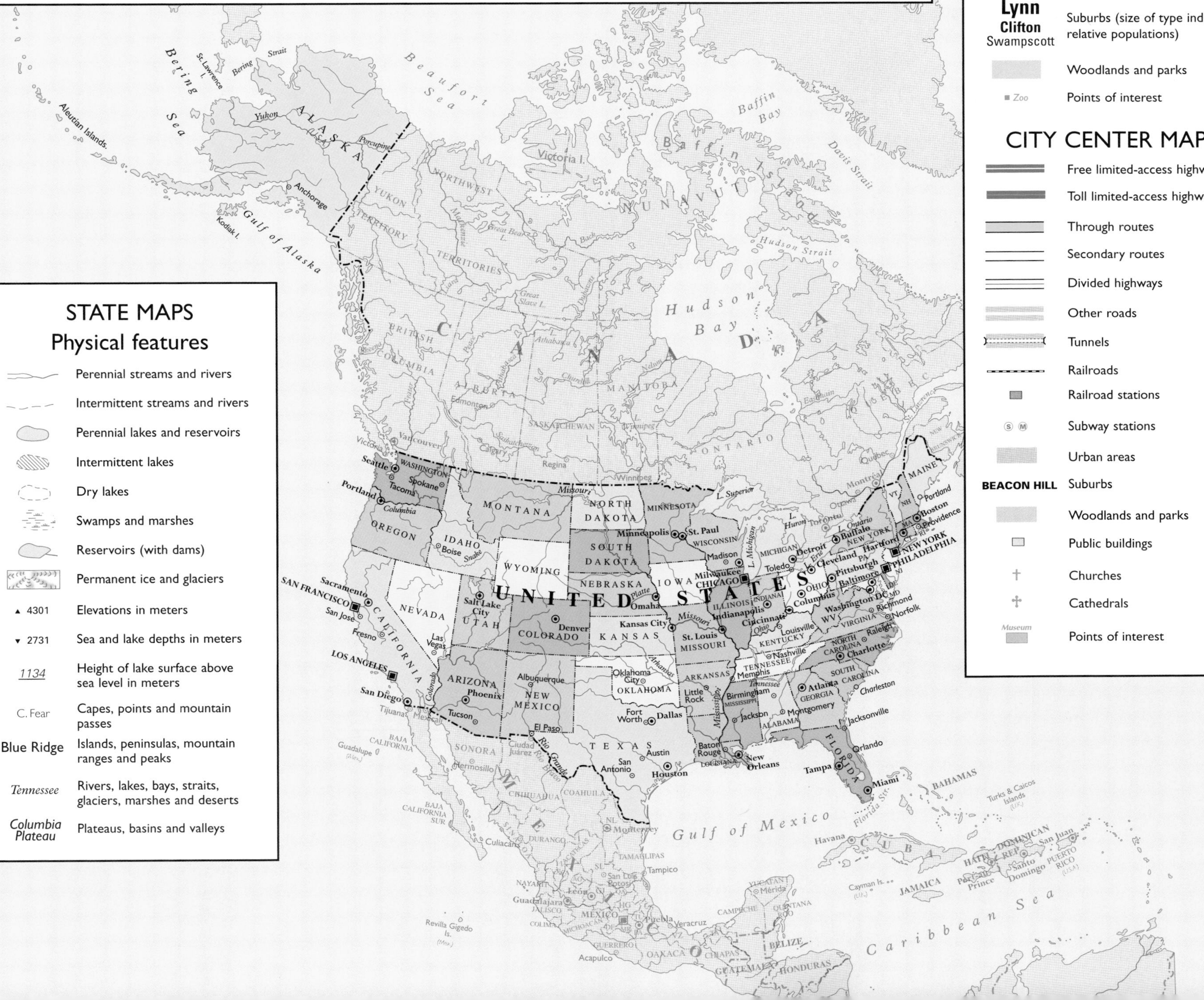

STATE MAPS

Physical features

	Perennial streams and rivers
	Intermittent streams and rivers
	Perennial lakes and reservoirs
	Intermittent lakes
	Dry lakes
	Swamps and marshes
	Reservoirs (with dams)
	Permanent ice and glaciers
▲ 4301	Elevations in meters
▼ 2731	Sea and lake depths in meters
1134	Height of lake surface above sea level in meters
C. Fear	Capes, points and mountain passes
Blue Ridge	Islands, peninsulas, mountain ranges and peaks
Tennessee	Rivers, lakes, bays, straits, glaciers, marshes and deserts
Columbia Plateau	Plateaus, basins and valleys

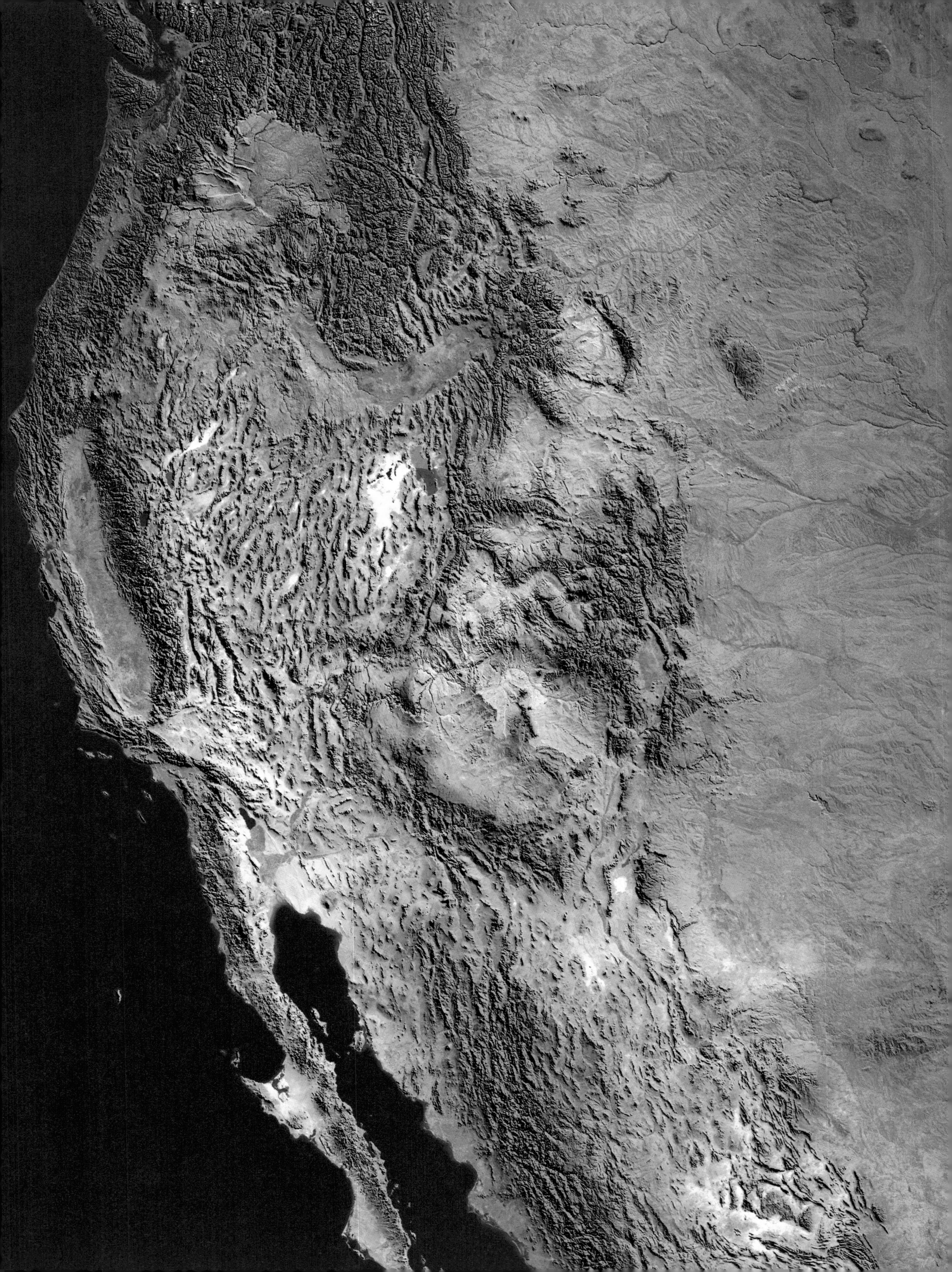

100 0 100 200 300 400 500 km
100 0 50 100 150 200 250 300 350 miles
1:9 600 000
1 2 3 4 5 6
A B C D
H J
15 16 17 4 5 6
Projection: Albers' Equal Area with two standard parallels
West from Greenwich
PACIFIC OCEAN
BRITISH COLUMBIA
ALBERTA
SASKATCHEWAN
CANADA
MANITOBA
WASHINGTON
OREGON
IDAHO
MONTANA
WYOMING
NORTH DAKOTA
SOUTH DAKOTA
NEBRASKA
KANSAS
OKLAHOMA
TEXAS
NEW MEXICO
ARIZONA
UTAH
COLORADO
NEVADA
CALIFORNIA
MEXICO
SONORA
CHIHUAHUA
COAHUILA
DURANGO
BAJA CALIFORNIA
BAJA CALIFORNIA SUR
Great Basin
Rocky Mountains
Coast Ranges
Sierra Nevada
Cascade Range
Columbia Plateau
Snake River Plain
Great Plains
High Plains
Colorado Plateau
Front Range
Sierra Madre
Bolsón de Mapimí
Llano Estacado
Edwards Plateau
Golfo de California
Baja California
Sonoran Desert
Mojave Desert
Great Salt Lake Desert
Calgary
Vancouver
Victoria
Seattle
Tacoma
Olympia
Spokane
Portland
Salem
Eugene
Boise
Sacramento
San Francisco
San Jose
Oakland
Fresno
Los Angeles
San Diego
San Bernardino
Las Vegas
Reno
Carson City
Salt Lake City
Phoenix
Tucson
Albuquerque
Denver
Colorado Springs
Pueblo
Cheyenne
Casper
Billings
Helena
Great Falls
Missoula
Bismarck
Pierre
Rapid City
Regina
Saskatoon
Lethbridge
Medicine Hat
El Paso
Ciudad Juárez
Tijuana
Mexicali
Hermosillo
Chihuahua
Torreón
Monterrey
Amarillo
Lubbock
San Angelo
Abilene
Midland
Odessa
Laredo
Nuevo Laredo
McAllen
HAWAI'I
1:8 000 000
Kaua'i
Ni'ihau
O'ahu
Honolulu
Moloka'i
Lāna'i
Maui
Kaho'olawe
Hawai'i
Hilo
Kailua
Mauna Kea 4205
Mauna Loa 4169
Kīlauea
Pāhala
Hawaiian Islands
Kauai Channel
'Alenuihāhā Channel
PACIFIC OCEAN

CANADA
ONTARIO
QUEBEC
NEW BRUNSWICK
Lake Winnipeg
Lake Superior
Lake Michigan
Lake Huron
Lake Erie
Lake Ontario
Winnipeg
Thunder Bay
Sault Ste. Marie
Sudbury
OTTAWA
MONTRÉAL
Québec
TORONTO
Hamilton
London
MINNESOTA
WISCONSIN
MICHIGAN
IOWA
ILLINOIS
INDIANA
OHIO
PENNSYLVANIA
NEW YORK
VERMONT
NEW HAMPSHIRE
MAINE
MASS.
CONN.
R.I.
NEW JERSEY
DEL.
MARYLAND
WEST VIRGINIA
VIRGINIA
KENTUCKY
TENNESSEE
NORTH CAROLINA
SOUTH CAROLINA
GEORGIA
ALABAMA
MISSISSIPPI
LOUISIANA
ARKANSAS
MISSOURI
FLORIDA
New England
Midwest
MINNEAPOLIS
ST. PAUL
MILWAUKEE
CHICAGO
DETROIT
CLEVELAND
COLUMBUS
INDIANAPOLIS
CINCINNATI
PITTSBURGH
BUFFALO
BOSTON
PROVIDENCE
NEW YORK
PHILADELPHIA
BALTIMORE
WASHINGTON D.C.
NORFOLK
Richmond
Charlotte
Raleigh
ATLANTA
Birmingham
Memphis
Nashville
Louisville
KANSAS CITY
ST. LOUIS
Tulsa
Oklahoma City
DALLAS
HOUSTON
NEW ORLEANS
Jacksonville
ORLANDO
TAMPA
St. Petersburg
MIAMI
BAHAMAS
Nassau
ATLANTIC OCEAN
GULF OF MEXICO
Straits of Florida
Appalachian Mts.
COPYRIGHT PHILIP'S

1:4 800 000
50 0 50 100 150 200 km
50 0 50 100 150 miles
LAKE SUPERIOR
LAKE HURON
LAKE MICHIGAN
LAKE ERIE
LAKE ONTARIO
Georgian Bay
ONTARIO
QUEBEC
NEW YORK
PENNSYLVANIA
OHIO
INDIANA
ILLINOIS
MICHIGAN
WISCONSIN
KENTUCKY
WEST VIRGINIA
VIRGINIA
MARYLAND
DELAWARE
NEW JERSEY
VERMONT
NEW HAMPSHIRE
MASS.
CONN.
R.I.
CHICAGO
DETROIT
TORONTO
MONTREAL
OTTAWA
BOSTON
NEW YORK
PHILADELPHIA
BALTIMORE
WASHINGTON D.C.
PITTSBURGH
CLEVELAND
COLUMBUS
CINCINNATI
INDIANAPOLIS
MILWAUKEE
BUFFALO
Chesapeake Bay
Delaware Bay
56

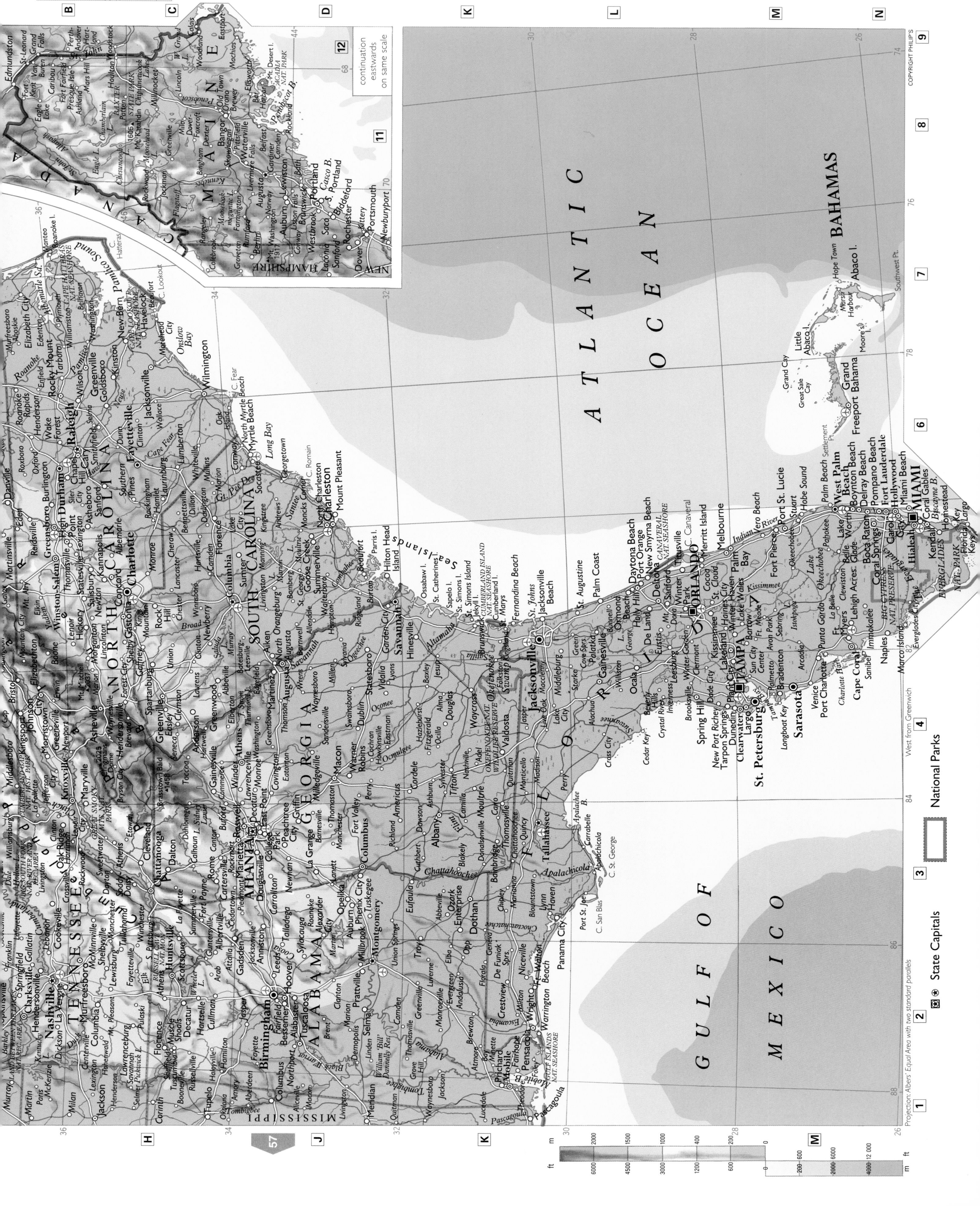
ATLANTIC OCEAN
GULF OF MEXICO
BAHAMAS
TENNESSEE
NORTH CAROLINA
SOUTH CAROLINA
GEORGIA
ALABAMA
FLORIDA
MAINE
NEW HAMPSHIRE
CANADA
MISSISSIPPI
Atlanta
Raleigh
Columbia
Nashville
Montgomery
Tallahassee
Augusta
Orlando
Tampa
Jacksonville
Miami
Charlotte
Charleston
Savannah
Birmingham
Wilmington
Portland
continuation eastwards on same scale
State Capitals
National Parks
West from Greenwich
Projection: Albers' Equal Area with two standard parallels
COPYRIGHT PHILIP'S
57

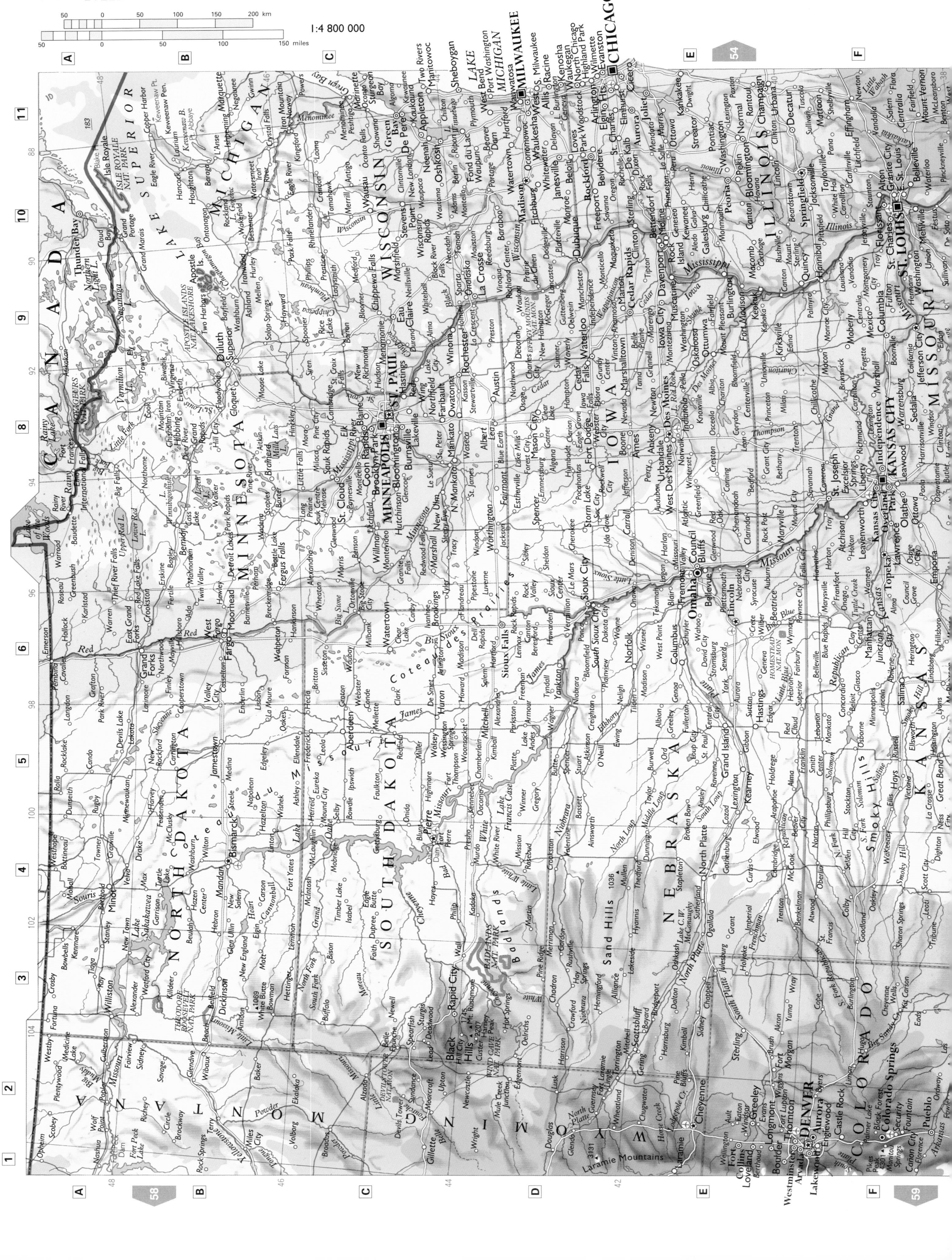
1:4 800 000
50 0 50 100 150 200 km
50 0 50 100 150 miles
A
B
C
D
E
F
54
58
59
CANADA
NORTH DAKOTA
SOUTH DAKOTA
MINNESOTA
WISCONSIN
MICHIGAN
IOWA
ILLINOIS
NEBRASKA
KANSAS
MISSOURI
COLORADO
WYOMING
MONTANA
LAKE SUPERIOR
LAKE MICHIGAN
CHICAGO
MILWAUKEE
MINNEAPOLIS
ST. PAUL
ST. LOUIS
KANSAS CITY
DENVER
Omaha
Des Moines
Sioux Falls
Bismarck
Pierre
Lincoln
Topeka
Cheyenne
Madison
Springfield
Jefferson City
Sand Hills
Badlands
Laramie Mountains
Smoky Hills
Mississippi
Missouri

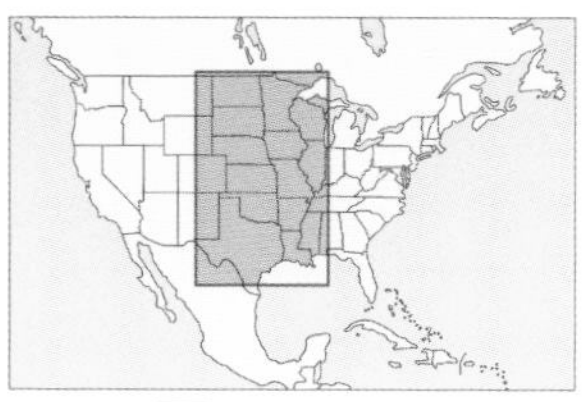

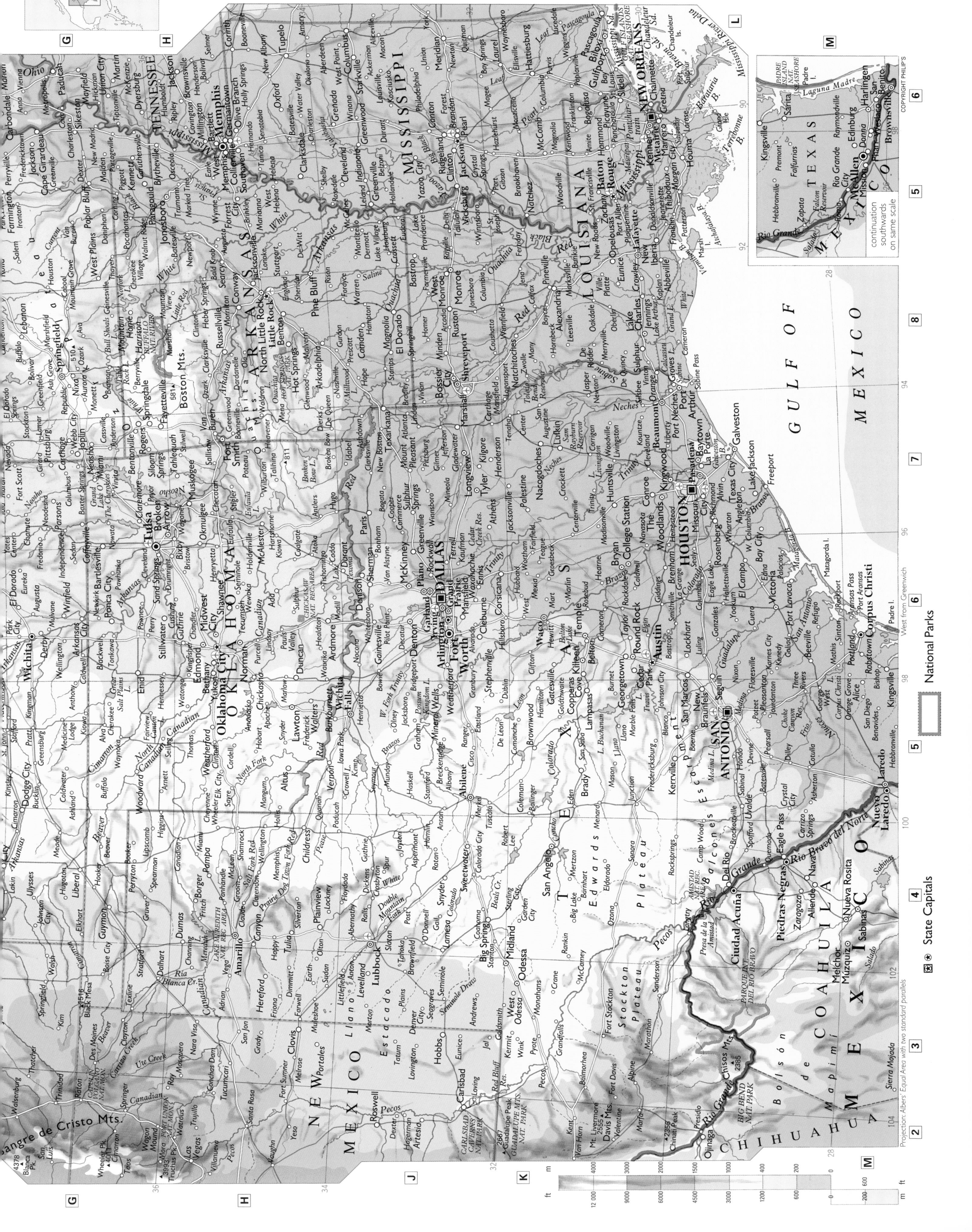
OKLAHOMA
ARKANSAS
MISSISSIPPI
LOUISIANA
TEXAS
NEW MEXICO
TENNESSEE
MEXICO
COAHUILA
CHIHUAHUA
GULF OF MEXICO
Llano Estacado
Edwards Plateau
Stockton Plateau
Balcones Escarpment
Bolsón de Mapimí
Ouachita Mts.
Boston Mts.
Sangre de Cristo Mts.
Chisos Mts.
Oklahoma City
Little Rock
Jackson
Baton Rouge
Austin
Dallas
Houston
San Antonio
New Orleans
Memphis
Tulsa
Fort Worth
Corpus Christi
El Paso
Amarillo
Lubbock
Shreveport
Wichita
State Capitals
National Parks
continuation southwards on same scale
Projection: Albers' Equal Area with two standard parallels
West from Greenwich
COPYRIGHT PHILIP'S

50 0 50 100 150 200 km

1:4 800 000

50 0 50 100 150 miles

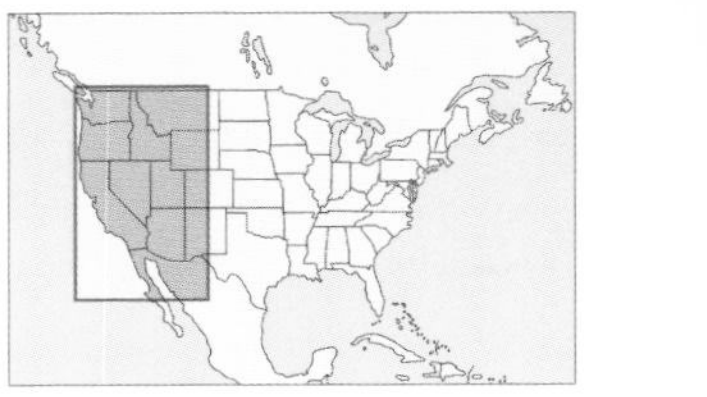

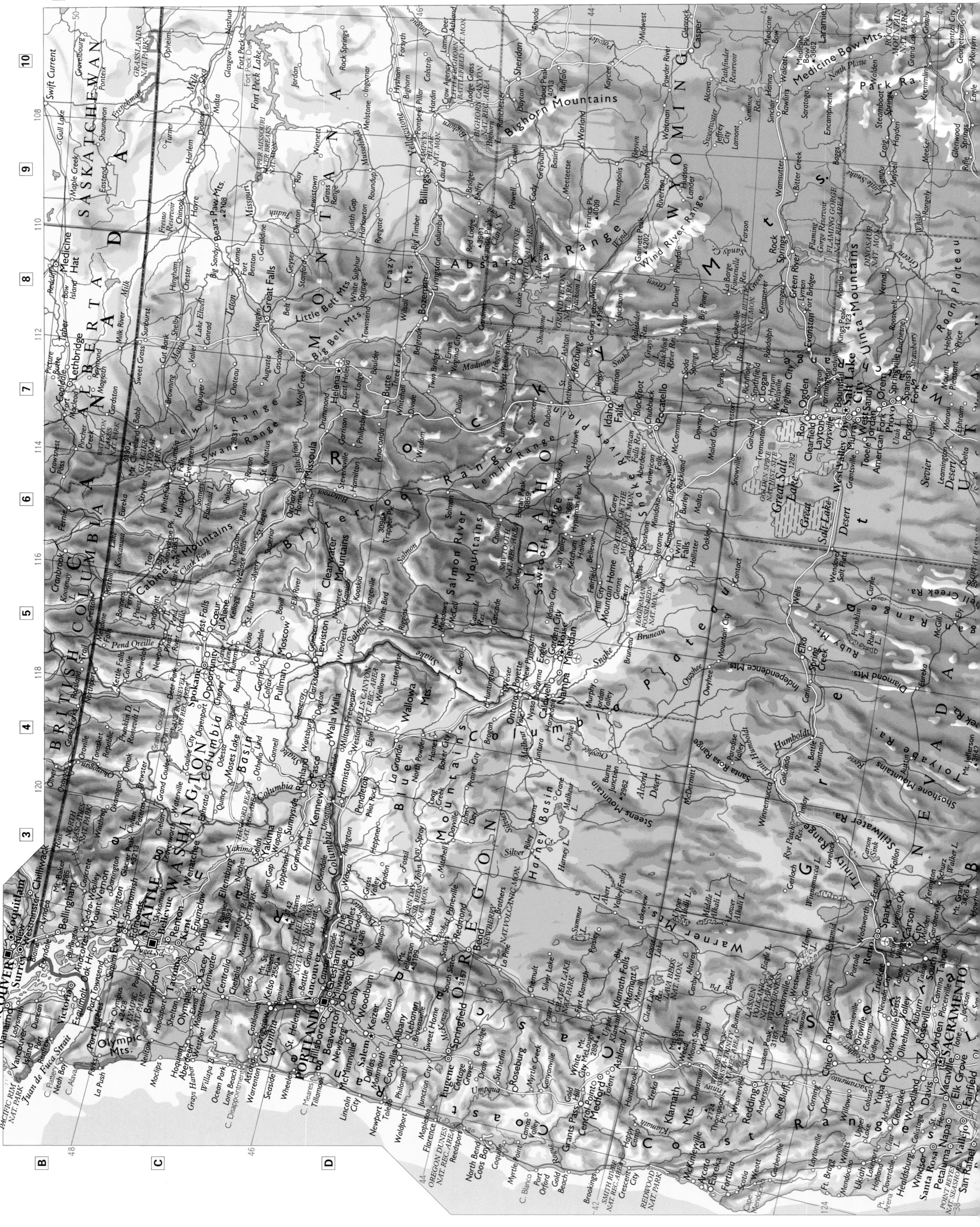

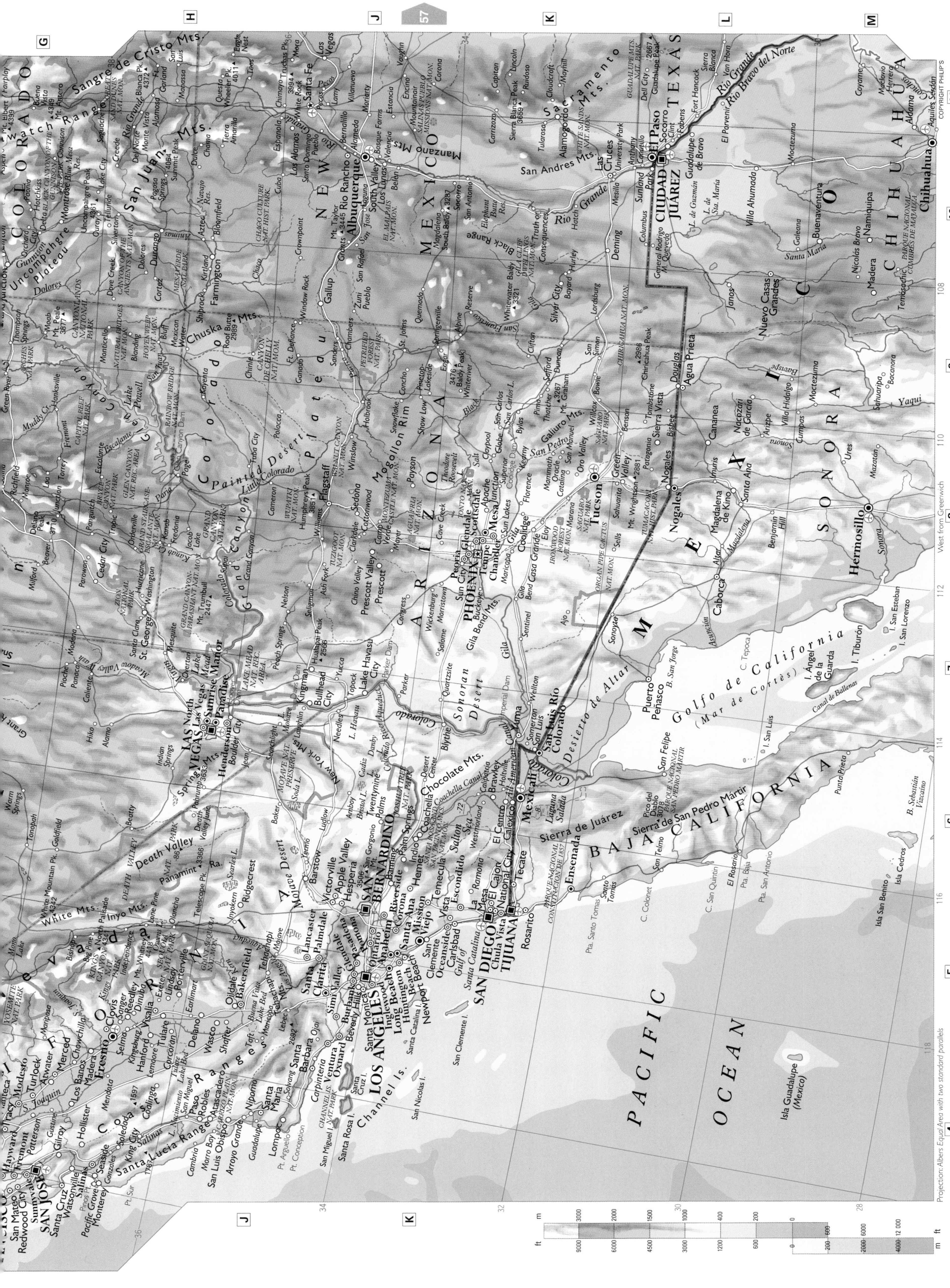
PACIFIC OCEAN
COLORADO
NEW MEXICO
ARIZONA
TEXAS
CHIHUAHUA
SONORA
MEXICO
BAJA CALIFORNIA
Colorado Plateau
Golfo de California (Mar de Cortès)
Sangre de Cristo Mts.
San Juan Mts.
Sacramento Mts.
Mojave Desert
Sonoran Desert
Painted Desert
Grand Canyon
Death Valley
LOS ANGELES
SAN DIEGO
TIJUANA
SAN JOSE
PHOENIX
Tucson
Albuquerque
Santa Fe
El Paso
CIUDAD JUÁREZ
Chihuahua
Hermosillo
Mexicali
LAS VEGAS
Fresno
Bakersfield
SAN BERNARDINO
Flagstaff
Channel Is.
Isla Guadalupe (Mexico)
State Capitals
National Parks
West from Greenwich
Projection: Albers Equal Area with two standard parallels
COPYRIGHT PHILIP'S

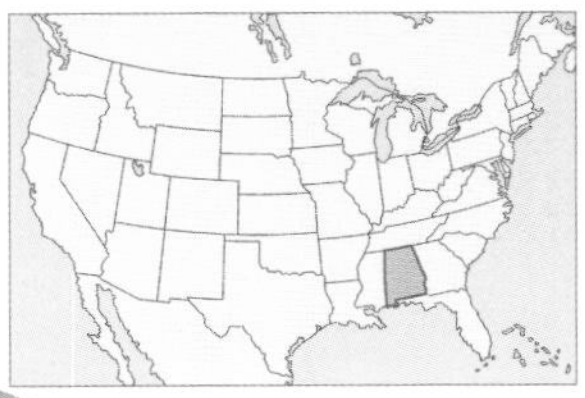

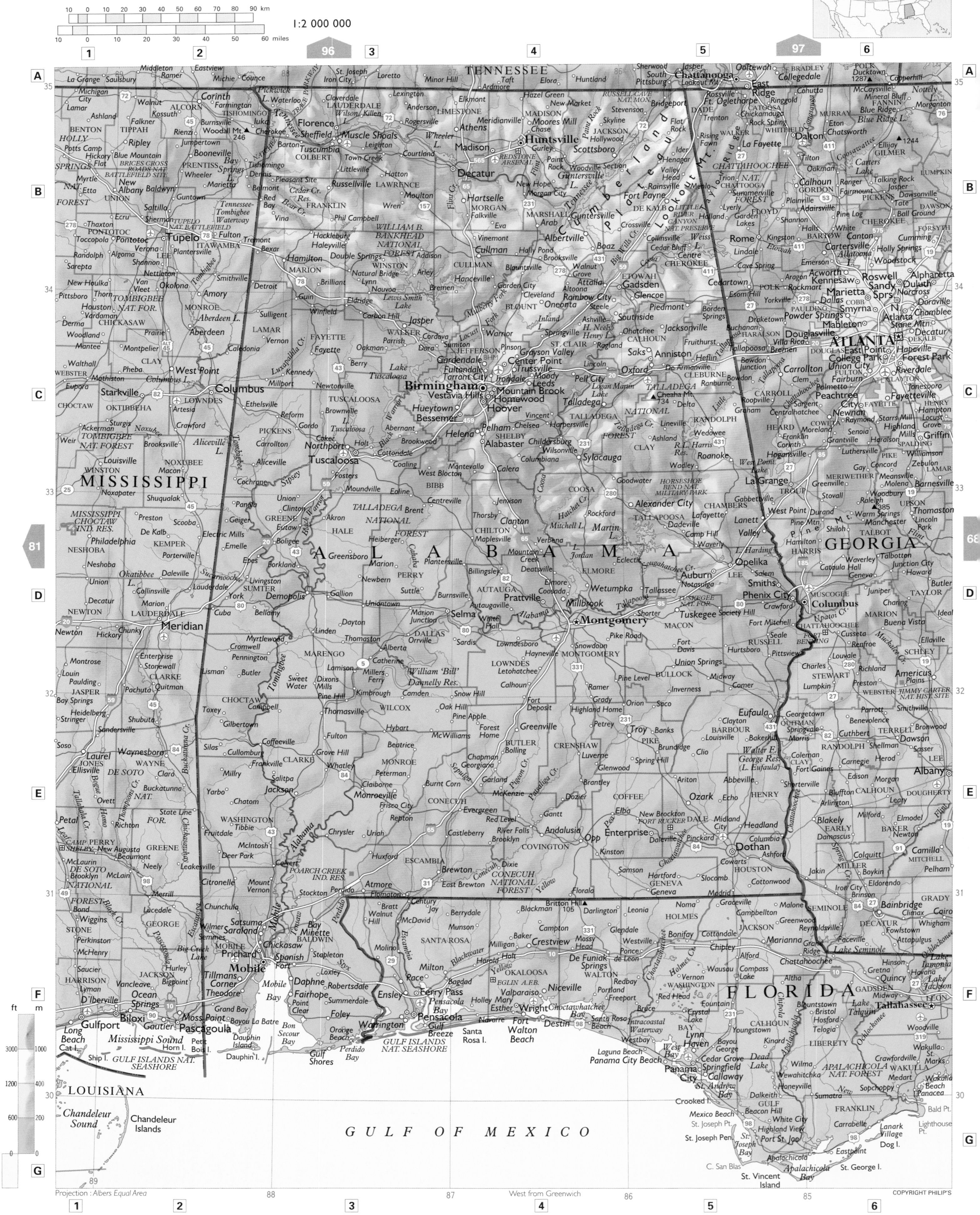

1:2 000 000
km
miles
TENNESSEE
MISSISSIPPI
ALABAMA
GEORGIA
FLORIDA
LOUISIANA
GULF OF MEXICO
Birmingham
Montgomery
Huntsville
Mobile
Tuscaloosa
Decatur
Gadsden
Anniston
Auburn
Opelika
Dothan
Florence
Selma
Chattanooga
Atlanta
Columbus
Tallahassee
Pensacola
Meridian
Tupelo
Gulfport
Biloxi
Pascagoula
Panama City
TALLADEGA NATIONAL FOREST
CONECUH NATIONAL FOREST
WILLIAM B. BANKHEAD NATIONAL FOREST
Mississippi Sound
GULF ISLANDS NAT. SEASHORE
Projection : Albers Equal Area
West from Greenwich
COPYRIGHT PHILIP'S

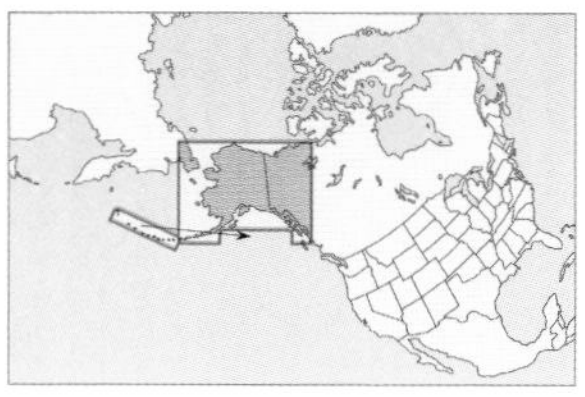

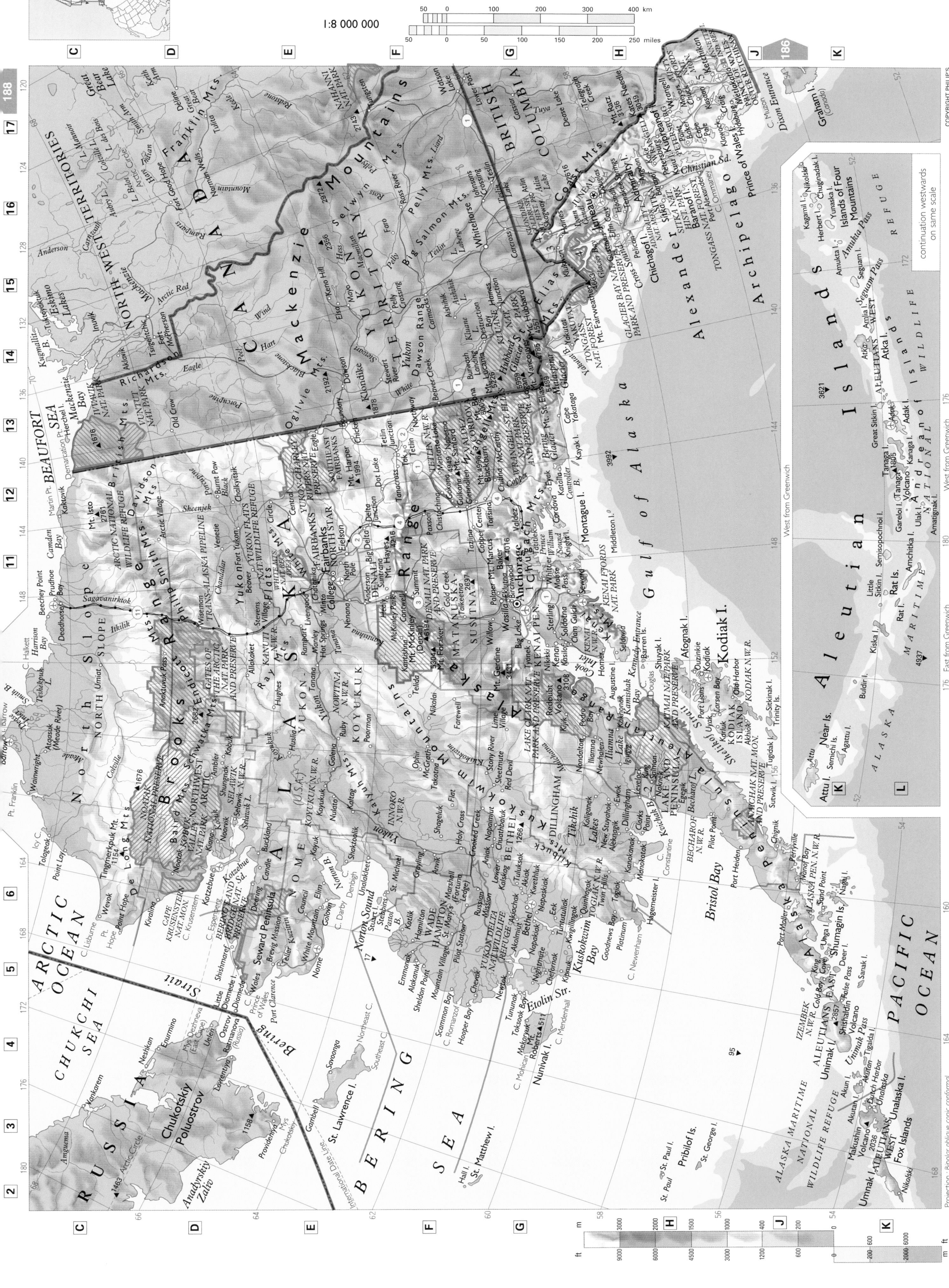
1:8 000 000
ARCTIC OCEAN
BEAUFORT SEA
CHUKCHI SEA
BERING SEA
PACIFIC OCEAN
Gulf of Alaska
Bristol Bay
Norton Sound
Bering Strait
RUSSIA
CANADA
ALASKA
NORTHWEST TERRITORIES
YUKON TERRITORY
BRITISH COLUMBIA
Brooks Range
North Slope
Alaska Range
Mackenzie Mountains
Alexander Archipelago
Aleutian Islands
Alaska Peninsula
Kodiak I.
Anchorage
Fairbanks
Juneau
Nome
Whitehorse
Chukotskiy Poluostrov
Seward Peninsula
St. Lawrence I.
Pribilof Is.
continuation westwards on same scale
1 ANCHORAGE
2 BRISTOL BAY
3 HAINES
4 SKAGWAY-HOONAH-ANGOON
5 KETCHIKAN GATEWAY
Projection: Bipolar oblique conic conformal
COPYRIGHT PHILIP'S

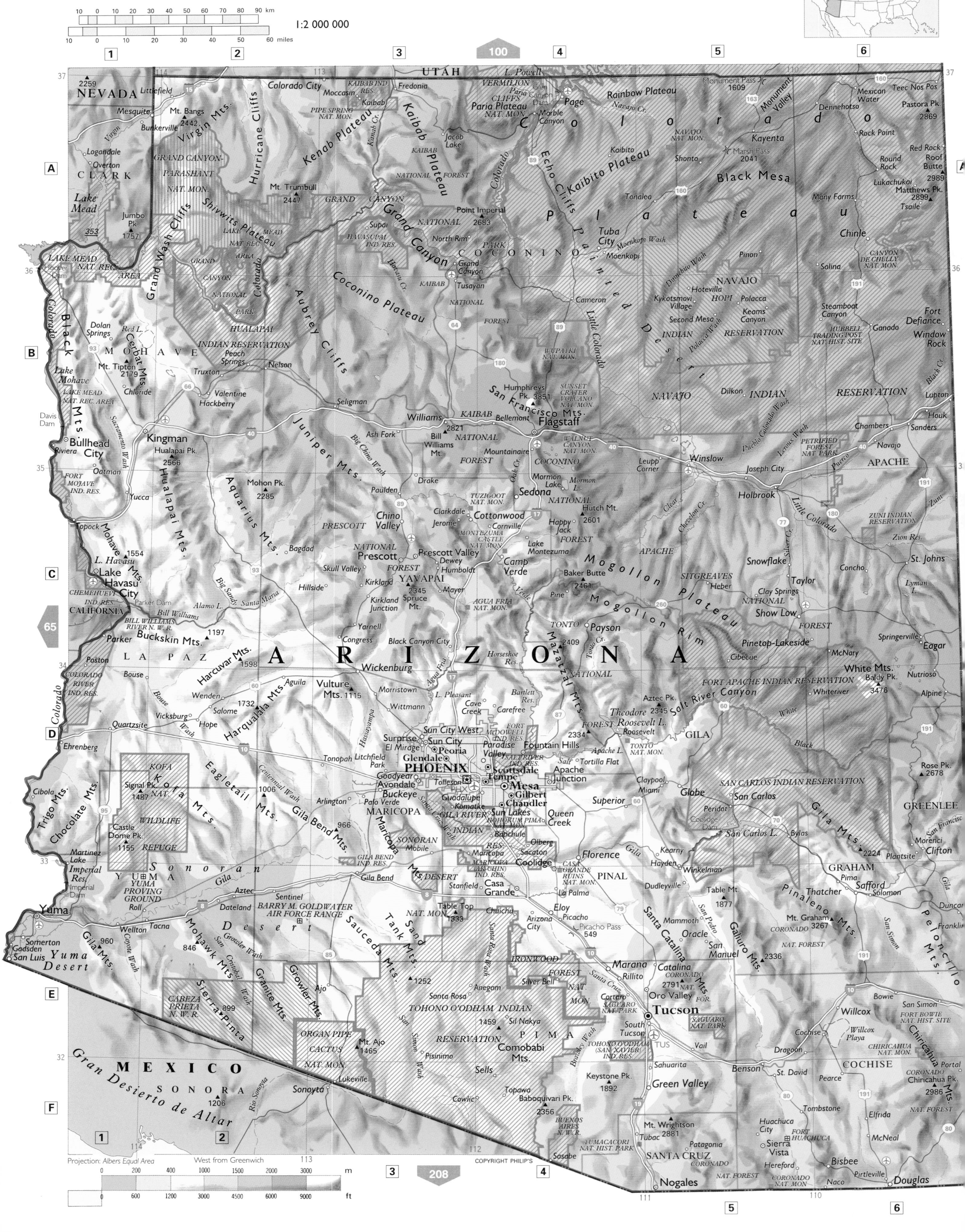

1:2 000 000
km
miles
UTAH
NEVADA
CALIFORNIA
MEXICO
SONORA
Gran Desierto de Altar
ARIZONA
Colorado Plateau
L. Powell
Page
Glen Canyon Dam
Paria Plateau
VERMILION CLIFFS NAT. MON.
Marble Canyon
Rainbow Plateau
Navajo Cr.
Monument Pass 1609
Monument Valley
Mexican Water
Teec Nos Pos
Dennehotso
Pastora Pk. 2869
Rock Point
Red Rock
Round Rock
Roof Butte 2989
Lukachukai
Matthews Pk. 2899
Tsaile
Many Farms
Chinle
CANYON DE CHELLY NAT. MON.
Kayenta
NAVAJO NAT. MON.
Marsh Pass 2041
Shonto
Kaibito
Kaibito Plateau
Black Mesa
Tonalea
Echo Cliffs
Painted Desert
Tuba City
Moenkopi
Moenkopi Wash
Pinon
Salina
Colorado City
Moccasin
KAIBAB IND. RES.
Kaibab
Fredonia
PIPE SPRING NAT. MON.
Kanab Cr.
Kenab Plateau
Kaibab Plateau
Jacob Lake
KAIBAB NATIONAL FOREST
Littlefield
Mesquite
Bunkerville
Mt. Bangs 2442
Virgin Mts.
Virgin
GRAND CANYON-PARASHANT NAT. MON.
Hurricane Cliffs
Mt. Trumbull 2447
Shivwits Plateau
Grand Wash Cliffs
Logandale
Overton
CLARK
Lake Mead
Jumbo Pk. 1757
LAKE MEAD NAT. REC. AREA
Hoover Dam
GRAND CANYON NATIONAL PARK
Grand Canyon
Point Imperial 2683
North Rim
Supai
HAVASUPAI IND. RES.
Havasu Cr.
Tusayan
COCONINO
Coconino Plateau
Aubrey Cliffs
Cameron
Little Colorado
Dinnebito Wash
NAVAJO
HOPI
Hotevilla
Kykotsmovi Village
Polacca
Second Mesa
Keams Canyon
INDIAN RESERVATION
Steamboat Canyon
HUBBELL TRADING POST NAT. HIST. SITE
Ganado
Fort Defiance
Window Rock
Dolan Springs
Red L.
MOHAVE
Cerbat Mts.
Mt. Tipton 2179
Chloride
HUALAPAI INDIAN RESERVATION
Peach Springs
Truxton
Nelson
Valentine
Hackberry
Black Mts.
Lake Mohave
LAKE MEAD NAT. REC. AREA
Davis Dam
Bullhead City
Riviera
Kingman
Sacramento Wash
Hualapai Pk. 2566
Hualapai Mts.
Oatman
FORT MOJAVE IND. RES.
Yucca
Topock
Mohave Mts.
L. Havasu 1554
Lake Havasu City
CHEMEHUEVI IND. RES.
Parker Dam
Seligman
Williams
Bill Williams Mt. 2821
KAIBAB NATIONAL FOREST
Bellemont
Flagstaff
San Francisco Mts.
Humphreys Pk. 3851
SUNSET CRATER VOLCANO NAT. MON.
WUPATKI NAT. MON.
WALNUT CANYON NAT. MON.
Mountainaire
Ash Fork
Juniper Mts.
Big Chino Wash
Aquarius Mts.
Mohon Pk. 2285
Drake
Paulden
Sedona
Mormon Lake
COCONINO NATIONAL FOREST
Hutch Mt. 2601
Leupp Corner
Winslow
Joseph City
Holbrook
PETRIFIED FOREST NAT. PARK
Chambers
Navajo
Sanders
Houk
Lupton
APACHE
Dilkon
NAVAJO INDIAN RESERVATION
Pueblo Colorado Wash
Chino Valley
PRESCOTT NATIONAL FOREST
Clarkdale
Jerome
Cottonwood
Cornville
TUZIGOOT NAT. MON.
MONTEZUMA CASTLE NAT. MON.
Happy Jack
Lake Montezuma
Camp Verde
Prescott
Prescott Valley
Dewey
Humboldt
Skull Valley
Kirkland
YAVAPAI
Spruce Mt. 2345
Mayer
Kirkland Junction
Hillside
Bagdad
Big Sandy
Santa Maria
Alamo L.
Bill Williams
BILL WILLIAMS RIVER N.W.R.
Mogollon Plateau
Mogollon Rim
Baker Butte 2461
Pine
Payson
TONTO
Heber
SITGREAVES NATIONAL FOREST
Clay Springs
Show Low
Snowflake
Taylor
Concho
St. Johns
Lyman L.
Zion Res.
ZUNI INDIAN RESERVATION
Little Colorado
Pinetop-Lakeside
Cibecue
McNary
Springerville
Eagar
White Mts.
Baldy Pk. 3476
Nutrioso
Alpine
FORT APACHE INDIAN RESERVATION
Whiteriver
Salt River Canyon
AGUA FRIA NAT. MON.
Yarnell
Congress
Black Canyon City
Parker
Buckskin Mts. 1197
LA PAZ
Poston
COLORADO RIVER IND. RES.
Bouse
Harcuvar Mts. 1598
Wenden
Salome
Wickenburg
Aguila
Vulture Mts. 1115
Morristown
Wittmann
Harquahala Mts. 1732
Vicksburg
Hope
Quartzsite
Ehrenberg
L. Pleasant
Cave Creek
Carefree
Horseshoe Res.
Bartlett Res.
Mazatzal Mts. 2409
Aztec Pk. 2345
Theodore Roosevelt L.
Roosevelt
TONTO NAT. MON.
GILA
Sun City West
Sun City
Surprise
El Mirage
Peoria
Glendale
PHOENIX
Paradise Valley
Scottsdale
Tempe
Mesa
Gilbert
Chandler
Fountain Hills
FORT McDOWELL IND. RES.
SALT RIVER IND. RES.
Tortilla Flat
Apache Junction
Apache L.
Tonopah
Litchfield Park
Goodyear
Avondale
Tolleson
Buckeye
Palo Verde
Arlington
Guadalupe
Komatke
GILA RIVER INDIAN RES.
Sun Lakes
Queen Creek
Superior
Claypool
Miami
Globe
SAN CARLOS INDIAN RESERVATION
San Carlos
Peridot
Coolidge Dam
San Carlos L.
Bylas
Gila Mts. 2224
Rose Pk. 2678
GREENLEE
Morenci
Clifton
Plantsite
San Francisco
KOFA NAT. WILDLIFE REFUGE
Kofa Mts.
Signal Pk. 1487
Castle Dome Pk. 1155
Eagletail Mts.
Centennial Wash
Gila Bend Mts. 966
MARICOPA
Maricopa
Maricopa Mts.
SONORAN DESERT
Mobile
GILA BEND IND. RES.
Gila Bend
Sacaton
Olberg
Coolidge
CASA GRANDE RUINS NAT. MON.
Florence
PINAL
Kearny
Hayden
Winkelman
Dudleyville
Table Mt. 1877
GRAHAM
Pima
Safford
Thatcher
Solomon
Pinaleno Mts.
Mt. Graham 3267
CORONADO NAT. FOREST
Stanfield
Casa Grande
Eloy
Picacho
Picacho Pass 549
Arizona City
Table Top 1333
Chuichu
Santa Rosa Wash
Sand Tank Mts.
Sauceda Mts.
Cibola
Trigo Mts.
Chocolate Mts.
Martinez Lake
Imperial Res.
Imperial Dam
YUMA PROVING GROUND
Roll
Sonoran Desert
Gila
Aztec
Sentinel
Dateland
BARRY M. GOLDWATER AIR FORCE RANGE
Yuma
Wellton
Tacna
Somerton
Gadsden
San Luis
Yuma Desert
Gila Mts. 960
Mohawk Mts. 846
Growler Wash
Granite Mts.
Growler Mts.
Ajo
CABEZA PRIETA N.W.R.
Sierra Pinta 899
ORGAN PIPE CACTUS NAT. MON.
Mt. Ajo 1465
Lukeville
Sonoyta
Rio Sonoyta
1206
TOHONO O'ODHAM INDIAN RESERVATION
PIMA
Santa Rosa
Anegam
1252
Sil Nakya 1459
Pisinimo
Comobabi Mts.
Sells
Topawa
Cowlic
Baboquivari Pk. 2356
BUENOS AIRES N.W.R.
Sasabe
IRONWOOD FOREST NAT. MON.
Silver Bell
Marana
Rillito
Santa Cruz
SAGUARO NAT. PARK
Tucson
South Tucson
TOHONO O'ODHAM (SAN XAVIER) IND. RES.
Catalina
Oro Valley
Santa Catalina Mts. 2791
Mammoth
Oracle
San Manuel
San Pedro
Galiuro Mts. 2336
Vail
Sahuarita
Green Valley
Keystone Pk. 1892
Mt. Wrightson 2881
Tubac
TUMACACORI NAT. HIST. PARK
Patagonia
SANTA CRUZ
Nogales
CORONADO NAT. FOREST
Benson
St. David
Huachuca City
FORT HUACHUCA
Sierra Vista
Hereford
Tombstone
Dragoon
Cochise
Willcox
Willcox Playa
Bowie
San Simon
FORT BOWIE NAT. HIST. SITE
Chiricahua Mts.
CHIRICAHUA NAT. MON.
COCHISE
Pearce
Chiricahua Pk. 2986
Portal
Elfrida
McNeal
Bisbee
Pirtleville
Naco
Douglas
Peloncillo Mts.
Duncan
Franklin
Projection: Albers Equal Area
West from Greenwich
COPYRIGHT PHILIP'S

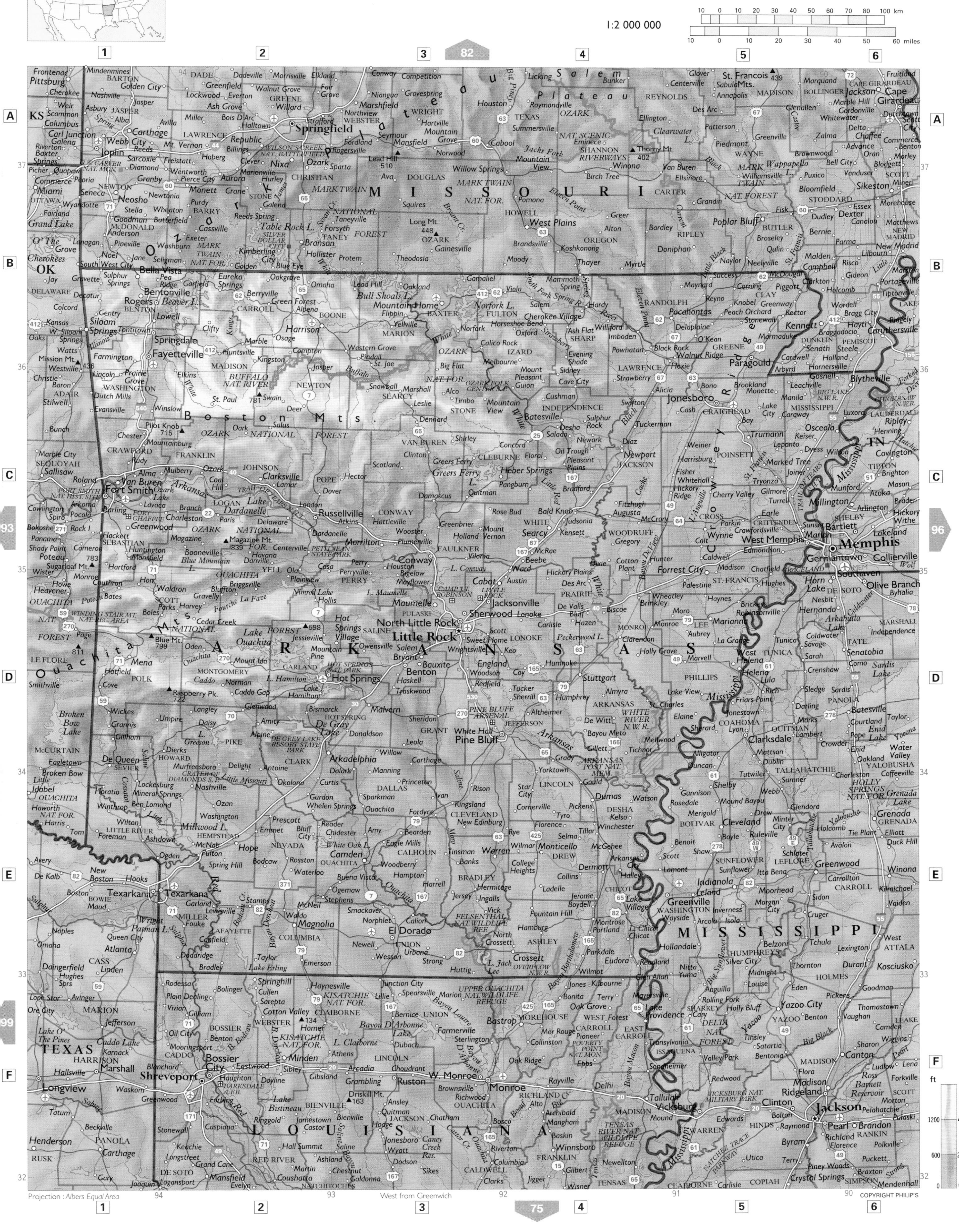
1:2 000 000
10 0 10 20 30 40 50 60 70 80 100 km
10 0 10 20 30 40 50 60 miles
1 2 3 4 5 6
A B C D E F
82
75
93
96
99
MISSOURI
ARKANSAS
MISSISSIPPI
LOUISIANA
TEXAS
KS
OK
TN
Salem Plateau
Ozark Plateau
Boston Mts.
Ouachita Mts.
Springfield
Joplin
Fort Smith
Fayetteville
Little Rock
North Little Rock
Hot Springs
Pine Bluff
Jonesboro
Memphis
Texarkana
El Dorado
Shreveport
Monroe
Jackson
Greenville
Mississippi
Arkansas
Red
White
Ouachita
ft m
1200 400
600 200
0 0
Projection : Albers Equal Area
94 93 West from Greenwich 92 91 90
COPYRIGHT PHILIP'S

1:2 000 000

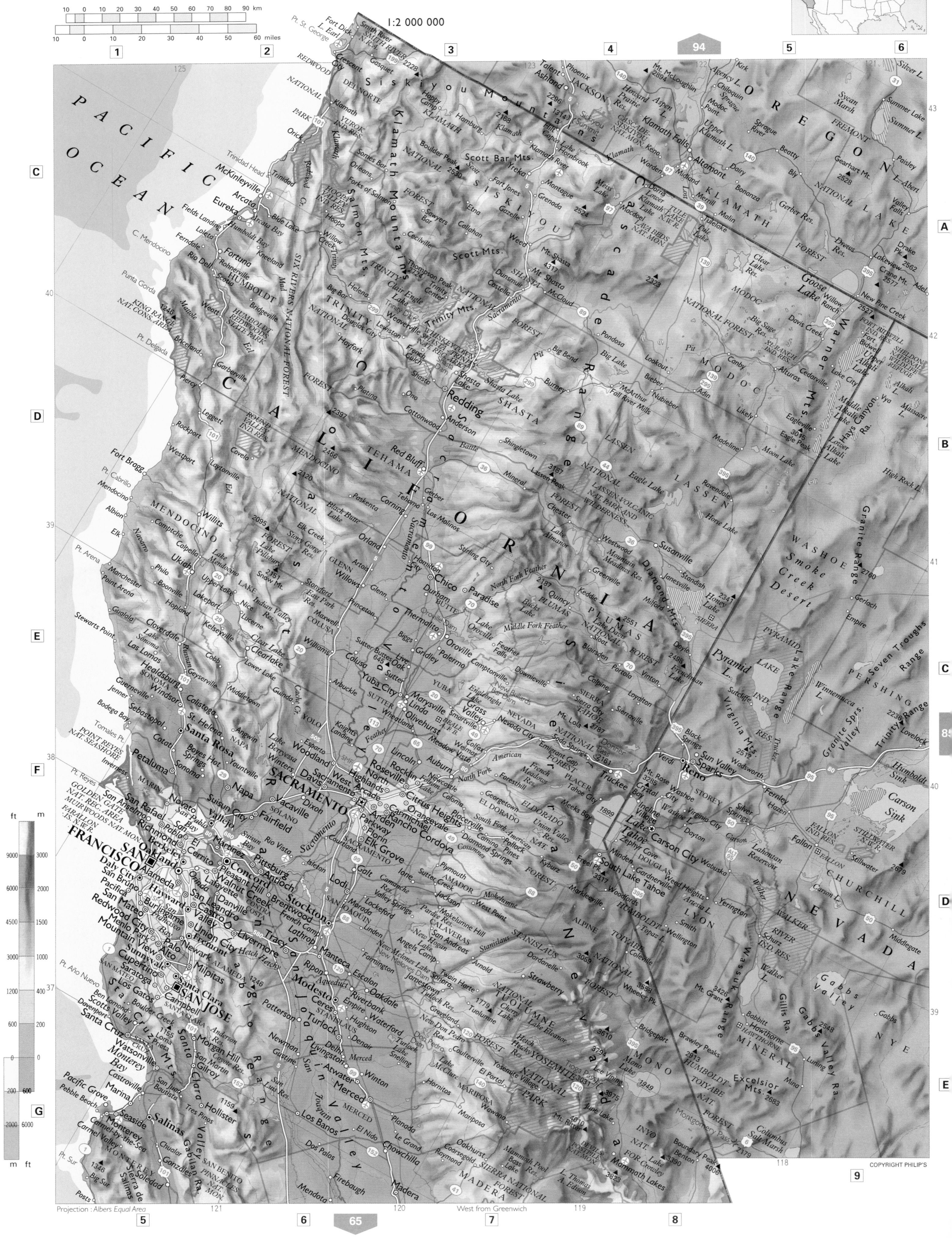

94
85
65

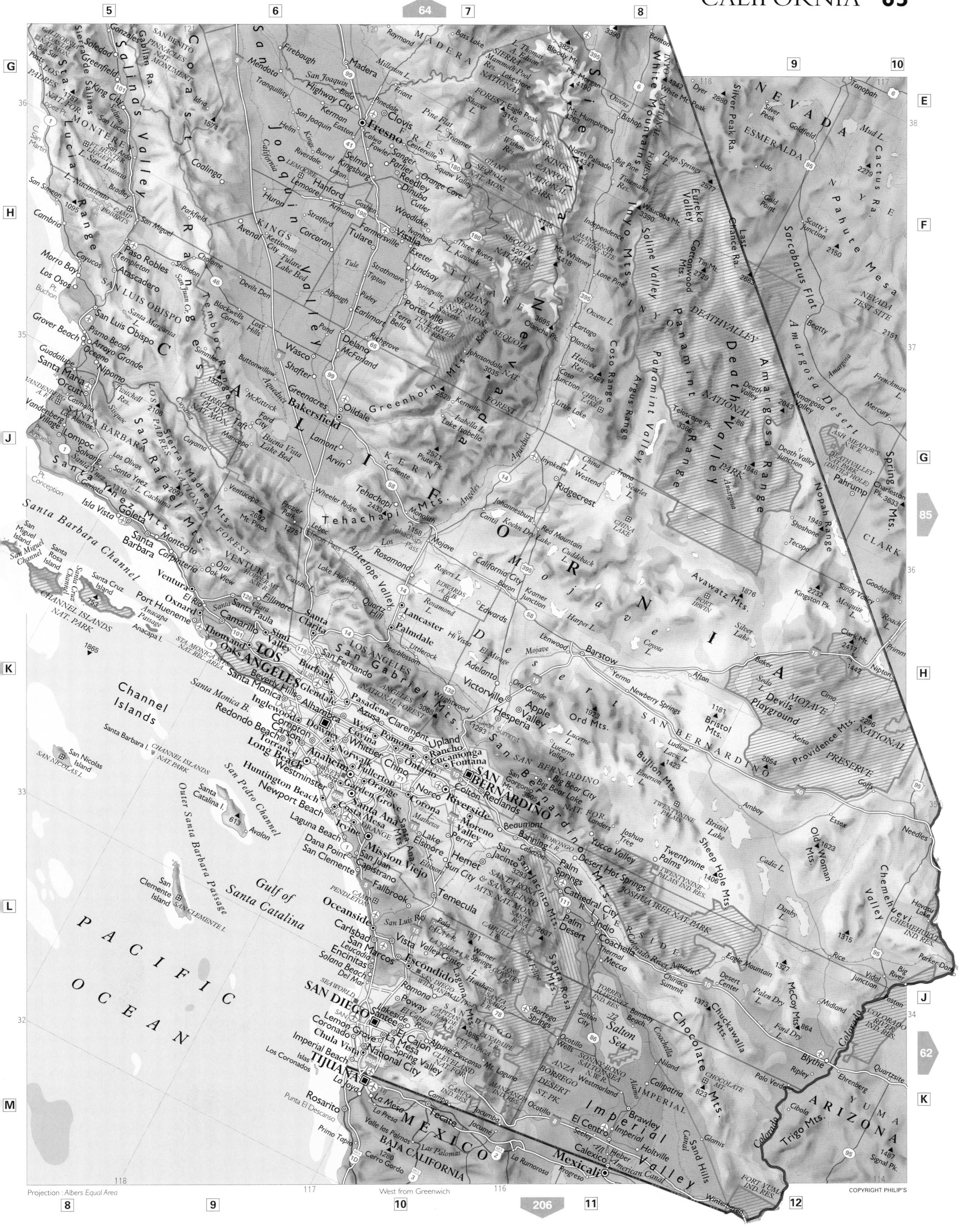
64
85
62
206
PACIFIC OCEAN
NEVADA
ARIZONA
MEXICO
BAJA CALIFORNIA
CALIFORNIA
Channel Islands
CHANNEL ISLANDS NAT. PARK
Santa Barbara Channel
Gulf of Santa Catalina
San Pedro Channel
Santa Catalina I.
San Clemente Island
San Nicolas Island
Santa Cruz Island
Santa Rosa Island
San Miguel Island
San Joaquin Valley
Salinas Valley
Coast Ranges
Sierra Nevada
Tehachapi Mts.
San Gabriel Mts.
San Bernardino Mts.
Santa Lucia Range
Temblor Range
Sierra Madre Mts.
Santa Ynez Mts.
Mojave Desert
Death Valley
DEATH VALLEY NATIONAL PARK
Panamint Range
Amargosa Range
Inyo Mts.
White Mountains
Coso Range
Argus Range
Owens L.
Salton Sea
Imperial Valley
Chocolate Mts.
Chuckawalla Mts.
Providence Mts.
MOJAVE NATIONAL PRESERVE
JOSHUA TREE NAT. PARK
KINGS CANYON NATIONAL PARK
SEQUOIA NAT. PARK
ANZA BORREGO DESERT ST. PK.
Fresno
Bakersfield
LOS ANGELES
SAN BERNARDINO
SAN DIEGO
TIJUANA
Mexicali
Santa Barbara
Ventura
Oxnard
Lancaster
Palmdale
Barstow
Victorville
Riverside
Palm Springs
Indio
El Centro
Blythe
Needles
Long Beach
Santa Ana
Anaheim
Oceanside
Escondido
San Luis Obispo
Paso Robles
Santa Maria
Lompoc
Visalia
Tulare
Hanford
Porterville
Delano
Madera
Coalinga
Ridgecrest
Bishop
Lone Pine
Pahrump
Tonopah
COPYRIGHT PHILIP'S

1:2 000 000

10 0 10 20 30 40 50 60 70 80 100 km

10 0 10 20 30 40 50 60 miles

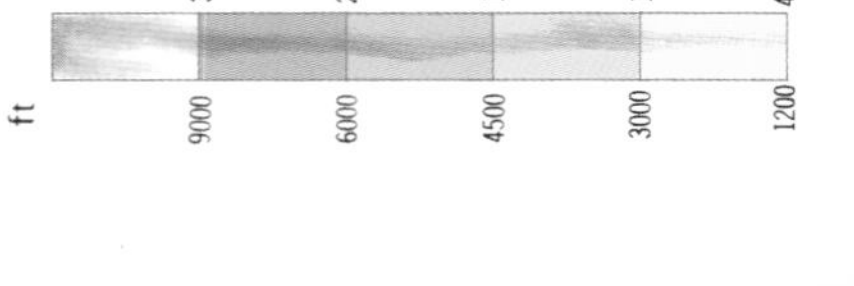

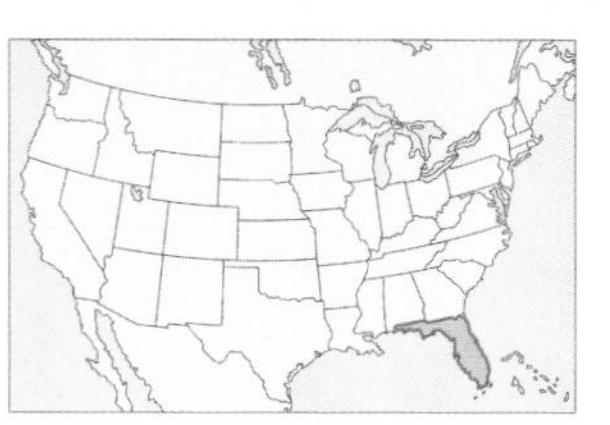

See page 78 for Connecticut and page 77 for Delaware and District of Columbia

1:2 000 000

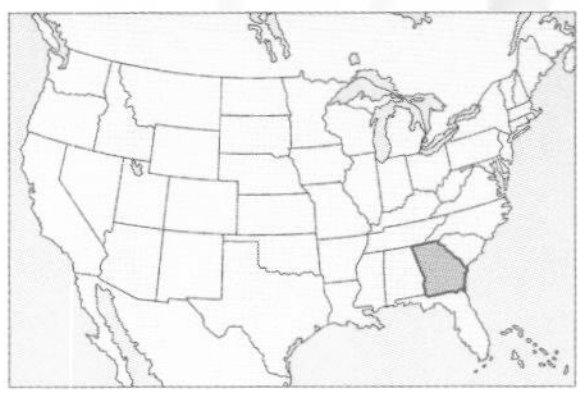

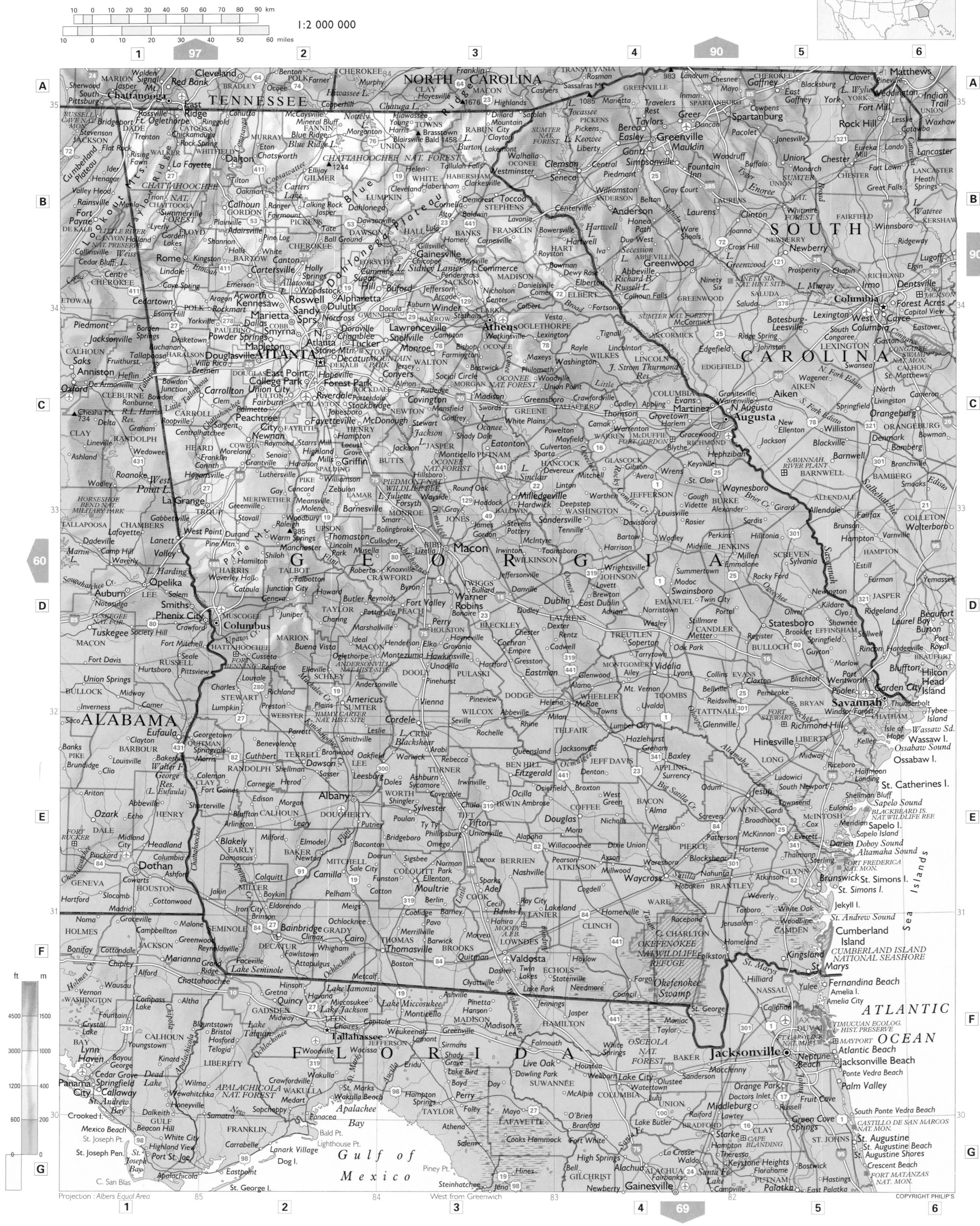

1:2 000 000
km
miles
NORTH CAROLINA
TENNESSEE
SOUTH CAROLINA
GEORGIA
ALABAMA
FLORIDA
ATLANTIC OCEAN
Gulf of Mexico
Sea Islands
ATLANTA
Athens
Augusta
Macon
Columbus
Savannah
Albany
Valdosta
Brunswick
Dalton
Rome
Gainesville
Marietta
Chattanooga
Greenville
Spartanburg
Columbia
Anderson
Aiken
Tallahassee
Jacksonville
Dothan
Opelika
Auburn
Phenix City
Eufaula
Okefenokee Swamp
OKEFENOKEE NAT. WILDLIFE REFUGE
CHATTAHOOCHEE NAT. FOREST
CUMBERLAND ISLAND NATIONAL SEASHORE
APALACHICOLA NAT. FOREST
OSCEOLA NAT. FOREST
Projection : Albers Equal Area
West from Greenwich
COPYRIGHT PHILIP'S
ft
m

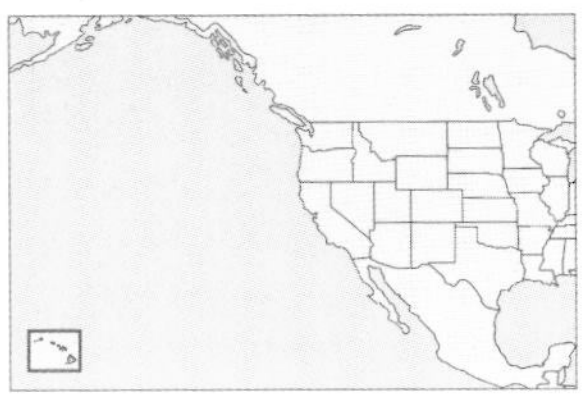

1:2 000 000

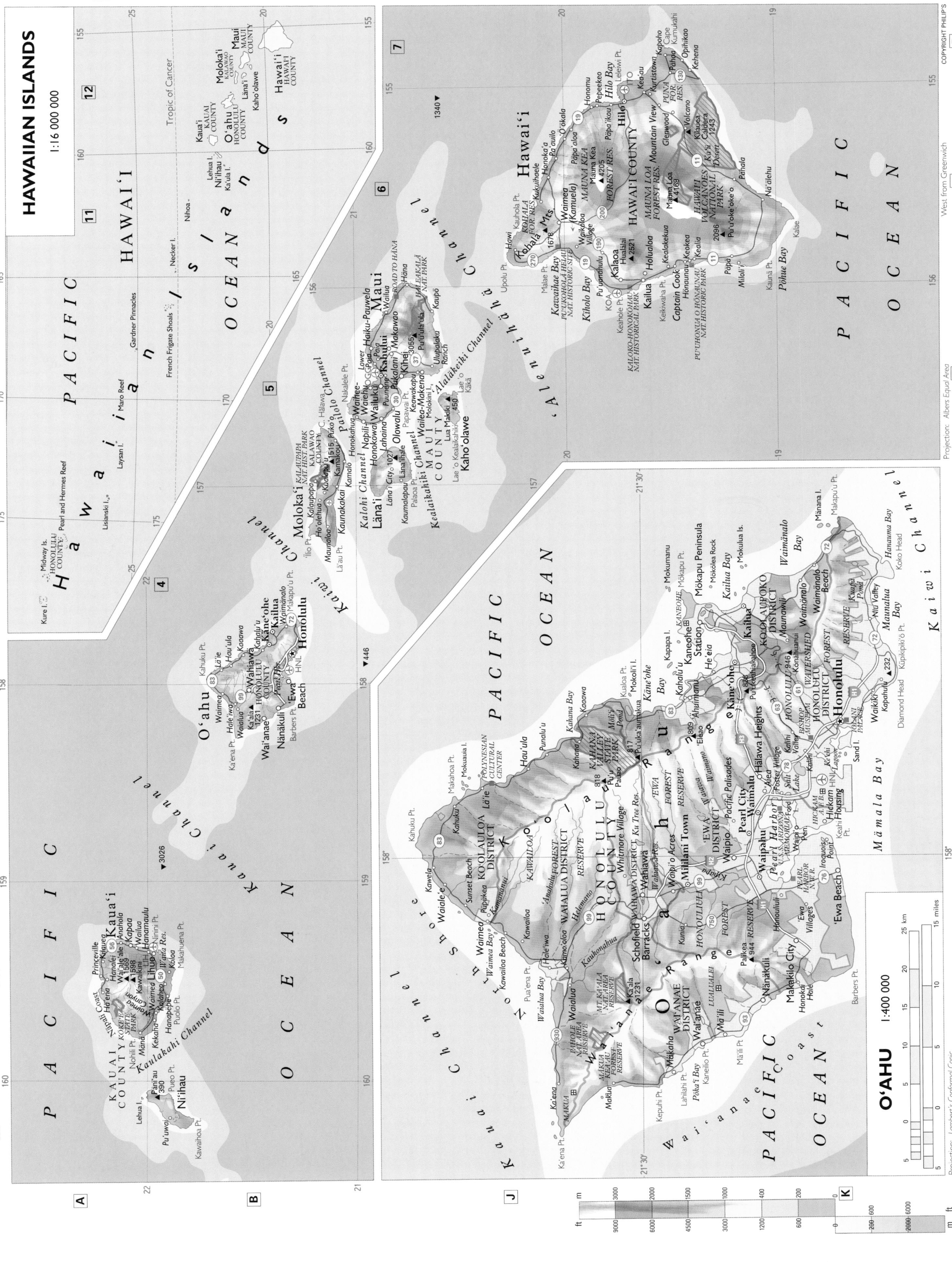
HAWAIIAN ISLANDS
1:16 000 000
PACIFIC
OCEAN
HAWAIʻI
Hawaiian Islands
Tropic of Cancer
Midway Is.
Kure I.
Pearl and Hermes Reef
Lisianski I.
Laysan I.
Maro Reef
Gardner Pinnacles
French Frigate Shoals
Necker I.
Nihoa
Kauaʻi
Niʻihau
Oʻahu
Molokaʻi
Lānaʻi
Maui
Kahoʻolawe
Hawaiʻi
Kauaʻi Channel
Kaiwi Channel
Kalohi Channel
Pailolo Channel
Alenuihāhā Channel
ʻAlalākeiki Channel
Kealaikahiki Channel
Kaulakahi Channel
Honolulu
Hilo
Kailua
Lihue
Kahului
Wailuku
Lahaina
Kaunakakai
Lānaʻi City
Mauna Kea
Mauna Loa
Kilauea Caldera
HAWAIʻI VOLCANOES NATIONAL PARK
HALEAKALĀ NAT. PARK
HAWAIʻI COUNTY
MAUI COUNTY
KAUAI COUNTY
HONOLULU COUNTY
OʻAHU
1:400 000
North Shore
Waiʻanae Coast
Koʻolau Range
Waiʻanae Range
Pearl Harbor
Kāneʻohe Bay
Kailua Bay
Waimānalo Bay
Māmala Bay
Schofield Barracks
Wahiawā
Mililani Town
Pearl City
Waipahu
ʻEwa Beach
Kāneʻohe
Waimānalo
Diamond Head
Koko Head
Kaʻena Pt.
Barbers Pt.
Makapuʻu Pt.
Kahuku Pt.
Projection: Albers Equal Area
Projection: Lambert's Conformal Conic
West from Greenwich
COPYRIGHT PHILIP'S

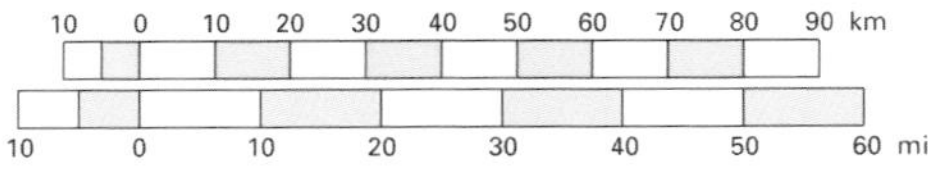
10 0 10 20 30 40 50 60 70 80 90 km
10 0 10 20 30 40 50 60 miles
1:2 000 000

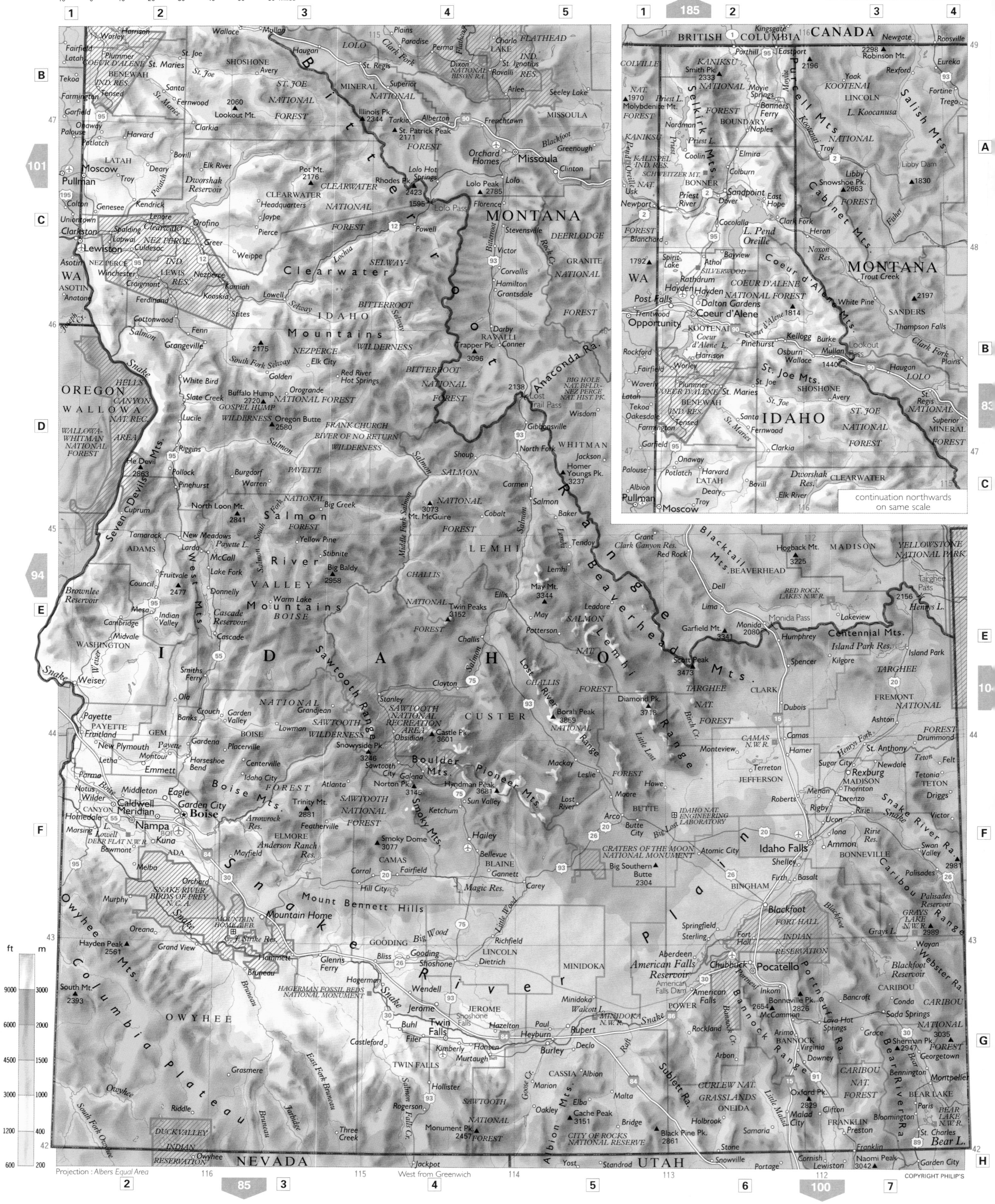
IDAHO
MONTANA
OREGON
WA
NEVADA
UTAH
BRITISH COLUMBIA
CANADA
YELLOWSTONE NATIONAL PARK
Bitterroot Range
Clearwater Mountains
Salmon River Mountains
Boise Mts.
Sawtooth Range
Lost River Range
Lemhi Range
Beaverhead Mts.
Seven Devils Mts.
West Mts.
Centennial Mts.
Snake River Plain
Snake River
Mount Bennett Hills
Owyhee Mts.
Columbia Plateau
Pioneer Mts.
Smoky Mts.
Boulder Mts.
Bannock Range
Portneuf Ra.
Caribou Range
Snake River Ra.
Bear River Ra.
Sublett Ra.
Albion Mts.
Selkirk Mts.
Purcell Mts.
Cabinet Mts.
Salish Mts.
Coeur d'Alene Mts.
St. Joe Mts.
Bitterroot Mts.
Anaconda Ra.
Blacktail Mts.
HELLS CANYON
WALLOWA-WHITMAN NATIONAL FOREST
FRANK CHURCH RIVER OF NO RETURN WILDERNESS
SELWAY-BITTERROOT WILDERNESS
GOSPEL HUMP WILDERNESS
SAWTOOTH NATIONAL RECREATION AREA
CRATERS OF THE MOON NATIONAL MONUMENT
HAGERMAN FOSSIL BEDS NATIONAL MONUMENT
CITY OF ROCKS NATIONAL RESERVE
IDAHO NAT. ENGINEERING LABORATORY
SNAKE RIVER BIRDS OF PREY N.C.A.
MOUNTAIN HOME A.F.B.
DUCK VALLEY INDIAN RESERVATION
FORT HALL INDIAN RESERVATION
NEZ PERCE IND. RES.
COEUR D'ALENE IND. RES.
CURLEW NAT. GRASSLANDS
Borah Peak 3859
Castle Pk. 3601
Hyndman Peak 3681
Diamond Pk. 3718
Scott Peak 3473
He Devil 2863
Trapper Pk. 3096
Lolo Pass
Lost Trail Pass
Monida Pass
Targhee Pass
Boise
Nampa
Caldwell
Meridian
Idaho Falls
Pocatello
Twin Falls
Lewiston
Moscow
Coeur d'Alene
Sandpoint
Missoula
American Falls Reservoir
Palisades Reservoir
Bear L.
Henrys L.
Pend Oreille L.
Dworshak Reservoir
Cascade Reservoir
Brownlee Reservoir
C.J. Strike Res.
continuation northwards on same scale
Projection : Albers Equal Area
West from Greenwich
COPYRIGHT PHILIP'S

1:2 000 000

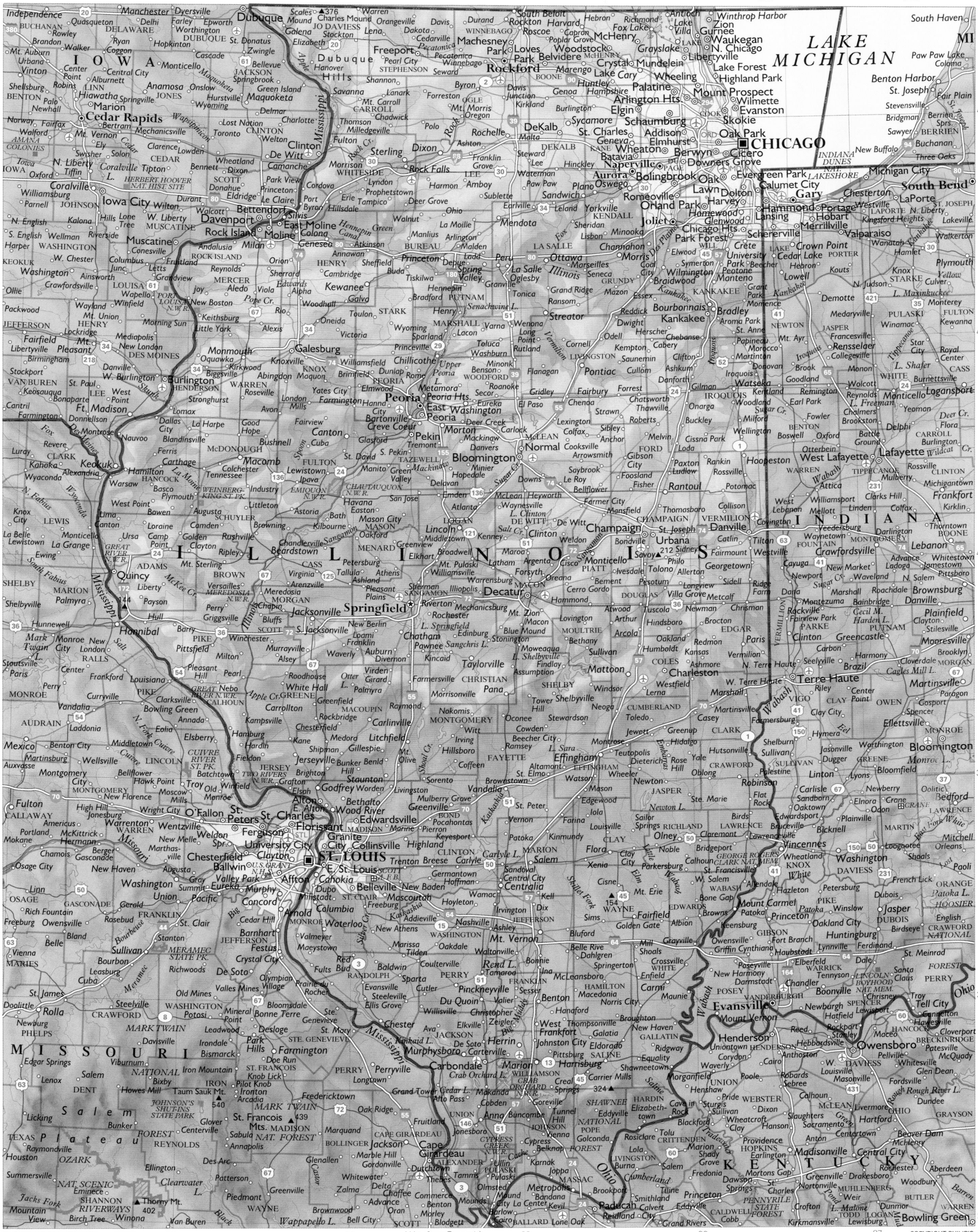

Projection : Albers Equal Area

West from Greenwich

COPYRIGHT PHILIP'S

103 96 72 73 82

10 0 10 20 30 40 50 60 70 80 90 km

10 0 10 20 30 40 50 60 miles

1:2 000 000

79

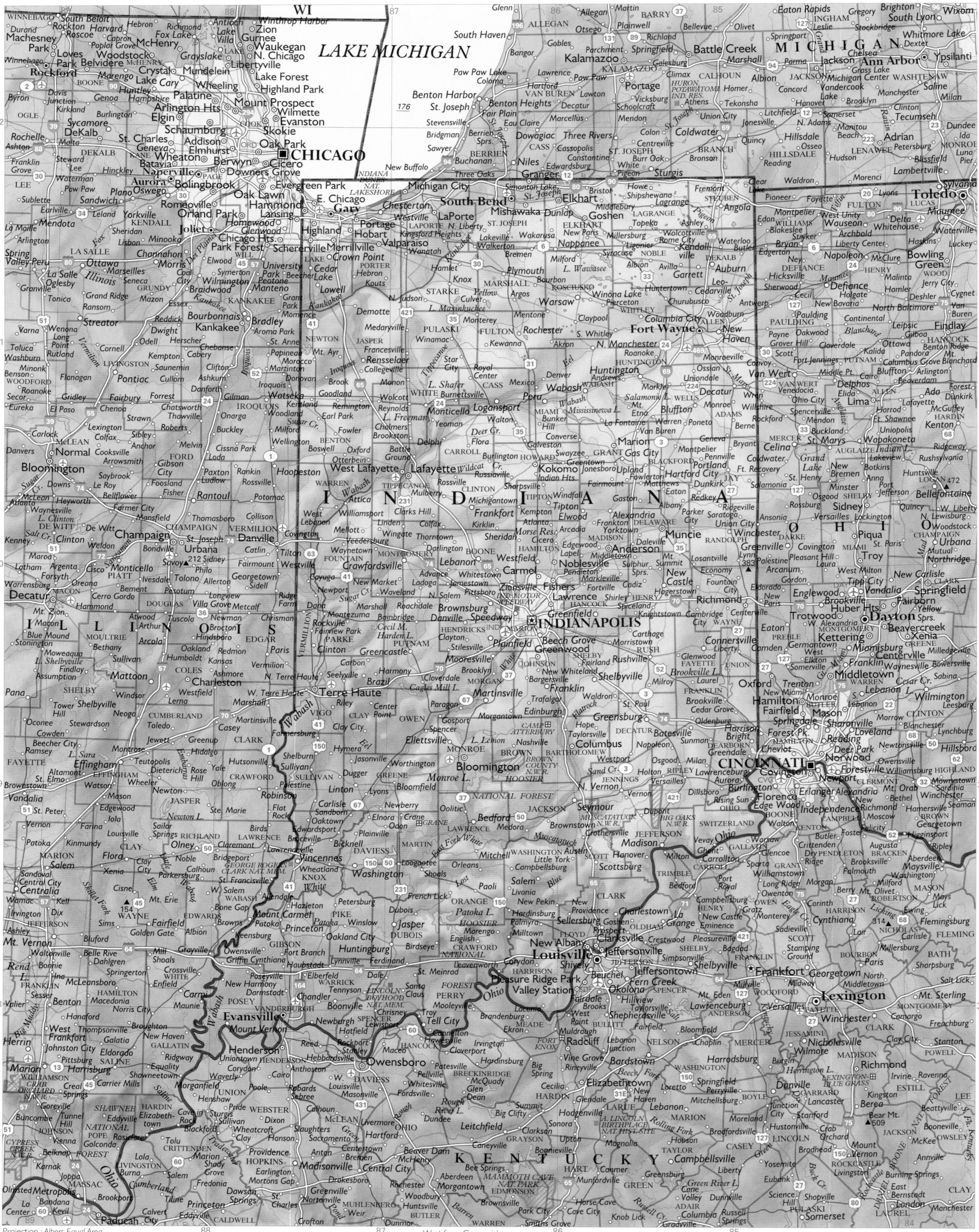

71
92

Projection : Albers Equal Area

West from Greenwich

96
97

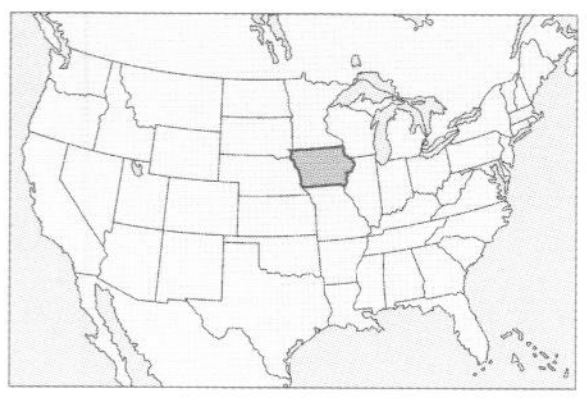

1:2 000 000

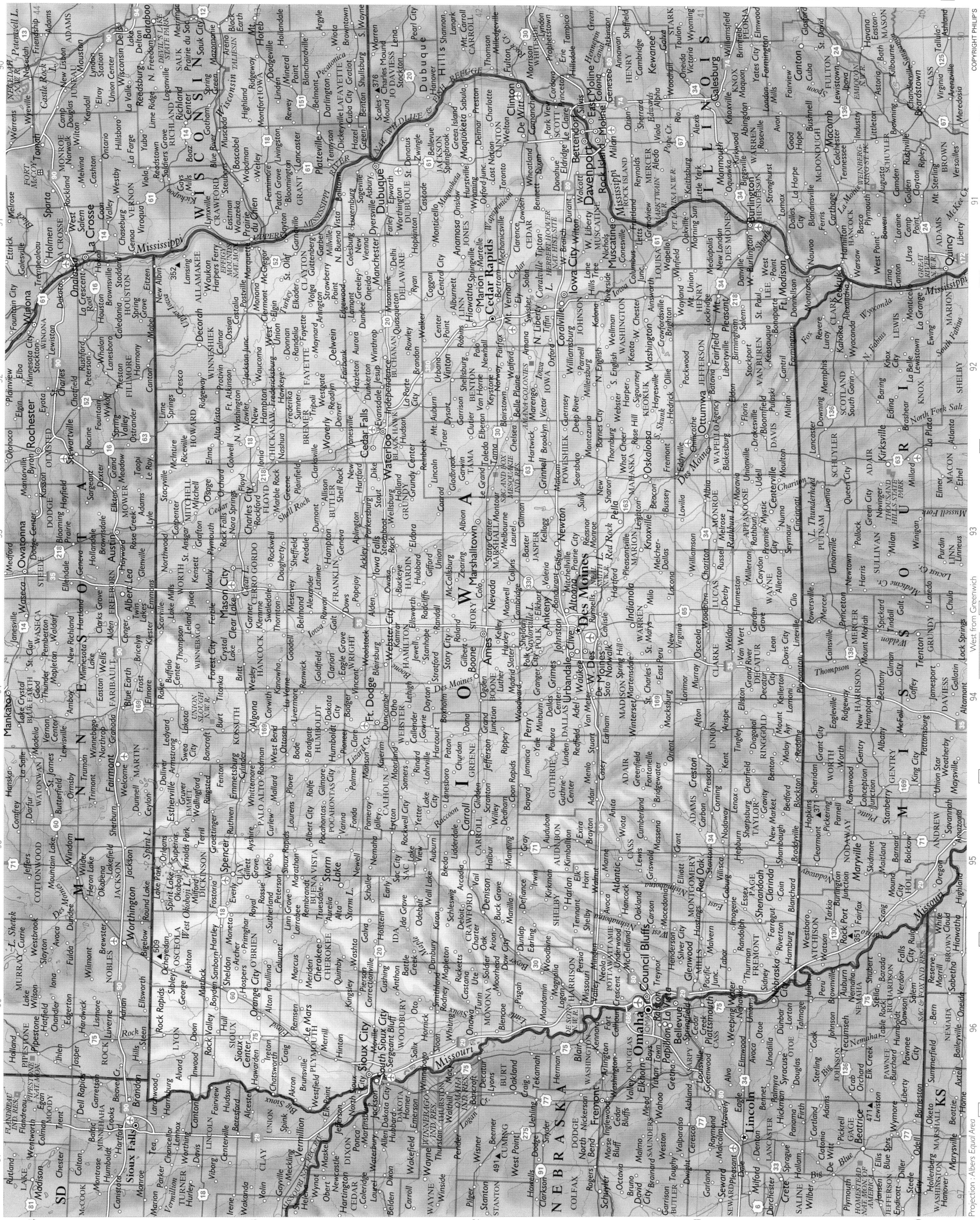

Projection : Albers Equal Area

10 0 10 20 30 40 50 60 70 80 90 km

10 0 10 20 30 40 50 60 miles

1:2 000 000

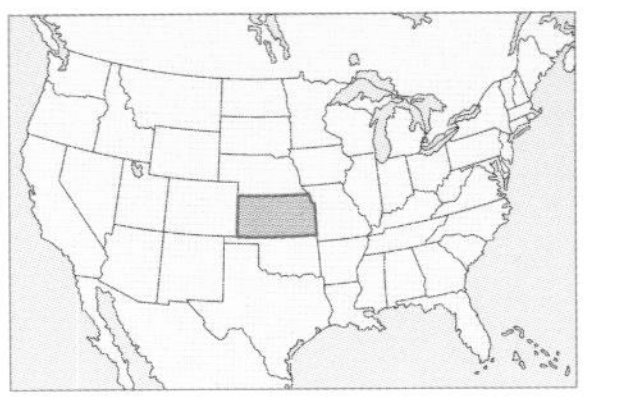

See page 96 for Kentucky

1:2 000 000

10 0 10 20 30 40 50 60 70 80 100 km

10 0 10 20 30 40 50 60 miles

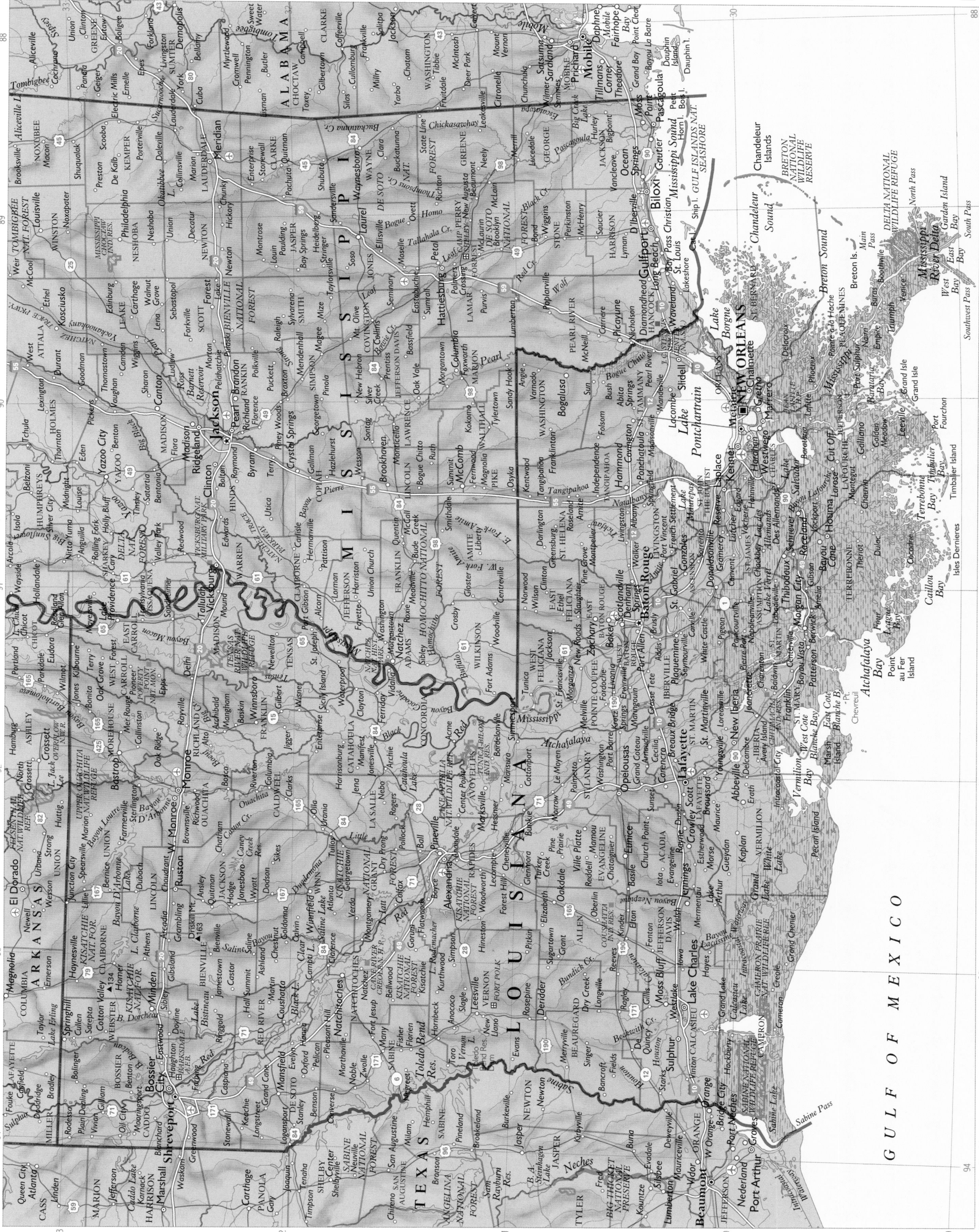

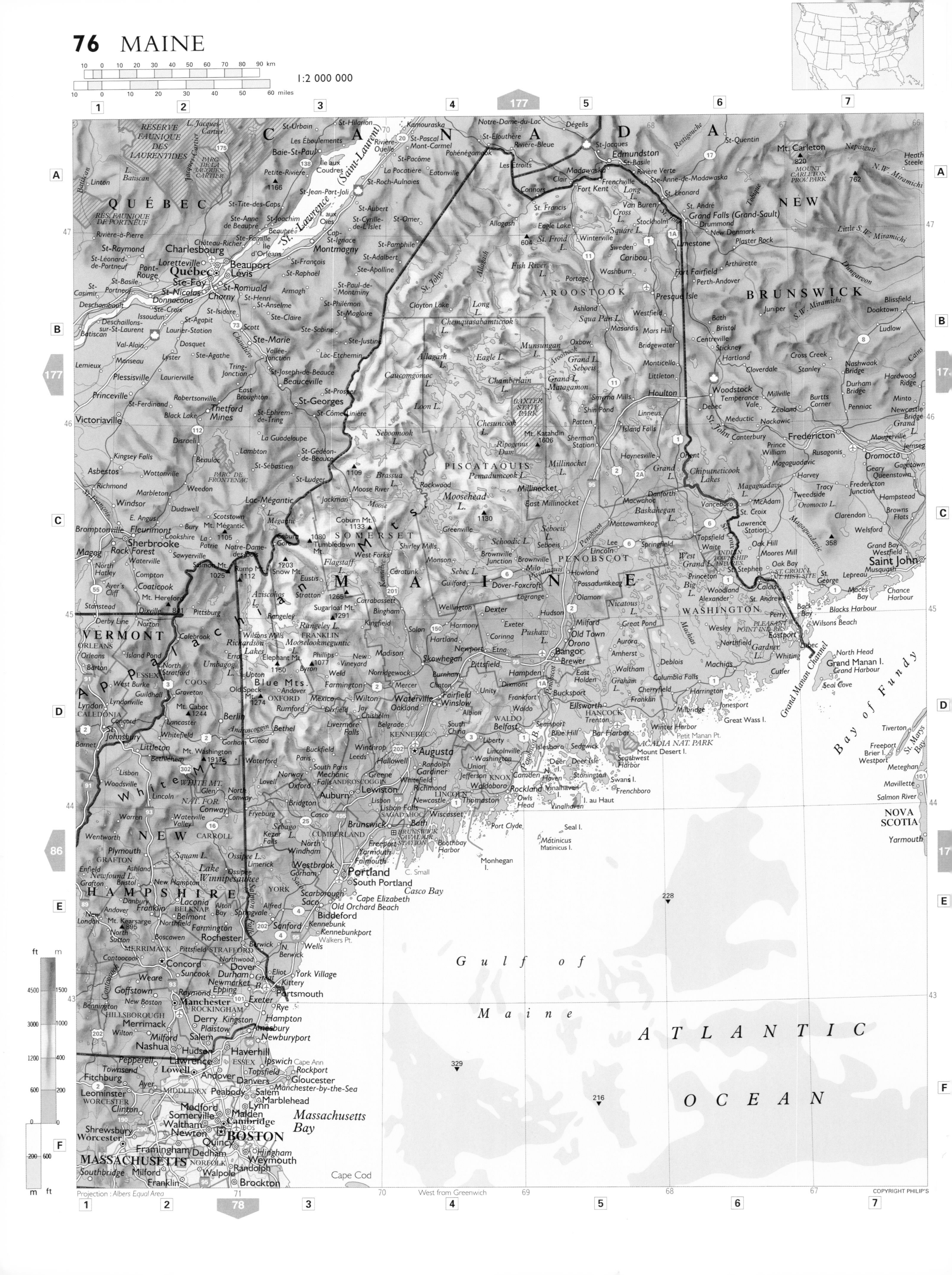
1:2 000 000
10 0 10 20 30 40 50 60 70 80 90 km
10 0 10 20 30 40 50 60 miles
1 2 3 4 5 6 7
A B C D E F
177
78
86
C A N A D A
QUÉBEC
NEW BRUNSWICK
MAINE
VERMONT
NEW HAMPSHIRE
MASSACHUSETTS
NOVA SCOTIA
Appalachian Mts
White Mts
AROOSTOOK
PISCATAQUIS
SOMERSET
PENOBSCOT
WASHINGTON
HANCOCK
WALDO
KNOX
LINCOLN
KENNEBEC
FRANKLIN
OXFORD
ANDROSCOGGIN
SAGADAHOC
CUMBERLAND
YORK
Gulf of Maine
ATLANTIC OCEAN
Bay of Fundy
Massachusetts Bay
Casco Bay
Grand Manan Channel
St. Lawrence (Saint-Laurent)
St. John
Allagash
Penobscot
Kennebec
Androscoggin
Moosehead L.
Chesuncook L.
Chamberlain L.
Eagle L.
Sebago L.
Rangeley L.
Mooselookmeguntic L.
Lake Winnipesaukee
BAXTER STATE PARK
Mt. Katahdin 1606
ACADIA NAT. PARK
Mount Desert I.
Mt. Washington 1917
Augusta
Portland
South Portland
Bangor
Lewiston
Auburn
Brunswick
Bath
Waterville
Skowhegan
Presque Isle
Caribou
Houlton
Millinocket
East Millinocket
Calais
Eastport
Lubec
Ellsworth
Bar Harbor
Belfast
Rockland
Camden
Biddeford
Saco
Sanford
Kittery
York Village
Old Town
Orono
Brewer
Fort Kent
Madawaska
Edmundston
Grand Falls (Grand-Sault)
Woodstock
Fredericton
Saint John
St. Stephen
Québec
Lévis
Sherbrooke
Thetford Mines
Victoriaville
St-Georges
Lac-Mégantic
Concord
Manchester
Nashua
Portsmouth
Dover
Lowell
Lawrence
Haverhill
BOSTON
Gloucester
Salem
Lynn
Cambridge
Quincy
Worcester
Fitchburg
Brockton
Cape Cod
Cape Ann
Cape Elizabeth
Old Orchard Beach
Monhegan I.
Matinicus I.
Vinalhaven
Grand Manan I.
Yarmouth
Projection : Albers Equal Area
West from Greenwich
71 70 69 68 67
47 46 45 44 43
ft m
4500 1500
3000 1000
1200 400
600 200
200 600
COPYRIGHT PHILIP'S

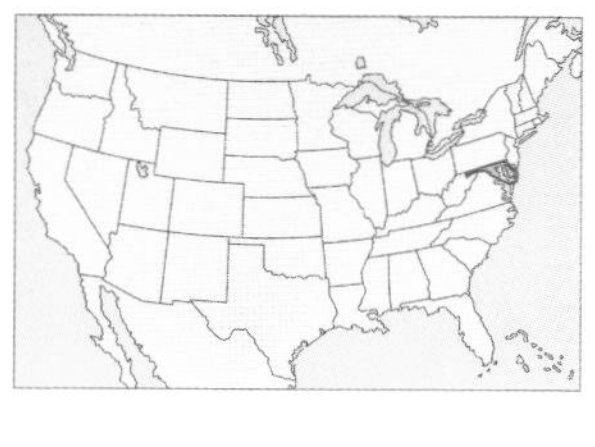

1:1 000 000

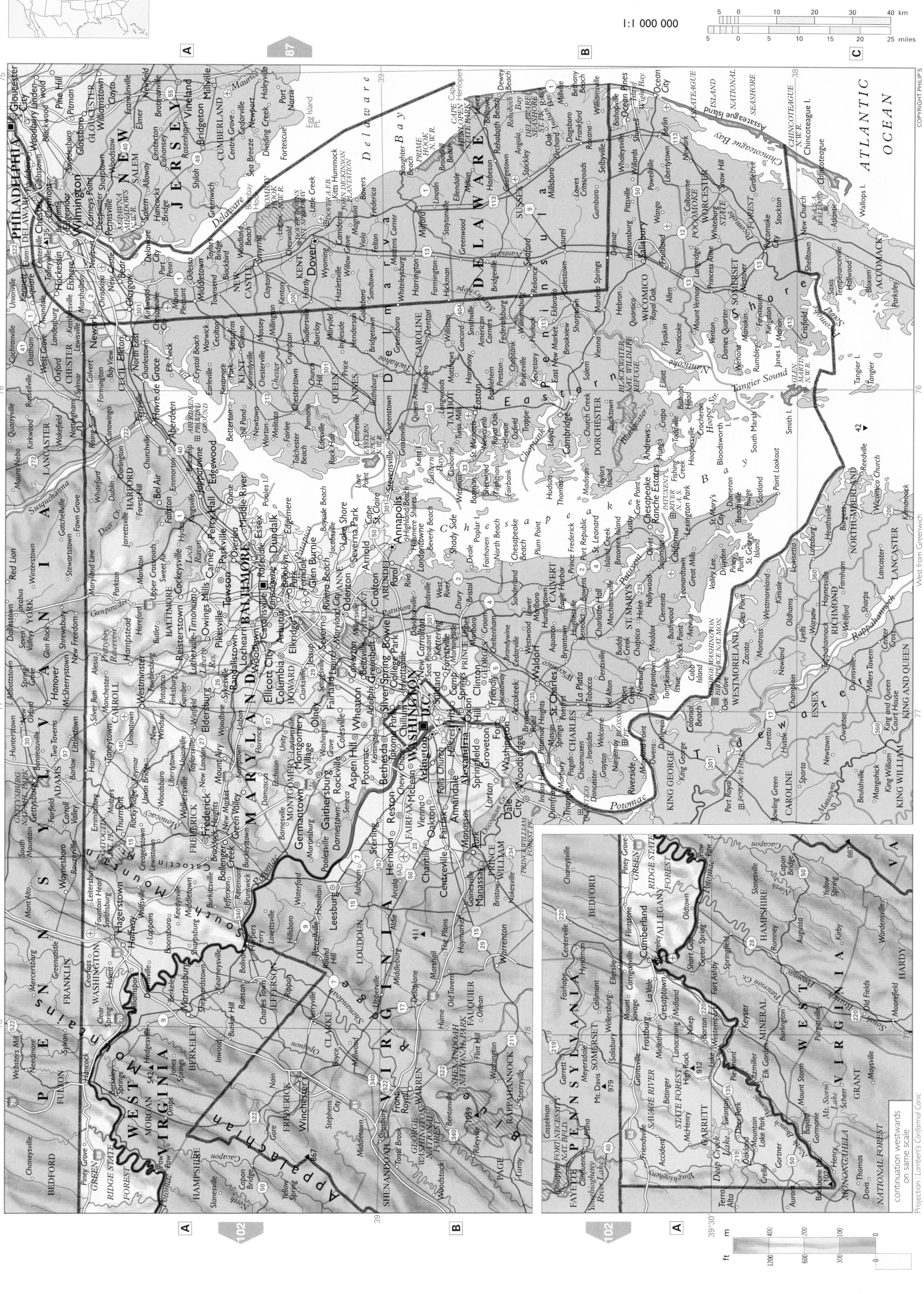
MARYLAND
DELAWARE
WASHINGTON D.C.
PENNSYLVANIA
NEW JERSEY
VIRGINIA
WEST VIRGINIA
ATLANTIC OCEAN
Chesapeake Bay
Delaware Bay
Delmarva Peninsula
Philadelphia
Wilmington
Dover
Baltimore
Annapolis
Frederick
Hagerstown
Salisbury
Ocean City
Cumberland
Alexandria
Arlington
Potomac
Underlined settlements give their name to the county in which they stand.
continuation westwards on same scale
Projection: Lambert's Conformal Conic
COPYRIGHT PHILIP'S
West from Greenwich

MASSACHUSETTS, CONNECTICUT AND RHODE ISLAND

1:1 000 000

5 0 10 20 30 40 km

5 0 5 10 15 20 25 miles

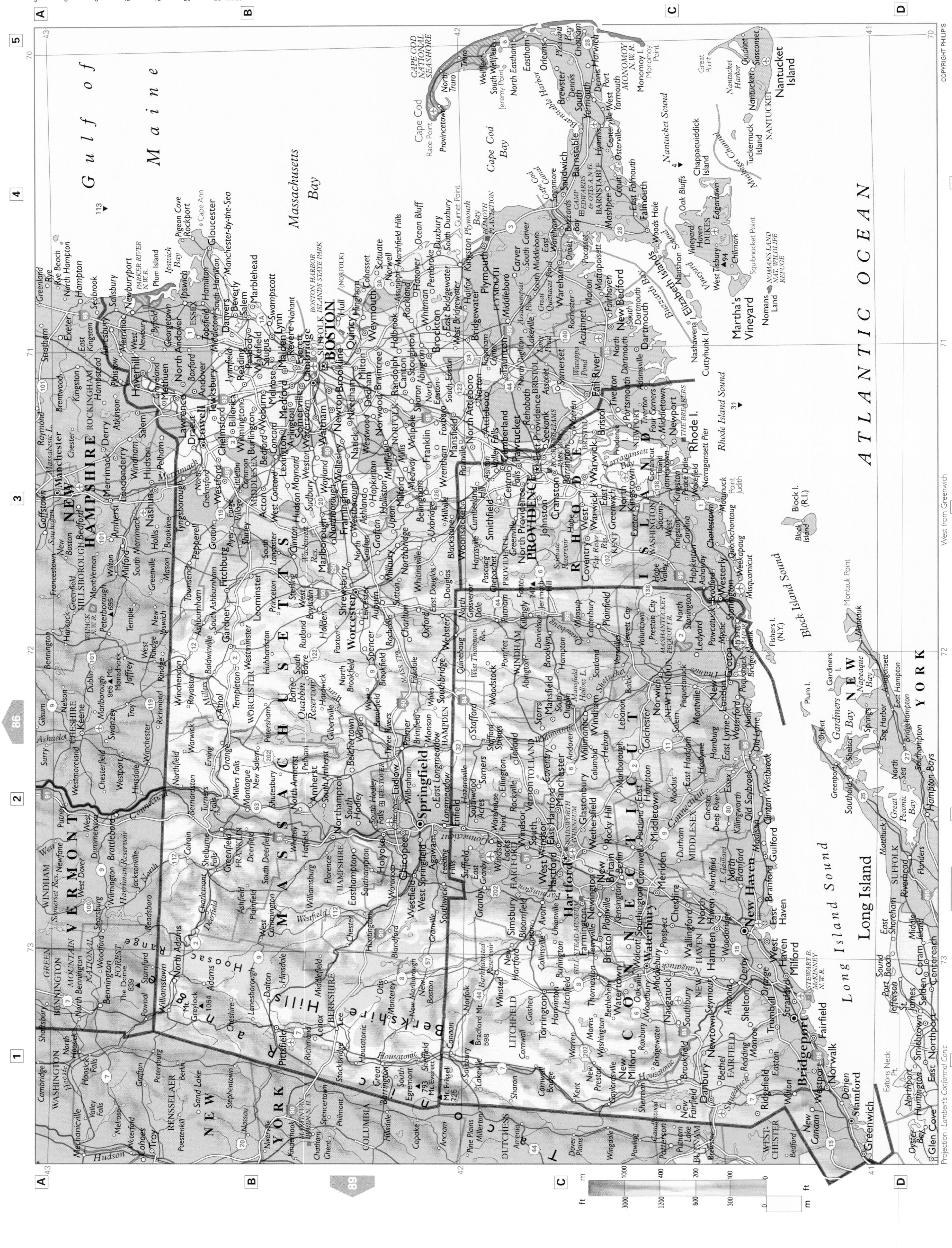

1:2 000 000

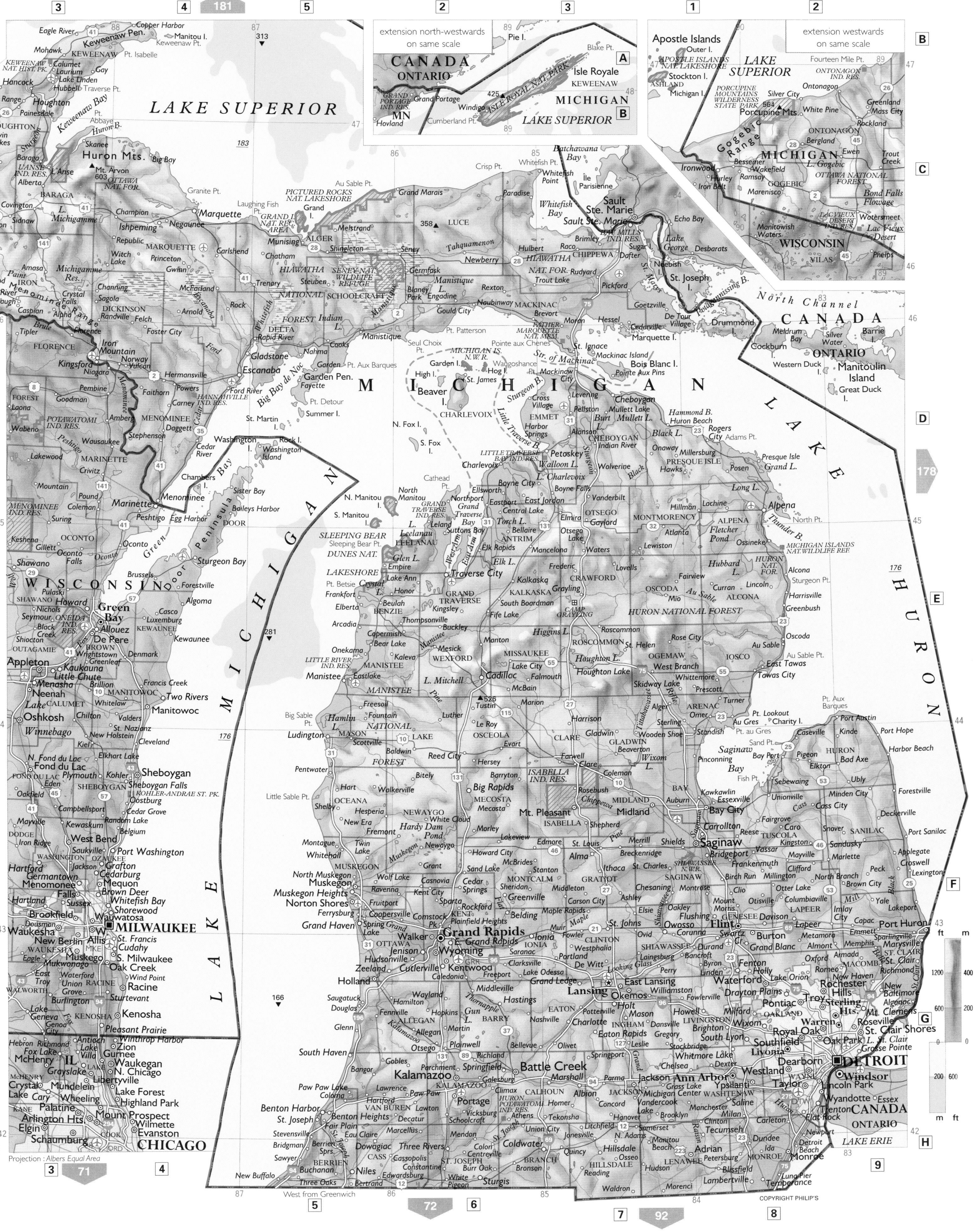
LAKE SUPERIOR
LAKE MICHIGAN
LAKE HURON
LAKE ERIE
MICHIGAN
WISCONSIN
CANADA
ONTARIO
North Channel
Manitoulin Island
Isle Royale
Apostle Islands
extension north-westwards on same scale
extension westwards on same scale
Keweenaw Pen.
Huron Mts.
Marquette
Sault Ste. Marie
Escanaba
Green Bay
Traverse City
Alpena
Saginaw Bay
Saginaw
Bay City
Midland
Flint
Port Huron
Lansing
Grand Rapids
Kalamazoo
Battle Creek
Jackson
Ann Arbor
DETROIT
Windsor
MILWAUKEE
CHICAGO
HURON NATIONAL FOREST
HIAWATHA NATIONAL FOREST
SLEEPING BEAR DUNES NAT. LAKESHORE
PICTURED ROCKS NAT. LAKESHORE
Str. of Mackinac
Door Peninsula
Projection : Albers Equal Area
West from Greenwich
COPYRIGHT PHILIP'S

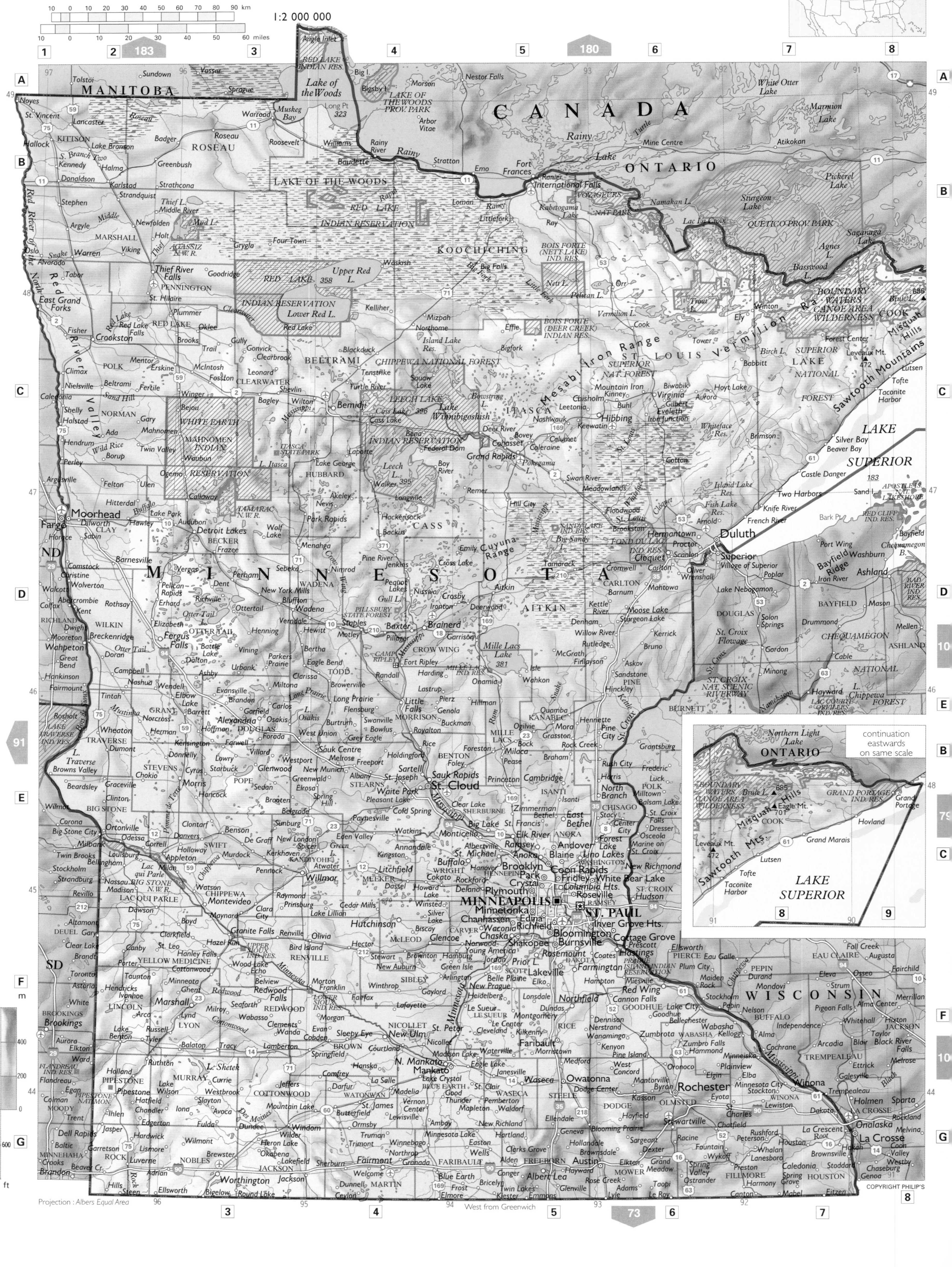
1:2 000 000
km
miles
183
180
CANADA
MANITOBA
ONTARIO
Lake of the Woods
Angle Inlet
RED LAKE INDIAN RES.
LAKE OF THE WOODS PROV. PARK
Rainy Lake
Fort Frances
International Falls
VOYAGEURS NAT. PARK
QUETICO PROV. PARK
BOUNDARY WATERS CANOE AREA WILDERNESS
LAKE OF THE WOODS
RED LAKE INDIAN RESERVATION
Upper Red L.
Lower Red L.
KOOCHICHING
BOIS FORTE (NETT LAKE) IND. RES.
BOIS FORTE (DEER CREEK) INDIAN RES.
ROSEAU
KITTSON
MARSHALL
PENNINGTON
Thief River Falls
RED LAKE
POLK
Crookston
East Grand Forks
BELTRAMI
CLEARWATER
Bemidji
CHIPPEWA NATIONAL FOREST
LEECH LAKE INDIAN RESERVATION
Lake Winnibigoshish
Leech L.
ITASCA
Grand Rapids
Mesabi Iron Range
Hibbing
Virginia
Ely
ST. LOUIS
SUPERIOR NAT. FOREST
Vermilion Range
COOK
LAKE
Sawtooth Mountains
LAKE SUPERIOR
Duluth
Superior
NORMAN
MAHNOMEN
WHITE EARTH INDIAN RESERVATION
ITASCA STATE PARK
HUBBARD
CASS
Cuyuna Range
Moorhead
Fargo
CLAY
BECKER
Detroit Lakes
ND
WILKIN
OTTER TAIL
Fergus Falls
WADENA
CROW WING
Brainerd
AITKIN
Mille Lacs Lake
CARLTON
PINE
M I N N E S O T A
MORRISON
TODD
DOUGLAS
Alexandria
GRANT
TRAVERSE
STEVENS
POPE
STEARNS
St. Cloud
BENTON
MILLE LACS
KANABEC
ISANTI
CHISAGO
SHERBURNE
ANOKA
WRIGHT
HENNEPIN
MINNEAPOLIS
ST. PAUL
RAMSEY
WASHINGTON
BIG STONE
SWIFT
KANDIYOHI
Willmar
MEEKER
CHIPPEWA
LAC QUI PARLE
YELLOW MEDICINE
RENVILLE
MCLEOD
CARVER
SCOTT
DAKOTA
SD
LINCOLN
LYON
Marshall
REDWOOD
SIBLEY
NICOLLET
LE SUEUR
RICE
GOODHUE
WABASHA
WINONA
OLMSTED
Rochester
DODGE
STEELE
WASECA
BLUE EARTH
Mankato
BROWN
New Ulm
WATONWAN
COTTONWOOD
MURRAY
PIPESTONE
ROCK
NOBLES
Worthington
JACKSON
MARTIN
FARIBAULT
FREEBORN
Albert Lea
MOWER
Austin
FILLMORE
HOUSTON
La Crosse
WISCONSIN
DOUGLAS
BAYFIELD
ASHLAND
BURNETT
POLK
ST. CROIX
PIERCE
PEPIN
BUFFALO
TREMPEALEAU
JACKSON
EAU CLAIRE
Mississippi
Minnesota
Red River of the North
St. Croix
continuation eastwards on same scale
Northern Light Lake
GRAND PORTAGE IND. RES.
Grand Portage
Grand Marais
Misquah Hills
Sawtooth Mts.
LAKE SUPERIOR
91
73
Projection : Albers Equal Area
West from Greenwich

1:2 000 000

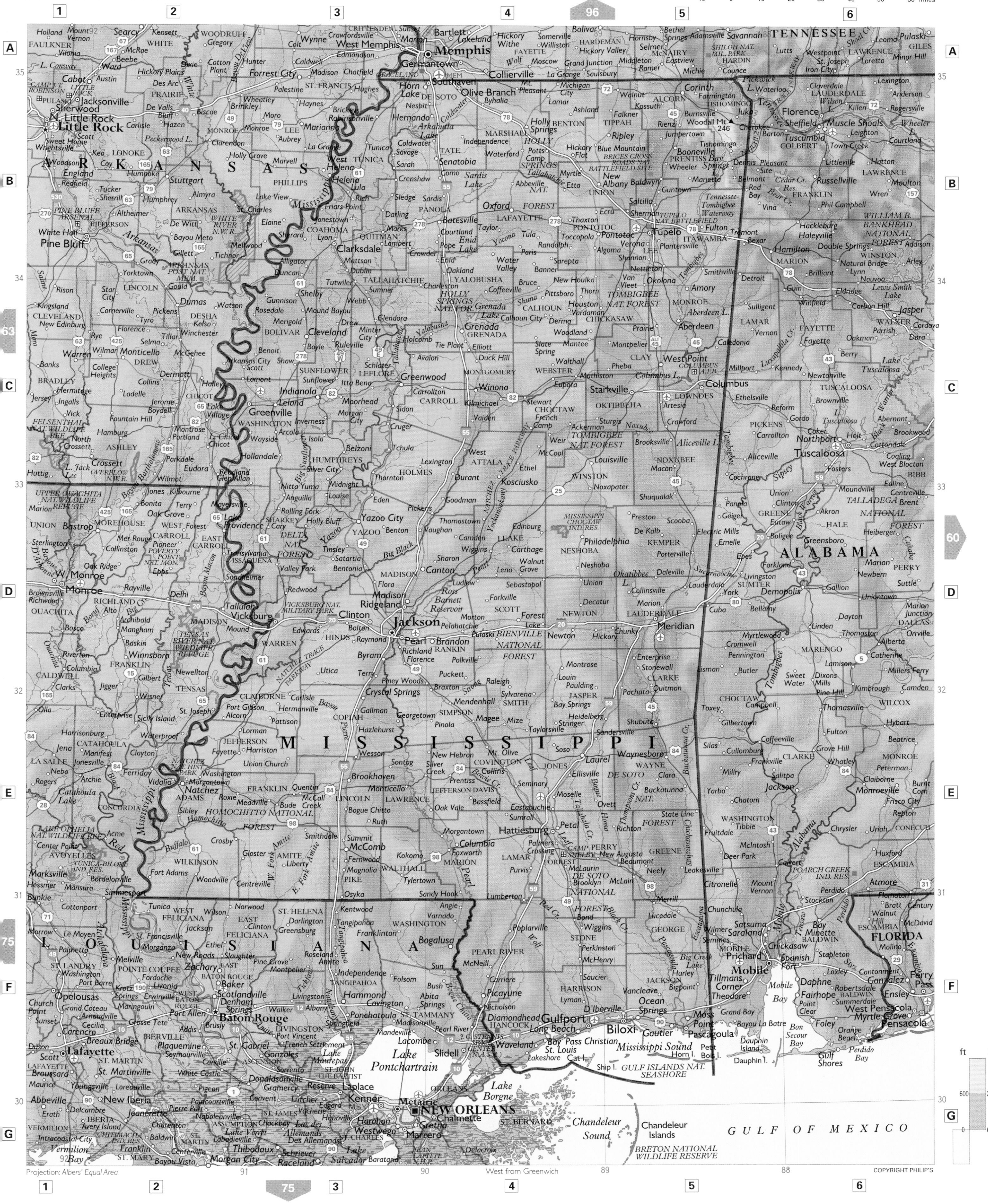
MISSISSIPPI
ALABAMA
TENNESSEE
ARKANSAS
LOUISIANA
FLORIDA
Memphis
Jackson
NEW ORLEANS
Baton Rouge
Mobile
Gulfport
Biloxi
Pensacola
Tuscaloosa
Meridian
Hattiesburg
Vicksburg
Natchez
Greenville
Tupelo
Columbus
Little Rock
Pine Bluff
Monroe
Lafayette
Lake Pontchartrain
Lake Borgne
Mississippi Sound
Chandeleur Sound
Chandeleur Islands
Mobile Bay
GULF OF MEXICO
GULF ISLANDS NAT. SEASHORE
BRETON NATIONAL WILDLIFE RESERVE
Mississippi
Tombigbee
Yazoo
Pearl
Projection: Albers' Equal Area
West from Greenwich
COPYRIGHT PHILIP'S
10 0 10 20 30 40 50 60 70 80 100 km
10 0 10 20 30 40 50 60 miles
ft m
600 200
0 0

1:2 000 000

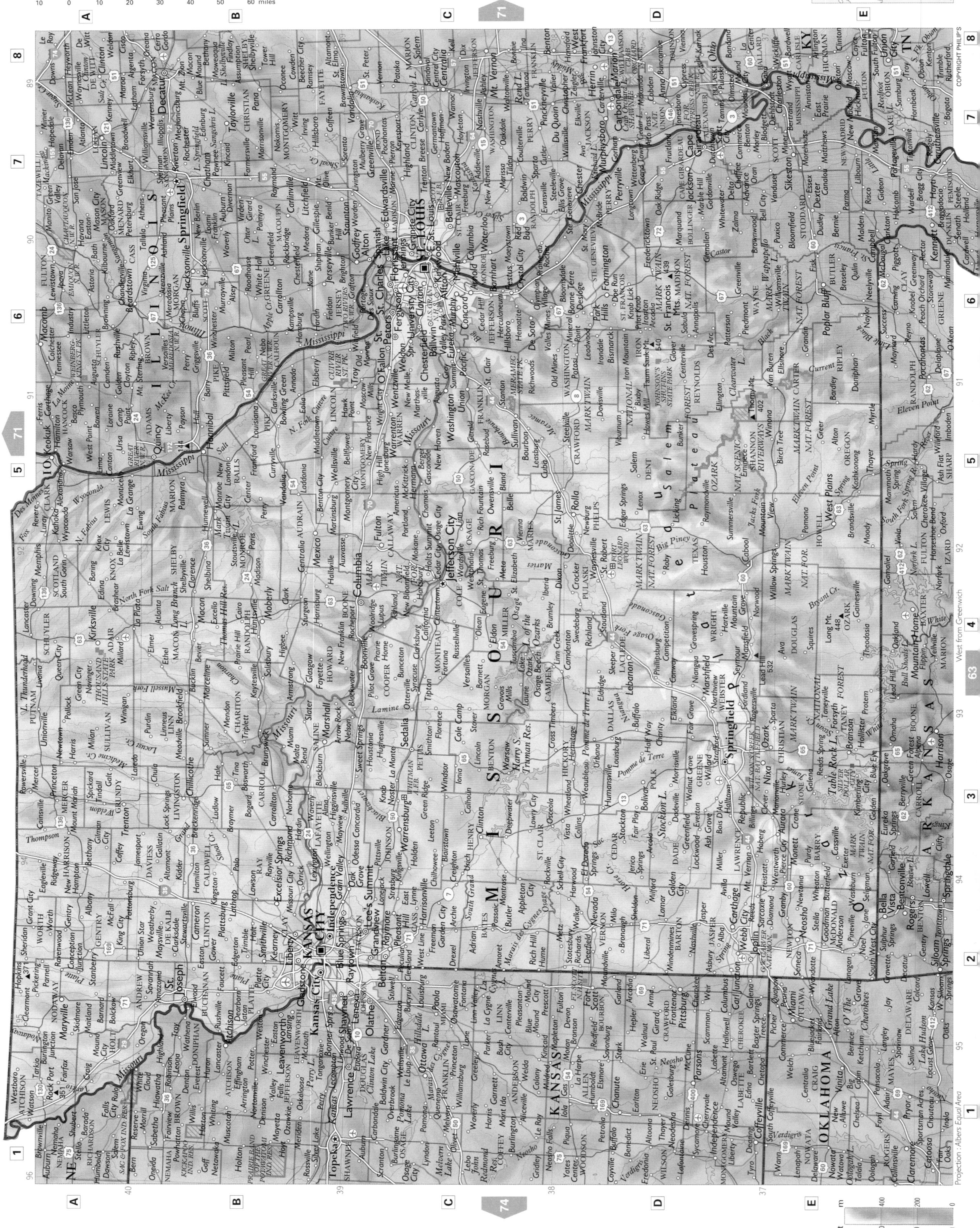

MISSOURI
ILLINOIS
KANSAS
OKLAHOMA
ARKANSAS
Jefferson City
Kansas City
St. Louis
Springfield
Projection : Albers Equal Area
COPYRIGHT PHILIP'S
West from Greenwich

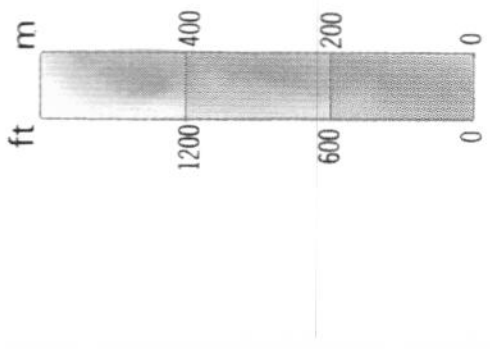

ft
m

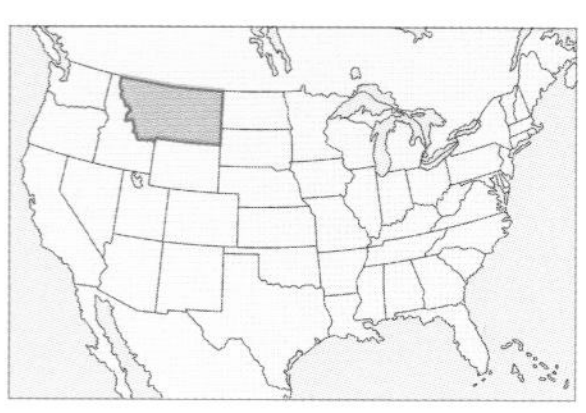

1:3 000 000

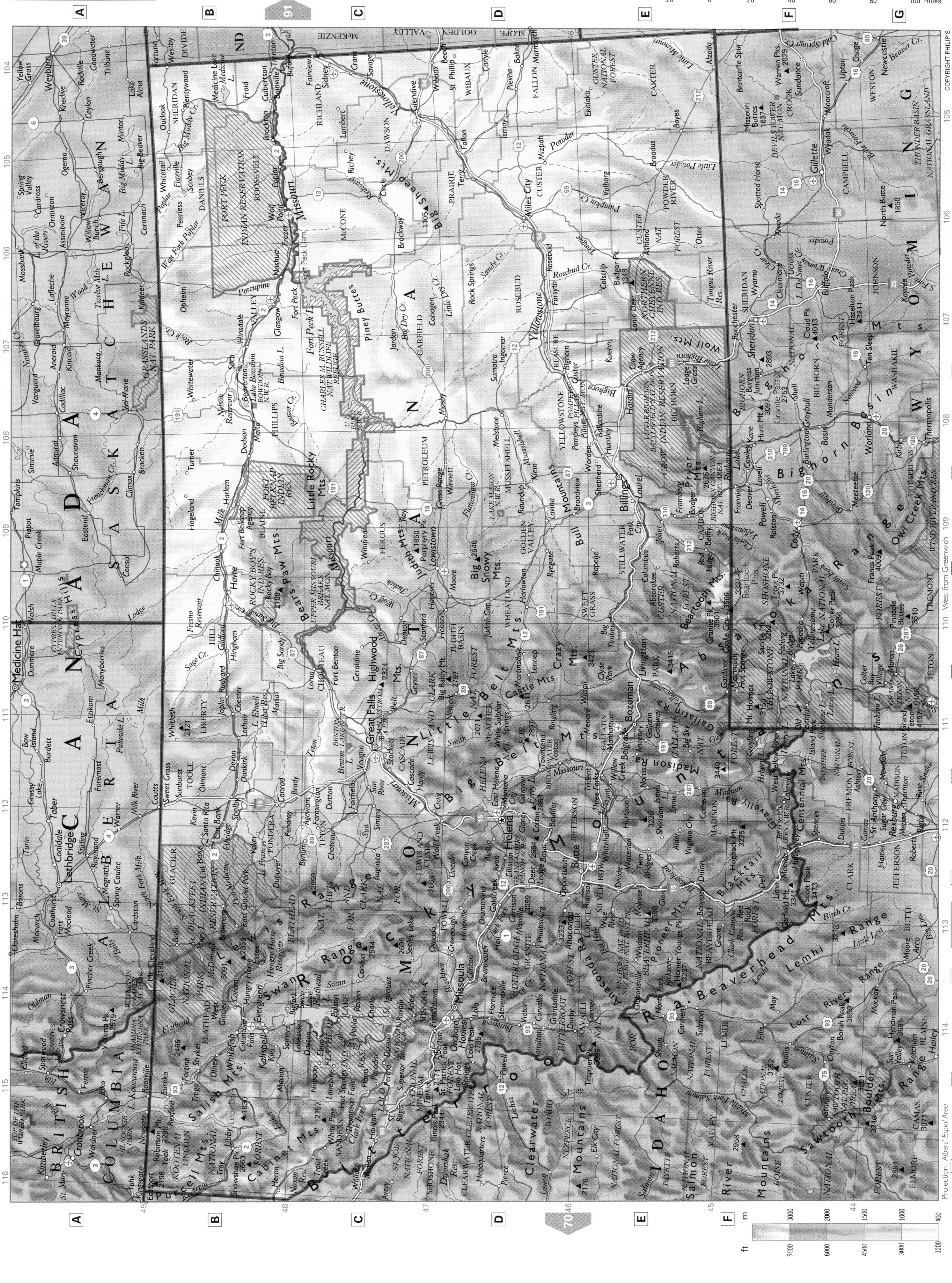
MONTANA
IDAHO
WYOMING
ALBERTA
SASKATCHEWAN
BRITISH COLUMBIA
Helena
Billings
Great Falls
Missoula
Bozeman
Butte
Havre
Miles City
Kalispell
Lewistown
Glendive
Medicine Hat
Lethbridge
Sheridan
Cody
Yellowstone
Missouri
Fort Peck L.
Little Rocky Mts.
Bears Paw Mts.
Big Snowy Mts.
Crazy Mts.
Absaroka Range
Beartooth Mts.
Bighorn Mts.
Bitterroot Range
Beaverhead Mts.
Lemhi Range
Lost River Range
Sawtooth Range
Clearwater Mountains
Salmon River Mountains
Cabinet Mts.
Purcell Mts.
Salish Mts.
Swan Range
Big Belt Mts.
Little Belt Mts.
Madison Range
Gallatin Range
Big Horn Basin
Owl Creek Mts.
Wolf Mts.
Big Sheep Mts.
Piney Buttes
Projection: Albers' Equal Area
COPYRIGHT PHILIP'S
West from Greenwich
km
miles
m
ft

1:2 000 000

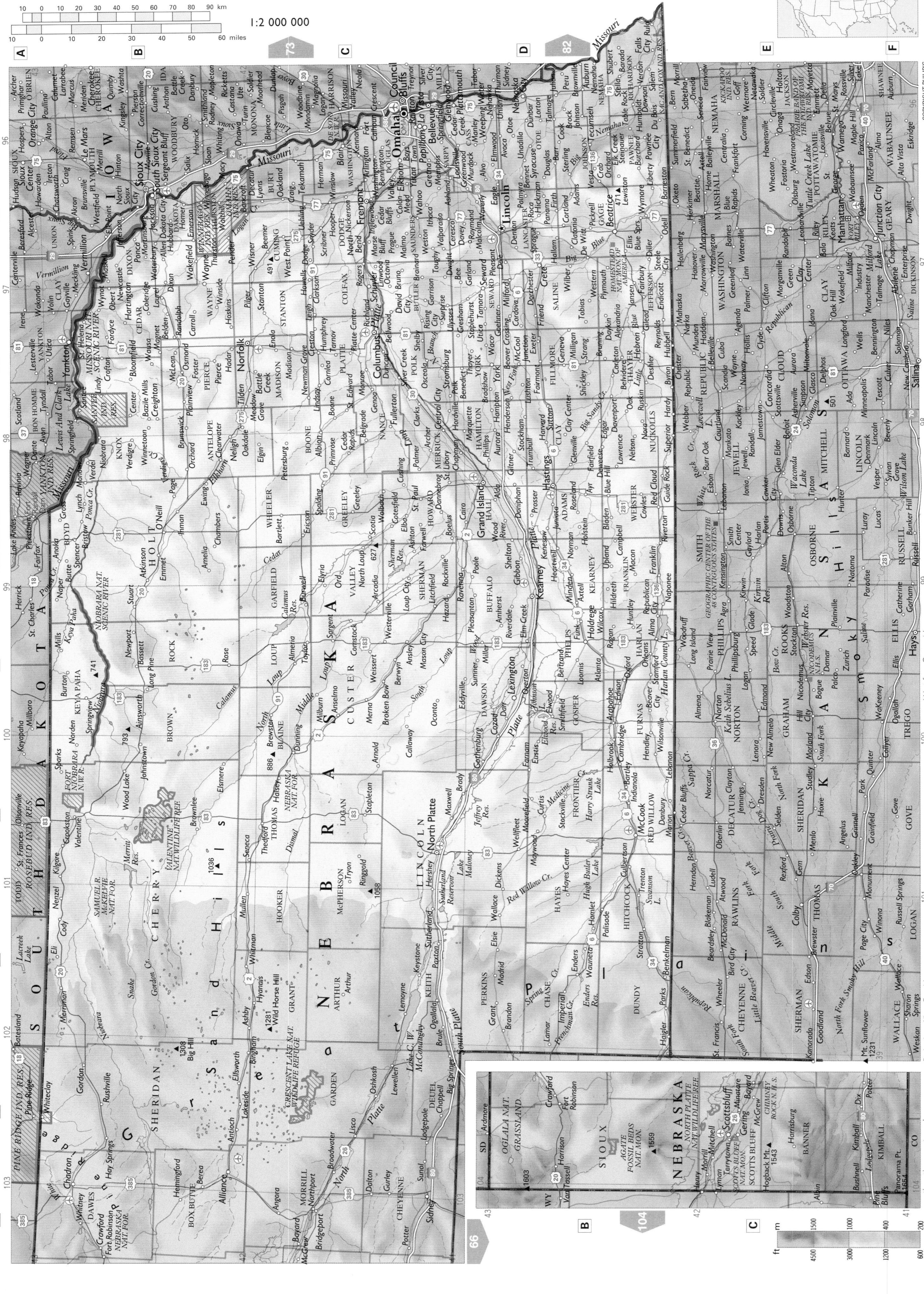
SOUTH DAKOTA
IOWA
NEBRASKA
KANSAS
Missouri
Platte
Sand Hills
Smoky Hills
Lincoln
Omaha
Council Bluffs
Sioux City
Grand Island
Kearney
Hastings
North Platte
Scottsbluff
Salina
Manhattan
Junction City
Columbus
Norfolk
Beatrice
Fremont
Lexington
McCook
Alliance
Chadron
Valentine
O'Neill
Yankton
Hays
West from Greenwich
Projection: Albers Equal Area
continuation westwards on same scale

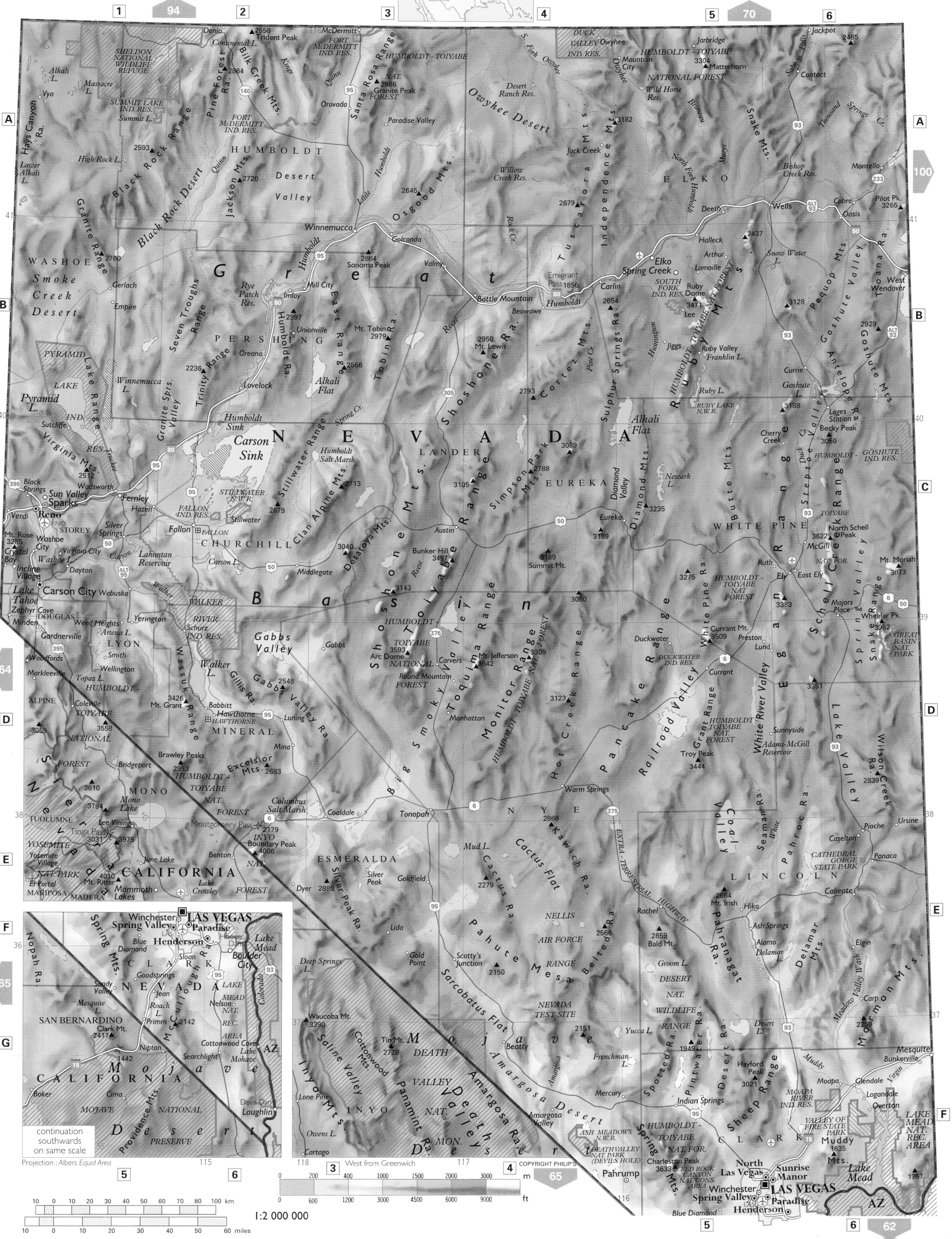

GREAT BASIN
NEVADA
CALIFORNIA
AZ
HUMBOLDT
PERSHING
WASHOE
LANDER
EUREKA
ELKO
WHITE PINE
CHURCHILL
STOREY
DOUGLAS
LYON
MINERAL
ESMERALDA
NYE
LINCOLN
CLARK
MONO
INYO
TUOLUMNE
MARIPOSA
MADERA
SAN BERNARDINO
ALPINE
LAS VEGAS
Las Vegas
North Las Vegas
Sunrise Manor
Winchester
Spring Valley
Paradise
Henderson
Boulder City
Carson City
Reno
Sparks
Sun Valley
Elko
Spring Creek
Winnemucca
Ely
East Ely
Fallon
Tonopah
Hawthorne
Yerington
Fernley
Lovelock
Battle Mountain
Wells
West Wendover
Mesquite
Pahrump
Laughlin
Jackpot
Caliente
Pioche
Austin
Eureka
Goldfield
Beatty
Black Rock Desert
Smoke Creek Desert
Carson Sink
Humboldt Sink
Pyramid L.
Walker L.
Lake Tahoe
Lake Mead
Mono Lake
Owyhee Desert
Amargosa Desert
Mojave Desert
Death Valley
Ruby Mts.
Snake Range
Toiyabe Range
Toquima Range
Monitor Range
Shoshone Mts.
Schell Creek Range
Egan Range
Spring Mts.
Sheep Range
Desatoya Mts.
Stillwater Range
Wassuk Range
Excelsior Mts.
Silver Peak Ra.
Kawich Ra.
Belted Ra.
Pahute Mesa
Cactus Flat
Sarcobatus Flat
NELLIS AIR FORCE RANGE
NEVADA TEST SITE
DESERT NAT. WILDLIFE RANGE
GREAT BASIN NAT. PARK
HUMBOLDT - TOIYABE NATIONAL FOREST
DEATH VALLEY NAT. PARK
LAKE MEAD NAT. REC. AREA
VALLEY OF FIRE STATE PARK
CATHEDRAL GORGE STATE PARK
SHELDON NATIONAL WILDLIFE REFUGE
PYRAMID LAKE IND. RES.
WALKER RIVER IND. RES.
FORT McDERMITT IND. RES.
DUCK VALLEY IND. RES.
SOUTH FORK IND. RES.
MOAPA RIVER IND. RES.
Wheeler Pk. 3982
Boundary Peak 4006
EXTRA-TERRESTRIAL HIGHWAY
continuation southwards on same scale
Projection : Albers Equal Area
West from Greenwich
COPYRIGHT PHILIP'S
1:2 000 000
0 200 400 1000 1500 2000 3000 m
0 600 1200 3000 4500 6000 9000 ft
10 0 10 20 30 40 50 60 70 80 100 km
10 0 10 20 30 40 50 60 miles

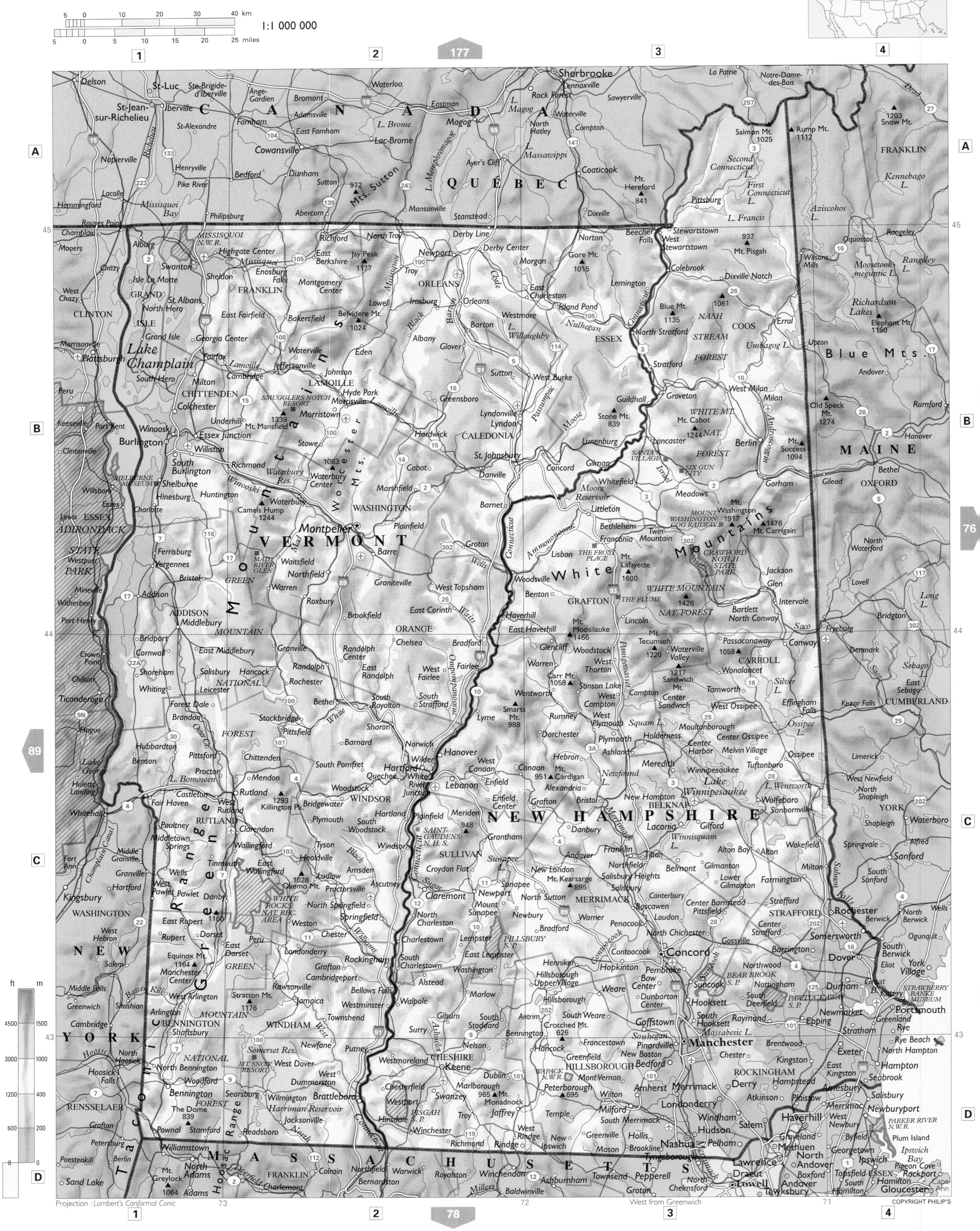

1:1 000 000
km
miles
177
78
89
76
C A N A D A
Q U É B E C
VERMONT
NEW HAMPSHIRE
M A I N E
M A S S A C H U S E T T S
N E W
Y O R K
Sherbrooke
Lennoxville
Magog
Rock Forest
Waterville
Compton
North Hatley
L. Massawippi
Coaticook
Ayer's Cliff
Stanstead
Mansonville
Sutton
Mts. Sutton
Cowansville
Lac-Brome
L. Brome
Bromont
Waterloo
Eastman
Farnham
Granby
Dunham
Bedford
Pike River
Henryville
Napierville
St-Jean-sur-Richelieu
Iberville
St-Luc
Ste-Brigide-d'Iberville
Ange-Gardien
St-Alexandre
Delson
Lacolle
Hemmingford
Missisquoi Bay
Philipsburg
Abercorn
Rouses Point
Champlain
Mooers
Alburg
Swanton
Highgate Center
Richford
North Troy
Jay Peak
Newport
Derby Line
Derby Center
Morgan
Troy
Enosburg Falls
Sheldon
St. Albans
Montgomery Center
Franklin
Orleans
Barton
Irasburg
Lowell
Belvidere Mt.
Bakersfield
East Fairfield
Georgia Center
Grand Isle
North Hero
Isle La Motte
Chazy
West Chazy
Clinton
Plattsburgh
Morrisonville
Lake Champlain
South Hero
Fairfax
Cambridge
Lamoille
Jeffersonville
Johnson
Eden
Waterville
Albany
Glover
Hyde Park
Morrisville
Morristown
Smugglers Notch Resort
Mt. Mansfield
Underhill
Milton
Chittenden
Colchester
Winooski
Burlington
Essex Junction
Williston
South Burlington
Shelburne
Shelburne Museum
Hinesburg
Huntington
Richmond
Waterbury
Waterbury Res.
Waterbury Center
Stowe
Worcester Mts.
Camels Hump
Montpelier
Barre
Washington
Marshfield
Plainfield
Cabot
Hardwick
Greensboro
Caledonia
Lyndonville
Lyndon
St. Johnsbury
Danville
Barnet
Sutton
West Burke
Willoughby
Island Pond
East Charleston
Westmore
Nulhegan
Essex
Lunenburg
Concord
Guildhall
Maidstone
Gilman
Groton
Wells
West Topsham
Northfield
Waitsfield
Mad River Glen
Warren
Roxbury
Graniteville
Brookfield
East Corinth
Orange
Chelsea
Randolph
Randolph Center
East Randolph
Bradford
Fairlee
West Fairlee
Ompompanoosuc
South Strafford
South Royalton
Sharon
Bethel
Rochester
Granville
Hancock
Salisbury
Middlebury
East Middlebury
Bristol
Vergennes
Ferrisburg
Addison
Westport
Elizabethtown
Essex
Willsboro
Charlotte
Lewis
Adirondack State Park
Port Henry
Witherbee
Mineville
Bridport
Cornwall
Shoreham
Crown Point
Ticonderoga
Whiting
Leicester
Forest Dale
Brandon
Pittsford
Chittenden
Stockbridge
Pittsfield
Hubbardton
Benson
Proctor
L. Bomoseen
Castleton
Fair Haven
West Rutland
Rutland
Mendon
Killington Pk.
Bridgewater
Woodstock
Quechee
Hartford
White River Junction
Norwich
Wilder
Hanover
Lebanon
West Canaan
Enfield
Enfield Center
Plainfield
Meriden
Saint-Gaudens N.H.S.
Grantham
Windsor
Hartland
South Woodstock
Plymouth
Clarendon
Wallingford
East Wallingford
Ludlow
Okemo Mt.
Tyson
Healdville
Proctorsville
Amsden
Ascutney
Springfield
North Springfield
Weston
Chester
Londonderry
Grafton
Cambridgeport
Rockingham
Bellows Falls
Westminster
Townshend
Jamaica
Rawsonville
Danby
Dorset
East Dorset
Manchester
Manchester Center
Equinox Mt.
Peru
Stratton Mt.
Arlington
West Arlington
Shaftsbury
Bennington
North Bennington
Woodford
Searsburg
Wilmington
Harriman Reservoir
Jacksonville
Readsboro
Stamford
Pownal
The Dome
Somerset Res.
Mt. Snow Resort
West Dover
Dummerston
Brattleboro
Putney
Newfane
West Dummerston
Windham
Poultney
Middletown Springs
Wells
Tinmouth
Pawlet
West Pawlet
Granville
Middle Granville
Hartford
Fort Ann
Whitehall
Kingsbury
Washington
Salem
West Hebron
Rupert
East Rupert
Cambridge
Greenwich
Shushan
Hoosick Falls
North Hoosick
Rensselaer
Grafton
Petersburg
Berlin
Poestenkill
Sand Lake
Mt. Greylock
Williamstown
North Adams
Adams
Charlemont
Colrain
Franklin
Northfield
Bernardston
Warwick
Royalston
Winchendon
Hoosac Range
Taconic Mts.
Green Mountains
Green Mountain National Forest
White Rocks Nat. Rec. Area
Champlain Canal
Lake George
Huletts Landing
Hague
Beecher Falls
Stewartstown
West Stewartstown
Colebrook
Pittsburg
First Connecticut L.
Second Connecticut L.
L. Francis
Mt. Pisgah
Dixville Notch
Dixville
Norton
Gore Mt.
Lemington
Mt. Hereford
Salmon Mt.
Rump Mt.
North Stratford
Stratford
Blue Mt.
Nash Stream Forest
Coos
Errol
Umbagog L.
Upton
Groveton
West Milan
Milan
White Mt. National Forest
Mt. Cabot
Lancaster
Stone Mt.
Berlin
Gorham
Santa's Village
Six Gun City
Whitefield
Jefferson
Meadows
Moore Reservoir
Littleton
Bethlehem
Franconia
Twin Mountain
Mount Washington Cog Railway
Mt. Washington
Mt. Carrigain
White Mountains
Crawford Notch State Park
The Frost Place
Lisbon
Mt. Lafayette
Jackson
Glen
Woodsville
Benton
Grafton
The Flume
Lincoln
Intervale
Bartlett
North Conway
White Mountain Nat. Forest
Haverhill
East Haverhill
Mt. Moosilauke
Glencliff
Woodstock
Warren
West Thorton
Mt. Tecumseh
Waterville Valley
Passaconaway
Conway
Carroll
Wonalancet
Sandwich
Carr Mt.
Stinson Lake
Wentworth
Campton
Center Sandwich
Tamworth
West Ossipee
Effingham Falls
Ossipee
Ossipee L.
Smarts Mt.
Lyme
Rumney
Dorchester
West Plymouth
Plymouth
Squam L.
Holderness
Moultonborough
Center Ossipee
Center Harbor
Melvin Village
Ashland
Hebron
Canaan
Mt. Cardigan
Alexandria
Newfound L.
Bristol
Meredith
Winnipesaukee
Lake Winnipesaukee
Tuftonboro
L. Wentworth
Wolfeboro
Sanbornville
New Hampton
Belknap
Laconia
Gilford
Winnisquam L.
Danbury
Franklin
Tilton
Northfield
Alton Bay
Alton
Wakefield
Milton
Farmington
Belmont
Gilmanton
Lower Gilmanton
Andover
New London
Salisbury
Salisbury Heights
Mt. Kearsarge
Sunapee
Sunapee L.
Newport
Croydon Flat
Claremont
Sullivan
North Charleston
Charlestown
South Charleston
Mount Sunapee
North Sutton
Newbury
Merrimack
Warner
Boscawen
Canterbury
Center Barnstead
Pittsfield
Strafford
Penacook
Loudon
North Chichester
Gossville
Contoocook
Concord
Henniker
Hopkinton
Hillsborough
Hillsborough Upper Village
Pembroke
Suncook
Bow Center
Dunbarton Center
Weare
South Weare
Bear Brook S.P.
Northwood
Nottingham
Pawtuckaway S.P.
Barrington
Rochester
Somersworth
Dover
Durham
Newmarket
Portsmouth
Kittery
Strawbery Banke Museum
Greenland
Rye
Rye Beach
North Hampton
Hampton
Stratham
Exeter
Epping
Raymond
Hooksett
South Hooksett
Goffstown
Manchester
Candia
Deerfield
South Deerfield
Auburn
Chester
Brentwood
Kingston
East Kingston
Seabrook
Rockingham
Hampstead
Derry
Londonderry
Windham
Atkinson
Plaistow
Salem
Amesbury
Salisbury
Newburyport
Merrimac
West Newbury
Haverhill
Hudson
Pelham
Nashua
Hollis
Brookline
Mason
Greenville
New Ipswich
Rindge
Jaffrey
Mt. Monadnock
Marlborough
Dublin
Harrisville
Peterborough
Temple
Wilton
Milford
Amherst
Merrimack
Bedford
New Boston
Mont Vernon
Francestown
Greenfield
Wapack N.W.R.
Hancock
Antrim
Bennington
Crotched Mt.
Hillsborough
Stoddard
South Stoddard
Nelson
Gilsum
Surry
Keene
Cheshire
Westmoreland
Swanzey
Chesterfield
Westport
Hinsdale
Pisgah S.P.
Winchester
Troy
Richmond
Fitzwilliam
Marlow
Alstead
Walpole
Washington
Lempster
East Lempster
Pillsbury S.P.
Bradford
Gorham
Bethel
Gilead
Oxford
Rumford
Hanover
Andover
Old Speck Mt.
Mt. Success
Mahoosuc
Blue Mts.
Franklin
Rangeley
Rangeley L.
Oquossoc
Mooselookmeguntic L.
Richardson Lakes
Elephant Mt.
Wilsons Mills
Aziscohos L.
Kennebago L.
Snow Mt.
North Waterford
Lovell
Bridgton
Long L.
Fryeburg
Denmark
Sebago L.
East Sebago
Cumberland
Kezar Falls
Limerick
Cornish
West Newfield
North Shapleigh
Shapleigh
York
Waterboro
Alfred
Springvale
Sanford
South Sanford
North Berwick
Berwick
Wells
Ogunquit
South Berwick
Eliot
York Village
Parker River N.W.R.
Plum Island
Ipswich Bay
Byfield
Georgetown
Ipswich
Rowley
Essex
Topsfield
Boxford
Andover
North Andover
Lawrence
Methuen
Groveland
Dracut
Lowell
Tewksbury
Chelmsford
North Chelmsford
Tyngsborough
Massabesic L.
Pepperell
Townsend
Groton
Ashburnham
Baldwinville
Hamilton
South Hamilton
Gloucester
Rockport
Pigeon Cove
Cape Ann
Essex
La Patrie
Notre-Dame-des-Bois
Sawyerville
Projection : Lambert's Conformal Conic
West from Greenwich
COPYRIGHT PHILIP'S

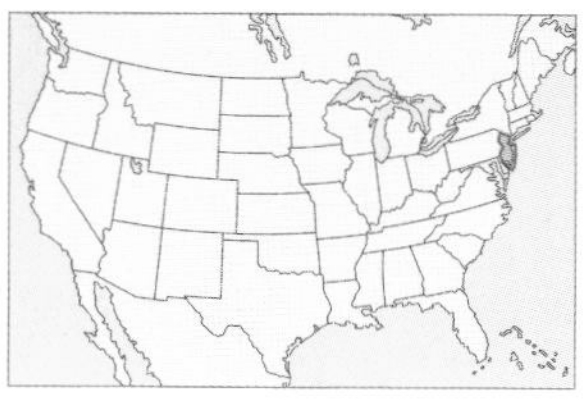

1:1 000 000

5 0 10 20 30 40 km

5 0 5 10 15 20 25 miles

89

78

95

77

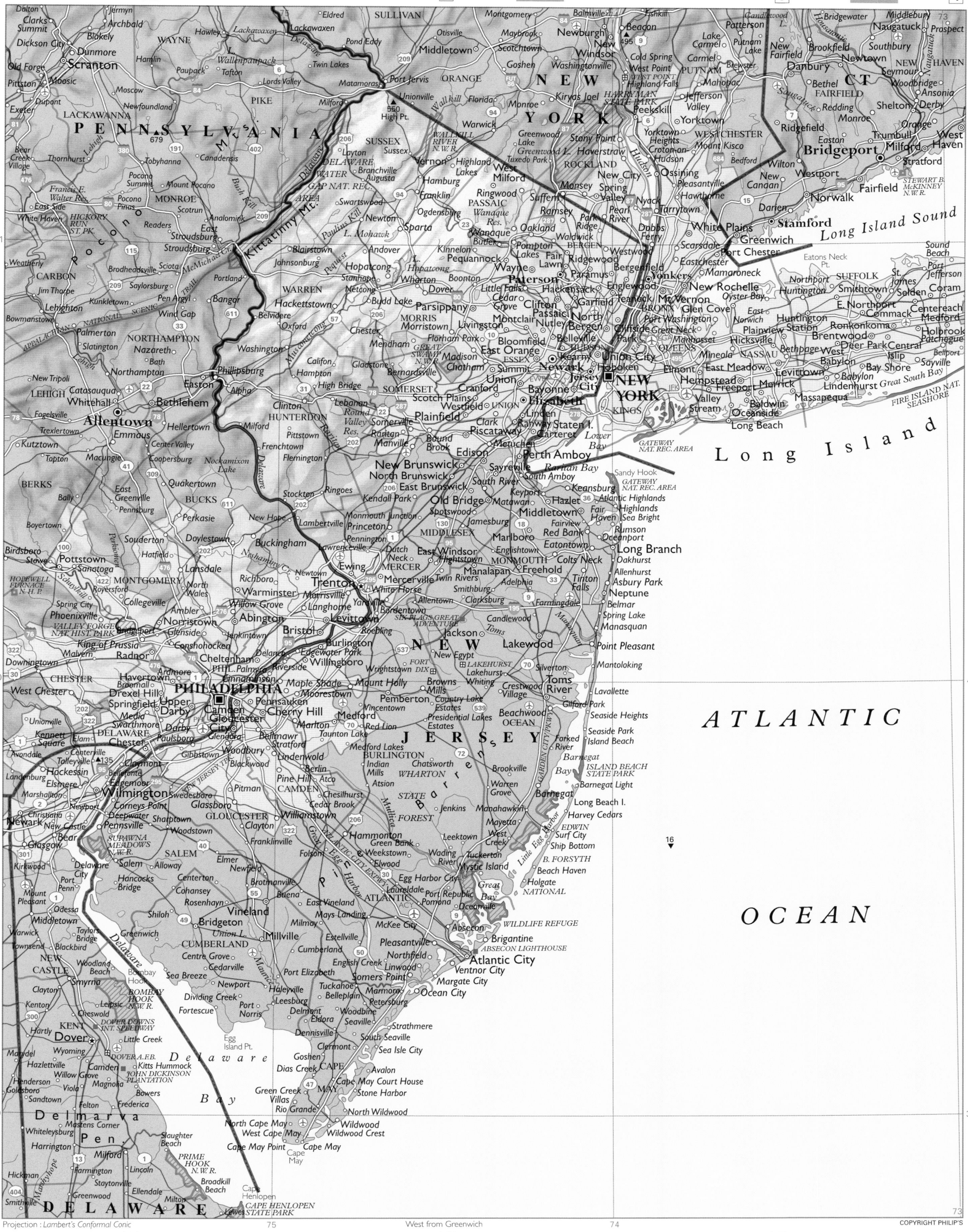

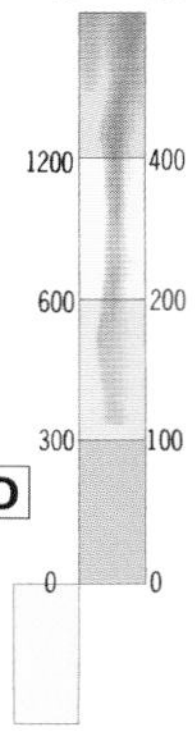

10 0 10 20 30 40 50 60 70 80 100 km

10 0 10 20 30 40 50 60 miles

1:2 100 000

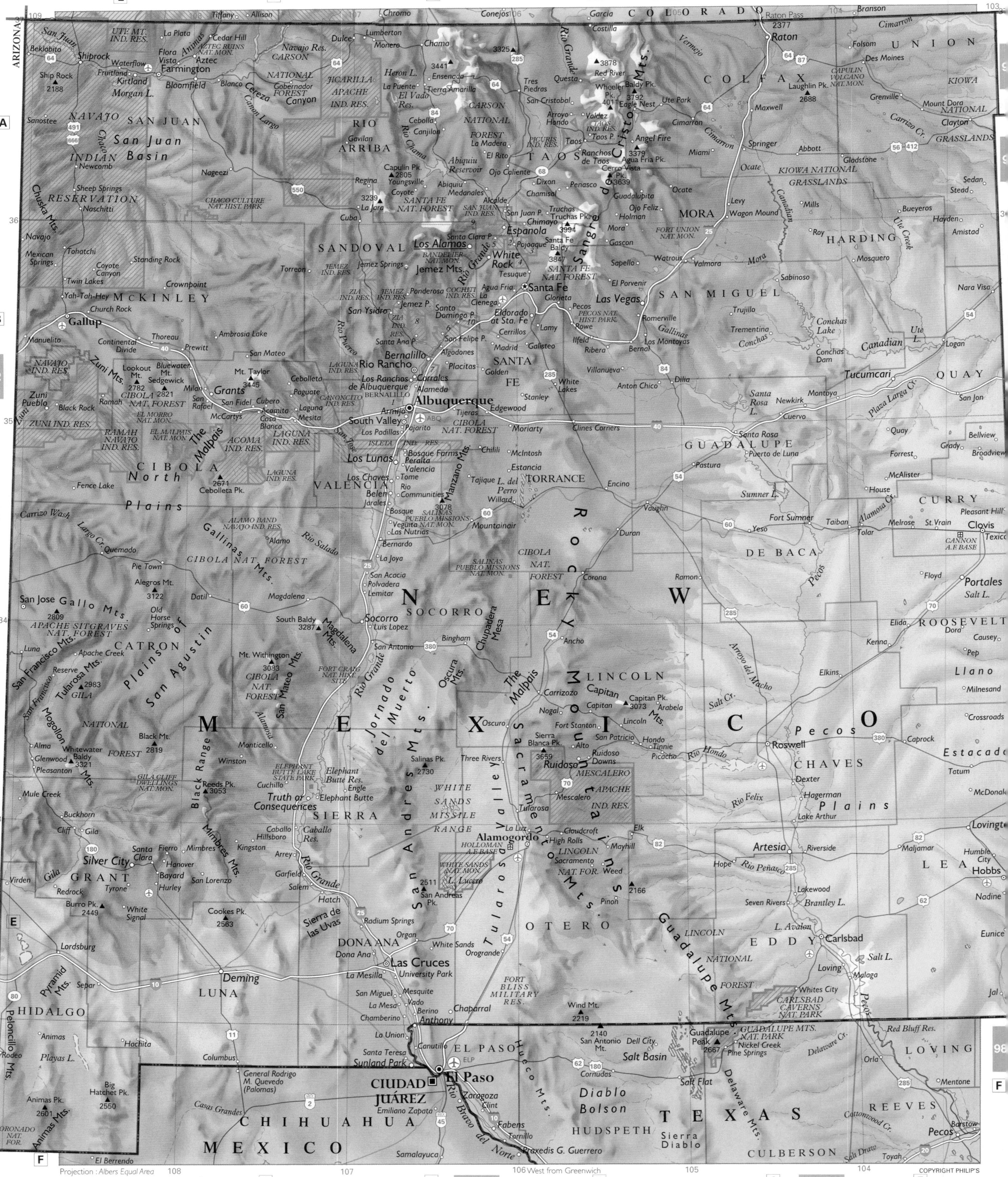

m	400	1000	1500	2000	3000	m
ft	1200	3000	4500	6000	9000	ft

Underlined settlements give their name to the county in which they stand.

1 PETROGLYPH NAT. MON.
2 POJOAQUE IND. RES.
3 NAMBE IND. RES.
4 TESUQUE IND. RES.
5 SAN ILDEFONSO IND. RES.
6 SAN FELIPE IND. RES.
7 SANDIA IND. RES.
8 SANTA ANA IND. RES.
9 SANTA CLARA IND. RES.
10 SANTO DOMINGO IND. RES.

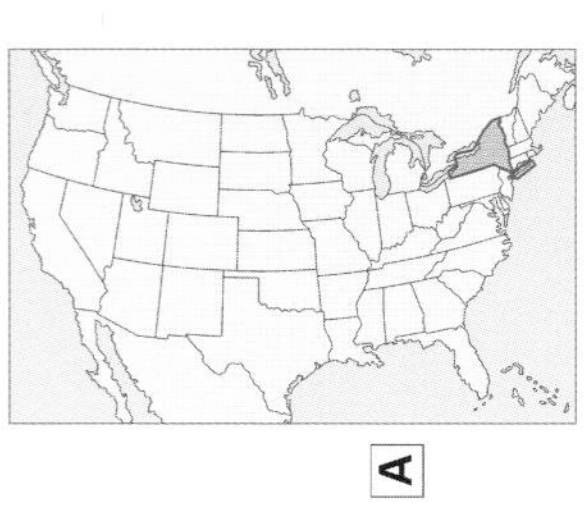

1:2 000 000

10 0 10 20 30 40 50 60 70 80 100 km

10 0 10 20 30 40 50 60 miles

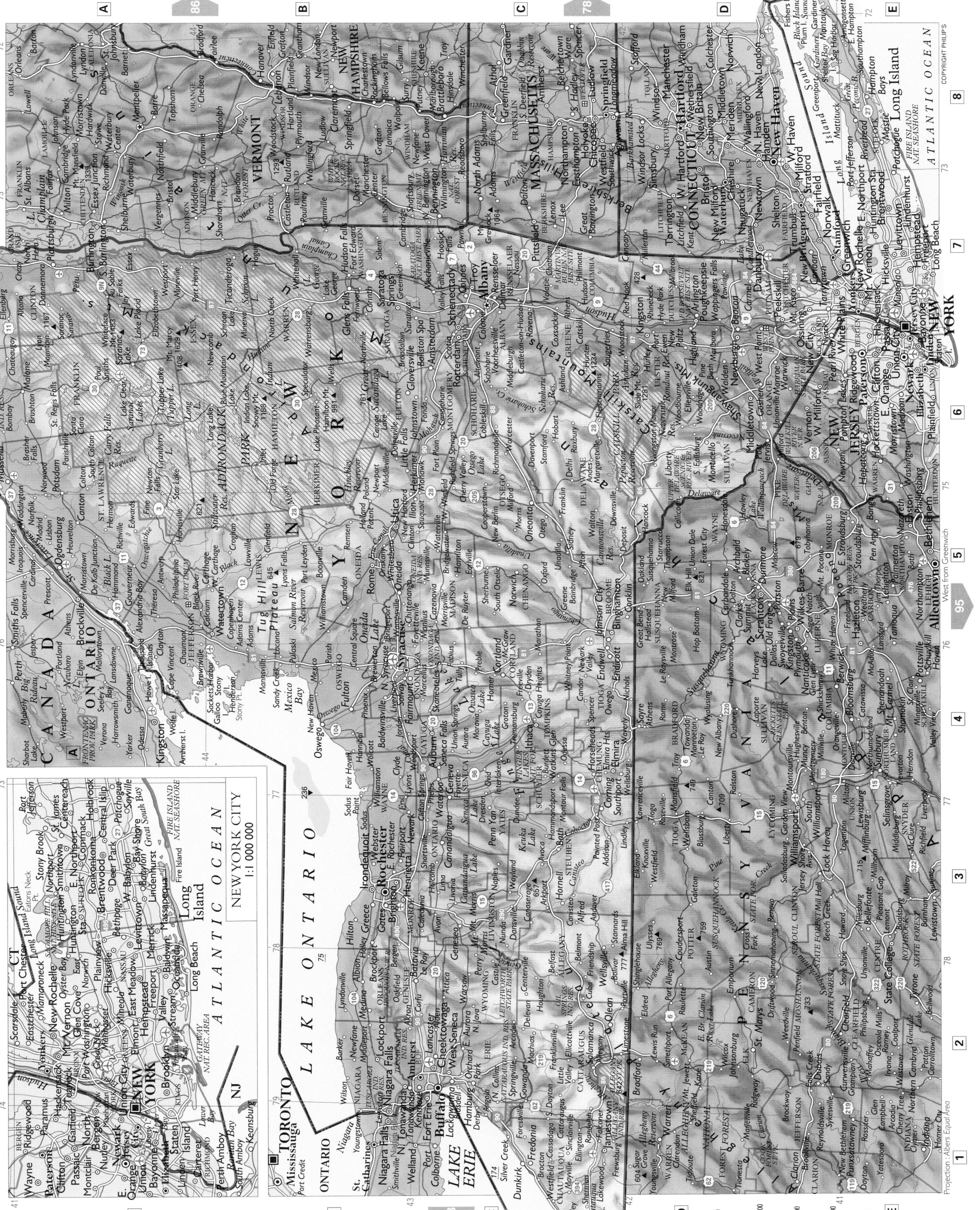

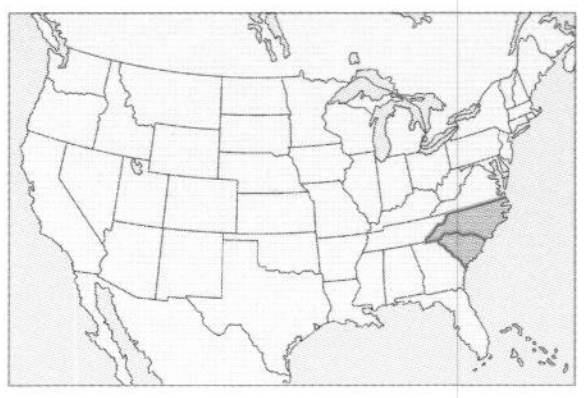

1:2 400 000

10 0 10 20 30 40 50 60 70 80 90 100 km

10 0 10 20 30 40 50 60 70 miles

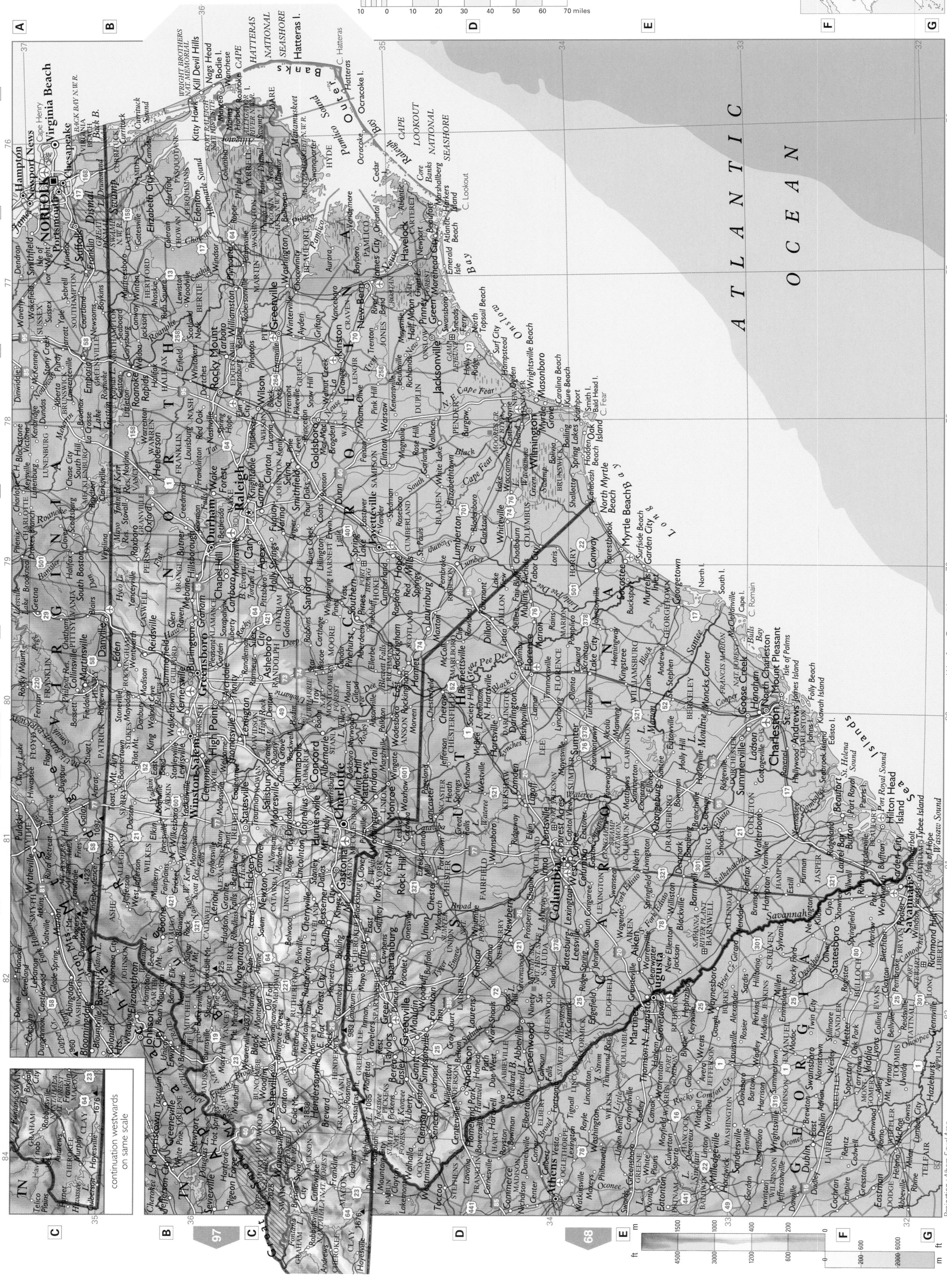

1:2 400 000
10 0 10 20 30 40 50 km
10 0 10 20 30 miles
SASKATCHEWAN
C A N A D A
MANITOBA
MONTANA
N O R T H D A K O T A
S O U T H D A K O T A
N E B R A S K A
MN
Williston
Minot
Lake Sakawea
Devils Lake
Grand Forks
Fargo
West Fargo
Moorhead
Jamestown
Valley City
Dickinson
Mandan
Bismarck
FORT BERTHOLD INDIAN RESERVATION
THEODORE ROOSEVELT NAT. PARK
STANDING ROCK INDIAN RESERVATION
CHEYENNE RIVER INDIAN RESERVATION
SPIRIT LAKE IND. RES.
LAKE TRAVERSE (SISSETON) IND. RES.
Aberdeen
Watertown
Brookings
Huron
Pierre
Lake Oahe
Rapid City
Black Hills
Mitchell
Sioux Falls
Yankton
Vermillion
PINE RIDGE INDIAN RESERVATION
ROSEBUD INDIAN RESERVATION
Missouri
Red River of the North
Big Sioux
Projection: Albers Equal Area
West from Greenwich
COPYRIGHT PHILIPS
400 1000 1500 2000 m
1200 3000 4500 6000 ft

10 0 10 20 30 40 50 60 70 80 90 km

10 0 10 20 30 40 50 60 miles

1:2 000 000

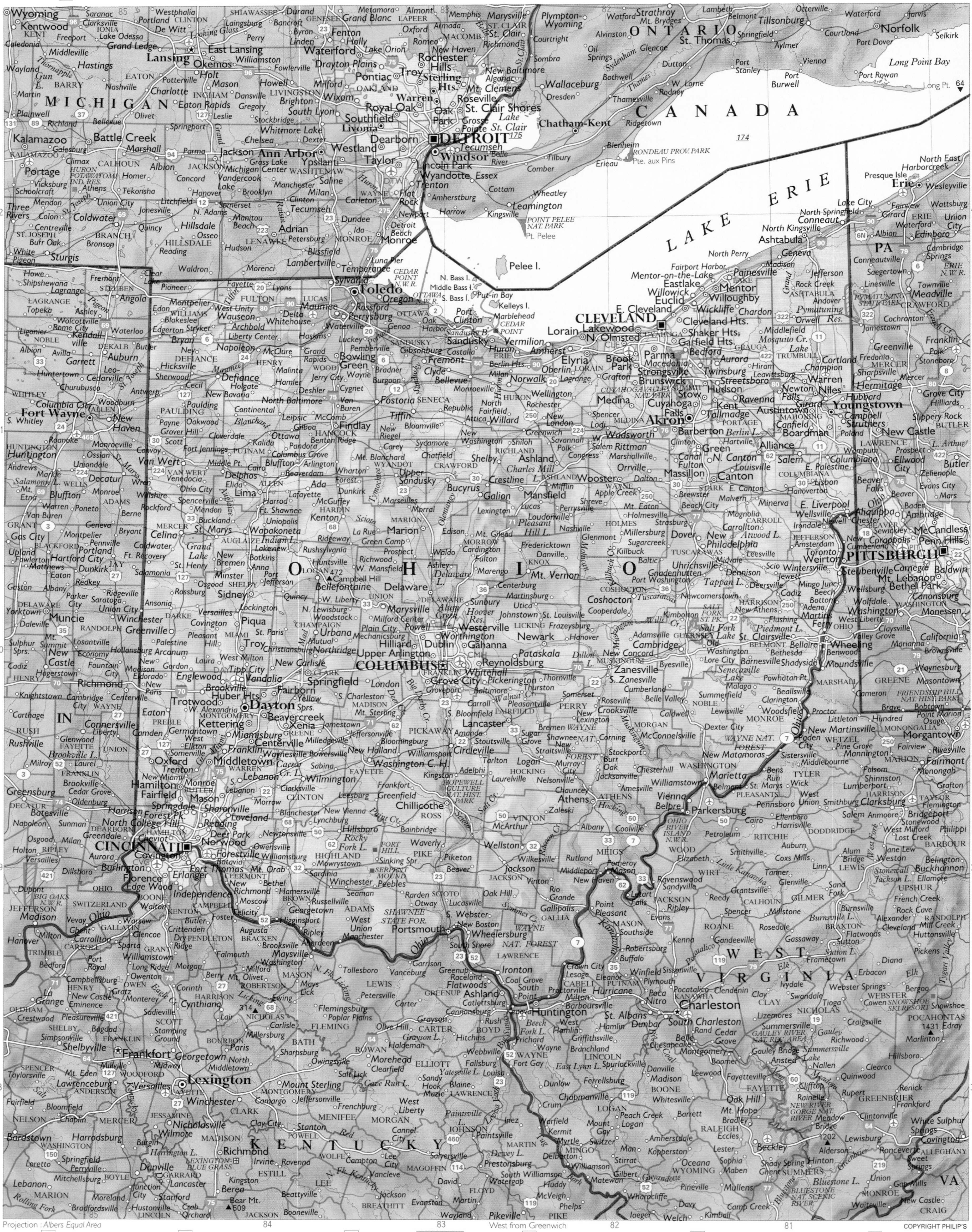

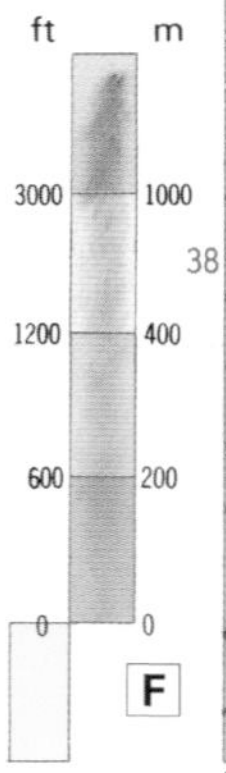

1:2 000 000

10 0 10 20 30 40 50 60 70 80 100 km
10 0 10 20 30 40 50 60 miles

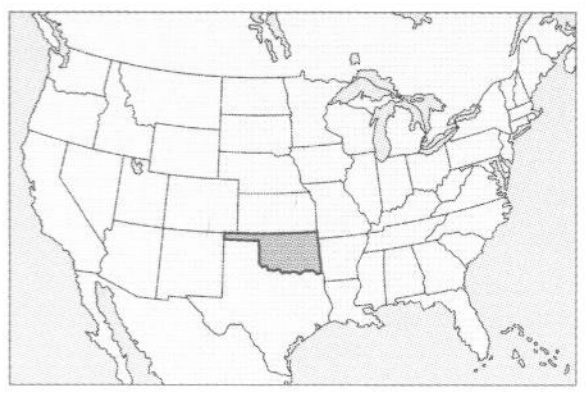

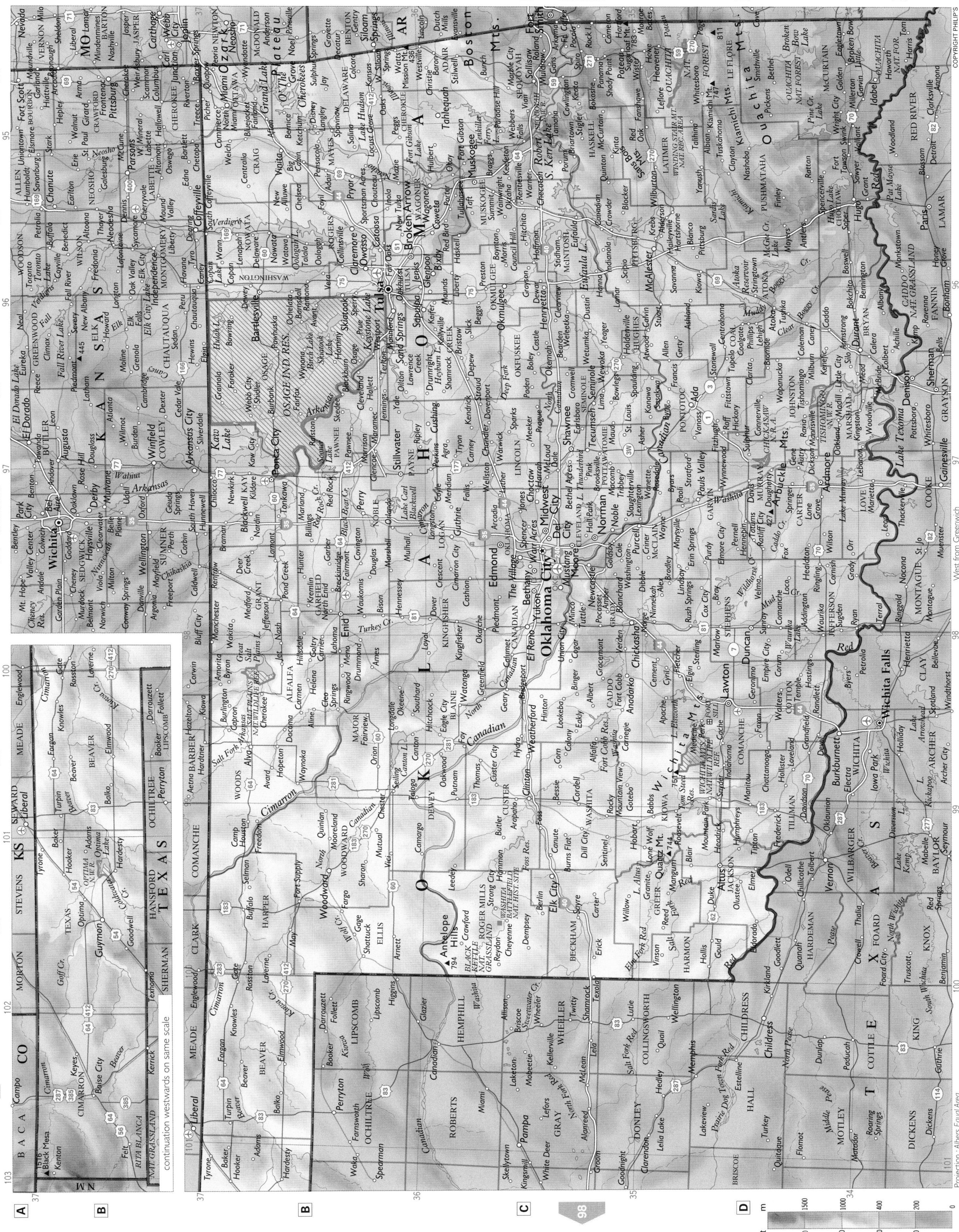

63
74
99
98

10 0 10 20 30 40 50 60 70 80 90 km

1:2 000 000

10 0 10 20 30 40 50 60 miles

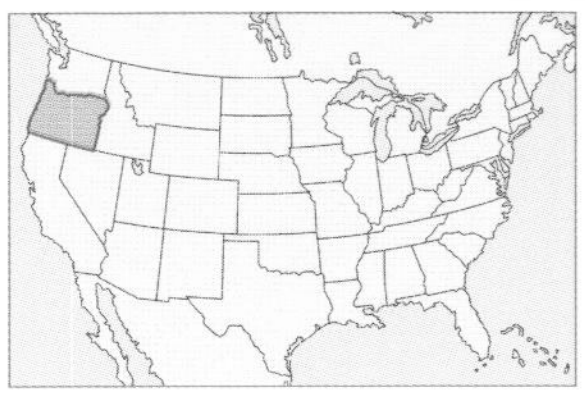

See page 78 for Rhode Island, page 90 for South Carolina and page 91 for South Dakota

1:2 000 000

km	10	0	10	20	30	40	50	60	70	80	100
miles	10	0	10	20	30	40	50	60			

Underlined settlements give their name to the county in which they stand.

West from Greenwich

Projection: Albers Equal Area

1. HOPEWELL FURNACE NAT. HIST. PARK
2. VALLEY FORGE NAT. HIST. PARK
3. ALLEGHENY PORTAGE RAILROAD NAT. HIST. SITE

m	1000	400	200	0
ft	3000	1200	600	0

77 89 92 102

10 0 10 20 30 40 50 60 70 80 90 km

10 0 10 20 30 40 50 60 miles

1:2 000 000

See page 78 for Rhode Island, page 90 for South Carolina and page 91 for South Dakota

1 2 3 71 4 5 72 6

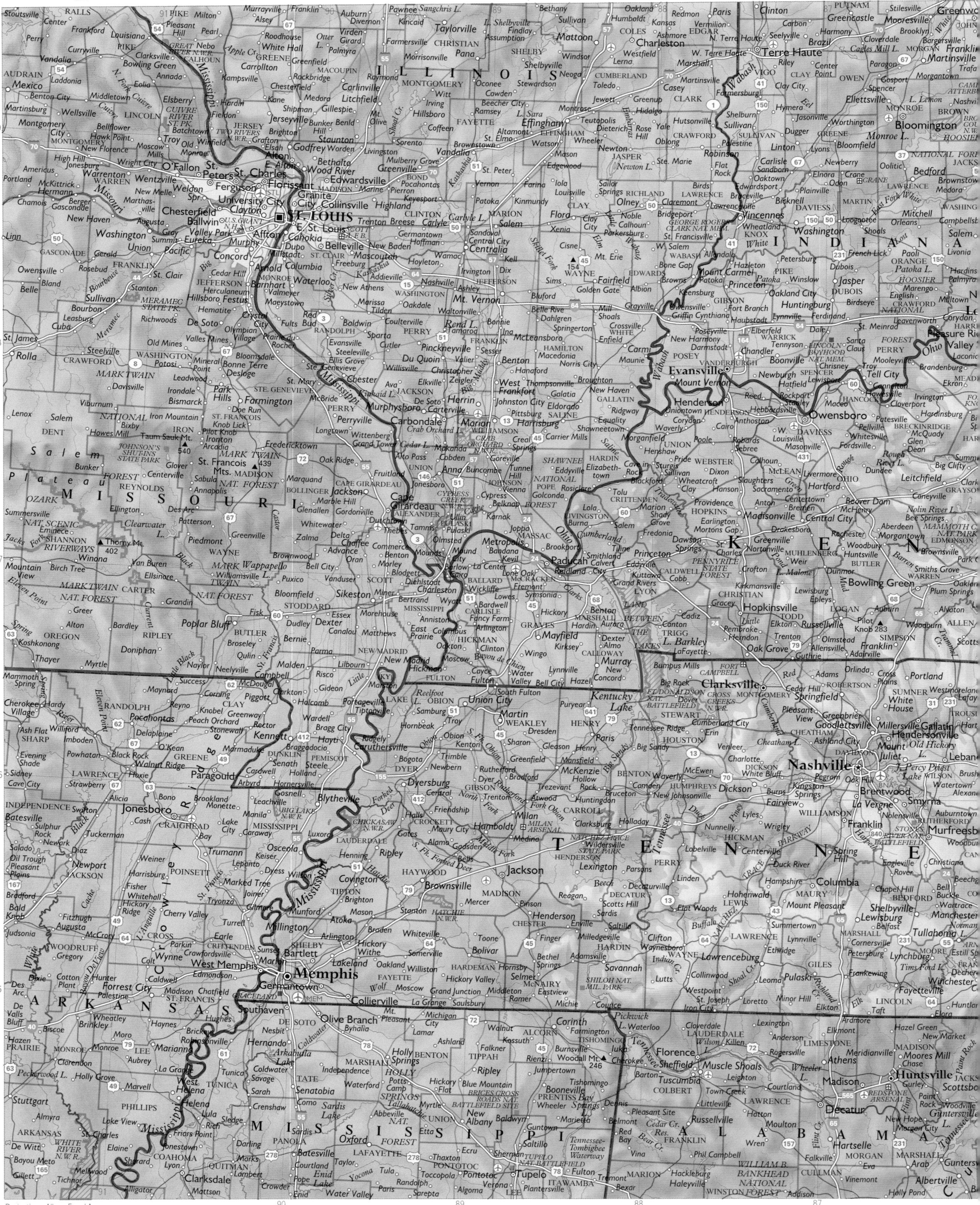

82
63

Projection : Albers Equal Area

1 2 3 81 4 5 60 6

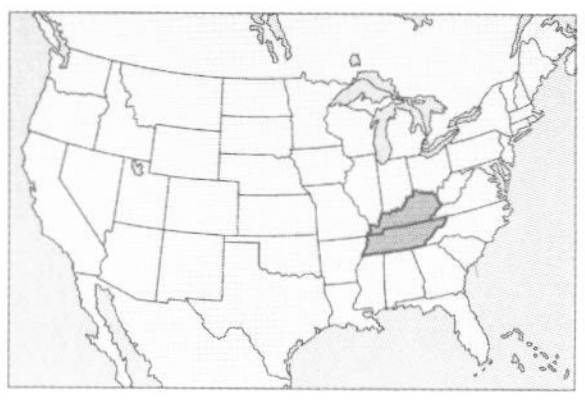

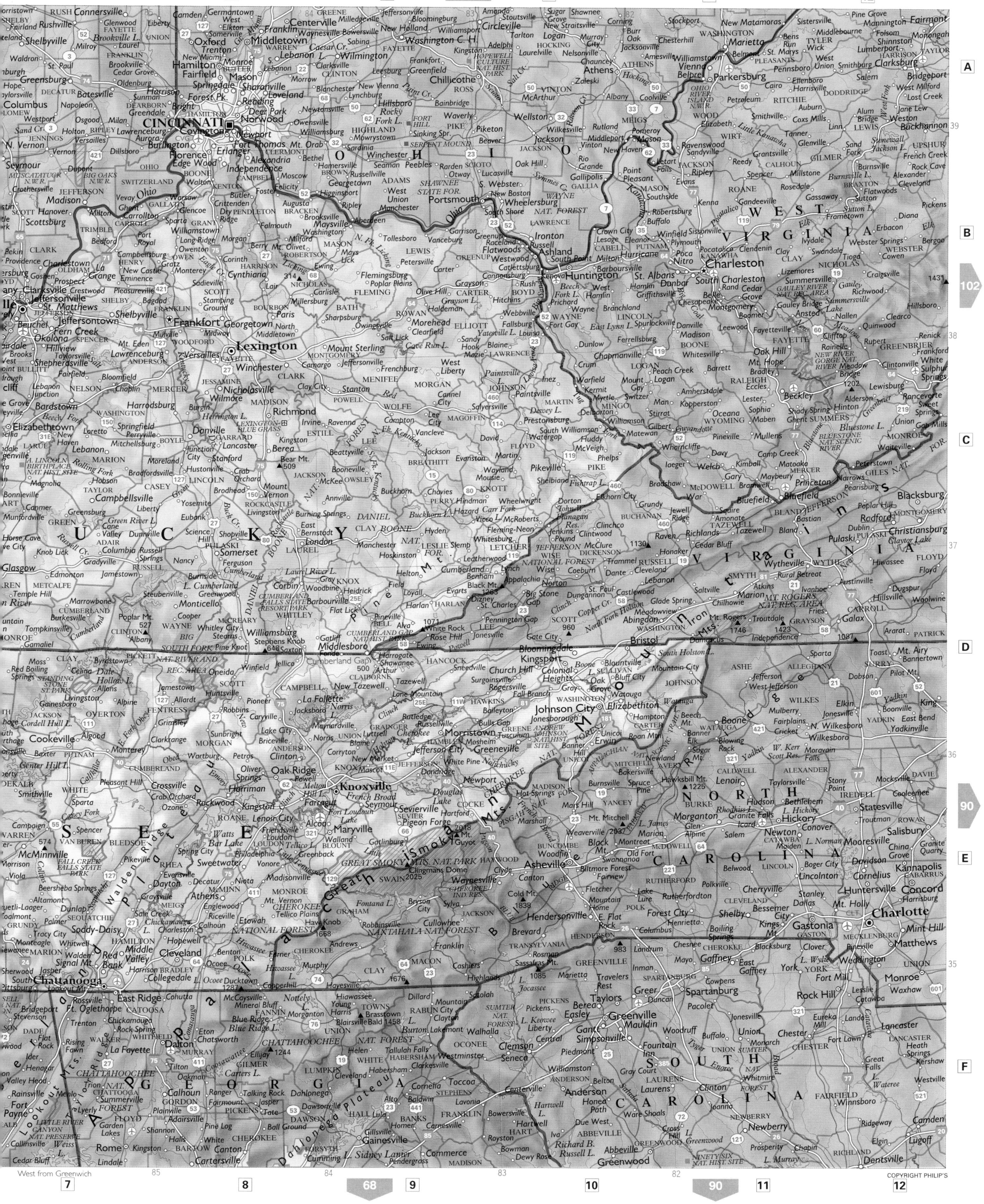
7
8
9
92
10
11
12
A
B
C
D
E
F
102
90
68
90
39
38
37
36
35
85
84
83
82
West from Greenwich
OHIO
WEST VIRGINIA
KENTUCKY
VIRGINIA
TENNESSEE
NORTH CAROLINA
SOUTH CAROLINA
GEORGIA
Appalachian Mts.
Cumberland Plateau
Blue Ridge
Great Smoky Mts.
CINCINNATI
Lexington
Frankfort
Louisville
Charleston
Huntington
Knoxville
Chattanooga
Asheville
Charlotte
Greenville
Spartanburg
Bristol
Johnson City
Kingsport
Parkersburg
Dalton
Gainesville

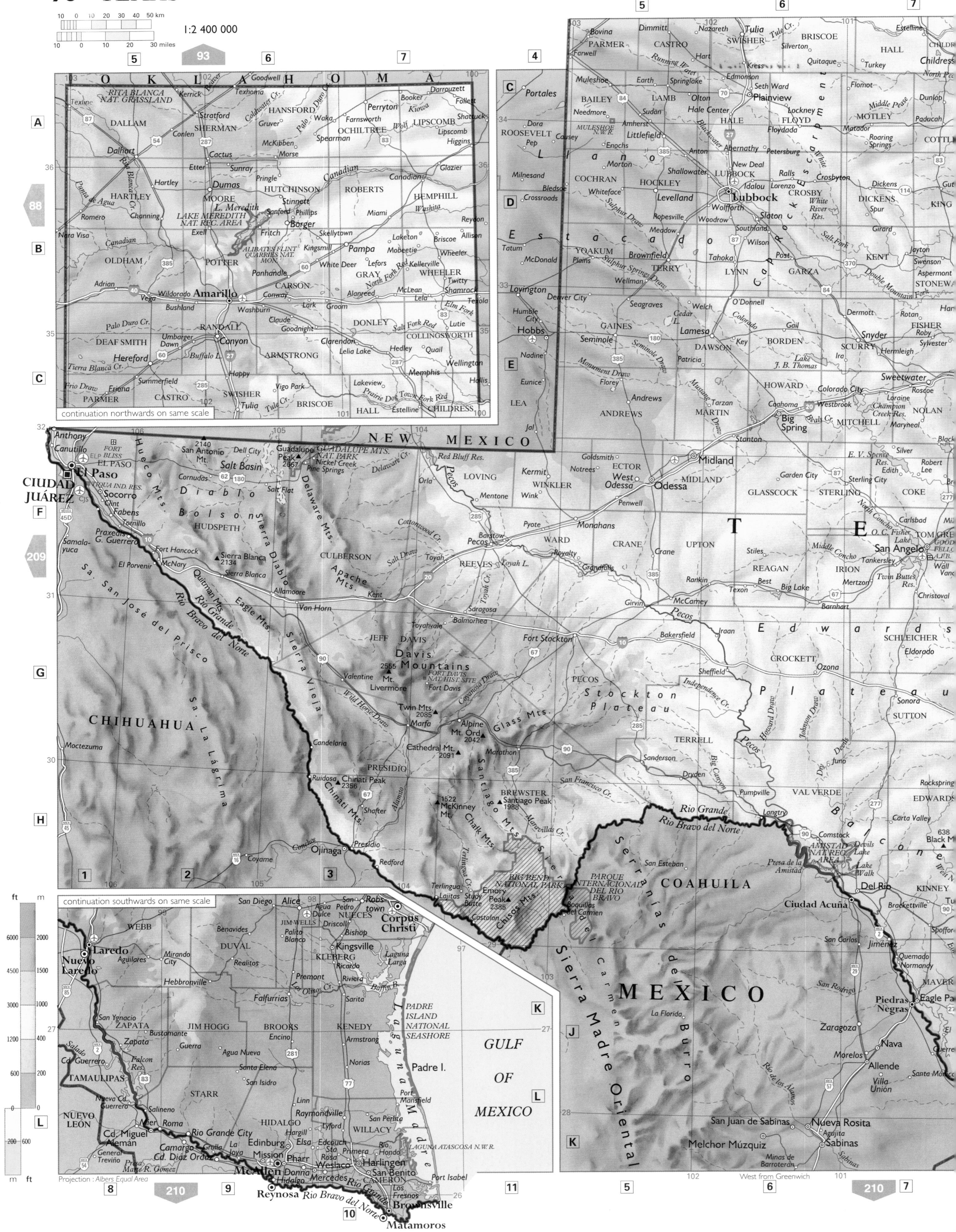

1:2 400 000
10 0 10 20 30 40 50 km
10 0 10 20 30 miles
93
88
209
210
continuation northwards on same scale
continuation southwards on same scale
O K L A H O M A
N E W M E X I C O
T E X A S
MEXICO
CHIHUAHUA
COAHUILA
TAMAULIPAS
NUEVO LEON
GULF OF MEXICO
RITA BLANCA NAT. GRASSLAND
DALLAM
HANSFORD
OCHILTREE
LIPSCOMB
SHERMAN
HUTCHINSON
ROBERTS
HEMPHILL
HARTLEY
MOORE
OLDHAM
POTTER
CARSON
GRAY
WHEELER
DEAF SMITH
RANDALL
ARMSTRONG
DONLEY
COLLINGSWORTH
PARMER
CASTRO
SWISHER
BRISCOE
HALL
CHILDRESS
Dalhart
Dumas
Amarillo
Canyon
Hereford
Borger
Pampa
Perryton
Spearman
Stratford
Texhoma
Goodwell
Booker
Darrouzett
Follett
Higgins
Canadian
Shamrock
Wellington
Memphis
Clarendon
Tulia
LAKE MEREDITH NAT. REC. AREA
L. Meredith
ALIBATES FLINT QUARRIES NAT. MON.
Palo Duro Cr.
Prairie Dog Town Fork Red
Salt Fork Red
North Fork Red
Portales
Roosevelt
Hobbs
LEA
Lovington
Eunice
Jal
Ll a n o E s t a c a d o
BAILEY
LAMB
HALE
FLOYD
MOTLEY
COCHRAN
HOCKLEY
LUBBOCK
CROSBY
DICKENS
KING
YOAKUM
TERRY
LYNN
GARZA
KENT
STONEWALL
GAINES
DAWSON
BORDEN
SCURRY
FISHER
ANDREWS
MARTIN
HOWARD
MITCHELL
NOLAN
LOVING
WINKLER
ECTOR
MIDLAND
GLASSCOCK
STERLING
COKE
WARD
CRANE
UPTON
REAGAN
IRION
TOM GREEN
REEVES
CULBERSON
HUDSPETH
JEFF DAVIS
PECOS
CROCKETT
SCHLEICHER
SUTTON
TERRELL
VAL VERDE
EDWARDS
KINNEY
PRESIDIO
BREWSTER
Muleshoe
Littlefield
Plainview
Lubbock
Levelland
Slaton
Brownfield
Lamesa
Seminole
Snyder
Sweetwater
Colorado City
Big Spring
Midland
Odessa
Monahans
Kermit
Pecos
San Angelo
Fort Stockton
Ozona
Sonora
Del Rio
Ciudad Acuña
Eagle Pass
Piedras Negras
El Paso
CIUDAD JUÁREZ
Van Horn
Sierra Blanca
Alpine
Marfa
Fort Davis
Presidio
Ojinaga
Davis Mountains
Mt. Livermore 2555
Guadalupe Peak 2667
GUADALUPE MTS. NAT. PARK
Hueco Mts.
Diablo Bolson
Sierra Diablo
Delaware Mts.
Apache Mts.
Quitman Mts.
Eagle Mts.
Sierra Vieja
Chinati Mts.
Chinati Peak 2356
Glass Mts.
Santiago Mts.
Chalk Mts.
Chisos Mts.
Emory Peak 2385
BIG BEND NATIONAL PARK
PARQUE INTERNACIONAL DEL RIO BRAVO
AMISTAD NAT. REC. AREA
Stockton Plateau
Edwards Plateau
Balcones Escarpment
Caprock Escarpment
Rio Grande
Rio Bravo del Norte
Pecos
Devils
Serranías del Burro
Sierra del Carmen
Sierra Madre Oriental
Sa. San José del Prisco
Sa. La Lágrima
Nueva Rosita
Sabinas
Melchor Múzquiz
San Juan de Sabinas
Zaragoza
Allende
Nava
Morelos
Jiménez
Laredo
Nuevo Laredo
Corpus Christi
Alice
Kingsville
Robstown
Falfurrias
Hebbronville
Zapata
Rio Grande City
Roma
Edinburg
McAllen
Mission
Pharr
Weslaco
Harlingen
San Benito
Brownsville
Matamoros
Reynosa
Port Isabel
Port Mansfield
Raymondville
Padre I.
PADRE ISLAND NATIONAL SEASHORE
Laguna Madre
WEBB
DUVAL
JIM WELLS
NUECES
KLEBERG
ZAPATA
JIM HOGG
BROOKS
KENEDY
STARR
HIDALGO
WILLACY
CAMERON
ft m
6000 2000
4500 1500
3000 1000
1200 400
600 200
0 0
200 600
Projection : Albers Equal Area
West from Greenwich

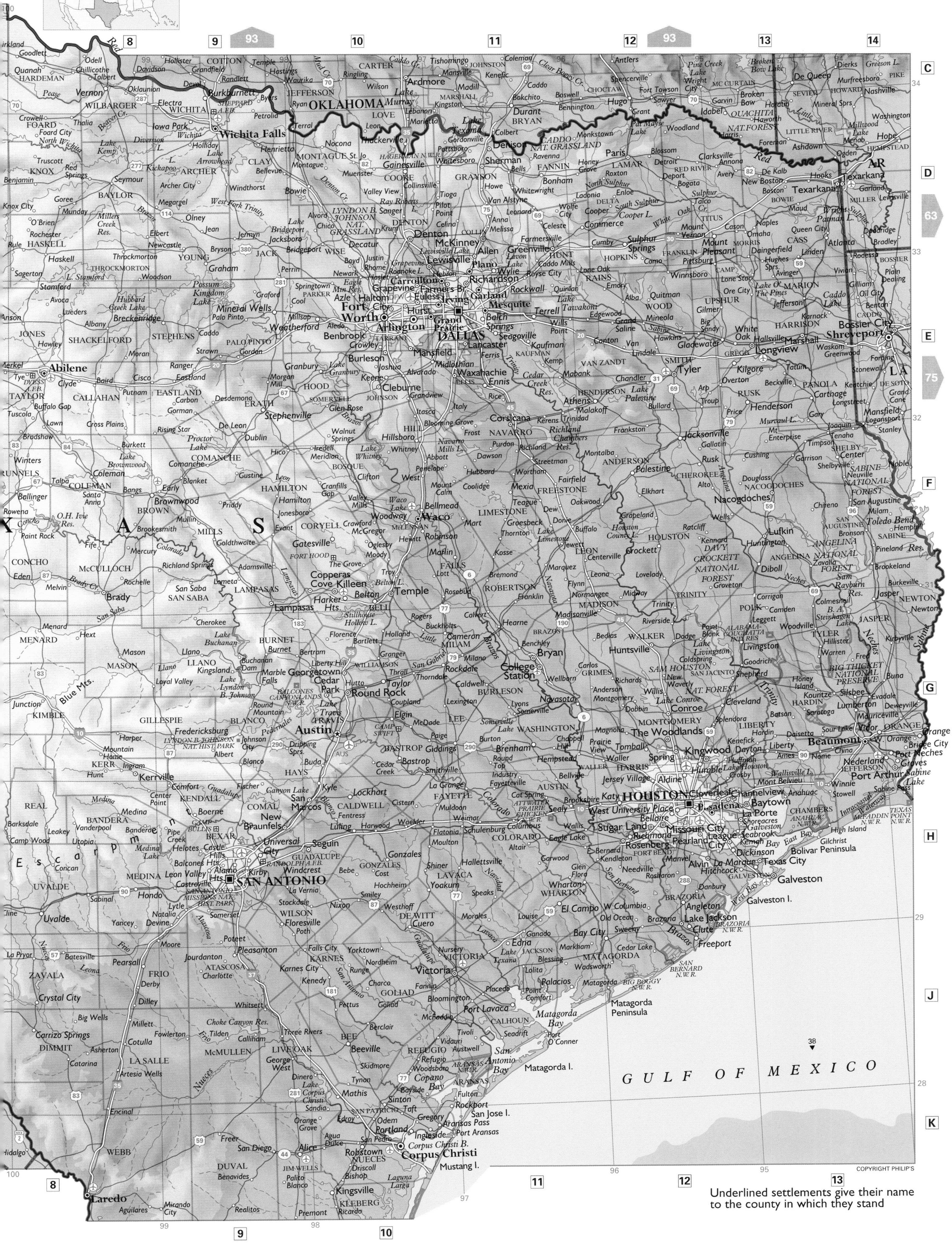

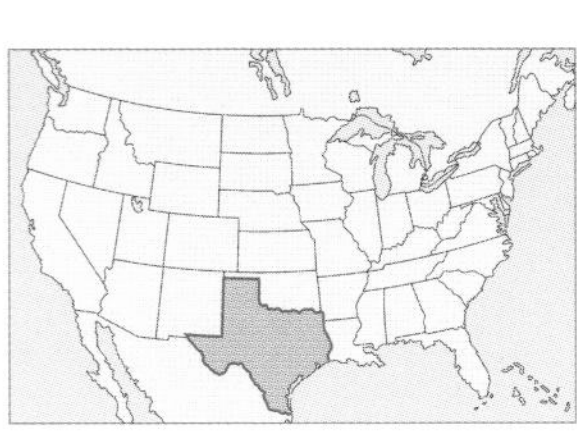

Underlined settlements give their name to the county in which they stand

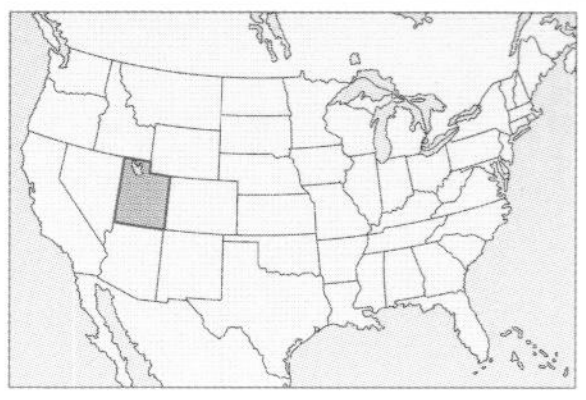

10 0 10 20 30 40 50 60 70 80 90 km

10 0 10 20 30 40 50 60 miles

1:2 000 000

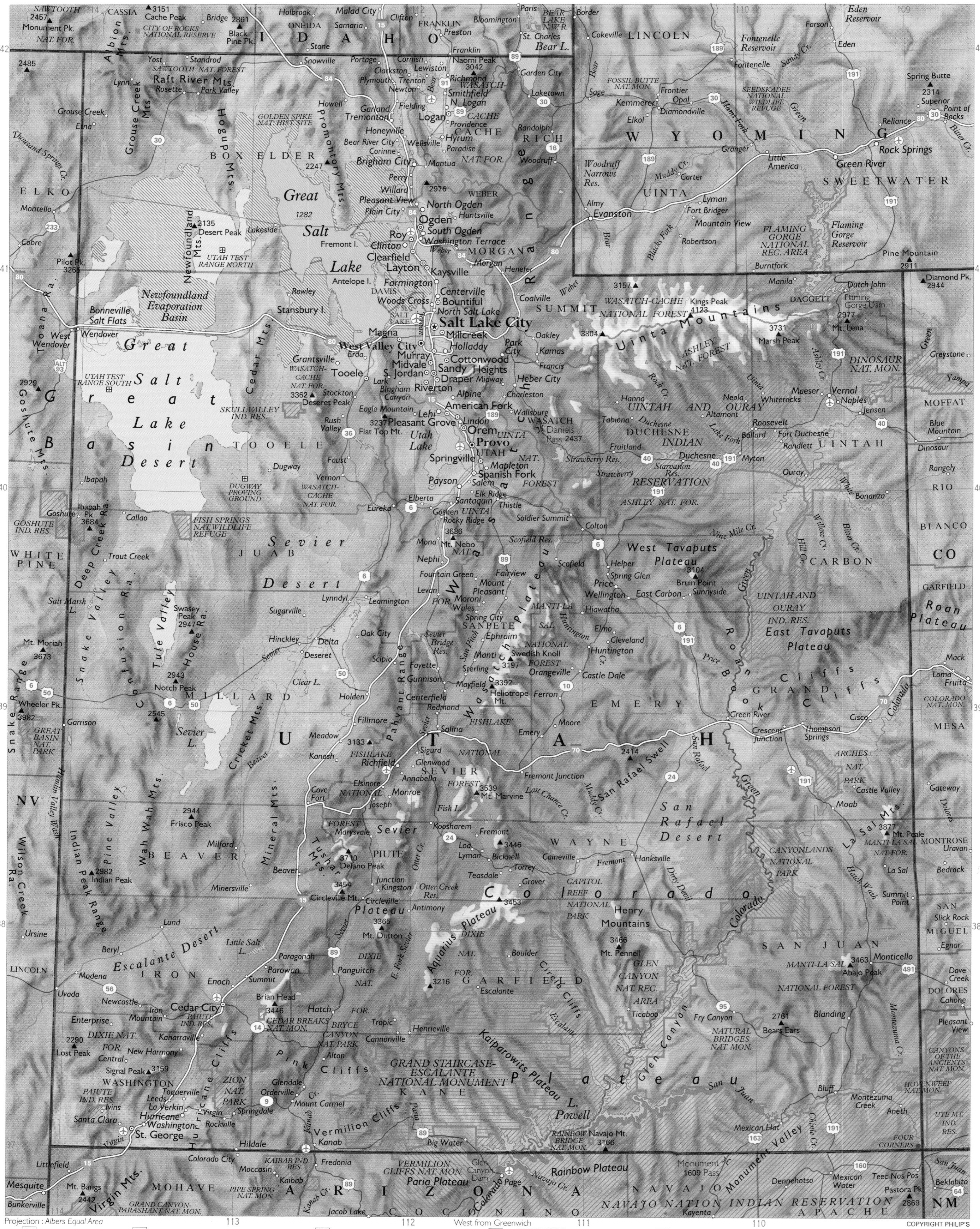

See page 86 for Vermont and page 102 for Virginia

1:2 000 000

10 0 10 20 30 40 50 60 70 80 100 km

10 0 10 20 30 40 50 60 miles

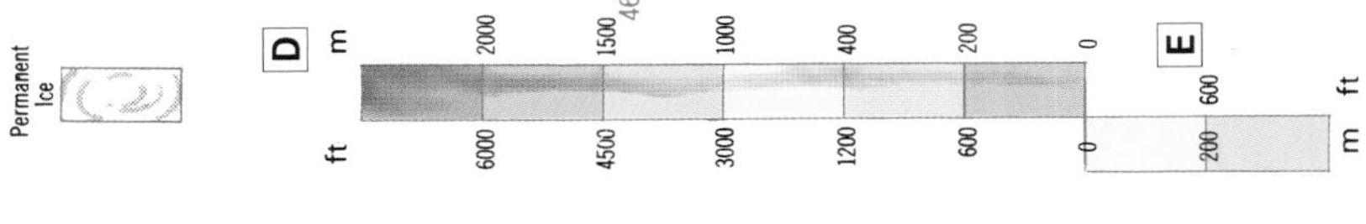

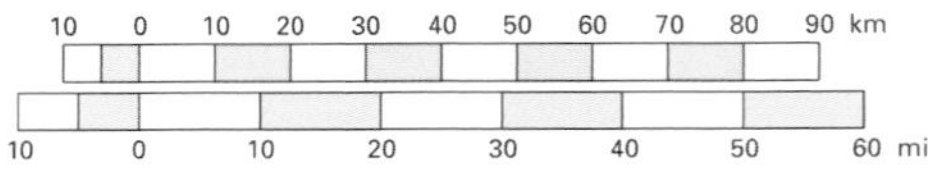

1:2 000 000

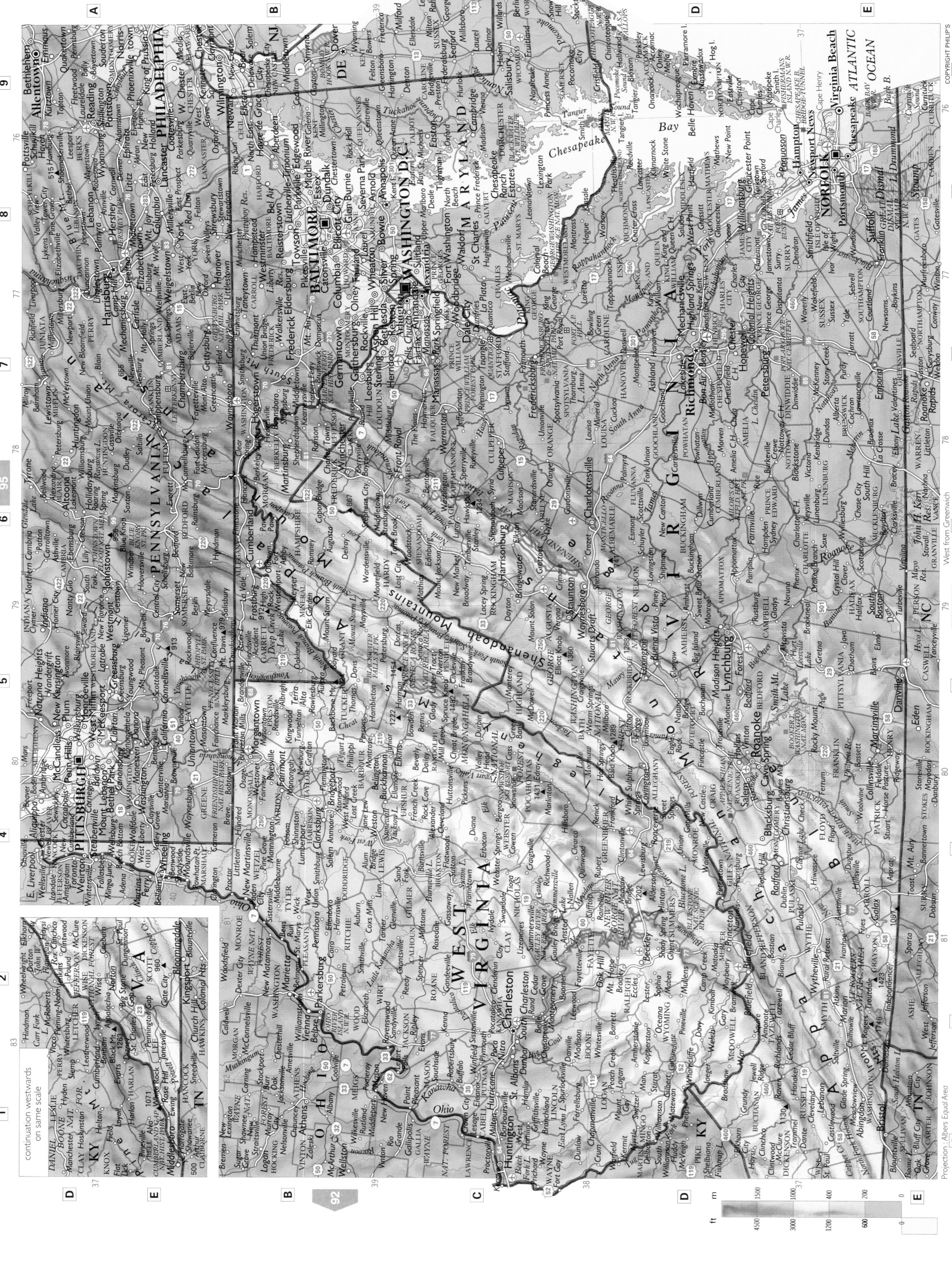

Projection: Albers Equal Area

West from Greenwich

1:2 000 000

10 0 10 20 30 40 50 60 70 80 100 km

10 0 10 20 30 40 50 60 miles

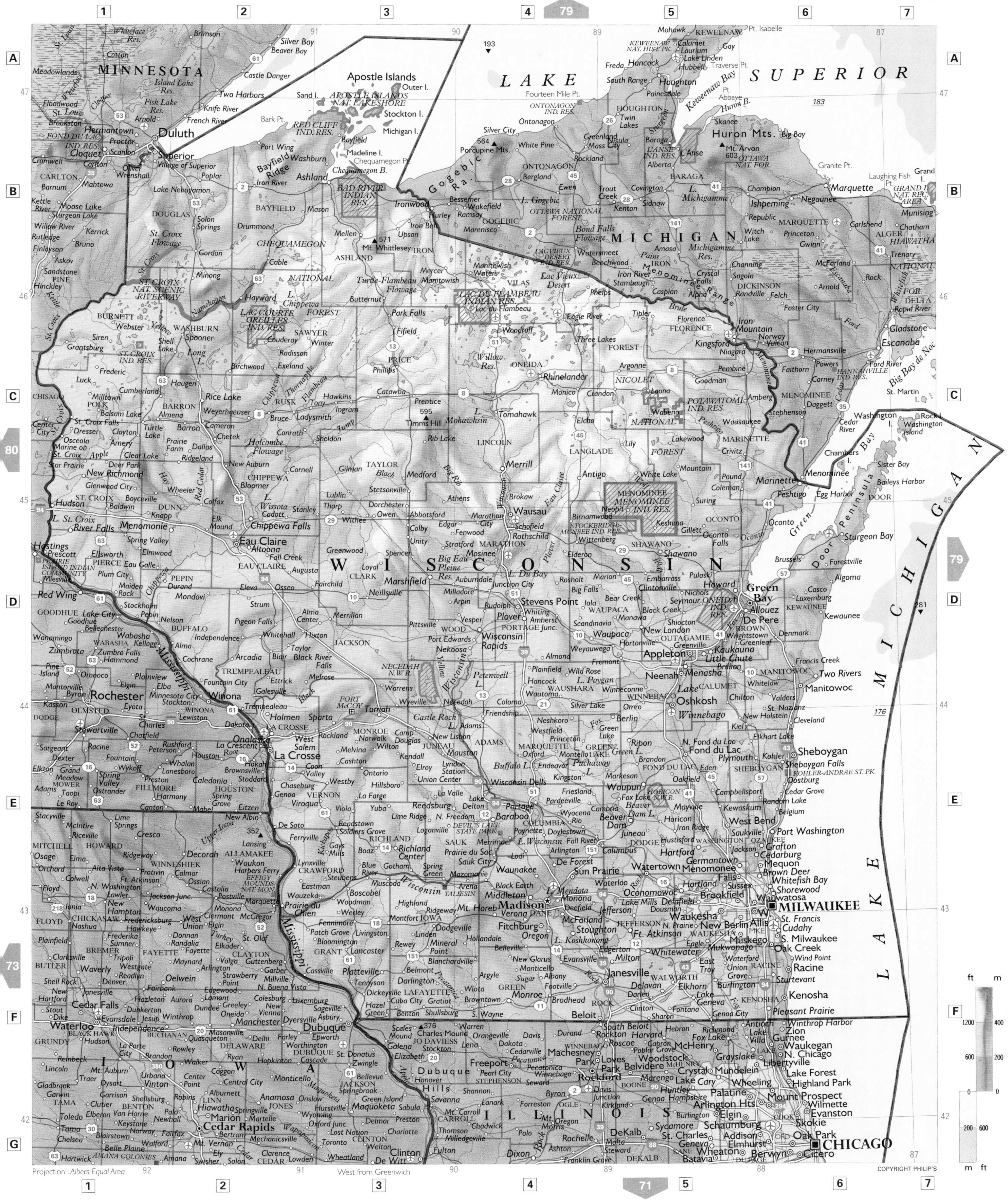

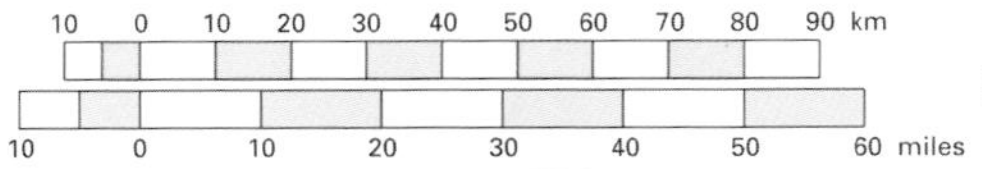
10 0 10 20 30 40 50 60 70 80 90 km
10 0 10 20 30 40 50 60 miles
1:2 000 000

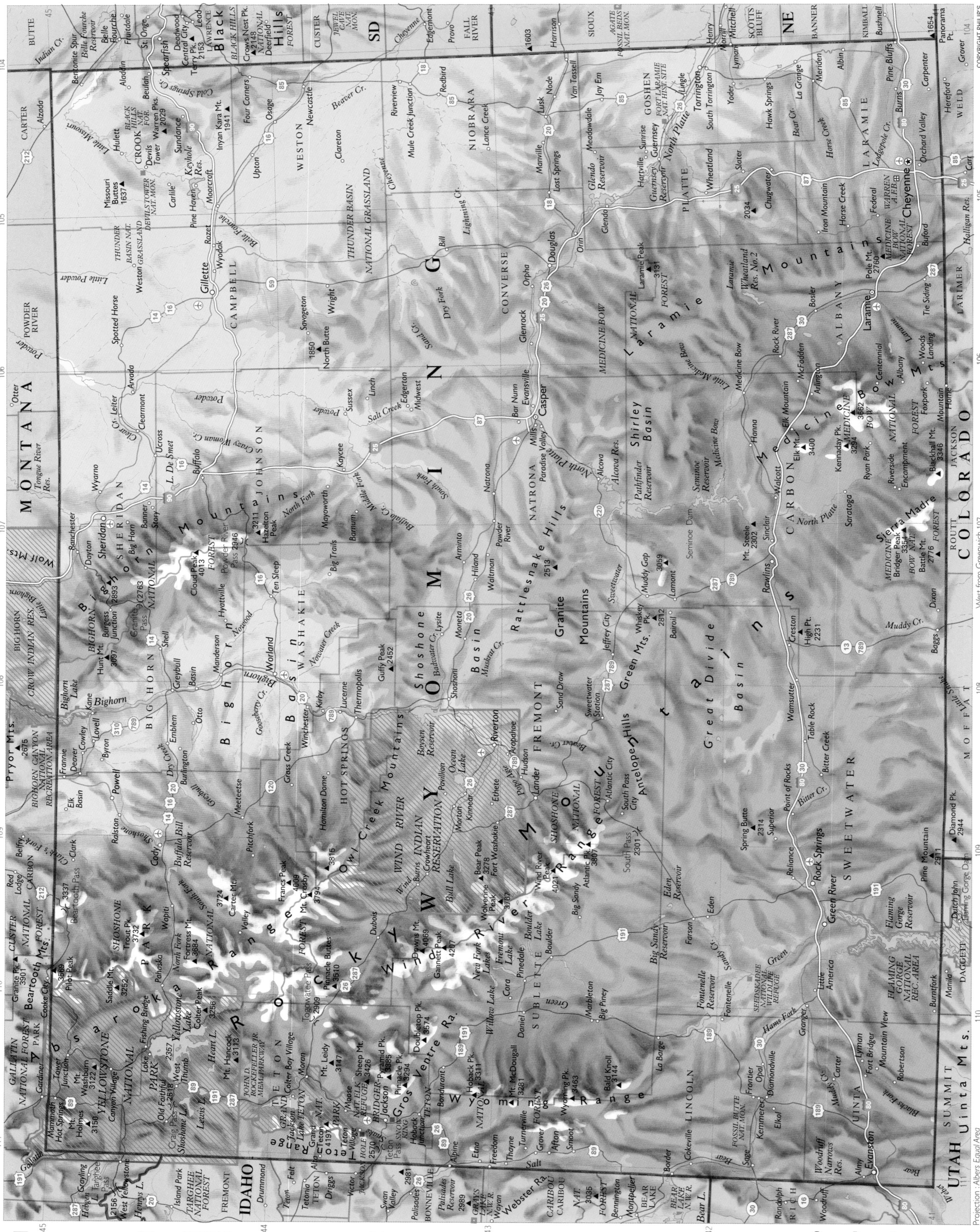
MONTANA
IDAHO
UTAH
COLORADO
SD
NE
WYOMING
Cheyenne
Casper
Laramie
Sheridan
Gillette
Cody
Rock Springs
Rawlins
Evanston
Riverton
Lander
Douglas
Yellowstone Lake
Bighorn Mountains
Wind River Range
Laramie Mountains
Medicine Bow Mts.
Uinta Mts.
Great Divide Basin
Projection: Albers Equal Area
West from Greenwich 107
COPYRIGHT PHILIP'S

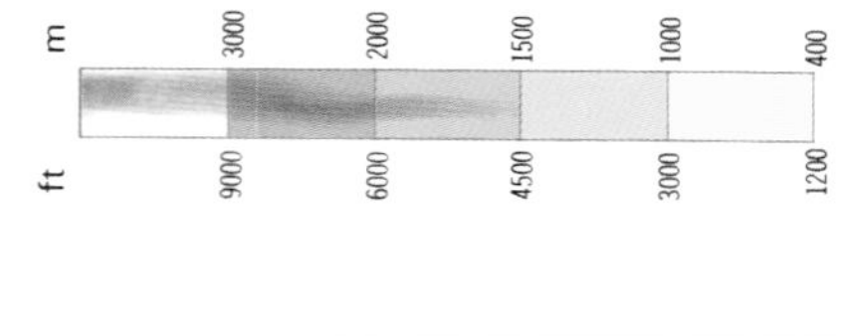
m
3000
2000
1500
1000
400
ft
9000
6000
4500
3000
1200

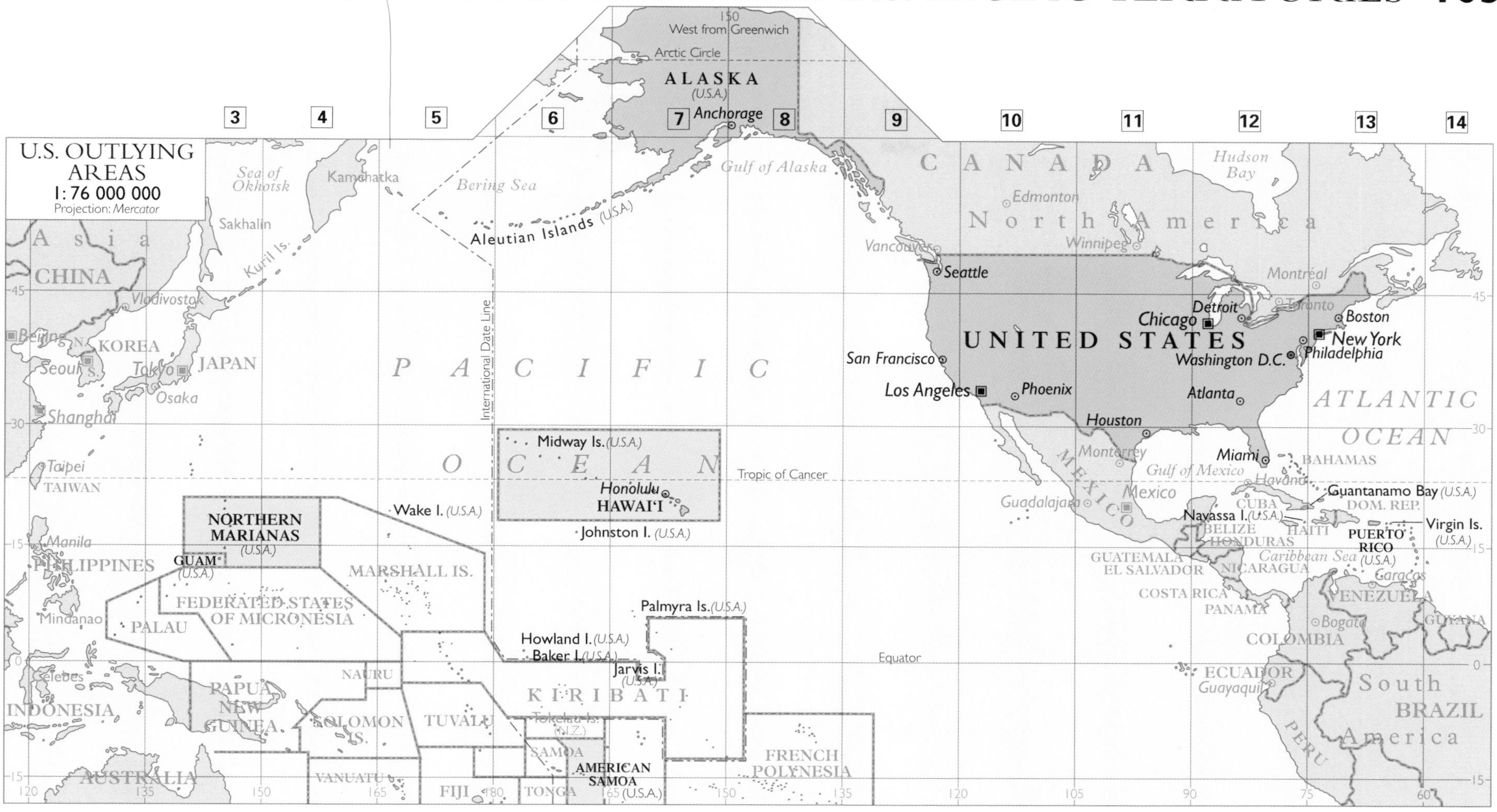

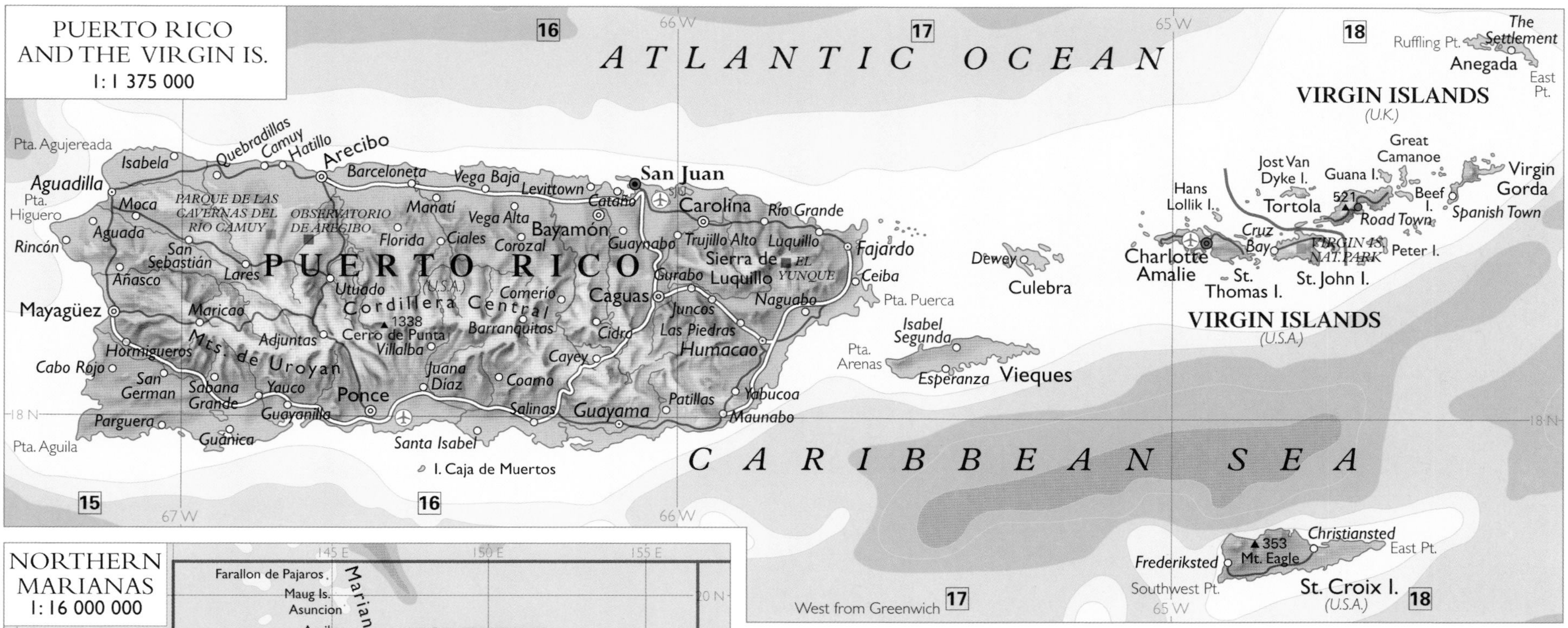

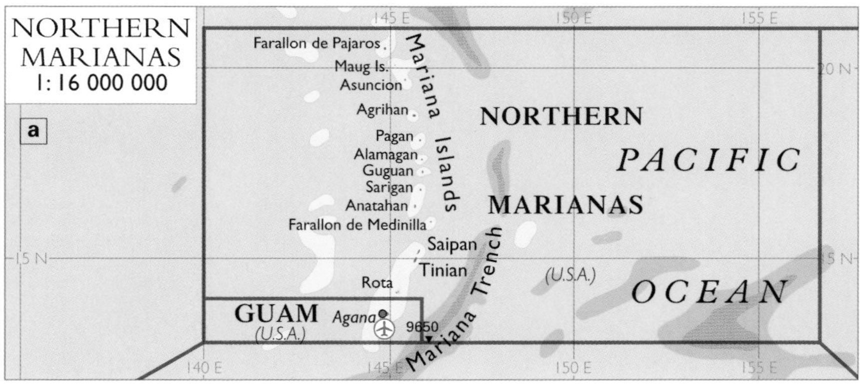

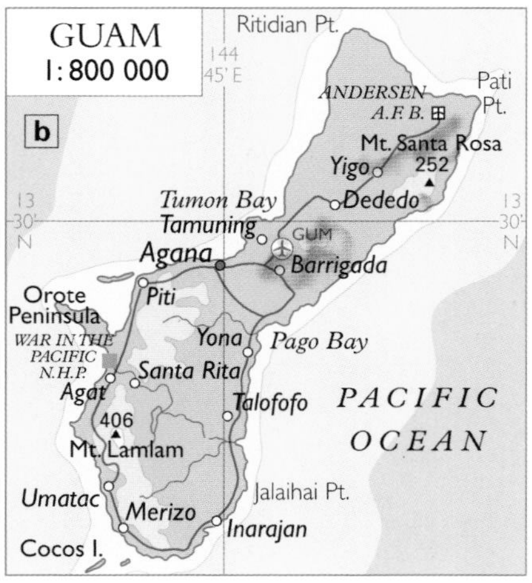

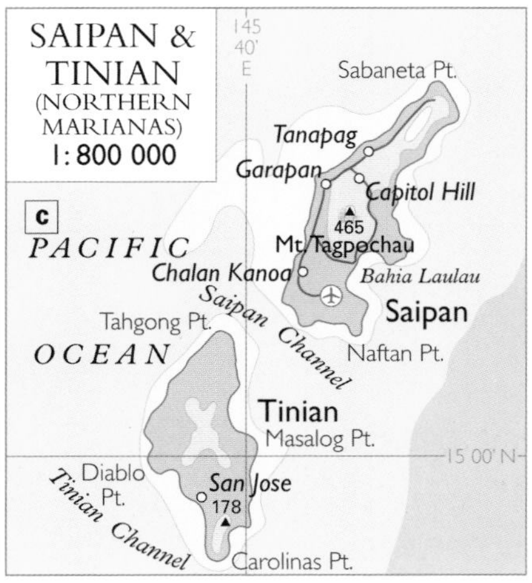

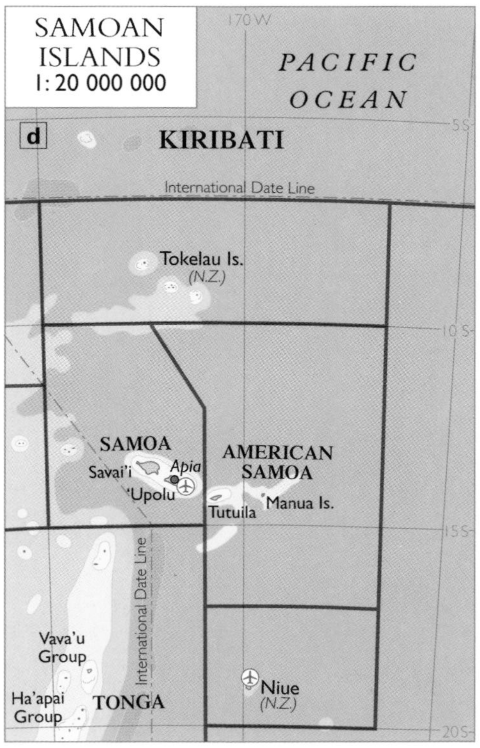

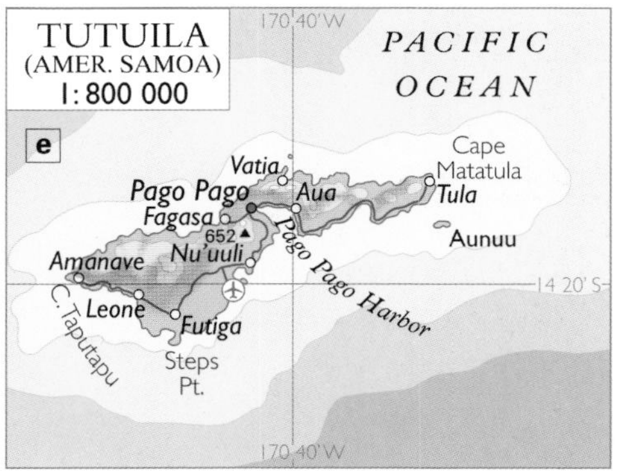

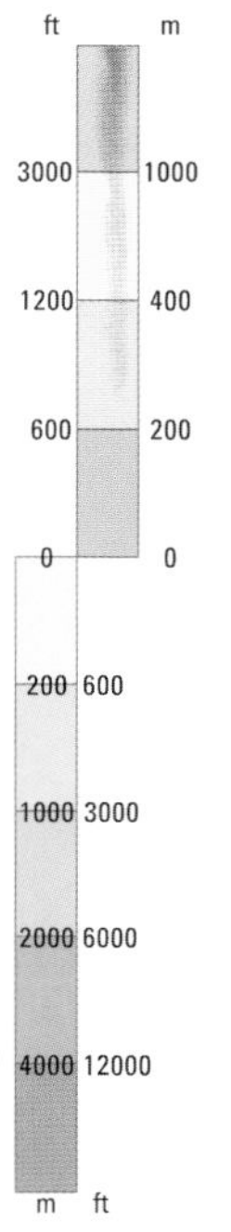

COPYRIGHT PHILIP'S

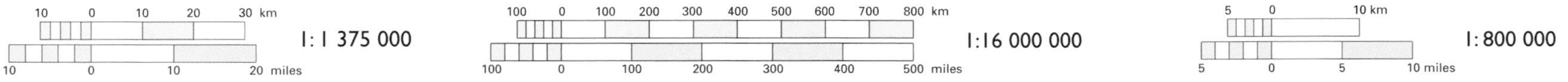

ATLANTA

0 km 5
0 miles 3

CENTRAL BOSTON

0 km 1
0 miles 0.5

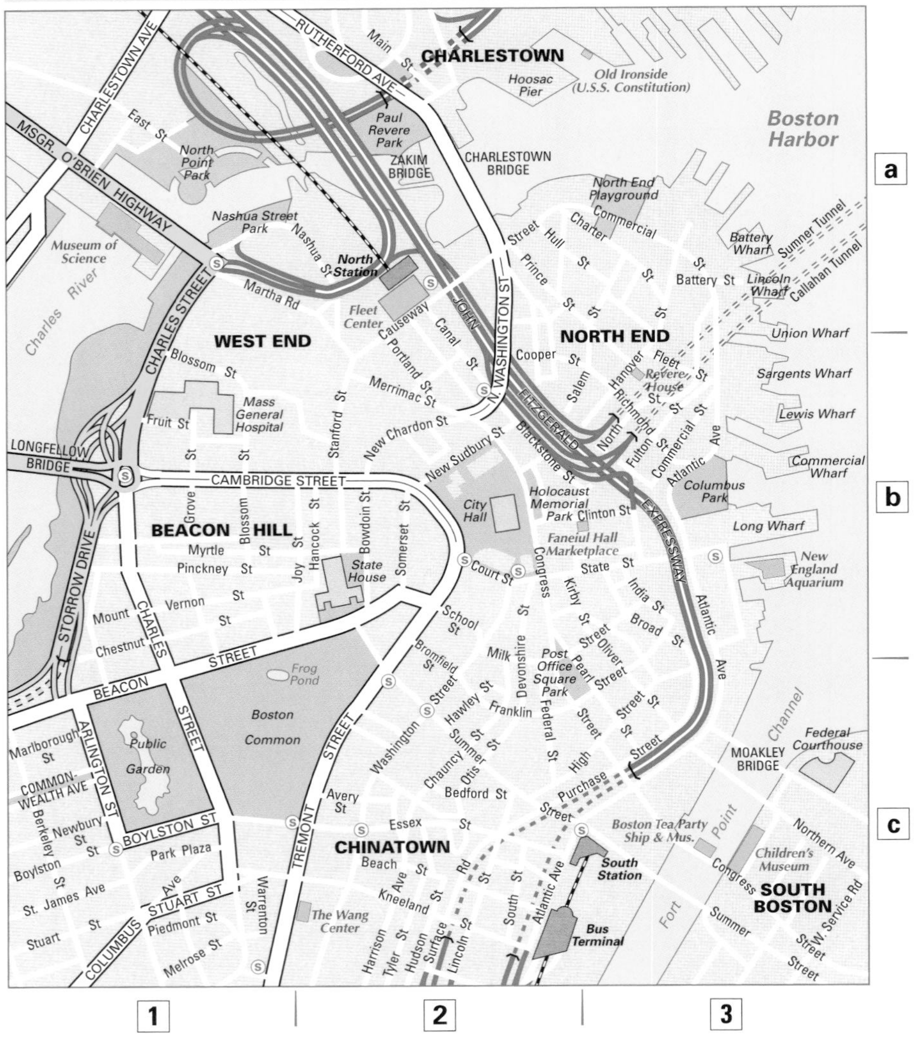

BOSTON

0 km 5
0 miles 3

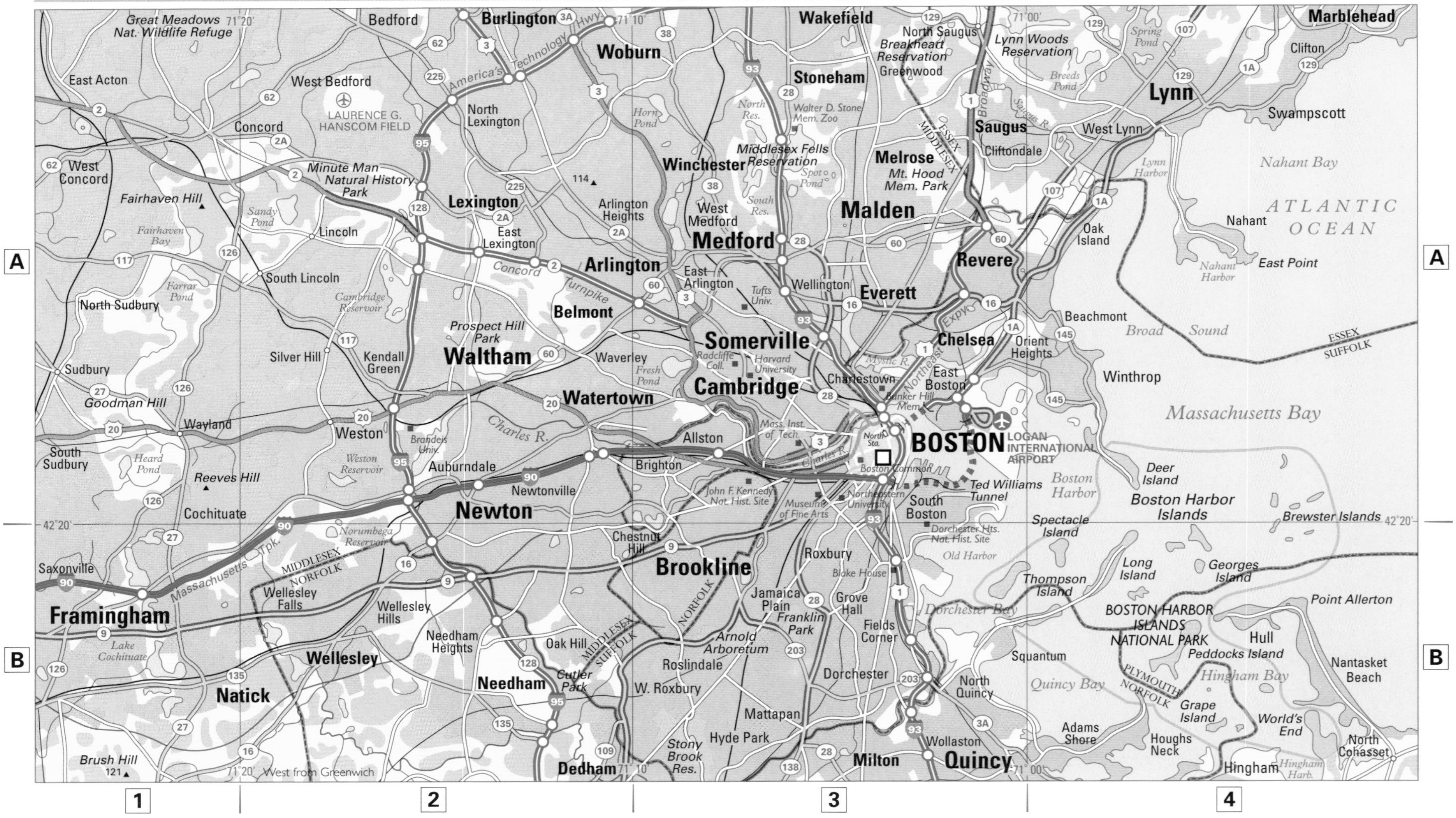

BALTIMORE

CHARLOTTE

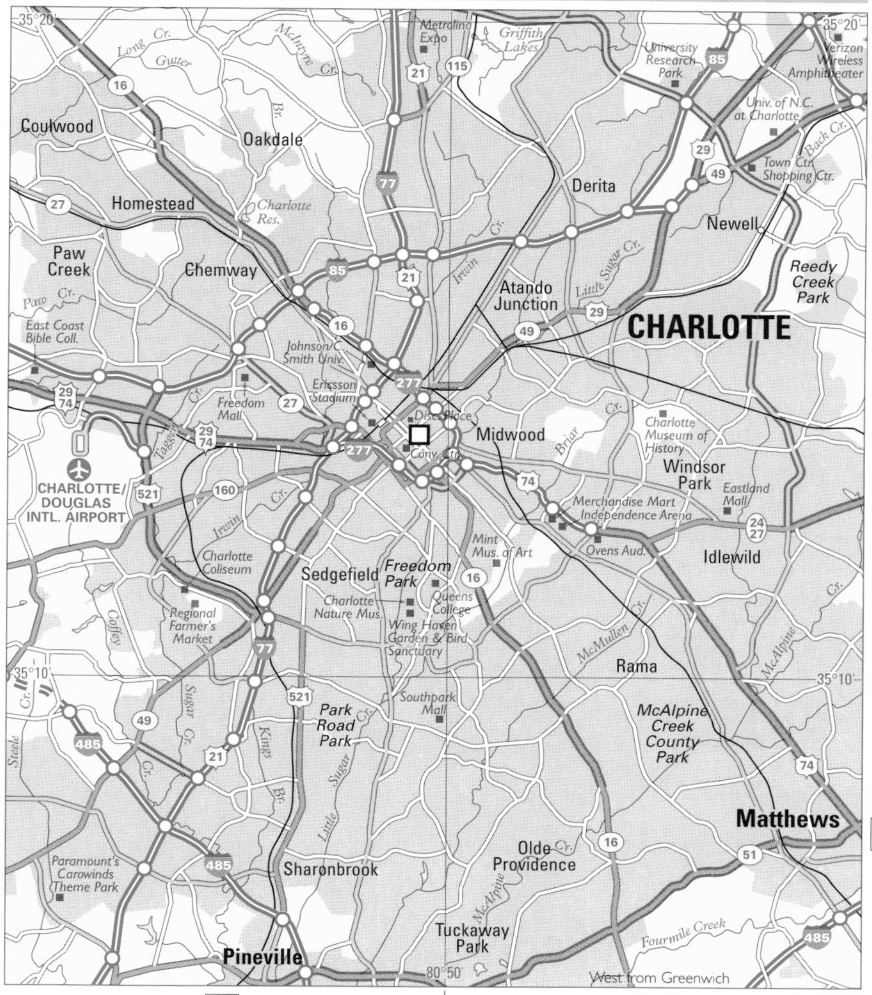

CINCINNATI

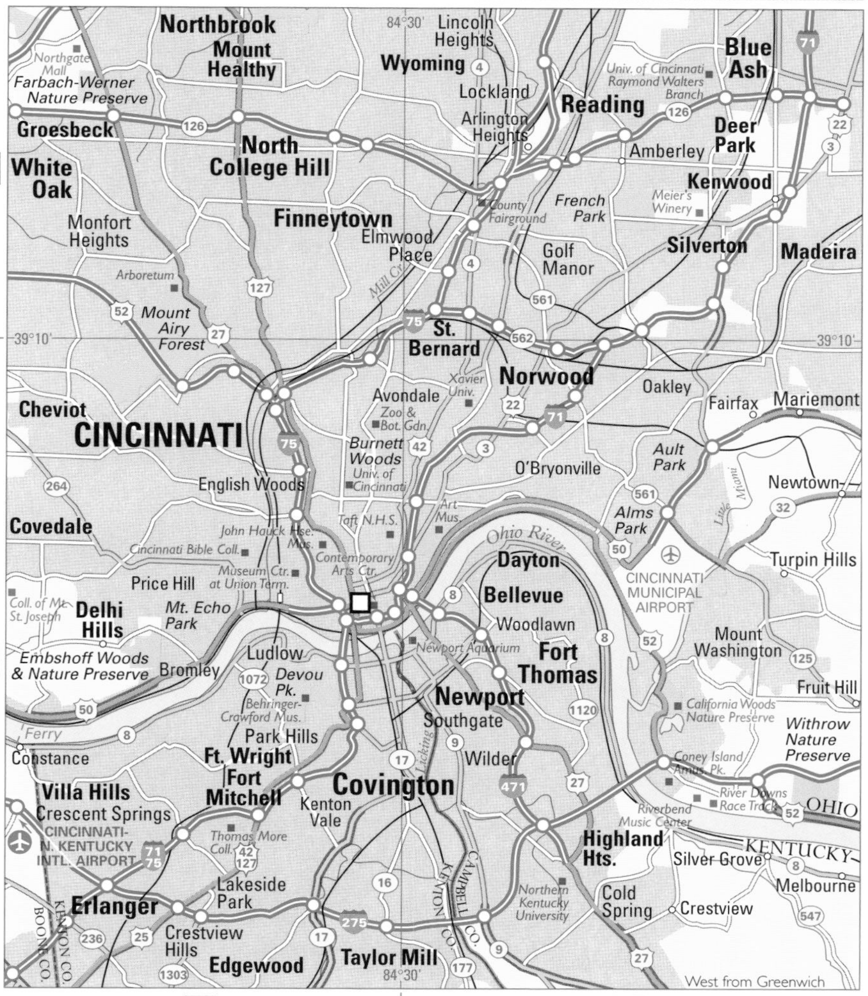

CLEVELAND

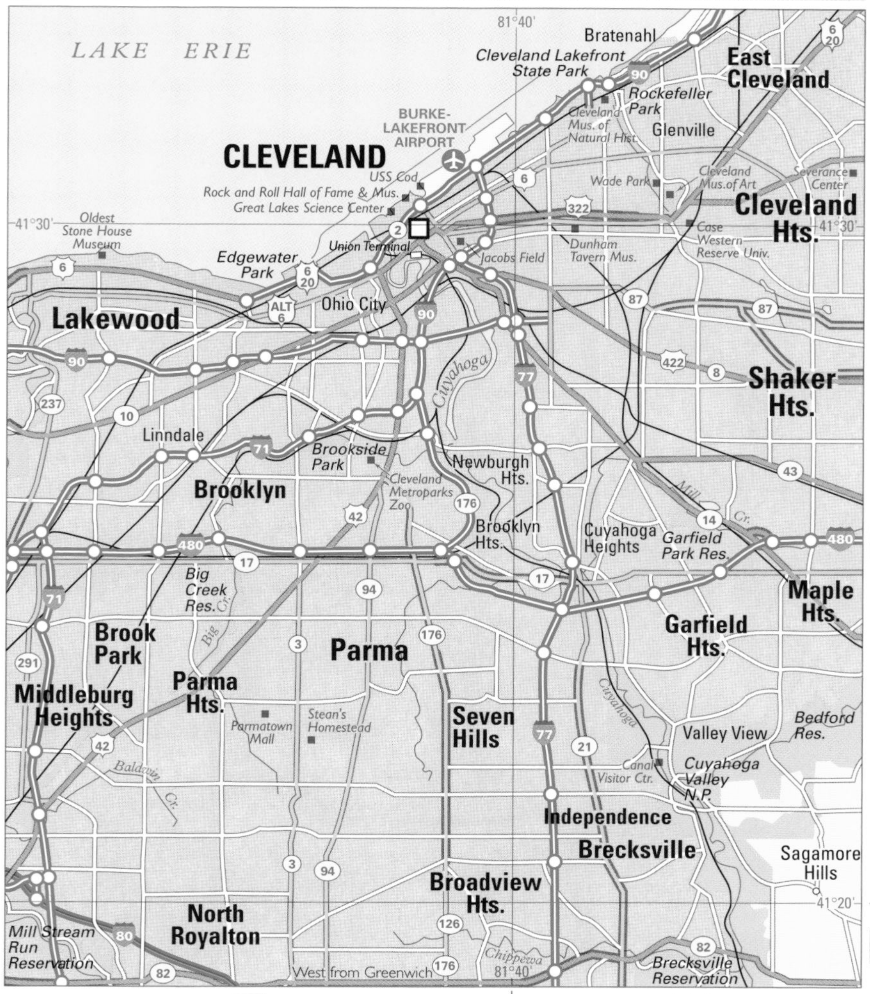

CHICAGO

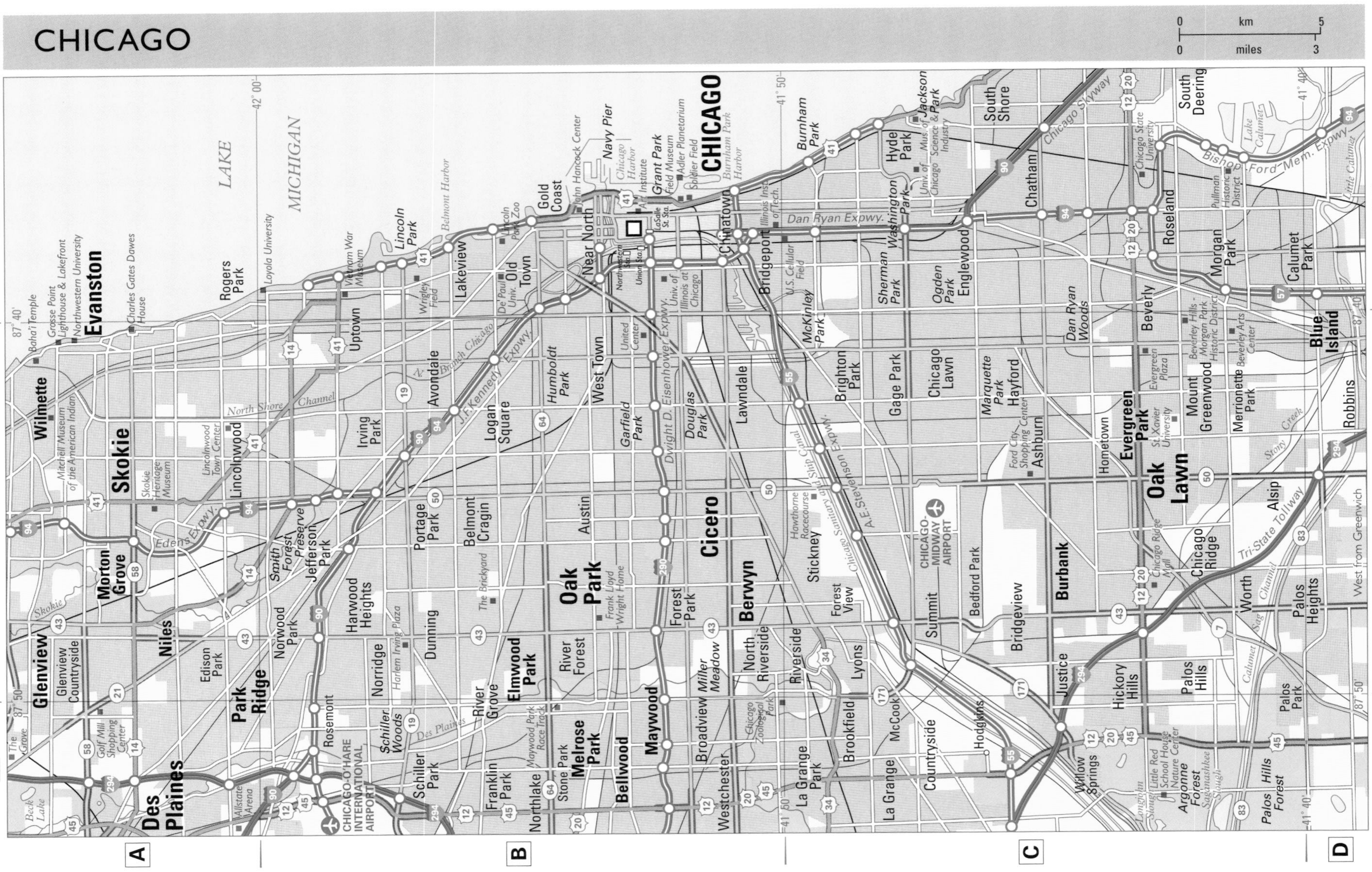

CENTRAL CHICAGO

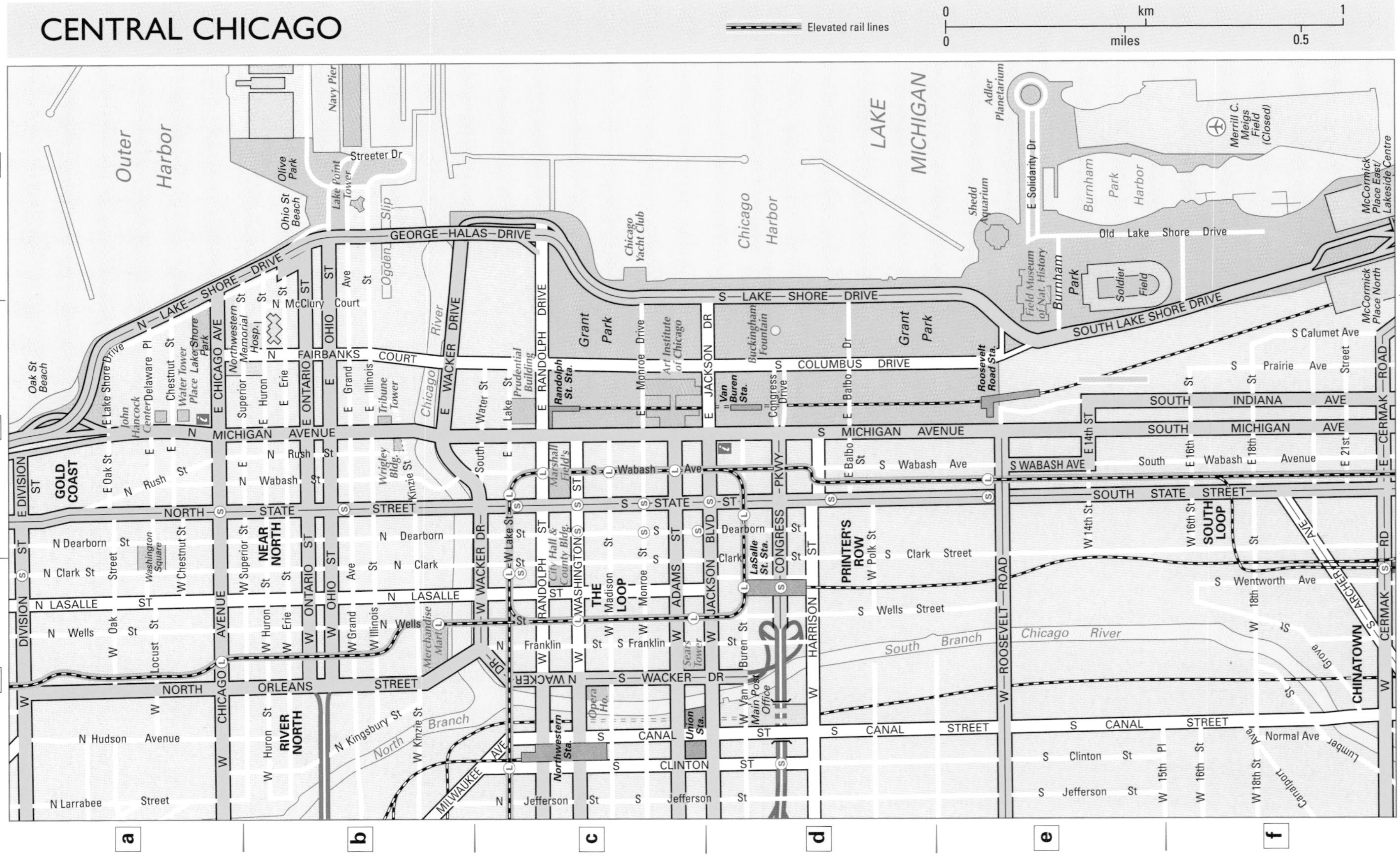

DALLAS – FORT WORTH

0 km 5
0 miles 3

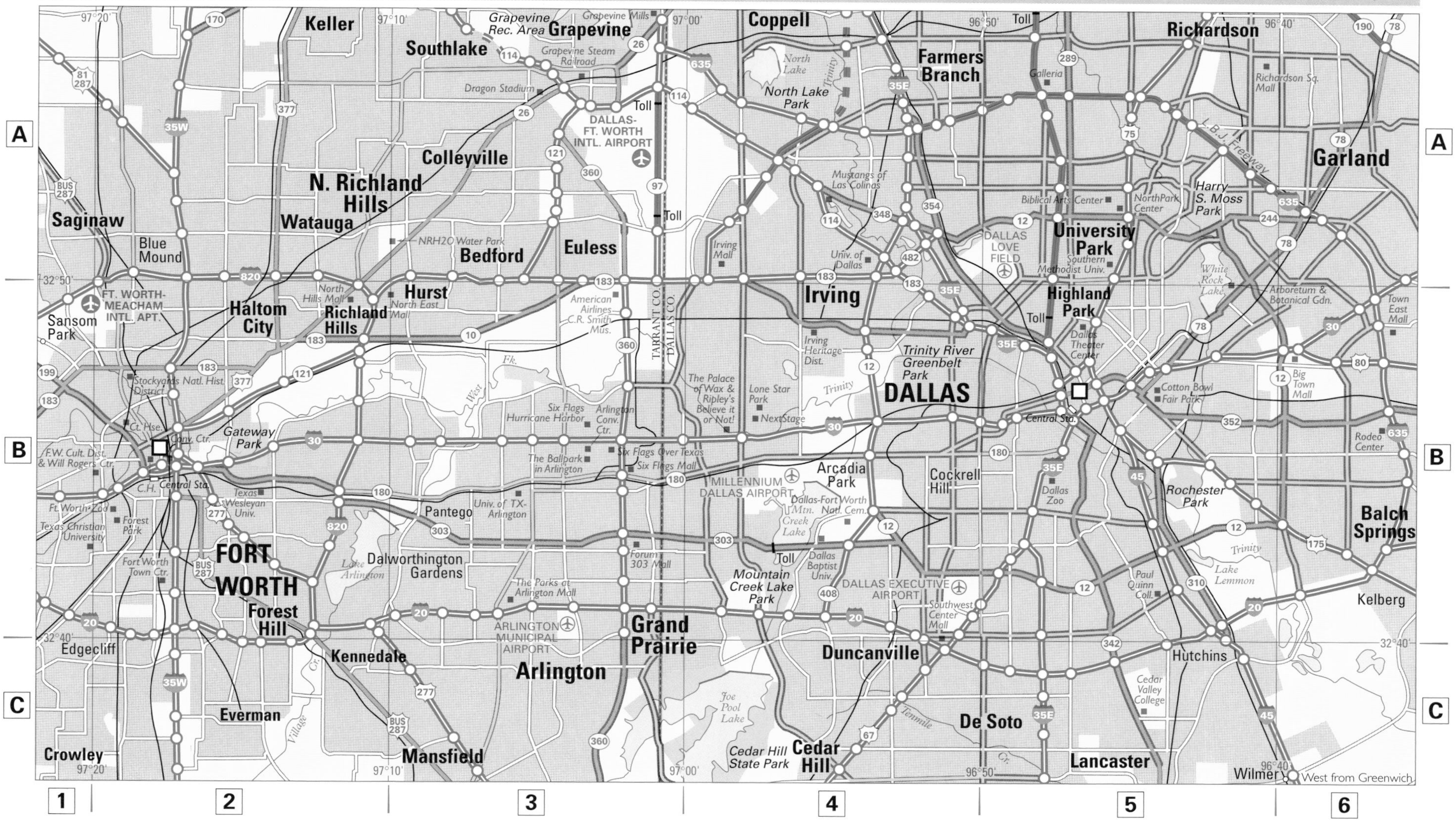

DENVER

0 km 5
0 miles 3

DETROIT

0 km 5
0 miles 3

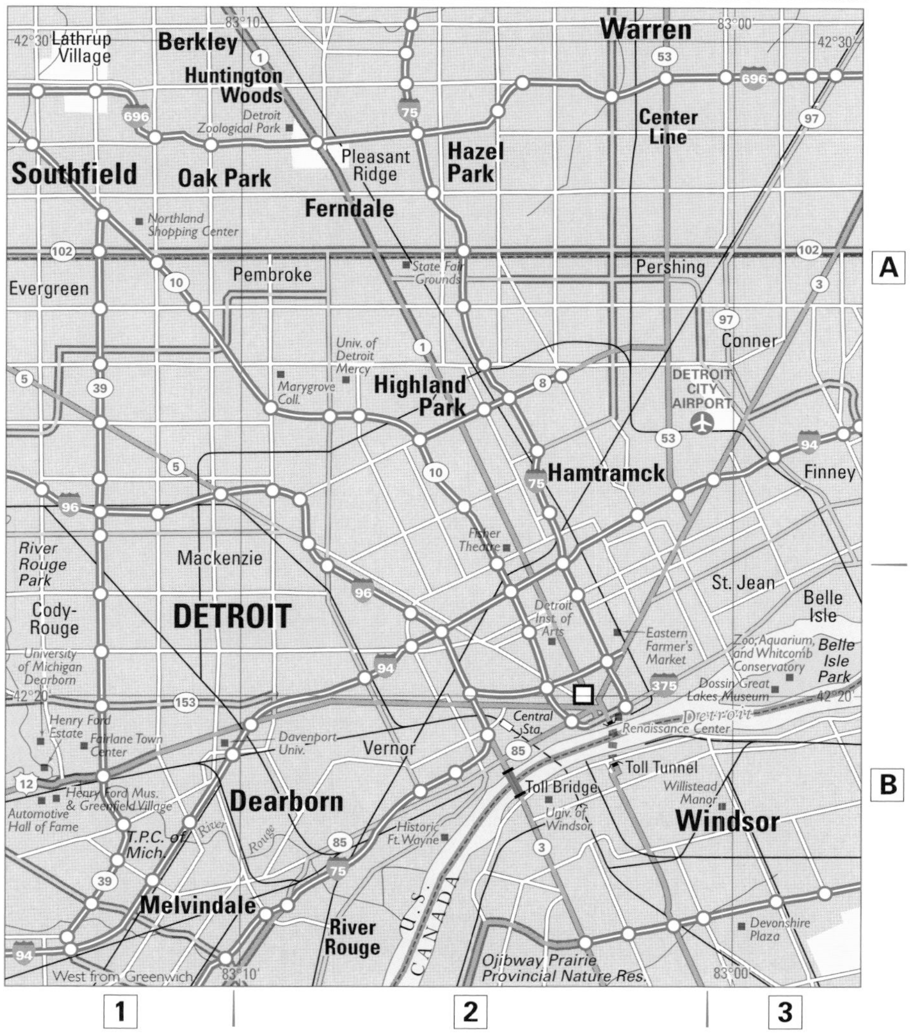

HOUSTON

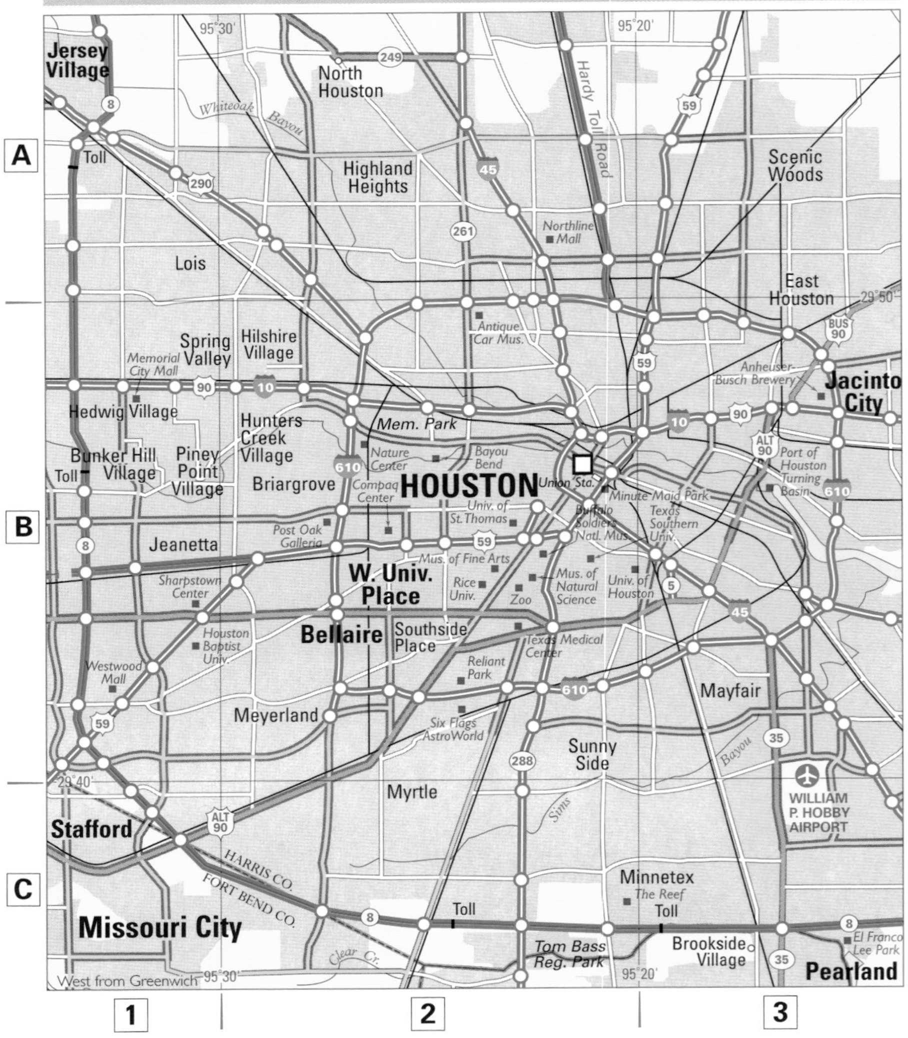

INDIANAPOLIS

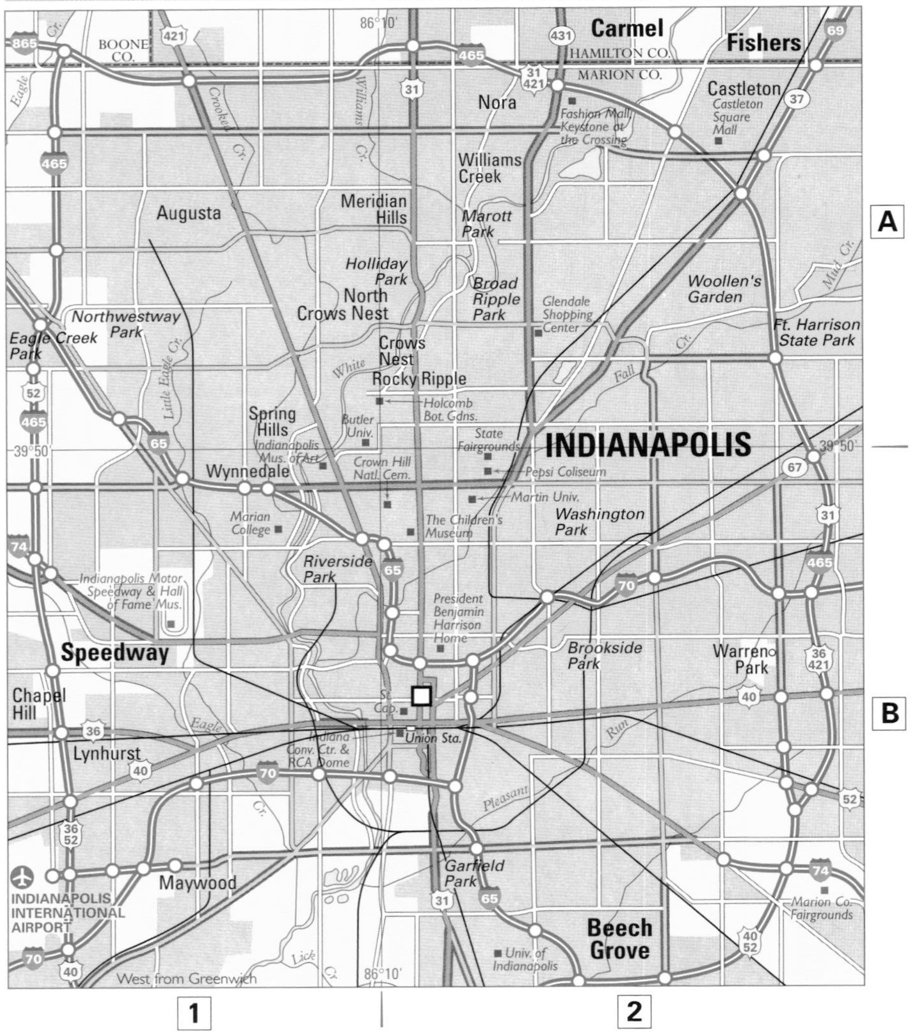

LAS VEGAS

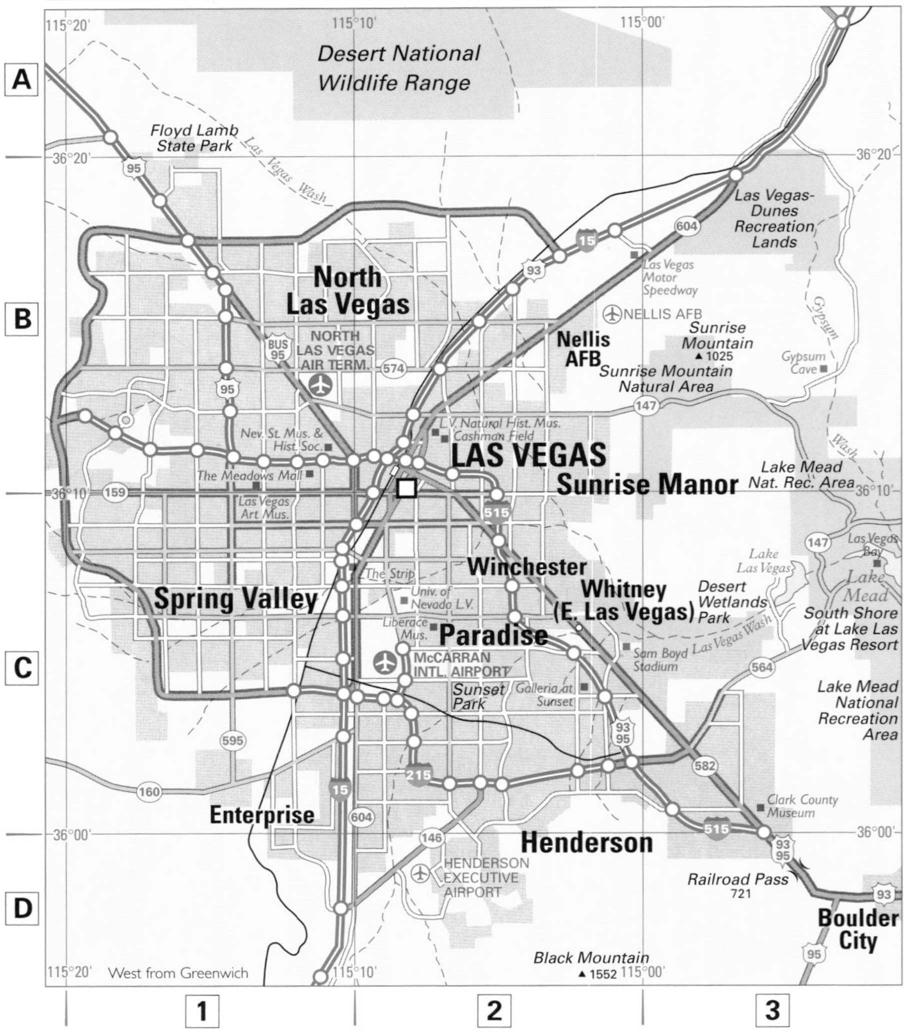

CENTRAL LOS ANGELES

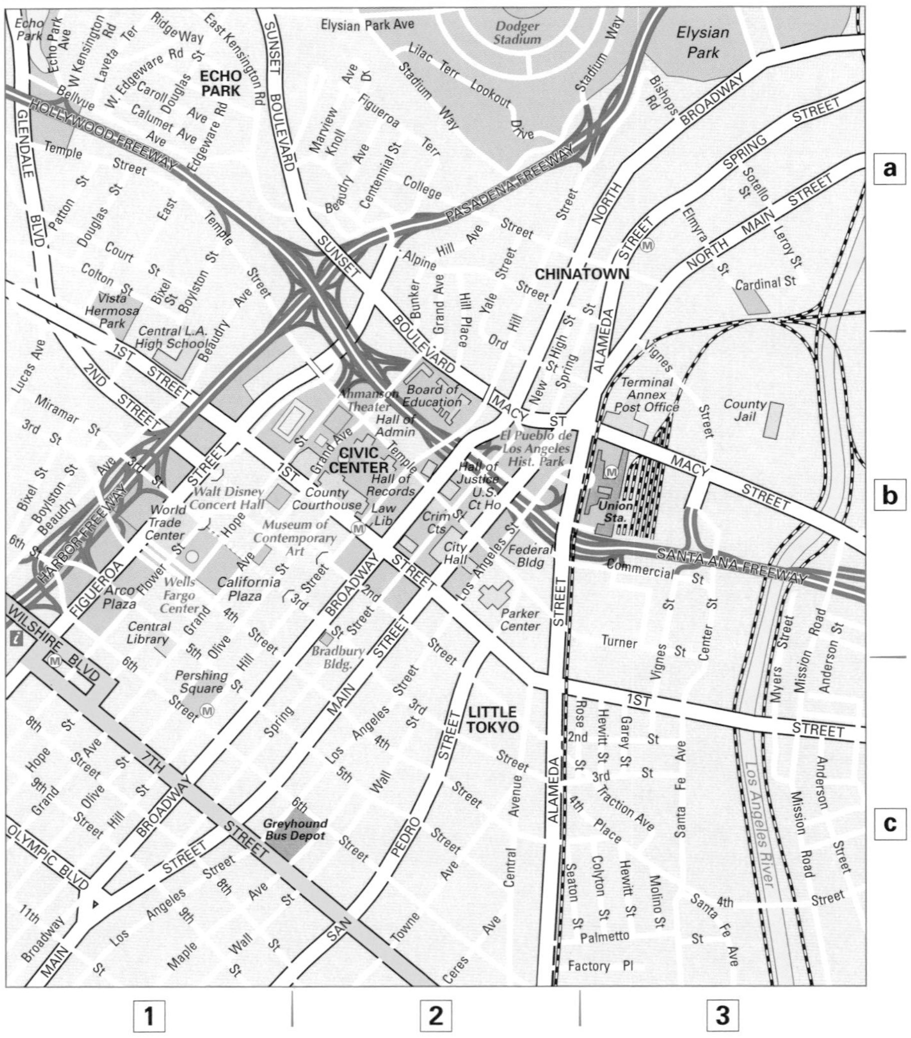

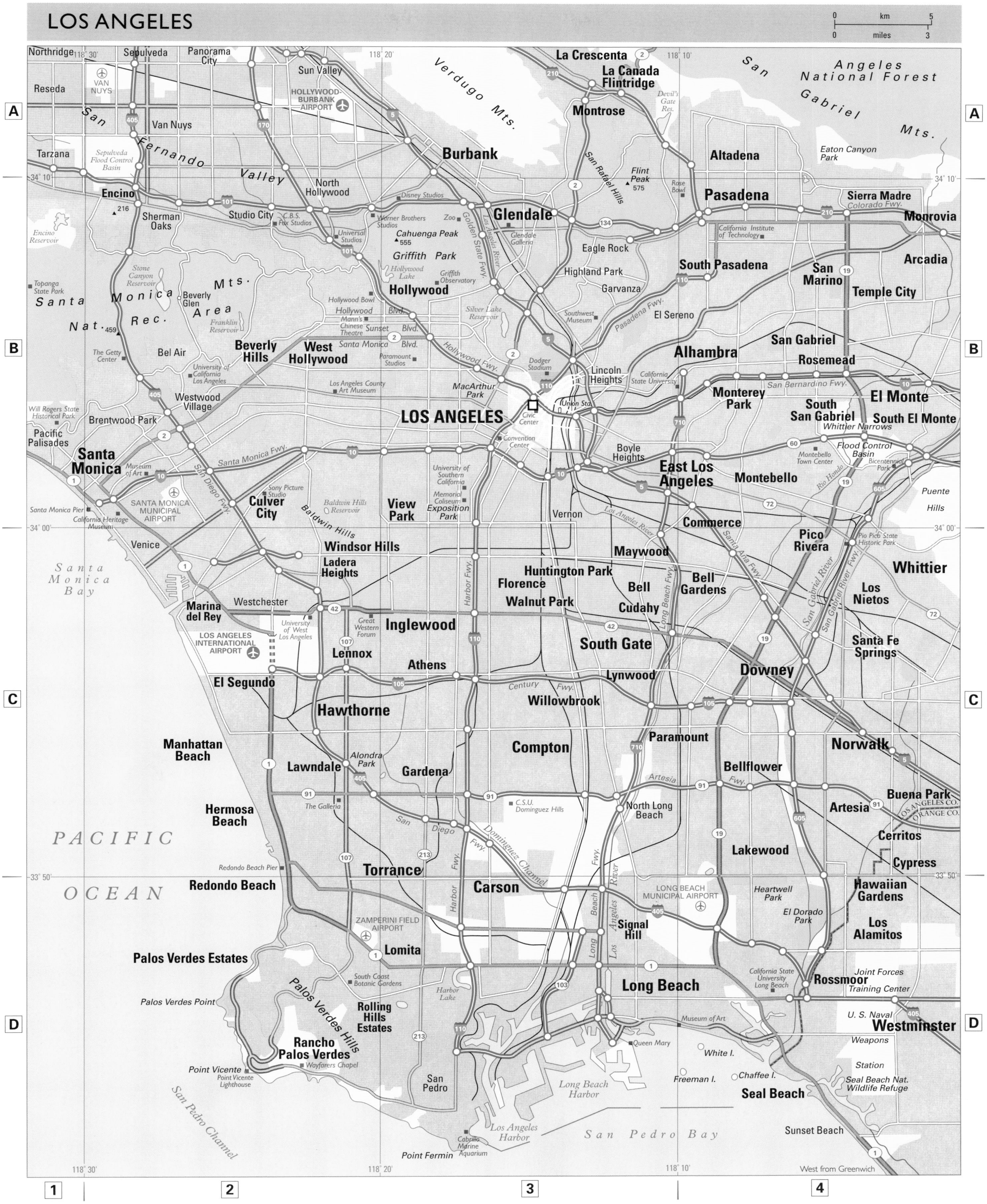
LOS ANGELES
0 km 5
0 miles 3
A
B
C
D
1
2
3
4
118° 30'
118° 20'
118° 10'
34° 10'
34° 00'
33° 50'
Northridge
Sepulveda
Panorama City
Sun Valley
La Crescenta
La Canada Flintridge
Angeles National Forest
San Gabriel Mts.
Verdugo Mts.
Reseda
VAN NUYS
HOLLYWOOD BURBANK AIRPORT
Montrose
Devil's Gate Res.
San Fernando Valley
Van Nuys
Burbank
Altadena
Eaton Canyon Park
Tarzana
Sepulveda Flood Control Basin
San Rafael Hills
Flint Peak 575
North Hollywood
Rose Bowl
Pasadena
Encino
216
Disney Studios
Sierra Madre
Colorado Fwy.
Sherman Oaks
Studio City
C.B.S. Fox Studios
Warner Brothers Studios
Zoo
Glendale
Monrovia
Encino Reservoir
Universal Studios
Cahuenga Peak 555
Glendale Galleria
California Institute of Technology
Eagle Rock
Griffith Park
Golden State Fwy.
Los Angeles River
South Pasadena
Arcadia
Topanga State Park
Stone Canyon Reservoir
Hollywood Lake
Griffith Observatory
Highland Park
San Marino
Santa Monica Mts. Nat. Rec. Area
Beverly Glen
Hollywood
Garvanza
Temple City
Hollywood Bowl
Hollywood Blvd.
Silver Lake Reservoir
Pasadena Fwy.
El Sereno
Franklin Reservoir
Mann's Chinese Theatre
Sunset Blvd.
Southwest Museum
459
The Getty Center
Bel Air
Beverly Hills
West Hollywood
Santa Monica Blvd.
Hollywood Fwy.
San Gabriel
Alhambra
Rosemead
Paramount Studios
Dodger Stadium
Lincoln Heights
University of California Los Angeles
California State University
San Bernardino Fwy.
Los Angeles County Art Museum
MacArthur Park
Monterey Park
El Monte
Will Rogers State Historical Park
Westwood Village
Union Sta.
South San Gabriel
South El Monte
Pacific Palisades
Brentwood Park
LOS ANGELES
Civic Center
Whittier Narrows
Convention Center
Flood Control Basin
Montebello Town Center
Boyle Heights
Santa Monica
Santa Monica Fwy.
Museum of Art
Bicentennial Park
University of Southern California
East Los Angeles
Montebello
Rio Hondo
Puente Hills
Sony Picture Studio
Memorial Coliseum
Exposition Park
San Diego Fwy.
Culver City
Baldwin Hills Reservoir
View Park
Santa Monica Pier
SANTA MONICA MUNICIPAL AIRPORT
California Heritage Museum
Vernon
Los Angeles River
Commerce
Baldwin Hills
Pio Pico State Historic Park
Pico Rivera
Venice
Windsor Hills
Maywood
Santa Ana Fwy.
Whittier
Santa Monica Bay
Ladera Heights
Huntington Park
Florence
Bell
Bell Gardens
Harbor Fwy.
Long Beach Fwy.
San Gabriel River
San Gabriel River Fwy.
Los Nietos
Marina del Rey
Westchester
Walnut Park
Cudahy
University of West Los Angeles
Great Western Forum
Inglewood
LOS ANGELES INTERNATIONAL AIRPORT
South Gate
Santa Fe Springs
Lennox
Athens
Downey
El Segundo
Lynwood
Century Fwy.
Willowbrook
Hawthorne
Manhattan Beach
Paramount
Norwalk
Compton
Alondra Park
Lawndale
Gardena
Bellflower
Artesia Fwy.
Buena Park
The Galleria
C.S.U. Dominguez Hills
North Long Beach
Artesia
LOS ANGELES CO.
ORANGE CO.
Hermosa Beach
San Diego Fwy.
Dominguez Channel
Cerritos
PACIFIC OCEAN
Lakewood
Cypress
Redondo Beach Pier
Torrance
Redondo Beach
Carson
LONG BEACH MUNICIPAL AIRPORT
Heartwell Park
Hawaiian Gardens
El Dorado Park
ZAMPERINI FIELD AIRPORT
Signal Hill
Los Alamitos
Palos Verdes Estates
Lomita
Joint Forces Training Center
Palos Verdes Hills
South Coast Botanic Gardens
Long Beach
California State University Long Beach
Rossmoor
Palos Verdes Point
Harbor Lake
Rolling Hills Estates
Museum of Art
U. S. Naval Weapons Station
Westminster
Rancho Palos Verdes
Queen Mary
White I.
Point Vicente
Point Vicente Lighthouse
Wayfarers Chapel
Freeman I.
Chaffee I.
Seal Beach Nat. Wildlife Refuge
San Pedro
Long Beach Harbor
Seal Beach
San Pedro Channel
Los Angeles Harbor
San Pedro Bay
Sunset Beach
Cabrillo Marine Aquarium
Point Fermin
West from Greenwich

MEMPHIS

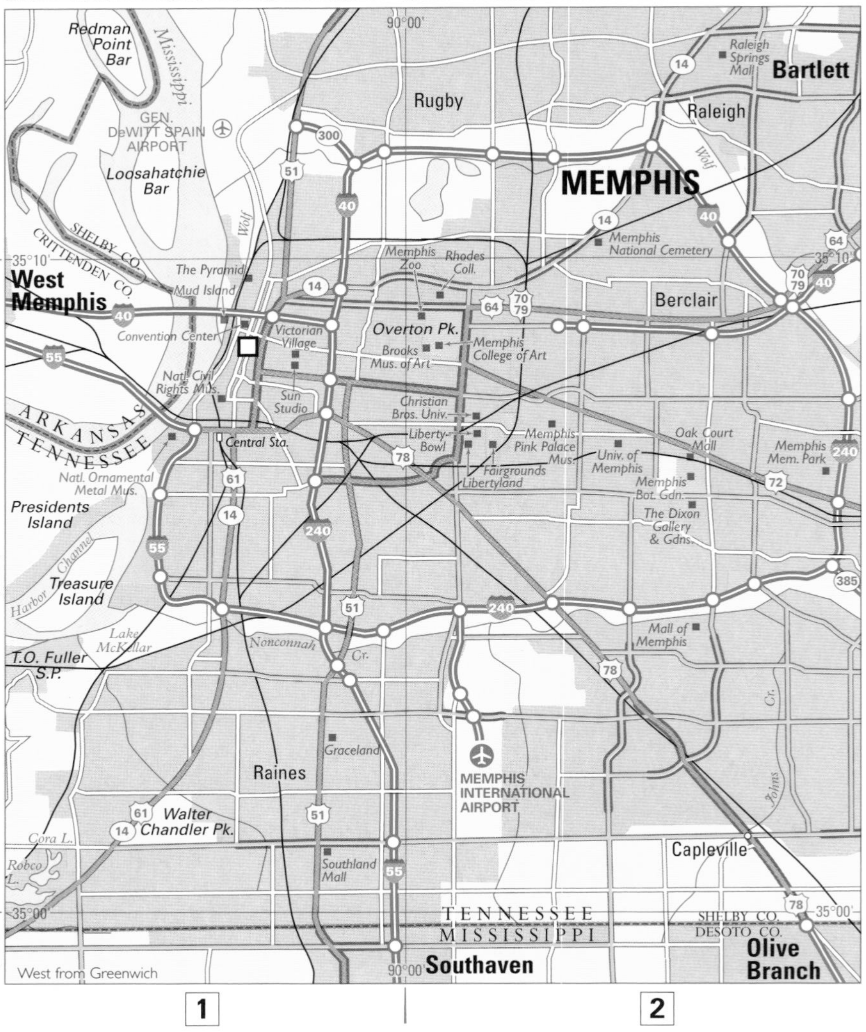

MILWAUKEE

MIAMI – FORT LAUDERDALE

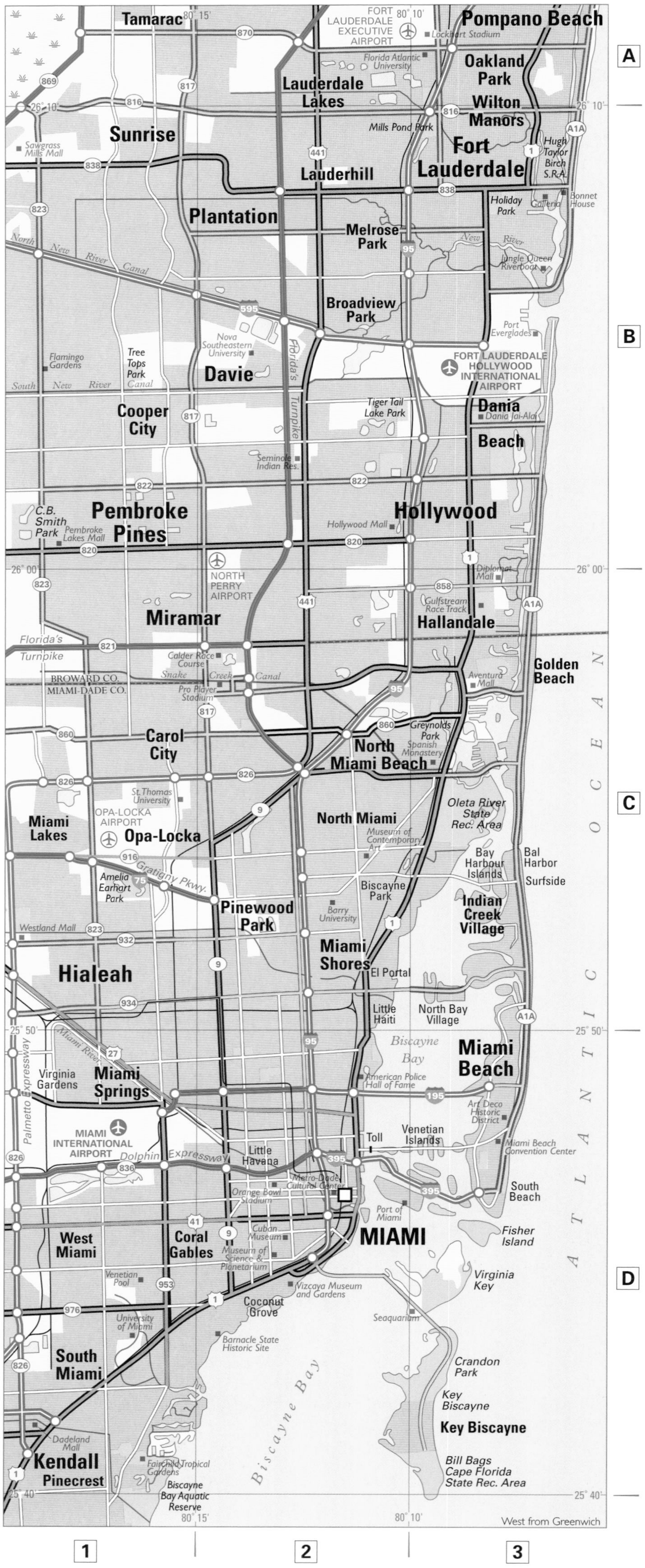

MINNEAPOLIS – ST. PAUL

0 km 5
0 miles 3

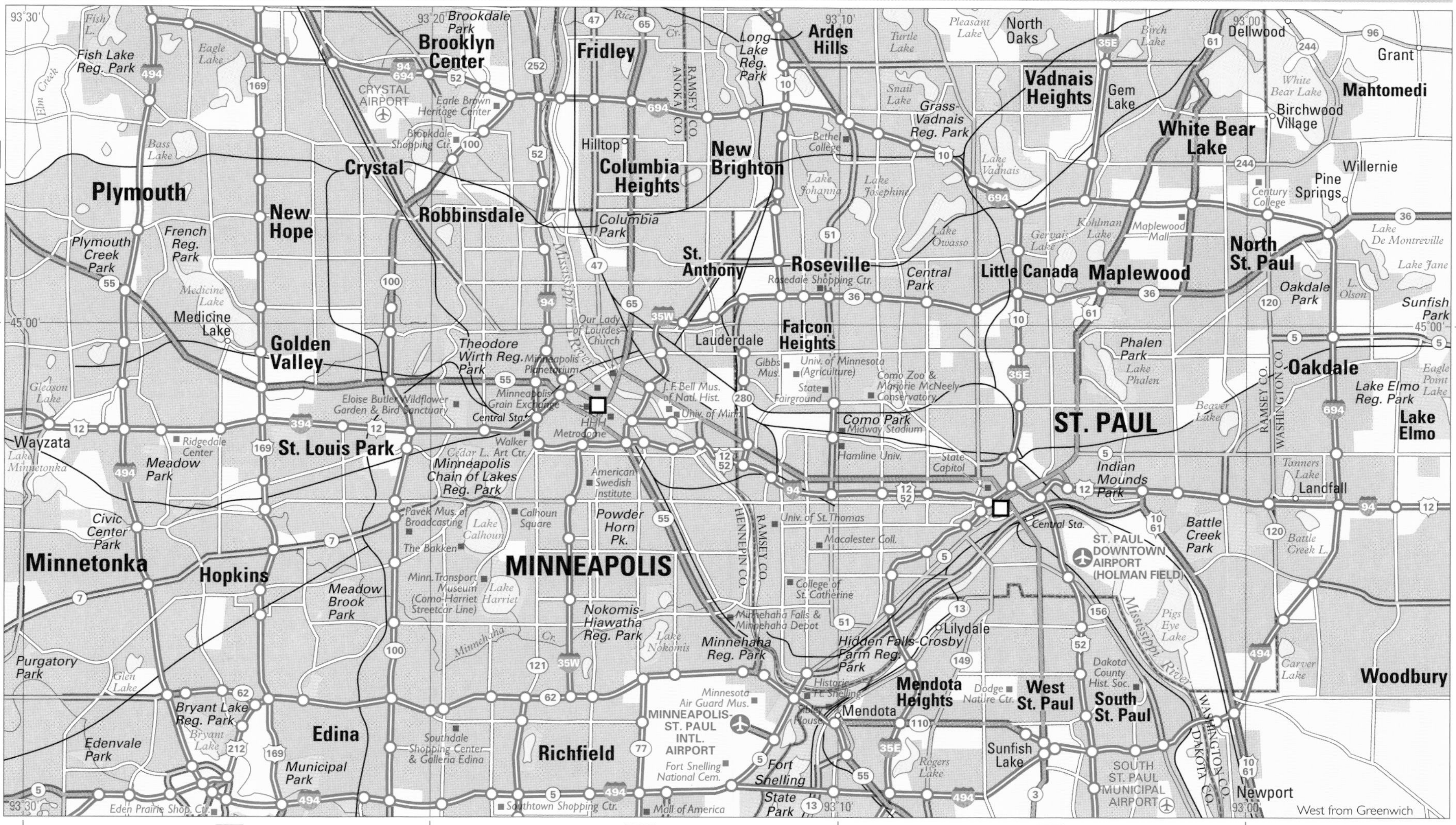

NEW ORLEANS

0 km 10
0 miles 6

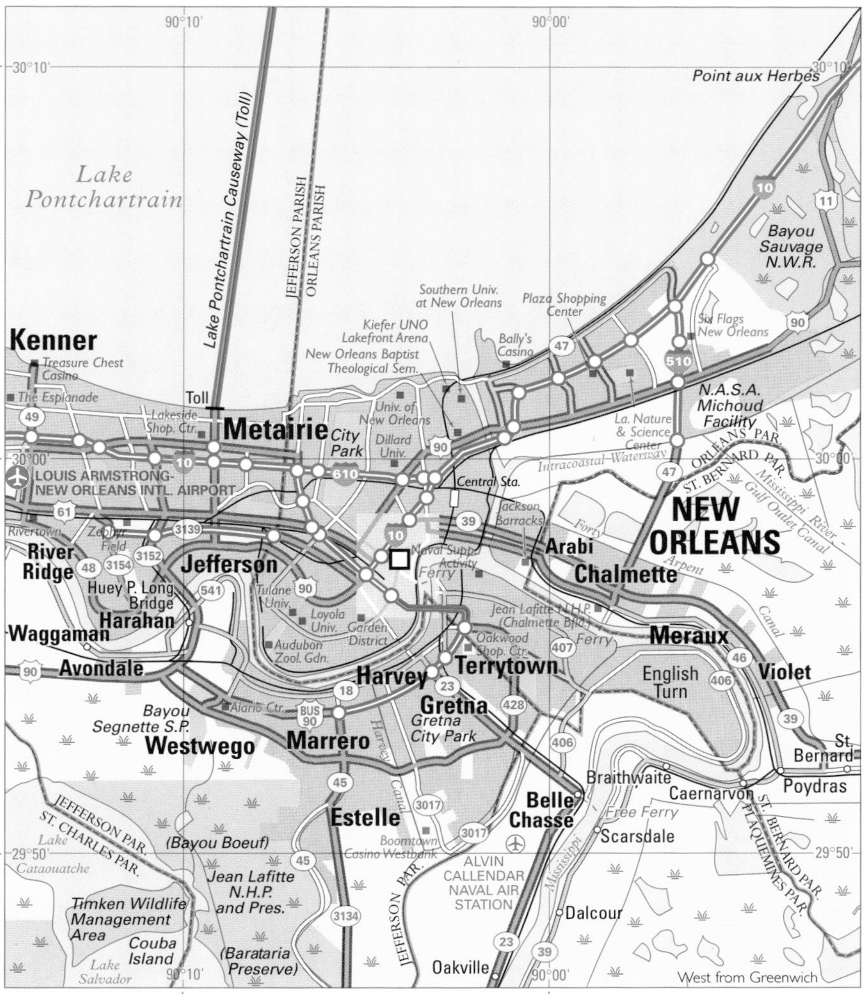

CENTRAL NEW ORLEANS

0 km 0.5
0 miles 0.25

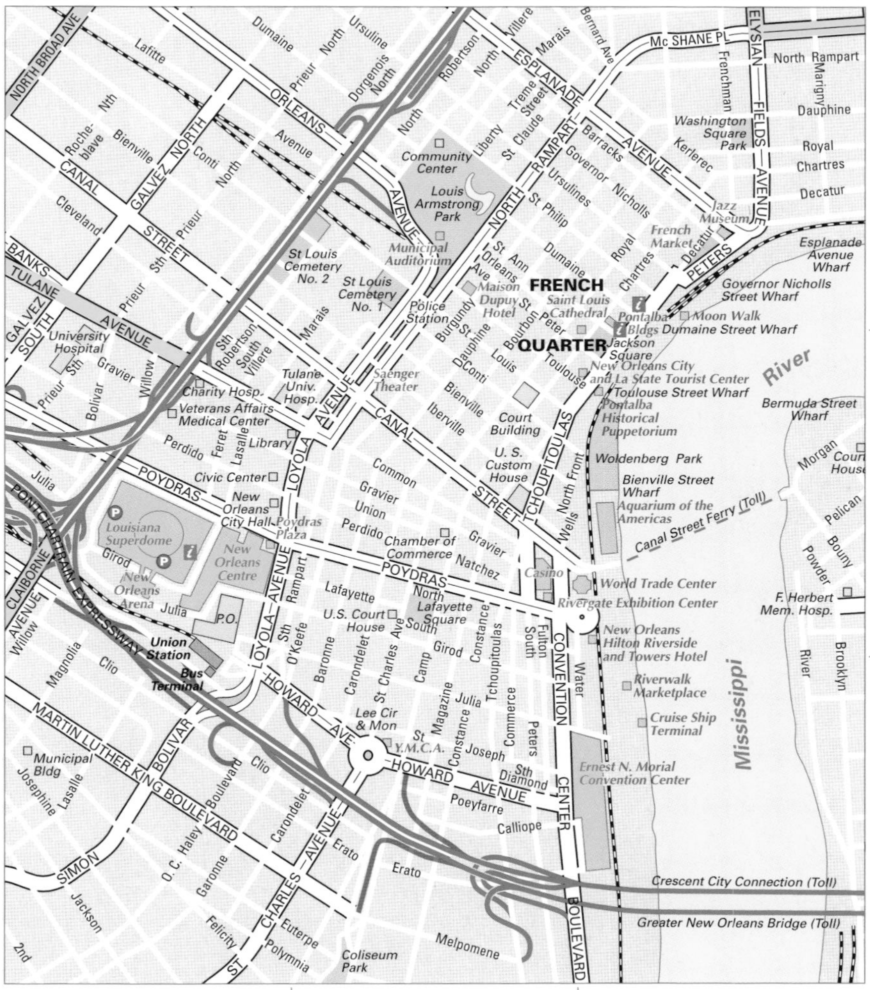

NEW YORK

0 km 5
0 miles 3
West from Greenwich
LONG ISLAND SOUND
ATLANTIC OCEAN
NEW YORK
Manhattan
Brooklyn
Queens
Bronx
Staten Island
Yonkers
New Rochelle
Mount Vernon
Jersey City
Newark
Elizabeth
Bayonne
Hoboken
Union City
Paterson
Passaic
Hackensack
Hempstead
Long Beach
Glen Cove
Port Washington
JFK INTERNATIONAL AIRPORT
LA GUARDIA AIRPORT
NEWARK LIBERTY INTL. AIRPORT
TETERBORO AIRPORT
Hudson River
East River
Upper New York Bay
Lower New York Bay
Jamaica Bay
Central Park
Flushing Meadows-Corona Park
Gateway National Recreation Area
Jacob Riis Park
Garden State Pkwy.
New Jersey Tpk.
Long Island Expwy.
Cross Island Pkwy.
Verrazano Narrows Bridge
George Washington Bridge
A B C
1 2 3 4 5

CENTRAL NEW YORK

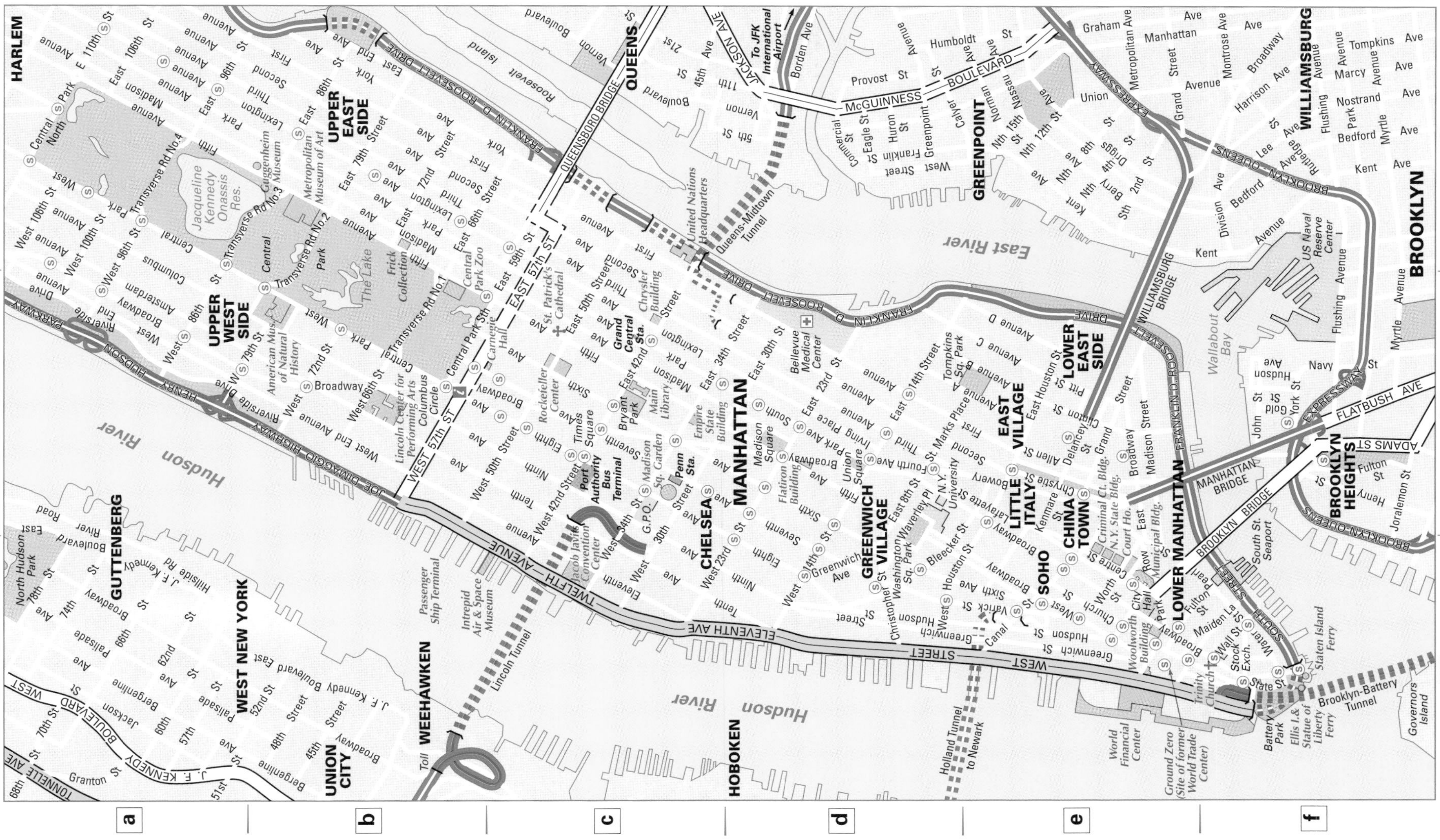

NORFOLK

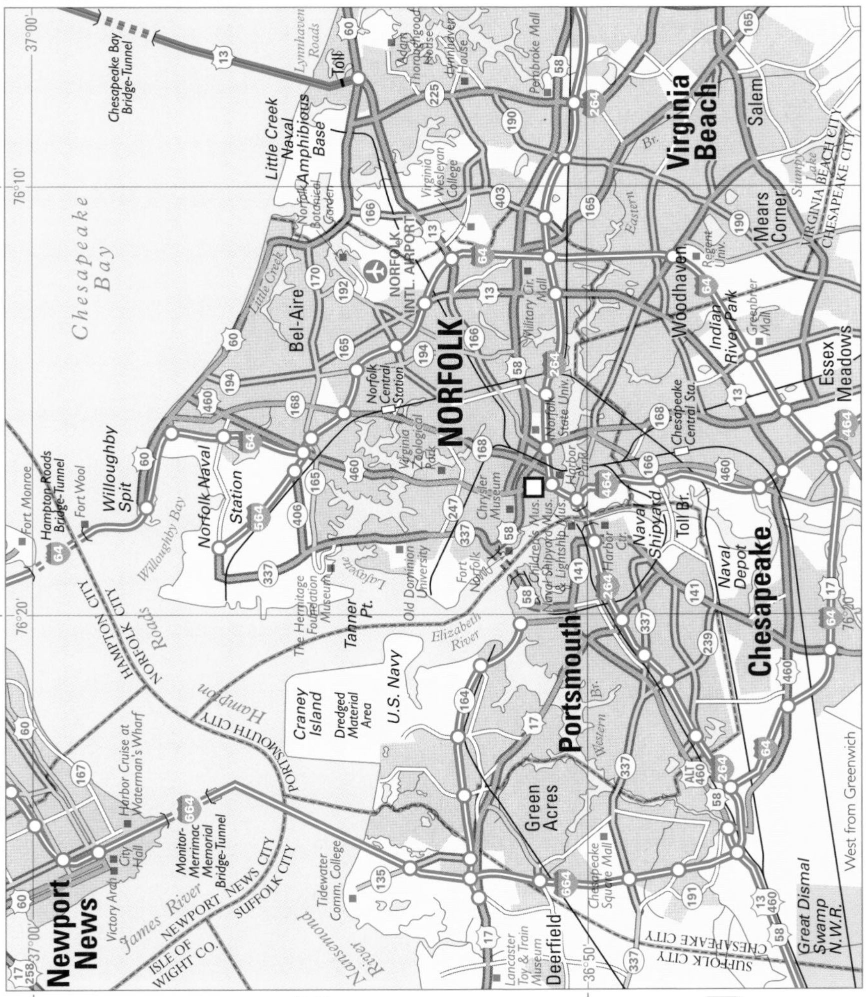

ORLANDO

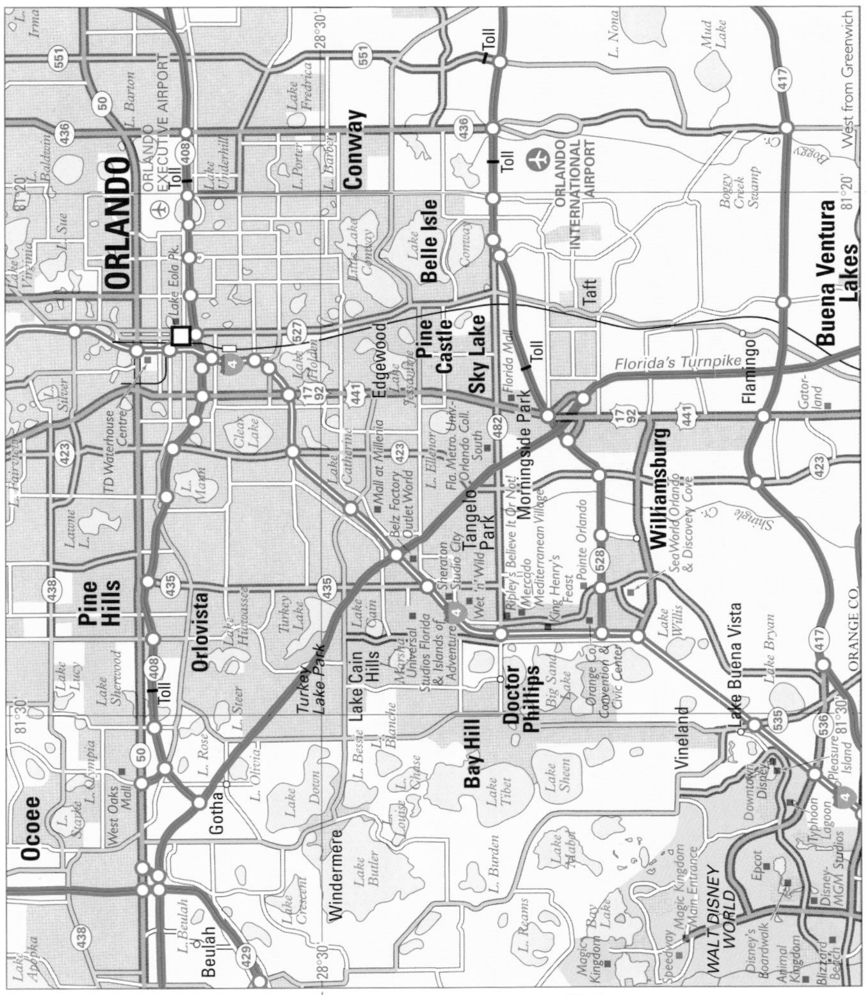

PHILADELPHIA

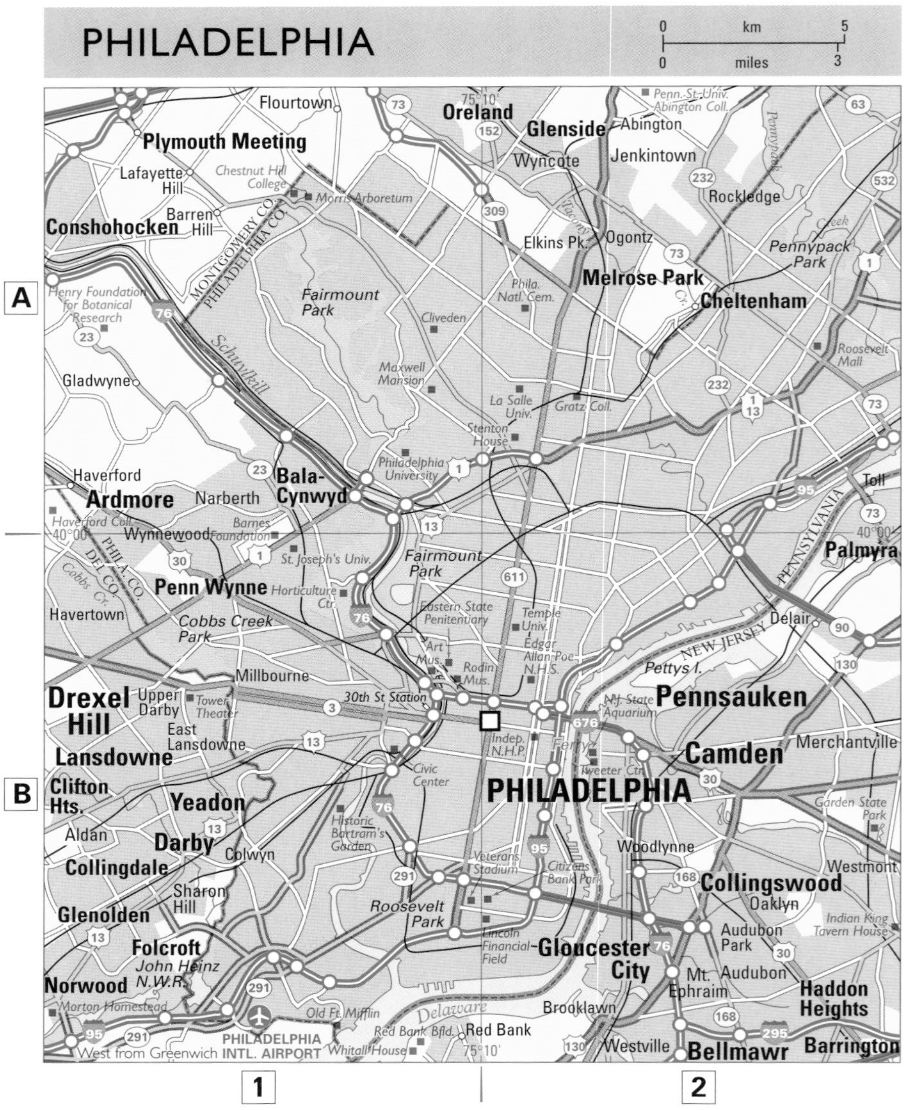

PHOENIX

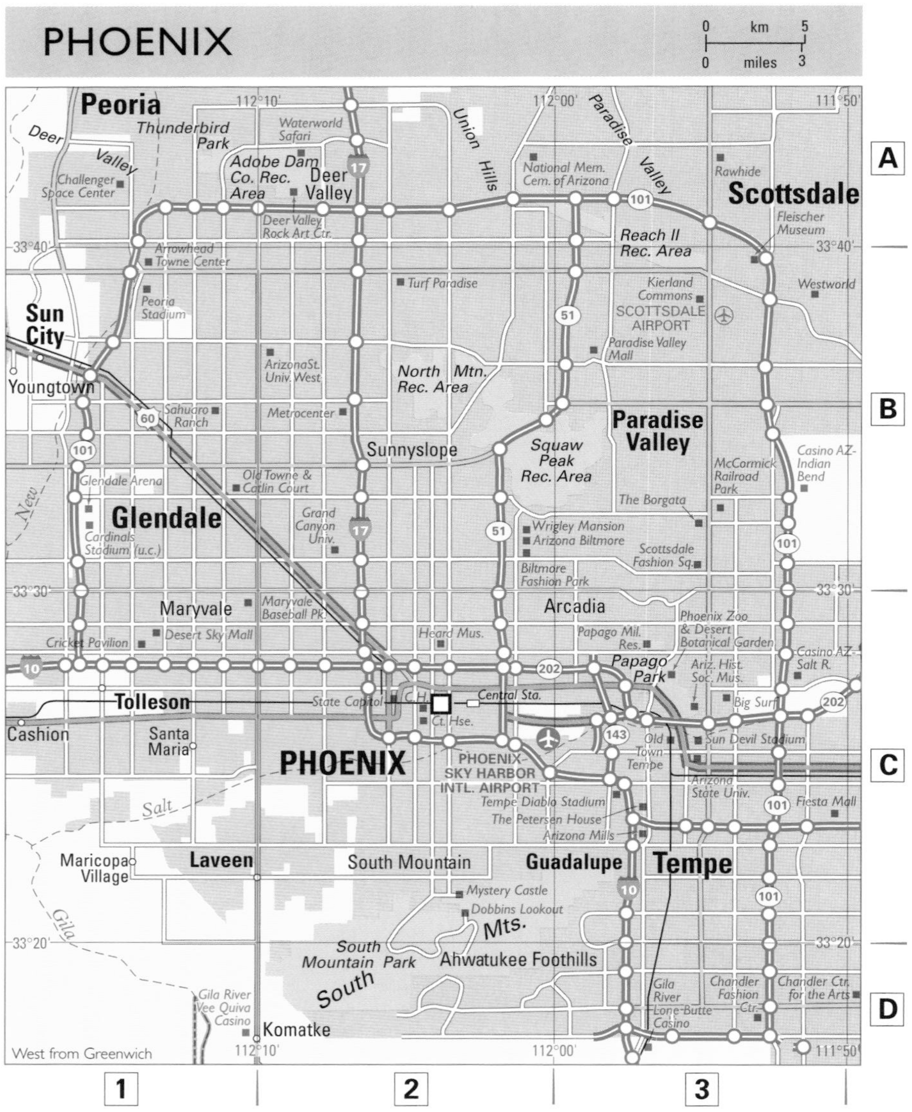

PITTSBURGH

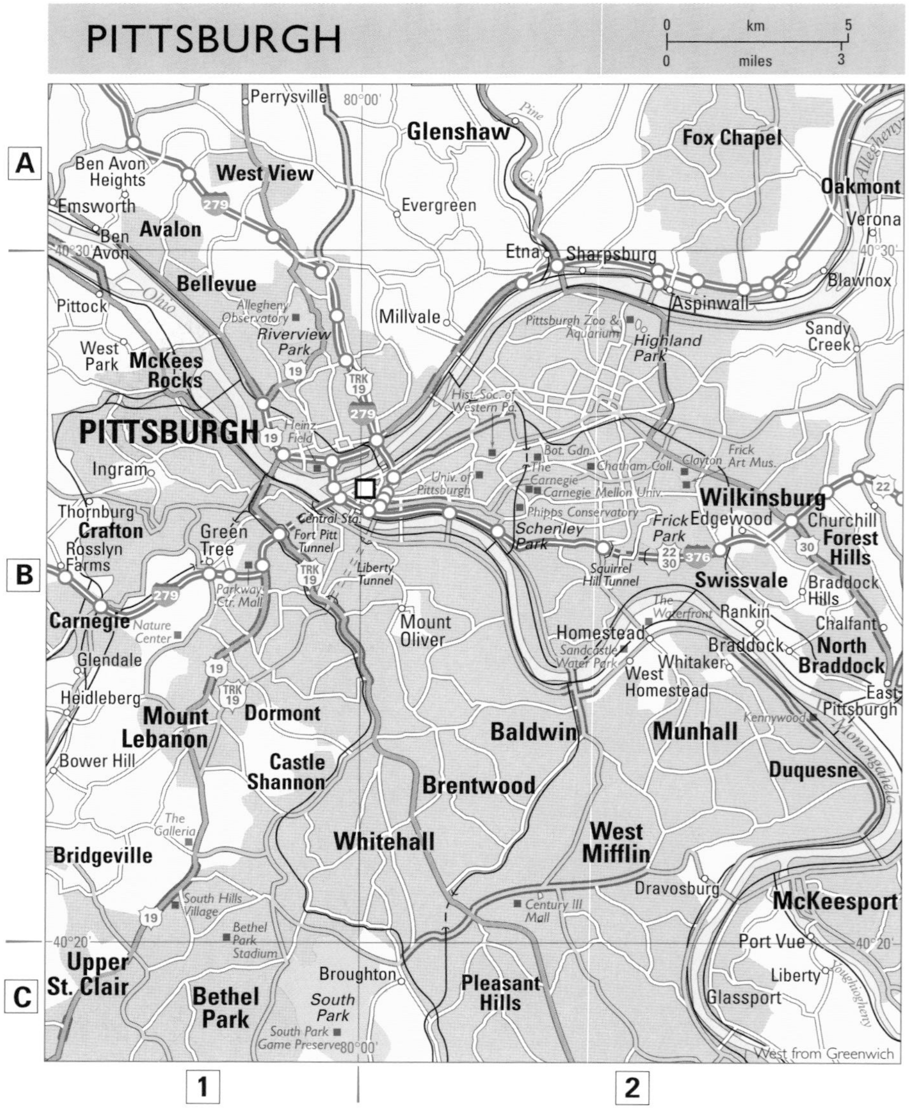

PORTLAND

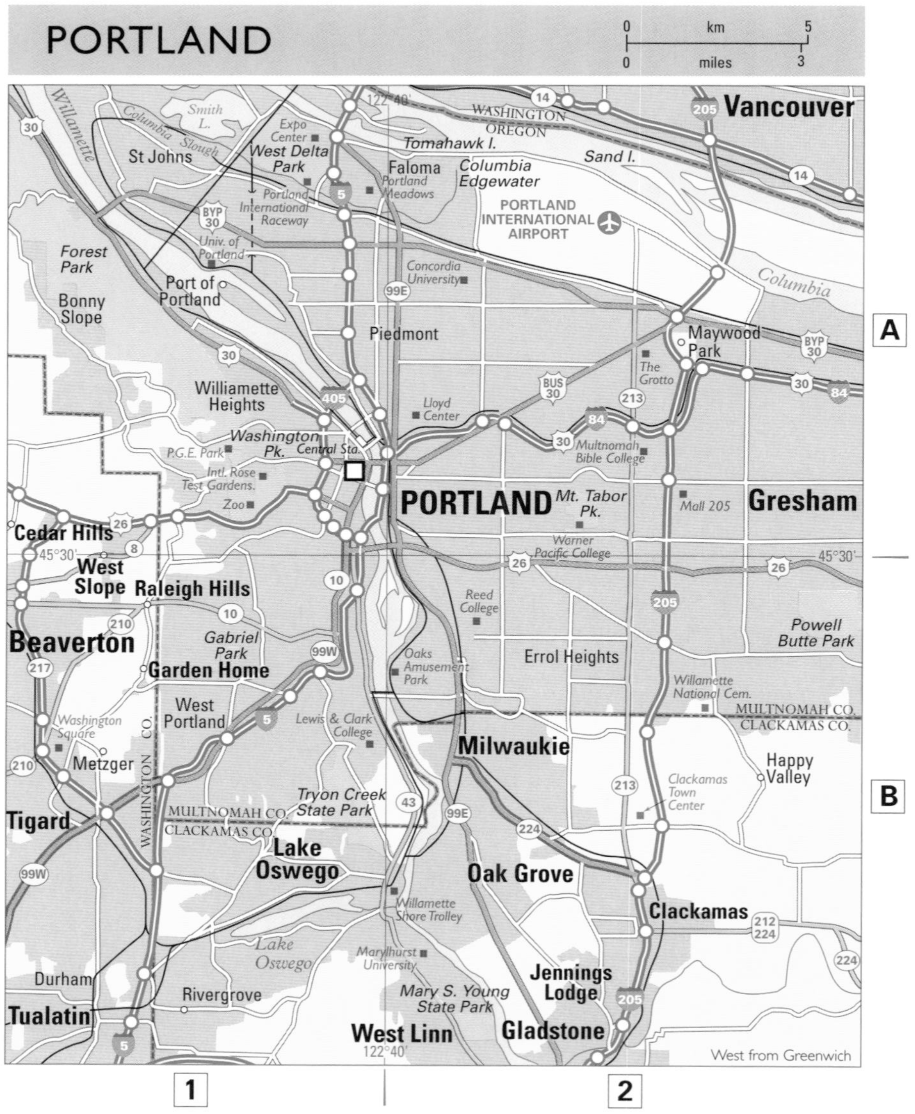

ST. LOUIS

0 km 5
0 miles 3

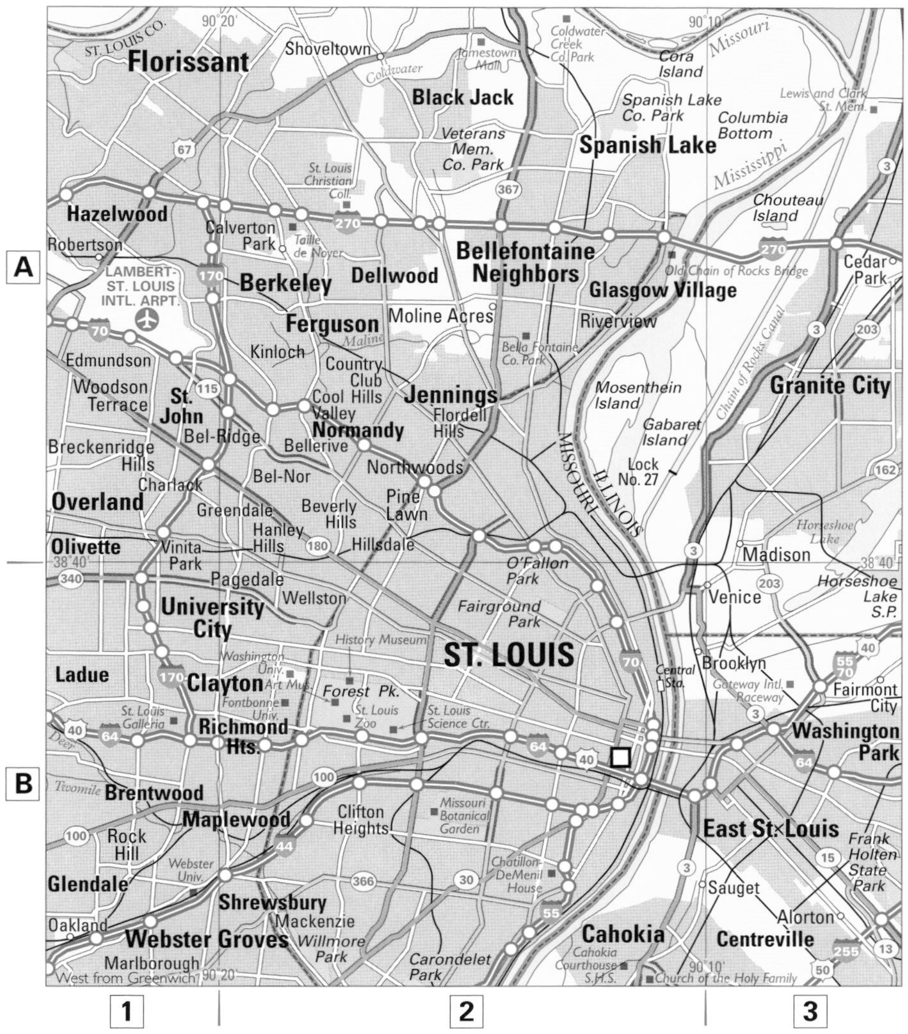

SALT LAKE CITY

0 km 5
0 miles 3

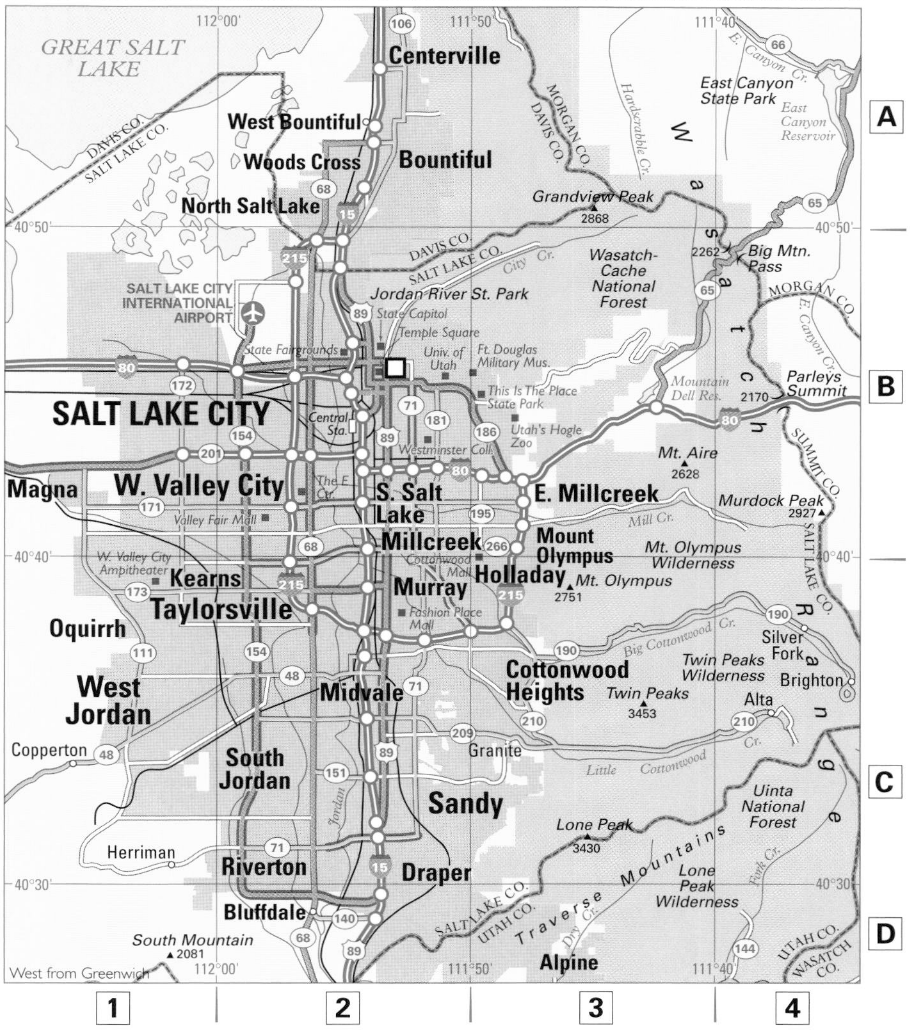

SAN ANTONIO

0 km 5
0 miles 3

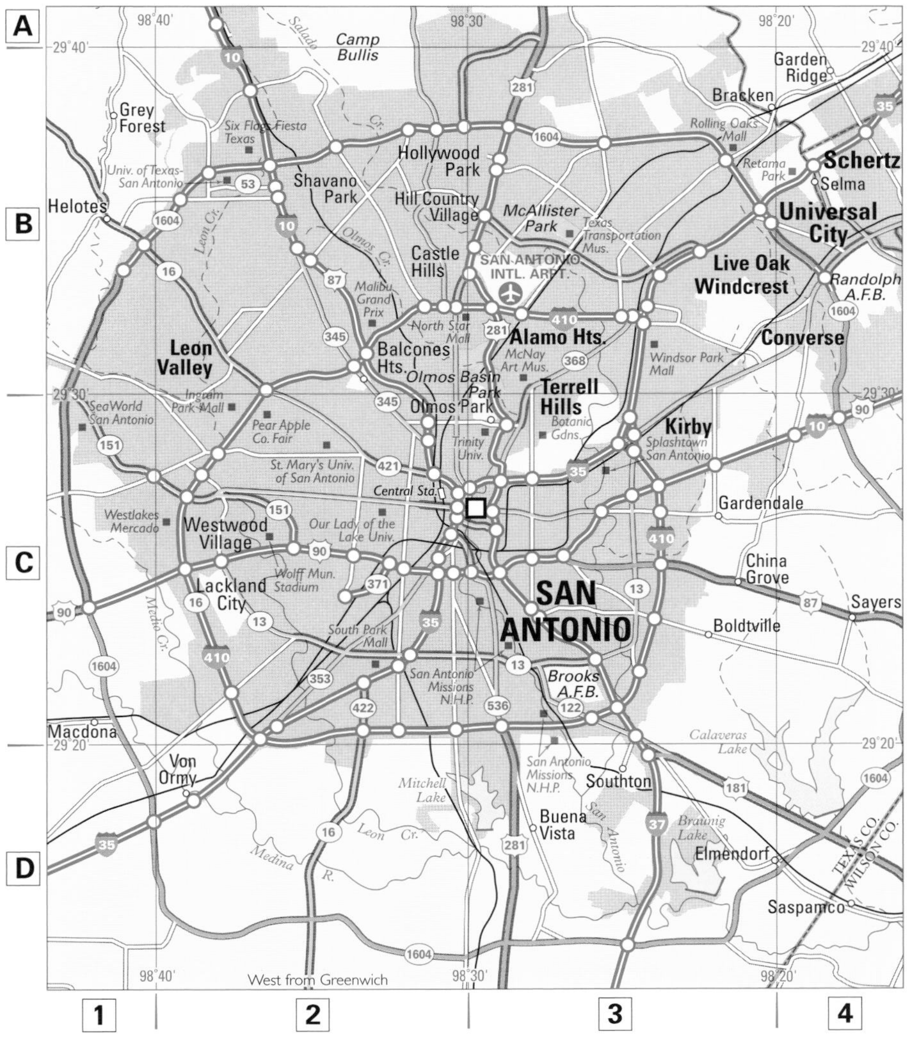

SAN DIEGO

0 km 5
0 miles 3

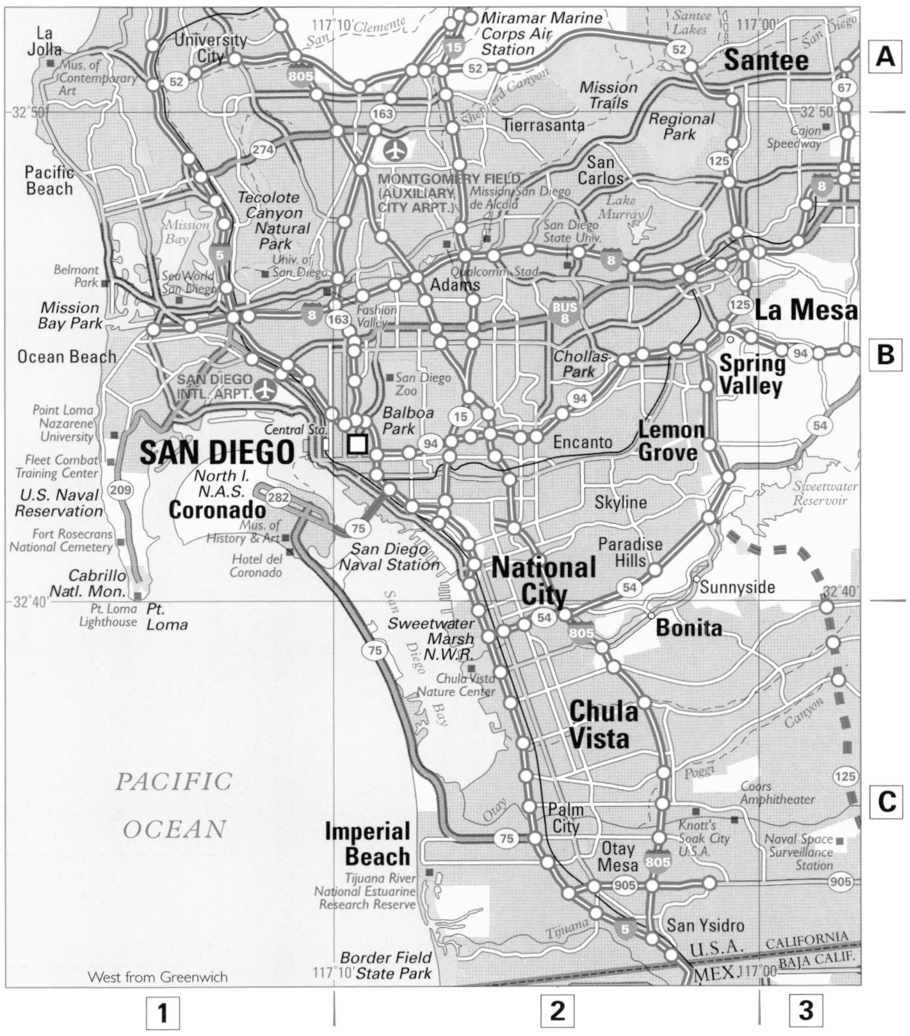

SAN FRANCISCO

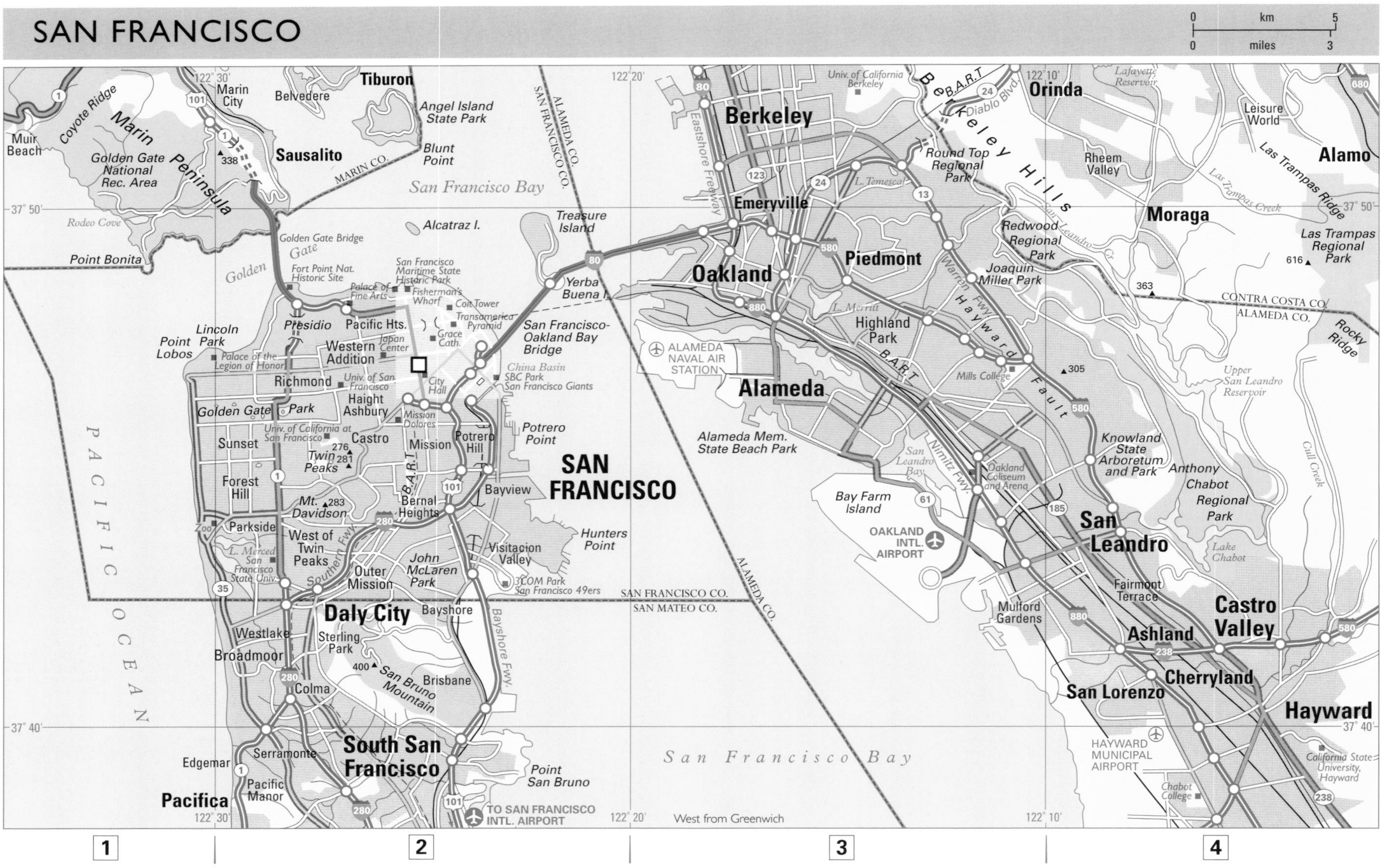

CENTRAL SAN FRANCISCO

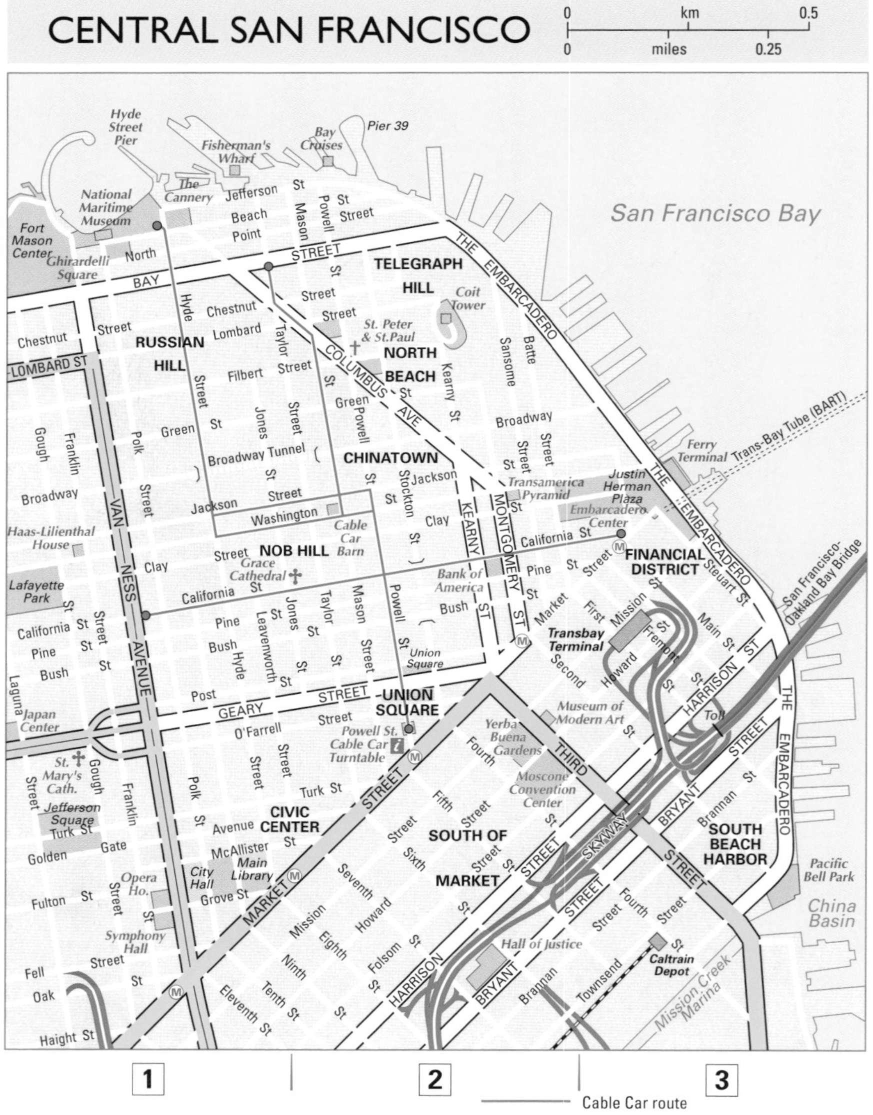

SEATTLE

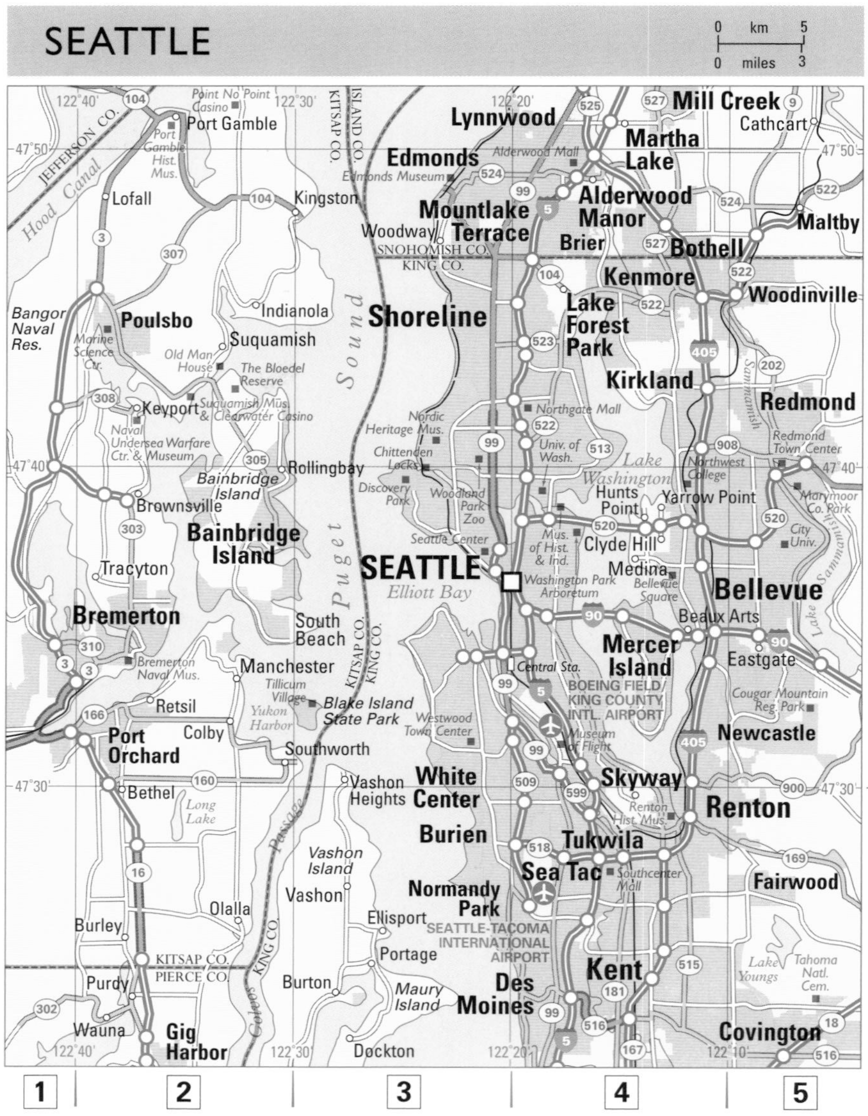

TAMPA & ST. PETERSBURG

CENTRAL WASHINGTON

WASHINGTON

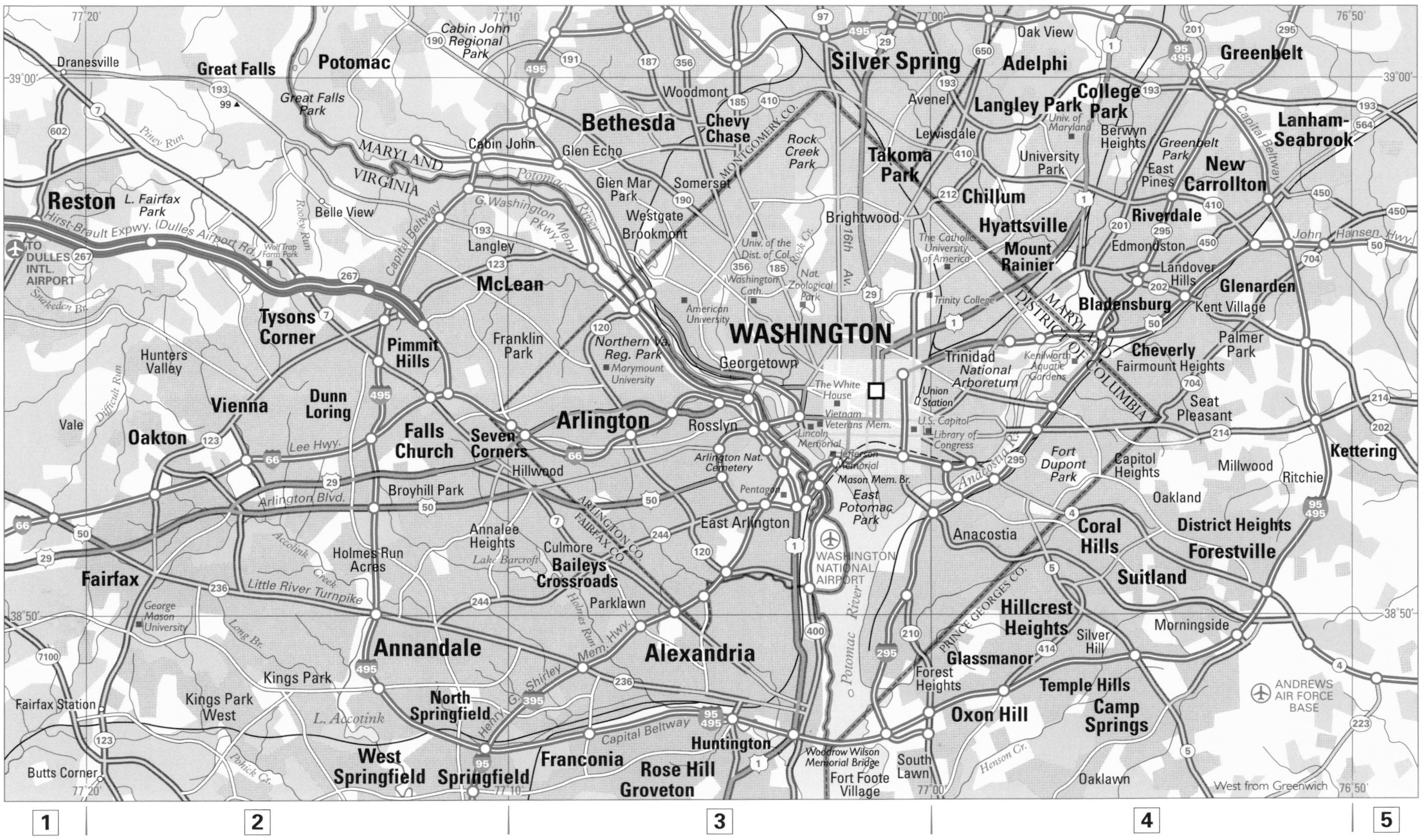

Alabama

Statehood: December 14, 1819
Nickname: The Heart of Dixie
State bird: Yellowhammer
State flower: Camellia
State tree: Southern pine
State motto: We dare defend our rights
State capital: Montgomery
Population of capital: 201,568 (2000)

Settled by the French in 1702, this Southeastern state in the chief cotton-growing region of the United States was acquired by Britain in 1763. Originally, Creek and Choctaw territory, most of Alabama was ceded to the fledgling country after the American Revolution (1776–83), and it was admitted into the Union as the 22nd state in 1819. Following secession in 1861 as one of the original six states of the Confederacy, Alabama was readmitted to the Union in 1868. Birmingham is the largest metropolis and a major center for manufacturing as well as telecommunications. In the 1960s, the civil rights movement took shape in Birmingham and Montgomery. Huntsville and Mobile are the other main cities in this state of 67 counties.

The Northern part of the state lies in the heavily wooded Appalachian Highlands, which have coal, iron ore, and other mineral deposits, while much of the rest of Alabama's geography consists of swampland on the Gulf coastal plain, crossed by a wide strip of rich, fertile soil. The Mobile River, its tributaries, and the canalized Tombigbee River form the chief river system. The principal crops are peanuts, soybeans, and corn, with cotton decreasingly important. Industries include chemicals, textiles, electronics, metal, and paper products.

A crimson St. Andrew's cross on a white background, the state flag of Alabama is patterned after the Confederate flag and was adopted in 1895.

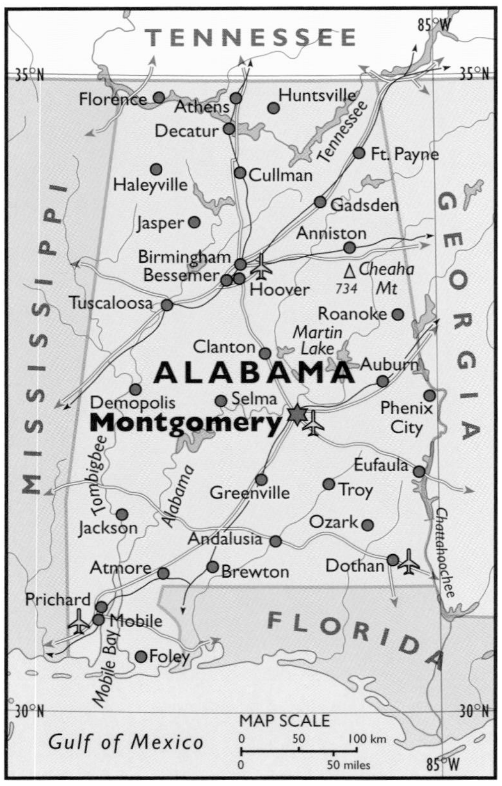

Montgomery

Made state capital in 1847, Montgomery later became the first capital of the Confederate States of America. Jefferson Davis was inaugurated president and occupied the first white house of the Confederacy here near the confluence of the Coosa and Tallapoosa rivers. It subsequently grew in importance and in the 1950s, was the scene of the beginnings of the civil-rights movement. It was in this city in the southeastern part of the state that Rosa Parks refused to give up her seat on a segregated city bus, sparking a bus boycott led by the Rev. Martin Luther King, Jr. Textiles, fertilizers, furniture, air conditioning and heating unit manufacturing comprise the local industry.

Alabama at a Glance

People	**Alabama**	**USA**
Population, 2003 estimate	4,500,752	290,809,777
Population percent change, April 1, 2000–July 1, 2001	1.2	1.2
Population, 2000	4,447,100	281,421,906
Persons under 5 years old, percent, 2000	6.7%	6.8%
Persons under 18 years old, percent, 2000	25.3%	25.7%
Persons 65 years old and over, percent, 2000	13.0%	12.4%
Female persons, percent, 2000	51.7%	50.9%
White persons, percent, 2000 (a)	71.1%	75.1%
African American persons, percent, 2000 (a)	26.0%	12.3%
Native American persons, percent, 2000 (a)	0.5%	0.9%
Asian persons, percent, 2000 (a)	0.7%	3.6%
Native Hawaiian and Other Pacific Islander, percent, 2000 (a)	Z	0.1%
Persons of Hispanic or Latino origin, percent, 2000 (b)	1.7%	12.5%
White persons, not of Hispanic/Latino origin, percent, 2000	70.3%	69.1%
Foreign born persons, percent, 2000	2.0%	11.1%
Language other than English spoken at home, percent age 5+, 2000	3.9%	17.9%
High school graduates, percent of persons age 25+, 2000	75.3%	80.4%
Bachelor's degree or higher, percent of persons age 25+, 2000	19.0%	24.4%
Persons with a disability, age 5+, 2000	945,705	49,746,248
Homeownership rate, 2000	72.5%	66.2%
Median value of owner-occupied housing units, 2000	$85,100	$119,600
Households, 2000	1,737,080	105,480,101
Persons per household, 2000	2.49	2.59
Median household money income, 1999	$34,135	$41,994
Per capita money income, 1999	$18,189	$21,587
Persons below poverty, percent, 1999	16.1%	12.4%
Business	**Alabama**	**USA**
Private nonfarm establishments, 1999	100,507	7,008,444
Private nonfarm employment, 1999	1,633,909	110,705,661
Private nonfarm employment, percent change 1990–99	21.7%	18.4%
Nonemployer establishments, 1999	219,932	16,152,604
Manufacturers shipments, 1997 ($1,000)	67,970,076	3,842,061,405
Retail sales, 1997 ($1,000)	36,623,327	2,460,886,012
Retail sales per capita, 1997	$8,477	$9,190
Minority-owned firms, percent of total, 1997	9.9%	14.6%
Women-owned firms, percent of total, 1997	24.4%	26.0%
Federal funds and grants, 2001 ($1,000)	31,700,462	1,763,896,019
Local government employment – full-time equivalent, 1997	175,369	10,227,429
Geography	**Alabama**	**USA**
Land area, 2000 (square miles)	50,744	3,537,438
Persons per square mile, 2000	87.6	79.6

(a) Includes persons reporting only one race.
(b) Hispanics may be of any race, so also are included in applicable race categories.
Z: Value greater than zero but less than half unit of measure shown.

Source: U.S. Census Bureau State & County QuickFacts

Alaska

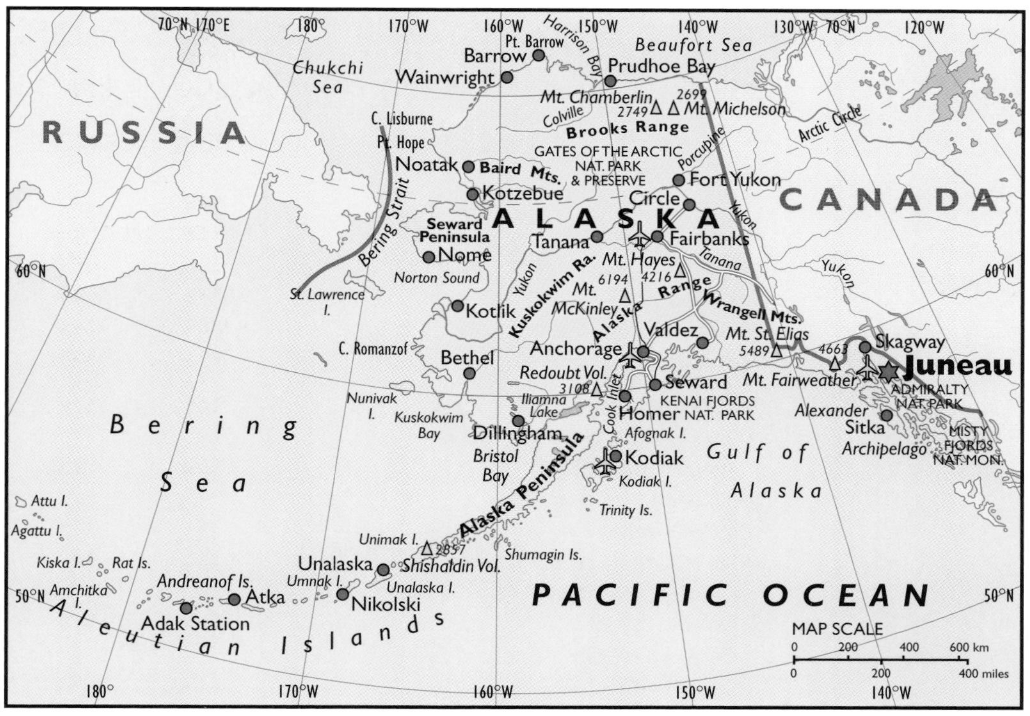

Statehood: January 3, 1959
Nickname: The Last Frontier
State bird: Willow ptarmigan
State flower: Forget-me-not
State tree: Sitka spruce
State motto: North to the future
State capital: Juneau
Population of capital: 30,711 (2000)

Separated from the rest of continental United States by the Canadian province of British Columbia, and from Russia by the Bering Strait, Alaska is the westernmost, northernmost, and easternmost state because the furthest Aleutian Islands cross the 180th meridian. Until Captain James Cook explored the region in search of a Northwest Passage, the maritime lifestyle of the Aleut, Athabaskan, and Inuit people remained unknown to Europeans. In 1867 the United States purchased Alaska from Russia for $7.2 million dollars. Fishing initially drew settlers and in the decade following the gold rush of the 1890s the population doubled. Alaska, partitioned into 25 census divisions, became the 49th state of the Union in 1959. The capital Juneau is considerably smaller than Fairbanks or Anchorage.

About twenty-five percent of the state lies inside the Arctic Circle and Alaska has more coastline than the rest of the states combined. Despite its latitude, however, glaciers only cover about five percent of Alaska. Between the Brooks Range and the Coast Range, the Alaska mountains include Mount McKinley (Denali), the highest peak in North America. The chief river is the Yukon. The Alaskan economy is based on fish, natural gas, timber, quartz, and (primarily) oil. Numerous national parks such as Glacier Bay encourage tourism. Because of its strategic position and oil reserves, Alaska has been developed as a military area linked to the rest of the United States via the 1,500 mile-long (2,450 km) Alaska Highway. Although by far the largest state by area in the U.S., it has the third smallest population after Wyoming and Vermont. Native Americans (mainly Inuit-Aleut) account for approximately fifteen percent of the total population.

The flag was adopted when Alaska gained its statehood. The blue field represents the sea, the sky and the mountain lakes while the stars in the shape of the Big Dipper allude to the state's gold resources. The eighth and largest star stands for the North Star, conveying Alaska's geographic position.

Juneau

A seaport on the Gastineau Channel, Juneau grew rapidly after the 1880 discovery of gold by the town's namesake, Joseph Juneau, and another prospector, Richard Harris. Made capital of the Alaska territory in 1900, the city is home to mining, timber, salmon canning, and tourist industries.

Alaska at a Glance

People	Alaska	USA
Population, 2003 estimate	648,818	290,809,777
Population percent change, April 1, 2000–July 1, 2001	1.3%	1.2%
Population, 2000	626,932	281,421,906
Persons under 5 years old, percent, 2000	7.6%	6.8%
Persons under 18 years old, percent, 2000	30.4%	25.7%
Persons 65 years old and over, percent, 2000	5.7%	12.4%
Female persons, percent, 2000	48.3%	50.9%
White persons, percent, 2000 (a)	69.3%	75.1%
African American persons, percent, 2000 (a)	3.5%	12.3%
Native American persons, percent, 2000 (a)	15.6%	0.9%
Asian persons, percent, 2000 (a)	4.0%	3.6%
Native Hawaiian and Other Pacific Islander, percent, 2000 (a)	0.5%	0.1%
Persons of Hispanic or Latino origin, percent, 2000 (b)	4.1%	12.5%
White persons, not of Hispanic/Latino origin, percent, 2000	67.6%	69.1%
Foreign born persons, percent, 2000	5.9%	11.1%
Language other than English spoken at home, percent age 5+, 2000	14.3%	17.9%
High school graduates, percent of persons age 25+, 2000	88.3%	80.4%
Bachelor's degree or higher, percent of persons age 25+, 2000	24.7%	24.4%
Persons with a disability, age 5+, 2000	83,220	49,746,248
Homeownership rate, 2000	62.5%	66.2%
Median value of owner-occupied housing units, 2000	$144,200	$119,600
Households, 2000	221,600	105,480,101
Persons per household, 2000	2.74	2.59
Median household money income, 1999	$51,571	$41,994
Per capita money income, 1999	$22,660	$21,587
Persons below poverty, percent, 1999	9.4%	12.4%
Business	**Alaska**	**USA**
Private nonfarm establishments, 1999	18,433	7,008,444
Private nonfarm employment, 1999	198,459	110,705,661
Private nonfarm employment, percent change 1990–99	25.8%	18.4%
Nonemployer establishments, 1999	48,441	16,152,604
Manufacturers shipments, 1997 ($1,000)	3,304,952	3,842,061,405
Retail sales, 1997 ($1,000)	6,251,372	2,460,886,012
Retail sales per capita, 1997	$10,268	$9,190
Minority-owned firms, percent of total, 1997	16.7%	14.6%
Women-owned firms, percent of total, 1997	25.9%	26.0%
Federal funds and grants, 2001 ($1,000)	6,403,171	1,763,896,019
Local government employment – full-time equivalent, 1997	23,132	10,227,429
Geography	**Alaska**	**USA**
Land area, 2000 (square miles)	571,951	3,537,438
Persons per square mile, 2000	1.1	79.6

(a) Includes persons reporting only one race.
(b) Hispanics may be of any race, so also are included in applicable race categories.
Z: Value greater than zero but less than half unit of measure shown.

Source: U.S. Census Bureau State & County QuickFacts

Arizona

Statehood: February 14, 1912
Nickname: The Grand Canyon State
State bird: Cactus wren
State flower: Saguaro (giant cactus)
State tree: Paloverde
State motto: God enriches
State capital: Phoenix
Population of capital: 1,321,045 (2000)

Bordering Mexico in the southwestern part of the country, Arizona became the 48th state of the Union in 1912 after 64 years as a territory when Mexico yielded most of the land presently within its boundaries to the United States at the end of the Mexican War (1846–48). Today the state is made up of 15 counties; many like Apache, Navajo and Yuma have taken the names of the Indian tribes that once claimed the land as their own. Most of the largest cities, with the exception of Tucson, cluster around the capital in the south.

The Colorado Plateau occupies the northern part of the state, and is cut by many steep canyons, most notably the Grand Canyon, through which the Colorado River flows. Arizona's mineral resources, grazing and farmland have long been mainstays of the economy and while mining and agriculture are still important, manufacturing has been the most profitable sector since the 1950s. The state has many scenic attractions including the Petrified Forest, Fort Apache, Hoover Dam, as well as the reconstructed London Bridge at Lake Havasu and tourism is now a major source of income. Arizona also has one of the largest Native American populations in the nation (255,879 in 2000) with Indian reservations comprising twenty-eight percent of the land area. Between 1990 and 1998, Arizona's population grew by 30 percent, one of the fastest rates in the country.

Full of symbolism, Arizona's flag displays thirteen rays of red and gold that simultaneously represent the setting sun and the original colonies. The colors themselves reflect those of Spain, while the blue on the bottom half of the banner matches that on the national flag. The star at the center borrows its color from the state's chief mineral. It was adopted in 1917.

Phoenix

Founded on the Salt River in 1870, the city expanded after agriculture in the area had been made possible by using water from the river for irrigation. It became the capital in 1889 and computer parts, aircraft, fabricated metals, machinery, textiles, clothing, and food products are now the leading industries along with many high-tech companies. The dry climate makes Phoenix a popular winter resort.

Arizona at a Glance

People	Arizona	USA
Population, 2003 estimate	5,580,811	290,809,777
Population percent change, April 1, 2000–July 1, 2001	3.4%	1.2%
Population, 2000	5,130,632	281,421,906
Persons under 5 years old, percent, 2000	7.5%	6.8%
Persons under 18 years old, percent, 2000	26.6%	25.7%
Persons 65 years old and over, percent, 2000	13.0%	12.4%
Female persons, percent, 2000	50.1%	50.9%
White persons, percent, 2000 (a)	75.5%	75.1%
African American persons, percent, 2000 (a)	3.1%	12.3%
Native American persons, percent, 2000 (a)	5.0%	0.9%
Asian persons, percent, 2000 (a)	1.8%	3.6%
Native Hawaiian and Other Pacific Islander, percent, 2000 (a)	0.1%	0.1%
Persons of Hispanic or Latino origin, percent, 2000 (b)	25.3%	12.5%
White persons, not of Hispanic/Latino origin, percent, 2000	63.8%	69.1%
Foreign born persons, percent, 2000	12.8%	11.1%
Language other than English spoken at home, percent age 5+, 2000	25.9%	17.9%
High school graduates, percent of persons age 25+, 2000	81.0%	80.4%
Bachelor's degree or higher, percent of persons age 25+, 2000	23.5%	24.4%
Persons with a disability, age 5+, 2000	902,252	49,746,248
Homeownership rate, 2000	68.0%	66.2%
Median value of owner-occupied housing units, 2000	$121,300	$119,600
Households, 2000	1,901,327	105,480,101
Persons per household, 2000	2.64	2.59
Median household money income, 1999	$40,558	$41,994
Per capita money income, 1999	$20,275	$21,587
Persons below poverty, percent, 1999	13.9%	12.4%

Business	Arizona	USA
Private nonfarm establishments, 1999	112,545	7,008,444
Private nonfarm employment, 1999	1,838,277	110,705,661
Private nonfarm employment, percent change 1990–99	48.7%	18.4%
Nonemployer establishments, 1999	260,743	16,152,604
Manufacturers shipments, 1997 ($1,000)	43,030,348	3,842,061,405
Retail sales, 1997 ($1,000)	43,960,933	2,460,886,012
Retail sales per capita, 1997	$9,657	$9,190
Minority-owned firms, percent of total, 1997	13.2%	14.6%
Women-owned firms, percent of total, 1997	27.0%	26.0%
Federal funds and grants, 2001 ($1,000)	30,375,935	1,763,896,019
Local government employment – full-time equivalent, 1997	165,331	10,227,429

Geography	Arizona	USA
Land area, 2000 (square miles)	113,635	3,537,438
Persons per square mile, 2000	45.2	79.6

(a) Includes persons reporting only one race.
(b) Hispanics may be of any race, so also are included in applicable race categories.
Z: Value greater than zero but less than half unit of measure shown.

Source: U.S. Census Bureau State & County QuickFacts

Arkansas

Statehood: June 15, 1836
Nickname: The Land of Opportunity
State bird: Mockingbird
State flower: Apple Blossom
State tree: Pine tree
State motto: The people rule
State capital: Little Rock
Population of capital: 183,133 (2000)

Bounded on the East by the Mississippi River, Arkansas was acquired as part of the Louisiana Purchase in 1803 and was admitted to the Union as the 25th state in 1836. The Quapaw people, called the Arkansea by other local tribes, give their name to the state. Arkansas was one of the 11 Confederate states during the American Civil War. Despite containing 75 counties, Arkansas has few large cities; Fort Smith and Pine Bluff are only a fraction of the size of the capital.

In the East and South the land is low and flat, providing excellent farmland for cotton, rice, and soybeans. The hilly, higher land in the northwest, including the Ouachita Mountains and the Ozark Plateau meets the plains of the state at Little Rock. Like all of the state's rivers, the principal waterway, the Arkansas, drains into the Mississippi. Forests are extensive and economically important. Bauxite processing, timber and chemicals are the main industries. Noted for its resistance to black equality in the 1960s, former president Bill Clinton served five terms as governor of Arkansas. Hot Springs National Park, America's most famous mineral water spa, and the oldest area in the National Park system, has long been a destination for tourists and health seekers.

The diamond design of the flag adopted by Arkansas in 1913 is meant to recall the state's unique status as the only producer of the precious gem in the country. The 25 stars around the diamond point to the timing of Arkansas's statehood. Of the stars in the center, the uppermost signifies its membership in the Confederate States of America, while the three below stand for Spain, France and the United States.

Little Rock

Founded on the banks of the river by the same name in 1814, Arkansas's largest city became the state capital in 1821. French explorers began calling the spot Little Rock to distinguish it from other outcroppings further up the river. In 1957, federal troops enforced a U.S. Supreme Court ruling against racial segregation in schools. The main industries are electronics, textiles and consumer goods.

Arkansas at a Glance

People	Arkansas	USA
Population, 2003 estimate	2,725,714	290,809,777
Population percent change, April 1, 2000–July 1, 2001	0.7%	1.2%
Population, 2000	2,673,400	281,421,906
Persons under 5 years old, percent, 2000	6.8%	6.8%
Persons under 18 years old, percent, 2000	25.4%	25.7%
Persons 65 years old and over, percent, 2000	14.0%	12.4%
Female persons, percent, 2000	51.2%	50.9%
White persons, percent, 2000 (a)	80.0%	75.17%
African American persons, percent, 2000 (a)	15.7%	12.3%
Native American persons, percent, 2000 (a)	0.7%	0.9%
Asian persons, percent, 2000 (a)	0.8%	3.6%
Native Hawaiian and Other Pacific Islander, percent, 2000 (a)	0.1%	0.1%
Persons of Hispanic or Latino origin, percent, 2000 (b)	3.2%	12.5%
White persons, not of Hispanic/Latino origin, percent, 2000	78.6%	69.1%
Foreign born persons, percent, 2000	2.8%	11.1%
Language other than English spoken at home, percent age 5+, 2000	5.0%	17.9%
High school graduates, percent of persons age 25+, 2000	75.3%	80.4%
Bachelor's degree or higher, percent of persons age 25+, 2000	16.7%	24.4%
Persons with a disability, age 5+, 2000	576,471	49,746,248
Homeownership rate, 2000	69.4%	66.2%
Median value of owner-occupied housing units, 2000	$72,800	$119,600
Households, 2000	1,042,696	105,480,101
Persons per household, 2000	2.49	2.59
Median household money income, 1999	$32,182	$41,994
Per capita money income, 1999	$16,904	$21,587
Persons below poverty, percent, 1999	15.8%	12.4%
Business	**Arkansas**	**USA**
Private nonfarm establishments, 1999	62,737	7,008,444
Private nonfarm employment, 1999	954,948	110,705,661
Private nonfarm employment, percent change 1990–99	27.2%	18.4%
Nonemployer establishments, 1999	151,948	16,152,604
Manufacturers shipments, 1997 ($1,000)	45,185,963	3,842,061,405
Retail sales, 1997 ($1,000)	21,643,695	2,460,886,012
Retail sales per capita, 1997	$8,575	$9,190
Minority-owned firms, percent of total, 1997	6.7%	14.6%
Women-owned firms, percent of total, 1997	22.0%	26.0%
Federal funds and grants, 2001 ($1,000)	16,632,110	1,763,896,019
Local government employment – full-time equivalent, 1997	90,806	10,227,429
Geography	**Arkansas**	**USA**
Land area, 2000 (square miles)	52,068	3,537,438
Persons per square mile, 2000	51.3	79.6

(a) Includes persons reporting only one race.
(b) Hispanics may be of any race, so also are included in applicable race categories.
Z: Value greater than zero but less than half unit of measure shown.

Source: U.S. Census Bureau State & County QuickFacts

California

Statehood: September 9, 1850
Nickname: The Golden State
State bird: California valley quail
State flower: Golden poppy
State tree: California redwood
State motto: Eureka!
State capital: Sacramento
Population of capital: 407,018 (2000)

The largest state by population and the third largest in area, California sits on the Pacific coast of the United States. The Spanish explored the coast in 1542, but the first European settlement did not appear until 1769, with the founding of a Franciscan mission at San Diego. The area became part of Mexico, and huge cattle ranches were established. Settlers later migrated from the East and, during the Mexican War, United States forces occupied California in 1846, which was ceded to the United States at the war's end. After gold was discovered at Sutter's Mill in 1848, the Gold Rush swelled the population from 15,000 to 250,000 in just four years and California joined the Union as the 31st state. In the 20th century, the discovery of oil and development of service industries encouraged further growth. Sacramento, as state capital nonetheless ranks behind Los Angeles, San Diego, San Jose, San Francisco, and Oakland in size. Fifty-eight counties divide the state.

In the West, coastal ranges run North to South, paralleled by the Sierra Nevada Mountains in the East; between them lies the fertile Central Valley, drained by the Sacramento and San Joaquin Rivers. Death Valley and the Mojave Desert occupy the Southeast. California is the leading producer of many crops, including a wide variety of fruits and vegetables but poultry, fishing, and dairy produce are also important farming activities. Forests cover approximately forty percent of the land and support a sizable timber industry. Deposits of oil, natural gas, and a variety of ores are valuable in manufacturing, the largest economic sector. Vital industries include aircraft, aerospace equipment, electronic components, entertainment, missiles, wine, and tourism.

Patterned after the flag flown by American settlers revolting against Mexico in 1846, the state flag was adopted in 1911. The single red star is meant to reflect the lone star of Texas and the grizzly bear was chosen due to its predominance at the time.

Sacramento

An inland port on the Sacramento River in central California, Sacramento was the focal point of the 1848 gold rush, and became the state capital in 1854. A 43 mi (69 km) channel links the city to an arm of San Francisco Bay, and it also benefits from a large U.S. Army depot and the McClellan Air Base. Industries of note are missile development, transportation equipment, food processing, and building materials.

California at a Glance

People	California	USA
Population, 2003 estimate	35,484,453	290,809,777
Population percent change, April 1, 2000–July 1, 2001	1.9%	1.2%
Population, 2000	33,871,648	281,421,906
Persons under 5 years old, percent, 2000	7.3%	6.8%
Persons under 18 years old, percent, 2000	27.3%	25.7%
Persons 65 years old and over, percent, 2000	10.6%	12.4%
Female persons, percent, 2000	50.2%	50.9%
White persons, percent, 2000 (a)	59.5%	75.1%
African American persons, percent, 2000 (a)	6.7%	12.3%
Native American persons, percent, 2000 (a)	1.0%	0.9%
Asian persons, percent, 2000 (a)	10.9%	3.6%
Native Hawaiian and Other Pacific Islander, percent, 2000 (a)	0.3%	0.1%
Persons of Hispanic or Latino origin, percent, 2000 (b)	32.4%	12.5%
White persons, not of Hispanic/Latino origin, percent, 2000	46.7%	69.1%
Foreign born persons, percent, 2000	26.2%	11.1%
Language other than English spoken at home, percent age 5+, 2000	39.5%	17.9%
High school graduates, percent of persons age 25+, 2000	76.8%	80.4%
Bachelor's degree or higher, percent of persons age 25+, 2000	26.6%	24.4%
Persons with a disability, age 5+, 2000	5,923,361	49,746,248
Homeownership rate, 2000	56.9%	66.2%
Median value of owner-occupied housing units, 2000	$211,500	$119,600
Households, 2000	11,502,870	105,480,101
Persons per household, 2000	2.87	2.59
Median household money income, 1999	$47,493	$41,994
Per capita money income, 1999	$22,711	$21,587
Persons below poverty, percent, 1999	14.2%	12.4%

Business	California	USA
Private nonfarm establishments, 1999	784,935	7,008,444
Private nonfarm employment, 1999	12,356,363	110,705,661
Private nonfarm employment, percent change 1990–99	9.2%	18.4%
Nonemployer establishments, 1999	2,050,809	16,152,604
Manufacturers shipments, 1997 ($1,000)	379,612,443	3,842,061,405
Retail sales, 1997 ($1,000)	263,118,346	2,460,886,012
Retail sales per capita, 1997	$8,167	$9,190
Minority-owned firms, percent of total, 1997	28.8%	14.6%
Women-owned firms, percent of total, 1997	27.3%	26.0%
Federal funds and grants, 2001 ($1,000)	188,516,866	1,763,896,019
Local government employment – full-time equivalent, 1997	1,194,169	10,227,429

Geography	California	USA
Land area, 2000 (square miles)	155,959	3,537,438
Persons per square mile, 2000	217.2	79.6

(a) Includes persons reporting only one race.
(b) Hispanics may be of any race, so also are included in applicable race categories.
Z: Value greater than zero but less than half unit of measure shown.

Source: U.S. Census Bureau State & County QuickFacts

Colorado

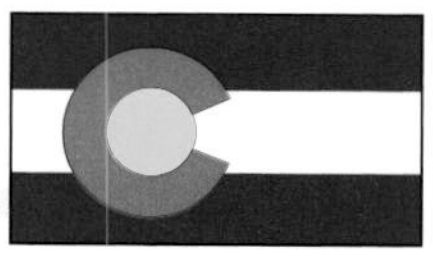

Statehood: August 1, 1876
Nickname: Centennial State
State bird: Lark bunting
State flower: White and lavender columbine
State tree: Colorado blue spruce
State motto: Nothing without the deity
State capital: Denver
Population of capital: 554,636 (2000)

The United States acquired the eastern portion of this Western state from France in the Louisiana Purchase and Mexico relinquished the remainder after the Mexican War (1848). The discovery of gold and silver encouraged immigration, and Colorado became a territory in 1861. Major cities include Colorado Springs, Boulder, Ft. Collins, and Pueblo as well as Denver, the seat of government, and fall along the eastern edge of the Rocky Mountains. The state's 63 counties allude to its history with Spanish (Huerfano, Mesa), English (Kit Carson, Fremont), and Native American (Arapahoe, Cheyenne) names.

It is the highest state in the U.S., with an average elevation of 6,800 ft (2,073 m) and over 1,000 peaks over 10,000 ft (3,048 m) within its borders. The Rocky Mountains cover the western half of the state, and the Great Plains occupy the east. Major rivers are the Colorado, the Río Grande, the Arkansas, and the South Platte. Agricultural activity includes sheep and cattle rearing on the Plains and sugar beet, corn and hay farming aided by irrigation. Key industries are transportation and electrical equipment, mining, telecommunications, chemicals and tourism at sites like Rocky Mountain National Park and Mesa Verde National Park.

Consisting of three alternating stripes of equal width, the state flag's colors are meant to evoke the blue sky and the white snow. Adopted in 1911, the red "C" in the center stands for the name Spanish explorers gave the reddish hued Colorado River. The golden circle within the letter symbolizes gold.

Denver

Resting at the foot of the Rocky Mountains at an altitude of 5,280 ft (1,608 m), Denver is nicknamed the "Mile High City." Founded in 1858, it became state capital in 1867. Like other western cities, its prosperity was boosted with the discovery of gold and silver, along with the construction of the Denver Pacific Railroad in 1870. Denver is the site of many government agencies, including a U.S. Mint and other places of note are the Denver Art Museum, the Boettcher Botanical Gardens. After World War II, Denver's dramatic growth and high altitude led to serious pollution problems. Exploitation of oil deposits created further growth in the 1970s, but the worldwide slump in prices in the early 1980s temporarily caused the economy to stagnate. Denver International Airport, one of the largest in the world, and the city's proximity to the Rockies as well as the Aspen ski resort have turned the capital into a major tourist center. Denver is a processing, shipping, and distribution center that many high-technology industries, especially aerospace and electronics, also call home.

Colorado at a Glance

People	Colorado	USA
Population, 2003 estimate	4,550,688	290,809,777
Population percent change, April 1, 2000–July 1, 2001	2.7%	1.2%
Population, 2000	4,301,261	281,421,906
Persons under 5 years old, percent, 2000	6.9%	6.8%
Persons under 18 years old, percent, 2000	25.6%	25.7%
Persons 65 years old and over, percent, 2000	9.7%	12.4%
Female persons, percent, 2000	49.6%	50.9%
White persons, percent, 2000 (a)	82.8%	75.1%
African American persons, percent, 2000 (a)	3.8%	12.3%
Native American persons, percent, 2000 (a)	1.0%	0.9%
Asian persons, percent, 2000 (a)	2.2%	3.6%
Native Hawaiian and Other Pacific Islander, percent, 2000 (a)	0.1%	0.1%
Persons of Hispanic or Latino origin, percent, 2000 (b)	17.1%	12.5%
White persons, not of Hispanic/Latino origin, percent, 2000	74.5%	69.1%
Foreign born persons, percent, 2000	8.6%	11.1%
Language other than English spoken at home, percent age 5+, 2000	15.1%	17.9%
High school graduates, percent of persons age 25+, 2000	86.9%	80.4%
Bachelor's degree or higher, percent of persons age 25+, 2000	32.7%	24.4%
Persons with a disability, age 5+, 2000	638,654	49,746,248
Homeownership rate, 2000	67.3%	66.2%
Median value of owner-occupied housing units, 2000	$166,600	$119,600
Households, 2000	1,658,238	105,480,101
Persons per household, 2000	2.53	2.59
Median household money income, 1999	$47,203	$41,994
Per capita money income, 1999	$24,049	$21,587
Persons below poverty, percent, 1999	9.3%	12.4%
Business	**Colorado**	**USA**
Private nonfarm establishments, 1999	133,743	7,008,444
Private nonfarm employment, 1999	1,821,717	110,705,661
Private nonfarm employment, percent change 1990–99	46.0%	18.4%
Nonemployer establishments, 1999	325,432	16,152,604
Manufacturers shipments, 1997 ($1,000)	40,012,820	3,842,061,405
Retail sales, 1997 ($1,000)	40,536,034	2,460,886,012
Retail sales per capita, 1997	$10,417	$9,190
Minority-owned firms, percent of total, 1997	9.0%	14.6%
Women-owned firms, percent of total, 1997	28.0%	26.0%
Federal funds and grants, 2001 ($1,000)	24,344,658	1,763,896,019
Local government employment – full-time equivalent, 1997	153,146	10,227,429
Geography	**Colorado**	**USA**
Land area, 2000 (square miles)	103,718	3,537,438
Persons per square mile, 2000	41.5	79.6

(a) Includes persons reporting only one race.
(b) Hispanics may be of any race, so also are included in applicable race categories.
Z: Value greater than zero but less than half unit of measure shown.

Source: U.S. Census Bureau State & County QuickFacts

Connecticut

Statehood: January 9, 1788
Nickname: Constitution state
State bird: Robin
State flower: Mountain laurel
State tree: White oak
State motto: He who transplanted still sustains
State capital: Hartford
Population of capital: 121,578 (2000)

The English first settled one of the original Thirteen Colonies, Connecticut, in the 1630s. Puritans flocked to the area, and in 1662 the colony received a charter from King Charles II. Connecticut was the fifth state to ratify the Constitution and was admitted to the Union in 1788. By chance, numerous inventions came into being in Connecticut, from the Algonquin word *quinnitukqut*, or beside the long tidal river, around the time of the Industrial Revolution. Eli Whitney and Samuel Colt perfected firearms manufacturing here and Noah Webster published the first American dictionary in New Haven in 1806. The state capital and largest city is Hartford, followed by Stamford, Bridgeport and New Haven. Only eight counties divide this small state.

The Connecticut River, the longest waterway in New England, separates the western and eastern highlands. The state economy is based primarily on manufacturing but fishing is also important. Industries include transport equipment, machinery, chemicals, and metallurgy. Dairy produce, eggs and tobacco are the main farm products. Mystic Seaport, once a shipyard of considerable importance, has restored many of its 18th- and 19th-century buildings and now attracts thousands of visitors annually. Connecticut is also one of the most heavily suburbanized states in the country.

A white shield on a field of blue, the flag bears the state motto under three grapevines that represent the first settlements of English colonists who moved from Massachusetts in the 1630s. In 1895, these "transplanted" citizens of Connecticut adopted the flag flown today.

Hartford

Dozens of insurance companies, the first of which opened in 1794, have their headquarters here along the Connecticut River. Founded by Dutch settlers in 1623, Hartford is also home to the oldest continually published newspaper in the United States, the Hartford *Courant* that began in 1764 as the Connecticut Courant. Manufactures include precision instruments, electrical equipment and computers as well as firearms.

Connecticut at a Glance

People	Connecticut	USA
Population, 2003 estimate	3,483,372	290,809,777
Population percent change, April 1, 2000–July 1, 2001	0.6%	1.2%
Population, 2000	3,405,565	281,421,906
Persons under 5 years old, percent, 2000	6.6%	6.8%
Persons under 18 years old, percent, 2000	24.7%	25.7%
Persons 65 years old and over, percent, 2000	13.8%	12.4%
Female persons, percent, 2000	51.6%	50.9%
White persons, percent, 2000 (a)	81.6%	75.1%
African American persons, percent, 2000 (a)	9.1%	12.3%
Native American persons, percent, 2000 (a)	0.3%	0.9%
Asian persons, percent, 2000 (a)	2.4%	3.6%
Native Hawaiian and Other Pacific Islander, percent, 2000 (a)	Z	0.1%
Persons of Hispanic or Latino origin, percent, 2000 (b)	9.4%	12.5%
White persons, not of Hispanic/Latino origin, percent, 2000	77.5%	69.1%
Foreign born persons, percent, 2000	10.9%	11.1%
Language other than English spoken at home, percent age 5+, 2000	18.3%	17.9%
High school graduates, percent of persons age 25+, 2000	84.0%	80.4%
Bachelor's degree or higher, percent of persons age 25+, 2000	31.4%	24.4%
Persons with a disability, age 5+, 2000	546,813	49,746,248
Homeownership rate, 2000	66.8%	66.2%
Median value of owner-occupied housing units, 2000	$166,900	$119,600
Households, 2000	1,301,670	105,480,101
Persons per household, 2000	2.53	2.59
Median household money income, 1999	$53,935	$41,994
Per capita money income, 1999	$28,766	$21,587
Persons below poverty, percent, 1999	7.9%	12.4%

Business	Connecticut	USA
Private nonfarm establishments, 1999	92,454	7,008,444
Private nonfarm employment, 1999	1,530,539	110,705,661
Private nonfarm employment, percent change 1990–99	3.3%	18.4%
Nonemployer establishments, 1999	211,724	16,152,604
Manufacturers shipments, 1997 ($1,000)	46,938,210	3,842,061,405
Retail sales, 1997 ($1,000)	34,938,893	2,460,886,012
Retail sales per capita, 1997	$10,690	$9,190
Minority-owned firms, percent of total, 1997	7.2%	14.6%
Women-owned firms, percent of total, 1997	25.5%	26.0%
Federal funds and grants, 2001 ($1,000)	22,741,764	1,763,896,019
Local government employment – full-time equivalent, 1997	104,338	10,227,429

Geography	Connecticut	USA
Land area, 2000 (square miles)	4,845	3,537,438
Persons per square mile, 2000	702.9	79.6

(a) Includes persons reporting only one race.
(b) Hispanics may be of any race, so also are included in applicable race categories.
Z: Value greater than zero but less than half unit of measure shown.

Source: U.S. Census Bureau State & County QuickFacts

Delaware

Statehood: December 7, 1787
Nickname: The First State
State bird: Blue hen chicken
State flower: Peach blossom
State tree: American holly
State motto: Liberty and independence
State capital: Dover
Population of capital: 32,135 (2000)

Discovered by Henry Hudson in 1609, this state on the Atlantic coast, occupying a peninsula between Chesapeake and Delaware Bays was named for the British Governor of Virginia, Baron De la Warr. Settled by Swedes in 1638, the Dutch, under Peter Stuyvesant, conquered the territory by 1655. Although the Dutch briefly recaptured Delaware in 1673, it was effectively under English control from 1664 to 1776. One of the original thirteen states, it was also the first to ratify the Constitution in 1789. Despite being a slave state, it maintained a fragile loyalty to the Union during the Civil War. The two largest cities, Wilmington and Newark, lie within the megalopolis on the northeastern seaboard and are clustered in the northernmost of Delaware's three counties.

After Rhode Island, Delaware is the second smallest state by area, and most of its land is coastal plain. Tidal marshes teeming with wildlife opposite New Jersey give way to sandy beaches in the south. The highest point in the state is only about 440 ft (135 m) above sea level.

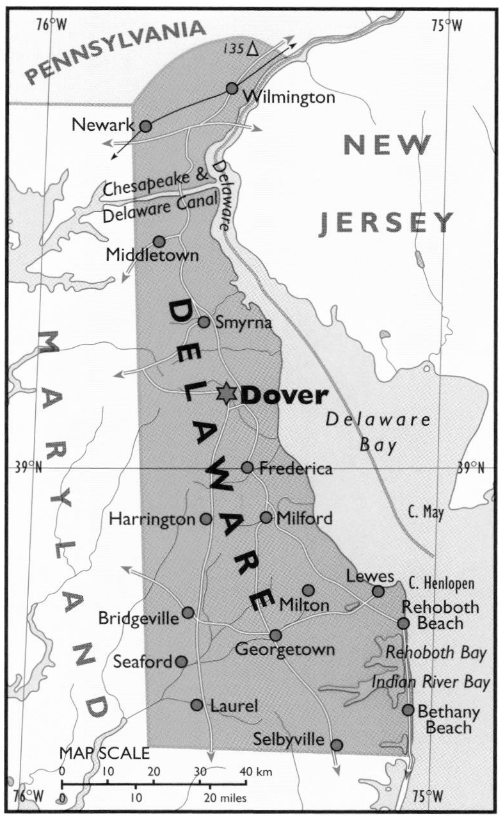

Emptying into the Atlantic, the Delaware River, an important shipping route from Philadelphia, forms part of the eastern boundary. Industries include chemicals, rubber, plastics, and metallurgy while agricultural products include cereal crops, soya, poultry, and dairy goods.

Delaware's flag, adopted in 1913, proudly displays the date on which it became the first state against the blue and buff colors that George Washington wore as general of the continental army. Within the central diamond, a farmer, an ox, wheat, and corn affirm the importance of agriculture in the history of the state while the soldier and the ship are symbols of the Revolution and commerce. The state motto appears between the two standing figures.

Dover

Founded in 1683, Dover was laid out by William Penn alongside the St. Jones River in 1717 and has been state capital since 1777. Dover contains fine examples of Georgian architecture and serves as a shipping and canning center for the surrounding agricultural region. It is also the site of Dover Air Force Base. Industries include lumber, paints, paper, synthetic polymers, adhesives, and chemicals.

Delaware at a Glance

People	Delaware	USA
Population, 2003 estimate	817,491	290,809,777
Population percent change, April 1, 2000–July 1, 2001	1.6%	1.2%
Population, 2000	783,600	281,421,906
Persons under 5 years old, percent, 2000	6.6%	6.8%
Persons under 18 years old, percent, 2000	24.8%	25.7%
Persons 65 years old and over, percent, 2000	13.0%	12.4%
Female persons, percent, 2000	51.4%	50.9%
White persons, percent, 2000 (a)	74.6%	75.1%
African American persons, percent, 2000 (a)	19.2%	12.3%
Native American persons, percent, 2000 (a)	0.3%	0.9%
Asian persons, percent, 2000 (a)	2.1%	3.6%
Native Hawaiian and Other Pacific Islander, percent, 2000 (a)	Z	0.1%
Persons of Hispanic or Latino origin, percent, 2000 (b)	4.8%	12.5%
White persons, not of Hispanic/Latino origin, percent, 2000	72.5%	69.1%
Foreign born persons, percent, 2000	5.7%	11.1%
Language other than English spoken at home, percent age 5+, 2000	9.5%	17.9%
High school graduates, percent of persons age 25+, 2000	82.6%	80.4%
Bachelor's degree or higher, percent of persons age 25+, 2000	25.0%	24.4%
Persons with a disability, age 5+, 2000	131,794	49,746,248
Homeownership rate, 2000	72.3%	66.2%
Median value of owner-occupied housing units, 2000	$130,400	$119,600
Households, 2000	298,736	105,480,101
Persons per household, 2000	2.54	2.59
Median household money income, 1999	$47,381	$41,994
Per capita money income, 1999	$23,305	$21,587
Persons below poverty, percent, 1999	9.2%	12.4%

Business	Delaware	USA
Private nonfarm establishments, 1999	23,381	7,008,444
Private nonfarm employment, 1999	360,735	110,705,661
Private nonfarm employment, percent change 1990–99	16.0%	18.4%
Nonemployer establishments, 1999	39,181	16,152,604
Manufacturers shipments, 1997 ($1,000)	13,397,302	3,842,061,405
Retail sales, 1997 ($1,000)	8,236,970	2,460,886,012
Retail sales per capita, 1997	$11,206	$9,190
Minority-owned firms, percent of total, 1997	9.4%	14.6%
Women-owned firms, percent of total, 1997	24.1%	26.0%
Federal funds and grants, 2001 ($1,000)	4,245,638	1,763,896,019
Local government employment – full-time equivalent, 1997	18,865	10,227,429

Geography	Delaware	USA
Land area, 2000 (square miles)	1,954	3,537,438
Persons per square mile, 2000	401.1	79.6

(a) Includes persons reporting only one race.
(b) Hispanics may be of any race, so also are included in applicable race categories.
Z: Value greater than zero but less than half unit of measure shown.

Source: U.S. Census Bureau State & County QuickFacts

Florida

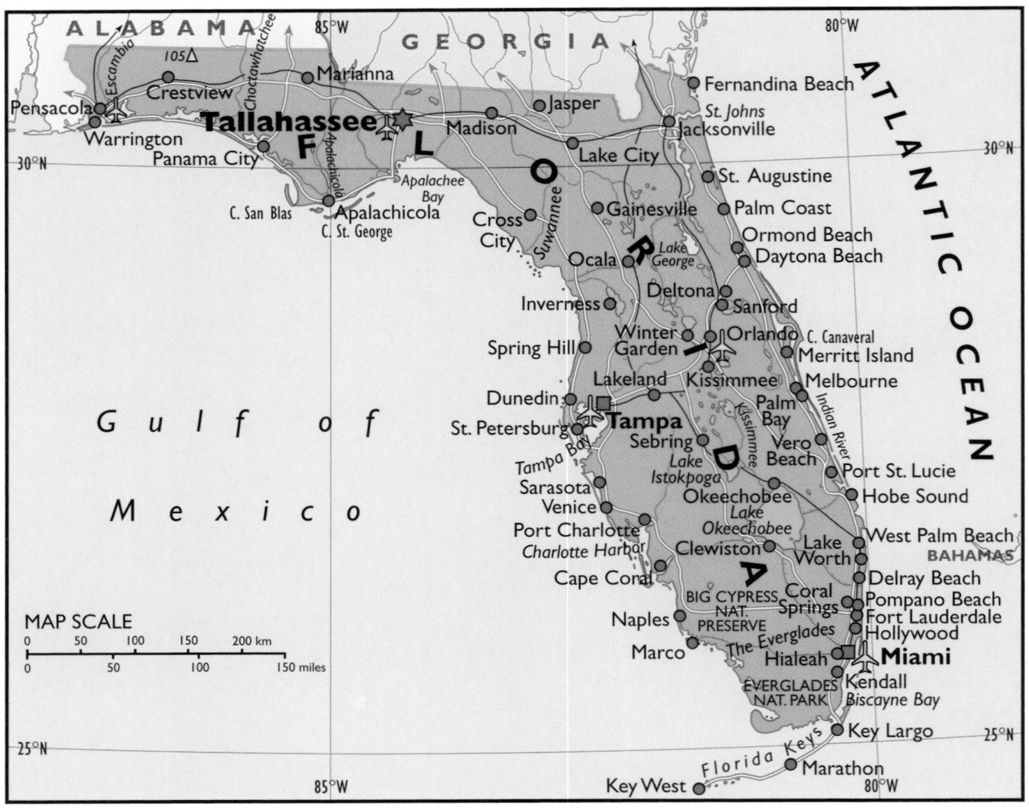

Statehood: March 3, 1845
Nickname: Sunshine State
State bird: Mockingbird
State flower: Orange blossom
State tree: Sabal palm
State motto: In God we trust
State capital: Tallahassee
Population of capital: 150,624 (2000)

Occupying a peninsula and adjoining mainland between the Atlantic Ocean and the Gulf of Mexico in the extreme Southeast of the United States, Florida was first visited by Europeans in 1513. The Spanish built the first permanent European settlement in the United States at St. Augustine on the northwestern coast. Its 17th-century walls stand as the oldest masonry fort in the nation. The land then passed to the English at the end of the French and Indian Wars (1689–1763) before returning to Spain in 1783. In 1819, the United States purchased Florida and in nearly twenty years, settlers forced the majority of the native Seminole population to move west. Although the state seceded from the Union in 1861, it was little affected by the Civil War. It developed rapidly after 1880, when forest clearing and drainage schemes were begun. The most populous cities in this state of 67 counties are Jacksonville, Orlando, Tampa, St. Petersburg and Miami, where Florida's historic ties with Cuba are particularly evident.

Much of Florida forms a long peninsula with tens of thousands of lakes, many rivers, and vast areas of wetland, the largest of which is the Everglades. Lake Okeechobee, the biggest lake in the southern United States feeds into the 40-mile wide marsh populated with a diverse array of rare flora and fauna. Stretching west from its southern tip, a chain of small coral islands known as Florida Keys is North America's largest reef system and one of the three biggest attractions in the state along with Everglades National Park and Walt Disney World in Orlando. Aside from tourism that attracts close to 50 million visitors each year, major industry concentrates on the John F. Kennedy Space Center at Cape Canaveral. Chief agricultural products are citrus fruits, sugarcane, and vegetables.

A red diagonal cross frames the state seal on Florida's flag. Adopted in 1899, the central seal depicts a steamboat sailing in front of the sun, a sabal palm (the state tree), as well as a Seminole woman scattering flowers. The image is encircled by the state motto.

Tallahassee

First discovered by Europeans in 1539, Tallahassee was the site of a Spanish mission before becoming the capital of Florida Territory in 1824. During the American Civil War, it was the only Confederate capital city east of the Mississippi River that was not captured by the Union army. Florida State University and Florida A & M University are located here along with businesses associated with chemicals, timber, paper, and tourism.

Florida at a Glance

People	Florida	USA
Population, 2003 estimate	17,019,068	290,809,777
Population percent change, April 1, 2000–July 1, 2001	2.6%	1.2%
Population, 2000	15,982,378	281,421,906
Persons under 5 years old, percent, 2000	5.9%	6.8%
Persons under 18 years old, percent, 2000	22.8%	25.7%
Persons 65 years old and over, percent, 2000	17.6%	12.4%
Female persons, percent, 2000	51.2%	50.9%
White persons, percent, 2000 (a)	78.0%	75.1%
African American persons, percent, 2000 (a)	14.6%	12.3%
Native American persons, percent, 2000 (a)	0.3%	0.9%
Asian persons, percent, 2000 (a)	1.7%	3.6%
Native Hawaiian and Other Pacific Islander, percent, 2000 (a)	0.1%	0.1%
Persons of Hispanic or Latino origin, percent, 2000 (b)	16.8%	12.5%
White persons, not of Hispanic/Latino origin, percent, 2000	65.4%	69.1%
Foreign born persons, percent, 2000	16.7%	11.1%
Language other than English spoken at home, percent age 5+, 2000	23.1%	17.9%
High school graduates, percent of persons age 25+, 2000	79.9%	80.4%
Bachelor's degree or higher, percent of persons age 25+, 2000	22.3%	24.4%
Persons with a disability, age 5+, 2000	3,274,566	49,746,248
Homeownership rate, 2000	70.1%	66.2%
Median value of owner-occupied housing units, 2000	$105,500	$119,600
Households, 2000	6,337,929	105,480,101
Persons per household, 2000	2.46	2.59
Median household money income, 1999	$38,819	$41,994
Per capita money income, 1999	$21,557	$21,587
Persons below poverty, percent, 1999	12.5%	12.4%

Business	Florida	USA
Private nonfarm establishments, 1999	424,089	7,008,444
Private nonfarm employment, 1999	5,954,982	110,705,661
Private nonfarm employment, percent change 1990–99	29.3%	18.4%
Nonemployer establishments, 1999	1,031,053	16,152,604
Manufacturers shipments, 1997 ($1,000)	77,477,510	3,842,061,405
Retail sales, 1997 ($1,000)	151,191,241	2,460,886,012
Retail sales per capita, 1997	$10,297	$9,190
Minority-owned firms, percent of total, 1997	22.0%	14.6%
Women-owned firms, percent of total, 1997	25.9%	26.0%
Federal funds and grants, 2001 ($1,000)	99,998,376	1,763,896,019
Local government employment – full-time equivalent, 1997	543,525	10,227,429

Geography	Florida	USA
Land area, 2000 (square miles)	53,927	3,537,438
Persons per square mile, 2000	296.4	79.6

(a) Includes persons reporting only one race.
(b) Hispanics may be of any race, so also are included in applicable race categories.
Z: Value greater than zero but less than half unit of measure shown.

Source: U.S. Census Bureau State & County QuickFacts

Georgia

Statehood: January 2, 1788
Nickname: Empire state of the South
State bird: Brown thrasher
State flower: Cherokee rose
State tree: Live oak
State motto: Wisdom, justice and moderation
State capital: Atlanta
Population of capital: 416,474 (2000)

First settled in 1732 and named after King George II, Georgia, on the Atlantic coast of the Southeast, was one of the original six states of the Confederacy in the Civil War. Ravaged by the armies of General William T. Sherman in 1864, Georgia was readmitted to the Union in 1870. Before the war broke out however, the discovery of gold at Dahlonega in 1828 sparked the first gold rush and prompted the government to establish a mint in Lumpkin County, one of 159 counties in the state. Outside of the Atlanta metropolitan area, where nearly half of the state's residents live, the other major cities are Columbus, Macon, and Savannah, the location of Georgia's first settlement.

A broad coastal plain encompasses the south and east of the state while the center consists of the hilly Piedmont. The Blue Ridge Mountains and the Appalachian, drained by the Savannah, Ogeechee, and Altamaha Rivers lie beyond the Piedmont in the North. Cotton, once the chief crop, has declined in favor of tobacco, peaches, peanuts, livestock, and poultry. Textiles have been a major industry, but chemicals, paper and timber, and the manufacture of ships, aircraft and truck bodies are becoming increasingly significant. The Confederate Memorial at Stone Mountain, Okefenokee National Wildlife Refuge and the Little White House at Warm Springs attract tourists to Georgia.

Georgia's new state flag, adopted in 2003, abandoned the Confederate banner in favor of three red and white stripes with the state seal in the upper left corner against a blue field. Three pillars supporting an arch on the seal represent the three branches of government while the thirteen stars that encircle it refer to the state's position as one of the original colonies. The man with a drawn sword drawn defends the Constitution, whose principles are wisdom, justice and moderation.

Atlanta

Creek and Cherokee land until the early 1800s, the city of Terminus, as it was known, was founded in 1837 at the eastern end of the Western and Atlantic Railroad. It became Marthasville in 1843, Atlanta two years later, and the permanent state capital in 1887. It served as a Confederate supply depot and communications center during the American Civil War and on September 2, 1864 fell to General Sherman, whose army razed the city. Atlanta was rapidly rebuilt and soon recovered its importance as a transport and cotton manufacturing center. Now the headquarters of Coca-Cola, Atlanta also contains the High Museum of Art and Emory University. The textile, chemicals, iron and steel, and electronics industries dominate the local economy.

Georgia at a Glance

People	Georgia	USA
Population, 2003 estimate	8,684,715	290,809,777
Population percent change, April 1, 2000–July 1, 2001	2.4%	1.2%
Population, 2000	8,186,453	281,421,906
Persons under 5 years old, percent, 2000	7.3%	6.8%
Persons under 18 years old, percent, 2000	26.5%	25.7%
Persons 65 years old and over, percent, 2000	9.6%	12.4%
Female persons, percent, 2000	50.8%	50.9%
White persons, percent, 2000 (a)	65.1%	75.1%
African American persons, percent, 2000 (a)	28.7%	12.3%
Native American persons, percent, 2000 (a)	0.3%	0.9%
Asian persons, percent, 2000 (a)	2.1%	3.6%
Native Hawaiian and Other Pacific Islander, percent, 2000 (a)	0.1%	0.1%
Persons of Hispanic or Latino origin, percent, 2000 (b)	5.3%	12.5%
White persons, not of Hispanic/Latino origin, percent, 2000	62.6%	69.1%
Foreign born persons, percent, 2000	7.1%	11.1%
Language other than English spoken at home, percent age 5+, 2000	9.9%	17.9%
High school graduates, percent of persons age 25+, 2000	78.6%	80.4%
Bachelor's degree or higher, percent of persons age 25+, 2000	24.3%	24.4%
Persons with a disability, age 5+, 2000	1,456,812	49,746,248
Homeownership rate, 2000	67.5%	66.2%
Median value of owner-occupied housing units, 2000	$111,200	$119,600
Households, 2000	3,006,369	105,480,101
Persons per household, 2000	2.65	2.59
Median household money income, 1999	$42,433	$41,994
Per capita money income, 1999	$21,154	$21,587
Persons below poverty, percent, 1999	13.0%	12.4%

Business	Georgia	USA
Private nonfarm establishments, 1999	197,759	7,008,444
Private nonfarm employment, 1999	3,363,797	110,705,661
Private nonfarm employment, percent change 1990–99	34.6%	18.4%
Nonemployer establishments, 1999	452,567	16,152,604
Manufacturers shipments, 1997 ($1,000)	124,526,834	3,842,061,405
Retail sales, 1997 ($1,000)	72,212,484	2,460,886,012
Retail sales per capita, 1997	$9,646	$9,190
Minority-owned firms, percent of total, 1997	15.6%	14.6%
Women-owned firms, percent of total, 1997	25.6%	26.0%
Federal funds and grants, 2001 ($1,000)	47,320,410	1,763,896,019
Local government employment – full-time equivalent, 1997	324,480	10,227,429

Geography	Georgia	USA
Land area, 2000 (square miles)	57,906	3,537,438
Persons per square mile, 2000	141.4	79.6

(a) Includes persons reporting only one race.
(b) Hispanics may be of any race, so also are included in applicable race categories.
Z: Value greater than zero but less than half unit of measure shown.

Source: U.S. Census Bureau State & County QuickFacts

Hawai'i

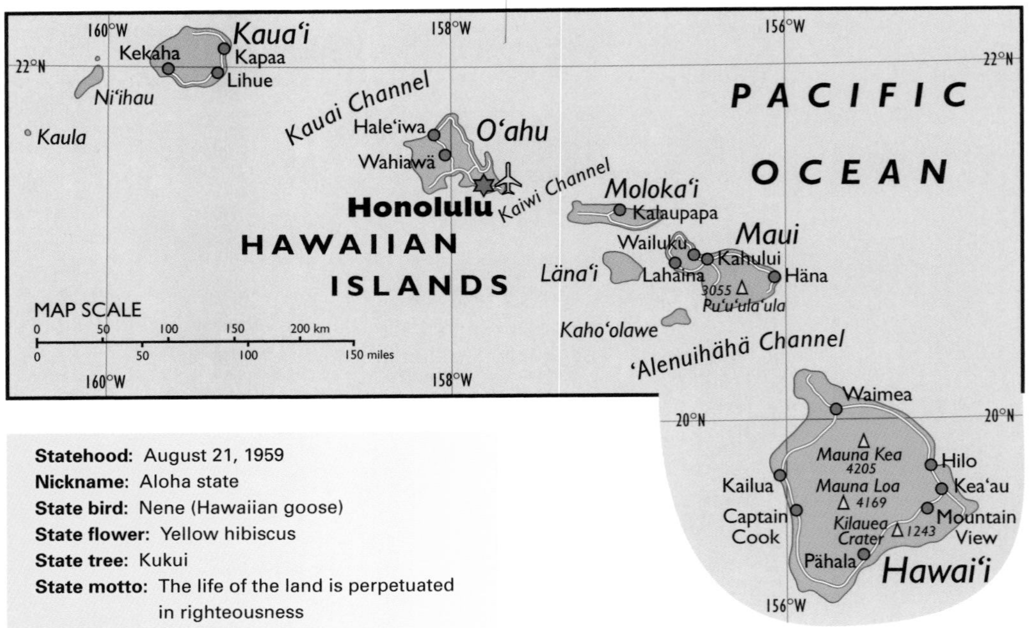

Statehood: August 21, 1959
Nickname: Aloha state
State bird: Nene (Hawaiian goose)
State flower: Yellow hibiscus
State tree: Kukui
State motto: The life of the land is perpetuated in righteousness
State capital: Honolulu
Population of capital: 371,657 (2000)

Southwest of California and separated from the continental United States by 2,400 miles of ocean, Hawai'i is comprised of 137 volcanic islands and atolls altogether. Settled by Polynesians in the 9th century, dubbed the Sandwich Islands by Captain James Cook, and unified under King Kamehameha in the late 18th century, Hawai'i then endured missionaries, disease and sugarcane plantations before becoming a republic in 1894. It was not until 1898 that Hawai'i became a U.S. territory, and statehood was not achieved until 1959, 18 years after the bombing of Pearl Harbor on December 7, 1941. Although there are eight major islands, divided into five counties, three out of four Hawaiians and the capital city can be found on Oahu.

A tropical paradise to tourists worldwide, Hawai'i is home to Mount Waialele, the wettest place on Earth. The moist climate as well as Hawai'i's geographic and reproductive isolation, means that ninety percent of the flowering plants found there today do not grow naturally any other place on Earth. Nevertheless, it is interesting to note that none of the flora or fauna is native to the islands; they were all carried from elsewhere by wind or water. Natural vegetation aside, Hawai'i is a land of volcanic beaches and smoking craters, and in fact, Hawai'i, the largest island, continues to grow in size due to volcanoes such as Kilauea island, the most active on the planet. The world's tallest sea cliffs at 3,250 ft (990 m) can be found on the of Molokai. Surfing or *hele nalu* (wave sliding) as it is known in Hawaiian, is the signature sport of the islands, first introduced to the world by Duke Kahanamoku in the early 1900s. The biggest industries are tourism and agriculture, which concentrates on sugarcane, bananas, pineapple, taro and macadamia nuts, as well as coffee and cattle to a lesser degree. As for manufacturing, food products, clothing and refined petroleum are particularly important to the economy of this state.

The red, white and blue stripes on the state flag represent the eight main islands and the Union Jack of Great Britain is emblazoned in the upper left corner to honor Hawai'i's friendship with the British. The flag was adopted in 1959.

Honolulu

A key port of entry for both people and commercial goods, Honolulu handles approximately eight million tons of cargo each year. Honolulu became the capital of the kingdom of Hawai'i in 1845 and remained the capital after the annexation of the islands under President McKinley. Landmarks include the Iolani Palace (the only royal residence on U.S. soil), Waikiki Beach, the USS *Arizona* Memorial at Pearl Harbor, and Diamond Head Crater. The headquarters of the U.S. Navy's Pacific fleet can be found here, as well as several colleges and universities. Tourism is the most important economic activity, followed by sugar refining and pineapple canning.

Hawai'i at a Glance

People	Hawai'i	USA
Population, 2003 estimate	1,257,608	290,809,777
Population percent change, April 1, 2000–July 1, 2001	1.1%	1.2%
Population, 2000	1,211,537	281,421,906
Persons under 5 years old, percent, 2000	6.5%	6.8%
Persons under 18 years old, percent, 2000	24.4%	25.7%
Persons 65 years old and over, percent, 2000	13.3%	12.4%
Female persons, percent, 2000	49.8%	50.9%
White persons, percent, 2000 (a)	24.3%	75.1%
African American persons, percent, 2000 (a)	1.8%	12.3%
Native American persons, percent, 2000 (a)	0.3%	0.9%
Asian persons, percent, 2000 (a)	41.6%	3.6%
Native Hawaiian and Other Pacific Islander, percent, 2000 (a)	9.4%	0.1%
Persons of Hispanic or Latino origin, percent, 2000 (b)	7.2%	12.5%
White persons, not of Hispanic/Latino origin, percent, 2000	22.9%	69.1%
Foreign born persons, percent, 2000	17.5%	11.1%
Language other than English spoken at home, percent age 5+, 2000	26.6%	17.9%
High school graduates, percent of persons age 25+, 2000	84.6%	80.4%
Bachelor's degree or higher, percent of persons age 25+, 2000	26.2%	24.4%
Persons with a disability, age 5+, 2000	199,819	49,746,248
Homeownership rate, 2000	56.5%	66.2%
Median value of owner-occupied housing units, 2000	$272,700	$119,600
Households, 2000	403,240	105,480,101
Persons per household, 2000	2.92	2.59
Median household money income, 1999	$49,820	$41,994
Per capita money income, 1999	$21,525	$21,587
Persons below poverty, percent, 1999	10.7%	12.4%

Business	Hawai'i	USA
Private nonfarm establishments, 1999	29,569	7,008,444
Private nonfarm employment, 1999	419,047	110,705,661
Private nonfarm employment, percent change 1990–99	–3.1%	18.4%
Nonemployer establishments, 1999	72,610	16,152,604
Manufacturers shipments, 1997 ($1,000)	3,192,532	3,842,061,405
Retail sales, 1997 ($1,000)	11,317,752	2,460,886,012
Retail sales per capita, 1997	$9,516	$9,190
Minority-owned firms, percent of total, 1997	57.7%	14.6%
Women-owned firms, percent of total, 1997	27.5%	26.0%
Federal funds and grants, 2001 ($1,000)	9,722,242	1,763,896,019
Local government employment – full-time equivalent, 1997	14,319	10,227,429

Geography	Hawai'i	USA
Land area, 2000 (square miles)	6,423	3,537,438
Persons per square mile, 2000	188.6	79.6

(a) Includes persons reporting only one race.
(b) Hispanics may be of any race, so also are included in applicable race categories.
Z: Value greater than zero but less than half unit of measure shown.

Source: U.S. Census Bureau State & County QuickFacts

Idaho

Statehood: July 3, 1890
Nickname: Gem state
State bird: Mountain bluebird
State flower: Mock orange
State tree: Western white pine
State motto: It is forever
State capital: Boise
Population of capital: 185,787 (2000)

The discovery of gold in 1860 brought many immigrants to this northwestern state, although Mormons established the first permanent settlement at Franklin in the same year. Idaho was admitted to the Union as the 43rd state in 1890 and soon began to develop its resources. Pocatello and Idaho Falls in the southern part of the state follow Boise, the most populous city. The names of the 44 counties are often taken from the native tribes such as the Shoshone, Kootenai and the Nez Perce, who resisted the early white communities until 1877.

The terrain is dominated by the Rocky Mountains, including the Bitterroot Range and is drained chiefly by the Snake River, whose waters are used for irrigation and to generate hydroelectricity. In addition to cattle raising, the agricultural economy relies of the production of hay, wheat and sugar beet, and potatoes in particular. Lumbering and the mining of silver, lead, cobalt, mercury, antimony and zinc are the largest industries. The state's tourist destinations are primarily natural attractions: Craters of the Moon and Hagerman Fossil Beds National Monuments, Nez Perce National Historic Park, Sun Valley ski resort and City of Rocks National Reserve.

Carrying the state seal on a blue field, Idaho's state flag was adopted in 1907. Within the seal, a woman holding the scales of justice represents liberty and equality while the miner alludes to the state's wealth of mineral resources. The elk, conifer and cornucopias stand for wildlife, timber and agriculture respectively.

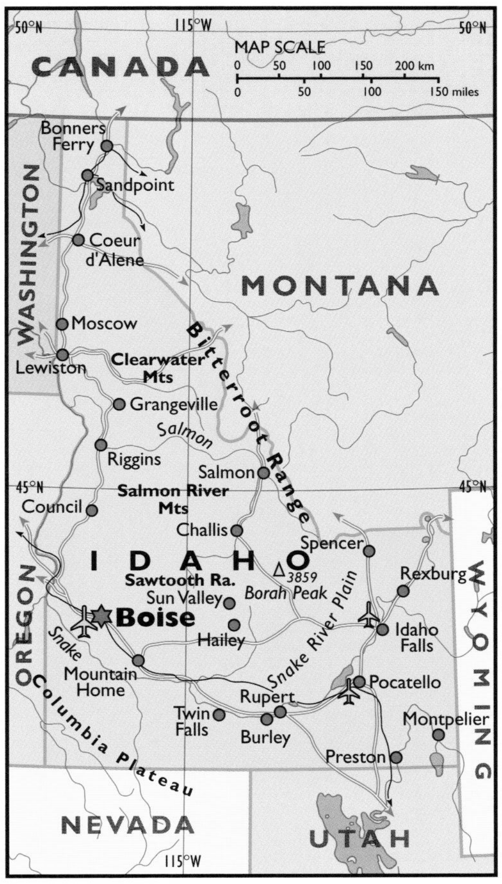

Boise

Founded in the Boise River valley in 1863 as a supply post for gold miners, the state capital is now a trade center for the agricultural region of southwestern Idaho and eastern Oregon. Farming yields sugar beets, potatoes, wheat, alfalfa, and onions and steel, sheet metal, furniture, electrical equipment, and timber products are the main industrial commodities. Despite its French name, Boise is home to the only Basque Museum in the United States.

Idaho at a Glance

People	Idaho	USA
Population, 2003 estimate	1,366,332	290,809,777
Population percent change, April 1, 2000–July 1, 2001	2.1%	1.2%
Population, 2000	1,293,953	281,421,906
Persons under 5 years old, percent, 2000	7.5%	6.8%
Persons under 18 years old, percent, 2000	28.5%	25.7%
Persons 65 years old and over, percent, 2000	11.3%	12.4%
Female persons, percent, 2000	49.9%	50.9%
White persons, percent, 2000 (a)	91.0%	75.1%
African American persons, percent, 2000 (a)	0.4%	12.3%
Native American persons, percent, 2000 (a)	1.4%	0.9%
Asian persons, percent, 2000 (a)	0.9%	3.6%
Native Hawaiian and Other Pacific Islander, percent, 2000 (a)	0.1%	0.1%
Persons of Hispanic or Latino origin, percent, 2000 (b)	7.9%	12.5%
White persons, not of Hispanic/Latino origin, percent, 2000	88.0%	69.1%
Foreign born persons, percent, 2000	5.0%	11.1%
Language other than English spoken at home, percent age 5+, 2000	9.3%	17.9%
High school graduates, percent of persons age 25+, 2000	84.7%	80.4%
Bachelor's degree or higher, percent of persons age 25+, 2000	21.7%	24.4%
Persons with a disability, age 5+, 2000	200,498	49,746,248
Homeownership rate, 2000	72.4%	66.2%
Median value of owner-occupied housing units, 2000	$106,300	$119,600
Households, 2000	469,645	105,480,101
Persons per household, 2000	2.69	2.59
Median household money income, 1999	$37,572	$41,994
Per capita money income, 1999	$17,841	$21,587
Persons below poverty, percent, 1999	11.8%	12.4%
Business	**Idaho**	**USA**
Private nonfarm establishments, 1999	36,975	7,008,444
Private nonfarm employment, 1999	434,461	110,705,661
Private nonfarm employment, percent change 1990–99	44.7%	18.4%
Nonemployer establishments, 1999	83,083	16,152,604
Manufacturers shipments, 1997 ($1,000)	16,952,872	3,842,061,405
Retail sales, 1997 ($1,000)	11,649,609	2,460,886,012
Retail sales per capita, 1997	$9,623	$9,190
Minority-owned firms, percent of total, 1997	4.7%	14.6%
Women-owned firms, percent of total, 1997	23.5%	26.0%
Federal funds and grants, 2001 ($1,000)	7,528,906	1,763,896,019
Local government employment – full-time equivalent, 1997	46,035	10,227,429
Geography	**Idaho**	**USA**
Land area, 2000 (square miles)	82,747	3,537,438
Persons per square mile, 2000	15.6	79.6

(a) Includes persons reporting only one race.
(b) Hispanics may be of any race, so also are included in applicable race categories.
Z: Value greater than zero but less than half unit of measure shown.

Source: U.S. Census Bureau State & County QuickFacts

Illinois

Statehood: December 3, 1818
Nickname: Prairie state
State bird: Cardinal
State flower: Native violet
State tree: Oak
State motto: State sovereignty, national union
State capital: Springfield
Population of capital: 111,454 (2000)

The French, attracted by the fur trade, first explored Illinois, on the eastern bank of the Mississippi River, in 1673. Ceded to the British in 1763, it was occupied by American troops during the American Revolution and became a state in 1818. By the early 19th century, nearly all of the Sauk, Fox and Illinois people living in the area had vanished and with the advent of the railroad in the latter part of the century, the population surged.

A massive fire in October of 1871 destroyed most of Chicago's wooden buildings, but the city quickly recovered. The steel plow, barbed wire and the Pullman sleeping car, accomplishments of innovative citizens, were invented here. After the transport and distribution center of Chicago, Peoria, Rockford, and the capital are the largest cities in this state of 102 counties.

Generally flat, the land is drained by rivers flowing to the Mississippi in the west like the Rock, the Illinois and the Kaskaskia. While much of the economy activity is located in northern Illinois, the state has fertile soil that supports crops such as corn, soybeans, hay, oats, and barley and livestock farming is also important. Coal and other mineral deposits are found in the south. The Art Institute of Chicago, the Sears Tower, the Frank Lloyd Wright Home and Studio and many other tourist attractions, with the exception of Lincoln Home National Historic Site, are clustered in the Windy City.

Featuring a simple design, the state seal occupies most of the white background of the flag of Illinois. The laurel and the rising sun represent progress on this banner, adopted in 1915.

Springfield

Founded in 1818, this landlocked city became state capital in 1837. It was named for a spring on the land of its first resident, Elisha Kelly. Abraham Lincoln lived here for 17 years before he left to occupy the White House. The center of a fertile farming area, Springfield's industries include machinery, consumer goods, electronics, and fertilizers.

Illinois at a Glance

People	**Illinois**	**USA**
Population, 2003 estimate	12,653,544	290,809,777
Population percent change, April 1, 2000–July 1, 2001	0.5%	1.2%
Population, 2000	12,419,293	281,421,906
Persons under 5 years old, percent, 2000	7.1%	6.8%
Persons under 18 years old, percent, 2000	26.1%	25.7%
Persons 65 years old and over, percent, 2000	12.1%	12.4%
Female persons, percent, 2000	51.0%	50.9%
White persons, percent, 2000 (a)	73.5%	75.1%
African American persons, percent, 2000 (a)	15.1%	12.3%
Native American persons, percent, 2000 (a)	0.2%	0.9%
Asian persons, percent, 2000 (a)	3.4%	3.6%
Native Hawaiian and Other Pacific Islander, percent, 2000 (a)	Z	0.1%
Persons of Hispanic or Latino origin, percent, 2000 (b)	12.3%	12.5%
White persons, not of Hispanic/Latino origin, percent, 2000	67.8%	69.1%
Foreign born persons, percent, 2000	12.3%	11.1%
Language other than English spoken at home, percent age 5+, 2000	19.2%	17.9%
High school graduates, percent of persons age 25+, 2000	81.4%	80.4%
Bachelor's degree or higher, percent of persons age 25+, 2000	26.1%	24.4%
Persons with a disability, age 5+, 2000	1,999,717	49,746,248
Homeownership rate, 2000	67.3%	66.2%
Median value of owner-occupied housing units, 2000	$130,800	$119,600
Households, 2000	4,591,779	105,480,101
Persons per household, 2000	2.63	2.59
Median household money income, 1999	$46,590	$41,994
Per capita money income, 1999	$23,104	$21,587
Persons below poverty, percent, 1999	10.7%	12.4%
Business	**Illinois**	**USA**
Private nonfarm establishments, 1999	306,899	7,008,444
Private nonfarm employment, 1999	5,342,675	110,705,661
Private nonfarm employment, percent change 1990–99	15.0%	18.4%
Nonemployer establishments, 1999	665,553	16,152,604
Manufacturers shipments, 1997 ($1,000)	200,019,991	3,842,061,405
Retail sales, 1997 ($1,000)	108,002,177	2,460,886,012
Retail sales per capita, 1997	$8,992	$9,190
Minority-owned firms, percent of total, 1997	12.5%	14.6%
Women-owned firms, percent of total, 1997	27.2%	26.0%
Federal funds and grants, 2001 ($1,000)	65,035,608	1,763,896,019
Local government employment – full-time equivalent, 1997	459,893	10,227,429
Geography	**Illinois**	**USA**
Land area, 2000 (square miles)	55,584	3,537,438
Persons per square mile, 2000	223.4	79.6

(a) Includes persons reporting only one race.
(b) Hispanics may be of any race, so also are included in applicable race categories.
Z: Value greater than zero but less than half unit of measure shown.

Source: U.S. Census Bureau State & County QuickFacts

Indiana

Statehood: December 11, 1816
Nickname: Hoosier state
State bird: Cardinal
State flower: Peony
State tree: Tulip tree
State motto: Crossroads of America
State capital: Indianapolis
Population of capital: 791,926 (2000)

Indiana, located in the Midwest, was explored by the French in the early 18th century, and ceded to the British in 1763. It passed to the United States after the American Revolution and the westward flow of trappers, traders and farmers pushed the Miami, Potawatomi, Delaware and other native peoples out of the territory. The state remained a rural area until the late 19th century when steel mills and oil refineries attracted immigrants from Eastern Europe. Indianapolis is by far the largest city, but Gary, South Bend, Fort Wayne and Evansville are also sizable urban areas. Known as the Hoosier State, Indiana is divided into 92 counties.

Glacial advances during the last ice age left the northern portion of the state low, flat and interspersed with small bodies of water and deposited dark, fertile soil across the center of Indiana. Access via interstate highways, long-distance railroads, and major waterways ensures efficient distribution of the state's agricultural and manufacturing products. The area is a rich farming region and the development of heavy industry in the northwest has also made Indiana a leading producer of machinery. Industries include grain, soybeans, livestock, coal, limestone, steel, electrical machinery, and motor vehicles. Indiana Dunes National Lakeshore, Lincoln Boyhood National Memorial, Turkey Run State Park and George Rogers Clark National Historic Park are among the major landmarks.

A gold flaming torch, symbol of liberty and enlightenment, occupies most of the flag adopted in 1917. Nineteen stars, the largest of which represents the state itself, are arranged in a circular fashion on a blue field.

Indianapolis

Built on a specially selected site on the White River in central Indiana, Indianapolis became the state capital in 1825 and resembles the wheel pattern used in the design of Washington, D.C. It is home to the Motor Speedway, where the Indianapolis 500 motor race has been held each year since 1911. The city is the major cereal and livestock market in a fertile agricultural area and its industries include electronic equipment, vehicle parts, pharmaceuticals, as well as printing and publishing.

Indiana at a Glance

People	Indiana	USA
Population, 2003 estimate	6,195,643	290,809,777
Population percent change, April 1, 2000–July 1, 2001	0.6%	1.2%
Population, 2000	6,080,485	281,421,906
Persons under 5 years old, percent, 2000	7.0%	6.8%
Persons under 18 years old, percent, 2000	25.9%	25.7%
Persons 65 years old and over, percent, 2000	12.4%	12.4%
Female persons, percent, 2000	51.0%	50.9%
White persons, percent, 2000 (a)	87.5%	75.1%
African American persons, percent, 2000 (a)	8.4%	12.3%
Native American persons, percent, 2000 (a)	0.3%	0.9%
Asian persons, percent, 2000 (a)	1.0%	3.6%
Native Hawaiian and Other Pacific Islander, percent, 2000 (a)	Z	0.1%
Persons of Hispanic or Latino origin, percent, 2000 (b)	3.5%	12.5%
White persons, not of Hispanic/Latino origin, percent, 2000	85.8%	69.1%
Foreign born persons, percent, 2000	3.1%	11.1%
Language other than English spoken at home, percent age 5+, 2000	6.4%	17.9%
High school graduates, percent of persons age 25+, 2000	82.1%	80.4%
Bachelor's degree or higher, percent of persons age 25+, 2000	19.4%	24.4%
Persons with a disability, age 5+, 2000	1,054,757	49,746,248
Homeownership rate, 2000	71.4%	66.2%
Median value of owner-occupied housing units, 2000	$94,300	$119,600
Households, 2000	2,336,306	105,480,101
Persons per household, 2000	2.53	2.59
Median household money income, 1999	$41,567	$41,994
Per capita money income, 1999	$20,397	$21,587
Persons below poverty, percent, 1999	9.5%	12.4%
Business	**Indiana**	**USA**
Private nonfarm establishments, 1999	146,528	7,008,444
Private nonfarm employment, 1999	2,580,408	110,705,661
Private nonfarm employment, percent change 1990–99	20.0%	18.4%
Nonemployer establishments, 1999	312,840	16,152,604
Manufacturers shipments, 1997 ($1,000)	142,270,702	3,842,061,405
Retail sales, 1997 ($1,000)	57,241,650	2,460,886,012
Retail sales per capita, 1997	$9,748	$9,190
Minority-owned firms, percent of total, 1997	5.5%	14.6%
Women-owned firms, percent of total, 1997	25.9%	26.0%
Federal funds and grants, 2001 ($1,000)	32,166,145	1,763,896,019
Local government employment – full-time equivalent, 1997	220,747	10,227,429
Geography	**Indiana**	**USA**
Land area, 2000 (square miles)	35,867	3,537,438
Persons per square mile, 2000	169.5	79.6

(a) Includes persons reporting only one race.
(b) Hispanics may be of any race, so also are included in applicable race categories.
Z: Value greater than zero but less than half unit of measure shown.

Source: U.S. Census Bureau State & County QuickFacts

Iowa

Statehood: December 28, 1846
Nickname: Hawkeye state
State bird: Eastern goldfinch
State flower: Wild rose
State tree: Oak
State motto: Our liberties we prize and our rights we will maintain
State capital: Des Moines
Population of capital: 198,682 (2000)

Located in the Midwest between the Missouri and Mississippi Rivers, Iowa was first explored by Europeans in 1673 and claimed for France by La Salle in 1682. The region inhabited by the Iowa people was sold to the U.S. in the Louisiana Purchase of 1803 and admitted to the Union in 1846 as the 29th state.

Industrial development was encouraged after World War II and today the Mesquakie tribe is the only native community remaining within state borders. Once characterized by small farming communities, the expansion of agribusiness has steadily encouraged those living in the nation's breadbasket to move to urban areas. Des Moines, Davenport, Cedar Rapids and Sioux City are the largest cities in a state with 99 counties.

Originally prairie that was plowed to create farmland, the region is known for its deep, fertile topsoil. Hilly topography along the Nebraska border contrasts with millions of acres of fields in the east. Nearly ninety percent of the land is farmed, corn, soybean and other cereals being the dominant cash crops, and Iowa stands second only to Texas in the raising of prime cattle. Industries, too, revolve around agriculture and include food processing as well as farm machinery. Fort Dodge Historical Museum, the Amana Colonies, Herbert Hoover National Historic Site, Effigy Mounds National Monument and Living History Farms are some of the main sites of interest.

Adopted in 1921, the Iowa flag shows an eagle with a banner bearing the state motto in its beak. Vertical red, white and blue stripes appear behind the bird.

Des Moines

Near the confluence of the Des Moines and Raccoon Rivers, Des Moines was founded in 1843 as a military garrison, and is now an industrial and transportation center for the Corn Belt. Named either for the native burial mounds or the Trappist Monks that lived at the mouth of the river, the city's industries include mechanical and aerospace engineering, chemical production, insurance, and plastic products.

Iowa at a Glance

People	Iowa	USA
Population, 2003 estimate	2,944,062	290,809,777
Population percent change, April 1, 2000–July 1, 2001	–0.1%	1.2%
Population, 2000	2,926,324	281,421,906
Persons under 5 years old, percent, 2000	6.4%	6.8%
Persons under 18 years old, percent, 2000	25.1%	25.7%
Persons 65 years old and over, percent, 2000	14.9%	12.4%
Female persons, percent, 2000	50.9%	50.9%
White persons, percent, 2000 (a)	93.9%	75.1%
African American persons, percent, 2000 (a)	2.1%	12.3%
Native American persons, percent, 2000 (a)	0.3%	0.9%
Asian persons, percent, 2000 (a)	1.3%	3.6%
Native Hawaiian and Other Pacific Islander, percent, 2000 (a)	Z	0.1%
Persons of Hispanic or Latino origin, percent, 2000 (b)	2.8%	12.5%
White persons, not of Hispanic/Latino origin, percent, 2000	92.6%	69.1%
Foreign born persons, percent, 2000	3.1%	11.1%
Language other than English spoken at home, percent age 5+, 2000	5.8%	17.9%
High school graduates, percent of persons age 25+, 2000	86.1%	80.4%
Bachelor's degree or higher, percent of persons age 25+, 2000	21.2%	24.4%
Persons with a disability, age 5+, 2000	446,665	49,746,248
Homeownership rate, 2000	72.3%	66.2%
Median value of owner-occupied housing units, 2000	$82,500	$119,600
Households, 2000	1,149,276	105,480,101
Persons per household, 2000	2.46	2.59
Median household money income, 1999	$39,469	$41,994
Per capita money income, 1999	$19,674	$21,587
Persons below poverty, percent, 1999	9.1%	12.4%

Business	Iowa	USA
Private nonfarm establishments, 1999	81,213	7,008,444
Private nonfarm employment, 1999	1,239,354	110,705,661
Private nonfarm employment, percent change 1990–99	23.0%	18.4%
Nonemployer establishments, 1999	169,753	16,152,604
Manufacturers shipments, 1997 ($1,000)	62,413,687	3,842,061,405
Retail sales, 1997 ($1,000)	26,723,822	2,460,886,012
Retail sales per capita, 1997	$9,362	$9,190
Minority-owned firms, percent of total, 1997	2.3%	14.6%
Women-owned firms, percent of total, 1997	25.3%	26.0%
Federal funds and grants, 2001 ($1,000)	17,401,265	1,763,896,019
Local government employment – full-time equivalent, 1997	112,667	10,227,429

Geography	Iowa	USA
Land area, 2000 (square miles)	55,869	3,537,438
Persons per square mile, 2000	52.4	79.6

(a) Includes persons reporting only one race.
(b) Hispanics may be of any race, so also are included in applicable race categories.
Z: Value greater than zero but less than half unit of measure shown.

Source: U.S. Census Bureau State & County QuickFacts

Kansas

Statehood: January 29, 1861
Nickname: Sunflower state
State bird: Western meadowlark
State flower: Sunflower
State tree: Cottonwood
State motto: To the stars through difficulties
State capital: Topeka
Population of capital: 122,377 (2000)

First visited by Spanish explorers in the 16th century, Kansas passed from France to the new United States under the Louisiana Purchase of 1803. It was Native American territory until 1854, when the creation of the Territory of Kansas opened up Wichita, Pawnee, Kansas and Osage lands for settlement. The Oregon and Sante Fe Trails, along with several others, pass through Kansas and carried thousands farther west. Those that stopped were forced to choose between becoming a free state or a slave state following the passage of the Kansas-Nebraska Act in 1854. After seven years of violent conflict, earning it the nickname of "Bleeding Kansas," the territory was admitted to the Union as a free state in 1861. Clustered in the east, Wichita, and Kansas City in addition to Topeka, are the four sizable metropolitan areas. Divided into 102 counties, Kansans elected the country's first female mayor.

Part of the Great Plains, the landscape rises from prairie in the east to semiarid high plains in the west and is drained by the Kansas, Smoky Hill, Arkansas and Neosho Rivers. The country's leading producer of wheat, Kansas also grows corn, hay, sugar beets and sorghum in abundance. Beginning in the 1860s cattle raising became economically significant along with manufacturing at the turn of the century. Industries include aircraft equipment, chemicals, petroleum products, and machinery. The Eisenhower Center, Dodge City, the cowboy capital, and Fort Scott and Fort Larned National Historic Sites are the some of the main tourist draws.

The state seal, depicting the sun rising over a farmer plowing his field, a steamboat on the river, a wagon train and a buffalo hunt, sits in the center of a deep blue background. Thirty-four stars within the seal mark the entrance of Kansas into the Union as the 34th state. The sunflower at the top of the flag adopted in 1927 refers to the state flower.

Topeka

West of Kansas City on the Kansas River, Topeka was founded in 1854 by settlers from New England, and became the state capital seven years later. A major transport center for cattle and wheat. The city was once the general headquarters for the Atchison, Topeka and Santa Fe Railroad. The Menninger Clinic, world famous for its treatment of mental illness, is located in the city. Printing, rubber goods, grain milling, steel products, and footwear all contribute significantly to the local economy.

Kansas at a Glance

People	**Kansas**	**USA**
Population, 2003 estimate	2,723,507	290,809,777
Population percent change, April 1, 2000–July 1, 2001	0.2%	1.2%
Population, 2000	2,688,418	281,421,906
Persons under 5 years old, percent, 2000	7.0%	6.8%
Persons under 18 years old, percent, 2000	26.5%	25.7%
Persons 65 years old and over, percent, 2000	13.3%	12.4%
Female persons, percent, 2000	50.6%	50.9%
White persons, percent, 2000 (a)	86.1%	75.1%
African American persons, percent, 2000 (a)	5.7%	12.3%
Native American persons, percent, 2000 (a)	0.9%	0.9%
Asian persons, percent, 2000 (a)	1.7%	3.6%
Native Hawaiian and Other Pacific Islander, percent, 2000 (a)	Z	0.1%
Persons of Hispanic or Latino origin, percent, 2000 (b)	7.0%	12.5%
White persons, not of Hispanic/Latino origin, percent, 2000	83.1%	69.1%
Foreign born persons, percent, 2000	5.0%	11.1%
Language other than English spoken at home, percent age 5+, 2000	8.7%	17.9%
High school graduates, percent of persons age 25+, 2000	86.0%	80.4%
Bachelor's degree or higher, percent of persons age 25+, 2000	25.8%	24.4%
Persons with a disability, age 5+, 2000	429,687	49,746,248
Homeownership rate, 2000	69.2%	66.2%
Median value of owner-occupied housing units, 2000	$83,500	$119,600
Households, 2000	1,037,891	105,480,101
Persons per household, 2000	2.51	2.59
Median household money income, 1999	$40,624	$41,994
Per capita money income, 1999	$20,506	$21,587
Persons below poverty, percent, 1999	9.9%	12.4%
Business	**Kansas**	**USA**
Private nonfarm establishments, 1999	74,486	7,008,444
Private nonfarm employment, 1999	1,111,884	110,705,661
Private nonfarm employment, percent change 1990–99	24.4%	18.4%
Nonemployer establishments, 1999	155,052	16,152,604
Manufacturers shipments, 1997 ($1,000)	46,296,431	3,842,061,405
Retail sales, 1997 ($1,000)	22,571,918	2,460,886,012
Retail sales per capita, 1997	$8,627	$9,190
Minority-owned firms, percent of total, 1997	5.5%	14.6%
Women-owned firms, percent of total, 1997	25.6%	26.0%
Federal funds and grants, 2001 ($1,000)	16,698,766	1,763,896,019
Local government employment – full-time equivalent, 1997	118,302	10,227,429
Geography	**Kansas**	**USA**
Land area, 2000 (square miles)	81,815	3,537,438
Persons per square mile, 2000	32.9	79.6

(a) Includes persons reporting only one race.
(b) Hispanics may be of any race, so also are included in applicable race categories.
Z: Value greater than zero but less than half unit of measure shown.

Source: U.S. Census Bureau State & County QuickFacts

Kentucky

Statehood: June 1, 1792
Nickname: Bluegrass state
State bird: Kentucky cardinal
State flower: Goldenrod
State tree: Tulip poplar
State motto: United we stand, divided we fall
State capital: Frankfort
Population of capital: 27,741 (2000)

Ceded to Britain by France in 1763, the territory now known as Kentucky was a fertile hunting ground for the Chicksaw, Cherokee and the Shawnee. Admitted to the Union in 1792, its loyalties were divided at the outbreak of the Civil War, and both sides invaded the state. A growing interest in coal, oil, and especially horse racing slowly helped the state recover economically, as did roads linking it to Cincinnati in the north and Nashville in the south. The dense grass that blooms each spring has given the state its nickname and its most enduring tradition: the Kentucky Derby. Since 1875 three-year-old horses have been racing around the one-mile track at Churchill Downs the first Saturday in May. Sectioned into 120 counties, Kentucky has two major cities, Louisville and Lexington.

Most of the state is rolling plain drained by the Ohio, Kentucky and Tennessee Rivers. In the southeast, the Pine Mountains, part of the Cumberlands, dominate the rugged appalachian plateau region. Tobacco is the chief crop, followed by hay, corn, and soybeans. Kentucky is noted for breeding thoroughbred racehorses and cattle raising to a lesser degree. Industries include electrical equipment, machinery, chemicals, and metals. Kentucky is also one of the major bituminous coal producers in the United States. Mammoth Cave National Park, Big South Fork National River and Recreation Area, Cumberland Gap National Historic Park, Abraham Lincoln Birthplace National Historic Site, and Shaker Village are some of the tourist attractions in Kentucky.

A frontiersman and a statesman embrace on Kentucky's flag, enacting the state motto. Adopted in 1918, sprigs of Goldenrod and the words "Commonwealth of Kentucky" placed against a blue background encircle the central image.

Frankfort

First settled in 1779, Frankfort was made the capital in 1792 as a compromise to the larger cities it lies between. Notable buildings here along the Kentucky River include the campus of Kentucky State College, "Liberty Hall," reportedly designed by Thomas Jefferson, and the Old Capitol. Tobacco, textiles, electronic parts, and furniture follow whisky distilling in their economic importance to the capital of the Bluegrass State.

Kentucky at a Glance

People	Kentucky	USA
Population, 2003 estimate	4,117,827	290,809,777
Population percent change, April 1, 2000–July 1, 2001	0.6%	1.2%
Population, 2000	4,041,769	281,421,906
Persons under 5 years old, percent, 2000	6.6%	6.8%
Persons under 18 years old, percent, 2000	24.6%	25.7%
Persons 65 years old and over, percent, 2000	12.5%	12.4%
Female persons, percent, 2000	51.1%	50.9%
White persons, percent, 2000 (a)	90.1%	75.1%
African American persons, percent, 2000 (a)	7.3%	12.3%
Native American persons, percent, 2000 (a)	0.2%	0.9%
Asian persons, percent, 2000 (a)	0.7%	3.6%
Native Hawaiian and Other Pacific Islander, percent, 2000 (a)	Z	0.1%
Persons of Hispanic or Latino origin, percent, 2000 (b)	1.5%	12.5%
White persons, not of Hispanic/Latino origin, percent, 2000	89.3%	69.1%
Foreign born persons, percent, 2000	2.0%	11.1%
Language other than English spoken at home, percent age 5+, 2000	3.9%	17.9%
High school graduates, percent of persons age 25+, 2000	74.1%	80.4%
Bachelor's degree or higher, percent of persons age 25+, 2000	17.1%	24.4%
Persons with a disability, age 5+, 2000	874,156	49,746,248
Homeownership rate, 2000	70.8%	66.2%
Median value of owner-occupied housing units, 2000	$86,700	$119,600
Households, 2000	1,590,647	105,480,101
Persons per household, 2000	2.47	2.59
Median household money income, 1999	$33,672	$41,994
Per capita money income, 1999	$18,093	$21,587
Persons below poverty, percent, 1999	15.8%	12.4%
Business	**Kentucky**	**USA**
Private nonfarm establishments, 1999	89,946	7,008,444
Private nonfarm employment, 1999	1,469,315	110,705,661
Private nonfarm employment, percent change 1990–99	23.9%	18.4%
Nonemployer establishments, 1999	222,304	16,152,604
Manufacturers shipments, 1997 ($1,000)	86,636,107	3,842,061,405
Retail sales, 1997 ($1,000)	33,332,675	2,460,886,012
Retail sales per capita, 1997	$8,530	$9,190
Minority-owned firms, percent of total, 1997	4.5%	14.6%
Women-owned firms, percent of total, 1997	23.4%	26.0%
Federal funds and grants, 2001 ($1,000)	25,835,136	1,763,896,019
Local government employment – full-time equivalent, 1997	134,740	10,227,429
Geography	**Kentucky**	**USA**
Land area, 2000 (square miles)	39,728	3,537,438
Persons per square mile, 2000	101.7	79.6

(a) Includes persons reporting only one race.
(b) Hispanics may be of any race, so also are included in applicable race categories.
Z: Value greater than zero but less than half unit of measure shown.

Source: U.S. Census Bureau State & County QuickFacts

Louisiana

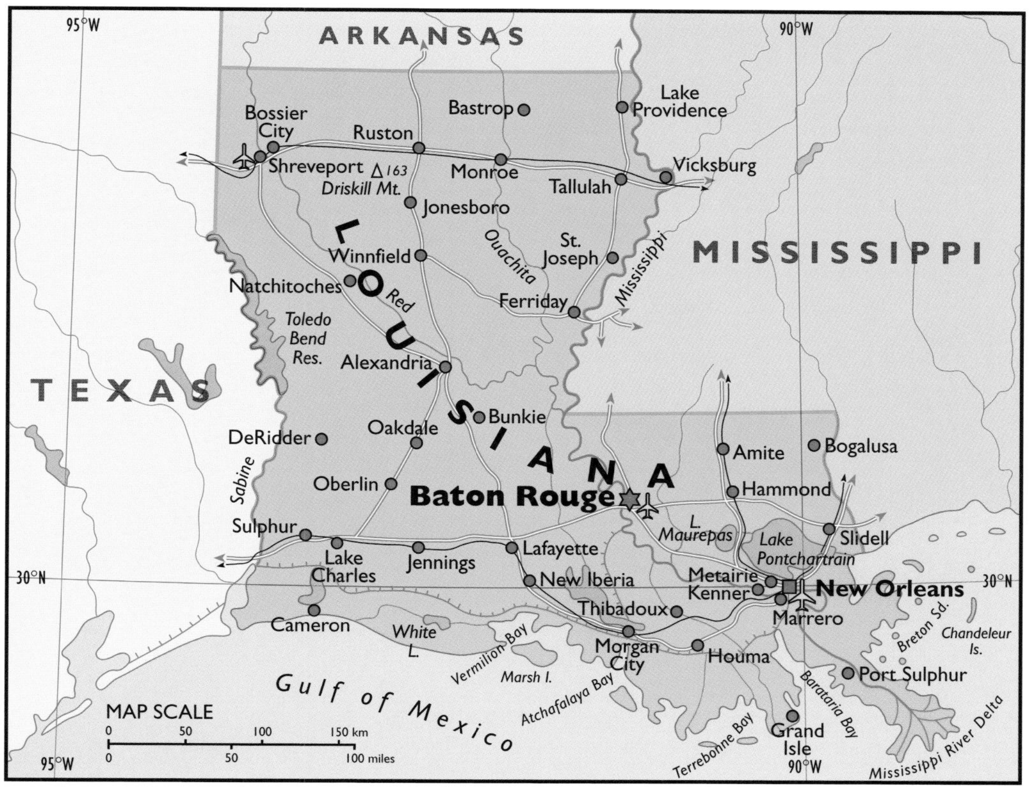

Statehood: April 30, 1812
Nickname: Pelican State
State bird: Brown pelican
State flower: Magnolia
State tree: Bald cypress
State motto: Union, Justice and Confidence
State capital: Baton Rouge
Population of capital: 227,818 (2000)

Around 1699, French colonists wrested control from Atapaka and Chitimacha Indians, founded Louisiana on the Gulf of Mexico and named it for their king, Louis XIV. Regained by France in 1800 after spending time under the Spanish crown, Napoleon then sold the territory to Thomas Jefferson three years later. It joined the Confederacy at the start of the Civil War, but was readmitted to the Union in 1868. The discovery of oil and natural gas in the early 20th century provided a great boost to the economy. Racial discrimination, however, left the large African-American community—approximately one third of the population—politically powerless until the 1960s. New Orleans, Shreveport, Monroe, Alexandria and Lafayette are the major cities to be found among 64 parishes, or county-like administrative divisions.

Louisiana consists of two main regions: the Mississippi alluvial plain and the Gulf coastal plain. The Mississippi Delta in the southeast covers close to 13,000 square miles (33,700 sq km), about one quarter of the state's total area. And at 7,721 miles (12,426 km) long, the tidal shoreline and the multitude of waterways have converted nearly fifteen percent of the state into swamp. The subtropical climate and low-lying land combined with heavy rainfall make this region prone to flooding. Although almost half of the state is forested, north of the marshes, prairies stretch to the Texas border. A leading producer of soybeans, sweet potatoes, rice, cotton and sugarcane, Louisiana is one of the nation's leading mineral producers. Petroleum and coal account for more than ninety-five percent of mining income. Fishing is another major industry, particularly shrimps and crayfish. The French Quarter in New Orleans, Jean Lafitte National Historic Park and the Poverty Point National Monument attract the most tourists.

Exemplifying the state's role as a guardian of its people and resources, a mother pelican and her nest dominate the flag. The only other element interrupting the blue field is a banner carrying the state motto.

Baton Rouge

Founded on the Mississippi River in 1719 by French colonists, Baton Rouge was named after a red post marking the dividing line between two Indian tribes. Ceded to Britain by France in 1763, and to the United States with the Louisiana Purchase, it became the state capital in 1849. The city contains both Louisiana State University and Southern University, and is the site of many food-processing industries as well as a large petrochemical complex. Other industries include natural gas, chemicals, plastics, pharmaceuticals and seafood.

Louisiana at a Glance

People	Louisiana	USA
Population, 2003 estimate	4,496,334	290,809,777
Population percent change, April 1, 2000–July 1, 2001	–0.1%	1.2%
Population, 2000	4,468,976	281,421,906
Persons under 5 years old, percent, 2000	7.1%	6.8%
Persons under 18 years old, percent, 2000	27.3%	25.7%
Persons 65 years old and over, percent, 2000	11.6%	12.4%
Female persons, percent, 2000	51.6%	50.9%
White persons, percent, 2000 (a)	63.9%	75.1%
African American persons, percent, 2000 (a)	32.5%	12.3%
Native American persons, percent, 2000 (a)	0.6%	0.9%
Asian persons, percent, 2000 (a)	1.2%	3.6%
Native Hawaiian and Other Pacific Islander, percent, 2000 (a)	Z	0.1%
Persons of Hispanic or Latino origin, percent, 2000 (b)	2.4%	12.5%
White persons, not of Hispanic/Latino origin, percent, 2000	62.5%	69.1%
Foreign born persons, percent, 2000	2.6%	11.1%
Language other than English spoken at home, percent age 5+, 2000	9.2%	17.9%
High school graduates, percent of persons age 25+, 2000	74.8%	80.4%
Bachelor's degree or higher, percent of persons age 25+, 2000	18.7%	24.4%
Persons with a disability, age 5+, 2000	880,047	49,746,248
Homeownership rate, 2000	67.9%	66.2%
Median value of owner-occupied housing units, 2000	$85,000	$119,600
Households, 2000	1,656,053	105,480,101
Persons per household, 2000	2.62	2.59
Median household money income, 1999	$32,566	$41,994
Per capita money income, 1999	$16,912	$21,587
Persons below poverty, percent, 1999	19.6%	12.4%

Business	Louisiana	USA
Private nonfarm establishments, 1999	101,020	7,008,444
Private nonfarm employment, 1999	1,579,949	110,705,661
Private nonfarm employment, percent change 1990–99	24.3%	18.4%
Nonemployer establishments, 1999	228,628	16,152,604
Manufacturers shipments, 1997 ($1,000)	80,423,978	3,842,061,405
Retail sales, 1997 ($1,000)	35,807,894	2,460,886,012
Retail sales per capita, 1997	$8,229	$9,190
Minority-owned firms, percent of total, 1997	14.1%	14.6%
Women-owned firms, percent of total, 1997	23.9%	26.0%
Federal funds and grants, 2001 ($1,000)	27,816,445	1,763,896,019
Local government employment – full-time equivalent, 1997	169,976	10,227,429

Geography	Louisiana	USA
Land area, 2000 (square miles)	43,562	3,537,438
Persons per square mile, 2000	102.6	79.6

(a) Includes persons reporting only one race.
(b) Hispanics may be of any race, so also are included in applicable race categories.
Z: Value greater than zero but less than half unit of measure shown.

Source: U.S. Census Bureau State & County QuickFacts

Maine

Statehood: March 15, 1820
Nickname: Pine Tree State
State bird: Chickadee
State flower: White pine cone and flower
State tree: White pine
State motto: I direct
State capital: Augusta
Population of capital: 18,560 (2000)

Inhabited by Algonquin and Abenaki Indians, Maine was explored by John Cabot in 1498 although Vikings are thought to have landed on the coast much earlier. The first British settlement, Fort St. George, was established in 1607 but quickly abandoned and firm colonization began in the 1620s as the rest of New England was populated. French and Native American resistance hindered further British settlement and in 1652 it fell under the administration of the Massachusetts Bay Company before becoming part of Massachusetts proper in 1691. It was not until 1820 however, that Maine entered the Union as the 23rd state. Portland, Lewiston and Bangor are the largest cities in this sparsely populated state of 16 counties.

The landscape is generally rolling country with the thickly wooded Longfellow Mountains in the west and more than 2,000 lakes scattered across the landscape. The biggest rivers are the St. John, the Penobscot, the Kennebec, and the St. Croix. Initial economic development was steady, based on numerous ports and its timber resources for shipbuilding. With poor soil, a short growing season, geographic remoteness, and three-quarters of Maine forested, the major economic sector at present is the manufacture of paper and wood products. Broiler chickens and blueberries are the major agricultural products while lobsters are the mainstay of the modern fishing industry. Tourism has also become important as East Coast urbanites seek the natural beauty found at places such as Acadia National Park, earning Maine another nickname: "vacationland."

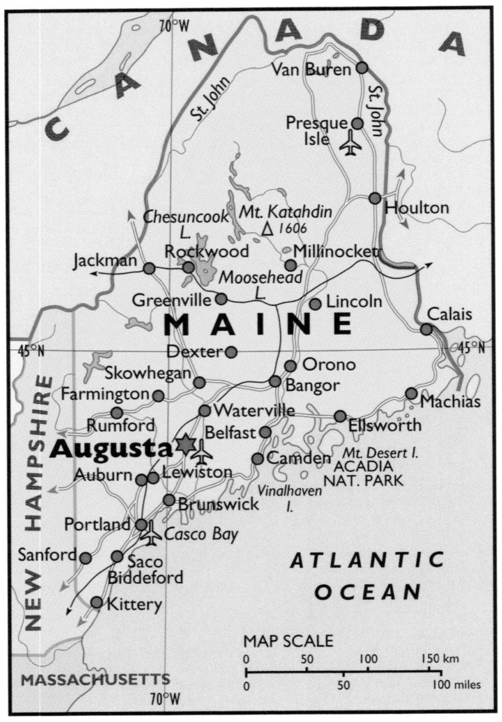

The flag adopted in 1909 displays the coat of arms against a blue background. The sailor and the farmer illustrate the first occupations in the state and the North Star above the moose and the state tree pictured symbolizes the motto.

Augusta

Founded by settlers from Plymouth as a trading post in 1628, Augusta, on the Kennebec River, was incorporated in 1797. A dam built across the river in 1837 led to a shift in Augusta's industry from shipping to the manufacture of textiles, paper, steel, and more recently, computers and electronics. The city also benefits from tourists passing through on their way to scenic vacation spots further up the Maine coast.

Maine at a Glance

People	Maine	USA
Population, 2003 estimate	1,305,728	290,809,777
Population percent change, April 1, 2000–July 1, 2001	0.9%	1.2%
Population, 2000	1,274,923	281,421,906
Persons under 5 years old, percent, 2000	5.5%	6.8%
Persons under 18 years old, percent, 2000	23.6%	25.7%
Persons 65 years old and over, percent, 2000	14.4%	12.4%
Female persons, percent, 2000	51.3%	50.9%
White persons, percent, 2000 (a)	96.9%	75.1%
African American persons, percent, 2000 (a)	0.5%	12.3%
Native American persons, percent, 2000 (a)	0.6%	0.9%
Asian persons, percent, 2000 (a)	0.7%	3.6%
Native Hawaiian and Other Pacific Islander, percent, 2000 (a)	Z	0.1%
Persons of Hispanic or Latino origin, percent, 2000 (b)	0.7%	12.5%
White persons, not of Hispanic/Latino origin, percent, 2000	96.5%	69.1%
Foreign born persons, percent, 2000	2.9%	11.1%
Language other than English spoken at home, percent age 5+, 2000	7.8%	17.9%
High school graduates, percent of persons age 25+, 2000	85.4%	80.4%
Bachelor's degree or higher, percent of persons age 25+, 2000	22.9%	24.4%
Persons with a disability, age 5+, 2000	237,910	49,746,248
Homeownership rate, 2000	71.6%	66.2%
Median value of owner-occupied housing units, 2000	$98,700	$119,600
Households, 2000	518,200	105,480,101
Persons per household, 2000	2.39	2.59
Median household money income, 1999	$37,240	$41,994
Per capita money income, 1999	$19,533	$21,587
Persons below poverty, percent, 1999	10.9%	12.4%
Business	**Maine**	**USA**
Private nonfarm establishments, 1999	38,878	7,008,444
Private nonfarm employment, 1999	475,149	110,705,661
Private nonfarm employment, percent change 1990–99	12.1%	18.4%
Nonemployer establishments, 1999	96,884	16,152,604
Manufacturers shipments, 1997 ($1,000)	14,097,609	3,842,061,405
Retail sales, 1997 ($1,000)	12,737,087	2,460,886,012
Retail sales per capita, 1997	$10,229	$9,190
Minority-owned firms, percent of total, 1997	2.2%	14.6%
Women-owned firms, percent of total, 1997	24.0%	26.0%
Federal funds and grants, 2001 ($1,000)	8,180,498	1,763,896,019
Local government employment – full-time equivalent, 1997	46,260	10,227,429
Geography	**Maine**	**USA**
Land area, 2000 (square miles)	30,862	3,537,438
Persons per square mile, 2000	41.3	79.6

(a) Includes persons reporting only one race.
(b) Hispanics may be of any race, so also are included in applicable race categories.
Z: Value greater than zero but less than half unit of measure shown.

Source: U.S. Census Bureau State & County QuickFacts

Maryland & Washington, D.C.

Maryland

District of Columbia

Statehood: April 28, 1788
Nickname: Old Line State
State bird: Baltimore Oriole
State flower: Black Eyed Susan
State tree: White Oak
State motto: Manly deeds, womanly words
State capital: Annapolis
Population of capital: 35, 838 (2000)

The first European settlements here on the Atlantic coast were founded circa 1634 but dozens of Indian groups like the Susquehannock, Patuxent, Assateague and Potomac, had hunted and fished Maryland's waterways for centuries. One of the original Thirteen Colonies, its citizens were active in the cause for independence. During the Civil War, Maryland was one of the border states that did not secede from the Union, but its citizens served on both sides of the conflict. Baltimore, the largest city, forms its own administrative division along with 23 counties.

The Alleghenies mark the western half of the state but the Chesapeake Bay and its coastal marshlands dominate Maryland geography. Cattle and poultry are the most important livestock while corn, hay, tobacco and soybeans are the chief crops. Industries include iron and steel, shipbuilding, transport equipment (particularly aircraft), chemical, electrical machinery, and fishing. Harper's Ferry National Park, Chesapeake and Ohio Canal National Park, Antietam National Battlefield and the Goddard Space Flight Center attract the most visitors.

The state flag borrows its design from two English families. The Crosslands coat of arms bore the red and white design, while the Calverts, a black and yellow. It was adopted in 1904.

Annapolis

A port at the mouth of the Severn River on the Chesapeake Bay, Annapolis, named in honor of Queen Anne, was founded in 1649 by Puritans from Virginia, and in 1694 was laid out as the state capital. The site of the signing of the peace treaty ending the American Revolution, it has many buildings dating from the colonial period. George Bancroft founded the U.S. Naval Academy here in 1845. Local industries such as seafood packing, sail and boat-making rely on the Chesapeake Bay and the Atlantic.

Washington, D.C.

The nation's capital, the District of Columbia occupies the eastern bank of the Potomac River, yet its metropolitan area extends far into the neighboring states of Maryland and Virginia. The site was chosen as the seat of government in 1791, and the French engineer Pierre Charles L'Enfant planned the city. Construction of the White House began in 1793, and the Capitol building the following year. In 1800, Congress moved from Philadelphia to Washington, but during the War of 1812, the British occupied the city and burned many public buildings, including the White House and the Capitol. The main governmental buildings for the legislative, judicial, and administrative center of the country include the Library of Congress, the Pentagon, the Supreme Court, and the Capitol which contains the senate and the House of Representatives.

Maryland & DC at a Glance

People	MD	DC	USA
Population, 2003 estimate	5,508,909	563,384	290,809,777
Population percent change, April 1, 2000–July 1, 2001	1.5%	0.0%	1.2%
Population, 2000	5,296,486	572,059	281,421,906
Persons under 5 years old, percent, 2000	6.7%	5.7%	6.8%
Persons under 18 years old, percent, 2000	25.6%	20.1%	25.7%
Persons 65 years old and over, percent, 2000	11.3%	12.2%	12.4%
Female persons, percent, 2000	51.7%	52.9%	50.9%
White persons, percent, 2000 (a)	64.0%	30.8%	75.1%
African American persons, percent, 2000 (a)	27.9%	60.0%	12.3%
Native American persons, percent, 2000 (a)	0.3%	0.3%	0.9%
Asian persons, percent, 2000 (a)	4.0%	2.7%	3.6%
Native Hawaiian and Other Pacific Islander, percent, 2000 (a)	Z	0.1%	0.1%
Persons of Hispanic or Latino origin, percent, 2000 (b)	4.3%	7.9%	12.5%
White persons, not of Hispanic/Latino origin, percent, 2000	62.1%	27.8%	69.1%
Foreign born persons, percent, 2000	9.8%	12.9%	11.1%
Language other than English spoken at home, percent age 5+, 2000	12.6%	16.8%	17.9%
High school graduates, percent of persons age 25+, 2000	83.8%	77.8%	80.4%
Bachelor's degree or higher, percent of persons age 25+, 2000	31.4%	39.1%	24.4%
Persons with a disability, age 5+, 2000	854,345	115,980	49,746,248
Homeownership rate, 2000	67.7%	40.8%	66.2%
Median value of owner-occupied housing units, 2000	$146,000	$157,200	$119,600
Households, 2000	1,980,859	248,338	105,480,101
Persons per household, 2000	2.61	2.16	2.59
Median household money income, 1999	$52,868	$40,127	$41,994
Per capita money income, 1999	$25,614	$28,659	$21,587
Persons below poverty, percent, 1999	8.5%	20.2%	12.4%
Business	**MD**	**DC**	**USA**
Private nonfarm establishments, 1999	127,431	19,469	7,008,444
Private nonfarm employment, 1999	1,988,950	404,372	110,705,661
Private nonfarm employment, percent change 1990–99	9.8%	–5.3%	18.4%
Nonemployer establishments, 1999	307,535	31,486	16,152,604
Manufacturers shipments, 1997 ($1,000)	36,505,948	320,234	3,842,061,405
Retail sales, 1997 ($1,000)	46,428,206	2,788,831	2,460,886,012
Retail sales per capita, 1997	$9,116	$5,274	$9,190
Minority-owned firms, percent of total, 1997	20.6%	33.6%	14.6%
Women-owned firms, percent of total, 1997	28.9%	30.9%	26.0%
Federal funds and grants, 2001 ($1,000)	48,163,883	30,940,658	1,763,896,019
Local government employment – full-time equivalent, 1997	171,635	46,246	10,227,429
Geography	**MD**	**DC**	**USA**
Land area, 2000 (square miles)	9,774	61	3,537,438
Persons per square mile, 2000	541.9	9,316.4	79.6

(a) Includes persons reporting only one race.
(b) Hispanics may be of any race, so also are included in applicable race categories.
Z: Value greater than zero but less than half unit of measure shown.

Source: U.S. Census Bureau State & County QuickFacts

Massachusetts

Statehood: February 6, 1788
Nickname: Bay State
State bird: Chickadee
State flower: Mayflower
State tree: American elm
State motto: By the sword we seek peace, but peace only under liberty
State capital: Boston
Population of capital: 589,141 (2000)

The Pilgrims founded the Plymouth Colony, the first settlement in New England, in 1620 on Massachusetts Bay. English Puritans, led by John Winthrop, established the city of Boston in 1630, and it became the center of the Massachusetts Bay Colony. The state played a leading role in events leading up to the American Revolution, and was the scene of the first major armed conflict at the Battle of Bunker Hill. Massachusetts prospered after achieving statehood in 1788 and 14 counties were eventually created. Apart from Boston, the biggest cities are Worcester, Springfield, Cambridge, and New Bedford.

The eastern portion of the state is a low-lying coastal plain while the Connecticut River valley and the Berkshire hills mark the uplands of the interior. The principal rivers are the Housatonic, Merrimack, and the Connecticut, New England's longest waterway. A once highly industrialized region, Massachusetts is one of the most densely populated states in the nation. Agricultural produce includes cranberries, tobacco, hay, vegetables, and dairy products. Manufacturing centers around the Boston metropolitan area; electronic equipment, plastics, footwear, paper, machinery, metal and rubber goods, printing and publishing, and fishing are the largest employers.

The state flag features a blue shield emblazoned with a Massachuset Indian on a white field. The state motto appears in Latin on the banner around the shield. The white star in the upper left corner represents the state as one of the original thirteen while the arm and sword above symbolizes the first part of the motto.

Boston

A principal seaport at the mouth of the Charles River on Massachusetts Bay, Boston is the largest city in New England. By 1700, Boston was the largest city in the British American colonies and the largest port in the British Empire outside the mother country. It had the first free public school (1635), the first public library (1653), as well as the first newspaper (1707) in the Americas. The city lay at the heart of the struggle for American independence. Faneuil Hall (1742), a meeting place for the revolutionaries, is known as the "Cradle of Liberty," and incidents such as the Boston Massacre (1770) and the Boston Tea Party (1773) were early warnings of American resistance to British rule. In the 19th century, Boston was the center of Transcendentalism, the first truly distinctive national cultural movement, and remains the world headquarters for the Church of Christian Science. The first subway system in the United States opened in Boston in 1895. Historic sites include Paul Revere's House, the oldest wooden building in Boston, the Old South Meeting House, the State Capitol built by Charles Bulfinch, Boston Athenaeum, and the Museum of Fine Arts. Printing and publishing, health care, banking and insurance, shipbuilding, electronics, fishing, and clothing manufacturing are the key industries.

Massachusetts at a Glance

People	Massachusetts	USA
Population, 2003 estimate	6,433,422	290,809,777
Population percent change, April 1, 2000–July 1, 2001	0.5%	1.2%
Population, 2000	6,349,097	281,421,906
Persons under 5 years old, percent, 2000	6.3%	6.8%
Persons under 18 years old, percent, 2000	23.6%	25.7%
Persons 65 years old and over, percent, 2000	13.5%	12.4%
Female persons, percent, 2000	51.8%	50.9%
White persons, percent, 2000 (a)	84.5%	75.1%
African American persons, percent, 2000 (a)	5.4%	12.3%
Native American persons, percent, 2000 (a)	0.2%	0.9%
Asian persons, percent, 2000 (a)	3.8%	3.6%
Native Hawaiian and Other Pacific Islander, percent, 2000 (a)	Z	0.1%
Persons of Hispanic or Latino origin, percent, 2000 (b)	6.8%	12.5%
White persons, not of Hispanic/Latino origin, percent, 2000	81.9%	69.1%
Foreign born persons, percent, 2000	12.2%	11.1%
Language other than English spoken at home, percent age 5+, 2000	18.7%	17.9%
High school graduates, percent of persons age 25+, 2000	84.8%	80.4%
Bachelor's degree or higher, percent of persons age 25+, 2000	33.2%	24.4%
Persons with a disability, age 5+, 2000	1,084,746	49,746,248
Homeownership rate, 2000	61.7%	66.2%
Median value of owner-occupied housing units, 2000	$185,700	$119,600
Households, 2000	2,443,580	105,480,101
Persons per household, 2000	2.51	2.59
Median household money income, 1999	$50,502	$41,994
Per capita money income, 1999	$25,952	$21,587
Persons below poverty, percent, 1999	9.3%	12.4%

Business	Massachusetts	USA
Private nonfarm establishments, 1999	173,267	7,008,444
Private nonfarm employment, 1999	2,971,052	110,705,661
Private nonfarm employment, percent change 1990–99	7.2%	18.4%
Nonemployer establishments, 1999	404,333	16,152,604
Manufacturers shipments, 1997 ($1,000)	77,876,576	3,842,061,405
Retail sales, 1997 ($1,000)	58,578,048	2,460,886,012
Retail sales per capita, 1997	$9,579	$9,190
Minority-owned firms, percent of total, 1997	7.3%	14.6%
Women-owned firms, percent of total, 1997	26.6%	26.0%
Federal funds and grants, 2001 ($1,000)	44,178,642	1,763,896,019
Local government employment – full-time equivalent, 1997	213,917	10,227,429

Geography	Massachusetts	USA
Land area, 2000 (square miles)	7,840	3,537,438
Persons per square mile, 2000	809.8	79.6

(a) Includes persons reporting only one race.
(b) Hispanics may be of any race, so also are included in applicable race categories.
Z: Value greater than zero but less than half unit of measure shown.

Source: U.S. Census Bureau State & County QuickFacts

Michigan

Statehood: January 26, 1837
Nickname: Wolverine State
State bird: Robin
State flower: Apple blossom
State tree: White pine
State motto: If you seek a pleasant peninsula, look around you
State capital: Lansing
Population of capital: 119,128 (2000)

First explored by the French in the 17th century, who traded for furs with the Chippewa, Ottawa and Potawatomi, this region bordered by four of the Great Lakes was surrendered to Britain after the Seven Years' War. The British finally left the area in 1796, and Michigan became a territory shortly thereafter, achieving full statehood in 1837. In 1825 the opening of the Erie Canal aided its growth, but the real industrial boom came with the development of the motor vehicle industry in the early 20th century. The largest cities are Detroit, Grand Rapids, Warren, Flint, Lansing, Sterling, Ann Arbor and Livonia. The Wolverine State is divided into 83 counties.

Michigan is made up of two peninsulas separated by the Straits of Mackinac, connecting Lakes Michigan and Huron. The Upper Peninsula has swampland on its northeastern shores and the Huron Mountains in the west. The rocky landscape yields natural resources like copper, iron ore and timber. The abundantly forested Lower Peninsula also contains deposits of oil, gypsum, sandstone, and limestone. In the south, near Battle Creek, cereal crops are cultivated and livestock rearing is important. The Lower Peninsula also holds most of Michigan's population. Industries include motor vehicles, primary and fabricated metals, chemicals, and food products. The appeal of the lakes and the natural beauty of places like Mackinac Island, Isle Royale National Park (the largest isle in Lake Superior) and Pictured Rocks National Lakeshore attract numerous visitors each summer.

An elk, a moose and an eagle hold a shield emblazoned with the Latin word *Tuebor* (I will defend) on the state flag. Set against a blue background the shield contains an image of a man standing on a peninsula with one hand raised in a gesture of peace and the other holding a rifle, in reference to defense. The mottoes of the nation and the state appear above and below the shield respectively. Michigan adopted their flag in 1911.

Lansing

This city in southern Michigan was first settled in the 1840s, it was made the state capital in 1847. Lansing didn't start to grow significantly until Ransom Eli Olds started manufacturing and selling his Oldsmobiles here along the Grand River in 1897. Lansing continues to produce motor vehicles, metal goods, machinery, plastic products and building materials. East Lansing is the home to one of the state's two premier universities, Michigan State University.

Michigan at a Glance

People	Michigan	USA
Population, 2003 estimate	10,079,985	290,809,777
Population percent change, April 1, 2000–July 1, 2001	0.5%	1.2%
Population, 2000	9,938,444	281,421,906
Persons under 5 years old, percent, 2000	6.8%	6.8%
Persons under 18 years old, percent, 2000	26.1%	25.7%
Persons 65 years old and over, percent, 2000	12.3%	12.4%
Female persons, percent, 2000	51.0%	50.9%
White persons, percent, 2000 (a)	80.2%	75.1%
African American persons, percent, 2000 (a)	14.2%	12.3%
Native American persons, percent, 2000 (a)	0.6%	0.9%
Asian persons, percent, 2000 (a)	1.8%	3.6%
Native Hawaiian and Other Pacific Islander, percent, 2000 (a)	Z	0.1%
Persons of Hispanic or Latino origin, percent, 2000 (b)	3.3%	12.5%
White persons, not of Hispanic/Latino origin, percent, 2000	78.6%	69.1%
Foreign born persons, percent, 2000	5.3%	11.1%
Language other than English spoken at home, percent age 5+, 2000	8.4%	17.9%
High school graduates, percent of persons age 25+, 2000	83.4%	80.4%
Bachelor's degree or higher, percent of persons age 25+, 2000	21.8%	24.4%
Persons with a disability, age 5+, 2000	1,711,231	49,746,248
Homeownership rate, 2000	73.8%	66.2%
Median value of owner-occupied housing units, 2000	$115,600	$119,600
Households, 2000	3,785,661	105,480,101
Persons per household, 2000	2.56	2.59
Median household money income, 1999	$44,667	$41,994
Per capita money income, 1999	$22,168	$21,587
Persons below poverty, percent, 1999	10.5%	12.4%
Business	**Michigan**	**USA**
Private nonfarm establishments, 1999	236,456	7,008,444
Private nonfarm employment, 1999	3,996,300	110,705,661
Private nonfarm employment, percent change 1990–99	17.1%	18.4%
Nonemployer establishments, 1999	506,038	16,152,604
Manufacturers shipments, 1997 ($1,000)	214,900,655	3,842,061,405
Retail sales, 1997 ($1,000)	93,706,078	2,460,886,012
Retail sales per capita, 1997	$9,576	$9,190
Minority-owned firms, percent of total, 1997	7.6%	14.6%
Women-owned firms, percent of total, 1997	27.2%	26.0%
Federal funds and grants, 2001 ($1,000)	51,632,490	1,763,896,019
Local government employment – full-time equivalent, 1997	332,671	10,227,429
Geography	**Michigan**	**USA**
Land area, 2000 (square miles)	56,804	3,537,438
Persons per square mile, 2000	175	79.6

(a) Includes persons reporting only one race.
(b) Hispanics may be of any race, so also are included in applicable race categories.
Z: Value greater than zero but less than half unit of measure shown.

Source: U.S. Census Bureau State & County QuickFacts

Minnesota

Statehood: May 11, 1858
Nickname: Gopher State
State bird: Common loon
State flower: Pink and white lady-slipper
State tree: Norway pine
State motto: Star of the North
State capital: St. Paul
Population of capital: 287,151 (2000)

French fur trader Daniel Greysolon, sieur Duluth reached this area along the existing Canadian border in 1679 and found it inhabited by Dakota and Ojibwa Indians. After the French and Indian War (1754–63), the land east of the Mississippi passed to Britain, then to the U.S. following the Revolutionary War. The lands west of the Mississippi were among those acquired with the Louisiana Purchase. Organized as a territory in 1849, Minnesota acquired statehood in 1858 and over time 87 counties took shape. Minneapolis, sitting on the same side of the river as the capital, and Duluth, the westernmost Atlantic seaport, are the major cities.

The state's terrain varies from the southern prairies to the northern forests. Northeast of Lake Itasca, the source of the Mississippi, lie several smaller mountain chains: the Misquah Hills and the Mesabi and Vermillion Ranges, which hold small deposits of iron ore. The numerous lakes in the north empty into the Mississippi, Minnesota, and St. Croix Rivers. Many farms raise beef and dairy cattle while wheat and corn are the major crops. Since the 1950s, manufacturing has replaced agriculture as the main economic activity. Industries include electronic equipment, machinery, paper products, chemicals, printing and publishing. Tourists to the Land of 10,000 Lakes who don't stop at the Mall of America often visit Voyageurs National Park, Mississippi National River and Recreational Area in addition to the Pipestone and Grand Portage National Monuments.

Nineteen stars surround the seal on the state flag of Minnesota. Within the seal a wreath of lady slippers, the state flower, encloses an image of a farmer plowing and a Native American on horseback, representing the state's heritage. The year Minnesota became the 32nd state appears above while 1819, the year Ft. Snelling was established on the present site of Minneapolis, and 1893, the year the original flag was adopted, flank the seal. The largest star on this current flag, adopted in 1957, stands for the North Star.

St. Paul

In 1849 the town formerly known as Pig's Eye, after a local saloon, was made capital of the Minnesota territory. When Minnesota joined the Union in 1858, St. Paul became the state capital, developing rapidly as a river port and transportation center on the eastern bank of the Mississippi. Today it is a major manufacturing and distribution hub with industries ranging from computers and electronics, to printing and automobile assembly.

Minnesota at a Glance

People	Minnesota	USA
Population, 2003 estimate	5,059,375	290,809,777
Population percent change, April 1, 2000–July 1, 2001	1.1%	1.2%
Population, 2000	4,919,479	281,421,906
Persons under 5 years old, percent, 2000	6.7%	6.8%
Persons under 18 years old, percent, 2000	26.2%	25.7%
Persons 65 years old and over, percent, 2000	12.1%	12.4%
Female persons, percent, 2000	50.5%	50.9%
White persons, percent, 2000 (a)	89.4%	75.1%
African American persons, percent, 2000 (a)	3.5%	12.3%
Native American persons, percent, 2000 (a)	1.1%	0.9%
Asian persons, percent, 2000 (a)	2.9%	3.6%
Native Hawaiian and Other Pacific Islander, percent, 2000 (a)	Z	0.1%
Persons of Hispanic or Latino origin, percent, 2000 (b)	2.9%	12.5%
White persons, not of Hispanic/Latino origin, percent, 2000	88.2%	69.1%
Foreign born persons, percent, 2000	5.3%	11.1%
Language other than English spoken at home, percent age 5+, 2000	8.5%	17.9%
High school graduates, percent of persons age 25+, 2000	87.9%	80.4%
Bachelor's degree or higher, percent of persons age 25+, 2000	27.4%	24.4%
Persons with a disability, age 5+, 2000	679,236	49,746,248
Homeownership rate, 2000	74.6%	66.2%
Median value of owner-occupied housing units, 2000	$122,400	$119,600
Households, 2000	1,895,127	105,480,101
Persons per household, 2000	2.52	2.59
Median household money income, 1999	$47,111	$41,994
Per capita money income, 1999	$23,198	$21,587
Persons below poverty, percent, 1999	7.9%	12.4%

Business	Minnesota	USA
Private nonfarm establishments, 1999	137,305	7,008,444
Private nonfarm employment, 1999	2,338,642	110,705,661
Private nonfarm employment, percent change 1990–99	27.6%	18.4%
Nonemployer establishments, 1999	313,444	16,152,604
Manufacturers shipments, 1997 ($1,000)	76,244,894	3,842,061,405
Retail sales, 1997 ($1,000)	48,097,982	2,460,886,012
Retail sales per capita, 1997	$10,260	$9,190
Minority-owned firms, percent of total, 1997	3.7%	14.6%
Women-owned firms, percent of total, 1997	26.4%	26.0%
Federal funds and grants, 2001 ($1,000)	24,935,394	1,763,896,019
Local government employment – full-time equivalent, 1997	188,845	10,227,429

Geography	Minnesota	USA
Land area, 2000 (square miles)	79,610	3,537,438
Persons per square mile, 2000	61.8	79.6

(a) Includes persons reporting only one race.
(b) Hispanics may be of any race, so also are included in applicable race categories.
Z: Value greater than zero but less than half unit of measure shown.

Source: U.S. Census Bureau State & County QuickFacts

Mississippi

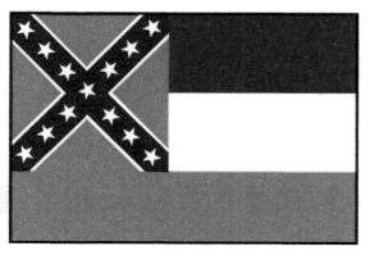

Statehood: December 10, 1817
Nickname: Magnolia State
State bird: Mockingbird
State flower: Magnolia
State tree: Magnolia
State motto: By valor and arms
State capital: Jackson
Population of capital: 184,256 (2000)

Hernando de Soto of Spain first wandered through the region in the early 1540s, but the French coastal settlements allowed them to claim the semitropical land on the Gulf of Mexico in 1682. Louisiana passed to the British after the French and Indian War and in 1798, when the U.S. government established the Territory of Mississippi, the Choctaw and other tribes were displaced by incoming settlers. The 29th state seceded from the Union in 1861 and was the site of several Civil War battles. Haunted by the legacy of slavery, racial segregation lasted until the 1960s, when the state was a focus of the civil rights movement. The capital and largest city is Jackson and other major cities are Meridian, Biloxi, Vicksburg, and Laurel. This low-lying state is broken into 82 counties.

The topography slopes westward from Alabama and the hills in the northeast to the delta, a fertile plain between the Mississippi and Yazoo Rivers. Pine forests cover most of the southern part of the state as far as the sandy coastal plain. Primarily an agricultural state, Mississippi is among the leading producers of cotton in the U.S. but hay, peanuts, pecans, rice and soybeans have grown in importance, as has dairy farming. Valuable reserves of oil and natural gas exist in small quantities. Other industries include clothing, wood products, and chemicals. Vicksburg National Military Park, Tupelo National Battlefield, the Mississippi Petrified Forest and the Natchez Trace Parkway are a few of the best-known landmarks.

The Mississippi flag, with three broad stripes of blue, white and red, still bears the confederate "southern cross" in the upper left corner. The stars stand for each of the eleven states in the Confederate States of America, in addition to Kentucky and Missouri. The flag was adopted in 1894.

Jackson

Located in southwestern Mississippi, Jason was established as a trading post in the 1790s by Louis LeFleur, a French Canadian. Later assuming the name of President Andrew Jackson, the city on the Pearl River was chosen as state capital in 1821. Glass, furniture, textiles, and more recently natural gas are some of the primary industries.

Mississippi at a Glance

People	Mississippi	USA
Population, 2003 estimate	2,881,281	290,809,777
Population percent change, April 1, 2000–July 1, 2001	0.5%	1.2%
Population, 2000	2,844,658	281,421,906
Persons under 5 years old, percent, 2000	7.2%	6.8%
Persons under 18 years old, percent, 2000	27.3%	25.7%
Persons 65 years old and over, percent, 2000	12.1%	12.4%
Female persons, percent, 2000	51.7%	50.9%
White persons, percent, 2000 (a)	61.4%	75.1%
African American persons, percent, 2000 (a)	36.3%	12.3%
Native American persons, percent, 2000 (a)	0.4%	0.9%
Asian persons, percent, 2000 (a)	0.7%	3.6%
Native Hawaiian and Other Pacific Islander, percent, 2000 (a)	Z	0.1%
Persons of Hispanic or Latino origin, percent, 2000 (b)	1.4%	12.5%
White persons, not of Hispanic/Latino origin, percent, 2000	60.7%	69.1%
Foreign born persons, percent, 2000	1.4%	11.1%
Language other than English spoken at home, percent age 5+, 2000	3.6%	17.9%
High school graduates, percent of persons age 25+, 2000	72.9%	80.4%
Bachelor's degree or higher, percent of persons age 25+, 2000	16.9%	24.4%
Persons with a disability, age 5+, 2000	607,570	49,746,248
Homeownership rate, 2000	72.3%	66.2%
Median value of owner-occupied housing units, 2000	$71,400	$119,600
Households, 2000	1,046,434	105,480,101
Persons per household, 2000	2.63	2.59
Median household money income, 1999	$31,330	$41,994
Per capita money income, 1999	$15,853	$21,587
Persons below poverty, percent, 1999	19.9%	12.4%
Business	**Mississippi**	**USA**
Private nonfarm establishments, 1999	59,834	7,008,444
Private nonfarm employment, 1999	948,883	110,705,661
Private nonfarm employment, percent change 1990–99	31.2%	18.4%
Nonemployer establishments, 1999	130,932	16,152,604
Manufacturers shipments, 1997 ($1,000)	39,658,260	3,842,061,405
Retail sales, 1997 ($1,000)	20,774,508	2,460,886,012
Retail sales per capita, 1997	$7,605	$9,190
Minority-owned firms, percent of total, 1997	13.1%	14.6%
Women-owned firms, percent of total, 1997	22.8%	26.0%
Federal funds and grants, 2001 ($1,000)	20,211,644	1,763,896,019
Local government employment – full-time equivalent, 1997	122,256	10,227,429
Geography	**Mississippi**	**USA**
Land area, 2000 (square miles)	46,907	3,537,438
Persons per square mile, 2000	60.6	79.6

(a) Includes persons reporting only one race.
(b) Hispanics may be of any race, so also are included in applicable race categories.
Z: Value greater than zero but less than half unit of measure shown.

Source: U.S. Census Bureau State & County QuickFacts

Missouri

Statehood: August 10, 1821
Nickname: "Show me" State
State bird: Eastern bluebird
State flower: Hawthorn
State tree: Flowering dogwood
State motto: The welfare of the people
State capital: Jefferson City
Population of capital: 39,636 (2000)

The French were the first Europeans to settle this area west of the Mississippi River in the mid-18th century, lured by stories from the Osage and Shawnee Indians of precious metals. In 1812, shortly after acquiring this midwestern region as part of the Louisiana Purchase, the U.S. government established the Missouri Territory, and it became a major corridor for westward migration. In 1821 Missouri was admitted to the Union without restrictions on slavery, where it remained throughout the prolonged conflict. A year before the violence of the Civil War bitterly divided the sympathies of its citizens the first Pony Express rider departed St. Joseph for California. St. Louis, Kansas City, Independence, Columbia and Springfield have the largest populations in this state of 114 counties.

Geographically, Missouri is divided into two parts: north of the Missouri River farmers grow corn, cotton and vegetables and raise livestock in prairie country. South of the river are the foothills and the Ozark Plateau. A small wheat-growing area is in the southwest and in the southeast the Missouri, Mississippi, and Ohio Rivers converge to create a floodplain crowded with cotton fields. The chief mineral resources are coal, lead, zinc, and iron ore. Missouri's economy is based on manufacturing for example, transportation equipment, food processing, chemicals, printing and publishing, fabricated metals, as well as electrical machinery. Wilson's Creek National Battlefield, George Washington Carver National Monument and the Harry S. Truman and Ulysses S. Grant National Historic Sites and the 630-foot Gateway Arch in St. Louis bring many sightseers to the "Show Me" state.

Demonstrating its loyalty to the Union, the Missouri state flag adopted a red, white and blue design in 1913. The coat of arms, placed in the center of the flag, shows two grizzly bears symbolizing strength and bravery supporting a shield with additional references to the state and the Federal government. Twenty-four stars around the seal signify Missouri's position as the 24th state.

Jefferson City

Chosen as state capital in 1821 and named after the nation's third president, Jefferson City lies on the Missouri River. The Capitol building (1911–18) contains a number of finely painted murals by Thomas Hart Benton and N. C. Wyeth. The production of shoes, clothing, dairy products, and electrical appliances drives the local economy.

Missouri at a Glance

People	Missouri	USA
Population, 2003 estimate	5,704,484	290,809,777
Population percent change, April 1, 2000–July 1, 2001	0.6%	1.2%
Population, 2000	5,595,211	281,421,906
Persons under 5 years old, percent, 2000	6.6%	6.8%
Persons under 18 years old, percent, 2000	25.5%	25.7%
Persons 65 years old and over, percent, 2000	13.5%	12.4%
Female persons, percent, 2000	51.4%	50.9%
White persons, percent, 2000 (a)	84.9%	75.1%
African American persons, percent, 2000 (a)	11.2%	12.3%
Native American persons, percent, 2000 (a)	0.4%	0.9%
Asian persons, percent, 2000 (a)	1.1%	3.6%
Native Hawaiian and Other Pacific Islander, percent, 2000 (a)	0.1%	0.1%
Persons of Hispanic or Latino origin, percent, 2000 (b)	2.1%	12.5%
White persons, not of Hispanic/Latino origin, percent, 2000	83.8%	69.1%
Foreign born persons, percent, 2000	2.7%	11.1%
Language other than English spoken at home, percent age 5+, 2000	5.1%	17.9%
High school graduates, percent of persons age 25+, 2000	81.3%	80.4%
Bachelor's degree or higher, percent of persons age 25+, 2000	21.6%	24.4%
Persons with a disability, age 5+, 2000	973,637	49,746,248
Homeownership rate, 2000	70.3%	66.2%
Median value of owner-occupied housing units, 2000	$89,900	$119,600
Households, 2000	2,194,594	105,480,101
Persons per household, 2000	2.48	2.59
Median household money income, 1999	$37,934	$41,994
Per capita money income, 1999	$19,936	$21,587
Persons below poverty, percent, 1999	11.7%	12.4%

Business	Missouri	USA
Private nonfarm establishments, 1999	144,874	7,008,444
Private nonfarm employment, 1999	2,350,965	110,705,661
Private nonfarm employment, percent change 1990–99	16.8%	18.4%
Nonemployer establishments, 1999	310,678	16,152,604
Manufacturers shipments, 1997 ($1,000)	93,115,478	3,842,061,405
Retail sales, 1997 ($1,000)	51,269,881	2,460,886,012
Retail sales per capita, 1997	$9,482	$9,190
Minority-owned firms, percent of total, 1997	6.5%	14.6%
Women-owned firms, percent of total, 1997	25.2%	26.0%
Federal funds and grants, 2001 ($1,000)	39,190,881	1,763,896,019
Local government employment – full-time equivalent, 1997	201,609	10,227,429

Geography	Missouri	USA
Land area, 2000 (square miles)	68,886	3,537,438
Persons per square mile, 2000	81.2	79.6

(a) Includes persons reporting only one race.
(b) Hispanics may be of any race, so also are included in applicable race categories.
Z: Value greater than zero but less than half unit of measure shown.

Source: U.S. Census Bureau State & County QuickFacts

Montana

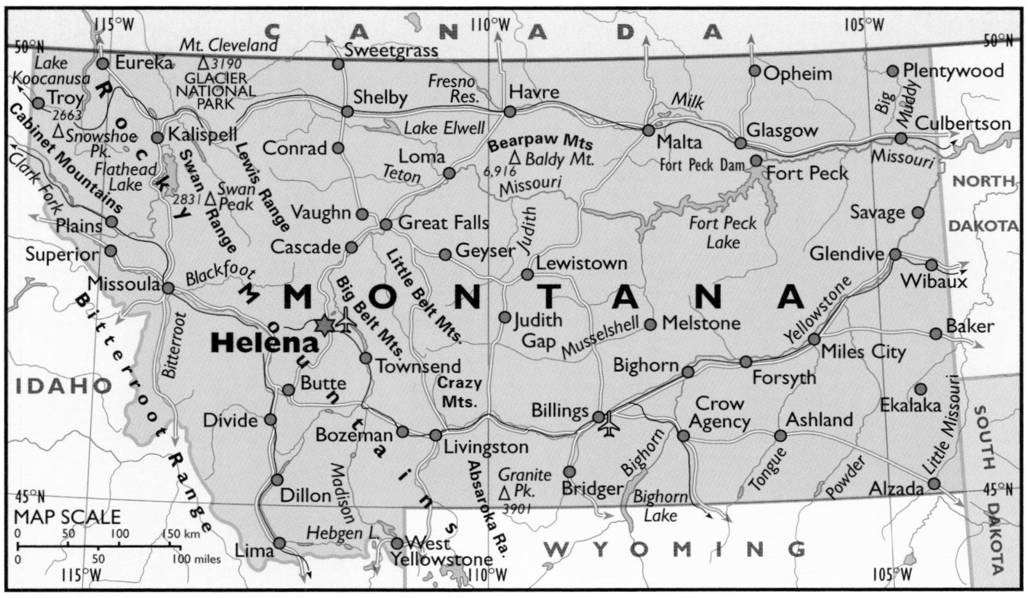

Statehood: November 8, 1889
Nickname: Treasure State
State bird: Western meadowlark
State flower: Bitterroot
State tree: Ponderosa pine
State motto: Gold and silver
State capital: Helena
Population of capital: 25,780 (2000)

Until the United States acquired this northwestern area in the Louisiana Purchase, Montana was relatively unexplored yet supported an array of indigenous cultures such as the Crow, Blackfoot, Cheyenne and Flathead. Although Lewis and Clark followed the Missouri River through the region en route to the Pacific Ocean in 1805, boomtowns did not appear until mid-century. The discovery of gold in 1852 brought a rush of immigrants and the Territory of Montana was organized in 1864. The opening of the Northern Pacific Railroad in 1883 provided a stimulus to further growth and development. With the exception of Billings, the other cities—Helena, Missoula and Great Falls—are concentrated in the west where some of the smallest of the 56 counties are also located.

The western section of Montana is dominated by dozens of mountain ranges, collectively called the Rocky Mountains, whereas the east is part of the Great Plains, drained by the Missouri and Yellowstone Rivers. Sheep and cattle are raised on the wide prairie (Big Sky Country), and the main crops: wheat, hay, barley, and sugar beet are grown in the same terrain using irrigation. The Rocky Mountains have large mineral deposits including copper, silver, gold, zinc, lead, and manganese. Oil, natural gas, and coal are found in the southeast. Industries include timber, food processing, and petroleum products but tourism is also important to the state economy. Yellowstone and Glacier National Park, as well as Custer Battlefield National Monument lure millions of visitors to Montana's frontier.

Beneath the word Montana against a blue background, the image of mountain peaks and the Great Falls alludes to the state's remote terrain. The centralized seal also contains mining and farming implements together with the Spanish state motto: *Oro y plata*.

Helena

Dubbed Last Chance by prospecting settlers in about 1864, Helena's population by 1868 had grown to 7,500 and $16 million worth of gold had been mined in the surrounding area. In 1875 this city in the western part of the state was made the capital of the Montana Territory, becoming the state capital in 1889. Mineral smelting is still a prominent industry here alongside the production of consumer goods, concrete and sheet metal products.

Montana at a Glance

People	**Montana**	**USA**
Population, 2003 estimate	917,621	290,809,777
Population percent change, April 1, 2000–July 1, 2001	0.2%	1.2%
Population, 2000	902,195	281,421,906
Persons under 5 years old, percent, 2000	6.1%	6.8%
Persons under 18 years old, percent, 2000	25.5%	25.7%
Persons 65 years old and over, percent, 2000	13.4%	12.4%
Female persons, percent, 2000	50.2%	50.9%
White persons, percent, 2000 (a)	90.6%	75.1%
African American persons, percent, 2000 (a)	0.3%	12.3%
Native American persons, percent, 2000 (a)	6.2%	0.9%
Asian persons, percent, 2000 (a)	0.5%	3.6%
Native Hawaiian and Other Pacific Islander, percent, 2000 (a)	0.1%	0.1%
Persons of Hispanic or Latino origin, percent, 2000 (b)	2.0%	12.5%
White persons, not of Hispanic/Latino origin, percent, 2000	89.5%	69.1%
Foreign born persons, percent, 2000	1.8%	11.1%
Language other than English spoken at home, percent age 5+, 2000	5.2%	17.9%
High school graduates, percent of persons age 25+, 2000	87.2%	80.4%
Bachelor's degree or higher, percent of persons age 25+, 2000	24.4%	24.4%
Persons with a disability, age 5+, 2000	145,732	49,746,248
Homeownership rate, 2000	69.1%	66.2%
Median value of owner-occupied housing units, 2000	$99,500	$119,600
Households, 2000	358,667	105,480,101
Persons per household, 2000	2.45	2.59
Median household money income, 1999	$33,024	$41,994
Per capita money income, 1999	$17,151	$21,587
Persons below poverty, percent, 1999	14.6%	12.4%
Business	**Montana**	**USA**
Private nonfarm establishments, 1999	31,365	7,008,444
Private nonfarm employment, 1999	288,358	110,705,661
Private nonfarm employment, percent change 1990–99	30.0%	18.4%
Nonemployer establishments, 1999	69,327	16,152,604
Manufacturers shipments, 1997 ($1,000)	4,866,279	3,842,061,405
Retail sales, 1997 ($1,000)	7,779,112	2,460,886,012
Retail sales per capita, 1997	$8,853	$9,190
Minority-owned firms, percent of total, 1997	3.6%	14.6%
Women-owned firms, percent of total, 1997	23.9%	26.0%
Federal funds and grants, 2001 ($1,000)	6,617,863	1,763,896,019
Local government employment – full-time equivalent, 1997	32,676	10,227,429
Geography	**Montana**	**USA**
Land area, 2000 (square miles)	145,552	3,537,438
Persons per square mile, 2000	6.2	79.6

(a) Includes persons reporting only one race.
(b) Hispanics may be of any race, so also are included in applicable race categories.
Z: Value greater than zero but less than half unit of measure shown.

Source: U.S. Census Bureau State & County QuickFacts

Nebraska

Statehood: March 1, 1867
Nickname: The Cornhusker State
State bird: Western meadowlark
State flower: Goldenrod
State tree: Cottonwood
State motto: Equality before the law
State capital: Lincoln
Population of capital: 225,581 (2000)

This region was acquired under the Louisiana Purchase of 1803 and was unexplored until the Lewis and Clark Expedition passed through the Great Plains in 1804. The Oto Indian word for the Platte River, *nebrathka*, meaning "flat water" appeared in publications shortly before the territory of Nebraska was officially created. By the time admittance to the Union occurred in 1867, hundreds of thousands of pioneers were using the Oregon Trail to cross the state on their way west. Omaha, the largest city, and the majority of the total population have remained near the Missouri River, which forms the eastern border with Iowa and Missouri. A few of the 93 counties in Nebraska take their names from tribes like the Cheyenne and the Pawnee that once roamed the vast grasslands.

The land rises gradually from the east to the foothills of the Rocky Mountains in the west, and is drained chiefly by the Platte River, a tributary of the Missouri. The eastern half of the state is devoted to agriculture where farmers grow grain and raise cattle and pigs. Nebraska's economy is overwhelmingly agricultural. Industries include food processing, oil, and sand, gravel, and stone quarrying. The Homestead, Scotts Bluff and Agate Fossil Beds National Monuments, and Chimney Rock National Historic Site, visible from miles away, are the main landmarks.

The state seal of Nebraska, in gold, rests on the blue field of the flag adopted in 1925. Inside the seal, a steamboat ascending the Missouri River, a smith with hammer and anvil, a settler's cabin, sheaves of wheat and stalks of corn, and finally a train heading towards the Rocky Mountains in the background symbolize the mechanical arts, agriculture and transportation. The state motto floats above the scene.

Lincoln

Founded in 1856 as Lancaster, its name was changed in honor of Abraham Lincoln. The city was made state capital when Nebraska joined the Union in 1867 and it is currently the second-largest city in the state. Home to the University of Nebraska, Lincoln is a center for livestock and grain, and more recently, finance and insurance. Food processing, automotive part production and construction material manufacturing are among the key industries based in and around Lincoln.

Nebraska at a Glance

People	Nebraska	USA
Population, 2003 estimate	1,739,291	290,809,777
Population percent change, April 1, 2000–July 1, 2001	0.1%	1.2%
Population, 2000	1,711,263	281,421,906
Persons under 5 years old, percent, 2000	6.8%	6.8%
Persons under 18 years old, percent, 2000	26.3%	25.7%
Persons 65 years old and over, percent, 2000	13.6%	12.4%
Female persons, percent, 2000	50.7%	50.9%
White persons, percent, 2000 (a)	89.6%	75.1%
African American persons, percent, 2000 (a)	4.0%	12.3%
Native American persons, percent, 2000 (a)	0.9%	0.9%
Asian persons, percent, 2000 (a)	1.3%	3.6%
Native Hawaiian and Other Pacific Islander, percent, 2000 (a)	Z	0.1%
Persons of Hispanic or Latino origin, percent, 2000 (b)	5.5%	12.5%
White persons, not of Hispanic/Latino origin, percent, 2000	87.3%	69.1%
Foreign born persons, percent, 2000	4.4%	11.1%
Language other than English spoken at home, percent age 5+, 2000	7.9%	17.9%
High school graduates, percent of persons age 25+, 2000	86.6%	80.4%
Bachelor's degree or higher, percent of persons age 25+, 2000	23.7%	24.4%
Persons with a disability, age 5+, 2000	250,534	49,746,248
Homeownership rate, 2000	67.4%	66.2%
Median value of owner-occupied housing units, 2000	$88,000	$119,600
Households, 2000	666,184	105,480,101
Persons per household, 2000	2.49	2.59
Median household money income, 1999	$39,250	$41,994
Per capita money income, 1999	$19,613	$21,587
Persons below poverty, percent, 1999	9.7%	12.4%
Business	**Nebraska**	**USA**
Private nonfarm establishments, 1999	48,968	7,008,444
Private nonfarm employment, 1999	733,905	110,705,661
Private nonfarm employment, percent change 1990–99	25.0%	18.4%
Nonemployer establishments, 1999	102,137	16,152,604
Manufacturers shipments, 1997 ($1,000)	27,859,177	3,842,061,405
Retail sales, 1997 ($1,000)	16,529,333	2,460,886,012
Retail sales per capita, 1997	$9,981	$9,190
Minority-owned firms, percent of total, 1997	3.3%	14.6%
Women-owned firms, percent of total, 1997	24.1%	26.0%
Federal funds and grants, 2001 ($1,000)	10,771,411	1,763,896,019
Local government employment – full-time equivalent, 1997	75,377	10,227,429
Geography	**Nebraska**	**USA**
Land area, 2000 (square miles)	76,872	3,537,438
Persons per square mile, 2000	22.3	79.6

(a) Includes persons reporting only one race.
(b) Hispanics may be of any race, so also are included in applicable race categories.
Z: Value greater than zero but less than half unit of measure shown.

Source: U.S. Census Bureau State & County QuickFacts

Nevada

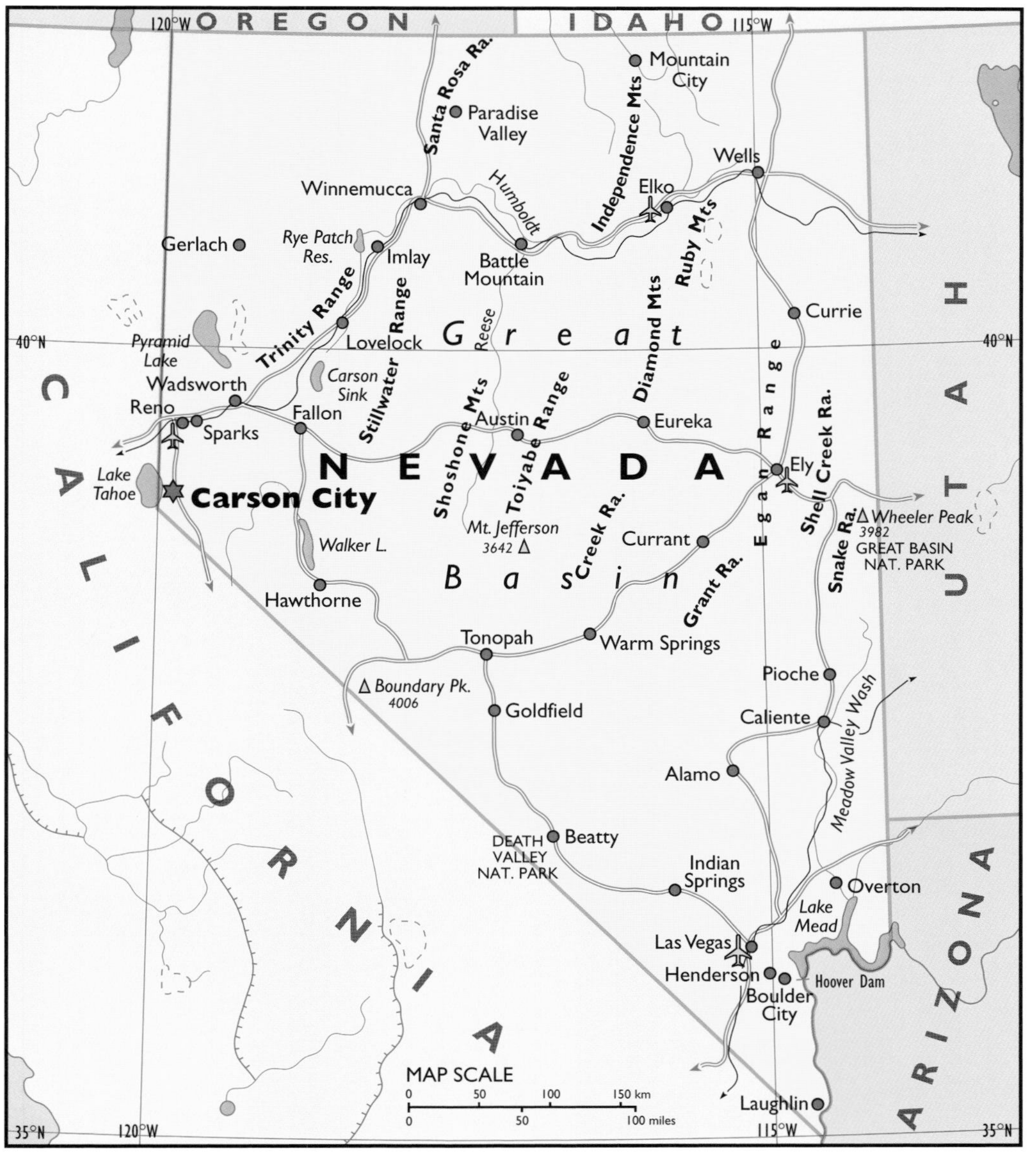

Statehood: October 31, 1864
Nickname: The Silver State
State bird: Mountain bluebird
State flower: Sagebrush
State tree: Pine nut
State motto: All for our country
State capital: Carson City
Population of capital: 52,547 (2000)

The United States acquired this western region in 1848 at the end of the Mexican War. When gold and silver were found in 1859, settlers flocked to the mountainous terrain inhabited by the Shoshone, Paiute and Washoe Indians. Nevada became the 36th state five years later. Mormon Station (now Genoa) just across the California border was the first permanent town, yet Las Vegas and Reno have evolved into the most populous cities since the legalization of gambling. Sixteen counties and the independent capital make up the state's administrative divisions.

Much of the state lies in the Great Basin, but the Sierra Nevada chain rises steeply from its western edge. Despite the Oasis created by Lake Mead in the southeast, Nevada's extremely dry climate and steep slopes have hindered the development of an agricultural economy. Hay and alfalfa are principal crops, sheep and cattle grazing are also important to the farming sector and additional wealth comes from mineral deposits of copper, lead, silver, gold, zinc, and tungsten. In Las Vegas and Reno, gambling and tourism provide the biggest source of revenue. Other less significant industries include chemicals, timber, electrical machinery, and glass products. In addition to glittering casinos, visitors are drawn to Nevada to see Lake Tahoe, the Hoover Dam, Great Basin National Park, and dusty, lonely ghost towns.

Nevada's blue flag displays a simple silver star, above which the words "Battle Born" allude to its entrance into the Union during the Civil War. The flag was adopted in 1929 and also depicts a half wreath of sagebrush, the state flower.

Carson City

The capital of Nevada, located south of Reno, grew rapidly after silver was discovered at the Comstock Lode in 1859. Nestled between Lake Tahoe and the Pine Nut Mountains, Carson City was named for Kit Carson, a legendary scout and frontiersman. Gambling is the main industry.

Nevada at a Glance

People	Nevada	USA
Population, 2003 estimate	2,241,154	290,809,777
Population percent change, April 1, 2000–July 1, 2001	5.4%	1.2%
Population, 2000	1,998,257	281,421,906
Persons under 5 years old, percent, 2000	7.3%	6.8%
Persons under 18 years old, percent, 2000	25.6%	25.7%
Persons 65 years old and over, percent, 2000	11.0%	12.4%
Female persons, percent, 2000	49.1%	50.9%
White persons, percent, 2000 (a)	75.2%	75.1%
African American persons, percent, 2000 (a)	6.8%	12.3%
Native American persons, percent, 2000 (a)	1.3%	0.9%
Asian persons, percent, 2000 (a)	4.5%	3.6%
Native Hawaiian and Other Pacific Islander, percent, 2000 (a)	0.4%	0.1%
Persons of Hispanic or Latino origin, percent, 2000 (b)	19.7%	12.5%
White persons, not of Hispanic/Latino origin, percent, 2000	65.2%	69.1%
Foreign born persons, percent, 2000	15.8%	11.1%
Language other than English spoken at home, percent age 5+, 2000	23.1%	17.9%
High school graduates, percent of persons age 25+, 2000	80.7%	80.4%
Bachelor's degree or higher, percent of persons age 25+, 2000	18.2%	24.4%
Persons with a disability, age 5+, 2000	375,910	49,746,248
Homeownership rate, 2000	60.9%	66.2%
Median value of owner-occupied housing units, 2000	$142,000	$119,600
Households, 2000	751,165	105,480,101
Persons per household, 2000	2.62	2.59
Median household money income, 1999	$44,581	$41,994
Per capita money income, 1999	$21,989	$21,587
Persons below poverty, percent, 1999	10.5%	12.4%

Business	Nevada	USA
Private nonfarm establishments, 1999	46,890	7,008,444
Private nonfarm employment, 1999	854,358	110,705,661
Private nonfarm employment, percent change 1990–99	59.2%	18.4%
Nonemployer establishments, 1999	106,416	16,152,604
Manufacturers shipments, 1997 ($1,000)	6,361,782	3,842,061,405
Retail sales, 1997 ($1,000)	18,220,790	2,460,886,012
Retail sales per capita, 1997	$10,874	$9,190
Minority-owned firms, percent of total, 1997	11.7%	14.6%
Women-owned firms, percent of total, 1997	25.7%	26.0%
Federal funds and grants, 2001 ($1,000)	9,623,557	1,763,896,019
Local government employment – full-time equivalent, 1997	56,607	10,227,429

Geography	Nevada	USA
Land area, 2000 (square miles)	109,826	3,537,438
Persons per square mile, 2000	18.2	79.6

(a) Includes persons reporting only one race.
(b) Hispanics may be of any race, so also are included in applicable race categories.
Z: Value greater than zero but less than half unit of measure shown.

Source: U.S. Census Bureau State & County QuickFacts

New Hampshire

Statehood: June 21, 1788
Nickname: The Granite State
State bird: Purple finch
State flower: Purple lilac
State tree: White birch
State motto: Live free or die
State capital: Concord
Population of capital: 40,687 (2000)

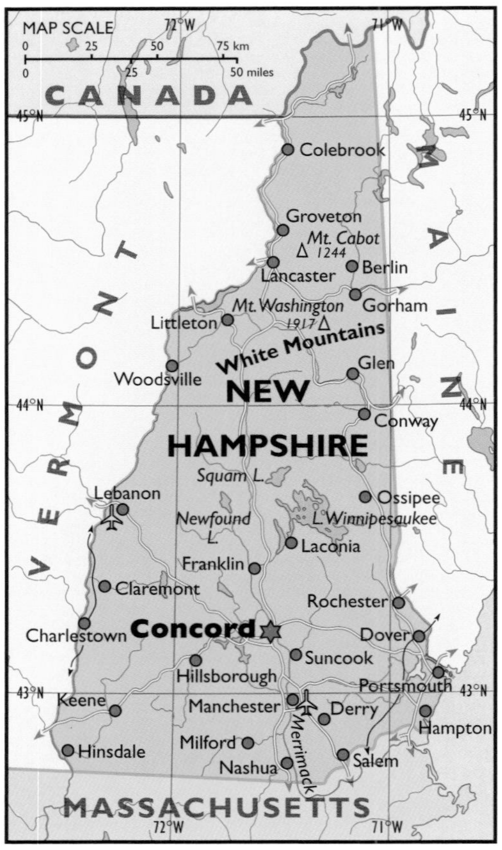

The first settlements in New Hampshire were made in 1623, along its small coastline. Early colonists interacted with the Pennacook and Abenaki tribes who relied on ocean resources for their way of life. Shipbuilding, weaving and granite mining brought the state considerable wealth in the 18th and 19th centuries and the beautifully restored mansions in the southeast reflect this prosperous period. In a state with just ten counties, Manchester and Nashua in the south are the largest cities.

Much of the land is mountainous and forested. Mount Washington, the tallest peak in the White Mountains, is known for its fierce winds, which have been recorded at speeds of over 200 miles per hour. The principal rivers are the Connecticut, which forms the border with Vermont, and the Merrimack, fed by countless smaller tributaries and more than 1,000 lakes. Characteristic of the northeast, farming is restricted by poor, stony soil and is mostly concentrated in the Connecticut Valley. Dairy and garden produce, hay, apples, and potatoes are the chief agricultural products. New Hampshire was formerly highly industrialized and relies on some hydroelectric power. Industries include electrical machinery, paper and wood products, printing and publishing, leather goods, and textiles. The Green Mountain Railroad, the Saint-Gaudens National Historic Site, and Canterbury Shaker Village encourage tourists to explore the history of the Granite State.

Surrounded by a wreath of laurel leaves and nine stars symbolizing its place as the 9th state to enter the United States, the seal appears in the center of the blue New Hampshire flag. Adopted in 1909, the centralized seal shows the frigate *Raleigh*, built at Portsmouth in 1776, one of the first 13 warships the Continental Congress commissioned for a new American navy.

Concord

Founded as a trading post on the Merrimack River, Concord was settled in 1727. It was the scene of New Hampshire's ratification of the Constitution as the ninth and deciding state in June of 1788, and designated state capital in 1808. Quarries north of the city produced the white granite used for the construction of the Library of Congress in Washington, D.C. and the Museum of Modern Art in New York City. A center for insurance and metal manufacturing, its industries include electrical equipment, publishing and printing.

New Hampshire at a Glance

People	New Hampshire	USA
Population, 2003 estimate	1,287,687	290,809,777
Population percent change, April 1, 2000–July 1, 2001	1.9%	1.2%
Population, 2000	1,235,786	281,421,906
Persons under 5 years old, percent, 2000	6.1%	6.8%
Persons under 18 years old, percent, 2000	25.0%	25.7%
Persons 65 years old and over, percent, 2000	12.0%	12.4%
Female persons, percent, 2000	50.8%	50.9%
White persons, percent, 2000 (a)	96.0%	75.1%
African American persons, percent, 2000 (a)	0.7%	12.3%
Native American persons, percent, 2000 (a)	0.2%	0.9%
Asian persons, percent, 2000 (a)	1.3%	3.6%
Native Hawaiian and Other Pacific Islander, percent, 2000 (a)	Z	0.1%
Persons of Hispanic or Latino origin, percent, 2000 (b)	1.7%	12.5%
White persons, not of Hispanic/Latino origin, percent, 2000	95.1%	69.1%
Foreign born persons, percent, 2000	4.4%	11.1%
Language other than English spoken at home, percent age 5+, 2000	8.3%	17.9%
High school graduates, percent of persons age 25+, 2000	87.4%	80.4%
Bachelor's degree or higher, percent of persons age 25+, 2000	28.7%	24.4%
Persons with a disability, age 5+, 2000	193,893	49,746,248
Homeownership rate, 2000	69.7%	66.2%
Median value of owner-occupied housing units, 2000	$133,300	$119,600
Households, 2000	474,606	105,480,101
Persons per household, 2000	2.53	2.59
Median household money income, 1999	$49,467	$41,994
Per capita money income, 1999	$23,844	$21,587
Persons below poverty, percent, 1999	6.5%	12.4%

Business	New Hampshire	USA
Private nonfarm establishments, 1999	37,180	7,008,444
Private nonfarm employment, 1999	528,902	110,705,661
Private nonfarm employment, percent change 1990–99	20.3%	18.4%
Nonemployer establishments, 1999	86,589	16,152,604
Manufacturers shipments, 1997 ($1,000)	19,813,107	3,842,061,405
Retail sales, 1997 ($1,000)	15,812,027	2,460,886,012
Retail sales per capita, 1997	$13,477	$9,190
Minority-owned firms, percent of total, 1997	2.8%	14.6%
Women-owned firms, percent of total, 1997	23.6%	26.0%
Federal funds and grants, 2001 ($1,000)	6,313,708	1,763,896,019
Local government employment – full-time equivalent, 1997	38,830	10,227,429

Geography	New Hampshire	USA
Land area, 2000 (square miles)	8,968	3,537,438
Persons per square mile, 2000	137.8	79.6

(a) Includes persons reporting only one race.
(b) Hispanics may be of any race, so also are included in applicable race categories.
Z: Value greater than zero but less than half unit of measure shown.

Source: U.S. Census Bureau State & County QuickFacts

New Jersey

Statehood: December 18, 1787
Nickname: The Garden State
State bird: Eastern goldfinch
State flower: Purple violet
State tree: Red oak
State motto: Liberty and prosperity
State capital: Trenton
Population of capital: 85,403 (2000)

Settlement of New Jersey, ancestral home of the Leni-Lenape Indians, began in the 1620s, when the Dutch founded the colony of New Netherland (later New York) on the Atlantic coast. In 1664, the British acquired the territory from the Netherlands, and separated the land between the Hudson and Delaware Rivers, naming it after the island of Jersey in the English Channel. The third state to ratify the Constitution in 1787, New Jersey introduced the world to the first steam-powered locomotive, the electric telegraph, the boardwalk, the picture postcard and the incandescent electric bulb. Divided into 21 counties, the state currently has one of the highest population densities in the U.S. with the majority of its citizens living in urban areas such as Newark, Elizabeth, Jersey City, and Paterson.

The Kittatinny Mountains in the north of the state form part of the Appalachian highland region and southeast of the Appalachians lie the fertile Piedmont plains. Pine and oak forests, cedar swamps and marshes characterize the southernmost section of the state. More than half of the state is coastal plain and the white sandy beaches of its barrier islands beckon vacationers each summer. The agricultural economy relies on variety of crops as well as cattle and poultry raising. New Jersey is overwhelmingly industrial, however, and chemicals, pharmaceuticals, rubber goods, textiles, electronic equipment, missile components, copper smelting, and oil refining number among the most important industries. Principal landmarks include the Delaware Water Gap, Edison National Historic Site, Morristown National Historic Park, and Pinelands National Reserve.

A variation of the state seal, the flag was adopted in 1896 and displays the coat of arms against a buff background. Three plows on the shield in the center symbolize agriculture, as does the horse head above. Ceres, the Roman goddess of grain, holding a cornucopia, and Liberty, carrying the liberty cap on her staff, stand on either side of the shield. The helmet denotes New Jersey's sovereignty and the banner beneath the coat of arms bears the year of independence along with the state motto.

Trenton

Located on the Delaware River, the state capital was first settled by English Quakers in the 1670s. The city takes its name from William Trent, a wealthy colonial merchant who became New Jersey's first Chief Justice in 1723. A monument in Trenton commemorates the 1776 battle in which George Washington crossed the frozen Delaware River to defeat Hessian troops during the American Revolution. Once thriving industries include ceramics, automobile parts, plastics, metal products, rubber goods, and textiles.

New Jersey at a Glance

People	**New Jersey**	**USA**
Population, 2003 estimate	8,638,396	290,809,777
Population percent change, April 1, 2000–July 1, 2001	0.8%	1.2%
Population, 2000	8,414,350	281,421,906
Persons under 5 years old, percent, 2000	6.7%	6.8%
Persons under 18 years old, percent, 2000	24.8%	25.7%
Persons 65 years old and over, percent, 2000	13.2%	12.4%
Female persons, percent, 2000	51.5%	50.9%
White persons, percent, 2000 (a)	72.6%	75.1%
African American persons, percent, 2000 (a)	13.6%	12.3%
Native American persons, percent, 2000 (a)	0.2%	0.9%
Asian persons, percent, 2000 (a)	5.7%	3.6%
Native Hawaiian and Other Pacific Islander, percent, 2000 (a)	Z	0.1%
Persons of Hispanic or Latino origin, percent, 2000 (b)	13.3%	12.5%
White persons, not of Hispanic/Latino origin, percent, 2000	66.0%	69.1%
Foreign born persons, percent, 2000	17.5%	11.1%
Language other than English spoken at home, percent age 5+, 2000	25.5%	17.9%
High school graduates, percent of persons age 25+, 2000	82.1%	80.4%
Bachelor's degree or higher, percent of persons age 25+, 2000	29.8%	24.4%
Persons with a disability, age 5+, 2000	1,389,811	49,746,248
Homeownership rate, 2000	65.6%	66.2%
Median value of owner-occupied housing units, 2000	$170,800	$119,600
Households, 2000	3,064,645	105,480,101
Persons per household, 2000	2.68	2.59
Median household money income, 1999	$55,146	$41,994
Per capita money income, 1999	$27,006	$21,587
Persons below poverty, percent, 1999	8.5%	12.4%
Business	**New Jersey**	**USA**
Private nonfarm establishments, 1999	231,823	7,008,444
Private nonfarm employment, 1999	3,440,721	110,705,661
Private nonfarm employment, percent change 1990–99	6.8%	18.4%
Nonemployer establishments, 1999	471,485	16,152,604
Manufacturers shipments, 1997 ($1,000)	97,060,800	3,842,061,405
Retail sales, 1997 ($1,000)	79,914,892	2,460,886,012
Retail sales per capita, 1997	$9,922	$9,190
Minority-owned firms, percent of total, 1997	15.6%	14.6%
Women-owned firms, percent of total, 1997	23.7%	26.0%
Federal funds and grants, 2001 ($1,000)	46,239,529	1,763,896,019
Local government employment – full-time equivalent, 1997	298,363	10,227,429
Geography	**New Jersey**	**USA**
Land area, 2000 (square miles)	7,417	3,537,438
Persons per square mile, 2000	1,134.4	79.6

(a) Includes persons reporting only one race.
(b) Hispanics may be of any race, so also are included in applicable race categories.
Z: Value greater than zero but less than half unit of measure shown.

Source: U.S. Census Bureau State & County QuickFacts

New Mexico

Statehood: January 16, 1912
Nickname: The Land of Enchantment
State bird: Roadrunner
State flower: Yucca flower
State tree: Pine nut
State motto: It grows as it goes
State capital: Santa Fe
Population of capital: 62,203 (2000)

Soon after Francisco Coronado crossed into present-day New Mexico in 1540, the first permanent Spanish settlers followed suit, competing with Navajo, Apache, Zuni, and Kiowa tribes for land. The U.S. acquired this southwestern region with the Mexican Cession and the Texas annexation, adding the last piece with the Gadsden Purchase in 1853. In 1912, New Mexico entered the Union as the 47th state. Heavily involved in energy research, the first atomic bomb was detonated near Alamogordo in 1945. Although Santa Fe gained its foothold in the north before Albuquerque, the metropolis on the river has surpassed the population of the capital city. Thirty-two counties divide the state.

The Sangre de Cristo and the Sierra Nacimiento Mountains in the north flank the Río Grande, which runs north to south through the state. Semiarid plains typify the south and southwest and the remaining terrain includes colorful desert, forested mountains, and stark mesa. The Pecos and Río Grande Rivers provide irrigation for fields of cotton, hay, and wheat. Dairy produce and chili peppers are also rather important to agriculture. A large proportion of the state's wealth comes from mineral deposits, including uranium, manganese, copper, silver, turquoise, oil, coal, and natural gas. Carlsbad Caverns National Park and Chaco Culture National Historic Park are perennially fascinating destinations for tourists.

Adopted in 1925, the New Mexico state flag borrows its red and yellow colors from Spain and the sun symbol from the Zia people. Four groups of four rays represent the cardinal directions, the seasons, the hours of the day, and the stages of life.

Santa Fe

The oldest capital city in the country, Santa Fe was founded at the foot of the Sangre de Cristo Mountains circa 1609 by the Spanish, and served as a center of trade for more than 200 years. Mexico's independence in 1821 opened trade with the United States and the city functioned as the western terminus of the Santa Fe Trail. In 1846, U.S. troops captured the city, and in 1850 the region became an official territory. Today, it is primarily an administrative, tourist, and resort center.

New Mexico at a Glance

People	New Mexico	USA
Population, 2003 estimate	1,874,614	290,809,777
Population percent change, April 1, 2000–July 1, 2001	0.6%	1.2%
Population, 2000	1,819,046	281,421,906
Persons under 5 years old, percent, 2000	7.2%	6.8%
Persons under 18 years old, percent, 2000	28.0%	25.7%
Persons 65 years old and over, percent, 2000	11.7%	12.4%
Female persons, percent, 2000	50.8%	50.9%
White persons, percent, 2000 (a)	66.8%	75.1%
African American persons, percent, 2000 (a)	1.9%	12.3%
Native American persons, percent, 2000 (a)	9.5%	0.9%
Asian persons, percent, 2000 (a)	1.1%	3.6%
Native Hawaiian and Other Pacific Islander, percent, 2000 (a)	0.1%	0.1%
Persons of Hispanic or Latino origin, percent, 2000 (b)	42.1%	12.5%
White persons, not of Hispanic/Latino origin, percent, 2000	44.7%	69.1%
Foreign born persons, percent, 2000	8.2%	11.1%
Language other than English spoken at home, percent age 5+, 2000	36.5%	17.9%
High school graduates, percent of persons age 25+, 2000	78.9%	80.4%
Bachelor's degree or higher, percent of persons age 25+, 2000	23.5%	24.4%
Persons with a disability, age 5+, 2000	338,430	49,746,248
Homeownership rate, 2000	70.0%	66.2%
Median value of owner-occupied housing units, 2000	$108,100	$119,600
Households, 2000	677,971	105,480,101
Persons per household, 2000	2.63	2.59
Median household money income, 1999	$34,133	$41,994
Per capita money income, 1999	$17,261	$21,587
Persons below poverty, percent, 1999	18.4%	12.4%

Business	New Mexico	USA
Private nonfarm establishments, 1999	42,918	7,008,444
Private nonfarm employment, 1999	541,386	110,705,661
Private nonfarm employment, percent change 1990–99	29.5%	18.4%
Nonemployer establishments, 1999	99,319	16,152,604
Manufacturers shipments, 1997 ($1,000)	17,906,091	3,842,061,405
Retail sales, 1997 ($1,000)	14,984,454	2,460,886,012
Retail sales per capita, 1997	$8,697	$9,190
Minority-owned firms, percent of total, 1997	28.5%	14.6%
Women-owned firms, percent of total, 1997	29.4%	26.0%
Federal funds and grants, 2001 ($1,000)	16,586,876	1,763,896,019
Local government employment – fulltime equivalent, 1997	69,941	10,227,429

Geography	New Mexico	USA
Land area, 2000 (square miles)	121,356	3,537,438
Persons per square mile, 2000	15	79.6

(a) Includes persons reporting only one race.
(b) Hispanics may be of any race, so also are included in applicable race categories.
Z: Value greater than zero but less than half unit of measure shown.

Source: U.S. Census Bureau State & County QuickFacts

New York

New York at a Glance

People	New York	USA
Population, 2003 estimate	19,190,115	290,809,777
Population percent change, April 1, 2000–July 1, 2001	0.2%	1.2%
Population, 2000	18,976,457	281,421,906
Persons under 5 years old, percent, 2000	6.5%	6.8%
Persons under 18 years old, percent, 2000	24.7%	25.7%
Persons 65 years old and over, percent, 2000	12.9%	12.4%
Female persons, percent, 2000	51.8%	50.9%
White persons, percent, 2000 (a)	67.9%	75.1%
African American persons, percent, 2000 (a)	15.9%	12.3%
Native American persons, percent, 2000 (a)	0.4%	0.9%
Asian persons, percent, 2000 (a)	5.5%	3.6%
Native Hawaiian and Other Pacific Islander, percent, 2000 (a)	Z	0.1%
Persons of Hispanic or Latino origin, percent, 2000 (b)	15.1%	12.5%
White persons, not of Hispanic/Latino origin, percent, 2000	62.0%	69.1%
Foreign born persons, percent, 2000	20.4%	11.1%
Language other than English spoken at home, percent age 5+, 2000	28.0%	17.9%
High school graduates, percent of persons age 25+, 2000	79.1%	80.4%
Bachelor's degree or higher, percent of persons age 25+, 2000	27.4%	24.4%
Persons with a disability, age 5+, 2000	3,606,147	49,746,248
Homeownership rate, 2000	53.0%	66.2%
Median value of owner-occupied housing units, 2000	$148,700	$119,600
Households, 2000	7,056,860	105,480,101
Persons per household, 2000	2.61	2.59
Median household money income, 1999	$43,393	$41,994
Per capita money income, 1999	$23,389	$21,587
Persons below poverty, percent, 1999	14.6%	12.4%

Business	New York	USA
Private nonfarm establishments, 1999	485,954	7,008,444
Private nonfarm employment, 1999	7,135,960	110,705,661
Private nonfarm employment, percent change 1990–99	0.9%	18.4%
Nonemployer establishments, 1999	1,168,595	16,152,604
Manufacturers shipments, 1997 ($1,000)	146,720,195	3,842,061,405
Retail sales, 1997 ($1,000)	139,303,944	2,460,886,012
Retail sales per capita, 1997	$7,678	$9,190
Minority-owned firms, percent of total, 1997	19.6%	14.6%
Women-owned firms, percent of total, 1997	26.1%	26.0%
Federal funds and grants, 2001 ($1,000)	116,366,112	1,763,896,019
Local government employment – full-time equivalent, 1997	860,168	10,227,429

Geography	New York	USA
Land area, 2000 (square miles)	47,214	3,537,438
Persons per square mile, 2000	401.9	79.6

(a) Includes persons reporting only one race.
(b) Hispanics may be of any race, so also are included in applicable race categories.
Z: Value greater than zero but less than half unit of measure shown.

Source: U.S. Census Bureau State & County QuickFacts

Statehood: July 26, 1788
Nickname: The Empire State
State bird: Bluebird
State flower: Rose
State tree: Sugar maple
State motto: Ever upward
State capital: Albany
Population of capital: 95,658 (2000)

Although Giovanni da Verrazano sailed past Manhattan Island in 1524, Henry Hudson explored New York Bay, and in 1609 sailed up the river that now bears his name. The Dutch established New Netherland colony in the Hudson Valley, but in 1664, this Algonquin and Iroquois land bounded by Canada, the Great Lakes and the Atlantic Ocean was seized by the British and renamed for the duke of York, eventually becoming one of the original Thirteen Colonies. The opening of the Erie Canal in 1825 was an enormous stimulus to New York's growth. New York City is by far the largest city in this state of 62 counties.

Much of the state is mountainous, the Adirondacks in the northeast and the Catskills in the southeast being the principal ranges. The west consists of the rolling Appalachian Plateau sloping down to Lake Ontario and the St. Lawrence River Valley. The Hudson and its tributary, the Mohawk, are the chief rivers. Throughout the history of the United States, New York's economic strength and large population have given it great influence in national affairs and for a time made it the leading manufacturing and commercial state in the country. Agricultural production concentrates on cattle, fruit and vegetable farming. Industries include clothing, chemicals, processed foods, communications, finance, advertising and publishing.

The coat of arms appears on the state flag against a dark blue background. Liberty and Justice flank a shield that bears an image of the sun rising over the Hudson. The eagle resting on a globe above the shield represents the western hemisphere and the crown at the feet of Liberty denotes independence from the English throne.

Albany

The Dutch settled here along the Hudson River in 1614 and Albany replaced New York as state capital in 1797. An administrative center with fine old buildings, it developed in the 1820s with the building of the Erie Canal, linking it to the Great Lakes, and remains an important river port. The largest industries are paper, brewing, machine tools, metal products, and textiles.

North Carolina

Statehood: November 21, 1789
Nickname: The Tar Heel State
State bird: Cardinal
State flower: Flowering dogwood
State tree: Pine
State motto: To be, rather than to seem
State capital: Raleigh
Population of capital: 276,093 (2000)

The first English colony in North America was founded in 1585 on Roanoke Island off the Atlantic coast of the eastern seaboard. Thwarted by a resistant native population, a second group of colonists had mysterious disappeared by the time a supply ship returned in 1590 and permanent settlers did not move into the region from Virginia until the 1650s. Finally subduing the Tuscarora and Roanoke Indians, among others, North Carolina was the 12th state to join the Union and the last state to secede. Coincidentally, brothers Wilbur and Orville Wright found success not far from this failed community, and watched as their flyer, the first powered aircraft, took flight in December of 1903 in Kitty Hawk. Charlotte, Winston-Salem, Greensboro, Wilmington and the Research Triangle encompassing Durham, Chapel Hill and Raleigh are the largest urban areas. The pine forests that still cover many of the state's 100 counties produced large quantities of tar, pitch and turpentine, as well as the unusual nickname.

North Carolina's low-lying coastal plain is characterized by swamps and forested dunes. Its hilly western edge rises steadily towards the Tennessee border to form the highest mountain ranges in the eastern U.S., the Blue Ridge and Great Smoky Mountains. The leading producer of tobacco in the U.S., North Carolina farms also raise corn, soybeans, peanuts, pigs, turkeys and chickens. Industries include textiles, timber, fishing, tourism, electrical machinery, and chemicals. Mineral

resources include phosphate, feldspar, mica and kaolin. Beaches along the Outer Banks, Cape Hatteras and Cape Lookout National Seashores, along with Blue Ridge National Parkway, Old Salem and Biltmore, the largest private home in the country, encourage tourism in North Carolina.

The two dates on the red, white and blue state flag adopted in 1885 display two declarations of independence. Above the white star is a gilt scroll reading May 20, 1775, when Mecklenberg County declared its independence from Great Britain. On April 12, 1776, North Carolina voted for independence at the Constitutional Convention.

Raleigh

Founded in the east central part of the state in 1792 as the capital, Raleigh was named for Sir Walter Raleigh, the poet, courtier and adventurer who fought against the Spanish Armada after colony on Roanoke Island failed. Historically at the center of the cotton and tobacco trade, its modern industries include food processing, textiles, chemicals, and electronic equipment. A number of colleges and universities cluster in and around Raleigh.

North Carolina at a Glance

People	North Carolina	USA
Population, 2003 estimate	8,407,248	290,809,777
Population percent change, April 1, 2000–July 1, 2001	1.7%	1.2%
Population, 2000	8,049,313	281,421,906
Persons under 5 years old, percent, 2000	6.7%	6.8%
Persons under 18 years old, percent, 2000	24.4%	25.7%
Persons 65 years old and over, percent, 2000	12.0%	12.4%
Female persons, percent, 2000	51.0%	50.9%
White persons, percent, 2000 (a)	72.1%	75.1%
African American persons, percent, 2000 (a)	21.6%	12.3%
Native American persons, percent, 2000 (a)	1.2%	0.9%
Asian persons, percent, 2000 (a)	1.4%	3.6%
Native Hawaiian and Other Pacific Islander, percent, 2000 (a)	Z	0.1%
Persons of Hispanic or Latino origin, percent, 2000 (b)	4.7%	12.5%
White persons, not of Hispanic/Latino origin, percent, 2000	70.2%	69.1%
Foreign born persons, percent, 2000	5.3%	11.1%
Language other than English spoken at home, percent age 5+, 2000	8.0%	17.9%
High school graduates, percent of persons age 25+, 2000	78.1%	80.4%
Bachelor's degree or higher, percent of persons age 25+, 2000	22.5%	24.4%
Persons with a disability, age 5+, 2000	1,540,365	49,746,248
Homeownership rate, 2000	69.4%	66.2%
Median value of owner-occupied housing units, 2000	$108,300	$119,600
Households, 2000	3,132,013	105,480,101
Persons per household, 2000	2.49	2.59
Median household money income, 1999	$39,184	$41,994
Per capita money income, 1999	$20,307	$21,587
Persons below poverty, percent, 1999	12.3%	12.4%
Business	**North Carolina**	**USA**
Private nonfarm establishments, 1999	201,706	7,008,444
Private nonfarm employment, 1999	3,324,155	110,705,661
Private nonfarm employment, percent change 1990–99	24.1%	18.4%
Nonemployer establishments, 1999	445,159	16,152,604
Manufacturers shipments, 1997 ($1,000)	161,900,477	3,842,061,405
Retail sales, 1997 ($1,000)	72,356,763	2,460,886,012
Retail sales per capita, 1997	$9,740	$9,190
Minority-owned firms, percent of total, 1997	10.8%	14.6%
Women-owned firms, percent of total, 1997	24.5%	26.0%
Federal funds and grants, 2001 ($1,000)	44,557,095	1,763,896,019
Local government employment – full-time equivalent, 1997	293,505	10,227,429
Geography	**North Carolina**	**USA**
Land area, 2000 (square miles)	48,711	3,537,438
Persons per square mile, 2000	165.2	79.6

(a) Includes persons reporting only one race.
(b) Hispanics may be of any race, so also are included in applicable race categories.
Z: Value greater than zero but less than half unit of measure shown.

Source: U.S. Census Bureau State & County QuickFacts

North Dakota & South Dakota

North Dakota

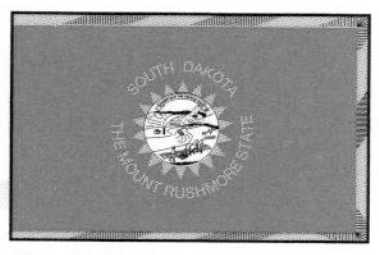
South Dakota

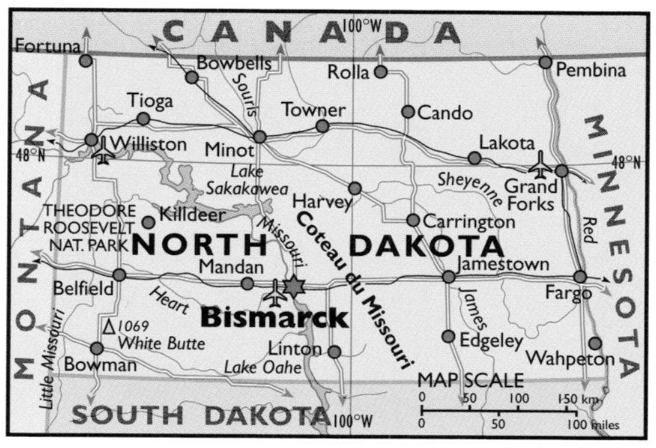

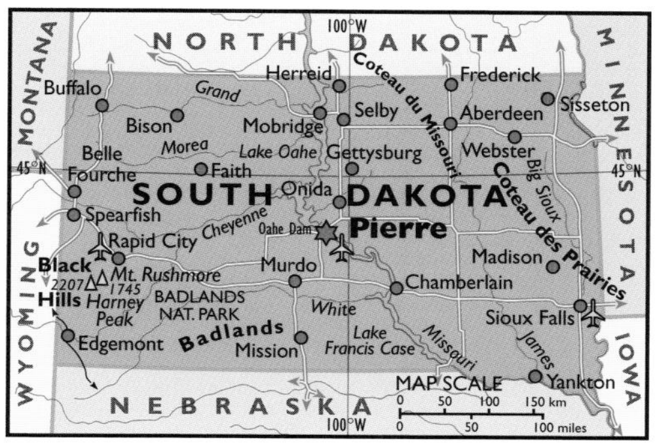

Statehood: November 2, 1889
Nickname: The Flickertail State
State bird: Western meadowlark
State flower: Wild prairie rose
State tree: American elm
State motto: Liberty and union, now and forever, one and inseparable
State capital: Bismarck
Population of capital: 55,532 (2000)

French explorers first ventured into the northern territory occupied by the Mandan, Hidatsa, Arikara and Sioux (Dakota) tribes in 1738. The United States acquired the western half of the area from France in the Louisiana Purchase, and the rest from Britain in 1818, when the boundary with Canada was fixed. Dakota was later divided into North and South Dakota, which both entered the Union in 1889. Fargo and Grand Forks, both just across the Minnesota state line, are the largest cities. North Dakota is divided into 53 counties. The region is low-lying and drained by the Missouri and Red Rivers. The most prominent geographical feature however is the windswept Badlands in the western part of the state. Wheat, barley, rye, oats, sunflowers, and flaxseed are the chief crops. Cattle raising, as well as coal, petroleum, and natural gas mining are key important economic activities.

Bismarck

Bismarck, overlooking the Missouri River, originated in the 1830s, became a distribution center for grain and cattle and was later an important stop on the Northern Pacific Railroad. By borrowing the name of the German Chancellor, residents hoped to attract German capital to use in railroad construction. Livestock raising, dairying, and woodworking are the largest employers. The University of Mary and Bismarck State College are also here, adding to the population.

Statehood: November 2, 1889
Nickname: The Sunshine State
State bird: Ring-necked pheasant
State flower: American pasqueflower
State tree: Black Hills spruce
State motto: Under God the people rule
State capital: Pierre
Population of capital: 13,876 (2000)

French trappers claimed this region on the northern Plains for France in the 1740s, and the U.S. acquired part of the land in 1803. The Dakota Territory was formed in 1861 and in 1874, the discovery of gold in the Black Hills led to an increase in population, subsequently causing the territory to be divided into two states. In 1890, the war that pitted Sioux and Cheyenne against the U.S. Army came to an end at Wounded Knee. Partitioned into 66 counties, today the largest populations can be found in Sioux Falls and Rapid City. The land rises gradually from the east to the Black Hills (featuring Mount Rushmore) in the west and the Badlands in the southwest, with the Missouri River bisecting the state. One-fifth of the area west of the Missouri River is semiarid plain, mostly covered by Native American Reservations, while the remainder is divided into large cattle and sheep ranches. Agriculture is a dominant economic activity; major crops include wheat, corn, oats, sunflowers and soybeans. The largest producer of gold in the country, South Dakota also mines tin, beryllium, stone, sand, and gravel. Industry is concentrated in meatpacking and food processing.

Pierre

Originally the capital of the Aricara Indians, and also on the Missouri River opposite Fort Pierre, Pierre started as a trading post in the early 19th century before being converted into a railroad terminus in 1880. It became the permanent state capital in 1904 and its economy is based on government services and agriculture.

The Dakotas at a Glance

People	ND	SD	USA
Population, 2003 estimate	633,837	764,309	290,809,777
Population percent change, April 1, 2000–July 1, 2001	–1.2%	0.2%	1.2%
Population, 2000	642,200	754,844	281,421,906
Persons under 5 years old, percent, 2000	6.1%	6.8%	6.8%
Persons under 18 years old, percent, 2000	25.0%	26.8%	25.7%
Persons 65 years old and over, percent, 2000	14.7%	14.3%	12.4%
Female persons, percent, 2000	50.1%	50.4%	50.9%
White persons, percent, 2000 (a)	92.4%	88.7%	75.1%
African American persons, percent, 2000 (a)	0.6%	0.6%	12.3%
Native American persons, percent, 2000 (a)	4.9%	8.3%	0.9%
Asian persons, percent, 2000 (a)	0.6%	0.6%	3.6%
Native Hawaiian and Other Pacific Islander, percent, 2000 (a)	Z	Z	0.1%
Persons of Hispanic or Latino origin, percent, 2000 (b)	1.2%	1.4%	12.5%
White persons, not of Hispanic/Latino origin, percent, 2000	91.7%	88.0%	69.1%
Foreign born persons, percent, 2000	1.9%	1.8%	11.1%
Language other than English spoken at home, percent age 5+, 2000	6.3%	6.5%	17.9%
High school graduates, percent of persons age 25+, 2000	83.9%	84.6%	80.4%
Bachelor's degree or higher, percent of persons age 25+, 2000	22.0%	21.5%	24.4%
Persons with a disability, age 5+, 2000	97,817	114,619	49,746,248
Homeownership rate, 2000	66.6%	68.2%	66.2%
Median value of owner-occupied housing units, 2000	$74,400	$79,600	$119,600
Households, 2000	257,152	290,245	105,480,101
Persons per household, 2000	2.41	2.5	2.59
Median household money income, 1999	$34,604	$35,282	$41,994
Per capita money income, 1999	$17,769	$17,562	$21,587
Persons below poverty, percent, 1999	11.9%	13.2%	12.4%
Business	**ND**	**SD**	**USA**
Private nonfarm establishments, 1999	20,380	23,693	7,008,444
Private nonfarm employment, 1999	250,292	295,139	110,705,661
Private nonfarm employment, percent change 1990–99	27.3%	37.2%	18.4%
Nonemployer establishments, 1999	38,921	47,469	16,152,604
Manufacturers shipments, 1997 ($1,000)	5,115,890	12,305,468	3,842,061,405
Retail sales, 1997 ($1,000)	6,702,134	11,707,133	2,460,886,012
Retail sales per capita, 1997	$10,457	$16,018	$9,190
Minority-owned firms, percent of total, 1997	2.8%	2.5%	14.6%
Women-owned firms, percent of total, 1997	22.5%	21.5%	26.0%
Federal funds and grants, 2001 ($1,000)	5,948,331	5,806,982	1,763,896,019
Local government employment – full-time equivalent, 1997	21,221	26,567	10,227,429
Geography	**ND**	**SD**	**USA**
Land area, 2000 (square miles)	68,976	75,885	3,537,438
Persons per square mile, 2000	9.3	9.9	79.6

(a) Includes persons reporting only one race.
(b) Hispanics may be of any race, so also are included in applicable race categories.
Z: Value greater than zero but less than half unit of measure shown.

Source: U.S. Census Bureau State & County QuickFacts

Ohio

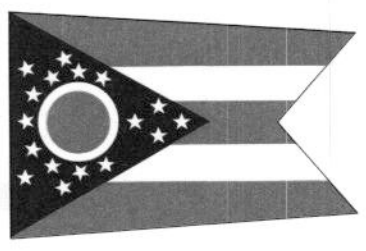

Statehood: March 1, 1803
Nickname: The Buckeye State
State bird: Cardinal
State flower: Scarlet carnation
State tree: Buckeye
State motto: With God, all things are possible
State capital: Columbus
Population of capital: 711,470 (2000)

As the first residents of Ohio, the Hopewell and Adena people built elaborate earthen mounds resembling animals and geometric shapes. The British likely encountered examples of ancient architecture when they acquired the land south of Lake Erie at the end of the French and Indian War. Ceded to the U.S. after the American Revolution, Ohio became part of Northwest Territory in 1787, joining the Union in 1803. Heavy migration from New England in the 19th century allowed industry to take hold, and railways and factories soon interrupted rural landscapes. The largest cities in this state of 88 counties include Columbus, the capital, along with Cleveland, Cincinnati, Toledo, Akron and Dayton.

Mostly low-lying with wooded hills in the south, the Buckeye State is intersected by numerous rivers, chiefly the Ohio, Scioto, Miami and Muskingum. Ohio's larger farms produce hay, corn, wheat, soybeans, and dairy foods, and cattle and pigs are raised. The state is highly industrialized and Ohio produces sandstone, oil, natural gas, clay, salt, lime, and gravel. Its lake ports handle large amounts of copper ore, coal and oil. Industries include vehicle and aircraft manufacturing, transportation equipment, and primary and fabricated metals. Cedar Point, the Rock and Roll Hall of Fame, the Cuyahoga Valley National Recreation Area, the homes of several presidents and numerous acclaimed museums number among the most popular tourist attractions.

The only state with a two-pointed pennant, Ohio adopted its unique flag in 1902. Seventeen stars represent Ohio as the 17th state, while the white "O," set against a blue field, stands for both the Buckeye and the Native American name of the state. The colors were chosen to match the stars and stripes of Old Glory, the flag of the United States.

Columbus

Founded in 1812, Columbus grew rapidly alongside the Scioto River with the arrival of the railroad in 1850. A major transport, industrial and trading center for a rich agricultural region, Columbus also has numerous universities and colleges including Ohio State University. The Battelle Memorial Institute (1929) conducts scientific, technological and economic research. The home offices of many machinery, aircraft, printing and publishing industries can be found in Columbus.

Ohio at a Glance

People	Ohio	USA
Population, 2003 estimate	11,435,798	290,809,777
Population percent change, April 1, 2000–July 1, 2001	0.2%	1.2%
Population, 2000	11,353,140	281,421,906
Persons under 5 years old, percent, 2000	6.6%	6.8%
Persons under 18 years old, percent, 2000	25.4%	25.7%
Persons 65 years old and over, percent, 2000	13.3%	12.4%
Female persons, percent, 2000	51.4%	50.9%
White persons, percent, 2000 (a)	85.0%	75.1%
African American persons, percent, 2000 (a)	11.5%	12.3%
Native American persons, percent, 2000 (a)	0.2%	0.9%
Asian persons, percent, 2000 (a)	1.2%	3.6%
Native Hawaiian and Other Pacific Islander, percent, 2000 (a)	Z	0.1%
Persons of Hispanic or Latino origin, percent, 2000 (b)	1.9%	12.5%
White persons, not of Hispanic/Latino origin, percent, 2000	84.0%	69.1%
Foreign born persons, percent, 2000	3.0%	11.1%
Language other than English spoken at home, percent age 5+, 2000	6.1%	17.9%
High school graduates, percent of persons age 25+, 2000	83.0%	80.4%
Bachelor's degree or higher, percent of persons age 25+, 2000	21.1%	24.4%
Persons with a disability, age 5+, 2000	1,909,489	49,746,248
Homeownership rate, 2000	69.1%	66.2%
Median value of owner-occupied housing units, 2000	$103,700	$119,600
Households, 2000	4,445,773	105,480,101
Persons per household, 2000	2.49	2.59
Median household money income, 1999	$40,956	$41,994
Per capita money income, 1999	$21,003	$21,587
Persons below poverty, percent, 1999	10.6%	12.4%
Business	**Ohio**	**USA**
Private nonfarm establishments, 1999	270,766	7,008,444
Private nonfarm employment, 1999	4,867,368	110,705,661
Private nonfarm employment, percent change 1990–99	14.6%	18.4%
Nonemployer establishments, 1999	591,150	16,152,604
Manufacturers shipments, 1997 ($1,000)	241,902,924	3,842,061,405
Retail sales, 1997 ($1,000)	102,938,830	2,460,886,012
Retail sales per capita, 1997	$9,181	$9,190
Minority-owned firms, percent of total, 1997	6.3%	14.6%
Women-owned firms, percent of total, 1997	26.2%	26.0%
Federal funds and grants, 2001 ($1,000)	61,704,785	1,763,896,019
Local government employment – full-time equivalent, 1997	421,092	10,227,429
Geography	**Ohio**	**USA**
Land area, 2000 (square miles)	40,948	3,537,438
Persons per square mile, 2000	277.3	79.6

(a) Includes persons reporting only one race.
(b) Hispanics may be of any race, so also are included in applicable race categories.
Z: Value greater than zero but less than half unit of measure shown.

Source: U.S. Census Bureau State & County QuickFacts

Oklahoma

Statehood: November 16, 1907
Nickname: The Sooner State
State bird: Scissor-tailed flycatcher
State flower: Mistletoe
State tree: Redbud
State motto: Labor conquers all things
State capital: Oklahoma City
Population of capital: 506,132 (2000)

Formerly hunting grounds for the Osage, Arapaho, Comanche and Apache tribes, much of the area that would become Oklahoma was acquired by the U.S. from France in the Louisiana Purchase of 1803. Designated as an Indian territory in 1834, hundreds of thousands of Native Americans living east of the Mississippi were relocated to Oklahoma. In 1889, after the discovery of valuable oil and coal deposits, and pressured by a rapidly expanding population, the government sponsored a land rush. Desperate for fields to farm, thousands of homesteaders clamored to claim parcels of land shortly after noon on April 22nd. The Sooners, as people who jumped the gun were called, earned the state the nickname that lasts to this day. In the 1930s, the newly formed state was one of those hardest hit by the Dust Bowl phenomenon. Apart from Oklahoma City, the other important city is Tulsa. Seventy-seven counties break the state into administrative divisions.

Starting with Black Mesa in the western panhandle, which scrapes against the foothills of the Rockies, Oklahoma extends across the Great Plains to the Ouachita Mountains and their numerous lakes, spilling over the state boundary from neighboring Arkansas. The river by the same name, running through the northeastern corner of the state and the Red River, forming the southern border with Texas, are Oklahoma's main waterways. Wheat and cotton are the leading crops, but livestock generates more revenue and the capital city continues to be one of the world's largest cattle markets. Although many minerals exist within Oklahoma's borders, oil and natural gas form the basis of Oklahoma's economic wealth. Landmarks include the Chicksaw National Recreation Area, the National Cowboy Hall of Fame, the Will Rogers Home and Memorial and the Cherokee Cultural Center.

A calumet pipe and an olive branch, symbols of peace, cross an Osage warrior's shield on the state flag. Set against a sky blue background, the shield is adorned with eagle feathers and small crosses that represent stars. Oklahoma's flag was adopted in 1925.

Oklahoma City

The capital and largest city of Oklahoma is located in the center of the state on the North Canadian River. The area was settled in 1889 and the city made the state capital in 1910, prospering with the discovery of one of the country's richest oil deposits in 1928. It was the site of a terrorist bomb in April 1995, which killed 168 people and injured 400 others. Industries include oil-refining, meatpacking, grain milling, cotton processing, steel products, electronic equipment, and aircraft manufacturing.

Oklahoma at a Glance

People	Oklahoma	USA
Population, 2003 estimate	3,511,532	290,809,777
Population percent change, April 1, 2000–July 1, 2001	0.3%	1.2%
Population, 2000	3,450,654	281,421,906
Persons under 5 years old, percent, 2000	6.8%	6.8%
Persons under 18 years old, percent, 2000	25.9%	25.7%
Persons 65 years old and over, percent, 2000	13.2%	12.4%
Female persons, percent, 2000	50.9%	50.9%
White persons, percent, 2000 (a)	76.2%	75.1%
African American persons, percent, 2000 (a)	7.6%	12.3%
Native American persons, percent, 2000 (a)	7.9%	0.9%
Asian persons, percent, 2000 (a)	1.4%	3.6%
Native Hawaiian and Other Pacific Islander, percent, 2000 (a)	0.1%	0.1%
Persons of Hispanic or Latino origin, percent, 2000 (b)	5.2%	12.5%
White persons, not of Hispanic/Latino origin, percent, 2000	74.1%	69.1%
Foreign born persons, percent, 2000	3.8%	11.1%
Language other than English spoken at home, percent age 5+, 2000	7.4%	17.9%
High school graduates, percent of persons age 25+, 2000	80.6%	80.4%
Bachelor's degree or higher, percent of persons age 25+, 2000	20.3%	24.4%
Persons with a disability, age 5+, 2000	676,098	49,746,248
Homeownership rate, 2000	68.4%	66.2%
Median value of owner-occupied housing units, 2000	$70,700	$119,600
Households, 2000	1,342,293	105,480,101
Persons per household, 2000	2.49	2.59
Median household money income, 1999	$33,400	$41,994
Per capita money income, 1999	$17,646	$21,587
Persons below poverty, percent, 1999	14.7%	12.4%
Business	**Oklahoma**	**USA**
Private nonfarm establishments, 1999	84,854	7,008,444
Private nonfarm employment, 1999	1,171,356	110,705,661
Private nonfarm employment, percent change 1990–99	24.5%	18.4%
Nonemployer establishments, 1999	217,991	16,152,604
Manufacturers shipments, 1997 ($1,000)	37,453,197	3,842,061,405
Retail sales, 1997 ($1,000)	27,065,555	2,460,886,012
Retail sales per capita, 1997	$8,166	$9,190
Minority-owned firms, percent of total, 1997	10.2%	14.6%
Women-owned firms, percent of total, 1997	24.0%	26.0%
Federal funds and grants, 2001 ($1,000)	22,671,563	1,763,896,019
Local government employment – full-time equivalent, 1997	129,462	10,227,429
Geography	**Oklahoma**	**USA**
Land area, 2000 (square miles)	68,667	3,537,438
Persons per square mile, 2000	50.3	79.6

(a) Includes persons reporting only one race.
(b) Hispanics may be of any race, so also are included in applicable race categories.
Z: Value greater than zero but less than half unit of measure shown.

Source: U.S. Census Bureau State & County QuickFacts

Oregon

Statehood: February 14, 1859
Nickname: The Beaver State
State bird: Western meadowlark
State flower: Oregon grape
State tree: Douglas fir
State motto: She flies with her own wings
State capital: Salem
Population of capital: 136,924 (2000)

The Hudson Bay Company set up outposts here on the Pacific coast in the 1790s, and from 1842, the fur trade and the Oregon Trail brought more settlers. The Oregon Territory was formed in 1848, and was admitted to the Union in 1859. The major cities, Portland and Eugene, as well as the state capital line up along the Willamette River in the northwest. Some of the state's 36 counties, such as Tillamook and Umatilla, take the name of the indigenous people who inhabited them before European explorers arrived.

The Columbia River to the north marks the boundary with Washington, while the Columbia Plateau in the east separates the state from neighboring Idaho. The forested slopes of the Coast Ranges and the Cascade Range, containing Mt. Hood, the highest peak, dominate the state. Between the two lies the fertile Willamette Valley. Agricultural revenue comes from cattle, dairy produce, wheat, fruit and salmon farming. Oregon's coastal conifers produce more than twenty percent of the softwood timber logged in the United States. Whereas the Oregon Trail brought many pioneers to the state in the 19th century, Crater Lake National Park, the John Day Fossil Beds and the Oregon Shakespeare Festival bring tourists to Oregon today.

The 33 stars around the seal on the blue state flag signify that Oregon was the 33rd state. Adopted in 1925, the blue flag has a different image on each side. The shield on the front depicts the setting sun over the Pacific, a plow, a pickaxe and wheat, symbols of the state's natural resources, and a covered wagon emerging from a forest. A beaver, the state animal appears on the reverse.

Salem

Founded in 1840 by Methodist missionaries, Salem was made territorial capital in 1851 and state capital in 1859. The industries clustered here on the Willamette River include timber, paper, textiles, food canning, meat packing, and high-technology equipment.

Oregon at a Glance

People	Oregon	USA
Population, 2003 estimate	3,559,596	290,809,777
Population percent change, April 1, 2000–July 1, 2001	1.5%	1.2%
Population, 2000	3,421,399	281,421,906
Persons under 5 years old, percent, 2000	6.5%	6.8%
Persons under 18 years old, percent, 2000	24.7%	25.7%
Persons 65 years old and over, percent, 2000	12.8%	12.4%
Female persons, percent, 2000	50.4%	50.9%
White persons, percent, 2000 (a)	86.6%	75.1%
African American persons, percent, 2000 (a)	1.6%	12.3%
Native American persons, percent, 2000 (a)	1.3%	0.9%
Asian persons, percent, 2000 (a)	3.0%	3.6%
Native Hawaiian and Other Pacific Islander, percent, 2000 (a)	0.2%	0.1%
Persons of Hispanic or Latino origin, percent, 2000 (b)	8.0%	12.5%
White persons, not of Hispanic/Latino origin, percent, 2000	83.5%	69.1%
Foreign born persons, percent, 2000	8.5%	11.1%
Language other than English spoken at home, percent age 5+, 2000	12.1%	17.9%
High school graduates, percent of persons age 25+, 2000	85.1%	80.4%
Bachelor's degree or higher, percent of persons age 25+, 2000	25.1%	24.4%
Persons with a disability, age 5+, 2000	593,301	49,746,248
Homeownership rate, 2000	64.3%	66.2%
Median value of owner-occupied housing units, 2000	$152,100	$119,600
Households, 2000	1,333,723	105,480,101
Persons per household, 2000	2.51	2.59
Median household money income, 1999	$40,916	$41,994
Per capita money income, 1999	$20,940	$21,587
Persons below poverty, percent, 1999	11.6%	12.4%

Business	Oregon	USA
Private nonfarm establishments, 1999	99,945	7,008,444
Private nonfarm employment, 1999	1,332,403	110,705,661
Private nonfarm employment, percent change 1990–99	31.0%	18.4%
Nonemployer establishments, 1999	212,334	16,152,604
Manufacturers shipments, 1997 ($1,000)	47,665,990	3,842,061,405
Retail sales, 1997 ($1,000)	33,396,849	2,460,886,012
Retail sales per capita, 1997	$10,297	$9,190
Minority-owned firms, percent of total, 1997	6.2%	14.6%
Women-owned firms, percent of total, 1997	27.6%	26.0%
Federal funds and grants, 2001 ($1,000)	18,401,222	1,763,896,019
Local government employment – full-time equivalent, 1997	117,999	10,227,429

Geography	Oregon	USA
Land area, 2000 (square miles)	95,997	3,537,438
Persons per square mile, 2000	35.6	79.6

(a) Includes persons reporting only one race.
(b) Hispanics may be of any race, so also are included in applicable race categories.
Z: Value greater than zero but less than half unit of measure shown.

Source: U.S. Census Bureau State & County QuickFacts

Pennsylvania

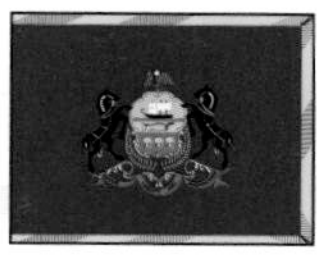

Statehood: December 12, 1787
Nickname: The Keystone State
State bird: Ruffed grouse
State flower: Mountain laurel
State tree: Hemlock
State motto: Virtue, liberty, and independence
State capital: Harrisburg
Population of capital: 48,950 (2000)

Swedish and Dutch settlements were made in the Middle Atlantic along the Delaware River in the mid-17th century but by 1664, the English controlled the area. William Penn received a charter from Charles II for the region and chose a Latin name, "Penn's Woods." One of the 13 original states, the Declaration of Independence was signed and the Constitution ratified in Philadelphia, which was also the national capital from 1790 to 1800. The Union victory at the Battle of Gettysburg in July 1863 was a turning point in the Civil War. The Keystone State introduced the first labor union, the first commercial oil well and the first limited access expressway in the United States. Pennsylvania's large population is concentrated in its largest cities: Philadelphia, Pittsburgh, Scranton, Allentown, Lancaster, Erie and Harrisburg. Sixty-seven counties fall within the state's borders.

Apart from small low-lying areas in the northwest and southeast, Pennsylvania is composed of mountain ridges and rolling hills with narrow valleys. The Delaware, Susquehanna and Allegheny Rivers are the longest in the state. Farming is concentrated to the south and east of the Alleghenies and the Appalachians where the principal crops are cereals, tobacco, potatoes, and fruit, besides some dairy farming. Pennsylvania has rich deposits of coal and iron ore and has long been a producer of steel, which today accounts for a decreasing percentage of the country's total output. Industries include chemicals, cement, electrical machinery, and metal goods. With an abundance of historic places, Gettysburg National Military Park, Valley Forge National Historic Park, Steamtown National Historic Site, and Independence National Park in Philadelphia are just some of the top attractions.

The Pennsylvania State Legislature adopted its flag in 1907. It displays the coat of arms on a blue background held by two horses and an eagle. Within the seal a tall ship, a plow and three bundles of wheat are pictured. A stalk of corn and an olive branch appear above the state motto.

Harrisburg

John Harris built a trading post here on the Susquehanna River in 1718, and by 1785 his son had established a town. Later the scene of the Harrisburg Convention, it became the state capital in 1812. When a disaster at the Three Mile Island power plant was narrowly avoided in 1979, the U.S. reassessed its nuclear safety standards. The local textile, machinery, and electronic equipment industries are no longer overshadowed by the chocolate production in nearby Hershey.

Pennsylvania at a Glance

People	**Pennsylvania**	**USA**
Population, 2003 estimate	12,365,455	290,809,777
Population percent change, April 1, 2000–July 1, 2001	0.0%	1.2%
Population, 2000	12,281,054	281,421,906
Persons under 5 years old, percent, 2000	5.9%	6.8%
Persons under 18 years old, percent, 2000	23.8%	25.7%
Persons 65 years old and over, percent, 2000	15.6%	12.4%
Female persons, percent, 2000	51.7%	50.9%
White persons, percent, 2000 (a)	85.4%	75.1%
African American persons, percent, 2000 (a)	10.0%	12.3%
Native American persons, percent, 2000 (a)	0.1%	0.9%
Asian persons, percent, 2000 (a)	1.8%	3.6%
Native Hawaiian and Other Pacific Islander, percent, 2000 (a)	Z	0.1%
Persons of Hispanic or Latino origin, percent, 2000 (b)	3.2%	12.5%
White persons, not of Hispanic/Latino origin, percent, 2000	84.1%	69.1%
Foreign born persons, percent, 2000	4.1%	11.1%
Language other than English spoken at home, percent age 5+, 2000	8.4%	17.9%
High school graduates, percent of persons age 25+, 2000	81.9%	80.4%
Bachelor's degree or higher, percent of persons age 25+, 2000	22.4%	24.4%
Persons with a disability, age 5+, 2000	2,111,771	49,746,248
Homeownership rate, 2000	71.3%	66.2%
Median value of owner-occupied housing units, 2000	$97,000	$119,600
Households, 2000	4,777,003	105,480,101
Persons per household, 2000	2.48	2.59
Median household money income, 1999	$40,106	$41,994
Per capita money income, 1999	$20,880	$21,587
Persons below poverty, percent, 1999	11.0%	12.4%
Business	**Pennsylvania**	**USA**
Private nonfarm establishments, 1999	293,491	7,008,444
Private nonfarm employment, 1999	4,986,591	110,705,661
Private nonfarm employment, percent change 1990–99	8.4%	18.4%
Nonemployer establishments, 1999	614,594	16,152,604
Manufacturers shipments, 1997 ($1,000)	172,193,216	3,842,061,405
Retail sales, 1997 ($1,000)	109,948,462	2,460,886,012
Retail sales per capita, 1997	$9,150	$9,190
Minority-owned firms, percent of total, 1997	5.9%	14.6%
Women-owned firms, percent of total, 1997	24.2%	26.0%
Federal funds and grants, 2001 ($1,000)	79,310,064	1,763,896,019
Local government employment – full-time equivalent, 1997	365,556	10,227,429
Geography	**Pennsylvania**	**USA**
Land area, 2000 (square miles)	44,817	3,537,438
Persons per square mile, 2000	274	79.6

(a) Includes persons reporting only one race.
(b) Hispanics may be of any race, so also are included in applicable race categories.
Z: Value greater than zero but less than half unit of measure shown.

Source: U.S. Census Bureau State & County QuickFacts

Rhode Island

Statehood: May 29, 1790
Nickname: Ocean State
State bird: Rhode Island Red
State flower: Violet
State tree: Red maple
State motto: Hope
State capital: Providence
Population of capital: 173,618 (2000)

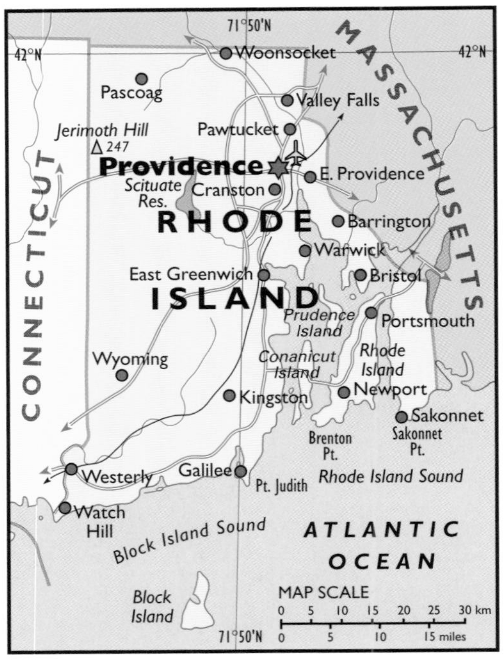

Located on the Atlantic coast, Rhode Island is the smallest U.S. state with only five counties. People from Massachusetts seeking religious freedom, led by Roger Williams, first settled the region in 1636, purchasing land from the Narragansett and other local tribes. It was granted a royal charter in 1663 and was occupied by British troops during the American Revolution after declaring independence before any of the other colonies. Despite being the first state to outlaw slavery, during the 18th century, Rhode Island merchants amassed fortunes participating in the Triangle Trade. By the 19th century, however, manufacturing had evolved into the most profitable business. Warwick, Pawtucket, and Cranston are scattered around the largest city and capital, Providence.

Rhode Island's low-lying position on the coast has left it vulnerable to hurricanes and flooding throughout its history. The highest point in the state, Jeremoth Hill, is a mere 812 feet above sea level. Much of the landscape is forested, dotted with small lakes as well as some dairy and poultry farms. Potatoes, hay, apples, oats, and corn are the chief crops, but fishing is a more significant source of revenue. Lobster, clams, Atlantic cod and flounder are a few of the products that contribute to an established maritime industry. Other industries include textiles, fabricated metals, silverware, machinery, electrical equipment and tourism. Visitors often stop at The Breakers, a famous seaside mansion built for Cornelius Vanderbilt, Samuel Slater's cotton mill in Pawtucket, and Touro Synagogue, the oldest in the country.

Featuring a rather simple design, the Rhode Island flag places an anchor ringed by thirteen stars representing the original colonies on a white background. The state motto appears on a blue ribbon beneath the image. It was adopted in 1897.

Providence

Providence was founded in 1636 as a refuge for religious dissenters from Massachusetts and became a port on Providence Bay in northeastern Rhode Island, enjoying great prosperity through trade with the West Indies. The city played an active role in the War for Independence and the Industrial Revolution and is now a center for jewelry, electrical equipment, silverware, machine tools, and plastic manufacturing. More than ten colleges are in Providence.

Rhode Island at a Glance

People	Rhode Island	USA
Population, 2003 estimate	1,076,164	290,809,777
Population percent change, April 1, 2000–July 1, 2001	1.0%	1.2%
Population, 2000	1,048,319	281,421,906
Persons under 5 years old, percent, 2000	6.1%	6.8%
Persons under 18 years old, percent, 2000	23.6%	25.7%
Persons 65 years old and over, percent, 2000	14.5%	12.4%
Female persons, percent, 2000	52.0%	50.9%
White persons, percent, 2000 (a)	85.0%	75.1%
African American persons, percent, 2000 (a)	4.5%	12.3%
Native American persons, percent, 2000 (a)	0.5%	0.9%
Asian persons, percent, 2000 (a)	2.3%	3.6%
Native Hawaiian and Other Pacific Islander, percent, 2000 (a)	0.1%	0.1%
Persons of Hispanic or Latino origin, percent, 2000 (b)	8.7%	12.5%
White persons, not of Hispanic/Latino origin, percent, 2000	81.9%	69.1%
Foreign born persons, percent, 2000	11.4%	11.1%
Language other than English spoken at home, percent age 5+, 2000	20.0%	17.9%
High school graduates, percent of persons age 25+, 2000	78.0%	80.4%
Bachelor's degree or higher, percent of persons age 25+, 2000	25.6%	24.4%
Persons with a disability, age 5+, 2000	195,806	49,746,248
Homeownership rate, 2000	60.0%	66.2%
Median value of owner-occupied housing units, 2000	$133,000	$119,600
Households, 2000	408,424	105,480,101
Persons per household, 2000	2.47	2.59
Median household money income, 1999	$42,090	$41,994
Per capita money income, 1999	$21,688	$21,587
Persons below poverty, percent, 1999	11.9%	12.4%
Business	**Rhode Island**	**USA**
Private nonfarm establishments, 1999	28,240	7,008,444
Private nonfarm employment, 1999	405,445	110,705,661
Private nonfarm employment, percent change 1990–99	3.0%	18.4%
Nonemployer establishments, 1999	57,664	16,152,604
Manufacturers shipments, 1997 ($1,000)	10,482,011	3,842,061,405
Retail sales, 1997 ($1,000)	7,505,754	2,460,886,012
Retail sales per capita, 1997	$7,605	$9,190
Minority-owned firms, percent of total, 1997	5.9%	14.6%
Women-owned firms, percent of total, 1997	24.6%	26.0%
Federal funds and grants, 2001 ($1,000)	6,988,588	1,763,896,019
Local government employment – full-time equivalent, 1997	29,102	10,227,429
Geography	**Rhode Island**	**USA**
Land area, 2000 (square miles)	1,045	3,537,438
Persons per square mile, 2000	1,003.2	79.6

(a) Includes persons reporting only one race.
(b) Hispanics may be of any race, so also are included in applicable race categories.
Z: Value greater than zero but less than half unit of measure shown.

Source: U.S. Census Bureau State & County QuickFacts

South Carolina

Statehood: May 23, 1788
Nickname: The Palmetto State
State bird: Carolina wren
State flower: Carolina jessamine
State tree: Palmetto
State motto: Prepared in mind and resources
State capital: Columbia
Population of capital: 116,278 (2000)

Although a Spanish expedition explored the coastline more than 100 years earlier, the English were the first Europeans to permanently settle the area beginning in 1663. South Carolina became a royal province in 1729, and a plantation society evolved based on rice, indigo, and cotton, compelling Catawba, Yamasee and other native peoples to fight or move westward. One of the original 13 states, it was the first to secede from the Union, and the opening shots of the Civil War were fired at Fort Sumter. In 1865, Union troops devastated South Carolina, leaving a long road ahead towards reconstruction and racial equality. The state capital and largest city is Columbia, followed by Greenville and Charleston, the main port. South Carolina has 46 counties.

The land rises from the swampy coastal plain to the rolling hills of the Piedmont plateau, jutting up against the Blue Ridge Mountains in the northwest. Many rivers, including the Savannah, which forms most of the Georgia border, drain the region and once powered textile mills whose operation depended on sprawling cotton plantations. Today major crops include tobacco, soybeans, corn, sweet potatoes, peaches and peanuts. Timber and fishing are other sources of employment, but tourism is now the state's second biggest source of income after textiles and clothing. Resorts such as Myrtle Beach and Hilton Head attract tourists seeking relaxation, while Fort Sumter National Monument, Cowpens National Battlefield appeal to people fascinated by the state's military history.

South Carolina's Revolutionary War recruits often wore a silver crescent moon, a shape that graces the State flag, on their hats. At the center of the blue flag adopted in 1861 is a palmetto, which refers to the resilience of the fort on Sullivan Island built from the tough logs of this tree.

Columbia

At the junction of the Broad and Saluda Rivers in the center of the state, Columbia was founded as the capital in 1786, a compromise between two different economic realities in the Piedmont and on the coast. Nearly destroyed by General William Sherman on his march to the sea, it is home to the University of South Carolina, Columbia College, Allen University and the Woodrow Wilson Museum. Textile, paper, pharmaceutical and electronic equipment manufacturers are located within the city limits along with a number of notable antebellum houses.

South Carolina at a Glance

People	**South Carolina**	**USA**
Population, 2003 estimate	4,147,152	290,809,777
Population percent change, April 1, 2000–July 1, 2001	1.3%	1.2%
Population, 2000	4,012,012	281,421,906
Persons under 5 years old, percent, 2000	6.6%	6.8%
Persons under 18 years old, percent, 2000	25.2%	25.7%
Persons 65 years old and over, percent, 2000	12.1%	12.4%
Female persons, percent, 2000	51.4%	50.9%
White persons, percent, 2000 (a)	67.2%	75.1%
African American persons, percent, 2000 (a)	29.5%	12.3%
Native American persons, percent, 2000 (a)	0.3%	0.9%
Asian persons, percent, 2000 (a)	0.9%	3.6%
Native Hawaiian and Other Pacific Islander, percent, 2000 (a)	Z	0.1%
Persons of Hispanic or Latino origin, percent, 2000 (b)	2.4%	12.5%
White persons, not of Hispanic/Latino origin, percent, 2000	66.1%	69.1%
Foreign born persons, percent, 2000	2.9%	11.1%
Language other than English spoken at home, percent age 5+, 2000	5.2%	17.9%
High school graduates, percent of persons age 25+, 2000	76.3%	80.4%
Bachelor's degree or higher, percent of persons age 25+, 2000	20.4%	24.4%
Persons with a disability, age 5+, 2000	810,857	49,746,248
Homeownership rate, 2000	72.2%	66.2%
Median value of owner-occupied housing units, 2000	$94,900	$119,600
Households, 2000	1,533,854	105,480,101
Persons per household, 2000	2.53	2.59
Median household money income, 1999	$37,082	$41,994
Per capita money income, 1999	$18,795	$21,587
Persons below poverty, percent, 1999	14.1%	12.4%

Business	**South Carolina**	**USA**
Private nonfarm establishments, 1999	96,440	7,008,444
Private nonfarm employment, 1999	1,561,727	110,705,661
Private nonfarm employment, percent change 1990–99	23.3%	18.4%
Nonemployer establishments, 1999	200,265	16,152,604
Manufacturers shipments, 1997 ($1,000)	70,797,020	3,842,061,405
Retail sales, 1997 ($1,000)	33,634,264	2,460,886,012
Retail sales per capita, 1997	$8,874	$9,190
Minority-owned firms, percent of total, 1997	11.8%	14.6%
Women-owned firms, percent of total, 1997	24.7%	26.0%
Federal funds and grants, 2001 ($1,000)	24,674,761	1,763,896,019
Local government employment – full-time equivalent, 1997	143,952	10,227,429

Geography	**South Carolina**	**USA**
Land area, 2000 (square miles)	30,109	3,537,438
Persons per square mile, 2000	133.2	79.6

(a) Includes persons reporting only one race.
(b) Hispanics may be of any race, so also are included in applicable race categories.
Z: Value greater than zero but less than half unit of measure shown.

Source: U.S. Census Bureau State & County QuickFacts

Tennessee

Statehood: June 1, 1796
Nickname: The Volunteer State
State bird: Mockingbird
State flower: Iris
State tree: Tulip-poplar
State motto: Agriculture and commerce
State capital: Nashville
Population of capital: 569,891 (2000)

The first European to enter the area in 1540 was a Spaniard, Hernando De Soto. The French followed a century later, but their claim was ceded to Britain in 1763, and the first permanent settlement between the Appalachian Mountains and the Mississippi River was established in 1769. Taking its name from a Yuchi word *tana-see*, which translates as "meeting place," Tennessee became the 16th State of the Union in 1796. Andrew Jackson forcibly relocated most of the large population of Cherokee to Oklahoma by 1839. Tennessee's enthusiastic response to the request for volunteers during the Mexican War (1846–48) earned it the nickname of the "Volunteer State," and during the Civil War, it was the site of more than 400 battles, many of which, like Shiloh and Chattanooga, were among the bloodiest. The last state to secede, in 1866 it became the first Southern state to be readmitted to the Union.

A melting pot for American music from blues to rockabilly, Tennessee has also been influenced by Christian fundamentalism, and the teaching of evolution was banned throughout its 95 counties from 1925 to 1967. In addition to the capital, the main cities are Memphis, Chattanooga, and Knoxville.

The Great Smoky Mountains, part of the Appalachian chain, and the Cumberland Plateau dominate the east while the fertile floodplains of west Tennessee, a production center for cotton, tobacco and soybeans, are defined by the Mississippi and Tennessee Rivers. Central Tennessee is a bluegrass region famed for its horse breeding and livestock rearing. Mineral deposits include zinc and coal and major industries include chemicals, automobile assembly, electrical equipment, foodstuffs, and tourism. Great Smoky Mountains National Park, Cherokee National Forest, Big South Fork National River and Recreation Area, Fort Donelson and Stones River National Battlefields, and the Shiloh, Chickamauga, and Chattanooga National Military Parks are the chief landmarks.

Adopted in 1905 and echoing the colors of the national flag, the state flag is crimson with a central blue circle containing three stars. Bound together in an unbroken circle they represent three regions: mountains in the east, highlands in the middle and lowlands in the west. A blue bar relieves some of the sameness of the red field when the flag hangs limp.

Nashville

A port on the Cumberland River, Fort Nasborough was settled in 1779 and changed its name before becoming the state capital in 1843. During the Civil War, it was the scene of a decisive Union victory. The city merged with Davidson County in 1963 and is now the center of country music, and home of the Country Music Hall of Fame, the Grand Ole Opry House and an entertainment complex called Opryland USA. Seat of several institutions of highter education, Nashville has many neo-classical buildings and the music and publishing industries are key to the economy.

Tennessee at a Glance

People	Tennessee	USA
Population, 2003 estimate	5,841,748	290,809,777
Population percent change, April 1, 2000–July 1, 2001	0.9%	1.2%
Population, 2000	5,689,283	281,421,906
Persons under 5 years old, percent, 2000	6.6%	6.8%
Persons under 18 years old, percent, 2000	24.6%	25.7%
Persons 65 years old and over, percent, 2000	12.4%	12.4%
Female persons, percent, 2000	51.3%	50.9%
White persons, percent, 2000 (a)	80.2%	75.1%
African American persons, percent, 2000 (a)	16.4%	12.3%
Native American persons, percent, 2000 (a)	0.3%	0.9%
Asian persons, percent, 2000 (a)	1.0%	3.6%
Native Hawaiian and Other Pacific Islander, percent, 2000 (a)	Z	0.1%
Persons of Hispanic or Latino origin, percent, 2000 (b)	2.2%	12.5%
White persons, not of Hispanic/Latino origin, percent, 2000	79.2%	69.1%
Foreign born persons, percent, 2000	2.8%	11.1%
Language other than English spoken at home, percent age 5+, 2000	4.8%	17.9%
High school graduates, percent of persons age 25+, 2000	75.9%	80.4%
Bachelor's degree or higher, percent of persons age 25+, 2000	19.6%	24.4%
Persons with a disability, age 5+, 2000	1,149,693	49,746,248
Homeownership rate, 2000	69.9%	66.2%
Median value of owner-occupied housing units, 2000	$93,000	$119,600
Households, 2000	2,232,905	105,480,101
Persons per household, 2000	2.48	2.59
Median household money income, 1999	$36,360	$41,994
Per capita money income, 1999	$19,393	$21,587
Persons below poverty, percent, 1999	13.5%	12.4%

Business	Tennessee	USA
Private nonfarm establishments, 1999	131,116	7,008,444
Private nonfarm employment, 1999	2,338,780	110,705,661
Private nonfarm employment, percent change 1990–99	25.1%	18.4%
Nonemployer establishments, 1999	335,266	16,152,604
Manufacturers shipments, 1997 ($1,000)	98,503,080	3,842,061,405
Retail sales, 1997 ($1,000)	50,813,221	2,460,886,012
Retail sales per capita, 1997	$9,448	$9,190
Minority-owned firms, percent of total, 1997	7.8%	14.6%
Women-owned firms, percent of total, 1997	24.0%	26.0%
Federal funds and grants, 2001 ($1,000)	36,757,793	1,763,896,019
Local government employment – full-time equivalent, 1997	194,274	10,227,429

Geography	Tennessee	USA
Land area, 2000 (square miles)	41,217	3,537,438
Persons per square mile, 2000	138	79.6

(a) Includes persons reporting only one race.
(b) Hispanics may be of any race, so also are included in applicable race categories.
Z: Value greater than zero but less than half unit of measure shown.

Source: U.S. Census Bureau State & County QuickFacts

Texas

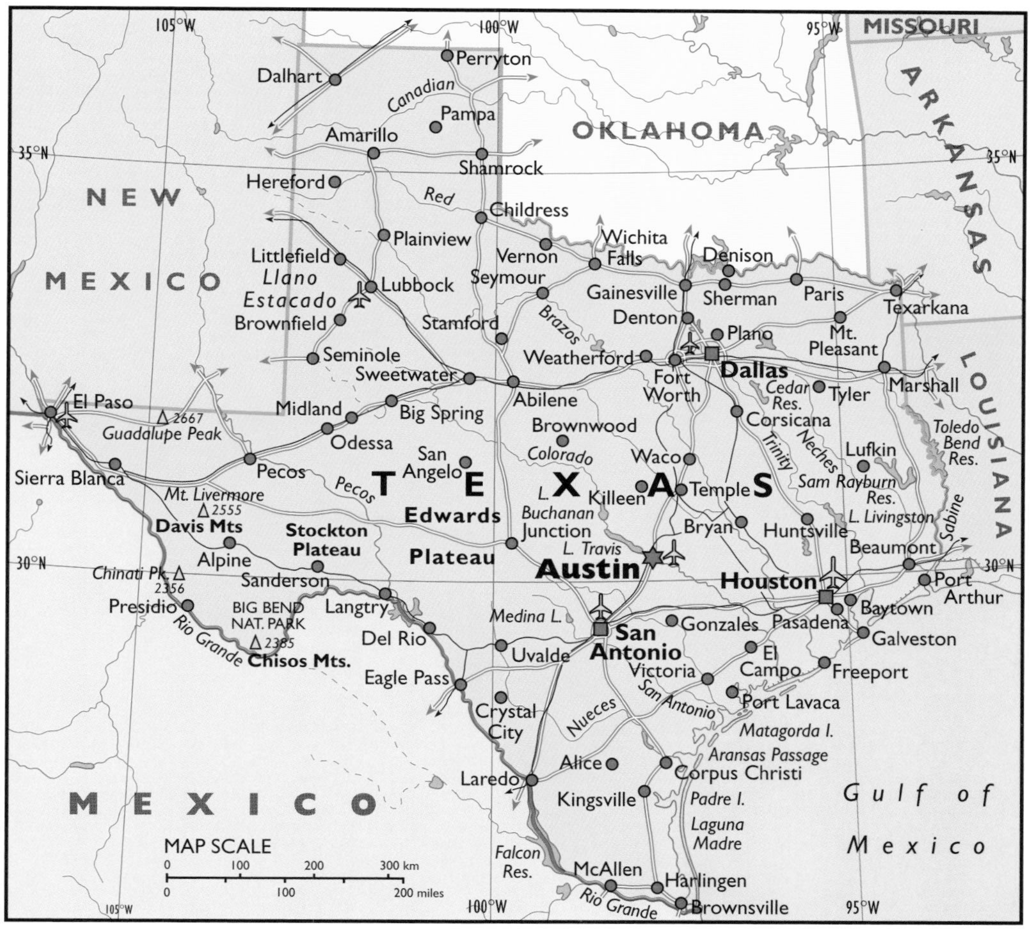

Statehood: December 29, 1845
Nickname: The Lone Star State
State bird: Mockingbird
State flower: Bluebonnet
State tree: Pecan
State motto: Friendship
State capital: Austin
Population of capital: 656,562 (2000)

Spaniards explored the region bounded by the Gulf of Mexico and the Río Grande in the early 16th century, and it became part of the colony of Mexico. Missionaries tried with limited success to convert Caddo, Concho and other Native American groups to Christianity and by the time Mexico achieved independence in 1821, many Americans had begun to settle in Texas. In 1836, they revolted against Mexican rule, rallied around a defeat at the Alamo, forced the army to surrender, and established the Republic of Texas. The following year, the U.S. recognized Sam Houston's republic and Texas was admitted to the Union as the 28th state. In 1873, the invention of barbed wire brought the short-lived era of cowboys and cattle drives to an end. Austin and most of the other major cities including Fort Worth, San Antonio, Dallas, and Houston are in the east. The second largest state in the country has 254 counties, many with names alluding to a persistent Hispanic influence.

Beginning with the southeast, the Texas terrain moves from barrier islands to cypress swamps, past pine-covered hills and the cliffs of the Balcones Escarpment across an expansive prairie to end at the New Mexico border with the Llano Estacado. Cotton, rice and citrus fruits are key cash crops and the timber industry contributes noticeably to the economy. Millions of cattle and sheep roam the rangeland of the Río Grande Valley, from where the land rises into the Davis and Guadalupe Mountains of West Texas and the Great Plains area of the Panhandle in the north. Rich oil and gas fields, some of which are offshore, anchor the state's economy. Other mainstay industries include oil refining, food processing, aircraft manufacturing, and telecommunications. Big Bend and Guadeloupe National Parks, the Johnson Space Center in Houston, and Padre Island National Seashore are some of the many attractions to be found in Texas.

The red, white and blue flag of Texas reflects the colors of the national banner representing bravery, purity and loyalty respectively. It was adopted in 1839.

Austin

Settled as Waterloo in 1835, the city was renamed four years later for Stephen Austin, the "father of Texas." A number of fine examples of 19th-century architecture, including the Capitol building were built here on the Colorado River. The market center for a farming and ranching area, Austin, as a location for high-tech electronics, furniture, machinery, building materials, and food processing industries, hosts national conventions.

Texas at a Glance

People	Texas	USA
Population, 2003 estimate	22,118,509	290,809,777
Population percent change, April 1, 2000–July 1, 2001	2.3%	1.2%
Population, 2000	20,851,820	281,421,906
Persons under 5 years old, percent, 2000	7.8%	6.8%
Persons under 18 years old, percent, 2000	28.2%	25.7%
Persons 65 years old and over, percent, 2000	9.9%	12.4%
Female persons, percent, 2000	50.4%	50.9%
White persons, percent, 2000 (a)	71.0%	75.1%
African American persons, percent, 2000 (a)	11.5%	12.3%
Native American persons, percent, 2000 (a)	0.6%	0.9%
Asian persons, percent, 2000 (a)	2.7%	3.6%
Native Hawaiian and Other Pacific Islander, percent, 2000 (a)	0.1%	0.1%
Persons of Hispanic or Latino origin, percent, 2000 (b)	32.0%	12.5%
White persons, not of Hispanic/Latino origin, percent, 2000	52.4%	69.1%
Foreign born persons, percent, 2000	13.9%	11.1%
Language other than English spoken at home, percent age 5+, 2000	31.2%	17.9%
High school graduates, percent of persons age 25+, 2000	75.7%	80.4%
Bachelor's degree or higher, percent of persons age 25+, 2000	23.2%	24.4%
Persons with a disability, age 5+, 2000	3,605,542	49,746,248
Homeownership rate, 2000	63.8%	66.2%
Median value of owner-occupied housing units, 2000	$82,500	$119,600
Households, 2000	7,393,354	105,480,101
Persons per household, 2000	2.74	2.59
Median household money income, 1999	$39,927	$41,994
Per capita money income, 1999	$19,617	$21,587
Persons below poverty, percent, 1999	15.4%	12.4%

Business	Texas	USA
Private nonfarm establishments, 1999	467,087	7,008,444
Private nonfarm employment, 1999	7,763,815	110,705,661
Private nonfarm employment, percent change 1990–99	32.4%	18.4%
Nonemployer establishments, 1999	1,236,927	16,152,604
Manufacturers shipments, 1997 ($1,000)	297,657,003	3,842,061,405
Retail sales, 1997 ($1,000)	182,516,112	2,460,886,012
Retail sales per capita, 1997	$9,430	$9,190
Minority-owned firms, percent of total, 1997	23.9%	14.6%
Women-owned firms, percent of total, 1997	25.0%	26.0%
Federal funds and grants, 2001 ($1,000)	112,530,383	1,763,896,019
Local government employment – full-time equivalent, 1997	850,380	10,227,429

Geography	Texas	USA
Land area, 2000 (square miles)	261,797	3,537,438
Persons per square mile, 2000	79.6	79.6

(a) Includes persons reporting only one race.
(b) Hispanics may be of any race, so also are included in applicable race categories.
Z: Value greater than zero but less than half unit of measure shown.

Source: U.S. Census Bureau State & County QuickFacts

Utah

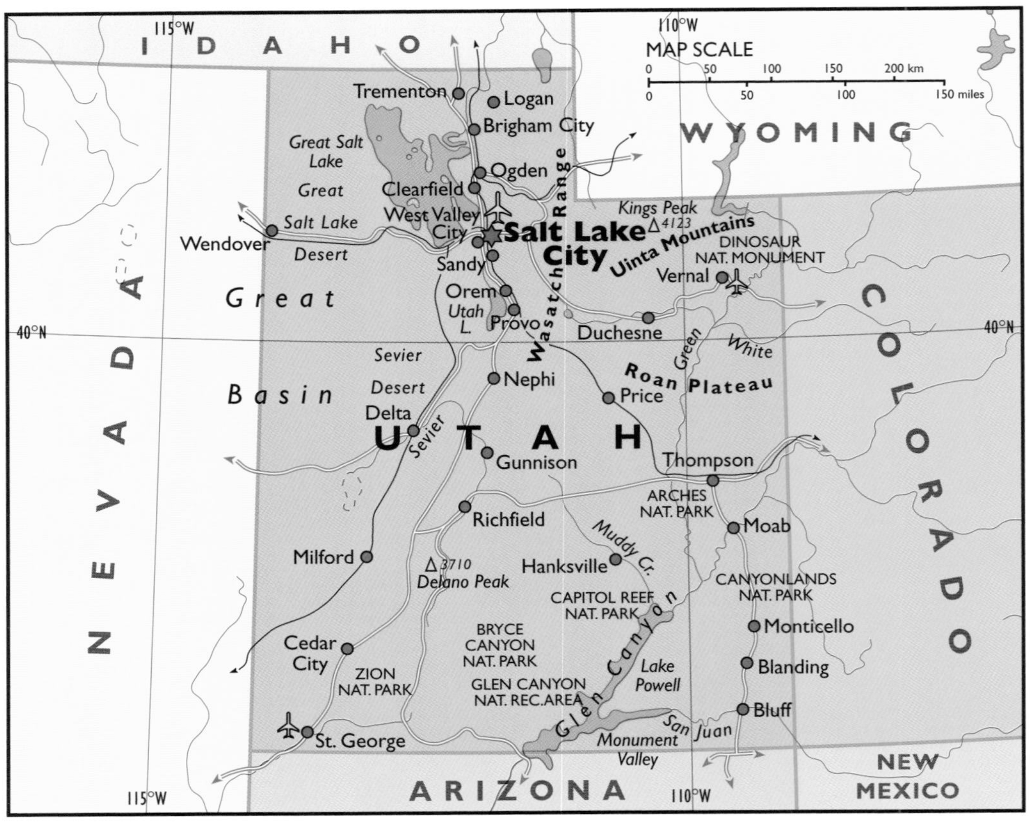

Statehood: January 4, 1896
Nickname: The Beehive State
State bird: Sea gull
State flower: Sego lily
State tree: Blue spruce
State motto: Industry
State capital: Salt Lake City
Population of capital: 181,743 (2000)

The Ute and Shoshone, replacing the Anasazi, lived among the mesas, plateaus and sandy wastes for centuries before the first Spaniards crossed into their territory. Another part of the region given to the U.S. at the end of the Mexican War, Utah was admitted to the Union in 1896. The influence of the Church of Jesus Christ of the Latter-Day Saints is strong in the state, and in 1857–58 there were conflicts between federal troops and the Mormons. Mining, then the transcontinental railroad, which was completed at Promontory in 1869, altered the peaceful religious community. Salt Lake City, the capital and single largest city in the state, is very close to the two other cities: Provo and Ogden. Divided into 29 sizable counties, Utah retains much of the wilderness encountered by Spanish explorers Escalante and Dominguez.

In the north, the Wasatch Range separates the mountainous east from the Great Basin, which includes the Great Salt Lake. Although large rivers such as the Green, the Colorado and Sevier run through the state and hay, barley, wheat, beans, and sugar beet are grown with the aid of irrigation, the semiarid climate hinders widespread agriculture. The chief farming activity is livestock raising. Mining is also important: there are rich deposits of copper, petroleum, coal, molybdenum, silver, lead, and gold. With many ski resorts, monuments, and national parks like Canyonlands, Arches, Grand Staircase and Zion, tourism is vital to the economy.

The state flag, adopted in 1913, shows two dates: 1847, the year Mormon settlers arrived, and 1896, the year Utah was added as the 45th state. Beneath the protective wings of a bald eagle, symbol of the United States, the seal rests in the center of the blue flag, displaying a beehive for industry (the state motto), and the sego lily for peace.

Salt Lake City

Founded southeast of Great Salt Lake in 1847 by Brigham Young, Salt Lake City, the world headquarters of the Mormon Church, grew rapidly to become capital of the territory and then the state of Utah. Zinc, gold, silver, lead, and copper are mined in the surrounding Wasatch Range. The city has developed into a headquarters for industries as varied as missiles, rocket engines, oil-refining, tourism, printing and publishing.

Utah at a Glance

People	Utah	USA
Population, 2003 estimate	2,351,467	290,809,777
Population percent change, April 1, 2000–July 1, 2001	1.6%	1.2%
Population, 2000	2,233,169	281,421,906
Persons under 5 years old, percent, 2000	9.4%	6.8%
Persons under 18 years old, percent, 2000	32.2%	25.7%
Persons 65 years old and over, percent, 2000	8.5%	12.4%
Female persons, percent, 2000	49.9%	50.9%
White persons, percent, 2000 (a)	89.2%	75.1%
African American persons, percent, 2000 (a)	0.8%	12.3%
Native American persons, percent, 2000 (a)	1.3%	0.9%
Asian persons, percent, 2000 (a)	1.7%	3.6%
Native Hawaiian and Other Pacific Islander, percent, 2000 (a)	0.7%	0.1%
Persons of Hispanic or Latino origin, percent, 2000 (b)	9.0%	12.5%
White persons, not of Hispanic/Latino origin, percent, 2000	85.3%	69.1%
Foreign born persons, percent, 2000	7.1%	11.1%
Language other than English spoken at home, percent age 5+, 2000	12.5%	17.9%
High school graduates, percent of persons age 25+, 2000	87.7%	80.4%
Bachelor's degree or higher, percent of persons age 25+, 2000	26.1%	24.4%
Persons with a disability, age 5+, 2000	298,686	49,746,248
Homeownership rate, 2000	71.5%	66.2%
Median value of owner-occupied housing units, 2000	$146,100	$119,600
Households, 2000	701,281	105,480,101
Persons per household, 2000	3.13	2.59
Median household money income, 1999	$45,726	$41,994
Per capita money income, 1999	$18,185	$21,587
Persons below poverty, percent, 1999	9.4%	12.4%

Business	Utah	USA
Private nonfarm establishments, 1999	53,809	7,008,444
Private nonfarm employment, 1999	889,355	110,705,661
Private nonfarm employment, percent change 1990–99	55.8%	18.4%
Nonemployer establishments, 1999	134,513	16,152,604
Manufacturers shipments, 1997 ($1,000)	24,014,379	3,842,061,405
Retail sales, 1997 ($1,000)	19,964,601	2,460,886,012
Retail sales per capita, 1997	$9,666	$9,190
Minority-owned firms, percent of total, 1997	5.1%	14.6%
Women-owned firms, percent of total, 1997	24.8%	26.0%
Federal funds and grants, 2001 ($1,000)	11,377,441	1,763,896,019
Local government employment – full-time equivalent, 1997	63,884	10,227,429

Geography	Utah	USA
Land area, 2000 (square miles)	82,144	3,537,438
Persons per square mile, 2000	27.2	79.6

(a) Includes persons reporting only one race.
(b) Hispanics may be of any race, so also are included in applicable race categories.
Z: Value greater than zero but less than half unit of measure shown.

Source: U.S. Census Bureau State & County QuickFacts

Vermont

Statehood: March 4, 1791
Nickname: The Green Mountain State
State bird: Hermit thrush
State flower: Red clover
State tree: Sugar maple
State motto: Freedom and unity
State capital: Montpelier
Population of capital: 8,035 (2000)

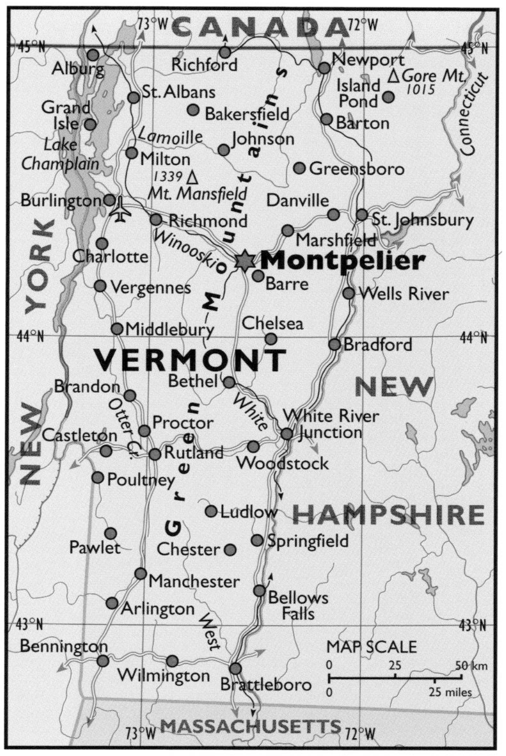

Traveling south from Québec in 1609, Samuel de Champlain discovered the lake that now bears his name, but permanent European settlements in the region did not appear until 1724. These first farms and villages probably interacted with Iroquois and Mahican people who hunted and fished in the same territory. Land grant disputes with New Hampshire and New York persisted for many years until Vermont declared its independence in 1777, retaining this unrecognized status until it was finally admitted to the Union in 1791. Perhaps in response to the growing popularity of winter sports, an enterprising Vermonter built the first ski tow in Woodstock, near the Ottauquechee River and the birthplace of Calvin Coolidge. Burlington is the major city in this state of 14 counties.

The Green Mountains range north to south, and dominate the terrain. Lake Champlain, the largest in New England, separates the state from New York, forming most of the western border of Vermont. The Connecticut River runs along the entire border with New Hampshire. Heavily forested with limited arable land, dairy farming is by far the most important agricultural activity in Vermont. Mineral resources include granite, slate, marble and asbestos while the biggest industries include pulp and paper production, food processing, computer component manufacturing, and maple syrup production. Outdoor enthusiasts might travel to the state to ski at Stowe or Killington or hike the undeveloped wilderness and return home having learned about Vermont's history from the Bennington Museum or the Billings Farm.

The Vermont coat of arms shows a pine tree, a cow and sheaves of grain in the foreground and the Green Mountains behind them. A stag's head is positioned at the top of the shield with the motto below. Vermont adopted the image for its deep blue flag in 1923.

Montpelier

First settled in the 1780s, Montpelier became state capital in 1805. Admiral George Dewey, who defeated the Spanish at Manilsa Bay in 1898, was born in the city limits. Tourism, machinery, granite quarrying, timber, maple sugar and syrup, and plastics industries can be found here at the confluence of the Winooski and North Branch Rivers.

Vermont at a Glance

People	Vermont	USA
Population, 2003 estimate	619,107	290,809,777
Population percent change, April 1, 2000–July 1, 2001	0.7%	1.2%
Population, 2000	608,827	281,421,906
Persons under 5 years old, percent, 2000	5.6%	6.8%
Persons under 18 years old, percent, 2000	24.2%	25.7%
Persons 65 years old and over, percent, 2000	12.7%	12.4%
Female persons, percent, 2000	51.0%	50.9%
White persons, percent, 2000 (a)	96.8%	75.1%
African American persons, percent, 2000 (a)	0.5%	12.3%
Native American persons, percent, 2000 (a)	0.4%	0.9%
Asian persons, percent, 2000 (a)	0.9%	3.6%
Native Hawaiian and Other Pacific Islander, percent, 2000 (a)	Z	0.1%
Persons of Hispanic or Latino origin, percent, 2000 (b)	0.9%	12.5%
White persons, not of Hispanic/Latino origin, percent, 2000	96.2%	69.1%
Foreign born persons, percent, 2000	3.8%	11.1%
Language other than English spoken at home, percent age 5+, 2000	5.9%	17.9%
High school graduates, percent of persons age 25+, 2000	86.4%	80.4%
Bachelor's degree or higher, percent of persons age 25+, 2000	29.4%	24.4%
Persons with a disability, age 5+, 2000	97,167	49,746,248
Homeownership rate, 2000	70.6%	66.2%
Median value of owner-occupied housing units, 2000	$111,500	$119,600
Households, 2000	240,634	105,480,101
Persons per household, 2000	2.44	2.59
Median household money income, 1999	$40,856	$41,994
Per capita money income, 1999	$20,625	$21,587
Persons below poverty, percent, 1999	9.4%	12.4%
Business	**Vermont**	**USA**
Private nonfarm establishments, 1999	21,598	7,008,444
Private nonfarm employment, 1999	246,320	110,705,661
Private nonfarm employment, percent change 1990–99	14.4%	18.4%
Nonemployer establishments, 1999	49,696	16,152,604
Manufacturers shipments, 1997 ($1,000)	7,803,041	3,842,061,405
Retail sales, 1997 ($1,000)	5,898,646	2,460,886,012
Retail sales per capita, 1997	$10,020	$9,190
Minority-owned firms, percent of total, 1997	3.1%	14.6%
Women-owned firms, percent of total, 1997	25.2%	26.0%
Federal funds and grants, 2001 ($1,000)	3,733,752	1,763,896,019
Local government employment – full-time equivalent, 1997	17,841	10,227,429
Geography	**Vermont**	**USA**
Land area, 2000 (square miles)	9,250	3,537,438
Persons per square mile, 2000	65.8	79.6

(a) Includes persons reporting only one race.
(b) Hispanics may be of any race, so also are included in applicable race categories.
Z: Value greater than zero but less than half unit of measure shown.

Source: U.S. Census Bureau State & County QuickFacts

Virginia

Statehood: June 25, 1788
Nickname: Old Dominion
State bird: Cardinal
State flower: Dogwood flower
State tree: Dogwood
State motto: This always to tyrants
State capital: Richmond
Population of capital: 197,790 (2000)

The first permanent British settlement in North America was at Jamestown in 1607. Overcoming disease, harsh weather and violent confrontations with the Mattaponi, Chickahominy, Monacan and Rappahannock tribes, Virginia evolved into an aristocratic plantation society based on vast tobacco holdings. Virginia's military and political leaders were at the forefront of the Revolution and during the Civil War Richmond acted as the capital of the Confederacy. The main battleground of the war with over 400 engagements and the location of General Lee's surrender to General Grant at Appomattox, Virginia gained readmittance to the Union in 1870. More than 110 years later, citizens of Old Dominion elected the country's first black governor. The majority of the population is distributed between Virginia's largest cities: Alexandria, Richmond, Newport News, and Norfolk. Forty-one independent cities and 95 counties, many named after places in England lie within state borders.

The most northerly of the southern states, Virginia's geography is split between coastal plain and the Appalachian Plateau. In the west, the Piedmont rises to the Blue Ridge Mountains, where extensive forests and limestone caves add to the natural beauty. An important part of the state economy, Virginia's farms yield tobacco, peanuts, grain, vegetables, and fruits as well as some livestock. Industries include chemicals, shipbuilding, fishing, and transportation equipment. Stone, sand, and gravel are quarried but coal is the most important mineral deposit. The homes of numerous statesmen (Virginia is also known as the Mother of Presidents), historic Jamestown and Williamsburg, numerous Civil War battlefields, and Skyline Drive in the Blue Ridge Mountains make this state a popular tourist destination.

Set on a blue field, the two figures, triumphant Virtue and defeated Tyranny pictured inside the seal enact the state motto. The Virginia Legislature adopted the flag in 1931.

Richmond

Settlers arrived here on the James River in about 1637 but the town served as a trading post before it was made state capital in 1780. Previous capitals at Jamestown and Williamsburg were short lived. In 1775 Patrick Henry, a fiery delegate who attended the Continental Congress uttered his famous words "Give me liberty or give me death," at St. John's Church in Richmond. During the Civil War, it became capital of the Confederate States until it fell to Union forces in 1865 after a prolonged siege. The tobacco industry has been an important source of revenue since the colonial period, joined more recently by metal product, textile, clothing, chemical, and publishing companies. Today large schools such as the University of Richmond and Virgina Commonwealth University share space downtown with numerous landmarks.

Virginia at a Glance

People	Virginia	USA
Population, 2003 estimate	7,386,330	290,809,777
Population percent change, April 1, 2000–July 1, 2001	1.5%	1.2%
Population, 2000	7,078,515	281,421,906
Persons under 5 years old, percent, 2000	6.5%	6.8%
Persons under 18 years old, percent, 2000	24.6%	25.7%
Persons 65 years old and over, percent, 2000	11.2%	12.4%
Female persons, percent, 2000	51.0%	50.9%
White persons, percent, 2000 (a)	72.3%	75.1%
African American persons, percent, 2000 (a)	19.6%	12.3%
Native American persons, percent, 2000 (a)	0.3%	0.9%
Asian persons, percent, 2000 (a)	3.7%	3.6%
Native Hawaiian and Other Pacific Islander, percent, 2000 (a)	0.1%	0.1%
Persons of Hispanic or Latino origin, percent, 2000 (b)	4.7%	12.5%
White persons, not of Hispanic/Latino origin, percent, 2000	70.2%	69.1%
Foreign born persons, percent, 2000	8.1%	11.1%
Language other than English spoken at home, percent age 5+, 2000	11.1%	17.9%
High school graduates, percent of persons age 25+, 2000	81.5%	80.4%
Bachelor's degree or higher, percent of persons age 25+, 2000	29.5%	24.4%
Persons with a disability, age 5+, 2000	1,155,083	49,746,248
Homeownership rate, 2000	68.1%	66.2%
Median value of owner-occupied housing units, 2000	$125,400	$119,600
Households, 2000	2,699,173	105,480,101
Persons per household, 2000	2.54	2.59
Median household money income, 1999	$46,677	$41,994
Per capita money income, 1999	$23,975	$21,587
Persons below poverty, percent, 1999	9.6%	12.4%

Business	Virginia	USA
Private nonfarm establishments, 1999	173,550	7,008,444
Private nonfarm employment, 1999	2,791,977	110,705,661
Private nonfarm employment, percent change 1990–99	20.3%	18.4%
Nonemployer establishments, 1999	360,974	16,152,604
Manufacturers shipments, 1997 ($1,000)	83,814,009	3,842,061,405
Retail sales, 1997 ($1,000)	62,569,924	2,460,886,012
Retail sales per capita, 1997	$9,293	$9,190
Minority-owned firms, percent of total, 1997	14.9%	14.6%
Women-owned firms, percent of total, 1997	27.5%	26.0%
Federal funds and grants, 2001 ($1,000)	71,257,343	1,763,896,019
Local government employment – full-time equivalent, 1997	253,219	10,227,429

Geography	Virginia	USA
Land area, 2000 (square miles)	39,594	3,537,438
Persons per square mile, 2000	178.8	79.6

(a) Includes persons reporting only one race.
(b) Hispanics may be of any race, so also are included in applicable race categories.
Z: Value greater than zero but less than half unit of measure shown.

Source: U.S. Census Bureau State & County QuickFacts

Washington

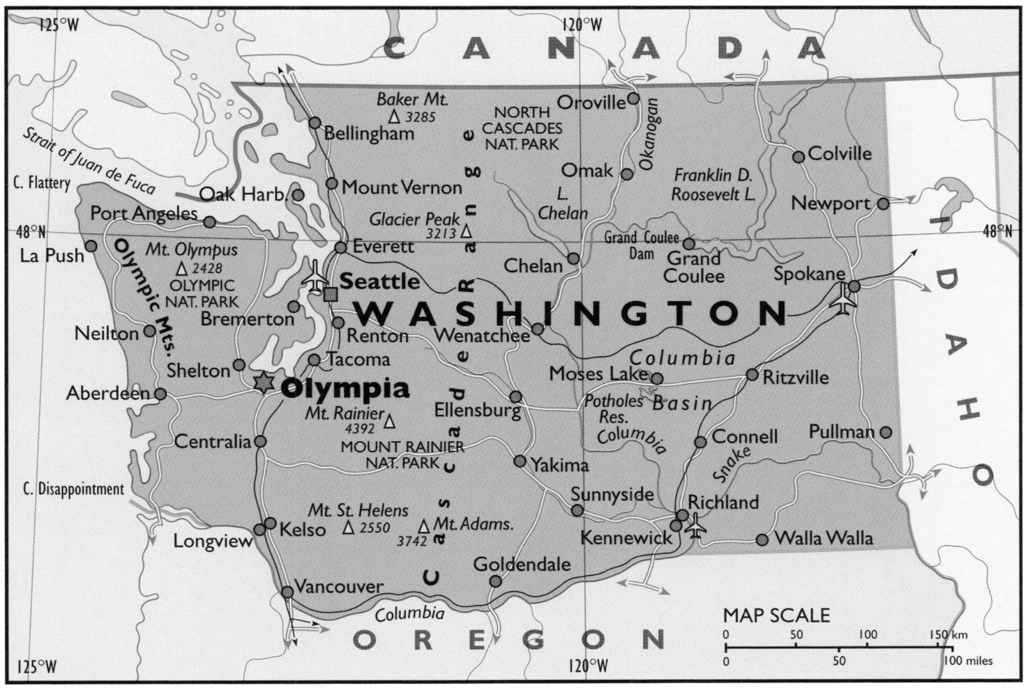

Statehood:	November 11, 1889
Nickname:	The Evergreen State
State bird:	Willow goldfinch
State flower:	Coast rhododendron
State tree:	Western hemlock
State motto:	Alki (Chinook word for "by and by")
State capital:	Olympia
Population of capital:	42,514 (2000)

Spanish explorers discovered the mouth of the Columbia River in 1775 and in 1792, British navigator George Vancouver mapped Puget Sound. Robert Gray sailed down the Sound and established the U.S. claim to the region. The Lewis and Clark Expedition, then the establishment of an American Fur Company trading post in 1811 strengthened this claim. From 1821 to 1846, the Hudson Bay Company administered the region, which was still inhabited by dozens of tribes like the Makah, Tulalip, Spokane, and Yakima. A treaty with the British fixed the boundary with Canada, and in 1847 most of the present state became part of the Oregon Territory. In 1853, Washington Territory was created and exploitation of its forests and fisheries attracted settlement. Spokane, on Hangman Creek in the east, along with Seattle and Tacoma, which hug the western shore, are the most populous cities. Washington is divided into 39 counties.

The Columbia Plateau, the volcanic Cascade Range, including Mount Rainier and Mount St. Helens, and Puget Sound dominate Washington's geography. The coastal region to the west of the range is one of the wettest areas in the country, supporting a dense temperate rain forest. In contrast, the region to the east of the Cascades is mostly treeless plain with low rainfall. An important wheat-producing area, the plateau is dependent on irrigation from the Columbia River, which is also one of the world's best sources of hydroelectricity. Washington is the leading producer of apples in the U.S.; other commercial activities include food processing, timber, aluminum, aerospace, and computer technology. Mounts Rainier and St. Helens, North Cascades National Park, the Whitman Mission and Fort Vancouver National Historic Site stand as examples of Washington's rich history and natural beauty.

The green background of the state flag represents the large fir, spruce and cedar forests in Washington. The centralized seal, showing George Washington, makes the flag the only banner in the nation with a picture of a president.

Olympia

A port on the southern tip of the Puget Sound, Olympia was made capital of Washington Territory in 1853. Development was spurred with the coming of the railroad in the 1880s and its port was expanded during both World Wars. Agriculture, food canning, brewing, oyster fishing, and lumbering generate the most revenue for the city.

Washington at a Glance

People	**Washington**	**USA**
Population, 2003 estimate	6,131,445	290,809,777
Population percent change, April 1, 2000–July 1, 2001	1.6%	1.2%
Population, 2000	5,894,121	281,421,906
Persons under 5 years old, percent, 2000	6.7%	6.8%
Persons under 18 years old, percent, 2000	25.7%	25.7%
Persons 65 years old and over, percent, 2000	11.2%	12.4%
Female persons, percent, 2000	50.2%	50.9%
White persons, percent, 2000 (a)	81.8%	75.1%
African American persons, percent, 2000 (a)	3.2%	12.3%
Native American persons, percent, 2000 (a)	1.6%	0.9%
Asian persons, percent, 2000 (a)	5.5%	3.6%
Native Hawaiian and Other Pacific Islander, percent, 2000 (a)	0.4%	0.1%
Persons of Hispanic or Latino origin, percent, 2000 (b)	7.5%	12.5%
White persons, not of Hispanic/Latino origin, percent, 2000	78.9%	69.1%
Foreign born persons, percent, 2000	10.4%	11.1%
Language other than English spoken at home, percent age 5+, 2000	14.0%	17.9%
High school graduates, percent of persons age 25+, 2000	87.1%	80.4%
Bachelor's degree or higher, percent of persons age 25+, 2000	27.7%	24.4%
Persons with a disability, age 5+, 2000	981,007	49,746,248
Homeownership rate, 2000	64.6%	66.2%
Median value of owner-occupied housing units, 2000	$168,300	$119,600
Households, 2000	2,271,398	105,480,101
Persons per household, 2000	2.53	2.59
Median household money income, 1999	$45,776	$41,994
Per capita money income, 1999	$22,973	$21,587
Persons below poverty, percent, 1999	10.6%	12.4%

Business	**Washington**	**USA**
Private nonfarm establishments, 1999	162,932	7,008,444
Private nonfarm employment, 1999	2,209,129	110,705,661
Private nonfarm employment, percent change 1990–99	25.4%	18.4%
Nonemployer establishments, 1999	321,766	16,152,604
Manufacturers shipments, 1997 ($1,000)	78,852,486	3,842,061,405
Retail sales, 1997 ($1,000)	52,472,866	2,460,886,012
Retail sales per capita, 1997	$9,363	$9,190
Minority-owned firms, percent of total, 1997	9.6%	14.6%
Women-owned firms, percent of total, 1997	27.5%	26.0%
Federal funds and grants, 2001 ($1,000)	36,903,358	1,763,896,019
Local government employment – full-time equivalent, 1997	185,152	10,227,429

Geography	**Washington**	**USA**
Land area, 2000 (square miles)	66,544	3,537,438
Persons per square mile, 2000	88.6	79.6

(a) Includes persons reporting only one race.
(b) Hispanics may be of any race, so also are included in applicable race categories.
Z: Value greater than zero but less than half unit of measure shown.

Source: U.S. Census Bureau State & County QuickFacts

West Virginia

Statehood: June 20, 1863
Nickname: The Mountain State
State bird: Cardinal
State flower: Rhododendron
State tree: Sugar maple
State motto: Mountaineers are always free
State capital: Charleston
Population of capital: 53,421 (2000)

In 1727, Germans established the first settlement at New Mecklenburg (now Shepherdstown) in the Appalachian Mountains. This land lay at the edge of the territory claimed by the Adena mound building culture and several structures survive today. English settlers crossing the Appalachian and Allegheny Mountains led to the French and Indian War. The region was then part of Virginia, but political and economic disagreements especially regarding slavery arose between western Virginians and the dominant eastern inhabitants. When Virginia seceded in May 1861 to join the Confederacy, there was much opposition in the west, and West Virginia was admitted to the Union as the 35th state. Charleston, Morgantown, Huntington and Wheeling contain the majority of West Virginia's population, the rest of which is dispersed across 55 counties.

West Virginia, mountainous and rugged, has two narrow projections: the Northern Panhandle extending north between Ohio and Pennsylvania and the Eastern Panhandle cutting between Maryland and Virginia. Harpers Ferry in the eastern corner lies on the bank of the Potomac River, which forms much of the state's northern border while the Ohio River forms most of the western border. Hay, tobacco, corn, and apples are the principal crops, but West Virginia also has rich mineral deposits, and is the leading producer of bituminous coal in the U.S. Some sixty-five percent of the land is forested. Industries include glass, chemicals, steel, machinery, and tourism, drawing people to Harpers Ferry, Blackwater Falls State Park, or any of the various caverns in the west.

Adopted in 1929, the state flag depicts a miner and a farmer standing in front of a pair of rifles and a red liberty cap that demonstrate their readiness to fight for freedom. The date of West Virginia's statehood is shown on a rock in the center of the seal and rhododendron, the state flower, surrounds the image. The white flag has a blue border.

Charleston

At the junction of the Elk and Kanawha Rivers, Charleston grew around Fort Lee in the 1780s. It is an important trade and transport center for the industrialized Kanawha Valley. A center for salt production in the 19th century, local industry has since shifted to concentrate on chemicals, glass, metallurgy, timber, and oil, gas, and coal in particular. Daniel Boone lived here at the end of the 18th century.

West Virginia at a Glance

People	West Virginia	USA
Population, 2003 estimate	1,810,354	290,809,777
Population percent change, April 1, 2000–July 1, 2001	–0.4%	1.2%
Population, 2000	1,808,344	281,421,906
Persons under 5 years old, percent, 2000	5.6%	6.8%
Persons under 18 years old, percent, 2000	22.3%	25.7%
Persons 65 years old and over, percent, 2000	15.3%	12.4%
Female persons, percent, 2000	51.4%	50.9%
White persons, percent, 2000 (a)	95.0%	75.1%
African American persons, percent, 2000 (a)	3.2%	12.3%
Native American persons, percent, 2000 (a)	0.2%	0.9%
Asian persons, percent, 2000 (a)	0.5%	3.6%
Native Hawaiian and Other Pacific Islander, percent, 2000 (a)	Z	0.1%
Persons of Hispanic or Latino origin, percent, 2000 (b)	0.7%	12.5%
White persons, not of Hispanic/Latino origin, percent, 2000	94.6%	69.1%
Foreign born persons, percent, 2000	1.1%	11.1%
Language other than English spoken at home, percent age 5+, 2000	2.7%	17.9%
High school graduates, percent of persons age 25+, 2000	75.2%	80.4%
Bachelor's degree or higher, percent of persons age 25+, 2000	14.8%	24.4%
Persons with a disability, age 5+, 2000	410,781	49,746,248
Homeownership rate, 2000	75.2%	66.2%
Median value of owner-occupied housing units, 2000	$72,800	$119,600
Households, 2000	736,481	105,480,101
Persons per household, 2000	2.4	2.59
Median household money income, 1999	$29,696	$41,994
Per capita money income, 1999	$16,477	$21,587
Persons below poverty, percent, 1999	17.9%	12.4%
Business	**West Virginia**	**USA**
Private nonfarm establishments, 1999	41,451	7,008,444
Private nonfarm employment, 1999	545,495	110,705,661
Private nonfarm employment, percent change 1990–99	13.1%	18.4%
Nonemployer establishments, 1999	81,212	16,152,604
Manufacturers shipments, 1997 ($1,000)	18,293,309	3,842,061,405
Retail sales, 1997 ($1,000)	14,057,933	2,460,886,012
Retail sales per capita, 1997	$7,743	$9,190
Minority-owned firms, percent of total, 1997	3.8%	14.6%
Women-owned firms, percent of total, 1997	27.1%	26.0%
Federal funds and grants, 2001 ($1,000)	12,540,808	1,763,896,019
Local government employment – full-time equivalent, 1997	59,926	10,227,429
Geography	**West Virginia**	**USA**
Land area, 2000 (square miles)	24,078	3,537,438
Persons per square mile, 2000	75.1	79.6

(a) Includes persons reporting only one race.
(b) Hispanics may be of any race, so also are included in applicable race categories.
Z: Value greater than zero but less than half unit of measure shown.

Source: U.S. Census Bureau State & County QuickFacts

Wisconsin

Statehood: May 29, 1848
Nickname: The Badger State
State bird: Robin
State flower: Wood violet
State tree: Sugar maple
State motto: Forward
State capital: Madison
Population of capital: 208,054 (2000)

Explorer Jean Nicolet claimed the region for France in 1634, but Britain seized the land southwest of the Great Lakes and east of the Mississippi River in 1763. At the end of the Revolutionary War, Britain ceded it to the United States but settlement of the rugged hills between Lake Superior and Lake Michigan was slow. In 1836, the U.S. government established the Territory of Wisconsin. The first state to establish primary elections, Wisconsin also contains the birthplace of the Ringling Brothers Circus at Baraboo. Madison, Milwaukee and Green Bay are the largest metropolitan areas in the Badger State. The names of many of Wisconsin's native tribes are preserved in the designations given to its waterways and its 72 counties: Winnebago, Menominee, Kickapoo and Oneida.

Primarily rolling plain, Wisconsin's landscape is dotted with numerous glacial lakes as it slopes gradually down from the Gogebic range in the north. Meandering rivers such as the St. Croix, the Chippewa, and state's namesake, have carved the terrain into interesting rock formations. Wisconsin is the leading producer of milk, butter, and cheese in the nation with hundreds of factories statewide. The chief crops are hay, corn, oats, fruit, and vegetables. Wisconsin's most valuable resource however, is timber—forty-five percent of the land is forested. Zinc, lead, copper, iron, sand, and gravel mining in the north along with food processing, farm machinery manufacturing, brewing, and tourism are the primary sources of employment. Numerous landmarks like the Apostle Islands National Lakeshore, the St. Croix National Scenic Riverway, the National Railroad Museum and the Wisconsin Maritime Museum encourage sightseers to visit the state more than once.

A seal replete with symbolism sits between the word "Wisconsin" and the date of statehood, "1848," on the blue state flag. Divided into quarters, the coat of arms displays representations of mining, sailing, manufacturing and agriculture. A sailor and a miner stand on either side, with a badger, the state animal, above. Beneath the scene a cornucopia and a stack of lead stand for the state's resources.

Madison

On an isthmus between Lakes Mendota and Monona, Madison was founded as the state capital in 1836, named for President James Madison, and incorporated as a city in 1856. The second-largest urban area in Wisconsin is an educational and manufacturing center in a dairy-farming region. The production of medical equipment, along with agricultural machinery, meat and dairy products, supports the economy.

Wisconsin at a Glance

People	Wisconsin	USA
Population, 2003 estimate	5,472,299	290,809,777
Population percent change, April 1, 2000–July 1, 2001	0.7%	1.2%
Population, 2000	5,363,675	281,421,906
Persons under 5 years old, percent, 2000	6.4%	6.8%
Persons under 18 years old, percent, 2000	25.5%	25.7%
Persons 65 years old and over, percent, 2000	13.1%	12.4%
Female persons, percent, 2000	50.6%	50.9%
White persons, percent, 2000 (a)	88.9%	75.1%
African American persons, percent, 2000 (a)	5.7%	12.3%
Native American persons, percent, 2000 (a)	0.9%	0.9%
Asian persons, percent, 2000 (a)	1.7%	3.6%
Native Hawaiian and Other Pacific Islander, percent, 2000 (a)	Z	0.1%
Persons of Hispanic or Latino origin, percent, 2000 (b)	3.6%	12.5%
White persons, not of Hispanic/Latino origin, percent, 2000	87.3%	69.1%
Foreign born persons, percent, 2000	3.6%	11.1%
Language other than English spoken at home, percent age 5+, 2000	7.3%	17.9%
High school graduates, percent of persons age 25+, 2000	85.1%	80.4%
Bachelor's degree or higher, percent of persons age 25+, 2000	22.4%	24.4%
Persons with a disability, age 5+, 2000	790,917	49,746,248
Homeownership rate, 2000	68.4%	66.2%
Median value of owner-occupied housing units, 2000	$112,200	$119,600
Households, 2000	2,084,544	105,480,101
Persons per household, 2000	2.5	2.59
Median household money income, 1999	$43,791	$41,994
Per capita money income, 1999	$21,271	$21,587
Persons below poverty, percent, 1999	8.7%	12.4%

Business	Wisconsin	USA
Private nonfarm establishments, 1999	139,646	7,008,444
Private nonfarm employment, 1999	2,368,404	110,705,661
Private nonfarm employment, percent change 1990–99	21.5%	18.4%
Nonemployer establishments, 1999	264,657	16,152,604
Manufacturers shipments, 1997 ($1,000)	117,382,992	3,842,061,405
Retail sales, 1997 ($1,000)	50,520,463	2,460,886,012
Retail sales per capita, 1997	$9,715	$9,190
Minority-owned firms, percent of total, 1997	3.7%	14.6%
Women-owned firms, percent of total, 1997	24.4%	26.0%
Federal funds and grants, 2001 ($1,000)	26,645,345	1,763,896,019
Local government employment – full-time equivalent, 1997	201,633	10,227,429

Geography	Wisconsin	USA
Land area, 2000 (square miles)	54,310	3,537,438
Persons per square mile, 2000	98.8	79.6

(a) Includes persons reporting only one race.
(b) Hispanics may be of any race, so also are included in applicable race categories.
Z: Value greater than zero but less than half unit of measure shown.

Source: U.S. Census Bureau State & County QuickFacts

Wyoming

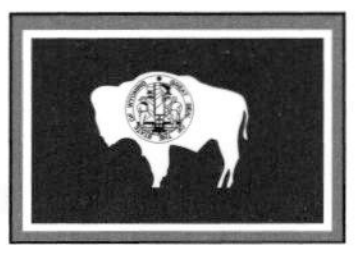

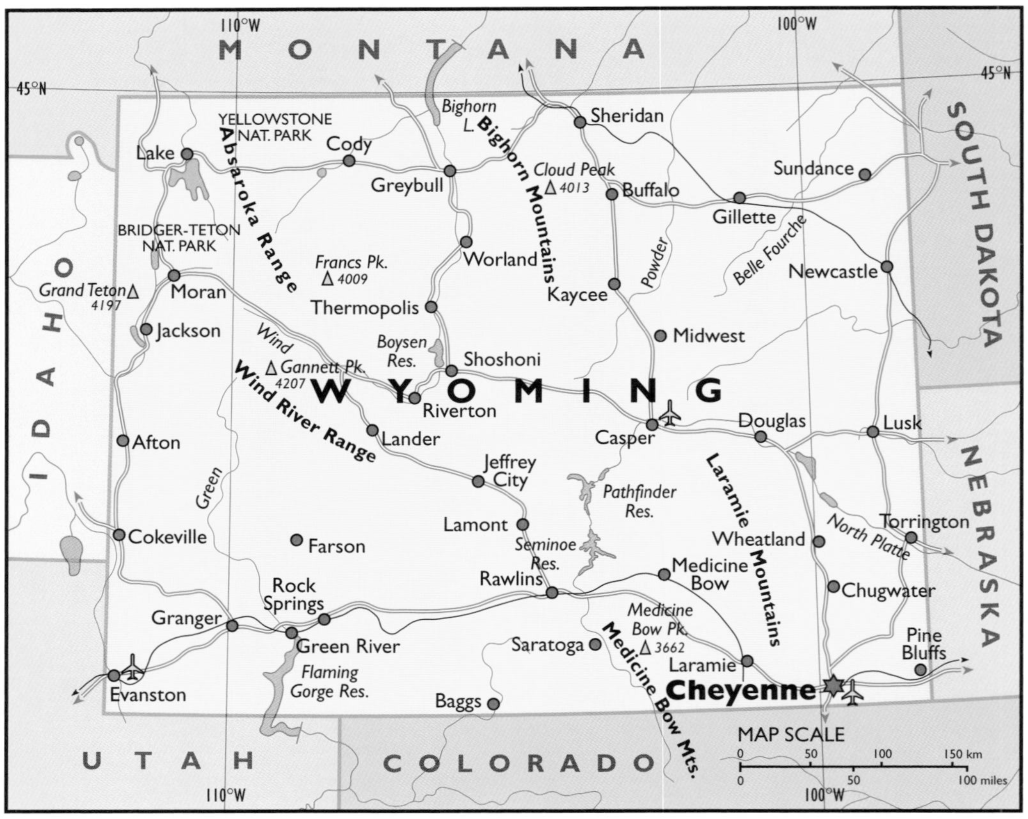

Statehood: July 10, 1890
Nickname: The Equality State
State bird: Meadowlark
State flower: Indian paintbrush
State tree: Cottonwood
State motto: Equal rights
State capital: Cheyenne
Population of capital: 53,001 (2000)

Beginning with the Louisiana Purchase of 1803, the U.S. gradually acquired the entire territory of Wyoming through treaties. The fur trade aided 19th-century development, as did westward migration along the Oregon Trail. The 1860s marked the first dramatic arrival of new settlers, first with the Bozeman Trail, and then with the arrival of the railroad in 1868. While the state did relocate most of the Native American population to reservations by the 1870s, it also passed the first equal rights laws in the nation, ensuring women could vote and hold office. The next 20 years were marked by a rise of vigilante groups formed to deal with cattle rustlers and outlaws. In 1890, Wyoming became the 44th state of the Union. Ranked last in population in the nation, the cities of Cheyenne, Casper and Laramie contain less than half a million inhabitants combined. Wyoming is divided into 23 counties.

Steep mountains and 10 million acres of forest dominate the landscape of Wyoming. The Wind River, and Absaroka ranges, as part of the Rockies cross the state from northwest to southeast offering a route west to pioneers at South Pass. In the east lie the rolling grasslands of high plains country. The north of the state where the Crow, Sioux, and Cheyenne hunted buffalo, is also primarily tall grass plain. Today, fertile farmland and cattle ranches cover the same country. Many rivers, including the North Platte and the Snake, flow down from the mountains. While cattle ranching, sheep, and wheat farming remain important to the economy, Wyoming is a top oil-producing state. Other important mineral resources include coal, bentonite and uranium. Tourism is a vital industry, with the state's natural beauty annually attracting more than seven million visitors. Yellowstone, the largest National Park in the country, occupies the entire northwestern corner of the state. Grand Teton National Park, Devil's Tower National Monument and Fort Laramie National Historic Site also compel tourists to linger in Wyoming.

The state seal is branded on the white silhouette of a buffalo on Wyoming's flag, adopted in 1917. It shows a woman, representing equal rights, with a rancher and a miner on either side. A banner curling around two columns reads: Livestock, Grains, Mines, and Oil. The red border refers to Native Americans and the blood of pioneers.

Cheyenne

Founded in 1867 as a banking and transportation center for freight and livestock, Cheyenne gained a degree of fame due to its connections with figures such as Buffalo Bill, Calamity Jane, and Wild Bill Hickock. Logging, packing plants, and oil refineries have risen in economic importance in the 20th century.

Wyoming at a Glance

People	Wyoming	USA
Population, 2003 estimate	501,242	290,809,777
Population percent change, April 1, 2000–July 1, 2001	0.1%	1.2%
Population, 2000	493,782	281,421,906
Persons under 5 years old, percent, 2000	6.3%	6.8%
Persons under 18 years old, percent, 2000	26.1%	25.7%
Persons 65 years old and over, percent, 2000	11.7%	12.4%
Female persons, percent, 2000	49.7%	50.9%
White persons, percent, 2000 (a)	92.1%	75.1%
African American persons, percent, 2000 (a)	0.8%	12.3%
Native American persons, percent, 2000 (a)	2.3%	0.9%
Asian persons, percent, 2000 (a)	0.6%	3.6%
Native Hawaiian and Other Pacific Islander, percent, 2000 (a)	0.1%	0.1%
Persons of Hispanic or Latino origin, percent, 2000 (b)	6.4%	12.5%
White persons, not of Hispanic/Latino origin, percent, 2000	88.9%	69.1%
Foreign born persons, percent, 2000	2.3%	11.1%
Language other than English spoken at home, percent age 5+, 2000	6.4%	17.9%
High school graduates, percent of persons age 25+, 2000	87.9%	80.4%
Bachelor's degree or higher, percent of persons age 25+, 2000	21.9%	24.4%
Persons with a disability, age 5+, 2000	77,143	49,746,248
Homeownership rate, 2000	70.0%	66.2%
Median value of owner-occupied housing units, 2000	$96,600	$119,600
Households, 2000	193,608	105,480,101
Persons per household, 2000	2.48	2.59
Median household money income, 1999	$37,892	$41,994
Per capita money income, 1999	$19,134	$21,587
Persons below poverty, percent, 1999	11.4%	12.4%

Business	Wyoming	USA
Private nonfarm establishments, 1999	17,909	7,008,444
Private nonfarm employment, 1999	169,188	110,705,661
Private nonfarm employment, percent change 1990–99	28.1%	18.4%
Nonemployer establishments, 1999	35,195	16,152,604
Manufacturers shipments, 1997 ($1,000)	2,955,070	3,842,061,405
Retail sales, 1997 ($1,000)	4,530,537	2,460,886,012
Retail sales per capita, 1997	$9,438	$9,190
Minority-owned firms, percent of total, 1997	4.3%	14.6%
Women-owned firms, percent of total, 1997	22.6%	26.0%
Federal funds and grants, 2001 ($1,000)	3,583,585	1,763,896,019
Local government employment – full-time equivalent, 1997	27,423	10,227,429

Geography	Wyoming	USA
Land area, 2000 (square miles)	97,100	3,537,438
Persons per square mile, 2000	5.1	79.6

(a) Includes persons reporting only one race.
(b) Hispanics may be of any race, so also are included in applicable race categories.
Z: Value greater than zero but less than half unit of measure shown.

Source: U.S. Census Bureau State & County QuickFacts

CANADA

PROVINCIAL MAPS

Settlements
(number of inhabitants)

TORONTO	Over 2,000,000
MONTRÉAL	1,000,000 – 2,000,000
Winnipeg	500,000 – 1,000,000
Windsor	250,000 – 500,000
Kitchener	100,000 – 250,000
Brantford	50,000 – 100,000
St. Thomas	20,000 – 50,000
Elliot Lake	10,000 – 20,000
Elmira	5,000 – 10,000
Palmerston	Less than 5,000
	Urban areas

Communications

Limited-access highways

Principal highways

Secondary highways

Trans-Canada highway

27 Provincial route numbers

Principal railroads

Other railroads

Railroad tunnels

YYZ Principal airports (with location identifiers)

Other airports

Physical features

Perennial streams and rivers

Perennial lakes and reservoirs

Intermittent lakes

Reservoirs (with dams)

Permanent ice and glaciers

▲ 4301 Elevations in meters

▼ 2731 Sea and lake depths in meters

1134 Height of lake surface above sea level in meters

C.Rich Capes, waterfalls, points and mountain passes

Great Duck I. Islands, peninsulas, mountain ranges and peaks

Cape Breton Island Regions, coasts and large islands

Ottawa Rivers, lakes, bays, straits, channels and glaciers

Administration

International boundaries

Provincial boundaries

National parks

Provincial parks and national wildlife areas

PRINCE EDWARD ISLAND Names of provinces and territories

OTTAWA National capital

CITY MAPS

Free limited-access highways (with interchange)

Toll limited-access highways

Tunnels

Primary divided highways

Primary undivided highways

Secondary divided highways

Secondary undivided highways

Other roads

Trans-Canada route numbers

19 Canadian autoroute numbers

27 Provincial route numbers

Railroads

Gare Windsor Principal railroad stations

Principal airports

Other airports

City centers

City center map coverage

Urban areas

Verdun Hampstead Chicot Suburbs (size of type indicates relative populations)

Woodlands and parks

Zoo Points of interest

CITY CENTER MAPS

Free limited-access highways

Toll limited-access highways

Through routes

Secondary routes

Divided highways

Other roads

Tunnels

Railroads

Union Station Railroad stations

S M Subway stations

Urban areas

ST.-LOUIS Suburbs

Woodlands and parks

Public buildings

† Churches

Cathedrals

Museum Points of interest

1:2 000 000
km
miles
NEWFOUNDLAND AND LABRADOR
QUÉBEC
Gulf of St. Lawrence
Île d'Anticosti
Détroit de Jaques-Cartier
Détroit d'Honguedo
St. Lawrence (Saint-Laurent)
Péninsule de la Gaspésie
Monts Chic-Chocs
Notre-Dame
Sept-Îles
Port-Cartier
Havre-St-Pierre
Natashquan
Baie-Comeau
Matane
Gaspé
Labrador City
Fermont
Wabush
Mont Wright
Gagnon
Clarke City
Moisie
Rivière-Pentecôte
Godbout
Franquelin
Mingan
Longue-Pointe-de-Mingan
Rivière-St-Jean
Magpie
Rivière-au-Tonnerre
Sheldrake
Rivière-aux-Graines
Manitou
Rivière-Pigou
Baie-Johan-Beetz
Aguanish
Pointe-Parent
Kegaska
Musquaro
La Romaine
Wolf Bay
Étamamiou
Pointe-à-Maurier
Harrington Harbour
Port-Menier
Baie-Ste-Claire
Baie-du-Renard
Rivière-de-la-Chaloupe
Waco
Percé
Chandler
Pabos Mills
Grande-Rivière
Cap-des-Rosiers
Douglastown
Murdochville
Ste-Anne-des-Monts
Tourelle
Cap-Chat
Les Méchins
Amqui
Causapscal
Mts. Groulx
1104
941
984
1049
1268
1149
RÉS. DE PARC NAT. DE L'ARCHIPEL-DE-MINGAN
RÉS. FAUNIQUE DE L'ÎLE-ANTICOSTI
RÉSERVE FAUNIQUE DE PORT-CARTIER-SEPT-ÎLES
PARC NAT. DE FORILLON
PARC DE LA GASPÉSIE
RÉS. FAUNIQUE DES CHIC-CHOCS
RÉS. FAUNIQUE DE MATANE
RÉS. FAUNIQUE DE DUNIÈRE
RÉS. FAUNIQUE DE PORT-DANIEL
174
175
177

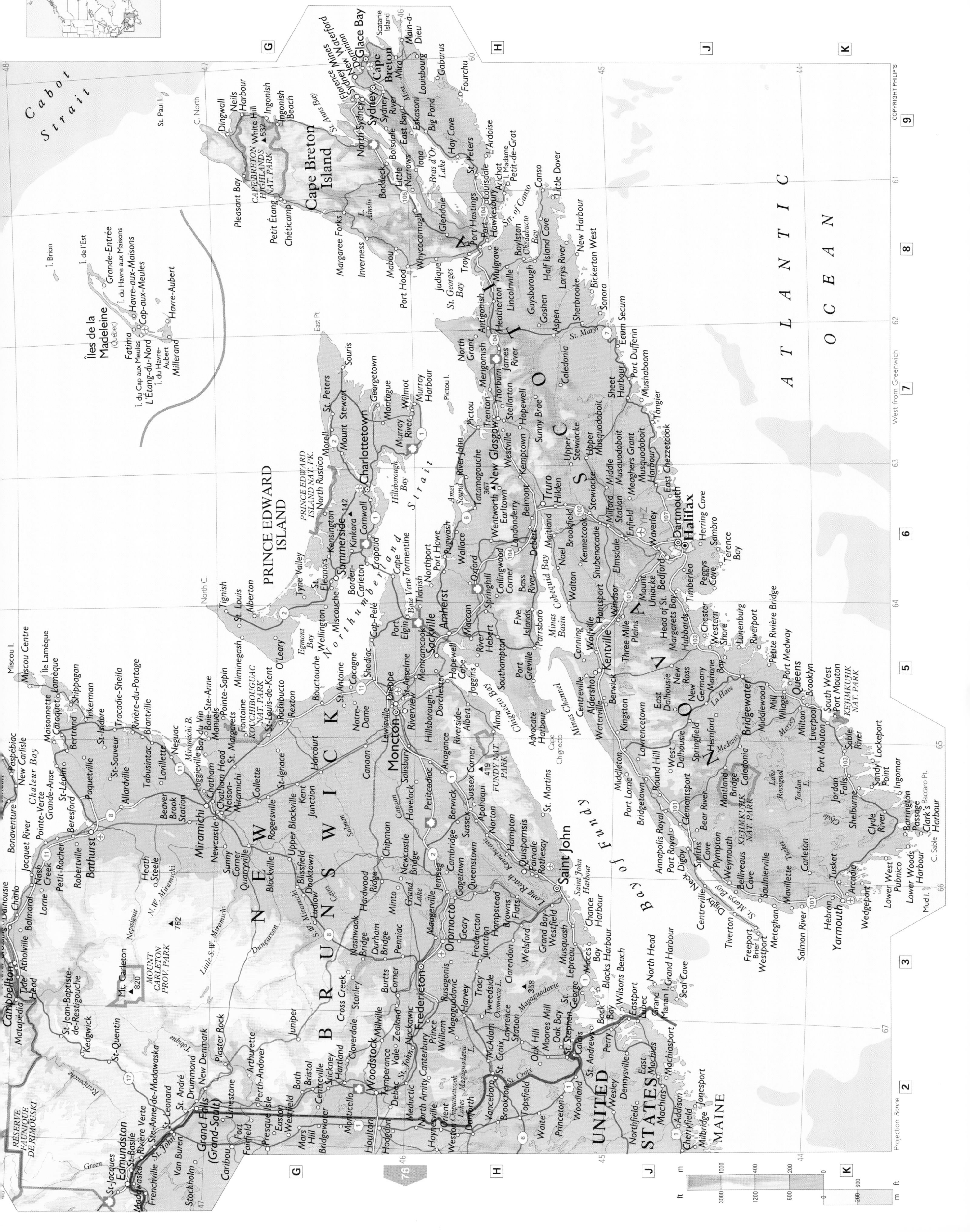
Cabot Strait
Gulf of St. Lawrence
Îles de la Madeleine
(Québec)
Grande-Entrée
Havre-aux-Maisons
Cap-aux-Meules
Havre-Aubert
Fatima
L'Étang-du-Nord
Millerand
Î. Brion
Î. de l'Est
St. Paul I.
C. North
Cape Breton Island
CAPE BRETON HIGHLANDS NAT. PARK
Cape Breton
Dingwall
Neils Harbour
White Hill
Ingonish
Ingonish Beach
Pleasant Bay
Petit Étang
Chéticamp
Margaree Forks
Inverness
Mabou
Port Hood
Whycocomagh
Baddeck
Little Narrows
Iona
Bras d'Or Lake
Lake Ainslie
St. Anns Bay
North Sydney
Sydney
Sydney Mines
Florence
New Waterford
New Victoria
Dominion
Glace Bay
Scatarie Island
Main-à-Dieu
Louisbourg
Gabarus
Fourchu
Mira
Eskasoni
Big Pond
East Bay
Boisdale
Hay Cove
St. Peters
L'Ardoise
Louisdale
Arichat
Petit-de-Grat
I. Madame
Port Hastings
Port Hawkesbury
Str. of Canso
Canso
Little Dover
Glendale
Judique
St. Georges Bay
Troy
Mulgrave
Antigonish
Heatherton
Lincolnville
Boylston
Guysborough
Chedabucto Bay
Half Island Cove
Larrys River
New Harbour
Bickerton West
Sherbrooke
Sonora
Goshen
Aspen
St. Marys
Ecum Secum
Port Dufferin
Mushaboom
Sheet Harbour
Tangier
Caledonia
North Grant
Merigomish
Thorburn
James River
Pictou
Trenton
New Glasgow
Stellarton
Westville
Hopewell
Sunny Brae
Kemptown
Upper Stewiacke
Upper Musquodoboit
Middle Musquodoboit
Meaghers Grant
Musquodoboit Harbour
East Chezzetcook
River John
Tatamagouche
Wentworth
Earltown
Londonderry
Belmont
Truro
Hilden
Stewiacke
Milford Station
Enfield
Brookfield
Maitland
Noel
Kennetcook
Shubenacadie
Elmsdale
Waverley
Dartmouth
Halifax
Herring Cove
Sambro
Terence Bay
Peggys Cove
Timberlea
Bedford
Mount Uniacke
Head of St. Margarets Bay
Hubbards
Chester
Western Shore
Lunenburg
Riverport
Petite Rivière Bridge
Port Medway
Mahone Bay
New Ross
New Germany
Bridgewater
La Have
Mill Village
Queens
Brooklyn
Liverpool
Milton
South West Port Mouton
KEJIMKUJIK NAT. PARK
Port Mouton
Sable River
Lockeport
Jordan Falls
Shelburne
Sandy Point
Ingomar
Barrington Passage
Clark's Harbour
Baccaro Pt.
C. Sable
Clyde River
Lower West Pubnico
Lower Woods Harbour
Tusket
Arcadia
Wedgeport
Yarmouth
Hebron
Salmon River
Carleton
Mavillette
Meteghan
Saulnierville
Belliveaus Cove
Weymouth
Plympton
Smiths Cove
Digby
Digby Neck
St. Marys Bay
Centreville
Tiverton
Freeport
Westport
Brier I.
Annapolis Royal
Port Royal
Clementsport
Bear River
Maitland Bridge
Caledonia
Bridgetown
Port Lorne
Middleton
Round Hill
West Dalhousie
Springfield
Hemford
Lawrencetown
Kingston
East Dalhousie
Berwick
Waterville
Aldershot
Kentville
Wolfville
Canning
Windsor
Hantsport
Three Mile Plains
Walton
Minas Basin
Minas Channel
Cobequid Bay
Parrsboro
Five Islands
Bass River
Debert
Port Greville
Advocate Harbour
Cape Chignecto
Southampton
River Hebert
Springhill
Oxford
Collingwood Corner
Maccan
Amherst
Joggins
Chignecto Bay
Pugwash
Wallace
Port Howe
Northport
Tidnish
Amet Sound
Northumberland Strait
PRINCE EDWARD ISLAND
PRINCE EDWARD ISLAND NAT. PK.
Tignish
St. Louis
Alberton
North C.
O'Leary
Tyne Valley
St. Eleanors
Summerside
Kensington
Kinkora
Borden-Carleton
Crapaud
Cornwall
Charlottetown
North Rustico
Hillsborough Bay
Morell
Mount Stewart
St. Peters
Souris
East Pt.
Georgetown
Montague
Murray River
Murray Harbour
Wilmot
Pictou I.
Egmont Bay
Wellington
Miscouche
Cape Tormentine
Port Elgin
Baie Verte
Sackville
Memramcook
St.-Anselme
Dieppe
Moncton
Riverview
Shediac
Cap-Pelé
Cocagne
Notre-Dame
Bouctouche
St.-Antoine
Rexton
Richibucto
St.-Louis-de-Kent
KOUCHIBOUGUAC NAT. PARK
Pointe-Sapin
Miminegash
Baie-Ste-Anne
Escuminac
Neguac
Miramichi B.
Brantville
Rivière-du-Portage
Tracadie-Sheila
Inkerman
Shippagan
Lamèque
Île Lamèque
Miscou Centre
Miscou I.
Caraquet
Maisonnette
Bertrand
St-Isidore
Paquetville
St-Sauveur
Allardville
Tabusintac
Lavillette
Loggieville
Chatham
Chatham Head
Miramichi
Nelson-Miramichi
Newcastle
Manuels
St. Margarets
Collette
St.-Ignace
Harcourt
Rogersville
Kent Junction
Canaan
Salisbury
Petitcodiac
Anagance
Hillsborough
Dorchester
Riverside-Albert
Hopewell Cape
Alma
FUNDY NAT. PARK
Sussex Corner
Sussex
Apohaqui
Norton
Hampton
Havelock
Berwick
Cambridge
Gagetown
Queenstown
Jemseg
Chipman
Newcastle Bridge
Grand Lake
Minto
Hardwood Ridge
Doaktown
Blissfield
Blackville
Upper Blackville
Quarryville
Sunny Corner
Ludlow
Boiestown
NEW BRUNSWICK
Bay of Fundy
Saint John
Quispamsis
Rothesay
Fairvale
St. Martins
Kennebecasis
Long Reach
Grand Bay-Westfield
Musquash
Chance Harbour
Lepreau
Maces Bay
Blacks Harbour
St. George
Wilsons Beach
North Head
Grand Harbour
Seal Cove
Grand Manan I.
Eastport
Lubec
Campobello I.
St. Andrews
St. Stephen
Calais
Oak Bay
Moores Mill
Oak Hill
Lawrence Station
St. Croix
McAdam
Tweedside
Harvey
Magaguadavic
Rusagonis
Oromocto
Fredericton
Fredericton Junction
Hampstead
Browns Flats
Welsford
Clarendon
Geary
Maugerville
Penniac
Durham Bridge
Nashwaak Bridge
Stanley
Cross Creek
Burtts Corner
Millville
Nackawic
Zealand
Prince William
Canterbury
Woodstock
Hartland
Bath
Florenceville
Centreville
Bristol
Perth-Andover
Arthurette
Plaster Rock
Juniper
Tobique
New Denmark
Drummond
Grand Falls (Grand-Sault)
Limestone
St. André
St. Leonard
Ste-Anne-de-Madawaska
Rivière Verte
St-Basile
Edmundston
St-Jacques
Madawaska
Frenchville
Van Buren
Stockholm
Caribou
Fort Fairfield
Presque Isle
Easton
Westfield
Mars Hill
Bridgewater
Monticello
Houlton
Hodgdon
Debec
Meductic
North Amity
Haynesville
Orient
Weston
Danforth
Vanceboro
Brookton
Topsfield
Waite
Princeton
Woodland
Wesley
Dennysville
Machias
Machiasport
Jonesport
Northfield
Addison
Cherryfield
Milbridge
UNITED STATES
MAINE
RÉSERVE FAUNIQUE DE RIMOUSKI
Green
St-Quentin
Kedgwick
St-Jean-Baptiste-de-Restigouche
Matapédia
Campbellton
Tide Head
Atholville
Dalhousie
Charlo
Balmoral
Jacquet River
Nash Creek
Lorne
Belledune
Petit-Rocher
Robertville
Bathurst
Beresford
Pointe-Verte
Grande-Anse
St-Léolin
New Carlisle
Bonaventure
Paspébiac
Chaleur Bay
Mt. Carleton 820
MOUNT CARLETON PROV. PARK
Nepisiguit
N.W. Miramichi
S.W. Miramichi
Little S.W. Miramichi
Dungarvon
Heath Steele
ATLANTIC OCEAN
NOVA SCOTIA
Projection: Bonne
West from Greenwich
COPYRIGHT PHILIP'S
76
ft m
3000 1000
1200 400
600 200
0 0
200 600

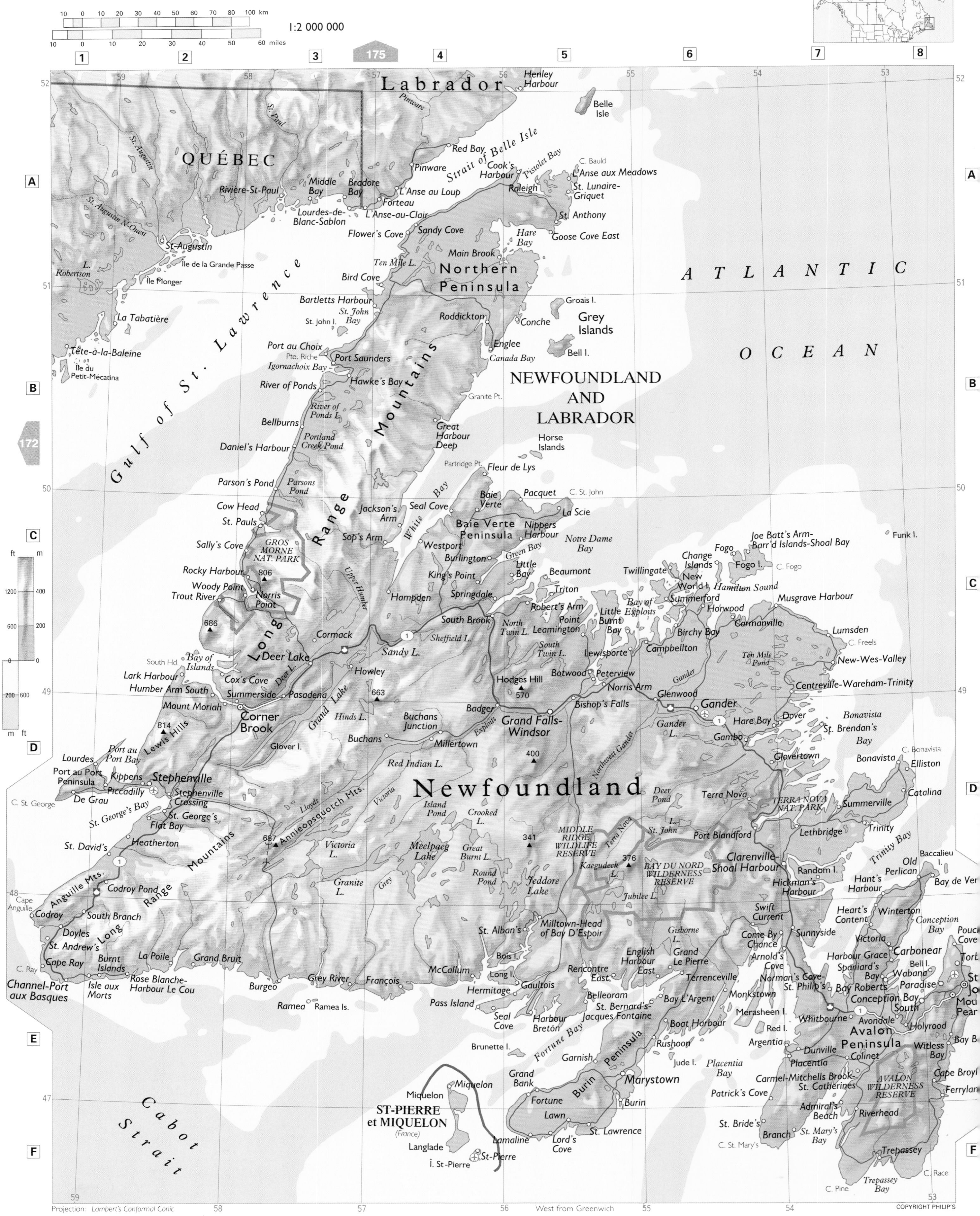

1:2 000 000
Projection: Lambert's Conformal Conic
West from Greenwich
COPYRIGHT PHILIP'S
175
172
Labrador
QUÉBEC
NEWFOUNDLAND AND LABRADOR
ATLANTIC OCEAN
Gulf of St. Lawrence
Cabot Strait
Strait of Belle Isle
Newfoundland
Northern Peninsula
Long Range Mountains
Baie Verte Peninsula
Burin Peninsula
Avalon Peninsula
Anguille Mts.
Annieopsquotch Mts.
Lewis Hills
GROS MORNE NAT. PARK
TERRA NOVA NAT. PARK
MIDDLE RIDGE WILDLIFE RESERVE
BAY DU NORD WILDERNESS RESERVE
AVALON WILDERNESS RESERVE
ST-PIERRE et MIQUELON
(France)
Henley Harbour
Belle Isle
Red Bay
Pinware
Cook's Harbour
Pistolet Bay
C. Bauld
L'Anse aux Meadows
Raleigh
St. Lunaire-Griquet
St. Anthony
Goose Cove East
Hare Bay
Main Brook
Rivière-St-Paul
Middle Bay
Bradore Bay
L'Anse au Loup
Forteau
L'Anse-au-Clair
Lourdes-de-Blanc-Sablon
Flower's Cove
Sandy Cove
St-Augustin
Île de la Grande Passe
Île Monger
L. Robertson
La Tabatière
Tête-à-la-Baleine
Île du Petit-Mécatina
Ten Mile L.
Bird Cove
Bartletts Harbour
St. John Bay
St. John I.
Roddickton
Conche
Groais I.
Grey Islands
Bell I.
Englee
Canada Bay
Port au Choix
Pte. Riche
Igornachoix Bay
Port Saunders
Hawke's Bay
River of Ponds
River of Ponds L.
Granite Pt.
Bellburns
Portland Creek Pond
Great Harbour Deep
Horse Islands
Daniel's Harbour
Partridge Pt.
Fleur de Lys
Parson's Pond
Parsons Pond
Cow Head
St. Pauls
Jackson's Arm
Seal Cove
White Bay
Baie Verte
Pacquet
C. St. John
La Scie
Sop's Arm
Nippers Harbour
Notre Dame Bay
Sally's Cove
Westport
Burlington
Green Bay
Little Bay
Rocky Harbour
806
Woody Point
Trout River
Norris Point
Upper Humber
King's Point
Hampden
Springdale
Beaumont
Triton
Twillingate
Change Islands
Fogo
Fogo I.
C. Fogo
Joe Batt's Arm-Barr'd Islands-Shoal Bay
Funk I.
New World I.
Hamilton Sound
Summerford
Horwood
Musgrave Harbour
Bay of Exploits
Robert's Arm
Little Burnt Bay
Point Leamington
Carmanville
686
South Brook
North Twin L.
Sheffield L.
Birchy Bay
Lumsden
C. Freels
Cormack
Deer Lake
Sandy L.
South Twin L.
Lewisporte
Campbellton
Ten Mile Pond
New-Wes-Valley
South Hd.
Bay of Islands
Howley
Botwood
Peterview
Gander
Lark Harbour
Cox's Cove
Deer L.
Hodges Hill
570
Norris Arm
Glenwood
Centreville-Wareham-Trinity
Humber Arm South
Summerside
Pasadena
663
Bishop's Falls
Gander
Badger
Grand Falls-Windsor
Mount Moriah
Corner Brook
Grand Lake
Hinds L.
Buchans Junction
Exploits
Gander L.
Hare Bay
Dover
Bonavista Bay
St. Brendan's
814
Buchans
Millertown
Northwest Gander
Gambo
Glover I.
Port au Port Bay
Red Indian L.
400
Glovertown
C. Bonavista
Bonavista
Elliston
Lourdes
Port au Port Peninsula
Kippens
Stephenville
Stephenville Crossing
Piccadilly
Catalina
C. St. George
De Grau
St. George's Bay
St. George's
Flat Bay
Lloyds
Victoria
Island Pond
Crooked L.
Deer Pond
Terra Nova
Summerville
St. John L.
Port Blandford
Trinity
Lethbridge
Trinity Bay
Baccalieu I.
St. David's
Heatherton
687
Victoria L.
Meelpaeg Lake
Great Burnt L.
341
Kaegudeck L.
376
Clarenville-Shoal Harbour
Random I.
Old Perlican
Hant's Harbour
Bay de Verde
Codroy Pond
Round Pond
Granite L.
Grey
Jeddore Lake
Jubilee L.
Hickman's Harbour
Cape Anguille
Codroy
South Branch
Swift Current
Heart's Content
Winterton
Conception Bay
Doyles
St. Alban's
Milltown-Head of Bay D'Espoir
Gisborne L.
Come By Chance
Sunnyside
Victoria
Carbonear
Pouch Cove
St. Andrew's
C. Ray
Cape Ray
Burnt Islands
La Poile
Grand Bruit
English Harbour East
Grand Le Pierre
Arnold's Cove
Harbour Grace
Spaniard's Bay
Bell I.
Bois I.
Long I.
McCallum
Rencontre East
Terrenceville
Norman's Cove-St. Philip's
Bay Roberts
Wabana
Paradise
Channel-Port aux Basques
Isle aux Morts
Rose Blanche-Harbour Le Cou
Burgeo
Grey River
François
Hermitage
Gaultois
Belleoram
Monkstown
Conception Bay South
Ramea
Ramea Is.
Pass Island
St. Bernard's-Jacques Fontaine
Bay L'Argent
Merasheen I.
Whitbourne
Avondale
Holyrood
Seal Cove
Harbour Breton
Boat Harbour
Red I.
Bay Bulls
Brunette I.
Fortune Bay
Rushoon
Argentia
Dunville
Witless Bay
Garnish
Jude I.
Placentia Bay
Placentia
Colinet
Grand Bank
Miquelon
Marystown
Carmel-Mitchells Brook-St. Catherines
Cape Broyle
Ferryland
Fortune
Burin
Patrick's Cove
Lawn
Admiral's Beach
Riverhead
Lamaline
Lord's Cove
St. Lawrence
St. Bride's
Branch
St. Mary's Bay
Langlade
St-Pierre
Î. St-Pierre
C. St. Mary's
Trepassey
C. Race
C. Pine
Trepassey Bay

1:5 600 000

50 0 50 100 150 200 250 300 km

50 0 50 100 150 200 miles

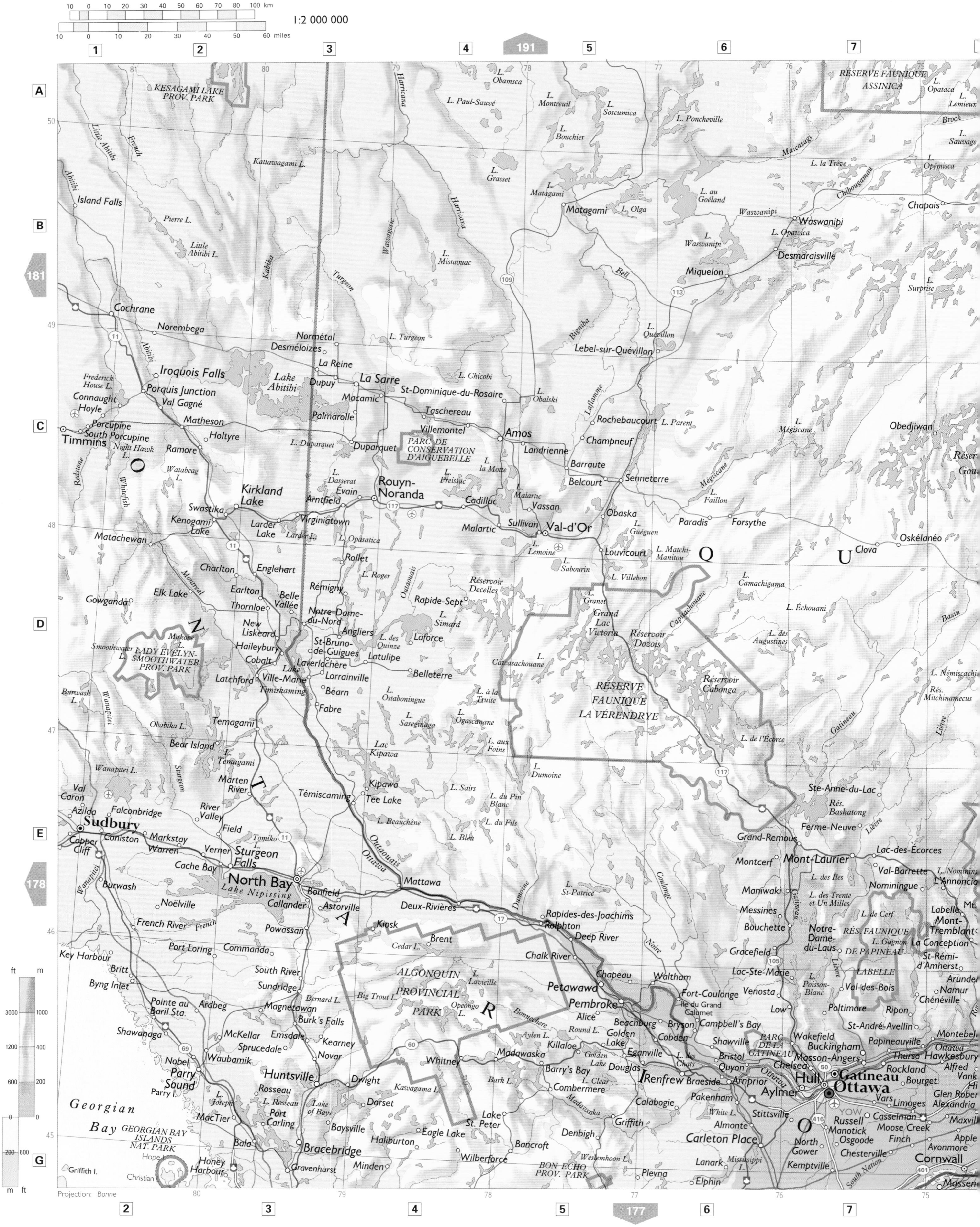

1:2 000 000
km
miles
191
181
178
177
Projection: Bonne
ft
m
KESAGAMI LAKE PROV. PARK
RESERVE FAUNIQUE ASSINICA
L. Obamsca
L. Paul-Sauvé
L. Montreuil
L. Soscumica
L. Poncheville
L. Opataca
L. Lemieux
Brock
L. Sauvage
Little Abitibi
French
Abitibi
Harricana
Kattawagami L.
L. Bouchier
L. Grasset
Maicasagi
L. la Trêve
L. Opémisca
Chibougamau
Island Falls
L. Matagami
Matagami
L. Olga
L. au Goéland
Waswanipi
Chapais
Pierre L.
Little Abitibi L.
Kabika
Wawagosic
L. Mistaouac
L. Waswanipi
L. Opawica
Desmaraisville
Bell
Miquelon
Turgeon
L. Surprise
Cochrane
Norembega
Normétal
Desméloizes
L. Turgeon
Bigniba
L. Quévillon
Lebel-sur-Quévillon
La Reine
Iroquois Falls
Frederick House L.
Lake Abitibi
Dupuy
La Sarre
L. Chicobi
St-Dominique-du-Rosaire
L. Obalski
Laflamme
Connaught
Porquis Junction
Val Gagné
Hoyle
Macamic
Palmarolle
Taschereau
Rochebaucourt
L. Parent
L. Mégiscane
Obedjiwan
Matheson
Porcupine
South Porcupine
Timmins
Night Hawk L.
Holtyre
Villemontel
Amos
Champneuf
Ramore
L. Duparquet
Duparquet
PARC DE CONSERVATION D'AIGUEBELLE
Landrienne
Redstone
Whitefish
Watabeag L.
L. la Motte
Barraute
Mégiscane
Réser
Gou
Rouyn-Noranda
L. Dasserat
Évain
L. Preissac
Belcourt
Senneterre
L. Faillon
Kirkland Lake
Swastika
Arntfield
Cadillac
L. Malartic
Vassan
Kenogami Lake
Larder Lake
Virginiatown
Malartic
Sullivan
Val-d'Or
Obaska
Paradis
Forsythe
Matachewan
L. Opasatica
L. Guéguen
Oskélanéo
Clova
L. Lemoine
L. Sabourin
Louvicourt
L. Matchi-Manitou
Charlton
Englehart
Rollet
L. Roger
Réservoir Decelles
L. Villebon
Capitachouane
L. Camachigama
Montreal
Earlton
Rémigny
Ottawa
Rapide-Sept
L. Granet
Gowganda
Elk Lake
Thornloe
Belle Vallée
Notre-Dame-du-Nord
L. Simard
Grand Lac Victoria
Réservoir Dozois
L. Échouani
Bazin
New Liskeard
Angliers
Laforce
L. des Quinze
Maskobe L.
LADY EVELYN-SMOOTHWATER PROV. PARK
Smoothwater L.
Haileybury
Cobalt
St-Bruno-de-Guigues
Latulipe
L. Cawasachouane
L. des Augustines
Laverlochère
Belleterre
Latchford
Ville-Marie
Lake Timiskaming
Lorrainville
RESERVE FAUNIQUE LA VÉRENDRYE
Réservoir Cabonga
L. Némiscachi
Burwash L.
Wanapitei
Béarn
L. Ostaboningue
L. à la Truite
Rés. Mitchinamecus
Fabre
L. Saseginaga
L. Ogascanane
Gatineau
Lièvre
Obabika L.
Temagami
L. aux Foins
L. de l'Écorce
Bear Island
L. Temagami
Lac Kipawa
L. Dumoine
Wanapitei L.
Sturgeon
Marten River
Kipawa
Tee Lake
L. Sairs
L. du Pin Blanc
Ste-Anne-du-Lac
Val Caron
Falconbridge
River Valley
Témiscaming
Rés. Baskatong
Azilda
Sudbury
L. Beauchêne
L. du Fils
Ferme-Neuve
Coniston
Field
Tomiko L.
L. Bleu
Grand-Remous
Copper Cliff
Markstay
Warren
Verner
Sturgeon Falls
Mont-Laurier
Lac-des-Écorces
Montcerf
Cache Bay
North Bay
Lake Nipissing
Mattawa
Coulonge
Val-Barrette
L. Nominingue
L'Annonciation
Burwash
Bonfield
Callander
Dumoine
L. St-Patrice
Maniwaki
L. des Îles
Nominingue
Noëlville
Astorville
Deux-Rivières
Rapides-des-Joachims
L. des Trente et Un Milles
Messines
Labelle
Mt.
French River
Powassan
Kiosk
Rolphton
Deep River
Bouchette
L. de Cerf
Mont-Tremblant
Brent
Cedar L.
Noire
Notre-Dame-du-Laus
RÉS. FAUNIQUE DE PAPINEAU-LABELLE
L. Gagnon
La Conception
Port Loring
Commanda
Chalk River
Gracefield
St-Rémi-d'Amherst
Key Harbour
ALGONQUIN PROVINCIAL PARK
L. Lavieille
Chapeau
Waltham
Lac-Ste-Marie
Arundel
Britt
South River
Sundridge
Petawawa
Fort-Coulonge
Venosta
L. Poisson-Blanc
Val-des-Bois
Namur
Byng Inlet
Big Trout L.
Opeongo L.
Pembroke
Île du Grand Calumet
Low
Chénéville
Pointe au Baril Sta.
Ardbeg
Bernard L.
Magnetawan
Bonnechere
Alice
Poltimore
Ripon
Burk's Falls
Beachburg
Bryson
Campbell's Bay
St-André-Avellin
Shawanaga
Round L.
Golden Lake
Cobden
PARC DE LA GATINEAU
Wakefield
Buckingham
Papineauville
Montebello
McKellar
Emsdale
Kearney
Aylen L.
Killaloe
Shawville
Masson-Angers
Thurso
Hawkesbury
Spruceedale
Novar
Madawaska
Eganville
L. des Chats
Bristol
Quyon
Nobel
Waubamik
Parry Sound
Parry I.
Huntsville
Whitney
Golden Lake
Barry's Bay
Douglas
Renfrew
Braeside
Arnprior
Hull
Gatineau
Ottawa
Bourget
Alfred
Vank
Dwight
Kawagama L.
Bark L.
L. Clear
Combermere
Aylmer
Glen Robertson
Rosseau
L. Rosseau
Port Carling
Dorset
Madawaska
Calabogie
Pakenham
Vars
Limoges
Alexandria
Georgian Bay
L. Joseph
Lake of Bays
Lake St. Peter
White L.
Stittsville
YOW
Russell
Casselman
Moose Creek
Maxville
MacTier
Baysville
Griffith
Almonte
Manotick
Osgoode
Finch
GEORGIAN BAY ISLANDS NAT. PARK
Haliburton
Eagle Lake
Denbigh
Carleton Place
North Gower
Apple Hill
Avonmore
Bala
Bracebridge
Bancroft
Wilberforce
Weslemkoon L.
Lanark
Mississippi
Chesterville
Cornwall
Hope I.
Honey Harbour
Gravenhurst
Minden
BON ECHO PROV. PARK
Plevna
Kemptville
South Nation
Griffith I.
Christian I.
Elphin
Massena
O
N
T
A
R
I
O
Q
U

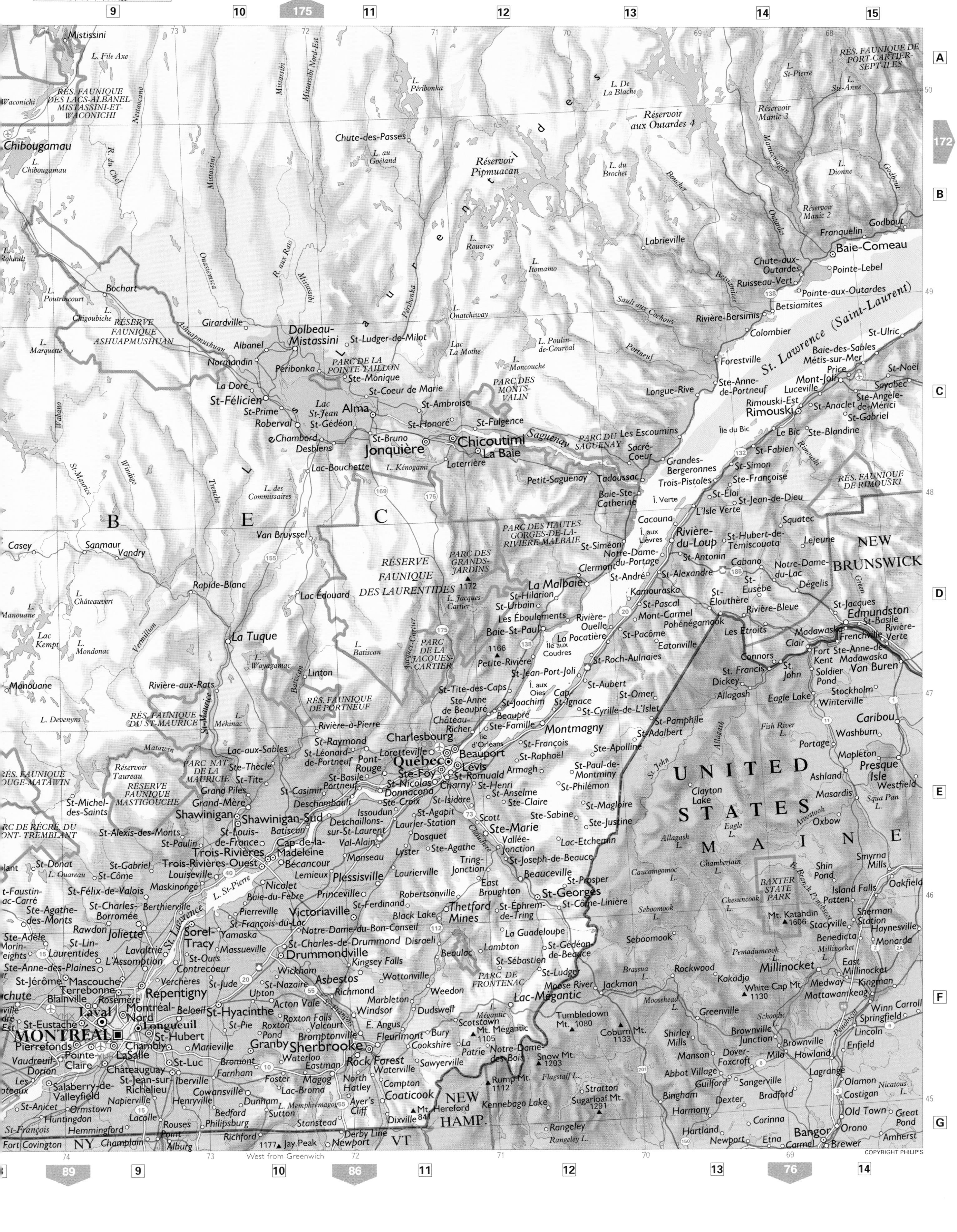
9
10
175
11
12
13
14
15
A
B
C
D
E
F
G
172
89
86
76
74
73
72
71
70
69
68
50
49
48
47
46
45
West from Greenwich
COPYRIGHT PHILIP'S
Mistissini
L. File Axe
RÉS. FAUNIQUE DES LACS-ALBANEL-MISTASSINI-ET-WACONICHI
Waconichi
Chibougamau
L. Chibougamau
R. du Chef
Mistassibi
Mistassibi Nord-Est
Mistassini
L. Péribonka
Chute-des-Passes
L. au Goéland
Réservoir Pipmuacan
L. De La Blache
Réservoir aux Outardes 4
Réservoir Manic 3
L. St-Pierre
L. Ste-Anne
RÉS. FAUNIQUE DE PORT-CARTIER-SEPT-ÎLES
L. du Brochet
L. Dionne
Godbout
Réservoir Manic 2
Manicouagan
Outardes
Boucher
Labrieville
Franquelin
Baie-Comeau
Chute-aux-Outardes
Pointe-Lebel
Ruisseau-Vert
Pointe-aux-Outardes
Betsiamites
Rivière-Bersimis
Colombier
St. Lawrence (Saint-Laurent)
Sault aux Cochons
L. Itomamo
L. Rowray
L. Onatchiway
Péribonka
R. aux Rats
Ouasiemsca
Bochart
L. Poutrincourt
L. Chigoubiche
RÉSERVE FAUNIQUE ASHUAPMUSHUAN
Ashuapmushuan
Girardville
Albanel
Dolbeau-Mistassini
St-Ludger-de-Milot
L. Marquette
Normandin
Péribonka
PARC DE LA POINTE-TAILLON
Ste-Monique
La Doré
St-Félicien
St-Prime
Roberval
Chambord
Desbiens
Lac St-Jean
Alma
St-Gédéon
St-Coeur de Marie
St-Ambroise
St-Honoré
St-Fulgence
St-Bruno
Jonquière
Chicoutimi
La Baie
Laterrière
L. Kénogami
Lac-Bouchette
Saguenay
PARC DU SAGUENAY
Petit-Saguenay
Tadoussac
Les Escoumins
Sacré-Coeur
Grandes-Bergeronnes
Baie-Ste-Catherine
Longue-Rive
Portneuf
Forestville
Ste-Anne-de-Portneuf
L. Poulin-de-Courval
Lac La Mothe
L. Moncouche
PARC DES MONTS-VALIN
Baie-des-Sables
Métis-sur-Mer
St-Ulric
Price
Mont-Joli
St-Noël
Sayabec
Luceville
Rimouski-Est
Rimouski
St-Anaclet
Ste-Angèle-de-Mérici
St-Gabriel
Île du Bic
Le Bic
Ste-Blandine
St-Fabien
St-Simon
Ste-Françoise
Trois-Pistoles
St-Éloi
St-Jean-de-Dieu
L'Isle Verte
Î. Verte
RÉS. FAUNIQUE DE RIMOUSKI
Squatec
Cacouna
Rivière-du-Loup
Î. aux Lièvres
St-Hubert-de-Témiscouata
St-Antonin
Cabano
Lejeune
Notre-Dame-du-Lac
NEW BRUNSWICK
Dégelis
St-Alexandre
St-André
Notre-Dame-du-Portage
St-Siméon
Clermont
PARC DES HAUTES-GORGES-DE-LA-RIVIÈRE-MALBAIE
PARC DES GRANDS-JARDINS
RÉSERVE FAUNIQUE DES LAURENTIDES
La Malbaie
St-Hilarion
St-Urbain
Les Éboulements
Baie-St-Paul
Kamouraska
St-Pascal
Mont-Carmel
Rivière-Ouelle
St-Éleuthère
Pohénégamook
Rivière-Bleue
Ste-Eusèbe
St-Jacques
Edmundston
Ste-Basile
Rivière-Verte
Madawaska
Frenchville
Clair
Fort Kent
Ste-Anne-de-Madawaska
Soldier Pond
Van Buren
La Pocatière
Île aux Coudres
St-Pacôme
Eatonville
Les Étroits
St-Roch-Aulnaies
Petite-Rivière
St-Jean-Port-Joli
St-Aubert
Connors
St. Francis
St. John
Dickey
Allagash
Eagle Lake
Stockholm
Winterville
Caribou
Î. aux Oies
Cap-St-Ignace
St-Omer
St-Cyrille-de-L'Islet
Casey
Sanmaur
Vandry
Van Bruyssel
Rapide-Blanc
L. Châteauvert
Manouane
Lac Kempt
L. Mondonac
Vermillion
La Tuque
Lac Édouard
L. Jacques-Cartier
L. Batiscan
PARC DE LA JACQUES-CARTIER
Jacques-Cartier
Linton
L. Wayagamac
Batiscan
RÉS. FAUNIQUE DE PORTNEUF
St-Tite-des-Caps
Ste-Anne de Beaupré
St-Joachim
Beaupré
Château-Richer
Île d'Orléans
Ste-Famille
Montmagny
St-Pamphile
St-Adalbert
Fish River L.
Washburn
Portage
Mapleton
Presque Isle
Ashland
Westfield
Manouane
Rivière-aux-Rats
L. Devenyns
RÉS. FAUNIQUE DU ST-MAURICE
L. Mékinac
St-Maurice
Rivière-à-Pierre
St-Raymond
Charlesbourg
Loretteville
Québec
Beauport
Lévis
St-Léonard-de-Portneuf
Pont-Rouge
Ste-Foy
St-Romuald
St-Nicolas
Charny
Donnacona
St-François
St-Raphaël
Armagh
Ste-Apolline
St-Paul-de-Montminy
St-Philémon
UNITED STATES
MAINE
Clayton Lake
Eagle L.
Masardis
Squa Pan L.
Oxbow
Aroostook
Lac-aux-Sables
PARC NAT. DE LA MAURICIE
Ste-Thècle
Ste-Tite
Réservoir Taureau
RÉSERVE FAUNIQUE MASTIGOUCHE
RÉS. FAUNIQUE ROUGE-MATAWIN
Matawin
Grand Piles
Grand-Mère
St-Michel-des-Saints
Shawinigan
Shawinigan-Sud
St-Casimir
Ste-Basile
Portneuf
Deschambault
Ste-Croix
St-Isidore
St-Henri
Ste-Anselme
Ste-Claire
Ste-Sabine
St-Magloire
Ste-Justine
St-Agapit
Issoudun
Scott
Ste-Marie
Chaudière
Laurier-Station
Deschaillons-sur-St-Laurent
St-Louis-de-France
Batiscan
St-Alexis-des-Monts
PARC DE RÉCRÉ. DU MONT-TREMBLANT
St-Paulin
Trois-Rivières
Cap-de-la-Madeleine
Val-Alain
Dosquet
Vallée-Jonction
St-Joseph-de-Beauce
Lac-Etchemin
Allagash L.
Chamberlain L.
Trois-Rivières-Ouest
Bécancour
Manseau
Lyster
Ste-Agathe
Tring-Jonction
Beauceville
St-Prosper
Caucomgomoc L.
BAXTER STATE PARK
E. Branch Penobscot
Smyrna Mills
Shin Pond
Oakfield
St-Donat
L. Ouareau
St-Gabriel
St-Côme
Louiseville
Lemieux
Plessisville
Laurierville
East Broughton
St-Georges
St-Côme-Linière
Island Falls
Patten
Maskinongé
St-Félix-de-Valois
St-Faustin-Lac-Carré
L. St-Pierre
Nicolet
Baie-du-Febvre
Princeville
Robertsonville
Thetford Mines
St-Éphrem-de-Tring
Chesuncook L.
Seboomook L.
Mt. Katahdin 1606
Sherman Station
Haynesville
Ste-Agathe-des-Monts
Ste-Charles-Borromée
Berthierville
Pierreville
St-François-du-Lac
Victoriaville
St-Ferdinand
Black Lake
Stacyville
Benedicta
Monarda
Rawdon
Joliette
Sorel-Tracy
Yamaska
Notre-Dame-du-Bon-Conseil
La Guadeloupe
Seboomook
Millinocket
Ste-Adèle
St-Lin-Laurentides
Lavaltrie
Massueville
St-Charles-de-Drummond
Disraeli
Lambton
St-Gédéon-de-Beauce
Pemadumcook L.
Ste-Anne-des-Plaines
L'Assomption
St-Ours
Contrecoeur
Drummondville
Kingsey Falls
Beaulac
St-Sébastien
St-Jérôme
Mascouche
Terrebonne
Verchères
Wickham
Asbestos
Wottonville
PARC DE FRONTENAC
St-Ludger
Moose River
Jackman
Brassua L.
Rockwood
Kokadjo
White Cap Mt. 1130
East Millinocket
Medway
Kingman
Mattawamkeag
Blainville
Rosemère
Repentigny
St-Jude
St-Nazaire
Upton
Richmond
Marbleton
Weedon
Lac-Mégantic
Moosehead L.
Greenville
Winn
Carroll
Laval
Montréal-Nord
Beloeil
St-Hyacinthe
Acton Vale
Windsor
Dudswell
L. Mégantic
Tumbledown Mt. 1080
Schoodic
Springfield
Lincoln
St-Eustache
MONTRÉAL
Longueuil
St-Hubert
St-Pie
Roxton Falls
Roxton Pond
Valcourt
E. Angus
Scotstown
Mt. Mégantic 1105
Coburn Mt. 1133
Shirley Mills
Brownville Junction
Brownville
Enfield
Pierrefonds
Chambly
Marieville
Granby
Sherbrooke
Bromptonville
Fleurimont
Bury
Cookshire
La Patrie
Notre-Dame-des-Bois
Manson
Dover-Foxcroft
Milo
Howland
Vaudreuil-Dorion
Pointe-Claire
LaSalle
Châteauguay
St-Luc
Bromont
Waterloo
Eastman
Rock Forest
Sawyerville
Snow Mt. 1203
Abbot Village
Lagrange
Les Coteaux
Salaberry-de-Valleyfield
St-Jean-sur-Richelieu
Iberville
Farnham
Foster
Magog
North Hatley
Waterville
Compton
Rump Mt. 1112
Flagstaff L.
Guilford
Sangerville
Olamon
Nicatous L.
Napierville
Henryville
Cowansville
Lac-Brome
Ayer's Cliff
Coaticook
NEW HAMP.
Stratton
Sugarloaf Mt. 1291
Bingham
Dexter
Bradford
Costigan
St-Anicet
Ormstown
Huntingdon
Dunham
Sutton
L. Memphrémagog
Bedford
Philipsburg
Mt. Hereford 841
Dixville
Kennebago Lake
Harmony
Old Town
Great Pond
Lacolle
St-François
Hemmingford
Rouses Point
Stanstead
Derby Line
Rangeley
Rangeley L.
Corinna
Orono
Bangor
Amherst
Fort Covington
NY
Champlain
Alburg
Richford
Jay Peak 1177
Newport
VT
Hartland
Newport
Etna
Carmel
Brewer

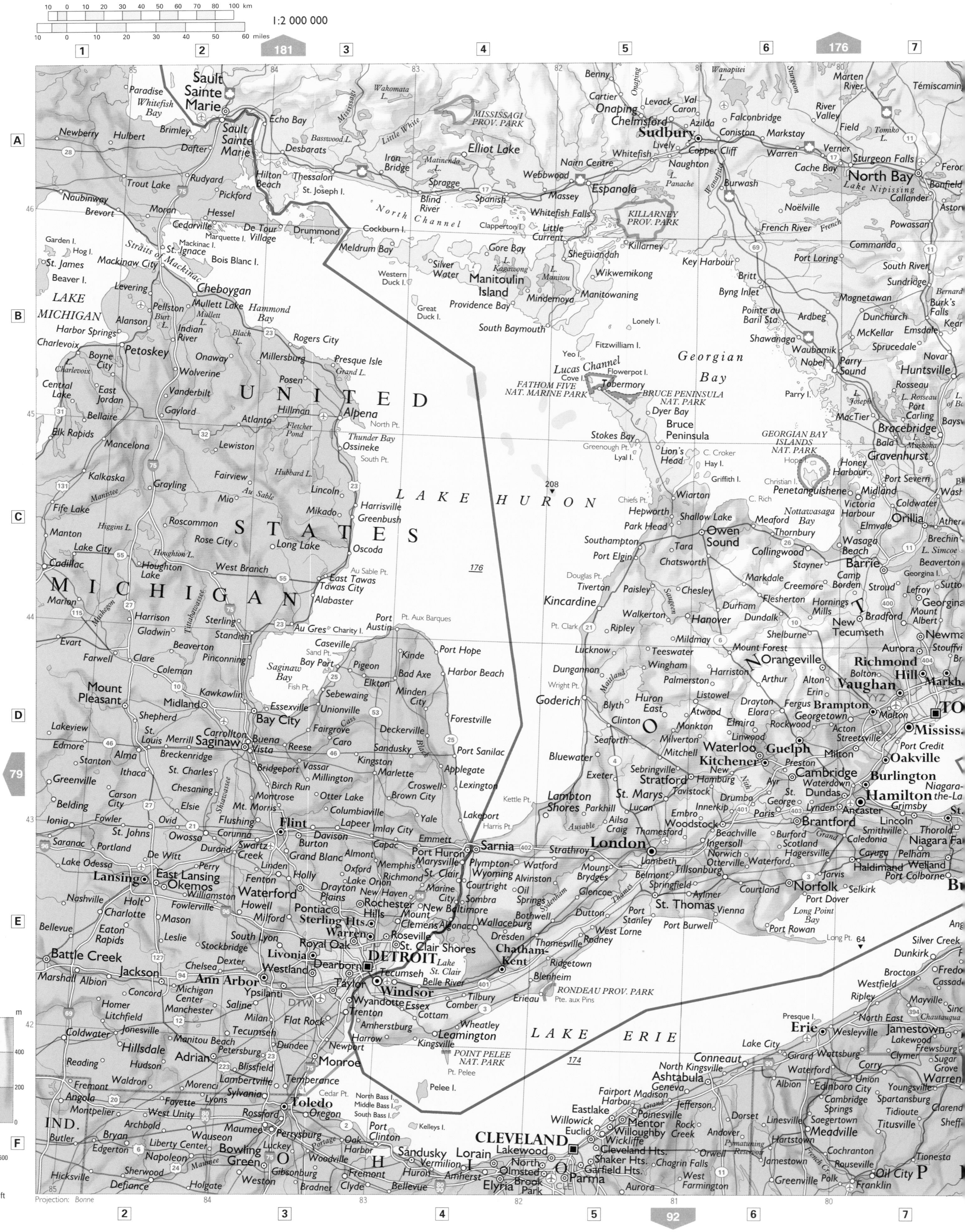
1:2 000 000
10 0 10 20 30 40 50 60 70 80 100 km
10 0 10 20 30 40 50 60 miles
181
176
92
79
Projection: Bonne
Sault Sainte Marie
Paradise
Whitefish Bay
Echo Bay
MISSISSAGI PROV. PARK
Elliot Lake
Desbarats
Thessalon
Iron Bridge
Blind River
Spragge
Spanish
Massey
Webbwood
Espanola
Nairn Centre
Whitefish
Lively
Copper Cliff
Sudbury
Chelmsford
Onaping
Cartier
Benny
Levack
Val Caron
Azilda
Falconbridge
Coniston
Markstay
Warren
Verner
Sturgeon Falls
North Bay
Lake Nipissing
Callander
Bonfield
Field
River Valley
Marten River
Témiscaming
Cache Bay
Naughton
Burwash
Noëlville
French River
Powassan
Commanda
Port Loring
Key Harbour
Britt
Byng Inlet
South River
Sundridge
Magnetawan
Burk's Falls
Pointe au Baril Sta.
Ardbeg
Dunchurch
McKellar
Emsdale
Shawanaga
Waubamik
Nobel
Parry Sound
Spruceda1e
Huntsville
Novar
Rosseau
Parry I.
Port Carling
MacTier
Bracebridge
Bala
Gravenhurst
Honey Harbour
Port Severn
GEORGIAN BAY ISLANDS NAT. PARK
Penetanguishene
Midland
Coldwater
Victoria Harbour
Orillia
Elmvale
Wasaga Beach
Barrie
Brechin
Beaverton
Stroud
Lefroy
Bradford
Newmarket
Aurora
Richmond Hill
Vaughan
Markham
Brampton
Malton
Mississauga
Oakville
Burlington
Hamilton
Grimsby
Lincoln
Niagara Falls
Welland
Port Colborne
Haldimand
Caledonia
Ancaster
Brantford
Paris
Cambridge
Guelph
Kitchener
Waterloo
Milton
Georgetown
Orangeville
Shelburne
Collingwood
Stayner
Creemore
Thornbury
Meaford
Owen Sound
Tara
Chatsworth
Southampton
Port Elgin
Paisley
Chesley
Hanover
Walkerton
Durham
Dundalk
Kincardine
Tiverton
Ripley
Lucknow
Teeswater
Wingham
Mildmay
Harriston
Palmerston
Listowel
Arthur
Mount Forest
Goderich
Dungannon
Blyth
Clinton
Seaforth
Huron East
Mitchell
Stratford
St. Marys
Exeter
Bluewater
Lambton Shores
Parkhill
Lucan
London
Woodstock
Ingersoll
Tillsonburg
St. Thomas
Aylmer
Port Stanley
Port Burwell
Long Point Bay
Port Rowan
Norfolk
Simcoe
Port Dover
Sarnia
Petrolia
Strathroy
Watford
Wyoming
Chatham-Kent
Wallaceburg
Dresden
Ridgetown
Blenheim
Erieau
RONDEAU PROV. PARK
Tilbury
Windsor
Tecumseh
Belle River
Essex
Amherstburg
Kingsville
Leamington
Wheatley
POINT PELEE NAT. PARK
Pt. Pelee
Pelee I.
LAKE ERIE
LAKE HURON
Georgian Bay
North Channel
Manitoulin Island
Gore Bay
Little Current
Sheguiandah
Wikwemikong
Manitowaning
Mindemoya
Providence Bay
South Baymouth
Killarney
KILLARNEY PROV. PARK
Tobermory
FATHOM FIVE NAT. MARINE PARK
BRUCE PENINSULA NAT. PARK
Bruce Peninsula
Lion's Head
Wiarton
Cockburn I.
Drummond I.
St. Joseph I.
Meldrum Bay
Silver Water
UNITED STATES
MICHIGAN
LAKE MICHIGAN
Straits of Mackinac
Mackinaw City
St. Ignace
Cheboygan
Bois Blanc I.
Beaver I.
Petoskey
Harbor Springs
Charlevoix
Boyne City
Gaylord
Onaway
Rogers City
Presque Isle
Alpena
Thunder Bay
Ossineke
Harrisville
Oscoda
East Tawas
Tawas City
Grayling
Roscommon
Houghton Lake
West Branch
Cadillac
Standish
Au Gres
Saginaw Bay
Bay City
Midland
Saginaw
Mount Pleasant
Clare
Caseville
Port Austin
Harbor Beach
Bad Axe
Sandusky
Port Sanilac
Lexington
Port Huron
Marysville
Flint
Lapeer
Owosso
Lansing
East Lansing
Okemos
Jackson
Battle Creek
Ann Arbor
Ypsilanti
Pontiac
Waterford
Rochester Hills
Sterling Hts.
Warren
Royal Oak
Livonia
Westland
Dearborn
DETROIT
Taylor
Wyandotte
Trenton
Monroe
Adrian
Toledo
Oregon
Sandusky
Port Clinton
Lorain
Elyria
CLEVELAND
Lakewood
Parma
Euclid
Mentor
Painesville
Ashtabula
Conneaut
Erie
Meadville
Jamestown
Dunkirk
Oil City
Franklin
IND.
OHIO
Angola
Hillsdale
Coldwater
Defiance
Bowling Green
Fremont
Vermilion
Huron
Port Dover
LAKE HURON
208
176
174
64

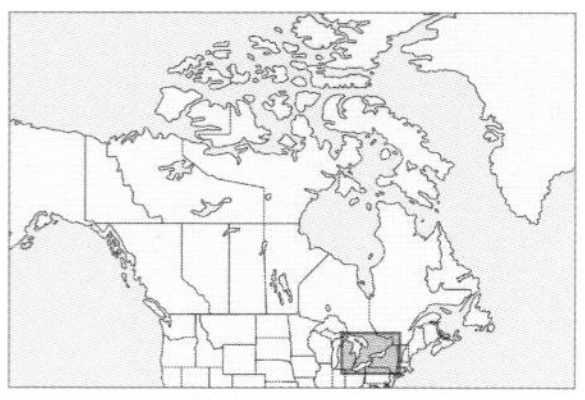

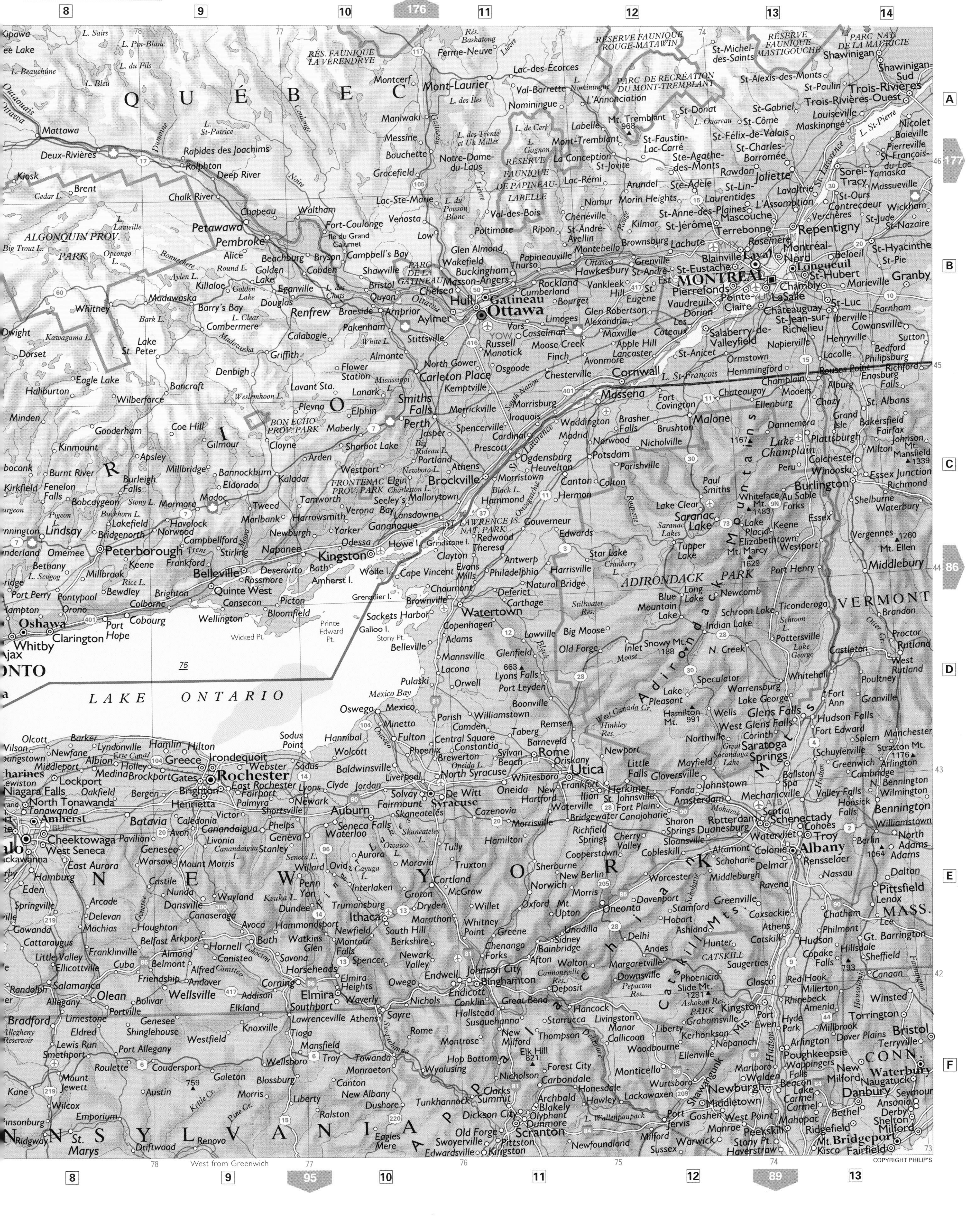

8
9
10
176
11
12
13
14
A
B
C
D
E
F
177
86
95
89
QUÉBEC
ONTARIO
NEW YORK
PENNSYLVANIA
VERMONT
MASS.
CONN.
LAKE ONTARIO
ADIRONDACK PARK
Adirondack Mountains
Appalachian Mts.
Catskill Mts.
ALGONQUIN PROV. PARK
RÉS. FAUNIQUE LA VERENDRYE
RESERVE FAUNIQUE ROUGE-MATAWIN
RÉSERVE FAUNIQUE MASTIGOUCHE
PARC NAT. DE LA MAURICIE
PARC DE RÉCRÉATION DU MONT-TREMBLANT
RÉSERVE FAUNIQUE DE PAPINEAU-LABELLE
PARC DE LA GATINEAU
BON ECHO PROV. PARK
FRONTENAC PROV. PARK
ST LAWRENCE IS. NAT. PARK
Ottawa
Gatineau
Hull
MONTRÉAL
Laval
Longueuil
Kingston
Peterborough
Oshawa
Whitby
Rochester
Syracuse
Utica
Rome
Albany
Schenectady
Troy
Binghamton
Scranton
Elmira
Ithaca
Watertown
Burlington
Plattsburgh
Trois-Rivières
Cornwall
Brockville
Belleville
Pembroke
Petawawa
Mont-Laurier
Shawinigan
Saratoga Springs
Glens Falls
Kingston
Newburgh
Poughkeepsie
Danbury
Waterbury
Bridgeport
Pittsfield
Bennington
Rutland
Middlebury
Lake Champlain
Oneida L.
Seneca L.
Cayuga L.
West from Greenwich
COPYRIGHT PHILIP'S

191
183
80
103
79

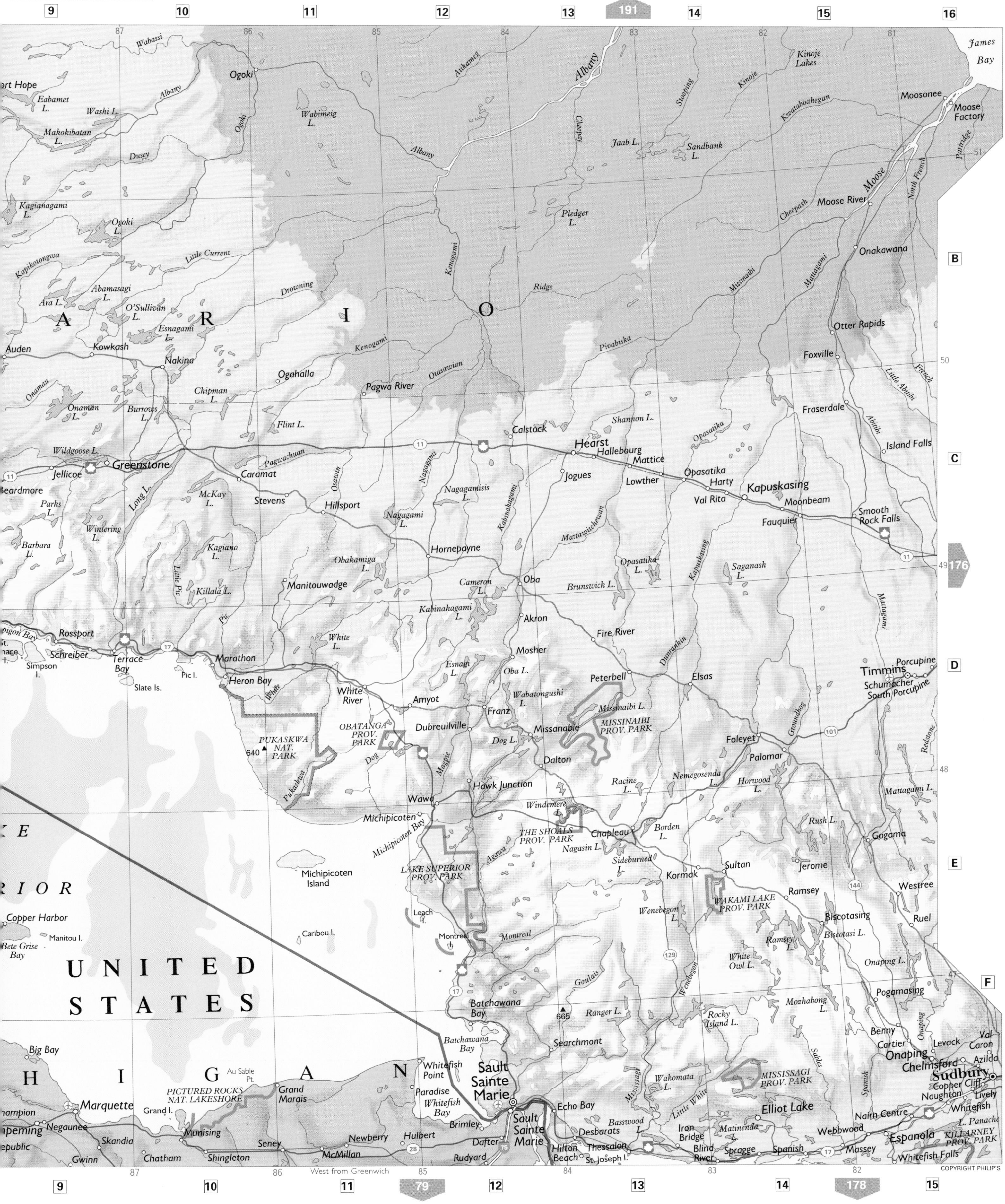
9
10
11
12
13
191
14
15
16
James Bay
Moosonee
Moose Factory
Partridge
Kinoje Lakes
Kinoje
Kwataboahegan
Sandbank L.
Jaab L.
Stooping
Cheepay
Albany
Attikameg
Wabassi
Ogoki
Port Hope
Eabamet L.
Washi L.
Makokibatan L.
Dusey
Wabimeig L.
Kagianagami L.
Ogoki L.
Kapikotongwa
Little Current
Abamasagi L.
Ara L.
O'Sullivan L.
Esnagami L.
Drowning
Kenogami
Ridge
Pledger L.
Cheepash
Moose River
Moose
North French
Onakawana
Missinaibi
Mattagami
O
N
T
A
R
I
O
Auden
Kowkash
Nakina
Ogahalla
Pagwa River
Otasawian
Pivabiska
Otter Rapids
Foxville
Little Abitibi
French
Onaman
Onaman L.
Chipman L.
Burrows L.
Flint L.
Calstock
Shannon L.
Fraserdale
Abitibi
Island Falls
Wildgoose L.
Jellicoe
Greenstone
Pagwachuan
Caramat
Hearst
Hallebourg
Mattice
Opasatika
Harty
Kapuskasing
Jogues
Lowther
Val Rita
Moonbeam
Smooth Rock Falls
Fauquier
Beardmore
Parks L.
Long L.
McKay L.
Stevens
Hillsport
Nagagami
Nagagamisis L.
Nagagami L.
Kabinakagami
Mattawitchewan
Kapuskasing
Wintering L.
Barbara L.
Kagiano L.
Hornepayne
Obakamiga L.
Opasatika L.
Saganash L.
Little Pic
Killala L.
Manitouwadge
Cameron L.
Oba
Brunswick L.
Kabinakagami L.
Akron
Pic
White L.
Fire River
Dunrankin
Nipigon Bay
Rossport
Schreiber
Terrace Bay
Simpson I.
Slate Is.
Pic I.
Marathon
Heron Bay
White
Esnagi L.
Oba L.
Mosher
Peterbell
Elsas
Timmins
Porcupine
Schumacher
South Porcupine
White River
Amyot
Wabatongushi L.
Franz
Missinaibi L.
MISSINAIBI PROV. PARK
Missanabie
OBATANGA PROV. PARK
Dubreuilville
Dog L.
Foleyet
Groundhog
PUKASKWA NAT. PARK
640
Dog
Magpie
Dalton
Palomar
Redstone
Pukaskwa
Hawk Junction
Racine L.
Nemegosenda L.
Horwood L.
Mattagami L.
Wawa
Windemere L.
Michipicoten
Michipicoten Bay
THE SHOALS PROV. PARK
Chapleau
Borden L.
Rush L.
Gogama
Nagasin L.
Sideburned L.
Kormak
Sultan
Jerome
Michipicoten Island
LAKE SUPERIOR PROV. PARK
Agawa
Westree
WAKAMI LAKE PROV. PARK
Ramsey
Wenebegon L.
Biscotasing
Ruel
Biscotasi L.
Leach I.
Caribou I.
Montreal I.
Montreal
Ramsey L.
White Owl L.
Onaping L.
Copper Harbor
Manitou I.
Bete Grise Bay
UNITED STATES
Wenebegon
Goulais
Pogamasing
Batchawana Bay
665
Ranger L.
Mozhabong L.
Rocky Island L.
Benny
Cartier
Onaping
Levack
Val Caron
Azilda
Chelmsford
Sudbury
Copper Cliff
Naughton
Lively
Whitefish
Batchawana Bay
Searchmont
Sables
Spanish
Big Bay
MICHIGAN
Au Sable Pt.
Whitefish Point
Sault Sainte Marie
Mississagi
Wakomata L.
MISSISSAGI PROV. PARK
Little White
Elliot Lake
PICTURED ROCKS NAT. LAKESHORE
Grand Marais
Paradise
Whitefish Bay
Marquette
Grand I.
Echo Bay
Champion
Negaunee
Ishpeming
Republic
Munising
Skandia
Gwinn
Chatham
Shingleton
Seney
Newberry
McMillan
Hulbert
Brimley
Dafter
Rudyard
Sault Sainte Marie
Basswood L.
Desbarats
Hilton Beach
Thessalon
St. Joseph I.
Iron Bridge
Blind River
Matinenda L.
Spragge
Spanish
Webbwood
Nairn Centre
Massey
Espanola
L. Panache
KILLARNEY PROV. PARK
Whitefish Falls
West from Greenwich
COPYRIGHT PHILIP'S
79
178
B
C
D
E
F
176

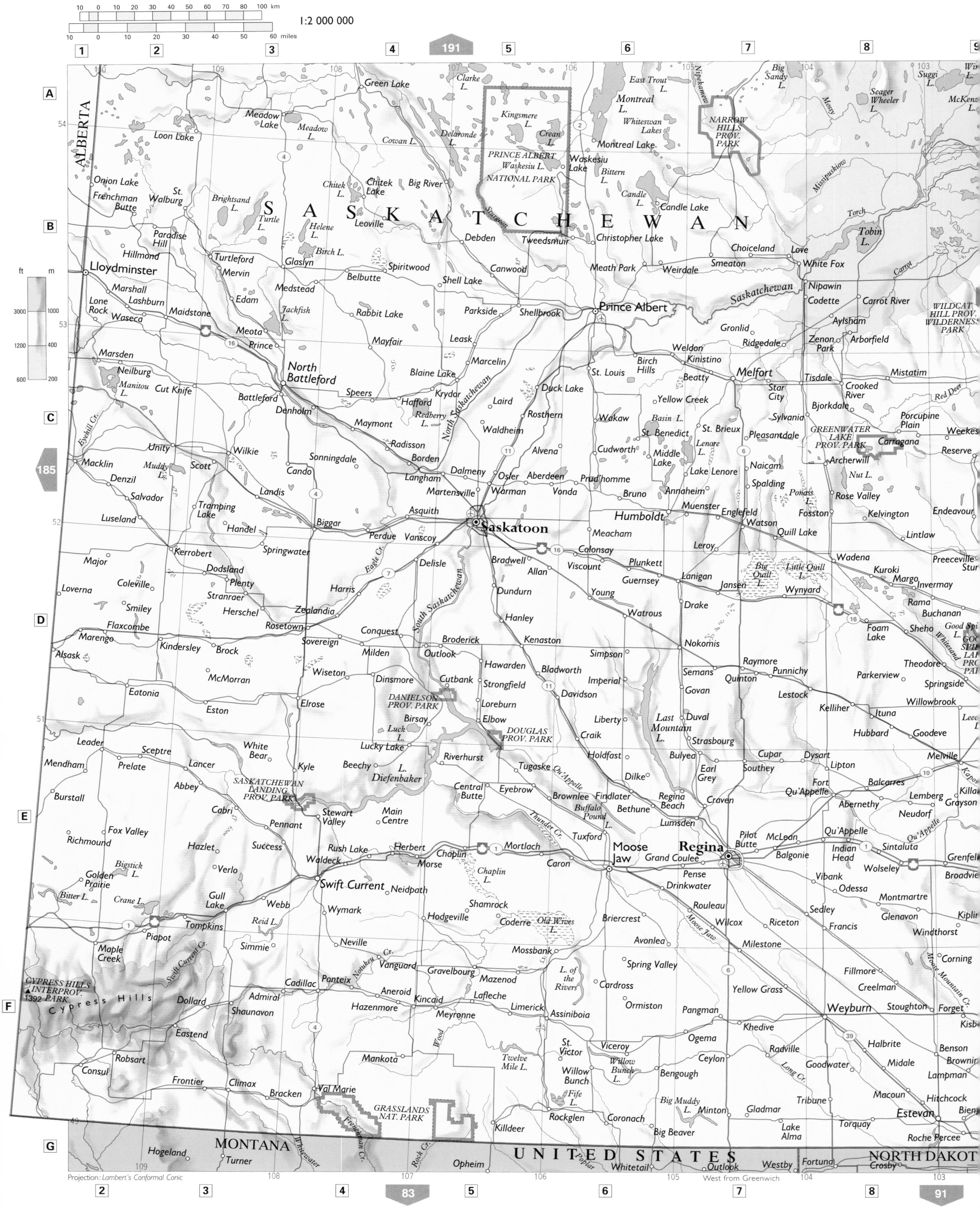
1:2 000 000
10 0 10 20 30 40 50 60 70 80 100 km
10 0 10 20 30 40 50 60 miles
1 2 3 4 5 6 7 8
191
A B C D E F G
185
ft m
3000 1000
1200 400
600 200
ALBERTA
SASKATCHEWAN
Green Lake
Clarke L.
Kingsmere L.
Crean L.
PRINCE ALBERT NATIONAL PARK
Waskesiu L.
Waskesiu Lake
East Trout L.
Montreal L.
Whiteswan Lakes
Montreal Lake
Bittern L.
Candle L.
Candle Lake
Big Sandy L.
NARROW HILLS PROV. PARK
Seager Wheeler L.
Suggi L.
Meadow Lake
Meadow L.
Cowan L.
Delaronde L.
Loon Lake
Onion Lake
Frenchman Butte
St. Walburg
Brightsand L.
Chitek L.
Chitek Lake
Big River
Turtle L.
Helene L.
Leoville
Birch L.
Paradise Hill
Hillmond
Lloydminster
Turtleford
Mervin
Glaslyn
Spiritwood
Debden
Tweedsmuir
Christopher Lake
Choiceland
Love
White Fox
Tobin L.
Torch
Carrot
Smeaton
Weirdale
Meath Park
Canwood
Shell Lake
Belbutte
Medstead
Marshall
Lashburn
Edam
Lone Rock
Waseca
Maidstone
Jackfish L.
Rabbit Lake
Parkside
Shellbrook
Prince Albert
Saskatchewan
Nipawin
Codette
Carrot River
WILDCAT HILL PROV. WILDERNESS PARK
Aylsham
Zenon Park
Arborfield
Gronlid
Ridgedale
Meota
Prince
Mayfair
Leask
Marsden
Neilburg
Manitou L.
Cut Knife
North Battleford
Blaine Lake
Marcelin
Birch Hills
Weldon
Kinistino
Melfort
Tisdale
Mistatim
Battleford
Speers
Hafford
Krydor
Duck Lake
St. Louis
Beatty
Star City
Crooked River
Red Deer
Denholm
Redberry L.
Laird
Rosthern
Yellow Creek
Sylvania
Bjorkdale
Porcupine Plain
Eyehill Cr.
Maymont
North Saskatchewan
Waldheim
Wakaw
Basin L.
St. Benedict
St. Brieux
Pleasantdale
GREENWATER LAKE PROV. PARK
Carragana
Weekes
Unity
Wilkie
Radisson
Alvena
Cudworth
Lenore L.
Middle Lake
Reserve
Macklin
Muddy L.
Scott
Borden
Naicam
Archerwill
Denzil
Cando
Sonningdale
Dalmeny
Osler
Aberdeen
Prud'homme
Lake Lenore
Spalding
Nut L.
Langham
Salvador
Tramping Lake
Landis
Martensville
Warman
Vonda
Bruno
Annaheim
Ponass L.
Rose Valley
Asquith
Muenster
Englefeld
Humboldt
Fosston
Kelvington
Endeavour
Luseland
Handel
Biggar
Saskatoon
Meacham
Watson
Quill Lake
Lintlaw
Perdue
Vanscoy
Kerrobert
Springwater
Eagle Cr.
Colonsay
Leroy
Delisle
Bradwell
Viscount
Plunkett
Big Quill L.
Little Quill L.
Wadena
Preeceville
Major
Dodsland
Plenty
Allan
Lanigan
Kuroki
Margo
Invermay
Coleville
Harris
Guernsey
Jansen
Wynyard
Loverna
Stranraer
Dundurn
Young
Smiley
Herschel
Zealandia
South Saskatchewan
Drake
Rama
Watrous
Buchanan
Hanley
Flaxcombe
Rosetown
Conquest
Good Spirit L.
Marengo
Foam Lake
Sheho
Whitesand
Kindersley
Brock
Sovereign
Broderick
Kenaston
Nokomis
Alsask
Milden
Outlook
Simpson
Hawarden
Bladworth
Raymore
Theodore
Wiseton
Semans
Quinton
Punnichy
McMorran
Dinsmore
Cutbank
Strongfield
Imperial
Parkerview
Springside
Eatonia
Davidson
Govan
Lestock
DANIELSON PROV. PARK
Loreburn
Willowbrook
Eston
Elrose
Kelliher
Ituna
Birsay
Elbow
Liberty
Last Mountain L.
Duval
Luck L.
DOUGLAS PROV. PARK
Craik
Strasbourg
Hubbard
Goodeve
Leader
Sceptre
White Bear
Lucky Lake
Holdfast
Bulyea
Cupar
Dysart
Melville
Mendham
Prelate
Lancer
Kyle
Beechy
L. Diefenbaker
Riverhurst
Tugaske
Qu'Appelle
Earl Grey
Southey
Lipton
Abbey
SASKATCHEWAN LANDING PROV. PARK
Central Butte
Eyebrow
Dilke
Fort Qu'Appelle
Balcarres
Burstall
Brownlee
Findlater
Regina Beach
Craven
Abernethy
Lemberg
Grayson
Cabri
Stewart Valley
Main Centre
Buffalo Pound L.
Bethune
Neudorf
Thunder Cr.
Pennant
Lumsden
Fox Valley
Tuxford
Pilot Butte
McLean
Qu'Appelle
Richmound
Hazlet
Success
Rush Lake
Herbert
Chaplin
Mortlach
Moose Jaw
Regina
Indian Head
Sintaluta
Grenfell
Waldeck
Morse
Caron
Grand Coulee
Balgonie
Wolseley
Bigstick L.
Verlo
Chaplin L.
Golden Prairie
Swift Current
Neidpath
Pense
Drinkwater
Vibank
Odessa
Broadview
Bitter L.
Crane L.
Gull Lake
Webb
Wymark
Shamrock
Rouleau
Montmartre
Sedley
Kipling
Reid L.
Hodgeville
Coderre
Old Wives L.
Briercrest
Wilcox
Riceton
Glenavon
Francis
Windthorst
Piapot
Tompkins
Swift Current Cr.
Simmie
Neville
Mossbank
Moose Jaw
Avonlea
Milestone
Maple Creek
Notukeu Cr.
Vanguard
Spring Valley
Corning
CYPRESS HILLS INTERPROV. PARK
1392
Cypress Hills
Cadillac
Ponteix
Gravelbourg
Mazenod
L. of the Rivers
Cardross
Fillmore
Creelman
Moose Mountain Cr.
Dollard
Admiral
Aneroid
Kincaid
Lafleche
Yellow Grass
Hazenmore
Limerick
Assiniboia
Ormiston
Pangman
Weyburn
Stoughton
Forget
Shaunavon
Meyronne
Khedive
Kisbey
Eastend
Wood
St. Victor
Viceroy
Ogema
Halbrite
Benson
Willow Bunch L.
Radville
Midale
Browning
Robsart
Mankota
Twelve Mile L.
Ceylon
Goodwater
Long Cr.
Consul
Willow Bunch
Bengough
Lampman
Frontier
Climax
Fife L.
Tribune
Macoun
Hitchcock
Bracken
Val Marie
Big Muddy L.
Minton
Gladmar
Estevan
Bienfait
GRASSLANDS NAT. PARK
Rockglen
Coronach
Torquay
Killdeer
Lake Alma
Big Beaver
Roche Percee
Frenchman Cr.
Whitewater
Hogeland
MONTANA
Rock Cr.
UNITED STATES
NORTH DAKOTA
Turner
Opheim
Poplar
Whitetail
Outlook
Westby
Fortuna
Crosby
Projection: Lambert's Conformal Conic
West from Greenwich
54 53 52 51 49
110 109 108 107 106 105 104 103
83
91

10
11
12
13
191
14
15
16
17
A
B
C
D
E
F
G
Goose L.
Simonhouse
GRASS RIVER PROV. PARK
Kiskitto L.
Kiskittogisu L.
Molson L.
Nelson
Minago
Namew L.
Cormorant L.
Cormorant
North Moose L.
Talbot L.
Wanless
CLEARWATER LAKE PROV. PARK
Cumberland L.
Cumberland House
William L.
Playgreen L.
Norway House
Stevenson L.
Island Lake
The Pas
South Moose L.
Limestone Bay
Bigstone L.
Moose Lake
Eagle I.
Gunisao
Gunisao L.
Cantin L.
Saskatchewan
Westray
M A N I T O B A
Belanger
Cedar L.
Horse I.
Lake Winnipeg
Hudwin L.
Otosquen
Overflowing
Grand Rapids
Mukutawa
253
Poplar River
Elliot L.
Leaf L.
Easterville
Long Point
Poplar
Spruce I.
217
Charron L.
Red Deer L.
Dawson Bay
Lake Winnipegosis
Grand I.
Katimik L.
Kaweenakumik L.
ONTARIO
Hudson Bay
Barrows
Pelican Rapids
Mafeking
Porcupine Hills
Reindeer I.
Berens River
Poplar
Bellsite
Swan L.
Birch I.
Chitek L.
Berens I.
Berens
Little Grand Rapids
Fishing L.
823
Pelican L.
Commissioner I.
Birch River
Swan
Bowsman
Duck Bay
Waterhen L.
Sturgeon Bay
Family L.
Swan River
Minitonas
Cowan
Skownan
Dauphin River
Kenville
Camperville
Matheson Island
Bloodvein
Hyas
Arran
Benito
Gypsumville
Moose I.
Pine Dock
Sasaginnigak L.
Norquay
Pelly
Pine River
L. St. Martin
DUCK MOUNTAIN PROV. PARK
Fairford
Fisher Bay
Bloodvein
ATIKAKI PROV. WILDERNESS PARK
Canora
Winnipegosis
Crane River
Portage Bay
Gammon
180
Kamsack
Baldy Mt. 831
Fork River
Fisher River
Veregin
Ethelbert
Steep Rock
Grahamdale
HECLA/GRINDSTONE PROV. PARK
San Clara
Rorketon
Black I.
Rhein
Togo
Sifton
Dauphin L.
Hodgson
Manigotagan
Ashern
Bissett
Yorkton
Wroxton
Roblin
Grandview
Dauphin
Ste. Rose du Lac
Dog L.
Fisher Branch
Riverton
Hecla I.
Manigotagan L.
MacNutt
Gilbert Plains
Ochre River
Vogar
Arborg
217
Saltcoats
Shellmouth
Laurier
Poplarfield
Victoria Beach
NOPIMING PROV. PARK
Bredenbury
Churchbridge
RIDING MOUNTAIN NAT. PARK
Silver Ridge
Eriksdale
Fort Alexander
Langenburg
Russell
McCreary
Lake Manitoba
Lundar
Fraserwood
Gimli
Pine Falls
Angusville
750
Great Falls
Dubuc
Rossburn
Kelwood
Amaranth
Oak Point
Inwood
Winnipeg Beach
Beaconia
Winnipeg
Esterhazy
Stockholm
Spy Hill
Binscarth
Onanole
Sandy Bay
Lac du Bonnet
Lac du Bonnet
Pointe du Bois
Elphinstone
Erickson
Glenella
St. Laurent
Teulon
Tantallon
Shoal Lake
Langruth
Petersfield
St-Lazare
Plumas
Eden
Balmoral
Birtle
Rocanville
Clanwilliam
248
Argyle
Seven Sisters Falls
Pinawa
Delta Beach
Stonewall
Selkirk
Whitewood
Arden
Gladstone
Woodlands
WHITESHELL PROV. PARK
Wapella
McAuley
Minnedosa
Stony Mountain
Tyndall
Neepawa
Grosse Isle
Beausejour
Poplar Point
Hamiota
Rapid City
Westbourne
Rivercrest
Whitemouth
Moosomin
Oak River
Marquette
Oakbank
Miniota
Brookdale
MacGregor
St. Eustache
Winnipeg
YWG
Elma
Rennie
Fleming
Rivers
Anola
Elkhorn
Portage la Prairie
St. François Xavier
Kennedy
Wawota
Sidney
Lorette
Reynolds
Virden
Alexander
Brandon
Carberry
Assiniboine
Starbuck
Grande Pointe
Maryfield
St. Anne
Waugh
MOOSE MOUNTAIN PROV. PARK
Oak Lake
SPRUCE WOODS PROV. PARK
St. Claude
Ste. Agathe
Niverville
La Broquerie
Whitemouth
Cromer
Treherne
Notre Dame de Lourdes
Brunkild
Carlyle
Souris
Wawanesa
Morris
Steinbach
Redvers
Reston
Cypress River
Sperling
St. Pierre -Jolys
Grunthal
Arcola
Manor
Antler
Glenboro
Carman
Roseisle
Lowe Farm
St. Malo
Woodridge
Whitemouth L.
Souris
Belmont
Morris
Hartney
Somerset
Roland
Rat
Tilston
Elgin
Ninette
Baldur
Lake of the Woods
Alida
Napinka
Plum Coulee
St. Jean Baptiste
Vassar
Pilot Mound
Manitou
Thornhill
Dominion City
Sundown
Souris
Boissevain
Morden
Winkler
Altona
Sprague
Alameda
Oxbow
Antler
Melita
Killarney
Crystal City
Red
Tolstoi
Pierson
Deloraine
Reinland
Gretna
Emerson
Frobisher
Glen Ewen
Carnduff
TURTLE MT. PROV. PARK
Cartwright
Snowflake
Pembina
Neche
Pembina
Humboldt
Lancaster
Roseau
North Portal
Waskada
St. John
Hansboro
Sarles
Hannah
Walhalla
Bathgate
MINNESOTA
Malung
766
Turtle Mts
NORTH DAKOTA
Wales
Cavalier
Hallock
Lake Bronson
Portal
Sherwood
Antler
Souris
Calvin
Akra
Hamilton
Greenbush
Flaxton
Westhope
Landa
Bottineau
Belcourt
Rolla
Rocklake
Langdon

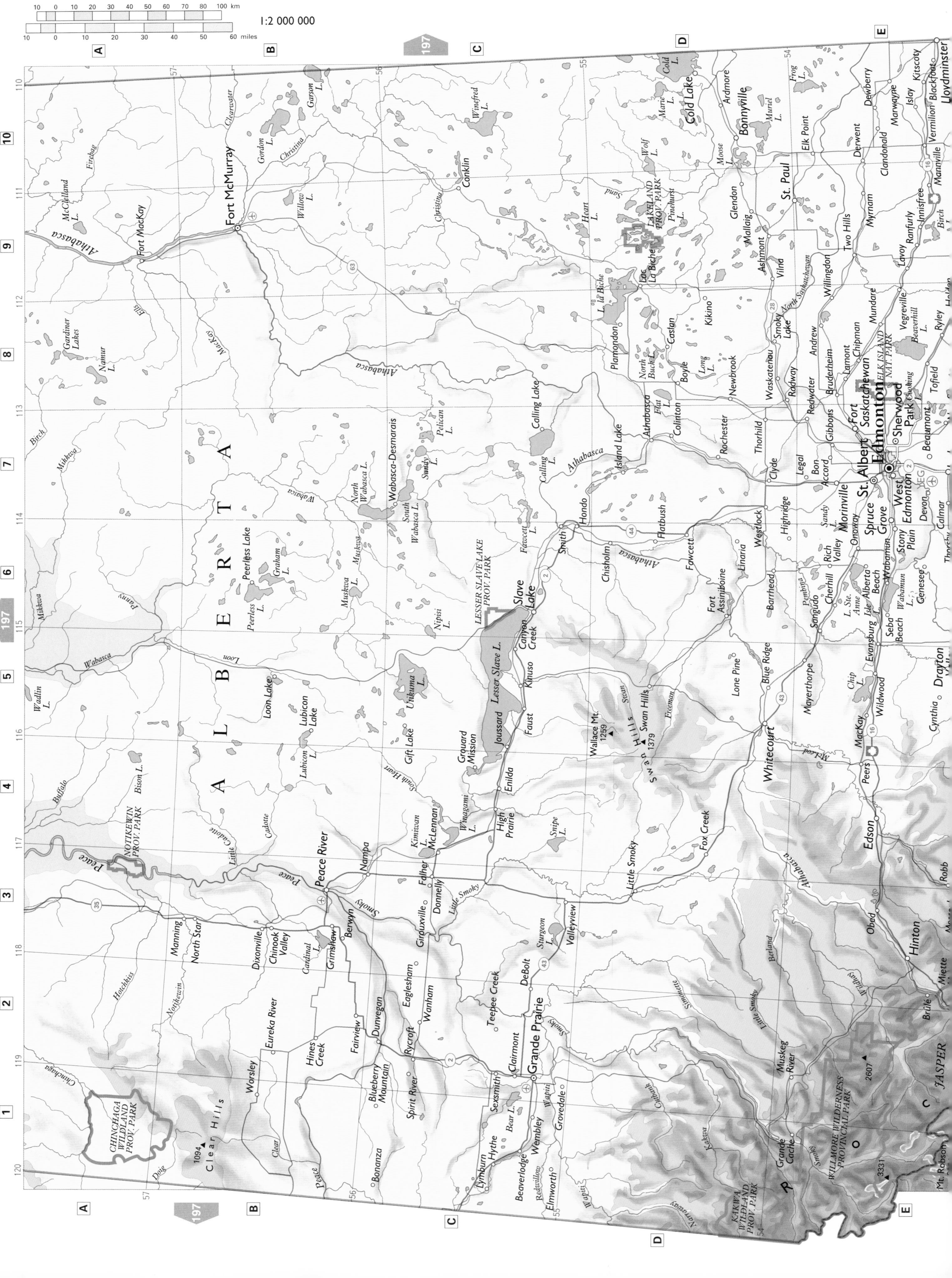
1:2 000 000
10 0 10 20 30 40 50 60 70 80 100 km
10 0 10 20 30 40 50 60 miles
A
B
C
D
E
197
ALBERTA
Fort McMurray
Fort MacKay
Athabasca
Conklin
Cold Lake
Bonnyville
St. Paul
Lac La Biche
LAKELAND PROV. PARK
Lloydminster
Vermilion
Mannville
Innisfree
Vegreville
Two Hills
Smoky Lake
Waskatenau
Redwater
Fort Saskatchewan
ELK ISLAND NAT. PARK
Sherwood Park
Edmonton
St. Albert
West Edmonton
Spruce Grove
Stony Plain
Devon
Beaumont
Morinville
Westlock
Barrhead
Athabasca
Island Lake
Calling Lake
Boyle
Colinton
Plamondon
Wabasca-Desmarais
North Wabasca L.
South Wabasca L.
Peerless Lake
Loon Lake
Lubicon Lake
Gift Lake
Grouard Mission
Slave Lake
LESSER SLAVE LAKE PROV. PARK
Lesser Slave L.
Canyon Creek
Kinuso
Faust
Joussard
Enilda
High Prairie
Smith
Hondo
Chisholm
Flatbush
Fawcett
Fort Assiniboine
Swan Hills
Wallace Mt. 1259
Whitecourt
Blue Ridge
Lone Pine
Mayerthorpe
Evansburg
Wildwood
Drayton Valley
MacKay
Peers
Edson
Obed
Hinton
Brûlé
JASPER
Robb
Peace River
NOTIKEWIN PROV. PARK
Manning
North Star
Dixonville
Chinook Valley
Grimshaw
Berwyn
Nampa
McLennan
Falher
Donnelly
Girouxville
Eaglesham
Wanham
Dunvegan
Fairview
Hines Creek
Eureka River
Worsley
Rycroft
Spirit River
Blueberry Mountain
Bonanza
Grande Prairie
Clairmont
Sexsmith
Wembley
Beaverlodge
Hythe
Lymburn
Grovedale
DeBolt
Valleyview
Little Smoky
Fox Creek
Teepee Creek
Grande Cache
Muskeg River
WILLMORE WILDERNESS PROVINCIAL PARK
KAKWA WILDLAND PROV. PARK
CHINCHAGA WILDLAND PROV. PARK
Clear Hills
Mt. Robson

UNITED STATES
MONTANA
IDAHO
WASHINGTON
BRITISH COLUMBIA
Calgary
Medicine Hat
Lethbridge
Red Deer
Drumheller
Brooks
Banff
Canmore
Cochrane
Airdrie
Okotoks
High River
Olds
Innisfail
Lacombe
Wetaskiwin
Camrose
Wainwright
Stettler
Taber
Coaldale
Fort Macleod
Crowsnest Pass
Cranbrook
Kimberley
Nelson
Castlegar
Trail
Revelstoke
Golden
Jasper
Fernie
Sparwood
Invermere
Nakusp
Rocky Mountain House
Sylvan Lake
Strathmore
Cypress Hills
CYPRESS HILLS INTERPROVINCIAL PARK
DINOSAUR PROV. PARK
WATERTON LAKES NAT. PARK
GLACIER NATIONAL PARK
BANFF NATIONAL PARK
JASPER NATIONAL PARK
YOHO NAT. PARK
KOOTENAY NAT. PARK
GLACIER NAT. PARK
MOUNT REVELSTOKE NAT. PARK
HEAD-SMASHED-IN BUFFALO JUMP
Cariboo Mountains
Mt. Assiniboine 3618
Mt. Columbia 3747
Mt. Brazeau 3470
Mt. Sir Sandford 3522
Crowsnest Pass 1357
Yellowhead Pass 1131
Red Deer
Bow
Oldman
S. Saskatchewan
Milk
Columbia
Kootenay
North Saskatchewan
Athabasca
West from Greenwich
Projection: Lambert's Conformal Conic
COPYRIGHT PHILIP'S
Permanent ice
m
ft
3000
2000
1500
1000
400
200
9000
6000
4500
3000
1200
600
182
187
83
70
101
F
G
H
J
K
2
3
4
5
6
7
8
9
10

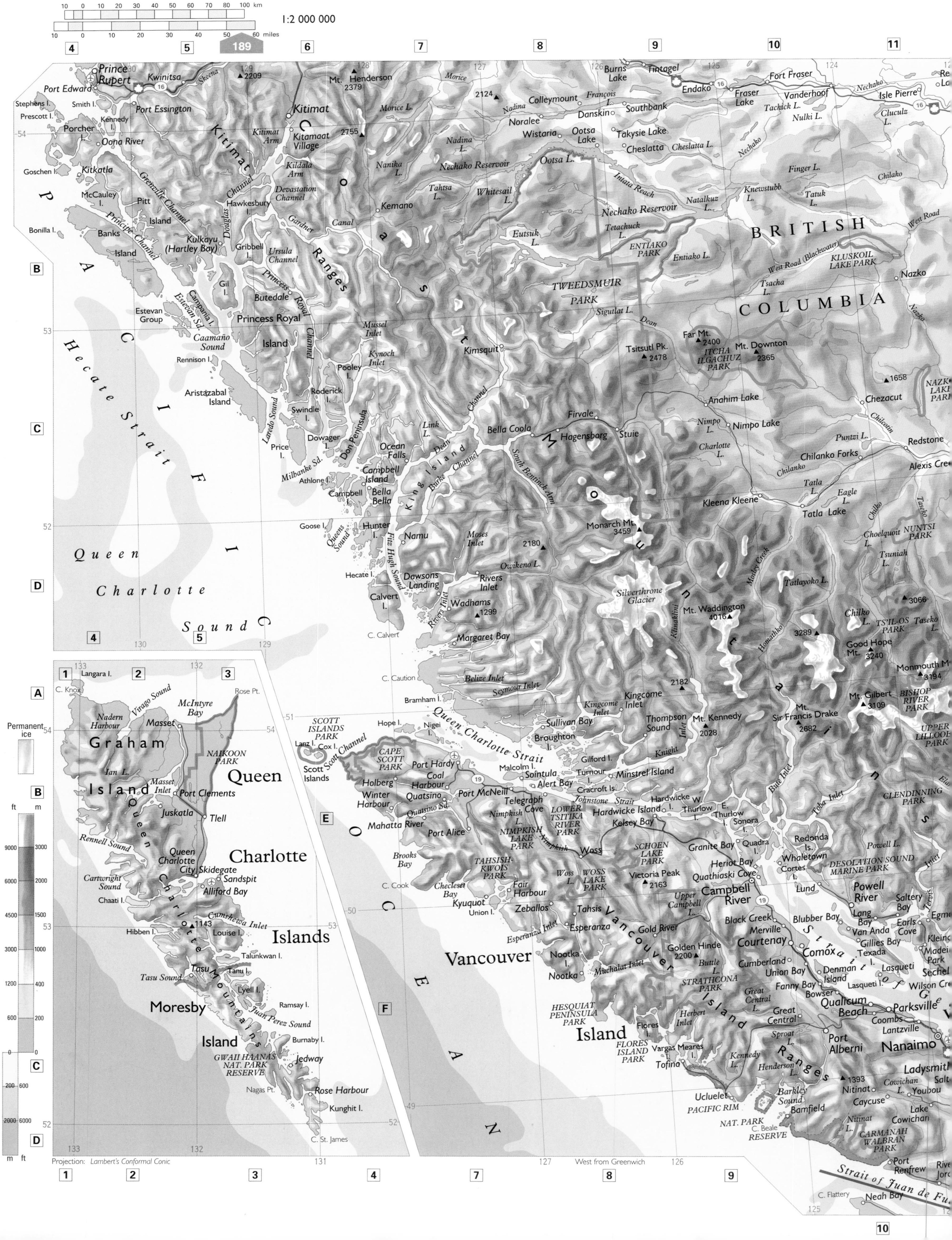
1:2 000 000
km
miles
189
Prince Rupert
Port Edward
Kwinitsa
Skeena
Port Essington
Stephens I.
Smith I.
Prescott I.
Porcher I.
Kennedy I.
Oona River
Goschen I.
Kitkatla
McCauley I.
Pitt Island
Banks Island
Bonilla I.
Kitimat
Kitimat Arm
Kitamaat Village
Kildala Arm
Devastation Channel
Hawkesbury I.
Douglas Channel
Grenville Channel
Principe Channel
Kulkayu (Hartley Bay)
Gribbell I.
Ursula Channel
Gardner Canal
Kemano
Gil I.
Campania I.
Estevan Sd.
Estevan Group
Butedale
Princess Royal Channel
Princess Royal Island
Caamaño Sound
Rennison I.
Aristazabal Island
Laredo Sound
Mussel Inlet
Kynoch Inlet
Pooley I.
Roderick I.
Swindle I.
Price I.
Dowager I.
Don Peninsula
Milbanke Sd.
Athlone I.
Campbell I.
Campbell Island
Ocean Falls
Bella Bella
Hunter I.
Goose I.
Queens Sound
Namu
Fitz Hugh Sound
Hecate I.
Calvert I.
C. Calvert
Dawsons Landing
Rivers Inlet
Wadhams
1299
Moses Inlet
Owikeno L.
2180
Kimsquit
Link L.
Dean Channel
King Island
Burke Channel
Bella Coola
Hagensborg
Firvale
Stuie
South Bentinck Arm
Monarch Mt. 3459
Silverthrone Glacier
Mt. Waddington 4016
Coast Mountains
Coast Ranges
Mt. Henderson 2379
2209
2755
2124
Morice L.
Morice
Nanika L.
Nadina L.
Nadina
Tahtsa L.
Whitesail L.
Eutsuk L.
Nechako Reservoir
Ootsa L.
Ootsa Lake
Wistaria
Noralee
Colleymount
Danskin
François L.
Southbank
Takysie Lake
Cheslatta
Cheslatta L.
Intata Reach
Natalkuz L.
Tetachuck L.
ENTIAKO PARK
Entiako L.
TWEEDSMUIR PARK
Sigutlat L.
Dean
Burns Lake
Tintagel
Endako
Fraser Lake
Fort Fraser
Vanderhoof
Nechako
Isle Pierre
Tachick L.
Nulki L.
Cluculz L.
Finger L.
Knewstubb L.
Tatuk L.
Chilako
West Road
West Road (Blackwater)
KLUSKOIL LAKE PARK
BRITISH COLUMBIA
Tsacha L.
Nazko
Far Mt. 2400
Mt. Downton 2365
ITCHA ILGACHUZ PARK
Tsitsutl Pk. 2478
1658
Anahim Lake
Chezacut
Nimpo L.
Nimpo Lake
Charlotte L.
Puntzi L.
Chilcotin
Redstone
Chilanko Forks
Chilanko
Alexis Cre
Tatla L.
Tatla Lake
Kleena Kleene
Eagle L.
Chilko
Taseko
Choelquoit L.
NUNTSI PARK
Tsuniah L.
Mosley Creek
Tatlayoko L.
Chilko L.
TS'IL-OS PARK
3066
3289
Good Hope Mt. 3240
Homathko
Klinaklini
Monmouth M 3194
Mt. Gilbert 3109
BISHOP RIVER PARK
Mt. Sir Francis Drake 2682
UPPER LILLOOET PARK
2182
Margaret Bay
Belize Inlet
Seymour Inlet
C. Caution
Bramham I.
Kingcome Inlet
Kingcome
Sullivan Bay
Thompson Sound
Mt. Kennedy 2028
Broughton I.
Knight Inlet
Gilford I.
Queen Charlotte Strait
SCOTT ISLANDS PARK
Hope I.
Nigei I.
Lanz I.
Cox I.
Scott Channel
Scott Islands
CAPE SCOTT PARK
Port Hardy
Coal Harbour
Holberg
Winter Harbour
Quatsino
Quatsino Sd.
Port McNeill
Malcolm I.
Sointula
Alert Bay
Telegraph Cove
Turnour I.
Minstrel Island
Cracroft Is.
Johnstone Strait
Hardwicke I.
Hardwicke Island
W. Thurlow I.
E. Thurlow I.
Sonora I.
Kelsey Bay
LOWER TSITIKA RIVER PARK
Nimpkish
Nimpkish L.
NIMPKISH LAKE PARK
Mahatta River
Port Alice
Brooks Bay
TAHSISH-KWOIS PARK
SCHOEN LAKE PARK
Woss
Woss L.
WOSS LAKE PARK
Victoria Peak 2163
Bute Inlet
Toba Inlet
CLENDINNING PARK
Redonda Is.
Whaletown
Cortes I.
DESOLATION SOUND MARINE PARK
Powell L.
Quadra I.
Granite Bay
Heriot Bay
Quathiaski Cove
Campbell River
Upper Campbell L.
Lund
Powell River
Saltery Bay
C. Cook
Checleset Bay
Kyuquot
Union I.
Fair Harbour
Zeballos
Tahsis
Esperanza Inlet
Esperanza
Gold River
Golden Hinde 2200
Buttle L.
Nootka I.
Nootka
Muchalat Inlet
STRATHCONA PARK
Black Creek
Merville
Courtenay
Comox
Cumberland
Union Bay
Blubber Bay
Lang Bay
Van Anda
Earls Cove
Gillies Bay
Texada I.
Denman Island
Lasqueti I.
Lasqueti
Fanny Bay
Bowser
Qualicum Beach
Parksville
Strait of Georgia
Vancouver Island
Vancouver Island Ranges
Great Central L.
Great Central
HESQUIAT PENINSULA PARK
Herbert Inlet
Flores I.
FLORES ISLAND PARK
Vargas I.
Meares I.
Tofino
Kennedy L.
Sproat L.
Port Alberni
Coombs
Lantzville
Nanaimo
Ladysmith
Henderson L.
Ucluelet
PACIFIC RIM NAT. PARK RESERVE
Barkley Sound
Bamfield
1393
Nitinat
Cowichan L.
Youbou
Caycuse
Nitinat L.
Cowichan Lake
C. Beale
CARMANAH WALBRAN PARK
Port Renfrew
Strait of Juan de Fuca
C. Flattery
Neah Bay
PACIFIC OCEAN
Hecate Strait
Queen Charlotte Sound
Langara I.
C. Knox
Virago Sound
Nadern Harbour
McIntyre Bay
Rose Pt.
Masset
NAIKOON PARK
Graham Island
Ian L.
Masset Inlet
Port Clements
Juskatla
Tlell
Rennell Sound
Queen Charlotte City
Skidegate
Sandspit
Alliford Bay
Cartwright Sound
Chaati I.
Cumshewa Inlet
Hibben I.
Louise I.
1143
Talunkwan I.
Tasu Sound
Tasu
Tanu I.
Lyell I.
Ramsay I.
Juan Perez Sound
Moresby Island
Burnaby I.
Jedway
GWAII HAANAS NAT. PARK RESERVE
Nagas Pt.
Rose Harbour
Kunghit I.
C. St. James
Queen Charlotte Islands
Queen Charlotte Mountains
Permanent ice
ft
m
Projection: Lambert's Conformal Conic
West from Greenwich

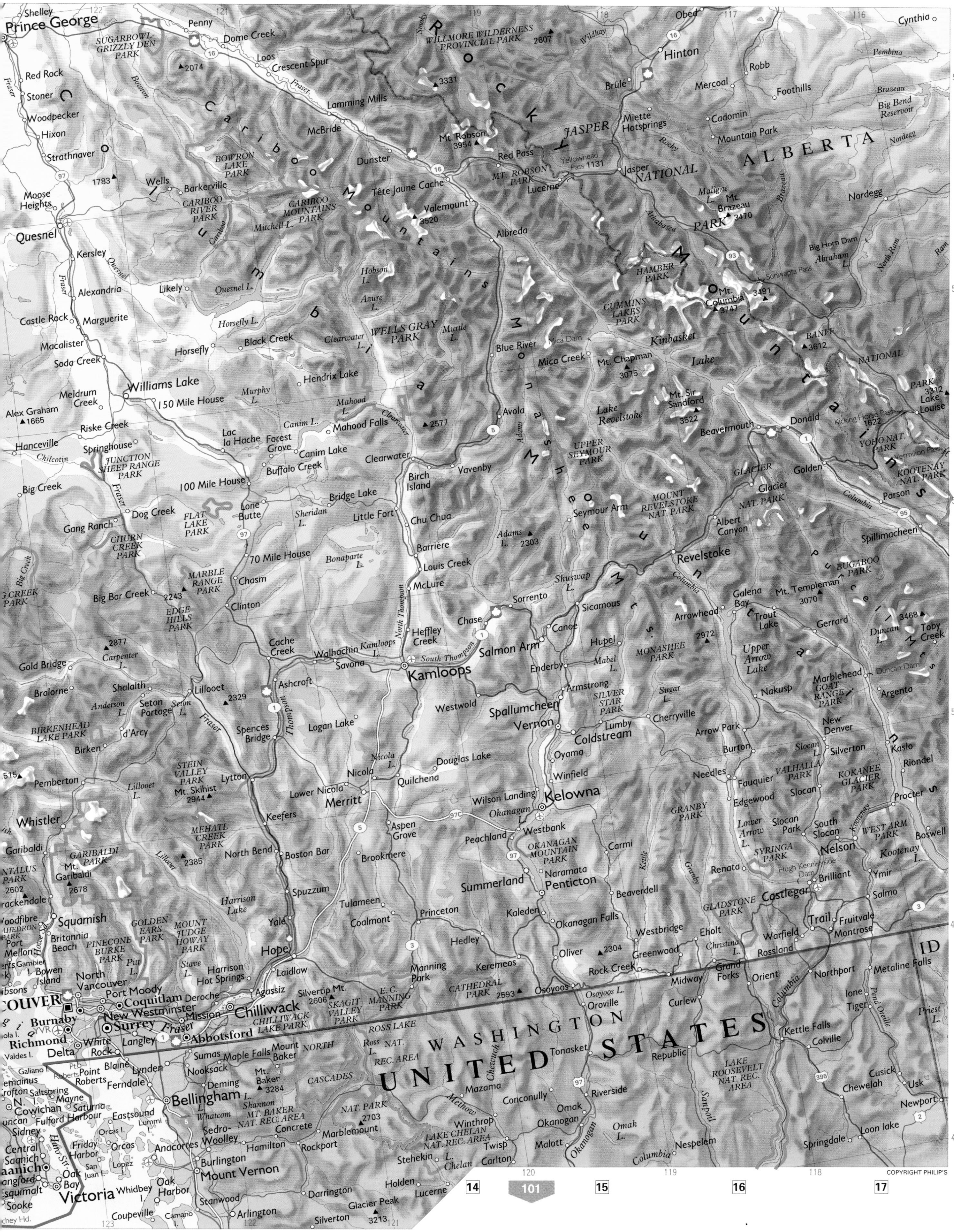
12
13
14
15
16
17
189
18
19
B
C
D
E
F
G
185
101
11
Prince George
Shelley
Penny
Dome Creek
SUGARBOWL-GRIZZLY DEN PARK
Loos
Crescent Spur
Red Rock
Stoner
Woodpecker
Hixon
Strathnaver
Lamming Mills
McBride
Dunster
Tête Jaune Cache
Valemount
Wells
Barkerville
BOWRON LAKE PARK
CARIBOO RIVER PARK
CARIBOO MOUNTAINS PARK
Mitchell L.
Moose Heights
Quesnel
Kersley
Alexandria
Likely
Quesnel L.
Castle Rock
Marguerite
Macalister
Soda Creek
Horsefly
Horsefly L.
Black Creek
Hendrix Lake
Williams Lake
150 Mile House
Murphy L.
Meldrum Creek
Alex Graham
Riske Creek
Hanceville
Chilcotin
Springhouse
JUNCTION SHEEP RANGE PARK
Big Creek
100 Mile House
Lac la Hache
Forest Grove
Canim Lake
Canim L.
Buffalo Creek
Mahood L.
Mahood Falls
Clearwater
Dog Creek
Gang Ranch
FLAT LAKE PARK
Lone Butte
CHURN CREEK PARK
70 Mile House
Bridge Lake
Sheridan L.
Little Fort
Chu Chua
Birch Island
Vavenby
Barrière
Louis Creek
McLure
Bonaparte L.
Chasm
MARBLE RANGE PARK
Big Bar Creek
Clinton
EDGE HILLS PARK
Cache Creek
Walhachin
Savona
Kamloops
Ashcroft
Heffley Creek
Chase
Sorrento
Salmon Arm
Shuswap L.
Gold Bridge
Carpenter L.
Bralorne
Shalalth
Anderson L.
Seton Portage
Seton L.
Lillooet
BIRKENHEAD LAKE PARK
d'Arcy
Birken
Spences Bridge
Logan Lake
Westwold
Pemberton
STEIN VALLEY PARK
Mt. Skihist
Lytton
Nicola L.
Nicola
Quilchena
Douglas Lake
Lower Nicola
Merritt
Whistler
Garibaldi
GARIBALDI PARK
Mt. Garibaldi
MEHATL CREEK PARK
Keefers
North Bend
Boston Bar
Aspen Grove
Brookmere
Squamish
Britannia Beach
GOLDEN EARS PARK
MOUNT JUDGE HOWAY PARK
PINECONE BURKE PARK
Harrison Lake
Spuzzum
Yale
Hope
Tulameen
Coalmont
Princeton
Hedley
Keremeos
Manning Park
E.C. MANNING PARK
Harrison Hot Springs
Laidlaw
Agassiz
Silvertip Mt.
SKAGIT VALLEY PARK
North Vancouver
Port Moody
Coquitlam
Deroche
Mission
Chilliwack
CHILLIWACK LAKE PARK
New Westminster
Burnaby
Surrey
Abbotsford
Richmond
Delta
White Rock
Langley
Bowen Island
Sumas
Maple Falls
Mount Baker
Blaine
Lynden
Point Roberts
Ferndale
Nooksack
Deming
Mt. Baker
Bellingham
Shannon L.
Whatcom L.
MT. BAKER NAT. REC. AREA
Sedro-Woolley
Concrete
Rockport
Marblemount
Hamilton
Burlington
Mount Vernon
Anacortes
Oak Harbor
Whidbey I.
Stanwood
Arlington
Darrington
Coupeville
Camano I.
Silverton
Glacier Peak
Victoria
Saanich
Sidney
Oak Bay
Sooke
Cowichan
Saltspring
Mayne
Saturna
Fulford Harbour
Eastsound
Orcas
Friday Harbor
San Juan I.
Lopez
Haro Str.
Galiano I.
Valdes I.
ROSS LAKE NAT. REC. AREA
NORTH CASCADES NAT. PARK
Ross L.
Mazama
Winthrop
Twisp
Stehekin
LAKE CHELAN NAT. REC. AREA
Chelan L.
Carlton
Holden
Lucerne
Conconully
Omak
Okanogan
Malott
Omak L.
Riverside
Tonasket
Oroville
Osoyoos
Osoyoos L.
Oliver
Okanagan Falls
Kaleden
Penticton
Naramata
Summerland
Peachland
Westbank
Kelowna
Okanagan L.
OKANAGAN MOUNTAIN PARK
Wilson Landing
Winfield
Oyama
Vernon
Coldstream
Lumby
Spallumcheen
Armstrong
Enderby
Mabel L.
SILVER STAR PARK
Sugar L.
Cherryville
Canoe
Sicamous
Hupel
MONASHEE PARK
Carmi
Beaverdell
Westbridge
Rock Creek
Greenwood
Midway
Grand Forks
Eholt
Christina L.
Curlew
Republic
CATHEDRAL PARK
WASHINGTON
UNITED STATES
Nespelem
Columbia
Sanpoil
LAKE ROOSEVELT NAT. REC. AREA
Kettle Falls
Colville
Orient
Northport
Metaline Falls
Ione
Tiger
Pend Oreille
Priest L.
Cusick
Usk
Chewelah
Newport
Springdale
Loon lake
ID
Rossland
Warfield
Trail
Fruitvale
Montrose
Castlegar
GLADSTONE PARK
Renata
Brilliant
Hugh Keenleyside Dam
Nelson
Ymir
Salmo
Kootenay L.
WEST ARM PARK
South Slocan
Slocan Park
Lower Arrow L.
SYRINGA PARK
Edgewood
Fauquier
Needles
GRANBY PARK
Granby
Kettle
VALHALLA PARK
Slocan
Slocan L.
Silverton
New Denver
KOKANEE GLACIER PARK
Kaslo
Riondel
Procter
Boswell
Burton
Arrow Park
Nakusp
Upper Arrow Lake
Marblehead
GOAT RANGE PARK
Argenta
Duncan Dam
Duncan L.
Toby Creek
Trout Lake
Gerrard
Galena Bay
Mt. Templeman
BUGABOO PARK
Arrowhead
Revelstoke
Albert Canyon
MOUNT REVELSTOKE NAT. PARK
Seymour Arm
Adams L.
Adams
UPPER SEYMOUR PARK
Lake Revelstoke
Mt. Sir Sandford
Mica Creek
Mica Dam
Mt. Chapman
Kinbasket Lake
Beavermouth
Donald
Golden
Glacier
GLACIER NAT. PARK
Parson
Spillimacheen
KOOTENAY NAT. PARK
YOHO NAT. PARK
Kicking Horse Pass
Vermilion Pass
Lake Louise
BANFF NATIONAL PARK
Avola
Blue River
Birch Island
WELLS GRAY PARK
Clearwater L.
Murtle L.
Hobson L.
Azure L.
Albreda
CUMMINS LAKES PARK
HAMBER PARK
Mt. Columbia
Sunwapta Pass
Abraham L.
Big Horn Dam
North Ram
Ram
Nordegg
Mt. Brazeau
Maligne L.
JASPER NATIONAL PARK
Jasper
Yellowhead Pass
Lucerne
Red Pass
MT. ROBSON PARK
Mt. Robson
WILLMORE WILDERNESS PROVINCIAL PARK
Smoky
Wildhay
Obed
Hinton
Brûlé
Miette Hotsprings
Cadomin
Mountain Park
Mercoal
Robb
Foothills
Pembina
Brazeau
Big Bend Reservoir
Cynthia
ALBERTA
Rocky Mountains
Cariboo Mountains
Columbia Mountains
Monashee Mountains
Selkirk Mountains
Purcell Mountains
Fraser
Thompson
North Thompson
South Thompson
Athabasca
Columbia
Okanagan
Similkameen
Methow
Chewuch
COPYRIGHT PHILIP'S

1:6 400 000

ARCTIC OCEAN
Beaufort Sea
Canada Basin
Northwind Ridge
Summer extent of sea ice
North Magnetic Pole 2004
Sverdrup Islands
Ellesmere Island
Axel Heiberg Island
Devon Island
Queen Elizabeth Islands
Parry Islands
Melville Island
Bathurst Island
Cornwallis Island
Somerset Island
Prince of Wales Island
Boothia Peninsula
Victoria Island
Banks Island
King William Island
Prince Patrick I.
Ellef Ringnes I.
Amund Ringnes I.
Borden I.
Mackenzie King I.
Brock I.
Emerald I.
Byam Martin I.
Stefansson Island
Prince Gustaf Adolf Sea
Parry Channel
Viscount Melville Sound
M'Clure Strait
M'Clintock Channel
Lancaster Sound
Barrow Strait
Peel Sound
Prince Regent Inlet
Franklin Strait
James Ross Str.
Rae Strait
Victoria Str.
Queen Maud Gulf
Dease Strait
Coronation G.
Dolphin and Union Str.
Amundsen Gulf
Prince of Wales Str.
Prince Albert Sd.
Mackenzie Bay
Liverpool Bay
Franklin Bay
Darnley Bay
Cambridge Bay (Ikaluktutiak)
Resolute (Qausuittuq)
Kugluktuk (Coppermine)
Bathurst Inlet (Kingaok)
Umingmaktok (Bay Chimo)
Gjoa Haven (Uqsuqtuuq)
Holman
Paulatuk
Tuktoyaktuk
Inuvik
Aklavik
Fort McPherson
Tsiigehtchic (Arctic Red River)
Old Crow
Sachs Harbour
Kaktovik
Prudhoe Bay
Camden Bay
AULAVIK NAT. PARK
TUKTUT NOGAIT NAT. PARK
IVVAVIK NAT. PARK
VUNTUT NAT. PARK
ARCTIC NAT. WILDLIFE REFUGE
ALASKA (USA)
NUNAVUT
Richardson Mts.
British Mts.
Philip Smith Mts.
Melville Hills
Mackenzie
Arctic Circle
Permanent ice
m
ft

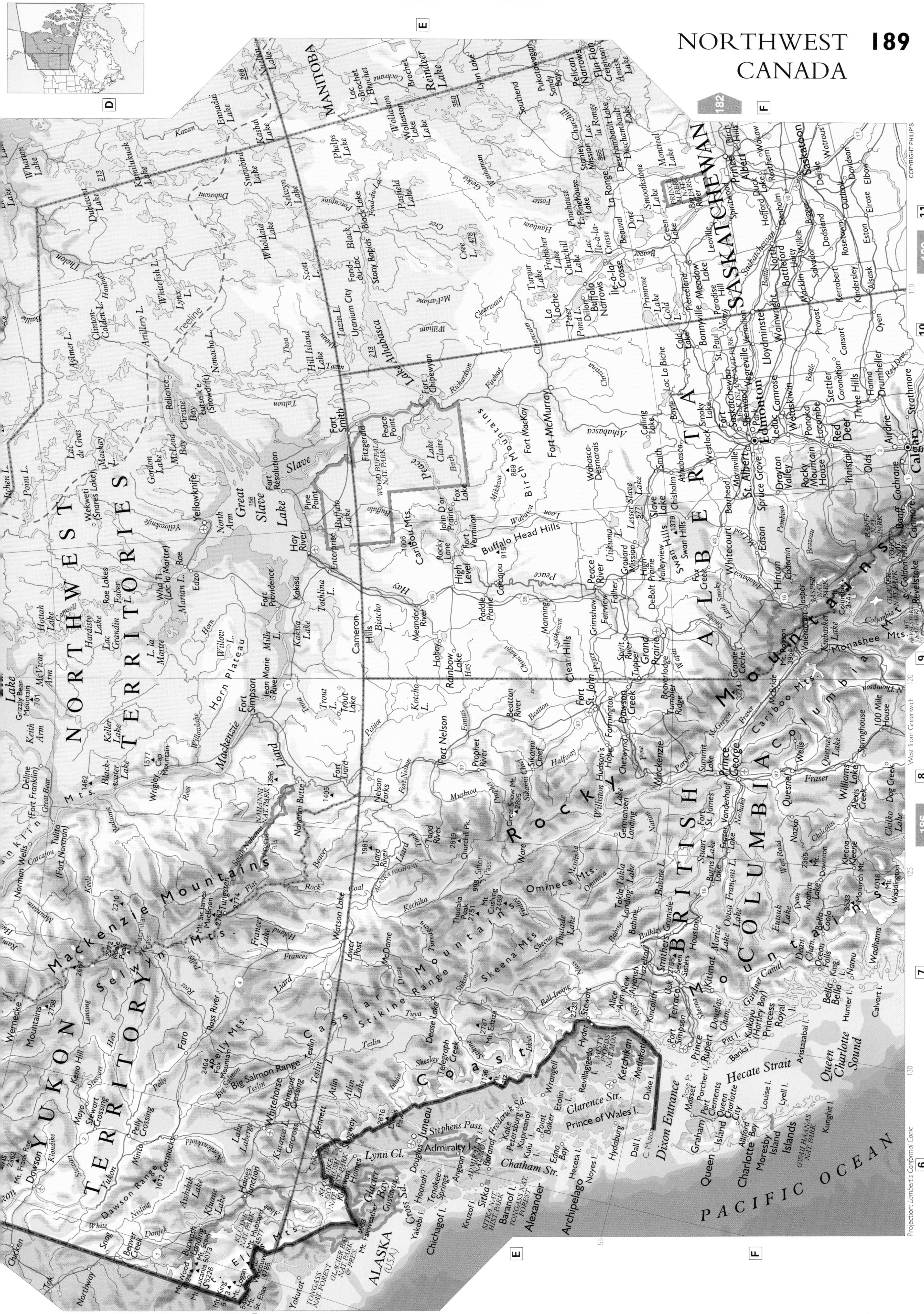
NORTHWEST TERRITORIES
YUKON TERRITORY
BRITISH COLUMBIA
ALBERTA
SASKATCHEWAN
MANITOBA
ALASKA (USA)
PACIFIC OCEAN
Great Slave Lake
Great Bear Lake
Lake Athabasca
Rocky Mountains
Mackenzie Mountains
Coast Mountains
Cassiar Mountains
Selwyn Mts.
Columbia Mts.
Caribou Mts.
Horn Plateau
Edmonton
Calgary
Saskatoon
Yellowknife
Whitehorse
Prince George
Prince Rupert
Juneau
Dawson
Fort McMurray
Fort Simpson
Fort Nelson
Fort Smith
Hay River
Grande Prairie
Red Deer
Lloydminster
North Battleford
Prince Albert
Queen Charlotte Islands
Queen Charlotte Sound
Hecate Strait
Dixon Entrance
Alexander Archipelago
Prince of Wales I.
WOOD BUFFALO NAT. PARK
Treeline
182
185
186
187
West from Greenwich
Projection: Lambert's Conformal Conic
COPYRIGHT PHILIPS

50 0 50 100 150 200 250 300 km
50 0 50 100 150 200 miles
1:6 400 000
B
C
D
Davis Strait
GREENLAND
(KALAALLIT NUNAAT)
(Denmark)
BAFFIN BAY
2136
2469
Melville Bugt
Lauge Koch Kyst
Knud Rasmussen Land
Upernavik
Kangersuatsiaq
Nuussuaq (Kraulshavn)
Steenstrup Gletscher
Uummannaq (Dundas) (Thule Air Base)
Kap York
Kap Atholl
Qaanaaq (Thule)
Qeqertarsuaq
Siorapaluk
Kap Alexander
Inglefield Land
Washington Land
Hall Land
Kane Basin
Nares Strait
Smith Sound
Robeson Chan.
Alert
C. Columbia
QUTTINIRPAAQ NAT. PARK
Lake Hazen
United States Range
British Empire Range
Barbeau Pk.
2616
Judge Daly Promontory
Archer Fiord
Agassiz Ice Cap
2210
Bache Peninsula
Pim I.
Ellesmere Island
Prince of Wales Icefield
2347
Talbot Inlet
Smith Bay
Clarence Hd.
Coburg I.
C. Parker
C. Sherard
Grise Fiord (Aujuittuq)
Devon Ice Cap
1951
Devon Island
Lancaster Sound
Jones Sound
Bear Bay
1494
Hoved I.
Bjorne Pen.
Baumann Fd.
Eureka Sd.
Eureka
Stor I.
Bay Fiord
Raanes Peninsula
Fosheim Peninsula
Cañon Fiord
Greely Fiord
Otto Fiord
Yelverton B.
Phillips In.
Nansen Sound
Axel Heiberg Island
Princess Margaret Range
2210 Outlook Pk.
C. Thomas Hubbard
Sverdrup Channel
Sverdrup Islands
Massey Sd.
Haig-Thomas I.
Norwegian Bay
Graham I.
Buckingham I.
North Kent I.
Cornwall I.
Belcher Channel
Table I.
Grinnell Peninsula
Amund Ringnes I.
Hassel Sound
Meighen I.
Peary Channel
Ellef Ringnes I.
King Christian I.
Summer extent of sea ice
Penny Str.
Queens Chan.
Baillie-Hamilton I.
Wellington Chan.
Cornwallis Island
Resolute (Qausuittuq)
Griffith I.
Bathurst Island
Helena I.
Maclean Str.
C. Isachsen
North Magnetic Pole 2004
Prince Gustaf Adolf Sea
Cameron I.
Ile Vanier
Massey I.
Alexander I.
Austin Chan.
Lougheed I.
Byam Martin Channel
Byam Martin I.
Byam Ch.
Queen Elizabeth Islands
Parry Islands
ARCTIC OCEAN
Borden I.
Wilkins Str.
Mackenzie King I.
Hazen Str.
Brock I.
Ballantyne Str.
Emerald I.
Hecla and Griper Bay
Melville Island
776
Liddon G.
Dundas Peninsula
C. Hay
Viscount Melville Sound
Parry Sound
Prince Patrick I.
Hardinge Bay
Crozier Chan.
Eglinton I.
Kellett Str.
Cape Russell
M'Clure Strait
Lands End
Dyer B.
Mercy Bay
NORTHWEST TERR.
Passage Pt.
Peel Pt.
Richard Collinson In.
Wynniatt Bay
Shaler Mountains
655
Victoria Island
Tahoe Lake
Washburn Lake
Stefansson Island
Goldsmith Ch.
Killan I.
Storkerson Pen.
Hadley Bay
Zeta Lake
Minto Hd.
Ommanney Bay
M'Clintock Channel
Norway Bay
C. Michelsen
Collinson Peninsula
Albert Edward Bay
Ferguson Lake
Cambridge Bay (Ikaluktutiak)
Jenny Lind I.
Melbourne I.
Queen Maud Gulf
Royal Geographical Society Is.
Admiralty I.
Victoria Str.
Larsen Sound
Gatesheads I.
C. Felix
King William Island
Gjoa Haven (Uqsuqtuuq)
Adelaide Peninsula
Sherman Basin
McNaughton Lake
Kent Peninsula
Melville Sd.
Elu Inlet
Umingmaktok (Bay Chimo)
Bathurst Inlet (Kingaok)
Bathurst In.
Arctic Sd.
Dease Strait
Coronation G.
Richardson Is.
Krusenstern
Wollaston Peninsula
George I.
Hood
Burnside
Prince of Wales Island
Prescott I.
Lowther I.
Russell I.
Peel Sound
Barrow Strait
Somerset Island
Creswell B.
Fitzgerald B.
C. Scoresby
Bellot Str.
Franklin Strait
Boothia Peninsula
573
James Ross Str.
Rae Strait
Shepherd B.
Chantrey In.
Murchison
Taloyoak (Spence Bay)
Kugaaruk (Pelly Bay)
Pelly B.
Simpson Peninsula
Lord Mayor B.
Gulf of Boothia
Crown Prince Frederik I.
C. Englefield
C. Chapman
Committee Bay
Wales I.
Bernier Bay
Prince Regent Inlet
Lancaster Sound
Parry Channel
Brodeur Peninsula
549
Admiralty In.
C. Crawford
Nanisivik
Arctic Bay (Ikpiarjuk)
Borden Peninsula
SIRMILIK NAT. PARK
Bylot Island
1951
C. Liverpool
Eclipse Sound
Pond Inlet (Mittimatalik)
Navy Board In.
Oqiivik
1905
Nova Zembla I.
Buchan G.
C. Adair
Baffin
Gifford
Fury and Hecla Strait
Erichsen Lake
Igloolik (Iglulik)
Hall Beach (Sanirajak)
Jens Munk I.
Hall L.
Melville
Parry B.
Nina Bang L.
Steensby Inlet
Koch I.
Rowley I.
Bray I.
North Spicer I.
South Spicer I.
Foley I.
Prince Charles I.
Baird Pen.
Gillian L.
Air Force I.
Flint L.
Barnes Ice Cap
Conn Lake
Bieler Lake
1905
Clyde River (Kangiqtugaapik)
C. Hewett
Henry Kater Pen.
C. Henry Kater
C. Raper
Home Bay
Ekalugad Fiord
Qikiqtarjuaq (Broughton Island)
AUYUITTUQ NAT. PARK
Penny Ice Cap
Cumberland Pen.
C. Dyer
Hantzsch
14
15
16
7
6
5
4
3
2
1
40
45
50
55
70
75
90
95
100
105
110
115
120
125
130
188
Permanent ice
m 1500 1000 400 200 0
ft 4500 3000 1200 600 0
0 200 600 2000 6000 4000 12000 6000 18000 8000 24000 m ft

ANTIC OCEAN
Hoare Bay
C. Mercy
Cumberland Sound
Lemieux Islands
Hall Peninsula
Pangnirtung (Panniqtuuq)
Frobisher B.
Loks Land
Resolution I.
Gabriel Strait
Iqaluit (Frobisher Bay)
Everett Mts.
Meta Incognita Peninsula
McKeand
Kimmirut (Lake Harbour)
Big I.
Killiniq
C. Chidley
NEWF. & LAB.
Torngat Mts.
Akpatok I.
Ungava Bay
C. Hopes Advance
Quaqtaq
Payne B.
Hopes Advance B.
Gyrfalcon Is.
Kangirsuk
Aupaluk
Kuujjuaq
Koksoak
Caniapiscau
Melèzes
Lac Faribault
Lac Tassialouc
Lac Payne
Lac Le Roy
Lac Bacqueville
Lac Minto
Lac Clairvigny
Lac des Loups Marins
Lac à l'Eau Claire
Lac D'Iberville
Lac Bienville
Lac Guillaume-Delisle
Petite r. de la Baleine
Grande r. de la Baleine
Nastapoka
Nastapoka Islands
Treeline
Kuujjuarapik
Q U É B E C
Péninsule d'Ungava
Mts. de Puvirnituq
Lac Nantais
Lac Klotz
Lac Couture
Arnaud
Kangiqsujuaq
Salluit
Ivujivik
Akulivik
Puvirnituq
B. de Puvirnituq
B. Kovik
B. Kogaluc
Kogaluc
Mosquito B.
Smith I.
Inukjuak
Hopewell Is.
King George Is.
Bakers Dozen Is.
Sanikiluaq
Belcher Islands
Sleeper Is.
Ottawa Is.
Long I.
Pte. Louis-XIV
C. Henrietta Maria
Chisasibi
La Grande
Rés. La Grande Deux
Rés. La Grande Trois
Rés. La Grande Quatre
Rés. Opinaca
Opinaca
Lac Sakami
Sakami
Wemindji
Eastmain
Lac Rossignol
Lac Naococane
Lac Plétipi
L. Caniapiscau
North Twin I.
South Twin I.
Trodely I.
Charlton I.
James Bay
Akimiski I.
Fort Albany
Albany
Attawapiskat
Sutton Lake
Wabuk Pt.
Peawanuck
Winisk
Webequie
Ekwan
Fort Severn
Severn
Big Trout Lake
Shibogama L.
Sachigo L.
Bearskin Lake
Sandy Lake
North Caribou L.
O N T A R I O
Hudson Strait
Charles I.
Salisbury I.
Nottingham I.
Digges Is.
Mansel I.
C. Wolstenholme
Fair Ness
C. de Nouvelle-France
Great Plain of the Koukdjuak
Nettilling Lake
Amadjuak Lake
Mingo L.
Bowman B.
Chorkbak Inlet
Tessik L.
Foxe Peninsula
Cape Dorset (Kingait)
Garnet Bay
Arctic Circle
C. Dominion
C. Dorchester
Mill I.
Foxe Basin
Foxe Channel
C. Wilson
Winter I.
Lyon Inlet
Vansittart I.
Frozen Str.
White I.
Repulse Bay (Naujaat)
Rae Isthmus
Southampton Island
Coral Harbour (Salliq)
Bell Peninsula
South Bay
Coats I.
Evans Strait
Fisher Strait
Roes Welcome Sound
Bay of Gods Mercy
C. Low
C. Southampton
Wager Bay
C. Fullerton
C. Kendall
Daly Bay
Chesterfield Inlet (Igluligaarjuk)
Chesterfield In.
Rankin Inlet (Kangiqliniq)
Marble I.
Whale Cove (Tikirarjuaq)
Bibby I.
Dawson Inlet
Maguse Pt.
Arviat (Eskimo Point)
HUDSON BAY
C. Tatnam
C. Churchill
Churchill
WAPUSK NAT. PARK
Bylot
Weir River
Gillam
Sundance
Nelson
Split Lake
Split L.
Thompson
Nelson House
Shamattawa
Kaskattama
Black Duck
Gods
Hayes
Knee Lake
Gods Lake
Oxford Lake
Sipiwesk Lake
Cross Lake
Norway House
Garden Hill
Island Lake
Berens River
Little Grand Rapids
Lake Winnipeg
Grand Rapids
Lake Winnipegosis
Cedar Lake
Gypsumville
The Pas
Cranberry Portage
Flin Flon
Creighton
Sandy Bay
Pukatawagan
Lynn Lake
Leaf Rapids
Granville Lake
South Indian Lake
Southern Indian L.
Big Sand L.
Northern Indian L.
Tadoule Lake
Stony L.
Seal
North Knife
North Knife L.
Churchill
Caribou
Nejanilini Lake
Nueltin Lake
Kasba Lake
Snowbird Lake
Ennadai Lake
Kazan
Thlewiaza
Tha-anne
South Henik L.
Maguse Lake
Kaminak Lake
Kaminuriak L. (Qamanirjuaq L.)
Yathkyed Lake
Baker Lake (Qamani'tuaaq)
Baker L.
Quoich
Tehek Lake
Schultz Lake
Aberdeen Lake
Garry Lake
Pelly Lake
Beverly Lake
Wharton Lake
Mallery Lake
Tulemalu Lake
Angikuni Lake
Kamilukuak Lake
Dubawnt Lake
Dubawnt
Thelon
Back
Aylmer L.
Clinton-Colden L.
Hanbury
Lac Brochet
Brochet
Reindeer Lake
Cochrane
Burntwood
Snow Lake
Grass
Minago
Poplar
Gunisao
Curtis Lake
Brown Lake
Armit Lake
Baker Lake
Jan Calder Lake
N U N A V U T
B a f f i n I s l a n d
M A N I T O B A
625
642
257
1135
West from Greenwich
Projection: Lambert's Conformal Conic
COPYRIGHT PHILIP'S
E
F
G
6
7
8
9
10
11
175
180
183
189
55
60
65
75
85
90
95
100
213
217
252
268
391

MONTRÉAL

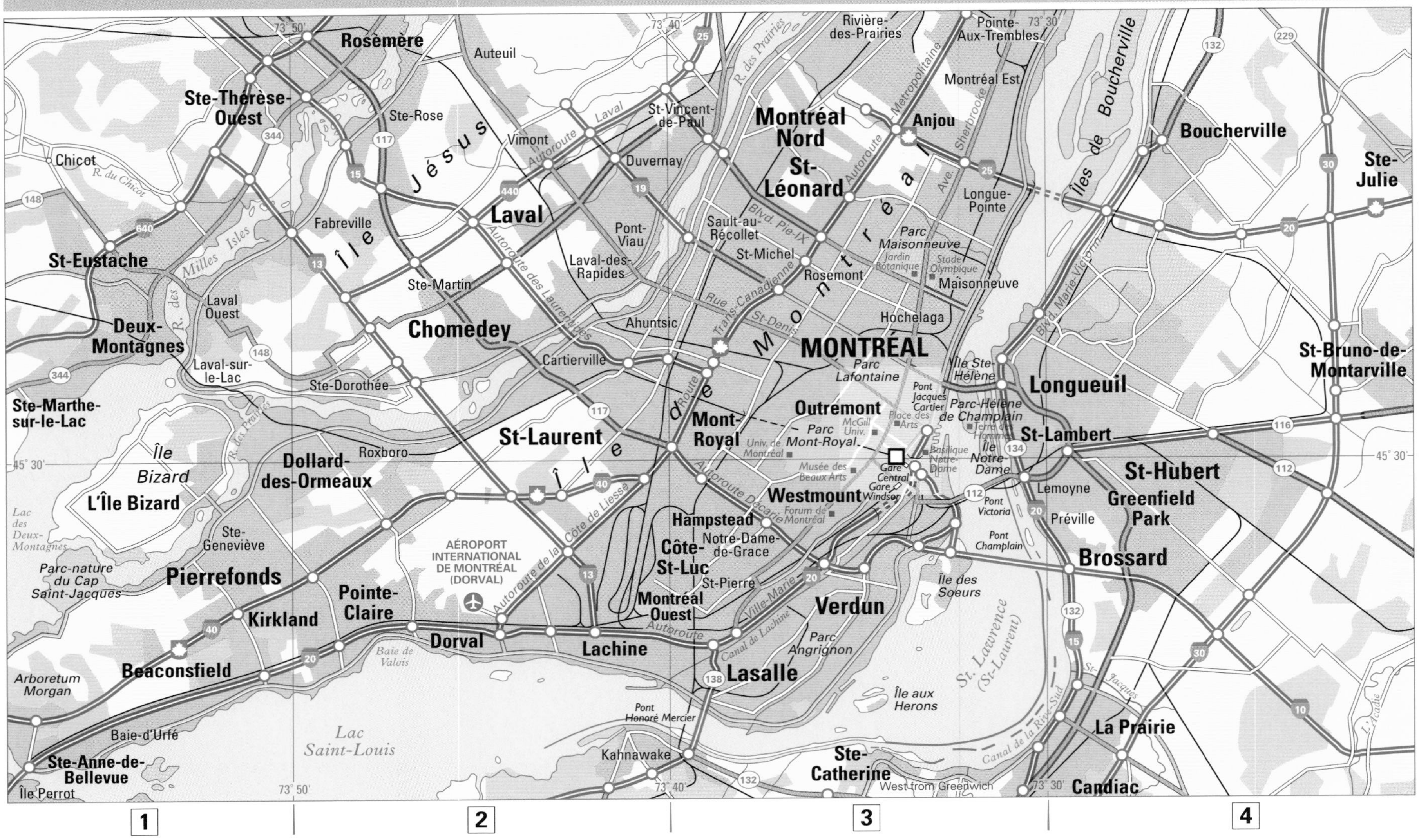

CENTRAL MONTRÉAL

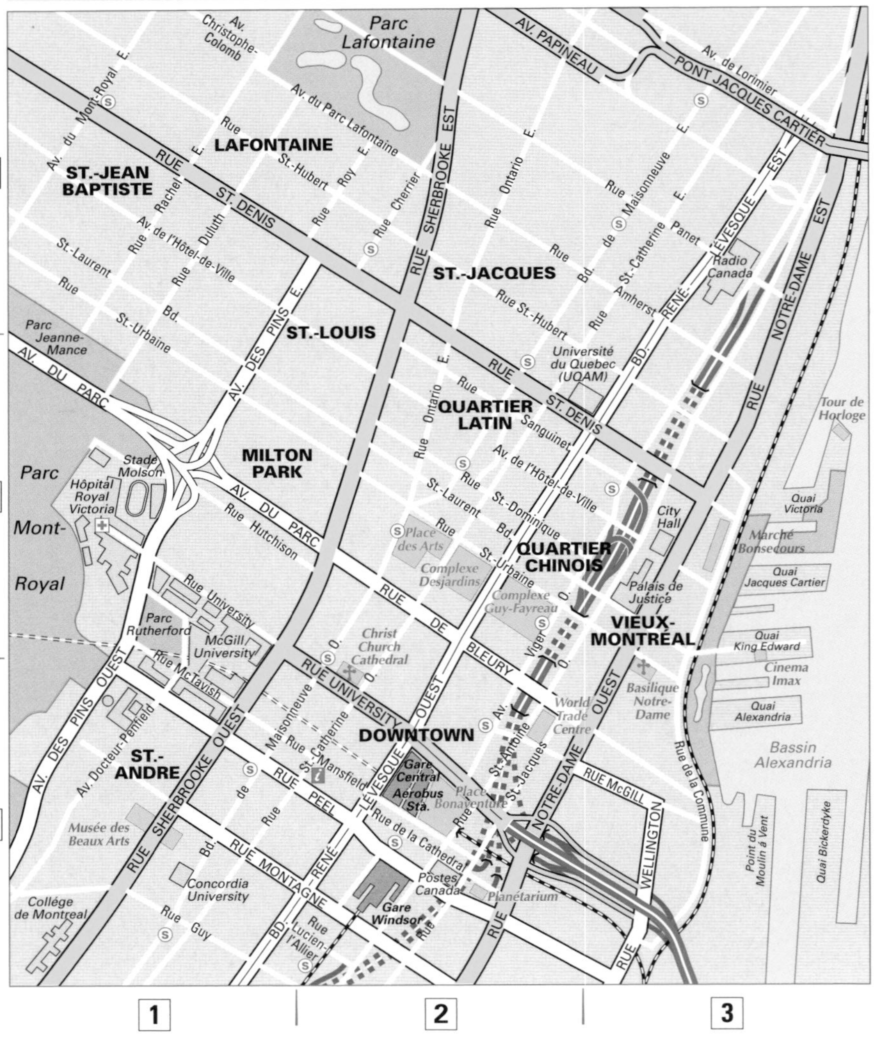

OTTAWA

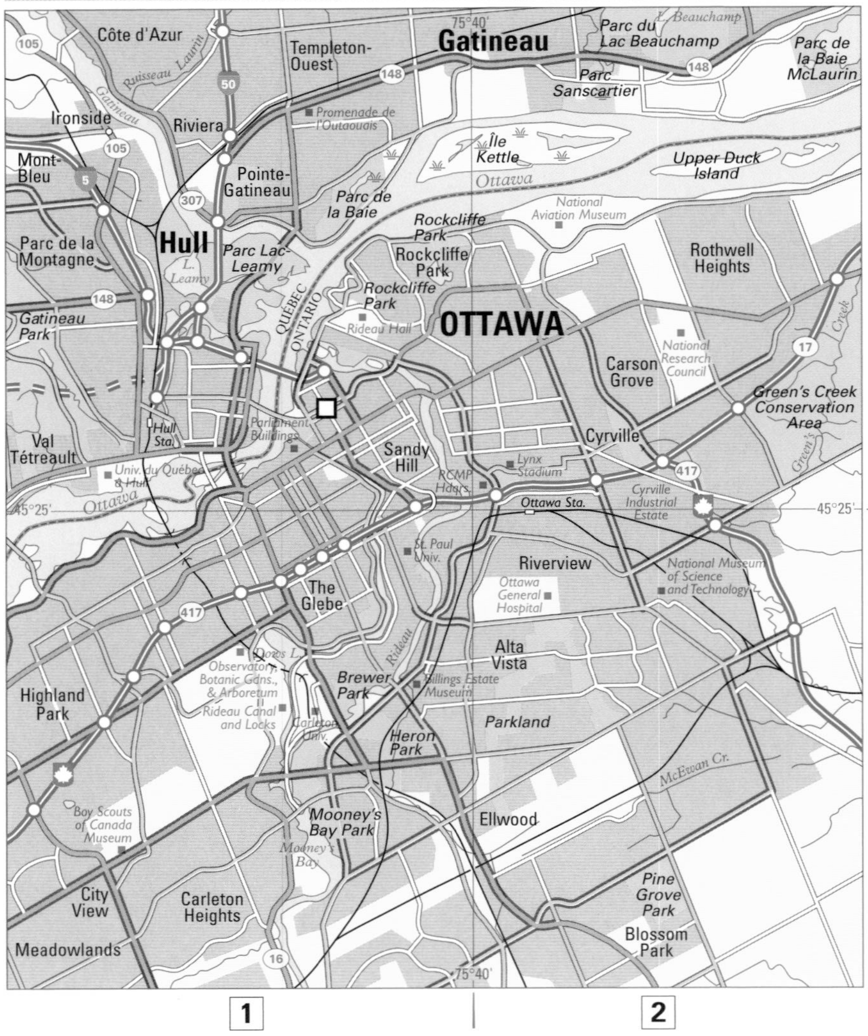

TORONTO

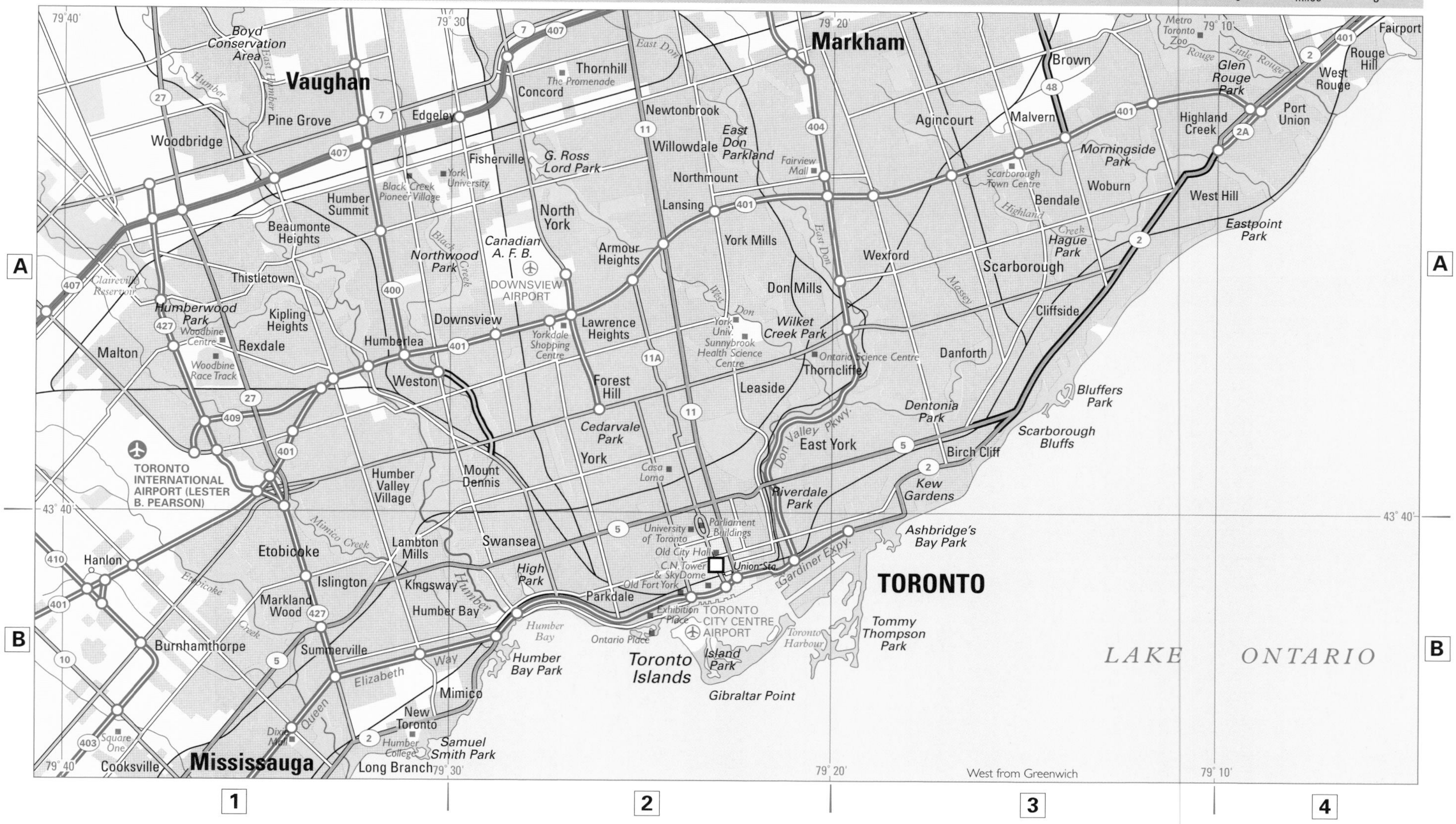

CENTRAL TORONTO

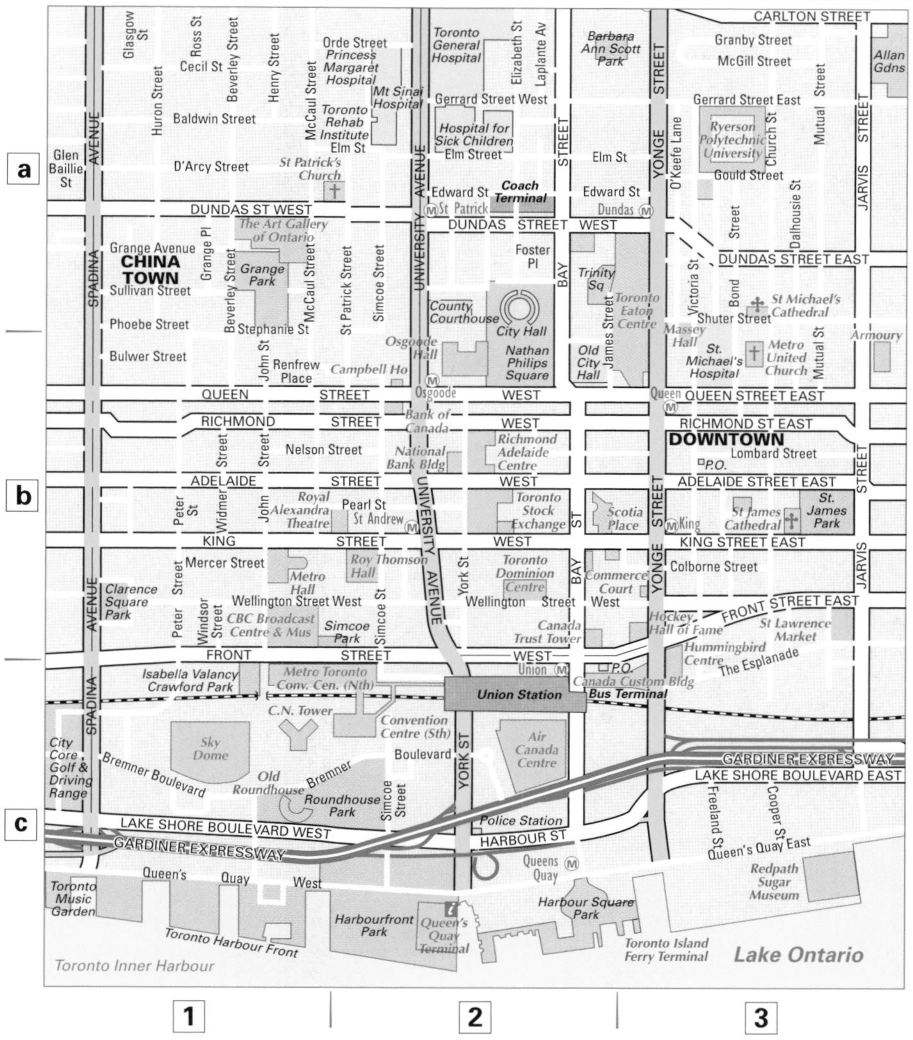

VANCOUVER

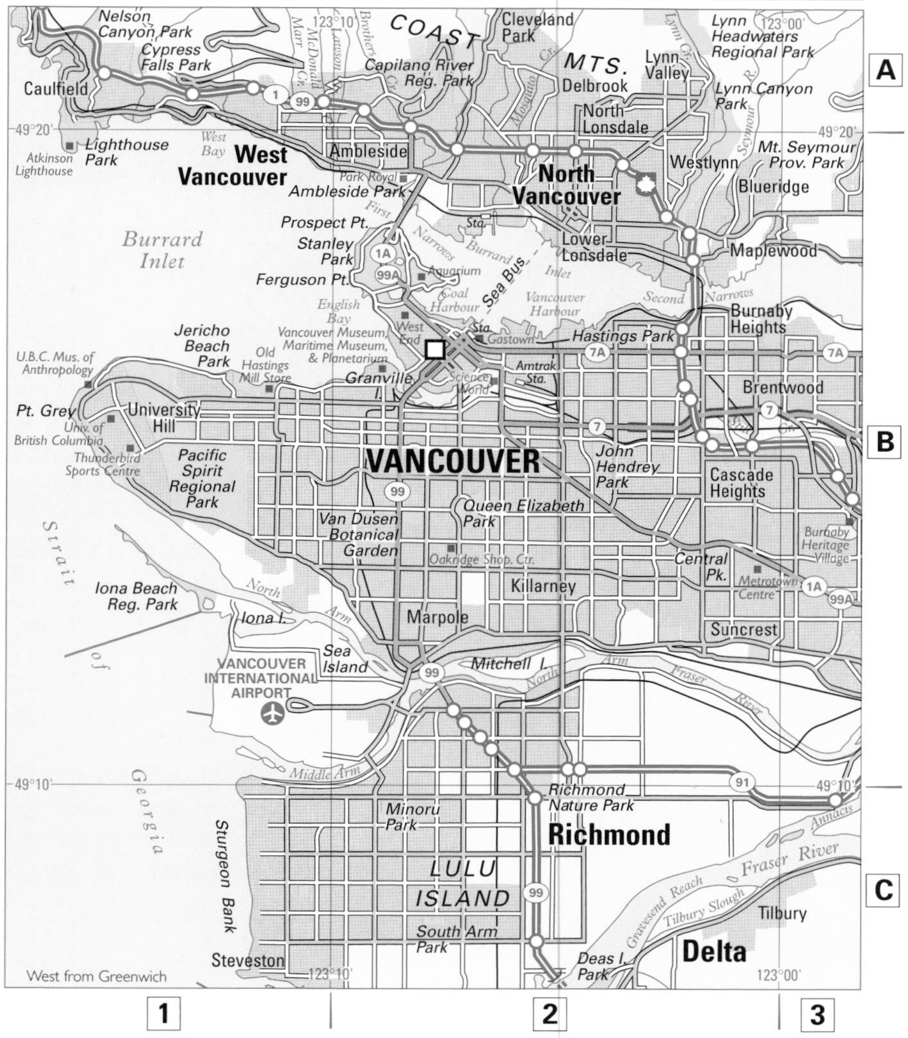

Alberta

Confederation date:
September 1, 1905
Provincial bird:
Great horned owl
Provincial flower:
Wild rose
Provincial tree:
Lodgepole pine
Provincial motto:
Strong and free
Provincial capital:
Edmonton
Population of capital:
666,104 (2001)

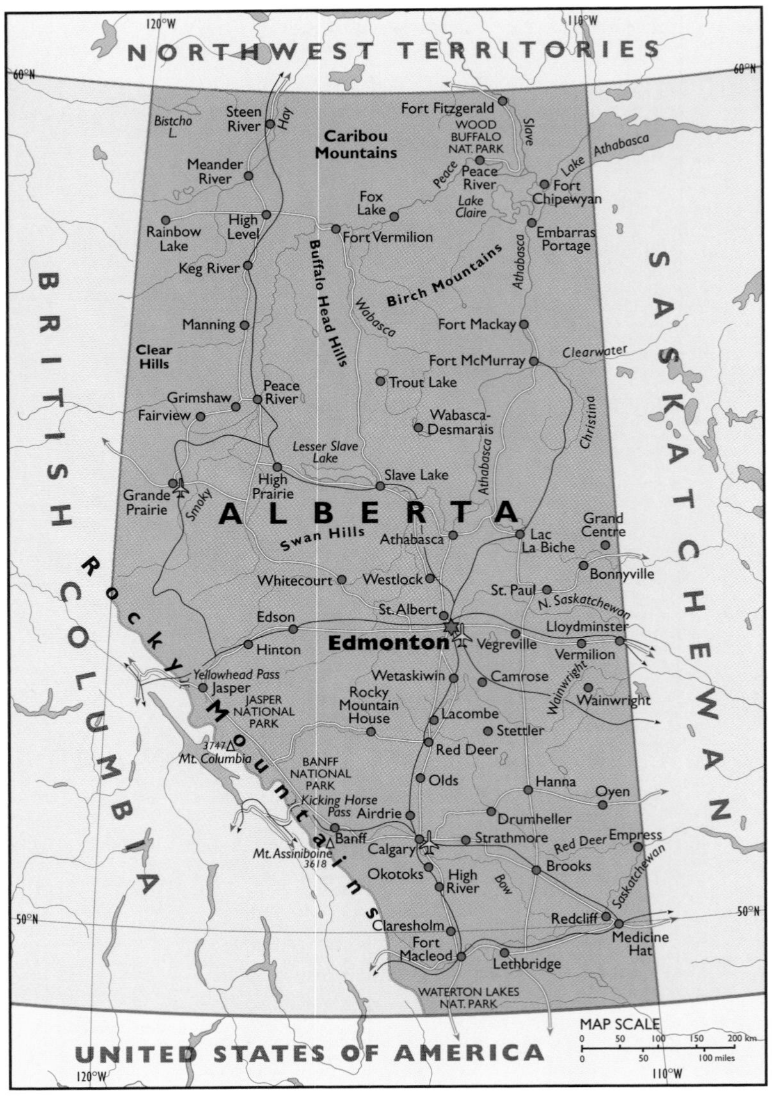

The area known today as Alberta was carved out of Rupert's Land, a vast territory granted to the Hudson's Bay Company by Charles II of England in 1670. Fur traders encountered the indigenous Beaver, Sarsi and Blackfoot Nations during the nineteenth century. In 1870 the government of Canada acquired the region. European settlement was slow and based mainly on extensive cattle ranching until completion of the Canadian Pacific Railway brought growing numbers of immigrant settlers in the 1890s. Alberta (named after Queen Victoria's fourth daughter) attained provincial status in 1905. Today, nearly half of the population lives in either Calgary, the rapidly growing corporate center of the oil industry or Edmonton, the provincial capital.

Characterized by grassland in the south and forested plains to the north, Alberta is the westernmost of Canada's three Prairie Provinces. Rivers such as the Athabasca and Peace flow northwards into the Mackenzie while the North and South Saskatchewan Rivers rise in the Rocky Mountain snow-pack and eventually drain east into the Hudson Bay. Prairie soils support the cultivation of wheat, barley and oilseeds with assistance from irrigation in the south. Alberta raises more cattle than any other province with immense feedlots in the Lethbridge area. Large oil and natural gas fields in central Alberta and the massive Athabascan oil sands deposits northeast of Edmonton have been a major stimulus to the economy and a source of provincial wealth—Alberta is the only province with no provincial sales tax. Notable manufacturing industries include petrochemicals, food processing, and forest products. World Heritage sites such as Head-Smashed-In Buffalo Jump and national parks such as Banff and Jasper attract tourists and skiers worldwide.

Edmonton

The "Gateway to the North," Edmonton is the northernmost major city in North America, and the sixth-largest in Canada. Founded by the Hudson's Bay Company in 1795, it was incorporated as a city in 1904 and became the capital of the newly formed province of Alberta a year later. Edmonton boomed after the discovery of oil in nearby Leduc in 1947 and downtown Edmonton sprouted a skyline in the 1960s. Edmonton's energy-based industries support the exploration, extraction and refining of coal, petroleum and natural gas.

Alberta at a Glance

People	**Alberta**	**Canada**
Total population, 2001 Census	2,974,810	30,007,090
Persons under 5 years old, percent, 2001	6.3%	5.7%
Persons under 18 years old, percent, 2001	25.3%	23.2%
Persons 65 years old and over, percent, 2001	10.4%	13.0%
Female persons, percent, 2001	50.0%	51.0%
Immigrant population, percent, 2001	14.7%	18.2%
Total population by home language	2,941,150	29,639,035
English language, percent, 2001 (a)	84.9%	61.0%
French language, percent, 2001 (a)	0.3%	19.5%
Non-official languages, percent, 2001 (a)	4.1%	5.6%
Total Aboriginal identity population, percent, 2001	5.3%	3.3%
Total Non-Aboriginal population, percent, 2001	93.6%	95.5%
Less than high school graduation certificate, percent persons 15+, 2001	30.6%	31.3%
High school graduates and/or some postsecondary, percent persons 15+, 2001	24.1%	24.9%
Trade certificate or diploma, percent persons 15+, 2001	12.8%	10.9%
College certificate, percent persons 15+, 2001	15.4%	15.0%
University diploma or degree, percent persons 15+, 2001	17.1%	17.9%
Homes owned, percent, 2001	70.4%	65.8%
Homes rented, percent, 2001	28.9%	33.8%
Average value of dwelling $	159,698	162,709
Total number of families	811,285	8,371,020
Average number of persons per census family	3.0	3.0
Average individual income of persons 15 years and over $	31,350	29,768
Average family income $	71,399	66,160
Business	**Alberta**	**Canada**
Total labor force 15 years and over	1,681,980	15,576,565
Females in labor force 15 years and over as a percent of total	45.8	46.7
Agriculture, forestry, fishing and hunting employment, percent, 2001	5.0	3.6
Mining and oil and gas extraction employment, percent, 2001	5.1	1.1
Utilities and construction employment, percent, 2001	8.5	6.4
Manufacturing employment, percent, 2001	8.0	14.0
Trade, transportation and warehousing employment, percent, 2001	20.9	20.6
Producer services employment, percent, 2001	18.3	18.7
Educational, health and social services employment, percent, 2001	15.4	16.3
Arts, accommodation and other services employment, percent, 2001	14.1	13.5
Public administration employment, percent, 2001	4.6	5.8
Geography	**Alberta**	**Canada**
Land area, 2001 (square kilometers)	642,317	9,093,507
Persons per square kilometer, 2001	4.6	3.3

(a) Only language spoken at home. Does not include bilingual households.
Note: Industries are defined according to the 1997 North American Industry Classification System.
Source: Statistics Canada

British Columbia

Confederation date: July 20, 1871
Provincial bird: Steller's jay
Provincial flower: Pacific dogwood
Provincial tree: Western red cedar
Provincial motto: Splendor without diminishment
Provincial capital: Victoria
Population of capital: 74,125 (2001)

Due to the isolation imposed by its mountainous character, British Columbia had a wider variety of distinct native cultures than any other province. The Tsimshian, Haidan, Wakashan, and Athapaskan peoples were among the native groups occupying British Columbia when Sir Francis Drake became the first European to sight Canada's Pacific coast in 1578. Captain James Cook landed in 1778, and George Vancouver claimed British possession of the island that bears his name in 1794. The Oregon Treaty of 1846 defined the province's southern boundary and completion of the Canadian Pacific Railway between Montréal and the coast in 1885 was the impetus for rapid economic development. British Columbia's population is now concentrated in the Lower Mainland, the southwestern corner where Vancouver is located, and in Victoria, the capital.

Physiographically, British Columbia is divided into the Insular, Coastal, Columbia, and Rocky mountain ranges as well as rugged interior plateaus. From these impressive elevations, rivers such as the Fraser carry the abundant precipitation that falls in the province back to the Pacific Ocean, providing hydroelectric power. Plentiful mineral deposits include copper, silver, gold, lead, and zinc. Dairying and horticulture in the Fraser Valley, orchard fruit and viticulture in the Okanagan Valley and extensive cattle ranching in the interior are the chief farming activities. As three-quarters of the land is forested, British Columbia is Canada's largest source of wood fiber and a wide range of forest products industries manufacture for domestic consumption and export. The salmon and herring fishery is another traditional resource-based activity that remains significant in coastal communities. Numerous national and provincial parks and dozens of world-class ski resorts such as Whistler-Blackcomb attract visitors to British Columbia year round.

Victoria

In 1843, the Hudson's Bay Company established a trading post at Fort Victoria, near the southern tip of Vancouver Island. The community grew during the gold rushes of the 1850s, and in 1868 Victoria became the capital of the colony of British Columbia, joining Canada as a province three years later. Government services, tourism, high technology, forest products, and shipbuilding are the main engines of growth.

British Columbia at a Glance

People	British Columbia	Canada
Total population, 2001 Census	3,907,735	30,007,090
Persons under 5 years old, percent, 2001	5.3%	5.7%
Persons under 18 years old, percent, 2001	22.3%	23.2%
Persons 65 years old and over, percent, 2001	7.1%	13.0%
Female persons, percent, 2001	50.9%	51.0%
Immigrant population, percent, 2001	25.8%	18.2%
Total population by home language	38,68,875	29,639,035
English language, percent, 2001 (a)	77.5%	61.0%
French language, percent, 2001 (a)	0.2%	19.5%
Non-official languages, percent, 2001 (a)	8.7%	5.6%
Total Aboriginal identity population, percent, 2001	4.4%	3.3%
Total Non-Aboriginal population, percent, 2001	94.7%	95.5%
Less than high school graduation certificate, percent persons 15+, 2001	28.0%	31.3%
High school graduates and/or some postsecondary, percent persons 15+, 2001	25.6%	24.9%
Trade certificate or diploma, percent persons 15+, 2001	11.8%	10.9%
College certificate, percent persons 15+, 2001	15.3%	15.0%
University diploma or degree, percent persons 15+, 2001	19.2%	17.9%
Homes owned, percent, 2001	66.3%	25.4%
Homes rented, percent, 2001	33.4%	13.0%
Average value of dwelling $	230,645	162,709
Total number of families	1,086,035	8,371,020
Average number of persons per census family	2.9	3
Average individual income of persons 15 years and over $	29,613	29,768
Average family income $	64,821	66,160

Business	British Columbia	Canada
Total labor force 15 years and over	2,014,605	15,576,565
Females in labor force 15 years and over as a percent of total	47.1	46.7
Agriculture, forestry, fishing and hunting employment, percent, 2001	3.9	3.6
Mining and oil and gas extraction employment, percent, 2001	0.7	1.1
Utilities and construction employment, percent, 2001	6.5	6.4
Manufacturing employment, percent, 2001	9.6	14.0
Trade, transportation and warehousing employment, percent, 2001	21.3	20.6
Producer services employment, percent, 2001	20.0	18.7
Educational, health and social services employment, percent, 2001	16.9	16.3
Arts, accommodation and other services employment, percent, 2001	15.5	13.5
Public administration employment, percent, 2001	5.6	5.8

Geography	British Columbia	Canada
Land area, 2001 (square kilometers)	925,186	9,093,507
Persons per square kilometer, 2001	4.2	3.3

(a) Only language spoken at home. Does not include bilingual households.
Note: Industries are defined according to the 1997 North American Industry Classification System.
Source: Statistics Canada

Manitoba

Confederation date:
July 15, 1870
Provincial bird:
Great gray owl
Provincial flower:
Prairie crocus
Provincial tree:
White spruce
Provincial motto:
Glorious and free
Provincial capital:
Winnipeg
Population of capital:
619,544 (2001)

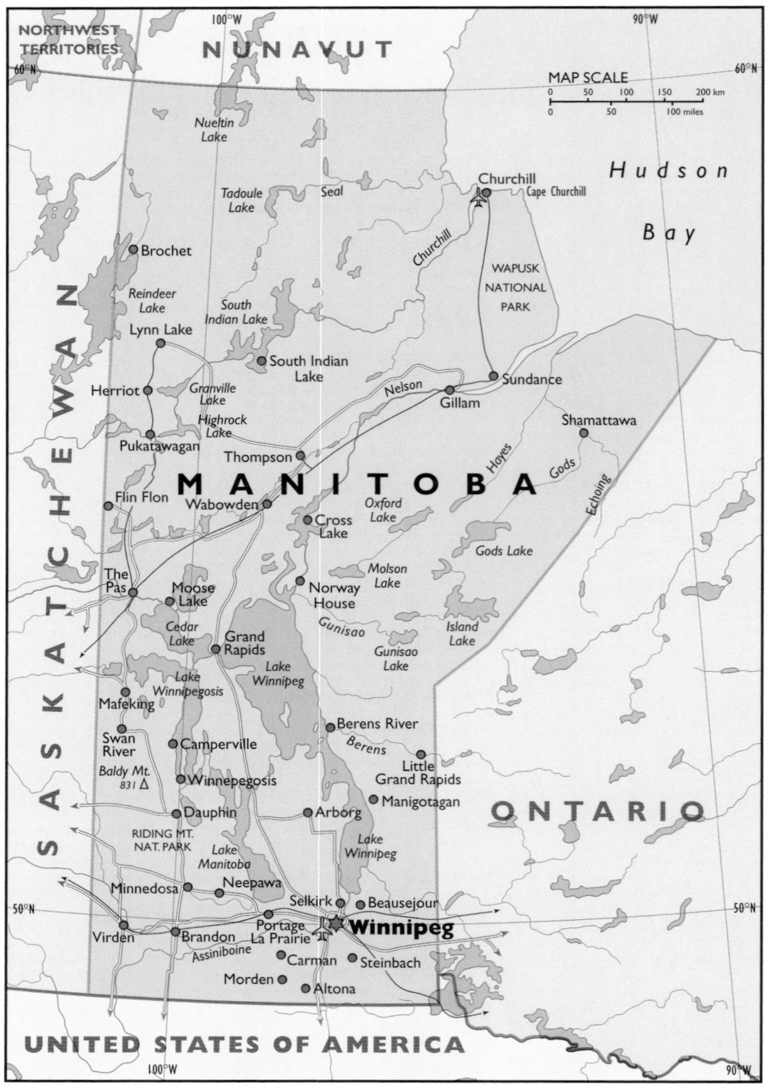

Manitoba at a Glance

People	Manitoba	Canada
Total population, 2001 Census	1,119,585	30,007,090
Persons under 5 years old, percent, 2001	6.3%	5.7%
Persons under 18 years old, percent, 2001	12.9%	23.2%
Persons 65 years old and over, percent, 2001	14.0%	13.0%
Female persons, percent, 2001	50.9%	51.0%
Immigrant population, percent, 2001	11.9%	18.2%
Total population by home language	1,103,695	29,639,035
English language, percent, 2001 (a)	80.6%	61.0%
French language, percent, 2001 (a)	0.8%	19.5%
Non-official languages, percent, 2001 (a)	3.9%	5.6%
Total Aboriginal identity population, percent, 2001	13.4%	3.3%
Total Non-Aboriginal population, percent, 2001	85.2%	95.5%
Less than high school graduation certificate, percent persons 15+, 2001	38.2%	31.3%
High school graduates and/or some postsecondary, percent persons 15+, 2001	22.7%	24.9%
Trade certificate or diploma, percent persons 15+, 2001	10.8%	10.9%
College certificate, percent persons 15+, 2001	13.1%	15.0%
University diploma or degree, percent persons 15+, 2001	15.3%	17.9%
Homes owned, percent, 2001	67.8%	65.8%
Homes rented, percent, 2001	29.8%	33.8%
Average value of dwelling $	97,670	162,709
Total number of families	302,850	8,371,020
Average number of persons per census family	3.0	3.0
Average individual income of persons 15 years and over $	26,416	29,768
Average family income $	59,005	66,160

Business	Manitoba	Canada
Total labor force 15 years and over	577,340	15,576,565
Females in labor force 15 years and over as a percent of total	46.8	46.7
Agriculture, forestry, fishing and hunting employment, percent, 2001	6.5	3.6
Mining and oil and gas extraction employment, percent, 2001	0.7	1.1
Utilities and construction employment, percent, 2001	6.2	6.4
Manufacturing employment, percent, 2001	11.8	14.0
Trade, transportation and warehousing employment, percent, 2001	20.5	20.6
Producer services employment, percent, 2001	14.3	18.7
Educational, health and social services employment, percent, 2001	19.8	16.3
Arts, accommodation and other services employment, percent, 2001	13.3	13.5
Public administration employment, percent, 2001	7.0	5.8

Geography	Manitoba	Canada
Land area, 2001 (square kilometers)	553,556	9,093,507
Persons per square kilometer, 2001	2.2	3.3

(a) Only language spoken at home. Does not include bilingual households.
Note: Industries are defined according to the 1997 North American Industry Classification System.
Source: Statistics Canada

Manitoba is the easternmost of Canada's Prairie Provinces and was created out of Rupert's Land which had been granted to the Hudson's Bay Company in 1670. Early European colonists found Assiniboin and Ojibwa tribes occupying the plains and Cree in the woodlands further north. In 1812, the Earl of Selkirk established the Red River Colony in what is now southern Manitoba. A new aboriginal group emerged from intermarriage between Native people and Europeans and by 1870, the Métis outnumbered the white settlers. Rupert's Land was transferred to Canada in 1870 and became Manitoba, Canada's fifth province. Outside of Winnipeg, most Manitobans are concentrated between the United States border and the Trans-Canada Highway.

In the south, the flat, low-lying terrain owes much to its origins as glacial Lake Agassiz and is prone to flooding in the spring. This grassland region contrasts with the bare, rocky upland of the Canadian Shield in central Manitoba, and the treeless tundra and permafrost of the far north. The Red and Assiniboine Rivers drain into Lake Winnipeg whose waters empty into Hudson Bay through the Nelson River. Manitoba's agricultural economy is best known for wheat but mixed grains, oilseed crops and intensive hog production are also important. In addition to extensive timber land, significant mineral deposits include copper and nickel in mining centers such as Flin Flon and Thompson. Some oil production is found in the southwestern corner of the province.

Winnipeg

Located at the confluence of the Red and Assiniboine Rivers, Winnipeg is "The Gateway to the West" as well as the capital of Manitoba. In 1738, French explorer Sieur de la Vérendrye founded Fort Rouge on the site of the present-day city. The settlement was later renamed Winnipeg, after the Cree word for muddy water, and today the city has more indigenous people than any other conurbation in Canada. As the key distribution center for Canada's Prairie West, Winnipeg's development kept pace with the rapid growth in railroad travel in the late nineteenth century and it became one of Canada's largest cities though its expansion has slowed in recent decades. Industrial activity includes grain storage, food processing, agricultural machinery, and transportation equipment. The Winnipeg Commodity Exchange is Canada's only agricultural futures and options exchange and forms the foundation for the city's function as a financial center.

New Brunswick

Confederation date: July 1, 1867
Provincial bird: Black-capped chickadee
Provincial flower: Purple violet
Provincial tree: Balsam fir
Provincial motto: Hope was restored
Provincial capital: Fredericton
Population of capital: 47,560 (2001)

Mi'kmaq and Malecite people occupied this part of Atlantic Canada before the French explorer Jacques Cartier arrived in 1534, paving the way for French settlement along the Bay of Fundy in a region that became known as Acadia in the seventeenth century. Acadia was ceded to Britain in 1713 and the population increased rapidly in 1783–84 when thousands of Loyalists fled the newly created United States and settled in the Saint John River Valley. The colony of New Brunswick was created to deal with the influx of Loyalists and in 1867, it joined Nova Scotia, Québec, and Ontario to form the Dominion of Canada. The capital is Fredericton while the largest cities are Saint John, a major port on the Bay of Fundy and Moncton, the cultural center for the French-speaking Acadian region. With one third of its people reporting French as their mother-tongue, New Brunswick is the only Canadian province to be officially bilingual.

Rising gradually from east to west, the Appalachian landscape of New Brunswick is drained by the Saint John and Miramichi rivers. Much of this rugged maritime province is forested with spruce, pine, and fir. Logging activities are an important source of employment in central New Brunswick and pulp and paper mills are a vital industry in many communities. Commercial potato production under contract to local frozen potato plants is the leading agricultural sector in the Saint John River valley while smaller mixed farms are found throughout the province. Metallic mineral extraction is concentrated near Bathurst which has become one of Canada's largest producers of lead and zinc ore which is exported for further processing.

Fredericton

In 1692, the fortified capital of Acadia was established at the junction of the Saint John and the Nashwaak rivers. Britain later acquired the territory, subduing both the native Maliseet people, who were allied with the French, and the Acadians. In 1785, Loyalists named the site after Frederick Augustus, second son of King George III. It became the capital of New Brunswick in the same year. Among Canada's smallest provincial capitals, Fredericton is a center for provincial government administration and home to the University of New Brunswick (founded in 1785). Computer software, forest products and construction material, along with footwear manufacturing contribute heavily to the local economy.

New Brunswick at a Glance

People	New Brunswick	Canada
Total population, 2001 Census	729,500	30,007,090
Persons under 5 years old, percent, 2001	5.2%	5.7%
Persons under 18 years old, percent, 2001	22.0%	23.2%
Persons 65 years old and over, percent, 2001	13.6%	13.0%
Female persons, percent, 2001	51.1%	51.0%
Immigrant population, percent, 2001	3.1%	18.2%
Total population by home language	719,710	29,639,035
English language, percent, 2001 (a)	63.8%	61.0%
French language, percent, 2001 (a)	32.4%	19.5%
Non-official languages, percent, 2001 (a)	1.6%	5.6%
Total Aboriginal identity population, percent, 2001	2.3%	3.3%
Total Non-Aboriginal population, percent, 2001	96.3%	95.5%
Less than high school graduation certificate, percent persons 15+, 2001	37.3%	31.3%
High school graduates and/or some postsecondary, percent persons 15+, 2001	24.4%	24.9%
Trade certificate or diploma, percent persons 15+, 2001	11.3%	10.9%
College certificate, percent persons 15+, 2001	13.8%	15.0%
University diploma or degree, percent persons 15+, 2001	13.2%	17.9%
Homes owned, percent, 2001	74.5%	65.8%
Homes rented, percent 2001	25.0%	33.8%
Average value of dwelling $	86,538	162,709
Total number of families	215,100	8,371,020
Average number of persons per census family	2.9	3.0
Average individual income of persons 15 years and over $	24,091	29,769
Average family income $	52,704	66,160

Business	New Brunswick	Canada
Total labor force 15 years and over	365,040	15,576,565
Females in labor force 15 years and over as a percent of total	46.9	46.7
Agriculture, forestry, fishing and hunting employment, percent, 2001	5.6	3.6
Mining and oil and gas extraction employment, percent, 2001	0.9	1.1
Utilities and construction employment, percent, 2001	7.4	6.4
Manufacturing employment, percent, 2001	12.6	14.0
Trade, transportation and warehousing employment, percent, 2001	20.2	20.6
Producer services employment, percent, 2001	14.3	18.7
Educational, health and social services employment, percent, 2001	17.6	16.3
Arts, accommodation and other services employment, percent, 2001	13.6	13.5
Public administration employment, percent, 2001	7.8	5.8

Geography	New Brunswick	Canada
Land area, 2001 (square kilometers)	71,450	9,093,507
Persons per square kilometer, 2001	10.2	3.3

(a) Only language spoken at home. Does not include bilingual households.
Note: Industries are defined according to the 1997 North American Industry Classification System.
Source: Statistics Canada

Newfoundland and Labrador

Confederation date:
March 31, 1949
Provincial bird:
Atlantic puffin
Provincial flower:
Pitcher plant
Provincial tree:
Black spruce
Provincial motto:
Seek ye first the kingdom of God
Provincial capital:
St. John's
Population of capital:
99,182 (2001)

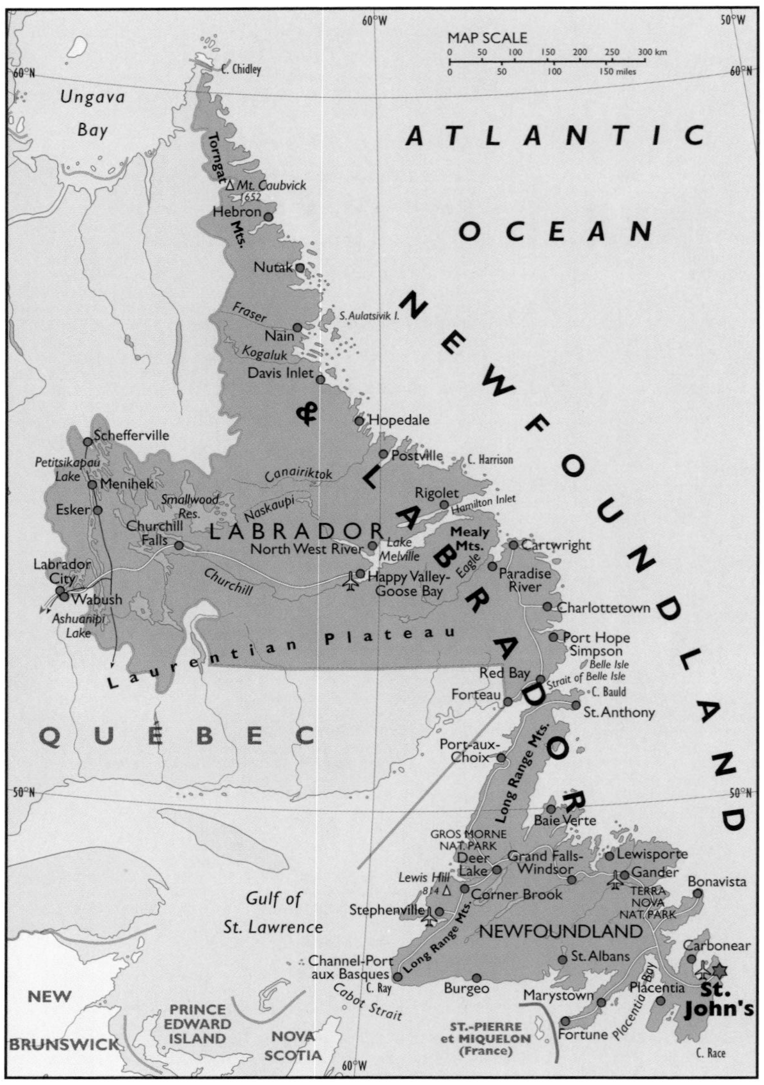

Comprising the island of Newfoundland and the mainland region of Labrador, the province once supported the fishing and sealing lifestyle of the aboriginal Beothuk people. Cree-speaking Innu people remain dominant in Labrador in five coastal communities. Archeological evidence suggests that Norsemen colonized L'Anse aux Meadows on the northern tip of Newfoundland. Occupied between 990 and 1050 CE, it is the earliest known European settlement in the western hemisphere. Retaining its status as a British colony until 1949, Newfoundland and Labrador is Canada's newest province.

Deep fiords and rocky headlands serrate the coastlines of Newfoundland and Labrador while the interior is largely a plateau covered with coniferous forest and numerous lakes and wetlands. The most notable feature in Labrador's rugged Canadian Shield topography is the spectacular coastal mountain ranges culminating with the Torngats in the far north. The rigorous climate, sparse population and lack of ground transportation facilities have hindered economic development in this region. However, open pit iron ore mines in the Labrador Trough near the Québec border have been a valuable resource since the 1950s. One of the largest nickel deposits in the world at Voisey Bay is poised for the development of a large scale commercial mine on the coast.

The foundation of Newfoundland's economy has been the cod fishery of The Grand Banks, the shallow waters extending east over the continental shelf. Overfishing and mismanagement of this valuable resource led to a decline in cod stocks and a moratorium was imposed in 1992 with disastrous consequences for many fishing communities. Offshore oil production began in 1997 with the Hibernia oil field some 200 miles east of St. John's and in 2002, the Terra Nova field came onstream.

St. John's

Sir Humphrey Gilbert founded an English colony at St. John's on the Avalon Peninsula in 1605. Due largely to its spectacular natural harbor, St. John's has long been a commercial hub and served as the capital of both colony and province. The traditional wood frame construction used throughout the city made St. John's vulnerable to fire and five separate conflagrations in the nineteenth century destroyed many of its oldest buildings. Guglielmo Marconi, inventor of radio communication, received the first transatlantic radio message on St. John's Signal Hill in 1901. Industrial activity includes transportation services, seafood processing, and services related to offshore oil exploration and production.

Newfoundland & Labrador at a Glance

People	Newfoundland & Labrador	Canada
Total population, 2001 Census	512,930	30,007,090
Persons under 5 years old, percent, 2001	4.8%	5.7%
Persons under 18 years old, percent, 2001	21.9%	23.2%
Persons 65 years old and over, percent, 2001	12.3%	13.0%
Female persons, percent, 2001	51.1%	51.0%
Immigrant population, percent, 2001	1.6%	18.2%
Total population by home language	508,075	29,639,035
English language, percent, 2001 (a)	97.4%	61.0%
French language, percent, 2001 (a)	0.40%	19.5%
Non-official languages, percent, 2001 (a)	1.1%	5.6%
Total Aboriginal identity population, percent, 2001	3.7%	3.3%
Total Non-Aboriginal population, percent, 2001	95.4%	95.5%
Less than high school graduation certificate, percent persons 15+, 2001	42.4%	31.3%
High school graduates and/or some postsecondary, percent persons 15+, 2001	18.6%	24.9%
Trade certificate or diploma, percent persons 15+, 2001	16.8%	10.9%
College certificate, percent persons 15+, 2001	10.9%	15.0%
University diploma or degree, percent persons 15+, 2001	11.3%	17.9%
Homes owned, percent, 2001	78.2%	65.8%
Homes rented, percent, 2001	21.8%	33.8%
Average value of dwelling $	76,283	162,709
Total number of families, 2001	154,380	8,371,020
Average number of persons per census family	2.9	3.0
Average individual income of persons 15 years and over $	22,620	29,768
Average family income $	49,679	66,160

Business	Newfoundland & Labrador	Canada
Total labor force 15 years and over	232,265	15,576,565
Females in labor force 15 years and over as a percent of total	46.7	46.7
Agriculture, forestry, fishing and hunting employment, percent, 2001	6.7	3.6
Mining and oil and gas extraction employment, percent, 2001	2.1	1.1
Utilities and construction employment, percent, 2001	7.4	6.4
Manufacturing employment, percent, 2001	10.3	14.0
Trade, transportation and warehousing employment, percent, 2001	20.7	20.6
Producer services employment, percent, 2001	11.3	18.7
Educational, health and social services employment, percent, 2001	19.5	16.3
Arts, accommodation and other services employment, percent, 2001	13.2	13.5
Public administration employment, percent, 2001	8.8	5.8

Geography	Newfoundland & Labrador	Canada
Land area, 2001 (square kilometers)	373,872	9,093,507
Persons per square kilometer, 2001	1.4	3.3

(a) Only language spoken at home. Does not include bilingual households.
Note: Industries are defined according to the 1997 North American Industry Classification System.
Source: Statistics Canada

Northwest Territories

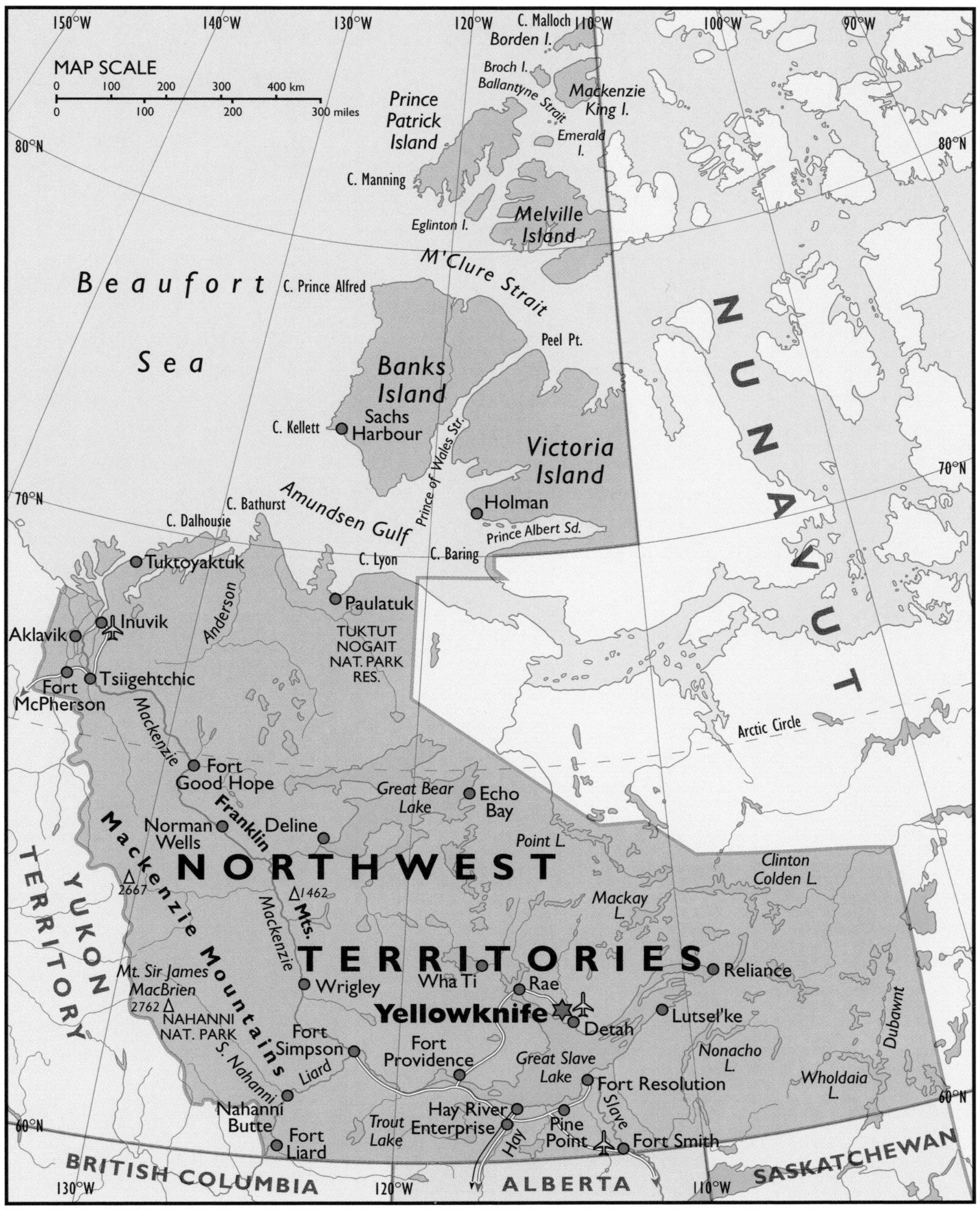

Confederation date: July 15, 1870
Territorial bird: Gyrfalcon
Territorial flower: Mountain avens
Territorial tree: Tamarack
Territorial motto: None
Territorial capital: Yellowknife
Population of capital: 16,541 (2001)

The Northwest Territories (NWT) is the second largest administrative division in the country. It includes much of Canada's western Arctic. Before European contact, Dene (Athapaskan) people occupied the Subarctic region while a chain of Inuit settlements stretched along the Arctic coastline. The Hudson's Bay Company acquired much of what became the NWT in 1670 and it was transferred to the Canadian government in 1870. In 1999, the eastern part of the NWT became the new territory of Nunavut.

Most commercial activity is found in the Mackenzie River Valley and around Great Slave Lake. To the northeast is sparsely inhabited taiga and tundra. Climatic limitations prevent large scale commercial agriculture or forestry thus economic development has only occurred at locations rich in minerals or favorably situated for transportation. Many of the highways are winter roads, open only when the ground is frozen. Gold is mined in the Yellowknife area and several diamond bearing kimberlite pipes are mined north of Great Slave Lake. Diamond production has grown rapidly since it began in 1998 and Canada has become the world's third largest producer of rough diamonds. An oilfield at Norman Wells is linked to northern Alberta's grid of oil pipelines. Significant oil and gas reserves in the Beaufort Sea await development but cannot be exploited until a pipeline is built.

Yellowknife

Yellowknife is the capital and largest settlement in the NWT. Located on Great Slave Lake, Yellowknife grew rapidly after the discovery of gold in the area in 1935 and is named for the copper knives traditionally used by the local Slavey people. Yellowknife is now principally an administrative center.

Northwest Territories at a Glance

People	**Northwest Territories**	**Canada**
Total population, 2001 Census	37,360	30,007,090
Persons under 5 years old, percent, 2001	8.1%	5.7%
Persons under 18 years old, percent, 2001	32.0%	23.2%
Persons over 65 years old, percent, 2001	4.4%	13.0%
Female persons	18,240	15,300,245
Immigrant population, percent, 2001	6.4%	18.2%
Total population by home language	37,100	29,639,035
English language, percent, 2001 (a)	80.6%	61.0%
French language, percent, 2001 (a)	0.5%	19.5%
Non-official languages, percent, 2001 (a)	3.9%	5.6%
Total Aboriginal identity population, percent, 2001	50.1%	3.3%
Total Non-Aboriginal population, percent, 2001	49.2%	95.5%
Less than high school graduation certificate, percent persons 15+, 2001	35.2%	31.3%
High school graduates and/or some postsecondary, percent persons 15+, 2001	20.9%	24.9%
Trade certificate or diploma, percent persons 15+, 2001	14.0%	10.9%
College certificate, percent persons 15+, 2001	14.7%	15.0%
University diploma or degree, percent persons 15+, 2001	15.2%	17.9%
Homes owned, percent, 2001	53.1%	65.8%
Homes rented, percent, 2001	45.6%	33.8%
Average value of dwelling $	139,384	162,709
Total number of families	9,700	8,371,020
Average number of persons per census family	3.3	3.0
Average individual income of persons 15 years and over $	35,012	29,768
Average family income $	75,102	66,160
Business	**Northwest Territories**	**Canada**
Total labor force 15 years and over	20,425	15,576,565
Females in labor force 15 years and over as a percent of total	46.5	46.7
Agriculture, forestry, fishing and hunting employment, percent, 2001	1.5	3.6
Mining and oil and gas extraction employment, percent, 2001	7.0	1.1
Utilities and construction employment, percent, 2001	9.0	6.4
Manufacturing employment, percent, 2001	1.3	14.0
Trade, transportation and warehousing employment, percent, 2001	18.1	20.6
Producer services employment, percent, 2001	13.4	18.7
Educational, health and social services employment, percent, 2001	17.4	16.3
Arts, accommodation and other services employment, percent, 2001	11.2	13.5
Public administration employment, percent, 2001	21.1	5.8
Geography	**Northwest Territories**	**Canada**
Land area, 2001 (square kilometers)	1,183,085	9,093,507
Persons per square kilometer, 2001	0.03	3.3

(a) Only language spoken at home. Does not include bilingual households.
Note: Industries are defined according to the 1997 North American Industry Classification System.
Source: Statistics Canada

Nova Scotia

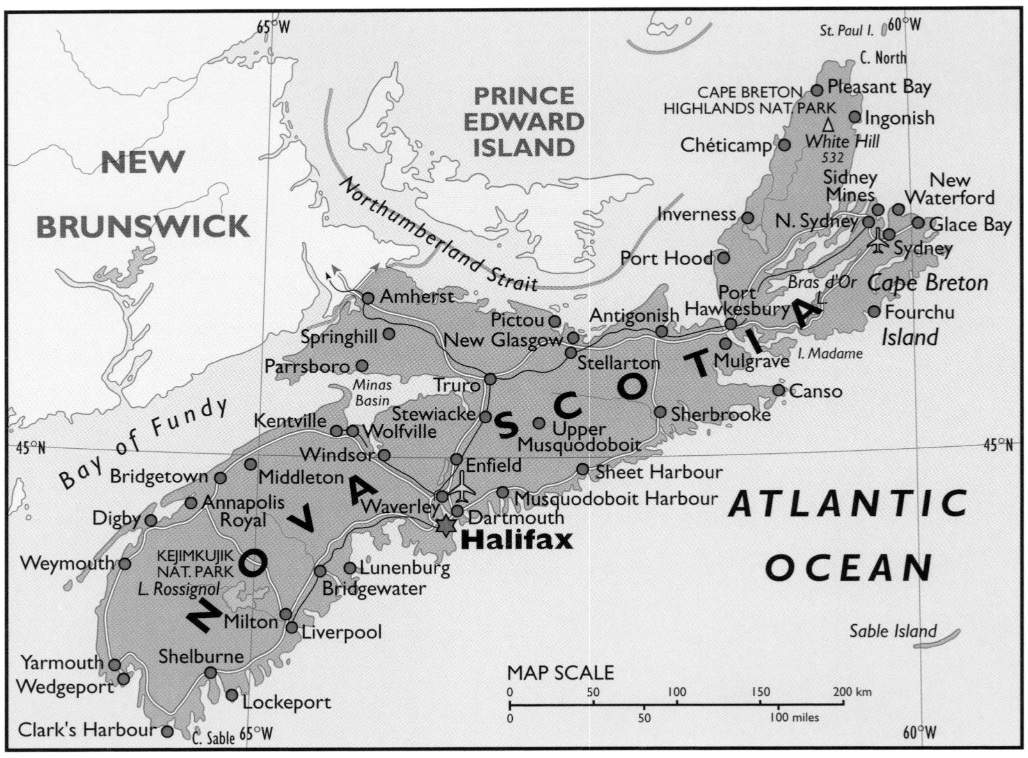

Confederation date: July 1, 1867
Provincial bird: Osprey
Provincial flower: Mayflower
Provincial tree: Red spruce
Provincial motto: One defends and the other conquers
Provincial capital: Halifax
Population of capital: 119,292 (2001)

Consisting of a mainland peninsula and adjacent Cape Breton Island, Nova Scotia is smaller than every province except Prince Edward Island. France established the first European settlement in Nova Scotia in 1605, beginning the displacement of the native Mi'kmaq and Malecite people. The mainland was awarded to Britain by treaty in 1713, and Cape Breton Island was captured from France in 1758. Nova Scotia joined New Brunswick, Québec and Ontario to form the Dominion of Canada in 1867.

Connected to the mainland by the low lying Isthmus of Chignecto, Nova Scotia's thin-soiled terrain reflects its geological origins as the weathered extension of the ancient Appalachian Mountains that extend into New Brunswick to the west from New England. Small scale mixed farming is found throughout the province but the Annapolis Valley, running parallel to the Bay of Fundy shore, is famous for its apple orchards. The Bay of Fundy itself is notable for the world's greatest tidal variation and the opportunities for generating massive quantities of electricity from tidal power are the subject of investigation. With the precipitous decline of coal mining in Nova Scotia and the closure of Cape Breton's primary iron and steel mill in Sydney, much of Nova Scotia's economy is linked to the Scotian Shelf. Shellfish such as scallops, crab and lobster are harvested at sea which supports shore-based industries such as ship and boat building and seafood processing for export. Offshore natural gas reservoirs near Sable Island have considerable potential but many technical, environmental and regulatory hurdles remain before extraction will be feasible. Pulp and paper mills, gypsum mining and processing, as well as three Michelin tire plants are locally significant.

Halifax

With the world's second largest natural harbor after Sydney, Australia, Halifax is the dominant metropolitan center in Atlantic Canada. In 1749, the British built the Citadel to defend the harbor and named it after the Earl of Halifax, who conceived the plan for the fortress. Halifax is Canada's oldest English-speaking city and the first to have a newspaper and an elected assembly. A vital naval base for the Allies in both World Wars, Halifax suffered the most devastating accidental explosion in history when an ammunition ship collided with another vessel in 1917, destroying much of the city. Now a commercial, administrative and educational center, it is the site of Dalhousie University and substantial naval dockyards. Fishing, ship repair, oil refining and administrative and government services employ the largest number of people within the city.

Nova Scotia at a Glance

People	Nova Scotia	Canada
Total population, 2001 Census	908,005	30,007,090
Persons under 5 years old, percent, 2001	5.2%	5.7%
Persons under 18 years old, percent, 2001	22.3%	23.2%
Persons over 65 years old, percent, 2001	13.9%	13.0%
Female persons	468,915	15,300,245
Immigrant population, percent, 2001	4.6%	18.2%
Total population by home language	897,570	29,639,035
English language, percent, 2001 (a)	92.8%	61.0%
French language, percent, 2001 (a)	1.1%	19.5%
Non-official languages, percent, 2001 (a)	0.7%	5.6%
Total Aboriginal identity population, percent, 2001	1.9%	3.3%
Total Non-Aboriginal population, percent, 2001	97.0%	95.5%
Less than high school graduation certificate, percent persons 15+, 2001	35.4%	31.3%
High school graduates and/or some postsecondary, percent persons 15+, 2001	19.4%	24.9%
Trade certificate or diploma, percent persons 15+, 2001	14.1%	10.9%
College certificate, percent persons 15+, 2001	14.7%	15.0%
University diploma or degree, percent persons 15+, 2001	16.5%	17.9%
Homes owned, percent, 2001	70.8%	65.8%
Homes rented, percent, 2001	28.8%	33.8%
Average value of dwelling $	101,515	162,709
Total number of families	262,910	8,371,020
Average number of persons per census family	2.9	3.0
Average individual income of persons 15 years and over $	25,297	29,768
Average family income	54,786	66,160

Business	Nova Scotia	Canada
Total labor force 15 years and over	442,425	15,576,565
Females in labor force 15 years and over as a percent of total	47.2	46.7
Agriculture, forestry, fishing and hunting employment, percent, 2001	5.2	3.6
Mining and oil and gas extraction employment, percent, 2001	0.8	1.1
Utilities and construction employment, percent, 2001	6.7	6.4
Manufacturing employment, percent, 2001	10.0	14.0
Trade, transportation and warehousing employment, percent, 2001	20.6	20.6
Producer services employment, percent, 2001	16.0	18.7
Educational, health and social services employment, percent, 2001	18.2	16.3
Arts, accommodation and other services employment, percent, 2001	14.0	13.5
Public administration employment, percent, 2001	8.5	5.8

Geography	Nova Scotia	Canada
Land area, 2001 (square kilometers)	53,338	9,093,507
Persons per square kilometer, 2001	17.0	3.3

(a) Only language spoken at home. Does not include bilingual households.
Note: Industries are defined according to the 1997 North American Industry Classification System.
Source: Statistics Canada

Nunavut

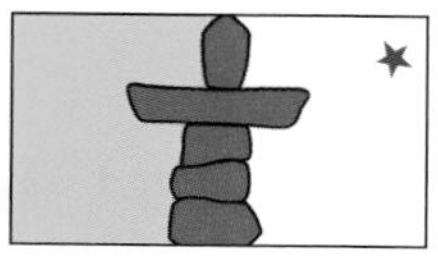

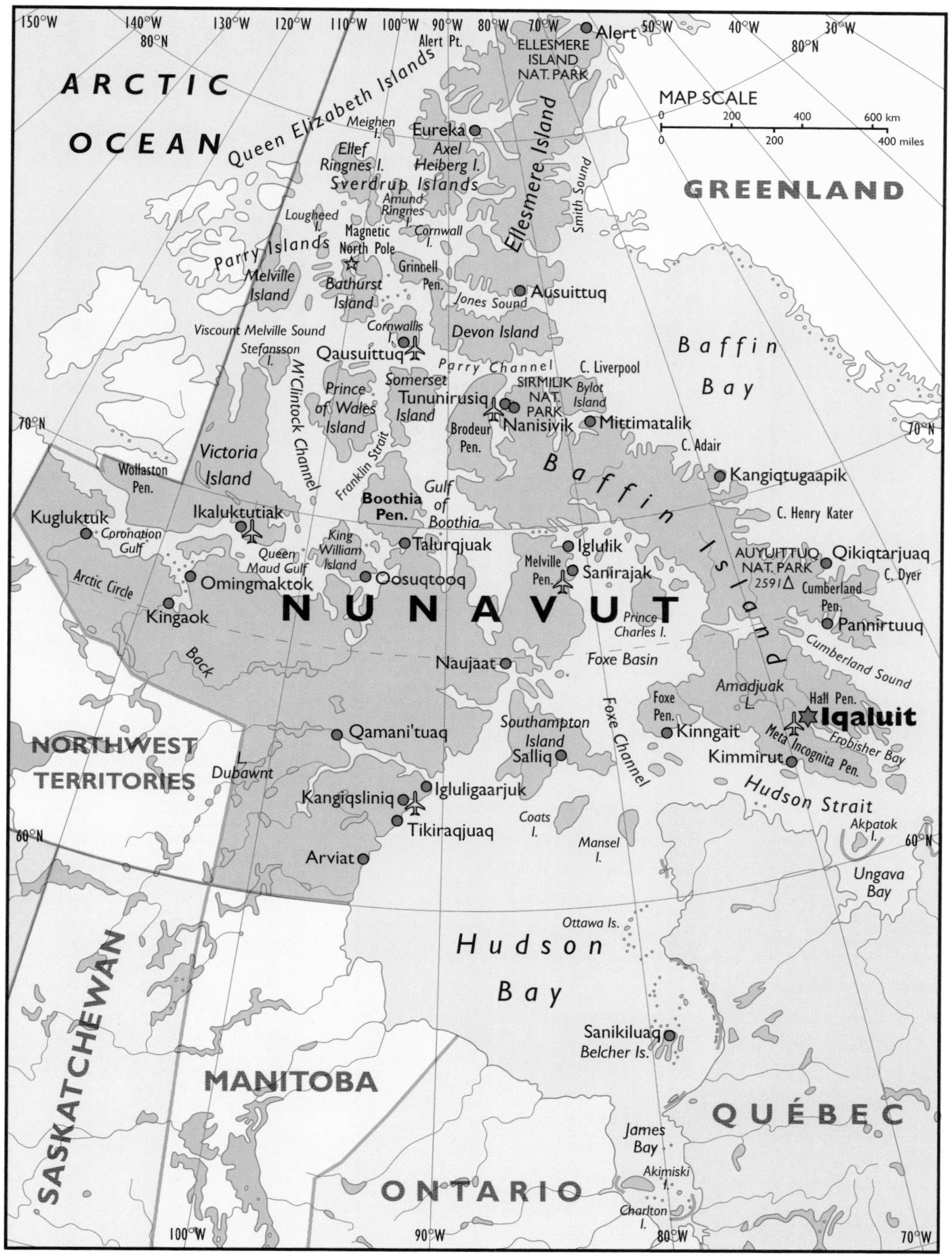

Confederation date: April 1, 1999
Provincial motto: Nunavut our strength
Provincial capital: Iqaluit
Population of capital: 5,236 (2001)

Once the eastern part of the Northwest Territories, Nunavut attained self-government in 1999 and covers approximately one-fifth of the Canadian landmass including a large area of the mainland west of Hudson Bay and fifty large islands that form Canada's Arctic Archipelago. Created as a part of a land claims agreement with the native Inuit, and with eighty-five percent of its population reporting Inuit ethnic origin in the 2001 census, Nunavut is unique as the only territorial unit in Canada where aboriginal peoples constitute a majority of the population.

Much of Nunavut is underlain by permafrost. The Arctic Cordillera, a band of mountains curving south from Ellesmere Island to Baffin Island, contains three large national parks. Large oil and gas fields have been discovered but challenges remain before these fossil fuels can be extracted for commercial gain. Consequently, Nunavut's economy is divided among the traditional subsistence economy of the Inuit, an administrative economy, and episodic ecotourism ventures that convey adventurous visitors to the high Arctic.

Iqaluit

Canada's smallest and northernmost capital, Iqaluit, three degrees south of the Arctic Circle, means "the place of many fish" in Inuktitut. As the Cold War intensified it became the logistical center for radar facilities defending North America from Russian bombers. In the 1960s, Iqaluit evolved into the center for federal government services in the Baffin region. Visitors to the largest community in Nunavut will find an igloo-shaped Anglican cathedral, the settlement's most distinctive landmark.

Nunavut at a Glance

People	Nunavut	Canada
Total population, 2001 Census	26,745	30,007,090
Persons under 5 years old, percent, 2001	12.5%	5.7%
Persons under 18 years old, percent, 2001	43.1%	23.2%
Persons 65 years old and over, percent, 2001	2.2%	13.0%
Female persons, percent, 2001	48.3%	51.0%
Immigrant population, percent, 2001	1.7%	18.2%
Total population by home language	26,665	29,639,035
English language, percent, 2001 (a)	24.9%	61.0%
French language, percent, 2001 (a)	0.4%	19.5%
Non-official languages, percent, 2001 (a)	28.3%	5.6%
Total Aboriginal identity population, percent, 2001	85.0%	3.3%
Total Non-Aboriginal population, percent, 2001	14.8%	95.5%
Less than high school graduation certificate, percent persons 15+, 2001	50.3%	31.3%
High school graduates and/or some postsecondary, percent persons 15+, 2001	18.6%	24.9%
Trade certificate or diploma, percent persons 15+, 2001	10.1%	10.9%
College certificate, percent persons 15+, 2001	12.4%	15.0%
University diploma or degree, percent persons 15+, 2001	8.6%	17.9%
Homes owned, percent, 2001	24.1%	65.8%
Homes rented, percent, 2001	75.8%	33.8%
Average value of dwelling $	165,383	162,709
Total number of families	6,360	8,371,020
Average number of persons per census family	3.8	3.0
Average individual income of persons 15 years and over $	26,924	29,768
Average family income $	52,624	66,160

Business	Nunavut	Canada
Total labor force 15 years and over	10,730	15,576,565
Females in labor force 15 years and over as a percent of total	46.0	46.7
Agriculture, forestry, fishing and hunting employment, percent, 2001	1.2	3.6
Mining and oil and gas extraction employment, percent, 2001	2.3	1.1
Utilities and construction employment, percent, 2001	8.9	6.4
Manufacturing employment, percent, 2001	1.7	14.0
Trade, transportation and warehousing employment, percent, 2001	18.7	20.6
Producer services employment, percent, 2001	9.9	18.7
Educational, health and social services employment, percent, 2001	23.2	16.3
Arts, accommodation and other services employment, percent, 2001	10.2	13.5
Public administration employment, percent, 2001	23.9	5.8

Geography	Nunavut	Canada
Land area, 2001 (square kilometers)	1,936,113	9,093,507
Persons per square kilometer, 2001	0.01	3.3

(a) Only language spoken at home. Does not include bilingual households.
Note: Industries are defined according to the 1997 North American Industry Classification System.
Source: Statistics Canada

Ontario

Confederation date: July 1, 1867
Provincial bird: Common loon
Provincial flower: White trillium
Provincial tree: Eastern white pine
Provincial motto: Loyal she began, loyal she remains
Provincial capital: Toronto
Population of capital: 2,481,494 (2001)

Ontario is Canada's most populous province. Trading posts were established in the region during the 17th century by French explorers and the area became part of New France, before Great Britain gained sovereignty over the territory in 1763. As the European immigrant population grew steadily, First Nations such as the Cree, Ojibwa, Ottawa and Huron were pushed to the north and west. Ontario was known as Upper Canada until 1841, when it joined with Québec to form the Province of Canada. In 1867, the Dominion of Canada was created, and the province of Ontario was established.

In the north the rocky, forested and mineral-rich Canadian Shield region blends into marshy lowlands bordering James Bay while in the south, agriculture, manufacturing and most urban areas are concentrated along the St. Lawrence River and in the Great Lakes lowlands. Cattle, dairy, and hog farms are the most common agricultural activities and the chief crops are tobacco, corn, fruits and vegetables. Ontario accounts for one third of Canada's metallic mineral production from numerous mines spread across the Canadian Shield. Motor vehicle assembly, primary metals, chemicals, machinery, and electrical products factories tend to cluster in the south near the major markets and the border with the United States. Ontario generates more manufacturing revenue than any other province but most of the largest manufacturing plants are foreign owned subsidiaries.

Toronto

Toronto, the provincial capital, has a metropolitan population of 4.7 million, making it Canada's largest urban area. Sited originally to take advantage of a portage route from Lake Ontario to Lake Simcoe, Toronto has become Canada's principal financial and cultural center. Toronto lies at the heart of the Golden Horseshoe, an industrial region that rings the western end of Lake Ontario and is home to nearly twenty percent of Canada's population. In 1615, French explorer Etienne Brulé became the first European to visit the area. Named York by John Graves Simcoe, it became the capital of Upper Canada in 1794. U. S. troops sacked the city twice during the War of 1812, and in 1834, York was renamed Toronto, the Huron word for meeting place. Visitors flock to see the Sky Dome stadium and the CN Tower, the world's tallest freestanding structure.

Ontario at a Glance

People	Ontario	Canada
Total population, 2001 Census	11,410,045	30,007,090
Persons under 5 years old, percent, 2001	5.9%	5.7%
Persons under 18 years old, percent, 2001	23.4%	23.2%
Persons 65 years old and over, percent, 2001	12.9%	13.0%
Female persons	5,832,990	51.0%
Immigrant population, percent, 2001	26.6%	18.2%
Total population by home language	11,285,550	29,639,035
English language, percent, 2001 (a)	74.1%	61.0%
French language, percent, 2001 (a)	1.4%	19.5%
Non-official languages, percent, 2001 (a)	7.9%	5.6%
Total Aboriginal identity population, percent, 2001	1.7%	3.3%
Total Non-Aboriginal population, percent, 2001	97.2%	95.5%
Less than high school graduation certificate, percent persons 15+, 2001	29.7%	31.3%
High school graduates and/or some postsecondary, percent persons 15+, 2001	25.6%	24.9%
Trade certificate or diploma, percent persons 15+, 2001	9.4%	10.9%
College certificate, percent persons 15+, 2001	15.7%	15.0%
University diploma or degree, percent persons 15+, 2001	19.6%	17.9%
Homes owned, percent, 2001	67.8%	65.8%
Homes rented, percent, 2001	32.0%	33.8%
Average value of dwelling $	199,884	162,709
Total number of families	3,190,990	8,371,020
Average number of persons per census family	3.0	3.0
Average individual income of persons 15 years and over $	32,865	29,768
Average family income $	73,849	66,160

Business	Ontario	Canada
Total labor force 15 years and over	5,992,765	15,576,565
Females in labor force 15 years and over as a percent of total	47.2	46.7
Agriculture, forestry, fishing and hunting employment, percent, 2001	2.1	3.6
Mining and oil and gas extraction employment, percent, 2001	0.4	1.1
Utilities and construction employment, percent, 2001	6.3	6.4
Manufacturing employment, percent, 2001	16.4	14.0
Trade, transportation and warehousing employment, percent, 2001	20.5	20.6
Producer services employment, percent, 2001	21.1	18.7
Educational, health and social services employment, percent, 2001	15.1	16.3
Arts, accommodation and other services employment, percent, 2001	12.9	13.5
Public administration employment, percent, 2001	5.2	5.8

Geography	Ontario	Canada
Land area, 2001 (square kilometers)	917,741	9,093,507
Persons per square kilometer, 2001	12.4	3.3

(a) Only language spoken at home. Does not include bilingual households.
Note: Industries are defined according to the 1997 North American Industry Classification System.
Source: Statistics Canada

Prince Edward Island

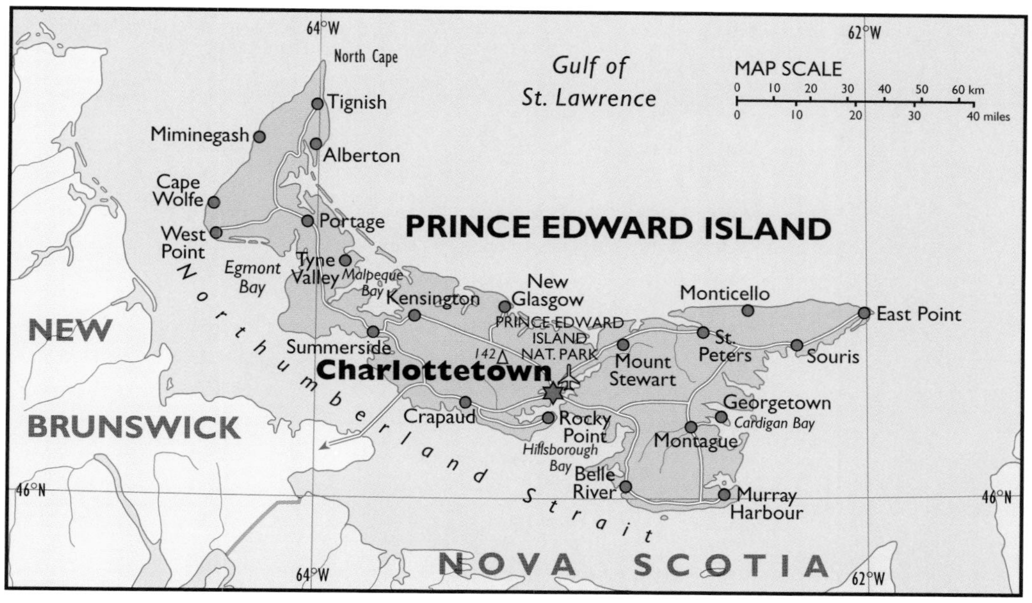

Confederation date: July 1, 1873
Provincial bird: Blue jay
Provincial flower: Pink Lady's Slipper
Provincial tree: Red oak
Provincial motto: The small under the protection of the great
Provincial capital: Charlottetown
Population of capital: 32,245 (2001)

In the early eighteenth century, French settlers were the first Europeans to colonize Prince Edward Island, then called Ile St-Jean, displacing the indigenous Mi'kmaq people. Ceded to Britain by the Treaty of Paris, the colony was renamed in 1799 after Prince Edward, the fourth son of George II and future father of Queen Victoria. Prince Edward Island became the seventh province of Canada in 1873, its smallest in both land area and population.

Prince Edward Island is known for the red sandstone which gives its soil and ocean beaches their characteristic ruddy color. The Northumberland Strait, which separates the island from mainland Nova Scotia and New Brunswick, supports a fishery rich in mollusks and crustaceans that are harvested for sale throughout Canada and New England. The eight mile-long Confederation Bridge over Northumberland Strait was completed in 1997, largely replacing the ferry service on which the island had always depended. Mixed agriculture, followed by tourism and fishing are the most important economic activities. Commercial potato production and horticulture are particularly notable in a province that styles itself as the "Garden of the Gulf."

Charlottetown

Charlottetown is the smallest of Canada's provincial capitals. Founded as Port La Joie by the French in 1720, it was formally laid out by the British in 1768 and named for the wife of King George III. The Charlottetown Conference of 1864 led to the Confederation of Canada in 1867. In 1992, the city hosted the signing of the Charlottetown Accord, which proposed amendments to the Canadian constitution that were ultimately rejected in a referendum. Attractions include the home of Lucy Maud Montgomery, author of the Anne of Green Gables books and Province House, the venue for the Charlottetown Conference.

Prince Edward Island at a Glance

People	Prince Edward Island	Canada
Total population, 2001 Census	135,290	30,007,090
Persons under 5 years old, percent, 2001	5.6%	5.7%
Persons under 18 years old, percent, 2001	24.3%	23.2%
Persons over 65 years old, percent, 2001	13.7%	13.0%
Female persons	51.4%	15,300,245
Immigrant population, percent, 2001	3.1%	18.2%
Total population by home language	133,385	29,639,035
English language, percent, 2001 (a)	93.8%	61.0%
French language, percent, 2001 (a)	1.2%	19.5%
Non-official languages, percent, 2001 (a)	0.2%	5.6%
Total Aboriginal identity population, percent, 2001	1.0%	3.3%
Total Non-Aboriginal population, percent, 2001	97.6%	95.5%
Less than high school graduation certificate, percent persons 15+, 2001	37.4%	31.3%
High school graduates and/or some postsecondary, percent persons 15+, 2001	21.5%	24.9%
Trade certificate or diploma, percent persons 15+, 2001	12.6%	10.9%
College certificate, percent persons 15+, 2001	14.9%	15.0%
University diploma or degree, percent persons 15+, 2001	13.7%	17.9%
Homes owned, percent, 2001	73.1%	65.8%
Homes rented, percent, 2001	26.6%	33.8%
Average value of dwelling $	100,657	162,709
Total number of families	38,420	8,371,020
Average number of persons per census family	3.0	3.0
Average individual income of persons 15 years and over $	23,709	29,768
Average family income $	53,958	66,160
Business	**Prince Edward Island**	**Canada**
Total labor force 15 years and over	72,930	15,576,565
Females in labor force 15 years and over as a percent of total	47.9	46.7
Agriculture, forestry, fishing and hunting employment, percent, 2001	13.0	3.6
Mining and oil and gas extraction employment, percent, 2001	0.3	1.1
Utilities and construction employment, percent, 2001	7.5	6.4
Manufacturing employment, percent, 2001	10.6	14.0
Trade, transportation and warehousing employment, percent, 2001	17.0	20.6
Producer services employment, percent, 2001	10.8	18.7
Educational, health and social services employment, percent, 2001	16.2	16.3
Arts, accommodation and other services employment, percent, 2001	15.0	13.5
Public administration employment, percent, 2001	9.7	5.8
Geography	**Prince Edward Island**	**Canada**
Land area, 2001 (square kilometers)	5,660	9,093,507
Persons per square kilometer, 2001	23.9	3.3

(a) Only language spoken at home. Does not include bilingual households.
Note: Industries are defined according to the 1997 North American Industry Classification System.
Source: Statistics Canada

Québec

Confederation date:
July 1, 1867
Provincial bird:
Snowy owl
Provincial flower:
Blue flag iris
Provincial tree:
Yellow birch
Provincial motto:
Je me souviens
Provincial capital:
Québec City
Population of capital:
169,076 (2001)

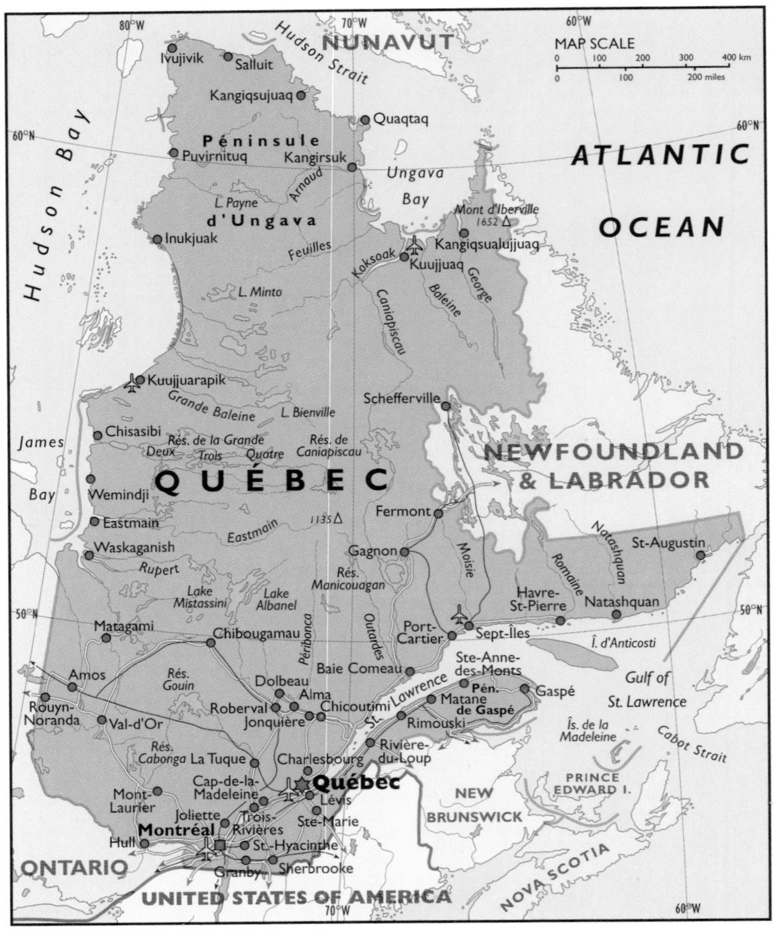

The largest province in area and second largest in population, much of Québec falls within the Canadian Shield. In 1535, Jacques Cartier landed in Iroquois territory in eastern Canada and a year later, sailed up the St. Lawrence River. French Canada was ceded to Britain in 1763, following the Seven Years' War, but it retained its distinctive culture. The Constitutional Act of 1791 separated the area into the colonies of Upper Canada and Lower Canada. With the establishment of the Dominion of Canada in 1867, Québec became a province. A sense of Québecois nationalism intensified during the 1960s Quiet Revolution and significant support developed for separatism. With just over eighty percent of the population reporting French as their mother tongue in 2001 and legislation in place to reinforce the dominant position of the French language, Québec is truly the "distinct society" within the Canadian federation. The capital is Québec and the largest city is Montréal.

Extending from the broad Ungava Peninsula to Lake Champlain and the New York State border, Québec is divided into three geographic regions. In the extreme north the plateaus and uplands of the Canadian Shield remain sparsely populated, while the forested slopes of the Notre Dame Mountains form the backbone of the Gaspé Peninsula. Squeezed in between, the lowlands on either side of the St. Lawrence River form the center of a diverse range of manufacturing centers and an agricultural base where most of the province's mixed farms and specialist dairy and hog producers are found. The many rivers flowing down off the Canadian Shield provide Québec with significant amounts of hydroelectricity to power pulp and paper mills and aluminum smelters in the Lac St-Jean region. Copper, iron, zinc, silver and gold are produced in remote northern mining communities while one of the world's largest asbestos deposits is found in the Appalachian region in the south.

Québec

Alqonquin for "where the river narrows," Vieux-Québec (Old Québec) has a commanding defensive site overlooking the St Lawrence. The Québec Bridge, the largest cantilevered bridge in the world, and the Pierre Laporte Bridge, Canada's longest suspension bridge span the river at this site where in 1608, French explorer Samuel de Champlain established the first permanent European settlement in Canada. The British captured the city from the French in the battle of the Plains of Abraham yet during the Revolutionary War, American troops were unsuccessful in their attempt to take the city. While the fur trade fueled the city's early growth, today Québec is an administrative, commercial, and financial center. Heavy manufacturing industries include shipbuilding and oil refining while printing and publishing as well as a vibrant tourism sector continue to loom large in the economy of the province.

Québec at a Glance

People	Québec	Canada
Total population, 2001 Census	7,237,480	30,007,090
Persons under 5 years old, percent, 2001	5.2%	5.7%
Persons under 18 years old, percent, 2001	22.2%	23.2%
Persons 65 years old and over, percent, 2001	13.3%	13.0%
Female persons	3,704,635	51.0%
Immigrant population, percent, 2001	9.8%	18.2%
Total population by home language	7,125,580	29,639,035
English language, percent, 2001 (a)	6.6%	61.0%
French language, percent, 2001 (a)	75.8%	19.5%
Non-official languages, percent, 2001 (a)	3.4%	5.6%
Total Aboriginal identity population, percent, 2001	1.1%	3.3%
Total Non-Aboriginal population, percent, 2001	97.4%	95.5%
Less than high school graduation certificate, percent persons 15+, 2001	31.7%	31.3%
High school graduates and/or some postsecondary, percent persons 15+, 2001	25.8%	24.9%
Trade certificate or diploma, percent persons 15+, 2001	10.8%	10.9%
College certificate, percent persons 15+, 2001	14.5%	15.0%
University diploma or degree, percent persons 15+, 2001	17.2%	17.9%
Homes owned, percent, 2001	57.9%	65.8%
Homes rented, percent, 2001	42.0%	33.8%
Average value of dwelling $	110,668	162,709
Total number of families	2,019,555	8,371,020
Average number of persons per census family	2.9	3.0
Average individual income of persons 15 years and over $	27125	29,768
Average family income $	59,297	66,160

Business	Québec	Canada
Total labor force 15 years and over	3,644,375	15,576,565
Females in labor force 15 years and over as a percent of total	46.2	46.7
Agriculture, forestry, fishing and hunting employment, percent, 2001	2.8	3.6
Mining and oil and gas extraction employment, percent, 2001	0.4	1.1
Utilities and construction employment, percent, 2001	5.3	6.4
Manufacturing employment, percent, 2001	17.6	14.0
Trade, transportation and warehousing employment, percent, 2001	20.7	20.6
Producer services employment, percent, 2001	17.1	18.7
Educational, health and social services employment, percent, 2001	16.8	16.3
Arts, accommodation and other services employment, percent, 2001	12.9	13.5
Public administration employment, percent, 2001	6.3	5.8

Geography	Québec	Canada
Land area, 2001 (square kilometers)	1,365,128	9,093,507
Persons per square kilometer, 2001	5.3	3.3

(a) Only language spoken at home. Does not include bilingual households.
Note: Industries are defined according to the 1997 North American Industry Classification System.
Source: Statistics Canada

Saskatchewan

Confederation date:
September 1, 1905
Provincial bird:
Sharp-tailed grouse
Provincial flower:
Western red lily
Provincial tree:
White birch
Provincial motto:
From many peoples, strength
Provincial capital:
Regina
Population of capital:
178,225 (2001)

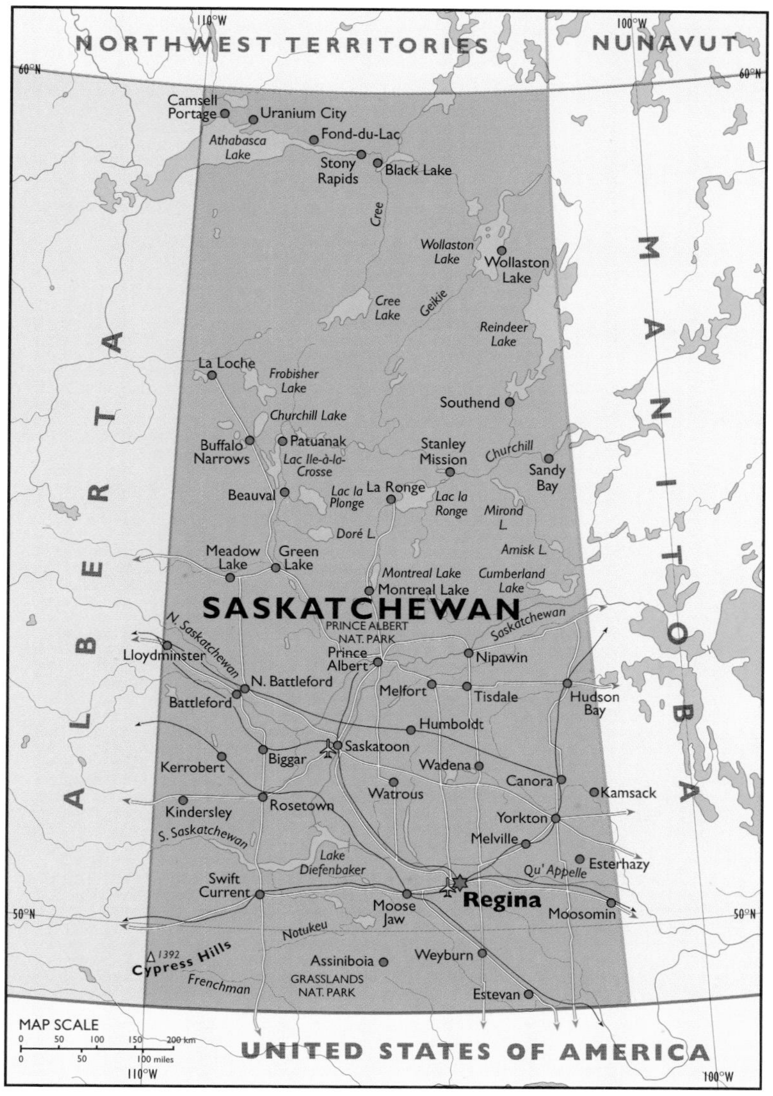

Straddling the fertile Great Plains and the lake-strewn Canadian Shield, the plains of Saskatchewan were originally occupied by First Nations people such as the Cree, Chipewyan, and Blackfoot. The first permanent European settlement was in 1774, but the pace of development was slow until the construction of the transcontinental Canadian Pacific Railway in 1885. Saskatchewan became a province in 1905 and its largest cities are Saskatoon and Regina, the capital.

The geography of Saskatchewan is divided quite sharply between the south and north. Southern Saskatchewan is a level grassland region on the Great Plains that is quite arid, especially in the southwest. This region supports extensive cultivation of wheat, other small grains, and oil seeds. Irrigation water is sourced from the Gardner Dam which creates Lake Diefenbaker from the waters of the South Saskatchewan River. The north becomes quite heavily forested as the Parkbelt grades into the rugged Canadian Shield country which is dotted with wetlands and lakes of which Lake Athabasca and Reindeer Lake are the largest.

Notable among the mineral deposits in the south are soft thermal coal used for pithead electrical generation near the American border, some oil and natural gas and the world's largest deposits of potash, which is used for fertilizer both domestically and overseas. In the north, underground hardrock mining produces uranium and a blend of copper, zinc, and gold in the Flin Flon area on the Manitoba border. Most industrial activity involves the processing and transshipment of raw materials.

Regina

An administrative, financial, trade, transportation, and service center for the surrounding grain-growing region, Regina is the second largest city in Saskatchewan after Saskatoon. Founded in 1882 as a railroad center, Regina is named using the Latin word for queen, in recognition of Queen Victoria. In 1883, it became capital of the Northwest Territories, and in 1905, capital of the newly formed province of Saskatchewan. In 1885 Louis Riel, leader of the Métis, was tried and executed for treason in Regina. Steel production based on scrap and oil refining are among the major manufacturing industries. However, most employment is based on public administration related to its status as provincial capital and headquarters for the Royal Canadian Mounted Police.

Saskatchewan at a Glance

People	**Saskatchewan**	**Canada**
Total population, 2001 Census	978,935	30,007,090
Persons under 5 years old, percent, 2001	6.2%	5.7%
Persons under 18 years old, percent, 2001	26.1%	23.2%
Persons 65 years old and over, percent, 2001	15.1%	13.0%
Female persons, percent, 2001	50.8%	51.0%
Immigrant population, percent, 2001	4.9%	18.2%
Total population by home language	963,150	29,639,035
English language, percent, 2001 (a)	89.7%	61.0%
French language, percent, 2001 (a)	0.2%	19.5%
Non-official languages, percent, 2001 (a)	1.9%	5.6%
Total Aboriginal identity population, percent, 2001	12.3%	3.3%
Total Non-Aboriginal population, percent, 2001	85.1%	95.5%
Less than high school graduation certificate, percentpersons 15+, 2001	39.4%	31.3%
High school graduates and/or some postsecondary, percent persons 15+, 2001	22.0%	24.9%
Trade certificate or diploma, percent persons 15+, 2001	12.5%	10.9%
College certificate, percent persons 15+, 2001	12.2%	15.0%
University diploma or degree, percent persons 15+, 2001	13.9%	17.9%
Homes owned, percent, 2001	70.8%	65.8%
Homes rented, percent, 2001	26.8%	33.8%
Average value of dwelling $	93,065	162,709
Total number of families	265,615	8,371,020
Average number of persons per census family	3.0	3.0
Average individual income of persons 15 years and over $	25,811	29,768
Average family income $	57,005	66,160

Business	**Saskatchewan**	**Canada**
Total labor force 15 years and over	504,015	15,576,565
Females in labor force 15 years and over as a percent of total	46.5	46.7
Agriculture, forestry, fishing and hunting employment, percent, 2001	14.4	3.6
Mining and oil and gas extraction employment, percent, 2001	2.9	1.1
Utilities and construction employment, percent, 2001	6.4	6.4
Manufacturing employment, percent, 2001	5.8	14.0
Trade, transportation and warehousing employment, percent, 2001	19.3	20.6
Producer services employment, percent, 2001	13.1	18.7
Educational, health and social services employment, percent, 2001	18.3	16.3
Arts, accommodation and other services employment, percent, 2001	13.5	13.5
Public administration employment, percent, 2001	6.2	5.8

Geography	**Saskatchewan**	**Canada**
Land area, 2001 (square kilometers)	591,670	9,093,507
Persons per square kilometer, 2001	1.6	3.3

(a) Only language spoken at home. Does not include bilingual households.
Note: Industries are defined according to the 1997 North American Industry Classification System.
Source: Statistics Canada

Yukon Territory

Confederation date:
June 13, 1898
Territorial bird:
Raven
Territorial flower:
Fireweed
Territorial tree:
Sub-alpine fir
Territorial motto:
None
Territorial capital:
Whitehorse
Population of capital:
19,058 (2001)

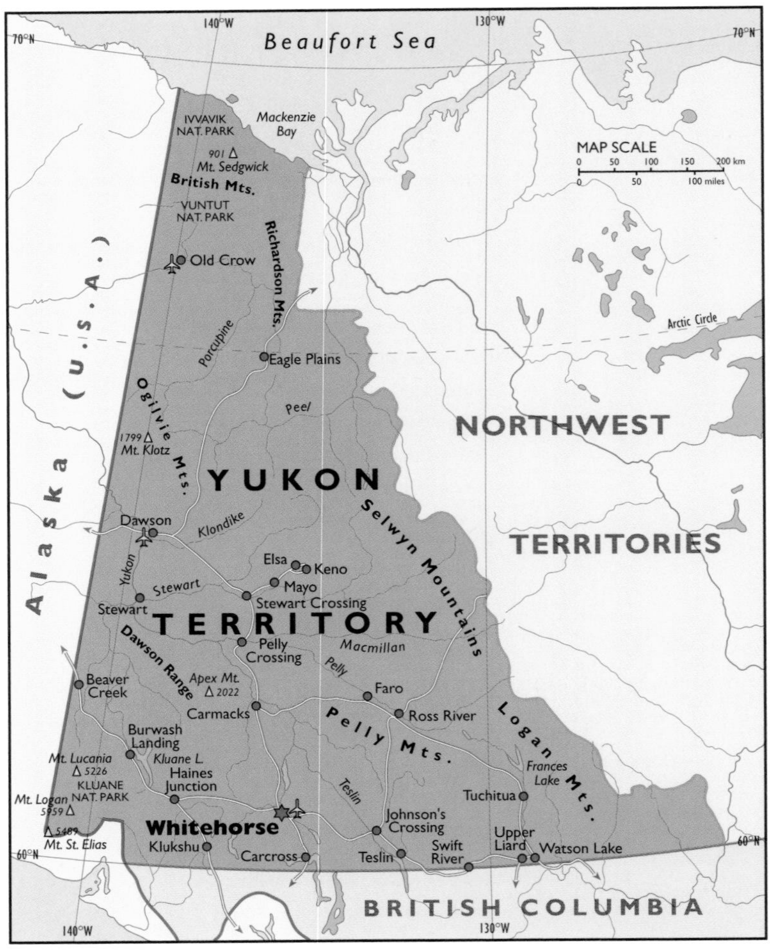

Fur traders from the Hudson's Bay Company first explored the Yukon Territory in the 1840s but settlement was sparse until 1897 when the Klondike Gold Rush saw the sudden influx of over 30,000 prospectors from the south. Their imprint remains in folklore and in the rusting remains of gold dredges and enormous piles of mine tailings. In 1993, the Canadian government agreed on the land claims made by some of the Yukon First Nations but other aboriginal land claims are still pending. The capital and largest settlement is Whitehorse.

The northern reaches of the province bordering the Beaufort Sea are generally low-lying. Further south, the Yukon's physiography is dominated by the western cordillera. Mount Logan, the highest peak in Canada, is in the southwestern corner of the Territory. The Yukon River, still famous for its gold-bearing gravel, drains much of the southern region through Alaska before reaching the Bering Sea. The principal industrial activity is mining and the lead and zinc mine in Faro is a major producer. A large underground gold mine operates in Dawson and hundreds of small-scale placer operations extract gold from river gravel. Forest products have some economic potential in the south but the most sustainable resource is the Yukon's pristine wilderness and spectacular natural beauty that supports eco-tourism and attracts outdoor enthusiasts to visit national parks such as Kluane, a World Heritage Site.

Whitehorse

Named for rapids on the Yukon River that resembled rearing white horses, Whitehorse developed rapidly during the Klondike Gold Rush and after the arrival of the narrow gauge railroad from Skagway, Alaska in 1900. Further growth took place during World War II when Whitehorse became a major U.S. military base and construction center for the Alaska Highway. Incorporated as a city in 1950, it became capital three years later. Whitehorse is the administration and transportation hub in the Yukon Territory and is home to two-thirds of all Yukon residents.

Yukon Territory at a Glance

People	**Yukon Territory**	**Canada**
Total population, 2001 Census	28,675	30,007,090
Persons under 5 years old, percent, 2001	5.9%	5.7%
Persons under 18 years old, percent, 2001	26.0%	23.2%
Persons over 65 years old, percent, 2001	6.0%	13.0%
Female persons	14230	15,300,245
Immigrant population, percent, 2001	10.5%	18.2%
Total population by home language	28,520	29,639,035
English language, percent, 2001 (a)	90.1%	61.0%
French language, percent, 2001 (a)	0.7%	19.5%
Non-official languages, percent, 2001 (a)	1.0%	5.6%
Total Aboriginal identity population, percent, 2001	22.8%	3.3%
Total Non-Aboriginal population, percent, 2001	76.7%	95.5%
Less than high school graduation certificate, percentpersons 15+, 2001	24.6%	31.3%
High school graduates and/or some postsecondary, percent persons 15+, 2001	23.5%	24.9%
Trade certificate or diploma, percent persons 15+, 2001	15.6%	10.9%
College certificate, percent persons 15+, 2001	17.6%	15.0%
University diploma or degree, percent persons 15+, 2001	18.6%	17.9%
Homes owned, percent, 2001	63.0%	65.8%
Homes rented, percent, 2001	31.3%	33.8%
Average value of dwelling $	140,447	162,709
Total number of families	7,815	8,371,020
Average number of persons per census family	3.0	3.0
Average individual income of persons 15 years and over $	31,917	29,768
Average family income $	69,564	66,160
Business	**Yukon Territory**	**Canada**
Total labor force 15 years and over	17,670	15,576,565
Females in labor force 15 years and over as a percent of total	48.7	46.7
Agriculture, forestry, fishing and hunting employment, percent, 2001	1.6	3.6
Mining and oil and gas extraction employment, percent, 2001	2.5	1.1
Utilities and construction employment, percent, 2001	8.7	6.4
Manufacturing employment, percent, 2001	2.2	14.0
Trade, transportation and warehousing employment, percent, 2001	17.2	20.6
Producer services employment, percent, 2001	14.7	18.7
Educational, health and social services employment, percent, 2001	15.6	16.3
Arts, accommodation and other services employment, percent, 2001	16.3	13.5
Public administration employment, percent, 2001	21.1	5.8
Geography	**Yukon Territory**	**Canada**
Land area, 2001 (square kilometers)	474,391	9,093,507
Persons per square kilometer, 2001	0.06	3.3

(a) Only language spoken at home. Does not include bilingual households.
Note: Industries are defined according to the 1997 North American Industry Classification System.
Source: Statistics Canada

MEXICO

STATE MAPS

Settlements
(number of inhabitants)

CIUDAD DE MÉXICO	Over 5,000,000
MONTERREY	2,000,000 – 5,000,000
ECATEPEC	1,000,000 – 2,000,000
Torreón	500,000 – 1,000,000
Gómez Palacio	250,000 – 500,000
Ciudad Lerdo	100,000 – 250,000
Ixcuintla	50,000 – 100,000
Tecuala	20,000 – 50,000
Santa Catarina	10,000 – 20,000
Ahualulco	5,000 – 10,000
San Lorenzo	Less than 5,000
	Urban areas

Communications

- Limited-access highways
- Principal highways
- Secondary highways
- Federal route numbers
- State route numbers
- Principal railroads
- Other railroads
- Railroad tunnels
- MEX Principal airports (with location identifiers)

Physical features

	Perennial streams and rivers
	Intermittent streams and rivers
	Perennial lakes and reservoirs
	Dry lakes
	Swamps and marshes
	Reservoirs (with dams)
▲ 4301	Elevations in meters
▼ 2731	Sea depths in meters
Punta el Morro	Capes, points and mountain passes
Islas Marías	Islands, peninsulas, mountain ranges and peaks
Mezquital	Rivers, lakes, bays, straits, marshes and deserts
Bolsón de Mapimí	Plateaus, basins and valleys

Administration

	International boundaries	COLIMA	State names
	State boundaries		National parks and selected nature reserves
CIUDAD DE MÉXICO	National capital	LA VENTA	Ruins and archeological sites

CITY MAPS

- Free limited-access highways (with interchange)
- Toll limited-access highways
- Tunnels
- Primary divided highways
- Primary undivided highways
- Secondary divided highways
- Secondary undivided highways
- Other roads
- Federal route numbers (MEX 40)
- State route numbers (67)
- Railroads
- Principal railroad stations
- Principal airports
- Other airports
- City centers
- City center map coverage
- Urban areas
- Tonalá / Santa Anita / El Quince — Suburbs (size of type indicates relative populations)
- Woodlands and parks
- *Planetario* — Points of interest

CITY CENTER MAPS

- Free limited-access highways
- Toll limited-access highways
- Through routes
- Secondary routes
- Divided highways
- Other roads
- Tunnels
- Railroads
- Estación FFCC Nacionales Buenavista — Railroad stations
- Subway stations
- Urban areas
- GUERRERO — Suburbs
- Woodlands and parks
- Public buildings
- Churches
- Cathedrals
- Biblioteca Nacional — Points of interest

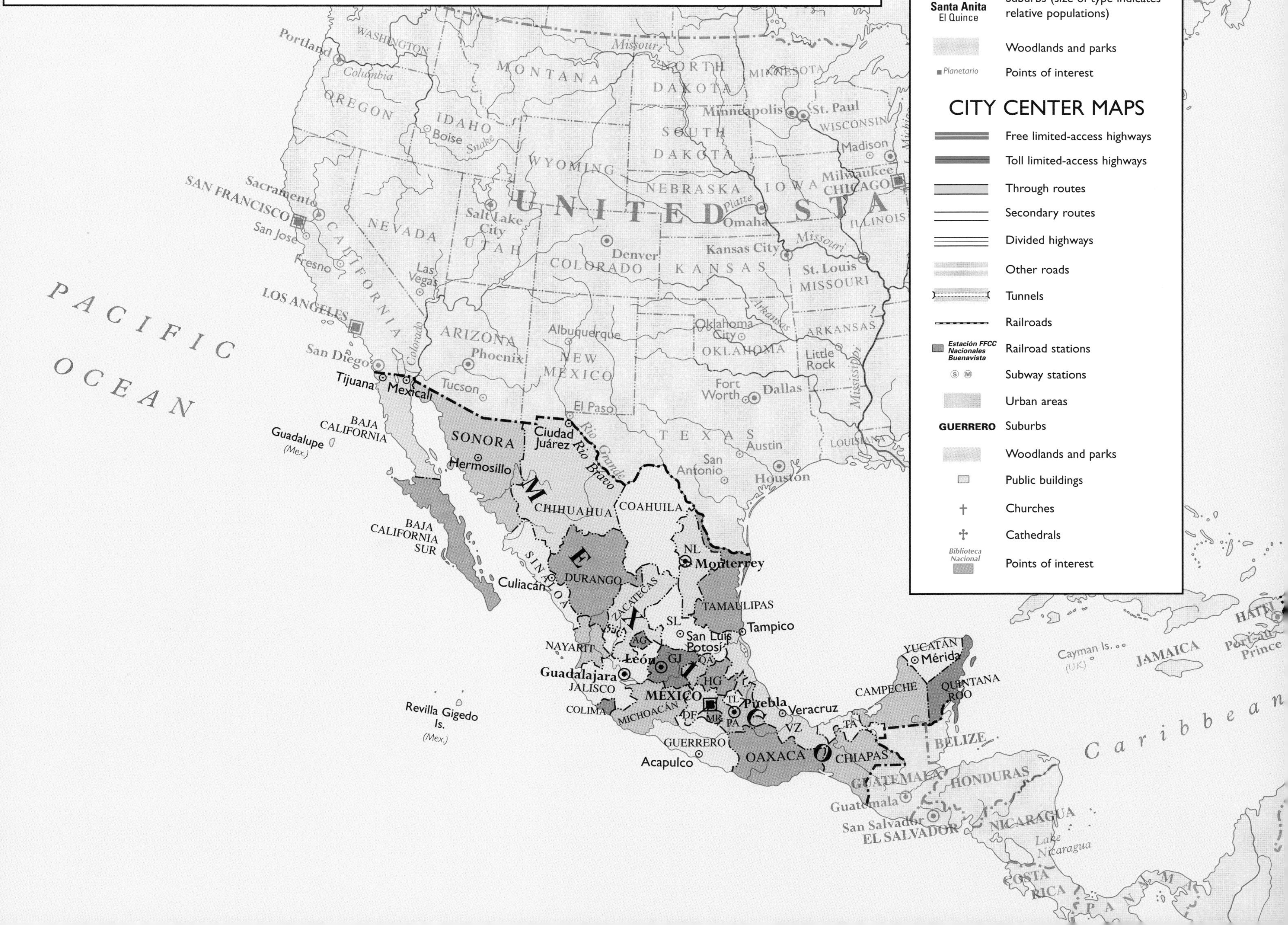

10 0 10 20 30 40 50 60 70 80 90 km

1:2 000 000

10 0 10 20 30 40 50 60 miles

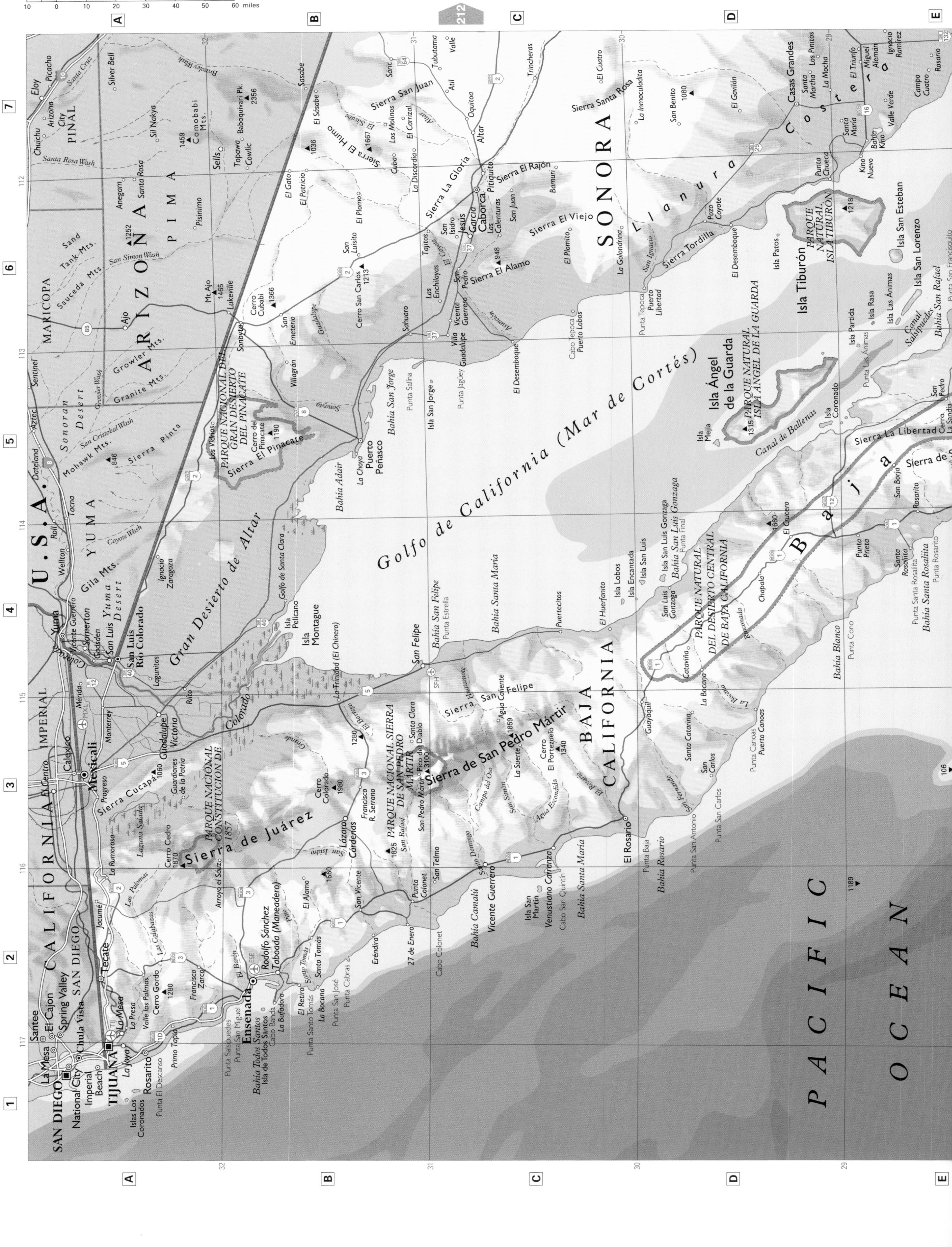

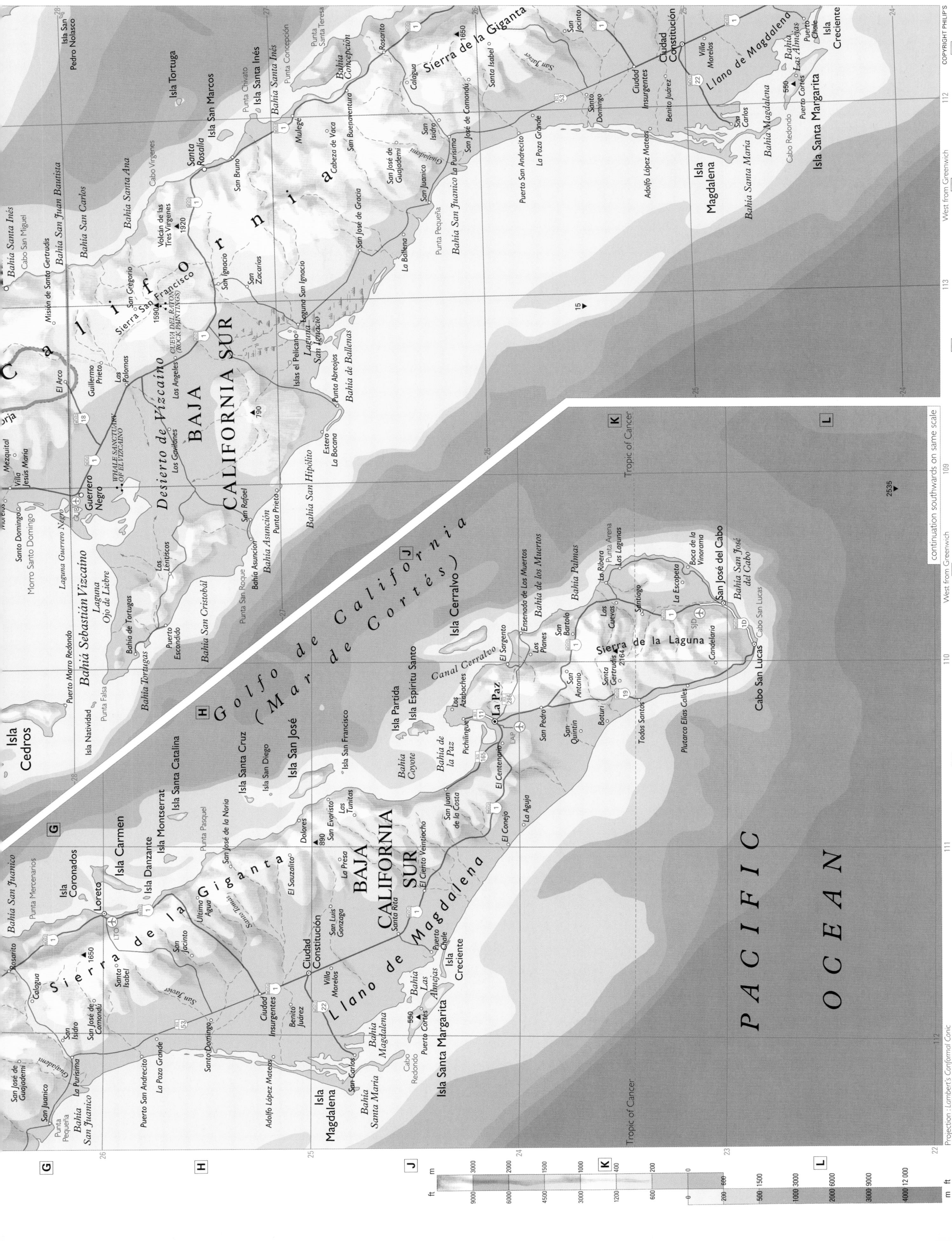
216
BAJA CALIFORNIA SUR
Golfo de California (Mar de Cortés)
PACIFIC OCEAN
Desierto de Vizcaíno
Sierra de la Giganta
Sierra de la Laguna
Llano de Magdalena
Sierra San Francisco
Isla Cedros
Isla Natividad
Bahía Sebastián Vizcaíno
Laguna Ojo de Liebre
Guerrero Negro
Villa Jesús María
Bahía Tortugas
Punta Eugenia
Bahía Asunción
Bahía San Hipólito
Punta Abreojos
Bahía de Ballenas
Laguna San Ignacio
San Ignacio
Volcán de las Tres Vírgenes
Santa Rosalía
Isla San Marcos
Isla Tortuga
Mulegé
Bahía Concepción
Isla Santa Inés
Loreto
Isla Coronados
Isla Carmen
Isla Danzante
Isla Montserrat
Isla Santa Catalina
Isla Santa Cruz
Isla San Diego
Isla San José
Isla San Francisco
Isla Partida
Isla Espíritu Santo
Isla Cerralvo
Canal Cerralvo
La Paz
Bahía de la Paz
El Sargento
Los Planes
Ensenada de los Muertos
Bahía de los Muertos
Bahía Palmas
La Ribera
Punta Arena
Los Lagunas
Santiago
Miraflores
La Escopeta
Boca de la Vinorama
San José del Cabo
Bahía San José del Cabo
Cabo San Lucas
Candelaria
Todos Santos
Plutarco Elías Calles
San Antonio
Santa Gertrudis
San Pedro
San Quintín
Baturi
El Centenario
El Conejo
La Aguja
San Juan de la Costa
Bahía Coyote
San Evaristo
Dolores
El Sauzalito
La Presa
Santa Rita
El Cielito Ventiocho
Ciudad Constitución
Ciudad Insurgentes
Villa Morelos
Benito Juárez
Isla Magdalena
Bahía Magdalena
Bahía Santa María
Isla Santa Margarita
Puerto Cortés
Bahía Las Almejas
Puerto Chale
Isla Creciente
Cabo Redondo
San Carlos
Adolfo López Mateos
Puerto San Andrecito
La Poza Grande
Santo Domingo
San Isidro
La Purísima
San José de Comondú
San Juanico
Bahía San Juanico
Punta Pequeña
Tropic of Cancer
West from Greenwich
continuation southwards on same scale
COPYRIGHT PHILIP'S
Projection : Lambert's Conformal Conic
ft
m
9000
6000
4500
3000
1200
600
200
500
1000
2000
3000
4000
1500
12 000

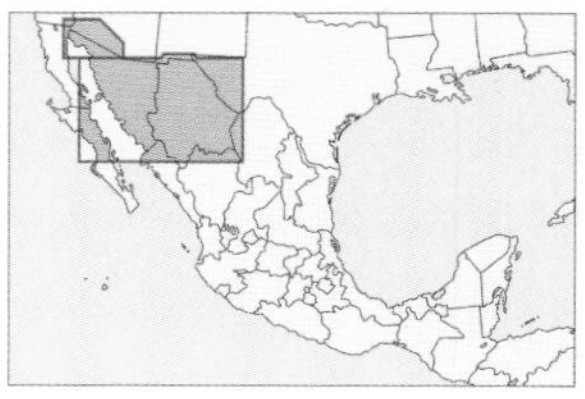

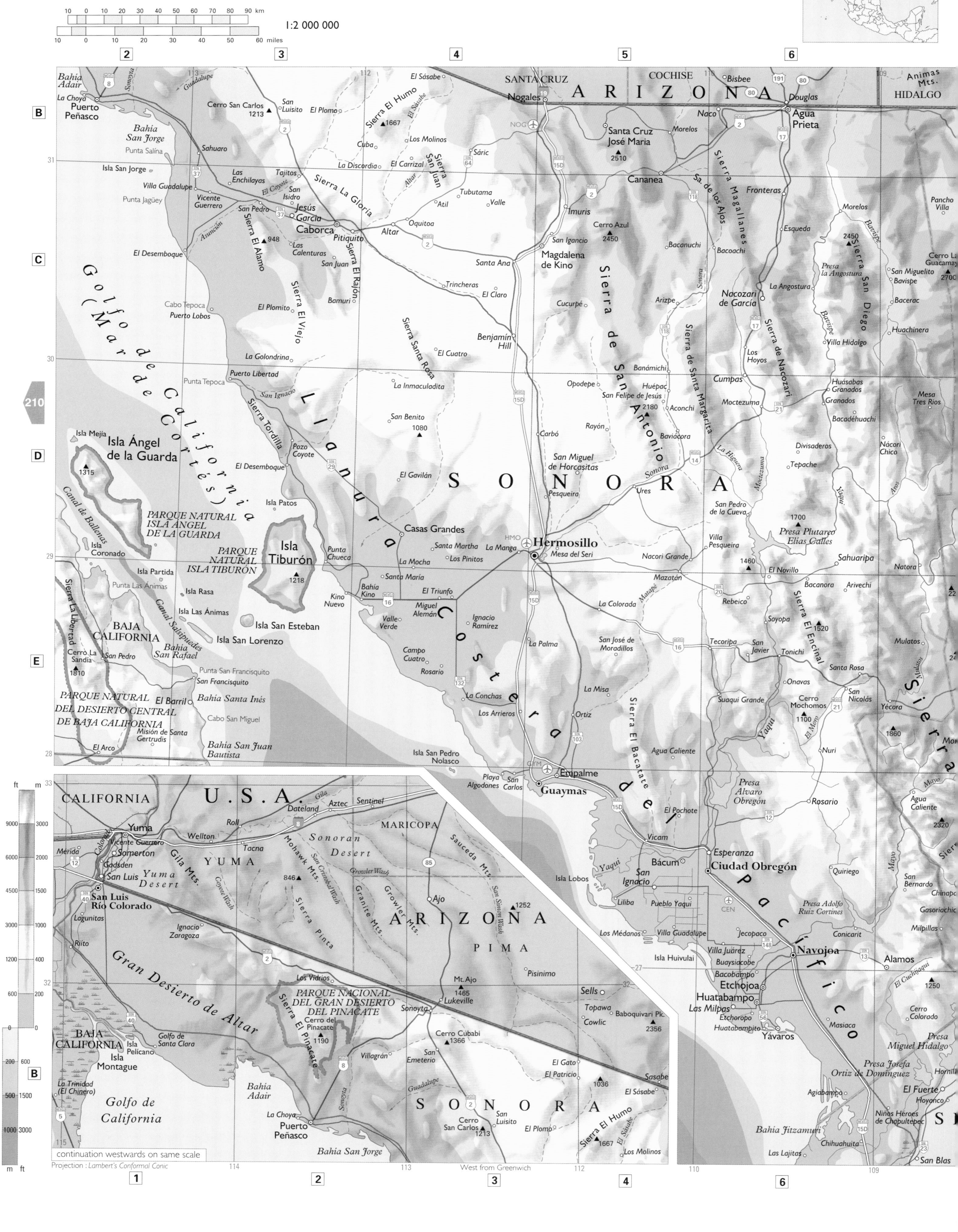
1:2 000 000
km
miles
ARIZONA
SONORA
SANTA CRUZ
COCHISE
HIDALGO
Animas Mts.
Nogales
Bisbee
Naco
Douglas
Agua Prieta
Bahía Adair
La Choya
Puerto Peñasco
Bahía San Jorge
Punta Salina
Isla San Jorge
Cerro San Carlos 1213
San Luisito
El Plomo
El Sásabe
Sierra El Humo
Cuba
Los Molinos
Sáric
La Discordia
El Carrizal
Sierra San Juan
Sahuaro
Villa Guadalupe
Punta Jagüey
Las Enchilayas
Tajitos
San Isidro
Vicente Guerrero
San Pedro
Jesús García
Caborca
Pitiquito
Altar
Oquitoa
Atil
Tubutama
Valle
Sierra La Gloria
Sierra El Álamo
Las Calenturas
San Juan
Sierra El Rajón
El Desemboque
Santa Cruz José María 2510
Cananea
Morelos
Fronteras
Imuris
Cerro Azul 2450
San Ignacio
Magdalena de Kino
Santa Ana
Bacanuchi
Bacoachi
Esqueda
Sierra Magallanes
Sa. de los Ajos
Golfo de California (Mar de Cortés)
Cabo Tepoca
Puerto Lobos
El Plomito
Bamuri
Sierra El Viejo
Trincheras
El Claro
Cucurpé
Arizpe
Nacozari de García
La Angostura
Presa la Angostura
Sierra San Diego
Bavispe
San Miguelito
Bacerac
Huachinera
Villa Hidalgo
Morelos
Pancho Villa
Cerro La Guacamaya 2700
Sierra de San Antonio
Sierra de Santa Margarita
Sierra de Nacozari
Los Hoyos
Benjamín Hill
El Cuatro
Sierra Santa Rosa
La Golondrina
Puerto Libertad
Punta Tepoca
La Inmaculadita
Llanura Costera del Pacífico
Banámichi
Huépac
Opodepe
San Felipe de Jesús
Aconchi
Cumpas
Moctezuma
Huásabas
Granados
Bacadéhuachi
Mesa Tres Ríos
Nácori Chico
Divisaderos
Tepache
San Benito 1080
Rayón
Carbó
Baviácora
Isla Mejía
Isla Ángel de la Guarda
1315
Sierra Tordilla
Pozo Coyote
El Desemboque
San Miguel de Horcasitas
Pesqueira
Ures
El Gavilán
Canal de Ballenas
PARQUE NATURAL ISLA ÁNGEL DE LA GUARDA
Isla Patos
Isla Tiburón
1218
PARQUE NATURAL ISLA TIBURÓN
Isla Coronado
Casas Grandes
Santa Martha
La Manga
Hermosillo
Mesa del Seri
Los Pinitos
Punta Chueca
La Mocha
Nacori Grande
Villa Pesqueira
San Pedro de la Cueva
Presa Plutarco Elías Calles
1700
Sahuaripa
Natora
Isla Partida
Punta Las Ánimas
Isla Rasa
Isla Las Ánimas
Sierra La Libertad
Canal Salsipuedes
Isla San Esteban
Isla San Lorenzo
Santa María
Bahía Kino
Kino Nuevo
El Triunfo
Miguel Alemán
Valle Verde
Ignacio Ramírez
La Colorada
Mazatán
El Novillo
Bacanora
Arivechi
Rebeico
Soyopa
Sierra El Encinal
1520
BAJA CALIFORNIA
Bahía San Rafael
Cerro La Sandía 1810
San Pedro
Punta San Francisquito
San Francisquito
Campo Cuatro
Rosario
La Palma
San José de Moradillos
Tecoripa
San Javier
Tonichi
Mulatos
Santa Rosa
Onavas
San Nicolás
Yécora
Suaqui Grande
Cerro Mochomos 1100
Nuri
1860
PARQUE NATURAL DEL DESIERTO CENTRAL DE BAJA CALIFORNIA
El Barril
Bahía Santa Inés
Cabo San Miguel
Misión de Santa Gertrudis
El Arco
Bahía San Juan Bautista
La Conchas
Los Arrieros
La Misa
Ortiz
Sierra El Bacatete
Agua Caliente
Isla San Pedro Nolasco
Playa Algodones
San Carlos
Empalme
Guaymas
Presa Alvaro Obregón
Rosario
El Pochote
Vicam
Esperanza
Ciudad Obregón
Bácum
San Ignacio
Isla Lobos
Liliba
Pueblo Yaqui
Quiriego
San Bernardo
Presa Adolfo Ruiz Cortines
Los Médanos
Villa Guadalupe
Jecopaco
Conicarit
Isla Huivulai
Villa Juárez
Buaysiacobe
Navojoa
Alamos
Bacobampo
Etchojoa
Huatabampo
Las Milpas
Etchoropo
Huatabampito
Yávaros
Masiaca
Cerro Colorado
Presa Miguel Hidalgo
Presa Josefa Ortiz de Domínguez
Agiabampo
El Fuerte
Hoyanco
Niños Héroes de Chapultepec
Bahía Jitzamuri
Chihuahuita
Las Lajitas
San Blas
Agua Caliente 2320
1250
CALIFORNIA
U.S.A.
Gila
Aztec
Sentinel
Dateland
Roll
Yuma
Wellton
Tacna
MARICOPA
Sonoran Desert
YUMA
Mérida
Vicente Guerrero
Somerton
Gadsden
San Luis
Yuma Desert
Gila Mts.
Mohawk Mts.
846
Sierra Pinta
Granite Mts.
Growler Mts.
Sauceda Mts.
Ajo
1252
PIMA
San Luis Río Colorado
Lagunitas
Ignacio Zaragoza
Riíto
Gran Desierto de Altar
Pisinimo
Los Vidrios
Mt. Ajo 1465
Lukeville
Sonoyta
Sells
Topawa
Cowlic
Baboquivari Pk. 2356
PARQUE NACIONAL DEL GRAN DESIERTO DEL PINACATE
Sierra El Pinacate
Cerro del Pinacate 1190
Cerro Cubabi 1366
BAJA CALIFORNIA
Isla Pelícano
Golfo de Santa Clara
Isla Montague
Villagrán
San Emeterio
El Gato
El Patricio
1036
Sasabe
El Sásabe
La Trinidad (El Chinero)
Golfo de California
Bahía Adair
continuation westwards on same scale
Projection: Lambert's Conformal Conic
West from Greenwich

NEW MEXICO
LUNA
DONA ANA
El Paso
CIUDAD JUÁREZ
General Rodrigo M. Quevedo (Palomas)
Cerro El Grande
Casas Grandes
Emiliano Zapata
Socorro
San Isidro
Fabens
Nuevo Cuauhtémoc
Guadalupe de Bravo
Samalayuca
Práxedis G. Guerrero
Fort Hancock
HUDSPETH
U.S.A.
CULBERSON
Sierra Diablo
Pecos
Toyah
REEVES
Apache Mts.
Kent
El Porvenir
Quitman Mts.
Rio Grande
Rio Bravo del Norte
Eagle Mts.
Van Horn
Saragosa
El Berrendo
Laguna de Guzmán
Guzmán
El Barreal
Laguna El Barreal
Laguna de Santa María
La Palotada
Ascensión
Sierra El Fresnal
Janos
El Mirador
Sierra San José del Prisco
El Consuelo
TEXAS
JEFF DAVIS
Davis Mountains
Mt. Livermore
Valentine
Sierra Vieja
Campo Cinco
Laguna Ojo del Diablo
Villa Ahumada
Los Juncos
Hidalgo
Lomas de Arena
Villa Ahumada y Anexas
Los Charcos
Progreso
Casas Grandes
Dublán
Nuevo Casas Grandes
PAQUIME
Juárez
Sierra La Lágrima
Sierra Pilares
Twin Mts.
Alpine
Glass Mts.
Marfa
Mt. Ord
Cathedral Mt.
Marathon
El Veinticuatro
Laguna La Vieja
El Carmen
Moctezuma
El Cuervo
El Llano
Sierra La Esperanza
PRESIDIO
Ignacio Zaragoza
Juan Mata Ortiz
Galeana
Benito Juárez
Las Cuatas
Ojo del Carrizo
Chinati Peak
Chinati Mts.
McKinney Mt.
Santiago Peak
Santiago Mts.
El Colorado
Ricardo Flores Magón
La Constitución
Buenaventura
San Lorenzo
La Trasquila
Sierra Las Tunas
Sierra El Nido
Santa Clara
Santa María
San Eduardo
Sierra El Peguis
Chalk Mts.
La Mesa del Huracán
CUERENTA CASAS
Ignacio Zaragoza
Sierra La Catarina
Presa el Tintero
Loma Blanca
Ojinaga
Presidio
BREWSTER
Las Varas
Laguna Encinillas
Los Prietos
Coyame
Cuchillo Parado
Sierra Matasaguas
Nogal
BIG BEND NATIONAL PARK
Emory Peak
Gómez Farías
Cruces
Laguna El Cuervo
Alamo Chapo
La Esmeralda
Madera
San José de Bavicora
Cerro Tres Picos
Namiquipa
Ojos Azules
Estación Colonias
Conchos
La Pinta
Benito Juárez
El Peñol
El Sauz
PARQUE NATURAL CAÑÓN DE SANTA ELENA
Manuel Benavides
ANASAZI
CHIHUAHUA
Lázaro Cárdenas
Plomosa
Maclovio Herrera
Oscar Soto Maynes
Luis L. León
Chilicote
Paso de San Antonio
San Antonio
Sirupa
Temosachic
Campo Sesenta y Uno
San José y Anexas
Presa Luis L. León
Chorreras
Polvorillas
Tres Ojitos
Matachic
PARQUE NACIONAL CUMBRES DE MAJALCA
Cumbres de Majalca
Aldama
Dolores
Cruces y Anexas
Los Alamos de Márquez
Bachíniva
Álvaro Obregón
Chihuahua
Aquiles Serdán
San Diego de Alcalá
Cocomorachic
Laguna Bustillos
Riva Palacio
El Becerro
Santa Fe
Tosanachic
Ciudad Guerrero
Presa Abraham González
Adolfo López Mateos
Julimes
El Salto
Anáhuac
San Miguel
Santa Anita
Tomochic
Cuauhtémoc
General Trias
La Perla
PARQUE NACIONAL CASCADAS DE BASASEACHIC
Cascadas de Basaseachic
Terrero
San Miguel
Cerro Prieto
Gran Morelos
Meoqui
Rosales
Delicias
Santa Isabel
Llanos de los Gigantes
Ocampo
Laguna de los Mexicanos
Cusihuiriachic
Santa Cruz
Presa Francisco I. Madero
El Orranteño
Texcoco
Hércules
La Capilla de los Remedios
Dr. Belisario Domínguez
Kilometro Noventa y Uno
Saucillo
Cajurichic
Tajirachic
La Joya
Ancón de Carros
El Alicante
Satevó
Estación Conchos
COAHUILA
San Juanito
Carichic
Santa María de Cuevas
San Pedro
La Cruz
Hormigas
San José de Carranza
Uruachic
Maguarichic
Bocoyna
San Francisco de Borja
Santa Gertrudis
Naica
Cenzontle
Sisoguichi
Creel
Monterde
Madre Occidental
San José Guacayvo
Panalachic
San José Baqueachi
Valerio
Monte Redondo
Ciudad Camargo
San Francisco de Conchos
Laguna Colorada
Las Norias
Guasizaco
Cusárare
La Libertad
La Boquilla del Conchos
Florido
Sierra Las Pampas
Las Pampas
Sierra El Diablo
Guazapares
San Rafael
Guaguachique
Urique
Nonoava
Presa la Boquilla
Valle de Zaragoza
Maravillas
Bolsón de Mapimí
Sierra Mojada
Boquilla de Abajo
Valle del Rosario
Parral
Búfalo
Santa Elena
PARQUE NATURAL BARRANCA DEL COBRE
Urique
Jiménez
La Providencia
Guimbalete
Laguna del Rey
Cerro La Casa Colorada
Rochéachic
Huejotitán
El Tule
San Antonio del Potrero
Villa López
División del Norte
Zona del Silencio
La Reforma
Batopilas
Buenavista
Balleza
La Magdalena
Hidalgo del Parral
Valle de Allende
Carrillo
Laguna Palomas
El Cinco
Fuerte
Tasajeras
San Miguel
Morelos
Guachochi
Cabórachi
El Porvenir
San Francisco del Oro
Santa Bárbara
Villa Matamoros
Torreón de Mata
Villa Coronado
Escalón
PARQUE NATURAL MAPIMÍ
Santa María de Mohovano
Choix
Guerachi
La Providencia
Guadalupe de Bahues
Ceballos
Las Tortugas
Las Palomas
El Caldillo
Orestes Pereyra
Villa Ocampo
Canutillo
Yecorato
Chinobampo
Baborigame
Los Loera
Verde
Turuachi
Cerro Prieto
El Diamante
San Fermín
Conejos
SINALOA
Presa Guillermo Blake Agular
Basonapita
Válgame Dios
Guadalupe y Calvo
Yerbitas
Sextín
DURANGO
Revolución
Villa Hidalgo
Sardinas
Potrero del Llano
El Jaralito
Tlahualilo de Zaragoza
La Lagunita
West from Greenwich
COPYRIGHT PHILIP'S
214
216

TEXAS
U.S.A.
COAHUILA
Balcones Escarpment
Serranías del Burro
Sierra del Carmen
Sierra Madre
Laguna Madre
Padre Island
SAN ANTONIO
Laredo
Nuevo Laredo
MONTERREY
Saltillo
Monclova
Piedras Negras
Eagle Pass
Del Rio
Ciudad Acuña
Brownsville
Matamoros
Reynosa
McAllen
Harlingen
Torreón
Gómez Palacio
Ciudad Lerdo
Región Lagunera
Desierto (Laguna) de Mayran
Río Grande
Río Bravo del Norte
VAL VERDE
EDWARDS
KINNEY
UVALDE
REAL
BANDERA
MEDINA
BEXAR
COMAL
GUADALUPE
CALDWELL
GONZALES
WILSON
DE WITT
KARNES
GOLIAD
BEE
ATASCOSA
FRIO
ZAVALA
MAVERICK
DIMMIT
LASALLE
McMULLEN
LIVE OAK
JIM WELLS
NUECES
KLEBERG
WEBB
DUVAL
BROOKS
KENEDY
JIM HOGG
ZAPATA
STARR
HIDALGO
WILLACY
CAMERON
BREWSTER
TERRELL
BIG BEND NATIONAL PARK
PARQUE NATURAL CINCO MANANTIALES
PARQUE NATURAL RIO SAN RODRIGO-EL BURRO
PARQUE NATURAL PRESA DE LA AMISTAD
PARQUE NACIONAL CUMBRES DE MONTERREY
PARQUE NATURAL CUATROCIÉNEGAS
PARQUE NATURAL SIERRA DE LA PAILA
Chisos Mts.
Chalk Mts.
Sierra La Gloria
Sierra Pájaros Azules
Sierra La Paila
Sierra San Marcos y Pinos
Sierra La Fragua
Sierra La Madera
Sierra Cristo
Sierra Obayos
Sierra Santa Rosa
Sierra Colorada
Sierra El Pino
Sierra de Tlahualilo
1:2 000 000
10 0 10 20 30 40 50 60 70 80 90 km
10 0 10 20 30 40 50 60 miles

213

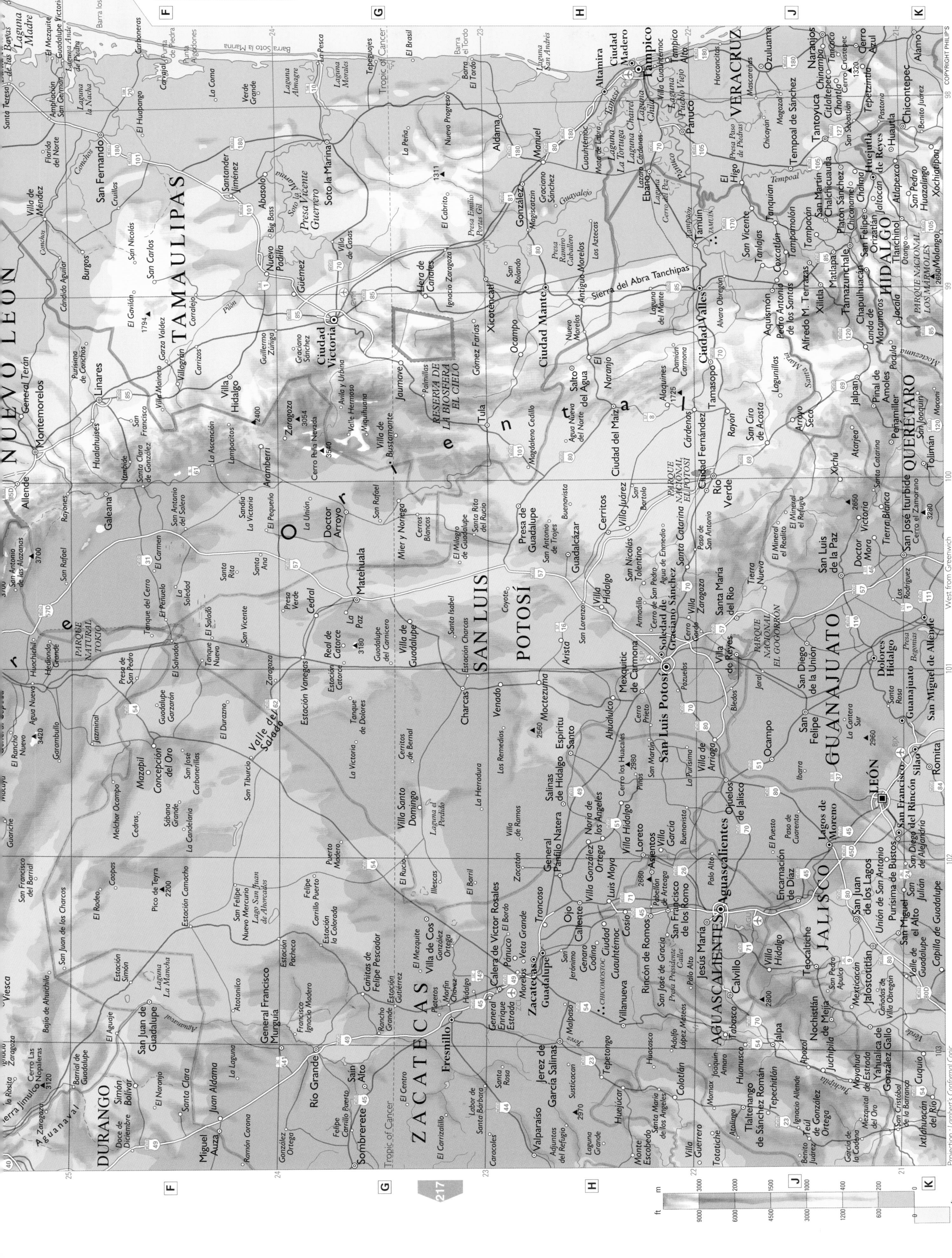
NUEVO LEÓN
TAMAULIPAS
SAN LUIS POTOSÍ
ZACATECAS
DURANGO
AGUASCALIENTES
JALISCO
GUANAJUATO
QUERÉTARO
HIDALGO
VERACRUZ
Tropic of Cancer
Ciudad Victoria
Tampico
Ciudad Madero
Altamira
Ciudad Mante
Ciudad Valles
San Luis Potosí
Matehuala
Aguascalientes
Zacatecas
Fresnillo
León
Linares
Montemorelos
Allende
Galeana
Sombrerete
San Fernando
Soto la Marina
RESERVA DE LA BIOSFERA EL CIELO
Sierra del Abra Tanchipas
West from Greenwich
Projection : Lambert's Conformal Conic
COPYRIGHT PHILIP'S
219
217

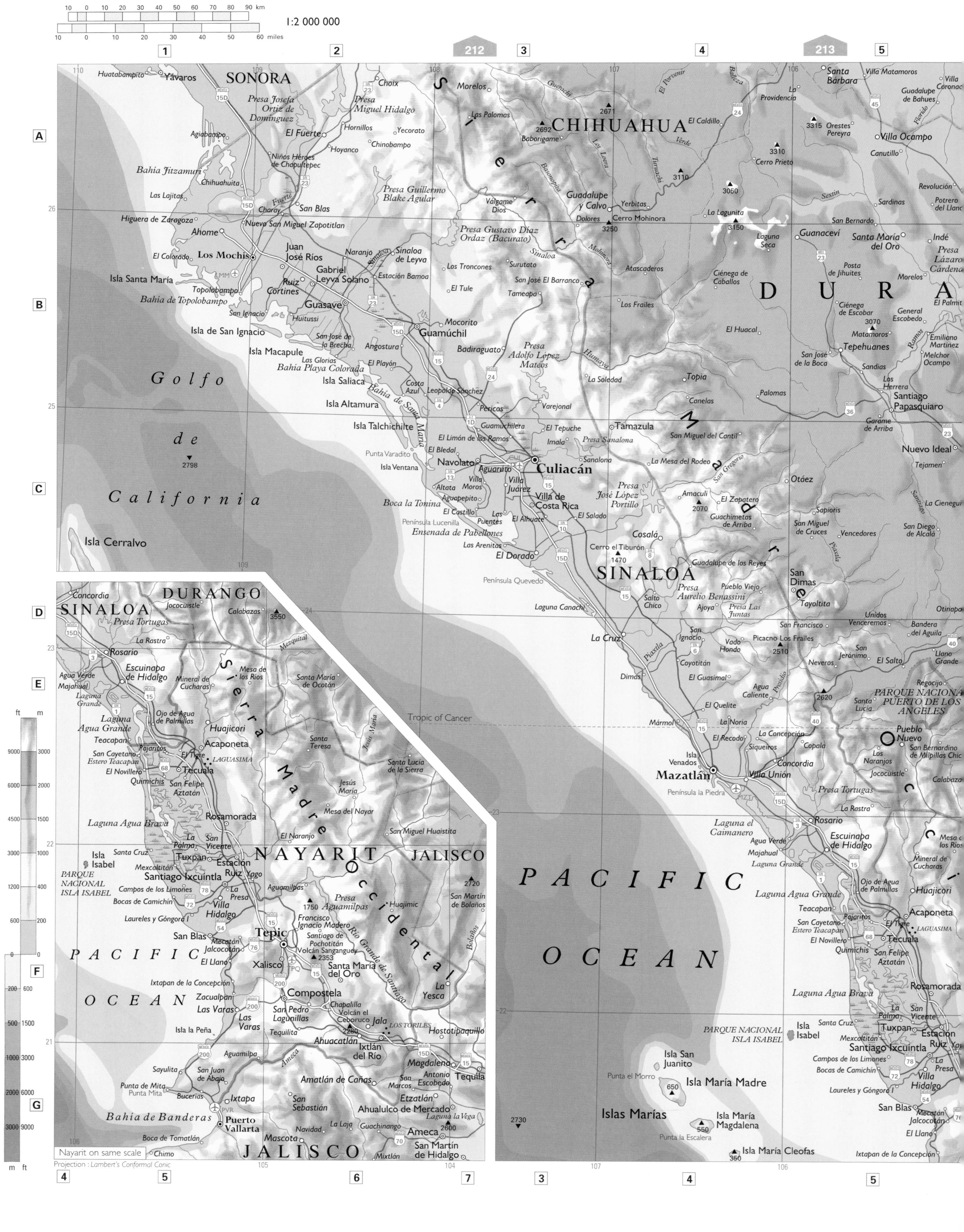
1:2 000 000
km
miles
212
213
SONORA
CHIHUAHUA
DURANGO
SINALOA
NAYARIT
JALISCO
Sierra Madre
Sierra Madre Occidental
Golfo de California
PACIFIC OCEAN
Tropic of Cancer
Huatabampito
Yavaros
Presa Josefa Ortiz de Domínguez
Presa Miguel Hidalgo
Choix
Morelos
Las Palomas
El Fuerte
Hornillos
Yecorato
Chinobampo
Agiabampo
Hoyanco
Niños Héroes de Chapultepec
Bahía Jitzamuri
Chihuahuita
Presa Guillermo Blake Aguilar
Las Lajitas
San Blas
Charay
Higuera de Zaragoza
Nuevo San Miguel Zapotitlan
Ahome
Los Mochis
El Colorado
Juan José Ríos
Naranjo
Sinaloa de Leyva
Gabriel Leyva Solano
Estación Bamoa
Isla Santa María
Ruiz Cortines
Topolobampo
Bahía de Topolobampo
Guasave
San Ignacio
Huitussi
Isla de San Ignacio
San José de la Brecha
Mocorito
Guamúchil
Isla Macapule
Angostura
Badiraguato
Las Glorias
Bahía Playa Colorada
El Playón
Isla Saliaca
Costa Azul
Leopoldo Sánchez
Bahía de Santa María
Isla Altamura
Pericos
Isla Talchichilte
Guamuchilera
El Limón de los Ramos
Punta Varadito
El Bledal
Isla Ventana
Navolato
Aguaruto
Culiacán
Altata
Villa Moros
Villa Juárez
Aguapepito
Boca la Tonina
Villa de Costa Rica
El Castillo
Las Puentes
El Alhuate
Península Lucenilla
Ensenada de Pabellones
Las Arenitas
El Dorado
Península Quevedo
Isla Cerralvo
Presa Gustavo Díaz Ordaz (Bacurato)
Los Troncones
El Tule
Surutato
San José El Barranco
Tameapa
Valgame Dios
Presa Adolfo López Mateos
Humaya
Varejonal
El Tepuche
Imala
Presa Sanalona
Sanalona
Tamazula
La Soledad
Topia
Canelas
Palomas
San Miguel del Cantil
La Mesa del Rodeo
Presa José López Portillo
Amaculi
El Zapatero
Guachimetas de Arriba
El Salado
Cosalá
Cerro el Tiburón
Guadalupe de los Reyes
Presa Aurelio Benassini
Pueblo Viejo
Salto Chico
Ajoya
Presa Las Juntas
Laguna Canachi
La Cruz
San Ignacio
Vado Hondo
Picacho Los Frailes
Coyotitán
Dimas
El Guasimal
Agua Caliente
El Quelite
Mármol
La Noria
El Recodo
La Concepción
Siqueiros
Copala
Isla Venados
Mazatlán
Concordia
Villa Unión
Península la Piedra
Presa Tortugas
Rosario
La Rastra
Laguna el Caimanero
Agua Verde
Escuinapa de Hidalgo
Majahual
Laguna Grande
Laguna Agua Grande
Teacapán
Baboriqame
Guadalupe y Calvo
Yerbitas
Dolores
Cerro Mohinora
Atascaderos
Los Frailes
El Caldillo
Providencia
Cerro Prieto
La Lagunita
Laguna Seca
Ciénega de Caballos
El Huacal
Santa Bárbara
Villa Matamoros
Guadalupe de Bahues
Orestes Pereyra
Villa Ocampo
Canutillo
Revolución
Sardinas
Potrero del Llano
San Bernardo
Guanaceví
Santa María del Oro
Indé
Posta de Jihuites
Morelos
Ciénega de Escobar
General Escobedo
Matamoros
Tepehuanes
Emiliano Martínez
Melchor Ocampo
San José de la Boca
Sandías
Los Herrera
Santiago Papasquiaro
Garame de Arriba
Nuevo Ideal
Tejamen
Otáez
Sapioris
San Miguel de Cruces
Vencedores
San Diego de Alcalá
San Dimas
Tayoltita
Unidos Venceremos
San Francisco
Bandera del Aguila
San Jerónimo
Neveros
El Salto
Llano Grande
Regocijo
PARQUE NACIONAL PUERTO DE LOS ANGELES
Santa Lucía
Pueblo Nuevo
Los Naranjos
San Bernardino de Milpillas Chico
Jocoocuistle
Mesa de los Ríos
Mineral de Cucharas
Ojo de Agua de Palmillas
Huajicori
Acaponeta
San Cayetano
Estero Teacapán
Pajaritos
El Tigre
LAGUASIMA
Tecuala
El Novillero
Quimichis
San Felipe Aztatán
Rosamorada
Laguna Agua Brava
La Palma
San Vicente
Isla Isabel
Santa Cruz
Tuxpan
Estación Ruiz
PARQUE NACIONAL ISLA ISABEL
Mexcaltitán
Santiago Ixcuintla
Yago
Campos de los Limones
La Presa
Bocas de Camichín
Villa Hidalgo
Laureles y Góngora
San Blas
Mecatán
Jalcocotán
El Llano
Ixtapan de la Concepción
Isla San Juanito
Punta el Morro
Isla María Madre
Islas Marías
Isla María Magdalena
Punta la Escalera
Isla María Cleofas
Concordia
Jocoocuistle
Calabazas
Presa Tortugas
La Rastra
Rosario
Santa María de Ocotán
Santa Teresa
Santa Lucía de la Sierra
Jesús María
Mesa del Nayar
El Naranjo
San Miguel Huaistita
Aguamilpas
Presa Aguamilpas
Huajimic
San Martín de Bolaños
Bolaños
Francisco Ignacio Madero
Santiago de Pochotitán
Volcán Sanganguey
Tepic
Xalisco
Santa María del Oro
Río Grande de Santiago
La Yesca
Compostela
Zacualpan
Las Varas
Chapalilla
Volcán el Ceboruco
San Pedro Lagunillas
Jala
LOS TORILES
Isla la Peña
Tequilita
Ahuacatlán
Ixtlán del Río
Hostotipaquillo
Aguamilpa
Ameca
Magdalena
Tequila
Sayulita
San Juan de Abajo
Amatlán de Cañas
Antonio Escobedo
San Marcos
Punta de Mita
Punta Mita
Bucerías
Ixtapa
San Sebastián
Etzatlán
Ahualulco de Mercado
Laguna la Vega
Bahía de Banderas
Puerto Vallarta
Navidad
La Laja
Guachinango
Boca de Tomatlán
Mascota
Chimo
Mixtlán
San Martín de Hidalgo
Nayarit on same scale
Projection : Lambert's Conformal Conic

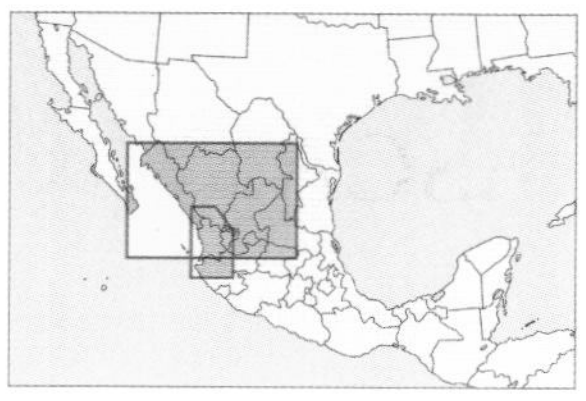

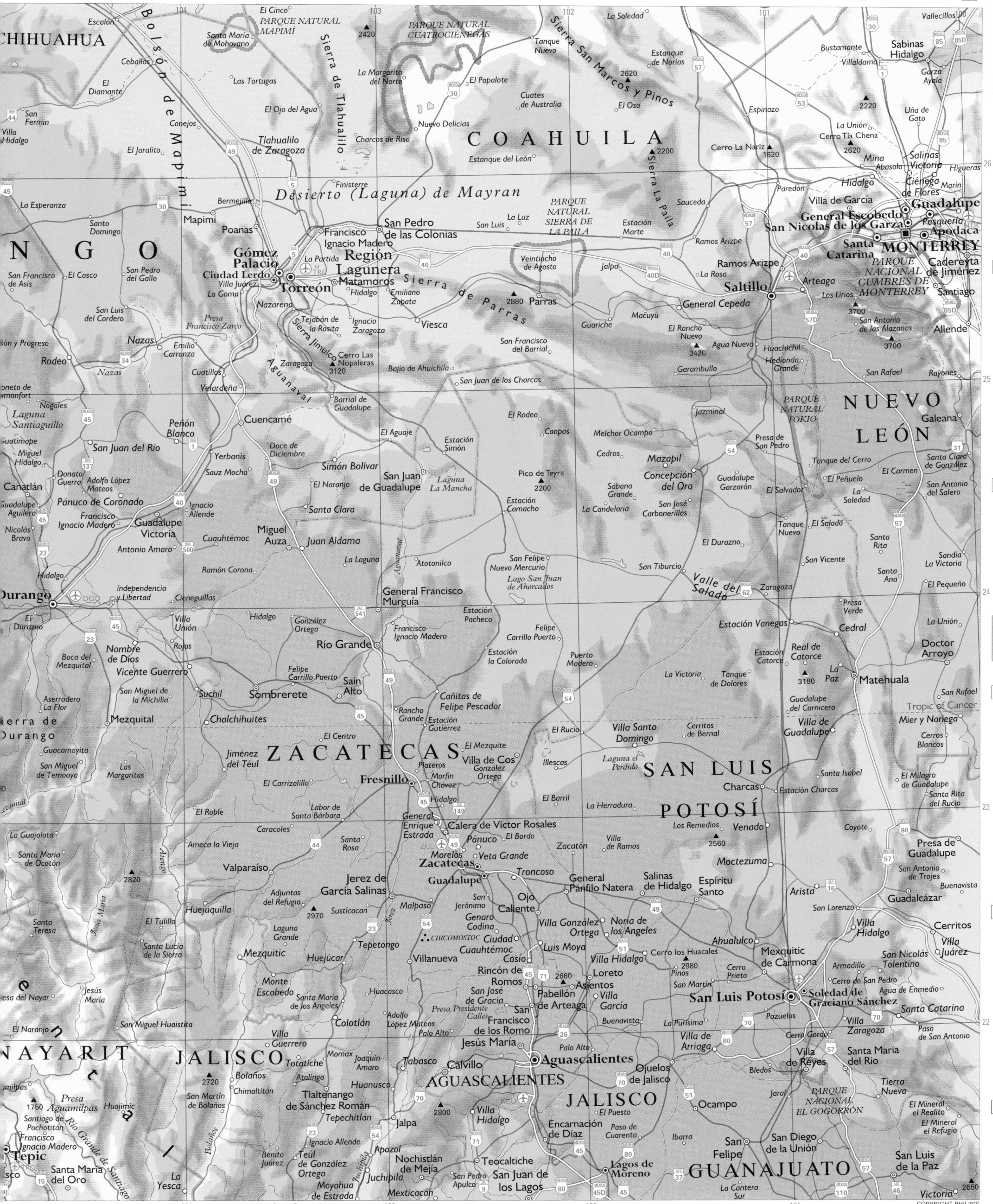
6
7
8
214
9
10
11
A
B
C
D
E
F
215
218
104
103
102
101
26
25
24
23
22
West from Greenwich
COPYRIGHT PHILIP'S
CHIHUAHUA
COAHUILA
NUEVO LEÓN
ZACATECAS
SAN LUIS POTOSÍ
NAYARIT
JALISCO
AGUASCALIENTES
GUANAJUATO
Bolsón de Mapimí
Sierra de Tlahualilo
Sierra San Marcos y Pinos
Sierra La Paila
Sierra de Parras
Sierra Jimulco
Aguanaval
Desierto (Laguna) de Mayran
Región Lagunera
PARQUE NATURAL MAPIMÍ
PARQUE NATURAL CUATROCIÉNEGAS
PARQUE NATURAL SIERRA DE LA PAILA
PARQUE NACIONAL CUMBRES DE MONTERREY
PARQUE NATURAL TOKIO
PARQUE NACIONAL EL GOGORRÓN
Valle del Salado
Tropic of Cancer
Escalón
Ceballos
El Diamante
San Fermín
Villa Hidalgo
El Cinco
Santa María de Mohovano
Las Tortugas
El Ojo del Agua
Conejos
Tlahualilo de Zaragoza
El Jaralito
La Esperanza
Bermejillo
Mapimí
Santo Domingo
Poanas
Gómez Palacio
Ciudad Lerdo
Villa Juárez
La Goma
Torreón
Matamoros
San Francisco de Asís
El Casco
San Pedro del Gallo
San Luis del Cordero
Nazareno
Presa Francisco Zarco
Nazas
Emilio Carranza
Rodeo
Cuatillos
Velardeña
Nogales
Laguna Santiaguillo
Peñón Blanco
Cuencamé
San Juan del Río
Yerbanis
Sauz Mocho
Donato Guerra
Adolfo López Mateos
Pánuco de Coronado
Canatlán
Francisco Ignacio Madero
Guadalupe Victoria
Ignacio Allende
Antonio Amaro
Cuauhtémoc
Miguel Auza
Juan Aldama
Nicolás Bravo
Ramón Corona
Hidalgo
Durango
DGO
Independencia y Libertad
Cieneguillas
El Durazno
Villa Unión
Rojas
Nombre de Dios
Vicente Guerrero
Boca del Mezquital
San Miguel de la Michilia
Súchil
Sombrerete
Aserradero La Flor
Mezquital
Chalchihuites
Sierra de Durango
Guacamayita
San Miguel de Temoaya
Las Margaritas
Jiménez del Téul
El Carrizalillo
El Roble
La Guajolota
Santa María de Ocotán
Caracoles
Ameca la Vieja
Valparaíso
Huejuquilla
Santa Teresa
Santa Lucía de la Sierra
Mezquitic
Jesús María
El Naranjo
San Miguel Huaistita
Bolaños
Chimaltitán
San Martín de Bolaños
Huajimic
Presa Aguamilpas
Santiago de Pochotitán
Tepic
Santa María del Oro
La Yesca
Río Grande de Santiago
Finisterre
Francisco Ignacio Madero
San Pedro de las Colonias
La Partida
Hidalgo
Emiliano Zapata
Tejabón de la Rosita
Ignacio Zaragoza
Viesca
Cerro Las Nopaleras
Zaragoza
Barrial de Guadalupe
Bajío de Ahuichila
San Juan de los Charcos
La Margarita del Norte
El Papalote
Tanque Nuevo
Estanque de Norias
Cuates de Australia
El Oso
Nuevo Delicias
Charcos de Risa
Estanque del León
La Soledad
San Luis
La Luz
Veintiocho de Agosto
Parras
Jalpa
Sauceda
Estación Marte
Guariche
Macuyú
El Rancho Nuevo
Agua Nueva
Garambullo
San Francisco del Barrial
Ramos Arizpe
La Rosa
Saltillo
SLW
Arteaga
General Cepeda
Los Lirios
San Antonio de las Alazanas
Allende
Santiago
Cadereyta de Jiménez
MONTERREY
Santa Catarina
General Escobedo
San Nicolás de los Garza
Guadalupe
Apodaca
Pesquería
Villa de García
Hidalgo
Paredón
Ciénega de Flores
Marín
Higueras
Salinas Victoria
Mina
Abasolo
Cerro Tía Chena
La Unión
Cerro La Nariz
Espinazo
Bustamante
Villaldama
Sabinas Hidalgo
Garza Ayala
Uña de Gato
Vallecillos
Huachichil
Hediondo Grande
San Rafael
Rayones
Galeana
Jazminal
Presa de San Pedro
Tanque del Cerro
El Peñuelo
El Carmen
Santa Clara de González
San Antonio del Salero
La Soledad
El Salvador
Guadalupe Garzarón
Mazapil
Concepción del Oro
Melchor Ocampo
Cedros
Sábana Grande
San José Carbonerillas
La Candelaria
Pico de Teyra
El Rodeo
Caopas
Estación Camacho
Estación Simón
El Aguaje
Doce de Diciembre
Simón Bolívar
San Juan de Guadalupe
El Naranjo
Laguna La Mancha
Santa Clara
La Laguna
Atotonilco
San Felipe Nuevo Mercurio
Lago San Juan de Ahorcados
San Tiburcio
El Durazno
Tanque Nuevo
El Salado
Santa Rita
San Vicente
Zaragoza
Sandía
La Victoria
Santa Ana
El Pequeño
Presa Verde
Cedral
La Unión
Doctor Arroyo
Estación Vanegas
Estación Catorce
Real de Catorce
La Paz
Matehuala
San Rafael
Guadalupe del Carnicero
Villa de Guadalupe
Mier y Noriega
Cerros Blancos
Santa Isabel
El Milagro de Guadalupe
Santa Rita del Rucio
Estación Charcas
Charcas
Cerritos de Bernal
Villa Santo Domingo
Laguna el Perdido
La Victoria
Tanque de Dolores
Puerto Madero
Felipe Carrillo Puerto
Estación la Colorada
Estación Pacheco
General Francisco Murguía
Francisco Ignacio Madero
Río Grande
González Ortega
Felipe Carrillo Puerto
Saín Alto
Cañitas de Felipe Pescador
Rancho Grande
Estación Gutiérrez
El Centro
El Rucio
El Mezquite
Villa de Cos
González Ortega
Plateros
Fresnillo
Morfín Chávez
Illescas
El Barril
La Herradura
Los Remedios
Venado
Labor de Santa Bárbara
Calera de Víctor Rosales
General Enrique Estrada
El Bordo
Pánuco
Veta Grande
Morelos
Zacatecas
ZCL
Guadalupe
Santa Rosa
Zacatón
Villa de Ramos
Moctezuma
Coyote
Presa de Guadalupe
San Antonio de Trojes
Buenavista
Guadalcázar
Arista
San Lorenzo
Villa Hidalgo
Cerritos
Villa Juárez
Jerez de García Salinas
Adjuntas del Refugio
Susticacán
Malpaso
San Jerónimo
Genaro Codina
Troncoso
Ojo Caliente
General Pánfilo Natera
Salinas de Hidalgo
Espíritu Santo
Villa González Ortega
Noria de los Ángeles
Luis Moya
Ciudad Cuauhtémoc
CHICOMOSTOC
Laguna Grande
Tepetongo
Huejúcar
Villanueva
Cosío
Rincón de Romos
Villa Hidalgo
Loreto
Asientos
Cerro los Huacales
Pinos
Cerro Prieto
San Martín
Ahualulco
Mexquitic de Carmona
Armadillo
San Nicolás Tolentino
Cerro de San Pedro
Agua de Enmedio
San Luis Potosí
Soledad de Graciano Sánchez
Santa Catarina
Villa Zaragoza
Paso de San Antonio
Pozuelos
Cerro Gordo
Villa de Reyes
Santa María del Río
Tierra Nueva
Bledos
Jaral
Monte Escobedo
Santa María de los Ángeles
Huacasco
Colotlán
Adolfo López Mateos
Presa Presidente Calles
San José de Gracia
Pabellón de Arteaga
Villa García
Buenavista
La Purísima
Villa de Arriaga
San Francisco de los Romo
Palo Alto
Jesús María
Aguascalientes
Ojuelos de Jalisco
Villa Guerrero
Totatiche
Momax
Joaquín Amaro
Tabasco
Calvillo
Atolinga
Tlaltenango de Sánchez Román
Tepechitlán
Huanusco
Jalpa
Villa Hidalgo
AGU
Encarnación de Díaz
El Puesto
Paso de Cuarenta
Ibarra
Ocampo
San Felipe
San Diego de la Unión
El Mineral el Realito
El Mineral el Refugio
Benito Juárez
Teúl de González Ortega
Ignacio Allende
Apozol
Nochistlán de Mejía
Juchipila
Moyahua de Estrada
Mexticacán
Teocaltiche
San Pedro Apulco
San Juan de los Lagos
Lagos de Moreno
La Cantera Sur
San Luis de la Paz
Victoria
2420
2620
2220
2620
1620
2200
2880
3420
3120
3700
3700
2200
3180
2560
2820
2970
2660
2980
2720
1750
2800
2650

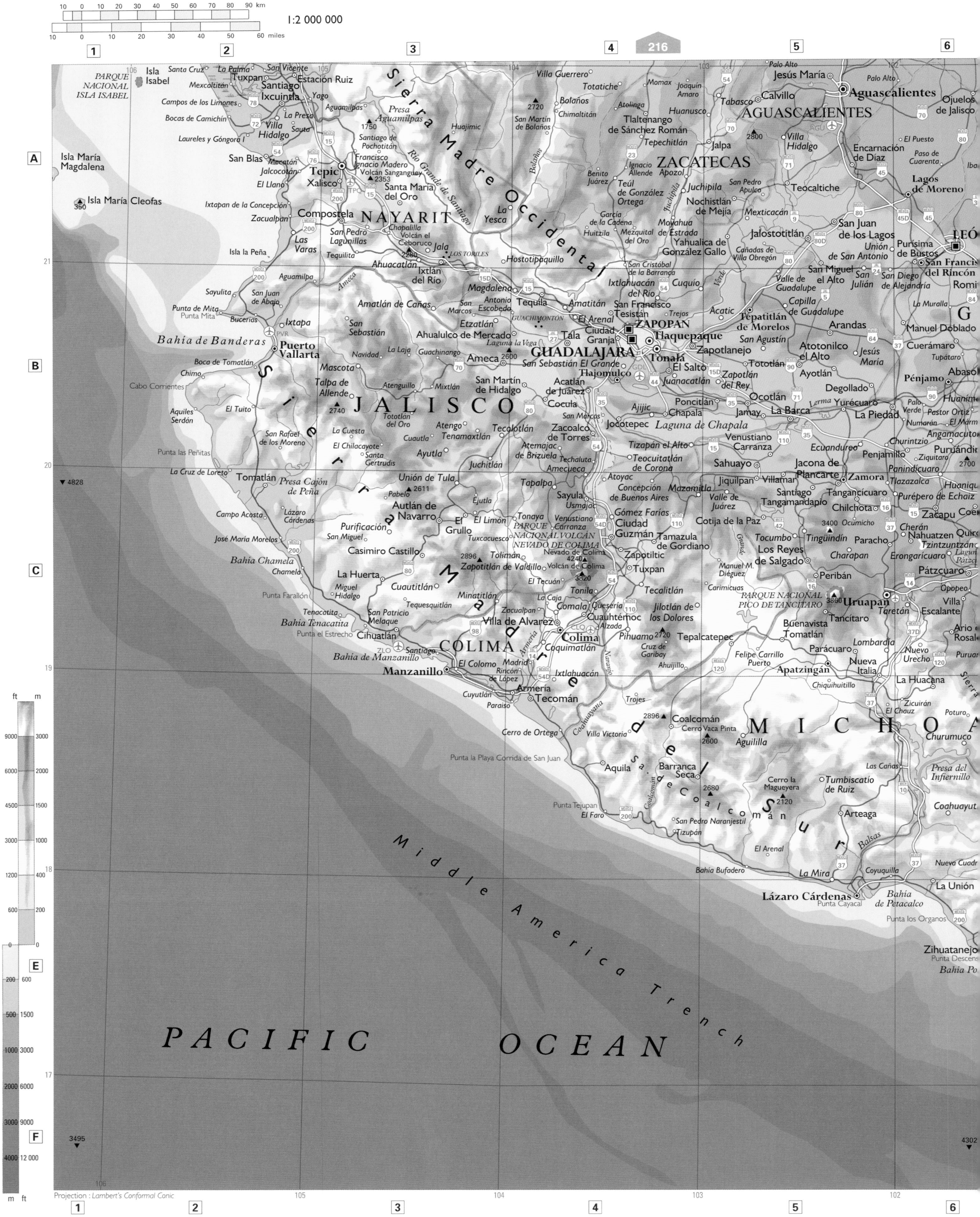
1:2 000 000
km
miles
216
PARQUE NACIONAL ISLA ISABEL
Isla Isabel
Santa Cruz
La Palma
San Vicente
Mexcaltitán
Tuxpan
Santiago Ixcuintla
Estación Ruiz
Yago
Campos de los Limones
Bocas de Camichín
La Presa
Villa Hidalgo
Sauta
Aguamilpas
Presa Aguamilpas
Laureles y Góngora
Isla María Magdalena
San Blas
Mecatán
Jalcocotán
El Llano
Tepic
Xalisco
Francisco Ignacio Madero
Volcán Sanganguey
Santiago de Pochotitán
Santa María del Oro
Isla María Cleofas
Ixtapan de la Concepción
Zacualpan
Compostela
NAYARIT
Las Varas
San Pedro Lagunillas
Chapalilla
Volcán el Ceboruco
Jala
LOS TORILES
Isla la Peña
Tequilita
Ahuacatlán
Ixtlán del Río
Aguamilpa
Sayulita
San Juan de Abajo
Punta de Mita
Punta Mita
Bucerías
Ixtapa
Bahía de Banderas
Puerto Vallarta
Boca de Tomatlán
Chimo
Cabo Corrientes
Aquiles Serdán
El Tuito
San Rafael de los Moreno
Punta las Peñitas
La Cruz de Loreto
Tomatlán
Presa Cajón de Peña
Campo Acosta
Lázaro Cárdenas
José María Morelos
Bahía Chamela
Chamela
Punta Farallón
Tenacatita
Bahía Tenacatita
Punta el Estrecho
Cihuatlán
Bahía de Manzanillo
Manzanillo
Santiago
El Colomo
Cuyutlán
Paraíso
Armería
Tecomán
Cerro de Ortega
Punta la Playa Corrida de San Juan
Punta Tejupan
El Faro
Sierra Madre Occidental
Río Grande de Santiago
Huajimic
Villa Guerrero
Totatiche
Bolaños
San Martín de Bolaños
Chimaltitán
La Yesca
Hostotipaquillo
Magdalena
Tequila
Amatitán
San Francisco Tesistán
ZAPOPAN
Tlaquepaque
Tonalá
GUADALAJARA
Ciudad Granja
Tala
GUACHIMONTÓN
El Arenal
Etzatlán
Ahualulco de Mercado
San Marcos
Antonio Escobedo
Amatlán de Cañas
San Sebastián
Navidad
La Laja
Guachinango
Mascota
Ameca
San Sebastián El Grande
Hajomulco
Talpa de Allende
Sierra Madre del Sur
JALISCO
Atenguillo
Mixtlán
San Martín de Hidalgo
Acatlán de Juárez
Cocula
Tototlán del Oro
La Cuesta
El Chilacayote
Santa Gertrudis
Cuautla
Atengo
Tenamaxtlán
Tecolotlán
Ayutla
Unión de Tula
Pabelo
Autlán de Navarro
El Grullo
El Limón
Purificación
San Miguel
Casimiro Castillo
La Huerta
Miguel Hidalgo
Cuautitlán
Tuxcacuesco
Tolimán
Zapotitlán de Vadillo
PARQUE NACIONAL VOLCÁN NEVADO DE COLIMA
Nevado de Colima
Volcán de Colima
El Tecuán
Minatitlán
Tequesquitlán
San Patricio Melaque
Zacualpan
Villa de Álvarez
Colima
COLIMA
Coquimatlán
Comala
Quesería
Cuauhtémoc
Alzada
Madrid
Rincón de López
Ixtlahuacán
Juchitlán
Tapalpa
Sayula
Usmajac
Atemajac de Brizuela
Techaluta
Amecueca
Zacoalco de Torres
San Marcos
Jocotepec
Ajijic
Chapala
Laguna de Chapala
Tizapán el Alto
Teocuitatlán de Corona
Atoyac
Concepción de Buenos Aires
Mazamitla
Gómez Farías
Ciudad Guzmán
Tamazula de Gordiano
Venustiano Carranza
Zapotiltic
Tuxpan
Tonila
Tecalitlán
Jilotlán de los Dolores
Pihuamo
Cruz de Garibay
Tepalcatepec
Ahuijillo
Trojes
Coalcomán
Cerro Vaca Pinta
Villa Victoria
Aquila
Barranca Seca
San Pedro Naranjestil
Tizupán
Aguililla
Cerro la Magueyera
Tumbiscatío de Ruiz
Arteaga
El Arenal
Bahía Bufadero
La Mira
Lázaro Cárdenas
Punta Cayacal
Bahía de Petacalco
Punta los Organos
La Unión
Coyuquilla
Nueva Cuadr
Zihuatanejo
Punta Descens
Bahía Po
Coahuayut
Presa del Infiernillo
Las Cañas
Churumuco
MICHOA
Poturo
Zicuirán
El Chauz
La Huacana
Nueva Italia
Apatzingán
Chiquihuitillo
Felipe Carrillo Puerto
Parácuaro
Lombardía
Buenavista Tomatlán
Nuevo Urecho
Tancítaro
Uruapan
Taretán
PARQUE NACIONAL PICO DE TANCÍTARO
Carimicuas
Manuel M. Diéguez
Peribán
Los Reyes de Salgado
Tocumbo
Tingüindín
Charapan
Paracho
Cotija de la Paz
Valle de Juárez
Santiago Tangamandapio
Jiquilpan
Villamar
Sahuayo
Jacona de Plancarte
Zamora
Tangancícuaro
Chilchota
Ocumicho
Erongarícuaro
Pátzcuaro
Opopeo
Villa Escalante
Zacapu
Cherán
Nahuatzen
Tzintzuntzan
Purépero de Echaiz
Tlazazalca
Panindícuaro
Zinapécuaro
Purúandiro
Churintzio
Penjamillo
Angamacutiro
Numarán
Pastor Ortiz
La Piedad
Yurécuaro
Ecuandureo
Venustiano Carranza
Degollado
Jamay
La Barca
Ocotlán
Poncitlán
Zapotlán del Rey
Juanacatlán
El Salto
Zapotlanejo
Tototlán
Atotonilco el Alto
Ayotlán
Arandas
Jesús María
Pénjamo
Cuerámaro
Manuel Doblado
Tepatitlán de Morelos
San Agustín
Acatic
Capilla de Guadalupe
Valle de Guadalupe
San Miguel el Alto
San Julián
San Diego de Alejandría
Unión de San Antonio
San Francisco del Rincón
Purísima de Bustos
La Muralla
Cuquío
Ixtlahuacán del Río
San Cristóbal de la Barranca
Yahualica de González Gallo
Cañadas de Villa Obregón
Jalostotitlán
San Juan de los Lagos
Lagos de Moreno
Mexticacán
Nochistlán de Mejía
Teocaltiche
Juchipila
Moyahua de Estrada
García de la Cadena
Mezquital del Oro
Huitzila
Teúl de González Ortega
Ignacio Allende
Apozol
ZACATECAS
Benito Juárez
Tlaltenango de Sánchez Román
Tepechitlán
Jalpa
Atolinga
Momax
Joaquín Amaro
Huanusco
Tabasco
Calvillo
Jesús María
AGUASCALIENTES
Aguascalientes
Palo Alto
Ojuelos de Jalisco
Encarnación de Díaz
El Puesto
Paso de Cuarenta
Villa Hidalgo
San Pedro Apulco
LEÓN
Middle America Trench
PACIFIC OCEAN
Projection : Lambert's Conformal Conic

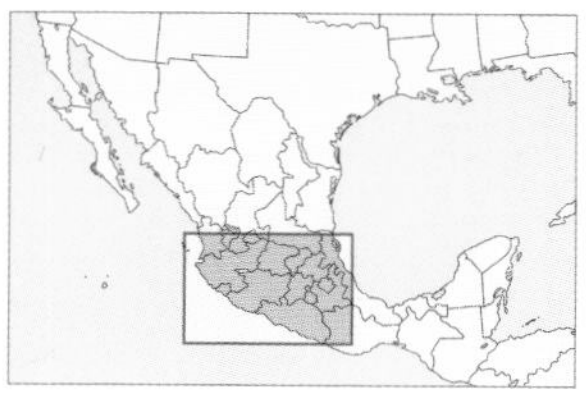

1. PARQUE NACIONAL CERRO DE LA ESTRELLA
2. PARQUE NACIONAL LA MARQUESA
3. PARQUE NACIONAL LAGUNAS DE ZEMPOALA
4. PARQUE NACIONAL DESIERTO DEL CARMEN

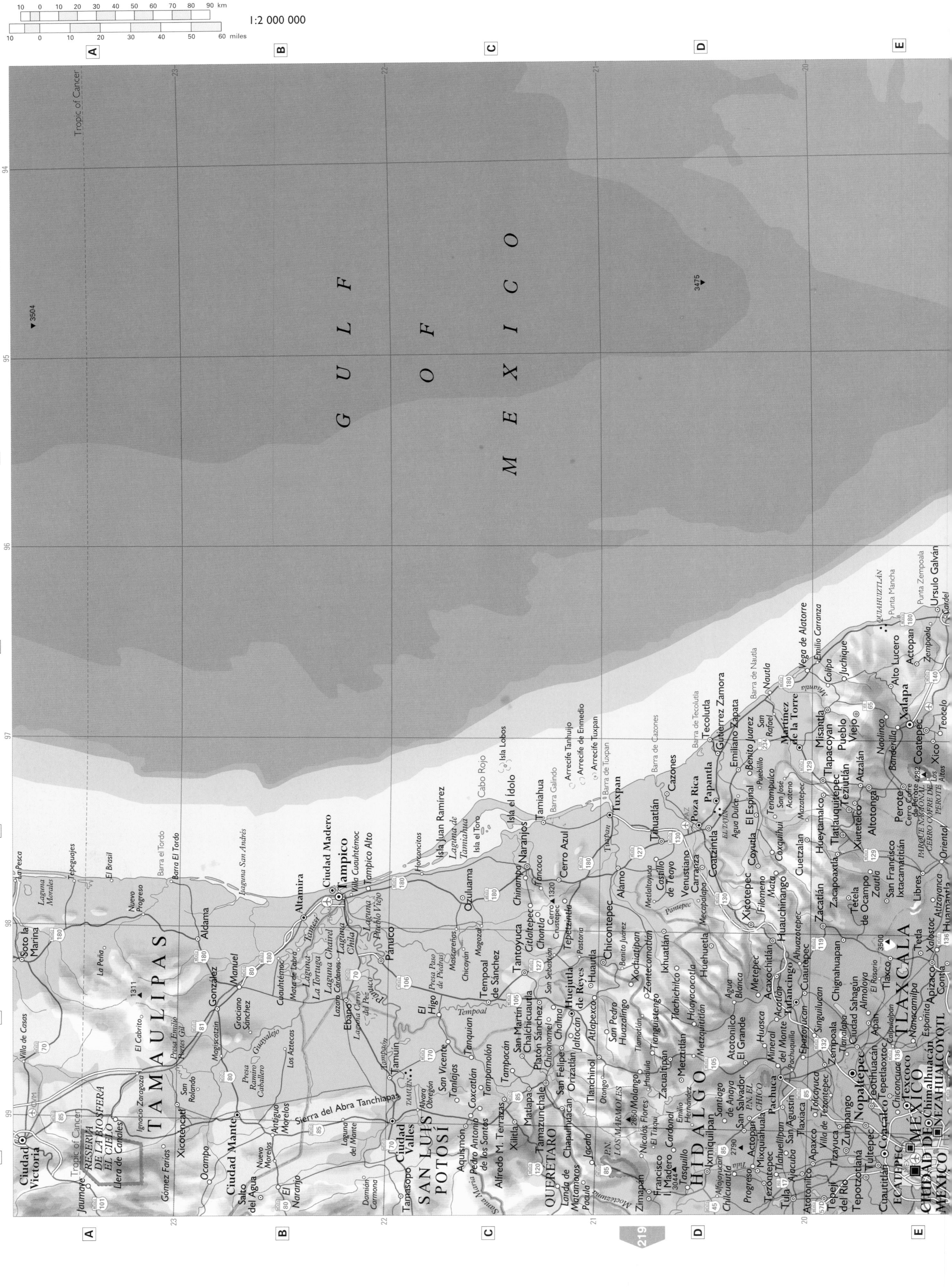
1:2 000 000
km
miles
Tropic of Cancer
GULF OF MEXICO
3504
3475
TAMAULIPAS
SAN LUIS POTOSÍ
QUERÉTARO
HIDALGO
TLAXCALA
MÉXICO
CIUDAD DE MÉXICO
Ciudad Victoria
Soto la Marina
Ciudad Mante
Ciudad Valles
Altamira
Ciudad Madero
Tampico
Pánuco
Tuxpan
Poza Rica
Papantla
Tamiahua
Cabo Rojo
Isla Lobos
Xalapa
Coatepec
Perote
Tlaxco
Apizaco
Pachuca
Tulancingo
Tula
Texcoco
Teotihuacán
Huejutla de Reyes
Tamazunchale
Sierra del Abra Tanchipa
Laguna de Tamiahua
Vega de Alatorre
Martínez de la Torre
Teziutlán
Zacatlán
Huauchinango
Xicotepec
Actopan
Ixmiquilpan
Nopaltepec
Zumpango
Ecatepec
Nezahualcóyotl
Chimalhuacán
Cerro Cofre de Perote 4282

219

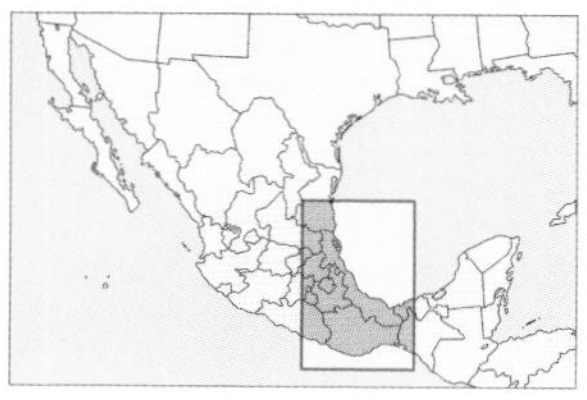

222
219
F
G
H
J
K
1
2
3
4
5
6
7
Bahía de Campeche
VERACRUZ
PUEBLA
MORELOS
GUERRERO
OAXACA
TABASCO
CHIAPAS
Istmo de Tehuantepec
Golfo de Tehuantepec
PACIFIC OCEAN
Middle America Trench
Sierra Madre del Sur
Sierra Madre de Chiapas
Región de los Chimalapas
Oaxaca
Puebla
Veracruz
Coatzacoalcos
Minatitlán
Acayucan
Juchitán de Zaragoza
Salina Cruz
Tehuantepec
Puerto Escondido
Pochutla
Tuxtepec
Orizaba
Córdoba
Tehuacán
Cuernavaca
Huajuapan de León
Tlaxiaco
Pinotepa Nacional
Tonalá
Arriaga
Cintalapa
Ixtepec
Matías Romero
Projection : Lambert's Conformal Conic
West from Greenwich
COPYRIGHT PHILIP'S

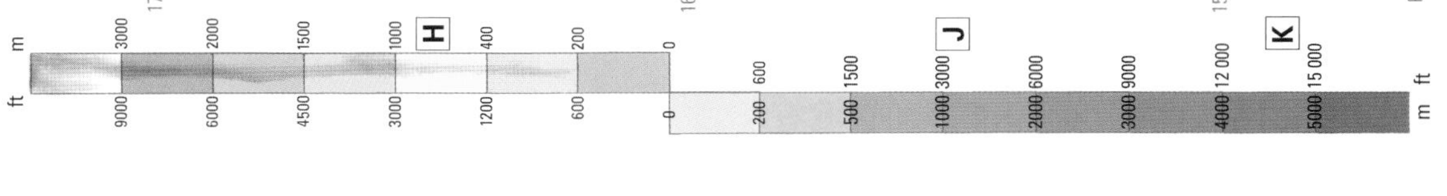
m
ft
3000
2000
1500
1000
400
200
0
9000
6000
4500
3000
1200
600
200
500
1000
2000
3000
4000
5000
600
1500
3000
6000
9000
12 000
15 000

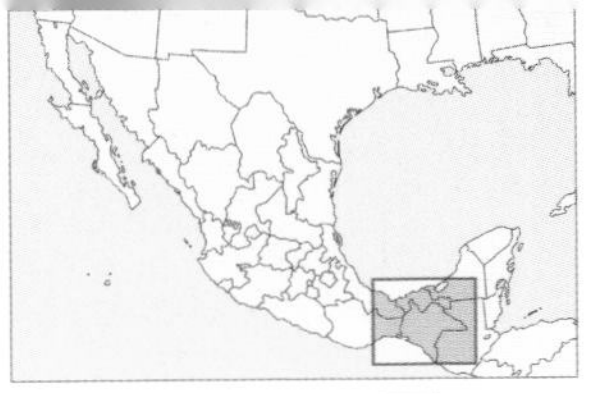

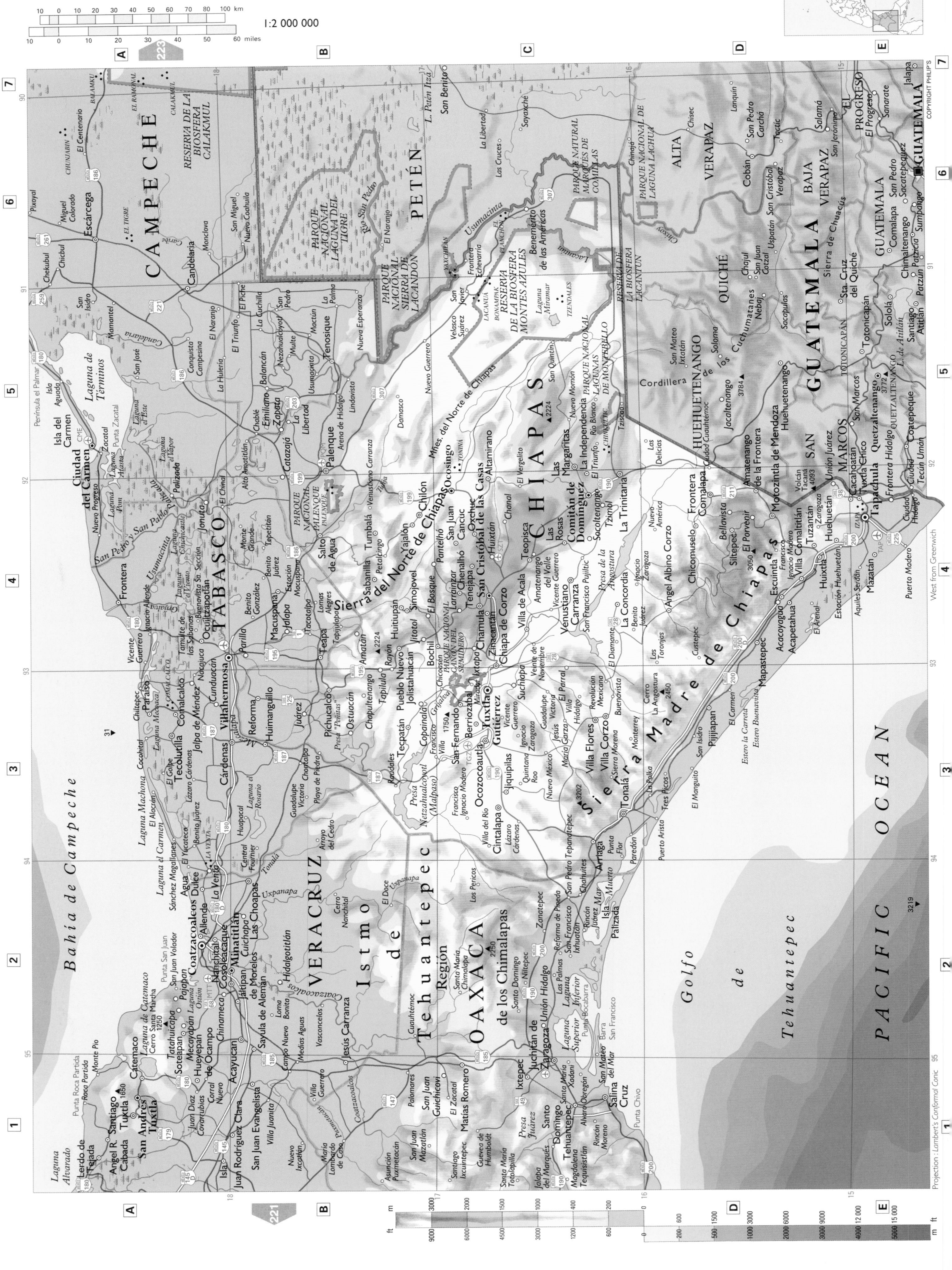
1:2 000 000
10 0 10 20 30 40 50 60 70 80 100 km
10 0 10 20 30 40 50 60 miles
Bahía de Campeche
CAMPECHE
RESERVA DE LA BIOSFERA CALAKMUL
Escárcega
Candelaria
Ciudad del Carmen
Isla del Carmen
Laguna de Términos
TABASCO
Villahermosa
Frontera
Cárdenas
Comalcalco
Paraíso
Macuspana
Teapa
Tenosique
Emiliano Zapata
Palenque
PARQUE NACIONAL PALENQUE
VERACRUZ
Coatzacoalcos
Minatitlán
Acayucan
San Andrés Tuxtla
Catemaco
Laguna de Catemaco
Istmo de Tehuantepec
OAXACA
Juchitán de Zaragoza
Salina Cruz
Santo Domingo Tehuantepec
Golfo de Tehuantepec
PACIFIC OCEAN
CHIAPAS
Tuxtla Gutiérrez
Chiapa de Corzo
San Cristóbal de las Casas
Comitán de Domínguez
Ocosingo
Tonalá
Arriaga
Tapachula
Sierra Madre de Chiapas
Sierra del Norte de Chiapas
Mtes. del Norte de Chiapas
PARQUE NACIONAL CAÑÓN DEL SUMIDERO
Presa Netzahualcóyotl (Malpaso)
RESERVA DE LA BIOSFERA MONTES AZULES
PARQUE NACIONAL LAGUNAS DE MONTEBELLO
PETÉN
PARQUE NACIONAL LAGUNA DEL TIGRE
PARQUE NACIONAL SIERRA DE LACANDÓN
GUATEMALA
HUEHUETENANGO
QUICHÉ
ALTA VERAPAZ
BAJA VERAPAZ
SAN MARCOS
Cobán
Quetzaltenango
Tajumulco 4220
Usumacinta
Grijalva
West from Greenwich
Projection: Lambert's Conformal Conic
COPYRIGHT PHILIP'S

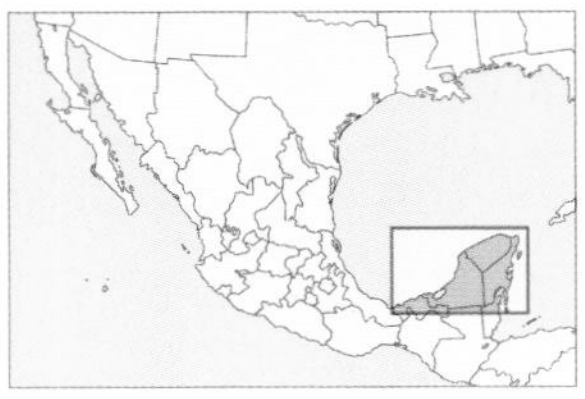

1:2 000 000

10 0 10 20 30 40 50 60 70 80 100 km

10 0 10 20 30 40 50 60 miles

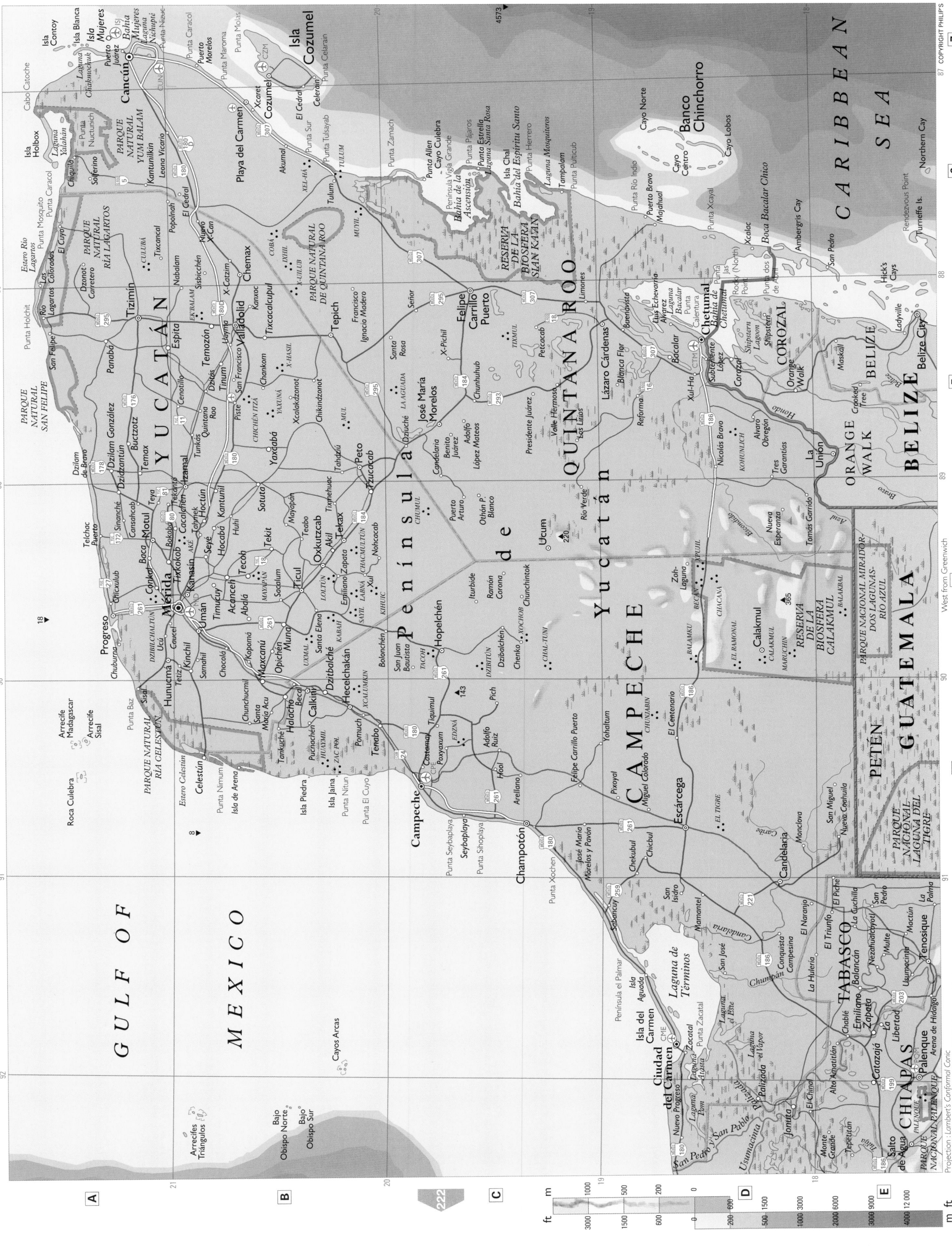

222

GUADALAJARA

0 km 5
0 miles 3

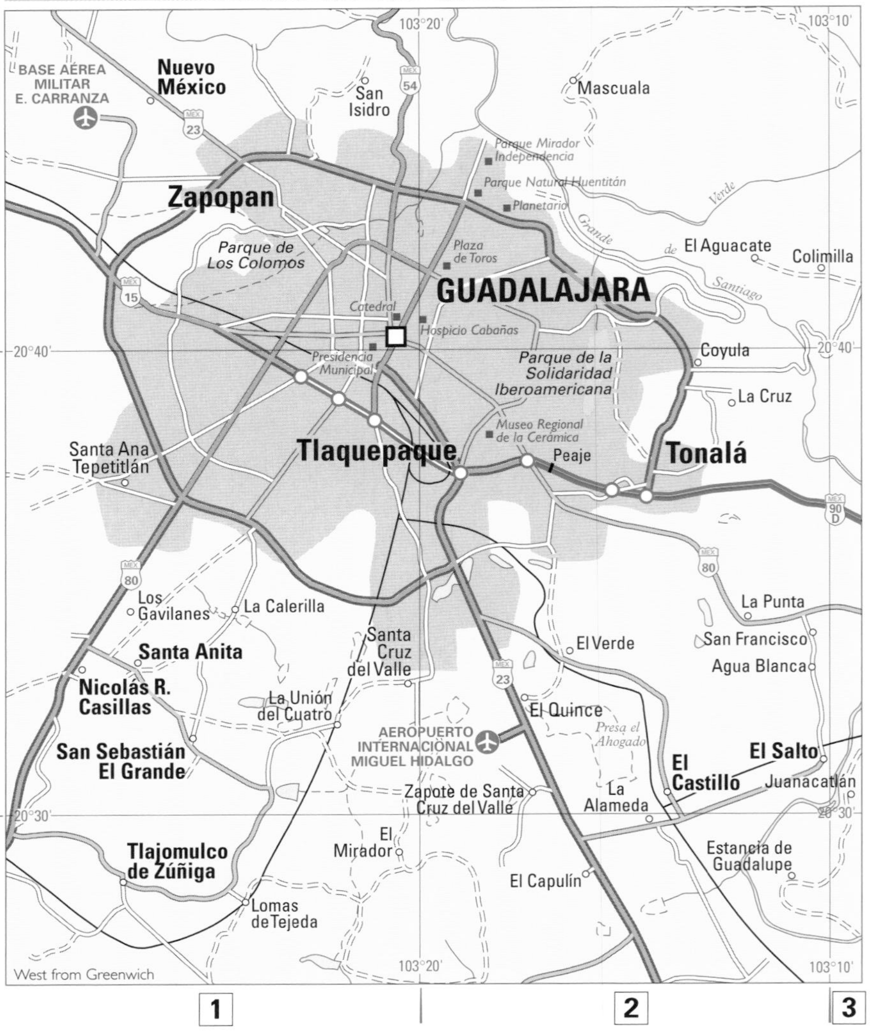

MONTERREY

0 km 5
0 miles 3

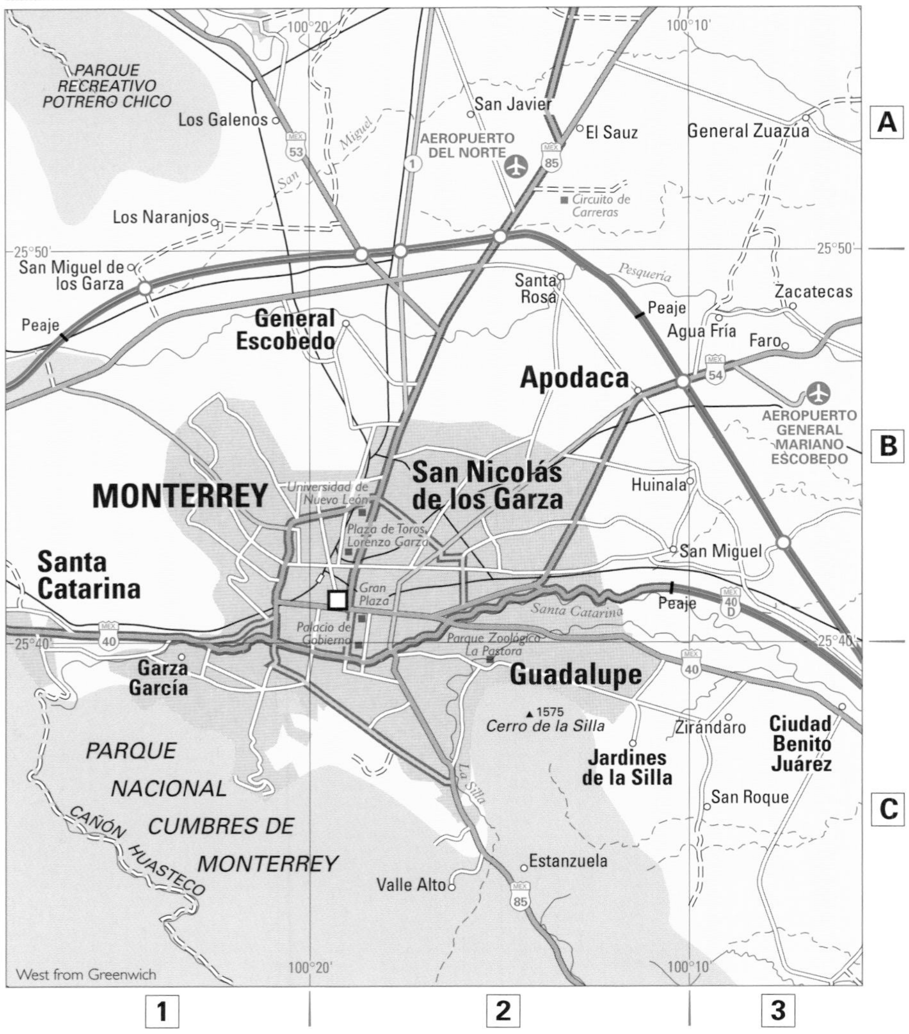

CENTRAL MEXICO CITY

0 km 1
0 miles 0.5

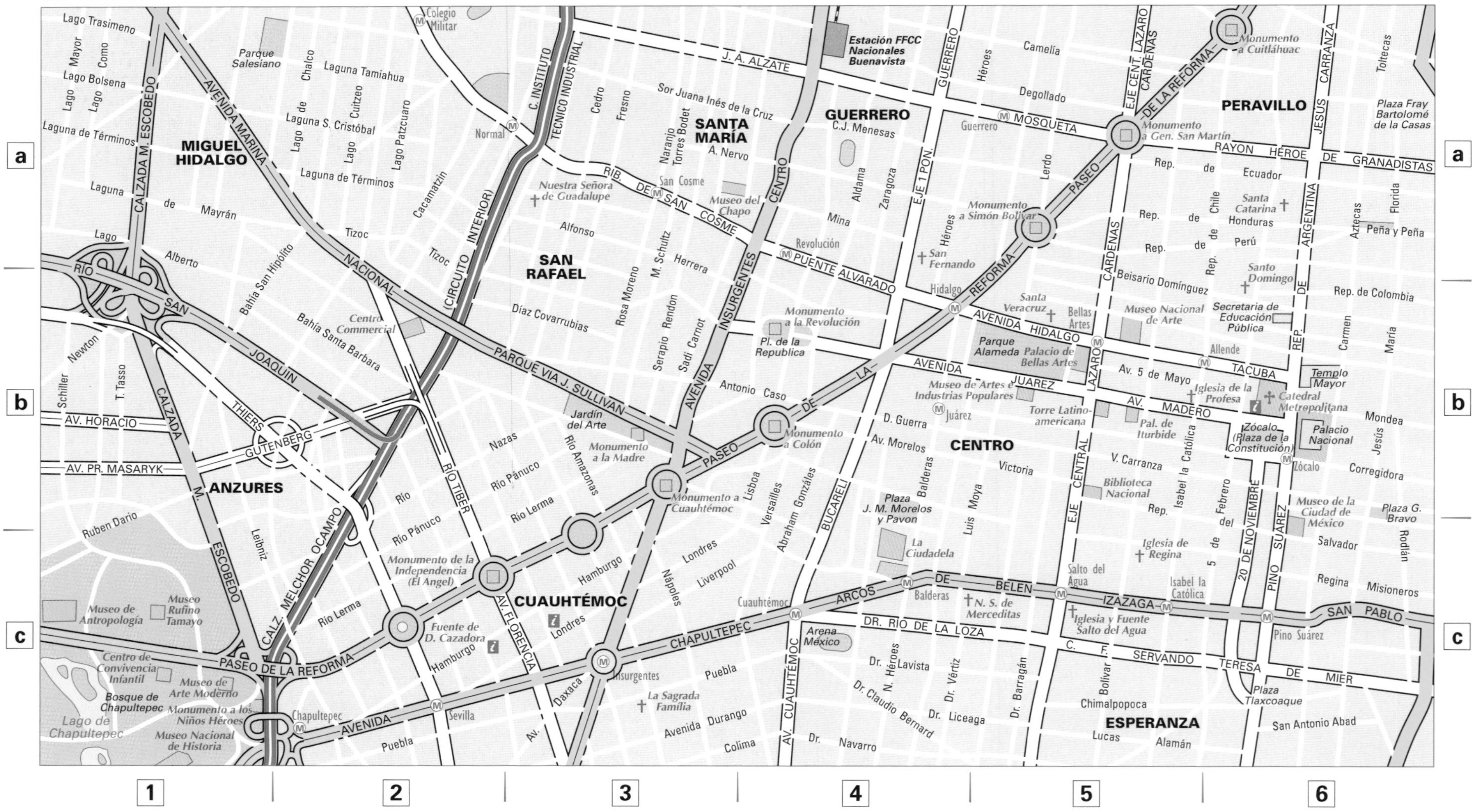

MEXICO CITY

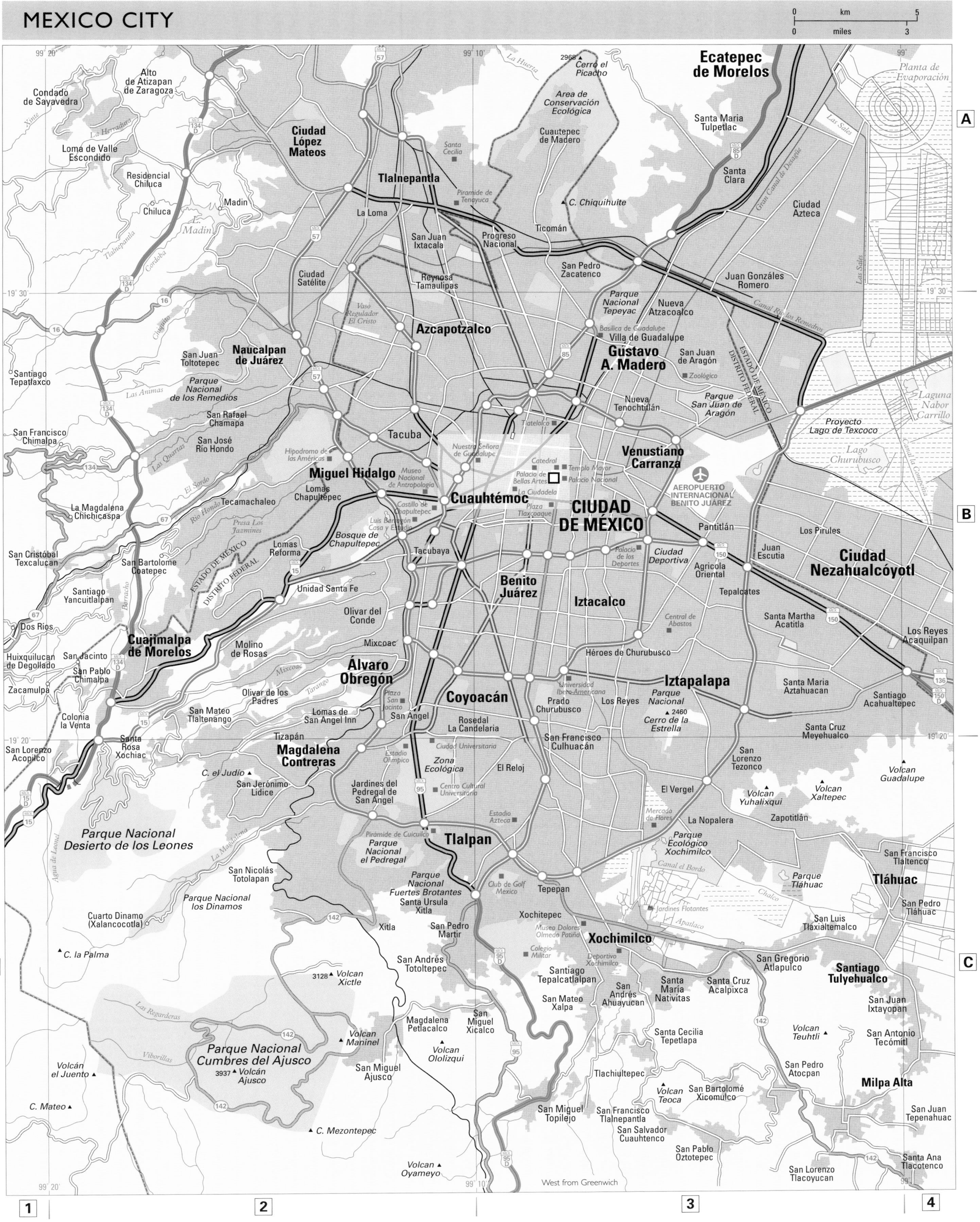
0 km 5
0 miles 3
99° 20'
99° 10'
99°
19° 30'
19° 20'
A
B
C
1
2
3
4
Condado de Sayavedra
Alto de Atizapan de Zaragoza
Loma de Valle Escondido
Residencial Chiluca
Chiluca
Madin
Ciudad López Mateos
Tlalnepantla
La Loma
San Juan Ixtacala
Progreso Nacional
Ticomán
Santa Cecilia
Pirámide de Tenayuca
2968 Cerro el Picacho
Area de Conservación Ecológica
Cuautepec de Madero
C. Chiquihuite
Ecatepec de Morelos
Santa Maria Tulpetlac
Santa Clara
Ciudad Azteca
Planta de Evaporación
Las Salas
Gran Canal de Desagüe
Juan Gonzáles Romero
Canal Río Los Remedios
Ciudad Satélite
Reynosa Tamaulipas
San Pedro Zacatenco
Parque Nacional Tepeyac
Nueva Atzacoalco
Vaso Regulador El Cristo
Azcapotzalco
Basílica de Guadalupe
Villa de Guadalupe
Gustavo A. Madero
San Juan de Aragón
Zoológico
Parque San Juan de Aragón
ESTADO DE MÉXICO
DISTRITO FEDERAL
Laguna Nabor Carrillo
Proyecto Lago de Texcoco
Lago Churubusco
Canal de la Compañía
Naucalpan de Juárez
San Juan Toltotepec
Santiago Tepatlaxco
Parque Nacional de los Remedios
Las Animas
San Rafael Chamapa
San José Rio Hondo
San Francisco Chimalpa
Las Cuartas
El Sordo
Nueva Tenochtitlán
Tlatelolco
Tacuba
Hipódromo de las Américas
Nuestra Señora de Guadalupe
Venustiano Carranza
Miguel Hidalgo
Museo Nacional de Antropología
Catedral
Templo Mayor
Palacio de Bellas Artes
Palacio Nacional
La Ciudadela
Cuauhtémoc
AEROPUERTO INTERNACIONAL BENITO JUÁREZ
Lomas Chapultepec
Tecamachaleo
La Magdalena Chichicaspa
Rio Hondo
Presa Los Jazmines
Castillo de Chapultepec
Luis Barragán Casa y Estudio
Bosque de Chapultepec
Plaza Tlaxcoaque
CIUDAD DE MÉXICO
Pantitlán
Los Pirules
San Cristóbal Texcalucan
San Bartolome Coatepec
Lomas Reforma
Tacubaya
Palacio de los Deportes
Ciudad Deportiva
Agrícola Oriental
Juan Escutia
Ciudad Nezahualcóyotl
Santiago Yancuitlalpan
Barranca
Unidad Santa Fe
Benito Juárez
Iztacalco
Tepalcates
Olivar del Conde
Central de Abastos
Santa Martha Acatitla
Dos Rios
Cuajimalpa de Morelos
Molino de Rosas
Mixcoac
Héroes de Churubusco
Los Reyes Acaquilpan
Huixquilucan de Degollado
San Jacinto
San Pablo Chimalpa
Zacamulpa
Álvaro Obregón
Universidad Ibero-Americana
Iztapalapa
Santa Maria Aztahuacan
Santiago Acahualtepec
Olivar de los Padres
Tarango
Plaza San Jacinto
Coyoacán
Prado Churubusco
Los Reyes
Parque Nacional
2460 Cerro de la Estrella
Colonia la Venta
San Mateo Tlaltenango
Lomas de San Angel Inn
San Angel
Rosedal La Candelaria
Santa Cruz Meyehualco
Santa Rosa Xochiac
San Lorenzo Acopilco
Tizapán
San Francisco Culhuacán
Magdalena Contreras
Estadio Olímpico
Ciudad Universitaria
Zona Ecológica
El Reloj
San Lorenzo Tezonco
Volcan Guadalupe
C. el Judío
San Jerónimo Lidice
Jardines del Pedregal de San Angel
Centro Cultural Universitario
El Vergel
Volcan Yuhalixqui
Volcan Xaltepec
Estadio Azteca
Mercado de Flores
La Nopalera
Zapotitlán
Parque Nacional Desierto de los Leones
Pirámide de Cuicuilco
Parque Nacional el Pedregal
Tlalpan
Parque Ecológico Xochimilco
San Francisco Tlaltenco
Agua de Leonal
La Magdalena
San Nicolás Totolapan
Parque Nacional Fuertes Brotantes
Club de Golf Mexico
Tepepan
Canal el Bordo
Parque Tláhuac
Tláhuac
Parque Nacional los Dinamos
Santa Ursula Xitla
Chalco
Jardines Flotantes
San Pedro Tláhuac
Cuarto Dinamo (Xalancocotla)
Xitla
San Pedro Martir
Xochitepec
Museo Dolores Olmedo Patiño
Xochimilco
Apatlaco
San Luis Tlaxialtemalco
C. la Palma
San Andrés Totoltepec
Colegio Militar
Deportivo Xochimilco
San Gregorio Atlapulco
Santiago Tulyehualco
3128 Volcan Xictle
Santiago Tepalcatlalpan
San Andrés Ahuayucan
Santa María Nativitas
Santa Cruz Acalpixca
San Juan Ixtayopan
Las Regaderas
San Mateo Xalpa
San Miguel Xicalco
Magdalena Petlacalco
Volcan Maninel
Santa Cecilia Tepetlapa
Volcan Teuhtli
San Antonio Tecómitl
Parque Nacional Cumbres del Ajusco
Viborillas
Volcan Ololizqui
Volcán el Juento
3937 Volcán Ajusco
San Miguel Ajusco
Tlachiultepec
San Pedro Atocpan
Volcan Teoca
San Bartolomé Xicomulco
Milpa Alta
C. Mateo
San Miguel Topilejo
San Francisco Tlalnepantla
San Juan Tepenahuac
C. Mezontepec
San Salvador Cuauhtenco
San Pablo Oztotepec
Volcan Oyameyo
San Lorenzo Tlacoyucan
Santa Ana Tlacotenco
West from Greenwich
La Huerta
Xinte
La Herradura
Tlalnepantla
Cordoba
Chiquito
Mixcoac
57
134 D
16
85
15
67
150
136
142
95
95 D

Baja California & Baja California Sur

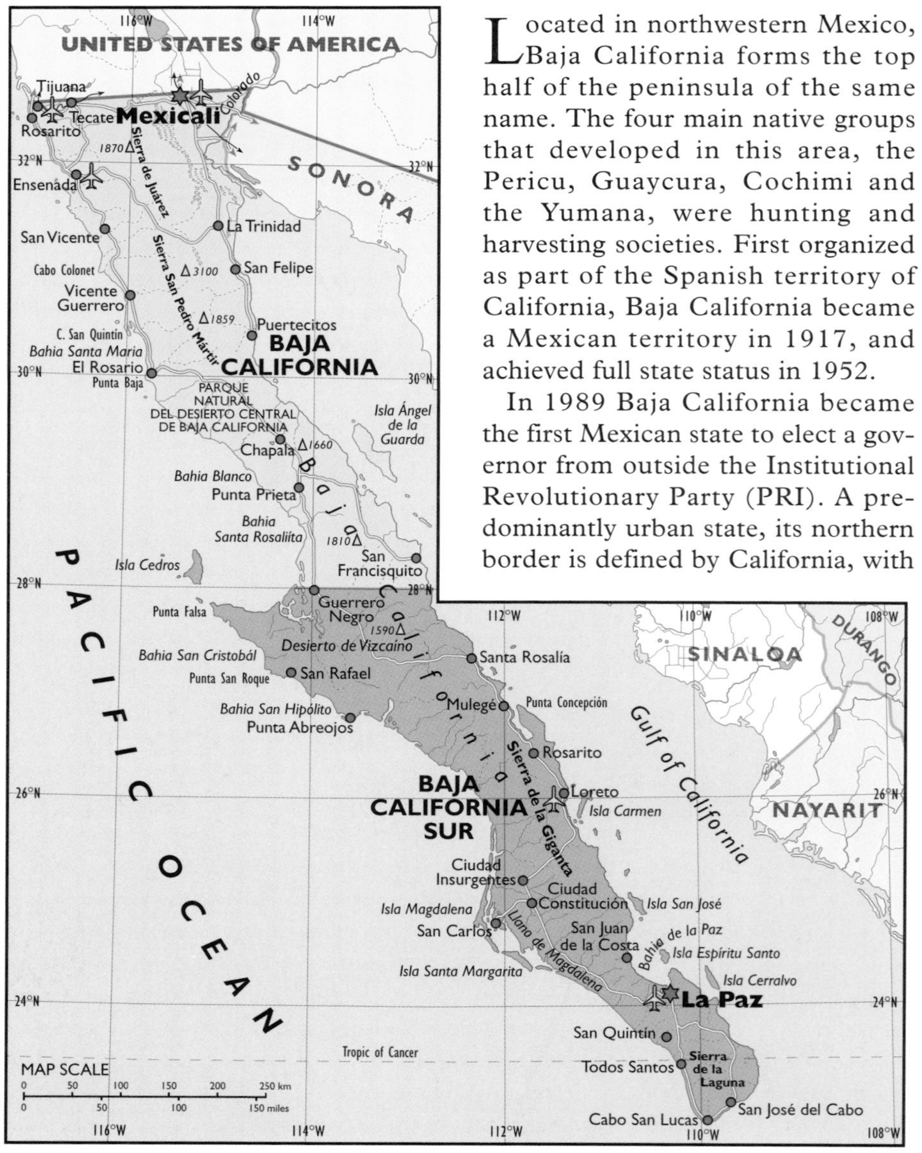

Located in northwestern Mexico, Baja California forms the top half of the peninsula of the same name. The four main native groups that developed in this area, the Pericu, Guaycura, Cochimi and the Yumana, were hunting and harvesting societies. First organized as part of the Spanish territory of California, Baja California became a Mexican territory in 1917, and achieved full state status in 1952.

In 1989 Baja California became the first Mexican state to elect a governor from outside the Institutional Revolutionary Party (PRI). A predominantly urban state, its northern border is defined by California, with the Pacific Ocean to the west and the Gulf of California on the east. The Colorado River forms the northeastern boundary with the state of Sonora. In a state with only five municipalities, Tijuana and Ensenada are the largest cities along with Mexicali, the capital. The northern border region of the state has a large concentration of *maquiladoras*, assembly plants for components made in the United States and overseas. Rapid industrial development in the twentieth century has brought environmental problems to this region. In addition to *maquiladoras*, limited cotton and wheat production, tourism from the United States as well as commercial fishing, generate the most income for Baja California.

Mexicali, the state capital of Baja California, sits opposite Calexico, California, northeast of the Sierra de Juárez mountains. It has many *maquiladoras*, serves as a trade center for the surrounding agricultural region, and employs a large percentage of the local population in tourist-related activities.

The southern half of the peninsula of Baja California is Baja California Sur, the least populated state in Mexico. It shares a native heritage with its northern neighbor, although separated by the Vizcaíno desert. In 1930 Baja California Sur separated from the territory of Baja California and later became a state of five municipalities in 1974. The state capital and largest city is La Paz followed by Loreto, while San José del Cabo and Cabo San Lucas on the southern tip of the peninsula are international tourist centers. To the east, the state includes several large islands such as Isla San José and Isla Espíritu Santo, both in the Gulf of California. Running parallel to the East Coast, the forested Sierra de la Giganta mountains fade into the fertile Magdalena Plain in the west.

Contrasting with its northern neighbor, Baja California Sur is predominantly agricultural. Cotton, olives, sugarcane, and wheat grow in the southern Santo Domingo Valley while tourism, tuna and sardine fishing, and salt processing comprise the chief industries.

Seeking an island rich in pearls, Hernán Cortés explored the area around La Paz in 1535, but its remote location, arid terrain and native resistance prevented any significant development for over a century. Now a fishing and pearling center, the state capital of Baja California Sur is also a popular winter resort for tourists lured to the beautiful beaches on the Bahía de la Paz.

Baja California & Baja California Sur at a Glance

People	BJ	BS	Mexico
Population, 2000	2,487,367	424,041	97,483,412
Population percent change, 1990–2000	4.1%	2.9%	1.8%
Persons under 5 years old, percent, 2000	10.8%	10.8%	10.9%
Persons under 15 years old, percent, 2000	30.4%	31.8%	33.4%
Persons 65 years old and over, percent, 2000	3.5%	3.9%	4.9%
Female persons, percent, 2000	49.6%	49.0%	51.2%
Percentage of population age 5+ that speaks Spanish, 2000	92.5%	93.1%	81.5%
Persons age 5+ that speak an indigenous language	37,685	5,353	6,044,547
Mixtec speakers, percent, 2000	31.7%	36.5%	7.4%
Zapotec speakers, percent, 2000	7.9%	11.3%	7.5%
Náhuatl speakers, percent, 2000	5.7%	18.4%	24.0%
Purepecha/Amuzgo speakers, percent, 2000	5.6%	2.4%	2% / 0.7%
Triqui speakers, percent, 2000	3.8%	2.1%	NA
Other indigenous language speakers, percent, 2000	19.2%	20.4%	4.2%
Completed primary education, percent of persons age 15+, 2000 (a)	18.0%	17.4%	19.4%
Completed post-primary education, percent of persons age 15+, 2000 (b)	23.0%	20.1%	19.1%
Persons with a disability	35,103	6,835	1,795,300

(a) Includes persons having passed 6 years of elementary school
(b) Includes persons having passed 3 years of high school
NA: Not available
Source: (INEGI) El Instituto Nacional de Estadística, Geografía e Informática

People (cont.)	BJ	BS	Mexico
Housing units, 2000	559,402	101,341	21,513,235
Units with floor other than earth, percent, 2000	95.8%	89.9%	86.7%
Units with durable roofing materials, percent, 2000	34.5%	58.5%	64.2%
Units with durable wall materials, percent, 2000	67.8%	82.4%	79.3%
Homeownership rate, 2000	72.4%	75.4%	78.3%
Households, 2000	568,090	107,009	22,268,916
Average number of persons per housing unit, 2000	4.1	4	4.4

Business	BJ	BS	Mexico
Agricultural employment, percent, 2003	4.8%	20.1%	NA
Industrial employment, percent, 2003	22.7%	9.9%	NA
Construction employment, percent, 2003	5.3%	4.4%	NA
Retail employment, percent, 2003	19.1%	16.7%	NA
Communication and transportation employment, percent, 2003	4.5%	4.3%	NA
Government employment, percent, 2003	4.0%	10.0%	NA
Social, financial and professional service employment, percent, 2003	14.0%	13.0%	NA
Service employment, percent, 2003	19.5%	21.6%	NA
Total workforce participation, percent, 2003	47.4%	48.4%	42.6%
Male workforce participation, percent, 2003	65.3%	67.3%	65.7%
Female workforce participation, percent, 2003	34.7%	32.7%	34.3%

Geography	BJ	BS	Mexico
Land area, 2000 (square kilometers)	71,505	73,948	1,958,200
Persons per square kilometer, 2000	35	6	50

Sinaloa & Sonora

A long and narrow state, Sinaloa consists primarily of a fertile coastal plain between the ocean and the Sierra Madre Occidental range. Indigenous groups such as the Cahitas, Tahues, and the Tortorames based their way of life on the local resources before Spanish conquest and Sinaloa became a state in 1830. The Fuerte and Sinaloa Rivers are the longest waterways in this state of 18 municipalities. Major cities like Los Mochis, Guasave and Guamúchil are clustered north of Culiacán Rosales, the capital.

Government subsidies and dam-building greatly enhanced agricultural output after World War II and today it is a top producer of vegetable and cereal crops. Sinaloa also falls within Mexico's leading fishing region along the Gulf of California and shrimp, sea bass and oysters are harvested commercially. With its appealing combination of natural beauty, colorful art and architecture and fascinating archeological remains, tourism is significant source of income for the state, notably in Mazatlán.

Originally a Colhua settlement, the modern city of Culiacán Rosales was founded on the River Culiacán, in western Mexico in 1531 by Spanish conquistador Nuño Beltran de Guzmán. The base for Francisco de Coronado's expedition to the Gulf of California in 1540, a railroad junction and a road hub on the western branch of the Pan-American Highway, the city is a commercial and trading center for the surrounding mining and agricultural area. As a tourist destination, Culiacán is noted for the Rosales Gardens of tropical plants.

The second largest Mexican state after Chihuahua, Sonora is named for the bell-like sound produced by striking the local marble deposits. Explored by Spain in the 1530s, Sonora became part of the northern frontier of the Viceroyalty of New Spain and achieved statehood in 1830. In the late nineteenth and early twentieth centuries, it was the scene of a prolonged rebellion by the Yaqui tribe. A state of seventy-two municipalities, Sonora includes a narrow coastal plain along the western coastline of the Gulf of California and a vast interior desert bordering Arizona and New Mexico known as the Gran Desierto. The state's major rivers, the Sonora, the Yaqui, and the Mayo, drain into the Pacific. After Hermosillo, the capital, the largest cities include Nogales, Agua Prieta, Ciudad Obregón, Guaymas, Navojoa, and San Luis Río Colorado. Sonora is the leading copper-mining center in Mexico and the most extensively irrigated region of the country growing cotton, grains, and winter vegetables. In addition to supporting businesses related to fishing, food processing and textiles, Sonora has many *maquiladoras*, or assembly plants, along the United States border.

Hermosillo, the state capital, was created at the entrance to the Sonora River gorge in 1700 for the resettlement of the Pima people. Today the city is a transportation hub surrounded by cattle, cotton and grain farming. Hermosillo is also developing into a major automobile assembly and parts producing center with its Ford assembly plant slated for massive expansion.

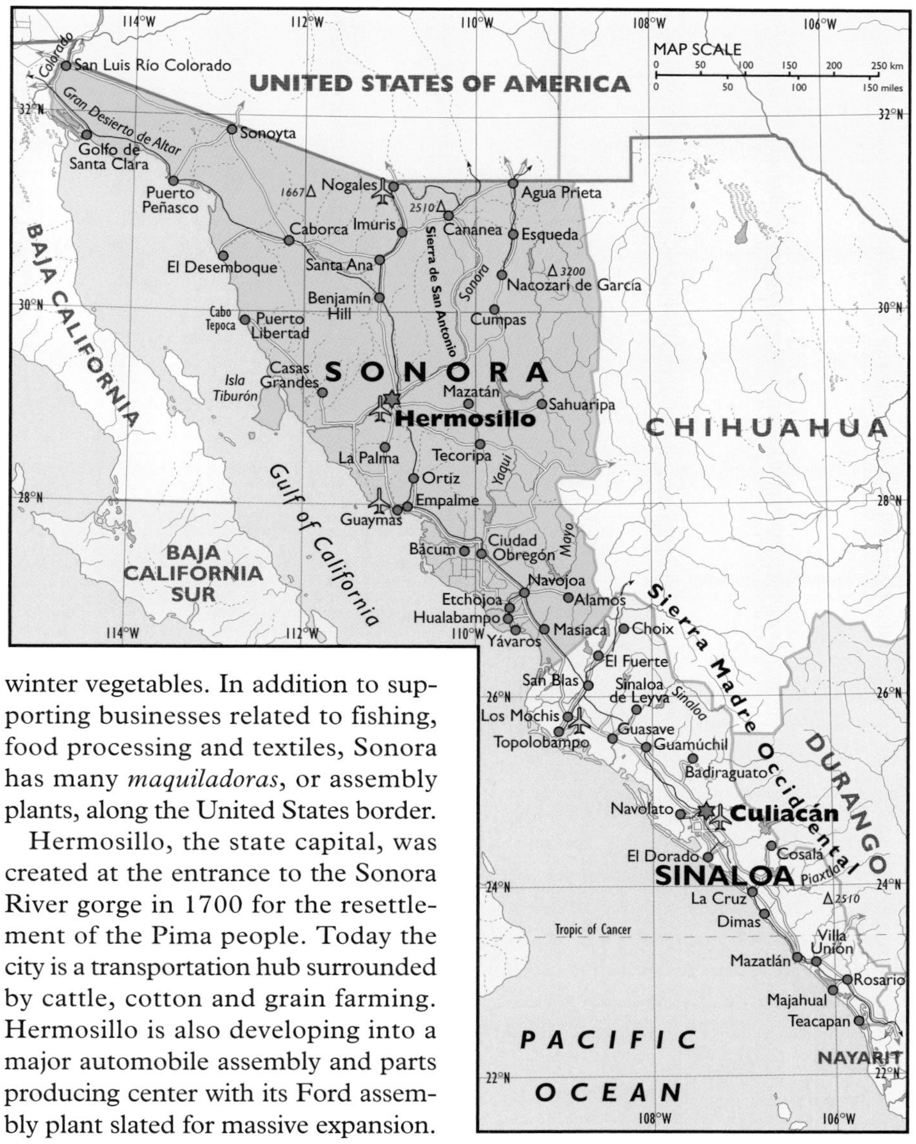

Sinaloa & Sonora at a Glance

People	**SI**	**SO**	**Mexico**
Population, 2000	2,536,844	2,216,969	97,483,412
Population percent change, 1990-2000	1.4%	2.0%	1.8%
Persons under 5 years old, percent, 2000	11.0%	11.0%	10.9%
Persons under 15 years old, percent, 2000	33.7%	32.4%	33.4%
Persons 65 years old and over, percent, 2000	4.9%	4.7%	4.9%
Female persons, percent, 2000	50.2%	49.9%	51.2%
Percentage of population age 5+ that speaks Spanish, 2000	84.5%	95.3%	81.5%
Persons age 5+ that speak an indigenous language	49,744	55,694	6,044,547
Mixteco/Mayo speakers, percent, 2000	27.6%	43.3%	7.4% / 0.5%
Mayo/Yaqui speakers, percent, 2000	13.8%	22.4%	0.5% / 0.2%
Náhuatl/Maya speakers, percent, 2000	13.0%	3.4%	24% / 13.2%
Zapoteco/Mixteco speakers, percent, 2000	10.1%	2.8%	7.5% / 7.4%
Tlapaneco/Náhuatl speakers, percent, 2000	5.8%	2.2%	1.6% / 24%
Other indigenous language speakers, percent, 2000	17.8%	10.3%	4.2%
Completed primary education, percent of persons age 15+, 2000 (a)	17.2%	16.5%	19.4%
Completed post-primary education, percent of persons age 15+, 2000 (b)	15.3%	21.1%	19.1%
Persons with a disability	48,370	42,022	1,795,300

(a) Includes persons having passed 6 years of elementary school
(b) Includes persons having passed 3 years of high school
NA: Not available
Source: (INEGI) El Instituto Nacional de Estadística, Geografía e Informática

People (cont.)	**SI**	**SO**	**Mexico**
Housing units, 2000	572,816	527,427	21,513,235
Units with floor other than earth, percent, 2000	86.2%	87.6%	86.7%
Units with durable roofing materials, percent, 2000	83.5%	59.4%	64.2%
Units with durable wall materials, percent, 2000	88.4%	80.9%	79.3%
Homeownership rate, 2000	83.3%	81.8%	78.3%
Households, 2000	585,943	535,743	22,268,916
Average number of persons per housing unit, 2000	4.4	4.1	4.4

Business	**SI**	**SO**	**Mexico**
Agricultural employment, percent, 2003	26.4%	11.2%	NA
Industrial employment, percent, 2003	10.8%	19.9%	NA
Construction employment, percent, 2003	5.7%	6.2%	NA
Retail employment, percent, 2003	21.6%	21.3%	NA
Communication and transportation employment, percent, 2003	2.8%	3.0%	NA
Government employment, percent, 2003	3.8%	6.1%	NA
Social, financial and professional service employment, percent, 2003	11.0%	13.1%	NA
Service employment, percent, 2003	17.3%	18.4%	NA
Total workforce participation, percent, 2003	44.9%	42.5%	42.6%
Male workforce participation, percent, 2003	64.0%	62.4%	65.7%
Female workforce participation, percent, 2003	36.0%	37.6%	34.3%

Geography	**SI**	**SO**	**Mexico**
Land area, 2000 (square kilometers)	58,328	182,052	1,958,200
Persons per square kilometer, 2000	44	12	50

Chihuahua & Coahuila

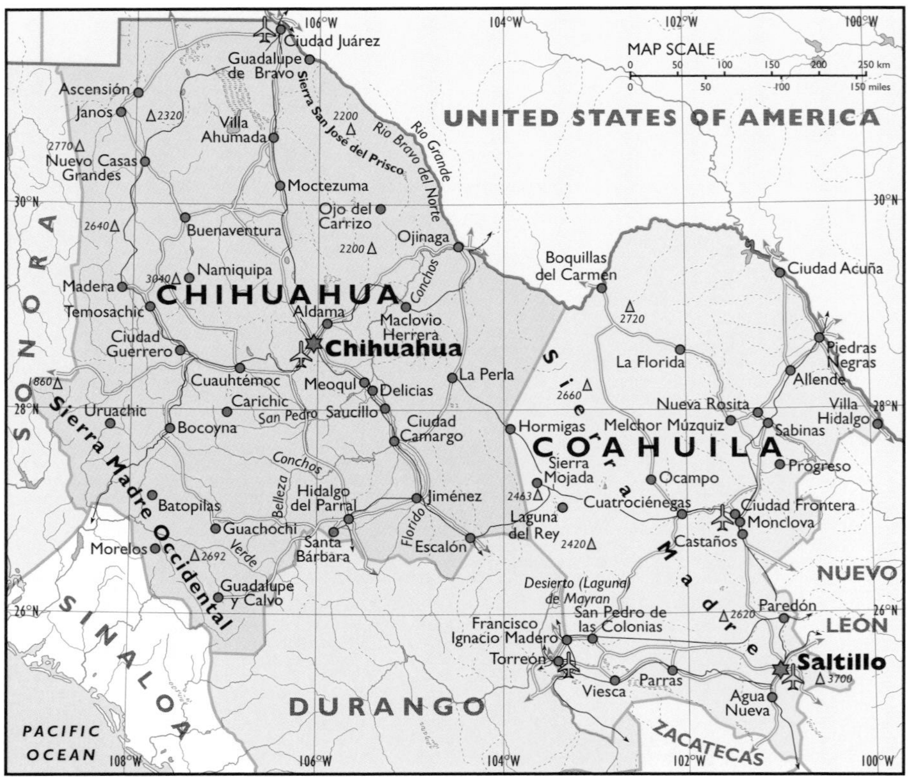

Situated on the northern part of the Mexican plateau, bordering the states of Texas and Arizona, Chihuahua is the largest state in Mexico and contains 67 municipalities. The modern population, which displaced the native Concho and Zacatec that first inhabited the area, is concentrated in large cities, particularly in Ojinaga and Ciudad Juárez along the Río Bravo, but also in the capital, Chihuahua. The climate and terrain vary from cool mountains in the west, where Basaseachic, the highest waterfall in the country can be found, to the arid Llanos de los Gigantes and the desert landscapes in the east. Mining, forestry, tourism, and cotton growing are the biggest industries.

The city and capital that gives its name to a small breed of dog was founded in 1709 at the heart of a rich mining and lumbering area. Chihuahua is also where Miguel Hidalgo y Costilla, father of Mexican independence, was executed in 1811.

Coahuila is Mexico's third largest state by area after Chihuahua and Sonora, filling the territory between the Río Bravo in the north and Durango and Zacatecas in the south. Settled by the Spanish in the 1570s, Coahuila and Texas were established as a single Mexican state in 1824 but Texas seceded to form the independent Republic of Texas in 1836. After the Mexican-American War, Mexico lost all of its territory north of the Río Grande to the U.S. and in 1868 Coahuila became a state of Mexico. Nearly 50 years later, the Mexican Revolution began in Coahuila. Split into 38 municipalities, Saltillo, the capital, is located in the south, a considerable distance from the other urban centers: Piedras Negras and Ciudad Acuña on the U.S. border. Largely an arid plateau region that is prone to drought, the rugged Sierra Madre Occidental range crosses the state from north to south. In addition to ferrous mining and metallurgy, Caohuila has two large assembly plants operated by Daimler-Chrysler and General Motors. In the southwest, the agricultural region of La Laguna is one of the most productive in Mexico.

Situated on a plateau of the Sierra Madre, the capital city was founded by the Spanish in 1575. Though formally established in 1907, the university in Saltillo upholds a tradition of learning dating back to 1591. The chief activities are cereal growing and stock raising, but the city also has commercial and industrial concerns, and is growing rapidly.

Chihuahua & Coahuila at a Glance

People	CI	CU	Mexico
Population, 2000	3,052,907	2,298,070	97,483,412
Population percent change, 1990- 2000	2.2%	1.5%	1.8%
Persons under 5 years old, percent, 2000	11.0%	11.0%	10.9%
Persons under 15 years old, percent, 2000	32.2%	32.4%	33.4%
Persons 65 years old and over, percent, 2000	4.5%	4.7%	4.9%
Female persons, percent, 2000	50.2%	50.4%	51.2%
Percentage of population age 5+ that speaks Spanish, 2000	80.2%	95.7%	81.5%
Persons age 5+ that speak an indigenous language	84,086	3,032	6,044,547
Tarahumara/Náhuatl speakers, percent, 2000	84.2%	24.7%	1.2% / 24%
Tepehuán/Mazahua speakers, percent, 2000	7.3%	10.4%	0.4% / 2.2%
Náhuatl/Maya speakers, percent, 2000	1.2%	6.9%	24% / 13.2%
Guarijio/Zapoteco speakers, percent, 2000	1.1%	5.6%	NA / 7.5%
Mazahua/Tarahumara speakers, percent, 2000	0.9%	5.5%	2.2% / 1.2%
Other indigenous language speakers, percent, 2000	3.8%	32.7%	4.2%
Completed primary education, percent of persons age 15+, 2000 (a)	24.4%	20.5%	19.4%
Completed post-primary education, percent of persons age 15+, 2000 (b)	20.0%	23.1%	19.1%
Persons with a disability	56,187	46,558	1,795,300

(a) Includes persons having passed 6 years of elementary school
(b) Includes persons having passed 3 years of high school
NA: Not available
Source: (INEGI) El Instituto Nacional de Estadística, Geografía e Informática

People (cont.)	CI	CU	Mexico
Housing units, 2000	773,379	539,169	21,513,235
Units with floor other than earth, percent, 2000	93.9%	95.6%	86.7%
Units with durable roofing materials, percent, 2000	49.8%	77.8%	64.2%
Units with durable wall materials, percent, 2000	67.9%	78.9%	79.3%
Homeownership rate, 2000	78.0%	78.2%	78.3%
Households, 2000	744,159	552,024	22,268,916
Average number of persons per housing unit, 2000	4	4.2	4.4

Business	CI	CU	Mexico
Agricultural employment, percent, 2003	12.2%	5.7%	NA
Industrial employment, percent, 2003	28.8%	29.6%	NA
Construction employment, percent, 2003	4.9%	5.1%	NA
Retail employment, percent, 2003	17.1%	18.9%	NA
Communication and transportation employment, percent, 2003	3.2%	4.6%	NA
Government employment, percent, 2003	4.7%	3.8%	NA
Social, financial and professional service employment, percent, 2003	12.1%	13.7%	NA
Service employment, percent, 2003	15.7%	18.5%	NA
Total workforce participation, percent, 2003	40.0%	39.2%	42.6%
Male workforce participation, percent, 2003	68.4%	67.5%	65.7%
Female workforce participation, percent, 2003	31.6%	32.5%	34.3%

Geography	CI	CU	Mexico
Land area, 2000 (square kilometers)	244,938	149,982	1,958,200
Persons per square kilometer, 2000	12	15	50

Nuevo León & Tamaulipas

During the Prehispanic period, the Huachichiles, Coahuiltecos, and the Azalapas were among the nomadic groups that peopled the territory that now falls within the borders of Nuevo León. The area became a state in 1824 and was occupied by U. S. troops under the command of Zachary Taylor during the Mexican-American War. The Sierra Madre Oriental range, most notably the peak of Cerro de la Silla, dominates the western part of Nuevo León, sheltering the major cities of Linares, Montemorelos and Monterrey, the capital. Cumbres de Monterrey, the largest national park in Mexico sits on the border of Coahuila while in the southeast an irrigated agricultural plateau allows livestock ample grazing land. Scrub and brush cover approximately two-thirds of the state and mining and ranching developed here during the Spanish colonial era. The nation's first radio station was built in Nuevo León in 1921 and today, with 51 municipalities, it is one of Mexico's most industrialized states largely due to the concentration of the nation's iron and steel industry in and around Monterrey.

Monterrey is Mexico's third largest city after Mexico City and Guadalajara. Founded by the Spanish in 1579, the state capital of Nuevo León is named after the Count of Monterrey, the Spanish viceroy of Mexico. Although Monterrey has many *maquiladoras*, its temperate climate also makes it a popular resort area.

Before the Spanish conquest in 1519, the Huastec people controlled most of this northeastern region. As with its neighbor to the west, Tamaulipas achieved statehood when Mexico became a republic in 1824 and its proximity to Texas involved it in the Texas Revolution (1836–37) and the Mexican-American War (1846–48). Many Franciscan missions were built here during the eighteenth century, several of which still survive. Tamaulipas is largely a coastal plain, drained by rivers such as the San Fernando, but the Sierra Madre Oriental dominates the south-central part of this state of 43 municipalities. At the heart of trade between Mexico and the United States, northern Tamaulipas is bordered by the Río Grande (known as the Río Bravo del Norte in Mexico) and the state of Texas. The cities of Nuevo Laredo, Reynosa, and Matamoros developed on the cross-border trade with their Texan counterparts, relying on many *maquiladora* assembly-plants in which imported components are assembled in Mexico and then exported to the United States. Tampico, at the southern tip of the

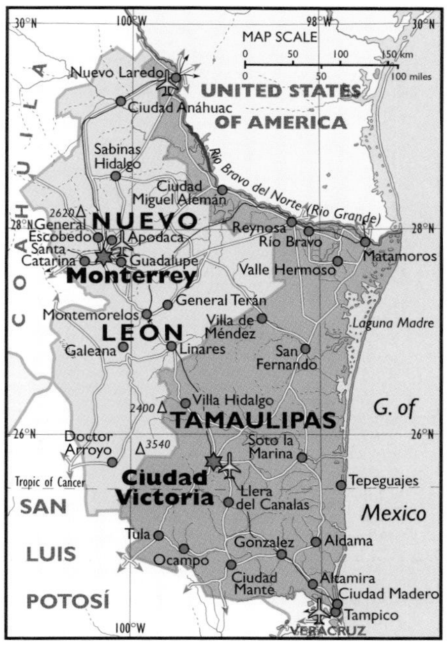

state, is a major industrial center and port on the Gulf of Mexico. In addition to cattle and hog production, industries include fishing, natural gas processing, petroleum refining, and petrochemicals.

Named after the first Mexican president, Guadalupe Victoria, and founded in 1750, Ciudad Victoria lies in the foothills of the Sierra Madre Oriental. The state capital of Tamaulipas is an agricultural and trading center, the hub for the four major highways in Tamaulipas and the seat of a university.

Nuevo León & Tamaulipas at a Glance

People	NL	TM	Mexico
Population, 2000	3,834,141	2,753,222	97,483,412
Population percent change, 1990-2000	2.1%	2.0%	1.8%
Persons under 5 years old, percent, 2000	10.3%	10.8%	10.9%
Persons under 15 years old, percent, 2000	29.7%	31.3%	33.4%
Persons 65 years old and over, percent, 2000	4.7%	5.0%	4.9%
Female persons, percent, 2000	50.2%	50.6%	51.2%
Percentage of population age 5+ that speaks Spanish, 2000	97.4%	96.8%	81.5%
Persons age 5+ that speak an indigenous language	15,446	17,118	6,044,547
Náhuatlspeakers, percent, 2000	53.8%	49.1%	24.0%
Huasteco speakers, percent, 2000	15.9%	23.9%	2.5%
Otomí/Totonaca speakers, percent, 2000	7.6%	7.7%	4.8% / 4%
Zapoteco/Otomí speakers, percent, 2000	4.0%	3.1%	7.5% / 4.8%
Mixteco/Mazahua speakers, percent, 2000	2.9%	2.7%	7.4% / 2.2%
Other indigenous language speakers, percent, 2000	11.1%	9.7%	4.2%
Completed primary education, percent of persons age 15+, 2000 (a)	17.1%	19.4%	19.4%
Completed post-primary education, percent of persons age 15+, 2000 (b)	24.7%	19.9%	19.1%
Persons with a disability	69,765	52,484	1,795,300

(a) Includes persons having passed 6 years of elementary school
(b) Includes persons having passed 3 years of high school
NA: Not available
Source: (INEGI) El Instituto Nacional de Estadística, Geografía e Informática

People (cont.)	NL	TM	Mexico
Housing units, 2000	878,600	677,489	21,513,235
Units with floor other than earth, percent, 2000	96.7%	91.5%	86.7%
Units with durable roofing materials, percent, 2000	85.7%	65.6%	64.2%
Units with durable wall materials, percent, 2000	93.7%	76.2%	79.3%
Homeownership rate, 2000	80.7%	75.0%	78.3%
Households, 2000	915,404	689,844	22,268,916
Average number of persons per housing unit, 2000	4.3	4	4.4

Business	NL	TM	Mexico
Agricultural employment, percent, 2003	4.1%	7.9%	NA
Industrial employment, percent, 2003	24.7%	22.9%	NA
Construction employment, percent, 2003	8.1%	9.2%	NA
Retail employment, percent, 2003	19.3%	18.4%	NA
Communication and transportation employment, percent, 2003	6.6%	5.9%	NA
Government employment, percent, 2003	3.1%	4.4%	NA
Social, financial and professional service employment, percent, 2003	16.6%	12.1%	NA
Service employment, percent, 2003	17.3%	17.8%	NA
Total workforce participation, percent, 2003	43.1%	42.0%	42.6%
Male workforce participation, percent, 2003	68.0%	67.7%	65.7%
Female workforce participation, percent, 2003	32.0%	32.3%	34.3%

Geography	NL	TM	Mexico
Land area, 2000 (square kilometers)	64,924	79,384	1,958,200
Persons per square kilometer, 2000	60	34	50

Aguascalientes & San Luis Potosí

Named for its numerous hot springs, or literally, "waters," Aguascalientes lies on Mexico's high central plateau. Originally occupied by the nomadic Chichimec, Aguascalientes became a state in 1857 and was the scene of some of the bloodiest confrontations in the Mexican Revolution. In 1914 the various military leaders of the revolution met in the Convention of Aguascalientes yet failed to reach an agreement, and warfare continued. The state capital and largest city is Aguascalientes and other cities include Asientos, Calvillo, and Jesús María.

Occupied by lush forests in the west, a wide valley in the Sierra Madre range divides this small state roughly into two parts. The eleven municipalities of Aguascalientes are predominantly rural. At the end of the twentieth century, it expanded rapidly as foreign investment developed the manufacturing base and now the production of electronics and automotive parts dominates the local industry.

Agricultural products based on irrigation include maize, wine, and fruit, while the mining of zinc, copper, and gold is still another important industrial activity. Tourists visiting the area will find theaters, sixteenth- and seventeenth-century churches, and museums devoted to art, history and bullfighting.

The Spanish founded the state capital of Aguascalientes in 1575 as a silver-mining town and a resting place for travelers. Now a health resort noted for its mineral springs, Aguascalientes is built over an ancient system of tunnels of advanced construction and unknown origin.

Separated from Aguascalientes by an extension of bordering Zacatecas, San Luis Potosí is the chief mining state of Mexico, with mines that have yielded gold, copper, zinc, bismuth, and especially silver since the eighteenth century. The richness of these mines, in tandem with a system of haciendas, necessitated a system of roads, which fostered further growth and development. Matehuala, Ciudad Valles, and San Luis Potosí, the state capital, are the most populous cities in this state of fifty-eight municipalities. Dominated by Mexico's central plateau, its rocky and arid conditions, primarily in the extreme northwest region known as El Salado, result in little farming, yet in contrast, the Pánuco River Valley in the southeast produces coffee, tobacco, and sugar.

Founded on the site of a Chichimec settlement by the Spanish in 1576, the capital city, San Luis Potosí, has numerous examples of fine colonial architecture. It is a mining and trade center for the surrounding agricultural area.

Aguascalientes & San Luis Potosí at a Glance

People	**AG**	**SL**	**Mexico**
Population, 2000	944,285	2,299,360	97,483,412
Population percent change, 1990-2000	2.7%	1.4%	1.8%
Persons under 5 years old, percent, 2000	12.3%	11.7%	10.9%
Persons under 15 years old, percent, 2000	36.2%	36.4%	33.4%
Persons 65 years old and over, percent, 2000	4.4%	5.6%	4.9%
Female persons, percent, 2000	51.7%	51.3%	51.2%
Percentage of population age 5+ that speaks Spanish, 2000	96.1%	88.7%	81.5%
Persons age 5+ that speak an indigenous language	1,244	235,253	6,044,547
Náhuatl speakers, percent, 2000	21.5%	58.9%	24.0%
Mazahua/Huasteco speakers, percent, 2000	8.8%	37.1%	2.2% / 2.5%
Otomí/Pame speakers, percent, 2000	8.6%	3.4%	4.8% / NA
Zapoteco/Otomí speakers, percent, 2000	6.8%	0.1%	7.5% / 4.8%
Huichol/Mixteco speakers, percent, 2000	5.1%	0.1%	0.5% / 7.4%
Other indigenous language speakers, percent, 2000	24.0%	0.3%	4.2%
Completed primary education, percent of persons age 15+, 2000 (a)	21.3%	19.1%	19.4%
Completed post-primary education, percent of persons age 15+, 2000 (b)	20.6%	18.5%	19.1%
Persons with a disability	17,021	48,190	1,795,300

(a) Includes persons having passed 6 years of elementary school
(b) Includes persons having passed 3 years of high school
NA: Not available
Source: (INEGI) El Instituto Nacional de Estadística, Geografía e Informática

People (cont.)	**AG**	**SL**	**Mexico**
Housing units, 2000	199,398	489,828	21,513,235
Units with floor other than earth, percent, 2000	97.0%	78.3%	86.7%
Units with durable roofing materials, percent, 2000	94.3%	66.9%	64.2%
Units with durable wall materials, percent, 2000	88.6%	70.2%	79.3%
Homeownership rate, 2000	75.7%	82.1%	78.3%
Households, 2000	329,552	307,698	22,268,916
Average number of persons per housing unit, 2000	4.7	4.6	4.4

Business	**AG**	**SL**	**Mexico**
Agricultural employment, percent, 2003	7.9%	29.3%	NA
Industrial employment, percent, 2003	23.7%	13.0%	NA
Construction employment, percent, 2003	7.1%	4.5%	NA
Retail employment, percent, 2003	19.4%	17.7%	NA
Communication and transportation employment, percent, 2003	3.6%	3.3%	NA
Government employment, percent, 2003	6.4%	4.3%	NA
Social, financial and professional service employment, percent, 2003	14.8%	12.0%	NA
Service employment, percent, 2003	17.1%	15.8%	NA
Total workforce participation, percent, 2003	40.1%	42.4%	42.6%
Male workforce participation, percent, 2003	64.4%	64.3%	65.7%
Female workforce participation, percent, 2003	35.6%	35.7%	34.3%

Geography	**AG**	**SL**	**Mexico**
Land area, 2000 (square kilometers)	5,471	63,068	1,958,200
Persons per square kilometer, 2000	168	38	50

Durango & Zacatecas

East of Sinaloa, Durango, the fourth largest state by area, is crowded with mountain chains such as the Sierra Espinazo del Diablo, the Sierra de la Magdalena, and the Sierra de Durango. Before the Spanish conquest and colonization, Huitchol, Tepehuano and Zacatec, among other tribes, resided in this territory. Revolutionary Pancho Villa, born Doroteo Arango in 1878, spent his childhood in the state. In western Durango, the Sierra Madre Occidental contains mineral deposits such as silver, gold, and lead while to the east, the arid plains provide excellent pastures, and many crops are cultivated in the fertile Nazas River Valley. Industries scattered among the thirty-nine municipalities include timber, tanning, textiles, and tourism. Beginning in the 1950s, Mexico was also a popular place to film Western movies and many Hollywood stars found their way to mountainous Durango. Bolsón de Mapimí, a large national reserve that is home to numerous endangered species of plants and animals can be found northeast of the state capital, Victoria de Durango.

Victoria de Durango, in the foothills of the Sierra Madre, is a major mining center and the capital of the state. Rich in iron ore, it was founded by the Spanish in 1563, as the capital of the colonial province of Nueva Viscaya, which consisted of the present-day Mexican states of Chihuahua and Durango. Also an important manufacturing and commercial center for the surrounding mining, agricultural, and forestry region, Durango is the seat of Juárez University of Durango State, established in 1856. Industries include iron foundries, textile mills, and sugar refineries.

Taking its name from the Náhuatl word for the type of grass native to the region, Zacatecas is another mountainous state on the high central plateau between the Sierra Madre Occidental and Sierra Madre Oriental ranges. In addition to the capital city, Zacatecas, the state contains several major cities such as Fresnillo de González Echeverría, Guadalupe, and Sombrerete within its 57 municipalities. Much like its neighbors, rich silver resources were discovered soon after the Spanish conquered the native Zacatecs, Caxcanes and Huachichiles in the early sixteenth century, and until the nineteenth century the state produced about one-fifth of the world's silver. This industry remains the principal source of state

income to this day. Agriculture is also an important economic activity, and Zacatecas is Mexico's leading producer of beans and chili peppers.

Founded by the Spanish in September of 1546, Zacatecas, began as a center for the surrounding silver-mining region and grew to become the state capital. The religious spirit and the wealth of its colonial inhabitants is reflected today in various examples of fine architecture scattered throughout the city, especially in the historic center, which was declared a UNESCO World Heritage site in 1993.

Durango & Zacatecas at a Glance

People	**DG**	**ZT**	**Mexico**
Population, 2000	1,448,661	1,353,610	97,483,412
Population percent change, 1990- 2000	0.7%	0.6%	1.8%
Persons under 5 years old, percent, 2000	11.7%	11.6%	10.9%
Persons under 15 years old, percent, 2000	35.8%	36.3%	33.4%
Persons 65 years old and over, percent, 2000	5.2%	6.2%	4.9%
Female persons, percent, 2000	51.0%	51.7%	51.2%
Percentage of population age 5+ that speaks Spanish, 2000	79.8%	90.1%	81.5%
Persons age 5+ that speak an indigenous language	24,934	1,837	6,044,547
Tepehuán speakers, percent, 2000	68.4%	19.5%	0.4%
Huichol speakers, percent, 2000	5.8%	18.0%	0.5%
Náhuatl speakers, percent, 2000	3.5%	18.0%	24.0%
Tarahumara/Otomí speakers, percent, 2000	1.8%	6.5%	1.2% / 4.8%
Cora/Mazahua speakers, percent, 2000	0.9%	5.5%	0.3% / 2.2
Other indigenous language speakers, percent, 2000	2.7%	18.7%	4.2%
Completed primary education, percent of persons age 15+, 2000 (a)	23.1%	23.2%	19.4%
Completed post-primary education, percent of persons age 15+, 2000 (b)	18.3%	15.6%	19.1%
Persons with a disability	32,052	32,229	1,795,300

(a) Includes persons having passed 6 years of elementary school
(b) Includes persons having passed 3 years of high school
NA: Not available
Source: (INEGI) El Instituto Nacional de Estadística, Geografía e Informática

People (cont.)	**DG**	**ZT**	**Mexico**
Housing units, 2000	322,288	298,217	21,513,235
Units with floor other than earth, percent, 2000	87.7%	91.4%	86.7%
Units with durable roofing materials, percent, 2000	70.0%	74.9%	64.2%
Units with durable wall materials, percent, 2000	56.0%	51.4%	79.3%
Homeownership rate, 2000	83.3%	80.7%	78.3%
Households, 2000	329,552	307,698	22,268,916
Average number of persons per housing unit, 2000	4.5	4.5	4.4

Business	**DG**	**ZT**	**Mexico**
Agricultural employment, percent, 2003	22.7%	27.8%	NA
Industrial employment, percent, 2003	17.7%	11.6%	NA
Construction employment, percent, 2003	5.6%	9.3%	NA
Retail employment, percent, 2003	16.9%	19.0%	NA
Communication and transportation employment, percent, 2003	4.5%	2.1%	NA
Government employment, percent, 2003	5.5%	5.3%	NA
Social, financial and professional service employment, percent, 2003	12.1%	12.3%	NA
Service employment, percent, 2003	14.4%	12.4%	NA
Total workforce participation, percent, 2003	36.5%	35.2%	42.6%
Male workforce participation, percent, 2003	69.8%	67.3%	65.7%
Female workforce participation, percent, 2003	30.2%	32.7%	34.3%

Geography	**DG**	**ZT**	**Mexico**
Land area, 2000 (square kilometers)	123,181	73,252	1,958,200
Persons per square kilometer, 2000	12	18	50

Colima, Jalisco & Nayarit

A small state on the Pacific coast in the west, Colima's ten municipalities, tucked between Jalisco and Michoacán, form seventy miles of coastal lowlands at the foothills of the Sierra Madre Occidental. The four Revillagigedo Islands, over a day's journey by sea from the port of Manzanillo, represent the most far-flung Mexican possession. Two volcanoes, Volcán de Fuego and Volcán de Colima in the Volcán Nevado de Colima National Park on the northern border with the state of Jalisco, dominate the skyline.

Growing some of Mexico's best coffee, the state economy is based largely on agriculture, but Colima is also a significant producer of iron. Food processing, tanning, tobacco, shoe manufacturing, and leather-working are several other large employers.

In 1523, Spanish explorer Gonzalo de Sandoval founded the city of Colima, naming it in honor of a former Nahua ruler. A processing center for the surrounding agricultural region, Spanish explorer Hernán Cortés pronounced it the third city of New Spain in 1527. A fine colonial cathedral and the State University can be found within the capital city's limits.

Meeting the Pacific Ocean in the west, Jalisco in central Mexico forms part of the nation's high central plateau. In 1529, the Spanish conquistador Nuño de Guzmán captured Jalisco and the Spanish conquest virtually extinguished the native population in the region. Occupied by the French during the wars of intervention, Spain regained the territory in 1866.

Jalisco was at the heart of Mexico's fight for independence, playing a prominent role in the Mexican Revolution, and the Cristero Rebellion (1926–29) against government attempts to restrict the power of the Catholic Church.

The Sierra Madre Occidental Range crosses the state north to south, tropical rainforests dominate the narrow coastal plain, and Lake Chapala, Mexico's largest lake, forms part of Jalisco's southeastern border with the state of Michoacán. Large cities such as Guadalajara, the political and economic capital, Puerto Vallarta, a popular tourist resort, and Ciudad Guzmán are scattered throughout the state in 124 municipalities.

Jalisco is the second largest producer of corn in Mexico but produces other agricultural goods including beans, wheat, rice, tobacco, and livestock. Processed foods, tequila and textiles are the major industries.

Guadalajara is the second-largest city in Mexico. Founded by the Spanish in 1531, it is known for its fine colonial architecture such as a cathedral and the governor's palace. Today, the capital is a major industrial center. Noted for its mountain scenery and mild climate, it is also a popular health resort and has been called Perla de Occidente or the Pearl of the West. Economic activity centers around engineering, textiles, and food processing, along with the production of intricate pottery and glassware.

Another state on the Pacific coast of western Mexico, Nayarit's landscape slopes upward from a coastal plain stretching from the ocean into the foothills of the Sierra Madre Occidental, which covers much of the eastern and southern parts of the state. Wetlands and the Agua Brava lagoon occupy the extreme northwest corner of the state and the major river is the Grande de Santiago. Among the twenty municipalities, San Blas, Tuxpan de Rodríguez Cano, and Ixtlán del Río rank with the capital, Tepic, as the most populous. The Marías Islands lie seventy-eight miles off the coast.

In the mid-1800s, Manuel Lozada led a native rebellion against Spanish rule in the region. Part of Jalisco for many years and a major battleground of the Mexican Revolution, Nayarit became a military district in 1867, a federal territory in 1884, and finally a state in 1917. A fertile agricultural region, Nayarit produces about three-quarters of Mexico's tobacco crop. In addition to tobacco, gold, silver, and lead mining, as well as forestry are important economically.

Resting at the base of Volcán Sanganguey on the Tepic River, Tepic, the capital, is dominated by sugar-refining and textile companies. Despite its status as a center of commerce, the capital city does retain some of its colonial character.

Colima, Jalisco & Nayarit at a Glance

People	CL	JA	NA	Mexico
Population, 2000	542,627	6,322,002	920,185	97,483,412
Population percent change, 1990–2000	1.6%	1.2%	2.9%	1.8%
Persons under 5 years old, percent, 2000	9.8%	11.1%	10.9%	10.9%
Persons under 15 years old, percent, 2000	30.9%	33.7%	34.3%	33.4%
Persons 65 years old and over, percent, 2000	4.9%	5.3%	5.9%	4.9%
Female persons, percent, 2000	50.6%	51.4%	50.4%	51.2%
Percentage of population age 5+ that speaks Spanish, 2000	90.6%	88.0%	79.4%	81.5%
Persons age 5+ that speak an indigenous language	2,932	39,259	37,206	6,044,547
Náhuatl/Huichol/Huichol speakers, percent, 2000	35.1%	28.0%	45.5%	NA
Purépecha/Náhuatl/Cora speakers, percent, 2000	17.3%	17.1%	41.1%	NA
Mixteco/Purépecha/Náhuatl speakers, percent, 2000	12.3%	7.8%	3.8%	NA
Zapoteco/Mixteco/Tepehuán speakers, percent, 2000	5.5%	3.7%	3.8%	NA
Mazahua/Otomí/Zapoteco speakers, percent, 2000	2.6%	3.0%	1.5%	NA
Other indigenous language speakers, percent, 2000	13.7%	11.7%	2.8%	4.2%
Completed primary education, percent of persons age 15+, 2000 (a)	18.2%	21.7%	16.4%	19.4%
Completed post-primary education, percent of persons age 15+, 2000 (b)	19.0%	19.2%	19.8%	19.1%
Persons with a disability	13,022	138,308	21,600	1,795,300

(a) Includes persons having passed 6 years of elementary school
(b) Includes persons having passed 3 years of high school
NA: Not available
Source: (INEGI) El Instituto Nacional de Estadística, Geografía e Informática

People (cont.)	CL	JA	NA	Mexico
Housing units, 2000	124,714	1,378,666	219,181	21,513,235
Units with floor other than earth, percent, 2000	88.5%	93.3%	88.2%	86.7%
Units with durable roofing materials, percent, 2000	61.1%	85.2%	67.3%	64.2%
Units with durable wall materials, percent, 2000	88.3%	87.7%	85.0%	79.3%
Homeownership rate, 2000	90.3%	69.3%	80.3%	78.3%
Households, 2000	128,295	1,441,069	222,953	22,268,916
Average number of persons per housing unit, 2000	4	4.5	4.2	4.4

Business	CL	JA	NA	Mexico
Agricultural employment, percent, 2003	11.8%	9.8%	25.6%	NA
Industrial employment, percent, 2003	12.2%	21.8%	10.8%	NA
Construction employment, percent, 2003	8.0%	5.0%	6.7%	NA
Retail employment, percent, 2003	20.1%	22.5%	19.5%	NA
Communication and transportation employment, percent, 2003	6.1%	3.4%	3.4%	NA
Government employment, percent, 2003	6.9%	3.0%	5.3%	NA
Social, financial and professional service employment, percent, 2003	13.4%	13.7%	11.9%	NA
Service employment, percent, 2003	21.4%	20.8%	16.8%	NA
Total workforce participation, percent, 2003	47.5%	44.4%	42.3%	42.6%
Male workforce participation, percent, 2003	62.7%	61.5%	64.2%	65.7%
Female workforce participation, percent, 2003	37.3%	38.5%	35.8%	34.3%

Geography	CL	JA	NA	Mexico
Land area, 2000 (square kilometers)	5,191	80,836	26,979	1,958,200
Persons per square kilometer, 2000	96	80	33	50

Guanajuato, Michoacán & Querétaro

A major center of the pre-Columbian Toltec civilization, the struggle for independence from Spain began in Guanajuato in 1810. The state witnessed some of the bloodiest battles of the Mexican Revolution, and likewise played a large role in the Cristero Rebellion (1926–29) against government attempts to restrict the power of the Catholic Church. It is one of Mexico's principal agricultural and mining states; one of the richest veins of silver was discovered near the present capital in 1558. The northernmost regions of this state in central Mexico are fairly mountainous, giving way to a fertile plateau region known as the Bajío—a major fruit-growing area fed by the principal river, the Lerma, in the south. It boasts many splendid examples of colonial architecture, including the Valenciana and San Augustín churches in the capital city, Guanajuato. Major cities scattered among the forty-six municipalities include León, Irapuato, Salamanca, Celaya, Pénjamo, and San Miguel de Allende. Gold, silver, mercury, and tin mining, along with the production of foodstuffs, leather goods, and clothing rank among the key economic activities.

Circled by barren hills in the northwestern portion of the state, Guanajuato is known for winding cobblestone streets and underground passageways. Diego Rivera, the famous muralist, was born here in 1886.

Stretching from the center of Mexico to the Pacific, two volcanic mountain ranges, running east to west, dominate the state of Michoacán: the Sierra Madre Occidental rises in the interior, while the Sierra del Coalcomán lies near the coast. Between the mountain ranges are the humid tropical lowlands known as the hot country or *tierra caliente*, through which flow the Balsas and Tepalcatepec Rivers. Lake Chapala, Mexico's largest lake, lies on the border with Jalisco. The Tarascan people inhabited this area until the Spanish conquest in the 1520s and their capital city, Tzintzuntzán, located in the center of the state near the popular resort of Lake Pátzcuaro, is an important archeological site. Other important cities include Zamora de Hidalgo, Tacámbaro, and Uruapan del Progreso. Michoacán is one of Mexico's leading producers of farming and forestry products, with many of its 113 municipalities generating cash crops such as cotton, corn, beans, and wheat. Hydroelectric plants aid the development of industry along the coast.

Over six thousand feet above sea level, Morelia, the state capital and cultural center of Michoacán, was founded in 1541 by the Spanish as Valladolid, and its name was changed in 1828 in honor of the revolutionary hero José María Morelos y Pavón. It is the site of the University of Michoacán (1539), one of the oldest educational institutions in the Western Hemisphere. The city is renowned for its colonial architecture and Spanish aqueduct. Morelia is a distribution and trade center for the surrounding region and food processing, as well as handicraft production provide income for much of the population.

One of the smaller states in central Mexico and similar to Guanajuato, Querétaro's 18 municipalities are also characterized by the rugged Sierra del Zamorano and the Sierra Gorda in the center and north of the state and the fertile Bajío in the south. The state capital and largest city is Querétaro followed by San Juan del Río, Amealco, and Cadereyta de Montes. Before the Spanish conquest in 1531, the Otomí tribe was the largest indigenous group populating Querétaro. The Spanish established the state's textile industry, and by the end of the eighteenth century the city of Querétaro was perhaps the largest producer of textiles in the Americas. It achieved statehood when Mexico became a republic in 1824. Today the manufacture of automobile and tractor parts, opal mining, and handicrafts contribute to the local economy.

The Spanish captured the Aztec city of Querétaro in 1531 and governed until Father Miguel Hidalgo planned an insurrection that would become a revolution in 1810. Acting as the nation's capital during the Mexican-American War between 1846 and 1848, the treaty ending the war was signed in Querétaro, the post-revolutionary Constitution of 1917 was drawn up in the city, and it was here that Emperor Maximilian was executed in 1867. Querétaro has a sixteenth-century cathedral, and is the site of the Autonomous University of Querétaro, founded in 1618. Cotton milling, tourism, food processing, and trade in opals are the largest sources of employment.

Guanajuato, Michoacán & Querétaro at a Glance

People	GJ	MG	QA	Mexico
Population, 2000	4,663,032	3,985,667	1,404,306	97,483,412
Population percent change, 1990–2000	1.6%	1.2%	2.9%	1.8%
Persons under 5 years old, percent, 2000	12.1%	11.4%	11.6%	10.9%
Persons under 15 years old, percent, 2000	36.6%	36.2%	35.8%	33.4%
Persons 65 years old and over, percent, 2000	5.0%	5.8%	4.1%	4.9%
Female persons, percent, 2000	52.1%	52.0%	51.5%	51.2%
Percentage of population age 5+ that speaks Spanish, 2000	92.8%	85.0%	90.6%	81.5%
Persons age 5+ that speak an indigenous language	10,689	121,849	25,269	6,044,547
Chichimeca jonaz/Purépecha/Otomí speakers, percent, 2000	13.4%	89.8%	87.4%	NA
Otomí/Náhuatl/Náhuatl speakers, percent, 2000	9.5%	3.9%	4.2%	NA
Náhuatl/Mazahua/Mazahua speakers, percent, 2000	8.6%	3.6%	1.3%	NA
Mazahua/Otomí/Zapoteco speakers, percent, 2000	5.9%	0.6%	0.9%	NA
Purépecha/Mixteco/Huasteco speakers, percent, 2000	3.9%	0.6%	0.5%	NA
Other indigenous language speakers, percent, 2000	11.3%	1.1%	3.4%	4.2%
Completed primary education, percent of persons age 15+, 2000 (a)	23.4%	20.2%	20.9%	19.4%
Completed post-primary education, percent of persons age 15+, 2000 (b)	17.3%	14.7%	21.1%	19.1%
Persons with a disability	88,103	85,165	22,165	1,795,300

(a) Includes persons having passed 6 years of elementary school
(b) Includes persons having passed 3 years of high school
NA: Not available
Source: (INEGI) El Instituto Nacional de Estadística, Geografía e Informática

People (cont.)	GJ	MG	QA	Mexico
Housing units, 2000	918,822	846,333	295,143	21,513,235
Units with floor other than earth, percent, 2000	90.0%	81.9%	90.8%	86.7%
Units with durable roofing materials, percent, 2000	71.4%	55.4%	72.7%	64.2%
Units with durable wall materials, percent, 2000	88.3%	69.5%	92.9%	79.3%
Homeownership rate, 2000	81.4%	80.5%	82.8%	78.3%
Households, 2000	990,119	887,958	310,098	22,268,916
Average number of persons per housing unit, 2000	5	4.6	4.7	4.4

Business	GJ	MG	QA	Mexico
Agricultural employment, percent, 2003	20.5%	28.9%	12.0%	NA
Industrial employment, percent, 2003	22.2%	13.1%	23.6%	NA
Construction employment, percent, 2003	5.9%	8.6%	10.6%	NA
Retail employment, percent, 2003	20.8%	17.7%	19.1%	NA
Communication and transportation employment, percent, 2003	2.7%	3.2%	4.2%	NA
Government employment, percent, 2003	2.6%	3.5%	4.1%	NA
Social, financial and professional service employment, percent, 2003	9.4%	8.9%	12.6%	NA
Service employment, percent, 2003	15.8%	16.1%	13.8%	NA
Total workforce participation, percent, 2003	37.8%	39.0%	43.3%	42.6%
Male workforce participation, percent, 2003	62.8%	67.1%	63.5%	65.7%
Female workforce participation, percent, 2003	37.2%	32.9%	36.5%	34.3%

Geography	GJ	MG	QA	Mexico
Land area, 2000 (square kilometers)	30,491	59,928	11,449	1,958,200
Persons per square kilometer, 2000	152	68	120	50

Puebla, Morelos & Tlaxcala

The eastern central region of Mexico was a vital part of the Aztec Empire, and the state of Puebla has many Mesoamerican archeological sites, most notably the Toltec pyramid at Cholula. In 1519, as part of their bloody campaign of conquest, the Spanish killed more than 3,000 residents of Cholula. Puebla achieved statehood when Mexico became a republic in 1824 and on May 5, 1862, General Ignacio Zaragoza led Mexican troops to victory over French invaders at the city of Puebla. Cinco de Mayo is now a public holiday. Aside from the state capital, other major cities include Atlixco, Teziutlán, and Tehuacán.

Topographically, this state of 217 municipalities is dominated by the Sierra Madre Oriental range, and a chain of volcanoes stretching across the center of the state. In the east is the volcanic peak of Pico de Orizaba (or Citlaltepetl), Mexico's highest mountain at 18,406 ft (5,610 m) while Popocatépetl and Iztaccihuatl occupy the northwest.

In the late nineteenth and early twentieth centuries, Puebla was a major center of textile manufacturing, and it continues to be a hub of industry, commerce, and services. Agriculture is, however, the major employer and the major crops are corn and cereal grains. Machinery, automobile, and textile production number among the main types of manufacturing.

Founded by the Spanish in 1532, Puebla de Zaragosa is one of the oldest European settlements in Mexico and, located on the route from Mexico City to the port of Veracruz, the city has always been of strategic importance. The U.S. army occupied the city during the Mexican-American War, and the French held it from 1862 until 1867. The seat of an archdiocese and home to the influential Palafoxian Seminary of Puebla, three universities also fall within city limits. The capital's historic center is an UNESCO World Heritage Site rich in colonial architecture, containing a sixteenth-century cathedral as well as numerous houses covered in tiles, known as *azulejos*.

Morelos in the south-central part of the country, is Mexico's third smallest state after Tlaxcala and the Distrito Federal, and the third most densely populated. It is named for the revolutionary hero José María Morelos y Pavón. The peasant revolutionary, Emiliano Zapata, was born in Morelos and is a local hero. Outside of Cuernavaca, the capital, Tepoztlán, Cuautla Morelos, Puente de Ixtla, and Yautepec constitute some of the largest cities among the state's thirty-three municipalities.

The terrain forms part of the central Mexican plateau with its mountains and semiarid valleys. In the extreme northwest of the state lies the southern flank of Popocatépetl. Today Morelos is one of Mexico's largest agricultural producers and its primary crops include sugarcane, corn, rice, beans, and wheat. The pyramids at El Tepozteco, Xochialco, and Teopancolco attract many tourists.

Just south of the Distrito Federal, Cuernavaca is the cultural and commercial center of Morelos. In 1535 Hernán Cortés built his palace here and the city's cathedral incorporates an important sixteenth-century Franciscan monastery. Many Mexican officials and foreign diplomats in Mexico City have holiday homes in Cuernavaca. Brewing and sugar refining are two of the main industries in a city that has become known for its many Spanish language schools.

In 1519, after suffering heavy losses, the Native American civilization of the Tlaxcalans surrendered to the Spanish conquistador Hernán Cortés, becoming the principal allies of the Spanish in the war against the Aztecs. The rugged Sierra Madre Oriental range dominates most of central Mexico and Tlaxcala is no different. The cities of Santa Ana Chiautempan, Apizaco, and Huamantla fall behind Tlaxcala, the capital as most populous urban areas out of the sixty municipalities in the state. A large national park, La Malinche, traditional bullfights, and impressive haciendas attract visitors to this small state where agriculture—mostly corn and barley—along with textile manufacturing play a large role in the economy.

Tlaxcala, the capital city on the Atoyac River that Cortés captured from the native Tlaxcalans boasts fine examples of Spanish colonial architecture, including the Church of San Francisco, completed in 1521 and reputedly the oldest Christian church in the Americas.

Puebla, Morelos & Tlaxcala at a Glance

People	**PU**	**MR**	**TL**	**Mexico**
Population, 2000	5,076,686	1,555,296	962,646	97,483,412
Population percent change, 1990–2000	2.1%	2.7%	2.4%	1.8%
Persons under 5 years old, percent, 2000	10.9%	10.4%	8.6%	10.9%
Persons under 15 years old, percent, 2000	35.5%	31.9%	26.0%	33.4%
Persons 65 years old and over, percent, 2000	5.3%	3.6%	5.8%	4.9%
Female persons, percent, 2000	51.8%	51.7%	51.2%	51.2%
Percentage of population age 5+ that speaks Spanish, 2000	84.5%	93.1%	95.0%	81.5%
Persons age 5+ that speak an indigenous language	565,509	30,896	26,662	6,044,547
Náhuatl speakers, percent, 2000	73.7%	60.4%	89.0%	NA
Totonaca/Mixteco/Totonaca speakers, percent, 2000	17.8%	12.3%	4.5%	NA
Popoluca/Tlapaneco/Otomí speakers, percent, 2000	2.6%	4.6%	3.1%	NA
Mazateco/Zapoteco speakers, percent, 2000	2.1%	2.0%	0.6%	NA
Mixteco/Otomí/Mixteco speakers, percent, 2000	1.5%	1.6%	0.5%	NA
Other indigenous language speakers, percent, 2000	2.3%	5.9%	1.7%	4.2%
Completed primary education, percent of persons age 15+, 2000 (a)	21.5%	17.3%	23.4%	19.4%
Completed post-primary education, percent of persons age 15+, 2000 (b)	16.6%	22.2%	22.9%	19.1%
Persons with a disability	82,833	30,195	12,498	1,795,300

(a) Includes persons having passed 6 years of elementary school
(b) Includes persons having passed 3 years of high school
NA: Not available
Source: (INEGI) El Instituto Nacional de Estadística, Geografía e Informática

People (cont.)	**PU**	**MR**	**TL**	**Mexico**
Housing units, 2000	1,028,692	354,035	193,288	21,513,235
Units with floor other than earth, percent, 2000	77.7%	86.7%	91.2%	86.7%
Units with durable roofing materials, percent, 2000	61.6%	67.1%	78.5%	64.2%
Units with durable wall materials, percent, 2000	78.2%	83.2%	81.2%	79.3%
Homeownership rate, 2000	79.0%	77.2%	84.6%	78.3%
Households, 2000	1,068,836	364,798	203,443	22,268,916
Average number of persons per housing unit, 2000	4.8	4.2	5.0	4.4

Business	**PU**	**MR**	**TL**	**Mexico**
Agricultural employment, percent, 2003	28.3%	10.8%	18.9%	NA
Industrial employment, percent, 2003	17.9%	14.3%	25.3%	NA
Construction employment, percent, 2003	6.3%	11.4%	10.2%	NA
Retail employment, percent, 2003	18.0%	19.0%	16.3%	NA
Communication and transportation employment, percent, 2003	3.1%	5.4%	3.6%	NA
Government employment, percent, 2003	2.8%	5.0%	4.9%	NA
Social, financial and professional service employment, percent, 2003	9.9%	13.3%	10.1%	NA
Service employment, percent, 2003	13.9%	20.7%	10.7%	NA
Total workforce participation, percent, 2003	43.0%	41.6%	41.9%	42.6%
Male workforce participation, percent, 2003	63.7%	64.5%	66.4%	65.7%
Female workforce participation, percent, 2003	36.3%	35.5%	33.6%	34.3%

Geography	**PU**	**MR**	**TL**	**Mexico**
Land area, 2000 (square kilometers)	33,902	4,950	4,016	1,958,200
Persons per square kilometer, 2000	148	318	241	50

Hidalgo, Mexico & Distrito Federal

A small state in central Mexico surrounded by six others, Hidalgo has ten locally recognized cultural areas such as the Huasteca and Valle del Mezquital, and eighty-four municipalities. The Spanish conquered the area in the early sixteenth century, and plundered the silver mines in the Mineral del Monte region. Hidalgo became a state in 1869 and continues to have a large indigenous population, most notably the Otomí. The state capital is Pachuca de Soto and other major cities include Tulancingo, Huejutla de Reyes, and Tula de Allende. Named for Miguel Hidalgo y Costilla, a leader in Mexico's struggle for independence from Spain, Hidalgo is split into two major geographic regions: the rugged Sierra Madre Oriental range in the north and the east, and the high central plateau in the southeast. The local economy is based on the mining of silver, gold, copper, manganese, and mercury. In addition to mining, meat and dairy production, cement production, and the manufacture of transportation equipment constitute the main industries. Once inhabited by the Huastec tribe the state has many important pre-Columbian archeological sites, including Tula, the capital of the Toltec civilization.

The Spanish founded the capital city of Pachuca de Soto in 1534 in the foothills of the Sierra Madre Oriental on the site of an ancient Toltec city. An administrative center for the state, it is also the site of a meteorological observatory, a university, a mining and metallurgy school, and a sixteenth-century convent. The main industry continues to be silver mining.

Virtually surrounding the Federal District, the state of Mexico was formed when the country became a republic in 1824. It is now the second most populous state in the country and includes 122 municipalities. In the northeast, not far from the remnants of Lake Texcoco, the body of water that once surrounded the Aztec capital, the pyramids of Teotihuacan are the country's most famous archeological site. Characterized by some of the highest peaks in the country, the crater of Xinantecatl or Nevado de Toluca containing two lakes called Sun and Moon, rises in the west and the volcanoes of Popocatépetl and Iztaccihuatl dominate the eastern part of the state. Two major rivers, the Lerma, and the Temascaltepec, run between the jagged system of volcanoes crossing the state, supporting wildlife in Nevado de Toluca National Park. Mexico is both a major industrial and agricultural region with industry concentrated along the highway between Toluca and Mexico City. An extensive network of canals and tunnels supply much of the drinking water for the vast metropolitan area of Mexico City.

The state capital sits at the foot of the extinct volcano of Nevado de Toluca, just southwest of Mexico City. Toluca de Lerdo was an Aztec pueblo before the Spanish conquest in the sixteenth century and became capital in 1830. It is the site of the Autonomous University of Mexico State as well as the El Calvario shrine that attracts many Catholic pilgrims. Industries include ceramic tile fabrication, handicrafts, silver, gold, and copper mining, and textile manufacturing.

The Distrito Federal (DF) contains Mexico City, the second most populous city in the world, which spills out into a horseshoe-shaped zona metropolitana that includes thirty-nine municipalities in the surrounding state of Mexico. Much of the city is sited on a dried-out lake bed in a volcanic basin which has become unstable as ground water has been drawn down, exacerbating the effect of frequent earthquakes. Many parts of the city suffer from overcrowding and a lack of adequate sanitary infrastructure. Air pollution from industry and automobile traffic is among the worst in the world and poses a health threat. Formerly the Aztec capital known as Tenochtitlan, it was destroyed by Hernán Cortés in 1521 and rebuilt as the capital of New Spain, governing Spain's New World colonies for the next 300 years. In 1847, during the Mexican-American War, U.S. troops occupied the city and in 1863, French troops conquered it, establishing Maximilian as emperor. Mexico was recaptured in 1867 by the republican forces of Benito Juárez. Between 1914 and 1915, the city was captured and lost three more times by the revolutionary forces of Emiliano Zapata and Francisco Villa. Today, Mexico City is also a major tourist center.

Hidalgo, Mexico & Distrito Federal at a Glance

People	HG	EM	DF	Mexico
Population, 2000	2,235,591	13,096,686	8,605,239	97,483,412
Population percent change, 1990–2000	1.7%	2.9%	0.4%	1.8%
Persons under 5 years old, percent, 2000	10.9%	10.4%	8.6%	10.9%
Persons under 15 years old, percent, 2000	35.5%	31.9%	26.0%	33.4%
Persons 65 years old and over, percent, 2000	5.3%	3.6%	5.8%	4.9%
Female persons, percent, 2000	51.6%	51.1%	52.2%	51.2%
Percentage of population age 5+ that speaks Spanish, 2000	81.4%	95.6%	97.1%	81.5%
Persons age 5+ that speak an indigenous language	339,866	361,972	141,710	6,044,547
Náhuatl/Mazahua/Náhuatl speakers, percent, 2000	65.2%	31.3%	26.4%	NA
Otomí speakers, percent, 2000	33.6%	28.8%	12.1%	NA
Tepehua/Náhuatl/Mixteco speakers, percent, 2000	0.5%	15.4%	11.3%	NA
Zapoteco/Mixteco/Zapoteco speakers, percent, 2000	0.1%	7.4%	10.0%	NA
Totonaca/Zapoteco/Mazahua speakers, percent, 2000	0.1%	4.6%	6.8%	NA
Other indigenous language speakers, percent, 2000	0.3%	10.5%	21.4%	4.2%
Completed primary education, percent of persons age 15+, 2000 (a)	20.3%	19.4%	15.5%	19.4%
Completed post-primary education, percent of persons age 15+, 2000 (b)	19.3%	24.0%	21.3%	19.1%
Persons with a disability	47,176	189,341	159,754	1,795,300

(a) Includes persons having passed 6 years of elementary school
(b) Includes persons having passed 3 years of high school
NA: Not available
Source: (INEGI) El Instituto Nacional de Estadística, Geografía e Informática

People (cont.)	HG	EM	DF	Mexico
Housing units, 2000	491,482	2,743,144	2,103,752	21,513,235
Units with floor other than earth, percent, 2000	82.0%	93.5%	98.8%	86.7%
Units with durable roofing materials, percent, 2000	62.0%	75.0%	87.3%	64.2%
Units with durable wall materials, percent, 2000	82.7%	90.9%	98.1%	79.3%
Homeownership rate, 2000	84.8%	79.0%	71.1%	78.3%
Households, 2000	503,151	2,848,992	2,180,243	22,268,916
Average number of persons per housing unit, 2000	4.5	4.6	4.0	4.4

Business	HG	EM	DF	Mexico
Agricultural employment, percent, 2003	30.6%	4.8%	0.2%	NA
Industrial employment, percent, 2003	14.9%	21.3%	15.3%	NA
Construction employment, percent, 2003	6.9%	8.7%	4.5%	NA
Retail employment, percent, 2003	17.2%	20.3%	20.3%	NA
Communication and transportation employment, percent, 2003	2.5%	7.0%	7.3%	NA
Government employment, percent, 2003	4.0%	5.2%	7.6%	NA
Social, financial and professional service employment, percent, 2003	9.6%	14.4%	25.0%	NA
Service employment, percent, 2003	14.3%	18.3%	19.5%	NA
Total workforce participation, percent, 2003	41.7%	42.1%	43.2%	42.6%
Male workforce participation, percent, 2003	62.2%	68.1%	61.1%	65.7%
Female workforce participation, percent, 2003	37.8%	31.9%	38.9%	34.3%

Geography	HG	EM	DF	Mexico
Land area, 2000 (square kilometers)	20,813	21,355	1,547	1,958,200
Persons per square kilometer, 2000	107	586	5799	50

Chiapas, Guerrero & Oaxaca

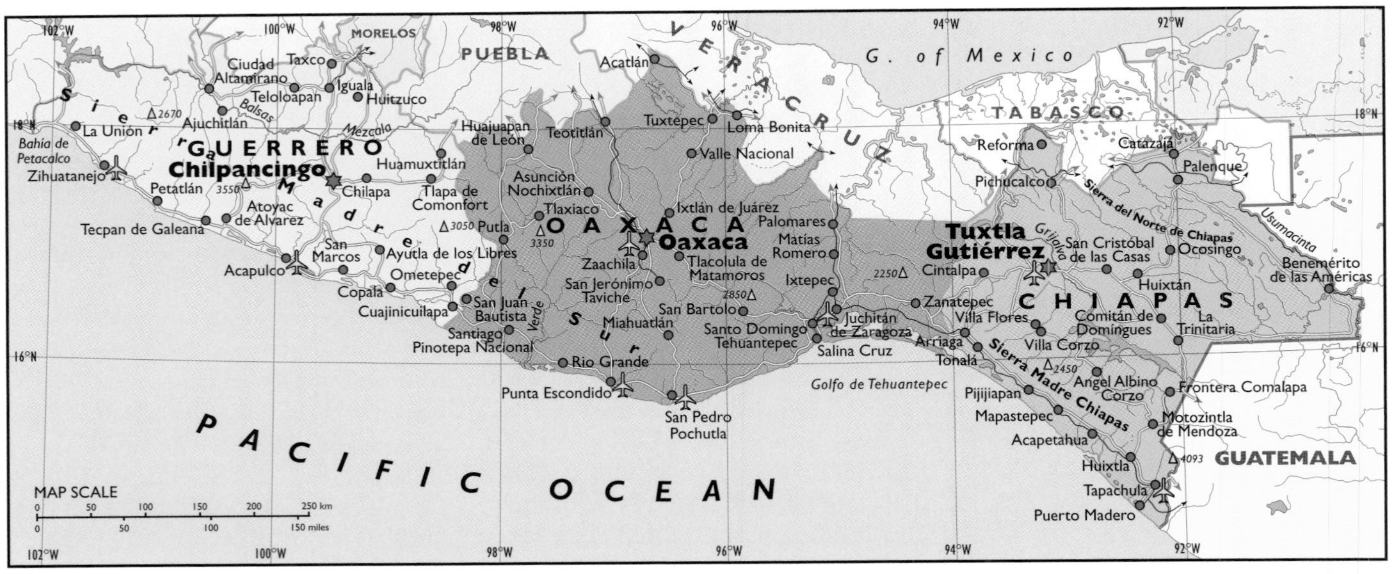

Located on the Pacific coast of southeastern Mexico, Chiapas is characterized by tropical rainforest and steep mountains. Plateaus surround the central valley of Chiapas between the Sierra Madre de Chiapas and the Sierra del Norte de Chiapas. The Usumacinta and Grijalva Rivers flow through the north of the state.

One of the most rural states in Mexico, Chiapas has a large Mayan population scattered throughout its 119 municipalities. Responding to the North American Free Trade Agreement, which did little to improve the lives of Mayan farmers in Chiapas, the Zapatista National Liberation Front led an armed uprising here in 1994. Coffee and cacao farming are economic staples for the economy as is the manufacture of furniture and jade products. The colonial architecture in San Cristóbal de las Casas and the ancient Maya city of Palenque attract tourists.

A center for cattle and timber trading, the capital of Chiapas, Tuxtla Gutiérrez, was named to honor Joaquin Miguel Gutiérrez, who campaigned to prevent the state from becoming part of Guatemala.

Named for Vicente Guerrero, a leader of the Mexican independence movement, Guerrero is one of Mexico's poorest and most rural states. The site of numerous pre-Columbian civilizations as well as the location of Mexico's formal declaration of independence, the Plan de Iguala, Guerrero became a state in 1849. The Sierra Madre del Sur range dominates the topography of an area that can be broadly divided into two major regions: the Costa Chica tropical coastal lowlands and drier, more temperate highlands. The Balsas River is the principal waterway, and its Infiernillo Dam creates one of Mexico's largest reservoirs on the border with the state of Michoacán. Divided into 76 municipalities, the capital is Chilpancingo de los Bravos. Livestock raising, tourism, mining, and forestry represent key economic activities.

Another poor, rural state on the coast, Oaxaca has the largest indigenous population in Mexico, constituting more than one-third of the state's total population. Zapotec culture flourished in Oaxaca from the 3rd to the 10th century before it was superseded by the Mixtec culture, which prospered until the Spanish conquest in 1521. Oaxaca became a state in 1824 and was the birthplace of two of Mexico's most influential presidents: Benito Juárez and Porfirio Díaz.

Oaxaca, the capital, along with larger cities like Juchitán de Zaragoza and Salina Cruz, attracts those in search of employment. The eastern portion of the state incorporates about half of the arid Isthmus of Tehuantepec, which connects central Mexico with the Yucatán Peninsula and Central America. The economy depends heavily on forestry and agriculture but handicrafts, tourism, and mining also contribute to the vitality of 570 municipalities.

Oaxaca is the capital of an agricultural state where coffee is the principal crop. Founded by the Aztecs, Oaxaca is a popular tourist base for exploring archeological sites such as Monte Albán, the center of Zapotec civilization. Renowned for its jewelry and hand-woven textiles, the city played a significant role in Mexico's struggle for independence.

Chiapas, Guerrero & Oaxaca at a Glance

People	CH	GR	OA	Mexico
Population, 2000	3,920,892	3,079,649	3,438,765	97,483,412
Population percent change, 1990–2000	2.0%	1.6%	1.3%	16.7%
Persons under 5 years old, percent, 2000	12.3%	12.7%	11.5%	10.9%
Persons under 15 years old, percent, 2000	38.0%	38.9%	37.8%	33.4%
Persons 65 years old and over, percent, 2000	3.6%	5.1%	5.9%	4.9%
Female persons, percent, 2000	50.5%	51.6%	52%	51.2%
Percentage of population age 5+ that speaks Spanish, 2000	61.2%	63.7%	79.0%	81.5%
Persons age 5+ that speak an indigenous language	809,592	367,110	1,120,312	6,044,547
Tzotzil/Nahuatl/Zapoteco speakers, percent, 2000	36.0%	37.2%	31.0%	NA
Tzeltal/Mixteco/Mixteco speakers, percent, 2000	34.4%	28.1%	21.5%	NA
Chol/Tlapaneco/Mazateco speakers, percent, 2000	17.4%	24.6%	15.6%	NA
Zoque/Amuzgo/Mixe speakers, percent, 2000	5.1%	9.4%	9.4%	NA
Tojolabal/Zapoteco/Chinanteco speakers, percent, 2000	4.7%	0.2%	9.3%	NA
Other indigenous language speakers, percent, 2000	2.3%	0.3%	13.2%	4.2
Completed primary education, percent of persons age 15+, 2000 (a)	17.5%	17.4%	20.9%	19.4%
Completed post-primary education, pct of persons age 15+, 2000 (b)	27.9%	35.3%	29.2%	46.9%
Persons with a disability	49,823	50,969	65,969	1,795,300

(a) Includes persons having passed 6 years of elementary school
(b) Includes persons having passed 3 years of high school
NA: Not available
Source: (INEGI) El Instituto Nacional de Estadística, Geografía e Informática

People (cont.)	CH	GR	OA	Mexico
Housing units, 2000	778,845	651,149	738,087	21,513,235
Units with floor other than earth, percent, 2000	61.9%	63.5%	60.6%	86.7%
Units with durable roofing materials, percent, 2000	23.3%	36.8%	33.0%	64.2%
Units with durable wall materials, percent, 2000	52.3%	51.3%	51.9%	79.3%
Homeownership rate, 2000	83.3%	84.0%	87.2%	78.3%
Households, 2000	808,149	674,177	763,292	22,268,916
Average number of persons per housing unit, 2000	4.9	4.7	4.6	4.4

Business	CH	GR	OA	Mexico
Agricultural employment, percent, 2003	35.5%	33.5%	39.9%	ND
Industrial employment, percent, 2003	12.3%	9.6%	14.3%	ND
Construction employment, percent, 2003	6.0%	6.0%	5.4%	ND
Retail employment, percent, 2003	15.5%	15.7%	16.1%	ND
Communication and transportation employment, percent, 2003	4.5%	4.3%	2.3%	ND
Government employment, percent, 2003	3.5%	4.9%	4.0%	ND
Social, financial and professional service employment, pct, 2003	9.3%	11.6%	8.2%	ND
Service employment, percent, 2003	13.4%	14.3%	9.8%	ND
Total workforce participation, percent, 2003	41.8%	38.6%	41.0%	42.6%
Male workforce participation, percent, 2003	69.8%	67.7%	63.7%	65.7%
Female workforce participation, percent, 2003	30.2%	32.3%	36.3%	34.3%

Geography	CH	GR	OA	Mexico
Land area, 2000 (square kilometers)	74,211	64,281	93,952	1,958,200
Persons per square kilometer, 2000	53	48	37	50

Tabasco & Veracruz

North of Chiapas on the Bay of Campeche, Tabasco's state capital and only major city among its seventeen municipalities is Villahermosa. Originally a center of the Olmec civilization, the Spanish explored the region in 1518, and Francisco de Montejo captured it from the Chol and Maya inhabitants in 1530. Largely an undeveloped alluvial floodplain with tropical forests, swamps, and lagoons, Tabasco averages more rainfall annually than any other Mexican state. The two principal waterways, the Grijalva and Usumacinta Rivers, divide the state into two hot and humid regions. It is the nation's leading producer of crude oil and natural gas. One of Mexico's largest oil fields, Cinco Presidentes, was discovered here in 1960. Sites of interest include La Venta, capital of the ancient Olmec Empire, ecological reserves such as Pantanos de Centla and Yumka, as well as numerous beaches.

Originally a small port between the Grijalva and Carrizal rivers, Villahermosa de San Juan Bautista grew to become a sizable city and the capital of Tabasco following the development of oil production and the advent of hydroelectric power.

Veracruz is a long and narrow state, the third largest by population, located between the coast of the Gulf of Mexico and the Sierra Madre Oriental mountain range. In 1519 Hernán Cortés landed at San Juan de Ulúa and systematically set about claiming the land for the Spanish crown. Of the pre-Columbian Olmec, Huastec, and Totonac cultures, only the ruins of their great cities and temples remain today at over 1,000 archeological sites. Veracruz achieved statehood when Mexico became an independent republic in 1824 and has since been divided into 210 municipalities. The state capital is Jalapa Enríquez (Xalapa) and other major cities include Veracruz, Coatzacoalcos, Tuxpan de Rodríguez Cano, Minatitlán, Orizaba, and Poza Rica. Consisting of a hot and flat coastal region and a forested highland plateau that includes Pico de Orizaba (Citlaltepetl), the highest peak in Mexico, the principal rivers in the state are the Pánuco, Tuxpan and the Tonalá. A leading manufacturing state, Veracruz also grows more rice than any other state and produces more than one-quarter of Mexico's petroleum—primarily through offshore drilling. Fishing is another valuable source of income as sea bass and red snapper can be found in abundance in the Gulf.

Sitting on the slopes of the Sierra Madre Oriental, Jalapa Enríquez gives its name to the medicinal purgative *jalap*, which is derived from a locally grown plant, the jalap bindweed. Conquered by Hernán Cortés in 1519, Jalapa later served as military base and today the capital city is a market center for local produce, particularly coffee and tobacco and, to a lesser degree, a tourist destination.

Tabasco & Veracruz at a Glance

People	TA	VZ	Mexico
Population, 2000	1,891,829	6,908,975	97,483,412
Population percent change, 1990–2000	2.3%	1.0%	1.8%
Persons under 5 years old, percent, 2000	11.3%	10.5%	10.9%
Persons under 15 years old, percent, 2000	35.5%	33.8%	33.4%
Persons 65 years old and over, percent, 2000	3.9%	5.4%	4.9%
Female persons, percent, 2000	50.6%	51.4%	51.2%
Percentage of population age 5+ that speaks Spanish, 2000	95.4%	85.7%	81.5%
Persons age 5+ that speak an indigenous language	62,027	633,372	6,044,547
Chontal de tabasco/Náhuatl speakers, percent, 2000	61.8%	53.4%	NA / 24%
Chol/Totonaca speakers, percent, 2000	16.2%	18.9%	2.7% / 4%
Tzeltal/Huasteco speakers, percent, 2000	3.1%	8.2%	4.7% / 2.5
Maya/Popoluca speakers, percent, 2000	2.0%	5.8%	13.2% / NA
Zapoteco/Zapoteco speakers, percent, 2000	1.8%	3.3%	7.5%
Other indigenous language speakers, percent, 2000	6.0%	10.3%	4.2%
Completed primary education, percent of persons age 15+, 2000 (a)	19.2%	18.6%	19.4%
Completed post-primary education, percent of persons age 15+, 2000 (b)	18.1%	15.0%	19.1%
Persons with a disability	38,558	137,267	1,795,300

(a) Includes persons having passed 6 years of elementary school
(b) Includes persons having passed 3 years of high school
NA: Not available
Source: (INEGI) El Instituto Nacional de Estadística, Geografía e Informática

People (cont.)	TA	VZ	Mexico
Housing units, 2000	410,388	1,597,311	21,513,235
Units with floor other than earth, percent, 2000	87.3%	73.7%	86.7%
Units with durable roofing materials, percent, 2000	29.6%	39.1%	64.2%
Units with durable wall materials, percent, 2000	78.3%	70.0%	79.3%
Homeownership rate, 2000	80.3%	79.9%	78.3%
Households, 2000	424,613	1,635,564	22,268,916
Average number of persons per housing unit, 2000	4.6	4.3	4.4
Business	**TA**	**VZ**	**Mexico**
Agricultural employment, percent, 2003	25.2%	30.3%	NA
Industrial employment, percent, 2003	13.5%	12.1%	NA
Construction employment, percent, 2003	6.1%	8.1%	NA
Retail employment, percent, 2003	15.9%	18.2%	NA
Communication and transportation employment, percent, 2003	3.6%	3.8%	NA
Government employment, percent, 2003	7.3%	2.8%	NA
Social, financial and professional service employment, percent, 2003	12.3%	10.0%	NA
Service employment, percent, 2003	16.1%	14.7%	NA
Total workforce participation, percent, 2003	42.0%	35.7%	42.6%
Male workforce participation, percent, 2003	70.7%	71.9%	65.7%
Female workforce participation, percent, 2003	29.3%	28.1%	34.3%
Geography	**TA**	**VZ**	**Mexico**
Land area, 2000 (square kilometers)	25,267	71,699	1,958,200
Persons per square kilometer, 2000	76	96	50

Campeche, Quintana Roo & Yucatán

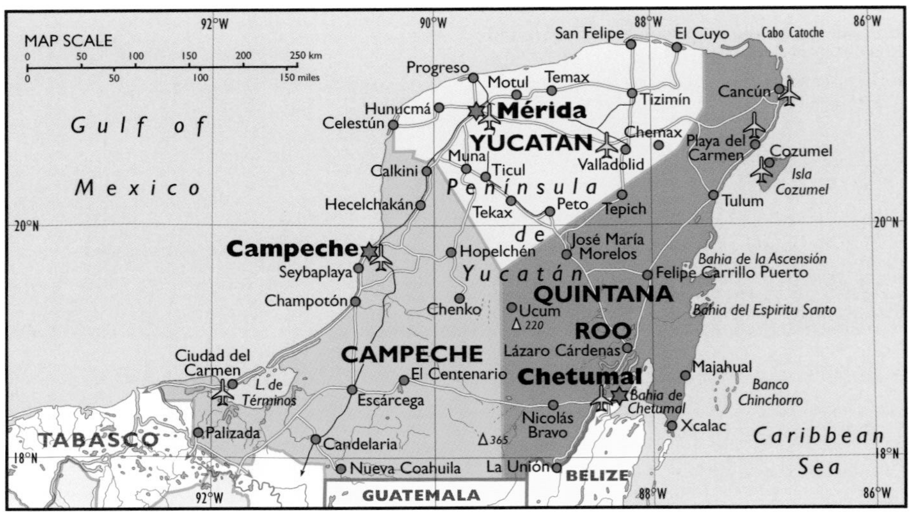

Bordering Guatemala in addition to three Mexican states, Campeche is divided into eleven municipalities that share a tropical climate on the Gulf of Mexico. Historically, the entire Yucatán Peninsula formed the core of the ancient Maya culture and dozens of once mighty cities such as Calakmul have been discovered within Campeche's borders. Traveling southeast from the coastal plain, the rainforests in the higher elevations continue to support a way of life Mayan speakers have practiced for thousands of years. The three largest rivers in the state, the Candelaria, Palizada, and the Chumpán empty into the Laguna de Términos, the nation's largest estuary. One of the least heavily populated states in the country, Ciudad del Carmen is the only sizable city apart from the capital. Fishing and agriculture in the north are key economic activities although offshore oilfields have become increasingly important.

Campeche is the capital city and a seaport on the Gulf coast. The site of a pre-Columbian town, it was settled by the Spanish in 1540 and the original stone walls built to defend against pirate attacks still survive. Cotton, sugarcane, cigars, hides, and tobacco are exported while cigars, chocolate, shoes, tanned leather products, and distilled beverages are made locally.

Occupying the eastern third of the Yucatán Peninsula in southeastern Mexico, Quintana Roo falls within a limestone plateau region, covered in dense tropical forests that include large stands of mahogany. This state with eight municipalities has a strong Maya heritage, with many important archeological sites, most notably Tulum on the coast. In 1517, the first Spanish explorers of Mexico landed at Cape Catoche, in northern Quintana Roo. The Caste War of the Yucatán began in 1847, and within six years the government defeated the Maya, many of whom fled into the remote forests of Quintana Roo, where they continued to wage a guerrilla war against the Mexican army until 1901. Quintana Roo became a federal territory a year later and a full state in 1974. Chetumal although the capital city, trails the beach resort of Cancún in population and tourism. Cozumel Island, located on the world's second largest coral reef is another world class tourist destination known for its beaches.

A smaller capital city on the shallow Chetumal Bay just north of Belize, Chetumal is especially vulnerable to hurricanes due to its location on the Caribbean Sea. Much of the traffic in local hardwoods moves through this free port.

The state of Yucatán occupies the northern third of the Yucatán peninsula. Low-lying terrain in this dry state is covered in most places with scrub and cactus thickets. Lacking any river systems, the only sources of water for the 106 municipalities are cenotes, wells that form naturally in the limestone. The state capital is Mérida, inland from Progreso on the Gulf of Mexico. Once the center of the Maya civilization, Yucatán was conquered by the Spanish in the 1540s yet several ancient cities such as Uxmal and Chichén Itzá stand as reminders of their ancient architects and act as beacons for a lucrative tourist industry. The region is a producer of *henequén*, a sisal hemp used for cordage and other principal products include tobacco, sugar, cotton, tropical fruit and seafood.

Founded in 1542 by Francisco de Montejo, Mérida, the capital of Yucatán, has many fine examples of Spanish colonial architecture, most notably its sixteenth-century cathedral. The largest city on the peninsula, it is the site of the Autonomous University of Yucatán which was established in 1624 and exports hides, chicle, and sisal, in addition to agricultural equipment. Tourism is the most significant source of revenue, followed by handicrafts and *henequén* production.

Campeche, Quintana Roo & Yucatán at a Glance

People	**CP**	**QR**	**YC**	**Mexico**
Population, 2000	690,689	874,963	1,658,210	97,483,412
Population percent change, 1990–2000	2.6%	5.8%	2.0%	1.8%
Persons under 5 years old, percent, 2000	10.9%	10.4%	8.6%	10.9%
Persons under 15 years old, percent, 2000	35.5%	31.9%	26.0%	33.4%
Persons 65 years old and over, percent, 2000	5.3%	3.6%	5.8%	4.9%
Female persons, percent, 2000	50.1%	48.8%	50.6%	51.2%
Percentage of population age 5+ that speaks Spanish, 2000	93.0%	91.7%	90.6%	81.5%
Persons age 5+ that speak an indigenous language	93,765	173,592	549,532	6,044,547
Maya speakers, percent, 2000	80.9%	94.2%	99.5%	13.2%
Chol/Kanjobal/Chol speakers, percent, 2000	9.4%	0.7%	0.1%	NA
Kanjobal/Náhuatl/Zapoteco speakers, percent, 2000	2.0%	0.7%	0.1%	NA
Tzeltal/Tzotzil/Mixe speakers, percent, 2000	1.8%	0.7%	0.1%	NA
Mame/Zapoteco/Náhuatl speakers, percent, 2000	1.3%	0.7%	0.0%	NA
Other indigenous language speakers, percent, 2000	4.1%	2.9%	0.2%	4.2%
Completed primary education, percent of persons age 15+, 2000 (a)	18.2%	17.2%	16.7%	19.4%
Completed post-primary education, percent of persons age 15+, 2000 (b)	15.4%	22.4%	15.8%	19.1%
Persons with a disability	15,778	12,186	47,774	1,795,300

(a) Includes persons having passed 6 years of elementary school
(b) Includes persons having passed 3 years of high school
NA: Not available
Source: (INEGI) El Instituto Nacional de Estadística, Geografía e Informática

People (cont.)	**CP**	**QR**	**YC**	**Mexico**
Housing units, 2000	156,125	210,482	371,242	21,513,235
Units with floor other than earth, percent, 2000	86.0%	90.0%	94.4%	86.7%
Units with durable roofing materials, percent, 2000	42.9%	65.7%	68.2%	64.2%
Units with durable wall materials, percent, 2000	68.7%	74.4%	84.8%	79.3%
Homeownership rate, 2000	83.3%	68.3%	84.7%	78.3%
Households, 2000	160,492	216,478	387,573	22,268,916
Average number of persons per housing unit, 2000	4.3	4.1	4.4	4.4

Business	**CP**	**QR**	**YC**	**Mexico**
Agricultural employment, percent, 2003	27.5%	9.5%	18.9%	NA
Industrial employment, percent, 2003	12.8%	8.4%	22.8%	NA
Construction employment, percent, 2003	9.6%	5.9%	4.9%	NA
Retail employment, percent, 2003	15.1%	19.4%	16.3%	NA
Communication and transportation employment, percent, 2003	3.0%	8.6%	4.1%	NA
Government employment, percent, 2003	6.6%	6.4%	5.0%	NA
Social, financial and professional service employment, percent, 2003	10.2%	11.7%	10.6%	NA
Service employment, percent, 2003	15.3%	30.1%	17.4%	NA
Total workforce participation, percent, 2003	45.5%	47.8%	45.8%	42.6%
Male workforce participation, percent, 2003	67.3%	70.0%	62.2%	65.7%
Female workforce participation, percent, 2003	32.7%	30.0%	37.8%	34.3%

Geography	**CP**	**QR**	**YC**	**Mexico**
Land area, 2000 (square kilometers)	50,812	50,212	38,402	1,958,200
Persons per square kilometer, 2000	12	21	42	50

INDEX

How to use the index

The index contains the names of the places and features shown on the maps covering the United States, Canada, and Mexico. Each name is followed by an additional entry in italics giving the state, province, region or country within which it is located. However, a name indexed to the large-scale city maps is followed by the name of the City Map within which it is located (e.g. Venice, Los Angeles).

The alphabetical order of names composed of two or more words is governed primarily by the first word and then by the second. This is an example of the rule:

Middle River, *MD, U.S.A.* **77 A4** 39 20N 76 27W
Middle River, *MN, U.S.A.* **80 B2** 48 26N 96 10W
Middle Valley, *TN, U.S.A.* **97 E7** 35 12N 85 11W
Middle Village, *NY, U.S.A.* **114 B3** 40 43N 73 52W
Middleboro, *MA, U.S.A.* **78 C4** 41 54N 70 55W

Physical features composed of a proper name (Erie) and a description (Lake) are positioned alphabetically by the proper name. The description is positioned after the proper name and is usually abbreviated:

Erie, L., *N. Amer.* **178 E5** 42 15N 81 0W

Where a description forms part of a settlement or administrative name, however, it is always written in full and put in its true alphabetical position:

Mount Olive, *IL, U.S.A.* **71 D4** 39 4N 89 44W

Names beginning with M' and Mc are indexed as if they were spelled Mac. Names beginning St. are alphabetized under Saint, but Sant', Santa and San are all spelled in full and are alphabetized accordingly.

The number in bold type that follows each name in the index refers to the number of the map page where that feature or place will be found. This is usually the largest scale at which the place or feature appears.

The letter and figure that are in bold type immediately after the page number give the grid square on the map page, within which the feature is situated. The letter represents the latitude and the figure the longitude. A lower-case letter immediately after the page number refers to an inset map on that page.

In some cases the feature itself may fall within the specified square, while the name is outside. This is usually the case only with features that are larger than a grid square.

The geographical coordinates that follow the letter-figure references give the latitude and longitude of each place. The first coordinate indicates latitude - the distance north or south of the Equator. The second coordinate indicates longitude - the distance east or west of the Greenwich Meridian. Both latitude and longitude are measures in degrees and minutes (there are 60 minutes in a degree).

The latitude is followed by N(orth) or S(outh) and the longitude by E(ast) or W(est).

Rivers are indexed to their mouths or confluences, and carry the symbol → after their names. The following symbols are also used in the index: ■ country, ▨ overseas territory or dependency, □ state or province, ☆ county, △ national park, ⌓ other park (national monuments and recreation areas, state and provincial parks, and wildlife reserves), and ✈ (DCA) principal airport (and location identifier).

Abbreviations

AK – Alaska
AL – Alabama
Amer. – America(n)
AR – Arkansas
AZ – Arizona
B. – Baie, Bahía, Bay
B.C. – British Columbia
Br. – British
C. – Cabo, Cap, Cape
CA – California
CO – Colorado
CT – Connecticut
DC – District of Columbia
DE – Delaware
E. – East
FL – Florida
G. – Golfe, Golfo, Gulf
GA – Georgia
Harb. – Harbor, Harbour
Hd. – Head
HI – Hawaii
Hts. – Heights
I.(s). – Île, Isla, Island, Isle
IA – Iowa
ID – Idaho
IL – Illinois
IN – Indiana
KS – Kansas
KY – Kentucky
L. – Lac, Lago, Lake
LA – Louisiana
MA – Massachusetts
Man. – Manitoba
MD – Maryland
ME – Maine
MI – Michigan
MN – Minnesota
MO – Missouri
MS – Mississippi
MT – Montana
Mt.(s). – Mont, Montaña, Mount, Mountain
N. – Nord, Norte, North, Northern
N.S. – Nova Scotia
N.W.T. – North West Territory
Nac. – Nacional
Nat. – National
NC – North Carolina
ND – North Dakota
NE – Nebraska
Nfld. & Lab. – Newfoundland and Labrador
NH – New Hampshire
NJ – New Jersey
NM – New Mexico
NV – Nevada
NY – New York
OH – Ohio
OK – Oklahoma
Ont. – Ontario
OR – Oregon
P. – Pass
P.E.I. – Prince Edward Island
PA – Pennsylvania
Pac. Oc. – Pacific Ocean
Pass. – Passage
Pen. – Peninsula, Péninsule
Pk. – Peak
Plat. – Plateau
Pt. – Point
Pta. – Punta
Qué – Québec
R. – Rio, River
Range – Range
Recr. – Recreational
Res. – Reserve, Reservoir
RI – Rhode Island
S. – South, Southern
Sa. – Serra, Sierra
Sask. – Saskatchewan
SC – South Carolina
SD – South Dakota
Sd. – Sound
Sprs. – Springs
St. – Saint
Sta. – Santa
Ste. – Sainte
Sto. – Santo
St-P. & M. – Saint Pierre et Miquelon
Str. – Strait, Stretto
Terr. – Territory, Territoire
TN – Tennessee
TX – Texas
UT – Utah
VA – Virginia
VT – Vermont
W. – West
WA – Washington
WI – Wisconsin
WV – West Virginia
WY – Wyoming

A

Abajo Peak, *UT, U.S.A.* **100 F6** 37 51N 109 27W
Abalá, *Yucatán, Mexico* **223 B4** 20 38N 89 41W
Abamasagi L., *Ont., Canada* **181 B9** 50 28N 87 15W
Abasolo, *Coahuila, Mexico* **214 C3** 27 12N 101 24W
Abasolo, *Guanajuato, Mexico* . . . **218 B6** 20 28N 101 32W
Abasolo, *Nuevo León, Mexico* . . . **214 E4** 25 58N 100 26W
Abasolo, *Tamaulipas, Mexico* **215 F6** 24 4N 98 22W
Abbaye, Pt., *MI, U.S.A.* **79 C3** 46 58N 88 8W
Abbeville, *AL, U.S.A.* **60 E5** 31 34N 85 15W
Abbeville, *GA, U.S.A.* **68 E3** 31 59N 83 18W
Abbeville, *LA, U.S.A.* **75 E3** 29 58N 92 8W
Abbeville, *MS, U.S.A.* **81 B4** 34 30N 89 30W
Abbeville, *SC, U.S.A.* **90 D3** 34 11N 82 23W
Abbeville County ☆, *SC, U.S.A.* . . **90 D3** 34 15N 82 30W
Abbey, *Sask., Canada* **182 E3** 50 44N 108 45W
Abbotsford, *B.C., Canada* **187 F12** 49 5N 122 20W
Abbotsford, *WI, U.S.A.* **103 D3** 44 57N 90 19W
Abbott, *NM, U.S.A.* **88 A6** 36 18N 104 16W
Abbott, *TX, U.S.A.* **99 F10** 31 53N 97 4W
Abbottstown, *PA, U.S.A.* **77 A4** 39 53N 76 59W
Abercorn, *Qué., Canada* **86 A2** 45 2N 72 40W
Abercrombie, *ND, U.S.A.* **91 D9** 46 27N 96 44W
Aberdeen, *Sask., Canada* **182 C5** 52 20N 106 8W
Aberdeen, *AL, U.S.A.* **81 C5** 33 49N 88 33W
Aberdeen, *ID, U.S.A.* **70 G6** 42 57N 112 50W
Aberdeen, *KY, U.S.A.* **96 C6** 37 15N 86 41W
Aberdeen, *MD, U.S.A.* **77 A4** 39 31N 76 10W
Aberdeen, *NC, U.S.A.* **90 C6** 35 8N 79 26W
Aberdeen, *SD, U.S.A.* **91 E7** 45 28N 98 29W
Aberdeen, *WA, U.S.A.* **101 D2** 46 59N 123 50W
Aberdeen L., *Nunavut, Canada* . . **191 E6** 64 30N 99 0W
Aberdeen L., *MS, U.S.A.* **81 C5** 33 50N 88 31W
Aberdeen Proving Ground, *MD, U.S.A.* **77 A4** 39 29N 76 10W
Abernant, *AL, U.S.A.* **60 C3** 33 17N 87 12W
Abernathy, *TX, U.S.A.* **98 D6** 33 50N 101 51W
Abernethy, *Sask., Canada* **182 E8** 50 45N 103 25W
Abert, L., *OR, U.S.A.* **94 E5** 42 38N 120 14W
Abilene, *KS, U.S.A.* **74 C6** 38 55N 97 13W
Abilene, *TX, U.S.A.* **99 E8** 32 28N 99 43W
Abingdon, *IL, U.S.A.* **71 C3** 40 48N 90 24W
Abingdon, *VA, U.S.A.* **102 E3** 36 43N 81 59W
Abington, *CT, U.S.A.* **78 C2** 41 52N 72 1W
Abington, *MA, U.S.A.* **78 B4** 42 6N 70 57W
Abington, *PA, U.S.A.* **87 B1** 40 7N 75 7W
Abiquiu, *NM, U.S.A.* **88 A4** 36 13N 106 19W
Abiquiu Res., *NM, U.S.A.* **88 A4** 36 16N 106 27W
Abita Springs, *LA, U.S.A.* **75 D5** 30 29N 90 2W
Abitau →, *Canada* **189 E11** 59 53N 109 3W
Abitibi →, *Ont., Canada* **181 A16** 51 3N 80 55W
Abitibi, L., *Ont., Canada* **176 C3** 48 40N 79 40W
Abra Tanchipas, Sa. del, *San Luis Potosí, Mexico* **215 H6** 22 15N 98 57W
Abraham González, Presa, *Chihuahua, Mexico* **213 E8** 28 28N 107 28W
Abraham L., *Alta., Canada* **185 F4** 52 15N 116 35W
Abraham Lincoln Birthplace Nat. Historic Site ⌂, *KY, U.S.A.* **97 C7** 37 32N 85 44W
Absaroka Range, *WY, U.S.A.* **104 B3** 44 45N 109 50W
Absarokee, *MT, U.S.A.* **83 E8** 45 31N 109 27W
Absecon, *NJ, U.S.A.* **87 C2** 39 26N 74 30W
Absecon Lighthouse, *NJ, U.S.A.* . **87 C2** 39 22N 74 27W
Acacoyagua, *Chiapas, Mexico* . . . **222 D4** 15 21N 92 39W
Acadia Nat. Park △, *ME, U.S.A.* . **76 D5** 44 20N 68 13W
Acadia Parish ☆, *LA, U.S.A.* **75 D3** 30 13N 92 22W
Acadia Valley, *Alta., Canada* **185 G10** 51 8N 110 13W
Acámbaro, *Guanajuato, Mexico* . . **219 B7** 20 2N 100 44W
Acambay, *México, Mexico* **219 C8** 19 58N 99 52W
Acancéh, *Yucatán, Mexico* **223 B4** 20 49N 89 27W
Acapetahua, *Chiapas, Mexico* . . . **222 D4** 15 17N 92 42W
Acapetlahuaya, *Guerrero, Mexico* **219 D7** 18 26N 100 4W
Acaponeta, *Nayarit, Mexico* **216 E5** 22 30N 105 22W
Acapulco, *Guerrero, Mexico* **219 F8** 16 51N 99 55W
Acatic, *Jalisco, Mexico* **218 B5** 20 47N 102 53W
Acatlán, *Hidalgo, Mexico* **219 B9** 20 9N 98 27W
Acatlán, *Oaxaca, Mexico* **221 F4** 18 32N 96 37W
Acatlán, *Puebla, Mexico* **221 F2** 18 12N 98 3W
Acatlán de Juárez, *Jalisco, Mexico* **218 B4** 20 26N 103 38W
Acatzingo, *Puebla, Mexico* **221 F3** 18 59N 97 47W
Acayucán, *Veracruz, Mexico* **221 G6** 17 57N 94 55W
Accident, *MD, U.S.A.* **77 A1** 39 38N 79 19W
Accokeek, *MD, U.S.A.* **77 B3** 38 40N 77 2W
Accomac, *VA, U.S.A.* **102 D9** 37 43N 75 40W
Accomack County ☆, *VA, U.S.A.* . **102 D9** 37 45N 75 40W
Accotink, L., *VA, U.S.A.* **119 C2** 38 47N 77 13W
Accotink Cr. →, *VA, U.S.A.* **119 B2** 38 51N 77 15W
Achille, *OK, U.S.A.* **93 E7** 33 50N 96 23W
Ackerman, *MS, U.S.A.* **81 C4** 33 19N 89 11W
Ackley, *IA, U.S.A.* **73 C5** 42 33N 93 3W
Acme, *Alta., Canada* **185 G7** 51 33N 113 30W
Acme, *LA, U.S.A.* **75 C4** 31 17N 91 49W
Acoma Indian Reservation, *NM, U.S.A.* **88 C3** 34 45N 107 30W
Acomita, *NM, U.S.A.* **88 B3** 35 3N 107 34W
Aconchi, *Sonora, Mexico* **212 D5** 29 50N 110 12W
Acteopan, *Puebla, Mexico* **221 F2** 18 47N 98 41W
Acton, *Ont., Canada* **178 D6** 43 38N 80 3W
Acton, *MA, U.S.A.* **78 B3** 42 29N 71 26W
Acton Vale, *Qué., Canada* **177 F10** 45 39N 72 34W
Actopan, *Hidalgo, Mexico* **219 B9** 20 16N 98 56W
Actopan, *Veracruz, Mexico* **220 E4** 19 30N 96 37W
Acuitzio del Canje, *Michoacan, Mexico* **219 C6** 19 29N 101 20W
Aculco, *México, Mexico* **219 B8** 20 7N 99 49W
Acushnet, *MA, U.S.A.* **78 C4** 41 41N 70 55W
Acuyo, *Michoacan, Mexico* **219 D6** 18 53N 101 11W
Acworth, *GA, U.S.A.* **68 B2** 34 4N 84 41W
Ada, *KS, U.S.A.* **74 B6** 39 9N 97 53W
Ada, *MN, U.S.A.* **80 C2** 47 18N 96 31W
Ada, *OH, U.S.A.* **92 C3** 40 46N 83 49W
Ada, *OK, U.S.A.* **93 D7** 34 46N 96 41W
Ada County ☆, *ID, U.S.A.* **70 F2** 43 30N 116 15W
Adair, *IA, U.S.A.* **73 D4** 41 30N 94 39W
Adair, *OK, U.S.A.* **93 B8** 36 26N 95 16W
Adair, B., *Sonora, Mexico* **212 B2** 31 30N 113 48W
Adair, C., *Nunavut, Canada* **190 C11** 71 30N 71 34W
Adair County ☆, *IA, U.S.A.* **73 D4** 41 20N 94 30W
Adair County ☆, *KY, U.S.A.* **97 C7** 37 5N 85 20W
Adair County ☆, *MO, U.S.A.* **82 A4** 40 10N 92 35W
Adair County ☆, *OK, U.S.A.* **93 C9** 35 55N 94 45W
Adairsville, *GA, U.S.A.* **68 B2** 34 22N 84 56W
Adairville, *KY, U.S.A.* **96 D6** 36 40N 86 51W
Adak, *AK, U.S.A.* **61 L3** 51 45N 176 45W
Adak I., *AK, U.S.A.* **61 L3** 51 45N 176 45W
Adams, *MA, U.S.A.* **78 B1** 42 38N 73 7W
Adams, *MN, U.S.A.* **80 G6** 43 34N 92 43W
Adams, *ND, U.S.A.* **91 B7** 48 25N 98 5W
Adams, *NY, U.S.A.* **89 B4** 43 49N 76 1W
Adams, *NE, U.S.A.* **84 D9** 40 28N 96 31W
Adams, *OK, U.S.A.* **93 B2** 36 45N 101 5W
Adams, *OR, U.S.A.* **94 B7** 45 46N 118 34W
Adams, *San Diego, U.S.A.* **117 B2** 32 45N 117 7W
Adams, *TN, U.S.A.* **96 D5** 36 35N 87 4W
Adams, *WI, U.S.A.* **103 E4** 43 57N 89 49W
Adams →, *B.C., Canada* **187 D15** 51 25N 119 27W
Adams, Mt., *WA, U.S.A.* **101 D4** 46 12N 121 30W
Adams Center, *NY, U.S.A.* **89 B5** 43 52N 76 0W
Adams County ☆, *CO, U.S.A.* . . . **66 C6** 39 50N 104 10W
Adams County ☆, *ID, U.S.A.* **70 E2** 45 0N 116 30W
Adams County ☆, *IL, U.S.A.* **71 D2** 40 0N 91 10W
Adams County ☆, *IN, U.S.A.* **72 C6** 40 45N 85 0W
Adams County ☆, *IA, U.S.A.* **73 D4** 41 0N 94 40W
Adams County ☆, *MS, U.S.A.* **81 E2** 31 23N 91 24W
Adams County ☆, *ND, U.S.A.* **91 D3** 46 0N 102 30W
Adams County ☆, *NE, U.S.A.* **84 D7** 40 30N 98 30W
Adams County ☆, *OH, U.S.A.* **92 E3** 38 48N 83 33W
Adams County ☆, *PA, U.S.A.* **95 E5** 39 50N 77 14W
Adams County ☆, *WA, U.S.A.* . . . **101 C7** 47 0N 118 30W
Adams County ☆, *WI, U.S.A.* **103 E4** 44 0N 89 50W
Adams L., *B.C., Canada* **187 D15** 51 10N 119 40W
Adams-McGill Res., *NV, U.S.A.* . . **85 D5** 38 22N 115 7W
Adams Park, *Atlanta, U.S.A.* **106 B2** 33 43N 84 27W
Adams Pt., *MI, U.S.A.* **79 D8** 45 25N 83 43W
Adams Shore, *Boston, U.S.A.* **106 B4** 42 15N 70 59W
Adamstown, *PA, U.S.A.* **95 D6** 40 15N 76 3W
Adamsville, *Qué., Canada* **86 A2** 45 17N 72 47W
Adamsville, *OH, U.S.A.* **92 C5** 40 4N 81 53W
Adamsville, *RI, U.S.A.* **78 C3** 41 30N 71 10W
Adamsville, *TN, U.S.A.* **96 E4** 35 14N 88 23W
Adamsville, *TX, U.S.A.* **99 F9** 31 18N 98 10W
Addieville, *IL, U.S.A.* **71 E4** 38 23N 89 29W
Addington, *OK, U.S.A.* **93 D6** 34 15N 97 58W
Addis, *LA, U.S.A.* **75 D4** 30 21N 91 16W
Addison, *AL, U.S.A.* **60 B3** 34 12N 87 11W
Addison, *IL, U.S.A.* **71 B5** 41 55N 88 0W
Addison, *NY, U.S.A.* **89 C3** 42 1N 77 14W
Addison, *OH, U.S.A.* **92 E4** 38 53N 82 9W
Addison, *VT, U.S.A.* **86 B1** 44 8N 73 20W
Addison County ☆, *VT, U.S.A.* . . **86 B1** 44 0N 73 15W
Addy, *WA, U.S.A.* **101 B8** 48 21N 117 50W
Adel, *GA, U.S.A.* **68 E3** 31 8N 83 25W
Adel, *IA, U.S.A.* **73 D4** 41 37N 94 1W
Adel, *OR, U.S.A.* **94 E6** 42 11N 119 54W
Adelaide Pen., *Nunavut, Canada* . **190 D6** 68 15N 97 30W
Adelanto, *CA, U.S.A.* **65 J9** 34 35N 117 22W
Adelphi, *MD, U.S.A.* **77 A4** 39 0N 76 58W
Adelphi, *OH, U.S.A.* **92 D4** 39 28N 82 45W
Adelphia, *NJ, U.S.A.* **87 B2** 40 13N 74 15W
Adena, *OH, U.S.A.* **92 C6** 40 13N 80 53W
Adin, *CA, U.S.A.* **64 B6** 41 12N 120 57W
Adirondack Mts., *NY, U.S.A.* **89 B7** 44 0N 74 0W
Adirondack Park ⌂, *NY, U.S.A.* . . **89 B6** 44 0N 74 20W
Adjuntas, *Puerto Rico* **105 G16** 18 10N 66 43W
Adjuntas del Refugio, *Zacatecas, Mexico* **217 E7** 22 39N 103 24W
Adlavik Is., *Nfld. & L., Canada* . . **175 C6** 55 0N 58 40W
Admiral, *Sask., Canada* **182 F3** 49 43N 108 1W
Admiral's Beach, *Nfld. & L., Canada* **174 E7** 47 1N 53 39W
Admiralty I., *N.W.T., Canada* **190 D5** 69 25N 101 10W
Admiralty I., *AK, U.S.A.* **61 H14** 57 30N 134 30W
Admiralty Inlet, *N.W.T., Canada* . **190 C8** 72 30N 86 0W
Admiralty Inlet, *WA, U.S.A.* **101 B3** 48 8N 122 58W
Admiralty Island Nat. Monument ⌂, *U.S.A.* **61 H14** 57 40N 134 10W
Adobe Creek Res., *CO, U.S.A.* . . . **66 D7** 38 14N 103 17W
Adobe Dam County Recreation Area, *Phoenix, U.S.A.* **116 A1** 33 41N 112 9W
Adolfo López Mateos, *Baja Calif. S., Mexico* **211 H6** 25 11N 112 8W
Adolfo López Mateos, *Chihuahua, Mexico* **213 E8** 28 28N 107 20W
Adolfo López Mateos, *Durango, Mexico* **217 C6** 24 32N 104 17W
Adolfo López Mateos, *Quintana Roo, Mexico* **223 C5** 19 37N 88 42W
Adolfo López Mateos, *Zacatecas, Mexico* **217 E7** 22 7N 103 1W
Adolfo López Mateos, Presa, *Sinaloa, Mexico* **216 B3** 25 10N 107 24W
Adolfo Ruiz, *Campeche, Mexico* . . **223 C3** 19 30N 90 21W
Adolfo Ruiz Cortines, Presa, *Sonora, Mexico* **212 F6** 27 15N 109 6W
Adrian, *GA, U.S.A.* **68 D4** 32 33N 82 35W
Adrian, *MI, U.S.A.* **79 H7** 41 54N 84 2W
Adrian, *MN, U.S.A.* **80 G3** 43 38N 95 56W
Adrian, *MO, U.S.A.* **82 C2** 38 24N 94 21W
Adrian, *OR, U.S.A.* **94 D8** 43 45N 117 4W
Adrian, *TX, U.S.A.* **98 B5** 35 16N 102 40W
Advance, *IN, U.S.A.* **72 D4** 40 0N 86 40W
Advance, *MO, U.S.A.* **82 D7** 37 6N 89 55W
Advocate Harbour, *N.S., Canada* . **173 H5** 45 20N 64 47W
Aetna, *KS, U.S.A.* **74 D5** 37 5N 98 58W
Affton, *MO, U.S.A.* **82 C6** 38 33N 90 20W
Afognak I., *AK, U.S.A.* **61 G9** 58 15N 152 30W
Afton, *CA, U.S.A.* **65 H10** 35 2N 116 23W
Afton, *IA, U.S.A.* **73 D4** 41 2N 94 12W
Afton, *NY, U.S.A.* **89 C5** 42 14N 75 32W
Afton, *OK, U.S.A.* **93 B9** 36 42N 94 58W
Afton, *WY, U.S.A.* **104 D2** 42 44N 110 56W
Agana, *Guam* . . . . **105 b** 13 28N 144 45 E
Agar, *SD, U.S.A.* **91 F5** 44 50N 100 5W
Agassiz, *B.C., Canada* **187 F13** 49 14N 121 46W
Agassiz Icecap, *Nunavut, Canada* **190 A10** 80 15N 76 0W
Agassiz Nat. Wildlife Refuge ⌂, *MN, U.S.A.* **80 B3** 48 21N 95 57W
Agassiz Pool, *MN, U.S.A.* **80 B3** 48 20N 95 59W
Agat, *Guam* . . . . **105 b** 13 25N 144 40 E
Agate, *CO, U.S.A.* **66 C7** 39 28N 103 57W
Agate Fossil Beds Nat. Monument ⌂, *NE, U.S.A.* **84 B2** 42 20N 103 50W
Agattu I., *AK, U.S.A.* . . . . **61 K1** 52 25N 173 35 E
Agawa →, *Ont., Canada* **181 E12** 47 23N 84 40W
Agawam, *MA, U.S.A.* **78 B2** 42 5N 72 37W
Agawam, *MT, U.S.A.* **83 C5** 48 0N 112 10W
Agency, *IA, U.S.A.* **73 E6** 41 0N 92 18W
Agency L., *OR, U.S.A.* **94 E4** 42 33N 121 58W
Agenda, *KS, U.S.A.* **74 B6** 39 43N 97 26W
Agiabampo, *Sonora, Mexico* **212 G6** 26 24N 109 8W
Agnes L., *Ont., Canada* **180 D5** 48 15N 91 20W
Agra, *KS, U.S.A.* **74 B4** 39 46N 99 7W
Agra, *OK, U.S.A.* **93 C7** 35 54N 96 53W
Agricola Oriental, *Distrito Federal, Mexico* **225 B3** 19 23N 99 4W
Agrihan, *N. Marianas* . . . . **105 a** 18 46N 145 40W
Agua Blanca, *Guadalajara, Mexico* **224 B2** 20 33N 103 10W
Agua Blanca, *Hidalgo, Mexico* . . . **219 B9** 20 22N 98 20W
Agua Brava, L. de, *Nayarit, Mexico* **216 E5** 22 10N 105 32W
Agua Caliente, *Baja Calif., Mexico* **210 C3** 30 40N 115 10W
Agua Caliente, *Chihuahua, Mexico* **212 F7** 27 55N 108 50W
Agua Caliente, *Sinaloa, Mexico* . . **216 D4** 23 36N 106 4W
Agua Caliente, *Sonora, Mexico* . . **212 E5** 28 5N 110 10W
Agua Caliente →, *Chihuahua, Mexico* **212 F7** 27 57N 108 30W
Agua de Enmedio, *San Luis Potosí, Mexico* **215 H4** 22 9N 100 15W
Agua Dulce, *Veracruz, Mexico* . . . **220 D3** 20 21N 97 17W
Agua Dulce, *Veracruz, Mexico* . . . **221 F6** 18 8N 94 8W
Agua Dulce, *TX, U.S.A.* **99 K10** 27 47N 97 55W
Agua Escondida →, *Baja Calif., Mexico* **210 C3** 30 31N 115 43W
Agua Fría, *Monterrey, Mexico* . . . **224 B3** 25 38N 100 10W
Agua Fria, *NM, U.S.A.* **88 B4** 35 39N 106 1W
Agua Fria →, *AZ, U.S.A.* **62 D3** 33 23N 112 22W
Agua Fria Nat. Monument ⌂, *U.S.A.* **59 J7** 34 14N 112 0W
Agua Fria Pk., *NM, U.S.A.* **88 A5** 36 22N 105 13W
Agua Grande, L., *Sinaloa, Mexico* **216 E5** 22 37N 105 40W
Agua Nueva, *Coahuila, Mexico* . . **215 E3** 25 12N 101 6W
Agua Nueva, *TX, U.S.A.* **98 L9** 26 54N 98 36W
Agua Nueva del Norte, *San Luis Potosí, Mexico* **215 H5** 22 37N 99 48W
Agua Prieta, *Sonora, Mexico* **212 B6** 31 18N 109 34W
Agua Verde, *Sinaloa, Mexico* **216 E5** 22 54N 105 59W
Agua Verde →, *Mexico* **214 C5** 27 50N 99 52W
Aguada, *Puerto Rico* **105 G15** 18 23N 67 11W
Aguadilla, *Puerto Rico* **105 G15** 18 26N 67 10W
Agualeguas, *Nuevo León, Mexico* . **214 D5** 26 18N 99 34W
Aguamilpa, *Nayarit, Mexico* **216 G5** 20 56N 105 2W
Aguamilpas, *Nayarit, Mexico* **216 F6** 21 47N 104 46W
Aguamilpas, Presa, *Nayarit, Mexico* **216 F6** 21 38N 104 37W
Aguanaval →, *Mexico* **217 C8** 25 28N 102 53W
Aguanaval, Sa., *Durango, Mexico* **217 B7** 25 3N 103 28W
Aguanish, *Qué., Canada* **175 C5** 50 14N 62 2W
Aguanus →, *Qué., Canada* **175 C5** 50 13N 62 5W
Aguapepito, *Sinaloa, Mexico* **216 C3** 24 35N 107 42W
Aguaruto, *Sinaloa, Mexico* **216 C3** 24 47N 107 29W
Aguascalientes, *Aguascalientes, Mexico* **217 F8** 21 53N 102 18W
Aguascalientes □, *Mexico* **217 F8** 22 0N 102 30W
Aguila, *AZ, U.S.A.* **62 D2** 33 57N 113 11W
Aguila, Punta, *Puerto Rico* **105 H15** 17 57N 67 13W
Aguilar, *CO, U.S.A.* **66 E6** 37 24N 104 39W
Aguilares, *TX, U.S.A.* **98 K8** 27 27N 99 5W
Aguililla, *Michoacan, Mexico* **218 D5** 18 44N 102 44W
Agujereada, Pta., *Puerto Rico* . . . **105 G15** 18 30N 67 8W
Ahome, *Sinaloa, Mexico* **216 B1** 25 55N 109 11W
Ahoskie, *NC, U.S.A.* **90 B9** 36 17N 76 59W
Ahuacatlán, *Nayarit, Mexico* **216 F6** 21 3N 104 29W
Ahuacuotzingo, *Guerrero, Mexico* **219 E9** 17 43N 98 59W
Ahualulco, *San Luis Potosí, Mexico* **215 H3** 22 24N 101 10W
Ahualulco de Mercado, *Jalisco, Mexico* **218 B4** 20 42N 103 59W
Ahuazotepec, *Puebla, Mexico* . . . **220 D2** 20 3N 98 9W
Ahuehuetitla, *Puebla, Mexico* . . . **221 F2** 18 12N 98 12W
Ahuijillo, *Jalisco, Mexico* **218 C4** 19 3N 103 5W
ʻĀhuimanu, *HI, U.S.A.* **69 K14** 21 26N 157 50W
Ahuntsic, *Montréal, Canada* **192 A2** 45 32N 73 41W
Ahwatukee Foothills, *Phoenix, U.S.A.* **116 D2** 33 20N 111 59W
ʻAiea, *HI, U.S.A.* **69 K14** 21 23N 157 56W
Aiguebelle, Parc de Conservation d' ⌂, *Qué., Canada* **176 C4** 48 30N 78 45W
Aiken, *SC, U.S.A.* **90 E4** 33 34N 81 43W
Aiken County ☆, *SC, U.S.A.* **90 E4** 33 30N 81 40W
Ailey, *GA, U.S.A.* **68 D4** 32 11N 82 34W
Aillik, *Nfld. & L., Canada* **175 B6** 55 11N 59 18W
Ailsa Craig, *Ont., Canada* **178 D5** 43 8N 81 33W
Ainslie, L., *N.S., Canada* **173 G8** 46 8N 61 11W
Ainsworth, *IA, U.S.A.* **73 D7** 41 17N 91 33W
Ainsworth, *NE, U.S.A.* **84 B6** 42 33N 99 52W
Air Force I., *Nunavut, Canada* . . . **190 D11** 67 58N 74 5W
Airdrie, *Alta., Canada* **185 G6** 51 18N 114 2W
Aire, Mt., *Salt Lake City, U.S.A.* . . **117 B3** 40 43N 111 41W
Airway Heights, *WA, U.S.A.* **101 C8** 47 39N 117 36W
Aishihik L., *Yukon, Canada* **189 D5** 61 26N 137 15W
Aitkin, *MN, U.S.A.* **80 D5** 46 32N 93 42W
Aitkin County ☆, *MN, U.S.A.* **80 D5** 46 30N 93 25W
Aix, Mt., *WA, U.S.A.* **101 D4** 46 47N 121 15W
Ajacuba, *Hidalgo, Mexico* **219 B8** 20 5N 99 8W
Ajalpan, *Puebla, Mexico* **221 F3** 18 22N 97 15W
Ajax, *Ont., Canada* **179 D7** 43 50N 79 1W
Ajijic, *Jalisco, Mexico* **218 B4** 20 18N 103 17W
Ajo, *AZ, U.S.A.* **62 E3** 32 22N 112 52W
Ajo Mt., *AZ, U.S.A.* **62 E3** 32 5N 112 45W
Ajos, Sa. de los, *Sonora, Mexico* . **212 C6** 30 57N 109 54W
Ajoxutla, *Puebla, Mexico* **221 F2** 18 15N 98 45W
Ajoya, *Sinaloa, Mexico* **216 C4** 24 7N 106 21W
Ajuchitlán, *Guerrero, Mexico* **219 D7** 18 10N 100 30W
Ajusco, Volcán, *Distrito Federal, Mexico* **225 C2** 19 12N 99 15W
Ak-Chin = Maricopa Indian Reservation, *AZ, U.S.A.* **62 E3** 33 0N 112 1W
Akamina-Kishinena Park ⌂, *B.C., Canada* **185 J6** 49 1N 114 12W
Akaska, *SD, U.S.A.* **91 E5** 45 20N 100 7W
Aké, *Yucatán, Mexico* **223 B4** 20 56N 89 18W
Akeley, *MN, U.S.A.* **80 C4** 47 0N 94 44W
Akhiok, *AK, U.S.A.* **61 H9** 56 57N 154 10W
Akiachak, *AK, U.S.A.* **61 F7** 60 55N 161 26W
Akiak, *AK, U.S.A.* **61 F7** 60 55N 161 13W
Akil, *Yucatán, Mexico* **223 B4** 20 15N 89 21W
Akimiski I., *Nunavut, Canada* **191 G9** 52 50N 81 30W
Aklavik, *N.W.T., Canada* **188 C5** 68 12N 135 0W
Akolmiut, *AK, U.S.A.* **61 F7** 60 55N 162 20W
Akpatok I., *Nunavut, Canada* **175 A4** 60 25N 68 8W
Akra, *ND, U.S.A.* **91 B8** 48 47N 97 44W
Akron, *Ont., Canada* **181 D12** 48 55N 84 7W
Akron, *AL, U.S.A.* **60 D3** 32 53N 87 45W
Akron, *CO, U.S.A.* **66 B7** 40 10N 103 13W
Akron, *IN, U.S.A.* **72 B4** 41 2N 86 1W
Akron, *IA, U.S.A.* **73 C2** 42 50N 96 33W
Akron, *NY, U.S.A.* **89 B2** 43 1N 78 30W
Akron, *OH, U.S.A.* **92 B5** 41 5N 81 31W
Akron, *PA, U.S.A.* **95 D6** 40 9N 76 12W
Akulivik, *Qué., Canada* **175 A2** 60 48N 78 12W
Akumal, *Quintana Roo, Mexico* . . **223 B6** 20 25N 87 18W
Akun I., *AK, U.S.A.* **61 J6** 54 11N 165 32W
Akutan, *AK, U.S.A.* **61 J6** 54 8N 165 46W
Akutan I., *AK, U.S.A.* **61 J6** 54 7N 165 55W
Alabama □, *U.S.A.* **60 D4** 33 0N 87 0W
Alabama →, *AL, U.S.A.* **60 E3** 31 8N 87 57W
Alabama-Coushatta Indian Reservation, *TX, U.S.A.* **99 G13** 30 43N 94 42W
Alabaster, *AL, U.S.A.* **60 C4** 33 15N 86 49W
Alachua, *FL, U.S.A.* **67 B6** 29 47N 82 30W
Alachua County ☆, *FL, U.S.A.* . . . **67 B6** 29 45N 82 20W
Aladdin, *WY, U.S.A.* **104 B8** 44 38N 104 11W
Alahuixtlán, *Guerrero, Mexico* . . . **219 D7** 18 36N 100 3W
Alakanuk, *AK, U.S.A.* **61 E6** 62 41N 164 37W
ʻAlalākeiki Channel, *HI, U.S.A.* . . **69 C5** 20 30N 156 30W
Alamagan, *N. Marianas* . . . . **105 a** 17 36N 145 50W
Alamance County ☆, *NC, U.S.A.* . . **90 C6** 36 0N 79 25W
Alameda, *Sask., Canada* **183 F9** 49 16N 102 17W
Alameda, *CA, U.S.A.* **64 F4** 37 46N 122 15W
Alameda, *NM, U.S.A.* **88 B4** 35 11N 106 37W
Alameda County ☆, *CA, U.S.A.* . . . **64 F5** 37 40N 121 50W
Alameda Memorial State Beach Park, *San Francisco, U.S.A.* . . . **118 B3** 37 45N 122 16W
Alameda Naval Air Station, *San Francisco, U.S.A.* **118 B3** 37 47N 122 19W
Alamito →, *TX, U.S.A.* **98 H3** 29 45N 104 18W
Alamo, *Veracruz, Mexico* **220 D3** 20 55N 97 41W
Alamo, *GA, U.S.A.* **68 D4** 32 9N 82 47W
Alamo, *ND, U.S.A.* **91 B2** 48 35N 103 28W
Alamo, *NM, U.S.A.* **88 C3** 34 25N 107 31W
Alamo, *NV, U.S.A.* **85 E5** 37 22N 115 10W
Alamo, *San Francisco, U.S.A.* **118 A4** 37 51N 122 1W
Alamo, *TN, U.S.A.* **96 E3** 35 47N 89 7W
Alamo →, *CA, U.S.A.* **65 K11** 33 13N 115 37W
Alamo Chapo, *Chihuahua, Mexico* **213 D11** 29 20N 104 23W
Alamo Heights, *TX, U.S.A.* **99 H9** 29 29N 98 27W
Alamo Indian Reservation, *NM, U.S.A.* **88 C3** 34 20N 107 30W
Alamo L., *AZ, U.S.A.* **62 C2** 34 10N 113 35W
Alamogordo, *NM, U.S.A.* **88 E5** 32 54N 105 57W
Alamos, *Sonora, Mexico* **212 F7** 27 1N 108 56W
Álamos, Río de los →, *Coahuila, Mexico* **214 C3** 27 53N 101 12W
Alamosa, *CO, U.S.A.* **66 E5** 37 28N 105 52W
Alamosa →, *CO, U.S.A.* **66 E5** 37 22N 105 46W
Alamosa →, *NM, U.S.A.* **88 D3** 33 25N 107 15W
Alamosa County ☆, *CO, U.S.A.* . . **66 E5** 37 40N 105 40W
Alamosa Cr. →, *NM, U.S.A.* **88 C6** 34 20N 104 10W
Alanreed, *TX, U.S.A.* **98 B7** 35 13N 100 44W
Alanson, *MI, U.S.A.* **79 D7** 45 27N 84 47W
Alapaha, *GA, U.S.A.* **68 E3** 31 23N 83 13W
Alapaha →, *GA, U.S.A.* **68 F3** 30 27N 83 6W
Alaquines, *San Luis Potosí, Mexico* **215 H5** 22 8N 99 36W
Alaska □, *U.S.A.* **61 D9** 64 0N 154 0W
Alaska, G. of, *Pac. Oc.* **61 G11** 58 0N 145 0W
Alaska Maritime Nat. Wildlife Refuge ⌂, *AK, U.S.A.* **61 L4** 52 0N 174 0W
Alaska Peninsula, *AK, U.S.A.* **61 H8** 56 0N 159 0W
Alaska Peninsula Nat. Wildlife Refuge ⌂, *AK, U.S.A.* **61 J8** 56 0N 159 0W
Alaska Range, *AK, U.S.A.* **61 E10** 62 50N 151 0W
Alava, C., *WA, U.S.A.* **101 B1** 48 10N 124 44W
Alba, *MO, U.S.A.* **82 D2** 37 14N 94 25W
Alba, *TX, U.S.A.* **99 E12** 32 48N 95 38W
Albanel, *Qué., Canada* **177 C10** 48 53N 72 27W
Albanel, L., *Qué., Canada* **175 C3** 50 55N 73 12W
Albany, *GA, U.S.A.* **68 E2** 31 35N 84 10W
Albany, *IN, U.S.A.* **72 C5** 40 18N 85 14W
Albany, *KY, U.S.A.* **97 D7** 36 42N 85 8W
Albany, *LA, U.S.A.* **75 D5** 30 30N 90 35W
Albany, *MN, U.S.A.* **80 E4** 45 38N 94 34W
Albany, *MO, U.S.A.* **82 A2** 40 15N 94 20W
Albany, *NY, U.S.A.* **89 C7** 42 39N 73 45W
Albany, *OH, U.S.A.* **92 D4** 39 14N 82 12W
Albany, *OK, U.S.A.* **93 E7** 33 53N 96 10W
Albany, *OR, U.S.A.* **94 C2** 44 38N 123 6W
Albany, *TX, U.S.A.* **99 E8** 32 44N 99 18W
Albany, *VT, U.S.A.* **86 B2** 44 43N 72 23W
Albany, *WI, U.S.A.* **103 F4** 42 42N 89 26W
Albany, *WY, U.S.A.* **104 E6** 41 11N 106 8W
Albany →, *Ont., Canada* **191 G9** 52 17N 81 31W
Albany County ☆, *NY, U.S.A.* . . . **89 C7** 42 30N 74 0W
Albany County ☆, *WY, U.S.A.* . . . **104 E7** 41 50N 105 40W
Albany International ✈ (ALB), *NY, U.S.A.* **89 C7** 42 45N 73 48W
Albemarle, *NC, U.S.A.* **90 C5** 35 21N 80 12W
Albemarle County ☆, *VA, U.S.A.* . **102 C6** 38 2N 78 30W
Albemarle Sd., *NC, U.S.A.* **90 B9** 36 5N 76 0W
Albert, *KS, U.S.A.* **74 C4** 38 27N 99 1W
Albert, *OK, U.S.A.* **93 C5** 35 14N 98 25W
Albert, *TX, U.S.A.* **99 G9** 30 13N 98 36W
Albert Canyon, *B.C., Canada* **187 D17** 51 8N 117 41W
Albert City, *IA, U.S.A.* **73 C4** 42 47N 94 57W
Albert Edward B., *Nunavut, Canada* **190 D5** 69 32N 102 25W
Albert Lea, *MN, U.S.A.* **80 G5** 43 39N 93 22W
Alberta, *AL, U.S.A.* **60 D3** 32 14N 87 25W
Alberta, *MI, U.S.A.* **79 C3** 46 39N 88 29W
Alberta, *VA, U.S.A.* **102 E7** 36 52N 77 53W
Alberta □, *Canada* **184 B4** 54 40N 115 0W
Alberta Beach, *Alta., Canada* **184 E6** 53 40N 114 21W
Alberton, *P.E.I., Canada* **173 G5** 46 50N 64 0W
Alberton, *MT, U.S.A.* **83 D3** 47 0N 114 29W
Albertson, *NY, U.S.A.* **114 B5** 40 46N 73 38W
Albertville, *AL, U.S.A.* **60 B4** 34 16N 86 13W
Albertville, *MN, U.S.A.* **80 E5** 45 14N 93 39W
Albia, *IA, U.S.A.* **73 D6** 41 2N 92 48W
Albin, *WY, U.S.A.* **104 E8** 41 25N 104 6W
Albino Zertuche, *Puebla, Mexico* . **221 F2** 18 1N 98 33W
Albion, *CA, U.S.A.* **64 D3** 39 14N 123 46W
Albion, *ID, U.S.A.* **70 G5** 42 25N 113 35W
Albion, *IL, U.S.A.* **71 E5** 38 23N 88 4W
Albion, *IN, U.S.A.* **72 B5** 41 24N 85 25W
Albion, *IA, U.S.A.* **73 C6** 42 7N 92 59W
Albion, *ME, U.S.A.* **76 D4** 44 32N 69 27W
Albion, *MI, U.S.A.* **79 G7** 42 15N 84 45W
Albion, *NY, U.S.A.* **89 B2** 43 15N 78 12W
Albion, *NE, U.S.A.* **84 C7** 41 42N 98 0W
Albion, *OK, U.S.A.* **93 D8** 34 40N 95 6W
Albion, *PA, U.S.A.* **95 C2** 41 53N 80 22W
Albion, *WA, U.S.A.* **101 D8** 46 48N 117 15W
Albion Mts., *ID, U.S.A.* **70 G5** 42 13N 113 43W
Albreda, *B.C., Canada* **187 C15** 52 35N 119 10W
Albright, *WV, U.S.A.* **102 B5** 39 30N 79 39W
Albuquerque, *NM, U.S.A.* **88 B4** 35 5N 106 39W
Albuquerque International ✈ (ABQ), *NM, U.S.A.* **88 B4** 35 3N 106 36W
Alburg, *VT, U.S.A.* **86 B1** 44 59N 73 18W
Alburnett, *IA, U.S.A.* **73 C7** 42 9N 91 37W
Alcalde, *NM, U.S.A.* **88 A4** 36 5N 106 3W
Alcatraz I., *San Francisco, U.S.A.* **118 B2** 37 49N 122 25W
Alcester, *SD, U.S.A.* **91 G9** 43 1N 96 38W
Alco, *AR, U.S.A.* **63 C3** 35 53N 92 22W
Alcoa, *TN, U.S.A.* **97 E9** 35 48N 83 59W
Alcolu, *SC, U.S.A.* **90 E5** 33 45N 80 13W
Alcoma, *FL, U.S.A.* **67 D7** 27 54N 81 29W
Alcona, *MI, U.S.A.* **79 E8** 44 45N 83 17W
Alcona County ☆, *MI, U.S.A.* **79 E8** 44 40N 83 40W
Alcorn, *MS, U.S.A.* **81 E2** 31 53N 91 8W
Alcorn County ☆, *MS, U.S.A.* **81 B5** 34 56N 88 31W
Alcova, *WY, U.S.A.* **104 D6** 42 34N 106 43W
Alcova Res., *WY, U.S.A.* **104 D6** 42 33N 106 43W
Alcozauca, *Guerrero, Mexico* **219 E9** 17 28N 98 23W
Alda, *NE, U.S.A.* **84 D7** 40 52N 98 28W
Aldama, *Chihuahua, Mexico* **213 E10** 28 51N 105 54W
Aldama, *Tamaulipas, Mexico* **215 H6** 22 55N 98 4W
Aldan, *PA, U.S.A.* **116 B1** 39 55N 75 17W
Alden, *IA, U.S.A.* **73 C5** 42 31N 93 23W
Alden, *KS, U.S.A.* **74 C5** 38 15N 98 19W
Alden, *MN, U.S.A.* **80 G5** 43 40N 93 34W
Alden, *NY, U.S.A.* **89 C2** 42 54N 78 30W
Aldene, *NJ, U.S.A.* **114 C1** 40 39N 74 16W
Alder, *MT, U.S.A.* **83 E5** 45 19N 112 6W
Alder L., *WA, U.S.A.* **101 D3** 46 48N 122 18W
Aldershot, *N.S., Canada* **173 H5** 45 6N 64 31W
Alderson, *OK, U.S.A.* **93 D8** 34 54N 95 41W
Alderson, *WV, U.S.A.* **102 D4** 37 44N 80 38W
Alderwood Manor, *Seattle, U.S.A.* **118 B4** 47 49N 122 16W
Aldie, *VA, U.S.A.* **77 B3** 38 59N 77 39W
Aldine, *TX, U.S.A.* **99 H12** 29 56N 95 23W
Aledo, *IL, U.S.A.* **71 B3** 41 12N 90 45W
Aledo, *TX, U.S.A.* **99 E10** 32 42N 97 36W
Alegros Mt., *NM, U.S.A.* **88 C2** 34 9N 108 11W
Aleknagik, *AK, U.S.A.* **61 G8** 59 17N 158 36W
ʻAlenuihāhā Channel, *HI, U.S.A.* . **69 C5** 20 30N 156 0W
Alert, *Nunavut, Canada* **190 A13** 83 2N 60 0W
Alert Bay, *B.C., Canada* **186 E8** 50 30N 126 55W
Alesia, *MD, U.S.A.* **77 A4** 39 43N 76 51W
Aleutian Is., *Pac. Oc.* **61 K3** 52 0N 175 0W
Aleutian Range, *AK, U.S.A.* **61 G9** 60 0N 154 0W
Aleutians East ☆, *AK, U.S.A.* **61 J7** 54 51N 163 25W
Aleutians West ☆, *AK, U.S.A.* . . . **61 K4** 52 15N 175 7W
Alex, *OK, U.S.A.* **93 D6** 34 55N 97 47W

Alex Graham, Mt., *B.C., Canada* . **187 C12** 52 4N 122 52W
Alexander, *Man., Canada* **183 F11** 49 49N 100 17W
Alexander, *GA, U.S.A.* **68 C5** 33 1N 81 53W
Alexander, *IA, U.S.A.* **73 C5** 42 48N 93 29W
Alexander, *KS, U.S.A.* **74 C4** 38 28N 99 33W
Alexander, *ME, U.S.A.* **76 C6** 45 5N 67 28W
Alexander, *ND, U.S.A.* **91 C2** 47 51N 103 39W
Alexander, *WV, U.S.A.* **102 C4** 38 47N 80 13W
Alexander Arch., *AK, U.S.A.* **61 J14** 56 0N 136 0W
Alexander City, *AL, U.S.A.* **60 D5** 32 56N 85 58W
Alexander County ☆, *IL, U.S.A.* . **71 F4** 37 10N 89 20W
Alexander County ☆, *NC, U.S.A.* **90 C4** 35 50N 81 10W
Alexander I., *Nunavut, Canada* . . **190 B5** 75 52N 102 37W
Alexandria, *B.C., Canada* **187 C12** 52 35N 122 27W
Alexandria, *Ont., Canada* **179 B12** 45 19N 74 38W
Alexandria, *IN, U.S.A.* **72 C5** 40 16N 85 41W
Alexandria, *KY, U.S.A.* **97 B8** 38 58N 84 23W
Alexandria, *LA, U.S.A.* **75 C3** 31 18N 92 27W
Alexandria, *MN, U.S.A.* **80 E3** 45 53N 95 22W
Alexandria, *MO, U.S.A.* **82 A5** 40 27N 91 28W
Alexandria, *NH, U.S.A.* **86 C3** 43 37N 71 47W
Alexandria, *NE, U.S.A.* **84 D8** 40 15N 97 23W
Alexandria, *PA, U.S.A.* **95 D4** 40 34N 78 6W
Alexandria, *SD, U.S.A.* **91 G8** 43 39N 97 47W
Alexandria, *TN, U.S.A.* **96 D6** 36 5N 86 2W
Alexandria, *VA, U.S.A.* **77 B3** 38 49N 77 5W
Alexandria Bay, *NY, U.S.A.* **89 A5** 44 20N 75 55W
Alexis, *IL, U.S.A.* **71 B3** 41 4N 90 33W
Alexis →, *Nfld. & L., Canada* . . . **175 C6** 52 33N 56 8W
Alexis Creek, *B.C., Canada* **186 C11** 52 10N 123 20W
Alfajayucan, *Hidalgo, Mexico* . . . **219 B8** 20 25N 99 20W
Alfalfa, *OK, U.S.A.* **93 C5** 35 13N 98 36W
Alfalfa County ☆, *OK, U.S.A.* . . . **93 B5** 36 45N 98 15W
Alford, *FL, U.S.A.* **67 A3** 30 42N 85 24W
Alfred, *Qué., Canada* **176 F8** 45 33N 74 52W
Alfred, *ME, U.S.A.* **76 E3** 43 29N 70 43W
Alfred, *NY, U.S.A.* **89 C3** 42 16N 77 48W
Alfredo M. Terrazas, *San Luis Potosí, Mexico* **215 J6** 21 28N 98 51W
Alfredo V. Bonfil, *Tamaulipas, Mexico* **214 E6** 25 33N 98 14W
Alger County ☆, *MI, U.S.A.* **79 C5** 46 20N 86 50W
Algodones, *NM, U.S.A.* **88 B4** 35 23N 106 29W
Algodones, Pta. de, *Tamaulipas, Mexico* **215 F7** 24 26N 97 45W
Algoma, *MS, U.S.A.* **81 B4** 34 11N 89 2W
Algoma, *WI, U.S.A.* **103 D6** 44 36N 87 26W
Algona, *IA, U.S.A.* **73 B4** 43 4N 94 14W
Algonac, *MI, U.S.A.* **79 G9** 42 37N 82 32W
Algonquin, *IL, U.S.A.* **71 A5** 42 10N 88 18W
Algonquin Prov. Park ⌂, *Ont., Canada* **179 B8** 45 50N 78 30W
Algood, *TN, U.S.A.* **97 D7** 36 12N 85 27W
Alhambra, *Alta., Canada* **185 F6** 52 20N 114 40W
Alhambra, *CA, U.S.A.* **65 J8** 34 5N 118 7W
Alibates Flint Quarries Nat. Monument ⌂, *TX, U.S.A.* **98 B6** 35 34N 101 41W
Alice, *Ont., Canada* **179 B9** 45 47N 77 14W
Alice, *ND, U.S.A.* **91 D8** 46 46N 97 33W
Alice, *TX, U.S.A.* **99 K9** 27 45N 98 5W
Alice, L., *ND, U.S.A.* **91 B6** 48 20N 99 7W
Alice Arm, *B.C., Canada* **189 E7** 55 29N 129 31W
Aliceville, *AL, U.S.A.* **60 C2** 33 8N 88 9W
Aliceville, *KS, U.S.A.* **74 C8** 38 9N 95 33W
Aliceville L., *U.S.A.* **81 C5** 33 15N 88 17W
Alicia, *AR, U.S.A.* **63 C4** 35 54N 91 5W
Alida, *Sask., Canada* **183 F10** 49 25N 101 55W
Aline, *OK, U.S.A.* **93 B5** 36 31N 98 27W
Aliquippa, *PA, U.S.A.* **95 D1** 40 37N 80 15W
Alix, *Alta., Canada* **185 F7** 52 24N 113 11W
Aljojuca, *Puebla, Mexico* **221 E3** 19 6N 97 31W
Alkali Flat, *NV, U.S.A.* **85 B3** 40 24N 117 21W
Alkali Flat, *NV, U.S.A.* **85 C5** 40 0N 115 58W
Alkali L., *NV, U.S.A.* **85 A1** 41 42N 119 51W
Alkali L., *OR, U.S.A.* **94 E5** 42 58N 120 2W
Alkaline L., *ND, U.S.A.* **91 D6** 46 40N 99 34W
All American Canal, *CA, U.S.A.* . . **65 L11** 32 45N 115 15W
Allagash, *ME, U.S.A.* **76 A4** 47 5N 69 3W
Allagash →, *ME, U.S.A.* **76 A4** 47 5N 69 3W
Allagash L., *ME, U.S.A.* **76 B4** 46 18N 69 35W
Allakaket, *AK, U.S.A.* **61 C9** 66 34N 152 39W
Allamakee County ☆, *IA, U.S.A.* . **73 B7** 43 15N 91 20W
Allamoore, *TX, U.S.A.* **98 F3** 31 5N 105 0W
Allan, *Sask., Canada* **182 D5** 51 53N 106 4W
Allan Water, *Ont., Canada* **180 B6** 50 14N 90 10W
Allard, L., *Qué., Canada* **172 C6** 50 32N 63 31W
Allardt, *TN, U.S.A.* **97 D8** 36 23N 84 53W
Allardville, *N.B., Canada* **173 F4** 47 28N 65 29W
Allatoona L., *GA, U.S.A.* **68 B2** 34 10N 84 44W
Allegan, *MI, U.S.A.* **79 G6** 42 32N 85 51W
Allegan County ☆, *MI, U.S.A.* . . . **79 G6** 42 35N 85 50W
Allegany, *NY, U.S.A.* **89 C2** 42 6N 78 30W
Allegany, *OR, U.S.A.* **94 D1** 43 26N 124 2W
Allegany County ☆, *MD, U.S.A.* . **77 A2** 39 40N 78 40W
Allegany County ☆, *NY, U.S.A.* . . **89 C3** 42 15N 78 0W
Allegany Indian Reservation, *NY, U.S.A.* **89 C2** 42 6N 78 55W
Allegany State Park ⌂, *NY, U.S.A.* **89 C2** 42 3N 78 48W
Alleghany County ☆, *NC, U.S.A.* **90 B4** 36 25N 81 10W
Alleghany County ☆, *VA, U.S.A.* . **102 D4** 37 50N 80 0W
Allegheny →, *PA, U.S.A.* **95 D2** 40 27N 80 1W
Allegheny County ☆, *PA, U.S.A.* . **95 D3** 40 25N 80 0W
Allegheny Mts., *WV, U.S.A.* **102 C4** 38 15N 80 10W
Allegheny Nat. Forest, *PA, U.S.A.* . **95 C3** 41 45N 79 5W
Allegheny Plateau, *PA, U.S.A.* . . . **95 C4** 41 30N 78 30W
Allegheny Portage Railroad Nat. Historic Site ⌂, *PA, U.S.A.* . . . **95 D4** 40 22N 78 51W
Allegheny Res., *PA, U.S.A.* **95 C4** 41 50N 79 0W
Allemands, L. des, *LA, U.S.A.* . . . **75 E5** 29 55N 90 35W
Allen, *KS, U.S.A.* **74 C7** 38 39N 96 10W
Allen, *MD, U.S.A.* **77 B5** 38 17N 75 42W
Allen, *NE, U.S.A.* **84 B9** 42 25N 96 51W
Allen, *OK, U.S.A.* **93 D7** 34 53N 96 25W
Allen, *SD, U.S.A.* **91 G4** 43 17N 101 56W
Allen, *TX, U.S.A.* **99 D11** 33 6N 96 40W
Allen County ☆, *IN, U.S.A.* **72 B5** 41 5N 85 5W
Allen County ☆, *KS, U.S.A.* **74 D8** 37 50N 95 15W
Allen County ☆, *KY, U.S.A.* **96 D6** 36 45N 86 10W
Allen County ☆, *OH, U.S.A.* **92 C2** 40 44N 84 6W
Allen Parish ☆, *LA, U.S.A.* **75 D3** 30 37N 92 46W
Allendale, *IL, U.S.A.* **71 E6** 38 32N 87 43W
Allendale, *SC, U.S.A.* **90 E4** 33 1N 81 18W
Allendale County ☆, *SC, U.S.A.* . . **90 E4** 33 0N 81 20W
Allende, *Coahuila, Mexico* **214 B4** 28 20N 100 51W
Allende, *Nuevo León, Mexico* **215 E4** 25 17N 100 1W
Allende, *Veracruz, Mexico* **221 F6** 18 4N 94 22W
Allenhurst, *NJ, U.S.A.* **87 B3** 40 15N 73 59W
Allensville, *KY, U.S.A.* **96 D5** 36 43N 87 4W
Allentown, *NJ, U.S.A.* **87 B2** 40 11N 74 35W
Allentown, *NY, U.S.A.* **114 B4** 40 47N 73 43W
Allentown, *PA, U.S.A.* **87 B1** 40 37N 75 29W
Allerton, *IL, U.S.A.* **71 D6** 39 55N 87 56W
Allerton, *IA, U.S.A.* **73 E5** 40 42N 93 22W
Allerton, Pt., *Boston, U.S.A.* **106 B4** 42 18N 70 52W
Alley Pond Park, *NY, U.S.A.* **114 B4** 40 44N 73 43W
Alliance, *Alta., Canada* **185 F9** 52 26N 111 47W
Alliance, *NE, U.S.A.* **84 B3** 42 6N 102 52W
Alliance, *OH, U.S.A.* **92 C5** 40 55N 81 6W
Alliford Bay, *B.C., Canada* **186 B3** 53 12N 131 58W
Alligator, *MS, U.S.A.* **81 B3** 34 6N 90 43W
Alligator →, *NC, U.S.A.* **90 C9** 35 55N 76 7W
Alligator Alley = Everglades Parkway, *FL, U.S.A.* **67 E7** 26 10N 81 0W
Alligator L. = New L., *NC, U.S.A.* **90 C9** 35 39N 76 21W
Allison, *CO, U.S.A.* **66 E3** 37 2N 107 29W
Allison, *IA, U.S.A.* **73 C6** 42 45N 92 48W
Allison, *TX, U.S.A.* **98 B7** 35 36N 100 6W
Alliston = New Tecumseth, *Ont., Canada* **178 C7** 44 9N 79 52W
Allons, *TN, U.S.A.* **97 D7** 36 27N 85 21W
Allouez, *WI, U.S.A.* **103 D5** 44 27N 88 4W
Alloway, *NJ, U.S.A.* **87 C1** 39 34N 75 22W
Allston, *Boston, U.S.A.* **106 A3** 42 21N 71 7W
Alluviaq Fjord, *Qué., Canada* **175 B4** 59 27N 65 10W
Allyn, *WA, U.S.A.* **101 C3** 47 23N 122 50W
Alma, *N.B., Canada* **173 H5** 45 36N 64 57W
Alma, *Qué., Canada* **177 C11** 48 35N 71 40W
Alma, *AR, U.S.A.* **63 C1** 35 29N 94 13W
Alma, *CO, U.S.A.* **66 C4** 39 17N 106 4W
Alma, *GA, U.S.A.* **68 E4** 31 33N 82 28W
Alma, *KS, U.S.A.* **74 B7** 39 1N 96 17W
Alma, *MI, U.S.A.* **79 F7** 43 23N 84 39W
Alma, *MO, U.S.A.* **82 B3** 39 6N 93 33W
Alma, *NM, U.S.A.* **88 D2** 33 23N 108 54W
Alma, *NE, U.S.A.* **84 D6** 40 6N 99 22W
Alma, *WI, U.S.A.* **103 D2** 44 20N 91 55W
Alma Center, *WI, U.S.A.* **103 D3** 44 26N 90 55W
Alma Hill, *NY, U.S.A.* **89 C3** 42 3N 78 0W
Almagre, L., *Tamaulipas, Mexico* . **215 G7** 23 48N 97 48W
Almanor, L., *CA, U.S.A.* **64 C5** 40 14N 121 9W
Almena, *KS, U.S.A.* **74 B4** 39 54N 99 43W
Almena, *WI, U.S.A.* **103 C1** 45 25N 92 2W
Almeria, *NE, U.S.A.* **84 C6** 41 50N 99 31W
Almira, *WA, U.S.A.* **101 C7** 47 43N 118 56W
Almo, *KY, U.S.A.* **96 D4** 36 42N 88 16W
Almoloya, *Hidalgo, Mexico* **219 C9** 19 44N 98 24W
Almon, *GA, U.S.A.* **68 C3** 33 37N 83 56W
Almond, *WI, U.S.A.* **103 D4** 44 16N 89 25W
Almont, *CO, U.S.A.* **66 D4** 38 40N 106 51W
Almont, *MI, U.S.A.* **79 G8** 42 55N 83 3W
Almont, *ND, U.S.A.* **91 D4** 46 44N 101 30W
Almonte, *Ont., Canada* **176 F6** 45 14N 76 12W
Alms Park, *OH, U.S.A.* **107 B2** 39 6N 84 25W
Almy, *WY, U.S.A.* **104 E2** 41 19N 111 0W
Almyra, *AR, U.S.A.* **63 D4** 34 24N 91 25W
Aloha, *OR, U.S.A.* **94 B3** 45 29N 122 52W
Alondra Park, *Los Angeles, U.S.A.* **111 C2** 33 52N 118 20W
Alorton, *IL, U.S.A.* **117 B3** 38 35N 90 7W
Alpaugh, *CA, U.S.A.* **65 H7** 35 53N 119 29W
Alpena, *AR, U.S.A.* **63 B2** 36 18N 93 18W
Alpena, *MI, U.S.A.* **79 D8** 45 4N 83 27W
Alpena, *SD, U.S.A.* **91 F7** 44 11N 98 22W
Alpena County ☆, *MI, U.S.A.* . . . **79 D8** 45 0N 83 40W
Alpha, *IL, U.S.A.* **71 B3** 41 12N 90 23W
Alpha, *MI, U.S.A.* **79 C3** 46 3N 88 23W
Alpha, *NJ, U.S.A.* **87 B1** 40 40N 75 9W
Alpharetta, *GA, U.S.A.* **68 B2** 34 5N 84 18W
Alpine, *AZ, U.S.A.* **62 D6** 33 51N 109 9W
Alpine, *AR, U.S.A.* **63 D2** 34 14N 93 23W
Alpine, *CA, U.S.A.* **65 L10** 32 50N 116 46W
Alpine, *NJ, U.S.A.* **114 A3** 40 57N 73 57W
Alpine, *TN, U.S.A.* **97 D7** 36 24N 85 13W
Alpine, *TX, U.S.A.* **98 G4** 30 22N 103 40W
Alpine, *UT, U.S.A.* **100 C4** 40 27N 111 46W
Alpine, *WY, U.S.A.* **104 C1** 43 11N 111 3W
Alpine County ☆, *CA, U.S.A.* . . . **64 E7** 38 40N 119 50W
Alpoyeca, *Guerrero, Mexico* **219 E9** 17 40N 98 31W
Alsask, *Sask., Canada* **182 D2** 51 21N 109 59W
Alsea →, *OR, U.S.A.* **94 C1** 44 26N 124 5W
Alsek →, *AK, U.S.A.* **189 E5** 59 10N 138 12W
Alsen, *ND, U.S.A.* **91 B7** 48 38N 98 42W
Alsey, *IL, U.S.A.* **71 D3** 39 34N 90 26W
Alsip, *Chicago, U.S.A.* **108 C2** 41 40N 87 44W
Alstead, *NH, U.S.A.* **86 C2** 43 9N 72 22W
Alta, *IA, U.S.A.* **73 C3** 42 40N 95 18W
Alta, *Salt Lake City, U.S.A.* **117 C4** 40 35N 111 38W
Alta, *WY, U.S.A.* **104 C1** 43 45N 111 2W
Alta Vista, *Ont., Canada* **192 B2** 45 23N 75 39W
Alta Vista, *IA, U.S.A.* **73 B6** 43 12N 92 25W
Alta Vista, *KS, U.S.A.* **74 C7** 38 52N 96 29W
Altadena, *Los Angeles, U.S.A.* . . . **111 A4** 34 11N 118 8W
Altair, *TX, U.S.A.* **99 H11** 29 34N 96 27W
Altamaha →, *GA, U.S.A.* **68 E5** 31 20N 81 20W
Altamaha Sound, *GA, U.S.A.* **68 E5** 31 19N 81 17W
Altamira, *Tamaulipas, Mexico* . . . **215 H7** 22 24N 97 55W
Altamirano, *Chiapas, Mexico* **222 C4** 16 53N 92 9W
Altamont, *IL, U.S.A.* **71 D5** 39 4N 88 45W
Altamont, *KS, U.S.A.* **74 D8** 37 12N 95 18W
Altamont, *MO, U.S.A.* **82 B2** 39 53N 94 5W
Altamont, *NY, U.S.A.* **89 C6** 42 42N 74 2W
Altamont, *OR, U.S.A.* **94 E4** 42 12N 121 44W
Altamont, *SD, U.S.A.* **91 F9** 44 50N 96 42W
Altamont, *TN, U.S.A.* **97 E7** 35 26N 85 44W
Altamont, *UT, U.S.A.* **100 C5** 40 22N 110 17W
Altamura, I., *Sinaloa, Mexico* **216 B2** 25 0N 108 10W
Altar, *Sonora, Mexico* **212 C4** 30 43N 111 44W
Altar →, *Sonora, Mexico* **212 C4** 30 39N 111 53W
Altar, Gran Desierto de, *Sonora, Mexico* **212 B1** 31 50N 114 10W
Altario, *Alta., Canada* **185 G10** 51 55N 110 9W
Altata, *Sinaloa, Mexico* **216 C3** 24 40N 107 55W
Altavista, *VA, U.S.A.* **102 D5** 37 6N 79 17W
Altepexi, *Puebla, Mexico* **221 F3** 18 24N 97 17W
Altha, *FL, U.S.A.* **67 A3** 30 34N 85 8W
Altheimer, *AR, U.S.A.* **63 D4** 34 19N 91 51W
Alto, *GA, U.S.A.* **68 B3** 34 28N 83 35W
Alto, *LA, U.S.A.* **75 B4** 32 22N 91 52W
Alto, *NM, U.S.A.* **88 D5** 33 23N 105 41W
Alto, *TX, U.S.A.* **99 F12** 31 39N 95 4W
Alto Amatitlán, *Tabasco, Mexico* . . **222 B5** 17 54N 91 47W
Alto de Atizapan de Zaragoza, *México, Mexico* **225 A2** 19 36N 99 18W
Alto Lucero, *Veracruz, Mexico* . . . **220 E4** 19 37N 96 43W
Alto Pass, *IL, U.S.A.* **71 F4** 37 34N 89 19W
Alton, *Ont., Canada* **178 D6** 43 54N 80 5W
Alton, *IL, U.S.A.* **71 E3** 38 53N 90 11W
Alton, *IA, U.S.A.* **73 C2** 42 59N 96 1W
Alton, *KS, U.S.A.* **74 B5** 39 28N 98 57W
Alton, *MO, U.S.A.* **82 E5** 36 42N 91 24W
Alton, *NH, U.S.A.* **86 C3** 43 27N 71 13W
Alton, *UT, U.S.A.* **100 F3** 37 26N 112 29W
Alton Bay, *NH, U.S.A.* **86 C3** 43 27N 71 13W
Altona, *Man., Canada* **183 F14** 49 6N 97 33W
Altona, *NY, U.S.A.* **89 A7** 44 53N 73 39W
Altoona, *AL, U.S.A.* **60 B4** 34 2N 86 20W
Altoona, *IA, U.S.A.* **73 D5** 41 39N 93 28W
Altoona, *KS, U.S.A.* **74 D8** 37 32N 95 40W
Altoona, *PA, U.S.A.* **95 D4** 40 31N 78 24W
Altoona, *WI, U.S.A.* **103 D2** 44 48N 91 26W
Altotonga, *Veracruz, Mexico* **220 E3** 19 46N 97 14W
Alturas, *CA, U.S.A.* **64 B6** 41 29N 120 32W
Altus, *OK, U.S.A.* **93 D4** 34 38N 99 20W
Altus, L., *OK, U.S.A.* **93 D4** 34 53N 99 18W
Alum Bridge, *WV, U.S.A.* **102 B4** 39 2N 80 40W
Alum Creek L., *OH, U.S.A.* **92 C4** 40 11N 82 57W
Alva, *FL, U.S.A.* **67 E7** 26 43N 81 37W
Alva, *KY, U.S.A.* **97 D9** 36 48N 83 25W
Alva, *OK, U.S.A.* **93 B5** 36 48N 98 40W
Alvarado, *Veracruz, Mexico* **221 F5** 18 46N 95 46W
Alvarado, *MN, U.S.A.* **80 B2** 48 10N 97 0W
Alvarado, *TX, U.S.A.* **99 E10** 32 24N 97 13W
Alvarado, L., *Veracruz, Mexico* . . **221 F5** 18 45N 95 50W
Alvaro Obregón, *Chihuahua, Mexico* **213 E9** 28 45N 106 55W
Alvaro Obregón, *Distrito Federal, Mexico* **225 B2** 19 22N 99 13W
Alvaro Obregón, *Michoacan, Mexico* **219 C6** 19 50N 101 5W
Alvaro Obregón, *Oaxaca, Mexico* **221 H6** 16 18N 95 4W
Alvaro Obregón, *Quintana Roo, Mexico* **223 D5** 18 16N 88 41W
Alvaro Obregón, *San Luis Potosí, Mexico* **215 J6** 21 51N 98 56W
Alvaro Obregón, Presa, *Sonora, Mexico* **212 F6** 27 52N 109 52W
Alvaton, *KY, U.S.A.* **96 D6** 36 53N 86 21W
Alvena, *Sask., Canada* **182 C5** 52 31N 106 1W
Alvin, *TX, U.S.A.* **99 H12** 29 26N 95 15W
Alvin Callendar Naval Air Station, *New Orleans, U.S.A.* **113 D2** 29 50N 90 1W
Alvinston, *Ont., Canada* **178 E5** 42 49N 81 52W
Alvo, *NE, U.S.A.* **84 D9** 40 52N 96 23W
Alvord, *IA, U.S.A.* **73 B2** 43 21N 96 18W
Alvord, *TX, U.S.A.* **99 D10** 33 22N 97 42W
Alvord Desert, *OR, U.S.A.* **94 E7** 42 30N 118 25W
Alvord L., *OR, U.S.A.* **94 E7** 42 23N 118 36W
Alzada, *Colima, Mexico* **218 C4** 19 14N 103 32W
Alzada, *MT, U.S.A.* **83 E13** 45 2N 104 25W
Amacueca, *Jalisco, Mexico* **218 B4** 20 1N 103 37W
Amaculi, *Durango, Mexico* **216 C4** 24 38N 106 37W
Amacuzac →, *Guerrero, Mexico* . . **219 E8** 17 53N 99 12W
Amadjuak L., *Nunavut, Canada* . . **191 E11** 65 0N 71 8W
Amador County ☆, *CA, U.S.A.* . . . **64 E6** 38 25N 120 45W
Amagansett, *NY, U.S.A.* **78 D2** 40 59N 72 9W
Amana, *IA, U.S.A.* **73 D7** 41 48N 91 52W
Amana Colonies, *IA, U.S.A.* **73 D7** 41 48N 91 56W
Amanave, *Amer. Samoa* . . . . **105 e** 14 20 S 170 50W
Amanda, *OH, U.S.A.* **92 D4** 39 39N 82 45W
Amaranth, *Man., Canada* **183 E13** 50 36N 98 43W
Amargosa →, *CA, U.S.A.* **65 G10** 36 14N 116 51W
Amargosa Desert, *U.S.A.* **85 F4** 36 40N 116 30W
Amargosa Range, *CA, U.S.A.* **65 G10** 36 20N 116 45W
Amargosa Valley, *NV, U.S.A.* **85 F4** 36 39N 116 24W
Amarillo, *TX, U.S.A.* **98 B6** 35 13N 101 50W
Amasa, *MI, U.S.A.* **79 C3** 46 14N 88 27W
Amatán, *Chiapas, Mexico* **222 B4** 17 21N 92 45W
Amatenango de la Frontera, *Chiapas, Mexico* **222 D3** 15 26N 92 7W
Amatenango del Valle, *Chiapas, Mexico* **222 C4** 16 31N 92 27W
Amatepec, *México, Mexico* **219 D7** 18 39N 100 9W
Amatignak I., *AK, U.S.A.* **61 L3** 51 16N 179 6W
Amatitán, *Jalisco, Mexico* **218 B4** 20 50N 103 43W
Amatlán de Cañas, *Nayarit, Mexico* **216 G6** 20 52N 104 27W
Amazonia, *MO, U.S.A.* **82 B2** 39 53N 94 54W
Amber, *OK, U.S.A.* **93 C6** 35 10N 97 53W
Amberg, *WI, U.S.A.* **103 C6** 45 30N 88 0W
Amberley, *OH, U.S.A.* **107 A2** 39 12N 84 25W
Ambler, *AK, U.S.A.* **61 C8** 67 5N 157 52W
Ambler, *PA, U.S.A.* **87 B1** 40 9N 75 13W
Ambleside, *Vancouver, Canada* . . . **193 B2** 49 19N 123 9W
Ambleside Park, *Vancouver, Canada* **193 B2** 49 19N 123 9W
Amboy, *CA, U.S.A.* **65 J11** 34 33N 115 45W
Amboy, *IL, U.S.A.* **71 B4** 41 44N 89 20W
Amboy, *MN, U.S.A.* **80 G4** 43 53N 94 10W
Ambridge, *PA, U.S.A.* **95 D2** 40 36N 80 14W
Ambrose, *GA, U.S.A.* **68 E3** 31 36N 83 1W
Ambrose, *ND, U.S.A.* **91 B2** 48 57N 103 29W
Ambrosia Lake, *NM, U.S.A.* **88 B3** 35 26N 107 54W
Amchitka I., *AK, U.S.A.* . . . . **61 L2** 51 32N 179 0 E
Amealco, *Querétaro, Mexico* **219 B7** 20 11N 100 9W
Ameca, *Jalisco, Mexico* **218 B3** 20 33N 104 2W
Ameca →, *Mexico* **218 B2** 20 41N 105 18W
Ameca la Vieja, *Zacatecas, Mexico* **217 E7** 22 56N 104 0W
Amecameca, *México, Mexico* **219 C9** 19 8N 98 46W
Amelia, *LA, U.S.A.* **75 E4** 29 40N 91 6W
Amelia, *NE, U.S.A.* **84 B7** 42 14N 98 55W
Amelia City, *FL, U.S.A.* **67 A7** 30 35N 81 28W
Amelia County ☆, *VA, U.S.A.* . . . **102 D7** 37 21N 77 59W
Amelia Court House, *VA, U.S.A.* . . **102 D7** 37 21N 77 59W
Amelia Earhart Park, *Miami, U.S.A.* **112 C1** 25 53N 80 16W
Amelia I., *FL, U.S.A.* **67 A7** 30 40N 81 25W
Amenia, *NY, U.S.A.* **78 C1** 41 51N 73 33W
American Corners, *MD, U.S.A.* . . . **77 B5** 38 47N 75 51W
American Falls, *ID, U.S.A.* **70 G6** 42 47N 112 51W
American Falls Dam, *ID, U.S.A.* . . **70 G6** 42 47N 112 52W
American Falls Res., *ID, U.S.A.* . . **70 G6** 42 47N 112 52W
American Fork, *UT, U.S.A.* **100 C4** 40 23N 111 48W
American Samoa ☑, *Pac. Oc.* . . . . **105 d** 14 20 S 170 40W
Americanos, Barra los, *Tamaulipas, Mexico* **215 F7** 24 48N 97 37W
Americus, *GA, U.S.A.* **68 D2** 32 4N 84 14W
Americus, *KS, U.S.A.* **74 C7** 38 30N 96 16W
Americus, *MO, U.S.A.* **82 C5** 38 47N 91 34W
Amery, *WI, U.S.A.* **103 C1** 45 19N 92 22W
Ames, *IA, U.S.A.* **73 C5** 42 2N 93 37W
Ames, *OK, U.S.A.* **93 B5** 36 15N 98 11W
Ames, *TX, U.S.A.* **99 G13** 30 3N 94 45W
Amesbury, *MA, U.S.A.* **78 B4** 42 51N 70 56W
Amesville, *OH, U.S.A.* **92 D5** 39 24N 81 57W
Amet Sound, *N.S., Canada* **173 H6** 45 47N 63 10W
Amherst, *N.S., Canada* **173 H5** 45 48N 64 8W
Amherst, *CO, U.S.A.* **66 B8** 40 41N 102 10W
Amherst, *ME, U.S.A.* **76 D5** 44 50N 68 22W
Amherst, *MA, U.S.A.* **78 B2** 42 23N 72 31W
Amherst, *NH, U.S.A.* **86 D3** 42 52N 71 38W
Amherst, *NY, U.S.A.* **89 C2** 42 59N 78 48W
Amherst, *NE, U.S.A.* **84 D6** 40 46N 99 16W
Amherst, *OH, U.S.A.* **92 B4** 41 24N 82 14W
Amherst, *TX, U.S.A.* **98 C5** 34 1N 102 25W
Amherst, *VA, U.S.A.* **102 D5** 37 35N 79 3W
Amherst County ☆, *VA, U.S.A.* . . **102 D5** 37 38N 79 5W
Amherst I., *Ont., Canada* **179 C10** 44 8N 76 43W
Amherst Junction, *WI, U.S.A.* . . . **103 D4** 44 28N 89 19W
Amherstburg, *Ont., Canada* **178 E3** 42 6N 83 6W
Amherstdale, *WV, U.S.A.* **102 D3** 37 47N 81 49W
Amidon, *ND, U.S.A.* **91 D2** 46 29N 103 19W
Amisk, *Alta., Canada* **185 F9** 52 33N 111 4W
Amisk L., *Sask., Canada* **189 F12** 54 35N 102 15W
Amistad, *NM, U.S.A.* **88 B7** 35 55N 103 9W
Amistad, Presa de la, *Coahuila, Mexico* **214 A3** 29 26N 101 3W
Amistad Nat. Recr. Area ⌂, *TX, U.S.A.* **98 H6** 29 32N 101 12W
Amistad Res., *TX, U.S.A.* **98 H6** 29 28N 101 4W
Amite, *LA, U.S.A.* **75 D5** 30 44N 90 30W
Amite →, *LA, U.S.A.* **75 D5** 30 18N 90 34W
Amite County ☆, *MS, U.S.A.* **81 E3** 31 10N 90 49W
Amity, *AR, U.S.A.* **63 D2** 34 16N 93 28W
Amity, *OR, U.S.A.* **94 B2** 45 7N 123 12W
Amlia I., *AK, U.S.A.* **61 K4** 52 4N 173 30W
Ammon, *ID, U.S.A.* **70 F7** 43 28N 111 58W
Ammonoosuc →, *NH, U.S.A.* **86 B2** 44 10N 72 2W
Amonate, *VA, U.S.A.* **102 D3** 37 12N 81 38W
Amoret, *MO, U.S.A.* **82 C2** 38 15N 94 35W
Amorita, *OK, U.S.A.* **93 B5** 36 56N 98 18W
Amory, *MS, U.S.A.* **81 C5** 33 59N 88 29W
Amos, *Qué., Canada* **176 C4** 48 35N 78 5W
Amozoc, *Puebla, Mexico* **221 E2** 19 1N 98 1W
Ampliación San Germán, *Tamaulipas, Mexico* **215 E6** 25 6N 98 3W
Amqui, *Qué., Canada* **172 E2** 48 28N 67 27W
Amsden, *VT, U.S.A.* **86 C2** 43 25N 72 30W
Amsterdam, *NY, U.S.A.* **89 C6** 42 56N 74 11W
Amsterdam, *OH, U.S.A.* **92 C6** 40 29N 80 56W
Amukta I., *AK, U.S.A.* **61 K5** 52 30N 171 16W
Amukta Pass, *AK, U.S.A.* **61 K5** 52 0N 171 0W
Amund Ringnes I., *Nunavut, Canada* **190 B6** 78 20N 96 25W
Amundsen Gulf, *Canada* **188 B8** 71 0N 124 0W
Amy, *AR, U.S.A.* **63 E3** 33 44N 92 49W
Amyot, *Ont., Canada* **181 D12** 48 29N 84 57W
Anacapa I., *CA, U.S.A.* **65 J7** 34 1N 119 26W
Anacoco, *LA, U.S.A.* **75 C2** 31 15N 93 21W
Anaconda, *MT, U.S.A.* **83 D5** 46 8N 112 57W
Anaconda Ra., *MT, U.S.A.* **83 E4** 45 30N 113 30W
Anacortes, *WA, U.S.A.* **101 B3** 48 30N 122 37W
Anacostia →, *Washington DC, U.S.A.* **119 B4** 38 52N 77 1W
Anacostia, *DC, U.S.A.* **119 B4** 38 51N 76 59W
Anadarko, *OK, U.S.A.* **93 C5** 35 4N 98 15W
Anaheim, *CA, U.S.A.* **65 K9** 33 50N 117 55W
Anahim Lake, *B.C., Canada* **186 C9** 52 28N 125 18W
Anahola, *HI, U.S.A.* **69 A2** 22 9N 159 19W
Anáhuac, *Chihuahua, Mexico* **213 E9** 28 28N 106 45W
Anáhuac, *Tamaulipas, Mexico* . . . **214 E7** 25 50N 97 48W
Anahuac, *TX, U.S.A.* **99 H13** 29 46N 94 41W
Anahuac Nat. Wildlife Refuge ⌂, *TX, U.S.A.* **99 H13** 29 34N 94 32W
'Anahulu →, *HI, U.S.A.* **69 J13** 21 37N 158 6W
Anaichak Nat. Monument and Preserve ⌂, *AK, U.S.A.* **61 H8** 56 50N 158 15W
Anaktuvuk Pass, *AK, U.S.A.* **61 B10** 68 8N 151 45W
Analomink, *PA, U.S.A.* **87 A1** 41 3N 75 13W
Anamoose, *ND, U.S.A.* **91 C5** 47 53N 100 15W
Anamosa, *IA, U.S.A.* **73 C7** 42 7N 91 17W
Anandale, *LA, U.S.A.* **75 C3** 31 16N 92 27W
Anasazi, *Chihuahua, Mexico* **213 D7** 29 8N 108 15W
Añasco, *Puerto Rico* **105 G15** 18 17N 67 8W
Anatahan, *N. Marianas* . . . . **105 a** 16 21N 145 40W
Anatone, *WA, U.S.A.* **101 D8** 46 8N 117 8W
Anceney, *MT, U.S.A.* **83 E6** 45 39N 111 21W
Ancho, *NM, U.S.A.* **88 D5** 33 56N 105 45W
Anchor, *IL, U.S.A.* **71 C5** 40 34N 88 32W
Anchorage, *AK, U.S.A.* **61 F10** 61 13N 149 54W
Anchorage ☆, *AK, U.S.A.* **61 F10** 61 10N 149 15W
Anchorage ✈ (ANC), *AK, U.S.A.* . **61 F10** 61 10N 150 0W
Ancón de Carros, *Chihuahua, Mexico* **213 F10** 27 58N 105 15W
Ancram, *NY, U.S.A.* **78 B1** 42 3N 73 38W
Andale, *KS, U.S.A.* **74 D6** 37 48N 97 38W
Andalusia, *AL, U.S.A.* **60 E4** 31 18N 86 29W
Andalusia, *IL, U.S.A.* **71 B3** 41 26N 90 43W
Ande de Piedra, L., *Tamaulipas, Mexico* **215 F7** 25 0N 97 49W
Andersen Air Force Base, *Guam* . . **105 b** 13 35N 144 55W
Anderson, *AL, U.S.A.* **60 B3** 34 55N 87 16W
Anderson, *AK, U.S.A.* **61 D10** 64 25N 149 15W
Anderson, *CA, U.S.A.* **64 C4** 40 27N 122 18W
Anderson, *IN, U.S.A.* **72 C5** 40 10N 85 41W
Anderson, *MO, U.S.A.* **82 E2** 36 39N 94 27W
Anderson, *SC, U.S.A.* **90 D3** 34 31N 82 39W
Anderson, *TX, U.S.A.* **99 G12** 30 29N 95 59W
Anderson →, *N.W.T., Canada* . . . **188 C7** 69 42N 129 0W
Anderson County ☆, *KS, U.S.A.* . . **74 C8** 38 15N 95 15W
Anderson County ☆, *KY, U.S.A.* . . **97 C8** 38 0N 85 0W
Anderson County ☆, *SC, U.S.A.* . . **90 D3** 34 30N 82 40W
Anderson County ☆, *TN, U.S.A.* . . **97 D8** 36 6N 84 8W
Anderson County ☆, *TX, U.S.A.* . . **99 F12** 31 46N 95 38W
Anderson L., *B.C., Canada* **187 E12** 50 37N 122 25W
Anderson Park, *Atlanta, U.S.A.* . . **106 B2** 33 45N 84 27W
Anderson Ranch Res., *ID, U.S.A.* . **70 F3** 43 22N 115 27W
Anderson Res., *CA, U.S.A.* **64 F5** 37 10N 121 38W
Andersonville, *GA, U.S.A.* **68 D2** 32 12N 84 9W
Andersonville Nat. Historic Site ⌂, *GA, U.S.A.* **68 D2** 32 12N 84 1W
Andes, *NY, U.S.A.* **89 C6** 42 12N 74 47W
Andes, L., *SD, U.S.A.* **91 G7** 43 11N 98 27W
Andover, *CT, U.S.A.* **78 C2** 41 44N 72 23W
Andover, *KS, U.S.A.* **74 D6** 37 43N 97 7W
Andover, *ME, U.S.A.* **76 D3** 44 38N 70 45W
Andover, *MA, U.S.A.* **78 B3** 42 40N 71 8W
Andover, *MN, U.S.A.* **80 E5** 45 17N 93 21W
Andover, *NH, U.S.A.* **86 C3** 43 26N 71 49W
Andover, *NJ, U.S.A.* **87 B2** 40 59N 74 45W
Andover, *NY, U.S.A.* **89 C3** 42 10N 77 48W
Andover, *OH, U.S.A.* **92 B6** 41 36N 80 34W
Andover, *SD, U.S.A.* **91 E8** 45 25N 97 54W
Andreanof Is., *AK, U.S.A.* **61 L4** 51 30N 176 0W
Andrew, *Alta., Canada* **184 E8** 53 53N 112 21W
Andrew County ☆, *MO, U.S.A.* . . . **82 B2** 40 0N 94 45W
Andrew Johnson Nat. Historic Site ⌂, *TN, U.S.A.* **97 D10** 36 10N 82 50W
Andrews, *IN, U.S.A.* **72 C5** 40 52N 85 36W
Andrews, *MD, U.S.A.* **77 B4** 38 20N 76 10W
Andrews, *NC, U.S.A.* **90 C2** 35 12N 83 49W
Andrews, *SC, U.S.A.* **90 E6** 33 27N 79 34W
Andrews, *TX, U.S.A.* **98 E5** 32 19N 102 33W
Andrews County ☆, *TX, U.S.A.* . . . **98 E5** 32 19N 102 33W
Androscoggin →, *ME, U.S.A.* **76 E4** 43 58N 69 52W
Androscoggin County ☆, *ME, U.S.A.* **76 D3** 44 5N 70 10W
Anegada, *Br. Virgin Is.* **105 G18** 18 45N 64 20W
Anegam, *AZ, U.S.A.* **62 E3** 32 22N 112 2W
Aneroid, *Sask., Canada* **182 F4** 49 43N 107 18W
Aneta, *ND, U.S.A.* **91 C8** 47 41N 97 59W
Aneth, *UT, U.S.A.* **100 F6** 37 13N 109 11W
Angamacutore, *Michoacan, Mexico* **218 B6** 20 8N 101 42W
Angangueo, *Michoacan, Mexico* . . . **219 C7** 19 37N 100 18W
Ange-Gardien, *Qué., Canada* **86 A2** 45 21N 72 56W
Ángel Albino Corzo, *Chiapas, Mexico* **222 D3** 15 55N 92 43W
Ángel de la Guarda, I., *Baja Calif., Mexico* **210 D5** 29 20N 113 25W
Angel Fire, *NM, U.S.A.* **88 A5** 36 24N 105 17W
Angel Island State Park ⌂, *San Francisco, U.S.A.* **118 A2** 37 52N 122 25W
Ángel R. Cabada, *Veracruz, Mexico* **221 F5** 18 36N 95 26W
Angeles Nat. Forest, *CA, U.S.A.* . . **65 J9** 34 15N 118 0W
Angelina →, *TX, U.S.A.* **99 G13** 30 54N 94 12W
Angelina County ☆, *TX, U.S.A.* . . **99 F13** 31 21N 94 44W
Angelina Nat. Forest, *TX, U.S.A.* . **99 F13** 31 7N 94 15W
Angels Camp, *CA, U.S.A.* **64 E6** 38 4N 120 32W
Angelus, *KS, U.S.A.* **74 B3** 39 11N 100 41W
Angie, *LA, U.S.A.* **75 D6** 30 58N 89 49W
Angier, *NC, U.S.A.* **90 C7** 35 31N 78 44W
Angikuni L., *Nunavut, Canada* . . . **191 E6** 62 12N 99 59W
Angle Inlet, *MN, U.S.A.* **80 A3** 49 21N 95 4W
Angleton, *TX, U.S.A.* **99 H12** 29 10N 95 26W
Angliers, *Qué., Canada* **176 D3** 47 33N 79 14W
Angola, *DE, U.S.A.* **77 B5** 38 40N 75 10W

Angola, *IN, U.S.A.* **72 B6** 41 38N 85 0W
Angola, *NY, U.S.A.* **89 C1** 42 38N 79 2W
Angoon, *AK, U.S.A.* **61 H14** 57 30N 134 35W
Angora, *NE, U.S.A.* **84 C2** 41 51N 103 8W
Angostura, *Sinaloa, Mexico* **216 B2** 25 22N 108 11W
Angostura, Presa de la, *Chiapas, Mexico* **222 C4** 16 10N 92 35W
Angostura, Presa de la, *Sonora, Mexico* **212 C6** 30 30N 109 22W
Angostura Res., *SD, U.S.A.* **91 G2** 43 21N 103 26W
Angrignon, Parc, *Montréal, Canada* **192 B3** 45 25N 73 36W
Anguilla, *MS, U.S.A.* **81 D3** 32 59N 90 50W
Anguille, C., *Nfld. & L., Canada* **174 E1** 47 55N 59 24W
Anguille Mts., *Nfld. & L., Canada* **174 E1** 48 0N 59 11W
Angus, *Ont., Canada* **178 C7** 44 19N 79 53W
Angusville, *Man., Canada* **183 E10** 50 44N 101 1W
Angwin, *CA, U.S.A.* **64 E4** 38 34N 122 26W
Aniak, *AK, U.S.A.* **61 F8** 61 35N 159 32W
Animas, *NM, U.S.A.* **88 F2** 31 57N 108 48W
Animas →, *NM, U.S.A.* **88 E2** 36 43N 108 13W
Animas Mts., *NM, U.S.A.* **88 F2** 31 33N 108 47W
Animas Peak, *NM, U.S.A.* **88 F2** 31 35N 108 47W
Anita, *IA, U.S.A.* **73 D4** 41 27N 94 46W
Anjou, *Montréal, Canada* **192 A3** 45 36N 73 33W
Ankeny, *IA, U.S.A.* **73 D5** 41 44N 93 36W
Anmoore, *WV, U.S.A.* **102 B4** 39 16N 80 18W
Ann, C., *MA, U.S.A.* **78 B4** 42 38N 70 35W
Ann Arbor, *MI, U.S.A.* **79 G8** 42 17N 83 45W
Anna, *IL, U.S.A.* **71 F4** 37 28N 89 15W
Anna, *OH, U.S.A.* **92 C2** 40 24N 84 11W
Anna, *TX, U.S.A.* **99 D11** 33 21N 96 33W
Anna, L., *VA, U.S.A.* **102 C7** 38 4N 77 45W
Annabella, *UT, U.S.A.* **100 E3** 38 43N 112 4W
Annada, *MO, U.S.A.* **82 B6** 39 16N 90 50W
Annadale, *NY, U.S.A.* **114 C2** 40 32N 74 10W
Annaheim, *Sask., Canada* **182 C7** 52 19N 104 49W
Annalee Heights, *VA, U.S.A.* **119 B2** 38 51N 77 10W
Annandale, *MN, U.S.A.* **80 E4** 45 16N 94 8W
Annandale, *VA, U.S.A.* **102 C7** 38 50N 77 11W
Annapolis, *MD, U.S.A.* **77 B4** 38 59N 76 30W
Annapolis, *MO, U.S.A.* **82 D6** 37 22N 90 42W
Annapolis Royal, *N.S., Canada* **173 J4** 44 44N 65 32W
Annawan, *IL, U.S.A.* **71 B4** 41 24N 89 55W
Anne Arundel County ☆, *MD, U.S.A.* **77 A4** 39 0N 76 40W
Annette Island Indian Reservation, *AK, U.S.A.* **61 J15** 55 9N 131 28W
Annieopsquotch Mts., *Nfld. & L., Canada* **174 D3** 48 20N 57 30W
Anniston, *AL, U.S.A.* **60 C5** 33 39N 85 50W
Anniston, *MO, U.S.A.* **82 E7** 36 50N 89 20W
Annona, *TX, U.S.A.* **99 D13** 33 35N 94 55W
Annville, *KY, U.S.A.* **97 C9** 37 19N 83 58W
Annville, *PA, U.S.A.* **95 D6** 40 20N 76 31W
Año Nuevo, Pt., *CA, U.S.A.* **64 F4** 37 7N 122 19W
Anoka, *MN, U.S.A.* **80 E5** 45 12N 93 23W
Anoka, *NE, U.S.A.* **84 B7** 42 57N 98 50W
Anoka County ☆, *MN, U.S.A.* **80 E5** 45 15N 93 15W
Anola, *Man., Canada* **183 F15** 49 53N 96 38W
Anselmo, *NE, U.S.A.* **84 C6** 41 37N 99 52W
Ansley, *LA, U.S.A.* **75 B3** 32 24N 92 42W
Ansley, *NE, U.S.A.* **84 C6** 41 18N 99 23W
Anson, *TX, U.S.A.* **99 E8** 32 45N 99 54W
Anson County ☆, *NC, U.S.A.* **90 D5** 35 0N 80 0W
Ansonia, *CT, U.S.A.* **78 C1** 41 21N 73 5W
Ansonia, *OH, U.S.A.* **92 C2** 40 13N 84 38W
Ansonville, *NC, U.S.A.* **90 C5** 35 6N 80 7W
Ansted, *WV, U.S.A.* **102 C3** 38 8N 81 6W
Antelope, *KS, U.S.A.* **74 C7** 38 26N 96 59W
Antelope, *OR, U.S.A.* **94 C5** 44 55N 120 43W
Antelope County ☆, *NE, U.S.A.* **84 B7** 42 15N 98 0W
Antelope Hills, *OK, U.S.A.* **93 C4** 35 55N 99 50W
Antelope Hills, *WY, U.S.A.* **104 D4** 42 20N 108 25W
Antelope I., *UT, U.S.A.* **100 C3** 40 51N 112 10W
Antelope Range, *NV, U.S.A.* **85 B6** 40 10N 114 30W
Antelope Res., *OR, U.S.A.* **94 E8** 42 54N 117 14W
Antero, Mt., *CO, U.S.A.* **66 D4** 38 41N 106 15W
Antero Res., *CO, U.S.A.* **66 D5** 38 56N 105 55W
Anthon, *IA, U.S.A.* **73 C3** 42 23N 95 52W
Anthony, *U.S.A.* **88 E4** 32 0N 106 36W
Anthony, *FL, U.S.A.* **67 B6** 29 18N 82 7W
Anthony, *KS, U.S.A.* **74 D5** 37 9N 98 2W
Anthony Chabot Regional Park ⌓, *San Francisco, U.S.A.* **118 B4** 37 51N 122 14W
Anthoston, *KY, U.S.A.* **96 C5** 37 46N 87 32W
Anticosti, Î. d', *Qué., Canada* **172 D6** 49 30N 63 0W
Antigo, *WI, U.S.A.* **103 C4** 45 9N 89 9W
Antigonish, *N.S., Canada* **173 H8** 45 38N 61 58W
Antiguo Morelos, *Tamaulipas, Mexico* **215 H5** 22 33N 99 5W
Antimony, *UT, U.S.A.* **100 E4** 38 7N 112 0W
Antioch, *CA, U.S.A.* **64 E5** 38 1N 121 48W
Antioch, *IL, U.S.A.* **71 A5** 42 29N 88 6W
Antioch, *NE, U.S.A.* **84 B3** 42 4N 102 35W
Antler, *Sask., Canada* **183 F10** 49 34N 101 27W
Antler, *ND, U.S.A.* **91 B4** 48 59N 101 17W
Antler →, *Man., Canada* **183 F10** 49 8N 101 0W
Antlers, *OK, U.S.A.* **93 D8** 34 14N 95 37W
Antoine, *AR, U.S.A.* **63 D2** 34 2N 93 25W
Anton, *CO, U.S.A.* **66 C7** 39 45N 103 13W
Anton, *KY, U.S.A.* **96 C5** 37 21N 87 24W
Anton, *TX, U.S.A.* **98 D5** 33 49N 102 10W
Anton Chico, *NM, U.S.A.* **88 B5** 35 12N 105 9W
Antón Lizardo, *Veracruz, Mexico* **221 E5** 19 3N 95 59W
Antón Lizardo, Pta., *Veracruz, Mexico* **221 E5** 19 1N 95 58W
Antonino, *KS, U.S.A.* **74 C4** 38 47N 99 24W
Antonio Amaro, *Durango, Mexico* **217 C6** 24 17N 104 2W
Antonio Escobedo, *Jalisco, Mexico* **218 B4** 20 46N 103 57W
Antonito, *CO, U.S.A.* **66 E5** 37 5N 106 0W
Antrim, *NH, U.S.A.* **86 C3** 43 2N 71 56W
Antrim County ☆, *MI, U.S.A.* **79 E6** 45 0N 85 10W
Antwerp, *NY, U.S.A.* **89 A5** 44 12N 75 37W
Antwerp, *OH, U.S.A.* **92 B2** 41 11N 84 45W
Anvik, *AK, U.S.A.* **61 E7** 62 39N 160 13W
Anza Borrego Desert State Park ⌓, *CA, U.S.A.* **65 L10** 33 0N 116 26W
Apache, *OK, U.S.A.* **93 D5** 34 54N 98 22W
Apache County ☆, *AZ, U.S.A.* **62 B6** 35 0N 109 30W
Apache Creek, *NM, U.S.A.* **88 D2** 33 50N 108 37W
Apache Junction, *AZ, U.S.A.* **62 D4** 33 25N 111 33W
Apache L., *AZ, U.S.A.* **62 D4** 33 36N 111 21W
Apache Mts., *TX, U.S.A.* **98 F3** 31 12N 104 35W
Apache Sitgreaves Nat. Forest, *AZ, U.S.A.* **62 C5** 34 30N 110 30W
Apalachee B., *FL, U.S.A.* **67 B5** 30 0N 84 0W
Apalachicola, *FL, U.S.A.* **67 B4** 29 43N 84 59W
Apalachicola →, *FL, U.S.A.* **67 B4** 29 43N 84 58W
Apalachicola B., *FL, U.S.A.* **67 B4** 29 40N 85 0W
Apalachicola Nat. Forest, *FL, U.S.A.* **67 A4** 30 10N 85 0W
Apan, *Hidalgo, Mexico* **219 C9** 19 43N 98 25W
Apango Mártir, *Guerrero, Mexico* **219 E8** 17 44N 99 20W
Apaseo el Alto, *Guanajuato, Mexico* **219 B7** 20 27N 100 37W
Apaseo el Grande, *Guanajuato, Mexico* **219 B7** 20 33N 100 41W
Apatzingán, *Michoacan, Mexico* **218 C5** 19 5N 102 21W
Apaxco, *México, Mexico* **219 C8** 19 59N 99 10W
Apaxtla, *Guerrero, Mexico* **219 D8** 18 8N 99 56W
Apex, *NC, U.S.A.* **90 C7** 35 44N 78 51W
Apishapa →, *CO, U.S.A.* **66 D7** 38 8N 103 57W
Apizaco, *Tlaxcala, Mexico* **219 C9** 19 25N 98 8W
Aplington, *IA, U.S.A.* **73 C6** 42 35N 92 53W
Apodaca, *Monterrey, Mexico* **224 B2** 25 46N 100 12W
Apodaca, *Nuevo León, Mexico* **214 E4** 25 46N 100 12W
Apohaqui, *N.B., Canada* **173 H4** 45 42N 65 36W
Apollo Beach, *Tampa, U.S.A.* **119 C4** 27 46N 82 24W
Apopka, *FL, U.S.A.* **67 C7** 28 40N 81 31W
Apopka, L., *FL, U.S.A.* **67 C7** 28 37N 81 37W
Apostle Is., *WI, U.S.A.* **103 A3** 47 0N 90 40W
Apostle Islands Nat. Lakeshore ⌓, *WI, U.S.A.* **103 B3** 46 55N 91 0W
Apozol, *Zacatecas, Mexico* **217 F7** 21 29N 103 6W
Appalachia, *VA, U.S.A.* **102 E2** 36 54N 82 47W
Appalachian Mts., *VA, U.S.A.* **53 C11** 38 0N 80 0W
Appalachian Nat. Scenic Trail ⌓, *U.S.A.* **68 B3** 34 44N 83 50W
Appanoose County ☆, *IA, U.S.A.* **73 E6** 40 45N 92 50W
Apple →, *IL, U.S.A.* **71 A3** 42 11N 90 14W
Apple →, *WI, U.S.A.* **103 C1** 45 9N 92 45W
Apple Creek, *OH, U.S.A.* **92 C5** 40 45N 81 51W
Apple Creek →, *IL, U.S.A.* **71 D3** 39 22N 90 37W
Apple Hill, *Ont., Canada* **179 B12** 45 13N 74 46W
Apple Valley, *CA, U.S.A.* **65 J9** 34 32N 117 14W
Applegate, *MI, U.S.A.* **79 F9** 43 21N 82 38W
Applegate, *OR, U.S.A.* **94 E2** 42 16N 123 10W
Appleton, *MN, U.S.A.* **80 E2** 45 12N 96 1W
Appleton, *WI, U.S.A.* **103 D5** 44 16N 88 25W
Appleton City, *MO, U.S.A.* **82 C2** 38 11N 94 2W
Appling, *GA, U.S.A.* **68 C4** 33 33N 82 19W
Appling County ☆, *GA, U.S.A.* **68 E4** 31 45N 82 15W
Appomattox, *VA, U.S.A.* **102 D6** 37 21N 78 50W
Appomattox →, *VA, U.S.A.* **102 D7** 37 19N 77 17W
Appomattox County ☆, *VA, U.S.A.* **102 D6** 37 21N 78 50W
Apsley, *Ont., Canada* **179 C8** 44 45N 78 6W
Aquarius Mts., *AZ, U.S.A.* **62 C2** 34 45N 113 20W
Aquarius Plateau, *UT, U.S.A.* **100 F4** 38 0N 111 40W
Aquasco, *MD, U.S.A.* **77 B4** 38 35N 76 43W
Aquila, *Michoacan, Mexico* **218 D4** 18 36N 103 30W
Aquiles Serdán, *Chiapas, Mexico* **222 E4** 14 55N 92 30W
Aquiles Serdán, *Chihuahua, Mexico* **213 E10** 28 36N 105 53W
Aquiles Serdán, *Jalisco, Mexico* **218 B2** 20 17N 105 37W
Aquiles Serdán, *Nuevo León, Mexico* **214 D5** 26 53N 99 43W
Aquismón, *San Luis Potosí, Mexico* **215 J5** 21 38N 99 2W
Ara L., *Ont., Canada* **181 B9** 50 33N 87 28W
Arab, *AL, U.S.A.* **60 B4** 34 19N 86 30W
Arabela, *NM, U.S.A.* **88 D5** 33 35N 105 10W
Arabi, *GA, U.S.A.* **68 E3** 31 50N 83 44W
Arabi, *New Orleans, U.S.A.* **113 C3** 29 57N 90 0W
Arago, C., *OR, U.S.A.* **94 D1** 43 20N 124 30W
Aragon, *GA, U.S.A.* **68 B1** 34 2N 85 3W
Aramberri, *Nuevo León, Mexico* **215 F5** 24 6N 99 49W
Arandas, *Jalisco, Mexico* **218 B5** 20 42N 102 21W
Aransas County ☆, *TX, U.S.A.* **99 J11** 28 5N 96 28W
Aransas Nat. Wildlife Refuge ⌓, *TX, U.S.A.* **99 J11** 28 14N 96 54W
Aransas Pass, *TX, U.S.A.* **99 K10** 27 55N 97 9W
Arapaho, *OK, U.S.A.* **93 C5** 35 34N 98 58W
Arapaho Nat. Forest, *CO, U.S.A.* **66 C4** 39 30N 106 15W
Arapahoe, *CO, U.S.A.* **66 D8** 38 51N 102 11W
Arapahoe, *NE, U.S.A.* **84 D6** 40 18N 99 54W
Arapahoe, *WY, U.S.A.* **104 D4** 42 58N 108 29W
Arapahoe County ☆, *CO, U.S.A.* **66 C6** 39 40N 104 15W
Ararat, *VA, U.S.A.* **102 E4** 36 36N 80 31W
Aratichanguio, *Guerrero, Mexico* **219 D6** 18 30N 101 21W
Arbon, *ID, U.S.A.* **70 G6** 42 27N 112 34W
Arbor Vitae, *Ont., Canada* **180 D2** 48 54N 94 18W
Arboretum Morgan, *Montréal, Canada* **192 B1** 45 24N 73 57W
Arborfield, *Sask., Canada* **182 B8** 53 6N 103 39W
Arborg, *Man., Canada* **183 E14** 50 54N 97 13W
Arbuckle, *CA, U.S.A.* **64 D4** 39 1N 122 3W
Arbuckle L., *FL, U.S.A.* **67 D7** 27 42N 81 24W
Arbuckle Mts., *OK, U.S.A.* **93 D6** 34 20N 97 10W
Arbutus, *MD, U.S.A.* **77 A4** 39 15N 76 42W
Arbyrd, *MO, U.S.A.* **82 E6** 36 3N 90 2W
Arc Dome, *NV, U.S.A.* **85 D3** 38 51N 117 22W
Arcade, *CA, U.S.A.* **64 E5** 38 38N 121 24W
Arcade, *GA, U.S.A.* **68 B3** 34 5N 83 34W
Arcade, *NY, U.S.A.* **89 C2** 42 32N 78 25W
Arcadia, *N.S., Canada* **173 K3** 43 50N 66 4W
Arcadia, *FL, U.S.A.* **67 D7** 27 13N 81 52W
Arcadia, *IN, U.S.A.* **72 C4** 40 11N 86 1W
Arcadia, *IA, U.S.A.* **73 C3** 42 5N 95 3W
Arcadia, *KS, U.S.A.* **74 D9** 37 38N 94 37W
Arcadia, *LA, U.S.A.* **75 B3** 32 33N 92 55W
Arcadia, *Los Angeles, U.S.A.* **111 B4** 34 7N 118 1W
Arcadia, *MI, U.S.A.* **79 E5** 44 30N 86 14W
Arcadia, *MO, U.S.A.* **82 D6** 37 35N 90 37W
Arcadia, *NE, U.S.A.* **84 C6** 41 25N 99 8W
Arcadia, *OK, U.S.A.* **93 C6** 35 40N 97 20W
Arcadia, *PA, U.S.A.* **95 D4** 40 47N 78 51W
Arcadia, *Phoenix, U.S.A.* **116 C3** 33 29N 111 58W
Arcadia, *WI, U.S.A.* **103 D2** 44 15N 91 30W
Arcadia Park, *Dallas-Fort Worth, U.S.A.* **109 B4** 32 44N 96 54W
Arcanum, *OH, U.S.A.* **92 D2** 39 59N 84 33W
Arcas, Cayos, *Campeche, Mexico* **223 B2** 20 12N 91 58W
Arcata, *CA, U.S.A.* **64 C2** 40 52N 124 5W
Arcata B., *CA, U.S.A.* **64 C2** 40 52N 124 5W
Arcelia, *Guerrero, Mexico* **219 D7** 18 17N 100 16W
Archbald, *PA, U.S.A.* **87 A1** 41 30N 75 32W
Archbold, *OH, U.S.A.* **92 B2** 41 31N 84 18W
Archdale, *NC, U.S.A.* **90 C6** 35 56N 79 57W
Archer, *FL, U.S.A.* **67 B6** 29 32N 82 32W
Archer, *IA, U.S.A.* **73 B3** 43 7N 95 45W
Archer, *NE, U.S.A.* **84 C7** 41 10N 98 8W
Archer City, *TX, U.S.A.* **99 D9** 33 36N 98 38W
Archer County ☆, *TX, U.S.A.* **99 D9** 33 35N 98 40W
Archer Fd., *Nunavut, Canada* **190 A12** 81 25N 67 0W
Archerwill, *Sask., Canada* **182 C8** 52 26N 103 51W
Arches Nat. Park △, *UT, U.S.A.* **100 E6** 38 45N 109 25W
Archibald, *LA, U.S.A.* **75 B4** 32 21N 91 47W
Archie, *LA, U.S.A.* **75 C4** 31 35N 91 58W
Archie, *MO, U.S.A.* **82 C2** 38 29N 94 21W
Archipel-de-Mingan, Réserve de Parc Nat. de l' ⌓, *Qué., Canada* **172 C6** 50 14N 63 37W
Archuleta County ☆, *CO, U.S.A.* **66 E4** 37 10N 107 0W
Arco, *ID, U.S.A.* **70 F5** 43 38N 113 18W
Arco, *MN, U.S.A.* **80 F2** 44 23N 96 11W
Arcola, *Sask., Canada* **183 F9** 49 40N 102 30W
Arcola, *IL, U.S.A.* **71 D5** 39 41N 88 19W
Arcola, *MS, U.S.A.* **81 C3** 33 16N 90 53W
Arcola, *MO, U.S.A.* **82 D3** 37 33N 93 53W
Arcola, *VA, U.S.A.* **77 B3** 38 57N 77 32W
Arctic Bay, *Nunavut, Canada* **190 C8** 73 1N 85 7W
Arctic Red →, *N.W.T., Canada* **188 C6** 67 26N 133 44W
Arctic Red River = Tsiigehtchic, *N.W.T., Canada* **188 C6** 67 15N 134 0W
Arctic Sd., *Nunavut, Canada* **190 D4** 67 32N 108 51W
Arctic Village, *AK, U.S.A.* **61 B11** 68 8N 145 32W
Ardbeg, *Ont., Canada* **178 B6** 45 38N 80 5W
Arden, *Man., Canada* **183 E12** 50 17N 99 16W
Arden, *Ont., Canada* **179 C10** 44 43N 76 56W
Arden, *CA, U.S.A.* **64 E5** 38 36N 121 33W
Arden Hills, *Minneapolis-St. Paul, U.S.A.* **113 A2** 45 3N 93 9W
Ardenvoir, *WA, U.S.A.* **101 C5** 47 44N 120 22W
Ardmore, *AL, U.S.A.* **60 B4** 34 59N 86 52W
Ardmore, *OK, U.S.A.* **93 D6** 34 10N 97 8W
Ardmore, *PA, U.S.A.* **95 D7** 40 2N 75 17W
Ardmore, *SD, U.S.A.* **91 G2** 43 1N 103 40W
Ardmore, *TN, U.S.A.* **96 F6** 35 0N 86 51W
Arecibo, *Puerto Rico* **105 G16** 18 29N 66 43W
Aredale, *IA, U.S.A.* **73 C5** 42 50N 93 0W
Arellano, *Campeche, Mexico* **223 C3** 19 24N 90 29W
Arena, *WI, U.S.A.* **103 E4** 43 10N 89 55W
Arena, Pt., *CA, U.S.A.* **64 E3** 38 57N 123 44W
Arena, Pta., *Baja Calif. S., Mexico* **211 K9** 23 34N 109 27W
Arena de Hidalgo, *Chiapas, Mexico* **222 B5** 17 27N 91 35W
Arenac County ☆, *MI, U.S.A.* **79 E8** 44 0N 83 55W
Arenas, Pta., *Puerto Rico* **105 G17** 18 7N 65 35W
Arenzville, *IL, U.S.A.* **71 D3** 39 53N 90 22W
Argenta = North Little Rock, *AR, U.S.A.* **63 D3** 34 45N 92 16W
Argenta, *B.C., Canada* **187 E18** 50 11N 116 56W
Argenta, *IL, U.S.A.* **71 D5** 39 59N 88 49W
Argentia, *Nfld. & L., Canada* **174 E7** 47 18N 53 58W
Argonia, *KS, U.S.A.* **74 D6** 37 16N 97 46W
Argonne, *WI, U.S.A.* **103 C5** 45 40N 88 53W
Argonne Forest, *Chicago, U.S.A.* **108 C1** 41 42N 87 53W
Argos, *IN, U.S.A.* **72 B4** 41 14N 86 15W
Arguello, Pt., *CA, U.S.A.* **65 J6** 34 35N 120 39W
Argus Range, *CA, U.S.A.* **65 G9** 36 10N 117 40W
Argusville, *ND, U.S.A.* **91 C9** 47 3N 96 56W
Argyle, *Man., Canada* **183 E14** 50 11N 97 27W
Argyle, *MN, U.S.A.* **80 B2** 48 20N 96 49W
Argyle, *WI, U.S.A.* **103 F4** 42 42N 89 52W
Arichat, *N.S., Canada* **173 H8** 45 31N 61 1W
Ariel, *WA, U.S.A.* **101 E3** 45 57N 122 34W
Arikaree →, *U.S.A.* **84 D4** 40 1N 101 56W
Arimo, *ID, U.S.A.* **70 G6** 42 34N 112 10W
Ario de Rosales, *Michoacan, Mexico* **218 C6** 19 12N 101 43W
Arion, *IA, U.S.A.* **73 D3** 41 57N 95 27W
Arispe, *IA, U.S.A.* **73 E4** 40 57N 94 13W
Arista, *San Luis Potosí, Mexico* **215 H4** 22 39N 100 50W
Aristazabal I., *B.C., Canada* **186 C5** 52 40N 129 10W
Ariton, *AL, U.S.A.* **60 E5** 31 36N 85 43W
Arivechi, *Sonora, Mexico* **212 E6** 28 56N 109 11W
Arizona □, *U.S.A.* **62 C4** 34 0N 112 0W
Arizona City, *AZ, U.S.A.* **62 E4** 32 45N 111 40W
Arizpe, *Sonora, Mexico* **212 C5** 30 20N 110 10W
Arkabutla L., *MS, U.S.A.* **81 B3** 34 46N 90 8W
Arkadelphia, *AR, U.S.A.* **63 D2** 34 7N 93 4W
Arkansas □, *U.S.A.* **63 D3** 35 0N 92 30W
Arkansas →, *AR, U.S.A.* **63 E4** 33 47N 91 4W
Arkansas City, *AR, U.S.A.* **63 E4** 33 37N 91 12W
Arkansas City, *KS, U.S.A.* **74 D6** 37 4N 97 2W
Arkansas County ☆, *AR, U.S.A.* **63 D4** 34 18N 91 20W
Arkansas Junction, *NM, U.S.A.* **88 E7** 32 42N 103 21W
Arkansas Post Nat. Memorial ⌓, *AR, U.S.A.* **63 D4** 34 1N 91 21W
Arkoma, *OK, U.S.A.* **93 C9** 35 21N 94 26W
Arkona, *Ont., Canada* **178 D5** 43 4N 81 50W
Arkport, *NY, U.S.A.* **89 C3** 42 24N 77 42W
Arlee, *MT, U.S.A.* **83 C3** 47 10N 114 5W
Arley, *AL, U.S.A.* **60 B3** 34 4N 87 13W
Arlington, *AZ, U.S.A.* **62 D3** 33 20N 112 46W
Arlington, *Baltimore, U.S.A.* **107 A1** 39 20N 76 41W
Arlington, *Boston, U.S.A.* **106 A2** 42 24N 71 10W
Arlington, *CO, U.S.A.* **66 D7** 38 20N 103 21W
Arlington, *GA, U.S.A.* **68 E2** 31 26N 84 44W
Arlington, *IL, U.S.A.* **71 B4** 41 29N 89 15W
Arlington, *IA, U.S.A.* **73 C7** 42 45N 91 40W
Arlington, *KS, U.S.A.* **74 D5** 37 54N 98 11W
Arlington, *KY, U.S.A.* **96 D3** 36 47N 89 1W
Arlington, *MA, U.S.A.* **78 B3** 42 25N 71 9W
Arlington, *MN, U.S.A.* **80 F4** 44 36N 94 5W
Arlington, *NY, U.S.A.* **89 D7** 41 42N 73 54W
Arlington, *NE, U.S.A.* **84 C9** 41 27N 96 21W
Arlington, *OH, U.S.A.* **92 C3** 40 54N 83 39W
Arlington, *OR, U.S.A.* **94 B5** 45 43N 120 12W
Arlington, *SD, U.S.A.* **91 F8** 44 22N 97 8W
Arlington, *TN, U.S.A.* **96 E3** 35 18N 89 40W
Arlington, *TX, U.S.A.* **99 E10** 32 44N 97 6W
Arlington, *VA, U.S.A.* **77 B3** 38 53N 77 7W
Arlington, *VT, U.S.A.* **86 C1** 43 5N 73 9W
Arlington, *WA, U.S.A.* **101 B3** 48 12N 122 8W
Arlington, *WI, U.S.A.* **103 E4** 43 20N 89 23W
Arlington, *WY, U.S.A.* **104 E6** 41 36N 106 12W
Arlington, L., *Dallas-Fort Worth, U.S.A.* **109 B2** 32 43N 97 11W
Arlington Heights, *Boston, U.S.A.* **106 A2** 42 25N 71 10W
Arlington Heights, *IL, U.S.A.* **71 A6** 42 5N 87 59W
Arlington Heights, *OH, U.S.A.* **107 A2** 39 12N 84 27W
Arlington Municipal ✕, *Dallas-Fort Worth, U.S.A.* **109 B3** 32 39N 97 5W
Arlington Nat. Cemetery, *VA, U.S.A.* **119 B3** 38 52N 77 4W
Arma, *KS, U.S.A.* **74 D9** 37 33N 94 42W
Armada, *MI, U.S.A.* **79 G9** 42 51N 82 53W
Armadillo, *San Luis Potosí, Mexico* **215 H4** 22 15N 100 39W
Armagh, *Qué., Canada* **177 E12** 46 41N 70 32W
Armería, *Colima, Mexico* **218 D4** 18 56N 103 58W
Armería →, *Colima, Mexico* **218 D4** 18 52N 103 59W
Armijo, *NM, U.S.A.* **88 B4** 35 4N 106 39W
Arminto, *WY, U.S.A.* **104 C6** 43 10N 106 49W
Armit L., *Nunavut, Canada* **191 E7** 64 10N 91 32W
Armona, *CA, U.S.A.* **65 G7** 36 19N 119 42W
Armour, *SD, U.S.A.* **91 G7** 43 19N 98 21W
Armstrong, *B.C., Canada* **187 E15** 50 25N 119 10W
Armstrong, *Ont., Canada* **180 B7** 50 18N 89 4W
Armstrong, *IA, U.S.A.* **73 B4** 43 24N 94 29W
Armstrong, *MO, U.S.A.* **82 B4** 39 16N 92 42W
Armstrong, *OK, U.S.A.* **93 D7** 34 3N 96 21W
Armstrong, *TX, U.S.A.* **98 L10** 26 56N 97 47W
Armstrong County ☆, *PA, U.S.A.* **95 D3** 40 45N 79 25W
Armstrong County ☆, *TX, U.S.A.* **98 C6** 35 0N 101 20W
Arnaud →, *Qué., Canada* **175 B4** 59 59N 69 46W
Arnaudville, *LA, U.S.A.* **75 D4** 30 24N 91 56W
Arnegard, *ND, U.S.A.* **91 C2** 47 49N 103 27W
Arnett, *OK, U.S.A.* **93 B4** 36 8N 99 46W
Arnold, *CA, U.S.A.* **64 E6** 38 15N 120 21W
Arnold, *MD, U.S.A.* **77 A4** 39 2N 76 30W
Arnold, *MI, U.S.A.* **79 C4** 46 3N 87 30W
Arnold, *MN, U.S.A.* **80 D6** 46 53N 92 5W
Arnold, *MO, U.S.A.* **82 C6** 38 26N 90 23W
Arnold, *NE, U.S.A.* **84 C5** 41 26N 100 12W
Arnold Arboretum, *Boston, U.S.A.* **106 B3** 42 18N 71 7W
Arnold Engineering Development Center, *TN, U.S.A.* **96 E6** 35 21N 86 2W
Arnolds Park, *IA, U.S.A.* **73 B3** 43 22N 95 8W
Arnprior, *Ont., Canada* **179 B10** 45 26N 76 21W
Arntfield, *Qué., Canada* **176 C3** 48 12N 79 15W
Arock, *OR, U.S.A.* **94 E8** 42 55N 117 32W
Aroma Park, *IL, U.S.A.* **71 B6** 41 5N 87 48W
Aroostook →, *ME, U.S.A.* **76 C6** 45 48N 67 45W
Aroostook County ☆, *ME, U.S.A.* **76 B5** 47 0N 69 0W
Aros →, *Sonora, Mexico* **212 D6** 29 30N 109 18W
Arp, *TX, U.S.A.* **99 E12** 32 14N 95 4W
Arpin, *WI, U.S.A.* **103 D3** 44 33N 90 2W
Arran, *Sask., Canada* **183 D10** 51 53N 101 43W
Arrey, *NM, U.S.A.* **88 E3** 32 48N 107 19W
Arriaga, *Chiapas, Mexico* **222 C3** 16 14N 93 54W
Arriba, *CO, U.S.A.* **66 C7** 39 17N 103 17W
Arrington, *KS, U.S.A.* **74 B8** 39 28N 95 32W
Arrow Cr. →, *MT, U.S.A.* **83 C8** 47 43N 109 50W
Arrow Park, *B.C., Canada* **187 E17** 50 6N 117 57W
Arrow Rock, *MO, U.S.A.* **82 B4** 39 4N 92 57W
Arrow Wood L., *ND, U.S.A.* **91 C7** 47 14N 98 50W
Arrowhead, *B.C., Canada* **187 E17** 50 40N 117 55W
Arrowhead, L., *TX, U.S.A.* **99 D9** 33 45N 98 25W
Arrowrock Res., *ID, U.S.A.* **70 F3** 43 36N 115 56W
Arrowsmith, *IL, U.S.A.* **71 C5** 40 27N 88 38W
Arrowwood, *Alta., Canada* **185 H7** 50 44N 113 9W
Arroyo del Cedro, *Veracruz, Mexico* **221 G7** 17 35N 93 54W
Arroyo del Macho →, *NM, U.S.A.* **88 D6** 33 49N 104 7W
Arroyo del Sáuz, *Baja Calif., Mexico* **210 A3** 32 1N 115 58W
Arroyo Grande, *CA, U.S.A.* **65 H6** 35 7N 120 35W
Arroyo Hondo, *NM, U.S.A.* **88 A5** 36 32N 105 40W
Arroyo Seco, *Querétaro, Mexico* **219 A8** 21 33N 99 42W
Artas, *SD, U.S.A.* **91 E6** 45 53N 99 49W
Arteaga, *Coahuila, Mexico* **214 E4** 25 28N 100 51W
Arteaga, *Michoacan, Mexico* **218 D5** 18 28N 102 25W
Artesia, *Los Angeles, U.S.A.* **111 C4** 33 51N 118 4W
Artesia, *MS, U.S.A.* **81 C5** 33 25N 88 39W
Artesia, *NM, U.S.A.* **88 E6** 32 51N 104 24W
Artesia L., *NV, U.S.A.* **85 D1** 38 56N 119 22W
Artesia Wells, *TX, U.S.A.* **99 J8** 28 17N 99 17W
Artesian, *SD, U.S.A.* **91 F8** 44 1N 97 55W
Arthur, *Ont., Canada* **178 D6** 43 50N 80 32W
Arthur, *IL, U.S.A.* **71 D5** 39 43N 88 28W
Arthur, *ND, U.S.A.* **91 C8** 47 6N 97 13W
Arthur, *NE, U.S.A.* **84 C4** 41 35N 101 41W
Arthur, *NV, U.S.A.* **85 B5** 40 48N 115 11W
Arthur, *TN, U.S.A.* **97 D9** 36 33N 83 40W
Arthur, L., *PA, U.S.A.* **95 D2** 40 58N 80 7W
Arthur County ☆, *NE, U.S.A.* **84 C4** 41 30N 101 40W
Arthur R. Marshall-Loxahatchee Nat. Wildlife Refuge ⌓, *FL, U.S.A.* **67 E8** 26 27N 80 14W
Arthurette, *N.B., Canada* **173 G2** 46 47N 67 29W
Artillery L., *N.W.T., Canada* **189 D11** 63 9N 107 52W
Artois, *CA, U.S.A.* **64 D4** 39 37N 122 12W
Arundel, *Qué., Canada* **176 F8** 45 58N 74 37W
Arundel Village, *Baltimore, U.S.A.* **107 B2** 39 13N 76 36W
Arvada, *CO, U.S.A.* **66 C5** 39 48N 105 5W
Arvada, *WY, U.S.A.* **104 B6** 44 39N 106 8W
Arvert L., *Nfld. & L., Canada* **172 A8** 52 18N 61 45W
Arviat, *Nunavut, Canada* **191 E7** 61 6N 93 59W
Arvin, *CA, U.S.A.* **65 H8** 35 12N 118 50W
Arvon, Mt., *MI, U.S.A.* **79 C3** 46 45N 88 9W
Asbury, *IA, U.S.A.* **73 C8** 42 31N 90 45W
Asbury, *MO, U.S.A.* **82 D2** 37 16N 94 36W
Asbury Park, *NJ, U.S.A.* **87 B2** 40 13N 74 1W
Ascensión, *Chihuahua, Mexico* **213 B8** 31 6N 107 59W
Ascensión, B. de la, *Quintana Roo, Mexico* **223 C6** 19 40N 87 30W
Ascension Parish ☆, *LA, U.S.A.* **75 D5** 30 14N 90 55W
Ascutney, *VT, U.S.A.* **86 C2** 43 24N 72 25W
Aserradero La Flor, *Durango, Mexico* **217 D6** 23 32N 104 43W
Ash Flat, *AR, U.S.A.* **63 B4** 36 13N 91 37W
Ash Fork, *AZ, U.S.A.* **62 B3** 35 13N 112 29W
Ash Grove, *MO, U.S.A.* **82 D3** 37 19N 93 35W
Ash Meadows Nat. Wildlife Refuge ⌓, *NV, U.S.A.* **85 F4** 36 25N 116 19W
Ash Springs, *NV, U.S.A.* **85 E5** 37 28N 115 12W
Ashaway, *RI, U.S.A.* **78 C3** 41 25N 71 47W
Ashburn, *Chicago, U.S.A.* **108 C2** 41 45N 87 43W
Ashburn, *GA, U.S.A.* **68 E3** 31 43N 83 39W
Ashburn, *VA, U.S.A.* **77 A3** 39 3N 77 29W
Ashburnham, *MA, U.S.A.* **78 B3** 42 38N 71 55W
Ashby, *MN, U.S.A.* **80 D3** 46 6N 95 49W
Ashby, *NE, U.S.A.* **84 B4** 42 1N 101 56W
Ashcroft, *B.C., Canada* **187 E13** 50 40N 121 20W
Ashdown, *AR, U.S.A.* **63 E1** 33 40N 94 8W
Ashe County ☆, *NC, U.S.A.* **90 B4** 36 25N 81 30W
Asheboro, *NC, U.S.A.* **90 C6** 35 43N 79 49W
Asher, *OK, U.S.A.* **93 D7** 34 59N 96 56W
Ashern, *Man., Canada* **183 D13** 51 11N 98 21W
Asherton, *TX, U.S.A.* **99 J8** 28 27N 99 46W
Asherville, *KS, U.S.A.* **74 B6** 39 24N 97 59W
Asheville, *NC, U.S.A.* **90 C3** 35 36N 82 33W
Ashfield, *MA, U.S.A.* **78 B2** 42 32N 72 48W
Ashford, *AL, U.S.A.* **60 E5** 31 11N 85 14W
Ashford, *WA, U.S.A.* **101 D3** 46 46N 122 2W
Ashkum, *IL, U.S.A.* **71 C6** 40 53N 87 57W
Ashland, *AL, U.S.A.* **60 C5** 33 16N 85 50W
Ashland, *IL, U.S.A.* **71 D3** 39 53N 90 1W
Ashland, *KS, U.S.A.* **74 D4** 37 11N 99 46W
Ashland, *KY, U.S.A.* **97 B10** 38 28N 82 38W
Ashland, *LA, U.S.A.* **75 B2** 32 9N 93 6W
Ashland, *ME, U.S.A.* **76 B5** 46 38N 68 24W
Ashland, *MA, U.S.A.* **78 B3** 42 16N 71 28W
Ashland, *MS, U.S.A.* **81 B4** 34 50N 89 11W
Ashland, *MO, U.S.A.* **82 C4** 38 47N 92 16W
Ashland, *MT, U.S.A.* **83 E11** 45 36N 106 16W
Ashland, *NH, U.S.A.* **86 C3** 43 42N 71 38W
Ashland, *NY, U.S.A.* **89 C6** 42 18N 74 20W
Ashland, *NE, U.S.A.* **84 C9** 41 3N 96 23W
Ashland, *OH, U.S.A.* **92 C4** 40 52N 82 19W
Ashland, *OK, U.S.A.* **93 D7** 34 46N 96 4W
Ashland, *OR, U.S.A.* **94 E3** 42 12N 122 43W
Ashland, *San Francisco, U.S.A.* **118 B4** 37 41N 122 6W
Ashland, *VA, U.S.A.* **102 D7** 37 46N 77 29W
Ashland, *WI, U.S.A.* **103 B3** 46 35N 90 53W
Ashland City, *TN, U.S.A.* **96 D5** 36 17N 87 4W
Ashland County ☆, *OH, U.S.A.* **92 C4** 40 52N 82 19W
Ashland County ☆, *WI, U.S.A.* **103 B3** 46 35N 90 45W
Ashley, *IL, U.S.A.* **71 E4** 38 20N 89 11W
Ashley, *IN, U.S.A.* **72 B5** 41 32N 85 4W
Ashley, *MI, U.S.A.* **79 F7** 43 11N 84 29W
Ashley, *ND, U.S.A.* **91 D6** 46 2N 99 22W
Ashley, *OH, U.S.A.* **92 C4** 40 25N 82 57W
Ashley County ☆, *AR, U.S.A.* **63 E4** 33 14N 91 48W
Ashley Cr. →, *UT, U.S.A.* **100 C6** 40 20N 109 17W
Ashley Nat. Forest, *UT, U.S.A.* **100 C5** 40 55N 110 0W
Ashmont, *Alta., Canada* **184 D9** 54 7N 111 35W
Ashmore, *IL, U.S.A.* **71 D5** 39 32N 88 1W
Ashokan Res., *NY, U.S.A.* **89 D6** 41 56N 74 13W
Ashtabula, *OH, U.S.A.* **92 B6** 41 52N 80 47W
Ashtabula, L., *ND, U.S.A.* **91 C7** 47 2N 98 0W
Ashtabula County ☆, *OH, U.S.A.* **92 B6** 41 40N 80 52W
Ashton, *ID, U.S.A.* **70 E7** 44 4N 111 27W
Ashton, *IL, U.S.A.* **71 B4** 41 52N 89 13W
Ashton, *IA, U.S.A.* **73 B3** 43 19N 95 47W
Ashton, *NE, U.S.A.* **84 C7** 41 15N 98 48W
Ashton, *RI, U.S.A.* **78 C3** 41 56N 71 26W
Ashton, *SD, U.S.A.* **91 F7** 44 59N 98 31W
Ashuanipi, L., *Nfld. & L., Canada* **175 C4** 52 45N 66 15W
Ashuapmushuan →, *Qué., Canada* **177 C10** 48 37N 72 20W
Ashuapmushuan, Réserve Faunique ⌓, *Qué., Canada* **177 B9** 49 5N 73 32W
Ashuelot →, *NH, U.S.A.* **86 D2** 42 46N 72 29W
Ashville, *AL, U.S.A.* **60 C4** 33 50N 86 15W

Ashville, *FL, U.S.A.* **67 A5** 30 37N 83 39W
Ashville, *PA, U.S.A.* **95 D4** 40 34N 78 33W
Ashwood, *OR, U.S.A.* **94 C5** 44 44N 120 45W
Asientos, *Aguascalientes, Mexico* **217 E8** 22 14N 102 5W
Askov, *MN, U.S.A.* **80 D6** 46 12N 92 47W
Asotin, *WA, U.S.A.* **101 D8** 46 20N 117 3W
Asotin County ☆, *WA, U.S.A.* **101 D8** 46 8N 117 8W
Aspen, *N.S., Canada* **173 H7** 45 18N 62 3W
Aspen, *CO, U.S.A.* **66 C4** 39 11N 106 49W
Aspen Grove, *B.C., Canada* **187 F14** 49 57N 120 37W
Aspen Hill, *MD, U.S.A.* **77 A3** 39 5N 77 5W
Aspen L., *OR, U.S.A.* **94 E3** 42 17N 122 0W
Aspermont, *TX, U.S.A.* **98 D7** 33 8N 100 14W
Aspinwall, *Pittsburgh, U.S.A.* **116 B2** 40 29N 79 54W
Asquith, *Sask., Canada* **182 C4** 52 8N 107 13W
Assaria, *KS, U.S.A.* **74 C6** 38 41N 97 36W
Assateague I., *MD, U.S.A.* **77 B5** 38 15N 75 10W
Assateague Island Nat. Seashore ⌂, *MD, U.S.A.* **77 B5** 38 15N 75 10W
Assawompset Pond, *MA, U.S.A.* **78 C4** 41 50N 70 55W
Assigny, L., *Nfld. & L., Canada* **172 A4** 52 0N 65 20W
Assiniboia, *Sask., Canada* **182 F6** 49 40N 105 59W
Assiniboine →, *Man., Canada* **183 F14** 49 53N 97 8W
Assinica, Réserve Faunique ⌂, *Qué., Canada* **176 A7** 50 37N 75 14W
Assinippi, *MA, U.S.A.* **78 B4** 42 10N 70 51W
Assonet, *MA, U.S.A.* **78 C3** 41 48N 71 4W
Assumption, *IL, U.S.A.* **71 D4** 39 31N 89 3W
Assumption Parish ☆, *LA, U.S.A.* **75 E4** 30 0N 91 0W
Astatula, *FL, U.S.A.* **67 C7** 28 43N 81 44W
Astoria, *IL, U.S.A.* **71 C3** 40 14N 90 21W
Astoria, *NY, U.S.A.* **114 B3** 40 46N 73 55W
Astoria, *OR, U.S.A.* **94 A2** 46 11N 123 50W
Astoria, *SD, U.S.A.* **91 F9** 44 34N 96 33W
Astorville, *Ont., Canada* **178 A7** 46 11N 79 17W
Asuncion, *N. Marianas* **105 a** 19 40N 145 24W
Asuncíon →, *Sonora, Mexico* **212 C3** 30 31N 113 0W
Asunción, B., *Baja Calif. S., Mexico* **211 F4** 27 6N 114 11W
Asunción Nochixtlán, *Oaxaca, Mexico* **221 G3** 17 28N 97 14W
Asunción Puxmetacán, *Oaxaca, Mexico* **221 G5** 17 15N 95 38W
Atacosa →, *TX, U.S.A.* **99 H9** 29 16N 98 44W
Atando Junction, *Charlotte, U.S.A.* **107 A2** 35 15N 80 49W
Atarjea, *Guanajuato, Mexico* **219 A8** 21 23N 99 52W
Atascadero, *CA, U.S.A.* **65 H6** 35 29N 120 40W
Atascosa County ☆, *TX, U.S.A.* **99 J9** 28 55N 98 33W
Atasta, L., *Campeche, Mexico* **223 D1** 18 35N 92 6W
Atchafalaya →, *LA, U.S.A.* **75 E4** 29 53N 91 28W
Atchafalaya B., *LA, U.S.A.* **75 E4** 29 25N 91 25W
Atchison, *KS, U.S.A.* **74 B8** 39 34N 95 7W
Atchison County ☆, *KS, U.S.A.* **74 B8** 39 30N 95 15W
Atchison County ☆, *MO, U.S.A.* **82 A1** 40 25N 95 25W
Atco, *NJ, U.S.A.* **87 C2** 39 46N 74 53W
Atemajac de Brizuela, *Jalisco, Mexico* **218 B4** 20 11N 103 42W
Atenango del Río, *Guerrero, Mexico* **219 D8** 18 5N 99 6W
Atenayuca, *Puebla, Mexico* **221 F3** 18 34N 97 44W
Atengo, *Jalisco, Mexico* **218 B3** 20 14N 104 14W
Atengo →, *Mexico* **217 E6** 21 50N 104 43W
Atenguillo, *Jalisco, Mexico* **218 B3** 20 25N 104 31W
Atexcal, *Puebla, Mexico* **221 F3** 18 25N 97 44W
Athabasca, *Alta., Canada* **184 D7** 54 45N 113 20W
Athabasca →, *Alta., Canada* **189 E10** 58 40N 110 50W
Athabasca, L., *Sask., Canada* **189 E11** 59 15N 109 15W
Athena, *FL, U.S.A.* **67 B5** 29 59N 83 30W
Athena, *OR, U.S.A.* **94 B7** 45 49N 118 30W
Athens, *Ont., Canada* **179 C11** 44 38N 75 57W
Athens, *AL, U.S.A.* **60 B4** 34 48N 86 58W
Athens, *GA, U.S.A.* **68 C3** 33 57N 83 23W
Athens, *IL, U.S.A.* **71 D4** 39 58N 89 44W
Athens, *LA, U.S.A.* **75 B2** 32 39N 93 1W
Athens, *Los Angeles, U.S.A.* **111 C3** 33 55N 118 16W
Athens, *MI, U.S.A.* **79 G6** 42 5N 85 14W
Athens, *NY, U.S.A.* **89 C7** 42 16N 73 49W
Athens, *OH, U.S.A.* **92 D4** 39 20N 82 6W
Athens, *PA, U.S.A.* **95 C6** 41 57N 76 31W
Athens, *TN, U.S.A.* **97 E8** 35 27N 84 36W
Athens, *TX, U.S.A.* **99 E12** 32 12N 95 51W
Athens, *WI, U.S.A.* **103 C3** 45 2N 90 5W
Athens County ☆, *OH, U.S.A.* **92 D4** 39 20N 82 6W
Atherley, *Ont., Canada* **178 C7** 44 37N 79 20W
Athlone I., *B.C., Canada* **186 C6** 52 11N 128 26W
Athol, *ID, U.S.A.* **70 B2** 47 57N 116 42W
Athol, *MA, U.S.A.* **78 B2** 42 36N 72 14W
Athol, *SD, U.S.A.* **91 E7** 45 1N 98 36W
Atholville, *N.B., Canada* **173 F3** 47 59N 66 43W
Aticonipi, L., *Qué., Canada* **172 B10** 51 52N 59 22W
Atikaki Prov. Wilderness Park ⌂, *Man., Canada* **183 D16** 51 30N 95 31W
Atikokan, *Ont., Canada* **180 D5** 48 45N 91 37W
Atikonak →, *Nfld. & L., Canada* **172 A4** 52 51N 65 16W
Atikonak L., *Nfld. & L., Canada* **175 C5** 52 40N 64 32W
Atil, *Sonora, Mexico* **212 C4** 30 52N 111 34W
Atka, *AK, U.S.A.* **61 K4** 52 12N 174 12W
Atka I., *AK, U.S.A.* **61 K4** 52 7N 174 30W
Atkins, *AR, U.S.A.* **63 C3** 35 14N 92 56W
Atkins, *VA, U.S.A.* **102 E3** 36 20N 81 25W
Atkinson, *GA, U.S.A.* **68 E5** 31 13N 81 47W
Atkinson, *IL, U.S.A.* **71 B3** 41 25N 90 1W
Atkinson, *NH, U.S.A.* **86 D3** 42 50N 71 9W
Atkinson, *NE, U.S.A.* **84 B7** 42 32N 98 59W
Atkinson County ☆, *GA, U.S.A.* **68 E4** 31 15N 82 50W
Atkinson Pt., *N.W.T., Canada* **188 C6** 69 57N 131 27W
Atlacomulco, *México, Mexico* **219 C8** 19 48N 99 53W
Atlamajalcingo del Monte, *Guerrero, Mexico* **219 E9** 17 19N 98 36W
Atlanta, *GA, U.S.A.* **68 C2** 33 45N 84 23W
Atlanta, *ID, U.S.A.* **70 F3** 43 48N 115 8W
Atlanta, *IL, U.S.A.* **71 C4** 40 16N 89 14W
Atlanta, *IN, U.S.A.* **72 C4** 40 13N 86 2W
Atlanta, *KS, U.S.A.* **74 D7** 37 26N 96 46W
Atlanta, *LA, U.S.A.* **75 C3** 31 48N 92 45W
Atlanta, *MI, U.S.A.* **79 E7** 45 0N 84 9W
Atlanta, *MO, U.S.A.* **82 B4** 39 54N 92 29W
Atlanta, *NE, U.S.A.* **84 D6** 40 22N 99 28W
Atlanta, *TX, U.S.A.* **99 D13** 33 7N 94 10W
Atlanta Hartsfield International ✈ (ATL), *GA, U.S.A.* **68 C2** 33 38N 84 26W
Atlantic, *IA, U.S.A.* **73 D3** 41 24N 95 1W
Atlantic, *NC, U.S.A.* **90 D9** 34 54N 76 20W
Atlantic, *VA, U.S.A.* **77 C5** 37 54N 75 30W
Atlantic Beach, *FL, U.S.A.* **67 A7** 30 20N 81 24W
Atlantic Beach, *NC, U.S.A.* **90 D9** 34 42N 76 44W
Atlantic Beach, *NY, U.S.A.* **114 C4** 40 35N 73 45W
Atlantic City, *NJ, U.S.A.* **87 C2** 39 21N 74 27W
Atlantic City, *WY, U.S.A.* **104 D4** 42 30N 108 45W
Atlantic County ☆, *NJ, U.S.A.* **87 C2** 39 30N 74 40W
Atlantic Highlands, *NJ, U.S.A.* **87 B2** 40 25N 74 3W
Atlantic Pk., *WY, U.S.A.* **104 D3** 42 37N 109 0W
Atlapexco, *Hidalgo, Mexico* **219 A9** 21 1N 98 20W
Atlin, *B.C., Canada* **189 E6** 59 31N 133 41W
Atlin, L., *B.C., Canada* **189 E6** 59 26N 133 45W
Atlixco, *Puebla, Mexico* **221 F2** 18 54N 98 26W
Atlixtac, *Guerrero, Mexico* **219 E9** 17 34N 98 56W
Atlzayanca, *Tlaxcala, Mexico* **219 C10** 19 25N 97 49W
Atmore, *AL, U.S.A.* **60 E3** 31 2N 87 29W
Atoka, *OK, U.S.A.* **93 D7** 34 23N 96 8W
Atoka, *TN, U.S.A.* **96 E3** 35 26N 89 47W
Atoka County ☆, *OK, U.S.A.* **93 D8** 34 25N 96 0W
Atoka Res., *OK, U.S.A.* **93 D7** 34 26N 96 5W
Atolinga, *Zacatecas, Mexico* **217 F7** 21 44N 103 28W
Atomic City, *ID, U.S.A.* **70 F6** 43 27N 112 49W
Atotonilco, *Hidalgo, Mexico* **219 B8** 20 1N 99 14W
Atotonilco, *Zacatecas, Mexico* **217 C8** 24 15N 102 45W
Atotonilco el Alto, *Jalisco, Mexico* **218 B5** 20 33N 102 31W
Atotonilco El Grande, *Hidalgo, Mexico* **219 B9** 20 17N 98 40W
Atoyac, *Jalisco, Mexico* **218 C4** 19 58N 103 32W
Atoyac →, *Puebla, Mexico* **221 F2** 18 10N 98 31W
Atoyac de Álvarez, *Guerrero, Mexico* **219 E7** 17 12N 100 26W
Atqasuk, *AK, U.S.A.* **61 A8** 70 28N 157 24W
Atqasuk →, *AK, U.S.A.* **61 A9** 70 52N 155 55W
Atsion, *NJ, U.S.A.* **87 C2** 39 44N 74 44W
Attala County ☆, *MS, U.S.A.* **81 C4** 33 4N 89 35W
Attalla, *AL, U.S.A.* **60 B4** 34 1N 86 6W
Attapulgus, *GA, U.S.A.* **68 F2** 30 45N 84 29W
Attawapiskat, *Ont., Canada* **191 G9** 52 56N 82 24W
Attawapiskat →, *Ont., Canada* **191 G9** 52 57N 82 18W
Attica, *IN, U.S.A.* **72 C3** 40 18N 87 15W
Attica, *KS, U.S.A.* **74 D5** 37 15N 98 13W
Attica, *NY, U.S.A.* **89 C2** 42 52N 78 17W
Attica, *OH, U.S.A.* **92 B4** 41 4N 82 53W
Attikamagen L., *Nfld. & L., Canada* **175 B4** 55 0N 66 30W
Attleboro, *MA, U.S.A.* **78 C3** 41 57N 71 17W
Attu, *AK, U.S.A.* **61 K1** 52 56N 173 15 E
Attu I., *AK, U.S.A.* **61 K1** 52 55N 172 55 E
Attwater Prairie Chicken Nat. Wildlife Refuge ⌂, *TX, U.S.A.* **99 H11** 29 43N 96 20W
Attwood →, *Ont., Canada* **180 A8** 51 15N 88 30W
Atwater, *CA, U.S.A.* **64 F6** 37 21N 120 37W
Atwater, *MN, U.S.A.* **80 E4** 45 8N 94 47W
Atwood, *Ont., Canada* **178 D5** 43 40N 81 1W
Atwood, *IL, U.S.A.* **71 D5** 39 48N 88 28W
Atwood, *KS, U.S.A.* **74 B2** 39 48N 101 3W
Atwood, *OK, U.S.A.* **93 D7** 34 57N 96 20W
Atwood, *TN, U.S.A.* **96 E4** 35 59N 88 41W
Atwood L., *OH, U.S.A.* **92 C5** 40 33N 81 13W
Atzala, *Puebla, Mexico* **221 F2** 18 34N 98 33W
Atzalán, *Veracruz, Mexico* **220 E3** 19 46N 97 13W
Au Gres, *MI, U.S.A.* **79 E8** 44 3N 83 42W
Au Sable, *MI, U.S.A.* **79 E8** 44 25N 83 20W
Au Sable →, *MI, U.S.A.* **79 E8** 44 25N 83 20W
Au Sable Forks, *NY, U.S.A.* **89 A7** 44 27N 73 41W
Au Sable Pt., *MI, U.S.A.* **79 C5** 46 40N 86 8W
Au Sable Pt., *MI, U.S.A.* **79 E8** 44 20N 83 20W
Aua, *Amer. Samoa* **105 e** 14 17 S 170 40W
Aubrey, *AR, U.S.A.* **63 D5** 34 43N 90 54W
Aubrey Cliffs, *AZ, U.S.A.* **62 B3** 35 45N 113 0W
Aubry L., *N.W.T., Canada* **188 C7** 67 23N 126 30W
Auburn, *AL, U.S.A.* **60 D5** 32 36N 85 29W
Auburn, *CA, U.S.A.* **64 E5** 38 54N 121 4W
Auburn, *GA, U.S.A.* **68 B3** 34 1N 83 50W
Auburn, *IL, U.S.A.* **71 D4** 39 36N 89 45W
Auburn, *IN, U.S.A.* **72 B5** 41 22N 85 4W
Auburn, *IA, U.S.A.* **73 C4** 42 15N 94 53W
Auburn, *KS, U.S.A.* **74 C8** 38 54N 95 49W
Auburn, *KY, U.S.A.* **96 D6** 36 52N 86 43W
Auburn, *ME, U.S.A.* **76 D3** 44 6N 70 14W
Auburn, *MA, U.S.A.* **78 B3** 42 12N 71 50W
Auburn, *MI, U.S.A.* **79 F7** 43 36N 84 4W
Auburn, *NY, U.S.A.* **89 C4** 42 56N 76 34W
Auburn, *NE, U.S.A.* **84 D10** 40 23N 95 51W
Auburn, *WV, U.S.A.* **102 B4** 39 6N 80 51W
Auburn, *WA, U.S.A.* **101 C3** 47 18N 122 14W
Auburndale, *Boston, U.S.A.* **106 A2** 42 20N 71 14W
Auburndale, *FL, U.S.A.* **67 C7** 28 4N 81 48W
Auburndale, *WI, U.S.A.* **103 D4** 44 38N 90 0W
Auburntown, *TN, U.S.A.* **96 E6** 35 57N 86 5W
Aucilla →, *FL, U.S.A.* **67 A5** 30 5N 83 59W
Auden, *Ont., Canada* **181 B9** 50 14N 87 53W
Audrain County ☆, *MO, U.S.A.* **82 B5** 39 10N 91 50W
Audubon, *IA, U.S.A.* **73 D4** 41 43N 94 56W
Audubon, *MN, U.S.A.* **80 D3** 46 52N 95 59W
Audubon, *PA, U.S.A.* **116 B2** 39 53N 79 4W
Audubon County ☆, *IA, U.S.A.* **73 D4** 41 40N 94 50W
Audubon L., *ND, U.S.A.* **91 C4** 47 36N 101 10W
Audubon Park, *PA, U.S.A.* **116 B2** 39 53N 79 5W
Auglaize →, *OH, U.S.A.* **92 B2** 41 17N 84 21W
Auglaize County ☆, *OH, U.S.A.* **92 C2** 40 34N 84 12W
Augusta, *AR, U.S.A.* **63 C4** 35 17N 91 22W
Augusta, *GA, U.S.A.* **68 C5** 33 28N 81 58W
Augusta, *IL, U.S.A.* **71 C3** 40 14N 90 57W
Augusta, *Indianapolis, U.S.A.* **110 A1** 39 53N 86 12W
Augusta, *KS, U.S.A.* **74 D7** 37 41N 96 59W
Augusta, *KY, U.S.A.* **97 B8** 38 47N 84 0W
Augusta, *ME, U.S.A.* **76 D4** 44 19N 69 47W
Augusta, *MO, U.S.A.* **82 C6** 38 34N 90 53W
Augusta, *MT, U.S.A.* **83 C5** 47 30N 112 24W
Augusta, *NJ, U.S.A.* **87 A2** 41 8N 74 44W
Augusta, *WV, U.S.A.* **77 A2** 39 18N 78 38W
Augusta, *WI, U.S.A.* **103 D2** 44 41N 91 7W
Augusta County ☆, *VA, U.S.A.* **102 C5** 38 9N 79 4W
Augustine I., *AK, U.S.A.* **61 G9** 59 22N 153 26W
Augustines, L. des, *Qué., Canada* **176 D7** 47 37N 75 56W
Aujuittuq = Grise Fiord, *Nunavut, Canada* **190 B9** 76 25N 82 57W
Aulavik Nat. Park △, *N.W.T., Canada* **188 B9** 73 42N 119 55W
Aullville, *MO, U.S.A.* **82 B3** 39 1N 93 41W
Aulneau Pen., *Ont., Canada* **180 C2** 49 23N 94 29W
Ault, *CO, U.S.A.* **66 B6** 40 35N 104 44W
Ault Park, *OH, U.S.A.* **107 B2** 39 4N 84 24W
Aumsville, *OR, U.S.A.* **94 C3** 44 50N 122 52W
Aunuu, *Amer. Samoa* **105 e** 14 17 S 170 33W
Aupaluk, *Qué., Canada* **175 B4** 59 18N 69 36W
Aurelia, *IA, U.S.A.* **73 C3** 42 43N 95 26W
Aurelio Benassini, Presa, *Sinaloa, Mexico* **216 C4** 24 9N 106 41W
Aurora, *CO, U.S.A.* **66 C6** 39 43N 104 49W
Aurora, *IL, U.S.A.* **71 B5** 41 45N 88 19W
Aurora, *IN, U.S.A.* **72 D6** 39 4N 84 54W
Aurora, *IA, U.S.A.* **73 C7** 42 37N 91 44W
Aurora, *KS, U.S.A.* **74 B6** 39 27N 97 32W
Aurora, *KY, U.S.A.* **96 D4** 36 47N 88 9W
Aurora, *ME, U.S.A.* **76 D5** 44 51N 68 20W
Aurora, *MN, U.S.A.* **80 C6** 47 32N 92 14W
Aurora, *MO, U.S.A.* **82 E3** 36 58N 93 43W
Aurora, *NC, U.S.A.* **90 C9** 35 18N 76 47W
Aurora, *NY, U.S.A.* **89 C4** 42 45N 76 42W
Aurora, *NE, U.S.A.* **84 D7** 40 52N 98 0W
Aurora, *OH, U.S.A.* **92 B5** 41 17N 81 20W
Aurora, *SD, U.S.A.* **91 F9** 44 17N 96 41W
Aurora, *WV, U.S.A.* **77 A1** 39 19N 79 33W
Aurora County ☆, *SD, U.S.A.* **91 G7** 43 43N 98 29W
Ausable →, *Ont., Canada* **178 D5** 43 19N 81 46W
Austin, *AR, U.S.A.* **63 D4** 35 0N 92 0W
Austin, *Chicago, U.S.A.* **108 B2** 41 53N 87 45W
Austin, *IN, U.S.A.* **72 E5** 38 45N 85 49W
Austin, *MN, U.S.A.* **80 G6** 43 40N 92 58W
Austin, *MT, U.S.A.* **83 D5** 46 39N 112 15W
Austin, *NV, U.S.A.* **85 C3** 39 30N 117 4W
Austin, *PA, U.S.A.* **95 C4** 41 38N 78 6W
Austin, *TX, U.S.A.* **99 G10** 30 17N 97 45W
Austin Bergstrom International ✈ (AUS), *TX, U.S.A.* **99 G10** 30 12N 97 41W
Austin Chan., *N.W.T., Canada* **190 B5** 75 35N 103 25W
Austin County ☆, *TX, U.S.A.* **99 H11** 29 57N 96 15W
Austintown, *OH, U.S.A.* **92 B6** 41 6N 80 48W
Austinville, *VA, U.S.A.* **102 E4** 36 51N 80 55W
Austwell, *TX, U.S.A.* **99 J11** 28 23N 96 51W
Autauga County ☆, *AL, U.S.A.* **60 D4** 32 26N 86 39W
Autaugaville, *AL, U.S.A.* **60 D4** 32 26N 86 39W
Auteuil, *Qué., Canada* **192 A2** 45 38N 73 46W
Auteuil, L. d', *Qué., Canada* **172 C8** 50 38N 61 17W
Autlán de Navarro, *Jalisco, Mexico* **218 C3** 19 46N 104 22W
Auxvasse, *MO, U.S.A.* **82 B5** 39 1N 91 54W
Auyuittuq Nat. Park △, *Nunavut, Canada* **190 D12** 67 30N 66 0W
Ava, *IL, U.S.A.* **71 F4** 37 53N 89 30W
Ava, *MO, U.S.A.* **82 E4** 36 57N 92 40W
Avalon, *CA, U.S.A.* **65 K8** 33 21N 118 20W
Avalon, *MS, U.S.A.* **81 C3** 33 39N 90 5W
Avalon, *NJ, U.S.A.* **87 C2** 39 6N 74 43W
Avalon, *Pittsburgh, U.S.A.* **116 A1** 40 30N 80 4W
Avalon, L., *NM, U.S.A.* **88 E6** 32 27N 104 15W
Avalon Pen., *Nfld. & L., Canada* **174 E7** 47 30N 53 20W
Avalon Wilderness Reserve ⌂, *Nfld. & L., Canada* **174 E7** 47 3N 53 15W
Avant, *OK, U.S.A.* **93 B7** 36 29N 96 4W
Avard, *OK, U.S.A.* **93 B5** 36 42N 98 47W
Avawatz Mts., *CA, U.S.A.* **65 H10** 35 40N 116 30W
Avenal, *CA, U.S.A.* **65 H6** 36 0N 120 8W
Avenel, *MD, U.S.A.* **119 B4** 38 59N 76 59W
Avenel, *NJ, U.S.A.* **114 C1** 40 34N 74 17W
Avenue, *MD, U.S.A.* **77 B4** 38 16N 76 46W
Avera, *GA, U.S.A.* **68 C4** 33 12N 82 32W
Avery, *ID, U.S.A.* **70 B3** 47 15N 115 49W
Avery, *TX, U.S.A.* **99 D13** 33 33N 94 47W
Avery County ☆, *NC, U.S.A.* **90 B4** 36 5N 82 0W
Avery Island, *LA, U.S.A.* **75 E4** 29 55N 91 54W
Avila y Urbina, *Tamaulipas, Mexico* **215 G5** 23 41N 99 36W
Avilla, *IN, U.S.A.* **72 B5** 41 22N 85 14W
Avilla, *MO, U.S.A.* **82 D2** 37 8N 94 8W
Avinger, *TX, U.S.A.* **99 E13** 32 54N 94 33W
Avis, *PA, U.S.A.* **95 C5** 41 11N 77 19W
Avoca, *IA, U.S.A.* **73 D3** 41 29N 95 20W
Avoca, *MN, U.S.A.* **80 G3** 43 57N 95 39W
Avoca, *NY, U.S.A.* **89 C3** 42 25N 77 25W
Avoca, *NE, U.S.A.* **84 D9** 40 48N 96 7W
Avoca, *TX, U.S.A.* **99 E8** 32 52N 99 43W
Avola, *B.C., Canada* **187 D15** 51 45N 119 19W
Avon, *CO, U.S.A.* **66 C4** 39 38N 106 31W
Avon, *CT, U.S.A.* **78 C2** 41 49N 72 50W
Avon, *IL, U.S.A.* **71 C3** 40 40N 90 26W
Avon, *MT, U.S.A.* **83 D5** 46 36N 112 36W
Avon, *NY, U.S.A.* **89 C3** 42 55N 77 45W
Avon, *SD, U.S.A.* **91 H7** 43 0N 98 4W
Avon Park, *FL, U.S.A.* **67 D7** 27 36N 81 31W
Avon Park Air Force Range, *FL, U.S.A.* **67 D7** 27 38N 81 33W
Avondale, *Nfld. & L., Canada* **174 E7** 47 25N 53 12W
Avondale, *AZ, U.S.A.* **62 D3** 33 26N 112 21W
Avondale, *Chicago, U.S.A.* **108 B2** 41 56N 87 41W
Avondale, *CO, U.S.A.* **66 D6** 38 14N 104 21W
Avondale, *New Orleans, U.S.A.* **113 C1** 29 54N 90 12W
Avondale, *OH, U.S.A.* **107 B1** 39 8N 84 29W
Avondale, *PA, U.S.A.* **77 A5** 39 50N 75 47W
Avonlea, *Sask., Canada* **182 E7** 50 0N 105 0W
Avonmore, *Ont., Canada* **176 F8** 45 10N 74 58W
Avonmore, *PA, U.S.A.* **95 D3** 40 32N 79 28W
Avoyelles Parish ☆, *LA, U.S.A.* **75 C3** 31 0N 92 0W
Axel Heiberg I., *Nunavut, Canada* **190 B7** 80 0N 90 0W
Axial, *CO, U.S.A.* **66 B3** 40 17N 107 47W
Axochiapan, *Morelos, Mexico* **219 D9** 18 30N 98 45W
Axson, *GA, U.S.A.* **68 E4** 31 17N 82 44W
Axtell, *KS, U.S.A.* **74 B7** 39 52N 96 15W
Axtell, *NE, U.S.A.* **84 D6** 40 29N 99 8W
Ayala, *Morelos, Mexico* **219 D9** 18 46N 98 59W
Ayden, *NC, U.S.A.* **90 C8** 35 28N 77 20W
Ayer, *MA, U.S.A.* **78 B3** 42 34N 71 35W
Ayer's Cliff, *Qué., Canada* **177 F10** 45 10N 72 3W
Aylen L., *Ont., Canada* **179 B9** 45 37N 77 51W
Aylmer, *Ont., Canada* **178 E6** 42 46N 80 59W
Aylmer, *Qué., Canada* **176 F7** 45 24N 75 51W
Aylmer, L., *N.W.T., Canada* **189 D10** 64 5N 108 30W
Aylsham, *Sask., Canada* **182 B8** 53 12N 103 49W
Ayotlán, *Jalisco, Mexico* **218 B5** 20 32N 102 19W
Ayotzintepec, *Oaxaca, Mexico* **221 G4** 17 41N 96 7W
Ayr, *Ont., Canada* **178 D6** 43 17N 80 27W
Ayr, *ND, U.S.A.* **91 C8** 47 3N 97 29W
Ayr, *NE, U.S.A.* **84 D7** 40 26N 98 26W
Ayshire, *IA, U.S.A.* **73 B4** 43 2N 94 50W
Ayutla, *Jalisco, Mexico* **218 B3** 20 7N 104 22W
Ayutla de los Libres, *Guerrero, Mexico* **219 F8** 16 54N 99 13W
Azcapotzalco, *Distrito Federal, Mexico* **225 B2** 19 28N 99 10W
Azilda, *Ont., Canada* **178 A5** 46 33N 81 6W
Aziscohos L., *ME, U.S.A.* **76 C3** 45 0N 71 0W
Azle, *TX, U.S.A.* **99 E10** 32 54N 97 32W
Azoyu, *Guerrero, Mexico* **219 F9** 16 46N 98 37W
Aztec, *AZ, U.S.A.* **62 E2** 32 49N 113 27W
Aztec, *NM, U.S.A.* **88 A3** 36 49N 107 59W
Aztec Peak, *AZ, U.S.A.* **62 D5** 33 49N 110 54W
Aztec Ruins Nat. Monument ⌂, *NM, U.S.A.* **88 A3** 36 50N 108 0W
Azul →, *Quintana Roo, Mexico* **223 E4** 17 54N 88 52W
Azul, Cerro, *Sonora, Mexico* **212 C5** 30 35N 110 35W
Azure L., *B.C., Canada* **187 C14** 52 23N 120 3W
Azusa, *CA, U.S.A.* **65 J9** 34 8N 117 52W

B

B.A. Steinhagen L., *TX, U.S.A.* **99 G13** 30 50N 94 15W
B. Everett Jordan L., *NC, U.S.A.* **90 C6** 35 30N 79 0W
Babb, *MT, U.S.A.* **83 B4** 48 51N 113 27W
Babbitt, *MN, U.S.A.* **80 C7** 47 41N 91 54W
Babbitt, *NV, U.S.A.* **85 D2** 38 32N 118 39W
Babbs, *OK, U.S.A.* **93 D4** 34 57N 99 3W
Babine, *B.C., Canada* **189 E7** 55 22N 126 37W
Babine →, *B.C., Canada* **189 E7** 55 45N 127 44W
Babine L., *B.C., Canada* **189 F7** 54 48N 126 0W
Baboquivari Peak, *AZ, U.S.A.* **62 F4** 31 46N 111 36W
Baborigame, *Chihuahua, Mexico* **213 G8** 26 27N 107 16W
Babson Park, *FL, U.S.A.* **67 D7** 27 49N 81 32W
Babylon, *NY, U.S.A.* **87 B3** 40 42N 73 19W
Baca, *Sinaloa, Mexico* **213 G7** 26 47N 108 28W
Baca, *Yucatán, Mexico* **223 A4** 21 6N 89 25W
Baca County ☆, *CO, U.S.A.* **66 E8** 37 15N 102 30W
Bacadéhuachi, *Sonora, Mexico* **212 D6** 29 44N 109 10W
Bacalar, *Quintana Roo, Mexico* **223 D5** 18 43N 88 27W
Bacalar, L., *Quintana Roo, Mexico* **223 D5** 18 43N 88 22W
Bacalar Chico, Boca, *Quintana Roo, Mexico* **223 D6** 18 12N 87 53W
Bacanora, *Sonora, Mexico* **212 E6** 28 59N 109 24W
Bacanuchi, *Sonora, Mexico* **212 C5** 30 38N 110 15W
Baccalieu I., *Nfld. & L., Canada* **174 D8** 48 8N 52 48W
Baccaro Pt., *N.S., Canada* **173 K4** 43 27N 65 28W
Bacerac, *Sonora, Mexico* **212 C7** 30 18N 108 50W
Bache Pen., *Nunavut, Canada* **190 B10** 79 8N 76 0W
Bachelor, Mt., *U.S.A.* **94 D4** 43 59N 121 41W
Bachíniva, *Chihuahua, Mexico* **213 E8** 28 45N 107 15W
Back →, *Canada* **191 D5** 65 10N 104 0W
Back B., *VA, U.S.A.* **102 E9** 36 35N 75 57W
Back Bay, *N.B., Canada* **173 H3** 45 3N 66 52W
Back Bay Nat. Wildlife Refuge ⌂, *VA, U.S.A.* **102 E9** 36 39N 75 56W
Backbone Mt., *MD, U.S.A.* **77 A1** 39 12N 79 28W
Backus, *MN, U.S.A.* **80 D4** 46 49N 94 31W
Bacoachi, *Sonora, Mexico* **212 C6** 30 38N 109 56W
Bacobampo, *Sonora, Mexico* **212 G6** 26 59N 109 40W
Bacon County ☆, *GA, U.S.A.* **68 E4** 31 30N 82 30W
Baconton, *GA, U.S.A.* **68 E2** 31 23N 84 10W
Bacqueville, L., *Qué., Canada* **175 B3** 58 7N 73 50W
Bácum, *Sonora, Mexico* **212 F5** 27 33N 110 5W
Bacurato = Gustavo Díaz Ordaz, Presa, *Sinaloa, Mexico* **216 B3** 25 55N 107 54W
Bad →, *SD, U.S.A.* **91 F5** 44 21N 100 22W
Bad Axe, *MI, U.S.A.* **79 F9** 43 48N 83 0W
Bad River Indian Reservation, *WI, U.S.A.* **103 B3** 46 30N 90 45W
Baddeck, *N.S., Canada* **173 G9** 46 6N 60 45W
Baden, *PA, U.S.A.* **95 D2** 40 38N 80 14W
Badger, *Nfld. & L., Canada* **174 D4** 49 0N 56 4W
Badger, *IA, U.S.A.* **73 C4** 42 37N 94 9W
Badger, *MN, U.S.A.* **80 B2** 48 47N 96 1W
Badger, *SD, U.S.A.* **91 F8** 44 29N 97 12W
Badger Cr. →, *CO, U.S.A.* **66 B7** 40 17N 103 42W
Badger Pk., *MT, U.S.A.* **83 E11** 45 40N 106 33W
Badger's Quay, *Nfld. & L., Canada* **174 C7** 49 7N 53 35W
Badin, *NC, U.S.A.* **90 C5** 35 24N 80 6W
Badin L., *NC, U.S.A.* **90 C5** 35 25N 80 6W
Badiraguato, *Sinaloa, Mexico* **216 B3** 25 22N 107 31W
Badlands, *SD, U.S.A.* **91 G3** 43 55N 102 30W
Badlands Nat. Park △, *SD, U.S.A.* **91 G3** 43 38N 102 56W
Badwater Cr. →, *WY, U.S.A.* **104 C4** 43 15N 107 8W
Baffin B., *N. Amer.* **190 C13** 72 0N 64 0W
Baffin B., *TX, U.S.A.* **98 K10** 27 18N 97 30W
Baffin I., *Nunavut, Canada* **190 C10** 68 0N 75 0W
Bagdad, *AZ, U.S.A.* **62 C2** 34 34N 113 13W
Bagdad, *FL, U.S.A.* **67 A1** 30 36N 87 2W
Bagdad, *KY, U.S.A.* **97 B7** 38 16N 85 3W
Baggs, *WY, U.S.A.* **104 E5** 41 2N 107 39W
Bagley, *MN, U.S.A.* **80 C3** 47 32N 95 24W
Bahía Asunción, *Baja Calif. S., Mexico* **211 F4** 27 9N 114 19W
Bahía Bufadero, *Michoacan, Mexico* **218 D5** 18 3N 102 45W
Bahía de Tortugas, *Baja Calif. S., Mexico* **211 F4** 27 43N 114 55W
Bahía Kino, *Sonora, Mexico* **212 E4** 28 47N 111 58W
Baie, Parc de la, *Qué., Canada* **192 A1** 45 27N 75 41W
Baie-Comeau, *Qué., Canada* **172 D1** 49 12N 68 10W
Baie-des-Sables, *Qué., Canada* **172 E2** 48 43N 67 54W
Baie-du-Febre, *Qué., Canada* **177 E10** 46 8N 72 43W
Baie-du-Poste = Mistissini, *Qué., Canada* **175 C3** 50 24N 73 56W
Baie-du-Renard, *Qué., Canada* **172 D8** 49 17N 61 50W
Baie-d'Urfé, *Montréal, Canada* **192 B1** 45 24N 73 53W
Baie-Johan-Beetz, *Qué., Canada* **172 C7** 50 17N 62 48W
Baie McLaurin, Parc de la, *Qué., Canada* **192 A2** 42 29N 75 35W
Baie-St-Paul, *Qué., Canada* **177 D12** 47 28N 70 32W
Baie-Ste-Anne, *N.B., Canada* **173 F5** 47 3N 64 58W
Baie-Ste-Catherine, *Qué., Canada* **177 C13** 48 6N 69 44W
Baie-Ste-Claire, *Qué., Canada* **172 D5** 49 54N 64 30W
Baie-Trinité, *Qué., Canada* **172 D2** 49 25N 67 20W
Baie Verte, *N.B., Canada* **173 G5** 46 1N 64 6W
Baie Verte, *Nfld. & L., Canada* **174 C4** 49 55N 56 12W
Baie Verte Pen., *Nfld. & L., Canada* **174 C4** 49 50N 56 30W
Bailey County ☆, *TX, U.S.A.* **98 C5** 34 0N 102 55W
Baileys Crossroads, *VA, U.S.A.* **119 B3** 38 50N 77 6W
Baileys Harbor, *WI, U.S.A.* **103 C6** 45 4N 87 8W
Baileyton, *TN, U.S.A.* **97 D10** 36 20N 82 50W
Baileyville, *KS, U.S.A.* **74 B7** 39 51N 96 11W
Baillie →, *Canada* **189 C12** 65 7N 104 36W
Baillie-Hamilton I., *Nunavut, Canada* **190 B7** 75 52N 94 35W
Bainbridge, *GA, U.S.A.* **68 F2** 30 55N 84 35W
Bainbridge, *IN, U.S.A.* **72 D4** 39 46N 86 49W
Bainbridge, *NY, U.S.A.* **89 C5** 42 18N 75 29W
Bainbridge, *OH, U.S.A.* **92 D3** 39 14N 83 16W
Bainbridge Island, *WA, U.S.A.* **101 C3** 47 38N 122 32W
Bainville, *MT, U.S.A.* **83 B13** 48 8N 104 13W
Baird, *TX, U.S.A.* **99 E8** 32 24N 99 24W
Baird Mts., *AK, U.S.A.* **61 C7** 67 0N 160 0W
Baird Pen., *N.W.T., Canada* **191 D10** 68 55N 76 4W
Bairoil, *WY, U.S.A.* **104 D5** 42 15N 107 33W
Baisley Pond, *NY, U.S.A.* **114 B4** 40 40N 73 47W
Baja, Pta., *Baja Calif., Mexico* **210 D3** 29 58N 115 49W
Baja California, *Mexico* **210 E5** 31 10N 115 12W
Baja California □, *Mexico* **210 C3** 30 0N 115 0W
Baja California Sur □, *Mexico* **211 H7** 25 50N 111 50W
Bajío de Ahuichila, *Coahuila, Mexico* **215 E2** 25 6N 102 37W
Bajo Obispo Norte, *Campeche, Mexico* **223 B1** 20 29N 92 9W
Bajo Obispo Sur, *Campeche, Mexico* **223 B1** 20 25N 92 9W
Baker, *CA, U.S.A.* **65 H10** 35 16N 116 4W
Baker, *FL, U.S.A.* **67 A2** 30 48N 86 41W
Baker, *ID, U.S.A.* **70 D5** 45 6N 113 44W
Baker, *LA, U.S.A.* **75 D4** 30 35N 91 10W
Baker, *MT, U.S.A.* **83 D13** 46 22N 104 17W
Baker, *ND, U.S.A.* **91 B6** 48 10N 99 39W
Baker, *OK, U.S.A.* **93 B2** 36 52N 101 1W
Baker, L., *Nunavut, Canada* **191 E6** 64 0N 96 0W
Baker, Mt., *WA, U.S.A.* **101 B4** 48 50N 121 49W
Baker Butte, *AZ, U.S.A.* **62 C4** 34 27N 111 22W
Baker City, *OR, U.S.A.* **94 C8** 44 47N 117 50W
Baker County ☆, *FL, U.S.A.* **67 A6** 30 20N 82 15W
Baker County ☆, *GA, U.S.A.* **68 E2** 31 20N 84 30W
Baker County ☆, *OR, U.S.A.* **94 C8** 44 40N 117 50W
Baker I., *Pac. Oc.* **105 D6** 0 10N 176 35W
Baker Lake, *Nunavut, Canada* **191 E6** 64 20N 96 3W
Bakerhill, *AL, U.S.A.* **60 E5** 31 47N 85 18W
Bakers Dozen Is., *Nunavut, Canada* **175 B2** 56 45N 78 45W
Bakersfield, *CA, U.S.A.* **65 H7** 35 23N 119 1W
Bakersfield, *TX, U.S.A.* **98 G5** 30 54N 102 18W
Bakersfield, *VT, U.S.A.* **86 B2** 44 45N 72 48W
Bakersville, *NC, U.S.A.* **90 B3** 36 1N 82 10W
Bal Harbor, *Miami, U.S.A.* **112 C3** 25 53N 80 7W
Bala, *Ont., Canada* **178 B7** 45 1N 79 37W
Bala, *KS, U.S.A.* **74 B7** 39 19N 96 57W
Bala-Cynwyd, *PA, U.S.A.* **116 A1** 40 0N 75 13W
Balakbal, *Campeche, Mexico* **223 E4** 17 53N 89 18W
Balamku, *Campeche, Mexico* **223 D4** 18 34N 89 54W
Balancán, *Tabasco, Mexico* **222 B5** 17 48N 91 32W
Balaton, *MN, U.S.A.* **80 F3** 44 14N 95 52W
Balboa Park, *San Diego, U.S.A.* **117 B2** 32 43N 117 8W
Balcarres, *Sask., Canada* **182 E8** 50 50N 103 35W
Balch Springs, *TX, U.S.A.* **99 E11** 32 43N 96 37W
Balcones Canyonlands Nat. Wildlife Refuge ⌂, *TX, U.S.A.* **99 G10** 30 33N 98 0W

Balcones Escarpment, *TX, U.S.A.* **98 H7** 29 30N 99 15W
Balcones Heights, *TX, U.S.A.* **99 H9** 29 29N 98 33W
Bald Head I., *NC, U.S.A.* **90 E8** 33 52N 77 59W
Bald Knob, *AR, U.S.A.* **63 C4** 35 19N 91 34W
Bald Knob, *VA, U.S.A.* **102 D5** 37 56N 79 51W
Bald Knoll, *WY, U.S.A.* **104 D2** 42 22N 110 28W
Bald Mt., *NV, U.S.A.* **85 E5** 37 27N 115 44W
Bald Mt., *OR, U.S.A.* **94 D4** 43 16N 121 21W
Bald Pt., *FL, U.S.A.* **67 B4** 29 57N 84 20W
Baldur, *Man., Canada* **183 F12** 49 23N 99 15W
Baldwin, *FL, U.S.A.* **67 A7** 30 18N 81 59W
Baldwin, *GA, U.S.A.* **68 B3** 34 30N 83 32W
Baldwin, *IL, U.S.A.* **71 E4** 38 11N 89 51W
Baldwin, *LA, U.S.A.* **75 E4** 29 50N 91 33W
Baldwin, *MI, U.S.A.* **79 F6** 43 54N 85 51W
Baldwin, *NY, U.S.A.* **87 B3** 40 39N 73 36W
Baldwin, *PA, U.S.A.* **95 D3** 40 21N 79 58W
Baldwin, *WI, U.S.A.* **103 D1** 44 58N 92 22W
Baldwin, L., *Orlando, U.S.A.* **115 A3** 28 34N 81 19W
Baldwin City, *KS, U.S.A.* **74 C8** 38 47N 95 11W
Baldwin County ☆, *AL, U.S.A.* **60 F3** 30 53N 87 46W
Baldwin County ☆, *GA, U.S.A.* **68 C3** 33 5N 83 10W
Baldwin Hills, *Los Angeles, U.S.A.* **111 B2** 34 0N 118 21W
Baldwin Hills Res., *Los Angeles, U.S.A.* **111 B2** 34 0N 118 21W
Baldwinsville, *NY, U.S.A.* **89 B4** 43 10N 76 20W
Baldwinville, *MA, U.S.A.* **78 B2** 42 37N 72 5W
Baldwyn, *MS, U.S.A.* **81 B5** 34 31N 88 38W
Baldy Mt., *Man., Canada* **183 D11** 51 28N 100 43W
Baldy Peak, *AZ, U.S.A.* **62 D6** 33 54N 109 34W
Baldy Pk., *NM, U.S.A.* **88 A5** 36 38N 105 13W
Baleine = Whale ➛, *Qué., Canada* **175 B4** 58 15N 67 40W
Baleine, Petite R. de la ➛, *Qué., Canada* **175 B2** 56 0N 76 45W
Baler, L., *WA, U.S.A.* **101 B4** 48 44N 121 38W
Balfour, *ND, U.S.A.* **91 C5** 47 57N 100 32W
Balgonie, *Sask., Canada* **182 E7** 50 29N 104 16W
Balko, *OK, U.S.A.* **93 B3** 36 38N 100 41W
Ball, *LA, U.S.A.* **75 C3** 31 25N 92 25W
Ball Ground, *GA, U.S.A.* **68 B2** 34 20N 84 23W
Ballantine, *MT, U.S.A.* **83 E9** 45 57N 108 9W
Ballantyne Str., *N.W.T., Canada* **188 A9** 77 35N 115 6W
Ballard, *UT, U.S.A.* **100 C6** 40 17N 109 57W
Ballard County ☆, *KY, U.S.A.* **96 D4** 37 0N 89 0W
Ballenas, B. de, *Baja Calif. S., Mexico* **211 G5** 26 45N 113 26W
Ballenas, Canal de, *Baja Calif., Mexico* **210 D5** 29 10N 113 29W
Ballenger Creek, *MD, U.S.A.* **77 A3** 39 22N 77 26W
Balleza, *Chihuahua, Mexico* **213 G9** 26 56N 106 21W
Balleza ➛, *Chihuahua, Mexico* **213 G9** 26 58N 106 20W
Ballinger, *TX, U.S.A.* **99 F8** 31 45N 99 57W
Ballston Spa, *NY, U.S.A.* **89 C7** 43 0N 73 51W
Balltown, *IA, U.S.A.* **73 C8** 42 38N 90 51W
Ballwin, *MO, U.S.A.* **82 C6** 38 36N 90 33W
Bally, *PA, U.S.A.* **95 D7** 40 24N 75 35W
Balmertown, *Ont., Canada* **180 A3** 51 4N 93 41W
Balmoral, *Man., Canada* **183 E14** 50 15N 97 19W
Balmorhea, *TX, U.S.A.* **98 G4** 30 59N 103 45W
Balmville, *NY, U.S.A.* **87 A2** 41 32N 74 1W
Balsam Lake, *WI, U.S.A.* **103 C1** 45 27N 92 27W
Balsas ➛, *Michoacan, Mexico* **218 E5** 17 55N 102 10W
Balsas del Norte, *Guerrero, Mexico* **219 E8** 18 0N 99 46W
Balta, *ND, U.S.A.* **91 B5** 48 10N 100 2W
Baltic, *CT, U.S.A.* **78 C2** 41 37N 72 5W
Baltic, *OH, U.S.A.* **92 C5** 40 26N 81 42W
Baltic, *SD, U.S.A.* **91 G9** 43 46N 96 44W
Baltimore, *MD, U.S.A.* **77 A4** 39 17N 76 36W
Baltimore, *OH, U.S.A.* **92 D4** 39 51N 82 36W
Baltimore County ☆, *MD, U.S.A.* **77 A4** 39 20N 76 40W
Baltimore Highlands, *Baltimore, U.S.A.* **107 B2** 39 13N 76 38W
Baltimore Washington International ✕ (BWI), *MD, U.S.A.* **77 A4** 39 11N 76 40W
Bamaji L., *Ont., Canada* **180 A5** 51 10N 91 25W
Bamberg, *SC, U.S.A.* **90 E4** 33 18N 81 2W
Bamberg County ☆, *SC, U.S.A.* **90 E5** 33 10N 81 0W
Bamfield, *B.C., Canada* **186 G9** 48 45N 125 10W
Bamuri, *Sonora, Mexico* **212 C3** 30 22N 112 5W
Banámichi, *Sonora, Mexico* **212 C5** 30 1N 110 10W
Bancroft, *Ont., Canada* **179 B9** 45 3N 77 51W
Bancroft, *ID, U.S.A.* **70 G7** 42 43N 111 53W
Bancroft, *IA, U.S.A.* **73 B4** 43 18N 94 13W
Bancroft, *LA, U.S.A.* **75 D2** 30 34N 93 41W
Bancroft, *MI, U.S.A.* **79 G7** 42 53N 84 4W
Bancroft, *NE, U.S.A.* **84 B9** 42 1N 96 34W
Banda, C., *Baja Calif., Mexico* **210 B2** 31 45N 116 45W
Bandana, *KY, U.S.A.* **96 C4** 37 9N 88 56W
Bandelier Nat. Monument ⌂, *NM, U.S.A.* **88 B4** 35 50N 106 25W
Bandera, *TX, U.S.A.* **99 H8** 29 44N 99 5W
Bandera County ☆, *TX, U.S.A.* **99 H8** 29 48N 99 15W
Bandera del Aguila, *Durango, Mexico* **216 D5** 23 55N 105 21W
Banderas, B. de, *Mexico* **218 B2** 20 40N 105 25W
Banderilla, *Veracruz, Mexico* **220 E4** 19 35N 96 56W
Bandon, *OR, U.S.A.* **94 D1** 43 7N 124 25W
Banff, *Alta., Canada* **185 G5** 51 10N 115 34W
Banff Nat. Park △, *Alta., Canada* **185 G4** 51 30N 116 15W
Bangor, *ME, U.S.A.* **76 D5** 44 48N 68 46W
Bangor, *MI, U.S.A.* **79 G5** 42 18N 86 7W
Bangor, *PA, U.S.A.* **87 B1** 40 52N 75 13W
Bangor Naval Reserve, *Seattle, U.S.A.* **118 B1** 47 43N 122 44W
Bangs, *TX, U.S.A.* **99 F8** 31 43N 99 8W
Bangs, Mt., *AZ, U.S.A.* **62 A2** 36 48N 113 51W
Banister ➛, *VA, U.S.A.* **102 E6** 36 42N 78 48W
Banks, *AL, U.S.A.* **60 E5** 31 49N 85 51W
Banks, *AR, U.S.A.* **63 E3** 33 35N 92 16W
Banks, *ID, U.S.A.* **70 E2** 44 5N 116 8W
Banks, *OR, U.S.A.* **94 B2** 45 37N 123 7W
Banks County ☆, *GA, U.S.A.* **68 B3** 34 30N 83 30W
Banks I., *B.C., Canada* **186 B4** 53 20N 130 0W
Banks I., *N.W.T., Canada* **188 B8** 73 15N 121 30W
Banks L., *GA, U.S.A.* **68 E3** 31 2N 83 6W
Banks L., *WA, U.S.A.* **101 C6** 47 47N 119 19W
Bannack, *MT, U.S.A.* **83 E5** 45 10N 112 59W
Banner, *MS, U.S.A.* **81 B4** 34 5N 89 23W
Banner, *WY, U.S.A.* **104 B6** 44 36N 106 52W
Banner County ☆, *NE, U.S.A.* **84 C2** 41 30N 103 40W
Banner Elk, *NC, U.S.A.* **90 B4** 36 10N 81 52W
Banner Hill, *TN, U.S.A.* **97 D10** 36 8N 82 25W
Bannertown, *NC, U.S.A.* **90 B5** 36 29N 80 35W
Banning, *CA, U.S.A.* **65 K10** 33 56N 116 53W
Bannock County ☆, *ID, U.S.A.* **70 G6** 42 30N 112 10W
Bannock Cr. ➛, *ID, U.S.A.* **70 G6** 42 53N 112 40W
Bannock Range, *ID, U.S.A.* **70 G6** 42 40N 112 30W
Bannockburn, *Ont., Canada* **179 C9** 44 39N 77 33W
Bantry, *ND, U.S.A.* **91 B5** 48 30N 100 37W
Bapchule, *AZ, U.S.A.* **62 D4** 33 12N 111 50W
Bar Harbor, *ME, U.S.A.* **76 D5** 44 23N 68 13W
Bar Nunn, *WY, U.S.A.* **104 D6** 42 55N 106 21W
Baraboo, *WI, U.S.A.* **103 E4** 43 28N 89 45W
Barachois-de-Malbaie, *Qué., Canada* **172 E5** 48 37N 64 17W
Barachois Pond Prov. Park ⌂, *Nfld. & L., Canada* **174 D2** 48 28N 58 15W
Barada, *NE, U.S.A.* **84 D10** 40 13N 95 35W
Baraga, *MI, U.S.A.* **79 C3** 46 47N 88 30W
Baraga County ☆, *MI, U.S.A.* **79 C3** 46 40N 88 20W
Baranof, *AK, U.S.A.* **61 H14** 57 5N 134 50W
Baranof I., *AK, U.S.A.* **61 H14** 57 0N 135 0W
Barataria, *LA, U.S.A.* **75 E5** 29 44N 90 8W
Barataria B., *LA, U.S.A.* **75 E6** 29 20N 89 55W
Barataria Preserve, *New Orleans, U.S.A.* **113 D2** 29 47N 90 7W
Barbara L., *Ont., Canada* **181 C9** 49 20N 87 47W
Barbeau Pk., *N.W.T., Canada* **190 A10** 81 54N 75 1W
Barbel, L., *Qué., Canada* **172 B1** 51 55N 68 13W
Barber, L., *Orlando, U.S.A.* **115 A3** 28 30N 81 19W
Barber County ☆, *KS, U.S.A.* **74 D5** 37 15N 98 40W
Barbers Pt., *HI, U.S.A.* **69 K13** 21 18N 158 7W
Barberton, *OH, U.S.A.* **92 B5** 41 1N 81 39W
Barberville, *FL, U.S.A.* **67 B7** 29 11N 81 26W
Barborview, *Baltimore, U.S.A.* **107 B2** 39 16N 76 31W
Barbour County ☆, *AL, U.S.A.* **60 E5** 31 53N 85 27W
Barbour County ☆, *WV, U.S.A.* **102 B4** 39 9N 80 3W
Barboursville, *WV, U.S.A.* **102 C2** 38 24N 82 18W
Barbourville, *KY, U.S.A.* **97 D9** 36 52N 83 53W
Barceloneta, *Puerto Rico* **105 G16** 18 27N 66 32W
Barclay, *MD, U.S.A.* **77 A5** 39 9N 75 52W
Barcroft, L., *VA, U.S.A.* **119 B3** 38 52N 77 9W
Bardley, *MO, U.S.A.* **82 E5** 36 42N 91 7W
Bardoux, L., *Qué., Canada* **172 B2** 51 9N 67 50W
Bardstown, *KY, U.S.A.* **97 C7** 37 49N 85 28W
Bardwell, *KY, U.S.A.* **96 D3** 36 52N 89 1W
Bare Mt., *WA, U.S.A.* **101 E3** 45 55N 122 4W
Bargersville, *IN, U.S.A.* **72 D4** 39 31N 86 10W
Baring, *MO, U.S.A.* **82 A4** 40 15N 92 12W
Baring, C., *N.W.T., Canada* **188 C9** 70 0N 117 30W
Bark L., *Ont., Canada* **176 F5** 45 27N 77 51W
Bark Pt., *WI, U.S.A.* **103 B2** 46 53N 91 11W
Barker, *NY, U.S.A.* **89 B2** 43 20N 78 33W
Barkerville, *B.C., Canada* **187 B13** 53 4N 121 31W
Barkhamsted Res., *CT, U.S.A.* **78 C2** 41 53N 72 58W
Barkley, L., *TN, U.S.A.* **96 C4** 37 1N 88 14W
Barkley Sound, *B.C., Canada* **186 G9** 48 50N 125 10W
Barksdale, *TX, U.S.A.* **99 H7** 29 44N 100 2W
Barksdale Air Force Base, *LA, U.S.A.* **75 B2** 32 29N 93 42W
Barling, *AR, U.S.A.* **63 C1** 35 20N 94 18W
Barlow, *KY, U.S.A.* **96 C3** 37 3N 89 3W
Barlow, *PA, U.S.A.* **77 A3** 39 45N 77 14W
Barnard, *KS, U.S.A.* **74 B5** 39 11N 98 3W
Barnard, *MO, U.S.A.* **82 A2** 40 10N 94 50W
Barnard, *VT, U.S.A.* **86 C2** 43 43N 72 38W
Barnegat, *NJ, U.S.A.* **87 C2** 39 45N 74 14W
Barnegat Bay, *NJ, U.S.A.* **87 C2** 39 45N 74 10W
Barnegat Light, *NJ, U.S.A.* **87 C2** 39 46N 74 6W
Barnes, *KS, U.S.A.* **74 B7** 39 43N 96 52W
Barnes City, *IA, U.S.A.* **73 D6** 41 31N 92 27W
Barnes County ☆, *ND, U.S.A.* **91 C7** 47 0N 98 0W
Barnes Icecap, *N.W.T., Canada* **190 D11** 70 0N 73 15W
Barneston, *NE, U.S.A.* **84 D9** 40 5N 96 38W
Barnesville, *GA, U.S.A.* **68 C2** 33 3N 84 9W
Barnesville, *MD, U.S.A.* **77 A3** 39 13N 77 23W
Barnesville, *MN, U.S.A.* **80 D2** 46 43N 96 28W
Barnesville, *OH, U.S.A.* **92 D5** 39 59N 81 11W
Barnet, *VT, U.S.A.* **86 B2** 44 18N 72 3W
Barnett, *MO, U.S.A.* **82 C4** 38 23N 92 41W
Barney, *GA, U.S.A.* **68 E3** 31 1N 83 31W
Barnhart, *MO, U.S.A.* **82 C6** 38 21N 90 24W
Barnhart, *TX, U.S.A.* **98 F6** 31 8N 101 10W
Barnsdall, *OK, U.S.A.* **93 B7** 36 34N 96 10W
Barnstable, *MA, U.S.A.* **78 C4** 41 42N 70 18W
Barnstable County ☆, *MA, U.S.A.* **78 C4** 41 40N 70 15W
Barnstable Harbor, *MA, U.S.A.* **78 C4** 41 43N 70 18W
Barnum, *MN, U.S.A.* **80 D6** 46 30N 92 42W
Barnum, *WY, U.S.A.* **104 C6** 43 40N 106 55W
Barnwell, *Alta., Canada* **185 J8** 49 46N 112 15W
Barnwell, *SC, U.S.A.* **90 E4** 33 15N 81 23W
Barnwell County ☆, *SC, U.S.A.* **90 E4** 33 15N 81 30W
Baron, *OK, U.S.A.* **93 C9** 35 55N 94 36W
Barons, *Alta., Canada* **185 H7** 50 0N 113 5W
Barques, Pt. Aux, *MI, U.S.A.* **79 E9** 44 4N 82 58W
Barques, Pt. Aux, *MI, U.S.A.* **79 D5** 45 48N 86 21W
Barra El Tordo, *Tamaulipas, Mexico* **215 G7** 23 3N 97 46W
Barranca del Cobre, Parque Natural ⌂, *Chihuahua, Mexico* **213 F8** 27 15N 107 45W
Barranca Seca, *Michoacan, Mexico* **218 D4** 18 31N 103 1W
Barranquitas, *Puerto Rico* **105 G16** 18 11N 66 19W
Barraute, *Qué., Canada* **176 C5** 48 26N 77 38W
Barre, *MA, U.S.A.* **78 B2** 42 25N 72 6W
Barre, *VT, U.S.A.* **86 B2** 44 12N 72 30W
Barren ➛, *KY, U.S.A.* **96 C6** 37 11N 86 37W
Barren County ☆, *KY, U.S.A.* **97 D7** 36 57N 85 57W
Barren Hill, *PA, U.S.A.* **116 A1** 40 5N 75 15W
Barren Is., *AK, U.S.A.* **61 G9** 58 55N 152 15W
Barren River L., *KY, U.S.A.* **96 D6** 36 54N 86 8W
Barrett, *MN, U.S.A.* **80 E3** 45 55N 95 53W
Barrett, *WV, U.S.A.* **102 D3** 37 53N 81 40W
Barrhead, *Alta., Canada* **184 D6** 54 10N 114 24W
Barrial de Guadalupe, *Coahuila, Mexico* **215 F1** 24 58N 103 12W
Barrie, *Ont., Canada* **178 C7** 44 24N 79 40W
Barriefield, *Ont., Canada* **179 C10** 44 14N 76 28W
Barrière, *B.C., Canada* **187 D14** 51 12N 120 7W
Barrigada, *Guam* **105 b** 13 28N 144 48W
Barril, L. el, *Tamaulipas, Mexico* **214 E7** 25 45N 97 18W
Barrineau Park, *FL, U.S.A.* **67 A1** 30 42N 87 26W
Barrington, *NH, U.S.A.* **86 C4** 43 12N 70 59W
Barrington, *NJ, U.S.A.* **116 B2** 39 51N 75 3W
Barrington, *RI, U.S.A.* **78 C3** 41 44N 71 18W
Barrington Passage, *N.S., Canada* **173 K4** 43 30N 65 38W
Barron, *WI, U.S.A.* **103 C2** 45 24N 91 51W
Barron County ☆, *WI, U.S.A.* **103 C2** 45 25N 91 50W
Barrow, *AK, U.S.A.* **61 A8** 71 18N 156 47W
Barrow, Pt., *AK, U.S.A.* **61 A8** 71 23N 156 29W
Barrow County ☆, *GA, U.S.A.* **68 C3** 34 0N 83 40W
Barrow Str., *Nunavut, Canada* **190 C7** 74 20N 95 0W
Barrows, *Man., Canada* **183 C10** 52 50N 101 27W
Barry, *IL, U.S.A.* **71 D2** 39 42N 91 2W
Barry County ☆, *MI, U.S.A.* **79 G6** 42 35N 85 25W
Barry County ☆, *MO, U.S.A.* **82 E3** 36 45N 93 45W
Barry M. Goldwater Air Force Range, *AZ, U.S.A.* **62 E2** 32 38N 113 3W
Barry's Bay, *Ont., Canada* **179 B9** 45 29N 77 41W
Barryton, *MI, U.S.A.* **79 F6** 43 45N 85 9W
Barstow, *CA, U.S.A.* **65 J9** 34 54N 117 1W
Barstow, *TX, U.S.A.* **98 F4** 31 28N 103 24W
Bartholomew, Bayou ➛, *LA, U.S.A.* **75 B3** 32 43N 92 4W
Bartholomew County ☆, *IN, U.S.A.* **72 D5** 39 10N 85 55W
Bartlesville, *OK, U.S.A.* **93 B8** 36 45N 95 59W
Bartlett, *KS, U.S.A.* **74 D8** 37 3N 95 13W
Bartlett, *NH, U.S.A.* **86 B3** 44 5N 71 17W
Bartlett, *NE, U.S.A.* **84 C7** 41 53N 98 33W
Bartlett, *TN, U.S.A.* **96 E3** 35 12N 89 52W
Bartlett, *TX, U.S.A.* **99 G10** 30 48N 97 26W
Bartlett Res., *AZ, U.S.A.* **62 D4** 33 49N 111 38W
Bartletts Harbour, *Nfld. & L., Canada* **174 B4** 50 57N 57 0W
Bartley, *NE, U.S.A.* **84 D5** 40 15N 100 18W
Barton, *AL, U.S.A.* **60 B3** 34 44N 87 54W
Barton, *MD, U.S.A.* **77 A1** 39 34N 79 2W
Barton, *ND, U.S.A.* **91 B5** 48 30N 100 11W
Barton, *VT, U.S.A.* **86 B2** 44 45N 72 11W
Barton ➛, *VT, U.S.A.* **86 B2** 44 53N 72 13W
Barton, L., *Orlando, U.S.A.* **115 A3** 28 33N 81 18W
Barton County ☆, *KS, U.S.A.* **74 C5** 38 30N 98 40W
Barton County ☆, *MO, U.S.A.* **82 D2** 37 30N 94 20W
Bartonville, *IL, U.S.A.* **71 C4** 40 39N 89 39W
Bartow, *FL, U.S.A.* **67 D7** 27 54N 81 50W
Bartow, *GA, U.S.A.* **68 D4** 32 53N 82 29W
Bartow County ☆, *GA, U.S.A.* **68 B2** 34 20N 84 50W
Barwick, *GA, U.S.A.* **68 F3** 30 54N 83 44W
Basalt, *CO, U.S.A.* **66 C3** 39 22N 107 2W
Basalt, *ID, U.S.A.* **70 F6** 43 19N 112 10W
Basaseachic, Cascadas de, *Chihuahua, Mexico* **213 E7** 28 10N 108 12W
Basco, *IL, U.S.A.* **71 C2** 40 20N 91 12W
Bashaw, *Alta., Canada* **185 F8** 52 35N 112 58W
Basile, *LA, U.S.A.* **75 D3** 30 29N 92 36W
Basin, *MT, U.S.A.* **83 D5** 46 16N 112 16W
Basin, *WY, U.S.A.* **104 B4** 44 23N 108 2W
Basin L., *Sask., Canada* **182 C6** 52 38N 105 17W
Basinger, *FL, U.S.A.* **67 D7** 27 23N 81 2W
Baskahegan L., *ME, U.S.A.* **76 C6** 45 30N 67 48W
Baskatong, Rés., *Qué., Canada* **176 E7** 46 46N 75 50W
Baskin, *LA, U.S.A.* **75 B4** 32 16N 91 45W
Basonopita ➛, *Chihuahua, Mexico* **213 G8** 26 1N 107 15W
Bass Lake, *CA, U.S.A.* **64 F7** 37 19N 119 33W
Bass Lake, *Minneapolis-St. Paul, U.S.A.* **113 A1** 45 3N 93 25W
Bass River, *Qué., Canada* **173 H6** 45 25N 63 47W
Bassano, *Alta., Canada* **185 H8** 50 48N 112 20W
Bassett, *NE, U.S.A.* **84 B6** 42 35N 99 32W
Bassett, *VA, U.S.A.* **102 E5** 36 46N 79 59W
Bassfield, *MS, U.S.A.* **81 E4** 31 30N 89 45W
Basswood L., *MN, U.S.A.* **80 B7** 48 7N 91 34W
Bastian, *VA, U.S.A.* **102 D3** 37 9N 81 9W
Bastille, L., *Qué., Canada* **172 B8** 51 46N 61 11W
Bastrop, *LA, U.S.A.* **75 B4** 32 47N 91 55W
Bastrop, *TX, U.S.A.* **99 G10** 30 7N 97 19W
Bastrop County ☆, *TX, U.S.A.* **99 G10** 30 10N 97 20W
Batavia, *IL, U.S.A.* **71 B5** 41 51N 88 19W
Batavia, *IA, U.S.A.* **73 E6** 41 0N 92 10W
Batavia, *NY, U.S.A.* **89 B2** 43 0N 78 11W
Batavia, *OH, U.S.A.* **92 D2** 39 5N 84 11W
Batchawana B., *Ont., Canada* **181 F12** 46 53N 84 30W
Batchawana Bay, *Ont., Canada* **181 F12** 46 55N 84 37W
Batchtown, *IL, U.S.A.* **71 D3** 39 2N 90 43W
Bates, *AR, U.S.A.* **63 D1** 34 55N 94 23W
Bates County ☆, *MO, U.S.A.* **82 C2** 38 15N 94 20W
Batesburg-Leesville, *SC, U.S.A.* **90 E4** 33 54N 81 33W
Batesland, *SD, U.S.A.* **91 G3** 43 8N 102 6W
Batesville, *AR, U.S.A.* **63 C4** 35 46N 91 39W
Batesville, *IN, U.S.A.* **72 D5** 39 18N 85 13W
Batesville, *MS, U.S.A.* **81 B4** 34 19N 89 57W
Batesville, *TX, U.S.A.* **99 J8** 28 58N 99 37W
Bath, *N.B., Canada* **173 G2** 46 31N 67 36W
Bath, *Ont., Canada* **179 C10** 44 11N 76 47W
Bath, *IL, U.S.A.* **71 C3** 40 11N 90 8W
Bath, *ME, U.S.A.* **76 E4** 43 55N 69 49W
Bath, *NY, U.S.A.* **89 C3** 42 20N 77 19W
Bath, *PA, U.S.A.* **87 B1** 40 44N 75 24W
Bath, *SD, U.S.A.* **91 E7** 45 28N 98 20W
Bath Beach, *NY, U.S.A.* **114 C2** 40 36N 74 0W
Bath County ☆, *KY, U.S.A.* **97 B9** 38 10N 83 45W
Bath County ☆, *VA, U.S.A.* **102 C5** 38 0N 79 50W
Bathgate, *ND, U.S.A.* **91 B8** 48 53N 97 29W
Bathurst, *N.B., Canada* **173 F4** 47 37N 65 43W
Bathurst, C., *N.W.T., Canada* **188 B7** 70 34N 128 0W
Bathurst I., *Nunavut, Canada* **190 B5** 76 0N 100 30W
Bathurst Inlet, *Nunavut, Canada* **188 C11** 66 50N 108 1W
Batiscan, *Qué., Canada* **177 E10** 46 30N 72 15W
Batiscan ➛, *Qué., Canada* **177 E10** 46 16N 72 15W
Batiscan, L., *Qué., Canada* **177 D11** 47 22N 71 55W
Baton Rouge, *LA, U.S.A.* **75 D4** 30 27N 91 11W
Batopilas, *Chihuahua, Mexico* **213 F8** 27 1N 107 44W
Batopilas ➛, *Chihuahua, Mexico* **213 G8** 26 51N 107 50W
Batson, *TX, U.S.A.* **99 G13** 30 15N 94 40W
Batten Kill ➛, *VT, U.S.A.* **86 C1** 43 6N 73 35W
Battle ➛, *Sask., Canada* **182 C3** 52 43N 108 15W
Battle ➛, *CA, U.S.A.* **64 C4** 40 21N 122 11W
Battle Creek, *IA, U.S.A.* **73 C3** 42 19N 95 36W
Battle Creek, *MI, U.S.A.* **79 G6** 42 19N 85 11W
Battle Creek, *NE, U.S.A.* **84 C8** 42 0N 97 36W
Battle Creek L., *Minneapolis-St. Paul, U.S.A.* **113 B4** 44 56N 92 58W
Battle Creek Park, *Minneapolis-St. Paul, U.S.A.* **113 B3** 44 56N 92 59W
Battle Ground, *IN, U.S.A.* **72 C4** 40 31N 86 50W
Battle Ground, *WA, U.S.A.* **101 E3** 45 47N 122 32W
Battle Harbour, *Nfld. & L., Canada* **175 C6** 52 16N 55 35W
Battle Lake, *MN, U.S.A.* **80 D3** 46 17N 95 43W
Battle Mountain, *NV, U.S.A.* **85 B4** 40 38N 116 56W
Battle Mt., *WY, U.S.A.* **104 E5** 41 2N 107 16W
Battleford, *Sask., Canada* **182 C3** 52 45N 108 15W
Baturi, *Baja Calif. S., Mexico* **211 K8** 23 35N 110 20W
Baudette, *MN, U.S.A.* **80 B4** 48 43N 94 36W
Bauld, C., *Nfld. & L., Canada* **174 A5** 51 38N 55 26W
Baumann Fiord, *Nunavut, Canada* **190 B8** 77 40N 85 35W
Bauxite, *AR, U.S.A.* **63 D3** 34 33N 92 30W
Bavaria, *KS, U.S.A.* **74 C6** 38 48N 97 45W
Baviácora, *Sonora, Mexico* **212 D5** 29 43N 110 9W
Bavispe, *Sonora, Mexico* **212 C7** 30 30N 108 54W
Bavispe ➛, *Sonora, Mexico* **212 D6** 29 15N 109 11W
Bawlf, *Alta., Canada* **185 F8** 52 55N 112 28W
Baxley, *GA, U.S.A.* **68 E4** 31 47N 82 21W
Baxter, *IA, U.S.A.* **73 D5** 41 49N 93 9W
Baxter, *MN, U.S.A.* **80 D4** 46 21N 94 17W
Baxter, *TN, U.S.A.* **97 D7** 36 9N 85 38W
Baxter County ☆, *AR, U.S.A.* **63 B3** 36 20N 92 23W
Baxter Estates, *NY, U.S.A.* **114 A4** 40 50N 73 41W
Baxter Springs, *KS, U.S.A.* **74 D9** 37 2N 94 44W
Baxter State Park ⌂, *U.S.A.* **76 B5** 46 5N 68 57W
Bay, *AR, U.S.A.* **63 C5** 35 45N 90 34W
Bay, L., *Orlando, U.S.A.* **115 A2** 28 25N 81 34W
Bay Bulls, *Nfld. & L., Canada* **174 E8** 47 19N 52 50W
Bay Chimo = Umingmaktok, *Nunavut, Canada* **190 D4** 67 41N 107 56W
Bay City, *MI, U.S.A.* **79 F8** 43 36N 83 54W
Bay City, *OR, U.S.A.* **94 B2** 45 31N 123 53W
Bay City, *TX, U.S.A.* **99 J12** 28 59N 95 58W
Bay County ☆, *FL, U.S.A.* **67 A3** 30 20N 85 45W
Bay County ☆, *MI, U.S.A.* **79 F7** 43 45N 84 5W
Bay de Verde, *Nfld. & L., Canada* **174 D8** 48 5N 52 54W
Bay du Nord Wilderness Reserve ⌂, *Nfld. & L., Canada* **174 D6** 48 5N 54 48W
Bay du Vin, *N.B., Canada* **173 F4** 47 2N 65 8W
Bay Farm Island, *San Francisco, U.S.A.* **118 B3** 37 43N 122 12W
Bay Fiord, *Nunavut, Canada* **190 B9** 78 55N 83 30W
Bay Harbour Islands, *Miami, U.S.A.* **112 C3** 25 53N 80 7W
Bay Hill, *Orlando, U.S.A.* **115 B1** 28 28N 81 30W
Bay L'Argent, *Nfld. & L., Canada* **174 E6** 47 33N 54 54W
Bay Mills Indian Reservation, *MI, U.S.A.* **79 C7** 46 25N 84 15W
Bay Minette, *AL, U.S.A.* **60 F3** 30 53N 87 46W
Bay Park, *NY, U.S.A.* **114 C5** 40 37N 73 40W
Bay Pines, *Tampa, U.S.A.* **119 C2** 27 48N 82 46W
Bay Port, *MI, U.S.A.* **79 F8** 43 51N 83 23W
Bay Ridge, *NY, U.S.A.* **114 C2** 40 37N 74 1W
Bay Roberts, *Nfld. & L., Canada* **174 E7** 47 36N 53 16W
Bay St. Louis, *MS, U.S.A.* **81 F4** 30 19N 89 20W
Bay Shore, *NY, U.S.A.* **87 B3** 40 43N 73 15W
Bay Springs, *MS, U.S.A.* **81 E4** 31 59N 89 17W
Bay Springs L., *MS, U.S.A.* **81 B5** 34 31N 88 20W
Bay View, *MD, U.S.A.* **77 A5** 39 39N 75 58W
Bayamón, *Puerto Rico* **105 G16** 18 24N 66 9W
Bayard, *IA, U.S.A.* **73 D4** 41 51N 94 33W
Bayard, *NM, U.S.A.* **88 E2** 32 46N 108 8W
Bayard, *NE, U.S.A.* **84 C2** 41 45N 103 20W
Bayard, *WV, U.S.A.* **77 A1** 39 16N 79 22W
Bayboro, *NC, U.S.A.* **90 C9** 35 9N 76 46W
Bayfield, *CO, U.S.A.* **66 E3** 37 14N 107 36W
Bayfield, *WI, U.S.A.* **103 B3** 46 49N 90 49W
Bayfield County ☆, *WI, U.S.A.* **103 B2** 46 25N 91 15W
Bayfield Ridge, *WI, U.S.A.* **103 B2** 46 45N 91 25W
Baylor County ☆, *TX, U.S.A.* **99 D8** 33 35N 99 16W
Bayonet Point, *FL, U.S.A.* **67 C6** 28 20N 82 41W
Bayonne, *NJ, U.S.A.* **87 B2** 40 40N 74 6W
Bayou Boeuf, *New Orleans, U.S.A.* **113 C2** 29 50N 90 5W
Bayou Cane, *LA, U.S.A.* **75 E5** 29 37N 90 45W
Bayou D'Arbonne L., *LA, U.S.A.* **75 B3** 32 43N 92 21W
Bayou de Chien ➛, *KY, U.S.A.* **96 D3** 36 35N 89 12W
Bayou DeView ➛, *AR, U.S.A.* **63 D4** 34 54N 91 8W
Bayou George, *FL, U.S.A.* **67 A3** 30 16N 85 33W
Bayou La Batre, *AL, U.S.A.* **60 F2** 30 24N 88 15W
Bayou Meto, *AR, U.S.A.* **63 D4** 34 13N 91 31W
Bayou Pierre ➛, *MS, U.S.A.* **81 E2** 31 55N 91 11W
Bayou Sauvage Nat. Wildlife Refuge ⌂, *New Orleans, U.S.A.* **113 B3** 30 1N 89 53W
Bayou Segnette State Park ⌂, *New Orleans, U.S.A.* **113 C1** 29 53N 90 10W
Bayou Vista, *LA, U.S.A.* **75 E4** 29 41N 91 16W
Bayport, *FL, U.S.A.* **67 C6** 28 32N 82 39W
Bays, L. of, *Ont., Canada* **178 B7** 45 15N 79 4W
Bayshore, *FL, U.S.A.* **67 E7** 26 43N 81 50W
Bayshore, *San Francisco, U.S.A.* **118 B2** 37 42N 122 24W
Bayside, *Ont., Canada* **179 C9** 44 7N 77 35W
Bayside, *Milwaukee, U.S.A.* **112 A2** 43 10N 87 54W
Bayside, *NY, U.S.A.* **114 B4** 40 46N 73 46W
Bayside, *TX, U.S.A.* **99 J10** 28 6N 97 13W
Bayside Beach, *MD, U.S.A.* **77 A4** 39 8N 76 27W
Baysville, *Ont., Canada* **178 B7** 45 9N 79 7W
Baytown, *TX, U.S.A.* **99 H13** 29 43N 94 59W
Bayview, *ID, U.S.A.* **70 B2** 47 59N 116 34W
Bayview, *San Francisco, U.S.A.* **118 B2** 37 44N 122 23W
Baz, Pta., *Yucatán, Mexico* **223 A3** 21 10N 90 5W
Bazaar, *KS, U.S.A.* **74 C7** 38 16N 96 32W
Bazile Mills, *NE, U.S.A.* **84 B8** 42 31N 97 53W
Bazin ➛, *Qué., Canada* **176 D7** 47 29N 75 22W
Bazine, *KS, U.S.A.* **74 C4** 38 27N 99 42W
Beach, *ND, U.S.A.* **91 D2** 46 58N 104 0W
Beach City, *OH, U.S.A.* **92 C5** 40 39N 81 35W
Beach Haven, *NJ, U.S.A.* **87 C2** 39 34N 74 14W
Beachburg, *Ont., Canada* **179 B10** 45 44N 76 51W
Beachmont, *Boston, U.S.A.* **106 A4** 42 23N 70 59W
Beachville, *Ont., Canada* **178 D6** 43 5N 80 49W
Beachville, *MD, U.S.A.* **77 B4** 38 8N 76 24W
Beachwood, *NJ, U.S.A.* **87 C2** 39 56N 74 12W
Beacon, *IA, U.S.A.* **73 D6** 41 17N 92 41W
Beacon, *NY, U.S.A.* **87 A3** 41 30N 73 58W
Beacon Hill, *FL, U.S.A.* **67 B3** 29 55N 85 23W
Beaconia, *Man., Canada* **183 E15** 50 25N 96 31W
Beaconsfield, *Qué., Canada* **192 B1** 45 26N 73 52W
Beadle County ☆, *SD, U.S.A.* **91 F7** 44 22N 98 13W
Beagle, *KS, U.S.A.* **74 C9** 38 25N 94 57W
Beale, C., *B.C., Canada* **186 G9** 48 47N 125 13W
Beale Air Force Base, *CA, U.S.A.* **64 D5** 39 7N 121 19W
Beallsville, *OH, U.S.A.* **92 D5** 39 51N 81 2W
Beals Cr. ➛, *TX, U.S.A.* **98 E7** 32 10N 100 51W
Beamsville, *Ont., Canada* **178 D7** 43 12N 79 28W
Bear, *DE, U.S.A.* **77 A5** 39 38N 75 39W
Bear ➛, *UT, U.S.A.* **100 B3** 41 30N 112 8W
Bear Bay, *Nunavut, Canada* **190 B8** 75 47N 87 0W
Bear Brook State Park ⌂, *NH, U.S.A.* **86 C3** 43 6N 71 21W
Bear Cr. ➛, *AL, U.S.A.* **60 C2** 33 11N 88 5W
Bear Cr. ➛, *WY, U.S.A.* **104 E8** 41 41N 104 13W
Bear Creek, *WI, U.S.A.* **103 D5** 44 32N 88 44W
Bear Creek ➛, *Baltimore, U.S.A.* **107 B2** 39 13N 76 30W
Bear Creek Village, *PA, U.S.A.* **87 A1** 41 11N 75 45W
Bear L., *Alta., Canada* **184 C1** 55 9N 119 4W
Bear L., *U.S.A.* **70 G7** 42 7N 111 19W
Bear L., *UT, U.S.A.* **100 B4** 41 59N 111 21W
Bear Lake, *MI, U.S.A.* **79 E5** 44 25N 86 9W
Bear Lake County ☆, *ID, U.S.A.* **70 G7** 42 10N 111 15W
Bear Lake Nat. Wildlife Refuge ⌂, *ID, U.S.A.* **70 G7** 42 10N 111 18W
Bear Mt., *KY, U.S.A.* **97 C8** 37 32N 84 16W
Bear Peak, *WY, U.S.A.* **104 C3** 43 4N 109 13W
Bear River, *N.S., Canada* **173 J4** 44 34N 65 39W
Bear River City, *UT, U.S.A.* **100 B3** 41 37N 112 8W
Bear River Range, *U.S.A.* **70 G7** 42 9N 111 36W
Bear Tooth Pass, *WY, U.S.A.* **104 B3** 44 58N 109 28W
Bearden, *AR, U.S.A.* **63 E3** 33 43N 92 37W
Bearden, *OK, U.S.A.* **93 C7** 35 21N 96 23W
Beardmore, *Ont., Canada* **181 C9** 49 36N 87 57W
Beardsley, *KS, U.S.A.* **74 B2** 39 49N 101 14W
Beardsley, *MN, U.S.A.* **80 E2** 45 33N 96 43W
Beardstown, *IL, U.S.A.* **71 C3** 40 1N 90 26W
Bearmouth, *MT, U.S.A.* **83 D4** 46 48N 113 20W
Béarn, *Qué., Canada* **176 D3** 47 17N 79 20W
Bearpaw Mts., *MT, U.S.A.* **83 B8** 48 12N 109 30W
Bears Ears, *UT, U.S.A.* **100 F6** 37 38N 109 51W
Bearskin Lake, *Ont., Canada* **191 G7** 53 58N 91 2W
Beartooth Mts., *MT, U.S.A.* **83 E8** 45 10N 109 30W
Beartooth Pass, *WY, U.S.A.* **104 B3** 44 58N 109 28W
Beatrice, *AL, U.S.A.* **60 E3** 31 44N 87 13W
Beatrice, *NE, U.S.A.* **84 D9** 40 16N 96 45W
Beattie, *KS, U.S.A.* **74 B7** 39 52N 96 25W
Beatton ➛, *B.C., Canada* **189 E8** 56 15N 120 45W
Beatton River, *B.C., Canada* **189 E8** 57 26N 121 20W
Beatty, *Sask., Canada* **182 C7** 52 54N 104 48W
Beatty, *NV, U.S.A.* **85 F4** 36 54N 116 46W
Beatty, *OR, U.S.A.* **94 E4** 42 27N 121 16W
Beattyville, *KY, U.S.A.* **97 C9** 37 35N 83 42W
Beauceville, *Qué., Canada* **177 E12** 46 13N 70 46W
Beaucham, L., *Qué., Canada* **192 A2** 45 29N 75 37W
Beauchêne, L., *Qué., Canada* **176 E4** 46 35N 78 55W
Beaufort, *NC, U.S.A.* **90 D9** 34 43N 76 40W
Beaufort, *SC, U.S.A.* **90 F5** 32 26N 80 40W
Beaufort County ☆, *NC, U.S.A.* **90 C9** 35 30N 76 50W
Beaufort County ☆, *SC, U.S.A.* **90 F5** 32 20N 80 50W
Beaufort Sea, *Arctic* **188 B4** 72 0N 140 0W
Beaulac, *Qué., Canada* **177 F11** 45 50N 71 23W
Beaumont, *Alta., Canada* **184 E7** 53 21N 113 25W
Beaumont, *Nfld. & L., Canada* **174 C5** 49 37N 55 41W
Beaumont, *CA, U.S.A.* **65 K10** 33 57N 116 59W
Beaumont, *MS, U.S.A.* **81 E5** 31 10N 88 55W
Beaumont, *TX, U.S.A.* **99 G13** 30 5N 94 6W
Beauport, *Qué., Canada* **177 E11** 46 52N 71 11W
Beaupré, *Qué., Canada* **177 D12** 47 3N 70 54W
Beauregard Parish ☆, *LA, U.S.A.* **75 D2** 30 39N 93 20W
Beausejour, *Man., Canada* **183 E15** 50 5N 96 35W
Beauval, *Sask., Canada* **189 E11** 55 9N 107 37W
Beaux Arts, *Seattle, U.S.A.* **118 C4** 47 35N 122 11W
Beaver, *AK, U.S.A.* **61 C11** 66 22N 147 24W

Beaver, *KS, U.S.A.* **74 C5** 38 38N 98 40W
Beaver, *OH, U.S.A.* **92 D4** 39 2N 82 50W
Beaver, *OK, U.S.A.* **93 B3** 36 49N 100 31W
Beaver, *OR, U.S.A.* **94 B2** 45 17N 123 49W
Beaver, *PA, U.S.A.* **95 D2** 40 42N 80 19W
Beaver, *UT, U.S.A.* **100 E3** 38 17N 112 38W
Beaver →, *B.C., Canada* **189 E8** 59 52N 124 20W
Beaver →, *Sask., Canada* **189 E11** 55 26N 107 45W
Beaver →, *OK, U.S.A.* **93 B4** 36 35N 99 30W
Beaver →, *UT, U.S.A.* **100 D3** 39 10N 112 57W
Beaver Bay, *MN, U.S.A.* **80 C7** 47 16N 91 18W
Beaver Brook Station, *N.B., Canada* **173 F4** 47 8N 65 36W
Beaver City, *NE, U.S.A.* **84 D6** 40 8N 99 50W
Beaver County ☆, *OK, U.S.A.* **93 B3** 36 45N 100 25W
Beaver County ☆, *PA, U.S.A.* **95 D2** 40 45N 80 20W
Beaver County ☆, *UT, U.S.A.* **100 E2** 38 20N 113 10W
Beaver Cr. →, *CO, U.S.A.* **66 B7** 40 20N 103 33W
Beaver Cr. →, *MT, U.S.A.* **83 B10** 48 27N 107 18W
Beaver Cr. →, *ND, U.S.A.* **91 D5** 46 15N 100 32W
Beaver Cr. →, *ND, U.S.A.* **91 C2** 47 20N 103 39W
Beaver Cr. →, *NE, U.S.A.* **84 D6** 40 7N 99 29W
Beaver Cr. →, *TX, U.S.A.* **99 D9** 33 53N 98 49W
Beaver Cr. →, *WY, U.S.A.* **104 D4** 42 58N 108 26W
Beaver Creek, *N.W.T., Canada* **189 D4** 63 0N 141 0W
Beaver Creek, *MN, U.S.A.* **80 G2** 43 37N 96 22W
Beaver Crossing, *NE, U.S.A.* **84 D8** 40 47N 97 17W
Beaver Dam, *KY, U.S.A.* **96 C6** 37 24N 86 52W
Beaver Dam, *WI, U.S.A.* **103 E5** 43 28N 88 50W
Beaver Dam L., *WI, U.S.A.* **103 E5** 43 31N 88 53W
Beaver Falls, *PA, U.S.A.* **95 D2** 40 46N 80 20W
Beaver I., *MI, U.S.A.* **79 D6** 45 40N 85 33W
Beaver L., *AR, U.S.A.* **63 B2** 36 25N 93 51W
Beaver Lake, *Minneapolis-St. Paul, U.S.A.* **113 B3** 44 59N 93 0W
Beavercreek, *OH, U.S.A.* **92 D2** 39 43N 84 11W
Beaverdam, *OH, U.S.A.* **92 C3** 40 50N 83 59W
Beaverdell, *B.C., Canada* **187 F15** 49 27N 119 6W
Beaverhead →, *MT, U.S.A.* **83 E5** 45 31N 112 21W
Beaverhead County ☆, *MT, U.S.A.* **83 E4** 45 5N 113 10W
Beaverhead Mts., *ID, U.S.A.* **70 E5** 45 0N 113 20W
Beaverhead Nat. Forest ⌂, *MT, U.S.A.* **83 E4** 45 10N 113 12W
Beaverhill L., *Alta., Canada* **184 E8** 53 27N 112 32W
Beaverlodge, *Alta., Canada* **184 C1** 55 11N 119 29W
Beavermouth, *B.C., Canada* **187 D17** 51 32N 117 23W
Beaverton, *Ont., Canada* **178 C7** 44 26N 79 9W
Beaverton, *MI, U.S.A.* **79 F7** 43 53N 84 29W
Beaverton, *MT, U.S.A.* **83 B10** 48 26N 107 15W
Beaverton, *OR, U.S.A.* **94 B3** 45 29N 122 48W
Beaverton, *Portland, U.S.A.* **116 B1** 45 29N 122 48W
Bebe, *TX, U.S.A.* **99 H10** 29 25N 97 38W
Becal, *Campeche, Mexico* **223 B3** 20 27N 90 2W
Becán, *Campeche, Mexico* **223 D4** 18 34N 89 31W
Bécancour, *Qué., Canada* **177 E10** 46 20N 72 26W
Becharof L., *AK, U.S.A.* **61 H8** 57 56N 156 23W
Becharof Nat. Wildlife Refuge ⌂, *AK, U.S.A.* **61 H8** 58 0N 156 15W
Beck L., *Chicago, U.S.A.* **108 A1** 42 4N 87 52W
Becker County ☆, *MN, U.S.A.* **80 D3** 46 50N 95 50W
Beckham County ☆, *OK, U.S.A.* **93 C4** 35 15N 99 40W
Beckley, *WV, U.S.A.* **102 D3** 37 47N 81 11W
Beckville, *TX, U.S.A.* **99 E13** 32 15N 94 27W
Beckwith Cr. →, *LA, U.S.A.* **75 D2** 30 13N 93 13W
Becky Pk., *NV, U.S.A.* **85 C6** 39 58N 114 36W
Bedford, *N.S., Canada* **173 J6** 44 44N 63 40W
Bedford, *Qué., Canada* **177 F10** 45 7N 72 59W
Bedford, *Dallas-Fort Worth, U.S.A.* **109 A3** 32 50N 97 8W
Bedford, *IN, U.S.A.* **72 E4** 38 52N 86 29W
Bedford, *IA, U.S.A.* **73 E4** 40 40N 94 44W
Bedford, *KY, U.S.A.* **97 B7** 38 36N 85 19W
Bedford, *MA, U.S.A.* **78 B3** 42 27N 71 15W
Bedford, *NH, U.S.A.* **86 D3** 42 55N 71 32W
Bedford, *NY, U.S.A.* **87 A3** 41 12N 73 39W
Bedford, *OH, U.S.A.* **92 B5** 41 23N 81 32W
Bedford, *PA, U.S.A.* **95 D4** 40 1N 78 30W
Bedford, *VA, U.S.A.* **102 D5** 37 20N 79 31W
Bedford County ☆, *PA, U.S.A.* **95 E4** 40 0N 78 30W
Bedford County ☆, *TN, U.S.A.* **96 E6** 35 29N 86 28W
Bedford County ☆, *VA, U.S.A.* **102 D5** 37 20N 79 31W
Bedford Park, *Chicago, U.S.A.* **108 C2** 41 46N 87 46W
Bedford Park, *NY, U.S.A.* **114 A3** 40 52N 73 52W
Bedford Reservation, *Cleveland, U.S.A.* **107 B2** 41 22N 81 33W
Bedford Stuyvesant, *NY, U.S.A.* **114 B3** 40 41N 73 56W
Bedias, *TX, U.S.A.* **99 G12** 30 47N 95 57W
Bedrock, *CO, U.S.A.* **66 D2** 38 19N 108 54W
Bee, *NE, U.S.A.* **84 C8** 41 0N 97 4W
Bee County ☆, *TX, U.S.A.* **99 J10** 28 24N 97 45W
Bee Ridge, *FL, U.S.A.* **67 D6** 27 17N 82 29W
Bee Springs, *KY, U.S.A.* **96 C6** 37 17N 86 17W
Beebe, *AR, U.S.A.* **63 C4** 35 4N 91 53W
Beech →, *TN, U.S.A.* **96 E4** 35 37N 88 2W
Beech Bottom, *WV, U.S.A.* **102 A4** 40 14N 80 39W
Beech Creek, *PA, U.S.A.* **95 C5** 41 5N 77 36W
Beech Fork →, *KY, U.S.A.* **97 C7** 37 46N 85 41W
Beech Fork L., *WV, U.S.A.* **102 C2** 38 18N 82 25W
Beech Grove, *IN, U.S.A.* **72 D4** 39 43N 86 5W
Beech Mountain, *NC, U.S.A.* **90 B4** 36 12N 81 53W
Beecher, *IL, U.S.A.* **71 B6** 41 21N 87 38W
Beecher City, *IL, U.S.A.* **71 D5** 39 11N 88 47W
Beecher Falls, *VT, U.S.A.* **86 A3** 45 1N 71 31W
Beechey Hd., *B.C., Canada* **187 G11** 48 10N 123 30W
Beechey Point, *AK, U.S.A.* **61 A10** 70 29N 149 9W
Beechgrove, *TN, U.S.A.* **96 E6** 35 38N 86 14W
Beechwood, *MI, U.S.A.* **79 C3** 46 10N 88 46W
Beechy, *Sask., Canada* **182 E4** 50 53N 107 24W
Beef I., *Br. Virgin Is.* **105 G18** 18 26N 64 30W
Beeler, *KS, U.S.A.* **74 C3** 38 26N 100 12W
Beemer, *NE, U.S.A.* **84 C9** 41 56N 96 48W
Beersheba Springs, *TN, U.S.A.* **97 E7** 35 28N 85 39W
Beeton, *Ont., Canada* **178 C7** 44 5N 79 47W
Beetz, L., *Qué., Canada* **172 C7** 50 34N 62 42W
Beeville, *TX, U.S.A.* **99 J10** 28 24N 97 45W
Beggs, *OK, U.S.A.* **93 C7** 35 45N 96 4W
Begonias, Presa, *Guanajuato, Mexico* **219 B7** 20 53N 100 51W
Beiseker, *Alta., Canada* **185 G7** 51 23N 113 32W
Bejacos, *México, Mexico* **219 D7** 18 46N 100 25W
Bejou, *MN, U.S.A.* **80 C3** 47 26N 95 59W
Beklabito, *NM, U.S.A.* **88 A1** 36 50N 109 1W
Bel Air, *Los Angeles, U.S.A.* **111 B2** 34 4N 118 27W
Bel Air, *MD, U.S.A.* **77 A4** 39 32N 76 21W
Bel Aire, *KS, U.S.A.* **74 D6** 37 46N 97 16W
Bel-Aire, *Norfolk, U.S.A.* **115 A2** 36 55N 76 13W
Bel Alton, *MD, U.S.A.* **77 B4** 38 28N 76 59W
Bel-Nor, *MO, U.S.A.* **117 A2** 38 42N 90 19W
Bel-Ridge, *MO, U.S.A.* **117 A2** 38 42N 90 19W
Bélanger, *Montréal, Canada* **192 A1** 45 35N 73 42W
Belanger →, *Man., Canada* **183 B14** 53 27N 97 41W
Belbutte, *Sask., Canada* **182 B4** 53 22N 107 49W
Belcamp, *MD, U.S.A.* **77 A4** 39 28N 76 14W
Belcher Chan., *Nunavut, Canada* **190 B6** 77 15N 95 0W
Belcher Is., *N.W.T., Canada* **175 B2** 56 15N 78 45W
Belchertown, *MA, U.S.A.* **78 B2** 42 17N 72 24W
Belcourt, *Qué., Canada* **176 C5** 48 24N 77 21W
Belcourt, *ND, U.S.A.* **91 B6** 48 50N 99 45W
Belden, *NE, U.S.A.* **84 B8** 42 25N 97 13W
Belding, *MI, U.S.A.* **79 F6** 43 6N 85 14W
Belen, *NM, U.S.A.* **88 C4** 34 40N 106 46W
Belews L., *NC, U.S.A.* **90 B5** 36 15N 80 5W
Belfair, *WA, U.S.A.* **101 C3** 47 27N 122 50W
Belfast, *ME, U.S.A.* **76 D4** 44 26N 69 1W
Belfast, *NY, U.S.A.* **89 C2** 42 21N 78 7W
Belfast, *TN, U.S.A.* **96 E6** 35 25N 86 42W
Belfield, *ND, U.S.A.* **91 D2** 46 53N 103 12W
Belfry, *MT, U.S.A.* **83 E8** 45 9N 109 1W
Belgium, *WI, U.S.A.* **103 E6** 43 30N 87 51W
Belgrade, *ME, U.S.A.* **76 D4** 44 27N 69 50W
Belgrade, *MN, U.S.A.* **80 E3** 45 27N 95 0W
Belgrade, *MT, U.S.A.* **83 E6** 45 47N 111 11W
Belgrade, *NE, U.S.A.* **84 C7** 41 28N 98 4W
Belhaven, *NC, U.S.A.* **90 C9** 35 33N 76 37W
Belington, *WV, U.S.A.* **102 B5** 39 2N 79 56W
Belize Inlet, *B.C., Canada* **186 D7** 51 8N 127 20W
Belknap, *IL, U.S.A.* **71 F5** 37 19N 88 56W
Belknap County ☆, *NH, U.S.A.* **86 C3** 43 30N 71 30W
Bell, *FL, U.S.A.* **67 B6** 29 45N 82 52W
Bell, *Los Angeles, U.S.A.* **111 C3** 33 58N 118 11W
Bell →, *Qué., Canada* **176 B5** 49 48N 77 38W
Bell Buckle, *TN, U.S.A.* **96 E6** 35 35N 86 21W
Bell City, *KY, U.S.A.* **96 D3** 36 31N 88 30W
Bell City, *MO, U.S.A.* **82 D7** 37 1N 89 49W
Bell County ☆, *KY, U.S.A.* **97 D9** 36 45N 83 40W
Bell County ☆, *TX, U.S.A.* **99 F10** 31 3N 97 28W
Bell Gardens, *Los Angeles, U.S.A.* **111 C3** 33 58N 118 9W
Bell I., *Nfld. & L., Canada* **174 E8** 47 38N 52 58W
Bell I., *Nfld. & L., Canada* **174 B5** 50 46N 55 35W
Bell-Irving →, *B.C., Canada* **189 E7** 56 12N 129 5W
Bell L., *Ont., Canada* **180 C6** 49 48N 90 58W
Bell Peninsula, *Nunavut, Canada* **191 E9** 63 50N 82 0W
Bell Ranch, *NM, U.S.A.* **88 B6** 35 32N 104 6W
Bella Bella, *B.C., Canada* **186 C6** 52 10N 128 10W
Bella Coola, *B.C., Canada* **186 C8** 52 25N 126 40W
Bella Vista, *AR, U.S.A.* **63 B1** 36 28N 94 16W
Bellaire, *MI, U.S.A.* **79 E6** 44 59N 85 13W
Bellaire, *NY, U.S.A.* **114 B4** 40 42N 73 45W
Bellaire, *OH, U.S.A.* **92 C6** 40 1N 80 45W
Bellaire, *TX, U.S.A.* **99 H12** 29 42N 95 27W
Bellamy, *AL, U.S.A.* **60 D2** 32 27N 88 8W
Bellavista, *Chiapas, Mexico* **222 D3** 15 35N 92 13W
Bellburns, *Nfld. & L., Canada* **174 B3** 50 20N 57 32W
Belle, *MO, U.S.A.* **82 C5** 38 17N 91 43W
Belle, *WV, U.S.A.* **102 C3** 38 14N 81 33W
Belle →, *MI, U.S.A.* **79 G9** 42 43N 82 30W
Belle-Chasse, *LA, U.S.A.* **113 C3** 29 51N 90 0W
Belle Fourche, *SD, U.S.A.* **91 F2** 44 40N 103 51W
Belle Fourche →, *SD, U.S.A.* **91 F3** 44 26N 102 18W
Belle Fourche Res., *SD, U.S.A.* **91 F2** 44 44N 103 41W
Belle Glade, *FL, U.S.A.* **67 E8** 26 41N 80 40W
Belle Harbor, *NY, U.S.A.* **114 C3** 40 34N 73 51W
Belle Haven, *VA, U.S.A.* **102 D9** 37 33N 75 49W
Belle Isle, *Nfld. & L., Canada* **174 A5** 51 57N 55 25W
Belle Isle, *FL, U.S.A.* **67 C7** 28 27N 81 12W
Belle Isle, *MI, U.S.A.* **109 A3** 42 20N 82 58W
Belle Isle, Str. of, *Nfld. & L., Canada* **174 A4** 51 30N 56 30W
Belle Isle Park, *MI, U.S.A.* **109 A3** 42 20N 82 58W
Belle Plaine, *IA, U.S.A.* **73 D6** 41 54N 92 17W
Belle Plaine, *KS, U.S.A.* **74 D6** 37 24N 97 17W
Belle Plaine, *MN, U.S.A.* **80 F5** 44 37N 93 46W
Belle Rive, *IL, U.S.A.* **71 E5** 38 14N 88 45W
Belle River, *Ont., Canada* **178 E4** 42 18N 82 43W
Belle Valley, *OH, U.S.A.* **92 D5** 39 47N 81 33W
Belle View, *VA, U.S.A.* **119 B2** 38 57N 77 14W
Belleair, *Tampa, U.S.A.* **119 B2** 27 56N 82 48W
Belleair Beach, *Tampa, U.S.A.* **119 B1** 27 55N 82 50W
Belleair Bluffs, *Tampa, U.S.A.* **119 B2** 27 55N 82 49W
Belleair Shore, *Tampa, U.S.A.* **119 B1** 27 54N 82 50W
Bellechester, *MN, U.S.A.* **80 F6** 44 22N 92 31W
Bellefontaine, *OH, U.S.A.* **92 C3** 40 22N 83 46W
Bellefontaine Neighbors, *MO, U.S.A.* **117 A2** 38 44N 90 13W
Bellefonte, *DE, U.S.A.* **77 A5** 39 47N 75 30W
Bellefonte, *PA, U.S.A.* **95 D5** 40 55N 77 47W
Bellemont, *AZ, U.S.A.* **62 B4** 35 14N 111 50W
Belleoram, *Nfld. & L., Canada* **174 E5** 47 31N 55 25W
Belleplain, *NJ, U.S.A.* **87 C2** 39 11N 74 46W
Bellerive, *MO, U.S.A.* **117 A2** 38 42N 90 18W
Bellerose, *NY, U.S.A.* **114 B4** 40 43N 73 42W
Belleterre, *Qué., Canada* **176 D4** 47 25N 78 41W
Belleview, *FL, U.S.A.* **67 B6** 29 4N 82 3W
Belleville, *Ont., Canada* **179 C9** 44 10N 77 23W
Belleville, *IL, U.S.A.* **71 E4** 38 31N 89 59W
Belleville, *KS, U.S.A.* **74 B6** 39 50N 97 38W
Belleville, *NJ, U.S.A.* **87 B2** 40 47N 74 9W
Belleville, *WI, U.S.A.* **103 F4** 42 52N 89 32W
Bellevue, *ID, U.S.A.* **70 F4** 43 28N 114 16W
Bellevue, *IA, U.S.A.* **73 C8** 42 16N 90 26W
Bellevue, *KY, U.S.A.* **107 B2** 39 6N 84 28W
Bellevue, *MD, U.S.A.* **77 B4** 38 42N 76 11W
Bellevue, *MI, U.S.A.* **79 G6** 42 27N 85 1W
Bellevue, *NE, U.S.A.* **84 C10** 41 9N 95 54W
Bellevue, *OH, U.S.A.* **92 B4** 41 17N 82 51W
Bellevue, *Pittsburgh, U.S.A.* **116 B1** 40 29N 80 3W
Bellevue, *TX, U.S.A.* **99 D9** 33 38N 98 1W
Bellevue, *WA, U.S.A.* **101 C3** 47 37N 122 12W
Bellflower, *IL, U.S.A.* **71 C5** 40 20N 88 32W
Bellflower, *Los Angeles, U.S.A.* **111 C4** 33 52N 118 6W
Bellflower, *MO, U.S.A.* **82 B5** 39 0N 91 21W
Bellin = Kangirsuk, *Qué., Canada* **175 A4** 60 0N 70 0W
Bellingham, *MA, U.S.A.* **78 B3** 42 5N 71 28W
Bellingham, *MN, U.S.A.* **80 E2** 45 8N 96 17W
Bellingham, *WA, U.S.A.* **101 B3** 48 46N 122 29W
Belliveaus Cove, *N.S., Canada* **173 J3** 44 23N 66 4W
Bellmawr, *NJ, U.S.A.* **87 C2** 39 52N 75 5W
Bellmead, *TX, U.S.A.* **99 F10** 31 35N 97 6W
Bellot Str., *Nunavut, Canada* **190 C7** 71 59N 94 48W
Bellows Falls, *VT, U.S.A.* **86 C2** 43 8N 72 27W
Bellport, *NY, U.S.A.* **87 B4** 40 46N 72 56W
Bells, *TN, U.S.A.* **96 E3** 35 43N 89 5W
Bells, *TX, U.S.A.* **99 D11** 33 37N 96 25W
Bells Corners, *Ont., Canada* **179 B11** 45 19N 75 50W
Bellsite, *Man., Canada* **183 C10** 52 15N 101 4W
Belltown, *DE, U.S.A.* **77 B5** 38 45N 75 11W
Bellview, *NM, U.S.A.* **88 C7** 34 49N 103 7W
Bellville, *GA, U.S.A.* **68 D5** 32 9N 81 59W
Bellville, *TX, U.S.A.* **99 H11** 29 57N 96 15W
Bellvue, *CO, U.S.A.* **66 B5** 40 38N 105 10W
Bellwood, *Chicago, U.S.A.* **108 B1** 41 52N 87 53W
Bellwood, *LA, U.S.A.* **75 C2** 31 32N 93 12W
Bellwood, *NE, U.S.A.* **84 C8** 41 21N 97 14W
Bellwood, *PA, U.S.A.* **95 D4** 40 36N 78 20W
Belly →, *Alta., Canada* **185 J7** 49 46N 113 2W
Belmar, *NJ, U.S.A.* **87 B2** 40 11N 74 2W
Belmond, *IA, U.S.A.* **73 C5** 42 51N 93 37W
Belmont, *Man., Canada* **183 F12** 49 25N 99 27W
Belmont, *N.S., Canada* **173 H6** 45 25N 63 23W
Belmont, *Ont., Canada* **178 E5** 42 53N 81 5W
Belmont, *Boston, U.S.A.* **106 A2** 42 23N 71 10W
Belmont, *KS, U.S.A.* **74 D6** 37 32N 97 56W
Belmont, *MS, U.S.A.* **81 B5** 34 31N 88 13W
Belmont, *NH, U.S.A.* **86 C3** 43 27N 71 29W
Belmont, *NY, U.S.A.* **89 C2** 42 14N 78 2W
Belmont, *WV, U.S.A.* **102 B3** 39 23N 81 16W
Belmont, *WI, U.S.A.* **103 F3** 42 44N 90 20W
Belmont County ☆, *OH, U.S.A.* **92 C5** 40 1N 81 4W
Belmont Cragin, *Chicago, U.S.A.* **108 B2** 41 55N 87 45W
Belmont Harbor, *Chicago, U.S.A.* **108 B3** 41 56N 87 38W
Beloeil, *Qué., Canada* **177 F9** 45 34N 73 12W
Beloit, *KS, U.S.A.* **74 B5** 39 28N 98 6W
Beloit, *WI, U.S.A.* **103 F4** 42 31N 89 2W
Belot, L., *N.W.T., Canada* **188 C7** 66 53N 126 16W
Belpre, *KS, U.S.A.* **74 D4** 37 57N 99 6W
Belpre, *OH, U.S.A.* **92 D5** 39 17N 81 34W
Belt, *MT, U.S.A.* **83 C7** 47 23N 110 55W
Belted Ra., *NV, U.S.A.* **85 E4** 37 22N 116 8W
Belton, *MO, U.S.A.* **82 C2** 38 49N 94 32W
Belton, *SC, U.S.A.* **90 D3** 34 31N 82 30W
Belton, *TX, U.S.A.* **99 F10** 31 3N 97 28W
Belton L., *TX, U.S.A.* **99 F10** 31 6N 97 28W
Beltrami, *MN, U.S.A.* **80 C2** 47 33N 96 32W
Beltrami County ☆, *MN, U.S.A.* **80 C4** 47 45N 94 50W
Beltsville, *MD, U.S.A.* **77 A4** 39 2N 76 54W
Belvedere, *Atlanta, U.S.A.* **106 B3** 33 45N 84 16W
Belvedere, *San Francisco, U.S.A.* **118 A2** 37 52N 122 27W
Belvidere, *IL, U.S.A.* **71 A5** 42 15N 88 50W
Belvidere, *NJ, U.S.A.* **87 B1** 40 50N 75 5W
Belvidere, *NE, U.S.A.* **84 D8** 40 15N 97 33W
Belvidere, *SD, U.S.A.* **91 G4** 43 50N 101 16W
Belvidere Mt., *VT, U.S.A.* **86 B2** 44 46N 72 33W
Belview, *MN, U.S.A.* **80 F3** 44 36N 95 20W
Belvue, *KS, U.S.A.* **74 B7** 39 13N 96 11W
Belwood, *NC, U.S.A.* **90 C4** 35 29N 81 31W
Belzoni, *MS, U.S.A.* **81 C3** 33 11N 90 29W
Bement, *IL, U.S.A.* **71 D5** 39 55N 88 34W
Bemidji, *MN, U.S.A.* **80 C4** 47 28N 94 53W
Bemis, *WV, U.S.A.* **102 C5** 38 49N 79 45W
Ben Avon, *Pittsburgh, U.S.A.* **116 A1** 40 30N 80 5W
Ben Avon Heights, *Pittsburgh, U.S.A.* **116 A1** 40 30N 80 4W
Ben Hill County ☆, *GA, U.S.A.* **68 E3** 31 45N 83 10W
Ben Lomond, *AR, U.S.A.* **63 E1** 33 50N 94 7W
Ben Lomond, *CA, U.S.A.* **64 F4** 37 5N 122 5W
Bena, *MN, U.S.A.* **80 C4** 47 21N 94 12W
Benavides, *TX, U.S.A.* **98 K9** 27 36N 98 25W
Benbrook, *TX, U.S.A.* **99 E10** 32 41N 97 28W
Benchley, *TX, U.S.A.* **99 G11** 30 45N 96 27W
Bend, *OR, U.S.A.* **94 C4** 44 4N 121 19W
Benedict, *KS, U.S.A.* **74 D8** 37 38N 95 45W
Benedict, *MD, U.S.A.* **77 B4** 38 31N 76 41W
Benedict, *NE, U.S.A.* **84 D8** 41 0N 97 36W
Benemérito de las Américas, *Chiapas, Mexico* **222 C6** 16 31N 90 38W
Benevolence, *GA, U.S.A.* **68 E2** 31 53N 84 44W
Benewah County ☆, *ID, U.S.A.* **70 B2** 47 5N 116 35W
Bengough, *Sask., Canada* **182 F6** 49 25N 105 10W
Benham, *KY, U.S.A.* **97 D10** 36 58N 82 57W
Benito, *Man., Canada* **183 D10** 51 55N 101 33W
Benito González, *Tabasco, Mexico* **222 B4** 17 52N 92 42W
Benito Juárez, *Baja Calif. S., Mexico* **211 H7** 25 7N 111 50W
Benito Juárez, *Chiapas, Mexico* **222 C4** 16 2N 92 49W
Benito Juárez, *Chihuahua, Mexico* **213 D9** 29 10N 106 58W
Benito Juárez, *Chihuahua, Mexico* **213 C9** 30 10N 106 53W
Benito Juárez, *Distrito Federal, Mexico* **225 B3** 19 23N 99 9W
Benito Juárez, *Guerrero, Mexico* **219 D7** 18 17N 100 28W
Benito Juárez, *Quintana Roo, Mexico* **223 C5** 19 42N 88 47W
Benito Juárez, *Tabasco, Mexico* **222 A3** 18 10N 93 54W
Benito Juárez, *Tabasco, Mexico* **222 B4** 17 50N 92 32W
Benito Juárez, *Veracruz, Mexico* **220 D3** 20 18N 97 9W
Benito Juárez, *Veracruz, Mexico* **220 D2** 20 54N 98 11W
Benito Juárez, *Zacatecas, Mexico* **217 F7** 21 30N 103 34W
Benito Juárez, Aeropuerto Int. ✕, *Distrito Federal, Mexico* **225 B3** 19 25N 99 5W
Benito Juárez, Parque Nacional △, *Oaxaca, Mexico* **221 G4** 17 8N 96 43W
Benjamin, *TX, U.S.A.* **99 D8** 33 35N 99 48W
Benjamín Hill, *Sonora, Mexico* **212 C4** 30 9N 111 7W
Benkelman, *NE, U.S.A.* **84 D4** 40 3N 101 32W
Benld, *IL, U.S.A.* **71 D4** 39 6N 89 48W
Bennet, *NE, U.S.A.* **84 D9** 40 41N 96 30W
Bennett, *B.C., Canada* **189 E6** 59 51N 135 0W
Bennett, *CO, U.S.A.* **66 C6** 39 46N 104 26W
Bennett, *IA, U.S.A.* **73 D8** 41 43N 90 59W
Bennett County ☆, *SD, U.S.A.* **91 G4** 43 5N 101 45W
Bennettsville, *SC, U.S.A.* **90 D6** 34 37N 79 41W
Bennington, *ID, U.S.A.* **70 G7** 42 24N 111 19W
Bennington, *KS, U.S.A.* **74 B6** 39 2N 97 36W
Bennington, *NH, U.S.A.* **86 C3** 43 0N 71 55W
Bennington, *NE, U.S.A.* **84 C9** 41 22N 96 9W
Bennington, *OK, U.S.A.* **93 E7** 34 0N 96 2W
Bennington, *VT, U.S.A.* **86 D1** 42 53N 73 12W
Bennington County ☆, *VT, U.S.A.* **86 D1** 43 0N 73 10W
Benny, *Ont., Canada* **178 A5** 46 47N 81 38W
Benoit, *MS, U.S.A.* **81 C2** 33 39N 91 1W
Bens Run, *WV, U.S.A.* **102 B3** 39 28N 81 6W
Bensley, *VA, U.S.A.* **102 D7** 37 27N 77 27W
Benson, *Sask., Canada* **182 F8** 49 27N 103 1W
Benson, *AZ, U.S.A.* **62 F5** 31 58N 110 18W
Benson, *IL, U.S.A.* **71 C4** 40 51N 89 7W
Benson, *LA, U.S.A.* **75 C2** 31 52N 93 42W
Benson, *MN, U.S.A.* **80 E3** 45 19N 95 36W
Benson, *NC, U.S.A.* **90 C7** 35 23N 78 33W
Benson, *VT, U.S.A.* **86 C1** 43 42N 73 18W
Benson County ☆, *ND, U.S.A.* **91 B6** 48 5N 99 25W
Bensonhurst, *NY, U.S.A.* **114 C3** 40 35N 73 59W
Bent County ☆, *CO, U.S.A.* **66 E7** 38 0N 103 0W
Bentley, *Alta., Canada* **185 F6** 52 28N 114 4W
Bentley, *KS, U.S.A.* **74 D6** 37 54N 97 31W
Bentleyville, *PA, U.S.A.* **95 D2** 40 7N 80 1W
Benton, *AR, U.S.A.* **63 D3** 34 34N 92 35W
Benton, *CA, U.S.A.* **64 F8** 37 48N 118 32W
Benton, *IL, U.S.A.* **71 E5** 38 0N 88 55W
Benton, *IA, U.S.A.* **73 E4** 40 42N 94 22W
Benton, *KS, U.S.A.* **74 D6** 37 47N 97 7W
Benton, *KY, U.S.A.* **96 D4** 36 52N 88 21W
Benton, *LA, U.S.A.* **75 B2** 32 42N 93 44W
Benton, *MS, U.S.A.* **81 D3** 32 50N 90 16W
Benton, *MO, U.S.A.* **82 D7** 37 6N 89 34W
Benton, *NH, U.S.A.* **86 B3** 44 8N 71 55W
Benton, *PA, U.S.A.* **95 C6** 41 12N 76 23W
Benton, *TN, U.S.A.* **97 E8** 35 10N 84 39W
Benton, *WI, U.S.A.* **103 F3** 42 34N 90 23W
Benton City, *MO, U.S.A.* **82 B5** 39 8N 91 46W
Benton City, *WA, U.S.A.* **101 D6** 46 16N 119 29W
Benton County ☆, *AR, U.S.A.* **63 B1** 36 22N 94 13W
Benton County ☆, *IN, U.S.A.* **72 C3** 40 35N 87 20W
Benton County ☆, *IA, U.S.A.* **73 C6** 42 0N 92 0W
Benton County ☆, *MN, U.S.A.* **80 E5** 45 45N 94 0W
Benton County ☆, *MS, U.S.A.* **81 B4** 34 50N 89 11W
Benton County ☆, *MO, U.S.A.* **82 C3** 38 20N 93 15W
Benton County ☆, *OR, U.S.A.* **94 C2** 44 30N 123 20W
Benton County ☆, *TN, U.S.A.* **96 D4** 36 4N 88 6W
Benton County ☆, *WA, U.S.A.* **101 D6** 46 25N 119 25W
Benton Harbor, *MI, U.S.A.* **79 G5** 42 6N 86 27W
Benton Heights, *MI, U.S.A.* **79 G5** 42 7N 86 24W
Benton L., *MT, U.S.A.* **83 C6** 47 40N 111 20W
Benton Lake Nat. Wildlife Refuge ⌂, *MT, U.S.A.* **83 C6** 47 40N 111 20W
Benton Ridge, *OH, U.S.A.* **92 C3** 41 0N 83 48W
Bentonia, *MS, U.S.A.* **81 D3** 32 38N 90 22W
Bentonite Spur, *WY, U.S.A.* **104 B8** 44 52N 104 9W
Bentonville, *AR, U.S.A.* **63 B1** 36 22N 94 13W
Bentonville, *VA, U.S.A.* **77 B2** 38 50N 78 19W
Bent's Old Fort Nat. Historic Site ⌂, *CO, U.S.A.* **66 D7** 38 6N 103 5W
Benwood, *WV, U.S.A.* **102 A4** 40 1N 80 44W
Benzie County ☆, *MI, U.S.A.* **79 E5** 44 40N 86 0W
Beowawe, *NV, U.S.A.* **85 B4** 40 35N 116 29W
Berclair, *TN, U.S.A.* **112 B2** 35 8N 89 54W
Berclair, *TX, U.S.A.* **99 J10** 28 32N 97 36W
Berea, *KY, U.S.A.* **97 C8** 37 34N 84 17W
Berea, *NE, U.S.A.* **84 B3** 42 13N 102 59W
Berea, *SC, U.S.A.* **90 D3** 34 50N 82 25W
Berens →, *Man., Canada* **183 C14** 52 25N 97 2W
Berens I., *Man., Canada* **183 C14** 52 18N 97 18W
Berens River, *Man., Canada* **183 C14** 52 25N 97 0W
Beresford, *N.B., Canada* **173 F4** 47 42N 65 42W
Beresford, *SD, U.S.A.* **91 G9** 43 5N 96 47W
Bergen, *NY, U.S.A.* **89 B3** 43 5N 77 57W
Bergen County ☆, *NJ, U.S.A.* **87 B2** 41 0N 74 10W
Bergenfield, *NJ, U.S.A.* **87 B3** 40 55N 73 59W
Berger, *MO, U.S.A.* **82 C5** 38 41N 91 20W
Bergland, *MI, U.S.A.* **79 C2** 46 36N 89 34W
Bergoo, *WV, U.S.A.* **102 C4** 38 29N 80 18W
Bering Glacier, *AK, U.S.A.* **61 F12** 60 20N 143 30W
Bering Land Bridge Nat. Preserve ⌂, *AK, U.S.A.* **61 C6** 66 20N 165 0W
Bering Strait, *Pac. Oc.* **61 D5** 65 30N 169 0W
Berino, *NM, U.S.A.* **88 E4** 32 4N 106 37W
Berkeley, *CA, U.S.A.* **64 F4** 37 51N 122 16W
Berkeley, *MO, U.S.A.* **117 A2** 38 45N 90 19W
Berkeley County ☆, *SC, U.S.A.* **90 E6** 33 15N 80 0W
Berkeley County ☆, *WV, U.S.A.* **102 B7** 39 27N 77 58W
Berkeley Hills, *San Francisco, U.S.A.* **118 A3** 37 52N 122 14W
Berkeley Springs, *WV, U.S.A.* **77 A2** 39 38N 78 14W
Berkley, *MI, U.S.A.* **109 A1** 43 30N 83 11W
Berks County ☆, *PA, U.S.A.* **95 D6** 40 25N 76 0W
Berkshire County ☆, *MA, U.S.A.* **78 B1** 42 25N 73 15W
Berkshire Hills, *MA, U.S.A.* **78 B1** 42 20N 73 10W
Berland →, *Alta., Canada* **184 D4** 54 0N 116 50W
Berlin = Kitchener, *Ont., Canada* **178 D6** 43 27N 80 29W
Berlin, *CT, U.S.A.* **78 C2** 41 37N 72 45W
Berlin, *GA, U.S.A.* **68 E3** 31 4N 83 37W
Berlin, *MD, U.S.A.* **77 B5** 38 20N 75 13W
Berlin, *ND, U.S.A.* **91 D7** 46 23N 98 29W
Berlin, *NH, U.S.A.* **86 B3** 44 28N 71 11W
Berlin, *NJ, U.S.A.* **87 C2** 39 48N 74 56W
Berlin, *NY, U.S.A.* **78 B1** 42 42N 73 22W
Berlin, *OK, U.S.A.* **93 C4** 35 27N 99 36W
Berlin, *PA, U.S.A.* **95 E4** 39 55N 78 57W
Berlin, *WI, U.S.A.* **103 E5** 43 58N 88 57W
Berlin Heights, *OH, U.S.A.* **92 B4** 41 20N 82 30W
Berlin L., *OH, U.S.A.* **92 B5** 41 3N 81 0W
Bermejillo, *Durango, Mexico* **217 B7** 25 53N 103 37W
Bermen, L., *Qué., Canada* **175 C4** 53 35N 68 55W
Bern, *KS, U.S.A.* **74 B8** 39 58N 95 58W
Bernal, *NM, U.S.A.* **88 B5** 35 24N 105 19W
Bernal Heights, *San Francisco, U.S.A.* **118 B2** 37 44N 122 24W
Bernalillo, *NM, U.S.A.* **88 B4** 35 18N 106 33W
Bernalillo County ☆, *NM, U.S.A.* **88 B4** 35 0N 106 45W
Bernard I., *N.W.T., Canada* **188 B8** 73 36N 124 14W
Bernard L., *Ont., Canada* **178 B7** 45 45N 79 23W
Bernardo, *NM, U.S.A.* **88 C4** 34 25N 106 50W
Bernardston, *MA, U.S.A.* **78 B2** 42 40N 72 33W
Bernardsville, *NJ, U.S.A.* **87 B2** 40 43N 74 34W
Berne, *IN, U.S.A.* **72 C6** 40 39N 84 57W
Bernice, *LA, U.S.A.* **75 B3** 32 49N 92 39W
Bernice, *OK, U.S.A.* **93 B9** 36 34N 94 57W
Bernie, *MO, U.S.A.* **82 E7** 36 40N 89 58W
Bernier B., *N.W.T., Canada* **190 C8** 71 5N 88 15W
Berrien County ☆, *GA, U.S.A.* **68 E3** 31 15N 83 10W
Berrien County ☆, *MI, U.S.A.* **79 H5** 42 0N 86 25W
Berrien Springs, *MI, U.S.A.* **79 H5** 41 57N 86 20W
Berriozábal, *Chiapas, Mexico* **222 C3** 16 48N 93 16W
Berry, *AL, U.S.A.* **60 C3** 33 40N 87 36W
Berry, *KY, U.S.A.* **97 B8** 38 31N 84 23W
Berry Cr. →, *Alta., Canada* **185 H9** 50 50N 111 37W
Berrydale, *FL, U.S.A.* **67 A1** 30 53N 87 3W
Berryessa, L., *CA, U.S.A.* **64 E4** 38 31N 122 6W
Berryville, *AR, U.S.A.* **63 B2** 36 22N 93 34W
Berryville, *VA, U.S.A.* **77 A3** 39 9N 77 59W
Bertha, *MN, U.S.A.* **80 D3** 46 16N 95 4W
Berthierville, *Qué., Canada* **177 E9** 46 5N 73 10W
Berthold, *ND, U.S.A.* **91 B4** 48 19N 101 44W
Berthoud, *CO, U.S.A.* **66 B5** 40 19N 105 5W
Berthoud Pass, *CO, U.S.A.* **66 C5** 39 48N 105 47W
Bertie County ☆, *NC, U.S.A.* **90 B8** 36 0N 77 0W
Bertram, *IA, U.S.A.* **73 D7** 41 57N 91 32W
Bertram, *TX, U.S.A.* **99 G9** 30 45N 98 3W
Bertrand, *N.B., Canada* **173 F4** 47 45N 65 4W
Bertrand, *MI, U.S.A.* **79 H5** 41 47N 86 16W
Bertrand, *MO, U.S.A.* **82 E7** 36 55N 89 27W
Bertrand, *NE, U.S.A.* **84 D6** 40 32N 99 38W
Berwick, *N.B., Canada* **173 H4** 45 47N 65 36W
Berwick, *N.S., Canada* **173 H5** 45 3N 64 44W
Berwick, *LA, U.S.A.* **75 E4** 29 42N 91 13W
Berwick, *ME, U.S.A.* **76 E3** 43 16N 70 52W
Berwick, *ND, U.S.A.* **91 B5** 48 22N 100 15W
Berwick, *PA, U.S.A.* **95 C6** 41 3N 76 14W
Berwyn, *Alta., Canada* **184 B3** 56 9N 117 44W
Berwyn, *IL, U.S.A.* **71 B6** 41 50N 87 47W
Berwyn, *NE, U.S.A.* **84 C6** 41 21N 99 30W
Berwyn Heights, *MD, U.S.A.* **119 B4** 38 59N 76 55W
Beryl, *UT, U.S.A.* **100 F2** 37 54N 113 40W
Bessemer, *AL, U.S.A.* **60 C4** 33 24N 86 58W
Bessemer, *MI, U.S.A.* **79 C1** 46 29N 90 3W
Bessemer, *PA, U.S.A.* **95 D2** 40 59N 80 30W
Bessemer City, *NC, U.S.A.* **90 C4** 35 17N 81 17W
Bessie, *OK, U.S.A.* **93 C4** 35 23N 98 59W
Bessie, L., *Orlando, U.S.A.* **115 B1** 28 29N 81 31W
Best, *TX, U.S.A.* **98 F6** 31 13N 101 37W
Bethalto, *IL, U.S.A.* **71 E3** 38 55N 90 2W
Bethany, *Ont., Canada* **179 C8** 44 11N 78 34W
Bethany, *IL, U.S.A.* **71 D5** 39 39N 88 45W
Bethany, *MO, U.S.A.* **82 A2** 40 16N 94 2W
Bethany, *OK, U.S.A.* **93 C6** 35 31N 97 38W
Bethany Beach, *DE, U.S.A.* **77 B5** 38 32N 75 5W
Bethel, *AK, U.S.A.* **61 F7** 60 48N 161 45W
Bethel, *CT, U.S.A.* **78 C1** 41 22N 73 25W
Bethel, *ME, U.S.A.* **76 D3** 44 25N 70 47W
Bethel, *MN, U.S.A.* **80 E5** 45 24N 93 16W
Bethel, *NC, U.S.A.* **90 C8** 35 48N 77 22W
Bethel, *OH, U.S.A.* **92 E2** 38 58N 84 5W
Bethel, *OK, U.S.A.* **93 D9** 34 22N 94 51W
Bethel, *PA, U.S.A.* **95 D6** 40 28N 76 18W
Bethel, *Seattle, U.S.A.* **118 D2** 47 29N 122 37W
Bethel, *VT, U.S.A.* **86 C2** 43 50N 72 38W
Bethel ☆, *AK, U.S.A.* **61 F7** 60 45N 160 30W
Bethel Acres, *OK, U.S.A.* **93 C6** 35 22N 97 3W
Bethel Park, *PA, U.S.A.* **95 D2** 40 19N 80 2W
Bethel Springs, *TN, U.S.A.* **96 E4** 35 14N 88 36W
Bethesda, *MD, U.S.A.* **77 B3** 38 59N 77 6W
Bethesda, *NC, U.S.A.* **90 C7** 35 57N 78 50W
Bethesda, *OH, U.S.A.* **92 C5** 40 1N 81 4W
Bethlehem, *CT, U.S.A.* **78 C1** 41 38N 73 13W
Bethlehem, *MD, U.S.A.* **77 B5** 38 45N 75 57W
Bethlehem, *NC, U.S.A.* **90 C4** 35 50N 81 18W
Bethlehem, *NH, U.S.A.* **86 B3** 44 17N 71 41W
Bethlehem, *PA, U.S.A.* **87 B1** 40 37N 75 23W
Bethpage, *NY, U.S.A.* **87 B3** 40 44N 73 30W

Bethune, *Sask., Canada* **182 E6** 50 43N 105 13W
Bethune, *CO, U.S.A.* **66 C8** 39 18N 102 26W
Betsiamites, *Qué., Canada* **177 C14** 48 56N 68 40W
Betsiamites →, *Qué., Canada* **177 C14** 48 56N 68 38W
Betsie, Pt., *MI, U.S.A.* **79 E5** 44 41N 86 15W
Bettendorf, *IA, U.S.A.* **73 D8** 41 32N 90 30W
Betterton, *MD, U.S.A.* **77 A4** 39 22N 76 4W
Beulah, *CO, U.S.A.* **66 D6** 38 5N 104 59W
Beulah, *MI, U.S.A.* **79 E5** 44 38N 86 6W
Beulah, *ND, U.S.A.* **91 C4** 47 16N 101 47W
Beulah, *Orlando, U.S.A.* **115 A1** 28 32N 81 34W
Beulah, *WY, U.S.A.* **104 B8** 44 33N 104 5W
Beulah, L., *Orlando, U.S.A.* **115 A1** 28 32N 81 33W
Beulah Res., *OR, U.S.A.* **94 D7** 43 55N 118 9W
Beulahville, *NC, U.S.A.* **90 D8** 34 55N 77 46W
Beulahville, *VA, U.S.A.* **77 C3** 37 51N 77 11W
Beverly, *Chicago, U.S.A.* **108 C3** 41 42N 87 39W
Beverly, *KS, U.S.A.* **74 B6** 39 1N 97 58W
Beverly, *MA, U.S.A.* **78 B4** 42 33N 70 53W
Beverly, *WV, U.S.A.* **102 C5** 38 51N 79 53W
Beverly, *WA, U.S.A.* **101 D6** 46 50N 119 56W
Beverly Beach, *MD, U.S.A.* **77 B4** 38 53N 76 31W
Beverly Glen, *Los Angeles, U.S.A.* **111 B2** 34 6N 118 26W
Beverly Hills, *CA, U.S.A.* **65 J8** 34 5N 118 24W
Beverly Hills, *FL, U.S.A.* **67 C6** 28 55N 82 28W
Beverly Hills, *MO, U.S.A.* **117 A2** 38 42N 90 19W
Beverly L., *Nunavut, Canada* **191 E5** 64 36N 100 30W
Bevier, *MO, U.S.A.* **82 B4** 39 45N 92 34W
Bewdley, *Ont., Canada* **179 C8** 44 5N 78 19W
Bexar, *AL, U.S.A.* **60 B2** 34 11N 88 9W
Bexar County ☆, *TX, U.S.A.* **99 H9** 29 25N 98 30W
Bibb County ☆, *AL, U.S.A.* **60 D3** 32 57N 87 8W
Bibb County ☆, *GA, U.S.A.* **68 D3** 32 50N 83 45W
Bibby I., *Nunavut, Canada* **191 E7** 61 55N 93 0W
Bic, Île du, *Qué., Canada* **177 C14** 48 24N 68 52W
Biche, L. la, *Alta., Canada* **184 D8** 54 50N 112 3W
Bickerton West, *N.S., Canada* **173 H8** 45 6N 61 44W
Bicknell, *IN, U.S.A.* **72 E3** 38 47N 87 19W
Bicknell, *UT, U.S.A.* **100 E4** 38 20N 111 33W
Biddeford, *ME, U.S.A.* **76 E3** 43 30N 70 28W
Bieber, *CA, U.S.A.* **64 B5** 41 7N 121 8W
Bieler L., *Nunavut, Canada* **190 C11** 70 23N 73 5W
Bienfait, *Sask., Canada* **182 F9** 49 10N 102 50W
Bienville, *LA, U.S.A.* **75 B3** 32 22N 92 59W
Bienville, L., *Qué., Canada* **175 B3** 55 5N 72 40W
Bienville Nat. Forest, *MS, U.S.A.* **81 D4** 32 10N 89 25W
Bienville Parish ☆, *LA, U.S.A.* **75 B2** 32 20N 93 0W
Big →, *Nfld. & L., Canada* **175 C6** 54 50N 58 55W
Big →, *MO, U.S.A.* **82 C6** 38 28N 90 37W
Big Antelope Cr. →, *OR, U.S.A.* **94 E8** 42 28N 117 13W
Big B., *Nfld. & L., Canada* **175 B5** 55 43N 60 35W
Big Baldy, *ID, U.S.A.* **70 E3** 44 47N 115 13W
Big Baldy Mountain, *MT, U.S.A.* **83 D7** 46 59N 110 39W
Big Bar, *CA, U.S.A.* **64 C3** 40 45N 123 15W
Big Bar Creek, *B.C., Canada* **187 D12** 51 12N 122 7W
Big Bass, *Tamaulipas, Mexico* **215 F6** 24 2N 98 41W
Big Basswood L., *Ont., Canada* **178 A3** 46 25N 83 23W
Big Bay, *MI, U.S.A.* **79 C4** 46 49N 87 44W
Big Bay de Noc, *MI, U.S.A.* **79 D5** 45 45N 86 40W
Big Bear City, *CA, U.S.A.* **65 J10** 34 16N 116 51W
Big Bear Lake, *CA, U.S.A.* **65 J10** 34 15N 116 56W
Big Beaver, *Sask., Canada* **182 F6** 49 10N 105 10W
Big Belt Mts., *MT, U.S.A.* **83 D6** 46 30N 111 25W
Big Bend, *CA, U.S.A.* **64 B5** 41 1N 121 55W
Big Bend Dam, *SD, U.S.A.* **91 F6** 44 1N 99 23W
Big Bend Nat. Park ⌂, *TX, U.S.A.* **98 H4** 29 20N 103 5W
Big Black →, *MS, U.S.A.* **81 D2** 32 3N 91 4W
Big Blue →, *KS, U.S.A.* **74 B7** 39 35N 96 34W
Big Boggy Nat. Wildlife Refuge ⌂, *TX, U.S.A.* **99 J12** 28 17N 95 52W
Big Bow, *KS, U.S.A.* **74 D2** 37 34N 101 34W
Big Cabin, *OK, U.S.A.* **93 B8** 36 32N 95 14W
Big Canyon →, *TX, U.S.A.* **98 H6** 29 45N 101 48W
Big Chino Wash →, *AZ, U.S.A.* **62 C3** 34 52N 112 28W
Big Clifty, *KY, U.S.A.* **96 C6** 37 33N 86 9W
Big Coal →, *WV, U.S.A.* **102 C3** 38 16N 81 48W
Big Cr. →, *B.C., Canada* **187 D12** 51 42N 122 41W
Big Cr. →, *LA, U.S.A.* **75 B4** 32 10N 91 53W
Big Creek, *B.C., Canada* **187 D11** 51 43N 123 2W
Big Creek, *ID, U.S.A.* **70 D3** 45 8N 115 20W
Big Creek L., *AL, U.S.A.* **60 F2** 30 43N 88 20W
Big Creek Park ⌂, *B.C., Canada* **187 D11** 51 18N 123 10W
Big Creek Reservation, *Cleveland, U.S.A.* **107 B1** 41 26N 81 45W
Big Cypress Indian Reservation, *FL, U.S.A.* **67 E8** 26 18N 81 0W
Big Cypress Nat. Preserve ⌂, *FL, U.S.A.* **67 F7** 26 0N 81 10W
Big Darby Cr. →, *OH, U.S.A.* **92 D4** 39 37N 82 58W
Big Delta, *AK, U.S.A.* **61 D11** 64 10N 145 51W
Big Dry Creek, *MT, U.S.A.* **83 C11** 47 31N 106 17W
Big Eau Pleine Res., *WI, U.S.A.* **103 D4** 44 44N 89 46W
Big Falls, *MN, U.S.A.* **80 B5** 48 12N 93 48W
Big Falls, *WI, U.S.A.* **103 D4** 44 37N 89 1W
Big Flat, *AR, U.S.A.* **63 B3** 36 1N 92 24W
Big Fork →, *MN, U.S.A.* **80 B5** 48 31N 93 43W
Big Hatchet Peak, *NM, U.S.A.* **88 F2** 31 38N 108 24W
Big Hill, *NE, U.S.A.* **84 B3** 42 23N 102 5W
Big Hole →, *MT, U.S.A.* **83 E5** 45 34N 112 20W
Big Hole Nat. Battlefield-Nez Perce Nat. Historic Park ⌂, *MT, U.S.A.* **83 E4** 45 39N 113 39W
Big Horn, *WY, U.S.A.* **104 B6** 44 41N 106 59W
Big Horn County ☆, *MT, U.S.A.* **83 E10** 45 25N 107 45W
Big Horn County ☆, *WY, U.S.A.* **104 B4** 44 45N 108 0W
Big Horn Dam, *Alta., Canada* **185 F4** 52 20N 116 20W
Big Horn Mts. = Bighorn Mts., *WY, U.S.A.* **104 B6** 44 25N 107 0W
Big I., *Nunavut, Canada* **191 E11** 62 43N 70 43W
Big I., *Ont., Canada* **180 C2** 49 9N 94 40W
Big Island, *VA, U.S.A.* **102 D5** 37 32N 79 22W
Big L., *CA, U.S.A.* **64 B5** 41 7N 121 25W
Big L., *ME, U.S.A.* **76 C6** 45 11N 67 41W
Big Lake, *AK, U.S.A.* **61 F10** 61 20N 150 20W
Big Lake, *MN, U.S.A.* **80 E5** 45 20N 93 45W
Big Lake, *TX, U.S.A.* **98 F6** 31 12N 101 28W
Big Lake Nat. Wildlife Refuge ⌂, *AR, U.S.A.* **63 C5** 35 54N 90 7W
Big Lookout Mt., *OR, U.S.A.* **94 C8** 44 36N 117 17W
Big Lost →, *ID, U.S.A.* **70 F6** 43 50N 112 44W
Big Muddy →, *IL, U.S.A.* **71 F4** 37 33N 89 32W
Big Muddy Cr. →, *MT, U.S.A.* **83 B13** 48 8N 104 36W
Big Muddy Cr. →, *ND, U.S.A.* **91 D4** 46 37N 101 24W
Big Muddy L., *Sask., Canada* **182 F7** 49 10N 104 51W
Big Nemaha →, *NE, U.S.A.* **84 D10** 40 1N 95 32W
Big Oak Nat. Wildlife Refuge ⌂, *IN, U.S.A.* **72 E5** 38 56N 85 26W
Big Otter →, *VA, U.S.A.* **102 D5** 37 7N 79 23W
Big Pine, *CA, U.S.A.* **65 F8** 37 10N 118 17W
Big Pine Key, *FL, U.S.A.* **67 G7** 24 40N 81 21W
Big Piney, *WY, U.S.A.* **104 D2** 42 32N 110 7W
Big Pond, *N.S., Canada* **173 H9** 45 48N 60 32W
Big Quill L., *Sask., Canada* **182 D7** 51 55N 104 50W
Big Rapids, *MI, U.S.A.* **79 F6** 43 42N 85 29W
Big Rib →, *WI, U.S.A.* **103 D4** 44 56N 89 41W
Big Rideau L., *Ont., Canada* **179 C10** 44 40N 76 15W
Big River, *Sask., Canada* **182 B4** 53 50N 107 0W
Big Rock, *TN, U.S.A.* **96 D5** 36 35N 87 46W
Big Sable Pt., *MI, U.S.A.* **79 E5** 44 3N 86 1W
Big Sage Res., *CA, U.S.A.* **64 B6** 41 35N 120 38W
Big Salmon →, *Yukon, Canada* **189 D6** 61 52N 134 55W
Big Salmon Range, *Yukon, Canada* **189 D6** 61 10N 133 45W
Big Sand L., *Man., Canada* **191 F6** 57 45N 99 45W
Big Sand Lake, *Orlando, U.S.A.* **115 B2** 28 25N 81 29W
Big Sandy, *MT, U.S.A.* **83 B7** 48 11N 110 7W
Big Sandy, *TN, U.S.A.* **96 D4** 36 14N 88 5W
Big Sandy, *TX, U.S.A.* **99 E12** 32 35N 95 7W
Big Sandy, *WY, U.S.A.* **104 D3** 42 38N 109 28W
Big Sandy →, *U.S.A.* **97 B10** 38 25N 82 36W
Big Sandy →, *AZ, U.S.A.* **62 C2** 34 19N 113 31W
Big Sandy →, *TN, U.S.A.* **96 D4** 36 14N 88 5W
Big Sandy Cr. = Sandy Cr. →, *WY, U.S.A.* **104 E3** 41 51N 109 47W
Big Sandy Cr. →, *CO, U.S.A.* **66 D8** 38 7N 102 29W
Big Sandy Cr. →, *MT, U.S.A.* **83 B8** 48 34N 109 48W
Big Sandy Cr. →, *NE, U.S.A.* **84 D8** 40 13N 97 18W
Big Sandy L., *Sask., Canada* **182 A7** 54 27N 104 6W
Big Sandy L., *MN, U.S.A.* **80 D5** 46 46N 93 17W
Big Sandy Res., *WY, U.S.A.* **104 D3** 42 15N 109 26W
Big Satilla Cr. →, *GA, U.S.A.* **68 E4** 31 27N 82 3W
Big Sheep Mt., *MT, U.S.A.* **83 C12** 47 10N 105 40W
Big Sioux →, *SD, U.S.A.* **91 H9** 42 29N 96 27W
Big Sky, *MT, U.S.A.* **83 E6** 45 17N 111 22W
Big Smoky Valley, *NV, U.S.A.* **85 D3** 38 30N 117 10W
Big Snowy Mts., *MT, U.S.A.* **83 D8** 46 45N 109 30W
Big South Fork Nat. River and Recr. Area ⌂, *TN, U.S.A.* **55 G3** 36 27N 84 47W
Big Southern Butte, *ID, U.S.A.* **70 F5** 43 23N 113 1W
Big Spring, *KY, U.S.A.* **96 C6** 37 48N 86 9W
Big Spring, *TX, U.S.A.* **98 E6** 32 15N 101 28W
Big Springs, *NE, U.S.A.* **84 C3** 41 4N 102 5W
Big Stone City, *SD, U.S.A.* **91 E9** 45 18N 96 28W
Big Stone County ☆, *MN, U.S.A.* **80 E2** 45 25N 96 15W
Big Stone Gap, *VA, U.S.A.* **102 E2** 36 52N 82 47W
Big Stone L., *MN, U.S.A.* **80 E2** 45 18N 96 27W
Big Stone Nat. Wildlife Refuge ⌂, *MN, U.S.A.* **80 E2** 45 12N 96 4W
Big Sunflower →, *MS, U.S.A.* **81 D3** 32 40N 90 40W
Big Sur, *CA, U.S.A.* **64 G5** 36 15N 121 48W
Big Swamp →, *NC, U.S.A.* **90 D7** 34 28N 78 57W
Big Thicket Nat. Preserve ⌂, *TX, U.S.A.* **99 G13** 30 12N 94 7W
Big Timber, *MT, U.S.A.* **83 E8** 45 50N 109 57W
Big Trails, *WY, U.S.A.* **104 C5** 43 46N 107 19W
Big Trout L., *Ont., Canada* **179 B8** 45 46N 78 37W
Big Trout L., *Ont., Canada* **191 G7** 53 40N 90 0W
Big Trout Lake, *Ont., Canada* **191 G8** 53 45N 90 0W
Big Valley, *Alta., Canada* **185 F8** 52 2N 112 46W
Big Water, *UT, U.S.A.* **100 F4** 37 5N 111 40W
Big Wells, *TX, U.S.A.* **99 J8** 28 34N 99 34W
Big Wills Cr. →, *AL, U.S.A.* **60 C5** 33 59N 86 0W
Big Wood →, *ID, U.S.A.* **70 G4** 42 52N 114 54W
Bigelow, *AR, U.S.A.* **63 C3** 35 0N 92 38W
Bigelow, *MN, U.S.A.* **80 G3** 43 30N 95 42W
Bigfork, *MN, U.S.A.* **80 C5** 47 45N 93 39W
Bigfork, *MT, U.S.A.* **83 B3** 48 4N 114 4W
Biggar, *Sask., Canada* **182 C4** 52 4N 108 0W
Biggs, *CA, U.S.A.* **64 D5** 39 25N 121 43W
Biggs, *OR, U.S.A.* **94 B5** 45 40N 120 50W
Biggsville, *IL, U.S.A.* **71 C3** 40 51N 90 52W
Bighorn, *MT, U.S.A.* **83 D10** 46 10N 107 27W
Bighorn →, *MT, U.S.A.* **83 D10** 46 10N 107 28W
Bighorn Basin, *WY, U.S.A.* **104 B6** 44 15N 108 0W
Bighorn Canyon Nat. Recr. Area ⌂, *MT, U.S.A.* **83 E9** 45 10N 108 0W
Bighorn L., *U.S.A.* **104 B4** 44 55N 108 15W
Bighorn Mts., *WY, U.S.A.* **104 B6** 44 25N 107 0W
Bighorn Nat. Forest, *WY, U.S.A.* **104 B5** 44 50N 107 25W
Biglerville, *PA, U.S.A.* **95 E5** 39 56N 77 15W
Bigniba →, *Qué., Canada* **176 B5** 49 18N 77 20W
Bigot, L., *Qué., Canada* **172 C4** 50 50N 65 39W
Bigpoint, *MS, U.S.A.* **81 F5** 30 35N 88 29W
Bigsby I, *Ont., Canada* **180 C2** 49 4N 94 34W
Bigstick L., *Sask., Canada* **182 E2** 50 16N 109 20W
Bigstone L., *Man., Canada* **183 B16** 53 42N 95 44W
Bijou Cr. →, *CO, U.S.A.* **66 B6** 40 17N 104 0W
Bilk Creek Mts., *NV, U.S.A.* **85 A2** 41 50N 118 27W
Bill, *WY, U.S.A.* **104 C7** 43 14N 105 16W
Bill Baggs Cape Florida State Recr. Area ⌂, *Miami, U.S.A.* **112 D3** 25 40N 80 9W
Bill Williams →, *AZ, U.S.A.* **62 C1** 34 18N 114 4W
Bill Williams Mt., *AZ, U.S.A.* **62 B3** 35 12N 112 12W
Bill Williams River Nat. Wildlife Refuge ⌂, *AZ, U.S.A.* **62 C1** 34 20N 114 5W
Billerica, *MA, U.S.A.* **78 B3** 42 34N 71 16W
Billete, Cerro el, *Guerrero, Mexico* **219 D6** 18 11N 101 18W
Billings, *MO, U.S.A.* **82 D3** 37 4N 93 33W
Billings, *MT, U.S.A.* **83 E9** 45 47N 108 30W
Billings, *OK, U.S.A.* **93 B6** 36 32N 97 27W
Billings County ☆, *ND, U.S.A.* **91 C2** 47 0N 103 15W
Billingsley, *AL, U.S.A.* **60 D4** 32 40N 86 43W
Billy Chinook, L., *OR, U.S.A.* **94 C4** 44 36N 121 17W
Billy Clapp L., *WA, U.S.A.* **101 C6** 47 29N 119 20W
Biloxi, *MS, U.S.A.* **81 F5** 30 24N 88 53W
Biltmore Forest, *NC, U.S.A.* **90 C3** 35 34N 82 33W
Binford, *ND, U.S.A.* **91 C7** 47 34N 98 21W
Bingen, *WA, U.S.A.* **101 E4** 45 43N 121 28W
Binger, *OK, U.S.A.* **93 C5** 35 18N 98 21W
Bingham, *ME, U.S.A.* **76 C4** 45 3N 69 53W
Bingham, *NM, U.S.A.* **88 D4** 33 55N 106 21W
Bingham, *NE, U.S.A.* **84 B3** 42 1N 102 5W
Bingham Canyon, *UT, U.S.A.* **100 C3** 40 32N 112 9W
Bingham County ☆, *ID, U.S.A.* **70 F6** 43 15N 112 30W
Binghamton, *NY, U.S.A.* **89 C5** 42 6N 75 55W
Binscarth, *Man., Canada* **183 E10** 50 37N 101 17W
Biola, *CA, U.S.A.* **65 G6** 36 48N 120 1W
Birch →, *Alta., Canada* **189 E10** 58 28N 112 17W
Birch Bay, *WA, U.S.A.* **101 B3** 48 55N 122 45W
Birch Cr. →, *ID, U.S.A.* **70 F6** 43 51N 112 43W
Birch Hills, *Sask., Canada* **182 C6** 52 59N 105 25W
Birch I., *Man., Canada* **183 C12** 52 26N 99 54W
Birch Island, *B.C., Canada* **187 D15** 51 37N 119 54W
Birch L., *Alta., Canada* **184 E9** 53 19N 111 35W
Birch L., *Ont., Canada* **180 A4** 51 23N 92 18W
Birch L., *Sask., Canada* **182 B3** 53 27N 108 10W
Birch L., *MN, U.S.A.* **80 C7** 47 45N 91 51W
Birch L., *OK, U.S.A.* **93 B7** 36 30N 96 27W
Birch Lake, *Minneapolis-St. Paul, U.S.A.* **113 A3** 45 4N 93 2W
Birch Mts., *Alta., Canada* **189 E10** 57 30N 113 10W
Birch River, *Man., Canada* **183 C10** 52 24N 101 6W
Birch Run, *MI, U.S.A.* **79 F8** 43 15N 83 48W
Birch Tree, *MO, U.S.A.* **82 E5** 36 59N 91 30W
Birchwood, *AK, U.S.A.* **61 F10** 61 24N 149 28W
Birchwood, *WI, U.S.A.* **103 C2** 45 40N 91 33W
Birchwood Village, *Minneapolis-St. Paul, U.S.A.* **113 A4** 45 3N 92 58W
Birchy Bay, *Nfld. & L., Canada* **174 C6** 49 21N 54 44W
Bird City, *KS, U.S.A.* **74 B2** 39 45N 101 32W
Bird Cove, *Nfld. & L., Canada* **174 A4** 51 3N 56 56W
Bird Island, *MN, U.S.A.* **80 F4** 44 46N 94 54W
Birds, *IL, U.S.A.* **71 E6** 38 50N 87 40W
Birdsboro, *PA, U.S.A.* **87 B1** 40 16N 75 48W
Birdseye, *IN, U.S.A.* **72 E4** 38 19N 86 42W
Birdsville, *MD, U.S.A.* **77 B4** 38 54N 76 36W
Birken, *B.C., Canada* **187 E12** 50 28N 122 37W
Birkenhead Lake Park ⌂, *B.C., Canada* **187 E12** 50 35N 122 45W
Birmingham, *AL, U.S.A.* **60 C4** 33 31N 86 48W
Birmingham, *IA, U.S.A.* **73 E7** 40 53N 91 57W
Birmingham ✕ (BHM), *AL, U.S.A.* **60 C4** 33 34N 86 45W
Birnamwood, *WI, U.S.A.* **103 D4** 44 56N 89 13W
Biron, *Qué., Canada* **172 E3** 48 12N 66 16W
Birsay, *Sask., Canada* **182 D5** 51 6N 106 59W
Birtle, *Man., Canada* **183 E10** 50 30N 101 5W
Bisbee, *AZ, U.S.A.* **62 F6** 31 27N 109 55W
Bisbee, *ND, U.S.A.* **91 B6** 48 37N 99 23W
Biscay, *MN, U.S.A.* **80 F4** 44 50N 94 16W
Biscayne, Key, *FL, U.S.A.* **67 F8** 25 42N 80 10W
Biscayne B., *FL, U.S.A.* **67 F8** 25 40N 80 12W
Biscayne Bay Aquatic Reserve, *Miami, U.S.A.* **112 D1** 25 33N 80 13W
Biscayne Nat. Park ⌂, *FL, U.S.A.* **67 F8** 25 25N 80 12W
Biscayne Park, *Miami, U.S.A.* **112 C2** 25 52N 80 10W
Biscoe, *AR, U.S.A.* **63 D4** 34 49N 91 25W
Biscoe, *NC, U.S.A.* **90 C6** 35 22N 79 47W
Biscotasi L., *Ont., Canada* **181 E14** 47 22N 82 1W
Biscotasing, *Ont., Canada* **181 E14** 47 18N 82 9W
Bishop, *CA, U.S.A.* **65 F8** 37 22N 118 24W
Bishop, *GA, U.S.A.* **68 C3** 33 49N 83 26W
Bishop, *TX, U.S.A.* **98 K10** 27 35N 97 48W
Bishop Creek Res., *NV, U.S.A.* **85 A6** 41 15N 114 55W
Bishop Museum, *HI, U.S.A.* **69 K14** 21 20N 157 52W
Bishop River Park ⌂, *B.C., Canada* **186 E10** 50 55N 124 2W
Bishop's Falls, *Nfld. & L., Canada* **174 C5** 49 2N 55 30W
Bishops Head, *MD, U.S.A.* **77 B4** 38 16N 76 5W
Bishopville, *MD, U.S.A.* **77 B5** 38 22N 75 12W
Bishopville, *SC, U.S.A.* **90 D5** 34 13N 80 15W
Bismarck, *AR, U.S.A.* **63 D2** 34 19N 93 10W
Bismarck, *IL, U.S.A.* **71 C6** 40 16N 87 37W
Bismarck, *MO, U.S.A.* **82 D6** 37 46N 90 38W
Bismarck, *ND, U.S.A.* **91 D5** 46 48N 100 47W
Bison, *KS, U.S.A.* **74 C4** 38 31N 99 12W
Bison, *OK, U.S.A.* **93 B6** 36 12N 97 53W
Bison, *SD, U.S.A.* **91 E3** 45 31N 102 28W
Bison L., *Alta., Canada* **184 A4** 57 12N 116 8W
Bissett, *Man., Canada* **183 D16** 51 2N 95 41W
Bistcho L., *Alta., Canada* **189 E9** 59 45N 118 50W
Bistineau, L., *LA, U.S.A.* **75 B2** 32 20N 93 25W
Bitely, *MI, U.S.A.* **79 F6** 43 45N 85 52W
Bithlo, *FL, U.S.A.* **67 C7** 28 33N 81 6W
Bitter Cr. →, *UT, U.S.A.* **100 D6** 39 59N 109 19W
Bitter Cr. →, *WY, U.S.A.* **104 E3** 41 31N 109 27W
Bitter Creek, *WY, U.S.A.* **104 E4** 41 33N 108 33W
Bitter L., *Sask., Canada* **182 E2** 50 7N 109 48W
Bitter L., *SD, U.S.A.* **91 E8** 45 17N 97 19W
Bittern L., *Alta., Canada* **185 E7** 53 3N 113 5W
Bittern L., *Sask., Canada* **182 B6** 53 56N 105 45W
Bitterroot →, *MT, U.S.A.* **83 D3** 46 52N 114 7W
Bitterroot Nat. Forest, *ID, U.S.A.* **83 E3** 45 52N 114 10W
Bitterroot Range, *ID, U.S.A.* **70 D4** 46 0N 114 20W
Bittinger, *MD, U.S.A.* **77 A1** 39 37N 79 14W
Biwabik, *MN, U.S.A.* **80 C6** 47 32N 92 21W
Bixby, *MO, U.S.A.* **82 D5** 37 40N 91 7W
Bixby, *OK, U.S.A.* **93 C8** 35 57N 95 53W
Bizard, Île, *Qué., Canada* **192 B1** 45 29N 73 54W
Bjorkdale, *Sask., Canada* **182 C8** 52 43N 103 39W
Bjorne Pen., *Nunavut, Canada* **190 B8** 77 37N 87 0W
Blache, L. de la, *Qué., Canada* **177 A13** 50 5N 69 29W
Black →, *Ont., Canada* **178 C7** 44 42N 79 19W
Black →, *AK, U.S.A.* **61 C11** 66 42N 144 42W
Black →, *AZ, U.S.A.* **62 D5** 33 44N 110 13W
Black →, *AR, U.S.A.* **63 C4** 35 38N 91 20W
Black →, *LA, U.S.A.* **75 C4** 31 16N 91 50W
Black →, *MI, U.S.A.* **79 D7** 45 39N 84 31W
Black →, *MI, U.S.A.* **79 G9** 42 59N 82 27W
Black →, *NC, U.S.A.* **90 D7** 34 35N 78 16W
Black →, *NY, U.S.A.* **89 B4** 43 59N 76 4W
Black →, *SC, U.S.A.* **90 E6** 33 24N 79 15W
Black →, *VT, U.S.A.* **86 B2** 44 55N 72 13W
Black →, *VT, U.S.A.* **86 C2** 43 16N 72 27W
Black →, *WI, U.S.A.* **103 E2** 43 57N 91 22W
Black B., *Ont., Canada* **180 D8** 48 40N 88 25W
Black Bay Pen., *Ont., Canada* **180 D8** 48 38N 88 21W
Black Bear Cr. →, *OK, U.S.A.* **93 B7** 36 25N 96 38W
Black Butte L., *CA, U.S.A.* **64 D4** 39 49N 122 20W
Black Canyon City, *AZ, U.S.A.* **62 C3** 34 3N 112 5W
Black Canyon of the Gunnison Nat. Park ⌂, *CO, U.S.A.* **66 D3** 38 40N 107 35W
Black Cr. →, *AZ, U.S.A.* **62 B6** 35 16N 109 14W
Black Cr. →, *MS, U.S.A.* **81 F5** 30 39N 88 39W
Black Cr. →, *SC, U.S.A.* **90 D6** 34 18N 79 37W
Black Creek, *B.C., Canada* **186 F9** 49 49N 125 7W
Black Creek, *B.C., Canada* **187 C13** 52 18N 121 6W
Black Creek, *NC, U.S.A.* **90 C8** 35 38N 77 56W
Black Creek, *WI, U.S.A.* **103 D5** 44 29N 88 27W
Black Diamond = Pittsburg, *CA, U.S.A.* **64 E5** 38 2N 121 53W
Black Diamond, *Alta., Canada* **185 H6** 50 45N 114 14W
Black Diamond, *WA, U.S.A.* **101 C4** 47 19N 122 0W
Black Duck →, *Ont., Canada* **191 F8** 56 51N 89 2W
Black Earth, *WI, U.S.A.* **103 E4** 43 8N 89 45W
Black Forest, *CO, U.S.A.* **66 C6** 39 0N 104 43W
Black Hawk, *CO, U.S.A.* **66 C5** 39 48N 105 30W
Black Hawk, *SD, U.S.A.* **91 F2** 44 9N 103 19W
Black Hawk County ☆, *IA, U.S.A.* **73 C6** 42 25N 92 20W
Black Hills, *SD, U.S.A.* **91 F2** 44 0N 103 45W
Black Hills Nat. Forest, *SD, U.S.A.* **91 F2** 44 10N 103 50W
Black Hills Nat. Forest, *WY, U.S.A.* **104 C9** 44 35N 104 25W
Black I., *Man., Canada* **183 D15** 51 12N 96 30W
Black Jack, *MO, U.S.A.* **117 A2** 38 47N 90 16W
Black Kettle Nat. Grassland, *OK, U.S.A.* **93 C4** 35 45N 99 45W
Black L., *Sask., Canada* **189 E11** 59 12N 105 15W
Black L., *LA, U.S.A.* **75 C2** 31 57N 93 3W
Black L., *MI, U.S.A.* **79 D7** 45 28N 84 16W
Black L., *NY, U.S.A.* **89 A5** 44 31N 75 36W
Black Lake, *Qué., Canada* **177 E11** 46 1N 71 22W
Black Lake, *Sask., Canada* **189 E11** 59 11N 105 20W
Black Mesa, *AZ, U.S.A.* **62 A5** 36 30N 110 15W
Black Mesa, *OK, U.S.A.* **93 B1** 36 58N 102 58W
Black Mountain, *NC, U.S.A.* **90 C3** 35 37N 82 19W
Black Mt., *KY, U.S.A.* **97 D10** 36 54N 82 54W
Black Mt., *Las Vegas, U.S.A.* **110 D2** 35 55N 115 2W
Black Mt., *NM, U.S.A.* **88 D2** 33 23N 108 14W
Black Mt., *OR, U.S.A.* **94 B6** 45 13N 119 17W
Black Mt., *TX, U.S.A.* **98 H7** 29 38N 100 20W
Black Mts., *AZ, U.S.A.* **62 B1** 35 30N 114 30W
Black Pine Pk., *ID, U.S.A.* **70 G5** 42 8N 113 8W
Black Range, *NM, U.S.A.* **88 D3** 33 15N 107 50W
Black River, *NY, U.S.A.* **89 A5** 44 1N 75 48W
Black River Falls, *WI, U.S.A.* **103 D3** 44 18N 90 51W
Black Rock, *AR, U.S.A.* **63 B4** 36 7N 91 6W
Black Rock, *NM, U.S.A.* **88 B2** 35 5N 108 47W
Black Rock Desert, *NV, U.S.A.* **85 A2** 41 10N 118 50W
Black Rock Pt., *Nfld. & L., Canada* **175 A5** 60 2N 64 10W
Black Rock Range, *NV, U.S.A.* **85 A1** 41 20N 119 8W
Black Springs, *NV, U.S.A.* **85 C1** 39 37N 119 51W
Black Squirrel Cr. →, *CO, U.S.A.* **66 D6** 38 14N 104 21W
Black Sturgeon L., *Ont., Canada* **180 C8** 49 20N 88 53W
Black Warrior →, *AL, U.S.A.* **60 D3** 32 32N 87 51W
Blackbeard Island Nat. Wildlife Refuge ⌂, *GA, U.S.A.* **68 E5** 31 30N 81 12W
Blackbird, *DE, U.S.A.* **77 A5** 39 21N 75 40W
Blackburn, *MO, U.S.A.* **82 B3** 39 6N 93 29W
Blackburn, *OK, U.S.A.* **93 B7** 36 23N 96 38W
Blackburn, Mt., *AK, U.S.A.* **61 F12** 61 44N 143 26W
Blackduck, *MN, U.S.A.* **80 C4** 47 44N 94 33W
Blackfalds, *Alta., Canada* **185 F7** 52 23N 113 47W
Blackfeet Indian Reservation, *MT, U.S.A.* **83 B5** 48 45N 113 0W
Blackfoot, *Alta., Canada* **184 E10** 53 17N 110 10W
Blackfoot, *ID, U.S.A.* **70 F6** 43 11N 112 21W
Blackfoot →, *ID, U.S.A.* **70 F6** 43 8N 112 30W
Blackfoot →, *MT, U.S.A.* **83 D4** 46 52N 113 53W
Blackfoot Res., *ID, U.S.A.* **70 G7** 42 55N 111 39W
Blackfoot Res., *ID, U.S.A.* **70 G7** 43 0N 111 43W
Blackford, *KY, U.S.A.* **96 C5** 37 27N 87 56W
Blackford County ☆, *IN, U.S.A.* **72 C5** 40 30N 85 20W
Blackhall Mt., *WY, U.S.A.* **104 E6** 41 2N 106 41W
Blackhead, *Nfld. & L., Canada* **174 E8** 47 32N 52 39W
Blackhead Road, *Nfld. & L., Canada* **174 E8** 47 33N 52 43W
Blackman, *FL, U.S.A.* **67 A2** 30 56N 86 38W
Blacks Fork →, *WY, U.S.A.* **104 E3** 41 25N 109 37W
Blacks Harbour, *N.B., Canada* **173 H3** 45 3N 66 49W
Blacksburg, *SC, U.S.A.* **90 C4** 35 7N 81 31W
Blacksburg, *VA, U.S.A.* **102 D4** 37 14N 80 25W
Blackshear, *GA, U.S.A.* **68 E4** 31 18N 82 14W
Blackshear, L., *GA, U.S.A.* **68 E3** 31 51N 83 56W
Blackstone, *MA, U.S.A.* **78 B3** 42 1N 71 30W
Blackstone, *VA, U.S.A.* **102 D6** 37 5N 78 0W
Blackstone →, *Yukon, Canada* **188 C5** 65 51N 137 15W
Blacktail Mts., *MT, U.S.A.* **83 F5** 44 58N 112 35W
Blackville, *N.B., Canada* **173 G4** 46 44N 65 50W
Blackville, *SC, U.S.A.* **90 E4** 33 22N 81 16W
Blackwater = West Road →, *B.C., Canada* **186 B11** 53 18N 122 53W
Blackwater, *MO, U.S.A.* **82 C4** 38 59N 92 59W
Blackwater →, *VA, U.S.A.* **102 E8** 36 24N 76 55W
Blackwater →, *FL, U.S.A.* **67 A1** 30 36N 87 2W
Blackwater →, *MD, U.S.A.* **77 B4** 38 21N 76 1W
Blackwater →, *MO, U.S.A.* **82 C4** 38 56N 92 57W
Blackwater →, *TX, U.S.A.* **98 D7** 33 40N 100 47W
Blackwater Falls State Park ⌂, *WV, U.S.A.* **102 B5** 39 7N 79 30W
Blackwater L., *N.W.T., Canada* **189 D8** 64 0N 123 5W
Blackwater Nat. Wildlife Refuge ⌂, *MD, U.S.A.* **77 B4** 38 26N 76 5W
Blackwell, *OK, U.S.A.* **93 B6** 36 48N 97 17W
Blackwell, *TX, U.S.A.* **98 E7** 32 5N 100 19W
Blackwood, *NJ, U.S.A.* **87 C1** 39 48N 75 4W
Bladen, *NE, U.S.A.* **84 D7** 40 19N 98 36W
Bladen County ☆, *NC, U.S.A.* **90 D7** 34 30N 78 30W
Bladenboro, *NC, U.S.A.* **90 D7** 34 33N 78 48W
Bladensburg, *MD, U.S.A.* **119 B4** 38 55N 76 55W
Bladworth, *Sask., Canada* **182 D5** 51 22N 106 8W
Blain, *PA, U.S.A.* **95 D5** 40 20N 77 31W
Blaine, *KY, U.S.A.* **97 B10** 38 2N 82 51W
Blaine, *MN, U.S.A.* **80 E5** 45 10N 93 13W
Blaine, *TN, U.S.A.* **97 D9** 36 9N 83 42W
Blaine, *WA, U.S.A.* **101 B3** 48 59N 122 45W
Blaine County ☆, *ID, U.S.A.* **70 F4** 43 30N 114 0W
Blaine County ☆, *MT, U.S.A.* **83 B9** 48 20N 109 0W
Blaine County ☆, *NE, U.S.A.* **84 C6** 42 0N 100 0W
Blaine County ☆, *OK, U.S.A.* **93 C5** 35 50N 98 25W
Blaine Lake, *Sask., Canada* **182 C5** 52 51N 106 52W
Blainville, *Qué., Canada* **177 F9** 45 40N 73 52W
Blair, *NE, U.S.A.* **84 C9** 41 33N 96 8W
Blair, *OK, U.S.A.* **93 D4** 34 47N 99 20W
Blair, *WI, U.S.A.* **103 D2** 44 18N 91 14W
Blair County ☆, *PA, U.S.A.* **95 D4** 40 30N 78 20W
Blair Village, *Atlanta, U.S.A.* **106 C2** 33 40N 84 23W
Blairs, *VA, U.S.A.* **102 E5** 36 41N 79 23W
Blairsburg, *IA, U.S.A.* **73 C5** 42 29N 93 39W
Blairsden, *CA, U.S.A.* **64 D6** 39 47N 120 37W
Blairstown, *IA, U.S.A.* **73 D6** 41 55N 92 5W
Blairstown, *MO, U.S.A.* **82 C3** 38 34N 93 58W
Blairstown, *NJ, U.S.A.* **87 B2** 40 59N 74 57W
Blairsville, *GA, U.S.A.* **68 B3** 34 53N 83 58W
Blairsville, *PA, U.S.A.* **95 D3** 40 26N 79 16W
Blake Island State Park ⌂, *Seattle, U.S.A.* **118 C3** 47 32N 122 39W
Blake Pt., *MI, U.S.A.* **79 A3** 48 11N 88 25W
Blakely, *GA, U.S.A.* **68 E2** 31 23N 84 56W
Blakely, *PA, U.S.A.* **87 A1** 41 28N 75 37W
Blakeman, *KS, U.S.A.* **74 B2** 39 49N 101 7W
Blakesburg, *IA, U.S.A.* **73 E6** 40 58N 92 38W
Blakeslee, *OH, U.S.A.* **92 B2** 41 32N 84 44W
Blalock, *OR, U.S.A.* **94 B5** 45 42N 120 22W
Blanc-Sablon, *Qué., Canada* **174 A3** 51 24N 57 12W
Blanca, *CO, U.S.A.* **66 E5** 37 27N 105 31W
Blanca, I., *Quintana Roo, Mexico* **223 A7** 21 24N 86 51W
Blanca, Sierra, *TX, U.S.A.* **98 F2** 31 15N 105 26W
Blanca Flor, *Quintana Roo, Mexico* **223 D5** 18 51N 88 28W
Blanca Peak, *CO, U.S.A.* **66 E5** 37 35N 105 29W
Blanchard, *ID, U.S.A.* **70 A2** 48 1N 116 59W
Blanchard, *IA, U.S.A.* **73 E3** 40 35N 95 13W
Blanchard, *LA, U.S.A.* **75 B2** 32 35N 93 54W
Blanchard, *ND, U.S.A.* **91 C8** 47 21N 97 13W
Blanchard, *OK, U.S.A.* **93 C6** 35 8N 97 39W
Blanchard →, *OH, U.S.A.* **92 B2** 41 2N 84 18W
Blanchardville, *WI, U.S.A.* **103 F4** 42 49N 89 52W
Blanche, L., *Orlando, U.S.A.* **115 B1** 28 28N 81 30W
Blanchester, *OH, U.S.A.* **92 D3** 39 17N 83 59W
Blanco, *NM, U.S.A.* **88 A3** 36 43N 107 50W
Blanco, *OK, U.S.A.* **93 D8** 34 45N 95 46W
Blanco, *TX, U.S.A.* **99 G9** 30 6N 98 25W
Blanco →, *TX, U.S.A.* **99 H10** 29 51N 97 55W
Blanco, B., *Baja Calif., Mexico* **210 D4** 29 3N 114 43W
Blanco, C., *OR, U.S.A.* **94 E1** 42 51N 124 34W
Blanco County ☆, *TX, U.S.A.* **99 G9** 30 17N 98 25W
Bland, *MO, U.S.A.* **82 C5** 38 18N 91 38W
Bland, *VA, U.S.A.* **102 D3** 37 6N 81 7W
Bland County ☆, *VA, U.S.A.* **102 D3** 37 6N 81 7W
Blandford, *MA, U.S.A.* **78 B2** 42 11N 72 56W
Blanding, *UT, U.S.A.* **100 F6** 37 37N 109 29W
Blandinsville, *IL, U.S.A.* **71 C3** 40 33N 90 52W
Blaney Park, *MI, U.S.A.* **79 C6** 46 9N 85 55W
Blanket, *TX, U.S.A.* **99 F9** 31 49N 98 47W
Blasdell, *NY, U.S.A.* **89 C2** 42 48N 78 50W
Blawnox, *Pittsburgh, U.S.A.* **116 B2** 40 29N 79 51W
Bleckley County ☆, *GA, U.S.A.* **68 D3** 32 25N 83 15W
Bledos, *San Luis Potosí, Mexico* **215 J3** 21 50N 101 7W
Bledsoe, *TX, U.S.A.* **98 D4** 33 38N 103 1W
Bledsoe County ☆, *TN, U.S.A.* **97 E7** 35 36N 85 11W
Blencoe, *IA, U.S.A.* **73 D2** 41 56N 96 5W
Blenheim, *Ont., Canada* **178 E5** 42 20N 82 0W
Blessing, *TX, U.S.A.* **99 J11** 28 52N 96 13W
Bleu, L., *Qué., Canada* **176 E4** 46 35N 78 24W
Blewett Falls L., *NC, U.S.A.* **90 C6** 35 3N 79 54W
Blind River, *Ont., Canada* **178 A4** 46 10N 82 58W
Bliss, *ID, U.S.A.* **70 G4** 42 56N 114 57W
Blissfield, *N.B., Canada* **173 G3** 46 36N 66 5W
Blissfield, *MI, U.S.A.* **79 H8** 41 50N 83 52W
Blissfield, *OH, U.S.A.* **92 C5** 40 24N 81 58W
Blitchton, *GA, U.S.A.* **68 D5** 32 12N 81 26W
Block I., *RI, U.S.A.* **78 C3** 41 11N 71 35W
Block Island Sd., *RI, U.S.A.* **78 C3** 41 15N 71 40W
Blocker, *OK, U.S.A.* **93 C8** 35 4N 95 34W
Blockton, *IA, U.S.A.* **73 E4** 40 37N 94 29W
Blodgett, *MO, U.S.A.* **82 D6** 37 0N 89 32W
Bloodsworth I., *MD, U.S.A.* **77 B4** 38 10N 76 3W
Bloodvein →, *Man., Canada* **183 D15** 51 47N 96 43W

Bloody Mt., CA, U.S.A. **65 F8** 37 34N 118 54W
Bloom = Chicago Heights, IL, U.S.A. **71 B6** 41 30N 87 38W
Bloomer, WI, U.S.A. **103 C2** 45 6N 91 29W
Bloomfield, Nfld. & L., Canada **174 D7** 48 23N 53 54W
Bloomfield, Ont., Canada **179 D9** 43 59N 77 14W
Bloomfield, IN, U.S.A. **72 D4** 39 1N 86 57W
Bloomfield, IA, U.S.A. **73 E6** 40 45N 92 25W
Bloomfield, KY, U.S.A. **97 C7** 37 55N 85 19W
Bloomfield, MO, U.S.A. **82 E7** 36 53N 89 56W
Bloomfield, NJ, U.S.A. **87 B2** 40 48N 74 11W
Bloomfield, NM, U.S.A. **88 A3** 36 43N 107 59W
Bloomfield, NE, U.S.A. **84 B8** 42 36N 97 39W
Blooming Grove, TX, U.S.A. **99 E11** 32 6N 96 43W
Blooming Prairie, MN, U.S.A. **80 G5** 43 52N 93 3W
Bloomingburg, OH, U.S.A. **92 D3** 39 36N 83 24W
Bloomingdale, TN, U.S.A. **97 D10** 36 34N 82 32W
Bloomington, ID, U.S.A. **70 G7** 42 11N 111 24W
Bloomington, IL, U.S.A. **71 C4** 40 28N 89 0W
Bloomington, IN, U.S.A. **72 D4** 39 10N 86 32W
Bloomington, MN, U.S.A. **80 F5** 44 50N 93 17W
Bloomington, TX, U.S.A. **99 J11** 28 39N 96 54W
Bloomington, WI, U.S.A. **103 F3** 42 53N 90 55W
Bloomsburg, PA, U.S.A. **95 D6** 41 0N 76 27W
Bloomsdale, MO, U.S.A. **82 C6** 38 1N 90 13W
Bloomville, OH, U.S.A. **92 B3** 41 3N 83 1W
Blossburg, PA, U.S.A. **95 C5** 41 41N 77 4W
Blossom, TX, U.S.A. **99 D12** 33 40N 95 23W
Blossom Park, Ont., Canada **192 B2** 45 21N 75 37W
Blossom Point Proving Grounds, MD, U.S.A. **77 B3** 38 26N 77 5W
Blount County ☆, AL, U.S.A. **60 C4** 33 57N 86 28W
Blount County ☆, TN, U.S.A. **97 E9** 35 46N 83 58W
Blountstown, FL, U.S.A. **67 A3** 30 27N 85 3W
Blountsville, AL, U.S.A. **60 B4** 34 5N 86 35W
Blountville, TN, U.S.A. **97 D10** 36 32N 82 19W
Blowing Rock, NC, U.S.A. **90 B4** 36 8N 81 41W
Bloxom, VA, U.S.A. **77 C5** 37 50N 75 38W
Blubber Bay, B.C., Canada **186 F10** 49 47N 124 37W
Blue →, IN, U.S.A. **72 E4** 38 11N 86 19W
Blue Ash, OH, U.S.A. **107 A2** 39 13N 84 22W
Blue Cypress L., FL, U.S.A. **67 D8** 27 44N 80 45W
Blue Diamond, NV, U.S.A. **85 F5** 36 3N 115 24W
Blue Earth, MN, U.S.A. **80 G4** 43 38N 94 6W
Blue Earth County ☆, MN, U.S.A. **80 F5** 44 5N 94 0W
Blue Eye, MO, U.S.A. **82 E3** 36 30N 93 24W
Blue Hill, ME, U.S.A. **76 D5** 44 25N 68 35W
Blue Hill, NE, U.S.A. **84 D7** 40 20N 98 27W
Blue Island, Chicago, U.S.A. **108 D2** 41 40N 87 40W
Blue Knob, PA, U.S.A. **95 D4** 40 17N 78 34W
Blue Knob State Park ⌓, PA, U.S.A. **95 D4** 40 16N 78 34W
Blue Lake, CA, U.S.A. **64 C3** 40 53N 123 59W
Blue Mesa Res., CO, U.S.A. **66 D3** 38 28N 107 20W
Blue Mound, Dallas-Fort Worth, U.S.A. **109 A2** 32 51N 97 20W
Blue Mound, IL, U.S.A. **71 D4** 39 42N 89 7W
Blue Mound, KS, U.S.A. **74 C9** 38 5N 95 0W
Blue Mountain, CO, U.S.A. **66 B2** 40 15N 108 52W
Blue Mountain, MS, U.S.A. **81 B4** 34 40N 89 2W
Blue Mountain L., AR, U.S.A. **63 C2** 35 2N 93 53W
Blue Mountain Lake, NY, U.S.A. **89 B6** 43 51N 74 27W
Blue Mountain Pass, OR, U.S.A. **94 E8** 42 18N 117 49W
Blue Mt., AR, U.S.A. **63 D1** 34 41N 94 3W
Blue Mt., NH, U.S.A. **86 B3** 44 47N 71 28W
Blue Mt., PA, U.S.A. **95 D6** 40 30N 76 20W
Blue Mts., ME, U.S.A. **76 D3** 44 50N 70 35W
Blue Mts., OR, U.S.A. **94 C7** 45 0N 118 20W
Blue Mts., TX, U.S.A. **99 G8** 30 34N 99 27W
Blue Rapids, KS, U.S.A. **74 B7** 39 41N 96 39W
Blue Ridge, Alta., Canada **184 D5** 54 8N 115 22W
Blue Ridge, GA, U.S.A. **68 B2** 34 52N 84 20W
Blue Ridge, VA, U.S.A. **102 E4** 36 40N 80 50W
Blue Ridge L., GA, U.S.A. **68 B2** 34 53N 84 17W
Blue Ridge Mts., NC, U.S.A. **53 C10** 36 30N 80 15W
Blue Ridge Parkway, VA, U.S.A. **102 E4** 36 40N 80 39W
Blue River, B.C., Canada **187 C15** 52 6N 119 18W
Blue River, OR, U.S.A. **94 C3** 44 9N 122 20W
Blue River, WI, U.S.A. **103 E3** 43 11N 90 34W
Blue Springs, MO, U.S.A. **82 B2** 39 1N 94 17W
Blue Springs, NE, U.S.A. **84 D9** 40 8N 96 40W
Blueberry Mountain, Alta., Canada **184 C1** 55 56N 119 9W
Bluefield, VA, U.S.A. **102 D3** 37 15N 81 17W
Bluefield, WV, U.S.A. **102 D3** 37 16N 81 13W
Bluejacket, OK, U.S.A. **93 B8** 36 48N 95 4W
Bluejoint L., OR, U.S.A. **94 E6** 42 42N 119 38W
Bluenose L., N.W.T., Canada **188 C9** 68 30N 119 35W
Blueridge, Vancouver, Canada **193 B2** 49 19N 122 59W
Bluestone →, WV, U.S.A. **102 D4** 37 37N 80 55W
Bluestone L., WV, U.S.A. **102 D4** 37 38N 80 53W
Bluestone Nat. Scenic River ⌓, WV, U.S.A. **102 D4** 37 33N 81 0W
Bluewater, Ont., Canada **178 D5** 43 28N 81 36W
Bluewater, NM, U.S.A. **88 B3** 35 15N 107 59W
Bluff, UT, U.S.A. **100 F6** 37 17N 109 33W
Bluff City, AR, U.S.A. **63 E2** 33 43N 93 8W
Bluff City, KS, U.S.A. **74 D6** 37 5N 97 53W
Bluff City, TN, U.S.A. **97 D10** 36 28N 82 16W
Bluffdale, Salt Lake City, U.S.A. **117 D2** 40 29N 111 56W
Bluffs, IL, U.S.A. **71 D3** 39 45N 90 32W
Bluffton, Alta., Canada **185 F6** 52 45N 114 17W
Bluffton, AR, U.S.A. **63 D2** 34 54N 93 36W
Bluffton, GA, U.S.A. **68 E2** 31 31N 84 52W
Bluffton, IN, U.S.A. **72 C5** 40 44N 85 11W
Bluffton, MN, U.S.A. **80 D3** 46 28N 95 14W
Bluffton, OH, U.S.A. **92 C3** 40 54N 83 54W
Bluffton, SC, U.S.A. **90 F5** 32 14N 80 52W
Bluford, IL, U.S.A. **71 E5** 38 20N 88 45W
Blumenau = Stettler, Alta., Canada **185 F8** 52 19N 112 40W
Blunt, SD, U.S.A. **91 F6** 44 31N 99 59W
Blunt Pt., San Francisco, U.S.A. **118 A2** 37 51N 122 25W
Bly, OR, U.S.A. **94 E4** 42 24N 121 3W
Blyn, WA, U.S.A. **101 B2** 48 1N 123 0W
Blyth, Ont., Canada **178 D5** 43 44N 81 26W
Blythe, CA, U.S.A. **65 K12** 33 37N 114 36W
Blythe, GA, U.S.A. **68 C4** 33 17N 82 12W
Blytheville, AR, U.S.A. **63 C6** 35 56N 89 55W
Boalsburg, PA, U.S.A. **95 D5** 40 47N 77 49W
Boardman, OH, U.S.A. **92 B6** 41 2N 80 40W
Boardman, OR, U.S.A. **94 B6** 45 51N 119 43W
Boardman Bombing Range, OR, U.S.A. **94 B6** 45 48N 119 45W
Boardwalk, NY, U.S.A. **114 C4** 40 34N 73 49W
Boat Harbour, Nfld. & L., Canada **174 E6** 47 24N 54 50W
Boaz, AL, U.S.A. **60 B4** 34 12N 86 10W
Boaz, WI, U.S.A. **103 E3** 43 20N 90 32W
Bobcaygeon, Ont., Canada **179 C8** 44 33N 78 33W
Bobtown, PA, U.S.A. **95 E3** 39 46N 79 59W
Boca de la Vinorama, Baja Calif. S., Mexico **211 K9** 23 11N 109 29W
Boca de Tomatlán, Jalisco, Mexico **218 B2** 20 31N 105 19W
Boca del Mezquital, Durango, Mexico **217 D6** 23 46N 104 27W
Boca del Río, Veracruz, Mexico **221 E4** 19 5N 96 4W
Boca Grande, FL, U.S.A. **67 E6** 26 45N 82 16W
Boca Raton, FL, U.S.A. **67 E8** 26 21N 80 5W
Bocabarra, Pta., Oaxaca, Mexico **221 H6** 16 17N 94 48W
Bocas de Camichín, Nayarit, Mexico **216 F5** 21 44N 105 29W
Bochart, Qué., Canada **177 B9** 49 10N 73 30W
Bochil, Chiapas, Mexico **222 C4** 16 59N 92 55W
Bock, MN, U.S.A. **80 E5** 45 47N 93 33W
Bocoyna, Chihuahua, Mexico **213 F8** 27 52N 107 35W
Bodcau, Bayou →, LA, U.S.A. **75 B2** 32 13N 93 30W
Bodcaw, AR, U.S.A. **63 E2** 33 33N 93 25W
Bode, IA, U.S.A. **73 C4** 42 52N 94 17W
Bodega Bay, CA, U.S.A. **64 E3** 38 20N 123 3W
Bodie I., NC, U.S.A. **90 C10** 35 54N 75 35W
Boeing Field = King County International ✕, Seattle, U.S.A. **118 C4** 47 31N 122 18W
Boelus, NE, U.S.A. **84 C7** 41 5N 98 43W
Boerne, TX, U.S.A. **99 H9** 29 47N 98 44W
Bogalusa, LA, U.S.A. **75 D6** 30 47N 89 52W
Bogard, MO, U.S.A. **82 B3** 39 27N 93 32W
Bogata, TX, U.S.A. **99 D12** 33 28N 95 13W
Boger City, NC, U.S.A. **90 C4** 35 28N 81 13W
Boggy Creek Swamp, Orlando, U.S.A. **115 B2** 28 22N 81 19W
Bogota, NJ, U.S.A. **114 A2** 40 52N 74 2W
Bogota, TN, U.S.A. **96 D3** 36 10N 89 26W
Bogue, KS, U.S.A. **74 B4** 39 22N 99 41W
Bogue Chitto, MS, U.S.A. **81 E3** 31 26N 90 27W
Bogue Chitto →, LA, U.S.A. **75 D6** 30 34N 89 50W
Bogue Homo →, MS, U.S.A. **81 E5** 31 10N 88 55W
Boiling Spring Lakes, NC, U.S.A. **90 D7** 34 2N 78 4W
Boiling Springs, NC, U.S.A. **90 C4** 35 15N 81 40W
Bois, L. des, N.W.T., Canada **188 C7** 66 50N 125 9W
Bois Blanc I., MI, U.S.A. **79 D7** 45 46N 84 27W
Bois D'Arc, MO, U.S.A. **82 D3** 37 16N 93 30W
Bois de Sioux →, ND, U.S.A. **91 D9** 46 16N 96 36W
Bois Forte (Deer Creek) Indian Reservation, MN, U.S.A. **80 C5** 47 48N 93 23W
Bois Forte (Nett Lake) Indian Reservation, MN, U.S.A. **80 B5** 48 5N 93 5W
Bois I., Nfld. & L., Canada **174 E5** 47 44N 56 0W
Boisdale, N.S., Canada **173 G9** 46 6N 60 30W
Boise, ID, U.S.A. **70 F2** 43 37N 116 13W
Boise →, ID, U.S.A. **70 F1** 43 49N 117 1W
Boise ✕ (BOI), ID, U.S.A. **70 F2** 43 34N 116 14W
Boise City, OK, U.S.A. **93 B1** 36 44N 102 31W
Boise County ☆, ID, U.S.A. **70 E3** 44 0N 115 45W
Boise Mts., ID, U.S.A. **70 F3** 43 45N 115 30W
Boise Nat. Forest, ID, U.S.A. **70 E3** 44 5N 115 30W
Boissevain, Man., Canada **183 F11** 49 15N 100 5W
Boistfort Pk., WA, U.S.A. **101 D2** 46 29N 123 12W
Bokchito, OK, U.S.A. **93 D7** 34 1N 96 9W
Bokobá, Yucatán, Mexico **223 B4** 20 59N 89 13W
Bokoshe, OK, U.S.A. **93 C9** 35 11N 94 47W
Bolaños, Jalisco, Mexico **217 F7** 21 41N 103 47W
Bolaños →, Mexico **218 A3** 21 12N 104 5W
Bolckow, MO, U.S.A. **82 A2** 40 7N 94 50W
Boldtville, San Antonio, U.S.A. **117 C3** 29 21N 98 21W
Boles, AR, U.S.A. **63 D1** 34 47N 94 3W
Boley, OK, U.S.A. **93 C7** 35 29N 96 29W
Boligee, AL, U.S.A. **60 D2** 32 45N 88 2W
Bolingbroke, GA, U.S.A. **68 D3** 32 57N 83 48W
Bolingbrook, IL, U.S.A. **71 B5** 41 42N 88 4W
Bolinger, LA, U.S.A. **75 B2** 32 57N 93 41W
Bolivar, MO, U.S.A. **82 D3** 37 37N 93 25W
Bolivar, NY, U.S.A. **89 C2** 42 4N 78 10W
Bolivar, TN, U.S.A. **96 E4** 35 12N 89 0W
Bolivar, WV, U.S.A. **77 A3** 39 19N 77 45W
Bolivar, Mt., OR, U.S.A. **94 E2** 42 51N 123 56W
Bolivar County ☆, MS, U.S.A. **81 C3** 33 50N 90 43W
Bolivar Peninsula, TX, U.S.A. **99 H13** 29 27N 94 39W
Bolivia, NC, U.S.A. **90 D7** 34 4N 78 9W
Bolling, AL, U.S.A. **60 E4** 31 43N 86 42W
Bollinger County ☆, MO, U.S.A. **82 D6** 37 20N 90 0W
Bolonchén, Campeche, Mexico **223 B4** 20 1N 89 45W
Bolton, Ont., Canada **178 D7** 43 54N 79 45W
Bolton, Atlanta, U.S.A. **106 B2** 33 48N 84 28W
Bolton, MS, U.S.A. **81 D3** 32 21N 90 28W
Bombay, NY, U.S.A. **89 A6** 44 56N 74 34W
Bombay Hook, DE, U.S.A. **77 A5** 39 21N 75 30W
Bombay Hook Nat. Wildlife Refuge ⌓, DE, U.S.A. **77 A5** 39 16N 75 27W
Bomoseen, L., VT, U.S.A. **86 C1** 43 39N 73 13W
Bon Accord, Alta., Canada **184 E7** 53 50N 113 25W
Bon Air, VA, U.S.A. **102 D7** 37 31N 77 34W
Bon Echo Prov. Park ⌓, Ont., Canada **179 C9** 44 55N 77 16W
Bon Homme County ☆, SD, U.S.A. **91 G8** 43 0N 97 50W
Bon Secour B., AL, U.S.A. **60 F3** 30 15N 87 58W
Bona, Mt., AK, U.S.A. **61 F12** 61 23N 141 45W
Bonaire, GA, U.S.A. **68 D3** 32 33N 83 36W
Bonampak, Chiapas, Mexico **222 C5** 16 44N 91 5W
Bonanza, Alta., Canada **184 C1** 55 55N 119 49W
Bonanza, CO, U.S.A. **66 D4** 38 18N 106 8W
Bonanza, OR, U.S.A. **94 E4** 42 12N 121 24W
Bonanza, UT, U.S.A. **100 C6** 40 1N 109 11W
Bonanza Pk., WA, U.S.A. **101 B5** 48 14N 120 52W
Bonaparte, IA, U.S.A. **73 E7** 40 42N 91 48W
Bonaparte, Mt., WA, U.S.A. **101 B6** 48 45N 119 8W
Bonaparte L., B.C., Canada **187 D14** 51 15N 120 34W
Bonaventure, N.B., Canada **173 E4** 48 5N 65 32W
Bonavista, Nfld. & L., Canada **174 D7** 48 40N 53 5W
Bonavista, C., Nfld. & L., Canada **174 D7** 48 42N 53 5W
Bonavista B., Nfld. & L., Canada **174 D7** 48 45N 53 25W
Bond, CO, U.S.A. **66 C4** 39 53N 106 42W
Bond, MS, U.S.A. **81 F4** 30 54N 89 10W
Bond County ☆, IL, U.S.A. **71 E4** 38 50N 89 25W
Bond Falls Flowage, MI, U.S.A. **79 C2** 46 30N 89 15W
Bondurant, IA, U.S.A. **73 D5** 41 42N 93 28W
Bondurant, WY, U.S.A. **104 C2** 43 12N 110 24W
Bondville, IL, U.S.A. **71 C5** 40 7N 88 22W
Bone Gap, IL, U.S.A. **71 E6** 38 27N 88 0W
Bonetraill, ND, U.S.A. **91 B2** 48 26N 103 51W
Bonfield, Ont., Canada **178 A7** 46 14N 79 9W
Bonham, TX, U.S.A. **99 D11** 33 35N 96 11W
Bonifay, FL, U.S.A. **67 A3** 30 47N 85 41W
Bonilla, SD, U.S.A. **91 F7** 44 35N 98 30W
Bonilla I., B.C., Canada **186 B4** 53 28N 130 37W
Bonita, LA, U.S.A. **75 B4** 32 55N 91 40W
Bonita, San Diego, U.S.A. **117 C2** 32 39N 117 1W
Bonita, Pt., San Francisco, U.S.A. **118 B1** 37 48N 122 31W
Bonita Springs, FL, U.S.A. **67 E7** 26 21N 81 47W
Bonne Terre, MO, U.S.A. **82 D6** 37 55N 90 33W
Bonneauville, PA, U.S.A. **77 A3** 39 49N 77 8W
Bonnechere →, Ont., Canada **179 B9** 45 35N 77 50W
Bonner County ☆, ID, U.S.A. **70 A2** 48 20N 116 30W
Bonner Springs, KS, U.S.A. **74 B9** 39 4N 94 53W
Bonners Ferry, ID, U.S.A. **70 A2** 48 42N 116 19W
Bonnet, Lac du, Man., Canada **183 E16** 50 22N 95 55W
Bonnet Plume →, Yukon, Canada **188 C6** 65 56N 134 56W
Bonneville County ☆, ID, U.S.A. **70 F7** 43 20N 111 20W
Bonneville Dam, U.S.A. **94 B4** 45 38N 121 56W
Bonneville Pk., ID, U.S.A. **70 G6** 42 46N 112 8W
Bonneville Salt Flats, UT, U.S.A. **100 C2** 40 45N 113 50W
Bonney Lake, WA, U.S.A. **101 C3** 47 11N 122 11W
Bonnie, IL, U.S.A. **71 E5** 38 12N 88 54W
Bonnieville, KY, U.S.A. **97 C7** 37 23N 85 54W
Bonny Res., CO, U.S.A. **66 C8** 39 37N 102 11W
Bonny Slope, Portland, U.S.A. **116 A1** 45 32N 122 46W
Bonnyville, Alta., Canada **184 D10** 54 20N 110 45W
Bono, AR, U.S.A. **63 C5** 35 55N 90 48W
Book Cliffs, CO, U.S.A. **66 C2** 39 20N 108 45W
Book Cliffs, UT, U.S.A. **100 D6** 39 20N 109 0W
Booker, TX, U.S.A. **98 A7** 36 27N 100 32W
Booker T. Washington Nat. Monument ⌓, VA, U.S.A. **102 D5** 37 7N 79 44W
Boomer, WV, U.S.A. **102 C3** 38 9N 81 17W
Boone, CO, U.S.A. **66 D6** 38 15N 104 15W
Boone, IA, U.S.A. **73 C5** 42 4N 93 53W
Boone, NC, U.S.A. **90 B4** 36 13N 81 41W
Boone, NE, U.S.A. **84 C8** 41 38N 97 55W
Boone →, IA, U.S.A. **73 C5** 42 19N 93 56W
Boone County ☆, AR, U.S.A. **63 B2** 36 14N 93 7W
Boone County ☆, IL, U.S.A. **71 A4** 42 20N 89 50W
Boone County ☆, IN, U.S.A. **72 C4** 40 5N 86 30W
Boone County ☆, IA, U.S.A. **73 D5** 42 0N 94 0W
Boone County ☆, KY, U.S.A. **97 B8** 38 55N 84 45W
Boone County ☆, MO, U.S.A. **82 B4** 39 0N 92 20W
Boone County ☆, NE, U.S.A. **84 C8** 41 40N 98 0W
Boone County ☆, WV, U.S.A. **102 C3** 38 0N 81 49W
Boone L., TN, U.S.A. **97 D10** 36 26N 82 26W
Boones Mill, VA, U.S.A. **102 D5** 37 7N 79 57W
Booneville, AR, U.S.A. **63 C2** 35 8N 93 55W
Booneville, KY, U.S.A. **97 C9** 37 29N 83 41W
Booneville, MS, U.S.A. **81 B5** 34 39N 88 34W
Boonsboro, MD, U.S.A. **77 A3** 39 30N 77 39W
Boonton, NJ, U.S.A. **87 B2** 40 54N 74 25W
Boonville, CA, U.S.A. **64 D3** 39 1N 123 22W
Boonville, IN, U.S.A. **72 E3** 38 3N 87 16W
Boonville, MO, U.S.A. **82 C4** 38 58N 92 44W
Boonville, NC, U.S.A. **90 B5** 36 14N 80 43W
Boonville, NY, U.S.A. **89 B5** 43 29N 75 20W
Boothbay Harbor, ME, U.S.A. **76 E4** 43 51N 69 38W
Boothia, Gulf of, Nunavut, Canada **190 C7** 71 0N 90 0W
Boothia Pen., Nunavut, Canada **190 C7** 71 0N 94 0W
Boothville, LA, U.S.A. **75 E6** 29 20N 89 25W
Boquilla, Presa la, Chihuahua, Mexico **213 F10** 27 31N 105 30W
Boquilla de Abajo, Chihuahua, Mexico **213 F9** 27 22N 106 31W
Boquillas, TX, U.S.A. **98 H5** 29 11N 102 58W
Boquillas del Carmen, Coahuila, Mexico **214 A2** 29 17N 102 53W
Borah Peak, ID, U.S.A. **70 E5** 44 8N 113 47W
Bordeaux, TN, U.S.A. **96 D6** 36 12N 86 50W
Bordelonville, LA, U.S.A. **75 C4** 31 6N 91 55W
Borden, Sask., Canada **182 C4** 52 27N 107 14W
Borden-Carleton, P.E.I., Canada **173 G6** 46 18N 63 47W
Borden County ☆, TX, U.S.A. **98 E6** 32 46N 101 27W
Borden I., Canada **188 A10** 78 30N 111 30W
Borden L., Ont., Canada **181 E13** 47 50N 83 17W
Borden Pen., Nunavut, Canada **190 C9** 73 0N 83 0W
Borden Springs, AL, U.S.A. **60 C5** 33 56N 85 28W
Bordentown, NJ, U.S.A. **87 B2** 40 9N 74 43W
Border, WY, U.S.A. **104 D1** 42 11N 111 3W
Border Field State Park ⌓, San Diego, U.S.A. **117 C2** 32 32N 117 7W
Bordulac, ND, U.S.A. **91 C7** 47 23N 98 58W
Borger, TX, U.S.A. **98 B6** 35 39N 101 24W
Borgne, L., LA, U.S.A. **75 D6** 30 1N 89 42W
Boron, CA, U.S.A. **65 H9** 35 0N 117 39W
Borrego Springs, CA, U.S.A. **65 K10** 33 15N 116 23W
Borup, MN, U.S.A. **80 C2** 47 11N 96 30W
Boscawen, NH, U.S.A. **86 C3** 43 19N 71 37W
Bosco, LA, U.S.A. **75 B3** 32 17N 92 5W
Boscobel, WI, U.S.A. **103 E3** 43 8N 90 42W
Bosencheve, Parque Nacional △, Mexico **219 C7** 19 26N 100 14W
Bosler, WY, U.S.A. **104 E7** 41 35N 105 42W
Bosque, NM, U.S.A. **88 C4** 34 34N 106 47W
Bosque County ☆, TX, U.S.A. **99 F10** 31 56N 97 39W
Bosque Farms, NM, U.S.A. **88 B4** 35 51N 106 42W
Bossier City, LA, U.S.A. **75 B2** 32 31N 93 44W
Bossier Parish ☆, LA, U.S.A. **75 B2** 32 42N 93 44W
Boston, GA, U.S.A. **68 F3** 30 47N 83 47W
Boston, MA, U.S.A. **78 B3** 42 22N 71 3W
Boston, TX, U.S.A. **99 D13** 33 27N 94 25W
Boston Bar, B.C., Canada **187 F13** 49 52N 121 30W
Boston Harbor, Boston, U.S.A. **106 A4** 42 20N 70 58W
Boston Harbor Islands Nat. Park △, Boston, U.S.A. **106 B4** 42 18N 70 57W
Boston Logan International ✕ (BOS), MA, U.S.A. **78 B3** 42 22N 71 1W
Boston Mts., AR, U.S.A. **63 C2** 35 42N 93 15W
Bostwick, FL, U.S.A. **67 B7** 29 46N 81 38W
Bostwick, GA, U.S.A. **68 C3** 33 44N 83 31W
Boswell, B.C., Canada **187 F18** 49 28N 116 45W
Boswell, IN, U.S.A. **72 C3** 40 31N 87 23W
Boswell, OK, U.S.A. **93 D8** 34 2N 95 52W
Boswell, PA, U.S.A. **95 D3** 40 10N 79 2W
Bosworth, MO, U.S.A. **82 B3** 39 28N 93 20W
Botetourt County ☆, VA, U.S.A. **102 D5** 37 32N 79 41W
Bothell, Seattle, U.S.A. **118 B4** 47 45N 122 12W
Bothell, WA, U.S.A. **101 C3** 47 45N 122 12W
Bothwell, Ont., Canada **178 E5** 42 38N 81 52W
Botkins, OH, U.S.A. **92 C2** 40 28N 84 11W
Bottineau, ND, U.S.A. **91 B5** 48 50N 100 27W
Bottineau County ☆, ND, U.S.A. **91 B5** 48 55N 101 0W
Botwood, Nfld. & L., Canada **174 C5** 49 6N 55 23W
Boucher →, Qué., Canada **177 B13** 49 10N 69 6W
Boucherville, Montréal, Canada **192 A4** 45 36N 73 28W
Boucherville, Îs. de, Montréal, Canada **192 A4** 45 36N 73 28W
Bouchette, Qué., Canada **176 E7** 46 12N 75 57W
Bouchier, L., Qué., Canada **176 A5** 50 6N 77 48W
Bouctouche, N.B., Canada **173 G5** 46 30N 64 45W
Boulder, CO, U.S.A. **66 B5** 40 1N 105 17W
Boulder, MT, U.S.A. **83 D5** 46 14N 112 7W
Boulder, UT, U.S.A. **100 F4** 37 55N 111 25W
Boulder, WY, U.S.A. **104 D3** 42 45N 109 43W
Boulder City, NV, U.S.A. **85 G6** 35 58N 114 49W
Boulder County ☆, CO, U.S.A. **66 B5** 40 10N 105 15W
Boulder Creek, CA, U.S.A. **64 F4** 37 7N 122 7W
Boulder Dam = Hoover Dam, U.S.A. **62 A1** 36 1N 114 44W
Boulder L., WY, U.S.A. **104 D3** 42 51N 109 40W
Boulder Mts., ID, U.S.A. **70 F4** 43 53N 114 30W
Boulder Peak, CA, U.S.A. **64 B3** 41 35N 123 5W
Bound Brook, NJ, U.S.A. **87 B2** 40 34N 74 32W
Boundary, AK, U.S.A. **61 D12** 64 5N 141 1W
Boundary County ☆, ID, U.S.A. **70 A2** 48 45N 116 25W
Boundary Peak, NV, U.S.A. **85 E2** 37 51N 118 21W
Boundary Waters Canoe Area Wilderness ⌓, MN, U.S.A. **80 C7** 47 57N 91 13W
Bountiful, UT, U.S.A. **100 C4** 40 53N 111 52W
Bourbeuse →, MO, U.S.A. **82 C6** 38 24N 90 53W
Bourbon, IN, U.S.A. **72 B4** 41 18N 86 7W
Bourbon, MO, U.S.A. **82 C5** 38 9N 91 15W
Bourbon County ☆, KS, U.S.A. **74 D9** 37 45N 94 45W
Bourbon County ☆, KY, U.S.A. **97 B8** 38 10N 84 15W
Bourbonnais, IL, U.S.A. **71 B6** 41 9N 87 52W
Bourget, Ont., Canada **176 F7** 45 26N 75 9W
Bouse, AZ, U.S.A. **62 D1** 33 56N 114 0W
Bouse Wash →, AZ, U.S.A. **62 C1** 34 3N 114 20W
Bovey, MN, U.S.A. **80 C5** 47 18N 93 25W
Bovill, ID, U.S.A. **70 C2** 46 51N 116 24W
Bovina, TX, U.S.A. **98 C5** 34 31N 102 53W
Bow, WA, U.S.A. **101 B3** 48 34N 122 24W
Bow →, Alta., Canada **185 J9** 49 57N 111 41W
Bow Center, NH, U.S.A. **86 C3** 43 10N 71 34W
Bow Cr. →, KS, U.S.A. **74 B4** 39 39N 99 8W
Bow Island, Alta., Canada **185 J9** 49 50N 111 23W
Bow Mar, Denver, U.S.A. **109 C1** 39 37N 105 2W
Bow Pass, Alta., Canada **185 G4** 51 43N 116 30W
Bowbells, ND, U.S.A. **91 B3** 48 48N 102 15W
Bowden, Alta., Canada **185 G6** 51 55N 114 2W
Bowden, WV, U.S.A. **102 C5** 38 55N 79 43W
Bowdle, SD, U.S.A. **91 E6** 45 27N 99 39W
Bowdoin L., MT, U.S.A. **83 B10** 48 25N 107 41W
Bowdoin Nat. Wildlife Refuge ⌓, MT, U.S.A. **83 B10** 48 24N 107 39W
Bowdon, GA, U.S.A. **68 C1** 33 32N 85 15W
Bowdon, ND, U.S.A. **91 C6** 47 28N 99 43W
Bowdon Junction, GA, U.S.A. **68 C1** 33 40N 85 9W
Bowen, IL, U.S.A. **71 C2** 40 14N 91 4W
Bowen Island, B.C., Canada **187 F11** 49 23N 123 20W
Bowens, MD, U.S.A. **77 B4** 38 30N 76 8W
Bower Hill, Pittsburgh, U.S.A. **116 B1** 40 22N 80 5W
Bowers, DE, U.S.A. **77 A5** 39 4N 75 24W
Bowersville, GA, U.S.A. **68 B3** 34 23N 83 5W
Bowersville, OH, U.S.A. **92 D3** 39 35N 83 44W
Bowie, AZ, U.S.A. **62 E6** 32 19N 109 29W
Bowie, CO, U.S.A. **66 D3** 38 55N 107 33W
Bowie, MD, U.S.A. **77 B4** 39 0N 76 47W
Bowie, TX, U.S.A. **99 D10** 33 34N 97 51W
Bowie County ☆, TX, U.S.A. **99 D13** 33 27N 94 25W
Bowie Cr. →, MS, U.S.A. **81 E4** 31 24N 89 27W
Bowlegs, OK, U.S.A. **93 C7** 35 9N 96 40W
Bowling Green, FL, U.S.A. **67 D7** 27 38N 81 50W
Bowling Green, KY, U.S.A. **96 D6** 36 59N 86 27W
Bowling Green, MO, U.S.A. **82 B5** 39 21N 91 12W
Bowling Green, OH, U.S.A. **92 B3** 41 23N 83 39W
Bowling Green, VA, U.S.A. **77 B3** 38 3N 77 21W
Bowlus, MN, U.S.A. **80 E4** 45 49N 94 24W
Bowman, GA, U.S.A. **68 B3** 34 12N 83 2W
Bowman, ND, U.S.A. **91 D2** 46 11N 103 24W
Bowman, SC, U.S.A. **90 E5** 33 21N 80 41W
Bowman B., Nunavut, Canada **191 D11** 65 30N 73 40W
Bowman County ☆, ND, U.S.A. **91 D2** 46 0N 103 30W
Bowman-Haley Lake, ND, U.S.A. **91 E2** 45 59N 103 14W
Bowmanstown, PA, U.S.A. **87 B1** 40 48N 75 40W
Bowmanville = Clarington, Ont., Canada **179 D8** 43 55N 78 41W
Bowmont, ID, U.S.A. **70 F2** 43 27N 116 32W
Bowring, OK, U.S.A. **93 B7** 36 53N 96 7W
Bowron →, B.C., Canada **187 A13** 54 3N 121 50W
Bowron Lake Park ⌓, B.C., Canada **187 B13** 53 10N 121 5W
Bowser, B.C., Canada **186 F10** 49 27N 124 40W
Bowsman, Man., Canada **183 C10** 52 14N 101 12W
Bowstring L., MN, U.S.A. **80 C5** 47 33N 93 55W
Box Butte County ☆, NE, U.S.A. **84 B2** 42 15N 103 0W
Box Elder, SD, U.S.A. **91 F2** 44 7N 103 4W
Box Elder County ☆, UT, U.S.A. **100 B3** 41 30N 113 0W
Boxelder →, SD, U.S.A. **91 F3** 44 1N 102 27W
Boxelder Cr. →, SD, U.S.A. **91 E2** 45 59N 103 57W
Boxford, MA, U.S.A. **78 B4** 42 40N 71 0W
Boxholm, IA, U.S.A. **73 C4** 42 10N 94 6W
Boy River, MN, U.S.A. **80 C4** 47 10N 94 7W
Boyce, LA, U.S.A. **75 C3** 31 23N 92 40W
Boyce, VA, U.S.A. **77 A2** 39 6N 78 4W
Boyceville, WI, U.S.A. **103 C1** 45 3N 92 2W
Boyd, FL, U.S.A. **67 A5** 30 11N 83 37W
Boyd, MN, U.S.A. **80 F3** 44 51N 95 54W
Boyd, TX, U.S.A. **99 D10** 33 5N 97 34W
Boyd County ☆, KY, U.S.A. **97 B10** 38 20N 82 40W
Boyd County ☆, NE, U.S.A. **84 B7** 42 50N 98 40W
Boyd L., Qué., Canada **175 C2** 52 46N 76 42W
Boydell, AR, U.S.A. **63 E4** 33 22N 91 29W
Boyden, IA, U.S.A. **73 B3** 43 12N 96 0W
Boydton, VA, U.S.A. **102 E6** 36 40N 78 24W
Boyer →, IA, U.S.A. **73 D3** 41 27N 95 55W
Boyertown, PA, U.S.A. **87 B1** 40 20N 75 38W
Boyes, MT, U.S.A. **83 E12** 45 16N 105 2W
Boyes Hot Springs, CA, U.S.A. **64 E4** 38 19N 122 29W
Boykin, GA, U.S.A. **68 E2** 31 6N 84 41W
Boykins, VA, U.S.A. **102 E7** 36 35N 77 12W
Boyle, Alta., Canada **184 D8** 54 35N 112 49W
Boyle, MS, U.S.A. **81 C3** 33 42N 90 44W
Boyle County ☆, KY, U.S.A. **97 C8** 37 35N 84 55W
Boyle Heights, Los Angeles, U.S.A. **111 B3** 34 1N 118 12 E
Boylston, N.S., Canada **173 H8** 45 26N 61 30W
Boyne City, MI, U.S.A. **79 D6** 45 13N 85 1W
Boyne Falls, MI, U.S.A. **79 D7** 45 10N 84 55W
Boynton, OK, U.S.A. **93 C8** 35 39N 95 39W
Boynton Beach, FL, U.S.A. **67 E8** 26 32N 80 4W
Boys Town, NE, U.S.A. **84 C9** 41 16N 96 8W
Boysen Res., WY, U.S.A. **104 C4** 43 25N 108 11W
Bozeman, MT, U.S.A. **83 E6** 45 41N 111 2W
Bozman, MD, U.S.A. **77 B4** 38 46N 76 16W
Bracebridge, Ont., Canada **178 B7** 45 2N 79 19W
Bracey, VA, U.S.A. **102 E6** 36 36N 78 9W
Bracken, Sask., Canada **182 F3** 49 11N 108 6W
Bracken, San Antonio, U.S.A. **117 B3** 29 36N 98 19W
Bracken County ☆, KY, U.S.A. **97 B8** 38 40N 84 5W
Brackendale, B.C., Canada **187 F11** 49 48N 123 8W
Brackettville, TX, U.S.A. **98 H7** 29 19N 100 25W
Braddock, ND, U.S.A. **91 D5** 46 34N 100 6W
Braddock, Pittsburgh, U.S.A. **116 B2** 40 24N 79 52W
Braddock Heights, MD, U.S.A. **77 A3** 39 25N 77 30W
Braddock Hills, Pittsburgh, U.S.A. **116 B2** 40 25N 79 51W
Braddyville, IA, U.S.A. **73 E3** 40 35N 95 2W
Braden, TN, U.S.A. **96 E3** 35 23N 89 34W
Bradenton, FL, U.S.A. **67 D6** 27 30N 82 34W
Bradford, Ont., Canada **178 C7** 44 7N 79 34W
Bradford, AR, U.S.A. **63 C4** 35 25N 91 27W
Bradford, IL, U.S.A. **71 B4** 41 11N 89 39W
Bradford, NH, U.S.A. **86 C3** 43 17N 71 56W
Bradford, PA, U.S.A. **95 C4** 41 58N 78 38W
Bradford, RI, U.S.A. **78 C3** 41 24N 71 45W
Bradford, TN, U.S.A. **96 D4** 36 5N 88 49W
Bradford, VT, U.S.A. **86 C2** 43 59N 72 9W
Bradford County ☆, FL, U.S.A. **67 B6** 30 0N 82 15W
Bradford County ☆, PA, U.S.A. **95 C6** 41 50N 76 30W
Bradford Mt., CT, U.S.A. **78 C1** 41 59N 73 18W
Bradfordsville, KY, U.S.A. **97 C7** 37 30N 85 9W
Bradgate, IA, U.S.A. **73 C4** 42 48N 94 25W
Bradley, AR, U.S.A. **63 E2** 33 6N 93 39W
Bradley, CA, U.S.A. **65 H6** 35 52N 120 48W
Bradley, IL, U.S.A. **71 B6** 41 9N 87 52W
Bradley, OK, U.S.A. **93 D6** 34 53N 97 42W
Bradley, SD, U.S.A. **91 E8** 45 5N 97 39W
Bradley, WV, U.S.A. **102 C3** 38 9N 81 43W
Bradley County ☆, AR, U.S.A. **63 E3** 33 27N 92 10W
Bradley County ☆, TN, U.S.A. **97 E8** 35 10N 84 53W
Bradley International, Hartford ✕ (BDL), CT, U.S.A. **78 C2** 41 56N 72 41W
Bradley Junction, FL, U.S.A. **67 D7** 27 48N 81 59W
Bradner, OH, U.S.A. **92 B3** 41 20N 83 26W
Bradore Bay, Qué., Canada **174 A3** 51 27N 57 18W
Bradshaw, NE, U.S.A. **84 D8** 40 53N 97 45W
Bradshaw, TX, U.S.A. **99 E8** 32 6N 99 54W
Bradshaw, WV, U.S.A. **102 D3** 37 21N 81 48W
Bradwell, Sask., Canada **182 D5** 51 57N 106 14W
Brady, MT, U.S.A. **83 B6** 48 2N 111 51W
Brady, NE, U.S.A. **84 C5** 41 1N 100 22W
Brady, TX, U.S.A. **99 F8** 31 9N 99 20W
Brady Cr. →, TX, U.S.A. **99 F9** 31 8N 98 59W
Braeside, Ont., Canada **176 F6** 45 28N 76 24W
Bragg City, MO, U.S.A. **82 E7** 36 16N 89 55W
Bragg Creek, Alta., Canada **185 H6** 50 57N 114 35W

Braggadocio, *MO, U.S.A.* **82 E7** 36 11N 89 50W
Braggs, *OK, U.S.A.* **93 C8** 35 40N 95 12W
Bragg's Spur = West Memphis, *AR, U.S.A.* **63 C5** 35 8N 90 11W
Braham, *MN, U.S.A.* **80 E5** 45 44N 93 10W
Braidwood, *IL, U.S.A.* **71 B5** 41 16N 88 13W
Brainard, *NE, U.S.A.* **84 C9** 41 11N 97 0W
Brainerd, *MN, U.S.A.* **80 D4** 46 22N 94 12W
Braintree, *MA, U.S.A.* **78 B4** 42 13N 71 0W
Braithwaite, *New Orleans, U.S.A.* **113 C3** 29 51N 89 56W
Bralorne, *B.C., Canada* **187 E12** 50 50N 122 50W
Braman, *OK, U.S.A.* **93 B6** 36 56N 97 20W
Bramham I., *B.C., Canada* **186 D7** 51 4N 127 34W
Brampton, *Ont., Canada* **178 D7** 43 45N 79 45W
Brampton, *ND, U.S.A.* **91 D8** 46 0N 97 52W
Bramwell, *WV, U.S.A.* **102 D3** 37 20N 81 19W
Branch, *Nfld. & L., Canada* **174 F7** 46 53N 53 57W
Branch, *AR, U.S.A.* **63 C2** 35 18N 93 57W
Branch County ☆, *MI, U.S.A.* **79 H6** 41 50N 85 5W
Branchland, *WV, U.S.A.* **102 C2** 38 13N 82 12W
Branchville, *NJ, U.S.A.* **87 A2** 41 9N 74 45W
Branchville, *SC, U.S.A.* **90 E5** 33 15N 80 49W
Brandenburg, *KY, U.S.A.* **96 C6** 38 0N 86 10W
Brandon, *Man., Canada* **183 F12** 49 50N 99 57W
Brandon, *CO, U.S.A.* **66 D8** 38 27N 102 26W
Brandon, *FL, U.S.A.* **67 D6** 27 56N 82 17W
Brandon, *IA, U.S.A.* **73 C7** 42 19N 92 0W
Brandon, *MN, U.S.A.* **80 E3** 45 58N 95 36W
Brandon, *MS, U.S.A.* **81 D4** 32 16N 89 59W
Brandon, *NE, U.S.A.* **84 D4** 40 48N 101 55W
Brandon, *SD, U.S.A.* **91 G9** 43 35N 96 35W
Brandon, *VT, U.S.A.* **86 C1** 43 48N 73 6W
Brandon, *WI, U.S.A.* **103 E5** 43 44N 88 47W
Brandonville, *WV, U.S.A.* **102 B5** 39 40N 79 37W
Brandsville, *MO, U.S.A.* **82 E5** 36 39N 91 42W
Brandt, *SD, U.S.A.* **91 F9** 44 40N 96 38W
Brandy Pk., *OR, U.S.A.* **94 E2** 42 36N 123 53W
Brandywine, *MD, U.S.A.* **77 B4** 38 42N 76 51W
Brandywine, *WV, U.S.A.* **102 C5** 38 38N 79 15W
Branford, *CT, U.S.A.* **78 C2** 41 17N 72 49W
Branford, *FL, U.S.A.* **67 B6** 29 58N 82 56W
Branson, *CO, U.S.A.* **66 E7** 37 1N 103 53W
Branson, *MO, U.S.A.* **82 E3** 36 39N 93 13W
Brantford, *Ont., Canada* **178 D6** 43 10N 80 15W
Brantford, *ND, U.S.A.* **91 C7** 47 36N 98 55W
Brantley, *AL, U.S.A.* **60 E4** 31 35N 86 16W
Brantley County ☆, *GA, U.S.A.* **68 E5** 31 10N 82 0W
Brantley L., *NM, U.S.A.* **88 E6** 32 32N 104 22W
Brantville, *N.B., Canada* **173 F5** 47 22N 64 58W
Bras d'Or L., *N.S., Canada* **173 H9** 45 50N 60 50W
Brashear, *MO, U.S.A.* **82 A4** 40 9N 92 23W
Brasher Falls, *NY, U.S.A.* **89 A6** 44 49N 74 47W
Brasstown Bald, *GA, U.S.A.* **68 B3** 34 53N 83 49W
Brassua L., *ME, U.S.A.* **76 C4** 45 40N 69 55W
Bratenahl, *Cleveland, U.S.A.* **107 A2** 41 32N 81 37W
Bratt, *FL, U.S.A.* **67 A1** 30 58N 87 26W
Brattleboro, *VT, U.S.A.* **86 D2** 42 51N 72 34W
Braunig Lake, *San Antonio, U.S.A.* **117 D3** 29 14N 98 22W
Brave, *PA, U.S.A.* **95 E2** 39 44N 80 16W
Bravo del Norte, Rio = Grande, Rio →, *N. Amer.* **98 M10** 25 58N 97 9W
Brawley, *CA, U.S.A.* **65 L11** 32 59N 115 31W
Brawley Peaks, *NV, U.S.A.* **85 D2** 38 15N 118 55W
Brawley Wash →, *AZ, U.S.A.* **62 E4** 32 34N 111 26W
Braxton, *MS, U.S.A.* **81 D4** 32 1N 89 58W
Braxton County ☆, *WV, U.S.A.* **102 C4** 38 43N 80 39W
Bray, *OK, U.S.A.* **93 D6** 34 38N 97 49W
Bray I., *Nunavut, Canada* **190 D10** 69 16N 77 0W
Braymer, *MO, U.S.A.* **82 B3** 39 35N 93 48W
Brayton, *IA, U.S.A.* **73 D4** 41 33N 94 56W
Brazeau →, *Alta., Canada* **185 F5** 52 55N 115 14W
Brazeau, Mt., *Alta., Canada* **185 F3** 52 33N 117 21W
Brazeau Res., *Alta., Canada* **185 F5** 52 59N 115 30W
Brazil, *IN, U.S.A.* **72 D3** 39 32N 87 8W
Brazoria, *TX, U.S.A.* **99 H12** 29 3N 95 34W
Brazoria County ☆, *TX, U.S.A.* **99 H12** 29 10N 95 26W
Brazoria Nat. Wildlife Refuge ⌓, *TX, U.S.A.* **99 H12** 29 3N 95 15W
Brazos →, *TX, U.S.A.* **99 J12** 28 53N 95 23W
Brazos County ☆, *TX, U.S.A.* **99 G11** 30 40N 96 22W
Breakheart Reservation, *Boston, U.S.A.* **106 A3** 42 28N 71 1W
Breaks Interstate Park ⌓, *U.S.A.* **97 C10** 37 17N 82 18W
Breathitt County ☆, *KY, U.S.A.* **97 C9** 37 30N 83 20W
Breaux Bridge, *LA, U.S.A.* **75 D4** 30 16N 91 54W
Brechin, *Ont., Canada* **178 C7** 44 32N 79 10W
Breckenridge, *CO, U.S.A.* **66 C4** 39 29N 106 3W
Breckenridge, *MI, U.S.A.* **79 F7** 43 24N 84 29W
Breckenridge, *MN, U.S.A.* **80 D2** 46 16N 96 35W
Breckenridge, *MO, U.S.A.* **82 B3** 39 46N 93 48W
Breckenridge, *TX, U.S.A.* **99 E9** 32 45N 98 54W
Breckenridge Hills, *MO, U.S.A.* **117 A1** 38 42N 90 22W
Breckinridge, *OK, U.S.A.* **93 B6** 36 26N 97 44W
Breckinridge County ☆, *KY, U.S.A.* **96 C6** 37 45N 86 25W
Brecksville, *Cleveland, U.S.A.* **107 B2** 41 19N 81 37W
Brecksville Reservation, *Cleveland, U.S.A.* **107 C2** 41 18N 81 36W
Breda, *IA, U.S.A.* **73 C4** 42 11N 94 59W
Bredenbury, *Sask., Canada* **183 E9** 50 57N 102 3W
Breeds Pond, *Boston, U.S.A.* **106 A4** 42 28N 70 58W
Breese, *IL, U.S.A.* **71 E4** 38 37N 89 32W
Breezy Point, *NY, U.S.A.* **114 C3** 40 33N 73 56W
Bremen, *AL, U.S.A.* **60 C4** 33 59N 86 58W
Bremen, *GA, U.S.A.* **68 C1** 33 43N 85 9W
Bremen, *IN, U.S.A.* **72 B4** 41 27N 86 9W
Bremen, *KY, U.S.A.* **96 C5** 37 22N 87 13W
Bremen, *OH, U.S.A.* **92 D4** 39 42N 82 26W
Bremer County ☆, *IA, U.S.A.* **73 C6** 42 50N 92 20W
Bremerton, *WA, U.S.A.* **101 C3** 47 34N 122 37W
Bremond, *TX, U.S.A.* **99 F11** 31 10N 96 41W
Brenham, *TX, U.S.A.* **99 G11** 30 10N 96 24W
Brent, *Ont., Canada* **179 A8** 46 2N 78 29W
Brent, *AL, U.S.A.* **60 D3** 32 56N 87 10W
Brentwood, *Vancouver, Canada* **193 B2** 49 16N 122 59W
Brentwood, *CA, U.S.A.* **64 F5** 37 56N 121 42W
Brentwood, *MO, U.S.A.* **117 B1** 38 37N 90 20W
Brentwood, *NH, U.S.A.* **86 D3** 42 58N 71 6W
Brentwood, *NY, U.S.A.* **87 B3** 40 47N 73 15W
Brentwood, *Pittsburgh, U.S.A.* **116 B2** 40 21N 79 58W
Brentwood, *TN, U.S.A.* **96 D6** 36 2N 86 47W
Brentwood Park, *Los Angeles, U.S.A.* **111 B2** 34 3N 118 29W
Breton, *Alta., Canada* **185 E6** 53 7N 114 28W
Breton Is., *LA, U.S.A.* **75 E6** 29 13N 89 12W
Breton Nat. Wildlife Refuge ⌓, *LA, U.S.A.* **75 E7** 29 50N 88 50W
Breton Sd., *LA, U.S.A.* **75 E6** 29 35N 89 15W
Brevard, *NC, U.S.A.* **90 C3** 35 14N 82 44W
Brevard County ☆, *FL, U.S.A.* **67 C8** 28 20N 80 45W
Brevig Mission, *AK, U.S.A.* **61 D6** 65 20N 166 29W
Brevort, *MI, U.S.A.* **79 C6** 46 1N 85 2W
Brewer, *ME, U.S.A.* **76 D5** 44 48N 68 46W
Brewer Park, *Ont., Canada* **192 B1** 45 23N 75 41W
Brewerton, *NY, U.S.A.* **89 B4** 43 14N 76 9W
Brewster, *KS, U.S.A.* **74 B2** 39 22N 101 23W
Brewster, *MA, U.S.A.* **78 C4** 41 46N 70 5W
Brewster, *MN, U.S.A.* **80 G3** 43 42N 95 28W
Brewster, *NY, U.S.A.* **87 A3** 41 24N 73 36W
Brewster, *NE, U.S.A.* **84 C6** 41 56N 99 52W
Brewster, *OH, U.S.A.* **92 C5** 40 43N 81 36W
Brewster, *WA, U.S.A.* **101 B6** 48 6N 119 47W
Brewster County ☆, *TX, U.S.A.* **98 H4** 30 0N 103 0W
Brewton, *AL, U.S.A.* **60 E3** 31 7N 87 4W
Brewton, *GA, U.S.A.* **68 D4** 32 36N 82 48W
Brian Head, *UT, U.S.A.* **100 F3** 37 41N 112 50W
Briargrove, *Houston, U.S.A.* **110 B2** 29 44N 95 29W
Briartown, *OK, U.S.A.* **93 C8** 35 18N 95 14W
Briceland, *CA, U.S.A.* **64 C3** 40 7N 123 54W
Bricelyn, *MN, U.S.A.* **80 G5** 43 34N 93 49W
Brices Cross Roads Nat. Battlefield Site ⌓, *MS, U.S.A.* **81 B5** 34 30N 88 44W
Briceville, *TN, U.S.A.* **97 D8** 36 11N 84 11W
Brickeys, *AR, U.S.A.* **63 D5** 34 52N 90 36W
Briçonnet, L., *Qué., Canada* **172 B9** 51 27N 60 10W
Bridge, *ID, U.S.A.* **70 G5** 42 8N 113 20W
Bridge, *OR, U.S.A.* **94 D2** 43 1N 124 0W
Bridge City, *TX, U.S.A.* **99 G14** 30 1N 93 51W
Bridge Lake, *B.C., Canada* **187 D14** 51 29N 120 43W
Bridgeboro, *GA, U.S.A.* **68 E3** 31 24N 83 59W
Bridgehampton, *NY, U.S.A.* **78 D2** 40 56N 72 18W
Bridgenorth, *Ont., Canada* **179 C8** 44 23N 78 23W
Bridgeport, *Ont., Canada* **178 D6** 43 29N 80 29W
Bridgeport, *AL, U.S.A.* **60 B5** 34 57N 85 43W
Bridgeport, *CA, U.S.A.* **64 E7** 38 15N 119 14W
Bridgeport, *Chicago, U.S.A.* **108 B3** 41 50N 87 38W
Bridgeport, *CT, U.S.A.* **78 C1** 41 11N 73 12W
Bridgeport, *IL, U.S.A.* **71 E6** 38 43N 87 46W
Bridgeport, *MI, U.S.A.* **79 F8** 43 22N 83 53W
Bridgeport, *NY, U.S.A.* **89 B5** 43 9N 75 58W
Bridgeport, *NE, U.S.A.* **84 C2** 41 40N 103 6W
Bridgeport, *OK, U.S.A.* **93 C5** 35 33N 98 23W
Bridgeport, *TX, U.S.A.* **99 D10** 33 13N 97 45W
Bridgeport, *WV, U.S.A.* **102 B4** 39 17N 80 15W
Bridgeport, *WA, U.S.A.* **101 C6** 48 0N 119 40W
Bridgeport, L., *TX, U.S.A.* **99 D10** 33 13N 97 50W
Bridger, *MT, U.S.A.* **83 E9** 45 18N 108 55W
Bridger Peak, *WY, U.S.A.* **104 E5** 41 11N 107 2W
Bridger-Teton Nat. Forest, *WY, U.S.A.* **104 C2** 43 5N 110 5W
Bridgeton, *NJ, U.S.A.* **87 D1** 39 26N 75 14W
Bridgetown, *N.S., Canada* **173 J4** 44 55N 65 18W
Bridgetown, *MD, U.S.A.* **77 A5** 39 2N 75 53W
Bridgeview, *Chicago, U.S.A.* **108 C2** 41 45N 87 48W
Bridgeville, *CA, U.S.A.* **64 C3** 40 25N 123 50W
Bridgeville, *DE, U.S.A.* **77 B5** 38 45N 75 36W
Bridgeville, *Pittsburgh, U.S.A.* **116 B1** 40 21N 80 6W
Bridgewater, *N.S., Canada* **173 J5** 44 25N 64 31W
Bridgewater, *CT, U.S.A.* **78 C1** 41 32N 73 22W
Bridgewater, *IA, U.S.A.* **73 D4** 41 15N 94 40W
Bridgewater, *ME, U.S.A.* **76 B6** 46 25N 67 51W
Bridgewater, *MA, U.S.A.* **78 C4** 41 59N 70 58W
Bridgewater, *NY, U.S.A.* **89 C5** 42 53N 75 15W
Bridgewater, *SD, U.S.A.* **91 G8** 43 33N 97 30W
Bridgewater, *VA, U.S.A.* **102 C5** 38 23N 78 59W
Bridgewater, *VT, U.S.A.* **86 C2** 43 35N 72 38W
Bridgman, *MI, U.S.A.* **79 H5** 41 57N 86 33W
Bridgton, *ME, U.S.A.* **76 D3** 44 3N 70 42W
Bridport, *VT, U.S.A.* **86 C1** 43 58N 73 20W
Brier, *Seattle, U.S.A.* **118 B4** 47 47N 122 16W
Brier Cr. →, *GA, U.S.A.* **68 D5** 32 44N 81 26W
Brier I., *N.S., Canada* **173 J3** 44 16N 66 22W
Briercrest, *Sask., Canada* **182 E6** 50 10N 105 16W
Brigantine, *NJ, U.S.A.* **87 C2** 39 24N 74 22W
Briggsdale, *CO, U.S.A.* **66 B6** 40 38N 104 20W
Briggsville, *AR, U.S.A.* **63 D2** 34 56N 93 30W
Brigham City, *UT, U.S.A.* **100 B3** 41 31N 112 1W
Bright, *IN, U.S.A.* **72 D6** 39 13N 84 51W
Brighton, *Ont., Canada* **179 C9** 44 2N 77 44W
Brighton, *Boston, U.S.A.* **106 A3** 42 21N 71 9W
Brighton, *CO, U.S.A.* **66 C6** 39 59N 104 49W
Brighton, *FL, U.S.A.* **67 D7** 27 14N 81 6W
Brighton, *IL, U.S.A.* **71 D3** 39 2N 90 8W
Brighton, *IA, U.S.A.* **73 D7** 41 10N 91 49W
Brighton, *MI, U.S.A.* **79 G8** 42 32N 83 47W
Brighton, *NY, U.S.A.* **89 B3** 43 8N 77 34W
Brighton, *Salt Lake City, U.S.A.* **117 C4** 40 36N 111 34W
Brighton, *TN, U.S.A.* **96 E3** 35 29N 89 43W
Brighton Indian Reservation, *FL, U.S.A.* **67 D7** 27 0N 81 15W
Brighton Park, *Chicago, U.S.A.* **108 C2** 41 48N 87 41W
Brightsand L., *Sask., Canada* **182 B3** 53 36N 108 53W
Brightwood, *DC, U.S.A.* **119 B3** 38 57N 77 1W
Brilliant, *B.C., Canada* **187 F17** 49 19N 117 38W
Brilliant, *AL, U.S.A.* **60 B3** 34 1N 87 46W
Brillion, *WI, U.S.A.* **103 D5** 44 11N 88 4W
Brimfield, *IL, U.S.A.* **71 C4** 40 50N 89 53W
Brimfield, *MA, U.S.A.* **78 B2** 42 7N 72 12W
Brimley, *MI, U.S.A.* **79 C7** 46 24N 84 34W
Brimson, *MN, U.S.A.* **80 C7** 47 17N 91 52W
Brinkley, *AR, U.S.A.* **63 D4** 34 53N 91 12W
Brinnon, *WA, U.S.A.* **101 C3** 47 41N 122 54W
Brinsmade, *ND, U.S.A.* **91 B6** 48 11N 99 19W
Brinson, *GA, U.S.A.* **68 F2** 30 59N 84 44W
Brion, Î., *Qué., Canada* **173 F8** 47 46N 61 26W
Brisbane, *San Francisco, U.S.A.* **118 B2** 37 40N 122 23W
Briscoe, *TX, U.S.A.* **98 B7** 35 35N 100 17W
Briscoe County ☆, *TX, U.S.A.* **98 C6** 34 28N 101 19W
Bristol, *N.B., Canada* **173 G2** 46 28N 67 35W
Bristol, *Qué., Canada* **176 F6** 45 32N 76 28W
Bristol, *CO, U.S.A.* **66 D8** 38 7N 102 19W
Bristol, *CT, U.S.A.* **78 C2** 41 40N 72 57W
Bristol, *FL, U.S.A.* **67 A4** 30 26N 84 59W
Bristol, *IN, U.S.A.* **72 B5** 41 43N 85 49W
Bristol, *MD, U.S.A.* **77 B4** 38 47N 76 40W
Bristol, *NH, U.S.A.* **86 C3** 43 36N 71 44W
Bristol, *PA, U.S.A.* **87 B2** 40 6N 74 51W
Bristol, *RI, U.S.A.* **78 C3** 41 40N 71 16W
Bristol, *SD, U.S.A.* **91 E8** 45 21N 97 45W
Bristol, *TN, U.S.A.* **97 D10** 36 36N 82 11W
Bristol, *VA, U.S.A.* **102 E2** 36 36N 82 11W
Bristol, *VT, U.S.A.* **86 B1** 44 8N 73 5W
Bristol B., *AK, U.S.A.* **61 H8** 58 0N 160 0W
Bristol Bay ☆, *AK, U.S.A.* **61 G8** 58 45N 156 50W
Bristol County ☆, *MA, U.S.A.* **78 C3** 41 45N 71 0W
Bristol County ☆, *RI, U.S.A.* **78 C3** 41 40N 71 20W
Bristol L., *CA, U.S.A.* **65 J11** 34 28N 115 41W
Bristol Mts., *CA, U.S.A.* **65 J11** 34 30N 115 50W
Bristow, *NE, U.S.A.* **84 B7** 42 51N 98 35W
Bristow, *OK, U.S.A.* **93 C7** 35 50N 96 23W
Bristow, *VA, U.S.A.* **77 B3** 38 43N 77 32W
Britannia Beach, *B.C., Canada* **187 F11** 49 38N 123 12W
British Columbia □, *Canada* **186 B10** 55 0N 125 15W
British Empire Range, *Nunavut, Canada* **190 A10** 82 21N 77 30W
British Mts., *N. Amer.* **188 C4** 68 50N 140 0W
British Virgin Is. ☒, *W. Indies* **105 G18** 18 30N 64 30W
Britt, *Ont., Canada* **178 B6** 45 46N 80 34W
Britt, *IA, U.S.A.* **73 B5** 43 6N 93 48W
Britton, *SD, U.S.A.* **91 E8** 45 48N 97 45W
Britton Hill, *FL, U.S.A.* **67 A2** 30 59N 86 17W
Broad →, *GA, U.S.A.* **68 C4** 33 59N 82 39W
Broad →, *SC, U.S.A.* **90 D4** 34 1N 81 4W
Broad Ripple Park, *Indianapolis, U.S.A.* **110 A2** 39 52N 86 7W
Broad Sd., *Boston, U.S.A.* **106 A4** 42 23N 70 56W
Broadalbin, *NY, U.S.A.* **89 B6** 43 4N 74 12W
Broadback →, *Qué., Canada* **175 C2** 51 21N 78 52W
Broadbent, *OR, U.S.A.* **94 D1** 43 1N 124 9W
Broadhurst, *GA, U.S.A.* **68 E5** 31 28N 81 55W
Broadkill Beach, *DE, U.S.A.* **77 B5** 38 47N 75 10W
Broadmoor, *San Francisco, U.S.A.* **118 B2** 37 41N 122 29W
Broadus, *MT, U.S.A.* **83 E12** 45 27N 105 25W
Broadview, *Sask., Canada* **182 E9** 50 22N 102 35W
Broadview, *Chicago, U.S.A.* **108 B1** 41 51N 87 52W
Broadview, *MT, U.S.A.* **83 D9** 46 6N 108 53W
Broadview, *NM, U.S.A.* **88 C7** 34 49N 103 13W
Broadview Heights, *Cleveland, U.S.A.* **107 B1** 41 18N 81 41W
Broadview Park, *Miami, U.S.A.* **112 B2** 26 5N 80 12W
Broadwater, *NE, U.S.A.* **84 C3** 41 36N 102 51W
Broadwater County ☆, *MT, U.S.A.* **83 D6** 46 25N 111 30W
Broadway, *VA, U.S.A.* **102 C6** 38 37N 78 48W
Broadwell, *IL, U.S.A.* **71 C4** 40 4N 89 27W
Brochet, *Man., Canada* **191 F5** 57 53N 101 40W
Brochet, L., *Man., Canada* **191 F5** 58 36N 101 35W
Brochet, L. du, *Qué., Canada* **177 B13** 49 40N 69 37W
Brock, *Sask., Canada* **182 D3** 51 26N 108 43W
Brock, *NE, U.S.A.* **84 D10** 40 29N 95 58W
Brock →, *Qué., Canada* **176 A7** 50 0N 75 5W
Brock I., *N.W.T., Canada* **188 A10** 77 52N 114 19W
Brocket, *ND, U.S.A.* **91 B7** 48 13N 98 21W
Brockport, *NY, U.S.A.* **89 B3** 43 13N 77 56W
Brockton, *MA, U.S.A.* **78 B3** 42 5N 71 1W
Brockton, *MT, U.S.A.* **83 B13** 48 9N 104 55W
Brockville, *Ont., Canada* **179 C11** 44 35N 75 41W
Brockway, *MT, U.S.A.* **83 C12** 47 18N 105 45W
Brockway, *PA, U.S.A.* **95 C4** 41 15N 78 47W
Brocton, *IL, U.S.A.* **71 D6** 39 43N 87 56W
Brocton, *NY, U.S.A.* **89 C1** 42 23N 79 26W
Broderick, *Sask., Canada* **182 D5** 51 30N 106 55W
Brodeur Pen., *Nunavut, Canada* **190 C8** 72 30N 88 10W
Brodhead, *KY, U.S.A.* **97 C8** 37 24N 84 25W
Brodhead, *WI, U.S.A.* **103 F4** 42 37N 89 22W
Brodheadsville, *PA, U.S.A.* **87 B1** 40 55N 75 24W
Brodnax, *VA, U.S.A.* **102 E6** 36 43N 78 2W
Brogan, *OR, U.S.A.* **94 C8** 44 15N 117 31W
Brogden, *NC, U.S.A.* **90 C7** 35 18N 78 2W
Brokaw, *WI, U.S.A.* **103 C4** 45 2N 89 39W
Broken Arrow, *OK, U.S.A.* **93 B8** 36 3N 95 48W
Broken Bow, *NE, U.S.A.* **84 C6** 41 24N 99 38W
Broken Bow, *OK, U.S.A.* **93 D9** 34 2N 94 44W
Broken Bow Lake, *OK, U.S.A.* **93 D9** 34 9N 94 40W
Bromide, *OK, U.S.A.* **93 D7** 34 24N 96 31W
Bromley, *OH, U.S.A.* **107 B1** 39 4N 84 33W
Bromont, *Qué., Canada* **177 F10** 45 17N 72 39W
Bromptonville, *Qué., Canada* **177 F11** 45 28N 71 57W
Bronaugh, *MO, U.S.A.* **82 D2** 37 41N 94 28W
Bronson, *FL, U.S.A.* **67 B6** 29 27N 82 39W
Bronson, *KS, U.S.A.* **74 D8** 37 54N 95 4W
Bronson, *MI, U.S.A.* **79 H6** 41 52N 85 12W
Bronson, *TX, U.S.A.* **99 F13** 31 21N 94 1W
Bronte, *TX, U.S.A.* **98 F7** 31 53N 100 18W
Bronwood, *GA, U.S.A.* **68 E2** 31 50N 84 22W
Bronx, *NY, U.S.A.* **114 B3** 40 51N 73 52W
Bronx County ☆, *NY, U.S.A.* **89 E7** 40 50N 73 52W
Bronxville, *NY, U.S.A.* **114 A4** 40 56N 73 49W
Brooch, L., *Qué., Canada* **172 C2** 50 45N 67 59W
Brook, *IN, U.S.A.* **72 C3** 40 52N 87 22W
Brook Park, *OH, U.S.A.* **92 B5** 41 23N 81 48W
Brookdale, *Man., Canada* **183 E12** 50 3N 99 34W
Brookdale Park, *Minneapolis-St. Paul, U.S.A.* **113 A2** 45 3N 93 20W
Brooke County ☆, *WV, U.S.A.* **102 A4** 40 16N 80 37W
Brookeland, *TX, U.S.A.* **99 F14** 31 10N 94 0W
Brookesmith, *TX, U.S.A.* **99 F8** 31 33N 99 7W
Brookfield, *N.S., Canada* **173 H6** 45 15N 63 17W
Brookfield, *Chicago, U.S.A.* **108 C1** 41 48N 87 50W
Brookfield, *MA, U.S.A.* **78 B2** 42 13N 72 6W
Brookfield, *MO, U.S.A.* **82 B3** 39 47N 93 4W
Brookfield, *VT, U.S.A.* **86 B2** 44 4N 72 38W
Brookfield, *WI, U.S.A.* **103 E5** 43 4N 88 9W
Brookhaven, *Atlanta, U.S.A.* **106 A2** 33 52N 84 19W
Brookhaven, *MS, U.S.A.* **81 E3** 31 35N 90 26W
Brookings, *OR, U.S.A.* **94 E1** 42 3N 124 17W
Brookings, *SD, U.S.A.* **91 F9** 44 19N 96 48W
Brookings County ☆, *SD, U.S.A.* **91 F9** 44 19N 96 48W
Brookland = West Columbia, *SC, U.S.A.* **90 E4** 33 59N 81 4W
Brookland, *AR, U.S.A.* **63 C5** 35 54N 90 35W
Brooklandville, *Baltimore, U.S.A.* **107 A1** 39 25N 76 40W
Brooklawn, *NJ, U.S.A.* **116 B2** 39 52N 75 7W
Brooklet, *GA, U.S.A.* **68 D5** 32 23N 81 40W
Brookline, *MA, U.S.A.* **78 B3** 42 19N 71 8W
Brookline, *NH, U.S.A.* **86 D3** 42 44N 71 40W
Brooklyn, *N.S., Canada* **173 J5** 44 3N 64 42W
Brooklyn, *AL, U.S.A.* **60 E4** 31 16N 86 46W
Brooklyn, *Cleveland, U.S.A.* **107 B1** 41 26N 81 44W
Brooklyn, *CT, U.S.A.* **78 C3** 41 47N 71 57W
Brooklyn, *IL, U.S.A.* **117 B3** 38 39N 90 10W
Brooklyn, *IN, U.S.A.* **72 D4** 39 32N 86 22W
Brooklyn, *IA, U.S.A.* **73 D6** 41 44N 92 27W
Brooklyn, *MI, U.S.A.* **79 G7** 42 7N 84 15W
Brooklyn, *MS, U.S.A.* **81 E4** 31 3N 89 11W
Brooklyn, *NY, U.S.A.* **89 E7** 40 37N 73 57W
Brooklyn, *WA, U.S.A.* **101 D2** 46 47N 123 31W
Brooklyn Center, *Minneapolis-St. Paul, U.S.A.* **113 A2** 45 4N 93 19W
Brooklyn Heights, *Cleveland, U.S.A.* **107 B1** 41 23N 81 41W
Brooklyn Heights, *New York, U.S.A.* **114 B3** 40 41N 73 59W
Brooklyn Park, *MD, U.S.A.* **77 A4** 39 13N 76 37W
Brooklyn Park, *MN, U.S.A.* **80 E5** 45 6N 93 23W
Brookmere, *B.C., Canada* **187 F14** 49 52N 120 53W
Brookmont, *MD, U.S.A.* **119 B3** 38 57N 77 7W
Brookneal, *VA, U.S.A.* **102 D6** 37 3N 78 57W
Brookport, *IL, U.S.A.* **71 F5** 37 8N 88 38W
Brooks, *Alta., Canada* **185 H9** 50 35N 111 55W
Brooks, *KY, U.S.A.* **97 B7** 38 4N 85 43W
Brooks, *MN, U.S.A.* **80 C3** 47 49N 96 0W
Brooks Air Force Base, *San Antonio, U.S.A.* **117 C3** 29 20N 98 25W
Brooks B., *B.C., Canada* **186 E7** 50 15N 127 55W
Brooks County ☆, *GA, U.S.A.* **68 F3** 30 50N 83 45W
Brooks County ☆, *TX, U.S.A.* **98 K9** 27 0N 98 5W
Brooks Range, *AK, U.S.A.* **61 C9** 68 0N 152 0W
Brookshire, *TX, U.S.A.* **99 H12** 29 47N 95 57W
Brookside Park, *Cleveland, U.S.A.* **107 B1** 41 27N 81 43W
Brookside Park, *Indianapolis, U.S.A.* **110 B2** 39 47N 86 6W
Brookside Village, *Houston, U.S.A.* **110 C3** 29 35N 95 13W
Brookston, *IN, U.S.A.* **72 C4** 40 36N 86 52W
Brookston, *MN, U.S.A.* **80 D6** 46 52N 92 36W
Brooksville, *AL, U.S.A.* **60 B4** 34 10N 86 29W
Brooksville, *FL, U.S.A.* **67 C6** 28 33N 82 23W
Brooksville, *KY, U.S.A.* **97 B8** 38 41N 84 4W
Brooksville, *MS, U.S.A.* **81 C5** 33 14N 88 35W
Brooksville, *OK, U.S.A.* **93 C7** 35 12N 96 58W
Brookview, *MD, U.S.A.* **77 B5** 38 35N 75 48W
Brookville, *IN, U.S.A.* **72 D5** 39 25N 85 1W
Brookville, *KS, U.S.A.* **74 C6** 38 46N 97 52W
Brookville, *NJ, U.S.A.* **87 C2** 39 44N 74 18W
Brookville, *OH, U.S.A.* **92 D2** 39 50N 84 24W
Brookville, *PA, U.S.A.* **95 C3** 41 10N 79 5W
Brookville L., *IN, U.S.A.* **72 D5** 39 28N 85 0W
Brookwood, *AL, U.S.A.* **60 C3** 33 17N 87 18W
Broome County ☆, *NY, U.S.A.* **89 C5** 42 5N 75 45W
Broomes Island, *MD, U.S.A.* **77 B4** 38 25N 76 33W
Broomfield, *CO, U.S.A.* **66 C5** 39 55N 105 5W
Brooten, *MN, U.S.A.* **80 E3** 45 30N 95 8W
Broseley, *MO, U.S.A.* **82 E6** 36 40N 90 15W
Brosewere Bay, *NY, U.S.A.* **114 C4** 40 37N 73 42W
Brossard, *Montréal, Canada* **192 B4** 45 27N 73 28W
Brothers, *OR, U.S.A.* **94 D5** 43 49N 120 36W
Brotmanville, *NJ, U.S.A.* **87 C1** 39 33N 75 3W
Broughton, *IL, U.S.A.* **71 F5** 37 56N 88 27W
Broughton, *Pittsburgh, U.S.A.* **116 C2** 40 19N 79 59W
Broughton I., *B.C., Canada* **186 E8** 50 48N 126 42W
Broughton Island = Qikiqtarjuaq, *Nunavut, Canada* **190 D13** 67 33N 63 0W
Broussard, *LA, U.S.A.* **75 D4** 30 9N 91 58W
Broward County ☆, *FL, U.S.A.* **67 E8** 26 15N 80 30W
Browerville, *MN, U.S.A.* **80 D4** 46 5N 94 52W
Brown, Pt., *WA, U.S.A.* **101 D1** 46 56N 124 10W
Brown City, *MI, U.S.A.* **79 F9** 43 13N 82 59W
Brown County ☆, *IL, U.S.A.* **71 D3** 39 55N 90 45W
Brown County ☆, *IN, U.S.A.* **72 D4** 39 10N 86 15W
Brown County ☆, *KS, U.S.A.* **74 B8** 39 45N 95 30W
Brown County ☆, *MN, U.S.A.* **80 F4** 44 10N 94 50W
Brown County ☆, *NE, U.S.A.* **84 B6** 42 30N 100 0W
Brown County ☆, *OH, U.S.A.* **92 E3** 38 55N 83 59W
Brown County ☆, *SD, U.S.A.* **91 E7** 45 37N 98 19W
Brown County ☆, *TX, U.S.A.* **99 F9** 31 43N 98 59W
Brown County ☆, *WI, U.S.A.* **103 D6** 44 30N 88 0W
Brown County State Park ⌓, *IN, U.S.A.* **72 D4** 39 7N 86 16W
Brown Deer, *WI, U.S.A.* **103 E6** 43 9N 87 57W
Brown Deer Park, *Milwaukee, U.S.A.* **112 B2** 43 9N 87 57W
Brown L., *Nunavut, Canada* **191 D7** 65 54N 91 15W
Brownell, *KS, U.S.A.* **74 C4** 38 38N 99 45W
Brownfield, *TX, U.S.A.* **98 D5** 33 11N 102 17W
Browning, *Sask., Canada* **182 F9** 49 27N 102 38W
Browning, *IL, U.S.A.* **71 C3** 40 8N 90 22W
Browning, *MT, U.S.A.* **83 B4** 48 34N 113 1W
Brownlee, *Sask., Canada* **182 E5** 50 43N 106 1W
Brownlee, *NE, U.S.A.* **84 B5** 42 17N 100 37W
Brownlee Res., *ID, U.S.A.* **70 E2** 44 50N 116 54W
Browns, *IL, U.S.A.* **71 E6** 38 23N 87 59W
Browns Flats, *N.B., Canada* **173 H3** 45 28N 66 7W
Browns Mills, *NJ, U.S.A.* **87 C2** 39 58N 74 34W
Browns Park Nat. Wildlife Refuge ⌓, *CO, U.S.A.* **66 B2** 40 50N 108 55W
Browns Valley, *MN, U.S.A.* **80 E2** 45 36N 96 50W
Brownsburg, *IN, U.S.A.* **72 D4** 39 51N 86 24W
Brownsdale, *MN, U.S.A.* **80 G6** 43 45N 92 52W
Brownstown, *IL, U.S.A.* **71 E5** 39 0N 88 57W
Brownstown, *IN, U.S.A.* **72 E4** 38 53N 86 3W
Brownsville, *KY, U.S.A.* **96 C6** 37 12N 86 16W
Brownsville, *LA, U.S.A.* **75 B3** 32 29N 92 9W
Brownsville, *MN, U.S.A.* **80 G7** 43 42N 91 17W
Brownsville, *OR, U.S.A.* **94 C3** 44 24N 122 59W
Brownsville, *PA, U.S.A.* **95 D3** 40 1N 79 53W
Brownsville, *Seattle, U.S.A.* **118 C2** 47 39N 122 36W
Brownsville, *TN, U.S.A.* **96 E3** 35 36N 89 16W
Brownsville, *TX, U.S.A.* **98 M10** 25 54N 97 30W
Brownton, *MN, U.S.A.* **80 F4** 44 44N 94 21W
Browntown, *WI, U.S.A.* **103 F4** 42 35N 89 48W
Brownville, *AL, U.S.A.* **60 C3** 33 24N 87 52W
Brownville, *ME, U.S.A.* **76 C4** 45 18N 69 2W
Brownville, *NY, U.S.A.* **89 A4** 44 0N 75 59W
Brownville, *NE, U.S.A.* **84 D10** 40 24N 95 40W
Brownville Junction, *ME, U.S.A.* **76 C4** 45 21N 69 3W
Brownwood, *MO, U.S.A.* **82 D7** 37 5N 89 57W
Brownwood, *TX, U.S.A.* **99 F9** 31 43N 98 59W
Brownwood, L., *TX, U.S.A.* **99 F8** 31 50N 99 0W
Broxton, *GA, U.S.A.* **68 E4** 31 38N 82 53W
Broyhill Park, *VA, U.S.A.* **119 B2** 38 52N 77 12W
Bruce, *Alta., Canada* **185 E8** 53 10N 112 2W
Bruce, *FL, U.S.A.* **67 A3** 30 28N 85 58W
Bruce, *MS, U.S.A.* **81 C4** 33 59N 89 21W
Bruce, *SD, U.S.A.* **91 F9** 44 26N 96 54W
Bruce, *WI, U.S.A.* **103 C2** 45 28N 91 16W
Bruce L., *Ont., Canada* **180 B3** 50 49N 93 20W
Bruce Pen., *Ont., Canada* **178 B5** 45 0N 81 30W
Bruce Peninsula Nat. Park △, *Ont., Canada* **178 B5** 45 14N 81 36W
Bruceton, *TN, U.S.A.* **96 D4** 36 3N 88 15W
Bruceton Mills, *WV, U.S.A.* **102 B5** 39 40N 79 38W
Bruceville, *IN, U.S.A.* **72 E3** 38 46N 87 25W
Bruceville, *MD, U.S.A.* **77 B5** 38 40N 75 59W
Bruderheim, *Alta., Canada* **184 E8** 53 47N 112 56W
Bruin Pt., *UT, U.S.A.* **100 D5** 39 39N 110 21W
Brûlé, *Alta., Canada* **184 E3** 53 15N 117 58W
Brule, *NE, U.S.A.* **84 C4** 41 6N 101 53W
Brule →, *WI, U.S.A.* **103 C5** 45 57N 88 12W
Brûlé, L., *Nfld. & L., Canada* **172 A6** 52 30N 63 40W
Brule County ☆, *SD, U.S.A.* **91 G6** 43 45N 99 0W
Brule L., *MN, U.S.A.* **80 D8** 46 58N 90 50W
Brumley, *MO, U.S.A.* **82 C4** 38 5N 92 29W
Brundidge, *AL, U.S.A.* **60 E5** 31 43N 85 49W
Bruneau, *ID, U.S.A.* **70 G3** 42 53N 115 48W
Bruneau →, *ID, U.S.A.* **70 G3** 42 56N 115 57W
Brunette I., *Nfld. & L., Canada* **174 E5** 47 16N 55 55W
Bruning, *NE, U.S.A.* **84 D8** 40 20N 97 34W
Brunkild, *Man., Canada* **183 F14** 49 36N 97 35W
Bruno, *Sask., Canada* **182 C6** 52 20N 105 30W
Bruno, *MN, U.S.A.* **80 D6** 46 17N 92 40W
Bruno, *NE, U.S.A.* **84 C9** 41 17N 96 58W
Brunson, *SC, U.S.A.* **90 F4** 32 56N 81 11W
Brunsville, *IA, U.S.A.* **73 C2** 42 49N 96 16W
Brunswick, *GA, U.S.A.* **68 E5** 31 10N 81 30W
Brunswick, *ME, U.S.A.* **76 E4** 43 55N 69 58W
Brunswick, *MD, U.S.A.* **77 A3** 39 19N 77 38W
Brunswick, *MO, U.S.A.* **82 B3** 39 26N 93 8W
Brunswick, *NE, U.S.A.* **84 B8** 42 20N 97 58W
Brunswick, *OH, U.S.A.* **92 B5** 41 14N 81 51W
Brunswick County ☆, *NC, U.S.A.* **90 D7** 34 0N 78 20W
Brunswick County ☆, *VA, U.S.A.* **102 E7** 36 46N 77 51W
Brunswick L., *Ont., Canada* **181 D13** 48 58N 83 23W
Brunswick Naval Air Station, *ME, U.S.A.* **76 E4** 43 53N 69 57W
Brush, *CO, U.S.A.* **66 B7** 40 15N 103 37W
Brush Creek, *TN, U.S.A.* **96 D6** 36 7N 86 2W
Brush Hill, *Boston, U.S.A.* **106 B1** 42 15N 71 22W
Brushton, *NY, U.S.A.* **89 A6** 44 50N 74 31W
Brusly, *LA, U.S.A.* **75 D4** 30 23N 91 14W
Brussels, *WI, U.S.A.* **103 D6** 44 44N 87 37W
Bryan, *OH, U.S.A.* **92 B2** 41 28N 84 33W
Bryan, *TX, U.S.A.* **99 G11** 30 40N 96 22W
Bryan, L., *Orlando, U.S.A.* **115 B2** 28 22N 81 29W
Bryan County ☆, *GA, U.S.A.* **68 D5** 32 0N 81 30W
Bryan County ☆, *OK, U.S.A.* **93 E7** 34 0N 96 15W
Bryans Road, *MD, U.S.A.* **77 B3** 38 38N 77 4W
Bryant, *AR, U.S.A.* **63 D3** 34 36N 92 29W
Bryant, *IN, U.S.A.* **72 C6** 40 32N 84 58W
Bryant, *SD, U.S.A.* **91 F8** 44 35N 97 28W
Bryant Cr. →, *MO, U.S.A.* **82 E4** 36 36N 92 17W
Bryant Lake, *Minneapolis-St. Paul, U.S.A.* **113 B1** 44 52N 93 25W
Bryant Lake Regional Park ⌓, *Minneapolis-St. Paul, U.S.A.* **113 B1** 44 52N 93 25W
Bryantown, *MD, U.S.A.* **77 B4** 38 33N 76 52W

Bryce Canyon Nat. Park △, *UT, U.S.A.* **100 F3** 37 30N 112 10W
Bryson, *Qué., Canada* **176 F6** 45 41N 76 37W
Bryson, *TX, U.S.A.* **99 D9** 33 10N 98 23W
Bryson City, *NC, U.S.A.* **90 C2** 35 26N 83 27W
Buaysiacobe, *Sonora, Mexico* **212 F6** 27 5N 109 43W
Bucerias, *Nayarit, Mexico* **216 G5** 20 46N 105 20W
Buchan G., *Nunavut, Canada* **190 C11** 71 45N 74 20W
Buchanan, *Sask., Canada* **182 D9** 51 40N 102 45W
Buchanan, *GA, U.S.A.* **68 C1** 33 48N 85 11W
Buchanan, *MI, U.S.A.* **79 H5** 41 50N 86 22W
Buchanan, *ND, U.S.A.* **91 C7** 47 4N 98 50W
Buchanan, *VA, U.S.A.* **102 D5** 37 32N 79 41W
Buchanan, L., *TX, U.S.A.* **99 G9** 30 45N 98 25W
Buchanan County ☆, *IA, U.S.A.* **73 C7** 42 30N 91 50W
Buchanan County ☆, *MO, U.S.A.* **82 B2** 39 40N 94 50W
Buchanan County ☆, *VA, U.S.A.* **102 D2** 37 17N 82 6W
Buchanan Dam, *TX, U.S.A.* **99 G9** 30 45N 98 25W
Buchans, *Nfld. & L., Canada* **174 D4** 48 50N 56 52W
Buchans Junction, *Nfld. & L., Canada* **174 D4** 48 51N 56 28W
Buchon, Pt., *CA, U.S.A.* **65 H6** 35 15N 120 54W
Buck Cr. →, *KY, U.S.A.* **97 D8** 36 59N 84 29W
Buck Grove, *IA, U.S.A.* **73 D3** 41 55N 95 23W
Buck L., *Alta., Canada* **185 F6** 52 59N 114 46W
Buck Lake, *Alta., Canada* **185 F6** 52 57N 114 47W
Buckatunna, *MS, U.S.A.* **81 E5** 31 32N 88 32W
Buckatunna Cr. →, *MS, U.S.A.* **81 E5** 31 30N 88 32W
Buckeye, *AZ, U.S.A.* **62 D3** 33 22N 112 35W
Buckeye, *IA, U.S.A.* **73 C5** 42 25N 93 23W
Buckeystown, *MD, U.S.A.* **77 A3** 39 20N 77 26W
Buckfield, *ME, U.S.A.* **76 D3** 44 17N 70 22W
Buckhannon, *WV, U.S.A.* **102 C4** 39 0N 80 8W
Buckhead, *Atlanta, U.S.A.* **106 A2** 33 51N 84 24W
Buckholts, *TX, U.S.A.* **99 G10** 30 52N 97 7W
Buckhorn, *KY, U.S.A.* **97 C9** 37 21N 83 28W
Buckhorn, *NM, U.S.A.* **88 D2** 33 2N 108 42W
Buckhorn L., *Ont., Canada* **179 C8** 44 29N 78 23W
Buckhorn L., *KY, U.S.A.* **97 C9** 37 21N 83 28W
Buckingham, *Qué., Canada* **176 F7** 45 37N 75 24W
Buckingham, *CO, U.S.A.* **66 B7** 40 37N 103 58W
Buckingham, *PA, U.S.A.* **87 B1** 40 19N 75 4W
Buckingham, *VA, U.S.A.* **102 D6** 37 33N 78 33W
Buckingham County ☆, *VA, U.S.A.* **102 D6** 37 40N 78 40W
Buckingham I., *Nunavut, Canada* **190 B7** 77 12N 91 0W
Buckland, *AK, U.S.A.* **61 D7** 65 59N 161 8W
Buckland, *OH, U.S.A.* **92 C2** 40 37N 84 16W
Buckley, *IL, U.S.A.* **71 C5** 40 36N 88 2W
Buckley, *MI, U.S.A.* **79 E6** 44 30N 85 41W
Buckley, *WA, U.S.A.* **101 C3** 47 10N 122 2W
Bucklin, *KS, U.S.A.* **74 D4** 37 33N 99 38W
Bucklin, *MO, U.S.A.* **82 B4** 39 47N 92 53W
Buckman, *MN, U.S.A.* **80 E4** 45 54N 94 6W
Bucks County ☆, *PA, U.S.A.* **95 D7** 40 15N 75 10W
Bucks L., *CA, U.S.A.* **64 D5** 39 54N 121 12W
Buckskin Mts., *AZ, U.S.A.* **62 C2** 34 10N 113 50W
Bucksport, *ME, U.S.A.* **76 D5** 44 34N 68 47W
Bucksport, *SC, U.S.A.* **90 E6** 33 40N 79 6W
Bucktown, *MD, U.S.A.* **77 B4** 38 25N 76 3W
Bucoda, *WA, U.S.A.* **101 D3** 46 48N 122 52W
Buctzotz, *Yucatán, Mexico* **223 A5** 21 12N 88 47W
Bucyrus, *KS, U.S.A.* **74 C9** 38 44N 94 44W
Bucyrus, *ND, U.S.A.* **91 D3** 46 4N 102 47W
Bucyrus, *OH, U.S.A.* **92 C4** 40 48N 82 59W
Buda, *IL, U.S.A.* **71 B4** 41 20N 89 41W
Buda, *TX, U.S.A.* **99 G10** 30 5N 97 51W
Budd Lake, *NJ, U.S.A.* **87 B2** 40 52N 74 44W
Budds Creek, *MD, U.S.A.* **77 B4** 38 23N 76 51W
Bude, *MS, U.S.A.* **81 E3** 31 28N 90 51W
Buechel, *KY, U.S.A.* **97 B7** 38 12N 85 39W
Buena, *NJ, U.S.A.* **87 C2** 39 31N 74 56W
Buena Park, *CA, U.S.A.* **111 C4** 33 52N 117 59W
Buena Ventura Lakes, *Orlando, U.S.A.* **115 B2** 28 21N 81 21W
Buena Vista, *AR, U.S.A.* **63 E3** 33 29N 92 57W
Buena Vista, *CO, U.S.A.* **66 D4** 38 51N 106 8W
Buena Vista, *GA, U.S.A.* **68 D2** 32 19N 84 31W
Buena Vista, *San Antonio, U.S.A.* **117 D3** 29 16N 98 27W
Buena Vista, *VA, U.S.A.* **102 D5** 37 44N 79 21W
Buena Vista County ☆, *IA, U.S.A.* **73 C3** 42 45N 95 10W
Buena Vista Lake Bed, *CA, U.S.A.* **65 H7** 35 12N 119 18W
Buenaventura, *Chihuahua, Mexico* **213 D8** 29 51N 107 29W
Buenavista, *Chiapas, Mexico* **222 C3** 16 18N 93 10W
Buenavista, *Chihuahua, Mexico* **213 G8** 26 59N 107 36W
Buenavista, *Guerrero, Mexico* **219 D8** 18 27N 99 25W
Buenavista, *Quintana Roo, Mexico* **223 D5** 18 54N 88 15W
Buenavista, *San Luis Potosí, Mexico* **215 H4** 22 37N 100 7W
Buenavista, *Zacatecas, Mexico* **217 E9** 22 4N 101 44W
Buenavista, Estero, *Chiapas, Mexico* **222 D3** 15 49N 93 10W
Buenavista Sa. Sección, *Tabasco, Mexico* **222 A4** 18 12N 92 44W
Buenavista Tomatlán, *Michoacan, Mexico* **218 C5** 19 12N 102 36W
Buenos Aires Nat. Wildlife Refuge ⌓, *AZ, U.S.A.* **62 F4** 31 30N 111 30W
Bueyeros, *NM, U.S.A.* **88 B7** 35 59N 103 41W
Búfalo, *Chihuahua, Mexico* **213 F10** 27 18N 105 10W
Buffalo, *KS, U.S.A.* **74 D8** 37 42N 95 42W
Buffalo, *MN, U.S.A.* **80 E5** 45 10N 93 53W
Buffalo, *MO, U.S.A.* **82 D3** 37 39N 93 6W
Buffalo, *ND, U.S.A.* **91 D8** 46 55N 97 33W
Buffalo, *NY, U.S.A.* **89 C2** 42 53N 78 53W
Buffalo, *OK, U.S.A.* **93 B4** 36 50N 99 38W
Buffalo, *SC, U.S.A.* **90 D4** 34 43N 81 41W
Buffalo, *SD, U.S.A.* **91 E2** 45 35N 103 33W
Buffalo, *TX, U.S.A.* **99 F11** 31 28N 96 4W
Buffalo, *WV, U.S.A.* **102 C3** 38 37N 81 59W
Buffalo, *WY, U.S.A.* **104 B6** 44 21N 106 42W
Buffalo →, *Alta., Canada* **189 D9** 60 5N 115 5W
Buffalo →, *AR, U.S.A.* **63 B3** 36 10N 92 26W
Buffalo →, *MN, U.S.A.* **80 C2** 47 6N 96 49W
Buffalo →, *MS, U.S.A.* **81 E2** 31 4N 91 34W
Buffalo →, *TN, U.S.A.* **96 E5** 36 0N 87 50W
Buffalo Bill Res., *WY, U.S.A.* **104 B3** 44 30N 109 11W
Buffalo Center, *IA, U.S.A.* **73 B5** 43 23N 93 57W
Buffalo County ☆, *NE, U.S.A.* **84 D6** 40 50N 99 0W
Buffalo County ☆, *SD, U.S.A.* **91 G6** 44 0N 99 5W
Buffalo County ☆, *WI, U.S.A.* **103 D2** 44 20N 91 50W
Buffalo Cr. →, *WY, U.S.A.* **104 C6** 43 36N 106 52W
Buffalo Creek, *B.C., Canada* **187 D13** 51 44N 121 9W
Buffalo Creek, *CO, U.S.A.* **66 C5** 39 23N 105 17W
Buffalo Gap, *SD, U.S.A.* **91 G2** 43 30N 103 19W
Buffalo Gap, *TX, U.S.A.* **99 E8** 32 17N 99 50W
Buffalo Gap Nat. Grassland, *SD, U.S.A.* **91 G2** 43 7N 103 30W
Buffalo Head Hills, *Alta., Canada* **189 E9** 57 25N 115 55W
Buffalo Hump, *ID, U.S.A.* **70 D3** 45 37N 115 42W
Buffalo L., *Alta., Canada* **185 F8** 52 27N 112 54W
Buffalo L., *N.W.T., Canada* **189 D9** 60 12N 115 25W
Buffalo L., *TX, U.S.A.* **98 C5** 34 52N 102 12W
Buffalo L., *WI, U.S.A.* **103 E4** 43 47N 89 25W
Buffalo Narrows, *Sask., Canada* **189 E11** 55 51N 108 29W
Buffalo Nat. River ⌓, *AR, U.S.A.* **63 B3** 36 14N 92 36W
Buffalo Niagara International ✕ (BUF), *NY, U.S.A.* **89 C2** 42 56N 78 44W
Buffalo Pound L., *Sask., Canada* **182 E6** 50 39N 105 30W
Buford, *GA, U.S.A.* **68 B3** 34 10N 84 0W
Buford, *ND, U.S.A.* **91 C2** 48 0N 103 59W
Buford, *WY, U.S.A.* **104 E7** 41 7N 105 18W
Bugaboo Park ⌓, *B.C., Canada* **187 E18** 50 48N 116 49W
Buhl, *ID, U.S.A.* **70 G4** 42 36N 114 46W
Buhl, *MN, U.S.A.* **80 C6** 47 30N 92 45W
Buhler, *KS, U.S.A.* **74 C6** 38 8N 97 46W
Buies Creek, *NC, U.S.A.* **90 C7** 35 25N 78 44W
Buit, L., *Qué., Canada* **172 C6** 50 59N 63 13W
Buldir I., *AK, U.S.A.* **61 K1** 52 21N 175 56 E
Bulkley →, *B.C., Canada* **189 E7** 55 15N 127 40W
Bull Cr. →, *SD, U.S.A.* **91 E2** 45 40N 103 18W
Bull L., *WY, U.S.A.* **104 C3** 43 13N 109 3W
Bull Mts., *MT, U.S.A.* **83 D9** 46 8N 109 0W
Bull Shoals L., *AR, U.S.A.* **63 B3** 36 22N 92 35W
Bullard, *GA, U.S.A.* **68 D3** 32 38N 83 30W
Bullard, *TX, U.S.A.* **99 E12** 32 8N 95 19W
Bullhead, *SD, U.S.A.* **91 E4** 45 46N 101 5W
Bullhead City, *AZ, U.S.A.* **62 B1** 35 8N 114 32W
Bullion Mts., *CA, U.S.A.* **65 J10** 34 40N 116 10W
Bullitt County ☆, *KY, U.S.A.* **97 C7** 38 0N 85 40W
Bulloch County ☆, *GA, U.S.A.* **68 D5** 32 20N 81 45W
Bullock County ☆, *AL, U.S.A.* **60 D5** 32 9N 85 43W
Bulls B., *SC, U.S.A.* **90 F6** 32 59N 79 35W
Bulls Gap, *TN, U.S.A.* **97 D9** 36 15N 83 5W
Bully Cr. →, *OR, U.S.A.* **94 D8** 43 58N 117 14W
Bulyea, *Sask., Canada* **182 E7** 50 59N 104 52W
Bumpus Mills, *TN, U.S.A.* **96 D5** 36 36N 87 50W
Buna, *TX, U.S.A.* **99 G14** 30 26N 93 58W
Bunceton, *MO, U.S.A.* **82 C4** 38 47N 92 48W
Bunch, *OK, U.S.A.* **93 C9** 35 41N 94 46W
Buncombe, *IL, U.S.A.* **71 F5** 37 27N 88 58W
Buncombe County ☆, *NC, U.S.A.* **90 C3** 35 30N 82 30W
Bundick Cr. →, *LA, U.S.A.* **75 D3** 30 36N 92 57W
Bunker, *MO, U.S.A.* **82 D5** 37 27N 91 13W
Bunker Hill, *IL, U.S.A.* **71 D4** 39 3N 89 57W
Bunker Hill, *IN, U.S.A.* **72 C4** 40 40N 86 6W
Bunker Hill, *KS, U.S.A.* **74 C5** 38 53N 98 42W
Bunker Hill, *NV, U.S.A.* **85 C3** 39 15N 117 8W
Bunker Hill, *OR, U.S.A.* **94 D1** 43 22N 124 12W
Bunker Hill, *WV, U.S.A.* **77 A2** 39 20N 78 3W
Bunker Hill Village, *Houston, U.S.A.* **110 B1** 29 46N 95 31W
Bunkerville, *NV, U.S.A.* **85 F6** 36 46N 114 8W
Bunkie, *LA, U.S.A.* **75 D3** 30 57N 92 11W
Bunnell, *FL, U.S.A.* **67 B7** 29 28N 81 16W
Buras, *LA, U.S.A.* **75 E6** 29 22N 89 32W
Burbank, *CA, U.S.A.* **65 J8** 34 12N 118 18W
Burbank, *Chicago, U.S.A.* **108 C2** 41 44N 87 46W
Burbank, *OK, U.S.A.* **93 B7** 36 42N 96 44W
Burbank, *WA, U.S.A.* **101 D6** 46 12N 119 1W
Burbank ✕ (BUR), *CA, U.S.A.* **65 J8** 34 12N 118 21W
Burchard, *NE, U.S.A.* **84 D9** 40 9N 96 21W
Burden, *KS, U.S.A.* **74 D7** 37 19N 96 45W
Burden, L., *Orlando, U.S.A.* **115 B1** 28 27N 81 33W
Burdett, *Alta., Canada* **185 J9** 49 50N 111 32W
Burdett, *KS, U.S.A.* **74 C4** 38 12N 99 32W
Burdett, *NY, U.S.A.* **89 C4** 42 25N 76 51W
Burdick, *KS, U.S.A.* **74 C7** 38 34N 96 51W
Bureau County ☆, *IL, U.S.A.* **71 B4** 41 25N 89 30W
Burford, *Ont., Canada* **178 D6** 43 7N 80 27W
Burgaw, *NC, U.S.A.* **90 D8** 34 33N 77 56W
Burgdorf, *ID, U.S.A.* **70 D3** 45 17N 115 55W
Burgeo, *Nfld. & L., Canada* **174 E3** 47 37N 57 38W
Burgess, *VA, U.S.A.* **77 C4** 37 53N 76 21W
Burgess Junction, *WY, U.S.A.* **104 B5** 44 46N 107 32W
Burgin, *KY, U.S.A.* **97 C8** 37 45N 84 46W
Burgoon, *OH, U.S.A.* **92 B3** 41 16N 83 15W
Burgos, *Tamaulipas, Mexico* **215 F6** 24 57N 98 47W
Burien, *WA, U.S.A.* **101 C3** 47 28N 122 20W
Burin, *Nfld. & L., Canada* **174 E5** 47 1N 55 14W
Burin Peninsula, *Nfld. & L., Canada* **174 E5** 47 0N 55 40W
Burkburnett, *TX, U.S.A.* **99 C9** 34 6N 98 34W
Burke, *ID, U.S.A.* **70 B3** 47 31N 115 49W
Burke, *SD, U.S.A.* **91 G6** 43 10N 99 18W
Burke Chan., *B.C., Canada* **186 C7** 52 10N 127 30W
Burke County ☆, *GA, U.S.A.* **68 C4** 33 0N 82 0W
Burke County ☆, *NC, U.S.A.* **90 C4** 35 45N 81 40W
Burke County ☆, *ND, U.S.A.* **91 B3** 48 55N 102 30W
Burke-Lakefront ✕, *Cleveland, U.S.A.* **107 A1** 41 31N 81 41W
Burkesville, *KY, U.S.A.* **97 D7** 36 48N 85 22W
Burkett, *TX, U.S.A.* **99 E8** 32 0N 99 8W
Burkettsville, *OH, U.S.A.* **92 C2** 40 21N 84 39W
Burkeville, *TX, U.S.A.* **99 F14** 31 0N 93 40W
Burkeville, *VA, U.S.A.* **102 D6** 37 11N 78 12W
Burkittsville, *MD, U.S.A.* **77 A3** 39 22N 77 38W
Burk's Falls, *Ont., Canada* **178 B7** 45 37N 79 24W
Burleigh County ☆, *ND, U.S.A.* **91 C5** 47 0N 100 30W
Burleigh Falls, *Ont., Canada* **179 C8** 44 33N 78 12W
Burleson, *TX, U.S.A.* **99 E10** 32 33N 97 19W
Burleson County ☆, *TX, U.S.A.* **99 G11** 30 32N 96 42W
Burley, *ID, U.S.A.* **70 G5** 42 32N 113 48W
Burley, *Seattle, U.S.A.* **118 D2** 47 25N 122 37W
Burlingame, *CA, U.S.A.* **64 F4** 37 35N 122 21W
Burlingame, *KS, U.S.A.* **74 C8** 38 45N 95 50W
Burlington, *Nfld. & L., Canada* **174 C4** 49 45N 56 1W
Burlington, *Ont., Canada* **178 D7** 43 18N 79 45W
Burlington, *CO, U.S.A.* **66 C8** 39 18N 102 16W
Burlington, *CT, U.S.A.* **78 C2** 41 46N 72 58W
Burlington, *IL, U.S.A.* **71 A5** 42 3N 88 33W
Burlington, *IN, U.S.A.* **72 C4** 40 29N 86 24W
Burlington, *IA, U.S.A.* **73 E7** 40 49N 91 14W
Burlington, *KS, U.S.A.* **74 C8** 38 12N 95 45W
Burlington, *KY, U.S.A.* **97 A8** 39 2N 84 43W
Burlington, *MA, U.S.A.* **78 B3** 42 30N 71 13W
Burlington, *NC, U.S.A.* **90 B6** 36 6N 79 26W
Burlington, *ND, U.S.A.* **91 B4** 48 17N 101 26W
Burlington, *NJ, U.S.A.* **87 B2** 40 4N 74 51W
Burlington, *OK, U.S.A.* **93 B5** 36 54N 98 25W
Burlington, *VT, U.S.A.* **86 B1** 44 29N 73 12W
Burlington, *WV, U.S.A.* **77 A2** 39 20N 78 55W
Burlington, *WA, U.S.A.* **101 B3** 48 28N 122 20W
Burlington, *WI, U.S.A.* **103 F5** 42 41N 88 17W
Burlington, *WY, U.S.A.* **104 B4** 44 27N 108 26W
Burlington County ☆, *NJ, U.S.A.* **87 C2** 39 50N 74 45W
Burlington Junction, *MO, U.S.A.* **82 A1** 40 27N 95 4W
Burna, *KY, U.S.A.* **96 C4** 37 15N 88 22W
Burnaby, *B.C., Canada* **187 F12** 49 16N 122 57W
Burnaby Heights, *Vancouver, Canada* **193 B2** 49 17N 123 0W
Burnaby I., *B.C., Canada* **186 C3** 52 25N 131 19W
Burnet, *TX, U.S.A.* **99 G9** 30 45N 98 14W
Burnet County ☆, *TX, U.S.A.* **99 G9** 30 45N 98 15W
Burnett County ☆, *WI, U.S.A.* **103 C1** 45 50N 92 20W
Burnett Woods, *OH, U.S.A.* **107 B1** 39 8N 84 31W
Burnettsville, *IN, U.S.A.* **72 C4** 40 46N 86 36W
Burney, *CA, U.S.A.* **64 C5** 40 53N 121 40W
Burnham, *ME, U.S.A.* **76 D4** 44 42N 69 26W
Burnham, *PA, U.S.A.* **95 D5** 40 38N 77 34W
Burnham Park, *Chicago, U.S.A.* **108 C3** 41 49N 87 36W
Burnham Park Harbor, *Chicago, U.S.A.* **108 B3** 41 51N 87 36W
Burning Springs, *KY, U.S.A.* **97 C9** 37 15N 83 49W
Burns, *CO, U.S.A.* **66 C4** 39 52N 106 53W
Burns, *KS, U.S.A.* **74 C7** 38 5N 96 53W
Burns, *OR, U.S.A.* **94 D6** 43 35N 119 3W
Burns, *TN, U.S.A.* **96 D5** 36 3N 87 19W
Burns, *WY, U.S.A.* **104 E8** 41 12N 104 21W
Burns Flat, *OK, U.S.A.* **93 C4** 35 21N 99 10W
Burns Junction, *OR, U.S.A.* **94 E8** 42 47N 117 51W
Burns Lake, *B.C., Canada* **186 A9** 54 14N 125 45W
Burns Paiute Indian Reservation, *OR, U.S.A.* **94 D6** 43 35N 119 6W
Burnside, *KY, U.S.A.* **97 D8** 36 59N 84 36W
Burnside →, *Nunavut, Canada* **188 C11** 66 51N 108 4W
Burnsville, *AL, U.S.A.* **60 D4** 32 28N 86 53W
Burnsville, *MN, U.S.A.* **80 F5** 44 47N 93 17W
Burnsville, *MS, U.S.A.* **81 B5** 34 51N 88 19W
Burnsville, *NC, U.S.A.* **90 C3** 35 55N 82 18W
Burnsville, *WV, U.S.A.* **102 C4** 38 52N 80 40W
Burnsville L., *WV, U.S.A.* **102 C4** 38 50N 80 37W
Burnt →, *OR, U.S.A.* **94 C8** 44 22N 117 14W
Burnt, L., *Nfld. & L., Canada* **175 C5** 53 35N 64 4W
Burnt Corn, *AL, U.S.A.* **60 E3** 31 33N 87 10W
Burnt Islands, *Nfld. & L., Canada* **174 E2** 47 36N 58 53W
Burnt Paw, *AK, U.S.A.* **61 C12** 66 54N 143 44W
Burnt River, *Ont., Canada* **179 C8** 44 41N 78 42W
Burntfork, *WY, U.S.A.* **104 E3** 41 2N 109 59W
Burntwood →, *Man., Canada* **191 F6** 56 8N 96 34W
Burr, *NE, U.S.A.* **84 D9** 40 33N 96 19W
Burr Oak, *KS, U.S.A.* **74 B5** 39 52N 98 18W
Burr Oak, *MI, U.S.A.* **79 H6** 41 51N 85 19W
Burr Oak, *OH, U.S.A.* **92 D4** 39 33N 82 4W
Burrel, *CA, U.S.A.* **65 G7** 36 29N 119 59W
Burris, *WY, U.S.A.* **104 C3** 43 22N 109 16W
Burro, Serranías del, *Coahuila, Mexico* **214 B2** 28 56N 102 5W
Burro Pk., *NM, U.S.A.* **88 E2** 32 35N 108 26W
Burrows L., *Ont., Canada* **181 C10** 49 57N 86 44W
Burrton, *KS, U.S.A.* **74 C6** 38 2N 97 41W
Burstall, *Sask., Canada* **182 E2** 50 39N 109 54W
Burt, *IA, U.S.A.* **73 B4** 43 12N 94 13W
Burt County ☆, *NE, U.S.A.* **84 C9** 41 50N 96 15W
Burt L., *MI, U.S.A.* **79 D7** 45 28N 84 40W
Burton, *B.C., Canada* **187 F17** 50 0N 117 53W
Burton, *MI, U.S.A.* **79 G8** 43 0N 83 40W
Burton, *NE, U.S.A.* **84 B6** 42 55N 99 35W
Burton, *SC, U.S.A.* **90 F5** 32 26N 80 43W
Burton, *Seattle, U.S.A.* **118 D3** 47 23N 122 27W
Burton, *TX, U.S.A.* **99 G11** 30 11N 96 42W
Burton, L., *Qué., Canada* **175 C2** 54 45N 78 20W
Burton, L., *GA, U.S.A.* **68 B3** 34 50N 83 33W
Burtrum, *MN, U.S.A.* **80 E4** 45 52N 94 41W
Burtts Corner, *N.B., Canada* **173 G3** 46 3N 66 52W
Burwash, *Ont., Canada* **178 A6** 46 14N 80 51W
Burwash Landing, *Yukon, Canada* **189 D5** 61 21N 139 0W
Burwell, *NE, U.S.A.* **84 C6** 41 47N 99 8W
Bury, *Qué., Canada* **177 F11** 45 28N 71 30W
Bush, *LA, U.S.A.* **75 D6** 30 36N 89 54W
Bush City, *KS, U.S.A.* **74 C8** 38 13N 95 9W
Bush Kill →, *PA, U.S.A.* **87 A1** 41 5N 75 0W
Bushland, *TX, U.S.A.* **98 B5** 35 11N 102 4W
Bushnell, *FL, U.S.A.* **67 C6** 28 40N 82 7W
Bushnell, *IL, U.S.A.* **71 C3** 40 33N 90 31W
Bushnell, *NE, U.S.A.* **84 C2** 41 14N 103 54W
Bushong, *KS, U.S.A.* **74 C7** 38 39N 96 15W
Bushton, *KS, U.S.A.* **74 C5** 38 31N 98 24W
Bushwick, *NY, U.S.A.* **114 B3** 40 41N 73 54W
Bushwood, *MD, U.S.A.* **77 B4** 38 18N 76 47W
Bussey, *IA, U.S.A.* **73 D6** 41 12N 92 53W
Bustamante, *Nuevo León, Mexico* **214 D4** 26 33N 100 30W
Bustamante, Pta., *TX, U.S.A.* **98 L8** 27 0N 99 7W
Bustillos, L., *Chihuahua, Mexico* **213 E9** 28 33N 106 45W
Bute Inlet, *B.C., Canada* **186 E10** 50 40N 124 53W
Butedale, *B.C., Canada* **186 B6** 53 8N 128 42W
Butler, *AL, U.S.A.* **60 D2** 32 5N 88 13W
Butler, *GA, U.S.A.* **68 D2** 32 33N 84 14W
Butler, *IN, U.S.A.* **72 B6** 41 26N 84 52W
Butler, *KY, U.S.A.* **97 B8** 38 47N 84 22W
Butler, *MD, U.S.A.* **77 A4** 39 35N 76 45W
Butler, *Milwaukee, U.S.A.* **112 B1** 43 6N 88 4W
Butler, *MO, U.S.A.* **82 C2** 38 16N 94 20W
Butler, *NJ, U.S.A.* **87 B2** 41 0N 74 20W
Butler, *OK, U.S.A.* **93 C4** 35 38N 99 11W
Butler, *PA, U.S.A.* **95 D3** 40 52N 79 54W
Butler, L., *Orlando, U.S.A.* **115 B1** 28 29N 81 33W
Butler County ☆, *AL, U.S.A.* **60 E4** 31 50N 86 38W
Butler County ☆, *IA, U.S.A.* **73 C6** 42 45N 92 45W
Butler County ☆, *KS, U.S.A.* **74 D7** 37 45N 96 45W
Butler County ☆, *KY, U.S.A.* **96 C6** 37 10N 86 45W
Butler County ☆, *MO, U.S.A.* **82 E6** 36 45N 90 25W
Butler County ☆, *NE, U.S.A.* **84 C8** 41 15N 97 0W
Butler County ☆, *OH, U.S.A.* **92 D2** 39 24N 84 34W
Butler County ☆, *PA, U.S.A.* **95 C3** 41 0N 80 0W
Butner, *NC, U.S.A.* **90 B7** 36 8N 78 45W
Butte, *MT, U.S.A.* **83 D5** 46 0N 112 32W
Butte, *ND, U.S.A.* **91 C5** 47 50N 100 40W
Butte, *NE, U.S.A.* **84 B7** 42 58N 98 51W
Butte City, *ID, U.S.A.* **70 F5** 43 37N 113 15W
Butte County ☆, *CA, U.S.A.* **64 D5** 39 40N 121 45W
Butte County ☆, *ID, U.S.A.* **70 F5** 43 50N 113 0W
Butte County ☆, *SD, U.S.A.* **91 F2** 45 0N 103 30W
Butte Falls, *OR, U.S.A.* **94 E3** 42 33N 122 34W
Butte Mts., *NV, U.S.A.* **85 C5** 39 50N 115 5W
Butter Cr. →, *OR, U.S.A.* **94 B6** 45 45N 119 20W
Butterfield, *MN, U.S.A.* **80 G4** 43 58N 94 48W
Butterfield, *MO, U.S.A.* **82 E3** 36 45N 93 54W
Butternut, *WI, U.S.A.* **103 B3** 46 1N 90 30W
Buttle L., *B.C., Canada* **186 F9** 49 42N 125 33W
Button Is., *Nfld. & L., Canada* **175 A5** 60 38N 64 40W
Buttonwillow, *CA, U.S.A.* **65 H7** 35 24N 119 28W
Butts Corner, *VA, U.S.A.* **119 C2** 38 46N 77 19W
Butts County ☆, *GA, U.S.A.* **68 C3** 33 20N 84 0W
Buxton, *ND, U.S.A.* **91 C8** 47 36N 97 6W
Buzzards B., *MA, U.S.A.* **78 C4** 41 30N 70 45W
Buzzards Bay, *MA, U.S.A.* **78 C4** 41 45N 70 37W
Byam Ch., *Nunavut, Canada* **190 B4** 75 15N 105 15W
Byam Martin Chan., *Nunavut, Canada* **190 B4** 76 15N 105 45W
Byam Martin I., *Nunavut, Canada* **190 B5** 75 15N 104 15W
Byars, *OK, U.S.A.* **93 D6** 34 53N 97 3W
Byers, *CO, U.S.A.* **66 C6** 39 43N 104 14W
Byers, *KS, U.S.A.* **74 D5** 37 48N 98 52W
Byers, *TX, U.S.A.* **99 C9** 34 4N 98 11W
Byesville, *OH, U.S.A.* **92 D5** 39 58N 81 32W
Byfield, *MA, U.S.A.* **78 B4** 42 46N 70 57W
Byhalia, *MS, U.S.A.* **81 B4** 34 52N 89 41W
Bylas, *AZ, U.S.A.* **62 D5** 33 8N 110 7W
Bylot, *Man., Canada* **191 F7** 58 25N 94 8W
Bylot I., *Nunavut, Canada* **190 C10** 73 13N 78 34W
Byng, *OK, U.S.A.* **93 D7** 34 50N 96 42W
Byng Inlet, *Ont., Canada* **178 B6** 45 46N 80 33W
Bynum, *MT, U.S.A.* **83 C5** 47 59N 112 19W
Byram, *MS, U.S.A.* **81 D3** 32 11N 90 15W
Byrdstown, *TN, U.S.A.* **97 D7** 36 34N 85 8W
Byron, *GA, U.S.A.* **68 D3** 32 39N 83 46W
Byron, *IL, U.S.A.* **71 A4** 42 8N 89 15W
Byron, *ME, U.S.A.* **76 D3** 44 43N 70 38W
Byron, *MI, U.S.A.* **79 G8** 42 49N 83 57W
Byron, *MN, U.S.A.* **80 F6** 44 2N 92 41W
Byron, *NE, U.S.A.* **84 D8** 40 0N 97 46W
Byron, *OK, U.S.A.* **93 B5** 36 54N 98 18W
Byron, *WY, U.S.A.* **104 B4** 44 48N 108 30W

C

C.J. Strike Res., *ID, U.S.A.* **70 G3** 42 59N 115 58W
C.W. McConaughy, L., *NE, U.S.A.* **84 C4** 41 14N 101 40W
Caamaño Sd., *B.C., Canada* **186 C5** 52 55N 129 25W
Caballo, *NM, U.S.A.* **88 E3** 32 59N 107 18W
Caballo Res., *NM, U.S.A.* **88 E3** 32 54N 107 18W
Cabano, *Qué., Canada* **177 D14** 47 40N 68 56W
Cabarrus County ☆, *NC, U.S.A.* **90 C5** 35 20N 80 30W
Cabazon, *CA, U.S.A.* **65 K10** 33 55N 116 47W
Cabazon, *CA, U.S.A.* **65 K10** 33 55N 116 47W
Cabell County ☆, *WV, U.S.A.* **102 C2** 38 26N 82 8W
Cabery, *IL, U.S.A.* **71 C5** 41 0N 88 12W
Cabeza de Vaca, *Baja Calif. S., Mexico* **211 G6** 26 44N 112 5W
Cabeza Prieta Nat. Wildlife Refuge ⌓, *AZ, U.S.A.* **62 E2** 32 15N 113 20W
Cabin Branch →, *Baltimore, U.S.A.* **107 B2** 39 12N 76 34W
Cabin John, *MD, U.S.A.* **119 B2** 38 58N 77 10W
Cabin John Regional Park ⌓, *MD, U.S.A.* **119 A2** 39 0N 77 10W
Cabinet Mts., *MT, U.S.A.* **83 B2** 48 10N 115 50W
Cable, *WI, U.S.A.* **103 B2** 46 13N 91 17W
Cabo Rojo, *Puerto Rico* **105 G15** 18 5N 67 9W
Cabo San Lucas, *Baja Calif. S., Mexico* **211 L9** 22 53N 109 54W
Cabonga, Réservoir, *Qué., Canada* **176 D6** 47 20N 76 40W
Cabool, *MO, U.S.A.* **82 D4** 37 7N 92 6W
Cabórachi, *Chihuahua, Mexico* **213 G9** 26 49N 106 58W
Caborca, *Sonora, Mexico* **212 C3** 30 37N 112 6W
Cabot, *AR, U.S.A.* **63 D3** 34 59N 92 1W
Cabot, *VT, U.S.A.* **86 B2** 44 23N 72 18W
Cabot, Mt., *NH, U.S.A.* **86 B3** 44 30N 71 25W
Cabras, Pta., *Baja Calif., Mexico* **210 B2** 31 23N 116 32W
Cabri, *Sask., Canada* **182 E3** 50 35N 108 25W
Cabrillo, Pt., *CA, U.S.A.* **64 D3** 39 21N 123 50W
Cabrillo Nat. Monument ⌓, *San Diego, U.S.A.* **117 B1** 32 40N 117 14W
Cacahoatán, *Chiapas, Mexico* **222 E4** 14 59N 92 10W
Cacalchén, *Yucatán, Mexico* **223 B4** 20 59N 89 14W
Cacapon →, *WV, U.S.A.* **77 A2** 39 37N 78 16W
Cache, *OK, U.S.A.* **93 D5** 34 38N 98 38W
Cache →, *AR, U.S.A.* **63 D4** 34 43N 91 20W
Cache →, *IL, U.S.A.* **71 F4** 37 4N 89 10W
Cache Bay, *Ont., Canada* **178 A6** 46 22N 80 0W
Cache County ☆, *UT, U.S.A.* **100 B4** 41 40N 111 45W
Cache Cr. →, *CA, U.S.A.* **64 E5** 38 42N 121 42W
Cache Creek, *B.C., Canada* **187 E13** 50 48N 121 19W
Cache la Poudre →, *CO, U.S.A.* **66 B6** 40 25N 104 36W
Cache Peak, *ID, U.S.A.* **70 G5** 42 11N 113 40W
Cachuma, L., *CA, U.S.A.* **65 J7** 34 35N 119 59W
Cacouna, *Qué., Canada* **177 D13** 47 55N 69 30W
Cactus, *TX, U.S.A.* **98 A6** 36 4N 101 59W
Cactus Flat, *NV, U.S.A.* **85 E4** 37 45N 116 40W
Cactus Ra., *NV, U.S.A.* **85 E4** 37 40N 116 50W
Cadboro Bay, *B.C., Canada* **187 G11** 48 28N 123 17W
Caddo, *OK, U.S.A.* **93 D7** 34 7N 96 16W
Caddo, *TX, U.S.A.* **99 E9** 32 43N 98 40W
Caddo →, *AR, U.S.A.* **63 D2** 34 10N 93 3W
Caddo County ☆, *OK, U.S.A.* **93 C5** 35 10N 98 20W
Caddo Cr. →, *OK, U.S.A.* **93 D7** 34 14N 96 59W
Caddo Gap, *AR, U.S.A.* **63 D2** 34 24N 93 37W
Caddo L., *LA, U.S.A.* **75 B2** 32 43N 93 55W
Caddo Mills, *TX, U.S.A.* **99 D11** 33 4N 96 14W
Caddo Nat. Grassland, *TX, U.S.A.* **99 D12** 33 44N 95 57W
Caddo Parish ☆, *LA, U.S.A.* **75 B2** 32 45N 93 58W
Caddoa, *CO, U.S.A.* **66 D8** 38 4N 102 56W
Cadereyta, *Querétaro, Mexico* **219 B8** 20 42N 99 49W
Cadereyta de Jiménez, *Nuevo León, Mexico* **214 E5** 25 36N 100 0W
Cadillac, *Qué., Canada* **176 C4** 48 14N 78 23W
Cadillac, *Sask., Canada* **182 F4** 49 44N 107 44W
Cadillac, *MI, U.S.A.* **79 E6** 44 15N 85 24W
Cadiz, *IN, U.S.A.* **72 D5** 39 57N 85 29W
Cadiz, *KY, U.S.A.* **96 D5** 36 52N 87 50W
Cadiz, *OH, U.S.A.* **92 C6** 40 22N 81 0W
Cadiz L., *CA, U.S.A.* **65 J11** 34 18N 115 24W
Cadley, *GA, U.S.A.* **68 C4** 33 32N 82 40W
Cadomin, *Alta., Canada* **185 E3** 53 2N 117 20W
Cadott, *WI, U.S.A.* **103 D2** 44 57N 91 9W
Cadotte →, *Alta., Canada* **184 B3** 56 43N 117 10W
Cadwell, *GA, U.S.A.* **68 D3** 32 20N 83 3W
Caernarvon, *New Orleans, U.S.A.* **113 C3** 29 51N 89 54W
Cagles Mill L., *IN, U.S.A.* **72 D4** 39 29N 86 55W
Caguas, *Puerto Rico* **105 G16** 18 14N 66 2W
Cahaba →, *AL, U.S.A.* **60 D3** 32 20N 87 5W
Cahokia, *IL, U.S.A.* **71 E3** 38 34N 90 11W
Cahone, *CO, U.S.A.* **66 E2** 37 39N 108 49W
Cahuenga Pk., *Los Angeles, U.S.A.* **111 B3** 34 8N 118 19 E
Cahuilla Indian Reservation, *CA, U.S.A.* **65 K10** 33 31N 116 43W
Caillou B., *LA, U.S.A.* **75 E5** 29 3N 91 0W
Cain, L., *Orlando, U.S.A.* **115 B2** 28 28N 81 28W
Caineville, *UT, U.S.A.* **100 E4** 38 20N 111 1W
Cains →, *N.B., Canada* **173 G4** 46 40N 65 47W
Cainsville, *MO, U.S.A.* **82 A3** 40 26N 93 47W
Cairo, *GA, U.S.A.* **68 F2** 30 52N 84 13W
Cairo, *IL, U.S.A.* **71 F4** 37 0N 89 11W
Cairo, *KY, U.S.A.* **96 C5** 37 42N 87 39W
Cairo, *MO, U.S.A.* **82 B4** 39 31N 92 27W
Cairo, *NE, U.S.A.* **84 C7** 41 0N 98 36W
Cairo, *OH, U.S.A.* **92 C2** 40 50N 84 5W
Cairo, *WV, U.S.A.* **102 B3** 39 13N 81 9W
Caja de Muertos, I., *Puerto Rico* **105 H16** 17 54N 66 32W
Cajón de Peña, Presa, *Jalisco, Mexico* **218 C2** 19 58N 105 6W
Cajon Summit, *CA, U.S.A.* **65 J9** 34 21N 117 27W
Cajurichic, *Chihuahua, Mexico* **213 E7** 28 7N 108 11W
Calabash, *NC, U.S.A.* **90 E7** 33 53N 78 34W
Calabazas, *Durango, Mexico* **216 D5** 23 13N 105 3W
Calabogie, *Ont., Canada* **179 B10** 45 18N 76 43W
Caladesi Island State Park ⌓, *Tampa, U.S.A.* **119 A2** 28 1N 82 49W
Calagua, *Baja Calif. S., Mexico* **211 G7** 26 20N 111 50W
Calais, *ME, U.S.A.* **76 C6** 45 11N 67 17W
Calakmul, *Campeche, Mexico* **223 D4** 18 15N 89 55W
Calakmul, Reserva de la Biosfera ⌓, *Campeche, Mexico* **223 D4** 18 30N 89 55W
Calamus →, *NE, U.S.A.* **84 C6** 41 48N 99 9W
Calamus Res., *NE, U.S.A.* **84 C6** 41 50N 99 13W
Calapooia →, *OR, U.S.A.* **94 C2** 44 38N 123 8W
Calaveras County ☆, *CA, U.S.A.* **64 E6** 38 15N 120 40W
Calaveras Lake, *San Antonio, U.S.A.* **117 C4** 29 16N 98 18W
Calcasieu →, *LA, U.S.A.* **75 D2** 30 5N 93 20W
Calcasieu L., *LA, U.S.A.* **75 E2** 29 55N 93 18W
Calcasieu Parish ☆, *LA, U.S.A.* **75 D2** 30 14N 93 23W
Calcium, *NY, U.S.A.* **89 A5** 44 1N 75 51W
Caldwell, *AR, U.S.A.* **63 C5** 35 5N 90 49W
Caldwell, *ID, U.S.A.* **70 F2** 43 40N 116 41W
Caldwell, *KS, U.S.A.* **74 D6** 37 2N 97 37W
Caldwell, *NJ, U.S.A.* **114 A1** 40 50N 74 16W
Caldwell, *OH, U.S.A.* **92 D5** 39 45N 81 31W
Caldwell, *TX, U.S.A.* **99 G11** 30 32N 96 42W
Caldwell County ☆, *KY, U.S.A.* **96 C5** 37 10N 87 50W

Caldwell County ☆, *MO, U.S.A.* **82 B3** 39 40N 94 0W
Caldwell County ☆, *NC, U.S.A.* **90 C4** 36 0N 81 30W
Caldwell County ☆, *TX, U.S.A.* **99 H10** 29 53N 97 40W
Caldwell Parish ☆, *LA, U.S.A.* **75 B3** 32 0N 92 0W
Caledonia, *N.S., Canada* **173 H7** 45 17N 62 33W
Caledonia, *N.S., Canada* **173 J4** 44 22N 65 2W
Caledonia, *Ont., Canada* **178 D7** 43 7N 79 58W
Caledonia, *MI, U.S.A.* **79 G6** 42 47N 85 31W
Caledonia, *MN, U.S.A.* **80 G7** 43 38N 91 30W
Caledonia, *MS, U.S.A.* **81 C5** 33 41N 88 20W
Caledonia, *ND, U.S.A.* **91 C9** 47 28N 96 53W
Caledonia, *NY, U.S.A.* **89 C3** 42 58N 77 51W
Caledonia County ☆, *VT, U.S.A.* **86 B2** 44 30N 72 10W
Calentura, Pta., *Quintana Roo, Mexico* **223 D5** 18 30N 88 7W
Calera, *AL, U.S.A.* **60 C4** 33 6N 86 45W
Calera, *OK, U.S.A.* **93 E7** 33 52N 96 29W
Calera de Víctor Rosales, *Zacatecas, Mexico* **217 E8** 22 57N 102 42W
Calexico, *CA, U.S.A.* **65 L11** 32 40N 115 30W
Calfkiller →, *TN, U.S.A.* **97 E7** 35 49N 85 29W
Calgary, *Alta., Canada* **185 G6** 51 0N 114 10W
Calgary ✕ (YYC), *Alta., Canada* **185 G6** 51 4N 114 1W
Calhan, *CO, U.S.A.* **66 C6** 39 2N 104 18W
Calhoun, *AL, U.S.A.* **60 D4** 32 3N 86 33W
Calhoun, *GA, U.S.A.* **68 B2** 34 30N 84 57W
Calhoun, *IL, U.S.A.* **71 E5** 38 39N 88 3W
Calhoun, *KY, U.S.A.* **96 C5** 37 32N 87 16W
Calhoun, *MO, U.S.A.* **82 C3** 38 28N 93 38W
Calhoun, *TN, U.S.A.* **97 E8** 35 18N 84 45W
Calhoun, L., *Minneapolis-St. Paul, U.S.A.* **113 B2** 44 56N 93 18W
Calhoun City, *MS, U.S.A.* **81 C4** 33 51N 89 19W
Calhoun County ☆, *AL, U.S.A.* **60 C4** 33 47N 86 0W
Calhoun County ☆, *AR, U.S.A.* **63 E3** 33 35N 92 31W
Calhoun County ☆, *FL, U.S.A.* **67 A3** 30 30N 85 15W
Calhoun County ☆, *GA, U.S.A.* **68 E2** 31 30N 84 35W
Calhoun County ☆, *IL, U.S.A.* **71 D3** 39 10N 90 40W
Calhoun County ☆, *IA, U.S.A.* **73 C4** 42 25N 94 40W
Calhoun County ☆, *MI, U.S.A.* **79 G7** 42 15N 85 0W
Calhoun County ☆, *MS, U.S.A.* **81 C4** 33 56N 89 20W
Calhoun County ☆, *SC, U.S.A.* **90 E5** 33 45N 80 50W
Calhoun County ☆, *TX, U.S.A.* **99 J11** 28 37N 96 38W
Calhoun County ☆, *WV, U.S.A.* **102 C3** 38 55N 81 6W
Calhoun Falls, *SC, U.S.A.* **90 D3** 34 6N 82 36W
Calico Rock, *AR, U.S.A.* **63 B3** 36 7N 92 9W
Caliente, *CA, U.S.A.* **65 H8** 35 17N 118 38W
Caliente, *NV, U.S.A.* **85 E6** 37 37N 114 31W
Califon, *NJ, U.S.A.* **87 B2** 40 42N 74 50W
California, *MD, U.S.A.* **77 B4** 38 18N 76 32W
California, *MO, U.S.A.* **82 C4** 38 38N 92 34W
California, *PA, U.S.A.* **95 D3** 40 4N 79 54W
California □, *U.S.A.* **64 F7** 37 30N 119 30W
California, Baja, T.N. = Baja California □, *Mexico* **210 C3** 30 0N 115 0W
California, Baja, T.S. = Baja California Sur □, *Mexico* **211 H7** 25 50N 111 50W
California, G. de, *Mexico* **211 F7** 27 0N 111 0W
California Aqueduct, *CA, U.S.A.* **65 K9** 33 52N 117 12W
California City, *CA, U.S.A.* **65 H9** 35 10N 117 55W
California Coastal Nat. Monument ⌓, *CA, U.S.A.* **65 G5** 36 19N 121 46W
California Inst. of Tech., *Los Angeles, U.S.A.* **111 B4** 34 8N 118 8W
California State University, *Los Angeles, U.S.A.* **111 B3** 34 4N 118 10W
Calio, *ND, U.S.A.* **91 B7** 48 38N 98 56W
Calion, *AR, U.S.A.* **63 E3** 33 20N 92 32W
Calipatria, *CA, U.S.A.* **65 K11** 33 8N 115 31W
Calistoga, *CA, U.S.A.* **64 E4** 38 35N 122 35W
Calkiní, *Campeche, Mexico* **223 B3** 20 22N 90 3W
Callahan, *CA, U.S.A.* **64 B4** 41 18N 122 48W
Callahan, *FL, U.S.A.* **67 A7** 30 34N 81 50W
Callahan County ☆, *TX, U.S.A.* **99 E8** 32 24N 99 24W
Callander, *Ont., Canada* **178 A7** 46 13N 79 22W
Callao, *UT, U.S.A.* **100 D2** 39 54N 113 43W
Callaway, *FL, U.S.A.* **67 A3** 30 8N 85 36W
Callaway, *MN, U.S.A.* **80 D3** 46 59N 95 54W
Callaway, *NE, U.S.A.* **84 C6** 41 18N 99 56W
Callaway County ☆, *MO, U.S.A.* **82 C5** 38 50N 91 50W
Callender, *IA, U.S.A.* **73 C4** 42 22N 94 17W
Callicoon, *NY, U.S.A.* **89 D5** 41 46N 75 3W
Calliham, *TX, U.S.A.* **99 J9** 28 29N 98 21W
Callimont, *PA, U.S.A.* **77 A2** 39 48N 78 55W
Calling L., *Alta., Canada* **184 C7** 55 15N 113 20W
Calling Lake, *Alta., Canada* **184 C7** 55 15N 113 12W
Calloway County ☆, *KY, U.S.A.* **96 D4** 36 40N 88 15W
Calmar, *Alta., Canada* **184 E7** 53 16N 113 49W
Calmar, *IA, U.S.A.* **73 B7** 43 11N 91 52W
Caloosahatchee →, *FL, U.S.A.* **67 E6** 26 31N 82 1W
Calpella, *CA, U.S.A.* **64 D3** 39 14N 123 12W
Calpine, *CA, U.S.A.* **64 D6** 39 40N 120 27W
Calpulalpán, *Tlaxcala, Mexico* **219 C9** 19 35N 98 35W
Calstock, *Ont., Canada* **181 C12** 49 47N 84 9W
Caltepec, *Puebla, Mexico* **221 F3** 18 11N 97 28W
Calumet, *IA, U.S.A.* **73 C3** 42 57N 95 33W
Calumet, *MI, U.S.A.* **79 B3** 47 14N 88 27W
Calumet, *MN, U.S.A.* **80 C5** 47 19N 93 17W
Calumet, *OK, U.S.A.* **93 C5** 35 36N 98 7W
Calumet City, *IL, U.S.A.* **71 B6** 41 37N 87 32W
Calumet County ☆, *WI, U.S.A.* **103 D5** 44 5N 88 10W
Calumet Park, *Chicago, U.S.A.* **108 C3** 41 40N 87 39W
Calumet Sag Channel →, *Chicago, U.S.A.* **108 C2** 41 40N 87 47W
Calvert, *AL, U.S.A.* **60 E2** 31 9N 88 1W
Calvert, *MD, U.S.A.* **77 A5** 39 42N 75 58W
Calvert, *TX, U.S.A.* **99 G11** 30 59N 96 40W
Calvert C., *B.C., Canada* **186 D7** 51 25N 127 53W
Calvert City, *KY, U.S.A.* **96 C4** 37 2N 88 21W
Calvert County ☆, *MD, U.S.A.* **77 B4** 38 30N 76 35W
Calvert I., *B.C., Canada* **186 D6** 51 30N 128 0W
Calverton, *MD, U.S.A.* **77 A4** 39 3N 76 56W
Calverton Park, *MO, U.S.A.* **117 A2** 38 45N 90 18W
Calvillo, *Aguascalientes, Mexico* **217 F8** 21 51N 102 43W
Calvin, *LA, U.S.A.* **75 C3** 31 58N 92 47W
Calvin, *ND, U.S.A.* **91 B7** 48 51N 98 56W
Calvin, *OK, U.S.A.* **93 D7** 34 58N 96 15W
Calwa, *CA, U.S.A.* **65 G7** 36 42N 119 46W
Camachigama, L., *Qué., Canada* **176 D6** 47 50N 76 19W
Camak, *GA, U.S.A.* **68 C4** 33 27N 82 39W
Camalú, B., *Baja Calif., Mexico* **210 C2** 30 47N 116 5W
Camanche, *IA, U.S.A.* **73 D8** 41 47N 90 15W
Camanche Res., *CA, U.S.A.* **64 E5** 38 14N 121 1W
Camano I., *WA, U.S.A.* **101 B3** 48 0N 122 30W
Camargo, *Tamaulipas, Mexico* **214 D6** 26 19N 98 50W
Camargo, *KY, U.S.A.* **97 C9** 38 0N 83 53W
Camargo, *OK, U.S.A.* **93 B4** 36 1N 99 17W
Camarillo, *CA, U.S.A.* **65 J7** 34 13N 119 2W
Camarón →, *Veracruz, Mexico* **221 F5** 18 50N 95 55W
Camas, *ID, U.S.A.* **70 E6** 44 0N 112 13W
Camas, *WA, U.S.A.* **101 E3** 45 35N 122 24W
Camas County ☆, *ID, U.S.A.* **70 F4** 43 30N 114 50W
Camas Nat. Wildlife Refuge ⌓, *ID, U.S.A.* **70 F6** 43 57N 112 15W
Camas Valley, *OR, U.S.A.* **94 D2** 43 2N 123 40W
Cambria, *CA, U.S.A.* **65 H5** 35 34N 121 5W
Cambria, *WI, U.S.A.* **103 E4** 43 33N 89 7W
Cambria County ☆, *PA, U.S.A.* **95 D4** 40 30N 78 52W
Cambria Heights, *NY, U.S.A.* **114 B4** 40 41N 73 44W
Cambridge, *N.B., Canada* **173 H4** 45 50N 65 58W
Cambridge, *Ont., Canada* **178 D6** 43 23N 80 15W
Cambridge, *ID, U.S.A.* **70 E2** 44 34N 116 41W
Cambridge, *IL, U.S.A.* **71 B3** 41 18N 90 12W
Cambridge, *IA, U.S.A.* **73 D5** 41 54N 93 32W
Cambridge, *KS, U.S.A.* **74 D7** 37 19N 96 40W
Cambridge, *MA, U.S.A.* **78 B3** 42 23N 71 7W
Cambridge, *MD, U.S.A.* **77 B4** 38 34N 76 5W
Cambridge, *MN, U.S.A.* **80 E5** 45 34N 93 13W
Cambridge, *NY, U.S.A.* **78 A1** 43 2N 73 22W
Cambridge, *NE, U.S.A.* **84 D5** 40 17N 100 10W
Cambridge, *OH, U.S.A.* **92 C5** 40 2N 81 35W
Cambridge, *VT, U.S.A.* **86 B2** 44 39N 72 53W
Cambridge Bay = Ikaluktutiak, *Nunavut, Canada* **190 D4** 69 10N 105 0W
Cambridge City, *IN, U.S.A.* **72 D5** 39 49N 85 10W
Cambridge Res., *Boston, U.S.A.* **106 A2** 42 24N 71 16W
Cambridge Springs, *PA, U.S.A.* **95 C2** 41 48N 80 4W
Cambridgeport, *VT, U.S.A.* **86 C2** 43 10N 72 35W
Camden, *AL, U.S.A.* **60 E3** 31 59N 87 17W
Camden, *AR, U.S.A.* **63 E3** 33 35N 92 50W
Camden, *DE, U.S.A.* **77 A5** 39 7N 75 33W
Camden, *IL, U.S.A.* **71 C3** 40 9N 90 46W
Camden, *ME, U.S.A.* **76 D4** 44 13N 69 4W
Camden, *MS, U.S.A.* **81 D4** 32 47N 89 50W
Camden, *NC, U.S.A.* **90 B9** 36 20N 76 10W
Camden, *NJ, U.S.A.* **87 C1** 39 55N 75 7W
Camden, *NY, U.S.A.* **89 B5** 43 20N 75 45W
Camden, *OH, U.S.A.* **92 D2** 39 38N 84 39W
Camden, *SC, U.S.A.* **90 D5** 34 16N 80 36W
Camden, *TN, U.S.A.* **96 D4** 36 4N 88 6W
Camden, *TX, U.S.A.* **99 G13** 30 55N 94 44W
Camden Bay, *AK, U.S.A.* **61 A11** 70 10N 145 15W
Camden County ☆, *GA, U.S.A.* **68 F5** 31 0N 81 45W
Camden County ☆, *MO, U.S.A.* **82 C4** 38 0N 92 45W
Camden County ☆, *NC, U.S.A.* **90 B9** 36 20N 76 15W
Camden County ☆, *NJ, U.S.A.* **87 C2** 39 45N 75 0W
Camdenton, *MO, U.S.A.* **82 C4** 38 1N 92 45W
Camels Hump, *VT, U.S.A.* **86 B2** 44 19N 72 53W
Cameron, *AZ, U.S.A.* **62 B4** 35 53N 111 25W
Cameron, *LA, U.S.A.* **75 E2** 29 48N 93 20W
Cameron, *MO, U.S.A.* **82 B2** 39 44N 94 14W
Cameron, *MT, U.S.A.* **83 E6** 45 13N 111 41W
Cameron, *OK, U.S.A.* **93 C9** 35 8N 94 32W
Cameron, *SC, U.S.A.* **90 E5** 33 34N 80 43W
Cameron, *TX, U.S.A.* **99 G11** 30 51N 96 59W
Cameron, *WV, U.S.A.* **102 B4** 39 50N 80 34W
Cameron, *WI, U.S.A.* **103 C2** 45 25N 91 44W
Cameron County ☆, *PA, U.S.A.* **95 C4** 41 30N 78 5W
Cameron County ☆, *TX, U.S.A.* **98 L10** 26 12N 97 42W
Cameron Hills, *Alta., Canada* **189 E9** 59 48N 118 0W
Cameron I., *Nunavut, Canada* **190 B5** 76 30N 103 50W
Cameron L., *Ont., Canada* **181 C12** 49 1N 84 17W
Cameron Parish ☆, *LA, U.S.A.* **75 E2** 29 58N 93 10W
Cameron Prairie Nat. Wildlife Refuge ⌓, *LA, U.S.A.* **75 E2** 29 50N 93 12W
Camilla, *GA, U.S.A.* **68 E2** 31 14N 84 12W
Camino, *CA, U.S.A.* **64 E6** 38 44N 120 41W
Camp Atterbury, *IN, U.S.A.* **72 D4** 39 20N 86 4W
Camp Blanding Training Site, *FL, U.S.A.* **67 B7** 29 56N 81 57W
Camp Borden, *Ont., Canada* **178 C7** 44 18N 79 56W
Camp Bullis, *TX, U.S.A.* **99 H9** 29 38N 98 34W
Camp Coulter = Powell, *WY, U.S.A.* **104 B4** 44 45N 108 46W
Camp County ☆, *TX, U.S.A.* **99 E13** 33 0N 94 59W
Camp Creek, *WV, U.S.A.* **102 D3** 37 30N 81 6W
Camp Crook, *SD, U.S.A.* **91 E2** 45 33N 103 59W
Camp Douglas, *WI, U.S.A.* **103 E3** 43 55N 90 16W
Camp Edwards and Otis A.N.G. Base, *MA, U.S.A.* **78 C4** 41 39N 70 32W
Camp Grayling, *MI, U.S.A.* **79 E7** 44 37N 84 47W
Camp Hill, *AL, U.S.A.* **60 D5** 32 48N 85 39W
Camp Hill, *PA, U.S.A.* **95 D6** 40 14N 76 55W
Camp Houston, *OK, U.S.A.* **93 B4** 36 49N 99 7W
Camp J.T. Robinson, *AR, U.S.A.* **63 D3** 34 52N 92 21W
Camp Lejeune Marine Corps Base, *NC, U.S.A.* **90 D8** 34 43N 77 22W
Camp Pendleton, *CA, U.S.A.* **65 K9** 33 13N 117 24W
Camp Point, *IL, U.S.A.* **71 C2** 40 3N 91 4W
Camp Ripley, *MN, U.S.A.* **80 D4** 46 9N 94 22W
Camp Roberts, *CA, U.S.A.* **65 H6** 35 47N 120 48W
Camp Shelby Training Site, *MS, U.S.A.* **81 E4** 31 11N 89 15W
Camp Springs, *MD, U.S.A.* **77 B4** 38 48N 76 55W
Camp Swift, *TX, U.S.A.* **99 G10** 30 18N 97 20W
Camp Verde, *AZ, U.S.A.* **62 C4** 34 34N 111 51W
Camp Wood, *TX, U.S.A.* **99 H7** 29 40N 100 1W
Campaign, *TN, U.S.A.* **97 E7** 35 46N 85 38W
Campania I., *B.C., Canada* **186 B5** 53 5N 129 25W
Campbell, *AL, U.S.A.* **60 E3** 31 55N 87 59W
Campbell, *CA, U.S.A.* **64 F5** 37 17N 121 57W
Campbell, *FL, U.S.A.* **67 C7** 28 16N 81 27W
Campbell, *MN, U.S.A.* **80 D2** 46 6N 96 24W
Campbell, *MO, U.S.A.* **82 E6** 36 30N 90 4W
Campbell, *NE, U.S.A.* **84 D7** 40 18N 98 44W
Campbell, *OH, U.S.A.* **92 B6** 41 5N 80 37W
Campbell County ☆, *KY, U.S.A.* **97 B8** 38 55N 84 20W
Campbell County ☆, *SD, U.S.A.* **91 E6** 45 55N 100 0W
Campbell County ☆, *TN, U.S.A.* **97 D8** 36 23N 84 7W
Campbell County ☆, *VA, U.S.A.* **102 D5** 37 15N 79 5W
Campbell County ☆, *WY, U.S.A.* **104 B7** 44 15N 105 30W
Campbell Hill, *OH, U.S.A.* **92 C3** 40 22N 83 43W
Campbell I., *B.C., Canada* **186 C6** 52 7N 128 12W
Campbell Island, *B.C., Canada* **186 C6** 52 8N 128 12W
Campbell River, *B.C., Canada* **186 E9** 50 5N 125 20W
Campbellford, *Ont., Canada* **179 C9** 44 18N 77 48W
Campbell's Bay, *Qué., Canada* **176 F6** 45 44N 76 36W
Campbellsburg, *IN, U.S.A.* **72 E4** 38 39N 86 16W
Campbellsburg, *KY, U.S.A.* **97 B7** 38 31N 85 12W
Campbellsport, *WI, U.S.A.* **103 E5** 43 36N 88 17W
Campbellsville, *KY, U.S.A.* **97 C7** 37 21N 85 20W
Campbellton, *N.B., Canada* **173 F3** 47 57N 66 43W
Campbellton, *Nfld. & L., Canada* **174 C6** 49 17N 54 56W
Campbellton, *FL, U.S.A.* **67 A3** 30 57N 85 24W
Campeche, *Campeche, Mexico* **223 C3** 19 51N 90 32W
Campeche □, *Mexico* **223 D3** 19 0N 90 30W
Camperville, *Man., Canada* **183 D11** 51 59N 100 9W
Campion, *CO, U.S.A.* **66 B5** 40 21N 105 5W
Campo, *CO, U.S.A.* **66 E8** 37 6N 102 35W
Campo Acosta, *Jalisco, Mexico* **218 C2** 19 45N 105 15W
Campo Cinco, *Chihuahua, Mexico* **213 C8** 30 47N 107 55W
Campo Cuatro, *Sonora, Mexico* **212 E4** 28 32N 111 35W
Campo del Oso →, *Baja Calif., Mexico* **210 C3** 30 49N 115 39W
Campo Indian Reservation, *CA, U.S.A.* **65 L10** 32 37N 116 23W
Campo Nuevo, *Veracruz, Mexico* **221 G5** 17 43N 95 5W
Campo Sesenta y Uno, *Chihuahua, Mexico* **213 E9** 28 54N 106 40W
Campos de los Limones, *Nayarit, Mexico* **216 F5** 21 47N 105 26W
Campti, *LA, U.S.A.* **75 C2** 31 54N 93 7W
Campton, *FL, U.S.A.* **67 A2** 30 53N 86 31W
Campton, *GA, U.S.A.* **68 C3** 33 52N 83 43W
Campton, *KY, U.S.A.* **97 C9** 37 44N 83 33W
Campton, *NH, U.S.A.* **86 C3** 43 50N 71 39W
Camptonville, *CA, U.S.A.* **64 D5** 39 27N 121 3W
Campville, *FL, U.S.A.* **67 B6** 29 40N 82 7W
Camrose, *Alta., Canada* **185 E8** 53 0N 112 50W
Camsell →, *N.W.T., Canada* **189 C9** 65 40N 118 7W
Camuy, *Puerto Rico* **105 G16** 18 29N 66 51W
Canaan, *N.B., Canada* **173 G4** 46 15N 65 4W
Canaan, *CT, U.S.A.* **78 B1** 42 2N 73 20W
Canaan, *NH, U.S.A.* **86 C2** 43 40N 72 1W
Canaan →, *N.B., Canada* **173 H4** 45 55N 65 47W
Canada B., *Nfld. & L., Canada* **174 B4** 50 43N 56 8W
Canada Basin, *Arctic* **188 A3** 80 0N 145 0W
Cañadas de Villa Orbregón, *Jalisco, Mexico* **218 A5** 21 7N 102 40W
Canadensis, *PA, U.S.A.* **87 A1** 41 12N 75 15W
Canadian, *OK, U.S.A.* **93 C8** 35 11N 95 39W
Canadian, *TX, U.S.A.* **98 B7** 35 55N 100 23W
Canadian →, *OK, U.S.A.* **93 C8** 35 28N 95 3W
Canadian County ☆, *OK, U.S.A.* **93 C6** 35 35N 98 0W
Canajoharie, *NY, U.S.A.* **89 C6** 42 54N 74 35W
Canal Flats, *B.C., Canada* **185 H5** 50 10N 115 48W
Canal Fulton, *OH, U.S.A.* **92 C5** 40 53N 81 36W
Canal Point, *FL, U.S.A.* **67 E8** 26 52N 80 38W
Canalou, *MO, U.S.A.* **82 E7** 36 46N 89 41W
Canandaigua, *NY, U.S.A.* **89 C3** 42 54N 77 17W
Canandaigua L., *NY, U.S.A.* **89 C3** 42 47N 77 19W
Cananea, *Sonora, Mexico* **212 C5** 31 0N 110 18W
Canarsie, *NY, U.S.A.* **114 C3** 40 38N 73 53W
Canaseraga, *NY, U.S.A.* **89 C3** 42 27N 77 45W
Canatlán, *Durango, Mexico* **217 C6** 24 31N 104 47W
Canaveral, C., *FL, U.S.A.* **67 C8** 28 27N 80 32W
Canaveral Nat. Seashore ⌓, *FL, U.S.A.* **67 C8** 28 28N 80 34W
Canby, *CA, U.S.A.* **64 B6** 41 27N 120 52W
Canby, *MN, U.S.A.* **80 F2** 44 43N 96 16W
Canby, *OR, U.S.A.* **94 B3** 45 16N 122 42W
Cancún, *Quintana Roo, Mexico* **223 A7** 21 8N 86 44W
Cancún ✕ (CUN), *Quintana Roo, Mexico* **223 C7** 19 1N 86 54W
Candela, *Coahuila, Mexico* **214 D4** 26 50N 100 40W
Candelaria, *Baja Calif. S., Mexico* **211 K8** 23 4N 110 0W
Candelaria, *Campeche, Mexico* **223 D2** 18 18N 91 21W
Candelaria, *Quintana Roo, Mexico* **223 C5** 19 45N 88 59W
Candelaria, *TX, U.S.A.* **98 G3** 30 8N 104 41W
Candelaria →, *Campeche, Mexico* **223 D2** 18 38N 91 15W
Candelaria Loxicha, *Oaxaca, Mexico* **221 J4** 15 56N 96 32W
Candiac, *Montréal, Canada* **192 B4** 45 23N 73 29W
Cándido Aguilar, *Tamaulipas, Mexico* **215 E6** 25 3N 98 47W
Candle, *AK, U.S.A.* **61 D7** 65 55N 161 56W
Candle L., *Sask., Canada* **182 B6** 53 50N 105 18W
Candle Lake, *Sask., Canada* **182 B6** 53 45N 105 15W
Candler County ☆, *GA, U.S.A.* **68 D4** 32 30N 82 0W
Candlewood, *NJ, U.S.A.* **87 B2** 40 9N 74 10W
Candlewood, L., *CT, U.S.A.* **78 C1** 41 30N 73 27W
Cando, *Sask., Canada* **182 C3** 52 23N 108 14W
Cando, *ND, U.S.A.* **91 B6** 48 32N 99 12W
Candor, *NC, U.S.A.* **90 C6** 35 18N 79 45W
Candor, *NY, U.S.A.* **89 C4** 42 14N 76 21W
Cane River Creole Nat. Historical Park ⌓, *LA, U.S.A.* **75 C2** 31 40N 93 1W
Cane Valley, *KY, U.S.A.* **97 C7** 37 11N 85 19W
Canelas, *Durango, Mexico* **216 B4** 25 7N 106 34W
Caney, *KS, U.S.A.* **74 D8** 37 1N 95 56W
Caney, *OK, U.S.A.* **93 D7** 34 14N 96 13W
Caney →, *U.S.A.* **74 E8** 36 20N 95 42W
Caney Creek Res., *LA, U.S.A.* **75 B3** 32 13N 92 30W
Caney Fork →, *TN, U.S.A.* **97 D7** 36 15N 85 57W
Caneyville, *KY, U.S.A.* **96 C6** 37 26N 86 29W
Canfield, *AR, U.S.A.* **63 E2** 33 11N 93 38W
Canfield, *OH, U.S.A.* **92 B6** 41 2N 80 46W
Caniapiscau →, *Qué., Canada* **175 B4** 56 40N 69 30W
Caniapiscau, L. de, *Qué., Canada* **175 C4** 54 10N 69 55W
Canim, L., *B.C., Canada* **187 D14** 51 45N 120 50W
Canim Lake, *B.C., Canada* **187 D14** 51 47N 120 54W
Canisteo, *NY, U.S.A.* **89 C3** 42 16N 77 36W
Canisteo →, *NY, U.S.A.* **89 C3** 42 7N 77 8W
Canistota, *SD, U.S.A.* **91 G8** 43 36N 97 18W
Cañitas de Felipe Pescador, *Zacatecas, Mexico* **217 D8** 23 36N 102 43W
Canjilon, *NM, U.S.A.* **88 A4** 36 29N 106 26W
Canmer, *KY, U.S.A.* **97 C7** 37 17N 85 46W
Canmore, *Alta., Canada* **185 G5** 51 7N 115 18W
Cannel City, *KY, U.S.A.* **97 C9** 37 47N 83 17W
Cannelton, *IN, U.S.A.* **72 F4** 37 55N 86 45W
Canning, *N.S., Canada* **173 H5** 45 9N 64 25W
Cannington, *Ont., Canada* **179 C7** 44 20N 79 2W
Cannon Air Force Base, *NM, U.S.A.* **88 B6** 35 23N 104 12W
Cannon Ball, *ND, U.S.A.* **91 D5** 46 25N 100 38W
Cannon Beach, *OR, U.S.A.* **94 B2** 45 54N 123 58W
Cannon County ☆, *TN, U.S.A.* **96 E6** 35 50N 86 4W
Cannon Falls, *MN, U.S.A.* **80 F6** 44 31N 92 54W
Cannonball →, *ND, U.S.A.* **91 D5** 46 26N 100 35W
Cannonsburg, *KY, U.S.A.* **97 B10** 38 23N 82 42W
Cannonsville Res., *NY, U.S.A.* **89 C5** 42 4N 75 22W
Cannonville, *UT, U.S.A.* **100 F3** 37 34N 112 3W
Canoas, Pta., *Baja Calif., Mexico* **210 D3** 29 26N 115 12W
Canobie Lake, *NH, U.S.A.* **86 D3** 42 49N 71 15W
Canoe, *B.C., Canada* **187 E15** 50 45N 119 13W
Cañon City, *CO, U.S.A.* **66 D5** 38 27N 105 14W
Cañón de Río Blanco, Parque Nacional △, *Puebla, Mexico* **221 F3** 18 40N 97 20W
Cañón de Santa Elena, Parque Natural △, *Madag.* **214 B1** 28 57N 103 15W
Cañón del Sumidero, Parque Nacional △, *Chiapas, Mexico* **222 C3** 16 51N 93 8W
Cañon Fiord, *Nunavut, Canada* **190 B9** 80 0N 82 35W
Canon Largo →, *NM, U.S.A.* **88 A3** 36 43N 107 49W
Canoncito Indian Reservation, *NM, U.S.A.* **88 B3** 35 10N 107 0W
Canonsburg, *PA, U.S.A.* **95 D2** 40 16N 80 11W
Canoochee →, *GA, U.S.A.* **68 E5** 31 59N 81 19W
Canora, *Sask., Canada* **183 D9** 51 40N 102 30W
Canova, *SD, U.S.A.* **91 G8** 43 53N 97 30W
Cansahcab, *Yucatán, Mexico* **223 A4** 21 10N 89 6W
Canso, *N.S., Canada* **173 H9** 45 20N 61 0W
Canso, Str. of, *N.S., Canada* **173 H8** 45 37N 61 22W
Canterbury = Invermere, *B.C., Canada* **185 H4** 50 30N 116 2W
Canterbury, *N.B., Canada* **173 H2** 45 53N 67 29W
Canterbury, *CT, U.S.A.* **78 C3** 41 41N 71 57W
Canterbury, *NH, U.S.A.* **86 C3** 43 20N 71 34W
Cantin L., *Man., Canada* **183 B16** 53 25N 95 10W
Canton, *Baltimore, U.S.A.* **107 B2** 39 16N 76 34W
Canton, *CT, U.S.A.* **78 C2** 41 49N 72 54W
Canton, *GA, U.S.A.* **68 B2** 34 14N 84 29W
Canton, *IL, U.S.A.* **71 C3** 40 33N 90 2W
Canton, *KS, U.S.A.* **74 C6** 38 23N 97 26W
Canton, *KY, U.S.A.* **96 D5** 36 48N 87 58W
Canton, *MA, U.S.A.* **78 B3** 42 9N 71 9W
Canton, *MN, U.S.A.* **80 G7** 43 32N 91 56W
Canton, *MS, U.S.A.* **81 D3** 32 37N 90 2W
Canton, *MO, U.S.A.* **82 A5** 40 8N 91 32W
Canton, *NC, U.S.A.* **90 C3** 35 32N 82 50W
Canton, *NY, U.S.A.* **89 A5** 44 36N 75 10W
Canton, *OH, U.S.A.* **92 C5** 40 48N 81 23W
Canton, *OK, U.S.A.* **93 B5** 36 3N 98 35W
Canton, *PA, U.S.A.* **95 C6** 41 39N 76 51W
Canton, *SD, U.S.A.* **91 G9** 43 18N 96 35W
Canton, *TX, U.S.A.* **99 E12** 32 33N 95 52W
Canton L., *OK, U.S.A.* **93 B5** 36 6N 98 35W
Cantonment, *FL, U.S.A.* **67 A1** 30 37N 87 20W
Cantril, *IA, U.S.A.* **73 E6** 40 39N 92 4W
Cantwell, *AK, U.S.A.* **61 E10** 63 24N 148 57W
Canute, *OK, U.S.A.* **93 C4** 35 25N 99 17W
Canutillo, *Durango, Mexico* **216 A5** 26 22N 105 25W
Canutillo, *TX, U.S.A.* **98 F1** 31 55N 106 36W
Canwood, *Sask., Canada* **182 B5** 53 22N 106 36W
Canyon, *TX, U.S.A.* **98 C6** 34 59N 101 55W
Canyon City, *OR, U.S.A.* **94 C7** 44 23N 118 57W
Canyon County ☆, *ID, U.S.A.* **70 F2** 43 35N 116 50W
Canyon Creek, *Alta., Canada* **184 C5** 55 22N 115 5W
Canyon Creek, *MT, U.S.A.* **83 D5** 46 49N 112 16W
Canyon De Chelly Nat. Monument ⌓, *AZ, U.S.A.* **62 A6** 36 10N 109 20W
Canyon Ferry L., *MT, U.S.A.* **83 D6** 46 39N 111 44W
Canyon L., *TX, U.S.A.* **99 H9** 29 52N 98 12W
Canyon Village, *WY, U.S.A.* **104 B2** 44 46N 110 32W
Canyonlands Nat. Park △, *UT, U.S.A.* **100 E6** 38 15N 110 0W
Canyons of the Ancients Nat. Monument ⌓, *CO, U.S.A.* **66 E2** 37 30N 108 55W
Canyonville, *OR, U.S.A.* **94 E2** 42 56N 123 17W
Caopacho →, *Qué., Canada* **172 B3** 51 18N 66 18W
Caopacho, L., *Qué., Canada* **172 A3** 52 0N 66 9W
Caopas, *Zacatecas, Mexico* **217 C8** 24 18N 102 10W
Caotibi, L., *Qué., Canada* **172 C2** 50 45N 67 34W
Cap-aux-Meules, *Qué., Canada* **173 F8** 47 23N 61 52W
Cap-aux-Meules, Î. du, *Qué., Canada* **173 F8** 47 23N 61 54W
Cap-Chat, *Qué., Canada* **172 D3** 49 6N 66 40W
Cap-de-la-Madeleine, *Qué., Canada* **177 E10** 46 22N 72 31W
Cap-des-Rosiers, *Qué., Canada* **172 E5** 48 52N 64 13W
Cap-d'Espoir, *Qué., Canada* **172 E5** 48 26N 64 20W
Cap Mt., *N.W.T., Canada* **189 D8** 63 24N 123 12W
Cap-Pelé, *N.B., Canada* **173 G5** 46 13N 64 18W
Cap Rock Escarpment, *TX, U.S.A.* **98 D6** 33 50N 101 11W
Cap-St-Ignace, *Qué., Canada* **177 D12** 47 2N 70 28W
Cap-Seize, *Qué., Canada* **172 D3** 49 1N 66 24W
Cap-Saint-Jacques, Parc-nature du, *Montréal, Canada* **192 B1** 45 28N 73 55W
Capa, *SD, U.S.A.* **91 F5** 44 7N 100 59W
Capac, *MI, U.S.A.* **79 F9** 43 1N 82 56W
Cape Breton, *N.S., Canada* **173 G9** 46 0N 60 19W
Cape Breton Highlands Nat. Park △, *N.S., Canada* **173 G9** 46 50N 60 40W
Cape Breton I., *N.S., Canada* **173 G9** 46 0N 60 30W
Cape Broyle, *Nfld. & L., Canada* **174 E8** 47 6N 52 57W
Cape Canaveral, *FL, U.S.A.* **67 C8** 28 24N 80 36W
Cape Canaveral Air Station, *FL, U.S.A.* **67 C8** 28 28N 80 34W
Cape Charles, *VA, U.S.A.* **102 D8** 37 16N 76 1W
Cape Cod B., *MA, U.S.A.* **78 C4** 41 50N 70 20W
Cape Cod Nat. Seashore ⌓, *MA, U.S.A.* **78 C4** 41 56N 70 6W
Cape Coral, *FL, U.S.A.* **67 E7** 26 33N 81 57W
Cape Dorset, *Nunavut, Canada* **191 E10** 64 14N 76 32W
Cape Elizabeth, *ME, U.S.A.* **76 E3** 43 34N 70 12W
Cape Fear →, *NC, U.S.A.* **90 E7** 33 53N 78 1W
Cape Girardeau, *MO, U.S.A.* **82 D7** 37 19N 89 32W
Cape Girardeau County ☆, *MO, U.S.A.* **82 D7** 37 25N 89 40W
Cape Hatteras Nat. Seashore ⌓, *NC, U.S.A.* **90 C10** 35 30N 75 28W
Cape Henlopen State Park ⌓, *DE, U.S.A.* **77 B5** 38 46N 75 5W
Cape I., *SC, U.S.A.* **90 E6** 33 2N 79 21W
Cape Krusenstern Nat. Monument ⌓, *U.S.A.* **61 C7** 67 30N 163 30W
Cape Lisburne = Wevok, *AK, U.S.A.* **61 B6** 68 53N 166 13W
Cape Lookout Nat. Seashore ⌓, *NC, U.S.A.* **90 C9** 35 45N 76 25W
Cape May, *NJ, U.S.A.* **87 D2** 38 56N 74 56W
Cape May County ☆, *NJ, U.S.A.* **87 C2** 39 10N 74 45W
Cape May Court House, *U.S.A.* **87 C2** 39 5N 74 50W
Cape May Point, *NJ, U.S.A.* **87 D2** 38 56N 74 58W
Cape Pole, *AK, U.S.A.* **61 J14** 55 58N 133 48W
Cape Ray, *Nfld. & L., Canada* **174 E1** 47 38N 59 17W
Cape St. Claire, *MD, U.S.A.* **77 A4** 39 3N 76 25W
Cape Scott Park △, *B.C., Canada* **186 E6** 50 45N 128 20W
Cape Tormentine, *N.B., Canada* **173 G6** 46 8N 63 47W
Cape Vincent, *NY, U.S.A.* **89 A4** 44 8N 76 20W
Cape Yakataga, *AK, U.S.A.* **61 F12** 60 4N 142 26W
Capilano River Regional Park, *Vancouver, Canada* **193 A2** 49 21N 122 7W
Capilla de Guadalupe, *Jalisco, Mexico* **218 B5** 20 50N 102 35W
Capitachouane →, *Qué., Canada* **176 D6** 47 40N 76 47W
Capitan, *NM, U.S.A.* **88 D5** 33 35N 105 35W
Capitan Grande Indian Reservation, *CA, U.S.A.* **65 L10** 32 54N 116 43W
Capitan Mts., *NM, U.S.A.* **88 D5** 33 36N 105 22W
Capitan Pk., *NM, U.S.A.* **88 D5** 33 36N 105 16W
Capitol Heights, *MD, U.S.A.* **119 B4** 38 53N 76 55W
Capitol Hill, *N. Marianas* **105 c** 15 13N 145 45W
Capitol Reef Nat. Park △, *UT, U.S.A.* **100 E4** 38 15N 111 10W
Capitol View, *SC, U.S.A.* **90 E5** 33 58N 80 55W
Capitola, *FL, U.S.A.* **67 A4** 30 27N 84 5W
Caplan, *N.B., Canada* **173 E4** 48 6N 65 40W
Capleville, *TN, U.S.A.* **112 B2** 35 1N 89 53W
Capon Bridge, *WV, U.S.A.* **77 A2** 39 18N 78 26W
Caprock, *NM, U.S.A.* **88 D7** 33 24N 103 43W
Capron, *IL, U.S.A.* **71 A5** 42 24N 88 44W
Capron, *OK, U.S.A.* **93 B5** 36 54N 98 35W
Captain Cook, *HI, U.S.A.* **69 D6** 19 30N 155 55W
Captiva, *FL, U.S.A.* **67 E6** 26 31N 82 11W
Capulin Pk., *NM, U.S.A.* **88 A4** 36 15N 106 46W
Capulin Volcano Nat. Monument ⌓, *U.S.A.* **88 A7** 36 47N 103 58W
Caracol, Pta., *Yucatán, Mexico* **223 A6** 21 32N 87 37W
Caracoles, *Zacatecas, Mexico* **217 E7** 22 59N 103 28W
Carácuaro, *Michoacan, Mexico* **219 C6** 19 1N 101 8W
Caramat, *Ont., Canada* **181 C10** 49 37N 86 9W
Caraquet, *N.B., Canada* **173 F5** 47 48N 64 57W
Caratunk, *ME, U.S.A.* **76 C4** 45 8N 69 59W
Caraway, *AR, U.S.A.* **63 C5** 35 46N 90 19W
Carberry, *Man., Canada* **183 F12** 49 50N 99 25W
Carbó, *Sonora, Mexico* **212 D5** 29 42N 110 58W
Carbon, *Alta., Canada* **185 G7** 51 30N 113 9W
Carbon, *IN, U.S.A.* **72 D3** 39 36N 87 6W
Carbon, *IA, U.S.A.* **73 D4** 41 3N 94 50W
Carbon, *TX, U.S.A.* **99 E9** 32 16N 98 50W
Carbon County ☆, *MT, U.S.A.* **83 E9** 45 10N 109 0W
Carbon County ☆, *PA, U.S.A.* **95 D7** 41 0N 75 50W
Carbon County ☆, *UT, U.S.A.* **100 D5** 39 40N 110 30W
Carbon County ☆, *WY, U.S.A.* **104 E6** 42 0N 107 0W
Carbon Hill, *AL, U.S.A.* **60 C3** 33 53N 87 32W
Carbonado, *WA, U.S.A.* **101 C3** 47 5N 122 3W
Carbondale, *CO, U.S.A.* **66 C3** 39 24N 107 13W
Carbondale, *IL, U.S.A.* **71 F4** 37 44N 89 13W
Carbondale, *KS, U.S.A.* **74 C8** 38 49N 95 41W
Carbondale, *PA, U.S.A.* **95 C7** 41 35N 75 30W
Carbonear, *Nfld. & L., Canada* **174 E7** 47 42N 53 13W
Carboneras, *Tamaulipas, Mexico* **215 F7** 24 38N 97 43W
Carcajou, *Alta., Canada* **189 E9** 57 47N 117 6W
Carcajou →, *N.W.T., Canada* **189 C7** 65 37N 128 43W

Carcross, *Yukon, Canada* **189 D6** 60 13N 134 45W
Cardel, *Veracruz, Mexico* **220 E4** 19 22N 96 21W
Cárdenas, *San Luis Potosí, Mexico* **215 H5** 22 0N 99 38W
Cárdenas, *Tabasco, Mexico* **222 B3** 17 59N 93 22W
Cardiff, *CO, U.S.A.* **66 C3** 39 31N 107 19W
Cardigan, Mt., *NH, U.S.A.* **86 C3** 43 40N 71 54W
Cardinal, *Ont., Canada* **179 C11** 44 47N 75 23W
Cardinal L., *Alta., Canada* **184 B3** 56 14N 117 44W
Cardington, *OH, U.S.A.* **92 C4** 40 30N 82 54W
Cardross, *Sask., Canada* **182 F6** 49 50N 105 40W
Cardston, *Alta., Canada* **185 J7** 49 15N 113 20W
Cardwell, *MO, U.S.A.* **82 E6** 36 3N 90 17W
Carefree, *AZ, U.S.A.* **62 D4** 33 50N 111 55W
Carencro, *LA, U.S.A.* **75 D3** 30 19N 92 3W
Carey, *ID, U.S.A.* **70 F5** 43 19N 113 57W
Carey, *OH, U.S.A.* **92 C3** 40 57N 83 23W
Carheil, L., *Qué., Canada* **172 A2** 52 40N 67 5W
Caribe →, *Campeche, Mexico* **223 D3** 18 7N 90 47W
Cariboo →, *B.C., Canada* **187 B13** 53 3N 121 20W
Cariboo Mountain Park △, *B.C., Canada* **187 C14** 52 53N 120 31W
Cariboo Mts., *B.C., Canada* **187 C14** 53 0N 121 0W
Cariboo River Park △, *B.C., Canada* **187 C13** 52 52N 121 12W
Caribou, *ME, U.S.A.* **76 B5** 46 52N 68 1W
Caribou →, *Man., Canada* **191 F6** 59 20N 94 44W
Caribou County ☆, *ID, U.S.A.* **70 G7** 42 50N 111 30W
Caribou I., *Ont., Canada* **181 E11** 47 22N 85 49W
Caribou L., *Ont., Canada* **180 B7** 50 25N 89 5W
Caribou Mts., *Alta., Canada* **189 E9** 59 12N 115 40W
Caribou Nat. Forest, *ID, U.S.A.* **70 G7** 42 50N 111 5W
Caribou Range, *ID, U.S.A.* **70 F7** 43 10N 111 15W
Carichic, *Chihuahua, Mexico* **213 F8** 27 56N 107 3W
Carimicuas, *Jalisco, Mexico* **218 C5** 19 27N 102 58W
Carl Blackwell, L., *OK, U.S.A.* **93 B6** 36 8N 97 11W
Carl Junction, *MO, U.S.A.* **82 D2** 37 11N 94 34W
Carleton = Borden, *Sask., Canada* **182 C4** 52 27N 107 14W
Carleton, *N.B., Canada* **173 E3** 48 5N 66 4W
Carleton, *N.S., Canada* **173 K4** 44 0N 65 56W
Carleton, *MI, U.S.A.* **79 G8** 42 4N 83 24W
Carleton, *NE, U.S.A.* **84 D8** 40 18N 97 41W
Carleton, Mt., *N.B., Canada* **173 F3** 47 23N 66 53W
Carleton Heights, *Ont., Canada* **192 B1** 45 21N 75 43W
Carleton Place, *Ont., Canada* **179 B10** 45 8N 76 9W
Carlile, *WY, U.S.A.* **104 B8** 44 29N 104 48W
Carlin, *NV, U.S.A.* **85 B4** 40 43N 116 7W
Carlinville, *IL, U.S.A.* **71 D4** 39 17N 89 53W
Carlisle, *AR, U.S.A.* **63 D4** 34 47N 91 45W
Carlisle, *IN, U.S.A.* **72 E3** 38 58N 87 24W
Carlisle, *IA, U.S.A.* **73 D5** 41 30N 93 29W
Carlisle, *KY, U.S.A.* **97 B8** 38 19N 84 1W
Carlisle, *MS, U.S.A.* **81 E3** 32 0N 90 47W
Carlisle, *PA, U.S.A.* **95 D5** 40 12N 77 12W
Carlisle, *WA, U.S.A.* **101 C1** 47 10N 124 6W
Carlisle County ☆, *KY, U.S.A.* **96 D4** 36 50N 89 0W
Carlock, *IL, U.S.A.* **71 C4** 40 35N 89 8W
Carlos, *MN, U.S.A.* **80 E3** 45 58N 95 18W
Carlos, *TX, U.S.A.* **99 G11** 30 36N 96 5W
Carlos A. Carrillo, *Veracruz, Mexico* **221 F5** 18 17N 95 49W
Carlsbad, *CA, U.S.A.* **65 K9** 33 10N 117 21W
Carlsbad, *NM, U.S.A.* **88 E6** 32 25N 104 14W
Carlsbad, *TX, U.S.A.* **98 F7** 31 36N 100 38W
Carlsbad Caverns Nat. Park △, *NM, U.S.A.* **88 E6** 32 10N 104 35W
Carlshend, *MI, U.S.A.* **79 C4** 46 19N 87 13W
Carlstadt, *NJ, U.S.A.* **114 A2** 40 50N 74 6W
Carlton, *MN, U.S.A.* **80 D6** 46 40N 92 25W
Carlton, *OR, U.S.A.* **94 B2** 45 18N 123 11W
Carlton County ☆, *MN, U.S.A.* **80 D6** 46 35N 92 50W
Carlyle, *Sask., Canada* **183 F9** 49 40N 102 20W
Carlyle, *IL, U.S.A.* **71 E4** 38 37N 89 22W
Carlyle, *MT, U.S.A.* **83 D13** 46 40N 104 4W
Carlyle L., *IL, U.S.A.* **71 E4** 38 37N 89 21W
Carmacks, *Yukon, Canada* **189 D5** 62 5N 136 16W
Carman, *Man., Canada* **183 F13** 49 30N 98 0W
Carmanah Walbran Park △, *B.C., Canada* **186 G10** 48 39N 124 39W
Carmangay, *Alta., Canada* **185 H7** 50 10N 113 10W
Carmanville, *Nfld. & L., Canada* **174 C6** 49 23N 54 19W
Carmel, *IN, U.S.A.* **72 D4** 39 58N 86 7W
Carmel, *NY, U.S.A.* **87 A3** 41 26N 73 41W
Carmel-by-the-Sea, *CA, U.S.A.* **64 G5** 36 33N 121 55W
Carmel-Michells Brook-St. Catherines, *Nfld. & L., Canada* **174 E7** 47 9N 53 29W
Carmel Valley, *CA, U.S.A.* **64 G5** 36 29N 121 43W
Carmen, *ID, U.S.A.* **70 D5** 45 15N 113 54W
Carmen, *OK, U.S.A.* **93 B5** 36 35N 98 28W
Carmen, I., *Baja Calif. S., Mexico* **211 H7** 25 57N 111 12W
Carmen, I. del, *Campeche, Mexico* **223 D2** 18 16N 91 48W
Carmen, L. el, *Tabasco, Mexico* **222 A3** 18 17N 93 48W
Carmen, Sa. del, *Coahuila, Mexico* **214 B2** 29 0N 102 28W
Carmi, *B.C., Canada* **187 F15** 49 36N 119 8W
Carmi, *IL, U.S.A.* **71 E5** 38 5N 88 10W
Carmichael, *CA, U.S.A.* **64 E5** 38 38N 121 19W
Carnduff, *Sask., Canada* **183 F10** 49 10N 101 50W
Carnegie, *GA, U.S.A.* **68 E2** 31 39N 84 47W
Carnegie, *OK, U.S.A.* **93 C5** 35 6N 98 36W
Carnegie, *PA, U.S.A.* **95 D2** 40 24N 80 5W
Carneiro, *KS, U.S.A.* **74 C5** 38 44N 98 2W
Carnesville, *GA, U.S.A.* **68 B3** 34 22N 83 14W
Carney, *MD, U.S.A.* **77 A4** 39 23N 76 31W
Carney, *MI, U.S.A.* **79 D4** 45 35N 87 34W
Carney, *OK, U.S.A.* **93 C6** 35 48N 97 1W
Carneys Point, *NJ, U.S.A.* **87 C1** 39 43N 75 28W
Carnwath →, *N.W.T., Canada* **188 C7** 68 26N 128 52W
Carnwood, *Alta., Canada* **185 E6** 53 11N 114 38W
Caro, *MI, U.S.A.* **79 F8** 43 29N 83 24W
Caroga Lake, *NY, U.S.A.* **89 B6** 43 8N 74 29W
Carol City, *FL, U.S.A.* **67 F8** 25 56N 80 14W
Carolina, *Puerto Rico* **105 G17** 18 23N 65 58W
Carolina, *RI, U.S.A.* **78 C3** 41 28N 71 40W
Carolina Beach, *NC, U.S.A.* **90 D8** 34 2N 77 54W
Carolinas Pt., *N. Marianas* **105 c** 14 55N 145 38W
Caroline, *Alta., Canada* **185 F6** 52 5N 114 45W
Caroline County ☆, *MD, U.S.A.* **77 B5** 38 50N 75 50W
Caroline County ☆, *VA, U.S.A.* **102 C7** 38 3N 77 21W
Caron, *Sask., Canada* **182 E6** 50 30N 105 50W
Caron, L., *Qué., Canada* **172 C2** 50 57N 67 44W
Carondelet Park, *MO, U.S.A.* **117 B2** 38 33N 90 15W
Carp, *NV, U.S.A.* **85 E6** 37 7N 114 29W
Carpenter, *IA, U.S.A.* **73 B5** 43 25N 93 1W
Carpenter, *WY, U.S.A.* **104 E8** 41 3N 104 22W
Carpenter L., *B.C., Canada* **187 E12** 50 53N 122 37W
Carpenterville, *OR, U.S.A.* **94 E1** 42 13N 124 17W
Carpinteria, *CA, U.S.A.* **65 J7** 34 24N 119 31W
Carpio, *ND, U.S.A.* **91 B4** 48 27N 101 43W
Carr, *CO, U.S.A.* **66 B6** 40 54N 104 53W
Carr Fork L., *KY, U.S.A.* **97 C9** 37 14N 83 2W
Carr Mt., *NH, U.S.A.* **86 C3** 43 52N 71 50W
Carrabassett, *ME, U.S.A.* **76 C3** 45 5N 70 13W
Carrabelle, *FL, U.S.A.* **67 B4** 29 51N 84 40W
Carragana, *Sask., Canada* **182 C8** 52 35N 103 6W
Carrboro, *NC, U.S.A.* **90 C6** 35 55N 79 5W
Carreta, Estero la, *Chiapas, Mexico* **222 D3** 15 33N 93 12W
Carrier, *OK, U.S.A.* **93 B5** 36 29N 98 2W
Carrier Mills, *IL, U.S.A.* **71 F5** 37 41N 88 38W
Carriere, *MS, U.S.A.* **81 F4** 30 37N 89 39W
Carrigain, Mt., *NH, U.S.A.* **86 B3** 44 6N 71 26W
Carrillo, *Chihuahua, Mexico* **213 G12** 26 54N 103 55W
Carrington, *ND, U.S.A.* **91 C6** 47 27N 99 8W
Carrizo Cr. →, *NM, U.S.A.* **88 A7** 36 55N 103 55W
Carrizo Plain Nat. Monument △, *U.S.A.* **65 H7** 35 11N 119 47W
Carrizo Springs, *TX, U.S.A.* **99 J8** 28 31N 99 52W
Carrizo Wash →, *U.S.A.* **88 C1** 34 36N 109 26W
Carrizos, *Tamaulipas, Mexico* **215 F5** 24 23N 99 16W
Carrizozo, *NM, U.S.A.* **88 D5** 33 38N 105 53W
Carroll, *IA, U.S.A.* **73 C4** 42 4N 94 52W
Carroll, *NE, U.S.A.* **84 B8** 42 17N 97 12W
Carroll, *OH, U.S.A.* **92 D4** 39 48N 82 43W
Carroll County ☆, *AR, U.S.A.* **63 B2** 36 22N 93 34W
Carroll County ☆, *GA, U.S.A.* **68 C1** 33 30N 85 10W
Carroll County ☆, *IL, U.S.A.* **71 A4** 42 0N 90 0W
Carroll County ☆, *IN, U.S.A.* **72 C4** 40 35N 86 35W
Carroll County ☆, *IA, U.S.A.* **73 C4** 42 0N 94 50W
Carroll County ☆, *KY, U.S.A.* **97 B7** 38 40N 85 5W
Carroll County ☆, *MD, U.S.A.* **77 A4** 39 30N 77 0W
Carroll County ☆, *MS, U.S.A.* **81 C4** 33 30N 89 55W
Carroll County ☆, *MO, U.S.A.* **82 B3** 39 25N 93 30W
Carroll County ☆, *NH, U.S.A.* **86 C3** 43 50N 71 45W
Carroll County ☆, *OH, U.S.A.* **92 C5** 40 34N 81 5W
Carroll County ☆, *TN, U.S.A.* **96 E4** 36 0N 88 26W
Carroll County ☆, *VA, U.S.A.* **102 E4** 36 55N 80 50W
Carroll Valley, *PA, U.S.A.* **77 A3** 39 44N 77 23W
Carrolls, *WA, U.S.A.* **101 D3** 46 4N 122 52W
Carrollton, *AL, U.S.A.* **60 C2** 33 16N 88 6W
Carrollton, *GA, U.S.A.* **68 C1** 33 35N 85 5W
Carrollton, *IL, U.S.A.* **71 D3** 39 18N 90 24W
Carrollton, *KY, U.S.A.* **97 B7** 38 41N 85 11W
Carrollton, *MI, U.S.A.* **79 F8** 43 28N 83 55W
Carrollton, *MS, U.S.A.* **81 C4** 33 30N 89 55W
Carrollton, *MO, U.S.A.* **82 B3** 39 22N 93 30W
Carrollton, *OH, U.S.A.* **92 C5** 40 34N 81 5W
Carrollton, *TX, U.S.A.* **99 E11** 32 57N 96 55W
Carrolltown, *PA, U.S.A.* **95 D4** 40 36N 78 43W
Carrollwood, *Tampa, U.S.A.* **119 A3** 28 2N 82 29W
Carrot →, *Sask., Canada* **183 B10** 53 50N 101 17W
Carrot River, *Sask., Canada* **182 B8** 53 17N 103 35W
Carry Falls Res., *NY, U.S.A.* **89 A6** 44 31N 74 45W
Carson, *CA, U.S.A.* **65 K8** 33 49N 118 16W
Carson, *IA, U.S.A.* **73 D3** 41 14N 95 25W
Carson, *ND, U.S.A.* **91 D4** 46 25N 101 34W
Carson, *WA, U.S.A.* **101 E4** 45 44N 121 49W
Carson →, *NV, U.S.A.* **85 C2** 39 45N 118 40W
Carson City, *MI, U.S.A.* **79 F7** 43 11N 84 51W
Carson City, *NV, U.S.A.* **85 C1** 39 10N 119 46W
Carson County ☆, *TX, U.S.A.* **98 B6** 35 20N 101 25W
Carson Grove, *Ont., Canada* **192 A2** 45 26N 75 37W
Carson L., *NV, U.S.A.* **85 C2** 39 18N 118 43W
Carson Nat. Forest, *NM, U.S.A.* **88 A4** 36 30N 106 15W
Carson Sink, *NV, U.S.A.* **85 C2** 39 50N 118 25W
Carstairs, *Alta., Canada* **185 G6** 51 34N 114 6W
Carta Valley, *TX, U.S.A.* **98 H7** 29 48N 100 41W
Cartago, *CA, U.S.A.* **65 G8** 36 19N 118 2W
Carter, *KY, U.S.A.* **97 B9** 38 26N 83 8W
Carter, *OK, U.S.A.* **93 C4** 35 13N 99 30W
Carter, *SD, U.S.A.* **91 G5** 43 23N 100 12W
Carter, *WY, U.S.A.* **104 E2** 41 26N 110 26W
Carter County ☆, *KY, U.S.A.* **97 B9** 38 20N 83 0W
Carter County ☆, *MO, U.S.A.* **82 E6** 37 0N 91 0W
Carter County ☆, *MT, U.S.A.* **83 E13** 45 30N 104 30W
Carter County ☆, *OK, U.S.A.* **93 D6** 34 15N 97 15W
Carter County ☆, *TN, U.S.A.* **97 D10** 36 17N 82 10W
Carter Mt., *WY, U.S.A.* **104 B3** 44 12N 109 25W
Carteret, *NJ, U.S.A.* **87 B2** 40 34N 74 13W
Carteret County ☆, *NC, U.S.A.* **90 D9** 34 50N 76 30W
Carters L., *GA, U.S.A.* **68 B2** 34 37N 84 40W
Cartersville, *GA, U.S.A.* **68 B2** 34 10N 84 48W
Cartersville, *VA, U.S.A.* **102 D6** 37 40N 78 6W
Carterville, *IL, U.S.A.* **71 F4** 37 46N 89 5W
Carthage, *AR, U.S.A.* **63 D3** 34 4N 92 33W
Carthage, *IL, U.S.A.* **71 C2** 40 25N 91 8W
Carthage, *IN, U.S.A.* **72 D5** 39 44N 85 34W
Carthage, *MS, U.S.A.* **81 D4** 32 44N 89 32W
Carthage, *MO, U.S.A.* **82 D2** 37 11N 94 19W
Carthage, *NC, U.S.A.* **90 C6** 35 21N 79 25W
Carthage, *NY, U.S.A.* **89 B5** 43 59N 75 37W
Carthage, *SD, U.S.A.* **91 F8** 44 10N 97 43W
Carthage, *TN, U.S.A.* **97 D7** 36 15N 85 57W
Carthage, *TX, U.S.A.* **99 E13** 32 9N 94 20W
Cartier, *Ont., Canada* **178 A5** 46 42N 81 33W
Cartierville, *Montréal, Canada* **192 A2** 45 31N 73 42W
Cartwright, *Man., Canada* **183 F12** 49 6N 99 20W
Cartwright, *Nfld. & L., Canada* **175 C6** 53 41N 56 58W
Cartwright Sd., *B.C., Canada* **186 B2** 53 13N 132 38W
Caruthersville, *MO, U.S.A.* **82 E7** 36 11N 89 39W
Carvajal, *Tamaulipas, Mexico* **215 F7** 24 30N 97 45W
Carver, *MA, U.S.A.* **78 C4** 41 53N 70 46W
Carver County ☆, *MN, U.S.A.* **80 F5** 44 50N 93 45W
Carver Lake, *Minneapolis-St. Paul, U.S.A.* **113 B4** 44 54N 92 58W
Carvers, *NV, U.S.A.* **85 D3** 38 47N 117 11W
Carville, *LA, U.S.A.* **75 D4** 30 13N 91 6W
Cary, *IL, U.S.A.* **71 A5** 42 13N 88 14W
Cary, *MS, U.S.A.* **81 D3** 32 49N 90 56W
Cary, *NC, U.S.A.* **90 C7** 35 47N 78 46W
Caryville, *TN, U.S.A.* **97 D8** 36 18N 84 13W
Casa, *AR, U.S.A.* **63 C2** 35 2N 93 3W
Casa Blanca, *NM, U.S.A.* **88 B3** 35 3N 107 28W
Casa de Piedra, Pta., *Guerrero, Mexico* **219 F9** 16 32N 98 52W
Casa Grande, *AZ, U.S.A.* **62 E4** 32 53N 111 45W
Casa Grande Ruins Nat. Monument △, *AZ, U.S.A.* **62 E4** 33 0N 111 30W
Casas Grandes, *Chihuahua, Mexico* **213 C8** 30 22N 107 57W
Casas Grandes, *Sonora, Mexico* **212 D4** 29 12N 111 43W
Casas Grandes →, *Chihuahua, Mexico* **213 B8** 31 22N 107 31W
Cascadas de Basaseachic, Parque Nacional △, *Chihuahua, Mexico* **213 E7** 28 10N 108 12W
Cascade, *CO, U.S.A.* **66 D6** 38 54N 104 58W
Cascade, *ID, U.S.A.* **70 E2** 44 31N 116 2W
Cascade, *IA, U.S.A.* **73 C8** 42 18N 91 0W
Cascade, *MT, U.S.A.* **83 C6** 47 16N 111 42W
Cascade County ☆, *MT, U.S.A.* **83 C6** 47 20N 111 30W
Cascade Head, *OR, U.S.A.* **94 B1** 45 3N 124 1W
Cascade Heights, *Vancouver, Canada* **193 B2** 49 15N 123 1W
Cascade Heights, *Atlanta, U.S.A.* **106 B2** 33 43N 84 26W
Cascade Locks, *OR, U.S.A.* **94 B4** 45 40N 121 54W
Cascade Ra., *WA, U.S.A.* **94 B4** 47 0N 121 30W
Cascade Res., *ID, U.S.A.* **70 E2** 44 32N 116 3W
Cascade-Siskiyou Nat. Monument △, *OR, U.S.A.* **94 E3** 42 5N 122 30W
Cascadia, *OR, U.S.A.* **94 C3** 44 24N 122 29W
Casco, *ME, U.S.A.* **76 E3** 44 0N 70 31W
Casco, *WI, U.S.A.* **103 D6** 44 34N 87 37W
Casco B., *ME, U.S.A.* **76 E4** 43 45N 70 0W
Caselton, *NV, U.S.A.* **85 E6** 37 55N 114 29W
Caseville, *MI, U.S.A.* **79 F8** 43 56N 83 16W
Casey, *Qué., Canada* **177 D8** 47 53N 74 11W
Casey, *IL, U.S.A.* **71 D6** 39 18N 87 59W
Casey, *IA, U.S.A.* **73 D4** 41 31N 94 32W
Casey County ☆, *KY, U.S.A.* **97 C8** 37 20N 85 0W
Cash, *AR, U.S.A.* **63 C5** 35 48N 90 56W
Cashie →, *NC, U.S.A.* **90 C9** 35 53N 76 49W
Cashiers, *NC, U.S.A.* **90 C2** 35 6N 83 6W
Cashion, *OK, U.S.A.* **93 C6** 35 48N 97 41W
Cashion, *Phoenix, U.S.A.* **116 C1** 33 26N 112 17W
Cashmere, *WA, U.S.A.* **101 C5** 47 31N 120 28W
Cashton, *WI, U.S.A.* **103 E3** 43 43N 90 47W
Casimiro Castillo, *Jalisco, Mexico* **218 C3** 19 38N 104 28W
Caslan, *Alta., Canada* **184 D8** 54 38N 112 31W
Casmalia, *CA, U.S.A.* **65 J6** 34 50N 120 32W
Casnovia, *MI, U.S.A.* **79 F6** 43 14N 85 48W
Cason, *TX, U.S.A.* **99 D13** 33 2N 94 49W
Casper, *WY, U.S.A.* **104 D6** 42 51N 106 19W
Caspian, *MI, U.S.A.* **79 C3** 46 4N 88 38W
Caspiana, *LA, U.S.A.* **75 B2** 32 17N 93 33W
Cass, *WV, U.S.A.* **102 C5** 38 24N 79 55W
Cass →, *MI, U.S.A.* **79 F8** 43 23N 83 59W
Cass City, *MI, U.S.A.* **79 F8** 43 36N 83 11W
Cass County ☆, *IL, U.S.A.* **71 D3** 40 0N 90 15W
Cass County ☆, *IN, U.S.A.* **72 C4** 40 45N 86 20W
Cass County ☆, *IA, U.S.A.* **73 D4** 41 20N 94 55W
Cass County ☆, *MI, U.S.A.* **79 H5** 41 50N 86 0W
Cass County ☆, *MN, U.S.A.* **80 D4** 47 0N 94 10W
Cass County ☆, *MO, U.S.A.* **82 C2** 38 40N 94 20W
Cass County ☆, *ND, U.S.A.* **91 D8** 47 0N 97 0W
Cass County ☆, *NE, U.S.A.* **84 D9** 40 50N 96 10W
Cass County ☆, *TX, U.S.A.* **99 D13** 33 1N 94 22W
Cass L., *MN, U.S.A.* **80 C4** 47 27N 94 29W
Cass Lake, *MN, U.S.A.* **80 C4** 47 23N 94 37W
Cassadaga, *NY, U.S.A.* **89 C1** 42 20N 79 19W
Casselberry, *FL, U.S.A.* **67 C7** 28 41N 81 20W
Casselman, *Ont., Canada* **176 F7** 45 19N 75 5W
Casselman, *PA, U.S.A.* **77 A1** 39 53N 79 13W
Casselton, *ND, U.S.A.* **91 D8** 46 54N 97 13W
Cassia County ☆, *ID, U.S.A.* **70 G5** 42 20N 113 30W
Cassiar Mts., *Canada* **189 E6** 59 30N 130 30W
Cassoday, *KS, U.S.A.* **74 C7** 38 3N 96 38W
Cassopolis, *MI, U.S.A.* **79 H5** 41 55N 86 1W
Cassville, *MO, U.S.A.* **82 E3** 36 41N 93 52W
Cassville, *PA, U.S.A.* **95 D4** 40 18N 78 2W
Cassville, *WI, U.S.A.* **103 F3** 42 43N 90 59W
Castaic L., *CA, U.S.A.* **65 J8** 34 32N 118 37W
Castalia, *IA, U.S.A.* **73 B7** 43 7N 91 41W
Castalia, *OH, U.S.A.* **92 B4** 41 24N 82 49W
Castamay, *Campeche, Mexico* **223 C3** 19 51N 90 27W
Castana, *IA, U.S.A.* **73 C3** 42 4N 95 55W
Castaños, *Coahuila, Mexico* **214 D3** 26 47N 101 25W
Castella, *CA, U.S.A.* **64 B4** 41 9N 122 19W
Castile, *NY, U.S.A.* **89 C2** 42 38N 78 3W
Castillo de San Marcos Nat. Monument △, *U.S.A.* **67 B7** 29 54N 81 19W
Castillo de Teayo, *Veracruz, Mexico* **220 D3** 20 44N 97 37W
Castle, *OK, U.S.A.* **93 C7** 35 28N 96 23W
Castle Dale, *UT, U.S.A.* **100 D4** 39 13N 111 1W
Castle Danger, *MN, U.S.A.* **80 C7** 47 7N 91 30W
Castle Dome Peak, *AZ, U.S.A.* **62 D1** 33 5N 114 9W
Castle Hayne, *NC, U.S.A.* **90 D8** 34 21N 77 54W
Castle Hills, *TX, U.S.A.* **99 H9** 29 31N 98 30W
Castle Mountain, *Alta., Canada* **185 G5** 51 16N 115 55W
Castle Mts., *MT, U.S.A.* **83 D7** 46 28N 110 46W
Castle Peak, *CO, U.S.A.* **66 C4** 39 1N 106 52W
Castle Pk., *ID, U.S.A.* **70 E4** 44 1N 114 42W
Castle Rock, *B.C., Canada* **187 C12** 52 32N 122 29W
Castle Rock, *CO, U.S.A.* **66 C6** 39 22N 104 51W
Castle Rock, *SD, U.S.A.* **91 F2** 44 57N 103 25W
Castle Rock, *WA, U.S.A.* **101 D3** 46 17N 122 54W
Castle Rock L., *WI, U.S.A.* **103 E4** 43 52N 89 57W
Castle Shannon, *Pittsburgh, U.S.A.* **116 B1** 40 21N 80 1W
Castle Valley, *UT, U.S.A.* **100 E6** 38 38N 109 25W
Castleberry, *AL, U.S.A.* **60 E3** 31 18N 87 1W
Castleford, *ID, U.S.A.* **70 G4** 42 31N 114 52W
Castlegar, *B.C., Canada* **187 F17** 49 20N 117 40W
Castleton, *Indianapolis, U.S.A.* **110 A2** 39 54N 86 3W
Castleton, *VT, U.S.A.* **86 C1** 43 37N 73 11W
Castleton Corners, *NY, U.S.A.* **114 C2** 40 36N 74 8W
Castleton-on-Hudson, *NY, U.S.A.* **89 C7** 42 32N 73 45W
Castlewood, *SD, U.S.A.* **91 F8** 44 44N 97 2W
Castlewood, *VA, U.S.A.* **102 E2** 36 53N 82 17W
Castolon, *TX, U.S.A.* **98 H4** 29 8N 103 31W
Castor, *Alta., Canada* **185 F9** 52 15N 111 50W
Castor, *LA, U.S.A.* **75 B2** 32 15N 93 10W
Castor →, *Qué., Canada* **175 C2** 53 24N 78 58W
Castor →, *MO, U.S.A.* **82 E7** 36 51N 89 44W
Castor Cr. →, *LA, U.S.A.* **75 C3** 31 47N 92 22W
Castro, *San Francisco, U.S.A.* **118 B2** 37 45N 122 26W
Castro County ☆, *TX, U.S.A.* **98 C5** 34 33N 102 19W
Castro Valley, *CA, U.S.A.* **64 F4** 37 41N 122 5W
Castroville, *CA, U.S.A.* **64 G5** 36 46N 121 45W
Castroville, *TX, U.S.A.* **99 H9** 29 21N 98 53W
Caswell County ☆, *NC, U.S.A.* **90 B6** 36 20N 79 15W
Cat I., *MS, U.S.A.* **81 F4** 30 14N 89 6W
Cat L., *Ont., Canada* **180 A5** 51 40N 91 50W
Cat Spring, *TX, U.S.A.* **99 H11** 29 51N 96 20W
Catahoula L., *LA, U.S.A.* **75 C3** 31 31N 92 7W
Catahoula Parish ☆, *LA, U.S.A.* **75 C4** 31 35N 91 58W
Catalina, *Nfld. & L., Canada* **174 D7** 48 31N 53 4W
Catalina, *AZ, U.S.A.* **62 E5** 32 30N 110 50W
Cataño, *Puerto Rico* **105 G16** 18 27N 66 7W
Cataouatche, L., *New Orleans, U.S.A.* **113 C1** 29 50N 90 14W
Cataract, *IN, U.S.A.* **72 D4** 39 30N 86 53W
Cataract L., *IN, U.S.A.* **72 D4** 39 29N 86 55W
Catarina, *TX, U.S.A.* **99 J8** 28 21N 99 37W
Catasauqua, *PA, U.S.A.* **87 B1** 40 39N 75 29W
Cataula, *GA, U.S.A.* **68 D2** 32 39N 84 52W
Cataviña, *Baja Calif., Mexico* **210 D4** 29 45N 114 45W
Catawba, *SC, U.S.A.* **90 D5** 34 51N 80 55W
Catawba, *WI, U.S.A.* **103 C3** 45 32N 90 32W
Catawba →, *SC, U.S.A.* **90 D5** 34 28N 80 53W
Catawba County ☆, *NC, U.S.A.* **90 C4** 35 40N 81 10W
Catawissa, *PA, U.S.A.* **95 D6** 40 57N 76 28W
Catazajá, *Chiapas, Mexico* **222 B4** 17 45N 92 1W
Catemaco, *Veracruz, Mexico* **221 F5** 18 25N 95 7W
Catemaco, L., *Veracruz, Mexico* **221 F5** 18 25N 95 5W
Cathay, *ND, U.S.A.* **91 C6** 47 33N 99 25W
Cathcart, *Seattle, U.S.A.* **118 A5** 47 50N 122 5W
Cathead Pt., *MI, U.S.A.* **79 D6** 45 11N 85 37W
Cathedral City, *CA, U.S.A.* **65 K10** 33 47N 116 28W
Cathedral Gorge State Park △, *NV, U.S.A.* **85 E6** 37 49N 114 25W
Cathedral Mt., *TX, U.S.A.* **98 G4** 30 11N 103 40W
Cathedral Park △, *B.C., Canada* **187 F14** 49 5N 120 0W
Catherine, *AL, U.S.A.* **60 D3** 32 11N 87 28W
Catherine, *KS, U.S.A.* **74 C4** 38 56N 99 13W
Catherine, L., *Orlando, U.S.A.* **115 B2** 28 30N 81 24W
Cathlamet, *WA, U.S.A.* **101 D2** 46 12N 123 23W
Catlettsburg, *KY, U.S.A.* **97 B10** 38 25N 82 36W
Catlin, *IL, U.S.A.* **71 C6** 40 4N 87 42W
Catlow Valley, *OR, U.S.A.* **94 E6** 42 20N 119 5W
Catoche, C., *Quintana Roo, Mexico* **223 A6** 21 35N 87 5W
Catoctin Mountain Park △, *MD, U.S.A.* **77 A3** 39 39N 77 28W
Catoctin Mt., *MD, U.S.A.* **77 A3** 39 35N 77 30W
Catonsville, *MD, U.S.A.* **77 A4** 39 16N 76 43W
Catoosa, *OK, U.S.A.* **93 B8** 36 11N 95 45W
Catoosa County ☆, *GA, U.S.A.* **68 B1** 34 50N 85 10W
Catron County ☆, *NM, U.S.A.* **88 D2** 34 0N 108 15W
Catskill, *NY, U.S.A.* **89 C7** 42 14N 73 52W
Catskill Mts., *NY, U.S.A.* **89 C6** 42 10N 74 25W
Catskill Park △, *U.S.A.* **89 C6** 42 8N 74 39W
Cattaraugus, *NY, U.S.A.* **89 C2** 42 20N 78 52W
Cattaraugus County ☆, *NY, U.S.A.* **89 C2** 42 30N 78 45W
Cattaraugus Indian Reservation, *NY, U.S.A.* **89 C2** 42 30N 79 0W
Caubvick, Mt. = Iberville, Mt. d', *Nfld. & L., Canada* **175 B5** 58 50N 63 50W
Caucel, *Yucatán, Mexico* **223 A4** 21 1N 89 43W
Cauchy, L., *Qué., Canada* **172 C9** 50 36N 60 46W
Caucomgomoc L., *ME, U.S.A.* **76 B4** 46 13N 69 36W
Caulfield, *B.C., Canada* **193 A1** 49 21N 123 14W
Causapscal, *Qué., Canada* **172 E2** 48 19N 67 12W
Causey, *NM, U.S.A.* **88 D7** 33 53N 103 8W
Cauthron, *AR, U.S.A.* **63 D1** 34 55N 94 18W
Caution C., *B.C., Canada* **186 D7** 51 10N 127 47W
Cavalier, *ND, U.S.A.* **91 B8** 48 48N 97 37W
Cavalier County ☆, *ND, U.S.A.* **91 B8** 48 55N 97 30W
Cave City, *AR, U.S.A.* **63 C4** 35 57N 91 33W
Cave City, *KY, U.S.A.* **97 C7** 37 8N 85 58W
Cave Creek, *AZ, U.S.A.* **62 D4** 33 50N 111 57W
Cave in Rock, *IL, U.S.A.* **71 F5** 37 28N 88 10W
Cave Junction, *OR, U.S.A.* **94 E2** 42 10N 123 39W
Cave Run L., *KY, U.S.A.* **97 B9** 38 5N 83 25W
Cave Spring, *GA, U.S.A.* **68 B1** 34 6N 85 20W
Cave Spring, *VA, U.S.A.* **102 D5** 37 47N 79 53W
Cavernas del Río Camuy, Parque de las △, *Puerto Rico* **105 G16** 18 20N 66 50W
Cawasachouane, L., *Qué., Canada* **176 D5** 47 27N 77 45W
Cawker City, *KS, U.S.A.* **74 B5** 39 31N 98 26W
Cayacal, Pta., *Michoacan, Mexico* **218 E5** 17 53N 102 10W
Cayce, *KY, U.S.A.* **96 D3** 36 33N 89 2W
Cayce, *SC, U.S.A.* **90 E4** 33 58N 81 4W
Caycuse, *B.C., Canada* **186 G10** 48 53N 124 22W
Cayey, *Puerto Rico* **105 G16** 18 7N 66 10W
Cayley, *Alta., Canada* **185 H7** 50 27N 113 51W
Cayucos, *CA, U.S.A.* **65 H6** 35 27N 120 54W
Cayuga, *Ont., Canada* **178 E7** 42 59N 79 50W
Cayuga, *IN, U.S.A.* **72 D3** 39 57N 87 28W
Cayuga, *ND, U.S.A.* **91 D8** 46 4N 97 23W
Cayuga County ☆, *NY, U.S.A.* **89 C4** 43 0N 76 35W
Cayuga Heights, *NY, U.S.A.* **89 C4** 42 28N 76 30W
Cayuga L., *NY, U.S.A.* **89 C4** 42 41N 76 41W
Cayuse, *OR, U.S.A.* **94 B7** 45 41N 118 33W
Cazenovia, *NY, U.S.A.* **89 C5** 42 56N 75 51W
Cazones, *Veracruz, Mexico* **220 D3** 20 43N 97 19W
Cazones, Barra de, *Veracruz, Mexico* **220 D3** 20 45N 97 10W
Cearfoss, *MD, U.S.A.* **77 A3** 39 42N 77 46W
Ceballos, *Durango, Mexico* **217 A6** 26 32N 104 9W
Cebolla, *NM, U.S.A.* **88 A4** 36 32N 106 29W
Cebolleta, *NM, U.S.A.* **88 B3** 35 12N 107 23W
Cecil, *GA, U.S.A.* **68 E3** 31 3N 83 24W
Cecil, *OH, U.S.A.* **92 B2** 41 13N 84 36W
Cecil, *OR, U.S.A.* **94 B6** 45 37N 119 58W
Cecil County ☆, *MD, U.S.A.* **77 A5** 39 30N 76 0W
Cecil M. Harden L., *IN, U.S.A.* **72 D3** 39 43N 87 4W
Cecilia, *KY, U.S.A.* **97 C7** 37 40N 85 57W
Cecilia, *LA, U.S.A.* **75 D4** 30 20N 91 51W
Cecilton, *MD, U.S.A.* **77 A5** 39 24N 75 52W
Cecilville, *CA, U.S.A.* **64 B3** 41 9N 123 8W
Cedar →, *IA, U.S.A.* **73 D7** 41 17N 91 21W
Cedar →, *MI, U.S.A.* **79 D4** 45 25N 87 26W
Cedar →, *NE, U.S.A.* **84 C8** 41 22N 97 56W
Cedar →, *WA, U.S.A.* **101 C3** 47 30N 122 13W
Cedar Bluff, *AL, U.S.A.* **60 B5** 34 13N 85 37W
Cedar Bluff, *VA, U.S.A.* **102 D3** 37 5N 81 46W
Cedar Bluff Res., *KS, U.S.A.* **74 C4** 38 47N 99 43W
Cedar Bluffs, *KS, U.S.A.* **74 B3** 39 59N 100 34W
Cedar Bluffs, *NE, U.S.A.* **84 C9** 41 24N 96 37W
Cedar Breaks Nat. Monument △, *UT, U.S.A.* **100 F3** 37 40N 112 50W
Cedar Brook, *NJ, U.S.A.* **87 C2** 39 43N 74 54W
Cedar Butte, *SD, U.S.A.* **91 G4** 43 35N 101 1W
Cedar City, *MO, U.S.A.* **82 C4** 38 36N 92 11W
Cedar City, *UT, U.S.A.* **100 F2** 37 41N 113 4W
Cedar County ☆, *IA, U.S.A.* **73 D7** 41 45N 91 10W
Cedar County ☆, *MO, U.S.A.* **82 D3** 37 45N 93 50W
Cedar County ☆, *NE, U.S.A.* **84 B8** 42 40N 97 15W
Cedar Cr. →, *ND, U.S.A.* **91 D4** 46 8N 101 19W
Cedar Creek, *AR, U.S.A.* **63 D2** 34 47N 93 51W
Cedar Creek, *NE, U.S.A.* **84 C9** 41 2N 96 6W
Cedar Creek, *TX, U.S.A.* **99 G10** 30 5N 97 30W
Cedar Creek Res., *AL, U.S.A.* **60 B3** 34 33N 87 59W
Cedar Creek Res., *TX, U.S.A.* **99 E11** 32 11N 96 4W
Cedar Falls, *IA, U.S.A.* **73 C6** 42 32N 92 27W
Cedar Grove, *Atlanta, U.S.A.* **106 C3** 33 40N 84 16W
Cedar Grove, *FL, U.S.A.* **67 A3** 30 10N 85 38W
Cedar Grove, *IN, U.S.A.* **72 D6** 39 22N 84 56W
Cedar Grove, *NJ, U.S.A.* **87 B2** 40 51N 74 13W
Cedar Grove, *WV, U.S.A.* **102 C3** 38 13N 81 26W
Cedar Grove, *WI, U.S.A.* **103 E6** 43 34N 87 49W
Cedar Grove Res., *NJ, U.S.A.* **114 A1** 40 51N 74 12W
Cedar Hill, *Dallas-Fort Worth, U.S.A.* **109 C4** 32 35N 96 57W
Cedar Hill, *MO, U.S.A.* **82 C6** 38 21N 90 39W
Cedar Hill, *NM, U.S.A.* **88 A3** 36 56N 107 53W
Cedar Hill, *TN, U.S.A.* **96 D5** 36 33N 87 0W
Cedar Hill State Park △, *Dallas-Fort Worth, U.S.A.* **109 C4** 32 36N 96 59W
Cedar Hills, *Portland, U.S.A.* **116 A1** 45 30N 122 47W
Cedar I., *NC, U.S.A.* **90 D9** 34 57N 76 20W
Cedar Key, *FL, U.S.A.* **67 B5** 29 8N 83 2W
Cedar L., *Man., Canada* **183 B11** 53 10N 100 0W
Cedar L., *Ont., Canada* **179 A8** 46 2N 78 30W
Cedar L., *IL, U.S.A.* **71 F4** 37 37N 89 18W
Cedar L., *TX, U.S.A.* **98 E5** 32 49N 102 17W
Cedar Lake, *IN, U.S.A.* **72 B3** 41 22N 87 26W
Cedar Lake, *Minneapolis-St. Paul, U.S.A.* **113 B2** 44 57N 93 19W
Cedar Lake, *TX, U.S.A.* **99 J12** 28 54N 95 38W
Cedar Mills, *MN, U.S.A.* **80 F4** 44 57N 94 31W
Cedar Mts., *UT, U.S.A.* **100 C3** 40 10N 112 30W
Cedar Park, *IL, U.S.A.* **117 A3** 38 45N 90 6W
Cedar Park, *TX, U.S.A.* **99 G10** 30 30N 97 49W
Cedar Point, *KS, U.S.A.* **74 C7** 38 16N 96 49W
Cedar Point Nat. Wildlife Refuge △, *OH, U.S.A.* **92 B3** 41 41N 83 19W
Cedar Point, *OH, U.S.A.* **92 B4** 41 29N 82 41W
Cedar Rapids, *IA, U.S.A.* **73 D7** 41 59N 91 40W
Cedar Rapids, *NE, U.S.A.* **84 C7** 41 34N 98 9W
Cedar River, *MI, U.S.A.* **79 D4** 45 25N 87 21W
Cedar River Nat. Grassland, *ND, U.S.A.* **91 E4** 46 0N 101 45W
Cedar Springs, *MI, U.S.A.* **79 F6** 43 13N 85 33W
Cedar Vale, *KS, U.S.A.* **74 D7** 37 6N 96 30W
Cedarburg, *WI, U.S.A.* **103 E6** 43 18N 87 59W
Cedaredge, *CO, U.S.A.* **66 D3** 38 54N 107 56W
Cedarhurst, *NY, U.S.A.* **114 C4** 40 37N 73 42W
Cedartown, *GA, U.S.A.* **68 B1** 34 1N 85 15W
Cedarville, *CA, U.S.A.* **64 B6** 41 32N 120 10W
Cedarville, *IL, U.S.A.* **71 A4** 42 23N 89 38W
Cedarville, *MD, U.S.A.* **77 B4** 38 40N 76 47W
Cedarville, *MI, U.S.A.* **79 D7** 46 0N 84 22W
Cedarville, *NJ, U.S.A.* **87 C1** 39 18N 75 12W
Cedarwood, *CO, U.S.A.* **66 E6** 37 57N 104 37W
Cedral, *San Luis Potosí, Mexico* **215 G4** 23 50N 100 45W
Cedro, Cerro, *Baja Calif., Mexico* **210 A3** 32 12N 115 59W
Cedros, *Zacatecas, Mexico* **217 C9** 24 41N 101 46W
Cedros, I., *Baja Calif., Mexico* **211 E3** 28 12N 115 15W

Ceiba, *Puerto Rico* **105 G17** 18 16N 65 39W
Celarain, Pta., *Quintana Roo, Mexico* **223 B7** 20 16N 86 59W
Celaya, *Guanajuato, Mexico* **219 B7** 20 31N 100 37W
Celerain, *Quintana Roo, Mexico* **223 B7** 20 18N 86 58W
Celeste, *TX, U.S.A.* **99 D11** 33 18N 96 12W
Celestún, *Yucatán, Mexico* **223 B3** 20 52N 90 24W
Celestún, Estero, *Yucatán, Mexico* **223 B3** 20 58N 90 22W
Celina, *OH, U.S.A.* **92 C2** 40 33N 84 35W
Celina, *TN, U.S.A.* **97 D7** 36 33N 85 30W
Celina, *TX, U.S.A.* **99 D11** 33 19N 96 47W
Cement, *OK, U.S.A.* **93 D5** 34 56N 98 8W
Cenotillo, *Yucatán, Mexico* **223 B5** 20 58N 88 37W
Centennial, *CO, U.S.A.* **66 C6** 39 34N 104 52W
Centennial, *WY, U.S.A.* **104 E6** 41 18N 106 8W
Centennial Mts., *ID, U.S.A.* **70 E7** 44 35N 111 55W
Centennial Wash →, *AZ, U.S.A.* **62 D3** 33 17N 112 48W
Center, *CO, U.S.A.* **66 E4** 37 45N 106 6W
Center, *GA, U.S.A.* **68 B3** 34 3N 83 25W
Center, *MO, U.S.A.* **82 B5** 39 30N 91 32W
Center, *ND, U.S.A.* **91 C4** 47 7N 101 18W
Center, *NE, U.S.A.* **84 B8** 42 37N 97 53W
Center, *TX, U.S.A.* **99 F13** 31 48N 94 11W
Center Barnstead, *NH, U.S.A.* **86 C3** 43 19N 71 15W
Center City, *MN, U.S.A.* **80 E6** 45 24N 92 49W
Center Cross, *VA, U.S.A.* **77 C4** 37 48N 76 47W
Center Harbor, *NH, U.S.A.* **86 C3** 43 42N 71 27W
Center Hill, *Atlanta, U.S.A.* **106 B2** 33 46N 84 29W
Center Hill, *FL, U.S.A.* **67 C6** 28 38N 82 3W
Center Hill L., *TN, U.S.A.* **97 D7** 36 6N 85 50W
Center Line, *MI, U.S.A.* **109 A2** 42 29N 83 1W
Center Ossipee, *NH, U.S.A.* **86 C3** 43 45N 71 9W
Center Point, *AL, U.S.A.* **60 C4** 33 38N 86 41W
Center Point, *IN, U.S.A.* **72 D3** 39 25N 87 4W
Center Point, *IA, U.S.A.* **73 C7** 42 12N 91 46W
Center Point, *LA, U.S.A.* **75 C3** 31 15N 92 13W
Center Point, *TX, U.S.A.* **99 H8** 29 57N 99 2W
Center Sandwich, *NH, U.S.A.* **86 C3** 43 39N 71 25W
Center Strafford, *NH, U.S.A.* **86 C3** 43 17N 71 10W
Center Valley, *PA, U.S.A.* **87 B1** 40 32N 75 24W
Centerburg, *OH, U.S.A.* **92 C4** 40 18N 82 42W
Centereach, *NY, U.S.A.* **78 D1** 40 52N 73 6W
Centerfield, *UT, U.S.A.* **100 D4** 39 8N 111 49W
Centertown, *KY, U.S.A.* **96 C6** 37 25N 86 59W
Centertown, *MO, U.S.A.* **82 C4** 38 38N 92 25W
Centertown, *TN, U.S.A.* **97 E7** 35 44N 85 55W
Centerville, *AR, U.S.A.* **63 C2** 35 7N 93 10W
Centerville, *CA, U.S.A.* **65 G7** 36 44N 119 30W
Centerville, *DE, U.S.A.* **77 A5** 39 49N 75 37W
Centerville, *ID, U.S.A.* **70 F3** 43 55N 115 53W
Centerville, *IN, U.S.A.* **72 D6** 39 49N 85 0W
Centerville, *IA, U.S.A.* **73 E6** 40 44N 92 52W
Centerville, *KS, U.S.A.* **74 C8** 38 13N 95 1W
Centerville, *LA, U.S.A.* **75 E4** 29 46N 91 26W
Centerville, *MO, U.S.A.* **82 D6** 37 26N 90 58W
Centerville, *NY, U.S.A.* **89 C2** 42 29N 78 15W
Centerville, *OH, U.S.A.* **92 D2** 39 38N 84 8W
Centerville, *PA, U.S.A.* **77 A2** 39 50N 78 39W
Centerville, *PA, U.S.A.* **95 C3** 41 44N 79 46W
Centerville, *PA, U.S.A.* **95 D3** 40 3N 79 59W
Centerville, *SC, U.S.A.* **90 D3** 34 32N 82 42W
Centerville, *SD, U.S.A.* **91 G9** 43 7N 96 58W
Centerville, *TN, U.S.A.* **96 E5** 35 47N 87 28W
Centerville, *TX, U.S.A.* **99 F12** 31 16N 95 59W
Centerville, *UT, U.S.A.* **100 C4** 40 55N 111 52W
Centinela, Picacho del, *Coahuila, Mexico* **214 A2** 29 14N 102 32W
Centrahoma, *OK, U.S.A.* **93 D7** 34 37N 96 21W
Central, *AK, U.S.A.* **61 D11** 65 35N 144 48W
Central, *SC, U.S.A.* **90 D3** 34 44N 82 47W
Central, *TN, U.S.A.* **96 E3** 35 48N 89 32W
Central, *UT, U.S.A.* **100 F2** 37 25N 113 38W
Central, Cordillera, *Puerto Rico* **105 G16** 18 8N 66 35W
Central Butte, *Sask., Canada* **182 E5** 50 48N 106 31W
Central City, *CO, U.S.A.* **66 C5** 39 48N 105 31W
Central City, *IL, U.S.A.* **71 E4** 38 33N 89 8W
Central City, *IA, U.S.A.* **73 C7** 42 12N 91 32W
Central City, *KY, U.S.A.* **96 C5** 37 18N 87 7W
Central City, *NE, U.S.A.* **84 C8** 41 7N 98 0W
Central City, *PA, U.S.A.* **95 D4** 40 7N 78 49W
Central City, *SD, U.S.A.* **91 F2** 44 22N 103 46W
Central Falls, *RI, U.S.A.* **78 C3** 41 54N 71 23W
Central Fournier, *Tabasco, Mexico* **222 B3** 17 52N 93 53W
Central Islip, *NY, U.S.A.* **87 B3** 40 47N 73 12W
Central Lake, *MI, U.S.A.* **79 D6** 45 4N 85 16W
Central Park, *Vancouver, Canada* **193 B2** 49 13N 123 1W
Central Park, *Minneapolis-St. Paul, U.S.A.* **113 A3** 45 1N 93 7W
Central Park, *New York, U.S.A.* **114 B3** 40 47N 73 58W
Central Park, *WA, U.S.A.* **101 D2** 46 58N 123 41W
Central Patricia, *Ont., Canada* **180 A6** 51 30N 90 9W
Central Point, *OR, U.S.A.* **94 E3** 42 23N 122 55W
Central Saanich, *B.C., Canada* **187 G11** 48 34N 123 25W
Central Square, *NY, U.S.A.* **89 B4** 43 17N 76 9W
Centralhatchee, *GA, U.S.A.* **68 C1** 33 22N 85 6W
Centralia, *IL, U.S.A.* **71 E4** 38 32N 89 8W
Centralia, *KS, U.S.A.* **74 B7** 39 44N 96 8W
Centralia, *MO, U.S.A.* **82 B4** 39 13N 92 8W
Centralia, *OK, U.S.A.* **93 B8** 36 48N 95 21W
Centralia, *WA, U.S.A.* **101 D3** 46 43N 122 58W
Centre, *AL, U.S.A.* **60 B5** 34 9N 85 41W
Centre County ☆, *PA, U.S.A.* **95 D5** 41 0N 78 0W
Centre Grove, *NJ, U.S.A.* **87 C1** 39 20N 75 8W
Centreville, *N.B., Canada* **173 G2** 46 26N 67 43W
Centreville, *N.S., Canada* **173 H5** 45 8N 64 32W
Centreville, *N.S., Canada* **173 J3** 44 33N 66 1W
Centreville, *AL, U.S.A.* **60 D3** 32 57N 87 8W
Centreville, *IL, U.S.A.* **117 B3** 38 34N 90 7W
Centreville, *MD, U.S.A.* **77 A4** 39 3N 76 4W
Centreville, *MI, U.S.A.* **79 H6** 41 55N 85 32W
Centreville, *MS, U.S.A.* **81 E2** 31 5N 91 4W
Centreville, *VA, U.S.A.* **77 B3** 38 50N 77 26W
Centreville-Wareham-Trinity, *Nfld. & L., Canada* **174 D7** 48 59N 53 59W
Centro, Cayo, *Quintana Roo, Mexico* **223 D6** 18 35N 87 20W
Century, *FL, U.S.A.* **67 A1** 30 58N 87 16W
Cenzontle, *Coahuila, Mexico* **214 C1** 27 43N 103 21W
Cerab Mts., *AZ, U.S.A.* **62 B1** 35 30N 114 10W
Cereal, *Alta., Canada* **185 G10** 51 25N 110 48W
Ceres, *CA, U.S.A.* **64 F6** 37 35N 120 57W
Ceresco, *NE, U.S.A.* **84 C9** 41 3N 96 39W
Cereze Canyon, *NM, U.S.A.* **88 A3** 36 39N 107 42W
Cerf, L. de, *Qué., Canada* **176 E7** 46 16N 75 30W
Cero del Pez, L., *San Luis Potosí, Mexico* **215 H6** 22 6N 98 28W
Cerralvo, *Nuevo León, Mexico* **214 D5** 26 6N 99 37W
Cerralvo, Canal, *Baja Calif. S., Mexico* **211 J9** 24 12N 110 0W
Cerralvo, I., *Baja Calif. S., Mexico* **211 J9** 24 15N 109 55W
Cerrillos, *NM, U.S.A.* **88 B4** 35 26N 106 8W
Cerritos, *San Luis Potosí, Mexico* **215 H4** 22 25N 100 16W
Cerritos, *Los Angeles, U.S.A.* **111 C4** 33 51N 118 3W
Cerritos de Bernal, *San Luis Potosí, Mexico* **215 G3** 23 23N 101 30W
Cerro Azul, *Veracruz, Mexico* **220 C3** 21 12N 97 44W
Cerro Cofre de Perote, Parque Nacional △, *Veracruz, Mexico* **220 E3** 19 30N 97 12W
Cerro Colorado, *Sonora, Mexico* **212 G7** 26 45N 108 50W
Cerro de la Estrella, *Distrito Federal, Mexico* **225 B3** 19 20N 99 5W
Cerro de la Estrella, Parque Nacional △, *Distrito Federal, Mexico* **219 C8** 19 23N 99 5W
Cerro de Ortega, *Colima, Mexico* **218 D4** 18 44N 103 43W
Cerro de San Pedro, *San Luis Potosí, Mexico* **215 H4** 22 3N 100 44W
Cerro del Pez, L., *Veracruz, Mexico* **220 B2** 22 9N 98 18W
Cerro Gordo, *San Luis Potosí, Mexico* **215 J4** 21 59N 100 48W
Cerro Gordo, *IL, U.S.A.* **71 D5** 39 53N 88 44W
Cerro Gordo County ☆, *IA, U.S.A.* **73 B5** 43 5N 93 15W
Cerro Mojarra, *Oaxaca, Mexico* **221 F4** 18 24N 96 35W
Cerro Nanchital, *Veracruz, Mexico* **221 G6** 17 30N 94 9W
Cerro Prieto, *Chihuahua, Mexico* **213 E8** 28 14N 107 9W
Cerro Prieto, *Durango, Mexico* **216 A4** 26 20N 106 13W
Cerro Prieto, *San Luis Potosí, Mexico* **215 H3** 22 13N 101 17W
Cerro Vista Peak, *NM, U.S.A.* **88 A5** 36 14N 105 25W
Cerros Blancos, *Nuevo León, Mexico* **215 G4** 23 21N 100 11W
Cesar Creek L., *OH, U.S.A.* **92 D2** 39 29N 84 3W
Ceylon, *Sask., Canada* **182 F7** 49 27N 104 36W
Ceylon, *MN, U.S.A.* **80 G4** 43 32N 94 38W
Chaati I., *B.C., Canada* **186 B2** 53 7N 132 30W
Chablé, *Tabasco, Mexico* **222 B5** 17 51N 91 46W
Chabot, L., *San Francisco, U.S.A.* **118 B4** 37 43N 122 7W
Chacaltianguis, *Veracruz, Mexico* **221 F5** 18 18N 95 51W
Chacana, *Campeche, Mexico* **223 D4** 18 29N 89 30W
Chackbay, *LA, U.S.A.* **75 E5** 29 53N 90 48W
Chacmultún, *Yucatán, Mexico* **223 B4** 20 8N 89 20W
Chaco →, *NM, U.S.A.* **88 A2** 36 46N 108 39W
Chaco Canyon Nat. Monument △, *NM, U.S.A.* **88 A3** 36 6N 108 0W
Chaco Culture Nat. Historical Park △, *U.S.A.* **88 A3** 36 3N 107 58W
Chacuaco →, *CO, U.S.A.* **66 E7** 37 34N 103 38W
Chadbourn, *NC, U.S.A.* **90 D7** 34 19N 78 50W
Chadron, *NE, U.S.A.* **84 B3** 42 50N 103 0W
Chadwick, *IL, U.S.A.* **71 A4** 42 1N 89 53W
Chaffee, *MO, U.S.A.* **82 D7** 37 11N 89 40W
Chaffee, *ND, U.S.A.* **91 D8** 46 46N 97 21W
Chaffee County ☆, *CO, U.S.A.* **66 D4** 38 45N 106 10W
Chaffee I., *Los Angeles, U.S.A.* **111 D4** 33 44N 118 8W
Chahuites, *Oaxaca, Mexico* **221 H6** 16 17N 94 11W
Chain of Lakes Regional Park △, *Minneapolis-St. Paul, U.S.A.* **113 B2** 44 56N 93 19W
Chairel, L., *Veracruz, Mexico* **220 B2** 22 19N 98 1W
Chaires, *FL, U.S.A.* **67 A4** 30 26N 84 7W
Chakmochuk, L., *Quintana Roo, Mexico* **223 A7** 21 20N 86 50W
Chakonipau, L., *Qué., Canada* **175 B4** 56 18N 68 30W
Chal, I., *Quintana Roo, Mexico* **223 C6** 19 20N 87 30W
Chal-Tuni, *Campeche, Mexico* **223 C4** 19 15N 89 57W
Chalan Kanoa, *N. Marianas* **105 c** 15 9N 145 42W
Chalchihuites, *Zacatecas, Mexico* **217 D7** 23 29N 103 53W
Chalco, *México, Mexico* **219 C9** 19 15N 98 54W
Chaleur B., *N.B., Canada* **173 F4** 47 55N 65 30W
Chalfant, *Pittsburgh, U.S.A.* **116 B2** 40 24N 79 50W
Chalk Mts., *TX, U.S.A.* **98 H4** 29 30N 103 18W
Chalk River, *Ont., Canada* **179 A9** 46 1N 77 27W
Chalkyitsik, *AK, U.S.A.* **61 C12** 66 39N 143 43W
Challis, *ID, U.S.A.* **70 E4** 44 30N 114 14W
Challis Nat. Forest, *ID, U.S.A.* **70 E5** 44 0N 113 40W
Chalmers, *IN, U.S.A.* **72 C4** 40 40N 86 52W
Chalmette, *LA, U.S.A.* **75 E6** 29 56N 89 57W
Chama, *CO, U.S.A.* **66 E5** 37 10N 105 23W
Chama, *NM, U.S.A.* **88 A4** 36 54N 106 35W
Chama →, *NM, U.S.A.* **88 A4** 36 10N 106 10W
Chamberino, *NM, U.S.A.* **88 E4** 32 3N 106 41W
Chamberlain, *SD, U.S.A.* **91 G6** 43 49N 99 20W
Chamberlain L., *ME, U.S.A.* **76 B4** 46 14N 69 19W
Chambers, *AZ, U.S.A.* **62 B6** 35 11N 109 26W
Chambers, *NE, U.S.A.* **84 B7** 42 12N 98 45W
Chambers County ☆, *AL, U.S.A.* **60 D5** 32 54N 85 24W
Chambers County ☆, *TX, U.S.A.* **99 H13** 29 47N 94 35W
Chambers I., *WI, U.S.A.* **103 C6** 45 11N 87 22W
Chambersburg, *PA, U.S.A.* **95 E5** 39 56N 77 40W
Chamblee, *GA, U.S.A.* **68 C2** 33 53N 84 18W
Chambly, *Qué., Canada* **177 F9** 45 27N 73 17W
Chambord, *Qué., Canada* **177 C10** 48 25N 72 6W
Chamela, *Jalisco, Mexico* **218 C2** 19 32N 105 5W
Chamela, B., *Jalisco, Mexico* **218 C2** 19 33N 105 7W
Chamisal, *NM, U.S.A.* **88 A5** 36 10N 105 44W
Chamois, *MO, U.S.A.* **82 C5** 38 41N 91 46W
Chamokane Cr. →, *WA, U.S.A.* **101 C8** 47 51N 117 51W
Champaign, *IL, U.S.A.* **71 C5** 40 7N 88 15W
Champaign County ☆, *IL, U.S.A.* **71 C5** 40 10N 88 10W
Champaign County ☆, *OH, U.S.A.* **92 C3** 40 7N 83 45W
Champdoré, L., *Qué., Canada* **175 B4** 55 55N 65 49W
Champion, *Alta., Canada* **185 H7** 50 14N 113 9W
Champion, *MI, U.S.A.* **79 C4** 46 31N 87 58W
Champion, *OH, U.S.A.* **92 B6** 41 19N 80 51W
Champion Creek Res., *TX, U.S.A.* **98 E7** 32 17N 100 52W
Champlain, *NY, U.S.A.* **86 B1** 44 59N 73 27W
Champlain, *VA, U.S.A.* **77 B3** 38 1N 77 0W
Champlain, L., *U.S.A.* **86 B1** 44 40N 73 20W
Champlain, Pont, *Montréal, Canada* **192 B3** 45 28N 73 31W
Champlain Canal, *NY, U.S.A.* **86 C1** 43 30N 73 27W
Champneuf, *Qué., Canada* **176 C5** 48 35N 77 30W
Champotón, *Campeche, Mexico* **223 C3** 19 21N 90 43W
Chamula, *Chiapas, Mexico* **222 C4** 16 47N 92 41W
Chanal, *Chiapas, Mexico* **222 C4** 16 43N 92 15W
Chance Harbour, *N.B., Canada* **173 H3** 45 7N 66 21W
Chancellor, *SD, U.S.A.* **91 G9** 43 22N 96 59W
Chandalar →, *AK, U.S.A.* **61 C11** 66 37N 146 0W
Chandeleur Is., *LA, U.S.A.* **75 E7** 29 55N 88 57W
Chandeleur Sd., *LA, U.S.A.* **75 E6** 29 55N 89 0W
Chandler, *Qué., Canada* **172 E5** 48 18N 64 46W
Chandler, *AZ, U.S.A.* **62 D4** 33 18N 111 50W
Chandler, *IN, U.S.A.* **72 E3** 38 3N 87 22W
Chandler, *MN, U.S.A.* **80 G3** 43 56N 95 57W
Chandler, *OK, U.S.A.* **93 C7** 35 42N 96 53W
Chandler, *TX, U.S.A.* **99 E12** 32 18N 95 29W
Chandlerville, *IL, U.S.A.* **71 C3** 40 3N 90 9W
Chaneysville, *PA, U.S.A.* **77 A2** 39 49N 78 29W
Change Islands, *Nfld. & L., Canada* **174 C6** 49 40N 54 25W
Chanhassen, *MN, U.S.A.* **80 F5** 44 55N 93 32W
Chankom, *Yucatán, Mexico* **223 B5** 20 33N 88 31W
Channahon, *IL, U.S.A.* **71 B5** 41 26N 88 14W
Channel Is., *CA, U.S.A.* **65 K7** 33 40N 119 15W
Channel Islands Nat. Park △, *CA, U.S.A.* **65 K7** 34 0N 119 24W
Channel-Port aux Basques, *Nfld. & L., Canada* **174 E1** 47 30N 59 9W
Channelview, *TX, U.S.A.* **99 H12** 29 47N 95 8W
Channing, *MI, U.S.A.* **79 C3** 46 9N 88 5W
Channing, *TX, U.S.A.* **98 B5** 35 41N 102 20W
Chantilly, *VA, U.S.A.* **77 B3** 38 54N 77 26W
Chantrey Inlet, *Nunavut, Canada* **190 D6** 67 48N 96 20W
Chanute, *KS, U.S.A.* **74 D8** 37 41N 95 27W
Chapais, *Qué., Canada* **176 B8** 49 47N 74 51W
Chapala, *Baja Calif., Mexico* **210 D4** 29 24N 114 22W
Chapala, *Jalisco, Mexico* **218 B4** 20 18N 103 12W
Chapala, L. de, *Jalisco, Mexico* **218 B5** 20 15N 103 0W
Chapalilla, *Nayarit, Mexico* **216 F6** 21 10N 104 38W
Chapantongo, *Hidalgo, Mexico* **219 B8** 20 17N 99 25W
Chaparral, *NM, U.S.A.* **88 E4** 32 4N 106 25W
Chapeau, *Qué., Canada* **176 F5** 45 54N 77 4W
Chapel Hill, *Indianapolis, U.S.A.* **110 B1** 39 46N 86 16W
Chapel Hill, *NC, U.S.A.* **90 C6** 35 55N 79 4W
Chapel Hill, *TN, U.S.A.* **96 E6** 35 38N 86 41W
Chapin = Edinburg, *TX, U.S.A.* **98 L9** 26 18N 98 10W
Chapin, *IL, U.S.A.* **71 D3** 39 46N 90 24W
Chapin, *SC, U.S.A.* **90 D4** 34 10N 81 21W
Chapleau, *Ont., Canada* **181 E13** 47 50N 83 24W
Chaplin, *Sask., Canada* **182 E5** 50 28N 106 40W
Chaplin, *KY, U.S.A.* **97 C7** 37 54N 85 13W
Chaplin L., *Sask., Canada* **182 E5** 50 22N 106 36W
Chapman, *AL, U.S.A.* **60 E4** 31 40N 86 43W
Chapman, *KS, U.S.A.* **74 C6** 38 58N 97 1W
Chapman, *NE, U.S.A.* **84 C7** 41 2N 98 10W
Chapman, Mt., *B.C., Canada* **187 D16** 51 56N 118 20W
Chapman C., *Nunavut, Canada* **190 D8** 69 17N 89 5W
Chapmanville, *WV, U.S.A.* **102 D2** 37 59N 82 1W
Chappaquiddick Island, *MA, U.S.A.* **78 C4** 41 22N 70 30W
Chappell, *NE, U.S.A.* **84 C3** 41 6N 102 28W
Chappell Hill, *TX, U.S.A.* **99 G11** 30 9N 96 15W
Chaptico, *MD, U.S.A.* **77 B4** 38 21N 76 49W
Chapulhuacán, *Hidalgo, Mexico* **219 A9** 21 10N 98 54W
Chapultenango, *Chiapas, Mexico* **222 B3** 17 19N 93 7W
Chapultepec, Bosque de, *Distrito Federal, Mexico* **225 B2** 19 25N 99 11W
Chapultepec, Castillo de, *Distrito Federal, Mexico* **225 B2** 19 25N 99 10W
Charapan, *Michoacan, Mexico* **218 C5** 19 37N 102 14W
Charay, *Sinaloa, Mexico* **216 A2** 26 1N 108 50W
Charcas, *San Luis Potosí, Mexico* **215 G3** 23 8N 101 7W
Charco, *TX, U.S.A.* **99 J10** 28 44N 97 37W
Charcos de Risa, *Coahuila, Mexico* **214 D1** 26 11N 103 7W
Chardon, *OH, U.S.A.* **92 B5** 41 35N 81 12W
Charenton, *LA, U.S.A.* **75 E4** 29 53N 91 32W
Charing, *GA, U.S.A.* **68 D2** 32 28N 84 22W
Chariton, *IA, U.S.A.* **73 D5** 41 1N 93 19W
Chariton →, *MO, U.S.A.* **82 B4** 39 19N 92 58W
Chariton County ☆, *MO, U.S.A.* **82 B4** 39 30N 93 0W
Charity, *MO, U.S.A.* **82 D3** 37 31N 93 1W
Charity I., *MI, U.S.A.* **79 E8** 44 2N 83 26W
Charlack, *MO, U.S.A.* **117 A1** 38 42N 90 20W
Charlemont, *MA, U.S.A.* **78 B2** 42 38N 72 52W
Charleroi, *PA, U.S.A.* **95 D3** 40 9N 79 57W
Charles, *GA, U.S.A.* **68 D2** 32 8N 84 50W
Charles →, *MA, U.S.A.* **78 B3** 42 22N 71 3W
Charles, C., *VA, U.S.A.* **102 D9** 37 7N 75 58W
Charles City, *IA, U.S.A.* **73 B6** 43 4N 92 41W
Charles City, *VA, U.S.A.* **102 D7** 37 21N 77 4W
Charles City County ☆, *VA, U.S.A.* **102 D7** 37 21N 77 4W
Charles County ☆, *MD, U.S.A.* **77 B3** 38 30N 77 0W
Charles I., *Nunavut, Canada* **191 E11** 62 39N 74 15W
Charles Mill L., *OH, U.S.A.* **92 C4** 40 45N 82 22W
Charles Mix County ☆, *SD, U.S.A.* **91 G7** 43 15N 98 42W
Charles Mound, *IL, U.S.A.* **71 A3** 42 30N 90 14W
Charles Town, *WV, U.S.A.* **77 A3** 39 17N 77 52W
Charlesbourg, *Qué., Canada* **177 E11** 46 51N 71 16W
Charleston, *AR, U.S.A.* **63 C1** 35 18N 94 5W
Charleston, *IL, U.S.A.* **71 D5** 39 30N 88 10W
Charleston, *MS, U.S.A.* **81 B3** 34 1N 90 4W
Charleston, *MO, U.S.A.* **82 E7** 36 55N 89 21W
Charleston, *NY, U.S.A.* **114 C1** 40 32N 74 14W
Charleston, *OR, U.S.A.* **94 D1** 43 20N 124 20W
Charleston, *SC, U.S.A.* **90 F6** 32 46N 79 56W
Charleston, *TN, U.S.A.* **97 E8** 35 17N 84 45W
Charleston, *UT, U.S.A.* **100 C4** 40 28N 111 28W
Charleston, *WV, U.S.A.* **102 C3** 38 21N 81 38W
Charleston County ☆, *SC, U.S.A.* **90 F5** 32 50N 80 0W
Charleston International ✈ (CHS), *SC, U.S.A.* **90 F5** 32 54N 80 2W
Charleston L., *Ont., Canada* **179 C10** 44 32N 76 0W
Charleston Peak, *NV, U.S.A.* **85 F5** 36 16N 115 42W
Charlestown, *Boston, U.S.A.* **106 A3** 42 22N 71 4W
Charlestown, *IN, U.S.A.* **72 E5** 38 27N 85 40W
Charlestown, *MD, U.S.A.* **77 A5** 39 35N 75 59W
Charlestown, *NH, U.S.A.* **86 C2** 43 14N 72 25W
Charlestown, *RI, U.S.A.* **78 C3** 41 23N 71 45W
Charlevoix, *MI, U.S.A.* **79 D6** 45 19N 85 16W
Charlevoix, L., *MI, U.S.A.* **79 D6** 45 16N 85 8W
Charlevoix County ☆, *MI, U.S.A.* **79 D6** 45 15N 85 10W
Charlo, *N.B., Canada* **173 F3** 47 59N 66 17W
Charlo, *MT, U.S.A.* **83 C3** 47 26N 114 10W
Charlotte, *IA, U.S.A.* **73 D8** 41 58N 90 28W
Charlotte, *MI, U.S.A.* **79 G7** 42 34N 84 50W
Charlotte, *NC, U.S.A.* **90 C5** 35 13N 80 50W
Charlotte, *TN, U.S.A.* **96 D5** 36 11N 87 21W
Charlotte, *TX, U.S.A.* **99 J9** 28 52N 98 43W
Charlotte, *VT, U.S.A.* **86 B1** 44 19N 73 16W
Charlotte Amalie, *U.S. Virgin Is.* **105 G18** 18 21N 64 56W
Charlotte County ☆, *FL, U.S.A.* **67 E7** 26 50N 82 0W
Charlotte County ☆, *VA, U.S.A.* **102 D6** 37 0N 78 55W
Charlotte Court House, *VA, U.S.A.* **102 D6** 37 3N 78 39W
Charlotte-Douglas International ✈ (CLT), *NC, U.S.A.* **90 C5** 35 12N 80 56W
Charlotte Hall, *MD, U.S.A.* **77 B4** 38 28N 76 45W
Charlotte Harbor, *FL, U.S.A.* **67 E6** 26 57N 82 4W
Charlotte L., *B.C., Canada* **186 C9** 52 12N 125 19W
Charlotte Res., *Charlotte, U.S.A.* **107 A1** 35 16N 80 53W
Charlottesville, *VA, U.S.A.* **102 C6** 38 2N 78 30W
Charlottetown, *P.E.I., Canada* **173 G6** 46 14N 63 8W
Charlton, *MA, U.S.A.* **78 B3** 42 8N 71 58W
Charlton County ☆, *GA, U.S.A.* **68 F4** 30 50N 82 10W
Charlton I., *N.W.T., Canada* **175 C2** 52 0N 79 20W
Charny, *Qué., Canada* **177 E11** 46 43N 71 15W
Charo, *Michoacan, Mexico* **219 C6** 19 45N 101 3W
Charron L., *Man., Canada* **183 C16** 52 44N 95 15W
Charter Oak, *IA, U.S.A.* **73 C3** 42 4N 95 36W
Chase, *B.C., Canada* **187 E15** 50 50N 119 41W
Chase, *AL, U.S.A.* **60 B4** 34 47N 86 33W
Chase, *KS, U.S.A.* **74 C5** 38 21N 98 21W
Chase, *MD, U.S.A.* **77 A4** 39 22N 76 22W
Chase, L., *Orlando, U.S.A.* **115 B1** 28 28N 81 31W
Chase City, *VA, U.S.A.* **102 E6** 36 48N 78 28W
Chase County ☆, *KS, U.S.A.* **74 C7** 38 15N 96 45W
Chase County ☆, *NE, U.S.A.* **84 D4** 40 30N 101 40W
Chaseburg, *WI, U.S.A.* **103 E2** 43 40N 91 6W
Chaseley, *ND, U.S.A.* **91 C6** 47 27N 99 49W
Chaska, *MN, U.S.A.* **80 F5** 44 47N 93 36W
Chasm, *B.C., Canada* **187 D13** 51 13N 121 30W
Chassahowitzka, *FL, U.S.A.* **67 C6** 28 43N 82 34W
Chataignier, *LA, U.S.A.* **75 D3** 30 34N 92 19W
Chatanika, *AK, U.S.A.* **61 D11** 65 7N 147 28W
Château-Richer, *Qué., Canada* **177 E11** 46 58N 71 1W
Chateaugay, *NY, U.S.A.* **89 A6** 44 56N 74 5W
Châteauguay, *Qué., Canada* **177 F9** 45 23N 73 45W
Châteauguay, L., *Qué., Canada* **175 B3** 56 26N 70 3W
Châteauvert, L., *Qué., Canada* **177 D9** 47 39N 73 56W
Chatfield, *AR, U.S.A.* **63 C5** 35 0N 90 24W
Chatfield, *MN, U.S.A.* **80 G6** 43 51N 92 11W
Chatfield, *OH, U.S.A.* **92 C4** 40 57N 82 57W
Chatfield State Park △, *Denver, U.S.A.* **109 C1** 39 32N 105 4W
Chatham = Chatham-Kent, *Ont., Canada* **178 E4** 42 24N 82 11W
Chatham = Miramichi, *N.B., Canada* **173 F4** 47 2N 65 28W
Chatham, *Chicago, U.S.A.* **108 C3** 41 45N 87 36W
Chatham, *IL, U.S.A.* **71 D4** 39 40N 89 42W
Chatham, *LA, U.S.A.* **75 B3** 32 18N 92 27W
Chatham, *MA, U.S.A.* **78 C5** 41 41N 69 58W
Chatham, *MI, U.S.A.* **79 C5** 46 21N 86 56W
Chatham, *NJ, U.S.A.* **87 B2** 40 44N 74 23W
Chatham, *NY, U.S.A.* **78 B1** 42 21N 73 36W
Chatham, *PA, U.S.A.* **77 A5** 39 51N 75 49W
Chatham, *VA, U.S.A.* **102 E5** 36 50N 79 24W
Chatham County ☆, *GA, U.S.A.* **68 E5** 32 0N 81 10W
Chatham County ☆, *NC, U.S.A.* **90 C6** 35 45N 79 10W
Chatham Head, *N.B., Canada* **173 G4** 47 0N 65 33W
Chatham-Kent, *Ont., Canada* **178 E4** 42 24N 82 11W
Chatham L., *TN, U.S.A.* **96 D5** 36 19N 87 13W
Chatom, *AL, U.S.A.* **60 E2** 31 28N 88 16W
Chats, L. des, *Ont., Canada* **176 F6** 45 30N 76 20W
Chatsworth, *Ont., Canada* **178 C6** 44 27N 80 54W
Chatsworth, *GA, U.S.A.* **68 B2** 34 46N 84 46W
Chatsworth, *IL, U.S.A.* **71 C5** 40 45N 88 18W
Chatsworth, *IA, U.S.A.* **73 C2** 42 55N 96 31W
Chatsworth, *NJ, U.S.A.* **87 C2** 39 49N 74 32W
Chattahoochee, *FL, U.S.A.* **67 A4** 30 42N 84 51W
Chattahoochee →, *GA, U.S.A.* **68 F2** 30 54N 84 57W
Chattahoochee County ☆, *GA, U.S.A.* **68 D2** 32 20N 84 50W
Chattahoochee Nat. Forest, *GA, U.S.A.* **68 B3** 34 50N 84 0W
Chattanooga, *OK, U.S.A.* **93 D5** 34 25N 98 39W
Chattanooga, *TN, U.S.A.* **97 E7** 35 3N 85 19W
Chattaroy, *WA, U.S.A.* **101 C8** 47 53N 117 21W
Chattolanee, *Baltimore, U.S.A.* **107 A1** 39 24N 76 44W
Chattooga County ☆, *GA, U.S.A.* **68 B1** 34 30N 85 15W
Chatuga L., *U.S.A.* **68 A3** 35 0N 83 40W
Chaudière →, *Qué., Canada* **177 E11** 46 45N 71 17W
Chaumont, *NY, U.S.A.* **89 A4** 44 4N 76 8W
Chauncey, *OH, U.S.A.* **92 D4** 39 24N 82 8W
Chautauqua, *KS, U.S.A.* **74 D7** 37 1N 96 11W
Chautauqua County ☆, *KS, U.S.A.* **74 D7** 37 15N 96 15W
Chautauqua County ☆, *NY, U.S.A.* **89 C1** 42 20N 79 15W
Chautauqua L., *NY, U.S.A.* **89 C1** 42 10N 79 24W
Chautauquan Nat. Wildlife Refuge △, *IL, U.S.A.* **71 C4** 40 23N 89 59W
Chauvin, *Alta., Canada* **185 F10** 52 45N 110 10W
Chauvin, *LA, U.S.A.* **75 E5** 29 26N 90 36W
Chaves County ☆, *NM, U.S.A.* **88 D6** 33 15N 104 30W
Chavies, *KY, U.S.A.* **97 C9** 37 21N 83 21W
Chavigny, L., *Qué., Canada* **175 B2** 58 12N 75 8W
Chazy, *NY, U.S.A.* **86 B1** 44 53N 73 26W
Cheaha Mt., *AL, U.S.A.* **60 C5** 33 29N 85 49W
Cheat Bridge, *WV, U.S.A.* **102 C5** 38 37N 79 52W
Cheatham County ☆, *TN, U.S.A.* **96 D5** 36 17N 87 4W
Chebanse, *IL, U.S.A.* **71 C6** 41 0N 87 54W
Cheboygan, *MI, U.S.A.* **79 D7** 45 39N 84 29W
Cheboygan County ☆, *MI, U.S.A.* **79 D7** 45 20N 84 30W
Check, *VA, U.S.A.* **102 D4** 37 2N 80 10W
Checleset B., *B.C., Canada* **186 E7** 50 5N 127 35W
Checotah, *OK, U.S.A.* **93 C8** 35 28N 95 31W
Chedabucto B., *N.S., Canada* **173 H8** 45 25N 61 8W
Cheektowaga, *NY, U.S.A.* **89 C2** 42 53N 78 45W
Cheepash →, *Ont., Canada* **181 A16** 51 3N 80 59W
Cheepay →, *Ont., Canada* **181 A13** 51 25N 83 26W
Cheeseman L., *Ont., Canada* **180 C7** 49 27N 89 20W
Cheeseman L., *CO, U.S.A.* **66 C5** 39 13N 105 16W
Chef, R. du →, *Qué., Canada* **177 B9** 49 21N 73 25W
Chefornak, *AK, U.S.A.* **61 F6** 60 13N 164 12W
Chehalis, *WA, U.S.A.* **101 D3** 46 40N 122 58W
Chehalis →, *WA, U.S.A.* **101 D2** 46 57N 123 50W
Chehalis Indian Reservation, *WA, U.S.A.* **101 D2** 46 49N 123 12W
Chekubul, *Campeche, Mexico* **223 D3** 18 51N 90 58W
Chelan, *WA, U.S.A.* **101 C5** 47 51N 120 1W
Chelan, L., *WA, U.S.A.* **101 B5** 48 11N 120 30W
Chelan County ☆, *WA, U.S.A.* **101 C5** 48 0N 120 30W
Chelan Falls, *WA, U.S.A.* **101 C6** 47 48N 119 59W
Chelatchie, *WA, U.S.A.* **101 E3** 45 55N 122 25W
Chelmsford, *MA, U.S.A.* **78 B3** 42 36N 71 21W
Chelsea, *Ont., Canada* **176 F7** 45 30N 75 47W
Chelsea, *AL, U.S.A.* **60 C4** 33 20N 86 38W
Chelsea, *Boston, U.S.A.* **106 A3** 42 23N 71 1W
Chelsea, *IA, U.S.A.* **73 D6** 41 55N 92 24W
Chelsea, *MI, U.S.A.* **79 G7** 42 19N 84 1W
Chelsea, *OK, U.S.A.* **93 B8** 36 32N 95 26W
Chelsea, *VT, U.S.A.* **86 C2** 43 59N 72 27W
Cheltenham, *MD, U.S.A.* **77 B4** 38 42N 76 50W
Cheltenham, *PA, U.S.A.* **116 A2** 40 33N 75 5W
Chemainus, *B.C., Canada* **187 G11** 48 55N 123 42W
Chemax, *Yucatán, Mexico* **223 B6** 20 39N 87 56W
Chemehuevi Indian Reservation, *CA, U.S.A.* **65 J12** 34 30N 114 25W
Chemquasabamticook L., *ME, U.S.A.* **76 B4** 46 30N 69 37W
Chemult, *OR, U.S.A.* **94 D4** 43 14N 121 47W
Chemung County ☆, *NY, U.S.A.* **89 C4** 42 10N 76 45W
Chemway, *Charlotte, U.S.A.* **107 A1** 35 16N 80 53W
Chenalhó, *Chiapas, Mexico* **222 C4** 16 53N 92 36W
Chenango →, *NY, U.S.A.* **89 C5** 42 6N 75 55W
Chenango County ☆, *NY, U.S.A.* **89 C5** 42 30N 75 40W
Chenes, Pointe aux, *MI, U.S.A.* **79 D7** 45 55N 84 54W
Chénéville, *Qué., Canada* **176 F7** 45 53N 75 3W
Cheney, *KS, U.S.A.* **74 D6** 37 38N 97 47W
Cheney, *WA, U.S.A.* **101 C8** 47 30N 117 35W
Cheney Res., *KS, U.S.A.* **74 D6** 37 43N 97 48W
Cheneyville, *LA, U.S.A.* **75 C3** 31 1N 92 17W
Chenil, L., *Qué., Canada* **172 B10** 51 51N 59 41W
Chenko, *Campeche, Mexico* **223 C4** 19 23N 89 48W
Chenoa, *IL, U.S.A.* **71 C5** 40 45N 88 43W
Chenoweth, *OR, U.S.A.* **94 B4** 45 37N 121 13W
Chepachet, *RI, U.S.A.* **78 C3** 41 55N 71 40W
Chequamegon B., *U.S.A.* **103 B3** 46 40N 90 51W
Chequamegon Nat. Forest, *WI, U.S.A.* **103 B3** 46 10N 91 0W
Chequamegon Pt., *WI, U.S.A.* **103 B3** 46 42N 90 45W
Cherán, *Michoacan, Mexico* **218 C6** 19 41N 101 57W
Cheraw, *CO, U.S.A.* **66 D7** 38 6N 103 31W
Cheraw, *SC, U.S.A.* **90 D6** 34 42N 79 53W
Cherhill, *Alta., Canada* **184 E6** 53 49N 114 41W
Cheriton, *VA, U.S.A.* **102 D9** 37 17N 75 58W
Cherokee, *AL, U.S.A.* **60 B3** 34 45N 87 58W
Cherokee, *IA, U.S.A.* **73 C3** 42 45N 95 33W
Cherokee, *KS, U.S.A.* **74 D9** 37 21N 94 49W
Cherokee, *OK, U.S.A.* **93 B5** 36 45N 98 21W
Cherokee, *TX, U.S.A.* **99 G9** 30 59N 98 43W
Cherokee County ☆, *AL, U.S.A.* **60 B5** 34 9N 85 41W
Cherokee County ☆, *GA, U.S.A.* **68 B2** 34 20N 84 20W
Cherokee County ☆, *IA, U.S.A.* **73 C3** 42 45N 95 35W
Cherokee County ☆, *KS, U.S.A.* **74 D9** 37 15N 94 45W
Cherokee County ☆, *NC, U.S.A.* **90 C1** 35 10N 84 10W
Cherokee County ☆, *OK, U.S.A.* **93 B9** 36 0N 95 0W
Cherokee County ☆, *SC, U.S.A.* **90 C4** 35 0N 81 40W
Cherokee County ☆, *TX, U.S.A.* **99 F12** 31 58N 95 17W
Cherokee Indian Reservation, *NC, U.S.A.* **90 C2** 35 30N 83 20W
Cherokee L., *TN, U.S.A.* **97 D9** 36 10N 83 30W
Cherokee Nat. Forest, *TN, U.S.A.* **97 E10** 36 0N 82 40W
Cherokee Village, *AR, U.S.A.* **63 B4** 36 18N 91 31W
Cherokees, Grand Lake O' The, *OK, U.S.A.* **93 B9** 36 28N 94 55W

Cherry County ☆, NE, U.S.A. **84 B4** 42 30N 101 0W
Cherry Cr. →, CO, U.S.A. **66 C6** 39 45N 104 1W
Cherry Cr. →, SD, U.S.A. **91 F4** 44 36N 101 30W
Cherry Creek, NV, U.S.A. **85 C6** 39 54N 114 53W
Cherry Creek, SD, U.S.A. **91 F4** 44 36N 101 30W
Cherry Creek L., Denver, U.S.A. **109 C2** 39 39N 104 51W
Cherry Creek State Park ⌂, Denver, U.S.A. **109 C2** 39 38N 104 51W
Cherry Hill, Baltimore, U.S.A. **107 B2** 39 15N 76 38W
Cherry Hill, NJ, U.S.A. **87 C1** 39 56N 75 2W
Cherry Hills Village, Denver, U.S.A. **109 C2** 39 38N 104 57W
Cherry L., CA, U.S.A. **64 F7** 37 59N 119 55W
Cherry Tree, PA, U.S.A. **95 D4** 40 44N 78 48W
Cherry Valley, AR, U.S.A. **63 C5** 35 24N 90 45W
Cherry Valley, NY, U.S.A. **89 C6** 42 48N 74 45W
Cherryfield, ME, U.S.A. **76 D6** 44 36N 67 56W
Cherryland, San Francisco, U.S.A. **118 B4** 37 40N 122 6W
Cherryvale, KS, U.S.A. **74 D8** 37 16N 95 33W
Cherryville, B.C., Canada **187 E16** 50 15N 118 37W
Cherryville, NC, U.S.A. **90 C4** 35 23N 81 23W
Chesaco Park, Baltimore, U.S.A. **107 B3** 39 18N 76 29W
Chesaning, MI, U.S.A. **79 F7** 43 11N 84 7W
Chesapeake, VA, U.S.A. **102 E8** 36 49N 76 16W
Chesapeake, WV, U.S.A. **102 C3** 38 13N 81 32W
Chesapeake B., VA, U.S.A. **102 C8** 38 0N 76 10W
Chesapeake Bay Bridge-Tunnel, VA, U.S.A. **102 D8** 37 2N 76 5W
Chesapeake Beach, MD, U.S.A. **77 B4** 38 41N 76 32W
Chesapeake City, MD, U.S.A. **77 A5** 39 32N 75 49W
Chesapeake Ranche Estates, MD, U.S.A. **77 B4** 38 21N 76 25W
Chesaw, WA, U.S.A. **101 B6** 48 57N 119 3W
Chesdin, L., VA, U.S.A. **102 D7** 37 20N 77 40W
Cheshire, CT, U.S.A. **78 C2** 41 30N 72 54W
Cheshire, MA, U.S.A. **78 B1** 42 34N 73 10W
Cheshire County ☆, NH, U.S.A. **86 D2** 43 0N 72 15W
Chesilhurst, NJ, U.S.A. **87 C2** 39 44N 74 52W
Cheslatta, B.C., Canada **186 B9** 53 48N 125 48W
Cheslatta L., B.C., Canada **186 B9** 53 49N 125 20W
Chesley, Ont., Canada **178 C5** 44 17N 81 5W
Chesnee, SC, U.S.A. **90 C4** 35 9N 81 52W
Chester, N.S., Canada **173 J5** 44 33N 64 15W
Chester, AR, U.S.A. **63 C1** 35 41N 94 11W
Chester, CA, U.S.A. **64 C5** 40 19N 121 14W
Chester, GA, U.S.A. **68 D3** 32 24N 83 9W
Chester, IL, U.S.A. **71 F4** 37 55N 89 49W
Chester, MA, U.S.A. **78 B2** 42 17N 72 59W
Chester, MT, U.S.A. **83 B7** 48 31N 110 58W
Chester, NH, U.S.A. **86 D3** 42 55N 71 15W
Chester, NJ, U.S.A. **87 B2** 40 47N 74 42W
Chester, NE, U.S.A. **84 D8** 40 1N 97 37W
Chester, OK, U.S.A. **93 B5** 36 13N 98 55W
Chester, PA, U.S.A. **77 A5** 39 51N 75 22W
Chester, SC, U.S.A. **90 D4** 34 43N 81 12W
Chester, SD, U.S.A. **91 G9** 43 54N 96 56W
Chester, VA, U.S.A. **102 D7** 37 21N 77 27W
Chester, VT, U.S.A. **86 C2** 43 16N 72 36W
Chester, WV, U.S.A. **102 A4** 40 37N 80 34W
Chester →, MD, U.S.A. **77 A4** 39 3N 76 16W
Chester County ☆, PA, U.S.A. **95 E7** 39 59N 75 50W
Chester County ☆, SC, U.S.A. **90 D4** 34 30N 81 10W
Chester County ☆, TN, U.S.A. **96 E4** 35 20N 88 45W
Chesterfield, IL, U.S.A. **71 D3** 39 15N 90 4W
Chesterfield, MO, U.S.A. **82 C6** 38 40N 90 35W
Chesterfield, NH, U.S.A. **86 D2** 42 52N 72 28W
Chesterfield, SC, U.S.A. **90 D5** 34 44N 80 5W
Chesterfield County ☆, SC, U.S.A. **90 D5** 34 30N 80 10W
Chesterfield County ☆, VA, U.S.A. **102 D7** 37 23N 77 31W
Chesterfield Court House, VA, U.S.A. **102 D7** 37 23N 77 31W
Chesterfield Inlet, Nunavut, Canada **191 E7** 63 30N 90 45W
Chesterhill, OH, U.S.A. **92 D5** 39 29N 81 52W
Chestermere, Alta., Canada **185 G7** 51 2N 113 49W
Chesterton, IN, U.S.A. **72 B3** 41 37N 87 4W
Chestertown, MD, U.S.A. **77 A4** 39 13N 76 4W
Chesterville, Ont., Canada **176 F7** 45 6N 75 14W
Chesterville, MD, U.S.A. **77 A5** 39 17N 75 55W
Chestnut, LA, U.S.A. **75 B2** 32 3N 93 1W
Chestnut Hill, Boston, U.S.A. **106 B2** 42 19N 71 10W
Chesuncook L., ME, U.S.A. **76 C4** 46 0N 69 21W
Cheswold, DE, U.S.A. **77 A5** 39 13N 75 35W
Chetco →, OR, U.S.A. **94 E1** 42 3N 124 16W
Chetek, WI, U.S.A. **103 C2** 45 19N 91 39W
Chéticamp, N.S., Canada **173 G9** 46 37N 60 59W
Chetopa, KS, U.S.A. **74 D8** 37 2N 95 5W
Chetumal, Quintana Roo, Mexico **223 D5** 18 30N 88 20W
Chetumal, B. de, Mexico **223 D5** 18 20N 88 5W
Chetwynd, B.C., Canada **189 E8** 55 45N 121 36W
Chevak, AK, U.S.A. **61 F6** 61 32N 165 35W
Chevelon Cr. →, AZ, U.S.A. **62 C5** 34 55N 110 35W
Cheverly, MD, U.S.A. **119 B4** 38 55N 76 54W
Cheviot, OH, U.S.A. **92 D2** 39 9N 84 36W
Chevreuil, Pt., LA, U.S.A. **75 E4** 29 31N 91 33W
Chevy Chase, MD, U.S.A. **77 B3** 38 59N 77 4W
Chewaucan →, OR, U.S.A. **94 E5** 42 31N 120 15W
Chewelah, WA, U.S.A. **101 B8** 48 17N 117 43W
Chewuch →, WA, U.S.A. **101 B5** 48 29N 120 11W
Cheyenne, OK, U.S.A. **93 C4** 35 37N 99 40W
Cheyenne, WY, U.S.A. **104 E8** 41 8N 104 49W
Cheyenne →, SD, U.S.A. **91 F4** 44 41N 101 18W
Cheyenne Bottoms, KS, U.S.A. **74 C5** 38 27N 98 40W
Cheyenne County ☆, CO, U.S.A. **66 D8** 38 50N 102 35W
Cheyenne County ☆, KS, U.S.A. **74 B2** 39 45N 101 45W
Cheyenne County ☆, NE, U.S.A. **84 C3** 41 15N 103 0W
Cheyenne River Indian Reservation, SD, U.S.A. **91 E4** 45 0N 101 0W
Cheyenne Wells, CO, U.S.A. **66 D8** 38 49N 102 21W
Chezacut, B.C., Canada **186 C10** 52 24N 124 1W
Chiapa de Corzo, Chiapas, Mexico **222 C4** 16 42N 93 0W
Chiapas □, Mexico **222 C4** 16 30N 92 30W
Chiapas, Sa. Madre de, Chiapas, Mexico **222 C3** 15 40N 93 0W
Chiautla, Puebla, Mexico **221 F2** 18 18N 98 36W
Chibougamau, Qué., Canada **177 B8** 49 56N 74 24W
Chibougamau →, Qué., Canada **176 B7** 49 42N 75 57W
Chibougamau, L., Qué., Canada **177 B8** 49 50N 74 20W
Chic-Chocs, Mts., Qué., Canada **172 E3** 48 55N 66 0W
Chic-Chocs, Réserve Faunique des ⌂, Qué., Canada **172 E3** 48 55N 66 20W
Chicago, IL, U.S.A. **71 B6** 41 52N 87 38W
Chicago Harbor, Chicago, U.S.A. **108 B3** 41 52N 87 36W
Chicago Heights, IL, U.S.A. **71 B6** 41 30N 87 38W
Chicago Lawn, Chicago, U.S.A. **108 C2** 41 47N 87 40W
Chicago-Midway ✕ (MDW), IL, U.S.A. **108 C2** 41 47N 87 45W
Chicago O'Hare International ✕ (ORD), IL, U.S.A. **108 B1** 41 59N 87 54W
Chicago Ridge, Chicago, U.S.A. **108 C2** 41 41N 87 46W
Chicago Sanitary and Ship Canal, Chicago, U.S.A. **108 C2** 41 49N 87 45W
Chicamuxen, MD, U.S.A. **77 B3** 38 33N 77 15W
Chicayán, Veracruz, Mexico **220 C2** 21 37N 98 6W
Chicbul, Campeche, Mexico **223 D3** 18 48N 90 44W
Chichagof I., AK, U.S.A. **61 H14** 57 30N 135 30W
Chichén-Itzá, Yucatán, Mexico **223 B5** 20 37N 88 35W
Chichicastle, L., Tabasco, Mexico **222 A4** 18 18N 92 28W
Chichihualco, Guerrero, Mexico **219 E8** 17 41N 99 39W
Chickahominy →, VA, U.S.A. **102 D8** 37 14N 76 53W
Chickamauga, GA, U.S.A. **68 B1** 34 52N 85 18W
Chickamauga L., TN, U.S.A. **97 E7** 35 6N 85 14W
Chickasaw, AL, U.S.A. **60 F2** 30 46N 88 5W
Chickasaw County ☆, IA, U.S.A. **73 B6** 43 5N 92 20W
Chickasaw County ☆, MS, U.S.A. **81 C5** 33 54N 89 0W
Chickasaw Nat. Recr. Area ⌂, OK, U.S.A. **93 D7** 34 26N 97 0W
Chickasaw Nat. Wildlife Refuge ⌂, TN, U.S.A. **96 E3** 35 49N 89 38W
Chickasawhay →, MS, U.S.A. **81 F5** 30 59N 88 44W
Chickasha, OK, U.S.A. **93 C6** 35 3N 97 58W
Chicken, AK, U.S.A. **61 D12** 64 5N 141 56W
Chico, CA, U.S.A. **64 D5** 39 44N 121 50W
Chico, TX, U.S.A. **99 D10** 33 18N 97 48W
Chico →, Chihuahua, Mexico **213 D7** 29 23N 108 29W
Chicoasén, Chiapas, Mexico **222 C3** 16 58N 93 6W
Chicobi, L., Qué., Canada **176 C4** 48 53N 78 30W
Chicomostoc, Zacatecas, Mexico **217 E8** 22 28N 102 46W
Chicomuselo, Chiapas, Mexico **222 D4** 15 46N 92 16W
Chiconcuac, México, Mexico **219 C9** 19 34N 98 54W
Chicontepec, Veracruz, Mexico **220 D2** 20 58N 98 10W
Chicopee, GA, U.S.A. **68 B3** 34 15N 83 51W
Chicopee, MA, U.S.A. **78 B2** 42 9N 72 37W
Chicopee →, MA, U.S.A. **78 B2** 42 9N 72 37W
Chicot, Montréal, Canada **192 A1** 45 35N 73 56W
Chicot, AR, U.S.A. **63 E4** 33 12N 91 17W
Chicot County ☆, AR, U.S.A. **63 E4** 33 12N 91 17W
Chicoutimi, Qué., Canada **177 C11** 48 28N 71 5W
Chicxulub, Yucatán, Mexico **223 A4** 21 17N 89 37W
Chidester, AR, U.S.A. **63 E2** 33 42N 93 1W
Chidley, C., Nfld. & L., Canada **175 A5** 60 23N 64 26W
Chief Joseph Dam, WA, U.S.A. **101 B6** 48 0N 119 38W
Chiefland, FL, U.S.A. **67 B6** 29 29N 82 52W
Chiefs Pt., Ont., Canada **178 C5** 44 41N 81 18W
Chietla, Puebla, Mexico **221 F2** 18 32N 98 35W
Chignahuapan, Puebla, Mexico **220 E2** 19 48N 98 2W
Chignecto, Cape, N.S., Canada **173 H5** 45 20N 64 57W
Chignecto B., N.B., Canada **173 H5** 45 30N 64 40W
Chignik, AK, U.S.A. **61 H8** 56 18N 158 24W
Chigoubiche, L., Qué., Canada **177 B9** 49 7N 73 30W
Chihuahua, Chihuahua, Mexico **213 E9** 28 38N 106 5W
Chihuahua □, Mexico **213 D9** 28 30N 106 0W
Chihuhuita, Sinaloa, Mexico **216 A1** 26 8N 109 4W
Chikaskia →, OK, U.S.A. **93 B6** 36 37N 97 15W
Chikindzonot, Yucatán, Mexico **223 B5** 20 20N 88 30W
Chila, L., Veracruz, Mexico **220 B3** 22 11N 97 58W
Chila de la Sal, Puebla, Mexico **221 F2** 18 7N 98 29W
Chila de las Flores, Puebla, Mexico **221 G3** 17 58N 97 52W
Chilako →, B.C., Canada **186 B11** 53 53N 122 57W
Chilanko →, B.C., Canada **186 C11** 52 7N 123 41W
Chilanko Forks, B.C., Canada **186 C10** 52 7N 124 5W
Chilapa, Guerrero, Mexico **219 E8** 17 36N 99 10W
Chilchota, Michoacan, Mexico **218 C5** 19 49N 102 6W
Chilcotin →, B.C., Canada **187 D12** 51 44N 122 23W
Chilcuautla, Hidalgo, Mexico **219 B8** 20 20N 99 14W
Childersburg, AL, U.S.A. **60 C4** 33 16N 86 21W
Childress, TX, U.S.A. **98 C7** 34 25N 100 13W
Childress County ☆, TX, U.S.A. **98 C7** 34 25N 100 15W
Chilhowee, MO, U.S.A. **82 C3** 38 36N 93 51W
Chilhowie, VA, U.S.A. **102 E3** 36 48N 81 41W
Chilicote, Chihuahua, Mexico **213 E11** 28 58N 104 52W
Chilili, NM, U.S.A. **88 C4** 34 53N 106 14W
Chilko →, B.C., Canada **186 D11** 52 0N 123 40W
Chilko L., B.C., Canada **186 D10** 51 20N 124 10W
Chilkoot Pass, N. Amer. **189 E5** 59 42N 135 14W
Chillicothe, IL, U.S.A. **71 C4** 40 55N 89 29W
Chillicothe, IA, U.S.A. **73 D6** 41 5N 92 32W
Chillicothe, MO, U.S.A. **82 B3** 39 48N 93 33W
Chillicothe, OH, U.S.A. **92 D4** 39 20N 82 59W
Chillicothe, TX, U.S.A. **99 C8** 34 15N 99 31W
Chilliwack, B.C., Canada **187 F13** 49 10N 121 54W
Chilliwack Lake Park ⌂, B.C., Canada **187 F13** 49 4N 121 26W
Chillum, MD, U.S.A. **119 B4** 38 57N 76 58W
Chillum, MD, U.S.A. **77 B4** 38 56N 76 58W
Chilmark, MA, U.S.A. **78 C4** 41 21N 70 45W
Chilocco, OK, U.S.A. **93 B6** 36 59N 97 4W
Chilón, Chiapas, Mexico **222 B4** 17 14N 92 15W
Chiloquin, OR, U.S.A. **94 E4** 42 35N 121 52W
Chilpancingo, Guerrero, Mexico **219 E8** 17 33N 99 30W
Chilson, NY, U.S.A. **86 C1** 43 53N 73 32W
Chiltepec, Tabasco, Mexico **222 A3** 18 25N 93 5W
Chilton, WI, U.S.A. **103 D5** 44 2N 88 10W
Chilton County ☆, AL, U.S.A. **60 D4** 32 51N 86 38W
Chiluca, México, Mexico **225 A2** 19 31N 99 17W
Chimalapas, Región de los, Oaxaca, Mexico **221 H6** 16 14N 94 30W
Chimalhuacán, México, Mexico **219 C9** 19 25N 98 57W
Chimaltitán, Jalisco, Mexico **217 F7** 21 35N 103 50W
Chimayo, NM, U.S.A. **88 B5** 36 0N 105 56W
Chimney Rock, CO, U.S.A. **66 E3** 37 13N 107 18W
Chimney Rock Nat. Historic Site ⌂, NE, U.S.A. **84 C2** 41 42N 103 21W
Chimo, Jalisco, Mexico **218 B2** 20 28N 105 35W
China, Nuevo León, Mexico **214 E5** 25 42N 99 14W
China, TX, U.S.A. **99 G13** 30 3N 94 20W
China Basin, San Francisco, U.S.A. **118 B2** 37 46N 122 23W
China Grove, NC, U.S.A. **90 C5** 35 34N 80 35W
China Grove, San Antonio, U.S.A. **117 C3** 29 23N 98 20W
China L., CA, U.S.A. **65 H9** 35 43N 117 20W
Chinameca, Veracruz, Mexico **221 F6** 18 1N 94 40W
Chinampa, Veracruz, Mexico **220 C3** 21 22N 97 43W
Chinati Mts., TX, U.S.A. **98 H3** 29 55N 104 30W
Chinati Peak, TX, U.S.A. **98 H3** 29 57N 104 29W
Chinatown, Chicago, U.S.A. **108 B3** 41 51N 87 37W
Chinchaga →, Alta., Canada **184 A1** 58 53N 118 20W
Chinchaga Wildland Prov. Park ⌂, Alta., Canada **184 A1** 57 10N 119 30W
Chinchorro, Banco, Quintana Roo, Mexico **223 D6** 18 35N 87 22W
Chincoteague, VA, U.S.A. **77 C5** 37 56N 75 23W
Chincoteague Bay, MD, U.S.A. **77 B5** 38 15N 75 15W
Chincoteague I., VA, U.S.A. **77 C5** 37 56N 75 22W
Chincoteague Nat. Wildlife Refuge ⌂, VA, U.S.A. **102 D9** 37 56N 75 19W
Chínipas, Chihuahua, Mexico **212 F7** 27 23N 108 32W
Chinkultic, Chiapas, Mexico **222 C5** 16 13N 91 52W
Chinle, AZ, U.S.A. **62 A6** 36 9N 109 33W
Chinle Cr. →, UT, U.S.A. **100 F6** 37 12N 109 43W
Chino, CA, U.S.A. **65 J9** 34 1N 117 41W
Chino Valley, AZ, U.S.A. **62 C3** 34 45N 112 27W
Chinobampo, Sinaloa, Mexico **216 A2** 26 26N 108 16W
Chinook, Alta., Canada **185 G10** 51 28N 110 59W
Chinook, MT, U.S.A. **83 B8** 48 35N 109 14W
Chinook, WA, U.S.A. **101 D2** 46 16N 123 57W
Chinook, L., OR, U.S.A. **94 C4** 44 33N 121 20W
Chinook Pass, WA, U.S.A. **101 D4** 46 52N 121 32W
Chinook Valley, Alta., Canada **184 B3** 56 29N 117 39W
Chip L., Alta., Canada **184 E5** 53 40N 115 23W
Chipley, FL, U.S.A. **67 A3** 30 47N 85 32W
Chipman, Alta., Canada **184 E8** 53 42N 112 38W
Chipman, N.B., Canada **173 G4** 46 6N 65 53W
Chipman L., Ont., Canada **181 C10** 49 58N 86 15W
Chipola →, FL, U.S.A. **67 A3** 30 1N 85 5W
Chippewa →, MI, U.S.A. **79 F7** 43 35N 84 17W
Chippewa →, MN, U.S.A. **80 F3** 44 56N 95 44W
Chippewa →, WI, U.S.A. **103 D1** 44 25N 92 5W
Chippewa, L., WI, U.S.A. **103 C2** 45 57N 91 12W
Chippewa County ☆, MI, U.S.A. **79 C7** 46 20N 84 40W
Chippewa County ☆, MN, U.S.A. **80 F3** 45 0N 95 35W
Chippewa County ☆, WI, U.S.A. **103 C2** 45 5N 91 20W
Chippewa Falls, WI, U.S.A. **103 D2** 44 56N 91 24W
Chippewa Nat. Forest, MN, U.S.A. **80 C4** 47 45N 94 0W
Chiputneticook Lakes, N. Amer. **173 H2** 45 35N 67 35W
Chiquihuite, Cerro, Distrito Federal, Mexico **225 A3** 19 32N 99 8W
Chiquihuitillo, Michoacan, Mexico **218 D5** 18 58N 102 20W
Chiquilá, Quintana Roo, Mexico **223 A6** 21 26N 87 20W
Chireno, TX, U.S.A. **99 F13** 31 30N 94 21W
Chiricahua Mts., AZ, U.S.A. **62 F6** 32 0N 109 15W
Chiricahua Nat. Monument ⌂, AZ, U.S.A. **62 E6** 32 0N 109 20W
Chiricahua Peak, AZ, U.S.A. **62 F6** 31 51N 109 18W
Chisago County ☆, MN, U.S.A. **80 E6** 45 30N 92 55W
Chisasibi, Qué., Canada **175 C2** 53 50N 79 0W
Chisholm, Alta., Canada **184 D6** 54 55N 114 10W
Chisholm, ME, U.S.A. **76 D3** 44 29N 70 12W
Chisholm, MN, U.S.A. **80 C6** 47 29N 92 53W
Chisos Mts., TX, U.S.A. **98 H4** 29 5N 103 15W
Chistochina, AK, U.S.A. **61 E11** 62 34N 144 40W
Chitek L., Man., Canada **183 C12** 52 25N 99 25W
Chitek L., Sask., Canada **182 B4** 53 45N 107 47W
Chitek Lake, Sask., Canada **182 B4** 53 45N 107 43W
Chitimacha Indian Reservation, LA, U.S.A. **75 D3** 30 33N 92 42W
Chitina, AK, U.S.A. **61 F11** 61 31N 144 26W
Chittenango, NY, U.S.A. **89 B5** 43 3N 75 52W
Chittenden, VT, U.S.A. **86 C2** 43 42N 72 55W
Chittenden County ☆, VT, U.S.A. **86 B1** 44 30N 73 10W
Chivato, Pta., Baja Calif. S., Mexico **211 F7** 27 5N 111 59W
Chivington, CO, U.S.A. **66 D8** 38 26N 102 32W
Chivo, Pta., Oaxaca, Mexico **221 H6** 16 1N 95 21W
Chloride, AZ, U.S.A. **62 B1** 35 25N 114 12W
Chochola, Yucatán, Mexico **223 B4** 20 45N 89 50W
Chocolate Mountain Naval Aerial Gunnery, CA, U.S.A. **65 K11** 33 14N 115 10W
Chocolate Mts., AZ, U.S.A. **62 D1** 33 15N 114 30W
Chocolate Mts., CA, U.S.A. **65 K11** 33 15N 115 15W
Chocowinity, NC, U.S.A. **90 C8** 35 31N 77 6W
Choctaw, OK, U.S.A. **93 C6** 35 31N 97 17W
Choctaw Bluff, AL, U.S.A. **60 E3** 31 22N 87 46W
Choctaw County ☆, AL, U.S.A. **60 E2** 32 0N 88 10W
Choctaw County ☆, MS, U.S.A. **81 C4** 33 19N 89 11W
Choctaw County ☆, OK, U.S.A. **93 D8** 34 0N 95 30W
Choctawhatchee →, FL, U.S.A. **67 A2** 30 25N 86 8W
Choctawhatchee B., FL, U.S.A. **67 A2** 30 20N 86 20W
Choelquoit L., B.C., Canada **186 D10** 51 42N 124 12W
Choiceland, Sask., Canada **182 B7** 53 29N 104 29W
Choix, Sinaloa, Mexico **216 A2** 26 43N 108 17W
Choke Canyon Res., TX, U.S.A. **99 J9** 28 30N 98 20W
Chokio, MN, U.S.A. **80 E2** 45 34N 96 10W
Chokoloskee, FL, U.S.A. **67 F7** 25 49N 81 22W
Chollas Park, San Diego, U.S.A. **117 B2** 32 44N 117 3W
Cholula, Puebla, Mexico **221 E2** 19 4N 98 18W
Chomedey, Qué., Canada **192 A2** 45 32N 73 45W
Chontalpa, Tabasco, Mexico **222 B3** 17 42N 93 31W
Chontla, Veracruz, Mexico **220 C3** 21 18N 97 55W
Choptank, MD, U.S.A. **77 B5** 38 41N 75 57W
Choptank →, MD, U.S.A. **77 B4** 38 38N 76 13W
Chorkbak Inlet, Nunavut, Canada **191 E11** 64 30N 74 25W
Chorreras, Chihuahua, Mexico **213 E10** 28 51N 105 17W
Choteau, MT, U.S.A. **83 C5** 47 49N 112 11W
Choudrant, LA, U.S.A. **75 B3** 32 32N 92 31W
Chouteau, OK, U.S.A. **93 B8** 36 11N 95 21W
Chouteau County ☆, MT, U.S.A. **83 C7** 47 55N 110 30W
Chouteau I., IL, U.S.A. **117 A3** 38 46N 90 8W
Chowan →, NC, U.S.A. **90 B9** 36 1N 76 40W
Chowan County ☆, NC, U.S.A. **90 B9** 36 10N 76 40W
Chowchilla, CA, U.S.A. **64 F6** 37 7N 120 16W
Chrisman, IL, U.S.A. **71 D6** 39 48N 87 41W
Chrisney, IN, U.S.A. **72 E3** 38 1N 87 2W
Christian County ☆, IL, U.S.A. **71 D4** 39 30N 89 15W
Christian County ☆, KY, U.S.A. **96 D5** 36 50N 87 30W
Christian County ☆, MO, U.S.A. **82 E3** 37 0N 93 10W
Christian I., Ont., Canada **176 G2** 44 50N 80 12W
Christian Sd., AK, U.S.A. **61 J14** 55 56N 134 40W
Christiana, DE, U.S.A. **77 A5** 39 40N 75 40W
Christiana, TN, U.S.A. **96 E6** 35 43N 86 24W
Christiansburg, OH, U.S.A. **92 C2** 40 3N 84 2W
Christiansburg, VA, U.S.A. **102 D4** 37 8N 80 25W
Christiansted, U.S. Virgin Is. **105 H18** 17 45N 64 42W
Christie, OK, U.S.A. **93 C9** 35 57N 94 42W
Christie B., N.W.T., Canada **189 D10** 62 32N 111 10W
Christina →, Alta., Canada **184 B9** 56 40N 111 3W
Christina, L., B.C., Canada **187 F16** 49 3N 118 12W
Christine, ND, U.S.A. **91 D9** 46 35N 96 48W
Christopher, IL, U.S.A. **71 F4** 37 59N 89 3W
Christopher Lake, Sask., Canada **182 B6** 53 32N 105 48W
Christoval, TX, U.S.A. **98 F7** 31 12N 100 30W
Chrome, NJ, U.S.A. **114 C1** 40 34N 74 13W
Chromo, CO, U.S.A. **66 E4** 37 2N 106 50W
Chrysler, AL, U.S.A. **60 E3** 31 18N 87 42W
Chu Chua, B.C., Canada **187 D14** 51 22N 120 10W
Chualar, CA, U.S.A. **64 G5** 36 34N 121 31W
Chuathbaluk, AK, U.S.A. **61 F8** 61 40N 159 15W
Chubbuck, ID, U.S.A. **70 G6** 42 55N 112 28W
Chuburna, Yucatán, Mexico **223 A4** 21 16N 89 49W
Chuckawalla Mts., CA, U.S.A. **65 K11** 33 30N 115 20W
Chugach Mts., AK, U.S.A. **61 F11** 60 45N 147 0W
Chuginadak I., AK, U.S.A. **61 K5** 52 50N 169 45W
Chugwater, WY, U.S.A. **104 E8** 41 46N 104 50W
Chuichu, AZ, U.S.A. **62 E4** 32 45N 111 47W
Chula, GA, U.S.A. **68 E3** 31 33N 83 32W
Chula, MO, U.S.A. **82 B3** 39 55N 93 29W
Chula, VA, U.S.A. **102 D7** 37 23N 77 54W
Chula Vista, CA, U.S.A. **65 L9** 32 38N 117 5W
Chumul, Yucatán, Mexico **223 C4** 19 48N 89 9W
Chunchintok, Campeche, Mexico **223 C4** 19 21N 89 40W
Chunchucmil, Yucatán, Mexico **223 B3** 20 39N 90 12W
Chunchula, AL, U.S.A. **60 F2** 30 55N 88 12W
Chunhuhub, Quintana Roo, Mexico **223 C5** 19 33N 88 41W
Chunjabin, Campeche, Mexico **223 D3** 18 45N 90 10W
Chunky, MS, U.S.A. **81 D5** 32 20N 88 56W
Chuntengo, Barra, Guerrero, Mexico **219 F8** 16 38N 99 8W
Chupadera Mesa, NM, U.S.A. **88 D4** 33 52N 106 14W
Church Creek, MD, U.S.A. **77 B4** 38 30N 76 10W
Church Hill, MD, U.S.A. **77 A5** 39 9N 75 59W
Church Hill, TN, U.S.A. **97 D10** 36 31N 82 43W
Church Point, LA, U.S.A. **75 D3** 30 24N 92 13W
Church Rock, NM, U.S.A. **88 B2** 35 32N 108 36W
Churchbridge, Sask., Canada **183 E10** 50 54N 101 54W
Churchill, Man., Canada **191 F7** 58 47N 94 11W
Churchill, Pittsburgh, U.S.A. **116 B2** 40 26N 79 50W
Churchill →, Man., Canada **191 F7** 58 47N 94 12W
Churchill →, Nfld. & L., Canada **175 C5** 53 19N 60 10W
Churchill, C., Man., Canada **191 F7** 58 46N 93 12W
Churchill County ☆, NV, U.S.A. **85 C2** 39 30N 118 20W
Churchill Falls, Nfld. & L., Canada **175 C5** 53 36N 64 19W
Churchill L., Ont., Canada **180 B5** 50 50N 91 10W
Churchill L., Sask., Canada **189 E11** 55 55N 108 20W
Churchill Pk., B.C., Canada **189 E7** 58 10N 125 10W
Churchs Ferry, ND, U.S.A. **91 B6** 48 16N 99 12W
Churchville, MD, U.S.A. **77 A4** 39 34N 76 15W
Churdan, IA, U.S.A. **73 C4** 42 9N 94 29W
Churintzio, Michoacan, Mexico **218 B5** 20 7N 102 3W
Churn Creek Park ⌂, B.C., Canada **187 D12** 51 25N 122 20W
Churubusco, IN, U.S.A. **72 B5** 41 14N 85 19W
Churubusco, L., México, Mexico **225 B3** 19 27N 99 1W
Churumuco, Michoacan, Mexico **218 D6** 18 40N 101 39W
Chuska Mts., NM, U.S.A. **88 A2** 36 15N 108 50W
Chute-aux-Outardes, Qué., Canada **177 B14** 49 7N 68 24W
Chute-des-Passes, Qué., Canada **177 B11** 49 52N 71 16W
Ciales, Puerto Rico **105 G16** 18 20N 66 28W
Cibecue, AZ, U.S.A. **62 C5** 34 2N 110 29W
Cibola, AZ, U.S.A. **62 D1** 33 17N 114 42W
Cibola County ☆, NM, U.S.A. **88 C2** 35 0N 108 0W
Cibola Nat. Forest, NM, U.S.A. **88 B2** 35 10N 108 15W
Cicero, IL, U.S.A. **71 B6** 41 51N 87 44W
Cicero, IN, U.S.A. **72 C4** 40 8N 86 1W
Cidra, Puerto Rico **105 G16** 18 11N 66 10W
Ciénega de Caballos, Durango, Mexico **216 B4** 25 41N 106 25W
Ciénega de Escobar, Durango, Mexico **216 B5** 25 37N 105 45W
Ciénega de Flores, Nuevo León, Mexico **214 E4** 25 57N 100 11W
Cieneguilla, Oaxaca, Mexico **221 G2** 17 45N 98 16W
Cieneguillas, Durango, Mexico **217 C6** 24 3N 104 3W
Cihuatlán, Jalisco, Mexico **218 C3** 19 14N 104 35W
Cima, CA, U.S.A. **65 H11** 35 14N 115 30W
Cimarron, KS, U.S.A. **74 D3** 37 48N 100 21W
Cimarron, NM, U.S.A. **88 A6** 36 31N 104 55W
Cimarron →, NM, U.S.A. **88 A6** 36 15N 104 30W
Cimarron →, OK, U.S.A. **93 B7** 36 10N 96 16W
Cimarron City, OK, U.S.A. **93 C6** 35 53N 97 36W
Cimarron County ☆, OK, U.S.A. **93 B1** 36 45N 102 30W
Cimarron Nat. Grassland, KS, U.S.A. **74 D1** 37 15N 102 2W
Cincinnati, IA, U.S.A. **73 E6** 40 38N 92 56W
Cincinnati, OH, U.S.A. **92 D2** 39 9N 84 27W
Cincinnati Municipal ✕, OH, U.S.A. **107 B2** 39 6N 84 25W
Cincinnati-Northern Kentucky International ✕ (CVG), KY, U.S.A. **97 A8** 39 3N 84 40W
Cinco Manantiales, Parque Natural ⌂, Coahuila, Mexico **214 B4** 28 30N 100 45W
Cintalapa, Chiapas, Mexico **222 C3** 16 44N 93 43W
Circle, AK, U.S.A. **61 D11** 65 50N 144 4W
Circle, MT, U.S.A. **83 C12** 47 25N 105 35W
Circle Cliffs, UT, U.S.A. **100 F4** 37 52N 111 15W
Circleville, KS, U.S.A. **74 B8** 39 31N 95 52W
Circleville, OH, U.S.A. **92 D4** 39 36N 82 57W
Circleville, UT, U.S.A. **100 E3** 38 10N 112 16W
Circleville, WV, U.S.A. **102 C5** 38 40N 79 30W
Circleville Mt., UT, U.S.A. **100 E3** 38 12N 112 24W
Cisco, IL, U.S.A. **71 C5** 40 1N 88 44W
Cisco, TX, U.S.A. **99 E9** 32 23N 98 59W
Cisco, UT, U.S.A. **100 E6** 38 58N 109 19W
Cisne, IL, U.S.A. **71 E5** 38 31N 88 26W
Cissna Park, IL, U.S.A. **71 C6** 40 34N 87 54W
Cistern, TX, U.S.A. **99 H10** 29 49N 97 13W
Citaltepec, Veracruz, Mexico **220 C3** 21 20N 97 52W
Citra, FL, U.S.A. **67 B6** 29 25N 82 7W
Citronelle, AL, U.S.A. **60 E2** 31 6N 88 14W
Citrus County ☆, FL, U.S.A. **67 C6** 28 45N 82 30W
Citrus Heights, CA, U.S.A. **64 E5** 38 42N 121 17W
Citrus Springs, FL, U.S.A. **67 B6** 29 2N 82 27W
City Island, NY, U.S.A. **114 A4** 40 50N 73 47W
City of Rocks Nat. Reserve ⌂, ID, U.S.A. **70 G5** 42 5N 113 42W
City Park, Denver, U.S.A. **109 B2** 39 44N 104 56W
City Park, New Orleans, U.S.A. **113 B2** 30 0N 90 5W
City View, Ont., Canada **192 B1** 45 21N 75 45W
Ciudad Acuña, Coahuila, Mexico **214 A4** 29 18N 100 55W
Ciudad Altamirano, Guerrero, Mexico **219 D7** 18 20N 100 40W
Ciudad Anáhuac, Nuevo León, Mexico **214 C4** 27 14N 100 7W
Ciudad Azteca, México, Mexico **225 A3** 19 31N 99 2W
Ciudad Benito Juárez, Monterrey, Mexico **224 C3** 25 37N 100 8W
Ciudad Camargo, Chihuahua, Mexico **213 F10** 27 40N 105 10W
Ciudad Constitución, Baja Calif. S., Mexico **211 J7** 25 0N 111 42W
Ciudad Cuauhtémoc, Chiapas, Mexico **222 D5** 15 37N 92 0W
Ciudad Cuauhtémoc, Zacatecas, Mexico **217 E8** 22 27N 102 20W
Ciudad de México, Distrito Federal, Mexico **219 C8** 19 24N 99 9W
Ciudad del Carmen, Campeche, Mexico **223 D2** 18 38N 91 50W
Ciudad del Maíz, San Luis Potosí, Mexico **215 H5** 22 24N 99 36W
Ciudad Delicias = Delicias, Chihuahua, Mexico **213 E10** 28 13N 105 28W
Ciudad Deportiva, Distrito Federal, Mexico **225 B3** 19 24N 99 5W
Ciudad Diaz Ordaz, Tamaulipas, Mexico **214 D6** 26 12N 98 28W
Ciudad Fernández, San Luis Potosí, Mexico **215 J4** 21 57N 100 4W
Ciudad Frontera, Coahuila, Mexico **214 D3** 26 56N 101 27W
Ciudad Granja, Jalisco, Mexico **218 B4** 20 39N 103 27W
Ciudad Guerrero, Chihuahua, Mexico **213 E8** 28 33N 107 30W
Ciudad Guerrero, Tamaulipas, Mexico **214 D5** 26 34N 99 15W
Ciudad Guzmán, Jalisco, Mexico **218 C4** 19 41N 103 29W
Ciudad Hidalgo, Chiapas, Mexico **222 E4** 14 41N 92 9W
Ciudad Hidalgo, Michoacan, Mexico **219 C7** 19 41N 100 34W
Ciudad Insurgentes, Baja Calif. S., Mexico **211 H7** 25 13N 111 48W
Ciudad Juárez, Chihuahua, Mexico **213 B9** 31 44N 106 29W
Ciudad Lerdo, Durango, Mexico **217 B7** 25 32N 103 32W
Ciudad López Mateos, México, Mexico **225 A2** 19 33N 99 15W
Ciudad Madero, Tamaulipas, Mexico **215 H7** 22 19N 97 50W
Ciudad Mante, Tamaulipas, Mexico **215 H6** 22 44N 98 59W
Ciudad Mendoza, Veracruz, Mexico **221 F3** 18 48N 97 11W
Ciudad Miguel Alemán, Tamaulipas, Mexico **214 D5** 26 23N 99 2W
Ciudad Nezahualcóyotl, México, Mexico **225 B3** 19 24N 99 1W
Ciudad Obregón, Sonora, Mexico **212 F6** 27 29N 109 56W
Ciudad Porfirio Díaz = Piedras Negras, Coahuila, Mexico **214 B4** 28 42N 100 31W
Ciudad Sahagún, Hidalgo, Mexico **219 C9** 19 52N 98 46W
Ciudad Satélite, México, Mexico **225 A2** 19 30N 99 13W
Ciudad Serdán, Puebla, Mexico **221 F3** 18 59N 97 27W
Ciudad Valles, San Luis Potosí, Mexico **215 J5** 21 59N 99 1W
Ciudad Victoria, Tamaulipas, Mexico **215 G5** 23 44N 99 8W
Civic Center Park, Minneapolis-St. Paul, U.S.A. **113 B1** 44 56N 93 27W
Clackamas, Portland, U.S.A. **116 B2** 45 24N 122 34W

Clackamas →, OR, U.S.A. 94 B3 45 22N 122 36W
Clackamas County ☆, OR, U.S.A. 94 B3 45 15N 122 15W
Claflin, KS, U.S.A. 74 C5 38 31N 98 32W
Claiborne, AL, U.S.A. 60 E3 31 33N 87 31W
Claiborne, MD, U.S.A. 77 B4 38 50N 76 17W
Claiborne, L., LA, U.S.A. 75 B3 32 45N 93 0W
Claiborne County ☆, MS, U.S.A. 81 E3 31 58N 90 59W
Claiborne County ☆, TN, U.S.A. 97 D9 36 27N 83 34W
Claiborne Parish ☆, LA, U.S.A. 75 B2 32 48N 93 4W
Clair Engle L., CA, U.S.A. 64 C4 40 48N 122 46W
Clairambault, L., Qué., Canada 175 C4 54 29N 69 0W
Claire, N.B., Canada 177 D14 47 15N 68 40W
Claire, L., Alta., Canada 189 E10 58 35N 112 5W
Clairmont, Alta., Canada 184 C2 55 16N 118 47W
Clairton, PA, U.S.A. 95 D3 40 18N 79 53W
Clallam Bay, WA, U.S.A. 101 B1 48 15N 124 16W
Clallam County ☆, WA, U.S.A. 101 C2 48 0N 124 0W
Clam Gulch, AK, U.S.A. 61 F10 60 15N 151 23W
Clan Alpine Mts., NV, U.S.A. 85 C3 39 40N 117 55W
Clancy, MT, U.S.A. 83 D6 46 28N 111 59W
Clandonald, Alta., Canada 184 E10 53 34N 110 44W
Clanton, AL, U.S.A. 60 D4 32 51N 86 38W
Clanwilliam, Man., Canada 183 E12 50 22N 99 49W
Clapperton I., Ont., Canada 178 A4 46 0N 82 14W
Clara, MS, U.S.A. 81 E5 31 35N 88 42W
Clara City, MN, U.S.A. 80 F3 44 57N 95 22W
Clare, IA, U.S.A. 73 C4 42 35N 94 21W
Clare, MI, U.S.A. 79 F7 43 49N 84 46W
Clare County ☆, MI, U.S.A. 79 F7 44 0N 84 50W
Claremont, CA, U.S.A. 65 J9 34 6N 117 43W
Claremont, IL, U.S.A. 71 E6 38 43N 87 58W
Claremont, NH, U.S.A. 86 C2 43 23N 72 20W
Claremont, SD, U.S.A. 91 E7 45 40N 98 1W
Claremont, VA, U.S.A. 102 D8 37 14N 76 58W
Claremore, OK, U.S.A. 93 B8 36 19N 95 36W
Clarence, IA, U.S.A. 73 D7 41 53N 91 4W
Clarence, LA, U.S.A. 75 C2 31 49N 93 2W
Clarence, MO, U.S.A. 82 B4 39 45N 92 16W
Clarence, Port, AK, U.S.A. 61 D6 65 15N 166 40W
Clarence Hd., Nunavut, Canada 190 B10 76 47N 77 47W
Clarendon, N.B., Canada 173 H3 45 29N 66 26W
Clarendon, AR, U.S.A. 63 D4 34 42N 91 19W
Clarendon, PA, U.S.A. 95 C3 41 47N 79 6W
Clarendon, TX, U.S.A. 98 C7 34 56N 100 53W
Clarendon County ☆, SC, U.S.A. 90 E5 33 45N 80 10W
Clarenville-Shoal Harbour, Nfld. & L., Canada 174 D6 48 10N 54 1W
Claresholm, Alta., Canada 185 H7 50 2N 113 33W
Clareton, WY, U.S.A. 104 C8 43 42N 104 42W
Clarinda, IA, U.S.A. 73 E3 40 44N 95 2W
Clarington, Ont., Canada 179 D8 43 55N 78 41W
Clarington, OH, U.S.A. 92 D6 39 46N 80 52W
Clarion, IA, U.S.A. 73 C5 42 44N 93 44W
Clarion, PA, U.S.A. 95 C3 41 13N 79 23W
Clarion →, PA, U.S.A. 95 C3 41 7N 79 41W
Clarion County ☆, PA, U.S.A. 95 C3 41 5N 79 40W
Clarissa, MN, U.S.A. 80 D4 46 8N 94 57W
Clarita, OK, U.S.A. 93 D7 34 29N 96 26W
Clark, MO, U.S.A. 82 B4 39 17N 92 21W
Clark, NJ, U.S.A. 87 B2 40 38N 74 18W
Clark, SD, U.S.A. 91 F8 44 53N 97 44W
Clark, WY, U.S.A. 104 B3 44 54N 109 9W
Clark, Pt., Ont., Canada 178 C5 44 4N 81 45W
Clark Canyon Res., MT, U.S.A. 83 F5 44 57N 112 56W
Clark County ☆, AR, U.S.A. 63 E2 33 55N 93 9W
Clark County ☆, ID, U.S.A. 70 E6 44 15N 112 30W
Clark County ☆, IL, U.S.A. 71 D6 39 20N 87 45W
Clark County ☆, IN, U.S.A. 72 E5 38 30N 85 40W
Clark County ☆, KS, U.S.A. 74 D4 37 15N 99 45W
Clark County ☆, KY, U.S.A. 97 C8 38 0N 84 10W
Clark County ☆, MO, U.S.A. 82 A5 40 25N 91 40W
Clark County ☆, NV, U.S.A. 85 F5 36 10N 115 10W
Clark County ☆, OH, U.S.A. 92 D3 39 55N 83 49W
Clark County ☆, SD, U.S.A. 91 F8 44 50N 97 44W
Clark County ☆, WA, U.S.A. 101 E3 45 55N 122 25W
Clark County ☆, WI, U.S.A. 103 D3 44 40N 90 40W
Clark Fork, ID, U.S.A. 70 A2 48 9N 116 11W
Clark Fork →, ID, U.S.A. 70 A2 48 9N 116 15W
Clark Mt., CA, U.S.A. 65 H11 35 32N 115 35W
Clarkdale, AZ, U.S.A. 62 C3 34 46N 112 3W
Clarke City, Qué., Canada 175 C4 50 12N 66 38W
Clarke County ☆, AL, U.S.A. 60 E3 31 42N 87 47W
Clarke County ☆, GA, U.S.A. 68 B3 34 0N 83 15W
Clarke County ☆, IA, U.S.A. 73 E5 41 0N 93 45W
Clarke County ☆, MS, U.S.A. 81 D5 32 2N 88 44W
Clarke County ☆, VA, U.S.A. 102 B7 39 9N 77 59W
Clarke L., Sask., Canada 182 A5 54 24N 106 54W
Clarkesville, GA, U.S.A. 68 B3 34 37N 83 31W
Clarkfield, MN, U.S.A. 80 F3 44 48N 95 48W
Clarkia, ID, U.S.A. 70 B2 47 1N 116 15W
Clarkrange, TN, U.S.A. 97 D7 36 11N 85 1W
Clarks, LA, U.S.A. 75 B3 32 2N 92 8W
Clarks, NE, U.S.A. 84 C8 41 13N 97 50W
Clarks →, KY, U.S.A. 96 C4 37 3N 88 33W
Clarks Fork Yellowstone →, WY, U.S.A. 83 E9 45 32N 108 50W
Clarks Grove, MN, U.S.A. 80 G5 43 46N 93 20W
Clark's Harbour, N.S., Canada 173 K4 43 25N 65 38W
Clarks Hill, IN, U.S.A. 72 C4 40 15N 86 43W
Clarks Hill L. = J. Strom Thurmond L., GA, U.S.A. 68 C4 33 40N 82 12W
Clarks Point, AK, U.S.A. 61 G8 58 51N 158 33W
Clarks Summit, PA, U.S.A. 87 A1 41 30N 75 42W
Clarksburg, MO, U.S.A. 82 C4 38 40N 92 40W
Clarksburg, NJ, U.S.A. 87 B2 40 12N 74 27W
Clarksburg, TN, U.S.A. 96 E4 35 52N 88 24W
Clarksburg, WV, U.S.A. 102 B4 39 17N 80 30W
Clarksdale, MS, U.S.A. 81 B3 34 12N 90 35W
Clarksdale, MO, U.S.A. 82 B2 39 49N 94 33W
Clarkson, KY, U.S.A. 96 C6 37 30N 86 13W
Clarkson, NE, U.S.A. 84 C8 41 43N 97 7W
Clarkston, UT, U.S.A. 100 B3 41 55N 112 3W
Clarkston, WA, U.S.A. 101 D8 46 25N 117 3W
Clarksville, AR, U.S.A. 63 C2 35 28N 93 28W
Clarksville, IN, U.S.A. 72 E5 38 17N 85 45W
Clarksville, IA, U.S.A. 73 C6 42 47N 92 40W
Clarksville, MD, U.S.A. 77 A4 39 12N 76 57W
Clarksville, MI, U.S.A. 79 G6 42 50N 85 15W
Clarksville, MO, U.S.A. 82 B6 39 22N 90 54W
Clarksville, OH, U.S.A. 92 D3 39 24N 83 59W
Clarksville, TN, U.S.A. 96 D5 36 32N 87 21W
Clarksville, TX, U.S.A. 99 D12 33 37N 95 3W
Clarksville, VA, U.S.A. 102 E6 36 37N 78 34W
Clarkton, NC, U.S.A. 90 D7 34 29N 78 39W
Clatonia, NE, U.S.A. 84 D9 40 28N 96 51W
Clatskanie, OR, U.S.A. 94 A2 46 6N 123 12W
Clatsop County ☆, OR, U.S.A. 94 A2 46 0N 123 45W
Claude, TX, U.S.A. 98 B6 35 7N 101 22W
Claxton, GA, U.S.A. 68 D5 32 10N 81 55W
Clay, KY, U.S.A. 96 C5 37 29N 87 49W
Clay, WV, U.S.A. 102 C3 38 28N 81 5W
Clay Center, KS, U.S.A. 74 B6 39 23N 97 8W
Clay Center, NE, U.S.A. 84 D7 40 32N 98 3W
Clay City, IL, U.S.A. 71 E5 38 41N 88 21W
Clay City, IN, U.S.A. 72 D3 39 17N 87 7W
Clay City, KY, U.S.A. 97 C9 37 52N 83 55W
Clay County ☆, AL, U.S.A. 60 C5 33 16N 85 50W
Clay County ☆, AR, U.S.A. 63 B5 36 19N 90 36W
Clay County ☆, FL, U.S.A. 67 B7 30 0N 81 45W
Clay County ☆, GA, U.S.A. 68 E2 31 30N 85 0W
Clay County ☆, IL, U.S.A. 71 E5 38 45N 88 30W
Clay County ☆, IN, U.S.A. 72 D3 39 20N 87 10W
Clay County ☆, IA, U.S.A. 73 B3 43 5N 95 10W
Clay County ☆, KS, U.S.A. 74 B6 39 20N 97 10W
Clay County ☆, KY, U.S.A. 97 C9 37 10N 83 45W
Clay County ☆, MN, U.S.A. 80 D2 46 50N 96 30W
Clay County ☆, MS, U.S.A. 81 C5 33 36N 88 39W
Clay County ☆, MO, U.S.A. 82 B2 39 20N 94 20W
Clay County ☆, NC, U.S.A. 90 C2 35 5N 83 45W
Clay County ☆, NE, U.S.A. 84 D7 40 30N 98 0W
Clay County ☆, SD, U.S.A. 91 H9 43 0N 97 0W
Clay County ☆, TN, U.S.A. 97 D7 36 33N 85 30W
Clay County ☆, TX, U.S.A. 99 D9 33 49N 98 12W
Clay County ☆, WV, U.S.A. 102 C3 38 28N 81 5W
Clay L., Ont., Canada 180 B3 50 3N 93 30W
Clay Springs, AZ, U.S.A. 62 C5 34 22N 110 18W
Claymont, DE, U.S.A. 77 A5 39 48N 75 27W
Claypool, AZ, U.S.A. 62 D5 33 25N 110 51W
Claypool, IN, U.S.A. 72 B5 41 8N 85 53W
Claysville, PA, U.S.A. 95 D2 40 7N 80 25W
Clayton, AL, U.S.A. 60 E5 31 53N 85 27W
Clayton, DE, U.S.A. 77 A5 39 17N 75 38W
Clayton, GA, U.S.A. 68 B3 34 53N 83 23W
Clayton, ID, U.S.A. 70 E4 44 16N 114 24W
Clayton, IL, U.S.A. 71 C3 40 2N 90 54W
Clayton, IN, U.S.A. 72 D4 39 41N 86 31W
Clayton, IA, U.S.A. 73 C7 42 54N 91 9W
Clayton, KS, U.S.A. 74 B3 39 44N 100 11W
Clayton, LA, U.S.A. 75 C4 31 43N 91 33W
Clayton, MO, U.S.A. 82 C6 38 38N 90 19W
Clayton, NC, U.S.A. 90 C7 35 39N 78 28W
Clayton, NJ, U.S.A. 87 C1 39 40N 75 6W
Clayton, NM, U.S.A. 88 A7 36 27N 103 11W
Clayton, NY, U.S.A. 89 A4 44 14N 76 5W
Clayton, OK, U.S.A. 93 D8 34 35N 95 21W
Clayton, WI, U.S.A. 103 C1 45 20N 92 10W
Clayton County ☆, GA, U.S.A. 68 C2 33 30N 84 20W
Clayton County ☆, IA, U.S.A. 73 C7 42 50N 91 20W
Clayton Lake, ME, U.S.A. 76 B4 46 36N 69 32W
Claytor L., VA, U.S.A. 102 D4 37 5N 80 35W
Cle Elum, WA, U.S.A. 101 C5 47 12N 120 56W
Clear →, Alta., Canada 184 B1 56 11N 119 42W
Clear →, AZ, U.S.A. 62 C5 34 59N 110 38W
Clear, L., Ont., Canada 179 B9 45 26N 77 12W
Clear, L., Orlando, U.S.A. 115 A2 28 31N 81 24W
Clear Boggy Cr. →, OK, U.S.A. 93 D8 34 3N 95 47W
Clear Cr. →, WY, U.S.A. 104 B6 44 53N 106 4W
Clear Creek County ☆, CO, U.S.A. 66 C5 39 40N 105 40W
Clear Hills, Canada 184 B1 56 40N 119 30W
Clear L., CA, U.S.A. 64 D4 39 2N 122 47W
Clear L., IA, U.S.A. 73 B5 43 8N 93 26W
Clear L., LA, U.S.A. 75 C3 31 53N 93 0W
Clear L., UT, U.S.A. 100 D3 39 7N 112 38W
Clear Lake, IN, U.S.A. 72 B6 41 44N 84 50W
Clear Lake, IA, U.S.A. 73 B5 43 8N 93 23W
Clear Lake, MN, U.S.A. 80 E5 45 27N 94 0W
Clear Lake, SD, U.S.A. 91 F9 44 45N 96 41W
Clear Lake, WI, U.S.A. 103 C1 45 15N 92 16W
Clear Lake Res., CA, U.S.A. 64 B5 41 56N 121 5W
Clear Spring, MD, U.S.A. 77 A3 39 39N 77 56W
Clearbrook, MN, U.S.A. 80 C3 47 42N 95 26W
Clearco, WV, U.S.A. 102 C4 38 6N 80 34W
Clearfield, IA, U.S.A. 73 E4 40 48N 94 29W
Clearfield, KY, U.S.A. 97 B9 38 10N 83 26W
Clearfield, PA, U.S.A. 95 C4 41 2N 78 27W
Clearfield, UT, U.S.A. 100 B3 41 7N 112 2W
Clearfield County ☆, PA, U.S.A. 95 D4 41 0N 78 35W
Clearlake, CA, U.S.A. 64 E4 38 57N 122 38W
Clearmont, MO, U.S.A. 82 A1 40 31N 95 2W
Clearmont, WY, U.S.A. 104 B6 44 38N 106 23W
Clearview, OK, U.S.A. 93 C7 35 24N 96 11W
Clearwater, B.C., Canada 187 D14 51 38N 120 2W
Clearwater, FL, U.S.A. 67 D6 27 59N 82 48W
Clearwater, KS, U.S.A. 74 D6 37 30N 97 30W
Clearwater, NE, U.S.A. 84 B7 42 10N 98 11W
Clearwater, SC, U.S.A. 90 E4 33 30N 81 54W
Clearwater →, Alta., Canada 184 B9 56 44N 111 23W
Clearwater →, Alta., Canada 185 F6 52 22N 114 57W
Clearwater →, B.C., Canada 187 D14 51 38N 120 3W
Clearwater →, ID, U.S.A. 70 C2 46 31N 116 33W
Clearwater →, MN, U.S.A. 80 C2 47 54N 96 16W
Clearwater Beach Island, Tampa, U.S.A. 119 A2 27 59N 82 49W
Clearwater County ☆, ID, U.S.A. 70 C3 46 50N 115 30W
Clearwater County ☆, MN, U.S.A. 80 C3 47 30N 95 20W
Clearwater L., B.C., Canada 187 C14 52 15N 120 13W
Clearwater L., MO, U.S.A. 82 D6 37 8N 90 47W
Clearwater Lake Prov. Park ⌓, Man., Canada 183 A10 54 0N 101 0W
Clearwater Mts., ID, U.S.A. 70 C3 46 5N 115 20W
Clearwater Nat. Forest, ID, U.S.A. 70 C3 46 40N 115 5W
Cleburne, TX, U.S.A. 99 E10 32 21N 97 23W
Cleburne County ☆, AL, U.S.A. 60 C5 33 39N 85 35W
Cleburne County ☆, AR, U.S.A. 63 C3 35 30N 92 2W
Clem, GA, U.S.A. 68 C1 33 32N 85 1W
Clements, KS, U.S.A. 74 C7 38 18N 96 44W
Clements, MD, U.S.A. 77 B4 38 18N 76 43W
Clements, MN, U.S.A. 80 F4 44 23N 95 3W
Clementsport, N.S., Canada 173 J4 44 40N 65 37W
Clemmons, NC, U.S.A. 90 B5 36 1N 80 23W
Clemson, SC, U.S.A. 90 D3 34 41N 82 50W
Clendenin, WV, U.S.A. 102 C3 38 29N 81 21W
Clendinning Park ⌓, B.C., Canada 186 E11 50 28N 123 44W
Cleo Springs, OK, U.S.A. 93 B5 36 26N 98 29W
Clermont, Qué., Canada 177 D12 47 41N 70 14W
Clermont, FL, U.S.A. 67 C7 28 33N 81 46W
Clermont, IA, U.S.A. 73 C7 43 0N 91 39W
Clermont, NJ, U.S.A. 87 C2 39 59N 74 48W
Clermont County ☆, OH, U.S.A. 92 D2 39 5N 84 11W
Cleveland, AL, U.S.A. 60 C4 33 59N 86 35W
Cleveland, GA, U.S.A. 68 B3 34 36N 83 46W
Cleveland, MN, U.S.A. 80 F5 44 19N 93 50W
Cleveland, MS, U.S.A. 81 C3 33 45N 90 43W
Cleveland, MO, U.S.A. 82 C2 38 41N 94 36W
Cleveland, ND, U.S.A. 91 D6 46 54N 99 6W
Cleveland, OH, U.S.A. 92 B5 41 29N 81 41W
Cleveland, OK, U.S.A. 93 B7 36 19N 96 28W
Cleveland, TN, U.S.A. 97 E8 35 10N 84 53W
Cleveland, TX, U.S.A. 99 G12 30 21N 95 5W
Cleveland, UT, U.S.A. 100 D5 39 21N 110 51W
Cleveland, VA, U.S.A. 102 E2 36 57N 82 9W
Cleveland, WV, U.S.A. 102 C4 38 44N 80 24W
Cleveland, WI, U.S.A. 103 E6 43 55N 87 45W
Cleveland, Mt., MT, U.S.A. 83 B4 48 56N 113 51W
Cleveland County ☆, AR, U.S.A. 63 E3 33 58N 92 11W
Cleveland County ☆, NC, U.S.A. 90 C4 35 20N 81 40W
Cleveland County ☆, OK, U.S.A. 93 C6 35 10N 97 20W
Cleveland Heights, OH, U.S.A. 92 B5 41 31N 81 33W
Cleveland Hopkins International ✕ (CLE), OH, U.S.A. 92 B5 41 25N 81 51W
Cleveland Nat. Forest, CA, U.S.A. 65 L10 32 45N 116 40W
Cleveland Park, Vancouver, Canada 193 A2 49 22N 123 6W
Clever, MO, U.S.A. 82 D3 37 2N 93 28W
Clewiston, FL, U.S.A. 67 E8 26 45N 80 56W
Cliff, NM, U.S.A. 88 E2 32 58N 108 37W
Clifford, MI, U.S.A. 79 F8 43 19N 83 11W
Clifford, ND, U.S.A. 91 C8 47 21N 97 24W
Cliffside Park, NJ, U.S.A. 87 B3 40 49N 73 59W
Clifftop, WV, U.S.A. 102 D4 38 0N 80 56W
Clifton, AZ, U.S.A. 62 D6 33 3N 109 18W
Clifton, Boston, U.S.A. 106 A4 42 29N 70 52W
Clifton, CO, U.S.A. 66 C2 39 7N 108 25W
Clifton, ID, U.S.A. 70 G7 42 11N 112 0W
Clifton, IL, U.S.A. 71 C6 40 56N 87 56W
Clifton, KS, U.S.A. 74 B6 39 34N 97 17W
Clifton, NJ, U.S.A. 87 B2 40 37N 74 4W
Clifton, TN, U.S.A. 96 E4 35 18N 88 1W
Clifton, TX, U.S.A. 99 F10 31 47N 97 35W
Clifton Forge, VA, U.S.A. 102 D5 37 49N 79 50W
Clifton Heights, MO, U.S.A. 117 B2 38 36N 90 17W
Clifton Heights, PA, U.S.A. 116 B1 39 55N 75 17W
Clifton Park, Baltimore, U.S.A. 107 B2 39 19N 76 34W
Clifton Springs, NY, U.S.A. 89 C3 42 58N 77 8W
Cliftondale, Boston, U.S.A. 106 A3 42 26N 71 0W
Clifty, AR, U.S.A. 63 B2 36 14N 93 48W
Climax, Sask., Canada 182 F3 49 10N 108 20W
Climax, CO, U.S.A. 66 C4 39 22N 106 11W
Climax, GA, U.S.A. 68 F2 30 53N 84 26W
Climax, KS, U.S.A. 74 D7 37 43N 96 13W
Climax, MI, U.S.A. 79 G6 42 14N 85 20W
Climax, MN, U.S.A. 80 C2 47 37N 96 49W
Clinch →, TN, U.S.A. 97 E8 35 53N 84 29W
Clinch County ☆, GA, U.S.A. 68 F4 31 0N 82 45W
Clinchco, VA, U.S.A. 102 D2 37 10N 82 22W
Cline, TX, U.S.A. 99 H7 29 15N 100 5W
Clines Corners, NM, U.S.A. 88 B5 35 1N 105 40W
Clingmans Dome, TN, U.S.A. 97 E9 35 34N 83 30W
Clint, TX, U.S.A. 98 F1 31 35N 106 14W
Clinton, B.C., Canada 187 D13 51 6N 121 35W
Clinton, Ont., Canada 178 D5 43 37N 81 32W
Clinton, AL, U.S.A. 60 D3 32 58N 88 0W
Clinton, AR, U.S.A. 63 C3 35 36N 92 28W
Clinton, CT, U.S.A. 78 C2 41 17N 72 32W
Clinton, IL, U.S.A. 71 C5 40 9N 88 57W
Clinton, IN, U.S.A. 72 D3 39 40N 87 24W
Clinton, IA, U.S.A. 73 D8 41 51N 90 12W
Clinton, KY, U.S.A. 96 D4 36 40N 89 0W
Clinton, LA, U.S.A. 75 D4 30 52N 91 1W
Clinton, ME, U.S.A. 76 D4 44 38N 69 30W
Clinton, MA, U.S.A. 78 B3 42 25N 71 41W
Clinton, MD, U.S.A. 77 B4 38 46N 76 54W
Clinton, MI, U.S.A. 79 G8 42 4N 83 58W
Clinton, MN, U.S.A. 80 E2 45 28N 96 26W
Clinton, MS, U.S.A. 81 D3 32 20N 90 20W
Clinton, MO, U.S.A. 82 C3 38 22N 93 46W
Clinton, MT, U.S.A. 83 D4 46 46N 113 43W
Clinton, NC, U.S.A. 90 C7 35 0N 78 22W
Clinton, NJ, U.S.A. 87 B2 40 38N 74 55W
Clinton, NY, U.S.A. 89 B5 43 3N 75 23W
Clinton, OH, U.S.A. 92 C5 40 56N 81 38W
Clinton, OK, U.S.A. 93 C5 35 31N 98 58W
Clinton, SC, U.S.A. 90 D4 34 29N 81 53W
Clinton, TN, U.S.A. 97 D8 36 6N 84 8W
Clinton, UT, U.S.A. 100 B3 41 8N 112 3W
Clinton, WA, U.S.A. 101 C3 47 59N 122 21W
Clinton, WI, U.S.A. 103 F5 42 34N 88 52W
Clinton, L., IL, U.S.A. 71 C5 40 15N 88 45W
Clinton Colden L., N.W.T., Canada 189 D11 63 58N 107 27W
Clinton County ☆, IL, U.S.A. 71 E4 38 35N 89 25W
Clinton County ☆, IN, U.S.A. 72 C4 40 20N 86 30W
Clinton County ☆, IA, U.S.A. 73 D8 41 55N 90 30W
Clinton County ☆, KY, U.S.A. 97 D7 36 45N 85 10W
Clinton County ☆, MI, U.S.A. 79 G7 42 55N 84 40W
Clinton County ☆, MO, U.S.A. 82 B2 39 35N 94 25W
Clinton County ☆, NY, U.S.A. 89 A7 44 50N 73 40W
Clinton County ☆, OH, U.S.A. 92 D3 39 27N 83 50W
Clinton County ☆, PA, U.S.A. 95 C5 41 10N 77 50W
Clinton L., KS, U.S.A. 74 C8 38 55N 95 20W
Clintonville, NY, U.S.A. 86 B1 44 28N 73 35W
Clintonville, WV, U.S.A. 102 D4 37 54N 80 36W
Clintonville, WI, U.S.A. 103 D5 44 37N 88 46W
Clintwood, VA, U.S.A. 102 D2 37 9N 82 28W
Clio, AL, U.S.A. 60 E5 31 43N 85 37W
Clio, IA, U.S.A. 73 E5 40 38N 93 27W
Clio, MI, U.S.A. 79 F8 43 11N 83 44W
Clio, SC, U.S.A. 90 D6 34 35N 79 33W
Clive, Alta., Canada 185 F7 52 28N 113 27W
Clive, IA, U.S.A. 73 D5 41 36N 93 43W
Clontarf, MN, U.S.A. 80 E3 45 23N 95 40W
Cloquet, MN, U.S.A. 80 D6 46 43N 92 28W
Cloquet →, MN, U.S.A. 80 D6 46 52N 92 35W
Cloud County ☆, KS, U.S.A. 74 B6 39 30N 97 45W
Cloud Peak, WY, U.S.A. 104 B5 44 23N 107 11W
Cloudcroft, NM, U.S.A. 88 E5 32 58N 105 45W
Clova, Qué., Canada 176 C7 48 7N 75 22W
Clover, SC, U.S.A. 90 C4 35 7N 81 14W
Clover, VA, U.S.A. 102 E6 36 50N 78 44W
Clover Pt., B.C., Canada 187 G11 48 24N 123 21W
Cloverdale, N.B., Canada 173 G2 46 17N 67 22W
Cloverdale, AL, U.S.A. 60 B3 34 56N 87 46W
Cloverdale, CA, U.S.A. 64 E3 38 48N 123 1W
Cloverdale, IN, U.S.A. 72 D4 39 31N 86 48W
Cloverdale, OH, U.S.A. 92 B2 41 1N 84 18W
Cloverleaf, TX, U.S.A. 99 H12 29 46N 95 10W
Cloverport, KY, U.S.A. 96 C6 37 50N 86 38W
Clovis, CA, U.S.A. 65 G7 36 49N 119 42W
Clovis, NM, U.S.A. 88 C7 34 24N 103 12W
Cloyne, Ont., Canada 179 C9 44 49N 77 11W
Cluculz L., B.C., Canada 186 B11 53 53N 123 33W
Clute, TX, U.S.A. 99 H12 29 1N 95 24W
Clutier, IA, U.S.A. 73 C6 42 4N 92 24W
Clyattville, GA, U.S.A. 68 F3 30 42N 83 19W
Clyde, Alta., Canada 184 D7 54 9N 113 39W
Clyde, KS, U.S.A. 74 B6 39 36N 97 24W
Clyde, NC, U.S.A. 90 C3 35 32N 82 55W
Clyde, NY, U.S.A. 89 B4 43 5N 76 52W
Clyde, OH, U.S.A. 92 B4 41 18N 82 59W
Clyde, TX, U.S.A. 99 E8 32 24N 99 30W
Clyde →, N.S., Canada 173 K4 43 35N 65 27W
Clyde →, VT, U.S.A. 86 B2 44 56N 72 13W
Clyde Hill, Seattle, U.S.A. 118 C4 47 37N 122 13W
Clyde Park, MT, U.S.A. 83 E7 45 52N 110 37W
Clyde River, N.S., Canada 173 K4 43 38N 65 29W
Clyde River, Nunavut, Canada 190 C12 70 30N 68 30W
Clymer, PA, U.S.A. 95 D3 40 40N 79 1W
Clyo, GA, U.S.A. 68 D5 32 29N 81 16W
Coacalco, México, Mexico 219 C8 19 37N 99 7W
Coachella, CA, U.S.A. 65 K10 33 41N 116 10W
Coachella Canal, CA, U.S.A. 65 L12 32 43N 114 57W
Coacoachou, L., Qué., Canada 172 C9 50 25N 60 14W
Coahoma, TX, U.S.A. 98 E6 32 18N 101 18W
Coahoma County ☆, MS, U.S.A. 81 B3 34 12N 90 35W
Coahuayana →, Mexico 218 D4 18 41N 103 45W
Coahuayutla, Michoacan, Mexico 218 D6 18 18N 101 43W
Coahuila □, Mexico 214 C2 27 20N 102 0W
Coal →, Canada 189 E7 59 39N 126 57W
Coal City, IL, U.S.A. 71 B5 41 17N 88 17W
Coal County ☆, OK, U.S.A. 93 D7 34 40N 96 15W
Coal Grove, OH, U.S.A. 92 E4 38 30N 82 39W
Coal Harbour, B.C., Canada 186 E7 50 36N 127 35W
Coal Harbour, Vancouver, Canada 193 B2 49 17N 123 8W
Coal Hill, AR, U.S.A. 63 C2 35 26N 93 40W
Coal Valley, NV, U.S.A. 85 E5 37 57N 115 18W
Coalcomán, Michoacan, Mexico 218 D4 18 47N 103 9W
Coalcomán →, Michoacan, Mexico 218 D4 18 14N 103 14W
Coalcomán, Sa. de, Michoacan, Mexico 218 E5 17 25N 102 55W
Coaldale, Alta., Canada 185 J8 49 45N 112 35W
Coaldale, CO, U.S.A. 66 D5 38 22N 105 45W
Coaldale, NV, U.S.A. 85 D3 38 2N 117 54W
Coalgate, OK, U.S.A. 93 D7 34 32N 96 13W
Coalhurst, Alta., Canada 185 J8 49 45N 112 56W
Coaling, AL, U.S.A. 60 C3 33 10N 87 20W
Coalinga, CA, U.S.A. 65 G6 36 9N 120 21W
Coalmont, B.C., Canada 187 F14 49 32N 120 42W
Coalmont, CO, U.S.A. 66 B4 40 34N 106 27W
Coalmont, TN, U.S.A. 97 E7 35 20N 85 42W
Coalport, PA, U.S.A. 95 D4 40 45N 78 32W
Coalville, UT, U.S.A. 100 C4 40 55N 111 24W
Coamo, Puerto Rico 105 G16 18 5N 66 22W
Coarsegold, CA, U.S.A. 64 F7 37 16N 119 42W
Coast Mts., B.C., Canada 186 B6 55 0N 129 20W
Coast Ranges, CA, U.S.A. 64 D4 39 0N 123 0W
Coast Ranges, OR, U.S.A. 94 D2 44 0N 123 40W
Coatepec, Veracruz, Mexico 220 E4 19 27N 96 58W
Coates, MN, U.S.A. 80 F5 44 43N 93 2W
Coatesville, PA, U.S.A. 95 E7 39 59N 75 50W
Coaticook, Qué., Canada 177 F11 45 10N 71 46W
Coats, KS, U.S.A. 74 D5 37 31N 98 50W
Coats, NC, U.S.A. 90 C7 35 25N 78 40W
Coats I., Nunavut, Canada 191 E9 62 30N 83 0W
Coatzacoalcos, Mexico 221 F6 18 7N 94 25W
Coatzacoalcos →, Veracruz, Mexico 221 F6 18 9N 94 24W
Coatzingo, Puebla, Mexico 221 F2 18 37N 98 11W
Coatzintla, Veracruz, Mexico 220 D3 20 29N 97 27W
Cobá, Quintana Roo, Mexico 223 B6 20 31N 87 45W
Cobalt, Ont., Canada 176 D3 47 25N 79 42W
Cobalt, ID, U.S.A. 70 D4 45 6N 114 14W
Cobaz, L., Qué., Canada 172 B9 51 15N 60 21W
Cobb, CA, U.S.A. 64 E4 38 49N 122 43W
Cobb, KY, U.S.A. 96 D5 36 59N 87 47W
Cobb County ☆, GA, U.S.A. 68 C2 33 50N 84 40W
Cobb Island, MD, U.S.A. 77 B4 38 16N 76 51W
Cobbs Creek Park, PA, U.S.A. 116 B1 39 58N 75 15W
Cobden, Ont., Canada 179 B10 45 38N 76 53W
Cobden, IL, U.S.A. 71 F4 37 32N 89 15W
Cobden, MN, U.S.A. 80 F4 44 17N 94 51W
Cobequid B., N.S., Canada 173 H6 45 21N 63 45W
Cobleskill, NY, U.S.A. 89 C6 42 41N 74 29W
Coboconk, Ont., Canada 179 C8 44 39N 78 48W
Cobourg, Ont., Canada 179 D8 43 58N 78 10W
Cobre, NV, U.S.A. 85 A6 41 7N 114 24W
Coburg, IA, U.S.A. 73 E3 40 55N 95 16W
Coburg, OR, U.S.A. 94 C2 44 8N 123 4W
Coburg I., N.W.T., Canada 190 B10 75 57N 79 26W
Coburn Gore, ME, U.S.A. 76 C3 45 23N 70 48W
Coburn Mt., ME, U.S.A. 76 C3 45 28N 70 6W
Cocagne, N.B., Canada 173 G5 46 20N 64 37W
Cochenour, Ont., Canada 180 A3 51 5N 93 48W
Cochise, AZ, U.S.A. 62 E6 32 7N 109 55W
Cochise County ☆, AZ, U.S.A. 62 F6 32 0N 109 30W
Cochiti Indian Reservation, NM, U.S.A. 88 B4 35 38N 106 22W
Cochituate, Boston, U.S.A. 106 A1 42 20N 71 21W
Cochituate, L., Boston, U.S.A. 106 B1 42 16N 71 21W
Cochran, GA, U.S.A. 68 D3 32 23N 83 21W
Cochran, VA, U.S.A. 102 E7 36 51N 77 54W
Cochran County ☆, TX, U.S.A. 98 D5 33 37N 102 48W
Cochrane, Alta., Canada 185 G6 51 11N 114 30W
Cochrane, Ont., Canada 176 B1 49 0N 81 0W
Cochrane, AL, U.S.A. 60 C2 33 4N 88 15W
Cochrane, WI, U.S.A. 103 D2 44 14N 91 50W
Cochrane →, Man., Canada 189 E12 57 53N 101 34W
Cochranton, PA, U.S.A. 95 C2 41 31N 80 3W
Cochranville, PA, U.S.A. 77 A5 39 54N 75 55W
Cockburn I., Ont., Canada 178 B3 45 55N 83 22W
Cocke County ☆, TN, U.S.A. 97 E9 35 58N 83 11W
Cockeysville, MD, U.S.A. 77 A4 39 29N 76 39W
Cockrell Hill, Dallas-Fort Worth, U.S.A. 109 B4 32 44N 96 53W
Cocoa, FL, U.S.A. 67 C8 28 21N 80 44W
Cocoa Beach, FL, U.S.A. 67 C8 28 19N 80 37W
Cocodrie, LA, U.S.A. 75 E5 29 15N 90 40W
Cocodrie, Bayou →, LA, U.S.A. 75 C4 31 11N 91 41W
Cocohital, Tabasco, Mexico 222 A3 18 23N 93 20W
Cocolalla, ID, U.S.A. 70 A2 48 6N 116 37W
Cocomorachic, Chihuahua, Mexico 213 E8 28 40N 107 55W
Coconino County ☆, AZ, U.S.A. 62 B4 36 0N 112 0W
Coconino Nat. Forest, AZ, U.S.A. 62 C4 34 45N 111 20W
Coconino Plateau, AZ, U.S.A. 62 B3 35 45N 112 40W
Coconut Grove, Miami, U.S.A. 112 D2 25 42N 80 15W
Cocos I., Guam 105 b 13 14N 144 39 E
Cocula, Guerrero, Mexico 219 D8 18 14N 99 40W
Cocula, Jalisco, Mexico 218 B4 20 23N 103 50W
Cod, C., MA, U.S.A. 78 B4 42 5N 70 10W
Cod I., Nfld. & L., Canada 175 B5 57 47N 61 47W
Coderre, Sask., Canada 182 E5 50 11N 106 31W
Codette, Sask., Canada 182 B7 53 16N 104 0W
Codington County ☆, SD, U.S.A. 91 F8 44 54N 97 7W
Codroy, Nfld. & L., Canada 174 E1 47 53N 59 24W
Codroy Pond, Nfld. & L., Canada 174 D2 48 4N 58 52W
Cody, NE, U.S.A. 84 B4 42 56N 101 15W
Cody, WY, U.S.A. 104 B3 44 32N 109 3W
Cody-Rouge, MI, U.S.A. 109 A1 42 21N 83 13W
Coe Hill, Ont., Canada 179 C9 44 52N 77 50W
Coeburn, VA, U.S.A. 102 E2 36 57N 82 28W
Coeneo, Michoacan, Mexico 218 C6 19 50N 101 35W
Coeur d'Alene, ID, U.S.A. 70 B2 47 41N 116 46W
Coeur d'Alene →, ID, U.S.A. 70 B2 47 28N 116 45W
Coeur d'Alene Indian Reservation, ID, U.S.A. 70 B2 47 10N 116 55W
Coeur d'Alene L., ID, U.S.A. 70 B2 47 32N 116 49W
Coeur d'Alene Mts., ID, U.S.A. 70 B2 47 45N 116 0W
Coeur d'Alene Nat. Forest, ID, U.S.A. 70 B2 47 55N 116 15W
Coffee County ☆, AL, U.S.A. 60 E5 31 23N 85 56W
Coffee County ☆, GA, U.S.A. 68 E4 31 30N 82 50W
Coffee County ☆, TN, U.S.A. 97 E6 35 29N 86 5W
Coffeen, IL, U.S.A. 71 D4 39 5N 89 24W
Coffeeville, AL, U.S.A. 60 E2 31 45N 88 5W
Coffeeville, MS, U.S.A. 81 C4 33 59N 89 41W
Coffey, MO, U.S.A. 82 A3 40 6N 94 0W
Coffey County ☆, KS, U.S.A. 74 C8 38 15N 95 45W
Coffeyville, KS, U.S.A. 74 D8 37 2N 95 37W
Cofre de Perote, Cerro, Veracruz, Mexico 220 E3 19 28N 97 0W
Cogar, OK, U.S.A. 93 C5 35 20N 98 8W
Cogdell, GA, U.S.A. 68 E4 31 10N 82 43W
Coggon, IA, U.S.A. 73 C7 42 17N 91 32W
Cogswell, ND, U.S.A. 91 D8 46 7N 97 47W
Cohagen, MT, U.S.A. 83 C11 47 3N 106 37W
Cohansey, NJ, U.S.A. 87 C1 39 21N 75 22W
Cohasset, MA, U.S.A. 78 B4 42 14N 70 48W
Cohasset, MN, U.S.A. 80 C5 47 16N 93 38W
Cohocton →, NY, U.S.A. 89 C3 42 9N 77 6W
Cohoes, NY, U.S.A. 78 B1 42 46N 73 42W
Cohutta, GA, U.S.A. 68 B2 34 58N 84 57W
Coin, IA, U.S.A. 73 E3 40 39N 95 14W
Coixtlahuaca, Oaxaca, Mexico 221 G3 17 45N 97 18W
Cokato, MN, U.S.A. 80 E4 45 5N 94 11W
Coke County ☆, TX, U.S.A. 98 F7 31 54N 100 29W
Coker, AL, U.S.A. 60 C3 33 15N 87 41W
Cokeville, WY, U.S.A. 104 D2 42 5N 110 57W

Colbert, *GA, U.S.A.* **68 B3** 34 2N 83 13W
Colbert, *OK, U.S.A.* **93 E7** 33 51N 96 30W
Colbert County ☆, *AL, U.S.A.* **60 B3** 34 44N 87 42W
Colborne, *Ont., Canada* **179 C9** 44 0N 77 53W
Colbourne, *MD, U.S.A.* **77 B5** 38 15N 75 26W
Colburn, *ID, U.S.A.* **70 A2** 48 24N 116 32W
Colby, *KS, U.S.A.* **74 B2** 39 24N 101 3W
Colby, *Seattle, U.S.A.* **118 C2** 47 31N 122 32W
Colby, *WI, U.S.A.* **103 D3** 44 55N 90 19W
Colchester, *CT, U.S.A.* **78 C2** 41 35N 72 20W
Colchester, *IL, U.S.A.* **71 C3** 40 25N 90 48W
Colchester, *VT, U.S.A.* **86 B1** 44 33N 73 9W
Colcord, *OK, U.S.A.* **93 B9** 36 16N 94 42W
Colcoyán de las Flores, *Oaxaca, Mexico* **221 G2** 17 17N 98 15W
Cold Bay, *AK, U.S.A.* **61 J7** 55 12N 162 42W
Cold L., *Alta., Canada* **184 D10** 54 33N 110 5W
Cold Lake, *Alta., Canada* **184 D10** 54 27N 110 10W
Cold Mt., *NC, U.S.A.* **90 C3** 35 25N 82 51W
Cold Spring, *KY, U.S.A.* **107 B2** 39 1N 84 26W
Cold Spring, *MN, U.S.A.* **80 E4** 45 27N 94 26W
Cold Spring, *NY, U.S.A.* **87 A3** 41 25N 73 57W
Cold Springs Cr. →, *WY, U.S.A.* **104 B8** 44 32N 104 6W
Coldspring, *TX, U.S.A.* **99 G12** 30 36N 95 8W
Coldstream, *B.C., Canada* **187 E15** 50 13N 119 11W
Coldwater, *Ont., Canada* **178 C7** 44 42N 79 40W
Coldwater, *KS, U.S.A.* **74 D4** 37 16N 99 20W
Coldwater, *MI, U.S.A.* **79 H6** 41 57N 85 0W
Coldwater, *MS, U.S.A.* **81 B4** 34 41N 89 59W
Coldwater, *OH, U.S.A.* **92 C2** 40 29N 84 38W
Coldwater →, *MS, U.S.A.* **81 B3** 34 10N 90 13W
Coldwater Cr. →, *OK, U.S.A.* **93 B2** 36 40N 101 10W
Cole, *OK, U.S.A.* **93 C6** 35 8N 97 33W
Cole Camp, *MO, U.S.A.* **82 C3** 38 28N 93 12W
Cole County ☆, *MO, U.S.A.* **82 C4** 38 30N 92 15W
Colebrook, *NH, U.S.A.* **86 B3** 44 54N 71 30W
Coleman, *FL, U.S.A.* **67 C6** 28 48N 82 4W
Coleman, *GA, U.S.A.* **68 E2** 31 40N 84 54W
Coleman, *MI, U.S.A.* **79 F7** 43 46N 84 35W
Coleman, *OK, U.S.A.* **93 D7** 34 16N 96 25W
Coleman, *TX, U.S.A.* **99 F8** 31 50N 99 26W
Coleman, *WI, U.S.A.* **103 C5** 45 4N 88 2W
Coleman County ☆, *TX, U.S.A.* **99 F8** 31 50N 99 30W
Colerain, *NC, U.S.A.* **90 B9** 36 12N 76 46W
Coleraine, *MN, U.S.A.* **80 C5** 47 17N 93 27W
Coleridge, *NE, U.S.A.* **84 B8** 42 30N 97 13W
Coles County ☆, *IL, U.S.A.* **71 D5** 39 30N 88 15W
Coles Point, *VA, U.S.A.* **77 B4** 38 9N 76 38W
Colesburg, *IA, U.S.A.* **73 C7** 42 38N 91 12W
Colesville, *MD, U.S.A.* **77 A4** 39 5N 77 0W
Coleville, *Sask., Canada* **182 D2** 51 43N 109 15W
Coleville, *CA, U.S.A.* **64 E7** 38 34N 119 30W
Colfax, *CA, U.S.A.* **64 D6** 39 6N 120 57W
Colfax, *IL, U.S.A.* **71 C5** 40 34N 88 37W
Colfax, *IN, U.S.A.* **72 C4** 40 12N 86 40W
Colfax, *IA, U.S.A.* **73 D5** 41 41N 93 14W
Colfax, *LA, U.S.A.* **75 C3** 31 31N 92 42W
Colfax, *ND, U.S.A.* **91 D9** 46 28N 96 53W
Colfax, *WA, U.S.A.* **101 D8** 46 53N 117 22W
Colfax, *WI, U.S.A.* **103 C2** 45 0N 91 44W
Colfax County ☆, *NM, U.S.A.* **88 A6** 36 30N 104 30W
Colfax County ☆, *NE, U.S.A.* **84 C8** 41 30N 97 0W
Colgate, *ND, U.S.A.* **91 C8** 47 15N 97 39W
Colima, *Colima, Mexico* **218 C4** 19 14N 103 43W
Colima □, *Mexico* **218 C4** 19 10N 104 0W
Colima, Nevado de, *Jalisco, Mexico* **218 C4** 19 33N 103 38W
Colima, Volcán de, *Mexico* **218 C4** 19 31N 103 38W
Colimilla, *Guadalajara, Mexico* **224 A2** 20 41N 103 12W
Colinet, *Nfld. & L., Canada* **174 E7** 47 13N 53 33W
Colinton, *Alta., Canada* **184 D7** 54 37N 113 15W
Colipa, *Veracruz, Mexico* **220 E4** 19 55N 96 42W
Collbran, *CO, U.S.A.* **66 C3** 39 14N 107 58W
College, *AK, U.S.A.* **61 D11** 64 52N 147 49W
College Corner, *OH, U.S.A.* **92 D2** 39 34N 84 49W
College Heights, *Alta., Canada* **185 F7** 52 28N 113 45W
College Heights, *AR, U.S.A.* **63 E4** 33 35N 91 48W
College Park, *GA, U.S.A.* **68 C2** 33 39N 84 27W
College Park, *MD, U.S.A.* **77 B4** 38 59N 76 55W
College Place, *WA, U.S.A.* **101 D7** 46 3N 118 23W
College Point, *NY, U.S.A.* **114 B3** 40 47N 73 50W
College Station, *TX, U.S.A.* **99 G11** 30 37N 96 21W
Collegedale, *TN, U.S.A.* **97 E7** 35 4N 85 3W
Collegeville, *IN, U.S.A.* **72 C3** 40 56N 87 9W
Collegeville, *PA, U.S.A.* **87 B1** 40 11N 75 27W
Colleton County ☆, *SC, U.S.A.* **90 F5** 33 0N 80 40W
Collette, *N.B., Canada* **173 G4** 46 47N 65 27W
Colleymount, *B.C., Canada* **186 A8** 54 2N 126 19W
Colleyville, *TX, U.S.A.* **109 A3** 32 52N 97 9W
Collier County ☆, *FL, U.S.A.* **67 E7** 26 0N 81 30W
Collierville, *TN, U.S.A.* **96 E3** 35 3N 89 40W
Collin County ☆, *TX, U.S.A.* **99 D11** 33 6N 96 40W
Collingdale, *PA, U.S.A.* **116 B1** 39 54N 75 16W
Collingswood, *U.S.A.* **116 B2** 39 55N 75 4W
Collingsworth County ☆, *TX, U.S.A.* **98 C7** 35 0N 100 15W
Collingwood, *Ont., Canada* **178 C6** 44 29N 80 13W
Collingwood Corner, *Qué., Canada* **173 H6** 45 37N 63 56W
Collins, *Ont., Canada* **180 B7** 50 17N 89 27W
Collins, *AR, U.S.A.* **63 E4** 33 32N 91 34W
Collins, *GA, U.S.A.* **68 D4** 32 11N 82 7W
Collins, *IA, U.S.A.* **73 D5** 41 54N 93 18W
Collins, *MS, U.S.A.* **81 E4** 31 39N 89 33W
Collins, *MO, U.S.A.* **82 D3** 37 54N 93 37W
Collins →, *TN, U.S.A.* **97 E7** 35 23N 85 34W
Collinson Pen., *N.W.T., Canada* **190 D5** 69 58N 101 24W
Collinston, *LA, U.S.A.* **75 B4** 32 41N 91 52W
Collinsville, *AL, U.S.A.* **60 B5** 34 16N 85 52W
Collinsville, *CT, U.S.A.* **78 C2** 41 49N 72 55W
Collinsville, *IL, U.S.A.* **71 E4** 38 40N 89 59W
Collinsville, *MS, U.S.A.* **81 D5** 32 30N 88 51W
Collinsville, *OK, U.S.A.* **93 B8** 36 22N 95 51W
Collinsville, *TX, U.S.A.* **99 D11** 33 34N 96 55W
Collinsville, *VA, U.S.A.* **102 E5** 36 43N 79 55W
Collinwood, *TN, U.S.A.* **96 E5** 35 10N 87 44W
Collison, *IL, U.S.A.* **71 C6** 40 14N 87 48W
Collyer, *KS, U.S.A.* **74 B3** 39 2N 100 7W
Colma, *San Francisco, U.S.A.* **118 B2** 37 40N 122 27W
Colman, *SD, U.S.A.* **91 G9** 43 59N 96 49W
Colmesneil, *TX, U.S.A.* **99 G13** 30 54N 94 25W
Colo, *IA, U.S.A.* **73 C5** 42 1N 93 19W
Coloma, *CA, U.S.A.* **64 E6** 38 48N 120 53W
Coloma, *MI, U.S.A.* **79 G5** 42 11N 86 19W
Coloma, *WI, U.S.A.* **103 D4** 44 2N 89 31W
Colombia, *Nuevo León, Mexico* **214 C5** 27 42N 99 45W
Colombier, *Qué., Canada* **177 C14** 48 52N 68 51W
Colome, *SD, U.S.A.* **91 G6** 43 16N 99 43W
Colón, *Querétaro, Mexico* **219 B7** 20 48N 100 3W
Colon, *MI, U.S.A.* **79 H6** 41 57N 85 19W
Colon, *NE, U.S.A.* **84 C9** 41 18N 96 37W
Colona, *CO, U.S.A.* **66 D3** 38 20N 107 47W
Colona, *IL, U.S.A.* **71 B3** 41 29N 90 21W
Colonet, C., *Baja Calif., Mexico* **210 C2** 30 57N 116 19W
Colonia, *NJ, U.S.A.* **114 C1** 40 34N 74 18W
Colonia la Venta, *Distrito Federal, Mexico* **225 B2** 19 20N 99 19W
Colonial Beach, *VA, U.S.A.* **77 B4** 38 15N 76 58W
Colonial Heights, *TN, U.S.A.* **97 D10** 36 29N 82 30W
Colonial Heights, *VA, U.S.A.* **102 D7** 37 15N 77 25W
Colonial Nat. Historical Park ⌂, *VA, U.S.A.* **102 D8** 37 13N 76 31W
Colonie, *NY, U.S.A.* **89 C7** 42 43N 73 50W
Colonsay, *Sask., Canada* **182 D6** 51 59N 105 52W
Colony, *KS, U.S.A.* **74 C8** 38 4N 95 22W
Colony, *OK, U.S.A.* **93 C5** 35 23N 98 41W
Colorada, L., *Coahuila, Mexico* **213 F12** 27 32N 103 40W
Colorado □, *U.S.A.* **66 C5** 39 30N 105 30W
Colorado →, *Baja Calif., Mexico* **210 B4** 31 54N 114 57W
Colorado →, *N. Amer.* **52 D4** 31 45N 114 40W
Colorado →, *TX, U.S.A.* **99 J12** 28 36N 95 59W
Colorado, Cerro, *Baja Calif., Mexico* **210 B3** 31 28N 115 32W
Colorado, Sa., *Coahuila, Mexico* **214 B2** 28 2N 102 13W
Colorado City, *AZ, U.S.A.* **62 A3** 36 59N 112 59W
Colorado City, *TX, U.S.A.* **98 E7** 32 24N 100 52W
Colorado County ☆, *TX, U.S.A.* **99 H11** 29 42N 96 33W
Colorado Nat. Monument ⌂, *CO, U.S.A.* **66 C2** 39 4N 108 42W
Colorado Plateau, *AZ, U.S.A.* **62 A5** 37 0N 111 0W
Colorado River Aqueduct, *CA, U.S.A.* **65 K9** 33 50N 117 23W
Colorado River Indian Reservation, *AZ, U.S.A.* **62 D1** 33 55N 114 25W
Colorado Springs, *CO, U.S.A.* **66 D6** 38 50N 104 49W
Colorado Springs Peterson Field ✕ (COS), *CO, U.S.A.* **66 D6** 38 49N 104 43W
Colotlán, *Jalisco, Mexico* **217 E7** 22 6N 103 16W
Colquitt, *GA, U.S.A.* **68 E2** 31 10N 84 44W
Colquitt County ☆, *GA, U.S.A.* **68 E3** 31 15N 83 50W
Colquitz, *B.C., Canada* **187 G11** 48 29N 123 24W
Colrain, *MA, U.S.A.* **78 B2** 42 41N 72 42W
Colstrip, *MT, U.S.A.* **83 E11** 45 53N 106 38W
Colt, *AR, U.S.A.* **63 C5** 35 8N 90 49W
Colter Bay Village, *WY, U.S.A.* **104 C2** 43 54N 110 38W
Colter Peak, *WY, U.S.A.* **104 B2** 44 18N 110 7W
Colton, *CA, U.S.A.* **65 J9** 34 4N 117 20W
Colton, *NY, U.S.A.* **89 A6** 44 33N 74 56W
Colton, *SD, U.S.A.* **91 G9** 43 47N 96 56W
Colton, *UT, U.S.A.* **100 D5** 39 51N 111 0W
Colton, *WA, U.S.A.* **101 D8** 46 34N 117 8W
Colts Neck, *NJ, U.S.A.* **87 B2** 40 17N 74 11W
Columbia, *AL, U.S.A.* **60 E5** 31 18N 85 7W
Columbia, *CT, U.S.A.* **78 C2** 41 42N 72 18W
Columbia, *IL, U.S.A.* **71 E3** 38 27N 90 12W
Columbia, *KY, U.S.A.* **97 C7** 37 6N 85 18W
Columbia, *LA, U.S.A.* **75 B3** 32 6N 92 5W
Columbia, *MD, U.S.A.* **77 A4** 39 14N 76 50W
Columbia, *MS, U.S.A.* **81 E4** 31 15N 89 50W
Columbia, *MO, U.S.A.* **82 C4** 38 57N 92 20W
Columbia, *NC, U.S.A.* **90 C9** 35 55N 76 15W
Columbia, *NJ, U.S.A.* **87 B1** 40 56N 75 6W
Columbia, *PA, U.S.A.* **95 D6** 40 2N 76 30W
Columbia, *SC, U.S.A.* **90 D4** 34 0N 81 2W
Columbia, *SD, U.S.A.* **91 E7** 45 37N 98 19W
Columbia, *TN, U.S.A.* **96 E5** 35 37N 87 2W
Columbia →, *N. Amer.* **101 D1** 46 15N 124 5W
Columbia, C., *Nunavut, Canada* **190 A12** 83 6N 69 57W
Columbia, District of □, *U.S.A.* **77 B4** 38 55N 77 0W
Columbia, Mt., *B.C., Canada* **187 C17** 52 8N 117 20W
Columbia Basin, *WA, U.S.A.* **101 D6** 46 45N 119 5W
Columbia Bottom, *MO, U.S.A.* **117 A3** 38 48N 90 9W
Columbia City, *IN, U.S.A.* **72 B5** 41 10N 85 29W
Columbia City, *OR, U.S.A.* **94 B3** 45 53N 122 49W
Columbia County ☆, *AR, U.S.A.* **63 E2** 33 16N 93 14W
Columbia County ☆, *FL, U.S.A.* **67 A6** 30 15N 82 40W
Columbia County ☆, *GA, U.S.A.* **68 C4** 33 30N 82 10W
Columbia County ☆, *NY, U.S.A.* **89 C7** 42 10N 73 40W
Columbia County ☆, *OR, U.S.A.* **94 B2** 45 55N 123 0W
Columbia County ☆, *PA, U.S.A.* **95 C6** 41 10N 76 20W
Columbia County ☆, *WA, U.S.A.* **101 D8** 46 19N 117 59W
Columbia County ☆, *WI, U.S.A.* **103 E4** 43 30N 89 20W
Columbia Edgewater, *Portland, U.S.A.* **116 A2** 45 35N 122 48W
Columbia Falls, *ME, U.S.A.* **76 D6** 44 39N 67 44W
Columbia Falls, *MT, U.S.A.* **83 B3** 48 23N 114 11W
Columbia Heights, *MN, U.S.A.* **80 E5** 45 2N 93 14W
Columbia L., *B.C., Canada* **185 H5** 50 15N 115 52W
Columbia Mts., *B.C., Canada* **187 D16** 51 0N 118 0W
Columbia Park, *Minneapolis-St. Paul, U.S.A.* **113 A2** 45 1N 93 15W
Columbia Plateau, *U.S.A.* **58 D5** 44 0N 117 30W
Columbia River Gorge Nat. Scenic Area ⌂, *WA, U.S.A.* **101 E4** 45 42N 121 55W
Columbia Road Res., *SD, U.S.A.* **91 E7** 45 40N 98 18W
Columbiana, *AL, U.S.A.* **60 C4** 33 11N 86 36W
Columbiana, *OH, U.S.A.* **92 C6** 40 53N 80 42W
Columbiana County ☆, *OH, U.S.A.* **92 C6** 40 46N 80 46W
Columbiaville, *MI, U.S.A.* **79 F8** 43 9N 83 25W
Columbine, *CO, U.S.A.* **66 B4** 40 56N 106 59W
Columbine Valley, *Denver, U.S.A.* **109 C1** 39 36N 105 1W
Columbus, *GA, U.S.A.* **68 D2** 32 28N 84 59W
Columbus, *IN, U.S.A.* **72 D5** 39 13N 85 55W
Columbus, *KS, U.S.A.* **74 D9** 37 10N 94 50W
Columbus, *KY, U.S.A.* **96 D3** 36 46N 89 6W
Columbus, *MS, U.S.A.* **81 C5** 33 30N 88 25W
Columbus, *MT, U.S.A.* **83 E8** 45 38N 109 15W
Columbus, *NC, U.S.A.* **90 C3** 35 15N 82 12W
Columbus, *ND, U.S.A.* **91 B3** 48 54N 102 47W
Columbus, *NM, U.S.A.* **88 F3** 31 50N 107 38W
Columbus, *NE, U.S.A.* **84 C8** 41 26N 97 22W
Columbus, *OH, U.S.A.* **92 D3** 39 58N 83 0W
Columbus, *TX, U.S.A.* **99 H11** 29 42N 96 33W
Columbus, *WI, U.S.A.* **103 E4** 43 21N 89 1W
Columbus Air Force Base, *MS, U.S.A.* **81 C5** 33 31N 88 28W
Columbus County ☆, *NC, U.S.A.* **90 D7** 34 15N 78 45W
Columbus Grove, *OH, U.S.A.* **92 C2** 40 55N 84 4W
Columbus Junction, *IA, U.S.A.* **73 D7** 41 17N 91 22W
Columbus L., *MS, U.S.A.* **81 C5** 33 31N 88 29W
Columbus Port Columbus International ✕ (CMH), *OH, U.S.A.* **92 D4** 40 0N 82 53W
Columbus Salt Marsh, *NV, U.S.A.* **85 D2** 38 5N 118 5W
Colusa, *CA, U.S.A.* **64 D4** 39 13N 122 1W
Colusa County ☆, *CA, U.S.A.* **64 D4** 39 15N 122 15W
Colville, *WA, U.S.A.* **101 B8** 48 33N 117 54W
Colville →, *AK, U.S.A.* **61 A10** 70 25N 150 30W
Colville →, *WA, U.S.A.* **101 B7** 48 37N 118 5W
Colville Indian Reservation, *WA, U.S.A.* **101 B7** 48 15N 119 0W
Colville L., *N.W.T., Canada* **188 C7** 67 2N 126 7W
Colville Lake, *N.W.T., Canada* **188 C7** 67 2N 126 7W
Colville Nat. Forest, *WA, U.S.A.* **101 B8** 48 50N 117 15W
Colvos Passage, *Seattle, U.S.A.* **118 D2** 47 29N 122 31W
Colwell, *IA, U.S.A.* **73 B6** 43 9N 92 36W
Colwich, *KS, U.S.A.* **74 D6** 37 47N 97 32W
Colwood, *B.C., Canada* **187 G11** 48 26N 123 29W
Colwyn, *PA, U.S.A.* **116 B1** 39 54N 75 15W
Comal County ☆, *TX, U.S.A.* **99 H9** 29 53N 98 25W
Comala, *Colima, Mexico* **218 C4** 19 19N 103 45W
Comalcalco, *Tabasco, Mexico* **222 A3** 18 16N 93 13W
Comanche, *OK, U.S.A.* **93 D6** 34 22N 97 58W
Comanche, *TX, U.S.A.* **99 F9** 31 54N 98 36W
Comanche County ☆, *KS, U.S.A.* **74 D4** 37 15N 99 15W
Comanche County ☆, *OK, U.S.A.* **93 D5** 34 40N 98 25W
Comanche County ☆, *TX, U.S.A.* **99 F9** 31 55N 98 35W
Comanche Nat. Grassland, *CO, U.S.A.* **66 E8** 37 20N 103 0W
Combahee →, *SC, U.S.A.* **90 F5** 32 31N 80 31W
Comber, *Ont., Canada* **178 E4** 42 14N 82 33W
Combermere, *Ont., Canada* **179 B9** 45 22N 77 37W
Come By Chance, *Nfld. & L., Canada* **174 E6** 47 51N 54 0W
Comer, *AL, U.S.A.* **60 D5** 32 2N 85 23W
Comer, *GA, U.S.A.* **68 B3** 34 4N 83 8W
Comerío, *Puerto Rico* **105 G16** 18 12N 66 12W
Cometa, Pta., *Oaxaca, Mexico* **221 J4** 15 41N 96 35W
Comfort, *TX, U.S.A.* **99 H9** 29 58N 98 55W
Comfrey, *MN, U.S.A.* **80 F4** 44 7N 94 54W
Comitán de Domínguez, *Chiapas, Mexico* **222 C4** 16 15N 92 8W
Commack, *NY, U.S.A.* **87 B3** 40 51N 73 18W
Commanda, *Ont., Canada* **178 B7** 45 57N 79 36W
Commerce, *GA, U.S.A.* **68 B3** 34 12N 83 28W
Commerce, *Los Angeles, U.S.A.* **111 B4** 34 0N 118 9W
Commerce, *MO, U.S.A.* **82 D7** 37 9N 89 27W
Commerce, *OK, U.S.A.* **93 B9** 36 56N 94 53W
Commerce, *TX, U.S.A.* **99 D12** 33 15N 95 54W
Commerce City, *CO, U.S.A.* **66 C6** 39 48N 104 56W
Commissaires, L. des, *Qué., Canada* **177 C10** 48 10N 72 16W
Commissioner I., *Man., Canada* **183 C14** 52 10N 97 16W
Committee B., *Nunavut, Canada* **190 D8** 68 30N 86 30W
Como, *CO, U.S.A.* **66 C5** 39 19N 105 54W
Como, *MS, U.S.A.* **81 B4** 34 31N 89 56W
Como, *TX, U.S.A.* **99 D12** 33 3N 95 28W
Como Park, *Minneapolis-St. Paul, U.S.A.* **113 B3** 44 58N 93 9W
Comobabi Mts., *AZ, U.S.A.* **62 E4** 32 0N 111 45W
Comonfort, *Guanajuato, Mexico* **219 B7** 20 43N 100 46W
Comox, *B.C., Canada* **186 F10** 49 42N 124 55W
Compass Lake, *FL, U.S.A.* **67 A3** 30 36N 85 24W
Compeer, *Alta., Canada* **185 G10** 51 52N 110 0W
Competition, *MO, U.S.A.* **82 D4** 37 29N 92 26W
Compostela, *Nayarit, Mexico* **216 F6** 21 14N 104 55W
Comptche, *CA, U.S.A.* **64 D3** 39 16N 123 35W
Compton, *Qué., Canada* **177 F11** 45 14N 71 49W
Compton, *AR, U.S.A.* **63 B2** 36 6N 93 18W
Compton, *CA, U.S.A.* **65 K8** 33 53N 118 13W
Comstock, *MN, U.S.A.* **80 D2** 46 40N 96 45W
Comstock, *NE, U.S.A.* **84 C6** 41 34N 99 15W
Comstock, *TX, U.S.A.* **98 H6** 29 41N 101 10W
Comstock Park, *MI, U.S.A.* **79 F6** 43 2N 85 40W
Conanicut I., *RI, U.S.A.* **78 C3** 41 32N 71 21W
Conasauga →, *GA, U.S.A.* **68 B2** 34 33N 84 55W
Concan, *TX, U.S.A.* **99 H8** 29 30N 99 43W
Concepción, B., *Baja Calif. S., Mexico* **211 G7** 26 39N 111 48W
Concepción, Pta., *Baja Calif. S., Mexico* **211 G7** 26 53N 111 50W
Concepción de Buenos Aires, *Jalisco, Mexico* **218 C4** 19 58N 103 16W
Concepción del Oro, *Zacatecas, Mexico* **217 C9** 24 38N 101 25W
Conception, Pt., *CA, U.S.A.* **65 J6** 34 27N 120 28W
Conception B., *Nfld. & L., Canada* **174 E8** 47 45N 53 0W
Conception Junction, *MO, U.S.A.* **82 A2** 40 16N 94 42W
Conchas →, *NM, U.S.A.* **88 B6** 35 23N 104 18W
Conchas Dam, *NM, U.S.A.* **88 B6** 35 22N 104 11W
Conchas Lake, *NM, U.S.A.* **88 B6** 35 23N 104 11W
Conche, *Nfld. & L., Canada* **174 B5** 50 55N 55 58W
Concheño →, *Chihuahua, Mexico* **213 E7** 28 3N 108 23W
Concho, *AZ, U.S.A.* **62 C6** 34 28N 109 36W
Concho →, *TX, U.S.A.* **99 F8** 31 34N 99 43W
Concho County ☆, *TX, U.S.A.* **99 F8** 31 13N 99 51W
Conchos →, *Chihuahua, Mexico* **213 D11** 29 35N 104 25W
Conchos →, *Tamaulipas, Mexico* **215 F7** 24 55N 97 38W
Conconully, *WA, U.S.A.* **101 B6** 48 34N 119 45W
Concord, *AR, U.S.A.* **63 C4** 35 40N 91 51W
Concord, *CA, U.S.A.* **64 F4** 37 59N 122 2W
Concord, *GA, U.S.A.* **68 C2** 33 5N 84 27W
Concord, *MA, U.S.A.* **78 B3** 42 27N 71 20W
Concord, *MD, U.S.A.* **77 B5** 38 38N 75 48W
Concord, *MI, U.S.A.* **79 G7** 42 11N 84 38W
Concord, *MO, U.S.A.* **82 C6** 38 32N 90 23W
Concord, *NC, U.S.A.* **90 C5** 35 25N 80 35W
Concord, *NH, U.S.A.* **86 C3** 43 12N 71 32W
Concord, *VT, U.S.A.* **86 B3** 44 26N 71 53W
Concordia, *Sinaloa, Mexico* **216 D4** 23 17N 106 4W
Concordia, *KS, U.S.A.* **74 B6** 39 34N 97 40W
Concordia, *MO, U.S.A.* **82 C3** 38 59N 93 34W
Concordia Parish ☆, *LA, U.S.A.* **75 C4** 31 38N 91 33W
Concrete, *WA, U.S.A.* **101 B4** 48 32N 121 45W
Conda, *ID, U.S.A.* **70 G7** 42 44N 111 32W
Condado de Sayavedra, *México, Mexico* **225 A2** 19 34N 99 20W
Conde, *SD, U.S.A.* **91 E7** 45 9N 98 6W
Condon, *MT, U.S.A.* **83 C4** 47 34N 113 45W
Condon, *OR, U.S.A.* **94 B5** 45 14N 120 11W
Conecuh →, *FL, U.S.A.* **67 A1** 30 58N 87 13W
Conecuh County ☆, *AL, U.S.A.* **60 E4** 31 26N 86 57W
Conecuh Nat. Forest, *AL, U.S.A.* **60 E4** 31 2N 86 45W
Conejos, *Durango, Mexico* **217 A7** 26 14N 103 53W
Conejos, *CO, U.S.A.* **66 E4** 37 5N 106 1W
Conejos →, *CO, U.S.A.* **66 E5** 37 18N 105 44W
Conejos County ☆, *CO, U.S.A.* **66 E4** 37 10N 106 10W
Conesville, *IA, U.S.A.* **73 D7** 41 23N 91 21W
Coneto de Comonfort, *Durango, Mexico* **217 C6** 24 58N 104 45W
Coney Island, *NY, U.S.A.* **114 C3** 40 34N 74 0W
Confluence, *PA, U.S.A.* **77 A1** 39 49N 79 21W
Confusion Range, *UT, U.S.A.* **100 D2** 39 20N 113 40W
Congaree →, *SC, U.S.A.* **90 E5** 33 44N 80 38W
Congaree Swamp Nat. Monument ⌂, *U.S.A.* **90 E5** 33 47N 80 47W
Conger, *MN, U.S.A.* **80 G5** 43 37N 93 32W
Congress, *AZ, U.S.A.* **62 C3** 34 9N 112 51W
Congress, *OH, U.S.A.* **92 C4** 40 56N 82 3W
Conicarit, *Sonora, Mexico* **212 F6** 27 12N 109 7W
Conifer, *CO, U.S.A.* **66 C5** 39 31N 105 18W
Coniston, *Ont., Canada* **178 A6** 46 29N 80 51W
Conkal, *Yucatán, Mexico* **223 A4** 21 4N 89 32W
Conklin, *Alta., Canada* **184 C9** 55 38N 111 5W
Conklin, *NY, U.S.A.* **89 C5** 42 2N 75 49W
Conlen, *TX, U.S.A.* **98 A5** 36 14N 102 15W
Conn L., *Nunavut, Canada* **190 C11** 70 32N 73 34W
Conneaut, *OH, U.S.A.* **92 B6** 41 57N 80 34W
Conneaut Lake, *PA, U.S.A.* **95 C2** 41 36N 80 18W
Conneautville, *PA, U.S.A.* **95 C2** 41 45N 80 22W
Connecticut □, *U.S.A.* **78 C2** 41 30N 72 45W
Connecticut →, *CT, U.S.A.* **78 C2** 41 16N 72 20W
Connell, *WA, U.S.A.* **101 D7** 46 40N 118 52W
Connellsville, *PA, U.S.A.* **95 D3** 40 1N 79 35W
Conner, *MI, U.S.A.* **109 A3** 42 26N 83 0W
Conner, *MT, U.S.A.* **83 E3** 45 56N 114 7W
Connersville, *IN, U.S.A.* **72 D5** 39 39N 85 8W
Connerville, *OK, U.S.A.* **93 D7** 34 27N 96 38W
Connors, *N.B., Canada* **177 D14** 47 10N 68 50W
Cono, Pta., *Baja Calif., Mexico* **210 E4** 28 59N 114 37W
Conover, *NC, U.S.A.* **90 C4** 35 42N 81 13W
Conowingo, *MD, U.S.A.* **77 A4** 39 40N 76 11W
Conquest, *Sask., Canada* **182 D4** 51 32N 107 14W
Conquista Campesina, *Campeche, Mexico* **223 D2** 18 10N 91 15W
Conrad, *IA, U.S.A.* **73 C6** 42 14N 92 52W
Conrad, *MT, U.S.A.* **83 B6** 48 10N 111 57W
Conrath, *WI, U.S.A.* **103 C2** 45 22N 91 2W
Conroe, *TX, U.S.A.* **99 G12** 30 19N 95 27W
Conroe, L., *TX, U.S.A.* **99 G12** 30 21N 95 37W
Consecon, *Ont., Canada* **179 D9** 44 0N 77 31W
Conshohocken, *PA, U.S.A.* **87 B1** 40 4N 75 18W
Consort, *Alta., Canada* **185 F10** 52 1N 110 46W
Constance, *KY, U.S.A.* **107 B1** 39 4N 84 38W
Constantine, *MI, U.S.A.* **79 H6** 41 50N 85 40W
Constantine, C., *AK, U.S.A.* **61 G8** 58 24N 158 54W
Constitución de 1857, Parque Nacional △, *Baja Calif., Mexico* **210 A3** 32 10N 116 2W
Constitution, *Atlanta, U.S.A.* **106 B2** 33 42N 84 20W
Consul, *Sask., Canada* **182 F2** 49 20N 109 30W
Contact, *NV, U.S.A.* **85 A6** 41 46N 114 45W
Contepec, *Michoacan, Mexico* **219 C7** 19 57N 100 9W
Continental, *OH, U.S.A.* **92 B2** 41 6N 84 16W
Continental Divide, *NM, U.S.A.* **88 B2** 35 25N 108 19W
Continental L., *NV, U.S.A.* **85 A2** 41 54N 118 43W
Contla, *Tlaxcala, Mexico* **219 C9** 19 20N 98 9W
Contoocook, *NH, U.S.A.* **86 C3** 43 12N 71 45W
Contoocook →, *NH, U.S.A.* **86 C3** 43 27N 71 35W
Contoy, I., *Quintana Roo, Mexico* **223 A7** 21 30N 86 48W
Contra Costa County ☆, *CA, U.S.A.* **64 F5** 37 50N 121 50W
Contrecoeur, *Qué., Canada* **177 F9** 45 51N 73 14W
Contreras, *NM, U.S.A.* **88 C4** 34 23N 106 49W
Controller B., *AK, U.S.A.* **61 F11** 60 7N 144 15W
Contwoyto L., *N.W.T., Canada* **189 C10** 65 42N 110 50W
Convent, *LA, U.S.A.* **75 D5** 30 1N 90 50W
Converse, *IN, U.S.A.* **72 C5** 40 35N 85 52W
Converse, *LA, U.S.A.* **75 C2** 31 47N 93 42W
Converse, *San Antonio, U.S.A.* **117 B4** 29 31N 98 18W
Converse County ☆, *WY, U.S.A.* **104 D7** 43 0N 105 45W
Convoy, *OH, U.S.A.* **92 C2** 40 55N 84 43W
Conway, *AR, U.S.A.* **63 C3** 35 5N 92 26W
Conway, *FL, U.S.A.* **67 C7** 28 30N 81 19W
Conway, *KS, U.S.A.* **74 C6** 38 22N 97 47W
Conway, *MO, U.S.A.* **82 D4** 37 30N 92 49W
Conway, *NC, U.S.A.* **90 B8** 36 26N 77 14W
Conway, *ND, U.S.A.* **91 B8** 48 14N 97 41W
Conway, *NH, U.S.A.* **86 C3** 43 59N 71 7W
Conway, *SC, U.S.A.* **90 E6** 33 51N 79 3W
Conway, *TX, U.S.A.* **98 B6** 35 13N 101 23W
Conway, L., *AR, U.S.A.* **63 D3** 34 58N 92 25W
Conway, L., *Orlando, U.S.A.* **115 B2** 28 28N 81 21W
Conway County ☆, *AR, U.S.A.* **63 C3** 35 10N 92 38W
Conway Springs, *KS, U.S.A.* **74 D6** 37 24N 97 39W
Conyers, *GA, U.S.A.* **68 C2** 33 40N 84 1W
Cook, *MN, U.S.A.* **80 C6** 47 51N 92 41W
Cook, *NE, U.S.A.* **84 D9** 40 31N 96 10W
Cook, C., *B.C., Canada* **186 E7** 50 8N 127 55W
Cook County ☆, *GA, U.S.A.* **68 E3** 31 10N 83 30W
Cook County ☆, *IL, U.S.A.* **71 B6** 41 50N 87 45W
Cook County ☆, *MN, U.S.A.* **80 C8** 47 50N 90 30W
Cook Forest State Park ⌂, *PA, U.S.A.* **95 C3** 41 19N 79 9W
Cook Inlet, *AK, U.S.A.* **61 G10** 60 0N 152 0W
Cooke City, *MT, U.S.A.* **83 E8** 45 1N 109 56W
Cooke County ☆, *TX, U.S.A.* **99 D10** 33 38N 97 8W
Cookes Peak, *NM, U.S.A.* **88 E3** 32 32N 107 44W
Cookeville, *TN, U.S.A.* **97 D7** 36 10N 85 30W
Cooking L., *Alta., Canada* **184 E7** 53 26N 113 2W
Cooks, *MI, U.S.A.* **79 D5** 45 55N 86 29W
Cooks Hammock, *FL, U.S.A.* **67 B5** 29 56N 83 17W
Cook's Harbour, *Nfld. & L., Canada* **174 A5** 51 36N 55 52W
Cookshire, *Qué., Canada* **177 F11** 45 25N 71 38W
Cooksville, *IL, U.S.A.* **71 C5** 40 33N 88 43W
Cool, *TX, U.S.A.* **99 E9** 32 49N 98 1W
Cool Valley, *MO, U.S.A.* **117 A2** 38 43N 90 18W
Cooleemee, *NC, U.S.A.* **90 C5** 35 49N 80 33W
Coolidge, *AZ, U.S.A.* **62 E4** 32 59N 111 31W
Coolidge, *GA, U.S.A.* **68 E3** 31 1N 83 52W
Coolidge, *KS, U.S.A.* **74 C1** 38 3N 102 1W
Coolidge, *TX, U.S.A.* **99 F11** 31 45N 96 39W
Coolidge Dam, *AZ, U.S.A.* **62 D5** 33 10N 110 32W
Coolin, *ID, U.S.A.* **70 A2** 48 29N 116 51W
Coolville, *OH, U.S.A.* **92 D5** 39 13N 81 48W
Coombs, *B.C., Canada* **186 F10** 49 18N 124 25W
Coon Rapids, *IA, U.S.A.* **73 D4** 41 53N 94 41W
Coon Rapids, *MN, U.S.A.* **80 E5** 45 9N 93 19W
Coon Valley, *WI, U.S.A.* **103 E2** 43 42N 91 1W
Cooper, *KY, U.S.A.* **97 D8** 36 46N 84 52W
Cooper, *TX, U.S.A.* **99 D12** 33 23N 95 42W
Cooper →, *SC, U.S.A.* **90 F6** 32 50N 79 56W
Cooper City, *Miami, U.S.A.* **112 B1** 26 3N 80 16W
Cooper County ☆, *MO, U.S.A.* **82 C4** 38 50N 92 45W
Cooper L., *TX, U.S.A.* **99 D12** 33 19N 95 42W
Cooperdale, *OH, U.S.A.* **92 C4** 40 13N 82 3W
Coopersburg, *PA, U.S.A.* **87 B1** 40 31N 75 23W
Cooperstown, *ND, U.S.A.* **91 C7** 47 27N 98 8W
Cooperstown, *NY, U.S.A.* **89 C6** 42 42N 74 56W
Coopersville, *MI, U.S.A.* **79 F6** 43 4N 85 57W
Coos Bay, *OR, U.S.A.* **94 D1** 43 22N 124 13W
Coos County ☆, *NH, U.S.A.* **86 B3** 44 40N 71 15W
Coos County ☆, *OR, U.S.A.* **94 D1** 43 15N 124 0W
Coosa →, *AL, U.S.A.* **60 D4** 32 30N 86 16W
Coosa County ☆, *AL, U.S.A.* **60 D4** 32 55N 86 13W
Coosada, *AL, U.S.A.* **60 D4** 32 29N 86 20W
Coosawattee →, *GA, U.S.A.* **68 B2** 34 35N 84 55W
Copainalá, *Chiapas, Mexico* **222 B3** 17 4N 93 18W
Copake, *NY, U.S.A.* **78 B1** 42 6N 73 33W
Copala, *Guerrero, Mexico* **219 F9** 16 39N 98 59W
Copala, *Sinaloa, Mexico* **216 D5** 23 23N 105 54W
Copalillo, *Guerrero, Mexico* **219 D8** 18 2N 99 3W
Copalis Beach, *WA, U.S.A.* **101 C1** 47 7N 124 10W
Copan, *OK, U.S.A.* **93 B8** 36 54N 95 56W
Copan L., *OK, U.S.A.* **93 B8** 36 58N 95 57W
Copanatoyac, *Guerrero, Mexico* **219 E9** 17 15N 98 45W
Copano B., *TX, U.S.A.* **99 J10** 28 5N 97 5W
Copco L., *CA, U.S.A.* **64 B4** 41 59N 122 20W
Cope, *CO, U.S.A.* **66 C8** 39 40N 102 51W
Copeland, *FL, U.S.A.* **67 F7** 25 57N 81 22W
Copeland, *KS, U.S.A.* **74 D3** 37 33N 100 38W
Copemish, *MI, U.S.A.* **79 E6** 44 29N 85 55W
Copenhagen, *NY, U.S.A.* **89 B5** 43 54N 75 41W
Copiah County ☆, *MS, U.S.A.* **81 E3** 31 52N 90 24W
Coppell, *Dallas-Fort Worth, U.S.A.* **109 A4** 32 57N 97 0W
Copper →, *AK, U.S.A.* **61 F11** 60 18N 145 3W
Copper Butte, *WA, U.S.A.* **101 B7** 48 42N 118 28W
Copper Canyon = Barranca del Cobre, Parque Natural ⌂, *Chihuahua, Mexico* **213 F8** 27 15N 107 45W
Copper Center, *AK, U.S.A.* **61 F11** 61 58N 145 18W
Copper City = Invermere, *B.C., Canada* **185 H4** 50 30N 116 2W
Copper Cliff, *Ont., Canada* **178 A5** 46 28N 81 4W
Copper Cr. →, *VA, U.S.A.* **102 E2** 36 40N 82 44W
Copper Harbor, *MI, U.S.A.* **79 B4** 47 28N 87 53W
Copperas Cove, *TX, U.S.A.* **99 F10** 31 8N 97 54W
Copperhill, *TN, U.S.A.* **97 E8** 35 0N 84 15W
Coppermine = Kugluktuk, *Nunavut, Canada* **188 C9** 67 50N 115 5W
Coppermine →, *Canada* **188 C9** 67 49N 116 4W
Copperton, *Salt Lake City, U.S.A.* **117 C1** 40 33N 112 4W
Coquille, *OR, U.S.A.* **94 D1** 43 11N 124 11W
Coquille →, *OR, U.S.A.* **94 D1** 43 7N 124 26W
Coquimatlán, *Colima, Mexico* **218 C4** 19 12N 103 48W

Coquitlam, *B.C., Canada* 187 F12 49 17N 122 45W
Cora, *WY, U.S.A.* 104 D3 42 56N 109 59W
Cora Island, *MO, U.S.A.* 117 A2 38 49N 90 11W
Cora L., *TN, U.S.A.* 112 B1 35 0N 90 7W
Coral Gables, *FL, U.S.A.* 67 F8 25 43N 80 16W
Coral Harbour, *Nunavut, Canada* 191 E9 64 8N 83 10W
Coral Hills, *MD, U.S.A.* 119 B4 38 51N 76 55W
Coral Springs, *FL, U.S.A.* 67 E8 26 16N 80 16W
Coralville, *IA, U.S.A.* 73 D7 41 40N 91 35W
Coralville L., *IA, U.S.A.* 73 D7 41 42N 91 33W
Coram, *MT, U.S.A.* 83 B3 48 25N 114 3W
Coram, *NY, U.S.A.* 87 B3 40 52N 73 0W
Coraopolis, *PA, U.S.A.* 95 D2 40 31N 80 10W
Corbin, *KS, U.S.A.* 74 D6 37 8N 97 33W
Corbin, *KY, U.S.A.* 97 D8 36 57N 84 6W
Corbin, *MT, U.S.A.* 83 D5 46 23N 112 4W
Corcoran, *CA, U.S.A.* 65 G7 36 6N 119 33W
Cordele, *GA, U.S.A.* 68 E3 31 58N 83 47W
Cordell, *OK, U.S.A.* 93 C5 35 17N 98 59W
Cordell Hull L., *TN, U.S.A.* 97 D7 36 17N 85 56W
Córdoba, *Veracruz, Mexico* 221 F4 18 53N 96 56W
Cordonal, *Hidalgo, Mexico* 219 B8 20 37N 99 7W
Cordova, *AL, U.S.A.* 60 C3 33 46N 87 11W
Cordova, *AK, U.S.A.* 61 F11 60 33N 145 45W
Cordova, *IL, U.S.A.* 71 B3 41 41N 90 19W
Cordova, *NE, U.S.A.* 84 D8 40 43N 97 21W
Core Banks, *NC, U.S.A.* 90 D9 34 45N 76 15W
Corfu, *NY, U.S.A.* 89 C2 42 58N 78 24W
Corinna, *ME, U.S.A.* 76 D4 44 55N 69 16W
Corinne, *UT, U.S.A.* 100 B3 41 33N 112 7W
Corinth, *GA, U.S.A.* 68 C2 33 14N 84 57W
Corinth, *KY, U.S.A.* 97 B8 38 30N 84 34W
Corinth, *MS, U.S.A.* 81 B5 34 56N 88 31W
Corinth, *NY, U.S.A.* 89 B7 43 15N 73 49W
Cormack, *Nfld. & L., Canada* 174 C3 49 18N 57 23W
Cormorant, *Man., Canada* 183 A11 54 14N 100 35W
Cormorant L., *Man., Canada* 183 A11 54 15N 100 50W
Corn, *OK, U.S.A.* 93 C5 35 24N 98 48W
Cornelia, *GA, U.S.A.* 68 B3 34 31N 83 32W
Cornelius, *NC, U.S.A.* 90 C5 35 29N 80 52W
Cornell, *IL, U.S.A.* 71 C5 41 0N 88 44W
Cornell, *WI, U.S.A.* 103 C2 45 10N 91 9W
Corner Brook, *Nfld. & L., Canada* 174 D3 48 57N 57 58W
Cornersville, *TN, U.S.A.* 96 E6 35 22N 86 50W
Cornerville, *AR, U.S.A.* 63 E4 33 51N 91 56W
Corning, *Sask., Canada* 182 F9 49 58N 102 58W
Corning, *AR, U.S.A.* 63 B5 36 25N 90 35W
Corning, *CA, U.S.A.* 64 D4 39 56N 122 11W
Corning, *IA, U.S.A.* 73 E4 40 59N 94 44W
Corning, *KS, U.S.A.* 74 B7 39 40N 96 2W
Corning, *NY, U.S.A.* 89 C3 42 9N 77 3W
Corning, *OH, U.S.A.* 92 D4 39 36N 82 5W
Cornish, *OK, U.S.A.* 93 D6 34 9N 97 36W
Cornish, *UT, U.S.A.* 100 B4 41 59N 111 57W
Cornlea, *NE, U.S.A.* 84 C8 41 41N 97 34W
Cornucopia, *OR, U.S.A.* 94 B8 45 0N 117 12W
Cornudas, *TX, U.S.A.* 98 F2 31 47N 105 28W
Cornville, *AZ, U.S.A.* 62 C4 34 43N 111 55W
Cornwall, *Ont., Canada* 179 B12 45 2N 74 44W
Cornwall, *P.E.I., Canada* 173 G6 46 14N 63 13W
Cornwall, *CT, U.S.A.* 78 C1 41 50N 73 20W
Cornwall, *PA, U.S.A.* 95 D6 40 17N 76 25W
Cornwall, *VT, U.S.A.* 86 C1 43 56N 73 13W
Cornwall Bridge, *CT, U.S.A.* 78 C1 41 49N 73 22W
Cornwall I., *Nunavut, Canada* 190 B7 77 37N 94 38W
Cornwallis I., *Nunavut, Canada* 190 B7 75 8N 95 0W
Cornwell, *FL, U.S.A.* 67 D7 27 23N 81 6W
Corona, *CA, U.S.A.* 65 K9 33 53N 117 34W
Corona, *NM, U.S.A.* 88 C5 34 15N 105 36W
Corona, *SD, U.S.A.* 91 E9 45 20N 96 46W
Coronach, *Sask., Canada* 182 F6 49 7N 105 31W
Coronado, *CA, U.S.A.* 65 L9 32 41N 117 10W
Coronado, I., *Baja Calif., Mexico* 210 D5 29 2N 113 31W
Coronado Nat. Forest, *AZ, U.S.A.* 62 E5 32 10N 110 20W
Coronado Nat. Monument △, *AZ, U.S.A.* 62 F5 31 20N 110 20W
Coronados, I., *Baja Calif. S., Mexico* 211 G7 26 5N 111 17W
Coronados, Is. Los, *Baja Calif., Mexico* 210 A1 32 26N 117 19W
Coronation, *Alta., Canada* 185 F9 52 5N 111 27W
Coronation Gulf, *Nunavut, Canada* 188 C10 68 25N 110 0W
Coroneo, *Guanajuato, Mexico* 219 B7 20 8N 100 20W
Corozal, *Puerto Rico* 105 G16 18 21N 66 19W
Corpus Christi, *TX, U.S.A.* 99 K10 27 47N 97 24W
Corpus Christi, L., *TX, U.S.A.* 99 J10 28 2N 97 52W
Corpus Christi B., *TX, U.S.A.* 99 K10 27 47N 97 22W
Corral, *ID, U.S.A.* 70 F4 43 21N 114 57W
Corral Nuevo, *Veracruz, Mexico* 221 F5 18 7N 95 8W
Corralejo, *Tamaulipas, Mexico* 215 F6 24 23N 99 0W
Corrales, *NM, U.S.A.* 88 B4 35 14N 106 36W
Correctionville, *IA, U.S.A.* 73 C2 42 29N 95 47W
Corregidora, *Querétaro, Mexico* 219 B7 20 32N 100 27W
Correll, *MN, U.S.A.* 80 E2 45 14N 96 10W
Corrientes, C., *Jalisco, Mexico* 218 B2 20 25N 105 42W
Corrigan, *TX, U.S.A.* 99 G13 31 0N 94 52W
Corriganville, *MD, U.S.A.* 77 A2 39 45N 78 17W
Corry, *PA, U.S.A.* 95 C3 41 55N 79 39W
Corryton, *TN, U.S.A.* 97 D9 36 9N 83 47W
Corsica, *SD, U.S.A.* 91 G7 43 25N 98 24W
Corsicana, *TX, U.S.A.* 99 E11 32 6N 96 28W
Corson County ☆, *SD, U.S.A.* 91 E4 45 55N 101 0W
Cortaro, *AZ, U.S.A.* 62 E4 32 21N 111 5W
Cortazar, *Guanajuato, Mexico* 219 B7 20 29N 100 56W
Cortés, Mar de = California, G. de, *Mexico* 211 F7 27 0N 111 0W
Cortes I., *B.C., Canada* 186 E10 50 7N 124 59W
Cortez, *CO, U.S.A.* 66 E2 37 21N 108 35W
Cortez Mts., *NV, U.S.A.* 85 B4 40 20N 116 20W
Cortland, *NY, U.S.A.* 89 C4 42 36N 76 11W
Cortland, *NE, U.S.A.* 84 D9 40 30N 96 42W
Cortland, *OH, U.S.A.* 92 B6 41 20N 80 44W
Cortland County ☆, *NY, U.S.A.* 89 C4 42 35N 76 5W
Corum, *OK, U.S.A.* 93 D5 34 22N 98 6W
Corunna, *Ont., Canada* 178 E4 42 53N 82 26W
Corunna, *MI, U.S.A.* 79 G7 42 59N 84 7W
Corvallis, *MT, U.S.A.* 83 D3 46 19N 114 7W
Corvallis, *OR, U.S.A.* 94 C2 44 34N 123 16W
Corvette, L. de la, *Qué., Canada* 175 C3 53 25N 74 3W
Corwin, *KS, U.S.A.* 74 D5 37 5N 98 18W
Corwith, *IA, U.S.A.* 73 C5 42 59N 93 57W
Corydon, *IN, U.S.A.* 72 E4 38 13N 86 7W
Corydon, *IA, U.S.A.* 73 E5 40 46N 93 19W
Corydon, *KY, U.S.A.* 96 C5 37 44N 87 43W
Coryell County ☆, *TX, U.S.A.* 99 F10 31 26N 97 45W
Cosalá, *Sinaloa, Mexico* 216 C4 24 23N 106 41W
Cosamaloapán, *Veracruz, Mexico* 221 F5 18 22N 95 49W
Coscomatepec, *Veracruz, Mexico* 221 E3 19 4N 97 2W
Coshocton, *OH, U.S.A.* 92 C5 40 16N 81 51W
Coshocton County ☆, *OH, U.S.A.* 92 C5 40 16N 81 51W
Cosío, *Aguascalientes, Mexico* 217 E8 22 21N 102 18W
Cosmopolis, *WA, U.S.A.* 101 D2 46 57N 123 46W
Coso Range, *CA, U.S.A.* 65 G9 36 9N 117 41W
Cosoleacaque, *Veracruz, Mexico* 221 G6 18 0N 94 37W
Cossatot →, *AR, U.S.A.* 63 E1 33 48N 94 9W
Cost, *TX, U.S.A.* 99 H10 29 26N 97 32W
Costa Azul, *Sinaloa, Mexico* 216 B2 25 7N 108 8W
Costa Mesa, *CA, U.S.A.* 65 K9 33 38N 117 55W
Costebelle, L., *Qué., Canada* 172 C7 50 19N 62 23W
Costera del Pacífico, Llanura, *Sonora, Mexico* 212 E4 29 0N 111 40W
Costilla, *NM, U.S.A.* 88 A5 36 59N 105 32W
Costilla County ☆, *CO, U.S.A.* 66 E5 37 15N 105 30W
Cosumnes →, *CA, U.S.A.* 64 E5 38 16N 121 26W
Cotati, *CA, U.S.A.* 64 E4 38 20N 122 42W
Côte d'Azur, *Qué., Canada* 192 A1 45 29N 75 44W
Côte-St-Luc, *Qué., Canada* 192 B3 45 28N 73 39W
Coteau des Prairies, *SD, U.S.A.* 91 E8 45 20N 97 50W
Coteau du Missouri, *ND, U.S.A.* 91 C5 47 0N 100 0W
Cotesfield, *NE, U.S.A.* 84 C7 41 22N 98 38W
Cotija de la Paz, *Michoacan, Mexico* 218 C5 19 49N 102 43W
Cottage Grove, *MN, U.S.A.* 80 F6 44 50N 92 57W
Cottage Grove, *OR, U.S.A.* 94 D2 43 48N 123 3W
Cottageville, *SC, U.S.A.* 90 F5 32 56N 80 29W
Cottam, *Ont., Canada* 178 E4 42 8N 82 45W
Cottle County ☆, *TX, U.S.A.* 98 D7 34 0N 100 18W
Cotton, *GA, U.S.A.* 68 E2 31 10N 84 4W
Cotton, *MN, U.S.A.* 80 C6 47 10N 92 28W
Cotton County ☆, *OK, U.S.A.* 93 D5 34 15N 98 20W
Cotton Plant, *AR, U.S.A.* 63 C4 35 0N 91 15W
Cotton Valley, *LA, U.S.A.* 75 B2 32 49N 93 25W
Cottondale, *AL, U.S.A.* 60 C3 33 11N 87 27W
Cottondale, *FL, U.S.A.* 67 A3 30 48N 85 23W
Cottonport, *LA, U.S.A.* 75 D3 30 59N 92 3W
Cottonwood, *AL, U.S.A.* 60 E5 31 3N 85 18W
Cottonwood, *AZ, U.S.A.* 62 C3 34 45N 112 1W
Cottonwood, *CA, U.S.A.* 64 C4 40 23N 122 17W
Cottonwood, *ID, U.S.A.* 70 C2 46 3N 116 21W
Cottonwood, *MN, U.S.A.* 80 F3 44 37N 95 41W
Cottonwood, *SD, U.S.A.* 91 G4 43 58N 101 54W
Cottonwood →, *KS, U.S.A.* 74 C7 38 23N 96 3W
Cottonwood →, *MN, U.S.A.* 80 F4 44 17N 94 25W
Cottonwood County ☆, *MN, U.S.A.* 80 F3 44 0N 95 10W
Cottonwood Cove, *NV, U.S.A.* 85 G6 35 29N 114 41W
Cottonwood Cr. →, *TX, U.S.A.* 98 F4 31 23N 103 46W
Cottonwood Falls, *KS, U.S.A.* 74 C7 38 22N 96 32W
Cottonwood Heights, *UT, U.S.A.* 100 C4 40 37N 111 48W
Cottonwood Mt., *OR, U.S.A.* 94 C8 44 10N 117 40W
Cottonwood Mts., *CA, U.S.A.* 65 G9 36 50N 117 40W
Cotuit, *MA, U.S.A.* 78 C4 41 37N 70 26W
Cotulla, *TX, U.S.A.* 99 J8 28 26N 99 14W
Couba Island, *New Orleans, U.S.A.* 113 D1 29 48N 90 12W
Couderay, *WI, U.S.A.* 103 C2 45 48N 91 18W
Coudersport, *PA, U.S.A.* 95 C4 41 46N 78 1W
Coudres, Île aux, *Qué., Canada* 177 D12 47 24N 70 23W
Cougar, *WA, U.S.A.* 101 D3 46 3N 122 18W
Cougar Res., *OR, U.S.A.* 94 C3 44 8N 122 14W
Coulee City, *WA, U.S.A.* 101 C6 47 37N 119 17W
Coulee Dam, *WA, U.S.A.* 101 C7 47 58N 118 58W
Coulee Dam Nat. Recr. Area = Lake Roosevelt Nat. Recr. Area △, *WA, U.S.A.* 101 B7 48 5N 118 14W
Coulonge →, *Qué., Canada* 176 F6 45 52N 76 46W
Coulterville, *CA, U.S.A.* 64 F6 37 43N 120 12W
Coulterville, *IL, U.S.A.* 71 E4 38 11N 89 36W
Coulwood, *Charlotte, U.S.A.* 107 A1 35 17N 80 56W
Counce, *TN, U.S.A.* 96 E4 35 3N 88 16W
Council, *AK, U.S.A.* 61 D7 64 53N 163 41W
Council, *GA, U.S.A.* 68 F4 30 37N 82 31W
Council, *ID, U.S.A.* 70 E2 44 44N 116 26W
Council Bluffs, *IA, U.S.A.* 73 D3 41 16N 95 52W
Council Grove, *KS, U.S.A.* 74 C7 38 40N 96 29W
Council Grove Lake, *KS, U.S.A.* 74 C7 38 41N 96 33W
Council Hill, *OK, U.S.A.* 93 C8 35 33N 95 42W
Country Club Hills, *MO, U.S.A.* 117 A2 38 43N 90 16W
Country Homes, *WA, U.S.A.* 101 C8 47 45N 117 24W
Country Lake Estates, *NJ, U.S.A.* 87 C2 39 55N 74 32W
Countryside, *Chicago, U.S.A.* 108 C1 41 47N 87 52W
Coupeaux, L., *Qué., Canada* 172 B6 51 27N 63 58W
Coupeville, *WA, U.S.A.* 101 B3 48 13N 122 41W
Coupland, *TX, U.S.A.* 99 G10 30 28N 97 23W
Courtenay, *B.C., Canada* 186 F9 49 45N 125 0W
Courtenay, *ND, U.S.A.* 91 C7 47 13N 98 34W
Courtland, *Ont., Canada* 178 E6 42 51N 80 38W
Courtland, *AL, U.S.A.* 60 B3 34 40N 87 19W
Courtland, *CA, U.S.A.* 64 E5 38 20N 121 34W
Courtland, *KS, U.S.A.* 74 B6 39 47N 97 54W
Courtland, *MN, U.S.A.* 80 F4 44 16N 94 20W
Courtland, *MS, U.S.A.* 81 B4 34 14N 89 57W
Courtland, *VA, U.S.A.* 102 E7 36 43N 77 4W
Courtright, *Ont., Canada* 178 E4 42 49N 82 28W
Courtright Res., *CA, U.S.A.* 65 F8 37 5N 118 58W
Coushatta, *LA, U.S.A.* 75 B2 32 1N 93 21W
Coushatta Indian Reservation, *LA, U.S.A.* 75 D3 30 31N 92 47W
Coutts, *Alta., Canada* 185 J9 49 0N 111 57W
Couture, L., *Qué., Canada* 175 A2 60 7N 75 20W
Cove, *AR, U.S.A.* 63 D1 34 26N 94 25W
Cove, *OR, U.S.A.* 94 B8 45 18N 117 49W
Cove Fort, *UT, U.S.A.* 100 E3 38 36N 112 35W
Cove I., *Ont., Canada* 178 B5 45 17N 81 44W
Cove Point, *MD, U.S.A.* 77 B4 38 23N 76 24W
Covedale, *OH, U.S.A.* 107 B1 39 7N 84 36W
Covelo, *CA, U.S.A.* 64 D3 39 48N 123 15W
Coventry, *CT, U.S.A.* 78 C2 41 48N 72 23W
Coventry, *RI, U.S.A.* 78 C3 41 41N 71 34W
Coverdale, *GA, U.S.A.* 68 E3 31 38N 83 58W
Covington, *GA, U.S.A.* 68 C3 33 36N 83 51W
Covington, *IN, U.S.A.* 72 C3 40 9N 87 24W
Covington, *KY, U.S.A.* 97 A8 39 5N 84 30W
Covington, *LA, U.S.A.* 75 D5 30 29N 90 6W
Covington, *MI, U.S.A.* 79 C3 46 33N 88 32W
Covington, *OH, U.S.A.* 92 C2 40 7N 84 21W
Covington, *OK, U.S.A.* 93 B6 36 18N 97 35W
Covington, *Seattle, U.S.A.* 118 D5 47 20N 122 6W
Covington, *TN, U.S.A.* 96 E3 35 34N 89 39W
Covington, *VA, U.S.A.* 102 D5 37 47N 79 59W
Covington County ☆, *AL, U.S.A.* 60 E4 31 18N 86 29W
Covington County ☆, *MS, U.S.A.* 81 E4 31 39N 89 33W
Cow Cr. →, *KS, U.S.A.* 74 D6 37 59N 97 50W
Cow Cr. →, *OR, U.S.A.* 94 E2 42 57N 123 22W
Cow Head, *Nfld. & L., Canada* 174 C3 49 55N 57 48W
Cowan, *Man., Canada* 183 C11 52 5N 100 45W
Cowan, *TN, U.S.A.* 96 E6 35 10N 86 1W
Cowan L., *Sask., Canada* 182 A4 54 0N 107 15W
Cowansville, *Qué., Canada* 177 F10 45 14N 72 46W
Coward, *SC, U.S.A.* 90 E6 33 58N 79 45W
Cowarts, *AL, U.S.A.* 60 E5 31 12N 85 18W
Cowden, *IL, U.S.A.* 71 D5 39 15N 88 52W
Cowdrey, *CO, U.S.A.* 66 B4 40 52N 106 19W
Cowen, *WV, U.S.A.* 102 C4 38 25N 80 34W
Coweta, *OK, U.S.A.* 93 C8 35 57N 95 39W
Coweta County ☆, *GA, U.S.A.* 68 C2 33 20N 84 50W
Cowichan L., *B.C., Canada* 186 G10 48 53N 124 17W
Cowles, *NE, U.S.A.* 84 D7 40 10N 98 27W
Cowley, *Alta., Canada* 185 J6 49 34N 114 5W
Cowley, *WY, U.S.A.* 104 B4 44 53N 108 28W
Cowley County ☆, *KS, U.S.A.* 74 D7 37 15N 96 45W
Cowlic, *AZ, U.S.A.* 62 F4 31 48N 111 59W
Cowlington, *OK, U.S.A.* 93 C9 35 17N 94 44W
Cowlitz →, *WA, U.S.A.* 101 D3 46 6N 122 55W
Cowlitz County ☆, *WA, U.S.A.* 101 D3 46 5N 122 50W
Cowpens, *SC, U.S.A.* 90 C4 35 1N 81 48W
Cox, *GA, U.S.A.* 68 E5 31 27N 81 34W
Cox City, *OK, U.S.A.* 93 D6 34 43N 97 44W
Cox I., *B.C., Canada* 186 E6 50 48N 128 36W
Coxcatlán, *Puebla, Mexico* 221 F3 18 16N 97 9W
Coxcatlán, *San Luis Potosí, Mexico* 215 J6 21 33N 98 55W
Coxquihui, *Veracruz, Mexico* 220 D3 20 11N 97 35W
Cox's Cove, *Nfld. & L., Canada* 174 C2 49 7N 58 5W
Coxs Mills, *WV, U.S.A.* 102 B4 39 3N 80 50W
Coxsackie, *NY, U.S.A.* 89 C7 42 21N 73 48W
Coy, *AR, U.S.A.* 63 D4 34 32N 91 53W
Coyame, *Chihuahua, Mexico* 213 D10 29 28N 105 6W
Coyanosa Draw →, *TX, U.S.A.* 98 F4 31 18N 103 6W
Coyle, *OK, U.S.A.* 93 C6 35 57N 97 14W
Coyoacán, *Distrito Federal, Mexico* 225 B2 19 21N 99 9W
Coyote, *San Luis Potosí, Mexico* 215 H4 22 54N 100 35W
Coyote, *NM, U.S.A.* 88 A4 36 10N 106 37W
Coyote, B., *Baja Calif. S., Mexico* 211 J8 24 30N 110 40W
Coyote Canyon, *NM, U.S.A.* 88 B2 35 46N 108 37W
Coyote L., *CA, U.S.A.* 65 H10 35 4N 116 46W
Coyote Res., *CA, U.S.A.* 64 F5 37 7N 121 33W
Coyote Ridge, *San Francisco, U.S.A.* 118 A1 37 51N 122 33W
Coyote Wash →, *AZ, U.S.A.* 62 E1 32 41N 114 8W
Coyotitán, *Sinaloa, Mexico* 216 D4 23 47N 106 35W
Coyuca de Benítez, *Guerrero, Mexico* 219 E7 17 2N 100 4W
Coyuca de Catalán, *Guerrero, Mexico* 219 D7 18 20N 100 39W
Coyula, *Guadalajara, Mexico* 224 B2 20 39N 103 13W
Coyuquilla, *Michoacan, Mexico* 218 D5 18 1N 102 2W
Coyutla, *Veracruz, Mexico* 220 D3 20 15N 97 38W
Coyville, *KS, U.S.A.* 74 D8 37 41N 95 54W
Cozad, *NE, U.S.A.* 84 D6 40 52N 99 59W
Cozumel, *Quintana Roo, Mexico* 223 B7 20 31N 86 55W
Cozumel, I. de, *Quintana Roo, Mexico* 223 B7 20 25N 86 55W
Crab Cr. →, *WA, U.S.A.* 101 C6 47 1N 119 19W
Crab Orchard, *KY, U.S.A.* 97 C8 37 28N 84 30W
Crab Orchard, *NE, U.S.A.* 84 D9 40 20N 96 25W
Crab Orchard, *TN, U.S.A.* 97 E8 35 55N 84 52W
Crab Orchard L., *IL, U.S.A.* 71 F4 37 43N 89 9W
Crab Orchard Nat. Wildlife Refuge △, *IL, U.S.A.* 71 F4 37 42N 89 4W
Crabtree, *OR, U.S.A.* 94 C3 44 38N 122 54W
Cracroft Is., *B.C., Canada* 186 E8 50 32N 126 25W
Crafton, *Pittsburgh, U.S.A.* 116 B1 40 26N 80 3W
Craig, *AK, U.S.A.* 61 J14 55 29N 133 9W
Craig, *CO, U.S.A.* 66 B3 40 31N 107 33W
Craig, *IA, U.S.A.* 73 C2 42 54N 96 19W
Craig, *MO, U.S.A.* 82 A1 40 12N 95 23W
Craig, *MT, U.S.A.* 83 C6 47 5N 111 58W
Craig, *NE, U.S.A.* 84 C9 41 47N 96 22W
Craig County ☆, *OK, U.S.A.* 93 B8 36 45N 95 10W
Craig County ☆, *VA, U.S.A.* 102 D4 37 25N 80 5W
Craig Pass, *WY, U.S.A.* 104 B2 44 26N 110 43W
Craigflower, *B.C., Canada* 187 G11 48 27N 123 26W
Craighead County ☆, *AR, U.S.A.* 63 C5 35 50N 90 42W
Craigmont, *ID, U.S.A.* 70 C2 46 15N 116 29W
Craigmyle, *Alta., Canada* 185 G8 51 40N 112 15W
Craigsville, *VA, U.S.A.* 102 C5 38 5N 79 23W
Craigsville, *WV, U.S.A.* 102 C4 38 20N 80 39W
Craik, *Sask., Canada* 182 D6 51 3N 105 49W
Cranberry L., *NY, U.S.A.* 89 A6 44 11N 74 50W
Cranberry Portage, *Man., Canada* 191 G5 54 35N 101 23W
Cranbrook, *B.C., Canada* 185 J5 49 30N 115 46W
Crandon, *WI, U.S.A.* 103 C5 45 34N 88 54W
Crandon Park, *Miami, U.S.A.* 112 D3 25 42N 80 9W
Crane, *IN, U.S.A.* 72 E4 38 54N 86 54W
Crane, *MO, U.S.A.* 82 E3 36 54N 93 34W
Crane, *MT, U.S.A.* 83 C13 47 35N 104 16W
Crane, *OR, U.S.A.* 94 D7 43 25N 118 35W
Crane, *TX, U.S.A.* 98 F5 31 24N 102 21W
Crane County ☆, *TX, U.S.A.* 98 F5 31 24N 102 21W
Crane L., *Sask., Canada* 182 E2 50 5N 109 5W
Crane Mt., *OR, U.S.A.* 94 E5 42 4N 120 13W
Crane Naval Weapons Support Center, *IN, U.S.A.* 72 E4 38 51N 86 50W
Crane Prairie Res., *OR, U.S.A.* 94 D4 43 45N 121 47W
Crane River, *Man., Canada* 183 D12 51 30N 99 14W
Craney Island, *Norfolk, U.S.A.* 115 A1 36 53N 76 21W
Cranfills Gap, *TX, U.S.A.* 99 F10 31 46N 97 50W
Cranford, *NJ, U.S.A.* 87 B2 40 40N 74 18W
Cranston, *RI, U.S.A.* 78 C3 41 47N 71 26W
Crapaud, *P.E.I., Canada* 173 G6 46 14N 63 30W
Crapo, *MD, U.S.A.* 77 B4 38 18N 76 9W
Crary, *ND, U.S.A.* 91 B7 48 4N 98 38W
Crater L., *OR, U.S.A.* 94 E3 42 56N 122 6W
Crater Lake, *OR, U.S.A.* 94 E3 42 54N 122 8W
Crater Lake Nat. Park △, *OR, U.S.A.* 94 E3 42 55N 122 10W
Crater of Diamonds State Park △, *AR, U.S.A.* 63 D2 34 2N 93 40W
Craters of the Moon Nat. Monument △, *ID, U.S.A.* 70 F5 43 25N 113 30W
Crauford, C., *N.W.T., Canada* 190 C9 73 44N 84 51W
Craven, *Sask., Canada* 182 E7 50 42N 104 49W
Craven, L., *Qué., Canada* 175 C2 54 20N 76 56W
Craven County ☆, *NC, U.S.A.* 90 C8 35 15N 77 10W
Crawford, *AL, U.S.A.* 60 D5 32 27N 85 11W
Crawford, *CO, U.S.A.* 66 D3 38 42N 107 37W
Crawford, *MS, U.S.A.* 81 C5 33 18N 88 37W
Crawford, *NE, U.S.A.* 84 B2 42 41N 103 25W
Crawford, *OK, U.S.A.* 93 C4 35 50N 99 48W
Crawford, *TX, U.S.A.* 99 F10 31 32N 97 27W
Crawford County ☆, *AR, U.S.A.* 63 C1 35 20N 94 18W
Crawford County ☆, *GA, U.S.A.* 68 D3 32 50N 84 0W
Crawford County ☆, *IL, U.S.A.* 71 D6 39 0N 87 45W
Crawford County ☆, *IN, U.S.A.* 72 E4 38 15N 86 25W
Crawford County ☆, *IA, U.S.A.* 73 C3 42 0N 95 20W
Crawford County ☆, *KS, U.S.A.* 74 D9 37 30N 94 45W
Crawford County ☆, *MI, U.S.A.* 79 E7 44 45N 84 40W
Crawford County ☆, *MO, U.S.A.* 82 D5 38 0N 91 20W
Crawford County ☆, *OH, U.S.A.* 92 C4 40 48N 82 59W
Crawford County ☆, *PA, U.S.A.* 95 C2 41 45N 80 0W
Crawford County ☆, *WI, U.S.A.* 103 E3 43 15N 90 50W
Crawford Notch State Park △, *NH, U.S.A.* 86 B3 44 11N 71 24W
Crawfordsville, *AR, U.S.A.* 63 C5 35 14N 90 20W
Crawfordsville, *IN, U.S.A.* 72 C4 40 2N 86 54W
Crawfordsville, *IA, U.S.A.* 73 D7 41 12N 91 32W
Crawfordville, *FL, U.S.A.* 67 A4 30 11N 84 23W
Crawfordville, *GA, U.S.A.* 68 C4 33 33N 82 54W
Crazy Horse Memorial, *SD, U.S.A.* 91 G2 43 49N 103 35W
Crazy Mts., *MT, U.S.A.* 83 D7 46 12N 110 20W
Crazy Woman Cr. →, *WY, U.S.A.* 104 B6 44 29N 106 8W
Creagerstown, *MD, U.S.A.* 77 A3 39 37N 77 22W
Creal Springs, *IL, U.S.A.* 71 F5 37 37N 88 50W
Crean L., *Sask., Canada* 182 A5 54 5N 106 9W
Creciente, I., *Baja Calif. S., Mexico* 211 J7 24 23N 111 42W
Cree →, *Sask., Canada* 189 E11 58 57N 105 47W
Cree L., *Sask., Canada* 189 E11 57 30N 106 30W
Creede, *CO, U.S.A.* 66 E4 37 51N 106 56W
Creedmoor, *NC, U.S.A.* 90 B7 36 7N 78 41W
Creek County ☆, *OK, U.S.A.* 93 C7 35 50N 96 20W
Creel, *Chihuahua, Mexico* 213 F8 27 45N 107 38W
Creelman, *Sask., Canada* 182 F8 49 49N 103 18W
Creemore, *Ont., Canada* 178 C6 44 19N 80 6W
Creighton, *Sask., Canada* 189 F12 54 45N 101 54W
Creighton, *MO, U.S.A.* 82 C3 38 30N 94 4W
Creighton, *NE, U.S.A.* 84 B8 42 28N 97 54W
Creighton, *SD, U.S.A.* 91 F3 44 15N 102 12W
Crellin, *MD, U.S.A.* 77 A1 39 25N 79 25W
Cremona, *Alta., Canada* 185 G6 51 33N 114 29W
Crenshaw, *MS, U.S.A.* 81 B3 34 30N 90 12W
Crenshaw County ☆, *AL, U.S.A.* 60 E4 31 43N 86 16W
Creole, *LA, U.S.A.* 75 E2 29 49N 93 7W
Cresaptown, *MD, U.S.A.* 77 A2 39 36N 78 50W
Cresbard, *SD, U.S.A.* 91 E7 45 10N 98 57W
Crescent, *IA, U.S.A.* 73 D3 41 22N 95 51W
Crescent, *OK, U.S.A.* 93 C6 35 57N 97 36W
Crescent, *OR, U.S.A.* 94 D4 43 28N 121 42W
Crescent, L., *Orlando, U.S.A.* 115 A1 28 30N 81 33W
Crescent, L., *WA, U.S.A.* 101 B2 48 4N 123 49W
Crescent Beach, *FL, U.S.A.* 67 B7 29 46N 81 15W
Crescent City, *CA, U.S.A.* 64 B2 41 45N 124 12W
Crescent City, *FL, U.S.A.* 67 B7 29 26N 81 31W
Crescent Junction, *UT, U.S.A.* 100 E6 38 57N 109 49W
Crescent L., *FL, U.S.A.* 67 B7 29 28N 81 30W
Crescent Lake, *OR, U.S.A.* 94 D4 43 30N 121 59W
Crescent Lake Nat. Wildlife Refuge △, *NE, U.S.A.* 84 C3 41 44N 102 19W
Crescent Springs, *KY, U.S.A.* 107 B1 39 3N 84 34W
Crescent Spur, *B.C., Canada* 187 B14 53 34N 120 42W
Cresco, *IA, U.S.A.* 73 B6 43 22N 92 7W
Cresskill, *NJ, U.S.A.* 114 A3 40 56N 73 57W
Cresson, *PA, U.S.A.* 95 D4 40 28N 78 36W
Crested Butte, *CO, U.S.A.* 66 D4 38 52N 106 59W
Crestline, *OH, U.S.A.* 92 C4 40 47N 82 44W
Creston, *B.C., Canada* 185 J4 49 10N 116 31W
Creston, *IA, U.S.A.* 73 D4 41 4N 94 22W
Creston, *NE, U.S.A.* 84 C8 41 42N 97 22W
Creston, *WA, U.S.A.* 101 C7 47 46N 118 31W
Creston, *WY, U.S.A.* 104 E5 41 42N 107 45W
Crestone, *CO, U.S.A.* 66 E5 37 56N 105 47W
Crestview, *FL, U.S.A.* 67 A2 30 46N 86 34W
Crestview, *KY, U.S.A.* 107 B2 39 1N 84 25W
Crestview Hills, *KY, U.S.A.* 107 B1 39 1N 84 35W
Crestwood, *KY, U.S.A.* 97 B7 38 19N 85 28W
Crestwood Village, *NJ, U.S.A.* 87 C2 39 56N 74 20W
Creswell, *OR, U.S.A.* 94 D2 43 55N 123 1W
Creswell B., *Nunavut, Canada* 190 C7 72 41N 93 25W
Crete, *IL, U.S.A.* 71 B6 41 27N 87 38W
Crete, *NE, U.S.A.* 84 D9 40 38N 96 58W
Creve Coeur, *IL, U.S.A.* 71 C4 40 39N 89 35W
Crewe, *VA, U.S.A.* 102 D6 37 10N 78 8W
Cricket, *NC, U.S.A.* 90 B4 36 11N 81 12W
Cricket Mts., *UT, U.S.A.* 100 E3 39 0N 112 58W
Crimora, *VA, U.S.A.* 102 C6 38 9N 78 51W
Criner, *OK, U.S.A.* 93 D6 34 58N 97 34W
Cripple Creek, *CO, U.S.A.* 66 D5 38 45N 105 11W
Crisfield, *MD, U.S.A.* 77 C5 37 59N 75 51W
Crisp County ☆, *GA, U.S.A.* 68 E3 31 50N 83 50W
Crisp Pt., *MI, U.S.A.* 79 C6 46 45N 85 16W
Cristo, Sa., *Coahuila, Mexico* 214 C3 27 23N 101 58W
Cristóbal Colón, *Tamaulipas, Mexico* 214 E6 25 36N 98 6W
Crittenden, *KY, U.S.A.* 97 B8 38 47N 84 36W
Crittenden County ☆, *AR, U.S.A.* 63 C5 35 14N 90 20W
Crittenden County ☆, *KY, U.S.A.* 96 C4 37 20N 88 5W
Crivitz, *WI, U.S.A.* 103 C5 45 14N 88 1W
Croatan Nat. Forest, *NC, U.S.A.* 90 D8 34 50N 77 5W
Crocheron, *MD, U.S.A.* 77 B4 38 15N 76 3W
Crocker, *MO, U.S.A.* 82 D4 37 57N 92 16W
Crockett, *TX, U.S.A.* 99 F12 31 19N 95 27W
Crockett County ☆, *TN, U.S.A.* 96 E3 35 49N 89 14W
Crockett County ☆, *TX, U.S.A.* 98 G6 30 45N 101 30W
Crofton, *B.C., Canada* 187 G11 48 52N 123 38W
Crofton, *KY, U.S.A.* 96 C5 37 3N 87 29W
Crofton, *MD, U.S.A.* 77 A4 39 1N 76 42W
Crofton, *NE, U.S.A.* 84 B8 42 44N 97 30W
Croghan, *NY, U.S.A.* 89 B5 43 54N 75 24W
Croix, L. La, *Ont., Canada* 180 D4 48 20N 92 15W
Croker, C., *Ont., Canada* 178 C6 44 58N 80 59W
Cromer, *Man., Canada* 183 F10 49 44N 101 14W
Cromwell, *AL, U.S.A.* 60 D2 32 14N 88 17W
Cromwell, *CT, U.S.A.* 78 C2 41 36N 72 39W
Cromwell, *MN, U.S.A.* 80 D6 46 41N 92 53W
Cromwell, *OK, U.S.A.* 93 C7 35 22N 96 29W
Crook, *CO, U.S.A.* 66 B8 40 52N 102 48W
Crook County ☆, *OR, U.S.A.* 94 C5 44 10N 120 20W
Crook County ☆, *WY, U.S.A.* 104 B8 44 44N 104 30W
Crooked →, *OR, U.S.A.* 94 C4 44 32N 121 16W
Crooked Creek, *AK, U.S.A.* 61 F8 61 52N 158 7W
Crooked I., *FL, U.S.A.* 67 B3 29 59N 85 31W
Crooked L., *Nfld. & L., Canada* 174 D4 48 24N 56 17W
Crooked L., *FL, U.S.A.* 67 D7 27 48N 81 35W
Crooked River, *Sask., Canada* 182 C8 52 51N 103 44W
Crooked River Nat. Grassland, *OR, U.S.A.* 94 C4 44 33N 121 7W
Crooks, *SD, U.S.A.* 91 G9 43 40N 96 49W
Crookston, *MN, U.S.A.* 80 C2 47 47N 96 37W
Crookston, *NE, U.S.A.* 84 B5 42 56N 100 45W
Crooksville, *OH, U.S.A.* 92 D4 39 46N 82 6W
Croom, *MD, U.S.A.* 77 B4 38 45N 76 46W
Cropsey, *IL, U.S.A.* 71 C5 40 37N 88 29W
Crosby, *MN, U.S.A.* 80 D5 46 29N 93 58W
Crosby, *MS, U.S.A.* 81 E2 31 17N 91 4W
Crosby, *ND, U.S.A.* 91 B2 48 55N 103 18W
Crosby, *TX, U.S.A.* 99 H12 29 55N 95 4W
Crosby, Mt., *WY, U.S.A.* 104 C3 43 52N 109 20W
Crosby County ☆, *TX, U.S.A.* 98 D6 33 40N 101 14W
Crosbyton, *TX, U.S.A.* 98 D6 33 40N 101 14W
Cross Anchor, *SC, U.S.A.* 90 D4 34 39N 81 51W
Cross City, *FL, U.S.A.* 67 B5 29 38N 83 7W
Cross County ☆, *AR, U.S.A.* 63 C5 35 14N 90 47W
Cross Creek, *N.B., Canada* 173 G3 46 19N 66 43W
Cross Creeks Nat. Wildlife Refuge △, *TN, U.S.A.* 96 D5 36 26N 87 42W
Cross Fork, *PA, U.S.A.* 95 C5 41 29N 77 49W
Cross Hill, *SC, U.S.A.* 90 D4 34 18N 81 59W
Cross L., *Man., Canada* 191 G6 54 45N 97 30W
Cross L., *ME, U.S.A.* 76 A5 47 7N 68 20W
Cross Lake, *Man., Canada* 191 G6 54 37N 97 47W
Cross Lake, *MN, U.S.A.* 80 D4 46 40N 94 7W
Cross Plains, *TN, U.S.A.* 96 D6 36 33N 86 42W
Cross Plains, *TX, U.S.A.* 99 E8 32 8N 99 11W
Cross Sound, *AK, U.S.A.* 61 G14 58 0N 135 0W
Cross Timbers, *MO, U.S.A.* 82 C3 38 1N 93 14W
Cross Village, *MI, U.S.A.* 79 D6 45 39N 85 2W
Crossett, *AR, U.S.A.* 63 E4 33 8N 91 58W
Crossfield, *Alta., Canada* 185 G6 51 25N 114 0W
Crossroads, *NM, U.S.A.* 88 D7 33 31N 103 20W
Crossville, *AL, U.S.A.* 60 B5 34 17N 86 0W
Crossville, *IL, U.S.A.* 71 E5 38 10N 88 4W
Crossville, *TN, U.S.A.* 97 E7 35 57N 85 2W
Croswell, *MI, U.S.A.* 79 F9 43 16N 82 37W
Crotched Mt., *NH, U.S.A.* 86 C3 43 0N 71 52W
Crothersville, *IN, U.S.A.* 72 E5 38 48N 85 50W
Croton-on-Hudson, *NY, U.S.A.* 87 A3 41 13N 73 54W
Crouch, *ID, U.S.A.* 70 E3 44 7N 115 58W
Crow Agency, *MT, U.S.A.* 83 E10 45 36N 107 28W
Crow Cr. →, *CO, U.S.A.* 66 B6 40 23N 104 29W
Crow Creek Indian Reservation, *SD, U.S.A.* 91 F6 44 0N 99 25W
Crow Indian Reservation, *MT, U.S.A.* 83 E10 45 25N 108 0W
Crow Wing →, *MN, U.S.A.* 80 D4 46 19N 94 20W
Crow Wing County ☆, *MN, U.S.A.* 80 D4 46 30N 94 0W
Crowder, *MS, U.S.A.* 81 B3 34 11N 90 8W
Crowder, *OK, U.S.A.* 93 C8 35 7N 95 40W
Crowell, *TX, U.S.A.* 99 D8 33 59N 99 43W

Crowheart, WY, U.S.A. **104 C3** 43 19N 109 12W
Crowley, CO, U.S.A. **66 D7** 38 12N 103 51W
Crowley, LA, U.S.A. **75 D3** 30 13N 92 22W
Crowley, TX, U.S.A. **99 E10** 32 34N 97 21W
Crowley, L., CA, U.S.A. **64 F8** 37 35N 118 42W
Crowley County ☆, CO, U.S.A. **66 D7** 38 15N 103 45W
Crowley Ridge, AR, U.S.A. **63 C5** 35 45N 90 45W
Crown City, OH, U.S.A. **92 E4** 38 36N 82 17W
Crown Point, IN, U.S.A. **72 B3** 41 25N 87 22W
Crown Point, NY, U.S.A. **86 C1** 43 57N 73 26W
Crown Prince Frederik I., Nunavut, Canada **190 C8** 70 2N 86 50W
Crownpoint, NM, U.S.A. **88 B2** 35 41N 108 9W
Crows Nest, Indianapolis, U.S.A. **110 A2** 39 51N 86 10W
Crows Nest Pk., SD, U.S.A. **91 F2** 44 3N 103 58W
Crowsnest Pass, Alta.-B.C., Canada **185 J6** 49 40N 114 40W
Croydon Flat, NH, U.S.A. **86 C2** 43 25N 72 12W
Crozet, VA, U.S.A. **102 C6** 38 4N 78 42W
Crozier Chan., N.W.T., Canada **188 A9** 76 10N 118 30W
Cruces, Chihuahua, Mexico **213 D8** 29 26N 107 24W
Cruces y Anexas, Chihuahua, Mexico **213 E11** 28 43N 104 17W
Cruger, MS, U.S.A. **81 C3** 33 19N 90 14W
Cruillas, Tamaulipas, Mexico **215 F6** 24 45N 98 31W
Crum, WV, U.S.A. **102 D2** 37 54N 82 27W
Crump L., OR, U.S.A. **94 E6** 42 17N 119 50W
Crumpton, MD, U.S.A. **77 A5** 39 14N 75 55W
Crustepec, Cerro, Veracruz, Mexico **220 C3** 21 13N 97 51W
Cruz Bay, U.S. Virgin Is. **105 G18** 18 20N 64 48W
Cruz Grande, Guerrero, Mexico **219 F8** 16 44N 99 8W
Cruz de Garibay, Jalisco, Mexico **218 C4** 19 9N 103 10W
Crystal, MN, U.S.A. **80 E5** 45 2N 93 21W
Crystal, ND, U.S.A. **91 B8** 48 36N 97 40W
Crystal →, CO, U.S.A. **66 C3** 39 25N 107 14W
Crystal ✈, Minneapolis-St. Paul, U.S.A. **113 A1** 45 3N 93 23W
Crystal B., FL, U.S.A. **67 C6** 28 50N 82 45W
Crystal Bay, NV, U.S.A. **85 C1** 39 15N 120 0W
Crystal Beach, MD, U.S.A. **77 A5** 39 26N 75 59W
Crystal City, Man., Canada **183 F13** 49 9N 98 57W
Crystal City, MO, U.S.A. **82 C6** 38 13N 90 23W
Crystal City, TX, U.S.A. **99 J8** 28 41N 99 50W
Crystal Falls, MI, U.S.A. **79 C3** 46 5N 88 20W
Crystal Hill, VA, U.S.A. **102 E6** 36 51N 78 55W
Crystal L., MI, U.S.A. **79 E5** 44 40N 86 10W
Crystal Lake, FL, U.S.A. **67 A3** 30 26N 85 42W
Crystal Lake, IL, U.S.A. **71 A5** 42 14N 88 19W
Crystal Lake, IA, U.S.A. **73 B5** 43 13N 93 47W
Crystal River, FL, U.S.A. **67 C6** 28 54N 82 35W
Crystal Springs, MS, U.S.A. **81 E3** 31 59N 90 21W
Cuajimalpa, Distrito Federal, Mexico **219 C8** 19 20N 99 16W
Cuajimalpa de Morelos, Distrito Federal, Mexico **225 B2** 19 21N 99 18W
Cuajinicuilapa, Guerrero, Mexico **219 F9** 16 28N 98 25W
Cualác, Guerrero, Mexico **219 E9** 17 46N 98 39W
Cuarto Dinamo, Distrito Federal, Mexico **225 C2** 19 15N 99 17W
Cuates de Australia, Coahuila, Mexico **214 D2** 26 18N 102 16W
Cuatillos, Durango, Mexico **217 B7** 25 6N 103 47W
Cuatrociénegas, Parque Natural ⌓, Coahuila, Mexico **214 D2** 26 37N 102 38W
Cuauhtémoc, Chihuahua, Mexico **213 E9** 28 25N 106 52W
Cuauhtémoc, Colima, Mexico **218 C4** 19 20N 103 36W
Cuauhtémoc, Durango, Mexico **217 C7** 24 24N 103 40W
Cuauhtémoc, México, Mexico **225 B3** 19 25N 99 9W
Cuauhtémoc, Oaxaca, Mexico **221 G6** 17 7N 94 54W
Cuauhtémoc, Tamaulipas, Mexico **215 H6** 22 32N 98 6W
Cuautepec, Guerrero, Mexico **219 F9** 16 14N 98 59W
Cuautepec, Hidalgo, Mexico **219 B9** 20 2N 98 18W
Cuautepec de Madero, Distrito Federal, Mexico **225 A3** 19 33N 99 8W
Cuautitlán, Jalisco, Mexico **218 C3** 19 26N 104 23W
Cuautitlán, México, Mexico **219 C8** 19 40N 99 11W
Cuautla, Jalisco, Mexico **218 B3** 20 11N 104 21W
Cuautla, Morelos, Mexico **219 D9** 18 48N 98 57W
Cub Hill, Baltimore, U.S.A. **107 A2** 39 24N 76 30W
Cuba, Sonora, Mexico **212 B4** 31 7N 111 56W
Cuba, AL, U.S.A. **60 D2** 32 26N 88 23W
Cuba, IL, U.S.A. **71 C3** 40 30N 90 12W
Cuba, KS, U.S.A. **74 B6** 39 48N 97 27W
Cuba, MO, U.S.A. **82 C5** 38 4N 91 24W
Cuba, NM, U.S.A. **88 A3** 36 1N 107 4W
Cuba, NY, U.S.A. **89 C2** 42 13N 78 17W
Cuba City, WI, U.S.A. **103 F3** 42 36N 90 26W
Cubabi, Cerro, Sonora, Mexico **212 B3** 31 44N 112 46W
Cubero, NM, U.S.A. **88 B3** 35 5N 107 31W
Cucapá, Sa., Baja Calif., Mexico **210 A3** 32 35N 115 40W
Cucharas →, CO, U.S.A. **66 E6** 37 55N 104 32W
Cuchillo, NM, U.S.A. **88 D3** 33 14N 107 22W
Cuchillo Parado, Chihuahua, Mexico **213 D11** 29 25N 104 52W
Cuckoo, VA, U.S.A. **102 D7** 37 57N 77 54W
Cucurpé, Sonora, Mexico **212 C5** 30 20N 110 43W
Cudahy, Los Angeles, U.S.A. **111 C3** 33 57N 118 11W
Cudahy, WI, U.S.A. **103 F6** 42 57N 87 51W
Cuddeback L., CA, U.S.A. **65 H9** 35 18N 117 29W
Cudworth, Sask., Canada **182 C6** 52 30N 105 44W
Cuencamé, Durango, Mexico **217 C7** 24 53N 103 42W
Cuerámaro, Guanajuato, Mexico **218 B6** 20 38N 101 41W
Cuerenta Casas, Chihuahua, Mexico **213 D7** 29 38N 108 12W
Cuernavaca, Morelos, Mexico **219 D8** 18 55N 99 15W
Cuero, TX, U.S.A. **99 H10** 29 6N 97 17W
Cuervo, NM, U.S.A. **88 B6** 35 2N 104 25W
Cuetzala, Guerrero, Mexico **219 D8** 18 8N 99 50W
Cuetzalán, Puebla, Mexico **220 D3** 20 2N 97 31W
Cuichapa, Veracruz, Mexico **221 G6** 17 59N 94 15W
Cuilapan, Oaxaca, Mexico **221 H4** 16 58N 96 46W
Cuitzeo, Michoacan, Mexico **219 C6** 19 59N 101 9W
Cuitzeo, L. de, Michoacan, Mexico **219 C6** 19 55N 101 5W
Cuivre →, MO, U.S.A. **82 C6** 38 56N 90 41W
Cuivre River State Park ⌓, MO, U.S.A. **82 B6** 39 2N 90 56W
Culberson County ☆, TX, U.S.A. **98 F3** 31 30N 104 30W
Culbertson, MT, U.S.A. **83 B13** 48 9N 104 31W
Culbertson, NE, U.S.A. **84 D5** 40 14N 100 50W
Culdesac, ID, U.S.A. **70 C2** 46 23N 116 40W
Culebra = Dewey, Puerto Rico **105 G17** 18 18N 65 18W
Culebra, Puerto Rico **105 G17** 18 19N 65 18W
Culebra, Cayo, Quintana Roo, Mexico **223 C6** 19 43N 87 30W
Culebra, Roca, Yucatán, Mexico **223 A3** 21 37N 90 30W
Culiacán, Mexico **216 C3** 24 50N 107 23W
Cullen, LA, U.S.A. **75 B2** 32 58N 93 27W
Cullison, KS, U.S.A. **74 D5** 37 38N 98 54W
Cullman, AL, U.S.A. **60 B4** 34 11N 86 51W
Cullman County ☆, AL, U.S.A. **60 B4** 34 11N 86 51W
Culloden, GA, U.S.A. **68 D2** 32 52N 84 6W
Cullom, IL, U.S.A. **71 C5** 40 53N 88 16W
Cullomburg, AL, U.S.A. **60 E2** 31 43N 88 18W
Cullowhee, NC, U.S.A. **90 C2** 35 19N 83 11W
Culmore, VA, U.S.A. **119 B3** 38 51N 77 8W
Culp Creek, OR, U.S.A. **94 D3** 43 42N 122 50W
Culpeper, VA, U.S.A. **102 C6** 38 30N 78 0W
Culpeper County ☆, VA, U.S.A. **102 C6** 38 28N 78 0W
Culubá, Yucatán, Mexico **223 A6** 21 6N 87 54W
Culver, IN, U.S.A. **72 B4** 41 13N 86 25W
Culver, KS, U.S.A. **74 C6** 38 58N 97 46W
Culver, OR, U.S.A. **94 C4** 44 32N 121 13W
Culver City, Los Angeles, U.S.A. **111 B2** 34 1N 118 24W
Culverton, GA, U.S.A. **68 C4** 33 19N 82 54W
Cumberland, B.C., Canada **186 F9** 49 40N 125 0W
Cumberland, Ont., Canada **179 B11** 45 29N 75 24W
Cumberland, IA, U.S.A. **73 D4** 41 16N 94 52W
Cumberland, KY, U.S.A. **97 D10** 36 59N 82 59W
Cumberland, MD, U.S.A. **77 A2** 39 39N 78 46W
Cumberland, NC, U.S.A. **90 C7** 35 0N 78 59W
Cumberland, NJ, U.S.A. **87 C1** 39 26N 75 14W
Cumberland, OH, U.S.A. **92 D5** 39 51N 81 40W
Cumberland, RI, U.S.A. **78 C3** 41 58N 71 26W
Cumberland, VA, U.S.A. **102 D6** 37 30N 78 15W
Cumberland, WI, U.S.A. **103 C1** 45 32N 92 1W
Cumberland →, U.S.A. **96 C4** 37 9N 88 25W
Cumberland, L., KY, U.S.A. **97 D7** 36 52N 85 9W
Cumberland City, TN, U.S.A. **96 D5** 36 23N 87 38W
Cumberland County ☆, IL, U.S.A. **71 D5** 39 15N 88 15W
Cumberland County ☆, KY, U.S.A. **97 D7** 36 45N 85 25W
Cumberland County ☆, ME, U.S.A. **76 E3** 43 50N 70 30W
Cumberland County ☆, NC, U.S.A. **90 D7** 35 0N 78 45W
Cumberland County ☆, NJ, U.S.A. **87 C1** 39 20N 75 10W
Cumberland County ☆, PA, U.S.A. **95 D5** 40 5N 77 10W
Cumberland County ☆, TN, U.S.A. **97 D7** 36 0N 85 0W
Cumberland County ☆, VA, U.S.A. **102 D6** 37 30N 78 15W
Cumberland Falls State Park ⌓, KY, U.S.A. **97 D8** 36 50N 84 20W
Cumberland Gap, KY, U.S.A. **97 D9** 36 36N 83 41W
Cumberland Gap Nat. Historical Park ⌓, KY, U.S.A. **97 D9** 36 36N 83 40W
Cumberland Hill, RI, U.S.A. **78 C3** 41 59N 71 28W
Cumberland House, Sask., Canada **183 B9** 53 58N 102 16W
Cumberland I., GA, U.S.A. **68 F5** 30 50N 81 25W
Cumberland Island Nat. Seashore ⌓, GA, U.S.A. **68 F5** 30 12N 81 24W
Cumberland L., Sask., Canada **183 A9** 54 3N 102 18W
Cumberland Pen., Nunavut, Canada **191 D13** 67 0N 64 0W
Cumberland Plateau, U.S.A. **97 E7** 36 0N 85 0W
Cumberland Pt., MI, U.S.A. **79 B2** 47 51N 89 14W
Cumberland Sd., Nunavut, Canada **190 D12** 65 30N 66 0W
Cumbres de Majalca, Parque Nacional △, Chihuahua, Mexico **213 E9** 28 48N 106 30W
Cumbres de Monterrey, Parque Nacional △, Nuevo León, Mexico **214 E4** 25 26N 100 25W
Cumbres del Ajusco, Parque Nacional △, Distrito Federal, Mexico **225 C2** 19 12N 99 15W
Cumby, TX, U.S.A. **99 D12** 33 8N 95 50W
Cuming County ☆, NE, U.S.A. **84 C9** 41 50N 96 40W
Cumming, GA, U.S.A. **68 B2** 34 12N 84 9W
Cummins Lakes Park ⌓, B.C., Canada **187 C16** 52 6N 118 3W
Cumpas, Sonora, Mexico **212 C6** 30 2N 109 48W
Cumshewa Inlet, B.C., Canada **186 B3** 53 3N 131 50W
Cunduacán, Tabasco, Mexico **222 A3** 18 4N 93 10W
Cunningham, KS, U.S.A. **74 D5** 37 39N 98 26W
Cupar, Sask., Canada **182 E7** 50 57N 104 10W
Cupertino, CA, U.S.A. **64 F4** 37 19N 122 2W
Cuprum, ID, U.S.A. **70 D2** 45 5N 116 41W
Cuquío, Jalisco, Mexico **218 B4** 20 55N 103 2W
Curecanti Nat. Recr. Area ⌓, CO, U.S.A. **66 D3** 38 24N 107 25W
Curlew, IA, U.S.A. **73 C4** 42 59N 94 44W
Curlew, WA, U.S.A. **101 B7** 48 53N 118 36W
Curlew Nat. Grasslands, ID, U.S.A. **70 G6** 42 13N 112 45W
Curran, MI, U.S.A. **79 E8** 44 43N 83 48W
Currant, NV, U.S.A. **85 D5** 38 44N 115 28W
Currant Mt., NV, U.S.A. **85 D5** 38 55N 115 25W
Current →, AR, U.S.A. **63 B5** 36 15N 90 55W
Currie, MN, U.S.A. **80 F3** 44 3N 95 40W
Currie, NV, U.S.A. **85 B6** 40 16N 114 45W
Currituck, NC, U.S.A. **90 B9** 36 27N 76 1W
Currituck County ☆, NC, U.S.A. **90 B10** 36 20N 76 0W
Currituck Sd., NC, U.S.A. **90 B10** 36 20N 75 52W
Curry County ☆, NM, U.S.A. **88 C7** 34 30N 103 15W
Curry County ☆, OR, U.S.A. **94 E1** 42 20N 124 20W
Curryville, MO, U.S.A. **82 B5** 39 21N 91 21W
Curtin, OR, U.S.A. **94 D2** 43 43N 123 12W
Curtis, AR, U.S.A. **63 E2** 34 0N 93 2W
Curtis, NE, U.S.A. **84 D5** 40 38N 100 31W
Curtis Bay, Baltimore, U.S.A. **107 B2** 39 13N 76 33W
Curtis Creek →, Baltimore, U.S.A. **107 B2** 39 13N 76 33W
Curtis L., Nunavut, Canada **191 D8** 66 41N 89 10W
Curwensville, PA, U.S.A. **95 D4** 40 58N 78 32W
Cusárare, Chihuahua, Mexico **213 F8** 27 37N 107 35W
Cushing, IA, U.S.A. **73 C3** 42 28N 95 41W
Cushing, NE, U.S.A. **84 C7** 41 19N 98 22W
Cushing, OK, U.S.A. **93 C7** 35 59N 96 46W
Cushing, TX, U.S.A. **99 F13** 31 49N 94 51W
Cushing, Mt., B.C., Canada **189 E7** 57 35N 126 57W
Cushman, AR, U.S.A. **63 C4** 35 53N 91 45W
Cushman, OR, U.S.A. **94 D1** 43 59N 124 3W
Cushman, L., WA, U.S.A. **101 C2** 47 25N 123 13W
Cusick, WA, U.S.A. **101 B8** 48 20N 117 18W
Cusihuiriáchic, Chihuahua, Mexico **213 E9** 28 14N 106 50W
Cusseta, GA, U.S.A. **68 D2** 32 18N 84 47W
Cusson, Pte., Qué., Canada **175 A2** 60 23N 77 46W
Custepec, Chiapas, Mexico **222 D3** 15 43N 92 58W
Custer, MT, U.S.A. **83 D10** 46 8N 107 33W
Custer, SD, U.S.A. **91 G2** 43 46N 103 36W
Custer, WA, U.S.A. **101 B3** 48 55N 122 38W
Custer City, OK, U.S.A. **93 C5** 35 40N 98 53W
Custer County ☆, CO, U.S.A. **66 D5** 38 10N 105 20W
Custer County ☆, ID, U.S.A. **70 E4** 44 0N 114 0W
Custer County ☆, MT, U.S.A. **83 D12** 46 25N 105 30W
Custer County ☆, NE, U.S.A. **84 C6** 41 30N 99 40W
Custer County ☆, OK, U.S.A. **93 C5** 35 40N 99 0W
Custer County ☆, SD, U.S.A. **91 G2** 43 50N 103 30W
Custer Nat. Forest, MT, U.S.A. **83 E8** 45 15N 109 50W
Custer Nat. Forest, SD, U.S.A. **91 E2** 45 30N 103 15W
Custer State Park ⌓, SD, U.S.A. **91 G2** 43 42N 103 22W
Cut Bank, MT, U.S.A. **83 B5** 48 38N 112 20W
Cut Bank Cr. →, MT, U.S.A. **83 B5** 48 29N 112 14W
Cut Bank Cr. →, ND, U.S.A. **91 B5** 48 10N 100 45W
Cut Knife, Sask., Canada **182 C2** 52 45N 109 1W
Cut Off, LA, U.S.A. **75 E5** 29 33N 90 20W
Cutbank, Sask., Canada **182 D5** 51 18N 106 51W
Cutbank →, Alta., Canada **184 D2** 54 43N 118 32W
Cuthbert, GA, U.S.A. **68 E2** 31 46N 84 48W
Cutler, CA, U.S.A. **65 G7** 36 31N 119 17W
Cutler, IL, U.S.A. **71 E4** 38 2N 89 34W
Cutler, ME, U.S.A. **76 D6** 44 40N 67 12W
Cutler Park, Boston, U.S.A. **106 B2** 42 17N 71 12W
Cutler Ridge, FL, U.S.A. **67 F8** 25 35N 80 20W
Cutlerville, MI, U.S.A. **79 G6** 42 50N 85 40W
Cuttyhunk I., MA, U.S.A. **78 C4** 41 25N 70 56W
Cutzamala, Guerrero, Mexico **219 D7** 18 28N 100 34W
Cutzamala →, Mexico **219 D7** 18 22N 100 39W
Cuyahoga →, Cleveland, U.S.A. **107 B1** 41 30N 81 41W
Cuyahoga County ☆, OH, U.S.A. **92 B5** 41 23N 81 43W
Cuyahoga Falls, OH, U.S.A. **92 B5** 41 8N 81 29W
Cuyahoga Heights, Cleveland, U.S.A. **107 B2** 41 26N 81 39W
Cuyahoga Valley Nat. Park △, U.S.A. **92 B5** 41 14N 81 33W
Cuyama →, CA, U.S.A. **65 J6** 34 58N 120 38W
Cuyamaca State Park ⌓, CA, U.S.A. **65 L10** 32 56N 116 33W
Cuyapaipe Indian Reservation, CA, U.S.A. **65 L10** 32 51N 116 23W
Cuyuna Range, MN, U.S.A. **80 D5** 46 25N 93 30W
Cuyutlán, Colima, Mexico **218 D3** 18 55N 104 4W
Cygnet, OH, U.S.A. **92 B3** 41 14N 83 39W
Cylinder, IA, U.S.A. **73 B4** 43 5N 94 33W
Cynthia, Alta., Canada **184 E5** 53 17N 115 25W
Cynthiana, IN, U.S.A. **72 E3** 38 11N 87 43W
Cynthiana, KY, U.S.A. **97 B8** 38 23N 84 18W
Cypress, IL, U.S.A. **71 F4** 37 22N 89 1W
Cypress, Los Angeles, U.S.A. **111 C4** 33 49N 118 2W
Cypress Creek Nat. Wildlife Refuge ⌓, IL, U.S.A. **71 F4** 37 18N 89 8W
Cypress Falls Park, Vancouver, Canada **193 A1** 49 21N 123 12W
Cypress Hills Interprovincial Park ⌓, Sask., Canada **182 F2** 49 40N 109 30W
Cypress River, Man., Canada **183 F12** 49 34N 99 5W
Cyril, OK, U.S.A. **93 D5** 34 54N 98 12W
Cyrus, MN, U.S.A. **80 E3** 45 37N 95 44W
Cyrville, Ont., Canada **192 A2** 45 25N 75 38W
Czar, Alta., Canada **185 F10** 52 27N 110 50W

D

Dacoma, OK, U.S.A. **93 B5** 36 40N 98 34W
Dacono, CO, U.S.A. **66 B6** 40 5N 104 56W
Dacula, GA, U.S.A. **68 C3** 33 59N 83 54W
Dade City, FL, U.S.A. **67 C6** 28 22N 82 11W
Dade County ☆, GA, U.S.A. **68 B1** 34 53N 85 31W
Dade County ☆, MO, U.S.A. **82 D3** 37 25N 93 50W
Dadeville, AL, U.S.A. **60 D5** 32 50N 85 46W
Dadeville, MO, U.S.A. **82 D3** 37 29N 93 41W
Dafter, MI, U.S.A. **79 C7** 46 22N 84 26W
Daggett, MI, U.S.A. **79 D4** 45 28N 87 36W
Daggett County ☆, UT, U.S.A. **100 C6** 40 55N 109 30W
Dagsboro, DE, U.S.A. **77 B5** 38 33N 75 15W
Dahlgren, IL, U.S.A. **71 E5** 38 12N 88 41W
Dahlgren, VA, U.S.A. **77 B3** 38 20N 77 3W
Dahlonega, GA, U.S.A. **68 B3** 34 32N 83 59W
Dahlonega Plat., GA, U.S.A. **68 B2** 34 10N 84 20W
Dailey, WV, U.S.A. **102 C5** 38 48N 79 54W
Daingerfield, TX, U.S.A. **99 D13** 33 2N 94 44W
Dairy, OR, U.S.A. **94 E4** 42 14N 121 31W
Daisetta, TX, U.S.A. **99 G13** 30 7N 94 39W
Daisy, AR, U.S.A. **63 D2** 34 14N 93 45W
Daisy, WA, U.S.A. **101 B7** 48 22N 118 10W
Dakota, IL, U.S.A. **71 A4** 42 23N 89 32W
Dakota, MN, U.S.A. **80 G7** 43 55N 91 22W
Dakota City, IA, U.S.A. **73 C4** 42 43N 94 12W
Dakota City, NE, U.S.A. **84 B9** 42 25N 96 25W
Dakota County ☆, MN, U.S.A. **80 F5** 44 45N 93 0W
Dakota County ☆, NE, U.S.A. **84 B9** 42 30N 96 30W
Dalark, AR, U.S.A. **63 D3** 34 2N 92 53W
Dalcour, New Orleans, U.S.A. **113 D3** 29 48N 89 59W
Dale, IN, U.S.A. **72 E4** 38 10N 86 59W
Dale, OK, U.S.A. **93 C6** 35 24N 97 3W
Dale City, VA, U.S.A. **102 C7** 38 38N 77 19W
Dale City, VA, U.S.A. **102 C7** 38 38N 77 18W
Dale County ☆, AL, U.S.A. **60 E5** 31 28N 85 39W
Dale Hollow L., TN, U.S.A. **97 D7** 36 32N 85 27W
Daleville, AL, U.S.A. **60 E5** 31 19N 85 43W
Daleville, IN, U.S.A. **72 C5** 40 7N 85 33W
Daleville, MS, U.S.A. **81 D5** 32 34N 88 41W
Dalhart, TX, U.S.A. **98 A5** 36 4N 102 31W
Dalhousie, N.B., Canada **173 E3** 48 5N 66 26W
Dalhousie, C., N.W.T., Canada **188 B7** 70 15N 129 40W
Dalkeith, FL, U.S.A. **67 A3** 30 0N 85 9W
Dallam County ☆, TX, U.S.A. **98 A5** 36 15N 102 30W
Dallas, GA, U.S.A. **68 C2** 33 55N 84 51W
Dallas, NC, U.S.A. **90 C4** 35 19N 81 11W
Dallas, OR, U.S.A. **94 C2** 44 55N 123 19W
Dallas, PA, U.S.A. **95 C7** 41 20N 75 58W
Dallas, SD, U.S.A. **91 G6** 43 14N 99 31W
Dallas, TX, U.S.A. **99 E11** 32 47N 96 48W
Dallas, WI, U.S.A. **103 C2** 45 16N 91 51W
Dallas Center, IA, U.S.A. **73 D5** 41 41N 93 58W
Dallas City, IL, U.S.A. **71 C2** 40 38N 91 10W
Dallas County ☆, AL, U.S.A. **60 D3** 32 25N 87 1W
Dallas County ☆, AR, U.S.A. **63 E3** 33 59N 92 38W
Dallas County ☆, IA, U.S.A. **73 D4** 41 40N 94 0W
Dallas County ☆, MO, U.S.A. **82 D3** 37 40N 93 0W
Dallas County ☆, TX, U.S.A. **99 E11** 32 50N 96 50W
Dallas-Fort Worth International ✈ (DFW), Dallas-Fort Worth, U.S.A. **109 A3** 32 53N 97 2W
Dallastown, PA, U.S.A. **77 A4** 39 54N 76 38W
Dalmeny, Sask., Canada **182 C5** 52 20N 106 46W
Dalton, Ont., Canada **181 D12** 48 11N 84 1W
Dalton, GA, U.S.A. **68 B2** 34 46N 84 58W
Dalton, MA, U.S.A. **78 B1** 42 28N 73 11W
Dalton, MN, U.S.A. **80 D3** 46 10N 95 55W
Dalton, NE, U.S.A. **84 C3** 41 25N 102 58W
Dalton, OH, U.S.A. **92 C5** 40 48N 81 42W
Dalton, PA, U.S.A. **87 A1** 41 32N 75 44W
Dalton Gardens, ID, U.S.A. **70 B2** 47 44N 116 46W
Dalworthington Gardens, Dallas-Fort Worth, U.S.A. **109 B3** 32 42N 97 9W
Daly B., Nunavut, Canada **191 E8** 64 0N 89 45W
Daly City, CA, U.S.A. **64 F4** 37 42N 122 27W
Damar, KS, U.S.A. **74 B4** 39 19N 99 35W
Damasco, Chiapas, Mexico **222 B5** 17 10N 91 36W
Damascus, AR, U.S.A. **63 C3** 35 22N 92 25W
Damascus, GA, U.S.A. **68 E2** 31 18N 84 43W
Damascus, MD, U.S.A. **77 A3** 39 17N 77 12W
Damascus, VA, U.S.A. **102 E3** 36 38N 81 47W
Dameron, MD, U.S.A. **77 B4** 38 10N 76 22W
Dames Quarter, MD, U.S.A. **77 B5** 38 11N 75 54W
Damián Carmona, San Luis Potosí, Mexico **215 H5** 22 6N 99 17W
Dan →, VA, U.S.A. **102 E6** 36 42N 78 50W
Dan Ryan Woods, Chicago, U.S.A. **108 C2** 41 44N 87 40W
Dana, IN, U.S.A. **72 D3** 39 48N 87 30W
Dana, IA, U.S.A. **73 C4** 42 6N 94 14W
Dana, L., Qué., Canada **175 C2** 50 53N 77 20W
Dana Point, CA, U.S.A. **65 K9** 33 28N 117 42W
Danbury, CT, U.S.A. **78 C1** 41 24N 73 28W
Danbury, IA, U.S.A. **73 C3** 42 14N 95 43W
Danbury, NC, U.S.A. **90 B5** 36 25N 80 12W
Danbury, NH, U.S.A. **86 C3** 43 32N 71 52W
Danbury, NE, U.S.A. **84 D5** 40 3N 100 25W
Danbury, TX, U.S.A. **99 H12** 29 14N 95 21W
Danby, VT, U.S.A. **86 C2** 43 20N 72 59W
Danby L., CA, U.S.A. **65 J11** 34 13N 115 5W
Dandridge, TN, U.S.A. **97 D9** 36 1N 83 25W
Dane County ☆, WI, U.S.A. **103 E4** 43 0N 89 29W
Danforth, IL, U.S.A. **71 C6** 40 49N 87 59W
Danforth, ME, U.S.A. **76 C6** 45 40N 67 52W
Danforth Hills, CO, U.S.A. **66 B2** 40 15N 108 0W
Dania Beach, Miami, U.S.A. **112 B3** 26 3N 80 8W
Daniel, WY, U.S.A. **104 D2** 42 52N 110 4W
Daniel Boone Nat. Forest, KY, U.S.A. **97 C8** 37 30N 84 10W
Daniels County ☆, MT, U.S.A. **83 B12** 48 40N 105 20W
Daniel's Harbour, Nfld. & L., Canada **174 B3** 50 13N 57 35W
Daniels Pass, UT, U.S.A. **100 C4** 40 18N 111 10W
Danielson, CT, U.S.A. **78 C3** 41 48N 71 53W
Danielson Prov. Park ⌓, Sask., Canada **182 D5** 51 16N 106 50W
Danielsville, GA, U.S.A. **68 B3** 34 8N 83 13W
Danish West Indies = Virgin Is. (U.S.) ☒, W. Indies **105 G18** 18 20N 65 0W
Dannebrog, NE, U.S.A. **84 C7** 41 7N 98 33W
Dannemora, NY, U.S.A. **89 A7** 44 43N 73 44W
Danskin, B.C., Canada **186 B9** 53 59N 125 47W
Dansville, MI, U.S.A. **79 G7** 42 34N 84 19W
Dansville, NY, U.S.A. **89 C3** 42 34N 77 42W
Dante, SD, U.S.A. **91 G7** 43 2N 98 11W
Dante, VA, U.S.A. **102 E2** 36 59N 82 18W
Danvers, IL, U.S.A. **71 C4** 40 32N 89 10W
Danvers, MA, U.S.A. **78 B4** 42 34N 70 56W
Danvers, MN, U.S.A. **80 E3** 45 17N 95 45W
Danville, AR, U.S.A. **63 C2** 35 3N 93 24W
Danville, CA, U.S.A. **64 F5** 37 49N 122 0W
Danville, GA, U.S.A. **68 D3** 32 37N 83 15W
Danville, IL, U.S.A. **71 C6** 40 8N 87 37W
Danville, IN, U.S.A. **72 D4** 39 46N 86 32W
Danville, IA, U.S.A. **73 E7** 40 52N 91 19W
Danville, KS, U.S.A. **74 D6** 37 17N 97 54W
Danville, KY, U.S.A. **97 C8** 37 39N 84 46W
Danville, OH, U.S.A. **92 C4** 40 27N 82 16W
Danville, PA, U.S.A. **95 D6** 40 58N 76 37W
Danville, VA, U.S.A. **102 E5** 36 36N 79 23W
Danville, VT, U.S.A. **86 B2** 44 25N 72 9W
Danville, WV, U.S.A. **102 C3** 38 5N 81 50W
Danville, WA, U.S.A. **101 B7** 48 59N 118 30W
Danzante, I., Baja Calif. S., Mexico **211 H7** 25 47N 111 17W
Daphne, AL, U.S.A. **60 F3** 30 36N 87 54W
D'Arbonne, Bayou →, LA, U.S.A. **75 B3** 32 34N 92 7W
Darby, MT, U.S.A. **83 D3** 46 1N 114 11W
Darby, PA, U.S.A. **87 C1** 39 55N 75 13W
Darby, C., AK, U.S.A. **61 D7** 64 19N 162 47W
D'Arcy, B.C., Canada **187 E12** 50 33N 122 29W
Dardanelle, AR, U.S.A. **63 C2** 35 13N 93 9W
Dardanelle, CA, U.S.A. **64 E7** 38 20N 119 50W
Dardanelle, L., AR, U.S.A. **63 C2** 35 14N 93 10W
Dare County ☆, NC, U.S.A. **90 C10** 35 45N 75 40W
Darfur, MN, U.S.A. **80 F4** 44 3N 94 50W
Darien, CT, U.S.A. **78 C1** 41 5N 73 28W
Darien, GA, U.S.A. **68 E5** 31 23N 81 26W
Darien, WI, U.S.A. **103 F5** 42 36N 88 43W
Dark Cove, Nfld. & L., Canada **174 D6** 48 47N 54 13W
Darke County ☆, OH, U.S.A. **92 C2** 40 6N 84 38W
Darling, MS, U.S.A. **81 B3** 34 22N 90 16W
Darling, L., ND, U.S.A. **91 B4** 48 27N 101 35W
Darlington, FL, U.S.A. **67 A2** 30 57N 86 3W
Darlington, IN, U.S.A. **72 C4** 40 6N 86 47W
Darlington, LA, U.S.A. **75 D5** 30 53N 90 47W
Darlington, MD, U.S.A. **77 A4** 39 38N 76 12W
Darlington, SC, U.S.A. **90 D6** 34 18N 79 52W
Darlington, WI, U.S.A. **103 F3** 42 41N 90 7W
Darlington County ☆, SC, U.S.A. **90 D6** 34 20N 80 0W
Darmstadt, IN, U.S.A. **72 E3** 38 6N 87 35W
Darnestown, MD, U.S.A. **77 A3** 39 6N 77 18W
Darnley B., N.W.T., Canada **188 C8** 69 30N 123 30W
Darr, NE, U.S.A. **84 D6** 40 49N 99 53W
Darrington, WA, U.S.A. **101 B4** 48 15N 121 36W
Darrouzett, TX, U.S.A. **98 A7** 36 27N 100 20W
Dartmouth, N.S., Canada **173 J6** 44 40N 63 30W
Dartmouth, MA, U.S.A. **78 C3** 41 34N 71 1W
Dartmouth →, Qué., Canada **172 E5** 48 53N 64 34W
Dasher, GA, U.S.A. **68 F3** 30 45N 83 13W
Dassel, MN, U.S.A. **80 E4** 45 5N 94 19W
Dasserat, L., Qué., Canada **176 C3** 48 16N 79 25W
Dateland, AZ, U.S.A. **62 E2** 32 48N 113 33W
Datil, NM, U.S.A. **88 C3** 34 9N 107 51W
Daulnay, N.B., Canada **173 F4** 47 25N 65 28W
Dauphin, Man., Canada **183 D11** 51 9N 100 5W
Dauphin County ☆, PA, U.S.A. **95 D6** 40 20N 76 55W
Dauphin I., AL, U.S.A. **60 F2** 30 15N 88 11W
Dauphin Island, AL, U.S.A. **60 F2** 30 15N 88 7W
Dauphin L., Man., Canada **183 D12** 51 20N 99 45W
Dauphin River, Man., Canada **183 D13** 51 58N 98 4W
Davenport, CA, U.S.A. **64 F4** 37 1N 122 12W
Davenport, FL, U.S.A. **67 C7** 28 10N 81 36W
Davenport, IA, U.S.A. **73 D8** 41 32N 90 35W
Davenport, ND, U.S.A. **91 D8** 46 43N 97 4W
Davenport, NY, U.S.A. **89 C6** 42 28N 74 51W
Davenport, NE, U.S.A. **84 D8** 40 19N 97 49W
Davenport, OK, U.S.A. **93 C7** 35 42N 96 46W
Davenport, WA, U.S.A. **101 C7** 47 39N 118 9W
Davey, NE, U.S.A. **84 D9** 40 59N 96 40W
David, KY, U.S.A. **97 C10** 37 36N 82 54W
David City, NE, U.S.A. **84 C8** 41 15N 97 8W
David's Island, NY, U.S.A. **114 A4** 40 53N 73 46W
Davidson, Sask., Canada **182 D6** 51 16N 105 59W
Davidson, NC, U.S.A. **90 C5** 35 30N 80 51W
Davidson, OK, U.S.A. **93 D4** 34 14N 99 5W
Davidson, Mt., San Francisco, U.S.A. **118 B2** 37 44N 122 27W
Davidson County ☆, NC, U.S.A. **90 C5** 35 45N 80 10W
Davidson County ☆, TN, U.S.A. **96 D6** 36 10N 86 47W
Davidson Mts., AK, U.S.A. **61 B12** 68 41N 142 22W
Davidsonville, MD, U.S.A. **77 B4** 38 55N 76 38W
Davie, FL, U.S.A. **67 E8** 26 3N 80 14W
Davie County ☆, NC, U.S.A. **90 C5** 35 50N 80 30W
Daviess County ☆, IN, U.S.A. **72 E3** 38 40N 87 5W
Daviess County ☆, KY, U.S.A. **96 C5** 37 40N 87 5W
Daviess County ☆, MO, U.S.A. **82 B3** 40 0N 94 0W
Davis, CA, U.S.A. **64 E5** 38 33N 121 44W
Davis, IL, U.S.A. **71 A4** 42 25N 89 25W
Davis, OK, U.S.A. **93 D6** 34 30N 97 7W
Davis, SD, U.S.A. **91 G9** 43 16N 96 59W
Davis, WV, U.S.A. **77 A1** 39 8N 79 28W
Davis, Lake, CA, U.S.A. **64 D6** 39 53N 120 29W
Davis, Mt., PA, U.S.A. **95 E3** 39 48N 79 10W
Davis City, IA, U.S.A. **73 E5** 40 38N 93 49W
Davis County ☆, IA, U.S.A. **73 E6** 40 45N 92 25W
Davis County ☆, UT, U.S.A. **100 C3** 41 0N 112 15W
Davis Creek, CA, U.S.A. **64 B6** 41 44N 120 22W
Davis Dam, U.S.A. **62 B1** 35 12N 114 34W
Davis Inlet, Nfld. & L., Canada **175 B5** 55 50N 60 59W
Davis Island, Tampa, U.S.A. **119 B4** 27 55N 82 27W
Davis Junction, IL, U.S.A. **71 A4** 42 6N 89 6W
Davis Mts., TX, U.S.A. **98 G4** 30 50N 103 55W
Davis Str., N. Amer. **190 D14** 65 0N 58 0W
Davisboro, GA, U.S.A. **68 D4** 32 59N 82 36W
Davison, MI, U.S.A. **79 F8** 43 2N 83 31W
Davison County ☆, SD, U.S.A. **91 G7** 43 40N 98 2W
Davisville, MO, U.S.A. **82 D5** 37 49N 91 11W
Davy, WV, U.S.A. **102 D3** 37 29N 81 39W
Davy Crockett Nat. Forest, TX, U.S.A. **99 F12** 31 12N 95 2W
Dawes County ☆, NE, U.S.A. **84 B2** 42 45N 103 0W
Dawn, TX, U.S.A. **98 C5** 34 55N 102 12W
Dawson, Yukon, Canada **189 D5** 64 10N 139 30W

Dawson, GA, U.S.A. 68 E2 31 46N 84 27W
Dawson, MN, U.S.A. 80 F2 44 56N 96 3W
Dawson, ND, U.S.A. 91 D6 46 52N 99 45W
Dawson, NE, U.S.A. 84 D10 40 8N 95 50W
Dawson, TX, U.S.A. 99 F11 31 54N 96 43W
Dawson B., Man., Canada 183 C11 52 53N 100 49W
Dawson County ☆, GA, U.S.A. 68 B2 34 25N 84 10W
Dawson County ☆, MT, U.S.A. 83 C13 47 15N 105 0W
Dawson County ☆, NE, U.S.A. 84 D6 40 50N 99 50W
Dawson County ☆, TX, U.S.A. 98 E6 32 44N 101 58W
Dawson Creek, B.C., Canada 189 E8 55 45N 120 15W
Dawson Inlet, Nunavut, Canada 191 E7 61 50N 93 25W
Dawson Range, Yukon, Canada 189 D5 62 35N 138 20W
Dawson Springs, KY, U.S.A. 96 C5 37 10N 87 41W
Dawsonville, GA, U.S.A. 68 B2 34 25N 84 7W
Day, FL, U.S.A. 67 A5 30 12N 83 17W
Day County ☆, SD, U.S.A. 91 E8 45 20N 97 31W
Daykin, NE, U.S.A. 84 D8 40 21N 97 18W
Daysland, Alta., Canada 185 F8 52 50N 112 20W
Dayton, AL, U.S.A. 60 D3 32 21N 87 38W
Dayton, IA, U.S.A. 73 C4 42 16N 94 4W
Dayton, KY, U.S.A. 107 B2 39 6N 84 28W
Dayton, MT, U.S.A. 83 C3 47 52N 114 17W
Dayton, NV, U.S.A. 85 C1 39 14N 119 36W
Dayton, OH, U.S.A. 92 D2 39 45N 84 12W
Dayton, PA, U.S.A. 95 D3 40 53N 79 15W
Dayton, TN, U.S.A. 97 E7 35 30N 85 1W
Dayton, TX, U.S.A. 99 G13 30 3N 94 54W
Dayton, VA, U.S.A. 102 C6 38 25N 78 56W
Dayton, WA, U.S.A. 101 D8 46 19N 117 59W
Dayton, WY, U.S.A. 104 B5 44 53N 107 16W
Dayton International ✕ (DAY), OH, U.S.A. 92 D2 39 54N 84 13W
Daytona Beach, FL, U.S.A. 67 B7 29 13N 81 1W
Dayville, OR, U.S.A. 94 C6 44 28N 119 32W
Dazey, ND, U.S.A. 91 C7 47 11N 98 12W
De Armanville, AL, U.S.A. 60 C5 33 38N 85 45W
De Baca County ☆, NM, U.S.A. 88 C6 34 15N 104 30W
De Bary, FL, U.S.A. 67 C7 28 54N 81 18W
De Beque, CO, U.S.A. 66 C2 39 20N 108 13W
De Forest, WI, U.S.A. 103 E4 43 15N 89 20W
De Funiak Springs, FL, U.S.A. 67 A2 30 43N 86 7W
De Graff, MN, U.S.A. 80 E3 45 16N 95 28W
De Grau, Nfld. & L., Canada 174 D1 48 29N 59 9W
De Gray L., AR, U.S.A. 63 D2 34 13N 93 7W
De Gray Lake Resort State Park ⌓, AR, U.S.A. 63 D2 34 15N 93 10W
De Kalb, MS, U.S.A. 81 D5 32 46N 88 39W
De Kalb, TX, U.S.A. 99 D13 33 31N 94 37W
De Kalb County ☆, AL, U.S.A. 60 B5 34 26N 85 43W
De Kalb County ☆, MO, U.S.A. 82 B2 39 50N 94 25W
De Kalb Junction, NY, U.S.A. 89 A5 44 30N 75 17W
De Land, FL, U.S.A. 67 B7 29 2N 81 18W
De Leon, TX, U.S.A. 99 E9 32 7N 98 32W
De Leon Springs, FL, U.S.A. 67 B7 29 7N 81 21W
De Long Mts., AK, U.S.A. 61 B7 68 10N 163 30W
De Montreville, L., Minneapolis-St. Paul, U.S.A. 113 A4 45 1N 92 56W
De Morbihan, L., Qué., Canada 172 B7 51 50N 62 54W
De Pere, WI, U.S.A. 103 D5 44 27N 88 4W
De Queen, AR, U.S.A. 63 D1 34 2N 94 21W
De Quincy, LA, U.S.A. 75 D2 30 27N 93 26W
De Ruyter, NY, U.S.A. 89 C5 42 46N 75 53W
De Smet, SD, U.S.A. 91 F8 44 23N 97 33W
De Smet, L., WY, U.S.A. 104 B6 44 29N 106 45W
De Soto, Dallas-Fort Worth, U.S.A. 109 C5 32 35N 96 51W
De Soto, IL, U.S.A. 71 F4 37 49N 89 14W
De Soto, IA, U.S.A. 73 D4 41 32N 94 1W
De Soto, KS, U.S.A. 74 C9 38 59N 94 58W
De Soto, MO, U.S.A. 82 C6 38 8N 90 34W
De Soto, WI, U.S.A. 103 E2 43 25N 91 12W
De Soto City, FL, U.S.A. 67 D7 27 27N 81 24W
De Soto County ☆, FL, U.S.A. 67 D7 27 15N 81 45W
De Soto County ☆, MS, U.S.A. 81 B3 34 53N 90 1W
De Soto Nat. Forest, MS, U.S.A. 81 E4 31 0N 89 0W
De Soto Nat. Memorial ⌓, FL, U.S.A. 67 D6 27 31N 82 39W
De Soto Nat. Wildlife Refuge △, IA, U.S.A. 73 D2 41 30N 96 1W
De Soto Parish ☆, LA, U.S.A. 75 B2 32 2N 93 43W
De Tour Village, MI, U.S.A. 79 C8 46 0N 83 56W
De Valls Bluff, AR, U.S.A. 63 D4 34 47N 91 28W
De Witt, AR, U.S.A. 63 D4 34 18N 91 20W
De Witt, IL, U.S.A. 71 C5 40 11N 88 47W
De Witt, IA, U.S.A. 73 D8 41 49N 90 33W
De Witt, MI, U.S.A. 79 G7 42 51N 84 34W
De Witt, NE, U.S.A. 84 D9 40 24N 96 55W
De Witt County ☆, IL, U.S.A. 71 C5 40 10N 88 55W
De Witt County ☆, TX, U.S.A. 99 H10 29 6N 97 17W
Dead L., FL, U.S.A. 67 A3 30 10N 85 10W
Deadhorse, AK, U.S.A. 61 A10 70 11N 148 27W
Deadman B., FL, U.S.A. 67 B5 29 30N 83 30W
Deadwood, SD, U.S.A. 91 F2 44 23N 103 44W
Deaf Smith County ☆, TX, U.S.A. 98 C5 35 0N 102 30W
Deale, MD, U.S.A. 77 B4 38 47N 76 33W
Dean →, B.C., Canada 186 C8 52 49N 126 58W
Dean Chan., B.C., Canada 186 C7 52 30N 127 15W
Dearborn, MI, U.S.A. 79 G8 42 19N 83 10W
Dearborn, MO, U.S.A. 82 B2 39 32N 94 46W
Dearborn County ☆, IN, U.S.A. 72 D6 39 10N 85 0W
Dearing, KS, U.S.A. 74 D8 37 4N 95 43W
Deary, ID, U.S.A. 70 C2 46 48N 116 32W
Deas Island Park, Vancouver, Canada 193 C2 49 7N 123 4W
Dease →, B.C., Canada 189 E7 59 56N 128 32W
Dease Arm, N.W.T., Canada 188 C9 66 52N 119 37W
Dease Inlet, AK, U.S.A. 61 A9 71 2N 155 26W
Dease Lake, B.C., Canada 189 E6 58 25N 130 6W
Dease Str., Nunavut, Canada 190 D4 68 50N 107 30W
Death Valley, CA, U.S.A. 65 G10 36 15N 116 50W
Death Valley Junction, CA, U.S.A. 65 G10 36 20N 116 25W
Death Valley Nat. Park △, U.S.A. 65 G9 36 29N 117 6W
Deatsville, AL, U.S.A. 60 D4 32 37N 86 24W
Deaver, WY, U.S.A. 104 B4 44 54N 108 36W
Debden, Sask., Canada 182 B5 53 30N 106 50W
Debec, N.B., Canada 173 G2 46 4N 67 41W
Debert, N.S., Canada 173 H6 45 26N 63 28W
Deblois, ME, U.S.A. 76 D5 44 45N 68 1W
DeBolt, Alta., Canada 184 C2 55 12N 118 1W
Decatur, AL, U.S.A. 60 B4 34 36N 86 59W
Decatur, AR, U.S.A. 63 B1 36 20N 94 28W
Decatur, GA, U.S.A. 68 C2 33 46N 84 16W
Decatur, IL, U.S.A. 71 D5 39 51N 88 57W
Decatur, IN, U.S.A. 72 C6 40 50N 84 56W
Decatur, MI, U.S.A. 79 G6 42 7N 85 58W
Decatur, MS, U.S.A. 81 D4 32 26N 89 7W
Decatur, NE, U.S.A. 84 C9 42 0N 96 15W
Decatur, TN, U.S.A. 97 E8 35 31N 84 47W
Decatur, TX, U.S.A. 99 D10 33 14N 97 35W
Decatur City, IA, U.S.A. 73 E5 40 45N 93 50W
Decatur County ☆, GA, U.S.A. 68 F2 31 0N 84 30W
Decatur County ☆, IN, U.S.A. 72 D5 39 15N 85 30W
Decatur County ☆, IA, U.S.A. 73 E5 40 45N 93 45W
Decatur County ☆, KS, U.S.A. 74 B3 39 45N 100 20W
Decatur County ☆, TN, U.S.A. 96 E4 35 35N 88 7W
Decaturville, TN, U.S.A. 96 E4 35 35N 88 7W
Decelles, Rés., Qué., Canada 176 D4 47 42N 78 8W
Déception, B., Qué., Canada 175 A3 62 8N 74 41W
Deception, Mt., WA, U.S.A. 101 C2 47 49N 123 14W
Decherd, TN, U.S.A. 96 E6 35 13N 86 5W
Deckerville, MI, U.S.A. 79 F9 43 32N 82 44W
Declo, ID, U.S.A. 70 G5 42 32N 113 40W
Decorah, IA, U.S.A. 73 B7 43 18N 91 48W
Dededo, Guam 105 b 13 31N 144 50W
Dedham, Boston, U.S.A. 106 B2 42 15N 71 10W
Dedham, IA, U.S.A. 73 D4 41 55N 94 49W
Dedham, MA, U.S.A. 78 B3 42 15N 71 10W
Dee, OR, U.S.A. 94 D4 43 35N 121 37W
Deep →, NC, U.S.A. 90 C6 35 36N 79 3W
Deep Cr. →, SD, U.S.A. 91 E3 45 11N 102 15W
Deep Creek L., MD, U.S.A. 77 A1 39 31N 79 24W
Deep Creek Range, UT, U.S.A. 100 D2 39 50N 113 50W
Deep Fork →, OK, U.S.A. 93 C8 35 28N 95 50W
Deep River, CT, U.S.A. 78 C2 41 23N 72 26W
Deep River, IA, U.S.A. 73 D6 41 35N 92 22W
Deep Run →, Baltimore, U.S.A. 107 B1 37 24N 76 40W
Deep Springs L., CA, U.S.A. 65 F8 37 20N 118 3W
Deepstep, GA, U.S.A. 68 C4 33 1N 82 58W
Deepwater, MO, U.S.A. 82 C3 38 16N 93 47W
Deepwater, NJ, U.S.A. 87 C1 39 41N 75 29W
Deer, AR, U.S.A. 63 C2 35 50N 93 13W
Deer, L., Nfld. & L., Canada 174 C3 49 6N 57 35W
Deer Cr. →, IN, U.S.A. 72 C4 40 34N 86 41W
Deer Cr. →, MD, U.S.A. 77 A4 39 40N 76 10W
Deer Cr. →, OH, U.S.A. 92 D3 39 27N 83 0W
Deer Creek, IL, U.S.A. 71 C4 40 38N 89 20W
Deer Creek, OK, U.S.A. 93 B6 36 48N 97 31W
Deer Flat Nat. Wildlife Refuge ⌓, ID, U.S.A. 70 F2 43 18N 116 35W
Deer Grove, IL, U.S.A. 71 B4 41 37N 89 42W
Deer I., AK, U.S.A. 61 J7 54 55N 162 18W
Deer I., Boston, U.S.A. 106 A4 42 21N 70 57W
Deer I., ME, U.S.A. 76 D5 44 13N 68 41W
Deer Isle, ME, U.S.A. 76 D5 44 14N 68 41W
Deer Lake, Nfld. & L., Canada 174 C3 49 11N 57 27W
Deer Lodge, MT, U.S.A. 83 D5 46 24N 112 44W
Deer Lodge County ☆, MT, U.S.A. 83 E4 46 0N 113 0W
Deer Park, AL, U.S.A. 60 E2 31 13N 88 19W
Deer Park, FL, U.S.A. 67 C8 28 6N 80 54W
Deer Park, MD, U.S.A. 77 A1 39 25N 79 18W
Deer Park, NY, U.S.A. 87 B3 40 46N 73 20W
Deer Park, OH, U.S.A. 92 D2 39 12N 84 23W
Deer Park, WA, U.S.A. 101 C8 47 57N 117 28W
Deer Park, WI, U.S.A. 103 C1 45 11N 92 23W
Deer Pond, Nfld. & L., Canada 174 D6 48 30N 54 45W
Deer River, MN, U.S.A. 80 C5 47 20N 93 48W
Deer Trail, CO, U.S.A. 66 C6 39 37N 104 2W
Deer Valley, Phoenix, U.S.A. 116 A2 33 41N 112 8W
Deer Valley, Phoenix, U.S.A. 116 A1 33 43N 112 12W
Deerfield, KS, U.S.A. 74 D2 37 59N 101 8W
Deerfield, MA, U.S.A. 78 B2 42 33N 72 36W
Deerfield, MO, U.S.A. 82 D2 37 50N 94 30W
Deerfield, Norfolk, U.S.A. 115 A1 36 50N 76 27W
Deerfield, SD, U.S.A. 91 F2 44 1N 103 50W
Deerfield, WI, U.S.A. 103 E4 43 3N 89 5W
Deerfield →, MA, U.S.A. 78 B2 42 35N 72 35W
Deerfield Beach, FL, U.S.A. 67 E8 26 19N 80 6W
Deering, AK, U.S.A. 61 C7 66 4N 162 42W
Deering, ND, U.S.A. 91 B4 48 24N 101 3W
Deerlodge Nat. Forest, MT, U.S.A. 83 D4 46 20N 113 30W
Deersville, OH, U.S.A. 92 C5 40 18N 81 11W
Deerwood, MN, U.S.A. 80 D5 46 29N 93 54W
Deeth, NV, U.S.A. 85 A5 41 4N 115 17W
Defiance, IA, U.S.A. 73 D3 41 49N 95 20W
Defiance, OH, U.S.A. 92 B2 41 17N 84 22W
Defiance County ☆, OH, U.S.A. 92 B2 41 23N 84 32W
Dégelis, Qué., Canada 177 D14 47 30N 68 35W
Degollado, Jalisco, Mexico 218 B5 20 28N 102 9W
DeKalb, IL, U.S.A. 71 B5 41 56N 88 46W
DeKalb County ☆, GA, U.S.A. 68 C2 33 45N 84 14W
DeKalb County ☆, IL, U.S.A. 71 B5 41 50N 88 45W
DeKalb County ☆, IN, U.S.A. 72 B6 41 25N 85 0W
DeKalb County ☆, TN, U.S.A. 97 E7 35 58N 85 51W
Del City, OK, U.S.A. 93 C6 35 26N 97 26W
Del Mar, CA, U.S.A. 65 L9 32 58N 117 16W
Del Norte, CO, U.S.A. 66 E4 37 41N 106 21W
Del Norte County ☆, CA, U.S.A. 64 B3 41 40N 124 0W
Del Rio, TX, U.S.A. 98 H7 29 22N 100 54W
Delacroix, LA, U.S.A. 75 E6 29 46N 89 45W
Delafield, WI, U.S.A. 103 E5 43 4N 88 24W
Delair, NJ, U.S.A. 116 B2 39 58N 75 3W
Delamar L., NV, U.S.A. 85 E6 37 19N 114 57W
Delanco, NJ, U.S.A. 87 B2 40 3N 74 57W
Delano, CA, U.S.A. 65 H7 35 46N 119 15W
Delano, MN, U.S.A. 80 E5 45 2N 93 47W
Delano Peak, UT, U.S.A. 100 E3 38 22N 112 22W
Delaplaine, AR, U.S.A. 63 B5 36 14N 90 44W
Delaplane, VA, U.S.A. 77 B3 38 55N 77 55W
Delaronde L., Sask., Canada 182 A4 54 3N 107 3W
Delavan, IL, U.S.A. 71 C4 40 22N 89 33W
Delavan, KS, U.S.A. 74 C7 38 40N 96 49W
Delavan, WI, U.S.A. 103 F5 42 38N 88 39W
Delaware, AR, U.S.A. 63 C2 35 17N 93 19W
Delaware, OH, U.S.A. 92 C3 40 18N 83 4W
Delaware, OK, U.S.A. 93 B8 36 47N 95 39W
Delaware □, U.S.A. 77 B5 39 0N 75 20W
Delaware →, DE, U.S.A. 77 A5 39 15N 75 20W
Delaware B., DE, U.S.A. 77 A5 39 0N 75 10W
Delaware City, DE, U.S.A. 77 A5 39 35N 75 36W
Delaware County ☆, IN, U.S.A. 72 C5 40 15N 85 25W
Delaware County ☆, IA, U.S.A. 73 C7 42 30N 91 20W
Delaware County ☆, NY, U.S.A. 89 D6 42 15N 75 0W
Delaware County ☆, OH, U.S.A. 92 C3 40 18N 83 4W
Delaware County ☆, OK, U.S.A. 93 B9 36 25N 94 50W
Delaware County ☆, PA, U.S.A. 95 E7 39 55N 75 23W
Delaware Cr. →, U.S.A. 98 E3 32 2N 104 0W
Delaware Mts., TX, U.S.A. 98 F3 31 45N 104 50W
Delaware Seashore State Park ⌓, DE, U.S.A. 77 B5 38 39N 75 4W
Delaware Water Gap Nat. Recr. Area ⌓, NJ, U.S.A. 87 A2 41 10N 74 55W
Delbarton, WV, U.S.A. 102 D2 37 43N 82 11W
Delbrook, Vancouver, Canada 193 A2 49 21N 123 5W
Delburne, Alta., Canada 185 F7 52 12N 113 14W
Delcambre, LA, U.S.A. 75 E4 29 57N 91 58W
Delevan, NY, U.S.A. 89 C2 42 29N 78 29W
Delgada, Pt., CA, U.S.A. 64 C2 40 2N 124 5W
Delhi, CA, U.S.A. 64 F6 37 26N 120 46W
Delhi, IA, U.S.A. 73 C7 42 26N 91 20W
Delhi, LA, U.S.A. 75 B4 32 28N 91 30W
Delhi, NY, U.S.A. 89 C6 42 17N 74 55W
Delhi Hills, OH, U.S.A. 107 B1 39 5N 84 36W
Delia, Alta., Canada 185 G8 51 38N 112 23W
Delia, KS, U.S.A. 74 B8 39 15N 95 59W
Delicias, Chihuahua, Mexico 213 E10 28 13N 105 28W
Delight, AR, U.S.A. 63 D2 34 2N 93 31W
Déline, N.W.T., Canada 189 C8 65 11N 123 25W
Delisle, Sask., Canada 182 D4 51 55N 107 8W
Dell, MT, U.S.A. 83 F5 44 44N 112 42W
Dell City, TX, U.S.A. 98 F2 31 56N 105 12W
Dell Rapids, SD, U.S.A. 91 G9 43 50N 96 43W
Dellwood, Minneapolis-St. Paul, U.S.A. 113 A4 45 6N 92 57W
Dellwood, MO, U.S.A. 117 A2 38 44N 90 17W
Delmar, DE, U.S.A. 77 B5 38 27N 75 35W
Delmar, IA, U.S.A. 73 C8 42 0N 90 37W
Delmar, NY, U.S.A. 89 C7 42 37N 73 50W
Delmarva Peninsula, MD, U.S.A. 77 B5 38 45N 75 45W
Delmont, NJ, U.S.A. 87 C2 39 13N 74 57W
Delmont, SD, U.S.A. 91 G7 43 16N 98 10W
Deloit, IA, U.S.A. 73 C3 42 6N 95 19W
Deloraine, Man., Canada 183 F11 49 15N 100 29W
Delphi, IN, U.S.A. 72 C4 40 36N 86 41W
Delphos, KS, U.S.A. 74 B6 39 17N 97 46W
Delphos, OH, U.S.A. 92 C2 40 51N 84 21W
Delray, WV, U.S.A. 102 B6 39 12N 78 36W
Delray Beach, FL, U.S.A. 67 E8 26 28N 80 4W
Delson, Qué., Canada 86 A1 45 22N 73 33W
Delta, B.C., Canada 187 F11 49 5N 123 5W
Delta, AL, U.S.A. 60 C5 33 26N 85 42W
Delta, CO, U.S.A. 66 D2 38 44N 108 4W
Delta, MO, U.S.A. 82 D7 37 12N 89 44W
Delta, OH, U.S.A. 92 B3 41 34N 84 0W
Delta, UT, U.S.A. 100 D3 39 21N 112 35W
Delta Beach, Man., Canada 183 E13 50 11N 98 19W
Delta County ☆, CO, U.S.A. 66 D3 38 50N 107 50W
Delta County ☆, MI, U.S.A. 79 D5 46 0N 87 0W
Delta County ☆, TX, U.S.A. 99 D12 33 23N 95 42W
Delta Junction, AK, U.S.A. 61 D11 64 2N 145 44W
Delta Nat. Forest, MS, U.S.A. 81 D3 32 50N 90 55W
Delta Nat. Wildlife Refuge ⌓, LA, U.S.A. 75 E6 29 15N 89 15W
Deltona, FL, U.S.A. 67 C7 28 54N 81 16W
Demarcation Pt., AK, U.S.A. 61 B12 69 41N 141 18W
Deming, NM, U.S.A. 88 E3 32 16N 107 46W
Deming, WA, U.S.A. 101 B3 48 50N 122 13W
Demopolis, AL, U.S.A. 60 D3 32 31N 87 50W
Demorest, GA, U.S.A. 68 B3 34 34N 83 33W
Demotte, IN, U.S.A. 72 B3 41 12N 87 12W
Dempsey, OK, U.S.A. 93 C4 35 31N 99 49W
Denair, CA, U.S.A. 64 F6 37 32N 120 48W
Denali = McKinley, Mt., AK, U.S.A. 61 E10 63 4N 151 0W
Denali ☆, AK, U.S.A. 61 F10 61 13N 149 52W
Denali Nat. Park and Preserve △, AK, U.S.A. 61 E10 63 30N 152 0W
Denbigh, Ont., Canada 179 B9 45 8N 77 15W
Denbigh, ND, U.S.A. 91 B5 48 19N 100 35W
Denbigh, C., AK, U.S.A. 61 D7 64 23N 161 32W
Dendron, VA, U.S.A. 102 D8 37 3N 76 56W
Denham, MN, U.S.A. 80 D6 46 22N 92 57W
Denham Springs, LA, U.S.A. 75 D5 30 29N 90 57W
Denhoff, ND, U.S.A. 91 C5 47 29N 100 16W
Denholm, Sask., Canada 182 C3 52 39N 108 1W
Denio, NV, U.S.A. 85 A2 41 59N 118 38W
Denison, IA, U.S.A. 73 C3 42 1N 95 21W
Denison, KS, U.S.A. 74 B8 39 24N 95 38W
Denison, TX, U.S.A. 99 D11 33 45N 96 33W
Denman Island, B.C., Canada 186 F10 49 33N 124 48W
Denmark, KS, U.S.A. 74 B5 39 5N 98 17W
Denmark, ME, U.S.A. 76 E2 43 58N 70 48W
Denmark, SC, U.S.A. 90 E4 33 19N 81 9W
Denmark, WI, U.S.A. 103 D6 44 21N 87 50W
Dennard, AR, U.S.A. 63 C3 35 46N 92 31W
Dennehotso, AZ, U.S.A. 62 A6 36 51N 109 51W
Dennis, KS, U.S.A. 74 D8 37 21N 95 25W
Dennis, MA, U.S.A. 78 C4 41 44N 70 12W
Dennis, MS, U.S.A. 81 B5 34 34N 88 14W
Dennis Port, MA, U.S.A. 78 C4 41 39N 70 8W
Dennison, MN, U.S.A. 80 F5 44 25N 93 2W
Dennison, OH, U.S.A. 92 C5 40 24N 81 19W
Dennisville, NJ, U.S.A. 87 C2 39 12N 74 49W
Dent, MN, U.S.A. 80 D3 46 33N 95 43W
Dent County ☆, MO, U.S.A. 82 D5 37 35N 91 30W
Denton, GA, U.S.A. 68 E4 31 44N 82 42W
Denton, KS, U.S.A. 74 B8 39 44N 95 16W
Denton, MD, U.S.A. 77 B5 38 53N 75 50W
Denton, MT, U.S.A. 83 C8 47 19N 109 57W
Denton, NC, U.S.A. 90 C5 35 38N 80 6W
Denton, NE, U.S.A. 84 D9 40 44N 96 51W
Denton, TX, U.S.A. 99 D10 33 13N 97 8W
Denton County ☆, TX, U.S.A. 99 D10 33 15N 97 10W
Denton Cr. →, TX, U.S.A. 99 E11 32 58N 96 57W
Dentsville, MD, U.S.A. 77 B4 38 28N 76 51W
Dentsville, SC, U.S.A. 90 D5 34 4N 80 58W
Denver, CO, U.S.A. 66 C6 39 42N 104 59W
Denver, IN, U.S.A. 72 C4 40 52N 86 5W
Denver, IA, U.S.A. 73 C6 42 40N 92 20W
Denver, PA, U.S.A. 95 D6 40 14N 76 8W
Denver City, TX, U.S.A. 98 E5 32 58N 102 50W
Denver County ☆, CO, U.S.A. 66 C6 39 45N 105 0W
Denver International ✕ (DEN), CO, U.S.A. 66 C6 39 52N 104 40W
Denwood = Wainwright, Alta., Canada 185 F10 52 50N 110 50W
Denzil, Sask., Canada 182 C2 52 14N 109 39W
Depew, OK, U.S.A. 93 C7 35 48N 96 31W
Depoe Bay, OR, U.S.A. 94 C1 44 49N 124 4W
Deport, TX, U.S.A. 99 D12 33 32N 95 19W
Deposit, NY, U.S.A. 89 C5 42 4N 75 25W
Depue, IL, U.S.A. 71 B4 41 19N 89 19W
Derby, CT, U.S.A. 78 C1 41 19N 73 5W
Derby, IA, U.S.A. 73 E5 40 56N 93 27W
Derby, KS, U.S.A. 74 D6 37 33N 97 16W
Derby, NY, U.S.A. 89 C2 42 41N 78 58W
Derby, TX, U.S.A. 99 J8 28 46N 99 8W
Derby Center, VT, U.S.A. 86 B2 44 57N 72 8W
Derby Line, VT, U.S.A. 86 B2 45 0N 72 6W
Deridder, LA, U.S.A. 75 D2 30 51N 93 17W
Derita, Charlotte, U.S.A. 107 A2 35 17N 80 47W
Derma, MS, U.S.A. 81 C4 33 51N 89 17W
Dermott, AR, U.S.A. 63 E4 33 32N 91 26W
Dermott, TX, U.S.A. 98 E6 32 51N 101 1W
Dernieres, Isles, LA, U.S.A. 75 E5 29 2N 90 50W
Deroche, B.C., Canada 187 F12 49 12N 122 4W
Derry, NH, U.S.A. 86 D3 42 53N 71 19W
Derwent, Alta., Canada 184 E10 53 41N 110 58W
Des Allemands, LA, U.S.A. 75 E5 29 49N 90 28W
Des Arc, AR, U.S.A. 63 D4 34 58N 91 30W
Des Arc, MO, U.S.A. 82 D6 37 17N 90 38W
Des Lacs, ND, U.S.A. 91 B4 48 16N 101 34W
Des Lacs →, ND, U.S.A. 91 B5 48 17N 100 20W
Des Lacs Nat. Wildlife Refuge ⌓, ND, U.S.A. 91 B3 48 46N 102 6W
Des Moines, IA, U.S.A. 73 D5 41 35N 93 37W
Des Moines, NM, U.S.A. 88 A7 36 46N 103 50W
Des Moines, WA, U.S.A. 101 C3 47 24N 122 19W
Des Moines →, IA, U.S.A. 73 E7 40 23N 91 25W
Des Moines ✕ (DSM), IA, U.S.A. 73 D5 41 32N 93 40W
Des Moines County ☆, IA, U.S.A. 73 E7 40 55N 91 10W
Des Plaines, IL, U.S.A. 71 A6 42 2N 87 54W
Des Plaines →, IL, U.S.A. 71 B5 41 23N 88 15W
Desatoya Mts., NV, U.S.A. 85 C3 39 20N 117 40W
Desbarats, Ont., Canada 178 A3 46 20N 83 56W
Desbiens, Qué., Canada 177 C11 48 25N 71 57W
Descanso, CA, U.S.A. 65 L10 32 51N 116 37W
Descenso, Pta., Michoacan, Mexico 218 E6 17 38N 101 35W
Deschaillons-sur-St-Laurent, Qué., Canada 177 E10 46 32N 72 7W
Deschambault, Qué., Canada 177 E11 46 39N 71 56W
Deschambault L., Sask., Canada 189 F12 54 50N 103 30W
Deschambault Lake, Sask., Canada 189 F12 54 55N 103 22W
Deschênes, Qué., Canada 176 F7 45 23N 75 48W
Deschutes →, OR, U.S.A. 94 B5 45 38N 120 55W
Deschutes County ☆, OR, U.S.A. 94 D4 44 0N 121 30W
Deschutes Nat. Forest, OR, U.S.A. 94 D4 43 40N 121 20W
Desdemona, TX, U.S.A. 99 E9 32 16N 98 33W
Deseret, UT, U.S.A. 100 D3 39 17N 112 39W
Deseret Peak, UT, U.S.A. 100 C3 40 28N 112 38W
Deseronto, Ont., Canada 179 C9 44 12N 77 3W
Desert Center, CA, U.S.A. 65 K11 33 43N 115 24W
Desert Hot Springs, CA, U.S.A. 65 K10 33 58N 116 30W
Desert L., NV, U.S.A. 85 F5 36 59N 115 14W
Desert Nat. Wildlife Range ⌓, NV, U.S.A. 85 E5 37 8N 115 52W
Desert Peak, UT, U.S.A. 100 B2 41 11N 113 22W
Desert Ra., NV, U.S.A. 85 F5 36 55N 115 25W
Desert Ranch Res., NV, U.S.A. 85 A4 41 42N 116 33W
Desert Valley, NV, U.S.A. 85 A2 41 10N 118 5W
Desert Wetlands Park, Las Vegas, U.S.A. 110 C3 36 7N 115 2W
Desha, AR, U.S.A. 63 C4 35 44N 91 41W
Desha County ☆, AR, U.S.A. 63 E4 33 48N 91 16W
Deshler, NE, U.S.A. 84 D8 40 9N 97 44W
Deshler, OH, U.S.A. 92 B3 41 13N 83 54W
Desierto Central de Baja California, Parque Natural del ⌓, Baja Calif., Mexico 210 D4 29 40N 114 50W
Desierto de los Leones, Parque Nacional △, Distrito Federal, Mexico 225 C2 19 18N 99 19W
Desierto del Carmen, Parque Nacional △, México, Mexico 219 D8 18 54N 99 37W
Desloge, MO, U.S.A. 82 D6 37 51N 90 32W
Desmarais, Alta., Canada 184 C7 55 56N 113 49W
Desmaraisville, Qué., Canada 176 B6 49 32N 76 9W
Desméloizes, Qué., Canada 176 C3 48 57N 79 29W
Desolation Sound Marine Park ⌓, B.C., Canada 186 E10 50 5N 124 25W
Destin, FL, U.S.A. 67 A2 30 24N 86 30W
Detour, Pt., MI, U.S.A. 79 D5 45 40N 86 40W
Detroit, AL, U.S.A. 60 B2 34 2N 88 10W
Detroit, MI, U.S.A. 79 G8 42 19N 83 12W
Detroit, OR, U.S.A. 94 C3 44 42N 122 9W
Detroit, TX, U.S.A. 99 D12 33 40N 95 16W
Detroit Beach, MI, U.S.A. 79 H8 41 56N 83 19W
Detroit City ✕, MI, U.S.A. 79 G8 42 24N 83 0W
Detroit Lakes, MN, U.S.A. 80 D3 46 49N 95 51W
Detroit Metropolitan Wayne County ✕ (DTW), MI, U.S.A. 79 G8 42 13N 83 21W
Deuel County ☆, NE, U.S.A. 84 C3 41 10N 102 20W
Deuel County ☆, SD, U.S.A. 91 F9 44 45N 96 41W
Deux-Loutres, L. aux, Qué., Canada 172 B7 51 31N 62 28W
Deux-Montagnes, Qué., Canada 192 A1 45 32N 73 53W
Deux-Montagnes, L. des, Montréal, Canada 192 B1 45 27N 74 0W
Devastation Chan., B.C., Canada 186 B6 53 40N 128 50W
Devenyns, L., Qué., Canada 177 D9 47 5N 73 50W
Devereux, GA, U.S.A. 68 C3 33 13N 83 5W
Devils Den, CA, U.S.A. 65 H7 35 46N 119 58W
Devil's Gate Res., Qué., Canada 111 A2 34 11N 118 10W
Devils Hole = Death Valley Nat. Park △, U.S.A. 65 G9 36 29N 117 6W
Devils L., ND, U.S.A. 91 B7 48 2N 98 58W
Devils L., TX, U.S.A. 98 H7 29 34N 100 59W
Devils Lake, ND, U.S.A. 91 B7 48 7N 98 52W
Devil's Lake State Park ⌓, WI, U.S.A. 103 E4 43 25N 89 42W
Devils Paw, B.C., Canada 189 E6 58 47N 134 0W
Devils Playground, CA, U.S.A. 65 J11 35 0N 115 50W
Devils Postpile Nat. Monument ⌓, CA, U.S.A. 64 F7 37 37N 119 5W
Devils Tower, WY, U.S.A. 104 B8 44 35N 104 42W
Devils Tower Nat. Monument △, WY, U.S.A. 104 B8 44 48N 104 55W
Devine, TX, U.S.A. 99 H9 29 8N 98 54W
Devol, OK, U.S.A. 93 D5 34 11N 98 35W
Devon, Alta., Canada 184 E7 53 24N 113 44W
Devon, KS, U.S.A. 74 D9 37 55N 94 49W
Devon, MT, U.S.A. 83 B6 48 28N 111 29W
Devon I., Nunavut, Canada 190 B8 75 10N 85 0W
Devon Ice Cap, Nunavut, Canada 190 B9 75 20N 82 30W
Devou Park, KY, U.S.A. 107 B1 39 4N 84 32W
Dew, TX, U.S.A. 99 F11 31 36N 96 9W
Dewar, OK, U.S.A. 93 C8 35 28N 95 56W
Dewberry, Alta., Canada 184 E10 53 35N 110 32W
Deweese, NE, U.S.A. 84 D7 40 21N 98 8W
Dewey, Puerto Rico 105 G17 18 18N 65 18W
Dewey, AZ, U.S.A. 62 C3 34 32N 112 15W
Dewey, OK, U.S.A. 93 B8 36 48N 95 56W
Dewey Beach, DE, U.S.A. 77 B5 38 42N 75 5W
Dewey County ☆, OK, U.S.A. 93 C5 36 0N 99 0W
Dewey County ☆, SD, U.S.A. 91 E5 45 0N 101 0W
Dewey L., KY, U.S.A. 97 C10 37 44N 82 44W
Deweyville, TX, U.S.A. 99 G14 30 18N 93 45W
Dewy Rose, GA, U.S.A. 68 B4 34 10N 82 57W
Dexter, GA, U.S.A. 68 D3 32 27N 83 4W
Dexter, KS, U.S.A. 74 D7 37 11N 96 43W
Dexter, KY, U.S.A. 96 D4 36 44N 88 17W
Dexter, ME, U.S.A. 76 C4 45 1N 69 18W
Dexter, MI, U.S.A. 79 G8 42 20N 83 53W
Dexter, MN, U.S.A. 80 G6 43 43N 92 42W
Dexter, MO, U.S.A. 82 E7 36 48N 89 57W
Dexter, NM, U.S.A. 88 D6 33 12N 104 22W
Dexter City, OH, U.S.A. 92 D5 39 39N 81 28W
Diablo, WA, U.S.A. 101 B4 48 58N 121 8W
Diablo, Pico del, Baja Calif., Mexico 210 B3 31 1N 115 28W
Diablo, Sierra, TX, U.S.A. 98 F3 31 15N 105 0W
Diablo Bolson, TX, U.S.A. 98 F2 31 45N 105 25W
Diablo Pt., N. Marianas 105 c 15 0N 145 35W
Diablo Range, CA, U.S.A. 64 F5 37 20N 121 25W
Diagonal, IA, U.S.A. 73 E4 40 49N 94 20W
Diamond, MO, U.S.A. 82 E2 36 59N 94 19W
Diamond, L., OR, U.S.A. 94 D3 43 10N 122 9W
Diamond City, Alta., Canada 185 J8 49 48N 112 51W
Diamond Head, HI, U.S.A. 69 K14 21 16N 157 49W
Diamond Lake, OR, U.S.A. 94 D3 43 11N 122 8W
Diamond Mts., CA, U.S.A. 64 C6 40 16N 120 33W
Diamond Mts., NV, U.S.A. 85 C5 39 40N 115 50W
Diamond Pk., CO, U.S.A. 66 B2 40 59N 108 50W
Diamond Pk., ID, U.S.A. 70 E5 44 9N 113 5W
Diamond Springs, CA, U.S.A. 64 E6 38 42N 120 49W
Diamond Valley, NV, U.S.A. 85 C5 39 46N 115 58W
Diamondhead, MS, U.S.A. 81 F4 30 24N 89 22W
Diamondville, WY, U.S.A. 104 E2 41 47N 110 32W
Diana, WV, U.S.A. 102 C4 38 34N 80 27W
Diana B., Qué., Canada 175 A4 61 20N 70 0W
Dias Creek, NJ, U.S.A. 87 C2 39 8N 74 53W
Diaz, AR, U.S.A. 63 C4 35 38N 91 16W
Dibble, OK, U.S.A. 93 C6 35 2N 97 38W
D'Iberville, MS, U.S.A. 81 F5 30 26N 88 54W
Diboll, TX, U.S.A. 99 F13 31 11N 94 47W
Dickens, NE, U.S.A. 84 D4 40 49N 101 2W
Dickens, TX, U.S.A. 98 D7 33 37N 100 50W
Dickens County ☆, TX, U.S.A. 98 D7 33 40N 100 50W
Dickenson County ☆, VA, U.S.A. 102 D2 37 10N 82 22W
Dickey, ND, U.S.A. 91 D7 46 32N 98 27W
Dickey County ☆, ND, U.S.A. 91 D7 46 2N 98 30W
Dickeyville, WI, U.S.A. 103 F3 42 38N 90 36W
Dickinson, ND, U.S.A. 91 D3 46 53N 102 47W
Dickinson, TX, U.S.A. 99 H12 29 28N 95 3W
Dickinson County ☆, IA, U.S.A. 73 B3 43 20N 95 10W
Dickinson County ☆, KS, U.S.A. 74 C6 38 50N 97 10W
Dickinson County ☆, MI, U.S.A. 79 C4 46 0N 87 50W

Dupo, *IL, U.S.A.* **71 E3** 38 31N 90 13W
Dupont, *Denver, U.S.A.* **109 A2** 39 50N 104 54W
Dupont, *IN, U.S.A.* **72 E5** 38 53N 85 31W
Dupont, *PA, U.S.A.* **87 A1** 41 20N 75 45W
DuPont, *WA, U.S.A.* **101 C3** 47 6N 122 38W
Dupree, *SD, U.S.A.* **91 E4** 45 4N 101 35W
Dupuy, *Qué., Canada* **176 C3** 48 50N 79 21W
Dupuyer, *MT, U.S.A.* **83 B5** 48 13N 112 30W
Duquesne, *Pittsburgh, U.S.A.* **116 B2** 40 22N 79 51W
Duran, *NM, U.S.A.* **88 C5** 34 28N 105 24W
Durand, *GA, U.S.A.* **68 D2** 32 55N 84 46W
Durand, *IL, U.S.A.* **71 A4** 42 26N 89 20W
Durand, *MI, U.S.A.* **79 G8** 42 55N 83 59W
Durand, *WI, U.S.A.* **103 D2** 44 38N 91 58W
Durango, *Mexico* **217 C6** 24 3N 104 39W
Durango, *CO, U.S.A.* **66 E3** 37 16N 107 53W
Durango □, *Mexico* **216 C5** 24 50N 105 20W
Durant, *IA, U.S.A.* **73 D8** 41 36N 90 54W
Durant, *MS, U.S.A.* **81 C4** 33 4N 89 51W
Durant, *OK, U.S.A.* **93 E7** 33 59N 96 25W
Durbin, *WV, U.S.A.* **102 C5** 38 33N 79 50W
Durham, *Ont., Canada* **178 C6** 44 10N 80 49W
Durham, *CA, U.S.A.* **64 D5** 39 39N 121 48W
Durham, *CT, U.S.A.* **78 C2** 41 29N 72 41W
Durham, *KS, U.S.A.* **74 C6** 38 30N 97 15W
Durham, *NC, U.S.A.* **90 C7** 35 59N 78 54W
Durham, *NH, U.S.A.* **86 C4** 43 8N 70 56W
Durham, *Portland, U.S.A.* **116 B1** 45 24N 122 45W
Durham Bridge, *N.B., Canada* **173 G3** 46 7N 66 36W
Durham County ☆, *NC, U.S.A.* **90 C7** 36 0N 78 55W
Durkee, *OR, U.S.A.* **94 C8** 44 35N 117 30W
Durocher, L., *Qué., Canada* **172 C8** 50 52N 61 12W
Dusey →, *Ont., Canada* **181 A10** 51 11N 86 21W
Dushore, *PA, U.S.A.* **95 C6** 41 31N 76 24W
Duson, *LA, U.S.A.* **75 D3** 30 14N 92 11W
Dustin, *OK, U.S.A.* **93 C7** 35 12N 96 1W
Dusty, *WA, U.S.A.* **101 D8** 46 51N 117 38W
Dutch Harbor, *AK, U.S.A.* **61 K6** 53 53N 166 32W
Dutch John, *UT, U.S.A.* **100 C6** 40 55N 109 24W
Dutch Mills, *AR, U.S.A.* **63 C1** 35 52N 94 29W
Dutch Neck, *NJ, U.S.A.* **87 B2** 40 17N 74 40W
Dutchess County ☆, *NY, U.S.A.* **89 D7** 41 45N 73 45W
Dutchtown, *MO, U.S.A.* **82 D7** 37 18N 89 42W
Dutton, *Ont., Canada* **178 E5** 42 39N 81 30W
Dutton, *MT, U.S.A.* **83 C6** 47 51N 111 43W
Dutton, Mt., *UT, U.S.A.* **100 E3** 38 1N 112 13W
Duval, *Sask., Canada* **182 D7** 51 9N 104 59W
Duval County ☆, *FL, U.S.A.* **67 A7** 30 30N 81 30W
Duval County ☆, *TX, U.S.A.* **99 K9** 27 50N 98 30W
Duvall, *WA, U.S.A.* **101 C4** 47 45N 121 59W
Duvernay, *Qué., Canada* **192 A2** 45 35N 73 40W
Duxbury, *MA, U.S.A.* **78 B4** 42 2N 70 40W
Dwight, *Ont., Canada* **176 F3** 45 20N 79 1W
Dwight, *IL, U.S.A.* **71 B5** 41 5N 88 26W
Dwight, *KS, U.S.A.* **74 C7** 38 50N 96 38W
Dwight, *ND, U.S.A.* **91 D9** 46 18N 96 44W
Dwight, *NE, U.S.A.* **84 C8** 41 5N 97 1W
Dworshak Res., *ID, U.S.A.* **70 C2** 46 48N 116 0W
Dyer, *NV, U.S.A.* **85 E2** 37 41N 118 5W
Dyer, *TN, U.S.A.* **96 D4** 36 4N 88 59W
Dyer, C., *Nunavut, Canada* **190 D13** 66 37N 61 16W
Dyer B., *N.W.T., Canada* **188 A8** 75 53N 121 42W
Dyer County ☆, *TN, U.S.A.* **96 D3** 36 0N 89 25W
Dyersburg, *TN, U.S.A.* **96 D3** 36 3N 89 23W
Dyersville, *IA, U.S.A.* **73 C7** 42 29N 91 8W
Dyess, *AR, U.S.A.* **63 C5** 35 35N 90 13W
Dyess Air Force Base, *TX, U.S.A.* **99 E8** 32 25N 99 51W
Dyke, *VA, U.S.A.* **102 C6** 38 15N 78 32W
Dyment, *Ont., Canada* **180 C4** 49 37N 92 18W
Dysart, *Sask., Canada* **182 E7** 50 57N 104 2W
Dysart, *IA, U.S.A.* **73 C6** 42 10N 92 18W
Dzibalchén, *Campeche, Mexico* **223 C4** 19 31N 89 45W
Dzibilchaltún, *Yucatán, Mexico* **223 A4** 21 10N 89 35W
Dzibitún, *Campeche, Mexico* **223 C4** 19 33N 89 56W
Dzidzantún, *Yucatán, Mexico* **223 A4** 21 15N 89 3W
Dzilam de Bravo, *Yucatán, Mexico* **223 A5** 21 24N 88 53W
Dzilam González, *Yucatán, Mexico* **223 A5** 21 17N 88 56W
Dzitás, *Yucatán, Mexico* **223 B5** 20 51N 88 31W
Dzitbalché, *Campeche, Mexico* **223 B3** 20 19N 90 3W
Dzonot Carretero, *Yucatán, Mexico* **223 A6** 21 25N 87 53W
Dzuiché, *Quintana Roo, Mexico* **223 C5** 19 54N 88 48W

E

E.C. Manning Park ⌓, *B.C., Canada* **187 F14** 49 5N 120 45W
E. Carranza, Base Aérea Militar, *Guadalajara, Mexico* **224 A1** 20 45N 103 27W
E.G. Simmons Park, *Tampa, U.S.A.* **119 C4** 27 46N 82 28W
E.V. Spence Res., *TX, U.S.A.* **98 F7** 31 58N 100 40W
Eabamet L., *Ont., Canada* **181 A9** 51 30N 87 46W
Eads, *CO, U.S.A.* **66 D8** 38 29N 102 47W
Eagar, *AZ, U.S.A.* **62 C6** 34 6N 109 17W
Eagle, *AK, U.S.A.* **61 D12** 64 47N 141 12W
Eagle, *CO, U.S.A.* **66 C4** 39 39N 106 50W
Eagle, *ID, U.S.A.* **70 F2** 43 42N 116 21W
Eagle, *NE, U.S.A.* **84 D9** 40 49N 96 26W
Eagle, *WI, U.S.A.* **103 F5** 42 53N 88 29W
Eagle →, *Nfld. & L., Canada* **175 C6** 53 36N 57 26W
Eagle →, *CO, U.S.A.* **66 C3** 39 39N 107 4W
Eagle, Mt., *U.S. Virgin Is.* **105 H18** 17 46N 64 49W
Eagle Bend, *MN, U.S.A.* **80 D3** 46 10N 95 2W
Eagle Butte, *SD, U.S.A.* **91 F4** 45 0N 101 10W
Eagle City, *OK, U.S.A.* **93 C5** 35 56N 98 35W
Eagle County ☆, *CO, U.S.A.* **66 C4** 39 40N 106 50W
Eagle Cr. →, *Sask., Canada* **182 C4** 52 20N 107 30W
Eagle Cr. →, *KY, U.S.A.* **97 B7** 38 36N 85 4W
Eagle Creek Park, *Indianapolis, U.S.A.* **110 A1** 39 52N 86 18W
Eagle Grove, *IA, U.S.A.* **73 C5** 42 40N 93 54W
Eagle Harbor, *MD, U.S.A.* **77 B4** 38 35N 76 40W
Eagle I., *Man., Canada* **183 B13** 53 40N 98 55W
Eagle L., *B.C., Canada* **186 D10** 51 55N 124 23W
Eagle L., *Ont., Canada* **180 C3** 49 42N 93 13W
Eagle L., *CA, U.S.A.* **64 C6** 40 39N 120 45W
Eagle L., *ME, U.S.A.* **76 B4** 46 20N 69 22W
Eagle Lake, *Ont., Canada* **179 B8** 45 8N 78 29W
Eagle Lake, *ME, U.S.A.* **76 A5** 47 3N 68 36W
Eagle Lake, *MN, U.S.A.* **80 F5** 44 10N 93 53W
Eagle Lake, *Minneapolis-St. Paul, U.S.A.* **113 A1** 45 4N 93 24W
Eagle Lake, *TX, U.S.A.* **99 H11** 29 35N 96 20W
Eagle Mills, *AR, U.S.A.* **63 E3** 33 41N 92 43W
Eagle Mountain, *CA, U.S.A.* **65 K11** 33 49N 115 27W
Eagle Mountain, *UT, U.S.A.* **100 C3** 40 19N 112 0W
Eagle Mountain Res., *TX, U.S.A.* **99 E10** 32 53N 97 28W
Eagle Mt., *MN, U.S.A.* **80 C8** 47 54N 90 34W
Eagle Mts., *TX, U.S.A.* **98 G2** 30 55N 105 5W
Eagle Nest, *NM, U.S.A.* **88 A5** 36 33N 105 16W
Eagle Nest Butte, *SD, U.S.A.* **91 G4** 43 27N 101 39W
Eagle Pass, *TX, U.S.A.* **98 J7** 28 43N 100 30W
Eagle Peak, *CA, U.S.A.* **64 B6** 41 17N 120 12W
Eagle Pk., *CA, U.S.A.* **65 F7** 37 5N 119 1W
Eagle Point, *OR, U.S.A.* **94 E3** 42 28N 122 48W
Eagle Point Lake, *Minneapolis-St. Paul, U.S.A.* **113 B4** 44 58N 92 54W
Eagle River, *Ont., Canada* **180 C3** 49 47N 93 12W
Eagle River, *MI, U.S.A.* **79 B3** 47 25N 88 18W
Eagle River, *WI, U.S.A.* **103 C4** 45 55N 89 15W
Eagle Rock, *Los Angeles, U.S.A.* **111 B3** 34 8N 118 12 E
Eagle Rock, *VA, U.S.A.* **102 D5** 37 38N 79 48W
Eaglehead L., *Ont., Canada* **180 C7** 49 2N 89 12W
Eaglesham, *Alta., Canada* **184 C3** 55 47N 117 53W
Eagletail Mts., *AZ, U.S.A.* **62 D2** 33 20N 113 30W
Eagletown, *OK, U.S.A.* **93 D9** 34 2N 94 34W
Eagleville, *CA, U.S.A.* **64 B6** 41 19N 120 7W
Eagleville, *MO, U.S.A.* **82 A3** 40 28N 93 59W
Eagleville, *TN, U.S.A.* **96 E6** 35 45N 86 39W
Eakly, *OK, U.S.A.* **93 C5** 35 18N 98 34W
Ear Falls, *Ont., Canada* **180 B3** 50 38N 93 13W
Earl, L., *CA, U.S.A.* **64 B2** 41 50N 124 11W
Earl Grey, *Sask., Canada* **182 E7** 50 57N 104 43W
Earl Park, *IN, U.S.A.* **72 C3** 40 42N 87 25W
Earle, *AR, U.S.A.* **63 C5** 35 16N 90 28W
Earleville, *MD, U.S.A.* **77 A5** 39 24N 75 54W
Earlham, *IA, U.S.A.* **73 D4** 41 30N 94 7W
Earlimart, *CA, U.S.A.* **65 H7** 35 53N 119 16W
Earling, *IA, U.S.A.* **73 D3** 41 28N 95 46W
Earlington, *KY, U.S.A.* **96 C5** 37 16N 87 30W
Earls Cove, *B.C., Canada* **186 F10** 49 45N 124 0W
Earlsboro, *OK, U.S.A.* **93 C7** 35 19N 96 47W
Earlton, *KS, U.S.A.* **74 D8** 37 35N 95 28W
Earltown, *N.S., Canada* **173 H6** 45 35N 63 8W
Earlville, *IL, U.S.A.* **71 B5** 41 35N 88 55W
Earlville, *NY, U.S.A.* **89 C5** 42 44N 75 33W
Early, *IA, U.S.A.* **73 C3** 42 28N 95 9W
Early, *TX, U.S.A.* **99 F9** 31 46N 98 58W
Early County ☆, *GA, U.S.A.* **68 E2** 31 20N 84 50W
Earth, *TX, U.S.A.* **98 C5** 34 14N 102 24W
Easley, *SC, U.S.A.* **90 D3** 34 50N 82 36W
East →, *NY, U.S.A.* **87 B3** 40 48N 73 48W
East Acton, *Boston, U.S.A.* **106 A1** 42 28N 71 24W
East Alton, *IL, U.S.A.* **71 E3** 38 53N 90 7W
East Angus, *Qué., Canada* **177 F11** 45 30N 71 40W
East Arlington, *Boston, U.S.A.* **106 A3** 42 24N 71 8W
East Arlington, *VA, U.S.A.* **119 B3** 38 51N 77 4W
East Arm Grand Traverse B., *MI, U.S.A.* **79 E6** 44 50N 85 30W
East Atlantic Beach, *NY, U.S.A.* **114 C4** 40 35N 73 42W
East Aurora, *NY, U.S.A.* **89 C2** 42 46N 78 37W
East B., *LA, U.S.A.* **75 E6** 29 0N 89 15W
East B., *TX, U.S.A.* **99 H13** 29 30N 94 35W
East Baton Rouge Parish ☆, *LA, U.S.A.* **75 D4** 30 30N 91 20W
East Bay, *N.S., Canada* **173 G9** 46 1N 60 25W
East Bend, *NC, U.S.A.* **90 B5** 36 13N 80 31W
East Berkshire, *VT, U.S.A.* **86 B2** 44 56N 72 42W
East Berlin, *PA, U.S.A.* **95 E6** 39 56N 76 59W
East Bernard, *TX, U.S.A.* **99 H11** 29 32N 96 4W
East Bernstadt, *KY, U.S.A.* **97 C8** 37 9N 84 12W
East Bethel, *MN, U.S.A.* **80 E5** 45 19N 93 12W
East Boston, *Boston, U.S.A.* **106 A3** 42 22N 71 1W
East Brady, *PA, U.S.A.* **95 D3** 40 59N 79 37W
East Branch Clarion River L., *PA, U.S.A.* **95 C4** 41 35N 78 35W
East Brewton, *AL, U.S.A.* **60 E3** 31 5N 87 4W
East Bridgewater, *MA, U.S.A.* **78 B4** 42 2N 70 58W
East Broughton, *Qué., Canada* **177 E11** 46 14N 71 5W
East Brunswick, *NJ, U.S.A.* **87 B2** 40 25N 74 23W
East Canton, *OH, U.S.A.* **92 C5** 40 47N 81 17W
East Canyon Res., *Salt Lake City, U.S.A.* **117 A4** 40 55N 111 36W
East Canyon State Park ⌓, *Salt Lake City, U.S.A.* **117 A4** 40 54N 111 35W
East Carbon, *UT, U.S.A.* **100 D5** 39 35N 110 25W
East Carroll Parish ☆, *LA, U.S.A.* **75 B4** 32 45N 91 15W
East Charleston, *VT, U.S.A.* **86 B3** 44 49N 71 59W
East Chezzetcook, *N.S., Canada* **173 J6** 44 43N 63 14W
East Chicago, *IN, U.S.A.* **72 B3** 41 38N 87 27W
East Cleveland, *OH, U.S.A.* **92 B5** 41 31N 81 34W
East Corinth, *VT, U.S.A.* **86 B2** 44 5N 72 12W
East Cote Blanche B., *LA, U.S.A.* **75 E4** 29 34N 91 38W
East Dalhousie, *N.S., Canada* **173 J5** 44 43N 64 48W
East Dismal Swamp, *NC, U.S.A.* **90 C9** 35 43N 76 41W
East Dorset, *VT, U.S.A.* **86 C2** 43 13N 73 0W
East Douglas, *MA, U.S.A.* **78 B3** 42 4N 71 43W
East Dublin, *GA, U.S.A.* **68 D4** 32 32N 82 52W
East Dubuque, *IL, U.S.A.* **71 A3** 42 30N 90 39W
East Elmhurst, *NY, U.S.A.* **114 B3** 40 45N 73 52W
East Ely, *NV, U.S.A.* **85 C6** 39 15N 114 53W
East Fairfield, *VT, U.S.A.* **86 B2** 44 47N 72 51W
East Farnham, *Qué., Canada* **86 A2** 45 14N 72 46W
East Feliciana Parish ☆, *LA, U.S.A.* **75 D4** 30 47N 91 8W
East Flat Rock, *NC, U.S.A.* **90 C3** 35 17N 82 25W
East Fork Amite →, *LA, U.S.A.* **81 E3** 31 0N 90 50W
East Fork Bruneau →, *ID, U.S.A.* **70 G3** 42 34N 115 38W
East Fork Obey →, *TN, U.S.A.* **97 D7** 36 27N 85 7W
East Fork Sevier →, *UT, U.S.A.* **100 E3** 38 14N 112 12W
East Fork White →, *IN, U.S.A.* **72 E3** 38 33N 87 14W
East Fultonham, *OH, U.S.A.* **92 D4** 39 51N 82 8W
East Gaffney, *SC, U.S.A.* **90 C4** 35 5N 81 38W
East Glacier Park, *MT, U.S.A.* **83 B4** 48 27N 113 13W
East Granby, *CT, U.S.A.* **78 C2** 41 57N 72 44W
East Grand Forks, *MN, U.S.A.* **80 C1** 47 56N 97 1W
East Grand Rapids, *MI, U.S.A.* **79 G6** 42 58N 85 37W
East Greenville, *PA, U.S.A.* **87 B1** 40 24N 75 30W
East Greenwich, *RI, U.S.A.* **78 C3** 41 40N 71 27W
East Haddam, *CT, U.S.A.* **78 C2** 41 27N 72 28W
East Hampton, *CT, U.S.A.* **78 C2** 41 35N 72 31W
East Hampton, *NY, U.S.A.* **89 E8** 40 58N 72 11W
East Hartford, *CT, U.S.A.* **78 C2** 41 46N 72 39W
East Haven, *CT, U.S.A.* **78 C2** 41 17N 72 52W
East Haverhill, *NH, U.S.A.* **86 B3** 44 3N 71 58W
East Helena, *MT, U.S.A.* **83 D6** 46 35N 111 56W
East Hills, *NY, U.S.A.* **114 B5** 40 47N 73 37W
East Holden, *ME, U.S.A.* **76 D5** 44 44N 68 38W
East Hope, *ID, U.S.A.* **70 A2** 48 14N 116 17W
East Houston, *Houston, U.S.A.* **110 A3** 29 49N 95 16W
East Jordan, *MI, U.S.A.* **79 D6** 45 10N 85 7W
East Kingston, *NH, U.S.A.* **86 D3** 42 54N 71 2W
East Lansdowne, *PA, U.S.A.* **116 B1** 39 56N 75 15W
East Lansing, *MI, U.S.A.* **79 G7** 42 44N 84 29W
East Las Vegas = Whitney, *NV, U.S.A.* **85 F5** 36 4N 115 5W
East Lempster, *NH, U.S.A.* **86 C2** 43 13N 72 13W
East Lexington, *Boston, U.S.A.* **106 A2** 42 25N 71 12W
East Liberty, *OH, U.S.A.* **92 C3** 40 20N 83 35W
East Livermore = Livermore Falls, *ME, U.S.A.* **76 D3** 44 29N 70 11W
East Liverpool, *OH, U.S.A.* **92 C6** 40 37N 80 35W
East Longmeadow, *MA, U.S.A.* **78 B2** 42 4N 72 31W
East Los Angeles, *Los Angeles, U.S.A.* **111 B3** 34 1N 118 10W
East Lyme, *CT, U.S.A.* **78 C2** 41 22N 72 13W
East Lynn L., *WV, U.S.A.* **102 C2** 38 10N 82 23W
East Lynne, *MO, U.S.A.* **82 C2** 38 40N 94 14W
East Main = Eastmain, *Qué., Canada* **175 C2** 52 10N 78 30W
East Meadow, *NY, U.S.A.* **87 B3** 40 43N 73 34W
East Middlebury, *VT, U.S.A.* **86 C1** 43 58N 73 6W
East Millcreek, *Salt Lake City, U.S.A.* **117 B3** 40 42N 111 48W
East Millinocket, *ME, U.S.A.* **76 C5** 45 38N 68 35W
East Milwaukee = Shorewood, *WI, U.S.A.* **103 E6** 43 5N 87 53W
East Moline, *IL, U.S.A.* **71 B3** 41 32N 90 26W
East Naples, *FL, U.S.A.* **67 E7** 26 8N 81 46W
East New Market, *MD, U.S.A.* **77 B5** 38 36N 75 56W
East New York, *NY, U.S.A.* **114 B3** 40 40N 73 53W
East Newark, *NJ, U.S.A.* **114 B1** 40 45N 74 9W
East Nishnabotna →, *IA, U.S.A.* **73 E3** 40 39N 95 38W
East Northport, *NY, U.S.A.* **78 D1** 40 53N 73 20W
East Norwich, *NY, U.S.A.* **87 B3** 40 51N 73 32W
East Olympia, *WA, U.S.A.* **101 D3** 46 58N 122 50W
East Orange, *NJ, U.S.A.* **87 B2** 40 46N 74 12W
East Palatka, *FL, U.S.A.* **67 B7** 29 39N 81 36W
East Palestine, *OH, U.S.A.* **92 C6** 40 50N 80 33W
East Park Res., *CA, U.S.A.* **64 D4** 39 37N 122 31W
East Paterson, *NJ, U.S.A.* **114 A2** 40 54N 74 9W
East Peoria, *IL, U.S.A.* **71 C4** 40 40N 89 34W
East Peru, *IA, U.S.A.* **73 D5** 41 14N 93 56W
East Petersburg, *PA, U.S.A.* **95 D6** 40 6N 76 21W
East Pines, *MD, U.S.A.* **119 B4** 38 57N 76 54W
East Pittsburgh, *Pittsburgh, U.S.A.* **116 B2** 40 23N 79 50W
East Point, *GA, U.S.A.* **68 C2** 33 41N 84 25W
East Potomac Park, *Washington DC, U.S.A.* **119 B3** 38 52N 77 1W
East Prairie, *MO, U.S.A.* **82 E7** 36 47N 89 23W
East Prospect, *PA, U.S.A.* **95 E6** 39 58N 76 32W
East Providence, *RI, U.S.A.* **78 C3** 41 49N 71 23W
East Pt., *Br. Virgin Is.* **105 G18** 18 40N 64 18W
East Pt., *N.S., Canada* **173 G8** 46 27N 61 58W
East Pt., *U.S. Virgin Is.* **105 H18** 17 45N 64 34W
East Pt., *Boston, U.S.A.* **106 A4** 42 25N 70 54W
East Randolph, *VT, U.S.A.* **86 C2** 43 56N 72 33W
East Range, *NV, U.S.A.* **85 B3** 40 30N 117 57W
East Ridge, *TN, U.S.A.* **97 F7** 34 59N 85 13W
East River →, *NY, U.S.A.* **114 B3** 40 44N 73 58W
East Rochester, *NY, U.S.A.* **89 B3** 43 7N 77 29W
East Rockaway, *NY, U.S.A.* **114 C4** 40 38N 73 40W
East Rockingham, *NC, U.S.A.* **90 D6** 34 55N 79 49W
East Rupert, *VT, U.S.A.* **86 C1** 43 16N 73 8W
East Rutherford, *NJ, U.S.A.* **114 A2** 40 50N 74 5W
East St. Louis, *IL, U.S.A.* **71 E3** 38 37N 90 9W
East Sebago, *ME, U.S.A.* **86 C4** 43 51N 70 38W
East Shoreham, *NY, U.S.A.* **78 D2** 40 57N 72 53W
East Side, *PA, U.S.A.* **87 A1** 41 4N 75 46W
East Spring Cr. →, *CO, U.S.A.* **66 C8** 39 30N 102 30W
East Stroudsburg, *PA, U.S.A.* **95 C7** 41 1N 75 11W
East Tavaputs Plateau, *UT, U.S.A.* **100 D6** 39 40N 109 40W
East Tawas, *MI, U.S.A.* **79 E8** 44 17N 83 29W
East Thurlow I., *B.C., Canada* **186 E9** 50 24N 125 25W
East Trout L., *Sask., Canada* **182 A6** 54 22N 105 5W
East Troy, *WI, U.S.A.* **103 F5** 42 47N 88 24W
East Vineland, *NJ, U.S.A.* **87 C2** 39 30N 74 55W
East Wallingford, *VT, U.S.A.* **86 C2** 43 25N 72 54W
East Wareham, *MA, U.S.A.* **78 C4** 41 46N 70 40W
East Wenatchee, *WA, U.S.A.* **101 C5** 47 25N 120 18W
East Williston, *NY, U.S.A.* **114 B5** 40 45N 73 38W
East Youngstown = Campbell, *OH, U.S.A.* **92 B6** 41 5N 80 37W
Eastabuchie, *MS, U.S.A.* **81 E4** 31 26N 89 17W
Eastchester, *NY, U.S.A.* **87 B3** 40 57N 73 49W
Eastchester Bay, *NY, U.S.A.* **114 A4** 40 50N 73 48W
Eastend, *Sask., Canada* **182 F3** 49 32N 108 50W
Eastern Bay, *MD, U.S.A.* **77 B4** 38 50N 76 15W
Eastern Neck Nat. Wildlife Refuge ⌓, *MD, U.S.A.* **77 A4** 39 2N 76 14W
Eastern Shore, *MD, U.S.A.* **77 B5** 38 30N 75 50W
Easterville, *Man., Canada* **183 B12** 53 8N 99 49W
Eastgate, *Seattle, U.S.A.* **118 C5** 47 34N 122 9W
Eastham, *MA, U.S.A.* **78 C5** 41 50N 69 58W
Easthampton, *MA, U.S.A.* **78 B2** 42 16N 72 40W
Eastlake, *MI, U.S.A.* **79 E5** 44 15N 86 18W
Eastlake, *OH, U.S.A.* **92 B5** 41 40N 81 26W
Eastland, *TX, U.S.A.* **99 E9** 32 24N 98 49W
Eastland County ☆, *TX, U.S.A.* **99 E9** 32 25N 98 50W
Eastmain, *Qué., Canada* **175 C2** 52 10N 78 30W
Eastmain →, *Qué., Canada* **175 C2** 52 27N 78 26W
Eastman, *Qué., Canada* **177 F10** 45 18N 72 19W
Eastman, *GA, U.S.A.* **68 D3** 32 12N 83 11W
Eastman, *WI, U.S.A.* **103 E2** 43 10N 91 1W
Easton, *CA, U.S.A.* **65 G7** 36 39N 119 47W
Easton, *CT, U.S.A.* **78 C1** 41 15N 73 18W
Easton, *IL, U.S.A.* **71 C4** 40 14N 89 50W
Easton, *KS, U.S.A.* **74 B8** 39 21N 95 7W
Easton, *MD, U.S.A.* **77 B4** 38 47N 76 5W
Easton, *MN, U.S.A.* **80 G5** 43 46N 93 54W
Easton, *MO, U.S.A.* **82 B2** 39 43N 94 39W
Easton, *PA, U.S.A.* **87 B1** 40 41N 75 13W
Easton, *WA, U.S.A.* **101 C4** 47 14N 121 11W
Eastover, *NC, U.S.A.* **90 C7** 35 6N 78 47W
Eastover, *SC, U.S.A.* **90 E5** 33 52N 80 41W
Eastpoint, *FL, U.S.A.* **67 B4** 29 44N 84 53W
Eastport, *ID, U.S.A.* **70 A2** 48 59N 116 10W
Eastport, *ME, U.S.A.* **76 D6** 44 56N 67 0W
Eastport, *MI, U.S.A.* **79 D6** 45 8N 85 21W
Eastsound, *WA, U.S.A.* **101 B3** 48 42N 122 55W
Eastview, *TN, U.S.A.* **96 E4** 35 5N 88 33W
Eastville, *VA, U.S.A.* **102 D9** 37 21N 75 57W
Eastwood, *LA, U.S.A.* **75 B2** 32 33N 93 34W
Eaton, *CO, U.S.A.* **66 B6** 40 32N 104 42W
Eaton, *IN, U.S.A.* **72 C5** 40 21N 85 21W
Eaton, *OH, U.S.A.* **92 D2** 39 45N 84 38W
Eaton Canyon Park, *Los Angeles, U.S.A.* **111 A3** 34 10N 118 5W
Eaton County ☆, *MI, U.S.A.* **79 G7** 42 35N 84 50W
Eaton Rapids, *MI, U.S.A.* **79 G7** 42 31N 84 39W
Eatonia, *Sask., Canada* **182 D2** 51 13N 109 25W
Eatons Neck Pt., *NY, U.S.A.* **78 D1** 40 57N 73 24W
Eatonton, *GA, U.S.A.* **68 C3** 33 20N 83 23W
Eatontown, *NJ, U.S.A.* **87 B2** 40 19N 74 4W
Eatonville, *Qué., Canada* **177 D13** 47 20N 69 41W
Eatonville, *WA, U.S.A.* **101 D3** 46 52N 122 16W
Eau Claire, *MI, U.S.A.* **79 H5** 41 59N 86 18W
Eau Claire, *WI, U.S.A.* **103 D2** 44 49N 91 30W
Eau Claire →, *WI, U.S.A.* **103 D4** 44 55N 89 35W
Eau-Claire, L. à l', *Nfld. & L., Canada* **172 A4** 52 36N 65 50W
Eau Claire, L. à l', *Qué., Canada* **175 B3** 56 10N 74 25W
Eau Claire County ☆, *WI, U.S.A.* **103 D2** 44 45N 91 20W
Eau Galle, *WI, U.S.A.* **103 D1** 44 42N 92 1W
Ebano, *San Luis Potosí, Mexico* **215 H6** 22 13N 98 24W
Ebensburg, *PA, U.S.A.* **95 D4** 40 29N 78 44W
Ebey's Landing Nat. Historical Reserve ⌓, *WA, U.S.A.* **101 B3** 48 12N 122 41W
Ebony, *VA, U.S.A.* **102 E7** 36 37N 77 59W
Ecatepec de Morelos, *México, Mexico* **219 C8** 19 36N 99 3W
Ecatzingo, *México, Mexico* **219 D9** 18 58N 98 45W
Eccles, *WV, U.S.A.* **102 D3** 37 47N 81 16W
Echeconnee →, *GA, U.S.A.* **68 D3** 32 38N 83 36W
Echo, *AL, U.S.A.* **60 E5** 31 29N 85 28W
Echo, *MN, U.S.A.* **80 F3** 44 37N 95 25W
Echo, *OR, U.S.A.* **94 B6** 45 45N 119 12W
Echo Bay, *N.W.T., Canada* **189 C9** 66 5N 117 55W
Echo Bay, *Ont., Canada* **178 A2** 46 29N 84 4W
Echo Bay, *NY, U.S.A.* **114 A4** 40 54N 73 44W
Echo Cliffs, *AZ, U.S.A.* **62 A4** 36 40N 111 35W
Echols County ☆, *GA, U.S.A.* **68 F4** 30 45N 83 0W
Échouani, L., *Qué., Canada* **176 D7** 47 46N 75 42W
Eckley, *CO, U.S.A.* **66 B8** 40 7N 102 29W
Eckville, *Alta., Canada* **185 F6** 52 21N 114 22W
Eclectic, *AL, U.S.A.* **60 D4** 32 38N 86 2W
Eclipse Sd., *Nunavut, Canada* **190 C10** 72 38N 79 0W
Economy = Ambridge, *PA, U.S.A.* **95 D2** 40 36N 80 14W
Economy, *IN, U.S.A.* **72 D5** 39 59N 85 5W
Écorce, L. de l', *Qué., Canada* **176 D6** 47 5N 76 24W
Ecru, *MS, U.S.A.* **81 B4** 34 21N 89 2W
Ector County ☆, *TX, U.S.A.* **98 F5** 31 46N 102 31W
Ecuandureo, *Michoacan, Mexico* **218 B5** 20 10N 102 11W
Ecueils, Pte. aux, *Qué., Canada* **175 B2** 59 47N 77 50W
Ecum Secum, *N.S., Canada* **173 J7** 44 58N 62 8W
Edam, *Sask., Canada* **182 B3** 53 11N 108 46W
Edberg, *Alta., Canada* **185 F8** 52 47N 112 47W
Edcouch, *TX, U.S.A.* **98 L10** 26 18N 97 58W
Eddy County ☆, *ND, U.S.A.* **91 C7** 47 50N 99 0W
Eddy County ☆, *NM, U.S.A.* **88 E6** 32 30N 104 20W
Eddyville, *IL, U.S.A.* **71 F5** 37 30N 88 35W
Eddyville, *IA, U.S.A.* **73 D6** 41 9N 92 38W
Eddyville, *KY, U.S.A.* **96 C4** 37 3N 88 4W
Eddyville, *NE, U.S.A.* **84 C6** 41 1N 99 38W
Eden = Bar Harbor, *ME, U.S.A.* **76 D5** 44 23N 68 13W
Eden, *Man., Canada* **183 E12** 50 23N 99 28W
Eden, *MS, U.S.A.* **81 D3** 32 59N 90 20W
Eden, *NC, U.S.A.* **90 B6** 36 29N 79 53W
Eden, *SD, U.S.A.* **91 E8** 45 37N 97 25W
Eden, *TX, U.S.A.* **99 F8** 31 13N 99 51W
Eden, *VT, U.S.A.* **86 B2** 44 42N 72 33W
Eden, *WI, U.S.A.* **103 E5** 43 42N 88 22W
Eden, *WY, U.S.A.* **104 D3** 42 3N 109 26W
Eden Res., *WY, U.S.A.* **104 D3** 42 14N 109 21W
Eden Valley, *MN, U.S.A.* **80 E4** 45 19N 94 33W
Edenton, *NC, U.S.A.* **90 B9** 36 4N 76 39W
Edenvale Park, *Minneapolis-St. Paul, U.S.A.* **113 B1** 44 52N 93 27W
Edesville, *MD, U.S.A.* **77 A4** 39 9N 76 13W
Edgar, *NE, U.S.A.* **84 D8** 40 22N 97 58W
Edgar, *WI, U.S.A.* **103 D4** 44 55N 89 59W
Edgar County ☆, *IL, U.S.A.* **71 D6** 39 40N 87 45W
Edgar Springs, *MO, U.S.A.* **82 D5** 37 42N 91 52W
Edgard, *LA, U.S.A.* **75 D5** 30 3N 90 34W
Edgartown, *MA, U.S.A.* **78 C4** 41 23N 70 31W
Edge Hills Park ⌓, *B.C., Canada* **187 D13** 51 2N 121 52W
Edgecliff, *Dallas-Fort Worth, U.S.A.* **109 C1** 32 39N 97 20W
Edgecombe County ☆, *NC, U.S.A.* **90 C8** 35 50N 77 30W
Edgefield, *SC, U.S.A.* **90 E4** 33 47N 81 56W
Edgefield County ☆, *SC, U.S.A.* **90 E4** 33 50N 82 0W
Edgeley, *ND, U.S.A.* **91 D7** 46 22N 98 43W
Edgemar, *San Francisco, U.S.A.* **118 C2** 37 39N 122 29W
Edgemere, *MD, U.S.A.* **77 A4** 39 14N 76 27W
Edgemont, *SD, U.S.A.* **91 G2** 43 18N 103 50W
Edgemoor, *DE, U.S.A.* **77 A5** 39 45N 75 30W
Edgerton, *Alta., Canada* **185 F10** 52 45N 110 27W
Edgerton, *KS, U.S.A.* **74 C8** 38 46N 95 1W
Edgerton, *MN, U.S.A.* **80 G2** 43 53N 96 8W
Edgerton, *MO, U.S.A.* **82 B2** 39 30N 94 38W
Edgerton, *OH, U.S.A.* **92 B2** 41 27N 84 45W
Edgerton, *WI, U.S.A.* **103 F4** 42 50N 89 4W
Edgerton, *WY, U.S.A.* **104 C6** 43 25N 106 15W
Edgewater, *B.C., Canada* **185 H4** 50 42N 116 5W
Edgewater, *Denver, U.S.A.* **109 B1** 39 45N 105 3W
Edgewater, *FL, U.S.A.* **67 C8** 28 59N 80 54W
Edgewater Park, *Cleveland, U.S.A.* **107 B1** 41 29N 81 43W
Edgewater Park, *NJ, U.S.A.* **87 B2** 40 4N 74 54W
Edgewood, *B.C., Canada* **187 F16** 49 47N 118 8W
Edgewood, *IL, U.S.A.* **71 E5** 38 55N 88 40W
Edgewood, *IN, U.S.A.* **72 D4** 39 41N 86 8W
Edgewood, *IA, U.S.A.* **73 C7** 42 39N 91 24W
Edgewood, *KY, U.S.A.* **97 A8** 39 1N 84 34W
Edgewood, *MD, U.S.A.* **77 A4** 39 25N 76 18W
Edgewood, *NM, U.S.A.* **88 B4** 35 4N 106 11W
Edgewood, *Orlando, U.S.A.* **115 B2** 28 29N 81 22W
Edgewood, *Pittsburgh, U.S.A.* **116 B2** 40 25N 79 52W
Edgewood, *TX, U.S.A.* **99 E12** 32 42N 95 53W
Edina, *MN, U.S.A.* **80 F5** 44 53N 93 20W
Edina, *MO, U.S.A.* **82 A4** 40 10N 92 11W
Edinboro, *PA, U.S.A.* **95 C2** 41 52N 80 8W
Edinburg, *IL, U.S.A.* **71 D4** 39 39N 89 23W
Edinburg, *MS, U.S.A.* **81 D4** 32 48N 89 20W
Edinburg, *ND, U.S.A.* **91 B8** 48 30N 97 52W
Edinburg, *TX, U.S.A.* **98 L9** 26 18N 98 10W
Edinburg, *VA, U.S.A.* **102 C6** 38 49N 78 34W
Edinburgh, *IN, U.S.A.* **72 D5** 39 21N 85 58W
Edison, *GA, U.S.A.* **68 E2** 31 34N 84 44W
Edison, *NJ, U.S.A.* **87 B2** 40 31N 74 25W
Edison, *NE, U.S.A.* **84 D6** 40 17N 99 47W
Edison, *OH, U.S.A.* **92 C4** 40 33N 82 52W
Edison Park, *Chicago, U.S.A.* **108 A2** 42 1N 87 48W
Edisto →, *SC, U.S.A.* **90 F5** 32 29N 80 21W
Edisto I., *SC, U.S.A.* **90 F5** 32 35N 80 20W
Edith, *TX, U.S.A.* **98 F7** 31 54N 100 37W
Edmond, *KS, U.S.A.* **74 B4** 39 37N 99 50W
Edmond, *OK, U.S.A.* **93 C6** 35 39N 97 29W
Edmonds, *WA, U.S.A.* **101 C3** 47 48N 122 22W
Edmondson, *AR, U.S.A.* **63 C5** 35 6N 90 19W
Edmondston, *MD, U.S.A.* **119 B4** 38 56N 76 54W
Edmonson, *TX, U.S.A.* **98 C6** 34 17N 101 54W
Edmonson County ☆, *KY, U.S.A.* **96 C6** 37 10N 86 15W
Edmonton, *Alta., Canada* **184 E7** 53 30N 113 30W
Edmonton, *KY, U.S.A.* **97 D7** 36 59N 85 37W
Edmonton International ✕ (YEG), *Alta., Canada* **184 E7** 53 21N 113 38W
Edmore, *MI, U.S.A.* **79 F6** 43 25N 85 3W
Edmore, *ND, U.S.A.* **91 B7** 48 25N 98 27W
Edmunds County ☆, *SD, U.S.A.* **91 E6** 45 27N 99 20W
Edmundson, *MO, U.S.A.* **117 A1** 38 44N 90 21W
Edmundston, *N.B., Canada* **173 F1** 47 23N 68 20W
Edna, *KS, U.S.A.* **74 D8** 37 4N 95 22W
Edna, *TX, U.S.A.* **99 J11** 28 59N 96 39W
Edon, *OH, U.S.A.* **92 B2** 41 33N 84 46W
Edray, *WV, U.S.A.* **102 C4** 38 16N 80 6W
Edroy, *TX, U.S.A.* **99 K10** 27 59N 97 41W
Edson, *Alta., Canada* **184 E4** 53 35N 116 28W
Edson, *KS, U.S.A.* **74 B2** 39 20N 101 33W
Edwall, *WA, U.S.A.* **101 C8** 47 30N 117 57W
Edward Arthur Patterson L., *ND, U.S.A.* **91 D3** 46 51N 102 51W
Edward I., *Ont., Canada* **180 D8** 48 22N 88 37W
Edwards, *CA, U.S.A.* **65 J9** 34 50N 117 40W
Edwards, *MS, U.S.A.* **81 D3** 32 20N 90 36W
Edwards, *NY, U.S.A.* **89 A5** 44 20N 75 15W
Edwards →, *IL, U.S.A.* **71 B3** 41 9N 90 59W
Edwards Air Force Base, *CA, U.S.A.* **65 J9** 34 52N 117 56W
Edwards County ☆, *IL, U.S.A.* **71 E5** 38 25N 88 5W
Edwards County ☆, *KS, U.S.A.* **74 D4** 37 50N 99 15W
Edwards County ☆, *TX, U.S.A.* **98 G7** 30 10N 100 13W
Edwards Plateau, *TX, U.S.A.* **98 G6** 30 45N 101 20W
Edwardsburg, *MI, U.S.A.* **79 H5** 41 48N 86 6W
Edwardsport, *IN, U.S.A.* **72 E3** 38 49N 87 15W
Edwardsville, *IL, U.S.A.* **71 E4** 38 49N 89 58W
Edziza, Mt., *B.C., Canada* **189 E6** 57 44N 130 40W
Edzná, *Campeche, Mexico* **223 C3** 19 35N 90 19W
Edzo, *N.W.T., Canada* **189 D9** 62 49N 116 4W
Eek, *AK, U.S.A.* **61 F7** 60 14N 162 2W
Eel →, *CA, U.S.A.* **64 C2** 40 38N 124 20W

Eel →, *IN, U.S.A.* **72 D4** 39 7N 86 57W
Eel →, *IN, U.S.A.* **72 C4** 40 45N 86 22W
Eel River Crossing, *N.B., Canada* **173 E3** 48 1N 66 25W
Effie, *MN, U.S.A.* **80 C5** 47 50N 93 38W
Effigy Mounds Nat. Monument ⌓, *IA, U.S.A.* **73 B7** 43 5N 91 11W
Effingham, *IL, U.S.A.* **71 D5** 39 7N 88 33W
Effingham, *KS, U.S.A.* **74 B8** 39 31N 95 24W
Effingham County ☆, *GA, U.S.A.* **68 D5** 32 20N 81 15W
Effingham County ☆, *IL, U.S.A.* **71 D5** 39 5N 88 35W
Effingham Falls, *NH, U.S.A.* **86 C3** 43 47N 71 5W
Egan, *SD, U.S.A.* **91 G9** 44 0N 96 37W
Egan Range, *NV, U.S.A.* **85 C6** 39 35N 114 55W
Eganville, *Ont., Canada* **179 B9** 45 32N 77 5W
Egegik, *AK, U.S.A.* **61 G8** 58 13N 157 22W
Egeland, *ND, U.S.A.* **91 B6** 48 38N 99 6W
Egg Harbor, *WI, U.S.A.* **103 C6** 45 3N 87 17W
Egg Harbor City, *NJ, U.S.A.* **87 C2** 39 32N 74 39W
Egg Island Pt., *NJ, U.S.A.* **87 C1** 39 11N 75 8W
Eglin Air Force Base, *FL, U.S.A.* **67 A2** 30 28N 86 32W
Eglinton I., *N.W.T., Canada* **188 A9** 75 48N 118 30W
Egmont, *B.C., Canada* **186 F11** 49 45N 123 56W
Egmont B., *P.E.I., Canada* **173 G5** 46 29N 64 6W
Egmont Channel, *Tampa, U.S.A.* **119 D2** 27 36N 82 47W
Egmont Key State Park, *Tampa, U.S.A.* **119 D2** 27 36N 82 46W
Egnar, *CO, U.S.A.* **66 E2** 37 55N 108 56W
Eholt, *B.C., Canada* **187 F16** 49 10N 118 34W
Ehrenberg, *AZ, U.S.A.* **62 D1** 33 36N 114 31W
Eielson, *AK, U.S.A.* **61 D11** 64 40N 147 4W
Eitzen, *MN, U.S.A.* **80 G7** 43 31N 91 28W
Ejutla, *Jalisco, Mexico* **218 C3** 19 54N 104 10W
Ejutla, *Oaxaca, Mexico* **221 H4** 16 34N 96 44W
Ekalaka, *MT, U.S.A.* **83 E13** 45 53N 104 33W
Ekalugad Fiord, *Nunavut, Canada* **190 D12** 68 46N 68 37W
Ek'Balam, *Yucatán, Mexico* **223 B5** 20 52N 88 9W
Ekka I., *N.W.T., Canada* **188 C8** 66 19N 122 29W
Eklutna, *AK, U.S.A.* **61 F10** 61 27N 149 22W
Ekron, *KY, U.S.A.* **96 C6** 37 56N 86 11W
Ekwan →, *Ont., Canada* **191 G9** 53 12N 82 15W
Ekwok, *AK, U.S.A.* **61 G8** 59 22N 157 30W
El Abandonado, *Coahuila, Mexico* **214 C2** 27 49N 102 11W
El Aguacate, *Guadalajara, Mexico* **224 A2** 20 42N 103 12W
El Aguaje, *Coahuila, Mexico* **215 F2** 24 47N 103 56W
El Ahogado, Presa, *Guadalajara, Mexico* **224 B2** 20 32N 103 16W
El Alacrán, *Tabasco, Mexico* **222 A3** 18 21N 93 41W
El Alamo, *Baja Calif., Mexico* **210 B2** 31 34N 116 2W
El Alamo, *Nuevo León, Mexico* **214 D5** 26 29N 99 46W
El Alamo, Sa., *Sonora, Mexico* **212 C3** 30 35N 112 35W
El Alhuate, *Sinaloa, Mexico* **216 C3** 24 30N 107 21W
El Alicante, *Coahuila, Mexico* **214 C1** 27 56N 103 34W
El Arco, *Baja Calif. S., Mexico* **211 E5** 28 1N 113 25W
El Arenal, *Chiapas, Mexico* **222 D3** 15 10N 92 42W
El Arenal, *Jalisco, Mexico* **218 B4** 20 46N 103 39W
El Arenal, *Michoacan, Mexico* **218 D5** 18 7N 102 38W
El Bacatete, Sa., *Sonora, Mexico* **212 F5** 27 54N 110 19W
El Barón →, *Baja Calif., Mexico* **210 B2** 31 50N 116 40W
El Barreal, *Chihuahua, Mexico* **213 B8** 31 17N 107 10W
El Barreal, L., *Chihuahua, Mexico* **213 B9** 31 7N 107 0W
El Barrego →, *Baja Calif., Mexico* **210 B3** 31 25N 114 52W
El Barril, *Baja Calif., Mexico* **211 E6** 28 18N 112 55W
El Barril, *San Luis Potosí, Mexico* **215 G2** 23 2N 102 8W
El Becerro, *Chihuahua, Mexico* **213 E11** 28 37N 104 39W
El Berrendo, *Chihuahua, Mexico* **213 B7** 31 20N 108 25W
El Bledal, *Sinaloa, Mexico* **216 C3** 24 49N 107 49W
El Bordo, *Zacatecas, Mexico* **217 E8** 22 54N 102 23W
El Bosque, *Chiapas, Mexico* **222 B4** 17 4N 92 44W
El Brasil, *Tamaulipas, Mexico* **215 G7** 23 20N 97 46W
El Cabrito, *Tamaulipas, Mexico* **215 G6** 23 11N 98 29W
El Caimanero, L., *Sinaloa, Mexico* **216 E4** 23 0N 106 7W
El Cajon, *CA, U.S.A.* **65 L10** 32 48N 116 58W
El Caldillo, *Chihuahua, Mexico* **213 G9** 26 31N 106 23W
El Camarón, *Oaxaca, Mexico* **221 H4** 16 34N 96 2W
El Campo, *TX, U.S.A.* **99 H11** 29 12N 96 16W
El Capitan Res., *CA, U.S.A.* **65 L10** 32 53N 116 49W
El Capulín, *Guadalajara, Mexico* **224 C2** 20 28N 103 16W
El Caracol, Presa, *Guerrero, Mexico* **219 E8** 17 57N 99 54W
El Carmen, *Chiapas, Mexico* **222 D3** 15 34N 93 7W
El Carmen, *Nuevo León, Mexico* **215 F4** 24 36N 100 28W
El Carmen, R. →, *Chihuahua, Mexico* **213 C9** 30 42N 106 29W
El Carrizal, *Guerrero, Mexico* **219 E7** 17 53N 100 56W
El Carrizal, *Sonora, Mexico* **212 B4** 31 5N 111 42W
El Carrizalillo, *Zacatecas, Mexico* **217 D7** 23 12N 103 22W
El Casco, *Durango, Mexico* **217 B6** 25 34N 104 35W
El Castillo, *Guadalajara, Mexico* **224 B2** 20 30N 103 14W
El Castillo, *Sinaloa, Mexico* **216 C3** 24 32N 107 43W
El Ceboruco, Volcán, *Nayarit, Mexico* **216 F6** 21 9N 104 30W
El Cedral, *Quintana Roo, Mexico* **223 B6** 20 21N 87 0W
El Cedral, *Quintana Roo, Mexico* **223 B6** 20 56N 87 32W
El Centenario, *Baja Calif. S., Mexico* **211 J8** 24 5N 110 26W
El Centenario, *Campeche, Mexico* **223 D3** 18 39N 90 17W
El Centro, *Zacatecas, Mexico* **217 D7** 23 22N 103 18W
El Centro, *CA, U.S.A.* **65 L11** 32 48N 115 34W
El Cerrito, *CA, U.S.A.* **64 F4** 37 55N 122 19W
El Chauz, *Michoacan, Mexico* **218 D5** 18 52N 102 2W
El Chico, Parque Nacional △, *Hidalgo, Mexico* **219 B9** 20 12N 98 43W
El Chilacayote, *Jalisco, Mexico* **218 B3** 20 8N 104 39W
El Chinal, *Tabasco, Mexico* **222 A4** 18 2N 92 8W
El Chinero = La Trinidad, *Baja Calif., Mexico* **210 B3** 31 24N 115 5W
El Cielo, Reserva de la Biosfera ⌓, *Tamaulipas, Mexico* **215 G5** 23 18N 99 12W
El Ciento Veintiocho, *Baja Calif. S., Mexico* **211 J7** 24 29N 111 15W
El Cimatario, Parque Nacional △, *Querétaro, Mexico* **219 B7** 20 30N 100 21W
El Cinco, *Coahuila, Mexico* **214 D1** 26 47N 103 27W
El Claro, *Sonora, Mexico* **212 C4** 30 22N 111 12W
El Colomo, *Colima, Mexico* **218 C3** 19 2N 104 15W
El Colorado, *Chihuahua, Mexico* **213 D7** 29 53N 108 53W
El Colorado, *Sinaloa, Mexico* **216 B1** 25 46N 109 19W
El Conejo, *Baja Calif. S., Mexico* **211 J8** 24 7N 110 59W
El Consuelo, *Chihuahua, Mexico* **213 C10** 30 47N 105 43W
El Control, *Tamaulipas, Mexico* **214 E7** 25 57N 97 48W
El Coyote, *Veracruz, Mexico* **221 F4** 18 37N 96 18W
El Coyote →, *Sonora, Mexico* **212 C3** 30 48N 112 37W
El Coyote, L., *Coahuila, Mexico* **214 C1** 27 13N 103 15W
El Crucero, *Baja Calif., Mexico* **210 D4** 29 15N 114 10W
El Cuatro, *Sonora, Mexico* **212 C4** 30 7N 111 33W
El Cuchijaqui →, *Sonora, Mexico* **212 G7** 26 35N 108 48W
El Cuchillo, Presa, *Nuevo León, Mexico* **214 E5** 25 37N 99 20W
El Cuervo, *Chihuahua, Mexico* **213 C10** 30 14N 105 10W
El Cuervo, L., *Chihuahua, Mexico* **213 D10** 29 17N 105 57W
El Cuyo, *Yucatán, Mexico* **223 A6** 21 31N 87 41W
El Cuyo, Pta., *Campeche, Mexico* **223 B3** 20 5N 90 29W
El Descanso, Pta., *Baja Calif., Mexico* **210 A1** 32 17N 117 4W
El Desemboque, *Sonora, Mexico* **212 C2** 30 33N 113 1W
El Desemboque, *Sonora, Mexico* **212 D3** 29 30N 112 27W
El Diablo, Sa., *Chihuahua, Mexico* **213 F11** 27 16N 104 10W
El Diamante, *Chiapas, Mexico* **222 C4** 16 6N 92 52W
El Diamante, *Durango, Mexico* **217 A6** 26 23N 104 20W
El Doce, *Veracruz, Mexico* **221 G6** 17 14N 94 13W
El Dorado, *Sinaloa, Mexico* **216 C3** 24 17N 107 21W
El Dorado, *AR, U.S.A.* **63 E3** 33 12N 92 40W
El Dorado, *KS, U.S.A.* **74 D7** 37 49N 96 52W
El Dorado County ☆, *CA, U.S.A.* **64 E6** 38 45N 120 40W
El Dorado L., *KS, U.S.A.* **74 D7** 37 51N 96 49W
El Dorado Park, *Los Angeles, U.S.A.* **111 D4** 33 48N 118 5W
El Dorado Springs, *MO, U.S.A.* **82 D2** 37 52N 94 1W
El Durazno, *Durango, Mexico* **217 D6** 23 58N 104 44W
El Durazno, *Zacatecas, Mexico* **217 C9** 24 15N 101 11W
El Encinal, Sa., *Sonora, Mexico* **212 E6** 28 45N 109 20W
El Espinal, *Veracruz, Mexico* **220 D3** 20 16N 97 24W
El Espíritu →, *Guerrero, Mexico* **219 D7** 18 19N 100 39W
El Este, L., *Campeche, Mexico* **223 D2** 18 25N 91 49W
El Faro, *Michoacan, Mexico* **218 D4** 18 20N 103 29W
El Fresnal, Sa., *Chihuahua, Mexico* **213 C8** 31 0N 107 40W
El Fuerte, *Sinaloa, Mexico* **216 A2** 26 25N 108 39W
El Gato, *Sonora, Mexico* **212 B3** 31 38N 112 0W
El Gato →, *Coahuila, Mexico* **214 C4** 27 29N 100 55W
El Gavilán, *Sonora, Mexico* **212 D4** 29 28N 111 45W
El Gavilán, *Tamaulipas, Mexico* **215 F6** 24 42N 98 59W
El Gogorrón, Parque Nacional △, *San Luis Potosí, Mexico* **215 J4** 21 49N 100 57W
El Golpe, *Tabasco, Mexico* **222 A3** 18 20N 93 30W
El Grande, Cerro, *Chihuahua, Mexico* **213 B8** 31 37N 107 59W
El Grullo, *Jalisco, Mexico* **218 C3** 19 48N 104 13W
El Guasimal, *Sinaloa, Mexico* **216 D4** 23 43N 106 18W
El Higo, *Veracruz, Mexico* **220 C2** 21 46N 98 28W
El Huacal, *Durango, Mexico* **216 B4** 25 27N 106 10W
El Huapango, *Tamaulipas, Mexico* **215 F6** 24 38N 98 8W
El Huerfanito, *Baja Calif., Mexico* **210 C4** 30 8N 114 39W
El Humo, Sa., *Sonora, Mexico* **212 B4** 31 20N 111 50W
El Indio, *TX, U.S.A.* **98 J7** 28 31N 100 19W
El Jaralito, *Durango, Mexico* **217 A6** 26 7N 104 10W
El Jilguero, *Guerrero, Mexico* **219 E7** 17 31N 100 2W
El Juento, Volcán, *México, Mexico* **225 C2** 19 13N 99 20W
El Limón, *Jalisco, Mexico* **218 C3** 19 49N 104 11W
El Limón de los Ramos, *Sinaloa, Mexico* **216 C3** 24 54N 107 32W
El Limón de Papatzingán, *Michoacan, Mexico* **219 C7** 19 5N 100 46W
El Llano, *Nayarit, Mexico* **216 F5** 21 24N 105 11W
El Llano →, *Chihuahua, Mexico* **213 C10** 30 15N 105 6W
El Malpais Nat. Monument ⌓, *U.S.A.* **88 C2** 34 53N 108 0W
El Manguito, *Chiapas, Mexico* **222 D3** 15 45N 93 31W
El Mármol, *Guanajuato, Mexico* **218 B6** 20 14N 101 44W
El Mezquital, *Baja Calif. S., Mexico* **211 E5** 28 17N 113 50W
El Mezquite, *Tamaulipas, Mexico* **215 E7** 25 4N 97 44W
El Mezquite, *Zacatecas, Mexico* **217 D8** 23 20N 102 37W
El Milagro de Guadalupe, *San Luis Potosí, Mexico* **215 G4** 23 8N 100 26W
El Mineral el Realito, *Guanajuato, Mexico* **219 A7** 21 37N 100 14W
El Mineral el Refugio, *Guanajuato, Mexico* **219 A7** 21 35N 100 11W
El Mirador, *Chihuahua, Mexico* **213 C8** 30 52N 107 7W
El Mirador, *Guadalajara, Mexico* **224 C1** 20 29N 103 20W
El Mirage, *AZ, U.S.A.* **62 D3** 33 36N 112 19W
El Mirage L., *CA, U.S.A.* **65 J9** 34 39N 117 37W
El Monte, *Los Angeles, U.S.A.* **111 B4** 34 3N 118 1W
El Moro →, *Sonora, Mexico* **212 E6** 28 20N 109 37W
El Morro Nat. Monument ⌓, *NM, U.S.A.* **88 B2** 35 2N 108 21W
El Naranjo, *Campeche, Mexico* **223 D2** 18 2N 91 7W
El Naranjo, *Durango, Mexico* **217 C7** 24 37N 103 21W
El Naranjo, *Nayarit, Mexico* **216 E6** 22 1N 104 53W
El Naranjo, *San Luis Potosí, Mexico* **215 H5** 22 30N 99 21W
El Nido, *CA, U.S.A.* **64 F6** 37 8N 120 29W
El Nido, Sa., *Chihuahua, Mexico* **213 D9** 29 33N 106 48W
El Novillero, *Nayarit, Mexico* **216 E5** 22 21N 105 39W
El Novillo, *Sonora, Mexico* **212 E6** 28 59N 109 37W
El Ocotito, *Guerrero, Mexico* **219 E8** 17 15N 99 34W
El Ojo del Agua, *Coahuila, Mexico* **214 D1** 26 20N 103 17W
El Oro, *México, Mexico* **219 C7** 19 51N 100 7W
El Orranteño, *Chihuahua, Mexico* **213 E10** 28 10N 105 20W
El Oso, *Coahuila, Mexico* **214 D3** 26 17N 101 46W
El Palmito, *Durango, Mexico* **216 B5** 25 38N 105 1W
El Papalote, *Coahuila, Mexico* **214 D2** 26 27N 102 32W
El Parral, *Chiapas, Mexico* **222 C3** 16 22N 93 0W
El Paso = Derby, *KS, U.S.A.* **74 D6** 37 33N 97 16W
El Paso, *IL, U.S.A.* **71 C4** 40 44N 89 1W
El Paso, *TX, U.S.A.* **98 F1** 31 45N 106 29W
El Paso County ☆, *CO, U.S.A.* **66 D6** 38 50N 104 30W
El Paso County ☆, *TX, U.S.A.* **98 F1** 31 55N 106 5W
El Paso International ✈ (ELP), *TX, U.S.A.* **98 F1** 31 48N 106 23W
El Patricio, *Sonora, Mexico* **212 B3** 31 34N 112 0W
El Pedregal, Parque Nacional △, *Distrito Federal, Mexico* **225 C2** 19 18N 99 12W
El Peguis, Sa., *Chihuahua, Mexico* **213 D11** 29 40N 104 48W
El Peñol, *Chihuahua, Mexico* **213 D9** 29 9N 106 14W
El Peñuelo, *Nuevo León, Mexico* **215 F4** 24 33N 100 44W
El Pequeño, *Nuevo León, Mexico* **215 F4** 24 4N 100 15W
El Picacho, Cerro, *Distrito Federal, Mexico* **225 A3** 19 37N 99 8W
El Piche, *Tabasco, Mexico* **222 B5** 17 55N 91 1W
El Pinacate, Sa., *Sonora, Mexico* **212 B2** 31 45N 113 35W
El Pino, Sa., *Coahuila, Mexico* **214 B1** 28 15N 103 5W
El Planchón, *Chiapas, Mexico* **222 C6** 16 36N 90 41W
El Playón, *Sinaloa, Mexico* **216 B2** 25 16N 108 11W
El Plomito, *Sonora, Mexico* **212 C3** 30 18N 112 22W
El Plomo, *Sonora, Mexico* **212 B3** 31 15N 112 4W
El Pochote, *Sonora, Mexico* **212 F5** 27 46N 110 8W
El Portal, *CA, U.S.A.* **64 F7** 37 41N 119 47W
El Portal, *Miami, U.S.A.* **112 C2** 25 51N 80 11W
El Porvenir, *Chiapas, Mexico* **222 D3** 15 27N 92 16W
El Porvenir, *Chihuahua, Mexico* **213 B10** 31 15N 105 51W
El Porvenir, *NM, U.S.A.* **88 B5** 35 43N 105 25W
El Porvenir →, *Chihuahua, Mexico* **213 G9** 26 59N 106 20W
El Potosí, Parque Nacional △, *San Luis Potosí, Mexico* **215 J5** 21 59N 99 58W
El Progreso, *Coahuila, Mexico* **214 A3** 29 19N 101 39W
El Puesto, *Jalisco, Mexico* **218 A6** 21 37N 101 58W
El Quelite, *Sinaloa, Mexico* **216 D4** 23 32N 106 28W
El Quince, *Guadalajara, Mexico* **224 B2** 20 32N 103 17W
El Rajón, Sa., *Sonora, Mexico* **212 C3** 30 30N 112 2W
El Ramonal, *Campeche, Mexico* **223 D4** 18 22N 89 55W
El Rancho Nuevo, *Coahuila, Mexico* **215 E3** 25 17N 101 21W
El Recodo, *Sinaloa, Mexico* **216 D4** 23 24N 106 14W
El Reloj, *Distrito Federal, Mexico* **225 C3** 19 19N 99 9W
El Reno, *OK, U.S.A.* **93 C6** 35 32N 97 57W
El Retiro, *Baja Calif., Mexico* **210 B2** 31 38N 116 40W
El Rio, *CA, U.S.A.* **65 J7** 34 14N 119 10W
El Rito, *NM, U.S.A.* **88 A4** 36 21N 106 11W
El Roble, *Zacatecas, Mexico* **217 D7** 23 4N 103 57W
El Rodeo, *Zacatecas, Mexico* **217 C8** 24 53N 102 11W
El Rosario, *Baja Calif., Mexico* **210 C3** 30 1N 115 45W
El Rosario, *Oaxaca, Mexico* **221 H3** 16 52N 97 59W
El Rosario, *Tlaxcala, Mexico* **219 C9** 19 40N 98 13W
El Rosario →, *Baja Calif., Mexico* **210 C3** 30 2N 115 48W
El Rucio, *Zacatecas, Mexico* **217 D9** 23 23N 102 0W
El Sabinal, Parque Nacional △, *Nuevo León, Mexico* **214 D5** 26 2N 99 40W
El Salado, *Coahuila, Mexico* **214 A3** 29 38N 101 45W
El Salado, *San Luis Potosí, Mexico* **215 F4** 24 18N 100 52W
El Salado, *Sinaloa, Mexico* **216 C3** 24 30N 107 10W
El Salto, *Chihuahua, Mexico* **213 E7** 28 30N 108 20W
El Salto, *Durango, Mexico* **216 D5** 23 47N 105 22W
El Salto, *Jalisco, Mexico* **218 B4** 20 31N 103 10W
El Salvador, *Zacatecas, Mexico* **217 C10** 24 31N 100 51W
El Sargento, *Baja Calif. S., Mexico* **211 J8** 24 3N 110 1W
El Sásabe, *Sonora, Mexico* **212 B4** 31 27N 111 31W
El Sásabe →, *Sonora, Mexico* **212 C4** 30 50N 111 50W
El Sauz, *Chihuahua, Mexico* **213 D9** 29 3N 106 15W
El Sauz, *Monterrey, Mexico* **224 A2** 25 52N 100 12W
El Sauzalito, *Baja Calif. S., Mexico* **211 H7** 25 7N 111 2W
El Segundo, *Los Angeles, U.S.A.* **111 C2** 33 55N 118 24W
El Sereno, *Los Angeles, U.S.A.* **111 B3** 34 6N 118 10 E
El Socorro, *Coahuila, Mexico* **214 C2** 27 40N 102 18W
El Tajin, *Veracruz, Mexico* **220 D3** 20 27N 97 22W
El Tecuán, *Jalisco, Mexico* **218 C4** 19 28N 103 43W
El Tepuche, *Sinaloa, Mexico* **216 C3** 24 56N 107 21W
El Tigre, *Campeche, Mexico* **223 D3** 18 16N 90 33W
El Tigre, *Nayarit, Mexico* **216 E5** 22 30N 105 21W
El Tixqui, *Hidalgo, Mexico* **219 B8** 20 44N 99 6W
El Triunfo, *Chiapas, Mexico* **222 C4** 16 12N 91 51W
El Triunfo, *Sonora, Mexico* **212 E4** 28 52N 111 26W
El Triunfo, *Tabasco, Mexico* **222 B5** 17 56N 91 9W
El Tuito, *Jalisco, Mexico* **218 B2** 20 19N 105 22W
El Tule, *Chihuahua, Mexico* **213 F9** 27 3N 106 16W
El Tule, *Coahuila, Mexico* **214 B3** 28 31N 101 31W
El Tule, *Sinaloa, Mexico* **216 B3** 25 39N 107 54W
El Tulillo, *Zacatecas, Mexico* **217 E6** 22 31N 104 7W
El Vado Res., *NM, U.S.A.* **88 A4** 36 36N 106 44W
El Veinticuatro, *Chihuahua, Mexico* **213 C10** 30 18N 105 55W
El Veladero, Parque Nacional △, *Guerrero, Mexico* **219 F8** 16 54N 99 52W
El Verde, *Guadalajara, Mexico* **224 B2** 20 33N 103 16W
El Vergel, *Distrito Federal, Mexico* **225 C3** 19 18N 99 5W
El Vergelito, *Chiapas, Mexico* **222 C4** 16 34N 92 4W
El Viejo, Sa., *Sonora, Mexico* **212 C3** 30 15N 112 20W
El Vizcaíno, *Baja Calif. S., Mexico* **211 F5** 27 46N 114 0W
El Yucateco, *Tabasco, Mexico* **222 A2** 18 12N 94 1W
El Yunque, *Puerto Rico* **105 G17** 18 19N 65 48W
El Zacatal, *Oaxaca, Mexico* **221 H6** 16 57N 95 11W
El Zapatero, *Durango, Mexico* **216 C4** 24 36N 106 23W
Elaho →, *B.C., Canada* **186 E11** 50 7N 123 23W
Elaine, *AR, U.S.A.* **63 D5** 34 19N 90 51W
Elam, *PA, U.S.A.* **77 A5** 39 51N 75 32W
Elba, *AL, U.S.A.* **60 E4** 31 25N 86 4W
Elba, *ID, U.S.A.* **70 G5** 42 14N 113 34W
Elba, *MN, U.S.A.* **80 F6** 44 5N 92 1W
Elba, *NE, U.S.A.* **84 C7** 41 17N 98 34W
Elberfeld, *IN, U.S.A.* **72 E3** 38 10N 87 27W
Elberon, *IA, U.S.A.* **73 C6** 42 0N 92 19W
Elbert, *CO, U.S.A.* **66 C6** 39 13N 104 32W
Elbert, *TX, U.S.A.* **99 D9** 33 15N 99 0W
Elbert, Mt., *CO, U.S.A.* **66 C4** 39 7N 106 27W
Elbert County ☆, *CO, U.S.A.* **66 C6** 39 20N 104 15W
Elbert County ☆, *GA, U.S.A.* **68 B4** 34 10N 82 50W
Elberta, *MI, U.S.A.* **79 E5** 44 37N 86 14W
Elberta, *UT, U.S.A.* **100 D4** 39 57N 111 57W
Elberton, *GA, U.S.A.* **68 B4** 34 7N 82 52W
Elbing, *KS, U.S.A.* **74 C6** 38 3N 97 8W
Elbow, *Sask., Canada* **182 D5** 51 7N 106 35W
Elbow →, *Alta., Canada* **185 G6** 51 3N 114 2W
Elbow Lake, *MN, U.S.A.* **80 E3** 45 59N 95 58W
Elcho, *WI, U.S.A.* **103 C4** 45 26N 89 11W
Elderon, *WI, U.S.A.* **103 D4** 44 47N 89 15W
Eldersburg, *MD, U.S.A.* **77 A4** 39 24N 76 57W
Eldon, *IA, U.S.A.* **73 E6** 40 55N 92 13W
Eldon, *MO, U.S.A.* **82 C4** 38 21N 92 35W
Eldon, *WA, U.S.A.* **101 C2** 47 33N 123 3W
Eldora, *IA, U.S.A.* **73 C5** 42 22N 93 5W
Eldora, *NJ, U.S.A.* **87 C2** 39 12N 74 52W
Eldorado = Echo Bay, *N.W.T., Canada* **189 C9** 66 5N 117 55W
Eldorado, *Ont., Canada* **179 C9** 44 35N 77 31W
Eldorado, *IL, U.S.A.* **71 F5** 37 49N 88 26W
Eldorado, *MD, U.S.A.* **77 B5** 38 37N 75 48W
Eldorado, *OH, U.S.A.* **92 D2** 39 54N 84 41W
Eldorado, *OK, U.S.A.* **93 D4** 34 28N 99 39W
Eldorado, *TX, U.S.A.* **98 G7** 30 52N 100 36W
Eldorado at Santa Fe, *NM, U.S.A.* **88 B5** 35 32N 105 56W
Eldorado Nat. Forest, *CA, U.S.A.* **64 E6** 38 50N 120 20W
Eldorendo, *GA, U.S.A.* **68 E2** 31 3N 84 39W
Eldred, *NY, U.S.A.* **87 A2** 41 32N 74 53W
Eldred, *PA, U.S.A.* **95 C4** 41 58N 78 23W
Eldridge, *AL, U.S.A.* **60 C3** 33 55N 87 37W
Eldridge, *IA, U.S.A.* **73 D8** 41 39N 90 35W
Eldridge, *MO, U.S.A.* **82 D4** 37 50N 92 45W
Eldridge, *ND, U.S.A.* **91 D7** 46 54N 98 51W
Eleanor, *WV, U.S.A.* **102 C3** 38 32N 81 56W
Eleanor, L., *CA, U.S.A.* **64 F7** 37 59N 119 53W
Eleao, *HI, U.S.A.* **69 K14** 21 27N 157 52W
Electra, *TX, U.S.A.* **99 C9** 34 2N 98 55W
Electra L., *CO, U.S.A.* **66 E3** 37 33N 107 48W
Electric City, *WA, U.S.A.* **101 C6** 47 56N 119 2W
Electric Mills, *MS, U.S.A.* **81 D5** 32 46N 88 28W
Elephant Butte, *NM, U.S.A.* **88 D3** 33 9N 107 11W
Elephant Butte Lake State Park ⌓, *NM, U.S.A.* **88 D3** 33 38N 107 1W
Elephant Butte Res., *NM, U.S.A.* **88 D3** 33 9N 107 11W
Elephant Mt., *ME, U.S.A.* **86 B4** 44 46N 70 47W
Eleva, *WI, U.S.A.* **103 D2** 44 35N 91 28W
Eleven Point →, *AR, U.S.A.* **63 B4** 36 9N 91 5W
Elevenmile Canyon Res., *CO, U.S.A.* **66 D5** 38 54N 105 29W
Elfin Cove, *AK, U.S.A.* **61 G13** 58 12N 136 22W
Elfrida, *AZ, U.S.A.* **62 F6** 31 41N 109 41W
Elgin, *Man., Canada* **183 F11** 49 27N 100 16W
Elgin, *Ont., Canada* **179 C10** 44 36N 76 13W
Elgin, *IL, U.S.A.* **71 A5** 42 2N 88 17W
Elgin, *IA, U.S.A.* **73 C7** 42 57N 91 38W
Elgin, *KS, U.S.A.* **74 E7** 37 0N 96 17W
Elgin, *MN, U.S.A.* **80 F6** 44 8N 92 15W
Elgin, *ND, U.S.A.* **91 D4** 46 24N 101 51W
Elgin, *NE, U.S.A.* **84 C7** 41 59N 98 5W
Elgin, *NV, U.S.A.* **85 E6** 37 21N 114 32W
Elgin, *OK, U.S.A.* **93 D5** 34 47N 98 18W
Elgin, *OR, U.S.A.* **94 B8** 45 34N 117 55W
Elgin, *SC, U.S.A.* **90 D5** 34 10N 80 48W
Elgin, *TX, U.S.A.* **99 G10** 30 21N 97 22W
Eli, *NE, U.S.A.* **84 B4** 42 57N 101 29W
Elida, *NM, U.S.A.* **88 D7** 33 57N 103 39W
Elida, *OH, U.S.A.* **92 C2** 40 47N 84 12W
Elim, *AK, U.S.A.* **61 D7** 64 37N 162 15W
Eliot, *ME, U.S.A.* **76 E3** 43 7N 70 47W
Elizabeth, *CO, U.S.A.* **66 C6** 39 22N 104 36W
Elizabeth, *IL, U.S.A.* **71 A3** 42 19N 90 13W
Elizabeth, *LA, U.S.A.* **75 D3** 30 52N 92 48W
Elizabeth, *MN, U.S.A.* **80 D2** 46 23N 96 8W
Elizabeth, *NJ, U.S.A.* **87 B2** 40 39N 74 12W
Elizabeth, *WV, U.S.A.* **102 B3** 39 4N 81 24W
Elizabeth, C., *WA, U.S.A.* **101 C1** 47 21N 124 19W
Elizabeth City, *NC, U.S.A.* **90 B9** 36 18N 76 14W
Elizabeth Islands, *MA, U.S.A.* **78 C4** 41 27N 70 47W
Elizabeth River →, *Norfolk, U.S.A.* **115 A1** 36 52N 76 20W
Elizabethton, *TN, U.S.A.* **97 D10** 36 21N 82 13W
Elizabethtown, *IL, U.S.A.* **71 F5** 37 27N 88 18W
Elizabethtown, *KY, U.S.A.* **97 C7** 37 42N 85 52W
Elizabethtown, *NC, U.S.A.* **90 D7** 34 38N 78 37W
Elizabethtown, *NY, U.S.A.* **89 A7** 44 13N 73 36W
Elizabethtown, *PA, U.S.A.* **95 D6** 40 9N 76 36W
Elizabethville, *PA, U.S.A.* **95 D6** 40 33N 76 49W
Elk, *CA, U.S.A.* **64 D3** 39 8N 123 43W
Elk, *NM, U.S.A.* **88 E5** 32 57N 105 20W
Elk →, *B.C., Canada* **185 J5** 49 11N 115 14W
Elk →, *U.S.A.* **60 B3** 34 46N 87 16W
Elk →, *KS, U.S.A.* **74 D8** 37 15N 95 41W
Elk →, *MD, U.S.A.* **77 A4** 39 26N 76 1W
Elk →, *WV, U.S.A.* **102 C3** 38 21N 81 38W
Elk Basin, *WY, U.S.A.* **104 B4** 44 59N 108 52W
Elk City, *ID, U.S.A.* **70 D3** 45 50N 115 26W
Elk City, *KS, U.S.A.* **74 D8** 37 18N 95 55W
Elk City, *OK, U.S.A.* **93 C4** 35 25N 99 25W
Elk City Lake, *KS, U.S.A.* **74 D8** 37 17N 95 47W
Elk County ☆, *KS, U.S.A.* **74 D7** 37 30N 96 15W
Elk County ☆, *PA, U.S.A.* **95 C4** 41 35N 78 45W
Elk Cr. →, *SD, U.S.A.* **91 F3** 44 15N 102 22W
Elk Creek, *CA, U.S.A.* **64 D4** 39 36N 122 32W
Elk Creek, *NE, U.S.A.* **84 D9** 40 17N 96 8W
Elk Falls, *KS, U.S.A.* **74 D7** 37 22N 96 11W
Elk Garden, *WV, U.S.A.* **77 A1** 39 23N 79 9W
Elk Grove, *CA, U.S.A.* **64 E5** 38 25N 121 22W
Elk Hill, *PA, U.S.A.* **95 C7** 41 42N 75 32W
Elk Horn, *IA, U.S.A.* **73 D3** 41 36N 95 3W
Elk Island Nat. Park △, *Alta., Canada* **184 E8** 53 35N 112 59W
Elk L., *MI, U.S.A.* **79 E6** 44 50N 85 20W
Elk Lake, *Ont., Canada* **176 D2** 47 40N 80 25W
Elk Lakes Park ⌓, *B.C., Canada* **185 H5** 50 30N 115 10W
Elk Mound, *WI, U.S.A.* **103 D2** 44 52N 91 42W
Elk Mountain, *WY, U.S.A.* **104 E6** 41 41N 106 25W
Elk Mt., *WY, U.S.A.* **104 E6** 41 38N 106 32W
Elk Neck, *MD, U.S.A.* **77 A5** 39 31N 75 57W
Elk Point, *Alta., Canada* **184 E10** 53 54N 110 55W
Elk Point, *SD, U.S.A.* **91 H9** 42 41N 96 41W
Elk Rapids, *MI, U.S.A.* **79 E6** 44 54N 85 25W
Elk Ridge, *UT, U.S.A.* **100 C4** 40 1N 111 41W
Elk River, *ID, U.S.A.* **70 C2** 46 47N 116 11W
Elk River, *MN, U.S.A.* **80 E5** 45 18N 93 35W
Elk Springs, *CO, U.S.A.* **66 B2** 40 21N 108 27W
Elkader, *IA, U.S.A.* **73 C7** 42 51N 91 24W
Elkford, *B.C., Canada* **185 J6** 49 52N 114 53W
Elkhart, *IL, U.S.A.* **71 C4** 40 1N 89 29W
Elkhart, *IN, U.S.A.* **72 B5** 41 41N 85 58W
Elkhart, *IA, U.S.A.* **73 D5** 41 48N 93 31W
Elkhart, *KS, U.S.A.* **74 D2** 37 0N 101 54W
Elkhart, *TX, U.S.A.* **99 F12** 31 38N 95 35W
Elkhart County ☆, *IN, U.S.A.* **72 B5** 41 35N 85 50W
Elkhart Lake, *WI, U.S.A.* **103 E5** 43 50N 88 1W
Elkhorn, *Man., Canada* **183 F10** 49 59N 101 14W
Elkhorn, *NE, U.S.A.* **84 C9** 41 17N 96 14W
Elkhorn, *WI, U.S.A.* **103 F5** 42 40N 88 33W
Elkhorn →, *NE, U.S.A.* **84 C9** 41 8N 96 19W
Elkhorn City, *KY, U.S.A.* **97 C10** 37 18N 82 21W
Elkin, *NC, U.S.A.* **90 B5** 36 15N 80 51W
Elkins, *AR, U.S.A.* **63 B2** 36 0N 94 0W
Elkins, *NM, U.S.A.* **88 D6** 33 42N 104 4W
Elkins, *WV, U.S.A.* **102 C5** 38 55N 79 51W
Elkins Park, *PA, U.S.A.* **116 A2** 40 4N 75 7W
Elkland, *MO, U.S.A.* **82 D3** 37 27N 93 2W
Elkland, *PA, U.S.A.* **95 C5** 41 59N 77 19W
Elkmont, *AL, U.S.A.* **60 B4** 34 56N 86 58W
Elko, *B.C., Canada* **185 J5** 49 20N 115 10W
Elko, *GA, U.S.A.* **68 D3** 32 20N 83 42W
Elko, *MN, U.S.A.* **80 F5** 44 34N 93 19W
Elko, *NV, U.S.A.* **85 B5** 40 50N 115 46W
Elko County ☆, *NV, U.S.A.* **85 A5** 41 10N 115 20W
Elkol, *WY, U.S.A.* **104 E2** 41 43N 110 37W
Elkridge, *Baltimore, U.S.A.* **107 B1** 39 12N 76 42W
Elkridge, *MD, U.S.A.* **77 A5** 39 36N 75 50W
Elkton, *KY, U.S.A.* **96 D5** 36 49N 87 9W
Elkton, *MI, U.S.A.* **79 F8** 43 49N 83 11W
Elkton, *MN, U.S.A.* **80 G6** 43 40N 92 42W
Elkton, *OR, U.S.A.* **94 D2** 43 38N 123 34W
Elkton, *SD, U.S.A.* **91 F9** 44 14N 96 29W
Elkton, *TN, U.S.A.* **96 E6** 35 3N 86 53W
Elkton, *VA, U.S.A.* **102 C6** 38 25N 78 37W
Elkville, *IL, U.S.A.* **71 F4** 37 55N 89 14W
Ellamore, *WV, U.S.A.* **102 C4** 38 55N 80 5W
Ellaville, *GA, U.S.A.* **68 D2** 32 14N 84 19W
Ellef Ringnes I., *Nunavut, Canada* **190 B5** 78 30N 102 2W
Ellenboro, *WV, U.S.A.* **102 B3** 39 16N 81 3W
Ellenburg, *NY, U.S.A.* **89 A7** 44 54N 73 48W
Ellendale, *DE, U.S.A.* **77 B5** 38 48N 75 26W
Ellendale, *MN, U.S.A.* **80 G5** 43 52N 93 18W
Ellendale, *ND, U.S.A.* **91 D7** 46 0N 98 32W
Ellenor, L., *Orlando, U.S.A.* **115 B2** 28 28N 81 25W
Ellensburg, *WA, U.S.A.* **101 D5** 46 59N 120 34W
Ellenton, *GA, U.S.A.* **68 E3** 31 11N 83 35W
Ellenville, *NY, U.S.A.* **89 D6** 41 43N 74 24W
Ellerbe, *NC, U.S.A.* **90 C6** 35 4N 79 46W
Ellesmere I., *Nunavut, Canada* **190 B10** 79 30N 80 0W
Ellesmere Island = Quttinirpaaq Nat. Park △, *Nunavut, Canada* **190 A11** 82 13N 72 13W
Ellettsville, *IN, U.S.A.* **72 D4** 39 14N 86 38W
Ellice →, *Nunavut, Canada* **190 D5** 68 2N 103 58W
Ellicott City, *MD, U.S.A.* **77 A4** 39 16N 76 48W
Ellicottville, *NY, U.S.A.* **89 C2** 42 17N 78 40W
Ellijay, *GA, U.S.A.* **68 B2** 34 42N 84 29W
Ellington, *CT, U.S.A.* **78 C2** 41 54N 72 28W
Ellington, *MO, U.S.A.* **82 D6** 37 14N 90 58W
Ellington, *NY, U.S.A.* **89 C1** 42 13N 79 7W
Ellinwood, *KS, U.S.A.* **74 C5** 38 21N 98 35W
Elliot L., *Man., Canada* **183 C16** 52 54N 95 18W
Elliot Lake, *Ont., Canada* **178 A4** 46 25N 82 35W
Elliott, *IA, U.S.A.* **73 D3** 41 9N 95 10W
Elliott, *MD, U.S.A.* **77 B5** 38 38N 75 59W
Elliott, *MS, U.S.A.* **81 C4** 33 41N 89 45W
Elliott, *ND, U.S.A.* **91 D8** 46 24N 97 49W
Elliott Bay, *Seattle, U.S.A.* **118 C3** 47 36N 122 21W
Elliott County ☆, *KY, U.S.A.* **97 B9** 38 5N 83 5W
Elliott Key, *FL, U.S.A.* **67 F8** 25 27N 80 12W
Elliott Knob, *VA, U.S.A.* **102 C5** 38 10N 79 19W
Ellis, *ID, U.S.A.* **70 E4** 44 42N 114 3W
Ellis, *KS, U.S.A.* **74 C4** 38 56N 99 34W
Ellis, *NE, U.S.A.* **84 D9** 40 13N 96 53W
Ellis County ☆, *KS, U.S.A.* **74 C4** 38 45N 99 15W
Ellis County ☆, *OK, U.S.A.* **93 B4** 36 20N 99 50W
Ellis County ☆, *TX, U.S.A.* **99 E11** 32 24N 96 51W
Ellis Grove, *IL, U.S.A.* **71 E4** 38 1N 89 55W
Ellis I., *NJ, U.S.A.* **114 B2** 40 41N 74 2W
Ellisport, *Seattle, U.S.A.* **118 D3** 47 25N 122 26W
Elliston, *Nfld. & L., Canada* **174 D7** 48 38N 53 3W
Elliston, *MT, U.S.A.* **83 D5** 46 33N 112 26W
Ellisville, *MS, U.S.A.* **81 E4** 31 36N 89 12W
Elloree, *SC, U.S.A.* **90 E5** 33 32N 80 34W
Ells →, *Alta., Canada* **184 A9** 57 18N 111 40W
Ellsinore, *MO, U.S.A.* **82 E6** 36 56N 90 45W
Ellston, *IA, U.S.A.* **73 E4** 40 51N 94 7W
Ellsworth, *IA, U.S.A.* **73 C5** 42 19N 93 35W
Ellsworth, *KS, U.S.A.* **74 C5** 38 44N 98 14W
Ellsworth, *ME, U.S.A.* **76 D5** 44 33N 68 25W
Ellsworth, *MI, U.S.A.* **79 D6** 45 10N 85 15W
Ellsworth, *MN, U.S.A.* **80 G2** 43 31N 96 1W

Ellsworth, *NE, U.S.A.* **84 B3** 42 4N 102 17W
Ellsworth, *SD, U.S.A.* **91 F2** 44 9N 103 4W
Ellsworth, *WI, U.S.A.* **103 D1** 44 44N 92 29W
Ellsworth County ☆, *KS, U.S.A.* **74 C5** 38 45N 98 15W
Ellwood, *Ont., Canada* **192 B2** 45 22N 75 40W
Ellwood City, *PA, U.S.A.* **95 D2** 40 52N 80 17W
Ellzey, *FL, U.S.A.* **67 B6** 29 19N 82 48W
Elm →, *ND, U.S.A.* **91 C9** 47 17N 96 20W
Elm →, *SD, U.S.A.* **91 F3** 44 21N 102 42W
Elm City, *NC, U.S.A.* **90 C8** 35 48N 77 52W
Elm Cr. →, *TX, U.S.A.* **99 J8** 28 42N 99 59W
Elm Creek, *NE, U.S.A.* **84 D6** 40 43N 99 22W
Elm Fork Red →, *U.S.A.* **93 D4** 34 53N 99 19W
Elm Grove, *Milwaukee, U.S.A.* **112 B1** 43 2N 88 4W
Elm L., *SD, U.S.A.* **91 E7** 45 51N 98 42W
Elma, *Man., Canada* **183 F16** 49 52N 95 55W
Elma, *IA, U.S.A.* **73 B6** 43 15N 92 26W
Elma, *WA, U.S.A.* **101 C2** 47 0N 123 25W
Elmdale, *KS, U.S.A.* **74 C7** 38 22N 96 39W
Elmendorf, *San Antonio, U.S.A.* **117 D3** 29 15N 98 19W
Elmer, *MO, U.S.A.* **82 B4** 39 57N 92 39W
Elmer, *NJ, U.S.A.* **87 C1** 39 36N 75 10W
Elmer, *OK, U.S.A.* **93 D4** 34 29N 99 21W
Elmer City, *WA, U.S.A.* **101 B7** 48 0N 118 58W
Elmhurst, *IL, U.S.A.* **71 B6** 41 53N 87 56W
Elmhurst, *NY, U.S.A.* **114 B3** 40 44N 73 53W
Elmira, *Ont., Canada* **178 D6** 43 36N 80 33W
Elmira, *ID, U.S.A.* **70 A2** 48 29N 116 27W
Elmira, *MI, U.S.A.* **79 D7** 45 4N 84 51W
Elmira, *NY, U.S.A.* **89 C4** 42 6N 76 48W
Elmira Heights, *NY, U.S.A.* **89 C4** 42 8N 76 50W
Elmo, *KS, U.S.A.* **74 C6** 38 41N 97 14W
Elmo, *MT, U.S.A.* **83 C3** 47 50N 114 21W
Elmo, *UT, U.S.A.* **100 D5** 39 23N 110 49W
Elmo, *VA, U.S.A.* **102 E5** 36 41N 79 7W
Elmodel, *GA, U.S.A.* **68 E2** 31 21N 84 29W
Elmont, *NY, U.S.A.* **87 B3** 40 42N 73 42W
Elmore, *AL, U.S.A.* **60 D4** 32 32N 86 19W
Elmore, *MN, U.S.A.* **80 G4** 43 30N 94 5W
Elmore City, *OK, U.S.A.* **93 D6** 34 37N 97 24W
Elmore County ☆, *AL, U.S.A.* **60 D4** 32 32N 86 13W
Elmore County ☆, *ID, U.S.A.* **70 F3** 43 30N 115 30W
Elmsdale, *N.S., Canada* **173 J6** 44 58N 63 30W
Elmvale, *Ont., Canada* **178 C7** 44 35N 79 52W
Elmwood, *IL, U.S.A.* **71 C4** 40 47N 89 58W
Elmwood, *NE, U.S.A.* **84 D9** 40 50N 96 18W
Elmwood, *OK, U.S.A.* **93 B3** 36 37N 100 31W
Elmwood, *WI, U.S.A.* **103 D1** 44 47N 92 9W
Elmwood Park, *Chicago, U.S.A.* **108 B2** 41 55N 87 48W
Elmwood Park, *NJ, U.S.A.* **114 A2** 40 54N 74 7W
Elmwood Place, *OH, U.S.A.* **107 A2** 39 11N 84 29W
Elmworth, *Alta., Canada* **184 C1** 55 3N 119 37W
Elnora, *Alta., Canada* **185 G7** 51 59N 113 12W
Elnora, *IN, U.S.A.* **72 E3** 38 53N 87 5W
Elora, *Ont., Canada* **178 D6** 43 41N 80 26W
Elora, *TN, U.S.A.* **96 E6** 35 1N 86 21W
Eloxochitlán, *Puebla, Mexico* **221 F4** 18 31N 96 57W
Eloy, *AZ, U.S.A.* **62 E4** 32 45N 111 33W
Elphin, *Ont., Canada* **179 C10** 44 55N 76 37W
Elphinstone, *Man., Canada* **183 E11** 50 32N 100 30W
Elrosa, *MN, U.S.A.* **80 E4** 45 34N 94 57W
Elrose, *Sask., Canada* **182 D3** 51 12N 108 0W
Elroy, *WI, U.S.A.* **103 E3** 43 45N 90 16W
Elsa, *TX, U.S.A.* **98 L10** 26 18N 97 59W
Elsah, *IL, U.S.A.* **71 E3** 38 57N 90 22W
Elsas, *Ont., Canada* **181 D14** 48 32N 82 55W
Elsberry, *MO, U.S.A.* **82 B6** 39 10N 90 47W
Elsie, *MI, U.S.A.* **79 F7** 43 5N 84 23W
Elsie, *NE, U.S.A.* **84 D4** 40 51N 101 23W
Elsie, *OR, U.S.A.* **94 B2** 45 52N 123 36W
Elsinore, *UT, U.S.A.* **100 E3** 38 41N 112 9W
Elsinore, L., *CA, U.S.A.* **65 K9** 33 40N 117 21W
Elsmere, *DE, U.S.A.* **77 A5** 39 44N 75 35W
Elsmere, *NE, U.S.A.* **84 B5** 42 10N 100 11W
Elsmore, *KS, U.S.A.* **74 D8** 37 48N 95 9W
Elsworth, L., *OK, U.S.A.* **93 D5** 34 49N 98 22W
Eltinville, *NY, U.S.A.* **114 C1** 40 33N 74 10W
Elton, *LA, U.S.A.* **75 D4** 30 29N 91 42W
Eltopia, *WA, U.S.A.* **101 D6** 46 27N 119 1W
Elu Inlet, *Nunavut, Canada* **190 D4** 68 30N 106 5W
Elverson, *PA, U.S.A.* **95 D7** 40 9N 75 50W
Elwell, L. = Tiber Res., *MT, U.S.A.* **83 B6** 48 19N 111 6W
Elwood, *IL, U.S.A.* **71 B5** 41 24N 88 7W
Elwood, *IN, U.S.A.* **72 C5** 40 17N 85 50W
Elwood, *KS, U.S.A.* **74 B9** 39 45N 94 52W
Elwood, *NJ, U.S.A.* **87 C2** 39 35N 74 43W
Elwood, *NE, U.S.A.* **84 D6** 40 36N 99 52W
Elwood Res., *NE, U.S.A.* **84 D6** 40 42N 99 55W
Ely, *IA, U.S.A.* **73 D7** 41 52N 91 35W
Ely, *MN, U.S.A.* **80 C7** 47 55N 91 51W
Ely, *NV, U.S.A.* **85 C6** 39 15N 114 54W
Elyria, *KS, U.S.A.* **74 C6** 38 17N 97 38W
Elyria, *NE, U.S.A.* **84 C7** 41 41N 99 0W
Elyria, *OH, U.S.A.* **92 B4** 41 22N 82 7W
Emanuel County ☆, *GA, U.S.A.* **68 D4** 32 40N 82 20W
Embarras →, *IL, U.S.A.* **71 E6** 38 39N 87 37W
Embarrass, *WI, U.S.A.* **103 D5** 44 40N 88 42W
Emblem, *WY, U.S.A.* **104 B4** 44 30N 108 23W
Embro, *Ont., Canada* **178 D6** 43 9N 80 54W
Embshoff Woods & Nature Preserve ⌂, *OH, U.S.A.* **107 B1** 39 5N 84 34W
Emden, *IL, U.S.A.* **71 C4** 40 18N 89 29W
Emelle, *AL, U.S.A.* **60 D2** 32 44N 88 19W
Emerado, *ND, U.S.A.* **91 C8** 47 55N 97 22W
Emerald I., *N.W.T., Canada* **188 A10** 76 48N 114 10W
Emerald Isle, *NC, U.S.A.* **90 D9** 34 41N 76 57W
Emeril, *Qué., Canada* **175 D2** 47 26N 75 47W
Emerson, *Man., Canada* **183 F14** 49 0N 97 10W
Emerson, *AR, U.S.A.* **63 E2** 33 6N 93 11W
Emerson, *GA, U.S.A.* **68 B2** 34 8N 84 45W
Emerson, *NE, U.S.A.* **84 B9** 42 17N 96 44W
Emerson L., *CA, U.S.A.* **65 J10** 34 27N 116 23W
Emery, *SD, U.S.A.* **91 G8** 43 36N 97 37W
Emery, *UT, U.S.A.* **100 E4** 38 55N 111 15W
Emery County ☆, *UT, U.S.A.* **100 D4** 39 0N 110 45W
Emeryville, *San Francisco, U.S.A.* **118 A3** 37 49N 122 17W
Emigrant Gap, *CA, U.S.A.* **64 D6** 39 19N 120 38W
Emigrant Pass, *NV, U.S.A.* **85 B4** 40 39N 116 16W
Emiliano Martínez, *Durango, Mexico* **216 B5** 25 26N 105 14W
Emiliano Zapata, *Chiapas, Mexico* **222 B5** 17 45N 91 46W
Emiliano Zapata, *Chihuahua, Mexico* **213 B9** 31 35N 106 28W
Emiliano Zapata, *Coahuila, Mexico* **214 E2** 25 29N 102 56W
Emiliano Zapata, *Veracruz, Mexico* **220 D3** 20 21N 97 8W
Emiliano Zapata, *Yucatán, Mexico* **223 B4** 20 13N 89 28W
Emilio Carranza, *Durango, Mexico* **217 B7** 25 15N 103 55W
Emilio Carranza, *Veracruz, Mexico* **220 E4** 19 58N 96 35W
Emilio Hernández, *Hidalgo, Mexico* **219 B9** 20 32N 98 59W
Emilio Portes Gil, Presa, *Tamaulipas, Mexico* **215 H6** 22 58N 98 46W
Emily, *MN, U.S.A.* **80 D5** 46 44N 93 58W
Eminece, *MO, U.S.A.* **82 D5** 37 9N 91 21W
Eminence, *KY, U.S.A.* **97 B7** 38 22N 85 11W
Emiquon Nat. Wildlife Refuge ⌂, *IL, U.S.A.* **71 C3** 40 20N 90 7W
Emlenton, *PA, U.S.A.* **95 C3** 41 11N 79 43W
Emmalane, *GA, U.S.A.* **68 D5** 32 46N 82 0W
Emmaus, *PA, U.S.A.* **87 B1** 40 32N 75 30W
Emmet, *AR, U.S.A.* **63 E2** 33 44N 93 28W
Emmet, *NE, U.S.A.* **84 B7** 42 29N 98 49W
Emmet County ☆, *IA, U.S.A.* **73 B4** 43 20N 94 40W
Emmet County ☆, *MI, U.S.A.* **79 D7** 45 30N 84 55W
Emmetsburg, *IA, U.S.A.* **73 B4** 43 7N 94 41W
Emmett, *ID, U.S.A.* **70 F2** 43 52N 116 30W
Emmett, *KS, U.S.A.* **74 B7** 39 19N 96 3W
Emmett, *MI, U.S.A.* **79 G9** 42 59N 82 46W
Emmitsburg, *MD, U.S.A.* **77 A3** 39 42N 77 20W
Emmonak, *AK, U.S.A.* **61 E6** 62 47N 164 31W
Emmons, *MN, U.S.A.* **80 G5** 43 30N 93 29W
Emmons County ☆, *ND, U.S.A.* **91 D5** 46 20N 100 10W
Emmorton, *MD, U.S.A.* **77 A4** 39 30N 76 20W
Emo, *Ont., Canada* **180 D3** 48 38N 93 50W
Emory, *TX, U.S.A.* **99 E12** 32 52N 95 46W
Emory →, *TN, U.S.A.* **97 E8** 35 53N 84 30W
Emory Peak, *TX, U.S.A.* **98 H4** 29 15N 103 18W
Empalme, *Sonora, Mexico* **212 F5** 27 58N 110 51W
Empire, *CA, U.S.A.* **64 F6** 37 38N 120 54W
Empire, *CO, U.S.A.* **66 C5** 39 46N 105 41W
Empire, *GA, U.S.A.* **68 D3** 32 21N 83 18W
Empire, *LA, U.S.A.* **75 E6** 29 23N 89 36W
Empire, *MI, U.S.A.* **79 E5** 44 49N 86 4W
Empire, *NV, U.S.A.* **85 B1** 40 35N 119 21W
Empire City, *OK, U.S.A.* **93 D5** 34 25N 98 2W
Empire Res., *CO, U.S.A.* **66 B6** 40 16N 104 12W
Emporia, *KS, U.S.A.* **74 C7** 38 25N 96 11W
Emporia, *VA, U.S.A.* **102 E7** 36 42N 77 32W
Emporium, *PA, U.S.A.* **95 C4** 41 31N 78 14W
Empress, *Alta., Canada* **185 H10** 50 57N 110 0W
Emsdale, *Ont., Canada* **176 F3** 45 32N 79 19W
Emsworth, *Pittsburgh, U.S.A.* **116 A1** 40 30N 80 5W
Encampment, *WY, U.S.A.* **104 E6** 41 12N 106 47W
Encantada, I., *Baja Calif., Mexico* **210 D4** 30 0N 114 30W
Encanto, *San Diego, U.S.A.* **117 B2** 32 42N 117 2W
Encarnación de Díaz, *Jalisco, Mexico* **218 A5** 21 31N 102 14W
Encinal, *TX, U.S.A.* **99 J8** 28 2N 99 21W
Encinillas, L., *Chihuahua, Mexico* **213 D9** 29 29N 106 20W
Encinitas, *CA, U.S.A.* **65 K9** 33 3N 117 17W
Encino, *Los Angeles, U.S.A.* **111 B2** 34 9N 118 28W
Encino, *NM, U.S.A.* **88 C5** 34 39N 105 28W
Encino, *TX, U.S.A.* **98 L9** 26 56N 98 8W
Encino Res., *Los Angeles, U.S.A.* **111 B1** 34 8N 118 30W
Endako, *B.C., Canada* **186 A9** 54 6N 125 2W
Endeavor, *WI, U.S.A.* **103 E4** 43 43N 89 28W
Endeavour, *Sask., Canada* **182 C9** 52 10N 102 39W
Enderby, *B.C., Canada* **187 E15** 50 35N 119 10W
Enderlin, *ND, U.S.A.* **91 D8** 46 38N 97 36W
Enders, *NE, U.S.A.* **84 D4** 40 27N 101 32W
Enders Res., *NE, U.S.A.* **84 D4** 40 25N 101 31W
Endicott, *NY, U.S.A.* **89 C4** 42 6N 76 4W
Endicott, *NE, U.S.A.* **84 D8** 40 5N 97 6W
Endicott, *WA, U.S.A.* **101 D8** 46 56N 117 41W
Endicott Mts., *AK, U.S.A.* **61 C9** 68 0N 152 0W
Endwell, *NY, U.S.A.* **89 C4** 42 6N 76 2W
Enfield, *N.S., Canada* **173 J6** 44 56N 63 32W
Enfield, *CT, U.S.A.* **78 C2** 41 58N 72 36W
Enfield, *IL, U.S.A.* **71 E5** 38 6N 88 20W
Enfield, *NC, U.S.A.* **90 B8** 36 11N 77 41W
Enfield, *NH, U.S.A.* **86 C2** 43 39N 72 9W
Enfield Center, *NH, U.S.A.* **86 C2** 43 38N 72 8W
Engadine, *MI, U.S.A.* **79 C6** 46 7N 85 34W
England, *AR, U.S.A.* **63 D4** 34 33N 91 58W
Engle, *NM, U.S.A.* **88 D3** 33 4N 107 2W
Englebright L., *CA, U.S.A.* **64 D5** 39 14N 121 16W
Englee, *Nfld. & L., Canada* **174 B4** 50 45N 56 5W
Englefeld, *Sask., Canada* **182 C7** 52 10N 104 39W
Englefield, C., *N.W.T., Canada* **190 D8** 69 49N 85 34W
Englehart, *Ont., Canada* **176 D3** 47 49N 79 52W
Englewood, *Chicago, U.S.A.* **108 C3** 41 46N 87 38W
Englewood, *CO, U.S.A.* **66 C6** 39 38N 104 59W
Englewood, *FL, U.S.A.* **67 E6** 26 58N 82 21W
Englewood, *KS, U.S.A.* **74 D4** 37 2N 99 59W
Englewood, *NJ, U.S.A.* **87 B3** 40 54N 73 58W
Englewood, *OH, U.S.A.* **92 D2** 39 53N 84 18W
Englewood, *TN, U.S.A.* **97 E8** 35 26N 84 29W
Englewood Cliffs, *NJ, U.S.A.* **114 A3** 40 53N 73 59W
English, *IN, U.S.A.* **72 E4** 38 20N 86 28W
English →, *Ont., Canada* **180 C5** 49 12N 91 5W
English B., *B.C., Canada* **193 B2** 49 17N 123 10W
English Creek, *NJ, U.S.A.* **87 C2** 39 20N 74 42W
English Harbour East, *Nfld. & L., Canada* **174 E6** 47 38N 54 54W
English River, *Ont., Canada* **180 C6** 49 14N 91 0W
English Turn, *New Orleans, U.S.A.* **113 C3** 29 53N 89 27W
English Woods, *OH, U.S.A.* **107 B1** 39 8N 84 33W
Englishtown, *NJ, U.S.A.* **87 B2** 40 18N 74 22W
Enid, *MS, U.S.A.* **81 B4** 34 7N 89 56W
Enid, *OK, U.S.A.* **93 B6** 36 24N 97 53W
Enid L., *MS, U.S.A.* **81 B4** 34 9N 89 54W
Enilda, *Alta., Canada* **184 C4** 55 25N 116 18W
Enloe, *TX, U.S.A.* **99 D12** 33 26N 95 39W
Enmedio, Arrecife de, *Veracruz, Mexico* **220 C3** 21 6N 97 13W
Ennadai L., *Nunavut, Canada* **191 E5** 60 58N 101 20W
Ennis, *MT, U.S.A.* **83 E6** 45 21N 111 44W
Ennis, *TX, U.S.A.* **99 E11** 32 20N 96 38W
Ennis L., *MT, U.S.A.* **83 E6** 45 26N 111 41W
Enoch, *UT, U.S.A.* **100 F2** 37 47N 113 2W
Enochs, *TX, U.S.A.* **98 D5** 33 52N 102 46W
Enola, *NE, U.S.A.* **84 C8** 41 54N 97 28W
Enoree →, *SC, U.S.A.* **90 D4** 34 26N 81 25W
Enosburg Falls, *VT, U.S.A.* **86 B2** 44 55N 72 48W
Ensenada, *Baja Calif., Mexico* **210 B2** 31 52N 116 37W
Ensenada, *NM, U.S.A.* **88 A4** 36 44N 106 32W
Ensenada de los Muertos, *Baja Calif. S., Mexico* **211 K9** 23 59N 109 51W
Ensign, *KS, U.S.A.* **74 D3** 37 39N 100 14W
Ensley, *FL, U.S.A.* **67 A1** 30 31N 87 16W
Enterprise, *N.W.T., Canada* **189 D9** 60 47N 115 45W
Enterprise, *AL, U.S.A.* **60 E5** 31 19N 85 51W
Enterprise, *KS, U.S.A.* **74 C6** 38 54N 97 7W
Enterprise, *LA, U.S.A.* **75 C4** 31 54N 91 53W
Enterprise, *Las Vegas, U.S.A.* **110 C1** 36 3N 115 14W
Enterprise, *MS, U.S.A.* **81 D5** 32 10N 88 49W
Enterprise, *OR, U.S.A.* **94 B8** 45 25N 117 17W
Enterprise, *UT, U.S.A.* **100 F2** 37 34N 113 43W
Entiako L., *B.C., Canada* **186 B9** 53 13N 125 31W
Entiako Park ⌂, *B.C., Canada* **186 B9** 53 15N 125 26W
Entiat, *WA, U.S.A.* **101 C5** 47 40N 120 13W
Enumclaw, *WA, U.S.A.* **101 C4** 47 12N 121 59W
Enville, *TN, U.S.A.* **96 E4** 35 23N 88 26W
Eolia, *MO, U.S.A.* **82 B5** 39 14N 91 1W
Eoline, *AL, U.S.A.* **60 D3** 32 59N 87 8W
Epatlán, *Puebla, Mexico* **221 F2** 18 38N 98 22W
Epazoyucan, *Hidalgo, Mexico* **219 B9** 20 2N 98 38W
Epes, *AL, U.S.A.* **60 D2** 32 42N 88 7W
Ephraim, *UT, U.S.A.* **100 D4** 39 22N 111 35W
Ephrata, *PA, U.S.A.* **95 D6** 40 11N 76 11W
Ephrata, *WA, U.S.A.* **101 C6** 47 19N 119 33W
Epleys, *KY, U.S.A.* **96 D6** 36 56N 86 56W
Epping, *ND, U.S.A.* **91 B2** 48 17N 103 21W
Epping, *NH, U.S.A.* **86 C3** 43 2N 71 4W
Eppley Airfield, Omaha ✕ (OMA), *NE, U.S.A.* **84 C10** 41 18N 95 53W
Epps, *LA, U.S.A.* **75 B4** 32 36N 91 29W
Epworth, *IA, U.S.A.* **73 C8** 42 27N 90 56W
Equality, *IL, U.S.A.* **71 F5** 37 44N 88 20W
Equinox Mt., *VT, U.S.A.* **86 C1** 43 11N 73 9W
Erath, *LA, U.S.A.* **75 E3** 29 58N 92 2W
Erath County ☆, *TX, U.S.A.* **99 E9** 32 13N 98 12W
Erbacon, *WV, U.S.A.* **102 C4** 38 31N 80 35W
Erda, *UT, U.S.A.* **100 C3** 40 37N 112 18W
Eréndira, *Baja Calif., Mexico* **210 B2** 31 17N 116 22W
Erhard, *MN, U.S.A.* **80 D2** 46 29N 96 6W
Éric L., *Qué., Canada* **172 B4** 51 55N 65 36W
Erichsen L., *Nunavut, Canada* **190 C9** 70 40N 80 41W
Erick, *OK, U.S.A.* **93 C4** 35 13N 99 52W
Erickson, *Man., Canada* **183 E12** 50 30N 99 55W
Ericson, *NE, U.S.A.* **84 C7** 41 47N 98 41W
Eridu, *FL, U.S.A.* **67 A5** 30 18N 83 45W
Erie, *CO, U.S.A.* **66 B5** 40 3N 105 3W
Erie, *IL, U.S.A.* **71 B3** 41 39N 90 5W
Erie, *KS, U.S.A.* **74 D8** 37 34N 95 15W
Erie, *ND, U.S.A.* **91 C8** 47 7N 97 23W
Erie, *PA, U.S.A.* **95 B2** 42 8N 80 5W
Erie, L., *N. Amer.* **178 E5** 42 15N 81 0W
Erie Canal, *NY, U.S.A.* **89 B2** 43 5N 78 43W
Erie County ☆, *NY, U.S.A.* **89 C2** 42 50N 78 45W
Erie County ☆, *OH, U.S.A.* **92 B4** 41 24N 82 33W
Erie County ☆, *PA, U.S.A.* **95 C2** 42 0N 80 0W
Erie Nat. Wildlife Refuge ⌂, *PA, U.S.A.* **95 C3** 41 36N 79 58W
Erieau, *Ont., Canada* **178 E5** 42 16N 81 57W
Eriksdale, *Man., Canada* **183 E13** 50 52N 98 7W
Erin, *Ont., Canada* **178 D6** 43 45N 80 7W
Erin, *TN, U.S.A.* **96 D5** 36 19N 87 42W
Erin Springs, *OK, U.S.A.* **93 D6** 34 49N 97 36W
Erlandson, L., *Qué., Canada* **175 B4** 57 3N 68 28W
Erlanger, *KY, U.S.A.* **97 A8** 39 1N 84 36W
Erling, L., *AR, U.S.A.* **63 E2** 33 3N 93 32W
Erongarícuaro, *Michoacan, Mexico* **218 C6** 19 35N 101 43W
Errol, *NH, U.S.A.* **86 B3** 44 47N 71 8W
Errol Heights, *Portland, U.S.A.* **116 B2** 45 28N 122 36W
Erskine, *Alta., Canada* **185 F8** 52 20N 112 53W
Erskine, *MN, U.S.A.* **80 C2** 47 40N 96 0W
Erving, *MA, U.S.A.* **78 B2** 42 36N 72 24W
Erwin, *NC, U.S.A.* **90 C7** 35 20N 78 41W
Erwin, *SD, U.S.A.* **91 F8** 44 29N 97 27W
Erwin, *TN, U.S.A.* **97 D10** 36 9N 82 25W
Erwinville, *LA, U.S.A.* **75 D4** 30 32N 91 24W
Esbon, *KS, U.S.A.* **74 B5** 39 49N 98 26W
Escalante, *UT, U.S.A.* **100 F4** 37 47N 111 36W
Escalante →, *UT, U.S.A.* **100 F5** 37 24N 110 57W
Escalante Desert, *UT, U.S.A.* **100 F2** 37 50N 113 20W
Escalón, *Chihuahua, Mexico* **213 G11** 26 45N 104 20W
Escalon, *CA, U.S.A.* **64 F6** 37 48N 121 0W
Escambia →, *FL, U.S.A.* **67 A1** 30 32N 87 11W
Escambia County ☆, *AL, U.S.A.* **60 E3** 31 7N 87 4W
Escambia County ☆, *FL, U.S.A.* **67 A1** 30 30N 87 30W
Escanaba, *MI, U.S.A.* **79 D4** 45 45N 87 4W
Escanaba →, *MI, U.S.A.* **79 D4** 45 47N 87 3W
Escárcega, *Campeche, Mexico* **223 D3** 18 37N 90 43W
Escatawpa →, *MS, U.S.A.* **81 F5** 30 26N 88 33W
Escobedo, *Coahuila, Mexico* **214 A2** 29 16N 102 9W
Escobedo, *Guanajuato, Mexico* **219 B7** 20 39N 100 45W
Escondido, *CA, U.S.A.* **65 K9** 33 7N 117 5W
Escondido →, *Quintana Roo, Mexico* **223 D5** 18 30N 88 35W
Escuinapa de Hidalgo, *Sinaloa, Mexico* **216 E5** 22 51N 105 48W
Escuintla, *Chiapas, Mexico* **222 D3** 15 20N 92 38W
Eskasoni, *N.S., Canada* **173 H9** 45 56N 60 36W
Esker, *Nfld. & L., Canada* **175 C4** 53 53N 66 25W
Eskimo Lakes, *N.W.T., Canada* **188 C6** 69 15N 132 17W
Eskimo Point = Arviat, *Nunavut, Canada* **191 E7** 61 6N 93 59W
Eskridge, *KS, U.S.A.* **74 C7** 38 52N 96 6W
Esmeralda County ☆, *NV, U.S.A.* **85 E3** 37 50N 117 45W
Esmond, *ND, U.S.A.* **91 B6** 48 2N 99 46W
Esmont, *VA, U.S.A.* **102 D6** 37 50N 78 37W
Esnagami L., *Ont., Canada* **181 B10** 50 19N 86 51W
Esnagi L., *Ont., Canada* **181 D12** 48 36N 84 33W
Esom Hill, *GA, U.S.A.* **68 C1** 33 57N 85 23W
Españita, *Tlaxcala, Mexico* **219 C9** 19 28N 98 24W
Espanola, *Ont., Canada* **178 A5** 46 15N 81 46W
Espanola, *FL, U.S.A.* **67 B7** 29 31N 81 19W
Espanola, *NM, U.S.A.* **88 B4** 35 59N 106 5W
Esparto, *CA, U.S.A.* **64 E4** 38 42N 122 1W
Espenberg, C., *AK, U.S.A.* **61 C7** 66 33N 163 36W
Esperanza, *B.C., Canada* **186 F8** 49 52N 126 43W
Esperanza, *Puebla, Mexico* **221 F3** 18 52N 97 24W
Esperanza, *Sonora, Mexico* **212 F6** 27 35N 109 56W
Esperanza, *Puerto Rico* **105 G17** 18 6N 65 28W
Esperanza Inlet, *B.C., Canada* **186 F8** 49 51N 126 55W
Espinazo, *Nuevo León, Mexico* **214 D3** 26 16N 101 6W
Espíritu Santo, *Zacatecas, Mexico* **217 E9** 22 36N 101 27W
Espíritu Santo, B. del, *Quintana Roo, Mexico* **223 C6** 19 20N 87 35W
Espíritu Santo, I., *Baja Calif. S., Mexico* **211 J8** 24 30N 110 22W
Espita, *Yucatán, Mexico* **223 A5** 21 1N 88 19W
Esqueda, *Sonora, Mexico* **212 C6** 30 46N 109 31W
Esquimalt, *B.C., Canada* **187 G11** 48 26N 123 25W
Essex, *Ont., Canada* **178 E4** 42 10N 82 49W
Essex, *CA, U.S.A.* **65 J11** 34 44N 115 15W
Essex, *CT, U.S.A.* **78 C2** 41 21N 72 24W
Essex, *IL, U.S.A.* **71 B5** 41 11N 88 11W
Essex, *IA, U.S.A.* **73 E3** 40 50N 95 18W
Essex, *MD, U.S.A.* **77 A4** 39 19N 76 29W
Essex, *MO, U.S.A.* **82 E7** 36 50N 89 8W
Essex, *MT, U.S.A.* **83 B4** 48 17N 113 37W
Essex, *NY, U.S.A.* **86 B1** 44 19N 73 21W
Essex County ☆, *MA, U.S.A.* **78 B4** 42 35N 70 50W
Essex County ☆, *NJ, U.S.A.* **87 B2** 40 45N 74 15W
Essex County ☆, *NY, U.S.A.* **89 A7** 44 0N 73 40W
Essex County ☆, *VA, U.S.A.* **102 D8** 37 56N 76 52W
Essex County ☆, *VT, U.S.A.* **86 B3** 44 45N 71 45W
Essex Fells, *NJ, U.S.A.* **114 B1** 40 49N 74 17W
Essex Junction, *VT, U.S.A.* **86 B1** 44 29N 73 7W
Essex Meadows, *Norfolk, U.S.A.* **115 B2** 36 45N 76 14W
Essexville, *MI, U.S.A.* **79 F8** 43 37N 83 50W
Est, Î. de l', *Qué., Canada* **173 F8** 47 37N 61 23W
Estacada, *OR, U.S.A.* **94 B3** 45 17N 122 20W
Estación Bamoa, *Sinaloa, Mexico* **216 B2** 25 42N 108 21W
Estación Camacho, *Zacatecas, Mexico* **217 C8** 24 25N 102 18W
Estación Catorce, *San Luis Potosí, Mexico* **215 G4** 23 41N 100 58W
Estación Charcas, *San Luis Potosí, Mexico* **215 G3** 23 7N 101 2W
Estación Colonias, *Chihuahua, Mexico* **213 D10** 29 12N 105 22W
Estación Conchos, *Chihuahua, Mexico* **213 F10** 27 57N 105 18W
Estación Gutiérrez, *Zacatecas, Mexico* **217 D8** 23 28N 102 46W
Estación Huehuetán, *Chiapas, Mexico* **222 D3** 15 1N 92 24W
Estación la Colorada, *Zacatecas, Mexico* **217 D8** 23 47N 102 24W
Estación Macuspana, *Tabasco, Mexico* **222 B4** 17 38N 92 32W
Estación Marte, *Coahuila, Mexico* **214 E3** 25 42N 101 45W
Estación Pacheco, *Zacatecas, Mexico* **217 D8** 24 0N 102 28W
Estación Ruiz, *Nayarit, Mexico* **216 F5** 21 56N 105 8W
Estación Simón, *Durango, Mexico* **217 C8** 24 42N 102 35W
Estación Vanegas, *San Luis Potosí, Mexico* **215 G4** 23 52N 100 57W
Estancia, *NM, U.S.A.* **88 C4** 34 46N 106 4W
Estanque de Norias, *Coahuila, Mexico* **214 D3** 26 29N 101 35W
Estanque del Léon, *Coahuila, Mexico* **214 D2** 26 5N 102 12W
Estanzuela, *Monterrey, Mexico* **224 C2** 25 36N 100 14W
Estelle, *New Orleans, U.S.A.* **113 C2** 29 50N 90 6W
Estelline, *SD, U.S.A.* **91 F9** 44 35N 96 54W
Estelline, *TX, U.S.A.* **98 C7** 34 33N 100 26W
Estellville, *NJ, U.S.A.* **87 C2** 39 23N 74 45W
Esterhazy, *Sask., Canada* **183 E9** 50 37N 102 5W
Estero, *FL, U.S.A.* **67 E7** 26 26N 81 49W
Estes Park, *CO, U.S.A.* **66 B5** 40 23N 105 31W
Estevan, *Sask., Canada* **182 F9** 49 10N 102 59W
Estevan Group, *B.C., Canada* **186 B5** 53 3N 129 38W
Estevan Sd., *B.C., Canada* **186 B5** 53 5N 129 34W
Estherville, *IA, U.S.A.* **73 B4** 43 24N 94 50W
Estherwood, *LA, U.S.A.* **75 D3** 30 11N 92 28W
Estill, *SC, U.S.A.* **90 F4** 32 45N 81 15W
Estill County ☆, *KY, U.S.A.* **97 C9** 37 40N 84 0W
Estill Springs, *TN, U.S.A.* **96 E6** 35 16N 86 8W
Eston, *Sask., Canada* **182 D3** 51 8N 108 40W
Estrecho, Pta. el, *Jalisco, Mexico* **218 C3** 19 20N 104 47W
Estrella, Pta., *Baja Calif., Mexico* **210 C4** 30 57N 114 45W
Étamamiou, *Qué., Canada* **175 C6** 50 18N 59 59W
Étang-du-Nord, L., *Qué., Canada* **173 F8** 47 22N 61 57W
Etchison, *MD, U.S.A.* **77 A3** 39 15N 77 8W
Etchojoa, *Sonora, Mexico* **212 G6** 26 55N 109 38W
Ethan, *SD, U.S.A.* **91 G8** 43 33N 97 59W
Ethel, *LA, U.S.A.* **75 D4** 30 47N 91 8W
Ethel, *MS, U.S.A.* **81 C4** 33 7N 89 28W
Ethel, *MO, U.S.A.* **82 B4** 39 54N 92 45W
Ethelbert, *Man., Canada* **183 D11** 51 32N 100 25W
Ethelsville, *AL, U.S.A.* **60 C2** 33 25N 88 13W
Ethete, *WY, U.S.A.* **104 C4** 43 2N 108 46W
Ethridge, *MT, U.S.A.* **83 B5** 48 34N 112 8W
Ethridge, *TN, U.S.A.* **96 E5** 35 19N 87 18W
Etna, *CA, U.S.A.* **64 B4** 41 27N 122 54W
Etna, *ME, U.S.A.* **76 D4** 44 49N 69 7W
Etna, *Pittsburgh, U.S.A.* **116 B2** 40 30N 79 56W
Etna, *UT, U.S.A.* **100 B2** 41 40N 113 58W
Etna, *WY, U.S.A.* **104 C2** 43 5N 111 0W
Etolin Strait, *AK, U.S.A.* **61 F6** 60 20N 165 15W
Eton, *GA, U.S.A.* **68 B2** 34 50N 84 46W
Etowah, *TN, U.S.A.* **97 E8** 35 20N 84 32W
Etowah →, *GA, U.S.A.* **68 B1** 34 15N 85 10W
Etowah County ☆, *AL, U.S.A.* **60 B5** 34 0N 86 0W
Etta, *MS, U.S.A.* **81 B4** 34 28N 89 14W
Etter, *TX, U.S.A.* **98 A6** 36 3N 101 59W
Ettrick, *WI, U.S.A.* **103 D2** 44 10N 91 16W
Etzatlán, *Jalisco, Mexico* **218 B3** 20 46N 104 5W
Etzikom, *Alta., Canada* **185 J9** 49 29N 111 6W
Eubank, *KY, U.S.A.* **97 C8** 37 17N 84 40W
Euclid, *OH, U.S.A.* **92 B5** 41 34N 81 32W
Eudistes, L. des, *Qué., Canada* **172 C4** 50 30N 65 15W
Eudora, *AR, U.S.A.* **63 E4** 33 7N 91 16W
Eudora, *KS, U.S.A.* **74 C8** 38 57N 95 6W
Eufaula, *AL, U.S.A.* **60 E5** 31 54N 85 9W
Eufaula, *OK, U.S.A.* **93 C8** 35 17N 95 35W
Eufaula L., *OK, U.S.A.* **93 C8** 35 18N 95 21W
Eugene, *MO, U.S.A.* **82 C4** 38 21N 92 24W
Eugene, *OR, U.S.A.* **94 C2** 44 5N 123 4W
Euless, *TX, U.S.A.* **99 E10** 32 50N 97 4W
Eulonia, *GA, U.S.A.* **68 E5** 31 32N 81 26W
Eunice, *LA, U.S.A.* **75 D3** 30 30N 92 25W
Eunice, *NM, U.S.A.* **88 E7** 32 26N 103 10W
Eupora, *MS, U.S.A.* **81 C4** 33 32N 89 16W
Eureka, *Nunavut, Canada* **190 A8** 80 0N 85 56W
Eureka, *CA, U.S.A.* **64 C2** 40 47N 124 9W
Eureka, *IL, U.S.A.* **71 C4** 40 43N 89 16W
Eureka, *KS, U.S.A.* **74 D7** 37 49N 96 17W
Eureka, *MO, U.S.A.* **82 C6** 38 30N 90 38W
Eureka, *MT, U.S.A.* **83 B2** 48 53N 115 3W
Eureka, *NV, U.S.A.* **85 C5** 39 31N 115 58W
Eureka, *SD, U.S.A.* **91 E6** 45 46N 99 38W
Eureka, *UT, U.S.A.* **100 D3** 39 58N 112 7W
Eureka, *WA, U.S.A.* **101 D7** 46 18N 118 37W
Eureka County ☆, *NV, U.S.A.* **85 C4** 40 0N 116 10W
Eureka Mill, *SC, U.S.A.* **90 D4** 34 43N 81 12W
Eureka River, *Alta., Canada* **184 B2** 56 27N 118 44W
Eureka Sd., *Nunavut, Canada* **190 B8** 79 0N 85 0W
Eureka Springs, *AR, U.S.A.* **63 B2** 36 24N 93 44W
Eureka Valley, *CA, U.S.A.* **65 F9** 37 7N 117 42W
Eustis, *FL, U.S.A.* **67 C7** 28 51N 81 41W
Eustis, *ME, U.S.A.* **76 C3** 45 13N 70 29W
Eustis, *NE, U.S.A.* **84 D5** 40 40N 100 2W
Eustis, L., *FL, U.S.A.* **67 C7** 28 50N 81 44W
Eutaw, *AL, U.S.A.* **60 D3** 32 50N 87 53W
Eutawville, *SC, U.S.A.* **90 E5** 33 24N 80 21W
Eutimias, *Coahuila, Mexico* **214 B2** 28 19N 102 45W
Eutsuk L., *B.C., Canada* **186 B8** 53 20N 126 45W
Eva, *AL, U.S.A.* **60 B4** 34 20N 86 46W
Evadale, *TX, U.S.A.* **99 G13** 30 21N 94 5W
Évain, *Qué., Canada* **176 C3** 48 14N 79 8W
Evan, *MN, U.S.A.* **80 F4** 44 21N 94 50W
Evangeline, *LA, U.S.A.* **75 D3** 30 16N 92 34W
Evangeline Parish ☆, *LA, U.S.A.* **75 D3** 30 47N 92 25W
Evans, *CO, U.S.A.* **66 B6** 40 23N 104 41W
Evans, *GA, U.S.A.* **68 C4** 33 32N 82 8W
Evans, *LA, U.S.A.* **75 D2** 30 59N 93 30W
Evans, *WV, U.S.A.* **102 C3** 38 49N 81 47W
Evans, L., *Qué., Canada* **175 C2** 50 50N 77 0W
Evans, Mt., *CO, U.S.A.* **66 C5** 39 35N 105 39W
Evans City, *PA, U.S.A.* **95 D2** 40 46N 80 4W
Evans County ☆, *GA, U.S.A.* **68 D5** 32 10N 81 55W
Evans Str., *Nunavut, Canada* **191 E9** 63 15N 82 0W
Evansburg, *Alta., Canada* **184 E6** 53 36N 114 59W
Evansdale, *IA, U.S.A.* **73 C6** 42 30N 92 17W
Evanston, *IL, U.S.A.* **71 A6** 42 3N 87 40W
Evanston, *KY, U.S.A.* **97 C9** 37 28N 83 2W
Evanston, *WY, U.S.A.* **104 E2** 41 16N 110 58W
Evansville, *AR, U.S.A.* **63 C1** 35 48N 94 30W
Evansville, *IL, U.S.A.* **71 E4** 38 5N 89 56W
Evansville, *IN, U.S.A.* **72 F3** 37 58N 87 35W
Evansville, *MN, U.S.A.* **80 D3** 46 0N 95 41W
Evansville, *WI, U.S.A.* **103 F4** 42 47N 89 18W
Evansville, *WY, U.S.A.* **104 D6** 42 52N 106 16W
Evant, *TX, U.S.A.* **99 F9** 31 29N 98 9W
Evart, *MI, U.S.A.* **79 F6** 43 54N 85 2W
Evarts, *KY, U.S.A.* **97 D9** 36 52N 83 12W
Eveleth, *MN, U.S.A.* **80 C6** 47 28N 92 32W
Evelyn, *LA, U.S.A.* **75 C2** 31 59N 93 27W
Evening Shade, *AR, U.S.A.* **63 B4** 36 4N 91 37W
Evensville, *TN, U.S.A.* **97 E8** 35 34N 84 57W
Everest, *KS, U.S.A.* **74 B8** 39 41N 95 26W
Everett, *GA, U.S.A.* **68 E5** 31 24N 81 38W
Everett, *MA, U.S.A.* **78 B3** 42 24N 71 3W
Everett, *PA, U.S.A.* **95 D4** 40 1N 78 23W
Everett, *WA, U.S.A.* **101 C3** 47 59N 122 12W
Everett, Mt., *MA, U.S.A.* **78 B1** 42 6N 73 26W
Everett Mts., *N.W.T., Canada* **191 E12** 62 45N 67 12W
Everglades, The, *FL, U.S.A.* **67 F8** 25 50N 81 0W
Everglades City, *FL, U.S.A.* **67 F7** 25 52N 81 23W

Everglades Nat. Park △, FL, U.S.A. 67 F8 25 30N 81 0W
Everglades Parkway, FL, U.S.A. 67 E7 26 10N 81 0W
Evergreen, AL, U.S.A. 60 E4 31 26N 86 57W
Evergreen, CO, U.S.A. 66 C5 39 38N 105 19W
Evergreen, MI, U.S.A. 109 A1 42 26N 86 12W
Evergreen, MT, U.S.A. 83 B3 48 14N 114 17W
Evergreen, Pittsburgh, U.S.A. 116 A2 40 30N 79 59W
Evergreen Park, IL, U.S.A. 71 B6 41 43N 87 42W
Everly, IA, U.S.A. 73 B3 43 10N 95 19W
Everman, Dallas-Fort Worth, U.S.A. 109 C2 32 37N 97 17W
Everson, WA, U.S.A. 101 B3 48 55N 122 20W
Everton, MO, U.S.A. 82 D3 37 21N 93 42W
'Ewa Beach, HI, U.S.A. 69 K13 21 19N 158 1W
'Ewa District, HI, U.S.A. 69 K14 21 25N 158 0W
'Ewa Forest Reserve, HI, U.S.A. 69 K14 21 27N 157 53W
'Ewa Villages, HI, U.S.A. 69 K13 21 20N 158 3W
Ewan, WA, U.S.A. 101 C8 47 7N 117 44W
Ewen, MI, U.S.A. 79 C2 46 32N 89 17W
Ewing, KY, U.S.A. 97 B9 38 26N 83 52W
Ewing, MO, U.S.A. 82 A5 40 6N 91 43W
Ewing, NJ, U.S.A. 87 B2 40 15N 74 48W
Ewing, NE, U.S.A. 84 B7 42 16N 98 21W
Ewing, VA, U.S.A. 102 E1 36 38N 83 26W
Excello, MO, U.S.A. 82 B4 39 38N 92 29W
Excelsior Mts., NV, U.S.A. 85 D2 38 15N 118 10W
Excelsior Springs, MO, U.S.A. 82 B2 39 20N 94 13W
Exeland, WI, U.S.A. 103 C2 45 40N 91 15W
Exell, TX, U.S.A. 98 B6 35 38N 101 59W
Exeter, Ont., Canada 178 D5 43 21N 81 29W
Exeter, CA, U.S.A. 65 G7 36 18N 119 9W
Exeter, ME, U.S.A. 76 D4 44 58N 69 9W
Exeter, MO, U.S.A. 82 E3 36 40N 93 56W
Exeter, NH, U.S.A. 86 D4 42 59N 70 57W
Exeter, NE, U.S.A. 84 D8 40 39N 97 27W
Exeter, PA, U.S.A. 87 A1 41 19N 75 49W
Exeter, RI, U.S.A. 78 C3 41 35N 71 32W
Exira, IA, U.S.A. 73 D4 41 35N 94 52W
Exmore, VA, U.S.A. 102 D9 37 32N 75 50W
Experiment = Highland Mills, GA, U.S.A. 68 C2 33 17N 84 17W
Exploits, B. of, Nfld. & L., Canada 174 C6 49 20N 55 0W
Exposition Park, Los Angeles, U.S.A. 111 B3 34 0N 118 17W
Exshaw, Alta., Canada 185 G5 51 3N 115 9W
Eyak, AK, U.S.A. 61 F11 60 32N 145 36W
Eyebrow, Sask., Canada 182 E5 50 48N 106 9W
Eyehill Cr. →, Alta., Canada 185 F10 52 14N 110 0W
Eyota, MN, U.S.A. 80 G6 43 59N 92 14W
Ezequiel Montes, Querétaro, Mexico 219 B8 20 40N 99 53W

F

F.D. Roosevelt Nat. Historic Site ⌓, NY, U.S.A. 89 D7 41 46N 73 56W
Fabens, TX, U.S.A. 98 F1 31 30N 106 10W
Faber L., N.W.T., Canada 189 D9 63 56N 117 15W
Fabius, NY, U.S.A. 89 C5 42 50N 75 59W
Fabre, Qué., Canada 176 D3 47 12N 79 22W
Fabreville, Qué., Canada 192 A2 45 34N 73 51W
Faceville, GA, U.S.A. 68 F2 30 45N 84 38W
Fagasa, Amer. Samoa 105 e 14 17 S 170 43W
Faillon, L., Qué., Canada 176 C6 48 21N 76 39W
Fair Bluff, NC, U.S.A. 90 D6 34 19N 79 2W
Fair Grove, MO, U.S.A. 82 D3 37 23N 93 9W
Fair Harbour, B.C., Canada 186 E7 50 4N 127 10W
Fair Haven, NJ, U.S.A. 87 B2 40 22N 74 2W
Fair Haven, NY, U.S.A. 89 B4 43 19N 76 42W
Fair Haven, VT, U.S.A. 86 C1 43 36N 73 16W
Fair Lawn, NJ, U.S.A. 87 B2 40 55N 74 7W
Fair Ness, Nunavut, Canada 191 E11 63 24N 72 5W
Fair Oaks, OK, U.S.A. 93 B8 36 17N 95 50W
Fair Plain, MI, U.S.A. 79 G5 42 5N 86 27W
Fair Play, MO, U.S.A. 82 D3 37 38N 93 35W
Fairbank, IA, U.S.A. 73 C6 42 38N 92 3W
Fairbank, MD, U.S.A. 77 B4 38 41N 76 20W
Fairbanks, AK, U.S.A. 61 D11 64 51N 147 43W
Fairbanks, FL, U.S.A. 67 B6 29 44N 82 16W
Fairbanks North Star ☆, AK, U.S.A. 61 D11 64 50N 146 25W
Fairborn, OH, U.S.A. 92 D2 39 49N 84 2W
Fairburn, GA, U.S.A. 68 C2 33 34N 84 35W
Fairburn, SD, U.S.A. 91 G2 43 41N 103 13W
Fairbury, IL, U.S.A. 71 C5 40 45N 88 31W
Fairbury, NE, U.S.A. 84 D8 40 8N 97 11W
Fairchance, PA, U.S.A. 95 E3 39 49N 79 45W
Fairchild, WI, U.S.A. 103 D3 44 36N 90 58W
Fairchild Air Force Base, WA, U.S.A. 101 C8 47 38N 117 35W
Fairdale, KY, U.S.A. 97 B7 38 6N 85 46W
Fairdale, ND, U.S.A. 91 B7 48 30N 98 14W
Fairfax, IA, U.S.A. 73 D7 41 55N 91 47W
Fairfax, MN, U.S.A. 80 F4 44 32N 94 43W
Fairfax, MO, U.S.A. 82 A1 40 20N 95 24W
Fairfax, OH, U.S.A. 107 B2 39 8N 84 23W
Fairfax, OK, U.S.A. 93 B7 36 34N 96 42W
Fairfax, SC, U.S.A. 90 F4 32 59N 81 15W
Fairfax, SD, U.S.A. 91 G7 43 2N 98 54W
Fairfax, VA, U.S.A. 77 B3 38 50N 77 19W
Fairfax, VT, U.S.A. 86 B1 44 40N 73 1W
Fairfax County ☆, VA, U.S.A. 102 C7 38 51N 77 18W
Fairfax Station, VA, U.S.A. 119 C2 38 48N 77 19W
Fairfield, AL, U.S.A. 55 J2 33 29N 86 55W
Fairfield, CA, U.S.A. 64 E4 38 15N 122 3W
Fairfield, CT, U.S.A. 78 C1 41 9N 73 16W
Fairfield, ID, U.S.A. 70 F4 43 21N 114 44W
Fairfield, IL, U.S.A. 71 E5 38 23N 88 22W
Fairfield, IA, U.S.A. 73 E7 40 56N 91 57W
Fairfield, KY, U.S.A. 97 C7 37 56N 85 23W
Fairfield, ME, U.S.A. 76 D4 44 35N 69 36W
Fairfield, MT, U.S.A. 83 C6 47 37N 111 59W
Fairfield, ND, U.S.A. 91 C2 47 8N 103 14W
Fairfield, NJ, U.S.A. 114 A1 40 53N 74 18W
Fairfield, NE, U.S.A. 84 D7 40 26N 98 6W
Fairfield, OH, U.S.A. 92 D2 39 20N 84 34W
Fairfield, PA, U.S.A. 77 A3 39 47N 77 22W
Fairfield, TX, U.S.A. 99 F11 31 44N 96 10W
Fairfield, WA, U.S.A. 101 C8 47 23N 117 10W
Fairfield County ☆, CT, U.S.A. 78 C1 41 15N 73 20W
Fairfield County ☆, OH, U.S.A. 92 D4 39 43N 82 36W
Fairfield County ☆, SC, U.S.A. 90 D4 34 25N 81 10W
Fairford, Man., Canada 183 D13 51 37N 98 38W
Fairground Park, MO, U.S.A. 117 B2 38 39N 90 13W
Fairgrove, MI, U.S.A. 79 F8 43 32N 83 33W
Fairhaven, MA, U.S.A. 78 C4 41 39N 70 55W
Fairhaven, MD, U.S.A. 77 B4 38 45N 76 34W
Fairhaven Bay, Boston, U.S.A. 106 A1 42 25N 71 21W
Fairhaven Hill, Boston, U.S.A. 106 A1 42 26N 71 20W
Fairhope, AL, U.S.A. 60 F3 30 31N 87 54W
Fairhope, PA, U.S.A. 77 A2 39 50N 78 48W
Fairland, IN, U.S.A. 72 D5 39 35N 85 52W
Fairland, MD, U.S.A. 77 A4 39 5N 76 57W
Fairland, OK, U.S.A. 93 B9 36 45N 94 51W
Fairlee, MD, U.S.A. 77 A4 39 13N 76 10W
Fairlee, VT, U.S.A. 86 C2 43 54N 72 9W
Fairmont, MN, U.S.A. 80 G4 43 39N 94 28W
Fairmont, NC, U.S.A. 90 D6 34 30N 79 7W
Fairmont, NE, U.S.A. 84 D8 40 38N 97 35W
Fairmont, OK, U.S.A. 93 B6 36 21N 97 43W
Fairmont, WV, U.S.A. 102 B4 39 29N 80 9W
Fairmont City, IL, U.S.A. 117 B3 38 38N 90 3W
Fairmont Terrace, San Francisco, U.S.A. 118 B4 37 42N 122 6W
Fairmount, GA, U.S.A. 68 B2 34 26N 84 42W
Fairmount, IL, U.S.A. 71 C6 40 3N 87 56W
Fairmount, IN, U.S.A. 72 C5 40 25N 85 39W
Fairmount, MD, U.S.A. 77 B5 38 6N 75 48W
Fairmount, ND, U.S.A. 91 D9 46 3N 96 36W
Fairmount, NY, U.S.A. 89 B4 43 5N 76 12W
Fairmount Heights, MD, U.S.A. 119 B4 38 54N 76 54W
Fairmount Park, PA, U.S.A. 116 A1 40 1N 75 11W
Fairplains, NC, U.S.A. 90 B4 36 12N 81 9W
Fairplay, CO, U.S.A. 66 C4 39 15N 106 2W
Fairport, NY, U.S.A. 89 B3 43 6N 77 27W
Fairport Harbor, OH, U.S.A. 92 B5 41 45N 81 17W
Fairtown, Baltimore, U.S.A. 107 B2 39 16N 76 31W
Fairvale, N.B., Canada 173 H4 45 25N 66 0W
Fairview, Alta., Canada 184 B2 56 5N 118 25W
Fairview, N.S., Canada 173 J6 44 40N 63 38W
Fairview, IL, U.S.A. 71 C3 40 38N 90 10W
Fairview, KS, U.S.A. 74 B8 39 50N 95 44W
Fairview, MI, U.S.A. 79 E7 44 44N 84 3W
Fairview, MT, U.S.A. 83 C13 47 51N 104 3W
Fairview, NC, U.S.A. 90 C3 35 31N 82 24W
Fairview, NJ, U.S.A. 114 B3 40 48N 73 59W
Fairview, NJ, U.S.A. 87 B2 40 23N 74 5W
Fairview, OK, U.S.A. 93 B5 36 16N 98 29W
Fairview, OR, U.S.A. 94 B3 45 32N 122 26W
Fairview, PA, U.S.A. 95 B2 42 2N 80 15W
Fairview, SD, U.S.A. 91 G9 43 13N 96 29W
Fairview, TN, U.S.A. 96 E5 35 59N 87 7W
Fairview, UT, U.S.A. 100 D4 39 38N 111 26W
Fairview, WV, U.S.A. 102 B4 39 36N 80 15W
Fairview, L., Orlando, U.S.A. 115 A2 28 35N 81 24W
Fairview Park, IN, U.S.A. 72 D3 39 41N 87 25W
Fairweather, Mt., AK, U.S.A. 61 G13 58 55N 137 32W
Fairwood, Seattle, U.S.A. 118 D5 47 26N 122 9W
Faison, NC, U.S.A. 90 C7 35 7N 78 8W
Faith, SD, U.S.A. 91 E3 45 2N 102 2W
Faithorn, MI, U.S.A. 79 D4 45 41N 87 45W
Fajardo, Puerto Rico 105 G17 18 20N 65 39W
Falcon, CO, U.S.A. 66 D6 38 56N 104 37W
Falcon, C., OR, U.S.A. 94 B2 45 46N 123 59W
Falcon Heights, Minneapolis-St. Paul, U.S.A. 113 B2 44 59N 93 10W
Falcon I., Ont., Canada 180 C2 49 23N 94 45W
Falcon Res., TX, U.S.A. 98 L8 26 34N 99 10W
Falconbridge, Ont., Canada 178 A6 46 35N 80 45W
Falconer, NY, U.S.A. 89 C1 42 7N 79 12W
Falfurrias, TX, U.S.A. 98 K9 27 14N 98 9W
Falher, Alta., Canada 184 C3 55 44N 117 15W
Falkner, MS, U.S.A. 81 B5 34 51N 88 56W
Falkville, AL, U.S.A. 60 B4 34 22N 86 55W
Fall →, KS, U.S.A. 74 D8 37 24N 95 40W
Fall Branch, TN, U.S.A. 97 D10 36 25N 82 37W
Fall Creek, WI, U.S.A. 103 D2 44 46N 91 17W
Fall Creek Falls State Park ⌓, TN, U.S.A. 97 E7 35 39N 85 20W
Fall River, KS, U.S.A. 74 D7 37 36N 96 2W
Fall River, MA, U.S.A. 78 C3 41 43N 71 10W
Fall River, WI, U.S.A. 103 E4 43 23N 89 3W
Fall River County ☆, SD, U.S.A. 91 G2 43 10N 103 30W
Fall River Lake, KS, U.S.A. 74 D7 37 39N 96 4W
Fall River Mills, CA, U.S.A. 64 B5 41 3N 121 26W
Fallasbee, WV, U.S.A. 102 A4 40 20N 80 36W
Fallbrook, CA, U.S.A. 65 K9 33 23N 117 15W
Fallis, OK, U.S.A. 93 C6 35 45N 97 7W
Fallon, MT, U.S.A. 83 D12 46 50N 105 8W
Fallon, NV, U.S.A. 85 C2 39 28N 118 47W
Fallon County ☆, MT, U.S.A. 83 D13 46 20N 104 30W
Fallon Indian Reservation, NV, U.S.A. 85 C2 39 25N 118 45W
Fallon N.A.S., NV, U.S.A. 85 C2 39 27N 118 44W
Falls Church, VA, U.S.A. 77 B3 38 53N 77 12W
Falls City, NE, U.S.A. 84 D10 40 3N 95 36W
Falls City, OR, U.S.A. 94 C2 44 52N 123 26W
Falls City, TX, U.S.A. 99 J9 28 59N 98 1W
Falls County ☆, TX, U.S.A. 99 F11 31 18N 96 54W
Falls Creek, PA, U.S.A. 95 C4 41 9N 78 48W
Falls L., NC, U.S.A. 90 C7 35 57N 78 35W
Fallsburg, KY, U.S.A. 97 B10 38 11N 82 40W
Fallstaff, Baltimore, U.S.A. 107 A1 39 22N 76 42W
Fallston, MD, U.S.A. 77 A4 39 31N 76 25W
Falmouth, FL, U.S.A. 67 A5 30 21N 83 8W
Falmouth, KY, U.S.A. 97 B8 38 41N 84 20W
Falmouth, ME, U.S.A. 76 E3 43 44N 70 14W
Falmouth, MA, U.S.A. 78 C4 41 33N 70 37W
Falmouth, MI, U.S.A. 79 E6 44 15N 85 5W
Falmouth, VA, U.S.A. 102 C7 38 20N 77 28W
Faloma, Portland, U.S.A. 116 A2 45 36N 122 40W
Falsa, Pta., Baja Calif. S., Mexico 211 F3 27 51N 115 3W
False Pass, AK, U.S.A. 61 J7 54 51N 163 25W
Falun, KS, U.S.A. 74 C6 38 40N 97 46W
Family L., Man., Canada 183 D16 51 54N 95 27W
Fancy Farm, KY, U.S.A. 96 D4 36 48N 88 47W
Fannin County ☆, GA, U.S.A. 68 B2 34 50N 84 15W
Fannin County ☆, TX, U.S.A. 99 D11 33 35N 96 11W
Fanny Bay, B.C., Canada 186 F10 49 37N 124 48W
Fanshawe, OK, U.S.A. 93 D9 34 57N 94 55W
Far Mt., B.C., Canada 186 C9 52 47N 125 20W
Far Rockaway, NY, U.S.A. 114 C4 40 36N 73 45W
Farallón, Pta., Jalisco, Mexico 218 C2 19 22N 105 2W
Farallon de Medinilla, N. Marianas 105 a 16 1N 146 4W
Farallon de Pajaros, N. Marianas 105 a 20 32N 144 54W
Farallon Islands Nat. Wildlife Refuge ⌓, CA, U.S.A. 64 F3 37 44N 123 2W
Farbach-Werner Nature Preserve ⌓, OH, U.S.A. 107 A1 39 14N 84 35W
Farewell, AK, U.S.A. 61 E9 62 31N 153 54W
Fargo, GA, U.S.A. 68 F4 30 41N 82 34W
Fargo, ND, U.S.A. 91 D9 46 53N 96 48W
Fargo, OK, U.S.A. 93 B4 36 22N 99 37W
Faribault, MN, U.S.A. 80 F5 44 18N 93 16W
Faribault, L., Qué., Canada 175 B3 59 3N 71 58W
Faribault County ☆, MN, U.S.A. 80 G5 43 45N 94 0W
Faride, L., Qué., Canada 172 C10 50 58N 59 55W
Farina, IL, U.S.A. 71 E5 38 50N 88 46W
Farley, IA, U.S.A. 73 C7 42 27N 91 0W
Farmer City, IL, U.S.A. 71 C5 40 15N 88 39W
Farmers Branch, TX, U.S.A. 99 E11 32 55N 96 53W
Farmersburg, IN, U.S.A. 72 D3 39 15N 87 23W
Farmersville, CA, U.S.A. 65 G7 36 18N 119 12W
Farmersville, IL, U.S.A. 71 D4 39 27N 89 39W
Farmersville, TX, U.S.A. 99 D11 33 10N 96 22W
Farmerville, LA, U.S.A. 75 B3 32 47N 92 24W
Farmingdale, NJ, U.S.A. 87 B2 40 12N 74 10W
Farmington, B.C., Canada 189 E8 55 54N 120 30W
Farmington, AR, U.S.A. 63 B1 36 3N 94 15W
Farmington, CA, U.S.A. 64 F6 37 55N 120 59W
Farmington, DE, U.S.A. 77 B5 38 52N 75 35W
Farmington, GA, U.S.A. 68 C3 33 47N 83 26W
Farmington, IL, U.S.A. 71 C3 40 42N 90 0W
Farmington, IA, U.S.A. 73 E7 40 38N 91 44W
Farmington, ME, U.S.A. 76 D3 44 40N 70 9W
Farmington, MD, U.S.A. 77 A4 39 42N 76 4W
Farmington, MN, U.S.A. 80 F5 44 38N 93 8W
Farmington, MS, U.S.A. 81 B5 34 56N 88 27W
Farmington, MO, U.S.A. 82 D6 37 47N 90 25W
Farmington, MT, U.S.A. 83 C5 47 53N 112 10W
Farmington, NH, U.S.A. 86 C3 43 24N 71 4W
Farmington, NM, U.S.A. 88 A2 36 44N 108 12W
Farmington, UT, U.S.A. 100 C4 40 59N 111 53W
Farmington, WA, U.S.A. 101 C8 47 5N 117 3W
Farmington →, CT, U.S.A. 78 C2 41 51N 72 38W
Farmville, NC, U.S.A. 90 C8 35 36N 77 35W
Farmville, VA, U.S.A. 102 D6 37 18N 78 24W
Farnam, NE, U.S.A. 84 D5 40 42N 100 13W
Farner, TN, U.S.A. 97 E8 35 9N 84 19W
Farnham, Qué., Canada 177 F10 45 17N 72 59W
Farnham, VA, U.S.A. 77 C4 37 53N 76 38W
Farnsworth, TX, U.S.A. 98 A7 36 19N 100 58W
Faro, Yukon, Canada 189 D6 62 11N 133 22W
Faro, Monterrey, Mexico 224 B3 25 48N 100 9W
Farragut, IA, U.S.A. 73 E3 40 43N 95 29W
Farragut, TN, U.S.A. 97 E8 35 53N 84 9W
Farrar Pond, Boston, U.S.A. 106 A1 42 24N 71 21W
Farrell, PA, U.S.A. 95 C2 41 13N 80 30W
Farson, WY, U.S.A. 104 D3 42 7N 109 26W
Farwell, MI, U.S.A. 79 F7 43 50N 84 52W
Farwell, MN, U.S.A. 80 E3 45 45N 95 37W
Farwell, NE, U.S.A. 84 C7 41 13N 98 38W
Farwell, TX, U.S.A. 98 C4 34 23N 103 2W
Father Marquette Nat. Memorial, MI, U.S.A. 79 D7 45 55N 84 46W
Fathom Five Nat. Marine Park ⌓, Ont., Canada 178 B5 45 17N 81 40W
Fatima, Qué., Canada 173 F8 47 24N 61 53W
Faucett, MO, U.S.A. 82 B2 39 36N 94 48W
Faulk County ☆, SD, U.S.A. 91 E6 45 0N 99 0W
Faulkner County ☆, AR, U.S.A. 63 C3 35 10N 92 16W
Faulkton, SD, U.S.A. 91 E6 45 2N 99 8W
Fauquier, B.C., Canada 187 F16 49 52N 118 5W
Fauquier, Ont., Canada 181 C14 49 18N 82 3W
Fauquier County ☆, VA, U.S.A. 102 C7 38 43N 77 48W
Faust, Alta., Canada 184 C5 55 19N 115 38W
Faust, UT, U.S.A. 100 C3 40 11N 112 24W
Fawcett, Alta., Canada 184 D6 54 32N 114 5W
Fawcett L., Alta., Canada 184 C7 55 19N 113 53W
Fawn →, Ont., Canada 191 F8 55 20N 87 35W
Fawn Grove, PA, U.S.A. 77 A4 39 44N 76 27W
Faxon, OK, U.S.A. 93 D5 34 28N 98 35W
Fay, OK, U.S.A. 93 C5 35 49N 98 39W
Fayette, AL, U.S.A. 60 C3 33 41N 87 50W
Fayette, IA, U.S.A. 73 C7 42 51N 91 48W
Fayette, MI, U.S.A. 79 D5 45 43N 86 40W
Fayette, MS, U.S.A. 81 E2 31 43N 91 4W
Fayette, MO, U.S.A. 82 B4 39 9N 92 41W
Fayette, NY, U.S.A. 89 C4 42 49N 76 49W
Fayette, OH, U.S.A. 92 B2 41 40N 84 20W
Fayette, UT, U.S.A. 100 D4 39 14N 111 51W
Fayette County ☆, AL, U.S.A. 60 C3 33 41N 87 50W
Fayette County ☆, GA, U.S.A. 68 C2 33 25N 84 30W
Fayette County ☆, IL, U.S.A. 71 E4 39 0N 89 0W
Fayette County ☆, IN, U.S.A. 72 D5 39 35N 85 10W
Fayette County ☆, IA, U.S.A. 73 C7 42 50N 91 50W
Fayette County ☆, KY, U.S.A. 97 B8 38 0N 84 30W
Fayette County ☆, OH, U.S.A. 92 D3 39 32N 83 26W
Fayette County ☆, PA, U.S.A. 95 E3 40 0N 79 40W
Fayette County ☆, TN, U.S.A. 96 E3 35 15N 89 21W
Fayette County ☆, TX, U.S.A. 99 H11 29 54N 96 52W
Fayette County ☆, WV, U.S.A. 102 D3 37 59N 81 9W
Fayetteville, AR, U.S.A. 63 B1 36 4N 94 10W
Fayetteville, GA, U.S.A. 68 C2 33 27N 84 27W
Fayetteville, NC, U.S.A. 90 C7 35 3N 78 53W
Fayetteville, NY, U.S.A. 89 B5 43 2N 76 0W
Fayetteville, PA, U.S.A. 95 E5 39 55N 77 33W
Fayetteville, TN, U.S.A. 96 E6 35 9N 86 34W
Fayetteville, TX, U.S.A. 99 H11 29 54N 96 41W
Fayetteville, WV, U.S.A. 102 C3 38 3N 81 6W
Fear, C., NC, U.S.A. 90 E8 33 50N 77 58W
Feather →, CA, U.S.A. 64 E5 38 47N 121 36W
Feather Falls, CA, U.S.A. 64 D5 39 36N 121 16W
Featherville, ID, U.S.A. 70 F3 43 37N 115 15W
Federal, WY, U.S.A. 104 E7 41 16N 105 7W
Federal Dam, MN, U.S.A. 80 C4 47 15N 94 14W
Federal Heights, CO, U.S.A. 66 C5 39 51N 104 59W
Federal Way, WA, U.S.A. 101 C3 47 18N 122 19W
Federalsburg, MD, U.S.A. 77 B5 38 42N 75 47W
Feeding Hills, MA, U.S.A. 78 B2 42 4N 72 41W
Felch, MI, U.S.A. 79 C4 46 0N 87 50W
Felda, FL, U.S.A. 67 E7 26 34N 81 26W
Felicity, OH, U.S.A. 92 E2 38 51N 84 6W
Felipe Carrillo Puerto, Campeche, Mexico 223 C3 19 7N 90 32W
Felipe Carrillo Puerto, Michoacan, Mexico 218 C5 19 7N 102 43W
Felipe Carrillo Puerto, Quintana Roo, Mexico 223 C5 19 38N 88 3W
Felipe Carrillo Puerto, Zacatecas, Mexico 217 D8 23 51N 102 6W
Felix →, NM, U.S.A. 88 D6 33 5N 104 25W
Felix, C., Nunavut, Canada 190 D6 69 54N 97 58W
Fellsmere, FL, U.S.A. 67 D8 27 46N 80 36W
Felsenthal Nat. Wildlife Refuge ⌓, AR, U.S.A. 63 E3 33 9N 92 10W
Felt, ID, U.S.A. 70 F7 43 52N 111 11W
Felt, OK, U.S.A. 93 B1 36 34N 102 48W
Felton, DE, U.S.A. 77 A5 39 1N 75 35W
Felton, MN, U.S.A. 80 C2 47 5N 96 30W
Felton, PA, U.S.A. 77 A4 39 51N 76 34W
Fence Lake, NM, U.S.A. 88 C2 34 40N 108 40W
Fenelon Falls, Ont., Canada 179 C8 44 32N 78 45W
Fenn, ID, U.S.A. 70 D2 45 58N 116 16W
Fennimore, WI, U.S.A. 103 F3 42 59N 90 39W
Fennville, MI, U.S.A. 79 G5 42 36N 86 6W
Fenton, IA, U.S.A. 73 B4 43 13N 94 26W
Fenton, LA, U.S.A. 75 D3 30 22N 92 55W
Fenton, MI, U.S.A. 79 G8 42 48N 83 42W
Fentress, TX, U.S.A. 99 H10 29 45N 97 47W
Fentress County ☆, TN, U.S.A. 97 D8 36 25N 85 0W
Fenwood, WI, U.S.A. 103 D3 44 52N 90 1W
Ferdinand, ID, U.S.A. 70 C2 46 9N 116 24W
Ferdinand, IN, U.S.A. 72 E4 38 14N 86 52W
Fergus, Ont., Canada 178 D6 43 43N 80 24W
Fergus County ☆, MT, U.S.A. 83 C8 47 30N 109 10W
Fergus Falls, MN, U.S.A. 80 D2 46 17N 96 4W
Ferguson, KY, U.S.A. 97 C8 37 3N 84 36W
Ferguson, MO, U.S.A. 82 C6 38 44N 90 18W
Ferguson Lake, Nunavut, Canada 190 D4 69 25N 105 15W
Ferguson Pt., Vancouver, Canada 193 B2 49 18N 123 9W
Ferintosh, Alta., Canada 185 F8 52 46N 112 58W
Ferland, Ont., Canada 180 B8 50 19N 88 27W
Ferme-Neuve, Qué., Canada 176 E7 46 42N 75 27W
Fermin, Pt., Los Angeles, U.S.A. 111 D3 33 42N 118 17W
Fermont, Qué., Canada 175 C4 52 47N 67 5W
Fern Creek, KY, U.S.A. 97 B7 38 9N 85 36W
Fern Ridge L., OR, U.S.A. 94 C2 44 7N 123 18W
Fernandina Beach, FL, U.S.A. 67 A7 30 40N 81 27W
Ferndale, CA, U.S.A. 64 C2 40 35N 124 16W
Ferndale, MD, U.S.A. 77 A4 39 10N 76 38W
Ferndale, MI, U.S.A. 109 A2 42 27N 83 8W
Ferndale, WA, U.S.A. 101 B3 48 51N 122 36W
Fernie, B.C., Canada 185 J5 49 30N 115 5W
Fernley, NV, U.S.A. 85 C1 39 36N 119 15W
Fernwood, ID, U.S.A. 70 B2 47 7N 116 24W
Fernwood, MS, U.S.A. 81 E3 31 11N 90 27W
Fernwood, NY, U.S.A. 89 B7 43 17N 73 40W
Feronia, Ont., Canada 178 A7 46 22N 79 19W
Ferrellsburg, WV, U.S.A. 102 C2 38 2N 82 6W
Ferriday, LA, U.S.A. 75 C4 31 38N 91 33W
Ferris, IL, U.S.A. 71 C2 40 28N 91 10W
Ferris, TX, U.S.A. 99 E11 32 32N 96 40W
Ferrisburg, VT, U.S.A. 86 B1 44 12N 73 15W
Ferron, UT, U.S.A. 100 D4 39 5N 111 8W
Ferrum, VA, U.S.A. 102 E4 36 55N 80 1W
Ferry County ☆, WA, U.S.A. 101 B7 48 30N 118 30W
Ferry Pass, FL, U.S.A. 67 A1 30 31N 87 13W
Ferryland, Nfld. & L., Canada 174 E8 47 2N 52 53W
Ferrysburg, MI, U.S.A. 79 F5 43 5N 86 13W
Ferryville, WI, U.S.A. 103 E2 43 21N 91 6W
Fertile, IA, U.S.A. 73 B5 43 16N 93 25W
Fertile, MN, U.S.A. 80 C2 47 32N 96 17W
Fessenden, ND, U.S.A. 91 C6 47 39N 99 38W
Festus, MO, U.S.A. 82 C6 38 13N 90 24W
Feuilles →, Qué., Canada 175 B3 58 47N 70 4W
Feuilles, B. aux, Qué., Canada 175 B4 58 55N 69 20W
Field, Ont., Canada 178 A6 46 31N 80 1W
Field, KY, U.S.A. 97 D9 36 54N 83 36W
Fieldale, VA, U.S.A. 102 E5 36 42N 79 56W
Fielding, UT, U.S.A. 100 B3 41 49N 112 7W
Fieldon, IL, U.S.A. 71 D3 39 7N 90 30W
Fields, LA, U.S.A. 75 D2 30 32N 93 35W
Fields, OR, U.S.A. 94 E7 42 16N 118 40W
Fields Corner, Boston, U.S.A. 106 B3 42 18N 71 3W
Fields Landing, CA, U.S.A. 64 C2 40 44N 124 13W
Fierro, NM, U.S.A. 88 E2 32 51N 108 5W
Fife, TX, U.S.A. 99 F8 31 24N 99 22W
Fife L., Sask., Canada 182 F6 49 14N 105 53W
Fife Lake, MI, U.S.A. 79 E6 44 35N 85 21W
Fifield, WI, U.S.A. 103 C3 45 53N 90 25W
File Axe, L., Qué., Canada 177 A9 50 18N 73 34W
Filer, ID, U.S.A. 70 G4 42 34N 114 37W
Fillmore, Sask., Canada 182 F8 49 50N 103 25W
Fillmore, CA, U.S.A. 65 J8 34 24N 118 55W
Fillmore, UT, U.S.A. 100 E3 38 58N 112 20W
Fillmore County ☆, MN, U.S.A. 80 G7 43 40N 92 0W
Fillmore County ☆, NE, U.S.A. 84 D8 40 30N 97 40W
Filomeno Mata, Veracruz, Mexico 220 D3 20 12N 97 42W
Fils, L. du, Qué., Canada 176 E4 46 37N 78 7W
Final, Pta., Baja Calif., Mexico 210 D4 29 47N 114 19W
Fincastle, VA, U.S.A. 102 D5 37 30N 79 53W
Finch, Ont., Canada 176 F7 45 11N 75 7W
Findlater, Sask., Canada 182 E6 50 47N 105 24W
Findlay, IL, U.S.A. 71 D5 39 31N 88 45W
Findlay, OH, U.S.A. 92 B3 41 2N 83 39W
Fine, NY, U.S.A. 89 A5 44 15N 75 8W
Fingal, ND, U.S.A. 91 D8 46 46N 97 47W
Finger, TN, U.S.A. 96 E4 35 22N 88 36W
Finger Lakes, NY, U.S.A. 89 C4 42 40N 76 30W
Finger Lakes Nat. Forest, NY, U.S.A. 89 C4 42 31N 76 47W
Finisterre, Coahuila, Mexico 214 E1 25 59N 103 14W
Finksburg, MD, U.S.A. 77 A4 39 30N 76 54W
Finlay →, B.C., Canada 189 E7 57 0N 125 10W
Finlayson, MN, U.S.A. 80 D6 46 12N 92 55W
Finley, ND, U.S.A. 91 C8 47 31N 97 50W
Finley, OK, U.S.A. 93 D8 34 20N 95 30W
Finmark, Ont., Canada 180 D7 48 35N 89 45W
Finney, MI, U.S.A. 109 A3 42 24N 82 55W
Finney County ☆, KS, U.S.A. 74 C3 38 0N 100 40W
Finneytown, OH, U.S.A. 107 A1 39 12N 84 31W
Fire I., NY, U.S.A. 89 E7 40 40N 73 11W
Fire Island Nat. Seashore ⌓, NY, U.S.A. 87 B3 40 38N 73 8W
Fire River, Ont., Canada 181 D13 48 47N 83 21W
Firebag →, Alta., Canada 184 A9 57 45N 111 21W
Firebaugh, CA, U.S.A. 65 G6 36 52N 120 27W
First Connecticut L., NH, U.S.A. 86 A3 45 5N 71 15W
Firth, ID, U.S.A. 70 F6 43 18N 112 11W
Firth, NE, U.S.A. 84 D9 40 33N 96 37W
Firvale, B.C., Canada 186 C8 52 27N 126 13W
Fischer, TX, U.S.A. 99 H9 29 58N 98 16W
Fish L., UT, U.S.A. 100 E4 38 33N 111 42W
Fish Lake, Minneapolis-St. Paul, U.S.A. 113 A1 45 5N 93 27W
Fish Lake Regional Park ⌓, Minneapolis-St. Paul, U.S.A. 113 A1 45 5N 93 27W
Fish Lake Res., MN, U.S.A. 80 D6 46 57N 92 17W
Fish Pt., MI, U.S.A. 79 F8 43 44N 83 31W
Fish River L., ME, U.S.A. 76 B5 46 50N 68 47W
Fish Springs Nat. Wildlife Refuge ⌓, UT, U.S.A. 100 D2 39 51N 113 22W
Fisheating Cr. →, FL, U.S.A. 67 E7 26 57N 81 7W
Fisher, AR, U.S.A. 63 C5 35 30N 90 58W
Fisher, IL, U.S.A. 71 C5 40 19N 88 21W
Fisher, LA, U.S.A. 75 C2 31 30N 93 28W
Fisher, MN, U.S.A. 80 C2 47 48N 96 48W
Fisher →, MT, U.S.A. 83 B2 48 22N 115 19W
Fisher B., Man., Canada 183 D14 51 35N 97 13W
Fisher Branch, Man., Canada 183 D14 51 5N 97 13W
Fisher County ☆, TX, U.S.A. 98 E7 32 45N 100 23W
Fisher Island, Miami, U.S.A. 112 D3 25 45N 80 8W
Fisher River, Man., Canada 183 D14 51 25N 97 21W
Fisher Str., N.W.T., Canada 191 E9 63 15N 83 30W
Fishermans Island Nat. Wildlife Refuge ⌓, VA, U.S.A. 102 D9 37 6N 75 57W
Fishers, IN, U.S.A. 72 D4 39 57N 86 0W
Fishers I., NY, U.S.A. 78 C4 41 15N 72 0W
Fishers Peak, CO, U.S.A. 66 E6 37 6N 104 28W
Fishing Bridge, WY, U.S.A. 104 B2 44 29N 110 22W
Fishing Creek, MD, U.S.A. 77 B4 38 20N 76 14W
Fishing Creek →, NC, U.S.A. 90 C8 35 56N 77 31W
Fishing L., Man., Canada 183 C16 52 10N 95 24W
Fishkill, NY, U.S.A. 87 A3 41 32N 73 54W
Fishlake Nat. Forest, UT, U.S.A. 100 E3 38 40N 112 20W
Fishtrap L., KY, U.S.A. 97 C10 37 25N 82 26W
Fisk, MO, U.S.A. 82 E6 36 47N 90 12W
Fiskdale, MA, U.S.A. 78 B2 42 7N 72 7W
Fitchburg, MA, U.S.A. 78 B3 42 35N 71 48W
Fitchburg, WI, U.S.A. 103 F4 42 58N 89 28W
Fittstown, OK, U.S.A. 93 D7 34 37N 96 38W
Fitz Hugh Sd., B.C., Canada 186 D7 51 40N 127 55W
Fitzgerald, Alta., Canada 189 E10 59 51N 111 36W
Fitzgerald, GA, U.S.A. 68 E3 31 43N 83 15W
Fitzgerald B., Nunavut, Canada 190 C8 72 9N 89 45W
Fitzhugh, AR, U.S.A. 63 C4 35 22N 91 19W
Fitzhugh, OK, U.S.A. 93 D7 34 40N 96 46W
Fitzwilliam I., Ont., Canada 178 B5 45 30N 81 45W
Five Islands, N.S., Canada 173 H5 45 23N 64 7W
Flagler, CO, U.S.A. 66 C7 39 18N 103 4W
Flagler Beach, FL, U.S.A. 67 B7 29 29N 81 8W
Flagler County ☆, FL, U.S.A. 67 B7 29 30N 81 20W
Flagstaff, AZ, U.S.A. 62 B4 35 12N 111 39W
Flagstaff L., ME, U.S.A. 76 C3 45 12N 70 18W
Flagstaff L., OR, U.S.A. 94 E6 42 35N 119 45W
Flaherty I., N.W.T., Canada 175 B2 56 15N 79 15W
Flambeau →, WI, U.S.A. 103 C2 45 18N 91 14W
Flaming Gorge Dam, UT, U.S.A. 100 C6 40 55N 109 25W
Flaming Gorge Nat. Recr. Area ⌓, WY, U.S.A. 104 E3 41 10N 109 25W

Flaming Gorge Res., *WY, U.S.A.* **104 E3** 41 10N 109 25W
Flamingo, *FL, U.S.A.* **67 F8** 25 8N 80 57W
Flamingo, *Orlando, U.S.A.* **115 B2** 28 22N 81 22W
Flanagan, *IL, U.S.A.* **71 C5** 40 53N 88 52W
Flanders, *NY, U.S.A.* **78 D2** 40 54N 72 37W
Flandreau, *SD, U.S.A.* **91 F9** 44 3N 96 36W
Flasher, *ND, U.S.A.* **91 D4** 46 27N 101 14W
Flat, *AK, U.S.A.* **61 E8** 62 28N 158 1W
Flat ➞, *N.W.T., Canada* **189 D7** 61 33N 125 18W
Flat ➞, *MI, U.S.A.* **79 G6** 42 56N 85 20W
Flat ➞, *NC, U.S.A.* **90 B7** 36 5N 78 49W
Flat Bay, *Nfld. & L., Canada* **174 D2** 48 24N 58 36W
Flat L., *Alta., Canada* **184 D8** 54 38N 112 54W
Flat Lake Park △, *B.C., Canada* **187 D13** 51 30N 121 31W
Flat Lick, *KY, U.S.A.* **97 D9** 36 50N 83 46W
Flat River Res., *RI, U.S.A.* **78 C3** 41 42N 71 37W
Flat Rock, *AL, U.S.A.* **60 B5** 34 46N 85 42W
Flat Rock, *IL, U.S.A.* **71 E6** 38 54N 87 40W
Flat Rock, *MI, U.S.A.* **79 G8** 42 6N 83 17W
Flat Top Mt., *UT, U.S.A.* **100 C3** 40 22N 112 11W
Flat Tops, The, *CO, U.S.A.* **66 C3** 39 50N 107 10W
Flat Woods, *TN, U.S.A.* **96 E5** 35 29N 87 50W
Flatbush, *Alta., Canada* **184 D6** 54 42N 114 9W
Flatbush, *NY, U.S.A.* **114 C3** 40 39N 73 56W
Flathead ➞, *MT, U.S.A.* **83 C3** 47 22N 114 47W
Flathead County ☆, *MT, U.S.A.* **83 B4** 48 15N 113 30W
Flathead Indian Reservation, *MT, U.S.A.* **83 C3** 47 35N 114 30W
Flathead L., *MT, U.S.A.* **83 C3** 47 51N 114 8W
Flathead Nat. Forest, *MT, U.S.A.* **83 C4** 47 50N 113 18W
Flatonia, *TX, U.S.A.* **99 H10** 29 41N 97 7W
Flatrock ➞, *IN, U.S.A.* **72 D5** 39 12N 85 56W
Flattery, C., *WA, U.S.A.* **101 B1** 48 23N 124 29W
Flatwillow Cr. ➞, *MT, U.S.A.* **83 D10** 46 56N 107 55W
Flatwoods, *KY, U.S.A.* **97 B10** 38 31N 82 43W
Flatwoods, *LA, U.S.A.* **75 C3** 31 24N 92 52W
Flatwoods, *WV, U.S.A.* **102 C4** 38 43N 80 39W
Flaxcombe, *Sask., Canada* **182 D2** 51 29N 109 36W
Flaxton, *ND, U.S.A.* **91 B3** 48 54N 102 24W
Flaxville, *MT, U.S.A.* **83 B12** 48 48N 105 11W
Fleetwood, *PA, U.S.A.* **95 D7** 40 27N 75 49W
Fleischmanns, *NY, U.S.A.* **89 C6** 42 10N 74 32W
Fleming, *Sask., Canada* **183 E10** 50 4N 101 31W
Fleming, *CO, U.S.A.* **66 B8** 40 41N 102 50W
Fleming County ☆, *KY, U.S.A.* **97 B9** 38 20N 83 40W
Fleming-Neon, *KY, U.S.A.* **97 C10** 37 12N 82 42W
Flemingsburg, *KY, U.S.A.* **97 B9** 38 25N 83 45W
Flemington, *NJ, U.S.A.* **87 B2** 40 31N 74 52W
Flemington, *WV, U.S.A.* **102 B4** 39 16N 80 8W
Flensburg, *MN, U.S.A.* **80 E4** 45 57N 94 32W
Flesherton, *Ont., Canada* **178 C6** 44 16N 80 33W
Fletcher = Aurora, *CO, U.S.A.* **66 C6** 39 43N 104 49W
Fletcher, *NC, U.S.A.* **90 C3** 35 26N 82 30W
Fletcher, *OK, U.S.A.* **93 D5** 34 50N 98 15W
Fletcher Pond, *MI, U.S.A.* **79 D8** 45 1N 83 47W
Fleur de Lys, *Nfld. & L., Canada* **174 B4** 50 7N 56 8W
Fleur-de-May, L., *Nfld. & L., Canada* **172 B4** 52 0N 65 5W
Fleurimont, *Qué., Canada* **177 F11** 45 24N 71 51W
Flin Flon, *Man., Canada* **189 F12** 54 46N 101 53W
Flint, *MI, U.S.A.* **79 F8** 43 1N 83 41W
Flint ➞, *AL, U.S.A.* **60 B4** 34 30N 86 30W
Flint ➞, *GA, U.S.A.* **68 F2** 30 57N 84 34W
Flint Cr. ➞, *AL, U.S.A.* **60 B4** 34 35N 86 56W
Flint Hill, *VA, U.S.A.* **77 B2** 38 46N 78 6W
Flint Hills, *KS, U.S.A.* **74 D7** 38 0N 96 40W
Flint L., *Nunavut, Canada* **190 D11** 69 16N 74 15W
Flint L., *Ont., Canada* **181 C11** 49 52N 85 53W
Flint Pk., *Los Angeles, U.S.A.* **111 B3** 34 9N 118 11 E
Flintstone, *MD, U.S.A.* **77 A2** 39 42N 78 34W
Flippin, *AR, U.S.A.* **63 B3** 36 17N 92 36W
Flomaton, *AL, U.S.A.* **60 E3** 31 0N 87 16W
Flomot, *TX, U.S.A.* **98 C7** 34 14N 100 59W
Floodwood, *MN, U.S.A.* **80 D6** 46 56N 92 55W
Flora, *IL, U.S.A.* **71 E5** 38 40N 88 29W
Flora, *IN, U.S.A.* **72 C4** 40 33N 86 31W
Flora, *MS, U.S.A.* **81 D3** 32 33N 90 19W
Flora, *OR, U.S.A.* **94 B8** 45 54N 117 19W
Flora Vista, *NM, U.S.A.* **88 A2** 36 48N 108 3W
Florahome, *FL, U.S.A.* **67 B7** 29 44N 81 54W
Floral, *AR, U.S.A.* **63 C4** 35 36N 91 45W
Floral City, *FL, U.S.A.* **67 C6** 28 45N 82 17W
Floral Park, *NY, U.S.A.* **114 B4** 40 43N 73 42W
Florala, *AL, U.S.A.* **60 E4** 31 0N 86 20W
Flordell Hills, *MO, U.S.A.* **117 A2** 38 43N 90 15W
Florence, *N.S., Canada* **173 G9** 46 16N 60 16W
Florence, *AL, U.S.A.* **60 B3** 34 48N 87 41W
Florence, *AZ, U.S.A.* **62 D4** 33 2N 111 23W
Florence, *AR, U.S.A.* **63 E4** 33 46N 91 39W
Florence, *CO, U.S.A.* **66 D5** 38 23N 105 8W
Florence, *KS, U.S.A.* **74 C7** 38 15N 96 56W
Florence, *KY, U.S.A.* **97 B8** 39 0N 84 38W
Florence, *Los Angeles, U.S.A.* **111 C3** 33 57N 118 13W
Florence, *MA, U.S.A.* **78 B2** 42 20N 72 40W
Florence, *MD, U.S.A.* **77 A3** 39 20N 77 8W
Florence, *MS, U.S.A.* **81 D3** 32 9N 90 8W
Florence, *MO, U.S.A.* **82 C4** 38 35N 92 59W
Florence, *MT, U.S.A.* **83 D3** 46 38N 114 5W
Florence, *OR, U.S.A.* **94 D1** 43 58N 124 7W
Florence, *SC, U.S.A.* **90 D6** 34 12N 79 46W
Florence, *SD, U.S.A.* **91 E8** 45 3N 97 20W
Florence, *TX, U.S.A.* **99 G10** 30 51N 97 48W
Florence, *WI, U.S.A.* **103 C5** 45 56N 88 15W
Florence County ☆, *SC, U.S.A.* **90 D6** 34 0N 79 45W
Florence County ☆, *WI, U.S.A.* **103 C5** 45 50N 88 20W
Flores I., *B.C., Canada* **186 F8** 49 20N 126 10W
Flores Island Park △, *B.C., Canada* **186 F8** 49 17N 126 11W
Floresville, *TX, U.S.A.* **99 H9** 29 8N 98 10W
Florey, *TX, U.S.A.* **98 E5** 32 27N 102 36W
Florham Park, *NJ, U.S.A.* **87 B2** 40 47N 74 23W
Florida, *Puerto Rico* **105 G16** 18 22N 66 34W
Florida, *NY, U.S.A.* **87 A2** 41 20N 74 21W
Florida □, *U.S.A.* **67 D7** 28 0N 82 0W
Florida B., *U.S.A.* **67 F8** 25 0N 80 45W
Florida City, *FL, U.S.A.* **67 F8** 25 27N 80 29W
Florida del Norte, *Tamaulipas, Mexico* **215 E6** 25 7N 98 13W
Florida Keys, *FL, U.S.A.* **67 G8** 24 40N 81 0W
Florido ➞, *Chihuahua, Mexico* **213 F10** 27 43N 105 10W
Florien, *LA, U.S.A.* **75 C2** 31 27N 93 28W
Florin, *CA, U.S.A.* **64 E5** 38 30N 121 24W
Floris, *IA, U.S.A.* **73 E6** 40 52N 92 20W
Florissant, *MO, U.S.A.* **82 C6** 38 47N 90 19W
Florissant Fossil Beds Nat. Monument △, *CO, U.S.A.* **66 D5** 38 54N 105 17W
Flourtown, *PA, U.S.A.* **116 A1** 40 6N 75 12W
Flower Hill, *NY, U.S.A.* **114 B4** 40 48N 73 40W
Flower Station, *Ont., Canada* **179 B10** 45 10N 76 41W
Flower's Cove, *Nfld. & L., Canada* **174 A4** 51 14N 56 46W
Floyd, *IA, U.S.A.* **73 B6** 43 8N 92 44W
Floyd, *NM, U.S.A.* **88 C7** 34 13N 103 35W
Floyd, *VA, U.S.A.* **102 E4** 36 55N 80 19W
Floyd ➞, *IA, U.S.A.* **73 C2** 42 29N 96 23W
Floyd County ☆, *GA, U.S.A.* **68 B1** 34 15N 85 10W
Floyd County ☆, *IN, U.S.A.* **72 E5** 38 20N 85 55W
Floyd County ☆, *IA, U.S.A.* **73 B6** 43 5N 92 45W
Floyd County ☆, *KY, U.S.A.* **97 C10** 37 30N 82 45W
Floyd County ☆, *TX, U.S.A.* **98 C6** 34 0N 101 15W
Floyd County ☆, *VA, U.S.A.* **102 E4** 36 58N 80 25W
Floyd Lamb State Park, *Las Vegas, U.S.A.* **110 A1** 36 19N 115 15W
Floydada, *TX, U.S.A.* **98 D6** 33 59N 101 20W
Flume, The, *NH, U.S.A.* **86 B3** 44 6N 71 41W
Flushing, *MI, U.S.A.* **79 F8** 43 4N 83 51W
Flushing, *NY, U.S.A.* **114 B4** 40 45N 73 49W
Flushing, *OH, U.S.A.* **92 C5** 40 9N 81 4W
Flushing Meadows Corona Park, *NY, U.S.A.* **114 B3** 40 44N 73 50W
Fluvanna County ☆, *VA, U.S.A.* **102 D6** 37 52N 78 16W
Flynn, *TX, U.S.A.* **99 F11** 31 9N 96 8W
Foam Lake, *Sask., Canada* **182 D8** 51 40N 103 32W
Foard City, *TX, U.S.A.* **99 D8** 33 53N 99 48W
Foard County ☆, *TX, U.S.A.* **99 D8** 33 59N 99 43W
Fogelsville, *PA, U.S.A.* **87 B1** 40 35N 75 38W
Fogo, *Nfld. & L., Canada* **174 C6** 49 43N 54 17W
Fogo, C., *Nfld. & L., Canada* **174 C7** 49 40N 54 0W
Fogo I., *Nfld. & L., Canada* **174 C6** 49 40N 54 5W
Foins, L. aux, *Qué., Canada* **176 D4** 47 5N 78 11W
Folcroft, *PA, U.S.A.* **116 B1** 39 53N 75 17W
Foley, *AL, U.S.A.* **60 F3** 30 24N 87 41W
Foley, *FL, U.S.A.* **67 A5** 30 4N 83 32W
Foley, *MN, U.S.A.* **80 E5** 45 40N 93 55W
Foley I., *N.W.T., Canada* **190 D10** 68 32N 75 5W
Foleyet, *Ont., Canada* **181 D14** 48 15N 82 25W
Folkston, *GA, U.S.A.* **68 F4** 30 50N 82 0W
Follett, *TX, U.S.A.* **98 A7** 36 26N 100 8W
Folly Beach, *SC, U.S.A.* **90 F6** 32 39N 79 56W
Folsom, *LA, U.S.A.* **75 D5** 30 38N 90 11W
Folsom, *NJ, U.S.A.* **87 C2** 39 38N 74 51W
Folsom, *NM, U.S.A.* **88 A7** 36 51N 103 55W
Folsom, *WV, U.S.A.* **102 B4** 39 28N 80 31W
Folsom L., *CA, U.S.A.* **64 E5** 38 42N 121 9W
Fond-du-Lac, *Sask., Canada* **189 E11** 59 19N 107 12W
Fond du Lac, *WI, U.S.A.* **103 E5** 43 47N 88 27W
Fond-du-Lac ➞, *Sask., Canada* **189 E11** 59 17N 106 0W
Fond du Lac County ☆, *WI, U.S.A.* **103 E5** 43 40N 88 30W
Fond du Lac Indian Reservation, *MN, U.S.A.* **80 D6** 46 45N 92 40W
Fonda, *IA, U.S.A.* **73 C4** 42 35N 94 51W
Fonda, *NY, U.S.A.* **89 C6** 42 57N 74 22W
Fonde, *KY, U.S.A.* **97 D9** 36 36N 83 53W
Fontaine, *N.B., Canada* **173 G5** 46 51N 64 58W
Fontana, *CA, U.S.A.* **65 J9** 34 6N 117 26W
Fontana, *KS, U.S.A.* **74 C9** 38 25N 94 51W
Fontana, *WI, U.S.A.* **103 F5** 42 33N 88 35W
Fontana L., *NC, U.S.A.* **90 C2** 35 27N 83 48W
Fontanelle, *IA, U.S.A.* **73 D4** 41 17N 94 34W
Fontas ➞, *B.C., Canada* **189 E8** 58 14N 121 48W
Fonteneau, L., *Qué., Canada* **172 B8** 51 55N 61 30W
Fontenelle, *WY, U.S.A.* **104 E2** 41 59N 110 3W
Fontenelle Res., *WY, U.S.A.* **104 D2** 42 1N 110 3W
Foosland, *IL, U.S.A.* **71 C5** 40 22N 88 26W
Foothills, *Alta., Canada* **185 E4** 53 4N 116 47W
Footville, *WI, U.S.A.* **103 F4** 42 40N 89 12W
Forada, *MN, U.S.A.* **80 E3** 45 48N 95 21W
Foraker, *OK, U.S.A.* **93 B7** 36 52N 96 34W
Foraker, Mt., *AK, U.S.A.* **61 E10** 62 58N 151 24W
Forbes, *ND, U.S.A.* **91 E7** 45 57N 98 47W
Forbing, *LA, U.S.A.* **75 B2** 32 24N 93 44W
Ford, *KS, U.S.A.* **74 D4** 37 38N 99 45W
Ford ➞, *MI, U.S.A.* **79 D4** 45 41N 87 9W
Ford City, *CA, U.S.A.* **65 H7** 35 9N 119 27W
Ford City, *PA, U.S.A.* **95 D3** 40 46N 79 32W
Ford County ☆, *IL, U.S.A.* **71 C5** 40 30N 88 10W
Ford County ☆, *KS, U.S.A.* **74 D4** 37 45N 100 0W
Ford Dry L., *CA, U.S.A.* **65 K12** 33 37N 114 59W
Ford I., *HI, U.S.A.* **69 K14** 21 22N 157 58W
Ford River, *MI, U.S.A.* **79 D4** 45 41N 87 8W
Fording, *B.C., Canada* **185 H6** 50 12N 114 52W
Fordland, *MO, U.S.A.* **82 D4** 37 9N 92 57W
Fordoche, *LA, U.S.A.* **75 D4** 30 36N 91 37W
Fords Prairie, *WA, U.S.A.* **101 D3** 46 44N 122 59W
Fordsville, *KY, U.S.A.* **96 C6** 37 38N 86 43W
Fordville, *ND, U.S.A.* **91 B8** 48 13N 97 48W
Fordyce, *AR, U.S.A.* **63 E3** 33 49N 92 25W
Fordyce, *NE, U.S.A.* **84 B8** 42 42N 97 22W
Foreman, *AR, U.S.A.* **63 E1** 33 43N 94 24W
Foremost, *Alta., Canada* **185 J9** 49 26N 111 34W
Forest, *LA, U.S.A.* **75 B4** 32 47N 91 25W
Forest, *MS, U.S.A.* **81 D4** 32 22N 89 29W
Forest, *OH, U.S.A.* **92 C3** 40 48N 83 31W
Forest, *VA, U.S.A.* **102 D5** 37 22N 79 17W
Forest ➞, *ND, U.S.A.* **91 B8** 48 21N 97 9W
Forest Acres, *SC, U.S.A.* **90 D5** 34 1N 80 58W
Forest Center, *MN, U.S.A.* **80 C7** 47 48N 91 19W
Forest City, *IA, U.S.A.* **73 B5** 43 16N 93 39W
Forest City, *NC, U.S.A.* **90 C4** 35 20N 81 52W
Forest City, *PA, U.S.A.* **95 C7** 41 39N 75 28W
Forest County ☆, *PA, U.S.A.* **95 C3** 41 30N 79 10W
Forest County ☆, *WI, U.S.A.* **103 C5** 45 35N 88 45W
Forest Dale, *VT, U.S.A.* **86 C1** 43 48N 73 4W
Forest Grove, *B.C., Canada* **187 D13** 51 46N 121 5W
Forest Grove, *OR, U.S.A.* **94 B2** 45 31N 123 7W
Forest Heights, *MD, U.S.A.* **119 C3** 38 48N 77 0W
Forest Hill, *Dallas-Fort Worth, U.S.A.* **109 B2** 32 40N 97 16W
Forest Hill, *LA, U.S.A.* **75 C3** 31 3N 92 32W
Forest Hill, *MD, U.S.A.* **77 A4** 39 35N 76 23W
Forest Hill, *San Francisco, U.S.A.* **118 B2** 37 45N 122 27W
Forest Hills, *NY, U.S.A.* **114 B3** 40 42N 73 51W
Forest Hills, *Pittsburgh, U.S.A.* **116 B2** 40 25N 79 51W
Forest Home, *AL, U.S.A.* **60 E4** 31 52N 86 50W
Forest Lake, *MN, U.S.A.* **80 E6** 45 17N 92 59W
Forest Park, *Chicago, U.S.A.* **108 B2** 41 51N 87 47W
Forest Park, *GA, U.S.A.* **68 C2** 33 37N 84 22W
Forest Park, *MO, U.S.A.* **117 B2** 38 38N 90 16W
Forest Park, *OH, U.S.A.* **92 D2** 39 17N 84 30W
Forest Park, *Portland, U.S.A.* **116 A1** 45 34N 122 46W
Forest River, *ND, U.S.A.* **91 B8** 48 13N 97 28W
Forest View, *Chicago, U.S.A.* **108 C2** 41 48N 87 47W
Forestbrook, *SC, U.S.A.* **90 E7** 33 43N 78 58W
Forestburg, *Alta., Canada* **185 F8** 52 35N 112 1W
Foresthill, *CA, U.S.A.* **64 D6** 39 1N 120 49W
Foreston, *MN, U.S.A.* **80 E5** 45 44N 93 43W
Forestville, *Qué., Canada* **177 C13** 48 48N 69 2W
Forestville, *MD, U.S.A.* **77 B4** 38 50N 76 52W
Forestville, *MI, U.S.A.* **79 F9** 43 40N 82 37W
Forestville, *NY, U.S.A.* **89 C1** 42 28N 79 10W
Forestville, *OH, U.S.A.* **92 D2** 39 4N 84 20W
Forestville, *WI, U.S.A.* **103 D6** 44 41N 87 29W
Forgan, *OK, U.S.A.* **93 B3** 36 54N 100 32W
Forge Village, *MA, U.S.A.* **78 B3** 42 35N 71 29W
Forget, *Sask., Canada* **182 F9** 49 39N 102 52W
Forillon, Parc Nat. du △, *Qué., Canada* **172 E5** 48 46N 64 12W
Fork River, *Man., Canada* **183 D11** 51 31N 100 1W
Fork Union, *VA, U.S.A.* **102 D6** 37 46N 78 16W
Forked Deer ➞, *TN, U.S.A.* **96 E3** 35 56N 89 35W
Forked River, *NJ, U.S.A.* **87 C2** 39 50N 74 12W
Forkland, *AL, U.S.A.* **60 D3** 32 39N 87 53W
Forks, *WA, U.S.A.* **101 C1** 47 57N 124 23W
Forks of Salmon, *CA, U.S.A.* **64 B3** 41 16N 123 19W
Forkville, *MS, U.S.A.* **81 D4** 32 28N 89 40W
Forman, *ND, U.S.A.* **91 D8** 46 7N 97 38W
Forrest, *IL, U.S.A.* **71 C5** 40 45N 88 25W
Forrest, *NM, U.S.A.* **88 C7** 34 48N 103 36W
Forrest City, *AR, U.S.A.* **63 C5** 35 1N 90 47W
Forrest County ☆, *MS, U.S.A.* **81 E4** 31 10N 89 13W
Forreston, *IL, U.S.A.* **71 A4** 42 8N 89 35W
Forsyth, *GA, U.S.A.* **68 C3** 33 2N 83 56W
Forsyth, *IL, U.S.A.* **71 D5** 39 56N 88 57W
Forsyth, *MO, U.S.A.* **82 E3** 36 41N 93 6W
Forsyth, *MT, U.S.A.* **83 D11** 46 16N 106 41W
Forsyth County ☆, *GA, U.S.A.* **68 B2** 34 15N 84 5W
Forsyth County ☆, *NC, U.S.A.* **90 B5** 36 10N 80 15W
Forsythe, *Qué., Canada* **176 C6** 48 14N 76 26W
Fort A.P. Hill Military Res., *VA, U.S.A.* **102 C7** 38 7N 77 13W
Fort Adams, *MS, U.S.A.* **81 E2** 31 5N 91 33W
Fort Albany, *Ont., Canada* **191 G9** 52 15N 81 35W
Fort Alexander, *Man., Canada* **183 E15** 50 36N 96 17W
Fort Ann, *NY, U.S.A.* **86 C1** 43 25N 73 29W
Fort Apache Indian Reservation, *AZ, U.S.A.* **62 D6** 33 50N 110 0W
Fort Ashby, *WV, U.S.A.* **77 A2** 39 30N 78 46W
Fort Assiniboine, *Alta., Canada* **184 D6** 54 20N 114 45W
Fort Atkinson, *IA, U.S.A.* **73 B7** 43 9N 91 56W
Fort Atkinson, *WI, U.S.A.* **103 F5** 42 56N 88 50W
Fort Belknap Agency, *MT, U.S.A.* **83 B9** 48 29N 108 45W
Fort Belknap Indian Reservation, *MT, U.S.A.* **83 B9** 48 20N 108 40W
Fort Bend County ☆, *TX, U.S.A.* **99 H12** 29 34N 95 49W
Fort Benning Military Reservation, *GA, U.S.A.* **68 D2** 32 21N 84 48W
Fort Benton, *MT, U.S.A.* **83 C7** 47 49N 110 40W
Fort Berthold Indian Reservation, *ND, U.S.A.* **91 C3** 47 45N 102 15W
Fort Bidwell, *CA, U.S.A.* **64 B6** 41 52N 120 9W
Fort Bidwell Indian Reservation, *CA, U.S.A.* **64 B6** 41 52N 120 12W
Fort Bliss Military Reservation, *U.S.A.* **88 F4** 31 49N 106 25W
Fort Bowie Nat. Historic Site △, *AZ, U.S.A.* **62 E6** 32 9N 109 22W
Fort Bragg, *CA, U.S.A.* **64 D3** 39 26N 123 48W
Fort Bragg Military Reservation, *NC, U.S.A.* **90 C6** 35 9N 79 0W
Fort Branch, *IN, U.S.A.* **72 E3** 38 15N 87 35W
Fort Bridger, *WY, U.S.A.* **104 E2** 41 19N 110 23W
Fort Calhoun, *NE, U.S.A.* **84 C9** 41 27N 96 2W
Fort Campbell, *TN, U.S.A.* **96 D5** 36 38N 87 26W
Fort Caroline Nat. Memorial △, *U.S.A.* **67 A7** 30 23N 81 30W
Fort Chaffee, *AR, U.S.A.* **63 C1** 35 19N 94 18W
Fort Chipewyan, *Alta., Canada* **189 E10** 58 42N 111 8W
Fort Clatsop Nat. Memorial △, *U.S.A.* **94 A2** 46 8N 123 53W
Fort Cobb, *OK, U.S.A.* **93 C5** 35 6N 98 26W
Fort Cobb Res., *OK, U.S.A.* **93 C5** 35 10N 98 27W
Fort Coffee, *OK, U.S.A.* **93 C9** 35 17N 94 35W
Fort Collins, *CO, U.S.A.* **66 B5** 40 35N 105 5W
Fort-Coulonge, *Qué., Canada* **176 F6** 45 50N 76 45W
Fort Craig Nat. Historic Site △, *NM, U.S.A.* **88 D4** 33 38N 106 59W
Fort Davis, *AL, U.S.A.* **60 D5** 32 15N 85 43W
Fort Davis, *TX, U.S.A.* **98 G4** 30 35N 103 54W
Fort Davis Nat. Historic Site △, *TX, U.S.A.* **98 G4** 30 35N 103 54W
Fort De Soto, *Tampa, U.S.A.* **119 D2** 27 36N 82 44W
Fort De Soto Park, *Tampa, U.S.A.* **119 D2** 27 37N 82 43W
Fort Defiance, *AZ, U.S.A.* **62 B6** 35 45N 109 5W
Fort Deposit, *AL, U.S.A.* **60 E4** 31 59N 86 35W
Fort Dick, *CA, U.S.A.* **64 B2** 41 52N 124 9W
Fort Dodge, *IA, U.S.A.* **73 C4** 42 30N 94 11W
Fort Donelson Nat. Battlefield △, *TN, U.S.A.* **96 D5** 36 29N 87 51W
Fort Drum, *FL, U.S.A.* **67 D8** 27 32N 80 48W
Fort Drum Military Reservation, *NY, U.S.A.* **89 A5** 44 10N 75 35W
Fort Duchesne, *UT, U.S.A.* **100 C6** 40 17N 109 52W
Fort Dupont Park, *DC, U.S.A.* **119 B4** 38 52N 76 56W
Fort Edward, *NY, U.S.A.* **89 B7** 43 16N 73 35W
Fort Eustis, *VA, U.S.A.* **102 D8** 37 7N 76 34W
Fort Fairfield, *ME, U.S.A.* **76 B6** 46 46N 67 50W
Fort Foote Village, *MD, U.S.A.* **119 C3** 38 46N 77 1W
Fort Frances, *Ont., Canada* **180 D3** 48 36N 93 24W
Fort Franklin = Déline, *N.W.T., Canada* **189 C8** 65 11N 123 25W
Fort Fraser, *B.C., Canada* **186 A10** 54 4N 124 33W
Fort Frederica Nat. Monument △, *GA, U.S.A.* **68 E5** 31 13N 81 23W
Fort Gaines, *GA, U.S.A.* **68 E1** 31 36N 85 3W
Fort Garland, *CO, U.S.A.* **66 E5** 37 26N 105 26W
Fort Gay, *WV, U.S.A.* **102 C2** 38 7N 82 36W
Fort George = Chisasibi, *Qué., Canada* **175 C2** 53 50N 79 0W
Fort George = Prince George, *B.C., Canada* **187 B12** 53 55N 122 50W
Fort Gibson, *OK, U.S.A.* **93 C8** 35 48N 95 15W
Fort Gibson L., *OK, U.S.A.* **93 C8** 35 52N 95 14W
Fort Good Hope, *N.W.T., Canada* **188 C7** 66 14N 128 40W
Fort Gordon Military Reservation, *GA, U.S.A.* **68 C4** 33 25N 82 10W
Fort Hall, *ID, U.S.A.* **70 F6** 43 2N 112 26W
Fort Hall Indian Reservation, *ID, U.S.A.* **70 F6** 43 2N 112 5W
Fort Hancock, *TX, U.S.A.* **98 F2** 31 18N 105 51W
Fort Hill, *OH, U.S.A.* **92 D2** 39 7N 84 49W
Fort Hood Military Reservation, *TX, U.S.A.* **99 F10** 31 8N 97 33W
Fort Hope, *Ont., Canada* **181 A9** 51 30N 88 0W
Fort Huachuca, *AZ, U.S.A.* **62 F5** 31 35N 110 20W
Fort Hunter Liggett, *CA, U.S.A.* **65 H5** 35 58N 121 12W
Fort Irwin, *CA, U.S.A.* **65 H10** 35 16N 116 41W
Fort Jackson Military Reservation, *SC, U.S.A.* **90 D5** 34 3N 80 55W
Fort Jennings, *OH, U.S.A.* **92 C2** 40 54N 84 18W
Fort Jesup, *LA, U.S.A.* **75 C2** 31 37N 93 24W
Fort Jones, *CA, U.S.A.* **64 B4** 41 36N 122 51W
Fort Kent, *ME, U.S.A.* **76 A5** 47 15N 68 36W
Fort Klamath, *OR, U.S.A.* **94 E3** 42 42N 122 0W
Fort Knox Military Reservation, *KY, U.S.A.* **96 C6** 37 55N 86 5W
Fort Laramie, *WY, U.S.A.* **104 D8** 42 13N 104 31W
Fort Larned Nat. Historic Site △, *KS, U.S.A.* **74 C4** 38 11N 99 13W
Fort Lauderdale, *FL, U.S.A.* **67 E8** 26 7N 80 8W
Fort Lauderdale Executive ✕, *Miami, U.S.A.* **112 A2** 26 11N 80 10W
Fort Lauderdale-Hollywood International ✕ (FLL), *FL, U.S.A.* **67 E8** 26 4N 80 10W
Fort Lawn, *SC, U.S.A.* **90 D5** 34 42N 80 54W
Fort Leavenworth, *KS, U.S.A.* **74 B9** 39 23N 94 56W
Fort Lee, *NJ, U.S.A.* **114 A3** 40 50N 73 58W
Fort Leonard Wood Military Reservation, *MO, U.S.A.* **82 D4** 37 48N 92 10W
Fort Lewis Military Reservation, *WA, U.S.A.* **101 C3** 47 3N 122 35W
Fort Liard, *N.W.T., Canada* **189 D8** 60 14N 123 30W
Fort Loudon, *PA, U.S.A.* **95 E5** 39 54N 77 54W
Fort Loudoun L., *TN, U.S.A.* **97 E8** 35 47N 84 15W
Fort Lupton, *CO, U.S.A.* **66 B6** 40 5N 104 49W
Fort McCoy, *WI, U.S.A.* **103 D3** 44 0N 90 41W
Fort McDermitt Indian Reservation, *OR, U.S.A.* **94 E8** 41 56N 117 43W
Fort McDowell Indian Reservation, *AZ, U.S.A.* **62 D4** 33 40N 111 50W
Fort MacKay, *Alta., Canada* **184 A9** 57 12N 111 41W
Fort Macleod, *Alta., Canada* **185 J7** 49 45N 113 30W
Fort McMurray, *Alta., Canada* **184 B9** 56 44N 111 7W
Fort McPherson, *N.W.T., Canada* **188 C6** 67 30N 134 55W
Fort Madison, *IA, U.S.A.* **73 E7** 40 38N 91 27W
Fort Matanzas Nat. Monument △, *U.S.A.* **67 B7** 29 43N 81 14W
Fort Meade, *FL, U.S.A.* **67 D7** 27 45N 81 48W
Fort Mill, *SC, U.S.A.* **90 C5** 35 2N 80 57W
Fort Mitchell, *AL, U.S.A.* **60 D5** 32 20N 85 1W
Fort Mitchell, *KY, U.S.A.* **107 B1** 39 3N 84 32W
Fort Mohave Indian Reservation, *AZ, U.S.A.* **62 C1** 34 55N 114 35W
Fort Morgan, *CO, U.S.A.* **66 B7** 40 15N 103 48W
Fort Myers, *FL, U.S.A.* **67 E7** 26 39N 81 52W
Fort Myers Beach, *FL, U.S.A.* **67 E7** 26 26N 81 52W
Fort Myers S.W. Florida Regional ✕ (RSW), *FL, U.S.A.* **67 E7** 26 32N 81 45W
Fort Myers Shores, *FL, U.S.A.* **67 E7** 26 43N 81 45W
Fort Necessity Nat. Battlefield △, *PA, U.S.A.* **95 E3** 39 49N 79 36W
Fort Nelson, *B.C., Canada* **189 E8** 58 50N 122 44W
Fort Nelson ➞, *B.C., Canada* **189 E8** 59 32N 124 0W
Fort Niobrara Nat. Wildlife Refuge △, *NE, U.S.A.* **84 B5** 42 54N 100 28W
Fort Norman = Tulita, *N.W.T., Canada* **189 D7** 64 57N 125 30W
Fort Oglethorpe, *GA, U.S.A.* **68 B1** 34 57N 85 16W
Fort Payne, *AL, U.S.A.* **60 B5** 34 26N 85 43W
Fort Peck, *MT, U.S.A.* **83 B11** 48 1N 106 27W
Fort Peck Dam, *MT, U.S.A.* **83 C11** 48 0N 106 26W
Fort Peck Indian Reservation, *MT, U.S.A.* **83 B12** 48 30N 105 30W
Fort Peck L., *MT, U.S.A.* **83 C11** 48 0N 106 26W
Fort Pierce, *FL, U.S.A.* **67 D8** 27 27N 80 20W
Fort Pierre, *SD, U.S.A.* **91 F5** 44 21N 100 22W
Fort Pierre Nat. Grassland, *SD, U.S.A.* **91 F5** 44 10N 100 12W
Fort Plain, *NY, U.S.A.* **89 C6** 42 56N 74 37W
Fort Polk Military Reservation, *LA, U.S.A.* **75 C2** 31 2N 93 13W
Fort Providence, *N.W.T., Canada* **189 D9** 61 3N 117 40W
Fort Qu'Appelle, *Sask., Canada* **182 E8** 50 45N 103 50W
Fort Raleigh Nat. Historic Site △, *NC, U.S.A.* **90 C10** 35 56N 75 43W
Fort Randall Dam, *SD, U.S.A.* **91 G7** 43 4N 98 34W
Fort Ransom, *ND, U.S.A.* **91 D8** 46 31N 97 56W
Fort Recovery, *OH, U.S.A.* **92 C2** 40 25N 84 47W
Fort Resolution, *N.W.T., Canada* **189 D10** 61 10N 113 40W
Fort Riley, *KS, U.S.A.* **74 B7** 39 10N 96 42W
Fort Ripley, *MN, U.S.A.* **80 D4** 46 10N 94 22W
Fort Robinson, *NE, U.S.A.* **84 B2** 42 40N 103 28W
Fort Rucker Military Reservation, *AL, U.S.A.* **60 E5** 31 20N 85 43W
Fort Rupert = Waskaganish, *Qué., Canada* **175 C2** 51 30N 78 40W
Fort St. James, *B.C., Canada* **189 F8** 54 30N 124 10W
Fort St. John, *B.C., Canada* **189 E8** 56 15N 120 50W
Fort Saskatchewan, *Alta., Canada* **184 E7** 53 40N 113 15W
Fort Scott, *KS, U.S.A.* **74 D9** 37 50N 94 42W
Fort Scott Nat. Historic Site △, *KS, U.S.A.* **74 D9** 37 51N 94 42W
Fort Severn, *Ont., Canada* **191 F8** 56 0N 87 40W
Fort Shawnee, *OH, U.S.A.* **92 C2** 40 42N 84 7W
Fort Sill Military Res., *OK, U.S.A.* **93 D5** 34 41N 98 30W
Fort Simpson, *N.W.T., Canada* **189 D8** 61 45N 121 15W
Fort Smith, *Alta., Canada* **189 D10** 60 0N 111 51W
Fort Smith, *AR, U.S.A.* **63 C1** 35 23N 94 25W
Fort Smith Nat. Historic Site △, *AR, U.S.A.* **63 C1** 35 23N 94 26W
Fort Snelling State Park △, *Minneapolis-St. Paul, U.S.A.* **113 B2** 44 53N 93 10W
Fort Stanton, *NM, U.S.A.* **88 D5** 33 30N 105 31W
Fort Stewart Military Reservation, *GA, U.S.A.* **68 E5** 31 52N 81 37W
Fort Stockton, *TX, U.S.A.* **98 G5** 30 53N 102 53W
Fort Sumner, *NM, U.S.A.* **88 C6** 34 28N 104 15W
Fort Supply, *OK, U.S.A.* **93 B4** 36 35N 99 35W
Fort Thomas, *KY, U.S.A.* **97 A8** 39 4N 84 26W
Fort Thompson, *SD, U.S.A.* **91 F6** 44 3N 99 26W
Fort Totten, *ND, U.S.A.* **91 C7** 47 59N 99 0W
Fort Totten Indian Reservation = Spirit Lake Indian Reservation, *ND, U.S.A.* **91 C7** 47 58N 99 0W
Fort Towson, *OK, U.S.A.* **93 D8** 34 1N 95 10W
Fort Union Nat. Monument △, *U.S.A.* **88 B5** 35 54N 105 1W
Fort Union Trading Post Nat. Historic Site △, *ND, U.S.A.* **91 B1** 48 1N 104 1W
Fort Valley, *GA, U.S.A.* **68 D3** 32 33N 83 53W
Fort Vancouver Nat. Historic Site △, *WA, U.S.A.* **101 E3** 45 37N 122 39W
Fort Vermilion, *Alta., Canada* **189 E9** 58 24N 116 0W
Fort Walton Beach, *FL, U.S.A.* **67 A2** 30 25N 86 36W
Fort Washakie, *WY, U.S.A.* **104 C4** 43 0N 108 53W
Fort Washington, *MD, U.S.A.* **77 B3** 38 42N 77 3W
Fort Wayne, *IN, U.S.A.* **72 B5** 41 4N 85 9W
Fort White, *FL, U.S.A.* **67 B6** 29 55N 82 43W
Fort Worth, *TX, U.S.A.* **99 E10** 32 43N 97 19W
Fort Worth-Meacham International ✕, *Dallas-Fort Worth, U.S.A.* **109 B1** 32 49N 97 21W
Fort Wright, *KY, U.S.A.* **107 B1** 39 3N 84 32W
Fort Yates, *ND, U.S.A.* **91 D5** 46 5N 100 38W
Fort Yukon, *AK, U.S.A.* **61 C11** 66 34N 145 16W
Fort Yuma Indian Reservation, *CA, U.S.A.* **65 L12** 32 45N 114 35W
Forteau, *Nfld. & L., Canada* **174 A4** 51 28N 56 58W
Fortescue, *NJ, U.S.A.* **87 C1** 39 12N 75 12W
Fortín, *Veracruz, Mexico* **221 F4** 18 54N 97 0W
Fortin, L., *Qué., Canada* **172 C2** 50 50N 67 46W
Fortine, *MT, U.S.A.* **83 B3** 48 46N 114 54W
Fortress Mt., *WY, U.S.A.* **104 B3** 44 20N 109 48W
Fortsonia, *GA, U.S.A.* **68 B4** 34 1N 82 47W
Fortuna, *CA, U.S.A.* **64 C2** 40 36N 124 9W
Fortuna, *MO, U.S.A.* **82 C4** 38 34N 92 48W
Fortuna, *ND, U.S.A.* **91 B2** 48 55N 103 47W
Fortuna Ledge = Marshall, *AK, U.S.A.* **61 F7** 61 53N 162 5W
Fortune, *Nfld. & L., Canada* **174 E5** 47 4N 55 50W
Fortune B., *Nfld. & L., Canada* **174 E5** 47 30N 55 22W
Fortville, *IN, U.S.A.* **72 D5** 39 56N 85 51W
Fosheim Pen., *N.W.T., Canada* **190 B9** 80 0N 85 0W
Foss, *OK, U.S.A.* **93 C4** 35 27N 99 10W
Foss L., *OK, U.S.A.* **93 C4** 35 33N 99 11W
Fossil, *OR, U.S.A.* **94 B5** 45 0N 120 9W
Fossil Butte Nat. Monument △, *WY, U.S.A.* **104 E2** 41 50N 110 27W
Fossil L., *OR, U.S.A.* **94 D5** 43 19N 120 25W
Fosston, *Sask., Canada* **182 C8** 52 12N 103 49W
Fosston, *MN, U.S.A.* **80 C3** 47 35N 95 45W
Foster, *Qué., Canada* **177 F10** 45 17N 72 30W
Foster, *KY, U.S.A.* **97 B8** 38 48N 84 13W
Foster, *NE, U.S.A.* **84 B8** 42 16N 97 40W
Foster, *OR, U.S.A.* **94 C3** 44 25N 122 40W
Foster, *RI, U.S.A.* **78 C3** 41 47N 71 44W
Foster ➞, *Sask., Canada* **189 E11** 55 47N 105 49W

Foster City, MI, U.S.A. 79 D4 45 58N 87 45W
Foster County ☆, ND, U.S.A. 91 C7 47 30N 99 0W
Foster L., OR, U.S.A. 94 E6 42 59N 119 15W
Foster Village, HI, U.S.A. 69 K14 21 21N 157 55W
Fosters, AL, U.S.A. 60 C3 33 6N 87 41W
Fostoria, IA, U.S.A. 73 B3 43 15N 95 9W
Fostoria, KS, U.S.A. 74 B7 39 26N 96 30W
Fostoria, OH, U.S.A. 92 B3 41 10N 83 25W
Fouke, AR, U.S.A. 63 E2 33 16N 93 53W
Fountain, CO, U.S.A. 66 D6 38 41N 104 42W
Fountain, FL, U.S.A. 67 A3 30 29N 85 25W
Fountain, MI, U.S.A. 79 E5 44 3N 86 11W
Fountain, MN, U.S.A. 80 G6 43 45N 92 8W
Fountain City, IN, U.S.A. 72 D6 39 57N 84 55W
Fountain City, WI, U.S.A. 103 D2 44 8N 91 43W
Fountain County ☆, IN, U.S.A. 72 C3 40 5N 87 15W
Fountain Cr. →, CO, U.S.A. 66 D6 38 15N 104 36W
Fountain Green, UT, U.S.A. 100 D4 39 38N 111 38W
Fountain Head, MD, U.S.A. 77 A3 39 42N 77 42W
Fountain Hill, AR, U.S.A. 63 E4 33 21N 91 51W
Fountain Hills, AZ, U.S.A. 62 D4 33 37N 111 43W
Fountain Inn, SC, U.S.A. 90 D3 34 42N 82 12W
Fountain Run, KY, U.S.A. 97 D7 36 43N 85 57W
Four Corners, OR, U.S.A. 94 C3 44 56N 122 58W
Four Corners, WY, U.S.A. 104 B8 44 5N 104 8W
Four Corners, UT, U.S.A. 100 F6 37 0N 109 3W
Four League B., LA, U.S.A. 75 E4 29 10N 91 13W
Four Mountains, Is. of, AK, U.S.A. 61 K5 53 0N 170 0W
Four Oaks, NC, U.S.A. 90 C7 35 27N 78 26W
Four Town, MN, U.S.A. 80 B3 48 17N 95 20W
Fourchu, N.S., Canada 173 H9 45 43N 60 17W
Fourmont L., Nfld. & L., Canada 172 A9 52 5N 60 27W
Fournier, L., Qué., Canada 172 B4 51 33N 65 25W
Fourteen Mile Pt., MI, U.S.A. 79 B2 47 0N 89 10W
Fowblesburg, MD, U.S.A. 77 A4 39 34N 76 50W
Fowler, CA, U.S.A. 65 G7 36 38N 119 41W
Fowler, CO, U.S.A. 66 D6 38 8N 104 2W
Fowler, IN, U.S.A. 72 C3 40 37N 87 19W
Fowler, KS, U.S.A. 74 D3 37 23N 100 12W
Fowler, MI, U.S.A. 79 G7 43 0N 84 45W
Fowlerton, IN, U.S.A. 72 C5 40 25N 85 34W
Fowlerton, TX, U.S.A. 99 J9 28 28N 98 48W
Fowlerville, MI, U.S.A. 79 G7 42 40N 84 4W
Fowlstown, GA, U.S.A. 68 F2 30 48N 84 33W
Fox, OK, U.S.A. 93 D6 34 22N 97 30W
Fox →, IL, U.S.A. 71 B5 41 21N 88 50W
Fox →, MO, U.S.A. 82 A5 40 17N 91 30W
Fox →, WI, U.S.A. 103 D5 44 32N 88 0W
Fox Chapel, Pittsburgh, U.S.A. 116 A2 40 30N 79 52W
Fox Creek, Alta., Canada 184 D4 54 24N 116 48W
Fox Is., AK, U.S.A. 61 K6 53 0N 168 0W
Fox Lake, Alta., Canada 189 E10 58 28N 114 31W
Fox Lake, IL, U.S.A. 71 A5 42 24N 88 11W
Fox Lake, WI, U.S.A. 103 E5 43 34N 88 55W
Fox Mt., Yukon, Canada 189 D6 61 55N 133 22W
Fox Point, Milwaukee, U.S.A. 112 B2 43 9N 87 54W
Fox Pt., Milwaukee, U.S.A. 112 A2 43 10N 87 52W
Fox Valley, Sask., Canada 182 E2 50 30N 109 25W
Foxboro, MA, U.S.A. 78 B3 42 4N 71 16W
Foxe Basin, Nunavut, Canada 191 D10 66 0N 77 0W
Foxe Chan., Nunavut, Canada 191 E9 65 0N 80 0W
Foxe Pen., Nunavut, Canada 191 E10 65 0N 76 0W
Foxfield, Denver, U.S.A. 109 C3 39 35N 104 47W
Foxpark, WY, U.S.A. 104 E6 41 5N 106 9W
Foxville, Ont., Canada 181 B15 50 4N 81 38W
Foxworth, MS, U.S.A. 81 E4 31 14N 89 52W
Foyil, OK, U.S.A. 93 B8 36 26N 95 31W
Frametown, WV, U.S.A. 102 C4 38 38N 80 52W
Framingham, MA, U.S.A. 78 B3 42 18N 71 24W
Frances, WA, U.S.A. 101 D2 46 33N 123 30W
Frances →, Yukon, Canada 189 D7 60 16N 129 10W
Frances, L., MT, U.S.A. 83 B5 48 16N 112 13W
Frances L., Yukon, Canada 189 D7 61 23N 129 30W
Francestown, NH, U.S.A. 86 D3 42 58N 71 48W
Francesville, IN, U.S.A. 72 C4 40 59N 86 53W
Francis, Sask., Canada 182 E8 50 6N 103 52W
Francis, OK, U.S.A. 93 D7 34 52N 96 36W
Francis, UT, U.S.A. 100 C4 40 37N 111 17W
Francis, L., NH, U.S.A. 86 A3 45 2N 71 20W
Francis Case, L., SD, U.S.A. 91 G7 43 4N 98 34W
Francis Creek, WI, U.S.A. 103 D6 44 12N 87 44W
Francis E. Walter Res., PA, U.S.A. 87 A1 41 8N 75 44W
Francis Marion Nat. Forest, SC, U.S.A. 90 E6 33 10N 79 40W
Francisco Ignacio Madero, Chiapas, Mexico 222 D3 15 21N 92 24W
Francisco Ignacio Madero, Chiapas, Mexico 222 C3 16 48N 93 46W
Francisco Ignacio Madero, Coahuila, Mexico 214 E1 25 45N 103 20W
Francisco Ignacio Madero, Durango, Mexico 217 C6 24 26N 104 18W
Francisco Ignacio Madero, Hidalgo, Mexico 219 B8 20 45N 99 19W
Francisco Ignacio Madero, Nayarit, Mexico 216 F6 21 39N 104 50W
Francisco Ignacio Madero, Quintana Roo, Mexico 223 B5 20 9N 88 1W
Francisco Ignacio Madero, Zacatecas, Mexico 217 D8 23 55N 102 56W
Francisco Ignacio Madero, Presa, Chihuahua, Mexico 213 E10 28 10N 105 37W
Francisco R. Serrano, Baja Calif., Mexico 210 B3 31 20N 115 33W
Francisco Villa, Chiapas, Mexico 222 B3 17 0N 93 28W
Francisco Zarco, Baja Calif., Mexico 210 A2 32 8N 116 34W
Francisco Zarco, Presa, Durango, Mexico 217 B7 25 16N 103 47W
François, Nfld. & L., Canada 174 E4 47 35N 56 45W
François L., B.C., Canada 186 A9 54 0N 125 30W
Franconia, NH, U.S.A. 86 B3 44 14N 71 44W
Franconia, VA, U.S.A. 119 C3 38 47N 77 7W
Francs Pk., WY, U.S.A. 104 C3 43 58N 109 20W
Frank Church River of No Return Wilderness, ID, U.S.A. 70 E4 44 41N 114 25W
Frank Rae, Mt., Yukon, Canada 189 D5 64 28N 138 33W
Frankenmuth, MI, U.S.A. 79 F8 43 20N 83 44W
Frankewing, TN, U.S.A. 96 E6 35 12N 86 51W
Frankford, Ont., Canada 179 C9 44 12N 77 36W
Frankford, DE, U.S.A. 77 B5 38 31N 75 14W
Frankford, MO, U.S.A. 82 B5 39 29N 91 19W
Frankford, WV, U.S.A. 102 D4 37 56N 80 23W
Frankfort, IN, U.S.A. 72 C4 40 17N 86 31W
Frankfort, KS, U.S.A. 74 B7 39 42N 96 25W
Frankfort, KY, U.S.A. 97 B8 38 12N 84 52W
Frankfort, ME, U.S.A. 76 D5 44 37N 68 53W
Frankfort, MI, U.S.A. 79 E5 44 38N 86 14W
Frankfort, OH, U.S.A. 92 D3 39 24N 83 11W
Frankfort, SD, U.S.A. 91 F7 44 53N 98 18W
Franklin, AZ, U.S.A. 62 E6 32 41N 109 5W
Franklin, GA, U.S.A. 68 C1 33 17N 85 6W
Franklin, ID, U.S.A. 70 G7 42 1N 111 48W
Franklin, IL, U.S.A. 71 D3 39 37N 90 3W
Franklin, IN, U.S.A. 72 D4 39 29N 86 3W
Franklin, KS, U.S.A. 74 D9 37 32N 94 42W
Franklin, KY, U.S.A. 96 D6 36 43N 86 35W
Franklin, LA, U.S.A. 75 E4 29 48N 91 30W
Franklin, ME, U.S.A. 76 D5 44 35N 68 14W
Franklin, MA, U.S.A. 78 B3 42 5N 71 24W
Franklin, MN, U.S.A. 80 F4 44 32N 94 53W
Franklin, NC, U.S.A. 90 C2 35 11N 83 23W
Franklin, NH, U.S.A. 86 C3 43 27N 71 39W
Franklin, NJ, U.S.A. 87 A2 41 7N 74 35W
Franklin, NY, U.S.A. 89 C5 42 21N 75 10W
Franklin, NE, U.S.A. 84 D7 40 6N 98 57W
Franklin, OH, U.S.A. 92 D2 39 34N 84 18W
Franklin, PA, U.S.A. 95 C3 41 24N 79 50W
Franklin, TN, U.S.A. 96 E6 35 55N 86 52W
Franklin, TX, U.S.A. 99 F11 31 2N 96 29W
Franklin, VA, U.S.A. 102 E8 36 41N 76 56W
Franklin, WV, U.S.A. 102 C5 38 39N 79 20W
Franklin, Pt., AK, U.S.A. 61 A8 70 55N 158 48W
Franklin B., N.W.T., Canada 188 C7 69 45N 126 0W
Franklin County ☆, AL, U.S.A. 60 B3 34 21N 87 42W
Franklin County ☆, AR, U.S.A. 63 C2 35 29N 93 50W
Franklin County ☆, FL, U.S.A. 67 B4 29 50N 84 45W
Franklin County ☆, GA, U.S.A. 68 B3 34 20N 83 10W
Franklin County ☆, ID, U.S.A. 70 G7 42 10N 111 50W
Franklin County ☆, IL, U.S.A. 71 E4 38 0N 89 0W
Franklin County ☆, IN, U.S.A. 72 D5 39 25N 85 5W
Franklin County ☆, IA, U.S.A. 73 C5 42 45N 93 25W
Franklin County ☆, KS, U.S.A. 74 C8 38 30N 95 15W
Franklin County ☆, KY, U.S.A. 97 B8 38 15N 84 55W
Franklin County ☆, ME, U.S.A. 76 D3 45 0N 70 30W
Franklin County ☆, MA, U.S.A. 78 B2 42 30N 72 35W
Franklin County ☆, MS, U.S.A. 81 E3 31 28N 90 54W
Franklin County ☆, MO, U.S.A. 82 C5 38 25N 91 0W
Franklin County ☆, NC, U.S.A. 90 B7 36 0N 78 20W
Franklin County ☆, NY, U.S.A. 89 A6 44 30N 74 15W
Franklin County ☆, NE, U.S.A. 84 D7 40 15N 99 0W
Franklin County ☆, OH, U.S.A. 92 D3 40 0N 83 4W
Franklin County ☆, PA, U.S.A. 95 E5 39 56N 77 40W
Franklin County ☆, TN, U.S.A. 96 E6 35 10N 86 1W
Franklin County ☆, TX, U.S.A. 99 D12 33 11N 95 13W
Franklin County ☆, VA, U.S.A. 102 E5 37 0N 80 0W
Franklin County ☆, VT, U.S.A. 86 B2 44 50N 72 50W
Franklin County ☆, WA, U.S.A. 101 D7 46 30N 119 0W
Franklin D. Roosevelt L., WA, U.S.A. 101 B7 48 18N 118 9W
Franklin Grove, IL, U.S.A. 71 B4 41 51N 89 18W
Franklin L., Nunavut, Canada 191 D6 66 56N 96 3W
Franklin L., NV, U.S.A. 85 B5 40 25N 115 22W
Franklin Mts., N.W.T., Canada 189 C7 65 0N 125 0W
Franklin Parish ☆, LA, U.S.A. 75 B4 32 10N 91 43W
Franklin Park, Boston, U.S.A. 106 B3 42 18N 71 5W
Franklin Park, Chicago, U.S.A. 108 B1 41 55N 87 52W
Franklin Park, VA, U.S.A. 119 B3 38 55N 77 9W
Franklin Res., Los Angeles, U.S.A. 111 B2 34 5N 118 24W
Franklin River, B.C., Canada 186 F10 49 7N 124 48W
Franklin Square, NY, U.S.A. 114 B4 40 42N 73 40W
Franklin Str., Nunavut, Canada 190 C6 72 0N 96 0W
Franklinton, LA, U.S.A. 75 D5 30 51N 90 9W
Franklinton, NC, U.S.A. 90 B7 36 6N 78 27W
Franklinville, NJ, U.S.A. 87 C1 39 37N 75 5W
Franklinville, NY, U.S.A. 89 C2 42 20N 78 27W
Frankston, TX, U.S.A. 99 E12 32 3N 95 30W
Frankton, IN, U.S.A. 72 C5 40 13N 85 46W
Frankville, AL, U.S.A. 60 E2 31 39N 88 9W
Frannie, WY, U.S.A. 104 B4 44 58N 108 37W
Franquelin, Qué., Canada 172 D2 49 18N 67 54W
Franz, Ont., Canada 181 D12 48 25N 84 30W
Fraser, CO, U.S.A. 66 C5 39 57N 105 49W
Fraser →, B.C., Canada 187 F11 49 7N 123 11W
Fraser →, Nfld. & L., Canada 175 B5 56 39N 62 10W
Fraser Lake, B.C., Canada 186 A10 54 0N 124 50W
Fraserdale, Ont., Canada 181 C15 49 55N 81 37W
Fraserville = Rivière-du-Loup, Qué., Canada 177 D13 47 50N 69 30W
Fraserwood, Man., Canada 183 E14 50 38N 97 13W
Frazee, MN, U.S.A. 80 D3 46 44N 95 42W
Frazer, MT, U.S.A. 83 B11 48 3N 106 2W
Frazer, L., Ont., Canada 180 C8 49 15N 88 40W
Frazeysburg, OH, U.S.A. 92 C4 40 7N 82 7W
Frazier Park, CA, U.S.A. 65 J8 34 49N 118 56W
Fred, TX, U.S.A. 99 G13 30 34N 94 10W
Freda, MI, U.S.A. 79 B3 47 8N 88 49W
Frederic, MI, U.S.A. 79 E7 44 47N 84 45W
Frederic, WI, U.S.A. 103 C1 45 40N 92 28W
Frederica, DE, U.S.A. 77 A5 39 1N 75 28W
Frederick, CO, U.S.A. 66 B6 40 6N 104 56W
Frederick, MD, U.S.A. 77 A3 39 25N 77 25W
Frederick, OK, U.S.A. 93 D4 34 23N 99 1W
Frederick, SD, U.S.A. 91 E7 45 50N 98 31W
Frederick County ☆, MD, U.S.A. 77 A3 39 30N 77 25W
Frederick County ☆, VA, U.S.A. 102 B6 39 5N 78 13W
Fredericksburg, IA, U.S.A. 73 C6 42 58N 92 12W
Fredericksburg, TX, U.S.A. 99 G9 30 16N 98 52W
Fredericksburg, VA, U.S.A. 102 C7 38 18N 77 28W
Fredericksburg and Spotsylvania Nat. Military Park △, VA, U.S.A. 102 C7 38 18N 77 43W
Fredericktown, MO, U.S.A. 82 D6 37 34N 90 18W
Fredericktown, OH, U.S.A. 92 C4 40 29N 82 33W
Fredericton, N.B., Canada 173 H3 45 57N 66 40W
Fredericton Junction, N.B., Canada 173 H3 45 41N 66 40W
Frederika, IA, U.S.A. 73 C6 42 53N 92 19W
Frederiksted, U.S. Virgin Is. 105 H18 17 43N 64 53W
Fredonia, AZ, U.S.A. 62 A3 36 57N 112 32W
Fredonia, KS, U.S.A. 74 D8 37 32N 95 49W
Fredonia, KY, U.S.A. 96 C4 37 12N 88 4W
Fredonia, ND, U.S.A. 91 D6 46 20N 99 6W
Fredonia, NY, U.S.A. 89 C1 42 26N 79 20W
Fredonia, PA, U.S.A. 95 C2 41 19N 80 16W
Fredrica, L., Orlando, U.S.A. 115 A3 28 30N 81 18W
Freeborn County ☆, MN, U.S.A. 80 G5 43 40N 93 15W
Freeburg, IL, U.S.A. 71 E4 38 26N 89 55W
Freeburg, MO, U.S.A. 82 C5 38 19N 91 56W
Freedom, OK, U.S.A. 93 B4 36 46N 99 7W
Freedom, WY, U.S.A. 104 D1 42 59N 111 3W
Freedom Park, Charlotte, U.S.A. 107 A1 35 11N 80 50W
Freehold, NJ, U.S.A. 87 B2 40 16N 74 17W
Freel Pk., CA, U.S.A. 64 E7 38 51N 119 54W
Freeland, PA, U.S.A. 95 C7 41 1N 75 54W
Freels, C., Nfld. & L., Canada 174 C7 49 15N 53 30W
Freeman, MO, U.S.A. 82 C2 38 37N 94 30W
Freeman, SD, U.S.A. 91 G8 43 21N 97 26W
Freeman →, Alta., Canada 184 D6 54 19N 114 47W
Freeman, L., IN, U.S.A. 72 C4 40 42N 86 45W
Freeman I., Los Angeles, U.S.A. 111 D4 33 44N 118 9W
Freeport, N.S., Canada 173 J3 44 15N 66 20W
Freeport, FL, U.S.A. 67 A2 30 30N 86 8W
Freeport, IL, U.S.A. 71 A4 42 17N 89 36W
Freeport, KS, U.S.A. 74 D6 37 12N 97 51W
Freeport, ME, U.S.A. 76 E3 43 52N 70 6W
Freeport, MI, U.S.A. 79 G6 42 46N 85 19W
Freeport, MN, U.S.A. 80 E4 45 40N 94 42W
Freeport, NY, U.S.A. 87 B3 40 39N 73 35W
Freeport, PA, U.S.A. 95 D3 40 41N 79 41W
Freeport, TX, U.S.A. 99 J12 28 57N 95 21W
Freer, TX, U.S.A. 99 K9 27 53N 98 37W
Freesoil, MI, U.S.A. 79 E5 44 7N 86 14W
Freestone County ☆, TX, U.S.A. 99 F11 31 44N 96 10W
Freeville, NY, U.S.A. 89 C4 42 31N 76 21W
Frégate, L. de la, Qué., Canada 175 C3 53 15N 74 45W
Freistatt, MO, U.S.A. 82 D3 37 1N 93 54W
Fremont, CA, U.S.A. 64 F5 37 32N 121 57W
Fremont, IN, U.S.A. 72 B6 41 44N 84 56W
Fremont, IA, U.S.A. 73 D6 41 13N 92 26W
Fremont, KY, U.S.A. 96 D4 36 58N 88 37W
Fremont, MI, U.S.A. 79 F6 43 28N 85 57W
Fremont, NC, U.S.A. 90 C8 35 33N 77 58W
Fremont, NE, U.S.A. 84 C9 41 26N 96 30W
Fremont, OH, U.S.A. 92 B3 41 21N 83 7W
Fremont, UT, U.S.A. 100 E4 38 27N 111 37W
Fremont, WI, U.S.A. 103 D5 44 16N 88 52W
Fremont →, UT, U.S.A. 100 E5 38 24N 110 42W
Fremont County ☆, CO, U.S.A. 66 D5 38 30N 105 30W
Fremont County ☆, ID, U.S.A. 70 E7 44 15N 111 20W
Fremont County ☆, IA, U.S.A. 73 E3 40 45N 95 35W
Fremont County ☆, WY, U.S.A. 104 D4 43 0N 108 30W
Fremont I., UT, U.S.A. 100 B3 41 10N 112 21W
Fremont Junction, UT, U.S.A. 100 E4 38 45N 111 23W
Fremont L., WY, U.S.A. 104 D3 42 57N 109 48W
Fremont Nat. Forest, OR, U.S.A. 94 E5 42 20N 120 50W
French →, Ont., Canada 178 A6 46 2N 80 34W
French →, Ont., Canada 181 B16 50 40N 80 59W
French Broad →, NC, U.S.A. 90 C2 35 57N 83 51W
French Broad →, TN, U.S.A. 97 E9 35 58N 83 51W
French Camp, CA, U.S.A. 64 F5 37 53N 121 16W
French Camp, MS, U.S.A. 81 C4 33 18N 89 24W
French Creek, WV, U.S.A. 102 C4 38 53N 80 18W
French Creek →, PA, U.S.A. 95 C3 41 24N 79 50W
French Frigate Shoals, HI, U.S.A. 69 G10 23 45N 166 10W
French Gulch, CA, U.S.A. 64 C4 40 42N 122 38W
French Lick, IN, U.S.A. 72 E4 38 33N 86 37W
French Meadows Res., CA, U.S.A. 64 D6 39 10N 120 40W
French Park, OH, U.S.A. 107 A2 39 11N 84 25W
French Regional Park △, Minneapolis-St. Paul, U.S.A. 113 A1 45 2N 93 26W
French River, Ont., Canada 178 A6 46 2N 80 34W
French River, MN, U.S.A. 80 D7 46 54N 91 54W
French Settlement, LA, U.S.A. 75 D5 30 18N 90 47W
Frenchboro, ME, U.S.A. 76 D5 44 7N 68 22W
Frenchburg, KY, U.S.A. 97 C9 37 57N 83 38W
Frenchglen, OR, U.S.A. 94 E7 42 50N 118 55W
Frenchman Butte, Sask., Canada 182 B2 53 35N 109 38W
Frenchman Cr. →, N. Amer. 83 B10 48 31N 107 10W
Frenchman Cr. →, NE, U.S.A. 84 D5 40 14N 100 50W
Frenchman L., CA, U.S.A. 64 D6 39 54N 120 11W
Frenchman L., NV, U.S.A. 85 F5 36 48N 115 56W
Frenchtown, MT, U.S.A. 83 C3 47 1N 114 14W
Frenchtown, NJ, U.S.A. 87 B1 40 32N 75 4W
Frenchville, ME, U.S.A. 76 A5 47 17N 68 23W
Fresh Meadows, NY, U.S.A. 114 B4 40 44N 73 47W
Fresh Pond, Boston, U.S.A. 106 A3 42 22N 71 8W
Fresnillo, Zacatecas, Mexico 217 D8 23 10N 102 53W
Fresno, CA, U.S.A. 65 G7 36 44N 119 47W
Fresno County ☆, CA, U.S.A. 65 G7 36 40N 120 0W
Fresno Res., MT, U.S.A. 83 B8 48 36N 109 57W
Frewsburg, NY, U.S.A. 89 C1 42 3N 79 10W
Friant, CA, U.S.A. 65 G7 36 59N 119 43W
Friars Point, MS, U.S.A. 81 B3 34 22N 90 38W
Frick Park, Pittsburgh, U.S.A. 116 B2 40 25N 79 54W
Friday Harbor, WA, U.S.A. 101 B2 48 32N 123 1W
Fridley, MN, U.S.A. 80 E5 45 5N 93 15W
Friend, KS, U.S.A. 74 C3 38 16N 100 55W
Friend, NE, U.S.A. 84 D8 40 38N 97 17W
Friendly, MD, U.S.A. 77 B4 38 42N 76 59W
Friendship, NY, U.S.A. 89 C2 42 12N 78 8W
Friendship, TN, U.S.A. 96 E3 35 55N 89 14W
Friendship, WI, U.S.A. 103 E4 43 58N 89 49W
Friendship Hill Nat. Historic Site △, PA, U.S.A. 95 E3 39 47N 79 56W
Friendsville, MD, U.S.A. 77 A1 39 40N 79 24W
Friendsville, TN, U.S.A. 97 E8 35 46N 84 8W
Fries, VA, U.S.A. 102 E4 36 43N 80 59W
Friesland, WI, U.S.A. 103 E4 43 35N 89 4W
Frio →, TX, U.S.A. 99 J9 28 26N 98 11W
Frio County ☆, TX, U.S.A. 99 J8 28 54N 99 6W
Frio Draw →, TX, U.S.A. 98 C5 34 50N 102 19W
Friona, TX, U.S.A. 98 C5 34 38N 102 43W
Frisco, CO, U.S.A. 66 C4 39 35N 106 6W
Frisco City, AL, U.S.A. 60 E3 31 26N 87 24W
Frisco Peak, UT, U.S.A. 100 E2 38 31N 113 17W
Frissell, Mt., CT, U.S.A. 78 B1 42 3N 73 28W
Fritch, TX, U.S.A. 98 B6 35 38N 101 36W
Frobisher, Sask., Canada 183 F9 49 12N 102 26W
Frobisher B., Nunavut, Canada 191 E12 62 30N 66 0W
Frobisher Bay = Iqaluit, Nunavut, Canada 191 E12 63 44N 68 31W
Frobisher L., Sask., Canada 189 E11 56 20N 108 15W
Frog L., Alta., Canada 184 E10 53 55N 110 20W
Froid, MT, U.S.A. 83 B13 48 20N 104 30W
Fromberg, MT, U.S.A. 83 E9 45 24N 108 54W
Front Range, CO, U.S.A. 66 B5 40 25N 105 45W
Front Royal, VA, U.S.A. 77 B2 38 55N 78 12W
Frontenac, KS, U.S.A. 74 D9 37 27N 94 42W
Frontenac, Parc de △, Qué., Canada 177 F11 45 52N 71 13W
Frontenac Prov. Park △, Ont., Canada 179 C10 44 32N 76 30W
Frontera, Tabasco, Mexico 222 A4 18 32N 92 38W
Frontera Comalapa, Chiapas, Mexico 222 D4 15 42N 92 6W
Frontera Echeverría, Chiapas, Mexico 222 C6 16 49N 90 53W
Frontera Hidalgo, Chiapas, Mexico 222 E4 14 47N 92 10W
Fronteras, Sonora, Mexico 212 C6 30 56N 109 31W
Frontier, Sask., Canada 182 F3 49 12N 108 34W
Frontier, WY, U.S.A. 104 E2 41 49N 110 32W
Frontier County ☆, NE, U.S.A. 84 D5 40 30N 100 30W
Frost, MN, U.S.A. 80 G5 43 35N 93 56W
Frost, TX, U.S.A. 99 E11 32 5N 96 49W
Frost Place, The, NH, U.S.A. 86 B3 44 13N 71 45W
Frostburg, MD, U.S.A. 77 A2 39 39N 78 56W
Frostproof, FL, U.S.A. 67 D7 27 45N 81 32W
Frozen Str., Nunavut, Canada 191 D9 65 45N 84 20W
Fruit Cove, FL, U.S.A. 67 A7 30 7N 81 39W
Fruit Hill, OH, U.S.A. 107 B2 39 4N 84 21W
Fruita, CO, U.S.A. 66 C2 39 9N 108 44W
Fruitdale, AL, U.S.A. 60 E2 31 21N 88 25W
Fruitdale, SD, U.S.A. 91 F2 44 40N 103 42W
Fruithurst, AL, U.S.A. 60 C5 33 44N 85 26W
Fruitland, ID, U.S.A. 70 F2 44 0N 116 55W
Fruitland, IA, U.S.A. 73 D7 41 21N 91 8W
Fruitland, MD, U.S.A. 77 B5 38 19N 75 37W
Fruitland, MO, U.S.A. 82 D7 37 27N 89 38W
Fruitland, NM, U.S.A. 88 A2 36 44N 108 24W
Fruitland, UT, U.S.A. 100 C5 40 13N 110 50W
Fruitland Park, FL, U.S.A. 67 C7 28 51N 81 54W
Fruitport, MI, U.S.A. 79 F5 43 7N 86 9W
Fruitvale, B.C., Canada 187 F17 49 7N 117 33W
Fruitvale, ID, U.S.A. 70 E2 44 49N 116 26W
Fruitvale, WA, U.S.A. 101 D5 46 37N 120 33W
Fry Canyon, UT, U.S.A. 100 F5 37 38N 110 9W
Fry L., Ont., Canada 180 A5 51 14N 91 19W
Fryeburg, ME, U.S.A. 76 D3 44 1N 70 59W
Fuerte →, Sinaloa, Mexico 216 B1 25 54N 109 22W
Fuertes Brotantes, Parque Nacional △, Distrito Federal, Mexico 225 C2 19 17N 99 11W
Fulda, MN, U.S.A. 80 G3 43 53N 95 36W
Fulford = North Miami Beach, FL, U.S.A. 67 F8 25 55N 80 9W
Fulford Harbour, B.C., Canada 187 G11 48 47N 123 27W
Fullerton, Baltimore, U.S.A. 107 A2 39 22N 76 30W
Fullerton, CA, U.S.A. 65 K9 33 53N 117 56W
Fullerton, ND, U.S.A. 91 D7 46 10N 98 26W
Fullerton, NE, U.S.A. 84 C8 41 22N 97 58W
Fullerton, C., Nunavut, Canada 191 E8 63 58N 88 46W
Fulton, AL, U.S.A. 60 E3 31 47N 87 44W
Fulton, AR, U.S.A. 63 E2 33 37N 93 49W
Fulton, IL, U.S.A. 71 B3 41 52N 90 11W
Fulton, KS, U.S.A. 74 C9 38 1N 94 43W
Fulton, KY, U.S.A. 96 D4 36 30N 88 53W
Fulton, MS, U.S.A. 81 B5 34 16N 88 25W
Fulton, MO, U.S.A. 82 C5 38 52N 91 57W
Fulton, NY, U.S.A. 89 B4 43 19N 76 25W
Fulton, OH, U.S.A. 92 C4 40 28N 82 50W
Fulton, SD, U.S.A. 91 G8 43 44N 97 49W
Fulton, TX, U.S.A. 99 J10 28 4N 97 2W
Fulton County ☆, AR, U.S.A. 63 B4 36 22N 91 50W
Fulton County ☆, GA, U.S.A. 68 C2 33 40N 84 40W
Fulton County ☆, IL, U.S.A. 71 C3 40 30N 90 10W
Fulton County ☆, IN, U.S.A. 72 B4 41 5N 86 15W
Fulton County ☆, KY, U.S.A. 96 D3 36 32N 89 10W
Fulton County ☆, NY, U.S.A. 89 B6 43 10N 74 25W
Fulton County ☆, OH, U.S.A. 92 B2 41 33N 84 8W
Fulton County ☆, PA, U.S.A. 95 E4 39 55N 78 5W
Fultondale, AL, U.S.A. 60 C4 33 37N 86 48W
Fults, IL, U.S.A. 71 E3 38 10N 90 13W
Fundy, B. of, N.B., Canada 173 J3 45 0N 66 0W
Fundy Nat. Park △, N.B., Canada 173 H4 45 35N 65 10W
Funk, NE, U.S.A. 84 D6 40 28N 99 15W
Funk I., Nfld. & L., Canada 174 C7 49 45N 53 11W
Funston, GA, U.S.A. 68 E3 31 12N 83 52W
Fuquay-Varina, NC, U.S.A. 90 C7 35 35N 78 48W
Furman, SC, U.S.A. 90 F4 32 41N 81 11W
Furnas County ☆, NE, U.S.A. 84 D6 40 15N 100 0W
Fury and Hecla Str., Nunavut, Canada 190 D9 69 56N 84 0W
Futiga, Amer. Samoa 105 e 14 21 S 170 45W

G

Gabaret I., IL, U.S.A. 117 A2 38 42N 90 10W
Gabarus, N.S., Canada 173 H9 45 50N 60 9W
Gabbettville, GA, U.S.A. 68 D1 32 57N 85 8W
Gabbs, NV, U.S.A. 85 D3 38 52N 117 55W
Gabbs Valley, NV, U.S.A. 85 D2 38 51N 118 12W
Gabbs Valley Range, NV, U.S.A. 85 D2 38 34N 118 0W
Gabilan Range, CA, U.S.A. 64 G5 36 30N 121 15W
Gabriel Leyva Solano, Sinaloa, Mexico 216 B2 25 40N 108 38W
Gabriel Park, Portland, U.S.A. 116 B1 45 28N 122 43W
Gabriel Str., Nunavut, Canada 191 E12 61 45N 65 30W
Gabriola I., B.C., Canada 187 F11 49 9N 123 47W
Gackle, ND, U.S.A. 91 D6 46 38N 99 9W
Gadsden, AL, U.S.A. 60 B4 34 1N 86 1W
Gadsden, AZ, U.S.A. 62 E1 32 33N 114 47W
Gadsden, TN, U.S.A. 96 E4 35 47N 88 59W
Gadsden County ☆, FL, U.S.A. 67 A4 30 30N 84 35W
Gadsden Point, Tampa, U.S.A. 119 C4 27 49N 82 28W
Gaffney, SC, U.S.A. 90 C4 35 5N 81 39W
Gage, OK, U.S.A. 93 B4 36 19N 99 45W
Gage County ☆, NE, U.S.A. 84 D9 40 20N 96 45W
Gage Park, Chicago, U.S.A. 108 C2 41 47N 87 42W
Gagetown, N.B., Canada 173 H3 45 46N 66 10W
Gagnon, Qué., Canada 175 C4 51 50N 68 5W
Gagnon, L., Qué., Canada 176 E7 46 7N 75 7W
Gahanna, OH, U.S.A. 92 C4 40 1N 82 53W
Gail, TX, U.S.A. 98 E6 32 46N 101 27W
Gaillarbois, L., Qué., Canada 172 B2 52 0N 67 27W
Gaillard, L., CT, U.S.A. 78 C2 41 21N 72 46W
Gaines County ☆, TX, U.S.A. 98 E5 32 43N 102 39W
Gainesboro, TN, U.S.A. 97 D7 36 21N 85 39W
Gainesville, FL, U.S.A. 67 B6 29 40N 82 20W
Gainesville, GA, U.S.A. 68 B3 34 18N 83 50W
Gainesville, MO, U.S.A. 82 E4 36 36N 92 26W
Gainesville, TX, U.S.A. 99 D10 33 38N 97 8W
Gainesville, VA, U.S.A. 77 B3 38 48N 77 37W
Gaithersburg, MD, U.S.A. 77 A3 39 8N 77 12W
Gakona, AK, U.S.A. 61 E11 62 18N 145 18W
Galahad, Alta., Canada 185 F9 52 31N 111 56W
Galatia, IL, U.S.A. 71 F5 37 51N 88 37W
Galatia, KS, U.S.A. 74 C5 38 38N 98 58W
Galax, VA, U.S.A. 102 E4 36 40N 80 56W
Galeana, Chihuahua, Mexico 213 C8 30 7N 107 38W
Galeana, Nuevo León, Mexico 215 F4 24 50N 100 4W
Galena, AK, U.S.A. 61 D8 64 44N 156 56W
Galena, ID, U.S.A. 70 F4 43 52N 114 39W
Galena, IL, U.S.A. 71 A3 42 25N 90 26W
Galena, KS, U.S.A. 74 D9 37 4N 94 38W
Galena, MD, U.S.A. 77 A5 39 21N 75 53W
Galena, MO, U.S.A. 82 E3 36 48N 93 28W
Galena Bay, B.C., Canada 187 E17 50 40N 117 51W
Galera, Pta., Oaxaca, Mexico 221 J3 15 58N 97 42W
Galesburg, IL, U.S.A. 71 C3 40 57N 90 22W
Galesburg, KS, U.S.A. 74 D8 37 28N 95 21W
Galesburg, MI, U.S.A. 79 G6 42 17N 85 26W
Galesburg, ND, U.S.A. 91 C8 47 16N 97 24W
Galestown, MD, U.S.A. 77 B5 38 35N 75 42W
Galesville, WI, U.S.A. 103 D2 44 5N 91 21W
Galeton, CO, U.S.A. 66 B6 40 31N 104 35W
Galeton, PA, U.S.A. 95 C5 41 44N 77 39W
Galindo, Barra, Veracruz, Mexico 220 C3 21 14N 97 26W
Galion, OH, U.S.A. 92 C4 40 44N 82 47W
Galisteo, NM, U.S.A. 88 B5 35 24N 105 57W
Galiuro Mts., AZ, U.S.A. 62 E5 32 30N 110 20W
Gallatin, MO, U.S.A. 82 B3 39 55N 93 58W
Gallatin, TN, U.S.A. 96 D6 36 24N 86 27W
Gallatin, TX, U.S.A. 99 F12 31 54N 95 9W
Gallatin →, MT, U.S.A. 83 E6 45 56N 111 30W
Gallatin County ☆, IL, U.S.A. 71 F5 37 45N 88 15W
Gallatin County ☆, KY, U.S.A. 97 B8 38 45N 84 55W
Gallatin County ☆, MT, U.S.A. 83 E6 45 55N 111 15W
Gallatin Gateway, MT, U.S.A. 83 E6 45 35N 111 12W
Gallatin Nat. Forest, MT, U.S.A. 83 E6 45 15N 111 15W
Gallatin Range, U.S.A. 83 F7 44 55N 110 53W
Gallia County ☆, OH, U.S.A. 92 E4 38 49N 82 12W
Galliano, LA, U.S.A. 75 E5 29 26N 90 18W
Gallinas →, NM, U.S.A. 88 B6 35 0N 104 55W
Gallinas Mts., NM, U.S.A. 88 C3 34 25N 107 45W
Gallion, AL, U.S.A. 60 D3 32 30N 87 43W
Gallipolis, OH, U.S.A. 92 E4 38 49N 82 12W
Gallman, MS, U.S.A. 81 E3 31 56N 90 23W
Gallo Mts., NM, U.S.A. 88 C2 34 5N 108 35W
Galloo I., NY, U.S.A. 89 B4 43 55N 76 25W
Gallup, NM, U.S.A. 88 B2 35 32N 108 45W
Galt, CA, U.S.A. 64 E5 38 15N 121 18W
Galt, IA, U.S.A. 73 C5 42 42N 93 36W
Galt, MO, U.S.A. 82 A3 40 8N 93 23W
Galva, IL, U.S.A. 71 B3 41 10N 90 3W
Galva, IA, U.S.A. 73 C3 42 30N 95 25W
Galveston, IN, U.S.A. 72 C4 40 35N 86 11W
Galveston, TX, U.S.A. 99 H13 29 18N 94 48W
Galveston B., TX, U.S.A. 99 H13 29 36N 94 50W
Galveston County ☆, TX, U.S.A. 99 H12 29 28N 95 5W
Galveston I., TX, U.S.A. 99 H13 29 16N 94 51W
Gamaliel, AR, U.S.A. 63 B3 36 27N 92 14W

Glen Canyon Dam, AZ, U.S.A. 62 A4 36 57N 111 29W
Glen Canyon Nat. Recr. Area ⌓, UT, U.S.A. 100 F5 37 15N 111 0W
Glen Cove, NY, U.S.A. 78 D1 40 51N 73 38W
Glen Dean, KY, U.S.A. 96 C6 37 39N 86 32W
Glen Elder, KS, U.S.A. 74 B5 39 30N 98 18W
Glen Ewen, Sask., Canada 183 F9 49 12N 102 1W
Glen Flora, TX, U.S.A. 99 H11 29 21N 96 12W
Glen Head, NY, U.S.A. 114 B5 40 50N 73 37W
Glen L., MI, U.S.A. 79 E6 44 52N 85 59W
Glen Lake, Minneapolis-St. Paul, U.S.A. 113 B1 44 54N 93 27W
Glen Lyon, PA, U.S.A. 95 C6 41 10N 76 5W
Glen Mar Park, MD, U.S.A. 119 B3 38 57N 77 7W
Glen Martin Nat. Wildlife Refuge ⌓, MD, U.S.A. 77 C5 38 0N 76 0W
Glen Oaks, NY, U.S.A. 114 B4 40 44N 73 42W
Glen Raven, NC, U.S.A. 90 B6 36 31N 79 29W
Glen Ridge, NJ, U.S.A. 114 B1 40 48N 74 12W
Glen Rock, PA, U.S.A. 77 A4 39 48N 76 44W
Glen Rose, TX, U.S.A. 99 E10 32 14N 97 45W
Glen Ullin, ND, U.S.A. 91 D4 46 49N 101 50W
Glenallen, MO, U.S.A. 82 D6 37 19N 90 2W
Glenarden, MD, U.S.A. 119 B4 38 56N 76 51W
Glenavon, Sask., Canada 182 E8 50 12N 103 8W
Glenboro, Man., Canada 183 F12 49 33N 99 17W
Glenburn, ND, U.S.A. 91 B4 48 31N 101 13W
Glencliff, NH, U.S.A. 86 C3 43 58N 71 53W
Glencoe, Ont., Canada 178 E5 42 45N 81 43W
Glencoe, AL, U.S.A. 60 C5 33 57N 85 56W
Glencoe, KY, U.S.A. 97 B8 38 43N 84 49W
Glencoe, MN, U.S.A. 80 F4 44 46N 94 9W
Glencoe, OK, U.S.A. 93 B7 36 14N 96 56W
Glendale, N.S., Canada 173 H8 45 49N 61 18W
Glendale, AZ, U.S.A. 62 D3 33 32N 112 11W
Glendale, CA, U.S.A. 65 J8 34 9N 118 15W
Glendale, Denver, U.S.A. 109 B2 39 42N 104 55W
Glendale, FL, U.S.A. 67 A2 30 52N 86 7W
Glendale, KY, U.S.A. 97 C7 37 36N 85 54W
Glendale, Milwaukee, U.S.A. 112 B2 43 8N 87 56W
Glendale, MO, U.S.A. 117 B1 38 35N 90 22W
Glendale, NV, U.S.A. 85 F6 36 40N 114 34W
Glendale, OR, U.S.A. 94 E2 42 44N 123 26W
Glendale, Pittsburgh, U.S.A. 116 B1 40 23N 80 5W
Glendale, UT, U.S.A. 100 F3 37 19N 112 36W
Glendale L., PA, U.S.A. 95 D4 40 42N 78 32W
Glendevey, CO, U.S.A. 66 B5 40 48N 105 56W
Glendive, MT, U.S.A. 83 C13 47 7N 104 43W
Glendo, WY, U.S.A. 104 D7 42 30N 105 2W
Glendo Res., WY, U.S.A. 104 D8 42 29N 104 57W
Glendon, Alta., Canada 184 D9 54 15N 111 10W
Glendora, MS, U.S.A. 81 C3 33 50N 90 18W
Glendora, NJ, U.S.A. 87 C1 39 50N 75 4W
Glenella, Man., Canada 183 E12 50 33N 99 11W
Glenfield, ND, U.S.A. 91 C7 47 27N 98 34W
Glenfield, NY, U.S.A. 89 B5 43 43N 75 24W
Glenham, SD, U.S.A. 91 E5 45 32N 100 16W
Glenmont, OH, U.S.A. 92 C4 40 31N 82 6W
Glenmora, LA, U.S.A. 75 D3 30 59N 92 35W
Glenn, CA, U.S.A. 64 D4 39 31N 122 1W
Glenn, MI, U.S.A. 79 G5 42 31N 86 14W
Glenn County ☆, CA, U.S.A. 64 D4 39 40N 122 20W
Glennallen, AK, U.S.A. 61 E11 62 7N 145 33W
Glenns Ferry, ID, U.S.A. 70 G3 42 57N 115 18W
Glennville, GA, U.S.A. 68 E5 31 56N 81 56W
Glenolden, PA, U.S.A. 116 B1 39 54N 75 17W
Glenoma, WA, U.S.A. 101 D3 46 31N 122 10W
Glenpool, OK, U.S.A. 93 C7 35 58N 96 1W
Glenrock, WY, U.S.A. 104 D7 42 52N 105 52W
Glens Falls, NY, U.S.A. 89 B7 43 19N 73 39W
Glenshaw, Pittsburgh, U.S.A. 116 A2 40 31N 79 58W
Glenside, PA, U.S.A. 87 B1 40 6N 75 9W
Glenview, Chicago, U.S.A. 108 A2 42 3N 87 48W
Glenview Countryside, Chicago, U.S.A. 108 A2 42 3N 87 49W
Glenville, Cleveland, U.S.A. 107 A2 41 32N 81 37W
Glenville, MN, U.S.A. 80 G5 43 34N 93 17W
Glenville, NE, U.S.A. 84 D7 40 30N 98 15W
Glenville, WV, U.S.A. 102 C4 38 56N 80 50W
Glenwood, Alta., Canada 185 J7 49 21N 113 31W
Glenwood, Nfld. & L., Canada 174 C6 49 0N 54 58W
Glenwood, AL, U.S.A. 60 E4 31 40N 86 10W
Glenwood, AR, U.S.A. 63 D2 34 20N 93 33W
Glenwood, GA, U.S.A. 68 D4 32 11N 82 40W
Glenwood, HI, U.S.A. 69 D6 19 29N 155 9W
Glenwood, IL, U.S.A. 71 B6 41 33N 87 37W
Glenwood, IN, U.S.A. 72 D5 39 37N 85 18W
Glenwood, IA, U.S.A. 73 D3 41 3N 95 45W
Glenwood, MN, U.S.A. 80 E3 45 39N 95 23W
Glenwood, NM, U.S.A. 88 D2 33 19N 108 53W
Glenwood, OR, U.S.A. 94 B2 45 39N 123 16W
Glenwood, UT, U.S.A. 100 E4 38 46N 111 59W
Glenwood, WA, U.S.A. 101 D4 46 1N 121 17W
Glenwood City, WI, U.S.A. 103 C1 45 4N 92 10W
Glenwood Landing, NY, U.S.A. 114 B5 40 49N 73 38W
Glenwood Springs, CO, U.S.A. 66 C3 39 33N 107 19W
Glidden, IA, U.S.A. 73 C4 42 4N 94 44W
Glide, OR, U.S.A. 94 D2 43 18N 123 6W
Globe, AZ, U.S.A. 62 D5 33 24N 110 47W
Glorieta, NM, U.S.A. 88 B5 35 35N 105 46W
Gloster, MS, U.S.A. 81 E2 31 12N 91 1W
Gloucester, MA, U.S.A. 78 B4 42 37N 70 40W
Gloucester, VA, U.S.A. 102 D8 37 25N 76 32W
Gloucester City, NJ, U.S.A. 87 C1 39 53N 75 7W
Gloucester County ☆, NJ, U.S.A. 87 C1 39 40N 75 15W
Gloucester County ☆, VA, U.S.A. 102 D8 37 25N 76 32W
Gloucester Point, VA, U.S.A. 102 D8 37 15N 76 30W
Glover, MO, U.S.A. 82 D6 37 29N 90 42W
Glover, VT, U.S.A. 86 B2 44 42N 72 12W
Glover I., Nfld. & L., Canada 174 D3 48 46N 57 43W
Gloversville, NY, U.S.A. 89 B6 43 3N 74 21W
Glynn County ☆, GA, U.S.A. 68 E5 31 10N 81 30W
Gnadenhutten, OH, U.S.A. 92 C5 40 22N 81 26W
Goat Range Park ⌓, B.C., Canada 187 E17 50 17N 117 17W
Gobernador, NM, U.S.A. 88 A3 36 43N 107 21W
Gobles, MI, U.S.A. 79 G6 42 22N 85 53W
Godbout, Qué., Canada 172 D2 49 20N 67 38W
Godbout →, Qué., Canada 172 D2 49 19N 67 36W
Goddard, KS, U.S.A. 74 D6 37 39N 97 34W
Goderich, Ont., Canada 178 D5 43 45N 81 41W
Godfrey, GA, U.S.A. 68 C3 33 27N 83 30W
Godfrey, IL, U.S.A. 71 E3 38 58N 90 11W
Gods →, Man., Canada 191 F7 56 22N 92 51W
Gods L., Man., Canada 191 G7 54 40N 94 15W
Gods Mercy, B. of, Nunavut, Canada 191 E8 63 30N 86 10W
Goehner, NE, U.S.A. 84 D8 40 50N 97 13W
Goéland, L. au, Qué., Canada 176 B6 49 50N 76 48W
Goélands, L. aux, Qué., Canada 175 B5 55 27N 64 17W
Goessel, KS, U.S.A. 74 C6 38 15N 97 21W
Goetzville, MI, U.S.A. 79 C7 46 3N 84 5W
Goff, KS, U.S.A. 74 B8 39 40N 95 56W
Goff Cr. →, OK, U.S.A. 93 B2 36 43N 101 29W
Goffs, CA, U.S.A. 65 J11 34 55N 115 4W
Goffstown, NH, U.S.A. 86 C3 43 1N 71 36W
Gogama, Ont., Canada 181 E15 47 35N 81 43W
Gogebic, L., MI, U.S.A. 79 C2 46 30N 89 35W
Gogebic County ☆, MI, U.S.A. 79 C2 46 25N 89 45W
Gogebic Range, MI, U.S.A. 79 C2 46 40N 89 40W
Gogebic Range, WA, U.S.A. 101 C4 47 51N 121 42W
Golconda, IL, U.S.A. 71 F5 37 22N 88 29W
Golconda, NV, U.S.A. 85 B3 40 58N 117 30W
Gold Beach, OR, U.S.A. 94 E1 42 25N 124 25W
Gold Coast, Chicago, U.S.A. 108 B3 41 54N 87 37W
Gold Creek, AK, U.S.A. 61 E10 62 46N 149 41W
Gold Hill, OR, U.S.A. 94 E2 42 26N 123 3W
Gold Point, NV, U.S.A. 85 E3 37 21N 117 22W
Gold River, B.C., Canada 186 F8 49 46N 126 3W
Goldcreek, MT, U.S.A. 83 D5 46 35N 112 55W
Golden, B.C., Canada 187 D18 51 20N 116 59W
Golden, ID, U.S.A. 70 D3 45 49N 115 41W
Golden, IL, U.S.A. 71 C2 40 7N 91 1W
Golden, MO, U.S.A. 82 E3 36 31N 93 39W
Golden, NM, U.S.A. 88 B4 35 16N 106 13W
Golden, OK, U.S.A. 93 D9 34 2N 94 54W
Golden Beach, Miami, U.S.A. 112 C3 25 57N 80 7W
Golden Bridge, B.C., Canada 187 E12 50 51N 122 50W
Golden City, MO, U.S.A. 82 D2 37 24N 94 5W
Golden Ears Park ⌓, B.C., Canada 187 F12 49 30N 122 25W
Golden Gate, CA, U.S.A. 118 B2 37 48N 122 29W
Golden Gate, FL, U.S.A. 67 E7 26 11N 81 42W
Golden Gate, IL, U.S.A. 71 E5 38 22N 88 12W
Golden Gate Bridge, San Francisco, U.S.A. 118 B2 37 49N 122 28W
Golden Gate Nat. Recr. Area ⌓, CA, U.S.A. 64 F4 37 51N 122 31W
Golden Gate Park, San Francisco, U.S.A. 118 B2 37 46N 122 28W
Golden Hinde, B.C., Canada 186 F9 49 40N 125 44W
Golden Lake, Ont., Canada 176 F5 45 34N 77 21W
Golden Meadow, LA, U.S.A. 75 E5 29 24N 90 16W
Golden Prairie, Sask., Canada 182 E2 50 13N 109 37W
Golden Spike Nat. Historic Site ⌓, U.S.A. 100 B3 41 37N 112 33W
Golden Valley, Minneapolis-St. Paul, U.S.A. 113 B1 44 59N 93 21W
Golden Valley, ND, U.S.A. 91 C3 47 17N 102 4W
Golden Valley County ☆, MT, U.S.A. 83 D8 46 30N 109 15W
Golden Valley County ☆, ND, U.S.A. 91 D2 47 0N 103 58W
Goldendale, WA, U.S.A. 101 E5 45 49N 120 50W
Goldfield, IA, U.S.A. 73 C5 42 44N 93 55W
Goldfield, NV, U.S.A. 85 E3 37 42N 117 14W
Goldonna, LA, U.S.A. 75 B3 32 1N 92 54W
Goldsboro, MD, U.S.A. 77 A5 39 2N 75 47W
Goldsboro, NC, U.S.A. 90 C8 35 23N 77 59W
Goldsby, OK, U.S.A. 93 C6 35 9N 97 28W
Goldsmith, TX, U.S.A. 98 F5 31 59N 102 37W
Goldsmith Ch., Nunavut, Canada 190 C4 73 10N 106 5W
Goldston, NC, U.S.A. 90 C6 35 36N 79 20W
Goldthwaite, TX, U.S.A. 99 F9 31 27N 98 34W
Goleta, CA, U.S.A. 65 J7 34 27N 119 50W
Golf Manor, OH, U.S.A. 107 A2 39 11N 84 26W
Golfo de Santa Clara, Sonora, Mexico 212 B1 31 45N 114 33W
Goliad, TX, U.S.A. 99 J10 28 40N 97 23W
Goliad County ☆, TX, U.S.A. 99 J10 28 45N 97 25W
Golovin, AK, U.S.A. 61 D7 64 33N 163 2W
Goltry, OK, U.S.A. 93 B5 36 32N 98 9W
Golva, ND, U.S.A. 91 D2 46 44N 103 59W
Gómez Farías, Chihuahua, Mexico 213 D8 29 17N 107 44W
Gómez Farías, Jalisco, Mexico 218 C4 19 47N 103 29W
Gómez Farías, Tamaulipas, Mexico 215 G5 23 3N 99 9W
Gómez Palacio, Durango, Mexico 217 B7 25 34N 103 30W
Gonvick, MN, U.S.A. 80 C3 47 44N 95 31W
Gonzales, CA, U.S.A. 64 G5 36 30N 121 26W
Gonzales, LA, U.S.A. 75 D5 30 14N 90 55W
Gonzales, TX, U.S.A. 99 H10 29 30N 97 27W
Gonzales County ☆, TX, U.S.A. 99 H10 29 26N 97 32W
González, Tamaulipas, Mexico 215 H6 22 48N 98 25W
Gonzalez, FL, U.S.A. 67 A1 30 35N 87 17W
González Ortega, Zacatecas, Mexico 217 D8 23 11N 102 28W
González Ortega, Zacatecas, Mexico 217 D7 23 58N 103 26W
Goochland, VA, U.S.A. 102 D7 37 41N 77 53W
Goochland County ☆, VA, U.S.A. 102 D7 37 41N 77 53W
Good Hope, IL, U.S.A. 71 C3 40 33N 90 41W
Good Hope Mt., B.C., Canada 186 D10 51 9N 124 10W
Good Spirit L., Sask., Canada 182 D9 51 34N 102 40W
Good Spirit Lake Prov. Park ⌓, Sask., Canada 182 D9 51 31N 102 41W
Good Thunder, MN, U.S.A. 80 F4 44 0N 94 4W
Goodell, IA, U.S.A. 73 C5 42 55N 93 37W
Gooderham, Ont., Canada 179 C8 44 54N 78 21W
Goodeve, Sask., Canada 182 D8 51 4N 103 10W
Goodfellow Air Force Base, TX, U.S.A. 98 F7 31 25N 100 25W
Goodhue, MN, U.S.A. 80 F6 44 24N 92 37W
Goodhue County ☆, MN, U.S.A. 80 F6 44 25N 92 45W
Gooding, ID, U.S.A. 70 G4 42 56N 114 43W
Gooding County ☆, ID, U.S.A. 70 F4 43 0N 115 0W
Goodland, IN, U.S.A. 72 C3 40 46N 87 18W
Goodland, KS, U.S.A. 74 B2 39 21N 101 43W
Goodlett, TX, U.S.A. 99 C8 34 20N 99 53W
Goodlettsville, TN, U.S.A. 96 D6 36 19N 86 43W
Goodman, MS, U.S.A. 81 D4 32 58N 89 55W
Goodman, MO, U.S.A. 82 E2 36 44N 94 25W
Goodman, WI, U.S.A. 103 C5 45 38N 88 21W
Goodman Hill, Boston, U.S.A. 106 A1 42 22N 71 23W
Goodnews Bay, AK, U.S.A. 61 G7 59 7N 161 35W
Goodnight, TX, U.S.A. 98 B6 35 2N 101 11W
Goodrich, CO, U.S.A. 66 B6 40 20N 104 7W
Goodrich, ND, U.S.A. 91 C5 47 29N 100 8W
Goodrich, TX, U.S.A. 99 G13 30 36N 94 57W
Goodridge, MN, U.S.A. 80 B3 48 9N 95 48W
Goodsprings, NV, U.S.A. 85 G5 35 50N 115 26W
Goodwater, Sask., Canada 182 F8 49 24N 103 42W
Goodwater, AL, U.S.A. 60 C4 33 4N 86 3W
Goodwell, OK, U.S.A. 93 B2 36 36N 101 38W
Goodyear, AZ, U.S.A. 62 D3 33 26N 112 21W
Goose →, Nfld. & L., Canada 175 C5 53 20N 60 35W
Goose →, ND, U.S.A. 91 C9 47 28N 96 52W
Goose Cove East, Nfld. & L., Canada 174 A5 51 18N 55 38W
Goose Creek, SC, U.S.A. 90 F5 32 59N 80 2W
Goose I., B.C., Canada 186 D6 51 57N 128 26W
Goose L., Man., Canada 183 A10 54 28N 101 30W
Goose L., CA, U.S.A. 64 B6 41 56N 120 26W
Gooseberry Cr. →, WY, U.S.A. 104 C4 43 55N 108 3W
Gorda, Punta, CA, U.S.A. 64 C2 40 16N 124 22W
Gordo, AL, U.S.A. 60 C3 33 19N 87 54W
Gordo, Cerro, Baja Calif., Mexico 210 A2 32 17N 116 42W
Gordon, GA, U.S.A. 68 C3 32 54N 83 20W
Gordon, NE, U.S.A. 84 B3 42 48N 102 12W
Gordon, OH, U.S.A. 92 D2 39 56N 84 31W
Gordon, TX, U.S.A. 99 E9 32 33N 98 22W
Gordon, WI, U.S.A. 103 B2 46 15N 91 48W
Gordon County ☆, GA, U.S.A. 68 B2 34 30N 84 50W
Gordon Cr. →, NE, U.S.A. 84 B5 42 49N 100 40W
Gordon Hd., B.C., Canada 187 G11 48 29N 123 18W
Gordon L., Alta., Canada 184 B10 56 30N 110 25W
Gordon L., N.W.T., Canada 189 D10 63 5N 113 11W
Gordonsville, TN, U.S.A. 97 D7 36 10N 85 56W
Gordonsville, VA, U.S.A. 102 C6 38 9N 78 11W
Gordonville, MO, U.S.A. 82 D7 37 19N 89 41W
Gordonville, TX, U.S.A. 99 D11 33 48N 96 51W
Gore, VA, U.S.A. 77 A2 39 16N 78 20W
Gore Bay, Ont., Canada 178 B4 45 57N 82 28W
Gore Mt., VT, U.S.A. 86 B3 44 55N 71 48W
Gore Range, CO, U.S.A. 66 C4 39 50N 106 25W
Goree, TX, U.S.A. 99 D8 33 28N 99 31W
Goreville, IL, U.S.A. 71 F5 37 33N 88 58W
Gorham, IL, U.S.A. 71 F4 37 43N 89 29W
Gorham, KS, U.S.A. 74 C4 38 53N 99 1W
Gorham, ME, U.S.A. 76 E3 43 41N 70 26W
Gorham, NH, U.S.A. 86 B3 44 23N 71 10W
Gorman, NC, U.S.A. 90 B7 36 2N 78 49W
Gorman, TX, U.S.A. 99 E9 32 12N 98 41W
Gortner, MD, U.S.A. 77 A1 39 20N 79 24W
Gorum, LA, U.S.A. 75 C3 31 26N 92 56W
Goschen I., B.C., Canada 186 B4 53 48N 130 33W
Goshen, N.S., Canada 173 H8 45 23N 61 59W
Goshen, CA, U.S.A. 65 G7 36 21N 119 25W
Goshen, CT, U.S.A. 78 C1 41 50N 73 14W
Goshen, IN, U.S.A. 72 B5 41 35N 85 50W
Goshen, KY, U.S.A. 97 B7 38 24N 85 34W
Goshen, NJ, U.S.A. 87 C2 39 8N 74 51W
Goshen, NY, U.S.A. 87 A2 41 24N 74 20W
Goshen, OR, U.S.A. 94 D2 43 58N 123 2W
Goshen, UT, U.S.A. 100 D4 39 57N 111 54W
Goshen County ☆, WY, U.S.A. 104 D8 42 0N 104 10W
Goshute, UT, U.S.A. 100 D1 39 53N 114 0W
Goshute Indian Reservation, NV, U.S.A. 85 C6 39 50N 114 5W
Goshute L., NV, U.S.A. 85 B6 40 9N 114 42W
Goshute Mts., NV, U.S.A. 85 B6 40 15N 114 19W
Goshute Valley, NV, U.S.A. 85 B6 40 45N 114 20W
Gosnell, AR, U.S.A. 63 C6 35 58N 89 58W
Gospel Hump Wilderness, ID, U.S.A. 70 D3 45 34N 115 46W
Gosper County ☆, NE, U.S.A. 84 D6 40 30N 99 50W
Gosport, IN, U.S.A. 72 D4 39 21N 86 40W
Gossville, NH, U.S.A. 86 C3 43 12N 71 22W
Gotebo, OK, U.S.A. 93 C5 35 4N 98 53W
Gotha, Orlando, U.S.A. 115 A1 28 31N 81 31W
Gotham, WI, U.S.A. 103 E3 43 13N 90 18W
Gothenburg, NE, U.S.A. 84 D5 40 56N 100 10W
Gough, GA, U.S.A. 68 C4 33 6N 82 14W
Gough L., Alta., Canada 185 F8 52 2N 112 28W
Gouin, Rés., Qué., Canada 176 C8 48 35N 74 40W
Goulais →, Ont., Canada 181 F12 46 43N 84 27W
Gould, AR, U.S.A. 63 E4 33 59N 91 34W
Gould, OK, U.S.A. 93 D4 34 40N 99 47W
Gould City, MI, U.S.A. 79 C6 46 6N 85 42W
Goulds, Nfld. & L., Canada 174 E8 47 29N 52 46W
Goulds, FL, U.S.A. 67 F8 25 33N 80 23W
Gouverneur, NY, U.S.A. 89 A5 44 20N 75 28W
Govan, Sask., Canada 182 D7 51 20N 105 0W
Gove, KS, U.S.A. 74 C3 38 58N 100 29W
Gove County ☆, KS, U.S.A. 74 C3 38 50N 100 30W
Governors I., NY, U.S.A. 114 B2 40 41N 74 1W
Govans, Baltimore, U.S.A. 107 A2 39 23N 76 36W
Gowanda, NY, U.S.A. 89 C2 42 28N 78 56W
Gower, MO, U.S.A. 82 B2 39 37N 94 36W
Gowrie, IA, U.S.A. 73 C4 42 17N 94 17W
Goyelle, L., Qué., Canada 172 C9 50 47N 60 45W
Grace, ID, U.S.A. 70 G7 42 35N 111 44W
Gracefield, Qué., Canada 176 E6 46 6N 76 3W
Graceland, TN, U.S.A. 96 E2 35 3N 90 1W
Gracemont, OK, U.S.A. 93 C5 35 11N 98 16W
Graceville, FL, U.S.A. 67 A3 30 58N 85 31W
Graceville, MN, U.S.A. 80 E2 45 34N 96 26W
Gracewood, GA, U.S.A. 68 C4 33 22N 82 2W
Gracey, KY, U.S.A. 96 D5 36 53N 87 40W
Graciano Sánchez, Tamaulipas, Mexico 215 H6 22 39N 98 32W
Graciano Sánchez, Tamaulipas, Mexico 215 G5 23 55N 99 17W
Grady, AL, U.S.A. 60 E4 31 59N 86 3W
Grady, AR, U.S.A. 63 D4 34 5N 91 42W
Grady, NM, U.S.A. 88 C7 34 49N 103 19W
Grady, OK, U.S.A. 93 D6 34 1N 97 40W
Grady County ☆, GA, U.S.A. 68 F2 30 50N 84 15W
Grady County ☆, OK, U.S.A. 93 C6 35 0N 97 50W
Gradyville, KY, U.S.A. 97 C7 37 4N 85 25W
Graettinger, IA, U.S.A. 73 B4 43 14N 94 45W
Graford, TX, U.S.A. 99 E9 32 56N 98 14W
Grafton, IL, U.S.A. 71 E3 38 58N 90 26W
Grafton, IA, U.S.A. 73 B5 43 20N 93 4W
Grafton, MA, U.S.A. 78 B3 42 12N 71 41W
Grafton, ND, U.S.A. 91 B8 48 25N 97 25W
Grafton, NH, U.S.A. 86 C3 43 34N 71 57W
Grafton, NY, U.S.A. 78 B1 42 46N 73 27W
Grafton, OH, U.S.A. 92 B4 41 16N 82 4W
Grafton, VT, U.S.A. 86 C2 43 10N 72 37W
Grafton, WV, U.S.A. 102 B4 39 21N 80 2W
Grafton, WI, U.S.A. 103 E6 43 19N 87 57W
Grafton County ☆, NH, U.S.A. 86 C3 43 50N 71 45W
Graham, Ont., Canada 180 C6 49 20N 90 30W
Graham, GA, U.S.A. 68 E4 31 50N 82 30W
Graham, NC, U.S.A. 90 B6 36 5N 79 25W
Graham, TX, U.S.A. 99 D9 33 6N 98 35W
Graham, Mt., AZ, U.S.A. 62 E6 32 42N 109 52W
Graham County ☆, AZ, U.S.A. 62 E6 33 0N 110 0W
Graham County ☆, KS, U.S.A. 74 B4 39 20N 99 45W
Graham County ☆, NC, U.S.A. 90 C2 35 20N 83 50W
Graham I., B.C., Canada 186 B2 53 40N 132 30W
Graham I., Nunavut, Canada 190 B7 77 25N 90 30W
Graham L., Alta., Canada 184 B6 56 35N 114 33W
Graham L., ME, U.S.A. 76 D5 44 39N 68 24W
Grahamdale, Man., Canada 183 D13 51 23N 98 30W
Grain Valley, MO, U.S.A. 82 B2 39 1N 94 12W
Grainfield, KS, U.S.A. 74 B3 39 7N 100 28W
Grainger County ☆, TN, U.S.A. 97 D9 36 17N 83 31W
Grainola, OK, U.S.A. 93 B7 36 57N 96 39W
Grambling, LA, U.S.A. 75 B3 32 32N 92 43W
Gramercy, LA, U.S.A. 75 D5 30 4N 90 42W
Grampian, PA, U.S.A. 95 D4 40 58N 78 37W
Gran Morelos, Chihuahua, Mexico 213 E9 28 15N 106 30W
Granada, CO, U.S.A. 66 D8 38 4N 102 19W
Granada, MN, U.S.A. 80 G4 43 42N 94 21W
Granados, Sonora, Mexico 212 D6 29 52N 109 20W
Granbury, TX, U.S.A. 99 E10 32 27N 97 47W
Granbury, L, TX, U.S.A. 99 E10 32 22N 97 41W
Granby, Qué., Canada 177 F10 45 25N 72 45W
Granby, CO, U.S.A. 66 B5 40 5N 105 56W
Granby, CT, U.S.A. 78 C2 41 57N 72 47W
Granby, MO, U.S.A. 82 E2 36 55N 94 15W
Granby →, B.C., Canada 187 F16 49 2N 118 27W
Granby, L., CO, U.S.A. 66 B5 40 9N 105 52W
Granby Park ⌓, B.C., Canada 187 F16 49 44N 118 27W
Grand →, Ont., Canada 178 E7 42 51N 79 34W
Grand →, MI, U.S.A. 79 F5 43 4N 86 15W
Grand →, MO, U.S.A. 82 B3 39 23N 93 7W
Grand →, OH, U.S.A. 92 B5 41 44N 81 17W
Grand →, SD, U.S.A. 91 E5 45 40N 100 45W
Grand Bank, Nfld. & L., Canada 174 E5 47 6N 55 48W
Grand Bay, AL, U.S.A. 60 F2 30 29N 88 21W
Grand Bay-Westfield, N.B., Canada 173 H3 45 18N 66 12W
Grand Blanc, MI, U.S.A. 79 G8 42 56N 83 38W
Grand Bruit, Nfld. & L., Canada 174 E2 47 40N 58 14W
Grand Calumet, Île du, Qué., Canada 176 F6 45 44N 76 41W
Grand Cane, LA, U.S.A. 75 B2 32 5N 93 49W
Grand Canyon, AZ, U.S.A. 62 A3 36 3N 112 9W
Grand Canyon Nat. Park △, AZ, U.S.A. 62 A3 36 15N 112 30W
Grand Canyon-Parashant Nat. Monument ⌓, AZ, U.S.A. 62 A2 36 30N 113 45W
Grand Chenier, LA, U.S.A. 75 E3 29 46N 92 58W
Grand Coteau, LA, U.S.A. 75 D3 30 25N 92 3W
Grand Coulee, Sask., Canada 182 E7 50 26N 104 49W
Grand Coulee, WA, U.S.A. 101 C6 47 57N 119 0W
Grand Coulee Dam, WA, U.S.A. 101 C7 47 57N 118 59W
Grand County ☆, CO, U.S.A. 66 B4 40 10N 106 15W
Grand County ☆, UT, U.S.A. 100 D6 39 0N 109 30W
Grand Falls, N.B., Canada 173 F1 47 3N 67 44W
Grand Falls-Windsor, Nfld. & L., Canada 174 D5 48 56N 55 40W
Grand Forks, B.C., Canada 187 G16 49 0N 118 30W
Grand Forks, ND, U.S.A. 91 C8 47 55N 97 3W
Grand Forks County ☆, ND, U.S.A. 91 C8 47 55N 97 22W
Grand Harbour, N.B., Canada 173 J3 44 41N 66 46W
Grand Haven, MI, U.S.A. 79 F5 43 4N 86 13W
Grand I., Man., Canada 183 C11 52 51N 100 0W
Grand I., LA, U.S.A. 75 E6 29 10N 90 0W
Grand I., MI, U.S.A. 79 C5 46 31N 86 40W
Grand Island, NE, U.S.A. 84 D7 40 55N 98 21W
Grand Island Nat. Recr. Area ⌓, MI, U.S.A. 79 C5 46 31N 86 40W
Grand Isle, LA, U.S.A. 75 E6 29 14N 90 0W
Grand Isle, VT, U.S.A. 86 B1 44 43N 73 18W
Grand Isle County ☆, VT, U.S.A. 86 B1 44 50N 73 17W
Grand Junction, CO, U.S.A. 66 C2 39 4N 108 33W
Grand Junction, IA, U.S.A. 73 C4 42 2N 94 14W
Grand Junction, TN, U.S.A. 96 E3 35 3N 89 11W
Grand L., N.B., Canada 173 H3 45 57N 66 7W
Grand L., Nfld. & L., Canada 174 D3 49 0N 57 30W
Grand L., Nfld. & L., Canada 175 C5 53 40N 60 30W
Grand L., LA, U.S.A. 75 E3 29 55N 92 47W
Grand L., ME, U.S.A. 76 C6 45 40N 67 50W
Grand L., MI, U.S.A. 79 D8 45 18N 83 30W
Grand L., OH, U.S.A. 92 C2 40 32N 84 25W
Grand Lac Victoria, Qué., Canada 176 D5 47 35N 77 35W
Grand Lake, CO, U.S.A. 66 B5 40 15N 105 49W
Grand Lake, LA, U.S.A. 75 D2 30 2N 93 17W
Grand Lake Matagamon, ME, U.S.A. 76 B5 46 12N 68 47W
Grand Lake Seboeis, ME, U.S.A. 76 B5 46 18N 68 39W
Grand Le Pierre, Nfld. & L., Canada 174 E6 47 41N 54 47W
Grand Ledge, MI, U.S.A. 79 G7 42 45N 84 45W
Grand Manan Channel, ME, U.S.A. 76 D7 44 40N 67 0W
Grand Manan I., N.B., Canada 173 J3 44 45N 66 52W
Grand Marais, Canada 180 E6 47 45N 90 25W
Grand Marais, MI, U.S.A. 79 C6 46 40N 85 59W
Grand Marais, MN, U.S.A. 80 C8 47 45N 90 20W
Grand Meadow, MN, U.S.A. 80 G6 43 42N 92 34W
Grand-Mère, Qué., Canada 177 E10 46 36N 72 40W
Grand Mesa, CO, U.S.A. 66 D2 39 0N 108 15W
Grand Mesa Nat. Forest, CO, U.S.A. 66 C3 39 20N 107 50W
Grand Piles, Qué., Canada 177 E10 46 40N 72 40W
Grand Portage, MN, U.S.A. 80 C9 47 58N 89 41W
Grand Portage Indian Reservation, MN, U.S.A. 80 C9 47 55N 89 50W
Grand Prairie, TX, U.S.A. 99 E11 32 44N 96 59W
Grand Rapids = Wisconsin Rapids, WI, U.S.A. 103 D4 44 23N 89 49W
Grand Rapids, Man., Canada 183 B12 53 12N 99 19W
Grand Rapids, MI, U.S.A. 79 G6 42 58N 85 40W
Grand Rapids, MN, U.S.A. 80 C5 47 14N 93 31W
Grand Rapids, OH, U.S.A. 92 B3 41 25N 83 52W
Grand Rapids ✕ (GRR), MI, U.S.A. 79 G6 42 53N 85 31W
Grand-Remous, Qué., Canada 176 E7 46 37N 75 54W
Grand Ridge, FL, U.S.A. 67 A3 30 43N 85 1W
Grand Ridge, IL, U.S.A. 71 B5 41 14N 88 50W
Grand River, IA, U.S.A. 73 E5 40 49N 93 58W
Grand River Nat. Grassland, SD, U.S.A. 91 E3 45 47N 102 30W
Grand Rivers, KY, U.S.A. 96 C4 37 1N 88 14W
Grand Ronde, OR, U.S.A. 94 B2 45 4N 123 37W
Grand Ronde →, U.S.A. 101 D8 46 5N 117 0W
Grand Saline, TX, U.S.A. 99 E12 32 41N 95 43W
Grand Staircase-Escalante Nat. Monument ⌓, UT, U.S.A. 100 F4 37 25N 111 33W
Grand Teton, WY, U.S.A. 104 C2 43 54N 110 50W
Grand Teton Nat. Park △, WY, U.S.A. 104 C2 43 50N 110 50W
Grand Tower, IL, U.S.A. 71 F4 37 38N 89 30W
Grand Traverse B., MI, U.S.A. 79 D6 45 5N 85 35W
Grand Traverse County ☆, MI, U.S.A. 79 E6 44 40N 85 35W
Grand Traverse Indian Reservation, MI, U.S.A. 79 D6 45 4N 85 40W
Grand View, ID, U.S.A. 70 G2 42 59N 116 6W
Grand Wash Cliffs, AZ, U.S.A. 62 A2 36 0N 113 50W
Grande →, Baja Calif., Mexico 210 B3 31 50N 115 15W
Grande →, Jalisco, Mexico 218 C5 19 26N 102 44W
Grande →, Oaxaca, Mexico 221 G4 17 43N 96 56W
Grande, L., Sinaloa, Mexico 216 E5 22 46N 105 53W
Grande, Rio →, N. Amer. 98 M10 25 58N 97 9W
Grande-Anse, N.B., Canada 173 F4 47 48N 65 11W
Grande Baleine, R. de la →, Qué., Canada 175 B2 55 16N 77 47W
Grande Cache, Alta., Canada 184 E1 53 53N 119 8W
Grande-Cascapédia, Qué., Canada 172 E4 48 15N 65 54W
Grande-Entrée, Qué., Canada 173 F8 47 30N 61 40W
Grande-Passe, I. de la, Qué., Canada 175 C6 51 10N 58 35W
Grande Pointe, Man., Canada 183 F14 49 46N 97 3W
Grande Prairie, Alta., Canada 184 C2 55 10N 118 50W
Grande-Rivière, Qué., Canada 172 E5 48 26N 64 30W
Grande Ronde →, OR, U.S.A. 94 A9 46 5N 116 59W
Grande Ronde Indian Reservation, OR, U.S.A. 94 B2 45 8N 123 40W
Grande-Vallée, Qué., Canada 172 D4 49 14N 65 8W
Grandes-Bergeronnes, Qué., Canada 177 C13 48 16N 69 35W
Grandfalls, TX, U.S.A. 98 F5 31 20N 102 51W
Grandfield, OK, U.S.A. 93 D5 34 14N 98 41W
Grandin, MO, U.S.A. 82 E6 36 50N 90 50W
Grandin, ND, U.S.A. 91 C9 47 14N 97 0W
Grandin, L., N.W.T., Canada 189 D9 63 59N 119 0W
Grandjean, ID, U.S.A. 70 E3 44 9N 115 10W
Grandmesnil, L., Qué., Canada 172 B2 51 19N 67 33W
Grands-Jardins, Parc des ⌓, Qué., Canada 177 D12 47 41N 70 51W
Grandview, Man., Canada 183 D11 51 10N 100 42W
Grandview, IA, U.S.A. 73 D7 41 17N 91 11W
Grandview, MO, U.S.A. 82 C2 38 53N 94 32W
Grandview, TX, U.S.A. 99 E10 32 16N 97 11W
Grandview, WA, U.S.A. 101 D6 46 15N 119 54W
Grandview Peak, Salt Lake City, U.S.A. 117 A3 40 51N 111 45W
Granet, L., Qué., Canada 176 D5 47 47N 77 31W
Granger, IN, U.S.A. 72 B4 41 45N 86 7W
Granger, IA, U.S.A. 73 D5 41 46N 93 50W
Granger, TX, U.S.A. 99 G10 30 43N 97 26W
Granger, WA, U.S.A. 101 D5 46 21N 120 11W

Granger, WY, U.S.A. 104 E3 41 35N 109 58W
Grangeville, ID, U.S.A. 70 D2 45 56N 116 7W
Granisle, B.C., Canada 189 F7 54 53N 126 13W
Granite, CO, U.S.A. 66 C4 39 3N 106 16W
Granite, OK, U.S.A. 93 D4 34 58N 99 23W
Granite, OR, U.S.A. 94 C7 44 49N 118 25W
Granite, Salt Lake City, U.S.A. 117 C3 40 34N 111 48W
Granite Bay, B.C., Canada 186 E9 50 14N 125 18W
Granite City, IL, U.S.A. 71 E3 38 42N 90 8W
Granite County ☆, MT, U.S.A. 83 D4 46 25N 113 30W
Granite Falls, MN, U.S.A. 80 F3 44 49N 95 33W
Granite Falls, NC, U.S.A. 90 C4 35 48N 81 26W
Granite Falls, WA, U.S.A. 101 B4 48 5N 121 58W
Granite L., Nfld. & L., Canada 174 D3 48 10N 57 5W
Granite Mts., AZ, U.S.A. 62 E2 32 20N 113 20W
Granite Mts., WY, U.S.A. 104 D5 42 45N 107 40W
Granite Pass, WY, U.S.A. 104 B5 44 38N 107 30W
Granite Peak, NV, U.S.A. 85 A3 41 40N 117 35W
Granite Pk., MT, U.S.A. 83 E8 45 10N 109 48W
Granite Pt., Nfld. & L., Canada 174 B4 50 31N 56 17W
Granite Pt., MI, U.S.A. 79 C4 46 47N 87 36W
Granite Quarry, NC, U.S.A. 90 C5 35 37N 80 26W
Granite Range, NV, U.S.A. 85 B1 40 55N 119 25W
Granite Springs Valley, NV, U.S.A. 85 B2 40 9N 118 57W
Graniteville, NY, U.S.A. 114 C2 40 37N 74 8W
Graniteville, SC, U.S.A. 90 E4 33 34N 81 49W
Graniteville, VT, U.S.A. 86 B2 44 8N 72 29W
Grannis, AR, U.S.A. 63 D1 34 14N 94 20W
Grano, ND, U.S.A. 91 B4 48 37N 101 35W
Grant, CO, U.S.A. 66 C5 39 28N 105 40W
Grant, FL, U.S.A. 67 D8 27 56N 80 32W
Grant, IA, U.S.A. 73 D4 41 9N 94 59W
Grant, LA, U.S.A. 75 D3 30 47N 92 57W
Grant, MI, U.S.A. 79 F6 43 20N 85 51W
Grant, Minneapolis-St. Paul, U.S.A. 113 A4 45 5N 92 34W
Grant, MT, U.S.A. 83 E4 45 1N 113 4W
Grant, NE, U.S.A. 84 D4 40 50N 101 43W
Grant, OK, U.S.A. 93 E8 33 57N 95 31W
Grant, Mt., NV, U.S.A. 85 D2 38 34N 118 48W
Grant City, MO, U.S.A. 82 A2 40 29N 94 25W
Grant County ☆, AR, U.S.A. 63 D3 34 19N 92 24W
Grant County ☆, IN, U.S.A. 72 C5 40 30N 85 40W
Grant County ☆, KS, U.S.A. 74 D2 37 30N 101 15W
Grant County ☆, KY, U.S.A. 97 B8 38 35N 84 35W
Grant County ☆, MN, U.S.A. 80 E2 45 55N 96 0W
Grant County ☆, ND, U.S.A. 91 D4 46 15N 101 30W
Grant County ☆, NM, U.S.A. 88 E2 33 0N 108 30W
Grant County ☆, NE, U.S.A. 84 C4 41 50N 101 45W
Grant County ☆, OK, U.S.A. 93 B6 36 50N 97 45W
Grant County ☆, OR, U.S.A. 94 C7 44 30N 119 0W
Grant County ☆, SD, U.S.A. 91 E9 45 12N 96 47W
Grant County ☆, WV, U.S.A. 102 B5 39 4N 79 4W
Grant County ☆, WA, U.S.A. 101 C6 47 10N 119 30W
Grant County ☆, WI, U.S.A. 103 F3 42 50N 90 45W
Grant-Kohrs Ranch Nat. Historic Site ⌓, MT, U.S.A. 83 D5 46 25N 112 45W
Grant Parish ☆, LA, U.S.A. 75 C3 31 32N 92 25W
Grant Park, Chicago, U.S.A. 108 B3 41 52N 87 37W
Grant Park, IL, U.S.A. 71 B6 41 14N 87 39W
Grant Range, NV, U.S.A. 85 D5 38 30N 115 25W
Grantham, NH, U.S.A. 86 C2 43 29N 72 8W
Grants, NM, U.S.A. 88 B3 35 9N 107 52W
Grants Pass, OR, U.S.A. 94 E2 42 26N 123 19W
Grantsburg, WI, U.S.A. 103 C1 45 47N 92 41W
Grantsdale, MT, U.S.A. 83 D3 46 12N 114 9W
Grantsville, MD, U.S.A. 77 A1 39 42N 79 12W
Grantsville, UT, U.S.A. 100 C3 40 36N 112 28W
Grantsville, WV, U.S.A. 102 C3 38 55N 81 6W
Grantville, GA, U.S.A. 68 C2 33 14N 84 50W
Granum, Alta., Canada 185 J7 49 52N 113 30W
Granville, IL, U.S.A. 71 B4 41 16N 89 14W
Granville, MA, U.S.A. 78 B2 42 4N 72 52W
Granville, ND, U.S.A. 91 B5 48 16N 100 47W
Granville, NY, U.S.A. 86 C1 43 24N 73 16W
Granville, OH, U.S.A. 92 C4 40 4N 82 31W
Granville, VT, U.S.A. 86 C2 43 58N 72 51W
Granville County ☆, NC, U.S.A. 90 B7 36 20N 78 40W
Granville I., Vancouver, Canada 193 B2 49 16N 123 8W
Granville L., Man., Canada 191 F5 56 18N 100 30W
Grape I., Boston, U.S.A. 106 B4 42 16N 70 55W
Grapeland, TX, U.S.A. 99 F12 31 30N 95 29W
Grapevine, TX, U.S.A. 99 E10 32 56N 97 4W
Grapevine L., TX, U.S.A. 99 E10 32 58N 97 4W
Grapevine Recr. Area, Dallas-Fort Worth, U.S.A. 109 A3 32 58N 97 3W
Gras, L. de, N.W.T., Canada 189 D10 64 30N 110 30W
Grasmere, ID, U.S.A. 70 G3 42 23N 115 53W
Grasonville, MD, U.S.A. 77 B4 38 57N 76 13W
Grass Creek, WY, U.S.A. 104 C4 43 56N 108 39W
Grass Hassock Channel, NY, U.S.A. 114 C4 40 36N 73 47W
Grass Lake, MI, U.S.A. 79 G7 42 15N 84 13W
Grass Range, MT, U.S.A. 83 C9 47 2N 108 48W
Grass River Prov. Park ⌓, Man., Canada 183 A11 54 40N 100 50W
Grass-Vadnais Regional Park, Minneapolis-St. Paul, U.S.A. 113 A3 45 4N 93 7W
Grass Valley, CA, U.S.A. 64 D5 39 13N 121 4W
Grass Valley, OR, U.S.A. 94 B5 45 22N 120 47W
Grasset, L., Qué., Canada 176 B4 49 55N 78 10W
Grasslands Nat. Park △, Sask., Canada 182 F4 49 11N 107 38W
Grasston, MN, U.S.A. 80 E5 45 48N 93 9W
Grassy Bay, NY, U.S.A. 114 C4 40 38N 73 48W
Grassy Butte, ND, U.S.A. 91 C2 47 24N 103 15W
Grassy Lake, Alta., Canada 185 J9 49 49N 111 43W
Gratiot, WI, U.S.A. 103 F3 42 35N 90 1W
Gratiot County ☆, MI, U.S.A. 79 F7 43 15N 84 40W
Gratz, KY, U.S.A. 97 B8 38 28N 84 57W
Gravel →, Qué., Canada 172 C3 50 2N 66 55W
Gravelbourg, Sask., Canada 182 F5 49 50N 106 35W
Gravelly, AR, U.S.A. 63 D2 34 53N 93 41W
Gravelly Ra., MT, U.S.A. 83 F6 44 49N 111 52W
Gravenhurst, Ont., Canada 176 G3 44 52N 79 20W
Graves County ☆, KY, U.S.A. 96 D4 36 45N 88 40W
Gravesend, NY, U.S.A. 114 C3 40 36N 73 56W
Gravette, AR, U.S.A. 63 B1 36 25N 94 27W
Gravity, IA, U.S.A. 73 E4 40 46N 94 45W
Gravois Mills, MO, U.S.A. 82 C4 38 19N 92 49W
Gray, GA, U.S.A. 68 C3 33 1N 83 32W
Gray, IA, U.S.A. 73 D4 41 49N 94 59W
Gray, KY, U.S.A. 97 D9 36 57N 84 0W
Gray, TN, U.S.A. 97 D10 36 25N 82 29W
Gray County ☆, KS, U.S.A. 74 D3 37 40N 100 20W
Gray County ☆, TX, U.S.A. 98 B7 35 26N 100 48W
Gray Court, SC, U.S.A. 90 D3 34 36N 82 7W
Gray Hawk, KY, U.S.A. 97 C9 37 24N 83 56W
Gray Summit, MO, U.S.A. 82 C6 38 29N 90 49W
Grayland, WA, U.S.A. 101 D1 46 49N 124 6W
Grayling, AK, U.S.A. 61 E7 62 57N 160 3W
Grayling, MI, U.S.A. 79 E7 44 40N 84 43W
Grays Harbor, WA, U.S.A. 101 D1 46 58N 124 5W
Grays Harbor County ☆, WA, U.S.A. 101 C2 47 15N 123 45W
Grays L., ID, U.S.A. 70 F7 43 4N 111 26W
Grays Lake Nat. Wildlife Refuge ⌓, ID, U.S.A. 70 F7 43 4N 111 26W
Grays River, WA, U.S.A. 101 D2 46 21N 123 37W
Grayslake, IL, U.S.A. 71 A5 42 21N 88 2W
Grayson, Sask., Canada 182 E9 50 45N 102 40W
Grayson, KY, U.S.A. 97 B10 38 20N 82 57W
Grayson, OK, U.S.A. 93 C8 35 32N 95 51W
Grayson County ☆, KY, U.S.A. 96 C6 37 25N 86 20W
Grayson County ☆, TX, U.S.A. 99 D11 33 38N 96 36W
Grayson County ☆, VA, U.S.A. 102 E3 36 40N 81 10W
Grayson L., KY, U.S.A. 97 B10 38 15N 82 59W
Grayson Valley, AL, U.S.A. 60 C4 33 39N 86 38W
Graysville, TN, U.S.A. 97 E7 35 27N 85 8W
Grayton, MD, U.S.A. 77 B3 38 26N 77 13W
Grayville, IL, U.S.A. 71 E5 38 16N 88 0W
Great B., NH, U.S.A. 86 C4 43 5N 70 53W
Great Barrington, MA, U.S.A. 78 B1 42 12N 73 22W
Great Basin, NV, U.S.A. 85 C4 40 0N 117 0W
Great Basin Nat. Park △, NV, U.S.A. 85 D6 38 56N 114 15W
Great Bay, NJ, U.S.A. 87 C2 39 30N 74 25W
Great Bear →, N.W.T., Canada 189 C8 65 0N 124 0W
Great Bear L., N.W.T., Canada 189 C8 65 30N 120 0W
Great Bend, KS, U.S.A. 74 C5 38 22N 98 46W
Great Bend, ND, U.S.A. 91 D9 46 9N 96 48W
Great Bend, PA, U.S.A. 95 C7 41 58N 75 45W
Great Burnt L., Nfld. & L., Canada 174 D4 48 20N 56 20W
Great Camanoe, Br. Virgin Is. 105 G18 18 30N 64 35W
Great Central, B.C., Canada 186 F9 49 20N 125 10W
Great Central L., B.C., Canada 186 F9 49 22N 125 10W
Great Dismal Swamp Nat. Wildlife Refuge ⌓, VA, U.S.A. 102 E8 36 35N 76 28W
Great Divide Basin, WY, U.S.A. 104 D5 42 0N 108 0W
Great Duck I., Ont., Canada 178 B4 45 40N 82 57W
Great Egg Harbor →, NJ, U.S.A. 87 C2 39 18N 74 40W
Great Falls, Man., Canada 183 E15 50 27N 96 1W
Great Falls, MT, U.S.A. 83 C6 47 30N 111 17W
Great Falls, SC, U.S.A. 90 D5 34 34N 80 54W
Great Falls, VA, U.S.A. 119 B2 38 59N 77 17W
Great Falls Park, MD, U.S.A. 119 B2 38 59N 77 14W
Great Kills, NY, U.S.A. 114 C2 40 33N 74 9W
Great Kills Harbor, NY, U.S.A. 114 C2 40 32N 74 8W
Great Kills Park, NY, U.S.A. 114 C2 40 32N 74 7W
Great L., NC, U.S.A. 90 D8 34 49N 77 2W
Great Meadows Nat. Wildlife Refuge ⌓, Boston, U.S.A. 106 A1 42 28N 71 19W
Great Miami →, OH, U.S.A. 92 D2 39 7N 84 49W
Great Miami →, OH, U.S.A. 92 D2 39 6N 84 49W
Great Mills, MD, U.S.A. 77 B4 38 14N 76 30W
Great Neck, NY, U.S.A. 87 B3 40 47N 73 44W
Great Peconic B., NY, U.S.A. 78 D2 40 57N 72 30W
Great Pee Dee →, SC, U.S.A. 90 E6 33 21N 79 10W
Great Plains Res., CO, U.S.A. 66 D8 38 15N 102 43W
Great Pond, ME, U.S.A. 76 D5 44 57N 68 19W
Great Pt., MA, U.S.A. 78 C4 41 24N 70 3W
Great Quittacas Pond, MA, U.S.A. 78 C4 41 48N 70 54W
Great River Nat. Wildlife Refuge ⌓, IL, U.S.A. 71 D3 39 27N 90 58W
Great Sacandaga L., NY, U.S.A. 89 B6 43 6N 74 16W
Great Salt L., UT, U.S.A. 100 B3 41 15N 112 40W
Great Salt Lake Desert, UT, U.S.A. 100 C2 40 50N 113 30W
Great Salt Plains L., OK, U.S.A. 93 B5 36 45N 98 8W
Great Sand Dunes Nat. Monument ⌓, CO, U.S.A. 66 E5 37 48N 105 45W
Great Sandy Desert, OR, U.S.A. 94 D5 43 35N 120 15W
Great Sitkin I., AK, U.S.A. 61 K3 52 3N 176 6W
Great Slave L., N.W.T., Canada 189 D9 61 23N 115 38W
Great Smoky Mountains Nat. Park △, TN, U.S.A. 90 C2 35 40N 83 40W
Great Smoky Mts., TN, U.S.A. 90 C2 35 40N 83 40W
Great Snow Mt., B.C., Canada 189 E8 57 26N 124 0W
Great South Bay, NY, U.S.A. 87 B3 40 40N 73 15W
Great Wass I., ME, U.S.A. 76 D6 44 29N 67 36W
Great Whale River = Kuujjuarapik, Qué., Canada 175 B2 55 20N 77 35W
Great White Heron Nat. Wildlife Refuge ⌓, FL, U.S.A. 67 G7 24 45N 81 10W
Greater Buffalo International ✕ (BUF), NY, U.S.A. 89 C2 42 56N 78 44W
Greater Sudbury = Sudbury, Ont., Canada 178 A5 46 30N 81 0W
Greece, NY, U.S.A. 89 B3 43 13N 77 41W
Greeley, CO, U.S.A. 66 B6 40 25N 104 42W
Greeley, IA, U.S.A. 73 C7 42 35N 91 21W
Greeley, KS, U.S.A. 74 C8 38 22N 95 8W
Greeley, NE, U.S.A. 84 C7 41 33N 98 32W
Greeley County ☆, KS, U.S.A. 74 C2 38 30N 101 45W
Greeley County ☆, NE, U.S.A. 84 C7 41 30N 98 30W
Greely Fd., Nunavut, Canada 190 A9 80 30N 85 0W
Green, KS, U.S.A. 74 B6 39 26N 97 0W
Green, OH, U.S.A. 92 C5 40 57N 81 29W
Green →, N.B., Canada 173 F1 47 18N 68 9W
Green →, IL, U.S.A. 71 B3 41 28N 90 23W
Green →, KY, U.S.A. 96 C5 37 54N 87 30W
Green →, ND, U.S.A. 91 D3 46 52N 102 35W
Green →, UT, U.S.A. 100 E6 38 11N 109 53W
Green →, WA, U.S.A. 101 C3 47 28N 122 15W
Green Acres, Norfolk, U.S.A. 115 A1 36 50N 76 24W
Green B., Nfld. & L., Canada 174 C5 49 45N 55 55W
Green B., WI, U.S.A. 103 D6 45 0N 87 30W
Green Bank, NJ, U.S.A. 87 C2 39 40N 74 36W
Green Bank, WV, U.S.A. 102 C5 38 25N 79 50W
Green Bay, WI, U.S.A. 103 D6 44 31N 88 0W
Green Camp, OH, U.S.A. 92 C3 40 32N 83 13W
Green City, MO, U.S.A. 82 A4 40 16N 92 57W
Green County ☆, KY, U.S.A. 97 C7 37 15N 85 35W
Green County ☆, WI, U.S.A. 103 F4 42 45N 89 40W
Green Cove Springs, FL, U.S.A. 67 B7 29 59N 81 42W
Green Creek, NJ, U.S.A. 87 C2 39 3N 74 54W
Green Forest, AR, U.S.A. 63 B2 36 20N 93 26W
Green Island, IA, U.S.A. 73 C8 42 9N 90 20W
Green Isle, MN, U.S.A. 80 F4 44 41N 94 1W
Green L., MN, U.S.A. 80 E4 45 15N 94 54W
Green L., WI, U.S.A. 103 E5 43 49N 89 0W
Green Lake, Sask., Canada 182 A4 54 17N 107 47W
Green Lake, WI, U.S.A. 103 E5 43 51N 88 58W
Green Lake County ☆, WI, U.S.A. 103 E5 43 45N 89 0W
Green Mountain Nat. Forest, VT, U.S.A. 86 C2 44 0N 73 0W
Green Mts., VT, U.S.A. 86 C2 43 45N 72 45W
Green Mts., WY, U.S.A. 104 D5 42 23N 107 45W
Green Peter L., OR, U.S.A. 94 C3 44 26N 122 37W
Green Ridge, MO, U.S.A. 82 C3 38 37N 93 25W
Green Ridge State Forest, MD, U.S.A. 77 A2 39 36N 78 30W
Green River, UT, U.S.A. 100 E5 38 59N 110 10W
Green River, WY, U.S.A. 104 E3 41 32N 109 28W
Green River L., KY, U.S.A. 97 C7 37 15N 85 15W
Green Spring, WV, U.S.A. 77 A2 39 32N 78 37W
Green Swamp, FL, U.S.A. 67 C7 28 12N 81 46W
Green Swamp, NC, U.S.A. 90 D7 34 15N 78 25W
Green Tree, Pittsburgh, U.S.A. 116 B1 40 24N 80 2W
Green Valley, AZ, U.S.A. 62 F5 31 52N 110 56W
Green Valley, IL, U.S.A. 71 C4 40 24N 89 38W
Green Valley, MD, U.S.A. 77 A3 39 19N 77 18W
Greenacres, CA, U.S.A. 65 H7 35 23N 119 7W
Greenacres, FL, U.S.A. 67 E8 26 38N 80 7W
Greenback, TN, U.S.A. 97 E8 35 40N 84 10W
Greenbelt, MD, U.S.A. 119 A4 39 0N 76 52W
Greenbelt, MD, U.S.A. 77 A4 39 0N 76 53W
Greenbelt Park, MD, U.S.A. 119 B4 38 58N 76 53W
Greenbrier, AR, U.S.A. 63 C3 35 14N 92 23W
Greenbrier, TN, U.S.A. 96 D6 36 26N 86 48W
Greenbrier →, WV, U.S.A. 102 D4 37 39N 80 53W
Greenbrier County ☆, WV, U.S.A. 102 D4 37 56N 80 23W
Greenbush, MI, U.S.A. 79 E8 44 35N 83 19W
Greenbush, MN, U.S.A. 80 B2 48 42N 96 11W
Greencastle, IN, U.S.A. 72 D4 39 38N 86 52W
Greencastle, PA, U.S.A. 77 A3 39 47N 77 44W
Greendale, IN, U.S.A. 72 D6 39 7N 84 52W
Greendale, Milwaukee, U.S.A. 112 C2 42 56N 87 59W
Greendale, MO, U.S.A. 117 A2 38 41N 90 18W
Greene, IA, U.S.A. 73 C6 42 54N 92 48W
Greene, ME, U.S.A. 76 D3 44 12N 70 8W
Greene, NY, U.S.A. 89 C5 42 20N 75 46W
Greene County ☆, AL, U.S.A. 60 D3 32 50N 87 53W
Greene County ☆, AR, U.S.A. 63 B5 36 3N 90 29W
Greene County ☆, GA, U.S.A. 68 C3 33 30N 83 5W
Greene County ☆, IL, U.S.A. 71 D3 39 20N 90 20W
Greene County ☆, IN, U.S.A. 72 D4 39 0N 87 0W
Greene County ☆, IA, U.S.A. 73 C4 42 0N 94 25W
Greene County ☆, MS, U.S.A. 81 E5 31 10N 88 45W
Greene County ☆, MO, U.S.A. 82 D3 37 15N 93 20W
Greene County ☆, NC, U.S.A. 90 C8 35 30N 77 40W
Greene County ☆, NY, U.S.A. 89 C7 42 20N 74 0W
Greene County ☆, OH, U.S.A. 92 D3 39 41N 83 56W
Greene County ☆, PA, U.S.A. 95 E2 39 55N 80 5W
Greene County ☆, TN, U.S.A. 97 D10 36 10N 82 50W
Greene County ☆, VA, U.S.A. 102 C6 38 18N 78 26W
Greeneville, TN, U.S.A. 97 D10 36 10N 82 50W
Greenfield, CA, U.S.A. 65 G5 36 19N 121 15W
Greenfield, IL, U.S.A. 71 D3 39 21N 90 12W
Greenfield, IN, U.S.A. 72 D5 39 47N 85 46W
Greenfield, IA, U.S.A. 73 D4 41 18N 94 28W
Greenfield, MA, U.S.A. 78 B2 42 35N 72 36W
Greenfield, Milwaukee, U.S.A. 112 C1 42 57N 88 0W
Greenfield, MO, U.S.A. 82 D3 37 25N 93 51W
Greenfield, NH, U.S.A. 86 D3 42 55N 71 51W
Greenfield, OH, U.S.A. 92 D3 39 21N 83 23W
Greenfield, OK, U.S.A. 93 C5 35 44N 98 23W
Greenfield, TN, U.S.A. 96 D4 36 9N 88 48W
Greenfield Park, Montréal, Canada 192 B4 45 29N 73 28W
Greenfield Park, Milwaukee, U.S.A. 112 B1 43 0N 88 3W
Greenhorn, OR, U.S.A. 94 C7 44 42N 118 29W
Greenhorn Mts., CA, U.S.A. 65 H8 35 51N 118 34W
Greenland, MI, U.S.A. 79 C2 46 47N 89 6W
Greenland, NH, U.S.A. 86 C4 43 4N 70 50W
Greenleaf, KS, U.S.A. 74 B7 39 44N 96 59W
Greenlee County ☆, AZ, U.S.A. 62 D6 33 0N 109 15W
Greenough, MT, U.S.A. 83 D4 46 55N 113 25W
Greenough Pt., Ont., Canada 178 C5 44 58N 81 26W
Greenpoint, NY, U.S.A. 114 B3 40 43N 73 57W
Greenport, NY, U.S.A. 78 C2 41 6N 72 22W
Green's Creek Conservation Area, Ont., Canada 192 A2 45 25N 75 35W
Greensboro, AL, U.S.A. 60 D3 32 42N 87 36W
Greensboro, FL, U.S.A. 67 A4 30 34N 84 45W
Greensboro, GA, U.S.A. 68 C3 33 35N 83 11W
Greensboro, MD, U.S.A. 77 B5 38 58N 75 48W
Greensboro, NC, U.S.A. 90 B6 36 4N 79 48W
Greensboro, VT, U.S.A. 86 B2 44 36N 72 18W
Greensboro-High Point ✕ (GSO), NC, U.S.A. 90 B6 36 5N 79 56W
Greensburg, IN, U.S.A. 72 D5 39 20N 85 29W
Greensburg, KS, U.S.A. 74 D4 37 36N 99 18W
Greensburg, KY, U.S.A. 97 C7 37 16N 85 30W
Greensburg, LA, U.S.A. 75 D5 30 50N 90 40W
Greensburg, PA, U.S.A. 95 D3 40 18N 79 33W
Greenstone, Ont., Canada 181 C9 49 44N 87 10W
Greensville County ☆, VA, U.S.A. 102 E7 36 42N 77 32W
Greentown, IN, U.S.A. 72 C5 40 29N 85 58W
Greenup, IL, U.S.A. 71 D5 39 15N 88 10W
Greenup, KY, U.S.A. 97 B10 38 35N 82 50W
Greenup County ☆, KY, U.S.A. 97 B10 38 30N 83 0W
Greenview, IL, U.S.A. 71 C4 40 5N 89 44W
Greenville, AL, U.S.A. 60 E4 31 50N 86 38W
Greenville, CA, U.S.A. 64 C6 40 8N 120 57W
Greenville, FL, U.S.A. 67 A5 30 28N 83 38W
Greenville, GA, U.S.A. 68 C2 33 2N 84 43W
Greenville, IL, U.S.A. 71 E4 38 53N 89 25W
Greenville, KY, U.S.A. 96 C5 37 12N 87 11W
Greenville, ME, U.S.A. 76 C4 45 28N 69 35W
Greenville, MI, U.S.A. 79 F6 43 11N 85 15W
Greenville, MS, U.S.A. 81 C2 33 24N 91 4W
Greenville, MO, U.S.A. 82 D6 37 8N 90 27W
Greenville, NC, U.S.A. 90 C8 35 37N 77 23W
Greenville, NH, U.S.A. 86 D3 42 46N 71 49W
Greenville, OH, U.S.A. 92 C2 40 6N 84 38W
Greenville, PA, U.S.A. 95 C1 41 24N 80 23W
Greenville, RI, U.S.A. 78 C3 41 52N 71 33W
Greenville, SC, U.S.A. 90 D3 34 51N 82 24W
Greenville, TX, U.S.A. 99 D11 33 8N 96 7W
Greenville, WI, U.S.A. 103 D5 44 18N 88 32W
Greenville County ☆, SC, U.S.A. 90 D3 34 50N 82 20W
Greenwald, MN, U.S.A. 80 E4 45 36N 94 52W
Greenwater L., Ont., Canada 180 D6 48 34N 90 26W
Greenwater Lake Prov. Park ⌓, Sask., Canada 182 C8 52 32N 103 30W
Greenway, AR, U.S.A. 63 B5 36 21N 90 13W
Greenwich, CT, U.S.A. 78 C1 41 2N 73 38W
Greenwich, NJ, U.S.A. 87 C1 39 24N 75 21W
Greenwich, NY, U.S.A. 89 B7 43 5N 73 30W
Greenwich, OH, U.S.A. 92 B4 41 2N 82 31W
Greenwich Village, New York, U.S.A. 114 B3 40 44N 73 59W
Greenwood, B.C., Canada 187 F16 49 10N 118 40W
Greenwood, AR, U.S.A. 63 C1 35 13N 94 16W
Greenwood, Boston, U.S.A. 106 A3 42 29N 71 2W
Greenwood, DE, U.S.A. 77 B5 38 49N 75 35W
Greenwood, FL, U.S.A. 67 A3 30 52N 85 10W
Greenwood, IN, U.S.A. 72 D4 39 37N 86 7W
Greenwood, KY, U.S.A. 97 D8 36 53N 84 30W
Greenwood, LA, U.S.A. 75 B2 32 27N 93 58W
Greenwood, MS, U.S.A. 81 C3 33 31N 90 11W
Greenwood, NE, U.S.A. 84 D9 40 58N 96 27W
Greenwood, SC, U.S.A. 90 D3 34 12N 82 10W
Greenwood, WI, U.S.A. 103 D3 44 46N 90 36W
Greenwood, L., SC, U.S.A. 90 D4 34 11N 81 54W
Greenwood Cemetery, NY, U.S.A. 114 C3 40 39N 73 59W
Greenwood County ☆, KS, U.S.A. 74 D7 37 45N 96 15W
Greenwood County ☆, SC, U.S.A. 90 D3 34 10N 82 5W
Greenwood L., U.S.A. 87 A2 41 10N 74 20W
Greenwood Village, CO, U.S.A. 66 C6 39 37N 104 57W
Greenwook Lake, NY, U.S.A. 87 A2 41 13N 74 18W
Greer, ID, U.S.A. 70 C2 46 24N 116 11W
Greer, MO, U.S.A. 82 E5 36 46N 91 21W
Greer, SC, U.S.A. 90 D3 34 56N 82 14W
Greer County ☆, OK, U.S.A. 93 D4 35 0N 99 35W
Greers Ferry, AR, U.S.A. 63 C3 35 35N 92 11W
Greers Ferry L., AR, U.S.A. 63 C3 35 32N 92 10W
Greeson, L., AR, U.S.A. 63 D2 34 9N 93 43W
Gregg County ☆, TX, U.S.A. 99 E13 32 30N 94 44W
Gregory, AR, U.S.A. 63 C4 35 9N 91 21W
Gregory, MI, U.S.A. 79 G7 42 28N 84 5W
Gregory, SD, U.S.A. 91 G6 43 14N 99 26W
Gregory, TX, U.S.A. 99 K10 27 56N 97 18W
Gregory County ☆, SD, U.S.A. 91 G6 43 11N 99 18W
Grenada, CA, U.S.A. 64 B4 41 39N 122 31W
Grenada, MS, U.S.A. 81 C4 33 47N 89 49W
Grenada County ☆, MS, U.S.A. 81 C4 33 47N 89 49W
Grenada L., MS, U.S.A. 81 C4 33 50N 89 47W
Grenfell, Sask., Canada 182 E9 50 30N 102 56W
Grenola, KS, U.S.A. 74 D7 37 21N 96 27W
Grenora, ND, U.S.A. 91 B2 48 37N 103 56W
Grenville, Qué., Canada 176 F8 45 37N 74 36W
Grenville, NM, U.S.A. 88 A7 36 36N 103 37W
Grenville, SD, U.S.A. 91 E8 45 28N 97 23W
Grenville Chan., B.C., Canada 186 B5 53 40N 129 46W
Gres, Pt. au, MI, U.S.A. 79 F8 43 59N 83 41W
Gresham, NE, U.S.A. 84 C8 41 2N 97 24W
Gresham, OR, U.S.A. 94 B3 45 29N 122 25W
Gresham Park, Atlanta, U.S.A. 106 B2 33 43N 84 20W
Gressitt, VA, U.S.A. 102 D8 37 29N 76 43W
Gresston, GA, U.S.A. 68 D3 32 17N 83 15W
Gretna, Man., Canada 183 F14 49 1N 97 34W
Gretna, FL, U.S.A. 67 A4 30 37N 84 40W
Gretna, LA, U.S.A. 75 E5 29 54N 90 3W
Gretna, NE, U.S.A. 84 C9 41 8N 96 15W
Gretna, VA, U.S.A. 102 E5 36 57N 79 22W
Gretna City Park, New Orleans, U.S.A. 113 C2 29 54N 90 3W
Grey →, Nfld. & L., Canada 174 E3 47 34N 57 6W
Grey, Pt., B.C., Canada 193 B1 49 17N 123 14W
Grey Eagle, MN, U.S.A. 80 E4 45 50N 94 45W
Grey Forest, San Antonio, U.S.A. 117 B1 29 36N 98 40W
Grey Is., Nfld. & L., Canada 174 B5 50 50N 55 35W
Grey River, Nfld. & L., Canada 174 E3 47 35N 57 6W
Greybull, WY, U.S.A. 104 B4 44 30N 108 3W
Greybull →, WY, U.S.A. 104 B4 44 28N 108 3W
Greylock, Mt., MA, U.S.A. 78 B1 42 38N 73 10W
Greynolds Park, Miami, U.S.A. 112 C3 25 56N 80 9W
Greystone, CO, U.S.A. 66 B2 40 37N 108 41W
Gribbell I., B.C., Canada 186 B5 53 23N 129 0W
Gridley, CA, U.S.A. 64 D5 39 22N 121 42W
Gridley, IL, U.S.A. 71 C5 40 45N 88 53W
Gridley, KS, U.S.A. 74 C8 38 6N 95 53W
Griffin, GA, U.S.A. 68 C2 33 15N 84 16W
Griffin, IN, U.S.A. 72 E3 38 12N 87 55W
Griffin, L., FL, U.S.A. 67 C7 28 52N 81 51W
Griffith, Ont., Canada 179 B9 45 15N 77 10W
Griffith I., Nunavut, Canada 190 C6 74 35N 95 30W
Griffith I., Ont., Canada 178 C6 44 50N 80 55W
Griffith Lakes, Charlotte, U.S.A. 107 A2 35 19N 80 48W
Griffith Park, Los Angeles, U.S.A. 111 B3 34 8N 118 17W
Griffithsville, WV, U.S.A. 102 C3 38 14N 81 59W
Grifton, NC, U.S.A. 90 C8 35 23N 77 26W
Griggs County ☆, ND, U.S.A. 91 C7 47 34N 98 21W
Griggsville, IL, U.S.A. 71 D3 39 43N 90 43W
Grijalva →, Tabasco, Mexico 222 A4 18 36N 92 39W
Grimes, IA, U.S.A. 73 D5 41 41N 93 47W
Grimes County ☆, TX, U.S.A. 99 G12 30 29N 95 59W
Grimsby, Ont., Canada 178 D7 43 12N 79 34W
Grimshaw, Alta., Canada 184 B3 56 10N 117 40W
Grimsley, TN, U.S.A. 97 D8 36 16N 84 59W
Grindstone I., Ont., Canada 179 C10 44 43N 76 14W
Grinnell, IA, U.S.A. 73 D6 41 45N 92 43W
Grinnell, KS, U.S.A. 74 B3 39 6N 100 38W
Grinnell Pen., Nunavut, Canada 190 B6 76 40N 95 0W
Grise Fiord, Nunavut, Canada 190 B9 76 25N 82 57W
Griswold, IA, U.S.A. 73 D3 41 14N 95 8W
Grizzly Bear Mt., N.W.T., Canada 189 C8 65 20N 121 0W
Groais I., Nfld. & L., Canada 174 B5 50 55N 55 35W
Groesbeck, OH, U.S.A. 107 A1 39 13N 84 35W
Groesbeck, TX, U.S.A. 99 F11 31 31N 96 32W
Gronlid, Sask., Canada 182 B7 53 6N 104 28W
Groom, TX, U.S.A. 98 B6 35 12N 101 6W
Groom L., NV, U.S.A. 85 E5 37 17N 115 48W
Gros-Morne, Qué., Canada 172 D4 49 15N 65 34W
Gros Morne Nat. Park △, Nfld. & L., Canada 174 C3 49 40N 57 50W
Gros Ventre Range, WY, U.S.A. 104 C2 43 12N 110 22W
Gross, NE, U.S.A. 84 B7 42 57N 98 34W
Grosse Isle, Man., Canada 183 E14 50 4N 97 27W
Grosse Pointe, MI, U.S.A. 79 G9 42 24N 82 56W
Grosse Tete, LA, U.S.A. 75 D4 30 25N 91 26W
Grosses-Roches, Qué., Canada 172 E2 48 57N 67 5W
Groswater B., Nfld. & L., Canada 175 C6 54 20N 57 40W
Groton, CT, U.S.A. 78 C2 41 21N 72 5W
Groton, MA, U.S.A. 78 B3 42 37N 71 34W
Groton, NY, U.S.A. 89 C4 42 36N 76 22W
Groton, SD, U.S.A. 91 E7 45 27N 98 6W
Groton, VT, U.S.A. 86 B2 44 12N 72 12W
Grottoes, VA, U.S.A. 102 C6 38 16N 78 50W
Grouard Mission, Alta., Canada 184 C4 55 33N 116 9W
Groundhog →, Ont., Canada 181 D14 48 45N 82 58W
Grouse Creek, UT, U.S.A. 100 B2 41 42N 113 53W
Grouse Creek Mts., UT, U.S.A. 100 B2 41 30N 113 50W
Grovania, GA, U.S.A. 68 D3 32 22N 83 40W
Grove, OK, U.S.A. 93 B9 36 36N 94 46W
Grove City, OH, U.S.A. 92 D3 39 53N 83 6W
Grove City, PA, U.S.A. 95 C2 41 10N 80 5W
Grove Hall, Boston, U.S.A. 106 B3 42 18N 71 4W
Grove Hill, AL, U.S.A. 60 E3 31 42N 87 47W
Grove Park, Atlanta, U.S.A. 106 B2 33 46N 84 26W
Grovedale, Alta., Canada 184 C2 55 3N 118 52W
Groveland, CA, U.S.A. 64 F6 37 50N 120 14W
Groveland, FL, U.S.A. 67 C7 28 34N 81 51W
Groveland, MA, U.S.A. 78 B3 42 46N 71 2W
Groveport, OH, U.S.A. 92 D4 39 51N 82 53W
Grover, CO, U.S.A. 66 B6 40 52N 104 14W
Grover, UT, U.S.A. 100 E4 38 14N 111 21W
Grover, WY, U.S.A. 104 D2 42 48N 110 56W
Grover Beach, CA, U.S.A. 65 H6 35 7N 120 37W
Grover Hill, OH, U.S.A. 92 B2 41 1N 84 29W
Groves, TX, U.S.A. 99 H14 29 57N 93 54W
Grovespring, MO, U.S.A. 82 D4 37 24N 92 37W
Groveton, NH, U.S.A. 86 B3 44 36N 71 31W
Groveton, TX, U.S.A. 99 F12 31 4N 95 8W
Groveton, VA, U.S.A. 77 B3 38 46N 77 6W
Grovetown, GA, U.S.A. 68 C4 33 27N 82 12W
Growler Mts., AZ, U.S.A. 62 E3 32 15N 113 0W
Growler Wash →, AZ, U.S.A. 62 E2 32 40N 113 30W
Gruetli-Leager, TN, U.S.A. 97 E7 35 22N 85 37W
Grulla, TX, U.S.A. 98 L9 26 16N 98 39W
Grundy, VA, U.S.A. 102 D2 37 17N 82 6W
Grundy Center, IA, U.S.A. 73 C6 42 22N 92 47W
Grundy County ☆, IL, U.S.A. 71 B5 41 20N 88 25W
Grundy County ☆, IA, U.S.A. 73 C6 42 25N 92 45W
Grundy County ☆, MO, U.S.A. 82 A3 40 5N 93 30W
Grundy County ☆, TN, U.S.A. 97 E7 35 26N 85 44W
Grundy Prov. Park ⌓, Ont., Canada 178 B6 45 58N 80 30W
Grunthal, Man., Canada 183 F15 49 24N 96 51W
Gruver, IA, U.S.A. 73 B4 43 24N 94 42W
Gruver, TX, U.S.A. 98 A6 36 16N 101 24W
Grygla, MN, U.S.A. 80 B3 48 18N 95 37W
Grymes Hill, NY, U.S.A. 114 C2 40 36N 74 6W
Guacamayita, Durango, Mexico 217 D6 23 21N 104 29W
Guachimetas de Arriba, Durango, Mexico 216 C4 24 28N 106 12W
Guachimontón, Jalisco, Mexico 218 B4 20 43N 103 51W
Guachinango, Jalisco, Mexico 218 B3 20 34N 104 23W
Guachochi, Chihuahua, Mexico 213 G8 26 48N 107 7W
Guadalajara, Jalisco, Mexico 218 B4 20 40N 103 20W
Guadalajara ✕ (GDL), Jalisco, Mexico 218 B4 20 38N 103 22W
Guadalcázar, San Luis Potosí, Mexico 215 H4 22 37N 100 24W

Guadalupe, *Nuevo León, Mexico* **214 E4** 25 41N 100 15W
Guadalupe, *Puebla, Mexico* **221 F2** 18 5N 98 6W
Guadalupe, *Zacatecas, Mexico* **217 E8** 22 45N 102 31W
Guadalupe, *AZ, U.S.A.* **62 D4** 33 22N 111 57W
Guadalupe, *CA, U.S.A.* **65 J6** 34 58N 120 34W
Guadalupe →, *Sonora, Mexico* **212 B2** 31 23N 113 6W
Guadalupe →, *TX, U.S.A.* **99 J11** 28 27N 96 47W
Guadalupe, Estancia de, *Guadalajara, Mexico* **224 C2** 20 28N 103 11W
Guadalupe, Volcan, *Distrito Federal, Mexico* **225 C4** 19 19N 99 0W
Guadalupe Aguilera, *Durango, Mexico* **217 C6** 24 30N 104 43W
Guadalupe County ☆, *NM, U.S.A.* **88 C6** 35 0N 104 45W
Guadalupe County ☆, *TX, U.S.A.* **99 H10** 29 34N 97 58W
Guadalupe de Bahues, *Chihuahua, Mexico* **213 G10** 26 37N 105 11W
Guadalupe de Bravo, *Chihuahua, Mexico* **213 B9** 31 23N 106 7W
Guadalupe de los Reyes, *Sinaloa, Mexico* **216 C4** 24 15N 106 32W
Guadalupe del Carnicero, *San Luis Potosí, Mexico* **215 G4** 23 28N 100 58W
Guadalupe Garzarón, *Zacatecas, Mexico* **217 C9** 24 36N 101 12W
Guadalupe Mountains Nat. Park △, *TX, U.S.A.* **98 F3** 31 40N 104 30W
Guadalupe Mts., *NM, U.S.A.* **88 E6** 32 15N 105 0W
Guadalupe Peak, *TX, U.S.A.* **98 F3** 31 50N 104 52W
Guadalupe Victoria, *Baja Calif., Mexico* **210 A3** 32 29N 115 7W
Guadalupe Victoria, *Chiapas, Mexico* **222 C3** 16 27N 93 7W
Guadalupe Victoria, *Durango, Mexico* **217 C6** 24 27N 104 7W
Guadalupe Victoria, *Puebla, Mexico* **220 E3** 19 18N 97 18W
Guadalupe Victoria, *Tabasco, Mexico* **222 B3** 17 37N 93 34W
Guadalupe Victoria, *Tamaulipas, Mexico* **215 E7** 25 0N 97 45W
Guadalupe y Calvo, *Chihuahua, Mexico* **213 G9** 26 6N 106 58W
Guadalupita, *NM, U.S.A.* **88 A5** 36 8N 105 14W
Guaguachique, *Chihuahua, Mexico* **213 F8** 27 22N 107 42W
Guajademi →, *Baja Calif. S., Mexico* **211 G6** 26 33N 112 5W
Guajardo, *Tamaulipas, Mexico* **214 E7** 25 23N 97 23W
Guaje, L. el, *Coahuila, Mexico* **214 C1** 28 0N 103 14W
Gualala, *CA, U.S.A.* **64 E3** 38 46N 123 32W
Guam ☑, *Pac. Oc.* **105 b** 13 27N 144 45 E
Guam Antonio B. Won Pat International ✕ (GUM), *Guam* **105 D3** 13 29N 144 48 E
Guamúchil, *Sinaloa, Mexico* **216 B2** 25 28N 108 6W
Guamuchilera, *Sinaloa, Mexico* **216 C3** 24 56N 107 43W
Guana I., *Br. Virgin Is.* **105 G18** 18 30N 64 30W
Guanacevi, *Durango, Mexico* **216 B5** 25 56N 105 57W
Guanajuato, *Guanajuato, Mexico* **219 A6** 21 1N 101 15W
Guanajuato ☐, *Mexico* **219 B7** 21 0N 101 0W
Guánica, *Puerto Rico* **105 H16** 17 58N 66 55W
Guano L., *OR, U.S.A.* **94 E6** 42 11N 119 32W
Guardianes de la Patria, *Baja Calif., Mexico* **210 A3** 32 12N 115 36W
Guariche, *Coahuila, Mexico* **215 E3** 25 19N 101 49W
Guasave, *Sinaloa, Mexico* **216 B2** 25 34N 108 27W
Guasizaco, *Chihuahua, Mexico* **213 F7** 27 39N 108 27W
Guatimape, *Durango, Mexico* **217 C6** 24 47N 104 55W
Guayalejo →, *Tamaulipas, Mexico* **215 H6** 22 25N 98 29W
Guayama, *Puerto Rico* **105 H16** 17 59N 66 7W
Guayameo, *Guerrero, Mexico* **219 D6** 18 12N 101 19W
Guayanilla, *Puerto Rico* **105 G16** 18 1N 66 47W
Guayaquil, *Baja Calif., Mexico* **210 D3** 29 59N 115 4W
Guaymas, *Sonora, Mexico* **212 F5** 27 56N 110 54W
Guaynabo, *Puerto Rico* **105 G16** 18 22N 66 7W
Guazapares, *Chihuahua, Mexico* **213 F7** 27 22N 108 15W
Guéguen, L., *Qué., Canada* **176 C5** 48 6N 77 13W
Guelph, *Ont., Canada* **178 D6** 43 35N 80 20W
Güémez, *Tamaulipas, Mexico* **215 G6** 23 56N 99 0W
Guerachi →, *Chihuahua, Mexico* **213 G8** 26 45N 107 32W
Guerneville, *CA, U.S.A.* **64 E3** 38 30N 123 0W
Guernsey, *Sask., Canada* **182 D6** 51 53N 105 11W
Guernsey, *IA, U.S.A.* **73 D6** 41 39N 92 21W
Guernsey, *WY, U.S.A.* **104 D8** 42 16N 104 45W
Guernsey County ☆, *OH, U.S.A.* **92 C5** 40 2N 81 35W
Guernsey Res., *WY, U.S.A.* **104 D8** 42 17N 104 46W
Guerra, *TX, U.S.A.* **98 L9** 26 53N 98 54W
Guerrero, *Coahuila, Mexico* **214 B4** 28 20N 100 23W
Guerrero ☐, *Mexico* **219 E8** 17 40N 100 0W
Guerrero Negro, *Baja Calif. S., Mexico* **211 F4** 27 57N 114 2W
Guerrero Negro, L., *Baja Calif. S., Mexico* **211 E4** 28 2N 114 2W
Guevea de Humboldt, *Oaxaca, Mexico* **221 H6** 16 48N 95 22W
Gueydan, *LA, U.S.A.* **75 D3** 30 2N 92 31W
Guffey, *CO, U.S.A.* **66 D5** 38 45N 105 31W
Guffy Peak, *WY, U.S.A.* **104 C5** 43 29N 107 54W
Guguan, *N. Marianas* **105 a** 17 18N 145 51W
Guide Rock, *NE, U.S.A.* **84 D7** 40 4N 98 20W
Guildhall, *VT, U.S.A.* **86 B3** 44 34N 71 34W
Guilford, *CT, U.S.A.* **78 C2** 41 17N 72 41W
Guilford, *ME, U.S.A.* **76 C4** 45 10N 69 23W
Guilford County ☆, *NC, U.S.A.* **90 B6** 36 10N 79 45W
Guillaume-Delisle, L., *Qué., Canada* **175 B2** 56 15N 76 17W
Guillermo Blake Agular, Presa, *Sinaloa, Mexico* **216 A2** 26 10N 108 17W
Guillermo Prieto, *Baja Calif. S., Mexico* **211 F5** 27 50N 113 19W
Guillermo Zúñiga, *Tamaulipas, Mexico* **215 G5** 24 0N 99 12W
Guimbalete, *Chihuahua, Mexico* **213 F12** 27 2N 103 44W
Guin, *AL, U.S.A.* **60 C3** 33 58N 87 55W
Guinda, *CA, U.S.A.* **64 E4** 38 50N 122 12W
Guines, L., *Nfld. & L., Canada* **172 A8** 52 8N 61 25W
Guion, *AR, U.S.A.* **63 C4** 35 56N 91 57W
Gulf City, *Tampa, U.S.A.* **119 C4** 27 42N 82 27W
Gulf County ☆, *FL, U.S.A.* **67 B3** 29 50N 85 15W
Gulf Hammock, *FL, U.S.A.* **67 B6** 29 15N 82 43W
Gulf Islands Nat. Seashore ⌓, *AL, U.S.A.* **67 A1** 30 10N 87 10W
Gulf Shores, *AL, U.S.A.* **60 F3** 30 17N 87 41W
Gulfport, *FL, U.S.A.* **67 D6** 27 44N 82 42W
Gulfport, *MS, U.S.A.* **81 F4** 30 22N 89 6W
Gulkana, *AK, U.S.A.* **61 E11** 62 16N 145 23W
Gull →, *Ont., Canada* **180 C7** 49 45N 89 0W
Gull L., *Alta., Canada* **185 F6** 52 34N 114 0W
Gull L., *MN, U.S.A.* **80 D4** 46 25N 94 21W
Gull Lake, *Sask., Canada* **182 E3** 50 10N 108 29W
Gullivan B., *FL, U.S.A.* **67 F5** 25 45N 81 40W
Gully, *MN, U.S.A.* **80 C3** 47 46N 95 37W
Gumboro, *DE, U.S.A.* **77 B5** 38 28N 75 22W
Gun L., *MI, U.S.A.* **79 G6** 42 36N 85 31W
Gunisao →, *Man., Canada* **183 B14** 53 56N 97 53W
Gunisao L., *Man., Canada* **183 B15** 53 33N 96 15W
Gunnison, *CO, U.S.A.* **66 D4** 38 33N 106 56W
Gunnison, *MS, U.S.A.* **81 C3** 33 57N 90 57W
Gunnison, *UT, U.S.A.* **100 D4** 39 9N 111 49W
Gunnison →, *CO, U.S.A.* **66 C2** 39 4N 108 35W
Gunnison, Mt., *CO, U.S.A.* **66 D3** 38 49N 107 23W
Gunnison County ☆, *CO, U.S.A.* **66 D4** 38 40N 107 0W
Gunnison Nat. Forest, *CO, U.S.A.* **66 D4** 38 30N 107 0W
Gunpowder →, *MD, U.S.A.* **77 A4** 39 20N 76 20W
Guntersville, *AL, U.S.A.* **60 B4** 34 21N 86 18W
Guntersville L., *AL, U.S.A.* **60 B4** 34 25N 86 23W
Guntown, *MS, U.S.A.* **81 B5** 34 27N 88 40W
Gurabo, *Puerto Rico* **105 G17** 18 16N 65 58W
Gurdon, *AR, U.S.A.* **63 E2** 33 55N 93 9W
Gurley, *AL, U.S.A.* **60 B4** 34 42N 86 23W
Gurley, *NE, U.S.A.* **84 C3** 41 19N 102 58W
Gurnee, *IL, U.S.A.* **71 A6** 42 22N 87 55W
Gurnet Point, *MA, U.S.A.* **78 B4** 42 1N 70 34W
Gustavo A. Madero, *Distrito Federal, Mexico* **225 B3** 19 29N 99 8W
Gustavo Díaz Ordaz, Presa, *Sinaloa, Mexico* **216 B3** 25 55N 107 54W
Gustavus, *AK, U.S.A.* **61 G14** 58 25N 135 44W
Gustine, *CA, U.S.A.* **64 F5** 37 16N 121 0W
Gustine, *TX, U.S.A.* **99 F9** 31 51N 98 24W
Guthrie, *KY, U.S.A.* **96 D5** 36 39N 87 10W
Guthrie, *OK, U.S.A.* **93 C6** 35 53N 97 25W
Guthrie, *TX, U.S.A.* **98 D7** 33 37N 100 19W
Guthrie Center, *IA, U.S.A.* **73 D4** 41 41N 94 30W
Guthrie County ☆, *IA, U.S.A.* **73 D4** 41 40N 94 30W
Gutiérrez Zamora, *Veracruz, Mexico* **220 D3** 20 27N 97 5W
Guttenberg, *IA, U.S.A.* **73 C7** 42 47N 91 6W
Guttenberg, *NJ, U.S.A.* **114 B2** 40 48N 74 0W
Guyandotte →, *WV, U.S.A.* **102 C2** 38 26N 82 23W
Guymon, *OK, U.S.A.* **93 B2** 36 41N 101 29W
Guyot, Mt., *TN, U.S.A.* **97 E9** 35 42N 83 15W
Guysborough, *N.S., Canada* **173 H8** 45 23N 61 30W
Guyton, *GA, U.S.A.* **68 D5** 32 20N 81 24W
Guzmán, L. de, *Chihuahua, Mexico* **213 B8** 31 20N 107 30W
Gwaii Haanas Nat. Park Reserve △, *B.C., Canada* **186 C3** 52 21N 131 26W
Gwinn, *MI, U.S.A.* **79 C4** 46 19N 87 27W
Gwinner, *ND, U.S.A.* **91 D8** 46 14N 97 40W
Gwinnett County ☆, *GA, U.S.A.* **68 C2** 34 0N 84 0W
Gwynns Falls Park, *Baltimore, U.S.A.* **107 B1** 39 18N 76 41W
Gypsum, *CO, U.S.A.* **66 C4** 39 39N 106 57W
Gypsum, *KS, U.S.A.* **74 C6** 38 42N 97 26W
Gypsumville, *Man., Canada* **183 D13** 51 45N 98 40W

H

H. Neely Henry L., *AL, U.S.A.* **60 C4** 33 55N 86 2W
Haakon County ☆, *SD, U.S.A.* **91 F4** 44 25N 101 35W
Habay, *Alta., Canada* **189 E9** 58 50N 118 44W
Habersham, *GA, U.S.A.* **68 B3** 34 36N 83 34W
Habersham County ☆, *GA, U.S.A.* **68 B3** 34 40N 83 30W
Hachita, *NM, U.S.A.* **88 F2** 31 55N 108 19W
Hackberry, *AZ, U.S.A.* **62 B2** 35 22N 113 44W
Hackberry, *LA, U.S.A.* **75 D2** 30 0N 93 17W
Hackensack, *MN, U.S.A.* **80 D4** 46 56N 94 31W
Hackensack, *NJ, U.S.A.* **87 B2** 40 52N 74 4W
Hackensack →, *New York, U.S.A.* **114 B2** 40 42N 74 7W
Hackett, *AR, U.S.A.* **63 C1** 35 11N 94 25W
Hackettstown, *NJ, U.S.A.* **87 B2** 40 51N 74 50W
Hackleburg, *AL, U.S.A.* **60 B3** 34 17N 87 50W
Hadar, *NE, U.S.A.* **84 B8** 42 6N 97 27W
Haddam, *KS, U.S.A.* **74 B6** 39 52N 97 18W
Haddock, *GA, U.S.A.* **68 C3** 33 2N 83 26W
Haddon Heights, *NJ, U.S.A.* **116 B2** 39 52N 75 3W
Hadlyme, *CT, U.S.A.* **78 C2** 41 25N 72 25W
Hā'ena, *HI, U.S.A.* **69 A2** 22 14N 159 34W
Hafford, *Sask., Canada* **182 C4** 52 43N 107 21W
Hagemeister I., *AK, U.S.A.* **61 G7** 58 39N 160 54W
Hagensborg, *B.C., Canada* **186 C8** 52 23N 126 32W
Hagerman, *ID, U.S.A.* **70 G4** 42 49N 114 54W
Hagerman, *NM, U.S.A.* **88 D6** 33 7N 104 20W
Hagerman Fossil Beds Nat. Monument ⌓, *U.S.A.* **70 G4** 42 48N 114 57W
Hagerman Nat. Wildlife Refuge ⌓, *TX, U.S.A.* **99 D11** 33 43N 96 47W
Hagerstown, *IN, U.S.A.* **72 D5** 39 55N 85 10W
Hagerstown, *MD, U.S.A.* **77 A3** 39 39N 77 43W
Hagersville, *Ont., Canada* **178 E6** 42 58N 80 3W
Hague, *ND, U.S.A.* **91 D6** 46 2N 99 59W
Hague, *NY, U.S.A.* **86 C1** 43 45N 73 30W
Hague, *VA, U.S.A.* **102 C8** 38 4N 76 39W
Hahira, *GA, U.S.A.* **68 F3** 30 59N 83 22W
Hahnville, *LA, U.S.A.* **75 E5** 29 59N 90 25W
Haig-Thomas I., *Nunavut, Canada* **190 B7** 78 14N 94 30W
Haight-Ashbury, *San Francisco, U.S.A.* **118 B2** 37 46N 122 26W
Haigler, *NE, U.S.A.* **84 D4** 40 1N 101 56W
Haiku-Pauwela, *HI, U.S.A.* **69 C5** 20 56N 156 19W
Hailey, *ID, U.S.A.* **70 F4** 43 31N 114 19W
Haileybury, *Ont., Canada* **176 D3** 47 30N 79 38W
Haileyville, *OK, U.S.A.* **93 D8** 34 51N 95 35W
Haines, *AK, U.S.A.* **61 G14** 59 14N 135 26W
Haines, *OR, U.S.A.* **94 C8** 44 55N 117 56W
Haines ☆, *AK, U.S.A.* **61 G14** 59 15N 135 30W
Haines City, *FL, U.S.A.* **67 C7** 28 7N 81 38W
Haines Junction, *Yukon, Canada* **189 D5** 60 45N 137 30W
Hainesport, *NJ, U.S.A.* **87 C2** 39 59N 74 50W
Haiwee Res., *CA, U.S.A.* **65 G9** 36 8N 117 57W
Halachó, *Yucatán, Mexico* **223 B3** 20 29N 90 5W
Hālawa, C., *HI, U.S.A.* **69 B5** 21 10N 156 43W
Hālawa Heights, *HI, U.S.A.* **69 K14** 21 23N 157 55W
Halbrite, *Sask., Canada* **182 F8** 49 30N 103 33W
Halbur, *IA, U.S.A.* **73 D4** 42 0N 94 59W
Haldeman, *KY, U.S.A.* **97 B9** 38 15N 83 19W
Haldimand, *Ont., Canada* **178 E7** 42 59N 79 52W
Hale, *CO, U.S.A.* **66 C8** 39 38N 102 9W
Hale, *MO, U.S.A.* **82 B3** 39 36N 93 20W
Hale Center, *TX, U.S.A.* **98 C6** 34 4N 101 51W
Hale County ☆, *AL, U.S.A.* **60 D3** 32 42N 87 36W
Hale County ☆, *TX, U.S.A.* **98 C6** 34 0N 101 55W
Haleakalā Nat. Park △, *HI, U.S.A.* **69 C5** 20 40N 156 15W
Haledon, *NJ, U.S.A.* **114 A1** 40 56N 74 11W
Hale'iwa, *HI, U.S.A.* **69 J13** 21 36N 158 6W
Hales Corners, *Milwaukee, U.S.A.* **112 C1** 42 56N 88 2W
Halethorpe, *MD, U.S.A.* **77 A4** 39 14N 76 40W
Haley, *ND, U.S.A.* **91 E2** 45 58N 103 7W
Haleyville, *AL, U.S.A.* **60 B3** 34 14N 87 37W
Haleyville, *NJ, U.S.A.* **87 C1** 39 17N 75 2W
Half Island Cove, *N.S., Canada* **173 H8** 45 21N 61 12W
Half Moon, *NC, U.S.A.* **90 D8** 34 50N 77 28W
Half Way, *MO, U.S.A.* **82 D3** 37 37N 93 15W
Halfmoon Landing, *GA, U.S.A.* **68 E5** 31 42N 81 16W
Halfway, *MD, U.S.A.* **77 A3** 39 37N 77 46W
Halfway, *OR, U.S.A.* **94 C8** 44 53N 117 7W
Halfway →, *B.C., Canada* **189 E8** 56 12N 121 32W
Haliburton, *Ont., Canada* **179 B8** 45 3N 78 30W
Halifax, *N.S., Canada* **173 J6** 44 38N 63 35W
Halifax, *MA, U.S.A.* **78 C4** 41 59N 70 52W
Halifax, *NC, U.S.A.* **90 B8** 36 20N 77 35W
Halifax, *VA, U.S.A.* **102 E6** 36 46N 78 56W
Halifax County ☆, *NC, U.S.A.* **90 B8** 36 15N 77 40W
Halifax County ☆, *VA, U.S.A.* **102 E6** 36 55N 79 0W
Halifax International ✕ (YHZ), *N.S., Canada* **173 J6** 44 50N 63 30W
Halkett, C., *AK, U.S.A.* **61 A9** 70 48N 152 11W
Halkirk, *Alta., Canada* **185 F8** 52 17N 112 9W
Hall, *MT, U.S.A.* **83 D4** 46 35N 113 12W
Hall Beach = Sanirajak, *Nunavut, Canada* **190 D9** 68 46N 81 12W
Hall County ☆, *GA, U.S.A.* **68 B3** 34 15N 83 50W
Hall County ☆, *NE, U.S.A.* **84 D7** 40 45N 98 30W
Hall County ☆, *TX, U.S.A.* **98 C7** 34 30N 100 35W
Hall I., *AK, U.S.A.* **61 F4** 60 40N 173 6W
Hall L., *Nunavut, Canada* **190 D9** 68 41N 82 17W
Hall Land, *Greenland* **190 A13** 81 30N 61 0W
Hall Park, *OK, U.S.A.* **93 C6** 35 14N 97 24W
Hall Pen., *Nunavut, Canada* **191 E12** 63 30N 66 0W
Hall Summit, *LA, U.S.A.* **75 B2** 32 11N 93 18W
Hallam, *NE, U.S.A.* **84 D9** 40 32N 96 47W
Hallandale, *FL, U.S.A.* **67 F8** 25 58N 80 8W
Hallebourg, *Ont., Canada* **181 C13** 49 40N 83 31W
Halleck, *NV, U.S.A.* **85 B5** 40 57N 115 27W
Hallett, *OK, U.S.A.* **93 B7** 36 19N 96 35W
Hallettsville, *TX, U.S.A.* **99 H11** 29 27N 96 57W
Halley, *AR, U.S.A.* **63 E4** 33 32N 91 20W
Halliday, *ND, U.S.A.* **91 C3** 47 21N 102 20W
Halligan Res., *CO, U.S.A.* **66 B5** 40 53N 105 20W
Hallock, *MN, U.S.A.* **80 B2** 48 47N 96 57W
Hallowell, *KS, U.S.A.* **74 D9** 37 10N 95 0W
Hallowell, *ME, U.S.A.* **76 D4** 44 17N 69 47W
Halls, *GA, U.S.A.* **68 B2** 34 18N 84 56W
Halls, *TN, U.S.A.* **96 E3** 35 53N 89 24W
Halls Summit, *KS, U.S.A.* **74 C8** 38 21N 95 41W
Hallstead, *PA, U.S.A.* **95 C7** 41 58N 75 45W
Hallsville, *MO, U.S.A.* **82 B4** 39 7N 92 13W
Hallsville, *TX, U.S.A.* **99 E13** 32 30N 94 35W
Halltown, *MO, U.S.A.* **82 D3** 37 12N 93 38W
Hallwood, *VA, U.S.A.* **77 C5** 37 53N 75 36W
Halma, *MN, U.S.A.* **80 B2** 48 40N 96 36W
Halsey, *NE, U.S.A.* **84 C5** 41 54N 100 16W
Halsey, *OR, U.S.A.* **94 C2** 44 23N 123 7W
Halstad, *MN, U.S.A.* **80 C2** 47 21N 96 50W
Halstead, *KS, U.S.A.* **74 D6** 38 0N 97 31W
Haltom City, *TX, U.S.A.* **99 E10** 32 47N 97 16W
Hamber Park ⌓, *B.C., Canada* **187 C17** 52 20N 118 0W
Hamberg, *ND, U.S.A.* **91 C6** 47 46N 99 31W
Hamblen County ☆, *TN, U.S.A.* **97 D9** 36 13N 83 18W
Hambleton, *WV, U.S.A.* **102 B5** 39 5N 79 39W
Hamburg, *AR, U.S.A.* **63 E4** 33 14N 91 48W
Hamburg, *CA, U.S.A.* **64 B3** 41 47N 123 4W
Hamburg, *CT, U.S.A.* **78 C2** 41 23N 72 21W
Hamburg, *IL, U.S.A.* **71 D3** 39 14N 90 43W
Hamburg, *IA, U.S.A.* **73 E3** 40 36N 95 39W
Hamburg, *MN, U.S.A.* **80 F5** 44 44N 93 58W
Hamburg, *NJ, U.S.A.* **87 A2** 41 9N 74 35W
Hamburg, *NY, U.S.A.* **89 C2** 42 43N 78 50W
Hamburg, *PA, U.S.A.* **95 D7** 40 33N 75 59W
Hamden, *CT, U.S.A.* **78 C2** 41 23N 72 54W
Hamer, *ID, U.S.A.* **70 F6** 43 56N 112 12W
Hamersville, *OH, U.S.A.* **92 E3** 38 55N 83 59W
Hamilton = Churchill →, *Nfld. & L., Canada* **175 C5** 53 19N 60 10W
Hamilton, *Ont., Canada* **178 D7** 43 15N 79 50W
Hamilton, *AL, U.S.A.* **60 B3** 34 9N 87 59W
Hamilton, *AK, U.S.A.* **61 E7** 62 54N 163 53W
Hamilton, *Baltimore, U.S.A.* **107 A2** 39 21N 76 33W
Hamilton, *CO, U.S.A.* **66 B3** 40 22N 107 37W
Hamilton, *GA, U.S.A.* **68 D2** 32 45N 84 53W
Hamilton, *IL, U.S.A.* **71 C2** 40 24N 91 21W
Hamilton, *KS, U.S.A.* **74 D7** 37 59N 96 10W
Hamilton, *MA, U.S.A.* **78 B4** 42 38N 70 51W
Hamilton, *MI, U.S.A.* **79 G6** 42 41N 86 0W
Hamilton, *MO, U.S.A.* **82 B2** 39 45N 94 0W
Hamilton, *MT, U.S.A.* **83 D3** 46 15N 114 10W
Hamilton, *ND, U.S.A.* **91 B8** 48 48N 97 24W
Hamilton, *NY, U.S.A.* **89 C5** 42 50N 75 33W
Hamilton, *OH, U.S.A.* **92 D2** 39 24N 84 34W
Hamilton, *OR, U.S.A.* **94 C6** 44 44N 119 18W
Hamilton, *TX, U.S.A.* **99 F9** 31 42N 98 7W
Hamilton, *VA, U.S.A.* **77 A3** 39 8N 77 40W
Hamilton, *WA, U.S.A.* **101 B4** 48 31N 121 59W
Hamilton, L., *AR, U.S.A.* **63 D2** 34 26N 93 2W
Hamilton City, *CA, U.S.A.* **64 D4** 39 45N 122 1W
Hamilton County ☆, *FL, U.S.A.* **67 A6** 30 30N 83 0W
Hamilton County ☆, *IL, U.S.A.* **71 E5** 38 5N 88 30W
Hamilton County ☆, *IN, U.S.A.* **72 C4** 40 5N 86 5W
Hamilton County ☆, *IA, U.S.A.* **73 C5** 42 20N 93 40W
Hamilton County ☆, *KS, U.S.A.* **74 D2** 38 0N 101 45W
Hamilton County ☆, *NY, U.S.A.* **89 B6** 43 30N 74 30W
Hamilton County ☆, *NE, U.S.A.* **84 D8** 40 45N 98 0W
Hamilton County ☆, *OH, U.S.A.* **92 D2** 39 13N 84 33W
Hamilton County ☆, *TN, U.S.A.* **97 E7** 35 17N 85 10W
Hamilton County ☆, *TX, U.S.A.* **99 F9** 31 40N 98 8W
Hamilton Dome, *WY, U.S.A.* **104 C4** 43 46N 108 35W
Hamilton Mt., *NY, U.S.A.* **89 B6** 43 25N 74 22W
Hamilton Sound, *Nfld. & L., Canada* **174 C6** 49 35N 54 15W
Hamiota, *Man., Canada* **183 E11** 50 11N 100 38W
Hamler, *OH, U.S.A.* **92 B2** 41 14N 84 2W
Hamlet, *IN, U.S.A.* **72 B4** 41 23N 86 35W
Hamlet, *NC, U.S.A.* **90 D6** 34 53N 79 42W
Hamlet, *NE, U.S.A.* **84 D4** 40 23N 101 14W
Hamlin, *PA, U.S.A.* **87 A1** 41 24N 75 24W
Hamlin, *TX, U.S.A.* **98 E7** 32 53N 100 8W
Hamlin, *WV, U.S.A.* **102 C2** 38 17N 82 6W
Hamlin County ☆, *SD, U.S.A.* **91 F8** 44 40N 97 13W
Hamlin L., *MI, U.S.A.* **79 E5** 44 3N 86 28W
Hamlin Valley Wash →, *U.S.A.* **100 E1** 38 42N 114 4W
Hammel Arverne, *NY, U.S.A.* **114 C4** 40 36N 73 48W
Hammett, *ID, U.S.A.* **70 G3** 42 57N 115 28W
Hammon, *OK, U.S.A.* **93 C4** 35 38N 99 23W
Hammond, *IL, U.S.A.* **71 D5** 39 48N 88 36W
Hammond, *IN, U.S.A.* **72 B3** 41 38N 87 30W
Hammond, *LA, U.S.A.* **75 D5** 30 30N 90 28W
Hammond, *MN, U.S.A.* **80 F6** 44 13N 92 23W
Hammond, *NY, U.S.A.* **89 A5** 44 27N 75 42W
Hammond B., *MI, U.S.A.* **79 D7** 45 31N 84 5W
Hammondsport, *NY, U.S.A.* **89 C3** 42 25N 77 13W
Hammonton, *NJ, U.S.A.* **87 C2** 39 39N 74 48W
Hampden, *Nfld. & L., Canada* **174 C4** 49 33N 56 51W
Hampden, *Denver, U.S.A.* **109 C2** 39 39N 104 52W
Hampden, *ME, U.S.A.* **76 D5** 44 44N 68 51W
Hampden, *ND, U.S.A.* **91 B7** 48 32N 98 40W
Hampden County ☆, *MA, U.S.A.* **78 B2** 42 10N 72 35W
Hampden Sydney, *VA, U.S.A.* **102 D6** 37 14N 78 28W
Hampshire, *IL, U.S.A.* **71 A5** 42 6N 88 32W
Hampshire, *TN, U.S.A.* **96 E5** 35 36N 87 18W
Hampshire County ☆, *MA, U.S.A.* **78 B2** 42 15N 72 35W
Hampshire County ☆, *WV, U.S.A.* **102 B6** 39 18N 78 38W
Hampstead, *Montréal, Canada* **192 B3** 45 28N 73 37W
Hampstead, *N.B., Canada* **173 H3** 45 37N 66 5W
Hampstead, *MD, U.S.A.* **77 A4** 39 37N 76 51W
Hampstead, *NC, U.S.A.* **90 D8** 34 22N 77 44W
Hampstead, *NH, U.S.A.* **86 D3** 42 51N 71 10W
Hampton, *N.B., Canada* **173 H4** 45 32N 65 51W
Hampton, *Ont., Canada* **179 D8** 43 58N 78 45W
Hampton, *AR, U.S.A.* **63 E3** 33 32N 92 28W
Hampton, *Baltimore, U.S.A.* **107 A2** 39 25N 76 35W
Hampton, *CT, U.S.A.* **78 C2** 41 47N 72 3W
Hampton, *FL, U.S.A.* **67 B6** 29 52N 82 8W
Hampton, *GA, U.S.A.* **68 C2** 33 23N 84 17W
Hampton, *IA, U.S.A.* **73 C5** 42 45N 93 13W
Hampton, *MN, U.S.A.* **80 F6** 44 37N 93 0W
Hampton, *NH, U.S.A.* **86 D4** 42 57N 70 50W
Hampton, *NJ, U.S.A.* **87 B2** 40 42N 74 58W
Hampton, *NE, U.S.A.* **84 D8** 40 53N 97 53W
Hampton, *OR, U.S.A.* **94 D5** 43 40N 120 14W
Hampton, *SC, U.S.A.* **90 F4** 32 52N 81 7W
Hampton, *TN, U.S.A.* **97 D10** 36 17N 82 10W
Hampton, *VA, U.S.A.* **102 D8** 37 2N 76 21W
Hampton Bays, *NY, U.S.A.* **78 D2** 40 53N 72 30W
Hampton County ☆, *SC, U.S.A.* **90 F4** 32 50N 81 10W
Hampton Roads, *Norfolk, U.S.A.* **115 A1** 36 57N 76 21W
Hampton Springs, *FL, U.S.A.* **67 A5** 30 5N 83 40W
Hams Fork →, *WY, U.S.A.* **104 E3** 41 35N 109 57W
Hamtramck, *MI, U.S.A.* **109 A2** 42 23N 83 2W
Hāna, *HI, U.S.A.* **69 C6** 20 45N 155 59W
Hanaford, *IL, U.S.A.* **71 F5** 37 57N 88 50W
Hanahan, *SC, U.S.A.* **90 F6** 32 55N 80 0W
Hanalei, *HI, U.S.A.* **69 A2** 22 12N 159 30W
Hanamaulu, *HI, U.S.A.* **69 B2** 21 59N 159 22W
Hanapēpē, *HI, U.S.A.* **69 B2** 21 55N 159 35W
Hanauma B., *HI, U.S.A.* **69 K14** 21 15N 157 40W
Hanbury →, *N.W.T., Canada* **189 D12** 63 37N 104 34W
Hanceville, *B.C., Canada* **187 D11** 51 55N 123 2W
Hanceville, *AL, U.S.A.* **60 B4** 34 4N 86 46W
Hancock, *IA, U.S.A.* **73 D3** 41 24N 95 21W
Hancock, *MD, U.S.A.* **77 A2** 39 42N 78 11W
Hancock, *MI, U.S.A.* **79 B3** 47 8N 88 35W
Hancock, *MN, U.S.A.* **80 E3** 45 30N 95 48W
Hancock, *NH, U.S.A.* **86 D3** 42 57N 71 58W
Hancock, *NY, U.S.A.* **89 D5** 41 57N 75 17W
Hancock, *VT, U.S.A.* **86 C2** 43 56N 72 51W
Hancock, *WI, U.S.A.* **103 D4** 44 8N 89 31W
Hancock, Mt., *WY, U.S.A.* **104 B2** 44 9N 110 25W
Hancock County ☆, *GA, U.S.A.* **68 C4** 33 20N 83 0W
Hancock County ☆, *IL, U.S.A.* **71 C2** 40 25N 91 10W
Hancock County ☆, *IN, U.S.A.* **72 D5** 39 50N 85 45W
Hancock County ☆, *IA, U.S.A.* **73 B5** 43 5N 93 45W
Hancock County ☆, *KY, U.S.A.* **96 C6** 37 50N 86 45W
Hancock County ☆, *ME, U.S.A.* **76 D5** 44 30N 68 30W
Hancock County ☆, *MS, U.S.A.* **81 F4** 30 17N 89 23W
Hancock County ☆, *OH, U.S.A.* **92 B3** 41 2N 83 40W
Hancock County ☆, *TN, U.S.A.* **97 D9** 36 32N 83 13W
Hancock County ☆, *WV, U.S.A.* **102 A4** 40 30N 80 35W
Hancocks Bridge, *NJ, U.S.A.* **87 C1** 39 31N 75 28W
Hand County ☆, *SD, U.S.A.* **91 F7** 44 31N 98 59W
Handel, *Sask., Canada* **182 C3** 52 4N 108 42W
Hanford, *CA, U.S.A.* **65 G7** 36 20N 119 39W
Hanford, *WA, U.S.A.* **101 D6** 46 37N 119 19W
Hanford Reach Nat. Monument ⌓, *U.S.A.* **101 D6** 46 40N 119 30W
Hanford Site, U.S. Dept. of Energy, *WA, U.S.A.* **101 D6** 46 35N 119 23W
Hangman Cr. →, *WA, U.S.A.* **101 C8** 47 40N 117 27W
Hankinson, *ND, U.S.A.* **91 D9** 46 4N 96 54W
Hanksville, *UT, U.S.A.* **100 E5** 38 22N 110 43W
Hanley, *Sask., Canada* **182 D5** 51 38N 106 26W
Hanley Falls, *MN, U.S.A.* **80 F3** 44 42N 95 37W
Hanley Hills, *MO, U.S.A.* **117 A2** 38 41N 90 19W
Hanna, *Alta., Canada* **185 G9** 51 40N 111 54W
Hanna, *IN, U.S.A.* **72 B4** 41 25N 86 47W
Hanna, *LA, U.S.A.* **75 C2** 31 58N 93 21W
Hanna, *OK, U.S.A.* **93 C8** 35 12N 95 53W
Hanna, *UT, U.S.A.* **100 C5** 40 26N 110 48W
Hanna, *WY, U.S.A.* **104 E6** 41 52N 106 34W
Hanna City, *IL, U.S.A.* **71 C4** 40 42N 89 48W
Hannaford, *ND, U.S.A.* **91 C7** 47 19N 98 11W
Hannah, *ND, U.S.A.* **91 B7** 48 58N 98 42W
Hannahville Indian Reservation, *MI, U.S.A.* **79 D4** 45 43N 87 25W
Hannibal, *MO, U.S.A.* **82 B5** 39 42N 91 22W
Hannibal, *NY, U.S.A.* **89 B4** 43 19N 76 35W
Hannover, *ND, U.S.A.* **91 C4** 47 7N 101 26W
Hanover, *Ont., Canada* **178 C5** 44 9N 81 2W
Hanover, *Baltimore, U.S.A.* **107 B1** 39 11N 76 43W
Hanover, *IL, U.S.A.* **71 A3** 42 15N 90 17W
Hanover, *IN, U.S.A.* **72 E5** 38 43N 85 28W
Hanover, *KS, U.S.A.* **74 B7** 39 54N 96 53W
Hanover, *ME, U.S.A.* **86 B4** 44 30N 70 42W
Hanover, *MA, U.S.A.* **78 B4** 42 7N 70 49W
Hanover, *MI, U.S.A.* **79 G7** 42 6N 84 33W
Hanover, *MN, U.S.A.* **80 E5** 45 10N 93 40W
Hanover, *MT, U.S.A.* **83 C8** 47 7N 109 33W
Hanover, *NH, U.S.A.* **86 C2** 43 42N 72 17W
Hanover, *NM, U.S.A.* **88 E2** 32 48N 108 6W
Hanover, *OH, U.S.A.* **92 C4** 40 4N 82 16W
Hanover, *PA, U.S.A.* **77 A4** 39 48N 76 59W
Hanover, *VA, U.S.A.* **102 D7** 37 46N 77 22W
Hanover County ☆, *VA, U.S.A.* **102 D7** 37 46N 77 29W
Hanoverton, *OH, U.S.A.* **92 C6** 40 45N 80 56W
Hans Lollik I., *U.S. Virgin Is.* **105 G18** 18 24N 64 53W
Hansboro, *ND, U.S.A.* **91 B6** 48 57N 99 23W
Hansen, *ID, U.S.A.* **70 G4** 42 32N 114 18W
Hansen Park, *Milwaukee, U.S.A.* **112 B1** 43 4N 88 1W
Hansford County ☆, *TX, U.S.A.* **98 A6** 36 10N 101 30W
Hanska, *MN, U.S.A.* **80 F4** 44 9N 94 30W
Hanson, *FL, U.S.A.* **67 A5** 30 34N 83 21W
Hanson, *KY, U.S.A.* **96 C5** 37 25N 87 29W
Hanson County ☆, *SD, U.S.A.* **91 G8** 43 40N 97 47W
Hanston, *KS, U.S.A.* **74 C4** 38 7N 99 43W
Hant's Harbour, *Nfld. & L., Canada* **174 D7** 48 1N 53 16W
Hantsport, *N.S., Canada* **173 H5** 45 4N 64 11W
Hantzsch →, *Nunavut, Canada* **190 D11** 67 32N 72 25W
Hapeville, *GA, U.S.A.* **68 C2** 33 39N 84 24W
Happy, *TX, U.S.A.* **98 C6** 34 45N 101 52W
Happy Camp, *CA, U.S.A.* **64 B3** 41 48N 123 23W
Happy Jack, *AZ, U.S.A.* **62 C4** 34 45N 111 24W
Happy Valley, *Portland, U.S.A.* **116 B2** 45 26N 122 31W
Happy Valley-Goose Bay, *Nfld. & L., Canada* **175 C5** 53 15N 60 20W
Harahan, *LA, U.S.A.* **75 E5** 29 56N 90 12W
Haralson, *GA, U.S.A.* **68 C2** 33 14N 84 34W
Haralson County ☆, *GA, U.S.A.* **68 C1** 33 45N 85 10W
Harbeson, *DE, U.S.A.* **77 B5** 38 43N 75 17W
Harbor, L., *Los Angeles, U.S.A.* **111 D3** 33 47N 118 17W
Harbor Beach, *MI, U.S.A.* **79 F9** 43 51N 82 39W
Harbor Bluffs, *Tampa, U.S.A.* **119 B2** 24 54N 87 49W
Harbor Hills, *NY, U.S.A.* **114 B4** 40 47N 73 44W
Harbor Springs, *MI, U.S.A.* **79 D7** 45 26N 85 0W
Harborcreek, *PA, U.S.A.* **95 B3** 42 10N 79 57W
Harbour, *OR, U.S.A.* **94 E1** 42 3N 124 16W
Harbour Breton, *Nfld. & L., Canada* **174 E5** 47 29N 55 50W
Harbour Deep, *Nfld. & L., Canada* **174 B4** 50 25N 56 32W
Harbour Grace, *Nfld. & L., Canada* **174 E7** 47 40N 53 22W
Harbour Heights, *FL, U.S.A.* **67 E7** 26 59N 82 0W
Harcones, *Nuevo León, Mexico* **214 C4** 27 10N 100 25W
Harcourt, *N.B., Canada* **173 G4** 46 27N 65 15W
Harcourt, *IA, U.S.A.* **73 C4** 42 16N 94 11W
Harcuvar Mts., *AZ, U.S.A.* **62 D2** 34 0N 113 30W
Hardee County ☆, *FL, U.S.A.* **67 D7** 27 30N 81 45W
Hardeeville, *SC, U.S.A.* **90 F4** 32 17N 81 5W
Hardeman County ☆, *TN, U.S.A.* **96 E4** 35 6N 89 0W
Hardeman County ☆, *TX, U.S.A.* **99 C8** 34 20N 99 50W
Hardesty, *OK, U.S.A.* **93 B2** 36 37N 101 12W
Hardin, *IL, U.S.A.* **71 D3** 39 10N 90 37W
Hardin, *KY, U.S.A.* **96 D4** 36 46N 88 18W

Hardin, MO, U.S.A. 82 B3 39 16N 93 50W
Hardin, MT, U.S.A. 83 E10 45 44N 107 37W
Hardin, TX, U.S.A. 99 G13 30 9N 94 44W
Hardin County ☆, IL, U.S.A. 71 F5 37 30N 88 15W
Hardin County ☆, IA, U.S.A. 73 C5 42 25N 93 15W
Hardin County ☆, KY, U.S.A. 96 C6 37 40N 86 0W
Hardin County ☆, OH, U.S.A. 92 C3 40 42N 83 47W
Hardin County ☆, TN, U.S.A. 96 E4 35 14N 88 15W
Hardin County ☆, TX, U.S.A. 99 G13 30 22N 94 19W
Harding, MN, U.S.A. 80 D4 46 7N 94 2W
Harding, L., AL, U.S.A. 60 D5 32 40N 85 5W
Harding County ☆, NM, U.S.A. 88 B7 36 0N 104 0W
Harding County ☆, SD, U.S.A. 91 E2 45 30N 103 30W
Hardinge B., N.W.T., Canada 188 A8 76 28N 121 40W
Hardinsburg, IN, U.S.A. 72 E4 38 28N 86 17W
Hardinsburg, KY, U.S.A. 96 C6 37 47N 86 28W
Hardisty, Alta., Canada 185 F9 52 40N 111 18W
Hardisty L., N.W.T., Canada 189 D9 64 37N 117 45W
Hardman, OR, U.S.A. 94 B6 45 10N 119 41W
Hardtner, KS, U.S.A. 74 D5 37 1N 98 39W
Hardwick, GA, U.S.A. 68 C3 33 4N 83 14W
Hardwick, MA, U.S.A. 78 B2 42 21N 72 12W
Hardwick, MN, U.S.A. 80 G2 43 47N 96 12W
Hardwick, VT, U.S.A. 86 B2 44 30N 72 22W
Hardwicke I., B.C., Canada 186 E9 50 27N 125 50W
Hardwicke Island, B.C., Canada 186 E9 50 26N 125 55W
Hardwood Ridge, N.B., Canada 173 G3 46 10N 66 1W
Hardy, AR, U.S.A. 63 B4 36 19N 91 29W
Hardy, MT, U.S.A. 83 C6 47 12N 111 47W
Hardy, NE, U.S.A. 84 D8 40 1N 97 56W
Hardy County ☆, WV, U.S.A. 102 C6 39 0N 78 50W
Hardy Dam Pond, MI, U.S.A. 79 F6 43 30N 85 37W
Hare B., Nfld. & L., Canada 174 A5 51 15N 55 45W
Hare Bay, Nfld. & L., Canada 174 D6 48 51N 54 1W
Hare Indian ➜, N.W.T., Canada 188 C7 66 17N 128 37W
Harford County ☆, MD, U.S.A. 77 A4 39 35N 76 25W
Hargill, TX, U.S.A. 98 L9 26 27N 98 1W
Harker Heights, TX, U.S.A. 99 F10 31 5N 97 40W
Harkers Island, NC, U.S.A. 90 D9 34 42N 76 34W
Harlan, IA, U.S.A. 73 D3 41 39N 95 19W
Harlan, KS, U.S.A. 74 B5 39 36N 98 46W
Harlan, KY, U.S.A. 97 D9 36 51N 83 19W
Harlan County ☆, KY, U.S.A. 97 D9 36 50N 83 15W
Harlan County ☆, NE, U.S.A. 84 D6 40 15N 99 30W
Harlan County Lake, NE, U.S.A. 84 D6 40 4N 99 13W
Harlem, FL, U.S.A. 67 E8 26 44N 80 57W
Harlem, GA, U.S.A. 68 C4 33 25N 82 19W
Harlem, MT, U.S.A. 83 B9 48 32N 108 47W
Harlem, New York, U.S.A. 114 B3 40 48N 73 56W
Harleyville, SC, U.S.A. 90 E5 33 13N 80 27W
Harlingen, TX, U.S.A. 98 L10 26 12N 97 42W
Harlowton, MT, U.S.A. 83 D8 46 26N 109 50W
Harman, WV, U.S.A. 102 C5 38 55N 79 32W
Harmon, IL, U.S.A. 71 B4 41 43N 89 33W
Harmon County ☆, OK, U.S.A. 93 D4 34 45N 99 50W
Harmon L., Ont., Canada 180 C6 49 56N 90 13W
Harmony, IN, U.S.A. 72 D3 39 32N 87 4W
Harmony, ME, U.S.A. 76 D4 44 58N 69 33W
Harmony, MD, U.S.A. 77 B5 38 47N 75 53W
Harmony, MN, U.S.A. 80 G6 43 34N 92 1W
Harnett County ☆, NC, U.S.A. 90 C7 35 20N 78 50W
Harney, MD, U.S.A. 77 A3 39 44N 77 13W
Harney, L., FL, U.S.A. 67 C7 28 45N 81 3W
Harney Basin, OR, U.S.A. 94 D6 43 0N 119 30W
Harney County ☆, OR, U.S.A. 94 D6 43 0N 119 0W
Harney L., OR, U.S.A. 94 D6 43 14N 119 8W
Harney Peak, SD, U.S.A. 91 G2 43 52N 103 32W
Haro Str., B.C., Canada 187 G11 48 30N 123 15W
Harold, FL, U.S.A. 67 A2 30 40N 86 53W
Harp L., Nfld. & L., Canada 175 B5 55 5N 61 50W
Harper = Costa Mesa, CA, U.S.A. 65 K9 33 38N 117 55W
Harper, IA, U.S.A. 73 D6 41 22N 92 3W
Harper, KS, U.S.A. 74 D5 37 17N 98 1W
Harper, OR, U.S.A. 94 D8 43 52N 117 37W
Harper, TX, U.S.A. 99 G8 30 18N 99 15W
Harper, Mt., AK, U.S.A. 61 D12 64 14N 143 51W
Harper County ☆, KS, U.S.A. 74 D5 37 15N 98 0W
Harper County ☆, OK, U.S.A. 93 B4 36 50N 99 40W
Harper L., CA, U.S.A. 65 H9 35 2N 117 17W
Harpers Ferry, IA, U.S.A. 73 B7 43 12N 91 9W
Harpers Ferry, WV, U.S.A. 77 A3 39 20N 77 44W
Harpers Ferry Nat. Historical Park ⌂, WV, U.S.A. 102 B7 39 19N 77 45W
Harpersville, AL, U.S.A. 60 C4 33 21N 86 26W
Harpeth ➜, TN, U.S.A. 96 D5 36 18N 87 10W
Harqualala Mts., AZ, U.S.A. 62 D2 33 45N 113 20W
Harrah, OK, U.S.A. 93 C6 35 29N 97 10W
Harrah, WA, U.S.A. 101 D5 46 24N 120 33W
Harrell, AR, U.S.A. 63 E3 33 31N 92 24W
Harricana ➜, Qué., Canada 176 A3 50 56N 79 32W
Harriet, L., Minneapolis-St. Paul, U.S.A. 113 B2 44 55N 93 18W
Harriman, TN, U.S.A. 97 E8 35 56N 84 33W
Harriman Res., VT, U.S.A. 86 D2 42 48N 72 55W
Harriman State Park ⌂, NY, U.S.A. 89 D6 41 13N 74 5W
Harrington, DE, U.S.A. 77 B5 38 56N 75 35W
Harrington, ME, U.S.A. 76 D6 44 37N 67 49W
Harrington, WA, U.S.A. 101 C7 47 29N 118 15W
Harrington Harbour, Qué., Canada 175 C6 50 31N 59 30W
Harris, Sask., Canada 182 D4 51 44N 107 35W
Harris, KS, U.S.A. 74 C8 38 19N 95 26W
Harris, MN, U.S.A. 80 E6 45 35N 92 58W
Harris, MO, U.S.A. 82 A3 40 18N 93 21W
Harris, OK, U.S.A. 93 E9 33 45N 94 44W
Harris, L., FL, U.S.A. 67 C7 28 47N 81 49W
Harris County ☆, GA, U.S.A. 68 D2 32 40N 84 50W
Harris County ☆, TX, U.S.A. 99 H12 29 46N 95 22W
Harris Pt., Ont., Canada 178 D4 43 6N 82 9W
Harrisburg, AR, U.S.A. 63 C5 35 34N 90 43W
Harrisburg, IL, U.S.A. 71 F5 37 44N 88 32W
Harrisburg, MO, U.S.A. 82 B4 39 9N 92 28W
Harrisburg, NC, U.S.A. 90 C5 35 19N 80 39W
Harrisburg, NE, U.S.A. 84 C2 41 33N 103 44W
Harrisburg, OR, U.S.A. 94 C2 44 16N 123 10W
Harrisburg, PA, U.S.A. 95 D6 40 16N 76 53W
Harrisburg, SD, U.S.A. 91 G9 43 26N 96 42W
Harrison, AR, U.S.A. 63 B2 36 14N 93 7W
Harrison, GA, U.S.A. 68 D4 32 50N 82 43W
Harrison, ID, U.S.A. 70 B2 47 27N 116 47W
Harrison, MI, U.S.A. 79 E7 44 1N 84 48W
Harrison, MT, U.S.A. 83 E6 45 42N 111 47W
Harrison, NE, U.S.A. 84 B2 42 41N 103 53W
Harrison, OH, U.S.A. 92 D2 39 16N 84 49W
Harrison, C., Nfld. & L., Canada 175 C6 54 55N 57 55W
Harrison Bay, AK, U.S.A. 61 A10 70 40N 151 0W
Harrison County ☆, IN, U.S.A. 72 E4 38 10N 86 10W
Harrison County ☆, IA, U.S.A. 73 D3 41 40N 95 50W
Harrison County ☆, KY, U.S.A. 97 B8 38 25N 84 20W
Harrison County ☆, MS, U.S.A. 81 F4 30 30N 89 7W
Harrison County ☆, MO, U.S.A. 82 A3 40 20N 94 0W
Harrison County ☆, OH, U.S.A. 92 C5 40 18N 81 11W
Harrison County ☆, TX, U.S.A. 99 E13 32 33N 94 23W
Harrison County ☆, WV, U.S.A. 102 B4 39 17N 80 30W
Harrison Hot Springs, B.C., Canada 187 F13 49 18N 121 47W
Harrison L., B.C., Canada 187 F13 49 33N 121 50W
Harrisonburg, LA, U.S.A. 75 C4 31 46N 91 49W
Harrisonburg, VA, U.S.A. 102 C6 38 27N 78 52W
Harrisonville, MO, U.S.A. 82 C2 38 39N 94 21W
Harriston, Ont., Canada 178 D6 43 57N 80 53W
Harriston, MS, U.S.A. 81 E2 31 44N 91 2W
Harrisville, MI, U.S.A. 79 E8 44 39N 83 17W
Harrisville, NY, U.S.A. 89 A5 44 9N 75 19W
Harrisville, RI, U.S.A. 78 C3 41 58N 71 41W
Harrisville, WV, U.S.A. 102 B3 39 13N 81 3W
Harrod, OH, U.S.A. 92 C3 40 43N 83 56W
Harrodsburg, KY, U.S.A. 97 C8 37 46N 84 51W
Harrogate, TN, U.S.A. 97 D9 36 35N 83 40W
Harrold, SD, U.S.A. 91 F6 44 31N 99 44W
Harrow, Ont., Canada 178 E4 42 2N 82 55W
Harrowsmith, Ont., Canada 179 C10 44 24N 76 40W
Harry S. Moss Park, Dallas-Fort Worth, U.S.A. 109 A5 32 53N 96 44W
Harry S. Truman Res., MO, U.S.A. 82 C3 38 16N 93 24W
Harry Strunk L., NE, U.S.A. 84 D5 40 23N 100 13W
Hart, MI, U.S.A. 79 F5 43 42N 86 22W
Hart, TX, U.S.A. 98 C5 34 23N 102 7W
Hart ➜, Yukon, Canada 188 C5 65 51N 136 22W
Hart County ☆, GA, U.S.A. 68 B4 34 15N 83 0W
Hart County ☆, KY, U.S.A. 97 C7 37 20N 85 50W
Hart Island, NY, U.S.A. 114 A4 40 51N 73 46W
Hart L., OR, U.S.A. 94 E6 42 25N 119 51W
Hart Mt., OR, U.S.A. 94 E6 42 23N 119 53W
Hartell, Alta., Canada 185 H6 50 36N 114 14W
Hartfield, VA, U.S.A. 102 D8 37 33N 76 27W
Hartford, AL, U.S.A. 60 E5 31 6N 85 42W
Hartford, AR, U.S.A. 63 C1 35 1N 94 23W
Hartford, CT, U.S.A. 78 C2 41 46N 72 41W
Hartford, GA, U.S.A. 68 D3 32 17N 83 28W
Hartford, IA, U.S.A. 73 D5 41 28N 93 24W
Hartford, KY, U.S.A. 96 C6 37 27N 86 55W
Hartford, MI, U.S.A. 79 G5 42 13N 86 10W
Hartford, NY, U.S.A. 86 C1 43 22N 73 24W
Hartford, SD, U.S.A. 91 G9 43 38N 96 57W
Hartford, TN, U.S.A. 97 E9 35 49N 83 9W
Hartford, VT, U.S.A. 86 C2 43 40N 72 20W
Hartford, WI, U.S.A. 103 E5 43 19N 88 22W
Hartford Bradley International ✈ (BDL), CT, U.S.A. 78 C2 41 56N 72 41W
Hartford City, IN, U.S.A. 72 C5 40 27N 85 22W
Hartford County ☆, CT, U.S.A. 78 C2 41 45N 72 45W
Hartington, NE, U.S.A. 84 B8 42 37N 97 16W
Hartland, N.B., Canada 173 G2 46 20N 67 32W
Hartland, ME, U.S.A. 76 D4 44 53N 69 27W
Hartland, MN, U.S.A. 80 G5 43 48N 93 29W
Hartland, VT, U.S.A. 86 C2 43 32N 72 24W
Hartland, WI, U.S.A. 103 E5 43 6N 88 21W
Hartley, IA, U.S.A. 73 B3 43 11N 95 29W
Hartley, TX, U.S.A. 98 B5 35 53N 102 24W
Hartley Bay, B.C., Canada 186 B5 53 25N 129 15W
Hartley County ☆, TX, U.S.A. 98 B5 35 50N 102 30W
Hartline, WA, U.S.A. 101 C6 47 41N 119 6W
Hartly, DE, U.S.A. 77 A5 39 10N 75 43W
Hartman, CO, U.S.A. 66 D8 38 7N 102 13W
Hartney, Man., Canada 183 F11 49 30N 100 35W
Hartsburg, MO, U.S.A. 82 C4 38 42N 92 19W
Hartsel, CO, U.S.A. 66 C5 39 1N 105 48W
Hartselle, AL, U.S.A. 60 B4 34 27N 86 56W
Hartsfield-Atlanta International ✈ (ATL), GA, U.S.A. 68 C2 33 38N 84 26W
Hartshorne, OK, U.S.A. 93 D8 34 51N 95 34W
Hartsville, SC, U.S.A. 90 D5 34 23N 80 4W
Hartsville, TN, U.S.A. 96 D6 36 24N 86 10W
Hartville, MO, U.S.A. 82 D4 37 15N 92 31W
Hartville, OH, U.S.A. 92 C5 40 58N 81 20W
Hartville, WY, U.S.A. 104 D8 42 20N 104 44W
Hartwell, GA, U.S.A. 68 B4 34 21N 82 56W
Hartwell L., SC, U.S.A. 90 D3 34 21N 82 49W
Hartwick, IA, U.S.A. 73 D6 41 47N 92 21W
Harty, Ont., Canada 181 C14 49 29N 82 41W
Harvard, ID, U.S.A. 70 C2 46 55N 116 44W
Harvard, IL, U.S.A. 71 A5 42 25N 88 37W
Harvard, NE, U.S.A. 84 D7 40 37N 98 6W
Harvard, Mt., CO, U.S.A. 66 B4 38 56N 106 19W
Harvard University, Boston, U.S.A. 106 A3 42 22N 71 7W
Harvey, N.B., Canada 173 H2 45 43N 67 1W
Harvey, AR, U.S.A. 63 D2 34 51N 93 47W
Harvey, IL, U.S.A. 71 B6 41 36N 87 50W
Harvey, ND, U.S.A. 91 C6 47 47N 99 56W
Harvey, New Orleans, U.S.A. 113 C2 29 54N 90 4W
Harvey Cedars, NJ, U.S.A. 87 C2 39 43N 74 11W
Harvey County ☆, KS, U.S.A. 74 C6 38 0N 97 30W
Harveys Lake, PA, U.S.A. 95 C6 41 23N 76 1W
Harveyville, KS, U.S.A. 74 C8 38 47N 95 58W
Harwich, MA, U.S.A. 78 C4 41 41N 70 5W
Harwinton, CT, U.S.A. 78 C1 41 46N 73 4W
Harwood, MO, U.S.A. 82 D2 37 57N 94 9W
Harwood, TX, U.S.A. 99 H10 29 40N 97 30W
Harwood Heights, Chicago, U.S.A. 108 B2 41 57N 87 46W
Harwood Park, Baltimore, U.S.A. 107 B1 39 11N 76 44W
Hasbrouck Heights, NJ, U.S.A. 114 A2 40 51N 74 6W
Haskell, AR, U.S.A. 63 D3 34 30N 92 38W
Haskell, OK, U.S.A. 93 C8 35 50N 95 40W
Haskell, TX, U.S.A. 99 D8 33 10N 99 44W
Haskell County ☆, KS, U.S.A. 74 D3 37 30N 100 45W
Haskell County ☆, OK, U.S.A. 93 C8 35 10N 95 10W
Haskell County ☆, TX, U.S.A. 99 D8 33 12N 99 44W
Haskins, OH, U.S.A. 92 B3 41 28N 83 42W
Haslet, TX, U.S.A. 99 E10 32 59N 97 21W
Hassayampa ➜, AZ, U.S.A. 62 D3 33 19N 112 42W
Hassel Sd., Nunavut, Canada 190 B6 78 18N 98 46W
Hastings, Ont., Canada 179 C9 44 18N 77 57W
Hastings, FL, U.S.A. 67 B7 29 43N 81 31W
Hastings, IA, U.S.A. 73 D3 41 1N 95 30W
Hastings, MI, U.S.A. 79 G6 42 39N 85 17W
Hastings, MN, U.S.A. 80 F6 44 44N 92 51W
Hastings, NE, U.S.A. 84 D7 40 35N 98 23W
Hastings, OK, U.S.A. 93 D5 34 14N 98 7W
Hastings Park, Vancouver, Canada 193 B2 49 17N 123 3W
Hasty, CO, U.S.A. 66 D8 38 7N 102 58W
Haswell, CO, U.S.A. 66 D7 38 27N 103 10W
Hat Cr. ➜, SD, U.S.A. 91 G2 43 15N 103 37W
Hatch, NM, U.S.A. 88 E3 32 40N 107 9W
Hatch, UT, U.S.A. 100 F3 37 39N 112 26W
Hatch Wash ➜, UT, U.S.A. 100 E6 38 35N 109 35W
Hatchet Cr. ➜, AL, U.S.A. 60 D4 32 51N 86 27W
Hatchie ➜, TN, U.S.A. 96 E3 35 35N 89 53W
Hatchie Nat. Wildlife Refuge ⌂, TN, U.S.A. 96 E3 35 30N 89 13W
Hatchineha, L., FL, U.S.A. 67 C7 28 2N 81 25W
Hatfield, AR, U.S.A. 63 D1 34 29N 94 23W
Hatfield, IN, U.S.A. 72 F3 37 54N 87 14W
Hatfield, MA, U.S.A. 78 B2 42 22N 72 36W
Hatfield, MN, U.S.A. 80 G2 43 58N 96 12W
Hatfield, PA, U.S.A. 87 B1 40 17N 75 18W
Hatillo, Puerto Rico 105 G16 18 29N 66 50W
Hatteras, NC, U.S.A. 90 C10 35 13N 75 42W
Hatteras, C., NC, U.S.A. 90 C10 35 14N 75 32W
Hatteras I., NC, U.S.A. 90 C10 35 30N 75 28W
Hattiesburg, MS, U.S.A. 81 E4 31 20N 89 17W
Hattieville, AR, U.S.A. 63 C3 35 17N 92 47W
Hatton, AL, U.S.A. 60 B3 34 34N 87 25W
Hatton, ND, U.S.A. 91 C8 47 38N 97 27W
Hatton, WA, U.S.A. 101 D7 46 47N 118 50W
Haubstadt, IN, U.S.A. 72 E3 38 12N 87 34W
Haugan, MT, U.S.A. 83 C2 47 23N 115 24W
Haugen, WI, U.S.A. 103 C2 45 37N 91 46W
Haughton, LA, U.S.A. 75 B2 32 32N 93 30W
Haultain ➜, Sask., Canada 189 E11 55 51N 106 46W
Hauser, OR, U.S.A. 94 D1 43 30N 124 13W
Haut, I. au, ME, U.S.A. 76 D5 44 3N 68 38W
Hautes-Gorges-de-la-Rivière-Malbaie, Parc des ⌂, Qué., Canada 177 D12 47 56N 70 31W
Hau'ula, HI, U.S.A. 69 J14 21 37N 157 55W
Havana, AR, U.S.A. 63 C2 35 7N 93 32W
Havana, FL, U.S.A. 67 A4 30 37N 84 25W
Havana, IL, U.S.A. 71 C3 40 18N 90 4W
Havana, KS, U.S.A. 74 D8 37 6N 95 57W
Havana, ND, U.S.A. 91 E8 45 57N 97 37W
Havasu, L., AZ, U.S.A. 62 C1 34 18N 114 28W
Havasu Cr. ➜, AZ, U.S.A. 62 A3 36 19N 112 46W
Havasupai Indian Reservation, AZ, U.S.A. 62 A3 36 15N 112 35W
Havelock, N.B., Canada 173 G4 46 2N 65 24W
Havelock, Ont., Canada 179 C9 44 26N 77 53W
Havelock, NC, U.S.A. 90 D9 34 53N 76 54W
Havelock, ND, U.S.A. 91 D3 46 29N 102 45W
Haven, KS, U.S.A. 74 D6 37 54N 97 47W
Havensville, KS, U.S.A. 74 B7 39 31N 96 5W
Haverford, PA, U.S.A. 116 A1 40 0N 75 17W
Haverhill, FL, U.S.A. 67 E8 26 42N 80 7W
Haverhill, MA, U.S.A. 78 B3 42 47N 71 5W
Haverhill, NH, U.S.A. 86 B2 44 3N 72 4W
Haverstraw, NY, U.S.A. 87 A3 41 12N 73 58W
Havertown, PA, U.S.A. 87 C1 39 58N 75 18W
Haviland, KS, U.S.A. 74 D4 37 37N 99 6W
Havre, MT, U.S.A. 83 B8 48 33N 109 41W
Havre-Aubert, Qué., Canada 173 F8 47 12N 61 56W
Havre-Aubert, Î., Qué., Canada 173 F8 47 13N 61 57W
Havre-aux-Maisons, Qué., Canada 173 F8 47 24N 61 49W
Havre-aux-Maisons, Î. du, Qué., Canada 173 F8 47 25N 61 47W
Havre de Grace, MD, U.S.A. 77 A4 39 33N 76 6W
Havre-St.-Pierre, Qué., Canada 175 C5 50 18N 63 33W
Haw ➜, NC, U.S.A. 90 C6 35 36N 79 3W
Haw Knob, NC, U.S.A. 90 C1 35 19N 84 2W
Hawai'i, HI, U.S.A. 69 D6 19 30N 155 30W
Hawai'i □, HI, U.S.A. 69 D5 19 30N 156 30W
Hawai'i County ☆, HI, U.S.A. 69 D6 19 30N 155 30W
Hawai'i Volcanoes Nat. Park △, HI, U.S.A. 69 D6 19 25N 155 18W
Hawaiian Gardens, Los Angeles, U.S.A. 111 D4 33 49N 118 4W
Hawaiian Is., Pac. Oc. 69 G12 20 30N 156 0W
Hawarden, Sask., Canada 182 D5 51 25N 106 36W
Hawarden, IA, U.S.A. 73 B2 43 0N 96 29W
Hawesville, KY, U.S.A. 96 C6 37 54N 86 45W
Hawi, HI, U.S.A. 69 C6 20 14N 155 50W
Hawk Junction, Ont., Canada 181 D12 48 5N 84 38W
Hawk Point, MO, U.S.A. 82 C5 38 58N 91 8W
Hawk Springs, WY, U.S.A. 104 E8 41 47N 104 16W
Hawke's Bay, Nfld. & L., Canada 174 B3 50 36N 57 10W
Hawkesbury I., B.C., Canada 186 B5 53 37N 129 3W
Hawkeye, IA, U.S.A. 73 C7 42 56N 91 57W
Hawkins, TX, U.S.A. 99 E12 32 35N 95 12W
Hawkins, WI, U.S.A. 103 C3 45 31N 90 43W
Hawkins County ☆, TN, U.S.A. 97 D9 36 24N 83 1W
Hawkinsville, GA, U.S.A. 68 D3 32 17N 83 28W
Hawks, MI, U.S.A. 79 D8 45 18N 83 53W
Hawksbill, VA, U.S.A. 102 C6 38 34N 78 27W
Hawksbill Mt., NC, U.S.A. 90 C4 35 55N 81 53W
Hawley, MN, U.S.A. 80 D2 46 53N 96 19W
Hawley, PA, U.S.A. 87 A1 41 28N 75 11W
Hawley, TX, U.S.A. 99 E8 32 37N 99 49W
Haworth, OK, U.S.A. 93 E9 33 51N 94 39W
Hawthorne, FL, U.S.A. 67 B6 29 36N 82 5W
Hawthorne, Los Angeles, U.S.A. 111 C2 33 54N 118 21W
Hawthorne, NY, U.S.A. 87 A3 41 6N 73 48W
Hawthorne, NV, U.S.A. 85 D2 38 32N 118 38W
Hawthorne Army Depot, NV, U.S.A. 85 D2 38 29N 118 39W
Haxtun, CO, U.S.A. 66 B8 40 39N 102 38W
Hay, WA, U.S.A. 101 D8 46 41N 117 55W
Hay ➜, Alta., Canada 189 D9 60 50N 116 26W
Hay ➜, WI, U.S.A. 103 D2 44 59N 91 51W
Hay, C., N.W.T., Canada 188 B10 74 25N 113 0W
Hay Cove, N.S., Canada 173 H9 45 45N 60 44W
Hay I., Ont., Canada 178 C6 44 53N 80 58W
Hay Lakes, Alta., Canada 185 E7 53 12N 113 2W
Hay River, N.W.T., Canada 189 D9 60 51N 115 44W
Hay Springs, NE, U.S.A. 84 B3 42 41N 102 41W
Hayden, AZ, U.S.A. 62 D5 33 0N 110 47W
Hayden, CO, U.S.A. 66 B3 40 30N 107 16W
Hayden, ID, U.S.A. 70 B2 47 46N 116 47W
Hayden, NM, U.S.A. 88 B7 35 59N 103 16W
Hayden Peak, ID, U.S.A. 70 G2 42 59N 116 40W
Hayes, LA, U.S.A. 75 D3 30 7N 92 55W
Hayes, SD, U.S.A. 91 F4 44 23N 101 1W
Hayes ➜, Man., Canada 191 F7 57 3N 92 12W
Hayes ➜, Nunavut, Canada 191 D6 67 8N 95 17W
Hayes, Mt., AK, U.S.A. 61 E11 63 37N 146 43W
Hayes Center, NE, U.S.A. 84 D4 40 31N 101 1W
Hayes County ☆, NE, U.S.A. 84 D4 40 30N 101 0W
Hayesville, IA, U.S.A. 73 D6 41 16N 92 15W
Hayesville, NC, U.S.A. 90 C2 35 3N 83 49W
Hayesville, OR, U.S.A. 94 C3 44 59N 122 59W
Hayfield, MN, U.S.A. 80 G6 43 53N 92 51W
Hayford, Chicago, U.S.A. 108 C2 41 45N 87 42W
Hayford Peak, NV, U.S.A. 85 F6 36 39N 115 12W
Hayfork, CA, U.S.A. 64 C3 40 33N 123 11W
Haylow, GA, U.S.A. 68 F4 30 50N 82 54W
Haymarket, VA, U.S.A. 77 B3 38 49N 77 38W
Haynes, AR, U.S.A. 63 D5 34 54N 90 47W
Haynes, ND, U.S.A. 91 E3 45 59N 102 28W
Haynesville, LA, U.S.A. 75 B2 32 58N 93 8W
Haynesville, ME, U.S.A. 76 C6 45 50N 67 59W
Haynesville, VA, U.S.A. 77 C4 37 57N 76 40W
Hayneville, AL, U.S.A. 60 D4 32 11N 86 35W
Hayneville, GA, U.S.A. 68 D3 32 23N 83 37W
Hays, Alta., Canada 185 H9 50 6N 111 48W
Hays, KS, U.S.A. 74 C4 38 53N 99 20W
Hays Canyon Ra., NV, U.S.A. 85 A1 41 25N 119 53W
Hays County ☆, TX, U.S.A. 99 H10 29 59N 97 53W
Haysi, VA, U.S.A. 102 D2 37 12N 82 18W
Haystack Peak, UT, U.S.A. 100 D2 39 50N 113 55W
Haysville, KS, U.S.A. 74 D6 37 34N 97 21W
Hayti, MO, U.S.A. 82 E7 36 14N 89 44W
Hayti, SD, U.S.A. 91 F8 44 40N 97 13W
Hayward, CA, U.S.A. 64 F4 37 40N 122 4W
Hayward, MN, U.S.A. 80 G5 43 39N 93 15W
Hayward, WI, U.S.A. 103 B2 46 1N 91 29W
Hayward Municipal ✈, San Francisco, U.S.A. 118 C4 37 39N 122 7W
Haywood County ☆, NC, U.S.A. 90 C3 35 30N 83 0W
Haywood County ☆, TN, U.S.A. 96 E3 35 36N 89 16W
Hazard, KY, U.S.A. 97 C9 37 15N 83 12W
Hazard, NE, U.S.A. 84 C6 41 6N 99 9W
Hazardville, CT, U.S.A. 78 C2 41 59N 72 32W
Hazel, KY, U.S.A. 96 D4 36 30N 88 20W
Hazel, SD, U.S.A. 91 F8 44 46N 97 23W
Hazel ➜, VA, U.S.A. 102 C7 38 33N 77 51W
Hazel Green, AL, U.S.A. 60 B4 34 56N 86 34W
Hazel Green, WI, U.S.A. 103 F3 42 32N 90 26W
Hazel Park, MI, U.S.A. 109 A2 42 27N 83 6W
Hazel Run, MN, U.S.A. 80 F3 44 45N 95 43W
Hazelton, B.C., Canada 189 E7 55 20N 127 42W
Hazelton, ID, U.S.A. 70 G4 42 36N 114 8W
Hazelton, KS, U.S.A. 74 D5 37 5N 98 24W
Hazelton, ND, U.S.A. 91 D5 46 29N 100 17W
Hazelton Peak, WY, U.S.A. 104 B5 44 6N 107 3W
Hazelwood, MO, U.S.A. 117 A1 38 47N 90 22W
Hazen, AR, U.S.A. 63 D4 34 47N 91 35W
Hazen, ND, U.S.A. 91 C4 47 18N 101 38W
Hazen, NV, U.S.A. 85 C1 39 34N 119 3W
Hazen, L., Nunavut, Canada 190 A11 81 47N 71 1W
Hazen Str., Canada 188 A11 77 15N 109 0W
Hazenmore, Sask., Canada 182 F4 49 42N 107 8W
Hazlehurst, GA, U.S.A. 68 E4 31 52N 82 36W
Hazlehurst, MS, U.S.A. 81 E3 31 52N 90 24W
Hazlet, Sask., Canada 182 E3 50 24N 108 36W
Hazlet, NJ, U.S.A. 87 B2 40 25N 74 12W
Hazleton, IN, U.S.A. 72 E3 38 29N 87 33W
Hazleton, IA, U.S.A. 73 C7 42 37N 91 54W
Hazleton, PA, U.S.A. 95 D7 40 57N 75 59W
Hazlettville, DE, U.S.A. 77 A5 39 5N 75 40W
He Devil, ID, U.S.A. 70 D2 45 21N 116 33W
Head of St. Margarets Bay, N.S., Canada 173 J6 44 41N 63 55W
Headland, AL, U.S.A. 60 E5 31 21N 85 21W
Headquarters, ID, U.S.A. 70 C3 46 38N 115 48W
Headrick, OK, U.S.A. 93 D4 34 38N 99 9W
Healdsburg, CA, U.S.A. 64 E4 38 37N 122 52W
Healdton, OK, U.S.A. 93 D6 34 14N 97 29W
Healdville, VT, U.S.A. 86 C2 43 25N 72 45W
Healy, AK, U.S.A. 61 E10 63 52N 148 58W
Healy, KS, U.S.A. 74 C3 38 36N 100 37W
Heard County ☆, GA, U.S.A. 68 C1 33 15N 85 0W
Heard Pond, Boston, U.S.A. 106 A1 42 20N 71 23W
Hearne, TX, U.S.A. 99 G11 30 53N 96 36W
Hearst, Ont., Canada 181 C13 49 40N 83 41W
Heart ➜, ND, U.S.A. 91 D5 46 46N 100 50W
Heart L., Alta., Canada 184 C9 55 2N 111 30W
Heart L., WY, U.S.A. 104 B2 44 16N 110 29W
Heart's Content, Nfld. & L., Canada 174 E7 47 54N 53 27W
Heartwell, NE, U.S.A. 84 D7 40 34N 98 47W
Heartwell Park, Los Angeles, U.S.A. 111 D4 33 49N 118 6W
Heath, Pte., Qué., Canada 172 D8 49 8N 61 40W
Heath Springs, SC, U.S.A. 90 D5 34 36N 80 40W
Heath Steele, N.B., Canada 173 F3 47 17N 66 5W
Heatherton, N.S., Canada 173 H8 45 35N 61 47W
Heatherton, Nfld. & L., Canada 174 D2 48 17N 58 45W
Heatherwood = Edson, Alta., Canada 184 E4 53 35N 116 28W
Heathsville, VA, U.S.A. 77 C4 37 55N 76 29W
Heavener, OK, U.S.A. 93 D9 34 53N 94 36W
Hebbardsville, KY, U.S.A. 96 C5 37 47N 87 23W
Hebbronville, TX, U.S.A. 98 K9 27 18N 98 41W
Heber, AZ, U.S.A. 62 C5 34 26N 110 36W
Heber, CA, U.S.A. 65 L11 32 44N 115 32W
Heber City, UT, U.S.A. 100 C4 40 31N 111 25W
Heber Springs, AR, U.S.A. 63 C3 35 30N 92 2W
Hebert, Sask., Canada 182 E4 50 30N 107 10W
Hebgen L., MT, U.S.A. 83 F6 44 52N 111 20W
Hebo, OR, U.S.A. 94 B2 45 14N 123 52W
Hebron, N.S., Canada 173 K3 43 53N 66 5W
Hebron, Nfld. & L., Canada 175 B5 58 5N 62 30W
Hebron, CT, U.S.A. 78 C2 41 39N 72 22W
Hebron, IL, U.S.A. 71 A5 42 28N 88 26W
Hebron, IN, U.S.A. 72 B3 41 19N 87 12W
Hebron, MD, U.S.A. 77 B5 38 25N 75 41W
Hebron, ND, U.S.A. 91 D3 46 54N 102 3W
Hebron, NH, U.S.A. 86 C3 43 42N 71 48W
Hebron, NE, U.S.A. 84 D8 40 10N 97 35W
Hebron, TX, U.S.A. 99 D11 33 2N 96 52W
Hebron Fd., Nfld. & L., Canada 175 B5 58 9N 62 45W
Hecate I., B.C., Canada 186 D7 51 42N 128 0W
Hecate Str., B.C., Canada 186 B4 53 10N 130 30W
Hecelchakán, Campeche, Mexico 223 B3 20 10N 90 8W
Hecla, SD, U.S.A. 91 E7 45 53N 98 9W
Hecla and Griper B., Canada 188 A11 76 0N 109 35W
Hecla-Grindstone Prov. Park ⌂, Man., Canada 183 D15 51 15N 96 45W
Hecla I., Man., Canada 183 D15 51 10N 96 43W
Hector, AR, U.S.A. 63 C3 35 28N 92 59W
Hector, MN, U.S.A. 80 F4 44 45N 94 43W
Hedgesville, WV, U.S.A. 77 A3 39 31N 77 58W
Hedionda Grande, Coahuila, Mexico 215 E4 25 7N 100 51W
Hedley, B.C., Canada 187 F14 49 22N 120 4W
Hedley, TX, U.S.A. 98 C7 34 52N 100 39W
Hedley B., N.W.T., Canada 190 C4 72 31N 108 12W
Hedrick, IA, U.S.A. 73 D6 41 11N 92 19W
Hedwig Village, Houston, U.S.A. 110 B1 29 46N 95 31W
He'eia, HI, U.S.A. 69 K14 21 25N 157 48W
Heffley Creek, B.C., Canada 187 E14 50 52N 120 16W
Heflin, AL, U.S.A. 60 C5 33 39N 85 35W
Heiberger, AL, U.S.A. 60 D3 32 46N 87 17W
Heidelberg, MN, U.S.A. 80 F5 44 30N 93 38W
Heidelberg, MS, U.S.A. 81 E5 31 53N 88 59W
Heidelberg, Pittsburgh, U.S.A. 116 B1 40 23N 80 5W
Heidrick, KY, U.S.A. 97 D9 36 52N 83 54W
Height of the Rockies Park ⌂, B.C., Canada 185 H5 50 30N 115 15W
Heisler, Alta., Canada 185 F8 52 41N 112 13W
Heizer, KS, U.S.A. 74 C5 38 25N 98 53W
Helemano ➜, HI, U.S.A. 69 J13 21 35N 158 7W
Helen, GA, U.S.A. 68 B3 34 42N 83 44W
Helen, MD, U.S.A. 77 B4 38 22N 76 42W
Helena, AL, U.S.A. 60 C4 33 18N 86 51W
Helena, AR, U.S.A. 63 D5 34 32N 90 36W
Helena, CA, U.S.A. 64 C3 40 47N 123 8W
Helena, GA, U.S.A. 68 D4 32 5N 82 55W
Helena, MT, U.S.A. 83 D5 46 36N 112 2W
Helena, OK, U.S.A. 93 B5 36 33N 98 16W
Helena I., Nunavut, Canada 190 B5 76 39N 101 4W
Helena Nat. Forest, MT, U.S.A. 83 D6 46 30N 111 30W
Helene L., Sask., Canada 182 B3 53 33N 108 12W
Heliotrope Mt., UT, U.S.A. 100 D4 39 7N 111 27W
Helix, OR, U.S.A. 94 B7 45 51N 118 39W
Hell Cr. ➜, CO, U.S.A. 66 C8 39 30N 102 30W
Hellertown, PA, U.S.A. 87 B1 40 35N 75 21W
Hells Canyon, OR, U.S.A. 94 B9 45 10N 116 50W
Hells Canyon Nat. Recr. Area ⌂, OR, U.S.A. 94 B8 45 30N 117 45W
Helmville, MT, U.S.A. 83 D5 46 52N 112 58W
Helotes, TX, U.S.A. 99 H9 29 34N 98 41W
Helper, UT, U.S.A. 100 D5 39 41N 110 51W
Helton, KY, U.S.A. 97 D9 36 58N 83 24W
Hematite, MO, U.S.A. 82 C6 38 12N 90 29W
Hemet, CA, U.S.A. 65 K10 33 45N 116 58W
Hemford, N.S., Canada 173 J5 44 30N 64 47W
Hemingford, NE, U.S.A. 84 B2 42 19N 103 4W
Hemingway, SC, U.S.A. 90 E6 33 45N 79 27W
Hemmingford, Qué., Canada 177 F9 45 3N 73 35W
Hemphill, TX, U.S.A. 99 F14 31 20N 93 51W
Hemphill County ☆, TX, U.S.A. 98 B7 35 55N 100 15W
Hempstead, NY, U.S.A. 87 B3 40 42N 73 37W
Hempstead, TX, U.S.A. 99 G11 30 6N 96 5W
Hempstead County ☆, AR, U.S.A. 63 E2 33 40N 93 36W
Hempstead Harbor, NY, U.S.A. 114 A5 40 49N 73 39W
Henagar, AL, U.S.A. 60 B5 34 38N 85 46W
Henderson, GA, U.S.A. 68 D3 32 21N 83 47W

Henderson, IA, U.S.A. 73 D3 41 8N 95 26W
Henderson, KY, U.S.A. 96 C5 37 50N 87 35W
Henderson, MD, U.S.A. 77 A5 39 6N 75 47W
Henderson, NC, U.S.A. 90 B7 36 20N 78 25W
Henderson, NE, U.S.A. 84 D8 40 47N 97 49W
Henderson, NV, U.S.A. 85 F6 36 2N 114 58W
Henderson, TN, U.S.A. 96 E4 35 26N 88 38W
Henderson, TX, U.S.A. 99 E13 32 9N 94 48W
Henderson, Mt., B.C., Canada 186 A6 54 16N 128 4W
Henderson County ☆, IL, U.S.A. 71 C3 40 50N 90 55W
Henderson County ☆, KY, U.S.A. 96 C5 37 45N 87 35W
Henderson County ☆, NC, U.S.A. 90 C3 35 15N 82 30W
Henderson County ☆, TN, U.S.A. 96 E4 35 39N 88 24W
Henderson County ☆, TX, U.S.A. 99 E12 32 12N 95 51W
Henderson Executive ✕, Las Vegas, U.S.A. 110 D2 35 59N 115 8W
Hendersonville, NC, U.S.A. 90 C3 35 19N 82 28W
Hendersonville, TN, U.S.A. 96 D6 36 18N 86 37W
Hendley, NE, U.S.A. 84 D6 40 8N 99 58W
Hendricks, MN, U.S.A. 80 F2 44 30N 96 25W
Hendricks County ☆, IN, U.S.A. 72 D4 39 45N 86 30W
Hendrix Lake, B.C., Canada 187 C14 52 5N 120 48W
Hendrum, MN, U.S.A. 80 C2 47 16N 96 49W
Hendry County ☆, FL, U.S.A. 67 E7 26 30N 81 20W
Henefer, UT, U.S.A. 100 B4 41 1N 111 30W
Henlopen, C., DE, U.S.A. 77 B5 38 48N 75 6W
Hennepin, IL, U.S.A. 71 B4 41 15N 89 21W
Hennepin, OK, U.S.A. 93 D6 34 31N 97 21W
Hennepin Canal, IL, U.S.A. 71 B3 41 29N 90 12W
Hennepin County ☆, MN, U.S.A. 80 E5 45 0N 93 30W
Hennessey, OK, U.S.A. 93 B6 36 6N 97 54W
Henniker, NH, U.S.A. 86 C3 43 11N 71 50W
Henning, IL, U.S.A. 71 C6 40 18N 87 42W
Henning, MN, U.S.A. 80 D3 46 19N 95 27W
Henning, TN, U.S.A. 96 E3 35 41N 89 34W
Henrico County ☆, VA, U.S.A. 102 D7 37 33N 77 20W
Henrietta, NC, U.S.A. 90 C4 35 15N 81 48W
Henrietta, NY, U.S.A. 89 B3 43 4N 77 37W
Henrietta, TX, U.S.A. 99 D9 33 49N 98 12W
Henrietta Maria, C., Ont., Canada 191 F9 55 9N 82 20W
Henriette, MN, U.S.A. 80 E5 45 53N 93 7W
Henrieville, UT, U.S.A. 100 F4 37 30N 112 0W
Henry, IL, U.S.A. 71 B4 41 7N 89 22W
Henry, NE, U.S.A. 84 C1 41 58N 104 4W
Henry, SD, U.S.A. 91 F8 44 53N 97 28W
Henry, TN, U.S.A. 96 D4 36 12N 88 25W
Henry, C., VA, U.S.A. 102 E8 36 56N 76 1W
Henry County ☆, AL, U.S.A. 60 E5 31 34N 85 15W
Henry County ☆, GA, U.S.A. 68 C2 33 25N 84 5W
Henry County ☆, IL, U.S.A. 71 B3 41 20N 90 10W
Henry County ☆, IN, U.S.A. 72 D5 39 55N 85 25W
Henry County ☆, IA, U.S.A. 73 D7 41 0N 91 30W
Henry County ☆, KY, U.S.A. 97 B7 38 25N 85 10W
Henry County ☆, MO, U.S.A. 82 C3 38 25N 93 45W
Henry County ☆, OH, U.S.A. 92 B2 41 19N 84 2W
Henry County ☆, TN, U.S.A. 96 D4 36 18N 88 19W
Henry County ☆, VA, U.S.A. 102 E5 36 50N 79 56W
Henry Kater, C., N.W.T., Canada 190 D12 69 8N 66 30W
Henry Kater Pen., Nunavut, Canada 190 D12 69 23N 68 4W
Henry Mts., UT, U.S.A. 100 E5 38 0N 110 50W
Henryetta, OK, U.S.A. 93 C8 35 27N 95 59W
Henrys Fork ➛, ID, U.S.A. 70 F7 43 57N 111 45W
Henrys Lake, ID, U.S.A. 70 E7 44 36N 111 21W
Henryville, Qué., Canada 177 F9 45 8N 73 11W
Henshaw, KY, U.S.A. 96 C4 37 37N 88 3W
Henshaw, L., CA, U.S.A. 65 K10 33 15N 116 45W
Hensler, ND, U.S.A. 91 C4 47 16N 101 5W
Henson Cr. ➛, MD, U.S.A. 119 C4 38 47N 76 58W
Hepburn, IA, U.S.A. 73 E3 40 51N 95 1W
Hephzibah, GA, U.S.A. 68 C4 33 19N 82 6W
Hepler, KS, U.S.A. 74 D9 37 40N 94 58W
Heppner, OR, U.S.A. 94 B6 45 21N 119 33W
Hepworth, Ont., Canada 178 C5 44 37N 81 9W
Herbert Hoover Nat. Historic Site ⌂, IA, U.S.A. 73 D7 41 40N 91 21W
Herbert I., AK, U.S.A. 61 K5 52 45N 170 7W
Herbert Inlet, B.C., Canada 186 F9 49 20N 125 58W
Herbes, Point aux, New Orleans, U.S.A. 113 B3 30 9N 89 51W
Herculaneum, MO, U.S.A. 82 C6 38 16N 90 23W
Hércules, Coahuila, Mexico 213 E12 28 6N 103 46W
Hereford, AZ, U.S.A. 62 F5 31 26N 110 6W
Hereford, CO, U.S.A. 66 B6 40 57N 104 18W
Hereford, MD, U.S.A. 77 A4 39 35N 76 40W
Hereford, TX, U.S.A. 98 C5 34 49N 102 24W
Hereford, Mt., Qué., Canada 177 F11 45 5N 71 36W
Herington, KS, U.S.A. 74 C7 38 40N 96 57W
Heriot Bay, B.C., Canada 186 E9 50 7N 125 13W
Herkimer, KS, U.S.A. 74 B7 39 54N 96 43W
Herkimer, NY, U.S.A. 89 B6 43 2N 74 59W
Herkimer County ☆, NY, U.S.A. 89 B6 43 0N 75 0W
Herman, MN, U.S.A. 80 E2 45 49N 96 9W
Herman, NE, U.S.A. 84 C9 41 40N 96 13W
Hermann, MO, U.S.A. 82 C5 38 42N 91 27W
Hermansville, MI, U.S.A. 79 D4 45 42N 87 36W
Hermantown, MN, U.S.A. 80 D6 46 50N 92 15W
Hermanville, MS, U.S.A. 81 E3 31 58N 90 50W
Hermiston, OR, U.S.A. 94 B6 45 51N 119 17W
Hermitage, Nfld. & L., Canada 174 E5 47 33N 55 56W
Hermitage, AR, U.S.A. 63 E3 33 27N 92 10W
Hermitage, MO, U.S.A. 82 D3 37 56N 93 19W
Hermitage, PA, U.S.A. 95 C2 41 14N 80 27W
Hermleigh, TX, U.S.A. 98 E7 32 38N 100 46W
Hermon, NY, U.S.A. 89 A5 44 28N 75 14W
Hermosa, SD, U.S.A. 91 G2 43 50N 103 12W
Hermosa Beach, Los Angeles, U.S.A. 111 C2 33 51N 118 23W
Hermosillo, Sonora, Mexico 212 D5 29 10N 111 0W
Hernando, FL, U.S.A. 67 C6 28 54N 82 23W
Hernando, MS, U.S.A. 81 B3 34 50N 90 0W
Hernando County ☆, FL, U.S.A. 67 C6 28 35N 82 30W
Herndon, KS, U.S.A. 74 B3 39 55N 100 47W
Herndon, KY, U.S.A. 96 D5 36 44N 87 34W
Herndon, PA, U.S.A. 95 D6 40 43N 76 51W
Herndon, VA, U.S.A. 102 C7 38 58N 77 23W
Herod, GA, U.S.A. 68 E2 31 42N 84 26W
Héroes de Churubusco, Distrito Federal, Mexico 225 B3 19 21N 99 6W
Heroica Caborca = Caborca, Sonora, Mexico 212 C3 30 37N 112 6W
Heroica Nogales = Nogales, Sonora, Mexico 212 B5 31 20N 110 56W
Heron, MT, U.S.A. 83 B2 48 3N 115 57W
Heron Bay, Ont., Canada 181 D10 48 40N 86 25W
Heron L., NM, U.S.A. 88 A4 36 41N 106 43W
Heron Lake, MN, U.S.A. 80 G3 43 48N 95 19W
Herons, Ont., Canada 192 B1 45 23N 75 41W
Herons, Î. aux, Montréal, Canada 192 B3 45 25N 73 34W
Herreid, SD, U.S.A. 91 E5 45 50N 100 4W
Herrero, Pta., Quintana Roo, Mexico 223 C6 19 17N 87 27W
Herrick, SD, U.S.A. 91 G6 43 7N 99 11W
Herricks, NY, U.S.A. 114 B5 40 45N 73 40W
Herriman, Salt Lake City, U.S.A. 117 C1 40 30N 112 1W
Herrin, IL, U.S.A. 71 F4 37 48N 89 2W
Herring Cove, N.S., Canada 173 J6 44 34N 63 34W
Herring Run Park, Baltimore, U.S.A. 107 B2 39 19N 76 33W
Herrington L., KY, U.S.A. 97 C8 37 45N 84 44W
Herschel, Sask., Canada 182 D3 51 38N 108 21W
Herschel I., Yukon, Canada 188 C5 69 35N 139 5W
Herscher, IL, U.S.A. 71 B5 41 3N 88 6W
Hersey, MI, U.S.A. 79 F6 43 51N 85 27W
Hershey, NE, U.S.A. 84 C5 41 10N 101 0W
Hershey, PA, U.S.A. 95 D6 40 17N 76 39W
Hershey Park, PA, U.S.A. 95 D6 40 17N 76 39W
Hertford, NC, U.S.A. 90 B9 36 11N 76 28W
Hertford County ☆, NC, U.S.A. 90 B9 36 20N 77 0W
Hesperia, CA, U.S.A. 65 J9 34 25N 117 18W
Hesperia, MI, U.S.A. 79 F5 43 34N 86 3W
Hesperus, CO, U.S.A. 66 E2 37 17N 108 2W
Hesquiat Peninsula Park ⌂, B.C., Canada 186 F8 49 26N 126 31W
Hess ➛, Yukon, Canada 189 D6 63 33N 133 59W
Hessel, MI, U.S.A. 79 C7 46 0N 84 26W
Hessmer, LA, U.S.A. 75 C3 31 3N 92 8W
Hesston, KS, U.S.A. 74 C6 38 8N 97 26W
Hetch Hetchy Aqueduct, CA, U.S.A. 64 F4 37 29N 122 19W
Hetch Hetchy Res., CA, U.S.A. 64 F7 37 57N 119 47W
Hettinger, ND, U.S.A. 91 D3 46 0N 102 42W
Hettinger County ☆, ND, U.S.A. 91 D3 46 25N 102 30W
Heuvelton, NY, U.S.A. 89 A5 44 37N 75 25W
Hewett, C., Nunavut, Canada 190 C12 70 16N 67 45W
Hewins, KS, U.S.A. 74 D7 37 3N 96 25W
Hewitt, MN, U.S.A. 80 D3 46 20N 95 5W
Hewitt, TX, U.S.A. 99 F10 31 28N 97 12W
Hewlett Neck, NY, U.S.A. 114 C4 40 37N 73 41W
Hext, TX, U.S.A. 99 G8 30 52N 99 32W
Heyburn, ID, U.S.A. 70 G5 42 34N 113 46W
Heyburn L., OK, U.S.A. 93 C7 35 57N 96 18W
Heyworth, IL, U.S.A. 71 C5 40 19N 88 59W
Hialeah, FL, U.S.A. 67 F8 25 51N 80 16W
Hiattville, KS, U.S.A. 74 D9 37 43N 94 52W
Hiawassa, L., Orlando, U.S.A. 115 A2 28 33N 81 28W
Hiawassee, GA, U.S.A. 68 B3 34 58N 83 46W
Hiawatha, IA, U.S.A. 73 C7 42 2N 91 41W
Hiawatha, KS, U.S.A. 74 B8 39 51N 95 32W
Hiawatha, UT, U.S.A. 100 D4 39 29N 111 1W
Hiawatha Nat. Forest, MI, U.S.A. 79 C5 46 15N 86 40W
Hibben I., B.C., Canada 186 C2 53 0N 132 18W
Hibbing, MN, U.S.A. 80 C6 47 25N 92 56W
Hickam Air Force Base, HI, U.S.A. 69 K14 21 20N 157 56W
Hickam Housing, HI, U.S.A. 69 K14 21 21N 157 57W
Hickman, DE, U.S.A. 77 B5 38 50N 75 42W
Hickman, KY, U.S.A. 96 D3 36 34N 89 11W
Hickman, NE, U.S.A. 84 D9 40 37N 96 38W
Hickman County ☆, KY, U.S.A. 96 D4 36 40N 89 0W
Hickman County ☆, TN, U.S.A. 96 E5 35 47N 87 28W
Hickman's Harbour, Nfld. & L., Canada 174 D7 48 6N 53 44W
Hickok, KS, U.S.A. 74 D2 37 34N 101 14W
Hickory, KY, U.S.A. 96 D4 36 48N 88 40W
Hickory, MS, U.S.A. 81 D4 32 19N 89 2W
Hickory, NC, U.S.A. 90 C4 35 44N 81 21W
Hickory, OK, U.S.A. 93 D7 34 33N 96 52W
Hickory, L., NC, U.S.A. 90 C4 35 49N 81 12W
Hickory County ☆, MO, U.S.A. 82 D3 37 55N 93 15W
Hickory Flat, MS, U.S.A. 81 B4 34 37N 89 11W
Hickory Hills, Chicago, U.S.A. 108 C2 41 43N 87 49W
Hickory Plains, AR, U.S.A. 63 D4 34 59N 91 44W
Hickory Ridge, AR, U.S.A. 63 C5 35 24N 90 58W
Hickory Run State Park ⌂, PA, U.S.A. 95 C7 41 2N 75 41W
Hickory Valley, TN, U.S.A. 96 E3 35 9N 89 8W
Hickory Withe, TN, U.S.A. 96 E3 35 14N 89 35W
Hicksville, NY, U.S.A. 87 B3 40 46N 73 32W
Hicksville, OH, U.S.A. 92 B2 41 18N 84 46W
Hico, TX, U.S.A. 99 F9 31 59N 98 2W
Hidalgo, Chihuahua, Mexico 213 C8 30 33N 107 54W
Hidalgo, Coahuila, Mexico 214 E1 25 29N 103 9W
Hidalgo, Durango, Mexico 217 C6 24 9N 104 35W
Hidalgo, Nuevo León, Mexico 214 E4 25 59N 100 27W
Hidalgo, Zacatecas, Mexico 217 D8 23 5N 102 43W
Hidalgo, Zacatecas, Mexico 217 D7 23 59N 103 40W
Hidalgo, IL, U.S.A. 71 D5 39 9N 88 9W
Hidalgo, TX, U.S.A. 98 L9 26 6N 98 16W
Hidalgo □, Mexico 219 B9 20 30N 99 0W
Hidalgo County ☆, NM, U.S.A. 88 F2 32 0N 108 45W
Hidalgo County ☆, TX, U.S.A. 98 L9 26 25N 98 10W
Hidalgo del Parral, Chihuahua, Mexico 213 G10 26 56N 105 40W
Hidalgotitlán, Veracruz, Mexico 221 G6 17 47N 94 38W
Hidden Falls-Crosby Farm Regional Park ⌂, Minneapolis-St. Paul, U.S.A. 113 B3 44 54N 93 9W
Higbee, MO, U.S.A. 82 B4 39 19N 92 31W
Higgins, TX, U.S.A. 98 A7 36 7N 100 2W
Higgins L., MI, U.S.A. 79 E7 44 29N 84 43W
Higginsport, OH, U.S.A. 92 E3 38 47N 83 58W
Higginsville, MO, U.S.A. 82 B3 39 4N 93 43W
High Bridge, NJ, U.S.A. 87 B2 40 40N 74 54W
High Desert, OR, U.S.A. 94 D5 43 40N 120 20W
High Hill, MO, U.S.A. 82 C5 38 53N 91 23W
High I., MI, U.S.A. 79 D6 45 44N 85 41W
High Island, TX, U.S.A. 99 H13 29 34N 94 24W
High Level, Alta., Canada 189 E9 58 31N 117 8W
High Point, NC, U.S.A. 90 C5 35 57N 80 0W
High Point, Tampa, U.S.A. 119 B2 27 54N 82 42W
High Prairie, Alta., Canada 184 C4 55 30N 116 30W
High Pt., NJ, U.S.A. 87 A2 41 19N 74 40W
High Pt., WY, U.S.A. 104 E5 41 37N 107 43W
High River, Alta., Canada 185 H7 50 30N 113 50W
High Rock L., NC, U.S.A. 90 C5 35 36N 80 14W
High Rock L., NV, U.S.A. 85 A1 41 17N 119 17W
High Rolls, NM, U.S.A. 88 E5 32 57N 105 50W
High Springs, FL, U.S.A. 67 B6 29 50N 82 36W
Highgate Center, VT, U.S.A. 86 B1 44 56N 73 3W
Highland, CA, U.S.A. 65 J9 34 8N 117 13W
Highland, IL, U.S.A. 71 E4 38 44N 89 41W
Highland, IN, U.S.A. 72 B3 41 33N 87 28W
Highland, KS, U.S.A. 74 B8 39 52N 95 16W
Highland, NY, U.S.A. 89 D7 41 43N 73 58W
Highland, WI, U.S.A. 103 E3 43 3N 90 22W
Highland Beach, MD, U.S.A. 77 B4 38 56N 76 28W
Highland City, FL, U.S.A. 67 D7 27 58N 81 53W
Highland County ☆, OH, U.S.A. 92 D3 39 12N 83 37W
Highland County ☆, VA, U.S.A. 102 C5 38 25N 79 35W
Highland Falls, NY, U.S.A. 87 A3 41 22N 73 58W
Highland Heights, Houston, U.S.A. 110 A2 29 51N 95 25W
Highland Heights, KY, U.S.A. 107 B2 39 1N 84 27W
Highland Hills, IL, U.S.A. 71 B5 41 51N 88 1W
Highland Home, AL, U.S.A. 60 E4 31 57N 86 19W
Highland Lakes, NJ, U.S.A. 87 A2 41 11N 74 28W
Highland Mills, GA, U.S.A. 68 C2 33 17N 84 17W
Highland Park, Ont., Canada 192 B1 45 22N 75 45W
Highland Park, Dallas-Fort Worth, U.S.A. 109 B5 32 50N 96 47W
Highland Park, IL, U.S.A. 71 A6 42 11N 87 48W
Highland Park, Los Angeles, U.S.A. 111 B3 34 7N 118 13 E
Highland Park, MI, U.S.A. 109 A2 42 24N 83 5W
Highland Park, Pittsburgh, U.S.A. 116 B2 40 28N 79 55W
Highland Park, San Francisco, U.S.A. 118 B3 37 47N 122 13W
Highland Springs, VA, U.S.A. 102 D7 37 33N 77 20W
Highland View, FL, U.S.A. 67 B3 29 50N 85 19W
Highlands = Fort Thomas, KY, U.S.A. 97 A8 39 4N 84 26W
Highlands, NC, U.S.A. 90 C2 35 3N 83 12W
Highlands, NJ, U.S.A. 87 B3 40 24N 73 59W
Highlands County ☆, FL, U.S.A. 67 D7 27 20N 81 20W
Highlands Ranch, Denver, U.S.A. 109 C2 39 33N 104 58W
Highlandtown, Baltimore, U.S.A. 107 B2 39 17N 76 34W
Highmore, SD, U.S.A. 91 F6 44 31N 99 27W
Highridge, Alta., Canada 184 D6 54 3N 114 8W
Hightstown, NJ, U.S.A. 87 B2 40 16N 74 31W
Highway City, CA, U.S.A. 65 G7 36 49N 119 43W
Highwood Mts., MT, U.S.A. 83 C7 47 30N 110 30W
Higuera de Zaragoza, Sinaloa, Mexico 216 B1 25 59N 109 18W
Higueras, Nuevo León, Mexico 214 E5 25 27N 100 0W
Higuero, Pta., Puerto Rico 105 G15 18 22N 67 16W
Hiko, NV, U.S.A. 85 E5 37 32N 115 14W
Hiland, WY, U.S.A. 104 C5 43 7N 107 21W
Hilda, Alta., Canada 185 H10 50 28N 110 3W
Hildale, UT, U.S.A. 100 F3 37 0N 112 58W
Hilden, N.S., Canada 173 H6 45 18N 63 18W
Hildreth, NE, U.S.A. 84 D6 40 20N 99 3W
Hilgard, OR, U.S.A. 94 B7 45 21N 118 14W
Hill City, ID, U.S.A. 70 F3 43 18N 115 3W
Hill City, KS, U.S.A. 74 B4 39 22N 99 51W
Hill City, MN, U.S.A. 80 D5 46 59N 93 36W
Hill City, SD, U.S.A. 91 G2 43 56N 103 35W
Hill Country Village, San Antonio, U.S.A. 117 B2 29 34N 98 29W
Hill County ☆, MT, U.S.A. 83 B7 48 40N 110 0W
Hill County ☆, TX, U.S.A. 99 E10 32 1N 97 8W
Hill Cr. ➛, UT, U.S.A. 100 D6 39 55N 109 40W
Hill Island L., N.W.T., Canada 189 D11 60 30N 109 50W
Hill Spring, Alta., Canada 185 J7 49 17N 113 38W
Hill-Stead Museum, CT, U.S.A. 78 C2 41 43N 72 49W
Hillcrest Heights, MD, U.S.A. 77 B4 38 49N 76 57W
Hilliard, FL, U.S.A. 67 A7 30 41N 81 55W
Hilliard, OH, U.S.A. 92 C3 40 2N 83 10W
Hilliards, PA, U.S.A. 95 C3 41 5N 79 50W
Hillister, TX, U.S.A. 99 G13 30 40N 94 23W
Hillman, MI, U.S.A. 79 D8 45 4N 83 54W
Hillman, MN, U.S.A. 80 E5 46 0N 93 53W
Hillmond, Sask., Canada 182 B2 53 26N 109 41W
Hillrose, CO, U.S.A. 66 B7 40 20N 103 31W
Hills, IA, U.S.A. 73 D7 41 33N 91 32W
Hills, MN, U.S.A. 80 G2 43 32N 96 21W
Hills Creek L., OR, U.S.A. 94 D3 43 43N 122 26W
Hillsboro = Deerfield Beach, FL, U.S.A. 67 E8 26 19N 80 6W
Hillsboro, GA, U.S.A. 68 C3 33 11N 83 38W
Hillsboro, IL, U.S.A. 71 D4 39 9N 89 29W
Hillsboro, KS, U.S.A. 74 C6 38 21N 97 12W
Hillsboro, MD, U.S.A. 77 B5 38 55N 75 50W
Hillsboro, MO, U.S.A. 82 C6 38 14N 90 34W
Hillsboro, ND, U.S.A. 91 C8 47 26N 97 3W
Hillsboro, NM, U.S.A. 88 E3 32 55N 107 34W
Hillsboro, OH, U.S.A. 92 D3 39 12N 83 37W
Hillsboro, OR, U.S.A. 94 B3 45 31N 122 59W
Hillsboro, TX, U.S.A. 99 E10 32 1N 97 8W
Hillsboro, VA, U.S.A. 77 A3 39 12N 77 43W
Hillsboro, WV, U.S.A. 102 C4 38 8N 80 13W
Hillsboro, WI, U.S.A. 103 E3 43 39N 90 21W
Hillsboro Canal, FL, U.S.A. 67 E8 26 30N 80 15W
Hillsborough, N.B., Canada 173 H5 45 55N 64 39W
Hillsborough, NC, U.S.A. 90 B6 36 5N 79 7W
Hillsborough, NH, U.S.A. 86 C3 43 7N 71 54W
Hillsborough B., P.E.I., Canada 173 G6 46 8N 63 5W
Hillsborough Bay, Tampa, U.S.A. 119 B4 27 50N 82 26W
Hillsborough County ☆, FL, U.S.A. 67 D6 27 50N 82 20W
Hillsborough County ☆, NH, U.S.A. 86 D3 42 50N 71 45W
Hillsborough Land = Belle Glade, FL, U.S.A. 67 E8 26 41N 80 40W
Hillsborough Upper Village, NH, U.S.A. 86 C3 43 9N 71 58W
Hillsdale, IL, U.S.A. 71 B3 41 37N 90 11W
Hillsdale, KS, U.S.A. 74 C9 38 40N 94 51W
Hillsdale, MI, U.S.A. 79 H7 41 56N 84 38W
Hillsdale, MO, U.S.A. 117 A2 38 41N 90 17W
Hillsdale, NY, U.S.A. 78 B1 42 11N 73 32W
Hillsdale, OK, U.S.A. 93 B6 36 34N 97 59W
Hillsdale County ☆, MI, U.S.A. 79 H7 41 50N 84 40W
Hillside, AZ, U.S.A. 62 C3 34 25N 112 55W
Hillside, NJ, U.S.A. 87 B2 40 42N 74 13W
Hillside, NY, U.S.A. 114 B4 40 42N 73 47W
Hillside Manor, NY, U.S.A. 114 B4 40 45N 73 40W
Hillsmere Shores, MD, U.S.A. 77 B4 38 56N 76 32W
Hillsport, Ont., Canada 181 C11 49 27N 85 34W
Hillsville, VA, U.S.A. 102 E4 36 46N 80 44W
Hilltonia, GA, U.S.A. 68 D5 32 53N 81 40W
Hilltop, Minneapolis-St. Paul, U.S.A. 113 A2 45 3N 93 14W
Hillview, KY, U.S.A. 97 B7 38 5N 85 49W
Hillwood, VA, U.S.A. 119 B3 38 52N 77 9W
Hilo, HI, U.S.A. 69 D6 19 44N 155 5W
Hilo ✕ (ITO), HI, U.S.A. 69 D6 19 43N 155 2W
Hilo B., HI, U.S.A. 69 D6 19 45N 155 5W
Hilshire Village, Houston, U.S.A. 110 B2 29 47N 95 29W
Hilt, CA, U.S.A. 64 B4 41 50N 122 37W
Hilton, NY, U.S.A. 89 B3 43 17N 77 48W
Hilton Beach, Ont., Canada 178 A3 46 15N 83 53W
Hilton Head Island, SC, U.S.A. 90 F5 32 13N 80 45W
Hinckley, IL, U.S.A. 71 B5 41 46N 88 38W
Hinckley, MN, U.S.A. 80 D6 46 1N 92 56W
Hinckley, UT, U.S.A. 100 D3 39 20N 112 40W
Hinckley Res., NY, U.S.A. 89 B5 43 19N 75 7W
Hindman, KY, U.S.A. 97 C10 37 20N 82 59W
Hinds County ☆, MS, U.S.A. 81 D3 32 16N 90 25W
Hinds L., Nfld. & L., Canada 174 D4 48 58N 57 0W
Hindsboro, IL, U.S.A. 71 D5 39 41N 88 8W
Hines, FL, U.S.A. 67 B5 29 45N 83 14W
Hines, OR, U.S.A. 94 D6 43 34N 119 5W
Hines Creek, Alta., Canada 184 B2 56 20N 118 40W
Hinesburg, VT, U.S.A. 86 B1 44 18N 73 6W
Hineston, LA, U.S.A. 75 C3 31 9N 92 46W
Hinesville, GA, U.S.A. 68 E5 31 51N 81 36W
Hingham, MA, U.S.A. 78 B4 42 14N 70 54W
Hingham, MT, U.S.A. 83 B7 48 33N 110 25W
Hingham B., Boston, U.S.A. 106 B4 42 17N 70 56W
Hingham Harbor, Boston, U.S.A. 106 B4 42 15N 70 53W
Hinsdale, MA, U.S.A. 78 B1 42 26N 73 8W
Hinsdale, MT, U.S.A. 83 B10 48 24N 107 5W
Hinsdale, NH, U.S.A. 86 D2 42 47N 72 29W
Hinsdale County ☆, CO, U.S.A. 66 E3 37 50N 107 20W
Hinson, FL, U.S.A. 67 A4 30 39N 84 25W
Hinton, Alta., Canada 184 E3 53 26N 117 34W
Hinton, IA, U.S.A. 73 C2 42 38N 96 18W
Hinton, OK, U.S.A. 93 C5 35 28N 98 21W
Hinton, WV, U.S.A. 102 D4 37 40N 80 54W
Hiram, OH, U.S.A. 92 B5 41 19N 81 9W
Hitchcock, Sask., Canada 182 F8 49 14N 103 7W
Hitchcock, OK, U.S.A. 93 C5 35 58N 98 21W
Hitchcock, SD, U.S.A. 91 F7 44 38N 98 25W
Hitchcock, TX, U.S.A. 99 H12 29 21N 95 1W
Hitchcock County ☆, NE, U.S.A. 84 D4 40 15N 101 0W
Hitchins, KY, U.S.A. 97 B10 38 17N 82 55W
Hitchita, OK, U.S.A. 93 C8 35 31N 95 44W
Hitterdal, MN, U.S.A. 80 D2 46 59N 96 16W
Hiwassee, VA, U.S.A. 102 E4 36 58N 80 43W
Hiwassee ➛, TN, U.S.A. 97 E8 35 19N 84 47W
Hiwassee L., NC, U.S.A. 90 C1 35 9N 84 11W
Hixon, B.C., Canada 187 B12 53 25N 122 35W
Hixton, WI, U.S.A. 103 D2 44 23N 91 1W
Hoare B., Nunavut, Canada 191 D13 65 17N 62 30W
Hoback Junction, WY, U.S.A. 104 C2 43 19N 110 44W
Hoback Pk., WY, U.S.A. 104 C2 43 5N 110 34W
Hobart, IN, U.S.A. 72 B3 41 32N 87 15W
Hobart, NY, U.S.A. 89 C6 42 22N 74 40W
Hobart, OK, U.S.A. 93 C4 35 1N 99 6W
Hobbs, NM, U.S.A. 88 E7 32 42N 103 8W
Hobe Sound, FL, U.S.A. 67 D8 27 4N 80 8W
Hoberg, MO, U.S.A. 82 D3 37 4N 93 51W
Hoboken, GA, U.S.A. 68 E4 31 11N 82 8W
Hoboken, NJ, U.S.A. 87 B2 40 44N 74 3W
Hobson, KY, U.S.A. 97 C7 37 25N 85 22W
Hobson, MT, U.S.A. 83 C8 47 0N 109 52W
Hobson L., B.C., Canada 187 C14 52 35N 120 15W
Hocabá, Yucatán, Mexico 223 B4 20 49N 89 15W
Hochelaga, Montréal, Canada 192 A3 45 32N 73 33W
Hochheim, TX, U.S.A. 99 H10 29 19N 97 17W
Hockessin, DE, U.S.A. 77 A5 39 47N 75 42W
Hocking, OH, U.S.A. 92 D5 39 12N 81 45W
Hocking County ☆, OH, U.S.A. 92 D4 39 32N 82 25W
Hockley = Levelland, TX, U.S.A. 98 D5 33 35N 102 23W
Hockley County ☆, TX, U.S.A. 98 D5 33 35N 102 23W
Hoctún, Yucatán, Mexico 223 B4 20 52N 89 12W
Hodge, LA, U.S.A. 75 B3 32 17N 92 43W
Hodgeman County ☆, KS, U.S.A. 74 C4 38 0N 100 0W
Hodgenville, KY, U.S.A. 97 C7 37 34N 85 44W
Hodges, SC, U.S.A. 90 D3 34 17N 82 15W
Hodges Hill, Nfld. & L., Canada 174 C5 49 4N 55 53W
Hodgeville, Sask., Canada 182 E5 50 7N 106 58W
Hodgkins, Chicago, U.S.A. 108 C1 41 46N 87 53W
Hodgson, Man., Canada 183 D14 51 13N 97 36W
Hoehne, CO, U.S.A. 66 E6 37 17N 104 23W
Hoffman, IL, U.S.A. 71 E4 38 32N 89 16W
Hoffman, MN, U.S.A. 80 E3 45 50N 95 48W
Hoffman, OK, U.S.A. 93 C8 35 29N 95 51W
Hoffman I., NY, U.S.A. 114 C2 40 34N 74 3W
Hog I., MI, U.S.A. 79 D6 45 48N 85 22W
Hog I., VA, U.S.A. 102 D9 37 26N 75 42W
Hogansville, GA, U.S.A. 68 C2 33 10N 84 55W
Hogback Mt., MT, U.S.A. 83 F5 44 54N 112 7W
Hogback Mt., NE, U.S.A. 84 C2 41 44N 103 42W
Hogeland, MT, U.S.A. 83 B9 48 51N 108 40W
Hogup Mts., UT, U.S.A. 100 B2 41 30N 113 7W
Hoh ➛, WA, U.S.A. 101 C1 47 45N 124 29W
Hoh Indian Reservation, WA, U.S.A. 101 C1 47 44N 124 25W
Hohenwald, TN, U.S.A. 96 E5 35 33N 87 33W
Hohokam Pima Nat. Monument ⌂, AZ, U.S.A. 62 D4 33 11N 111 56W
Hoisington, KS, U.S.A. 74 C5 38 31N 98 47W
Hokah, MN, U.S.A. 80 G7 43 46N 91 21W
Hoke County ☆, NC, U.S.A. 90 C6 35 0N 79 15W
Holberg, B.C., Canada 186 E6 50 40N 128 0W
Holbox, I., Quintana Roo, Mexico 223 A6 21 33N 87 15W
Holbrook, AZ, U.S.A. 62 C5 34 54N 110 10W
Holbrook, ID, U.S.A. 70 G6 42 10N 112 39W
Holbrook, MA, U.S.A. 78 B3 42 9N 71 1W
Holbrook, NY, U.S.A. 87 B3 40 49N 73 5W
Holbrook, NE, U.S.A. 84 D5 40 18N 100 1W
Holchit, Pta., Yucatán, Mexico 223 A5 21 37N 88 8W
Holcomb, KS, U.S.A. 74 D3 37 59N 100 59W
Holcomb, MS, U.S.A. 81 C4 33 46N 89 59W
Holcomb, MO, U.S.A. 82 E6 36 24N 90 2W
Holcomb, NY, U.S.A. 89 C3 42 54N 77 25W
Holcombe Flowage, WI, U.S.A. 103 C2 45 13N 91 8W
Holden, Alta., Canada 184 E8 53 13N 112 11W
Holden, MA, U.S.A. 78 B3 42 21N 71 52W
Holden, MO, U.S.A. 82 C3 38 43N 94 0W
Holden, UT, U.S.A. 100 D3 39 6N 112 16W
Holden, L., Orlando, U.S.A. 115 B2 28 30N 81 23W
Holden Beach, NC, U.S.A. 90 E7 33 55N 78 15W
Holdenville, OK, U.S.A. 93 C7 35 5N 96 24W
Holder, FL, U.S.A. 67 C6 28 58N 82 25W
Holderness, NH, U.S.A. 86 C3 43 43N 71 37W
Holdfast, Sask., Canada 182 E6 50 58N 105 25W
Holdingford, MN, U.S.A. 80 E4 45 44N 94 28W
Holdrege, NE, U.S.A. 84 D6 40 26N 99 23W
Holgate, NJ, U.S.A. 87 C2 39 33N 74 15W
Holgate, OH, U.S.A. 92 B2 41 15N 84 8W
Holiday, FL, U.S.A. 67 C6 28 11N 82 44W
Holiday Park, Miami, U.S.A. 112 B3 26 8N 80 7W
Holinshead L., Ont., Canada 180 C7 49 39N 89 40W
Holladay, TN, U.S.A. 96 E4 35 52N 88 9W
Holladay, UT, U.S.A. 100 C4 40 40N 111 49W
Holland, AR, U.S.A. 63 C3 35 10N 92 16W
Holland, GA, U.S.A. 68 B1 34 21N 85 22W
Holland, IA, U.S.A. 73 C6 42 24N 92 48W
Holland, MI, U.S.A. 79 G5 42 47N 86 7W
Holland, MN, U.S.A. 80 F2 44 6N 96 11W
Holland, MO, U.S.A. 82 E7 36 3N 89 52W
Holland, TX, U.S.A. 99 G10 30 53N 97 24W
Holland Patent, NY, U.S.A. 89 B5 43 15N 75 15W
Hollandale, MN, U.S.A. 80 G5 43 46N 93 12W
Hollandale, MS, U.S.A. 81 C3 33 10N 90 51W
Hollandale, WI, U.S.A. 103 F4 42 53N 89 56W
Hollansburg, OH, U.S.A. 92 D2 39 59N 84 50W
Hollenberg, KS, U.S.A. 74 B7 39 58N 96 59W
Holley, FL, U.S.A. 67 A2 30 27N 86 54W
Holley, NY, U.S.A. 89 B2 43 14N 78 2W
Holley, OR, U.S.A. 94 C3 44 21N 122 47W
Holliday, TX, U.S.A. 99 D9 33 49N 98 42W
Holliday Park, Indianapolis, U.S.A. 110 A2 39 52N 86 9W
Hollidaysburg, PA, U.S.A. 95 D4 40 26N 78 24W
Hollins, VA, U.S.A. 102 D5 37 20N 79 57W
Hollis, AR, U.S.A. 63 D2 34 52N 93 7W
Hollis, KS, U.S.A. 74 B6 39 38N 97 33W
Hollis, NH, U.S.A. 86 D3 42 45N 71 36W
Hollis, NY, U.S.A. 114 B4 40 42N 73 46W
Hollis, OK, U.S.A. 93 D4 34 41N 99 55W
Hollister, CA, U.S.A. 64 G5 36 51N 121 24W
Hollister, ID, U.S.A. 70 G4 42 21N 114 35W
Hollister, MO, U.S.A. 82 E3 36 38N 93 12W
Hollister, OK, U.S.A. 93 D5 34 21N 98 52W
Holliston, MA, U.S.A. 78 B3 42 12N 71 26W
Holloman Air Force Base, NM, U.S.A. 88 E4 32 50N 106 4W
Hollow Rock, TN, U.S.A. 96 D4 36 2N 88 16W
Holloway, MN, U.S.A. 80 E3 45 15N 95 55W
Holly, CO, U.S.A. 66 D8 38 3N 102 7W
Holly, MI, U.S.A. 79 G8 42 48N 83 38W
Holly Bluff, MS, U.S.A. 81 D3 32 49N 90 43W
Holly Grove, AR, U.S.A. 63 D4 34 36N 91 12W
Holly Hill, FL, U.S.A. 67 B7 29 16N 81 3W
Holly Hill, SC, U.S.A. 90 E5 33 19N 80 25W
Holly Pond, AL, U.S.A. 60 B4 34 10N 86 37W
Holly Ridge, NC, U.S.A. 90 D8 34 30N 77 33W
Holly Springs, GA, U.S.A. 68 B2 34 10N 84 30W
Holly Springs, MS, U.S.A. 81 B4 34 46N 89 27W
Holly Springs, NC, U.S.A. 90 C7 35 39N 78 50W
Holly Springs Nat. Forest, MS, U.S.A. 81 B4 34 44N 89 8W
Hollywood, AL, U.S.A. 60 B5 34 44N 85 59W
Hollywood, CA, U.S.A. 111 B3 34 5N 118 19W

Hollywood, FL, U.S.A. **67 E8** 26 0N 80 8W
Hollywood, MD, U.S.A. **77 B4** 38 21N 76 34W
Hollywood, SC, U.S.A. **90 F5** 32 44N 80 15W
Hollywood-Burbank ✕, Los Angeles, U.S.A. **111 A2** 34 12N 118 22W
Hollywood Lake, Los Angeles, U.S.A. **111 B3** 34 5N 118 20W
Hollywood Park, San Antonio, U.S.A. **117 B3** 29 36N 98 29W
Holman, N.W.T., Canada **188 B9** 70 44N 117 44W
Holman, NM, U.S.A. **88 A5** 36 2N 105 23W
Holman Field = St. Paul Downtown ✕, Minneapolis-St. Paul, U.S.A. **113 B3** 44 56N 93 3W
Holmen, WI, U.S.A. **103 E2** 43 58N 91 15W
Holmes, Mt., WY, U.S.A. **104 B2** 44 49N 110 51W
Holmes Beach, FL, U.S.A. **67 D6** 27 31N 82 43W
Holmes County ☆, FL, U.S.A. **67 A3** 30 50N 85 45W
Holmes County ☆, MS, U.S.A. **81 C3** 33 7N 90 3W
Holmes County ☆, OH, U.S.A. **92 C5** 40 33N 81 55W
Holmes Cr. →, FL, U.S.A. **67 A3** 30 30N 85 50W
Holmes Run Acres, VA, U.S.A. **119 B2** 38 51N 77 13W
Holmesville, OH, U.S.A. **92 C5** 40 38N 81 56W
Holopaw, FL, U.S.A. **67 C7** 28 8N 81 5W
Holstein, IA, U.S.A. **73 C3** 42 29N 95 33W
Holstein, NE, U.S.A. **84 D7** 40 28N 98 39W
Holston →, TN, U.S.A. **97 E9** 35 58N 83 51W
Holt, AL, U.S.A. **60 C3** 33 14N 87 29W
Holt, FL, U.S.A. **67 A2** 30 43N 86 45W
Holt, MI, U.S.A. **79 G7** 42 39N 84 31W
Holt, MN, U.S.A. **80 B2** 48 18N 96 11W
Holt, MO, U.S.A. **82 B2** 39 27N 94 21W
Holt County ☆, MO, U.S.A. **82 A1** 40 5N 95 10W
Holt County ☆, NE, U.S.A. **84 B7** 42 30N 98 45W
Holton, Nfld. & L., Canada **175 C6** 54 31N 57 12W
Holton, IN, U.S.A. **72 D5** 39 5N 85 23W
Holton, KS, U.S.A. **74 B8** 39 28N 95 44W
Holts Summit, MO, U.S.A. **82 C4** 38 38N 92 7W
Holtville, CA, U.S.A. **65 L11** 32 49N 115 23W
Holualoa, HI, U.S.A. **69 D6** 19 37N 155 57W
Holy Cross, AK, U.S.A. **61 E8** 62 12N 159 46W
Holyoke, CO, U.S.A. **66 B8** 40 35N 102 18W
Holyoke, MA, U.S.A. **78 B2** 42 12N 72 37W
Holyrood, Nfld. & L., Canada **174 E7** 47 27N 53 8W
Holyrood, KS, U.S.A. **74 C5** 38 35N 98 25W
Homathko →, B.C., Canada **186 D10** 51 0N 124 56W
Home, KS, U.S.A. **74 B7** 39 51N 96 31W
Home B., Nunavut, Canada **190 D12** 68 40N 67 10W
Homedale, ID, U.S.A. **70 F2** 43 37N 116 56W
Homeland, GA, U.S.A. **68 F4** 30 51N 82 1W
Homeland Park, SC, U.S.A. **90 D3** 34 28N 82 40W
Homer, AK, U.S.A. **61 G10** 59 39N 151 33W
Homer, GA, U.S.A. **68 B3** 34 20N 83 30W
Homer, LA, U.S.A. **75 B2** 32 48N 93 4W
Homer, MI, U.S.A. **79 G7** 42 9N 84 49W
Homer, NY, U.S.A. **89 C4** 42 38N 76 11W
Homer, NE, U.S.A. **84 B9** 42 19N 96 29W
Homer City, PA, U.S.A. **95 D3** 40 32N 79 10W
Homer Youngs Pk., MT, U.S.A. **83 E4** 45 19N 113 41W
Homerville, GA, U.S.A. **68 E4** 31 2N 82 45W
Homestead, Charlotte, U.S.A. **107 A1** 35 17N 80 54W
Homestead, FL, U.S.A. **67 F8** 25 28N 80 29W
Homestead, OR, U.S.A. **94 B9** 45 2N 116 51W
Homestead, Pittsburgh, U.S.A. **116 B2** 40 24N 79 54W
Homestead Nat. Monument of America △, NE, U.S.A. **84 D9** 40 17N 96 50W
Hometown, Chicago, U.S.A. **108 C2** 41 44N 87 42W
Homewood, AL, U.S.A. **60 C4** 33 29N 86 47W
Homewood, IL, U.S.A. **71 B6** 41 34N 87 40W
Hominy, OK, U.S.A. **93 B7** 36 25N 96 24W
Homochitto →, MS, U.S.A. **81 E2** 31 13N 91 32W
Homochitto Nat. Forest, MS, U.S.A. **81 E3** 31 15N 90 45W
Homosassa Springs, FL, U.S.A. **67 C6** 28 48N 82 35W
Hon, AR, U.S.A. **63 D1** 34 56N 94 11W
Honaker, VA, U.S.A. **102 D3** 37 1N 81 59W
Hōnaunau, HI, U.S.A. **69 D6** 19 26N 155 55W
Hondo, Alta., Canada **184 C6** 55 4N 114 2W
Hondo, NM, U.S.A. **88 D5** 33 24N 105 16W
Hondo, TX, U.S.A. **99 H8** 29 21N 99 9W
Hondo →, NM, U.S.A. **88 D6** 33 20N 104 25W
Hondo, Rio →, Belize **223 D5** 18 25N 88 21W
Hondo, Rio →, Los Angeles, U.S.A. **111 B4** 34 2N 118 15W
Honea Path, SC, U.S.A. **90 D3** 34 27N 82 24W
Honesdale, PA, U.S.A. **95 C7** 41 34N 75 16W
Honey Brook, PA, U.S.A. **95 D7** 40 6N 75 55W
Honey Grove, TX, U.S.A. **99 D12** 33 35N 95 55W
Honey Harbour, Ont., Canada **178 C7** 44 52N 79 49W
Honey Island, TX, U.S.A. **99 G13** 30 24N 94 27W
Honey L., CA, U.S.A. **64 C6** 40 15N 120 19W
Honeyville, FL, U.S.A. **67 A3** 30 3N 85 11W
Honeyville, UT, U.S.A. **100 B3** 41 38N 112 4W
Honga, MD, U.S.A. **77 B4** 38 19N 76 14W
Honguedo, Détroit d', Qué., Canada **172 D6** 49 15N 64 0W
Honoka'a, HI, U.S.A. **69 C6** 20 5N 155 28W
Honokahua, HI, U.S.A. **69 B5** 21 0N 156 40W
Honokai Hale, HI, U.S.A. **69 K13** 21 20N 158 6W
Honolulu, HI, U.S.A. **69 K14** 21 19N 157 52W
Honolulu District, HI, U.S.A. **69 K14** 21 19N 157 46W
Honolulu International ✕ (HNL), HI, U.S.A. **69 K14** 21 19N 157 55W
Honolulu Watershed Forest Reserve, HI, U.S.A. **69 K14** 21 21N 157 48W
Honomu, HI, U.S.A. **69 D6** 19 52N 155 7W
Honor, MI, U.S.A. **79 E5** 44 40N 86 1W
Honoré Mercier, Pont, Montréal, Canada **192 B3** 45 24N 73 39W
Honouliuli, HI, U.S.A. **69 K13** 21 22N 158 2W
Honouliuli Forest Reserve, HI, U.S.A. **69 K13** 21 25N 158 4W
Honu'apo B., HI, U.S.A. **69 D6** 19 5N 155 33W
Hood →, Nunavut, Canada **188 C11** 67 26N 108 53W
Hood, Mt., OR, U.S.A. **94 B4** 45 23N 121 42W
Hood Canal, WA, U.S.A. **101 C2** 47 35N 123 0W
Hood County ☆, TX, U.S.A. **99 E10** 32 27N 97 47W
Hood River, OR, U.S.A. **94 B4** 45 43N 121 31W
Hood River County ☆, OR, U.S.A. **94 B4** 45 30N 121 20W
Hoodsport, WA, U.S.A. **101 C2** 47 24N 123 9W
Hooker, OK, U.S.A. **93 B2** 36 52N 101 13W
Hooker County ☆, NE, U.S.A. **84 C4** 41 50N 101 0W
Hooker L., Ont., Canada **180 B5** 50 35N 91 1W
Hooks, TX, U.S.A. **99 D13** 33 28N 94 16W
Hooksett, NH, U.S.A. **86 C3** 43 5N 71 30W
Hool, Campeche, Mexico **223 C3** 19 31N 90 27W
Ho'olehua, HI, U.S.A. **69 B4** 21 10N 157 5W
Hoonah, AK, U.S.A. **61 G14** 58 7N 135 27W
Hoopa, CA, U.S.A. **64 B3** 41 3N 123 41W
Hoopa Valley Indian Reservation, CA, U.S.A. **64 B3** 41 10N 123 45W
Hooper, CO, U.S.A. **66 E5** 37 45N 105 53W
Hooper, NE, U.S.A. **84 C9** 41 37N 96 33W
Hooper, WA, U.S.A. **101 D7** 46 45N 118 9W
Hooper Bay, AK, U.S.A. **61 F6** 61 32N 166 6W
Hooper Str., MD, U.S.A. **77 B4** 38 15N 76 5W
Hoopersville, MD, U.S.A. **77 B4** 38 16N 76 11W
Hoopeston, IL, U.S.A. **71 C6** 40 28N 87 40W
Hoople, ND, U.S.A. **91 B8** 48 32N 97 38W
Hoosac Range, U.S.A. **78 B1** 42 45N 73 2W
Hoosic →, NY, U.S.A. **86 D1** 42 56N 73 40W
Hoosick Falls, NY, U.S.A. **78 B1** 42 54N 73 21W
Hoosier Nat. Forest, IN, U.S.A. **72 E4** 38 30N 86 35W
Hoover, AL, U.S.A. **60 C4** 33 24N 86 49W
Hoover Dam, U.S.A. **62 A1** 36 1N 114 44W
Hoover Dam, NV, U.S.A. **85 F6** 36 1N 114 44W
Hoover Res., OH, U.S.A. **92 C4** 40 7N 82 53W
Hooversville, PA, U.S.A. **95 D4** 40 9N 78 55W
Hop Bottom, PA, U.S.A. **95 C7** 41 42N 75 46W
Hopatcong, NJ, U.S.A. **87 B2** 40 55N 74 40W
Hopatcong, L., NJ, U.S.A. **87 B2** 40 57N 74 38W
Hope, B.C., Canada **187 F13** 49 25N 121 25W
Hope, AZ, U.S.A. **62 D2** 33 43N 113 42W
Hope, AR, U.S.A. **63 E2** 33 40N 93 36W
Hope, IN, U.S.A. **72 D5** 39 18N 85 46W
Hope, KS, U.S.A. **74 C6** 38 41N 97 5W
Hope, ND, U.S.A. **91 C8** 47 19N 97 43W
Hope, NM, U.S.A. **88 E6** 32 49N 104 44W
Hope, RI, U.S.A. **78 C3** 41 44N 71 34W
Hope, Pt., AK, U.S.A. **61 B6** 68 21N 166 47W
Hope I., B.C., Canada **186 E7** 50 55N 127 53W
Hope I., Ont., Canada **178 C6** 44 55N 80 11W
Hope Mills, NC, U.S.A. **90 D7** 34 59N 78 57W
Hope Valley, RI, U.S.A. **78 C3** 41 30N 71 43W
Hopedale, Nfld. & L., Canada **175 B5** 55 28N 60 13W
Hopedale, IL, U.S.A. **71 C4** 40 25N 89 25W
Hopelawn, NJ, U.S.A. **114 C1** 40 31N 74 17W
Hopelchén, Campeche, Mexico **223 C4** 19 46N 89 51W
Hopes Advance C., Qué., Canada **175 A4** 61 4N 69 34W
Hopes Advance B., Qué., Canada **175 B4** 59 20N 69 40W
Hopeton, OK, U.S.A. **93 B5** 36 41N 98 40W
Hopewell, N.S., Canada **173 H7** 45 29N 62 42W
Hopewell, TN, U.S.A. **97 E8** 35 14N 84 53W
Hopewell, VA, U.S.A. **102 D7** 37 18N 77 17W
Hopewell Cape, N.B., Canada **173 H5** 45 51N 64 35W
Hopewell Culture Nat. Historical Park △, OH, U.S.A. **92 D4** 39 17N 82 55W
Hopewell Furnace Nat. Historical Park △, PA, U.S.A. **95 D7** 40 12N 75 47W
Hopewell Is., Nunavut, Canada **191 F10** 58 24N 78 10W
Hopi Indian Reservation, AZ, U.S.A. **62 B5** 35 45N 110 30W
Hopkins, MI, U.S.A. **79 G6** 42 37N 85 46W
Hopkins, Minneapolis-St. Paul, U.S.A. **113 B1** 44 55N 93 27W
Hopkins, MO, U.S.A. **82 A2** 40 33N 94 49W
Hopkins County ☆, KY, U.S.A. **96 C5** 37 20N 87 30W
Hopkins County ☆, TX, U.S.A. **99 D12** 33 8N 95 36W
Hopkinsville, KY, U.S.A. **96 D5** 36 52N 87 29W
Hopkinton, IA, U.S.A. **73 C7** 42 21N 91 15W
Hopkinton, MA, U.S.A. **78 B3** 42 14N 71 31W
Hopkinton, NH, U.S.A. **86 C3** 43 12N 71 41W
Hopkinton, RI, U.S.A. **78 C3** 41 28N 71 48W
Hopland, CA, U.S.A. **64 E3** 38 58N 123 7W
Hoquiam, WA, U.S.A. **101 D2** 46 59N 123 53W
Horace, KS, U.S.A. **74 C2** 38 29N 101 47W
Horace, ND, U.S.A. **91 D9** 46 45N 96 54W
Horatio, AR, U.S.A. **63 E1** 33 56N 94 21W
Horconcitos, Veracruz, Mexico **220 C3** 21 51N 97 43W
Hordville, NE, U.S.A. **84 C8** 41 5N 97 53W
Horicon, WI, U.S.A. **103 E5** 43 27N 88 38W
Horicon Nat. Wildlife Refuge △, WI, U.S.A. **103 E5** 43 35N 88 38W
Hormigas, Coahuila, Mexico **213 F12** 27 46N 103 56W
Hormigueros, Puerto Rico **105 G15** 18 8N 67 8W
Horn →, N.W.T., Canada **189 D9** 61 30N 118 1W
Horn I., MS, U.S.A. **81 F5** 30 14N 88 39W
Horn Lake, MS, U.S.A. **81 B3** 34 58N 90 2W
Horn Plateau, N.W.T., Canada **189 D9** 62 15N 119 15W
Horn Pond, Boston, U.S.A. **106 A2** 42 28N 71 9W
Hornaday →, N.W.T., Canada **188 C8** 69 19N 123 48W
Hornbeak, TN, U.S.A. **96 D3** 36 20N 89 18W
Hornbeck, LA, U.S.A. **75 C2** 31 20N 93 24W
Hornbrook, CA, U.S.A. **64 B4** 41 55N 122 33W
Hornell, NY, U.S.A. **89 C3** 42 20N 77 40W
Hornepayne, Ont., Canada **181 C12** 49 14N 84 48W
Hornersville, MO, U.S.A. **82 E6** 36 3N 90 7W
Hornick, IA, U.S.A. **73 C2** 42 14N 96 6W
Hornillos, Sinaloa, Mexico **216 A2** 26 28N 108 27W
Hornings Mills, Ont., Canada **178 C6** 44 9N 80 12W
Hornitos, CA, U.S.A. **64 F6** 37 30N 120 14W
Hornsby, TN, U.S.A. **96 E4** 35 14N 88 50W
Horry County ☆, SC, U.S.A. **90 E7** 33 50N 79 0W
Horse →, CO, U.S.A. **66 D7** 38 5N 103 19W
Horse Cave, KY, U.S.A. **97 C7** 37 11N 85 54W
Horse Cr. →, FL, U.S.A. **67 D7** 27 6N 81 58W
Horse Cr. →, MO, U.S.A. **82 D3** 37 46N 93 53W
Horse Cr. →, WY, U.S.A. **104 E7** 41 57N 103 58W
Horse Creek, WY, U.S.A. **104 E7** 41 25N 105 11W
Horse Creek Res., CO, U.S.A. **66 D7** 38 10N 103 24W
Horse Heaven Hills, WA, U.S.A. **101 D6** 46 3N 119 30W
Horse I., Man., Canada **183 B12** 53 20N 99 6W
Horse Is., Nfld. & L., Canada **174 B5** 50 15N 55 50W
Horse L., CA, U.S.A. **64 C6** 40 40N 120 31W
Horse Pasture, VA, U.S.A. **102 E5** 36 38N 79 57W
Horsefly, B.C., Canada **187 C13** 52 20N 121 25W
Horsefly L., B.C., Canada **187 C13** 52 25N 121 0W
Horsehead L., ND, U.S.A. **91 C6** 47 3N 99 47W
Horseheads, NY, U.S.A. **89 C4** 42 10N 76 49W
Horseshoe Bend, AR, U.S.A. **63 B4** 36 14N 91 46W
Horseshoe Bend, ID, U.S.A. **70 F2** 43 55N 116 12W
Horseshoe Bend Nat. Military Park △, AL, U.S.A. **60 D5** 32 59N 85 44W
Horseshoe Lake, IL, U.S.A. **117 A3** 38 41N 90 5W
Horseshoe Lake State Park △, IL, U.S.A. **117 B3** 38 41N 90 5W
Horseshoe Res., AZ, U.S.A. **62 C4** 34 2N 111 42W
Hortense, GA, U.S.A. **68 E5** 31 20N 81 57W
Horton, KS, U.S.A. **74 B8** 39 40N 95 32W
Horton →, N.W.T., Canada **188 C7** 69 56N 126 52W
Horton L., N.W.T., Canada **188 C8** 67 29N 122 31W
Hortonville, WI, U.S.A. **103 D5** 44 20N 88 38W
Horwood, Nfld. & L., Canada **174 C6** 49 27N 54 32W
Horwood L., Ont., Canada **181 D14** 48 5N 82 20W
Hosford, FL, U.S.A. **67 A4** 30 23N 84 48W
Hoskins, NE, U.S.A. **84 B8** 42 7N 97 18W
Hoskins, OR, U.S.A. **94 C2** 44 41N 123 28W
Hoskinston, KY, U.S.A. **97 C9** 37 5N 83 24W
Hosmer, SD, U.S.A. **91 E6** 45 34N 99 28W
Hospers, IA, U.S.A. **73 B3** 43 4N 95 54W
Hostotipaquillo, Jalisco, Mexico **218 A3** 21 4N 104 4W
Hot Creek Range, NV, U.S.A. **85 D4** 38 40N 116 20W
Hot Spring County ☆, AR, U.S.A. **63 D3** 34 14N 92 55W
Hot Springs = Truth or Consequences, NM, U.S.A. **88 D3** 33 8N 107 15W
Hot Springs, AR, U.S.A. **63 D2** 34 31N 93 3W
Hot Springs, MT, U.S.A. **83 C3** 47 37N 114 40W
Hot Springs, NC, U.S.A. **90 C3** 35 54N 82 50W
Hot Springs, SD, U.S.A. **91 G2** 43 26N 103 29W
Hot Springs, VA, U.S.A. **102 D5** 38 0N 79 50W
Hot Springs County ☆, WY, U.S.A. **104 C4** 43 55N 108 30W
Hot Springs Nat. Park △, AR, U.S.A. **63 D2** 34 31N 93 3W
Hot Springs Village, AR, U.S.A. **63 D3** 34 40N 93 0W
Hot Sulphur Springs, CO, U.S.A. **66 B4** 40 4N 106 6W
Hotchkiss, CO, U.S.A. **66 D3** 38 48N 107 43W
Hotchkiss →, Alta., Canada **184 A3** 57 2N 117 28W
Hotevilla, AZ, U.S.A. **62 B5** 35 56N 110 41W
Hottah L., N.W.T., Canada **189 C9** 65 4N 118 30W
Houck, AZ, U.S.A. **62 B6** 35 20N 109 10W
Houghs Neck, Boston, U.S.A. **106 B4** 42 15N 70 57W
Houghton, MI, U.S.A. **79 B3** 47 7N 88 34W
Houghton, NY, U.S.A. **89 C2** 42 25N 78 10W
Houghton County ☆, MI, U.S.A. **79 C3** 47 0N 88 45W
Houghton L., MI, U.S.A. **79 E7** 44 21N 84 44W
Houghton Lake, MI, U.S.A. **79 E7** 44 18N 84 45W
Houlton, ME, U.S.A. **76 B6** 46 8N 67 51W
Houma, LA, U.S.A. **75 E5** 29 36N 90 43W
Housatonic, MA, U.S.A. **78 B1** 42 16N 73 22W
Housatonic →, CT, U.S.A. **78 C1** 41 10N 73 7W
House, NM, U.S.A. **88 C7** 34 39N 103 54W
House Range, UT, U.S.A. **100 D2** 39 30N 113 20W
Houston, B.C., Canada **189 F7** 54 25N 126 39W
Houston, AR, U.S.A. **63 C3** 35 2N 92 42W
Houston, FL, U.S.A. **67 A6** 30 15N 82 54W
Houston, MN, U.S.A. **80 G7** 43 46N 91 34W
Houston, MS, U.S.A. **81 C4** 33 54N 89 0W
Houston, MO, U.S.A. **82 D5** 37 22N 91 58W
Houston, TX, U.S.A. **99 H12** 29 45N 95 21W
Houston →, LA, U.S.A. **75 D2** 30 16N 93 13W
Houston, L., TX, U.S.A. **99 H12** 29 55N 95 8W
Houston County ☆, AL, U.S.A. **60 E5** 31 11N 85 14W
Houston County ☆, GA, U.S.A. **68 D3** 32 20N 83 45W
Houston County ☆, MN, U.S.A. **80 G7** 43 35N 91 30W
Houston County ☆, TN, U.S.A. **96 D5** 36 19N 87 42W
Houston County ☆, TX, U.S.A. **99 F12** 31 19N 95 27W
Houston County L., TX, U.S.A. **99 F12** 31 25N 95 35W
Houston George Bush Intercontinental ✕ (IAH), TX, U.S.A. **99 H12** 29 59N 95 20W
Houston William P. Hobby ✕ (HOU), TX, U.S.A. **99** 29 38N 95 16W
Houstonia, MO, U.S.A. **82 C3** 38 54N 93 22W
Hoved I., Nunavut, Canada **190 B8** 77 32N 85 9W
Hoven, SD, U.S.A. **91 E6** 45 15N 99 47W
Hovenweep Nat. Monument △, CO, U.S.A. **66 E2** 37 20N 109 0W
Hovland, MN, U.S.A. **80 C9** 47 51N 89 58W
Howard, CO, U.S.A. **66 D5** 38 27N 105 50W
Howard, GA, U.S.A. **68 D2** 32 36N 84 23W
Howard, KS, U.S.A. **74 D7** 37 28N 96 16W
Howard, PA, U.S.A. **95 C5** 41 1N 77 40W
Howard, SD, U.S.A. **91 F8** 44 1N 97 32W
Howard, WI, U.S.A. **103 D5** 44 33N 88 4W
Howard Beach, NY, U.S.A. **114 C3** 40 39N 73 50W
Howard City, MI, U.S.A. **79 F6** 43 24N 85 28W
Howard County ☆, AR, U.S.A. **63 D1** 34 7N 94 1W
Howard County ☆, IN, U.S.A. **72 C4** 40 30N 86 10W
Howard County ☆, IA, U.S.A. **73 B6** 43 20N 92 20W
Howard County ☆, MD, U.S.A. **77 A4** 39 15N 77 0W
Howard County ☆, MO, U.S.A. **82 B4** 39 10N 92 40W
Howard County ☆, NE, U.S.A. **84 C7** 41 15N 98 30W
Howard County ☆, TX, U.S.A. **98 E6** 32 15N 101 28W
Howard Draw →, TX, U.S.A. **98 G6** 30 10N 101 35W
Howard Hanson Res., WA, U.S.A. **101 C4** 47 17N 121 47W
Howard Lake, MN, U.S.A. **80 E4** 45 4N 94 4W
Howard Prairie L., OR, U.S.A. **94 E3** 42 13N 122 22W
Howe, ID, U.S.A. **70 F5** 43 48N 113 0W
Howe, IN, U.S.A. **72 B5** 41 43N 85 25W
Howe, OK, U.S.A. **93 D9** 34 57N 94 38W
Howe, TX, U.S.A. **99 D11** 33 30N 96 37W
Howe I., Ont., Canada **179 C10** 44 16N 76 17W
Howe Sd., B.C., Canada **187 F11** 49 35N 123 15W
Howell, MI, U.S.A. **79 G8** 42 36N 83 56W
Howell, UT, U.S.A. **100 B3** 41 48N 112 27W
Howell County ☆, MO, U.S.A. **82 E5** 36 45N 91 50W
Howells, NE, U.S.A. **84 C9** 41 44N 97 0W
Howes, SD, U.S.A. **91 F3** 44 37N 102 3W
Howes Mill, MO, U.S.A. **82 D5** 37 38N 91 16W
Howland, ME, U.S.A. **76 C5** 45 14N 68 40W
Howland I., Pac. Oc. **105 D6** 0 48N 176 38W
Howley, Nfld. & L., Canada **174 C3** 49 12N 57 2W
Hoxie, AR, U.S.A. **63 B5** 36 3N 90 59W
Hoxie, KS, U.S.A. **74 B3** 39 21N 100 26W
Hoyanco, Sinaloa, Mexico **216 A2** 26 22N 108 36W
Hoyleton, IL, U.S.A. **71 E4** 38 27N 89 16W
Hoyt, CO, U.S.A. **66 B6** 40 1N 104 5W
Hoyt, KS, U.S.A. **74 B8** 39 15N 95 43W
Hoyt Lakes, MN, U.S.A. **80 C6** 47 32N 92 8W
Huacales, Cerro los, Zacatecas, Mexico **217 E9** 22 21N 101 30W
Huacasco, Jalisco, Mexico **217 E7** 22 13N 103 6W
Huachichil, Coahuila, Mexico **215 E4** 25 11N 100 50W
Huachinera, Sonora, Mexico **212 C7** 30 9N 108 55W
Huachuca City, AZ, U.S.A. **62 F5** 31 34N 110 21W
Huajicori, Nayarit, Mexico **216 E5** 22 44N 105 21W
Huajimic, Nayarit, Mexico **216 F6** 21 42N 104 20W
Huajuapán de León, Oaxaca, Mexico **221 G3** 17 48N 97 46W
Huajumbaro, Michoacan, Mexico **219 C7** 19 52N 100 36W
Hualahuises, Nuevo León, Mexico **215 F5** 24 53N 99 41W
Hualālai, HI, U.S.A. **69 D6** 19 42N 155 52W
Hualapai Indian Reservation, AZ, U.S.A. **62 B2** 35 45N 113 20W
Hualapai Mts., AZ, U.S.A. **62 C2** 34 45N 113 45W
Hualapai Peak, AZ, U.S.A. **62 B2** 35 5N 113 54W
Hualula, Hidalgo, Mexico **219 B9** 20 45N 98 47W
Huamantla, Tlaxcala, Mexico **219 C10** 19 19N 97 56W
Huamuxtitlán, Guerrero, Mexico **219 E9** 17 49N 98 34W
Huandacareó, Michoacan, Mexico **219 C6** 19 59N 101 17W
Huanímaro, Guanajuato, Mexico **218 B6** 20 23N 101 31W
Huaniqueo, Michoacan, Mexico **218 C6** 19 55N 101 31W
Huanusco, Zacatecas, Mexico **217 F8** 21 46N 102 59W
Huapacal, Tabasco, Mexico **222 B3** 17 55N 93 45W
Huásabas Granados, Sonora, Mexico **212 D6** 29 57N 109 18W
Huasca, Hidalgo, Mexico **219 B9** 20 12N 98 34W
Huasteco, Cañón, Monterrey, Mexico **224 C1** 25 30N 100 21W
Huatabampo, Sonora, Mexico **212 G6** 26 50N 109 38W
Huatamote →, Baja Calif., Mexico **210 C4** 30 50N 114 43W
Huatusco, Veracruz, Mexico **221 E4** 19 9N 96 57W
Huauchinango, Puebla, Mexico **220 D2** 20 12N 98 3W
Huautla, Hidalgo, Mexico **219 A9** 21 3N 98 16W
Huautla, Oaxaca, Mexico **221 F4** 18 8N 96 51W
Huayacocotla, Veracruz, Mexico **220 D2** 20 33N 98 29W
Huaymil, Campeche, Mexico **223 B3** 20 27N 90 25W
Hubbard, Sask., Canada **182 B8** 51 8N 103 22W
Hubbard, IA, U.S.A. **73 C5** 42 18N 93 18W
Hubbard, NE, U.S.A. **84 B9** 42 23N 96 36W
Hubbard, OH, U.S.A. **92 B6** 41 9N 80 34W
Hubbard, OR, U.S.A. **94 B3** 45 11N 122 48W
Hubbard, TX, U.S.A. **99 F11** 31 51N 96 48W
Hubbard, Mt., N. Amer. **189 D5** 60 19N 139 4W
Hubbard County ☆, MN, U.S.A. **80 C4** 47 10N 94 50W
Hubbard Creek L., TX, U.S.A. **99 E9** 32 50N 98 58W
Hubbard L., MI, U.S.A. **79 E8** 44 49N 83 34W
Hubbards, N.S., Canada **173 J5** 44 38N 64 4W
Hubbardston, MA, U.S.A. **78 B3** 42 28N 72 0W
Hubbardton, VT, U.S.A. **86 C1** 43 42N 73 12W
Hubbell, MI, U.S.A. **79 B3** 47 10N 88 26W
Hubbell, NE, U.S.A. **84 D8** 40 1N 97 29W
Hubbell Trading Post Nat. Historic Site △, AZ, U.S.A. **62 B6** 35 43N 109 33W
Huber Heights, OH, U.S.A. **92 D2** 39 50N 84 5W
Huddy, KY, U.S.A. **97 C10** 37 36N 82 17W
Hudson, Ont., Canada **180 B4** 50 6N 92 9W
Hudson, CO, U.S.A. **66 B6** 40 4N 104 39W
Hudson, FL, U.S.A. **67 C6** 28 22N 82 42W
Hudson, IA, U.S.A. **73 C6** 42 24N 92 28W
Hudson, KS, U.S.A. **74 C5** 38 6N 98 40W
Hudson, ME, U.S.A. **76 C5** 45 0N 68 53W
Hudson, MA, U.S.A. **78 B3** 42 23N 71 34W
Hudson, MD, U.S.A. **77 B4** 38 36N 76 15W
Hudson, MI, U.S.A. **79 H7** 41 51N 84 21W
Hudson, NC, U.S.A. **90 C4** 35 51N 81 30W
Hudson, NH, U.S.A. **86 D3** 42 46N 71 26W
Hudson, NY, U.S.A. **89 C7** 42 15N 73 46W
Hudson, OH, U.S.A. **92 B5** 41 14N 81 26W
Hudson, SD, U.S.A. **91 G9** 43 8N 96 27W
Hudson, WI, U.S.A. **103 D1** 44 58N 92 45W
Hudson, WY, U.S.A. **104 D4** 42 54N 108 35W
Hudson →, NY, U.S.A. **89 E6** 40 42N 74 2W
Hudson, L., OK, U.S.A. **93 B8** 36 14N 95 11W
Hudson Bay, Nunavut, Canada **191 E8** 60 0N 86 0W
Hudson Bay, Sask., Canada **183 C9** 52 51N 102 23W
Hudson County ☆, NJ, U.S.A. **87 B2** 40 45N 74 5W
Hudson Falls, NY, U.S.A. **89 B7** 43 18N 73 35W
Hudson Str., Nunavut, Canada **191 E11** 62 0N 70 0W
Hudson's Hope, B.C., Canada **189 E8** 56 0N 121 54W
Hudsonville, MI, U.S.A. **79 G6** 42 52N 85 52W
Hudspeth County ☆, TX, U.S.A. **98 F2** 31 30N 105 30W
Hudwin L., Man., Canada **183 B16** 53 12N 95 41W
Hueco Mts., TX, U.S.A. **98 F2** 31 53N 105 58W
Huehuetán, Chiapas, Mexico **222 D4** 15 5N 92 22W
Huehuetla, Hidalgo, Mexico **219 B9** 20 28N 98 3W
Huehuetlán el Chico, Puebla, Mexico **221 F2** 18 44N 98 10W
Huejotitán, Chihuahua, Mexico **213 F9** 27 4N 106 12W
Huejotzingo, Puebla, Mexico **221 F2** 19 10N 98 24W
Huejúcar, Jalisco, Mexico **217 E7** 22 21N 103 13W
Huejuquilla, Jalisco, Mexico **217 E7** 22 36N 103 52W
Huejutla de Reyes, Hidalgo, Mexico **219 A9** 21 8N 98 25W
Hueneme = Port Hueneme, CA, U.S.A. **65 J7** 34 7N 119 12W
Huépac, Sonora, Mexico **212 D5** 29 54N 110 10W
Huerfano →, CO, U.S.A. **66 D6** 38 14N 104 15W
Huerfano County ☆, CO, U.S.A. **66 E6** 37 40N 104 50W
Huetamo, Michoacan, Mexico **219 D7** 18 35N 100 53W
Hueyapán de Ocampo, Veracruz, Mexico **221 F5** 18 7N 95 9W
Hueytamalco, Puebla, Mexico **220 E3** 19 57N 97 27W
Hueytown, AL, U.S.A. **60 C4** 33 27N 86 59W
Huffman, TX, U.S.A. **99 G12** 30 1N 95 6W
Hugh Butler L., NE, U.S.A. **84 D5** 40 21N 100 39W
Hugh Taylor Birch State Recr. Area △, Miami, U.S.A. **112 B3** 26 8N 80 6W
Hughes, AK, U.S.A. **61 C9** 66 3N 154 15W
Hughes, AR, U.S.A. **63 D5** 34 57N 90 28W
Hughes County ☆, OK, U.S.A. **93 C7** 35 0N 96 15W
Hughes County ☆, SD, U.S.A. **91 F6** 44 30N 100 0W
Hughes Springs, TX, U.S.A. **99 E13** 33 0N 94 38W
Hughesville, MD, U.S.A. **77 B4** 38 32N 76 47W
Hughesville, MO, U.S.A. **82 C3** 38 50N 93 18W
Hughesville, PA, U.S.A. **95 C6** 41 14N 76 44W
Hughson, CA, U.S.A. **64 F6** 37 36N 120 52W
Hugo, CO, U.S.A. **66 C7** 39 8N 103 28W
Hugo, OK, U.S.A. **93 D8** 34 1N 95 31W
Hugo L., OK, U.S.A. **93 D8** 34 3N 95 27W
Hugoton, KS, U.S.A. **74 D2** 37 11N 101 21W
Huguenot, NY, U.S.A. **114 C1** 40 32N 74 11W
Huguenot Park, NY, U.S.A. **114 C1** 40 33N 74 11W
Huhi, Yucatán, Mexico **223 B4** 20 43N 89 10W
Huichapán, Hidalgo, Mexico **219 B8** 20 23N 99 39W
Huimanguillo, Tabasco, Mexico **222 B3** 17 51N 93 23W
Huimilpan, Querétaro, Mexico **219 B7** 20 22N 100 17W
Huinala, Monterrey, Mexico **224 B3** 25 44N 100 11W
Huitiupán, Chiapas, Mexico **222 B4** 17 13N 92 39W
Huitussi, Sinaloa, Mexico **216 B2** 25 30N 108 31W
Huitzila, Zacatecas, Mexico **218 A4** 21 12N 103 37W
Huitzuco, Guerrero, Mexico **219 D8** 18 18N 99 21W
Huivulai, I., Sonora, Mexico **212 F6** 27 3N 109 59W
Huixquilucan de Degollado, México, Mexico **225 B1** 19 23N 99 27W
Huixtán, Chiapas, Mexico **222 C4** 16 46N 92 27W
Huixtla, Chiapas, Mexico **222 D4** 15 9N 92 28W
Hulah L., OK, U.S.A. **93 B7** 36 56N 96 5W
Hulbert, MI, U.S.A. **79 C6** 46 21N 85 9W
Hulbert, OK, U.S.A. **93 C8** 35 56N 95 9W
Hulett, WY, U.S.A. **104 B8** 44 41N 104 36W
Huletts Landing, NY, U.S.A. **86 C1** 43 38N 73 30W
Hull, Qué., Canada **176 F7** 45 26N 75 43W
Hull, FL, U.S.A. **67 D7** 27 7N 81 56W
Hull, IL, U.S.A. **71 D2** 39 43N 91 13W
Hull, IA, U.S.A. **73 B2** 43 11N 96 8W
Hull, MA, U.S.A. **78 B4** 42 18N 70 54W
Humacao, Puerto Rico **105 G17** 18 9N 65 50W
Humansville, MO, U.S.A. **82 D3** 37 48N 93 35W
Humaya →, Mexico **216 C3** 24 49N 107 24W
Humber Arm South, Nfld. & L., Canada **174 C2** 49 1N 58 7W
Humble, TX, U.S.A. **99 H12** 30 0N 95 18W
Humble City, NM, U.S.A. **88 E7** 32 47N 103 13W
Humboldt, Sask., Canada **182 C6** 52 15N 105 9W
Humboldt, AZ, U.S.A. **62 C3** 34 30N 112 14W
Humboldt, IL, U.S.A. **71 D5** 39 36N 88 19W
Humboldt, IA, U.S.A. **73 C4** 42 44N 94 13W
Humboldt, KS, U.S.A. **74 D8** 37 49N 95 26W
Humboldt, NE, U.S.A. **84 D10** 40 10N 95 57W
Humboldt, SD, U.S.A. **91 G8** 43 39N 97 5W
Humboldt, TN, U.S.A. **96 E4** 35 50N 88 55W
Humboldt →, NV, U.S.A. **85 C2** 39 59N 118 36W
Humboldt B., CA, U.S.A. **64 C2** 40 45N 124 10W
Humboldt County ☆, CA, U.S.A. **64 C3** 40 50N 124 0W
Humboldt County ☆, IA, U.S.A. **73 C4** 42 50N 94 10W
Humboldt County ☆, NV, U.S.A. **85 A2** 41 20N 118 10W
Humboldt Nat. Forest, NV, U.S.A. **85 A5** 41 35N 115 30W
Humboldt Park, Chicago, U.S.A. **108 B2** 41 54N 87 42W
Humboldt Peak, CO, U.S.A. **66 E5** 37 59N 105 33W
Humboldt Range, NV, U.S.A. **85 B2** 40 20N 118 10W
Humboldt Redwoods State Park △, CA, U.S.A. **64 C3** 40 19N 123 59W
Humboldt Salt Marsh, NV, U.S.A. **85 C3** 39 50N 117 55W
Humboldt Sink, NV, U.S.A. **85 B2** 40 1N 118 38W
Humboldt-Toiyabe Nat. Forest, NV, U.S.A. **85 D4** 38 40N 117 0W
Hume, MO, U.S.A. **82 C2** 38 6N 94 34W
Hume, VA, U.S.A. **77 B3** 38 50N 78 0W
Hume →, N.W.T., Canada **188 C7** 66 1N 129 8W
Humeston, IA, U.S.A. **73 E5** 40 52N 93 30W
Humnoke, AR, U.S.A. **63 D4** 34 33N 91 45W
Humphrey, AR, U.S.A. **63 D4** 34 25N 91 43W
Humphrey, ID, U.S.A. **70 E6** 44 29N 112 14W
Humphrey, NE, U.S.A. **84 C8** 41 42N 97 29W
Humphreys, OK, U.S.A. **93 D4** 34 33N 99 14W
Humphreys, Mt., CA, U.S.A. **65 F8** 37 17N 118 40W
Humphreys County ☆, MS, U.S.A. **81 C3** 33 10N 90 30W
Humphreys County ☆, TN, U.S.A. **96 D5** 36 5N 87 48W
Humphreys Peak, AZ, U.S.A. **62 B4** 35 21N 111 41W
Hundred, WV, U.S.A. **102 B4** 39 41N 80 28W
Hundred and Fifty Mile House, B.C., Canada **187 C13** 52 7N 121 57W

Hundred Mile House, B.C., Canada 187 D13 51 38N 121 18W
Hungry Horse, MT, U.S.A. 83 B3 48 23N 114 4W
Hungry Horse Res., MT, U.S.A. 83 B3 48 21N 114 1W
Hunnewell, KS, U.S.A. 74 D6 37 1N 97 25W
Hunnewell, MO, U.S.A. 82 B5 39 40N 91 52W
Hunt, TX, U.S.A. 99 G8 30 4N 99 20W
Hunt County ☆, TX, U.S.A. 99 D11 33 8N 96 7W
Hunt Mt., WY, U.S.A. 104 B5 44 55N 107 59W
Hunter, AR, U.S.A. 63 C4 35 3N 91 8W
Hunter, KS, U.S.A. 74 B5 39 14N 98 24W
Hunter, ND, U.S.A. 91 C8 47 12N 97 13W
Hunter, NY, U.S.A. 89 C6 42 13N 74 13W
Hunter, OK, U.S.A. 93 B6 36 34N 97 40W
Hunter I., B.C., Canada 186 D6 51 55N 128 0W
Hunterdon County ☆, NJ, U.S.A. 87 B2 40 30N 75 0W
Hunters, WA, U.S.A. 101 B7 48 7N 118 12W
Hunters Creek Village, Houston, U.S.A. 110 B2 29 46N 95 30W
Hunters Pt., San Francisco, U.S.A. 118 B2 37 43N 122 21W
Hunters Valley, VA, U.S.A. 119 B2 38 54N 77 17W
Hunterstown, PA, U.S.A. 77 A3 39 53N 77 10W
Huntersville, NC, U.S.A. 90 C5 35 25N 80 51W
Huntertown, IN, U.S.A. 72 B5 41 14N 85 10W
Huntingburg, IN, U.S.A. 72 E4 38 18N 86 57W
Huntingdon, Qué., Canada 177 F8 45 6N 74 10W
Huntingdon, PA, U.S.A. 95 D4 40 30N 78 1W
Huntingdon, TN, U.S.A. 96 E4 36 0N 88 26W
Huntingdon County ☆, PA, U.S.A. 95 D5 40 15N 78 0W
Huntington = Shelton, CT, U.S.A. 78 C1 41 19N 73 5W
Huntington, AR, U.S.A. 63 C1 35 5N 94 16W
Huntington, IN, U.S.A. 72 C5 40 53N 85 30W
Huntington, MA, U.S.A. 78 B2 42 14N 72 53W
Huntington, NY, U.S.A. 78 D1 40 52N 73 26W
Huntington, OR, U.S.A. 94 C8 44 21N 117 16W
Huntington, TX, U.S.A. 99 F13 31 17N 94 34W
Huntington, UT, U.S.A. 100 D5 39 20N 110 58W
Huntington, VA, U.S.A. 119 C3 38 47N 77 4W
Huntington, VT, U.S.A. 86 B2 44 22N 72 58W
Huntington, WV, U.S.A. 102 C2 38 25N 82 27W
Huntington →, NV, U.S.A. 85 B5 40 37N 115 43W
Huntington →, UT, U.S.A. 100 D5 39 9N 110 55W
Huntington Beach, CA, U.S.A. 65 K8 33 40N 118 5W
Huntington County ☆, IN, U.S.A. 72 C5 40 50N 85 30W
Huntington Park, Los Angeles, U.S.A. 111 C3 33 58N 118 13W
Huntington Station, NY, U.S.A. 87 B3 40 51N 73 25W
Huntington Woods, MI, U.S.A. 109 A1 42 28N 83 10W
Huntingtown, MD, U.S.A. 77 B4 38 37N 76 37W
Huntland, TN, U.S.A. 96 E6 35 3N 86 16W
Huntley, IL, U.S.A. 71 A5 42 10N 88 26W
Huntley, MT, U.S.A. 83 E9 45 54N 108 19W
Huntley, NE, U.S.A. 84 D6 40 13N 99 18W
Hunts Point, Seattle, U.S.A. 118 C4 47 38N 122 13W
Huntsville, Ont., Canada 178 B7 45 20N 79 14W
Huntsville, AL, U.S.A. 60 B4 34 44N 86 35W
Huntsville, AR, U.S.A. 63 B2 36 5N 93 44W
Huntsville, KY, U.S.A. 96 C6 37 10N 86 53W
Huntsville, MO, U.S.A. 82 B4 39 26N 92 33W
Huntsville, OH, U.S.A. 92 C3 40 26N 83 48W
Huntsville, TN, U.S.A. 97 D8 36 25N 84 29W
Huntsville, TX, U.S.A. 99 G12 30 43N 95 33W
Huntsville, UT, U.S.A. 100 B4 41 16N 111 46W
Hunucmá, Yucatán, Mexico 223 A4 21 1N 89 52W
Hupel, B.C., Canada 187 E16 50 37N 118 44W
Hurdsfield, ND, U.S.A. 91 C6 47 26N 99 55W
Hurley, MS, U.S.A. 81 F5 30 40N 88 30W
Hurley, MO, U.S.A. 82 E3 36 56N 93 30W
Hurley, NM, U.S.A. 88 E2 32 42N 108 8W
Hurley, NY, U.S.A. 89 D6 41 55N 74 4W
Hurley, SD, U.S.A. 91 G8 43 17N 97 5W
Hurley, WI, U.S.A. 103 B3 46 27N 90 11W
Hurlock, MD, U.S.A. 77 B5 38 38N 75 52W
Huron, CA, U.S.A. 65 G6 36 12N 120 6W
Huron, KS, U.S.A. 74 B8 39 38N 95 21W
Huron, OH, U.S.A. 92 B4 41 24N 82 33W
Huron, SD, U.S.A. 91 F7 44 22N 98 13W
Huron →, MI, U.S.A. 79 G8 42 2N 83 11W
Huron, L., MI, U.S.A. 178 C4 44 30N 82 40W
Huron Bay, MI, U.S.A. 79 C3 46 54N 88 13W
Huron Beach, MI, U.S.A. 79 D7 45 30N 84 6W
Huron County ☆, MI, U.S.A. 79 F9 43 50N 83 0W
Huron County ☆, OH, U.S.A. 92 B4 41 15N 82 37W
Huron East, Ont., Canada 178 D5 43 37N 81 18W
Huron Mts., MI, U.S.A. 79 C4 46 50N 88 0W
Huron Nat. Forest, MI, U.S.A. 79 E8 44 30N 84 0W
Huron Potawatomi Indian Reservation, MI, U.S.A. 79 G6 42 5N 85 16W
Hurricane, UT, U.S.A. 100 F2 37 11N 113 17W
Hurricane, WV, U.S.A. 102 C2 38 26N 82 1W
Hurricane Cliffs, AZ, U.S.A. 62 A2 36 45N 113 20W
Hurricane L., ND, U.S.A. 91 B6 48 26N 99 31W
Hurst, TX, U.S.A. 99 E10 32 49N 97 10W
Hurstville, IA, U.S.A. 73 C8 42 6N 90 41W
Hurt, VA, U.S.A. 102 D5 37 6N 79 18W
Hurtsboro, AL, U.S.A. 60 D5 32 15N 85 25W
Huslia, AK, U.S.A. 61 D8 65 41N 156 24W
Hussar, Alta., Canada 185 G8 51 3N 112 41W
Hustisford, WI, U.S.A. 103 E5 43 21N 88 36W
Hustle, VA, U.S.A. 77 B3 38 3N 77 4W
Hustonville, KY, U.S.A. 97 C8 37 28N 84 49W
Husum, WA, U.S.A. 101 E4 45 48N 121 29W
Hutch Mt., AZ, U.S.A. 62 C4 34 47N 111 22W
Hutchins, Dallas-Fort Worth, U.S.A. 109 C5 32 38N 96 42W
Hutchinson, KS, U.S.A. 74 C6 38 5N 97 56W
Hutchinson, MN, U.S.A. 80 F4 44 54N 94 22W
Hutchinson County ☆, SD, U.S.A. 91 G8 43 25N 97 48W
Hutchinson County ☆, TX, U.S.A. 98 B6 35 50N 101 30W
Hutsonville, IL, U.S.A. 71 D6 39 7N 87 40W
Hutte Sauvage, L. de la, Qué., Canada 175 B5 56 15N 64 45W
Huttig, AR, U.S.A. 63 E3 33 2N 92 11W
Hutto, TX, U.S.A. 99 G10 30 33N 97 33W
Hutton, MD, U.S.A. 77 A1 39 25N 79 28W
Huttonsville, WV, U.S.A. 102 C5 38 43N 79 59W
Huxford, AL, U.S.A. 60 E3 31 13N 87 28W
Huxley, IA, U.S.A. 73 D5 41 54N 93 36W
Huyett, MD, U.S.A. 77 A3 39 40N 77 20W
Hyak, WA, U.S.A. 101 C4 47 24N 121 24W
Hyannis, MA, U.S.A. 78 C4 41 39N 70 17W
Hyannis, NE, U.S.A. 84 C4 42 0N 101 46W
Hyas, Sask., Canada 183 D9 51 54N 102 16W
Hyattsville, MD, U.S.A. 77 B4 38 57N 76 57W
Hyattville, WY, U.S.A. 104 B5 44 15N 107 36W
Hybart, AL, U.S.A. 60 E3 31 50N 87 23W
Hyco L., NC, U.S.A. 90 B6 36 31N 79 3W
Hydaburg, AK, U.S.A. 61 J14 55 15N 132 50W
Hyde County ☆, NC, U.S.A. 90 C9 35 30N 76 20W
Hyde County ☆, SD, U.S.A. 91 F6 44 31N 99 27W
Hyde Park, Boston, U.S.A. 106 B3 42 15N 71 7W
Hyde Park, Chicago, U.S.A. 108 C3 41 47N 87 35W
Hyde Park, NY, U.S.A. 89 D7 41 47N 73 56W
Hyde Park, VT, U.S.A. 86 B2 44 36N 72 37W
Hyden, KY, U.S.A. 97 C9 37 10N 83 22W
Hydes, MD, U.S.A. 77 A4 39 30N 76 29W
Hydro, OK, U.S.A. 93 C5 35 33N 98 39W
Hygiene, CO, U.S.A. 66 B5 40 11N 105 11W
Hyland →, Canada 189 E7 59 52N 128 12W
Hymera, IN, U.S.A. 72 D3 39 11N 87 18W
Hymers, Ont., Canada 180 D7 48 18N 89 43W
Hyndman, PA, U.S.A. 77 A2 39 49N 78 43W
Hyndman Peak, ID, U.S.A. 70 F4 43 45N 114 8W
Hyrum, UT, U.S.A. 100 B4 41 38N 111 51W
Hysham, MT, U.S.A. 83 D10 46 18N 107 14W
Hythe, Alta., Canada 184 C1 55 20N 119 33W

I

Iaeger, WV, U.S.A. 102 D3 37 28N 81 49W
Iamonia L., FL, U.S.A. 67 A4 30 38N 84 14W
Ian Calder L., Nunavut, Canada 191 D6 66 28N 97 22W
Ian L., B.C., Canada 186 B2 53 50N 132 45W
Iatan, MO, U.S.A. 82 B2 39 29N 94 59W
Iatt L., LA, U.S.A. 75 C3 31 35N 92 40W
Ibapah, UT, U.S.A. 100 C2 40 2N 113 59W
Ibapah Pk., UT, U.S.A. 100 C2 40 2N 113 53W
Ibarra, Guanajuato, Mexico 218 A6 21 29N 101 33W
Iberia, MO, U.S.A. 82 C4 38 5N 92 18W
Iberia Parish ☆, LA, U.S.A. 75 D4 30 1N 91 49W
Iberville, Qué., Canada 177 F9 45 19N 73 17W
Iberville, Lac d', Qué., Canada 175 B5 55 55N 73 15W
Iberville, Mt. d', Nfld. & L., Canada 175 B5 58 50N 63 50W
Iberville Parish ☆, LA, U.S.A. 75 D4 30 17N 91 14W
Icard, NC, U.S.A. 90 C4 35 44N 81 28W
Ice Harbor Dam, WA, U.S.A. 101 D7 46 15N 118 53W
Icy C., AK, U.S.A. 61 A7 70 20N 161 52W
Ida, MI, U.S.A. 79 H8 41 55N 83 34W
Ida County ☆, IA, U.S.A. 73 C3 42 25N 95 30W
Ida Grove, IA, U.S.A. 73 C3 42 21N 95 28W
Idabel, OK, U.S.A. 93 E9 33 54N 94 50W
Idaho □, U.S.A. 70 E4 45 0N 115 0W
Idaho City, ID, U.S.A. 70 F3 43 50N 115 50W
Idaho County ☆, ID, U.S.A. 70 D3 45 35N 115 30W
Idaho Falls, ID, U.S.A. 70 F6 43 30N 112 2W
Idaho Nat. Engineering Laboratory, ID, U.S.A. 70 F6 43 38N 112 45W
Idaho Springs, CO, U.S.A. 66 C5 39 45N 105 31W
Idalia, CO, U.S.A. 66 C8 39 42N 102 18W
Idalou, TX, U.S.A. 98 D6 33 40N 101 41W
Idana, KS, U.S.A. 74 B6 39 22N 97 16W
Idanha, OR, U.S.A. 94 C3 44 42N 122 5W
Ideal, GA, U.S.A. 68 D2 32 22N 84 11W
Ideal, SD, U.S.A. 91 G6 43 33N 99 54W
Ider, AL, U.S.A. 60 B5 34 43N 85 41W
Idlewild, Charlotte, U.S.A. 107 A2 35 11N 80 44W
Idolo, I. del, Veracruz, Mexico 220 C3 21 25N 97 27W
Idria, CA, U.S.A. 65 G6 36 25N 120 41W
Igiugig, AK, U.S.A. 61 G9 59 20N 155 55W
Igloolik, Nunavut, Canada 190 D9 69 20N 81 49W
Igluligaarjuk = Chesterfield Inlet, Nunavut, Canada 191 E7 63 30N 90 45W
Iglulik = Igloolik, Nunavut, Canada 190 D9 69 20N 81 49W
Ignace, Ont., Canada 180 C5 49 30N 91 40W
Ignacio, CO, U.S.A. 66 E3 37 7N 107 38W
Ignacio Allende, Durango, Mexico 217 C7 24 28N 104 0W
Ignacio Allende, Tabasco, Mexico 222 A4 18 21N 92 51W
Ignacio Allende, Zacatecas, Mexico 217 F7 21 30N 103 24W
Ignacio de la Llave, Veracruz, Mexico 221 F5 18 43N 95 59W
Ignacio Ramirez, Sonora, Mexico 212 E4 28 43N 111 20W
Ignacio Zaragoza, Chiapas, Mexico 222 C4 16 1N 92 35W
Ignacio Zaragoza, Chiapas, Mexico 222 C3 16 35N 93 21W
Ignacio Zaragoza, Chihuahua, Mexico 213 C7 30 12N 108 18W
Ignacio Zaragoza, Chihuahua, Mexico 213 D8 29 40N 107 43W
Ignacio Zaragoza, Coahuila, Mexico 215 E1 25 21N 103 9W
Ignacio Zaragoza, Sonora, Mexico 212 A1 32 18N 114 12W
Ignacio Zaragoza, Tamaulipas, Mexico 215 G6 23 12N 98 46W
Igornachoix Bay, Nfld. & L., Canada 174 B3 50 40N 57 25W
Iguala, Guerrero, Mexico 219 D8 18 21N 99 32W
Igualapa, Guerrero, Mexico 219 F9 16 44N 98 36W
Ihlen, MN, U.S.A. 80 G2 43 55N 96 22W
Ikaluktutiak, Nunavut, Canada 190 D4 69 10N 105 0W
Ikparjuk = Arctic Bay, Nunavut, Canada 190 C8 73 1N 85 7W
Île-à-la-Crosse, Sask., Canada 189 E11 55 27N 107 53W
Île-à-la-Crosse, Lac, Sask., Canada 189 E11 55 40N 107 45W
Île-Anticosti, Réserve Faunique de l' ⌓, Qué., Canada 172 D7 49 30N 62 50W
Île-Perrot, Qué., Canada 192 B1 45 22N 73 57W
Îles, L. des, Qué., Canada 176 E7 46 20N 75 18W
Ilfeld, NM, U.S.A. 88 B5 35 25N 105 34W
Iliamna, AK, U.S.A. 61 G9 59 45N 154 55W
Iliamna L., AK, U.S.A. 61 G9 59 30N 155 0W
Iliff, CO, U.S.A. 66 B7 40 45N 103 4W
ʻIlio Pt., HI, U.S.A. 69 B4 21 13N 157 16W
Ilion, NY, U.S.A. 89 B5 43 1N 75 2W
Illescas, San Luis Potosí, Mexico 215 G2 23 13N 102 7W
Illinois □, U.S.A. 71 C4 40 15N 89 30W
Illinois →, IL, U.S.A. 71 E3 38 58N 90 28W
Illinois →, OK, U.S.A. 93 C8 35 30N 95 5W
Illinois →, OR, U.S.A. 94 E1 42 33N 124 3W
Illinois Peak, U.S.A. 83 C2 47 2N 115 4W
Illiopolis, IL, U.S.A. 71 D4 39 51N 89 15W
Illukotat →, Qué., Canada 175 A2 60 48N 78 11W
Ilwaco, WA, U.S.A. 101 D1 46 19N 124 3W
Imala, Sinaloa, Mexico 216 C3 24 53N 107 13W
Imbler, OR, U.S.A. 94 B8 45 28N 117 58W
Imboden, AR, U.S.A. 63 B4 36 12N 91 11W
Imlay, NV, U.S.A. 85 B2 40 40N 118 9W
Imlay City, MI, U.S.A. 79 F8 43 2N 83 5W
Immokalee, FL, U.S.A. 67 E7 26 25N 81 25W
Imnaha, OR, U.S.A. 94 B9 45 34N 116 50W
Imnaha →, OR, U.S.A. 94 B9 45 49N 116 46W
Imogene, IA, U.S.A. 73 E3 40 53N 95 29W
Imperial, Sask., Canada 182 D6 51 21N 105 28W
Imperial, CA, U.S.A. 65 L11 32 51N 115 34W
Imperial, NE, U.S.A. 84 D4 40 31N 101 39W
Imperial, Pt., AZ, U.S.A. 62 A4 36 15N 111 57W
Imperial Beach, CA, U.S.A. 65 L9 32 35N 117 6W
Imperial County ☆, CA, U.S.A. 65 K11 33 0N 115 20W
Imperial Dam, AZ, U.S.A. 62 E1 32 55N 114 25W
Imperial Res., AZ, U.S.A. 62 E1 32 53N 114 28W
Imperial Valley, CA, U.S.A. 65 L11 33 0N 115 30W
Imuris, Sonora, Mexico 212 C5 30 47N 110 52W
Ina, IL, U.S.A. 71 E5 38 9N 88 54W
Inarajan, Guam 105 b 13 16N 144 45 E
Inchelium, WA, U.S.A. 101 B7 48 18N 118 12W
Incline Village, NV, U.S.A. 85 C1 39 10N 119 58W
Indé, Durango, Mexico 216 B5 25 54N 105 13W
Independence, CA, U.S.A. 65 G8 36 48N 118 12W
Independence, Cleveland, U.S.A. 107 B2 41 22N 81 38W
Independence, IA, U.S.A. 73 C7 42 28N 91 54W
Independence, KS, U.S.A. 74 D8 37 14N 95 42W
Independence, KY, U.S.A. 97 B8 38 57N 84 33W
Independence, LA, U.S.A. 75 D5 30 38N 90 30W
Independence, MS, U.S.A. 81 B4 34 42N 89 49W
Independence, MO, U.S.A. 82 B2 39 6N 94 25W
Independence, OR, U.S.A. 94 C2 44 51N 123 11W
Independence, VA, U.S.A. 102 E3 36 37N 81 9W
Independence, WI, U.S.A. 103 D2 44 22N 91 25W
Independence County ☆, AR, U.S.A. 63 C4 35 46N 91 39W
Independence Cr. →, TX, U.S.A. 98 G6 30 27N 101 44W
Independence Mts., NV, U.S.A. 85 A4 41 20N 116 0W
Independence Pass, CO, U.S.A. 66 C4 39 7N 106 33W
Independencia y Libertad, Durango, Mexico 217 C6 24 2N 104 19W
Index, WA, U.S.A. 101 C4 47 50N 121 33W
Indiahoma, OK, U.S.A. 93 D5 34 37N 98 45W
Indialantic, FL, U.S.A. 67 C8 28 6N 80 34W
Indian →, FL, U.S.A. 67 D8 27 59N 80 34W
Indian Cr. →, SD, U.S.A. 91 F2 44 39N 103 19W
Indian Cr. →, TN, U.S.A. 96 E4 35 23N 88 9W
Indian Creek Village, Miami, U.S.A. 112 C3 25 52N 80 8W
Indian Harbour, Nfld. & L., Canada 175 C6 54 27N 57 13W
Indian Harbour Beach, FL, U.S.A. 67 C8 28 10N 80 35W
Indian Head, Sask., Canada 182 E8 50 30N 103 41W
Indian Head, MD, U.S.A. 77 B3 38 38N 77 12W
Indian Heights, IN, U.S.A. 72 C4 40 26N 86 10W
Indian L., MI, U.S.A. 79 D5 45 59N 86 20W
Indian L., NY, U.S.A. 89 B6 43 42N 74 19W
Indian L., OH, U.S.A. 92 C3 40 30N 83 53W
Indian Lake, NY, U.S.A. 89 B6 43 47N 74 16W
Indian Mills, NJ, U.S.A. 87 C2 39 48N 74 46W
Indian Mounds Park, Minneapolis-St. Paul, U.S.A. 113 B3 44 56N 93 3W
Indian Peak, UT, U.S.A. 100 E2 38 16N 113 53W
Indian Peak Range = Needle Range, UT, U.S.A. 100 E2 38 25N 113 55W
Indian River, MI, U.S.A. 79 D7 45 25N 84 37W
Indian River Bay, DE, U.S.A. 77 B5 38 36N 75 4W
Indian River County ☆, FL, U.S.A. 67 D8 27 40N 80 45W
Indian River Park, Norfolk, U.S.A. 115 B2 36 48N 76 13W
Indian River Shores, FL, U.S.A. 67 D8 27 43N 80 23W
Indian Rock, WA, U.S.A. 101 E5 45 59N 120 49W
Indian Rocks Beach, FL, U.S.A. 67 D6 27 52N 82 51W
Indian Shores, Tampa, U.S.A. 119 B1 27 51N 82 50W
Indian Springs, NV, U.S.A. 85 F5 36 35N 115 40W
Indian Township Indian Reservation, ME, U.S.A. 76 C6 45 18N 67 34W
Indian Trail, NC, U.S.A. 90 C5 35 5N 80 40W
Indian Valley, ID, U.S.A. 70 E2 44 33N 116 26W
Indian Valley Res., CA, U.S.A. 64 D4 39 5N 122 32W
Indian Village, KS, U.S.A. 74 D8 37 5N 95 38W
Indiana, PA, U.S.A. 95 D3 40 37N 79 9W
Indiana □, U.S.A. 72 C5 40 0N 86 0W
Indiana County ☆, PA, U.S.A. 95 D3 40 45N 79 0W
Indiana Dunes Nat. Lakeshore ⌓, IN, U.S.A. 72 B3 41 40N 87 0W
Indianapolis, IN, U.S.A. 72 D4 39 46N 86 9W
Indianapolis International ✕ (IND), IN, U.S.A. 72 D4 39 43N 86 17W
Indianola, IA, U.S.A. 73 D5 41 22N 93 34W
Indianola, MS, U.S.A. 81 C3 33 27N 90 39W
Indianola, NE, U.S.A. 84 D5 40 14N 100 25W
Indianola, OK, U.S.A. 93 C8 35 10N 95 46W
Indianola, Seattle, U.S.A. 118 B2 47 44N 122 31W
Indiantown, FL, U.S.A. 67 D8 27 1N 80 28W
Indio, CA, U.S.A. 65 K10 33 43N 116 13W
Industry, IL, U.S.A. 71 C3 40 20N 90 36W
Industry, KS, U.S.A. 74 B6 39 8N 97 10W
Industry, TX, U.S.A. 99 H11 29 58N 96 30W
Inez, KY, U.S.A. 97 C10 37 52N 82 32W
Inferior, L., Oaxaca, Mexico 221 H6 16 20N 94 40W
Infiernillo, Presa del, Michoacan, Mexico 218 D6 18 35N 101 50W
Ingalls, AR, U.S.A. 63 E3 33 23N 92 9W
Ingalls, KS, U.S.A. 74 D3 37 50N 100 27W
Ingersoll, Ont., Canada 178 D6 43 4N 80 55W
Ingham County ☆, MI, U.S.A. 79 G7 42 35N 84 30W
Ingleside, MD, U.S.A. 77 A5 39 6N 75 53W
Ingleside, TX, U.S.A. 99 K10 27 53N 97 13W
Inglewood, CA, U.S.A. 65 K8 33 58N 118 21W
Inglewood, Los Angeles, U.S.A. 111 C3 33 57N 118 19W
Inglewood, NE, U.S.A. 84 C9 41 25N 96 30W
Inglis, FL, U.S.A. 67 B6 29 2N 82 40W
Ingomar, N.S., Canada 173 K4 43 34N 65 22W
Ingomar, MT, U.S.A. 83 D10 46 35N 107 23W
Ingonish, N.S., Canada 173 G9 46 42N 60 18W
Ingonish Beach, N.S., Canada 173 G9 46 38N 60 25W
Ingram, Pittsburgh, U.S.A. 116 B1 40 26N 80 4W
Ingram, TX, U.S.A. 99 G8 30 5N 99 14W
Ingram, WI, U.S.A. 103 C3 45 31N 90 49W
Inkerman, N.B., Canada 173 F5 47 40N 64 49W
Inklin →, N. Amer. 189 E6 58 50N 133 10W
Inkom, ID, U.S.A. 70 G6 42 48N 112 15W
Inkster, ND, U.S.A. 91 B8 48 9N 97 39W
Inland L., AL, U.S.A. 60 C4 33 50N 86 30W
Inlet, NY, U.S.A. 89 B6 43 45N 74 48W
Inman, KS, U.S.A. 74 C6 38 14N 97 47W
Inman, NE, U.S.A. 84 B7 42 23N 98 32W
Inman, SC, U.S.A. 90 C3 35 3N 82 5W
Innerkip, Ont., Canada 178 D6 43 13N 80 42W
Innetalling I., N.W.T., Canada 175 B2 56 0N 79 0W
Innisfail, Alta., Canada 185 F7 52 2N 113 57W
Innisfree, Alta., Canada 184 E9 53 22N 111 32W
Innoko Nat. Wildlife Refuge ⌓, AK, U.S.A. 61 E8 63 20N 158 25W
Inola, OK, U.S.A. 93 B8 36 9N 95 31W
Inoucdjouac = Inukjuak, Qué., Canada 175 B2 58 25N 78 15W
Insurgente J. M. Morelos y Pavón, Parque Nacional △, Michoacan, Mexico 219 C7 19 36N 100 57W
Intata Reach, B.C., Canada 186 B9 53 38N 125 30W
Intercession City, FL, U.S.A. 67 C7 28 16N 81 31W
Interior, SD, U.S.A. 91 G4 43 44N 101 59W
Interlachen, FL, U.S.A. 67 B7 29 37N 81 53W
Interlaken, NY, U.S.A. 89 C4 42 37N 76 44W
International Falls, MN, U.S.A. 80 B5 48 36N 93 25W
International Peace Garden, ND, U.S.A. 91 B5 49 0N 100 4W
Intervale, NH, U.S.A. 86 B3 44 6N 71 8W
Intracoastal City, LA, U.S.A. 75 E3 29 47N 92 9W
Inukjuak, Qué., Canada 175 B2 58 25N 78 15W
Inuvik, N.W.T., Canada 188 C6 68 16N 133 40W
Inver Grove Heights, MN, U.S.A. 80 F5 44 51N 93 1W
Invermay, Sask., Canada 182 D8 51 48N 103 9W
Invermere, B.C., Canada 185 H4 50 30N 116 2W
Inverness, N.S., Canada 173 G8 46 15N 61 19W
Inverness, AL, U.S.A. 60 D5 32 1N 85 45W
Inverness, Baltimore, U.S.A. 107 B3 39 15N 76 29W
Inverness, CA, U.S.A. 64 E4 38 6N 122 51W
Inverness, FL, U.S.A. 67 C6 28 50N 82 20W
Inverness, MS, U.S.A. 81 C3 33 21N 90 35W
Inwood, Man., Canada 183 E14 50 30N 97 30W
Inwood, IA, U.S.A. 73 B2 43 19N 96 26W
Inwood, NY, U.S.A. 114 C4 40 37N 73 44W
Inwood, WV, U.S.A. 77 A2 39 21N 78 2W
Inyan Kara Mt., WY, U.S.A. 104 B8 44 13N 104 21W
Inyo County ☆, CA, U.S.A. 65 G9 36 30N 117 40W
Inyo Mts., CA, U.S.A. 65 G9 36 40N 118 0W
Inyo Nat. Forest, U.S.A. 65 F8 37 30N 118 15W
Inyokern, CA, U.S.A. 65 H9 35 39N 117 49W
Iola, IL, U.S.A. 71 E5 38 50N 88 38W
Iola, KS, U.S.A. 74 D8 37 55N 95 24W
Iola, WI, U.S.A. 103 D4 44 30N 89 8W
Iolani Palace, HI, U.S.A. 69 K14 21 18N 157 51W
Iona, N.S., Canada 173 H9 45 58N 60 48W
Iona, ID, U.S.A. 70 F7 43 32N 111 56W
Iona, MN, U.S.A. 80 G3 43 55N 95 47W
Iona, SD, U.S.A. 91 G6 43 33N 99 26W
Iona Beach Regional Park, Vancouver, Canada 193 B1 49 13N 123 12W
Iona I., Vancouver, Canada 193 B1 49 13N 123 12W
Ione, CA, U.S.A. 64 E6 38 21N 120 56W
Ione, OR, U.S.A. 94 B6 45 30N 119 50W
Ione, WA, U.S.A. 101 B8 48 45N 117 25W
Ionia, IA, U.S.A. 73 B6 43 2N 92 27W
Ionia, KS, U.S.A. 74 B5 39 40N 98 21W
Ionia, MI, U.S.A. 79 G6 42 59N 85 4W
Ionia, MO, U.S.A. 82 C3 38 30N 93 19W
Ionia County ☆, MI, U.S.A. 79 G6 42 55N 85 5W
Iosco County ☆, MI, U.S.A. 79 E8 44 20N 83 40W
Iota, LA, U.S.A. 75 D3 30 20N 92 30W
Iowa, LA, U.S.A. 75 D2 30 14N 93 1W
Iowa □, U.S.A. 73 C5 42 18N 93 30W
Iowa →, IA, U.S.A. 73 D7 41 10N 91 1W
Iowa City, IA, U.S.A. 73 D7 41 40N 91 32W
Iowa County ☆, IA, U.S.A. 73 D6 41 40N 92 0W
Iowa County ☆, WI, U.S.A. 103 F3 43 0N 90 10W
Iowa Falls, IA, U.S.A. 73 C5 42 31N 93 16W
Iowa Indian Reservation, U.S.A. 74 B8 39 59N 95 21W
Iowa Park, TX, U.S.A. 99 D9 33 57N 98 40W
Ipava, IL, U.S.A. 71 C3 40 21N 90 19W
Ipswich, MA, U.S.A. 78 B4 42 41N 70 50W
Ipswich, SD, U.S.A. 91 E6 45 27N 99 2W
Ipswich B., MA, U.S.A. 78 B4 42 41N 70 42W
Iqaluit, Nunavut, Canada 191 E12 63 44N 68 31W
Ira, TX, U.S.A. 98 E6 32 35N 101 0W
Iraan, TX, U.S.A. 98 G6 30 55N 101 54W
Irapuato, Guanajuato, Mexico 219 B6 20 41N 101 28W
Irasburg, VT, U.S.A. 86 B1 44 18N 73 47W
Iredell, TX, U.S.A. 99 F10 31 59N 97 52W
Iredell County ☆, NC, U.S.A. 90 C5 35 45N 80 50W
Irene, SD, U.S.A. 91 G8 43 5N 97 9W
Ireton, IA, U.S.A. 73 C2 42 58N 96 19W
Irimbo, Michoacan, Mexico 219 C7 19 43N 100 29W
Irion County ☆, TX, U.S.A. 98 F7 31 15N 101 0W
Irish, Mt., NV, U.S.A. 85 E5 37 39N 115 24W
Irma, Alta., Canada 185 F9 52 55N 111 14W
Irma, L., Orlando, U.S.A. 115 A3 28 35N 81 16W
Irmo, SC, U.S.A. 90 D4 34 5N 81 11W
Iron Belt, WI, U.S.A. 103 B3 46 24N 90 19W
Iron Bridge, Ont., Canada 178 A3 46 17N 83 14W
Iron City, GA, U.S.A. 68 E2 31 1N 84 49W
Iron City, TN, U.S.A. 96 E5 35 1N 87 35W
Iron County ☆, MI, U.S.A. 79 C3 46 15N 88 35W
Iron County ☆, MO, U.S.A. 82 D6 37 30N 90 40W
Iron County ☆, UT, U.S.A. 100 F2 37 50N 113 20W
Iron County ☆, WI, U.S.A. 103 B3 46 15N 90 15W
Iron Junction, MN, U.S.A. 80 C6 47 25N 92 36W
Iron Mountain, MI, U.S.A. 79 D3 45 49N 88 4W
Iron Mountain, MO, U.S.A. 82 D6 37 42N 90 39W
Iron Mountain, UT, U.S.A. 100 F2 37 37N 113 23W
Iron Mountain, WY, U.S.A. 104 E7 41 33N 105 13W
Iron Mts., VA, U.S.A. 102 E3 36 40N 81 45W
Iron Ridge, WI, U.S.A. 103 E5 43 24N 88 32W
Iron River, MI, U.S.A. 79 C3 46 6N 88 39W
Iron River, WI, U.S.A. 103 B2 46 34N 91 24W
Iron Springs, Alta., Canada 185 J8 49 56N 112 41W
Irondale, AL, U.S.A. 60 C4 33 32N 86 42W
Irondale, MO, U.S.A. 82 D6 37 50N 90 41W
Irondale, OH, U.S.A. 92 C6 40 34N 80 44W
Irondequoit, NY, U.S.A. 89 B3 43 13N 77 35W
Ironside, Ont., Canada 192 A1 45 28N 75 44W
Ironside, OR, U.S.A. 94 C8 44 19N 117 57W
Ironsides, MD, U.S.A. 77 B3 38 30N 77 12W
Ironton, MN, U.S.A. 80 D5 46 28N 93 59W
Ironton, MO, U.S.A. 82 D6 37 36N 90 38W
Ironton, OH, U.S.A. 92 E4 38 32N 82 41W
Ironwood, MI, U.S.A. 79 C1 46 27N 90 9W
Ironwood Forest Nat. Monument ⌓, U.S.A. 62 E4 32 32N 111 28W
Iroquois, Ont., Canada 179 C11 44 51N 75 19W
Iroquois, IL, U.S.A. 71 C6 40 50N 87 35W
Iroquois, SD, U.S.A. 91 F8 44 22N 97 51W
Iroquois →, N.W.T., Canada 188 C7 68 5N 129 26W
Iroquois →, IN, U.S.A. 72 B3 41 5N 87 49W
Iroquois County ☆, IL, U.S.A. 71 C6 40 45N 87 50W
Iroquois Falls, Ont., Canada 176 C2 48 46N 80 41W
Iroquois Nat. Wildlife Refuge ⌓, NY, U.S.A. 89 B2 43 7N 78 21W
Iroquois Point, HI, U.S.A. 69 K14 21 19N 157 58W
Irricana, Alta., Canada 185 G7 51 19N 113 37W
Irrigon, OR, U.S.A. 94 B6 45 54N 119 30W
Irvine, CA, U.S.A. 65 K9 33 41N 117 46W
Irvine, KY, U.S.A. 97 C9 37 42N 83 58W
Irving, IL, U.S.A. 71 D4 39 12N 89 24W
Irving, TX, U.S.A. 99 E11 32 48N 96 56W
Irving Park, Chicago, U.S.A. 108 B2 41 57N 87 42W
Irvington, IL, U.S.A. 71 E4 38 26N 89 10W
Irvington, KY, U.S.A. 96 C6 37 53N 86 17W
Irvington, NJ, U.S.A. 114 B1 40 43N 74 14W
Irvona, PA, U.S.A. 95 D4 40 46N 78 33W
Irwin, IA, U.S.A. 73 D3 41 47N 95 12W
Irwin County ☆, GA, U.S.A. 68 E3 31 40N 83 15W
Irwinton, GA, U.S.A. 68 D3 32 49N 83 10W
Irwinville, GA, U.S.A. 68 E3 31 39N 83 23W
Isabel, KS, U.S.A. 74 D5 37 28N 98 33W
Isabel, SD, U.S.A. 91 E4 45 24N 101 26W
Isabel, I., Nayarit, Mexico 216 F5 21 51N 105 55W
Isabel Segunda, Puerto Rico 105 G17 18 9N 65 27W
Isabela, Puerto Rico 105 G15 18 30N 67 2W
Isabella County ☆, MI, U.S.A. 79 F7 43 40N 84 50W
Isabella Indian Reservation, MI, U.S.A. 79 F7 43 36N 84 42W
Isabella L., CA, U.S.A. 65 H8 35 39N 118 28W
Isabelle, Pt., MI, U.S.A. 79 B4 47 21N 87 56W
Isachsen, C., Nunavut, Canada 190 B4 79 20N 105 28W
Isanti, MN, U.S.A. 80 E5 45 29N 93 15W
Isanti County ☆, MN, U.S.A. 80 E5 45 30N 93 15W
Ishpeming, MI, U.S.A. 79 C4 46 29N 87 40W
Iskut →, B.C., Canada 189 E6 56 45N 131 49W
Isla, Veracruz, Mexico 221 F5 18 4N 95 33W
Isla Aguada, Campeche, Mexico 223 D2 18 47N 91 28W
Isla Ángel de la Guarda, Parque Natural ⌓, Baja Calif., Mexico 210 D5 29 30N 113 30W
Isla de Arena, Campeche, Mexico 223 B3 20 42N 90 26W
Isla Isabel, Parque Nacional △, Nayarit, Mexico 216 F5 21 54N 105 58W
Isla la Peña, Nayarit, Mexico 216 F5 21 3N 105 16W
Isla Vista, CA, U.S.A. 65 J7 34 25N 119 53W
Islamorada, FL, U.S.A. 67 G8 24 56N 80 37W
Island Beach, NJ, U.S.A. 87 C2 39 50N 74 5W
Island Beach State Park ⌓, NJ, U.S.A. 87 C2 39 51N 74 5W
Island Channel, NY, U.S.A. 114 C3 40 36N 73 53W
Island City, OR, U.S.A. 94 B7 45 20N 118 3W
Island County ☆, WA, U.S.A. 101 B3 48 10N 122 35W
Island Creek, MD, U.S.A. 77 B4 38 27N 76 35W
Island Falls, Ont., Canada 176 B1 49 35N 81 20W
Island Falls, ME, U.S.A. 76 B5 46 1N 68 16W

Island Heights, NJ, U.S.A. **87 C2** 39 57N 74 9W
Island L., Man., Canada **191 G7** 53 47N 94 25W
Island Lake, Alta., Canada **184 D7** 54 51N 113 33W
Island Lake Res., MN, U.S.A. **80 C6** 47 0N 92 14W
Island Lake Res., MN, U.S.A. **80 C4** 47 48N 94 19W
Island Park, ID, U.S.A. **70 E7** 44 24N 111 19W
Island Park, NY, U.S.A. **114 C5** 40 36N 73 39W
Island Park Res., ID, U.S.A. **70 E7** 44 25N 111 24W
Island Pond, Nfld. & L., Canada **174 D4** 48 25N 56 23W
Island Pond, VT, U.S.A. **86 B3** 44 49N 71 53W
Islands, B. of, Nfld. & L., Canada **174 C2** 49 11N 58 15W
Islay, Alta., Canada **184 E10** 53 24N 110 33W
Isle, MN, U.S.A. **80 D5** 46 8N 93 28W
Isle aux Morts, Nfld. & L., Canada **174 E2** 47 35N 59 0W
Isle L., Alta., Canada **184 E6** 53 38N 114 44W
Isle La Motte, VT, U.S.A. **86 B1** 44 52N 73 18W
Isle of Hope, GA, U.S.A. **68 E5** 31 58N 81 5W
Isle of Palms, SC, U.S.A. **90 F6** 32 47N 79 48W
Isle of Wight, VA, U.S.A. **102 E8** 36 54N 76 43W
Isle of Wight Bay, MD, U.S.A. **77 B5** 38 22N 75 6W
Isle of Wight County ☆, VA, U.S.A. **102 E8** 36 54N 76 43W
Isle Pierre, B.C., Canada **186 B11** 53 57N 123 16W
Isle Royale Nat. Park △, MI, U.S.A. **79 A3** 48 0N 88 55W
Isles, L. des, Ont., Canada **180 C7** 49 10N 89 40W
Islesboro I., ME, U.S.A. **76 D5** 44 19N 68 54W
Isleta Indian Reservation, NM, U.S.A. **88 C4** 34 55N 106 45W
Isleton, CA, U.S.A. **64 E5** 38 10N 121 37W
Ismay, MT, U.S.A. **83 D13** 46 30N 104 48W
Isola, MS, U.S.A. **81 C3** 33 16N 90 35W
Israel →, NH, U.S.A. **86 B3** 44 29N 71 35W
Issaquah, WA, U.S.A. **101 C3** 47 32N 122 2W
Issaquena County ☆, MS, U.S.A. **81 D2** 32 54N 91 3W
Issoudun, Qué., Canada **177 E11** 46 35N 71 38W
Issue, MD, U.S.A. **77 B4** 38 16N 76 53W
Isto, Mt., AK, U.S.A. **61 B12** 69 12N 143 48W
Istokpoga, L., FL, U.S.A. **67 D7** 27 23N 81 17W
Italy, TX, U.S.A. **99 E11** 32 11N 96 53W
Itasca, TX, U.S.A. **99 E10** 32 10N 97 9W
Itasca, L., MN, U.S.A. **80 C3** 47 13N 95 12W
Itasca County ☆, MN, U.S.A. **80 C5** 47 25N 93 25W
Itasca State Park ⌂, MN, U.S.A. **80 C3** 47 12N 95 12W
Itawamba County ☆, MS, U.S.A. **81 B5** 34 16N 88 25W
Itcha Ilgachuz Park ⌂, B.C., Canada **186 C10** 52 42N 124 58W
Itchen L., N.W.T., Canada **189 C10** 65 35N 112 25W
Ithaca, MI, U.S.A. **79 F7** 43 18N 84 36W
Ithaca, NY, U.S.A. **89 C4** 42 27N 76 30W
Ithaca, NE, U.S.A. **84 C9** 41 10N 96 33W
Itkilik →, AK, U.S.A. **61 A10** 70 9N 150 56W
Itomamo, L., Qué., Canada **177 B12** 49 11N 70 28W
Itta Bena, MS, U.S.A. **81 C3** 33 30N 90 20W
Ituna, Sask., Canada **182 D8** 51 10N 103 24W
Iturbide, Campeche, Mexico **223 C4** 19 40N 89 37W
Iturbide, Nuevo León, Mexico **215 F5** 24 44N 99 54W
Itxlahuacán del Río, Jalisco, Mexico **218 B4** 20 52N 103 18W
Iuka, KS, U.S.A. **74 D5** 37 44N 98 44W
Iuka, MS, U.S.A. **81 B5** 34 49N 88 12W
Iva, SC, U.S.A. **90 D3** 34 19N 82 40W
Ivan, AR, U.S.A. **63 E3** 33 55N 92 26W
Ivanhoe, CA, U.S.A. **65 G7** 36 23N 119 13W
Ivanhoe, MN, U.S.A. **80 F2** 44 28N 96 15W
Ivanhoe, VA, U.S.A. **102 E4** 36 50N 80 58W
Ivanof Bay, AK, U.S.A. **61 J8** 55 54N 159 29W
Ivesdale, IL, U.S.A. **71 D5** 39 57N 88 28W
Ivins, UT, U.S.A. **100 F2** 37 10N 113 41W
Ivor, VA, U.S.A. **102 E8** 36 54N 76 54W
Ivujivik, Qué., Canada **175 A2** 62 24N 77 55W
Ivvavik Nat. Park △, Yukon, Canada **188 C5** 69 6N 139 30W
Ivydale, WV, U.S.A. **102 C3** 38 32N 81 2W
Ixcamilpa, Puebla, Mexico **221 F2** 18 3N 98 41W
Ixcapuzalco, Guerrero, Mexico **219 D8** 18 32N 99 53W
Ixcateopan, Guerrero, Mexico **219 D8** 18 30N 99 46W
Ixcatepec, Guerrero, Mexico **219 D7** 18 32N 100 6W
Ixhil, Quintana Roo, Mexico **223 B6** 20 27N 87 54W
Ixhuatlán, Veracruz, Mexico **220 D2** 20 42N 98 0W
Ixmiquilpan, Hidalgo, Mexico **219 B8** 20 29N 99 14W
Ixtaczoquitlán, Veracruz, Mexico **221 F3** 18 52N 97 3W
Ixtalahuite, Pta., Oaxaca, Mexico **221 J4** 15 40N 96 30W
Ixtapa, Chiapas, Mexico **222 C4** 16 48N 92 55W
Ixtapa, Jalisco, Mexico **218 B2** 20 42N 105 11W
Ixtapaluca, México, Mexico **219 C9** 19 18N 98 53W
Ixtapán de la Concepción, Nayarit, Mexico **216 F5** 21 19N 105 10W
Ixtapán de la Sal, México, Mexico **219 D8** 18 50N 99 41W
Ixtapán del Oro, México, Mexico **219 C7** 19 16N 100 16W
Ixtepec, Oaxaca, Mexico **221 H5** 16 34N 95 6W
Ixtlahuaca, México, Mexico **219 C8** 19 34N 99 46W
Ixtlahuacán, Colima, Mexico **218 D4** 18 59N 103 45W
Ixtlán de Juárez, Oaxaca, Mexico **221 G4** 17 20N 96 30W
Ixtlán del Río, Nayarit, Mexico **216 F6** 21 2N 104 22W
Izamal, Yucatán, Mexico **223 B4** 20 56N 89 1W
Izapa, Chiapas, Mexico **222 E4** 14 58N 92 11W
Izard County ☆, AR, U.S.A. **63 B4** 36 4N 91 54W
Izembek Nat. Wildlife Refuge ⌂, AK, U.S.A. **61 J7** 55 15N 162 45W
Iztacalco, Distrito Federal, Mexico **225 B3** 19 23N 99 5W
Iztaccihuatl y Popocatépetl, Parque Nacional △, Mexico **221 E2** 19 10N 98 38W
Iztapalapa, Distrito Federal, Mexico **225 B3** 19 21N 99 6W
Izúcar de Matamoros, Puebla, Mexico **221 F2** 18 36N 98 28W

J

J.B. Thomas, L., TX, U.S.A. **98 E6** 32 36N 101 8W
J. Clark Salyer Nat. Wildlife Reserve ⌂, ND, U.S.A. **91 B5** 48 37N 100 40W
J.F.K. International ✈ (JFK), NY, U.S.A. **89 E7** 40 38N 73 47W
J. Percy Priest L., TN, U.S.A. **96 D6** 36 9N 86 37W
J. Strom Thurmond L., GA, U.S.A. **68 C4** 33 40N 82 12W
Jaab L., Ont., Canada **181 A14** 51 10N 82 58W
Jacala, Hidalgo, Mexico **219 A8** 21 1N 99 11W
Jacinto City, TX, U.S.A. **110 B3** 29 46N 95 14W
Jack County ☆, TX, U.S.A. **99 D9** 33 13N 98 10W
Jack Creek, NV, U.S.A. **85 A4** 41 30N 116 6W
Jack Lee, L., AR, U.S.A. **63 E3** 33 15N 92 8W
Jackfish L., Sask., Canada **182 B3** 53 9N 108 29W
Jackman, ME, U.S.A. **76 C3** 45 37N 70 15W
Jackpot, NV, U.S.A. **85 A6** 41 59N 114 40W
Jacks Fork →, MO, U.S.A. **82 D5** 37 12N 91 18W
Jacksboro, TN, U.S.A. **97 D8** 36 20N 84 11W
Jacksboro, TX, U.S.A. **99 D9** 33 13N 98 10W
Jackson, AL, U.S.A. **60 E3** 31 31N 87 53W
Jackson, CA, U.S.A. **64 E6** 38 21N 120 46W
Jackson, GA, U.S.A. **68 C3** 33 20N 83 57W
Jackson, KY, U.S.A. **97 C9** 37 33N 83 23W
Jackson, LA, U.S.A. **75 D4** 30 50N 91 13W
Jackson, MI, U.S.A. **79 G7** 42 15N 84 24W
Jackson, MN, U.S.A. **80 G3** 43 37N 95 1W
Jackson, MS, U.S.A. **81 D3** 32 18N 90 12W
Jackson, MO, U.S.A. **82 D7** 37 23N 89 40W
Jackson, MT, U.S.A. **83 E4** 45 23N 113 28W
Jackson, NC, U.S.A. **90 B8** 36 23N 77 25W
Jackson, NH, U.S.A. **86 B3** 44 10N 71 11W
Jackson, NJ, U.S.A. **87 B2** 40 6N 74 23W
Jackson, NE, U.S.A. **84 B9** 42 27N 96 34W
Jackson, OH, U.S.A. **92 D4** 39 3N 82 39W
Jackson, SC, U.S.A. **90 E4** 33 20N 81 47W
Jackson, TN, U.S.A. **96 E4** 35 37N 88 49W
Jackson, WI, U.S.A. **103 E5** 43 19N 88 10W
Jackson, WY, U.S.A. **104 C2** 43 29N 110 46W
Jackson County ☆, AL, U.S.A. **60 B4** 34 40N 86 2W
Jackson County ☆, AR, U.S.A. **63 C4** 35 38N 91 16W
Jackson County ☆, CO, U.S.A. **66 B4** 40 45N 106 20W
Jackson County ☆, FL, U.S.A. **67 A3** 30 45N 85 15W
Jackson County ☆, GA, U.S.A. **68 B3** 34 10N 83 30W
Jackson County ☆, IL, U.S.A. **71 F4** 37 45N 89 25W
Jackson County ☆, IN, U.S.A. **72 E4** 38 55N 86 0W
Jackson County ☆, IA, U.S.A. **73 C8** 42 10N 90 35W
Jackson County ☆, KS, U.S.A. **74 B8** 39 20N 95 45W
Jackson County ☆, KY, U.S.A. **97 C8** 37 25N 84 0W
Jackson County ☆, MI, U.S.A. **79 G7** 42 15N 84 30W
Jackson County ☆, MN, U.S.A. **80 G3** 43 40N 95 10W
Jackson County ☆, MS, U.S.A. **81 F5** 30 32N 88 42W
Jackson County ☆, MO, U.S.A. **82 C2** 39 0N 94 20W
Jackson County ☆, NC, U.S.A. **90 C2** 35 20N 83 10W
Jackson County ☆, OH, U.S.A. **92 D4** 39 3N 82 39W
Jackson County ☆, OK, U.S.A. **93 D4** 34 30N 99 25W
Jackson County ☆, OR, U.S.A. **94 E3** 42 20N 122 45W
Jackson County ☆, SD, U.S.A. **91 G4** 43 45N 101 45W
Jackson County ☆, TN, U.S.A. **97 D7** 36 21N 85 39W
Jackson County ☆, TX, U.S.A. **99 J11** 28 59N 96 39W
Jackson County ☆, WV, U.S.A. **102 C3** 38 49N 81 43W
Jackson County ☆, WI, U.S.A. **103 D3** 44 20N 90 45W
Jackson Heights, NY, U.S.A. **114 B3** 40 44N 73 53W
Jackson Hole, WY, U.S.A. **104 C2** 43 36N 110 51W
Jackson Junction, IA, U.S.A. **73 B6** 43 7N 92 2W
Jackson L., FL, U.S.A. **67 A4** 30 30N 84 17W
Jackson L., GA, U.S.A. **68 C3** 33 19N 83 50W
Jackson L., WY, U.S.A. **104 C2** 43 52N 110 36W
Jackson Mts., NV, U.S.A. **85 A2** 41 15N 118 30W
Jackson Parish ☆, LA, U.S.A. **75 B3** 32 15N 92 43W
Jackson Park, Chicago, U.S.A. **108 C3** 41 46N 87 34W
Jackson Park, Milwaukee, U.S.A. **112 C2** 42 57N 87 57W
Jackson Res., CO, U.S.A. **66 B6** 40 22N 104 6W
Jackson's Arm, Nfld. & L., Canada **174 C4** 49 52N 56 47W
Jacksonville, AL, U.S.A. **60 C5** 33 49N 85 46W
Jacksonville, AR, U.S.A. **63 D3** 34 52N 92 7W
Jacksonville, FL, U.S.A. **67 A7** 30 20N 81 39W
Jacksonville, GA, U.S.A. **68 E4** 31 49N 82 59W
Jacksonville, IL, U.S.A. **71 D3** 39 44N 90 14W
Jacksonville, NC, U.S.A. **90 D8** 34 45N 77 26W
Jacksonville, OH, U.S.A. **92 D4** 39 29N 82 5W
Jacksonville, OR, U.S.A. **94 E3** 42 19N 122 57W
Jacksonville, TX, U.S.A. **99 F12** 31 58N 95 17W
Jacksonville, VT, U.S.A. **86 D2** 42 47N 72 49W
Jacksonville Beach, FL, U.S.A. **67 A7** 30 17N 81 24W
Jacksonville International ✈ (JAX), FL, U.S.A. **67 A7** 30 30N 81 41W
Jacob Lake, AZ, U.S.A. **62 A3** 36 43N 112 13W
Jacob Riis Park, NY, U.S.A. **114 C3** 40 33N 73 52W
Jacobsville, MD, U.S.A. **77 A4** 39 7N 76 31W
Jacobus, PA, U.S.A. **77 A4** 39 52N 76 42W
Jacomulco, Veracruz, Mexico **220 E4** 19 20N 96 44W
Jacona de Plancarte, Michoacan, Mexico **218 C5** 19 57N 102 16W
Jacques-Cartier, Montréal, Canada **192 A3** 45 31N 73 27W
Jacques-Cartier →, Qué., Canada **177 E11** 46 40N 71 45W
Jacques-Cartier, Dét. de, Qué., Canada **175 C5** 50 0N 63 30W
Jacques-Cartier, L., Qué., Canada **177 D11** 47 35N 71 13W
Jacques-Cartier, Mt., Qué., Canada **177 E4** 48 57N 66 0W
Jacques-Cartier, Parc de ⌂, Qué., Canada **177 D11** 47 15N 71 33W
Jacquet River, N.B., Canada **173 F3** 47 55N 66 0W
Jacumba, CA, U.S.A. **65 L10** 32 37N 116 11W
Jacumé, Baja Calif., Mexico **210 A2** 32 36N 116 10W
Jaffrey, NH, U.S.A. **86 D2** 42 49N 72 2W
Jagüey, Pta., Sonora, Mexico **212 C2** 30 47N 113 12W
Jaina, I., Campeche, Mexico **223 B3** 20 15N 90 30W
Jakin, GA, U.S.A. **68 E2** 31 6N 84 59W
Jal, NM, U.S.A. **88 E7** 32 7N 103 12W
Jala, Nayarit, Mexico **216 F6** 21 6N 104 26W
Jalaihai Pt., Guam **105 b** 13 18N 144 46W
Jalapa, Oaxaca, Mexico **221 F4** 18 4N 96 32W
Jalapa, Tabasco, Mexico **222 B4** 17 43N 92 49W
Jalapa del Marques, Oaxaca, Mexico **221 H5** 16 26N 95 25W
Jalapa Enríquez = Xalapa, Veracruz, Mexico **220 E4** 19 32N 96 55W
Jalcocotán, Nayarit, Mexico **216 F5** 21 28N 105 7W
Jalisco □, Mexico **218 B4** 20 20N 103 40W
Jalostotitlán, Jalisco, Mexico **218 A5** 21 12N 102 28W
Jalpa, Coahuila, Mexico **214 E3** 25 34N 101 45W
Jalpa, Zacatecas, Mexico **217 F8** 21 38N 102 58W
Jalpa de Méndez, Tabasco, Mexico **222 A3** 18 11N 93 4W
Jalpan, Querétaro, Mexico **219 A8** 21 14N 99 29W
Jáltipan de Morelos, Veracruz, Mexico **221 G6** 17 58N 94 43W
Jaltocán, Hidalgo, Mexico **219 A9** 21 8N 98 32W
Jamaica, IA, U.S.A. **73 D4** 41 51N 94 18W
Jamaica, VT, U.S.A. **86 C2** 43 13N 72 46W
Jamaica B., NY, U.S.A. **89 E7** 40 36N 73 50W
Jamaica Plain, Boston, U.S.A. **106 B3** 42 18N 71 6W
Jamapa, Veracruz, Mexico **221 E4** 19 3N 96 25W
Jamay, Jalisco, Mexico **218 B5** 20 18N 102 43W
James, GA, U.S.A. **68 D3** 32 58N 83 29W
James →, U.S.A. **91 H8** 42 52N 97 18W
James →, MO, U.S.A. **82 E3** 36 45N 93 30W
James →, VA, U.S.A. **102 E8** 36 56N 76 27W
James, L., NC, U.S.A. **90 C4** 35 44N 81 54W
James B., Nunavut, Canada **191 G9** 54 0N 80 0W
James City, NC, U.S.A. **90 C8** 35 5N 77 2W
James City County ☆, VA, U.S.A. **102 D8** 37 16N 76 40W
James Island, SC, U.S.A. **90 F6** 32 45N 79 55W
James River, N.S., Canada **173 H7** 45 35N 62 7W
James Ross Str., Nunavut, Canada **190 A13** 69 40N 96 10W
Jamesburg, NJ, U.S.A. **87 B2** 40 21N 74 27W
Jamesport, MO, U.S.A. **82 B3** 39 58N 93 48W
Jamestown = Wawa, Ont., Canada **181 E12** 47 59N 84 47W
Jamestown, CA, U.S.A. **64 F6** 37 57N 120 25W
Jamestown, IN, U.S.A. **72 D4** 39 56N 86 38W
Jamestown, KS, U.S.A. **74 B6** 39 36N 97 52W
Jamestown, KY, U.S.A. **97 D7** 36 59N 85 4W
Jamestown, LA, U.S.A. **75 B2** 32 21N 93 13W
Jamestown, ND, U.S.A. **91 D7** 46 54N 98 42W
Jamestown, NY, U.S.A. **89 C1** 42 6N 79 14W
Jamestown, OH, U.S.A. **92 D3** 39 39N 83 33W
Jamestown, PA, U.S.A. **95 C2** 41 29N 80 27W
Jamestown, RI, U.S.A. **78 C3** 41 30N 71 22W
Jamestown, TN, U.S.A. **97 D8** 36 26N 84 56W
Jamestown, VA, U.S.A. **102 D5** 37 12N 79 46W
Jamestown Res., ND, U.S.A. **91 D7** 46 56N 98 43W
Jamesville, NC, U.S.A. **90 C9** 35 49N 76 54W
Jamieson, OR, U.S.A. **94 C8** 44 11N 117 26W
Jane, MO, U.S.A. **82 E2** 36 33N 94 18W
Jane, L., Minneapolis-St. Paul, U.S.A. **113 A4** 45 1N 92 55W
Jane Lew, WV, U.S.A. **102 B4** 39 7N 80 25W
Janes I., DE, U.S.A. **77 C5** 38 0N 75 51W
Janesville, CA, U.S.A. **64 C6** 40 18N 120 32W
Janesville, IA, U.S.A. **73 C6** 42 39N 92 28W
Janesville, MN, U.S.A. **80 F5** 44 7N 93 42W
Janesville, WI, U.S.A. **103 F4** 42 41N 89 1W
Janos, Chihuahua, Mexico **213 C7** 30 54N 108 10W
Jansen, Sask., Canada **182 D7** 51 54N 104 45W
Jansen, CO, U.S.A. **66 E6** 37 9N 104 32W
Jansen, NE, U.S.A. **84 D8** 40 11N 97 5W
Jantetelco, Morelos, Mexico **219 D9** 18 34N 98 46W
Jaral, Guanajuato, Mexico **219 A6** 21 41N 101 1W
Jaral del Progreso, Guanajuato, Mexico **219 B6** 20 23N 101 5W
Jarales, NM, U.S.A. **88 C4** 34 37N 106 46W
Jarbidge, NV, U.S.A. **85 A5** 41 52N 115 26W
Jarbidge →, ID, U.S.A. **70 G3** 42 20N 115 39W
Jarboesville = Lexington Park, MD, U.S.A. **77 B4** 38 16N 76 27W
Jardines de la Silla, Monterrey, Mexico **224 C2** 25 38N 100 11W
Jarratt, VA, U.S.A. **102 E7** 36 48N 77 28W
Jarrettsville, MD, U.S.A. **77 A4** 39 36N 76 29W
Jarvis, Ont., Canada **178 E6** 42 53N 80 6W
Jarvis I., Pac. Oc. **105 E7** 0 15 S 160 5W
Jas Punta, Quintana Roo, Mexico **223 D6** 18 25N 87 56W
Jasonville, IN, U.S.A. **72 D3** 39 10N 87 12W
Jasper, Alta., Canada **185 F2** 52 55N 118 5W
Jasper, Ont., Canada **179 C11** 44 52N 75 57W
Jasper, AL, U.S.A. **60 C3** 33 50N 87 17W
Jasper, AR, U.S.A. **63 B2** 36 1N 93 11W
Jasper, FL, U.S.A. **67 A6** 30 31N 82 57W
Jasper, GA, U.S.A. **68 B2** 34 28N 84 26W
Jasper, IN, U.S.A. **72 E4** 38 24N 86 56W
Jasper, MN, U.S.A. **80 G2** 43 51N 96 24W
Jasper, MO, U.S.A. **82 D2** 37 20N 94 18W
Jasper, TN, U.S.A. **97 E7** 35 5N 85 38W
Jasper, TX, U.S.A. **99 G13** 30 56N 94 1W
Jasper County ☆, GA, U.S.A. **68 C3** 33 20N 83 45W
Jasper County ☆, IL, U.S.A. **71 E5** 39 0N 88 10W
Jasper County ☆, IN, U.S.A. **72 B3** 41 0N 87 5W
Jasper County ☆, IA, U.S.A. **73 D5** 41 40N 93 0W
Jasper County ☆, MS, U.S.A. **81 D4** 32 2N 89 2W
Jasper County ☆, MO, U.S.A. **82 D2** 37 10N 94 20W
Jasper County ☆, SC, U.S.A. **90 F4** 32 30N 81 0W
Jasper County ☆, TX, U.S.A. **99 G14** 30 40N 93 54W
Jasper Nat. Park △, Alta., Canada **185 F2** 52 50N 118 8W
Jatate →, Chiapas, Mexico **222 C5** 16 15N 91 17W
Jaumave, Tamaulipas, Mexico **215 G5** 23 25N 99 23W
Java, SD, U.S.A. **91 E6** 45 30N 99 53W
Java, VA, U.S.A. **102 E5** 36 50N 79 14W
Jay, FL, U.S.A. **67 A1** 30 57N 87 9W
Jay, ME, U.S.A. **76 D3** 44 30N 70 13W
Jay, NY, U.S.A. **89 A7** 44 20N 73 45W
Jay, OK, U.S.A. **93 B9** 36 25N 94 48W
Jay County ☆, IN, U.S.A. **72 C6** 40 25N 85 0W
Jay Em, WY, U.S.A. **104 D8** 42 28N 104 22W
Jay Peak, VT, U.S.A. **86 B2** 44 55N 72 32W
Jaype, ID, U.S.A. **70 C3** 46 32N 115 50W
Jayton, TX, U.S.A. **98 D7** 33 15N 100 34W
Jazminal, Coahuila, Mexico **215 F3** 24 52N 101 24W
Jean, NV, U.S.A. **85 G5** 35 47N 115 20W
Jean, TX, U.S.A. **99 D9** 33 18N 98 37W
Jean Lafitte Nat. Historical Park ⌂, LA, U.S.A. **75 E5** 29 51N 90 9W
Jean Marie River, N.W.T., Canada **189 D8** 61 32N 120 38W
Jeanerette, LA, U.S.A. **75 E4** 29 55N 91 40W
Jeanetta, Houston, U.S.A. **110 B1** 29 43N 95 31W
Jeanette L., Ont., Canada **180 A4** 51 5N 92 56W
Jecopaco, Sonora, Mexico **212 F6** 27 12N 109 46W
Jeddore L., Nfld. & L., Canada **174 D5** 48 3N 55 55W
Jedway, B.C., Canada **186 C3** 52 17N 131 14W
Jeff Davis County ☆, GA, U.S.A. **68 E4** 31 50N 82 45W
Jeff Davis County ☆, TX, U.S.A. **98 G3** 30 55N 104 5W
Jeffers, MN, U.S.A. **80 F3** 44 3N 95 12W
Jefferson, CO, U.S.A. **66 C5** 39 23N 105 48W
Jefferson, GA, U.S.A. **68 B3** 34 7N 83 35W
Jefferson, IA, U.S.A. **73 C4** 42 1N 94 23W
Jefferson, ME, U.S.A. **76 D4** 44 13N 69 27W
Jefferson, MD, U.S.A. **77 A3** 39 22N 77 32W
Jefferson, NC, U.S.A. **90 B4** 36 25N 81 28W
Jefferson, New Orleans, U.S.A. **113 C2** 29 57N 90 9W
Jefferson, OH, U.S.A. **92 B6** 41 44N 80 46W
Jefferson, OK, U.S.A. **93 B6** 36 43N 97 48W
Jefferson, OR, U.S.A. **94 C2** 44 43N 123 1W
Jefferson, SC, U.S.A. **90 D5** 34 39N 80 23W
Jefferson, SD, U.S.A. **91 H9** 42 36N 96 34W
Jefferson, TX, U.S.A. **99 E13** 32 46N 94 21W
Jefferson, WI, U.S.A. **103 E5** 43 0N 88 48W
Jefferson →, MT, U.S.A. **83 E6** 45 56N 111 31W
Jefferson, Mt., NV, U.S.A. **85 D4** 38 47N 116 56W
Jefferson, Mt., OR, U.S.A. **94 C4** 44 41N 121 48W
Jefferson City, MO, U.S.A. **82 C4** 38 34N 92 10W
Jefferson City, TN, U.S.A. **97 D9** 36 7N 83 30W
Jefferson County ☆, AL, U.S.A. **60 C4** 33 31N 86 48W
Jefferson County ☆, AR, U.S.A. **63 D3** 34 13N 92 1W
Jefferson County ☆, CO, U.S.A. **66 C5** 39 40N 105 15W
Jefferson County ☆, FL, U.S.A. **67 A5** 30 20N 84 0W
Jefferson County ☆, GA, U.S.A. **68 C4** 33 10N 82 25W
Jefferson County ☆, ID, U.S.A. **70 F6** 43 50N 112 20W
Jefferson County ☆, IL, U.S.A. **71 E5** 38 20N 88 55W
Jefferson County ☆, IN, U.S.A. **72 E5** 38 40N 85 25W
Jefferson County ☆, IA, U.S.A. **73 D7** 41 0N 92 0W
Jefferson County ☆, KS, U.S.A. **74 B8** 39 15N 95 30W
Jefferson County ☆, KY, U.S.A. **97 B7** 38 10N 85 40W
Jefferson County ☆, MS, U.S.A. **81 E2** 31 43N 91 4W
Jefferson County ☆, MO, U.S.A. **82 C6** 38 15N 90 30W
Jefferson County ☆, MT, U.S.A. **83 D6** 46 8N 112 0W
Jefferson County ☆, NY, U.S.A. **89 A4** 44 0N 76 0W
Jefferson County ☆, NE, U.S.A. **84 D8** 40 15N 97 10W
Jefferson County ☆, OH, U.S.A. **92 C6** 40 25N 80 54W
Jefferson County ☆, OK, U.S.A. **93 D6** 34 10N 97 50W
Jefferson County ☆, OR, U.S.A. **94 C4** 44 40N 121 10W
Jefferson County ☆, PA, U.S.A. **95 C4** 41 5N 79 0W
Jefferson County ☆, TN, U.S.A. **97 D9** 36 7N 83 30W
Jefferson County ☆, TX, U.S.A. **99 H13** 29 55N 94 15W
Jefferson County ☆, WV, U.S.A. **102 B7** 39 17N 77 52W
Jefferson County ☆, WA, U.S.A. **101 C2** 47 50N 123 45W
Jefferson County ☆, WI, U.S.A. **103 F5** 43 0N 88 45W
Jefferson Davis County ☆, MS, U.S.A. **81 E4** 31 36N 89 52W
Jefferson Davis Parish ☆, LA, U.S.A. **75 D3** 30 14N 92 49W
Jefferson Nat. Forest, VA, U.S.A. **102 D3** 37 10N 81 15W
Jefferson Parish ☆, LA, U.S.A. **75 E5** 29 44N 90 8W
Jefferson Park, Chicago, U.S.A. **108 B2** 41 58N 87 46W
Jefferson Valley, NY, U.S.A. **87 A3** 41 20N 73 47W
Jeffersonton, VA, U.S.A. **102 C7** 38 38N 77 55W
Jeffersontown, KY, U.S.A. **97 B7** 38 12N 85 35W
Jeffersonville, GA, U.S.A. **68 D3** 32 41N 83 20W
Jeffersonville, IN, U.S.A. **72 E5** 38 17N 85 44W
Jeffersonville, KY, U.S.A. **97 C9** 37 59N 83 51W
Jeffersonville, OH, U.S.A. **92 D3** 39 39N 83 34W
Jeffersonville, VT, U.S.A. **86 B2** 44 40N 72 50W
Jeffrey City, WY, U.S.A. **104 D5** 42 30N 107 49W
Jeffrey Res., NE, U.S.A. **84 D5** 40 58N 100 24W
Jekyll I., GA, U.S.A. **68 E5** 31 4N 81 25W
Jellico, TN, U.S.A. **97 D8** 36 33N 84 8W
Jellicoe, Ont., Canada **181 C9** 49 40N 87 30W
Jemez Indian Reservation, NM, U.S.A. **88 B4** 35 40N 106 50W
Jemez Mts., NM, U.S.A. **88 B4** 35 45N 106 30W
Jemez Pueblo, NM, U.S.A. **88 B4** 35 37N 106 44W
Jemez Springs, NM, U.S.A. **88 B4** 35 46N 106 42W
Jemison, AL, U.S.A. **60 D4** 32 58N 86 45W
Jemseg, N.B., Canada **173 H3** 45 50N 66 7W
Jena, FL, U.S.A. **67 B5** 29 40N 83 22W
Jena, LA, U.S.A. **75 C3** 31 41N 92 8W
Jenison, MI, U.S.A. **79 G6** 42 54N 85 47W
Jenkins, KY, U.S.A. **97 C10** 37 10N 82 38W
Jenkins, MN, U.S.A. **80 D4** 46 39N 94 20W
Jenkins, NJ, U.S.A. **87 C2** 39 42N 74 32W
Jenkins County ☆, GA, U.S.A. **68 D5** 32 45N 82 0W
Jenkintown, PA, U.S.A. **87 B1** 40 5N 75 7W
Jenks, OK, U.S.A. **93 B8** 36 1N 95 58W
Jenner, CA, U.S.A. **64 E3** 38 27N 123 7W
Jennings, FL, U.S.A. **67 A5** 30 36N 83 6W
Jennings, KS, U.S.A. **74 B3** 39 41N 100 18W
Jennings, LA, U.S.A. **75 D3** 30 13N 92 40W
Jennings, MO, U.S.A. **82 C6** 38 43N 90 15W
Jennings, OK, U.S.A. **93 B7** 36 11N 96 34W
Jennings County ☆, IN, U.S.A. **72 D5** 39 0N 85 40W
Jennings Lodge, Portland, U.S.A. **116 B2** 45 23N 122 36W
Jenny Lind I., Nunavut, Canada **190 D5** 68 43N 101 58W
Jens Munk I., Nunavut, Canada **190 D9** 69 39N 80 4W
Jensen, UT, U.S.A. **100 C6** 40 22N 109 20W
Jensen Beach, FL, U.S.A. **67 D8** 27 15N 80 14W
Jerauld County ☆, SD, U.S.A. **91 F7** 44 0N 98 45W
Jerécuaro, Guanajuato, Mexico **219 B7** 20 9N 100 31W
Jeremy Point, MA, U.S.A. **78 C4** 41 53N 70 4W
Jerez →, Zacatecas, Mexico **217 E7** 22 18N 103 13W
Jerez de García Salinas, Zacatecas, Mexico **217 E8** 22 39N 103 0W
Jericho Beach Park, Vancouver, Canada **193 B1** 49 16N 123 2W
Jerico Springs, MO, U.S.A. **82 D2** 37 37N 94 1W
Jerimoth Hill, RI, U.S.A. **78 C3** 41 51N 71 47W
Jermyn, PA, U.S.A. **87 A1** 41 32N 75 33W
Jermyn, TX, U.S.A. **99 D9** 33 16N 98 23W
Jerome, Ont., Canada **181 E14** 47 37N 82 14W
Jerome, AZ, U.S.A. **62 C3** 34 45N 112 7W
Jerome, AR, U.S.A. **63 E4** 33 24N 91 28W
Jerome, ID, U.S.A. **70 G4** 42 44N 114 31W
Jerome County ☆, ID, U.S.A. **70 G4** 42 42N 114 15W
Jerry City, OH, U.S.A. **92 B3** 41 15N 83 36W
Jersey, AR, U.S.A. **63 E3** 33 26N 92 19W
Jersey, GA, U.S.A. **68 C3** 33 43N 83 47W
Jersey City, NJ, U.S.A. **87 B2** 40 42N 74 4W
Jersey County ☆, IL, U.S.A. **71 D3** 39 5N 90 20W
Jersey Shore, PA, U.S.A. **95 C5** 41 12N 77 15W
Jersey Village, TX, U.S.A. **99 H12** 29 53N 95 33W
Jerseyside, Nfld. & L., Canada **174 E7** 47 16N 53 58W
Jerseyville, IL, U.S.A. **71 D3** 39 7N 90 20W
Jerusalem, OK, U.S.A. **93 B5** 36 0N 98 16W
Jervis Inlet, B.C., Canada **186 F11** 50 0N 123 57W
Jessamine, L., Orlando, U.S.A. **115 B2** 28 28N 81 23W
Jessamine County ☆, KY, U.S.A. **97 C8** 37 50N 84 35W
Jessieville, AR, U.S.A. **63 D2** 34 42N 93 4W
Jessup, MD, U.S.A. **77 A4** 39 9N 76 46W
Jesup, GA, U.S.A. **68 E5** 31 36N 81 53W
Jesup, IA, U.S.A. **73 C6** 42 29N 92 4W
Jesup, L., FL, U.S.A. **67 C7** 28 43N 81 14W
Jésus, Î., Montréal, Canada **192 A2** 45 36N 73 44W
Jesús Carranza, Veracruz, Mexico **221 G5** 17 26N 95 2W
Jesús Garcia, Sonora, Mexico **212 C3** 30 45N 112 23W
Jesús María, Aguascalientes, Mexico **217 F8** 21 57N 102 20W
Jesús María, Jalisco, Mexico **218 B5** 20 37N 102 7W
Jesús María, Nayarit, Mexico **216 E6** 22 14N 104 31W
Jesús María →, Mexico **216 F6** 21 57N 104 31W
Jesús María Garza, Chiapas, Mexico **222 C3** 16 22N 93 18W
Jet, OK, U.S.A. **93 B5** 36 40N 98 11W
Jetmore, KS, U.S.A. **74 C4** 38 4N 99 54W
Jewel Cave Nat. Monument ⌂, SD, U.S.A. **91 G2** 43 45N 103 48W
Jewell, IA, U.S.A. **73 C5** 42 20N 93 39W
Jewell, KS, U.S.A. **74 B5** 39 40N 98 10W
Jewell County ☆, KS, U.S.A. **74 B5** 39 45N 98 10W
Jewell Ridge, VA, U.S.A. **102 D3** 37 11N 81 47W
Jewett, IL, U.S.A. **71 D5** 39 13N 88 15W
Jewett, OH, U.S.A. **92 C5** 40 22N 81 2W
Jewett, TX, U.S.A. **99 F11** 31 22N 96 9W
Jewett City, CT, U.S.A. **78 C3** 41 36N 71 59W
Jicarilla Indian Reservation, NM, U.S.A. **88 A4** 36 45N 107 0W
Jigger, LA, U.S.A. **75 B4** 32 2N 91 45W
Jiggs, NV, U.S.A. **85 B5** 40 26N 115 40W
Jilotlán de los Dolores, Jalisco, Mexico **218 C4** 19 12N 103 13W
Jim Hogg County ☆, TX, U.S.A. **98 K9** 27 0N 98 45W
Jim Thorpe, PA, U.S.A. **87 B1** 40 52N 75 44W
Jim Wells County ☆, TX, U.S.A. **99 K9** 28 0N 98 0W
Jiménez, Chihuahua, Mexico **213 F11** 27 8N 104 54W
Jiménez, Coahuila, Mexico **214 A4** 29 2N 100 41W
Jiménez del Téul, Zacatecas, Mexico **217 D7** 23 15N 103 47W
Jimmy Carter Nat. Historic Site ⌂, GA, U.S.A. **68 D2** 32 2N 84 25W
Jimulco, Sa., Coahuila, Mexico **215 E1** 25 15N 103 19W
Jiquilpan, Michoacan, Mexico **218 C5** 19 59N 102 43W
Jiquipilas, Chiapas, Mexico **222 C3** 16 40N 93 39W
Jitotol, Chiapas, Mexico **222 B4** 17 2N 92 52W
Jitzamuri, B., Mexico **216 A1** 26 15N 109 16W
Jiutepec, Morelos, Mexico **219 D8** 18 53N 99 10W
Jo Daviess County ☆, IL, U.S.A. **71 A3** 42 20N 90 10W
Joanna, SC, U.S.A. **90 D4** 34 25N 81 49W
Joaquin, TX, U.S.A. **99 F13** 31 58N 94 3W
Joaquín Amaro, Zacatecas, Mexico **217 F7** 21 56N 103 6W
Joaquin Miller Park, San Francisco, U.S.A. **118 B3** 37 48N 122 10W
Jocassee, L., SC, U.S.A. **90 D3** 34 58N 82 56W
Jococuistle, Durango, Mexico **216 D5** 23 15N 105 21W
Jocotepec, Jalisco, Mexico **218 B4** 20 18N 103 26W
Jocotitlán, México, Mexico **219 C8** 19 42N 99 48W
Joe Batt's Arm-Barr'd Islands-Shoal Bay, Nfld. & L., Canada **174 C6** 49 44N 54 10W
Joe Pool Lake, Dallas-Fort Worth, U.S.A. **109 C4** 32 38N 96 59W
Joes, CO, U.S.A. **66 C8** 39 39N 102 41W
Joffre, Mt., B.C., Canada **185 H5** 50 32N 115 13W
Joggins, N.S., Canada **173 H5** 45 42N 64 27W
Jogues, Ont., Canada **181 C13** 49 36N 83 45W
Johanna, L., Minneapolis-St. Paul, U.S.A. **113 A2** 45 2N 93 10W
Johannesburg, CA, U.S.A. **65 H9** 35 22N 117 38W
John C. Stennis Space Center, MS, U.S.A. **81 F4** 30 23N 89 37W
John D. Rockefeller Jr. Memorial Parkway, WY, U.S.A. **104 B2** 44 5N 110 44W
John Day, OR, U.S.A. **94 C7** 44 25N 118 57W
John Day →, OR, U.S.A. **94 B5** 45 44N 120 39W
John Day Dam, WA, U.S.A. **101 E5** 45 43N 120 41W
John Day Fossil Beds Nat. Monument ⌂, OR, U.S.A. **58 D4** 44 33N 119 38W

John Day Fossil Beds Nat. Monument Clarno ⌓, *OR, U.S.A.* **94 C5** 44 55N 120 28W
John Day Fossil Beds Nat. Monument Painted Hills ⌓, *OR, U.S.A.* **94 C5** 44 39N 120 15W
John Day Fossil Beds Nat. Monument Sheep Rock ⌓, *OR, U.S.A.* **94 C6** 44 33N 119 30W
John Dickinson Plantation, *DE, U.S.A.* **77 A5** 39 10N 75 31W
John D'Or Prairie, *Alta., Canada* **189 E9** 58 30N 115 8W
John F. Kennedy International, New York ✈ (JFK), *NY, U.S.A.* **89 E7** 40 38N 73 47W
John F. Kennedy Space Center, *U.S.A.* **67 C8** 28 40N 80 42W
John H. Kerr Res., *NC, U.S.A.* **90 B7** 36 36N 78 18W
John Heinz Nat. Wildlife Refuge ⌓, *PA, U.S.A.* **116 B1** 39 53N 75 17W
John Hendrey Park, *Vancouver, Canada* **193 B2** 49 15N 123 5W
John McLaren Park, *San Francisco, U.S.A.* **118 B2** 37 43N 122 24W
John Martin Res., *CO, U.S.A.* **66 D8** 38 4N 102 56W
John Redmond Res., *KS, U.S.A.* **74 C8** 38 14N 95 46W
John W. Flanagan Res., *VA, U.S.A.* **102 D2** 37 15N 82 22W
John Wayne, Santa Ana ✈ (SNA), *CA, U.S.A.* **65 K9** 33 41N 117 52W
Johns I., *SC, U.S.A.* **90 F5** 32 40N 80 10W
Johns I., *SC, U.S.A.* **90 F5** 32 47N 80 7W
Johnson, *NE, U.S.A.* **84 D10** 40 25N 96 0W
Johnson, *VT, U.S.A.* **86 B2** 44 38N 72 41W
Johnson City, *KS, U.S.A.* **74 D2** 37 34N 101 45W
Johnson City, *NY, U.S.A.* **89 C5** 42 7N 75 58W
Johnson City, *TN, U.S.A.* **97 D10** 36 19N 82 21W
Johnson City, *TX, U.S.A.* **99 G9** 30 17N 98 25W
Johnson County ☆, *AR, U.S.A.* **63 C2** 35 28N 93 28W
Johnson County ☆, *GA, U.S.A.* **68 D4** 32 45N 82 40W
Johnson County ☆, *IL, U.S.A.* **71 F5** 37 30N 88 50W
Johnson County ☆, *IN, U.S.A.* **72 D4** 39 30N 86 5W
Johnson County ☆, *IA, U.S.A.* **73 D7** 41 40N 91 35W
Johnson County ☆, *KS, U.S.A.* **74 C9** 38 45N 94 45W
Johnson County ☆, *KY, U.S.A.* **97 C10** 37 50N 82 50W
Johnson County ☆, *MO, U.S.A.* **82 C3** 38 45N 93 45W
Johnson County ☆, *NE, U.S.A.* **84 D9** 40 20N 96 15W
Johnson County ☆, *TN, U.S.A.* **97 D11** 36 29N 81 48W
Johnson County ☆, *TX, U.S.A.* **99 E10** 32 21N 97 23W
Johnson County ☆, *WY, U.S.A.* **104 B6** 44 0N 106 35W
Johnson Draw →, *TX, U.S.A.* **98 G6** 30 8N 101 7W
Johnson L., *NE, U.S.A.* **84 D6** 40 42N 99 49W
Johnsonburg, *NJ, U.S.A.* **87 B2** 40 58N 74 53W
Johnsonburg, *PA, U.S.A.* **95 C4** 41 29N 78 41W
Johnsondale, *CA, U.S.A.* **65 H8** 35 58N 118 32W
Johnsons Crossing, *Yukon, Canada* **189 D6** 60 29N 133 18W
Johnson's Shut-Ins State Park ⌓, *MO, U.S.A.* **82 D6** 37 32N 90 51W
Johnsonville, *SC, U.S.A.* **90 E6** 33 49N 79 27W
Johnston, *IA, U.S.A.* **73 D5** 41 40N 93 42W
Johnston, *RI, U.S.A.* **78 C3** 41 50N 71 30W
Johnston, *SC, U.S.A.* **90 E4** 33 50N 81 48W
Johnston City, *IL, U.S.A.* **71 F5** 37 49N 88 56W
Johnston County ☆, *NC, U.S.A.* **90 C7** 35 30N 78 20W
Johnston County ☆, *OK, U.S.A.* **93 D7** 34 20N 96 40W
Johnston I., *Pac. Oc.* **105 C6** 17 10N 169 8W
Johnstone Str., *B.C., Canada* **186 E8** 50 28N 126 0W
Johnstown, *CO, U.S.A.* **66 B6** 40 20N 104 54W
Johnstown, *NY, U.S.A.* **89 B6** 43 0N 74 22W
Johnstown, *NE, U.S.A.* **84 B5** 42 34N 100 3W
Johnstown, *OH, U.S.A.* **92 C4** 40 9N 82 41W
Johnstown, *PA, U.S.A.* **95 D4** 40 20N 78 55W
Johnstown Flood Nat. Memorial ⌓, *PA, U.S.A.* **95 D4** 40 20N 78 46W
Joice, *IA, U.S.A.* **73 B5** 43 22N 93 27W
Joiner, *AR, U.S.A.* **63 C5** 35 31N 90 9W
Joir →, *Qué., Canada* **172 B9** 51 59N 60 12W
Jojutla, *Morelos, Mexico* **219 D8** 18 37N 99 11W
Jolalpán, *Puebla, Mexico* **221 F2** 18 19N 98 50W
Joliet, *IL, U.S.A.* **71 B5** 41 32N 88 5W
Joliet, *MT, U.S.A.* **83 E9** 45 29N 108 58W
Joliette, *Qué., Canada* **177 E9** 46 3N 73 24W
Jolley, *IA, U.S.A.* **73 C4** 42 29N 94 43W
Jonacatepec, *Morelos, Mexico* **219 D9** 18 41N 98 48W
Jones, *LA, U.S.A.* **75 B4** 32 58N 91 39W
Jones, *OK, U.S.A.* **93 C6** 35 34N 97 17W
Jones County ☆, *GA, U.S.A.* **68 D3** 33 0N 83 30W
Jones County ☆, *IA, U.S.A.* **73 C7** 42 5N 91 5W
Jones County ☆, *MS, U.S.A.* **81 E4** 31 36N 89 12W
Jones County ☆, *NC, U.S.A.* **90 C8** 35 0N 77 30W
Jones County ☆, *SD, U.S.A.* **91 F5** 44 0N 100 50W
Jones County ☆, *TX, U.S.A.* **99 E8** 32 45N 99 54W
Jones Falls →, *Baltimore, U.S.A.* **107 A1** 39 18N 76 37W
Jones Sound, *Nunavut, Canada* **190 B8** 76 0N 85 0W
Jones Springs, *WV, U.S.A.* **77 A2** 39 29N 78 6W
Jonesboro, *AR, U.S.A.* **63 C5** 35 50N 90 42W
Jonesboro, *GA, U.S.A.* **68 C2** 33 31N 84 22W
Jonesboro, *IL, U.S.A.* **71 F4** 37 27N 89 16W
Jonesboro, *IN, U.S.A.* **72 C5** 40 29N 85 38W
Jonesboro, *LA, U.S.A.* **75 B3** 32 15N 92 43W
Jonesboro, *TX, U.S.A.* **99 F10** 31 37N 97 53W
Jonesborough, *TN, U.S.A.* **97 D10** 36 18N 82 29W
Jonesburg, *MO, U.S.A.* **82 C5** 38 51N 91 18W
Jonesport, *ME, U.S.A.* **76 D6** 44 32N 67 37W
Jonestown, *MS, U.S.A.* **81 B3** 34 19N 90 27W
Jonestown, *PA, U.S.A.* **95 D6** 40 25N 76 29W
Jonesville, *LA, U.S.A.* **75 C4** 31 38N 91 49W
Jonesville, *MI, U.S.A.* **79 H7** 41 59N 84 40W
Jonesville, *NC, U.S.A.* **90 B5** 36 14N 80 51W
Jonesville, *SC, U.S.A.* **90 D4** 34 50N 81 41W
Jonesville, *VA, U.S.A.* **102 E1** 36 41N 83 7W
Jonquière, *Qué., Canada* **177 C11** 48 27N 71 14W
Jonuta, *Tabasco, Mexico* **222 A4** 18 5N 92 8W
Joplin, *MO, U.S.A.* **82 D2** 37 6N 94 31W
Joplin, *MT, U.S.A.* **83 B7** 48 34N 110 46W
Joppa, *IL, U.S.A.* **71 F5** 37 12N 88 51W
Joppatowne, *MD, U.S.A.* **77 A4** 39 27N 76 21W
Joquicingo, *México, Mexico* **219 C8** 19 4N 99 32W
Jordan, *MN, U.S.A.* **80 F5** 44 40N 93 38W
Jordan, *MT, U.S.A.* **83 C11** 47 19N 106 55W
Jordan, *NY, U.S.A.* **89 B4** 43 4N 76 29W
Jordan →, *UT, U.S.A.* **100 C3** 40 49N 112 8W
Jordan, L., *N.S., Canada* **173 J4** 44 5N 65 14W
Jordan, L., *AL, U.S.A.* **60 D4** 32 37N 86 15W
Jordan Falls, *N.S., Canada* **173 K4** 43 49N 65 14W
Jordan River State Park ⌓, *Salt Lake City, U.S.A.* **117 B2** 40 47N 111 46W
Jordan Valley, *OR, U.S.A.* **94 E8** 42 59N 117 3W
Jornado del Muerto, *NM, U.S.A.* **88 D4** 33 15N 106 50W
José Azueta, *Veracruz, Mexico* **221 F5** 18 4N 95 43W
José López Portillo, Presa, *Sinaloa, Mexico* **216 C4** 24 36N 106 45W
José María Morelos, *Jalisco, Mexico* **218 C2** 19 39N 105 9W
José María Morelos, *Quintana Roo, Mexico* **223 C5** 19 45N 88 47W
José María Morelos y Pavón, *Campeche, Mexico* **223 C3** 19 5N 90 44W
Josefa Ortiz de Dominguez, Presa, *Sinaloa, Mexico* **216 A2** 26 30N 108 42W
Joseph, *OR, U.S.A.* **94 B8** 45 21N 117 14W
Joseph, *UT, U.S.A.* **100 E3** 38 38N 112 13W
Joseph, L., *Nfld. & L., Canada* **175 C4** 52 45N 65 18W
Joseph, L., *Ont., Canada* **176 F3** 45 10N 79 44W
Joseph, Petit lac, *Nfld. & L., Canada* **172 A4** 52 36N 65 5W
Joseph City, *AZ, U.S.A.* **62 C5** 34 57N 110 20W
Joseph Cr. →, *WA, U.S.A.* **101 D8** 46 3N 117 1W
Josephine, L., *Minneapolis-St. Paul, U.S.A.* **113 A3** 45 2N 93 9W
Josephine County ☆, *OR, U.S.A.* **94 E2** 42 20N 123 40W
Joshua, *TX, U.S.A.* **99 E10** 32 28N 97 23W
Joshua Tree, *CA, U.S.A.* **65 J10** 34 8N 116 19W
Joshua Tree Nat. Park △, *CA, U.S.A.* **65 K11** 33 55N 116 0W
Jost Van Dyke I., *Br. Virgin Is.* **105 G18** 18 29N 64 47W
Jourdanton, *TX, U.S.A.* **99 J9** 28 55N 98 33W
Joussard, *Alta., Canada* **184 C5** 55 22N 115 50W
Joy, *IL, U.S.A.* **71 B3** 41 12N 90 53W
Joy B., *Qué., Canada* **175 A3** 61 30N 72 0W
Joyce, *WA, U.S.A.* **101 B2** 48 8N 123 44W
Juab County ☆, *UT, U.S.A.* **100 D3** 39 40N 113 0W
Juan Aldama, *Zacatecas, Mexico* **217 C7** 24 19N 103 21W
Juan de Fuca, Str of., *B.C., Canada* **186 G10** 48 15N 124 0W
Juan de la Cruz Borrego, *Coahuila, Mexico* **214 B1** 28 5N 103 18W
Juan Diaz Covarrubias, *Veracruz, Mexico* **221 F5** 18 9N 95 11W
Juan Escutia, *México, Mexico* **225 B3** 19 25N 99 4W
Juan González Romero, *México, Mexico* **225 A3** 19 30N 99 3W
Juan Ixcaquixtla, *Puebla, Mexico* **221 F3** 18 27N 97 49W
Juan José Ríos, *Sinaloa, Mexico* **216 B2** 25 45N 108 49W
Juan Mata Ortiz, *Chihuahua, Mexico* **213 C7** 30 8N 108 4W
Juan Perez Sd., *B.C., Canada* **186 C3** 52 32N 131 30W
Juan Ramírez, I., *Veracruz, Mexico* **220 C3** 21 45N 97 28W
Juan Rodríguez Clara, *Veracruz, Mexico* **221 G5** 17 59N 95 25W
Juana Díaz, *Puerto Rico* **105 G16** 18 3N 66 31W
Juanacatlán, *Jalisco, Mexico* **218 B4** 20 31N 103 10W
Juárez, *Chiapas, Mexico* **222 B3** 17 39N 93 10W
Juárez, *Chihuahua, Mexico* **213 C7** 30 19N 108 5W
Juárez, *Coahuila, Mexico* **214 C4** 27 37N 100 44W
Juárez, Presa, *Oaxaca, Mexico* **221 H5** 16 30N 95 28W
Juárez, Sa. de, *Baja Calif., Mexico* **210 B3** 32 0N 115 50W
Jubilee L., *Nfld. & L., Canada* **174 D5** 48 3N 55 11W
Juchipila, *Zacatecas, Mexico* **217 F7** 21 25N 103 7W
Juchipila →, *Mexico* **218 A4** 21 4N 103 22W
Juchique, *Veracruz, Mexico* **220 E4** 19 51N 96 41W
Juchitán de Zaragoza, *Oaxaca, Mexico* **221 H5** 16 26N 95 1W
Juchitlán, *Guerrero, Mexico* **219 F9** 16 37N 98 52W
Juchitlán, *Jalisco, Mexico* **218 B3** 20 4N 104 5W
Jud, *ND, U.S.A.* **91 D7** 46 32N 98 54W
Jude I., *Nfld. & L., Canada* **174 E6** 47 15N 54 49W
Judge Daly Promontory, *Nunavut, Canada* **190 A12** 81 15N 67 0W
Judique, *N.S., Canada* **173 H8** 45 52N 61 30W
Judith →, *MT, U.S.A.* **83 C8** 47 44N 109 39W
Judith, Pt., *RI, U.S.A.* **78 C3** 41 22N 71 29W
Judith Basin County ☆, *MT, U.S.A.* **83 D7** 46 55N 110 10W
Judith Gap, *MT, U.S.A.* **83 D8** 46 41N 109 45W
Judith Mts., *MT, U.S.A.* **83 C8** 47 15N 109 20W
Judsonia, *AR, U.S.A.* **63 C4** 35 16N 91 38W
Julesburg, *CO, U.S.A.* **66 B8** 40 59N 102 16W
Julesburg Res., *CO, U.S.A.* **66 B8** 40 56N 102 38W
Julian, *NE, U.S.A.* **84 D10** 40 31N 95 52W
Julian, L., *Qué., Canada* **175 C2** 54 25N 77 57W
Juliette, L., *GA, U.S.A.* **68 C3** 33 2N 83 50W
Julimes, *Chihuahua, Mexico* **213 E10** 28 25N 105 27W
Jump →, *WI, U.S.A.* **103 C2** 45 17N 91 5W
Jumpertown, *MS, U.S.A.* **81 B5** 34 43N 88 40W
Juncos, *Puerto Rico* **105 G17** 18 14N 65 55W
Junction, *TX, U.S.A.* **99 G8** 30 29N 99 46W
Junction, *UT, U.S.A.* **100 E3** 38 14N 112 13W
Junction City, *GA, U.S.A.* **68 D2** 32 36N 84 28W
Junction City, *KS, U.S.A.* **74 B7** 39 2N 96 50W
Junction City, *KY, U.S.A.* **97 C8** 37 35N 84 48W
Junction City, *LA, U.S.A.* **75 B3** 33 0N 92 43W
Junction City, *OR, U.S.A.* **94 C2** 44 13N 123 12W
Junction City, *WI, U.S.A.* **103 D4** 44 35N 89 46W
Junction Sheep Range Park ⌓, *B.C., Canada* **187 D12** 51 48N 122 25W
June Lake, *CA, U.S.A.* **64 F7** 37 47N 119 4W
Juneau, *AK, U.S.A.* **61 G14** 58 18N 134 25W
Juneau, *WI, U.S.A.* **103 E5** 43 24N 88 42W
Juneau ☆, *AK, U.S.A.* **61 G14** 58 25N 134 20W
Juneau County ☆, *WI, U.S.A.* **103 E3** 43 50N 90 10W
Juneau Park, *Milwaukee, U.S.A.* **112 B2** 42 3N 87 53W
Jungapeo, *Michoacan, Mexico* **219 C7** 19 27N 100 29W
Juniata, *NE, U.S.A.* **84 D7** 40 35N 98 30W
Juniata →, *PA, U.S.A.* **95 D5** 40 24N 77 1W
Juniata County ☆, *PA, U.S.A.* **95 D5** 40 45N 77 5W
Junior, *WV, U.S.A.* **102 C5** 38 59N 79 57W
Juniper, *N.B., Canada* **173 G2** 46 33N 67 13W
Juniper, *GA, U.S.A.* **68 D2** 32 32N 84 36W
Juniper Mts., *AZ, U.S.A.* **62 B3** 35 10N 113 0W
Juno, *TX, U.S.A.* **98 G6** 30 8N 101 7W
Juno Beach, *FL, U.S.A.* **67 E8** 26 52N 80 3W
Juntura, *OR, U.S.A.* **94 D7** 43 45N 118 5W
Jupiter, *FL, U.S.A.* **67 E8** 26 57N 80 6W
Jupiter →, *Qué., Canada* **172 D6** 49 29N 63 37W
Juquila Mixes, *Oaxaca, Mexico* **221 H5** 16 58N 95 55W
Juskatla, *B.C., Canada* **186 B2** 53 37N 132 18W
Justice, *Chicago, U.S.A.* **108 C2** 41 44N 87 49W
Justin, *TX, U.S.A.* **99 D10** 33 5N 97 18W
Juventino Rosas, *Guanajuato, Mexico* **219 B7** 20 39N 101 0W

K

Kaaawa, *HI, U.S.A.* **69 J14** 21 33N 157 51W
Ka'ala, *HI, U.S.A.* **69 J13** 21 31N 158 9W
Ka'alu'alu B., *HI, U.S.A.* **69 E6** 18 58N 155 37W
Kabah, *Yucatán, Mexico* **223 B4** 20 15N 89 41W
Kabetogama L., *MN, U.S.A.* **80 B5** 48 28N 93 1W
Kabinakagami →, *Ont., Canada* **181 B12** 50 25N 84 20W
Kabinakagami L., *Ont., Canada* **181 D12** 48 54N 84 25W
Kachess L., *WA, U.S.A.* **101 C4** 47 20N 121 15W
Kackley, *KS, U.S.A.* **74 B6** 39 42N 97 51W
Kadiak I. = Kodiak I., *AK, U.S.A.* **61 H9** 57 30N 152 45W
Kadoka, *SD, U.S.A.* **91 G4** 43 50N 101 31W
Kaegudeck L., *Nfld. & L., Canada* **174 D5** 48 7N 55 12W
Ka'ena, *HI, U.S.A.* **69 J13** 21 34N 158 14W
Ka'ena Pt., *HI, U.S.A.* **69 J13** 21 35N 158 17W
Kagamil I., *AK, U.S.A.* **61 K5** 53 0N 169 43W
Kagawong L., *Ont., Canada* **178 B4** 45 54N 82 15W
Kagianagami L., *Ont., Canada* **181 B9** 50 57N 87 50W
Kagiano L., *Ont., Canada* **181 C10** 49 16N 86 26W
Kahalu'u, *HI, U.S.A.* **69 K14** 21 27N 157 50W
Kahana, *HI, U.S.A.* **69 J14** 21 34N 157 53W
Kahana B., *HI, U.S.A.* **69 J14** 21 35N 157 50W
Kahana Valley State Park ⌓, *HI, U.S.A.* **69 J14** 21 32N 157 53W
Kahlotus, *WA, U.S.A.* **101 D7** 46 39N 118 33W
Kahnawake, *Montréal, Canada* **192 B2** 45 24N 73 40W
Kahoka, *MO, U.S.A.* **82 A5** 40 25N 91 44W
Kaho'olawe, *HI, U.S.A.* **69 C5** 20 33N 156 37W
Kahuku, *HI, U.S.A.* **69 J14** 21 41N 157 57W
Kahuku Pt., *HI, U.S.A.* **69 J14** 21 43N 157 59W
Kahului, *HI, U.S.A.* **69 C5** 20 54N 156 28W
Kahului ✈ (OGG), *HI, U.S.A.* **69 C5** 20 54N 156 26W
Kaibab, *AZ, U.S.A.* **62 A3** 36 54N 112 44W
Kaibab Indian Reservation, *AZ, U.S.A.* **62 A3** 36 55N 112 40W
Kaibab Nat. Forest, *AZ, U.S.A.* **62 A3** 36 35N 112 15W
Kaibab Plateau, *AZ, U.S.A.* **62 A3** 36 45N 112 15W
Kaibito, *AZ, U.S.A.* **62 A4** 36 35N 111 4W
Kaibito Plateau, *AZ, U.S.A.* **62 A4** 36 30N 111 15W
Kailua, *HI, U.S.A.* **69 D6** 19 39N 155 59W
Kailua, *HI, U.S.A.* **69 K14** 21 24N 157 44W
Kailua B., *HI, U.S.A.* **69 K14** 21 25N 157 40W
Kaiparowits Plateau, *UT, U.S.A.* **100 F4** 37 30N 111 35W
Kaipokok B., *Nfld. & L., Canada* **175 C6** 54 54N 59 47W
Kaiwi Channel, *HI, U.S.A.* **69 K14** 21 15N 157 30W
Kaiyuh Mts., *AK, U.S.A.* **61 D8** 64 30N 158 0W
Kakabeka Falls, *Ont., Canada* **180 D7** 48 24N 89 37W
Kakagi L., *Ont., Canada* **180 C3** 49 13N 93 52W
Kake, *AK, U.S.A.* **61 H14** 56 59N 133 57W
Kakhonak, *AK, U.S.A.* **61 G9** 59 26N 154 51W
Kakisa, *N.W.T., Canada* **189 D9** 60 56N 117 25W
Kakisa L., *N.W.T., Canada* **189 D9** 60 56N 117 43W
Kaktovik, *AK, U.S.A.* **61 A12** 70 8N 143 38W
Kakwa →, *Alta., Canada* **184 D2** 54 37N 118 28W
Kakwa Wildland Prov. Park ⌓, *Alta., Canada* **184 D1** 54 5N 119 55W
Kaladar, *Ont., Canada* **179 C9** 44 37N 77 5W
Kalae, *HI, U.S.A.* **69 E6** 18 55N 155 41W
Kalaheo, *HI, U.S.A.* **69 B2** 21 56N 159 32W
Kalama, *WA, U.S.A.* **101 D3** 46 1N 122 51W
Kalamazoo, *MI, U.S.A.* **79 G6** 42 17N 85 35W
Kalamazoo →, *MI, U.S.A.* **79 G5** 42 40N 86 10W
Kalamazoo County ☆, *MI, U.S.A.* **79 G6** 42 15N 85 30W
Kalaoa, *HI, U.S.A.* **69 D6** 19 43N 155 58W
Kalaupapa, *HI, U.S.A.* **69 B5** 21 12N 156 59W
Kalaupapa Nat. Historical Park ⌓, *U.S.A.* **69 B5** 21 10N 156 59W
Kalawao County ☆, *HI, U.S.A.* **69 B5** 21 11N 156 58W
Kaleden, *B.C., Canada* **187 F15** 49 24N 119 36W
Kaleva, *MI, U.S.A.* **79 E5** 44 22N 86 1W
Kalida, *OH, U.S.A.* **92 C2** 40 59N 84 12W
Kalihi, *HI, U.S.A.* **69 K14** 21 20N 157 53W
Kalihi Valley, *HI, U.S.A.* **69 K14** 21 20N 157 52W
Kalispel Indian Reservation, *WA, U.S.A.* **101 B8** 48 23N 117 17W
Kalispell, *MT, U.S.A.* **83 B3** 48 12N 114 19W
Kalkaska, *MI, U.S.A.* **79 E6** 44 44N 85 11W
Kalkaska County ☆, *MI, U.S.A.* **79 E6** 44 45N 85 5W
Kalohi Channel, *HI, U.S.A.* **69 C5** 21 0N 157 0W
Kaloko-Honokōhau Nat. Historical Park ⌓, *U.S.A.* **69 D5** 19 40N 156 1W
Kalona, *IA, U.S.A.* **73 D7** 41 29N 91 43W
Kaltag, *AK, U.S.A.* **61 D8** 64 20N 158 43W
Kalvesta, *KS, U.S.A.* **74 C3** 38 4N 100 18W
Kamakou, *HI, U.S.A.* **69 B5** 21 7N 156 52W
Kamalō, *HI, U.S.A.* **69 B5** 21 3N 156 52W
Kamananui →, *HI, U.S.A.* **69 J13** 21 38N 158 4W
Kamas, *UT, U.S.A.* **100 C4** 40 38N 111 17W
Kamela, *OR, U.S.A.* **94 B7** 45 26N 118 24W
Kamiah, *ID, U.S.A.* **70 C2** 46 14N 116 2W
Kamilukuak L., *Nunavut, Canada* **191 E5** 62 22N 101 40W
Kaminak L., *Nunavut, Canada* **191 E7** 62 10N 95 0W
Kaminuriak L., *Nunavut, Canada* **191 E6** 62 57N 95 46W
Kamishak Bay, *AK, U.S.A.* **61 G9** 59 15N 153 45W
Kamloops, *B.C., Canada* **187 E14** 50 40N 120 20W
Kamloops L., *B.C., Canada* **187 E14** 50 45N 120 40W
Kamo'oloa, *HI, U.S.A.* **69 J13** 21 34N 158 7W
Kamouraska, *Qué., Canada* **177 D13** 47 34N 69 52W
Kampsville, *IL, U.S.A.* **71 D3** 39 18N 90 37W
Kamrar, *IA, U.S.A.* **73 C5** 42 24N 93 44W
Kamsack, *Sask., Canada* **183 D10** 51 34N 101 54W
Kamuela, *HI, U.S.A.* **69 C6** 20 1N 155 41W
Kanaaupscow, *Qué., Canada* **175 C2** 53 39N 77 9W
Kanaaupscow →, *Qué., Canada* **175 C2** 54 2N 76 30W
Kanab, *UT, U.S.A.* **100 F3** 37 3N 112 32W
Kanab Cr. →, *AZ, U.S.A.* **62 A3** 36 24N 112 38W
Kanabec County ☆, *MN, U.S.A.* **80 E5** 45 55N 93 20W
Kanaga I., *AK, U.S.A.* **61 L3** 51 45N 177 22W
Kanairiktok →, *Nfld. & L., Canada* **175 B5** 55 2N 60 18W
Kanakanak, *AK, U.S.A.* **61 G8** 59 0N 158 32W
Kanarraville, *UT, U.S.A.* **100 F2** 37 32N 113 11W
Kanasín, *Yucatán, Mexico* **223 B4** 20 56N 89 34W
Kanata, *Ont., Canada* **179 B11** 45 20N 75 59W
Kanawha, *IA, U.S.A.* **73 C5** 42 56N 93 48W
Kanawha →, *WV, U.S.A.* **102 C2** 38 50N 82 9W
Kanawha County ☆, *WV, U.S.A.* **102 C3** 38 21N 81 38W
Kandiyohi County ☆, *MN, U.S.A.* **80 E4** 45 10N 95 0W
Kane, *IL, U.S.A.* **71 D3** 39 11N 90 21W
Kane, *PA, U.S.A.* **95 C4** 41 40N 78 49W
Kane, *WY, U.S.A.* **104 B4** 44 51N 108 12W
Kane Basin, *Greenland* **190 B12** 79 1N 70 0W
Kane County ☆, *IL, U.S.A.* **71 B5** 41 50N 88 25W
Kane County ☆, *UT, U.S.A.* **100 F4** 37 15N 112 0W
Kaneilio Pt., *HI, U.S.A.* **69 K13** 21 27N 158 12W
Kāne'ohe, *HI, U.S.A.* **69 K14** 21 25N 157 48W
Kāne'ohe B., *HI, U.S.A.* **69 K14** 21 30N 157 50W
Kaneohe Marine Corps Air Station, *HI, U.S.A.* **69 K14** 21 27N 157 46W
Kangersuatsiaq, *Greenland* **190 C14** 72 23N 55 32W
Kangiqliniq = Rankin Inlet, *Nunavut, Canada* **191 E7** 62 30N 93 0W
Kangiqsualujjuaq, *Qué., Canada* **175 B4** 58 30N 65 59W
Kangiqsujuaq, *Qué., Canada* **175 A3** 61 30N 72 0W
Kangiqtugaapik = Clyde River, *Nunavut, Canada* **190 C12** 70 30N 68 30W
Kangirsuk, *Qué., Canada* **175 A4** 60 0N 70 0W
Kaniapiskau = Caniapiscau →, *Qué., Canada* **175 B4** 56 40N 69 30W
Kaniapiskau, L. = Caniapiscau, L. de, *Qué., Canada* **175 C4** 54 10N 69 55W
Kaniksu Nat. Forest, *ID, U.S.A.* **70 A2** 48 50N 116 30W
Kankakee, *IL, U.S.A.* **71 B6** 41 7N 87 52W
Kankakee →, *IL, U.S.A.* **71 B5** 41 23N 88 15W
Kankakee County ☆, *IL, U.S.A.* **71 B6** 41 10N 87 50W
Kannapolis, *NC, U.S.A.* **90 C5** 35 30N 80 37W
Kanopolis, *KS, U.S.A.* **74 C5** 38 43N 98 9W
Kanopolis Lake, *KS, U.S.A.* **74 C6** 38 37N 97 58W
Kanorado, *KS, U.S.A.* **74 B1** 39 20N 102 2W
Kanosh, *UT, U.S.A.* **100 E3** 38 48N 112 26W
Kansas, *IL, U.S.A.* **71 D6** 39 33N 87 56W
Kansas, *OK, U.S.A.* **93 B9** 36 12N 94 48W
Kansas □, *U.S.A.* **74 C5** 38 30N 99 0W
Kansas →, *KS, U.S.A.* **74 B9** 39 7N 94 37W
Kansas City, *KS, U.S.A.* **74 B9** 39 7N 94 38W
Kansas City, *MO, U.S.A.* **82 B2** 39 6N 94 35W
Kansas City International ✈ (MCI), *MO, U.S.A.* **82 B2** 39 18N 94 43W
Kantishna, *AK, U.S.A.* **61 E10** 63 31N 150 57W
Kantishna →, *AK, U.S.A.* **61 D10** 64 45N 149 58W
Kantunil, *Yucatán, Mexico* **223 B4** 20 48N 89 2W
Kantunilkin, *Quintana Roo, Mexico* **223 A6** 21 7N 87 28W
Kanuti Nat. Wildlife Refuge ⌓, *AK, U.S.A.* **61 C10** 66 25N 151 50W
Kanxoc, *Yucatán, Mexico* **223 B5** 20 6N 88 4W
Kapaa, *HI, U.S.A.* **69 A2** 22 5N 159 19W
Kapahulu, *HI, U.S.A.* **69 K14** 21 16N 157 49W
Kapapa I., *HI, U.S.A.* **69 K14** 21 29N 157 48W
Kapikotongwa →, *Ont., Canada* **181 B10** 50 39N 86 43W
Kaplan, *LA, U.S.A.* **75 E3** 30 0N 92 17W
Kapoho, *HI, U.S.A.* **69 D7** 19 30N 154 50W
Kaposvar Cr. →, *Sask., Canada* **183 E10** 50 31N 101 55W
Kapowsin, *WA, U.S.A.* **101 D3** 46 59N 122 13W
Kapuskasing, *Ont., Canada* **181 C14** 49 25N 82 30W
Kapuskasing →, *Ont., Canada* **181 C14** 49 49N 82 0W
Karlsruhe, *ND, U.S.A.* **91 B5** 48 6N 100 37W
Karlstad, *MN, U.S.A.* **80 B2** 48 35N 96 31W
Karluk, *AK, U.S.A.* **61 H9** 57 34N 154 28W
Karnack, *TX, U.S.A.* **99 E13** 32 40N 94 10W
Karnak, *IL, U.S.A.* **71 F5** 37 18N 88 58W
Karnes City, *TX, U.S.A.* **99 J10** 28 53N 97 54W
Karnes County ☆, *TX, U.S.A.* **99 J10** 28 49N 97 51W
Kasaan, *AK, U.S.A.* **61 J14** 55 32N 132 24W
Kasba L., *Nunavut, Canada* **189 D12** 60 20N 102 10W
Kashabowie, *Ont., Canada* **180 D6** 48 40N 90 26W
Kasilof, *AK, U.S.A.* **61 F10** 60 23N 151 18W
Kaskaskia →, *IL, U.S.A.* **71 F4** 37 58N 89 57W
Kaskattama →, *Man., Canada* **191 F7** 57 3N 90 4W
Kaslo, *B.C., Canada* **187 F18** 49 55N 116 55W
Kasson, *MN, U.S.A.* **80 F6** 44 2N 92 45W
Katahdin, Mt., *ME, U.S.A.* **76 C5** 45 54N 68 56W
Katalla, *AK, U.S.A.* **61 F11** 60 12N 144 31W
Kathleen, *FL, U.S.A.* **67 C6** 28 7N 82 2W
Kathryn, *ND, U.S.A.* **91 D8** 46 41N 97 58W
Katimik L., *Man., Canada* **183 C12** 52 53N 99 21W
Katmai Nat. Park and Preserve △, *AK, U.S.A.* **61 G9** 58 20N 155 0W
Katy, *TX, U.S.A.* **99 H12** 29 47N 95 49W
Ka'ū Desert, *HI, U.S.A.* **69 D6** 19 21N 155 19W
Kaua'i, *HI, U.S.A.* **69 A2** 22 3N 159 30W
Kaua'i Channel, *HI, U.S.A.* **69 B3** 21 45N 158 50W
Kauai Island Lihue Municipal ✈ (LIH), *HI, U.S.A.* **69 B2** 21 58N 159 20W
Kaufman, *TX, U.S.A.* **99 E11** 32 35N 96 19W
Kaufman County ☆, *TX, U.S.A.* **99 E11** 32 35N 96 20W
Kauhola Pt., *HI, U.S.A.* **69 C6** 20 15N 155 47W
Kaukauna, *WI, U.S.A.* **103 D5** 44 17N 88 17W
Kaukonahua →, *HI, U.S.A.* **69 J13** 21 35N 158 7W
Ka'ula I., *HI, U.S.A.* **69 B1** 21 40N 160 33W
Kaulakahi Channel, *HI, U.S.A.* **69 B2** 22 0N 159 55W
Kaumalapau, *HI, U.S.A.* **69 C5** 20 47N 156 59W
Kaunā Pt., *HI, U.S.A.* **69 D6** 19 2N 155 53W
Kaunakakai, *HI, U.S.A.* **69 B4** 21 6N 157 1W
Kaupō, *HI, U.S.A.* **69 C5** 20 38N 156 8W
Kaw City, *OK, U.S.A.* **93 B7** 36 46N 96 50W
Kaw L., *OK, U.S.A.* **93 B7** 36 50N 96 55W
Kawagama L., *Ont., Canada* **176 F4** 45 18N 78 45W
Kawaihae B., *HI, U.S.A.* **69 C6** 20 0N 155 50W
Kawaihoa Pt., *HI, U.S.A.* **69 B1** 21 47N 160 12W
Kawaikini, *HI, U.S.A.* **69 A2** 22 5N 159 29W
Kawailoa, *HI, U.S.A.* **69 J13** 21 36N 158 3W
Kawailoa Beach, *HI, U.S.A.* **69 J13** 21 37N 158 5W
Kawailoa Forest Reserve, *HI, U.S.A.* **69 J14** 21 37N 158 0W
Kawawachikamach, *Qué., Canada* **175 C4** 54 48N 66 50W
Kaweah, L., *CA, U.S.A.* **65 G8** 36 28N 118 52W
Kaweenakumik L., *Man., Canada* **183 C12** 52 50N 99 30W
Kawela, *HI, U.S.A.* **69 J13** 21 42N 158 1W
Kawick Ra., *NV, U.S.A.* **85 E4** 38 0N 116 25W
Kawkawlin, *MI, U.S.A.* **79 F8** 43 39N 83 57W
Kay County ☆, *OK, U.S.A.* **93 B6** 36 50N 97 5W
Kayak I., *AK, U.S.A.* **61 G11** 59 56N 144 23W
Kaycee, *WY, U.S.A.* **104 C6** 43 43N 106 38W
Kayenta, *AZ, U.S.A.* **62 A5** 36 44N 110 15W
Kaylor, *SD, U.S.A.* **91 G8** 43 11N 97 50W
Kaysville, *UT, U.S.A.* **100 B4** 41 2N 111 56W
Kazan →, *Nunavut, Canada* **191 E6** 64 2N 95 29W
Ke'au, *HI, U.S.A.* **69 D6** 19 37N 155 2W
Keachie, *LA, U.S.A.* **75 B2** 32 11N 93 54W
Keahi Pt., *HI, U.S.A.* **69 K14** 21 19N 157 59W
Keahole Pt., *HI, U.S.A.* **69 D5** 19 44N 156 4W
Kealaikahiki Channel, *HI, U.S.A.* **69 C5** 20 35N 156 50W
Kealakekua, *HI, U.S.A.* **69 D6** 19 31N 155 55W
Kealia, *HI, U.S.A.* **69 D6** 19 24N 155 53W
Keams Canyon, *AZ, U.S.A.* **62 B5** 35 49N 110 12W
Keansburg, *NJ, U.S.A.* **87 B2** 40 27N 74 8W
Kearney, *Ont., Canada* **178 B7** 45 33N 79 13W
Kearney, *MO, U.S.A.* **82 B2** 39 22N 94 22W
Kearney, *NE, U.S.A.* **84 D6** 40 42N 99 5W
Kearney County ☆, *NE, U.S.A.* **84 D7** 40 30N 99 0W
Kearneysville, *WV, U.S.A.* **77 A3** 39 23N 77 53W
Kearns, *Salt Lake City, U.S.A.* **117 C1** 40 39N 111 59W
Kearny, *AZ, U.S.A.* **62 D5** 33 3N 110 55W
Kearny, *NJ, U.S.A.* **87 B2** 40 46N 74 8W
Kearny County ☆, *KS, U.S.A.* **74 C2** 38 0N 101 15W
Kearsarge, Mt., *NH, U.S.A.* **86 C3** 43 22N 71 50W
Keating, *OR, U.S.A.* **94 C8** 44 53N 117 35W
Keats, *KS, U.S.A.* **74 B7** 39 14N 96 43W
Keawakapu, *HI, U.S.A.* **69 C5** 20 43N 156 27W
Kechika →, *B.C., Canada* **189 E7** 59 41N 127 12W
Keddie, *CA, U.S.A.* **64 C6** 40 1N 120 58W
Kedgwick, *N.B., Canada* **173 F2** 47 40N 67 20W
Keedysville, *MD, U.S.A.* **77 A3** 39 29N 77 40W
Keefers, *B.C., Canada* **187 E13** 50 1N 121 32W
Keefeton, *OK, U.S.A.* **93 C8** 35 36N 95 21W
Ke'ehi Lagoon, *HI, U.S.A.* **69 K14** 21 20N 157 54W
Keele →, *N.W.T., Canada* **189 D8** 64 25N 124 48W
Keele Pk., *Yukon, Canada* **189 D6** 63 26N 130 19W
Keene, *Ont., Canada* **179 C8** 44 15N 78 10W
Keene, *ND, U.S.A.* **91 C3** 47 56N 102 56W
Keene, *NH, U.S.A.* **86 D2** 42 56N 72 17W
Keene, *TX, U.S.A.* **99 E10** 32 24N 97 20W
Keenesburg, *CO, U.S.A.* **66 B6** 40 7N 104 31W
Keensburg, *IL, U.S.A.* **71 E6** 38 21N 87 52W
Keeseville, *NY, U.S.A.* **86 B1** 44 30N 73 39W
Keewatin, *MN, U.S.A.* **80 C5** 47 24N 93 5W
Keezhik L., *Ont., Canada* **180 A8** 51 45N 88 30W
Kegaska, *Qué., Canada* **175 C5** 50 9N 61 18W
Kégaska, L., *Qué., Canada* **172 C8** 50 20N 61 25W
Keglo B., *Qué., Canada* **175 B4** 58 40N 66 0W
Kehena, *HI, U.S.A.* **69 D7** 19 23N 154 55W
Keikiwaha Pt., *HI, U.S.A.* **69 D6** 19 31N 155 58W
Keiser, *AR, U.S.A.* **63 C5** 35 40N 90 6W
Keith Arm, *N.W.T., Canada* **189 D8** 64 20N 122 15W
Keith County ☆, *NE, U.S.A.* **84 C4** 41 15N 101 40W
Keith Sebelius L., *KS, U.S.A.* **74 B4** 39 48N 99 56W
Keithsburg, *IL, U.S.A.* **71 B3** 41 6N 90 56W
Keizer, *OR, U.S.A.* **94 C2** 44 57N 123 1W
Kejimkujik Nat. Park △, *N.S., Canada* **173 J4** 44 25N 65 25W
Kekaha, *HI, U.S.A.* **69 B2** 21 58N 159 43W
Kelberg, *Dallas-Fort Worth, U.S.A.* **109 B6** 32 42N 96 36W
Kell, *IL, U.S.A.* **71 E5** 38 30N 88 54W
Keller, *Dallas-Fort Worth, U.S.A.* **109 A2** 32 56N 97 15W
Keller, *GA, U.S.A.* **68 E5** 31 50N 81 15W
Keller, *WA, U.S.A.* **101 B7** 48 5N 118 41W
Keller L., *N.W.T., Canada* **189 D8** 63 57N 121 35W
Kellerton, *IA, U.S.A.* **73 E4** 40 43N 94 3W
Kellerville, *TX, U.S.A.* **98 B7** 35 22N 100 30W
Kellet →, *Nunavut, Canada* **190 D7** 68 20N 96 6W
Kellett, C., *N.W.T., Canada* **188 B7** 72 0N 126 0W

Kellett Str., *N.W.T., Canada* **188 A9** 75 45N 117 30W
Kelley, *IA, U.S.A.* **73 D5** 41 57N 93 40W
Kelleys I., *OH, U.S.A.* **92 B4** 41 36N 82 42W
Kelligrews, *Nfld. & L., Canada* **174 E7** 47 30N 53 1W
Kelliher, *Sask., Canada* **182 D8** 51 16N 103 44W
Kelliher, *MN, U.S.A.* **80 C4** 47 57N 94 27W
Kellogg, *ID, U.S.A.* **70 B2** 47 32N 116 7W
Kellogg, *IA, U.S.A.* **73 D6** 41 43N 92 54W
Kellogg, *MN, U.S.A.* **80 F7** 44 18N 91 59W
Kellyville, *OK, U.S.A.* **93 C7** 35 57N 96 13W
Kelowna, *B.C., Canada* **187 F15** 49 50N 119 25W
Kelsey Bay, *B.C., Canada* **186 E9** 50 25N 126 0W
Kelseyville, *CA, U.S.A.* **64 E4** 38 59N 122 50W
Kelso, *AR, U.S.A.* **63 E4** 33 48N 91 16W
Kelso, *WA, U.S.A.* **101 D3** 46 9N 122 54W
Kelvin I., *Ont., Canada* **180 C8** 49 51N 88 40W
Kelvington, *Sask., Canada* **182 C8** 52 10N 103 30W
Kelwood, *Man., Canada* **183 E12** 50 37N 99 28W
Kemah, *TX, U.S.A.* **99 H12** 29 33N 95 1W
Kemano, *B.C., Canada* **186 B7** 53 35N 128 0W
Kemblesville, *PA, U.S.A.* **77 A5** 39 45N 75 50W
Kemmerer, *WY, U.S.A.* **104 E2** 41 48N 110 32W
Kemp, *OK, U.S.A.* **93 E7** 33 46N 96 21W
Kemp, *TX, U.S.A.* **99 E11** 32 26N 96 14W
Kemp, L., *TX, U.S.A.* **99 D8** 33 46N 99 9W
Kemper County ☆, *MS, U.S.A.* **81 D5** 32 46N 88 39W
Kempt, L., *Qué., Canada* **177 D8** 47 25N 74 22W
Kempton, *IL, U.S.A.* **71 C5** 40 56N 88 14W
Kempton, *IN, U.S.A.* **72 C4** 40 17N 86 14W
Kemptown, *N.S., Canada* **173 H6** 45 28N 63 5W
Kemptown, *MD, U.S.A.* **77 A3** 39 20N 77 13W
Kemptville, *Ont., Canada* **179 B11** 45 0N 75 38W
Kenab Plateau, *AZ, U.S.A.* **62 A3** 36 40N 113 0W
Kenai, *AK, U.S.A.* **61 F10** 60 33N 151 16W
Kenai Fjords Nat. Park △, *AK, U.S.A.* **61 G10** 59 40N 149 50W
Kenai Mts., *AK, U.S.A.* **61 G10** 60 0N 150 0W
Kenai Nat. Wildlife Refuge ⌂, *AK, U.S.A.* **61 F10** 60 20N 150 30W
Kenai Peninsula ☆, *AK, U.S.A.* **61 F10** 60 25N 151 15W
Kenansville, *FL, U.S.A.* **67 D8** 27 53N 80 59W
Kenansville, *NC, U.S.A.* **90 D8** 34 58N 77 58W
Kenaston, *Sask., Canada* **182 D5** 51 30N 106 17W
Kenbridge, *VA, U.S.A.* **102 E6** 36 58N 78 8W
Kendall, *FL, U.S.A.* **67 F8** 25 40N 80 19W
Kendall, *KS, U.S.A.* **74 D2** 37 56N 101 33W
Kendall, *WI, U.S.A.* **103 E3** 43 48N 90 21W
Kendall, C., *Nunavut, Canada* **191 E8** 63 36N 87 12W
Kendall County ☆, *IL, U.S.A.* **71 B5** 41 35N 88 25W
Kendall County ☆, *TX, U.S.A.* **99 H9** 29 57N 98 48W
Kendall Green, *Boston, U.S.A.* **106 A2** 42 22N 71 16W
Kendall Park, *NJ, U.S.A.* **87 B2** 40 25N 74 34W
Kendallville, *IN, U.S.A.* **72 B5** 41 27N 85 16W
Kendleton, *TX, U.S.A.* **99 H12** 29 26N 96 0W
Kendrick, *FL, U.S.A.* **67 B6** 29 15N 82 10W
Kendrick, *ID, U.S.A.* **70 C2** 46 37N 116 39W
Kendrick, *OK, U.S.A.* **93 C7** 35 47N 96 46W
Kenedy, *TX, U.S.A.* **99 J10** 28 49N 97 51W
Kenedy County ☆, *TX, U.S.A.* **98 K10** 27 0N 97 40W
Kenefic, *OK, U.S.A.* **93 D7** 34 9N 96 22W
Kenefick, *TX, U.S.A.* **99 G13** 30 7N 94 52W
Kenesaw, *NE, U.S.A.* **84 D7** 40 37N 98 39W
Kenilworth, *NJ, U.S.A.* **114 B1** 40 40N 74 17W
Kenly, *NC, U.S.A.* **90 C7** 35 36N 78 7W
Kenmare, *ND, U.S.A.* **91 B3** 48 41N 102 5W
Kenmore, *NY, U.S.A.* **89 C2** 42 58N 78 52W
Kenmore, *Seattle, U.S.A.* **118 B4** 47 45N 122 14W
Kenna, *NM, U.S.A.* **88 D7** 33 51N 103 46W
Kenna, *WV, U.S.A.* **102 C3** 38 41N 81 40W
Kennaday Peak, *WY, U.S.A.* **104 E6** 41 27N 106 31W
Kennard, *NE, U.S.A.* **84 C9** 41 28N 96 12W
Kennard, *TX, U.S.A.* **99 F12** 31 22N 95 11W
Kennebago L., *ME, U.S.A.* **86 A4** 45 6N 70 44W
Kennebec, *SD, U.S.A.* **91 G6** 43 54N 99 52W
Kennebec →, *ME, U.S.A.* **76 E4** 43 45N 69 46W
Kennebec County ☆, *ME, U.S.A.* **76 D4** 44 20N 69 50W
Kennebecasis →, *N.B., Canada* **173 H3** 45 19N 66 4W
Kennebunk, *ME, U.S.A.* **76 E3** 43 23N 70 33W
Kennebunkport, *ME, U.S.A.* **76 E3** 43 21N 70 28W
Kennedale, *Dallas-Fort Worth, U.S.A.* **109 C2** 32 38N 97 13W
Kennedy, *Sask., Canada* **183 E9** 50 1N 102 21W
Kennedy, *AL, U.S.A.* **60 C3** 33 35N 87 59W
Kennedy, *MN, U.S.A.* **80 B2** 48 39N 96 54W
Kennedy, C. = Canaveral, C., *FL, U.S.A.* **67 C8** 28 27N 80 32W
Kennedy, Mt., *B.C., Canada* **186 E9** 50 50N 125 33W
Kennedy Entrance, *AK, U.S.A.* **61 G10** 59 1N 152 0W
Kennedy I., *B.C., Canada* **186 A4** 54 3N 130 11W
Kennedy L., *B.C., Canada* **186 F9** 49 3N 125 32W
Kennedy Space Center, *U.S.A.* **67 C8** 28 40N 80 42W
Kennedyville, *MD, U.S.A.* **77 A5** 39 18N 75 58W
Kenner, *LA, U.S.A.* **75 E5** 29 59N 90 14W
Kennesaw, *GA, U.S.A.* **68 B2** 34 1N 84 37W
Kennetcook, *Qué., Canada* **173 H6** 45 11N 63 44W
Kenneth City, *Tampa, U.S.A.* **119 C2** 27 48N 82 43W
Kennett, *MO, U.S.A.* **82 E6** 36 14N 90 3W
Kennett Square, *PA, U.S.A.* **77 A5** 39 51N 75 43W
Kennewick, *WA, U.S.A.* **101 D6** 46 12N 119 7W
Kenney, *IL, U.S.A.* **71 C4** 40 6N 89 5W
Keno, *OR, U.S.A.* **94 E4** 42 8N 121 56W
Keno Hill, *Yukon, Canada* **189 D5** 63 57N 135 18W
Kenogami →, *Ont., Canada* **181 A12** 51 6N 84 28W
Kénogami, L., *Qué., Canada* **177 C11** 48 20N 71 23W
Kenogami Lake, *Qué., Canada* **176 C2** 48 6N 80 12W
Kenora, *Ont., Canada* **180 C2** 49 47N 94 29W
Kenosha, *WI, U.S.A.* **103 F6** 42 35N 87 49W
Kenosha County ☆, *WI, U.S.A.* **103 F6** 42 35N 87 50W
Kenova, *WV, U.S.A.* **102 C2** 38 24N 82 35W
Kensal, *ND, U.S.A.* **91 C7** 47 18N 98 44W
Kensett, *AR, U.S.A.* **63 C4** 35 14N 91 40W
Kensett, *IA, U.S.A.* **73 B5** 43 21N 93 13W
Kensington, *P.E.I., Canada* **173 G6** 46 28N 63 34W
Kensington, *CT, U.S.A.* **78 C2** 41 38N 72 46W
Kensington, *KS, U.S.A.* **74 B4** 39 46N 99 2W
Kensington, *MD, U.S.A.* **77 A3** 39 2N 77 5W
Kensington, *MN, U.S.A.* **80 E3** 45 47N 95 42W
Kensington, *NY, U.S.A.* **114 C3** 40 38N 73 57W
Kent, *CT, U.S.A.* **78 C1** 41 44N 73 29W
Kent, *IA, U.S.A.* **73 E4** 40 57N 94 28W
Kent, *MN, U.S.A.* **80 D2** 46 26N 96 41W
Kent, *OH, U.S.A.* **92 B5** 41 9N 81 22W
Kent, *OR, U.S.A.* **94 B5** 45 12N 120 42W
Kent, *TX, U.S.A.* **98 F3** 31 4N 104 13W
Kent, *WA, U.S.A.* **101 C3** 47 22N 122 14W
Kent City, *MI, U.S.A.* **79 F6** 43 12N 85 45W
Kent County ☆, *DE, U.S.A.* **77 A5** 39 10N 75 30W
Kent County ☆, *MD, U.S.A.* **77 A5** 39 15N 76 0W
Kent County ☆, *MI, U.S.A.* **79 F6** 43 0N 85 35W
Kent County ☆, *RI, U.S.A.* **78 C3** 41 35N 71 40W
Kent County ☆, *TX, U.S.A.* **98 D7** 33 10N 100 45W
Kent I., *MD, U.S.A.* **77 B4** 38 57N 76 18W
Kent Junction, *N.B., Canada* **173 G4** 46 35N 65 20W
Kent Pen., *Nunavut, Canada* **190 D4** 68 30N 107 0W
Kent Village, *MD, U.S.A.* **119 B4** 38 55N 76 53W
Kentland, *IN, U.S.A.* **72 C3** 40 46N 87 27W
Kentmore Park, *MD, U.S.A.* **77 A5** 39 22N 75 58W
Kenton, *DE, U.S.A.* **77 A5** 39 14N 75 40W
Kenton, *MI, U.S.A.* **79 C3** 46 28N 88 54W
Kenton, *OH, U.S.A.* **92 C3** 40 39N 83 37W
Kenton, *OK, U.S.A.* **93 B1** 36 54N 102 58W
Kenton, *TN, U.S.A.* **96 D3** 36 12N 89 1W
Kenton County ☆, *KY, U.S.A.* **97 B8** 38 55N 84 32W
Kenton Vale, *KY, U.S.A.* **107 B1** 39 3N 84 31W
Kentucky □, *U.S.A.* **97 C8** 37 0N 84 0W
Kentucky →, *KY, U.S.A.* **97 B7** 38 41N 85 11W
Kentucky L., *KY, U.S.A.* **96 C4** 37 1N 88 16W
Kentville, *N.S., Canada* **173 H5** 45 6N 64 29W
Kentwood, *LA, U.S.A.* **75 D5** 30 56N 90 31W
Kentwood, *MI, U.S.A.* **79 G6** 42 52N 85 39W
Kenville, *Man., Canada* **183 D10** 52 0N 101 20W
Kenwood, *Baltimore, U.S.A.* **107 B2** 39 20N 76 30W
Kenwood, *OH, U.S.A.* **107 A2** 39 12N 84 22W
Kenyon, *MN, U.S.A.* **80 F6** 44 16N 92 59W
Keo, *AR, U.S.A.* **63 D3** 34 36N 92 1W
Keokuk, *IA, U.S.A.* **73 E7** 40 24N 91 24W
Keokuk County ☆, *IA, U.S.A.* **73 D6** 41 20N 92 10W
Keosauqua, *IA, U.S.A.* **73 E7** 40 44N 91 58W
Keota, *CO, U.S.A.* **66 B6** 40 42N 104 5W
Keota, *IA, U.S.A.* **73 D7** 41 22N 91 57W
Keota, *OK, U.S.A.* **93 C9** 35 15N 94 55W
Kepuhi Pt., *HI, U.S.A.* **69 K13** 21 29N 158 14W
Kerby, *OR, U.S.A.* **94 E2** 42 12N 123 39W
Keremeos, *B.C., Canada* **187 F15** 49 13N 119 50W
Kerens, *TX, U.S.A.* **99 E11** 32 8N 96 14W
Kerkhoven, *MN, U.S.A.* **80 E3** 45 12N 95 19W
Kerman, *CA, U.S.A.* **65 G6** 36 43N 120 4W
Kermit, *TX, U.S.A.* **98 F4** 31 52N 103 6W
Kermit, *WV, U.S.A.* **102 D2** 37 50N 82 24W
Kern →, *CA, U.S.A.* **65 H7** 35 16N 119 18W
Kern County ☆, *CA, U.S.A.* **65 H8** 35 20N 118 30W
Kern Park, *Milwaukee, U.S.A.* **112 B2** 43 5N 87 53W
Kernersville, *NC, U.S.A.* **90 B5** 36 7N 80 5W
Kernville, *CA, U.S.A.* **65 H8** 35 45N 118 26W
Kerr County ☆, *TX, U.S.A.* **99 G8** 30 0N 99 21W
Kerrick, *MN, U.S.A.* **80 D6** 46 20N 92 35W
Kerrick, *TX, U.S.A.* **98 A5** 36 30N 102 15W
Kerrobert, *Sask., Canada* **182 D2** 51 56N 109 8W
Kerrville, *TX, U.S.A.* **99 G8** 30 3N 99 8W
Kersey, *CO, U.S.A.* **66 B6** 40 23N 104 34W
Kershaw, *SC, U.S.A.* **90 D5** 34 33N 80 35W
Kershaw County ☆, *SC, U.S.A.* **90 D5** 34 20N 80 40W
Kersley, *B.C., Canada* **187 C12** 52 49N 122 25W
Keshena, *WI, U.S.A.* **103 D5** 44 53N 88 39W
Keswick = Georgina, *Ont., Canada* **178 C7** 44 15N 79 28W
Ketchikan, *AK, U.S.A.* **61 J15** 55 21N 131 39W
Ketchikan Gateway ☆, *AK, U.S.A.* **61 J15** 55 30N 131 25W
Ketchum, *ID, U.S.A.* **70 F4** 43 41N 114 22W
Ketchum, *OK, U.S.A.* **93 B8** 36 32N 95 1W
Kettering, *MD, U.S.A.* **77 B4** 38 53N 76 49W
Kettering, *OH, U.S.A.* **92 D2** 39 41N 84 10W
Kettle →, *N. Amer.* **187 G16** 48 41N 118 7W
Kettle →, *MN, U.S.A.* **80 E6** 45 52N 92 46W
Kettle, Île, *Qué., Canada* **192 A2** 45 28N 75 36W
Kettle Cr. →, *PA, U.S.A.* **95 C5** 41 18N 77 51W
Kettle Falls, *WA, U.S.A.* **101 B7** 48 37N 118 3W
Kettle Pt., *Ont., Canada* **178 D4** 43 13N 82 1W
Kettle River, *MN, U.S.A.* **80 D6** 46 29N 92 53W
Kettle River Range, *WA, U.S.A.* **101 B7** 48 30N 118 40W
Kettleman City, *CA, U.S.A.* **65 G7** 36 1N 119 58W
Keuka L., *NY, U.S.A.* **89 C3** 42 30N 77 9W
Kevil, *KY, U.S.A.* **96 C4** 37 5N 88 53W
Kevin, *MT, U.S.A.* **83 B6** 48 45N 111 58W
Kewanee, *IL, U.S.A.* **71 B4** 41 14N 89 56W
Kewanna, *IN, U.S.A.* **72 B4** 41 1N 86 25W
Kewaskum, *WI, U.S.A.* **103 E5** 43 31N 88 14W
Kewaunee, *WI, U.S.A.* **103 D6** 44 27N 87 31W
Kewaunee County ☆, *WI, U.S.A.* **103 D6** 44 30N 87 40W
Keweenaw B., *MI, U.S.A.* **79 C3** 47 0N 88 15W
Keweenaw County ☆, *MI, U.S.A.* **79 B3** 47 20N 88 5W
Keweenaw Nat. Historical Park ⌂, *MI, U.S.A.* **79 B3** 47 9N 88 33W
Keweenaw Pen., *MI, U.S.A.* **79 B3** 47 15N 88 15W
Keweenaw Pt., *MI, U.S.A.* **79 B4** 47 25N 87 43W
Key, *TX, U.S.A.* **98 E6** 32 44N 101 48W
Key Biscayne, *Miami, U.S.A.* **112 D3** 25 41N 80 9W
Key Colony Beach, *FL, U.S.A.* **67 G8** 24 45N 80 57W
Key Harbour, *Ont., Canada* **178 B6** 45 50N 80 45W
Key Largo, *FL, U.S.A.* **67 F8** 25 5N 80 27W
Key West, *FL, U.S.A.* **67 G7** 24 33N 81 48W
Key West Nat. Wildlife Refuge ⌂, *FL, U.S.A.* **67 G6** 24 33N 82 2W
Keya Paha →, *NE, U.S.A.* **84 B6** 42 54N 99 0W
Keya Paha County ☆, *NE, U.S.A.* **84 B6** 42 50N 99 40W
Keyapaha, *SD, U.S.A.* **91 G5** 43 7N 100 8W
Keyes, *OK, U.S.A.* **93 B1** 36 49N 102 15W
Keyesport, *IL, U.S.A.* **71 E4** 38 45N 89 17W
Keyhole Reservoir, *WY, U.S.A.* **104 B8** 44 21N 104 51W
Keymar, *MD, U.S.A.* **77 A3** 39 38N 77 14W
Keyport, *NJ, U.S.A.* **87 C3** 40 26N 74 12W
Keyport, *Seattle, U.S.A.* **118 B2** 47 42N 122 37W
Keyser, *WV, U.S.A.* **77 A2** 39 26N 78 59W
Keystone, *IA, U.S.A.* **73 D6** 42 0N 92 12W
Keystone, *NE, U.S.A.* **84 C4** 41 13N 101 35W
Keystone, *SD, U.S.A.* **91 G2** 43 54N 103 25W
Keystone Heights, *FL, U.S.A.* **67 B6** 29 47N 82 2W
Keystone L., *OK, U.S.A.* **93 B7** 36 15N 96 25W
Keystone Peak, *AZ, U.S.A.* **62 F4** 31 53N 111 13W
Keysville, *GA, U.S.A.* **68 C4** 33 14N 82 14W
Keysville, *VA, U.S.A.* **102 D6** 37 2N 78 29W
Keytesville, *MO, U.S.A.* **82 B4** 39 26N 92 56W
Kezar Falls, *ME, U.S.A.* **76 E3** 43 48N 70 53W
Khedive, *Sask., Canada* **182 F7** 49 37N 104 31W
Kiamichi →, *OK, U.S.A.* **93 E8** 33 58N 95 14W
Kiamichi Mt., *OK, U.S.A.* **93 D8** 34 38N 94 35W
Kiamichi Mts., *OK, U.S.A.* **93 D9** 34 37N 95 0W
Kiana, *AK, U.S.A.* **61 C7** 66 58N 160 26W
Kianuko Park ⌂, *B.C., Canada* **185 J4** 49 26N 116 28W
Kiawah Island, *SC, U.S.A.* **90 F5** 32 36N 80 5W
Kickapoo →, *WI, U.S.A.* **103 E3** 43 5N 90 53W
Kickapoo, L., *TX, U.S.A.* **99 D9** 33 40N 98 47W
Kickapoo Indian Reservation, *KS, U.S.A.* **74 B8** 39 40N 95 50W
Kicking Horse Pass, *B.C., Canada* **187 D18** 51 28N 116 16W
Kidder, *MO, U.S.A.* **82 B2** 39 47N 94 6W
Kidder County ☆, *ND, U.S.A.* **91 D6** 47 0N 99 55W
Kief, *ND, U.S.A.* **91 C5** 47 51N 100 31W
Kiefer, *OK, U.S.A.* **93 C7** 35 57N 96 4W
Kiel, *WI, U.S.A.* **103 E5** 43 55N 88 2W
Kiester, *MN, U.S.A.* **80 G5** 43 32N 93 43W
Kiglapait Mts., *Nfld. & L., Canada* **175 B5** 57 6N 61 22W
Kīhei, *HI, U.S.A.* **69 C5** 20 47N 156 28W
Kīholo B., *HI, U.S.A.* **69 D6** 19 50N 155 55W
Kihuic, *Yucatán, Mexico* **223 B4** 20 4N 89 32W
Kijik, *AK, U.S.A.* **61 F9** 60 20N 154 20W
Kikerk L., *Nunavut, Canada* **188 C10** 67 18N 113 12W
Kikino, *Alta., Canada* **184 D8** 54 27N 112 8W
Kikkertoksoak I., *N.W.T., Canada* **175 B4** 58 50N 65 50W
Kila, *MT, U.S.A.* **83 B3** 48 7N 114 27W
Kilauea, *HI, U.S.A.* **69 A2** 22 13N 159 25W
Kīlauea Caldera, *HI, U.S.A.* **69 D6** 19 25N 155 17W
Kilbourne, *IL, U.S.A.* **71 C3** 40 9N 90 1W
Kilbourne, *LA, U.S.A.* **75 B4** 33 0N 91 20W
Kilbride, *Nfld. & L., Canada* **174 E8** 47 32N 52 45W
Kilbuck Mts., *AK, U.S.A.* **61 F8** 60 36N 159 53W
Kildala Arm, *B.C., Canada* **186 B6** 53 50N 128 29W
Kildare, *GA, U.S.A.* **68 D5** 32 32N 81 27W
Kildare, *OK, U.S.A.* **93 B6** 36 48N 97 3W
Kilgore, *ID, U.S.A.* **70 E7** 44 24N 111 54W
Kilgore, *NE, U.S.A.* **84 B5** 42 56N 100 57W
Kilgore, *TX, U.S.A.* **99 E13** 32 23N 94 53W
Kilian I., *Nunavut, Canada* **190 C4** 73 35N 107 53W
Kilkenny, *MN, U.S.A.* **80 F5** 44 19N 93 34W
Kill Devil Hills, *NC, U.S.A.* **90 B10** 36 1N 75 39W
Kill Van Kull →, *New York, U.S.A.* **114 C2** 40 39N 74 5W
Killala L., *Ont., Canada* **181 C10** 49 5N 86 32W
Killaloe, *Ont., Canada* **176 F5** 45 33N 77 25W
Killaly, *Sask., Canada* **182 E9** 50 45N 102 50W
Killam, *Alta., Canada* **185 F9** 52 47N 111 51W
Killarney, *Man., Canada* **183 F12** 49 10N 99 40W
Killarney, *Ont., Canada* **178 B5** 45 55N 81 30W
Killarney, *Vancouver, Canada* **193 B2** 49 13N 123 2W
Killarney Prov. Park ⌂, *Ont., Canada* **178 A5** 46 2N 81 35W
Killbuck, *OH, U.S.A.* **92 C5** 40 30N 81 59W
Killbuck Cr. →, *OH, U.S.A.* **92 C5** 40 30N 81 59W
Killdeer, *Sask., Canada* **182 F5** 49 6N 106 22W
Killdeer, *ND, U.S.A.* **91 C3** 47 22N 102 45W
Killeen, *TX, U.S.A.* **99 F10** 31 7N 97 44W
Killen, *AL, U.S.A.* **60 B3** 34 52N 87 32W
Killingly, *CT, U.S.A.* **78 C3** 41 50N 71 55W
Killington Pk., *VT, U.S.A.* **86 C2** 43 36N 72 49W
Killingworth, *CT, U.S.A.* **78 C2** 41 21N 72 30W
Killiniq I., *Nfld. & L., Canada* **175 A5** 60 24N 64 37W
Kilmar, *Qué., Canada* **176 F8** 45 46N 74 37W
Kilmarnock, *VA, U.S.A.* **77 C4** 37 43N 76 23W
Kilmichael, *MS, U.S.A.* **81 C4** 33 27N 89 34W
Kilometro Noventa y Uno, *Chihuahua, Mexico* **213 E10** 28 7N 105 36W
Kim, *CO, U.S.A.* **66 E7** 37 15N 103 21W
Kimball, *NE, U.S.A.* **84 C2** 41 14N 103 40W
Kimball, *SD, U.S.A.* **91 G7** 43 45N 98 57W
Kimball, *WV, U.S.A.* **102 D3** 37 26N 81 30W
Kimball County ☆, *NE, U.S.A.* **84 C2** 41 15N 103 40W
Kimballton, *IA, U.S.A.* **73 D3** 41 38N 95 4W
Kimberley, *B.C., Canada* **185 J5** 49 40N 115 59W
Kimberling City, *MO, U.S.A.* **82 E3** 36 38N 93 25W
Kimberly, *ID, U.S.A.* **70 G4** 42 32N 114 22W
Kimberly, *OR, U.S.A.* **94 C6** 44 46N 119 39W
Kimble County ☆, *TX, U.S.A.* **99 G8** 30 29N 99 46W
Kimbolton, *OH, U.S.A.* **92 C5** 40 9N 81 34W
Kimbrough, *AL, U.S.A.* **60 D3** 32 2N 87 34W
Kimiwan L., *Alta., Canada* **184 C4** 55 45N 116 55W
Kimmirut, *Nunavut, Canada* **191 E12** 62 50N 69 50W
Kimsquit, *B.C., Canada* **186 C8** 52 45N 126 57W
Kinard, *FL, U.S.A.* **67 A3** 30 16N 85 15W
Kinbasket L., *B.C., Canada* **187 C16** 52 0N 118 10W
Kincaid, *Sask., Canada* **182 F4** 49 40N 107 0W
Kincaid, *IL, U.S.A.* **71 D4** 39 35N 89 25W
Kincaid, *KS, U.S.A.* **74 C8** 38 5N 95 9W
Kincardine, *Ont., Canada* **178 C5** 44 10N 81 40W
Kinchafoonee Cr. →, *GA, U.S.A.* **68 E2** 31 38N 84 10W
Kinchil, *Yucatán, Mexico* **223 B4** 20 55N 89 57W
Kincolith, *B.C., Canada* **189 F7** 55 0N 129 57W
Kinde, *MI, U.S.A.* **79 F9** 43 56N 83 0W
Kinder, *LA, U.S.A.* **75 D3** 30 29N 92 51W
Kinderhook, *NY, U.S.A.* **78 B1** 42 24N 73 42W
Kindersley, *Sask., Canada* **182 D2** 51 30N 109 10W
Kindred, *ND, U.S.A.* **91 D8** 46 39N 97 1W
King, *NC, U.S.A.* **90 B5** 36 17N 80 22W
King and Queen County ☆, *VA, U.S.A.* **102 D8** 37 40N 76 53W
King and Queen Court House, *VA, U.S.A.* **77 C4** 37 40N 76 53W
King Christian I., *Nunavut, Canada* **190 B5** 77 48N 101 40W
King City, *CA, U.S.A.* **65 G5** 36 13N 121 8W
King City, *MO, U.S.A.* **82 A2** 40 3N 94 31W
King County ☆, *TX, U.S.A.* **98 D7** 33 37N 100 19W
King County ☆, *WA, U.S.A.* **101 C4** 47 25N 121 40W
King County International ✕, *Seattle, U.S.A.* **118 C4** 47 31N 122 18W
King Cove, *AK, U.S.A.* **61 J7** 55 3N 162 19W
King George, *VA, U.S.A.* **77 B3** 38 16N 77 11W
King George County ☆, *VA, U.S.A.* **102 C7** 38 16N 77 11W
King George Is., *Nunavut, Canada* **175 B1** 57 20N 80 30W
King I., *B.C., Canada* **186 C7** 52 10N 127 40W
King of Prussia, *PA, U.S.A.* **87 B1** 40 5N 75 23W
King Range Nat. Conservation Area ⌂, *CA, U.S.A.* **64 C2** 40 10N 124 8W
King Salmon, *AK, U.S.A.* **61 G8** 58 42N 156 40W
King William, *VA, U.S.A.* **102 D7** 37 41N 77 1W
King William County ☆, *VA, U.S.A.* **102 D7** 37 41N 77 1W
King William I., *Nunavut, Canada* **190 D6** 69 10N 97 25W
Kingait = Cape Dorset, *Nunavut, Canada* **191 E10** 64 14N 76 32W
Kingaok = Bathurst Inlet, *Nunavut, Canada* **188 C11** 66 50N 108 1W
Kingcome Inlet, *B.C., Canada* **186 E8** 50 56N 126 29W
Kingfield, *ME, U.S.A.* **76 D3** 44 58N 70 9W
Kingfisher, *OK, U.S.A.* **93 C6** 35 52N 97 56W
Kingfisher County ☆, *OK, U.S.A.* **93 C6** 36 0N 98 0W
Kingman, *AZ, U.S.A.* **62 B1** 35 12N 114 4W
Kingman, *KS, U.S.A.* **74 D5** 37 39N 98 7W
Kingman County ☆, *KS, U.S.A.* **74 D5** 37 30N 98 5W
Kings →, *AR, U.S.A.* **63 B2** 36 30N 93 35W
Kings →, *CA, U.S.A.* **65 G7** 36 3N 119 50W
Kings →, *NV, U.S.A.* **85 A2** 41 31N 118 8W
Kings Canyon Nat. Park △, *CA, U.S.A.* **65 G8** 36 50N 118 40W
Kings County ☆, *CA, U.S.A.* **65 G7** 36 0N 119 50W
Kings County ☆, *NY, U.S.A.* **89 E7** 40 37N 73 55W
Kings Mountain, *NC, U.S.A.* **90 C4** 35 15N 81 20W
Kings Park, *VA, U.S.A.* **119 C2** 38 48N 77 17W
Kings Park West, *VA, U.S.A.* **119 C2** 38 48N 77 18W
Kings Peak, *UT, U.S.A.* **100 C5** 40 46N 110 23W
King's Point, *Nfld. & L., Canada* **174 C4** 49 35N 56 11W
King's Point, *NY, U.S.A.* **114 B4** 40 49N 73 44W
Kings Valley, *OR, U.S.A.* **94 C2** 44 42N 123 26W
Kingsburg, *CA, U.S.A.* **65 G7** 36 31N 119 33W
Kingsbury, *NY, U.S.A.* **86 C1** 43 22N 73 32W
Kingsbury County ☆, *SD, U.S.A.* **91 F8** 44 23N 97 33W
Kingsdown, *KS, U.S.A.* **74 D4** 37 32N 99 46W
Kingsey Falls, *Qué., Canada* **177 F10** 45 51N 72 4W
Kingsford, *MI, U.S.A.* **79 D3** 45 48N 88 4W
Kingsford Heights, *IN, U.S.A.* **72 B4** 41 29N 86 42W
Kingsgate, *B.C., Canada* **185 J4** 49 1N 116 11W
Kingsland, *AR, U.S.A.* **63 E3** 33 52N 92 18W
Kingsland, *GA, U.S.A.* **68 F5** 30 48N 81 41W
Kingsland, *TX, U.S.A.* **99 G9** 30 40N 98 26W
Kingsley, *IA, U.S.A.* **73 C3** 42 35N 95 58W
Kingsley, *MI, U.S.A.* **79 E6** 44 35N 85 32W
Kingsmere L., *Sask., Canada* **182 A5** 54 6N 106 27W
Kingsmill, *TX, U.S.A.* **98 B6** 35 29N 101 4W
Kingsport, *TN, U.S.A.* **97 D10** 36 33N 82 33W
Kingston, *N.S., Canada* **173 J5** 44 59N 64 57W
Kingston, *Ont., Canada* **179 C10** 44 14N 76 30W
Kingston, *AR, U.S.A.* **63 B2** 36 3N 93 31W
Kingston, *GA, U.S.A.* **68 B2** 34 14N 84 57W
Kingston, *KY, U.S.A.* **97 C8** 37 39N 84 15W
Kingston, *MA, U.S.A.* **78 B4** 42 0N 70 43W
Kingston, *MD, U.S.A.* **77 B5** 38 1N 75 46W
Kingston, *MI, U.S.A.* **79 F8** 43 25N 83 11W
Kingston, *MN, U.S.A.* **80 E4** 45 12N 94 19W
Kingston, *MO, U.S.A.* **82 B2** 39 39N 94 2W
Kingston, *NH, U.S.A.* **86 D3** 42 56N 71 3W
Kingston, *NM, U.S.A.* **88 E3** 32 55N 107 42W
Kingston, *NY, U.S.A.* **89 D7** 41 56N 73 59W
Kingston, *OH, U.S.A.* **92 D4** 39 28N 82 55W
Kingston, *OK, U.S.A.* **93 E7** 33 59N 96 45W
Kingston, *PA, U.S.A.* **95 C7** 41 16N 75 54W
Kingston, *Seattle, U.S.A.* **118 B3** 47 47N 122 29W
Kingston, *TN, U.S.A.* **97 E8** 35 52N 84 31W
Kingston, *UT, U.S.A.* **100 E3** 38 13N 112 11W
Kingston, *WI, U.S.A.* **103 E4** 43 42N 89 8W
Kingston Pk., *CA, U.S.A.* **65 H11** 35 44N 115 55W
Kingston Springs, *TN, U.S.A.* **96 D5** 36 6N 87 7W
Kingstree, *SC, U.S.A.* **90 E6** 33 40N 79 50W
Kingsville, *Ont., Canada* **178 E4** 42 2N 82 45W
Kingsville, *MD, U.S.A.* **77 A4** 39 27N 76 25W
Kingsville, *MO, U.S.A.* **82 C2** 38 45N 94 4W
Kingsville, *TX, U.S.A.* **98 K10** 27 31N 97 52W
Kingwood, *TX, U.S.A.* **99 G12** 30 2N 95 16W
Kingwood, *WV, U.S.A.* **102 B5** 39 28N 79 41W
Kinistino, *Sask., Canada* **182 C6** 52 57N 105 2W
Kinkaid L., *IL, U.S.A.* **71 F4** 37 40N 89 25W
Kinkora, *P.E.I., Canada* **173 G6** 46 19N 63 36W
Kinloch, *MO, U.S.A.* **117 A2** 38 44N 90 19W
Kinmount, *Ont., Canada* **179 C8** 44 48N 78 45W
Kinmundy, *IL, U.S.A.* **71 E5** 38 46N 88 51W
Kinnear, *WY, U.S.A.* **104 C4** 43 9N 108 41W
Kinnelon, *NJ, U.S.A.* **87 B2** 40 58N 74 22W
Kinney, *MN, U.S.A.* **80 C6** 47 31N 92 44W
Kinney County ☆, *TX, U.S.A.* **98 H7** 29 19N 100 25W
Kino Nuevo, *Sonora, Mexico* **212 E3** 28 52N 112 3W
Kinoje Lakes, *Ont., Canada* **181 A15** 51 35N 81 48W
Kinsale, *VA, U.S.A.* **77 B4** 38 2N 76 35W
Kinsley, *KS, U.S.A.* **74 D4** 37 55N 99 25W
Kinston, *AL, U.S.A.* **60 E4** 31 13N 86 10W
Kinston, *NC, U.S.A.* **90 C8** 35 16N 77 35W
Kinta, *OK, U.S.A.* **93 C8** 35 8N 95 14W
Kinuso, *Alta., Canada* **184 C5** 55 20N 115 25W
Kinzua, *OR, U.S.A.* **94 C5** 44 59N 120 3W
Kiosk, *Ont., Canada* **179 A8** 46 6N 78 53W
Kiowa, *CO, U.S.A.* **66 C6** 39 21N 104 28W
Kiowa, *KS, U.S.A.* **74 D5** 37 1N 98 29W
Kiowa, *OK, U.S.A.* **93 D8** 34 43N 95 54W
Kiowa County ☆, *CO, U.S.A.* **66 D8** 38 25N 102 50W
Kiowa County ☆, *KS, U.S.A.* **74 D4** 37 30N 99 15W
Kiowa County ☆, *OK, U.S.A.* **93 D5** 35 0N 99 0W
Kiowa Cr. →, *CO, U.S.A.* **66 B6** 40 20N 104 5W
Kiowa Cr. →, *OK, U.S.A.* **93 B4** 36 49N 99 55W
Kipapa →, *HI, U.S.A.* **69 K13** 21 24N 158 1W
Kipawa, *Qué., Canada* **176 E4** 46 47N 78 59W
Kipawa, L., *Qué., Canada* **176 E4** 46 50N 79 0W
Kipling, *Sask., Canada* **182 E9** 50 6N 102 38W
Kipnuk, *AK, U.S.A.* **61 G6** 59 56N 164 3W
Kipp, *KS, U.S.A.* **74 C6** 38 47N 97 27W
Kippens, *Nfld. & L., Canada* **174 D2** 48 33N 58 38W
Kiptopeke, *VA, U.S.A.* **102 D9** 37 8N 75 58W
Kirby, *TX, U.S.A.* **99 H9** 29 27N 98 23W
Kirby, *WV, U.S.A.* **77 A2** 39 11N 78 44W
Kirby, *WY, U.S.A.* **104 C4** 43 48N 108 11W
Kirbyville, *TX, U.S.A.* **99 G14** 30 40N 93 54W
Kirk, *CO, U.S.A.* **66 C8** 39 37N 102 36W
Kirk, *OR, U.S.A.* **94 E4** 42 45N 121 50W
Kirkfield, *Ont., Canada* **179 C8** 44 34N 78 59W
Kirkland, *Qué., Canada* **192 B1** 45 26N 73 52W
Kirkland, *AZ, U.S.A.* **62 C3** 34 25N 112 43W
Kirkland, *IL, U.S.A.* **71 A5** 42 6N 88 51W
Kirkland, *TX, U.S.A.* **99 C7** 34 23N 100 4W
Kirkland, *WA, U.S.A.* **101 C3** 47 40N 122 12W
Kirkland Junction, *AZ, U.S.A.* **62 C3** 34 22N 112 40W
Kirklin, *IN, U.S.A.* **72 C4** 40 12N 86 22W
Kirkman, *IA, U.S.A.* **73 D3** 41 44N 95 16W
Kirkmansville, *KY, U.S.A.* **96 C5** 37 1N 87 15W
Kirksey, *KY, U.S.A.* **96 D4** 36 42N 88 24W
Kirksville, *MO, U.S.A.* **82 A4** 40 12N 92 35W
Kirkwood, *DE, U.S.A.* **77 A5** 39 34N 75 42W
Kirkwood, *IL, U.S.A.* **71 C3** 40 52N 90 45W
Kirkwood, *MO, U.S.A.* **82 C6** 38 35N 90 24W
Kirkwood, *PA, U.S.A.* **77 A4** 39 51N 76 5W
Kiron, *IA, U.S.A.* **73 C3** 42 12N 95 20W
Kirtland, *NM, U.S.A.* **88 A2** 36 44N 108 21W
Kirwin, *KS, U.S.A.* **74 B4** 39 40N 99 7W
Kirwin Res., *KS, U.S.A.* **74 B4** 39 40N 99 8W
Kiryas Joel, *NY, U.S.A.* **87 A2** 41 21N 74 10W
Kisatchie, *LA, U.S.A.* **75 C2** 31 25N 93 10W
Kisatchie Nat. Forest, *LA, U.S.A.* **75 C3** 31 45N 92 30W
Kisbey, *Sask., Canada* **182 F9** 49 39N 102 40W
Kiska I., *AK, U.S.A.* ..... **61 L2** 51 59N 177 30 E
Kiskitto L., *Man., Canada* **183 A13** 54 16N 98 30W
Kiskittogisu L., *Man., Canada* **183 A13** 54 13N 98 20W
Kismet, *KS, U.S.A.* **74 D3** 37 12N 100 42W
Kissena Park, *NY, U.S.A.* **114 B4** 40 44N 73 48W
Kissimmee, *FL, U.S.A.* **67 C7** 28 18N 81 24W
Kissimmee →, *FL, U.S.A.* **67 D8** 27 9N 80 52W
Kissimmee, L., *FL, U.S.A.* **67 D7** 27 55N 81 17W
Kit Carson, *CO, U.S.A.* **66 D8** 38 46N 102 48W
Kit Carson County ☆, *CO, U.S.A.* **66 C8** 39 15N 102 30W
Kitamaat Village, *B.C., Canada* **186 B6** 53 59N 128 39W
Kitchener, *Ont., Canada* **178 D6** 43 27N 80 29W
Kitimat, *B.C., Canada* **186 A6** 54 3N 128 38W
Kitimat Arm, *B.C., Canada* **186 B6** 53 55N 128 42W
Kitimat Ranges, *B.C., Canada* **186 B5** 54 0N 129 15W
Kitkatla, *B.C., Canada* **186 B4** 53 47N 130 25W
Kitsap County ☆, *WA, U.S.A.* **101 C3** 47 30N 122 45W
Kitscoty, *Alta., Canada* **184 E10** 53 20N 110 20W
Kittanning, *PA, U.S.A.* **95 D3** 40 49N 79 31W
Kittatinny Mt., *NJ, U.S.A.* **87 A2** 41 19N 74 39W
Kittery, *ME, U.S.A.* **76 E3** 43 5N 70 45W
Kittery, *NH, U.S.A.* **86 C4** 43 5N 70 45W
Kittitas, *WA, U.S.A.* **101 D5** 46 59N 120 25W
Kittitas County ☆, *WA, U.S.A.* **101 C5** 47 10N 120 30W
Kitts Hummock, *DE, U.S.A.* **77 A5** 39 8N 75 25W
Kittson County ☆, *MN, U.S.A.* **80 B2** 48 50N 96 50W
Kitzmiller, *MD, U.S.A.* **77 A1** 39 23N 79 10W
Kivalina, *AK, U.S.A.* **61 C6** 67 44N 164 33W
Klamath, *CA, U.S.A.* **64 B2** 41 32N 124 2W
Klamath →, *CA, U.S.A.* **64 B2** 41 33N 124 5W
Klamath County ☆, *OR, U.S.A.* **94 E4** 42 40N 121 40W
Klamath Falls, *OR, U.S.A.* **94 E4** 42 13N 121 46W
Klamath Marsh, *OR, U.S.A.* **94 E4** 43 0N 121 40W
Klamath Mts., *CA, U.S.A.* **64 B3** 41 50N 123 20W
Klamath Nat. Forest, *CA, U.S.A.* **64 B3** 41 30N 123 20W
Klamath River, *CA, U.S.A.* **64 B3** 41 52N 123 12W
Klawock, *AK, U.S.A.* **61 J14** 55 33N 133 6W
Kleberg County ☆, *TX, U.S.A.* **98 K10** 27 31N 97 52W
Kleczkowski, L., *Qué., Canada* **172 C6** 50 48N 63 27W
Kleena Kleene, *B.C., Canada* **186 D10** 52 0N 124 59W
Klein, *MT, U.S.A.* **83 D9** 46 24N 108 33W
Kleindale, *B.C., Canada* **186 F11** 49 38N 123 58W
Klemme, *IA, U.S.A.* **73 B5** 43 1N 93 36W
Kletzsch Park, *Milwaukee, U.S.A.* **112 B2** 43 7N 87 55W
Klickitat, *WA, U.S.A.* **101 E4** 45 49N 121 9W
Klickitat →, *WA, U.S.A.* **101 E4** 45 42N 121 17W
Klickitat County ☆, *WA, U.S.A.* **101 E5** 45 55N 120 30W
Klinaklini →, *B.C., Canada* **186 D9** 51 21N 125 40W
Klondike →, *Yukon, Canada* **189 D5** 64 3N 139 26W
Klondike Goldrush Nat. Historical Park ⌂, *U.S.A.* **61 G14** 59 27N 135 19W
Klotz, L., *Qué., Canada* **175 A3** 60 32N 73 40W
Kluane L., *Yukon, Canada* **189 D5** 61 15N 138 40W

Kluane Nat. Park △, Yukon, Canada 189 D5 60 45N 139 30W
Klukwan, AK, U.S.A. 61 G14 59 24N 135 54W
Kluskoil Lake Park ⌓, B.C., Canada 186 B11 53 13N 123 54W
Knapp, WI, U.S.A. 103 D1 44 57N 92 5W
Knee L., Man., Canada 191 F7 55 3N 94 45W
Kneeland, CA, U.S.A. 64 C3 40 45N 123 59W
Knewstubb L., B.C., Canada 186 B10 53 33N 124 55W
Knierim, IA, U.S.A. 73 C4 42 27N 94 27W
Knife →, ND, U.S.A. 91 C4 47 17N 101 20W
Knife River, MN, U.S.A. 80 D7 46 57N 91 47W
Knife River Indian Village Nat. Historic Site ⌓, ND, U.S.A. 91 C4 47 20N 101 23W
Knight I., AK, U.S.A. 61 F11 60 21N 147 45W
Knight Inlet, B.C., Canada 186 E9 50 45N 125 40W
Knightdale, NC, U.S.A. 90 C7 35 47N 78 29W
Knights Landing, CA, U.S.A. 64 E5 38 48N 121 43W
Knightstown, IN, U.S.A. 72 D5 39 48N 85 32W
Knob Lake = Kawawachikamach, Qué., Canada 175 C4 54 48N 66 50W
Knob Lick, KY, U.S.A. 97 C7 37 5N 85 42W
Knob Lick, MO, U.S.A. 82 D6 37 41N 90 22W
Knob Noster, MO, U.S.A. 82 C3 38 46N 93 33W
Knobel, AR, U.S.A. 63 B5 36 19N 90 36W
Knott County ☆, KY, U.S.A. 97 C10 37 20N 83 0W
Knowland State Arboretum and Park ⌓, San Francisco, U.S.A. 118 B4 37 45N 122 7W
Knowles, OK, U.S.A. 93 B3 36 53N 100 12W
Knowlton, Qué., Canada 177 F10 45 13N 72 31W
Knox, IN, U.S.A. 72 B4 41 18N 86 37W
Knox, ND, U.S.A. 91 B6 48 20N 99 41W
Knox, PA, U.S.A. 95 C3 41 14N 79 32W
Knox, C., B.C., Canada 186 A1 54 11N 133 5W
Knox City, MO, U.S.A. 82 A4 40 9N 92 1W
Knox City, TX, U.S.A. 99 D8 33 25N 99 49W
Knox County ☆, IL, U.S.A. 71 C3 40 55N 90 10W
Knox County ☆, IN, U.S.A. 72 E3 38 40N 87 25W
Knox County ☆, KY, U.S.A. 97 D9 36 55N 83 50W
Knox County ☆, ME, U.S.A. 76 D4 44 5N 69 5W
Knox County ☆, MO, U.S.A. 82 A4 40 10N 92 10W
Knox County ☆, NE, U.S.A. 84 B8 42 40N 97 50W
Knox County ☆, OH, U.S.A. 92 C4 40 23N 82 29W
Knox County ☆, TN, U.S.A. 97 D9 36 0N 84 0W
Knox County ☆, TX, U.S.A. 99 D8 33 35N 99 48W
Knoxville, GA, U.S.A. 68 D3 32 47N 83 59W
Knoxville, IL, U.S.A. 71 C3 40 55N 90 17W
Knoxville, IA, U.S.A. 73 D5 41 19N 93 6W
Knoxville, PA, U.S.A. 95 C5 41 57N 77 27W
Knoxville, TN, U.S.A. 97 E9 35 58N 83 55W
Knoxville McGhee Tyson ✕ (TYS), TN, U.S.A. 97 E9 35 49N 83 59W
Koartac = Quaqtaq, Qué., Canada 175 A4 60 55N 69 40W
Kobuk, AK, U.S.A. 61 C8 66 55N 156 52W
Kobuk →, AK, U.S.A. 61 C7 66 54N 160 38W
Kobuk Valley Nat. Park △, AK, U.S.A. 61 C7 67 0N 160 0W
Koch I., Nunavut, Canada 190 D10 69 38N 78 20W
Kodiak, AK, U.S.A. 61 H9 57 47N 152 24W
Kodiak I., AK, U.S.A. 61 H9 57 30N 152 45W
Kodiak Island ☆, AK, U.S.A. 61 H9 57 20N 153 20W
Koehn Dry L., CA, U.S.A. 65 H9 35 20N 117 53W
Kofa Mts., AZ, U.S.A. 62 D2 33 15N 113 40W
Kofa Nat. Wildlife Refuge ⌓, AZ, U.S.A. 62 D2 33 15N 113 50W
Kogaluc →, Nfld. & L., Canada 175 B5 56 12N 61 44W
Kogaluc, B., Qué., Canada 175 B2 59 10N 78 40W
Kohala Forest Reserve, HI, U.S.A. 69 C6 20 9N 155 4W
Kohala Mts., HI, U.S.A. 69 C6 20 5N 155 45W
Kohler, WI, U.S.A. 103 E6 43 44N 87 47W
Kohlman Lake, Minneapolis-St. Paul, U.S.A. 113 A3 45 1N 93 3W
Kohunlich, Quintana Roo, Mexico 223 D5 18 22N 88 47W
Kokanee Glacier Park ⌓, B.C., Canada 187 F17 49 47N 117 10W
Kōke'e State Park ⌓, HI, U.S.A. 69 A2 22 6N 159 40W
Koko Head, HI, U.S.A. 69 K14 21 16N 157 43W
Kokomo, IN, U.S.A. 72 C4 40 29N 86 8W
Kokomo, MS, U.S.A. 81 E3 31 12N 90 0W
Koksoak →, Qué., Canada 175 B4 58 30N 68 10W
Koliganek, AK, U.S.A. 61 G8 59 48N 157 25W
Koloa, HI, U.S.A. 69 B2 21 55N 159 28W
Komatke, AZ, U.S.A. 62 D3 33 17N 112 10W
Kona ✕ (KOA), HI, U.S.A. 69 D5 19 44N 156 3W
Kōnāhuanui, HI, U.S.A. 69 K14 21 21N 157 47W
Konawa, OK, U.S.A. 93 D7 34 58N 96 45W
Koocanusa, L., B.C., Canada 185 J5 49 20N 115 15W
Koochiching County ☆, MN, U.S.A. 80 B5 48 15N 93 50W
Ko'olau Range, HI, U.S.A. 69 J14 21 35N 157 50W
Ko'olauloa District, HI, U.S.A. 69 J14 21 35N 157 55W
Ko'olaupoko District, HI, U.S.A. 69 K14 21 25N 157 50W
Koosharem, UT, U.S.A. 100 E4 38 31N 111 53W
Kooskia, ID, U.S.A. 70 C3 46 9N 115 59W
Kootenai →, ID, U.S.A. 70 A2 49 0N 116 30W
Kootenai County ☆, ID, U.S.A. 70 B2 47 45N 116 30W
Kootenai Nat. Forest, MT, U.S.A. 83 B2 48 30N 115 40W
Kootenay L., B.C., Canada 187 F18 49 45N 116 50W
Kootenay Nat. Park △, B.C., Canada 185 G4 51 0N 116 0W
Kopka →, Ont., Canada 180 B7 50 4N 89 1W
Kopomá, Yucatán, Mexico 223 B4 20 38N 89 55W
Kopperston, WV, U.S.A. 102 D3 37 45N 81 35W
Kormak, Ont., Canada 181 E14 47 38N 82 59W
Koroc →, Qué., Canada 175 B4 58 50N 65 50W
Korona, FL, U.S.A. 67 B7 29 25N 81 12W
Kosciusko, MS, U.S.A. 81 C4 33 4N 89 35W
Kosciusko County ☆, IN, U.S.A. 72 B5 41 15N 85 50W
Koshkonong, MO, U.S.A. 82 E5 36 36N 91 39W
Koshkonong L., WI, U.S.A. 103 F5 42 52N 88 58W
Kosse, TX, U.S.A. 99 F11 31 18N 96 38W
Kossuth, MS, U.S.A. 81 B5 34 52N 88 39W
Kossuth County ☆, IA, U.S.A. 73 B4 43 15N 94 10W
Kotcho L., B.C., Canada 189 E8 59 7N 121 12W
Kotlik, AK, U.S.A. 61 E7 63 2N 163 33W
Kotzebue, AK, U.S.A. 61 C7 66 53N 162 39W
Kotzebue Sound, AK, U.S.A. 61 C7 66 20N 163 0W
Kouchibouguac Nat. Park △, N.B., Canada 173 G5 46 50N 65 0W
Koukdjuak →, Nunavut, Canada 191 D11 66 43N 73 0W
Koukdjuak, Great Plain of the, Nunavut, Canada 191 D11 66 25N 72 50W
Kountze, TX, U.S.A. 99 G13 30 22N 94 19W
Kouts, IN, U.S.A. 72 B3 41 19N 87 2W
Kovik, B., Qué., Canada 175 A2 61 35N 77 36W
Kowkash, Ont., Canada 181 B9 50 20N 87 12W
Koyuk, AK, U.S.A. 61 D7 64 56N 161 9W
Koyukuk, AK, U.S.A. 61 D8 64 53N 157 42W
Koyukuk →, AK, U.S.A. 61 D8 64 55N 157 32W
Koyukuk Nat. Wildlife Refuge ⌓, AK, U.S.A. 61 D8 65 35N 156 30W
Kramer, ND, U.S.A. 91 B5 48 42N 100 43W
Kranzburg, SD, U.S.A. 91 F9 44 54N 96 55W
Krebs, OK, U.S.A. 93 D8 34 56N 95 43W
Kremlin, OK, U.S.A. 93 B6 36 33N 97 50W
Kremmling, CO, U.S.A. 66 B4 40 4N 106 24W
Kress, TX, U.S.A. 98 C6 34 22N 101 45W
Krotz Springs, LA, U.S.A. 75 D4 30 32N 91 45W
Krum, TX, U.S.A. 99 D10 33 16N 97 14W
Krusenstern, C., Nunavut, Canada 188 C10 68 24N 113 54W
Krusenstern, C., AK, U.S.A. 61 C7 67 8N 163 45W
Krydor, Sask., Canada 182 C4 52 47N 107 4W
Ku Tree Res., HI, U.S.A. 69 J13 21 30N 157 59W
Kualapu'u, HI, U.S.A. 69 B4 21 9N 157 2W
Kualoa Pt., HI, U.S.A. 69 J14 21 31N 157 50W
Kuapā Pond, HI, U.S.A. 69 K14 21 17N 157 43W
Kuehn, MT, U.S.A. 83 E10 45 49N 107 5W
Kugaaruk = Pelly Bay, Nunavut, Canada 190 D8 68 38N 89 50W
Kugluktuk, Nunavut, Canada 188 C9 67 50N 115 5W
Kugong I., N.W.T., Canada 175 B2 56 18N 79 50W
Kuiu I., AK, U.S.A. 61 H14 57 45N 134 10W
Kukuihaele, HI, U.S.A. 69 C6 20 5N 155 35W
Kukukus L., Ont., Canada 180 C5 49 47N 91 41W
Kulkayu = Hartley Bay, B.C., Canada 186 B5 53 25N 129 15W
Kulm, ND, U.S.A. 91 D7 46 18N 98 57W
Kumukahi, C., HI, U.S.A. 69 D7 19 31N 154 49W
Kuna, ID, U.S.A. 70 F2 43 30N 116 25W
Kunghit I., B.C., Canada 186 C3 52 6N 131 3W
Kunia, HI, U.S.A. 69 K13 21 28N 158 4W
Kunkletown, PA, U.S.A. 87 B1 40 51N 75 27W
Kūpikipiki'ō Pt., HI, U.S.A. 69 K14 21 15N 157 47W
Kupreanof I., AK, U.S.A. 61 H14 56 50N 133 30W
Kure I., HI, U.S.A. 69 F8 28 25N 178 25W
Kuroki, Sask., Canada 182 D8 51 52N 103 29W
Kurthwood, LA, U.S.A. 75 C2 31 20N 93 10W
Kurtistown, HI, U.S.A. 69 D6 19 36N 155 4W
Kusawa L., Yukon, Canada 189 D5 60 20N 136 13W
Kuskokwim →, AK, U.S.A. 61 F7 60 5N 162 25W
Kuskokwim B., AK, U.S.A. 61 G7 59 45N 162 25W
Kuskokwim Mts., AK, U.S.A. 61 E9 62 30N 156 0W
Kuttawa, KY, U.S.A. 96 C4 37 4N 88 7W
Kutztown, PA, U.S.A. 87 B1 40 31N 75 47W
Kuujjuaq, Qué., Canada 175 B4 58 6N 68 15W
Kuujjuarapik, Qué., Canada 175 B2 55 20N 77 35W
Kuzitrin →, AK, U.S.A. 61 D6 65 10N 165 25W
Kvichak B., AK, U.S.A. 61 G8 58 48N 157 30W
Kwataboahegan →, Ont., Canada 181 A16 51 9N 80 50W
Kwethluk, AK, U.S.A. 61 F7 60 49N 161 26W
Kwigillingok, AK, U.S.A. 61 G7 59 51N 163 8W
Kwinitsa, B.C., Canada 186 A5 54 19N 129 22W
Kyburz, CA, U.S.A. 64 E6 38 47N 120 18W
Kykotsmovi Village, AZ, U.S.A. 62 B5 35 52N 110 37W
Kyle, Sask., Canada 182 E3 50 50N 108 2W
Kyle, SD, U.S.A. 91 G3 43 26N 102 10W
Kyle, TX, U.S.A. 99 H10 29 59N 97 53W
Kynoch Inlet, B.C., Canada 186 C7 52 45N 128 0W
Kyuquot, B.C., Canada 186 E7 50 3N 127 25W

L

La Aguada, Quintana Roo, Mexico 223 C5 19 57N 88 32W
La Aguja, Baja Calif. S., Mexico 211 K8 23 59N 110 53W
La Alameda, Guadalajara, Mexico 224 C2 20 30N 103 15W
La Angostura, Sonora, Mexico 212 C6 30 26N 109 22W
La Angostura, Cerro, Chiapas, Mexico 222 D3 15 54N 93 10W
La Antigua, Veracruz, Mexico 220 E4 19 19N 96 19W
La Ascensión, Nuevo León, Mexico 215 F5 24 20N 99 55W
La Ballena, Baja Calif. S., Mexico 211 G6 26 22N 112 39W
La Barca, Jalisco, Mexico 218 B5 20 17N 102 34W
La Barge, WY, U.S.A. 104 D2 42 16N 110 12W
La Belle, FL, U.S.A. 67 E7 26 46N 81 26W
La Belle, MO, U.S.A. 82 A5 40 7N 91 55W
La Bocana, Baja Calif., Mexico 210 D4 29 42N 114 53W
La Bocana, Baja Calif., Mexico 210 B2 31 34N 116 41W
La Bocana →, Baja Calif., Mexico 210 D3 29 26N 115 7W
La Bocana, Estero, Baja Calif. S., Mexico 211 G5 26 47N 113 43W
La Boquilla →, Coahuila, Mexico 214 B1 29 11N 102 58W
La Boquilla del Conchos, Chihuahua, Mexico 213 F10 27 32N 105 21W
La Broquerie, Man., Canada 183 F15 49 25N 96 30W
La Bufadora, Baja Calif., Mexico 210 B2 31 45N 116 46W
La Caja, Colima, Mexico 218 C4 19 21N 103 47W
La Calerilla, Guadalajara, Mexico 224 B1 20 33N 103 24W
La Cañada, Querétaro, Mexico 219 B7 20 37N 100 19W
La Canada Flintridge, Los Angeles, U.S.A. 111 A2 34 11N 118 11W
La Candelaria, Zacatecas, Mexico 217 C9 24 28N 101 51W
La Cantera Sur, Guanajuato, Mexico 219 A6 21 17N 101 16W
La Capilla de los Remedios, Chihuahua, Mexico 213 E9 28 7N 106 57W
La Casa Colorada, Cerro, Chihuahua, Mexico 213 F7 27 4N 108 20W
La Catarina, Sa., Chihuahua, Mexico 213 D8 29 30N 107 40W
La Center, KY, U.S.A. 96 C4 37 4N 88 58W
La Center, WA, U.S.A. 101 E3 45 52N 122 40W
La Choya, Sonora, Mexico 212 B2 31 20N 113 40W
La Ciénega, Oaxaca, Mexico 221 H4 16 55N 96 47W
La Cienega, NM, U.S.A. 88 B4 35 34N 106 4W
La Cieneguita, Durango, Mexico 216 C5 24 34N 105 1W
La Colorada, Sonora, Mexico 212 E5 28 49N 110 36W
La Coma, Tamaulipas, Mexico 215 F7 24 17N 97 57W
La Compañía, Oaxaca, Mexico 221 H4 16 34N 96 49W
La Concepción, Sinaloa, Mexico 216 D4 23 23N 106 9W
La Conception, Qué., Canada 176 E8 46 9N 74 42W
La Conchas, Sonora, Mexico 212 E4 28 21N 111 20W
La Concordia, Chiapas, Mexico 222 C4 16 5N 92 38W
La Conner, WA, U.S.A. 101 B3 48 23N 122 30W
La Constitución, Chihuahua, Mexico 213 D9 29 55N 106 48W
La Crescent, MN, U.S.A. 80 G7 43 50N 91 18W
La Crescenta, Los Angeles, U.S.A. 111 A2 34 14N 118 14W
La Croix L., MN, U.S.A. 80 B6 48 20N 92 10W
La Crosse, FL, U.S.A. 67 B6 29 51N 82 24W
La Crosse, KS, U.S.A. 74 C4 38 32N 99 18W
La Crosse, VA, U.S.A. 102 E6 36 42N 78 6W
La Crosse, WA, U.S.A. 101 D8 46 49N 117 53W
La Crosse, WI, U.S.A. 103 E2 43 48N 91 15W
La Crosse County ☆, WI, U.S.A. 103 E2 44 0N 91 0W
La Cruz, Chihuahua, Mexico 213 F10 27 52N 105 12W
La Cruz, Guadalajara, Mexico 224 B2 20 39N 103 12W
La Cruz, Sinaloa, Mexico 216 D4 23 55N 106 54W
La Cruz de Loreto, Jalisco, Mexico 218 C2 20 0N 105 27W
La Cuchilla, Tabasco, Mexico 222 B5 17 49N 91 14W
La Cuesta, Jalisco, Mexico 218 B3 20 9N 104 49W
La Cygne, KS, U.S.A. 74 C9 38 21N 94 46W
La Cygnes L., KS, U.S.A. 74 C9 38 20N 94 39W
La Discordia, Sonora, Mexico 212 B4 31 1N 111 55W
La Doré, Qué., Canada 177 C10 48 43N 72 39W
La Encantada, Coahuila, Mexico 214 B2 28 35N 102 27W
La Encantada, Coahuila, Mexico 214 B2 28 22N 102 35W
La Escopeta, Baja Calif. S., Mexico 211 K9 23 14N 109 34W
La Esmeralda, Chihuahua, Mexico 213 D7 29 18N 108 25W
La Esperanza, Sa., Chihuahua, Mexico 213 C11 30 1N 104 52W
La Farge, WI, U.S.A. 103 E3 43 35N 90 38W
La Fayette, GA, U.S.A. 68 B1 34 42N 85 17W
La Fayette, KY, U.S.A. 96 D5 36 40N 87 40W
La Florida, Coahuila, Mexico 214 B2 28 37N 102 8W
La Follette, TN, U.S.A. 97 D8 36 23N 84 7W
La Fontaine, IN, U.S.A. 72 C5 40 40N 85 43W
La Fragua, Sa., Coahuila, Mexico 214 D2 26 45N 102 28W
La Galissonnière, L., Qué., Canada 172 B7 51 25N 62 0W
La Garita, CO, U.S.A. 66 E4 37 50N 106 15W
La Gloria, Sa., Coahuila, Mexico 214 D3 26 45N 101 10W
La Gloria, Sa., Sonora, Mexico 212 C3 30 50N 112 10W
La Golondrina, Sonora, Mexico 212 C3 30 3N 112 23W
La Goma, Durango, Mexico 217 B7 25 29N 103 42W
La Grande, OR, U.S.A. 94 B7 45 20N 118 5W
La Grande, WA, U.S.A. 101 D3 46 50N 122 19W
La Grande →, Qué., Canada 175 C2 53 50N 79 0W
La Grande Deux, Rés., Qué., Canada 175 C2 53 40N 76 55W
La Grande Quatre, Rés., Qué., Canada 175 C3 54 0N 73 15W
La Grande Trois, Rés., Qué., Canada 175 C2 53 46N 75 30W
La Grange, AR, U.S.A. 63 D5 34 39N 90 44W
La Grange, Chicago, U.S.A. 108 C1 41 48N 87 53W
La Grange, GA, U.S.A. 68 C1 33 2N 85 2W
La Grange, KY, U.S.A. 97 B7 38 25N 85 23W
La Grange, MO, U.S.A. 82 A5 40 3N 91 35W
La Grange, NC, U.S.A. 90 C8 35 19N 77 47W
La Grange, TN, U.S.A. 96 E3 35 3N 89 15W
La Grange, TX, U.S.A. 99 H11 29 54N 96 52W
La Grange, WY, U.S.A. 104 E8 41 38N 104 10W
La Grange Park, Chicago, U.S.A. 108 C1 41 49N 87 51W
La Guadeloupe, Qué., Canada 177 F12 45 57N 70 56W
La Guajolota, Durango, Mexico 217 E6 22 56N 104 52W
La Guardia, New York ✕ (LGA), NY, U.S.A. 89 E7 40 46N 73 52W
La Harpe, IL, U.S.A. 71 C3 40 35N 90 58W
La Harpe, KS, U.S.A. 74 D8 37 55N 95 18W
La Have →, N.S., Canada 173 J5 44 14N 64 20W
La Herradura, San Luis Potosí, Mexico 215 G3 23 1N 101 45W
La Higuera →, Sonora, Mexico 212 D6 29 21N 109 42W
La Huacana, Michoacan, Mexico 218 D6 18 58N 101 49W
La Huerta, Jalisco, Mexico 218 C3 19 29N 104 36W
La Hulería, Tabasco, Mexico 222 A5 17 59N 91 23W
La Independencia, Chiapas, Mexico 222 C4 16 15N 92 1W
La Inmaculadita, Sonora, Mexico 212 D4 29 55N 111 48W
La Jara, CO, U.S.A. 66 E5 37 16N 105 58W
La Jara, NM, U.S.A. 88 A4 36 5N 106 58W
La Jolla, San Diego, U.S.A. 117 A1 32 50N 117 16W
La Jolla Indian Reservation, CA, U.S.A. 65 K10 33 16N 116 52W
La Joya, Baja Calif., Mexico 210 A1 32 29N 117 1W
La Joya, Chihuahua, Mexico 213 E9 28 5N 106 16W
La Joya, NM, U.S.A. 88 C4 34 21N 106 51W
La Joya, TX, U.S.A. 98 L9 26 14N 98 27W
La Junta, CO, U.S.A. 66 E7 37 59N 103 33W
La Lágrima, Sa., Chihuahua, Mexico 213 C10 30 15N 105 20W
La Laguna, Guerrero, Mexico 219 E8 17 45N 99 45W
La Laguna, Zacatecas, Mexico 217 C7 24 15N 103 8W
La Lagunita, Durango, Mexico 216 A4 26 2N 106 29W
La Laja, Jalisco, Mexico 218 B3 20 35N 104 32W
La Leche, L., Coahuila, Mexico 214 C2 27 14N 102 53W
La Libertad, Chiapas, Mexico 222 B5 17 41N 91 43W
La Libertad, Chihuahua, Mexico 213 F9 27 37N 106 40W
La Libertad, Sa., Baja Calif., Mexico 210 E5 28 45N 114 0W
La Linda, Coahuila, Mexico 214 A2 29 26N 102 48W
La Loche, Sask., Canada 189 E11 56 29N 109 26W
La Loma, México, Mexico 225 A2 19 31N 99 11W
La Luz, Coahuila, Mexico 214 E2 25 47N 102 16W
La Luz, NM, U.S.A. 88 E5 32 59N 105 57W
La Madera, NM, U.S.A. 88 A4 36 23N 106 3W
La Madera, Sa., Coahuila, Mexico 214 C2 27 6N 102 30W
La Magdalena, Chihuahua, Mexico 213 G9 26 52N 106 20W
La Magdalena Chichicaspa, México, Mexico 225 B2 19 26N 99 19W
La Malbaie, Qué., Canada 177 D12 47 40N 70 10W
La Malinche, Parque Nacional △, Mexico 219 C9 19 15N 98 2W
La Mancha, L., Durango, Mexico 217 C8 24 37N 102 37W
La Manga, Sonora, Mexico 212 D4 29 8N 111 5W
La Margarita del Norte, Coahuila, Mexico 214 D2 26 27N 102 53W
La Marque, TX, U.S.A. 99 H13 29 23N 94 58W
La Marquesa, Parque Nacional △, México, Mexico 219 C8 19 20N 99 21W
La Martre, Qué., Canada 172 D3 49 12N 66 10W
La Martre, L., N.W.T., Canada 189 D9 63 15N 117 55W
La Mesa, Baja Calif., Mexico 210 A2 32 30N 116 57W
La Mesa, CA, U.S.A. 65 L9 32 46N 117 1W
La Mesa, NM, U.S.A. 88 E4 32 7N 106 42W
La Mesa del Huracán, Chihuahua, Mexico 213 D7 29 40N 108 15W
La Mesa del Rodeo, Durango, Mexico 216 C4 24 47N 106 46W
La Mesilla, NM, U.S.A. 88 E4 32 16N 106 48W
La Mira, Michoacan, Mexico 218 D5 18 0N 102 19W
La Misa, Sonora, Mexico 212 E5 28 23N 110 53W
La Mocha, Sonora, Mexico 212 D4 29 0N 111 40W
La Moille, IL, U.S.A. 71 B4 41 32N 89 17W
La Moine →, IL, U.S.A. 71 D3 39 59N 90 31W
La Monte, MO, U.S.A. 82 C3 38 46N 93 26W
La Mora, Coahuila, Mexico 214 C2 27 44N 102 30W
La Mora, Michoacan, Mexico 219 C7 19 20N 100 31W
La Mothe, L., Qué., Canada 177 C11 48 46N 71 9W
La Moure, ND, U.S.A. 91 D7 46 21N 98 18W
La Moure County ☆, ND, U.S.A. 91 D7 46 23N 98 29W
La Muralla, Guanajuato, Mexico 218 B6 20 48N 101 42W
La Nariz, Cerro, Coahuila, Mexico 214 D4 26 6N 100 59W
La Nopalera, Distrito Federal, Mexico 225 C3 19 18N 99 5W
La Noria, Sinaloa, Mexico 216 D4 23 30N 106 18W
La Paila, Sa., Coahuila, Mexico 214 E3 25 50N 101 36W
La Palma, Nayarit, Mexico 216 F5 21 59N 105 22W
La Palma, Sonora, Mexico 212 E5 28 40N 110 59W
La Palma, Tabasco, Mexico 222 B5 17 27N 91 7W
La Palma, AZ, U.S.A. 62 E4 32 53N 111 31W
La Palma, Cerro, Distrito Federal, Mexico 225 C2 19 15N 99 20W
La Palomas, Baja Calif. S., Mexico 211 F5 27 43N 113 25W
La Palotada →, Chihuahua, Mexico 213 B7 31 7N 108 3W
La Partida, Coahuila, Mexico 214 E1 25 36N 103 19W
La Patrie, Qué., Canada 177 F11 45 24N 71 15W
La Paz, Baja Calif. S., Mexico 211 J8 24 10N 110 18W
La Paz, San Luis Potosí, Mexico 215 G4 23 41N 100 42W
La Paz ☆, AZ, U.S.A. 62 D2 33 37N 113 53W
La Peña, Tamaulipas, Mexico 215 G6 23 22N 98 8W
La Perla, Chihuahua, Mexico 213 E11 28 18N 104 32W
La Pesca, Tamaulipas, Mexico 215 G7 23 46N 97 47W
La Piedad, Michoacan, Mexico 218 B6 20 21N 102 0W
La Pine, OR, U.S.A. 94 D4 43 40N 121 30W
La Pinta, Chihuahua, Mexico 213 D8 29 12N 107 40W
La Plant, SD, U.S.A. 91 E5 45 9N 100 39W
La Plata, MD, U.S.A. 77 B4 38 32N 76 59W
La Plata, MO, U.S.A. 82 A4 40 2N 92 29W
La Plata, NM, U.S.A. 88 A2 36 56N 108 12W
La Plata County ☆, CO, U.S.A. 66 E3 37 15N 107 50W
La Pocatière, Qué., Canada 177 D12 47 22N 70 2W
La Poile, Nfld. & L., Canada 174 E2 47 41N 58 24W
La Polka, Chiapas, Mexico 222 D3 15 57N 93 39W
La Porte, TX, U.S.A. 99 H12 29 40N 95 1W
La Porte City, IA, U.S.A. 73 C6 42 19N 92 12W
La Poza Grande, Baja Calif. S., Mexico 211 H6 25 50N 112 2W
La Prairie, Montréal, Canada 192 B4 45 25N 73 29W
La Presa, Baja Calif., Mexico 210 A2 32 28N 116 55W
La Presa, Baja Calif. S., Mexico 211 J7 24 51N 111 5W
La Presa, Nayarit, Mexico 216 F5 21 46N 105 13W
La Providencia, Coahuila, Mexico 214 C1 27 5N 103 31W
La Providencia, Durango, Mexico 216 A5 26 41N 105 59W
La Pryor, TX, U.S.A. 99 J8 28 57N 99 51W
La Puente, NM, U.S.A. 88 A4 36 42N 106 36W
La Punta, Guadalajara, Mexico 224 B2 20 34N 103 12W
La Purísima, Baja Calif. S., Mexico 211 G6 26 10N 112 4W
La Purisma, Zacatecas, Mexico 217 E9 22 4N 101 24W
La Push, WA, U.S.A. 101 C1 47 55N 124 38W
La Rastra, Sinaloa, Mexico 216 D5 23 4N 105 32W
La Reforma, Chihuahua, Mexico 213 G7 26 58N 108 9W
La Reine, Qué., Canada 176 C3 48 50N 79 30W
La Ribera, Baja Calif. S., Mexico 211 K9 23 35N 109 34W
La Romaine, Qué., Canada 175 C5 50 13N 60 40W
La Ronge, Sask., Canada 189 E11 55 5N 105 20W
La Rue, OH, U.S.A. 92 C3 40 35N 83 23W
La Rumorosa, Baja Calif., Mexico 210 A2 32 34N 116 6W
La Sal, UT, U.S.A. 100 E6 38 19N 109 14W
La Sal Mts., UT, U.S.A. 100 E6 38 30N 109 10W
La Salle, CO, U.S.A. 66 B6 40 21N 104 42W
La Salle, IL, U.S.A. 71 B4 41 20N 89 6W
La Salle, MN, U.S.A. 80 F4 44 4N 94 33W
La Salle County ☆, IL, U.S.A. 71 B5 41 20N 88 50W
La Salle County ☆, TX, U.S.A. 99 J8 28 26N 99 14W
La Salle Parish ☆, LA, U.S.A. 75 C3 31 41N 92 8W
La Sarre, Qué., Canada 176 C3 48 45N 79 15W
La Scie, Nfld. & L., Canada 174 C5 49 57N 55 36W
La Silla, Cerro de, Monterrey, Mexico 224 C2 25 37N 100 13W
La Soledad, Coahuila, Mexico 214 D3 26 48N 101 42W
La Soledad, Durango, Mexico 216 B3 25 14N 107 8W
La Soledad, Nuevo León, Mexico 215 F4 24 30N 100 34W
La Solidaridad Iberoamericana, Parque de, Guadalajara, Mexico 224 B2 20 39N 103 17W
La Suerte, Baja Calif., Mexico 210 C3 30 34N 115 19W
La Tabatière, Qué., Canada 174 B2 50 50N 58 58W
La Tinaja, Veracruz, Mexico 221 F4 18 45N 96 28W
La Trasquila, Chihuahua, Mexico 213 D8 29 45N 107 5W
La Trinidad, Baja Calif., Mexico 210 B3 31 24N 115 5W
La Trinitaria, Chiapas, Mexico 222 C4 16 7N 92 3W
La Tuque, Qué., Canada 177 D10 47 30N 72 50W
La Unión, Guerrero, Mexico 218 E6 17 58N 101 49W
La Unión, Nuevo León, Mexico 214 E6 25 45N 98 45W
La Unión, Nuevo León, Mexico 214 D4 26 11N 100 29W
La Unión, Nuevo León, Mexico 215 G4 23 51N 100 6W
La Unión, Quintana Roo, Mexico 223 E5 17 50N 88 50W
La Union, NM, U.S.A. 88 F4 31 57N 106 40W
La Unión del Cuatro, Guadalajara, Mexico 224 B1 20 31N 103 21W
La Vale, MD, U.S.A. 77 A2 39 40N 78 48W
La Valle, WI, U.S.A. 103 E3 43 35N 90 8W
La Venta, Tabasco, Mexico 222 A2 18 5N 94 3W
La Vérendrye, Réserve Faunique ⌓, Qué., Canada 176 D6 47 20N 76 40W
La Vergne, TN, U.S.A. 96 D6 36 1N 86 35W
La Verkin, UT, U.S.A. 100 F2 37 12N 113 16W
La Vernia, TX, U.S.A. 99 H9 29 21N 98 7W
La Veta, CO, U.S.A. 66 E6 37 31N 105 0W
La Victoria, San Luis Potosí, Mexico 215 G3 23 38N 101 23W
La Vieja, L., Chihuahua, Mexico 213 C8 30 15N 107 15W
La Vista, NE, U.S.A. 84 C9 41 11N 96 2W
La Yesca, Nayarit, Mexico 216 F6 21 19N 104 1W
Lā'au Pt., HI, U.S.A. 69 B4 21 6N 157 19W
Labadieville, LA, U.S.A. 75 E5 29 50N 90 57W
Laberge, L., Yukon, Canada 189 D5 61 11N 135 12W
Labette, KS, U.S.A. 74 D8 37 14N 95 11W
Labette County ☆, KS, U.S.A. 74 D8 37 15N 95 15W
Labná, Yucatán, Mexico 223 B4 20 9N 89 33W
Labor de Santa Bárbara, Zacatecas, Mexico 217 E7 23 0N 103 13W
Labrador, Nfld. & L., Canada 175 C5 53 20N 61 0W
Labrador City, Nfld. & L., Canada 175 C4 52 57N 66 55W
Labrieville, Qué., Canada 177 B13 49 18N 69 34W
Lac Allard, Qué., Canada 175 C5 50 33N 63 24W
Lac-au-Saumon, Qué., Canada 172 E2 48 25N 67 22W
Lac-aux-Sables, Qué., Canada 177 E10 46 51N 72 24W
Lac-Beauchamp, Parc du, Qué., Canada 192 A2 45 29N 75 37W
Lac-Bouchette, Qué., Canada 177 C10 48 16N 72 11W
Lac Brochet, Man., Canada 191 F5 58 37N 101 29W
Lac Courte Oreilles Indian Reservation, WI, U.S.A. 103 C2 45 50N 91 15W
Lac-des-Écorces, Qué., Canada 176 E7 46 34N 75 22W
Lac du Bonnet, Man., Canada 183 E15 50 15N 96 4W
Lac du Flambeau, WI, U.S.A. 103 C4 45 58N 89 53W
Lac du Flambeau Indian Reservation, WI, U.S.A. 103 B4 46 0N 89 50W
Lac Édouard, Qué., Canada 177 D10 47 40N 72 16W
Lac-Etchemin, Qué., Canada 177 E12 46 24N 70 30W
Lac La Biche, Alta., Canada 184 D9 54 45N 111 58W
Lac la Hache, B.C., Canada 187 D13 51 49N 121 27W
Lac la Martre = Wha Ti, N.W.T., Canada 189 D9 63 8N 117 16W
Lac-Leamy, Parc, Qué., Canada 192 A1 45 27N 75 43W
Lac-Mégantic, Qué., Canada 177 F12 45 35N 70 53W
Lac qui Parle County ☆, MN, U.S.A. 80 F2 44 55N 96 0W
Lac-Ste-Marie, Qué., Canada 176 F7 45 57N 75 57W
Lac Vieux Desert Indian Reservation, MI, U.S.A. 79 C2 46 10N 89 9W
Lacantún →, Chiapas, Mexico 222 C6 16 36N 90 39W
Lacanuá, Chiapas, Mexico 222 C6 16 41N 91 6W
Lacassine, Bayou →, LA, U.S.A. 75 D3 30 19N 92 53W
Lacey, WA, U.S.A. 101 C3 47 7N 122 49W
Lacey Spring, VA, U.S.A. 102 C6 38 32N 78 46W
Lachine, Qué., Canada 177 F9 45 26N 73 42W
Lachine, MI, U.S.A. 79 D8 45 4N 83 43W
Lachute, Qué., Canada 177 F8 45 39N 74 21W
Lackawanna, NY, U.S.A. 89 C2 42 50N 78 50W
Lackawanna →, PA, U.S.A. 87 A1 41 20N 75 48W
Lackawanna County ☆, PA, U.S.A. 95 C7 41 30N 75 50W
Lackawaxen →, PA, U.S.A. 87 A2 41 29N 74 59W
Lackland City, San Antonio, U.S.A. 117 C2 29 23N 98 38W
Laclede County ☆, MO, U.S.A. 82 D4 37 40N 92 35W
Laclu, Ont., Canada 180 C2 49 46N 94 41W
Lacolle, Qué., Canada 177 F9 45 5N 73 22W
Lacombe, Alta., Canada 185 F7 52 30N 113 44W
Lacombe, LA, U.S.A. 75 D6 30 19N 89 56W
Lacon, IL, U.S.A. 71 B4 41 2N 89 24W
Lacona, IA, U.S.A. 73 D5 41 12N 93 23W
Lacona, NY, U.S.A. 89 B4 43 39N 76 10W
Laconia, IN, U.S.A. 72 E4 38 2N 86 5W
Laconia, NH, U.S.A. 86 C3 43 32N 71 28W
Lacoochee, FL, U.S.A. 67 C6 28 28N 82 11W
Lacreek L., SD, U.S.A. 91 G4 43 7N 101 33W

Lacs-Albanel-Mistassini et Waconichi, Réserve Faunique des ⌓, Qué., Canada 177 A8 51 8N 74 25W
Ladd, IL, U.S.A. 71 B4 41 23N 89 13W
Ladder Cr. →, KS, U.S.A. 74 C3 38 45N 100 52W
Laddonia, MO, U.S.A. 82 B5 39 15N 91 39W
Ladelle, AR, U.S.A. 63 E4 33 28N 91 48W
Ladera Heights, Los Angeles, U.S.A. 111 C2 33 59N 118 22W
Ladoga, IN, U.S.A. 72 D4 39 55N 86 48W
Ladonia, TX, U.S.A. 99 D12 33 25N 95 57W
Ladson, SC, U.S.A. 90 F5 32 59N 80 6W
Ladue, MO, U.S.A. 117 B1 38 38N 90 22W
Lady Lake, FL, U.S.A. 67 C7 28 55N 81 55W
Ladysmith, B.C., Canada 186 G11 49 0N 123 49W
Ladysmith, WI, U.S.A. 103 C2 45 28N 91 12W
Lae 'o Kākā, HI, U.S.A. 69 C5 20 31N 156 33W
Lae 'o Kealaikahiki, HI, U.S.A. 69 C5 20 32N 156 42W
Lafayette, AL, U.S.A. 60 D5 32 54N 85 24W
Lafayette, CA, U.S.A. 64 F4 37 53N 122 7W
Lafayette, CO, U.S.A. 66 C5 39 58N 105 12W
Lafayette, IN, U.S.A. 72 C4 40 25N 86 54W
Lafayette, LA, U.S.A. 75 D3 30 14N 92 1W
Lafayette, MN, U.S.A. 80 F4 44 27N 94 24W
Lafayette, OH, U.S.A. 92 C3 40 46N 83 57W
Lafayette, OR, U.S.A. 94 B2 45 15N 123 7W
LaFayette, TN, U.S.A. 96 D6 36 31N 86 2W
Lafayette, Mt., NH, U.S.A. 86 B3 44 10N 71 38W
Lafayette County ☆, AR, U.S.A. 63 E2 33 22N 93 43W
Lafayette County ☆, FL, U.S.A. 67 B5 30 0N 83 0W
Lafayette County ☆, MS, U.S.A. 81 B4 34 22N 89 31W
Lafayette County ☆, MO, U.S.A. 82 B3 39 5N 93 45W
Lafayette County ☆, WI, U.S.A. 103 F3 42 35N 90 10W
Lafayette Hill, PA, U.S.A. 116 A1 40 4N 75 15W
Lafayette Parish ☆, LA, U.S.A. 75 D3 30 14N 92 1W
Lafayette Res., San Francisco, U.S.A. 118 A4 37 53N 122 8W
Lafitte, LA, U.S.A. 75 E5 29 40N 90 6W
Laflamme →, Qué., Canada 176 B5 49 17N 77 9W
Lafleche, Sask., Canada 182 F5 49 45N 106 40W
Lafontaine, KS, U.S.A. 74 D8 37 24N 95 51W
Laforce, Qué., Canada 176 D4 47 32N 78 44W
Lafourche, Bayou →, LA, U.S.A. 75 E5 29 5N 90 14W
Lafourche Parish ☆, LA, U.S.A. 75 E5 29 34N 90 23W
Lages Station, NV, U.S.A. 85 B6 40 4N 114 37W
Laggan = Lake Louise, Alta., Canada 185 G4 51 30N 116 10W
Lagona = Laguna Beach, CA, U.S.A. 65 K9 33 33N 117 47W
Lagos de Moreno, Jalisco, Mexico 218 A6 21 21N 101 55W
Lagrange, IN, U.S.A. 72 B5 41 39N 85 25W
Lagrange, ME, U.S.A. 76 C5 45 11N 68 54W
Lagrange, OH, U.S.A. 92 B4 41 14N 82 7W
Lagrange County ☆, IN, U.S.A. 72 B5 41 35N 85 25W
Laguashima, Nayarit, Mexico 216 E5 22 25N 105 17W
Laguna, NM, U.S.A. 88 B3 35 2N 107 25W
Laguna, Sa. de la, Baja Calif. S., Mexico 211 K9 23 35N 109 55W
Laguna Atascosa Nat. Wildlife Refuge ⌓, TX, U.S.A. 99 26 17N 97 23W
Laguna Beach, CA, U.S.A. 65 K9 33 33N 117 47W
Laguna Beach, FL, U.S.A. 67 A3 30 14N 85 55W
Laguna Canachi, Sinaloa, Mexico 216 C3 24 4N 107 6W
Laguna del Mante, San Luis Potosí, Mexico 215 H6 22 13N 98 59W
Laguna Grande, Zacatecas, Mexico 217 E7 22 27N 103 30W
Laguna Indian Reservation, NM, U.S.A. 88 C3 35 0N 107 20W
Laguna Mts., CA, U.S.A. 65 K10 33 0N 116 40W
Laguna San Ignacio, Baja Calif. S., Mexico 211 G5 26 54N 113 8W
Laguna Seca, Durango, Mexico 216 B4 25 53N 106 9W
Lagunas de Chacahua, Parque Nacional △, Oaxaca, Mexico 221 H3 16 47N 97 2W
Lagunas de Montebello, Parque Nacional △, Chiapas, Mexico 222 C5 16 4N 91 42W
Lagunas de Zempoala ⌓, México, Mexico 219 C8 19 6N 99 18W
Lagunera, Región, Coahuila, Mexico 214 E1 25 35N 103 3W
Lagunillas, Michoacan, Mexico 219 C6 19 4N 101 26W
Lagunillas, San Luis Potosí, Mexico 215 J5 21 34N 99 35W
Lagunitas, Sonora, Mexico 212 A1 32 20N 114 52W
Lahaina, HI, U.S.A. 69 C5 20 53N 156 41W
Lahilahi Pt., HI, U.S.A. 69 K13 21 28N 158 13W
Lahoma, OK, U.S.A. 93 B5 36 23N 98 5W
Lahontan Res., NV, U.S.A. 85 C1 39 28N 119 4W
Laidlaw, B.C., Canada 187 F13 49 20N 121 36W
Lā'ie, HI, U.S.A. 69 J14 21 39N 157 56W
Laingsburg, MI, U.S.A. 79 G7 42 54N 84 21W
Lair, KY, U.S.A. 97 B8 38 20N 84 18W
Laird, Sask., Canada 182 C5 52 43N 106 35W
Lajitas, TX, U.S.A. 98 H4 29 16N 103 46W
Lake, MS, U.S.A. 81 D4 32 21N 89 20W
Lake, WY, U.S.A. 104 B2 44 33N 110 24W
Lake Alfred, FL, U.S.A. 67 C7 28 6N 81 44W
Lake Alma, Sask., Canada 182 F7 49 9N 104 12W
Lake and Peninsula ☆, AK, U.S.A. 61 H8 57 0N 158 0W
Lake Andes, SD, U.S.A. 91 G7 43 9N 98 32W
Lake Ann, MI, U.S.A. 79 E6 44 43N 85 51W
Lake Arthur, LA, U.S.A. 75 D3 30 5N 92 41W
Lake Arthur, NM, U.S.A. 88 D6 33 0N 104 22W
Lake Benton, MN, U.S.A. 80 F2 44 15N 96 17W
Lake Bird, FL, U.S.A. 67 A5 30 14N 83 37W
Lake Bronson, MN, U.S.A. 80 B2 48 44N 96 40W
Lake Buena Vista, Orlando, U.S.A. 115 B1 28 23N 81 32W
Lake Butler, FL, U.S.A. 67 A6 30 1N 82 21W
Lake Cain Hills, Orlando, U.S.A. 115 B2 28 29N 81 28W
Lake Carmel, NY, U.S.A. 87 A3 41 28N 73 40W
Lake Charles, LA, U.S.A. 75 D2 30 14N 93 13W
Lake Chelan Nat. Recr. Area ⌓, WA, U.S.A. 101 B5 48 25N 120 52W
Lake City, AR, U.S.A. 63 C5 35 49N 90 26W
Lake City, CA, U.S.A. 64 B6 41 39N 120 13W
Lake City, CO, U.S.A. 66 D3 38 2N 107 19W
Lake City, FL, U.S.A. 67 A6 30 11N 82 38W
Lake City, IA, U.S.A. 73 C4 42 16N 94 44W
Lake City, KS, U.S.A. 74 D5 37 21N 98 49W
Lake City, MI, U.S.A. 79 E6 44 20N 85 13W
Lake City, MN, U.S.A. 80 F6 44 27N 92 16W
Lake City, PA, U.S.A. 95 B2 42 1N 80 21W
Lake City, SC, U.S.A. 90 E6 33 52N 79 45W
Lake City, TN, U.S.A. 97 D8 36 13N 84 9W
Lake Clark Nat. Park and Preserve △, AK, U.S.A. 61 F9 61 0N 154 0W
Lake Clear, NY, U.S.A. 89 A6 44 22N 74 14W
Lake County ☆, CA, U.S.A. 64 D4 39 5N 122 45W
Lake County ☆, CO, U.S.A. 66 C4 39 10N 106 20W
Lake County ☆, FL, U.S.A. 67 C7 28 45N 81 45W
Lake County ☆, IL, U.S.A. 71 A5 42 20N 88 0W
Lake County ☆, IN, U.S.A. 72 B3 41 25N 87 25W
Lake County ☆, MI, U.S.A. 79 F6 44 0N 85 50W
Lake County ☆, MN, U.S.A. 80 C7 47 30N 91 20W
Lake County ☆, MT, U.S.A. 83 C3 47 40N 114 10W
Lake County ☆, OH, U.S.A. 92 B5 41 40N 81 21W
Lake County ☆, OR, U.S.A. 94 C5 44 45N 120 20W
Lake County ☆, SD, U.S.A. 91 F8 44 0N 97 7W
Lake County ☆, TN, U.S.A. 96 D3 36 23N 89 29W
Lake Cowichan, B.C., Canada 186 G10 48 49N 124 3W
Lake Crystal, MN, U.S.A. 80 F4 44 6N 94 13W
Lake Delton, WI, U.S.A. 103 E4 43 35N 89 47W
Lake Elmo, Minneapolis-St. Paul, U.S.A. 113 B4 44 59N 92 54W
Lake Elmo Regional Park, Minneapolis-St. Paul, U.S.A. 113 B4 44 59N 92 55W
Lake Elsinore, CA, U.S.A. 65 K9 33 40N 117 20W
Lake Fairfax Park, VA, U.S.A. 119 B2 38 57N 77 19W
Lake Forest, IL, U.S.A. 71 A6 42 15N 87 50W
Lake Forest Park, Seattle, U.S.A. 118 B4 47 45N 122 16W
Lake Fork, ID, U.S.A. 70 E2 44 50N 116 5W
Lake Fork →, UT, U.S.A. 100 C5 40 13N 110 7W
Lake Geneva, WI, U.S.A. 103 F5 42 36N 88 26W
Lake George, CO, U.S.A. 66 D5 38 59N 105 22W
Lake George, MN, U.S.A. 80 C4 47 12N 94 59W
Lake George, NY, U.S.A. 89 B7 43 26N 73 43W
Lake Hamilton, AR, U.S.A. 63 D2 34 25N 93 6W
Lake Harbor, FL, U.S.A. 67 E8 26 42N 80 48W
Lake Harbour = Kimmirut, Nunavut, Canada 191 E12 62 50N 69 50W
Lake Havasu City, AZ, U.S.A. 62 C1 34 27N 114 22W
Lake Helen, FL, U.S.A. 67 C7 28 59N 81 14W
Lake Hill, B.C., Canada 187 G11 48 28N 123 22W
Lake Hughes, CA, U.S.A. 65 J8 34 41N 118 26W
Lake Isabella, CA, U.S.A. 65 H8 35 38N 118 28W
Lake Jackson, TX, U.S.A. 99 H12 29 3N 95 27W
Lake Lenore, Sask., Canada 182 C7 52 24N 104 59W
Lake Lenore Caves, WA, U.S.A. 101 C6 47 28N 119 31W
Lake Lillian, MN, U.S.A. 80 F4 44 57N 94 53W
Lake Linden, MI, U.S.A. 79 B3 47 11N 88 24W
Lake Louise, Alta., Canada 185 G4 51 30N 116 10W
Lake Lure, NC, U.S.A. 90 C3 35 25N 82 12W
Lake Mary, FL, U.S.A. 67 C7 28 46N 81 19W
Lake Mason Nat. Wildlife Refuge ⌓, MT, U.S.A. 83 D9 46 38N 108 44W
Lake Mead, NV, U.S.A. 85 F6 36 1N 114 44W
Lake Mead Nat. Recr. Area ⌓, AZ, U.S.A. 62 A1 36 30N 114 22W
Lake Meredith Nat. Recr. Area ⌓, TX, U.S.A. 98 B6 35 50N 101 50W
Lake Mills, IA, U.S.A. 73 B5 43 25N 93 32W
Lake Mills, WI, U.S.A. 103 E5 43 5N 88 55W
Lake Mohawk, NJ, U.S.A. 87 A2 41 1N 74 39W
Lake Montezuma, AZ, U.S.A. 62 C4 34 38N 111 47W
Lake Murray, San Diego, U.S.A. 117 B2 32 46N 117 2W
Lake Nebagamon, WI, U.S.A. 103 B2 46 31N 91 42W
Lake Norden, SD, U.S.A. 91 F8 44 35N 97 13W
Lake Odessa, MI, U.S.A. 79 G6 42 47N 85 8W
Lake of the Woods County ☆, MN, U.S.A. 80 B4 48 40N 94 50W
Lake of the Woods Prov. Park ⌓, Ont., Canada 180 C2 49 4N 94 31W
Lake Ophelia Nat. Wildlife Refuge ⌓, LA, U.S.A. 75 C4 31 15N 91 55W
Lake Orion, MI, U.S.A. 79 G8 42 47N 83 14W
Lake Oswego, OR, U.S.A. 94 B3 45 25N 122 40W
Lake Ozark, MO, U.S.A. 82 C4 38 12N 92 38W
Lake Park, FL, U.S.A. 67 E8 26 48N 80 3W
Lake Park, GA, U.S.A. 68 F3 30 41N 83 11W
Lake Park, IA, U.S.A. 73 B3 43 27N 95 19W
Lake Park, Milwaukee, U.S.A. 112 B2 43 4N 87 52W
Lake Park, MN, U.S.A. 80 D2 46 53N 96 6W
Lake Placid, FL, U.S.A. 67 D7 27 18N 81 22W
Lake Placid, NY, U.S.A. 89 A7 44 17N 73 59W
Lake Pleasant, NY, U.S.A. 89 B6 43 28N 74 25W
Lake Preston, SD, U.S.A. 91 F8 44 22N 97 23W
Lake Providence, LA, U.S.A. 75 B4 32 48N 91 10W
Lake Range, NV, U.S.A. 85 B1 40 10N 119 20W
Lake Roosevelt Nat. Recr. Area ⌓, WA, U.S.A. 101 B7 48 5N 118 14W
Lake St. Peter, Ont., Canada 179 B8 45 18N 78 2W
Lake Seminole Park, Tampa, U.S.A. 119 B2 27 51N 82 46W
Lake Shore, MD, U.S.A. 77 A4 39 7N 76 29W
Lake Stevens, WA, U.S.A. 101 B3 48 1N 122 4W
Lake Success, NY, U.S.A. 114 B4 40 46N 73 43W
Lake Superior Prov. Park ⌓, Ont., Canada 181 E12 47 45N 84 45W
Lake Traverse Indian Reservation, ND, U.S.A. 91 E8 46 0N 97 10W
Lake Valley, NV, U.S.A. 85 D6 38 20N 114 30W
Lake View, AR, U.S.A. 63 C5 35 54N 90 27W
Lake View, IA, U.S.A. 73 C3 42 18N 95 3W
Lake View, SC, U.S.A. 90 D6 34 21N 79 10W
Lake Villa, IL, U.S.A. 71 A5 42 25N 88 5W
Lake Village, AR, U.S.A. 63 E4 33 20N 91 17W
Lake Wales, FL, U.S.A. 67 D7 27 54N 81 35W
Lake Wilson, MN, U.S.A. 80 G3 43 59N 95 57W
Lake Worth, FL, U.S.A. 67 E8 26 37N 80 3W
Lakecreek, OR, U.S.A. 94 E3 42 26N 122 37W
Lakefield, Ont., Canada 179 C8 44 25N 78 16W
Lakefield, MN, U.S.A. 80 G3 43 41N 95 10W
Lakefront State Park ⌓, Cleveland, U.S.A. 107 A2 41 32N 81 39W
Lakehurst, NJ, U.S.A. 87 B2 40 1N 74 19W
Lakeland, FL, U.S.A. 67 C7 28 3N 81 57W
Lakeland, GA, U.S.A. 68 E3 31 2N 83 4W
Lakeland, TN, U.S.A. 96 E3 35 14N 89 44W
Lakeland Prov. Park ⌓, Alta., Canada 184 D9 54 45N 111 33W
Lakemont, GA, U.S.A. 68 B3 34 47N 83 25W
Lakemont, PA, U.S.A. 95 D4 40 28N 78 24W
Lakeport, CA, U.S.A. 64 D4 39 3N 122 55W
Lakeport, MI, U.S.A. 79 F9 43 7N 82 30W
Lakeshore, CA, U.S.A. 65 F7 37 15N 119 12W
Lakeshore, MS, U.S.A. 81 F4 30 15N 89 26W
Lakeside, CA, U.S.A. 65 L10 32 52N 116 55W
Lakeside, Denver, U.S.A. 109 B1 39 46N 105 3W
Lakeside, MT, U.S.A. 83 B3 48 1N 114 14W
Lakeside, NE, U.S.A. 84 B3 42 3N 102 26W
Lakeside, OR, U.S.A. 94 D1 43 35N 124 11W
Lakeside, UT, U.S.A. 100 B3 41 13N 112 52W
Lakeside, VA, U.S.A. 102 D7 37 37N 77 28W
Lakeside Park, KY, U.S.A. 107 B1 39 2N 84 34W
Laketon, TX, U.S.A. 98 B7 35 33N 100 38W
Laketown, UT, U.S.A. 100 B4 41 49N 111 19W
Lakeview, Chicago, U.S.A. 108 B3 41 56N 87 38W
Lakeview, MI, U.S.A. 79 F6 43 27N 85 17W
Lakeview, MT, U.S.A. 83 F6 44 36N 111 49W
Lakeview, OH, U.S.A. 92 C3 40 29N 83 56W
Lakeview, OR, U.S.A. 94 E5 42 11N 120 21W
Lakeview, TX, U.S.A. 98 C7 34 40N 100 42W
Lakeville, CT, U.S.A. 78 C1 41 58N 73 26W
Lakeville, IN, U.S.A. 72 B4 41 31N 86 16W
Lakeville, MA, U.S.A. 78 C4 41 50N 70 55W
Lakeville, MN, U.S.A. 80 F5 44 39N 93 14W
Lakewood, CO, U.S.A. 66 C5 39 42N 105 4W
Lakewood, Los Angeles, U.S.A. 111 C4 33 51N 118 7W
Lakewood, NJ, U.S.A. 87 B2 40 6N 74 13W
Lakewood, NM, U.S.A. 88 E6 32 38N 104 23W
Lakewood, NY, U.S.A. 89 C1 42 6N 79 19W
Lakewood, OH, U.S.A. 92 B5 41 28N 81 47W
Lakewood, WA, U.S.A. 101 B3 48 9N 122 13W
Lakewood, WA, U.S.A. 101 C3 47 11N 122 32W
Lakewood, WI, U.S.A. 103 C5 45 18N 88 31W
Lakewood Park, Atlanta, U.S.A. 106 B2 33 43N 84 24W
Lakewood Park, FL, U.S.A. 67 D8 27 33N 80 24W
Lakin, KS, U.S.A. 74 D2 37 57N 101 15W
Lakota, IA, U.S.A. 73 B4 43 23N 94 6W
Lakota, ND, U.S.A. 91 B7 48 2N 98 21W
Lamadrid, Coahuila, Mexico 214 C3 27 3N 101 47W
Lamaline, Nfld. & L., Canada 174 F5 46 52N 55 49W
Lamar, AR, U.S.A. 63 C2 35 27N 93 23W
Lamar, CO, U.S.A. 66 D8 38 5N 102 37W
Lamar, MS, U.S.A. 81 B4 34 55N 89 19W
Lamar, MO, U.S.A. 82 D2 37 30N 94 16W
Lamar, NE, U.S.A. 84 D4 40 34N 101 59W
Lamar, OK, U.S.A. 93 C7 35 6N 96 8W
Lamar, SC, U.S.A. 90 D5 34 10N 80 4W
Lamar County ☆, AL, U.S.A. 60 C2 33 45N 88 7W
Lamar County ☆, GA, U.S.A. 68 C2 33 5N 84 10W
Lamar County ☆, MS, U.S.A. 81 E4 31 9N 89 25W
Lamar County ☆, TX, U.S.A. 99 D12 33 40N 95 33W
Lamb County ☆, TX, U.S.A. 98 D5 34 0N 102 15W
Lambert, MS, U.S.A. 81 B3 34 12N 90 17W
Lambert, MT, U.S.A. 83 C13 47 41N 104 37W
Lambert-St. Louis International ✈ (STL), MO, U.S.A. 82 C6 38 45N 90 22W
Lamberton, MN, U.S.A. 80 F3 44 14N 95 16W
Lambertville, MI, U.S.A. 79 H8 41 46N 83 35W
Lambertville, NJ, U.S.A. 87 B2 40 22N 74 57W
Lambeth, Ont., Canada 178 E5 42 54N 81 18W
Lambton, Qué., Canada 177 F11 45 50N 71 5W
Lambton, C., N.W.T., Canada 188 B8 71 5N 123 9W
Lambton Shores, Ont., Canada 178 D5 43 10N 81 56W
Lame Deer, MT, U.S.A. 83 E11 45 37N 106 40W
Lamèque, N.B., Canada 173 F5 47 45N 64 38W
Lamèque I., N.B., Canada 173 F5 47 50N 64 38W
Lamesa, TX, U.S.A. 98 E6 32 44N 101 58W
Lamine →, MO, U.S.A. 82 C4 38 59N 92 51W
Lamison, AL, U.S.A. 60 D3 32 7N 87 34W
Lamlam, Mt., Guam 105 b 13 22N 144 41 E
Lamming Mills, B.C., Canada 187 B14 53 20N 120 15W
Lamoille, NV, U.S.A. 85 B5 40 44N 115 29W
Lamoille →, VT, U.S.A. 86 B1 44 38N 73 13W
Lamoille County ☆, VT, U.S.A. 86 B2 44 40N 72 40W
Lamona, WA, U.S.A. 101 C7 47 22N 118 29W
Lamoni, IA, U.S.A. 73 E5 40 37N 93 56W
Lamont, Alta., Canada 184 E8 53 46N 112 50W
Lamont, CA, U.S.A. 65 H8 35 15N 118 55W
Lamont, FL, U.S.A. 67 A5 30 23N 83 49W
Lamont, IA, U.S.A. 73 C7 42 36N 91 39W
Lamont, KS, U.S.A. 74 C7 38 7N 96 2W
Lamont, MS, U.S.A. 81 C2 33 32N 91 5W
Lamont, OK, U.S.A. 93 B6 36 42N 97 30W
Lamont, WA, U.S.A. 101 C8 47 12N 117 54W
Lamont, WY, U.S.A. 104 D5 42 13N 107 29W
Lampacitos, Nuevo León, Mexico 215 F5 24 14N 99 42W
Lampasas, TX, U.S.A. 99 F9 31 4N 98 11W
Lampasas →, TX, U.S.A. 99 G10 30 59N 97 24W
Lampasas County ☆, TX, U.S.A. 99 F9 31 5N 98 10W
Lampazos de Naranjo, Nuevo León, Mexico 214 C4 27 1N 100 31W
Lampman, Sask., Canada 182 F9 49 25N 102 50W
Lamy, NM, U.S.A. 88 B5 35 29N 105 53W
Lanagan, MO, U.S.A. 82 E2 36 37N 94 27W
Lāna'i, HI, U.S.A. 69 C5 20 50N 156 55W
Lāna'i City, HI, U.S.A. 69 C5 20 50N 156 55W
Lāna'ihale, HI, U.S.A. 69 C5 20 49N 156 53W
Lanark, Ont., Canada 176 F6 45 1N 76 22W
Lanark, IL, U.S.A. 71 A4 42 6N 89 50W
Lanark Village, FL, U.S.A. 67 B4 29 53N 84 36W
Lancaster, Ont., Canada 176 F8 45 10N 74 30W
Lancaster, CA, U.S.A. 65 J8 34 42N 118 8W
Lancaster, KS, U.S.A. 74 B8 39 34N 95 18W
Lancaster, KY, U.S.A. 97 C8 37 37N 84 35W
Lancaster, MN, U.S.A. 80 B2 48 52N 96 48W
Lancaster, MO, U.S.A. 82 A4 40 31N 92 32W
Lancaster, NH, U.S.A. 86 B3 44 29N 71 34W
Lancaster, NY, U.S.A. 89 C2 42 54N 78 40W
Lancaster, OH, U.S.A. 92 D4 39 43N 82 36W
Lancaster, PA, U.S.A. 95 D6 40 2N 76 19W
Lancaster, SC, U.S.A. 90 D5 34 43N 80 46W
Lancaster, TX, U.S.A. 99 E11 32 35N 96 45W
Lancaster, VA, U.S.A. 77 C4 37 46N 76 28W
Lancaster, WI, U.S.A. 103 F3 42 51N 90 43W
Lancaster County ☆, NE, U.S.A. 84 D9 40 45N 96 45W
Lancaster County ☆, PA, U.S.A. 95 E6 40 0N 76 19W
Lancaster County ☆, SC, U.S.A. 90 D5 34 40N 80 40W
Lancaster County ☆, VA, U.S.A. 102 D8 37 45N 76 30W
Lancaster Sd., Nunavut, Canada 190 C9 74 13N 84 0W
Lance Creek, WY, U.S.A. 104 C8 43 2N 104 39W
Lancer, Sask., Canada 182 E3 50 48N 108 53W
Land Between the Lakes Nat. Recr. Area ⌓, U.S.A. 96 D4 36 25N 88 0W
Land O'Lakes, FL, U.S.A. 67 C6 28 13N 82 27W
Landa, ND, U.S.A. 91 B5 48 54N 100 55W
Landa de Matamoros, Querétaro, Mexico 219 A8 21 13N 99 20W
Landenburg, PA, U.S.A. 77 A5 39 47N 75 46W
Lander, WY, U.S.A. 104 D4 42 50N 108 44W
Lander County ☆, NV, U.S.A. 85 C3 40 0N 117 0W
Landfall, Minneapolis-St. Paul, U.S.A. 113 B4 44 57N 92 58W
Landis, Sask., Canada 182 C3 52 12N 108 27W
Landis, NC, U.S.A. 90 C5 35 33N 80 37W
Lando, SC, U.S.A. 90 D4 34 46N 81 1W
Landover Hills, MD, U.S.A. 119 B4 38 56N 76 54W
Landrienne, Qué., Canada 176 C5 48 30N 77 50W
Landrum, SC, U.S.A. 90 C3 35 11N 82 11W
Lands End, N.W.T., Canada 190 B1 76 22N 122 37W
Lane, KS, U.S.A. 74 C8 38 26N 95 5W
Lane, SC, U.S.A. 90 E6 33 32N 79 53W
Lane, SD, U.S.A. 91 F7 44 4N 98 26W
Lane County ☆, KS, U.S.A. 74 C3 38 30N 100 30W
Lane County ☆, OR, U.S.A. 94 D2 44 0N 123 0W
Lanesboro, IA, U.S.A. 73 C4 42 11N 94 41W
Lanesboro, MN, U.S.A. 80 G7 43 43N 91 58W
Lanesborough, MA, U.S.A. 78 B1 42 31N 73 14W
Lanett, AL, U.S.A. 60 D5 32 52N 85 12W
Lang Bay, B.C., Canada 186 F10 49 45N 124 21W
Langara I., B.C., Canada 186 A1 54 14N 133 1W
Langdon, KS, U.S.A. 74 D5 37 51N 98 19W
Langdon, ND, U.S.A. 91 B7 48 45N 98 22W
Langenburg, Sask., Canada 183 E10 50 51N 101 43W
Langford, B.C., Canada 187 G11 48 27N 123 29W
Langford, SD, U.S.A. 91 E8 45 36N 97 50W
Langham, Sask., Canada 182 C5 52 22N 106 58W
Langhorne, PA, U.S.A. 87 B2 40 10N 74 55W
Langlade, St-P. & M. 174 F4 46 50N 56 20W
Langlade County ☆, WI, U.S.A. 103 C4 45 15N 89 10W
Langley, B.C., Canada 187 F12 49 7N 122 39W
Langley, AR, U.S.A. 63 D2 34 19N 93 51W
Langley, OK, U.S.A. 93 B8 36 28N 95 3W
Langley, VA, U.S.A. 119 B2 38 57N 77 11W
Langley, WA, U.S.A. 101 B3 48 2N 122 24W
Langley Park, MD, U.S.A. 119 B4 38 59N 76 58W
Langlois, OR, U.S.A. 94 E1 42 56N 124 27W
Langruth, Man., Canada 183 E13 50 23N 98 40W
Langston, OK, U.S.A. 93 C6 35 59N 97 18W
Langtry, TX, U.S.A. 98 H6 29 49N 101 34W
L'Anguille →, AR, U.S.A. 63 D5 34 44N 90 40W
Lanham, MD, U.S.A. 119 B4 38 59N 76 51W
Lanier County ☆, GA, U.S.A. 68 E3 31 0N 83 5W
Lanigan, Sask., Canada 182 D6 51 51N 105 2W
Lankin, ND, U.S.A. 91 B8 48 19N 97 55W
L'Annonciation, Qué., Canada 176 E8 46 25N 74 55W
Lansdale, PA, U.S.A. 87 B1 40 14N 75 17W
Lansdowne, Ont., Canada 179 C10 44 24N 76 1W
Lansdowne, MD, U.S.A. 77 A4 39 14N 76 39W
Lansdowne, PA, U.S.A. 116 B1 39 56N 75 16W
L'Anse, MI, U.S.A. 79 C3 46 45N 88 27W
L'Anse-au-Clair, Nfld. & L., Canada 174 A3 51 25N 57 5W
L'Anse au Loup, Nfld. & L., Canada 174 A4 51 32N 56 50W
L'Anse aux Meadows, Canada 174 A5 51 36N 55 32W
L'Anse Indian Reservation, MI, U.S.A. 79 C3 46 45N 88 20W
Lansford, ND, U.S.A. 91 B4 48 38N 101 23W
Lansford, PA, U.S.A. 95 D7 40 50N 75 53W
Lansing, IL, U.S.A. 71 B6 41 34N 87 33W
Lansing, IA, U.S.A. 73 B7 43 22N 91 13W
Lansing, KS, U.S.A. 74 B9 39 15N 94 54W
Lansing, MI, U.S.A. 79 G7 42 44N 84 33W
Lansing →, Yukon, Canada 189 D6 63 44N 133 28W
Lantana, FL, U.S.A. 67 E8 26 35N 80 3W
Lantzville, B.C., Canada 186 F10 49 15N 124 5W
Lanz I., B.C., Canada 186 E6 50 49N 128 41W
Laona, WI, U.S.A. 103 C5 45 34N 88 40W
Lapeer, MI, U.S.A. 79 F8 43 3N 83 19W
Lapeer County ☆, MI, U.S.A. 79 F8 43 5N 83 15W
Lapel, IN, U.S.A. 72 C5 40 4N 85 51W
Laplace, LA, U.S.A. 75 D5 30 4N 90 29W
LaPorte, IN, U.S.A. 72 B4 41 36N 86 43W
Laporte, MN, U.S.A. 80 C4 47 13N 94 45W
Laporte, PA, U.S.A. 95 C6 41 25N 76 30W
LaPorte County ☆, IN, U.S.A. 72 B4 41 30N 86 45W
Lappans, MD, U.S.A. 77 A3 39 33N 77 43W
Lapwai, ID, U.S.A. 70 C2 46 24N 116 48W
Laramie, WY, U.S.A. 104 E7 41 19N 105 35W
Laramie →, WY, U.S.A. 104 D8 42 13N 104 33W
Laramie County ☆, WY, U.S.A. 104 E8 41 15N 104 40W
Laramie Mts., WY, U.S.A. 104 E7 42 0N 105 30W
Laramie Pk., WY, U.S.A. 104 D7 42 17N 105 27W
Larchmont, NY, U.S.A. 114 A4 40 55N 73 45W
Larchwood, IA, U.S.A. 73 B2 43 27N 96 26W
Larder Lake, Ont., Canada 176 C3 48 5N 79 40W
Lardo, ID, U.S.A. 70 E2 44 55N 116 8W
L'Ardoise, N.S., Canada 173 H9 45 37N 60 45W
Laredo, MO, U.S.A. 82 A3 40 2N 93 27W
Laredo, TX, U.S.A. 98 K8 27 30N 99 30W
Laredo Sd., B.C., Canada 186 C6 52 30N 128 53W
Lares, Puerto Rico 105 G16 18 18N 66 53W
Larga, Laguna, TX, U.S.A. 99 K10 27 30N 97 25W
Largo, FL, U.S.A. 67 D6 27 54N 82 47W
Largo, Key, FL, U.S.A. 67 F8 25 15N 80 15W
Largo Cr. →, NM, U.S.A. 88 C2 34 30N 108 51W
Larimer County ☆, CO, U.S.A. 66 B5 40 40N 105 20W
Larimore, ND, U.S.A. 91 C8 47 54N 97 38W
Lark, ND, U.S.A. 91 D4 46 27N 101 24W
Lark, TX, U.S.A. 98 B6 35 12N 101 14W
Lark, UT, U.S.A. 100 C3 40 32N 112 6W
Lark Harbour, Nfld. & L., Canada 174 C2 49 6N 58 23W
Larkins = South Miami, FL, U.S.A. 67 F8 25 42N 80 17W
Larkspur, CO, U.S.A. 66 C6 39 14N 104 53W
Larned, KS, U.S.A. 74 C4 38 11N 99 6W
Larose, LA, U.S.A. 75 E5 29 34N 90 23W
Larrabee, IA, U.S.A. 73 C3 42 52N 95 33W
Larrainzar, Chiapas, Mexico 222 C4 16 53N 92 42W
Larrys River, N.S., Canada 173 H8 45 13N 61 23W
Larsen Bay, AK, U.S.A. 61 H9 57 32N 153 59W
Larsen Sound, Nunavut, Canada 190 C6 70 30N 98 45W
Larson, ND, U.S.A. 91 B3 48 53N 102 52W
Larue County ☆, KY, U.S.A. 97 C7 37 30N 85 40W
Larus L., Ont., Canada 180 A2 51 17N 94 40W
Las Almejas, B., Baja Calif. S., Mexico 211 J7 24 33N 111 42W
Las Animas, CO, U.S.A. 66 D7 38 4N 103 13W
Las Ánimas, I., Baja Calif., Mexico 210 E6 28 43N 112 58W
Las Ánimas, Pta., Baja Calif., Mexico 210 E5 28 51N 113 16W
Las Animas County ☆, CO, U.S.A. 66 E7 37 15N 104 0W
Las Arenitas, Sinaloa, Mexico 216 C3 24 22N 107 34W
Las Calabazas →, Baja Calif., Mexico 210 A2 32 18N 116 33W
Las Calenturas, Sonora, Mexico 212 C3 30 37N 112 22W
Las Cañas, Michoacan, Mexico 218 D6 18 34N 101 58W
Las Choapas, Veracruz, Mexico 221 G6 17 55N 94 7W
Las Coloradas, Yucatán, Mexico 223 A6 21 36N 87 59W
Las Cruces, NM, U.S.A. 88 E4 32 19N 106 47W
Las Cuatas, Chihuahua, Mexico 213 C10 30 3N 105 55W
Las Cuevas, Baja Calif. S., Mexico 211 K9 23 32N 109 41W
Las Delicias, Chiapas, Mexico 222 D5 15 58N 91 51W
Las Enchilayas, Sonora, Mexico 212 C3 30 55N 112 45W
Las Esperanza, Durango, Mexico 217 B6 25 52N 104 50W
Las Glorias, Sinaloa, Mexico 216 B2 25 17N 108 30W
Las Guacamayas, Cerro, Chihuahua, Mexico 212 C7 30 32N 108 38W
Las Herrera, Durango, Mexico 216 B5 25 10N 105 31W
Las Hormigas, Nuevo León, Mexico 214 E6 25 27N 98 39W
Las Juntas, Presa, Sinaloa, Mexico 216 D4 24 0N 106 18W
Las Lagunas, Baja Calif. S., Mexico 211 K9 23 31N 109 29W
Las Lajitas, Sinaloa, Mexico 216 A1 26 5N 109 22W
Las Lomas, CA, U.S.A. 64 E3 38 41N 123 8W
Las Margaritas, Chiapas, Mexico 222 C5 16 19N 91 59W
Las Margaritas, Durango, Mexico 217 D6 23 18N 104 17W
Las Mesas, Michoacan, Mexico 219 C7 19 4N 100 33W
Las Milpas, Sonora, Mexico 212 G6 26 48N 109 50W
Las Nopaleras, Cerro, Coahuila, Mexico 215 E1 25 8N 103 15W
Las Norias, Coahuila, Mexico 214 C1 27 33N 103 39W
Las Nutrias, NM, U.S.A. 88 C4 34 28N 106 46W
Las Palmas, Oaxaca, Mexico 221 H6 16 27N 94 35W
Las Palomas, Chihuahua, Mexico 213 G8 26 32N 107 50W
Las Palomas →, Baja Calif., Mexico 210 A2 32 18N 116 33W
Las Pampas, Chihuahua, Mexico 213 F11 27 30N 104 45W
Las Pampas, Sa., Chihuahua, Mexico 213 F11 27 20N 104 45W
Las Piedras, Puerto Rico 105 G17 18 11N 65 52W
Las Puentes, Sinaloa, Mexico 216 C3 24 31N 107 34W
Las Rosas, Chiapas, Mexico 222 C4 16 24N 92 23W
Las Toronjas, Chiapas, Mexico 222 D3 15 57N 92 59W
Las Tortugas, Durango, Mexico 217 A7 26 28N 103 45W
Las Trampas Regional Park, San Francisco, U.S.A. 118 B4 37 48N 122 2W
Las Trampas Ridge, San Francisco, U.S.A. 118 A4 37 48N 122 1W
Las Tunas, Sa., Chihuahua, Mexico 213 D8 29 40N 107 15W
Las Tunitas, Baja Calif. S., Mexico 211 J8 24 49N 110 50W
Las Varas, Chihuahua, Mexico 213 D7 29 30N 108 3W
Las Varas, Nayarit, Mexico 216 F5 21 10N 105 10W
Las Vegas, NM, U.S.A. 88 B5 35 36N 105 13W
Las Vegas, NV, U.S.A. 85 F5 36 10N 115 8W
Las Vegas, L., Las Vegas, U.S.A. 110 C3 36 8N 114 58W
Las Vegas Bay, Las Vegas, U.S.A. 110 C3 36 7N 114 51W
Las Vegas-Dunes Recreation Lands, Las Vegas, U.S.A. 110 B3 36 17N 114 55W
Las Vegas McCarran International ✈ (LAS), NV, U.S.A. 85 F5 36 5N 115 9W
Las Vigas, Guerrero, Mexico 219 F8 16 46N 99 14W
Lasalle, Montréal, Canada 192 B3 45 26N 73 37W
Lasalle, Qué., Canada 177 F9 45 26N 73 38W

Lashburn, *Sask., Canada* **182 B2** 53 10N 109 40W
Lasqueti, *B.C., Canada* **186 F10** 49 30N 124 21W
Lasqueti I., *B.C., Canada* **186 F10** 49 29N 124 16W
Lassen County ☆, *CA, U.S.A.* **64 C6** 40 45N 120 30W
Lassen Nat. Forest, *CA, U.S.A.* **64 C5** 40 30N 121 15W
Lassen Pk., *CA, U.S.A.* **64 C5** 40 29N 121 30W
Lassen Volcanic Nat. Park and Wilderness △, *CA, U.S.A.* **64 C5** 40 30N 121 20W
Last Chance, *CO, U.S.A.* **66 C7** 39 44N 103 36W
Last Chance Cr. →, *UT, U.S.A.* **100 E4** 38 38N 111 21W
Last Chance Range, *CA, U.S.A.* **65 G9** 36 55N 117 36W
Last Mountain L., *Sask., Canada* **182 D6** 51 5N 105 14W
Lastrup, *MN, U.S.A.* **80 D4** 46 2N 94 4W
Lata Mt., *Amer. Samoa* **105 f** 14 14 S 169 27W
Latah, *WA, U.S.A.* **101 C8** 47 17N 117 9W
Latah County ☆, *ID, U.S.A.* **70 C2** 46 45N 116 50W
Latchford, *Ont., Canada* **176 D3** 47 20N 79 50W
Laterrière, *Qué., Canada* **177 C11** 48 18N 71 7W
Latham, *IL, U.S.A.* **71 D4** 39 58N 89 10W
Latham, *KS, U.S.A.* **74 D7** 37 32N 96 38W
Lathrop, *CA, U.S.A.* **64 F5** 37 49N 121 16W
Lathrop, *MO, U.S.A.* **82 B2** 39 33N 94 20W
Lathrup Village, *MI, U.S.A.* **109 A1** 42 29N 83 13W
Latimer, *IA, U.S.A.* **73 C5** 42 46N 93 22W
Latimer, *KS, U.S.A.* **74 C7** 38 44N 96 51W
Latimer County ☆, *OK, U.S.A.* **93 D8** 34 50N 95 10W
Laton, *CA, U.S.A.* **65 G7** 36 26N 119 41W
Latrobe, *PA, U.S.A.* **95 D3** 40 19N 79 23W
Latta, *SC, U.S.A.* **90 D6** 34 21N 79 26W
Latulipe, *Qué., Canada* **176 D3** 47 26N 79 2W
Lauderdale, *Minneapolis-St. Paul, U.S.A.* **113 B2** 44 59N 93 12W
Lauderdale, *MS, U.S.A.* **81 D5** 32 31N 88 31W
Lauderdale County ☆, *AL, U.S.A.* **60 B3** 34 56N 87 46W
Lauderdale County ☆, *MS, U.S.A.* **81 D5** 32 22N 88 42W
Lauderdale County ☆, *TN, U.S.A.* **96 E3** 35 45N 89 23W
Lauderdale Lakes, *Miami, U.S.A.* **112 B1** 26 9N 80 12W
Lauderhill, *Miami, U.S.A.* **112 B2** 26 8N 80 12W
Lauge Koch Kyst, *Greenland* **190 B14** 75 45N 57 45W
Laughing Fish Pt., *MI, U.S.A.* **79 C4** 46 32N 87 1W
Laughlin, *NV, U.S.A.* **85 G6** 35 10N 114 34W
Laughlin Pk., *NM, U.S.A.* **88 A6** 36 40N 104 10W
Laulau, Bahia, *N. Marianas* **105 c** 15 8N 145 45W
Laura, *OH, U.S.A.* **92 D2** 39 59N 84 22W
Laurel, *DE, U.S.A.* **77 B5** 38 33N 75 34W
Laurel, *FL, U.S.A.* **67 D6** 27 8N 82 27W
Laurel, *IN, U.S.A.* **72 D5** 39 30N 85 11W
Laurel, *IA, U.S.A.* **73 D6** 41 53N 92 55W
Laurel, *MD, U.S.A.* **77 A4** 39 6N 76 51W
Laurel, *MS, U.S.A.* **81 E4** 31 41N 89 8W
Laurel, *MT, U.S.A.* **83 E9** 45 40N 108 46W
Laurel, *NE, U.S.A.* **84 B8** 42 26N 97 6W
Laurel Bay, *SC, U.S.A.* **90 F5** 32 27N 80 47W
Laurel County ☆, *KY, U.S.A.* **97 C8** 37 5N 84 10W
Laurel Hill, *PA, U.S.A.* **95 D3** 40 14N 79 6W
Laurel River L., *KY, U.S.A.* **97 D8** 36 57N 84 10W
Laureldale, *NJ, U.S.A.* **87 C2** 39 30N 74 41W
Laureldale, *PA, U.S.A.* **95 D7** 40 23N 75 55W
Laureles y Góngora I, *Nayarit, Mexico* **216 F5** 21 39N 105 23W
Laurelton, *NY, U.S.A.* **114 B4** 40 40N 73 45W
Laurelville, *OH, U.S.A.* **92 D4** 39 28N 82 44W
Laurence G. Hanscom Field, *Boston, U.S.A.* **106 A2** 42 28N 71 16W
Laurens, *IA, U.S.A.* **73 C4** 42 51N 94 52W
Laurens, *SC, U.S.A.* **90 D3** 34 30N 82 1W
Laurens County ☆, *GA, U.S.A.* **68 D4** 32 30N 83 0W
Laurens County ☆, *SC, U.S.A.* **90 D4** 34 30N 82 0W
Laurentides, Réserve Faunique des ⌂, *Qué., Canada* **177 D11** 47 45N 71 15W
Laurie, *MO, U.S.A.* **82 C4** 38 12N 92 50W
Laurier, *Man., Canada* **183 E12** 50 53N 99 33W
Laurier-Station, *Qué., Canada* **177 E11** 46 32N 71 38W
Laurierville, *Qué., Canada* **177 E11** 46 18N 71 39W
Laurinburg, *NC, U.S.A.* **90 D6** 34 47N 79 28W
Laurium, *MI, U.S.A.* **79 B3** 47 14N 88 27W
Lava Beds Nat. Monument ⌂, *CA, U.S.A.* **64 B5** 41 40N 121 30W
Lava Hot Springs, *ID, U.S.A.* **70 G6** 42 37N 112 1W
Lavaca, *AR, U.S.A.* **63 C1** 35 20N 94 10W
Lavaca →, *TX, U.S.A.* **99 J11** 28 41N 96 35W
Lavaca County ☆, *TX, U.S.A.* **99 H11** 29 27N 96 57W
Laval, *Qué., Canada* **177 F9** 45 34N 73 43W
Laval-des-Rapides, *Qué., Canada* **192 A2** 45 33N 73 42W
Laval Ouest, *Montréal, Canada* **192 A1** 45 33N 73 52W
Laval-sur-le-Lac, *Qué., Canada* **192 A1** 45 32N 73 52W
Lavallette, *NJ, U.S.A.* **87 C2** 39 58N 74 4W
Lavaltrie, *Qué., Canada* **177 F9** 45 53N 73 17W
Lavant Station, *Ont., Canada* **179 B10** 45 3N 76 42W
Laveen, *Phoenix, U.S.A.* **116 C1** 33 21N 112 12W
Laverlochère, *Qué., Canada* **176 D3** 47 26N 79 18W
Laverne, *OK, U.S.A.* **93 B4** 36 43N 99 54W
Lavic L., *CA, U.S.A.* **65 J10** 34 40N 116 21W
Lavieille, L., *Ont., Canada* **179 B8** 45 51N 78 14W
Lavillette, *N.B., Canada* **173 F4** 47 16N 65 18W
Lavina, *MT, U.S.A.* **83 D9** 46 18N 108 56W
Lavon L., *TX, U.S.A.* **99 D11** 33 2N 96 28W
Lavonia, *GA, U.S.A.* **68 B3** 34 26N 83 6W
Lavoy, *Alta., Canada* **184 E9** 53 27N 111 52W
Lawen, *OR, U.S.A.* **94 D7** 43 27N 118 48W
Lawler, *IA, U.S.A.* **73 B6** 43 4N 92 9W
Lawn, *Nfld. & L., Canada* **174 F5** 46 57N 55 35W
Lawn, *TX, U.S.A.* **99 E8** 32 8N 99 45W
Lawndale, *Chicago, U.S.A.* **108 B2** 41 50N 87 42W
Lawndale, *Los Angeles, U.S.A.* **111 C2** 33 53N 118 21W
Lawne L., *Orlando, U.S.A.* **115 A2** 28 33N 81 26W
Lawrence, *IN, U.S.A.* **72 D4** 39 50N 86 2W
Lawrence, *KS, U.S.A.* **74 C8** 38 58N 95 14W
Lawrence, *MA, U.S.A.* **78 B3** 42 43N 71 10W
Lawrence, *MI, U.S.A.* **79 G5** 42 13N 86 3W
Lawrence, *NY, U.S.A.* **114 C5** 40 36N 73 43W
Lawrence, *NE, U.S.A.* **84 D7** 40 18N 98 16W
Lawrence County ☆, *AL, U.S.A.* **60 B3** 34 29N 87 18W
Lawrence County ☆, *AR, U.S.A.* **63 B4** 36 0N 91 0W
Lawrence County ☆, *IL, U.S.A.* **71 E6** 38 45N 87 45W
Lawrence County ☆, *IN, U.S.A.* **72 E4** 38 50N 86 30W
Lawrence County ☆, *KY, U.S.A.* **97 B10** 38 5N 82 45W
Lawrence County ☆, *MS, U.S.A.* **81 E3** 31 33N 90 7W
Lawrence County ☆, *MO, U.S.A.* **82 D3** 37 10N 93 50W
Lawrence County ☆, *OH, U.S.A.* **92 E4** 38 32N 82 41W
Lawrence County ☆, *PA, U.S.A.* **95 D2** 41 0N 80 15W
Lawrence County ☆, *SD, U.S.A.* **91 F2** 44 23N 103 44W
Lawrence County ☆, *TN, U.S.A.* **96 E5** 35 14N 87 20W
Lawrence Creek, *OK, U.S.A.* **93 B7** 36 5N 96 26W
Lawrence J. Timmerman ✈, *Milwaukee, U.S.A.* **112 B1** 43 6N 88 2W
Lawrence Station, *N.B., Canada* **173 H2** 45 26N 67 11W
Lawrenceburg, *IN, U.S.A.* **72 D6** 39 6N 84 52W
Lawrenceburg, *KY, U.S.A.* **97 B8** 38 2N 84 54W
Lawrenceburg, *TN, U.S.A.* **96 E5** 35 14N 87 20W
Lawrencetown, *N.S., Canada* **173 J4** 44 53N 65 10W
Lawrenceville, *GA, U.S.A.* **68 C3** 33 57N 83 59W
Lawrenceville, *IL, U.S.A.* **71 E6** 38 44N 87 41W
Lawrenceville, *NJ, U.S.A.* **87 B2** 40 18N 74 44W
Lawrenceville, *PA, U.S.A.* **95 C5** 41 59N 77 8W
Lawrenceville, *VA, U.S.A.* **102 E7** 36 46N 77 51W
Lawson, *MO, U.S.A.* **82 B2** 39 26N 94 12W
Lawtey, *FL, U.S.A.* **67 A6** 30 3N 82 5W
Lawton, *MI, U.S.A.* **79 G6** 42 10N 85 50W
Lawton, *ND, U.S.A.* **91 B7** 48 18N 98 22W
Lawton, *OK, U.S.A.* **93 D5** 34 37N 98 25W
Lay, *CO, U.S.A.* **66 B3** 40 32N 107 53W
Laysan I., *HI, U.S.A.* **69 F9** 25 50N 171 50W
Layton, *FL, U.S.A.* **67 G8** 24 50N 80 47W
Layton, *NJ, U.S.A.* **87 A2** 41 13N 74 50W
Layton, *UT, U.S.A.* **100 B4** 41 4N 111 58W
Laytonsville, *MD, U.S.A.* **77 A3** 39 13N 77 9W
Laytonville, *CA, U.S.A.* **64 D3** 39 41N 123 29W
Lázaro Cárdenas, *Baja Calif., Mexico* **210 B3** 31 25N 115 43W
Lázaro Cárdenas, *Chiapas, Mexico* **222 C3** 16 39N 93 48W
Lázaro Cárdenas, *Chihuahua, Mexico* **213 D8** 29 7N 107 5W
Lázaro Cárdenas, *Jalisco, Mexico* **218 C2** 19 48N 105 9W
Lázaro Cárdenas, *Michoacan, Mexico* **218 E5** 17 55N 102 11W
Lázaro Cárdenas, *Quintana Roo, Mexico* **223 C5** 18 59N 88 13W
Lázaro Cárdenas, *Tabasco, Mexico* **222 A3** 18 10N 93 34W
Lázaro Cárdenas, *Veracruz, Mexico* **220 B2** 22 15N 98 8W
Lázaro Cárdenas, Presa, *Durango, Mexico* **216 B5** 25 36N 105 3W
Lazear, *CO, U.S.A.* **66 D3** 38 47N 107 47W
Le Bic, *Qué., Canada* **177 C14** 48 20N 68 41W
Le Breton, L., *Qué., Canada* **172 B9** 51 53N 60 9W
Le Center, *MN, U.S.A.* **80 F5** 44 23N 93 44W
Le Claire, *IA, U.S.A.* **73 D8** 41 36N 90 21W
Le Doré, L., *Qué., Canada* **172 B8** 51 17N 61 23W
Le Flore County ☆, *OK, U.S.A.* **93 D9** 35 0N 94 45W
Le Grand, *CA, U.S.A.* **64 F6** 37 14N 120 15W
Le Grand, *IA, U.S.A.* **73 C6** 42 0N 92 47W
Le Loup, *KS, U.S.A.* **74 C8** 38 42N 95 10W
Le Mars, *IA, U.S.A.* **73 C2** 42 47N 96 10W
Le Moyen, *LA, U.S.A.* **75 D3** 30 48N 92 4W
Le Raysville, *PA, U.S.A.* **95 C6** 41 51N 76 11W
Le Roy, *IL, U.S.A.* **71 C5** 40 21N 88 46W
Le Roy, *KS, U.S.A.* **74 C8** 38 5N 95 38W
Le Roy, *MI, U.S.A.* **79 E6** 44 2N 85 27W
Le Roy, *MN, U.S.A.* **80 G6** 43 31N 92 30W
Le Roy, *NY, U.S.A.* **89 C2** 42 58N 78 0W
Le Roy, *PA, U.S.A.* **95 C6** 41 41N 76 43W
Le Roy, L., *Qué., Canada* **175 B4** 55 10N 67 15W
Le Sueur, *MN, U.S.A.* **80 F5** 44 28N 93 55W
Le Sueur County ☆, *MN, U.S.A.* **80 F5** 44 20N 93 45W
Lea County ☆, *NM, U.S.A.* **88 E7** 32 50N 103 30W
Leach I., *Ont., Canada* **181 E12** 47 28N 84 57W
Leachville, *AR, U.S.A.* **63 C5** 35 56N 90 16W
Lead, *SD, U.S.A.* **91 F2** 44 21N 103 46W
Lead Hill, *AR, U.S.A.* **63 B3** 36 25N 92 55W
Lead Hill, *MO, U.S.A.* **82 D4** 37 6N 92 38W
Leadbetter Pt., *WA, U.S.A.* **101 D1** 46 39N 124 3W
Leader, *Sask., Canada* **182 E2** 50 50N 109 30W
Leadore, *ID, U.S.A.* **70 E5** 44 41N 113 21W
Leadpoint, *WA, U.S.A.* **101 B8** 48 55N 117 35W
Leadville, *CO, U.S.A.* **66 C4** 39 15N 106 18W
Leadwood, *MO, U.S.A.* **82 D6** 37 52N 90 36W
Leaf →, *MS, U.S.A.* **81 F5** 30 59N 88 44W
Leaf L., *Sask., Canada* **183 B9** 53 1N 102 8W
Leaf Rapids, *Man., Canada* **191 F6** 56 30N 99 59W
League City, *TX, U.S.A.* **99 H12** 29 31N 95 6W
Leake County ☆, *MS, U.S.A.* **81 D4** 32 42N 89 38W
Leakesville, *MS, U.S.A.* **81 E5** 31 9N 88 33W
Leakey, *TX, U.S.A.* **99 H8** 29 44N 99 46W
Leaksville = Eden, *NC, U.S.A.* **90 B6** 36 29N 79 53W
Lealman, *Tampa, U.S.A.* **119 C3** 27 49N 82 40W
Leamington, *Ont., Canada* **178 E4** 42 3N 82 36W
Leamington, *UT, U.S.A.* **100 D3** 39 32N 112 17W
Leamy, L., *Qué., Canada* **192 A1** 45 27N 75 43W
Leary, *GA, U.S.A.* **68 E2** 31 29N 84 31W
Leasburg, *MO, U.S.A.* **82 C5** 38 5N 91 18W
Leask, *Sask., Canada* **182 B5** 53 5N 106 45W
Leatherwood, *KY, U.S.A.* **97 C9** 37 2N 83 11W
Leavenworth, *IN, U.S.A.* **72 E4** 38 12N 86 21W
Leavenworth, *KS, U.S.A.* **74 B9** 39 19N 94 55W
Leavenworth, *WA, U.S.A.* **101 C5** 47 36N 120 40W
Leavenworth County ☆, *KS, U.S.A.* **74 B9** 39 15N 95 0W
Leavittsburg, *OH, U.S.A.* **92 B6** 41 14N 80 53W
Leawood, *KS, U.S.A.* **74 C9** 38 58N 94 37W
Lebam, *WA, U.S.A.* **101 D2** 46 34N 123 33W
Lebanon, *CT, U.S.A.* **78 C2** 41 38N 72 13W
Lebanon, *IN, U.S.A.* **72 C4** 40 3N 86 28W
Lebanon, *KS, U.S.A.* **74 B5** 39 49N 98 33W
Lebanon, *KY, U.S.A.* **97 C7** 37 34N 85 15W
Lebanon, *MO, U.S.A.* **82 D4** 37 41N 92 40W
Lebanon, *NH, U.S.A.* **86 C2** 43 39N 72 15W
Lebanon, *NE, U.S.A.* **84 D5** 40 3N 100 17W
Lebanon, *OH, U.S.A.* **92 D2** 39 26N 84 13W
Lebanon, *OK, U.S.A.* **93 E7** 33 59N 96 55W
Lebanon, *OR, U.S.A.* **94 C3** 44 32N 122 55W
Lebanon, *PA, U.S.A.* **95 D6** 40 20N 76 26W
Lebanon, *SD, U.S.A.* **91 E6** 45 4N 99 46W
Lebanon, *TN, U.S.A.* **96 D6** 36 12N 86 18W
Lebanon, *VA, U.S.A.* **102 E2** 36 54N 82 5W
Lebanon County ☆, *PA, U.S.A.* **95 D6** 40 20N 76 25W
Lebanon Junction, *KY, U.S.A.* **97 C7** 37 50N 85 44W
Lebanon State Forest, *NJ, U.S.A.* **87 C2** 39 53N 74 30W
Lebanon Station, *FL, U.S.A.* **67 B6** 29 10N 82 37W
Lebec, *CA, U.S.A.* **65 J8** 34 51N 118 52W
Lebel-sur-Quévillon, *Qué., Canada* **176 B6** 49 3N 76 59W
Lebo, *KS, U.S.A.* **74 C8** 38 25N 95 51W
Lecompte, *LA, U.S.A.* **75 C3** 31 6N 92 24W
Lecompton, *KS, U.S.A.* **74 B8** 39 3N 95 24W
Leduc, *Alta., Canada* **184 E7** 53 15N 113 30W
Ledyard, *IA, U.S.A.* **73 B4** 43 25N 94 10W
Lee, *FL, U.S.A.* **67 A5** 30 25N 83 18W
Lee, *IL, U.S.A.* **71 B5** 41 48N 88 56W
Lee, *ME, U.S.A.* **76 C5** 45 22N 68 17W
Lee, *MA, U.S.A.* **78 B1** 42 19N 73 15W
Lee, *NV, U.S.A.* **85 B5** 40 34N 115 36W
Lee City, *KY, U.S.A.* **97 C9** 37 44N 83 20W
Lee County ☆, *AL, U.S.A.* **60 D5** 32 39N 85 23W
Lee County ☆, *AR, U.S.A.* **63 D5** 34 46N 90 46W
Lee County ☆, *FL, U.S.A.* **67 E7** 26 30N 81 45W
Lee County ☆, *GA, U.S.A.* **68 E2** 31 45N 84 5W
Lee County ☆, *IL, U.S.A.* **71 B4** 41 45N 89 20W
Lee County ☆, *IA, U.S.A.* **73 E7** 40 40N 91 30W
Lee County ☆, *KY, U.S.A.* **97 C9** 37 35N 83 45W
Lee County ☆, *MS, U.S.A.* **81 B5** 34 16N 88 43W
Lee County ☆, *NC, U.S.A.* **90 C6** 35 30N 79 10W
Lee County ☆, *SC, U.S.A.* **90 D5** 34 10N 80 15W
Lee County ☆, *TX, U.S.A.* **99 G11** 30 17N 96 58W
Lee County ☆, *VA, U.S.A.* **102 E1** 36 45N 83 5W
Lee Vining, *CA, U.S.A.* **64 F7** 37 58N 119 7W
Leech L., *Sask., Canada* **182 D9** 51 5N 102 28W
Leech L., *MN, U.S.A.* **80 C4** 47 10N 94 24W
Leech Lake Indian Reservation, *MN, U.S.A.* **80 C4** 47 20N 94 10W
Leedey, *OK, U.S.A.* **93 C4** 35 52N 99 21W
Leeds, *AL, U.S.A.* **60 C4** 33 33N 86 33W
Leeds, *ME, U.S.A.* **76 D3** 44 18N 70 7W
Leeds, *ND, U.S.A.* **91 B6** 48 17N 99 27W
Leeds, *UT, U.S.A.* **100 F2** 37 14N 113 22W
Leeds, *UT, U.S.A.* **87 C2** 39 38N 74 26W
Leektown, *NJ, U.S.A.* **87 C2** 39 38N 74 26W
Leelanau County ☆, *MI, U.S.A.* **79 E6** 44 55N 85 50W
Leelanau L., *MI, U.S.A.* **79 E6** 44 55N 85 43W
Lee's Summit, *MO, U.S.A.* **82 C2** 38 55N 94 23W
Leesburg, *FL, U.S.A.* **67 C7** 28 49N 81 53W
Leesburg, *GA, U.S.A.* **68 E2** 31 44N 84 10W
Leesburg, *NJ, U.S.A.* **87 C2** 39 15N 74 59W
Leesburg, *OH, U.S.A.* **92 D3** 39 21N 83 33W
Leesburg, *VA, U.S.A.* **77 A3** 39 7N 77 34W
Leesport, *PA, U.S.A.* **95 D7** 40 27N 75 58W
Leesville, *LA, U.S.A.* **75 C2** 31 8N 93 16W
Leesville, *OH, U.S.A.* **92 C5** 40 27N 81 13W
Leesville L., *VA, U.S.A.* **102 D5** 37 5N 79 25W
Leeton, *MO, U.S.A.* **82 C3** 38 35N 93 42W
Leetonia, *MN, U.S.A.* **80 C6** 47 26N 92 59W
Leeville, *LA, U.S.A.* **75 E5** 29 15N 90 12W
Leewood, *WV, U.S.A.* **102 C3** 38 4N 81 27W
Leflore, *OK, U.S.A.* **93 D9** 34 54N 94 59W
Leflore County ☆, *MS, U.S.A.* **81 C3** 33 30N 90 20W
Lefors, *TX, U.S.A.* **98 B7** 35 26N 100 48W
Lefroy, *Ont., Canada* **178 C7** 44 16N 79 34W
Legal, *Alta., Canada* **184 D7** 53 55N 113 35W
Légère, *N.B., Canada* **173 F5** 47 25N 64 56W
Leggett, *CA, U.S.A.* **64 D3** 39 52N 123 43W
Leggett, *TX, U.S.A.* **99 G13** 30 49N 94 52W
Lehi, *UT, U.S.A.* **100 C4** 40 24N 111 51W
Lehigh, *IA, U.S.A.* **73 C4** 42 22N 94 3W
Lehigh, *KS, U.S.A.* **74 C6** 38 22N 97 18W
Lehigh, *OK, U.S.A.* **93 D7** 34 28N 96 13W
Lehigh →, *PA, U.S.A.* **87 B1** 40 41N 75 12W
Lehigh Acres, *FL, U.S.A.* **67 E7** 26 36N 81 39W
Lehigh County ☆, *PA, U.S.A.* **95 D7** 40 40N 75 50W
Lehighton, *PA, U.S.A.* **87 B1** 40 50N 75 43W
Lehr, *ND, U.S.A.* **91 D6** 46 17N 99 21W
Lehua I., *HI, U.S.A.* **69 A1** 22 1N 160 6W
Leicester, *MA, U.S.A.* **78 B3** 42 15N 71 55W
Leicester, *VT, U.S.A.* **86 C1** 43 50N 73 8W
Leidy, Mt., *WY, U.S.A.* **104 C2** 43 44N 110 24W
Leigh, *NE, U.S.A.* **84 C8** 41 42N 97 14W
Leighton, *AL, U.S.A.* **60 B3** 34 42N 87 32W
Leighton, *IA, U.S.A.* **73 D6** 41 20N 92 47W
Leipsic, *DE, U.S.A.* **77 A5** 39 14N 75 31W
Leipsic, *OH, U.S.A.* **92 B3** 41 6N 83 59W
Leisure City, *FL, U.S.A.* **67 F8** 25 30N 80 26W
Leitchfield, *KY, U.S.A.* **96 C6** 37 29N 86 18W
Leiter, *WY, U.S.A.* **104 B6** 44 43N 106 16W
Leitersburg, *MD, U.S.A.* **77 A3** 39 42N 77 37W
Leith, *ND, U.S.A.* **91 D4** 46 22N 101 38W
Lejeune, *Qué., Canada* **177 D14** 47 46N 68 34W
Lela, *TX, U.S.A.* **98 B7** 35 14N 100 21W
Leland, *IL, U.S.A.* **71 B5** 41 37N 88 48W
Leland, *IA, U.S.A.* **73 B5** 43 20N 93 38W
Leland, *MI, U.S.A.* **79 D6** 45 1N 85 45W
Leland, *MS, U.S.A.* **81 C3** 33 24N 90 54W
Leland, *NC, U.S.A.* **90 D7** 34 15N 78 3W
Leland, *WA, U.S.A.* **101 C3** 47 53N 122 53W
Leleiwi Pt., *HI, U.S.A.* **69 D7** 19 44N 155 0W
Lelia Lake, *TX, U.S.A.* **98 C7** 34 54N 100 46W
Lemberg, *Sask., Canada* **182 E8** 50 44N 103 12W
Lemhi, *ID, U.S.A.* **70 E5** 44 52N 113 38W
Lemhi →, *ID, U.S.A.* **70 D5** 45 12N 113 53W
Lemhi County ☆, *ID, U.S.A.* **70 E4** 45 0N 114 0W
Lemhi Ra., *ID, U.S.A.* **70 E5** 44 0N 113 0W
Lemieux, *Qué., Canada* **177 E10** 46 18N 72 7W
Lemieux, L., *Qué., Canada* **176 A8** 50 19N 74 38W
Lemieux Is., *N.W.T., Canada* **191 E13** 63 40N 64 20W
Lemington, *VT, U.S.A.* **86 B3** 44 51N 71 36W
Lemitar, *NM, U.S.A.* **88 C4** 34 10N 106 55W
Lemmon, *SD, U.S.A.* **91 E3** 45 57N 102 10W
Lemmon, L., *Dallas-Fort Worth, U.S.A.* **109 B5** 32 41N 96 44W
Lemoine, L., *Qué., Canada* **176 C5** 48 0N 78 0W
Lemon Grove, *CA, U.S.A.* **65 L9** 32 44N 117 1W
Lemont, *PA, U.S.A.* **95 D5** 40 48N 77 49W
Lemoore, *CA, U.S.A.* **65 G7** 36 18N 119 46W
Lemoyne, *Montréal, Canada* **192 B4** 45 29N 73 29W
Lemoyne, *NE, U.S.A.* **84 C4** 41 17N 101 49W
Lempster, *NH, U.S.A.* **86 C2** 43 15N 72 12W
Lena, *IL, U.S.A.* **71 A4** 42 23N 89 49W
Lena, *MS, U.S.A.* **81 D4** 32 36N 89 36W
Lena, Mt., *UT, U.S.A.* **100 C6** 40 50N 109 20W
Lenapah, *OK, U.S.A.* **93 B8** 36 51N 95 38W
Lenawee County ☆, *MI, U.S.A.* **79 H7** 41 50N 84 5W
Lenexa, *KS, U.S.A.* **74 C9** 38 57N 94 44W
Lennep, *MT, U.S.A.* **83 D7** 46 25N 110 33W
Lennox, *Los Angeles, U.S.A.* **111 C2** 33 56N 118 20W
Lennox, *SD, U.S.A.* **91 G9** 43 21N 96 53W
Lennoxville, *Qué., Canada* **86 A3** 45 22N 71 51W
Lenoir, *NC, U.S.A.* **90 C4** 35 55N 81 32W
Lenoir City, *TN, U.S.A.* **97 E8** 35 48N 84 16W
Lenoir County ☆, *NC, U.S.A.* **90 C8** 35 10N 77 40W
Lenora, *KS, U.S.A.* **74 B3** 39 37N 100 0W
Lenore, *ID, U.S.A.* **70 C2** 46 31N 116 33W
Lenore L., *Sask., Canada* **182 C7** 52 30N 104 59W
Lenox, *GA, U.S.A.* **68 E3** 31 16N 83 28W
Lenox, *IA, U.S.A.* **73 E4** 40 53N 94 34W
Lenox, *MA, U.S.A.* **78 B1** 42 22N 73 17W
Lenox, *MO, U.S.A.* **82 D5** 37 39N 91 46W
Lenwood, *CA, U.S.A.* **65 J9** 34 53N 117 7W
Leo-Cedarville, *IN, U.S.A.* **72 B5** 41 13N 85 1W
Leola, *AR, U.S.A.* **63 D3** 34 10N 92 35W
Leola, *SD, U.S.A.* **91 E7** 45 43N 98 56W
Leoma, *TN, U.S.A.* **96 E5** 35 10N 87 21W
Leominster, *MA, U.S.A.* **78 B3** 42 32N 71 46W
León, *Guanajuato, Mexico* **218 A6** 21 6N 101 41W
Leon, *IA, U.S.A.* **73 E5** 40 44N 93 45W
Leon, *KS, U.S.A.* **74 D7** 37 42N 96 46W
Leon, *OK, U.S.A.* **93 E6** 33 53N 97 26W
Leon, *TX, U.S.A.* **99 F10** 31 14N 97 28W
Leon →, *TX, U.S.A.* **99 F10** 31 14N 97 28W
Leon County ☆, *FL, U.S.A.* **67 A4** 30 30N 84 15W
Leon County ☆, *TX, U.S.A.* **99 F12** 31 16N 95 59W
Leon Springs, *TX, U.S.A.* **99 H9** 29 29N 98 39W
Leon Valley, *TX, U.S.A.* **99 H9** 29 29N 98 39W
Leona, *KS, U.S.A.* **74 B8** 39 47N 95 19W
Leona, *TX, U.S.A.* **99 F12** 31 9N 95 58W
Leona →, *TX, U.S.A.* **99 J8** 28 45N 99 11W
Leona Vicario, *Quintana Roo, Mexico* **223 B6** 21 0N 87 11W
Leonard, *MN, U.S.A.* **80 C3** 47 39N 95 16W
Leonard, *ND, U.S.A.* **91 D8** 46 39N 97 15W
Leonard, *TX, U.S.A.* **99 D11** 33 23N 96 15W
Leonardtown, *MD, U.S.A.* **77 B4** 38 17N 76 38W
Leonardville, *KS, U.S.A.* **74 B7** 39 22N 96 51W
Leone, *Amer. Samoa* **105 e** 14 23 S 170 48W
Leonia, *FL, U.S.A.* **67 A2** 30 55N 86 1W
Leonia, *NJ, U.S.A.* **114 A3** 40 51N 73 59W
Leopoldo Sánchez, *Sinaloa, Mexico* **216 B2** 25 7N 108 1W
Leoti, *KS, U.S.A.* **74 C2** 38 29N 101 21W
Leoville, *Sask., Canada* **182 B4** 53 39N 107 33W
Lepanto, *AR, U.S.A.* **63 C5** 35 37N 90 20W
Lepreau, *N.B., Canada* **173 H3** 45 10N 66 28W
Lerdo de Tejada, *Veracruz, Mexico* **221 F5** 18 37N 95 31W
Lerma →, *Mexico* **218 B5** 20 13N 102 46W
Lerna, *IL, U.S.A.* **71 D5** 39 25N 88 17W
Leroux Wash →, *AZ, U.S.A.* **62 C5** 34 50N 110 10W
Leroy, *Sask., Canada* **182 C7** 52 0N 104 44W
Léry, *Qué., Canada* **177 F9** 45 21N 73 48W
Les Coteaux, *Qué., Canada* **177 F8** 45 15N 74 13W
Les Éboulements, *Qué., Canada* **177 D12** 47 28N 70 21W
Les Escoumins, *Qué., Canada* **177 C13** 48 21N 69 24W
Les Étroits, *Qué., Canada* **177 D14** 47 24N 68 54W
Les Laurentides, *Qué., Canada* **177 D8** 47 13N 74 23W
Les Méchins, *Qué., Canada* **172 E3** 48 59N 66 59W
Les Notre-Dame, *Qué., Canada* **172 E2** 48 10N 68 0W
Lesage, *WV, U.S.A.* **102 C2** 38 30N 82 18W
Leslie, *AR, U.S.A.* **63 C3** 35 50N 92 34W
Leslie, *GA, U.S.A.* **68 E2** 31 57N 84 5W
Leslie, *ID, U.S.A.* **70 F5** 43 52N 113 28W
Leslie, *MI, U.S.A.* **79 G7** 42 27N 84 26W
Leslie County ☆, *KY, U.S.A.* **97 C9** 37 5N 83 25W
Leslieville, *Alta., Canada* **185 F6** 52 23N 114 36W
Lesser Slave L., *Alta., Canada* **184 C5** 55 30N 115 25W
Lesser Slave Lake Prov. Park ⌂, *Alta., Canada* **184 C6** 55 26N 114 49W
Lesslie, *SC, U.S.A.* **90 D5** 34 53N 80 57W
Lester, *WV, U.S.A.* **102 D3** 37 44N 81 18W
Lester B. Pearson International, Toronto ✈ (YYZ), *Ont., Canada* **178 D7** 43 46N 79 35W
Lestershire = Johnson City, *NY, U.S.A.* **89 C5** 42 7N 75 58W
Lesterville, *SD, U.S.A.* **91 G8** 43 2N 97 35W
Lestock, *Sask., Canada* **182 D8** 51 19N 103 59W
Letart Falls, *OH, U.S.A.* **92 E5** 38 54N 81 56W
Letcher, *SD, U.S.A.* **91 G7** 43 54N 98 8W
Letcher County ☆, *KY, U.S.A.* **97 C10** 37 5N 82 55W
Letchworth State Park ⌂, *NY, U.S.A.* **89 C2** 42 37N 78 0W
Letha, *ID, U.S.A.* **70 F2** 43 54N 116 39W
Lethbridge, *Alta., Canada* **185 J8** 49 45N 112 45W
Lethbridge, *Nfld. & L., Canada* **174 D7** 48 22N 53 52W
Letohatchee, *AL, U.S.A.* **60 D4** 32 8N 86 29W
Letterkenny Army Depot, *PA, U.S.A.* **95 D4** 40 2N 77 37W
Letts, *IA, U.S.A.* **73 D7** 41 20N 91 14W
Leucadia, *CA, U.S.A.* **65 K9** 33 4N 117 18W
Leupp Corner, *AZ, U.S.A.* **62 B5** 35 5N 110 52W
Leusoalii, *Amer. Samoa* **105 f** 14 14 S 169 25W
Levack, *Ont., Canada* **178 A5** 46 38N 81 23W
Levan, *UT, U.S.A.* **100 D4** 39 33N 111 52W
Leveaux Mt., *MN, U.S.A.* **80 C8** 47 37N 90 48W
Levelland, *TX, U.S.A.* **98 D5** 33 35N 102 23W
Levelock, *AK, U.S.A.* **61 G8** 59 7N 156 51W
Levering, *MI, U.S.A.* **79 D7** 45 38N 84 47W
Lévis, *Qué., Canada* **177 E11** 46 48N 71 9W
Levisa Fork →, *KY, U.S.A.* **97 B10** 38 8N 82 37W
Levittown = Willingboro, *NJ, U.S.A.* **87 B2** 40 3N 74 54W
Levittown, *NY, U.S.A.* **87 B3** 40 44N 73 31W
Levittown, *PA, U.S.A.* **87 B2** 40 9N 74 51W
Levy, *NM, U.S.A.* **88 A6** 36 5N 104 41W
Levy County ☆, *FL, U.S.A.* **67 B6** 29 15N 82 45W
Lewellen, *NE, U.S.A.* **84 C3** 41 20N 102 9W
Lewes, *DE, U.S.A.* **77 B5** 38 46N 75 9W
Lewis, *IA, U.S.A.* **73 D3** 41 18N 95 5W
Lewis, *KS, U.S.A.* **74 D4** 37 56N 99 15W
Lewis, *NY, U.S.A.* **86 B1** 44 17N 73 34W
Lewis →, *WA, U.S.A.* **101 E3** 45 51N 122 48W
Lewis, Mt., *NV, U.S.A.* **85 B4** 40 24N 116 52W
Lewis and Clark County ☆, *MT, U.S.A.* **83 C5** 47 25N 112 35W
Lewis and Clark L., *U.S.A.* **84 B8** 42 52N 97 48W
Lewis and Clark Nat. Forest, *MT, U.S.A.* **83 C5** 47 30N 112 55W
Lewis and Clark Nat. Historic Trail ⌂, *U.S.A.* **91 G6** 43 30N 99 20W
Lewis County ☆, *ID, U.S.A.* **70 C2** 46 15N 116 29W
Lewis County ☆, *KY, U.S.A.* **97 B9** 38 30N 83 25W
Lewis County ☆, *MO, U.S.A.* **82 A5** 40 5N 91 40W
Lewis County ☆, *NY, U.S.A.* **89 B5** 43 45N 75 30W
Lewis County ☆, *TN, U.S.A.* **96 E5** 35 33N 87 33W
Lewis County ☆, *WV, U.S.A.* **102 B4** 39 2N 80 28W
Lewis County ☆, *WA, U.S.A.* **101 D3** 46 30N 122 0W
Lewis Hills, *Nfld. & L., Canada* **174 D2** 48 48N 58 30W
Lewis L., *WY, U.S.A.* **104 B2** 44 18N 110 38W
Lewis Range, *MT, U.S.A.* **83 B4** 48 5N 113 5W
Lewis Run, *PA, U.S.A.* **95 C4** 41 52N 78 40W
Lewis Smith L., *AL, U.S.A.* **60 C3** 33 56N 87 6W
Lewisburg, *KY, U.S.A.* **96 D6** 36 59N 86 57W
Lewisburg, *OH, U.S.A.* **92 D2** 39 51N 84 33W
Lewisburg, *PA, U.S.A.* **95 D6** 40 58N 76 54W
Lewisburg, *TN, U.S.A.* **96 E6** 35 27N 86 48W
Lewisburg, *WV, U.S.A.* **102 D4** 37 48N 80 27W
Lewisdale, *MD, U.S.A.* **119 B4** 38 58N 76 59W
Lewisetta, *VA, U.S.A.* **77 B4** 38 0N 76 28W
Lewisport, *KY, U.S.A.* **96 C6** 37 56N 86 54W
Lewisporte, *Nfld. & L., Canada* **174 C5** 49 15N 55 3W
Lewiston, *CA, U.S.A.* **64 C4** 40 43N 122 48W
Lewiston, *ID, U.S.A.* **70 C1** 46 25N 117 1W
Lewiston, *ME, U.S.A.* **76 D3** 44 6N 70 13W
Lewiston, *MI, U.S.A.* **79 E7** 44 53N 84 18W
Lewiston, *MN, U.S.A.* **80 G7** 43 59N 91 52W
Lewiston, *NC, U.S.A.* **90 B8** 36 7N 77 10W
Lewiston, *NY, U.S.A.* **89 B1** 43 11N 79 3W
Lewiston, *NE, U.S.A.* **84 D9** 40 14N 96 25W
Lewiston, *UT, U.S.A.* **100 B4** 41 59N 111 51W
Lewiston Woodville, *NC, U.S.A.* **90 B8** 36 7N 77 11W
Lewistown, *IL, U.S.A.* **71 C3** 40 24N 90 9W
Lewistown, *MD, U.S.A.* **77 A3** 39 32N 77 25W
Lewistown, *MO, U.S.A.* **82 A5** 40 5N 91 49W
Lewistown, *MT, U.S.A.* **83 C8** 47 4N 109 26W
Lewistown, *PA, U.S.A.* **95 D5** 40 36N 77 34W
Lewisville, *N.B., Canada* **173 G5** 46 6N 64 46W
Lewisville, *AR, U.S.A.* **63 E2** 33 22N 93 35W
Lewisville, *MN, U.S.A.* **80 G4** 43 55N 94 26W
Lewisville, *NC, U.S.A.* **90 B5** 36 6N 80 25W
Lewisville, *OH, U.S.A.* **92 D5** 39 46N 81 13W
Lewisville, *TX, U.S.A.* **99 D11** 33 5N 97 0W
Lewisville, L., *TX, U.S.A.* **99 D11** 33 4N 96 58W
Lexington, *AL, U.S.A.* **60 B3** 34 58N 87 22W
Lexington, *GA, U.S.A.* **68 C3** 33 52N 83 7W
Lexington, *IL, U.S.A.* **71 C5** 40 39N 88 47W
Lexington, *KY, U.S.A.* **97 B8** 38 3N 84 30W
Lexington, *MA, U.S.A.* **78 B3** 42 25N 71 12W
Lexington, *MI, U.S.A.* **79 F9** 43 16N 82 32W
Lexington, *MS, U.S.A.* **81 C3** 33 7N 90 3W
Lexington, *MO, U.S.A.* **82 B3** 39 11N 93 52W
Lexington, *NC, U.S.A.* **90 C5** 35 49N 80 15W
Lexington, *NE, U.S.A.* **84 D6** 40 47N 99 45W
Lexington, *OH, U.S.A.* **92 C4** 40 41N 82 35W
Lexington, *OK, U.S.A.* **93 C6** 35 1N 97 20W
Lexington, *OR, U.S.A.* **94 B6** 45 27N 119 42W
Lexington, *SC, U.S.A.* **90 E4** 33 59N 81 11W
Lexington, *TN, U.S.A.* **96 E4** 35 39N 88 24W
Lexington, *TX, U.S.A.* **99 G10** 30 25N 97 1W
Lexington, *VA, U.S.A.* **102 D5** 37 47N 79 27W
Lexington, *WA, U.S.A.* **101 D3** 46 11N 122 54W
Lexington Blue Grass, *KY, U.S.A.* **97 C8** 37 43N 84 14W
Lexington County ☆, *SC, U.S.A.* **90 E4** 33 50N 81 10W
Lexington Park, *MD, U.S.A.* **77 B4** 38 16N 76 27W
Liard →, *Canada* **189 D8** 61 51N 121 18W
Liard River, *B.C., Canada* **189 E7** 59 25N 126 5W
Libby, *MT, U.S.A.* **83 B2** 48 23N 115 33W
Libby Dam, *MT, U.S.A.* **83 B2** 48 24N 115 19W
Liberal, *KS, U.S.A.* **74 D3** 37 3N 100 55W
Liberal, *MO, U.S.A.* **82 D2** 37 34N 94 31W
Liberty, *Sask., Canada* **182 D6** 51 8N 105 26W
Liberty, *IL, U.S.A.* **71 D2** 39 53N 91 6W
Liberty, *IN, U.S.A.* **72 D6** 39 38N 84 56W
Liberty, *KS, U.S.A.* **74 D8** 37 9N 95 36W
Liberty, *KY, U.S.A.* **97 C8** 37 19N 84 56W
Liberty, *ME, U.S.A.* **76 D4** 44 24N 69 18W
Liberty, *MS, U.S.A.* **81 E3** 31 10N 90 49W

Liberty, *MO, U.S.A.* **82 B2** 39 15N 94 25W
Liberty, *NC, U.S.A.* **90 C6** 35 51N 79 34W
Liberty, *NY, U.S.A.* **89 D6** 41 48N 74 45W
Liberty, *NE, U.S.A.* **84 D9** 40 5N 96 29W
Liberty, *OK, U.S.A.* **93 C8** 35 52N 95 59W
Liberty, *PA, U.S.A.* **95 C5** 41 34N 77 6W
Liberty, *Pittsburgh, U.S.A.* **116 C2** 40 19N 79 51W
Liberty, *SC, U.S.A.* **90 D3** 34 48N 82 42W
Liberty, *TN, U.S.A.* **97 D7** 36 1N 85 58W
Liberty, *TX, U.S.A.* **99 G13** 30 3N 94 48W
Liberty, *WA, U.S.A.* **101 C5** 47 14N 120 42W
Liberty Center, *OH, U.S.A.* **92 B2** 41 27N 84 1W
Liberty County ☆, *FL, U.S.A.* **67 A4** 30 15N 85 0W
Liberty County ☆, *GA, U.S.A.* **68 E5** 31 50N 81 30W
Liberty County ☆, *MT, U.S.A.* **83 B7** 48 40N 111 0W
Liberty County ☆, *TX, U.S.A.* **99 G13** 30 7N 94 52W
Liberty Hill, *TX, U.S.A.* **99 G10** 30 40N 97 55W
Liberty I., *NY, U.S.A.* **89 E6** 40 41N 74 2W
Liberty Res., *MD, U.S.A.* **77 A4** 39 23N 76 54W
Libertytown, *MD, U.S.A.* **77 A3** 39 30N 77 15W
Libertytown, *MD, U.S.A.* **77 B5** 38 18N 75 18W
Libertyville, *IL, U.S.A.* **71 A6** 42 18N 87 57W
Libertyville, *IA, U.S.A.* **73 E6** 40 57N 92 3W
Libres, *Puebla, Mexico* **220 E3** 19 28N 97 40W
Licking, *MO, U.S.A.* **82 D5** 37 30N 91 54W
Licking →, *KY, U.S.A.* **97 A8** 39 6N 84 30W
Licking County ☆, *OH, U.S.A.* **92 C4** 40 3N 82 24W
Lida, *NV, U.S.A.* **85 E3** 37 28N 117 30W
Lidderdale, *IA, U.S.A.* **73 C4** 42 8N 94 47W
Liddon G., *N.W.T., Canada* **188 A10** 75 3N 113 0W
Lidgerwood, *ND, U.S.A.* **91 D8** 46 5N 97 9W
Lido Beach, *NY, U.S.A.* **114 C5** 40 35N 73 37W
Liebenthal, *KS, U.S.A.* **74 C4** 38 39N 99 19W
Lièvre →, *Qué., Canada* **176 F7** 45 31N 75 26W
Lièvres, Î. aux, *Qué., Canada* **177 D13** 47 50N 69 44W
Lighthouse Park, *Vancouver, Canada* **193 B1** 49 20N 123 14W
Lighthouse Point, *FL, U.S.A.* **67 E8** 26 15N 80 7W
Lighthouse Pt., *FL, U.S.A.* **67 B4** 29 54N 84 21W
Lightning Cr. →, *WY, U.S.A.* **104 C8** 43 11N 104 44W
Lignite, *ND, U.S.A.* **91 B3** 48 53N 102 34W
Lignum, *VA, U.S.A.* **102 C7** 38 25N 77 50W
Ligonier, *IN, U.S.A.* **72 B5** 41 28N 85 35W
Ligonier, *PA, U.S.A.* **95 D3** 40 15N 79 14W
Lihue, *HI, U.S.A.* **69 B2** 21 59N 159 23W
Likely, *B.C., Canada* **187 C13** 52 37N 121 35W
Likely, *CA, U.S.A.* **64 B6** 41 14N 120 30W
Lilbourn, *MO, U.S.A.* **82 E7** 36 36N 89 37W
L'Île Bizard, *Montréal, Canada* **192 B1** 45 29N 73 52W
Liliba, *Sonora, Mexico* **212 F5** 27 19N 110 29W
Lillian L. = Le Doré, L., *Qué., Canada* **172 B8** 51 17N 61 23W
Lillie, *LA, U.S.A.* **75 B3** 32 56N 92 39W
Lillington, *NC, U.S.A.* **90 C7** 35 24N 78 49W
Lillooet, *B.C., Canada* **187 E13** 50 44N 121 57W
Lillooet →, *B.C., Canada* **187 F13** 49 15N 121 57W
Lillooet L., *B.C., Canada* **187 E12** 50 18N 122 35W
Lilly, *PA, U.S.A.* **95 D4** 40 26N 78 37W
Lily, *SD, U.S.A.* **91 E8** 45 11N 97 41W
Lily, *WI, U.S.A.* **103 C5** 45 18N 88 51W
Lilydale, *Minneapolis-St. Paul, U.S.A.* **113 B3** 44 54N 93 7W
Lima, *IL, U.S.A.* **71 C2** 40 11N 91 23W
Lima, *MT, U.S.A.* **83 F5** 44 38N 112 36W
Lima, *NY, U.S.A.* **89 C3** 42 55N 77 37W
Lima, *OH, U.S.A.* **92 C2** 40 44N 84 6W
Lima, *OK, U.S.A.* **93 C7** 35 10N 96 36W
Lime, *OR, U.S.A.* **94 C8** 44 24N 117 19W
Lime Ridge, *WI, U.S.A.* **103 E3** 43 28N 90 9W
Lime Springs, *IA, U.S.A.* **73 B6** 43 27N 92 17W
Lime Village, *AK, U.S.A.* **61 F9** 61 21N 155 28W
Limerick, *Sask., Canada* **182 F5** 49 39N 106 16W
Limerick, *ME, U.S.A.* **76 E3** 43 41N 70 48W
Limestone, *FL, U.S.A.* **67 D7** 27 22N 81 54W
Limestone, *ME, U.S.A.* **76 B6** 46 55N 67 50W
Limestone, *NY, U.S.A.* **89 C2** 42 2N 78 38W
Limestone, L., *TX, U.S.A.* **99 F11** 31 25N 96 22W
Limestone B., *Man., Canada* **183 B13** 53 50N 98 53W
Limestone County ☆, *AL, U.S.A.* **60 B4** 34 48N 86 58W
Limestone County ☆, *TX, U.S.A.* **99 F11** 31 39N 96 31W
Limestone Hill = Lackawanna, *NY, U.S.A.* **89 C2** 42 50N 78 50W
Limoges, *Ont., Canada* **176 F7** 45 20N 75 16W
Limon, *CO, U.S.A.* **66 C7** 39 16N 103 41W
Limones, *Quintana Roo, Mexico* **223 D5** 19 4N 88 12W
Linares, *Nuevo León, Mexico* **215 F5** 24 52N 99 34W
Linaria, *Alta., Canada* **184 D6** 54 19N 114 8W
Linch, *WY, U.S.A.* **104 C6** 43 37N 106 12W
Lincoln = Beamsville, *Ont., Canada* **178 D7** 43 12N 79 28W
Lincoln, *AL, U.S.A.* **60 C4** 33 37N 86 7W
Lincoln, *AR, U.S.A.* **63 C1** 35 57N 94 25W
Lincoln, *Boston, U.S.A.* **106 A2** 42 25N 71 18W
Lincoln, *CA, U.S.A.* **64 E5** 38 54N 121 17W
Lincoln, *DE, U.S.A.* **77 B5** 38 52N 75 25W
Lincoln, *IL, U.S.A.* **71 C4** 40 9N 89 22W
Lincoln, *IA, U.S.A.* **73 C6** 42 16N 92 42W
Lincoln, *KS, U.S.A.* **74 B5** 39 3N 98 9W
Lincoln, *ME, U.S.A.* **76 C5** 45 22N 68 30W
Lincoln, *MI, U.S.A.* **79 E8** 44 41N 83 25W
Lincoln, *MO, U.S.A.* **82 C3** 38 23N 93 20W
Lincoln, *MT, U.S.A.* **83 D5** 46 58N 112 41W
Lincoln, *ND, U.S.A.* **91 D5** 46 45N 100 44W
Lincoln, *NH, U.S.A.* **86 B3** 44 3N 71 40W
Lincoln, *NM, U.S.A.* **88 D5** 33 30N 105 23W
Lincoln, *NE, U.S.A.* **84 D9** 40 49N 96 41W
Lincoln, *WA, U.S.A.* **101 C7** 47 50N 118 25W
Lincoln Boyhood Nat. Memorial ⌂, *IN, U.S.A.* **72 E4** 38 7N 86 59W
Lincoln City, *OR, U.S.A.* **94 C1** 44 57N 124 1W
Lincoln County ☆, *AR, U.S.A.* **63 E4** 33 56N 91 51W
Lincoln County ☆, *CO, U.S.A.* **66 D7** 39 0N 103 20W
Lincoln County ☆, *GA, U.S.A.* **68 C4** 33 45N 82 20W
Lincoln County ☆, *ID, U.S.A.* **70 G4** 43 0N 114 0W
Lincoln County ☆, *KS, U.S.A.* **74 B5** 39 0N 98 10W
Lincoln County ☆, *KY, U.S.A.* **97 C8** 37 25N 84 40W
Lincoln County ☆, *ME, U.S.A.* **76 D4** 44 0N 69 30W
Lincoln County ☆, *MN, U.S.A.* **80 F2** 44 25N 96 10W
Lincoln County ☆, *MS, U.S.A.* **81 E3** 31 35N 90 26W
Lincoln County ☆, *MO, U.S.A.* **82 B5** 39 0N 91 0W
Lincoln County ☆, *MT, U.S.A.* **83 B2** 48 45N 115 30W
Lincoln County ☆, *NC, U.S.A.* **90 C4** 35 30N 81 10W
Lincoln County ☆, *NM, U.S.A.* **88 D5** 33 40N 105 30W
Lincoln County ☆, *NE, U.S.A.* **84 C4** 41 0N 101 0W
Lincoln County ☆, *NV, U.S.A.* **85 E6** 37 20N 115 0W
Lincoln County ☆, *OK, U.S.A.* **93 C7** 35 40N 96 50W
Lincoln County ☆, *OR, U.S.A.* **94 C2** 44 40N 123 50W
Lincoln County ☆, *SD, U.S.A.* **91 G9** 43 21N 96 53W
Lincoln County ☆, *TN, U.S.A.* **96 E6** 35 9N 86 34W
Lincoln County ☆, *WV, U.S.A.* **102 C3** 38 14N 81 59W
Lincoln County ☆, *WA, U.S.A.* **101 C7** 47 45N 118 30W
Lincoln County ☆, *WI, U.S.A.* **103 C4** 45 20N 89 45W
Lincoln County ☆, *WY, U.S.A.* **104 D2** 42 0N 110 30W
Lincoln Creek Parkway, *Milwaukee, U.S.A.* **112 B2** 43 6N 87 56W
Lincoln Heights, *Los Angeles, U.S.A.* **111 B3** 34 4N 118 12 E
Lincoln Heights, *OH, U.S.A.* **107 A2** 39 14N 84 27W
Lincoln Nat. Forest, *NM, U.S.A.* **88 E5** 32 45N 105 40W
Lincoln Parish ☆, *LA, U.S.A.* **75 B3** 32 32N 92 38W
Lincoln Park, *Chicago, U.S.A.* **108 B3** 41 57N 87 38W
Lincoln Park, *CO, U.S.A.* **66 D5** 38 25N 105 10W
Lincoln Park, *GA, U.S.A.* **68 D2** 32 52N 84 20W
Lincoln Park, *MI, U.S.A.* **79 G8** 42 15N 83 11W
Lincoln Park, *Milwaukee, U.S.A.* **112 B2** 43 6N 87 55W
Lincoln Park, *NJ, U.S.A.* **114 A1** 40 55N 74 18W
Lincoln Park, *San Francisco, U.S.A.* **118 B1** 37 47N 122 30W
Lincolnton, *GA, U.S.A.* **68 C4** 33 48N 82 29W
Lincolnton, *NC, U.S.A.* **90 C4** 35 29N 81 16W
Lincolnville, *N.S., Canada* **173 H8** 45 30N 61 33W
Lincolnville, *KS, U.S.A.* **74 C7** 38 30N 96 58W
Lincolnville, *ME, U.S.A.* **76 D4** 44 17N 69 1W
Lincolnwood, *Chicago, U.S.A.* **108 A2** 42 1N 87 43W
Lind, *WA, U.S.A.* **101 D7** 46 58N 118 37W
Linda, *CA, U.S.A.* **64 D5** 39 8N 121 34W
Lindale, *GA, U.S.A.* **68 B1** 34 11N 85 11W
Lindale, *TX, U.S.A.* **99 E12** 32 31N 95 25W
Lindavista, *Chiapas, Mexico* **222 B5** 17 24N 91 30W
Lindell Beach, *B.C., Canada* **187 F12** 49 2N 122 1W
Linden = Gladstone, *MO, U.S.A.* **82 B2** 39 13N 94 35W
Linden, *Alta., Canada* **185 G7** 51 36N 113 28W
Linden, *AL, U.S.A.* **60 D3** 32 18N 87 48W
Linden, *CA, U.S.A.* **64 E5** 38 1N 121 5W
Linden, *IN, U.S.A.* **72 C4** 40 11N 86 54W
Linden, *IA, U.S.A.* **73 D4** 41 39N 94 16W
Linden, *MI, U.S.A.* **79 G8** 42 49N 83 47W
Linden, *NJ, U.S.A.* **87 B2** 40 37N 74 14W
Linden, *TN, U.S.A.* **96 E5** 35 37N 87 50W
Linden, *TX, U.S.A.* **99 D13** 33 1N 94 22W
Linden, *WI, U.S.A.* **103 F3** 42 55N 90 16W
Lindenhurst, *NY, U.S.A.* **87 B3** 40 41N 73 23W
Lindenwold, *NJ, U.S.A.* **87 C2** 39 49N 74 59W
Lindley, *NY, U.S.A.* **89 C3** 42 1N 77 8W
Lindon, *CO, U.S.A.* **66 C7** 39 44N 103 24W
Lindon, *UT, U.S.A.* **100 C4** 40 21N 111 43W
Lindsay, *Ont., Canada* **179 C8** 44 22N 78 43W
Lindsay, *CA, U.S.A.* **65 G7** 36 12N 119 5W
Lindsay, *NE, U.S.A.* **84 C8** 41 42N 97 42W
Lindsay, *OK, U.S.A.* **93 D6** 34 50N 97 38W
Lindsborg, *KS, U.S.A.* **74 C6** 38 35N 97 40W
Lindy, *NE, U.S.A.* **84 B8** 42 44N 97 44W
Linesville, *PA, U.S.A.* **95 C2** 41 39N 80 26W
Lineville, *AL, U.S.A.* **60 C5** 33 19N 85 45W
Lineville, *IA, U.S.A.* **73 E5** 40 35N 93 32W
Lingle, *WY, U.S.A.* **104 D8** 42 8N 104 21W
Linglestown, *PA, U.S.A.* **95 D6** 40 20N 76 47W
Link L., *B.C., Canada* **186 C7** 52 25N 127 40W
Linn, *KS, U.S.A.* **74 B6** 39 41N 97 5W
Linn, *MO, U.S.A.* **82 C5** 38 29N 91 51W
Linn, *TX, U.S.A.* **98 L9** 26 34N 98 7W
Linn, *WV, U.S.A.* **102 B4** 39 0N 80 43W
Linn County ☆, *IA, U.S.A.* **73 C7** 42 5N 91 35W
Linn County ☆, *KS, U.S.A.* **74 C9** 38 15N 94 45W
Linn County ☆, *MO, U.S.A.* **82 B3** 39 50N 93 10W
Linn County ☆, *OR, U.S.A.* **94 C3** 44 30N 122 20W
Linn Creek, *MO, U.S.A.* **82 C4** 38 2N 92 43W
Linn Grove, *IA, U.S.A.* **73 C3** 42 53N 95 15W
Linn Valley, *KS, U.S.A.* **74 C9** 38 23N 94 42W
Linndale, *Cleveland, U.S.A.* **107 B1** 41 26N 81 46W
Linneus, *ME, U.S.A.* **76 B6** 46 3N 67 52W
Linneus, *MO, U.S.A.* **82 B3** 39 53N 93 11W
Lino Lakes, *MN, U.S.A.* **80 E5** 45 12N 93 6W
Linthicum, *Baltimore, U.S.A.* **107 B1** 39 12N 76 39W
Lintlaw, *Sask., Canada* **182 C8** 52 4N 103 14W
Linton, *Qué., Canada* **177 D10** 47 15N 72 16W
Linton, *GA, U.S.A.* **68 B4** 33 7N 83 0W
Linton, *IN, U.S.A.* **72 D3** 39 2N 87 10W
Linton, *ND, U.S.A.* **91 D5** 46 16N 100 14W
Linwood, *Ont., Canada* **178 D6** 43 35N 80 43W
Linwood, *KS, U.S.A.* **74 B8** 39 0N 95 2W
Linwood, *NJ, U.S.A.* **87 C2** 39 21N 74 34W
Linwood, *NE, U.S.A.* **84 C9** 41 25N 96 56W
Lion's Head, *Ont., Canada* **178 C5** 44 58N 81 15W
Lipscomb, *TX, U.S.A.* **98 A7** 36 14N 100 16W
Lipscomb County ☆, *TX, U.S.A.* **98 A7** 36 15N 100 15W
Lipton, *Sask., Canada* **182 E8** 50 54N 103 51W
Liquillo, Sierra de, *Puerto Rico* **105 G17** 18 20N 65 47W
Lisbon, *IL, U.S.A.* **71 B5** 41 29N 88 29W
Lisbon, *ME, U.S.A.* **76 D3** 44 2N 70 6W
Lisbon, *MD, U.S.A.* **77 A3** 39 20N 77 4W
Lisbon, *ND, U.S.A.* **91 D8** 46 27N 97 41W
Lisbon, *NH, U.S.A.* **86 B3** 44 13N 71 55W
Lisbon, *NY, U.S.A.* **89 A5** 44 44N 75 19W
Lisbon, *OH, U.S.A.* **92 C6** 40 46N 80 46W
Lisbon Falls, *ME, U.S.A.* **76 D3** 44 0N 70 4W
Lisco, *NE, U.S.A.* **84 C3** 41 30N 102 37W
Lisianski I., *HI, U.S.A.* **69 F9** 26 2N 174 0W
L'Isle Verte, *Qué., Canada* **177 C13** 48 1N 69 20W
Lisman, *AL, U.S.A.* **60 D2** 32 10N 88 15W
Lismore, *MN, U.S.A.* **80 G3** 43 45N 95 57W
Listowel, *Ont., Canada* **178 D6** 43 44N 80 58W
Litchfield, *CT, U.S.A.* **78 C1** 41 45N 73 11W
Litchfield, *IL, U.S.A.* **71 D4** 39 11N 89 39W
Litchfield, *MI, U.S.A.* **79 G7** 42 3N 84 46W
Litchfield, *MN, U.S.A.* **80 E4** 45 8N 94 32W
Litchfield, *NE, U.S.A.* **84 C6** 41 10N 99 9W
Litchfield County ☆, *CT, U.S.A.* **78 C1** 41 40N 73 15W
Litchfield Park, *AZ, U.S.A.* **62 D3** 33 30N 112 22W
Litchville, *ND, U.S.A.* **91 D7** 46 39N 98 12W
Lititz, *PA, U.S.A.* **95 D6** 40 9N 76 18W
Little →, *AR, U.S.A.* **63 E1** 33 45N 94 3W
Little →, *GA, U.S.A.* **68 F3** 30 46N 83 30W
Little →, *KY, U.S.A.* **96 D5** 36 51N 87 58W
Little →, *LA, U.S.A.* **75 C3** 31 40N 92 20W
Little →, *NC, U.S.A.* **90 C7** 35 18N 78 42W
Little →, *TN, U.S.A.* **97 E9** 35 53N 83 59W
Little →, *TX, U.S.A.* **99 G11** 30 51N 96 41W
Little Abitibi →, *Ont., Canada* **181 B15** 50 29N 81 32W
Little America, *WY, U.S.A.* **104 E3** 41 33N 109 52W
Little Arkansas →, *KS, U.S.A.* **74 D6** 37 41N 97 21W
Little Bay, *Nfld. & L., Canada* **174 C5** 49 36N 55 57W
Little Beaver Cr. →, *U.S.A.* **74 B2** 39 49N 101 2W
Little Belt Mts., *MT, U.S.A.* **83 D7** 46 40N 110 45W
Little Bighorn →, *MT, U.S.A.* **83 E10** 45 44N 107 34W
Little Bighorn Battlefield Nat. Monument ⌂, *MT, U.S.A.* **83 E10** 45 34N 107 25W
Little Black →, *AR, U.S.A.* **63 B5** 36 25N 90 49W
Little Blue →, *KS, U.S.A.* **74 B7** 39 42N 96 41W
Little Bow →, *Alta., Canada* **185 J8** 49 53N 112 29W
Little Burnt Bay, *Nfld. & L., Canada* **174 C5** 49 25N 55 5W
Little Cadotte →, *Alta., Canada* **184 B3** 56 41N 117 6W
Little Calumet →, *Chicago, U.S.A.* **108 D3** 41 39N 87 34W
Little Canada, *Minneapolis-St. Paul, U.S.A.* **113 A3** 45 1N 93 5W
Little Chute, *WI, U.S.A.* **103 D5** 44 17N 88 16W
Little City, *OK, U.S.A.* **93 D7** 34 5N 96 36W
Little Colorado →, *AZ, U.S.A.* **62 A4** 36 12N 111 48W
Little Creek, *DE, U.S.A.* **77 A5** 39 10N 75 27W
Little Creek Naval Amphibious Base, *Norfolk, U.S.A.* **115 A3** 36 54N 76 9W
Little Current, *Ont., Canada* **178 B5** 45 55N 82 0W
Little Current →, *Ont., Canada* **181 B12** 50 57N 84 36W
Little Diomede I., *AK, U.S.A.* **61 D5** 65 45N 168 56W
Little Dover, *N.S., Canada* **173 H8** 45 15N 61 3W
Little Dry Creek, *MT, U.S.A.* **83 C11** 47 21N 106 22W
Little Eagle, *SD, U.S.A.* **91 E5** 45 40N 100 49W
Little Egg Harbor →, *NJ, U.S.A.* **87 C2** 39 35N 74 18W
Little Falls, *MN, U.S.A.* **80 E4** 45 59N 94 22W
Little Falls, *NJ, U.S.A.* **87 B2** 40 52N 74 12W
Little Falls, *NY, U.S.A.* **89 B6** 43 3N 74 51W
Little Ferry, *NJ, U.S.A.* **114 A2** 40 50N 74 2W
Little Fork →, *MN, U.S.A.* **80 B5** 48 31N 93 35W
Little Fort, *B.C., Canada* **187 D14** 51 26N 120 13W
Little Goose Dam, *WA, U.S.A.* **101 D7** 46 35N 118 1W
Little Grand Rapids, *Man., Canada* **183 C16** 52 0N 95 29W
Little Haiti, *Miami, U.S.A.* **112 C2** 25 50N 80 11W
Little Havana, *Miami, U.S.A.* **112 D1** 25 47N 80 15W
Little Haw Cr. →, *FL, U.S.A.* **67 B7** 29 23N 81 24W
Little Humboldt →, *NV, U.S.A.* **85 A3** 41 1N 117 43W
Little Kanawha →, *WV, U.S.A.* **102 B3** 39 16N 81 34W
Little Lake, *CA, U.S.A.* **65 H9** 35 56N 117 55W
Little Lake Conway, *Orlando, U.S.A.* **115 B2** 28 29N 81 21W
Little Lost →, *ID, U.S.A.* **70 F6** 43 46N 112 58W
Little Mecatina = Petit-Mécatina →, *Qué., Canada* **175 C6** 50 40N 59 30W
Little Medicine Bow →, *WY, U.S.A.* **104 E6** 41 58N 106 17W
Little Menomonee River Parkway, *Milwaukee, U.S.A.* **112 B1** 43 4N 88 2W
Little Missouri →, *AR, U.S.A.* **63 E3** 33 49N 92 54W
Little Missouri →, *ND, U.S.A.* **91 C3** 47 36N 102 25W
Little Missouri Badlands, *ND, U.S.A.* **91 C2** 47 5N 103 45W
Little Muddy →, *ND, U.S.A.* **91 B2** 48 11N 103 36W
Little Narrows, *N.S., Canada* **173 H9** 45 59N 60 59W
Little Neck, *NY, U.S.A.* **114 B4** 40 45N 73 44W
Little Pee Dee →, *SC, U.S.A.* **90 E6** 33 42N 79 11W
Little Pic →, *Ont., Canada* **181 D10** 48 48N 86 37W
Little Powder →, *MT, U.S.A.* **83 E12** 45 28N 105 20W
Little Quill L., *Sask., Canada* **182 D7** 51 55N 104 5W
Little Red →, *AR, U.S.A.* **63 C4** 35 11N 91 27W
Little River, *KS, U.S.A.* **74 C5** 38 24N 98 1W
Little River Canyon Nat. Preserve ⌂, *AL, U.S.A.* **60 B5** 34 25N 85 37W
Little River County ☆, *AR, U.S.A.* **63 E1** 33 40N 94 8W
Little River Indian Reservation, *MI, U.S.A.* **79 E5** 44 16N 86 15W
Little Rock, *AR, U.S.A.* **63 D3** 34 45N 92 17W
Little Rock Air Force Base, *AR, U.S.A.* **63 D3** 34 54N 92 9W
Little Rocky Mts., *MT, U.S.A.* **83 C9** 47 55N 108 30W
Little Sable Pt., *MI, U.S.A.* **79 F5** 43 38N 86 33W
Little Salt L., *UT, U.S.A.* **100 F3** 37 55N 112 53W
Little Sioux →, *IA, U.S.A.* **73 D2** 41 48N 96 4W
Little Sitkin I., *AK, U.S.A.* **61 L2** 51 57N 178 31 E
Little Smoky →, *Alta., Canada* **184 D3** 54 44N 117 11W
Little Snake →, *CO, U.S.A.* **66 B2** 40 27N 108 26W
Little Tallapoosa →, *AL, U.S.A.* **68 C1** 33 19N 85 34W
Little Tennessee →, *TN, U.S.A.* **97 E8** 35 47N 84 16W
Little Traverse B., *MI, U.S.A.* **79 D6** 45 25N 85 10W
Little Traverse Bay Indian Reservation, *MI, U.S.A.* **79 D7** 45 20N 84 58W
Little Valley, *NY, U.S.A.* **89 C2** 42 15N 78 48W
Little Wabash →, *IL, U.S.A.* **71 F5** 37 55N 88 5W
Little White →, *Ont., Canada* **178 A3** 46 23N 83 20W
Little White →, *SD, U.S.A.* **91 G5** 43 40N 100 40W
Little Wood →, *ID, U.S.A.* **70 G4** 42 57N 114 21W
Little York, *IL, U.S.A.* **71 B3** 41 1N 90 45W
Little York, *IN, U.S.A.* **72 E5** 38 42N 85 54W
Littlefield, *AZ, U.S.A.* **62 A2** 36 53N 113 56W
Littlefield, *TX, U.S.A.* **98 D5** 33 55N 102 20W
Littlefork, *MN, U.S.A.* **80 B5** 48 24N 93 34W
Littlerock, *CA, U.S.A.* **65 J9** 34 31N 117 59W
Littlerock, *WA, U.S.A.* **101 D2** 46 54N 123 1W
Littlestown, *PA, U.S.A.* **77 A3** 39 45N 77 5W
Littleton, *CO, U.S.A.* **66 C5** 39 36N 105 0W
Littleton, *IL, U.S.A.* **71 C3** 40 14N 90 37W
Littleton, *ME, U.S.A.* **76 B6** 46 14N 67 51W
Littleton, *NC, U.S.A.* **90 B8** 36 26N 77 54W
Littleton, *NH, U.S.A.* **86 B3** 44 18N 71 46W
Littleton, *WV, U.S.A.* **102 B4** 39 42N 80 32W
Littleton Common, *MA, U.S.A.* **78 B3** 42 33N 71 28W
Littleville, *AL, U.S.A.* **60 B3** 34 36N 87 41W
Live Oak, *CA, U.S.A.* **64 D5** 39 17N 121 40W
Live Oak, *FL, U.S.A.* **67 A6** 30 18N 82 59W
Live Oak, *San Antonio, U.S.A.* **117 B3** 29 33N 98 20W
Live Oak County ☆, *TX, U.S.A.* **99 J9** 28 20N 98 7W
Lively, *Ont., Canada* **178 A5** 46 26N 81 9W
Livengood, *AK, U.S.A.* **61 D10** 65 32N 148 33W
Livermore, *CA, U.S.A.* **64 F5** 37 41N 121 47W
Livermore, *IA, U.S.A.* **73 C4** 42 52N 94 11W
Livermore, *KY, U.S.A.* **96 C5** 37 29N 87 8W
Livermore, Mt., *TX, U.S.A.* **98 G3** 30 38N 104 11W
Livermore Falls, *ME, U.S.A.* **76 D3** 44 29N 70 11W
Liverpool, *N.S., Canada* **173 J5** 44 5N 64 41W
Liverpool, *NY, U.S.A.* **89 B4** 43 6N 76 13W
Liverpool, *PA, U.S.A.* **95 D6** 40 34N 76 59W
Liverpool, C., *N.W.T., Canada* **190 C10** 73 38N 78 6W
Liverpool Bay, *N.W.T., Canada* **188 B7** 70 0N 128 0W
Livingston, *AL, U.S.A.* **60 D2** 32 35N 88 11W
Livingston, *CA, U.S.A.* **64 F6** 37 23N 120 43W
Livingston, *IL, U.S.A.* **71 E4** 38 58N 89 46W
Livingston, *KY, U.S.A.* **97 C8** 37 17N 84 13W
Livingston, *LA, U.S.A.* **75 D5** 30 30N 90 45W
Livingston, *MT, U.S.A.* **83 E7** 45 40N 110 34W
Livingston, *NJ, U.S.A.* **87 B2** 40 48N 74 19W
Livingston, *SC, U.S.A.* **90 E4** 33 38N 81 7W
Livingston, *TN, U.S.A.* **97 D7** 36 23N 85 19W
Livingston, *TX, U.S.A.* **99 G13** 30 43N 94 56W
Livingston, *WI, U.S.A.* **103 F3** 42 54N 90 26W
Livingston, L., *TX, U.S.A.* **99 G12** 30 50N 95 10W
Livingston County ☆, *IL, U.S.A.* **71 C5** 40 55N 88 50W
Livingston County ☆, *KY, U.S.A.* **96 C4** 37 10N 88 20W
Livingston County ☆, *MI, U.S.A.* **79 G8** 42 35N 83 55W
Livingston County ☆, *MO, U.S.A.* **82 B3** 39 50N 93 30W
Livingston County ☆, *NY, U.S.A.* **89 C3** 42 40N 77 45W
Livingston Manor, *NY, U.S.A.* **89 D6** 41 54N 74 50W
Livingston Parish ☆, *LA, U.S.A.* **75 D5** 30 30N 90 45W
Livingstone, *NJ, U.S.A.* **114 B1** 40 48N 74 17W
Livonia, *IN, U.S.A.* **72 E4** 38 33N 86 17W
Livonia, *LA, U.S.A.* **75 D4** 30 34N 91 33W
Livonia, *MI, U.S.A.* **79 G8** 42 23N 83 23W
Livonia, *MO, U.S.A.* **82 A4** 40 30N 92 42W
Livonia, *NY, U.S.A.* **89 C3** 42 49N 77 40W
Lizard Cr. →, *IA, U.S.A.* **73 C4** 42 30N 94 14W
Lizella, *GA, U.S.A.* **68 D3** 32 48N 83 49W
Lizemores, *WV, U.S.A.* **102 C3** 38 20N 81 11W
Llano, *TX, U.S.A.* **99 G9** 30 45N 98 41W
Llano →, *TX, U.S.A.* **99 G9** 30 39N 98 26W
Llano County ☆, *TX, U.S.A.* **99 G9** 30 45N 98 41W
Llano Estacado, *TX, U.S.A.* **98 D5** 33 30N 103 0W
Llano Grande, *Durango, Mexico* **216 D5** 23 27N 105 5W
Llera de Canales, *Tamaulipas, Mexico* **215 G5** 23 19N 99 1W
Lloydminster, *Sask., Canada* **182 B2** 53 17N 110 0W
Lloyds, *MD, U.S.A.* **77 B4** 38 36N 76 12W
Lloyds →, *Nfld. & L., Canada* **174 D3** 48 35N 57 15W
Loa, *UT, U.S.A.* **100 E4** 38 24N 111 39W
Loami, *IL, U.S.A.* **71 D4** 39 40N 89 51W
Lobelville, *TN, U.S.A.* **96 E5** 35 46N 87 47W
Lobos, Cayo, *Quintana Roo, Mexico* **223 D6** 18 22N 87 24W
Lobos, I., *Baja Calif., Mexico* **210 C4** 30 5N 114 30W
Lobos, I., *Sonora, Mexico* **212 F5** 27 20N 110 36W
Lobos, I., *Veracruz, Mexico* **220 C3** 21 28N 97 8W
Lobos, Pt., *San Francisco, U.S.A.* **118 B1** 37 46N 122 30W
Loch Raven, *MD, U.S.A.* **77 A4** 39 26N 76 33W
Lochbuie, *CO, U.S.A.* **66 C6** 40 0N 104 43W
Lochearn, *MD, U.S.A.* **77 A4** 39 20N 76 42W
Lochloosa L., *FL, U.S.A.* **67 B6** 29 30N 82 7W
Lochsa →, *ID, U.S.A.* **70 C3** 46 9N 115 36W
Lock Haven, *PA, U.S.A.* **95 C5** 41 8N 77 28W
Lock Springs, *MO, U.S.A.* **82 B3** 39 51N 93 47W
Lockeford, *CA, U.S.A.* **64 E5** 38 10N 121 9W
Lockeport, *N.S., Canada* **173 K4** 43 47N 65 4W
Lockesburg, *AR, U.S.A.* **63 E1** 33 58N 94 10W
Lockhart, *TX, U.S.A.* **99 H10** 29 53N 97 40W
Lockington, *OH, U.S.A.* **92 C2** 40 12N 84 14W
Lockland, *OH, U.S.A.* **107 A2** 39 13N 84 27W
Lockney, *TX, U.S.A.* **98 C6** 34 7N 101 27W
Lockport, *IL, U.S.A.* **71 B5** 41 35N 88 3W
Lockport, *LA, U.S.A.* **75 E5** 29 39N 90 33W
Lockport, *NY, U.S.A.* **89 B2** 43 10N 78 42W
Lockridge, *IA, U.S.A.* **73 E7** 40 59N 91 45W
Lockwood, *MO, U.S.A.* **82 D3** 37 23N 93 57W
Loco, *OK, U.S.A.* **93 D6** 34 19N 97 41W
Locust Cr. →, *MO, U.S.A.* **82 B3** 39 40N 93 17W
Locust Fork →, *AL, U.S.A.* **60 C3** 33 33N 87 11W
Locust Grove, *GA, U.S.A.* **68 C2** 33 21N 84 7W
Locust Grove, *OK, U.S.A.* **93 B8** 36 12N 95 10W
Locust Manor, *NY, U.S.A.* **114 B4** 40 41N 73 46W
Locust Valley, *NY, U.S.A.* **114 A5** 40 52N 73 35W
Loda, *IL, U.S.A.* **71 C5** 40 31N 88 4W
Lodge →, *MT, U.S.A.* **83 B8** 48 35N 109 12W
Lodge Grass, *MT, U.S.A.* **83 E10** 45 19N 107 22W
Lodgepole, *Alta., Canada* **185 E5** 53 6N 115 19W
Lodgepole, *NE, U.S.A.* **84 C3** 41 9N 102 38W
Lodgepole, *SD, U.S.A.* **91 E3** 45 48N 102 40W
Lodgepole →, *NE, U.S.A.* **84 C3** 41 2N 102 10W
Lodgepole Cr. →, *U.S.A.* **66 B8** 40 57N 102 23W
Lodi, *CA, U.S.A.* **64 E5** 38 8N 121 16W
Lodi, *NJ, U.S.A.* **114 A2** 40 52N 74 5W
Lodi, *OH, U.S.A.* **92 B4** 41 2N 82 1W
Lodi, *WI, U.S.A.* **103 E4** 43 19N 89 32W
Lofall, *Seattle, U.S.A.* **118 B2** 47 48N 122 39W
Log Lane Village, *CO, U.S.A.* **66 B7** 40 17N 103 51W
Logan, *IA, U.S.A.* **73 D3** 41 39N 95 47W
Logan, *KS, U.S.A.* **74 B4** 39 40N 99 34W
Logan, *NM, U.S.A.* **88 B7** 35 22N 103 25W
Logan, *OH, U.S.A.* **92 D4** 39 32N 82 25W
Logan, *UT, U.S.A.* **100 B4** 41 44N 111 50W
Logan, *WV, U.S.A.* **102 D3** 37 51N 81 59W
Logan, Mt., *Qué., Canada* **172 E3** 48 53N 66 38W
Logan, Mt., *Yukon, Canada* **189 D4** 60 34N 140 23W
Logan County ☆, *AR, U.S.A.* **63 C2** 35 18N 93 44W
Logan County ☆, *CO, U.S.A.* **66 B7** 40 45N 103 0W
Logan County ☆, *IL, U.S.A.* **71 B4** 41 10N 89 20W
Logan County ☆, *KS, U.S.A.* **74 C2** 39 0N 101 0W
Logan County ☆, *KY, U.S.A.* **96 D6** 36 50N 86 50W
Logan County ☆, *ND, U.S.A.* **91 D6** 46 28N 99 25W
Logan County ☆, *NE, U.S.A.* **84 C5** 41 30N 100 30W
Logan County ☆, *OH, U.S.A.* **92 C3** 40 22N 83 46W
Logan County ☆, *OK, U.S.A.* **93 C6** 36 0N 97 30W
Logan County ☆, *WV, U.S.A.* **102 D3** 37 58N 82 0W
Logan Cr. →, *NE, U.S.A.* **84 C9** 41 37N 96 30W
Logan I., *Ont., Canada* **180 B8** 50 7N 88 27W
Logan International, Boston ✈ (BOS), *MA, U.S.A.* **78 B3** 42 22N 71 1W
Logan Lake, *B.C., Canada* **187 E14** 50 30N 120 48W
Logan Martin L., *AL, U.S.A.* **60 C4** 33 26N 86 20W
Logan Square, *Chicago, U.S.A.* **108 B2** 41 55N 87 42W
Logandale, *NV, U.S.A.* **85 F6** 36 36N 114 29W
Logansport, *IN, U.S.A.* **72 C4** 40 45N 86 22W
Logansport, *LA, U.S.A.* **75 C2** 31 58N 94 0W
Loganton, *PA, U.S.A.* **95 C5** 41 2N 77 19W
Loganville, *WI, U.S.A.* **103 E3** 43 27N 90 2W
Loggieville, *N.B., Canada* **173 F4** 47 4N 65 23W
Logy Bay, *Nfld. & L., Canada* **174 E8** 47 38N 52 40W
Lohrville, *IA, U.S.A.* **73 C4** 42 17N 94 33W
Lois, *Houston, U.S.A.* **110 A1** 29 49N 95 30W
Loks Land, *Nunavut, Canada* **191 E13** 62 26N 64 38W
Lola, *KY, U.S.A.* **96 C4** 37 19N 88 18W
Lola, Mt., *CA, U.S.A.* **64 D6** 39 26N 120 22W
Loleta, *CA, U.S.A.* **64 C2** 40 38N 124 13W
Lolita, *TX, U.S.A.* **99 J11** 28 50N 96 33W
Lolo, *MT, U.S.A.* **83 D3** 46 45N 114 5W
Lolo Hot Springs, *MT, U.S.A.* **83 D3** 46 44N 114 32W
Lolo Nat. Forest, *MT, U.S.A.* **83 C3** 47 8N 114 40W
Lolo Pass, *U.S.A.* **70 C4** 46 38N 114 35W
Lolo Peak, *MT, U.S.A.* **83 D3** 46 41N 114 14W
Loltún, *Yucatán, Mexico* **223 B4** 20 15N 89 30W
Loma, *CO, U.S.A.* **66 C2** 39 12N 108 49W
Loma, *MT, U.S.A.* **83 C7** 47 56N 110 30W
Loma, *ND, U.S.A.* **91 B7** 48 38N 98 32W
Loma, Pt, *San Diego, U.S.A.* **117 C1** 32 42N 117 14W
Loma Blanca, *Chihuahua, Mexico* **213 D10** 29 38N 105 32W
Loma Bonita, *Oaxaca, Mexico* **221 F5** 18 7N 95 53W
Loma Bonita, *Veracruz, Mexico* **221 G6** 17 48N 94 48W
Loma de Valle Escondido, *México, Mexico* **225 A2** 19 33N 99 19W
Loma Prieta, *CA, U.S.A.* **64 F5** 37 6N 121 50W
Loman, *MN, U.S.A.* **80 B5** 48 31N 93 49W
Lomas Alegres, *Tabasco, Mexico* **222 B4** 17 34N 92 36W
Lomas Chapultepec, *Distrito Federal, Mexico* **225 B2** 19 25N 99 12W
Lomas de Arena, *Chihuahua, Mexico* **213 C11** 30 35N 104 56W
Lomas de San Angel Inn, *Distrito Federal, Mexico* **225 B2** 19 20N 99 13W
Lomas de Tejeda, *Guadalajara, Mexico* **224 C1** 20 28N 103 24W
Lomax, *IL, U.S.A.* **71 C2** 40 41N 91 4W
Lombardía, *Michoacan, Mexico* **218 C5** 19 8N 102 3W
Lometa, *TX, U.S.A.* **99 F9** 31 13N 98 24W
Lomita, *Los Angeles, U.S.A.* **111 D3** 33 47N 118 18W
Lomond, *Alta., Canada* **185 H8** 50 24N 112 36W
Lompoc, *CA, U.S.A.* **65 J6** 34 38N 120 28W
Lomus Reforma, *Distrito Federal, Mexico* **225 B2** 19 24N 99 14W
Lonaconing, *MD, U.S.A.* **77 A2** 39 34N 78 59W
London, *Ont., Canada* **178 E5** 42 59N 81 15W
London, *AR, U.S.A.* **63 C2** 35 20N 93 15W
London, *KY, U.S.A.* **97 C8** 37 8N 84 5W
London, *OH, U.S.A.* **92 D3** 39 53N 83 27W
London Mills, *IL, U.S.A.* **71 C3** 40 43N 90 11W
Londonderry, *Qué., Canada* **173 H6** 45 29N 63 36W
Londonderry, *NH, U.S.A.* **86 D3** 42 52N 71 22W
Londonderry, *OH, U.S.A.* **92 D4** 39 16N 82 48W
Londonderry, *VT, U.S.A.* **86 C2** 43 14N 72 48W
Londontowne, *MD, U.S.A.* **77 B4** 38 56N 76 33W
Lone Butte, *B.C., Canada* **187 D13** 51 33N 121 12W
Lone Grove, *OK, U.S.A.* **93 D6** 34 11N 97 14W
Lone Mountain, *TN, U.S.A.* **97 D9** 36 24N 83 35W
Lone Mt., *SD, U.S.A.* **91 E2** 45 23N 103 44W
Lone Oak, *KY, U.S.A.* **96 C4** 37 2N 88 40W
Lone Oak, *TX, U.S.A.* **99 E12** 33 0N 95 57W
Lone Peak, *Salt Lake City, U.S.A.* **117 C3** 40 31N 111 45W
Lone Peak Wilderness, *Salt Lake City, U.S.A.* **117 C3** 40 30N 111 42W
Lone Pine, *Alta., Canada* **184 D5** 54 18N 115 7W

Lone Pine, CA, U.S.A. **65 G8** 36 36N 118 4W
Lone Rock, Sask., Canada **182 B2** 53 3N 109 53W
Lone Star, TX, U.S.A. **99 E13** 32 55N 94 43W
Lone Tree, IA, U.S.A. **73 D7** 41 29N 91 26W
Lone Wolf, OK, U.S.A. **93 D4** 34 59N 99 15W
Lonejack, MO, U.S.A. **82 C2** 38 52N 94 10W
Lonely I., Ont., Canada **178 B5** 45 34N 81 28W
Lonepine, MT, U.S.A. **83 C3** 47 42N 114 38W
Lonerock, OR, U.S.A. **94 B6** 45 5N 119 53W
Long B., SC, U.S.A. **90 E7** 33 35N 78 45W
Long Beach, CA, U.S.A. **65 K8** 33 46N 118 11W
Long Beach, MS, U.S.A. **81 F4** 30 21N 89 9W
Long Beach, NY, U.S.A. **78 D1** 40 35N 73 39W
Long Beach, WA, U.S.A. **101 D1** 46 21N 124 3W
Long Beach Harbor, Los Angeles, U.S.A. **111 D3** 33 44N 118 13W
Long Beach I., NJ, U.S.A. **87 C2** 39 42N 74 6W
Long Beach Municipal ✕, Los Angeles, U.S.A. **111 D3** 33 49N 118 9W
Long Branch, NJ, U.S.A. **87 B3** 40 18N 74 0W
Long Branch L., MO, U.S.A. **82 B4** 39 50N 92 30W
Long Brook →, VA, U.S.A. **119 C2** 38 49N 77 15W
Long County ☆, GA, U.S.A. **68 E5** 31 45N 81 45W
Long Cr. →, Sask., Canada **182 F9** 49 7N 102 59W
Long Creek, OR, U.S.A. **94 C6** 44 43N 119 6W
Long I., Nfld. & L., Canada **174 E5** 47 34N 55 59W
Long I., Nunavut, Canada **175 C2** 54 50N 79 20W
Long I., Boston, U.S.A. **106 B4** 42 19N 70 59W
Long I., NY, U.S.A. **87 B3** 40 45N 73 30W
Long Island, KS, U.S.A. **74 B4** 39 57N 99 32W
Long Island City, NY, U.S.A. **114 B3** 40 45N 73 56W
Long Island Sd., NY, U.S.A. **78 C2** 41 10N 73 0W
Long L., Alta., Canada **184 D8** 54 22N 112 46W
Long L., Ont., Canada **181 C10** 49 30N 86 50W
Long L., ME, U.S.A. **76 A5** 47 13N 68 15W
Long L., ME, U.S.A. **76 B4** 46 43N 69 23W
Long L., ME, U.S.A. **86 B4** 44 2N 70 39W
Long L., MI, U.S.A. **79 D8** 45 13N 83 29W
Long L., ND, U.S.A. **91 D5** 46 44N 100 6W
Long L., NY, U.S.A. **89 A6** 44 1N 74 24W
Long L., WA, U.S.A. **101 C8** 47 50N 117 51W
Long L., WI, U.S.A. **103 C2** 45 40N 91 45W
Long Lake, NY, U.S.A. **89 B6** 43 58N 74 25W
Long Lake, Seattle, U.S.A. **118 D2** 47 29N 122 35W
Long Lake Regional Park ⌓, Minneapolis-St. Paul, U.S.A. **113 A2** 45 3N 93 11W
Long Mt., MO, U.S.A. **82 E4** 36 43N 92 31W
Long Pine, NE, U.S.A. **84 B6** 42 32N 99 42W
Long Point, IL, U.S.A. **71 B5** 41 0N 88 54W
Long Point B., Ont., Canada **178 E6** 42 40N 80 10W
Long Pond, MA, U.S.A. **78 C4** 41 48N 70 56W
Long Prairie, MN, U.S.A. **80 E4** 45 59N 94 52W
Long Prairie →, MN, U.S.A. **80 D4** 46 20N 94 36W
Long Pt, MN, U.S.A. **80 B4** 48 59N 94 59W
Long Pt., Man., Canada **183 B13** 53 2N 98 25W
Long Pt., Nfld. & L., Canada **174 D2** 48 47N 58 46W
Long Pt., Ont., Canada **178 E6** 42 35N 80 2W
Long Range Mts., Nfld. & L., Canada **174 C3** 49 30N 57 30W
Long Reach, N.B., Canada **173 H3** 45 28N 66 5W
Long Ridge, KY, U.S.A. **97 B8** 38 35N 84 49W
Long Valley, SD, U.S.A. **91 G4** 43 28N 101 29W
Longboat Key, FL, U.S.A. **67 D6** 27 23N 82 39W
Longbranch, WA, U.S.A. **101 C3** 47 13N 122 46W
Longdale, OK, U.S.A. **93 B5** 36 8N 98 33W
Longford, KS, U.S.A. **74 B6** 39 10N 97 20W
Longjohn Slough, Chicago, U.S.A. **108 C1** 41 42N 87 52W
Longlegged L., Ont., Canada **180 B2** 50 46N 94 8W
Longmeadow, MA, U.S.A. **78 B2** 42 3N 72 34W
Longmont, CO, U.S.A. **66 B5** 40 10N 105 6W
Longridge, MD, U.S.A. **77 B5** 38 16N 75 37W
Longs Pk., CO, U.S.A. **66 B5** 40 15N 105 37W
Longstreet, LA, U.S.A. **75 B2** 32 6N 93 57W
Longton, KS, U.S.A. **74 D7** 37 23N 96 5W
Longtown, MO, U.S.A. **82 D7** 37 40N 89 47W
Longue-Pointe, Montréal, Canada **192 A3** 45 35N 73 31W
Longue-Pointe-de-Mingan, Qué., Canada **172 C5** 50 16N 64 9W
Longue-Rive, Qué., Canada **177 C13** 48 33N 69 15W
Longueuil, Montréal, Canada **192 A4** 45 31N 73 29W
Longueuil, Qué., Canada **177 F9** 45 32N 73 30W
Longueuil-St-Hubert = St-Hubert, Qué., Canada **177 F9** 45 29N 73 25W
Longview, Alta., Canada **185 H6** 50 32N 114 10W
Longview, IL, U.S.A. **71 D5** 39 53N 88 4W
Longview, TX, U.S.A. **99 E13** 32 30N 94 44W
Longview, WA, U.S.A. **101 D3** 46 8N 122 57W
Longville, LA, U.S.A. **75 D2** 30 36N 93 14W
Longville, MN, U.S.A. **80 D4** 46 59N 94 13W
Longwood, FL, U.S.A. **67 C7** 28 42N 81 21W
Longwoods, MD, U.S.A. **77 B4** 38 52N 76 5W
Lonoke, AR, U.S.A. **63 D4** 34 47N 91 54W
Lonoke County ☆, AR, U.S.A. **63 D4** 34 47N 91 54W
Lonsdale, MN, U.S.A. **80 F5** 44 29N 93 26W
Loogootee, IN, U.S.A. **72 E4** 38 41N 86 55W
Lookeba, OK, U.S.A. **93 C5** 35 22N 98 22W
Looking Glass →, MI, U.S.A. **79 G7** 42 52N 84 54W
Lookout, CA, U.S.A. **64 B5** 41 13N 121 9W
Lookout, C., NC, U.S.A. **90 D9** 34 35N 76 32W
Lookout, C., OR, U.S.A. **94 B1** 45 20N 124 1W
Lookout, Pt., MI, U.S.A. **79 E8** 44 3N 83 35W
Lookout Mountain, TN, U.S.A. **97 F7** 34 59N 85 21W
Lookout Mt., AL, U.S.A. **60 B5** 34 20N 85 45W
Lookout Mt., ID, U.S.A. **70 B3** 47 5N 115 58W
Lookout Mt., NM, U.S.A. **88 B2** 35 13N 108 13W
Lookout Mt., OR, U.S.A. **94 C4** 44 21N 121 31W
Lookout Pass, U.S.A. **70 B3** 47 27N 115 42W
Lookout Point Res., OR, U.S.A. **94 D3** 43 55N 122 45W
Loomis, NE, U.S.A. **84 D6** 40 29N 99 31W
Loomis, WA, U.S.A. **101 B6** 48 49N 119 38W
Loon →, Alta., Canada **184 A5** 57 8N 115 3W
Loon L., ME, U.S.A. **76 B4** 46 8N 69 36W
Loon Lake, Alta., Canada **184 B5** 56 33N 115 24W
Loon Lake, Sask., Canada **182 A2** 54 2N 109 10W
Loon Lake, WA, U.S.A. **101 B8** 48 4N 117 38W
Loos, B.C., Canada **187 B14** 53 36N 120 42W
Loosahatchie Bar, TN, U.S.A. **112 A1** 35 11N 90 4W
Lopez I., WA, U.S.A. **101 B3** 48 29N 122 54W
Lopez Pt., CA, U.S.A. **65 G5** 36 1N 121 34W
Lorain, OH, U.S.A. **92 B4** 41 28N 82 11W
Lorain County ☆, OH, U.S.A. **92 B4** 41 14N 82 7W
Loraine, IL, U.S.A. **71 C2** 40 9N 91 13W
Loraine, TX, U.S.A. **98 E7** 32 25N 100 43W
Lord Mayor B., Nunavut, Canada **190 D7** 69 44N 92 2W
Lord's Cove, Nfld. & L., Canada **174 F5** 46 53N 55 40W
Lords Valley, PA, U.S.A. **87 A1** 41 22N 75 4W
Lordsburg, NM, U.S.A. **88 E2** 32 21N 108 43W
Lore City, OH, U.S.A. **92 D5** 39 59N 81 28W
Loreauville, LA, U.S.A. **75 D4** 30 3N 91 44W
Loreburn, Sask., Canada **182 D5** 51 13N 106 36W
Lorenzo, ID, U.S.A. **70 F7** 43 44N 111 52W
Lorenzo, TX, U.S.A. **98 D6** 33 40N 101 32W
Loreto, Baja Calif. S., Mexico **211 G7** 26 0N 111 21W
Loreto, Zacatecas, Mexico **217 E9** 22 16N 101 59W
Loretta, KS, U.S.A. **74 C4** 38 39N 99 12W
Lorette, Man., Canada **183 F15** 49 44N 96 52W
Loretteville, Qué., Canada **177 E11** 46 51N 71 21W
Loretto, KY, U.S.A. **97 C7** 37 38N 85 24W
Loretto, TN, U.S.A. **96 E5** 35 5N 87 26W
Loretto, VA, U.S.A. **77 B3** 38 5N 77 3W
Lorimor, IA, U.S.A. **73 D4** 41 8N 94 3W
Loris, SC, U.S.A. **90 D7** 34 4N 78 53W
Lorman, MS, U.S.A. **81 E2** 31 49N 91 3W
Lorne, N.B., Canada **173 F3** 47 53N 66 8W
Lorraine = Baker, MT, U.S.A. **83 D13** 46 22N 104 17W
Lorraine, KS, U.S.A. **74 C5** 38 34N 98 19W
Lorrainville, Qué., Canada **176 D3** 47 21N 79 23W
Lorton, NE, U.S.A. **84 D9** 40 35N 96 1W
Lorton, VA, U.S.A. **77 B3** 38 42N 77 14W
Los Alamitos, Los Angeles, U.S.A. **111 D4** 33 48N 118 4W
Los Alamos, CA, U.S.A. **65 J6** 34 44N 120 17W
Los Alamos, NM, U.S.A. **88 B4** 35 53N 106 19W
Los Alamos County ☆, NM, U.S.A. **88 B4** 35 55N 106 15W
Los Alamos de Márquez, Coahuila, Mexico **214 B1** 28 46N 103 28W
Los Aldamas, Nuevo León, Mexico **214 D5** 26 3N 99 11W
Los Altos, Veracruz, Mexico **220 E3** 19 27N 97 11W
Los Angeles, Baja Calif. S., Mexico **211 F5** 27 30N 113 18W
Los Angeles, CA, U.S.A. **65 J8** 34 4N 118 15W
Los Angeles →, Los Angeles, U.S.A. **111 D3** 33 47N 118 12W
Los Angeles Aqueduct, CA, U.S.A. **65 H8** 35 22N 118 5W
Los Angeles County ☆, CA, U.S.A. **65 J8** 34 20N 118 10W
Los Angeles Harbor, Los Angeles, U.S.A. **111 D3** 33 42N 118 16W
Los Angeles International ✕ (LAX), CA, U.S.A. **65 K8** 33 57N 118 25W
Los Arrieros, Sonora, Mexico **212 E4** 28 18N 111 2W
Los Azabaches, Baja Calif. S., Mexico **211 J8** 24 20N 110 15W
Los Aztecas, Tamaulipas, Mexico **215 H6** 22 30N 98 37W
Los Banos, CA, U.S.A. **64 F6** 37 4N 120 51W
Los Charcos →, Chihuahua, Mexico **213 C9** 30 33N 106 30W
Los Chaves, NM, U.S.A. **88 C4** 34 44N 106 44W
Los Colomos, Parque de, Guadalajara, Mexico **224 A1** 20 43N 103 23W
Los Coyotes Indian Reservation, CA, U.S.A. **65 K10** 33 17N 116 33W
Los Dinamos, Parque Nacional △, Distrito Federal, Mexico **225 C2** 19 16N 99 16W
Los Frailes, Durango, Mexico **216 B4** 25 37N 106 56W
Los Frailes, Picacho, Sinaloa, Mexico **216 D4** 23 53N 106 2W
Los Fresnos, TX, U.S.A. **98 L10** 26 4N 97 29W
Los Galenos, Monterrey, Mexico **224 A1** 25 53N 100 21W
Los Gatos, CA, U.S.A. **64 F5** 37 14N 121 59W
Los Gavilanes, Baja Calif. S., Mexico **211 F5** 27 32N 113 42W
Los Gavilanes, Guadalajara, Mexico **224 B1** 20 34N 103 26W
Los Herreras, Nuevo León, Mexico **214 E5** 25 55N 99 24W
Los Hoyos, Sonora, Mexico **212 C6** 30 10N 109 47W
Los Jazmines, Presa, Distrito Federal, Mexico **225 B2** 19 25N 99 15W
Los Juncos →, Chihuahua, Mexico **213 C9** 30 47N 106 42W
Los Lentiscos, Baja Calif. S., Mexico **211 F4** 27 32N 114 28W
Los Lirios, Coahuila, Mexico **214 E4** 25 23N 100 34W
Los Lirios, Quintana Roo, Mexico **223 C5** 19 4N 88 45W
Los Loera →, Chihuahua, Mexico **213 G8** 26 37N 107 13W
Los Lunas, NM, U.S.A. **88 C4** 34 48N 106 44W
Los Mármoles, Parque Nacional △, Hidalgo, Mexico **219 B8** 20 53N 99 12W
Los Médanos, Sonora, Mexico **212 F5** 27 10N 110 20W
Los Mochis, Sinaloa, Mexico **216 B2** 25 45N 108 57W
Los Molinos, Sonora, Mexico **212 B4** 31 9N 111 45W
Los Molinos, CA, U.S.A. **64 C4** 40 1N 122 6W
Los Montoyas, NM, U.S.A. **88 B5** 35 25N 105 12W
Los Naranjos, Durango, Mexico **216 D5** 23 21N 105 30W
Los Naranjos, Monterrey, Mexico **224 A1** 25 51N 100 22W
Los Naranjos, Veracruz, Mexico **221 F4** 18 21N 96 10W
Los Nietos, Los Angeles, U.S.A. **111 C4** 33 57N 118 4W
Los Novillos, Parque Nacional △, Coahuila, Mexico **214 A3** 29 22N 101 40W
Los Olivos, CA, U.S.A. **65 J6** 34 40N 120 7W
Los Olmos Cr. →, TX, U.S.A. **99 K10** 27 16N 97 44W
Los Osos, CA, U.S.A. **65 H5** 35 19N 120 50W
Los Padillas, NM, U.S.A. **88 C4** 34 57N 106 42W
Los Padres National Forest, CA, U.S.A. **65 J7** 34 40N 119 40W
Los Pericos, Oaxaca, Mexico **221 H6** 16 48N 94 7W
Los Pinitos, Sonora, Mexico **212 D4** 29 5N 111 28W
Los Pinos →, CO, U.S.A. **66 F3** 36 56N 107 36W
Los Pirules, México, Mexico **225 B3** 19 25N 99 2W
Los Planes, Baja Calif. S, Mexico **211 K9** 23 57N 109 58W
Los Prietos →, Chihuahua, Mexico **213 D9** 29 28N 106 21W
Los Ramones, Nuevo León, Mexico **214 E5** 25 42N 99 37W
Los Ranchos de Albuquerque, NM, U.S.A. **88 B4** 35 10N 106 39W
Los Remedios, San Luis Potosí, Mexico **215 H3** 22 55N 101 19W
Los Reyes, México, Mexico **225 B3** 19 21N 99 6W
Los Reyes Acaquilpan, México, Mexico **225 B4** 19 22N 98 59W
Los Reyes de Salgado, Michoacan, Mexico **218 C5** 19 35N 102 29W
Los Rodríguez, Guanajuato, Mexico **219 A7** 21 3N 100 38W
Los Sauces, Guerrero, Mexico **219 D8** 18 17N 99 50W
Los Toriles, Nayarit, Mexico **216 F6** 21 4N 104 20W
Los Troncones, Sinaloa, Mexico **216 B3** 25 45N 107 55W
Los Vidrios, Sonora, Mexico **212 A2** 32 2N 113 26W
Losantville, IN, U.S.A. **72 C5** 40 2N 85 11W
Lost →, IN, U.S.A. **72 E4** 38 33N 86 49W
Lost →, OR, U.S.A. **94 F4** 41 56N 121 30W
Lost →, WV, U.S.A. **102 B6** 39 4N 78 39W
Lost Brook Preserve, NJ, U.S.A. **114 A3** 40 56N 73 56W
Lost City, WV, U.S.A. **102 C6** 38 56N 78 50W
Lost Creek, WV, U.S.A. **102 B4** 39 10N 80 21W
Lost Hills, CA, U.S.A. **65 H7** 35 37N 119 41W
Lost Nation, IA, U.S.A. **73 D8** 41 58N 90 49W
Lost Peak, UT, U.S.A. **100 F2** 37 29N 113 55W
Lost River, ID, U.S.A. **70 F5** 43 41N 113 22W
Lost River Range, ID, U.S.A. **70 E5** 44 8N 113 47W
Lost Springs, KS, U.S.A. **74 C7** 38 34N 96 58W
Lost Springs, WY, U.S.A. **104 D8** 42 46N 104 56W
Lost Trail Pass, U.S.A. **70 D5** 45 42N 113 57W
Lostine, OR, U.S.A. **94 B8** 45 29N 117 26W
Lostwood, ND, U.S.A. **91 B3** 48 29N 102 25W
Lostwood Nat. Wildlife Reserve ⌓, ND, U.S.A. **91 B3** 48 40N 102 30W
Lothair, MT, U.S.A. **83 B6** 48 28N 111 14W
Lott, TX, U.S.A. **99 F10** 31 12N 97 2W
Lottsburg, VA, U.S.A. **77 C4** 37 58N 76 31W
Loudon, NH, U.S.A. **86 C3** 43 16N 71 27W
Loudon, TN, U.S.A. **97 E8** 35 45N 84 20W
Loudon County ☆, TN, U.S.A. **97 E8** 35 45N 84 20W
Loudonville, OH, U.S.A. **92 C4** 40 38N 82 14W
Loudoun County ☆, VA, U.S.A. **102 B7** 39 5N 77 50W
Lougheed, Alta., Canada **185 F9** 52 44N 111 33W
Lougheed I., Nunavut, Canada **190 B4** 77 26N 105 6W
Loughman, FL, U.S.A. **67 C7** 28 14N 81 34W
Louin, MS, U.S.A. **81 D4** 32 4N 89 16W
Louis Armstrong New Orleans International ✕ (MSY), LA, U.S.A. **75 E5** 30 0N 90 15W
Louis Creek, B.C., Canada **187 D14** 51 8N 120 7W
Louis XIV, Pte., Qué., Canada **175 C2** 54 37N 79 45W
Louisa, KY, U.S.A. **97 B10** 38 7N 82 36W
Louisa, VA, U.S.A. **102 C7** 38 1N 78 0W
Louisa County ☆, IA, U.S.A. **73 D7** 41 15N 91 15W
Louisa County ☆, VA, U.S.A. **102 D7** 38 1N 78 0W
Louisbourg, N.S., Canada **173 H10** 45 55N 60 0W
Louisburg, KS, U.S.A. **74 C9** 38 37N 94 41W
Louisburg, MN, U.S.A. **80 E2** 45 10N 96 10W
Louisburg, MO, U.S.A. **82 D3** 37 46N 93 8W
Louisburg, NC, U.S.A. **90 B7** 36 6N 78 18W
Louisdale, N.S., Canada **173 H8** 45 36N 61 4W
Louise, MS, U.S.A. **81 D3** 32 59N 90 35W
Louise, TX, U.S.A. **99 H11** 29 6N 96 24W
Louise, L., Orlando, U.S.A. **115 B1** 28 28N 81 32W
Louise I., B.C., Canada **186 C3** 52 55N 131 50W
Louiseville, Qué., Canada **177 E10** 46 20N 72 56W
Louisiana, MO, U.S.A. **82 B5** 39 27N 91 3W
Louisiana □, U.S.A. **75 D3** 30 50N 92 0W
Louisville, AL, U.S.A. **60 E5** 31 47N 85 33W
Louisville, CO, U.S.A. **66 C5** 39 59N 105 8W
Louisville, GA, U.S.A. **68 D4** 33 0N 82 25W
Louisville, IL, U.S.A. **71 E5** 38 46N 88 30W
Louisville, KS, U.S.A. **74 B7** 39 15N 96 18W
Louisville, KY, U.S.A. **97 B7** 38 15N 85 46W
Louisville, MS, U.S.A. **81 C4** 33 7N 89 3W
Louisville, NE, U.S.A. **84 D9** 41 0N 96 10W
Louisville, OH, U.S.A. **92 C5** 40 50N 81 16W
Louisville International ✕ (SDF), KY, U.S.A. **97 B7** 38 10N 85 44W
Loup →, NE, U.S.A. **84 C8** 41 24N 97 19W
Loup City, NE, U.S.A. **84 C7** 41 17N 98 58W
Loup County ☆, NE, U.S.A. **84 C6** 41 50N 99 30W
Loups Marins, Lacs des, Qué., Canada **175 B3** 56 30N 73 45W
Lourdes, Nfld. & L., Canada **174 D2** 48 39N 59 0W
Loutre, Bayou →, LA, U.S.A. **75 B3** 32 41N 92 8W
Louvale, GA, U.S.A. **68 D2** 32 10N 84 50W
Louvicourt, Qué., Canada **176 C5** 48 4N 77 23W
Louviers, CO, U.S.A. **66 C5** 39 28N 105 1W
Love, Sask., Canada **182 B7** 53 29N 104 10W
Love County ☆, OK, U.S.A. **93 E6** 34 0N 97 15W
Love Point, MD, U.S.A. **77 A4** 39 2N 76 19W
Lovelady, TX, U.S.A. **99 F12** 31 8N 95 27W
Loveland, CO, U.S.A. **66 B5** 40 24N 105 5W
Loveland, OH, U.S.A. **92 D2** 39 16N 84 16W
Loveland, OK, U.S.A. **93 D5** 34 18N 98 46W
Loveland Pass, CO, U.S.A. **66 C5** 39 40N 105 53W
Lovell, ME, U.S.A. **76 D3** 44 8N 70 54W
Lovell, WY, U.S.A. **104 B4** 44 50N 108 24W
Lovells, MI, U.S.A. **79 E7** 44 48N 84 29W
Lovelock, NV, U.S.A. **85 B2** 40 11N 118 28W
Loverna, Sask., Canada **182 D2** 51 40N 110 0W
Loves Park, IL, U.S.A. **71 A4** 42 19N 89 3W
Lovett, GA, U.S.A. **68 D4** 32 38N 82 46W
Lovettsville, VA, U.S.A. **77 A3** 39 16N 77 38W
Lovilia, IA, U.S.A. **73 D6** 41 8N 92 55W
Loving, NM, U.S.A. **88 E6** 32 17N 104 6W
Loving County ☆, TX, U.S.A. **98 F4** 31 42N 103 36W
Lovingston, VA, U.S.A. **102 D6** 37 46N 78 52W
Lovington, IL, U.S.A. **71 D5** 39 43N 88 38W
Lovington, NM, U.S.A. **88 E7** 32 57N 103 21W
Low, Qué., Canada **176 F7** 45 50N 75 58W
Low, C., N.W.T., Canada **191 E8** 63 7N 85 18W
Low Desert, OR, U.S.A. **94 D5** 43 27N 120 27W
Low L., Qué., Canada **175 B4** 55 54N 67 5W
Lowden, IA, U.S.A. **73 D8** 41 52N 90 56W
Lowe Farm, Man., Canada **183 F14** 49 21N 97 35W
Lowell, AR, U.S.A. **63 B1** 36 15N 94 8W
Lowell, FL, U.S.A. **67 B6** 29 20N 82 12W
Lowell, ID, U.S.A. **70 C3** 46 9N 115 36W
Lowell, IN, U.S.A. **72 B3** 41 18N 87 25W
Lowell, MA, U.S.A. **78 B3** 42 38N 71 19W
Lowell, OR, U.S.A. **94 D3** 43 55N 122 47W
Lowell, VT, U.S.A. **86 B2** 44 48N 72 27W
Lowell, L., ID, U.S.A. **70 F2** 43 35N 116 44W
Lower Alkali L., CA, U.S.A. **64 B6** 41 16N 120 2W
Lower Arrow L., B.C., Canada **187 F16** 49 40N 118 5W
Lower B., NY, U.S.A. **89 E6** 40 32N 74 5W
Lower Brule, SD, U.S.A. **91 F6** 44 5N 99 34W
Lower Brule Indian Reservation, SD, U.S.A. **91 F6** 44 5N 100 0W
Lower California = Baja California, Mexico **210 E5** 31 10N 115 12W
Lower Crab Cr. →, WA, U.S.A. **101 D6** 46 49N 119 55W
Lower Elwha Indian Reservation, WA, U.S.A. **101 B2** 48 8N 123 33W
Lower Gilmanton, NH, U.S.A. **86 C3** 43 24N 71 24W
Lower Granite L., WA, U.S.A. **101 D8** 46 26N 117 14W
Lower Kalskag, AK, U.S.A. **61 F7** 61 31N 160 22W
Lower Klamath L., CA, U.S.A. **64 B5** 41 57N 121 42W
Lower Lake, CA, U.S.A. **64 E4** 38 55N 122 37W
Lower Lonsdale, Vancouver, Canada **193 B2** 49 19N 123 4W
Lower Manitou L., Ont., Canada **180 C4** 49 15N 93 0W
Lower Marlboro, MD, U.S.A. **77 B4** 38 39N 76 41W
Lower Monumental Dam, WA, U.S.A. **101 D7** 46 32N 118 33W
Lower New York B. = Lower B., NY, U.S.A. **89 E6** 40 32N 74 5W
Lower Nicola, B.C., Canada **187 E14** 50 12N 120 54W
Lower Paia, HI, U.S.A. **69 C5** 20 55N 156 23W
Lower Post, B.C., Canada **189 E7** 59 58N 128 30W
Lower Red L., MN, U.S.A. **80 C4** 47 58N 95 0W
Lower Sioux Indian Reservation, MN, U.S.A. **80 F4** 44 32N 94 59W
Lower Suwannee Nat. Wildlife Refuge ⌓, FL, U.S.A. **67 B5** 29 20N 83 8W
Lower Tsitika River Park ⌓, B.C., Canada **186 E8** 50 27N 126 35W
Lower West Pubnico, N.S., Canada **173 K4** 43 38N 65 48W
Lower Woods Harbour, N.S., Canada **173 K4** 43 31N 65 44W
Lowes, KY, U.S.A. **96 D4** 36 53N 88 46W
Lowes Crossroads, DE, U.S.A. **77 B5** 38 34N 75 24W
Lowman, ID, U.S.A. **70 E3** 44 5N 115 37W
Lowmoor, VA, U.S.A. **102 D5** 37 47N 79 53W
Lowndes County ☆, AL, U.S.A. **60 D4** 32 11N 86 35W
Lowndes County ☆, GA, U.S.A. **68 F3** 30 50N 83 15W
Lowndes County ☆, MS, U.S.A. **81 C5** 33 30N 88 25W
Lowndesboro, AL, U.S.A. **60 D4** 32 17N 86 37W
Lowry, MN, U.S.A. **80 E3** 45 42N 95 31W
Lowry, SD, U.S.A. **91 E6** 45 20N 99 59W
Lowry City, MO, U.S.A. **82 C3** 38 8N 93 44W
Lowther, Ont., Canada **181 C13** 49 32N 83 2W
Lowther I., Nunavut, Canada **190 C6** 74 33N 97 30W
Lowville, NY, U.S.A. **89 B5** 43 47N 75 29W
Loxley, AL, U.S.A. **60 F3** 30 37N 87 45W
Loyal, OK, U.S.A. **93 C5** 35 59N 98 6W
Loyal, WI, U.S.A. **103 D3** 44 44N 90 30W
Loyal Valley, TX, U.S.A. **99 G9** 30 35N 99 0W
Loyall, KY, U.S.A. **97 D9** 36 51N 83 22W
Loyalton, CA, U.S.A. **64 D6** 39 41N 120 14W
Loyalton, SD, U.S.A. **91 E6** 45 17N 99 17W
Lu Verne, IA, U.S.A. **73 C4** 42 55N 94 5W
Lua Makiki, HI, U.S.A. **69 C5** 20 33N 156 37W
Lualualei Naval Reserve, HI, U.S.A. **69 K13** 21 27N 158 6W
Lubbock, TX, U.S.A. **98 D6** 33 35N 101 51W
Lubbock County ☆, TX, U.S.A. **98 D6** 33 35N 101 50W
Lubec, ME, U.S.A. **76 D7** 44 52N 66 59W
Lubicon L., Alta., Canada **184 B5** 56 23N 115 56W
Lubicon Lake, Alta., Canada **184 B5** 56 22N 115 52W
Lublin, WI, U.S.A. **103 C3** 45 5N 90 43W
Lucama, NC, U.S.A. **90 C7** 35 39N 78 0W
Lucan, Ont., Canada **178 D5** 43 11N 81 24W
Lucania, Mt., Yukon, Canada **189 D4** 61 1N 140 27W
Lucas, KS, U.S.A. **74 B5** 39 4N 98 32W
Lucas, KY, U.S.A. **96 D6** 36 53N 86 2W
Lucas, OH, U.S.A. **92 C4** 40 42N 82 25W
Lucas County ☆, IA, U.S.A. **73 E5** 41 0N 93 20W
Lucas County ☆, OH, U.S.A. **92 B3** 41 31N 83 48W
Lucasville, OH, U.S.A. **92 E4** 38 53N 82 59W
Luce County ☆, MI, U.S.A. **79 C6** 46 30N 85 30W
Lucedale, MS, U.S.A. **81 F5** 30 56N 88 35W
Lucenilla, Península, Sinaloa, Mexico **216 C3** 24 29N 107 46W
Lucerne = Lake Worth, FL, U.S.A. **67 E8** 26 37N 80 3W
Lucerne, B.C., Canada **187 C16** 52 52N 118 33W
Lucerne, CA, U.S.A. **64 D4** 39 6N 122 48W
Lucerne, CO, U.S.A. **66 B6** 40 29N 104 41W
Lucerne, WY, U.S.A. **104 C4** 43 44N 108 11W
Lucerne L., CA, U.S.A. **65 J10** 34 31N 116 58W
Lucerne Valley, CA, U.S.A. **65 J10** 34 27N 116 57W
Lucero, L., NM, U.S.A. **88 E4** 32 42N 106 27W
Luceville, Qué., Canada **177 C14** 48 32N 68 22W
Lucile, ID, U.S.A. **70 D2** 45 32N 116 18W
Luck, WI, U.S.A. **103 C1** 45 35N 92 29W
Luck L., Sask., Canada **182 D4** 51 5N 107 5W
Luckey, OH, U.S.A. **92 B3** 41 27N 83 29W
Lucknow, Ont., Canada **178 D5** 43 57N 81 31W
Lucky Lake, Sask., Canada **182 E4** 50 59N 107 8W
Lucy, L., Orlando, U.S.A. **115 A2** 28 34N 81 29W
Ludden, ND, U.S.A. **91 D7** 46 1N 98 7W
Ludell, KS, U.S.A. **74 B3** 39 52N 100 58W
Ludington, MI, U.S.A. **79 F5** 43 57N 86 27W
Ludlow, N.B., Canada **173 G3** 46 29N 66 21W
Ludlow, CA, U.S.A. **65 J10** 34 43N 116 10W
Ludlow, CO, U.S.A. **66 E6** 37 20N 104 35W
Ludlow, IL, U.S.A. **71 C5** 40 23N 88 8W
Ludlow, KY, U.S.A. **107 B1** 39 5N 84 32W
Ludlow, MA, U.S.A. **78 B2** 42 10N 72 29W
Ludlow, MS, U.S.A. **81 D4** 32 34N 89 43W
Ludlow, MO, U.S.A. **82 B3** 39 39N 93 42W
Ludlow, SD, U.S.A. **91 E2** 45 50N 103 23W
Ludlow, VT, U.S.A. **86 C2** 43 24N 72 42W
Ludowici, GA, U.S.A. **68 E5** 31 43N 81 45W
Lueders, TX, U.S.A. **99 E8** 32 48N 99 37W
Lufkin, TX, U.S.A. **99 F13** 31 21N 94 44W
Lugoff, SC, U.S.A. **90 D5** 34 13N 80 40W
Luis Echevarría Alvarez, Quintana Roo, Mexico **223 D5** 18 39N 88 14W
Luis L. León, Presa, Chihuahua, Mexico **213 E10** 28 57N 105 17W
Luis Lopez, NM, U.S.A. **88 D4** 33 59N 106 53W
Luis Moya, Zacatecas, Mexico **217 E8** 22 25N 102 15W
Luis Munoz Marin International, San Juan ✕ (SJU), Puerto Rico **105 G16** 18 26N 66 0W
Lukachukai, AZ, U.S.A. **62 A6** 36 25N 109 15W
Luke, MD, U.S.A. **77 A1** 39 30N 79 5W
Lukeville, AZ, U.S.A. **62 F3** 31 53N 112 49W
Lula, GA, U.S.A. **68 B3** 34 23N 83 40W
Lula, MS, U.S.A. **81 B3** 34 27N 90 29W
Luling, TX, U.S.A. **99 H10** 29 41N 97 39W
Lulu, FL, U.S.A. **67 A6** 30 7N 82 29W
Lulu I., B.C., Canada **193 C2** 49 10N 123 6W
Luma, Amer. Samoa **105 f** 14 16 S 169 33W
Lumber →, NC, U.S.A. **90 D6** 34 12N 79 10W
Lumber City, GA, U.S.A. **68 E4** 31 56N 82 41W
Lumberport, WV, U.S.A. **102 B4** 39 22N 80 21W
Lumberton, MS, U.S.A. **81 E4** 31 0N 89 27W
Lumberton, NC, U.S.A. **90 D7** 34 37N 79 0W
Lumberton, NM, U.S.A. **88 A4** 36 56N 106 56W
Lumberton, TX, U.S.A. **99 G13** 30 16N 94 12W
Lumby, B.C., Canada **187 E16** 50 15N 118 58W
Lummi Indian Reservation, WA, U.S.A. **101 B3** 48 52N 122 32W
Lumpkin, GA, U.S.A. **68 D2** 32 3N 84 48W
Lumpkin County ☆, GA, U.S.A. **68 B3** 34 40N 84 0W
Lumsden, Nfld. & L., Canada **174 C7** 49 19N 53 37W
Lumsden, Sask., Canada **182 E7** 50 39N 104 52W
Luna, NM, U.S.A. **88 D2** 33 49N 108 57W
Luna County ☆, NM, U.S.A. **88 E3** 32 15N 107 45W
Luna Pier, MI, U.S.A. **79 H8** 41 48N 83 29W
Lund, B.C., Canada **186 F10** 49 59N 124 45W
Lund, NV, U.S.A. **85 D5** 38 52N 115 0W
Lund, UT, U.S.A. **100 E2** 38 0N 113 26W
Lundar, Man., Canada **183 E13** 50 42N 98 2W
Lundbreck, Alta., Canada **185 J6** 49 35N 114 10W
Lunenburg, N.S., Canada **173 J5** 44 22N 64 18W
Lunenburg, VA, U.S.A. **102 E6** 36 58N 78 16W
Lunenburg, VT, U.S.A. **86 B3** 44 26N 71 42W
Lunenburg County ☆, VA, U.S.A. **102 E6** 36 58N 78 16W
Luning, NV, U.S.A. **85 D2** 38 30N 118 11W
Lupton, AZ, U.S.A. **62 B6** 35 21N 109 4W
Lupus, MO, U.S.A. **82 C4** 38 51N 92 27W
Luquillo, Puerto Rico **105 G17** 18 23N 65 43W
Luray, KS, U.S.A. **74 B5** 39 7N 98 41W
Luray, MO, U.S.A. **82 A5** 40 27N 91 53W
Luray, VA, U.S.A. **102 C6** 38 40N 78 28W
Lusby, MD, U.S.A. **77 B4** 38 22N 76 26W
Luseland, Sask., Canada **182 C2** 52 5N 109 24W
Lushton, NE, U.S.A. **84 D8** 40 43N 97 44W
Lusk, WY, U.S.A. **104 D8** 42 46N 104 27W
Lutcher, LA, U.S.A. **75 D5** 30 2N 90 42W
Luther, IA, U.S.A. **73 D5** 41 58N 93 49W
Luther, MI, U.S.A. **79 E6** 44 2N 85 41W
Luther, OK, U.S.A. **93 C6** 35 40N 97 12W
Luthersville, GA, U.S.A. **68 C2** 33 13N 84 45W
Lutherville, Baltimore, U.S.A. **107 A2** 39 25N 76 37W
Lutherville-Timonium, MD, U.S.A. **77 A4** 39 25N 76 38W
Lutie, TX, U.S.A. **98 B7** 35 1N 100 13W
Łutselk'e, N.W.T., Canada **189 D10** 62 24N 110 44W
Lutsen, MN, U.S.A. **80 C8** 47 39N 90 41W
Luttrell, TN, U.S.A. **97 D9** 36 12N 83 45W
Lutts, TN, U.S.A. **96 E5** 35 9N 87 56W
Lutz, FL, U.S.A. **67 C6** 28 9N 82 28W
Luverne, AL, U.S.A. **60 E4** 31 43N 86 16W
Luverne, MN, U.S.A. **80 G2** 43 39N 96 13W
Luverne, ND, U.S.A. **91 C8** 47 16N 97 55W
Luxapallila Cr. →, U.S.A. **81 C6** 33 27N 88 26W
Luxemburg, IA, U.S.A. **73 C7** 42 36N 91 5W
Luxemburg, WI, U.S.A. **103 D6** 44 33N 87 42W
Luxora, AR, U.S.A. **63 C6** 35 45N 89 56W
Luzerne County ☆, PA, U.S.A. **95 C7** 41 10N 76 0W
Lyal I., Ont., Canada **178 C5** 44 57N 81 24W
Lycan, CO, U.S.A. **66 E8** 37 37N 102 12W
Lycoming County ☆, PA, U.S.A. **95 C5** 41 20N 77 0W
Lyell I., B.C., Canada **186 C3** 52 40N 131 35W
Lyells, VA, U.S.A. **77 C4** 38 0N 76 44W
Lyerly, GA, U.S.A. **68 B1** 34 24N 85 24W
Lyford, TX, U.S.A. **98 L10** 26 25N 97 48W
Lykens, PA, U.S.A. **95 D6** 40 34N 76 42W

Lyle, MN, U.S.A. 80 G6 43 30N 92 57W
Lyles, TN, U.S.A. 96 E5 35 55N 87 21W
Lyman, MS, U.S.A. 81 F4 30 30N 89 7W
Lyman, NE, U.S.A. 84 C1 41 55N 104 2W
Lyman, UT, U.S.A. 100 E4 38 24N 111 35W
Lyman, WA, U.S.A. 101 B3 48 32N 122 4W
Lyman, WY, U.S.A. 104 E2 41 20N 110 18W
Lyman County ☆, SD, U.S.A. 91 G6 44 0N 100 0W
Lyman L., AZ, U.S.A. 62 C6 34 22N 109 23W
Lymburn, Alta., Canada 184 C1 55 21N 119 47W
Lyme, NH, U.S.A. 86 C2 43 48N 72 12W
Lynbrook, NY, U.S.A. 114 C4 40 39N 73 40W
Lynch, KY, U.S.A. 97 D10 36 58N 82 54W
Lynch, NE, U.S.A. 84 B7 42 50N 98 28W
Lynchburg, OH, U.S.A. 92 D3 39 15N 83 48W
Lynchburg, SC, U.S.A. 90 D5 34 3N 80 4W
Lynchburg, TN, U.S.A. 96 E6 35 17N 86 22W
Lynchburg, VA, U.S.A. 102 D5 37 25N 79 9W
Lynches ➔, SC, U.S.A. 90 E6 33 50N 79 22W
Lynd, MN, U.S.A. 80 F3 44 23N 95 54W
Lynden, WA, U.S.A. 101 B3 48 57N 122 27W
Lyndhurst, NJ, U.S.A. 114 B2 40 49N 74 7W
Lyndon, IL, U.S.A. 71 B4 41 43N 89 56W
Lyndon, KS, U.S.A. 74 C8 38 37N 95 41W
Lyndon, VT, U.S.A. 86 B2 44 31N 72 1W
Lyndon B. Johnson, L., TX, U.S.A. 99 G9 30 33N 98 20W
Lyndon B. Johnson Nat. Grassland, TX, U.S.A. 99 D10 33 25N 97 37W
Lyndon B. Johnson Nat. Historical Park ⌂, TX, U.S.A. 99 G9 30 15N 98 25W
Lyndon Station, WI, U.S.A. 103 E4 43 43N 89 54W
Lyndonville, NY, U.S.A. 89 B2 43 20N 78 23W
Lyndonville, VT, U.S.A. 86 B2 44 31N 72 1W
Lynhurst, Indianapolis, U.S.A. 110 B1 39 46N 86 14W
Lynn, AL, U.S.A. 60 B3 34 3N 87 33W
Lynn, IN, U.S.A. 72 C6 40 3N 84 56W
Lynn, MA, U.S.A. 78 B4 42 28N 70 57W
Lynn, UT, U.S.A. 100 B2 41 53N 113 45W
Lynn Canal, AK, U.S.A. 61 G14 58 50N 135 15W
Lynn Canyon Park, Vancouver, Canada 193 A2 42 20N 123 1W
Lynn County ☆, TX, U.S.A. 98 D6 33 10N 101 48W
Lynn Harbor, Boston, U.S.A. 106 A4 42 26N 70 56W
Lynn Haven, FL, U.S.A. 67 A3 30 15N 85 39W
Lynn Headwaters Regional Park, Vancouver, Canada 193 A2 49 22N 123 1W
Lynn Lake, Man., Canada 191 F5 56 51N 101 3W
Lynn Valley, Vancouver, Canada 193 A2 49 20N 123 2W
Lynn Woods Res., Boston, U.S.A. 106 A3 42 29N 71 0W
Lynndyl, UT, U.S.A. 100 D3 39 31N 112 22W
Lynne, FL, U.S.A. 67 B7 29 12N 81 55W
Lynnfield, MA, U.S.A. 78 B3 42 32N 71 3W
Lynnville, IN, U.S.A. 72 E3 38 12N 87 18W
Lynnville, KY, U.S.A. 96 D4 36 34N 88 34W
Lynnville, TN, U.S.A. 96 E5 35 23N 87 0W
Lynnwood, WA, U.S.A. 101 C3 47 49N 122 18W
Lynwood, Los Angeles, U.S.A. 111 C3 33 55N 118 12W
Lynx L., N.W.T., Canada 189 D11 62 25N 106 15W
Lynxville, WI, U.S.A. 103 E2 43 15N 91 2W
Lyon, MS, U.S.A. 81 B3 34 13N 90 33W
Lyon, C., N.W.T., Canada 188 C8 69 50N 122 57W
Lyon County ☆, IA, U.S.A. 73 B2 43 20N 96 10W
Lyon County ☆, KS, U.S.A. 74 C7 38 30N 96 10W
Lyon County ☆, KY, U.S.A. 96 D4 37 0N 88 5W
Lyon County ☆, MN, U.S.A. 80 F3 44 25N 95 50W
Lyon County ☆, NV, U.S.A. 85 D1 38 45N 119 10W
Lyon Inlet, Nunavut, Canada 191 D9 66 32N 83 53W
Lyon Mountain, NY, U.S.A. 89 A7 44 43N 73 55W
Lyons, Chicago, U.S.A. 108 C2 41 48N 87 49W
Lyons, CO, U.S.A. 66 B5 40 14N 105 16W
Lyons, GA, U.S.A. 68 D4 32 12N 82 19W
Lyons, IN, U.S.A. 72 E3 38 59N 87 5W
Lyons, KS, U.S.A. 74 C5 38 21N 98 12W
Lyons, NY, U.S.A. 89 B4 43 5N 77 0W
Lyons, NE, U.S.A. 84 C9 41 56N 96 28W
Lyons, OH, U.S.A. 92 B2 41 42N 84 4W
Lyons, OR, U.S.A. 94 C3 44 47N 122 37W
Lyons, TX, U.S.A. 99 G11 30 23N 96 34W
Lyons Falls, NY, U.S.A. 89 B5 43 37N 75 22W
Lysite, WY, U.S.A. 104 C5 43 16N 107 41W
Lyster, Qué., Canada 177 E11 46 22N 71 37W
Lytle, TX, U.S.A. 99 H9 29 14N 98 48W
Lytton, B.C., Canada 187 E13 50 13N 121 31W
Lytton, IA, U.S.A. 73 C4 42 25N 94 51W

M

Ma-Me-O Beach, Alta., Canada 185 F7 52 58N 113 59W
Mabank, TX, U.S.A. 99 E11 32 22N 96 6W
Mabel, MN, U.S.A. 80 G7 43 32N 91 46W
Mabel, L., Orlando, U.S.A. 115 B1 28 25N 81 32W
Mabel L., B.C., Canada 187 E16 50 35N 118 43W
Maben, WV, U.S.A. 102 D3 37 38N 81 23W
Maberly, Ont., Canada 179 C10 44 50N 76 32W
Mableton, GA, U.S.A. 68 C2 33 49N 84 35W
Mabou, N.S., Canada 173 G8 46 4N 61 29W
Mabton, WA, U.S.A. 101 D5 46 13N 120 0W
McAdam, N.B., Canada 173 H2 45 36N 67 20W
McAdoo, PA, U.S.A. 95 D7 40 55N 75 59W
McAlester, OK, U.S.A. 93 D8 34 56N 95 46W
Macalister, B.C., Canada 187 C12 52 27N 122 24W
McAlister, NM, U.S.A. 88 C7 34 42N 103 47W
McAllen, TX, U.S.A. 98 L9 26 12N 98 14W
McAllister Park, San Antonio, U.S.A. 117 B3 29 33N 98 23W
McAlpin, FL, U.S.A. 67 A6 30 8N 82 57W
McAlpine Creek County Park, Charlotte, U.S.A. 107 B2 35 9N 80 44W
MacAlpine L., N.W.T., Canada 191 D5 66 32N 102 45W
Macamic, Qué., Canada 176 C3 48 45N 79 0W
Macapule, I., Sinaloa, Mexico 216 B2 25 21N 108 40W
McArthur, CA, U.S.A. 64 B5 41 3N 121 24W
McArthur, OH, U.S.A. 92 D4 39 15N 82 29W
MacArthur Park, Los Angeles, U.S.A. 111 B3 34 3N 118 16W
Macaulay Pt., B.C., Canada 187 G11 48 25N 123 24W
McAuley, Man., Canada 183 E10 50 16N 101 23W
McBain, MI, U.S.A. 79 E6 44 12N 85 13W
McBee, SC, U.S.A. 90 D5 34 28N 80 15W
McBride, B.C., Canada 187 B14 53 20N 120 19W
McBride, MO, U.S.A. 82 D7 37 50N 89 50W
McBride, OK, U.S.A. 93 E7 33 54N 96 36W
McBrides, MI, U.S.A. 79 F6 43 21N 85 2W
McCall, ID, U.S.A. 70 E2 44 55N 116 6W
McCall Creek, MS, U.S.A. 81 E3 31 31N 90 42W
McCallsburg, IA, U.S.A. 73 C5 42 10N 93 23W
McCallum, Nfld. & L., Canada 174 E4 47 38N 56 14W
McCamey, TX, U.S.A. 98 F5 31 8N 102 14W
McCammon, ID, U.S.A. 70 G6 42 39N 112 12W
Maccan, N.S., Canada 173 H5 45 43N 64 15W
McCandless, PA, U.S.A. 95 D2 40 30N 80 4W
McCarran International, Las Vegas ✕ (LAS), NV, U.S.A. 85 F5 36 5N 115 9W
McCarthy, AK, U.S.A. 61 F12 61 26N 142 56W
McCarty Park, Milwaukee, U.S.A. 112 C1 42 59N 88 0W
McCartys, NM, U.S.A. 88 B3 35 4N 107 41W
McCauley I., B.C., Canada 186 B4 53 40N 130 15W
McCaysville, GA, U.S.A. 68 B2 34 59N 84 23W
McClain County ☆, OK, U.S.A. 93 D6 35 0N 97 30W
McClave, CO, U.S.A. 66 D8 38 8N 102 51W
McCleary, WA, U.S.A. 101 C2 47 3N 123 16W
McClelland, IA, U.S.A. 73 D3 41 20N 95 41W
McClelland L., Alta., Canada 184 A9 57 29N 111 20W
McClellanville, SC, U.S.A. 90 E6 33 5N 79 28W
Macclenny, FL, U.S.A. 67 A6 30 17N 82 7W
M'Clintock Chan., Nunavut, Canada 190 C5 72 0N 102 0W
McCloud, CA, U.S.A. 64 B4 41 15N 122 8W
McClure, OH, U.S.A. 92 B3 41 22N 83 57W
McClure, PA, U.S.A. 95 D5 40 42N 77 19W
McClure, VA, U.S.A. 102 D2 37 6N 82 23W
McClure, L., CA, U.S.A. 64 F6 37 35N 120 16W
M'Clure Str., N.W.T., Canada 188 B9 75 0N 119 0W
McClusky, ND, U.S.A. 91 C5 47 29N 100 27W
McColl, SC, U.S.A. 90 D6 34 40N 79 33W
McComb, MS, U.S.A. 81 E3 31 15N 90 27W
McComb, OH, U.S.A. 92 B3 41 7N 83 48W
McCone County ☆, MT, U.S.A. 83 C12 47 40N 105 50W
McConnell Air Force Base, KS, U.S.A. 74 D6 37 40N 97 16W
McConnellsburg, PA, U.S.A. 95 E5 39 56N 77 59W
McConnelsville, OH, U.S.A. 92 D5 39 39N 81 51W
McCook, Chicago, U.S.A. 108 C2 41 47N 87 49W
McCook, NE, U.S.A. 84 D5 40 12N 100 38W
McCook County ☆, SD, U.S.A. 91 G8 43 44N 97 23W
McCool, MS, U.S.A. 81 C4 33 12N 89 21W
McCool Junction, NE, U.S.A. 84 D8 40 45N 97 36W
McCormick, SC, U.S.A. 90 E3 33 55N 82 17W
McCormick County ☆, SC, U.S.A. 90 E3 33 50N 82 15W
McCoy, CO, U.S.A. 66 C4 39 55N 106 44W
McCracken, KS, U.S.A. 74 C4 38 36N 99 33W
McCracken County ☆, KY, U.S.A. 97 C4 37 5N 88 45W
McCreary, Man., Canada 183 E12 50 47N 99 29W
McCreary County ☆, KY, U.S.A. 97 D8 36 45N 84 30W
McCrory, AR, U.S.A. 63 C4 35 16N 91 12W
McCulloch County ☆, TX, U.S.A. 99 F8 31 9N 99 20W
McCullough Ra., NV, U.S.A. 85 G5 35 45N 115 5W
McCune, KS, U.S.A. 74 D8 37 21N 95 1W
McCurtain, OK, U.S.A. 93 C9 35 9N 94 58W
McCurtain County ☆, OK, U.S.A. 93 D9 34 10N 94 45W
McDade, TX, U.S.A. 99 G10 30 17N 97 14W
McDame, B.C., Canada 189 E7 59 44N 128 59W
McDavid, FL, U.S.A. 67 A1 30 52N 87 19W
McDermitt, NV, U.S.A. 85 A3 41 59N 117 43W
Macdiarmid, Ont., Canada 180 C8 49 26N 88 8W
MacDill Air Force Base, Tampa, U.S.A. 119 B3 27 50N 82 30W
Macdoel, CA, U.S.A. 64 B5 41 50N 122 0W
Macdona, San Antonio, U.S.A. 117 C1 29 19N 98 41W
McDonald, KS, U.S.A. 74 B2 39 47N 101 22W
McDonald, NM, U.S.A. 88 D7 33 9N 103 19W
McDonald, L., MT, U.S.A. 83 B4 48 35N 113 56W
McDonald Cartier International, Ottawa ✕ (YOW), Ont., Canada 179 B11 45 19N 75 40W
McDonald County ☆, MO, U.S.A. 82 E2 36 40N 94 20W
McDonough, GA, U.S.A. 68 C2 33 27N 84 9W
McDonough County ☆, IL, U.S.A. 71 C3 40 30N 90 40W
McDougal, AR, U.S.A. 63 B5 36 26N 90 23W
McDougall, Mt., WY, U.S.A. 104 D2 42 54N 110 36W
McDowell, VA, U.S.A. 102 C5 38 20N 79 29W
McDowell County ☆, NC, U.S.A. 90 C4 35 40N 82 0W
McDowell County ☆, WV, U.S.A. 102 D3 37 22N 81 33W
McDuffie County ☆, GA, U.S.A. 68 C4 33 20N 82 25W
Macedonia, IL, U.S.A. 71 E5 38 3N 88 42W
Macedonia, IA, U.S.A. 73 D3 41 12N 95 25W
Macedonia, OH, U.S.A. 92 B5 41 19N 81 31W
Maceo, KY, U.S.A. 96 C6 37 51N 87 0W
Maces Bay, N.B., Canada 173 H3 45 6N 66 29W
McEwen, TN, U.S.A. 96 D5 36 7N 87 38W
McFadden, WY, U.S.A. 104 E6 41 39N 106 8W
McFaddin, TX, U.S.A. 99 J10 28 33N 97 1W
McFaddin Nat. Wildlife Refuge ⌂, TX, U.S.A. 99 H13 29 39N 94 3W
McFall, MO, U.S.A. 82 A2 40 7N 94 13W
McFarland, CA, U.S.A. 65 H7 35 41N 119 14W
McFarland, KS, U.S.A. 74 B7 39 3N 96 14W
McFarland, MI, U.S.A. 79 C4 46 11N 87 15W
McFarland, WI, U.S.A. 103 E4 43 1N 89 17W
McFarlane ➔, Sask., Canada 189 E11 59 12N 107 58W
McGee Creek L., OK, U.S.A. 93 D8 34 22N 95 38W
McGehee, AR, U.S.A. 63 E4 33 38N 91 24W
McGhee Tyson, Knoxville ✕ (TYS), TN, U.S.A. 97 E9 35 49N 83 59W
McGill, NV, U.S.A. 85 C6 39 23N 114 47W
McGrath, AK, U.S.A. 61 E9 62 58N 155 36W
McGrath, MN, U.S.A. 80 D5 46 14N 93 16W
McGraw, NY, U.S.A. 89 C4 42 36N 76 8W
MacGregor, Man., Canada 183 F13 49 57N 98 48W
McGregor, IA, U.S.A. 73 B7 43 1N 91 11W
McGregor, ND, U.S.A. 91 B3 48 36N 102 56W
McGregor, TX, U.S.A. 99 F10 31 27N 97 24W
McGregor ➔, B.C., Canada 189 F8 54 11N 122 2W
McGregor L., Alta., Canada 185 H8 50 25N 112 52W
McGrew, NE, U.S.A. 84 C2 41 45N 103 25W
McGuffey, OH, U.S.A. 92 C3 40 42N 83 47W
McHenry, IL, U.S.A. 71 A5 42 21N 88 16W
McHenry, KY, U.S.A. 96 C6 37 22N 86 55W
McHenry, MD, U.S.A. 77 A1 39 36N 79 22W
McHenry, MS, U.S.A. 81 F4 30 43N 89 8W
McHenry, ND, U.S.A. 91 C7 47 35N 98 35W
McHenry County ☆, IL, U.S.A. 71 A5 42 20N 88 25W
McHenry County ☆, ND, U.S.A. 91 B5 48 20N 100 45W
Machesney Park, IL, U.S.A. 71 A4 42 21N 89 2W
Machias, ME, U.S.A. 76 D6 44 43N 67 28W
Machias, NY, U.S.A. 89 C2 42 25N 78 29W
Machias ➔, ME, U.S.A. 76 D6 44 43N 67 22W
Machona, L., Tabasco, Mexico 222 A3 18 20N 93 40W
McIntire, IA, U.S.A. 73 B6 43 26N 92 36W
McIntosh, AL, U.S.A. 60 E2 31 16N 88 2W
McIntosh, MN, U.S.A. 80 C3 47 38N 95 53W
McIntosh, NM, U.S.A. 88 C4 34 52N 106 3W
McIntosh, SD, U.S.A. 91 E4 45 55N 101 21W
McIntosh County ☆, GA, U.S.A. 68 E5 31 30N 81 25W
McIntosh County ☆, ND, U.S.A. 91 D6 46 2N 99 20W
McIntosh County ☆, OK, U.S.A. 93 C8 35 20N 95 40W
McIntyre, GA, U.S.A. 68 D3 32 51N 83 11W
McIntyre B., B.C., Canada 186 A3 54 5N 132 0W
Mack, CO, U.S.A. 66 C2 39 13N 108 52W
MacKay, Alta., Canada 184 E5 53 39N 115 35W
Mackay, ID, U.S.A. 70 F5 43 55N 113 37W
MacKay ➔, Alta., Canada 184 A9 57 10N 111 38W
MacKay L., N.W.T., Canada 189 D10 63 55N 110 25W
McKay L., Ont., Canada 181 C10 49 37N 86 25W
McKean County ☆, PA, U.S.A. 95 C4 41 50N 78 45W
McKeand ➔, Nunavut, Canada 191 D12 65 34N 67 55W
McKee, KY, U.S.A. 97 C9 37 25N 84 0W
McKee City, NJ, U.S.A. 87 C2 39 26N 74 37W
McKee Cr. ➔, IL, U.S.A. 71 D3 39 46N 90 36W
McKees Rocks, Pittsburgh, U.S.A. 116 B1 40 27N 80 3W
McKeesport, PA, U.S.A. 95 D3 40 20N 79 51W
McKellar, Ont., Canada 178 B7 45 30N 79 55W
McKenney, VA, U.S.A. 102 E7 36 59N 77 43W
Mackenzie, B.C., Canada 189 E8 55 20N 123 5W
McKenzie, AL, U.S.A. 60 E4 31 33N 86 43W
Mackenzie, MI, U.S.A. 109 A1 42 21N 83 9W
Mackenzie, MO, U.S.A. 117 B2 38 34N 90 19W
McKenzie, ND, U.S.A. 91 D5 46 50N 100 25W
McKenzie, TN, U.S.A. 96 D4 36 8N 88 31W
Mackenzie ➔, N.W.T., Canada 188 C6 69 10N 134 20W
McKenzie ➔, OR, U.S.A. 94 C2 44 7N 123 6W
Mackenzie Bay, Canada 188 C5 69 0N 137 30W
McKenzie Bridge, OR, U.S.A. 94 C3 44 11N 122 10W
McKenzie County ☆, ND, U.S.A. 91 C2 47 55N 103 30W
Mackenzie King I., N.W.T., Canada 188 A10 77 45N 111 0W
McKenzie L., Sask., Canada 182 A9 54 12N 102 30W
Mackenzie Mts., Canada 189 D7 64 0N 130 0W
McKibben, TX, U.S.A. 98 A6 36 8N 101 20W
Mackinac, Straits of, MI, U.S.A. 79 D7 45 50N 84 40W
Mackinac County ☆, MI, U.S.A. 79 C7 46 5N 85 0W
Mackinac Island, MI, U.S.A. 79 D7 45 51N 84 37W
Mackinaw, IL, U.S.A. 71 C4 40 32N 89 21W
Mackinaw ➔, IL, U.S.A. 71 C4 40 33N 89 44W
Mackinaw City, MI, U.S.A. 79 D7 45 47N 84 44W
McKinley, Mt., AK, U.S.A. 61 E10 63 4N 151 0W
McKinley County ☆, NM, U.S.A. 88 B2 35 30N 108 0W
McKinley Park, AK, U.S.A. 61 E10 63 44N 148 55W
McKinley Park, Chicago, U.S.A. 108 C2 41 49N 87 40W
McKinleyville, CA, U.S.A. 64 C2 40 57N 124 6W
McKinney, TX, U.S.A. 99 D11 33 12N 96 37W
McKinney Mt., TX, U.S.A. 98 H4 29 50N 103 47W
McKinnon, GA, U.S.A. 68 E5 31 25N 81 56W
McKittrick, MO, U.S.A. 82 C5 38 44N 91 27W
Macklin, Sask., Canada 182 C2 52 20N 109 56W
Macksburg, IA, U.S.A. 73 D4 41 13N 94 11W
Macksville, KS, U.S.A. 74 D5 37 58N 98 58W
McLain, MS, U.S.A. 81 E5 31 7N 88 50W
McLaughlin, SD, U.S.A. 91 E5 45 49N 100 49W
McLaurin, MS, U.S.A. 81 E4 31 10N 89 13W
McLean, Sask., Canada 182 E7 50 31N 104 4W
McLean, IL, U.S.A. 71 C4 40 19N 89 10W
McLean, NE, U.S.A. 84 B8 42 23N 97 28W
McLean, TX, U.S.A. 98 B7 35 14N 100 36W
McLean, VA, U.S.A. 77 B3 38 56N 77 10W
McLean County ☆, IL, U.S.A. 71 C5 40 30N 88 50W
McLean County ☆, KY, U.S.A. 96 C5 37 30N 87 15W
McLean County ☆, ND, U.S.A. 91 C4 47 30N 101 0W
Maclean Str., N.W.T., Canada 190 B5 77 30N 103 30W
McLeansboro, IL, U.S.A. 71 E5 38 6N 88 32W
McLellan Res., Denver, U.S.A. 109 C1 39 34N 105 1W
McLennan, Alta., Canada 184 C4 55 42N 116 50W
McLennan County ☆, TX, U.S.A. 99 F10 31 33N 97 9W
MacLeod = Fort Macleod, Alta., Canada 185 J7 49 45N 113 30W
McLeod, ND, U.S.A. 91 D8 46 24N 97 18W
McLeod ➔, Alta., Canada 184 D5 54 9N 115 44W
MacLeod, B., N.W.T., Canada 189 D10 62 53N 110 0W
McLeod County ☆, MN, U.S.A. 80 F4 44 50N 94 15W
McLoud, OK, U.S.A. 93 C6 35 26N 97 6W
McLoughlin, Mt., OR, U.S.A. 94 E3 42 27N 122 19W
McLouth, KS, U.S.A. 74 B8 39 12N 95 13W
Maclovio Herrera, Chihuahua, Mexico 213 D10 29 5N 105 8W
McLure, B.C., Canada 187 D14 51 2N 120 13W
McMichael Cr. ➔, PA, U.S.A. 87 B1 40 59N 75 11W
Macmillan Pass, Canada 189 D6 63 15N 130 2W
McMinn County ☆, TN, U.S.A. 97 E8 35 27N 84 36W
McMinnville, OR, U.S.A. 94 B2 45 13N 123 12W
McMinnville, TN, U.S.A. 97 E7 35 41N 85 46W
McMorran, Sask., Canada 182 D3 51 19N 108 42W
McMullen County ☆, TX, U.S.A. 99 J9 28 28N 98 33W
McMurray = Fort McMurray, Alta., Canada 184 B9 56 44N 111 7W
McMurray, WA, U.S.A. 101 B3 48 19N 122 14W
McNab, AR, U.S.A. 63 E2 33 40N 93 50W
McNairy County ☆, TN, U.S.A. 96 E4 35 10N 88 36W
McNary, AZ, U.S.A. 62 C6 34 4N 109 51W
McNary, TX, U.S.A. 98 F2 31 15N 105 48W
McNaughton L., Nunavut, Canada 190 D6 67 20N 98 25W
McNeal, AZ, U.S.A. 62 F6 31 36N 109 40W
McNeil, AR, U.S.A. 63 E2 33 21N 93 13W
McNeill, MS, U.S.A. 81 F4 30 40N 89 38W
MacNutt, Sask., Canada 183 D10 51 5N 101 36W
Macomb, IL, U.S.A. 71 C3 40 27N 90 40W
Macomb, OK, U.S.A. 93 C6 35 10N 97 0W
Macomb County ☆, MI, U.S.A. 79 G9 42 40N 83 0W
Macon, GA, U.S.A. 68 D3 32 51N 83 38W
Macon, IL, U.S.A. 71 D5 39 43N 89 0W
Macon, MS, U.S.A. 81 C5 33 7N 88 34W
Macon, MO, U.S.A. 82 B4 39 44N 92 28W
Macon, NE, U.S.A. 84 D7 40 13N 98 55W
Macon, Bayou ➔, LA, U.S.A. 75 C4 31 55N 91 33W
Macon County ☆, AL, U.S.A. 60 D5 32 25N 85 42W
Macon County ☆, GA, U.S.A. 68 D2 32 20N 84 0W
Macon County ☆, IL, U.S.A. 71 D5 39 50N 89 0W
Macon County ☆, MO, U.S.A. 82 B4 39 50N 92 30W
Macon County ☆, NC, U.S.A. 90 C2 35 15N 83 30W
Macon County ☆, TN, U.S.A. 96 D6 36 31N 86 2W
Maconi, Querétaro, Mexico 219 B8 20 50N 99 32W
Macoun, Sask., Canada 182 F8 49 19N 103 16W
Macoupin County ☆, IL, U.S.A. 71 D4 39 20N 89 55W
MacPherson = Kapuskasing, Ont., Canada 181 C14 49 25N 82 30W
McPherson, KS, U.S.A. 74 C6 38 22N 97 40W
McPherson County ☆, KS, U.S.A. 74 C6 38 20N 97 40W
McPherson County ☆, NE, U.S.A. 84 C4 41 30N 101 0W
McPherson County ☆, SD, U.S.A. 91 E6 45 46N 99 0W
McQuady, KY, U.S.A. 96 C6 37 42N 86 31W
McRae, AR, U.S.A. 63 C4 35 7N 91 49W
McRae, GA, U.S.A. 68 D4 32 4N 82 54W
McRoberts, KY, U.S.A. 97 C10 37 12N 82 40W
McSherrystown, PA, U.S.A. 77 A3 39 48N 77 1W
McTavish Arm, N.W.T., Canada 188 C9 66 6N 119 0W
MacTier, Ont., Canada 178 B7 45 8N 79 47W
Mactún, Tabasco, Mexico 222 B5 17 35N 91 17W
Macungie, PA, U.S.A. 87 B1 40 31N 75 33W
Macuspana, Tabasco, Mexico 222 B4 17 46N 92 36W
Macuyú, Coahuila, Mexico 215 E3 25 20N 101 37W
McVeigh, KY, U.S.A. 97 C10 37 32N 82 15W
McVeytown, PA, U.S.A. 95 D5 40 30N 77 45W
McVicar Arm, N.W.T., Canada 189 C8 65 20N 120 10W
McVille, ND, U.S.A. 91 C7 47 46N 98 11W
Macwahoc, ME, U.S.A. 76 C5 45 38N 68 16W
McWilliams, AL, U.S.A. 60 E3 31 50N 87 6W
Macy, NE, U.S.A. 84 B9 42 7N 96 21W
Mad ➔, CA, U.S.A. 64 C2 40 57N 124 7W
Mad ➔, OH, U.S.A. 92 D2 39 46N 84 12W
Mad ➔, VT, U.S.A. 86 B2 44 18N 72 41W
Mad River Glen, VT, U.S.A. 86 B2 44 12N 72 55W
Madagascar, Arrecife, Yucatán, Mexico 223 A3 21 29N 90 19W
Madame, I., N.S., Canada 173 H9 45 30N 60 58W
Madawaska, Ont., Canada 176 F5 45 30N 78 0W
Madawaska, ME, U.S.A. 76 A5 47 21N 68 20W
Madawaska ➔, Ont., Canada 179 B10 45 27N 76 21W
Maddock, ND, U.S.A. 91 C6 47 58N 99 32W
Maddox, MD, U.S.A. 77 B4 38 20N 76 48W
Maddox Cove, Nfld. & L., Canada 174 E8 47 28N 52 42W
Madeira, OH, U.S.A. 107 A2 39 11N 84 21W
Madeira Beach, FL, U.S.A. 67 D6 27 47N 82 47W
Madeira Park, B.C., Canada 186 F10 49 37N 124 0W
Madeleine ➔, Qué., Canada 172 D4 49 15N 65 19W
Madeleine, Îs. de la, Qué., Canada 173 F8 47 30N 61 40W
Madeleine-Centre, Qué., Canada 172 D4 49 15N 65 22W
Madelia, MN, U.S.A. 80 F4 44 3N 94 25W
Madeline, CA, U.S.A. 64 B6 41 3N 120 28W
Madeline I., WI, U.S.A. 103 B3 46 49N 90 42W
Madera, Chihuahua, Mexico 213 D7 29 12N 108 7W
Madera, CA, U.S.A. 65 G6 36 57N 120 3W
Madera County ☆, CA, U.S.A. 64 F7 37 15N 119 35W
Madill, OK, U.S.A. 93 D7 34 6N 96 46W
Madín, México, Mexico 225 A2 19 32N 99 16W
Madín, L., México, Mexico 225 A2 19 31N 99 16W
Madison, AL, U.S.A. 60 B4 34 42N 86 45W
Madison, AR, U.S.A. 63 C5 35 1N 90 43W
Madison, FL, U.S.A. 67 A5 30 28N 83 25W
Madison, GA, U.S.A. 68 C3 33 36N 83 28W
Madison, IL, U.S.A. 117 A3 38 40N 90 9W
Madison, IN, U.S.A. 72 E5 38 44N 85 23W
Madison, KS, U.S.A. 74 C7 38 8N 96 8W
Madison, ME, U.S.A. 76 D4 44 48N 69 53W
Madison, MD, U.S.A. 77 B4 38 30N 76 13W
Madison, MN, U.S.A. 80 E2 45 1N 96 11W
Madison, MS, U.S.A. 81 D3 32 28N 90 7W
Madison, MO, U.S.A. 82 B4 39 28N 92 13W
Madison, NC, U.S.A. 90 B6 36 23N 79 58W
Madison, NJ, U.S.A. 87 B2 40 46N 74 25W
Madison, NE, U.S.A. 84 C8 41 50N 97 27W
Madison, OH, U.S.A. 92 B5 41 46N 81 3W
Madison, SD, U.S.A. 91 G8 44 0N 97 7W
Madison, TN, U.S.A. 96 D6 36 16N 86 42W
Madison, VA, U.S.A. 102 C6 38 23N 78 15W
Madison, WV, U.S.A. 102 C3 38 4N 81 49W
Madison, WI, U.S.A. 103 E4 43 4N 89 24W
Madison ➔, MT, U.S.A. 83 E6 45 56N 111 31W
Madison County ☆, AL, U.S.A. 60 B4 34 44N 86 35W
Madison County ☆, AR, U.S.A. 63 B2 36 5N 93 44W
Madison County ☆, FL, U.S.A. 67 A5 30 30N 83 30W
Madison County ☆, GA, U.S.A. 68 B3 34 10N 83 10W
Madison County ☆, ID, U.S.A. 70 F7 43 55N 111 50W
Madison County ☆, IL, U.S.A. 71 E4 38 50N 89 55W
Madison County ☆, IN, U.S.A. 72 C5 40 10N 85 45W
Madison County ☆, IA, U.S.A. 73 D5 41 20N 94 0W
Madison County ☆, KY, U.S.A. 97 C8 37 40N 84 20W
Madison County ☆, MS, U.S.A. 81 D3 32 37N 90 2W
Madison County ☆, MO, U.S.A. 82 D6 37 30N 90 20W
Madison County ☆, MT, U.S.A. 83 E6 45 12N 112 0W
Madison County ☆, NC, U.S.A. 90 C3 35 50N 82 50W
Madison County ☆, NY, U.S.A. 89 C5 43 0N 75 45W
Madison County ☆, NE, U.S.A. 84 C8 41 50N 97 30W
Madison County ☆, OH, U.S.A. 92 D3 39 53N 83 27W
Madison County ☆, TN, U.S.A. 96 E4 35 37N 88 49W
Madison County ☆, TX, U.S.A. 99 G12 31 0N 96 0W
Madison County ☆, VA, U.S.A. 102 C6 38 23N 78 15W
Madison Heights, VA, U.S.A. 102 D5 37 25N 79 8W
Madison Lake, MN, U.S.A. 80 F5 44 12N 93 49W
Madison Mills, OH, U.S.A. 92 D3 39 39N 83 20W
Madison Parish ☆, LA, U.S.A. 75 B4 32 25N 91 11W
Madison Range, MT, U.S.A. 83 E6 45 15N 111 30W
Madisonville, KY, U.S.A. 96 C5 37 20N 87 30W
Madisonville, LA, U.S.A. 75 D5 30 24N 90 10W
Madisonville, TN, U.S.A. 97 E8 35 31N 84 22W
Madisonville, TX, U.S.A. 99 G12 30 57N 95 55W
Madoc, Ont., Canada 179 C9 44 30N 77 28W
Madras, OR, U.S.A. 94 C4 44 38N 121 8W
Madre, L., TX, U.S.A. 215 E7 25 15N 97 30W
Madre del Sur, Sa., Mexico 219 F8 17 0N 100 0W
Madre Occidental, Sierra, Mexico 216 C5 27 0N 107 0W
Madre Oriental, Sierra, Mexico 215 H5 25 0N 100 0W
Madrid, Colima, Mexico 218 C4 19 4N 103 52W
Madrid, AL, U.S.A. 60 E5 31 2N 85 24W
Madrid, IA, U.S.A. 73 D5 41 53N 93 49W
Madrid, NM, U.S.A. 88 B4 35 24N 106 9W
Madrid, NY, U.S.A. 89 A5 44 45N 75 8W
Madrid, NE, U.S.A. 84 D4 40 51N 101 33W
Madsen, Ont., Canada 180 B3 50 58N 93 55W
Maeser, UT, U.S.A. 100 C6 40 28N 109 35W
Maeystown, IL, U.S.A. 71 E3 38 13N 90 14W
Mafeking, Man., Canada 183 C10 52 40N 101 10W
Magaguadavic, N.B., Canada 173 H2 45 42N 67 12W
Magaguadavic ➔, N.B., Canada 173 H3 45 7N 66 54W
Magaguadavic L., N.B., Canada 173 H2 45 43N 67 12W
Magallanes, Sa., Sonora, Mexico 212 C6 30 50N 109 50W
Magazine, AR, U.S.A. 63 C2 35 9N 93 48W
Magazine Mt., AR, U.S.A. 63 C2 35 10N 93 41W
Magdalen Is. = Madeleine, Îs. de la, Qué., Canada 173 F8 47 30N 61 40W
Magdalena, Jalisco, Mexico 218 B4 20 55N 103 57W
Magdalena, NM, U.S.A. 88 C3 34 7N 107 15W
Magdalena, B., Baja Calif. S., Mexico 211 J7 24 35N 112 0W
Magdalena, I., Baja Calif. S., Mexico 211 J6 24 55N 112 15W
Magdalena, Llano de, Baja Calif. S., Mexico 211 J7 25 0N 111 25W
Magdalena Contreras, Distrito Federal, Mexico 225 C2 19 20N 99 13W
Magdalena de Kino, Sonora, Mexico 212 C5 30 38N 110 57W
Magdalena Jaltepec, Oaxaca, Mexico 221 G3 17 25N 97 13W
Magdalena Mts., NM, U.S.A. 88 D3 33 45N 107 15W
Magdalena Petlacalco, Distrito Federal, Mexico 225 C2 19 14N 99 11W
Magdalena Tequisistlán, Oaxaca, Mexico 221 H5 16 22N 95 45W
Magdaleno Cedillo, Tamaulipas, Mexico 215 H5 22 48N 99 56W
Magee, MS, U.S.A. 81 E4 31 52N 89 44W
Maggiore, L., Tampa, U.S.A. 119 C3 27 44N 82 39W
Magic Res., ID, U.S.A. 70 F4 43 15N 114 22W
Magiscatzin, Tamaulipas, Mexico 215 H6 22 48N 98 42W
Magna, UT, U.S.A. 100 C3 40 42N 112 6W
Magnet, NE, U.S.A. 84 B8 42 27N 97 28W
Magnetawan, Ont., Canada 178 B7 45 40N 79 39W
Magnetic Pole (North), Canada 190 B5 82 18N 113 24W
Magnolia, AR, U.S.A. 63 E2 33 16N 93 14W
Magnolia, DE, U.S.A. 77 A5 39 4N 75 29W
Magnolia, IA, U.S.A. 73 D3 41 42N 95 52W
Magnolia, KY, U.S.A. 97 C7 37 27N 85 45W
Magnolia, MS, U.S.A. 81 E3 31 9N 90 28W
Magnolia, NC, U.S.A. 90 D7 34 54N 78 3W
Magnolia, OH, U.S.A. 92 C5 40 39N 81 18W
Magnolia, TX, U.S.A. 99 G12 30 13N 95 45W
Magoffin County ☆, KY, U.S.A. 97 C9 37 45N 83 5W
Magog, Qué., Canada 177 F10 45 18N 72 9W
Magog, L., Qué., Canada 86 A2 45 18N 72 3W
Magozal, Veracruz, Mexico 220 C3 21 34N 97 59W
Magpie, Qué., Canada 172 C5 50 19N 64 30W
Magpie ➔, Ont., Canada 181 E12 47 56N 84 50W
Magpie ➔, Qué., Canada 172 C5 50 19N 64 27W
Magpie, L., Qué., Canada 172 B5 51 0N 64 41W
Magpie Ouest ➔, Qué., Canada 175 C5 52 0N 65 0W
Magrath, Alta., Canada 185 J8 49 25N 112 50W
Maguarichic, Chihuahua, Mexico 213 F8 27 50N 108 0W
Maguey, Cerro el, Guerrero, Mexico 219 E9 17 15N 98 51W
Magueyal, Coahuila, Mexico 214 C2 27 7N 102 51W

Maguse L., Nunavut, Canada 191 E6 61 37N 95 10W
Maguse Pt., Nunavut, Canada 191 E7 61 20N 93 50W
Mahaffey, PA, U.S.A. 95 D4 40 53N 78 44W
Mahanoy City, PA, U.S.A. 95 D6 40 49N 76 9W
Mahaska, KS, U.S.A. 74 B6 39 59N 97 20W
Mahaska County ☆, IA, U.S.A. 73 D6 41 20N 92 40W
Mahatta River, B.C., Canada 186 E7 50 22N 127 47W
Mahnomen, MN, U.S.A. 80 C3 47 19N 95 58W
Mahnomen County ☆, MN, U.S.A. 80 C3 47 20N 95 45W
Mahogany Mts., OR, U.S.A. 94 D8 43 14N 117 15W
Mahomet, IL, U.S.A. 71 C5 40 12N 88 24W
Mahone Bay, N.S., Canada 173 J5 44 27N 64 23W
Mahoning County ☆, OH, U.S.A. 92 B6 41 6N 80 48W
Mahood Falls, B.C., Canada 187 D14 51 50N 120 38W
Mahood L., B.C., Canada 187 D14 51 50N 120 23W
Mahopac, NY, U.S.A. 87 A3 41 22N 73 44W
Mahtomedi, Minneapolis-St. Paul, U.S.A. 113 A4 45 3N 92 57W
Mahtowa, MN, U.S.A. 80 D6 46 34N 92 38W
Maicasagi ➛, Qué., Canada 176 B6 49 58N 76 33W
Maiden, NC, U.S.A. 90 C4 35 35N 81 13W
Maiden Rock, WI, U.S.A. 103 D1 44 34N 92 18W
Maidstone, Sask., Canada 182 B2 53 5N 109 20W
Mā'ili, HI, U.S.A. 69 K13 21 25N 158 11W
Mā'ili Pt, HI, U.S.A. 69 K13 21 24N 158 11W
Main-à-Dieu, N.S., Canada 173 H10 46 0N 59 51W
Main Brook, Nfld. & L., Canada 174 A4 51 11N 56 1W
Main Centre, Sask., Canada 182 E4 50 35N 107 21W
Main Pass, LA, U.S.A. 75 E6 29 15N 89 14W
Maine □, U.S.A. 76 C5 45 20N 69 0W
Maisonnette, N.B., Canada 173 F4 47 49N 65 0W
Maissoneuve, Montréal, Canada 192 A3 45 32N 73 33W
Maitland, N.S., Canada 173 H6 45 19N 63 30W
Maitland, MO, U.S.A. 82 A1 40 12N 95 5W
Maitland Bridge, N.S., Canada 173 J4 44 27N 65 12W
Maizaga, Oaxaca, Mexico 221 F4 18 18N 96 34W
Majahual, Quintana Roo, Mexico 223 D6 18 43N 87 43W
Majahual, Sinaloa, Mexico 216 E4 22 48N 106 2W
Major, Sask., Canada 182 D2 51 52N 109 37W
Major County ☆, OK, U.S.A. 93 B5 36 15N 98 30W
Majors Place, NV, U.S.A. 85 C6 39 2N 114 35W
Makah Indian Reservation, WA, U.S.A. 101 B1 48 23N 124 29W
Mākaha, HI, U.S.A. 69 K13 21 29N 158 13W
Makahoa Pt., HI, U.S.A. 69 J14 21 41N 157 56W
Makahuena Pt., HI, U.S.A. 69 B2 21 52N 159 27W
Makakilo City, HI, U.S.A. 69 K13 21 22N 158 5W
Makanda, IL, U.S.A. 71 F4 37 37N 89 13W
Makapu'u Pt., HI, U.S.A. 69 K14 21 19N 157 39W
Makawao, HI, U.S.A. 69 C5 20 52N 156 17W
Makkovik, Nfld. & L., Canada 175 B6 55 10N 59 10W
Makokibatan L., Ont., Canada 181 A9 51 17N 87 20W
Makoti, ND, U.S.A. 91 C4 47 58N 101 48W
Makua, HI, U.S.A. 69 J13 21 32N 158 13W
Mākua Kea'au Forest Reserve, HI, U.S.A. 69 J13 21 30N 158 12W
Makua Military Reservation, HI, U.S.A. 69 J13 21 32N 158 14W
Makushin Volcano, AK, U.S.A. 61 K6 53 53N 166 55W
Malabar, FL, U.S.A. 67 D8 28 0N 80 34W
Malachi, Ont., Canada 180 C2 49 56N 94 59W
Malad City, ID, U.S.A. 70 G6 42 12N 112 15W
Malae Pt., HI, U.S.A. 69 C6 20 7N 155 53W
Malaga, NM, U.S.A. 88 E6 32 14N 104 4W
Malaga, OH, U.S.A. 92 D5 39 51N 81 9W
Malakoff, TX, U.S.A. 99 E11 32 10N 96 1W
Malartic, Qué., Canada 176 C4 48 9N 78 9W
Malartic, L., Qué., Canada 176 C4 48 15N 78 5W
Malaspina Glacier, AK, U.S.A. 61 G12 59 50N 140 30W
Malcolm, NE, U.S.A. 84 D9 40 54N 96 52W
Malcolm I., B.C., Canada 186 E8 50 38N 127 0W
Malcom, IA, U.S.A. 73 D6 41 43N 92 33W
Malden, IL, U.S.A. 71 B4 41 25N 89 22W
Malden, MA, U.S.A. 78 B3 42 26N 71 3W
Malden, MO, U.S.A. 82 E7 36 34N 89 57W
Maldonado, Pta., Guerrero, Mexico 221 H2 16 20N 98 33W
Malheur ➛, OR, U.S.A. 94 C9 44 4N 116 59W
Malheur County ☆, OR, U.S.A. 94 D8 43 15N 117 45W
Malheur L., OR, U.S.A. 94 D7 43 20N 118 48W
Malheur Nat. Forest, OR, U.S.A. 94 C6 44 10N 119 15W
Maligne L., Alta., Canada 185 F3 52 40N 117 31W
Malin, OR, U.S.A. 94 E4 42 1N 121 24W
Malinalco, México, Mexico 219 D8 19 0N 99 26W
Malinaltepec, Guerrero, Mexico 219 E9 17 3N 98 40W
Malinta, OH, U.S.A. 92 B2 41 19N 84 2W
Maljamar, NM, U.S.A. 88 E7 32 51N 103 46W
Mallaig, Alta., Canada 184 D9 54 13N 111 22W
Mallard, IA, U.S.A. 73 C4 42 56N 94 41W
Mallery L., Nunavut, Canada 191 E6 63 59N 98 23W
Mallorytown, Ont., Canada 179 C11 44 29N 75 53W
Malmo, NE, U.S.A. 84 C9 41 16N 96 43W
Malmstrom Air Force Base, MT, U.S.A. 83 C6 47 30N 111 11W
Malone, FL, U.S.A. 67 A3 30 57N 85 10W
Malone, NY, U.S.A. 89 A6 44 51N 74 18W
Malone, L., KY, U.S.A. 96 C5 37 5N 87 2W
Maloney, L., NE, U.S.A. 84 C5 41 3N 100 48W
Malott, WA, U.S.A. 101 B6 48 17N 119 42W
Maloy, IA, U.S.A. 73 E4 40 40N 94 25W
Malpais, The, NM, U.S.A. 88 D5 33 43N 105 56W
Malpaso, Zacatecas, Mexico 217 E8 22 37N 102 46W
Malpaso, Presa = Netzahualcóyotl, Presa, Chiapas, Mexico 222 B3 17 8N 93 35W
Malta, ID, U.S.A. 70 G5 42 18N 113 22W
Malta, IL, U.S.A. 71 B5 41 56N 88 52W
Malta, MT, U.S.A. 83 B10 48 21N 107 52W
Malta Bend, MO, U.S.A. 82 B3 39 12N 93 22W
Maltby, Seattle, U.S.A. 118 B5 47 48N 122 6W
Malvern, AR, U.S.A. 63 D3 34 22N 92 49W
Malvern, IA, U.S.A. 73 E3 41 0N 95 35W
Malvern, OH, U.S.A. 92 C5 40 42N 81 11W
Malvern, PA, U.S.A. 87 B1 40 2N 75 31W
Malverne, NY, U.S.A. 114 B4 40 40N 73 40W
Māmala B., HI, U.S.A. 69 K14 21 15N 157 55W
Mamantel, Campeche, Mexico 223 D2 18 33N 91 5W
Mamaroneck, NY, U.S.A. 87 B3 40 57N 73 44W
Mamaroneck Harbor, NY, U.S.A. 114 A4 40 56N 73 42W
Mameigwess L., Ont., Canada 180 C5 49 34N 91 49W
Mammoth, AZ, U.S.A. 62 E5 32 43N 110 39W
Mammoth Cave Nat. Park △, KY, U.S.A. 96 C6 37 8N 86 13W
Mammoth Hot Springs, WY, U.S.A. 104 B2 44 59N 110 42W
Mammoth Lakes, CA, U.S.A. 64 F8 37 39N 118 59W
Mammoth Pool Res., CA, U.S.A. 64 F7 37 20N 119 19W
Mammoth Spring, AR, U.S.A. 63 B4 36 30N 91 33W
Mamou, LA, U.S.A. 75 D3 30 38N 92 25W
Man, WV, U.S.A. 102 D3 37 45N 81 53W
Mānā, HI, U.S.A. 69 A2 22 2N 159 47W
Manahawkin, NJ, U.S.A. 87 C2 39 42N 74 16W
Manalapan, NJ, U.S.A. 87 B2 40 15N 74 24W
Mānana I., HI, U.S.A. 69 K14 21 20N 157 40W
Manasquan, NJ, U.S.A. 87 B2 40 8N 74 3W
Manasquan ➛, NJ, U.S.A. 87 B2 40 6N 74 2W
Manassa, CO, U.S.A. 66 E5 37 11N 105 56W
Manassas, VA, U.S.A. 77 B3 38 45N 77 29W
Manassas Park, VA, U.S.A. 77 B3 38 47N 77 28W
Manatee County ☆, FL, U.S.A. 67 D6 27 30N 82 30W
Manatí, Puerto Rico 105 G16 18 26N 66 29W
Manawa, WI, U.S.A. 103 D5 44 28N 88 55W
Mancelona, MI, U.S.A. 79 E6 44 54N 85 4W
Mancha, Pta., Veracruz, Mexico 220 E4 19 37N 96 22W
Manchester, CA, U.S.A. 64 E3 38 58N 123 41W
Manchester, CT, U.S.A. 78 C2 41 47N 72 31W
Manchester, GA, U.S.A. 68 D2 32 51N 84 37W
Manchester, IA, U.S.A. 73 C7 42 29N 91 27W
Manchester, KS, U.S.A. 74 B6 39 6N 97 19W
Manchester, KY, U.S.A. 97 C9 37 9N 83 46W
Manchester, MD, U.S.A. 77 A4 39 40N 76 53W
Manchester, MI, U.S.A. 79 G7 42 9N 84 2W
Manchester, NH, U.S.A. 86 D3 42 59N 71 28W
Manchester, OH, U.S.A. 92 E3 38 41N 83 36W
Manchester, OK, U.S.A. 93 C5 35 59N 98 2W
Manchester, Seattle, U.S.A. 118 C2 47 33N 122 32W
Manchester, TN, U.S.A. 96 E6 35 29N 86 5W
Manchester-by-the-Sea, MA, U.S.A. 78 B4 42 35N 70 46W
Manchester Center, VT, U.S.A. 86 C1 43 10N 73 4W
Mancos, CO, U.S.A. 66 E2 37 21N 108 18W
Mandan, ND, U.S.A. 91 D5 46 50N 100 54W
Mandaree, ND, U.S.A. 91 C3 47 43N 102 41W
Manderson, WY, U.S.A. 104 B5 44 16N 107 58W
Mandeville, LA, U.S.A. 75 D5 30 22N 90 4W
Mandinga, L., Veracruz, Mexico 221 F4 19 0N 96 4W
Maneadero = Rodolfo Sánchez Taboada, Baja Calif., Mexico 210 B2 31 45N 116 35W
Mangham, LA, U.S.A. 75 B4 32 19N 91 47W
Mango, FL, U.S.A. 67 D6 27 59N 82 18W
Mangohick, VA, U.S.A. 77 C3 37 49N 77 16W
Mangum, OK, U.S.A. 93 D4 34 53N 99 30W
Manhasset, NY, U.S.A. 87 B3 40 47N 73 42W
Manhasset Bay, NY, U.S.A. 114 B4 40 49N 73 43W
Manhasset Hills, NY, U.S.A. 114 B5 40 45N 73 40W
Manhattan, KS, U.S.A. 74 B7 39 11N 96 35W
Manhattan, MT, U.S.A. 83 E6 45 51N 111 20W
Manhattan, NY, U.S.A. 89 E7 40 48N 73 57W
Manhattan, NV, U.S.A. 85 D3 38 32N 117 4W
Manhattan Beach, Los Angeles, U.S.A. 111 C2 33 53N 118 24W
Manhattan Beach, NY, U.S.A. 114 C3 40 34N 73 56W
Manic 2, Rés., Qué., Canada 177 B14 49 30N 68 24W
Manic 3, Rés., Qué., Canada 177 B14 50 0N 68 40W
Manicouagan ➛, Qué., Canada 177 B14 49 30N 68 30W
Manicouagan, Rés., Qué., Canada 175 C4 51 5N 68 40W
Manifest, LA, U.S.A. 75 C4 31 43N 91 58W
Manigotagan, Man., Canada 183 D15 51 6N 96 18W
Manigotagan L., Man., Canada 183 E16 50 52N 95 37W
Manila, AR, U.S.A. 63 C5 35 53N 90 10W
Manila, UT, U.S.A. 100 C6 40 59N 109 43W
Manilla, IA, U.S.A. 73 D3 41 53N 95 14W
Maninel, Volcan, Distrito Federal, Mexico 225 C2 19 14N 99 12W
Manistee, MI, U.S.A. 79 E5 44 15N 86 19W
Manistee ➛, MI, U.S.A. 79 E5 44 15N 86 21W
Manistee County ☆, MI, U.S.A. 79 E5 44 20N 86 10W
Manistee Nat. Forest, MI, U.S.A. 79 E5 44 0N 86 0W
Manistique, MI, U.S.A. 79 D5 45 57N 86 15W
Manistique ➛, MI, U.S.A. 79 D5 45 57N 86 15W
Manistique L., MI, U.S.A. 79 C6 46 15N 85 46W
Manito, IL, U.S.A. 71 C4 40 26N 89 47W
Manitoba □, Man., Canada 183 B14 53 30N 97 0W
Manitoba, L., Man., Canada 183 E13 51 0N 98 45W
Manitou, Man., Canada 183 F13 49 15N 98 32W
Manitou, Qué., Canada 172 C4 50 18N 65 15W
Manitou, OK, U.S.A. 93 D5 34 30N 98 59W
Manitou ➛, Qué., Canada 172 C4 50 18N 65 15W
Manitou, L., Ont., Canada 178 B5 45 51N 82 0W
Manitou, L., Qué., Canada 175 C4 50 55N 65 17W
Manitou Beach, MI, U.S.A. 79 H7 41 58N 84 19W
Manitou I., MI, U.S.A. 79 B4 47 25N 87 37W
Manitou Is., MI, U.S.A. 54 C2 45 8N 86 0W
Manitou L., Sask., Canada 182 C2 52 43N 109 43W
Manitou Springs, CO, U.S.A. 66 D6 38 52N 104 55W
Manitoulin I., Ont., Canada 178 B4 45 40N 82 30W
Manitouwadge, Ont., Canada 181 C11 49 8N 85 48W
Manitowaning, Ont., Canada 178 B5 45 46N 81 49W
Manitowish, WI, U.S.A. 103 B3 46 8N 90 0W
Manitowish Waters, WI, U.S.A. 103 B4 46 9N 89 53W
Manitowoc, WI, U.S.A. 103 D6 44 5N 87 40W
Manitowoc County ☆, WI, U.S.A. 103 D6 44 10N 87 50W
Maniwaki, Qué., Canada 176 E7 46 23N 75 58W
Mankato, KS, U.S.A. 74 B5 39 47N 98 13W
Mankato, MN, U.S.A. 80 F4 44 10N 94 0W
Mankota, Sask., Canada 182 F4 49 25N 107 5W
Manley, NE, U.S.A. 84 D9 40 55N 96 10W
Manley Hot Springs, AK, U.S.A. 61 D10 65 0N 150 38W
Manlio Fabio Altamirano, Veracruz, Mexico 221 E4 19 5N 96 19W
Manlius, IL, U.S.A. 71 B4 41 27N 89 40W
Manlius, NY, U.S.A. 89 C5 43 0N 75 59W
Manly, IA, U.S.A. 73 B5 43 17N 93 12W
Mann, L., Orlando, U.S.A. 115 A2 28 32N 81 35W
Mannford, OK, U.S.A. 93 B7 36 8N 96 24W
Manning, Alta., Canada 184 B3 56 53N 117 39W
Manning, AR, U.S.A. 63 D3 34 1N 92 48W
Manning, IA, U.S.A. 73 D3 41 55N 95 3W
Manning, ND, U.S.A. 91 C3 47 14N 102 46W
Manning, SC, U.S.A. 90 E5 33 42N 80 13W
Manning Park, B.C., Canada 187 F14 49 4N 120 47W
Mannington, WV, U.S.A. 102 B4 39 32N 80 21W
Manns Harbor, NC, U.S.A. 90 C10 35 53N 75 46W
Mannsville, NY, U.S.A. 89 B4 43 43N 76 4W
Mannsville, OK, U.S.A. 93 D7 34 11N 96 53W
Mannville, Alta., Canada 184 E9 53 20N 111 10W
Manokin, MD, U.S.A. 77 B5 38 5N 75 55W
Manokotak, AK, U.S.A. 61 G8 58 58N 159 3W
Manor, Sask., Canada 183 F9 49 36N 102 5W
Manorhaven, NY, U.S.A. 114 A4 40 50N 73 42W
Manotick, Ont., Canada 179 B11 45 13N 75 41W
Manouane, Qué., Canada 177 D8 47 13N 74 23W
Manouane, L., Qué., Canada 175 C3 50 45N 70 45W
Manouane, L., Qué., Canada 177 D8 47 33N 74 6W
Manseau, Qué., Canada 177 E11 46 22N 72 0W
Mansel I., Nunavut, Canada 191 E10 62 0N 80 0W
Mansfield, AR, U.S.A. 63 C1 35 4N 94 15W
Mansfield, CT, U.S.A. 78 C2 41 46N 72 14W
Mansfield, GA, U.S.A. 68 C3 33 31N 83 44W
Mansfield, IL, U.S.A. 71 C5 40 13N 88 31W
Mansfield, LA, U.S.A. 75 B2 32 2N 93 43W
Mansfield, MA, U.S.A. 78 B3 42 2N 71 13W
Mansfield, MO, U.S.A. 82 D4 37 6N 92 35W
Mansfield, OH, U.S.A. 92 C4 40 45N 82 31W
Mansfield, PA, U.S.A. 95 C5 41 48N 77 5W
Mansfield, SD, U.S.A. 91 E7 45 15N 98 34W
Mansfield, TN, U.S.A. 96 D4 36 11N 88 17W
Mansfield, TX, U.S.A. 99 E10 32 33N 97 8W
Mansfield, WA, U.S.A. 101 C6 47 49N 119 38W
Mansfield, Mt., VT, U.S.A. 86 B2 44 33N 72 49W
Mansfield Hollow L., CT, U.S.A. 78 C2 41 45N 72 11W
Manson, IA, U.S.A. 73 C4 42 32N 94 32W
Manson, WA, U.S.A. 101 C5 47 53N 120 9W
Mansura, LA, U.S.A. 75 C3 31 4N 92 3W
Mantador, ND, U.S.A. 91 D9 46 10N 96 59W
Manteca, CA, U.S.A. 64 F5 37 48N 121 13W
Mantee, MS, U.S.A. 81 C4 33 44N 89 3W
Manteno, IL, U.S.A. 71 B6 41 15N 87 50W
Manteo, NC, U.S.A. 90 C10 35 55N 75 40W
Manter, KS, U.S.A. 74 D2 37 31N 101 53W
Manti, UT, U.S.A. 100 D4 39 16N 111 38W
Manti-la Sal Nat. Forest, UT, U.S.A. 100 F6 37 50N 109 50W
Mantoloking, NJ, U.S.A. 87 B2 40 4N 74 4W
Manton, MI, U.S.A. 79 E6 44 25N 85 24W
Mantorville, MN, U.S.A. 80 F6 44 5N 92 45W
Mantua, OH, U.S.A. 92 B5 41 17N 81 14W
Mantua, UT, U.S.A. 100 B4 41 30N 111 57W
Manua Is., Amer. Samoa 105 f 14 13 S 169 35W
Manuel, Tamaulipas, Mexico 215 H6 22 44N 98 19W
Manuel Benavides, Chihuahua, Mexico 213 D12 29 8N 103 55W
Manuel Doblado, Guanajuato, Mexico 218 B6 20 44N 101 56W
Manuel M. Diéguez, Jalisco, Mexico 218 C5 19 35N 102 55W
Manuelito, NM, U.S.A. 88 B2 35 24N 109 0W
Manuels, N.B., Canada 173 F5 47 3N 64 59W
Manvel, ND, U.S.A. 91 B8 48 5N 97 11W
Manvel, TX, U.S.A. 99 H12 29 28N 95 21W
Manville, NJ, U.S.A. 87 B2 40 33N 74 35W
Manville, WY, U.S.A. 104 D8 42 47N 104 37W
Many, LA, U.S.A. 75 C2 31 34N 93 29W
Many Farms, AZ, U.S.A. 62 A6 36 21N 109 37W
Many Island L., Alta., Canada 185 H10 50 8N 110 3W
Manyberries, Alta., Canada 185 J10 49 24N 110 42W
Manzanar Nat. Historic Site ⌓, CA, U.S.A. 65 G8 36 44N 118 9W
Manzanillo, Colima, Mexico 218 C3 19 3N 104 20W
Manzanillo, B. de, Colima, Mexico 218 C3 19 1N 104 27W
Manzanita, OR, U.S.A. 94 B2 45 43N 123 56W
Manzanita Indian Reservation, CA, U.S.A. 65 L10 32 45N 116 20W
Manzano Mts., NM, U.S.A. 88 C4 34 40N 106 20W
Manzanola, CO, U.S.A. 66 D7 38 6N 103 52W
Mapastepec, Chiapas, Mexico 222 D4 15 26N 92 54W
Mapimí, Durango, Mexico 217 B7 25 49N 103 51W
Mapimí, Bolsón de, Mexico 217 A6 27 0N 104 15W
Maple ➛, IA, U.S.A. 73 C3 42 0N 95 59W
Maple ➛, MI, U.S.A. 79 G7 42 59N 84 57W
Maple ➛, ND, U.S.A. 91 D9 46 56N 96 55W
Maple ➛, SD, U.S.A. 91 E7 45 48N 98 38W
Maple Bay, B.C., Canada 187 G11 48 48N 123 37W
Maple Creek, Sask., Canada 182 F2 49 55N 109 29W
Maple Falls, WA, U.S.A. 101 B3 48 56N 122 5W
Maple Heights, Cleveland, U.S.A. 107 B2 41 24N 81 33W
Maple Hill, KS, U.S.A. 74 B7 39 5N 96 2W
Maple Rapids, MI, U.S.A. 79 F7 43 6N 84 42W
Maple Shade, NJ, U.S.A. 87 C2 39 57N 74 58W
Maplesville, AL, U.S.A. 60 D4 32 47N 86 52W
Mapleton, IA, U.S.A. 73 C3 42 10N 95 47W
Mapleton, KS, U.S.A. 74 C9 38 1N 94 53W
Mapleton, MN, U.S.A. 80 G5 43 56N 93 57W
Mapleton, ND, U.S.A. 91 D8 46 53N 97 3W
Mapleton, OR, U.S.A. 94 C2 44 2N 123 52W
Mapleton, UT, U.S.A. 100 C4 40 8N 111 35W
Maplewood, Vancouver, Canada 193 B2 49 18N 123 0W
Maplewood, Minneapolis-St. Paul, U.S.A. 113 A3 44 59N 93 1W
Maplewood, MO, U.S.A. 117 B1 38 36N 90 19W
Maplewood, NJ, U.S.A. 114 B1 40 44N 74 16W
Maquoketa, IA, U.S.A. 73 C8 42 4N 90 40W
Maquoketa ➛, IA, U.S.A. 73 C8 42 11N 90 19W
Maquon, IL, U.S.A. 71 C3 40 48N 90 10W
Mar-Mac, NC, U.S.A. 90 C7 35 20N 78 3W
Mar Negro, L., Tamaulipas, Mexico 214 E7 25 53N 97 9W
Marais des Cygnes ➛, U.S.A. 82 C2 38 3N 94 17W
Maramec, OK, U.S.A. 93 B7 36 15N 96 41W
Marana, AZ, U.S.A. 62 E4 32 27N 111 13W
Marathon, Ont., Canada 181 D10 48 44N 86 23W
Marathon, FL, U.S.A. 67 G7 24 43N 81 5W
Marathon, IA, U.S.A. 73 C4 42 52N 94 59W
Marathon, NY, U.S.A. 89 C4 42 27N 76 2W
Marathon, TX, U.S.A. 98 G4 30 12N 103 15W
Marathon City, WI, U.S.A. 103 D4 44 56N 89 50W
Marathon County ☆, WI, U.S.A. 103 D4 44 50N 89 45W
Maravatío, Michoacan, Mexico 219 C7 19 54N 100 27W
Maravillas, Chihuahua, Mexico 213 F11 27 22N 104 29W
Maravillas Cr. ➛, TX, U.S.A. 98 H5 29 34N 102 47W
Marble, AR, U.S.A. 63 B2 36 8N 93 35W
Marble, CO, U.S.A. 66 C3 39 4N 107 12W
Marble Canyon, AZ, U.S.A. 62 A4 36 49N 111 38W
Marble City, OK, U.S.A. 93 C9 35 35N 94 49W
Marble Falls, TX, U.S.A. 99 G9 30 35N 98 16W
Marble Hill, MO, U.S.A. 82 D7 37 18N 89 58W
Marble I., Nunavut, Canada 191 E7 62 41N 91 8W
Marble Range Park ⌓, B.C., Canada 187 D13 51 11N 121 49W
Marble Rock, IA, U.S.A. 73 C6 42 58N 92 52W
Marblehead, B.C., Canada 187 E18 50 15N 116 58W
Marblehead, MA, U.S.A. 78 B4 42 29N 70 51W
Marblehead, OH, U.S.A. 92 B4 41 32N 82 44W
Marblemount, WA, U.S.A. 101 B4 48 32N 121 26W
Marbleton, Qué., Canada 177 F11 45 37N 71 35W
Marbleton, WY, U.S.A. 104 D2 42 34N 110 7W
Marbury, MD, U.S.A. 77 B3 38 35N 77 10W
Marceau, L., Qué., Canada 172 B3 51 25N 66 41W
Marcelin, Sask., Canada 182 C5 52 55N 106 47W
Marceline, MO, U.S.A. 82 B4 39 43N 92 57W
Marcellus, MI, U.S.A. 79 G6 42 2N 85 49W
Marcellus, NY, U.S.A. 89 C4 42 59N 76 20W
Marcellus, WA, U.S.A. 101 C7 47 14N 118 24W
Marco Island, FL, U.S.A. 67 F7 25 58N 81 44W
Marcola, OR, U.S.A. 94 C3 44 10N 122 54W
Marcus, IA, U.S.A. 73 C3 42 50N 95 48W
Marcus, WA, U.S.A. 101 B7 48 40N 118 4W
Marcus Baker, Mt., AK, U.S.A. 61 F11 61 26N 147 45W
Marcy, Mt., NY, U.S.A. 89 A7 44 7N 73 56W
Mardela Springs, MD, U.S.A. 77 B5 38 28N 75 45W
Marengo, Sask., Canada 182 D2 51 29N 109 47W
Marengo, IL, U.S.A. 71 A5 42 15N 88 37W
Marengo, IN, U.S.A. 72 E4 38 22N 86 21W
Marengo, IA, U.S.A. 73 D6 41 48N 92 4W
Marengo, OH, U.S.A. 92 C4 40 24N 82 49W
Marengo, WA, U.S.A. 101 C7 47 1N 118 12W
Marengo County ☆, AL, U.S.A. 60 D3 32 18N 87 48W
Marenisco, MI, U.S.A. 79 C2 46 23N 89 45W
Marfa, TX, U.S.A. 98 G3 30 19N 104 1W
Margaree Forks, N.S., Canada 173 G8 46 20N 61 5W
Margaret Bay, B.C., Canada 186 D7 51 20N 127 35W
Margaretville, NY, U.S.A. 89 C6 42 9N 74 39W
Margate, FL, U.S.A. 67 E8 26 15N 80 12W
Margate City, NJ, U.S.A. 87 C2 39 20N 74 30W
Margo, Sask., Canada 182 D8 51 49N 103 20W
Marguerite, B.C., Canada 187 C12 52 30N 122 25W
Maria, Qué., Canada 172 E4 48 10N 65 59W
María Cleofas, I., Nayarit, Mexico 216 F4 21 16N 106 14W
María Lombardo de Caso, Oaxaca, Mexico 221 G5 17 27N 95 27W
María Madre, I., Nayarit, Mexico 216 F4 21 35N 106 33W
María Magdalena, I., Nayarit, Mexico 216 F4 21 25N 106 24W
Marian, L., FL, U.S.A. 67 D7 27 53N 81 6W
Mariana Islands, N. Marianas 105 a 15 15N 145 48W
Mariana Trench, Pac. Oc. 105 a 13 0N 145 0 E
Marianna, AR, U.S.A. 63 D5 34 46N 90 46W
Marianna, FL, U.S.A. 67 A3 30 46N 85 14W
Marianna, PA, U.S.A. 95 D2 40 2N 80 6W
Marias ➛, MT, U.S.A. 83 C7 47 56N 110 30W
Marías, Is., Nayarit, Mexico 216 F4 21 25N 106 28W
Maricao, Puerto Rico 105 G16 18 11N 66 59W
Maricopa, AZ, U.S.A. 62 D3 33 4N 112 3W
Maricopa, CA, U.S.A. 65 H7 35 4N 119 24W
Maricopa County ☆, AZ, U.S.A. 62 D3 33 15N 112 30W
Maricopa Indian Reservation, AZ, U.S.A. 62 E3 33 0N 112 1W
Maricopa Mts., AZ, U.S.A. 62 D3 33 0N 112 30W
Maricopa Village, Phoenix, U.S.A. 116 C1 33 22N 112 14W
Maricourt, Qué., Canada 175 B3 56 34N 70 49W
Marie L., Alta., Canada 184 D10 54 38N 110 18W
Mariecourt = Kangiqsujuaq, Qué., Canada 175 A3 61 30N 72 0W
Mariemont, OH, U.S.A. 107 B2 39 8N 84 22W
Marienthal, KS, U.S.A. 74 C2 38 29N 101 13W
Marienville, PA, U.S.A. 95 C3 41 28N 79 8W
Maries ➛, MO, U.S.A. 82 C4 38 30N 92 1W
Maries County ☆, MO, U.S.A. 82 C5 38 10N 91 55W
Marietta, GA, U.S.A. 68 C2 33 57N 84 33W
Marietta, MS, U.S.A. 81 B5 34 30N 88 28W
Marietta, OH, U.S.A. 92 D5 39 25N 81 27W
Marietta, OK, U.S.A. 93 E6 33 56N 97 7W
Marietta, SC, U.S.A. 90 C3 35 1N 82 30W
Marietta, WA, U.S.A. 101 B3 48 47N 122 35W
Marieville, Qué., Canada 177 F9 45 26N 73 10W
Marín, Nuevo León, Mexico 214 E4 25 52N 100 3W
Marin City, San Francisco, U.S.A. 118 A1 37 52N 122 30W
Marin County ☆, CA, U.S.A. 64 E4 38 0N 122 45W
Marin Pen., San Francisco, U.S.A. 118 A1 37 50N 122 30W
Marina, CA, U.S.A. 64 G5 36 41N 121 48W
Marina del Rey, Los Angeles, U.S.A. 111 C2 33 58N 118 27W
Marine, IL, U.S.A. 71 E4 38 47N 89 47W
Marine on St. Croix, MN, U.S.A. 80 E6 45 12N 92 46W
Marine Park, NY, U.S.A. 114 C3 40 36N 73 55W
Marineland, FL, U.S.A. 67 B7 29 40N 81 13W
Mariners Harbor, NY, U.S.A. 114 C2 40 38N 74 9W
Marinette, WI, U.S.A. 103 C6 45 6N 87 38W
Marinette County ☆, WI, U.S.A. 103 C5 45 25N 88 10W
Maringouin, LA, U.S.A. 75 D4 30 29N 91 31W
Marion, AL, U.S.A. 60 D3 32 38N 87 19W
Marion, AR, U.S.A. 63 C5 35 13N 90 12W
Marion, ID, U.S.A. 70 G5 42 17N 113 55W
Marion, IL, U.S.A. 71 F5 37 44N 88 56W
Marion, IN, U.S.A. 72 C5 40 32N 85 40W
Marion, IA, U.S.A. 73 C7 42 2N 91 36W
Marion, KS, U.S.A. 74 C6 38 21N 97 1W
Marion, KY, U.S.A. 96 C4 37 20N 88 5W
Marion, LA, U.S.A. 75 B3 32 54N 92 15W
Marion, MA, U.S.A. 78 C4 41 42N 70 46W
Marion, MD, U.S.A. 77 B5 38 2N 75 46W
Marion, MI, U.S.A. 79 E6 44 6N 85 9W
Marion, MS, U.S.A. 81 D5 32 25N 88 39W
Marion, MT, U.S.A. 83 B3 48 6N 114 40W
Marion, NC, U.S.A. 90 C3 35 41N 82 1W
Marion, ND, U.S.A. 91 D7 46 37N 98 20W
Marion, NE, U.S.A. 84 D5 40 1N 100 29W
Marion, OH, U.S.A. 92 C3 40 35N 83 8W
Marion, SC, U.S.A. 90 D6 34 11N 79 24W
Marion, SD, U.S.A. 91 G8 43 25N 97 16W
Marion, VA, U.S.A. 102 E3 36 50N 81 31W
Marion, WI, U.S.A. 103 D5 44 39N 88 54W
Marion, L., SC, U.S.A. 90 E5 33 28N 80 10W
Marion County ☆, AL, U.S.A. 60 B3 34 9N 87 59W
Marion County ☆, AR, U.S.A. 63 B3 36 14N 92 41W
Marion County ☆, FL, U.S.A. 67 B7 29 15N 82 0W
Marion County ☆, GA, U.S.A. 68 D2 32 25N 84 35W
Marion County ☆, IL, U.S.A. 71 E5 38 40N 88 55W
Marion County ☆, IN, U.S.A. 72 D4 39 45N 86 10W
Marion County ☆, IA, U.S.A. 73 D5 41 20N 93 5W
Marion County ☆, KS, U.S.A. 74 C6 38 20N 97 0W
Marion County ☆, KY, U.S.A. 97 C7 37 30N 85 15W
Marion County ☆, MS, U.S.A. 81 E4 31 15N 89 50W
Marion County ☆, MO, U.S.A. 82 B5 39 50N 91 35W
Marion County ☆, OH, U.S.A. 92 C3 40 35N 83 8W
Marion County ☆, OR, U.S.A. 94 C3 44 50N 122 50W
Marion County ☆, SC, U.S.A. 90 D6 34 10N 79 20W
Marion County ☆, TN, U.S.A. 97 E7 35 5N 85 38W
Marion County ☆, TX, U.S.A. 99 E13 32 46N 94 21W
Marion County ☆, WV, U.S.A. 102 B4 39 29N 80 9W
Marion Junction, AL, U.S.A. 60 D3 32 26N 87 14W
Marion Lake, KS, U.S.A. 74 C6 38 22N 97 5W
Marionville, MO, U.S.A. 82 E3 37 0N 93 38W
Mariposa, CA, U.S.A. 64 F7 37 29N 119 58W
Mariposa County ☆, CA, U.S.A. 64 F7 37 30N 120 0W
Mariscala, Oaxaca, Mexico 221 G2 17 53N 98 7W
Marissa, IL, U.S.A. 71 E4 38 15N 89 45W
Mark Twain L., MO, U.S.A. 82 B5 39 28N 91 55W
Mark Twain Nat. Forest, MO, U.S.A. 82 E5 36 50N 92 0W
Mark Twain Nat. Wildlife Refuge ⌓, IA, U.S.A. 73 D7 41 17N 91 6W
Markdale, Ont., Canada 178 C6 44 19N 80 39W
Marked Tree, AR, U.S.A. 63 C5 35 32N 90 25W
Markerville, Alta., Canada 185 F6 52 7N 114 10W
Markesan, WI, U.S.A. 103 E5 43 42N 88 59W
Markham, Ont., Canada 178 D7 43 52N 79 16W
Markham, TX, U.S.A. 99 J11 28 58N 96 4W
Markle, IN, U.S.A. 72 C5 40 50N 85 20W
Markleeville, CA, U.S.A. 64 E7 38 42N 119 47W
Markleville, IN, U.S.A. 72 D5 39 59N 85 37W
Markleysburg, PA, U.S.A. 95 E3 39 44N 79 27W
Marks, MS, U.S.A. 81 B3 34 16N 90 16W
Marks Butte, CO, U.S.A. 66 B8 40 53N 102 23W
Markstay, Ont., Canada 178 A6 46 29N 80 32W
Marksville, LA, U.S.A. 75 C3 31 8N 92 4W
Marland, OK, U.S.A. 93 B6 36 34N 97 9W
Marlbank, Ont., Canada 179 C9 44 26N 77 6W
Marlboro, NJ, U.S.A. 87 B2 40 19N 74 15W
Marlboro, NY, U.S.A. 89 D7 41 36N 73 59W
Marlboro County ☆, SC, U.S.A. 90 D6 34 40N 79 40W
Marlborough, CT, U.S.A. 78 C2 41 38N 72 27W
Marlborough, MA, U.S.A. 78 B3 42 21N 71 33W
Marlborough, MO, U.S.A. 117 B1 38 34N 90 20W
Marlborough, NH, U.S.A. 86 D2 42 54N 72 13W
Marlette, MI, U.S.A. 79 F8 43 20N 83 5W
Marlin, TX, U.S.A. 99 F11 31 18N 96 54W
Marlin, WA, U.S.A. 101 C7 47 25N 118 59W
Marlinton, WV, U.S.A. 102 C4 38 13N 80 6W
Marlow, GA, U.S.A. 68 D5 32 16N 81 23W
Marlow, NH, U.S.A. 86 C2 43 9N 72 12W
Marlow, OK, U.S.A. 93 D6 34 39N 97 58W
Marlton, NJ, U.S.A. 87 C2 39 54N 74 55W
Marmaduke, AR, U.S.A. 63 B5 36 11N 90 23W
Marmarth, ND, U.S.A. 91 D2 46 18N 103 54W
Marmion L., Ont., Canada 180 D5 48 55N 91 20W
Mármol, Sinaloa, Mexico 216 D4 23 29N 106 36W
Marmora, Ont., Canada 179 C9 44 29N 77 41W
Marmora, NJ, U.S.A. 87 C2 39 16N 74 39W
Marne, IA, U.S.A. 73 C3 41 28N 95 6W
Maro Reef, HI, U.S.A. 69 F9 25 25N 170 35W
Maroa, IL, U.S.A. 71 C5 40 2N 88 57W
Maroma, Pta., Quintana Roo, Mexico 223 B7 20 44N 86 58W

Marott Park, *Indianapolis, U.S.A.* 110 A2 39 53N 86 8W
Marpole, *Vancouver, Canada* 193 B2 49 12N 123 8W
Marquand, *MO, U.S.A.* 82 D6 37 26N 90 10W
Marquelia, *Guerrero, Mexico* 219 F9 16 36N 98 48W
Marqués de Comillas, Parque Natural ⌂, *Chiapas, Mexico* 222 C6 16 16N 90 39W
Marquesas Keys, *FL, U.S.A.* 67 G6 24 35N 82 10W
Marquette, *Man., Canada* 183 E14 50 4N 97 44W
Marquette, *IA, U.S.A.* 73 B7 43 3N 91 11W
Marquette, *KS, U.S.A.* 74 C6 38 33N 97 50W
Marquette, *MI, U.S.A.* 79 C4 46 33N 87 24W
Marquette, *NE, U.S.A.* 84 D7 41 0N 98 1W
Marquette, L., *Qué., Canada* 177 C9 48 54N 73 54W
Marquette County ☆, *MI, U.S.A.* 79 C4 46 20N 87 30W
Marquette County ☆, *WI, U.S.A.* 103 E4 43 50N 89 25W
Marquette I., *MI, U.S.A.* 79 D7 45 58N 84 24W
Marquette Park, *Chicago, U.S.A.* 108 C2 41 46N 87 42W
Marquez, *TX, U.S.A.* 99 F11 31 14N 96 15W
Marrero, *LA, U.S.A.* 75 E5 29 53N 90 6W
Marrowbone, *KY, U.S.A.* 97 D7 36 50N 85 30W
Mars, *PA, U.S.A.* 95 D2 40 42N 80 1W
Mars Hill, *ME, U.S.A.* 76 B6 46 31N 67 52W
Mars Hill, *NC, U.S.A.* 90 C3 35 50N 82 33W
Marsden, *Sask., Canada* 182 C2 52 51N 109 49W
Marseilles, *IL, U.S.A.* 71 B5 41 20N 88 43W
Marseilles, *OH, U.S.A.* 92 C3 40 42N 83 24W
Marsh I., *LA, U.S.A.* 75 E4 29 34N 91 53W
Marsh Pass, *AZ, U.S.A.* 62 A5 36 36N 110 35W
Marsh Peak, *UT, U.S.A.* 100 C6 40 43N 109 50W
Marsha, L., *Orlando, U.S.A.* 115 B2 28 29N 81 29W
Marshall, *Sask., Canada* 182 B2 53 11N 109 47W
Marshall, *AK, U.S.A.* 61 F7 61 53N 162 5W
Marshall, *AR, U.S.A.* 63 C3 35 55N 92 38W
Marshall, *IL, U.S.A.* 71 D6 39 23N 87 42W
Marshall, *IN, U.S.A.* 72 D3 39 51N 87 11W
Marshall, *MI, U.S.A.* 79 G7 42 16N 84 58W
Marshall, *MN, U.S.A.* 80 F3 44 27N 95 47W
Marshall, *MO, U.S.A.* 82 B3 39 7N 93 12W
Marshall, *NC, U.S.A.* 90 C3 35 48N 82 41W
Marshall, *OK, U.S.A.* 93 B6 36 9N 97 38W
Marshall, *TX, U.S.A.* 99 E13 32 33N 94 23W
Marshall, *VA, U.S.A.* 77 B3 38 52N 77 51W
Marshall County ☆, *AL, U.S.A.* 60 B4 34 21N 86 18W
Marshall County ☆, *IL, U.S.A.* 71 B4 41 0N 89 20W
Marshall County ☆, *IN, U.S.A.* 72 B4 41 20N 86 15W
Marshall County ☆, *IA, U.S.A.* 73 D5 42 0N 93 0W
Marshall County ☆, *KS, U.S.A.* 74 B7 39 45N 96 30W
Marshall County ☆, *KY, U.S.A.* 96 D4 36 55N 88 20W
Marshall County ☆, *MN, U.S.A.* 80 B2 48 15N 96 15W
Marshall County ☆, *MS, U.S.A.* 81 B4 34 46N 89 27W
Marshall County ☆, *OK, U.S.A.* 93 D7 34 0N 96 50W
Marshall County ☆, *SD, U.S.A.* 91 E8 45 48N 97 45W
Marshall County ☆, *TN, U.S.A.* 96 E6 35 27N 86 48W
Marshall County ☆, *WV, U.S.A.* 102 B4 39 50N 80 34W
Marshallberg, *NC, U.S.A.* 90 D9 34 44N 76 31W
Marshallton, *DE, U.S.A.* 77 A5 39 44N 75 39W
Marshalltown, *IA, U.S.A.* 73 C6 42 3N 92 55W
Marshallville = Lewisporte, *Nfld. & L., Canada* 174 C5 49 15N 55 3W
Marshallville, *GA, U.S.A.* 68 D3 32 27N 83 56W
Marshallville, *OH, U.S.A.* 92 C5 40 54N 81 44W
Marshfield = Coos Bay, *OR, U.S.A.* 94 D1 43 22N 124 13W
Marshfield, *MO, U.S.A.* 82 D4 37 15N 92 54W
Marshfield, *VT, U.S.A.* 86 B2 44 20N 72 20W
Marshfield, *WI, U.S.A.* 103 D3 44 40N 90 10W
Marshfield Hills, *MA, U.S.A.* 78 B4 42 9N 70 44W
Marshville, *NC, U.S.A.* 90 C5 35 0N 80 25W
Marshyhope →, *MD, U.S.A.* 77 B5 38 32N 75 45W
Marsing, *ID, U.S.A.* 70 F2 43 33N 116 48W
Marsoui, *Qué., Canada* 172 D3 49 13N 66 4W
Marston, *MO, U.S.A.* 82 E7 36 31N 89 37W
Marston L., *Denver, U.S.A.* 109 C1 39 38N 105 3W
Mart, *TX, U.S.A.* 99 F11 31 33N 96 50W
Marte R. Gomez, Presa, *Tamaulipas, Mexico* 214 D6 26 10N 99 0W
Martelle, *IA, U.S.A.* 73 C7 42 1N 91 22W
Marten River, *Ont., Canada* 178 A7 46 44N 79 49W
Martensdale, *IA, U.S.A.* 73 D5 41 23N 93 45W
Martensville, *Sask., Canada* 182 C5 52 17N 106 40W
Martha Lake, *Seattle, U.S.A.* 118 A4 47 50N 122 14W
Martha's Vineyard, *MA, U.S.A.* 78 C4 41 25N 70 38W
Marthasville, *MO, U.S.A.* 82 C5 38 38N 91 4W
Marthaville, *LA, U.S.A.* 75 C2 31 44N 93 24W
Martin, *KY, U.S.A.* 97 C10 37 34N 82 45W
Martin, *LA, U.S.A.* 75 B2 32 5N 93 13W
Martin, *MI, U.S.A.* 79 G6 42 32N 85 39W
Martin, *ND, U.S.A.* 91 C5 47 50N 100 7W
Martin, *SD, U.S.A.* 91 G4 43 11N 101 44W
Martin, *TN, U.S.A.* 96 D4 36 21N 88 51W
Martin County ☆, *FL, U.S.A.* 67 D8 27 10N 80 20W
Martin County ☆, *IN, U.S.A.* 72 E4 38 40N 86 50W
Martin County ☆, *KY, U.S.A.* 97 C10 37 45N 82 30W
Martin County ☆, *MN, U.S.A.* 80 G4 43 40N 94 30W
Martin County ☆, *NC, U.S.A.* 90 C9 35 45N 77 0W
Martin County ☆, *TX, U.S.A.* 98 E6 32 18N 101 58W
Martin L., *AL, U.S.A.* 60 D5 32 41N 85 55W
Martin Pt., *AK, U.S.A.* 61 A12 70 8N 143 16W
Martin Van Buren Nat. Historic Site ⌂, *NY, U.S.A.* 89 C7 42 22N 73 42W
Martinecock, *NY, U.S.A.* 114 A5 40 51N 73 35W
Martinez, *CA, U.S.A.* 64 E4 38 1N 122 8W
Martinez, *GA, U.S.A.* 68 C4 33 31N 82 5W
Martínez de la Torre, *Veracruz, Mexico* 220 D3 20 4N 97 3W
Martinez Lake, *AZ, U.S.A.* 62 E1 32 59N 114 29W
Martins Ferry, *OH, U.S.A.* 92 C6 40 6N 80 44W
Martinsburg, *MD, U.S.A.* 77 A3 39 10N 77 28W
Martinsburg, *MO, U.S.A.* 82 B5 39 6N 91 39W
Martinsburg, *NE, U.S.A.* 84 B9 42 30N 96 50W
Martinsburg, *OH, U.S.A.* 92 C4 40 16N 82 21W
Martinsburg, *PA, U.S.A.* 95 D4 40 19N 78 20W
Martinsburg, *WV, U.S.A.* 77 A3 39 27N 77 58W
Martinsdale, *MT, U.S.A.* 83 D7 46 28N 110 18W
Martinsville, *IL, U.S.A.* 71 D6 39 20N 87 53W
Martinsville, *IN, U.S.A.* 72 D4 39 26N 86 25W
Martinsville, *VA, U.S.A.* 102 E5 36 41N 79 52W
Martinton, *IL, U.S.A.* 71 C6 40 55N 87 44W
Maruchin, *Campeche, Mexico* 223 D4 18 17N 89 53W
Marvel, *CO, U.S.A.* 66 E2 37 7N 108 8W
Marvell, *AR, U.S.A.* 63 D5 34 33N 90 55W
Marvin, *SD, U.S.A.* 91 E9 45 16N 96 55W
Marvine, Mt., *UT, U.S.A.* 100 E4 38 40N 111 39W
Marwayne, *Alta., Canada* 184 E10 53 32N 110 20W
Mary Esther, *FL, U.S.A.* 67 A2 30 25N 86 40W
Mary S. Young State Park ⌂, *Portland, U.S.A.* 116 B2 45 22N 122 37W
Marydel, *MD, U.S.A.* 77 A5 39 7N 75 45W
Maryen, L., *Qué., Canada* 172 B9 51 20N 60 28W
Maryfield, *Sask., Canada* 183 F10 49 50N 101 35W
Maryhill, *WA, U.S.A.* 101 E5 45 41N 120 49W
Maryland □, *U.S.A.* 77 A4 39 0N 76 30W
Maryland City, *MD, U.S.A.* 77 A4 39 6N 76 50W
Maryland Line, *MD, U.S.A.* 77 A4 39 43N 76 40W
Maryland Point, *MD, U.S.A.* 77 B3 38 22N 77 14W
Maryneal, *TX, U.S.A.* 98 E7 32 14N 100 27W
Marys →, *NV, U.S.A.* 85 A5 41 4N 115 16W
Marys Corner, *WA, U.S.A.* 101 D3 46 33N 122 49W
Mary's Harbour, *Nfld. & L., Canada* 175 C6 52 18N 55 51W
Marys Pk., *OR, U.S.A.* 94 C2 44 30N 123 33W
Marystown, *Nfld. & L., Canada* 174 E5 47 10N 55 10W
Marysvale, *UT, U.S.A.* 100 E3 38 27N 112 14W
Marysville, *CA, U.S.A.* 64 D5 39 9N 121 35W
Marysville, *KS, U.S.A.* 74 B7 39 51N 96 39W
Marysville, *MI, U.S.A.* 79 G9 42 54N 82 29W
Marysville, *OH, U.S.A.* 92 C3 40 14N 83 22W
Marysville, *PA, U.S.A.* 95 D6 40 21N 76 56W
Marysville, *WA, U.S.A.* 101 B3 48 3N 122 11W
Maryvale, *Phoenix, U.S.A.* 116 C1 33 30N 112 10W
Maryville, *MO, U.S.A.* 82 A2 40 21N 94 52W
Maryville, *TN, U.S.A.* 97 E9 35 46N 83 58W
Masalog Pt., *N. Marianas* 105 c 15 1N 145 40W
Masardis, *ME, U.S.A.* 76 B5 46 30N 68 22W
Masaryktown, *FL, U.S.A.* 67 C6 28 27N 82 27W
Mascareñas, *Veracruz, Mexico* 220 C2 21 40N 98 0W
Mascot, *TN, U.S.A.* 97 D9 36 4N 83 45W
Mascota, *Jalisco, Mexico* 218 B3 20 32N 104 49W
Mascouche, *Qué., Canada* 177 F9 45 45N 73 36W
Mascoutah, *IL, U.S.A.* 71 E4 38 29N 89 48W
Mascuala, *Guadalajara, Mexico* 224 A2 20 46N 103 17W
Mashantucket Pequot Indian Reservation, *CT, U.S.A.* 78 C3 41 27N 71 58W
Mashpee, *MA, U.S.A.* 78 C4 41 39N 70 29W
Masiaca, *Sonora, Mexico* 212 G6 26 45N 109 18W
Maskell, *NE, U.S.A.* 84 B9 42 41N 96 59W
Maskinongé, *Qué., Canada* 177 E9 46 14N 73 1W
Mason, *IL, U.S.A.* 71 E5 38 57N 88 38W
Mason, *MI, U.S.A.* 79 G7 42 35N 84 27W
Mason, *NH, U.S.A.* 86 D3 42 45N 71 47W
Mason, *OH, U.S.A.* 92 D2 39 22N 84 19W
Mason, *TN, U.S.A.* 96 E3 35 25N 89 32W
Mason, *TX, U.S.A.* 99 G8 30 45N 99 14W
Mason, *WV, U.S.A.* 102 B2 39 1N 82 2W
Mason, *WI, U.S.A.* 103 B2 46 26N 91 4W
Mason City, *IL, U.S.A.* 71 C4 40 12N 89 42W
Mason City, *IA, U.S.A.* 73 B5 43 9N 93 12W
Mason City, *NE, U.S.A.* 84 C6 41 13N 99 18W
Mason County ☆, *IL, U.S.A.* 71 C4 40 15N 89 50W
Mason County ☆, *KY, U.S.A.* 97 B9 38 35N 83 50W
Mason County ☆, *MI, U.S.A.* 79 F5 44 0N 86 15W
Mason County ☆, *TX, U.S.A.* 99 G8 30 45N 99 15W
Mason County ☆, *WV, U.S.A.* 102 C2 38 50N 82 8W
Mason County ☆, *WA, U.S.A.* 101 C2 47 20N 123 10W
Mason Springs, *MD, U.S.A.* 77 B3 38 36N 77 10W
Masonboro, *NC, U.S.A.* 90 D8 34 11N 77 51W
Masontown, *PA, U.S.A.* 95 E3 39 50N 79 54W
Masontown, *WV, U.S.A.* 102 B5 39 33N 79 48W
Masonville, *IA, U.S.A.* 73 C7 42 29N 91 36W
Maspeth, *NY, U.S.A.* 114 B3 40 43N 73 55W
Mass City, *MI, U.S.A.* 79 C2 46 46N 89 5W
Massabesic L., *NH, U.S.A.* 86 C3 43 0N 71 23W
Massac County ☆, *IL, U.S.A.* 71 F5 37 15N 88 45W
Massachusetts □, *U.S.A.* 78 B2 42 30N 72 0W
Massachusetts B., *MA, U.S.A.* 78 B4 42 25N 70 50W
Massacre L., *NV, U.S.A.* 85 A1 41 39N 119 36W
Massapequa, *NY, U.S.A.* 87 B3 40 41N 73 29W
Massawippi, L., *Qué., Canada* 86 A3 45 13N 72 0W
Massena, *IA, U.S.A.* 73 D4 41 15N 94 46W
Massena, *NY, U.S.A.* 89 A6 44 56N 74 54W
Masset, *B.C., Canada* 186 A2 54 2N 132 10W
Masset Inlet, *B.C., Canada* 186 B2 53 43N 132 20W
Massey, *Ont., Canada* 178 A4 46 12N 82 5W
Massey, *MD, U.S.A.* 77 A5 39 18N 75 49W
Massey I., *Nunavut, Canada* 190 B5 76 0N 103 0W
Massey Sd., *Nunavut, Canada* 190 B7 78 30N 94 0W
Massillon, *OH, U.S.A.* 92 C5 40 48N 81 32W
Masson-Angers, *Qué., Canada* 176 F7 45 32N 75 25W
Massueville, *Qué., Canada* 177 F10 45 55N 72 56W
Mastens Corner, *DE, U.S.A.* 77 B5 38 57N 75 37W
Masters, *CO, U.S.A.* 66 B6 40 18N 104 15W
Mastic, *NY, U.S.A.* 89 E8 40 47N 72 54W
Mastigouche, Réserve Faunique ⌂, *Qué., Canada* 177 E9 46 33N 73 41W
Mata de Labra, *Tamaulipas, Mexico* 215 H6 22 26N 98 7W
Matachic, *Chihuahua, Mexico* 213 E8 28 51N 107 45W
Matador, *TX, U.S.A.* 98 C7 34 1N 100 49W
Matagami, *Qué., Canada* 175 D2 49 45N 77 34W
Matagami, L., *Qué., Canada* 175 D2 49 50N 77 40W
Matagorda, *TX, U.S.A.* 99 J12 28 42N 95 58W
Matagorda B., *TX, U.S.A.* 99 J11 28 40N 96 12W
Matagorda County ☆, *TX, U.S.A.* 99 J12 29 0N 96 0W
Matagorda I., *TX, U.S.A.* 99 J11 28 15N 96 30W
Matagorda Peninsula, *TX, U.S.A.* 99 J12 28 38N 96 0W
Matamec, L., *Qué., Canada* 172 C4 50 21N 65 58W
Matamoros, *Coahuila, Mexico* 214 E1 25 32N 103 15W
Matamoros, *Durango, Mexico* 216 B5 25 27N 105 27W
Matamoros, *Tamaulipas, Mexico* 214 E7 25 53N 97 30W
Matane, *Qué., Canada* 172 E2 48 50N 67 33W
Matane →, *Qué., Canada* 172 E2 48 50N 67 35W
Matane, Réserve Faunique de ⌂, *Qué., Canada* 172 E3 48 40N 67 0W
Matanuska-Susitna ☆, *AK, U.S.A.* 61 E10 62 30N 150 0W
Matapé →, *Sonora, Mexico* 212 E5 28 15N 110 42W
Matapédia, *N.B., Canada* 173 F3 48 0N 66 59W
Matapédia, L., *Qué., Canada* 172 E2 48 35N 67 35W
Matasaguas, Sa., *Chihuahua, Mexico* 213 D11 29 20N 104 38W
Matatula, C., *Amer. Samoa* 105 e 14 15 S 170 33W
Matawan, *NJ, U.S.A.* 87 B2 40 25N 74 14W
Matawin →, *Qué., Canada* 177 E10 46 54N 72 56W
Matawin, Rés., *Qué., Canada* 177 E9 46 46N 73 50W
Matchi-Manitou, L., *Qué., Canada* 176 D5 48 0N 77 5W
Matehuala, *San Luis Potosí, Mexico* 215 G4 23 39N 100 39W
Mateo, Cerro, *Distrito Federal, Mexico* 225 C2 19 11N 99 19W
Matewan, *WV, U.S.A.* 102 D2 37 37N 82 10W
Matfield Green, *KS, U.S.A.* 74 C7 38 9N 96 31W
Matheson, *CO, U.S.A.* 66 C7 39 10N 103 59W
Matheson Island, *Man., Canada* 183 D15 51 45N 96 56W
Mathews, *VA, U.S.A.* 102 D8 37 26N 76 19W
Mathews, L., *CA, U.S.A.* 65 K9 33 51N 117 27W
Mathews County ☆, *VA, U.S.A.* 102 D8 37 26N 76 19W
Mathias, *WV, U.S.A.* 102 C6 38 53N 78 52W
Mathis, *TX, U.S.A.* 99 J10 28 6N 97 50W
Mathiston, *MS, U.S.A.* 81 C4 33 32N 89 7W
Matías Romero, *Oaxaca, Mexico* 221 H5 16 53N 95 2W
Matinenda L., *Ont., Canada* 178 A4 46 22N 82 57W
Matinicus, *ME, U.S.A.* 76 E5 43 52N 68 54W
Matinicus I., *ME, U.S.A.* 76 E5 43 52N 68 54W
Matlapa, *San Luis Potosí, Mexico* 215 J6 21 19N 98 49W
Matlock, *IA, U.S.A.* 73 B3 43 15N 95 56W
Matoaka, *WV, U.S.A.* 102 D3 37 25N 81 15W
Mattagami →, *Ont., Canada* 181 B15 50 43N 81 29W
Mattagami L., *Ont., Canada* 181 E15 47 54N 81 35W
Mattamuskeet, L., *NC, U.S.A.* 90 C9 35 30N 76 12W
Mattapan, *Boston, U.S.A.* 106 B3 42 16N 71 6W
Mattapoisett, *MA, U.S.A.* 78 C4 41 40N 70 49W
Mattaponi →, *VA, U.S.A.* 102 D8 37 31N 76 47W
Mattawa, *WA, U.S.A.* 101 D6 46 44N 119 54W
Mattawamkeag, *ME, U.S.A.* 76 C5 45 32N 68 21W
Mattawitchewan →, *Ont., Canada* 181 C13 49 52N 83 12W
Matterhorn, *NV, U.S.A.* 85 A5 41 49N 115 23W
Matthews, *IN, U.S.A.* 72 C5 40 23N 85 30W
Matthews, *MD, U.S.A.* 77 B5 38 49N 75 57W
Matthews, *MO, U.S.A.* 82 E7 36 46N 89 35W
Matthews, *NC, U.S.A.* 90 C5 35 7N 80 43W
Matthews Pk., *AZ, U.S.A.* 62 A6 36 20N 109 8W
Mattice, *Ont., Canada* 181 C13 49 40N 83 20W
Mattituck, *NY, U.S.A.* 78 D2 40 59N 72 32W
Mattole →, *CA, U.S.A.* 64 C2 40 18N 124 21W
Mattoon, *IL, U.S.A.* 71 D5 39 29N 88 23W
Mattson, *MS, U.S.A.* 81 B3 34 6N 90 31W
Matunuck, *RI, U.S.A.* 78 C3 41 23N 71 32W
Maud, *OK, U.S.A.* 93 C7 35 8N 96 46W
Maud, *TX, U.S.A.* 99 D13 33 20N 94 21W
Maug Is., *N. Marianas* 105 a 20 1N 145 13W
Maugerville, *N.B., Canada* 173 H3 45 52N 66 27W
Maui, *HI, U.S.A.* 69 C5 20 48N 156 20W
Mauldin, *SC, U.S.A.* 90 D3 34 47N 82 19W
Maumee, *OH, U.S.A.* 92 B3 41 34N 83 39W
Maumee →, *OH, U.S.A.* 92 B3 41 42N 83 28W
Maumelle, *AR, U.S.A.* 63 D3 34 52N 92 24W
Maumelle, L., *AR, U.S.A.* 63 D3 34 51N 92 29W
Mauna Kea, *HI, U.S.A.* 69 D6 19 50N 155 28W
Mauna Kea Forest Reserve, *HI, U.S.A.* 69 D6 19 52N 155 26W
Mauna Loa, *HI, U.S.A.* 69 D6 19 30N 155 35W
Mauna Loa Forest Reserve, *HI, U.S.A.* 69 D6 19 35N 155 33W
Maunabo, *Puerto Rico* 105 G17 18 1N 65 54W
Maunaloa, *HI, U.S.A.* 69 B4 21 8N 157 13W
Maunalua B., *HI, U.S.A.* 69 K14 21 15N 157 45W
Maunawili, *HI, U.S.A.* 69 K14 21 23N 157 46W
Maunie, *IL, U.S.A.* 71 E5 38 2N 88 3W
Maunoir, L., *N.W.T., Canada* 188 C8 67 30N 124 55W
Maupin, *OR, U.S.A.* 94 B4 45 11N 121 5W
Maurepas, L., *LA, U.S.A.* 75 D5 30 15N 90 30W
Maurice, *LA, U.S.A.* 75 D3 30 7N 92 7W
Maurice →, *NJ, U.S.A.* 87 C1 39 13N 75 2W
Mauriceville, *TX, U.S.A.* 99 G14 30 12N 93 52W
Mauricie, Parc Nat. de la △, *Qué., Canada* 177 E10 46 45N 73 0W
Maurine, *SD, U.S.A.* 91 E3 45 1N 102 35W
Maury →, *VA, U.S.A.* 102 D5 37 50N 79 25W
Maury City, *TN, U.S.A.* 96 E3 35 49N 89 14W
Maury County ☆, *TN, U.S.A.* 96 E5 35 37N 87 2W
Maury Island, *Seattle, U.S.A.* 118 D3 47 22N 122 25W
Mauston, *WI, U.S.A.* 103 E3 43 48N 90 5W
Maverick County ☆, *TX, U.S.A.* 98 J7 28 55N 100 8W
Mavillette, *N.S., Canada* 173 J3 44 6N 66 11W
Max, *ND, U.S.A.* 91 C4 47 49N 101 18W
Maxbass, *ND, U.S.A.* 91 B4 48 43N 101 9W
Maxcanú, *Yucatán, Mexico* 223 B4 20 35N 90 0W
Maxeys, *GA, U.S.A.* 68 C3 33 45N 83 11W
Maxinkuckee, L., *IN, U.S.A.* 72 B4 41 12N 86 24W
Maxton, *NC, U.S.A.* 90 D6 34 44N 79 21W
Maxville, *Ont., Canada* 176 F8 45 17N 74 51W
Maxville, *MT, U.S.A.* 83 D4 46 28N 113 14W
Maxwell, *CA, U.S.A.* 64 D4 39 17N 122 11W
Maxwell, *IA, U.S.A.* 73 D5 41 53N 93 24W
Maxwell, *NM, U.S.A.* 88 A6 36 32N 104 33W
Maxwell, *NE, U.S.A.* 84 C5 41 5N 100 31W
May, *ID, U.S.A.* 70 E5 44 36N 113 55W
May, *OK, U.S.A.* 93 B4 36 37N 99 45W
May, C., *NJ, U.S.A.* 87 D2 38 56N 74 58W
May Mt., *ID, U.S.A.* 70 E5 44 41N 113 50W
Mayagüez, *Puerto Rico* 105 G15 18 12N 67 9W
Mayapán, *Yucatán, Mexico* 223 B4 20 29N 89 11W
Mayapán, *Yucatán, Mexico* 223 B4 20 35N 89 29W
Maybell, *CO, U.S.A.* 66 B2 40 31N 108 5W
Maybeury, *WV, U.S.A.* 102 D3 37 22N 81 22W
Maybrook, *NY, U.S.A.* 87 A2 41 29N 74 13W
Mayer, *AZ, U.S.A.* 62 C3 34 24N 112 14W
Mayersville, *MS, U.S.A.* 81 D2 32 54N 91 3W
Mayerthorpe, *Alta., Canada* 184 E5 53 57N 115 8W
Mayes County ☆, *OK, U.S.A.* 93 B8 36 15N 95 10W
Mayesville, *SC, U.S.A.* 90 D5 34 0N 80 12W
Mayetta, *KS, U.S.A.* 74 B8 39 20N 95 43W
Mayetta, *NJ, U.S.A.* 87 C2 39 40N 74 18W
Mayfair, *Sask., Canada* 182 C4 52 58N 107 36W
Mayfair, *Houston, U.S.A.* 110 B3 29 41N 95 19W
Mayfield, *GA, U.S.A.* 68 C4 33 21N 82 48W
Mayfield, *ID, U.S.A.* 70 F3 43 25N 115 54W
Mayfield, *KS, U.S.A.* 74 D6 37 16N 97 33W
Mayfield, *KY, U.S.A.* 96 D4 36 44N 88 38W
Mayfield, *UT, U.S.A.* 100 D4 39 7N 111 43W
Mayflower, *AR, U.S.A.* 63 D3 34 57N 92 26W
Mayhill, *NM, U.S.A.* 88 E5 32 53N 105 29W
Maymont, *Sask., Canada* 182 C4 52 34N 107 42W
Maynard, *AR, U.S.A.* 63 B5 36 25N 90 54W
Maynard, *IA, U.S.A.* 73 C7 42 47N 91 53W
Maynard, *MA, U.S.A.* 78 B3 42 26N 71 27W
Maynard, *MN, U.S.A.* 80 F3 44 54N 95 28W
Maynardville, *TN, U.S.A.* 97 D9 36 15N 83 48W
Mayne, *B.C., Canada* 187 G11 48 52N 123 17W
Mayo, *Yukon, Canada* 189 D5 63 38N 135 57W
Mayo, *FL, U.S.A.* 67 A5 30 3N 83 10W
Mayo, *SC, U.S.A.* 90 C4 35 5N 81 52W
Mayo →, *Sonora, Mexico* 212 G6 26 45N 109 47W
Mayo Res., *NC, U.S.A.* 90 B7 36 32N 78 53W
Mayodan, *NC, U.S.A.* 90 B6 36 25N 79 58W
Mayoworth, *WY, U.S.A.* 104 C6 43 50N 106 47W
Mayport Naval Station, *FL, U.S.A.* 67 A7 30 24N 81 25W
Mayran, Desierto de, *Mexico* 214 E1 25 53N 103 8W
Mays Landing, *NJ, U.S.A.* 87 C2 39 27N 74 44W
Mays Lick, *KY, U.S.A.* 97 B9 38 31N 83 50W
Maysville, *GA, U.S.A.* 68 B3 34 15N 83 34W
Maysville, *KY, U.S.A.* 97 B9 38 39N 83 46W
Maysville, *MO, U.S.A.* 82 B2 39 53N 94 22W
Maysville, *NC, U.S.A.* 90 D8 34 54N 77 14W
Maysville, *OK, U.S.A.* 93 D6 34 49N 97 24W
Maysville, *WV, U.S.A.* 77 A1 39 7N 79 10W
Mayview, *MO, U.S.A.* 82 B3 39 3N 93 50W
Mayville, *MI, U.S.A.* 79 F8 43 20N 83 21W
Mayville, *ND, U.S.A.* 91 C8 47 30N 97 20W
Mayville, *NY, U.S.A.* 89 C1 42 15N 79 30W
Mayville, *WI, U.S.A.* 103 E5 43 30N 88 33W
Maywood, *Chicago, U.S.A.* 108 B1 41 52N 87 51W
Maywood, *Indianapolis, U.S.A.* 110 B1 39 43N 86 12W
Maywood, *Los Angeles, U.S.A.* 111 C3 33 59N 118 12W
Maywood, *NJ, U.S.A.* 114 A2 40 53N 74 3W
Maywood, *NE, U.S.A.* 84 D5 40 39N 100 37W
Maywood Park, *Portland, U.S.A.* 116 A2 45 33N 122 33W
Maza, *ND, U.S.A.* 91 B6 48 22N 99 12W
Mazama, *WA, U.S.A.* 101 B5 48 36N 120 24W
Mazamitla, *Jalisco, Mexico* 218 C4 19 55N 103 2W
Mazapil, *Zacatecas, Mexico* 217 C9 24 39N 101 34W
Mazatán, *Chiapas, Mexico* 222 E4 14 52N 92 27W
Mazatán, *Sonora, Mexico* 212 D6 29 0N 110 8W
Mazatepec, *Puebla, Mexico* 220 D3 20 2N 97 24W
Mazatlán, *Guerrero, Mexico* 219 E8 17 26N 99 28W
Mazatlán, *Sinaloa, Mexico* 216 D4 23 13N 106 25W
Mazatzal Mts., *AZ, U.S.A.* 62 D4 34 0N 111 30W
Mazenod, *Sask., Canada* 182 F5 49 52N 106 13W
Mazie, *KY, U.S.A.* 97 B10 38 2N 82 58W
Mazie, *OK, U.S.A.* 93 B8 36 6N 95 22W
Mazomanie, *WI, U.S.A.* 103 E4 43 11N 89 48W
Mazon, *IL, U.S.A.* 71 B5 41 14N 88 25W
Meacham, *Sask., Canada* 182 C6 52 6N 105 45W
Meacham, *OR, U.S.A.* 94 B7 45 31N 118 25W
Mead, *NE, U.S.A.* 84 C9 41 14N 96 29W
Mead, *OK, U.S.A.* 93 E7 34 0N 96 31W
Mead, *WA, U.S.A.* 101 C8 47 46N 117 21W
Mead, L., *U.S.A.* 62 A1 36 0N 114 44W
Meade = Atqasuk →, *AK, U.S.A.* 61 A9 70 52N 155 55W
Meade, *KS, U.S.A.* 74 D3 37 17N 100 20W
Meade County ☆, *KS, U.S.A.* 74 D3 37 15N 100 20W
Meade County ☆, *KY, U.S.A.* 96 C6 37 55N 86 10W
Meade County ☆, *SD, U.S.A.* 91 F3 44 30N 102 30W
Meade River = Atqasuk, *AK, U.S.A.* 61 A8 70 28N 157 24W
Meadow, *SD, U.S.A.* 91 E3 45 32N 102 13W
Meadow, *TX, U.S.A.* 98 D5 33 20N 102 12W
Meadow, *UT, U.S.A.* 100 E3 38 53N 112 24W
Meadow →, *WV, U.S.A.* 102 C4 38 12N 80 57W
Meadow Bridge, *WV, U.S.A.* 102 D4 37 52N 80 51W
Meadow Brook Park, *Minneapolis-St. Paul, U.S.A.* 113 B1 44 55N 93 21W
Meadow Grove, *NE, U.S.A.* 84 B8 42 2N 97 44W
Meadow L., *Sask., Canada* 182 A3 54 7N 108 20W
Meadow Lake, *Sask., Canada* 182 A3 54 10N 108 26W
Meadow Lake, *NY, U.S.A.* 114 B3 40 44N 73 50W
Meadow Park, *Minneapolis-St. Paul, U.S.A.* 113 B1 44 57N 93 26W
Meadow Valley Wash →, *NV, U.S.A.* 85 F6 36 40N 114 34W
Meadow Vista, *CA, U.S.A.* 64 D5 39 6N 121 1W
Meadowdale, *WY, U.S.A.* 104 D8 42 33N 104 42W
Meadowlands, *Ont., Canada* 192 B1 45 21N 75 45W
Meadowlands, *MN, U.S.A.* 80 C6 47 4N 92 44W
Meadows, *NH, U.S.A.* 86 B3 44 21N 71 28W
Meadowview, *VA, U.S.A.* 102 E3 36 46N 81 52W
Meadville, *MS, U.S.A.* 81 E3 31 28N 90 54W
Meadville, *MO, U.S.A.* 82 B3 39 47N 93 18W
Meadville, *PA, U.S.A.* 95 C2 41 39N 80 9W
Meaford, *Ont., Canada* 178 C6 44 36N 80 35W
Meagher County ☆, *MT, U.S.A.* 83 D6 46 40N 111 0W
Meaghers Grant, *N.S., Canada* 173 J6 44 55N 63 15W
Meander River, *Alta., Canada* 189 E9 59 2N 117 42W
Meansville, *GA, U.S.A.* 68 C2 33 3N 84 18W
Meares, C., *OR, U.S.A.* 58 D2 45 37N 124 0W
Meares I., *B.C., Canada* 186 F9 49 12N 125 50W
Mears Corner, *Norfolk, U.S.A.* 115 B2 36 46N 76 11W
Meath Park, *Sask., Canada* 182 B6 53 27N 105 22W
Mebane, *NC, U.S.A.* 90 B6 36 6N 79 16W
Mecapalapa, *Puebla, Mexico* 220 D3 20 32N 97 50W
Mecatán, *Nayarit, Mexico* 216 F5 21 32N 105 7W
Mecatina, Little →, *Nfld. & L., Canada* 172 A9 52 0N 60 15W
Mecayapán, *Veracruz, Mexico* 221 F6 18 13N 94 50W
Mecca, *CA, U.S.A.* 65 K10 33 34N 116 5W
Mechanic Falls, *ME, U.S.A.* 76 D3 44 7N 70 24W
Mechanicsburg, *IL, U.S.A.* 71 D4 39 49N 89 24W
Mechanicsburg, *OH, U.S.A.* 92 C3 40 4N 83 33W
Mechanicsburg, *PA, U.S.A.* 95 D5 40 13N 77 1W
Mechanicsville, *IA, U.S.A.* 73 D7 41 54N 91 16W
Mechanicsville, *MD, U.S.A.* 77 B4 38 26N 76 44W
Mechanicsville, *VA, U.S.A.* 102 D7 37 36N 77 22W
Mechanicville, *NY, U.S.A.* 78 B1 42 54N 73 41W
Mechanicville, *NY, U.S.A.* 89 C7 42 54N 73 41W
Mecklenburg County ☆, *NC, U.S.A.* 90 C5 35 10N 80 50W
Mecklenburg County ☆, *VA, U.S.A.* 102 E6 36 55N 78 20W
Meckling, *SD, U.S.A.* 91 H8 42 51N 97 4W
Mecoaca, L., *Tabasco, Mexico* 222 A3 18 22N 93 9W
Mecosta, *MI, U.S.A.* 79 F6 43 37N 85 14W
Mecosta County ☆, *MI, U.S.A.* 79 F6 43 35N 85 20W
Medanales, *NM, U.S.A.* 88 A4 36 11N 106 11W
Medart, *FL, U.S.A.* 67 A4 30 5N 84 23W
Medaryville, *IN, U.S.A.* 72 B4 41 5N 86 55W
Medellín, *Veracruz, Mexico* 221 E4 19 2N 96 7W
Medfield, *MA, U.S.A.* 78 B3 42 11N 71 18W
Medford, *MA, U.S.A.* 78 B3 42 25N 71 7W
Medford, *MN, U.S.A.* 80 F5 44 11N 93 15W
Medford, *NJ, U.S.A.* 87 C2 39 54N 74 50W
Medford, *NY, U.S.A.* 87 B3 40 49N 73 0W
Medford, *OK, U.S.A.* 93 B6 36 48N 97 44W
Medford, *OR, U.S.A.* 94 E3 42 19N 122 52W
Medford, *WI, U.S.A.* 103 C3 45 9N 90 20W
Medford Lakes, *NJ, U.S.A.* 87 C2 39 52N 74 48W
Media, *PA, U.S.A.* 87 C1 39 55N 75 23W
Mediapolis, *IA, U.S.A.* 73 E7 41 0N 91 10W
Medias Aguas, *Veracruz, Mexico* 221 G5 17 40N 95 2W
Medical Lake, *WA, U.S.A.* 101 C8 47 34N 117 41W
Medicine Bow, *WY, U.S.A.* 104 E6 41 54N 106 12W
Medicine Bow →, *WY, U.S.A.* 104 D6 42 0N 106 40W
Medicine Bow Mts., *U.S.A.* 66 B5 40 40N 106 0W
Medicine Bow Nat. Forest, *WY, U.S.A.* 104 E6 42 20N 105 38W
Medicine Bow Pk., *WY, U.S.A.* 58 F10 41 21N 106 19W
Medicine Cr. →, *MO, U.S.A.* 82 B3 39 43N 93 24W
Medicine Cr. →, *NE, U.S.A.* 84 D5 40 17N 100 10W
Medicine Hat, *Alta., Canada* 185 H10 50 0N 110 45W
Medicine L., *Minneapolis-St. Paul, U.S.A.* 113 A1 45 0N 93 25W
Medicine L., *MT, U.S.A.* 83 B13 48 28N 104 24W
Medicine Lake, *Minneapolis-St. Paul, U.S.A.* 113 A1 44 59N 93 24W
Medicine Lake, *MT, U.S.A.* 83 B13 48 30N 104 30W
Medicine Lodge, *KS, U.S.A.* 74 D5 37 17N 98 35W
Medicine Lodge →, *KS, U.S.A.* 74 E5 36 49N 98 20W
Medicine Park, *OK, U.S.A.* 93 D5 34 44N 98 30W
Medina, *ND, U.S.A.* 91 D6 46 54N 99 18W
Medina, *NY, U.S.A.* 89 B2 43 13N 78 23W
Medina, *OH, U.S.A.* 92 B5 41 8N 81 52W
Medina, *Seattle, U.S.A.* 118 C4 47 37N 122 13W
Medina, *TN, U.S.A.* 96 E4 35 48N 88 46W
Medina, *TX, U.S.A.* 99 H8 29 48N 99 15W
Medina →, *TX, U.S.A.* 99 H9 29 16N 98 29W
Medina County ☆, *OH, U.S.A.* 92 B5 41 8N 81 52W
Medina County ☆, *TX, U.S.A.* 99 H8 29 21N 99 9W
Medina L., *TX, U.S.A.* 99 H8 29 32N 98 56W
Medora, *IL, U.S.A.* 71 D3 39 11N 90 9W
Medora, *IN, U.S.A.* 72 E4 38 49N 86 10W
Medora, *ND, U.S.A.* 91 D2 46 55N 103 31W
Medstead, *Sask., Canada* 182 B3 53 19N 108 5W
Meductic, *N.B., Canada* 173 H2 46 0N 67 29W
Medway, *MA, U.S.A.* 78 B3 42 8N 71 24W
Medway →, *N.S., Canada* 173 J5 44 8N 64 36W
Meeker, *CO, U.S.A.* 66 B3 40 2N 107 55W
Meeker, *OK, U.S.A.* 93 C7 35 30N 96 54W
Meeker County ☆, *MN, U.S.A.* 80 E4 45 10N 94 30W
Meeks Bay, *CA, U.S.A.* 64 D6 39 2N 120 8W
Meelpaeg L., *Nfld. & L., Canada* 174 D4 48 20N 56 30W
Meeteetse, *WY, U.S.A.* 104 B4 44 9N 108 52W
Mégantic, L., *Qué., Canada* 177 F12 45 32N 70 53W
Mégantic, Mt., *Qué., Canada* 177 F11 45 28N 71 9W
Megargel, *TX, U.S.A.* 99 D9 33 27N 98 56W
Mégiscane →, *Qué., Canada* 176 C7 48 29N 75 38W
Mégiscane, L., *Qué., Canada* 176 C7 48 35N 75 55W
Megueyera, Cerro la, *Michoacan, Mexico* 218 D5 18 25N 102 34W
Mehatl Creek Park ⌂, *B.C., Canada* 187 E12 50 3N 122 2W
Meherrin →, *VA, U.S.A.* 102 E8 36 26N 76 57W
Mehlville, *MO, U.S.A.* 82 C6 38 30N 90 19W
Meighen I., *Nunavut, Canada* 190 A5 80 0N 99 30W
Meigs, *GA, U.S.A.* 68 E2 31 4N 84 6W

Meigs County ☆, *OH, U.S.A.* **92 D4** 39 3N 82 8W
Meigs County ☆, *TN, U.S.A.* **97 E8** 35 31N 84 47W
Meiss L., *CA, U.S.A.* **64 B4** 41 52N 122 4W
Mejía, I., *Baja Calif., Mexico* **210 D5** 29 36N 113 37W
Mékinac, L., *Qué., Canada* **177 D10** 47 3N 72 41W
Mekinock, *ND, U.S.A.* **91 B8** 48 1N 97 22W
Mekoryuk, *AK, U.S.A.* **61 F6** 60 23N 166 11W
Melba, *ID, U.S.A.* **70 F2** 43 23N 116 32W
Melbourne, *AR, U.S.A.* **63 B4** 36 4N 91 54W
Melbourne, *FL, U.S.A.* **67 C8** 28 5N 80 37W
Melbourne, *IA, U.S.A.* **73 D5** 41 57N 93 6W
Melbourne, *KY, U.S.A.* **107 B2** 39 1N 84 21W
Melbourne I., *Nunavut, Canada* **190 D5** 68 30N 104 45W
Melcher-Dallas, *IA, U.S.A.* **73 D5** 41 14N 93 15W
Melchor Múzquiz, *Coahuila, Mexico* **214 C3** 27 53N 101 31W
Melchor Ocampo, *Durango, Mexico* **216 B5** 25 22N 105 16W
Melchor Ocampo, *Nuevo León, Mexico* **214 D5** 26 4N 99 32W
Melchor Ocampo, *Zacatecas, Mexico* **217 C9** 24 51N 101 39W
Meldrum Bay, *Ont., Canada* **178 B3** 45 56N 83 6W
Meldrum Creek, *B.C., Canada* **187 C12** 52 6N 122 21W
Mélèzes ➝, *Qué., Canada* **175 B4** 57 40N 69 29W
Melfa, *VA, U.S.A.* **102 D9** 37 39N 75 45W
Melfort, *Sask., Canada* **182 C7** 52 50N 104 37W
Melissa, *TX, U.S.A.* **99 D11** 33 17N 96 34W
Melita, *Man., Canada* **183 F11** 49 15N 101 0W
Melitota, *MD, U.S.A.* **77 A4** 39 16N 76 9W
Mellen, *WI, U.S.A.* **103 B3** 46 20N 90 40W
Mellette, *SD, U.S.A.* **91 E7** 45 9N 98 30W
Mellette County ☆, *SD, U.S.A.* **91 G5** 43 35N 101 0W
Mellott, *IN, U.S.A.* **72 C3** 40 10N 87 9W
Mellwood, *AR, U.S.A.* **63 D5** 34 12N 90 56W
Melrose, *IA, U.S.A.* **73 E5** 40 59N 93 3W
Melrose, *MA, U.S.A.* **78 B3** 42 27N 71 2W
Melrose, *MN, U.S.A.* **80 E4** 45 40N 94 49W
Melrose, *MT, U.S.A.* **83 E5** 45 38N 112 41W
Melrose, *NM, U.S.A.* **88 C7** 34 26N 103 38W
Melrose, *NY, U.S.A.* **114 B3** 40 49N 73 55W
Melrose, *NY, U.S.A.* **78 B1** 42 51N 73 37W
Melrose, *WI, U.S.A.* **103 D2** 44 8N 91 1W
Melrose Park, *Chicago, U.S.A.* **108 B1** 41 53N 87 50W
Melrose Park, *Miami, U.S.A.* **112 B3** 26 6N 80 11W
Melrose Park, *PA, U.S.A.* **116 A2** 40 3N 75 7W
Melstone, *MT, U.S.A.* **83 D10** 46 36N 107 52W
Melstrand, *MI, U.S.A.* **79 C5** 46 28N 86 25W
Melton Hill L., *TN, U.S.A.* **97 E8** 35 53N 84 18W
Melvern, *KS, U.S.A.* **74 C8** 38 30N 95 38W
Melvern Lake, *KS, U.S.A.* **74 C8** 38 30N 95 50W
Melville, *Sask., Canada* **182 E9** 50 55N 102 50W
Melville, *LA, U.S.A.* **75 D4** 30 42N 91 45W
Melville, L., *Nfld. & L., Canada* **175 C6** 53 30N 60 0W
Melville Hills, *Canada* **188 C8** 68 57N 120 45W
Melville I., *Canada* **188 A10** 75 30N 112 0W
Melville Pen., *Nunavut, Canada* **190 D9** 68 0N 84 0W
Melville Sd., *Nunavut, Canada* **190 D4** 68 10N 107 0W
Melvin, *AL, U.S.A.* **60 E2** 31 55N 88 27W
Melvin, *IL, U.S.A.* **71 C5** 40 34N 88 15W
Melvin, *TX, U.S.A.* **99 F8** 31 12N 99 35W
Melvin Village, *NH, U.S.A.* **86 C3** 43 42N 71 28W
Melvina, *WI, U.S.A.* **103 E3** 43 48N 90 47W
Melvindale, *MI, U.S.A.* **109 B1** 42 13N 83 10W
Memorial Park, *Houston, U.S.A.* **110 B2** 29 45N 95 26W
Memphis, *FL, U.S.A.* **67 D6** 27 32N 82 34W
Memphis, *MI, U.S.A.* **79 G9** 42 54N 82 46W
Memphis, *MO, U.S.A.* **82 A4** 40 28N 92 10W
Memphis, *NE, U.S.A.* **84 C9** 41 6N 96 26W
Memphis, *TN, U.S.A.* **96 E2** 35 8N 90 2W
Memphis, *TX, U.S.A.* **98 C7** 34 44N 100 33W
Memphis International ✕ (MEM), *TN, U.S.A.* **96 E3** 35 3N 89 59W
Memphrémagog, L., *Qué., Canada* **177 F10** 45 8N 72 17W
Memramcook, *N.B., Canada* **173 J5** 45 58N 64 35W
Mena, *AR, U.S.A.* **63 D1** 34 35N 94 15W
Menahga, *MN, U.S.A.* **80 D3** 46 45N 95 6W
Menan, *ID, U.S.A.* **70 F7** 43 43N 111 59W
Menard, *MT, U.S.A.* **83 E6** 45 59N 111 10W
Menard, *TX, U.S.A.* **99 G8** 30 55N 99 47W
Menard County ☆, *IL, U.S.A.* **71 C4** 40 0N 89 50W
Menard County ☆, *TX, U.S.A.* **99 G8** 30 55N 99 45W
Ménascouagama, L., *Qué., Canada* **172 B8** 51 13N 61 52W
Menasha, *WI, U.S.A.* **103 D5** 44 13N 88 26W
Mendenhall, *MS, U.S.A.* **81 E4** 31 58N 89 52W
Mendenhall, C., *AK, U.S.A.* **61 G6** 59 45N 166 10W
Mendham, *Sask., Canada* **182 E2** 50 46N 109 40W
Mendham, *NJ, U.S.A.* **87 B2** 40 47N 74 36W
Mendocino, *CA, U.S.A.* **64 D3** 39 19N 123 48W
Mendocino, C., *CA, U.S.A.* **64 C2** 40 26N 124 25W
Mendocino, L., *CA, U.S.A.* **64 D3** 39 12N 123 11W
Mendocino County ☆, *CA, U.S.A.* **64 D3** 39 20N 123 20W
Mendocino Nat. Forest, *CA, U.S.A.* **64 D4** 39 45N 122 50W
Mendon, *MI, U.S.A.* **79 G6** 42 0N 85 27W
Mendon, *MO, U.S.A.* **82 B3** 39 36N 93 8W
Mendon, *OH, U.S.A.* **92 C2** 40 40N 84 31W
Mendon, *VT, U.S.A.* **86 C2** 43 40N 72 54W
Mendota, *CA, U.S.A.* **65 G6** 36 45N 120 23W
Mendota, *IL, U.S.A.* **71 B4** 41 33N 89 7W
Mendota, *Minneapolis-St. Paul, U.S.A.* **113 B3** 44 53N 93 9W
Mendota, L., *WI, U.S.A.* **103 E4** 43 7N 89 25W
Mendota Heights, *Minneapolis-St. Paul, U.S.A.* **113 B3** 44 53N 93 8W
Menifee County ☆, *KY, U.S.A.* **97 C9** 37 55N 83 35W
Menihek, *Nfld. & L., Canada* **175 C6** 54 28N 56 36W
Menihek L., *Nfld. & L., Canada* **175 C6** 54 0N 67 0W
Ménistouc, L., *Qué., Canada* **172 A3** 52 52N 66 29W
Menlo, *GA, U.S.A.* **68 B1** 34 29N 85 29W
Menlo, *IA, U.S.A.* **73 D4** 41 31N 94 24W
Menlo, *KS, U.S.A.* **74 B3** 39 21N 100 43W
Menlo, *WA, U.S.A.* **101 D2** 46 38N 123 39W
Menlo Park, *CA, U.S.A.* **64 F4** 37 27N 122 12W
Menlo Park Terrace, *NJ, U.S.A.* **114 C1** 40 33N 74 19W
Menno, *SD, U.S.A.* **91 G8** 43 14N 97 34W
Meno, *OK, U.S.A.* **93 B5** 36 23N 98 11W
Menominee, *MI, U.S.A.* **79 D4** 45 6N 87 37W
Menominee ➝, *U.S.A.* **103 C6** 45 6N 87 35W
Menominee County ☆, *MI, U.S.A.* **79 D4** 45 30N 87 40W
Menominee County ☆, *WI, U.S.A.* **103 C5** 45 0N 88 45W
Menominee Ind. Reservation, *WI, U.S.A.* **103 C5** 45 0N 88 45W
Menominee Ra., *MI, U.S.A.* **79 B3** 46 0N 88 10W
Menomonee Falls, *WI, U.S.A.* **103 E5** 43 10N 88 7W
Menomonie, *WI, U.S.A.* **103 D2** 44 53N 91 55W
Mentasta Lake, *AK, U.S.A.* **61 E12** 62 55N 143 45W
Mentone, *IN, U.S.A.* **72 B4** 41 10N 86 2W
Mentone, *TX, U.S.A.* **98 F4** 31 42N 103 36W
Mentor, *MN, U.S.A.* **80 C2** 47 42N 96 9W
Mentor, *OH, U.S.A.* **92 B5** 41 40N 81 21W
Mentor-on-the-Lake, *OH, U.S.A.* **92 B5** 41 43N 81 22W
Meoqui, *Chihuahua, Mexico* **213 E10** 28 17N 105 29W
Meota, *Sask., Canada* **182 B3** 53 2N 108 27W
Mequon, *WI, U.S.A.* **103 E6** 43 14N 87 59W
Mer Rouge, *LA, U.S.A.* **75 B4** 32 47N 91 48W
Meramec ➝, *MO, U.S.A.* **82 C6** 38 24N 90 21W
Meramec State Park ⌂, *MO, U.S.A.* **82 C5** 38 13N 91 5W
Merasheen I., *Nfld. & L., Canada* **174 E6** 47 25N 54 15W
Meraux, *New Orleans, U.S.A.* **113 C3** 29 55N 89 56W
Merced, *CA, U.S.A.* **64 F6** 37 18N 120 29W
Merced ➝, *CA, U.S.A.* **64 F6** 37 21N 120 59W
Merced, L., *San Francisco, U.S.A.* **118 B2** 37 43N 122 29W
Merced County ☆, *CA, U.S.A.* **64 F6** 37 15N 120 30W
Mercedes, *TX, U.S.A.* **98 L10** 26 9N 97 55W
Mercenarios, Pta., *Baja Calif. S., Mexico* **211 G7** 26 20N 111 23W
Mercer, *ME, U.S.A.* **76 D4** 44 41N 69 56W
Mercer, *MO, U.S.A.* **82 A3** 40 31N 93 32W
Mercer, *ND, U.S.A.* **91 C5** 47 29N 100 43W
Mercer, *PA, U.S.A.* **95 C2** 41 14N 80 15W
Mercer, *TN, U.S.A.* **96 E3** 35 29N 89 2W
Mercer, *WI, U.S.A.* **103 B3** 46 10N 90 4W
Mercer County ☆, *IL, U.S.A.* **71 B3** 41 15N 90 40W
Mercer County ☆, *KY, U.S.A.* **97 C8** 37 50N 84 50W
Mercer County ☆, *MO, U.S.A.* **82 A3** 40 25N 93 30W
Mercer County ☆, *ND, U.S.A.* **91 C4** 47 15N 102 0W
Mercer County ☆, *NJ, U.S.A.* **87 B2** 40 13N 74 40W
Mercer County ☆, *OH, U.S.A.* **92 C2** 40 33N 84 35W
Mercer County ☆, *PA, U.S.A.* **95 C2** 41 15N 80 10W
Mercer County ☆, *WV, U.S.A.* **102 D3** 37 22N 81 6W
Mercer Island, *WA, U.S.A.* **101 C3** 47 34N 122 13W
Mercersburg, *PA, U.S.A.* **77 A3** 39 50N 77 54W
Mercerville, *NJ, U.S.A.* **87 B2** 40 14N 74 41W
Merchantville, *NJ, U.S.A.* **116 B2** 39 56N 75 4W
Mercier, *Qué., Canada* **177 F9** 45 19N 73 45W
Mercoal, *Alta., Canada* **184 E3** 53 10N 117 5W
Mercury, *NV, U.S.A.* **85 F5** 36 40N 115 59W
Mercury, *TX, U.S.A.* **99 F8** 31 28N 99 10W
Mercy, C., *Nunavut, Canada* **191 E13** 65 0N 63 30W
Mercy B., *N.W.T., Canada* **188 B9** 74 5N 119 0W
Meredith, *CO, U.S.A.* **66 C4** 39 22N 106 44W
Meredith, *NH, U.S.A.* **86 C3** 43 39N 71 30W
Meredith, L., *CO, U.S.A.* **66 D7** 38 12N 103 43W
Meredith, L., *TX, U.S.A.* **98 B6** 35 43N 101 33W
Meredosia, *IL, U.S.A.* **71 D3** 39 50N 90 34W
Meredosia Nat. Wildlife Refuge ⌂, *IL, U.S.A.* **71 D3** 39 53N 90 34W
Mérida, *Baja Calif., Mexico* **210 A4** 32 41N 114 55W
Mérida, *Yucatán, Mexico* **223 B4** 20 58N 89 37W
Meriden, *CT, U.S.A.* **78 C2** 41 32N 72 48W
Meriden, *IA, U.S.A.* **73 C3** 42 48N 95 38W
Meriden, *KS, U.S.A.* **74 B8** 39 11N 95 34W
Meriden, *NH, U.S.A.* **86 C2** 43 36N 72 16W
Meriden, *WY, U.S.A.* **104 E8** 41 33N 104 19W
Meridian, *GA, U.S.A.* **68 E5** 31 27N 81 23W
Meridian, *ID, U.S.A.* **70 F2** 43 37N 116 24W
Meridian, *MS, U.S.A.* **81 D5** 32 22N 88 42W
Meridian, *OK, U.S.A.* **93 C6** 35 48N 97 15W
Meridian, *TX, U.S.A.* **99 F10** 31 56N 97 39W
Meridian Hills, *Indianapolis, U.S.A.* **110 A2** 39 53N 86 9W
Meridianville, *AL, U.S.A.* **60 B4** 34 51N 86 34W
Merigold, *MS, U.S.A.* **81 C3** 33 50N 90 43W
Merigomish, *N.S., Canada* **173 H7** 45 38N 62 26W
Meriwether County ☆, *GA, U.S.A.* **68 C2** 33 0N 84 40W
Merizo, *Guam* **105 b** 13 16N 144 40W
Merkel, *TX, U.S.A.* **99 E7** 32 28N 100 1W
Merlin, *OR, U.S.A.* **94 E2** 42 31N 123 25W
Mermentau, *LA, U.S.A.* **75 D3** 30 11N 92 35W
Merna, *NE, U.S.A.* **84 C6** 41 29N 99 46W
Merrick, *NY, U.S.A.* **87 B3** 40 40N 73 33W
Merrick County ☆, *NE, U.S.A.* **84 C7** 41 15N 98 0W
Merrickville, *Ont., Canada* **179 C11** 44 55N 75 50W
Merricourt, *ND, U.S.A.* **91 D7** 46 12N 98 46W
Merrill, *IA, U.S.A.* **73 C2** 42 43N 96 15W
Merrill, *MI, U.S.A.* **79 F7** 43 25N 84 20W
Merrill, *MS, U.S.A.* **81 F5** 30 59N 88 43W
Merrill, *OR, U.S.A.* **94 E4** 42 1N 121 36W
Merrill, *WI, U.S.A.* **103 C4** 45 11N 89 41W
Merrillan, *WI, U.S.A.* **103 D3** 44 27N 90 50W
Merrillville, *GA, U.S.A.* **68 F3** 30 57N 83 53W
Merrillville, *IN, U.S.A.* **72 B3** 41 29N 87 20W
Merrimac, *MA, U.S.A.* **78 B3** 42 50N 71 0W
Merrimac, *WI, U.S.A.* **103 E4** 43 22N 89 37W
Merrimack, *NH, U.S.A.* **86 D4** 42 49N 70 49W
Merrimack, *NH, U.S.A.* **86 D3** 42 52N 71 30W
Merrimack ➝, *MA, U.S.A.* **78 B4** 42 49N 70 49W
Merrimack County ☆, *NH, U.S.A.* **86 C3** 43 15N 71 45W
Merriman, *NE, U.S.A.* **84 B4** 42 55N 101 42W
Merrionette Park, *Chicago, U.S.A.* **108 C2** 41 41N 87 40W
Merritt, *B.C., Canada* **187 E14** 50 10N 120 45W
Merritt, *WA, U.S.A.* **101 C5** 47 47N 120 50W
Merritt, L., *San Francisco, U.S.A.* **118 B3** 37 48N 122 15W
Merritt Island, *FL, U.S.A.* **67 C8** 28 21N 80 42W
Merritt Island Nat. Wildlife Refuge ⌂, *FL, U.S.A.* **67 C8** 28 40N 80 42W
Merritt Res., *NE, U.S.A.* **84 B5** 42 38N 100 53W
Merry I., *N.W.T., Canada* **175 B2** 55 29N 77 31W
Merryville, *LA, U.S.A.* **75 D2** 30 45N 93 33W
Mersey ➝, *N.S., Canada* **173 J5** 44 2N 64 43W
Mershon, *GA, U.S.A.* **68 E4** 31 28N 82 15W
Mertzon, *TX, U.S.A.* **98 F7** 31 16N 100 49W
Merville, *B.C., Canada* **186 F9** 49 48N 125 3W
Mervin, *Sask., Canada* **182 B3** 53 20N 108 53W
Mesa, *AZ, U.S.A.* **62 D4** 33 25N 111 50W
Mesa, *CO, U.S.A.* **66 C2** 39 10N 108 8W
Mesa, *ID, U.S.A.* **70 E2** 44 38N 116 27W
Mesa, *WA, U.S.A.* **101 D6** 46 35N 119 0W
Mesa County ☆, *CO, U.S.A.* **66 C2** 39 0N 108 30W
Mesa de los Ríos, *Nayarit, Mexico* **216 E5** 22 50N 105 6W
Mesa del Nayar, *Nayarit, Mexico* **216 E6** 22 16N 104 35W
Mesa del Seri, *Sonora, Mexico* **212 D5** 29 8N 110 50W
Mesa Tres Rios, *Sonora, Mexico* **212 D7** 29 52N 108 44W
Mesa Verde, *CO, U.S.A.* **66 E2** 37 15N 108 45W
Mesa Verde Nat. Park △, *CO, U.S.A.* **66 E2** 37 11N 108 29W
Mesabi Iron Range, *MN, U.S.A.* **80 C6** 47 40N 92 45W
Mescalero, *NM, U.S.A.* **88 D5** 33 9N 105 46W
Mescalero Apache Indian Reservation, *NM, U.S.A.* **88 D5** 33 12N 105 40W
Meservey, *IA, U.S.A.* **73 C5** 42 55N 93 29W
Mesgouez, L., *Qué., Canada* **175 C2** 51 20N 75 0W
Mesick, *MI, U.S.A.* **79 E6** 44 24N 85 43W
Mesilinka ➝, *B.C., Canada* **189 E8** 56 6N 124 30W
Mesita, *CO, U.S.A.* **66 E5** 37 6N 105 36W
Mesita, *NM, U.S.A.* **88 B3** 35 1N 107 19W
Mesquite, *NM, U.S.A.* **88 E4** 32 10N 106 42W
Mesquite, *NV, U.S.A.* **85 E6** 36 48N 114 4W
Mesquite, *TX, U.S.A.* **99 E11** 32 46N 96 36W
Mesquite L., *CA, U.S.A.* **65 H11** 35 43N 115 35W
Messines, *Qué., Canada* **176 E6** 46 14N 76 2W
Meta, *MO, U.S.A.* **82 C4** 38 19N 92 10W
Meta Incognita Pen., *Nunavut, Canada* **191 E12** 62 45N 68 30W
Metairie, *LA, U.S.A.* **75 E5** 29 59N 90 9W
Metaline, *WA, U.S.A.* **101 B8** 48 51N 117 23W
Metaline Falls, *WA, U.S.A.* **101 B8** 48 52N 117 22W
Metamora, *IL, U.S.A.* **71 C4** 40 47N 89 22W
Metamora, *MI, U.S.A.* **79 G8** 42 57N 83 17W
Metamoras, *PA, U.S.A.* **87 A2** 41 22N 74 42W
Metcalf, *GA, U.S.A.* **68 F3** 30 43N 83 59W
Metcalf, *IL, U.S.A.* **71 D6** 39 48N 87 48W
Metcalfe County ☆, *KY, U.S.A.* **97 D7** 37 0N 85 40W
Meteghan, *N.S., Canada* **173 J3** 44 11N 66 10W
Metepec, *Hidalgo, Mexico* **219 B9** 20 14N 98 19W
Metepec, *México, Mexico* **219 C8** 19 15N 99 36W
Methow, *WA, U.S.A.* **101 B6** 48 8N 120 0W
Methow ➝, *WA, U.S.A.* **101 B6** 48 5N 119 56W
Methuen, *MA, U.S.A.* **78 B3** 42 44N 71 11W
Métis-sur-Mer, *Qué., Canada* **172 E2** 48 40N 67 59W
Metlakatla, *AK, U.S.A.* **61 J15** 55 8N 131 35W
Metlaltoyuca, *Puebla, Mexico* **220 D3** 20 44N 97 51W
Metlatonoc, *Guerrero, Mexico* **219 E9** 17 11N 98 20W
Metolius, *OR, U.S.A.* **94 C4** 44 35N 121 11W
Metropolis, *IL, U.S.A.* **71 F5** 37 9N 88 44W
Metter, *GA, U.S.A.* **68 D4** 32 24N 82 3W
Metuchen, *NJ, U.S.A.* **87 B2** 40 32N 74 22W
Metz, *MO, U.S.A.* **82 D2** 37 59N 94 27W
Metzger, *Portland, U.S.A.* **116 B1** 45 26N 122 45W
Metzquititlán, *Hidalgo, Mexico* **219 B9** 20 33N 98 37W
Metztitlán, *Hidalgo, Mexico* **219 B9** 20 36N 98 45W
Mexcaltepec, Cerro, *Guerrero, Mexico* **219 E9** 17 4N 98 53W
Mexcaltitán, *Nayarit, Mexico* **216 F5** 21 55N 105 31W
Mexia, *TX, U.S.A.* **99 F11** 31 41N 96 29W
Mexicali, *Mexico* **210 A3** 32 40N 115 30W
Mexican Hat, *UT, U.S.A.* **100 F6** 37 9N 109 52W
Mexican Springs, *NM, U.S.A.* **88 B2** 35 47N 108 50W
Mexican Water, *AZ, U.S.A.* **62 A6** 36 57N 109 32W
Mexicanos, L. de los, *Chihuahua, Mexico* **213 E9** 28 9N 106 57W
Mexico, *IN, U.S.A.* **72 C4** 40 49N 86 7W
Mexico, *ME, U.S.A.* **76 D3** 44 34N 70 33W
Mexico, *MO, U.S.A.* **82 B5** 39 10N 91 53W
Mexico, *NY, U.S.A.* **89 B4** 43 28N 76 14W
México □, *Mexico* **219 C8** 19 20N 99 30W
México, Ciudad de, *Distrito Federal, Mexico* **219 C8** 19 24N 99 9W
Mexico B., *NY, U.S.A.* **89 B4** 43 35N 76 20W
Mexico Beach, *FL, U.S.A.* **67 B3** 29 57N 85 25W
Mexico City International ✕ (MEX), *Distrito Federal, Mexico* **219 C8** 19 30N 99 7W
Mexquitic de Carmona, *San Luis Potosí, Mexico* **215 H3** 22 16N 101 7W
Mexticaćan, *Jalisco, Mexico* **218 A5** 21 13N 102 43W
Meyerland, *Houston, U.S.A.* **110 B2** 29 41N 95 28W
Meyers Chuck, *AK, U.S.A.* **61 J14** 55 45N 132 15W
Meyersdale, *PA, U.S.A.* **77 A1** 39 49N 79 2W
Meyronne, *Sask., Canada* **182 F5** 49 39N 106 50W
Mezacalapa ➝, *Tabasco, Mexico* **222 B3** 17 22N 93 23W
Mezcala ➝, *Guerrero, Mexico* **219 E8** 17 58N 99 42W
Mezontepec, Cerro, *Distrito Federal, Mexico* **225 C2** 19 11N 99 14W
Mezquital, *Durango, Mexico* **217 D6** 23 29N 104 23W
Mezquital, *Tamaulipas, Mexico* **215 E7** 25 15N 97 26W
Mezquital ➝, *Mexico* **216 E6** 22 54N 104 54W
Mezquital del Oro, *Zacatecas, Mexico* **218 A4** 21 10N 103 23W
Mezquitic, *Jalisco, Mexico* **217 E7** 22 23N 103 41W
Miacatlán, *Morelos, Mexico* **219 D8** 18 46N 99 17W
Miahuatlán, *Oaxaca, Mexico* **221 H4** 16 20N 96 36W
Miami, *AZ, U.S.A.* **62 D5** 33 24N 110 52W
Miami, *FL, U.S.A.* **67 F8** 25 46N 80 11W
Miami, *MO, U.S.A.* **82 B3** 39 19N 93 14W
Miami, *NM, U.S.A.* **88 A6** 36 21N 104 48W
Miami, *OK, U.S.A.* **93 B9** 36 53N 94 53W
Miami, *TX, U.S.A.* **98 B7** 35 42N 100 38W
Miami Beach, *FL, U.S.A.* **67 F8** 25 47N 80 7W
Miami Canal, *FL, U.S.A.* **67 E8** 26 30N 80 45W
Miami County ☆, *IN, U.S.A.* **72 C4** 40 45N 86 0W
Miami County ☆, *KS, U.S.A.* **74 C9** 38 30N 94 45W
Miami County ☆, *OH, U.S.A.* **92 C2** 40 9N 84 15W
Miami-Dade County ☆, *FL, U.S.A.* **67 F8** 25 30N 80 30W
Miami International ✕ (MIA), *FL, U.S.A.* **67 F8** 25 48N 80 17W
Miami Lakes, *Miami, U.S.A.* **112 C1** 25 54N 80 18W
Miami Shores, *FL, U.S.A.* **67 F8** 25 51N 80 11W
Miami Springs, *FL, U.S.A.* **67 F8** 25 49N 80 17W
Miamisburg, *OH, U.S.A.* **92 D2** 39 38N 84 17W
Mica Creek, *B.C., Canada* **187 C16** 52 2N 118 35W
Micanopy, *FL, U.S.A.* **67 B6** 29 30N 82 17W
Micco, *FL, U.S.A.* **67 D8** 27 53N 80 30W
Miccosukee, *FL, U.S.A.* **67 A4** 30 36N 84 3W
Miccosukee, L., *FL, U.S.A.* **67 A5** 30 33N 83 53W
Miccosukee Indian Reservation, *FL, U.S.A.* **67 F8** 25 46N 80 46W
Michelsen, C., *Nunavut, Canada* **190 C5** 70 42N 103 3W
Michie, *TN, U.S.A.* **96 E4** 35 3N 88 26W
Michigamme, L., *MI, U.S.A.* **79 C3** 46 32N 88 5W
Michigamme Res., *MI, U.S.A.* **79 C3** 46 10N 88 10W
Michigan, *ND, U.S.A.* **91 B7** 48 1N 98 7W
Michigan □, *U.S.A.* **79 F7** 44 0N 85 0W
Michigan, L., *U.S.A.* **79 F5** 44 0N 87 0W
Michigan, L., *MI, U.S.A.* **79 G7** 42 14N 84 20W
Michigan Center, *MI, U.S.A.* **72 B4** 41 43N 86 54W
Michigan City, *IN, U.S.A.* **81 B4** 34 59N 89 15W
Michigan City, *MS, U.S.A.* **103 B3** 46 53N 90 29W
Michigan I., *WI, U.S.A.*
Michigan Islands Nat. Wildlife Refuge ⌂, *MI, U.S.A.* **79 D6** 45 42N 85 50W
Michigantown, *IN, U.S.A.* **72 C4** 40 20N 86 24W
Michipicoten, *Ont., Canada* **181 E12** 47 55N 84 55W
Michipicoten B., *Ont., Canada* **181 E12** 47 53N 84 53W
Michipicoten I., *Ont., Canada* **181 E11** 47 40N 85 40W
Michoacán □, *Mexico* **218 C6** 19 10N 101 50W
Midale, *Sask., Canada* **182 F8** 49 25N 103 20W
Middle ➝, *MN, U.S.A.* **80 B1** 48 22N 97 5W
Middle Alkali L., *CA, U.S.A.* **64 B6** 41 27N 120 5W
Middle Bass I., *OH, U.S.A.* **92 B4** 41 41N 82 48W
Middle Bay, *Qué., Canada* **174 A3** 51 28N 57 30W
Middle Bay, *NY, U.S.A.* **114 C5** 40 37N 73 36W
Middle Branch ➝, *Baltimore, U.S.A.* **107 B2** 39 15N 76 37W
Middle Concho ➝, *TX, U.S.A.* **98 F7** 31 27N 100 25W
Middle Falls, *NY, U.S.A.* **86 C1** 43 6N 73 32W
Middle Fork Feather ➝, *CA, U.S.A.* **64 E5** 38 33N 121 30W
Middle Fork Forked Deer ➝, *TN, U.S.A.* **96 D3** 36 1N 89 13W
Middle Fork John Day ➝, *OR, U.S.A.* **94 C6** 44 45N 119 38W
Middle Fork Powder ➝, *WY, U.S.A.* **104 C6** 43 42N 106 34W
Middle Fork Sappa Cr. ➝, *KS, U.S.A.* **74 B3** 39 42N 100 51W
Middle Granville, *NY, U.S.A.* **86 C1** 43 26N 73 17W
Middle Island, *NY, U.S.A.* **78 D2** 40 53N 72 56W
Middle Lake, *Sask., Canada* **182 C6** 52 29N 105 18W
Middle Loup ➝, *NE, U.S.A.* **84 C7** 41 17N 98 24W
Middle Musquodoboit, *N.S., Canada* **173 H6** 45 3N 63 9W
Middle Pease ➝, *TX, U.S.A.* **98 C7** 34 15N 100 7W
Middle Point, *OH, U.S.A.* **92 C2** 40 51N 84 27W
Middle Ridge Wildlife Reserve ⌂, *Nfld. & L., Canada* **174 D5** 48 15N 55 16W
Middle River, *MD, U.S.A.* **77 A4** 39 20N 76 27W
Middle River, *MN, U.S.A.* **80 B2** 48 26N 96 10W
Middle Valley, *TN, U.S.A.* **97 E7** 35 12N 85 11W
Middle Village, *NY, U.S.A.* **114 B3** 40 43N 73 52W
Middleboro, *MA, U.S.A.* **78 C4** 41 54N 70 55W
Middlebourne, *WV, U.S.A.* **102 B4** 39 30N 80 54W
Middleburg, *FL, U.S.A.* **67 A7** 30 4N 81 52W
Middleburg, *PA, U.S.A.* **95 D5** 40 47N 77 3W
Middleburg, *VA, U.S.A.* **77 B3** 38 58N 77 44W
Middleburg Heights, *Cleveland, U.S.A.* **107 B1** 41 22N 81 48W
Middleburgh, *NY, U.S.A.* **89 C6** 42 36N 74 20W
Middlebury, *CT, U.S.A.* **78 C1** 41 32N 73 7W
Middlebury, *IN, U.S.A.* **72 B5** 41 41N 85 42W
Middlebury, *VT, U.S.A.* **86 B1** 44 1N 73 10W
Middlefield, *MA, U.S.A.* **78 B1** 42 20N 73 2W
Middlefield, *OH, U.S.A.* **92 B5** 41 28N 81 5W
Middlegate, *NV, U.S.A.* **85 C2** 39 17N 118 2W
Middleport, *NY, U.S.A.* **89 B2** 43 13N 78 29W
Middleport, *OH, U.S.A.* **92 D4** 39 0N 82 3W
Middlesboro, *KY, U.S.A.* **97 D9** 36 36N 83 43W
Middlesex, *NC, U.S.A.* **90 C7** 35 47N 78 12W
Middlesex County ☆, *CT, U.S.A.* **78 C2** 41 25N 72 30W
Middlesex County ☆, *MA, U.S.A.* **78 B3** 42 20N 71 15W
Middlesex County ☆, *NJ, U.S.A.* **87 B2** 40 30N 74 25W
Middlesex County ☆, *VA, U.S.A.* **102 D8** 37 36N 76 36W
Middlesex Fells Reservation, *Boston, U.S.A.* **106 A3** 42 27N 71 6W
Middleton, *N.S., Canada* **173 J4** 44 57N 65 4W
Middleton, *ID, U.S.A.* **70 F2** 43 42N 116 37W
Middleton, *MA, U.S.A.* **78 B3** 42 36N 71 1W
Middleton, *MI, U.S.A.* **79 F7** 43 11N 84 43W
Middleton, *TN, U.S.A.* **96 E4** 35 4N 88 53W
Middleton, *WI, U.S.A.* **103 E4** 43 6N 89 30W
Middleton I., *AK, U.S.A.* **61 G11** 59 26N 146 20W
Middletown, *CA, U.S.A.* **64 E4** 38 45N 122 37W
Middletown, *CT, U.S.A.* **78 C2** 41 34N 72 39W
Middletown, *DE, U.S.A.* **77 A5** 39 27N 75 43W
Middletown, *IL, U.S.A.* **71 C4** 40 11N 89 35W
Middletown, *IN, U.S.A.* **72 C5** 40 3N 85 32W
Middletown, *MD, U.S.A.* **77 A3** 39 27N 77 33W
Middletown, *MO, U.S.A.* **82 B5** 39 8N 91 25W
Middletown, *NJ, U.S.A.* **87 B2** 40 24N 74 8W
Middletown, *NY, U.S.A.* **87 A2** 41 27N 74 25W
Middletown, *OH, U.S.A.* **92 D2** 39 31N 84 24W
Middletown, *PA, U.S.A.* **95 D6** 40 12N 76 44W
Middletown, *RI, U.S.A.* **78 C3** 41 32N 71 17W
Middletown, *VA, U.S.A.* **77 A2** 39 2N 78 17W
Middletown Springs, *VT, U.S.A.* **86 C1** 43 28N 73 8W
Middleville, *MI, U.S.A.* **79 G6** 42 43N 85 28W
Middleville, *NY, U.S.A.* **89 B6** 43 8N 74 58W
Middlewood, *N.S., Canada* **173 J5** 44 14N 64 34W
Midland, *Ont., Canada* **178 C7** 44 45N 79 50W
Midland, *CA, U.S.A.* **65 K12** 33 52N 114 48W
Midland, *MD, U.S.A.* **77 A2** 39 37N 78 55W
Midland, *MI, U.S.A.* **79 F7** 43 37N 84 14W
Midland, *OR, U.S.A.* **94 E4** 42 8N 121 49W
Midland, *SD, U.S.A.* **91 F4** 44 4N 101 10W
Midland, *TX, U.S.A.* **98 F5** 32 0N 102 3W
Midland Beach, *NY, U.S.A.* **114 C2** 40 34N 74 6W
Midland City, *AL, U.S.A.* **60 E5** 31 19N 85 30W
Midland County ☆, *MI, U.S.A.* **79 F7** 43 35N 84 20W
Midland County ☆, *TX, U.S.A.* **98 F5** 32 0N 102 0W
Midlothian, *MD, U.S.A.* **77 A2** 39 40N 78 58W
Midlothian, *TX, U.S.A.* **99 E11** 32 30N 97 0W
Midlothian, *VA, U.S.A.* **102 D7** 37 30N 77 28W
Midnight, *MS, U.S.A.* **81 C3** 33 3N 90 35W
Midvale, *ID, U.S.A.* **70 E2** 44 28N 116 44W
Midvale, *OH, U.S.A.* **92 C5** 40 26N 81 23W
Midvale, *UT, U.S.A.* **100 C4** 40 36N 111 53W
Midville, *GA, U.S.A.* **68 D4** 32 49N 82 14W
Midway, *B.C., Canada* **187 F16** 49 1N 118 48W
Midway, *AL, U.S.A.* **60 D5** 32 5N 85 31W
Midway, *FL, U.S.A.* **67 A4** 30 30N 84 27W
Midway, *GA, U.S.A.* **68 E5** 31 48N 81 26W
Midway, *KY, U.S.A.* **97 B8** 38 9N 84 41W
Midway, *TX, U.S.A.* **99 F12** 31 2N 95 45W
Midway, *UT, U.S.A.* **100 C4** 40 31N 111 28W
Midwest, *U.S.A.* **53 B9** 42 0N 90 0W
Midwest, *WY, U.S.A.* **104 C6** 43 25N 106 16W
Midwest City, *OK, U.S.A.* **93 C6** 35 27N 97 24W
Midwood, *Charlotte, U.S.A.* **107 A2** 35 13N 80 48W
Mier, *Tamaulipas, Mexico* **214 D5** 26 26N 99 9W
Mier y Noriega, *Nuevo León, Mexico* **215 G4** 23 25N 100 7W
Miesville, *MN, U.S.A.* **80 F6** 44 36N 92 49W
Miette Hotsprings, *Alta., Canada* **184 E3** 53 8N 117 46W
Mifflin, *OH, U.S.A.* **92 C4** 40 46N 82 22W
Mifflin County ☆, *PA, U.S.A.* **95 D5** 40 45N 77 45W
Mifflinburg, *PA, U.S.A.* **95 D5** 40 55N 77 3W
Mifflintown, *PA, U.S.A.* **95 D5** 40 34N 77 24W
Miguel Alemán, *Sonora, Mexico* **212 E4** 28 50N 111 30W
Miguel Alemán, Presa, *Oaxaca, Mexico* **221 F4** 18 15N 96 32W
Miguel Auza, *Zacatecas, Mexico* **217 C7** 24 19N 103 25W
Miguel Hidalgo, *Durango, Mexico* **217 C6** 24 40N 104 43W
Miguel Hidalgo, *Jalisco, Mexico* **218 C3** 19 25N 104 54W
Miguel Hidalgo, *México, Mexico* **225 B2** 19 25N 99 12W
Miguel Hidalgo, Aeropuerto Internacional ✕, *Guadalajara, Mexico* **224 B2** 20 31N 103 19W
Miguel Hidalgo, Presa, *Sinaloa, Mexico* **216 A2** 26 30N 108 34W
Mikkalo, *OR, U.S.A.* **94 B5** 45 28N 120 14W
Mikkwa ➝, *Alta., Canada* **184 A6** 58 25N 114 46W
Milaca, *MN, U.S.A.* **80 E5** 45 45N 93 39W
Milam, *TX, U.S.A.* **99 F14** 31 26N 93 51W
Milam County ☆, *TX, U.S.A.* **99 G11** 30 51N 96 59W
Milan, *GA, U.S.A.* **68 D3** 32 1N 83 4W
Milan, *IL, U.S.A.* **71 B3** 41 27N 90 34W
Milan, *IN, U.S.A.* **72 D5** 39 7N 85 8W
Milan, *MI, U.S.A.* **79 G8** 42 5N 83 41W
Milan, *MN, U.S.A.* **80 E3** 45 7N 95 55W
Milan, *MO, U.S.A.* **82 A3** 40 12N 93 7W
Milan, *NH, U.S.A.* **86 B3** 44 36N 71 12W
Milan, *NM, U.S.A.* **88 B3** 35 9N 107 54W
Milan, *OH, U.S.A.* **92 B4** 41 18N 82 37W
Milan, *TN, U.S.A.* **96 E4** 35 55N 88 46W
Milan, *WA, U.S.A.* **101 C8** 47 58N 117 20W
Milan Arsenal, *TN, U.S.A.* **96 E4** 35 52N 88 43W
Milano, *TX, U.S.A.* **99 G11** 30 43N 96 52W
Milbank, *SD, U.S.A.* **91 E9** 45 13N 96 38W
Milbanke Sd., *B.C., Canada* **186 C6** 52 19N 128 33W
Milbridge, *ME, U.S.A.* **76 D6** 44 32N 67 53W
Milburn, *NE, U.S.A.* **84 C6** 41 43N 99 44W
Milburn, *OK, U.S.A.* **93 D7** 34 14N 96 33W
Milden, *Sask., Canada* **182 D4** 51 29N 107 32W
Mildmay, *Ont., Canada* **178 C5** 44 3N 81 7W
Mildred, *KS, U.S.A.* **74 C8** 38 1N 95 10W
Miles, *TX, U.S.A.* **98 F7** 31 36N 100 11W
Miles, *WA, U.S.A.* **101 C7** 47 55N 118 18W
Miles City, *MT, U.S.A.* **83 D12** 46 25N 105 51W
Milesburg, *PA, U.S.A.* **95 D5** 40 57N 77 47W
Milestone, *Sask., Canada* **182 F7** 49 59N 104 31W
Milford, *Baltimore, U.S.A.* **107 A1** 39 20N 76 44W
Milford, *CA, U.S.A.* **64 C6** 40 10N 120 22W
Milford, *CT, U.S.A.* **78 C1** 41 14N 73 3W
Milford, *DE, U.S.A.* **77 B5** 38 55N 75 26W
Milford, *GA, U.S.A.* **68 E2** 31 23N 84 33W
Milford, *IL, U.S.A.* **71 C6** 40 38N 87 42W
Milford, *IN, U.S.A.* **72 B5** 41 25N 85 51W
Milford, *IA, U.S.A.* **73 B3** 43 20N 95 9W
Milford, *KS, U.S.A.* **74 B7** 39 10N 96 55W
Milford, *KY, U.S.A.* **97 B8** 38 35N 84 9W
Milford, *ME, U.S.A.* **76 D5** 44 57N 68 39W
Milford, *MA, U.S.A.* **78 B3** 42 8N 71 31W
Milford, *MI, U.S.A.* **79 G8** 42 35N 83 36W

Milford, *MO, U.S.A.* **82 D2** 37 35N 94 9W
Milford, *NH, U.S.A.* **86 D3** 42 50N 71 39W
Milford, *NJ, U.S.A.* **87 B1** 40 34N 75 6W
Milford, *NY, U.S.A.* **89 C6** 42 35N 74 57W
Milford, *NE, U.S.A.* **84 D8** 40 47N 97 3W
Milford, *PA, U.S.A.* **87 A2** 41 19N 74 48W
Milford, *UT, U.S.A.* **100 E2** 38 24N 113 1W
Milford Center, *OH, U.S.A.* **92 C3** 40 11N 83 26W
Milford Lake, *KS, U.S.A.* **74 B7** 39 5N 96 54W
Milford Station, *N.S., Canada* **173 H6** 45 3N 63 26W
Mililani Town, *HI, U.S.A.* **69 K13** 21 28N 158 1W
Milk River, *Alta., Canada* **185 J8** 49 10N 112 5W
Mill →, *MI, U.S.A.* **79 F9** 43 2N 82 35W
Mill City, *NV, U.S.A.* **85 B2** 40 41N 118 4W
Mill City, *OR, U.S.A.* **94 C3** 44 45N 122 29W
Mill Creek, *WV, U.S.A.* **102 C5** 38 44N 79 58W
Mill Creek, *WA, U.S.A.* **101 C3** 47 51N 122 12W
Mill Hall, *PA, U.S.A.* **95 C5** 41 6N 77 29W
Mill I., *Nunavut, Canada* **191 E10** 63 58N 77 47W
Mill Shoals, *IL, U.S.A.* **71 E5** 38 15N 88 21W
Mill Stream Run Reservation, *Cleveland, U.S.A.* **107 C1** 41 19N 81 48W
Mill Village, *N.S., Canada* **173 J5** 44 9N 64 39W
Milladore, *WI, U.S.A.* **103 D4** 44 36N 89 51W
Millard, *MO, U.S.A.* **82 A4** 40 7N 92 33W
Millard County ☆, *UT, U.S.A.* **100 D3** 39 0N 113 0W
Millboro, *SD, U.S.A.* **91 G6** 43 4N 99 58W
Millboro, *VA, U.S.A.* **102 D5** 37 59N 79 36W
Millbourne, *PA, U.S.A.* **116 B1** 39 57N 75 15W
Millbridge, *Ont., Canada* **179 C9** 44 41N 77 36W
Millbrook, *Ont., Canada* **179 C8** 44 10N 78 29W
Millbrook, *AL, U.S.A.* **60 D4** 32 29N 86 22W
Millbrook, *NY, U.S.A.* **89 D7** 41 47N 73 42W
Millbury, *MA, U.S.A.* **78 B3** 42 12N 71 46W
Millcreek, *UT, U.S.A.* **100 C4** 40 41N 111 52W
Mille Lacs, L. des, *Ont., Canada* **180 D6** 48 45N 90 35W
Mille Lacs County ☆, *MN, U.S.A.* **80 E5** 45 50N 93 45W
Mille Lacs Indian Reservation, *MN, U.S.A.* **80 D5** 46 8N 93 45W
Mille Lacs L., *MN, U.S.A.* **80 D5** 46 15N 93 39W
Milledgeville, *GA, U.S.A.* **68 C3** 33 5N 83 14W
Milledgeville, *IL, U.S.A.* **71 B4** 41 58N 89 46W
Milledgeville, *OH, U.S.A.* **92 D3** 39 36N 83 35W
Milledgeville, *TN, U.S.A.* **96 E4** 35 22N 88 22W
Millen, *GA, U.S.A.* **68 D5** 32 48N 81 57W
Miller, *KS, U.S.A.* **74 C8** 38 38N 95 59W
Miller, *MO, U.S.A.* **82 D3** 37 13N 93 50W
Miller, *NE, U.S.A.* **84 D6** 40 56N 99 23W
Miller, *SD, U.S.A.* **91 F7** 44 31N 98 59W
Miller County ☆, *AR, U.S.A.* **63 E2** 33 10N 93 58W
Miller County ☆, *GA, U.S.A.* **68 E2** 31 10N 84 45W
Miller County ☆, *MO, U.S.A.* **82 C4** 38 15N 92 25W
Miller Meadow, *Chicago, U.S.A.* **108 B2** 41 51N 87 49W
Millerand, *Qué., Canada* **173 F8** 47 13N 61 59W
Millers →, *MA, U.S.A.* **78 B2** 42 35N 72 30W
Millers Creek Res., *TX, U.S.A.* **99 D8** 33 30N 99 20W
Millers Falls, *MA, U.S.A.* **78 B2** 42 35N 72 30W
Millers Ferry, *AL, U.S.A.* **60 D3** 32 6N 87 22W
Millers Tavern, *VA, U.S.A.* **77 C4** 37 50N 76 57W
Millersburg, *IN, U.S.A.* **72 B5** 41 32N 85 42W
Millersburg, *IA, U.S.A.* **73 D6** 41 34N 92 10W
Millersburg, *KY, U.S.A.* **97 B8** 38 18N 84 9W
Millersburg, *MI, U.S.A.* **79 D7** 45 20N 84 4W
Millersburg, *OH, U.S.A.* **92 C5** 40 33N 81 55W
Millersburg, *PA, U.S.A.* **95 D6** 40 32N 76 58W
Millersport, *OH, U.S.A.* **92 D4** 39 54N 82 32W
Millersville, *MD, U.S.A.* **77 A4** 39 4N 76 39W
Millersville, *PA, U.S.A.* **95 E6** 40 0N 76 22W
Millersville, *TN, U.S.A.* **96 D6** 36 22N 86 43W
Millerton, *IA, U.S.A.* **73 E5** 40 51N 93 18W
Millerton, *NY, U.S.A.* **78 C1** 41 57N 73 31W
Millerton, *OK, U.S.A.* **93 E8** 33 59N 95 1W
Millerton L., *CA, U.S.A.* **65 F7** 37 1N 119 41W
Millertown, *Nfld. & L., Canada* **174 D4** 48 49N 56 33W
Milles Isles, R. des →, *Montréal, Canada* **192 A1** 45 34N 73 50W
Millet, *Alta., Canada* **185 E7** 53 6N 113 28W
Millett, *TX, U.S.A.* **99 J8** 28 35N 99 12W
Millheim, *PA, U.S.A.* **95 D5** 40 54N 77 29W
Milligan, *FL, U.S.A.* **67 A2** 30 45N 86 38W
Milligan, *NE, U.S.A.* **84 D8** 40 30N 97 23W
Millington, *MD, U.S.A.* **77 A5** 39 16N 75 50W
Millington, *MI, U.S.A.* **79 F8** 43 17N 83 32W
Millington, *TN, U.S.A.* **96 E3** 35 20N 89 53W
Millinocket, *ME, U.S.A.* **76 C5** 45 39N 68 43W
Millinocket L., *ME, U.S.A.* **76 C5** 45 46N 68 48W
Millis, *MA, U.S.A.* **78 B3** 42 10N 71 22W
Millport, *AL, U.S.A.* **60 C2** 33 34N 88 5W
Millry, *AL, U.S.A.* **60 E2** 31 38N 88 19W
Mills, *NM, U.S.A.* **88 A6** 36 5N 104 15W
Mills, *NE, U.S.A.* **84 B6** 42 57N 99 27W
Mills, *WY, U.S.A.* **104 D6** 42 50N 106 22W
Mills County ☆, *IA, U.S.A.* **73 D3** 41 0N 95 35W
Mills County ☆, *TX, U.S.A.* **99 F9** 31 27N 98 34W
Mills L., *N.W.T., Canada* **189 D9** 61 30N 118 20W
Millsap, *TX, U.S.A.* **99 E9** 32 45N 98 1W
Millsboro, *DE, U.S.A.* **77 B5** 38 36N 75 18W
Millstadt, *IL, U.S.A.* **71 E3** 38 28N 90 6W
Millstone, *WV, U.S.A.* **102 C3** 38 48N 81 6W
Millstream, *N.B., Canada* **173 E2** 48 2N 67 2W
Milltown, *IN, U.S.A.* **72 E4** 38 21N 86 17W
Milltown, *SD, U.S.A.* **91 G8** 43 25N 97 48W
Milltown, *WI, U.S.A.* **103 C1** 45 32N 92 30W
Milltown-Head of Bay d'Espoir, *Nfld. & L., Canada* **174 E5** 47 56N 55 45W
Millvale, *Pittsburgh, U.S.A.* **116 B2** 40 28N 79 58W
Millville, *N.B., Canada* **173 G2** 46 8N 67 12W
Millville, *DE, U.S.A.* **77 B5** 38 35N 75 8W
Millville, *IA, U.S.A.* **73 C7** 42 42N 91 5W
Millville, *KY, U.S.A.* **97 B8** 38 8N 84 49W
Millville, *MA, U.S.A.* **78 B3** 42 2N 71 35W
Millville, *NJ, U.S.A.* **87 C1** 39 24N 75 2W
Millville, *PA, U.S.A.* **95 C6** 41 7N 76 32W
Millwood, *GA, U.S.A.* **68 E4** 31 16N 82 40W
Millwood, *MD, U.S.A.* **119 B4** 38 52N 76 52W
Millwood, *VA, U.S.A.* **77 A2** 39 4N 78 2W
Millwood, *WA, U.S.A.* **101 C8** 47 41N 117 17W
Millwood L., *AR, U.S.A.* **63 E2** 33 42N 93 58W
Milmay, *NJ, U.S.A.* **87 C2** 39 26N 74 52W
Milner, *CO, U.S.A.* **66 B3** 40 29N 107 1W
Milnesand, *NM, U.S.A.* **88 D7** 33 39N 103 20W
Milnor, *ND, U.S.A.* **91 D8** 46 16N 97 27W
Milo, *Alta., Canada* **185 H8** 50 34N 112 53W
Milo, *IA, U.S.A.* **73 D5** 41 17N 93 27W
Milo, *ME, U.S.A.* **76 C5** 45 15N 68 59W
Milo, *MO, U.S.A.* **82 D2** 37 45N 94 18W
Milo, *OR, U.S.A.* **94 E2** 42 56N 123 3W
Miloli'i, *HI, U.S.A.* **69 D6** 19 11N 155 55W
Milpa Alta, *Distrito Federal, Mexico* **225 C3** 19 11N 99 1W
Milpillas, *Chihuahua, Mexico* **212 F7** 27 13N 108 40W
Milpitas, *CA, U.S.A.* **64 F5** 37 26N 121 55W
Milroy, *IN, U.S.A.* **72 D5** 39 30N 85 28W
Milroy, *MN, U.S.A.* **80 F3** 44 25N 95 33W
Milroy, *PA, U.S.A.* **95 D5** 40 43N 77 35W
Milton, *N.S., Canada* **173 J5** 44 4N 64 45W
Milton, *Ont., Canada* **178 D7** 43 31N 79 53W
Milton, *DE, U.S.A.* **77 B5** 38 47N 75 19W
Milton, *FL, U.S.A.* **67 A1** 30 38N 87 3W
Milton, *IL, U.S.A.* **71 D3** 39 34N 90 39W
Milton, *IA, U.S.A.* **73 E6** 40 41N 92 10W
Milton, *KS, U.S.A.* **74 D6** 37 26N 97 46W
Milton, *KY, U.S.A.* **97 B7** 38 43N 85 22W
Milton, *MA, U.S.A.* **78 B3** 42 14N 71 2W
Milton, *ND, U.S.A.* **91 B7** 48 38N 98 3W
Milton, *NH, U.S.A.* **86 C4** 43 25N 70 59W
Milton, *PA, U.S.A.* **95 C6** 41 1N 76 51W
Milton, *VT, U.S.A.* **86 B1** 44 38N 73 7W
Milton, *WV, U.S.A.* **102 C2** 38 26N 82 8W
Milton, *WI, U.S.A.* **103 F5** 42 47N 88 56W
Milton-Freewater, *OR, U.S.A.* **94 B7** 45 56N 118 23W
Miltona, *MN, U.S.A.* **80 D3** 46 3N 95 18W
Miltonvale, *KS, U.S.A.* **74 B6** 39 21N 97 27W
Milverton, *Ont., Canada* **178 D6** 43 34N 80 55W
Milwaukee, *WI, U.S.A.* **103 E6** 43 2N 87 54W
Milwaukee Bay, *Milwaukee, U.S.A.* **112 B2** 43 1N 87 53W
Milwaukee County ☆, *WI, U.S.A.* **103 E6** 43 0N 88 0W
Milwaukee General Mitchell International ✕ (MKE), *WI, U.S.A.* **103 F6** 42 57N 87 54W
Milwaukie, *OR, U.S.A.* **94 B3** 45 26N 122 38W
Mimbres, *NM, U.S.A.* **88 E3** 32 51N 107 59W
Mimbres Mts., *NM, U.S.A.* **88 E3** 32 50N 107 45W
Miminegash, *P.E.I., Canada* **173 G5** 46 53N 64 14W
Miminiska L., *Ont., Canada* **180 A8** 51 35N 88 37W
Mims, *FL, U.S.A.* **67 C8** 28 40N 80 51W
Mina, *Nuevo León, Mexico* **214 D4** 26 1N 100 32W
Mina, *NV, U.S.A.* **85 D2** 38 24N 118 7W
Minago →, *Man., Canada* **183 A13** 54 33N 98 59W
Minaki, *Ont., Canada* **180 C2** 49 59N 94 40W
Minam, *OR, U.S.A.* **94 B8** 45 38N 117 43W
Minas Basin, *N.S., Canada* **173 H5** 45 20N 64 12W
Minas Channel, *N.S., Canada* **173 H5** 45 15N 64 45W
Minas de Barroterán, *Coahuila, Mexico* **214 C3** 27 41N 101 18W
Minatare, *NE, U.S.A.* **84 C2** 41 49N 103 30W
Minatitlán, *Colima, Mexico* **218 C3** 19 22N 104 4W
Minatitlán, *Veracruz, Mexico* **221 G6** 17 59N 94 31W
Minburn, *IA, U.S.A.* **73 D4** 41 45N 94 2W
Minco, *OK, U.S.A.* **93 C6** 35 19N 97 57W
Mindemoya, *Ont., Canada* **178 B4** 45 44N 82 10W
Minden, *Ont., Canada* **179 C8** 44 55N 78 43W
Minden, *IA, U.S.A.* **73 D3** 41 28N 95 32W
Minden, *LA, U.S.A.* **75 B2** 32 37N 93 17W
Minden, *NE, U.S.A.* **84 D7** 40 30N 98 57W
Minden, *NV, U.S.A.* **85 D1** 38 57N 119 46W
Minden City, *MI, U.S.A.* **79 F9** 43 40N 82 47W
Mindenmines, *MO, U.S.A.* **82 D2** 37 28N 94 35W
Minel, L. de la, *Qué., Canada* **172 C5** 50 51N 64 43W
Mine Centre, *Ont., Canada* **180 D4** 48 45N 92 37W
Minebank Run →, *Baltimore, U.S.A.* **107 A2** 39 25N 76 32W
Mineola, *NY, U.S.A.* **87 B3** 40 44N 73 38W
Mineola, *TX, U.S.A.* **99 E12** 32 40N 95 29W
Miner, *MO, U.S.A.* **82 E7** 36 53N 89 32W
Miner →, *Yukon, Canada* **188 C5** 66 30N 138 25W
Miner County ☆, *SD, U.S.A.* **91 F8** 44 1N 97 36W
Mineral, *CA, U.S.A.* **64 C5** 40 21N 121 36W
Mineral, *VA, U.S.A.* **102 C7** 38 1N 77 55W
Mineral, *WA, U.S.A.* **101 D3** 46 43N 122 11W
Mineral Bluff, *GA, U.S.A.* **68 B2** 34 55N 84 17W
Mineral County ☆, *CO, U.S.A.* **66 E4** 37 40N 106 50W
Mineral County ☆, *MT, U.S.A.* **83 C3** 47 4N 115 0W
Mineral County ☆, *NV, U.S.A.* **85 D2** 38 30N 118 25W
Mineral County ☆, *WV, U.S.A.* **102 B6** 39 21N 79 0W
Mineral de Cucharas, *Nayarit, Mexico* **216 E5** 22 49N 105 17W
Mineral del Monte, *Hidalgo, Mexico* **219 B9** 20 8N 98 40W
Mineral la Luz, *Coahuila, Mexico* **214 C3** 27 36N 101 29W
Mineral Mts., *UT, U.S.A.* **100 E3** 38 30N 112 45W
Mineral Point, *MO, U.S.A.* **82 D6** 37 57N 90 44W
Mineral Point, *WI, U.S.A.* **103 F3** 42 52N 90 11W
Mineral Springs, *AR, U.S.A.* **63 E2** 33 53N 93 55W
Mineral Wells, *TX, U.S.A.* **99 E9** 32 48N 98 7W
Minersville, *PA, U.S.A.* **95 D6** 40 41N 76 16W
Minersville, *UT, U.S.A.* **100 E3** 38 13N 112 56W
Minerva, *NY, U.S.A.* **89 B7** 43 47N 73 59W
Minerva, *OH, U.S.A.* **92 C5** 40 44N 81 6W
Mineville, *NY, U.S.A.* **89 A7** 44 6N 73 31W
Mingan, *Qué., Canada* **175 C5** 50 20N 64 0W
Mingan →, *Qué., Canada* **172 C6** 50 18N 63 59W
Mingan, Îles de, *Qué., Canada* **172 C6** 50 12N 63 35W
Mingo County ☆, *WV, U.S.A.* **102 D2** 37 43N 82 11W
Mingo Junction, *OH, U.S.A.* **92 C6** 40 19N 80 37W
Mingo L., *Nunavut, Canada* **191 E11** 64 35N 72 10W
Minidoka, *ID, U.S.A.* **70 G5** 42 45N 113 29W
Minidoka County ☆, *ID, U.S.A.* **70 G5** 42 50N 113 38W
Minidoka Nat. Wildlife Refuge ⌂, *ID, U.S.A.* **70 G5** 42 40N 113 23W
Minier, *IL, U.S.A.* **71 C4** 40 26N 89 19W
Miniota, *Man., Canada* **183 E10** 50 8N 101 2W
Minipi L., *Nfld. & L., Canada* **172 A9** 52 25N 60 45W
Miniss L., *Ont., Canada* **180 B6** 50 48N 90 50W
Minitonas, *Man., Canada* **183 C10** 52 5N 101 2W
Minneapolis, *KS, U.S.A.* **74 B6** 39 8N 97 42W
Minneapolis, *MN, U.S.A.* **80 F5** 44 57N 93 16W
Minneapolis-St. Paul International ✕ (MSP), *MN, U.S.A.* **80 F5** 44 53N 93 13W
Minnedosa, *Man., Canada* **183 E12** 50 14N 99 50W
Minnehaha County ☆, *SD, U.S.A.* **91 G9** 43 40N 96 49W
Minnehaha Regional Park ⌂, *Minneapolis-St. Paul, U.S.A.* **113 B2** 44 53N 93 12W
Minneiska, *MN, U.S.A.* **80 F7** 44 12N 91 52W
Minneola, *KS, U.S.A.* **74 D3** 37 26N 100 1W
Minneota, *MN, U.S.A.* **80 F3** 44 34N 95 59W
Minnesota □, *U.S.A.* **80 D4** 46 0N 94 15W
Minnesota →, *MN, U.S.A.* **80 F5** 44 54N 93 9W
Minnesota City, *MN, U.S.A.* **80 F7** 44 6N 91 46W
Minnesota Lake, *MN, U.S.A.* **80 G5** 43 51N 93 50W
Minnetex, *Houston, U.S.A.* **110 C2** 29 36N 95 21W
Minnetonka, *MN, U.S.A.* **80 F5** 44 55N 93 27W
Minnetonka, L., *Minneapolis-St. Paul, U.S.A.* **113 B1** 44 54N 93 38W
Minnewaukan, *ND, U.S.A.* **91 B6** 48 4N 99 15W
Minnitaki L., *Ont., Canada* **180 C4** 49 57N 92 10W
Minong, *WI, U.S.A.* **103 B2** 46 6N 91 49W
Minonk, *IL, U.S.A.* **71 C4** 40 54N 89 2W
Minooka, *IL, U.S.A.* **71 B5** 41 27N 88 16W
Minor Hill, *TN, U.S.A.* **96 E5** 35 4N 87 9W
Minoru Park, *Vancouver, Canada* **193 C2** 49 9N 123 9W
Minot, *ND, U.S.A.* **91 B4** 48 14N 101 18W
Minster, *OH, U.S.A.* **92 C2** 40 24N 84 23W
Minstrel Island, *B.C., Canada* **186 E8** 50 37N 126 18W
Mint Hill, *NC, U.S.A.* **90 C5** 35 13N 80 41W
Minter City, *MS, U.S.A.* **81 C3** 33 45N 90 19W
Minto, *N.B., Canada* **173 G3** 46 5N 66 5W
Minto, *AK, U.S.A.* **61 D10** 64 53N 149 10W
Minto, *ND, U.S.A.* **91 B8** 48 17N 97 22W
Minto, L., *Qué., Canada* **175 B3** 57 13N 75 0W
Minto Hd., *Nunavut, Canada* **190 C5** 73 5N 102 17W
Minto Inlet, *N.W.T., Canada* **188 B9** 71 20N 117 0W
Minton, *Sask., Canada* **182 F7** 49 10N 104 35W
Minturn, *CO, U.S.A.* **66 C4** 39 35N 106 26W
Minute Man Nat. Historic Park ⌂, *Boston, U.S.A.* **106 A2** 42 25N 71 16W
Minuteman Missile Nat. Historic Site ⌂, *SD, U.S.A.* **91 G3** 43 55N 102 8W
Mio, *MI, U.S.A.* **79 E7** 44 39N 84 8W
Miquelon, *Qué., Canada* **176 B6** 49 25N 76 27W
Miquelon, *St-P. & M.* **174 E4** 47 8N 56 22W
Miquihuana, *Tamaulipas, Mexico* **215 G5** 23 34N 99 47W
Mira, *N.S., Canada* **173 G10** 46 2N 59 58W
Mira →, *N.S., Canada* **173 G10** 46 2N 59 58W
Mirador, *Chiapas, Mexico* **222 C3** 16 49N 93 8W
Miramar, *FL, U.S.A.* **67 F8** 25 59N 80 13W
Miramar, L., *Chiapas, Mexico* **222 C5** 16 25N 91 15W
Miramichi, *N.B., Canada* **173 F4** 47 2N 65 28W
Miramichi, Little S.W. →, *N.B., Canada* **173 G4** 46 58N 65 40W
Miramichi, N.W. →, *N.B., Canada* **173 G4** 46 57N 65 50W
Miramichi, S.W. →, *N.B., Canada* **173 G4** 46 58N 65 38W
Miramichi B., *N.B., Canada* **173 F4** 47 15N 65 0W
Mirando City, *TX, U.S.A.* **98 K9** 27 26N 99 0W
Mirror, *Alta., Canada* **185 F7** 52 30N 113 7W
Misantla, *Veracruz, Mexico* **220 E4** 19 56N 96 50W
Miscou Centre, *N.B., Canada* **173 F5** 47 57N 64 34W
Miscou I., *N.B., Canada* **173 F5** 47 57N 64 31W
Miscouche, *P.E.I., Canada* **173 G6** 46 26N 63 52W
Misehkow →, *Ont., Canada* **180 A7** 51 26N 89 11W
Mishawaka, *IN, U.S.A.* **72 B4** 41 40N 86 11W
Misión de Santa Gertrudis, *Baja Calif., Mexico* **211 E5** 28 5N 113 4W
Misquah Hills, *MN, U.S.A.* **80 C8** 47 50N 90 30W
Misquamicut, *RI, U.S.A.* **78 C3** 41 20N 71 49W
Missanabie, *Ont., Canada* **181 D12** 48 20N 84 6W
Missaukee County ☆, *MI, U.S.A.* **79 E6** 44 20N 85 10W
Missinaibi →, *Ont., Canada* **181 B15** 50 43N 81 29W
Missinaibi L., *Ont., Canada* **181 D13** 48 23N 83 40W
Missinaibi Lake Prov. Park ⌂, *Ont., Canada* **181 D13** 48 25N 83 30W
Mission, *B.C., Canada* **187 F12** 49 10N 122 15W
Mission, *SD, U.S.A.* **91 G5** 43 18N 100 39W
Mission, *San Francisco, U.S.A.* **118 B2** 37 44N 122 25W
Mission, *TX, U.S.A.* **98 L9** 26 13N 98 20W
Mission Bay, *San Diego, U.S.A.* **117 B1** 32 46N 117 14W
Mission Bay Park, *San Diego, U.S.A.* **117 B1** 32 46N 117 13W
Mission Mt., *OK, U.S.A.* **93 B9** 36 2N 94 35W
Mission Ridge, *SD, U.S.A.* **91 F5** 44 42N 100 47W
Mission Trails Regional Park ⌂, *San Diego, U.S.A.* **117 A2** 32 47N 117 2W
Mission Viejo, *CA, U.S.A.* **65 K9** 33 36N 117 40W
Missipuskiow →, *Sask., Canada* **182 B8** 53 53N 103 18W
Missisicabi →, *Qué., Canada* **175 C2** 51 14N 79 31W
Missisquoi →, *VT, U.S.A.* **86 B1** 45 0N 73 8W
Missisquoi, B., *Qué., Canada* **86 A1** 45 2N 73 9W
Missisquoi B., *VT, U.S.A.* **86 A1** 45 0N 73 8W
Missisquoi Nat. Wildlife Refuge ⌂, *VT, U.S.A.* **86 B1** 44 57N 73 10W
Mississagi →, *Ont., Canada* **178 A3** 46 15N 83 9W
Mississagi Prov. Park ⌂, *Ont., Canada* **178 A4** 46 30N 82 40W
Mississauga, *Ont., Canada* **178 D7** 43 32N 79 35W
Mississinewa L., *IN, U.S.A.* **72 C5** 40 42N 85 52W
Mississippi □, *U.S.A.* **81 D4** 33 0N 90 0W
Mississippi →, *LA, U.S.A.* **75 E6** 29 9N 89 15W
Mississippi Choctaw Indian Reservation, *MS, U.S.A.* **81 D4** 32 48N 89 7W
Mississippi County ☆, *AR, U.S.A.* **63 C5** 35 45N 90 5W
Mississippi County ☆, *MO, U.S.A.* **82 E7** 36 50N 89 15W
Mississippi L., *Ont., Canada* **176 F6** 45 5N 76 10W
Mississippi River Delta, *LA, U.S.A.* **75 E6** 29 10N 89 15W
Mississippi Sd., *MS, U.S.A.* **81 F5** 30 20N 89 0W
Missoula, *MT, U.S.A.* **83 D3** 46 52N 114 1W
Missoula County ☆, *MT, U.S.A.* **83 C4** 47 4N 114 0W
Missouri □, *U.S.A.* **82 C4** 38 25N 92 30W
Missouri →, *MO, U.S.A.* **82 C6** 38 49N 90 7W
Missouri Buttes, *WY, U.S.A.* **104 B8** 44 37N 104 47W
Missouri City, *MO, U.S.A.* **82 B2** 39 14N 94 18W
Missouri City, *TX, U.S.A.* **99 H12** 29 37N 95 32W
Missouri Nat. Scenic River ⌂, *U.S.A.* **84 B8** 42 48N 97 25W
Missouri Valley, *IA, U.S.A.* **73 D3** 41 34N 95 53W
Mistanipisipou →, *Qué., Canada* **172 B8** 51 32N 61 50W
Mistaouac, L., *Qué., Canada* **176 B4** 49 25N 78 41W
Mistasin L., *Qué., Canada* **175 C2** 52 35N 78 33W
Mistassibi →, *Qué., Canada* **177 C10** 48 53N 72 13W
Mistassibi Nord-Est →, *Qué., Canada* **177 B11** 49 31N 71 56W
Mistassini →, *Qué., Canada* **177 C10** 48 42N 72 20W
Mistassini, L., *Qué., Canada* **175 C3** 51 0N 73 30W
Mistatim, *Sask., Canada* **182 C8** 52 52N 103 22W
Mistissini, *Qué., Canada* **175 C3** 50 24N 73 56W
Misty Fjords Nat. Monument ⌂, *AK, U.S.A.* **61 J15** 55 40N 130 40W
Mita, Pta., *Nayarit, Mexico* **216 G5** 20 47N 105 33W
Mitchell, *Ont., Canada* **178 D5** 43 28N 81 12W
Mitchell, *GA, U.S.A.* **68 C4** 33 13N 82 42W
Mitchell, *IN, U.S.A.* **72 E4** 38 44N 86 28W
Mitchell, *IA, U.S.A.* **73 B6** 43 19N 92 53W
Mitchell, *NE, U.S.A.* **84 C2** 41 57N 103 49W
Mitchell, *OR, U.S.A.* **94 C5** 44 34N 120 9W
Mitchell, *SD, U.S.A.* **91 G7** 43 43N 98 2W
Mitchell, L., *MI, U.S.A.* **79 E6** 44 15N 85 30W
Mitchell, Mt., *NC, U.S.A.* **90 C3** 35 46N 82 16W
Mitchell County ☆, *GA, U.S.A.* **68 E2** 31 15N 84 10W
Mitchell County ☆, *IA, U.S.A.* **73 B6** 43 20N 92 45W
Mitchell County ☆, *KS, U.S.A.* **74 B5** 39 30N 98 10W
Mitchell County ☆, *NC, U.S.A.* **90 B3** 36 5N 82 10W
Mitchell County ☆, *TX, U.S.A.* **98 E7** 32 24N 100 52W
Mitchell I., *B.C., Canada* **193 B2** 49 12N 123 5W
Mitchell L., *B.C., Canada* **187 C14** 52 52N 120 37W
Mitchell L., *AL, U.S.A.* **60 D4** 32 48N 86 27W
Mitchell Lake, *San Antonio, U.S.A.* **117 D3** 29 16N 98 29W
Mitchellsburg, *KY, U.S.A.* **97 C8** 37 36N 84 57W
Mitchellville, *IA, U.S.A.* **73 D5** 41 40N 93 22W
Mitchinamecus, Rés., *Qué., Canada* **176 D7** 47 19N 75 9W
Mitla, *Oaxaca, Mexico* **221 H4** 16 57N 96 24W
Mittimatalik = Pond Inlet, *Nunavut, Canada* **190 C10** 72 40N 77 0W
Mixcoac, *Distrito Federal, Mexico* **225 B2** 19 23N 99 11W
Mixistlán, *Oaxaca, Mexico* **221 G4** 17 6N 96 5W
Mixquiahuala, *Hidalgo, Mexico* **219 B8** 20 14N 99 13W
Mixtlán, *Jalisco, Mexico* **218 B3** 20 26N 104 25W
Mize, *MS, U.S.A.* **81 E4** 31 52N 89 33W
Mizpah, *MN, U.S.A.* **80 C4** 47 55N 94 12W
Mizpah, *MT, U.S.A.* **83 D12** 46 14N 105 16W
Moab, *UT, U.S.A.* **100 E6** 38 35N 109 33W
Moapa, *NV, U.S.A.* **85 F6** 36 40N 114 37W
Moapa River Indian Reservation, *NV, U.S.A.* **85 F6** 36 36N 114 45W
Mobeetie, *TX, U.S.A.* **98 B7** 35 31N 100 26W
Moberly, *MO, U.S.A.* **82 B4** 39 25N 92 26W
Mobile, *AL, U.S.A.* **60 F2** 30 41N 88 3W
Mobile, *AZ, U.S.A.* **62 D3** 33 3N 112 16W
Mobile →, *AL, U.S.A.* **60 F2** 30 39N 88 2W
Mobile B., *AL, U.S.A.* **60 F3** 30 30N 88 0W
Mobile County ☆, *AL, U.S.A.* **60 F2** 30 41N 88 3W
Mobridge, *SD, U.S.A.* **91 E5** 45 32N 100 26W
Moca, *Puerto Rico* **105 G15** 18 24N 67 10W
Moccasin, *AZ, U.S.A.* **62 A3** 36 55N 112 46W
Moccasin Gap, *VA, U.S.A.* **102 E2** 36 38N 82 33W
Mochomos, Cerro, *Sonora, Mexico* **212 E6** 28 20N 109 25W
Mocksville, *NC, U.S.A.* **90 C5** 35 54N 80 34W
Moclips, *WA, U.S.A.* **101 C1** 47 14N 124 13W
Mocorito, *Sinaloa, Mexico* **216 B3** 25 29N 107 55W
Moctezuma, *Chihuahua, Mexico* **213 C9** 30 12N 106 26W
Moctezuma, *San Luis Potosí, Mexico* **215 H3** 22 45N 101 5W
Moctezuma, *Sonora, Mexico* **212 D6** 29 48N 109 42W
Moctezuma →, *San Luis Potosí, Mexico* **219 A9** 21 59N 98 34W
Moctezuma →, *Sonora, Mexico* **212 D6** 29 9N 109 40W
Model, *CO, U.S.A.* **66 E6** 37 22N 104 15W
Modena, *UT, U.S.A.* **100 F2** 37 48N 113 56W
Modesto, *CA, U.S.A.* **64 F5** 37 39N 121 0W
Modoc, *GA, U.S.A.* **68 D4** 32 37N 82 19W
Modoc County ☆, *CA, U.S.A.* **64 B6** 41 40N 120 50W
Modoc Nat. Forest, *CA, U.S.A.* **64 B6** 41 30N 121 0W
Modoc Point, *OR, U.S.A.* **94 E4** 42 27N 121 52W
Moenkopi, *AZ, U.S.A.* **62 A4** 36 7N 111 13W
Moenkopi Wash →, *AZ, U.S.A.* **62 B4** 35 50N 111 20W
Moffat, *CO, U.S.A.* **66 E5** 37 58N 105 56W
Moffat County ☆, *CO, U.S.A.* **66 B2** 40 45N 108 10W
Mogollon Mts., *NM, U.S.A.* **88 D2** 33 25N 108 40W
Mogollon Plateau, *AZ, U.S.A.* **62 C5** 34 30N 111 0W
Mogollon Rim, *AZ, U.S.A.* **62 C5** 34 10N 110 50W
Mohall, *ND, U.S.A.* **91 B4** 48 46N 101 31W
Mohave, L., *U.S.A.* **62 B1** 35 12N 114 34W
Mohave County ☆, *AZ, U.S.A.* **62 B1** 35 0N 114 0W
Mohave Mts., *AZ, U.S.A.* **62 C1** 34 35N 114 20W
Mohawk, *MI, U.S.A.* **79 B3** 47 18N 88 21W
Mohawk, *NY, U.S.A.* **89 C6** 43 0N 75 0W
Mohawk →, *NY, U.S.A.* **89 C7** 42 47N 73 41W
Mohawk Mts., *AZ, U.S.A.* **62 E2** 32 30N 113 35W
Mohawksin, L., *WI, U.S.A.* **103 C4** 45 26N 89 43W
Mohican →, *OH, U.S.A.* **92 C4** 40 22N 82 10W
Mohican, C., *AK, U.S.A.* **61 F6** 60 12N 167 25W
Mohon Pk., *AZ, U.S.A.* **62 C2** 34 57N 113 9W
Moira →, *Ont., Canada* **179 C9** 44 21N 77 24W
Moisie, *Qué., Canada* **175 C4** 50 12N 66 1W
Moisie →, *Qué., Canada* **172 C3** 50 14N 66 5W
Mojave, *CA, U.S.A.* **65 H8** 35 3N 118 10W
Mojave →, *CA, U.S.A.* **65 H10** 35 6N 116 4W
Mojave Desert, *CA, U.S.A.* **65 H10** 35 0N 116 30W
Mojave Nat. Preserve ⌂, *U.S.A.* **65 H11** 35 7N 115 32W
Mojikit L., *Ont., Canada* **180 B8** 50 40N 88 15W
Mokane, *MO, U.S.A.* **82 C5** 38 41N 91 53W
Mōkapu Peninsula, *HI, U.S.A.* **69 K14** 21 25N 157 45W
Mokelumne →, *CA, U.S.A.* **64 E5** 38 13N 121 28W
Mokelumne Hill, *CA, U.S.A.* **64 E6** 38 18N 120 43W
Mōkōlea Rock, *HI, U.S.A.* **69 K14** 21 27N 157 44W
Mokuauia I., *HI, U.S.A.* **69 J14** 21 40N 157 56W
Mokulua Is., *HI, U.S.A.* **69 K14** 21 24N 157 42W
Mokumanu, *HI, U.S.A.* **69 K14** 21 28N 157 43W
Molalla, *OR, U.S.A.* **94 B3** 45 9N 122 35W
Molango, *Hidalgo, Mexico* **219 B9** 20 47N 98 43W
Molas, Pta., *Quintana Roo, Mexico* **223 B7** 20 35N 86 45W
Molena, *GA, U.S.A.* **68 C2** 33 1N 84 30W
Mōli'i Pond, *HI, U.S.A.* **69 J14** 21 31N 157 51W
Molina, *CO, U.S.A.* **66 C2** 39 11N 108 4W
Moline, *IL, U.S.A.* **71 B3** 41 30N 90 31W
Moline, *KS, U.S.A.* **74 D7** 37 22N 96 18W
Moline Acres, *MO, U.S.A.* **117 A2** 38 45N 90 15W
Molino, *FL, U.S.A.* **67 A1** 30 43N 87 20W
Molino de Rosas, *Distrito Federal, Mexico* **225 B2** 19 21N 99 14W
Moloka'i, *HI, U.S.A.* **69 B4** 21 8N 157 0W
Molokini I., *HI, U.S.A.* **69 C5** 20 38N 156 30W
Molson L., *Man., Canada* **183 A15** 54 22N 96 40W
Molybdenite Mt., *WA, U.S.A.* **101 B8** 48 42N 117 15W
Momax, *Zacatecas, Mexico* **217 F7** 21 55N 103 18W
Momence, *IL, U.S.A.* **71 B6** 41 10N 87 40W
Mona, *UT, U.S.A.* **100 D4** 39 49N 111 51W
Monadnock, Mt., *NH, U.S.A.* **86 D2** 42 52N 72 7W
Monahans, *TX, U.S.A.* **98 F5** 31 36N 102 54W
Monango, *ND, U.S.A.* **91 D7** 46 10N 98 36W
Monarch, *Alta., Canada* **185 J7** 49 48N 113 7W
Monarch, *SC, U.S.A.* **90 D4** 34 43N 81 36W
Monarch Mt., *B.C., Canada* **186 D9** 51 55N 125 57W
Monarch Pass, *CO, U.S.A.* **66 D4** 38 30N 106 20W
Monashee Mts., *B.C., Canada* **187 D16** 51 0N 118 43W
Monashee Pass, *B.C., Canada* **187 E16** 50 30N 118 15W
Moncks Corner, *SC, U.S.A.* **90 E5** 33 12N 80 1W
Monclova, *Campeche, Mexico* **223 D3** 18 4N 90 51W
Monclova, *Coahuila, Mexico* **214 D3** 26 54N 101 25W
Moncouche, L., *Qué., Canada* **177 C12** 48 45N 70 42W
Moncton, *N.B., Canada* **173 G5** 46 7N 64 51W
Mondamin, *IA, U.S.A.* **73 D2** 41 42N 96 1W
Mondonac, L., *Qué., Canada* **177 D9** 47 24N 73 58W
Mondovi, *WI, U.S.A.* **103 D2** 44 34N 91 40W
Monero, *NM, U.S.A.* **88 A4** 36 55N 106 52W
Monessen, *PA, U.S.A.* **95 D3** 40 9N 79 54W
Moneta, *IA, U.S.A.* **73 B3** 43 13N 95 24W
Moneta, *WY, U.S.A.* **104 C5** 43 9N 107 43W
Monett, *MO, U.S.A.* **82 E3** 36 55N 93 55W
Monette, *AR, U.S.A.* **63 C5** 35 53N 90 21W
Monfort Heights, *OH, U.S.A.* **107 A1** 39 11N 84 35W
Monhegan I., *ME, U.S.A.* **76 E4** 43 46N 69 19W
Moniac, *GA, U.S.A.* **68 F4** 30 31N 82 14W
Monico, *WI, U.S.A.* **103 C4** 45 35N 89 9W
Monida, *MT, U.S.A.* **83 F5** 44 34N 112 19W
Monida Pass, *U.S.A.* **70 E6** 44 34N 112 18W
Moniteau County ☆, *MO, U.S.A.* **82 C4** 38 35N 92 35W
Monitor, *Alta., Canada* **185 G10** 51 58N 110 34W
Monitor, *WA, U.S.A.* **101 C5** 47 29N 120 25W
Monitor Range, *NV, U.S.A.* **85 D4** 38 40N 116 40W
Monkstown, *Nfld. & L., Canada* **174 E6** 47 35N 54 26W
Monkstown, *TX, U.S.A.* **99 D12** 33 48N 95 56W
Monkton, *Ont., Canada* **178 D5** 43 35N 81 5W
Monkton, *MD, U.S.A.* **77 A4** 39 35N 76 37W
Monmouth, *IL, U.S.A.* **71 C3** 40 55N 90 39W
Monmouth, *OR, U.S.A.* **94 C2** 44 51N 123 14W
Monmouth County ☆, *NJ, U.S.A.* **87 B2** 40 15N 74 15W
Monmouth Junction, *NJ, U.S.A.* **87 B2** 40 23N 74 33W
Monmouth Mt., *B.C., Canada* **186 D11** 51 0N 123 47W
Mono County ☆, *CA, U.S.A.* **64 E7** 38 0N 119 0W
Mono L., *CA, U.S.A.* **64 E7** 38 1N 119 1W
Monocacy →, *MD, U.S.A.* **77 A3** 39 13N 77 27W
Monolith, *CA, U.S.A.* **65 H8** 35 7N 118 22W
Monomoy I., *MA, U.S.A.* **78 C5** 41 36N 69 59W
Monomoy Nat. Wildlife Refuge ⌂, *MA, U.S.A.* **78 C5** 41 29N 69 58W
Monomoy Point, *MA, U.S.A.* **78 C4** 41 33N 70 2W
Monon, *IN, U.S.A.* **72 C4** 40 52N 86 53W
Monona, *IA, U.S.A.* **73 B7** 43 3N 91 23W
Monona, *WI, U.S.A.* **103 E4** 43 4N 89 20W
Monona County ☆, *IA, U.S.A.* **73 D3** 42 0N 96 0W
Monongah, *WV, U.S.A.* **102 B4** 39 28N 80 13W
Monongahela, *PA, U.S.A.* **95 D3** 40 12N 79 56W
Monongahela →, *U.S.A.* **95 D2** 40 27N 80 1W
Monongahela Nat. Forest, *WV, U.S.A.* **102 C5** 38 30N 79 57W
Monongalia County ☆, *WV, U.S.A.* **102 B4** 39 39N 80 1W
Monowi, *NE, U.S.A.* **84 B7** 42 50N 98 20W
Monroe, *AR, U.S.A.* **63 D4** 34 44N 91 6W
Monroe, *GA, U.S.A.* **68 C3** 33 47N 83 43W
Monroe, *IN, U.S.A.* **72 C6** 40 45N 84 56W
Monroe, *IA, U.S.A.* **73 D5** 41 31N 93 6W

Monroe, LA, U.S.A. 75 B3 32 30N 92 7W
Monroe, MI, U.S.A. 79 H8 41 55N 83 24W
Monroe, NC, U.S.A. 90 D5 34 59N 80 33W
Monroe, NY, U.S.A. 87 A2 41 20N 74 11W
Monroe, NE, U.S.A. 84 C8 41 28N 97 36W
Monroe, OH, U.S.A. 92 D2 39 27N 84 22W
Monroe, OK, U.S.A. 93 D9 34 59N 94 30W
Monroe, OR, U.S.A. 94 C2 44 19N 123 18W
Monroe, SD, U.S.A. 91 G8 43 29N 97 13W
Monroe, UT, U.S.A. 100 E3 38 38N 112 7W
Monroe, VA, U.S.A. 102 D5 37 30N 79 8W
Monroe, WA, U.S.A. 101 C4 47 51N 121 58W
Monroe, WI, U.S.A. 103 F4 42 36N 89 38W
Monroe, L., FL, U.S.A. 67 C7 28 50N 81 19W
Monroe City, MO, U.S.A. 82 B5 39 39N 91 44W
Monroe County ☆, AL, U.S.A. 60 E3 31 31N 87 20W
Monroe County ☆, AR, U.S.A. 63 D4 34 42N 91 19W
Monroe County ☆, FL, U.S.A. 67 F7 25 30N 81 0W
Monroe County ☆, GA, U.S.A. 68 C3 33 0N 83 55W
Monroe County ☆, IL, U.S.A. 71 E3 38 15N 90 10W
Monroe County ☆, IN, U.S.A. 72 D4 39 10N 86 30W
Monroe County ☆, IA, U.S.A. 73 E6 41 0N 92 50W
Monroe County ☆, KY, U.S.A. 97 D7 36 45N 85 45W
Monroe County ☆, MI, U.S.A. 79 H8 41 50N 83 35W
Monroe County ☆, MS, U.S.A. 81 C5 33 49N 88 33W
Monroe County ☆, MO, U.S.A. 82 B5 39 30N 92 0W
Monroe County ☆, NY, U.S.A. 89 B3 43 10N 77 40W
Monroe County ☆, OH, U.S.A. 92 D5 39 46N 81 7W
Monroe County ☆, PA, U.S.A. 95 C7 41 0N 75 15W
Monroe County ☆, TN, U.S.A. 97 E8 35 31N 84 22W
Monroe County ☆, WV, U.S.A. 102 D4 37 36N 80 33W
Monroe County ☆, WI, U.S.A. 103 E3 43 50N 90 40W
Monroe L., IN, U.S.A. 72 D4 39 1N 86 31W
Monroeton, PA, U.S.A. 95 C6 41 43N 76 29W
Monroeville, AL, U.S.A. 60 E3 31 31N 87 20W
Monroeville, IN, U.S.A. 72 C6 40 59N 84 52W
Monroeville, OH, U.S.A. 92 B4 41 15N 82 42W
Monroeville, PA, U.S.A. 95 D3 40 26N 79 45W
Monrovia, Los Angeles, U.S.A. 111 B4 34 9N 118 1W
Monsey, NY, U.S.A. 87 A2 41 7N 74 4W
Monson, ME, U.S.A. 76 C4 45 17N 69 30W
Monson, MA, U.S.A. 78 B2 42 6N 72 19W
Mont Alto, PA, U.S.A. 77 A3 39 51N 77 34W
Mont Belvieu, TX, U.S.A. 99 H13 29 51N 94 53W
Mont-Bleu, Qué., Canada 192 A1 45 27N 75 45W
Mont-Carmel, Qué., Canada 177 D13 47 26N 69 52W
Mont Ida, KS, U.S.A. 74 C8 38 13N 95 22W
Mont-Joli, Qué., Canada 177 C14 48 37N 68 10W
Mont-Laurier, Qué., Canada 176 E7 46 35N 75 30W
Mont-Louis, Qué., Canada 172 D4 49 15N 65 44W
Mont-Royal, Montréal, Canada 192 A3 45 30N 73 38W
Mont St-Pierre, Qué., Canada 172 D4 49 13N 65 49W
Mont-Tremblant, Qué., Canada 176 E8 46 13N 74 36W
Mont-Tremblant, Parc de Récr.
du ⌓, Qué., Canada 177 E8 46 30N 74 30W
Mont Vernon, NH, U.S.A. 86 D3 42 50N 71 42W
Montagne, Parc de la, Qué.,
Canada 192 A1 45 27N 75 45W
Montague, P.E.I., Canada 173 G7 46 10N 62 39W
Montague, CA, U.S.A. 64 B4 41 44N 122 32W
Montague, MA, U.S.A. 78 B2 42 32N 72 32W
Montague, MI, U.S.A. 79 F5 43 25N 86 22W
Montague, TX, U.S.A. 99 D10 33 42N 97 48W
Montague, I., Baja Calif., Mexico 210 B4 31 45N 114 48W
Montague County ☆, TX, U.S.A. 99 D10 33 47N 97 44W
Montague I., AK, U.S.A. 61 G11 60 0N 147 30W
Montalba, TX, U.S.A. 99 F12 31 53N 95 44W
Montana □, U.S.A. 83 C7 47 0N 110 0W
Montana City, MT, U.S.A. 83 D6 46 32N 111 56W
Montauk, NY, U.S.A. 78 C3 41 3N 71 57W
Montauk Pt., NY, U.S.A. 78 C3 41 4N 71 51W
Montbello, Denver, U.S.A. 109 B3 39 47N 104 49W
Montcalm County ☆, MI, U.S.A. 79 F6 43 15N 85 10W
Montcerf, Qué., Canada 176 E6 46 32N 76 3W
Montcevelles, L., Qué., Canada 172 B9 51 7N 60 38W
Montclair, NJ, U.S.A. 87 B2 40 49N 74 12W
Monte Albán, Oaxaca, Mexico 221 G4 17 2N 96 46W
Monte Blanco, Veracruz, Mexico 221 F3 18 58N 97 2W
Monte Escobedo, Zacatecas,
Mexico 217 E7 22 18N 103 34W
Monte Grande, Tabasco, Mexico 222 B4 17 56N 92 16W
Monte Pio, Veracruz, Mexico 221 F5 18 38N 95 6W
Monte Redondo, Chihuahua,
Mexico 213 F10 27 38N 105 37W
Monte Vista, CO, U.S.A. 66 E4 37 35N 106 9W
Monteagle, TN, U.S.A. 97 E7 35 15N 85 50W
Montebello, Qué., Canada 176 F8 45 40N 74 55W
Montebello, Los Angeles, U.S.A. 111 B4 34 1N 118 8W
Montecito, CA, U.S.A. 65 J7 34 26N 119 40W
Montegut, LA, U.S.A. 75 E5 29 28N 90 33W
Montello, NV, U.S.A. 85 A6 41 16N 114 12W
Montello, WI, U.S.A. 103 E4 43 48N 89 20W
Montemorelos, Nuevo León,
Mexico 215 E5 25 12N 99 49W
Monterde, Sa., Chihuahua, Mexico 213 F7 27 45N 108 25W
Monterey, CA, U.S.A. 64 G5 36 37N 121 55W
Monterey, KY, U.S.A. 97 B8 38 25N 84 52W
Monterey, MA, U.S.A. 78 B1 42 11N 73 13W
Monterey, TN, U.S.A. 97 D7 36 9N 85 16W
Monterey, VA, U.S.A. 102 C5 38 25N 79 35W
Monterey B., CA, U.S.A. 64 G5 36 45N 122 0W
Monterey County ☆, CA, U.S.A. 65 G5 36 15N 121 20W
Monterey Park, Los Angeles,
U.S.A. 111 B4 34 3N 118 7W
Monterrey, Baja Calif., Mexico 210 A3 32 34N 115 4W
Monterrey, Chiapas, Mexico 222 C3 16 5N 93 23W
Monterrey, Nuevo León, Mexico 214 E4 25 40N 100 19W
Montes Azules, Reserva de la
Biosfera ⌓, Chiapas, Mexico 222 C5 16 30N 91 10W
Montesano, WA, U.S.A. 101 D2 46 59N 123 36W
Montevallo, AL, U.S.A. 60 C4 33 6N 86 52W
Montevideo, MN, U.S.A. 80 F3 44 57N 95 43W
Monteview, ID, U.S.A. 70 F6 43 56N 112 32W
Montezuma, GA, U.S.A. 68 D2 32 18N 84 2W
Montezuma, IN, U.S.A. 72 D3 39 48N 87 22W
Montezuma, IA, U.S.A. 73 D6 41 35N 92 32W
Montezuma, KS, U.S.A. 74 D3 37 36N 100 27W
Montezuma Castle Nat.
Monument ⌓, AZ, U.S.A. 62 C4 34 39N 111 45W
Montezuma County ☆, CO, U.S.A. 66 E2 37 20N 108 30W
Montezuma Cr. →, UT, U.S.A. 100 F6 37 17N 109 20W
Montezuma Creek, UT, U.S.A. 100 F6 37 16N 109 19W
Montfort, WI, U.S.A. 103 F3 42 58N 90 26W
Montgomery, AL, U.S.A. 60 D4 32 23N 86 19W
Montgomery, LA, U.S.A. 75 C3 31 40N 92 53W
Montgomery, MN, U.S.A. 80 F5 44 26N 93 35W
Montgomery, NY, U.S.A. 87 A2 41 32N 74 14W
Montgomery, PA, U.S.A. 95 C6 41 10N 76 53W
Montgomery, TX, U.S.A. 99 G12 30 23N 95 42W
Montgomery, WV, U.S.A. 102 C3 38 11N 81 19W
Montgomery Center, VT, U.S.A. 86 B1 44 53N 73 40W
Montgomery City, MO, U.S.A. 82 C5 38 59N 91 30W
Montgomery County ☆, AL,
U.S.A. 60 D4 32 15N 86 18W
Montgomery County ☆, AR,
U.S.A. 63 D2 34 34N 93 38W
Montgomery County ☆, GA,
U.S.A. 68 D4 32 15N 82 35W
Montgomery County ☆, IL, U.S.A. 71 D4 39 10N 89 30W
Montgomery County ☆, IN, U.S.A. 72 C4 40 5N 86 55W
Montgomery County ☆, IA, U.S.A. 73 D3 41 0N 95 10W
Montgomery County ☆, KS,
U.S.A. 74 D8 37 15N 95 45W
Montgomery County ☆, KY,
U.S.A. 97 B9 38 0N 83 55W
Montgomery County ☆, MD,
U.S.A. 77 A3 39 15N 77 15W
Montgomery County ☆, MS,
U.S.A. 81 C4 33 29N 89 44W
Montgomery County ☆, MO,
U.S.A. 82 C5 38 55N 91 30W
Montgomery County ☆, NC,
U.S.A. 90 C6 35 20N 79 50W
Montgomery County ☆, NY,
U.S.A. 89 C6 42 50N 74 30W
Montgomery County ☆, OH,
U.S.A. 92 D2 39 45N 84 12W
Montgomery County ☆, PA,
U.S.A. 95 D7 40 10N 75 10W
Montgomery County ☆, TN,
U.S.A. 96 D5 36 32N 87 21W
Montgomery County ☆, TX,
U.S.A. 99 G12 30 19N 95 27W
Montgomery County ☆, VA,
U.S.A. 102 D4 37 8N 80 25W
Montgomery Field, San Diego,
U.S.A. 117 B2 32 48N 117 8W
Montgomery Pass, NV, U.S.A. 85 E2 37 58N 118 20W
Montgomery Village, MD, U.S.A. 77 A3 39 12N 77 13W
Monticello, AR, U.S.A. 63 E4 33 38N 91 47W
Monticello, FL, U.S.A. 67 A5 30 33N 83 52W
Monticello, GA, U.S.A. 68 C3 33 18N 83 40W
Monticello, IL, U.S.A. 71 C5 40 1N 88 34W
Monticello, IN, U.S.A. 72 C4 40 45N 86 46W
Monticello, IA, U.S.A. 73 C7 42 15N 91 12W
Monticello, KY, U.S.A. 97 D8 36 50N 84 51W
Monticello, ME, U.S.A. 76 B6 46 19N 67 51W
Monticello, MN, U.S.A. 80 E5 45 18N 93 48W
Monticello, MS, U.S.A. 81 E3 31 33N 90 7W
Monticello, MO, U.S.A. 82 A5 40 7N 91 43W
Monticello, NM, U.S.A. 88 D3 33 24N 107 27W
Monticello, NY, U.S.A. 89 D6 41 39N 74 42W
Monticello, UT, U.S.A. 100 F6 37 52N 109 21W
Monticello, WI, U.S.A. 103 F4 42 45N 89 36W
Monticello, VA, U.S.A. 102 D6 38 0N 78 27W
Montmagny, Qué., Canada 177 E12 46 58N 70 34W
Montmartre, Sask., Canada 182 E8 50 14N 103 27W
Montmorency County ☆, MI,
U.S.A. 79 D7 45 0N 84 10W
Montour, ID, U.S.A. 70 F2 43 55N 116 20W
Montour, IA, U.S.A. 73 D6 41 59N 92 43W
Montour County ☆, PA, U.S.A. 95 D6 41 0N 76 40W
Montour Falls, NY, U.S.A. 89 C4 42 21N 76 51W
Montoursville, PA, U.S.A. 95 C6 41 15N 76 55W
Montoya, NM, U.S.A. 88 B6 35 6N 104 4W
Montpelier, ID, U.S.A. 70 G7 42 19N 111 18W
Montpelier, IN, U.S.A. 72 C5 40 33N 85 17W
Montpelier, LA, U.S.A. 75 D5 30 41N 90 39W
Montpelier, MS, U.S.A. 81 C5 33 43N 88 57W
Montpelier, ND, U.S.A. 91 D7 46 42N 98 35W
Montpelier, OH, U.S.A. 92 B2 41 35N 84 37W
Montpelier, VA, U.S.A. 102 D7 37 49N 77 41W
Montpelier, VT, U.S.A. 86 B2 44 16N 72 35W
Montréal, Qué., Canada 177 F9 45 30N 73 33W
Montreal →, Ont., Canada 181 E12 47 14N 84 39W
Montréal, Î. de, Qué., Canada 192 A3 45 30N 73 40W
Montréal, Université de, Montréal,
Canada 192 B3 45 29N 73 37W
Montréal Dorval International ✕
(YUL), Qué., Canada 177 F9 45 28N 73 44W
Montréal Est, Montréal, Canada 192 A3 45 37N 73 31W
Montreal I., Ont., Canada 181 E12 47 19N 84 44W
Montreal L., Sask., Canada 182 A6 54 20N 105 45W
Montreal Lake, Sask., Canada 182 A6 54 3N 105 46W
Montréal-Nord, Qué., Canada 177 F9 45 36N 73 36W
Montréal-Ouest, Montréal, Canada 192 B2 45 27N 73 39W
Montreat, NC, U.S.A. 90 C3 35 39N 82 15W
Montreuil, L., Qué., Canada 176 A5 50 12N 77 40W
Montrose, B.C., Canada 187 F17 49 5N 117 35W
Montrose, AR, U.S.A. 63 E4 33 18N 91 30W
Montrose, CO, U.S.A. 66 D3 38 29N 107 53W
Montrose, IL, U.S.A. 71 D5 39 10N 88 23W
Montrose, IA, U.S.A. 73 E7 40 31N 91 25W
Montrose, Los Angeles, U.S.A. 111 A2 34 12N 118 13W
Montrose, MI, U.S.A. 79 F8 43 11N 83 54W
Montrose, MS, U.S.A. 81 D4 32 8N 89 14W
Montrose, MO, U.S.A. 82 C3 38 16N 93 59W
Montrose, PA, U.S.A. 95 C7 41 50N 75 53W
Montrose, SD, U.S.A. 91 G8 43 42N 97 11W
Montrose, WV, U.S.A. 102 B5 39 4N 79 49W
Montrose County ☆, CO, U.S.A. 66 D2 38 30N 108 15W
Montross, VA, U.S.A. 77 B4 38 6N 76 50W
Monts, Pte. des, Qué., Canada 172 D2 49 20N 67 12W
Monts-Valin, Parc des ⌓, Qué.,
Canada 177 C12 48 37N 70 48W
Montserrat, I., Baja Calif. S.,
Mexico 211 H7 25 40N 111 5W
Montvale, VA, U.S.A. 102 D5 37 23N 79 44W
Montville, CT, U.S.A. 78 C2 41 27N 72 8W
Monument, CO, U.S.A. 66 C6 39 6N 104 52W
Monument, KS, U.S.A. 74 B2 39 6N 101 1W
Monument, OR, U.S.A. 94 C6 44 49N 119 25W
Monument Draw →, TX, U.S.A. 98 E5 32 29N 102 20W
Monument Pass, AZ, U.S.A. 62 A5 36 58N 110 5W
Monument Pk., ID, U.S.A. 70 G4 42 7N 114 14W
Monument Valley, U.S.A. 62 A5 36 56N 110 5W
Moodus, CT, U.S.A. 78 C2 41 30N 72 25W
Moody, AL, U.S.A. 60 C4 33 35N 86 29W
Moody, MO, U.S.A. 82 E5 36 32N 91 59W
Moody, TX, U.S.A. 99 F10 31 18N 97 21W
Moody Air Force Base, GA,
U.S.A. 68 F3 30 58N 83 12W
Moody County ☆, SD, U.S.A. 91 F9 44 3N 96 36W
Moodyville = North Vancouver,
B.C., Canada 187 F11 49 19N 123 4W
Mooers, NY, U.S.A. 86 B1 44 58N 73 35W
Mooleyville, KY, U.S.A. 96 B6 38 1N 86 28W
Moomaw, L., VA, U.S.A. 102 D5 37 57N 79 57W
Moon L., CA, U.S.A. 64 B6 41 10N 120 22W
Moon Res., OR, U.S.A. 94 D6 43 24N 119 24W
Moonachie, NJ, U.S.A. 114 A2 40 50N 74 2W
Moonbeam, Ont., Canada 181 C14 49 20N 82 10W
Mooney's Bay, Ont., Canada 192 B1 45 22N 75 41W
Mooney's Bay Park, Ont., Canada 192 B1 45 22N 75 41W
Moorcroft, WY, U.S.A. 104 B8 44 16N 104 57W
Moore, ID, U.S.A. 70 F5 43 44N 113 22W
Moore, MT, U.S.A. 83 D8 46 59N 109 42W
Moore, OK, U.S.A. 93 C6 35 20N 97 29W
Moore, TX, U.S.A. 99 H8 29 3N 99 1W
Moore, UT, U.S.A. 100 E4 38 58N 111 10W
Moore County ☆, NC, U.S.A. 90 C6 35 20N 79 20W
Moore County ☆, TN, U.S.A. 96 E6 35 17N 86 22W
Moore County ☆, TX, U.S.A. 98 B6 35 55N 101 59W
Moore Haven, FL, U.S.A. 67 E7 26 50N 81 6W
Moore Res., NH, U.S.A. 86 B3 44 20N 71 53W
Moorefield, NE, U.S.A. 84 D5 40 41N 100 24W
Moorefield, WV, U.S.A. 77 A2 39 4N 78 58W
Mooreland, OK, U.S.A. 93 B4 36 26N 99 12W
Moores Creek Nat. Battlefield ⌓,
NC, U.S.A. 90 D7 34 27N 78 7W
Moores Mill, N.B., Canada 173 H2 45 18N 67 17W
Moores Mill, AL, U.S.A. 60 B4 34 51N 86 31W
Moorestown, NJ, U.S.A. 87 C2 39 58N 74 57W
Mooresville, IN, U.S.A. 72 D4 39 37N 86 22W
Mooresville, NC, U.S.A. 90 C5 35 35N 80 48W
Mooreton, ND, U.S.A. 91 D9 46 16N 96 53W
Moorhead, IA, U.S.A. 73 D3 41 56N 95 51W
Moorhead, MN, U.S.A. 80 D2 46 53N 96 45W
Moorhead, MS, U.S.A. 81 C3 33 27N 90 30W
Mooringsport, LA, U.S.A. 75 B2 32 41N 93 58W
Moorland, IA, U.S.A. 73 C4 42 26N 94 18W
Moose, WY, U.S.A. 104 C2 43 39N 110 43W
Moose →, Ont., Canada 181 A16 51 20N 80 25W
Moose →, ME, U.S.A. 76 C4 45 41N 69 45W
Moose →, NY, U.S.A. 89 B5 43 38N 75 24W
Moose →, VT, U.S.A. 86 B2 44 24N 72 1W
Moose Creek, Ont., Canada 179 B12 45 15N 74 58W
Moose Factory, Ont., Canada 181 A16 51 16N 80 32W
Moose Heights, B.C., Canada 187 B12 53 4N 122 31W
Moose I., Man., Canada 183 D14 51 42N 97 10W
Moose Jaw, Sask., Canada 182 E6 50 24N 105 30W
Moose Jaw →, Sask., Canada 182 E6 50 34N 105 18W
Moose L., Alta., Canada 184 D10 54 15N 110 55W
Moose L., Man., Canada 183 B11 53 46N 100 8W
Moose Lake, MN, U.S.A. 80 D6 46 27N 92 46W
Moose Mountain Cr. →, Sask.,
Canada 182 F9 49 13N 102 12W
Moose Mountain Prov. Park ⌓,
Sask., Canada 183 F9 49 48N 102 25W
Moose Pass, AK, U.S.A. 61 F10 60 29N 149 22W
Moose River, Ont., Canada 181 B15 50 48N 81 17W
Moose River, ME, U.S.A. 76 C3 45 39N 70 16W
Moosehead L., ME, U.S.A. 76 C4 45 38N 69 40W
Mooselookmeguntic L., ME,
U.S.A. 76 D3 44 55N 70 49W
Moosic, PA, U.S.A. 87 A1 41 21N 75 44W
Moosilauke, Mt., NH, U.S.A. 86 B3 44 3N 71 40W
Moosomin, Sask., Canada 183 E10 50 9N 101 40W
Moosonee, Ont., Canada 181 A16 51 17N 80 39W
Moosup, CT, U.S.A. 78 C3 41 43N 71 53W
Mora, GA, U.S.A. 68 E4 31 25N 82 57W
Mora, MN, U.S.A. 80 E5 45 53N 93 18W
Mora, NM, U.S.A. 88 B5 35 58N 105 20W
Mora →, NM, U.S.A. 88 B6 35 35N 104 25W
Mora County ☆, NM, U.S.A. 88 B6 36 0N 104 58W
Morada, CA, U.S.A. 64 E5 38 2N 121 15W
Moraga, San Francisco, U.S.A. 118 B4 37 50N 122 7W
Morales, TX, U.S.A. 99 H11 29 8N 96 46W
Morales, L., Tamaulipas, Mexico 215 G7 23 35N 97 47W
Moran, KS, U.S.A. 74 D8 37 55N 95 10W
Moran, MI, U.S.A. 79 C7 46 0N 84 50W
Moran, TX, U.S.A. 99 E8 32 33N 99 10W
Moran, WY, U.S.A. 104 C2 43 50N 110 31W
Moravia, IA, U.S.A. 73 E6 40 53N 92 49W
Moravia, NY, U.S.A. 89 C4 42 43N 76 25W
Morden, Man., Canada 183 F13 49 15N 98 10W
Moreau →, SD, U.S.A. 91 E5 45 18N 100 43W
Morehead, KY, U.S.A. 97 B9 38 11N 83 26W
Morehead City, NC, U.S.A. 90 D9 34 43N 76 43W
Morehouse, MO, U.S.A. 82 E7 36 51N 89 41W
Morehouse Parish ☆, LA, U.S.A. 75 B4 32 47N 91 48W
Moreland, GA, U.S.A. 68 C2 33 17N 84 46W
Moreland, KY, U.S.A. 97 C8 37 30N 84 49W
Morelia, Michoacan, Mexico 219 C6 19 42N 101 7W
Morell, P.E.I., Canada 173 G7 46 25N 62 42W
Morelos, Baja Calif. S., Mexico 211 E4 28 19N 114 5W
Morelos, Chihuahua, Mexico 213 G8 26 42N 107 40W
Morelos, Coahuila, Mexico 214 C3 28 0N 101 43W
Morelos, Coahuila, Mexico 214 A2 29 6N 102 26W
Morelos, Coahuila, Mexico 214 B4 28 25N 100 53W
Morelos, Durango, Mexico 216 B5 25 45N 105 15W
Morelos, Sonora, Mexico 212 C6 30 50N 109 13W
Morelos, Sonora, Mexico 212 B5 31 12N 110 14W
Morelos, Zacatecas, Mexico 217 E8 22 53N 102 37W
Morelos □, Mexico 219 D9 18 45N 99 0W
Morenci, AZ, U.S.A. 62 D6 33 5N 109 22W
Morenci, MI, U.S.A. 79 H7 41 43N 84 13W
Moreno Valley, CA, U.S.A. 65 K9 33 56N 117 14W
Moresby I., B.C., Canada 186 C3 52 30N 131 40W
Morevain Falls, NC, U.S.A. 90 B4 36 6N 81 11W
Morfin Chávez, Zacatecas, Mexico 217 D8 23 11N 102 46W
Morgan, GA, U.S.A. 68 E2 31 32N 84 36W
Morgan, KY, U.S.A. 97 B8 38 36N 84 24W
Morgan, MN, U.S.A. 80 F4 44 25N 94 56W
Morgan, UT, U.S.A. 100 B4 41 2N 111 41W
Morgan, VT, U.S.A. 86 B1 44 53N 73 2W
Morgan, Mt., CA, U.S.A. 65 F8 37 31N 118 47W
Morgan City, AL, U.S.A. 60 B4 34 28N 86 34W
Morgan City, LA, U.S.A. 75 E4 29 42N 91 12W
Morgan City, MS, U.S.A. 81 C3 33 23N 90 21W
Morgan County ☆, AL, U.S.A. 60 B4 34 27N 86 56W
Morgan County ☆, CO, U.S.A. 66 B7 40 15N 103 50W
Morgan County ☆, GA, U.S.A. 68 C3 33 40N 83 25W
Morgan County ☆, IL, U.S.A. 71 D3 39 45N 90 10W
Morgan County ☆, IN, U.S.A. 72 D4 39 30N 86 25W
Morgan County ☆, KY, U.S.A. 97 C9 37 55N 83 15W
Morgan County ☆, MO, U.S.A. 82 C4 38 25N 92 50W
Morgan County ☆, OH, U.S.A. 92 D5 39 39N 81 51W
Morgan County ☆, TN, U.S.A. 97 D8 36 6N 84 36W
Morgan County ☆, UT, U.S.A. 100 B4 41 10N 111 45W
Morgan County ☆, WV, U.S.A. 102 B6 39 35N 78 16W
Morgan Hill, CA, U.S.A. 64 F5 37 8N 121 39W
Morgan L., NM, U.S.A. 88 A2 36 52N 108 41W
Morgan Mill, TX, U.S.A. 99 E9 32 23N 98 10W
Morgan Park, Chicago, U.S.A. 108 C3 41 41N 87 38W
Morganfield, KY, U.S.A. 96 C5 37 41N 87 55W
Morganton, GA, U.S.A. 68 B2 34 53N 84 15W
Morganton, NC, U.S.A. 90 C4 35 45N 81 41W
Morgantown, IN, U.S.A. 72 D4 39 22N 86 16W
Morgantown, KY, U.S.A. 96 C6 37 14N 86 41W
Morgantown, MD, U.S.A. 77 B4 38 21N 76 58W
Morgantown, MS, U.S.A. 81 E5 31 18N 88 55W
Morgantown, MS, U.S.A. 81 E2 31 34N 91 21W
Morgantown, OH, U.S.A. 92 D3 39 8N 83 12W
Morgantown, WV, U.S.A. 102 B5 39 38N 79 57W
Morganville, KS, U.S.A. 74 B6 39 28N 97 12W
Morganza, LA, U.S.A. 75 D4 30 44N 91 36W
Moriah, Mt., NV, U.S.A. 85 C6 39 17N 114 12W
Moriarty, NM, U.S.A. 88 C4 34 59N 106 3W
Morice →, B.C., Canada 186 A7 54 12N 127 5W
Morice L., B.C., Canada 186 B7 53 50N 127 40W
Morin-Heights, Qué., Canada 177 F8 45 54N 74 15W
Morinville, Alta., Canada 184 E7 53 49N 113 41W
Moris, Chihuahua, Mexico 212 E7 28 10N 108 32W
Morland, KS, U.S.A. 74 B3 39 21N 100 5W
Morley, MI, U.S.A. 79 F6 43 29N 85 27W
Morley, MO, U.S.A. 82 D7 37 3N 89 37W
Mormon L., AZ, U.S.A. 62 C4 34 57N 111 29W
Mormon Lake, AZ, U.S.A. 62 C4 34 55N 111 28W
Mormon Mts., NV, U.S.A. 85 F6 37 0N 114 0W
Morning Sun, IA, U.S.A. 73 D7 41 5N 91 15W
Morningside, MD, U.S.A. 77 B4 38 49N 76 53W
Morningside Park, Orlando, U.S.A. 115 B2 28 26N 81 24W
Moro, AR, U.S.A. 63 D5 34 48N 90 59W
Moro, OR, U.S.A. 94 B5 45 29N 120 44W
Moro →, AR, U.S.A. 63 E3 33 17N 92 21W
Morocco, IN, U.S.A. 72 C3 40 57N 87 27W
Moroleón, Guanajuato, Mexico 219 B6 20 8N 101 12W
Morongo Indian Reservation, CA,
U.S.A. 65 K10 33 57N 116 49W
Moroni, UT, U.S.A. 100 D4 39 32N 111 35W
Morral, OH, U.S.A. 92 C3 40 41N 83 13W
Morrill, KS, U.S.A. 74 B8 39 56N 95 42W
Morrill, NE, U.S.A. 84 C2 41 58N 103 56W
Morrill County ☆, NE, U.S.A. 84 C3 41 45N 103 0W
Morrilton, AR, U.S.A. 63 C3 35 9N 92 44W
Morrin, Alta., Canada 185 G8 51 40N 112 47W
Morris, Man., Canada 183 F14 49 25N 97 22W
Morris, CT, U.S.A. 78 C1 41 43N 73 15W
Morris, GA, U.S.A. 68 E2 31 48N 84 57W
Morris, IL, U.S.A. 71 B5 41 22N 88 26W
Morris, MN, U.S.A. 80 E3 45 35N 95 55W
Morris, NY, U.S.A. 89 C5 42 33N 75 15W
Morris, OK, U.S.A. 93 C8 35 36N 95 51W
Morris →, Man., Canada 183 F14 49 21N 97 21W
Morris County ☆, KS, U.S.A. 74 C7 38 30N 96 40W
Morris County ☆, NJ, U.S.A. 87 B2 40 45N 74 30W
Morris County ☆, TX, U.S.A. 99 D13 33 2N 94 44W
Morrisburg, Ont., Canada 179 C11 44 55N 75 7W
Morrison, IL, U.S.A. 71 B4 41 49N 89 58W
Morrison, OK, U.S.A. 93 B6 36 18N 97 1W
Morrison, TN, U.S.A. 97 E7 35 36N 85 55W
Morrison County ☆, MN, U.S.A. 80 E4 46 0N 94 10W
Morrisonville, IL, U.S.A. 71 D4 39 25N 89 27W
Morrisonville, NY, U.S.A. 86 B1 44 42N 73 34W
Morristown, AZ, U.S.A. 62 D3 33 51N 112 37W
Morristown, IN, U.S.A. 72 D5 39 40N 85 42W
Morristown, MN, U.S.A. 80 F5 44 14N 93 27W
Morristown, NJ, U.S.A. 87 B2 40 48N 74 29W
Morristown, NY, U.S.A. 89 A5 44 35N 75 39W
Morristown, SD, U.S.A. 91 E4 45 56N 101 43W
Morristown, TN, U.S.A. 97 D9 36 13N 83 18W
Morristown, VT, U.S.A. 86 B2 44 33N 72 37W
Morrisville, MO, U.S.A. 82 D3 37 29N 93 25W
Morrisville, NC, U.S.A. 90 C7 35 49N 78 50W
Morrisville, NY, U.S.A. 89 C5 42 53N 75 35W
Morrisville, PA, U.S.A. 87 B2 40 13N 74 47W
Morrisville, VT, U.S.A. 86 B2 44 34N 72 36W
Morro Bay, CA, U.S.A. 65 H6 35 22N 120 51W
Morro Santo Domingo,
Baja Calif. S., Mexico 211 E4 28 12N 114 8W
Morrow, LA, U.S.A. 75 D3 30 50N 92 5W
Morrow, OH, U.S.A. 92 D2 39 21N 84 8W
Morrow County ☆, OH, U.S.A. 92 C4 40 33N 82 50W
Morrow County ☆, OR, U.S.A. 94 B6 45 25N 119 40W
Morrowville, KS, U.S.A. 74 B6 39 51N 97 10W
Morse, Sask., Canada 182 E4 50 25N 107 3W
Morse, LA, U.S.A. 75 D3 30 17N 92 30W
Morse, TX, U.S.A. 98 A6 36 4N 101 29W
Morse Bluff, NE, U.S.A. 84 C9 41 26N 96 46W
Morse Res., IN, U.S.A. 72 C4 40 7N 86 3W
Morson, Ont., Canada 180 C2 49 6N 94 19W
Mortlach, Sask., Canada 182 E5 50 27N 106 4W
Morton, IL, U.S.A. 71 C4 40 37N 89 28W
Morton, MN, U.S.A. 80 F4 44 33N 94 59W
Morton, MS, U.S.A. 81 D4 32 21N 89 39W
Morton, TX, U.S.A. 98 D5 33 44N 102 46W
Morton, WA, U.S.A. 101 D3 46 34N 122 17W
Morton, WY, U.S.A. 104 C4 43 12N 108 46W
Morton County ☆, KS, U.S.A. 74 D2 37 15N 101 45W
Morton County ☆, ND, U.S.A. 91 D4 46 45N 101 30W
Morton Grove, Chicago, U.S.A. 108 A2 42 2N 87 46W
Mortons Gap, KY, U.S.A. 96 C5 37 14N 87 28W
Morven, GA, U.S.A. 68 F3 30 57N 83 30W
Morven, NC, U.S.A. 90 D5 34 52N 80 0W
Morven, VA, U.S.A. 102 D6 37 58N 78 28W
Mosby, MT, U.S.A. 83 C11 47 0N 107 52W
Mosca, CO, U.S.A. 66 E5 37 39N 105 52W
Moscow, ID, U.S.A. 70 C2 46 44N 117 0W
Moscow, KS, U.S.A. 74 D2 37 20N 101 12W
Moscow, KY, U.S.A. 96 D3 36 37N 89 2W
Moscow, OH, U.S.A. 92 E2 38 52N 84 14W
Moscow, PA, U.S.A. 87 A1 41 20N 75 31W
Moscow, TN, U.S.A. 96 E3 35 4N 89 24W
Moscow Mills, MO, U.S.A. 82 C6 38 57N 90 55W
Moselle, MS, U.S.A. 81 E4 31 30N 89 17W
Mosenthein Island, IL, U.S.A. 117 A2 38 43N 90 12W
Moses Inlet, B.C., Canada 186 D7 51 47N 127 23W
Moses Lake, WA, U.S.A. 101 C6 47 8N 119 17W
Moshannon State Forest, PA,
U.S.A. 95 C4 41 7N 78 29W
Mosheim, TN, U.S.A. 97 D10 36 11N 82 57W
Mosher, Ont., Canada 181 D12 48 42N 84 12W
Mosher, SD, U.S.A. 91 G5 43 28N 100 18W
Mosier, OR, U.S.A. 94 B4 45 41N 121 24W
Mosinee, WI, U.S.A. 103 D4 44 47N 89 43W
Mosley Cr. →, B.C., Canada 186 D10 51 18N 124 50W
Mosquero, NM, U.S.A. 88 B7 35 47N 103 58W
Mosquiteros, L., Quintana Roo,
Mexico 223 C6 19 12N 87 33W
Mosquito, Pta., Yucatán, Mexico 223 A6 21 34N 87 48W
Mosquito B., Qué., Canada 175 A2 61 10N 78 0W
Mosquito Creek L., OH, U.S.A. 92 B6 41 18N 80 46W
Moss, TN, U.S.A. 97 D7 36 36N 85 37W
Moss Bluff, LA, U.S.A. 75 D2 30 18N 93 11W
Moss Point, MS, U.S.A. 81 F5 30 25N 88 30W
Mossbank, Sask., Canada 182 F6 49 56N 105 56W
Mossy →, Sask., Canada 182 A9 54 5N 102 58W
Mossy Head, FL, U.S.A. 67 A2 30 45N 86 19W
Mossyrock, WA, U.S.A. 101 D3 46 32N 122 29W
Motley, MN, U.S.A. 80 D4 46 20N 94 40W
Motley County ☆, TX, U.S.A. 98 C7 34 1N 100 50W
Motor Speedway, IN, U.S.A. 72 D4 39 48N 86 14W
Motozintla de Mendoza, Chiapas,
Mexico 222 D4 15 22N 92 14W
Mott, ND, U.S.A. 91 D3 46 23N 102 20W
Motte, L. la, Qué., Canada 176 C4 48 20N 78 2W
Motters, MD, U.S.A. 77 A3 39 40N 77 20W
Motul, Yucatán, Mexico 223 A4 21 6N 89 17W
Mouchalagane →, Qué., Canada 175 C4 50 56N 68 41W
Moulton, AL, U.S.A. 60 B3 34 29N 87 18W
Moulton, IA, U.S.A. 73 E6 40 41N 92 41W
Moulton, TX, U.S.A. 99 H10 29 35N 97 9W
Moultonborough, NH, U.S.A. 86 C3 43 45N 71 10W
Moultrie, GA, U.S.A. 68 E3 31 11N 83 47W
Moultrie, L., SC, U.S.A. 90 E5 33 20N 80 5W
Moultrie County ☆, IL, U.S.A. 71 D5 39 40N 88 35W
Mound, LA, U.S.A. 75 B4 32 21N 91 1W
Mound Bayou, MS, U.S.A. 81 C3 33 53N 90 44W
Mound City, IL, U.S.A. 71 F4 37 5N 89 10W
Mound City, KS, U.S.A. 74 C9 38 8N 94 49W
Mound City, MO, U.S.A. 82 A1 40 7N 95 14W
Mound City, SD, U.S.A. 91 E5 45 44N 100 4W
Mound Valley, KS, U.S.A. 74 D8 37 12N 95 24W
Moundridge, KS, U.S.A. 74 C6 38 12N 97 31W
Mounds, IL, U.S.A. 71 F4 37 7N 89 12W
Mounds, OK, U.S.A. 93 C7 35 53N 96 4W
Moundsville, WV, U.S.A. 102 B4 39 55N 80 44W
Moundville, AL, U.S.A. 60 C3 33 1N 87 37W
Moundville, MO, U.S.A. 82 D2 37 46N 94 27W
Mount Airy, MD, U.S.A. 77 A3 39 23N 77 10W
Mount Airy, NC, U.S.A. 90 B5 36 31N 80 37W

Mount Airy Forest, *OH, U.S.A.* .. **107 A1** 39 9N 84 34W
Mount Albert, *Ont., Canada* **178 C7** 44 8N 79 19W
Mount Angel, *OR, U.S.A.* **94 B3** 45 4N 122 48W
Mount Assiniboine Park ⌂, *B.C., Canada* **185 H5** 50 53N 115 39W
Mount Auburn, *IA, U.S.A.* **73 C6** 42 15N 92 6W
Mount Ayr, *IN, U.S.A.* **72 C3** 40 57N 87 18W
Mount Ayr, *IA, U.S.A.* **73 E4** 40 43N 94 14W
Mount Baker Nat. Recr. Area ⌂, *WA, U.S.A.* **101 C4** 47 44N 121 48W
Mount Baker-Snoqualmie Nat. Forest, *WA, U.S.A.* **101 B4** 48 10N 121 15W
Mount Bennett Hills, *ID, U.S.A.* . **70 F3** 43 13N 115 5W
Mount Blanchard, *OH, U.S.A.* ... **92 C3** 40 54N 83 34W
Mount Brydges, *Ont., Canada* ... **178 E5** 42 54N 81 29W
Mount Calm, *TX, U.S.A.* **99 F11** 31 46N 96 53W
Mount Carleton Prov. Park ⌂, *N.B., Canada* **173 F3** 47 25N 66 55W
Mount Carmel, *IL, U.S.A.* **71 E6** 38 25N 87 46W
Mount Carmel, *PA, U.S.A.* **95 D6** 40 47N 76 26W
Mount Carmel, *UT, U.S.A.* **100 F3** 37 15N 112 40W
Mount Carroll, *IL, U.S.A.* **71 A4** 42 6N 89 59W
Mount Clemens, *MI, U.S.A.* **79 G9** 42 35N 82 53W
Mount Desert I., *ME, U.S.A.* **76 D5** 44 21N 68 20W
Mount Dora, *FL, U.S.A.* **67 C7** 28 48N 81 38W
Mount Dora, *NM, U.S.A.* **88 A7** 36 31N 103 29W
Mount Eaton, *OH, U.S.A.* **92 C5** 40 42N 81 42W
Mount Echo Park, *OH, U.S.A.* ... **107 B1** 39 5N 84 33W
Mount Eden, *KY, U.S.A.* **97 B7** 38 3N 85 9W
Mount Enterprise, *TX, U.S.A.* ... **99 F13** 31 55N 94 41W
Mount Ephraim, *NJ, U.S.A.* **116 B2** 39 52N 75 5W
Mount Erie, *IL, U.S.A.* **71 E5** 38 31N 88 14W
Mount Etna, *IN, U.S.A.* **72 C5** 40 45N 85 34W
Mount Forest, *Ont., Canada* **178 D6** 43 59N 80 43W
Mount Gay, *WV, U.S.A.* **102 D2** 37 51N 82 1W
Mount Gilead, *NC, U.S.A.* **90 C6** 35 13N 80 0W
Mount Gilead, *OH, U.S.A.* **92 C4** 40 33N 82 50W
Mount Greenwood, *Chicago, U.S.A.* **108 C2** 41 42N 87 42W
Mount Healthy, *OH, U.S.A.* **107 A1** 39 14N 84 32W
Mount Holly, *NC, U.S.A.* **90 C4** 35 18N 81 1W
Mount Holly, *NJ, U.S.A.* **87 C2** 39 59N 74 47W
Mount Holly Springs, *PA, U.S.A.* **95 D5** 40 7N 77 12W
Mount Hood Memorial Park ⌂, *Boston, U.S.A.* **106 A3** 42 26N 71 1W
Mount Hood Nat. Forest, *OR, U.S.A.* **94 B4** 45 15N 122 0W
Mount Hope, *KS, U.S.A.* **74 D6** 37 52N 97 40W
Mount Hope, *WV, U.S.A.* **102 D3** 37 54N 81 10W
Mount Horeb, *WI, U.S.A.* **103 E4** 43 1N 89 44W
Mount Ida, *AR, U.S.A.* **63 D2** 34 34N 93 38W
Mount Jackson, *VA, U.S.A.* **102 C6** 38 45N 78 39W
Mount Jewett, *PA, U.S.A.* **95 C4** 41 44N 78 39W
Mount Joy, *PA, U.S.A.* **95 D6** 40 7N 76 30W
Mount Judge Howay Park ⌂, *B.C., Canada* **187 F12** 49 30N 122 18W
Mount Juliet, *TN, U.S.A.* **96 D6** 36 12N 86 31W
Mount Ka'ala Nat. Area Reserve ⌂, *HI, U.S.A.* **69 J13** 21 31N 158 7W
Mount Kisco, *NY, U.S.A.* **87 A3** 41 12N 73 44W
Mount Laguna, *CA, U.S.A.* **65 L10** 32 52N 116 25W
Mount Lebanon, *PA, U.S.A.* **95 D2** 40 21N 80 2W
Mount Liberty, *OH, U.S.A.* **92 C4** 40 21N 82 38W
Mount McGuire, *ID, U.S.A.* **70 D4** 45 10N 114 36W
Mount McKinley = Denali Nat. Park and Preserve △, *AK, U.S.A.* **61 E10** 63 30N 152 0W
Mount Moriah, *Nfld. & L., Canada* **174 D2** 48 58N 58 2W
Mount Moriah, *MO, U.S.A.* **82 A3** 40 20N 93 48W
Mount Morris, *IL, U.S.A.* **71 A4** 42 3N 89 26W
Mount Morris, *MI, U.S.A.* **79 F8** 43 7N 83 42W
Mount Morris, *NY, U.S.A.* **89 C3** 42 44N 77 52W
Mount Morris L., *NY, U.S.A.* ... **89 C3** 42 44N 77 54W
Mount Nebo, *PA, U.S.A.* **77 A4** 39 53N 76 20W
Mount Olive, *IL, U.S.A.* **71 D4** 39 4N 89 44W
Mount Olive, *MS, U.S.A.* **81 E4** 31 46N 89 39W
Mount Olive, *NC, U.S.A.* **90 C7** 35 12N 78 4W
Mount Oliver, *Pittsburgh, U.S.A.* . **116 B2** 40 24N 79 59W
Mount Olivet, *KY, U.S.A.* **97 B8** 38 32N 84 2W
Mount Olympus, *Salt Lake City, U.S.A.* **117 B3** 40 41N 111 47W
Mount Olympus Wilderness, *Salt Lake City, U.S.A.* **117 B3** 40 39N 111 43W
Mount Orab, *OH, U.S.A.* **92 D3** 39 2N 83 55W
Mount Pearl, *Nfld. & L., Canada* . **174 E8** 47 31N 52 47W
Mount Pleasant, *AR, U.S.A.* **63 C4** 35 58N 91 45W
Mount Pleasant, *DE, U.S.A.* **77 A5** 39 32N 75 43W
Mount Pleasant, *IA, U.S.A.* **73 E7** 40 58N 91 33W
Mount Pleasant, *MI, U.S.A.* **79 F7** 43 36N 84 46W
Mount Pleasant, *MS, U.S.A.* **81 B4** 34 57N 89 31W
Mount Pleasant, *PA, U.S.A.* **95 D3** 40 9N 79 33W
Mount Pleasant, *SC, U.S.A.* **90 F6** 32 47N 79 52W
Mount Pleasant, *TN, U.S.A.* **96 E5** 35 32N 87 12W
Mount Pleasant, *TX, U.S.A.* **99 D13** 33 9N 94 58W
Mount Pleasant, *UT, U.S.A.* **100 D4** 39 33N 111 27W
Mount Pocono, *PA, U.S.A.* **87 A1** 41 7N 75 22W
Mount Prospect, *IL, U.S.A.* **71 A6** 42 4N 87 56W
Mount Pulaski, *IL, U.S.A.* **71 C4** 40 1N 89 17W
Mount Rainier, *MD, U.S.A.* **119 B4** 38 56N 76 57W
Mount Rainier Nat. Park △, *WA, U.S.A.* **101 D4** 46 55N 121 50W
Mount Revelstoke Nat. Park △, *B.C., Canada* **187 D16** 51 5N 118 30W
Mount Robson Park ⌂, *B.C., Canada* **187 C16** 53 0N 119 0W
Mount Rushmore Nat. Memorial ⌂, *SD, U.S.A.* **91 G2** 43 53N 103 27W
Mount St. Helens Nat. Volcanic Monument ⌂, *WA, U.S.A.* **101 D3** 46 14N 122 11W
Mount Savage, *MD, U.S.A.* **77 A2** 39 42N 78 53W
Mount Seymour Prov. Park ⌂, *Vancouver, Canada* **193 B3** 49 20N 123 0W
Mount Shasta, *CA, U.S.A.* **64 B4** 41 19N 122 19W
Mount Snow Resort, *VT, U.S.A.* . **86 D2** 42 58N 72 54W
Mount Solon, *VA, U.S.A.* **102 C5** 38 21N 79 5W
Mount Sterling, *IL, U.S.A.* **71 D3** 39 59N 90 45W
Mount Sterling, *KY, U.S.A.* **97 B9** 38 4N 83 56W
Mount Sterling, *OH, U.S.A.* **92 D3** 39 43N 83 16W
Mount Stewart, *P.E.I., Canada* ... **173 G7** 46 22N 62 52W
Mount Storm, *WV, U.S.A.* **77 A1** 39 17N 79 15W
Mount Storm L., *WV, U.S.A.* ... **77 A1** 39 13N 79 16W
Mount Summit, *IN, U.S.A.* **72 C5** 40 0N 85 23W
Mount Sunapee, *NH, U.S.A.* **86 C2** 43 19N 72 6W
Mount Tabor Park, *Portland, U.S.A.* **116 A2** 45 30N 122 35W
Mount Tolmie, *B.C., Canada* ... **187 G11** 48 28N 123 20W
Mount Uniacke, *N.S., Canada* .. **173 J6** 44 54N 63 50W
Mount Union, *IA, U.S.A.* **73 D7** 41 3N 91 23W
Mount Union, *PA, U.S.A.* **95 D5** 40 23N 77 53W
Mount Vernon, *AL, U.S.A.* **60 E2** 31 5N 88 1W
Mount Vernon, *AR, U.S.A.* **63 C3** 35 14N 92 8W
Mount Vernon, *GA, U.S.A.* **68 D4** 32 11N 82 36W
Mount Vernon, *IL, U.S.A.* **71 E5** 38 19N 88 55W
Mount Vernon, *IN, U.S.A.* **72 F3** 37 56N 87 54W
Mount Vernon, *IA, U.S.A.* **73 D7** 41 55N 91 23W
Mount Vernon, *KY, U.S.A.* **97 C8** 37 21N 84 21W
Mount Vernon, *MD, U.S.A.* **77 B3** 38 47N 77 6W
Mount Vernon, *MO, U.S.A.* **82 D3** 37 6N 93 49W
Mount Vernon, *NY, U.S.A.* **87 B3** 40 54N 73 49W
Mount Vernon, *OH, U.S.A.* **92 C4** 40 23N 82 29W
Mount Vernon, *OR, U.S.A.* **94 C6** 44 25N 119 7W
Mount Vernon, *SD, U.S.A.* **91 G7** 43 43N 98 16W
Mount Vernon, *TN, U.S.A.* **97 E8** 35 25N 84 22W
Mount Vernon, *TX, U.S.A.* **99 D12** 33 11N 95 13W
Mount Vernon, *WA, U.S.A.* **101 B3** 48 25N 122 20W
Mount Washington, *KY, U.S.A.* .. **107 B2** 38 3N 85 33W
Mount Washington Cog Railway, *NH, U.S.A.* **86 B3** 44 17N 71 21W
Mount Wolf, *PA, U.S.A.* **95 D6** 40 4N 76 43W
Mount Zion, *IL, U.S.A.* **71 D5** 39 46N 88 53W
Mountain, *ND, U.S.A.* **91 B8** 48 41N 97 52W
Mountain, *WI, U.S.A.* **103 C5** 45 11N 88 28W
Mountain →, *N.W.T., Canada* .. **189 C7** 65 41N 128 50W
Mountain Brook, *AL, U.S.A.* **60 C4** 33 30N 86 45W
Mountain City, *GA, U.S.A.* **68 B3** 34 55N 83 23W
Mountain City, *NV, U.S.A.* **85 A5** 41 50N 115 58W
Mountain City, *TN, U.S.A.* **97 D11** 36 29N 81 48W
Mountain Creek, *AL, U.S.A.* **60 D4** 32 43N 86 29W
Mountain Creek L., *Dallas-Fort Worth, U.S.A.* **109 B4** 32 43N 96 56W
Mountain Creek Lake Park, *Dallas-Fort Worth, U.S.A.* **109 B4** 32 41N 96 58W
Mountain Grove, *MO, U.S.A.* ... **82 D4** 37 8N 92 16W
Mountain Home, *AR, U.S.A.* **63 B3** 36 20N 92 23W
Mountain Home, *ID, U.S.A.* **70 F3** 43 8N 115 41W
Mountain Home, *NC, U.S.A.* **90 C3** 35 23N 82 30W
Mountain Home, *TX, U.S.A.* **99 G8** 30 10N 99 22W
Mountain Home, *WY, U.S.A.* ... **104 E6** 41 0N 106 10W
Mountain Home Air Force Base, *ID, U.S.A.* **70 F3** 43 3N 115 51W
Mountain Iron, *MN, U.S.A.* **80 C6** 47 32N 92 37W
Mountain Lake, *MN, U.S.A.* **80 G4** 43 57N 94 56W
Mountain Lake Park, *MD, U.S.A.* **77 A1** 39 24N 79 23W
Mountain Meadows Res., *CA, U.S.A.* **64 C6** 40 17N 120 49W
Mountain Park, *Alta., Canada* ... **185 F3** 52 55N 117 16W
Mountain Park, *OK, U.S.A.* **93 D5** 34 42N 98 57W
Mountain Pine, *AR, U.S.A.* **63 D2** 34 34N 93 10W
Mountain View, *Alta., Canada* ... **185 J7** 49 8N 113 36W
Mountain View, *AR, U.S.A.* **63 C3** 35 52N 92 7W
Mountain View, *CA, U.S.A.* **64 F4** 37 23N 122 5W
Mountain View, *Denver, U.S.A.* .. **109 B1** 39 46N 105 3W
Mountain View, *HI, U.S.A.* **69 D6** 19 33N 155 7W
Mountain View, *MO, U.S.A.* **82 D5** 37 0N 91 42W
Mountain View, *NJ, U.S.A.* **114 A1** 40 55N 74 15W
Mountain View, *OK, U.S.A.* **93 C5** 35 6N 98 45W
Mountain View, *WY, U.S.A.* **104 E2** 41 16N 110 20W
Mountain Village, *AK, U.S.A.* .. **61 E7** 62 5N 163 43W
Mountainair, *NM, U.S.A.* **88 C4** 34 31N 106 15W
Mountainaire, *AZ, U.S.A.* **62 B4** 35 5N 111 40W
Mountainburg, *AR, U.S.A.* **63 C1** 35 38N 94 10W
Mountlake Terrace, *WA, U.S.A.* . **101 C3** 47 47N 122 18W
Mountrail County ☆, *ND, U.S.A.* . **91 B3** 48 10N 102 30W
Mousie, *KY, U.S.A.* **97 C10** 37 25N 82 53W
Moville, *IA, U.S.A.* **73 C2** 42 29N 96 4W
Moweaqua, *IL, U.S.A.* **71 D4** 39 38N 89 1W
Mower County ☆, *MN, U.S.A.* ... **80 G6** 43 40N 92 45W
Mowrystown, *OH, U.S.A.* **92 D3** 39 2N 83 45W
Moxee City, *WA, U.S.A.* **101 D5** 46 33N 120 23W
Moyahua de Estrada, *Zacatecas, Mexico* **217 F7** 21 16N 103 11W
Moyers, *OK, U.S.A.* **93 D8** 34 19N 95 39W
Moyie Springs, *ID, U.S.A.* **70 A2** 48 44N 116 11W
Moylie →, *ID, U.S.A.* **70 A2** 48 43N 116 11W
Mozhabong L., *Ont., Canada* ... **181 F14** 46 58N 82 30W
Muchalat Inlet, *B.C., Canada* ... **186 F8** 49 38N 126 15W
Muckalee Cr. →, *GA, U.S.A.* **68 E2** 31 38N 84 9W
Mud →, *KY, U.S.A.* **96 C6** 37 13N 86 54W
Mud Butte, *SD, U.S.A.* **91 E3** 45 0N 102 54W
Mud Cr. →, *OK, U.S.A.* **93 E6** 33 55N 97 28W
Mud Cr. →, *SD, U.S.A.* **91 E7** 45 11N 98 24W
Mud I., *N.S., Canada* **173 K4** 43 28N 65 59W
Mud L., *NV, U.S.A.* **85 E3** 37 52N 117 4W
Mud L., *Orlando, U.S.A.* **115 B3** 28 23N 81 17W
Mud Lake Res., *SD, U.S.A.* **91 E7** 45 47N 98 15W
Muddy →, *NV, U.S.A.* **85 F6** 36 31N 114 24W
Muddy Boggy Cr. →, *OK, U.S.A.* **93 D8** 34 3N 95 47W
Muddy Cr. →, *UT, U.S.A.* **100 E5** 38 24N 110 42W
Muddy Cr. →, *WY, U.S.A.* **104 E3** 41 35N 109 58W
Muddy Creek Res., *CO, U.S.A.* .. **66 E7** 37 45N 103 15W
Muddy Gap, *WY, U.S.A.* **104 D5** 42 21N 107 28W
Muddy L., *Sask., Canada* **182 C2** 52 19N 109 6W
Muddy Mts., *NV, U.S.A.* **85 F6** 36 24N 114 39W
Muenster, *Sask., Canada* **182 C7** 52 12N 105 0W
Muenster, *TX, U.S.A.* **99 D10** 33 39N 97 23W
Muerto, Mar, *Oaxaca, Mexico* .. **221 H6** 16 10N 94 10W
Muertos, B. de los, *Baja Calif. S., Mexico* **211 K9** 23 55N 109 45W
Muhlenberg County ☆, *KY, U.S.A.* **96 C5** 37 10N 87 10W
Muir, *MI, U.S.A.* **79 F7** 43 0N 84 56W
Muir Beach, *San Francisco, U.S.A.* **118 A1** 37 51N 122 34W
Muir Woods Nat. Monument ⌂, *CA, U.S.A.* **64 F4** 37 55N 122 35W
Mujeres, B., *Quintana Roo, Mexico* **223 A7** 21 15N 86 46W
Mujeres, I., *Quintana Roo, Mexico* **223 A7** 21 13N 86 43W
Mukilteo, *WA, U.S.A.* **101 C3** 47 57N 122 18W
Mukutawa →, *Man., Canada* ... **183 B14** 53 10N 97 24W
Mukwonago, *WI, U.S.A.* **103 F5** 42 52N 88 20W
Mul, *Yucatán, Mexico* **223 B5** 20 10N 88 42W
Mulatos, *Sonora, Mexico* **212 E7** 28 39N 108 51W
Mulatos →, *Mexico* **212 E7** 28 58N 108 46W
Mulberry, *AR, U.S.A.* **63 C1** 35 30N 94 3W
Mulberry, *FL, U.S.A.* **67 D7** 27 54N 81 59W
Mulberry, *IN, U.S.A.* **72 C4** 40 21N 86 40W
Mulberry, *NC, U.S.A.* **90 B4** 36 14N 81 11W
Mulberry Fork →, *AL, U.S.A.* ... **60 C3** 33 33N 87 11W
Mulberry Grove, *IL, U.S.A.* **71 E4** 38 56N 89 16W
Mulchatna →, *AK, U.S.A.* **61 G8** 59 40N 157 7W
Muldoon, *TX, U.S.A.* **99 H10** 29 49N 97 4W
Muldraugh, *KY, U.S.A.* **97 C7** 37 56N 85 59W
Muldrow, *OK, U.S.A.* **93 C9** 35 24N 94 36W
Mule Creek, *NM, U.S.A.* **88 D2** 33 7N 108 57W
Mule Creek Junction, *WY, U.S.A.* **104 C8** 43 23N 104 13W
Mulegé, *Baja Calif. S., Mexico* ... **211 G7** 26 53N 111 59W
Muleshoe, *TX, U.S.A.* **98 C5** 34 13N 102 43W
Muleshoe Nat. Wildlife Refuge ⌂, *TX, U.S.A.* **98 D5** 33 58N 102 44W
Mulford Gardens, *San Francisco, U.S.A.* **118 B3** 37 42N 122 10W
Mulgrave, *N.S., Canada* **173 H8** 45 38N 61 31W
Mulhall, *OK, U.S.A.* **93 B6** 36 4N 97 25W
Mullan, *ID, U.S.A.* **70 B3** 47 28N 115 48W
Mullen, *NE, U.S.A.* **84 B4** 42 3N 101 1W
Mullens, *WV, U.S.A.* **102 D3** 37 35N 81 23W
Mullett L., *MI, U.S.A.* **79 D7** 45 31N 84 31W
Mullett Lake, *MI, U.S.A.* **79 D7** 45 34N 84 32W
Mullica →, *NJ, U.S.A.* **87 C2** 39 33N 74 25W
Mullin, *TX, U.S.A.* **99 F9** 31 33N 98 40W
Mullins, *SC, U.S.A.* **90 D6** 34 12N 79 15W
Mullinville, *KS, U.S.A.* **74 D4** 37 35N 99 29W
Multe, *Tabasco, Mexico* **222 B5** 17 41N 91 24W
Multnomah County ☆, *OR, U.S.A.* **94 B3** 45 30N 122 10W
Mulvane, *KS, U.S.A.* **74 D6** 37 29N 97 15W
Muna, *Yucatán, Mexico* **223 B4** 20 29N 89 43W
Muncie, *IN, U.S.A.* **72 C5** 40 12N 85 23W
Muncy, *PA, U.S.A.* **95 C6** 41 12N 76 47W
Mundare, *Alta., Canada* **184 E8** 53 35N 112 20W
Munday, *TX, U.S.A.* **99 D8** 33 27N 99 38W
Mundelein, *IL, U.S.A.* **71 A5** 42 16N 88 0W
Munden, *KS, U.S.A.* **74 B6** 39 55N 97 32W
Munford, *TN, U.S.A.* **96 E3** 35 27N 89 49W
Munfordville, *KY, U.S.A.* **97 C7** 37 16N 85 54W
Munhall, *Pittsburgh, U.S.A.* ... **116 B2** 40 23N 79 54W
Munich, *ND, U.S.A.* **91 B7** 48 40N 98 50W
Municipal Park, *Minneapolis-St. Paul, U.S.A.* ... **113 B1** 44 52N 93 22W
Munising, *MI, U.S.A.* **79 C5** 46 25N 86 40W
Munjor, *KS, U.S.A.* **74 C4** 38 49N 99 16W
Munnsville, *NY, U.S.A.* **89 C5** 42 59N 75 35W
Munsey Park, *NY, U.S.A.* **114 B4** 40 47N 73 40W
Munson, *Alta., Canada* **185 G8** 51 34N 112 45W
Munson, *FL, U.S.A.* **67 A2** 30 52N 86 52W
Munsungan L., *ME, U.S.A.* ... **76 B5** 46 22N 69 0W
Murchison →, *Nunavut, Canada* . **190 D7** 68 35N 93 35W
Murchison I., *Ont., Canada* **180 C8** 50 0N 88 21W
Murdo, *SD, U.S.A.* **91 G5** 43 53N 100 43W
Murdochville, *Qué., Canada* ... **172 E4** 48 58N 65 30W
Murdock, *KS, U.S.A.* **74 D6** 37 37N 97 56W
Murdock, *MN, U.S.A.* **80 E3** 45 13N 95 24W
Murdock, *NE, U.S.A.* **84 D9** 40 55N 96 17W
Murdock Peak, *Salt Lake City, U.S.A.* **117 B4** 40 41N 111 36W
Murfreesboro, *AR, U.S.A.* **63 D2** 34 4N 93 41W
Murfreesboro, *NC, U.S.A.* **90 B8** 36 27N 77 6W
Murfreesboro, *TN, U.S.A.* **96 E6** 35 51N 86 24W
Muriel L., *Alta., Canada* **184 D10** 54 9N 110 40W
Murphy, *ID, U.S.A.* **70 F2** 43 13N 116 33W
Murphy, *MO, U.S.A.* **82 C6** 38 29N 90 29W
Murphy, *NC, U.S.A.* **90 C1** 35 5N 84 2W
Murphy, *OR, U.S.A.* **94 E2** 42 21N 123 20W
Murphy L., *B.C., Canada* **187 C13** 52 3N 121 15W
Murphy's Station = Sunnyvale, *CA, U.S.A.* **64 F4** 37 23N 122 2W
Murphysboro, *IL, U.S.A.* **71 F4** 37 46N 89 20W
Murray, *IA, U.S.A.* **73 D5** 41 3N 93 57W
Murray, *KY, U.S.A.* **96 D4** 36 37N 88 19W
Murray, *UT, U.S.A.* **100 C4** 40 40N 111 53W
Murray, L., *OK, U.S.A.* **93 D6** 34 2N 97 3W
Murray, L., *SC, U.S.A.* **90 D4** 34 3N 81 13W
Murray City, *OH, U.S.A.* **92 D4** 39 31N 82 10W
Murray County ☆, *GA, U.S.A.* .. **68 B2** 34 50N 84 45W
Murray County ☆, *MN, U.S.A.* . **80 F3** 44 0N 95 45W
Murray County ☆, *OK, U.S.A.* .. **93 D6** 34 30N 97 0W
Murray Harbour, *P.E.I., Canada* . **173 H7** 46 0N 62 28W
Murray River, *P.E.I., Canada* ... **173 G7** 46 1N 62 37W
Murrayville, *IL, U.S.A.* **71 D3** 39 35N 90 15W
Murrells Inlet, *SC, U.S.A.* **90 E6** 33 33N 79 2W
Murtaugh, *ID, U.S.A.* **70 G4** 42 30N 114 10W
Murtle L., *B.C., Canada* **187 C15** 52 8N 119 38W
Murvaul L., *TX, U.S.A.* **99 E13** 32 2N 94 25W
Muscatatuck →, *IN, U.S.A.* ... **72 E4** 38 46N 86 10W
Muscatatuck Nat. Wildlife Refuge ⌂, *IN, U.S.A.* **72 E5** 38 56N 85 49W
Muscatine, *IA, U.S.A.* **73 D7** 41 25N 91 3W
Muscatine County ☆, *IA, U.S.A.* . **73 D7** 41 30N 91 0W
Muscle Shoals, *AL, U.S.A.* **60 B3** 34 45N 87 40W
Muscoda, *WI, U.S.A.* **103 E3** 43 11N 90 27W
Muscogee County ☆, *GA, U.S.A.* **68 D2** 32 30N 84 58W
Musconetcong →, *NJ, U.S.A.* .. **87 B1** 40 36N 75 11W
Muscotah, *KS, U.S.A.* **74 B8** 39 33N 95 31W
Musella, *GA, U.S.A.* **68 D2** 32 48N 84 2W
Musgrave Harbour, *Nfld. & L., Canada* **174 C7** 49 27N 53 58W
Mushaboom, *N.S., Canada* **173 J7** 44 51N 62 32W
Muskeg B., *MN, U.S.A.* **80 B3** 48 55N 95 10W
Muskeg L., *Ont., Canada* **180 C6** 49 0N 90 2W
Muskeg River, *Alta., Canada* ... **184 E2** 53 55N 118 39W
Muskeget Channel, *MA, U.S.A.* . **78 C4** 41 25N 70 25W
Muskego, *WI, U.S.A.* **103 F5** 42 55N 88 8W
Muskegon, *MI, U.S.A.* **79 F5** 43 14N 86 16W
Muskegon →, *MI, U.S.A.* **79 F5** 43 14N 86 21W
Muskegon County ☆, *MI, U.S.A.* . **79 F5** 43 15N 86 15W
Muskegon Heights, *MI, U.S.A.* .. **79 F5** 43 12N 86 16W
Muskingum →, *OH, U.S.A.* **92 C5** 40 3N 81 59W
Muskingum County ☆, *OH, U.S.A.* **92 D4** 39 56N 82 1W
Muskogee, *OK, U.S.A.* **93 C8** 35 45N 95 22W
Muskogee County ☆, *OK, U.S.A.* **93 C8** 35 40N 95 25W
Muskoka, L., *Ont., Canada* **178 C7** 45 0N 79 25W
Muskrat Cr. →, *WY, U.S.A.* ... **104 C4** 43 9N 108 12W
Muskwa →, *Alta., Canada* **184 B7** 56 15N 113 48W
Muskwa →, *B.C., Canada* **189 E8** 58 47N 122 48W
Muskwa L., *Alta., Canada* **184 B6** 56 9N 114 38W
Musquanousse, L., *Qué., Canada* . **172 C8** 50 22N 61 5W
Musquaro, *Qué., Canada* **172 C8** 50 10N 61 3W
Musquaro, L., *Qué., Canada* ... **175 C5** 50 38N 61 5W
Musquash, *N.B., Canada* **173 H3** 45 11N 66 19W
Musquodoboit Harbour, *N.S., Canada* **173 J6** 44 50N 63 9W
Mussel Fork →, *MO, U.S.A.* **82 B4** 39 26N 92 57W
Mussel Inlet, *B.C., Canada* **186 C6** 52 53N 128 7W
Musselshell →, *MT, U.S.A.* **83 C10** 47 21N 107 57W
Musselshell County ☆, *MT, U.S.A.* **83 D9** 46 35N 108 30W
Mustang, *OK, U.S.A.* **93 C6** 35 24N 97 42W
Mustang Draw →, *TX, U.S.A.* .. **98 F5** 31 58N 102 40W
Mustang I., *TX, U.S.A.* **99 K10** 27 52N 97 3W
Mustinka →, *MN, U.S.A.* **80 E2** 45 45N 96 38W
Mutual, *OH, U.S.A.* **92 C3** 40 5N 83 38W
Mutual, *OK, U.S.A.* **93 B4** 36 14N 99 9W
Muyil, *Quintana Roo, Mexico* ... **223 B6** 20 4N 87 37W
Muzon, C., *AK, U.S.A.* **61 J14** 54 40N 132 42W
Myakka →, *FL, U.S.A.* **67 E6** 26 56N 82 11W
Myakka City, *FL, U.S.A.* **67 D6** 27 21N 82 10W
Myerstown, *PA, U.S.A.* **95 D6** 40 22N 76 19W
Mylo, *ND, U.S.A.* **91 B6** 48 38N 99 37W
Myrnam, *Alta., Canada* **184 E9** 53 40N 111 14W
Myrtle, *Houston, U.S.A.* **110 C2** 29 39N 95 24W
Myrtle, *MS, U.S.A.* **81 B4** 34 34N 89 7W
Myrtle, *MO, U.S.A.* **82 E5** 36 31N 91 16W
Myrtle, *WV, U.S.A.* **102 D2** 37 46N 82 12W
Myrtle Beach, *SC, U.S.A.* **90 E7** 33 42N 78 53W
Myrtle Creek, *OR, U.S.A.* **94 D2** 43 1N 123 17W
Myrtle Grove, *FL, U.S.A.* **67 A1** 30 23N 87 17W
Myrtle Grove, *NC, U.S.A.* **90 D8** 34 8N 77 53W
Myrtle Point, *OR, U.S.A.* **94 D1** 43 4N 124 8W
Myrtlewood, *AL, U.S.A.* **60 D3** 32 16N 87 57W
Mystic, *CT, U.S.A.* **78 C3** 41 21N 71 58W
Mystic, *IA, U.S.A.* **73 E6** 40 47N 92 57W
Mystic →, *Boston, U.S.A.* **106 A3** 42 22N 71 3W
Mystic Island, *NJ, U.S.A.* **87 C2** 39 34N 74 22W
Mystic Seaport, *CT, U.S.A.* ... **78 C3** 41 22N 71 58W
Myton, *UT, U.S.A.* **100 C5** 40 12N 110 4W

N

N.A.S.A. Michoud Facility, *New Orleans, U.S.A.* **113 B3** 30 1N 89 55W
N.A.S.A. Space Center = John C. Stennis Space Center, *MS, U.S.A.* **81 F4** 30 23N 89 37W
N.A.S.A. Wallops I., *VA, U.S.A.* . **102 D9** 37 50N 75 30W
Nā'ālehu, *HI, U.S.A.* **69 D6** 19 4N 155 35W
Nabalam, *Yucatán, Mexico* **223 B5** 20 56N 88 1W
Nabesna, *AK, U.S.A.* **61 E12** 62 22N 143 0W
Nabisipi →, *Qué., Canada* **175 C5** 50 14N 62 13W
Nabor Carrillo, Laguna, *México, Mexico* **225 B4** 19 28N 98 59W
Nacajuca, *Tabasco, Mexico* **222 A3** 18 8N 93 1W
Nacha, L. la, *Tamaulipas, Mexico* **215 F7** 24 52N 97 51W
Naches, *WA, U.S.A.* **101 D5** 46 44N 120 42W
Naches →, *WA, U.S.A.* **101 D5** 46 38N 120 31W
Nachicapau, L., *Qué., Canada* ... **175 B4** 56 40N 68 5W
Nachvak Fd., *Nfld. & L., Canada* . **175 B5** 59 3N 63 45W
Nacimiento, L., *CA, U.S.A.* **65 H6** 35 46N 120 53W
Nackawic, *N.B., Canada* **173 H2** 45 59N 67 17W
Naco, *Sonora, Mexico* **212 B6** 31 20N 109 56W
Naco, *AZ, U.S.A.* **62 F6** 31 20N 109 57W
Nacogdoches, *TX, U.S.A.* **99 F13** 31 36N 94 39W
Nacogdoches County ☆, *TX, U.S.A.* **99 F13** 31 35N 94 40W
Nácori Chico, *Sonora, Mexico* ... **212 D7** 29 40N 108 57W
Nacori Grande, *Sonora, Mexico* .. **212 D5** 29 4N 110 3W
Nacozari de García, *Sonora, Mexico* **212 C6** 30 25N 109 38W
Nacupétaro, *Michoacan, Mexico* . **219 C6** 19 4N 101 10W
Nadadores, *Coahuila, Mexico* ... **214 C3** 27 3N 101 36W
Nadadores →, *Coahuila, Mexico* . **214 C4** 27 28N 100 43W
Nadern Harb., *B.C., Canada* **186 A2** 54 0N 132 36W
Nadina →, *B.C., Canada* **186 B8** 53 58N 126 30W
Nadina L., *B.C., Canada* **186 B7** 53 53N 127 2W
Nadine, *NM, U.S.A.* **88 E7** 32 37N 103 8W
Naftan Pt., *N. Marianas* ...... **105 c** 15 5N 145 45W
Nagagami →, *Ont., Canada* **181 C12** 49 40N 84 40W
Nagagami L., *Ont., Canada* **181 C11** 49 25N 85 1W
Nagagamisis L., *Ont., Canada* .. **181 C12** 49 28N 84 40W
Nagai I., *AK, U.S.A.* **61 J8** 55 5N 160 0W
Nagas Pt., *B.C., Canada* **186 C3** 52 12N 131 22W
Nagasin L., *Ont., Canada* **181 E13** 47 48N 83 50W
Nageezi, *NM, U.S.A.* **88 A3** 36 16N 107 45W
Nags Head, *NC, U.S.A.* **90 C10** 35 57N 75 38W
Naguabo, *Puerto Rico* **105 G17** 18 13N 65 44W
Nahanni Butte, *N.W.T., Canada* .. **189 D8** 61 2N 123 31W
Nahanni Nat. Park △, *N.W.T., Canada* **189 D8** 61 36N 125 41W
Nahant, *MA, U.S.A.* **78 B4** 42 25N 70 54W
Nahant B., *Boston, U.S.A.* **106 A4** 42 26N 70 54W
Nahant Harbor, *Boston, U.S.A.* .. **106 A4** 42 25N 70 55W
Nahma, *MI, U.S.A.* **79 D5** 45 50N 86 40W
Nahuatzen, *Michoacan, Mexico* .. **218 C6** 19 40N 101 55W
Nahunta, *GA, U.S.A.* **68 E5** 31 12N 81 59W
Naicá, *Chihuahua, Mexico* **213 F10** 27 53N 105 31W
Naicam, *Sask., Canada* **182 C7** 52 30N 104 30W
Naikoon Park ⌂, *B.C., Canada* .. **186 B3** 53 55N 131 55W
Nain, *Nfld. & L., Canada* **175 B5** 56 34N 61 40W
Nain, *VA, U.S.A.* **77 A2** 39 14N 78 12W
Nairn, *LA, U.S.A.* **75 E6** 29 26N 89 37W
Nairn Centre, *Ont., Canada* **178 A5** 46 20N 81 35W
Nakalele Pt., *HI, U.S.A.* **69 B5** 21 2N 156 35W
Nakina, *Ont., Canada* **181 B10** 50 10N 86 40W
Naknek, *AK, U.S.A.* **61 G8** 58 44N 157 1W
Nakusp, *B.C., Canada* **187 E17** 50 20N 117 45W
Nallen, *WV, U.S.A.* **102 C4** 38 7N 80 53W
Namakan L., *Ont., Canada* **180 D4** 48 27N 92 35W
Nambe Indian Reservation, *NM, U.S.A.* **88 B5** 35 52N 105 52W
Namekagon →, *WI, U.S.A.* **103 B1** 46 5N 92 6W
Namew L., *Sask., Canada* **183 A10** 54 14N 101 56W
Namiquipa, *Chihuahua, Mexico* .. **213 D8** 29 15N 107 25W
Nampa, *Alta., Canada* **184 B3** 56 2N 117 8W
Nampa, *ID, U.S.A.* **70 F2** 43 34N 116 34W
Namu, *B.C., Canada* **186 D7** 51 52N 127 50W
Namur, *Qué., Canada* **176 F8** 45 54N 74 56W
Namur L., *Alta., Canada* **184 A8** 57 25N 112 40W
Nanacamilpa, *Tlaxcala, Mexico* .. **219 C9** 19 45N 98 31W
Nanaimo, *B.C., Canada* **186 F11** 49 10N 124 0W
Nānākuli, *HI, U.S.A.* **69 K13** 21 24N 158 9W
Nance County ☆, *NE, U.S.A.* .. **84 C8** 41 25N 98 0W
Nanchital, *Veracruz, Mexico* ... **221 F6** 18 4N 94 24W
Nancy, *KY, U.S.A.* **97 C8** 37 4N 84 45W
Nanika L., *B.C., Canada* **186 B7** 53 47N 127 38W
Nanisivik, *Nunavut, Canada* ... **190 C9** 73 2N 84 33W
Nanjemoy, *MD, U.S.A.* **77 B3** 38 27N 77 13W
Nansen Sd., *Nunavut, Canada* .. **190 A7** 81 0N 91 0W
Nantahala Nat. Forest, *NC, U.S.A.* **90 C2** 35 15N 83 40W
Nantasket Beach, *Boston, U.S.A.* . **106 B4** 42 16N 70 52W
Nanticoke, *MD, U.S.A.* **77 B5** 38 16N 75 54W
Nanticoke, *PA, U.S.A.* **95 C6** 41 12N 76 0W
Nanticoke →, *MD, U.S.A.* **77 B5** 38 16N 75 56W
Nanton, *Alta., Canada* **185 H7** 50 21N 113 46W
Nantucket, *MA, U.S.A.* **78 C4** 41 17N 70 6W
Nantucket County ☆, *MA, U.S.A.* **78 C4** 41 15N 70 5W
Nantucket Harbor, *MA, U.S.A.* .. **78 C4** 41 17N 70 5W
Nantucket I., *MA, U.S.A.* **78 C4** 41 16N 70 5W
Nantucket Sd., *MA, U.S.A.* ... **78 C4** 41 30N 70 15W
Nanty Glo, *PA, U.S.A.* **95 D4** 40 28N 78 50W
Naocoane, L., *Qué., Canada* ... **175 C3** 52 50N 70 45W
Naolinco, *Veracruz, Mexico* **220 E4** 19 39N 96 53W
Naomi Peak, *UT, U.S.A.* **100 B4** 41 55N 111 41W
Napa, *CA, U.S.A.* **64 E4** 38 18N 122 17W
Napa County ☆, *CA, U.S.A.* ... **64 E4** 38 30N 122 20W
Napaimiut, *AK, U.S.A.* **61 F8** 61 33N 158 42W
Napakiak, *AK, U.S.A.* **61 F7** 60 42N 161 57W
Napaktulik L., *N.W.T., Canada* .. **188 C10** 65 30N 113 5W
Nāpali Coast, *HI, U.S.A.* **69 A2** 22 11N 159 39W
Napanee, *Ont., Canada* **179 C10** 44 15N 77 0W
Napartokh B., *Nfld. & L., Canada* **175 B5** 58 1N 62 43W
Napaskiak, *AK, U.S.A.* **61 F7** 60 43N 161 55W
Napavine, *WA, U.S.A.* **101 D3** 46 35N 122 54W
Napeague B., *NY, U.S.A.* **78 C2** 41 2N 72 2W
Naper, *NE, U.S.A.* **84 B6** 42 58N 99 6W
Naperville, *IL, U.S.A.* **71 B5** 41 46N 88 9W
Napierville, *Qué., Canada* **177 F9** 45 11N 73 25W
Napierville □, *Qué., Canada* ... **177 F9** 45 10N 73 30W
Napili-Honokowai, *HI, U.S.A.* .. **69 C5** 20 58N 156 39W
Napinka, *Man., Canada* **183 F11** 49 19N 100 50W
Naples, *FL, U.S.A.* **67 E7** 26 8N 81 48W
Naples, *ID, U.S.A.* **70 A2** 48 34N 116 24W
Naples, *NY, U.S.A.* **89 C3** 42 37N 77 24W
Naples, *TX, U.S.A.* **99 D13** 33 12N 94 41W
Naples, *UT, U.S.A.* **100 C6** 40 26N 109 30W
Naples Park, *FL, U.S.A.* **67 E7** 26 17N 81 46W
Napoleanville, *LA, U.S.A.* **75 E4** 29 56N 91 2W
Napoleon, *IN, U.S.A.* **72 D5** 39 12N 85 20W
Napoleon, *ND, U.S.A.* **91 D6** 46 30N 99 46W
Napoleon, *OH, U.S.A.* **92 B2** 41 23N 84 8W
Naponee, *NE, U.S.A.* **84 D6** 40 5N 99 9W
Nappanee, *IN, U.S.A.* **72 B5** 41 27N 86 0W
Nara Visa, *NM, U.S.A.* **88 B7** 35 37N 103 6W
Naramata, *B.C., Canada* **187 F15** 49 36N 119 35W
Naranjo, *Sinaloa, Mexico* **216 B2** 25 48N 108 31W
Naranjo →, *Jalisco, Mexico* ... **218 C4** 19 30N 103 37W
Naranjos, *Veracruz, Mexico* ... **220 C3** 21 21N 97 41W
Narberth, *PA, U.S.A.* **116 A1** 40 0N 75 13W
Nardin, *OK, U.S.A.* **93 B6** 36 48N 97 27W
Nares Str., *Arctic* **190 B12** 80 0N 70 0W
Narka, *KS, U.S.A.* **74 B6** 39 58N 97 26W
Narragansett Bay, *RI, U.S.A.* .. **78 C3** 41 36N 71 19W
Narragansett Pier, *RI, U.S.A.* .. **78 C3** 41 26N 71 27W
Narraway →, *Alta., Canada* **184 C1** 55 44N 119 55W

Narrow Hills Prov. Park ⌂, Sask., Canada **182 A7** 54 0N 104 37W
Narrows, VA, U.S.A. **102 D4** 37 20N 80 49W
Narrows, The, NY, U.S.A. **114 C2** 40 37N 74 3W
Naruna, VA, U.S.A. **102 D6** 37 6N 79 0W
Naschitti, NM, U.S.A. **88 A2** 36 4N 108 41W
Naselle, WA, U.S.A. **101 D2** 46 22N 123 49W
Nash, OK, U.S.A. **93 B5** 36 40N 98 3W
Nash County ☆, NC, U.S.A. **90 B8** 36 0N 78 0W
Nash Creek, N.B., Canada **173 F3** 47 56N 66 6W
Nash Stream Forest, NH, U.S.A. **86 B3** 44 42N 71 25W
Nashawena I., MA, U.S.A. **78 C4** 41 26N 70 53W
Nashoba, OK, U.S.A. **93 D8** 34 29N 95 13W
Nashua, IA, U.S.A. **73 C6** 42 57N 92 32W
Nashua, MN, U.S.A. **80 D2** 46 2N 96 19W
Nashua, MT, U.S.A. **83 B11** 48 8N 106 22W
Nashua, NH, U.S.A. **86 D3** 42 45N 71 28W
Nashville, AR, U.S.A. **63 E2** 33 57N 93 51W
Nashville, GA, U.S.A. **68 E3** 31 12N 83 15W
Nashville, IL, U.S.A. **71 E4** 38 21N 89 23W
Nashville, IN, U.S.A. **72 D4** 39 12N 86 15W
Nashville, KS, U.S.A. **74 D5** 37 27N 98 25W
Nashville, MI, U.S.A. **79 G6** 42 36N 85 5W
Nashville, MO, U.S.A. **82 D2** 37 23N 94 30W
Nashville, NC, U.S.A. **90 C8** 35 58N 77 58W
Nashville, OH, U.S.A. **92 C4** 40 36N 82 7W
Nashville, TN, U.S.A. **96 D6** 36 10N 86 47W
Nashville ✕ (BNA), TN, U.S.A. **96 D6** 36 7N 86 41W
Nashwaak Bridge, N.B., Canada **173 G3** 46 14N 66 37W
Nashwauk, MN, U.S.A. **80 C5** 47 23N 93 10W
Naskaupi →, Nfld. & L., Canada **175 C5** 53 47N 60 51W
Nass →, B.C., Canada **189 E7** 55 0N 129 40W
Nassau, MN, U.S.A. **80 E2** 45 4N 96 26W
Nassau, NY, U.S.A. **78 B1** 42 31N 73 37W
Nassau County ☆, FL, U.S.A. **67 A7** 30 40N 81 45W
Nassau County ☆, NY, U.S.A. **89 E7** 40 45N 73 40W
Nassawadox, VA, U.S.A. **102 D9** 37 28N 75 52W
Nastapoka →, Qué., Canada **175 B2** 56 55N 76 33W
Nastapoka, Is., Nunavut, Canada **175 B2** 56 55N 76 50W
Natal, B.C., Canada **185 J6** 49 43N 114 51W
Natalbany →, LA, U.S.A. **75 D5** 30 20N 90 30W
Natalia, TX, U.S.A. **99 H9** 29 11N 98 52W
Natalkuz L., B.C., Canada **186 B9** 53 36N 125 20W
Natashquan, Qué., Canada **175 C5** 50 14N 61 46W
Natashquan →, Qué., Canada **175 C5** 50 7N 61 50W
Natashquan, Pte., Qué., Canada **172 C8** 50 8N 61 40W
Natashquan-Est →, Qué., Canada **172 B8** 51 20N 61 40W
Natchez Nat. Historical Park ⌂, MS, U.S.A. **81 E2** 31 30N 91 23W
Natchez, LA, U.S.A. **75 C2** 31 41N 93 3W
Natchez, MS, U.S.A. **81 E2** 31 34N 91 24W
Natchez Trace Parkway, U.S.A. **81 D3** 31 37N 91 16W
Natchez Trace State Park ⌂, TN, U.S.A. **96 E4** 35 47N 88 17W
Natchitoches, LA, U.S.A. **75 C2** 31 46N 93 5W
Natchitoches Parish ☆, LA, U.S.A. **75 C2** 31 41N 93 3W
Nathrop, CO, U.S.A. **66 D4** 38 45N 106 5W
Natick, MA, U.S.A. **78 B3** 42 16N 71 19W
Nation →, B.C., Canada **189 E8** 55 30N 123 32W
National Bison Range ⌂, MT, U.S.A. **83 C3** 47 20N 114 14W
National City, CA, U.S.A. **65 L9** 32 40N 117 5W
National Elk Refuge ⌂, WY, U.S.A. **104 C2** 43 38N 110 35W
National Key Deer Refuge ⌂, FL, U.S.A. **67 G7** 24 43N 81 30W
Natividad, I., Baja Calif. S., Mexico **211 F3** 27 52N 115 11W
Natoma, KS, U.S.A. **74 B4** 39 11N 99 2W
Natora, Sonora, Mexico **212 D7** 29 2N 108 55W
Natrona, WY, U.S.A. **104 C8** 43 2N 104 49W
Natrona County ☆, WY, U.S.A. **104 D6** 43 0N 107 0W
Natrona Heights, PA, U.S.A. **95 D3** 40 37N 79 44W
Natural Bridge, AL, U.S.A. **60 B3** 34 6N 87 36W
Natural Bridge, VA, U.S.A. **102 D5** 37 38N 79 33W
Natural Bridges Nat. Monument ⌂, UT, U.S.A. **100 F5** 37 36N 110 0W
Naturita, CO, U.S.A. **66 D2** 38 14N 108 34W
Naubinway, MI, U.S.A. **79 C6** 46 6N 85 27W
Naucalpan de Juárez, México, Mexico **219 C8** 19 28N 99 14W
Naugatuck, CT, U.S.A. **78 C1** 41 30N 73 3W
Naugatuck →, CT, U.S.A. **78 C1** 41 18N 73 7W
Naughton, Ont., Canada **178 A5** 46 24N 81 12W
Naujaat = Repulse Bay, Nunavut, Canada **191 D8** 66 30N 86 30W
Nautla, Veracruz, Mexico **220 D4** 20 13N 96 47W
Nautla, Barra de, Veracruz, Mexico **220 D4** 20 15N 96 45W
Nauvoo, AL, U.S.A. **60 C3** 33 59N 87 29W
Nauvoo, IL, U.S.A. **71 C2** 40 33N 91 23W
Nava, Coahuila, Mexico **214 B4** 28 25N 100 45W
Navajo, AZ, U.S.A. **62 B6** 35 7N 109 32W
Navajo, NM, U.S.A. **88 B1** 35 54N 109 2W
Navajo County ☆, AZ, U.S.A. **62 B5** 36 0N 110 20W
Navajo Cr. →, AZ, U.S.A. **62 A4** 36 59N 111 24W
Navajo Indian Reservation, AZ, U.S.A. **62 B6** 35 20N 110 0W
Navajo Mt., UT, U.S.A. **100 F5** 37 2N 110 52W
Navajo Nat. Monument ⌂, AZ, U.S.A. **62 A5** 36 41N 110 32W
Navajo Res., NM, U.S.A. **88 A3** 36 48N 107 36W
Navarre, FL, U.S.A. **67 A2** 30 24N 86 52W
Navarro →, CA, U.S.A. **64 D3** 39 11N 123 45W
Navarro County ☆, TX, U.S.A. **99 E11** 32 6N 96 28W
Navarro Mills L., TX, U.S.A. **99 F11** 31 57N 96 42W
Navasota, TX, U.S.A. **99 G11** 30 23N 96 5W
Navasota →, TX, U.S.A. **99 G11** 30 21N 96 10W
Navidad, Jalisco, Mexico **218 B3** 20 34N 104 40W
Navidad →, TX, U.S.A. **99 J11** 28 50N 96 35W
Navojoa, Sonora, Mexico **212 F6** 27 6N 109 26W
Navolato, Sinaloa, Mexico **216 C3** 24 47N 107 42W
Navy Pier, Chicago, U.S.A. **108 B3** 41 53N 87 36W
Nayarit □, Mexico **216 F6** 22 0N 105 0W
Naylor, MO, U.S.A. **82 E6** 36 34N 90 36W
Nazareno, Durango, Mexico **214 E1** 25 23N 103 27W
Nazareth, PA, U.S.A. **87 B1** 40 44N 75 19W
Nazareth, TX, U.S.A. **98 C5** 34 33N 102 6W
Nazas, Durango, Mexico **217 B6** 25 14N 104 8W
Nazas →, Durango, Mexico **217 B6** 25 12N 104 12W
Nazko, B.C., Canada **186 B11** 53 1N 123 37W
Nazko →, B.C., Canada **186 B11** 53 7N 123 34W
Nazko Lake Park ⌂, B.C., Canada **186 C11** 52 26N 123 33W
Neah Bay, WA, U.S.A. **101 B1** 48 22N 124 37W
Neal, KS, U.S.A. **74 D7** 37 50N 96 5W
Neal Smith Nat. Wildlife Refuge ⌂, IA, U.S.A. **73 D5** 41 35N 93 15W
Nealtican, Puebla, Mexico **221 E2** 19 3N 98 25W
Near Is., AK, U.S.A. **61 K1** 52 30N 174 0 E
Near North, Chicago, U.S.A. **108 B3** 41 54N 87 38W
Nebo, IL, U.S.A. **71 D3** 39 27N 90 47W
Nebo, LA, U.S.A. **75 C3** 31 35N 92 9W
Nebo, Mt., UT, U.S.A. **100 D4** 39 49N 111 46W
Nebraska □, U.S.A. **84 C6** 41 30N 99 30W
Nebraska City, NE, U.S.A. **84 D10** 40 41N 95 52W
Nebraska Nat. Forest, NE, U.S.A. **84 B2** 42 45N 103 10W
Necedah, WI, U.S.A. **103 D3** 44 2N 90 4W
Necedah Nat. Wildlife Refuge ⌂, WI, U.S.A. **103 D3** 44 9N 90 11W
Nechako →, B.C., Canada **187 B12** 53 55N 122 42W
Nechako Res., B.C., Canada **186 B7** 53 42N 127 30W
Neche, ND, U.S.A. **91 B8** 48 59N 97 33W
Neches →, TX, U.S.A. **99 H14** 29 58N 93 51W
Necker I., HI, U.S.A. **69 G11** 23 35N 164 42W
Nederland, CO, U.S.A. **66 C5** 39 58N 105 31W
Nederland, TX, U.S.A. **99 H13** 29 59N 94 0W
Neebish I., MI, U.S.A. **79 C7** 46 16N 84 9W
Needham, MA, U.S.A. **78 B3** 42 17N 71 14W
Needham Heights, Boston, U.S.A. **106 B2** 42 17N 71 14W
Needle Range, UT, U.S.A. **100 E2** 38 25N 113 55W
Needles, B.C., Canada **187 F16** 49 53N 118 7W
Needles, CA, U.S.A. **65 J12** 34 51N 114 37W
Needmore, GA, U.S.A. **68 F4** 30 41N 82 43W
Needmore, PA, U.S.A. **77 A2** 39 51N 78 9W
Needmore, TX, U.S.A. **98 C5** 34 2N 102 45W
Needville, TX, U.S.A. **99 H12** 29 24N 95 50W
Neely, MS, U.S.A. **81 E5** 31 10N 88 45W
Neelyville, MO, U.S.A. **82 E6** 36 34N 90 30W
Neenah, WI, U.S.A. **103 D5** 44 11N 88 28W
Neepawa, Man., Canada **183 E12** 50 15N 99 30W
Negaunee, MI, U.S.A. **79 C4** 46 30N 87 36W
Negreet, LA, U.S.A. **75 C2** 31 28N 93 35W
Neguac, N.B., Canada **173 F4** 47 15N 65 5W
Nehalem, OR, U.S.A. **94 B2** 45 43N 123 54W
Nehalem →, OR, U.S.A. **94 B2** 45 40N 123 56W
Nehawka, NE, U.S.A. **84 D10** 40 50N 95 59W
Neidpath, Sask., Canada **182 E4** 50 12N 107 20W
Neihart, MT, U.S.A. **83 D7** 46 56N 110 44W
Neilburg, Sask., Canada **182 C2** 52 50N 109 38W
Neillsville, WI, U.S.A. **103 D3** 44 34N 90 36W
Neils Harbour, N.S., Canada **173 G9** 46 48N 60 20W
Neilton, WA, U.S.A. **101 C2** 47 25N 123 53W
Nejanilini L., Man., Canada **191 F6** 59 33N 97 48W
Nekoma, KS, U.S.A. **74 C4** 38 28N 99 27W
Nekoma, ND, U.S.A. **91 B7** 48 35N 98 22W
Nekoosa, WI, U.S.A. **103 D4** 44 19N 89 54W
Neligh, NE, U.S.A. **84 B7** 42 8N 98 2W
Nellis Air Force Base, Las Vegas, U.S.A. **110 B2** 36 14N 115 2W
Nellis Air Force Range Complex, NV, U.S.A. **85 E4** 37 15N 116 30W
Nelson, B.C., Canada **187 F17** 49 30N 117 20W
Nelson, AZ, U.S.A. **62 B2** 35 31N 113 19W
Nelson, MO, U.S.A. **82 C3** 38 59N 93 3W
Nelson, NH, U.S.A. **86 D2** 42 58N 72 8W
Nelson, NE, U.S.A. **84 D7** 40 12N 98 4W
Nelson, NV, U.S.A. **85 G6** 35 42N 114 49W
Nelson, WI, U.S.A. **103 D2** 44 25N 92 0W
Nelson →, Man., Canada **191 G6** 54 33N 98 2W
Nelson Canyon Park, Vancouver, Canada **193 A1** 49 22N 123 13W
Nelson County ☆, KY, U.S.A. **97 C7** 37 50N 85 30W
Nelson County ☆, ND, U.S.A. **91 C7** 48 0N 98 5W
Nelson County ☆, VA, U.S.A. **102 D6** 37 50N 78 52W
Nelson Forks, B.C., Canada **189 E8** 59 30N 124 0W
Nelson House, Man., Canada **191 F6** 55 47N 98 51W
Nelson-Miramichi, N.B., Canada **173 G4** 46 59N 65 34W
Nelson Res., MT, U.S.A. **83 B10** 48 30N 107 31W
Nelsonville, OH, U.S.A. **92 D4** 39 28N 82 13W
Nemah, WA, U.S.A. **101 D2** 46 31N 123 53W
Nemaha, IA, U.S.A. **73 C3** 42 31N 95 6W
Nemaha, NE, U.S.A. **84 D10** 40 20N 95 41W
Nemaha County ☆, KS, U.S.A. **74 B8** 39 45N 96 0W
Nemaha County ☆, NE, U.S.A. **84 D10** 40 20N 95 45W
Nemegosenda L., Ont., Canada **181 D13** 48 0N 83 7W
Némiscachingue, L., Qué., Canada **176 D8** 47 25N 74 30W
Nemiscau, Qué., Canada **175 C2** 51 18N 76 54W
Nemiscau, L., Qué., Canada **175 C2** 51 25N 76 40W
Nenana, AK, U.S.A. **61 D10** 64 34N 149 5W
Nenzel, NE, U.S.A. **84 B4** 42 56N 101 6W
Neodesha, KS, U.S.A. **74 D8** 37 25N 95 41W
Neoga, IL, U.S.A. **71 D5** 39 19N 88 27W
Neola, IA, U.S.A. **73 D3** 41 27N 95 37W
Neola, UT, U.S.A. **100 C5** 40 26N 110 2W
Neopit, WI, U.S.A. **103 D5** 44 59N 88 50W
Neosho, MO, U.S.A. **82 E2** 36 52N 94 22W
Neosho →, OK, U.S.A. **93 B8** 36 48N 95 18W
Neosho County ☆, KS, U.S.A. **74 D8** 37 30N 95 15W
Neosho Falls, KS, U.S.A. **74 D8** 37 59N 95 33W
Neosho Rapids, KS, U.S.A. **74 C8** 38 22N 95 59W
Nephi, UT, U.S.A. **100 D4** 39 43N 111 50W
Nepisiguit →, N.B., Canada **173 F4** 47 37N 65 38W
Neppel = Moses Lake, WA, U.S.A. **101 C6** 47 8N 119 17W
Neptune, NJ, U.S.A. **87 B2** 40 13N 74 2W
Neptune Beach, FL, U.S.A. **67 A7** 30 19N 81 24W
Néret, L., Qué., Canada **175 C3** 54 45N 70 44W
Nerstrand, MN, U.S.A. **80 F5** 44 20N 93 4W
Nesbit, MS, U.S.A. **81 B3** 34 53N 90 1W
Neshaminy Cr. →, PA, U.S.A. **87 B2** 40 4N 74 55W
Neshkoro, WI, U.S.A. **103 E4** 43 58N 89 13W
Neshoba, MS, U.S.A. **81 D4** 32 37N 89 8W
Neshoba County ☆, MS, U.S.A. **81 D4** 32 46N 89 7W
Nespelem, WA, U.S.A. **101 B7** 48 10N 118 59W
Ness City, KS, U.S.A. **74 C4** 38 27N 99 54W
Ness County ☆, KS, U.S.A. **74 C4** 38 30N 100 0W
Nestaocano →, Qué., Canada **177 B9** 49 38N 73 28W
Nestor Falls, Ont., Canada **180 C3** 49 7N 93 56W
Netarts, OR, U.S.A. **94 B2** 45 26N 123 57W
Netawaka, KS, U.S.A. **74 B8** 39 36N 95 43W
Netcong, NJ, U.S.A. **87 B2** 40 54N 74 42W
Nett L., MN, U.S.A. **80 B5** 48 7N 93 7W
Nettilling L., Nunavut, Canada **191 D11** 66 30N 71 0W
Nettleton, MS, U.S.A. **81 B5** 34 5N 88 37W
Netzahualcóyotl, Tabasco, Mexico **222 B5** 17 42N 91 27W
Netzahualcóyotl, Presa, Chiapas, Mexico **222 B3** 17 8N 93 35W
Neudorf, Sask., Canada **182 E8** 50 43N 103 1W
Neuse →, NC, U.S.A. **90 C9** 35 6N 76 29W
Neuville, TX, U.S.A. **99 F13** 31 41N 94 9W
Nevada, IA, U.S.A. **73 C5** 42 1N 93 27W
Nevada, MO, U.S.A. **82 D2** 37 51N 94 22W
Nevada □, U.S.A. **85 C4** 39 0N 117 0W
Nevada City, CA, U.S.A. **64 D5** 39 16N 121 1W
Nevada County ☆, AR, U.S.A. **63 E2** 33 36N 93 17W
Nevada County ☆, CA, U.S.A. **64 D5** 39 15N 121 0W
Nevado de Toluca, Parque Nacional △, México, Mexico **219 C8** 19 8N 99 45W
Neveros, Durango, Mexico **216 D5** 23 46N 105 44W
Neversink →, NY, U.S.A. **89 D6** 41 21N 74 42W
Neversink Res., NY, U.S.A. **89 D6** 41 48N 74 42W
Neville, Sask., Canada **182 F4** 49 58N 107 39W
Nevis, MN, U.S.A. **80 D4** 46 58N 94 51W
New →, FL, U.S.A. **67 B4** 29 50N 84 40W
New →, NC, U.S.A. **90 D8** 34 32N 77 20W
New →, TN, U.S.A. **97 D8** 36 25N 84 37W
New →, WV, U.S.A. **102 C3** 38 10N 81 12W
New Aiyansh, B.C., Canada **189 E7** 55 12N 129 4W
New Albany, IN, U.S.A. **72 E5** 38 18N 85 49W
New Albany, KS, U.S.A. **74 D8** 37 34N 95 56W
New Albany, MS, U.S.A. **81 B5** 34 29N 89 0W
New Albany, PA, U.S.A. **95 C6** 41 36N 76 27W
New Albin, IA, U.S.A. **73 B7** 43 30N 91 17W
New Alluwe, OK, U.S.A. **93 B8** 36 37N 95 29W
New Almelo, KS, U.S.A. **74 B3** 39 36N 100 7W
New Athens, IL, U.S.A. **71 E4** 38 19N 89 53W
New Athens, OH, U.S.A. **92 C5** 40 11N 81 0W
New Auburn, MN, U.S.A. **80 F4** 44 40N 94 14W
New Auburn, WI, U.S.A. **103 C2** 45 12N 91 33W
New Augusta, MS, U.S.A. **81 E4** 31 12N 89 2W
New Baden, IL, U.S.A. **71 E4** 38 32N 89 42W
New Baltimore, MI, U.S.A. **79 G9** 42 41N 82 44W
New Baltimore, PA, U.S.A. **95 E4** 39 59N 78 46W
New Barbadoes = Hackensack, NJ, U.S.A. **87 B2** 40 52N 74 4W
New Bavaria, OH, U.S.A. **92 B2** 41 12N 84 10W
New Bedford, MA, U.S.A. **78 C4** 41 38N 70 56W
New Berlin = North Canton, OH, U.S.A. **92 C5** 40 53N 81 24W
New Berlin, IL, U.S.A. **71 D4** 39 44N 89 55W
New Berlin, NY, U.S.A. **89 C5** 42 37N 75 20W
New Berlin, WI, U.S.A. **103 F5** 42 59N 88 6W
New Bern, NC, U.S.A. **90 C8** 35 7N 77 3W
New Bethlehem, PA, U.S.A. **95 D3** 41 0N 79 20W
New Bloomfield, MO, U.S.A. **82 C4** 38 43N 92 5W
New Bloomfield, PA, U.S.A. **95 D5** 40 25N 77 11W
New Boston, IL, U.S.A. **71 B3** 41 10N 91 0W
New Boston, MA, U.S.A. **78 B1** 42 6N 73 5W
New Boston, NH, U.S.A. **86 D3** 42 59N 71 41W
New Boston, OH, U.S.A. **92 E4** 38 45N 82 56W
New Boston, TX, U.S.A. **99 D13** 33 28N 94 25W
New Braunfels, TX, U.S.A. **99 H9** 29 42N 98 8W
New Bremen, OH, U.S.A. **92 C2** 40 26N 84 23W
New Brigden, Alta., Canada **185 G10** 51 42N 110 29W
New Brighton, Minneapolis-St. Paul, U.S.A. **113 A2** 45 3N 93 12W
New Brighton, NY, U.S.A. **114 C2** 40 38N 74 5W
New Britain, CT, U.S.A. **78 C2** 41 40N 72 47W
New Brockton, AL, U.S.A. **60 E5** 31 23N 85 56W
New Brookland = West Columbia, SC, U.S.A. **90 E4** 33 59N 81 4W
New Brunswick, NJ, U.S.A. **87 B2** 40 30N 74 27W
New Brunswick □, Canada **173 G3** 46 50N 66 30W
New Buffalo, MI, U.S.A. **79 H5** 41 47N 86 45W
New Bullards Bar Dam, CA, U.S.A. **64 D5** 39 24N 121 8W
New Cambria, KS, U.S.A. **74 C6** 38 53N 97 30W
New Canaan, CT, U.S.A. **78 C1** 41 9N 73 30W
New Canton, VA, U.S.A. **102 D6** 37 42N 78 18W
New Carlisle, N.B., Canada **173 E4** 48 1N 65 20W
New Carlisle, OH, U.S.A. **92 D2** 39 56N 84 2W
New Carrollton, MD, U.S.A. **119 B4** 38 58N 76 52W
New Carrollton, MD, U.S.A. **77 B4** 38 58N 76 53W
New Castle, CO, U.S.A. **66 C3** 39 34N 107 32W
New Castle, DE, U.S.A. **77 A5** 39 40N 75 34W
New Castle, IN, U.S.A. **72 D5** 39 55N 85 22W
New Castle, KY, U.S.A. **97 B7** 38 26N 85 10W
New Castle, PA, U.S.A. **95 D2** 41 0N 80 21W
New Castle, VA, U.S.A. **102 D4** 37 30N 80 7W
New Castle County ☆, DE, U.S.A. **77 A5** 39 30N 75 40W
New Church, VA, U.S.A. **77 C5** 37 59N 75 32W
New City, NY, U.S.A. **87 A3** 41 9N 73 59W
New Concord, KY, U.S.A. **96 D4** 36 33N 88 9W
New Concord, OH, U.S.A. **92 D5** 39 59N 81 54W
New Cumberland, WV, U.S.A. **102 A4** 40 30N 80 36W
New Deal, TX, U.S.A. **98 D6** 33 44N 101 50W
New Denmark, N.B., Canada **173 F2** 47 2N 67 38W
New Denver, B.C., Canada **187 F17** 50 0N 117 25W
New Don Pedro Res., CA, U.S.A. **64 F6** 37 43N 120 24W
New Dorp, NY, U.S.A. **114 C2** 40 34N 74 7W
New Dorp Beach, NY, U.S.A. **114 C2** 40 33N 74 6W
New Edinburg, AR, U.S.A. **63 E3** 33 46N 92 14W
New Effington, SD, U.S.A. **91 E9** 45 51N 96 55W
New Egypt, NJ, U.S.A. **87 B2** 40 4N 74 32W
New Ellenton, SC, U.S.A. **90 E4** 33 28N 81 41W
New England, U.S.A. **53 B12** 43 0N 71 0W
New England, ND, U.S.A. **91 D3** 46 32N 102 52W
New Era, MI, U.S.A. **79 F5** 43 34N 86 21W
New Fairfield, CT, U.S.A. **78 C1** 41 27N 73 14W
New Florence, MO, U.S.A. **82 C5** 38 55N 91 27W
New Florence, PA, U.S.A. **95 D3** 40 23N 79 5W
New Fork Lakes, WY, U.S.A. **104 C3** 43 6N 109 57W
New Franklin, MO, U.S.A. **82 B4** 39 1N 92 44W
New Freedom, PA, U.S.A. **77 A4** 39 44N 76 42W
New Germany, N.S., Canada **173 J5** 44 33N 64 43W
New Glarus, WI, U.S.A. **103 F4** 42 49N 89 38W
New Glasgow, N.S., Canada **173 H7** 45 35N 62 36W
New Hamburg, Ont., Canada **178 D6** 43 23N 80 42W
New Hampshire □, U.S.A. **86 C3** 44 0N 71 30W
New Hampton, IA, U.S.A. **73 B6** 43 3N 92 19W
New Hampton, MO, U.S.A. **82 A2** 40 16N 94 12W
New Hampton, NH, U.S.A. **86 C3** 43 36N 71 39W
New Hanover County ☆, NC, U.S.A. **90 D8** 34 15N 77 50W
New Harbour, N.S., Canada **173 H8** 45 13N 61 29W
New Harmony, IN, U.S.A. **72 E3** 38 8N 87 56W
New Harmony, UT, U.S.A. **100 F2** 37 29N 113 19W
New Hartford, CT, U.S.A. **78 C2** 41 53N 72 59W
New Hartford, IA, U.S.A. **73 C6** 42 34N 92 37W
New Hartford, NY, U.S.A. **89 B5** 43 4N 75 18W
New Haven, CT, U.S.A. **78 C2** 41 18N 72 55W
New Haven, IL, U.S.A. **71 F5** 37 55N 88 8W
New Haven, IN, U.S.A. **72 B5** 41 4N 85 1W
New Haven, KY, U.S.A. **97 C7** 37 40N 85 36W
New Haven, MI, U.S.A. **79 G9** 42 44N 82 48W
New Haven, MO, U.S.A. **82 C5** 38 37N 91 13W
New Haven, NY, U.S.A. **89 B4** 43 29N 76 19W
New Haven, WV, U.S.A. **102 C3** 38 59N 81 58W
New Haven County ☆, CT, U.S.A. **78 C2** 41 25N 72 50W
New Hebron, MS, U.S.A. **81 E4** 31 44N 89 59W
New Hogan L., CA, U.S.A. **64 E6** 38 9N 120 49W
New Holland, OH, U.S.A. **92 D3** 39 33N 83 15W
New Holland, PA, U.S.A. **95 D6** 40 6N 76 5W
New Holstein, WI, U.S.A. **103 E5** 43 57N 88 5W
New Hope, AL, U.S.A. **60 B4** 34 32N 86 24W
New Hope, Minneapolis-St. Paul, U.S.A. **113 A1** 45 2N 93 23W
New Hope, PA, U.S.A. **87 B2** 40 22N 74 57W
New Houlka, MS, U.S.A. **81 B4** 34 2N 89 1W
New Hyde Park, NY, U.S.A. **114 B4** 40 44N 73 41W
New Iberia, LA, U.S.A. **75 D4** 30 1N 91 49W
New Ipswich, NH, U.S.A. **86 D3** 42 46N 71 51W
New Jersey □, U.S.A. **87 B2** 40 0N 74 30W
New Johnsonville, TN, U.S.A. **96 D5** 36 1N 87 58W
New Kensington, PA, U.S.A. **95 D3** 40 34N 79 46W
New Kent, VA, U.S.A. **102 D8** 37 31N 76 59W
New Kent County ☆, VA, U.S.A. **102 D8** 37 31N 76 59W
New L., NC, U.S.A. **90 C9** 35 39N 76 21W
New Leipzig, ND, U.S.A. **91 D4** 46 22N 101 57W
New Lexington, OH, U.S.A. **92 D4** 39 43N 82 13W
New Lisbon, WI, U.S.A. **103 E3** 43 53N 90 10W
New Liskeard, Ont., Canada **176 D3** 47 31N 79 41W
New Llano, LA, U.S.A. **75 C2** 31 7N 93 16W
New London, CT, U.S.A. **78 C2** 41 22N 72 6W
New London, IA, U.S.A. **73 E7** 40 55N 91 24W
New London, MD, U.S.A. **77 A3** 39 25N 77 16W
New London, MN, U.S.A. **80 E4** 45 18N 94 56W
New London, MO, U.S.A. **82 B5** 39 35N 91 24W
New London, NH, U.S.A. **86 C3** 43 25N 71 59W
New London, OH, U.S.A. **92 B4** 41 5N 82 24W
New London, WI, U.S.A. **103 D5** 44 23N 88 45W
New London County ☆, CT, U.S.A. **78 C2** 41 30N 72 15W
New Madison, OH, U.S.A. **92 D2** 39 58N 84 43W
New Madrid, MO, U.S.A. **82 E7** 36 36N 89 32W
New Madrid County ☆, MO, U.S.A. **82 E7** 36 40N 89 35W
New Market, AL, U.S.A. **60 B4** 34 55N 86 26W
New Market, IN, U.S.A. **72 D4** 39 57N 86 55W
New Market, IA, U.S.A. **73 E4** 40 44N 94 54W
New Market, MD, U.S.A. **77 A3** 39 23N 77 16W
New Market, TN, U.S.A. **97 D9** 36 6N 83 33W
New Market, VA, U.S.A. **102 C6** 38 39N 78 40W
New Marlborough, MA, U.S.A. **78 B1** 42 7N 73 14W
New Martinsville, WV, U.S.A. **102 B4** 39 39N 80 52W
New Matamoras, OH, U.S.A. **92 D5** 39 31N 81 4W
New Meadows, ID, U.S.A. **70 E2** 44 58N 116 18W
New Melle, MO, U.S.A. **82 C6** 38 43N 90 53W
New Melones Dam, CA, U.S.A. **64 F6** 37 57N 120 32W
New Melones L., CA, U.S.A. **64 F6** 37 57N 120 31W
New Mexico □, U.S.A. **88 C5** 34 30N 106 0W
New Miami, OH, U.S.A. **92 D2** 39 26N 84 32W
New Milford, CT, U.S.A. **78 C1** 41 35N 73 25W
New Milford, PA, U.S.A. **95 C7** 41 52N 75 44W
New Munich, MN, U.S.A. **80 E4** 45 38N 94 45W
New Norway, Alta., Canada **185 F8** 52 52N 112 57W
New Orleans, LA, U.S.A. **75 E5** 29 57N 90 4W
New Orleans International ✕ (MSY), LA, U.S.A. **75 E5** 30 0N 90 15W
New Oxford, PA, U.S.A. **77 A3** 39 52N 77 4W
New Paltz, NY, U.S.A. **89 D6** 41 45N 74 5W
New Paris, IN, U.S.A. **72 B5** 41 30N 85 50W
New Paris, OH, U.S.A. **92 D2** 39 51N 84 48W
New Pekin, IN, U.S.A. **72 E4** 38 30N 86 0W
New Philadelphia, OH, U.S.A. **92 C5** 40 30N 81 27W
New Pine Creek, OR, U.S.A. **94 E5** 42 0N 120 18W
New Plymouth, ID, U.S.A. **70 F2** 43 58N 116 49W
New Point, VA, U.S.A. **102 D8** 37 21N 76 17W
New Port Richey, FL, U.S.A. **67 C6** 28 16N 82 43W
New Prague, MN, U.S.A. **80 F5** 44 32N 93 35W
New Preston, CT, U.S.A. **78 C1** 41 40N 73 21W
New Princeton, OR, U.S.A. **94 D7** 43 15N 118 35W
New Providence, IN, U.S.A. **72 E5** 38 28N 85 57W
New Raymer, CO, U.S.A. **66 B7** 40 36N 103 51W
New Richland, MN, U.S.A. **80 G5** 43 54N 93 30W
New Richmond, Qué., Canada **172 E4** 48 15N 65 45W
New Richmond, OH, U.S.A. **92 E2** 38 57N 84 17W
New Richmond, WI, U.S.A. **103 C1** 45 7N 92 32W
New Riegel, OH, U.S.A. **92 B3** 41 3N 83 19W
New River →, Miami, U.S.A. **112 B3** 26 6N 80 6W
New River Gorge Nat. River ⌂, WV, U.S.A. **102 D3** 37 53N 81 5W
New Roads, LA, U.S.A. **75 D4** 30 42N 91 26W
New Rochelle, NY, U.S.A. **87 B3** 40 55N 73 46W
New Rockford, ND, U.S.A. **91 C6** 47 41N 99 8W
New Ross, N.S., Canada **173 J5** 44 44N 64 27W
New Salem, MA, U.S.A. **78 B2** 42 30N 72 20W
New Salem, ND, U.S.A. **91 D4** 46 51N 101 25W
New Sarepta, Alta., Canada **184 E7** 53 16N 113 8W
New Sharon, IA, U.S.A. **73 D6** 41 28N 92 39W
New Smyrna Beach, FL, U.S.A. **67 B8** 29 1N 80 56W
New Springville, NY, U.S.A. **114 C2** 40 35N 74 9W
New Straitsville, OH, U.S.A. **92 D4** 39 35N 82 14W
New Stuyahok, AK, U.S.A. **61 G8** 59 29N 157 20W
New Tazewell, TN, U.S.A. **97 D9** 36 27N 83 36W
New Tecumseth, Ont., Canada **178 C7** 44 9N 79 52W
New Town, ND, U.S.A. **91 C3** 47 59N 102 30W
New Tripoli, PA, U.S.A. **87 B1** 40 41N 75 45W
New Tulsa, OK, U.S.A. **93 B8** 36 9N 95 48W
New Ulm, MN, U.S.A. **80 F4** 44 19N 94 28W
New Underwood, SD, U.S.A. **91 F3** 44 6N 102 50W
New Utrecht, NY, U.S.A. **114 C3** 40 36N 73 59W
New Vienna, IA, U.S.A. **73 C7** 42 33N 91 7W
New Vienna, OH, U.S.A. **92 D3** 39 19N 83 42W
New Vineyard, ME, U.S.A. **76 D3** 44 48N 70 7W
New Virginia, IA, U.S.A. **73 D5** 41 11N 93 44W
New Washington, OH, U.S.A. **92 C4** 40 58N 82 51W
New Waterford, N.S., Canada **173 G9** 46 13N 60 4W
New Waverly, TX, U.S.A. **99 G12** 30 32N 95 29W
New-Wes-Valley, Nfld. & L., Canada **174 C7** 49 8N 53 36W
New Westminster, B.C., Canada **187 F12** 49 13N 122 55W
New Whiteland, IN, U.S.A. **72 D4** 39 33N 86 5W
New Windsor, MD, U.S.A. **77 A3** 39 34N 77 9W
New Windsor, NY, U.S.A. **87 A2** 41 29N 74 1W
New World I., Nfld. & L., Canada **174 C6** 49 35N 54 40W
New York, NY, U.S.A. **89 E7** 40 43N 74 0W
New York □, U.S.A. **89 B5** 43 0N 75 0W
New York County ☆, NY, U.S.A. **89 E7** 40 45N 73 59W
New York J.F. Kennedy International ✕ (JFK), NY, U.S.A. **89 E7** 40 38N 73 47W
New York La Guardia ✕ (LGA), NY, U.S.A. **89 E7** 40 46N 73 52W
New York Mills, MN, U.S.A. **80 D3** 46 31N 95 22W
Newark, AR, U.S.A. **63 C4** 35 42N 91 27W
Newark, CA, U.S.A. **64 F4** 37 32N 122 2W
Newark, DE, U.S.A. **77 A5** 39 41N 75 46W
Newark, MD, U.S.A. **77 B5** 38 15N 75 17W
Newark, NJ, U.S.A. **87 B2** 40 44N 74 10W
Newark, NY, U.S.A. **89 B3** 43 3N 77 6W
Newark, OH, U.S.A. **92 C4** 40 3N 82 24W
Newark, TX, U.S.A. **99 D10** 33 0N 97 29W
Newark B., NJ, U.S.A. **114 B2** 40 40N 74 8W
Newark L., NV, U.S.A. **85 C5** 39 42N 115 44W
Newark Liberty International ✕ (EWR), NJ, U.S.A. **89 E6** 40 42N 74 10W
Newark Valley, NY, U.S.A. **89 C4** 42 14N 76 11W
Newaygo, MI, U.S.A. **79 F6** 43 25N 85 48W
Newaygo County ☆, MI, U.S.A. **79 F6** 43 30N 85 50W
Newberg, OR, U.S.A. **94 B3** 45 18N 122 58W
Newbern, AL, U.S.A. **60 D3** 32 36N 87 32W
Newbern, TN, U.S.A. **96 D3** 36 7N 89 16W
Newberry, FL, U.S.A. **67 B6** 29 39N 82 37W
Newberry, IN, U.S.A. **72 E3** 38 55N 87 1W
Newberry, MI, U.S.A. **79 C6** 46 21N 85 30W
Newberry, SC, U.S.A. **90 D4** 34 17N 81 37W
Newberry County ☆, SC, U.S.A. **90 D4** 34 20N 81 40W
Newberry Nat. Volcanic Monument △, OR, U.S.A. **94 D4** 43 43N 121 14W
Newberry Springs, CA, U.S.A. **65 J10** 34 50N 116 41W
Newboro L., Ont., Canada **179 C10** 44 38N 76 20W
Newbrook, Alta., Canada **184 D8** 54 24N 112 57W
Newburg, MD, U.S.A. **77 B4** 38 22N 76 37W
Newburg, MO, U.S.A. **82 D5** 37 55N 91 54W
Newburg, ND, U.S.A. **91 B5** 48 43N 100 55W
Newburg, PA, U.S.A. **95 D5** 40 8N 77 33W
Newburg, WV, U.S.A. **102 B5** 39 23N 79 51W
Newburgh, Ont., Canada **179 C10** 44 19N 76 52W
Newburgh, IN, U.S.A. **72 F3** 37 57N 87 24W
Newburgh, NY, U.S.A. **87 A2** 41 30N 74 1W
Newburgh Heights, Cleveland, U.S.A. **107 B1** 41 27N 81 39W
Newbury, NH, U.S.A. **86 C2** 43 19N 72 3W
Newburyport, MA, U.S.A. **78 B4** 42 49N 70 53W
Newcastle, N.B., Canada **173 F4** 47 1N 65 38W
Newcastle, CA, U.S.A. **64 E5** 38 53N 121 8W
Newcastle, ME, U.S.A. **76 D4** 44 2N 69 32W
Newcastle, NE, U.S.A. **84 B9** 42 39N 96 53W
Newcastle, OK, U.S.A. **93 C6** 35 15N 97 36W
Newcastle, Seattle, U.S.A. **118 C5** 47 32N 122 9W
Newcastle, TX, U.S.A. **99 D9** 33 12N 98 44W
Newcastle, UT, U.S.A. **100 F2** 37 40N 113 33W
Newcastle, WY, U.S.A. **104 C8** 43 50N 104 12W
Newcastle Bridge, N.B., Canada **173 G3** 46 5N 66 3W

Newcomb, MD, U.S.A. 77 B4 38 45N 76 12W
Newcomb, NM, U.S.A. 88 A2 36 17N 108 42W
Newcomb, NY, U.S.A. 89 B6 43 58N 74 10W
Newcomerstown, OH, U.S.A. 92 C5 40 16N 81 36W
Newell, AR, U.S.A. 63 E3 33 10N 92 45W
Newell, Charlotte, U.S.A. 107 A2 35 16N 80 44W
Newell, IA, U.S.A. 73 C3 42 36N 95 0W
Newell, SD, U.S.A. 91 F2 44 43N 103 25W
Newell, WV, U.S.A. 102 A4 40 37N 80 36W
Newell, L., Alta., Canada 185 H9 50 26N 111 55W
Newellton, LA, U.S.A. 75 B4 32 4N 91 14W
Newenham, C., AK, U.S.A. 61 G7 58 39N 162 11W
Newfane, NY, U.S.A. 89 B2 43 17N 78 43W
Newfane, VT, U.S.A. 86 D2 42 59N 72 39W
Newfield, NJ, U.S.A. 87 C1 39 33N 75 1W
Newfolden, MN, U.S.A. 80 B2 48 21N 96 20W
Newfound L., NH, U.S.A. 86 C3 43 40N 71 47W
Newfoundland, Canada 174 D4 49 0N 55 0W
Newfoundland, PA, U.S.A. 87 A1 41 18N 75 19W
Newfoundland & Labrador □, Canada 174 B5 53 0N 58 0W
Newfoundland Evaporation Basin, UT, U.S.A. 100 C2 40 50N 113 26W
Newfoundland Mts., UT, U.S.A. 100 B2 41 10N 113 20W
Newgate, B.C., Canada 185 J5 49 2N 115 12W
Newhalem, WA, U.S.A. 101 B4 48 40N 121 15W
Newhalen, AK, U.S.A. 61 G9 59 43N 154 54W
Newhall, IA, U.S.A. 73 D7 41 59N 91 59W
Newington, CT, U.S.A. 78 C2 41 43N 72 45W
Newington, GA, U.S.A. 68 D5 32 35N 81 30W
Newkirk, NM, U.S.A. 88 B6 35 4N 104 16W
Newkirk, OK, U.S.A. 93 B6 36 53N 97 3W
Newland, NC, U.S.A. 90 B4 36 5N 81 56W
Newland, VA, U.S.A. 77 B4 38 3N 76 52W
Newman, CA, U.S.A. 64 F5 37 19N 121 1W
Newman, IL, U.S.A. 71 D6 39 48N 87 59W
Newman Grove, NE, U.S.A. 84 C8 41 45N 97 47W
Newmans L., FL, U.S.A. 67 B6 29 40N 82 12W
Newmarket, Ont., Canada 178 C7 44 3N 79 28W
Newmarket, NH, U.S.A. 86 C4 43 5N 70 56W
Newnan, GA, U.S.A. 68 C2 33 23N 84 48W
Newport, Qué., Canada 172 E5 48 16N 64 45W
Newport, AR, U.S.A. 63 C4 35 37N 91 16W
Newport, DE, U.S.A. 77 A5 39 43N 75 37W
Newport, IN, U.S.A. 72 D3 39 53N 87 25W
Newport, KY, U.S.A. 97 A8 39 5N 84 29W
Newport, ME, U.S.A. 76 D4 44 50N 69 17W
Newport, MI, U.S.A. 79 H8 42 0N 83 19W
Newport, Minneapolis-St. Paul, U.S.A. 113 B4 44 52N 92 59W
Newport, NC, U.S.A. 90 D9 34 48N 76 52W
Newport, NH, U.S.A. 86 C2 43 22N 72 10W
Newport, NJ, U.S.A. 87 C1 39 18N 75 11W
Newport, NY, U.S.A. 89 B5 43 11N 75 1W
Newport, NE, U.S.A. 84 B6 42 36N 99 20W
Newport, OR, U.S.A. 94 C1 44 39N 124 3W
Newport, PA, U.S.A. 95 D5 40 29N 77 8W
Newport, RI, U.S.A. 78 C3 41 29N 71 19W
Newport, TN, U.S.A. 97 E9 35 58N 83 11W
Newport, VT, U.S.A. 86 B2 44 56N 72 13W
Newport, WA, U.S.A. 101 B8 48 11N 117 3W
Newport Beach, CA, U.S.A. 65 K9 33 37N 117 56W
Newport County ☆, RI, U.S.A. 78 C3 41 30N 71 20W
Newport News, VA, U.S.A. 102 E8 36 58N 76 25W
Newsoms, VA, U.S.A. 102 E7 36 38N 77 8W
Newtok, AK, U.S.A. 61 F6 60 56N 164 38W
Newton, Boston, U.S.A. 106 B2 42 19N 71 13W
Newton, GA, U.S.A. 68 E2 31 19N 84 20W
Newton, IL, U.S.A. 71 E5 38 59N 88 10W
Newton, IA, U.S.A. 73 D5 41 42N 93 3W
Newton, KS, U.S.A. 74 C6 38 3N 97 21W
Newton, MA, U.S.A. 78 B3 42 21N 71 12W
Newton, MS, U.S.A. 81 D4 32 19N 89 10W
Newton, NC, U.S.A. 90 C4 35 40N 81 13W
Newton, NJ, U.S.A. 87 A2 41 3N 74 45W
Newton, TX, U.S.A. 99 G14 30 51N 93 46W
Newton, UT, U.S.A. 100 B3 41 52N 112 0W
Newton County ☆, AR, U.S.A. 63 C2 35 50N 93 13W
Newton County ☆, GA, U.S.A. 68 C3 33 30N 83 50W
Newton County ☆, IN, U.S.A. 72 B3 41 0N 87 25W
Newton County ☆, MS, U.S.A. 81 D4 32 26N 89 7W
Newton County ☆, MO, U.S.A. 82 E2 36 55N 94 20W
Newton County ☆, TX, U.S.A. 99 G14 30 32N 93 49W
Newton Falls, NY, U.S.A. 89 A6 44 13N 74 59W
Newton Falls, OH, U.S.A. 92 B6 41 11N 80 59W
Newton L., IL, U.S.A. 71 E5 38 55N 88 15W
Newtonia, MO, U.S.A. 82 E2 36 53N 94 11W
Newtonsville, OH, U.S.A. 92 D2 39 11N 84 5W
Newtonville, AL, U.S.A. 60 C3 33 33N 87 48W
Newtonville, Boston, U.S.A. 106 A2 42 20N 71 11W
Newtown, Nfld. & L., Canada 174 C7 49 12N 53 31W
Newtown, CT, U.S.A. 78 C1 41 25N 73 19W
Newtown, MD, U.S.A. 77 A4 39 18N 76 9W
Newtown, MO, U.S.A. 82 A3 40 22N 93 20W
Newtown, OH, U.S.A. 107 B2 39 7N 84 21W
Newtown, PA, U.S.A. 87 B2 40 14N 74 57W
Newtown, VA, U.S.A. 77 C3 37 55N 77 8W
Newville, PA, U.S.A. 95 D5 40 10N 77 24W
Ney, OH, U.S.A. 92 B2 41 23N 84 32W
Nez Perce County ☆, ID, U.S.A. 70 C2 46 10N 116 55W
Nez Perce Indian Reservation, ID, U.S.A. 70 C2 46 15N 116 30W
Nezahualcóyotl, México, Mexico 219 C9 19 23N 99 0W
Nezperce, ID, U.S.A. 70 C2 46 14N 116 14W
Nezperce Nat. Forest, ID, U.S.A. 70 D3 45 50N 115 20W
Nezpique, Bayou →, LA, U.S.A. 75 D3 30 11N 92 34W
Niagara, ND, U.S.A. 91 C8 48 0N 97 54W
Niagara, WI, U.S.A. 103 C5 45 46N 88 0W
Niagara →, NY, U.S.A. 89 B1 43 16N 79 4W
Niagara County ☆, NY, U.S.A. 89 B2 43 15N 78 45W
Niagara Falls, Ont., Canada 178 D7 43 7N 79 5W
Niagara Falls, NY, U.S.A. 89 B1 43 5N 79 4W
Niagara-on-the-Lake, Ont., Canada 178 D7 43 15N 79 4W
Niangua, MO, U.S.A. 82 D4 37 23N 92 50W
Niangua →, MO, U.S.A. 82 C4 38 58N 92 48W
Niantic, CT, U.S.A. 78 C2 41 20N 72 11W
Niarada, MT, U.S.A. 83 C3 47 49N 114 36W
Nicatous L., ME, U.S.A. 76 C5 45 5N 68 9W
Nice, CA, U.S.A. 64 D4 39 7N 122 51W
Niceville, FL, U.S.A. 67 A2 30 31N 86 30W
Nicholas County ☆, KY, U.S.A. 97 B9 38 20N 84 0W
Nicholas County ☆, WV, U.S.A. 102 C4 38 17N 80 51W
Nicholasville, KY, U.S.A. 97 C8 37 53N 84 34W
Nicholls, GA, U.S.A. 68 E4 31 31N 82 38W
Nichols, IA, U.S.A. 73 D7 41 29N 91 19W
Nichols, NY, U.S.A. 89 C4 42 1N 76 22W
Nichols, SC, U.S.A. 90 D6 34 14N 79 9W
Nichols, WI, U.S.A. 103 D5 44 40N 88 28W
Nicholson, GA, U.S.A. 68 B3 34 7N 83 26W
Nicholson, MS, U.S.A. 81 F4 30 29N 89 43W
Nichupté, L., Quintana Roo, Mexico 223 A7 21 7N 86 47W
Nickel Creek, TX, U.S.A. 98 F3 31 55N 104 45W
Nickerson, KS, U.S.A. 74 C5 38 8N 98 5W
Nickerson, NE, U.S.A. 84 C9 41 32N 96 28W
Nicodemus, KS, U.S.A. 74 B4 39 24N 99 37W
Nicodemus Nat. Historic Site ⌓, KS, U.S.A. 74 B4 39 23N 99 37W
Nicola, B.C., Canada 187 E14 50 12N 120 40W
Nicola L., B.C., Canada 187 E14 50 10N 120 32W
Nicolás Bravo, Durango, Mexico 217 C6 24 29N 104 45W
Nicolás Bravo, Quintana Roo, Mexico 223 D5 18 29N 88 55W
Nicolás Flores, Hidalgo, Mexico 219 B8 20 46N 99 9W
Nicolás R. Casillas, Guadalajara, Mexico 224 B1 20 33N 103 28W
Nicolet, Qué., Canada 177 E10 46 17N 72 35W
Nicolet Nat. Forest, WI, U.S.A. 103 C5 45 35N 88 45W
Nicollet, MN, U.S.A. 80 F4 44 17N 94 11W
Nicollet County ☆, MN, U.S.A. 80 F4 44 20N 94 15W
Nielsville, MN, U.S.A. 80 C2 47 32N 96 49W
Nigei I., B.C., Canada 186 E7 50 53N 127 43W
Nighthawk, WA, U.S.A. 101 B6 48 58N 119 38W
Nightmute, AK, U.S.A. 61 F6 60 29N 164 44W
Nihoa, HI, U.S.A. 69 G11 23 6N 161 58W
Ni'ihau, HI, U.S.A. 69 B1 21 54N 160 9W
Nikep, MD, U.S.A. 77 A1 39 32N 79 1W
Nikiski, AK, U.S.A. 61 F10 61 41N 151 18W
Nikolai, AK, U.S.A. 61 E9 62 58N 154 10W
Nikolski, AK, U.S.A. 61 K5 52 56N 168 52W
Niland, CA, U.S.A. 65 K11 33 14N 115 31W
Niles, Chicago, U.S.A. 108 A2 42 1N 87 48W
Niles, KS, U.S.A. 74 C6 38 58N 97 28W
Niles, MI, U.S.A. 79 H5 41 50N 86 15W
Niles, OH, U.S.A. 92 B6 41 11N 80 46W
Niles Center = Skokie, IL, U.S.A. 71 A6 42 2N 87 43W
Niltepec, Oaxaca, Mexico 221 H6 16 34N 94 37W
Nimpkish →, B.C., Canada 186 E8 50 34N 126 58W
Nimpkish L., B.C., Canada 186 E8 50 25N 126 59W
Nimpkish Lake Park ⌓, B.C., Canada 186 E7 50 20N 127 0W
Nimpo L., B.C., Canada 186 C9 52 20N 125 10W
Nimpo Lake, B.C., Canada 186 C9 52 20N 125 9W
Nimrod, MN, U.S.A. 80 D4 46 38N 94 53W
Nimrod L., AR, U.S.A. 63 D2 34 57N 93 10W
Nimún, Pta., Campeche, Mexico 223 B3 20 46N 90 25W
Nina Bang L., Nunavut, Canada 190 C10 70 52N 79 24W
Ninaview, CO, U.S.A. 66 E7 37 39N 103 15W
Nine Mile Cr. →, UT, U.S.A. 100 D6 39 50N 109 53W
Ninette, Man., Canada 183 F12 49 24N 99 38W
Ninety Six, SC, U.S.A. 90 D3 34 11N 82 1W
Ninety Six Nat. Historical Site ⌓, SC, U.S.A. 90 D3 34 9N 82 1W
Ninini Pt., HI, U.S.A. 69 B2 21 58N 159 20W
Ninnekah, OK, U.S.A. 93 D6 34 57N 97 56W
Ninnescah →, KS, U.S.A. 74 D6 37 20N 97 10W
Niños Héroes de Chapultepec, Sinaloa, Mexico 216 A2 26 19N 108 54W
Niobrara, NE, U.S.A. 84 B7 42 45N 98 2W
Niobrara →, NE, U.S.A. 84 B7 42 46N 98 3W
Niobrara County ☆, WY, U.S.A. 104 C8 43 0N 104 25W
Niobrara Nat. Scenic River ⌓, NE, U.S.A. 84 B7 42 48N 98 7W
Nioman, Qué., Canada 175 C4 50 25N 66 5W
Niota, TN, U.S.A. 97 E8 35 31N 84 33W
Nipawin, Sask., Canada 182 B7 53 20N 104 0W
Nipekamew →, Sask., Canada 182 A7 54 59N 104 52W
Nipigon, Ont., Canada 180 C8 49 0N 88 17W
Nipigon →, Ont., Canada 180 D8 48 57N 88 14W
Nipigon, L., Ont., Canada 180 C8 49 50N 88 30W
Nipigon B., Ont., Canada 181 D9 48 53N 87 50W
Nipishish L., Nfld. & L., Canada 175 C5 54 12N 60 45W
Nipisi L., Alta., Canada 184 C6 55 47N 114 57W
Nipissing, L., Ont., Canada 178 A7 46 20N 80 0W
Nipissis →, Qué., Canada 175 C4 50 30N 66 5W
Nipissis, L., Qué., Canada 172 B3 51 2N 66 10W
Nipisso, L., Qué., Canada 172 C4 50 52N 65 50W
Nipomo, CA, U.S.A. 65 H6 35 3N 120 29W
Nippers Harbour, Nfld. & L., Canada 174 C5 49 48N 55 52W
Nipton, CA, U.S.A. 65 H11 35 28N 115 16W
Nisland, SD, U.S.A. 91 F2 44 40N 103 33W
Nisling →, Yukon, Canada 189 D5 62 29N 139 28W
Nisqually, WA, U.S.A. 101 C3 47 3N 122 42W
Nisqually →, WA, U.S.A. 101 C3 47 7N 122 42W
Nisswa, MN, U.S.A. 80 D4 46 31N 94 17W
Nisula, MI, U.S.A. 79 C3 46 46N 88 48W
Nitchequon, Qué., Canada 175 C3 53 10N 70 58W
Nith →, Ont., Canada 178 D6 43 12N 80 23W
Nitinat, B.C., Canada 186 G10 48 56N 124 29W
Nitinat L., B.C., Canada 186 G10 48 45N 124 45W
Nitro, WV, U.S.A. 102 C3 38 25N 81 51W
Nitta Yuma, MS, U.S.A. 81 C3 33 2N 90 51W
Nitun, Pta., Campeche, Mexico 223 B3 20 10N 90 29W
Niu Valley, HI, U.S.A. 69 K14 21 19N 157 44W
Niverville, Man., Canada 183 F14 49 36N 97 3W
Niverville, NY, U.S.A. 78 B1 42 26N 73 40W
Niwot, CO, U.S.A. 66 B5 40 6N 105 10W
Nixa, MO, U.S.A. 82 D3 37 3N 93 18W
Nixon, TX, U.S.A. 99 H10 29 16N 97 46W
Nizuc, Pta., Quintana Roo, Mexico 223 A7 21 2N 86 48W
Noank, CT, U.S.A. 78 C2 41 19N 72 1W
Noatak, AK, U.S.A. 61 C7 67 34N 162 58W
Noatak Nat. Preserve ⌓, AK, U.S.A. 61 B8 68 10N 160 0W
Nobel, Ont., Canada 178 B6 45 25N 80 6W
Noble, IL, U.S.A. 71 E5 38 42N 88 14W
Noble, LA, U.S.A. 75 C2 31 41N 93 41W
Noble, OK, U.S.A. 93 C6 35 8N 97 24W
Noble County ☆, IN, U.S.A. 72 B5 41 25N 85 25W
Noble County ☆, OH, U.S.A. 92 D5 39 45N 81 31W
Noble County ☆, OK, U.S.A. 93 B6 36 20N 97 10W
Nobleford, Alta., Canada 185 J7 49 53N 113 3W
Nobles County ☆, MN, U.S.A. 80 G3 43 45N 95 45W
Noblesville, IN, U.S.A. 72 C4 40 3N 86 1W
Nocatee, FL, U.S.A. 67 D7 27 10N 81 53W
Nochistlán de Mejía, Zacatecas, Mexico 217 F8 21 22N 102 51W
Nockamixon Lake, PA, U.S.A. 87 B1 40 28N 75 11W
Nocona, TX, U.S.A. 99 D10 33 47N 97 44W
Nodaway, IA, U.S.A. 73 E4 40 56N 94 54W
Nodaway →, MO, U.S.A. 82 B2 39 54N 94 58W
Nodaway County ☆, MO, U.S.A. 82 A2 40 20N 94 50W
Node, WY, U.S.A. 104 D8 42 43N 104 18W
Noel, Qué., Canada 173 H6 45 18N 63 45W
Noel, MO, U.S.A. 82 E2 36 33N 94 29W
Noëlville, Ont., Canada 178 A6 46 8N 80 26W
Nogal, NM, U.S.A. 88 D5 33 33N 105 42W
Nogal →, Chihuahua, Mexico 213 D11 29 25N 104 13W
Nogales, Durango, Mexico 217 C6 24 59N 104 43W
Nogales, Sonora, Mexico 212 B5 31 20N 110 56W
Nogales, Veracruz, Mexico 221 F3 18 49N 97 10W
Nogales, AZ, U.S.A. 62 F5 31 20N 110 56W
Nohcacab, Yucatán, Mexico 223 B4 20 2N 89 22W
Nohili Pt., HI, U.S.A. 69 A2 22 4N 159 47W
Noirclair, L., Qué., Canada 172 C9 50 38N 60 23W
Noire →, Qué., Canada 176 F6 45 54N 76 57W
Nokesville, VA, U.S.A. 77 B3 38 42N 77 35W
Nokomis, Sask., Canada 182 D7 51 35N 105 0W
Nokomis, FL, U.S.A. 67 D6 27 7N 82 27W
Nokomis, IL, U.S.A. 71 D4 39 18N 89 18W
Nokomis, L., Minneapolis-St. Paul, U.S.A. 113 B2 44 54N 93 14W
Nokomis-Hiawatha Regional Park ⌓, Minneapolis-St. Paul, U.S.A. 113 B2 44 55N 93 15W
Nolan County ☆, TX, U.S.A. 98 E7 32 28N 100 25W
Nolensville, TN, U.S.A. 96 E6 35 57N 86 40W
Nolichucky →, TN, U.S.A. 97 D9 36 5N 83 14W
Nolin River L., KY, U.S.A. 96 C6 37 17N 86 15W
Noma, FL, U.S.A. 67 A3 30 59N 85 37W
Nomans Land, MA, U.S.A. 78 C4 41 15N 70 49W
Nomans Land Nat. Wildlife Refuge ⌓, MA, U.S.A. 78 C4 41 15N 70 49W
Nombre de Dios, Durango, Mexico 217 D6 23 51N 104 14W
Nome, AK, U.S.A. 61 D6 64 30N 165 25W
Nome, ND, U.S.A. 91 D8 46 41N 97 49W
Nome, TX, U.S.A. 99 G13 30 2N 94 25W
Nome ☆, AK, U.S.A. 61 D7 64 50N 163 45W
Nominingue, Qué., Canada 176 E7 46 24N 75 2W
Nominingue, L., Qué., Canada 176 E8 46 26N 74 59W
Nona, L., Orlando, U.S.A. 115 B3 28 24N 81 16W
Nonacho L., N.W.T., Canada 189 D11 61 42N 109 40W
Nondalton, AK, U.S.A. 61 F9 60 0N 154 51W
Nonoava, Chihuahua, Mexico 213 F9 27 28N 106 44W
Nooksack, WA, U.S.A. 101 B3 48 56N 122 19W
Noonan, ND, U.S.A. 91 B2 48 54N 103 1W
Noorvik, AK, U.S.A. 61 C7 66 50N 161 3W
Nootka, B.C., Canada 186 F8 49 38N 126 38W
Nootka I., B.C., Canada 186 F8 49 32N 126 42W
Nopah Range, CA, U.S.A. 65 G10 36 10N 116 10W
Nopaltepec, México, Mexico 219 C9 19 47N 98 43W
Nopiming Prov. Park ⌓, Man., Canada 183 E16 50 30N 95 37W
Nora, Indianapolis, U.S.A. 110 A2 39 54N 86 8W
Nora, NE, U.S.A. 84 D8 40 10N 97 58W
Nora Springs, IA, U.S.A. 73 B6 43 9N 93 0W
Noralee, B.C., Canada 186 B8 53 59N 126 26W
Noranda = Rouyn-Noranda, Qué., Canada 176 C3 48 20N 79 0W
Norborne, MO, U.S.A. 82 B3 39 18N 93 40W
Norcatur, KS, U.S.A. 74 B3 39 50N 100 11W
Norco, CA, U.S.A. 65 K9 33 56N 117 33W
Norcross, GA, U.S.A. 68 C2 33 56N 84 13W
Norcross, MN, U.S.A. 80 E2 45 52N 96 12W
Nord, Grand L. du, Qué., Canada 172 C2 50 54N 67 6W
Nord, Petit L. du, Qué., Canada 172 C2 50 50N 67 10W
Nordegg, Alta., Canada 185 F4 52 29N 116 5W
Norden, NE, U.S.A. 84 B5 42 52N 100 5W
Nordenskiold →, Yukon, Canada 189 D5 62 6N 136 18W
Nordheim, TX, U.S.A. 99 J10 28 55N 97 37W
Nordman, ID, U.S.A. 70 A2 48 38N 116 57W
Norembega, Ont., Canada 176 C2 48 59N 80 43W
Norfolk, Ont., Canada 178 E6 42 50N 80 23W
Norfolk, CT, U.S.A. 78 C1 41 59N 73 12W
Norfolk, NY, U.S.A. 89 A5 44 50N 75 1W
Norfolk, NE, U.S.A. 84 B8 42 2N 97 25W
Norfolk, VA, U.S.A. 102 E8 36 50N 76 17W
Norfolk County ☆, MA, U.S.A. 78 B3 42 10N 71 20W
Norfolk International ✈ (ORF), VA, U.S.A. 102 E8 36 54N 76 12W
Norfork, AR, U.S.A. 63 B3 36 13N 92 17W
Norfork L., AR, U.S.A. 63 B3 36 15N 92 14W
Norge, OK, U.S.A. 93 D6 34 59N 98 0W
Noria de los Angeles, Zacatecas, Mexico 217 E9 22 27N 101 53W
Norias, TX, U.S.A. 98 L10 26 47N 97 47W
Norias del Caballo, Coahuila, Mexico 214 C1 27 43N 103 3W
Norlina, NC, U.S.A. 90 B7 36 27N 78 12W
Normal, IL, U.S.A. 71 C5 40 31N 88 59W
Norman, AR, U.S.A. 63 D2 34 27N 93 41W
Norman, NE, U.S.A. 84 D7 40 29N 98 48W
Norman, OK, U.S.A. 93 C6 35 13N 97 26W
Norman, L., NC, U.S.A. 90 C5 35 26N 80 57W
Norman County ☆, MN, U.S.A. 80 C2 47 20N 96 30W
Norman Park, GA, U.S.A. 68 E3 31 16N 83 41W
Norman Wells, N.W.T., Canada 189 C7 65 17N 126 51W
Normandin, Qué., Canada 177 C10 48 49N 72 31W
Normandy, MO, U.S.A. 117 A2 38 43N 90 17W
Normandy, TX, U.S.A. 98 J7 28 55N 100 36W
Normandy L., TN, U.S.A. 96 E6 35 28N 86 15W
Normandy Park, Seattle, U.S.A. 118 D3 47 26N 122 20W
Normangee, TX, U.S.A. 99 F11 31 2N 96 7W
Norman's Cove-St. Philip's, Nfld. & L., Canada 174 E7 47 33N 53 40W
Normétal, Qué., Canada 176 C3 49 0N 79 22W
Norphlet, AR, U.S.A. 63 E3 33 19N 92 40W
Norquay, Sask., Canada 183 D9 51 53N 102 5W
Norridge, Chicago, U.S.A. 108 B2 41 57N 87 49W
Norridgewock, ME, U.S.A. 76 D4 44 43N 69 47W
Norris, MT, U.S.A. 83 E6 45 34N 111 41W
Norris, SD, U.S.A. 91 G4 43 28N 101 12W
Norris, TN, U.S.A. 97 D8 36 12N 84 4W
Norris Arm, Nfld. & L., Canada 174 C5 49 5N 55 15W
Norris City, IL, U.S.A. 71 F5 37 59N 88 20W
Norris L., TN, U.S.A. 97 D8 36 14N 84 6W
Norris Point, Nfld. & L., Canada 174 C3 49 31N 57 53W
Norristown, GA, U.S.A. 68 D4 32 30N 82 30W
Norristown, PA, U.S.A. 87 B1 40 7N 75 21W
Norte, Aeropuerto del ✈, Monterrey, Mexico 224 A2 25 51N 100 14W
Norte, Cayo, Quintana Roo, Mexico 223 D6 18 45N 87 19W
Norte de Chiapas, Mts. del, Chiapas, Mexico 222 C5 16 50N 91 40W
Norte de Chiapas, Sa. del, Chiapas, Mexico 222 B4 17 15N 92 30W
North, SC, U.S.A. 90 E4 33 37N 81 6W
North →, Nfld. & L., Canada 175 B5 57 30N 61 50W
North →, MA, U.S.A. 78 B2 42 37N 72 44W
North →, WV, U.S.A. 77 A2 39 25N 78 25W
North, C., N.S., Canada 173 F9 47 2N 60 20W
North Adams, MA, U.S.A. 78 B1 42 42N 73 7W
North Adams, MI, U.S.A. 79 H7 41 58N 84 32W
North Amherst, MA, U.S.A. 78 B2 42 25N 72 32W
North Andover, MA, U.S.A. 78 B3 42 42N 71 8W
North Anna →, VA, U.S.A. 102 D7 37 48N 77 25W
North Arlington, NJ, U.S.A. 114 B2 40 47N 74 7W
North Arm, N.W.T., Canada 189 D10 62 0N 114 30W
North Atlanta, GA, U.S.A. 68 C2 33 52N 84 21W
North Attleboro, MA, U.S.A. 78 C3 41 59N 71 20W
North Augusta, SC, U.S.A. 90 E4 33 30N 81 59W
North Aulatsivik I., Nfld. & L., Canada 175 B5 59 46N 64 5W
North Baltimore, OH, U.S.A. 92 B3 41 11N 83 41W
North Bass I., OH, U.S.A. 92 B4 41 40N 82 56W
North Battleford, Sask., Canada 182 C3 52 50N 108 17W
North Bay, Ont., Canada 178 A7 46 20N 79 30W
North Bay Village, Miami, U.S.A. 112 C3 25 50N 80 9W
North Beach, MD, U.S.A. 77 B4 38 43N 76 32W
North Beach Peninsula, WA, U.S.A. 101 D1 46 30N 124 2W
North Belcher Is., N.W.T., Canada 175 B2 56 50N 79 50W
North Bend, B.C., Canada 187 F13 49 50N 121 27W
North Bend, NE, U.S.A. 84 C9 41 28N 96 47W
North Bend, OR, U.S.A. 94 D1 43 24N 124 14W
North Bend, WA, U.S.A. 101 C4 47 30N 121 47W
North Bennington, VT, U.S.A. 86 D1 42 56N 73 15W
North Bergen, NJ, U.S.A. 87 B2 40 48N 74 0W
North Berwick, ME, U.S.A. 76 E3 43 18N 70 44W
North Bonneville, WA, U.S.A. 101 E4 45 39N 121 57W
North Braddock, Pittsburgh, U.S.A. 116 B2 40 23N 79 50W
North Branch, MI, U.S.A. 79 F8 43 14N 83 12W
North Branch, MN, U.S.A. 80 E6 45 31N 92 59W
North Branch Chicago River →, Chicago, U.S.A. 108 B2 41 53N 87 42W
North Branch Elkhorn →, NE, U.S.A. 84 C8 41 59N 97 27W
North Branch Potomac →, U.S.A. 77 A2 39 32N 78 35W
North Branford, CT, U.S.A. 78 C2 41 20N 72 46W
North Brookfield, MA, U.S.A. 78 B2 42 16N 72 5W
North Brunswick, NJ, U.S.A. 87 B2 40 28N 74 28W
North Buck L., Alta., Canada 184 D8 54 41N 112 32W
North Buena Vista, IA, U.S.A. 73 C8 42 41N 90 58W
North Butte, WY, U.S.A. 104 C7 43 54N 105 57W
North C., N.B., Canada 173 F6 47 5N 64 0W
North Caldwell, NJ, U.S.A. 114 A1 40 51N 74 15W
North Canadian →, OK, U.S.A. 93 C8 35 22N 95 37W
North Canton, OH, U.S.A. 92 C5 40 53N 81 24W
North Cape May, NJ, U.S.A. 87 D2 38 59N 74 57W
North Caribou L., Ont., Canada 191 G7 52 50N 90 40W
North Carolina □, U.S.A. 90 C6 35 30N 80 0W
North Cascades Nat. Park △, WA, U.S.A. 101 B4 48 45N 121 10W
North Channel, Ont., Canada 178 A3 46 0N 83 0W
North Charleston, NH, U.S.A. 86 C2 43 18N 72 24W
North Charleston, SC, U.S.A. 90 F6 32 53N 79 58W
North Chelmsford, MA, U.S.A. 78 B3 42 38N 71 23W
North Chicago, IL, U.S.A. 71 A6 42 19N 87 51W
North Chichester, NH, U.S.A. 86 C3 43 15N 71 22W
North Cohasset, Boston, U.S.A. 106 B4 42 15N 70 50W
North College Hill, OH, U.S.A. 92 D2 39 13N 84 33W
North Collins, NY, U.S.A. 89 C2 42 36N 78 56W
North Concho →, TX, U.S.A. 98 F7 31 27N 100 25W
North Conway, NH, U.S.A. 86 B3 44 3N 71 8W
North Cowichan, B.C., Canada 187 G11 48 50N 123 41W
North Creek, NY, U.S.A. 89 B7 43 42N 73 59W
North Crossett, AR, U.S.A. 63 E4 33 10N 91 56W
North Crows Nest, Indianapolis, U.S.A. 110 A1 39 51N 86 9W
North Dakota □, U.S.A. 91 C5 47 30N 100 15W
North Dartmouth, MA, U.S.A. 78 C4 41 36N 70 59W
North Decatur, Atlanta, U.S.A. 106 B3 33 48N 84 17W
North Dighton, MA, U.S.A. 78 C3 41 50N 71 10W
North Druid Hills, GA, U.S.A. 106 B3 33 49N 84 17W
North East, MD, U.S.A. 77 A5 39 36N 75 57W
North East, PA, U.S.A. 95 B3 42 13N 79 50W
North East Cape Fear →, NC, U.S.A. 90 D8 34 11N 77 57W
North Eastham, MA, U.S.A. 78 C5 41 52N 69 59W
North Easton, MA, U.S.A. 78 B3 42 4N 71 6W
North English, IA, U.S.A. 73 D6 41 31N 92 5W
North Enid, OK, U.S.A. 93 B6 36 26N 97 52W
North Fabius →, MO, U.S.A. 82 B5 39 54N 91 30W
North Fairfield, OH, U.S.A. 92 B4 41 6N 82 37W
North Folk Holston →, VA, U.S.A. 102 E2 36 33N 82 19W
North Fond du Lac, WI, U.S.A. 103 E5 43 48N 88 29W
North Fork, ID, U.S.A. 70 D5 45 25N 113 59W
North Fork, Salt →, MO, U.S.A. 82 B5 39 26N 91 53W
North Fork American →, CA, U.S.A. 64 E6 38 57N 120 59W
North Fork Bad →, SD, U.S.A. 91 F4 44 2N 101 40W
North Fork Cimarron →, U.S.A. 74 D1 37 15N 102 9W
North Fork Cuivre →, MO, U.S.A. 82 B6 39 2N 90 59W
North Fork Edisto →, SC, U.S.A. 90 E5 33 16N 80 54W
North Fork Feather →, CA, U.S.A. 64 E5 38 33N 121 30W
North Fork Forked Deer →, TN, U.S.A. 96 E3 36 0N 89 26W
North Fork Grand →, SD, U.S.A. 91 E3 45 47N 102 16W
North Fork Humboldt →, NV, U.S.A. 85 B5 40 56N 115 32W
North Fork John Day →, OR, U.S.A. 94 C6 44 45N 119 38W
North Fork Kentucky →, KY, U.S.A. 97 C9 37 35N 83 40W
North Fork Licking →, KY, U.S.A. 97 B8 38 35N 84 12W
North Fork Moreau →, SD, U.S.A. 91 E3 45 9N 102 50W
North Fork Red →, OK, U.S.A. 93 D4 34 24N 99 14W
North Fork Shenandoah →, VA, U.S.A. 102 C6 38 59N 78 22W
North Fork Shoshone →, WY, U.S.A. 104 B3 44 29N 109 18W
North Fork Smoky Hill →, KS, U.S.A. 74 C2 38 54N 101 18W
North Fork Solomon →, KS, U.S.A. 74 B5 39 28N 98 26W
North Fork South Platte →, CO, U.S.A. 66 C5 39 25N 105 10W
North Fort Myers, FL, U.S.A. 67 E7 26 41N 81 53W
North Fox I., MI, U.S.A. 79 D6 45 29N 85 47W
North Freedom, WI, U.S.A. 103 E4 43 28N 89 52W
North French →, Ont., Canada 181 A16 51 10N 80 50W
North Gower, Ont., Canada 179 B11 45 8N 75 43W
North Grafton, MA, U.S.A. 78 B3 42 14N 71 42W
North Grant, N.S., Canada 173 H7 45 40N 62 2W
North Greenfield = West Allis, WI, U.S.A. 103 E6 43 1N 88 0W
North Grosvenor Dale, CT, U.S.A. 78 C3 41 59N 71 54W
North Hackensack, NJ, U.S.A. 114 A2 40 54N 74 2W
North Hampton, NH, U.S.A. 86 D4 42 57N 70 48W
North Hartsville, SC, U.S.A. 90 D5 34 24N 80 4W
North Hatley, Qué., Canada 177 F11 45 17N 71 58W
North Haven, CT, U.S.A. 78 C2 41 23N 72 52W
North Haven, ME, U.S.A. 76 D5 44 8N 68 53W
North Head, N.B., Canada 173 J3 44 46N 66 45W
North Head, Nfld. & L., Canada 174 E8 47 29N 52 38W
North Hero, VT, U.S.A. 86 B1 44 49N 73 18W
North Highlands, CA, U.S.A. 64 E5 38 40N 121 23W
North Hills, NY, U.S.A. 114 B5 40 46N 73 40W
North Hollywood, Los Angeles, U.S.A. 111 B2 34 9N 118 22W
North Hoosick, NY, U.S.A. 78 B1 42 55N 73 21W
North Houston, Houston, U.S.A. 110 A2 29 55N 95 30W
North I., SC, U.S.A. 90 E6 33 17N 79 11W
North Java, NY, U.S.A. 89 C2 42 41N 78 20W
North Judson, IN, U.S.A. 72 B4 41 13N 86 46W
North Kent I., Nunavut, Canada 190 B7 76 40N 90 8W
North Kingstown, RI, U.S.A. 78 C3 41 33N 71 28W
North Kingsville, OH, U.S.A. 92 B6 41 54N 80 42W
North Knife →, Man., Canada 191 F7 58 53N 94 45W
North Knife L., Man., Canada 191 F6 58 5N 97 4W
North L., Dallas-Fort Worth, U.S.A. 109 A4 32 56N 96 58W
North La Veta Pass, CO, U.S.A. 66 E5 37 36N 105 13W
North Lake Park, Dallas-Fort Worth, U.S.A. 109 A4 32 55N 96 58W
North Las Vegas, NV, U.S.A. 85 F5 36 11N 115 7W
North Las Vegas Air Terminal, Las Vegas, U.S.A. 110 B1 36 12N 115 11W
North Lewisburg, OH, U.S.A. 92 C3 40 13N 83 33W
North Lexington, Boston, U.S.A. 106 A2 42 28N 71 14W
North Liberty, IN, U.S.A. 72 B4 41 32N 86 26W
North Liberty, IA, U.S.A. 73 D7 41 45N 91 35W
North Little Rock, AR, U.S.A. 63 D3 34 45N 92 16W
North Logan, UT, U.S.A. 100 B4 41 46N 111 48W
North Long Beach, Los Angeles, U.S.A. 111 C3 33 51N 118 11W
North Lonsdale, B.C., Canada 193 A2 49 20N 123 4W

North Loon Mt., *ID, U.S.A.* **70 D3** 45 7N 115 52W
North Loup, *NE, U.S.A.* **84 C7** 41 30N 98 46W
North Loup →, *NE, U.S.A.* **84 C7** 41 17N 98 24W
North Magnetic Pole, *Canada* **190 B5** 82 18N 113 24W
North Manchester, *IN, U.S.A.* **72 B5** 41 0N 85 46W
North Manitou, *MI, U.S.A.* **79 D6** 45 7N 85 58W
North Manitou I., *MI, U.S.A.* **79 D5** 45 7N 86 1W
North Mankato, *MN, U.S.A.* **80 F4** 44 10N 94 2W
North Miami, *FL, U.S.A.* **67 F8** 25 53N 80 11W
North Miami, *OK, U.S.A.* **93 B9** 36 55N 94 53W
North Miami Beach, *FL, U.S.A.* **67 F8** 25 55N 80 9W
North Middletown, *KY, U.S.A.* **97 B8** 38 9N 84 7W
North Moose L., *Man., Canada* **183 A11** 54 4N 100 12W
North Mountain Recreation Area, *Phoenix, U.S.A.* **116 B2** 33 35N 112 4W
North Muskegon, *MI, U.S.A.* **79 F5** 43 15N 86 17W
North Myrtle Beach, *SC, U.S.A.* **90 E7** 33 48N 78 42W
North Naples, *FL, U.S.A.* **67 E7** 26 12N 81 48W
North New Hyde Park, *NY, U.S.A.* **114 B4** 40 44N 73 41W
North Oaks, *Minneapolis-St. Paul, U.S.A.* **113 A3** 45 6N 93 5W
North Ogden, *UT, U.S.A.* **100 B4** 41 19N 111 58W
North Olmsted, *OH, U.S.A.* **92 B5** 41 25N 81 56W
North Palisade, *CA, U.S.A.* **65 F8** 37 6N 118 31W
North Pass, *LA, U.S.A.* **75 E6** 29 12N 89 2W
North Pease →, *TX, U.S.A.* **98 C7** 34 15N 100 7W
North Pelham, *NY, U.S.A.* **114 A4** 40 54N 73 49W
North Perry, *OH, U.S.A.* **92 B5** 41 47N 81 9W
North Perry ✕, *Miami, U.S.A.* **112 B2** 26 0N 80 14W
North Plains, *NM, U.S.A.* **88 C2** 34 45N 108 10W
North Plains, *OR, U.S.A.* **94 B3** 45 37N 123 0W
North Platte, *NE, U.S.A.* **84 C5** 41 8N 100 46W
North Platte →, *NE, U.S.A.* **84 C5** 41 7N 100 42W
North Platte Nat. Wildlife Refuge ⌂, *NE, U.S.A.* **84 C2** 41 56N 103 29W
North Pole, *AK, U.S.A.* **61 D11** 64 45N 147 21W
North Port, *FL, U.S.A.* **67 D6** 27 3N 82 14W
North Portal, *Sask., Canada* **183 F9** 49 0N 102 33W
North Powder, *OR, U.S.A.* **94 B8** 45 2N 117 55W
North Prairie, *WI, U.S.A.* **103 F5** 42 56N 88 24W
North Providence, *RI, U.S.A.* **78 C3** 41 50N 71 25W
North Pt., *MI, U.S.A.* **79 D8** 45 2N 83 16W
North Quincy, *Boston, U.S.A.* **106 B3** 42 16N 71 1W
North Ram →, *Alta., Canada* **185 F6** 52 16N 114 38W
North Redington Beach, *Tampa, U.S.A.* **119 C2** 27 48N 82 49W
North Res., *Boston, U.S.A.* **106 A3** 42 27N 71 6W
North Richland Hills, *TX, U.S.A.* **109 A2** 32 50N 97 13W
North Rim, *AZ, U.S.A.* **62 A3** 36 12N 112 3W
North Riverside, *Chicago, U.S.A.* **108 B2** 41 50N 87 48W
North Royalton, *Cleveland, U.S.A.* **107 C1** 41 18N 81 43W
North Rustico, *P.E.I., Canada* **173 G6** 46 27N 63 19W
North St. Paul, *Minneapolis-St. Paul, U.S.A.* **113 A4** 45 5N 92 59W
North Salem, *IN, U.S.A.* **72 D4** 39 52N 86 39W
North Salt Lake, *UT, U.S.A.* **100 C4** 40 50N 111 54W
North Santiam →, *OR, U.S.A.* **94 C3** 44 41N 123 0W
North Saskatchewan →, *Sask., Canada* **182 B6** 53 15N 105 5W
North Saugus, *Boston, U.S.A.* **106 A3** 42 29N 71 0W
North Schell Peak, *NV, U.S.A.* **85 C6** 39 25N 114 36W
North Sea, *NY, U.S.A.* **78 D2** 40 56N 72 25W
North Shapleigh, *ME, U.S.A.* **86 C4** 43 36N 70 53W
North Shore, *HI, U.S.A.* **69 J13** 21 39N 158 30W
North Shore Channel →, *Chicago, U.S.A.* **108 B2** 41 58N 87 42W
North Sioux City, *SD, U.S.A.* **91 H9** 42 32N 96 29W
North Slope ☆, *AK, U.S.A.* **61 B9** 69 15N 152 0W
North Spicer I., *Nunavut, Canada* **190 D10** 68 33N 78 45W
North Springfield, *PA, U.S.A.* **95 C2** 41 59N 80 26W
North Springfield, *VA, U.S.A.* **119 C2** 38 48N 77 11W
North Springfield, *VT, U.S.A.* **86 C2** 43 20N 72 32W
North Star, *Alta., Canada* **184 B3** 56 51N 117 38W
North Stratford, *NH, U.S.A.* **86 B3** 44 45N 71 38W
North Sudbury, *Boston, U.S.A.* **106 A1** 42 24N 71 24W
North Sulphur →, *TX, U.S.A.* **99 D12** 33 23N 95 18W
North Sutton, *NH, U.S.A.* **86 C3** 43 22N 71 56W
North Sydney, *N.S., Canada* **173 G9** 46 12N 60 15W
North Syracuse, *NY, U.S.A.* **89 B4** 43 8N 76 7W
North Terre Haute, *IN, U.S.A.* **72 D3** 39 31N 87 22W
North Thompson →, *B.C., Canada* **187 E14** 50 40N 120 20W
North Tonawanda, *NY, U.S.A.* **89 B2** 43 2N 78 53W
North Troy, *VT, U.S.A.* **86 B2** 45 0N 72 24W
North Truro, *MA, U.S.A.* **78 B4** 42 2N 70 5W
North Twin I., *N.W.T., Canada* **175 C1** 53 20N 80 0W
North Twin L., *Nfld. & L., Canada* **174 C5** 49 16N 55 56W
North Umpqua →, *OR, U.S.A.* **94 D2** 43 16N 123 27W
North Union = Shaker Heights, *OH, U.S.A.* **92 B5** 41 28N 81 32W
North Valley Stream, *NY, U.S.A.* **114 B4** 40 41N 73 42W
North Vancouver, *B.C., Canada* **187 F11** 49 19N 123 4W
North Vernon, *IN, U.S.A.* **72 D5** 39 0N 85 38W
North Wabasca L., *Alta., Canada* **184 B7** 56 0N 113 55W
North Wales, *PA, U.S.A.* **87 B1** 40 13N 75 17W
North Washington, *IA, U.S.A.* **73 B6** 43 7N 92 25W
North Waterford, *ME, U.S.A.* **86 B4** 44 14N 70 46W
North West River, *Nfld. & L., Canada* **175 C5** 53 30N 60 10W
North Wichita →, *TX, U.S.A.* **99 D8** 33 43N 99 29W
North Wildwood, *NJ, U.S.A.* **87 D2** 39 0N 74 48W
North Wilkesboro, *NC, U.S.A.* **90 B4** 36 10N 81 9W
North Windham, *ME, U.S.A.* **76 E3** 43 50N 70 26W
North Wolf Cr. →, *SD, U.S.A.* **91 F7** 44 42N 98 46W
North Yakima = Yakima, *WA, U.S.A.* **101 D5** 46 36N 120 31W
Northampton, *MA, U.S.A.* **78 B2** 42 19N 72 38W
Northampton, *PA, U.S.A.* **87 B1** 40 41N 75 30W
Northampton County ☆, *NC, U.S.A.* **90 B8** 36 20N 77 30W
Northampton County ☆, *PA, U.S.A.* **95 D7** 40 50N 75 20W
Northampton County ☆, *VA, U.S.A.* **102 D9** 37 15N 75 55W
Northborough, *MA, U.S.A.* **78 B3** 42 19N 71 39W
Northbridge, *MA, U.S.A.* **78 B3** 42 9N 71 39W
Northbrook, *OH, U.S.A.* **107 A1** 39 14N 84 35W
Northeast C., *AK, U.S.A.* **61 E5** 63 18N 168 42W
Northern Cambria, *PA, U.S.A.* **95 D4** 40 40N 78 47W
Northern Cheyenne Indian Reservation, *MT, U.S.A.* **83 E11** 45 30N 106 40W
Northern Indian L., *Man., Canada* **191 F6** 57 20N 97 20W
Northern Light L., *Ont., Canada* **180 D6** 48 15N 90 39W
Northern Marianas ⊠, *Pac. Oc.* **105 a** 17 0N 145 0 E
Northfield, *ME, U.S.A.* **76 D6** 44 52N 67 34W
Northfield, *MA, U.S.A.* **78 B2** 42 42N 72 27W
Northfield, *MN, U.S.A.* **80 F5** 44 27N 93 9W
Northfield, *NH, U.S.A.* **86 C3** 43 26N 71 36W
Northfield, *NJ, U.S.A.* **87 C2** 39 22N 74 33W
Northfield, *VT, U.S.A.* **86 B2** 44 9N 72 40W
Northford, *CT, U.S.A.* **78 C2** 41 24N 72 48W
Northgate, *ND, U.S.A.* **91 B3** 48 59N 102 15W
Northglenn, *CO, U.S.A.* **66 C6** 39 53N 104 59W
Northlake, *Chicago, U.S.A.* **108 B1** 41 54N 87 53W
Northome, *MN, U.S.A.* **80 C4** 47 52N 94 17W
Northport, *Qué., Canada* **173 H6** 45 56N 63 52W
Northport, *AL, U.S.A.* **60 C3** 33 14N 87 35W
Northport, *MI, U.S.A.* **79 D6** 45 8N 85 37W
Northport, *NY, U.S.A.* **78 D1** 40 54N 73 21W
Northport, *NE, U.S.A.* **84 C2** 41 41N 103 5W
Northport, *WA, U.S.A.* **101 B8** 48 55N 117 48W
Northridge, *Los Angeles, U.S.A.* **111 A1** 34 13N 118 32W
Northridge, *OH, U.S.A.* **92 D3** 39 59N 83 46W
Northrop, *MN, U.S.A.* **80 G4** 43 44N 94 26W
Northumberland, *PA, U.S.A.* **95 D6** 40 54N 76 48W
Northumberland County ☆, *PA, U.S.A.* **95 D6** 40 55N 76 50W
Northumberland County ☆, *VA, U.S.A.* **102 D8** 37 55N 76 29W
Northumberland Str., *N.S., Canada* **173 G6** 46 20N 64 0W
Northview, *MO, U.S.A.* **82 D4** 37 17N 93 0W
Northville, *NY, U.S.A.* **89 B6** 43 13N 74 11W
Northville, *SD, U.S.A.* **91 E7** 45 9N 98 35W
Northway, *AK, U.S.A.* **61 E12** 62 58N 141 56W
Northwest Arctic ☆, *AK, U.S.A.* **61 C7** 66 50N 161 0W
Northwest Gander →, *Nfld. & L., Canada* **174 D5** 48 55N 55 2W
Northwest Territories □, *Alta., Canada* **189 D9** 63 0N 118 0W
Northwestway Park, *Indianapolis, U.S.A.* **110 A1** 39 52N 86 14W
Northwind Ridge, *Arctic* **188 A1** 77 50N 155 10W
Northwood, *IA, U.S.A.* **73 B5** 43 27N 93 13W
Northwood, *ND, U.S.A.* **91 C8** 47 44N 97 34W
Northwood, *NH, U.S.A.* **86 C3** 43 12N 71 9W
Northwoods, *MO, U.S.A.* **117 A2** 38 42N 90 17W
Norton, *N.B., Canada* **173 H4** 45 38N 65 42W
Norton, *KS, U.S.A.* **74 B4** 39 50N 99 53W
Norton, *MA, U.S.A.* **78 C3** 41 58N 71 11W
Norton, *VA, U.S.A.* **102 E2** 36 56N 82 38W
Norton, *VT, U.S.A.* **86 B3** 45 0N 71 48W
Norton B., *AK, U.S.A.* **61 D7** 64 45N 161 15W
Norton County ☆, *KS, U.S.A.* **74 B4** 39 45N 99 50W
Norton Pk., *ID, U.S.A.* **70 F4** 43 46N 114 39W
Norton Sd., *AK, U.S.A.* **61 E7** 63 50N 164 0W
Norton Shores, *MI, U.S.A.* **79 F5** 43 10N 86 16W
Nortonville, *KS, U.S.A.* **74 B8** 39 25N 95 20W
Nortonville, *KY, U.S.A.* **96 C5** 37 12N 87 27W
Norumbega Res., *Boston, U.S.A.* **106 B2** 42 19N 71 17W
Norwalk, *CA, U.S.A.* **65 K8** 33 54N 118 4W
Norwalk, *CT, U.S.A.* **78 C1** 41 7N 73 22W
Norwalk, *IA, U.S.A.* **73 D5** 41 29N 93 41W
Norwalk, *OH, U.S.A.* **92 B4** 41 15N 82 37W
Norwalk, *WI, U.S.A.* **103 E3** 43 50N 90 37W
Norway, *IA, U.S.A.* **73 D7** 41 54N 91 55W
Norway, *KS, U.S.A.* **74 B6** 39 42N 97 47W
Norway, *ME, U.S.A.* **76 D3** 44 13N 70 32W
Norway, *MI, U.S.A.* **79 D4** 45 47N 87 55W
Norway B., *Nunavut, Canada* **190 C5** 71 6N 104 28W
Norway House, *Man., Canada* **183 B14** 53 59N 97 50W
Norwegian B., *Nunavut, Canada* **190 B7** 77 30N 90 0W
Norwell, *MA, U.S.A.* **78 B4** 42 10N 70 48W
Norwich, *Ont., Canada* **178 E6** 42 59N 80 36W
Norwich, *CT, U.S.A.* **78 C2** 41 31N 72 5W
Norwich, *KS, U.S.A.* **74 D6** 37 27N 97 51W
Norwich, *NY, U.S.A.* **89 C5** 42 32N 75 32W
Norwich, *VT, U.S.A.* **86 C2** 43 42N 72 18W
Norwood, *Ont., Canada* **179 C9** 44 23N 77 59W
Norwood, *CO, U.S.A.* **66 D2** 38 8N 108 20W
Norwood, *LA, U.S.A.* **75 D4** 30 58N 91 6W
Norwood, *MA, U.S.A.* **78 B3** 42 12N 71 12W
Norwood, *MO, U.S.A.* **82 D4** 37 7N 92 24W
Norwood, *NC, U.S.A.* **90 C5** 35 14N 80 7W
Norwood, *NY, U.S.A.* **89 A6** 44 45N 75 0W
Norwood, *OH, U.S.A.* **92 D2** 39 9N 84 27W
Norwood, *PA, U.S.A.* **116 B1** 39 53N 75 18W
Norwood →, *WY, U.S.A.* **104 B5** 44 17N 107 58W
Norwood Park, *Chicago, U.S.A.* **108 B2** 41 59N 87 48W
Norwood-Young America, *MN, U.S.A.* **80 F5** 44 46N 93 55W
Norwoodville, *IA, U.S.A.* **73 D5** 41 39N 93 33W
Notasulga, *AL, U.S.A.* **60 D5** 32 34N 85 41W
Notch Peak, *UT, U.S.A.* **100 D2** 39 9N 113 25W
Notikewin →, *Alta., Canada* **184 A3** 57 2N 117 38W
Notikewin Prov. Park ⌂, *Alta., Canada* **184 A3** 57 14N 117 8W
Notre-Dame, *N.B., Canada* **173 G5** 46 18N 64 46W
Notre-Dame, Île, *Montréal, Canada* **192 A3** 45 29N 73 31W
Notre Dame B., *Nfld. & L., Canada* **174 C5** 49 45N 55 30W
Notre-Dame-de-Grace, *Montréal, Canada* **192 B3** 45 28N 73 38W
Notre-Dame-de-Koartac = Quaqtaq, *Qué., Canada* **175 A4** 60 55N 69 40W
Notre Dame de Lourdes, *Man., Canada* **183 F13** 49 32N 98 33W
Notre-Dame-des-Bois, *Qué., Canada* **177 F11** 45 24N 71 4W
Notre-Dame-d'Ivugivic = Ivujivik, *Qué., Canada* **175 A2** 62 24N 77 55W
Notre-Dame-du-Bon-Conseil, *Qué., Canada* **177 F10** 46 0N 72 21W
Notre-Dame-du-Laus, *Qué., Canada* **176 E7** 46 5N 75 37W
Notre-Dame-du-Nord, *Qué., Canada* **176 D3** 47 36N 79 30W
Notre-Dame-du-Portage, *Qué., Canada* **177 D13** 47 46N 69 37W
Notrees, *TX, U.S.A.* **98 F5** 31 55N 102 45W
Nottawasaga B., *Ont., Canada* **178 C6** 44 35N 80 15W
Nottaway = Senneterre, *Qué., Canada* **176 C5** 48 25N 77 15W
Nottaway →, *Qué., Canada* **175 C2** 51 22N 78 55W
Nottely L., *GA, U.S.A.* **68 B2** 34 58N 84 5W
Nottingham, *NH, U.S.A.* **86 C3** 43 7N 71 6W
Nottingham, *PA, U.S.A.* **77 A4** 39 45N 76 1W
Nottingham I., *Nunavut, Canada* **191 E10** 63 20N 77 55W
Nottoway →, *VA, U.S.A.* **102 E8** 36 33N 76 55W
Nottoway County ☆, *VA, U.S.A.* **102 D6** 37 8N 78 5W
Nottoway Court House, *VA, U.S.A.* **102 D6** 37 8N 78 5W
Notukeu Cr. →, *Sask., Canada* **182 F5** 49 56N 106 29W
Notus, *ID, U.S.A.* **70 F2** 43 43N 116 48W
Nouveau Comptoir = Wemindji, *Qué., Canada* **175 C2** 53 0N 78 49W
Nouvelle, *N.B., Canada* **173 E3** 48 8N 66 19W
Nouvelle →, *N.B., Canada* **173 E3** 48 7N 66 19W
Nouvelle France, C. de, *Qué., Canada* **175 A3** 62 27N 73 42W
Nova Scotia □, *Canada* **173 J5** 45 10N 63 0W
Nova Zembla I., *N.W.T., Canada* **190 C11** 72 11N 74 50W
Novar, *Ont., Canada* **178 B7** 45 27N 79 15W
Novato, *CA, U.S.A.* **64 E4** 38 6N 122 35W
Novinger, *MO, U.S.A.* **82 A4** 40 14N 92 43W
Nowata, *OK, U.S.A.* **93 B8** 36 42N 95 38W
Nowata County ☆, *OK, U.S.A.* **93 B8** 36 50N 95 40W
Nowater Cr. →, *WY, U.S.A.* **104 C5** 43 57N 108 0W
Nowitna Nat. Wildlife Refuge ⌂, *AK, U.S.A.* **61 D9** 64 40N 154 16W
Noxapater, *MS, U.S.A.* **81 C4** 33 1N 89 1W
Noxon Res., *MT, U.S.A.* **83 C2** 47 57N 115 44W
Noxubee →, *U.S.A.* **60 D2** 32 50N 88 10W
Noxubee County ☆, *MS, U.S.A.* **81 C5** 33 7N 88 34W
Noyes, *MN, U.S.A.* **80 B1** 49 0N 97 12W
Nubieber, *CA, U.S.A.* **64 B5** 41 6N 121 11W
Nuckolls County ☆, *NE, U.S.A.* **84 D8** 40 15N 98 0W
Nucla, *CO, U.S.A.* **66 D2** 38 16N 108 33W
Nuctunich, Pta., *Quintana Roo, Mexico* **223 A6** 21 27N 87 11W
Nueces →, *TX, U.S.A.* **99 K10** 27 51N 97 30W
Nueces County ☆, *TX, U.S.A.* **99 K10** 27 47N 97 40W
Nueltin L., *Canada* **191 E6** 60 30N 99 30W
Nueva Atzacoalco, *Distrito Federal, Mexico* **225 B3** 19 29N 99 4W
Nueva Ciudad Guerrero, *Tamaulipas, Mexico* **214 D5** 26 34N 99 12W
Nueva Cuadrilla, *Michoacan, Mexico* **218 D6** 18 4N 101 32W
Nueva Esperanza, *Quintana Roo, Mexico* **223 D4** 18 9N 89 9W
Nueva Esperanza, *Tabasco, Mexico* **222 B5** 17 20N 91 4W
Nueva Italia, *Michoacan, Mexico* **218 C5** 19 1N 102 6W
Nueva Rosita, *Coahuila, Mexico* **214 C3** 27 57N 101 13W
Nueva Tenochtitlán, *Distrito Federal, Mexico* **225 B3** 19 27N 99 5W
Nuevo América, *Chiapas, Mexico* **222 D3** 15 57N 92 26W
Nuevo Anáhuac, *Nuevo León, Mexico* **214 C4** 27 14N 100 9W
Nuevo Casas Grandes, *Chihuahua, Mexico* **213 C8** 30 25N 107 55W
Nuevo Coahuila, *Campeche, Mexico* **223 E3** 17 55N 90 51W
Nuevo Cuauhtémoc, *Chihuahua, Mexico* **213 B8** 31 30N 107 15W
Nuevo Delicias, *Coahuila, Mexico* **214 D2** 26 14N 102 48W
Nuevo Guerrero, *Chiapas, Mexico* **222 B5** 17 1N 91 19W
Nuevo Ideal, *Durango, Mexico* **216 C5** 24 55N 105 7W
Nuevo Ixcatlán, *Veracruz, Mexico* **221 G5** 17 38N 95 27W
Nuevo Laredo, *Tamaulipas, Mexico* **214 C5** 27 30N 99 31W
Nuevo León □, *Mexico* **215 E5** 25 20N 100 0W
Nuevo México, *Chiapas, Mexico* **222 C3** 16 27N 93 26W
Nuevo México, *Guadalajara, Mexico* **224 A1** 20 45N 103 26W
Nuevo Momón, *Chiapas, Mexico* **222 C5** 16 20N 91 44W
Nuevo Morelos, *Tamaulipas, Mexico* **215 H5** 22 32N 99 12W
Nuevo Padilla, *Tamaulipas, Mexico* **215 F6** 24 1N 98 47W
Nuevo Progreso, *Tamaulipas, Mexico* **214 D7** 26 3N 97 56W
Nuevo Progreso, *Tamaulipas, Mexico* **215 G7** 23 11N 97 56W
Nuevo Progresso, *Campeche, Mexico* **223 D1** 18 37N 92 17W
Nuevo Reforma, *Coahuila, Mexico* **214 C2** 27 28N 102 6W
Nuevo San Miguel Zapotitlán, *Sinaloa, Mexico* **216 B1** 25 56N 109 3W
Nuevo Urecho, *Michoacan, Mexico* **218 C6** 19 8N 101 53W
Nuevo X-Can, *Yucatán, Mexico* **223 B6** 20 51N 87 40W
Nulato, *AK, U.S.A.* **61 D8** 64 43N 158 6W
Nulhegan →, *VT, U.S.A.* **86 B3** 44 45N 71 38W
Nulki L., *B.C., Canada* **186 B10** 53 55N 124 7W
Numa, *IA, U.S.A.* **73 E6** 40 41N 92 59W
Numarán, *Michoacan, Mexico* **218 B6** 20 15N 101 56W
Nunaksaluk I., *Nfld. & L., Canada* **175 B5** 55 49N 60 20W
Nunavut □, *Canada* **190 C7** 66 0N 85 0W
Nunda, *NY, U.S.A.* **89 C3** 42 35N 77 56W
Nunda, *SD, U.S.A.* **91 F8** 44 10N 97 1W
Nungesser L., *Ont., Canada* **180 A3** 51 28N 93 30W
Nunivak I., *AK, U.S.A.* **61 F6** 60 10N 166 30W
Nunn, *CO, U.S.A.* **66 B6** 40 42N 104 47W
Nunnelly, *TN, U.S.A.* **96 E5** 35 52N 87 28W
Nuntsi Park ⌂, *B.C., Canada* **186 D11** 51 45N 123 47W
Nuri, *Sonora, Mexico* **212 E6** 28 5N 109 22W
Nursery, *TX, U.S.A.* **99 J10** 28 56N 97 6W
Nut L., *Sask., Canada* **182 C8** 52 22N 103 42W
Nutak, *Nfld. & L., Canada* **175 B5** 57 28N 61 59W
Nutley, *NJ, U.S.A.* **87 B2** 40 49N 74 9W
Nutrioso, *AZ, U.S.A.* **62 D6** 33 57N 109 13W
Nu'uuli, *Amer. Samoa* **105 e** 14 19 S 170 42W
Nuvuk Is., *Nfld. & L., Canada* **175 A2** 62 24N 78 3W
Nyack, *NY, U.S.A.* **87 A3** 41 5N 73 55W
Nye County ☆, *NV, U.S.A.* **85 E4** 38 0N 116 40W
Nyssa, *OR, U.S.A.* **94 D8** 43 53N 117 0W

O

O.C. Fisher L., *TX, U.S.A.* **98 F7** 31 29N 100 29W
O.H. Ivie Res., *TX, U.S.A.* **99 F8** 31 34N 99 41W
Oacoma, *SD, U.S.A.* **91 G6** 43 48N 99 24W
Oahe, L., *U.S.A.* **91 F5** 44 27N 100 24W
Oahe Dam, *SD, U.S.A.* **91 F5** 44 27N 100 24W
O'ahu, *HI, U.S.A.* **69 K14** 21 28N 157 58W
Oak, *NE, U.S.A.* **84 D8** 40 14N 97 54W
Oak Bay, *B.C., Canada* **187 G11** 48 26N 123 18W
Oak Bay, *N.B., Canada* **173 H2** 45 14N 67 12W
Oak Bluffs, *MA, U.S.A.* **78 C4** 41 27N 70 34W
Oak City, *UT, U.S.A.* **100 D3** 39 22N 112 20W
Oak Cr. →, *AZ, U.S.A.* **62 C4** 34 45N 111 55W
Oak Cr. →, *SD, U.S.A.* **91 E5** 45 35N 100 30W
Oak Creek, *CO, U.S.A.* **66 B4** 40 16N 106 57W
Oak Creek, *WI, U.S.A.* **103 F6** 42 52N 87 55W
Oak Grove, *Atlanta, U.S.A.* **106 A3** 33 50N 84 18W
Oak Grove, *KY, U.S.A.* **96 D5** 36 40N 87 26W
Oak Grove, *LA, U.S.A.* **75 B4** 32 52N 91 23W
Oak Grove, *MO, U.S.A.* **82 C2** 39 0N 94 8W
Oak Grove, *Portland, U.S.A.* **116 B2** 45 25N 122 38W
Oak Grove, *TN, U.S.A.* **97 D10** 36 25N 82 25W
Oak Grove, *VA, U.S.A.* **77 B4** 38 11N 77 0W
Oak Harbor, *OH, U.S.A.* **92 B3** 41 30N 83 9W
Oak Harbor, *WA, U.S.A.* **101 B3** 48 18N 122 39W
Oak Hill, *N.B., Canada* **173 H2** 45 20N 67 20W
Oak Hill, *AL, U.S.A.* **60 E3** 31 55N 87 5W
Oak Hill, *Boston, U.S.A.* **106 B2** 42 18N 71 10W
Oak Hill, *FL, U.S.A.* **67 C8** 28 52N 80 51W
Oak Hill, *KS, U.S.A.* **74 B6** 39 15N 97 21W
Oak Hill, *OH, U.S.A.* **92 E4** 38 54N 82 35W
Oak Hill, *TN, U.S.A.* **96 D6** 36 5N 86 47W
Oak Hill, *WV, U.S.A.* **102 D3** 37 59N 81 9W
Oak Island, *Boston, U.S.A.* **106 A4** 42 25N 70 59W
Oak Island, *NC, U.S.A.* **90 E7** 33 55N 78 10W
Oak Lake, *Man., Canada* **183 F11** 49 46N 100 38W
Oak Lawn, *IL, U.S.A.* **71 B6** 41 42N 87 45W
Oak Orchard, *DE, U.S.A.* **77 B5** 38 36N 75 12W
Oak Park, *GA, U.S.A.* **68 D4** 32 22N 82 19W
Oak Park, *IL, U.S.A.* **71 B6** 41 52N 87 47W
Oak Park, *MI, U.S.A.* **79 G8** 42 27N 83 10W
Oak Point, *Man., Canada* **183 E13** 50 30N 98 1W
Oak Ridge, *LA, U.S.A.* **75 B4** 32 38N 91 47W
Oak Ridge, *MO, U.S.A.* **82 D7** 37 30N 89 44W
Oak Ridge, *TN, U.S.A.* **97 D8** 36 1N 84 16W
Oak River, *Man., Canada* **183 E11** 50 8N 100 26W
Oak Vale, *MS, U.S.A.* **81 E4** 31 26N 89 58W
Oak Valley, *KS, U.S.A.* **74 D7** 37 20N 96 1W
Oak View, *CA, U.S.A.* **65 J7** 34 24N 119 18W
Oak View, *MD, U.S.A.* **119 A4** 39 1N 76 58W
Oakbank, *Man., Canada* **183 F15** 49 57N 96 51W
Oakboro, *NC, U.S.A.* **90 C5** 35 13N 80 20W
Oakdale, *Atlanta, U.S.A.* **106 A2** 33 51N 84 30W
Oakdale, *CA, U.S.A.* **64 F6** 37 46N 120 51W
Oakdale, *Charlotte, U.S.A.* **107 A1** 35 18N 80 53W
Oakdale, *IL, U.S.A.* **71 E4** 38 16N 89 30W
Oakdale, *LA, U.S.A.* **75 D3** 30 49N 92 40W
Oakdale, *Minneapolis-St. Paul, U.S.A.* **113 B4** 44 57N 92 57W
Oakdale, *NE, U.S.A.* **84 B8** 42 4N 97 58W
Oakdale Park, *Minneapolis-St. Paul, U.S.A.* **113 A4** 45 1N 92 57W
Oakes, *ND, U.S.A.* **91 D7** 46 8N 98 6W
Oakesdale, *WA, U.S.A.* **101 C8** 47 8N 117 15W
Oakfield, *GA, U.S.A.* **68 E3** 31 47N 83 58W
Oakfield, *NY, U.S.A.* **89 B2** 43 4N 78 16W
Oakfield, *WI, U.S.A.* **103 E5** 43 41N 88 33W
Oakford, *IL, U.S.A.* **71 C4** 40 6N 89 58W
Oakgrove, *AR, U.S.A.* **63 B2** 36 27N 93 26W
Oakhurst, *CA, U.S.A.* **64 F7** 37 19N 119 40W
Oakhurst, *NJ, U.S.A.* **87 B2** 40 16N 74 1W
Oakhurst, *OK, U.S.A.* **93 B7** 36 5N 96 4W
Oakland, *AR, U.S.A.* **63 B3** 36 28N 92 35W
Oakland, *CA, U.S.A.* **64 F4** 37 48N 122 18W
Oakland, *IL, U.S.A.* **71 D5** 39 39N 88 2W
Oakland, *IA, U.S.A.* **73 D3** 41 19N 95 23W
Oakland, *KY, U.S.A.* **96 C6** 37 2N 86 15W
Oakland, *ME, U.S.A.* **76 D4** 44 33N 69 43W
Oakland, *MD, U.S.A.* **119 B4** 38 53N 76 54W
Oakland, *MD, U.S.A.* **77 A1** 39 25N 79 24W
Oakland, *MS, U.S.A.* **81 B4** 34 3N 89 55W
Oakland, *MO, U.S.A.* **117 B1** 38 34N 90 23W
Oakland, *NJ, U.S.A.* **87 A2** 41 2N 74 14W
Oakland, *NE, U.S.A.* **84 C9** 41 50N 96 28W
Oakland, *OK, U.S.A.* **93 D7** 34 6N 96 49W
Oakland, *OR, U.S.A.* **94 D2** 43 25N 123 18W
Oakland, *PA, U.S.A.* **95 C7** 41 57N 75 37W
Oakland, *TN, U.S.A.* **96 E3** 35 14N 89 31W
Oakland City, *IN, U.S.A.* **72 E3** 38 20N 87 21W
Oakland County ☆, *MI, U.S.A.* **79 G8** 42 35N 83 20W
Oakland Gardens, *NY, U.S.A.* **114 B4** 40 44N 73 44W
Oakland International ✕ (OAK), *CA, U.S.A.* **64 F4** 37 43N 122 13W
Oakland Park, *FL, U.S.A.* **67 E8** 26 10N 80 7W
Oaklawn, *KS, U.S.A.* **74 D6** 37 36N 97 18W
Oaklawn, *MD, U.S.A.* **119 C4** 38 46N 76 56W
Oakley, *ID, U.S.A.* **70 G5** 42 15N 113 53W
Oakley, *KS, U.S.A.* **74 B3** 39 8N 100 51W
Oakley, *MI, U.S.A.* **79 F7** 43 9N 84 10W
Oakley, *OH, U.S.A.* **107 B2** 39 9N 84 25W
Oakley, *UT, U.S.A.* **100 C4** 40 43N 111 18W
Oaklyn, *PA, U.S.A.* **116 B2** 39 54N 79 5W
Oakman, *AL, U.S.A.* **60 C3** 33 43N 87 23W
Oakman, *GA, U.S.A.* **68 B2** 34 34N 84 43W
Oakmont, *Pittsburgh, U.S.A.* **116 A2** 40 31N 79 50W
Oakridge, *OR, U.S.A.* **94 D3** 43 45N 122 28W
Oaks, *OK, U.S.A.* **93 B9** 36 10N 94 51W
Oakton, *KY, U.S.A.* **96 D3** 36 40N 89 4W
Oakton, *VA, U.S.A.* **77 B3** 38 52N 77 18W
Oaktown, *IN, U.S.A.* **72 E3** 38 52N 87 27W
Oakville, *Ont., Canada* **178 D7** 43 27N 79 41W
Oakville, *CT, U.S.A.* **78 C1** 41 36N 73 5W
Oakville, *IA, U.S.A.* **73 D7** 41 6N 91 3W
Oakville, *New Orleans, U.S.A.* **113 D2** 29 46N 90 1W
Oakville, *WA, U.S.A.* **101 D2** 46 51N 123 14W
Oakwood, *NY, U.S.A.* **114 C2** 40 33N 74 6W
Oakwood, *OH, U.S.A.* **92 B2** 41 6N 84 23W
Oakwood, *OK, U.S.A.* **93 C5** 35 56N 98 42W
Oakwood, *PA, U.S.A.* **95 C2** 41 1N 80 23W
Oakwood, *TX, U.S.A.* **99 F12** 31 35N 95 51W
Oakwood Beach, *NY, U.S.A.* **114 C2** 40 33N 74 7W
Oark, *AR, U.S.A.* **63 C2** 35 41N 93 35W
Oasis, *NV, U.S.A.* **85 A6** 41 2N 114 29W
Oatman, *AZ, U.S.A.* **62 B1** 35 1N 114 19W
Oaxaca, *Oaxaca, Mexico* **221 G4** 17 3N 96 43W
Oaxaca □, *Mexico* **221 H4** 17 0N 96 30W
Oba, *Ont., Canada* **181 C12** 49 4N 84 7W
Oba L., *Ont., Canada* **181 D12** 48 40N 84 16W
Obakamiga L., *Ont., Canada* **181 C11** 49 9N 85 9W
Obalski, L., *Qué., Canada* **176 C5** 48 43N 77 58W
Obamsca, L., *Qué., Canada* **176 A4** 50 24N 78 16W
Obaska, *Qué., Canada* **176 C5** 48 13N 77 21W
Obatanga Prov. Park ⌂, *Ont., Canada* **181 D11** 48 20N 85 10W
Obayos, *Coahuila, Mexico* **214 C3** 27 26N 101 24W
Obayos, Sa., *Coahuila, Mexico* **214 C3** 27 35N 101 37W
Obed, *Alta., Canada* **184 E3** 53 30N 117 10W
Obed →, *TN, U.S.A.* **97 D8** 36 5N 84 39W
Obedjiwan, *Qué., Canada* **176 C8** 48 40N 74 56W
Oberlin, *KS, U.S.A.* **74 B3** 39 49N 100 32W
Oberlin, *LA, U.S.A.* **75 D3** 30 37N 92 46W
Oberlin, *OH, U.S.A.* **92 B4** 41 18N 82 13W
Oberon, *ND, U.S.A.* **91 C6** 47 55N 99 13W
Obert, *NE, U.S.A.* **84 B8** 42 41N 97 2W
Obion, *TN, U.S.A.* **96 D3** 36 16N 89 12W
Obion →, *TN, U.S.A.* **96 E3** 35 55N 89 39W
Obion County ☆, *TN, U.S.A.* **96 D3** 36 20N 89 10W
Oblong, *IL, U.S.A.* **71 D6** 39 0N 87 55W
Obonga L., *Ont., Canada* **180 C7** 49 57N 89 22W
O'Brien, *FL, U.S.A.* **67 A6** 30 2N 82 57W
O'Brien, *OR, U.S.A.* **94 E2** 42 4N 123 42W
O'Brien, *TX, U.S.A.* **99 D8** 33 23N 99 51W
O'Brien County ☆, *IA, U.S.A.* **73 B3** 43 5N 95 35W
O'Bryonville, *OH, U.S.A.* **107 B2** 39 8N 84 28W
Obscura, Sierra, *NM, U.S.A.* **88 D4** 33 45N 106 25W
Observatorio de Arecibo, *Puerto Rico* **105 G16** 18 21N 66 45W
Obsidian, *ID, U.S.A.* **70 E4** 44 5N 114 51W
Ocala, *FL, U.S.A.* **67 B6** 29 11N 82 8W
Ocampo, *Chihuahua, Mexico* **213 E7** 28 11N 108 23W
Ocampo, *Coahuila, Mexico* **214 C2** 27 20N 102 21W
Ocampo, *Guanajuato, Mexico* **219 A6** 21 39N 101 30W
Ocampo, *Tamaulipas, Mexico* **215 H5** 22 50N 99 20W
Ocate, *NM, U.S.A.* **88 A5** 36 11N 105 3W
Ocate →, *NM, U.S.A.* **88 A6** 36 10N 104 30W
Occoquan Cr. →, *VA, U.S.A.* **77 B3** 38 39N 77 14W
Ocean Beach, *San Diego, U.S.A.* **117 B1** 32 44N 117 15W
Ocean Bluff, *MA, U.S.A.* **78 B4** 42 6N 70 39W
Ocean City, *MD, U.S.A.* **77 B5** 38 20N 75 5W
Ocean City, *NJ, U.S.A.* **87 C2** 39 17N 74 35W
Ocean City, *WA, U.S.A.* **101 C1** 47 4N 124 10W
Ocean County ☆, *NJ, U.S.A.* **87 C2** 39 50N 74 15W
Ocean Falls, *B.C., Canada* **186 C7** 52 18N 127 48W
Ocean L., *WY, U.S.A.* **104 C4** 43 12N 108 36W
Ocean Park, *WA, U.S.A.* **101 D1** 46 30N 124 3W
Ocean Pines, *MD, U.S.A.* **77 B5** 38 24N 75 9W
Ocean Springs, *MS, U.S.A.* **81 F5** 30 25N 88 50W
Oceana, *WV, U.S.A.* **102 D3** 37 42N 81 38W
Oceana County ☆, *MI, U.S.A.* **79 F5** 43 40N 86 20W
Oceano, *CA, U.S.A.* **65 H6** 35 6N 120 37W
Oceanport, *NJ, U.S.A.* **87 B2** 40 19N 74 3W
Oceanside, *CA, U.S.A.* **65 K9** 33 12N 117 23W
Oceanside, *NY, U.S.A.* **87 B3** 40 38N 73 37W
Oceanville, *NJ, U.S.A.* **87 C2** 39 28N 74 28W
Ochelata, *OK, U.S.A.* **93 B8** 36 36N 95 59W
Ocheyedan, *IA, U.S.A.* **73 B3** 43 25N 95 32W
Ocheyedan Mound, *IA, U.S.A.* **73 B3** 43 24N 95 31W
Ochiltree County ☆, *TX, U.S.A.* **98 A7** 36 10N 100 55W
Ochlocknee, *GA, U.S.A.* **68 F2** 30 58N 84 3W
Ochlockonee →, *FL, U.S.A.* **67 B4** 29 59N 84 26W
Ochoco Mts., *OR, U.S.A.* **94 C5** 44 30N 120 35W

Ochoco Nat. Forest, *OR, U.S.A.* **94 C5** 44 20N 120 15W
Ochopee, *FL, U.S.A.* **67 F7** 25 54N 81 18W
Ochre River, *Man., Canada* **183 D12** 51 4N 99 47W
Ocilla, *GA, U.S.A.* **68 E3** 31 36N 83 15W
Ocmulgee →, *GA, U.S.A.* **68 E4** 31 58N 82 33W
Ocoee, *FL, U.S.A.* **67 C7** 28 34N 81 32W
Ocoee, *TN, U.S.A.* **97 E8** 35 7N 84 43W
Ocoee →, *TN, U.S.A.* **97 E8** 35 12N 84 39W
Ocoee, L., *TN, U.S.A.* **97 E8** 35 6N 84 39W
Oconee, *IL, U.S.A.* **71 D4** 39 17N 89 7W
Oconee →, *GA, U.S.A.* **68 E4** 31 58N 82 33W
Oconee, L., *GA, U.S.A.* **68 C3** 33 28N 83 15W
Oconee County ☆, *GA, U.S.A.* **68 C3** 33 50N 83 25W
Oconee County ☆, *SC, U.S.A.* **90 D2** 34 45N 83 0W
Oconee Nat. Forest, *GA, U.S.A.* **68 C3** 33 15N 83 45W
Oconomowoc, *WI, U.S.A.* **103 E5** 43 7N 88 30W
Oconto, *NE, U.S.A.* **84 C6** 41 9N 99 46W
Oconto, *WI, U.S.A.* **103 D6** 44 53N 87 52W
Oconto →, *WI, U.S.A.* **103 D6** 44 53N 87 50W
Oconto County ☆, *WI, U.S.A.* **103 D5** 45 0N 88 15W
Oconto Falls, *WI, U.S.A.* **103 D5** 44 52N 88 9W
Ocosingo, *Chiapas, Mexico* **222 C4** 16 53N 92 6W
Ocotlán, *Jalisco, Mexico* **218 B5** 20 21N 102 46W
Ocotlán, *Oaxaca, Mexico* **221 H4** 16 48N 96 40W
Ocoyucan, *Puebla, Mexico* **221 F2** 18 59N 98 17W
Ocozocoautla, *Chiapas, Mexico* **222 C3** 16 46N 93 22W
Ocracoke, *NC, U.S.A.* **90 C10** 35 7N 75 58W
Ocracoke I., *NC, U.S.A.* **90 C10** 35 10N 75 50W
Octavia, *NE, U.S.A.* **84 C8** 41 21N 97 4W
Ocuiltzapotlán, *Tabasco, Mexico* **222 A4** 18 8N 92 51W
Ocumicho, *Michoacan, Mexico* **218 C5** 19 46N 102 13W
Odebolt, *IA, U.S.A.* **73 C3** 42 19N 95 15W
Odell, *IL, U.S.A.* **71 B5** 41 0N 88 31W
Odell, *NE, U.S.A.* **84 D9** 40 3N 96 48W
Odell, *OR, U.S.A.* **94 B4** 45 38N 121 32W
Odell, *TX, U.S.A.* **99 C8** 34 21N 99 25W
Odem, *TX, U.S.A.* **99 K10** 27 57N 97 35W
Oden, *AR, U.S.A.* **63 D2** 34 37N 93 47W
Odenton, *MD, U.S.A.* **77 A4** 39 5N 76 42W
Odessa, *Ont., Canada* **179 C10** 44 17N 76 43W
Odessa, *Sask., Canada* **182 E8** 50 17N 103 47W
Odessa, *DE, U.S.A.* **77 A5** 39 27N 75 40W
Odessa, *MN, U.S.A.* **80 E2** 45 16N 96 20W
Odessa, *MO, U.S.A.* **82 C3** 39 0N 93 57W
Odessa, *NY, U.S.A.* **89 C4** 42 20N 76 47W
Odessa, *TX, U.S.A.* **98 F5** 31 52N 102 23W
Odessa, *WA, U.S.A.* **101 C7** 47 20N 118 41W
Odin, Mt., *Nunavut, Canada* **190 D12** 66 33N 65 26W
Odon, *IN, U.S.A.* **72 E4** 38 51N 86 59W
O'Donnell, *TX, U.S.A.* **98 E6** 32 58N 101 50W
Odum, *GA, U.S.A.* **68 E4** 31 40N 82 2W
Oelrichs, *SD, U.S.A.* **91 G2** 43 11N 103 14W
Oelwein, *IA, U.S.A.* **73 C7** 42 41N 91 55W
O'Fallon, *MO, U.S.A.* **82 C6** 38 49N 90 42W
O'Fallon Park, *MO, U.S.A.* **117 A2** 38 40N 90 13W
Offerle, *KS, U.S.A.* **74 D4** 37 54N 99 33W
Ofu, *Amer. Samoa* **105 f** 14 11 S 169 41W
Ogahalla, *Ont., Canada* **181 B11** 50 6N 85 51W
Ogallah, *KS, U.S.A.* **74 C4** 38 59N 99 44W
Ogallala, *NE, U.S.A.* **84 C4** 41 8N 101 43W
Ogascanane, L., *Qué., Canada* **176 D4** 47 5N 78 25W
Ogden, *AR, U.S.A.* **63 E1** 33 35N 94 3W
Ogden, *IA, U.S.A.* **73 C4** 42 2N 94 2W
Ogden, *KS, U.S.A.* **74 B7** 39 7N 96 43W
Ogden, *UT, U.S.A.* **100 B4** 41 13N 111 58W
Ogden Park, *Chicago, U.S.A.* **108 C2** 41 46N 87 39W
Ogdensburg, *NJ, U.S.A.* **87 A2** 41 5N 74 36W
Ogdensburg, *NY, U.S.A.* **89 A5** 44 42N 75 30W
Ogeechee →, *GA, U.S.A.* **68 E5** 31 50N 81 3W
Ogema, *Sask., Canada* **182 F7** 49 35N 104 55W
Ogema, *MN, U.S.A.* **80 C3** 47 6N 95 56W
Ogemaw, *AR, U.S.A.* **63 E2** 33 28N 93 2W
Ogemaw County ☆, *MI, U.S.A.* **79 E7** 44 15N 84 10W
Ogilvie, *MN, U.S.A.* **80 E5** 45 50N 93 26W
Ogilvie →, *Yukon, Canada* **188 C5** 65 51N 137 15W
Ogilvie Mts., *N.W.T., Canada* **189 D5** 65 0N 140 0W
Oglala, *SD, U.S.A.* **91 G3** 43 17N 102 44W
Oglala Nat. Grassland, *NE, U.S.A.* **84 B2** 42 55N 103 45W
Ogle County ☆, *IL, U.S.A.* **71 A4** 42 0N 89 20W
Oglesby, *IL, U.S.A.* **71 B4** 41 18N 89 4W
Oglesby, *TX, U.S.A.* **99 F10** 31 25N 97 30W
Oglethorpe, *GA, U.S.A.* **68 D2** 32 18N 84 4W
Oglethorpe County ☆, *GA, U.S.A.* **68 C4** 33 50N 83 0W
Ogoki, *Ont., Canada* **181 A11** 51 38N 85 58W
Ogoki →, *Ont., Canada* **181 A11** 51 38N 85 57W
Ogoki L., *Ont., Canada* **181 B9** 50 50N 87 10W
Ogoki Res., *Ont., Canada* **180 B8** 50 45N 88 15W
Ogontz, *PA, U.S.A.* **116 A2** 40 6N 75 6W
Ogunquit, *ME, U.S.A.* **86 C4** 43 15N 70 36W
O'Hare International, Chicago ✕ (ORD), *IL, U.S.A.* **108 B1** 41 59N 87 54W
Ohatchee, *AL, U.S.A.* **60 C5** 33 47N 86 0W
Ohio, *CO, U.S.A.* **66 D4** 38 34N 106 37W
Ohio, *IL, U.S.A.* **71 B4** 41 34N 89 28W
Ohio □, *U.S.A.* **92 C4** 40 15N 82 45W
Ohio →, *OH, U.S.A.* **96 D3** 36 59N 89 8W
Ohio City, *Cleveland, U.S.A.* **107 B1** 41 29N 81 42W
Ohio City, *OH, U.S.A.* **92 C2** 40 46N 84 37W
Ohio County ☆, *IN, U.S.A.* **72 E6** 38 55N 85 0W
Ohio County ☆, *KY, U.S.A.* **96 C6** 37 30N 86 50W
Ohio County ☆, *WV, U.S.A.* **102 A4** 40 6N 80 34W
Ohio River Islands Nat. Wildlife Refuge ⌓, *U.S.A.* **102 B3** 39 25N 81 12W
Ohiopyle, *PA, U.S.A.* **77 A1** 39 52N 79 30W
Ohiopyle State Park ⌓, *PA, U.S.A.* **95 E3** 39 50N 79 26W
Ohioville, *PA, U.S.A.* **95 D2** 40 41N 80 30W
Ohoopee →, *GA, U.S.A.* **68 E4** 31 54N 82 8W
Oies, Î. aux, *Qué., Canada* **177 D12** 47 4N 70 33W
Oil City, *LA, U.S.A.* **75 B2** 32 45N 93 58W
Oil City, *PA, U.S.A.* **95 C3** 41 26N 79 42W
Oil Springs, *Ont., Canada* **178 E4** 42 47N 82 7W
Oil Springs Indian Reservation, *NY, U.S.A.* **89 C2** 42 14N 78 18W
Oil Trough, *AR, U.S.A.* **63 C4** 35 38N 91 28W
Oildale, *CA, U.S.A.* **65 H7** 35 25N 119 1W
Oilmont, *MT, U.S.A.* **83 B6** 48 44N 111 51W
Oilton, *OK, U.S.A.* **93 B7** 36 5N 96 35W
Ojai, *CA, U.S.A.* **65 J7** 34 27N 119 15W
Ojinaga, *Chihuahua, Mexico* **213 D11** 29 34N 104 25W
Ojo Caliente, *Zacatecas, Mexico* **217 E8** 22 34N 102 15W
Ojo Caliente, *NM, U.S.A.* **88 A4** 36 18N 106 3W
Ojo de Agua de Palmillas, *Sinaloa, Mexico* **216 E5** 22 37N 105 37W
Ojo de Liebre, L., *Baja Calif. S., Mexico* **211 F4** 27 45N 114 15W
Ojo del Carrizo, *Chihuahua, Mexico* **213 D10** 29 58N 105 16W
Ojo del Diablo, L., *Chihuahua, Mexico* **213 C9** 30 40N 106 55W
Ojo Feliz, *NM, U.S.A.* **88 A5** 36 4N 105 7W
Ojo Sarco, *NM, U.S.A.* **88 A5** 36 7N 105 47W
Ojos Azules, *Chihuahua, Mexico* **213 D9** 29 18N 106 46W
Ojuelos de Jalisco, *Jalisco, Mexico* **218 A6** 21 51N 101 35W
Okabena, *MN, U.S.A.* **80 G3** 43 44N 95 19W
Okak, *Nfld. & L., Canada* **175 B5** 57 33N 61 58W
Okak Is., *Nfld. & L., Canada* **175 B5** 57 30N 61 30W
Okaloosa County ☆, *FL, U.S.A.* **67 A2** 30 30N 86 40W
Okanagan Falls, *B.C., Canada* **187 F15** 49 21N 119 34W
Okanagan L., *B.C., Canada* **187 F15** 50 0N 119 30W
Okanagan Mountain Park ⌓, *B.C., Canada* **187 F15** 49 45N 119 30W
Okanogan, *WA, U.S.A.* **101 B6** 48 22N 119 35W
Okanogan →, *WA, U.S.A.* **101 B6** 48 6N 119 44W
Okanogan County ☆, *WA, U.S.A.* **101 B6** 48 30N 120 0W
Okanogan Nat. Forest, *WA, U.S.A.* **101 B5** 48 30N 120 10W
Okarche, *OK, U.S.A.* **93 C6** 35 44N 97 58W
Okatibbee L., *MS, U.S.A.* **81 D5** 32 29N 88 48W
Okaton, *SD, U.S.A.* **91 G5** 43 53N 100 53W
Okay, *OK, U.S.A.* **93 C8** 35 51N 95 19W
O'Kean, *AR, U.S.A.* **63 B5** 36 10N 90 49W
Okeechobee, *FL, U.S.A.* **67 D8** 27 15N 80 50W
Okeechobee, L., *FL, U.S.A.* **67 E8** 27 0N 80 50W
Okeechobee County ☆, *FL, U.S.A.* **67 D8** 27 30N 81 0W
Okeene, *OK, U.S.A.* **93 B5** 36 7N 98 19W
Okefenokee Nat. Wildlife Refuge ⌓, *U.S.A.* **68 F4** 30 45N 82 18W
Okefenokee Swamp, *GA, U.S.A.* **68 F4** 30 40N 82 20W
Okemah, *OK, U.S.A.* **93 C7** 35 26N 96 19W
Okemo Mt., *VT, U.S.A.* **86 C2** 43 24N 72 45W
Okemos, *MI, U.S.A.* **79 G7** 42 43N 84 26W
Oketo, *KS, U.S.A.* **74 B7** 39 58N 96 36W
Okfuskee County ☆, *OK, U.S.A.* **93 C7** 35 25N 96 15W
Oklahoma □, *U.S.A.* **93 C6** 35 20N 97 30W
Oklahoma City, *OK, U.S.A.* **93 C6** 35 30N 97 30W
Oklahoma City Will Rogers ✕ (OKC), *OK, U.S.A.* **93 C6** 35 24N 97 36W
Oklahoma County ☆, *OK, U.S.A.* **93 C6** 35 35N 97 20W
Oklaunion, *TX, U.S.A.* **99 C8** 34 8N 99 9W
Oklawaha →, *FL, U.S.A.* **67 B7** 29 28N 81 41W
Oklawaha, L., *FL, U.S.A.* **67 B7** 29 30N 81 45W
Oklee, *MN, U.S.A.* **80 C3** 47 50N 95 51W
Okmulgee, *OK, U.S.A.* **93 C8** 35 37N 95 58W
Okmulgee County ☆, *OK, U.S.A.* **93 C8** 35 40N 96 0W
Okoboji, *IA, U.S.A.* **73 B3** 43 23N 95 8W
Okolona, *AR, U.S.A.* **63 E2** 34 0N 93 20W
Okolona, *KY, U.S.A.* **97 B7** 38 8N 85 41W
Okolona, *MS, U.S.A.* **81 B5** 34 0N 88 45W
Oktaha, *OK, U.S.A.* **93 C8** 35 35N 95 29W
Oktibbeha County ☆, *MS, U.S.A.* **81 C5** 33 28N 88 49W
Ola, *AR, U.S.A.* **63 C2** 35 2N 93 13W
Ola, *ID, U.S.A.* **70 E2** 44 11N 116 18W
Olalla, *Seattle, U.S.A.* **118 D2** 47 25N 122 32W
Olamon, *ME, U.S.A.* **76 C5** 45 7N 68 37W
Olancha, *CA, U.S.A.* **65 G8** 36 17N 118 1W
Olancha Pk., *CA, U.S.A.* **65 G8** 36 16N 118 7W
Olanta, *SC, U.S.A.* **90 E6** 33 56N 79 56W
Olathe, *CO, U.S.A.* **66 D3** 38 36N 107 59W
Olathe, *KS, U.S.A.* **74 C9** 38 53N 94 49W
Olberg, *AZ, U.S.A.* **62 D4** 33 6N 111 41W
Old Bridge, *NJ, U.S.A.* **87 B2** 40 25N 74 22W
Old Crow, *Yukon, Canada* **188 C5** 67 30N 139 55W
Old Faithful, *WY, U.S.A.* **104 B2** 44 28N 110 50W
Old Fields, *WV, U.S.A.* **77 A2** 39 8N 78 57W
Old Forge, *NY, U.S.A.* **89 B6** 43 43N 74 58W
Old Forge, *PA, U.S.A.* **87 A1** 41 22N 75 45W
Old Fort, *NC, U.S.A.* **90 C3** 35 38N 82 11W
Old Harbor, *AK, U.S.A.* **61 H9** 57 12N 153 18W
Old Harbor, *Boston, U.S.A.* **106 B3** 42 19N 71 1W
Old Hickory L., *TN, U.S.A.* **96 D6** 36 18N 86 40W
Old Horse Springs, *NM, U.S.A.* **88 D2** 33 55N 108 14W
Old Lyme, *CT, U.S.A.* **78 C2** 41 19N 72 20W
Old Mines, *MO, U.S.A.* **82 C6** 38 1N 90 45W
Old Monroe, *MO, U.S.A.* **82 C6** 38 56N 90 45W
Old Ocean, *TX, U.S.A.* **99 H12** 29 5N 95 45W
Old Orchard Beach, *ME, U.S.A.* **76 E3** 43 31N 70 23W
Old Perlican, *Nfld. & L., Canada* **174 D7** 48 5N 53 1W
Old Saybrook, *CT, U.S.A.* **78 C2** 41 18N 72 23W
Old Speck Mt., *ME, U.S.A.* **76 D3** 44 34N 70 57W
Old Tampa Bay, *Tampa, U.S.A.* **119 B3** 27 54N 82 35W
Old Tampa Bay Park, *Tampa, U.S.A.* **119 A3** 28 1N 82 38W
Old Tavern, *VA, U.S.A.* **77 B3** 38 50N 77 49W
Old Town, *Chicago, U.S.A.* **108 B3** 41 54N 87 37W
Old Town, *FL, U.S.A.* **67 B6** 29 36N 82 59W
Old Town, *ME, U.S.A.* **76 D5** 44 56N 68 39W
Old Washington, *OH, U.S.A.* **92 C5** 40 2N 81 27W
Old Wives L., *Sask., Canada* **182 E6** 50 5N 106 0W
Old Woman Mts., *CA, U.S.A.* **65 J11** 34 20N 115 0W
Olde Providence, *Charlotte, U.S.A.* **107 B2** 35 6N 80 47W
Oldenburg, *IN, U.S.A.* **72 D5** 39 21N 85 12W
Oldham, *SD, U.S.A.* **91 F8** 44 14N 97 19W
Oldham County ☆, *KY, U.S.A.* **97 B7** 38 25N 85 30W
Oldham County ☆, *TX, U.S.A.* **98 B5** 35 30N 102 30W
Oldhams, *VA, U.S.A.* **77 B4** 38 0N 76 40W
Oldman →, *Alta., Canada* **185 J9** 49 57N 111 42W
Olds, *Alta., Canada* **185 G6** 51 50N 114 10W
Oldsmar, *FL, U.S.A.* **67 C6** 28 2N 82 39W
Oldtown, *MD, U.S.A.* **77 A2** 39 33N 78 37W
Olean, *MO, U.S.A.* **82 C4** 38 25N 92 32W
Olean, *NY, U.S.A.* **89 C2** 42 5N 78 26W
O'Leary, *P.E.I., Canada* **173 G5** 46 42N 64 13W
Olentangy →, *OH, U.S.A.* **92 D3** 39 58N 83 2W
Oleta River State Rec. Area, *Miami, U.S.A.* **112 C3** 25 55N 80 8W
Olex, *OR, U.S.A.* **94 B5** 45 30N 120 11W
Olga, L., *Qué., Canada* **175 D2** 49 47N 77 15W
Olinalá, *Guerrero, Mexico* **219 E9** 17 47N 98 43W
Olivar de los Padres, *Distrito Federal, Mexico* **225 B2** 19 21N 99 14W
Olivar del Conde, *Distrito Federal, Mexico* **225 B2** 19 22N 99 12W
Olive Branch, *MS, U.S.A.* **81 B4** 34 57N 89 49W
Olive Hill, *KY, U.S.A.* **97 B9** 38 18N 83 13W
Olivehurst, *CA, U.S.A.* **64 D5** 39 6N 121 34W
Oliver, *B.C., Canada* **187 F15** 49 13N 119 37W
Oliver, *GA, U.S.A.* **68 D5** 32 31N 81 32W
Oliver, *WI, U.S.A.* **103 B1** 46 40N 92 12W
Oliver County ☆, *ND, U.S.A.* **91 C4** 47 2N 101 25W
Oliver Springs, *TN, U.S.A.* **97 D8** 36 3N 84 20W
Olivet, *KS, U.S.A.* **74 C8** 38 29N 95 45W
Olivet, *MD, U.S.A.* **77 B4** 38 20N 76 26W
Olivet, *MI, U.S.A.* **79 G7** 42 27N 84 56W
Olivet, *SD, U.S.A.* **91 G8** 43 14N 97 40W
Olivette, *MO, U.S.A.* **117 A1** 38 39N 90 22W
Olivia, *MN, U.S.A.* **80 F4** 44 47N 94 59W
Olivia, L., *Orlando, U.S.A.* **115 A1** 28 31N 81 29W
Olla, *LA, U.S.A.* **75 C3** 31 54N 92 14W
Ollie, *IA, U.S.A.* **73 D6** 41 12N 92 6W
Olmos Basin Park, *San Antonio, U.S.A.* **117 B2** 29 29N 98 28W
Olmos Park, *San Antonio, U.S.A.* **117 C2** 29 28N 98 28W
Olmstead, *KY, U.S.A.* **96 D5** 36 45N 87 1W
Olmsted, *IL, U.S.A.* **71 F4** 37 11N 89 5W
Olmsted County ☆, *MN, U.S.A.* **80 G6** 44 0N 92 30W
Olney, *IL, U.S.A.* **71 E5** 38 44N 88 5W
Olney, *MD, U.S.A.* **77 A3** 39 9N 77 4W
Olney, *MT, U.S.A.* **83 B3** 48 33N 114 35W
Olney, *TX, U.S.A.* **99 D9** 33 22N 98 45W
Olney Springs, *CO, U.S.A.* **66 D7** 38 10N 103 57W
Ololizqui, Volcan, *Distrito Federal, Mexico* **225 C2** 19 14N 99 11W
Olomane →, *Qué., Canada* **175 C5** 50 14N 60 37W
Olomatlán, *Puebla, Mexico* **221 G2** 17 57N 98 15W
Olosega, *Amer. Samoa* **105 f** 14 12 S 169 38W
Olowalu, *HI, U.S.A.* **69 C5** 20 49N 156 38W
Olpe, *KS, U.S.A.* **74 C7** 38 16N 96 10W
Olsburg, *KS, U.S.A.* **74 B7** 39 26N 96 37W
Olson, L., *Minneapolis-St. Paul, U.S.A.* **113 A4** 45 1N 92 56W
Olton, *TX, U.S.A.* **98 C5** 34 11N 102 8W
Olustee, *FL, U.S.A.* **67 A6** 30 12N 82 26W
Olustee, *OK, U.S.A.* **93 D4** 34 33N 99 25W
Olympia, *WA, U.S.A.* **101 C3** 47 3N 122 53W
Olympia, L., *Orlando, U.S.A.* **115 A1** 28 34N 81 31W
Olympian Village, *MO, U.S.A.* **82 C6** 38 8N 90 27W
Olympic Mts., *WA, U.S.A.* **101 C2** 47 55N 123 45W
Olympic Nat. Forest, *WA, U.S.A.* **101 C2** 47 25N 123 35W
Olympic Nat. Park △, *WA, U.S.A.* **101 B1** 48 16N 124 40W
Olympique, Stade, *Montréal, Canada* **192 A3** 45 33N 73 33W
Olympus, Mt., *Salt Lake City, U.S.A.* **117 C3** 40 39N 111 46W
Olympus, Mt., *WA, U.S.A.* **101 C2** 47 48N 123 43W
Omaha, *AR, U.S.A.* **63 B2** 36 27N 93 11W
Omaha, *NE, U.S.A.* **84 C10** 41 17N 95 58W
Omaha, *TX, U.S.A.* **99 D13** 33 11N 94 45W
Omaha Eppley Airfield ✕ (OMA), *NE, U.S.A.* **84 C10** 41 18N 95 53W
Omaha Indian Reservation, *NE, U.S.A.* **84 B9** 42 10N 96 30W
Omak, *WA, U.S.A.* **101 B6** 48 25N 119 31W
Omak L., *WA, U.S.A.* **101 B6** 48 17N 119 24W
Omak Mt., *WA, U.S.A.* **101 B6** 48 27N 119 18W
Omega, *GA, U.S.A.* **68 E3** 31 21N 83 36W
Omemee, *Ont., Canada* **179 C8** 44 18N 78 33W
Omemee, *ND, U.S.A.* **91 B5** 48 42N 100 22W
Omer, *MI, U.S.A.* **79 E8** 44 3N 83 51W
Ometepec, *Guerrero, Mexico* **219 F9** 16 41N 98 25W
Omineca →, *B.C., Canada* **189 E8** 56 3N 124 16W
Omineca Mts., *B.C., Canada* **189 E7** 56 30N 125 30W
Omitlán →, *Guerrero, Mexico* **219 E8** 17 6N 99 34W
Ommaney, C., *AK, U.S.A.* **61 H14** 56 10N 134 40W
Ommanney B., *N.W.T., Canada* **190 C5** 73 0N 101 0W
Ompompanoosuc →, *VT, U.S.A.* **86 C2** 43 45N 72 14W
Omps, *WV, U.S.A.* **77 A2** 39 30N 78 17W
Omro, *WI, U.S.A.* **103 D5** 44 2N 88 45W
Ona, *FL, U.S.A.* **67 D7** 27 29N 81 55W
Onaga, *KS, U.S.A.* **74 B7** 39 29N 96 10W
Onaka, *SD, U.S.A.* **91 E6** 45 12N 99 28W
Onakawana, *Ont., Canada* **181 B15** 50 36N 81 27W
Onalaska, *WI, U.S.A.* **103 E2** 43 53N 91 14W
Onaman →, *Ont., Canada* **181 C9** 49 59N 88 0W
Onaman L., *Ont., Canada* **181 C9** 50 0N 87 26W
Onamia, *MN, U.S.A.* **80 D5** 46 4N 93 40W
Onancock, *VA, U.S.A.* **102 D9** 37 43N 75 45W
Onanole, *Man., Canada* **183 E12** 50 37N 99 58W
Onaping, *Ont., Canada* **178 A5** 46 37N 81 25W
Onaping →, *Ont., Canada* **178 A5** 46 37N 81 18W
Onaping L., *Ont., Canada* **181 E15** 47 3N 81 30W
Onarga, *IL, U.S.A.* **71 C5** 40 43N 88 1W
Onatchiway, L., *Qué., Canada* **177 B11** 49 3N 71 5W
Onavas, *Sonora, Mexico* **212 E6** 28 31N 109 35W
Onawa, *IA, U.S.A.* **73 C2** 42 2N 96 6W
Onaway, *ID, U.S.A.* **70 C2** 46 56N 116 53W
Onaway, *MI, U.S.A.* **79 D7** 45 21N 84 14W
Oneco, *FL, U.S.A.* **67 D6** 27 25N 82 31W
Oneida, *IL, U.S.A.* **71 B3** 41 4N 90 13W
Oneida, *IA, U.S.A.* **73 C7** 42 33N 91 21W
Oneida, *KS, U.S.A.* **74 B8** 39 52N 95 56W
Oneida, *NY, U.S.A.* **89 B5** 43 6N 75 39W
Oneida, *TN, U.S.A.* **97 D8** 36 30N 84 31W
Oneida County ☆, *ID, U.S.A.* **70 G6** 42 10N 112 30W
Oneida County ☆, *NY, U.S.A.* **89 B5** 43 20N 75 30W
Oneida County ☆, *WI, U.S.A.* **103 C4** 45 40N 89 35W
Oneida Indian Reservation, *NY, U.S.A.* **89 B5** 43 1N 75 38W
Oneida Indian Reservation, *WI, U.S.A.* **103 D5** 44 25N 88 10W
Oneida L., *NY, U.S.A.* **89 B5** 43 12N 75 54W
O'Neill, *NE, U.S.A.* **84 B7** 42 27N 98 39W
Onekama, *MI, U.S.A.* **79 E5** 44 22N 86 12W
Oneonta, *AL, U.S.A.* **60 C4** 33 57N 86 28W
Oneonta, *NY, U.S.A.* **89 C5** 42 27N 75 4W
Onida, *SD, U.S.A.* **91 F5** 44 42N 100 4W
Onion Lake, *Sask., Canada* **182 B2** 53 43N 110 0W
Onley, *VA, U.S.A.* **102 D9** 37 41N 75 43W
Ono, *CA, U.S.A.* **64 C4** 40 29N 122 37W
Onondaga County ☆, *NY, U.S.A.* **89 B4** 43 0N 76 15W
Onondaga Indian Reservation, *NY, U.S.A.* **89 C4** 42 55N 76 10W
Onoway, *Alta., Canada* **184 E6** 53 42N 114 12W
Onset, *MA, U.S.A.* **78 C4** 41 45N 70 39W
Onslow, *IA, U.S.A.* **73 C7** 42 6N 91 1W
Onslow B., *NC, U.S.A.* **90 D8** 34 20N 77 15W
Onslow County ☆, *NC, U.S.A.* **90 D8** 34 50N 77 30W
Ontario, *CA, U.S.A.* **65 J9** 34 4N 117 39W
Ontario, *OR, U.S.A.* **94 C9** 44 2N 116 58W
Ontario, *WI, U.S.A.* **103 E3** 43 45N 90 35W
Ontario □, *Canada* **180 B6** 48 0N 83 0W
Ontario, L., *N. Amer.* **179 D9** 43 20N 78 0W
Ontario County ☆, *NY, U.S.A.* **89 C3** 42 50N 77 20W
Ontario International ✕ (ONT), *CA, U.S.A.* **65 J9** 34 3N 117 36W
Ontonagon, *MI, U.S.A.* **79 C2** 46 52N 89 19W
Ontonagon County ☆, *MI, U.S.A.* **79 C2** 46 40N 89 25W
Ontonagon Indian Reservation, *MI, U.S.A.* **79 C2** 46 29N 89 6W
'Ō'ōkala, *HI, U.S.A.* **69 C6** 20 1N 155 17W
Oolitic, *IN, U.S.A.* **72 E4** 38 54N 86 31W
Oologah, *OK, U.S.A.* **93 B8** 36 27N 95 43W
Oologah L., *OK, U.S.A.* **93 B8** 36 26N 95 41W
Oona River, *B.C., Canada* **186 B4** 53 57N 130 16W
Oostburg, *WI, U.S.A.* **103 E6** 43 37N 87 48W
Ootsa L., *B.C., Canada* **186 B8** 53 50N 126 2W
Ootsa Lake, *B.C., Canada* **186 B8** 53 50N 126 5W
Opa-Locka, *Miami, U.S.A.* **112 C1** 25 54N 80 15W
Opa-Locka ✕, *Miami, U.S.A.* **112 C1** 25 54N 80 16W
Opal, *WY, U.S.A.* **104 E2** 41 46N 110 20W
Opasatica, L., *Qué., Canada* **176 C3** 48 5N 79 18W
Opasatika, *Ont., Canada* **181 C14** 49 30N 82 50W
Opasatika →, *Ont., Canada* **181 B14** 50 25N 82 25W
Opasatika L., *Ont., Canada* **181 C13** 49 4N 83 6W
Opataca, L., *Qué., Canada* **176 A8** 50 22N 74 55W
Opawica, L., *Qué., Canada* **176 B7** 49 35N 75 55W
Opelika, *AL, U.S.A.* **60 D5** 32 39N 85 23W
Opelousas, *LA, U.S.A.* **75 D3** 30 32N 92 5W
Opémisca, L., *Qué., Canada* **175 D3** 49 56N 74 52W
Opeongo L., *Ont., Canada* **179 B8** 45 42N 78 23W
Opequon →, *WV, U.S.A.* **77 A3** 39 31N 77 52W
Opheim, *MT, U.S.A.* **83 B11** 48 51N 106 24W
Ophir, *AK, U.S.A.* **61 E8** 63 10N 156 31W
Ophir, *OR, U.S.A.* **94 E1** 42 34N 124 23W
Opichén, *Yucatán, Mexico* **223 B4** 20 33N 89 51W
Opihikao, *HI, U.S.A.* **69 D7** 19 26N 154 53W
Opinaca →, *Qué., Canada* **175 C2** 52 15N 78 2W
Opinaca, Rés., *Qué., Canada* **175 C2** 52 39N 76 20W
Opiscotéo, L., *Qué., Canada* **175 C4** 53 10N 68 10W
Opocopa, L., *Qué., Canada* **172 A3** 52 38N 66 35W
Opodepe, *Sonora, Mexico* **212 D5** 29 55N 110 39W
Opopeo, *Michoacan, Mexico* **218 C6** 19 25N 101 37W
Opp, *AL, U.S.A.* **60 E4** 31 17N 86 16W
Opportunity, *MT, U.S.A.* **83 D5** 46 6N 112 50W
Opportunity, *WA, U.S.A.* **101 C8** 47 39N 117 15W
Optima, *OK, U.S.A.* **93 B2** 36 46N 101 21W
Optima L., *OK, U.S.A.* **93 B2** 36 40N 101 8W
Optima Nat. Wildlife Refuge ⌓, *OK, U.S.A.* **93 B2** 36 48N 101 19W
Oquawka, *IL, U.S.A.* **71 C3** 40 56N 90 57W
Oquirrh, *Salt Lake City, U.S.A.* **117 C1** 40 37N 112 1W
Oquitoa, *Sonora, Mexico* **212 C4** 30 44N 111 41W
Oquossoc, *ME, U.S.A.* **86 B4** 44 58N 70 46W
Oracle, *AZ, U.S.A.* **62 E5** 32 37N 110 46W
Oran, *MO, U.S.A.* **82 D7** 37 5N 89 39W
Orange, *CA, U.S.A.* **65 K9** 33 47N 117 51W
Orange, *CT, U.S.A.* **78 C1** 41 17N 73 2W
Orange, *MA, U.S.A.* **78 B2** 42 35N 72 19W
Orange, *NJ, U.S.A.* **114 B1** 40 46N 74 13W
Orange, *TX, U.S.A.* **99 G14** 30 6N 93 44W
Orange, *VA, U.S.A.* **102 C6** 38 15N 78 7W
Orange Beach, *AL, U.S.A.* **60 F3** 30 18N 87 34W
Orange City, *FL, U.S.A.* **67 C7** 28 57N 81 18W
Orange City, *IA, U.S.A.* **73 B2** 43 0N 96 4W
Orange County ☆, *CA, U.S.A.* **65 K9** 33 30N 117 45W
Orange County ☆, *FL, U.S.A.* **67 C7** 28 30N 81 15W
Orange County ☆, *IN, U.S.A.* **72 E4** 38 30N 86 30W
Orange County ☆, *NC, U.S.A.* **90 B6** 36 0N 79 10W
Orange County ☆, *NY, U.S.A.* **89 D6** 41 20N 74 15W
Orange County ☆, *TX, U.S.A.* **99 G14** 30 12N 93 52W
Orange County ☆, *VA, U.S.A.* **102 C6** 38 15N 78 7W
Orange County ☆, *VT, U.S.A.* **86 B2** 44 0N 72 20W
Orange Cove, *CA, U.S.A.* **65 G7** 36 38N 119 19W
Orange Grove, *TX, U.S.A.* **99 K10** 27 58N 97 56W
Orange L., *FL, U.S.A.* **67 B6** 29 25N 82 13W
Orange Park, *FL, U.S.A.* **67 A7** 30 10N 81 42W
Orange Res., *NJ, U.S.A.* **114 B1** 40 45N 74 17W
Orangeburg, *SC, U.S.A.* **90 E5** 33 30N 80 52W
Orangeburg County ☆, *SC, U.S.A.* **90 E5** 33 20N 80 30W
Orangevale, *CA, U.S.A.* **64 E5** 38 41N 121 13W
Orangeville, *Ont., Canada* **178 D6** 43 55N 80 5W
Orangeville, *IL, U.S.A.* **71 A4** 42 28N 89 39W
Orangeville, *PA, U.S.A.* **95 C6** 41 5N 76 25W
Orangeville, *UT, U.S.A.* **100 D4** 39 14N 111 3W
Orbisonia, *PA, U.S.A.* **95 D5** 40 15N 77 54W
Orcas I., *WA, U.S.A.* **101 B3** 48 42N 122 56W
Orchard, *CO, U.S.A.* **66 B6** 40 20N 104 7W
Orchard, *ID, U.S.A.* **70 F2** 43 19N 116 2W
Orchard, *IA, U.S.A.* **73 B6** 43 14N 92 47W
Orchard, *NE, U.S.A.* **84 B7** 42 20N 98 15W
Orchard City, *CO, U.S.A.* **66 D3** 38 50N 107 58W
Orchard Homes, *MT, U.S.A.* **83 D3** 46 55N 114 4W
Orchard Mesa, *CO, U.S.A.* **66 C2** 39 3N 108 33W
Orchard Park, *NY, U.S.A.* **89 C2** 42 46N 78 45W
Orchard Valley, *WY, U.S.A.* **104 E8** 41 6N 104 49W
Orchards, *WA, U.S.A.* **101 E3** 45 40N 122 34W
Orcutt, *CA, U.S.A.* **65 J6** 34 52N 120 26W
Ord, *NE, U.S.A.* **84 C7** 41 36N 98 56W
Ord, Mt., *TX, U.S.A.* **98 G4** 30 18N 103 30W
Ord Mts., *CA, U.S.A.* **65 J10** 34 39N 116 45W
Orderville, *UT, U.S.A.* **100 F3** 37 17N 112 38W
Ordway, *CO, U.S.A.* **66 D7** 38 13N 103 46W
Ore City, *TX, U.S.A.* **99 E13** 32 48N 94 43W
Oreana, *ID, U.S.A.* **70 F2** 43 3N 116 24W
Oreana, *IL, U.S.A.* **71 D5** 39 56N 88 52W
Oreana, *NV, U.S.A.* **85 B2** 40 20N 118 19W
Oregon, *IL, U.S.A.* **71 A4** 42 1N 89 20W
Oregon, *MO, U.S.A.* **82 B1** 39 59N 95 9W
Oregon, *OH, U.S.A.* **92 B3** 41 38N 83 25W
Oregon, *WI, U.S.A.* **103 F4** 42 56N 89 23W
Oregon □, *U.S.A.* **94 D4** 44 0N 121 0W
Oregon Butte, *ID, U.S.A.* **70 D3** 45 31N 115 40W
Oregon Butte, *WA, U.S.A.* **101 D8** 46 7N 117 41W
Oregon Caves Nat. Monument ⌓, *OR, U.S.A.* **94 E2** 42 6N 123 24W
Oregon City, *OR, U.S.A.* **94 B3** 45 21N 122 36W
Oregon County ☆, *MO, U.S.A.* **82 E5** 36 40N 91 25W
Oregon Dunes Nat. Recr. Area ⌓, *OR, U.S.A.* **94 D1** 43 40N 124 10W
Oreland, *PA, U.S.A.* **116 A1** 40 7N 75 10W
Orem, *UT, U.S.A.* **100 C4** 40 19N 111 42W
Orestes Pereyra, *Durango, Mexico* **216 A5** 26 30N 105 39W
Organ, *NM, U.S.A.* **88 E4** 32 26N 106 36W
Organ Pipe Cactus Nat. Monument ⌓, *AZ, U.S.A.* **62 E3** 32 0N 112 52W
Organos, Pta. los, *Michoacan, Mexico* **218 E6** 17 50N 101 45W
Orick, *CA, U.S.A.* **64 B2** 41 17N 124 4W
Orient, *IA, U.S.A.* **73 D4** 41 12N 94 25W
Orient, *ME, U.S.A.* **76 C6** 45 49N 67 50W
Orient, *NY, U.S.A.* **78 C2** 41 8N 72 18W
Orient, *SD, U.S.A.* **91 F6** 44 54N 99 5W
Orient, *WA, U.S.A.* **101 B7** 48 52N 118 12W
Orient Heights, *Boston, U.S.A.* **106 A4** 42 23N 70 59W
Oriental, *Puebla, Mexico* **220 E3** 19 22N 97 37W
Oriental, *NC, U.S.A.* **90 C9** 35 2N 76 42W
Orillia, *Ont., Canada* **178 C7** 44 40N 79 24W
Orin, *WY, U.S.A.* **104 D7** 42 39N 105 12W
Orinda, *CA, U.S.A.* **64 F4** 37 52N 122 10W
Orion, *AL, U.S.A.* **60 E5** 31 58N 86 0W
Orion, *IL, U.S.A.* **71 B3** 41 21N 90 23W
Orion, *OK, U.S.A.* **93 B5** 36 13N 98 47W
Oriska, *ND, U.S.A.* **91 D8** 46 56N 97 47W
Oriskany, *NY, U.S.A.* **89 B5** 43 10N 75 20W
Orizaba, *Veracruz, Mexico* **221 F3** 18 51N 97 6W
Orizaba, Volcán Pico de, *Veracruz, Mexico* **221 F3** 18 58N 97 15W
Orla, *TX, U.S.A.* **98 F4** 31 50N 103 55W
Orland, *CA, U.S.A.* **64 D4** 39 45N 122 12W
Orland Park, *IL, U.S.A.* **71 B6** 41 38N 87 52W
Orlando, *FL, U.S.A.* **67 C7** 28 32N 81 22W
Orlando, *OK, U.S.A.* **93 B6** 36 9N 97 23W
Orlando Executive ✕, *Orlando, U.S.A.* **115 A2** 28 32N 81 20W
Orlando International ✕ (MCO), *FL, U.S.A.* **67 C7** 28 26N 81 19W
Orlean, *VA, U.S.A.* **77 B3** 38 45N 77 58W
Orleans, *CA, U.S.A.* **64 B3** 41 18N 123 32W
Orleans, *IN, U.S.A.* **72 E4** 38 40N 86 27W
Orleans, *IA, U.S.A.* **73 B3** 43 27N 95 6W
Orleans, *MA, U.S.A.* **78 C5** 41 47N 69 59W
Orleans, *NE, U.S.A.* **84 D6** 40 8N 99 27W
Orleans, *VT, U.S.A.* **86 B2** 44 49N 72 12W
Orléans, Î. d', *Qué., Canada* **177 E12** 46 54N 70 58W
Orleans County ☆, *NY, U.S.A.* **89 B2** 43 15N 78 10W
Orleans County ☆, *VT, U.S.A.* **86 B2** 44 45N 72 15W
Orleans Parish ☆, *LA, U.S.A.* **75 E5** 29 58N 90 4W
Orlinda, *TN, U.S.A.* **96 D6** 36 36N 86 43W
Orlovista, *Orlando, U.S.A.* **115 A2** 28 32N 81 27W
Ormiston, *Sask., Canada* **182 F6** 49 44N 105 24W
Ormond Beach, *FL, U.S.A.* **67 B7** 29 17N 81 3W
Ormond-by-the-Sea, *FL, U.S.A.* **67 B7** 29 21N 81 4W
Ormsby, *MN, U.S.A.* **80 G4** 43 51N 94 42W
Ormstown, *Qué., Canada* **177 F9** 45 8N 74 0W
Oro Grande, *CA, U.S.A.* **65 J9** 34 36N 117 20W
Oro Valley, *AZ, U.S.A.* **62 E5** 32 26N 110 58W
Orofino, *ID, U.S.A.* **70 C2** 46 29N 116 15W
Orogrande, *ID, U.S.A.* **70 D3** 45 42N 115 33W
Orogrande, *NM, U.S.A.* **88 E4** 32 24N 106 5W
Oromocto, *N.B., Canada* **173 H3** 45 54N 66 29W
Oromocto L., *N.B., Canada* **173 H3** 45 36N 67 0W
Orono, *Ont., Canada* **179 D8** 43 59N 78 37W
Orono, *ME, U.S.A.* **76 D5** 44 53N 68 40W
Oronoco, *MN, U.S.A.* **80 F6** 44 10N 92 32W

Orote Pen., *Guam* **105 b** 13 26N 144 38 E
Orovada, *NV, U.S.A.* **85 A3** 41 34N 117 47W
Oroville, *CA, U.S.A.* **64 D5** 39 31N 121 33W
Oroville, *WA, U.S.A.* **101 B6** 48 56N 119 26W
Oroville, L., *CA, U.S.A.* **64 D5** 39 33N 121 29W
Oroville Dam, *CA, U.S.A.* **64 D5** 39 33N 121 29W
Orpha, *WY, U.S.A.* **104 D7** 42 51N 105 30W
Orr, *MN, U.S.A.* **80 B6** 48 3N 92 50W
Orr, *OK, U.S.A.* **93 D6** 34 2N 97 32W
Orrick, *MO, U.S.A.* **82 B2** 39 13N 94 7W
Orrin, *ND, U.S.A.* **91 B5** 48 6N 100 10W
Orrville, *AL, U.S.A.* **60 B4** 34 40N 86 59W
Orrville, *OH, U.S.A.* **92 C5** 40 50N 81 46W
Orting, *WA, U.S.A.* **101 C3** 47 6N 122 12W
Ortiz, *Sonora, Mexico* **212 E5** 28 17N 110 43W
Ortley, *SD, U.S.A.* **91 E8** 45 20N 97 12W
Ortonville, *MN, U.S.A.* **80 E2** 45 19N 96 27W
Orwell, *OH, U.S.A.* **92 B6** 41 32N 80 52W
Osage, *AR, U.S.A.* **63 B2** 36 11N 93 24W
Osage, *IA, U.S.A.* **73 B6** 43 17N 92 49W
Osage, *OK, U.S.A.* **93 B7** 36 19N 96 24W
Osage, *WV, U.S.A.* **102 B4** 39 39N 80 1W
Osage, *WY, U.S.A.* **104 C8** 43 59N 104 25W
Osage →, *MO, U.S.A.* **82 C5** 38 36N 91 57W
Osage Beach, *MO, U.S.A.* **82 C4** 38 9N 92 37W
Osage City, *KS, U.S.A.* **74 C8** 38 38N 95 50W
Osage City, *MO, U.S.A.* **82 C4** 38 33N 92 2W
Osage County ☆, *KS, U.S.A.* **74 C8** 38 40N 95 40W
Osage County ☆, *MO, U.S.A.* **82 C5** 38 30N 91 45W
Osage County ☆, *OK, U.S.A.* **93 B7** 36 40N 96 30W
Osage Fork →, *MO, U.S.A.* **82 D4** 37 46N 92 26W
Osage Indian Reservation, *OK, U.S.A.* **93 B7** 36 35N 96 20W
Osakis, *MN, U.S.A.* **80 E3** 45 52N 95 9W
Osakis, L., *MN, U.S.A.* **80 E3** 45 54N 95 7W
Osawatomie, *KS, U.S.A.* **74 C9** 38 31N 94 57W
Osawin →, *Ont., Canada* **181 C11** 49 45N 85 19W
Osborne, *KS, U.S.A.* **74 B5** 39 26N 98 42W
Osborne County ☆, *KS, U.S.A.* **74 B5** 39 30N 98 45W
Osburn, *ID, U.S.A.* **70 B2** 47 30N 116 0W
Oscar Soto Maynes, *Chihuahua, Mexico* **213 D8** 29 3N 107 28W
Osceola, *AR, U.S.A.* **63 C6** 35 42N 89 58W
Osceola, *IA, U.S.A.* **73 D5** 41 2N 93 46W
Osceola, *MO, U.S.A.* **82 C3** 38 3N 93 42W
Osceola, *NE, U.S.A.* **84 C8** 41 11N 97 33W
Osceola, *WI, U.S.A.* **103 C1** 45 19N 92 42W
Osceola County ☆, *FL, U.S.A.* **67 C7** 28 0N 81 0W
Osceola County ☆, *IA, U.S.A.* **73 B3** 43 20N 95 35W
Osceola County ☆, *MI, U.S.A.* **79 F6** 44 0N 85 20W
Osceola Mills, *PA, U.S.A.* **95 D4** 40 51N 78 16W
Osceola Nat. Forest, *FL, U.S.A.* **67 A6** 30 20N 82 30W
Oscoda, *MI, U.S.A.* **79 E8** 44 26N 83 20W
Oscoda County ☆, *MI, U.S.A.* **79 E7** 44 40N 84 10W
Oscuro, *NM, U.S.A.* **88 D4** 33 29N 106 3W
Osgood, *IN, U.S.A.* **72 D5** 39 8N 85 18W
Osgood, *OH, U.S.A.* **92 C2** 40 20N 84 30W
Osgood Mts., *NV, U.S.A.* **85 A3** 41 10N 117 20W
Osgoode, *Ont., Canada* **179 B11** 45 8N 75 36W
Oshawa, *Ont., Canada* **179 D8** 43 50N 78 50W
Oshkosh, *NE, U.S.A.* **84 C3** 41 24N 102 21W
Oshkosh, *WI, U.S.A.* **103 D5** 44 1N 88 33W
Osierfield, *GA, U.S.A.* **68 E3** 31 40N 83 7W
Oskaloosa, *IA, U.S.A.* **73 D6** 41 18N 92 39W
Oskaloosa, *KS, U.S.A.* **74 B8** 39 13N 95 19W
Oskélanéo, *Qué., Canada* **176 C7** 48 5N 75 15W
Osler, *Sask., Canada* **182 C5** 52 22N 106 33W
Oslo, *MN, U.S.A.* **80 B1** 48 12N 97 8W
Osmond, *NE, U.S.A.* **84 B8** 42 22N 97 36W
Osnabrock, *ND, U.S.A.* **91 B7** 48 40N 98 9W
Osnaburgh House, *Ont., Canada* **180 A6** 51 14N 90 14W
Osnaburgh L., *Ont., Canada* **180 A6** 51 12N 90 9W
Osoyoos, *B.C., Canada* **187 F15** 49 0N 119 30W
Osoyoos L., *B.C., Canada* **187 G15** 49 0N 119 27W
Osprey, *FL, U.S.A.* **67 D6** 27 12N 82 29W
Ossabaw I., *GA, U.S.A.* **68 E5** 31 50N 81 5W
Ossabaw Sd., *GA, U.S.A.* **68 E5** 31 50N 81 6W
Osseo, *MI, U.S.A.* **79 H7** 41 53N 84 33W
Osseo, *WI, U.S.A.* **103 D2** 44 35N 91 13W
Ossian, *IN, U.S.A.* **72 C5** 40 53N 85 10W
Ossian, *IA, U.S.A.* **73 B7** 43 9N 91 46W
Ossineke, *MI, U.S.A.* **79 E8** 44 55N 83 26W
Ossining, *NY, U.S.A.* **87 A3** 41 10N 73 55W
Ossipee, *NH, U.S.A.* **86 C3** 43 41N 71 7W
Ossipee L., *NH, U.S.A.* **86 C3** 43 42N 71 10W
Ossokmanuan L., *Nfld. & L., Canada* **175 C5** 53 25N 65 0W
Ostaboningue, L., *Qué., Canada* **176 D4** 47 9N 78 53W
Ostego L., *MI, U.S.A.* **79 E7** 44 55N 84 42W
Osterville, *MA, U.S.A.* **78 C4** 41 38N 70 22W
Ostión, L., *Veracruz, Mexico* **221 F6** 18 11N 94 38W
Ostrander, *MN, U.S.A.* **80 G6** 43 37N 92 26W
Ostuacán, *Chiapas, Mexico* **222 B3** 17 22N 93 18W
O'Sullivan Dam, *WA, U.S.A.* **101 D6** 46 59N 119 16W
O'Sullivan L., *Ont., Canada* **181 B9** 50 25N 87 2W
Oswegatchie →, *NY, U.S.A.* **89 A5** 44 42N 75 30W
Oswego, *IL, U.S.A.* **71 B5** 41 41N 88 21W
Oswego, *KS, U.S.A.* **74 D8** 37 10N 95 6W
Oswego, *NY, U.S.A.* **89 B4** 43 27N 76 31W
Oswego →, *NY, U.S.A.* **89 B4** 43 27N 76 30W
Oswego, L., *Portland, U.S.A.* **116 B1** 45 25N 122 40W
Oswego County ☆, *NY, U.S.A.* **89 B4** 43 25N 76 10W
Osyka, *MS, U.S.A.* **81 E3** 31 0N 90 28W
Otáez, *Durango, Mexico* **216 C5** 24 42N 106 0W
Otatlán →, *Guerrero, Mexico* **219 E7** 17 59N 100 5W
Otay Mesa, *San Diego, U.S.A.* **117 C2** 32 40N 117 3W
Otego, *NY, U.S.A.* **89 C5** 42 24N 75 10W
Otelnuk, L., *Qué., Canada* **175 B4** 56 9N 68 12W
Otero County ☆, *CO, U.S.A.* **66 E7** 38 0N 103 45W
Otero County ☆, *NM, U.S.A.* **88 E5** 32 30N 105 45W
Oteros →, *Chihuahua, Mexico* **212 F7** 27 29N 108 30W
Othello, *WA, U.S.A.* **101 D6** 46 50N 119 10W
Otho, *IA, U.S.A.* **73 C4** 42 25N 94 9W
Othón P. Blanco, *Quintana Roo, Mexico* **223 C4** 19 35N 89 4W
Otinapa, *Durango, Mexico* **216 C5** 24 11N 105 2W
Otis, *CO, U.S.A.* **66 B8** 40 9N 102 58W
Otis, *KS, U.S.A.* **74 C4** 38 32N 99 3W
Otis, *MA, U.S.A.* **78 B1** 42 12N 73 6W
Otish, Mts., *Qué., Canada* **175 C3** 52 22N 70 30W
Otisville, *MI, U.S.A.* **79 F8** 43 10N 83 31W
Otisville, *NY, U.S.A.* **87 A2** 41 28N 74 32W
Oto, *IA, U.S.A.* **73 C3** 42 17N 95 54W
Otoe, *NE, U.S.A.* **84 D9** 40 43N 96 7W
Otoe County ☆, *NE, U.S.A.* **84 D9** 40 40N 96 0W
Otongo, *Hidalgo, Mexico* **219 B9** 20 58N 98 45W
Otosquen, *Sask., Canada* **183 B9** 53 17N 102 1W
Otsego, *MI, U.S.A.* **79 G6** 42 27N 85 42W
Otsego County ☆, *MI, U.S.A.* **79 D7** 45 0N 84 40W
Otsego County ☆, *NY, U.S.A.* **89 C6** 42 40N 75 0W
Otsego L., *NY, U.S.A.* **89 C6** 42 45N 74 52W
Ottawa = Outaouais →, *Qué., Canada* **177 F8** 45 27N 74 8W
Ottawa, *Ont., Canada* **179 B11** 45 26N 75 42W
Ottawa, *IL, U.S.A.* **71 B5** 41 21N 88 51W
Ottawa, *KS, U.S.A.* **74 C8** 38 37N 95 16W
Ottawa, *OH, U.S.A.* **92 B2** 41 1N 84 3W
Ottawa County ☆, *KS, U.S.A.* **74 B6** 39 15N 97 45W
Ottawa County ☆, *MI, U.S.A.* **79 G6** 42 50N 86 0W
Ottawa County ☆, *OH, U.S.A.* **92 B3** 41 30N 83 9W
Ottawa County ☆, *OK, U.S.A.* **93 B9** 36 50N 94 50W
Ottawa Is., *N.W.T., Canada* **175 B1** 59 35N 80 10W
Ottawa McDonald Cartier International ✕ (YOW), *Ont., Canada* **179 B11** 45 19N 75 40W
Ottawa Nat. Forest, *MI, U.S.A.* **79 C2** 46 30N 89 30W
Ottawa Nat. Wildlife Refuge ⌂, *OH, U.S.A.* **92 B3** 41 36N 83 13W
Otter, *MT, U.S.A.* **83 E11** 45 12N 106 12W
Otter Cr. →, *UT, U.S.A.* **100 E3** 38 10N 112 2W
Otter Cr. →, *VT, U.S.A.* **86 B1** 44 13N 73 17W
Otter Creek, *FL, U.S.A.* **67 B6** 29 19N 82 46W
Otter Creek Res., *UT, U.S.A.* **100 E3** 38 10N 112 1W
Otter Lake, *IL, U.S.A.* **71 D4** 39 28N 89 56W
Otter Lake, *MI, U.S.A.* **79 F8** 43 13N 83 28W
Otter Rapids, *Ont., Canada* **181 B15** 50 11N 81 39W
Otter Tail →, *MN, U.S.A.* **80 D2** 46 16N 96 36W
Otter Tail County ☆, *MN, U.S.A.* **80 D3** 46 20N 95 45W
Otter Tail L., *MN, U.S.A.* **80 D3** 46 24N 95 40W
Otterbein, *IN, U.S.A.* **72 C3** 40 29N 87 6W
Ottertail, *MN, U.S.A.* **80 D3** 46 26N 95 33W
Otterville, *Ont., Canada* **178 E6** 42 55N 80 36W
Otterville, *MO, U.S.A.* **82 C4** 38 42N 93 0W
Otto, *WY, U.S.A.* **104 B4** 44 24N 108 16W
Otto Fiord, *Nunavut, Canada* **190 A8** 81 2N 87 0W
Ottosen, *IA, U.S.A.* **73 C4** 42 54N 94 23W
Ottumwa, *IA, U.S.A.* **73 D6** 41 1N 92 25W
Otway, *OH, U.S.A.* **92 E3** 38 52N 83 11W
Otzoloapan, *México, Mexico* **219 D7** 19 0N 100 16W
Ouachita, *AR, U.S.A.* **63 E3** 33 51N 92 50W
Ouachita →, *LA, U.S.A.* **75 C4** 31 38N 91 49W
Ouachita, L., *AR, U.S.A.* **63 D2** 34 34N 93 12W
Ouachita County ☆, *AR, U.S.A.* **63 E3** 33 35N 92 50W
Ouachita Mts., *AR, U.S.A.* **93 D9** 34 30N 94 30W
Ouachita Nat. Forest, *AR, U.S.A.* **63 D2** 34 42N 93 48W
Ouachita Nat. Forest, *OK, U.S.A.* **93 D9** 34 50N 94 50W
Ouachita Parish ☆, *LA, U.S.A.* **75 B3** 32 30N 92 7W
Ouareau, L., *Qué., Canada* **177 E8** 46 17N 74 9W
Ouasiemsca →, *Qué., Canada* **177 B10** 49 0N 72 30W
Ouest, Pte. de l', *Qué., Canada* **172 D5** 49 52N 64 40W
Ouray, *CO, U.S.A.* **66 D3** 38 1N 107 40W
Ouray, *UT, U.S.A.* **100 C6** 40 6N 109 41W
Ouray County ☆, *CO, U.S.A.* **66 D3** 38 10N 107 45W
Outagamie County ☆, *WI, U.S.A.* **103 D5** 44 20N 88 30W
Outaouais →, *Qué., Canada* **177 F8** 45 27N 74 8W
Outardes →, *Qué., Canada* **177 A13** 50 20N 69 10W
Outardes →, *Qué., Canada* **175 D4** 49 24N 69 30W
Outardes 4, Rés. aux, *Qué., Canada* **177 A13** 50 11N 69 13W
Outer Banks, *U.S.A.* **90 C10** 35 54N 75 28W
Outer I. = Grande-Passe, I. de la, *Qué., Canada* **175 C6** 51 10N 58 35W
Outer I., *WI, U.S.A.* **103 A3** 47 2N 90 26W
Outer Mission, *San Francisco, U.S.A.* **118 B2** 37 43N 122 26W
Outer Santa Barbara Passage, *CA, U.S.A.* **65 K8** 33 15N 118 40W
Outlook, *Sask., Canada* **182 D4** 51 30N 107 0W
Outlook, *MT, U.S.A.* **83 B13** 48 53N 104 47W
Outlook Pk., *Nunavut, Canada* **190 B7** 79 45N 91 23W
Outremont, *Montréal, Canada* **192 A3** 45 31N 73 36W
Ouzinkie, *AK, U.S.A.* **61 H9** 57 56N 152 30W
Oval Pk., *WA, U.S.A.* **101 B5** 48 17N 120 25W
Ovando, *MT, U.S.A.* **83 C4** 47 1N 113 8W
Overbrook, *KS, U.S.A.* **74 C8** 38 47N 95 33W
Overflow Nat. Wildlife Refuge ⌂, *AR, U.S.A.* **63 E4** 33 4N 91 41W
Overflowing →, *Man., Canada* **183 B10** 53 8N 101 5W
Overland, *MO, U.S.A.* **117 A1** 38 42N 90 21W
Overland Park, *KS, U.S.A.* **74 C9** 38 58N 94 40W
Overlea, *MD, U.S.A.* **77 A4** 39 21N 76 31W
Overly, *ND, U.S.A.* **91 B5** 48 41N 100 9W
Overton, *NE, U.S.A.* **84 D6** 40 44N 99 32W
Overton, *NV, U.S.A.* **85 F6** 36 33N 114 27W
Overton, *TX, U.S.A.* **99 E13** 32 16N 94 59W
Overton County ☆, *TN, U.S.A.* **97 D7** 36 23N 85 19W
Overton Park, *TN, U.S.A.* **112 B2** 35 8N 89 59W
Ovett, *MS, U.S.A.* **81 E4** 31 29N 89 2W
Ovid, *CO, U.S.A.* **66 B8** 40 58N 102 23W
Ovid, *MI, U.S.A.* **79 F7** 43 1N 84 22W
Ovid, *NY, U.S.A.* **89 C4** 42 41N 76 49W
Oviedo, *FL, U.S.A.* **67 C7** 28 40N 81 13W
Owanka, *SD, U.S.A.* **91 F3** 44 1N 102 35W
Owasa, *IA, U.S.A.* **73 C5** 42 26N 93 12W
Owasco L., *NY, U.S.A.* **89 C4** 42 50N 76 31W
Owasso, *OK, U.S.A.* **93 B8** 36 16N 95 51W
Owasso, L., *Minneapolis-St. Paul, U.S.A.* **113 A3** 45 2N 93 7W
Owatonna, *MN, U.S.A.* **80 F5** 44 5N 93 14W
Owego, *NY, U.S.A.* **89 C4** 42 6N 76 16W
Owen, *WI, U.S.A.* **103 D3** 44 57N 90 33W
Owen County ☆, *IN, U.S.A.* **72 D4** 39 20N 86 50W
Owen County ☆, *KY, U.S.A.* **97 B8** 38 30N 84 50W
Owen Sound, *Ont., Canada* **178 C6** 44 35N 80 55W
Owens, *VA, U.S.A.* **77 B3** 38 20N 77 5W
Owens →, *CA, U.S.A.* **65 G9** 36 32N 117 59W
Owens L., *CA, U.S.A.* **65 G9** 36 26N 117 57W
Owensboro, *KY, U.S.A.* **96 C5** 37 46N 87 7W
Owensville, *AR, U.S.A.* **63 D3** 34 37N 92 49W
Owensville, *IN, U.S.A.* **72 E3** 38 16N 87 41W
Owensville, *MO, U.S.A.* **82 C5** 38 21N 91 30W
Owensville, *OH, U.S.A.* **92 D2** 39 7N 84 8W
Owenton, *KY, U.S.A.* **97 B8** 38 32N 84 50W
Owenton, *VA, U.S.A.* **77 C3** 37 53N 77 6W
Owikeno L., *B.C., Canada* **186 D8** 51 40N 126 50W
Owings Mills, *MD, U.S.A.* **77 A4** 39 25N 76 47W
Owingsville, *KY, U.S.A.* **97 B9** 38 9N 83 46W
Owl →, *Man., Canada* **191 F7** 57 51N 92 44W
Owl Creek Mts., *WY, U.S.A.* **104 C4** 43 40N 108 55W
Owls Head, *ME, U.S.A.* **76 D4** 44 5N 69 4W
Owosso, *MI, U.S.A.* **79 F7** 43 0N 84 10W
Owsley County ☆, *KY, U.S.A.* **97 C9** 37 25N 83 40W
Owyhee, *NV, U.S.A.* **85 A4** 41 57N 116 6W
Owyhee →, *OR, U.S.A.* **94 D8** 43 49N 117 2W
Owyhee, L., *OR, U.S.A.* **94 D8** 43 38N 117 14W
Owyhee County ☆, *ID, U.S.A.* **70 G2** 42 45N 116 0W
Owyhee Desert, *NV, U.S.A.* **85 A4** 41 40N 116 50W
Owyhee Mts., *ID, U.S.A.* **70 G2** 42 45N 116 20W
Ox Cr. →, *ND, U.S.A.* **91 B5** 48 35N 100 8W
Oxbow, *Sask., Canada* **183 F9** 49 14N 102 10W
Oxbow, *ME, U.S.A.* **76 B5** 46 25N 68 28W
Oxchuc, *Chiapas, Mexico* **222 C4** 16 47N 92 20W
Oxford, *Qué., Canada* **173 H6** 45 44N 63 52W
Oxford, *AL, U.S.A.* **60 C5** 33 36N 85 51W
Oxford, *AR, U.S.A.* **63 B4** 36 13N 91 56W
Oxford, *IN, U.S.A.* **72 C3** 40 31N 87 15W
Oxford, *IA, U.S.A.* **73 D7** 41 43N 91 47W
Oxford, *KS, U.S.A.* **74 D6** 37 17N 97 10W
Oxford, *LA, U.S.A.* **75 C2** 31 56N 93 38W
Oxford, *ME, U.S.A.* **76 D3** 44 8N 70 30W
Oxford, *MA, U.S.A.* **78 B3** 42 7N 71 52W
Oxford, *MD, U.S.A.* **77 B4** 38 41N 76 11W
Oxford, *MI, U.S.A.* **79 G8** 42 49N 83 16W
Oxford, *MS, U.S.A.* **81 B4** 34 22N 89 31W
Oxford, *NC, U.S.A.* **90 B7** 36 19N 78 35W
Oxford, *NY, U.S.A.* **89 C5** 42 27N 75 36W
Oxford, *NE, U.S.A.* **84 D6** 40 15N 99 38W
Oxford, *OH, U.S.A.* **92 D2** 39 31N 84 45W
Oxford, *PA, U.S.A.* **77 A5** 39 47N 75 59W
Oxford, *WI, U.S.A.* **103 E4** 43 47N 89 34W
Oxford County ☆, *ME, U.S.A.* **76 D3** 44 30N 70 30W
Oxford Junction, *IA, U.S.A.* **73 D8** 41 59N 90 57W
Oxford L., *Man., Canada* **191 G6** 54 51N 95 37W
Oxford Pk., *ID, U.S.A.* **70 G6** 42 16N 112 6W
Oxkutzcab, *Yucatán, Mexico* **223 B4** 20 18N 89 25W
Oxnard, *CA, U.S.A.* **65 J7** 34 12N 119 11W
Oxon Hill, *MD, U.S.A.* **77 B4** 38 48N 76 59W
Oyama, *B.C., Canada* **187 E15** 50 7N 119 22W
Oyameyo, Volcan, *Distrito Federal, Mexico* **225 C2** 19 11N 99 11W
Oyen, *Alta., Canada* **185 G10** 51 22N 110 28W
Oyster Bay, *NY, U.S.A.* **78 D1** 40 52N 73 32W
Oyster Harbour = Ladysmith, *B.C., Canada* **186 G11** 49 0N 123 49W
Ozan, *AR, U.S.A.* **63 E2** 33 51N 93 43W
Ozark, *AL, U.S.A.* **60 E5** 31 28N 85 39W
Ozark, *AR, U.S.A.* **63 C2** 35 29N 93 50W
Ozark, *MO, U.S.A.* **82 D3** 37 1N 93 12W
Ozark County ☆, *MO, U.S.A.* **82 E4** 36 40N 92 25W
Ozark Folk Center State Park ⌂, *AR, U.S.A.* **63 C3** 35 53N 92 7W
Ozark Lake, *AR, U.S.A.* **63 C1** 35 30N 94 10W
Ozark Nat. Forest, *AR, U.S.A.* **63 C2** 35 40N 93 20W
Ozark Nat. Scenic Riverways ⌂, *MO, U.S.A.* **82 D5** 37 25N 91 12W
Ozark Plateau, *MO, U.S.A.* **82 E3** 37 20N 91 40W
Ozarks, L. of the, *MO, U.S.A.* **82 C4** 38 12N 92 38W
Ozaukee County ☆, *WI, U.S.A.* **103 E6** 43 20N 88 0W
Ozawkie, *KS, U.S.A.* **74 B8** 39 14N 95 28W
Ozette, L., *WA, U.S.A.* **101 B1** 48 6N 124 38W
Ozette Indian Reservation, *WA, U.S.A.* **101 B1** 48 10N 124 43W
Ozona, *TX, U.S.A.* **98 G6** 30 43N 101 12W
Ozone, *TN, U.S.A.* **97 E8** 35 53N 84 49W
Ozone Park, *NY, U.S.A.* **114 B3** 40 40N 73 50W
Ozuluama, *Veracruz, Mexico* **220 C3** 21 40N 97 51W
Ozumba, *México, Mexico* **219 C9** 19 3N 98 46W

P

Pa'auilo, *HI, U.S.A.* **69 C6** 20 2N 155 22W
Pabellón de Arteaga, *Aguascalientes, Mexico* **217 E8** 22 10N 102 21W
Pabellónes, Ensenada de, *Sinaloa, Mexico* **216 C3** 24 27N 107 36W
Pabelo, *Jalisco, Mexico* **218 C3** 19 53N 104 39W
Pablo, *MT, U.S.A.* **83 C3** 47 36N 114 7W
Pabos Mills, *Qué., Canada* **172 E5** 48 19N 64 42W
Pace, *FL, U.S.A.* **67 A1** 30 36N 87 10W
Pachuca, *Hidalgo, Mexico* **219 B9** 20 7N 98 44W
Pachuquilla, *Hidalgo, Mexico* **219 B9** 20 5N 98 41W
Pachuta, *MS, U.S.A.* **81 D5** 32 2N 88 53W
Pacific, *MO, U.S.A.* **82 C6** 38 29N 90 45W
Pacific Beach, *San Diego, U.S.A.* **117 B1** 32 47N 117 14W
Pacific Beach, *WA, U.S.A.* **101 C1** 47 13N 124 12W
Pacific City = Huntington Beach, *CA, U.S.A.* **65 K8** 33 40N 118 5W
Pacific City, *OR, U.S.A.* **94 B2** 45 12N 123 57W
Pacific County ☆, *WA, U.S.A.* **101 D2** 46 30N 123 55W
Pacific Grove, *CA, U.S.A.* **64 G5** 36 38N 121 56W
Pacific Heights, *San Francisco, U.S.A.* **118 B2** 37 47N 112 26W
Pacific Junction, *IA, U.S.A.* **73 D3** 41 1N 95 48W
Pacific Manor, *San Francisco, U.S.A.* **118 C2** 37 38N 122 27W
Pacific Palisades, *HI, U.S.A.* **69 K14** 21 25N 157 58W
Pacific Palisades, *Los Angeles, U.S.A.* **111 B1** 34 2N 118 32W
Pacific Rim Nat. Park Reserve △, *B.C., Canada* **186 G10** 48 40N 124 45W
Pacific Spirit Regional Park, *Vancouver, Canada* **193 B1** 49 15N 123 3W
Pacifica, *CA, U.S.A.* **64 F4** 37 37N 122 27W
Packanack Lake, *NJ, U.S.A.* **114 A1** 40 56N 94 13W
Packenham, *Ont., Canada* **179 B10** 45 22N 76 25W
Packwood, *IA, U.S.A.* **73 D6** 41 8N 92 5W
Packwood, *WA, U.S.A.* **101 D4** 46 36N 121 40W
Pacolet, *SC, U.S.A.* **90 D4** 34 54N 81 46W
Pacquet, *Nfld. & L., Canada* **174 C5** 50 0N 55 53W
Pacula, *Hidalgo, Mexico* **219 A8** 21 3N 99 18W
Paddle Prairie, *Alta., Canada* **189 E9** 57 57N 117 29W
Paden, *OK, U.S.A.* **93 C7** 35 30N 96 34W
Paden City, *WV, U.S.A.* **102 B4** 39 36N 80 56W
Padre I., *TX, U.S.A.* **98 K10** 27 10N 97 25W
Padre Island Nat. Seashore ⌂, *U.S.A.* **98 K10** 27 0N 97 25W
Padroni, *CO, U.S.A.* **66 B7** 40 47N 103 10W
Paducah, *KY, U.S.A.* **96 C4** 37 5N 88 37W
Paducah, *TX, U.S.A.* **98 C7** 34 1N 100 18W
Pagan, *N. Marianas* **105 a** 18 7N 145 46W
Page, *AZ, U.S.A.* **62 A4** 36 57N 111 27W
Page, *ND, U.S.A.* **91 C8** 47 10N 97 34W
Page, *NE, U.S.A.* **84 B7** 42 26N 98 25W
Page, *OK, U.S.A.* **93 D9** 34 45N 94 40W
Page City, *KS, U.S.A.* **74 B2** 39 5N 101 9W
Page County ☆, *IA, U.S.A.* **73 E3** 40 45N 95 10W
Page County ☆, *VA, U.S.A.* **102 C6** 38 40N 78 28W
Pagedale, *MO, U.S.A.* **117 B2** 38 41N 90 18W
Pageland, *SC, U.S.A.* **90 D5** 34 46N 80 24W
Pago B., *Guam* **105 b** 13 25N 144 47W
Pago Pago, *Amer. Samoa* **105 e** 14 16 S 170 43W
Pago Pago Harbor, *Amer. Samoa* **105 e** 14 17 S 170 40W
Pagosa Springs, *CO, U.S.A.* **66 E3** 37 16N 107 1W
Paguate, *NM, U.S.A.* **88 B3** 35 8N 107 23W
Pagwa River, *Ont., Canada* **181 B11** 50 2N 85 14W
Pagwachuan →, *Ont., Canada* **181 B12** 50 12N 84 43W
Pāhala, *HI, U.S.A.* **69 D6** 19 12N 155 29W
Pahaska, *WY, U.S.A.* **104 B3** 44 30N 109 58W
Pāhoa, *HI, U.S.A.* **69 D7** 19 30N 154 57W
Pahokee, *FL, U.S.A.* **67 E8** 26 50N 80 40W
Pahrangat Ra., *NV, U.S.A.* **85 E5** 37 15N 115 20W
Pahroc Ra., *NV, U.S.A.* **85 E6** 37 35N 114 58W
Pahrump, *NV, U.S.A.* **85 F5** 36 12N 115 59W
Pahute Mesa, *NV, U.S.A.* **85 E4** 37 20N 116 45W
Pahvant Range, *UT, U.S.A.* **100 D3** 39 10N 112 5W
Paia, *HI, U.S.A.* **69 C5** 20 54N 156 22W
Paige, *TX, U.S.A.* **99 G10** 30 13N 97 7W
Pailolo Channel, *HI, U.S.A.* **69 B5** 21 0N 156 40W
Paimpont, L., *Qué., Canada* **172 C8** 50 28N 61 34W
Paincourtville, *LA, U.S.A.* **75 E4** 29 59N 91 3W
Painesdale, *MI, U.S.A.* **79 B3** 47 3N 88 40W
Painesville, *OH, U.S.A.* **92 B5** 41 43N 81 15W
Paint →, *MI, U.S.A.* **79 D3** 45 58N 88 15W
Paint Cr. →, *OH, U.S.A.* **92 D3** 39 15N 83 20W
Paint Hills = Wemindji, *Qué., Canada* **175 C2** 53 0N 78 49W
Paint Rock, *AL, U.S.A.* **60 B4** 34 40N 86 20W
Paint Rock, *TX, U.S.A.* **99 F8** 31 31N 99 55W
Paint Rock →, *AL, U.S.A.* **60 B4** 34 28N 86 28W
Painted Desert, *AZ, U.S.A.* **62 B5** 36 0N 111 0W
Painted Post, *NY, U.S.A.* **89 C3** 42 10N 77 6W
Paintsville, *KY, U.S.A.* **97 C10** 37 49N 82 48W
Paintsville L., *KY, U.S.A.* **97 C10** 37 50N 82 52W
Paisley, *Ont., Canada* **178 C5** 44 18N 81 16W
Paisley, *OR, U.S.A.* **94 E5** 42 42N 120 32W
Paiute Indian Reservation, *UT, U.S.A.* **100 F2** 37 10N 113 46W
Pajapán, *Veracruz, Mexico* **221 F6** 18 15N 94 42W
Pajarito, *NM, U.S.A.* **88 C4** 34 59N 106 42W
Pajaritos, *Nayarit, Mexico* **216 E5** 22 28N 105 32W
Pájaros, Pta., *Quintana Roo, Mexico* **223 C6** 19 36N 87 25W
Pájaros Azules, Sa., *Coahuila, Mexico* **214 C4** 27 3N 100 58W
Pakashkan L., *Ont., Canada* **180 C6** 49 21N 90 15W
Pakenham, *Ont., Canada* **176 F6** 45 18N 76 18W
Pakwash L., *Ont., Canada* **180 B3** 50 45N 93 30W
Pala, *CA, U.S.A.* **65 K9** 33 22N 117 5W
Pala Indian Reservation, *CA, U.S.A.* **65 K10** 33 22N 116 58W
Palacios, *TX, U.S.A.* **99 J11** 28 42N 96 13W
Palamos = General Rodrigo M. Quevedo, *Chihuahua, Mexico* **213 B8** 31 46N 107 37W
Palaoa Pt., *HI, U.S.A.* **69 C5** 20 44N 156 58W
Palatine, *IL, U.S.A.* **71 A5** 42 7N 88 3W
Palatka, *FL, U.S.A.* **67 B7** 29 39N 81 38W
Palco, *KS, U.S.A.* **74 B4** 39 15N 99 34W
Palen Dry L., *CA, U.S.A.* **65 K11** 33 46N 115 13W
Palenque, *Chiapas, Mexico* **222 B4** 17 29N 92 1W
Palenque, Parque Nacional △, *Chiapas, Mexico* **222 B4** 17 30N 92 3W
Palermo, *CA, U.S.A.* **64 D5** 39 26N 121 33W
Palermo, *ND, U.S.A.* **91 B3** 48 21N 102 14W
Palestine, *AR, U.S.A.* **63 D5** 34 58N 90 54W
Palestine, *IL, U.S.A.* **71 D6** 39 0N 87 37W
Palestine, *OH, U.S.A.* **92 C2** 40 3N 84 45W
Palestine, *TX, U.S.A.* **99 F12** 31 46N 95 38W
Palestine, L., *TX, U.S.A.* **99 E12** 32 6N 95 27W
Palikea, *HI, U.S.A.* **69 K13** 21 26N 158 6W
Palisade, *CO, U.S.A.* **66 C2** 39 7N 108 21W
Palisade, *NE, U.S.A.* **84 D4** 40 21N 101 7W
Palisades, *ID, U.S.A.* **70 F7** 43 21N 111 13W
Palisades, *WA, U.S.A.* **101 C6** 47 25N 119 54W
Palisades Park, *NJ, U.S.A.* **114 A2** 40 50N 74 1W
Palisades Res., *ID, U.S.A.* **70 F7** 43 20N 111 12W
Palito Blanco, *TX, U.S.A.* **98 K9** 27 35N 98 11W
Palizada, *Campeche, Mexico* **223 D1** 18 15N 92 5W
Palizada, I., *Oaxaca, Mexico* **221 H6** 16 9N 94 12W
Palm Bay, *FL, U.S.A.* **67 C8** 28 2N 80 35W
Palm Beach, *FL, U.S.A.* **67 E8** 26 43N 80 2W
Palm Beach County ☆, *FL, U.S.A.* **67 E8** 26 45N 80 20W
Palm Beach Gardens, *FL, U.S.A.* **67 E8** 26 49N 80 8W
Palm Beach International ✕ (PBI), *FL, U.S.A.* **67 E8** 26 41N 80 6W
Palm City, *San Diego, U.S.A.* **117 C2** 32 35N 117 5W
Palm Coast, *FL, U.S.A.* **67 B7** 29 35N 81 12W
Palm Desert, *CA, U.S.A.* **65 K10** 33 43N 116 22W
Palm Harbor, *FL, U.S.A.* **67 C6** 28 5N 82 46W
Palm Springs, *CA, U.S.A.* **65 K10** 33 50N 116 33W
Palm Valley, *FL, U.S.A.* **67 A7** 30 11N 81 23W
Palmar, Península el, *Campeche, Mexico* **223 D2** 18 50N 91 27W
Palmar Chico, *México, Mexico* **219 D7** 18 42N 100 22W
Palmar Grande, *México, Mexico* **219 D7** 18 36N 100 24W
Palmarolle, *Qué., Canada* **176 C3** 48 40N 79 12W
Palmas, B., *Baja Calif. S., Mexico* **211 K9** 23 40N 109 40W
Palmdale, *CA, U.S.A.* **65 J8** 34 35N 118 7W
Palmdale, *FL, U.S.A.* **67 E7** 26 57N 81 19W
Palmer, *AK, U.S.A.* **61 F10** 61 36N 149 7W
Palmer, *IA, U.S.A.* **73 C4** 42 38N 94 36W
Palmer, *KS, U.S.A.* **74 B6** 39 38N 97 8W
Palmer, *MA, U.S.A.* **78 B2** 42 9N 72 20W
Palmer, *NE, U.S.A.* **84 C7** 41 13N 98 15W
Palmer, *TN, U.S.A.* **97 E7** 35 21N 85 34W
Palmer Lake, *CO, U.S.A.* **66 C6** 39 7N 104 55W
Palmer Park, *MD, U.S.A.* **119 B4** 38 55N 76 52W
Palmers Crossing, *MS, U.S.A.* **81 E4** 31 16N 89 15W
Palmerston, *Ont., Canada* **178 D6** 43 50N 80 51W
Palmerton, *PA, U.S.A.* **87 B1** 40 48N 75 37W
Palmetto, *FL, U.S.A.* **67 D6** 27 31N 82 34W
Palmetto, *GA, U.S.A.* **68 C2** 33 31N 84 40W
Palmetto, *LA, U.S.A.* **75 D4** 30 43N 91 55W
Palmillas, *Tamaulipas, Mexico* **215 G5** 23 18N 99 33W
Palmyra, *IL, U.S.A.* **71 D4** 39 26N 90 0W
Palmyra, *IN, U.S.A.* **72 E4** 38 24N 86 7W
Palmyra, *MO, U.S.A.* **82 B5** 39 48N 91 32W
Palmyra, *NJ, U.S.A.* **87 B1** 40 0N 75 1W
Palmyra, *NE, U.S.A.* **84 D9** 40 42N 96 23W
Palmyra, *PA, U.S.A.* **95 D6** 40 18N 76 36W
Palmyra, *VA, U.S.A.* **102 D6** 37 52N 78 16W
Palmyra Is., *Pac. Oc.* **105 D7** 5 52N 162 5W
Palo, *IA, U.S.A.* **73 C7** 42 4N 91 48W
Palo Alto, *Aguascalientes, Mexico* **217 F9** 21 56N 101 59W
Palo Alto, *Aguascalientes, Mexico* **217 E8** 22 1N 102 41W
Palo Alto, *CA, U.S.A.* **64 F4** 37 27N 122 10W
Palo Alto County ☆, *IA, U.S.A.* **73 B4** 43 5N 94 40W
Palo Duro Cr. →, *TX, U.S.A.* **98 B6** 35 0N 101 55W
Palo Pinto, *TX, U.S.A.* **99 E9** 32 46N 98 18W
Palo Pinto County ☆, *TX, U.S.A.* **99 E9** 32 45N 98 20W
Palo Verde, *Guanajuato, Mexico* **218 B6** 20 20N 101 51W
Palo Verde, *AZ, U.S.A.* **62 D3** 33 21N 112 41W
Palo Verde, *CA, U.S.A.* **65 K12** 33 26N 114 44W
Palomar, *Ont., Canada* **181 D14** 48 10N 82 16W
Palomares, *Oaxaca, Mexico* **221 G5** 17 9N 95 4W
Palomas, *Durango, Mexico* **216 B4** 25 8N 106 10W
Palomas, L., *Chihuahua, Mexico* **213 G12** 26 48N 103 55W
Palos Heights, *Chicago, U.S.A.* **108 D2** 41 39N 87 47W
Palos Hills, *Chicago, U.S.A.* **108 C2** 41 42N 87 49W
Palos Hills Forest, *Chicago, U.S.A.* **108 C1** 41 40N 87 52W
Palos Park, *Chicago, U.S.A.* **108 C1** 41 40N 87 50W
Palos Verdes, Pt., *CA, U.S.A.* **111 D2** 33 46N 118 25W
Palos Verdes Estates, *Los Angeles, U.S.A.* **111 D2** 33 48N 118 23W
Palos Verdes Hills, *Los Angeles, U.S.A.* **111 D2** 33 44N 118 20W
Palouse, *WA, U.S.A.* **101 D8** 46 55N 117 4W
Palouse →, *WA, U.S.A.* **101 D7** 46 35N 118 13W
Pamlico →, *NC, U.S.A.* **90 C9** 35 20N 76 28W
Pamlico County ☆, *NC, U.S.A.* **90 C9** 35 10N 76 45W
Pamlico Sd., *NC, U.S.A.* **90 C10** 35 20N 76 0W
Pampa, *TX, U.S.A.* **98 B7** 35 32N 100 58W
Pamplico, *SC, U.S.A.* **90 E6** 34 0N 79 34W
Pamplin, *VA, U.S.A.* **102 D6** 37 16N 78 41W
Pamunkey →, *VA, U.S.A.* **102 D8** 37 32N 76 48W
Pana, *IL, U.S.A.* **71 D4** 39 23N 89 5W
Panabá, *Yucatán, Mexico* **223 A5** 21 17N 88 16W
Panaca, *NV, U.S.A.* **85 E6** 37 47N 114 23W
Panacea, *FL, U.S.A.* **67 A4** 30 2N 84 23W
Panache, L., *Ont., Canada* **178 A5** 46 15N 81 20W
Panalachic, *Chihuahua, Mexico* **213 F8** 27 40N 107 23W
Panama, *NE, U.S.A.* **84 D9** 40 36N 96 31W
Panama, *OK, U.S.A.* **93 C9** 35 10N 94 40W
Panama City, *FL, U.S.A.* **67 A3** 30 10N 85 40W
Panama City Beach, *FL, U.S.A.* **67 A3** 30 11N 85 48W
Panamint Range, *CA, U.S.A.* **65 G9** 36 20N 117 20W
Panamint Valley, *CA, U.S.A.* **65 G9** 36 15N 117 20W
Pancake Range, *NV, U.S.A.* **85 D5** 38 30N 115 50W
Pancho Villa, *Chihuahua, Mexico* **212 C7** 30 50N 108 40W

Pandora, *OH, U.S.A.* **92 C3** 40 57N 83 58W
Pangburn, *AR, U.S.A.* **63 C4** 35 26N 91 50W
Pangman, *Sask., Canada* **182 F7** 49 39N 104 40W
Pangnirtung, *Nunavut, Canada* **191 D12** 66 8N 65 43W
Panguitch, *UT, U.S.A.* **100 F3** 37 50N 112 26W
Panhandle, *TX, U.S.A.* **98 B6** 35 21N 101 23W
Pānī'au, *HI, U.S.A.* **69 B1** 21 56N 160 5W
Panindícuaro, *Michoacan, Mexico* **218 C6** 19 59N 101 46W
Pannirtuuq = Pangnirtung, *Nunavut, Canada* **191 D12** 66 8N 65 43W
Panny →, *Alta., Canada* **184 A6** 57 8N 114 51W
Panola, *AL, U.S.A.* **60 D2** 32 57N 88 16W
Panola County ☆, *MS, U.S.A.* **81 B4** 34 19N 89 57W
Panola County ☆, *TX, U.S.A.* **99 E13** 32 9N 94 20W
Panora, *IA, U.S.A.* **73 D4** 41 42N 94 22W
Panorama City, *Los Angeles, U.S.A.* **111 A2** 34 13N 118 26W
Panorama Pt., *NE, U.S.A.* **84 C1** 41 0N 104 2W
Pantego, *Dallas-Fort Worth, U.S.A.* **109 B3** 32 42N 97 9W
Pantelhó, *Chiapas, Mexico* **222 C4** 17 0N 92 28W
Panthersville, *Atlanta, U.S.A.* **106 B3** 33 43N 84 16W
Pantitlán, *Distrito Federal, Mexico* **225 B3** 19 24N 99 4W
Pánuco, *Veracruz, Mexico* **220 B2** 22 3N 98 10W
Pánuco, *Zacatecas, Mexico* **217 E8** 22 53N 102 31W
Pánuco →, *Veracruz, Mexico* **220 B3** 22 16N 97 47W
Pánuco de Coronado, *Durango, Mexico* **217 C6** 24 32N 104 20W
Paola, *KS, U.S.A.* **74 C9** 38 35N 94 53W
Paoli, *CO, U.S.A.* **66 B8** 40 37N 102 28W
Paoli, *IN, U.S.A.* **72 E4** 38 33N 86 28W
Paoli, *OK, U.S.A.* **93 D6** 34 50N 97 15W
Paonia, *CO, U.S.A.* **66 D3** 38 52N 107 36W
Pāpā, *HI, U.S.A.* **69 D6** 19 13N 155 52W
Pāpa'aloa, *HI, U.S.A.* **69 D6** 19 59N 155 13W
Papagayo →, *Guerrero, Mexico* **219 F8** 16 46N 99 43W
Papago Park, *Phoenix, U.S.A.* **116 C3** 33 27N 111 56W
Pāpa'ikou, *HI, U.S.A.* **69 D6** 19 47N 155 6W
Papaloapán →, *Veracruz, Mexico* **221 F5** 18 42N 95 38W
Papanoa, B., *Guerrero, Mexico* **219 E6** 17 20N 101 6W
Papanoa, Pta., *Guerrero, Mexico* **219 E6** 17 17N 101 4W
Papantla, *Veracruz, Mexico* **220 D3** 20 27N 97 19W
Papawai Pt., *HI, U.S.A.* **69 C5** 20 47N 156 32W
Papigochic →, *Chihuahua, Mexico* **213 D8** 29 9N 107 57W
Papillion, *NE, U.S.A.* **84 C9** 41 9N 96 3W
Papineau, *IL, U.S.A.* **71 C6** 40 58N 87 43W
Papineau-Labelle, Réserve Faunique de ⌂, *Qué., Canada* **176 E7** 46 10N 75 15W
Papineauville, *Qué., Canada* **176 F7** 45 37N 75 1W
Paquetville, *N.B., Canada* **173 F4** 47 40N 65 5W
Paquimé, *Chihuahua, Mexico* **213 C8** 30 20N 108 0W
Paracho, *Michoacan, Mexico* **218 C5** 19 39N 102 4W
Parachute, *CO, U.S.A.* **66 C2** 39 27N 108 3W
Parácuaro, *Guanajuato, Mexico* **219 B7** 20 9N 100 46W
Parácuaro, *Michoacan, Mexico* **218 C5** 19 7N 102 12W
Parade, *SD, U.S.A.* **91 E4** 45 1N 101 6W
Paradis, *Qué., Canada* **176 C6** 48 15N 76 35W
Paradise, *Nfld. & L., Canada* **174 E8** 47 32N 52 53W
Paradise, *CA, U.S.A.* **64 D5** 39 46N 121 37W
Paradise, *KS, U.S.A.* **74 B5** 39 7N 98 55W
Paradise, *MI, U.S.A.* **79 C6** 46 38N 85 2W
Paradise, *MT, U.S.A.* **83 C3** 47 23N 114 48W
Paradise, *NV, U.S.A.* **85 F5** 36 5N 115 8W
Paradise, *UT, U.S.A.* **100 B4** 41 34N 111 50W
Paradise →, *Nfld. & L., Canada* **175 C6** 53 27N 57 19W
Paradise Hill, *Sask., Canada* **182 B2** 53 32N 109 28W
Paradise Hill, *OK, U.S.A.* **93 C8** 35 40N 95 5W
Paradise Hills, *San Diego, U.S.A.* **117 B2** 32 40N 117 3W
Paradise Valley, *Alta., Canada* **185 E10** 53 2N 110 17W
Paradise Valley, *AZ, U.S.A.* **116 A3** 33 36N 112 0W
Paradise Valley, *AZ, U.S.A.* **62 D4** 33 31N 111 56W
Paradise Valley, *NV, U.S.A.* **85 A3** 41 30N 117 32W
Paradise Valley, *WY, U.S.A.* **104 D6** 42 49N 106 23W
Paragon, *IN, U.S.A.* **72 D4** 39 24N 86 34W
Paragonah, *UT, U.S.A.* **100 F3** 37 53N 112 46W
Paragould, *AR, U.S.A.* **63 B5** 36 3N 90 29W
Paraiso, *Colima, Mexico* **218 D4** 18 53N 103 58W
Paraíso, *Tabasco, Mexico* **222 A3** 18 24N 93 14W
Paraiso →, *Baja Calif. S., Mexico* **211 E4** 28 22N 114 5W
Paramount, *Los Angeles, U.S.A.* **111 C3** 33 53N 118 9W
Paramus, *NJ, U.S.A.* **87 B2** 40 56N 74 2W
Parás, *Nuevo León, Mexico* **214 D5** 26 30N 99 31W
Parchment, *MI, U.S.A.* **79 G6** 42 20N 85 34W
Parco = Sinclair, *WY, U.S.A.* **104 E5** 41 47N 107 7W
Pardee Res., *CA, U.S.A.* **64 E6** 38 16N 120 51W
Pardeeville, *WI, U.S.A.* **103 E4** 43 32N 89 18W
Paredón, *Chiapas, Mexico* **222 C3** 16 2N 93 52W
Paredón, *Coahuila, Mexico* **214 E4** 25 56N 100 58W
Parent, *Qué., Canada* **176 D8** 47 55N 74 35W
Parent, L., *Qué., Canada* **176 C5** 48 31N 77 1W
Parguera, *Puerto Rico* **105 H15** 17 59N 67 3W
Parham, *Ont., Canada* **179 C10** 44 39N 76 43W
Paria →, *AZ, U.S.A.* **62 A4** 36 52N 111 36W
Paria Plateau, *AZ, U.S.A.* **62 A4** 36 50N 111 50W
Paris, *Ont., Canada* **178 D6** 43 12N 80 25W
Paris, *AR, U.S.A.* **63 C2** 35 18N 93 44W
Paris, *ID, U.S.A.* **70 G7** 42 14N 111 24W
Paris, *IL, U.S.A.* **71 D6** 39 36N 87 42W
Paris, *KY, U.S.A.* **97 B8** 38 13N 84 15W
Paris, *ME, U.S.A.* **76 D3** 44 16N 70 30W
Paris, *MS, U.S.A.* **81 B4** 34 11N 89 27W
Paris, *MO, U.S.A.* **82 B5** 39 29N 92 0W
Paris, *TN, U.S.A.* **96 D4** 36 18N 88 19W
Paris, *TX, U.S.A.* **99 D12** 33 40N 95 33W
Parish, *NY, U.S.A.* **89 B4** 43 25N 76 8W
Parishville, *NY, U.S.A.* **89 A6** 44 38N 74 49W
Park, *KS, U.S.A.* **74 B3** 39 7N 100 22W
Park →, *ND, U.S.A.* **91 B8** 48 28N 97 9W
Park City, *KS, U.S.A.* **74 D6** 37 48N 97 20W
Park City, *KY, U.S.A.* **96 C6** 37 6N 86 3W
Park City, *MT, U.S.A.* **83 E9** 45 38N 108 55W
Park City, *UT, U.S.A.* **100 C4** 40 39N 111 30W
Park County ☆, *CO, U.S.A.* **66 C5** 39 0N 105 45W
Park County ☆, *MT, U.S.A.* **83 E7** 45 30N 110 30W
Park County ☆, *WY, U.S.A.* **104 B3** 44 30N 109 30W
Park Falls, *WI, U.S.A.* **103 C3** 45 56N 90 27W
Park Forest, *IL, U.S.A.* **71 B6** 41 29N 87 40W
Park Hills, *KY, U.S.A.* **107 B1** 39 4N 84 31W
Park Hills, *MO, U.S.A.* **82 D6** 37 51N 90 51W
Park Range, *CO, U.S.A.* **66 B4** 40 41N 106 41W
Park Rapids, *MN, U.S.A.* **80 D3** 46 55N 95 4W
Park Ridge, *Chicago, U.S.A.* **108 A1** 42 0N 87 50W
Park Ridge, *NJ, U.S.A.* **87 A2** 41 2N 74 2W
Park River, *ND, U.S.A.* **91 B8** 48 24N 97 45W
Park Road Park, *Charlotte, U.S.A.* **107 B1** 35 8N 80 51W
Park Valley, *UT, U.S.A.* **100 B2** 41 49N 113 20W
Park View, *IA, U.S.A.* **73 D8** 41 42N 90 33W
Parkchester, *NY, U.S.A.* **114 B3** 40 49N 73 50W
Parkdale, *AR, U.S.A.* **63 E4** 33 7N 91 33W
Parkdale, *CO, U.S.A.* **66 D5** 38 29N 105 23W
Parkdale, *OR, U.S.A.* **94 B4** 45 31N 121 36W
Parke County ☆, *IN, U.S.A.* **72 D3** 39 45N 87 10W
Parker, *AZ, U.S.A.* **62 C1** 34 9N 114 17W
Parker, *CO, U.S.A.* **66 C6** 39 31N 104 46W
Parker, *KS, U.S.A.* **74 C8** 38 18N 95 0W
Parker, *SD, U.S.A.* **91 G8** 43 24N 97 8W
Parker, *WA, U.S.A.* **101 D5** 46 30N 120 28W
Parker, C., *Nunavut, Canada* **190 B10** 75 13N 79 30W
Parker City, *IN, U.S.A.* **72 C5** 40 11N 85 12W
Parker County ☆, *TX, U.S.A.* **99 E10** 32 46N 97 48W
Parker Dam, *AZ, U.S.A.* **62 C1** 34 18N 114 8W
Parker River Nat. Wildlife Refuge ⌂, *MA, U.S.A.* **78 B4** 42 45N 70 49W
Parkers Prairie, *MN, U.S.A.* **80 D3** 46 9N 95 20W
Parkersburg, *IL, U.S.A.* **71 E5** 38 36N 88 3W
Parkersburg, *IA, U.S.A.* **73 C6** 42 35N 92 47W
Parkersburg, *WV, U.S.A.* **102 B3** 39 16N 81 34W
Parkerview, *Sask., Canada* **182 D8** 51 21N 103 18W
Parkerville, *KS, U.S.A.* **74 C7** 38 46N 96 40W
Parkesburg, *PA, U.S.A.* **95 E7** 39 58N 75 55W
Parkfield, *CA, U.S.A.* **65 H6** 35 54N 120 26W
Parkhill, *Ont., Canada* **178 D5** 43 15N 81 38W
Parkin, *AR, U.S.A.* **63 C5** 35 16N 90 34W
Parkland, *Ont., Canada* **192 B2** 45 23N 75 40W
Parkland, *WA, U.S.A.* **101 C3** 47 9N 122 26W
Parklawn, *VA, U.S.A.* **119 B3** 38 50N 77 7W
Parkrose, *OR, U.S.A.* **94 B3** 45 34N 122 33W
Parks, *AR, U.S.A.* **63 D2** 34 48N 93 58W
Parks, *NE, U.S.A.* **84 D4** 40 3N 101 44W
Parks L., *Ont., Canada* **181 C9** 49 27N 87 38W
Parkside, *Sask., Canada* **182 B5** 53 10N 106 33W
Parkside, *San Francisco, U.S.A.* **118 B2** 37 44N 122 29W
Parksley, *VA, U.S.A.* **77 C5** 37 47N 75 39W
Parkston, *SD, U.S.A.* **91 G8** 43 24N 97 59W
Parksville, *B.C., Canada* **186 F10** 49 20N 124 21W
Parkton, *MD, U.S.A.* **77 A4** 39 40N 76 40W
Parkville, *MD, U.S.A.* **77 A4** 39 22N 76 32W
Parkville, *NY, U.S.A.* **114 C3** 40 38N 73 57W
Parkway, *CA, U.S.A.* **64 E5** 38 32N 121 26W
Parle, L. qui, *MN, U.S.A.* **80 E3** 45 1N 95 52W
Parleys Summit, *Salt Lake City, U.S.A.* **117 B4** 40 45N 111 37W
Parlier, *CA, U.S.A.* **65 G7** 36 37N 119 32W
Parma, *ID, U.S.A.* **70 F2** 43 47N 116 57W
Parma, *MI, U.S.A.* **79 G7** 42 16N 84 36W
Parma, *MO, U.S.A.* **82 E7** 36 37N 89 48W
Parma, *OH, U.S.A.* **92 B5** 41 24N 81 43W
Parma Heights, *Cleveland, U.S.A.* **107 B1** 41 23N 81 45W
Parmelee, *SD, U.S.A.* **91 G4** 43 19N 101 2W
Parmer County ☆, *TX, U.S.A.* **98 C5** 34 38N 102 45W
Parnell, *IA, U.S.A.* **73 C7** 41 35N 92 0W
Parnell, *MO, U.S.A.* **82 A2** 40 26N 94 37W
Parol, *MD, U.S.A.* **77 B4** 38 59N 76 32W
Parowan, *UT, U.S.A.* **100 F3** 37 51N 112 50W
Parral →, *Chihuahua, Mexico* **213 F10** 27 39N 105 7W
Parramore I., *VA, U.S.A.* **102 D9** 37 32N 75 39W
Parras, *Coahuila, Mexico* **214 E2** 25 25N 102 11W
Parras, Sa. de, *Coahuila, Mexico* **214 E2** 25 24N 102 45W
Parrilla, *Tabasco, Mexico* **222 B4** 17 55N 92 55W
Parris I., *SC, U.S.A.* **90 F5** 32 20N 80 41W
Parrish, *AL, U.S.A.* **60 C3** 33 44N 87 17W
Parrish, *FL, U.S.A.* **67 D6** 27 35N 82 26W
Parrott, *GA, U.S.A.* **68 E2** 31 54N 84 31W
Parrsboro, *N.S., Canada* **173 H5** 45 30N 64 25W
Parry, C., *N.W.T., Canada* **188 B8** 70 20N 123 38W
Parry B., *Nunavut, Canada* **190 D9** 68 6N 81 40W
Parry Channel, *Nunavut, Canada* **190 C7** 74 15N 94 0W
Parry Is., *Canada* **188 A10** 77 0N 110 0W
Parry Pen., *N.W.T., Canada* **188 C8** 69 45N 124 45W
Parry Sound, *Ont., Canada* **178 B6** 45 20N 80 0W
Parshall, *CO, U.S.A.* **66 B4** 40 3N 106 11W
Parshall, *ND, U.S.A.* **91 C3** 47 57N 102 8W
Parsippany, *NJ, U.S.A.* **87 B2** 40 52N 74 26W
Parsnip →, *B.C., Canada* **189 E8** 55 10N 123 2W
Parson, *B.C., Canada* **187 D18** 51 5N 116 37W
Parsons, *KS, U.S.A.* **74 D8** 37 20N 95 16W
Parsons, *TN, U.S.A.* **96 E4** 35 39N 88 8W
Parsons, *WV, U.S.A.* **102 B5** 39 6N 79 41W
Parson's Pond, *Nfld. & L., Canada* **174 B3** 50 2N 57 43W
Parsonsburg, *MD, U.S.A.* **77 B5** 38 22N 75 28W
Partida, I., *Baja Calif., Mexico* **210 E5** 28 55N 113 5W
Partida, I., *Baja Calif. S., Mexico* **211 J8** 24 34N 110 24W
Partridge, *KS, U.S.A.* **74 D5** 37 58N 98 5W
Partridge →, *Ont., Canada* **181 A16** 51 19N 80 18W
Partridge Pt., *Nfld. & L., Canada* **174 B4** 50 10N 56 10W
Pasadena, *Nfld. & L., Canada* **174 C3** 49 1N 57 36W
Pasadena, *CA, U.S.A.* **65 J8** 34 9N 118 8W
Pasadena, *TX, U.S.A.* **99 H12** 29 43N 95 13W
Pasayten →, *N. Amer.* **101 A5** 49 9N 120 36W
Pascagoula, *MS, U.S.A.* **81 F5** 30 21N 88 33W
Pascagoula →, *MS, U.S.A.* **81 F5** 30 23N 88 37W
Pasco, *WA, U.S.A.* **101 D6** 46 14N 119 6W
Pasco County ☆, *FL, U.S.A.* **67 C6** 28 20N 82 30W
Pascoag, *RI, U.S.A.* **78 C3** 41 57N 71 42W
Pasfield L., *Sask., Canada* **189 E11** 58 24N 105 20W
Paskenta, *CA, U.S.A.* **64 D4** 39 53N 122 33W
Paso de Cuarenta, *Jalisco, Mexico* **218 A6** 21 31N 101 45W
Paso de Ovejas, *Veracruz, Mexico* **220 E4** 19 17N 96 26W
Paso de Piedras, Presa, *Veracruz, Mexico* **220 C2** 21 43N 98 8W
Paso de San Antonio, *Chihuahua, Mexico* **213 E12** 28 59N 103 45W
Paso de San Antonio, *San Luis Potosí, Mexico* **215 J4** 22 0N 100 22W
Paso del Macho, *Veracruz, Mexico* **221 F4** 18 58N 96 43W
Paso Robles, *CA, U.S.A.* **65 H6** 35 38N 120 41W
Paspébiac, *N.B., Canada* **173 E4** 48 3N 65 17W
Pasquel, Pta., *Baja Calif. S., Mexico* **211 H7** 25 31N 111 6W
Pasquotank County ☆, *NC, U.S.A.* **90 B9** 36 15N 76 10W
Pass Christian, *MS, U.S.A.* **81 F4** 30 19N 89 15W
Pass Island, *Nfld. & L., Canada* **174 E4** 47 30N 56 12W
Passaconaway, *NH, U.S.A.* **86 C3** 43 59N 71 22W
Passadumkeag, *ME, U.S.A.* **76 C5** 45 11N 68 37W
Passage Pt., *N.W.T., Canada* **188 B9** 73 29N 115 16W
Passaic, *MO, U.S.A.* **82 D2** 38 19N 94 21W
Passaic, *NJ, U.S.A.* **87 B2** 40 51N 74 7W
Passaic →, *NJ, U.S.A.* **114 B2** 40 42N 74 10W
Passaic County ☆, *NJ, U.S.A.* **87 B1** 41 0N 74 20W
Passumpsic →, *VT, U.S.A.* **86 B2** 44 18N 72 3W
Pasteur, L., *Qué., Canada* **172 C3** 50 13N 66 58W
Pastol B., *AK, U.S.A.* **61 E7** 63 7N 163 15W
Pastor Ortiz, *Guanajuato, Mexico* **218 B6** 20 18N 101 37W
Pastora Peak, *AZ, U.S.A.* **62 A6** 36 47N 109 10W
Pastoria, *Veracruz, Mexico* **220 C2** 21 5N 98 7W
Pastura, *NM, U.S.A.* **88 C6** 34 47N 104 57W
Pat Mayse L., *TX, U.S.A.* **99 D12** 33 51N 95 33W
Patagonia, *AZ, U.S.A.* **62 F5** 31 33N 110 45W
Patapsco, *MD, U.S.A.* **77 A4** 39 32N 76 54W
Patapsco →, *MD, U.S.A.* **77 A4** 39 10N 76 26W
Pataskala, *OH, U.S.A.* **92 C4** 40 0N 82 40W
Patch Grove, *WI, U.S.A.* **103 F3** 42 56N 90 58W
Patchogue, *NY, U.S.A.* **87 B3** 40 46N 73 1W
Pateros, *WA, U.S.A.* **101 B6** 48 3N 119 54W
Paterson, *NJ, U.S.A.* **87 B2** 40 54N 74 9W
Paterson, *WA, U.S.A.* **101 E6** 45 56N 119 36W
Patesville, *KY, U.S.A.* **96 C6** 37 47N 86 43W
Pathfinder Res., *WY, U.S.A.* **104 D6** 42 28N 106 51W
Pati Pt., *Guam* **105 b** 13 35N 144 57W
Patillas, *Puerto Rico* **105 G16** 18 1N 66 1W
Patoka, *IL, U.S.A.* **71 E4** 38 45N 89 6W
Patoka, *IN, U.S.A.* **72 E3** 38 24N 87 35W
Patoka →, *IN, U.S.A.* **72 E3** 38 24N 87 45W
Patoka L., *IN, U.S.A.* **72 E4** 38 20N 86 40W
Paton, *IA, U.S.A.* **73 C4** 42 10N 94 16W
Patos, I., *Sonora, Mexico* **212 D3** 29 17N 112 26W
Patricia, *TX, U.S.A.* **98 E5** 32 33N 102 1W
Patrick County ☆, *VA, U.S.A.* **102 E4** 36 55N 80 10W
Patrick's Cove, *Nfld. & L., Canada* **174 E6** 47 3N 54 7W
Patsaliga Cr. →, *AL, U.S.A.* **60 E4** 31 22N 86 31W
Patten, *ME, U.S.A.* **76 B5** 46 0N 68 38W
Patterson, *CA, U.S.A.* **64 F5** 37 28N 121 8W
Patterson, *GA, U.S.A.* **68 E4** 31 23N 82 8W
Patterson, *ID, U.S.A.* **70 E5** 44 32N 113 43W
Patterson, *LA, U.S.A.* **75 E4** 29 42N 91 18W
Patterson, *MO, U.S.A.* **82 D6** 37 11N 90 33W
Patterson, *NY, U.S.A.* **87 A3** 41 31N 73 36W
Patterson, Pt., *MI, U.S.A.* **79 D6** 45 58N 85 39W
Patterson Cr. →, *WV, U.S.A.* **77 A2** 39 34N 78 44W
Pattison, *MS, U.S.A.* **81 E3** 31 53N 90 53W
Patton = Monroeville, *PA, U.S.A.* **95 D3** 40 26N 79 45W
Patton, *PA, U.S.A.* **95 D4** 40 38N 78 39W
Pattonsburg, *MO, U.S.A.* **82 A2** 40 3N 94 8W
Patuxent →, *MD, U.S.A.* **77 B4** 38 18N 76 25W
Patuxent Nat. Wildlife Refuge ⌂, *MD, U.S.A.* **77 A4** 39 6N 76 48W
Patuxent River Naval Air Station, *MD, U.S.A.* **77 B4** 38 17N 76 27W
Pátzcuaro, *Michoacan, Mexico* **218 C6** 19 31N 101 38W
Pátzcuaro, L. de, *Michoacan, Mexico* **218 C6** 19 35N 101 40W
Paul, *ID, U.S.A.* **70 G5** 42 36N 113 47W
Paul I., *Nfld. & L., Canada* **175 B5** 56 30N 61 20W
Paul-Sauvé, L., *Qué., Canada* **176 A4** 50 15N 78 20W
Paul Smiths, *NY, U.S.A.* **89 A6** 44 26N 74 15W
Paulatuk, *N.W.T., Canada* **188 C8** 69 25N 124 0W
Paulden, *AZ, U.S.A.* **62 C3** 34 53N 112 28W
Paulding, *MS, U.S.A.* **81 D4** 32 2N 89 2W
Paulding, *OH, U.S.A.* **92 B2** 41 8N 84 35W
Paulding County ☆, *GA, U.S.A.* **68 C2** 34 0N 84 50W
Paulding County ☆, *OH, U.S.A.* **92 B2** 41 8N 84 35W
Paulina, *OR, U.S.A.* **94 C6** 44 8N 119 58W
Paulina Marsh, *OR, U.S.A.* **94 D4** 43 15N 121 0W
Paulina Pk., *OR, U.S.A.* **94 D4** 43 41N 121 15W
Paulins Kill →, *NJ, U.S.A.* **87 B1** 40 55N 75 5W
Paullina, *IA, U.S.A.* **73 C3** 42 59N 95 41W
Pauls Valley, *OK, U.S.A.* **93 D6** 34 44N 97 13W
Paulsboro, *NJ, U.S.A.* **87 C1** 39 50N 75 15W
Paupack, *PA, U.S.A.* **87 A1** 41 24N 75 12W
Pavillion, *WY, U.S.A.* **104 C4** 43 15N 108 42W
Pavo, *GA, U.S.A.* **68 F3** 30 58N 83 45W
Paw Creek, *NC, U.S.A.* **107 A1** 35 16N 80 56W
Paw Paw, *IL, U.S.A.* **71 B5** 41 41N 88 59W
Paw Paw, *MI, U.S.A.* **79 G6** 42 13N 85 53W
Paw Paw, *WV, U.S.A.* **77 A2** 39 32N 78 28W
Paw Paw Lake, *MI, U.S.A.* **79 G5** 42 13N 86 16W
Pawcatuck, *CT, U.S.A.* **78 C3** 41 22N 71 52W
Pawhuska, *OK, U.S.A.* **93 B7** 36 40N 96 20W
Pawlet, *VT, U.S.A.* **86 C1** 43 20N 73 12W
Pawling, *NY, U.S.A.* **78 C1** 41 34N 73 36W
Pawnee, *IL, U.S.A.* **71 D4** 39 36N 89 35W
Pawnee, *OK, U.S.A.* **93 B7** 36 20N 96 48W
Pawnee →, *KS, U.S.A.* **74 C4** 38 10N 99 6W
Pawnee City, *NE, U.S.A.* **84 D9** 40 7N 96 9W
Pawnee County ☆, *KS, U.S.A.* **74 C4** 38 10N 99 15W
Pawnee County ☆, *NE, U.S.A.* **84 D9** 40 10N 96 20W
Pawnee County ☆, *OK, U.S.A.* **93 B7** 36 20N 96 50W
Pawnee Cr. →, *CO, U.S.A.* **66 B7** 40 34N 103 14W
Pawnee Nat. Grassland, *CO, U.S.A.* **66 B6** 40 40N 104 20W
Pawnee Rock, *KS, U.S.A.* **74 C4** 38 16N 99 1W
Pawtuckaway State Park ⌂, *NH, U.S.A.* **86 C3** 43 7N 71 11W
Pawtucket, *RI, U.S.A.* **78 C3** 41 53N 71 23W
Paxico, *KS, U.S.A.* **74 B7** 39 4N 96 10W
Paxson, *AK, U.S.A.* **61 E11** 63 2N 145 30W
Paxton, *IL, U.S.A.* **71 C5** 40 27N 88 6W
Paxton, *MA, U.S.A.* **78 B3** 42 19N 71 56W
Paxton, *NE, U.S.A.* **84 C4** 41 7N 101 21W
Payette, *ID, U.S.A.* **70 E2** 44 5N 116 56W
Payette →, *ID, U.S.A.* **70 E2** 44 5N 116 57W
Payette County ☆, *ID, U.S.A.* **70 E2** 44 0N 116 55W
Payette L., *ID, U.S.A.* **70 E2** 44 55N 116 7W
Payette Nat. Forest, *ID, U.S.A.* **70 D3** 45 10N 115 30W
Payne, *OH, U.S.A.* **92 B2** 41 5N 84 44W
Payne, B., *Qué., Canada* **175 B4** 60 0N 69 43W
Payne, L., *Qué., Canada* **175 B3** 59 25N 74 0W
Payne Bay = Kangirsuk, *Qué., Canada* **175 A4** 60 0N 70 0W
Payne County ☆, *OK, U.S.A.* **93 B7** 36 5N 97 0W
Payne L., *Qué., Canada* **175 B2** 59 30N 74 30W
Paynesville, *MN, U.S.A.* **80 E4** 45 23N 94 43W
Payo Obispo = Chetumal, *Quintana Roo, Mexico* **223 D5** 18 30N 88 20W
Payson, *AZ, U.S.A.* **62 C4** 34 14N 111 20W
Payson, *IL, U.S.A.* **71 D2** 39 49N 91 15W
Payson, *UT, U.S.A.* **100 C4** 40 3N 111 44W
Paz, B. de la, *Baja Calif. S., Mexico* **211 J8** 24 9N 110 25W
Pe Ell, *WA, U.S.A.* **101 D2** 46 34N 123 18W
Pea →, *AL, U.S.A.* **60 E5** 31 1N 85 51W
Pea Ridge, *AR, U.S.A.* **63 B1** 36 27N 94 7W
Peabody, *KS, U.S.A.* **74 C6** 38 10N 97 7W
Peabody, *MA, U.S.A.* **78 B4** 42 31N 70 56W
Peace →, *Alta., Canada* **189 E10** 59 0N 111 25W
Peace →, *FL, U.S.A.* **67 E6** 26 56N 82 6W
Peace Dale, *RI, U.S.A.* **78 C3** 41 27N 71 30W
Peace Point, *Alta., Canada* **189 E10** 59 7N 112 27W
Peace River, *Alta., Canada* **184 B3** 56 15N 117 18W
Peach County ☆, *GA, U.S.A.* **68 D3** 32 30N 83 50W
Peach Creek, *WV, U.S.A.* **102 D3** 37 53N 81 59W
Peach Orchard, *AR, U.S.A.* **63 B5** 36 17N 90 40W
Peach Springs, *AZ, U.S.A.* **62 B2** 35 32N 113 25W
Peachland, *B.C., Canada* **187 F15** 49 47N 119 45W
Peachtree City, *GA, U.S.A.* **68 C2** 33 25N 84 35W
Peale, Mt., *UT, U.S.A.* **100 E6** 38 26N 109 14W
Pearblossom, *CA, U.S.A.* **65 J9** 34 30N 117 55W
Pearce, *AZ, U.S.A.* **62 F6** 31 54N 109 49W
Pearisburg, *VA, U.S.A.* **102 D4** 37 20N 80 44W
Pearl, *Ont., Canada* **180 D8** 48 40N 88 40W
Pearl, *IL, U.S.A.* **71 D3** 39 28N 90 38W
Pearl, *MS, U.S.A.* **81 D3** 32 18N 90 12W
Pearl →, *MS, U.S.A.* **81 F4** 30 11N 89 32W
Pearl and Hermes Reef, *HI, U.S.A.* **69 F8** 27 55N 175 45W
Pearl City, *HI, U.S.A.* **69 K14** 21 24N 157 59W
Pearl City, *IL, U.S.A.* **71 A4** 42 16N 89 50W
Pearl Harbor, *HI, U.S.A.* **69 K14** 21 21N 157 57W
Pearl Harbor Nat. Wildlife Refuge ⌂, *HI, U.S.A.* **69 K14** 21 23N 157 59W
Pearl River, *LA, U.S.A.* **75 D6** 30 23N 89 45W
Pearl River, *NY, U.S.A.* **87 A2** 41 4N 74 2W
Pearl River County ☆, *MS, U.S.A.* **81 F4** 30 40N 89 38W
Pearland, *TX, U.S.A.* **99 H12** 29 33N 95 17W
Pearsall, *TX, U.S.A.* **99 J8** 28 54N 99 6W
Pearson, *GA, U.S.A.* **68 E4** 31 18N 82 51W
Peary Chan., *Nunavut, Canada* **190 B5** 79 40N 101 30W
Pease, *MN, U.S.A.* **80 E5** 45 42N 93 39W
Pease →, *TX, U.S.A.* **99 C8** 34 12N 99 2W
Peawanuck, *Ont., Canada* **191 F8** 55 15N 85 12W
Pebble Beach, *CA, U.S.A.* **64 G5** 36 34N 121 57W
Pecan Island, *LA, U.S.A.* **75 E3** 29 39N 92 27W
Pecatonica, *IL, U.S.A.* **71 A4** 42 19N 89 22W
Pecatonica →, *IL, U.S.A.* **71 A4** 42 26N 89 12W
Peck, *MI, U.S.A.* **79 F9** 43 16N 82 49W
Peckerwood L., *AR, U.S.A.* **63 D4** 34 40N 91 30W
Pecos, *NM, U.S.A.* **88 B5** 35 35N 105 41W
Pecos, *TX, U.S.A.* **98 F4** 31 26N 103 30W
Pecos →, *TX, U.S.A.* **98 H6** 29 42N 101 22W
Pecos County ☆, *TX, U.S.A.* **98 G5** 30 53N 102 53W
Pecos Nat. Historical Park ⌂, *NM, U.S.A.* **88 B5** 35 33N 105 41W
Pecos Plains, *NM, U.S.A.* **88 D6** 33 15N 104 10W
Peculiar, *MO, U.S.A.* **82 C2** 38 43N 94 28W
Peddocks I., *Boston, U.S.A.* **106 B4** 42 17N 70 56W
Pedernales, *Michoacan, Mexico* **219 C6** 19 8N 101 28W
Pedernales →, *TX, U.S.A.* **99 G9** 30 26N 98 4W
Pedregal de San Angel, Jardines del, *Distrito Federal, Mexico* **225 C2** 19 19N 99 12W
Pedro Antonio de los Santos, *San Luis Potosí, Mexico* **215 J6** 21 36N 98 58W
Pedro Bay, *AK, U.S.A.* **61 G9** 59 47N 154 7W
Pee Dee = Great Pee Dee →, *SC, U.S.A.* **90 E6** 33 21N 79 10W
Peebles, *OH, U.S.A.* **92 E3** 38 57N 83 24W
Peekskill, *NY, U.S.A.* **87 A3** 41 17N 73 55W
Peel →, *Canada* **188 C6** 67 0N 135 0W
Peel Pt., *N.W.T., Canada* **188 B10** 73 22N 114 30W
Peel Sd., *Nunavut, Canada* **190 C6** 73 0N 96 0W
Peerless, *MT, U.S.A.* **83 B12** 48 47N 105 50W
Peerless L., *Alta., Canada* **184 B6** 56 40N 114 35W
Peerless Lake, *Alta., Canada* **184 B6** 56 37N 114 40W
Peers, *Alta., Canada* **184 E4** 53 40N 116 0W
Peetz, *CO, U.S.A.* **66 B7** 40 58N 103 7W
Peever, *SD, U.S.A.* **91 E9** 45 33N 96 57W
Peggs, *OK, U.S.A.* **93 B8** 36 5N 95 6W
Peggys Cove, *N.S., Canada* **173 J6** 44 30N 63 55W
Pegram, *TN, U.S.A.* **96 D5** 36 6N 87 3W
Pékans →, *Qué., Canada* **172 A3** 52 12N 66 49W
Pekin, *IL, U.S.A.* **71 C4** 40 35N 89 40W
Pekin, *ND, U.S.A.* **91 C7** 47 48N 98 20W
Pelahatchie, *MS, U.S.A.* **81 D4** 32 19N 89 48W
Pelee, Pt., *Ont., Canada* **178 F4** 41 54N 82 31W
Pelee I., *Ont., Canada* **178 F4** 41 47N 82 40W
Pelham, *Ont., Canada* **178 D7** 43 3N 79 21W
Pelham, *AL, U.S.A.* **60 C5** 33 44N 85 48W
Pelham, *GA, U.S.A.* **68 E2** 31 8N 84 9W
Pelham, *MA, U.S.A.* **78 B2** 42 24N 72 24W
Pelham, *NH, U.S.A.* **86 D3** 42 44N 71 20W
Pelham, *NY, U.S.A.* **114 A4** 40 54N 73 48W
Pelham Bay Park, *NY, U.S.A.* **114 A4** 40 51N 73 48W
Pelham Manor, *NY, U.S.A.* **114 A4** 40 53N 73 48W
Pelican, *AK, U.S.A.* **61 H13** 57 58N 136 14W
Pelican, *LA, U.S.A.* **75 C2** 31 53N 93 35W
Pélican, L. du, *Qué., Canada* **175 B3** 59 47N 73 35W
Pelican L., *Alta., Canada* **184 C7** 55 48N 113 15W
Pelican L., *Man., Canada* **183 C11** 52 28N 100 20W
Pelican L., *MN, U.S.A.* **80 B6** 48 4N 92 55W
Pelican Narrows, *Sask., Canada* **189 E12** 55 10N 102 56W
Pelican Rapids, *Man., Canada* **183 C11** 52 45N 100 42W
Pelican Rapids, *MN, U.S.A.* **80 D2** 46 34N 96 5W
Pelícano, I., *Sonora, Mexico* **212 B1** 31 45N 114 36W
Pelícano, Is. el, *Baja Calif. S., Mexico* **211 G5** 26 55N 113 10W
Pell City, *AL, U.S.A.* **60 C4** 33 35N 86 17W
Pella, *IA, U.S.A.* **73 D6** 41 25N 92 55W
Pellston, *MI, U.S.A.* **79 D7** 45 33N 84 47W
Pellville, *KY, U.S.A.* **96 C6** 37 45N 86 49W
Pelly, *Sask., Canada* **183 D10** 51 52N 101 56W
Pelly →, *Yukon, Canada* **189 D5** 62 47N 137 19W
Pelly B., *Nunavut, Canada* **190 D7** 68 53N 90 5W
Pelly Bay, *Nunavut, Canada* **190 D8** 68 38N 89 50W
Pelly Crossing, *N.W.T., Canada* **189 D5** 62 49N 136 34W
Pelly L., *Nunavut, Canada* **191 D5** 66 0N 102 0W
Pelly Mts., *Yukon, Canada* **189 D6** 61 40N 132 30W
Peloncillo Mts., *AZ, U.S.A.* **62 E6** 32 20N 109 20W
Pemadumcook L., *ME, U.S.A.* **76 C5** 45 42N 68 57W
Pemberton, *B.C., Canada* **187 E12** 50 25N 122 50W
Pemberton, *MN, U.S.A.* **80 F5** 44 1N 93 47W
Pemberton, *NJ, U.S.A.* **87 C2** 39 58N 74 41W
Pemberville, *OH, U.S.A.* **92 B3** 41 25N 83 28W
Pembina, *ND, U.S.A.* **91 B8** 48 58N 97 15W
Pembina →, *Alta., Canada* **184 D6** 54 45N 114 17W
Pembina →, *ND, U.S.A.* **91 B8** 48 58N 97 14W
Pembina County ☆, *ND, U.S.A.* **91 B8** 48 48N 97 37W
Pembine, *WI, U.S.A.* **103 C6** 45 38N 87 59W
Pembroke, *Ont., Canada* **179 B9** 45 50N 77 7W
Pembroke, *GA, U.S.A.* **68 D5** 32 8N 81 37W
Pembroke, *KY, U.S.A.* **96 D5** 36 47N 87 21W
Pembroke, *MA, U.S.A.* **78 B4** 42 5N 70 48W
Pembroke, *MI, U.S.A.* **109 A2** 42 26N 83 11W
Pembroke, *NC, U.S.A.* **90 D6** 34 41N 79 12W
Pembroke Pines, *FL, U.S.A.* **67 E8** 26 0N 80 13W
Pemigewasset →, *NH, U.S.A.* **86 C3** 43 26N 71 40W
Pemiscot County ☆, *MO, U.S.A.* **82 E7** 36 10N 89 50W
Pen Argyl, *PA, U.S.A.* **87 B1** 40 52N 75 16W
Peña Nevada, Cerro, *Nuevo León, Mexico* **215 G5** 23 46N 99 52W
Penacook, *NH, U.S.A.* **86 C3** 43 15N 71 40W
Penalosa, *KS, U.S.A.* **74 D5** 37 43N 98 19W
Peñamiller, *Querétaro, Mexico* **219 A8** 21 3N 99 49W
Penasco, *NM, U.S.A.* **88 A5** 36 10N 105 41W
Peñasco →, *NM, U.S.A.* **88 E6** 32 40N 104 25W
Pend Oreille →, *WA, U.S.A.* **101 A8** 49 4N 117 37W
Pend Oreille, L., *ID, U.S.A.* **70 A2** 48 10N 116 21W
Pend Oreille County ☆, *WA, U.S.A.* **101 B8** 48 30N 117 10W
Pender, *NE, U.S.A.* **84 B9** 42 7N 96 43W
Pender County ☆, *NC, U.S.A.* **90 D8** 34 30N 78 0W
Pendergrass, *GA, U.S.A.* **68 B3** 34 10N 83 41W
Pendleton, *IN, U.S.A.* **72 D5** 40 0N 85 45W
Pendleton, *OR, U.S.A.* **94 B7** 45 40N 118 47W
Pendleton County ☆, *KY, U.S.A.* **97 B8** 38 40N 84 20W
Pendleton County ☆, *WV, U.S.A.* **102 C5** 38 47N 79 17W
Pendroy, *MT, U.S.A.* **83 B5** 48 4N 112 18W
Penelope, *TX, U.S.A.* **99 F11** 31 52N 96 56W
Penetanguishene, *Nfld. & L., Canada* **174 E8** 47 36N 52 45W
Penetanguishene, *Ont., Canada* **178 C7** 44 50N 79 55W
Penfield, *PA, U.S.A.* **95 C4** 41 13N 78 35W
Penhold, *Alta., Canada* **185 F7** 52 8N 113 52W
Peñitas, Presa, *Chiapas, Mexico* **222 B3** 17 25N 93 27W
Peñitas, Pta. las, *Jalisco, Mexico* **218 B2** 20 4N 105 33W
Penjamillo, *Michoacan, Mexico* **218 B6** 20 6N 101 54W
Pénjamo, *Guanajuato, Mexico* **218 B6** 20 26N 101 44W
Penn = Penn Hills, *PA, U.S.A.* **95 D3** 40 28N 79 52W
Penn Hills, *PA, U.S.A.* **95 D3** 40 28N 79 52W
Penn Wynne, *PA, U.S.A.* **116 B1** 39 59N 75 16W
Penn Yan, *NY, U.S.A.* **89 C3** 42 40N 77 3W
Pennant, *Sask., Canada* **182 E3** 50 32N 108 14W
Pennell, Mt., *UT, U.S.A.* **100 F5** 37 58N 110 47W
Penniac, *N.B., Canada* **173 G3** 46 2N 66 34W
Pennington, *AL, U.S.A.* **60 D2** 32 13N 88 3W
Pennington, *NJ, U.S.A.* **87 B2** 40 19N 74 48W
Pennington County ☆, *MN, U.S.A.* **80 B3** 48 5N 96 0W
Pennington County ☆, *SD, U.S.A.* **91 G2** 44 0N 103 0W
Pennington Gap, *VA, U.S.A.* **102 E1** 36 46N 83 2W
Pennock, *MN, U.S.A.* **80 E3** 45 9N 95 10W
Penns Grove, *NJ, U.S.A.* **87 C1** 39 44N 75 28W
Pennsauken, *NJ, U.S.A.* **87 C1** 39 58N 75 3W
Pennsboro, *WV, U.S.A.* **102 B4** 39 17N 80 58W
Pennsburg, *PA, U.S.A.* **87 B1** 40 23N 75 29W
Pennsville, *NJ, U.S.A.* **87 C1** 39 39N 75 31W
Pennsylvania □, *U.S.A.* **95 D5** 40 45N 77 30W
Pennville, *IN, U.S.A.* **72 C5** 40 30N 85 9W

Penny, *B.C., Canada* **187 B13** 53 51N 121 20W
Penny Ice Cap, *Nunavut, Canada* **190 D12** 67 17N 66 13W
Penny Str., *Nunavut, Canada* **190 B6** 76 30N 97 0W
Pennypack Park, *PA, U.S.A.* **116 A2** 40 3N 75 2W
Pennyrile State Forest, *KY, U.S.A.* **96 C5** 37 11N 87 33W
Penobscot ➜, *ME, U.S.A.* **76 D5** 44 30N 68 48W
Penobscot B., *ME, U.S.A.* **76 D5** 44 35N 68 50W
Penobscot County ☆, *ME, U.S.A.* **76 C5** 45 0N 69 0W
Peñón Blanco, *Durango, Mexico* **217 C6** 24 47N 104 2W
Penrose, *CO, U.S.A.* **66 D5** 38 26N 105 1W
Pensacola, *FL, U.S.A.* **67 A1** 30 25N 87 13W
Pensacola, *OK, U.S.A.* **93 B8** 36 28N 95 7W
Pensacola B., *FL, U.S.A.* **67 A1** 30 25N 87 5W
Pense, *Sask., Canada* **182 E7** 50 25N 104 59W
Pentecôte ➜, *Qué., Canada* **172 D2** 49 46N 67 10W
Pentecôte, L., *Qué., Canada* **172 D2** 49 53N 67 20W
Penticton, *B.C., Canada* **187 F15** 49 30N 119 38W
Pentwater, *MI, U.S.A.* **79 F5** 43 47N 86 26W
Penwell, *TX, U.S.A.* **98 F5** 31 45N 102 36W
Peoria, *AZ, U.S.A.* **62 D3** 33 43N 112 14W
Peoria, *IL, U.S.A.* **71 C4** 40 42N 89 36W
Peoria, *OK, U.S.A.* **93 B9** 36 54N 94 41W
Peoria County ☆, *IL, U.S.A.* **71 C4** 40 45N 89 45W
Peoria Heights, *IL, U.S.A.* **71 C4** 40 45N 89 35W
Peotone, *IL, U.S.A.* **71 B6** 41 20N 87 48W
Pep, *NM, U.S.A.* **88 D7** 33 50N 103 20W
Pepacton Res., *NY, U.S.A.* **89 C6** 42 5N 74 58W
Pepeekeo, *HI, U.S.A.* **69 D6** 19 51N 155 6W
Pepin, *WI, U.S.A.* **103 D1** 44 27N 92 9W
Pepin County ☆, *WI, U.S.A.* **103 D1** 44 30N 92 10W
Pepperell, *MA, U.S.A.* **78 B3** 42 40N 71 35W
Pequannock, *NJ, U.S.A.* **87 B2** 40 57N 74 18W
Pequeña, Pta., *Baja Calif. S., Mexico* **211 G6** 26 15N 112 30W
Pequest ➜, *NJ, U.S.A.* **87 B1** 40 50N 75 5W
Pequop Mts., *NV, U.S.A.* **85 B6** 40 45N 114 40W
Pequot Lakes, *MN, U.S.A.* **80 D4** 46 36N 94 19W
Peralta, *NM, U.S.A.* **88 C4** 34 50N 106 41W
Percé, *Qué., Canada* **172 E5** 48 31N 64 13W
Perdido, *AL, U.S.A.* **60 E3** 31 0N 87 38W
Perdido ➜, *AL, U.S.A.* **60 F3** 30 27N 87 23W
Perdido, L. el, *San Luis Potosí, Mexico* **215 G3** 23 17N 101 43W
Perdido B., *AL, U.S.A.* **60 F3** 30 20N 87 30W
Perdue, *Sask., Canada* **182 C4** 52 4N 107 33W
Perham, *MN, U.S.A.* **80 D3** 46 36N 95 34W
Peribán, *Michoacan, Mexico* **218 C5** 19 30N 102 25W
Péribonka, *Qué., Canada* **177 C10** 48 46N 72 3W
Péribonka ➜, *Qué., Canada* **175 D3** 48 45N 72 5W
Péribonka, L., *Qué., Canada* **177 A11** 50 1N 71 10W
Pericos, *Sinaloa, Mexico* **216 B3** 25 3N 107 42W
Peridot, *AZ, U.S.A.* **62 D5** 33 18N 110 28W
Perkasie, *PA, U.S.A.* **87 B1** 40 22N 75 18W
Perkins, *GA, U.S.A.* **68 D5** 32 55N 81 57W
Perkins, *OK, U.S.A.* **93 C6** 35 58N 97 2W
Perkins County ☆, *NE, U.S.A.* **84 D4** 40 45N 101 45W
Perkins County ☆, *SD, U.S.A.* **91 E3** 45 30N 102 30W
Perkinston, *MS, U.S.A.* **81 F4** 30 47N 89 8W
Perkiomen ➜, *PA, U.S.A.* **87 B1** 40 7N 75 28W
Perley, *MN, U.S.A.* **80 C2** 47 11N 96 48W
Perma, *MT, U.S.A.* **83 C3** 47 22N 114 35W
Pernell, *OK, U.S.A.* **93 D6** 34 34N 97 31W
Perote, *Veracruz, Mexico* **220 E3** 19 34N 97 14W
Perquimans County ☆, *NC, U.S.A.* **90 B9** 36 10N 76 30W
Perrin, *TX, U.S.A.* **99 D9** 33 2N 98 4W
Perrine, *FL, U.S.A.* **67 F8** 25 36N 80 21W
Perris, *CA, U.S.A.* **65 K9** 33 47N 117 14W
Perro, L. del, *NM, U.S.A.* **88 C5** 34 41N 105 58W
Perry, *AR, U.S.A.* **63 C3** 35 3N 92 48W
Perry, *FL, U.S.A.* **67 A5** 30 7N 83 35W
Perry, *GA, U.S.A.* **68 D3** 32 28N 83 44W
Perry, *IL, U.S.A.* **71 D3** 39 47N 90 45W
Perry, *IA, U.S.A.* **73 D4** 41 51N 94 6W
Perry, *KS, U.S.A.* **74 B8** 39 5N 95 24W
Perry, *ME, U.S.A.* **76 D6** 44 58N 67 5W
Perry, *MI, U.S.A.* **79 G7** 42 50N 84 13W
Perry, *MO, U.S.A.* **82 B5** 39 26N 91 40W
Perry, *NY, U.S.A.* **89 C2** 42 43N 78 0W
Perry, *OK, U.S.A.* **93 B6** 36 17N 97 14W
Perry, *UT, U.S.A.* **100 B3** 41 28N 112 2W
Perry County ☆, *AL, U.S.A.* **60 D3** 32 38N 87 19W
Perry County ☆, *AR, U.S.A.* **63 D3** 35 0N 92 48W
Perry County ☆, *IL, U.S.A.* **71 E4** 38 5N 89 20W
Perry County ☆, *IN, U.S.A.* **72 E4** 38 5N 86 40W
Perry County ☆, *KY, U.S.A.* **97 C9** 37 15N 83 15W
Perry County ☆, *MS, U.S.A.* **81 E4** 31 12N 89 2W
Perry County ☆, *MO, U.S.A.* **82 D7** 37 45N 89 50W
Perry County ☆, *OH, U.S.A.* **92 D4** 39 43N 82 12W
Perry County ☆, *PA, U.S.A.* **95 D5** 40 35N 77 5W
Perry County ☆, *TN, U.S.A.* **96 E5** 35 39N 87 50W
Perry Hall, *MD, U.S.A.* **77 A4** 39 25N 76 28W
Perry Lake, *KS, U.S.A.* **74 B8** 39 7N 95 26W
Perrydale, *OR, U.S.A.* **94 B2** 45 3N 123 16W
Perrysburg, *OH, U.S.A.* **92 B3** 41 34N 83 38W
Perrysville, *OH, U.S.A.* **92 C4** 40 40N 82 19W
Perrysville, *Pittsburgh, U.S.A.* **116 A1** 40 32N 80 1W
Perryton, *TX, U.S.A.* **98 A7** 36 24N 100 48W
Perryville, *AK, U.S.A.* **61 J8** 55 55N 159 9W
Perryville, *AR, U.S.A.* **63 C3** 35 0N 92 48W
Perryville, *KY, U.S.A.* **97 C8** 37 39N 84 57W
Perryville, *MD, U.S.A.* **77 A4** 39 34N 76 4W
Perryville, *MO, U.S.A.* **82 D7** 37 43N 89 52W
Pershing, *MI, U.S.A.* **109 A2** 42 26N 83 3W
Pershing County ☆, *NV, U.S.A.* **85 B2** 40 20N 118 10W
Persia, *IA, U.S.A.* **73 D3** 41 35N 95 33W
Person County ☆, *NC, U.S.A.* **90 B7** 36 15N 79 0W
Perth, *Ont., Canada* **179 C10** 44 55N 76 15W
Perth, *KS, U.S.A.* **74 D6** 37 11N 97 31W
Perth, *ND, U.S.A.* **91 B6** 48 43N 99 28W
Perth Amboy, *NJ, U.S.A.* **87 B2** 40 30N 74 15W
Perth-Andover, *N.B., Canada* **173 G2** 46 44N 67 42W
Peru, *IL, U.S.A.* **71 B4** 41 20N 89 8W
Peru, *IN, U.S.A.* **72 C4** 40 45N 86 4W
Peru, *KS, U.S.A.* **74 D7** 37 5N 96 6W
Peru, *NY, U.S.A.* **86 B1** 44 35N 73 32W
Peru, *NE, U.S.A.* **84 D10** 40 29N 95 44W
Peru, *VT, U.S.A.* **86 C2** 43 14N 72 54W
Peshtigo, *WI, U.S.A.* **103 C6** 45 3N 87 45W
Peshtigo ➜, *WI, U.S.A.* **103 D6** 44 58N 87 40W
Pesotum, *IL, U.S.A.* **71 D5** 39 55N 88 16W
Pesqueira, *Sonora, Mexico* **212 D5** 29 23N 110 54W
Pesquería, *Nuevo León, Mexico* **214 E4** 25 45N 100 4W
Pesquería ➜, *Nuevo León, Mexico* **214 E5** 25 53N 99 11W
Petacalco, B. de, *Guerrero, Mexico* **218 E5** 17 57N 102 5W
Petal, *MS, U.S.A.* **81 E4** 31 21N 89 16W
Petalcingo, *Chiapas, Mexico* **222 B4** 17 17N 92 27W
Petaluma, *CA, U.S.A.* **64 E4** 38 14N 122 39W
Petatlán, *Guerrero, Mexico* **219 E6** 17 31N 101 16W
Petawawa, *Ont., Canada* **179 B9** 45 54N 77 17W
Petcacab, *Quintana Roo, Mexico* **223 C5** 19 16N 88 12W
Petenwell L., *WI, U.S.A.* **103 D3** 44 4N 90 1W
Peter I., *Br. Virgin Is.* **105 G18** 18 22N 64 35W
Peter Lougheed Prov. Park ⌓, *Alta., Canada* **185 H5** 50 42N 115 10W
Peter O. Knight ✈, *Tampa, U.S.A.* **119 B4** 27 54N 82 26W
Peter Pond L., *Sask., Canada* **189 E11** 55 55N 108 44W
Peterbell, *Ont., Canada* **181 D13** 48 36N 83 21W
Peterborough, *Ont., Canada* **179 C8** 44 20N 78 20W
Peterborough, *NH, U.S.A.* **86 D3** 42 53N 71 57W
Peterman, *AL, U.S.A.* **60 E3** 31 35N 87 16W
Peters, L., *Qué., Canada* **175 B3** 59 41N 70 53W
Petersburg, *AK, U.S.A.* **61 H14** 56 48N 132 58W
Petersburg, *IL, U.S.A.* **71 C4** 40 1N 89 51W
Petersburg, *IN, U.S.A.* **72 E3** 38 30N 87 17W
Petersburg, *MI, U.S.A.* **79 H8** 41 54N 83 43W
Petersburg, *ND, U.S.A.* **91 C7** 48 0N 98 0W
Petersburg, *NJ, U.S.A.* **87 C2** 39 15N 74 43W
Petersburg, *NY, U.S.A.* **78 B1** 42 44N 73 20W
Petersburg, *NE, U.S.A.* **84 C7** 41 51N 98 5W
Petersburg, *OH, U.S.A.* **92 C6** 40 55N 80 32W
Petersburg, *PA, U.S.A.* **95 D4** 40 34N 78 3W
Petersburg, *TN, U.S.A.* **96 E6** 35 19N 86 38W
Petersburg, *TX, U.S.A.* **98 D6** 33 52N 101 36W
Petersburg, *VA, U.S.A.* **102 D7** 37 14N 77 24W
Petersburg, *WV, U.S.A.* **102 B5** 39 1N 79 5W
Petersfield, *Man., Canada* **183 E15** 50 18N 96 58W
Petersham, *MA, U.S.A.* **78 B2** 42 29N 72 11W
Peterson, *IA, U.S.A.* **73 C3** 42 55N 95 21W
Peterson, *MN, U.S.A.* **80 G7** 43 47N 91 50W
Peterson Field, Colorado Springs ✈ (COS), *CO, U.S.A.* **66 D6** 38 49N 104 43W
Peterstown, *WV, U.S.A.* **102 D4** 37 24N 80 48W
Petersville, *KY, U.S.A.* **97 B9** 38 27N 83 30W
Peterview, *Nfld. & L., Canada* **174 C5** 49 7N 55 21W
Petit Bois I., *MS, U.S.A.* **81 F5** 30 12N 88 26W
Petit-Cap, *Qué, Canada* **172 D5** 49 3N 64 30W
Petit-de-Grat, *N.S., Canada* **173 H9** 45 30N 60 58W
Petit Étang, *N.S., Canada* **173 G9** 46 39N 60 58W
Petit Jean State Park ⌓, *AR, U.S.A.* **63 C3** 35 7N 92 56W
Petit Lac Manicouagan, *Qué., Canada* **172 B2** 51 25N 67 40W
Petit Manan Pt., *ME, U.S.A.* **76 D6** 44 24N 67 54W
Petit-Mécatina ➜, *Qué., Canada* **175 C6** 50 40N 59 30W
Petit-Mécatina, Î. du, *Qué., Canada* **175 C6** 50 30N 59 25W
Petit-Rocher, *N.B., Canada* **173 F4** 47 46N 65 43W
Petit-Saguenay, *Qué., Canada* **177 C12** 48 15N 70 4W
Petitcodiac, *N.B., Canada* **173 H4** 45 57N 65 11W
Petite-Rivière, *Qué., Canada* **177 D12** 47 20N 70 33W
Petite Rivière Bridge, *N.S., Canada* **173 J5** 44 14N 64 27W
Petitot ➜, *B.C., Canada* **189 D8** 60 14N 123 29W
Petitsikapau L., *Nfld. & L., Canada* **175 C4** 54 37N 66 25W
Petlalcingo, *Puebla, Mexico* **221 F3** 18 5N 97 54W
Peto, *Yucatán, Mexico* **223 B5** 20 8N 88 55W
Petoskey, *MI, U.S.A.* **79 D7** 45 22N 84 57W
Petrey, *AL, U.S.A.* **60 E4** 31 51N 86 13W
Petrified Forest Nat. Park △, *AZ, U.S.A.* **62 B6** 35 0N 109 30W
Petroglyph Nat. Monument ⌓, *NM, U.S.A.* **88 B4** 35 10N 106 43W
Petroleum, *WV, U.S.A.* **102 B3** 39 11N 81 16W
Petroleum County ☆, *MT, U.S.A.* **83 C9** 47 7N 108 25W
Petrolia, *Ont., Canada* **178 E4** 42 54N 82 9W
Petrolia, *KS, U.S.A.* **74 D8** 37 45N 95 29W
Petrolia, *TX, U.S.A.* **99 C9** 34 1N 98 14W
Petros, *TN, U.S.A.* **97 D8** 36 6N 84 27W
Pettibone, *ND, U.S.A.* **91 C6** 47 7N 99 31W
Pettis County ☆, *MO, U.S.A.* **82 C3** 38 40N 93 15W
Pettus, *TX, U.S.A.* **99 J10** 28 37N 97 48W
Petty Harbour Long Pond, *Nfld. & L., Canada* **174 E8** 47 31N 52 58W
Pettys Island, *NJ, U.S.A.* **116 B2** 39 57N 75 6W
Pfeifer, *KS, U.S.A.* **74 C4** 38 43N 99 10W
Phalen, L., *Minneapolis-St. Paul, U.S.A.* **113 B3** 44 59N 93 3W
Phalen Park, *Minneapolis-St. Paul, U.S.A.* **113 B3** 44 59N 93 3W
Pharr, *TX, U.S.A.* **98 L9** 26 12N 98 11W
Pheba, *MS, U.S.A.* **81 C5** 33 35N 88 57W
Phelps, *KY, U.S.A.* **97 C10** 37 32N 82 9W
Phelps, *NY, U.S.A.* **89 C3** 42 58N 77 3W
Phelps, *WI, U.S.A.* **103 B4** 46 4N 89 5W
Phelps County ☆, *MO, U.S.A.* **82 D5** 37 55N 91 45W
Phelps County ☆, *NE, U.S.A.* **84 D6** 40 30N 99 30W
Phelps L., *Sask., Canada* **189 E12** 59 15N 103 15W
Phelps L., *NC, U.S.A.* **90 C9** 35 46N 76 27W
Phenix, *VA, U.S.A.* **102 D6** 37 5N 78 45W
Phenix City, *AL, U.S.A.* **60 D5** 32 28N 85 0W
Phil Campbell, *AL, U.S.A.* **60 B3** 34 21N 87 42W
Philadelphia, *MS, U.S.A.* **81 D4** 32 46N 89 7W
Philadelphia, *NY, U.S.A.* **89 A5** 44 9N 75 43W
Philadelphia, *PA, U.S.A.* **87 C1** 39 57N 75 9W
Philadelphia, *TN, U.S.A.* **97 E8** 35 41N 84 24W
Philadelphia County ☆, *PA, U.S.A.* **95 E7** 39 57N 75 10W
Philadelphia International ✈ (PHL), *PA, U.S.A.* **116 B1** 39 51N 75 18W
Philip, *SD, U.S.A.* **91 F4** 44 2N 101 40W
Philip Smith Mts., *AK, U.S.A.* **61 C10** 68 0N 148 0W
Philippi, *WV, U.S.A.* **102 B4** 39 9N 80 3W
Philip's L., *OR, U.S.A.* **94 B2** 45 25N 123 13W
Philipsburg, *Qué., Canada* **177 F9** 45 2N 73 5W
Philipsburg, *MT, U.S.A.* **83 D4** 46 20N 113 18W
Philipsburg, *PA, U.S.A.* **95 D4** 40 54N 78 13W
Phillips, *ME, U.S.A.* **76 D3** 44 49N 70 21W
Phillips, *NE, U.S.A.* **84 D7** 40 54N 98 13W
Phillips, *OK, U.S.A.* **93 D7** 34 30N 96 12W
Phillips, *TX, U.S.A.* **98 B6** 35 42N 101 22W
Phillips, *WI, U.S.A.* **103 C3** 45 42N 90 24W
Phillips County ☆, *AR, U.S.A.* **63 D5** 34 19N 90 51W
Phillips County ☆, *CO, U.S.A.* **66 B8** 40 40N 102 20W
Phillips County ☆, *KS, U.S.A.* **74 B4** 39 45N 99 15W
Phillips County ☆, *MT, U.S.A.* **83 B10** 48 12N 108 0W
Phillips Inlet, *Nunavut, Canada* **190 A8** 82 5N 86 10W
Phillipsburg, *GA, U.S.A.* **68 E3** 31 25N 83 30W
Phillipsburg, *KS, U.S.A.* **74 B4** 39 45N 99 19W
Phillipsburg, *MO, U.S.A.* **82 D4** 37 33N 92 47W
Phillipsburg, *NJ, U.S.A.* **87 B1** 40 42N 75 12W
Philmont, *NY, U.S.A.* **89 C7** 42 15N 73 39W
Philo, *CA, U.S.A.* **64 D3** 39 4N 123 26W
Philo, *IL, U.S.A.* **71 C5** 40 1N 88 9W
Philomath, *GA, U.S.A.* **68 C4** 33 44N 82 59W
Philomath, *OR, U.S.A.* **94 C2** 44 32N 123 22W
Philpott Res., *VA, U.S.A.* **102 E4** 36 47N 80 2W
Phippsburg, *CO, U.S.A.* **66 B4** 40 14N 106 57W
Phoenix, *AZ, U.S.A.* **62 D3** 33 26N 112 4W
Phoenix, *LA, U.S.A.* **75 E6** 29 39N 89 56W
Phoenix, *NY, U.S.A.* **89 B4** 43 14N 76 18W
Phoenix, *OR, U.S.A.* **94 E3** 42 16N 122 49W
Phoenix Sky Harbour ✈ (PHX), *AZ, U.S.A.* **62 D3** 33 26N 112 5W
Phoenixville, *PA, U.S.A.* **87 B1** 40 8N 75 31W
Piapot, *Sask., Canada* **182 F2** 49 59N 109 8W
Piashti, L., *Qué., Canada* **172 C7** 50 29N 62 52W
Piatt County ☆, *IL, U.S.A.* **71 D5** 40 0N 88 35W
Piaxtla, *Puebla, Mexico* **221 F2** 18 12N 98 14W
Piaxtla ➜, *Sinaloa, Mexico* **216 D4** 23 42N 106 49W
Pic ➜, *Ont., Canada* **181 D10** 48 36N 86 18W
Pic I., *Ont., Canada* **181 D10** 48 43N 86 37W
Picacho, *AZ, U.S.A.* **62 E4** 32 43N 111 30W
Picacho, *NM, U.S.A.* **88 D5** 33 21N 105 9W
Picacho Pass, *AZ, U.S.A.* **62 E4** 32 40N 111 25W
Picachos, Sa. los, *Michoacan, Mexico* **218 D6** 18 50N 101 30W
Picayune, *MS, U.S.A.* **81 F4** 30 32N 89 41W
Piccadilly, *Nfld. & L., Canada* **174 D2** 48 34N 58 55W
Piceance Cr. ➜, *CO, U.S.A.* **66 B2** 40 5N 108 14W
Pich, *Campeche, Mexico* **223 C3** 19 31N 90 5W
Picher, *OK, U.S.A.* **93 B9** 36 59N 94 50W
Pichilingue, *Baja Calif. S., Mexico* **211 J8** 24 15N 110 20W
Pichucalco, *Chiapas, Mexico* **222 B3** 17 31N 93 4W
Pickaway County ☆, *OH, U.S.A.* **92 D4** 39 43N 82 59W
Pickens, *AR, U.S.A.* **63 E4** 33 51N 91 29W
Pickens, *MS, U.S.A.* **81 D4** 32 53N 89 58W
Pickens, *OK, U.S.A.* **93 D8** 34 23N 95 2W
Pickens, *SC, U.S.A.* **90 D3** 34 53N 82 42W
Pickens, *WV, U.S.A.* **102 C4** 38 39N 80 13W
Pickens County ☆, *AL, U.S.A.* **60 C2** 33 16N 88 6W
Pickens County ☆, *GA, U.S.A.* **68 B2** 34 30N 84 25W
Pickens County ☆, *SC, U.S.A.* **90 D3** 34 50N 82 45W
Pickerel L., *Ont., Canada* **180 D5** 48 40N 91 25W
Pickering, *MO, U.S.A.* **82 A2** 40 27N 94 49W
Pickerington, *OH, U.S.A.* **92 D4** 39 53N 82 45W
Pickett County ☆, *TN, U.S.A.* **97 D7** 36 34N 85 8W
Pickford, *MI, U.S.A.* **79 C7** 46 10N 84 22W
Pickle Lake, *Ont., Canada* **180 A6** 51 30N 90 12W
Pickrell, *NE, U.S.A.* **84 D9** 40 23N 96 44W
Pickstown, *SD, U.S.A.* **91 G7** 43 4N 98 32W
Pickwick L., *AL, U.S.A.* **60 A2** 35 4N 88 15W
Pico de Orizaba, Parque Nacional △, *Puebla, Mexico* **221 E3** 19 0N 97 20W
Pico de Tancítaro, Parque Nacional △, *Michoacan, Mexico* **218 C5** 19 21N 102 20W
Pico Rivera, *Los Angeles, U.S.A.* **111 C4** 33 59N 118 5W
Picton, *Ont., Canada* **179 C9** 44 1N 77 9W
Pictou, *N.S., Canada* **173 H7** 45 41N 62 42W
Pictou I., *N.S., Canada* **173 H7** 45 49N 62 33W
Picture Butte, *Alta., Canada* **185 J8** 49 55N 112 45W
Pictured Rocks Nat. Lakeshore ⌓, *MI, U.S.A.* **79 C5** 46 30N 86 30W
Picuris Indian Reservation, *NM, U.S.A.* **88 A5** 36 12N 105 48W
Pie I., *Ont., Canada* **180 D7** 48 15N 89 6W
Pie Town, *NM, U.S.A.* **88 C2** 34 18N 108 9W
Piedmont, *AL, U.S.A.* **60 C5** 33 55N 85 37W
Piedmont, *KS, U.S.A.* **74 D7** 37 37N 96 22W
Piedmont, *MO, U.S.A.* **82 D6** 37 9N 90 42W
Piedmont, *OK, U.S.A.* **93 C6** 35 39N 97 44W
Piedmont, *Portland, U.S.A.* **116 A1** 45 33N 122 40W
Piedmont, *SC, U.S.A.* **90 D3** 34 42N 82 28W
Piedmont, *SD, U.S.A.* **91 F2** 44 14N 103 24W
Piedmont, *San Francisco, U.S.A.* **118 B3** 37 49N 122 13W
Piedmont, *WV, U.S.A.* **77 A1** 39 29N 79 3W
Piedmont L., *OH, U.S.A.* **92 C5** 40 11N 81 13W
Piedmont Nat. Wildlife Refuge ⌓, *GA, U.S.A.* **68 C3** 33 8N 83 45W
Piedmont Park, *Atlanta, U.S.A.* **106 B2** 33 47N 84 22W
Piedra, I., *Campeche, Mexico* **223 B3** 20 23N 90 30W
Piedra, Península la, *Sinaloa, Mexico* **216 D4** 23 8N 106 21W
Piedra, Pta. de, *Tamaulipas, Mexico* **215 F7** 24 29N 97 45W
Piedras Negras, *Coahuila, Mexico* **214 B4** 28 42N 100 31W
Piedras Negras, *Veracruz, Mexico* **221 F4** 18 46N 96 11W
Piedritas, *Coahuila, Mexico* **214 B1** 28 46N 103 4W
Pierce, *CO, U.S.A.* **66 B6** 40 38N 104 45W
Pierce, *ID, U.S.A.* **70 C3** 46 30N 115 48W
Pierce, *NE, U.S.A.* **84 B8** 42 12N 97 32W
Pierce City, *MO, U.S.A.* **82 E3** 36 57N 94 0W
Pierce County ☆, *GA, U.S.A.* **68 E4** 31 20N 82 10W
Pierce County ☆, *ND, U.S.A.* **91 B5** 48 0N 100 0W
Pierce County ☆, *NE, U.S.A.* **84 B8** 42 20N 97 40W
Pierce County ☆, *WA, U.S.A.* **101 C3** 47 0N 122 0W
Pierce County ☆, *WI, U.S.A.* **103 D1** 44 45N 92 25W
Pierceland, *Sask., Canada* **189 F11** 54 20N 109 46W
Pierceton, *IN, U.S.A.* **72 B5** 41 12N 85 42W
Pierceville, *KS, U.S.A.* **74 D3** 37 53N 100 40W
Piercy, *CA, U.S.A.* **64 D3** 39 59N 123 48W
Pierpont, *SD, U.S.A.* **91 E8** 45 30N 97 50W
Pierre, *SD, U.S.A.* **91 F5** 44 22N 100 21W
Pierre Part, *LA, U.S.A.* **75 E4** 29 58N 91 12W
Pierrefonds, *Qué., Canada* **177 F9** 45 29N 73 51W
Pierreville, *Qué., Canada* **177 E10** 46 4N 72 49W
Pierron, *IL, U.S.A.* **71 E4** 38 47N 89 36W
Pierson, *Man., Canada* **183 F10** 49 11N 101 15W
Pierson, *FL, U.S.A.* **67 B7** 29 14N 81 28W
Pierson, *IA, U.S.A.* **73 C3** 42 33N 95 52W
Pierz, *MN, U.S.A.* **80 E4** 45 59N 94 6W
Pigeon, *LA, U.S.A.* **75 D4** 30 4N 91 17W
Pigeon, *MI, U.S.A.* **79 F8** 43 50N 83 16W
Pigeon ➜, *IN, U.S.A.* **72 B5** 41 47N 85 49W
Pigeon ➜, *TN, U.S.A.* **97 D9** 36 2N 83 17W
Pigeon Cove, *MA, U.S.A.* **78 B4** 42 41N 70 38W
Pigeon Cr. ➜, *AL, U.S.A.* **60 E4** 31 20N 86 42W
Pigeon Falls, *WI, U.S.A.* **103 D2** 44 26N 91 13W
Pigeon Forge, *TN, U.S.A.* **97 E9** 35 48N 83 33W
Pigeon L., *Alta., Canada* **185 E6** 53 1N 114 2W
Pigeon L., *Ont., Canada* **179 C8** 44 27N 78 30W
Pigg ➜, *VA, U.S.A.* **102 E5** 37 0N 79 29W
Piggott, *AR, U.S.A.* **63 B5** 36 23N 90 11W
Pigs Eye Lake, *Minneapolis-St. Paul, U.S.A.* **113 B3** 44 54N 93 1W
Pihuamo, *Jalisco, Mexico* **218 C4** 19 15N 103 23W
Pijijiapan, *Chiapas, Mexico* **222 D3** 15 42N 93 14W
Pike County ☆, *AL, U.S.A.* **60 E5** 31 48N 85 58W
Pike County ☆, *AR, U.S.A.* **63 D2** 34 14N 93 45W
Pike County ☆, *GA, U.S.A.* **68 C2** 33 5N 84 20W
Pike County ☆, *IL, U.S.A.* **71 D3** 39 35N 90 50W
Pike County ☆, *IN, U.S.A.* **72 E3** 38 25N 87 10W
Pike County ☆, *KY, U.S.A.* **97 C10** 37 30N 82 25W
Pike County ☆, *MS, U.S.A.* **81 E3** 31 15N 90 27W
Pike County ☆, *MO, U.S.A.* **82 B5** 39 20N 91 10W
Pike County ☆, *OH, U.S.A.* **92 D3** 39 4N 83 1W
Pike County ☆, *PA, U.S.A.* **95 C8** 41 20N 75 0W
Pike Nat. Forest, *CO, U.S.A.* **66 C5** 39 15N 105 20W
Pike River, *Qué., Canada* **86 A1** 45 4N 73 6W
Pike Road, *AL, U.S.A.* **60 D4** 32 17N 86 6W
Pikes Peak, *CO, U.S.A.* **66 D5** 38 50N 105 3W
Pikesville, *MD, U.S.A.* **77 A4** 39 22N 76 43W
Piketon, *OH, U.S.A.* **92 D3** 39 4N 83 1W
Pikeville, *KY, U.S.A.* **97 C10** 37 29N 82 31W
Pikeville, *NC, U.S.A.* **90 C8** 35 30N 77 59W
Pikeville, *TN, U.S.A.* **97 E7** 35 36N 85 11W
Pilares, Sa., *Chihuahua, Mexico* **213 C11** 30 20N 104 55W
Pilger, *NE, U.S.A.* **84 B8** 42 0N 97 3W
Pillager, *MN, U.S.A.* **80 D4** 46 20N 94 28W
Pillsbury, *ND, U.S.A.* **91 C8** 47 13N 97 48W
Pillsbury, L., *CA, U.S.A.* **64 D4** 39 25N 122 57W
Pillsbury State Forest, *MN, U.S.A.* **80 D4** 46 25N 94 26W
Pillsbury State Park ⌓, *NH, U.S.A.* **86 C2** 43 14N 72 6W
Pilón ➜, *Tamaulipas, Mexico* **215 G6** 23 58N 98 42W
Pilot Butte, *Sask., Canada* **182 E7** 50 28N 104 25W
Pilot Grove, *MO, U.S.A.* **82 C4** 38 53N 92 55W
Pilot Knob, *AR, U.S.A.* **63 C2** 35 42N 93 57W
Pilot Knob, *KY, U.S.A.* **96 D6** 36 50N 86 41W
Pilot Knob, *MO, U.S.A.* **82 D6** 37 40N 90 40W
Pilot Mound, *Man., Canada* **183 F13** 49 15N 98 54W
Pilot Mountain, *NC, U.S.A.* **90 B5** 36 23N 80 28W
Pilot Pk., *NV, U.S.A.* **85 A6** 41 1N 114 5W
Pilot Pk., *WY, U.S.A.* **104 B3** 44 58N 109 53W
Pilot Point, *AK, U.S.A.* **61 H8** 57 34N 157 35W
Pilot Point, *TX, U.S.A.* **99 D11** 33 24N 96 58W
Pilot Rock, *OR, U.S.A.* **94 B7** 45 29N 118 50W
Pilot Station, *AK, U.S.A.* **61 F7** 61 56N 162 53W
Pim I., *Nunavut, Canada* **190 B11** 78 44N 74 25W
Pima, *AZ, U.S.A.* **62 E6** 32 54N 109 50W
Pima County ☆, *AZ, U.S.A.* **62 E4** 32 0N 112 0W
Pimmit Hills, *VA, U.S.A.* **119 B2** 38 54N 77 12W
Pin-Blanc, L. du, *Qué., Canada* **176 E4** 46 45N 78 8W
Pinacate, Cerro del, *Sonora, Mexico* **212 B2** 31 45N 113 30W
Pinal County ☆, *AZ, U.S.A.* **62 E4** 33 0N 111 15W
Pinal de Amoles, *Querétaro, Mexico* **219 A8** 21 8N 99 42W
Pinaleno Mts., *AZ, U.S.A.* **62 E6** 32 45N 110 0W
Pinardville, *NH, U.S.A.* **86 D3** 42 59N 71 30W
Pinawa, *Man., Canada* **183 E16** 50 9N 95 50W
Pincher Creek, *Alta., Canada* **185 J7** 49 30N 113 57W
Pinckard, *AL, U.S.A.* **60 E5** 31 19N 85 33W
Pinckneyville, *IL, U.S.A.* **71 E4** 38 5N 89 23W
Pinconning, *MI, U.S.A.* **79 F8** 43 51N 83 58W
Pindall, *AR, U.S.A.* **63 B3** 36 4N 92 53W
Pine, *AZ, U.S.A.* **62 C4** 34 23N 111 27W
Pine, *OR, U.S.A.* **94 C8** 44 52N 117 5W
Pine ➜, *B.C., Canada* **189 E8** 56 8N 120 43W
Pine ➜, *MI, U.S.A.* **79 E6** 44 14N 85 54W
Pine ➜, *MI, U.S.A.* **79 F7** 43 35N 84 8W
Pine, C., *Nfld. & L., Canada* **174 F7** 46 37N 53 32W
Pine Apple, *AL, U.S.A.* **60 E4** 31 52N 87 0W
Pine Barrens, *NJ, U.S.A.* **87 C2** 39 30N 74 30W
Pine Bluff, *AR, U.S.A.* **63 D3** 34 13N 92 1W
Pine Bluff Arsenal, *AR, U.S.A.* **63 D3** 34 19N 92 6W
Pine Bluffs, *WY, U.S.A.* **104 E8** 41 11N 104 4W
Pine Bush, *NY, U.S.A.* **89 D6** 41 36N 74 17W
Pine Castle, *Orlando, U.S.A.* **115 B2** 28 28N 81 22W
Pine City, *MN, U.S.A.* **80 E6** 45 50N 92 59W
Pine City, *WA, U.S.A.* **101 C8** 47 12N 117 31W
Pine County ☆, *MN, U.S.A.* **80 D6** 46 5N 92 50W
Pine Cr. ➜, *NV, U.S.A.* **85 B4** 40 36N 116 12W
Pine Cr. ➜, *PA, U.S.A.* **95 C5** 41 10N 77 16W
Pine Creek L., *OK, U.S.A.* **93 D8** 34 7N 95 5W
Pine Dock, *Man., Canada* **183 D15** 51 38N 96 48W
Pine Falls, *Man., Canada* **183 E15** 50 34N 96 11W
Pine Flat L., *CA, U.S.A.* **65 G7** 36 50N 119 20W
Pine Forest Range, *NV, U.S.A.* **85 A2** 41 45N 118 50W
Pine Grove, *LA, U.S.A.* **75 D5** 30 43N 90 45W
Pine Grove, *PA, U.S.A.* **95 D6** 40 33N 76 23W
Pine Grove, *WV, U.S.A.* **102 B4** 39 34N 80 41W
Pine Grove Park, *Ont., Canada* **192 B2** 45 22N 75 37W
Pine Haven, *WY, U.S.A.* **104 B8** 44 21N 104 49W
Pine Hill, *AL, U.S.A.* **60 E3** 31 59N 87 35W
Pine Hills, *FL, U.S.A.* **67 C7** 28 33N 81 27W
Pine Hills, *NJ, U.S.A.* **87 C2** 39 47N 74 59W
Pine I., *FL, U.S.A.* **67 E6** 26 36N 82 7W
Pine Island, *MN, U.S.A.* **80 F6** 44 12N 92 39W
Pine Knot, *KY, U.S.A.* **97 D8** 36 39N 84 26W
Pine Lawn, *MO, U.S.A.* **117 A2** 38 41N 90 16W
Pine Level, *AL, U.S.A.* **60 D4** 32 4N 86 4W
Pine Level, *NC, U.S.A.* **90 C7** 35 31N 78 14W
Pine Log, *GA, U.S.A.* **68 B2** 34 21N 84 44W
Pine Mountain, *GA, U.S.A.* **68 D2** 32 49N 84 51W
Pine Mt., *GA, U.S.A.* **68 D2** 32 49N 84 50W
Pine Mt., *KY, U.S.A.* **97 D9** 37 0N 83 45W
Pine Mt., *WY, U.S.A.* **104 E3** 41 2N 109 1W
Pine Plains, *NY, U.S.A.* **78 B1** 42 59N 73 39W
Pine Point, *N.W.T., Canada* **189 D10** 60 50N 114 28W
Pine Prairie, *LA, U.S.A.* **75 D3** 30 47N 92 25W
Pine Ridge, *SD, U.S.A.* **91 G3** 43 2N 102 33W
Pine Ridge Indian Reservation, *SD, U.S.A.* **91 G3** 43 30N 102 0W
Pine River, *Man., Canada* **183 D11** 51 45N 100 30W
Pine River, *MN, U.S.A.* **80 D4** 46 43N 94 24W
Pine Springs, *Minneapolis-St. Paul, U.S.A.* **113 A4** 45 2N 92 57W
Pine Springs, *TX, U.S.A.* **98 F3** 31 54N 104 49W
Pine Valley, *UT, U.S.A.* **100 E2** 38 20N 113 45W
Pinebluff, *NC, U.S.A.* **90 C6** 35 6N 79 28W
Pinecone Burke Park ⌓, *B.C., Canada* **187 F12** 49 32N 122 41W
Pinecrest, *Miami, U.S.A.* **112 D1** 25 40N 80 18W
Pinedale, *CA, U.S.A.* **65 G7** 36 50N 119 48W
Pinedale, *WY, U.S.A.* **104 D3** 42 52N 109 52W
Pinehouse L., *Sask., Canada* **189 E11** 55 32N 106 35W
Pinehouse Lake, *Sask., Canada* **189 E11** 55 32N 106 35W
Pinehurst, *GA, U.S.A.* **68 D3** 32 12N 83 46W
Pinehurst, *ID, U.S.A.* **70 D2** 45 15N 116 20W
Pinehurst, *NC, U.S.A.* **90 C6** 35 12N 79 28W
Pinehurst L., *Alta., Canada* **184 D9** 54 39N 111 25W
Pineland, *TX, U.S.A.* **99 F14** 31 15N 93 58W
Pinellas County ☆, *FL, U.S.A.* **67 C6** 28 0N 82 45W
Pinellas Nat. Wildlife Refuge ⌓, *Tampa, U.S.A.* **119 C2** 27 39N 82 41W
Pinellas Park, *FL, U.S.A.* **67 D6** 27 50N 82 41W
Pinellas Point, *Tampa, U.S.A.* **119 C3** 27 42N 82 38W
Pines, Lake O' The, *TX, U.S.A.* **99 E13** 32 45N 94 30W
Pinetop-Lakeside, *AZ, U.S.A.* **62 C6** 34 9N 109 58W
Pinetops, *NC, U.S.A.* **90 C8** 35 46N 77 38W
Pinetta, *FL, U.S.A.* **67 A5** 30 36N 83 21W
Pineview, *GA, U.S.A.* **68 D3** 32 7N 83 30W
Pineville, *KY, U.S.A.* **97 D9** 36 46N 83 42W
Pineville, *LA, U.S.A.* **75 C3** 31 19N 92 26W
Pineville, *MO, U.S.A.* **82 E2** 36 36N 94 23W
Pineville, *NC, U.S.A.* **90 C5** 35 4N 80 53W
Pineville, *WV, U.S.A.* **102 D3** 37 35N 81 32W
Pinewood, *SC, U.S.A.* **90 E5** 33 44N 80 27W
Pinewood Park, *Miami, U.S.A.* **112 C2** 25 52N 80 13W
Piney ➜, *MO, U.S.A.* **82 D4** 37 54N 92 4W
Piney ➜, *TN, U.S.A.* **96 E5** 35 49N 87 34W
Piney Buttes, *MT, U.S.A.* **83 C11** 47 35N 106 45W
Piney Green, *NC, U.S.A.* **90 D8** 34 43N 77 19W
Piney Grove, *MD, U.S.A.* **77 A2** 39 42N 78 24W
Piney Point, *MD, U.S.A.* **77 B4** 38 9N 76 31W
Piney Point Village, *Houston, U.S.A.* **110 B1** 29 45N 95 31W
Piney Pt., *FL, U.S.A.* **67 B5** 29 46N 83 35W
Piney River, *VA, U.S.A.* **102 D5** 37 42N 79 1W
Piney Run ➜, *VA, U.S.A.* **119 B2** 38 58N 77 14W
Piney Woods, *MS, U.S.A.* **81 D3** 32 2N 90 0W
Pingree, *ND, U.S.A.* **91 C7** 47 10N 98 55W
Pink, *OK, U.S.A.* **93 C6** 35 18N 97 6W
Pink Cliffs, *UT, U.S.A.* **100 F3** 37 25N 112 20W
Pink Hill, *NC, U.S.A.* **90 C8** 35 3N 77 45W
Pinnacle Buttes, *WY, U.S.A.* **104 C3** 43 44N 109 57W
Pinnacle Peak, *WY, U.S.A.* **104 C2** 43 23N 110 32W
Pinnacles Nat. Monument ⌓, *CA, U.S.A.* **65 G5** 36 25N 121 12W
Pino ➜, *Baja Calif., Mexico* **210 B2** 31 44N 116 40W
Pinola, *MS, U.S.A.* **81 E4** 31 53N 89 58W
Pinon, *AZ, U.S.A.* **62 A5** 36 6N 110 13W
Pinon, *NM, U.S.A.* **88 E5** 32 37N 105 24W
Pinos, *Zacatecas, Mexico* **217 E9** 22 18N 101 34W
Pinos, Mt., *CA, U.S.A.* **65 J7** 34 50N 119 9W
Pinos Pt., *CA, U.S.A.* **59 H3** 36 38N 121 57W
Pins, Pte. aux, *Ont., Canada* **178 E5** 42 15N 81 51W
Pinson, *AL, U.S.A.* **60 C4** 33 41N 86 41W
Pinson, *TN, U.S.A.* **96 E4** 35 29N 88 43W
Pinta, Sierra, *AZ, U.S.A.* **62 E2** 32 15N 113 30W
Pintwater Ra., *NV, U.S.A.* **85 F5** 36 50N 115 34W
Pinware, *Nfld. & L., Canada* **174 A4** 51 37N 56 42W
Pinware ➜, *Nfld. & L., Canada* **174 A4** 51 39N 56 42W
Pioche, *NV, U.S.A.* **85 E6** 37 56N 114 27W
Pioneer, *IA, U.S.A.* **73 C4** 42 39N 94 23W
Pioneer, *LA, U.S.A.* **75 B4** 32 44N 91 26W

Pioneer, *OH, U.S.A.* **92 B2** 41 41N 84 33W
Pioneer, *TN, U.S.A.* **97 D8** 36 25N 84 19W
Pioneer Mts., *ID, U.S.A.* **70 F5** 43 38N 113 52W
Pioneer Mts., *MT, U.S.A.* **83 E5** 45 29N 112 58W
Pipe Creek, *TX, U.S.A.* **99 H9** 29 43N 98 56W
Pipe Spring Nat. Monument ⌂, *AZ, U.S.A.* **62 A3** 36 50N 112 55W
Pipestem L., *ND, U.S.A.* **91 D7** 46 57N 98 45W
Pipestone, *MN, U.S.A.* **80 F2** 44 0N 96 19W
Pipestone County ☆, *MN, U.S.A.* **80 F2** 44 0N 96 15W
Pipestone Cr. →, *Man., Canada* **183 F11** 49 38N 100 15W
Pipestone Nat. Monument ⌂, *MN, U.S.A.* **80 G2** 43 58N 96 14W
Pipmuacan, Rés., *Qué., Canada* **177 B12** 49 45N 70 30W
Piqua, *KS, U.S.A.* **74 D8** 37 56N 95 32W
Piqua, *OH, U.S.A.* **92 C2** 40 9N 84 15W
Pirtleville, *AZ, U.S.A.* **62 F6** 31 21N 109 34W
Piscataquis →, *ME, U.S.A.* **76 C5** 45 15N 68 58W
Piscataquis County ☆, *ME, U.S.A.* **76 C4** 46 0N 69 0W
Piscataway, *MD, U.S.A.* **77 B4** 38 42N 76 58W
Piscataway, *NJ, U.S.A.* **87 B2** 40 34N 74 27W
Pisek, *ND, U.S.A.* **91 B8** 48 19N 97 43W
Pisgah, *IA, U.S.A.* **73 D3** 41 50N 95 55W
Pisgah, *MD, U.S.A.* **77 B3** 38 32N 77 8W
Pisgah, Mt., *NH, U.S.A.* **86 B3** 44 59N 71 13W
Pisgah Nat. Forest, *NC, U.S.A.* **90 C3** 35 50N 82 0W
Pisgah State Park ⌂, *NH, U.S.A.* **86 D2** 42 50N 72 27W
Pisinimo, *AZ, U.S.A.* **62 E3** 32 2N 112 19W
Pismo Beach, *CA, U.S.A.* **65 H6** 35 9N 120 38W
Piste, *Yucatán, Mexico* **223 B5** 20 42N 88 35W
Pistol River, *OR, U.S.A.* **94 E1** 42 17N 124 24W
Pistolet B., *Nfld. & L., Canada* **174 A5** 51 35N 55 45W
Pit →, *CA, U.S.A.* **64 C4** 40 47N 122 6W
Pitchfork, *WY, U.S.A.* **104 B3** 44 6N 109 5W
Piti, *Guam* **105 b** 13 28N 144 41W
Pitiquito, *Sonora, Mexico* **212 C3** 30 41N 112 5W
Pitkin, *CO, U.S.A.* **66 D4** 38 37N 106 31W
Pitkin, *LA, U.S.A.* **75 D3** 30 56N 92 56W
Pitkin County ☆, *CO, U.S.A.* **66 C4** 39 10N 106 50W
Pitman, *NJ, U.S.A.* **87 C1** 39 44N 75 8W
Pitt County ☆, *NC, U.S.A.* **90 C8** 35 30N 77 20W
Pitt I., *B.C., Canada* **186 B5** 53 30N 129 50W
Pitt L., *B.C., Canada* **187 F12** 49 25N 122 32W
Pittock, *Pittsburgh, U.S.A.* **116 B1** 40 29N 80 5W
Pittsboro, *IN, U.S.A.* **72 D4** 39 52N 86 28W
Pittsboro, *MS, U.S.A.* **81 C4** 33 56N 89 20W
Pittsboro, *NC, U.S.A.* **90 C6** 35 43N 79 11W
Pittsburg, *CA, U.S.A.* **64 E5** 38 2N 121 53W
Pittsburg, *IL, U.S.A.* **71 F5** 37 47N 88 51W
Pittsburg, *KS, U.S.A.* **74 D9** 37 25N 94 42W
Pittsburg, *NH, U.S.A.* **86 A3** 45 3N 71 24W
Pittsburg, *OK, U.S.A.* **93 D8** 34 43N 95 52W
Pittsburg, *TX, U.S.A.* **99 D13** 33 0N 94 59W
Pittsburg County ☆, *OK, U.S.A.* **93 D8** 34 50N 95 50W
Pittsburgh, *PA, U.S.A.* **95 D2** 40 26N 79 58W
Pittsburgh International ✕ (PIT), *PA, U.S.A.* **95 D2** 40 29N 80 14W
Pittsfield, *IL, U.S.A.* **71 D3** 39 36N 90 49W
Pittsfield, *ME, U.S.A.* **76 D4** 44 47N 69 23W
Pittsfield, *MA, U.S.A.* **78 B1** 42 27N 73 15W
Pittsfield, *NH, U.S.A.* **86 C3** 43 18N 71 20W
Pittsfield, *VT, U.S.A.* **86 C2** 43 46N 72 48W
Pittsford, *VT, U.S.A.* **86 C1** 43 42N 73 3W
Pittston, *PA, U.S.A.* **87 A1** 41 19N 75 47W
Pittstown, *NJ, U.S.A.* **87 B2** 40 36N 74 56W
Pittsview, *AL, U.S.A.* **60 D5** 32 11N 85 10W
Pittsville, *MD, U.S.A.* **77 B5** 38 24N 75 52W
Pittsville, *MO, U.S.A.* **82 C3** 38 50N 94 0W
Pittsville, *WI, U.S.A.* **103 D3** 44 27N 90 8W
Pittsylvania County ☆, *VA, U.S.A.* **102 E5** 36 55N 79 15W
Piumafua Mt., *Amer. Samoa* **105 f** 14 11 S 169 37W
Piute County ☆, *UT, U.S.A.* **100 E3** 38 20N 112 10W
Piute Pk., *CA, U.S.A.* **65 H8** 35 27N 118 23W
Pivabiska →, *Ont., Canada* **181 B14** 50 13N 82 52W
Pixley, *CA, U.S.A.* **65 H7** 35 58N 119 18W
Pixoyal, *Campeche, Mexico* **223 D3** 18 56N 90 37W
Placedo, *TX, U.S.A.* **99 J11** 28 41N 96 50W
Placentia, *Nfld. & L., Canada* **174 E7** 47 20N 54 0W
Placentia B., *Nfld. & L., Canada* **174 E6** 47 0N 54 40W
Placer County ☆, *CA, U.S.A.* **64 D6** 39 10N 120 30W
Placeres del Oro, *Guerrero, Mexico* **219 D7** 18 15N 100 55W
Placerville, *CA, U.S.A.* **64 E6** 38 44N 120 48W
Placerville, *CO, U.S.A.* **66 D2** 38 1N 108 3W
Placerville, *ID, U.S.A.* **70 F3** 43 57N 115 57W
Placid, L., *FL, U.S.A.* **67 D7** 27 15N 81 22W
Placitas, *NM, U.S.A.* **88 B4** 35 18N 106 25W
Plain City, *OH, U.S.A.* **92 C3** 40 6N 83 16W
Plain City, *UT, U.S.A.* **100 B3** 41 18N 112 6W
Plain Dealing, *LA, U.S.A.* **75 B2** 32 54N 93 42W
Plainfield, *CT, U.S.A.* **78 C3** 41 41N 71 56W
Plainfield, *IN, U.S.A.* **72 D4** 39 42N 86 24W
Plainfield, *IA, U.S.A.* **73 C6** 42 51N 92 32W
Plainfield, *MA, U.S.A.* **78 B2** 42 31N 72 57W
Plainfield, *NH, U.S.A.* **86 C2** 43 32N 72 21W
Plainfield, *NJ, U.S.A.* **87 B2** 40 37N 74 25W
Plainfield, *VT, U.S.A.* **86 B2** 44 17N 72 26W
Plainfield, *WI, U.S.A.* **103 D4** 44 13N 89 30W
Plainfield Heights, *MI, U.S.A.* **79 F6** 43 1N 85 37W
Plains, *GA, U.S.A.* **68 D2** 32 2N 84 24W
Plains, *KS, U.S.A.* **74 D3** 37 16N 100 35W
Plains, *MT, U.S.A.* **83 C3** 47 28N 114 53W
Plains, *PA, U.S.A.* **95 C7** 41 15N 75 37W
Plains, *TX, U.S.A.* **98 D5** 33 11N 102 50W
Plainview, *AR, U.S.A.* **63 D2** 34 59N 93 18W
Plainview, *MN, U.S.A.* **80 F6** 44 10N 92 10W
Plainview, *NY, U.S.A.* **87 B3** 40 46N 73 29W
Plainview, *NE, U.S.A.* **84 B8** 42 21N 97 47W
Plainview, *TX, U.S.A.* **98 C6** 34 11N 101 43W
Plainville, *CT, U.S.A.* **78 C2** 41 41N 72 51W
Plainville, *GA, U.S.A.* **68 B1** 34 24N 85 2W
Plainville, *IN, U.S.A.* **72 E3** 38 48N 87 9W
Plainville, *KS, U.S.A.* **74 B4** 39 14N 99 18W
Plainville, *MA, U.S.A.* **78 B3** 42 0N 71 20W
Plainwell, *MI, U.S.A.* **79 G6** 42 27N 85 38W
Plaistow, *NH, U.S.A.* **86 D3** 42 50N 71 6W
Plamondon, *Alta., Canada* **184 D8** 54 51N 112 32W
Planada, *CA, U.S.A.* **64 F6** 37 16N 120 19W
Plandome, *NY, U.S.A.* **114 B4** 40 48N 73 42W
Plandome Heights, *NY, U.S.A.* **114 B4** 40 48N 73 42W
Plankinton, *SD, U.S.A.* **91 G7** 43 43N 98 29W
Plano, *IL, U.S.A.* **71 B5** 41 40N 88 32W
Plano, *TX, U.S.A.* **99 D11** 33 1N 96 42W
Plant City, *FL, U.S.A.* **67 C6** 28 1N 82 7W
Plantation, *FL, U.S.A.* **67 E8** 26 7N 80 14W
Plantersville, *AL, U.S.A.* **60 D4** 32 40N 86 56W
Plantersville, *MS, U.S.A.* **81 B5** 34 12N 88 40W
Plantón Sánchez, *Veracruz, Mexico* **220 C2** 21 17N 98 21W
Plantsite, *AZ, U.S.A.* **62 D6** 33 2N 109 21W
Plaquemine, *LA, U.S.A.* **75 D4** 30 17N 91 14W
Plaquemines Parish ☆, *LA, U.S.A.* **75 E6** 29 29N 89 42W
Plaster Rock, *N.B., Canada* **173 G2** 46 53N 67 22W
Plateros, *Zacatecas, Mexico* **217 D8** 23 13N 102 51W
Platina, *CA, U.S.A.* **64 C4** 40 22N 122 53W
Platinum, *AK, U.S.A.* **61 G7** 59 1N 161 49W
Platte, *SD, U.S.A.* **91 G7** 43 23N 98 51W
Platte →, *MO, U.S.A.* **82 B2** 39 16N 94 50W
Platte →, *NE, U.S.A.* **84 C10** 41 4N 95 53W
Platte Center, *NE, U.S.A.* **84 C8** 41 32N 97 29W
Platte City, *MO, U.S.A.* **82 B2** 39 22N 94 47W
Platte County ☆, *MO, U.S.A.* **82 B2** 39 20N 94 45W
Platte County ☆, *NE, U.S.A.* **84 C8** 41 30N 97 30W
Platte County ☆, *WY, U.S.A.* **104 D8** 42 0N 105 0W
Platteville, *CO, U.S.A.* **66 B6** 40 13N 104 49W
Platteville, *WI, U.S.A.* **103 F3** 42 44N 90 29W
Plattsburg, *MO, U.S.A.* **82 B2** 39 34N 94 27W
Plattsburgh, *NY, U.S.A.* **86 B1** 44 42N 73 28W
Plattsmouth, *NE, U.S.A.* **84 C10** 41 1N 95 53W
Playa Algodones, *Sonora, Mexico* **212 F4** 27 58N 111 8W
Playa Colorada, B., *Sinaloa, Mexico* **216 B2** 25 14N 108 22W
Playa Corrida de San Juan, Pta. la, *Michoacan, Mexico* **218 D4** 18 35N 103 42W
Playa de Piedra, *Tabasco, Mexico* **222 B3** 17 33N 93 26W
Playa del Carmen, *Quintana Roo, Mexico* **223 B6** 20 37N 87 4W
Playa Lauro Villar, *Tamaulipas, Mexico* **214 E7** 25 49N 97 8W
Playa Vicente, *Veracruz, Mexico* **221 G5** 17 50N 95 49W
Playas L., *NM, U.S.A.* **88 F2** 31 51N 108 35W
Playgreen L., *Man., Canada* **183 B13** 54 0N 98 15W
Plaza, *ND, U.S.A.* **91 B4** 48 1N 101 58W
Plaza, *WA, U.S.A.* **101 C8** 47 19N 117 23W
Plaza Larga Cr. →, *NM, U.S.A.* **88 B7** 35 10N 103 29W
Pleasant, L., *AZ, U.S.A.* **62 D3** 33 51N 112 16W
Pleasant, B., *MA, U.S.A.* **78 C5** 41 40N 69 57W
Pleasant Dale, *NE, U.S.A.* **84 D9** 40 48N 96 56W
Pleasant Gap, *PA, U.S.A.* **95 D5** 40 52N 77 44W
Pleasant Garden, *NC, U.S.A.* **90 C6** 35 58N 79 46W
Pleasant Grove, *UT, U.S.A.* **100 C4** 40 22N 111 44W
Pleasant Hill, *CA, U.S.A.* **64 F4** 37 57N 122 4W
Pleasant Hill, *IL, U.S.A.* **71 D3** 39 27N 90 52W
Pleasant Hill, *IA, U.S.A.* **73 D5** 41 35N 93 31W
Pleasant Hill, *LA, U.S.A.* **75 C2** 31 49N 93 31W
Pleasant Hill, *MO, U.S.A.* **82 C2** 38 47N 94 16W
Pleasant Hill, *NM, U.S.A.* **88 C7** 34 31N 103 4W
Pleasant Hill, *OH, U.S.A.* **92 C2** 40 3N 84 21W
Pleasant Hill, *TN, U.S.A.* **97 E7** 35 59N 85 12W
Pleasant Hill L., *OH, U.S.A.* **92 C4** 40 37N 82 19W
Pleasant Hills, *Pittsburgh, U.S.A.* **116 C2** 40 20N 79 57W
Pleasant Lake, *MN, U.S.A.* **80 E4** 45 30N 94 17W
Pleasant Lake, *Minneapolis-St. Paul, U.S.A.* **113 A3** 45 5N 93 5W
Pleasant Plains, *AR, U.S.A.* **63 C4** 35 33N 91 38W
Pleasant Plains, *IL, U.S.A.* **71 D4** 39 52N 89 55W
Pleasant Point Indian Reservation, *ME, U.S.A.* **76 D6** 44 57N 67 3W
Pleasant Prairie, *WI, U.S.A.* **103 F6** 42 33N 87 56W
Pleasant Ridge, *MI, U.S.A.* **109 A2** 42 28N 83 8W
Pleasant Site, *AL, U.S.A.* **60 B2** 34 33N 88 4W
Pleasant View, *CO, U.S.A.* **66 E2** 37 35N 108 46W
Pleasant View, *TN, U.S.A.* **96 D5** 36 24N 87 2W
Pleasant View, *UT, U.S.A.* **100 B3** 41 19N 112 0W
Pleasant View, *WA, U.S.A.* **101 D7** 46 29N 118 20W
Pleasantdale, *Sask., Canada* **182 C7** 52 35N 104 30W
Pleasanton, *IA, U.S.A.* **73 E5** 40 35N 93 45W
Pleasanton, *KS, U.S.A.* **74 C9** 38 11N 94 43W
Pleasanton, *NM, U.S.A.* **88 D2** 33 17N 108 53W
Pleasanton, *NE, U.S.A.* **84 D6** 40 58N 99 5W
Pleasanton, *TX, U.S.A.* **99 J9** 28 58N 98 29W
Pleasants County ☆, *WV, U.S.A.* **102 B3** 39 22N 81 12W
Pleasantville, *IA, U.S.A.* **73 D5** 41 23N 93 18W
Pleasantville, *NJ, U.S.A.* **87 C2** 39 24N 74 32W
Pleasantville, *NY, U.S.A.* **87 A3** 41 8N 73 48W
Pleasantville, *OH, U.S.A.* **92 D4** 39 49N 82 32W
Pleasure Ridge Park, *KY, U.S.A.* **97 B7** 38 9N 85 50W
Pleasureville, *KY, U.S.A.* **97 B7** 38 21N 85 7W
Pledger L., *Ont., Canada* **181 B13** 50 53N 83 42W
Plenty, *Sask., Canada* **182 D3** 51 47N 108 38W
Plentywood, *MT, U.S.A.* **83 B13** 48 47N 104 34W
Plessisville, *Qué., Canada* **177 E11** 46 14N 71 47W
Plétipi, L., *Qué., Canada* **175 C3** 51 44N 70 6W
Plevna, *Ont., Canada* **179 C10** 44 58N 76 59W
Plevna, *KS, U.S.A.* **74 D5** 37 59N 98 19W
Plevna, *MT, U.S.A.* **83 D13** 46 25N 104 31W
Plimoth Plantation, *MA, U.S.A.* **78 C4** 41 56N 70 37W
Plomosa, *Chihuahua, Mexico* **213 D10** 29 5N 105 15W
Plover, *IA, U.S.A.* **73 C4** 42 53N 94 38W
Plover, *WI, U.S.A.* **103 D4** 44 27N 89 32W
Plover →, *WI, U.S.A.* **103 D4** 44 29N 89 35W
Plum, *PA, U.S.A.* **95 D3** 40 29N 79 47W
Plum City, *WI, U.S.A.* **103 D1** 44 38N 92 11W
Plum Coulee, *Man., Canada* **183 F14** 49 11N 97 45W
Plum Cr. →, *SD, U.S.A.* **91 F5** 44 13N 100 45W
Plum I., *MA, U.S.A.* **78 B4** 42 45N 70 48W
Plum I., *NY, U.S.A.* **78 C2** 41 11N 72 12W
Plum Point, *MD, U.S.A.* **77 B4** 38 37N 76 32W
Plum Springs, *KY, U.S.A.* **96 D6** 37 0N 86 20W
Plumas, *Man., Canada* **183 E12** 50 23N 99 5W
Plumas County ☆, *CA, U.S.A.* **64 D5** 40 0N 121 0W
Plumas Nat. Forest, *CA, U.S.A.* **64 D6** 39 50N 120 40W
Plumerville, *AR, U.S.A.* **63 C3** 35 10N 92 38W
Plummer, *ID, U.S.A.* **70 B2** 47 20N 116 53W
Plummer, *MN, U.S.A.* **80 C2** 47 55N 96 3W
Plunkett, *Sask., Canada* **182 D6** 51 55N 105 27W
Plush, *OR, U.S.A.* **94 E6** 42 25N 119 54W
Plutarco Elías Calles, *Baja Calif. S., Mexico* **211 K8** 23 11N 110 9W
Plutarco Elías Calles, Presa del, *Sonora, Mexico* **212 D6** 29 10N 109 40W
Plymouth, *CA, U.S.A.* **64 E6** 38 29N 120 51W
Plymouth, *IL, U.S.A.* **71 C3** 40 18N 90 58W
Plymouth, *IN, U.S.A.* **72 B4** 41 21N 86 19W
Plymouth, *IA, U.S.A.* **73 B5** 43 15N 93 7W
Plymouth, *KS, U.S.A.* **74 C7** 38 25N 96 20W
Plymouth, *MA, U.S.A.* **78 C4** 41 57N 70 40W
Plymouth, *MN, U.S.A.* **80 E5** 45 1N 93 27W
Plymouth, *NC, U.S.A.* **90 C9** 35 52N 76 43W
Plymouth, *NH, U.S.A.* **86 C3** 43 46N 71 41W
Plymouth, *NE, U.S.A.* **84 D9** 40 18N 96 59W
Plymouth, *PA, U.S.A.* **95 C7** 41 14N 75 57W
Plymouth, *UT, U.S.A.* **100 B3** 41 53N 112 9W
Plymouth, *VT, U.S.A.* **86 C2** 43 34N 72 45W
Plymouth, *WI, U.S.A.* **103 E6** 43 45N 87 59W
Plymouth Bay, *MA, U.S.A.* **78 C4** 41 57N 70 37W
Plymouth County ☆, *IA, U.S.A.* **73 C2** 42 45N 96 10W
Plymouth County ☆, *MA, U.S.A.* **78 C4** 41 45N 70 45W
Plymouth Creek Park, *Minneapolis-St. Paul, U.S.A.* **113 A1** 45 1N 93 28W
Plymouth Meeting, *PA, U.S.A.* **116 A1** 40 6N 75 16W
Plympton, *N.S., Canada* **173 J4** 44 30N 65 55W
Plympton-Wyoming, *Ont., Canada* **178 D4** 43 1N 82 6W
Poanas, *Durango, Mexico* **217 B7** 25 46N 103 37W
Poarch Creek Indian Reservation, *AL, U.S.A.* **60 E3** 31 10N 87 35W
Poca, *WV, U.S.A.* **102 C3** 38 28N 81 49W
Pocahontas, *AR, U.S.A.* **63 B5** 36 16N 90 58W
Pocahontas, *IL, U.S.A.* **71 E4** 38 50N 89 33W
Pocahontas, *IA, U.S.A.* **73 C4** 42 44N 94 40W
Pocahontas County ☆, *IA, U.S.A.* **73 C4** 42 45N 94 40W
Pocahontas County ☆, *WV, U.S.A.* **102 C4** 38 10N 80 2W
Pocasset, *MA, U.S.A.* **78 C4** 41 41N 70 37W
Pocasset, *OK, U.S.A.* **93 C6** 35 12N 97 58W
Pocatalico, *WV, U.S.A.* **102 C3** 38 29N 81 40W
Pocatalico →, *WV, U.S.A.* **102 C3** 38 29N 81 49W
Pocatello, *ID, U.S.A.* **70 G6** 42 52N 112 27W
Pocola, *OK, U.S.A.* **93 C9** 35 14N 94 29W
Pocomoke →, *MD, U.S.A.* **77 C5** 37 58N 75 39W
Pocomoke City, *MD, U.S.A.* **77 B5** 38 5N 75 34W
Pocomoke Sd., *VA, U.S.A.* **77 C5** 37 50N 75 50W
Pocomoke State Forest, *MD, U.S.A.* **77 B5** 38 9N 75 32W
Pocono Mts., *PA, U.S.A.* **87 A1** 41 7N 75 22W
Pocono Pines, *PA, U.S.A.* **87 A1** 41 6N 75 27W
Pocono Summit, *PA, U.S.A.* **87 A1** 41 7N 75 23W
Poestenkill, *NY, U.S.A.* **78 B1** 42 41N 73 34W
Pogamasing, *Ont., Canada* **181 F15** 46 55N 81 50W
Pohénégamook, *Qué., Canada* **177 D13** 47 28N 69 13W
Pōhue B., *HI, U.S.A.* **69 E6** 19 0N 155 48W
Poinsett, L., *SD, U.S.A.* **91 F8** 44 34N 97 5W
Poinsett County ☆, *AR, U.S.A.* **63 C5** 35 34N 90 43W
Point Arena, *CA, U.S.A.* **64 E3** 38 55N 123 41W
Point au Fer I., *LA, U.S.A.* **75 E4** 29 18N 91 15W
Point Baker, *AK, U.S.A.* **61 H14** 56 21N 133 37W
Point Blank, *TX, U.S.A.* **99 G12** 30 45N 95 13W
Point Clear, *AL, U.S.A.* **60 F3** 30 28N 87 55W
Point Comfort, *TX, U.S.A.* **99 J11** 28 41N 96 33W
Point Hope, *AK, U.S.A.* **61 B6** 68 21N 166 47W
Point L., *N.W.T., Canada* **189 C10** 65 15N 113 4W
Point Lay, *AK, U.S.A.* **61 B7** 69 46N 163 3W
Point Leamington, *Nfld. & L., Canada* **174 C5** 49 20N 55 24W
Point Lookout, *MD, U.S.A.* **77 B4** 38 5N 76 18W
Point Marion, *PA, U.S.A.* **95 E3** 39 44N 79 54W
Point of Rocks, *WY, U.S.A.* **104 E4** 41 41N 108 47W
Point Pelee Nat. Park △, *Ont., Canada* **178 F4** 41 57N 82 31W
Point Pleasant, *NJ, U.S.A.* **87 B2** 40 5N 74 4W
Point Pleasant, *WV, U.S.A.* **102 C2** 38 51N 82 8W
Point Reyes Nat. Seashore ⌂, *CA, U.S.A.* **64 E4** 38 10N 122 55W
Point Roberts, *WA, U.S.A.* **101 B2** 48 59N 123 4W
Point Vicente Lighthouse, *Los Angeles, U.S.A.* **111 D2** 33 44N 118 24W
Pointe-à-la-Frégate, *Qué., Canada* **172 D5** 49 12N 64 55W
Pointe à la Hache, *LA, U.S.A.* **75 E6** 29 35N 89 48W
Pointe-à-Maurier, *Qué., Canada* **172 C10** 50 20N 59 48W
Pointe au Baril Station, *Ont., Canada* **178 B6** 45 35N 80 23W
Pointe-au-Pic = La Malbaie, *Qué., Canada* **177 D12** 47 40N 70 10W
Pointe-aux-Anglais, *Qué., Canada* **172 D2** 49 41N 67 10W
Pointe-aux-Outardes, *Qué., Canada* **177 B14** 49 3N 68 26W
Pointe Aux Pins, *MI, U.S.A.* **79 D7** 45 44N 84 29W
Pointe-Aux-Trembles, *Montréal, Canada* **192 A3** 45 38N 73 30W
Pointe-Claire, *Qué., Canada* **177 F9** 45 26N 73 50W
Pointe Coupee Parish ☆, *LA, U.S.A.* **75 D4** 30 36N 91 37W
Pointe du Bois, *Man., Canada* **183 E16** 50 18N 95 33W
Pointe-Gatineau, *Ont., Canada* **179 B11** 45 27N 75 41W
Pointe-Lebel, *Qué., Canada* **177 B14** 49 10N 68 12W
Pointe-Parent, *Qué., Canada* **172 C8** 50 8N 61 47W
Pointe-Sapin, *N.B., Canada* **173 G5** 46 58N 64 50W
Pointe-Taillon, Parc de la ⌂, *Qué., Canada* **177 C11** 48 42N 71 58W
Pointe-Verte, *N.B., Canada* **173 F4** 47 51N 65 46W
Poisson Blanc, L., *Qué., Canada* **176 F7** 46 0N 75 45W
Pojoaque, *NM, U.S.A.* **88 B4** 35 54N 106 1W
Pojoaque Indian Reservation, *NM, U.S.A.* **88 B4** 35 54N 106 1W
Pōka'ī B., *HI, U.S.A.* **69 K13** 21 27N 158 12W
Pokegama L., *MN, U.S.A.* **80 C5** 47 12N 93 35W
Polacca, *AZ, U.S.A.* **62 B5** 35 50N 110 23W
Polacca Wash →, *AZ, U.S.A.* **62 B5** 35 22N 110 50W
Poland, *NY, U.S.A.* **89 B5** 43 14N 75 4W
Poland, *OH, U.S.A.* **92 B6** 41 1N 80 37W
Pole Mt., *WY, U.S.A.* **104 E7** 41 14N 105 23W
Polk, *NE, U.S.A.* **84 C8** 41 5N 97 46W
Polk, *OH, U.S.A.* **92 C4** 40 57N 82 13W
Polk, *PA, U.S.A.* **95 C3** 41 22N 79 56W
Polk City, *FL, U.S.A.* **67 C7** 28 11N 81 49W
Polk City, *IA, U.S.A.* **73 D5** 41 46N 93 43W
Polk County ☆, *AR, U.S.A.* **63 D1** 34 35N 94 15W
Polk County ☆, *FL, U.S.A.* **67 D7** 28 0N 81 45W
Polk County ☆, *GA, U.S.A.* **68 B1** 34 0N 85 10W
Polk County ☆, *IA, U.S.A.* **73 D5** 41 40N 93 35W
Polk County ☆, *MN, U.S.A.* **80 C2** 47 40N 96 30W
Polk County ☆, *MO, U.S.A.* **82 D3** 37 35N 93 25W
Polk County ☆, *NC, U.S.A.* **90 C3** 35 15N 82 10W
Polk County ☆, *NE, U.S.A.* **84 C8** 41 15N 97 40W
Polk County ☆, *OR, U.S.A.* **94 C2** 44 55N 123 20W
Polk County ☆, *TN, U.S.A.* **97 E8** 35 10N 84 39W
Polk County ☆, *TX, U.S.A.* **99 G13** 30 43N 94 56W
Polk County ☆, *WI, U.S.A.* **103 C1** 45 30N 92 30W
Polkton, *NC, U.S.A.* **90 C5** 35 1N 80 12W
Polkville, *MS, U.S.A.* **81 D4** 32 11N 89 42W
Polkville, *NC, U.S.A.* **90 C4** 35 25N 81 39W
Pollock, *ID, U.S.A.* **70 D2** 45 19N 116 21W
Pollock, *LA, U.S.A.* **75 C3** 31 32N 92 25W
Pollock, *MO, U.S.A.* **82 A3** 40 21N 93 5W
Pollock, *SD, U.S.A.* **91 E5** 45 55N 100 17W
Pollock Pines, *CA, U.S.A.* **64 E6** 38 46N 120 34W
Polo, *IL, U.S.A.* **71 B4** 41 59N 89 35W
Polo, *MO, U.S.A.* **82 B2** 39 33N 94 3W
Polotitlán, *México, Mexico* **219 B8** 20 13N 99 49W
Polson, *MT, U.S.A.* **83 C3** 47 41N 114 9W
Poltimore, *Qué., Canada* **176 F7** 45 47N 75 43W
Polvadera, *NM, U.S.A.* **88 C4** 34 12N 106 55W
Polvorillas, *Chihuahua, Mexico* **213 E11** 28 48N 104 14W
Polynesian Cultural Center, *HI, U.S.A.* **69 J14** 21 38N 157 55W
Pom, L., *Campeche, Mexico* **223 D1** 18 35N 92 12W
Pomeroy, *IA, U.S.A.* **73 C4** 42 33N 94 41W
Pomeroy, *OH, U.S.A.* **92 D4** 39 2N 82 2W
Pomeroy, *WA, U.S.A.* **101 D8** 46 28N 117 36W
Pomfret, *CT, U.S.A.* **78 C3** 41 54N 71 58W
Pomfret, *MD, U.S.A.* **77 B3** 38 30N 77 2W
Pomme de Terre →, *MN, U.S.A.* **80 E2** 45 10N 96 5W
Pomme de Terre →, *MO, U.S.A.* **82 C3** 38 11N 93 25W
Pomme de Terre L., *MO, U.S.A.* **82 D3** 37 54N 93 19W
Pomona, *CA, U.S.A.* **65 J9** 34 4N 117 45W
Pomona, *KS, U.S.A.* **74 C8** 38 36N 95 27W
Pomona, *MD, U.S.A.* **77 A4** 39 10N 76 7W
Pomona, *MO, U.S.A.* **82 E5** 36 52N 91 55W
Pomona, *NJ, U.S.A.* **87 C2** 39 29N 74 35W
Pomona Lake, *KS, U.S.A.* **74 C8** 38 39N 95 34W
Pomona Park, *FL, U.S.A.* **67 B7** 29 30N 81 36W
Pompano Beach, *FL, U.S.A.* **67 E8** 26 14N 80 7W
Pompeys Pillar, *MT, U.S.A.* **83 E10** 45 59N 107 57W
Pompeys Pillar Nat. Monument ⌂, *U.S.A.* **58 D10** 46 0N 108 0W
Pompton Lakes, *NJ, U.S.A.* **87 B2** 41 0N 74 17W
Pomuch, *Campeche, Mexico* **223 B3** 20 8N 90 11W
Ponass L., *Sask., Canada* **182 C8** 52 16N 103 58W
Ponca, *NE, U.S.A.* **84 B9** 42 34N 96 43W
Ponca City, *OK, U.S.A.* **93 B6** 36 42N 97 5W
Ponca Cr. →, *NE, U.S.A.* **84 B7** 42 48N 98 5W
Ponce, *Puerto Rico* **105 G16** 18 1N 66 37W
Ponce de Leon, *FL, U.S.A.* **67 A3** 30 44N 85 56W
Ponce de Leon B., *FL, U.S.A.* **67 F7** 25 15N 81 10W
Ponce Inlet, *FL, U.S.A.* **67 B8** 29 6N 80 56W
Poncha Springs, *CO, U.S.A.* **66 D4** 38 31N 106 5W
Ponchatoula, *LA, U.S.A.* **75 D5** 30 26N 90 26W
Poncheville, L., *Qué., Canada* **175 C2** 50 10N 76 55W
Poncitlán, *Jalisco, Mexico* **218 B5** 20 22N 102 55W
Pond, *CA, U.S.A.* **65 H7** 35 43N 119 20W
Pond →, *KY, U.S.A.* **96 C5** 37 32N 87 21W
Pond Creek, *OK, U.S.A.* **93 B6** 36 40N 97 48W
Pond Eddy, *NY, U.S.A.* **87 A2** 41 26N 74 49W
Pond Inlet, *Nunavut, Canada* **190 C10** 72 40N 77 0W
Pondera County ☆, *MT, U.S.A.* **83 B5** 48 12N 112 30W
Ponderosa, *NM, U.S.A.* **88 B4** 35 40N 106 40W
Pondosa, *CA, U.S.A.* **64 B5** 41 12N 121 41W
Ponds, I. of, *Nfld. & L., Canada* **175 C6** 53 27N 55 52W
Poneto, *IN, U.S.A.* **72 C5** 40 39N 85 13W
Ponoka, *Alta., Canada* **185 F7** 52 42N 113 40W
Pont-Rouge, *Qué., Canada* **177 E11** 46 45N 71 42W
Pontchartrain, L., *LA, U.S.A.* **75 D5** 30 5N 90 5W
Ponte Vedra Beach, *FL, U.S.A.* **67 A7** 30 15N 81 23W
Ponteix, *Sask., Canada* **182 F4** 49 46N 107 29W
Pontiac, *IL, U.S.A.* **71 C5** 40 53N 88 38W
Pontiac, *MI, U.S.A.* **79 G8** 42 38N 83 18W
Pontotoc, *MS, U.S.A.* **81 B5** 34 15N 89 0W
Pontotoc County ☆, *MS, U.S.A.* **81 B5** 34 15N 89 0W
Pontotoc County ☆, *OK, U.S.A.* **93 D7** 34 45N 96 45W
Pontypool, *Ont., Canada* **179 C8** 44 6N 78 38W
Poole, *KY, U.S.A.* **96 C5** 37 38N 87 39W
Poole, *NE, U.S.A.* **84 D7** 40 59N 98 58W
Pooler, *GA, U.S.A.* **68 D5** 32 7N 81 15W
Pooles I., *MD, U.S.A.* **77 A4** 39 17N 76 16W
Poolesville, *MD, U.S.A.* **77 A3** 39 9N 77 25W
Pooley I., *B.C., Canada* **186 C6** 52 45N 128 15W
Poorman, *AK, U.S.A.* **61 D9** 64 5N 155 33W
Pope, *MS, U.S.A.* **81 B4** 34 13N 89 57W
Pope County ☆, *AR, U.S.A.* **63 C3** 35 28N 92 59W
Pope County ☆, *IL, U.S.A.* **71 F5** 37 25N 88 35W
Pope County ☆, *MN, U.S.A.* **80 E3** 45 40N 95 25W
Pope Cr. →, *IL, U.S.A.* **71 B3** 41 8N 90 58W
Popejoy, *IA, U.S.A.* **73 C5** 42 36N 93 26W
Popes Creek, *MD, U.S.A.* **77 B4** 38 24N 76 58W
Poplar, *MT, U.S.A.* **83 B12** 48 7N 105 12W
Poplar, *WI, U.S.A.* **103 B2** 46 35N 91 48W
Poplar →, *Man., Canada* **183 C14** 53 0N 97 19W
Poplar →, *MT, U.S.A.* **83 B12** 48 5N 105 11W
Poplar Bluff, *MO, U.S.A.* **82 E6** 36 46N 90 24W
Poplar Grove, *IL, U.S.A.* **71 A5** 42 22N 88 49W
Poplar Grove Nat. Cemetery, *VA, U.S.A.* **102 D7** 37 10N 77 26W
Poplar Head = Dothan, *AL, U.S.A.* **60 E5** 31 13N 85 24W
Poplar Hill, *VA, U.S.A.* **102 D4** 37 13N 80 44W
Poplar I., *MD, U.S.A.* **77 B4** 38 46N 76 23W
Poplar Mt., *KY, U.S.A.* **97 D7** 36 43N 85 3W
Poplar Plains, *KY, U.S.A.* **97 B9** 38 21N 83 41W
Poplar Point, *Man., Canada* **183 E14** 50 4N 97 59W
Poplar River, *Man., Canada* **183 C14** 52 59N 97 16W
Poplarfield, *Man., Canada* **183 E14** 50 53N 97 36W
Poplarville, *MS, U.S.A.* **81 F4** 30 51N 89 32W
Popo Agie →, *WY, U.S.A.* **104 C4** 43 1N 108 21W
Popocatépetl, Volcán, *Puebla, Mexico* **221 E2** 19 2N 98 38W
Popolnah, *Yucatán, Mexico* **223 B6** 21 0N 87 35W
Poquetanuck, *CT, U.S.A.* **78 C2** 41 29N 72 3W
Poquonock Bridge, *CT, U.S.A.* **78 C2** 41 19N 72 11W
Poquoson, *VA, U.S.A.* **102 D8** 37 8N 76 24W
Porcher I., *B.C., Canada* **186 B4** 53 50N 130 30W
Porcupine, *Ont., Canada* **176 C1** 48 30N 81 11W
Porcupine, *SD, U.S.A.* **91 G3** 43 14N 102 19W
Porcupine →, *Sask., Canada* **189 E12** 59 11N 104 46W
Porcupine →, *AK, U.S.A.* **61 C11** 66 34N 145 19W
Porcupine →, *MT, U.S.A.* **83 B11** 48 7N 106 20W
Porcupine Hills, *Canada* **183 C10** 52 33N 101 22W
Porcupine Mountains Wilderness State Park ⌂, *MI, U.S.A.* **79 C2** 46 47N 89 41W
Porcupine Mts., *MI, U.S.A.* **79 C3** 46 47N 89 44W
Porcupine Plain, *Sask., Canada* **182 C8** 52 36N 103 15W
Porphyry Pk., *MT, U.S.A.* **83 C8** 47 14N 109 18W
Porquis Junction, *Qué., Canada* **176 C2** 48 42N 80 47W
Port Alberni, *B.C., Canada* **186 F10** 49 14N 124 50W
Port Alexander, *AK, U.S.A.* **61 H14** 56 15N 134 38W
Port Alfred, *Qué., Canada* **177 C12** 48 18N 70 53W
Port Alice, *B.C., Canada* **186 E7** 50 20N 127 25W
Port Allegany, *PA, U.S.A.* **95 C4** 41 48N 78 17W
Port Allen, *LA, U.S.A.* **75 D4** 30 27N 91 12W
Port Angeles, *WA, U.S.A.* **101 B2** 48 7N 123 27W
Port Aransas, *TX, U.S.A.* **99 K10** 27 50N 97 4W
Port Arthur, *TX, U.S.A.* **99 H14** 29 54N 93 56W
Port au Choix, *Nfld. & L., Canada* **174 B3** 50 43N 57 22W
Port au Port, *Nfld. & L., Canada* **174 D2** 48 33N 58 43W
Port au Port B., *Nfld. & L., Canada* **174 D2** 48 40N 58 50W
Port au Port Pen., *Nfld. & L., Canada* **174 D2** 48 35N 59 0W
Port Austin, *MI, U.S.A.* **79 E8** 44 3N 83 1W
Port Barre, *LA, U.S.A.* **75 D4** 30 34N 91 57W
Port Blandford, *Nfld. & L., Canada* **174 D6** 48 20N 54 10W
Port Burwell, *Ont., Canada* **178 E6** 42 40N 80 48W
Port Byron, *IL, U.S.A.* **71 B3** 41 36N 90 20W
Port Carling, *Ont., Canada* **178 B7** 45 7N 79 35W
Port-Cartier, *Qué., Canada* **175 C4** 50 2N 66 50W
Port-Cartier-Sept-Îles, Réserve Faunique de ⌂, *Qué., Canada* **172 C2** 50 30N 67 20W
Port Charlotte, *FL, U.S.A.* **67 E6** 26 59N 82 6W
Port Chester, *NY, U.S.A.* **89 E7** 41 0N 73 40W
Port Clements, *B.C., Canada* **186 B2** 53 40N 132 10W
Port Clinton, *OH, U.S.A.* **92 B4** 41 31N 82 56W
Port Clyde, *ME, U.S.A.* **76 E4** 43 56N 69 16W
Port Colborne, *Ont., Canada* **178 E7** 42 50N 79 10W
Port Columbus International, Columbus ✕ (CMH), *OH, U.S.A.* **92 D4** 40 0N 82 53W
Port Credit, *Ont., Canada* **178 D7** 43 33N 79 35W
Port-Daniel, Réserve Faunique de ⌂, *Qué., Canada* **172 E5** 48 11N 64 58W
Port Dover, *Ont., Canada* **178 E6** 42 47N 80 12W
Port Dufferin, *N.S., Canada* **173 J7** 44 55N 62 23W
Port Edward, *B.C., Canada* **186 A4** 54 12N 130 10W
Port Edwards, *WI, U.S.A.* **103 D4** 44 21N 89 52W
Port Elgin, *N.B., Canada* **173 G5** 46 3N 64 5W
Port Elgin, *Ont., Canada* **178 C5** 44 25N 81 25W
Port Elizabeth, *NJ, U.S.A.* **87 C2** 39 19N 74 59W
Port Essington, *B.C., Canada* **186 A5** 54 9N 129 58W
Port Ewen, *NY, U.S.A.* **89 D7** 41 54N 73 59W
Port Fourchon, *LA, U.S.A.* **75 E5** 29 6N 90 11W
Port Gamble, *WA, U.S.A.* **101 C3** 47 51N 122 34W
Port Gibson, *MS, U.S.A.* **81 E3** 31 58N 90 59W
Port Greville, *N.S., Canada* **173 H5** 45 24N 64 33W
Port Hadlock, *WA, U.S.A.* **101 B3** 48 2N 122 45W
Port Hardy, *B.C., Canada* **186 E7** 50 41N 127 30W
Port Harrison = Inukjuak, *Qué., Canada* **175 B2** 58 25N 78 15W
Port Hastings, *N.S., Canada* **173 H8** 45 39N 61 24W
Port Hawkesbury, *N.S., Canada* **173 H8** 45 36N 61 22W
Port Heiden, *AK, U.S.A.* **61 H8** 56 55N 158 41W
Port Henry, *NY, U.S.A.* **86 B1** 44 3N 73 28W
Port Hood, *N.S., Canada* **173 G8** 46 0N 61 32W
Port Hope, *Ont., Canada* **179 D8** 43 56N 78 20W
Port Hope, *MI, U.S.A.* **79 F9** 43 57N 82 43W
Port Hope Simpson, *Nfld. & L., Canada* **175 C6** 52 33N 56 18W
Port Howe, *Qué., Canada* **173 H6** 45 51N 63 45W
Port Hueneme, *CA, U.S.A.* **65 J7** 34 7N 119 12W
Port Huron, *MI, U.S.A.* **79 G9** 42 58N 82 26W
Port Isabel, *TX, U.S.A.* **98 L10** 26 5N 97 12W
Port Jefferson, *NY, U.S.A.* **78 D1** 40 57N 73 3W

Port Jefferson, *OH, U.S.A.* **92 C2** 40 20N 84 6W
Port Jervis, *NY, U.S.A.* **87 A2** 41 22N 74 41W
Port Kent, *NY, U.S.A.* **86 B1** 44 32N 73 24W
Port Lavaca, *TX, U.S.A.* **99 J11** 28 37N 96 38W
Port Leyden, *NY, U.S.A.* **89 B5** 43 35N 75 21W
Port Lions, *AK, U.S.A.* **61 H9** 57 52N 152 53W
Port Loring, *Ont., Canada* **178 B6** 45 55N 80 0W
Port Lorne, *N.S., Canada* **173 J4** 44 57N 65 16W
Port Louisa Nat. Wildlife Refuge ⌓, *IL, U.S.A.* **71 B3** 41 6N 90 57W
Port Ludlow, *WA, U.S.A.* **101 C3** 47 56N 122 41W
Port McNeill, *B.C., Canada* **186 E7** 50 35N 127 6W
Port Mansfield, *TX, U.S.A.* **98 L10** 26 34N 97 26W
Port Mayaca, *FL, U.S.A.* **67 E8** 26 59N 80 36W
Port Medway, *N.S., Canada* **173 J5** 44 8N 64 35W
Port Mellon, *B.C., Canada* **187 F11** 49 32N 123 31W
Port-Menier, *Qué., Canada* **172 D5** 49 51N 64 15W
Port Moller, *AK, U.S.A.* **61 J7** 55 59N 160 34W
Port Moody, *B.C., Canada* **187 F12** 49 17N 122 51W
Port Mouton, *N.S., Canada* **173 K5** 43 58N 64 50W
Port Neches, *TX, U.S.A.* **99 H14** 30 0N 93 59W
Port Newark, *NJ, U.S.A.* **114 B2** 40 41N 74 7W
Port Norris, *NJ, U.S.A.* **87 C1** 39 15N 75 2W
Port Nouveau-Québec = Kangiqsualujjuaq, *Qué., Canada* **175 B4** 58 30N 65 59W
Port O'Connor, *TX, U.S.A.* **99 J11** 28 27N 96 24W
Port of Portland, *Portland, U.S.A.* **116 A1** 45 34N 122 43W
Port Orange, *FL, U.S.A.* **67 B8** 29 9N 80 59W
Port Orchard, *WA, U.S.A.* **101 C3** 47 32N 122 38W
Port Orford, *OR, U.S.A.* **94 E1** 42 45N 124 30W
Port Penn, *DE, U.S.A.* **77 A5** 39 31N 75 35W
Port Perry, *Ont., Canada* **179 C8** 44 6N 78 56W
Port Reading, *NJ, U.S.A.* **114 C1** 40 33N 74 15W
Port Renfrew, *B.C., Canada* **186 G10** 48 30N 124 20W
Port Republic, *MD, U.S.A.* **77 B4** 38 30N 76 33W
Port Republic, *NJ, U.S.A.* **87 C2** 39 31N 74 29W
Port Richey, *FL, U.S.A.* **67 C6** 28 16N 82 43W
Port Richmond, *NY, U.S.A.* **114 C2** 40 38N 74 7W
Port Rowan, *Ont., Canada* **178 E6** 42 40N 80 30W
Port Royal, *N.S., Canada* **173 J4** 44 43N 65 36W
Port Royal, *KY, U.S.A.* **97 B7** 38 33N 85 5W
Port Royal, *SC, U.S.A.* **90 F5** 32 23N 80 42W
Port Royal, *VA, U.S.A.* **77 B3** 38 10N 77 12W
Port Royal Sd., *SC, U.S.A.* **90 F5** 32 15N 80 40W
Port St. Joe, *FL, U.S.A.* **67 B3** 29 49N 85 18W
Port St. John, *FL, U.S.A.* **67 C8** 28 29N 80 47W
Port St. Lucie, *FL, U.S.A.* **67 D8** 27 18N 80 21W
Port Salerno, *FL, U.S.A.* **67 D8** 27 9N 80 12W
Port Sanilac, *MI, U.S.A.* **79 F9** 43 26N 82 33W
Port Saunders, *Nfld. & L., Canada* **174 B3** 50 40N 57 18W
Port Severn, *Ont., Canada* **178 C7** 44 48N 79 43W
Port Simpson, *B.C., Canada* **189 F6** 54 30N 130 20W
Port Stanley, *Ont., Canada* **178 E5** 42 40N 81 10W
Port Sulphur, *LA, U.S.A.* **75 E6** 29 29N 89 42W
Port Susan, *WA, U.S.A.* **101 B3** 48 5N 122 15W
Port Tobacco, *MD, U.S.A.* **77 B3** 38 27N 77 2W
Port Townsend, *WA, U.S.A.* **101 B3** 48 7N 122 45W
Port Vincent, *LA, U.S.A.* **75 D5** 30 20N 90 51W
Port Vue, *Pittsburgh, U.S.A.* **116 B2** 40 20N 79 52W
Port Washington, *NY, U.S.A.* **87 B3** 40 49N 73 41W
Port Washington, *OH, U.S.A.* **92 C5** 40 20N 81 31W
Port Washington, *WI, U.S.A.* **103 E6** 43 23N 87 53W
Port Washington North, *NY, U.S.A.* **114 A4** 40 50N 73 42W
Port Wentworth, *GA, U.S.A.* **68 D5** 32 9N 81 10W
Port Wing, *WI, U.S.A.* **103 B2** 46 47N 91 23W
Portage, *IN, U.S.A.* **72 B3** 41 34N 87 11W
Portage, *ME, U.S.A.* **76 B5** 46 46N 68 29W
Portage, *MI, U.S.A.* **79 G6** 42 12N 85 35W
Portage, *Seattle, U.S.A.* **118 D3** 47 24N 122 26W
Portage, *UT, U.S.A.* **100 B3** 41 59N 112 14W
Portage, *WI, U.S.A.* **103 E4** 43 33N 89 28W
Portage →, *OH, U.S.A.* **92 B3** 41 31N 83 5W
Portage B., *Man., Canada* **183 D13** 51 33N 98 50W
Portage County ☆, *OH, U.S.A.* **92 B5** 41 9N 81 15W
Portage County ☆, *WI, U.S.A.* **103 D4** 44 25N 89 30W
Portage la Prairie, *Man., Canada* **183 F13** 49 58N 98 18W
Portage Park, *Chicago, U.S.A.* **108 B2** 41 56N 87 45W
Portageville, *MO, U.S.A.* **82 E7** 36 26N 89 42W
Portal, *AZ, U.S.A.* **62 F6** 31 55N 109 9W
Portal, *GA, U.S.A.* **68 D5** 32 33N 81 56W
Portal, *ND, U.S.A.* **91 B3** 48 59N 102 33W
Portales, *NM, U.S.A.* **88 C7** 34 11N 103 20W
Porter, *MN, U.S.A.* **80 F2** 44 38N 96 10W
Porter, *OK, U.S.A.* **93 C8** 35 52N 95 31W
Porter, *WA, U.S.A.* **101 D2** 46 56N 123 18W
Porter, L., *Orlando, U.S.A.* **115 A3** 28 30N 81 19W
Porter County ☆, *IN, U.S.A.* **72 B3** 41 25N 87 5W
Porterville, *CA, U.S.A.* **65 G7** 36 4N 119 1W
Porterville, *MS, U.S.A.* **81 D5** 32 41N 88 28W
Portezuelo, Cerro El, *Baja Calif., Mexico* **210 C3** 30 22N 115 20W
Porthill, *ID, U.S.A.* **70 A2** 48 59N 116 30W
Portis, *KS, U.S.A.* **74 B5** 39 34N 98 41W
Portland, *Ont., Canada* **179 C10** 44 42N 76 12W
Portland, *AR, U.S.A.* **63 E4** 33 14N 91 31W
Portland, *CT, U.S.A.* **78 C2** 41 34N 72 38W
Portland, *FL, U.S.A.* **67 A2** 30 31N 86 12W
Portland, *IN, U.S.A.* **72 C6** 40 26N 84 59W
Portland, *ME, U.S.A.* **76 E3** 43 39N 70 16W
Portland, *MI, U.S.A.* **79 G7** 42 52N 84 54W
Portland, *MO, U.S.A.* **82 C5** 38 43N 91 43W
Portland, *ND, U.S.A.* **91 C8** 47 30N 97 22W
Portland, *OR, U.S.A.* **94 B3** 45 32N 122 37W
Portland, *PA, U.S.A.* **87 B1** 40 55N 75 6W
Portland, *TN, U.S.A.* **96 D6** 36 35N 86 31W
Portland, *TX, U.S.A.* **99 K10** 27 53N 97 20W
Portland Creek Pond, *Nfld. & L., Canada* **174 B3** 50 11N 57 32W
Portland International ✕ (PDX), *OR, U.S.A.* **94 B3** 45 35N 122 36W
Portland Prom., *Qué., Canada* **175 B2** 58 40N 78 33W
Portneuf, *Qué., Canada* **177 E11** 46 43N 71 55W
Portneuf →, *Qué., Canada* **177 C13** 48 38N 69 5W
Portneuf →, *ID, U.S.A.* **70 G6** 42 58N 112 35W
Portneuf, Réserve Faunique de ⌓, *Qué., Canada* **177 D10** 47 10N 72 25W
Portneuf Range, *ID, U.S.A.* **70 G7** 42 50N 112 0W
Portola, *CA, U.S.A.* **64 D6** 39 49N 120 28W
Portsmouth, *NH, U.S.A.* **86 C4** 43 5N 70 45W
Portsmouth, *OH, U.S.A.* **92 E4** 38 44N 82 57W
Portsmouth, *RI, U.S.A.* **78 C3** 41 36N 71 15W
Portsmouth, *VA, U.S.A.* **102 E8** 36 58N 76 23W
Portville, *NY, U.S.A.* **89 C2** 42 3N 78 20W
Porum, *OK, U.S.A.* **93 C8** 35 22N 95 16W
Posen, *MI, U.S.A.* **79 D8** 45 16N 83 42W
Posey County ☆, *IN, U.S.A.* **72 E3** 38 0N 87 50W
Poseyville, *IN, U.S.A.* **72 E3** 38 10N 87 47W
Possum Kingdom L., *TX, U.S.A.* **99 E9** 32 52N 98 26W
Post, *OR, U.S.A.* **94 C5** 44 10N 120 29W
Post, *TX, U.S.A.* **98 D6** 33 12N 101 23W
Post Falls, *ID, U.S.A.* **70 B2** 47 43N 116 57W
Posta de Jihuites, *Durango, Mexico* **216 B5** 25 44N 105 37W
Poste-de-la-Baleine = Kuujjuarapik, *Qué., Canada* **175 B2** 55 20N 77 35W
Poston, *AZ, U.S.A.* **62 C1** 34 0N 114 24W
Posts, *CA, U.S.A.* **64 G5** 36 14N 121 46W
Postville, *IA, U.S.A.* **73 B7** 43 5N 91 34W
Pot Mt., *ID, U.S.A.* **70 C3** 46 44N 115 24W
Potagannissing B., *MI, U.S.A.* **79 C8** 46 5N 83 50W
Potatch →, *ID, U.S.A.* **70 C2** 46 26N 116 47W
Potawatomi Indian Reservation, *WI, U.S.A.* **103 C5** 45 27N 88 35W
Poteau, *OK, U.S.A.* **93 C9** 35 3N 94 37W
Poteau →, *OK, U.S.A.* **93 C9** 35 23N 94 26W
Poteet, *TX, U.S.A.* **99 H9** 29 2N 98 35W
Poterdale, *GA, U.S.A.* **68 C3** 33 35N 83 54W
Poth, *TX, U.S.A.* **99 H9** 29 4N 98 5W
Potholes Res., *WA, U.S.A.* **101 D6** 46 59N 119 16W
Potlatch, *ID, U.S.A.* **70 C2** 46 55N 116 54W
Potomac, *IL, U.S.A.* **71 C6** 40 18N 87 48W
Potomac, *MD, U.S.A.* **77 A3** 38 59N 77 13W
Potomac →, *MD, U.S.A.* **77 B4** 38 0N 76 23W
Potomac Heights, *MD, U.S.A.* **77 B3** 38 36N 77 8W
Potosi, *MO, U.S.A.* **82 D6** 37 56N 90 47W
Potosí, B., *Michoacan, Mexico* **218 E6** 17 35N 101 35W
Potosí, Pta. el, *Guerrero, Mexico* **219 E6** 17 33N 101 27W
Potrero Chico, Parque Recreativo, *Monterrey, Mexico* **224 A1** 25 53N 100 26W
Potrero del Llano, *Durango, Mexico* **216 A5** 26 7N 105 13W
Potrero Hill, *San Francisco, U.S.A.* **118 B2** 37 45N 122 23W
Potrero Pt., *San Francisco, U.S.A.* **118 B2** 37 45N 122 22W
Potsdam, *NY, U.S.A.* **89 A6** 44 40N 74 59W
Pottawatomie County ☆, *KS, U.S.A.* **74 B7** 39 20N 96 15W
Pottawatomie County ☆, *OK, U.S.A.* **93 C7** 35 10N 97 0W
Pottawattamie County ☆, *IA, U.S.A.* **73 D3** 41 20N 95 30W
Potter, *KS, U.S.A.* **74 B8** 39 26N 95 9W
Potter, *NE, U.S.A.* **84 C2** 41 13N 103 19W
Potter County ☆, *PA, U.S.A.* **95 C5** 41 50N 78 0W
Potter County ☆, *SD, U.S.A.* **91 E6** 45 0N 100 0W
Potter County ☆, *TX, U.S.A.* **98 B6** 35 22N 101 50W
Potterville, *GA, U.S.A.* **68 D2** 32 31N 84 7W
Potterville, *MI, U.S.A.* **79 G7** 42 38N 84 45W
Potts Camp, *MS, U.S.A.* **81 B4** 34 39N 89 18W
Pottsboro, *TX, U.S.A.* **99 D11** 33 46N 96 40W
Pottstown, *PA, U.S.A.* **87 B1** 40 15N 75 39W
Pottsville, *PA, U.S.A.* **95 D6** 40 41N 76 12W
Poturo, *Michoacan, Mexico* **218 D6** 18 48N 101 38W
Potwin, *KS, U.S.A.* **74 D6** 37 56N 97 1W
Pouch Cove, *Nfld. & L., Canada* **174 E8** 47 46N 52 46W
Poughkeepsie, *NY, U.S.A.* **89 D7** 41 42N 73 56W
Poulan, *GA, U.S.A.* **68 E3** 31 31N 83 47W
Poulin-de-Courval, L., *Qué., Canada* **177 C12** 48 52N 70 27W
Poulsbo, *WA, U.S.A.* **101 C3** 47 44N 122 38W
Poultney, *VT, U.S.A.* **86 C1** 43 31N 73 14W
Pound, *VA, U.S.A.* **102 D2** 37 8N 82 36W
Pound, *WI, U.S.A.* **103 C5** 45 6N 88 2W
Poutrincourt, L., *Qué., Canada* **177 B8** 49 11N 74 7W
Poverty Point Nat. Monument ⌓, *LA, U.S.A.* **75 B4** 32 39N 91 24W
Povungnituk = Puvirnituq, *Qué., Canada* **175 A2** 60 2N 77 10W
Powassan, *Ont., Canada* **178 A7** 46 5N 79 25W
Poway, *CA, U.S.A.* **65 L9** 32 58N 117 2W
Powder →, *MT, U.S.A.* **83 D12** 46 45N 105 26W
Powder →, *OR, U.S.A.* **94 C8** 44 45N 117 3W
Powder Horn Park, *Minneapolis-St. Paul, U.S.A.* **113 B2** 44 56N 93 15W
Powder River, *WY, U.S.A.* **104 C6** 43 2N 106 59W
Powder River County ☆, *MT, U.S.A.* **83 E12** 45 20N 105 40W
Powder River Pass, *WY, U.S.A.* **104 B5** 44 9N 107 5W
Powder Springs, *GA, U.S.A.* **68 C2** 33 52N 84 41W
Powderhorn, *CO, U.S.A.* **66 D3** 38 17N 107 7W
Powell, *ID, U.S.A.* **70 C4** 46 35N 114 43W
Powell, *OH, U.S.A.* **92 C5** 40 18N 81 42W
Powell, *TN, U.S.A.* **97 D8** 36 2N 84 2W
Powell, *WY, U.S.A.* **104 B4** 44 45N 108 46W
Powell →, *TN, U.S.A.* **97 D9** 36 29N 83 52W
Powell, L., *UT, U.S.A.* **100 G4** 36 57N 111 29W
Powell Butte, *OR, U.S.A.* **94 C4** 44 15N 121 1W
Powell Butte Park, *Portland, U.S.A.* **116 B2** 45 29N 122 30W
Powell County ☆, *KY, U.S.A.* **97 C9** 37 50N 83 50W
Powell County ☆, *MT, U.S.A.* **83 D4** 47 0N 113 0W
Powell L., *B.C., Canada* **186 E10** 50 2N 124 25W
Powell River, *B.C., Canada* **186 F10** 49 50N 124 35W
Powellville, *MD, U.S.A.* **77 B5** 38 20N 75 22W
Powelton, *GA, U.S.A.* **68 C4** 33 26N 82 52W
Power County ☆, *ID, U.S.A.* **70 G6** 42 50N 112 50W
Power House = Drayton Valley, *Alta., Canada* **184 E6** 53 12N 114 58W
Powers, *MI, U.S.A.* **79 D4** 45 41N 87 32W
Powers, *OR, U.S.A.* **94 E1** 42 53N 124 4W
Powers Lake, *ND, U.S.A.* **91 B3** 48 34N 102 39W
Powersville, *MO, U.S.A.* **82 A3** 40 33N 93 15W
Poweshiek County ☆, *IA, U.S.A.* **73 D6** 41 40N 92 30W
Powhatan, *AR, U.S.A.* **63 B4** 36 5N 91 7W
Powhatan, *VA, U.S.A.* **102 D7** 37 32N 77 55W
Powhatan County ☆, *VA, U.S.A.* **102 D7** 37 32N 77 55W
Powhatan Point, *OH, U.S.A.* **92 D6** 39 52N 80 49W
Powhattan, *KS, U.S.A.* **74 B8** 39 46N 95 38W
Pownal, *VT, U.S.A.* **86 D1** 42 46N 73 14W
Poxyaxum, *Campeche, Mexico* **223 C3** 19 45N 90 20W
Poydras, *New Orleans, U.S.A.* **113 C3** 29 52N 89 53W
Poygan L., *WI, U.S.A.* **103 D5** 44 19N 88 50W
Poynette, *WI, U.S.A.* **103 E4** 43 24N 89 24W
Poza Rica, *Veracruz, Mexico* **220 D3** 20 33N 97 27W
Pozo Coyote, *Sonora, Mexico* **212 C3** 30 25N 112 55W
Pozuelos, *San Luis Potosí, Mexico* **215 H3** 22 6N 101 7W
Prado Churubusco, *Distrito Federal, Mexico* **225 B3** 19 20N 99 8W
Prague, *NE, U.S.A.* **84 C9** 41 19N 96 49W
Prague, *OK, U.S.A.* **93 C7** 35 29N 96 41W
Praires, R. des →, *Montréal, Canada* **192 A3** 45 38N 73 36W
Prairie, *MS, U.S.A.* **81 C5** 33 48N 88 40W
Prairie Band of the Potawatomi Indian Reservation, *KS, U.S.A.* **74 B8** 39 20N 95 52W
Prairie City, *IA, U.S.A.* **73 D5** 41 36N 93 14W
Prairie City, *OR, U.S.A.* **94 C7** 44 28N 118 43W
Prairie City, *SD, U.S.A.* **91 E3** 45 32N 102 48W
Prairie County ☆, *AR, U.S.A.* **63 D4** 34 47N 91 35W
Prairie County ☆, *MT, U.S.A.* **83 D12** 46 57N 105 30W
Prairie Dog Cr. →, *KS, U.S.A.* **74 B4** 40 0N 99 18W
Prairie Dog Town Fork Red →, *U.S.A.* **98 C7** 34 34N 99 58W
Prairie du Chien, *WI, U.S.A.* **103 E2** 43 3N 91 9W
Prairie du Rocher, *IL, U.S.A.* **71 E3** 38 5N 90 6W
Prairie du Sac, *WI, U.S.A.* **103 E4** 43 17N 89 43W
Prairie Farm, *WI, U.S.A.* **103 C2** 45 14N 91 59W
Prairie Grove, *AR, U.S.A.* **63 C1** 35 59N 94 19W
Prairie Hill, *MO, U.S.A.* **82 B4** 39 31N 92 44W
Prairie Home, *MO, U.S.A.* **82 C4** 38 49N 92 35W
Prairie Island Indian Reservation, *MN, U.S.A.* **80 F6** 44 39N 92 39W
Prairie View, *KS, U.S.A.* **74 B4** 39 50N 99 34W
Prairie View, *TX, U.S.A.* **99 G12** 30 6N 95 59W
Prairie Village, *KS, U.S.A.* **74 C9** 38 58N 94 38W
Pratt, *KS, U.S.A.* **74 D5** 37 39N 98 44W
Pratt County ☆, *KS, U.S.A.* **74 D5** 37 35N 98 45W
Prattville, *AL, U.S.A.* **60 D4** 32 28N 86 29W
Práxedis G. Guerrero, *Chihuahua, Mexico* **213 B9** 31 22N 106 0W
Preble, *NY, U.S.A.* **89 C4** 42 44N 76 9W
Preble County ☆, *OH, U.S.A.* **92 D2** 39 45N 84 38W
Preeceville, *Sask., Canada* **182 D9** 51 57N 102 40W
Preissac, L., *Qué., Canada* **176 C4** 48 20N 78 20W
Prelate, *Sask., Canada* **182 E2** 50 51N 109 24W
Premont, *TX, U.S.A.* **98 K9** 27 22N 98 7W
Prentice, *WI, U.S.A.* **103 C3** 45 33N 90 17W
Prentiss, *MS, U.S.A.* **81 E4** 31 36N 89 52W
Prentiss County ☆, *MS, U.S.A.* **81 B5** 34 39N 88 34W
Presa de Guadalupe, *San Luis Potosí, Mexico* **215 H4** 22 52N 100 8W
Presa de la Amistad, Parque Natural ⌓, *Coahuila, Mexico* **214 A3** 29 30N 101 15W
Presa de San Pedro, *Coahuila, Mexico* **215 F3** 24 41N 101 3W
Presa Verde, *San Luis Potosí, Mexico* **215 F4** 24 0N 100 42W
Prescott, *Ont., Canada* **179 C11** 44 45N 75 30W
Prescott, *AZ, U.S.A.* **62 C3** 34 33N 112 28W
Prescott, *AR, U.S.A.* **63 E2** 33 48N 93 23W
Prescott, *IA, U.S.A.* **73 D4** 41 1N 94 37W
Prescott, *KS, U.S.A.* **74 C9** 38 4N 94 42W
Prescott, *MI, U.S.A.* **79 E8** 44 11N 83 56W
Prescott, *OR, U.S.A.* **94 A3** 46 3N 122 53W
Prescott, *WA, U.S.A.* **101 D7** 46 18N 118 19W
Prescott, *WI, U.S.A.* **103 D1** 44 45N 92 48W
Prescott I., *B.C., Canada* **186 A4** 54 6N 130 37W
Prescott I., *Nunavut, Canada* **190 C6** 73 3N 96 50W
Prescott Nat. Forest, *AZ, U.S.A.* **62 C3** 34 30N 112 30W
Prescott Valley, *AZ, U.S.A.* **62 C3** 34 40N 112 18W
Presho, *SD, U.S.A.* **91 G5** 43 54N 100 3W
Presidente Calles, Presa, *Aguascalientes, Mexico* **217 E8** 22 9N 102 27W
Presidente Juárez, *Quintana Roo, Mexico* **223 C5** 19 18N 88 34W
Presidential Lakes Estates, *NJ, U.S.A.* **87 C2** 39 54N 74 35W
Presidents I., *TN, U.S.A.* **112 B1** 35 6N 90 6W
Presidio, *San Francisco, U.S.A.* **118 B2** 37 47N 122 27W
Presidio, *TX, U.S.A.* **98 H3** 29 34N 104 22W
Presidio County ☆, *TX, U.S.A.* **98 G3** 30 0N 104 0W
Presido →, *Sinaloa, Mexico* **216 D4** 23 6N 106 17W
Presque I., *PA, U.S.A.* **95 B2** 42 10N 80 6W
Presque Isle, *ME, U.S.A.* **76 B5** 46 41N 68 1W
Presque Isle, *MI, U.S.A.* **79 D8** 45 18N 83 29W
Presque Isle County ☆, *MI, U.S.A.* **79 D8** 45 15N 84 0W
Preston, *GA, U.S.A.* **68 D2** 32 4N 84 32W
Preston, *ID, U.S.A.* **70 G7** 42 6N 111 53W
Preston, *IA, U.S.A.* **73 C8** 42 3N 90 24W
Preston, *KS, U.S.A.* **74 D5** 37 46N 98 33W
Preston, *MD, U.S.A.* **77 B5** 38 43N 75 55W
Preston, *MN, U.S.A.* **80 G6** 43 40N 92 5W
Preston, *MS, U.S.A.* **81 D5** 32 53N 88 50W
Preston, *NV, U.S.A.* **85 D5** 38 55N 115 4W
Preston, *OK, U.S.A.* **93 C8** 35 43N 95 59W
Preston City, *CT, U.S.A.* **78 C2** 41 33N 72 57W
Preston County ☆, *WV, U.S.A.* **102 B5** 39 31N 79 48W
Prestonsburg, *KY, U.S.A.* **97 C10** 37 40N 82 47W
Pretty Prairie, *KS, U.S.A.* **74 D5** 37 47N 98 1W
Prettyboy Res., *MD, U.S.A.* **77 A4** 39 37N 76 43W
Préville, *Montréal, Canada* **192 B4** 45 28N 73 29W
Prewitt, *NM, U.S.A.* **88 B2** 35 22N 108 3W
Prewitt Res., *CO, U.S.A.* **66 B7** 40 26N 103 22W
Pribilof Is., *AK, U.S.A.* **61 H5** 57 0N 170 0W
Price, *Qué., Canada* **172 E1** 48 36N 68 7W
Price, *MD, U.S.A.* **77 A5** 39 6N 75 58W
Price, *TX, U.S.A.* **99 E13** 32 8N 94 57W
Price, *UT, U.S.A.* **100 D5** 39 36N 110 49W
Price →, *UT, U.S.A.* **100 D5** 39 10N 110 6W
Price County ☆, *WI, U.S.A.* **103 C3** 45 45N 90 20W
Price Hill, *OH, U.S.A.* **107 B1** 39 6N 84 34W
Price I., *B.C., Canada* **186 C6** 52 23N 128 41W
Prichard, *AL, U.S.A.* **60 F2** 30 44N 88 5W
Prichard, *WV, U.S.A.* **102 C2** 38 15N 82 36W
Priddy, *TX, U.S.A.* **99 F9** 31 41N 98 31W
Pride, *KY, U.S.A.* **96 C5** 37 34N 87 53W
Priest →, *ID, U.S.A.* **70 A2** 48 12N 116 54W
Priest L., *ID, U.S.A.* **70 A2** 48 35N 116 52W
Priest Rapids Dam, *WA, U.S.A.* **101 D6** 46 39N 119 54W
Priest River, *ID, U.S.A.* **70 A2** 48 11N 116 55W
Prime Hook Nat. Wildlife Refuge ⌓, *DE, U.S.A.* **77 B5** 38 55N 75 18W
Primera, *TX, U.S.A.* **98 L10** 26 13N 97 45W
Primghar, *IA, U.S.A.* **73 B3** 43 5N 95 38W
Primm, *NV, U.S.A.* **85 G5** 35 37N 115 23W
Primo Tapia, *Baja Calif., Mexico* **210 A2** 32 16N 116 54W
Primrose, *NE, U.S.A.* **84 C7** 41 38N 98 14W
Primrose L., *Sask., Canada* **189 F11** 54 55N 109 45W
Prince, *Sask., Canada* **182 C3** 52 58N 108 23W
Prince Albert, *Sask., Canada* **182 B6** 53 15N 105 50W
Prince Albert Nat. Park △, *Sask., Canada* **182 B5** 54 0N 106 25W
Prince Albert Pen., *N.W.T., Canada* **188 B9** 72 30N 116 0W
Prince Albert Sd., *N.W.T., Canada* **188 B9** 70 25N 115 0W
Prince Alfred, C., *N.W.T., Canada* **188 B8** 74 20N 124 40W
Prince Charles I., *Nunavut, Canada* **190 D10** 67 47N 76 12W
Prince Edward County ☆, *VA, U.S.A.* **102 D6** 37 15N 78 25W
Prince Edward I. □, *Canada* **173 G6** 46 20N 63 20W
Prince Edward Island Nat. Park △, *P.E.I., Canada* **173 G6** 46 26N 63 12W
Prince Edward Pt., *Ont., Canada* **179 D10** 43 56N 76 52W
Prince Frederick, *MD, U.S.A.* **77 B4** 38 33N 76 35W
Prince George, *B.C., Canada* **187 B12** 53 55N 122 50W
Prince George, *VA, U.S.A.* **102 D7** 37 13N 77 17W
Prince George County ☆, *VA, U.S.A.* **102 D7** 37 13N 77 17W
Prince Georges County ☆, *MD, U.S.A.* **77 B4** 38 45N 76 50W
Prince Gustaf Adolf Sea, *N.W.T., Canada* **190 B4** 78 30N 107 0W
Prince of Wales, C., *Qué, Canada* **175 A3** 61 37N 71 30W
Prince of Wales, C., *AK, U.S.A.* **61 D5** 65 36N 168 5W
Prince of Wales I., *Nunavut, Canada* **190 C6** 73 0N 99 0W
Prince of Wales I., *AK, U.S.A.* **61 J14** 55 47N 132 50W
Prince of Wales Icefield, *Nunavut, Canada* **190 B10** 78 15N 79 0W
Prince of Wales-Outer Ketchikan ☆, *AK, U.S.A.* **61 J15** 55 30N 132 0W
Prince of Wales Str., *N.W.T., Canada* **188 B9** 73 0N 117 0W
Prince Patrick I., *N.W.T., Canada* **188 A9** 77 0N 120 0W
Prince Regent Inlet, *Nunavut, Canada* **190 C8** 73 0N 90 0W
Prince Rupert, *B.C., Canada* **186 A4** 54 20N 130 20W
Prince William County ☆, *VA, U.S.A.* **102 C7** 38 45N 77 29W
Prince William Forest Park ⌓, *VA, U.S.A.* **102 C7** 38 35N 77 24W
Prince William Sd., *AK, U.S.A.* **61 F11** 60 40N 147 0W
Princess Anne, *MD, U.S.A.* **77 B5** 38 12N 75 42W
Princess Margaret Range, *N.W.T., Canada* **190 A7** 80 30N 92 0W
Princess Royal Chan., *B.C., Canada* **186 B6** 53 0N 128 31W
Princess Royal I., *B.C., Canada* **186 B6** 53 0N 128 40W
Princeton, *B.C., Canada* **187 F14** 49 27N 120 30W
Princeton, *AR, U.S.A.* **63 E3** 33 59N 92 38W
Princeton, *CA, U.S.A.* **64 D4** 39 24N 122 1W
Princeton, *IL, U.S.A.* **71 B4** 41 23N 89 28W
Princeton, *IN, U.S.A.* **72 E3** 38 21N 87 34W
Princeton, *IA, U.S.A.* **73 D8** 41 40N 90 20W
Princeton, *KS, U.S.A.* **74 C8** 38 29N 95 16W
Princeton, *KY, U.S.A.* **96 C5** 37 7N 87 53W
Princeton, *ME, U.S.A.* **76 C6** 45 13N 67 34W
Princeton, *MA, U.S.A.* **78 B3** 42 27N 71 55W
Princeton, *MI, U.S.A.* **79 C4** 46 17N 87 29W
Princeton, *MN, U.S.A.* **80 E5** 45 34N 93 35W
Princeton, *MO, U.S.A.* **82 A3** 40 24N 93 35W
Princeton, *NC, U.S.A.* **90 C7** 35 28N 78 10W
Princeton, *NJ, U.S.A.* **87 B2** 40 21N 74 39W
Princeton, *WV, U.S.A.* **102 D3** 37 22N 81 6W
Princeton, *WI, U.S.A.* **103 E4** 43 51N 89 8W
Princeville, *Qué., Canada* **177 E11** 46 10N 71 53W
Princeville, *HI, U.S.A.* **69 A2** 22 13N 159 29W
Princeville, *IL, U.S.A.* **71 C4** 40 56N 89 46W
Principe Chan., *B.C., Canada* **186 B4** 53 28N 130 0W
Prineville, *OR, U.S.A.* **94 C5** 44 18N 120 51W
Prineville Res., *OR, U.S.A.* **94 C5** 44 7N 120 47W
Pringle, *SD, U.S.A.* **91 G2** 43 37N 103 36W
Pringle, *TX, U.S.A.* **98 B6** 35 57N 101 27W
Prinsburg, *MN, U.S.A.* **80 F3** 44 56N 95 11W
Prior Lake, *MN, U.S.A.* **80 F5** 44 43N 93 25W
Pritchett, *CO, U.S.A.* **66 E8** 37 22N 102 52W
Procter, *B.C., Canada* **187 F18** 49 37N 116 57W
Proctor, *CO, U.S.A.* **66 B8** 40 48N 102 57W
Proctor, *MN, U.S.A.* **80 D6** 46 45N 92 14W
Proctor, *VT, U.S.A.* **86 C1** 43 40N 73 2W
Proctor, *WV, U.S.A.* **102 B4** 39 43N 80 49W
Proctor L., *TX, U.S.A.* **99 F9** 31 58N 98 29W
Proctorsville, *VT, U.S.A.* **86 C2** 43 23N 72 40W
Proctorville, *OH, U.S.A.* **92 E4** 38 26N 82 23W
Progreso, *Baja Calif., Mexico* **210 A3** 32 38N 115 40W
Progreso, *Chihuahua, Mexico* **213 C8** 30 25N 107 17W
Progreso, *Coahuila, Mexico* **214 C4** 27 28N 100 59W
Progreso, *Hidalgo, Mexico* **219 B8** 20 15N 99 12W
Progreso, *Yucatán, Mexico* **223 A4** 21 20N 89 40W
Progreso Nacional, *Distrito Federal, Mexico* **225 A3** 19 30N 99 9W
Promise City, *IA, U.S.A.* **73 E5** 40 45N 93 9W
Promontory Mts., *UT, U.S.A.* **100 B3** 41 40N 112 30W
Prophet →, *B.C., Canada* **189 E8** 58 48N 122 40W
Prophet River, *B.C., Canada* **189 E8** 58 6N 122 43W
Prophetstown, *IL, U.S.A.* **71 B4** 41 40N 89 56W
Prospect, *CT, U.S.A.* **78 C2** 41 30N 72 59W
Prospect, *KY, U.S.A.* **97 B7** 38 21N 85 37W
Prospect, *OH, U.S.A.* **92 C3** 40 27N 83 11W
Prospect, *OR, U.S.A.* **94 E3** 42 45N 122 29W
Prospect, *PA, U.S.A.* **95 D2** 40 54N 80 3W
Prospect Hill Park, *Boston, U.S.A.* **106 A2** 42 23N 71 13W
Prospect Park, *NJ, U.S.A.* **114 A1** 40 56N 74 10W
Prospect Park, *NY, U.S.A.* **114 C3** 40 39N 73 58W
Prospect Pt., *Vancouver, Canada* **193 B2** 49 19N 123 8W
Prosperity, *SC, U.S.A.* **90 D4** 34 12N 81 32W
Prosser, *NE, U.S.A.* **84 D7** 40 41N 98 34W
Prosser, *WA, U.S.A.* **101 D6** 46 12N 119 46W
Protection, *KS, U.S.A.* **74 D4** 37 12N 99 29W
Protem, *MO, U.S.A.* **82 E4** 36 32N 92 51W
Protivin, *IA, U.S.A.* **73 B6** 43 13N 92 6W
Providence, *Baltimore, U.S.A.* **107 A2** 39 25N 76 33W
Providence, *KY, U.S.A.* **96 C5** 37 24N 87 46W
Providence, *RI, U.S.A.* **78 C3** 41 49N 71 24W
Providence, *UT, U.S.A.* **100 B4** 41 43N 111 49W
Providence Bay, *Ont., Canada* **178 B4** 45 41N 82 15W
Providence County ☆, *RI, U.S.A.* **78 C3** 41 50N 71 40W
Providence Mts., *CA, U.S.A.* **65 H11** 35 10N 115 15W
Provincetown, *MA, U.S.A.* **78 B4** 42 3N 70 11W
Provo, *SD, U.S.A.* **91 G2** 43 12N 103 50W
Provo, *UT, U.S.A.* **100 C4** 40 14N 111 39W
Provost, *Alta., Canada* **185 F10** 52 25N 110 20W
Prowers County ☆, *CO, U.S.A.* **66 E8** 38 0N 102 30W
Prudence I., *RI, U.S.A.* **78 C3** 41 37N 71 19W
Prudhoe Bay, *AK, U.S.A.* **61 A10** 70 18N 148 22W
Prud'homme, *Sask., Canada* **182 C6** 52 20N 105 54W
Prue, *OK, U.S.A.* **93 B7** 36 15N 96 15W
Pryor, *OK, U.S.A.* **93 B8** 36 19N 95 19W
Pryor Mts., *MT, U.S.A.* **83 E9** 45 15N 108 30W
Pua'ena Pt., *HI, U.S.A.* **69 J13** 21 36N 158 6W
Puckaway L., *WI, U.S.A.* **103 E4** 43 45N 89 10W
Puckett, *MS, U.S.A.* **81 D4** 32 5N 89 47W
Pucnachén, *Campeche, Mexico* **223 B3** 20 22N 90 13W
Puebla, *Puebla, Mexico* **221 E2** 19 3N 98 12W
Puebla □, *Mexico* **221 F3** 18 50N 98 0W
Pueblillo, *Veracruz, Mexico* **220 D3** 20 15N 97 14W
Pueblo, *CO, U.S.A.* **66 D6** 38 16N 104 37W
Pueblo Colorado Wash →, *AZ, U.S.A.* **62 B5** 35 5N 110 22W
Pueblo County ☆, *CO, U.S.A.* **66 D6** 38 15N 104 30W
Pueblo Mt., *OR, U.S.A.* **94 E7** 42 6N 118 39W
Pueblo Mts., *OR, U.S.A.* **94 E7** 42 6N 118 43W
Pueblo Nuevo, *Durango, Mexico* **216 D5** 23 23N 105 23W
Pueblo Nuevo Jolistahuacán, *Chiapas, Mexico* **222 B4** 17 6N 92 53W
Pueblo Viejo, *Sinaloa, Mexico* **216 C4** 24 8N 106 9W
Pueblo Viejo, *Veracruz, Mexico* **220 E4** 19 48N 96 51W
Pueblo Viejo, L., *Veracruz, Mexico* **220 B3** 22 10N 97 53W
Pueblo West, *CO, U.S.A.* **66 D6** 38 20N 104 43W
Pueblo Yaqui, *Sonora, Mexico* **212 F5** 27 20N 110 2W
Puente de Ixtla, *Morelos, Mexico* **219 D8** 18 38N 99 19W
Puente Hills, *Los Angeles, U.S.A.* **111 B4** 33 59N 117 55W
Pueo Pt., *HI, U.S.A.* **69 B1** 21 54N 160 4W
Puerca, Pta., *Puerto Rico* **105 G17** 18 13N 65 36W
Puerco →, *AZ, U.S.A.* **62 C5** 34 54N 110 2W
Puerco →, *NM, U.S.A.* **88 C3** 34 22N 107 50W
Puertecitos, *Baja Calif., Mexico* **210 C4** 30 22N 114 40W
Puerto Ángel, *Oaxaca, Mexico* **221 J4** 15 40N 96 29W
Puerto Arista, *Chiapas, Mexico* **222 D3** 15 56N 93 48W
Puerto Arturo, *Quintana Roo, Mexico* **223 C4** 19 38N 89 5W
Puerto Bravo, *Quintana Roo, Mexico* **223 D6** 18 47N 87 40W
Puerto Canoas, *Baja Calif., Mexico* **210 D3** 29 26N 115 8W
Puerto Chale, *Baja Calif. S., Mexico* **211 J7** 24 26N 111 33W
Puerto Cortés, *Baja Calif. S., Mexico* **211 J7** 24 28N 111 51W
Puerto de Luna, *NM, U.S.A.* **88 B6** 35 50N 104 37W
Puerto del Gallo, *Guerrero, Mexico* **219 E7** 17 30N 100 11W
Puerto Escondido, *Baja Calif. S., Mexico* **211 F4** 27 35N 114 46W
Puerto Escondido, *Oaxaca, Mexico* **221 J3** 15 50N 97 3W
Puerto Juárez, *Quintana Roo, Mexico* **223 A7** 21 11N 86 49W
Puerto Libertad, *Sonora, Mexico* **212 D3** 29 55N 112 43W
Puerto Lobos, *Sonora, Mexico* **212 C3** 30 25N 112 55W
Puerto Madero, *Chiapas, Mexico* **222 E4** 14 44N 92 25W
Puerto Mexico = Coatzacoalcos, *Mexico* **221 F6** 18 7N 94 25W
Puerto Modero, *Zacatecas, Mexico* **217 D9** 23 43N 101 56W
Puerto Morelos, *Quintana Roo, Mexico* **223 B7** 20 50N 86 52W
Puerto Morro Redondo, *Baja Calif. S., Mexico* **211 E3** 28 2N 115 11W

Puerto Peñasco, *Sonora, Mexico* . **212 B2** 31 20N 113 33W
Puerto Rico ☒, *W. Indies* . **105 G16** 18 15N 66 45W
Puerto San Andrecito, *Baja Calif. S., Mexico* . **211 H6** 25 49N 112 8W
Puerto Vallarta, *Jalisco, Mexico* . **218 B2** 20 37N 105 15W
Puerto Vallarta ✈ (PVR), *Jalisco, Mexico* . **218 B2** 20 39N 105 15W
Puget Sound, *WA, U.S.A.* . **101 C3** 47 50N 122 30W
Pugwash, *Qué., Canada* . **173 H6** 45 51N 63 40W
Pukalani, *HI, U.S.A.* . **69 C5** 20 51N 156 20W
Pukaskwa →, *Ont., Canada* . **181 D11** 48 0N 85 53W
Pukaskwa Nat. Park △, *Ont., Canada* . **181 D11** 48 20N 86 0W
Pukatawagan, *Man., Canada* . **189 E12** 55 45N 101 20W
Pūko'o, *HI, U.S.A.* . **69 B5** 21 4N 156 48W
Pulaski, *IL, U.S.A.* . **71 F4** 37 12N 89 10W
Pulaski, *IA, U.S.A.* . **73 E6** 40 45N 92 12W
Pulaski, *MS, U.S.A.* . **81 D4** 32 16N 89 36W
Pulaski, *NY, U.S.A.* . **89 B4** 43 34N 76 8W
Pulaski, *TN, U.S.A.* . **96 E5** 35 12N 87 2W
Pulaski, *VA, U.S.A.* . **102 D4** 37 3N 80 47W
Pulaski, *WI, U.S.A.* . **103 D5** 44 41N 88 14W
Pulaski County ☆, *AR, U.S.A.* . **63 D3** 34 45N 92 20W
Pulaski County ☆, *GA, U.S.A.* . **68 D3** 32 15N 83 30W
Pulaski County ☆, *IL, U.S.A.* . **71 F4** 37 15N 89 5W
Pulaski County ☆, *IN, U.S.A.* . **72 B4** 41 0N 86 40W
Pulaski County ☆, *KY, U.S.A.* . **97 C8** 37 5N 84 35W
Pulaski County ☆, *MO, U.S.A.* . **82 D4** 37 50N 92 10W
Pulaski County ☆, *VA, U.S.A.* . **102 D4** 37 0N 80 45W
Pullman, *WA, U.S.A.* . **101 D8** 46 44N 117 10W
Púlpito, Pta., *Baja Calif. S., Mexico* **211 G7** 26 31N 111 28W
Pulticub, Pta., *Quintana Roo, Mexico* . **223 C6** 19 7N 87 32W
Pumphrey, *Baltimore, U.S.A.* . **107 B2** 39 13N 76 38W
Pumpkin Creek, *MT, U.S.A.* . **83 D12** 46 15N 105 45W
Pumpville, *TX, U.S.A.* . **98 H6** 29 53N 101 45W
Puna Forest Reserve, *HI, U.S.A.* . **69 D7** 19 26N 154 59W
Punalu'u, *HI, U.S.A.* . **69 J14** 21 35N 157 53W
Pungo →, *NC, U.S.A.* . **90 C9** 35 23N 76 33W
Pungo L., *NC, U.S.A.* . **90 C9** 35 42N 76 33W
Punnichy, *Sask., Canada* . **182 D7** 51 23N 104 18W
Punta, Cerro de, *Puerto Rico* . **105 G16** 18 10N 66 37W
Punta Abreojos, *Baja Calif. S., Mexico* . **211 G5** 26 42N 113 35W
Punta Allen, *Quintana Roo, Mexico* . **223 C6** 19 48N 87 28W
Punta Caracol, *Quintana Roo, Mexico* . **223 B7** 20 54N 86 51W
Punta Chueca, *Sonora, Mexico* . **212 D3** 29 1N 112 10W
Punta Colonet, *Baja Calif., Mexico* **210 B2** 31 5N 116 11W
Punta de Agua →, *TX, U.S.A.* . **98 B5** 35 32N 102 27W
Punta de Mita, *Nayarit, Mexico* . **216 G5** 20 46N 105 30W
Punta Estrella, *Quintana Roo, Mexico* . **223 C6** 19 34N 87 26W
Punta Flor, *Chiapas, Mexico* . **222 C3** 16 6N 93 58W
Punta Gorda, *FL, U.S.A.* . **67 E6** 26 56N 82 3W
Punta Prieta, *Baja Calif., Mexico* . **210 E4** 28 58N 114 17W
Punta Prieta, *Baja Calif. S., Mexico* **211 F4** 27 1N 114 1W
Punta Rassa, *FL, U.S.A.* . **67 E7** 26 26N 81 59W
Puntzi L., *B.C., Canada* . **186 C10** 52 12N 124 2W
Punxsatawney, *PA, U.S.A.* . **95 D4** 40 57N 78 59W
Puolo Pt., *HI, U.S.A.* . **69 B2** 21 54N 159 36W
Pūpūkea, *HI, U.S.A.* . **69 J13** 21 40N 158 3W
Purcell, *OK, U.S.A.* . **93 C6** 35 1N 97 22W
Purcell Mts., *U.S.A.* . **83 B2** 48 30N 116 0W
Purcellville, *VA, U.S.A.* . **77 A3** 39 8N 77 43W
Purdin, *MO, U.S.A.* . **82 B3** 39 57N 93 10W
Purdon, *TX, U.S.A.* . **99 F11** 31 57N 96 37W
Purdy, *MO, U.S.A.* . **82 E3** 36 49N 93 55W
Purdy, *OK, U.S.A.* . **93 D6** 34 43N 97 35W
Purdy, *Seattle, U.S.A.* . **118 D2** 47 23N 122 37W
Purdy, *VA, U.S.A.* . **102 E7** 36 49N 77 36W
Purépero de Echaiz, *Michoacan, Mexico* . **218 C6** 19 54N 102 0W
Purgatoire →, *CO, U.S.A.* . **66 D7** 38 4N 103 11W
Purgatory Park, *Minneapolis-St. Paul, U.S.A.* . **113 B1** 44 54N 93 30W
Purgitsville, *WV, U.S.A.* . **77 A2** 39 14N 78 55W
Purificación, *Jalisco, Mexico* . **218 C3** 19 43N 104 38W
Purísima de Bustos, *Guanajuato, Mexico* . **218 A6** 21 2N 101 55W
Purísima de Conchos, *Nuevo León, Mexico* . **215 F5** 24 55N 99 15W
Puruándiro, *Michoacan, Mexico* . **218 B6** 20 6N 101 32W
Puruarán, *Michoacan, Mexico* . **218 C6** 19 5N 101 32W
Purvis, *MS, U.S.A.* . **81 E4** 31 9N 89 25W
Puryear, *TN, U.S.A.* . **96 D4** 36 27N 88 20W
Pushaw L., *ME, U.S.A.* . **76 D5** 44 56N 68 48W
Pushmataha County ☆, *OK, U.S.A.* . **93 D8** 34 25N 95 20W
Put-in Bay, *OH, U.S.A.* . **92 B4** 41 39N 82 49W
Putla, *Oaxaca, Mexico* . **221 G3** 17 2N 97 56W
Putnam, *CT, U.S.A.* . **78 C3** 41 55N 71 55W
Putnam, *OK, U.S.A.* . **93 C5** 35 51N 98 58W
Putnam, *TX, U.S.A.* . **99 E8** 32 22N 99 12W
Putnam County ☆, *FL, U.S.A.* . **67 B7** 29 35N 81 45W
Putnam County ☆, *GA, U.S.A.* . **68 C3** 33 20N 83 15W
Putnam County ☆, *IL, U.S.A.* . **71 B4** 41 10N 89 15W
Putnam County ☆, *IN, U.S.A.* . **72 D4** 39 40N 86 50W
Putnam County ☆, *MO, U.S.A.* . **82 A4** 40 30N 93 0W
Putnam County ☆, *NY, U.S.A.* . **89 D7** 41 25N 73 45W
Putnam County ☆, *OH, U.S.A.* . **92 C2** 40 59N 84 12W
Putnam County ☆, *TN, U.S.A.* . **97 D7** 36 10N 85 30W
Putnam County ☆, *WV, U.S.A.* . **102 C3** 38 32N 81 54W
Putnam Lake, *NY, U.S.A.* . **78 C1** 41 28N 73 33W
Putney, *GA, U.S.A.* . **68 E2** 31 29N 84 8W
Putney, *SD, U.S.A.* . **91 E7** 45 34N 98 11W
Putney, *VT, U.S.A.* . **86 D2** 42 58N 72 31W
Putty Hill, *Baltimore, U.S.A.* . **107 A2** 39 22N 76 30W
Pu'uanahulu, *HI, U.S.A.* . **69 D6** 19 49N 155 51W
Pu'uhonua o Hōnaunau Nat. Historical Park ⌂, *U.S.A.* . **69 D6** 19 25N 155 54W
Pu'uka'aumakua, *HI, U.S.A.* . **69 J13** 21 30N 157 54W
Pu'ukeahiakahoe, *HI, U.S.A.* . **69 K14** 21 23N 157 49W
Pu'ukoholā Heiau Nat. Historic Site ⌂, *U.S.A.* . **69 C6** 20 1N 155 49W
P'u'ula'ula, *HI, U.S.A.* . **69 C5** 20 42N 156 15W
Puunene, *HI, U.S.A.* . **69 C5** 20 53N 156 23W
Pu'u'oke'oke'o, *HI, U.S.A.* . **69 D6** 19 13N 155 44W
Pu'uwai, *HI, U.S.A.* . **69 B1** 21 54N 160 12W
Puvirnituq, *Qué., Canada* . **175 A2** 60 2N 77 10W
Puvirnituq →, *Qué., Canada* . **175 A2** 60 3N 77 15W
Puvirnituq, B. de, *Qué., Canada* . **175 B2** 60 0N 77 30W
Puvirnituq, Mts. de, *Qué., Canada* **175 A2** 61 22N 75 5W
Puxico, *MO, U.S.A.* . **82 E6** 36 57N 90 10W
Puxmetacán →, *Oaxaca, Mexico* . **221 G5** 17 22N 95 36W
Puyallup, *WA, U.S.A.* . **101 C3** 47 12N 122 18W
Puyallup Indian Reservation, *WA, U.S.A.* . **101 C3** 47 14N 122 17W
Puyjalon, L., *Qué., Canada* . **172 C6** 50 30N 63 25W
Pymatuning Res., *OH, U.S.A.* . **92 B6** 41 30N 80 28W
Pymatuning State Park ⌂, *PA, U.S.A.* . **95 C2** 41 37N 80 24W
Pyote, *TX, U.S.A.* . **98 F4** 31 32N 103 8W
Pyramid L., *NV, U.S.A.* . **85 B1** 40 1N 119 35W
Pyramid Lake Indian Reservation, *NV, U.S.A.* . **85 B1** 40 20N 119 35W
Pyramid Mts., *NM, U.S.A.* . **88 E2** 32 12N 108 43W
Pyramid Pk., *WY, U.S.A.* . **104 C2** 43 27N 110 28W

Q

Qamanirjuaq L. = Kaminuriak L., *Nunavut, Canada* . **191 E6** 62 57N 95 46W
Qamani'tuaq = Baker Lake, *Nunavut, Canada* . **191 E6** 64 20N 96 3W
Qausuittuq = Resolute, *Nunavut, Canada* . **190 C7** 74 42N 94 54W
Qiajivik, *Nunavut, Canada* . **190 C10** 72 10N 75 54W
Qikiqtarjuaq, *Nunavut, Canada* . **190 D13** 67 33N 63 0W
Qikirtajuaq, I., *Qué., Canada* . **175 B4** 59 5N 69 15W
Qirniraujaq, Pte., *Qué., Canada* . **175 B4** 58 35N 68 1W
Quabbin Res., *MA, U.S.A.* . **78 B2** 42 20N 72 20W
Quadra I., *B.C., Canada* . **186 E9** 50 10N 125 15W
Quail, *TX, U.S.A.* . **98 C7** 34 55N 100 30W
Quakertown, *PA, U.S.A.* . **95 D7** 40 26N 75 21W
Qualicum Beach, *B.C., Canada* . **186 F10** 49 22N 124 26W
Quamba, *MN, U.S.A.* . **80 E5** 45 55N 93 10W
Quanah, *TX, U.S.A.* . **99 C8** 34 18N 99 44W
Quantico, *MD, U.S.A.* . **77 B5** 38 23N 75 44W
Quantico U.S.M.C. Base, *VA, U.S.A.* . **102 C7** 38 30N 77 17W
Quapaw, *OK, U.S.A.* . **93 B9** 36 58N 94 50W
Qu'Appelle, *Sask., Canada* . **182 E8** 50 33N 103 53W
Qu'Appelle →, *Sask., Canada* . **183 E10** 50 26N 101 19W
Quaqtaq, *Qué., Canada* . **175 A4** 60 55N 69 40W
Quarryville, *N.B., Canada* . **173 G4** 46 50N 65 47W
Quarryville, *PA, U.S.A.* . **77 A4** 39 54N 76 10W
Quartz Hill, *CA, U.S.A.* . **65 J8** 34 39N 118 13W
Quartz Mt., *OK, U.S.A.* . **93 D4** 34 54N 99 19W
Quartzsite, *AZ, U.S.A.* . **62 D1** 33 40N 114 13W
Quasqueton, *IA, U.S.A.* . **73 C7** 42 24N 91 46W
Quathiaski Cove, *B.C., Canada* . **186 E9** 50 3N 125 12W
Quatsino, *B.C., Canada* . **186 E7** 50 30N 127 40W
Quatsino Sd., *B.C., Canada* . **186 E7** 50 25N 127 58W
Quay, *NM, U.S.A.* . **88 C7** 34 56N 103 45W
Quay County ☆, *NM, U.S.A.* . **88 B7** 35 0N 103 30W
Québec, *Qué., Canada* . **177 E11** 46 52N 71 13W
Québec ☐, *Canada* . **176 C6** 48 0N 74 0W
Québec International ✈ (YQB), *Qué., Canada* . **177 E11** 46 51N 71 19W
Quebradillas, *Puerto Rico* . **105 G16** 18 29N 66 56W
Quechee, *VT, U.S.A.* . **86 C2** 43 40N 72 25W
Quechultenango, *Guerrero, Mexico* **219 E8** 17 25N 99 23W
Queen Anne, *MD, U.S.A.* . **77 B5** 38 55N 75 57W
Queen Annes County ☆, *MD, U.S.A.* . **77 A5** 39 10N 76 0W
Queen Charlotte City, *B.C., Canada* . **186 B2** 53 15N 132 2W
Queen Charlotte Is., *B.C., Canada* **186 B2** 53 20N 132 10W
Queen Charlotte Mts., *B.C., Canada* . **186 B2** 53 5N 132 15W
Queen Charlotte Sd., *B.C., Canada* **186 D5** 51 0N 128 0W
Queen City, *MO, U.S.A.* . **82 A4** 40 25N 92 34W
Queen City, *TX, U.S.A.* . **99 D13** 33 9N 94 9W
Queen Creek, *AZ, U.S.A.* . **62 D4** 33 15N 111 35W
Queen Elizabeth Is., *Canada* . **190 B3** 76 0N 95 0W
Queen Elizabeth Park, *Vancouver, Canada* . **193 B2** 49 15N 123 17W
Queen Maud G., *Nunavut, Canada* **190 D5** 68 15N 102 30W
Queens, *N.S., Canada* . **173 J5** 44 14N 65 0W
Queens, *NY, U.S.A.* . **114 B4** 40 44N 73 47W
Queens Chan., *Nunavut, Canada* . **190 B6** 76 11N 96 0W
Queens County ☆, *NY, U.S.A.* . **89 E7** 40 40N 73 50W
Queens Sd., *B.C., Canada* . **186 D6** 51 57N 128 20W
Queens Village, *NY, U.S.A.* . **114 B4** 40 43N 73 44W
Queensland, *GA, U.S.A.* . **68 E3** 31 46N 83 14W
Queenstown, *N.B., Canada* . **173 H3** 45 41N 66 7W
Queenstown, *MD, U.S.A.* . **77 B4** 38 59N 76 9W
Queets, *WA, U.S.A.* . **101 C1** 47 32N 124 19W
Queets →, *WA, U.S.A.* . **101 C1** 47 33N 124 21W
Quemado, *NM, U.S.A.* . **88 C2** 34 20N 108 30W
Quemado, *TX, U.S.A.* . **98 J7** 28 56N 100 37W
Quenemo, *KS, U.S.A.* . **74 C8** 38 35N 95 30W
Quentin, *MS, U.S.A.* . **81 E3** 31 30N 90 45W
Queréndaro, *Michoacan, Mexico* . **219 C7** 19 48N 100 53W
Querétaro, *Querétaro, Mexico* . **219 B7** 20 36N 100 23W
Querétaro ☐, *Mexico* . **219 B8** 21 0N 99 55W
Quesería, *Colima, Mexico* . **218 C4** 19 22N 103 35W
Quesnel, *B.C., Canada* . **187 C12** 53 0N 122 30W
Quesnel →, *B.C., Canada* . **187 C12** 52 58N 122 29W
Quesnel L., *B.C., Canada* . **187 C13** 52 30N 121 20W
Questa, *NM, U.S.A.* . **88 A5** 36 42N 105 36W
Quetico Prov. Park ⌂, *Ont., Canada* . **180 D5** 48 30N 91 45W
Quetzala →, *Guerrero, Mexico* . **219 F9** 16 35N 98 30W
Quevedo, Península, *Sinaloa, Mexico* . **216 C3** 24 10N 107 18W
Quévillon, L., *Qué., Canada* . **176 B6** 49 4N 76 57W
Quiahuiztlán, *Veracruz, Mexico* . **220 E4** 19 40N 96 25W
Quidi Vidi, *Nfld. & L., Canada* . **174 E8** 47 35N 52 41W
Quidnet, *MA, U.S.A.* . **78 C5** 41 18N 69 58W
Quilcene, *WA, U.S.A.* . **101 C3** 47 49N 122 53W
Quilchena, *B.C., Canada* . **187 E14** 50 10N 120 30W
Quileute Indian Reservation, *WA, U.S.A.* . **101 C1** 47 54N 124 37W
Quill Lake, *Sask., Canada* . **182 C7** 52 4N 104 15W
Quimby, *IA, U.S.A.* . **73 C3** 42 38N 95 38W
Quimichis, *Nayarit, Mexico* . **216 E5** 22 21N 105 32W
Quinault, *WA, U.S.A.* . **101 C2** 47 28N 123 51W
Quinault →, *WA, U.S.A.* . **101 C1** 47 21N 124 18W
Quinault Indian Reservation, *WA, U.S.A.* . **101 C1** 47 30N 124 5W
Quinby, *SC, U.S.A.* . **90 D6** 34 14N 79 44W
Quincy, *CA, U.S.A.* . **64 D6** 39 56N 120 57W
Quincy, *FL, U.S.A.* . **67 A4** 30 35N 84 34W
Quincy, *IL, U.S.A.* . **71 D2** 39 56N 91 23W
Quincy, *MA, U.S.A.* . **78 B4** 42 14N 71 0W
Quincy, *MI, U.S.A.* . **79 H7** 41 57N 84 53W
Quincy, *OH, U.S.A.* . **92 C3** 40 18N 83 58W
Quincy, *WA, U.S.A.* . **101 C6** 47 14N 119 51W
Quincy B., *Boston, U.S.A.* . **106 B4** 42 16N 70 59W
Quincy Res., *Denver, U.S.A.* . **109 C3** 39 38N 104 46W
Quinebaug, *CT, U.S.A.* . **78 B3** 42 1N 71 57W
Quinebaug →, *CT, U.S.A.* . **78 C2** 41 33N 72 3W
Quinhagak, *AK, U.S.A.* . **61 G7** 59 45N 161 54W
Quinlan, *OK, U.S.A.* . **93 B4** 36 27N 99 3W
Quinlan, *TX, U.S.A.* . **99 E11** 32 55N 96 8W
Quinn →, *NV, U.S.A.* . **85 B1** 40 53N 119 3W
Quintana Roo, *Chiapas, Mexico* . **222 C3** 16 40N 93 42W
Quintana Roo, *Yucatán, Mexico* . **223 B5** 20 52N 88 38W
Quintana Roo ☐, *Mexico* . **223 C5** 19 40N 88 30W
Quintana Roo, Parque Natural de ⌂, *Quintana Roo, Mexico* . **223 B6** 20 15N 87 45W
Quinte West, *Ont., Canada* . **179 C9** 44 10N 77 34W
Quinter, *KS, U.S.A.* . **74 B3** 39 4N 100 14W
Quinton, *Sask., Canada* . **182 D7** 51 23N 104 24W
Quinton, *OK, U.S.A.* . **93 C8** 35 7N 95 22W
Quinwood, *WV, U.S.A.* . **102 C4** 38 4N 80 42W
Quinze, L. des, *Qué., Canada* . **176 D3** 47 35N 79 5W
Quiriego, *Sonora, Mexico* . **212 F6** 27 31N 109 16W
Quiroga, *Michoacan, Mexico* . **218 C6** 19 40N 101 31W
Quitaque, *TX, U.S.A.* . **98 C6** 34 22N 101 4W
Quitman, *AR, U.S.A.* . **63 C3** 35 23N 92 13W
Quitman, *GA, U.S.A.* . **68 F3** 30 47N 83 34W
Quitman, *LA, U.S.A.* . **75 B3** 32 21N 92 43W
Quitman, *MS, U.S.A.* . **81 D5** 32 2N 88 44W
Quitman, *TX, U.S.A.* . **99 E12** 32 48N 95 27W
Quitman County ☆, *GA, U.S.A.* . **68 E2** 31 50N 85 0W
Quitman County ☆, *MS, U.S.A.* . **81 B3** 34 12N 90 17W
Quitman Mts., *TX, U.S.A.* . **98 F2** 31 0N 105 16W
Quivira Nat. Wildlife Refuge ⌂, *KS, U.S.A.* . **74 C5** 38 11N 98 31W
Qulin, *MO, U.S.A.* . **82 E6** 36 36N 90 15W
Quoich →, *Nunavut, Canada* . **191 E7** 64 0N 93 30W
Quonochontaug, *RI, U.S.A.* . **78 C3** 41 21N 71 43W
Qurlutuq →, *Qué., Canada* . **175 B4** 58 57N 66 50W
Quttinirpaaq Nat. Park △, *Nunavut, Canada* . **190 A11** 82 13N 72 13W
Quyon, *Qué., Canada* . **176 F6** 45 31N 76 14W

R

R.D. Bailey L., *WV, U.S.A.* . **102 D3** 37 36N 81 49W
Raanes Pen., *N.W.T., Canada* . **190 B8** 78 30N 85 45W
Rabbit Cr. →, *SD, U.S.A.* . **91 E3** 45 13N 102 10W
Rabbit Ears Pass, *CO, U.S.A.* . **66 B4** 40 23N 106 37W
Rabbit Lake, *Sask., Canada* . **182 B4** 53 8N 107 46W
Rabón, L. el, *Tamaulipas, Mexico* **214 E7** 25 27N 97 23W
Rabun County ☆, *GA, U.S.A.* . **68 B3** 34 50N 83 30W
Raccoon →, *IA, U.S.A.* . **73 D5** 41 35N 93 37W
Raccoon Cr. →, *OH, U.S.A.* . **92 C4** 40 2N 82 24W
Race, C., *Nfld. & L., Canada* . **174 F7** 46 40N 53 5W
Race Point, *MA, U.S.A.* . **78 B4** 42 4N 70 14W
Raceland, *KY, U.S.A.* . **97 B10** 38 32N 82 44W
Raceland, *LA, U.S.A.* . **75 E5** 29 44N 90 36W
Racepond, *GA, U.S.A.* . **68 E4** 31 1N 82 8W
Rachel, *NV, U.S.A.* . **85 E5** 37 39N 115 45W
Racine, *MN, U.S.A.* . **80 G6** 43 48N 92 31W
Racine, *WI, U.S.A.* . **103 F6** 42 44N 87 47W
Racine ☆, *WI, U.S.A.* . **103 F5** 42 45N 88 5W
Racine L., *Ont., Canada* . **181 D13** 48 2N 83 20W
Raco, *MI, U.S.A.* . **79 C7** 46 23N 84 43W
Radcliff, *KY, U.S.A.* . **97 C7** 37 51N 85 57W
Radcliffe, *IA, U.S.A.* . **73 C5** 42 20N 93 25W
Radford, *VA, U.S.A.* . **102 D4** 37 8N 80 34W
Radisson, *Sask., Canada* . **182 C4** 52 30N 107 20W
Radisson, *WI, U.S.A.* . **103 C2** 45 45N 91 14W
Radium, *KS, U.S.A.* . **74 C5** 38 12N 98 56W
Radium Hot Springs, *B.C., Canada* **185 H4** 50 35N 116 2W
Radium Springs, *NM, U.S.A.* . **88 E4** 32 30N 106 55W
Radnor, *OH, U.S.A.* . **92 C3** 40 23N 83 9W
Radnor, *PA, U.S.A.* . **87 B1** 40 3N 75 22W
Radville, *Sask., Canada* . **182 F7** 49 30N 104 15W
Radway, *Alta., Canada* . **184 D8** 54 4N 112 57W
Rae, *N.W.T., Canada* . **189 D9** 62 50N 116 3W
Rae →, *Nunavut, Canada* . **188 C9** 67 55N 115 31W
Rae Isthmus, *Nunavut, Canada* . **191 D8** 66 40N 87 30W
Rae Lakes, *N.W.T., Canada* . **189 D9** 64 7N 117 21W
Rae Str., *Nunavut, Canada* . **190 D7** 68 50N 94 51W
Raeford, *NC, U.S.A.* . **90 D6** 34 59N 79 13W
Rafael Delgado, *Veracruz, Mexico* **221 F3** 18 46N 97 1W
Raft →, *ID, U.S.A.* . **70 G5** 42 37N 113 15W
Raft River Mts., *UT, U.S.A.* . **100 B2** 41 55N 113 25W
Ragan, *NE, U.S.A.* . **84 D6** 40 19N 99 15W
Ragland, *AL, U.S.A.* . **60 C4** 33 45N 86 9W
Ragley, *LA, U.S.A.* . **75 D2** 30 30N 93 15W
Rago, *KS, U.S.A.* . **74 D5** 37 26N 98 4W
Rahway, *NJ, U.S.A.* . **87 B2** 40 36N 74 16W
Raiford, *FL, U.S.A.* . **67 A6** 30 4N 82 14W
Railroad Valley, *NV, U.S.A.* . **85 D5** 38 25N 115 40W
Rainbow Bridge Nat. Monument ⌂, *U.S.A.* . **100 F5** 37 5N 110 58W
Rainbow City, *AL, U.S.A.* . **60 C4** 33 57N 86 5W
Rainbow Lake, *Alta., Canada* . **189 E9** 58 30N 119 23W
Rainbow Plateau, *AZ, U.S.A.* . **62 A5** 36 55N 111 0W
Rainelle, *WV, U.S.A.* . **102 D4** 37 58N 80 47W
Raines, *TN, U.S.A.* . **112 B1** 35 2N 90 3W
Rainier, *WA, U.S.A.* . **101 D3** 46 53N 122 41W
Rainier, Mt., *WA, U.S.A.* . **101 D4** 46 52N 121 46W
Rains, *SC, U.S.A.* . **90 D6** 34 6N 79 19W
Rains County ☆, *TX, U.S.A.* . **99 E12** 32 52N 95 46W
Rainsburg, *PA, U.S.A.* . **95 E4** 39 54N 78 30W
Rainsville, *AL, U.S.A.* . **60 B5** 34 30N 85 50W
Rainy →, *Ont., Canada* . **180 D2** 48 43N 94 29W
Rainy →, *MN, U.S.A.* . **80 B4** 48 50N 94 42W
Rainy L., *Ont., Canada* . **180 D3** 48 42N 93 10W
Rainy River, *Ont., Canada* . **180 D2** 48 43N 94 29W
Raisin →, *MI, U.S.A.* . **79 H8** 41 54N 83 20W
Rake, *IA, U.S.A.* . **73 B5** 43 35N 93 50W
Raleigh, *Nfld. & L., Canada* . **174 A5** 51 34N 55 44W
Raleigh, *FL, U.S.A.* . **67 B6** 29 25N 82 32W
Raleigh, *GA, U.S.A.* . **68 D2** 32 56N 84 38W
Raleigh, *MS, U.S.A.* . **81 D4** 32 2N 89 30W
Raleigh, *NC, U.S.A.* . **90 C7** 35 47N 78 39W
Raleigh, *ND, U.S.A.* . **91 D4** 46 20N 101 20W
Raleigh, *TN, U.S.A.* . **112 A2** 35 12N 89 54W
Raleigh B., *NC, U.S.A.* . **90 D9** 34 50N 76 15W
Raleigh County ☆, *WV, U.S.A.* . **102 D3** 37 45N 81 10W
Raleigh-Durham International ✈ (RDU), *NC, U.S.A.* . **90 C7** 35 52N 78 47W
Raleigh Hills, *Portland, U.S.A.* . **116 B1** 45 28N 122 45W
Ralls, *TX, U.S.A.* . **98 D6** 33 41N 101 24W
Ralls County ☆, *MO, U.S.A.* . **82 B5** 39 30N 91 30W
Ralston, *Alta., Canada* . **185 H9** 50 15N 111 10W
Ralston, *NE, U.S.A.* . **84 C9** 41 12N 96 3W
Ralston, *OK, U.S.A.* . **93 B7** 36 30N 96 44W
Ralston, *PA, U.S.A.* . **95 C6** 41 30N 76 57W
Ralston, *WY, U.S.A.* . **104 B4** 44 43N 108 52W
Ram →, *Alta., Canada* . **185 F5** 52 23N 115 25W
Rama, *Sask., Canada* . **182 D9** 51 46N 103 0W
Rama, *Charlotte, U.S.A.* . **107 A2** 35 10N 80 46W
Ramah, *Nfld. & L., Canada* . **175 B5** 58 52N 63 15W
Ramah, *CO, U.S.A.* . **66 C6** 39 7N 104 10W
Ramah, *NM, U.S.A.* . **88 B2** 35 8N 108 29W
Ramah B., *Nfld. & L., Canada* . **175 B5** 58 52N 63 13W
Ramea, *Nfld. & L., Canada* . **174 E3** 47 31N 57 23W
Ramea Is., *Nfld. & L., Canada* . **174 E3** 47 31N 57 22W
Ramer, *AL, U.S.A.* . **60 D4** 32 3N 86 13W
Ramer, *TN, U.S.A.* . **96 E4** 35 4N 88 37W
Ramiro Caballero, Presa, *Tamaulipas, Mexico* . **215 H6** 22 37N 98 42W
Ramon, *NM, U.S.A.* . **88 C6** 34 14N 104 54W
Ramón Corona, *Campeche, Mexico* . **223 C4** 19 28N 89 28W
Ramón Corona, *Durango, Mexico* **217 C7** 24 13N 103 37W
Ramona, *CA, U.S.A.* . **65 K10** 33 2N 116 52W
Ramona, *KS, U.S.A.* . **74 C6** 38 36N 97 4W
Ramona, *OK, U.S.A.* . **93 B8** 36 32N 95 55W
Ramona, *SD, U.S.A.* . **91 F8** 44 7N 97 13W
Ramore, *Ont., Canada* . **176 C2** 48 30N 80 25W
Ramos →, *Durango, Mexico* . **216 B5** 25 32N 105 3W
Ramos Arizpe, *Coahuila, Mexico* **214 E3** 25 41N 101 23W
Ramos Arizpe, *Coahuila, Mexico* **214 E4** 25 33N 100 58W
Rampart, *AK, U.S.A.* . **61 D10** 65 30N 150 10W
Ramparts →, *N.W.T., Canada* . **188 C7** 66 11N 129 2W
Ramsay, *MI, U.S.A.* . **79 C2** 46 28N 90 0W
Ramsay, *MT, U.S.A.* . **83 D5** 46 1N 112 42W
Ramsay I., *B.C., Canada* . **186 C3** 52 33N 131 23W
Ramseur, *NC, U.S.A.* . **90 C6** 35 44N 79 39W
Ramsey, *Ont., Canada* . **181 E14** 47 25N 82 20W
Ramsey, *IL, U.S.A.* . **71 D4** 39 8N 89 7W
Ramsey, *MN, U.S.A.* . **80 E6** 45 15N 92 58W
Ramsey, *NJ, U.S.A.* . **87 A2** 41 4N 74 9W
Ramsey County ☆, *MN, U.S.A.* . **80 F5** 45 0N 93 5W
Ramsey County ☆, *ND, U.S.A.* . **91 B7** 48 15N 98 50W
Ramsey L., *Ont., Canada* . **181 E14** 47 13N 82 15W
Ranchester, *WY, U.S.A.* . **104 B5** 44 54N 107 10W
Rancho Cordova, *CA, U.S.A.* . **64 E5** 38 36N 121 18W
Rancho Cucamonga, *CA, U.S.A.* . **65 J9** 34 10N 117 30W
Rancho Grande, *Zacatecas, Mexico* **217 D8** 23 32N 102 57W
Rancho Palos Verdes, *Los Angeles, U.S.A.* . **111 D2** 33 44N 118 23W
Ranchos de Taos, *NM, U.S.A.* . **88 A5** 36 22N 105 37W
Rand, *CO, U.S.A.* . **66 B4** 40 27N 106 11W
Rand, *WV, U.S.A.* . **102 C3** 38 17N 81 34W
Randalia, *IA, U.S.A.* . **73 C7** 42 52N 91 53W
Randall, *IA, U.S.A.* . **73 C5** 42 14N 93 35W
Randall, *KS, U.S.A.* . **74 B5** 39 38N 98 3W
Randall, *MN, U.S.A.* . **80 D4** 46 5N 94 30W
Randall County ☆, *TX, U.S.A.* . **98 C6** 34 59N 101 55W
Randallstown, *MD, U.S.A.* . **77 A4** 39 22N 76 48W
Randle, *WA, U.S.A.* . **101 D4** 46 32N 121 57W
Randleman, *NC, U.S.A.* . **90 C6** 35 49N 79 48W
Randlett, *OK, U.S.A.* . **93 D5** 34 11N 98 28W
Randlett, *UT, U.S.A.* . **100 C6** 40 14N 109 48W
Randolph, *IA, U.S.A.* . **73 E3** 40 52N 95 34W
Randolph, *KS, U.S.A.* . **74 B7** 39 26N 96 46W
Randolph, *ME, U.S.A.* . **76 D4** 44 14N 69 46W
Randolph, *MA, U.S.A.* . **78 B3** 42 10N 71 2W
Randolph, *MS, U.S.A.* . **81 B4** 34 11N 89 10W
Randolph, *NY, U.S.A.* . **89 C2** 42 10N 78 59W
Randolph, *NE, U.S.A.* . **84 B8** 42 23N 97 22W
Randolph, *UT, U.S.A.* . **100 B4** 41 40N 111 11W
Randolph, *VT, U.S.A.* . **86 C2** 43 55N 72 40W
Randolph Air Force Base, *TX, U.S.A.* . **99 H9** 29 31N 98 16W
Randolph Center, *VT, U.S.A.* . **86 C2** 43 55N 72 37W
Randolph County ☆, *AL, U.S.A.* . **60 C5** 33 20N 85 25W
Randolph County ☆, *AR, U.S.A.* . **63 B5** 36 20N 91 0W
Randolph County ☆, *GA, U.S.A.* . **68 E2** 31 45N 84 45W
Randolph County ☆, *IL, U.S.A.* . **71 E4** 38 0N 89 50W
Randolph County ☆, *IN, U.S.A.* . **72 C6** 40 10N 85 0W
Randolph County ☆, *MO, U.S.A.* . **82 B4** 39 25N 92 30W
Randolph County ☆, *NC, U.S.A.* . **90 C6** 35 40N 79 50W
Randolph County ☆, *WV, U.S.A.* . **102 C5** 38 45N 80 0W
Random I., *Nfld. & L., Canada* . **174 D7** 48 8N 53 44W
Random Lake, *WI, U.S.A.* . **103 E6** 43 33N 87 58W
Randville, *MI, U.S.A.* . **79 C3** 46 0N 88 3W
Ranfurly, *Alta., Canada* . **184 E9** 53 25N 111 41W
Rangeley, *ME, U.S.A.* . **76 D3** 44 58N 70 39W
Rangeley L., *ME, U.S.A.* . **76 D3** 44 55N 70 43W
Rangely, *CO, U.S.A.* . **66 B2** 40 5N 108 48W
Ranger, *GA, U.S.A.* . **68 B2** 34 30N 84 43W
Ranger, *TX, U.S.A.* . **99 E9** 32 28N 98 41W
Ranger L., *Ont., Canada* . **181 F13** 46 52N 83 35W
Ranier, *MN, U.S.A.* . **80 B5** 48 36N 93 20W
Rankin, *IL, U.S.A.* . **71 C6** 40 28N 87 54W
Rankin, *Pittsburgh, U.S.A.* . **116 B2** 40 24N 79 52W
Rankin, *TX, U.S.A.* . **98 F6** 31 13N 101 56W
Rankin County ☆, *MS, U.S.A.* . **81 D4** 32 15N 90 0W
Rankin Inlet, *Nunavut, Canada* . **191 E7** 62 30N 93 0W
Ransom, *IL, U.S.A.* . **71 B5** 41 9N 88 39W
Ransom, *KS, U.S.A.* . **74 C4** 38 38N 99 58W
Ransom County ☆, *ND, U.S.A.* . **91 D8** 46 30N 97 40W
Ranson, *WV, U.S.A.* . **77 A3** 39 18N 77 52W
Rantoul, *IL, U.S.A.* . **71 C5** 40 19N 88 9W
Rantoul, *KS, U.S.A.* . **74 C8** 38 33N 95 7W
Rapelje, *MT, U.S.A.* . **83 E8** 45 58N 109 14W
Raper, C., *Nunavut, Canada* . **190 D12** 69 44N 67 6W
Rapid →, *MN, U.S.A.* . **80 B4** 48 42N 94 26W
Rapid City, *Man., Canada* . **183 E11** 50 7N 100 2W
Rapid City, *SD, U.S.A.* . **91 F2** 44 5N 103 14W
Rapid Cr. →, *SD, U.S.A.* . **91 G3** 43 54N 102 37W
Rapid River, *MI, U.S.A.* . **79 D5** 45 55N 86 58W
Rapidan →, *VA, U.S.A.* . **102 C7** 38 22N 77 37W
Rapide-Blanc, *Qué., Canada* . **177 D9** 47 48N 73 2W
Rapide-Sept, *Qué., Canada* . **176 D4** 47 46N 78 19W
Rapides-des-Joachims, *Qué., Canada* . **176 E5** 46 13N 77 43W
Rapides Parish ☆, *LA, U.S.A.* . **75 C3** 31 15N 92 30W
Rappahannock →, *VA, U.S.A.* . **77 C4** 37 34N 76 18W
Rappahannock County ☆, *VA, U.S.A.* . **102 C6** 38 40N 78 10W
Raquette →, *NY, U.S.A.* . **89 A6** 45 0N 74 42W
Rarden, *OH, U.S.A.* . **92 E3** 38 55N 83 12W
Raritan, *NJ, U.S.A.* . **87 B2** 40 34N 74 38W
Raritan →, *NJ, U.S.A.* . **87 B2** 40 29N 74 17W
Raritan Bay, *NJ, U.S.A.* . **87 B2** 40 27N 74 15W
Rasa, I., *Baja Calif., Mexico* . **210 E6** 28 50N 112 57W
Raspberry Pk., *AR, U.S.A.* . **63 D2** 34 23N 94 0W
Rat →, *Man., Canada* . **183 F14** 49 35N 97 10W
Rat I., *AK, U.S.A.* . **61 L2** 51 48N 178 15 E
Rat Islands, *AK, U.S.A.* . **61 L2** 52 0N 178 0 E
Ratcliff, *TX, U.S.A.* . **99 F12** 31 24N 95 8W
Rathbun, *IA, U.S.A.* . **73 E6** 40 50N 92 50W
Rathbun L., *IA, U.S.A.* . **73 E5** 40 54N 93 5W
Rathdrum, *ID, U.S.A.* . **70 B2** 47 49N 116 54W
Ratliff City, *OK, U.S.A.* . **93 D6** 34 25N 97 30W
Raton, *NM, U.S.A.* . **88 A6** 36 54N 104 24W
Raton, Cueva del, *Baja Calif. S., Mexico* . **211 F5** 27 32N 113 0W
Raton Pass, *U.S.A.* . **66 E6** 37 0N 104 30W
Rats, R. aux →, *Qué., Canada* . **177 C10** 48 53N 72 14W
Rattan, *OK, U.S.A.* . **93 D8** 34 12N 95 25W
Rattlesnake Cr. →, *OR, U.S.A.* . **94 E8** 42 44N 117 47W
Rattlesnake Hills, *WA, U.S.A.* . **101 D5** 46 31N 120 20W
Rattlesnake Hills, *WY, U.S.A.* . **104 D5** 42 45N 107 10W
Ratz, Mt., *B.C., Canada* . **189 E6** 57 23N 132 12W
Raudales, *Chiapas, Mexico* . **222 B3** 17 27N 93 39W
Ravalli, *MT, U.S.A.* . **83 C3** 47 17N 114 11W
Ravalli County ☆, *MT, U.S.A.* . **83 E3** 46 0N 114 0W
Raven, *VA, U.S.A.* . **102 D3** 37 5N 81 51W
Ravena, *NY, U.S.A.* . **89 C7** 42 28N 73 49W
Ravendale, *CA, U.S.A.* . **64 C6** 40 48N 120 22W
Ravenel, *SC, U.S.A.* . **90 F5** 32 46N 80 15W
Ravenna, *KY, U.S.A.* . **97 C9** 37 41N 83 57W
Ravenna, *MI, U.S.A.* . **79 F5** 43 11N 86 56W
Ravenna, *NE, U.S.A.* . **84 C7** 41 1N 98 55W
Ravenna, *OH, U.S.A.* . **92 B5** 41 9N 81 15W
Ravenna, *TX, U.S.A.* . **99 D11** 33 40N 96 15W
Ravenswood, *WV, U.S.A.* . **102 C3** 38 57N 81 46W
Ravenwood, *MO, U.S.A.* . **82 A2** 40 22N 94 41W
Ravia, *OK, U.S.A.* . **93 D7** 34 15N 96 45W
Ravinia, *SD, U.S.A.* . **91 G7** 43 8N 98 26W
Rawdon, *Qué., Canada* . **177 E9** 46 3N 73 40W
Rawlins, *WY, U.S.A.* . **104 E5** 41 47N 107 14W
Rawlins County ☆, *KS, U.S.A.* . **74 B2** 39 45N 101 0W
Rawsonville, *VT, U.S.A.* . **86 C2** 43 10N 72 50W
Ray, *MN, U.S.A.* . **80 B5** 48 25N 93 13W
Ray, *ND, U.S.A.* . **91 B2** 48 21N 103 10W
Ray, C., *Nfld. & L., Canada* . **174 E1** 47 33N 59 15W
Ray City, *GA, U.S.A.* . **68 E3** 31 5N 83 11W
Ray County ☆, *MO, U.S.A.* . **82 B3** 39 20N 94 0W
Ray Mts., *AK, U.S.A.* . **61 D10** 66 0N 152 0W
Ray Roberts L., *TX, U.S.A.* . **99 D10** 33 20N 97 2W
Rayle, *GA, U.S.A.* . **68 C4** 33 48N 82 54W

Raymond, *Alta., Canada* **185 J8** 49 30N 112 35W
Raymond, *CA, U.S.A.* **64 F7** 37 13N 119 54W
Raymond, *GA, U.S.A.* **68 C2** 33 20N 84 43W
Raymond, *IL, U.S.A.* **71 D4** 39 19N 89 34W
Raymond, *KS, U.S.A.* **74 C5** 38 17N 98 25W
Raymond, *MN, U.S.A.* **80 E3** 45 2N 95 14W
Raymond, *MS, U.S.A.* **81 D3** 32 16N 90 25W
Raymond, *NH, U.S.A.* **86 C3** 43 2N 71 11W
Raymond, *NE, U.S.A.* **84 D9** 40 57N 96 47W
Raymond, *SD, U.S.A.* **91 F8** 44 55N 97 56W
Raymond, *WA, U.S.A.* **101 D2** 46 41N 123 44W
Raymondville, *MO, U.S.A.* **82 D5** 37 20N 91 50W
Raymondville, *TX, U.S.A.* **98 L10** 26 29N 97 47W
Raymore, *Sask., Canada* **182 D7** 51 25N 104 31W
Raymore, *MO, U.S.A.* **82 C2** 38 48N 94 27W
Rayne, *LA, U.S.A.* **75 D3** 30 14N 92 16W
Raynham Center, *MA, U.S.A.* **78 C3** 41 55N 71 3W
Rayón, *Chiapas, Mexico* **222 B4** 17 12N 93 0W
Rayón, *San Luis Potosí, Mexico* **215 J5** 21 51N 99 40W
Rayón, *Sonora, Mexico* **212 D5** 29 43N 110 35W
Rayones, *Nuevo León, Mexico* **215 E4** 25 1N 100 5W
Raystown Branch →, *PA, U.S.A.* **95 D5** 40 27N 77 59W
Raystown L., *PA, U.S.A.* **95 D4** 40 25N 78 5W
Raytown, *MO, U.S.A.* **82 B2** 39 1N 94 28W
Rayville, *LA, U.S.A.* **75 B4** 32 29N 91 46W
Rayville, *MO, U.S.A.* **82 B2** 39 21N 94 4W
Reach II Recreation Area, *Phoenix, U.S.A.* **116 A3** 33 37N 111 53W
Reader, *AR, U.S.A.* **63 E2** 33 46N 93 6W
Reading, *KS, U.S.A.* **74 C8** 38 31N 95 58W
Reading, *MA, U.S.A.* **78 B3** 42 32N 71 6W
Reading, *MI, U.S.A.* **79 H7** 41 50N 84 45W
Reading, *OH, U.S.A.* **92 D2** 39 13N 84 26W
Reading, *PA, U.S.A.* **95 D7** 40 20N 75 56W
Readland, *AR, U.S.A.* **63 E4** 33 4N 91 13W
Readlyn, *IA, U.S.A.* **73 C6** 42 42N 92 14W
Readsboro, *VT, U.S.A.* **86 D2** 42 46N 72 57W
Readstown, *WI, U.S.A.* **103 E3** 43 27N 90 45W
Reagan, *TN, U.S.A.* **96 E4** 35 31N 88 20W
Reagan County ☆, *TX, U.S.A.* **98 F6** 31 25N 101 34W
Real County ☆, *TX, U.S.A.* **99 H8** 29 55N 99 55W
Real de Catorce, *San Luis Potosí, Mexico* **215 G4** 23 42N 100 54W
Realitos, *TX, U.S.A.* **98 K9** 27 27N 98 32W
Reams, L., *Orlando, U.S.A.* **115 B1** 28 26N 81 34W
Reardan, *WA, U.S.A.* **101 C8** 47 40N 117 53W
Reasnor, *IA, U.S.A.* **73 D5** 41 35N 93 1W
Rebecca, *GA, U.S.A.* **68 E3** 31 48N 83 29W
Rebeico, *Sonora, Mexico* **212 E6** 28 53N 109 45W
Rector, *AR, U.S.A.* **63 B5** 36 16N 90 17W
Red →, *U.S.A.* **75 C4** 31 1N 91 45W
Red →, *KY, U.S.A.* **97 C8** 37 51N 84 5W
Red →, *TN, U.S.A.* **96 D5** 36 32N 87 22W
Red Bank, *NJ, U.S.A.* **116 B1** 39 52N 75 10W
Red Bank, *NJ, U.S.A.* **87 B2** 40 21N 74 5W
Red Bank, *TN, U.S.A.* **97 E7** 35 7N 85 17W
Red Bay, *Nfld. & L., Canada* **174 A4** 51 44N 56 25W
Red Bay, *AL, U.S.A.* **60 B2** 34 27N 88 7W
Red Bird, *OK, U.S.A.* **93 C8** 35 54N 95 36W
Red Bluff, *CA, U.S.A.* **64 C4** 40 11N 122 15W
Red Bluff Res., *NM, U.S.A.* **88 F7** 31 54N 103 55W
Red Boiling Springs, *TN, U.S.A.* **97 D7** 36 32N 85 51W
Red Bud, *IL, U.S.A.* **71 E4** 38 13N 89 59W
Red Cedar →, *WI, U.S.A.* **103 D2** 44 42N 91 53W
Red Cliff, *CO, U.S.A.* **66 C4** 39 31N 106 22W
Red Cliff Ind. Reservation, *WI, U.S.A.* **103 B3** 46 50N 90 47W
Red Cloud, *NE, U.S.A.* **84 D7** 40 5N 98 32W
Red Cr. →, *MS, U.S.A.* **81 F5** 30 41N 88 40W
Red Deer, *Alta., Canada* **185 F7** 52 20N 113 50W
Red Deer →, *Alta., Canada* **185 H10** 50 58N 110 0W
Red Deer →, *Man., Canada* **183 C10** 52 53N 101 1W
Red Deer L., *Alta., Canada* **185 F7** 52 43N 113 2W
Red Deer L., *Man., Canada* **183 C10** 52 55N 101 20W
Red Devil, *AK, U.S.A.* **61 F8** 61 46N 157 19W
Red Feather Lakes, *CO, U.S.A.* **66 B5** 40 48N 105 35W
Red Head, *FL, U.S.A.* **67 A3** 30 29N 85 51W
Red Hills, *KS, U.S.A.* **74 D5** 37 40N 98 50W
Red Hook, *NY, U.S.A.* **89 D7** 41 55N 73 53W
Red I., *Nfld. & L., Canada* **174 E6** 47 23N 54 10W
Red Indian L., *Nfld. & L., Canada* **174 D3** 48 35N 57 0W
Red L., *Ont., Canada* **180 A3** 51 3N 93 49W
Red L., *AZ, U.S.A.* **62 B1** 35 40N 114 4W
Red L., *SD, U.S.A.* **91 G6** 43 44N 99 13W
Red Lake, *Ont., Canada* **180 A3** 51 3N 93 49W
Red Lake, *MN, U.S.A.* **80 C3** 47 53N 95 1W
Red Lake →, *MN, U.S.A.* **80 C1** 47 55N 97 1W
Red Lake County ☆, *MN, U.S.A.* **80 C3** 47 50N 96 0W
Red Lake Falls, *MN, U.S.A.* **80 C2** 47 53N 96 16W
Red Lake Indian Reservation, *MN, U.S.A.* **80 B4** 48 30N 94 30W
Red Lake Road, *Ont., Canada* **180 C3** 49 59N 93 25W
Red Level, *AL, U.S.A.* **60 E4** 31 24N 86 36W
Red Lion, *NJ, U.S.A.* **87 C2** 39 53N 74 45W
Red Lion, *PA, U.S.A.* **77 A4** 39 54N 76 36W
Red Lodge, *MT, U.S.A.* **83 E8** 45 11N 109 15W
Red Mountain, *CA, U.S.A.* **65 H9** 35 37N 117 38W
Red Oak, *IA, U.S.A.* **73 D3** 41 1N 95 14W
Red Oak, *NC, U.S.A.* **90 B8** 36 2N 77 54W
Red Oak, *OK, U.S.A.* **93 D8** 34 57N 95 5W
Red Pass, *B.C., Canada* **187 C15** 53 0N 119 0W
Red River, *NM, U.S.A.* **88 A5** 36 42N 105 22W
Red River County ☆, *TX, U.S.A.* **99 D12** 33 37N 95 3W
Red River Hot Springs, *ID, U.S.A.* **70 D3** 45 47N 115 12W
Red River of the North →, *N. Amer.* **183 F14** 49 0N 97 15W
Red River Parish ☆, *LA, U.S.A.* **75 B2** 32 1N 93 21W
Red River Valley, *MN, U.S.A.* **80 C2** 48 0N 96 50W
Red Rock, *B.C., Canada* **187 B12** 53 42N 122 40W
Red Rock, *Ont., Canada* **180 D8** 48 55N 88 15W
Red Rock, *AZ, U.S.A.* **62 A6** 36 36N 109 3W
Red Rock, *MT, U.S.A.* **83 F5** 44 55N 112 50W
Red Rock, *OK, U.S.A.* **93 B6** 36 28N 97 11W
Red Rock, L., *IA, U.S.A.* **73 D6** 41 22N 92 59W
Red Rock Canyon Nat. Conservation Area ⌓, *NV, U.S.A.* **85 F5** 36 6N 115 28W
Red Rock Cr. →, *OK, U.S.A.* **93 B7** 36 30N 96 59W
Red Rock Lakes Nat. Wildlife Refuge ⌓, *MT, U.S.A.* **83 F6** 44 38N 111 45W
Red Springs, *NC, U.S.A.* **90 D6** 34 49N 79 11W
Red Springs, *TX, U.S.A.* **99 D8** 33 37N 99 25W
Red Willow County ☆, *NE, U.S.A.* **84 D5** 40 15N 100 30W
Red Willow Cr. →, *NE, U.S.A.* **84 D5** 40 13N 100 29W
Red Wing, *MN, U.S.A.* **80 F6** 44 34N 92 31W
Redbay, *FL, U.S.A.* **67 A3** 30 35N 85 57W
Redberry L., *Sask., Canada* **182 C4** 52 45N 107 14W
Redbird, *WY, U.S.A.* **104 C8** 43 15N 104 17W
Redcliff, *Alta., Canada* **185 H10** 50 10N 110 50W
Reddell, *LA, U.S.A.* **75 D3** 30 40N 92 25W
Reddick, *FL, U.S.A.* **67 B6** 29 22N 82 12W
Reddick, *IL, U.S.A.* **71 B5** 41 6N 88 15W
Redding, *CA, U.S.A.* **64 C4** 40 35N 122 24W
Redding, *CT, U.S.A.* **78 C1** 41 18N 73 23W
Redding, *IA, U.S.A.* **73 E4** 40 36N 94 23W
Redding Ridge, *CT, U.S.A.* **78 C1** 41 19N 73 21W
Redditt, *Ont., Canada* **180 C2** 49 59N 94 24W
Redfield, *AR, U.S.A.* **63 D3** 34 27N 92 11W
Redfield, *IA, U.S.A.* **73 D4** 41 35N 94 12W
Redfield, *KS, U.S.A.* **74 D9** 37 50N 94 53W
Redfield, *SD, U.S.A.* **91 F7** 44 53N 98 31W
Redford, *TX, U.S.A.* **98 H3** 29 27N 104 11W
Redig, *SD, U.S.A.* **91 E2** 45 16N 103 33W
Redington Beach, *Tampa, U.S.A.* **119 C2** 27 48N 82 48W
Redington Shores, *Tampa, U.S.A.* **119 C2** 27 49N 82 49W
Redkey, *IN, U.S.A.* **72 C5** 40 21N 85 9W
Redlands, *CA, U.S.A.* **65 J9** 34 4N 117 11W
Redman Point Bar, *TN, U.S.A.* **112 A1** 35 13N 90 5W
Redmesa, *CO, U.S.A.* **66 E2** 37 6N 108 11W
Redmon, *IL, U.S.A.* **71 D6** 39 39N 87 52W
Redmond, *OR, U.S.A.* **94 C4** 44 17N 121 11W
Redmond, *UT, U.S.A.* **100 D4** 39 0N 111 52W
Redmond, *WA, U.S.A.* **101 C3** 47 40N 122 7W
Redonda Is., *B.C., Canada* **186 E10** 50 15N 124 50W
Redondo, Cabo, *Baja Calif. S., Mexico* **211 J6** 24 34N 112 5W
Redondo Beach, *CA, U.S.A.* **65 K8** 33 50N 118 23W
Redoubt Volcano, *AK, U.S.A.* **61 F9** 60 29N 152 45W
Redrock, *NM, U.S.A.* **88 E2** 32 41N 108 44W
Redstone, *B.C., Canada* **186 C11** 52 8N 123 42W
Redstone, *CO, U.S.A.* **66 C3** 39 11N 107 14W
Redstone →, *N.W.T., Canada* **189 D8** 64 17N 124 32W
Redstone Arsenal, *AL, U.S.A.* **60 B4** 34 35N 86 41W
Redstone Cr. →, *SD, U.S.A.* **91 F7** 44 4N 98 5W
Redvers, *Sask., Canada* **183 F10** 49 35N 101 40W
Redwater, *Alta., Canada* **184 E7** 53 55N 113 6W
Redwater →, *MT, U.S.A.* **83 B12** 48 3N 105 13W
Redwillow →, *Alta., Canada* **184 C1** 55 2N 119 18W
Redwood, *MS, U.S.A.* **81 D3** 32 29N 90 48W
Redwood →, *MN, U.S.A.* **80 F3** 44 34N 95 5W
Redwood City, *CA, U.S.A.* **64 F4** 37 30N 122 15W
Redwood County ☆, *MN, U.S.A.* **80 F3** 44 20N 95 15W
Redwood Cr. →, *CA, U.S.A.* **64 B2** 41 18N 124 5W
Redwood Falls, *MN, U.S.A.* **80 F3** 44 32N 95 7W
Redwood Nat. Park △, *CA, U.S.A.* **64 B2** 41 40N 124 5W
Redwood Regional Park ⌓, *San Francisco, U.S.A.* **118 B3** 37 48N 122 9W
Ree Heights, *SD, U.S.A.* **91 F6** 44 31N 99 12W
Reece, *KS, U.S.A.* **74 D7** 37 48N 96 27W
Reed, *KY, U.S.A.* **96 C5** 37 51N 87 21W
Reed, *OK, U.S.A.* **93 D4** 34 54N 99 42W
Reed City, *MI, U.S.A.* **79 F6** 43 53N 85 31W
Reeder, *ND, U.S.A.* **91 D3** 46 7N 102 57W
Reeders, *PA, U.S.A.* **87 A1** 41 1N 75 20W
Reedley, *CA, U.S.A.* **65 G7** 36 36N 119 27W
Reeds, *MO, U.S.A.* **82 D2** 37 7N 94 10W
Reeds Pk., *NM, U.S.A.* **88 D3** 33 9N 107 51W
Reeds Spring, *MO, U.S.A.* **82 E3** 36 45N 93 23W
Reedsburg, *WI, U.S.A.* **103 E3** 43 32N 90 0W
Reedsport, *OR, U.S.A.* **94 D1** 43 42N 124 6W
Reedsville, *WV, U.S.A.* **102 B5** 39 31N 79 48W
Reedville, *VA, U.S.A.* **77 C4** 37 51N 76 17W
Reedy, *WV, U.S.A.* **102 C3** 38 54N 81 26W
Reedy Creek Park, *Charlotte, U.S.A.* **107 A2** 35 16N 80 42W
Reelfoot L., *TN, U.S.A.* **96 D3** 36 25N 89 22W
Reese, *MI, U.S.A.* **79 F8** 43 27N 83 42W
Reese →, *NV, U.S.A.* **85 B3** 40 48N 117 4W
Reeves, *LA, U.S.A.* **75 D2** 30 31N 93 3W
Reeves County ☆, *TX, U.S.A.* **98 F4** 31 13N 103 45W
Reeves Hill, *Boston, U.S.A.* **106 A1** 42 20N 71 20W
Reform, *AL, U.S.A.* **60 C2** 33 23N 88 1W
Reforma, *Chiapas, Mexico* **222 B3** 17 56N 93 10W
Reforma, *Quintana Roo, Mexico* **223 D5** 18 45N 88 25W
Reforma de Pineda, *Oaxaca, Mexico* **221 H6** 16 24N 94 28W
Refugio, *TX, U.S.A.* **99 J10** 28 18N 97 17W
Refugio County ☆, *TX, U.S.A.* **99 J10** 28 14N 97 20W
Regan, *ND, U.S.A.* **91 C5** 47 10N 100 32W
Regent, *ND, U.S.A.* **91 D3** 46 25N 102 33W
Regina, *Sask., Canada* **182 E7** 50 27N 104 35W
Regina, *NM, U.S.A.* **88 A4** 36 11N 106 57W
Regina Beach, *Sask., Canada* **182 E7** 50 47N 105 0W
Register, *GA, U.S.A.* **68 D5** 32 22N 81 53W
Rego Park, *NY, U.S.A.* **114 B3** 40 43N 73 51W
Regocijo, *Durango, Mexico* **216 D5** 23 35N 105 11W
Rehoboth, *MA, U.S.A.* **78 C3** 41 50N 71 15W
Rehoboth, *NM, U.S.A.* **88 B2** 35 32N 108 39W
Rehoboth Bay, *DE, U.S.A.* **77 B5** 38 40N 75 6W
Rehoboth Beach, *DE, U.S.A.* **77 B5** 38 43N 75 5W
Reid L., *Sask., Canada* **182 E3** 50 0N 108 9W
Reid Lake, *B.C., Canada* **186 B11** 53 58N 123 6W
Reidland, *KY, U.S.A.* **96 C4** 37 1N 88 32W
Reidsville, *GA, U.S.A.* **68 D4** 32 6N 82 7W
Reidsville, *NC, U.S.A.* **90 B6** 36 21N 79 40W
Reinbeck, *IA, U.S.A.* **73 C6** 42 19N 92 36W
Reindeer I., *Man., Canada* **183 C14** 52 30N 98 0W
Reindeer L., *Sask., Canada* **189 E12** 57 15N 102 15W
Reinland, *Man., Canada* **183 F14** 49 2N 97 52W
Reisterstown, *MD, U.S.A.* **77 A4** 39 28N 76 50W
Reliance, *N.W.T., Canada* **189 D11** 63 0N 109 20W
Reliance, *DE, U.S.A.* **77 B5** 38 38N 75 43W
Reliance, *SD, U.S.A.* **91 G6** 43 53N 99 36W
Reliance, *WY, U.S.A.* **104 E3** 41 40N 109 12W
Rembrandt, *IA, U.S.A.* **73 C3** 42 50N 95 10W
Remedios, Parque Nacional de los △, *México, Mexico* **225 B2** 19 28N 99 17W
Remer, *MN, U.S.A.* **80 C5** 47 4N 93 55W
Rémigny, *Qué., Canada* **176 D3** 47 46N 79 12W
Remington, *IN, U.S.A.* **72 C3** 40 46N 87 9W
Remington, *VA, U.S.A.* **102 C7** 38 32N 77 49W
Remmel Mt., *WA, U.S.A.* **101 B5** 48 58N 120 9W
Remsen, *IA, U.S.A.* **73 C3** 42 49N 95 58W
Remsen, *NY, U.S.A.* **89 B5** 43 20N 75 11W
Renata, *B.C., Canada* **187 F16** 49 27N 118 7W
Rencontre East, *Nfld. & L., Canada* **174 E5** 47 38N 55 12W
Rend Lake, *IL, U.S.A.* **71 E5** 38 2N 88 58W
René-Levasseur, I., *Qué., Canada* **175 C4** 51 20N 68 40W
Renews, *Nfld. & L., Canada* **174 F8** 46 56N 52 56W
Renfrew, *Ont., Canada* **179 B10** 45 30N 76 40W
Renfroe, *GA, U.S.A.* **68 D2** 32 14N 84 43W
Renfrow, *OK, U.S.A.* **93 B6** 36 56N 97 39W
Renick, *WV, U.S.A.* **102 C4** 38 1N 80 22W
Renell Sd., *B.C., Canada* **186 B2** 53 23N 132 35W
Rennie, *Man., Canada* **183 F16** 49 51N 95 33W
Rennison I., *B.C., Canada* **186 C5** 52 50N 129 20W
Reno, *NV, U.S.A.* **85 C1** 39 31N 119 48W
Reno ✕ (RNO), *NV, U.S.A.* **85 C1** 39 30N 119 46W
Reno County ☆, *KS, U.S.A.* **74 C5** 38 0N 98 0W
Renovo, *PA, U.S.A.* **95 C5** 41 20N 77 45W
Rensselaer, *IN, U.S.A.* **72 C3** 40 57N 87 9W
Rensselaer, *NY, U.S.A.* **89 C7** 42 38N 73 45W
Rensselaer County ☆, *NY, U.S.A.* **89 C7** 42 40N 73 30W
Rentiesville, *OK, U.S.A.* **93 C8** 35 35N 95 30W
Renton, *WA, U.S.A.* **101 C3** 47 28N 122 12W
Rentz, *GA, U.S.A.* **68 D4** 32 25N 82 59W
Renville, *MN, U.S.A.* **80 F3** 44 48N 95 13W
Renville County ☆, *MN, U.S.A.* **80 F4** 44 45N 95 0W
Renville County ☆, *ND, U.S.A.* **91 B4** 48 37N 101 35W
Renwick, *IA, U.S.A.* **73 C5** 42 50N 93 59W
Repentigny, *Qué., Canada* **177 F9** 45 44N 73 28W
Repton, *AL, U.S.A.* **60 E3** 31 25N 87 14W
Republic, *KS, U.S.A.* **74 B6** 39 55N 97 49W
Republic, *MI, U.S.A.* **79 C4** 46 25N 87 59W
Republic, *MO, U.S.A.* **82 D3** 37 7N 93 29W
Republic, *OH, U.S.A.* **92 B3** 41 8N 83 1W
Republic, *WA, U.S.A.* **101 B7** 48 39N 118 44W
Republic County ☆, *KS, U.S.A.* **74 B6** 39 45N 97 40W
Republican →, *KS, U.S.A.* **74 B7** 39 4N 96 48W
Republican City, *NE, U.S.A.* **84 D6** 40 6N 99 13W
Repulse Bay, *Nunavut, Canada* **191 D8** 66 30N 86 30W
Reseda, *Los Angeles, U.S.A.* **111 A1** 34 12N 118 32W
Reserve, *Sask., Canada* **182 C9** 52 28N 102 39W
Reserve, *KS, U.S.A.* **74 B8** 39 59N 95 34W
Reserve, *LA, U.S.A.* **75 D5** 30 3N 90 33W
Reserve, *NM, U.S.A.* **88 D2** 33 43N 108 45W
Residencial Chiluca, *México, Mexico* **225 A2** 19 33N 99 17W
Resolute, *Nunavut, Canada* **190 C7** 74 42N 94 54W
Resolution I., *Nunavut, Canada* **191 E13** 61 30N 65 0W
Restigouche →, *N.B., Canada* **173 F2** 47 50N 67 0W
Reston, *Man., Canada* **183 F10** 49 33N 101 6W
Reston, *VA, U.S.A.* **77 B3** 38 57N 77 20W
Retsil, *Seattle, U.S.A.* **118 C2** 47 32N 122 36W
Reva, *SD, U.S.A.* **91 E2** 45 32N 103 5W
Revelstoke, *B.C., Canada* **187 E16** 51 0N 118 10W
Revere, *MA, U.S.A.* **78 B3** 42 25N 71 0W
Revere, *MO, U.S.A.* **82 A5** 40 35N 91 41W
Revillo, *SD, U.S.A.* **91 E9** 45 1N 96 34W
Revolución, *Durango, Mexico* **216 A5** 26 12N 105 6W
Revolución Mexicana, *Chiapas, Mexico* **222 C3** 16 10N 93 4W
Rewey, *WI, U.S.A.* **103 F3** 42 51N 90 24W
Rexburg, *ID, U.S.A.* **70 F7** 43 49N 111 47W
Rexford, *KS, U.S.A.* **74 B3** 39 28N 100 45W
Rexford, *MT, U.S.A.* **83 B2** 48 53N 115 12W
Rexton, *N.B., Canada* **173 G5** 46 39N 64 52W
Rexton, *MI, U.S.A.* **79 C6** 46 10N 85 14W
Rey, L. del, *Coahuila, Mexico* **214 C1** 27 1N 103 26W
Reydon, *OK, U.S.A.* **93 C4** 35 39N 99 55W
Reyes, Pt., *CA, U.S.A.* **64 F3** 38 0N 123 0W
Reyno, *AR, U.S.A.* **63 B5** 36 22N 90 45W
Reynolds, *Man., Canada* **183 F16** 49 40N 95 55W
Reynolds, *GA, U.S.A.* **68 D2** 32 33N 84 6W
Reynolds, *IL, U.S.A.* **71 B3** 41 20N 90 40W
Reynolds, *IN, U.S.A.* **72 C4** 40 45N 86 52W
Reynolds, *ND, U.S.A.* **91 C8** 47 40N 97 7W
Reynolds, *NE, U.S.A.* **84 D8** 40 4N 97 20W
Reynolds Channel, *NY, U.S.A.* **114 C4** 40 35N 73 40W
Reynolds County, *MO, U.S.A.* **82 D6** 37 20N 91 0W
Reynoldsburg, *OH, U.S.A.* **92 D4** 39 57N 82 48W
Reynoldsville, *GA, U.S.A.* **68 F2** 30 51N 84 47W
Reynoldsville, *PA, U.S.A.* **95 C4** 41 6N 78 53W
Reynosa, *Tamaulipas, Mexico* **214 D6** 26 7N 98 18W
Reynosa Tamaulipas, *Distrito Federal, Mexico* **225 A2** 19 30N 99 10W
Rhame, *ND, U.S.A.* **91 D2** 46 14N 103 39W
Rhea County ☆, *TN, U.S.A.* **97 E8** 35 30N 85 0W
Rheem Valley, *San Francisco, U.S.A.* **118 A4** 37 51N 122 7W
Rhein, *Sask., Canada* **183 D9** 51 25N 102 15W
Rhine, *GA, U.S.A.* **68 E3** 31 59N 83 12W
Rhinebeck, *NY, U.S.A.* **89 D7** 41 56N 73 55W
Rhinelander, *WI, U.S.A.* **103 C4** 45 38N 89 25W
Rhode Island, *RI, U.S.A.* **78 C3** 41 30N 71 15W
Rhode Island □, *U.S.A.* **78 C3** 41 40N 71 30W
Rhode Island Sd., *RI, U.S.A.* **78 C3** 41 20N 71 10W
Rhodes Pk., *ID, U.S.A.* **70 C4** 46 40N 114 47W
Rhodhiss L., *NC, U.S.A.* **90 C4** 35 47N 81 26W
Rhododendron, *OR, U.S.A.* **94 B4** 45 20N 121 55W
Rhome, *TX, U.S.A.* **99 D10** 33 3N 97 28W
Ría Celestún, Parque Natural ⌓, *Yucatán, Mexico* **223 A3** 21 0N 90 20W
Ría Lagartos, Parque Natural ⌓, *Yucatán, Mexico* **223 A6** 21 30N 87 45W
Rib Lake, *WI, U.S.A.* **103 C3** 45 19N 90 12W
Ribera, *NM, U.S.A.* **88 B5** 35 23N 105 27W
Ribstone Cr. →, *Alta., Canada* **185 F10** 52 52N 110 5W
Ricardo, *TX, U.S.A.* **98 K10** 27 25N 97 51W
Ricardo Flores Magón, *Chihuahua, Mexico* **213 D9** 29 56N 106 57W
Rice, *CA, U.S.A.* **65 J12** 34 5N 114 51W
Rice, *MN, U.S.A.* **80 E4** 45 45N 94 13W
Rice, *TX, U.S.A.* **99 E11** 32 14N 96 30W
Rice, *VA, U.S.A.* **102 D6** 37 17N 78 18W
Rice County ☆, *KS, U.S.A.* **74 C5** 38 25N 98 10W
Rice County ☆, *MN, U.S.A.* **80 F5** 44 20N 93 15W
Rice L., *Ont., Canada* **179 C8** 44 12N 78 10W
Rice Lake, *WI, U.S.A.* **103 C2** 45 30N 91 44W
Riceboro, *GA, U.S.A.* **68 E5** 31 44N 81 26W
Riceton, *Sask., Canada* **182 E7** 50 7N 104 19W
Riceville, *IA, U.S.A.* **73 B6** 43 22N 92 33W
Riceville, *TN, U.S.A.* **97 E8** 35 23N 84 42W
Rich, *MS, U.S.A.* **81 B3** 34 25N 90 27W
Rich, C., *Ont., Canada* **178 C6** 44 43N 80 38W
Rich County ☆, *UT, U.S.A.* **100 B4** 41 30N 111 10W
Rich Fountain, *MO, U.S.A.* **82 C5** 38 24N 91 53W
Rich Hill, *MO, U.S.A.* **82 C2** 38 6N 94 22W
Rich Square, *NC, U.S.A.* **90 B8** 36 16N 77 17W
Rich Valley, *Alta., Canada* **184 E6** 53 51N 114 21W
Richard B. Russell L., *GA, U.S.A.* **68 B4** 34 5N 82 38W
Richard Collinson Inlet, *N.W.T., Canada* **188 B10** 72 46N 113 54W
Richards, *MO, U.S.A.* **82 D2** 37 54N 94 33W
Richards, *TX, U.S.A.* **99 G12** 30 32N 95 51W
Richards I., *N.W.T., Canada* **188 C6** 68 0N 135 0W
Richardson, *TX, U.S.A.* **99 E11** 32 56N 96 43W
Richardson →, *Alta., Canada* **189 E10** 58 25N 111 14W
Richardson County ☆, *NE, U.S.A.* **84 D10** 40 15N 95 45W
Richardson Is., *Nunavut, Canada* **188 C10** 68 33N 110 45W
Richardson Lakes, *ME, U.S.A.* **76 D3** 44 46N 70 58W
Richardson Mts., *N.W.T., Canada* **188 C5** 68 20N 135 45W
Richardton, *ND, U.S.A.* **91 D3** 46 53N 102 19W
Richboro, *PA, U.S.A.* **87 B1** 40 13N 75 1W
Riche, Pte., *Nfld. & L., Canada* **174 B3** 50 42N 57 25W
Richelieu →, *Qué., Canada* **86 A1** 45 28N 73 18W
Richey, *MT, U.S.A.* **83 C12** 47 39N 105 4W
Richfield, *ID, U.S.A.* **70 F4** 43 3N 114 9W
Richfield, *KS, U.S.A.* **74 D2** 37 16N 101 47W
Richfield, *MN, U.S.A.* **80 F5** 44 53N 93 16W
Richfield, *PA, U.S.A.* **95 D5** 40 41N 77 7W
Richfield, *UT, U.S.A.* **100 E3** 38 46N 112 5W
Richfield Springs, *NY, U.S.A.* **89 C6** 42 51N 74 59W
Richford, *VT, U.S.A.* **86 B2** 45 0N 72 40W
Richgrove, *CA, U.S.A.* **65 H7** 35 48N 119 7W
Richibucto, *N.B., Canada* **173 G5** 46 42N 64 54W
Richland, *GA, U.S.A.* **68 D2** 32 5N 84 40W
Richland, *MI, U.S.A.* **79 G6** 42 22N 85 27W
Richland, *MS, U.S.A.* **81 D3** 32 14N 90 10W
Richland, *MO, U.S.A.* **82 D4** 37 51N 92 26W
Richland, *NE, U.S.A.* **84 C8** 41 26N 97 13W
Richland, *OR, U.S.A.* **94 C8** 44 46N 117 10W
Richland, *TX, U.S.A.* **99 F11** 31 57N 96 26W
Richland, *WA, U.S.A.* **101 D6** 46 17N 119 18W
Richland Center, *WI, U.S.A.* **103 E3** 43 21N 90 23W
Richland Chambers Res., *TX, U.S.A.* **99 F11** 32 0N 96 12W
Richland County ☆, *IL, U.S.A.* **71 E5** 38 45N 88 5W
Richland County ☆, *MT, U.S.A.* **83 C13** 47 48N 104 40W
Richland County ☆, *ND, U.S.A.* **91 D9** 46 15N 97 0W
Richland County ☆, *OH, U.S.A.* **92 C4** 40 45N 82 31W
Richland County ☆, *SC, U.S.A.* **90 D5** 34 10N 81 0W
Richland County ☆, *WI, U.S.A.* **103 E3** 43 20N 90 30W
Richland Cr. →, *TN, U.S.A.* **96 E6** 35 2N 86 56W
Richland Hills, *Dallas-Fort Worth, U.S.A.* **109 B2** 32 48N 97 13W
Richland Parish ☆, *LA, U.S.A.* **75 B4** 32 22N 91 52W
Richland Springs, *TX, U.S.A.* **99 F9** 31 16N 98 57W
Richlands, *NC, U.S.A.* **90 D8** 34 54N 77 34W
Richlands, *VA, U.S.A.* **102 D3** 37 6N 81 48W
Richmond, *B.C., Canada* **187 F11** 49 10N 123 7W
Richmond, *Ont., Canada* **179 B11** 45 11N 75 50W
Richmond, *Qué., Canada* **177 F10** 45 40N 72 9W
Richmond, *CA, U.S.A.* **64 F4** 37 56N 122 21W
Richmond, *IL, U.S.A.* **71 A5** 42 29N 88 18W
Richmond, *IN, U.S.A.* **72 D6** 39 50N 84 53W
Richmond, *KS, U.S.A.* **74 C8** 38 24N 95 15W
Richmond, *KY, U.S.A.* **97 C8** 37 45N 84 18W
Richmond, *ME, U.S.A.* **76 D4** 44 5N 69 48W
Richmond, *MI, U.S.A.* **79 G9** 42 49N 82 45W
Richmond, *MO, U.S.A.* **82 B3** 39 17N 93 58W
Richmond, *NH, U.S.A.* **86 D2** 42 45N 72 18W
Richmond, *San Francisco, U.S.A.* **118 B2** 37 46N 122 27W
Richmond, *TX, U.S.A.* **99 H12** 29 35N 95 46W
Richmond, *UT, U.S.A.* **100 B4** 41 56N 111 48W
Richmond, *VA, U.S.A.* **102 D7** 37 33N 77 27W
Richmond, *VT, U.S.A.* **86 B2** 44 24N 72 59W
Richmond ✕ (RIC), *VA, U.S.A.* **102 D7** 37 30N 77 19W
Richmond County ☆, *GA, U.S.A.* **68 C4** 33 15N 82 5W
Richmond County ☆, *NC, U.S.A.* **90 D6** 35 0N 79 45W
Richmond County ☆, *NY, U.S.A.* **89 E6** 40 40N 74 15W
Richmond County ☆, *VA, U.S.A.* **102 D8** 37 58N 76 46W
Richmond Heights, *FL, U.S.A.* **67 F8** 25 38N 80 23W
Richmond Heights, *MO, U.S.A.* **117 B2** 38 37N 90 19W
Richmond Hill, *Ont., Canada* **178 D7** 43 52N 79 27W
Richmond Hill, *GA, U.S.A.* **68 E5** 31 56N 81 18W
Richmond Hill, *NY, U.S.A.* **114 B3** 40 41N 73 51W
Richmond Nature Park, *Vancouver, Canada* **193 C2** 49 10N 123 7W
Richmond Valley, *NY, U.S.A.* **114 C1** 40 31N 74 13W
Richmondville, *NY, U.S.A.* **89 C6** 42 38N 74 34W
Richmound, *Sask., Canada* **182 E2** 50 27N 109 45W
Richton, *MS, U.S.A.* **81 E5** 31 16N 88 56W
Richville, *MN, U.S.A.* **80 D3** 46 31N 95 38W
Richville, *NY, U.S.A.* **89 A5** 44 25N 75 22W
Richwood, *LA, U.S.A.* **75 B3** 32 27N 92 5W
Richwood, *OH, U.S.A.* **92 C3** 40 26N 83 18W
Richwood, *WV, U.S.A.* **102 C4** 38 14N 80 32W
Richwoods, *MO, U.S.A.* **82 C6** 38 10N 90 50W
Ricketts, *IA, U.S.A.* **73 C3** 42 8N 95 35W
Ricketts Glen State Park ⌓, *PA, U.S.A.* **95 C6** 41 19N 76 16W
Rico, *CO, U.S.A.* **66 E2** 37 42N 108 2W
Riddle, *ID, U.S.A.* **70 G2** 42 11N 116 7W
Riddle, *OR, U.S.A.* **94 E2** 42 57N 123 22W
Rideau →, *Ont., Canada* **192 B1** 45 27N 75 42W
Riderwood, *Baltimore, U.S.A.* **107 A2** 39 24N 76 38W
Ridge, *MD, U.S.A.* **77 B4** 38 8N 76 24W
Ridge →, *Ont., Canada* **181 B12** 50 25N 84 20W
Ridge Farm, *IL, U.S.A.* **71 D6** 39 54N 87 39W
Ridge Spring, *SC, U.S.A.* **90 E4** 33 51N 81 40W
Ridgecrest, *CA, U.S.A.* **65 H9** 35 38N 117 40W
Ridgedale, *Sask., Canada* **182 B7** 53 0N 104 10W
Ridgefield, *CT, U.S.A.* **78 C1** 41 17N 73 30W
Ridgefield, *NJ, U.S.A.* **114 B2** 40 49N 74 0W
Ridgefield, *WA, U.S.A.* **101 E3** 45 49N 122 45W
Ridgefield Park, *NJ, U.S.A.* **114 A2** 40 52N 74 1W
Ridgeland, *MS, U.S.A.* **81 D3** 32 26N 90 8W
Ridgeland, *SC, U.S.A.* **90 F5** 32 29N 80 59W
Ridgeland, *WI, U.S.A.* **103 C2** 45 12N 91 54W
Ridgely, *TN, U.S.A.* **96 D3** 36 16N 89 29W
Ridgetown, *Ont., Canada* **178 E5** 42 26N 81 52W
Ridgeville, *IN, U.S.A.* **72 C5** 40 18N 85 2W
Ridgeville, *SC, U.S.A.* **90 E5** 33 6N 80 19W
Ridgeway, *IA, U.S.A.* **73 B7** 43 18N 91 59W
Ridgeway, *MO, U.S.A.* **82 A3** 40 23N 93 57W
Ridgeway, *OH, U.S.A.* **92 C3** 40 31N 83 35W
Ridgeway, *SC, U.S.A.* **90 D5** 34 18N 80 58W
Ridgeway, *VA, U.S.A.* **102 E5** 36 35N 79 52W
Ridgeway, *WI, U.S.A.* **103 E3** 43 1N 90 1W
Ridgewood, *NJ, U.S.A.* **87 B2** 40 59N 74 7W
Ridgewood, *NY, U.S.A.* **114 B3** 40 42N 73 53W
Ridgway, *CO, U.S.A.* **66 D3** 38 9N 107 46W
Ridgway, *IL, U.S.A.* **71 F5** 37 48N 88 16W
Ridgway, *PA, U.S.A.* **95 C4** 41 25N 78 44W
Riding Mountain Nat. Park △, *Man., Canada* **183 E11** 50 50N 100 0W
Rienzi, *MS, U.S.A.* **81 B5** 34 46N 88 32W
Rieth, *OR, U.S.A.* **94 B7** 45 40N 118 54W
Riffe L., *WA, U.S.A.* **101 D3** 46 32N 122 26W
Rifle, *CO, U.S.A.* **66 C3** 39 32N 107 47W
Rifle →, *MI, U.S.A.* **79 E8** 44 0N 83 49W
Rigby, *ID, U.S.A.* **70 F7** 43 40N 111 55W
Riggins, *ID, U.S.A.* **70 D2** 45 25N 116 19W
Rigolet, *Nfld. & L., Canada* **175 C6** 54 10N 58 23W
Rikers I., *NY, U.S.A.* **114 B3** 40 47N 73 53W
Riley, *IN, U.S.A.* **72 D3** 39 23N 87 18W
Riley, *KS, U.S.A.* **74 B7** 39 18N 96 50W
Riley, *OR, U.S.A.* **94 D6** 43 32N 119 28W
Riley County ☆, *KS, U.S.A.* **74 B7** 39 20N 96 40W
Rileyville, *VA, U.S.A.* **77 B2** 38 46N 78 23W
Rillito, *AZ, U.S.A.* **62 E4** 32 25N 111 9W
Rimbey, *Alta., Canada* **185 F6** 52 35N 114 15W
Rimersburg, *PA, U.S.A.* **95 C3** 41 3N 79 30W
Rimouski, *Qué., Canada* **177 C14** 48 27N 68 30W
Rimouski →, *Qué., Canada* **177 C14** 48 27N 68 32W
Rimouski, Réserve Faunique de ⌓, *Qué., Canada* **177 C14** 48 0N 68 15W
Rimouski-Est, *Qué., Canada* **177 C14** 48 28N 68 31W
Rimrock, *WA, U.S.A.* **101 D4** 46 40N 121 7W
Rinard, *IA, U.S.A.* **73 C4** 42 20N 94 29W
Rincón, *Puerto Rico* **105 G15** 18 20N 67 15W
Rincon, *GA, U.S.A.* **68 D5** 32 18N 81 14W
Rincón de las Bayas, B., *Tamaulipas, Mexico* **215 E7** 25 15N 97 45W
Rincón de López, *Colima, Mexico* **218 C4** 19 2N 103 56W
Rincón de Romos, *Aguascalientes, Mexico* **217 E8** 22 14N 102 18W
Rincón Juárez, *Oaxaca, Mexico* **221 H6** 16 17N 94 21W
Rincón Moreno, *Oaxaca, Mexico* **221 H6** 16 14N 95 28W
Rinconada →, *Baja Calif., Mexico* **210 D4** 29 17N 114 52W
Rindge, *NH, U.S.A.* **86 D2** 42 45N 72 1W
Rineyville, *KY, U.S.A.* **97 C7** 37 45N 85 58W
Ringgold, *GA, U.S.A.* **68 B1** 34 55N 85 7W
Ringgold, *LA, U.S.A.* **75 B2** 32 20N 93 17W
Ringgold, *NE, U.S.A.* **84 C5** 41 31N 100 47W
Ringgold County ☆, *IA, U.S.A.* **73 E4** 40 45N 94 15W
Ringling, *MT, U.S.A.* **83 D7** 46 16N 110 49W
Ringling, *OK, U.S.A.* **93 D6** 34 11N 97 36W
Ringoes, *NJ, U.S.A.* **87 B2** 40 26N 74 52W
Ringsted, *IA, U.S.A.* **73 B4** 43 18N 94 31W
Ringwood, *NJ, U.S.A.* **87 A2** 41 7N 74 15W
Ringwood, *OK, U.S.A.* **93 B5** 36 23N 98 15W
Rio, *IL, U.S.A.* **71 B3** 41 7N 90 24W
Rio, *WI, U.S.A.* **103 E4** 43 27N 89 14W
Rio Arriba County ☆, *NM, U.S.A.* **88 A4** 36 30N 106 45W
Río Blanco, *Chiapas, Mexico* **222 C5** 16 12N 91 38W
Rio Blanco, *CO, U.S.A.* **66 C3** 39 44N 107 57W
Rio Blanco County ☆, *CO, U.S.A.* **66 C2** 40 0N 108 15W
Río Bravo, *Tamaulipas, Mexico* **214 E6** 25 59N 98 6W
Rio Communities, *NM, U.S.A.* **88 C4** 34 40N 106 43W

Rio Dell, *CA, U.S.A.* **64 C2** 40 30N 124 6W
Río Grande, *Oaxaca, Mexico* **221 H3** 16 1N 97 37W
Río Grande, *Puebla, Mexico* **221 F2** 18 39N 98 20W
Río Grande, *Puerto Rico* **105 G17** 18 23N 65 50W
Rio Grande, *NJ, U.S.A.* **87 C2** 39 1N 74 53W
Rio Grande, *OH, U.S.A.* **92 E4** 38 56N 82 21W
Rio Grande →, *N. Amer.* **98 M10** 25 58N 97 9W
Rio Grande City, *TX, U.S.A.* **98 L9** 26 23N 98 49W
Rio Grande County ☆, *CO, U.S.A.* **66 E4** 37 40N 106 20W
Río Grande de Santiago →, *Nayarit, Mexico* **216 F5** 21 36N 105 26W
Rio Grande Nat. Forest, *CO, U.S.A.* **66 E4** 37 30N 106 30W
Rio Hondo, *TX, U.S.A.* **98 L10** 26 14N 97 35W
Río Indio, Pta., *Quintana Roo, Mexico* **223 D6** 18 50N 87 38W
Río Lagartos, *Yucatán, Mexico* **223 A5** 21 36N 88 10W
Río Lagartos, Estero, *Yucatán, Mexico* **223 A6** 21 37N 87 55W
Rio Rancho, *NM, U.S.A.* **88 B4** 35 14N 106 41W
Río San Rodrigo-El Burro, Parque Natural ⌂, *Coahuila, Mexico* **214 B3** 28 57N 101 53W
Río Verde, *Quintana Roo, Mexico* **223 C4** 19 5N 89 2W
Río Verde, *San Luis Potosí, Mexico* **215 J5** 21 56N 99 59W
Rio Vista, *CA, U.S.A.* **64 E5** 38 10N 121 42W
Riondel, *B.C., Canada* **187 F18** 49 46N 116 51W
Ripley, *Ont., Canada* **178 C5** 44 4N 81 35W
Ripley, *IL, U.S.A.* **71 C3** 40 1N 90 38W
Ripley, *MS, U.S.A.* **81 B5** 34 44N 88 57W
Ripley, *NY, U.S.A.* **89 C1** 42 16N 79 43W
Ripley, *OH, U.S.A.* **92 E3** 38 45N 83 51W
Ripley, *OK, U.S.A.* **93 B7** 36 1N 96 54W
Ripley, *TN, U.S.A.* **96 E3** 35 45N 89 32W
Ripley, *WV, U.S.A.* **102 C3** 38 49N 81 43W
Ripley County ☆, *IN, U.S.A.* **72 D5** 39 5N 85 15W
Ripley County ☆, *MO, U.S.A.* **82 E6** 36 40N 90 50W
Ripogenus Dam, *ME, U.S.A.* **76 C4** 45 53N 69 11W
Ripon, *Qué., Canada* **176 F7** 45 45N 75 10W
Ripon, *CA, U.S.A.* **64 F5** 37 44N 121 7W
Ripon, *WI, U.S.A.* **103 E5** 43 51N 88 50W
Rippey, *IA, U.S.A.* **73 D4** 41 56N 94 12W
Rippon, *WV, U.S.A.* **77 A3** 39 13N 77 54W
Ririe, *ID, U.S.A.* **70 F7** 43 38N 111 47W
Ririe Res., *ID, U.S.A.* **70 F7** 43 30N 111 43W
Risco, *MO, U.S.A.* **82 E7** 36 33N 89 49W
Rising City, *NE, U.S.A.* **84 C8** 41 12N 97 18W
Rising Fawn, *GA, U.S.A.* **68 B1** 34 46N 85 32W
Rising Star, *TX, U.S.A.* **99 E9** 32 6N 98 58W
Rising Sun, *IN, U.S.A.* **72 E6** 38 57N 84 51W
Rising Sun, *MD, U.S.A.* **77 A4** 39 42N 76 4W
Rison, *AR, U.S.A.* **63 E3** 33 58N 92 11W
Rita Blanca Cr. →, *TX, U.S.A.* **98 B5** 35 40N 102 29W
Rita Blanca Nat. Grassland, *TX, U.S.A.* **98 A5** 36 20N 102 30W
Ritchie, *MD, U.S.A.* **119 B4** 38 52N 76 51W
Ritchie County ☆, *WV, U.S.A.* **102 B3** 39 13N 81 3W
Ritchie L., *Nfld. & L., Canada* **172 A3** 52 58N 66 1W
Ritidian Pt., *Guam* **105 b** 13 39N 144 51 E
Ritter, Mt., *CA, U.S.A.* **64 F7** 37 41N 119 12W
Rittman, *OH, U.S.A.* **92 C5** 40 58N 81 47W
Ritzville, *WA, U.S.A.* **101 C7** 47 8N 118 23W
Riva, *MD, U.S.A.* **77 B4** 38 57N 76 35W
Riva Palacio, *Chihuahua, Mexico* **213 E9** 28 33N 106 30W
Rivanna →, *VA, U.S.A.* **102 D6** 37 45N 78 10W
Rive Sud, Canal de la, *Montréal, Canada* **192 B3** 45 24N 73 31W
River Edge, *NJ, U.S.A.* **114 A2** 40 56N 74 1W
River Falls, *AL, U.S.A.* **60 E4** 31 21N 86 32W
River Falls, *WI, U.S.A.* **103 D1** 44 52N 92 38W
River Forest, *Chicago, U.S.A.* **108 B2** 41 53N 87 49W
River Grove, *Chicago, U.S.A.* **108 B1** 41 55N 87 50W
River Hebert, *N.S., Canada* **173 H5** 45 42N 64 23W
River Hills, *Milwaukee, U.S.A.* **112 B2** 43 10N 87 55W
River John, *N.S., Canada* **173 H6** 45 45N 63 3W
River Jordan, *B.C., Canada* **186 G10** 48 26N 124 3W
River of Ponds, *Nfld. & L., Canada* **174 B3** 50 32N 57 24W
River of Ponds L., *Nfld. & L., Canada* **174 B3** 50 30N 57 20W
River Ridge, *New Orleans, U.S.A.* **113 C1** 29 57N 90 12W
River Rouge, *MI, U.S.A.* **109 B2** 42 16N 83 7W
River Rouge Park, *MI, U.S.A.* **109 A1** 42 18N 83 14W
River Valley, *Ont., Canada* **178 A6** 46 35N 80 11W
Riverbank, *CA, U.S.A.* **64 F6** 37 44N 120 56W
Rivercrest, *Man., Canada* **183 E14** 50 0N 97 3W
Riverdale, *CA, U.S.A.* **65 G7** 36 26N 119 52W
Riverdale, *GA, U.S.A.* **68 C2** 33 34N 84 25W
Riverdale, *MD, U.S.A.* **119 B4** 38 57N 76 54W
Riverdale, *ND, U.S.A.* **91 C4** 47 30N 101 22W
Riverdale, *NY, U.S.A.* **114 A3** 40 59N 74 17W
Riverdale, *NE, U.S.A.* **84 D6** 40 47N 99 10W
Rivergrove, *Portland, U.S.A.* **116 B1** 45 23N 122 43W
Riverhead, *Nfld. & L., Canada* **174 F7** 46 58N 53 31W
Riverhead, *NY, U.S.A.* **78 D2** 40 55N 72 40W
Riverhurst, *Sask., Canada* **182 E5** 50 55N 106 50W
Riverport, *N.S., Canada* **173 J5** 44 18N 64 20W
Rivers, *Man., Canada* **183 E11** 50 2N 100 14W
Rivers, L. of the, *Sask., Canada* **182 F6** 49 49N 105 44W
Rivers Inlet, *B.C., Canada* **186 D7** 51 42N 127 15W
Riverside, *CA, U.S.A.* **65 K9** 33 59N 117 22W
Riverside, *Chicago, U.S.A.* **108 C2** 41 49N 87 49W
Riverside, *IA, U.S.A.* **73 D7** 41 29N 91 35W
Riverside, *MD, U.S.A.* **77 B3** 38 22N 77 11W
Riverside, *NJ, U.S.A.* **87 B2** 40 2N 74 58W
Riverside, *NM, U.S.A.* **88 E6** 32 50N 104 17W
Riverside, *OR, U.S.A.* **94 D7** 43 32N 118 10W
Riverside, *TX, U.S.A.* **99 G12** 30 51N 95 24W
Riverside, *WA, U.S.A.* **101 B6** 48 30N 119 30W
Riverside, *WY, U.S.A.* **104 E6** 41 13N 106 47W
Riverside-Albert, *N.B., Canada* **173 H5** 45 42N 64 45W
Riverside County ☆, *CA, U.S.A.* **65 K11** 33 45N 116 0W
Riverside Park, *Indianapolis, U.S.A.* **110 B1** 39 48N 86 11W
Riverside Res., *CO, U.S.A.* **66 B6** 40 20N 104 15W
Riverton, *Man., Canada* **183 D14** 51 1N 97 0W
Riverton, *IL, U.S.A.* **71 D4** 39 51N 89 33W
Riverton, *IA, U.S.A.* **73 E3** 40 41N 95 34W
Riverton, *KS, U.S.A.* **74 D9** 37 5N 94 42W
Riverton, *LA, U.S.A.* **75 B3** 32 10N 92 6W
Riverton, *NE, U.S.A.* **84 D7** 40 5N 98 46W
Riverton, *OR, U.S.A.* **94 D1** 43 10N 124 16W
Riverton, *UT, U.S.A.* **100 C4** 40 31N 111 56W
Riverton, *WV, U.S.A.* **102 C5** 38 45N 79 26W
Riverton, *WY, U.S.A.* **104 C4** 43 2N 108 23W
Riverview, *N.B., Canada* **173 G5** 46 4N 64 48W
Riverview, *Ont., Canada* **192 B2** 45 24N 75 39W
Riverview, *FL, U.S.A.* **67 D6** 27 52N 82 20W
Riverview, *MO, U.S.A.* **117 A2** 38 44N 90 12W
Riverview, *WY, U.S.A.* **104 C8** 43 25N 104 12W
Riverview Park, *Pittsburgh, U.S.A.* **116 B1** 40 28N 80 1W
Rivesville, *WV, U.S.A.* **102 B4** 39 32N 80 7W
Riviera, *Qué., Canada* **192 A1** 45 28N 75 43W
Riviera, *AZ, U.S.A.* **62 B1** 35 4N 114 35W
Riviera, *TX, U.S.A.* **98 K10** 27 18N 97 49W
Riviera Beach, *FL, U.S.A.* **67 E8** 26 47N 80 3W
Riviera Beach, *MD, U.S.A.* **77 A4** 39 10N 76 31W
Rivière-à-Pierre, *Qué., Canada* **177 E10** 46 59N 72 11W
Rivière-au-Renard, *Qué., Canada* **172 E5** 48 59N 64 23W
Rivière-au-Tonnerre, *Qué., Canada* **172 C5** 50 16N 64 47W
Rivière-aux-Graines, *Qué., Canada* **172 C4** 50 17N 65 11W
Rivière-aux-Rats, *Qué., Canada* **177 D10** 47 13N 72 53W
Rivière-Bersimis, *Qué., Canada* **177 C14** 48 56N 68 42W
Rivière-Bleue, *Qué., Canada* **177 D13** 47 26N 69 3W
Rivière-de-la-Chaloupe, *Qué., Canada* **172 D7** 49 8N 62 32W
Rivière-des-Praires, *Montréal, Canada* **192 A3** 45 38N 73 34W
Rivière-du-Loup, *Qué., Canada* **177 D13** 47 50N 69 30W
Rivière-du-Portage, *N.B., Canada* **173 F5** 47 25N 64 56W
Rivière-Ouelle, *Qué., Canada* **177 D12** 47 26N 70 1W
Rivière-Pentecôte, *Qué., Canada* **172 D2** 49 57N 67 1W
Rivière-Pigou, *Qué., Canada* **172 C4** 50 16N 65 35W
Rivière-St-Jean, *Qué., Canada* **172 C5** 50 17N 64 19W
Rivière Verte, *N.B., Canada* **173 F1** 47 19N 68 9W
Rixeyville, *VA, U.S.A.* **102 C7** 38 35N 77 59W
Roach L., *NV, U.S.A.* **85 G5** 35 41N 115 22W
Roachdale, *IN, U.S.A.* **72 D4** 39 51N 86 48W
Road Town, *Br. Virgin Is.* **105 G18** 18 27N 64 37W
Roan Cliffs, *CO, U.S.A.* **66 C2** 39 20N 108 40W
Roan Cliffs, *UT, U.S.A.* **100 D6** 39 20N 109 40W
Roan Cr. →, *CO, U.S.A.* **66 C2** 39 20N 108 13W
Roan Mountain, *TN, U.S.A.* **97 D10** 36 12N 82 4W
Roan Plateau, *CO, U.S.A.* **66 C2** 39 35N 108 40W
Roan Plateau, *UT, U.S.A.* **100 D6** 39 20N 109 20W
Roanoake I., *NC, U.S.A.* **90 C10** 35 53N 75 39W
Roane County ☆, *TN, U.S.A.* **97 E8** 35 52N 84 31W
Roane County ☆, *WV, U.S.A.* **102 C3** 38 48N 81 21W
Roanoke, *AL, U.S.A.* **60 C5** 33 9N 85 22W
Roanoke, *IL, U.S.A.* **71 C4** 40 48N 89 12W
Roanoke, *IN, U.S.A.* **72 C5** 40 58N 85 22W
Roanoke, *TX, U.S.A.* **99 D10** 33 0N 97 10W
Roanoke, *VA, U.S.A.* **102 D5** 37 16N 79 56W
Roanoke →, *NC, U.S.A.* **90 C9** 35 57N 76 42W
Roanoke County ☆, *VA, U.S.A.* **102 D5** 37 16N 79 56W
Roanoke I., *NC, U.S.A.* **90 C10** 35 55N 75 40W
Roanoke Rapids, *NC, U.S.A.* **90 B8** 36 28N 77 40W
Roanoke Rapids L., *NC, U.S.A.* **90 B8** 36 29N 77 40W
Roaring Spring, *PA, U.S.A.* **95 D4** 40 20N 78 24W
Roaring Springs, *TX, U.S.A.* **98 D7** 33 54N 100 52W
Robards, *KY, U.S.A.* **96 C5** 37 41N 87 33W
Robb, *Alta., Canada* **184 E4** 53 13N 116 58W
Robbins, *Chicago, U.S.A.* **108 D2** 41 38N 87 42W
Robbins, *NC, U.S.A.* **90 C6** 35 26N 79 35W
Robbins, *TN, U.S.A.* **97 D8** 36 21N 84 35W
Robbinsdale, *Minneapolis-St. Paul, U.S.A.* **113 A2** 45 1N 93 19W
Robbinsville, *NC, U.S.A.* **90 C2** 35 19N 83 48W
Robco L., *TN, U.S.A.* **112 B1** 35 0N 90 7W
Robe-Noire, L. de la, *Qué., Canada* **172 C7** 50 42N 62 42W
Robersonville, *NC, U.S.A.* **90 C8** 35 50N 77 15W
Robert E. Lee Park, *Baltimore, U.S.A.* **107 A2** 39 23N 76 39W
Robert Lee, *TX, U.S.A.* **98 F7** 31 54N 100 29W
Robert S. Kerr L., *OK, U.S.A.* **93 C9** 35 21N 94 47W
Roberta, *GA, U.S.A.* **68 D2** 32 43N 84 1W
Roberts, *ID, U.S.A.* **70 F6** 43 43N 112 8W
Roberts, *IL, U.S.A.* **71 C5** 40 37N 88 11W
Roberts, *MT, U.S.A.* **83 E8** 45 22N 109 10W
Roberts, Mt., *AK, U.S.A.* **61 F6** 60 2N 166 16W
Robert's Arm, *Nfld. & L., Canada* **174 C5** 49 29N 55 49W
Roberts County ☆, *SD, U.S.A.* **91 E9** 45 33N 96 57W
Roberts County ☆, *TX, U.S.A.* **98 B7** 35 55N 100 55W
Roberts Creek, *B.C., Canada* **187 F11** 49 26N 123 38W
Robertsdale, *AL, U.S.A.* **60 F3** 30 33N 87 43W
Robertson, *MO, U.S.A.* **117 A1** 38 44N 90 22W
Robertson, *WY, U.S.A.* **104 E2** 41 11N 110 25W
Robertson County ☆, *KY, U.S.A.* **97 B8** 38 30N 84 5W
Robertson County ☆, *TN, U.S.A.* **96 D6** 36 31N 86 53W
Robertson County ☆, *TX, U.S.A.* **99 F11** 31 2N 96 29W
Robertsonville, *Qué., Canada* **177 E11** 46 9N 71 13W
Robertsville, *NJ, U.S.A.* **87 B2** 40 21N 74 17W
Robertville, *N.B., Canada* **173 F4** 47 42N 65 46W
Roberval, *Qué., Canada* **177 C10** 48 32N 72 15W
Robeson Chan., *N. Amer.* **190 A13** 82 0N 61 30W
Robeson County ☆, *NC, U.S.A.* **90 D6** 34 30N 79 10W
Robesonia, *PA, U.S.A.* **95 D6** 40 21N 76 8W
Robins, *IA, U.S.A.* **73 C7** 42 4N 91 40W
Robinson, *IL, U.S.A.* **71 E6** 39 0N 87 44W
Robinson, *KS, U.S.A.* **74 B8** 39 49N 95 25W
Robinson, *ND, U.S.A.* **91 C6** 47 9N 99 47W
Robinson, *TX, U.S.A.* **99 F10** 31 28N 97 7W
Robinson, L., *SC, U.S.A.* **90 D5** 34 30N 80 12W
Robinson Mt., *MT, U.S.A.* **83 B2** 48 58N 115 25W
Robinsonville, *MS, U.S.A.* **81 B3** 34 49N 90 19W
Roblin, *Man., Canada* **183 D10** 51 14N 101 21W
Robsart, *Sask., Canada* **182 F2** 49 23N 109 17W
Robson, Mt., *B.C., Canada* **187 B15** 53 10N 119 10W
Robstown, *TX, U.S.A.* **99 K10** 27 47N 97 40W
Roby, *MO, U.S.A.* **82 D4** 37 31N 92 8W
Roby, *TX, U.S.A.* **98 E7** 32 45N 100 23W
Roca, *NE, U.S.A.* **84 D9** 40 39N 96 40W
Roca Partida, *Veracruz, Mexico* **221 F5** 18 42N 95 5W
Roca Partida, Pta., *Veracruz, Mexico* **221 F5** 18 42N 95 10W
Rocanville, *Sask., Canada* **183 E10** 50 23N 101 42W
Rochdale, *MA, U.S.A.* **78 B3** 42 12N 71 54W
Roche Percee, *Sask., Canada* **182 F9** 49 4N 102 48W
Rochéachic, *Chihuahua, Mexico* **213 F8** 27 5N 107 12W
Rochebaucourt, *Qué., Canada* **176 C5** 48 41N 77 30W
Rochelle, *GA, U.S.A.* **68 E3** 31 57N 83 27W
Rochelle, *IL, U.S.A.* **71 B4** 41 56N 89 4W
Rochelle, *TX, U.S.A.* **99 F8** 31 14N 99 13W
Rochelle Park, *NJ, U.S.A.* **114 A2** 40 54N 74 4W
Rocheport, *MO, U.S.A.* **82 C4** 38 59N 92 34W
Rochester, *Alta., Canada* **184 D7** 54 22N 113 27W
Rochester, *IL, U.S.A.* **71 D4** 39 45N 89 32W
Rochester, *IN, U.S.A.* **72 B4** 41 4N 86 13W
Rochester, *KY, U.S.A.* **96 C6** 37 13N 86 53W
Rochester, *MA, U.S.A.* **78 C4** 41 44N 70 49W
Rochester, *MN, U.S.A.* **80 F6** 44 1N 92 28W
Rochester, *NH, U.S.A.* **86 C4** 43 18N 70 59W
Rochester, *NY, U.S.A.* **89 B3** 43 10N 77 37W
Rochester, *OH, U.S.A.* **92 B4** 41 8N 82 18W
Rochester, *TX, U.S.A.* **99 D8** 33 19N 99 51W
Rochester, *VT, U.S.A.* **86 C2** 43 52N 72 49W
Rochester, *WA, U.S.A.* **101 D2** 46 49N 123 6W
Rochester Hills, *MI, U.S.A.* **79 G8** 42 41N 83 8W
Rochester Park, *Dallas-Fort Worth, U.S.A.* **109 B5** 32 43N 96 44W
Rock, *MI, U.S.A.* **79 C4** 46 4N 87 10W
Rock →, *Yukon, Canada* **189 D7** 66 7N 127 7W
Rock →, *IL, U.S.A.* **71 B3** 41 29N 90 37W
Rock Cave, *WV, U.S.A.* **102 C4** 38 50N 80 21W
Rock County ☆, *MN, U.S.A.* **80 G2** 43 45N 96 15W
Rock County ☆, *NE, U.S.A.* **84 B6** 42 30N 99 30W
Rock County ☆, *WI, U.S.A.* **103 F4** 42 45N 89 10W
Rock Cr. →, *DC, U.S.A.* **119 B3** 38 54N 77 3W
Rock Cr. →, *IL, U.S.A.* **71 B3** 41 42N 90 3W
Rock Cr. →, *MT, U.S.A.* **83 D4** 46 43N 113 40W
Rock Cr. →, *MT, U.S.A.* **83 B10** 48 27N 107 6W
Rock Cr. →, *NV, U.S.A.* **85 B4** 40 39N 116 55W
Rock Cr. →, *OR, U.S.A.* **94 B5** 45 34N 120 25W
Rock Cr. →, *SD, U.S.A.* **91 G8** 43 44N 97 58W
Rock Cr. →, *UT, U.S.A.* **100 C5** 40 17N 110 30W
Rock Creek, *B.C., Canada* **187 F16** 49 4N 119 0W
Rock Creek, *MN, U.S.A.* **80 E6** 45 45N 92 58W
Rock Creek, *OH, U.S.A.* **92 B6** 41 40N 80 52W
Rock Creek Butte, *OR, U.S.A.* **94 C7** 44 49N 118 7W
Rock Creek Park, *DC, U.S.A.* **119 B3** 38 56N 77 2W
Rock Falls, *IL, U.S.A.* **71 B4** 41 47N 89 41W
Rock Falls, *IA, U.S.A.* **73 B4** 43 13N 93 5W
Rock Forest, *Qué., Canada* **177 F11** 45 21N 71 59W
Rock Hall, *MD, U.S.A.* **77 A4** 39 8N 76 14W
Rock Hill, *MO, U.S.A.* **117 B1** 38 36N 90 22W
Rock Hill, *SC, U.S.A.* **90 D4** 34 56N 81 1W
Rock I., *WI, U.S.A.* **103 C7** 45 25N 86 49W
Rock Island, *IL, U.S.A.* **71 B3** 41 30N 90 34W
Rock Island, *OK, U.S.A.* **93 C9** 35 10N 94 28W
Rock Island, *WA, U.S.A.* **101 C5** 47 22N 120 8W
Rock Island County ☆, *IL, U.S.A.* **71 B3** 41 25N 90 30W
Rock Island Dam, *WA, U.S.A.* **101 C5** 47 23N 120 4W
Rock L., *ND, U.S.A.* **91 B6** 48 50N 99 12W
Rock L., *WA, U.S.A.* **101 C8** 47 11N 117 41W
Rock Point, *AZ, U.S.A.* **62 A6** 36 43N 109 38W
Rock Point, *MD, U.S.A.* **77 B4** 38 16N 76 50W
Rock Port, *MO, U.S.A.* **82 A1** 40 25N 95 31W
Rock Rapids, *IA, U.S.A.* **73 B2** 43 26N 96 10W
Rock River, *WY, U.S.A.* **104 E7** 41 44N 105 58W
Rock Spring, *GA, U.S.A.* **68 B1** 34 50N 85 14W
Rock Springs, *MT, U.S.A.* **83 D11** 46 49N 106 15W
Rock Springs, *WY, U.S.A.* **104 E3** 41 35N 109 14W
Rock Valley, *IA, U.S.A.* **73 B2** 43 12N 96 18W
Rockaway Beach, *OR, U.S.A.* **94 B2** 45 37N 123 57W
Rockaway Inlet, *NY, U.S.A.* **114 C3** 40 34N 73 54W
Rockaway Pt., *NY, U.S.A.* **114 C3** 40 33N 73 54W
Rockbridge, *IL, U.S.A.* **71 D3** 39 16N 90 12W
Rockbridge County ☆, *VA, U.S.A.* **102 D5** 37 55N 79 20W
Rockcastle →, *KY, U.S.A.* **97 D8** 36 58N 84 21W
Rockcastle County ☆, *KY, U.S.A.* **97 C8** 37 20N 84 20W
Rockcliffe Park, *Ont., Canada* **192 A1** 45 27N 75 41W
Rockdale, *TX, U.S.A.* **99 G11** 30 39N 97 0W
Rockdale County ☆, *GA, U.S.A.* **68 C2** 33 40N 84 0W
Rockefeller Park, *Cleveland, U.S.A.* **107 A2** 41 31N 81 37W
Rockford, *AL, U.S.A.* **60 D4** 32 53N 86 13W
Rockford, *IL, U.S.A.* **71 A4** 42 16N 89 6W
Rockford, *IA, U.S.A.* **73 B6** 43 3N 92 57W
Rockford, *MI, U.S.A.* **79 F6** 43 7N 85 34W
Rockford, *MN, U.S.A.* **80 E5** 45 5N 93 44W
Rockford, *OH, U.S.A.* **92 C2** 40 41N 84 39W
Rockford, *WA, U.S.A.* **101 C8** 47 27N 117 8W
Rockglen, *Sask., Canada* **182 F6** 49 11N 105 57W
Rockham, *SD, U.S.A.* **91 F7** 44 55N 98 49W
Rockingham, *NC, U.S.A.* **90 D6** 34 57N 79 46W
Rockingham, *VT, U.S.A.* **86 C2** 43 11N 72 29W
Rockingham County ☆, *NC, U.S.A.* **90 B6** 36 20N 79 50W
Rockingham County ☆, *NH, U.S.A.* **86 D3** 43 0N 71 10W
Rockingham County ☆, *VA, U.S.A.* **102 C6** 38 27N 78 52W
Rocklake, *ND, U.S.A.* **91 B6** 48 47N 99 15W
Rockland, *Ont., Canada* **176 F7** 45 33N 75 17W
Rockland, *ID, U.S.A.* **70 G6** 42 34N 112 53W
Rockland, *ME, U.S.A.* **76 D4** 44 6N 69 7W
Rockland, *MA, U.S.A.* **78 B4** 42 8N 70 55W
Rockland, *MI, U.S.A.* **79 C2** 46 44N 89 11W
Rockland, *WI, U.S.A.* **103 E3** 43 54N 90 55W
Rockland County ☆, *NY, U.S.A.* **89 D6** 41 10N 74 5W
Rockledge, *FL, U.S.A.* **67 C8** 28 20N 80 43W
Rockledge, *PA, U.S.A.* **116 A2** 40 4N 75 5W
Rocklin, *CA, U.S.A.* **64 E5** 38 48N 121 14W
Rockmart, *GA, U.S.A.* **68 B1** 34 0N 85 3W
Rockport, *CA, U.S.A.* **64 D3** 39 44N 123 49W
Rockport, *IN, U.S.A.* **72 F3** 37 53N 87 3W
Rockport, *MA, U.S.A.* **78 B4** 42 39N 70 37W
Rockport, *TX, U.S.A.* **99 J10** 28 2N 97 3W
Rockport, *WA, U.S.A.* **101 B4** 48 29N 121 36W
Rocksprings, *TX, U.S.A.* **98 G7** 30 1N 100 13W
Rockton, *IL, U.S.A.* **71 A4** 42 27N 89 4W
Rockville, *CT, U.S.A.* **78 C2** 41 52N 72 28W
Rockville, *IN, U.S.A.* **72 D3** 39 46N 87 14W
Rockville, *MD, U.S.A.* **77 A3** 39 5N 77 9W
Rockville, *MO, U.S.A.* **82 C2** 38 4N 94 5W
Rockville, *NE, U.S.A.* **84 C7** 41 7N 98 50W
Rockville, *UT, U.S.A.* **100 F2** 37 10N 113 2W
Rockville Centre, *NY, U.S.A.* **114 C5** 40 39N 73 38W
Rockwall, *TX, U.S.A.* **99 E11** 32 56N 96 28W
Rockwall County ☆, *TX, U.S.A.* **99 E11** 32 56N 96 28W
Rockwell, *IA, U.S.A.* **73 C5** 42 59N 93 11W
Rockwell, *NC, U.S.A.* **90 C5** 35 33N 80 25W
Rockwell City, *IA, U.S.A.* **73 C4** 42 24N 94 38W
Rockwood, *Ont., Canada* **178 D6** 43 37N 80 8W
Rockwood, *ME, U.S.A.* **76 C4** 45 41N 69 45W
Rockwood, *PA, U.S.A.* **95 E3** 39 55N 79 9W
Rockwood, *TN, U.S.A.* **97 E8** 35 52N 84 41W
Rocky, *OK, U.S.A.* **93 C4** 35 9N 99 3W
Rocky →, *Alta., Canada* **185 E3** 53 8N 117 59W
Rocky →, *NC, U.S.A.* **90 C6** 35 37N 79 9W
Rocky →, *NC, U.S.A.* **90 C5** 35 9N 80 5W
Rocky Boy, *MT, U.S.A.* **83 B8** 48 16N 109 47W
Rocky Boy's Indian Reservation, *MT, U.S.A.* **83 B8** 48 25N 109 30W
Rocky Comfort Cr. →, *GA, U.S.A.* **68 D4** 32 59N 82 25W
Rocky Ford, *CO, U.S.A.* **66 D7** 38 3N 103 43W
Rocky Ford, *GA, U.S.A.* **68 D5** 32 40N 81 50W
Rocky Fork L., *OH, U.S.A.* **92 D3** 39 11N 83 26W
Rocky Harbour, *Nfld. & L., Canada* **174 C3** 49 36N 57 55W
Rocky Hill, *CT, U.S.A.* **78 C2** 41 40N 72 39W
Rocky Island L., *Ont., Canada* **181 F14** 46 55N 83 0W
Rocky Lane, *Alta., Canada* **189 E9** 58 31N 116 22W
Rocky Mount, *NC, U.S.A.* **90 C8** 35 57N 77 48W
Rocky Mount, *VA, U.S.A.* **102 D5** 37 12N 79 57W
Rocky Mountain Arsenal Nat. Wildlife Area ⌂, *Denver, U.S.A.* **109 A2** 39 50N 104 50W
Rocky Mountain House, *Alta., Canada* **185 F6** 52 22N 114 55W
Rocky Mountain Nat. Park △, *CO, U.S.A.* **66 B5** 40 25N 105 45W
Rocky Mts., *N. Amer.* **189 E8** 49 0N 115 0W
Rocky Reach Dam, *WA, U.S.A.* **101 C5** 47 32N 120 18W
Rocky Ridge, *MD, U.S.A.* **77 A3** 39 38N 77 20W
Rocky Ridge, *San Francisco, U.S.A.* **118 B4** 37 48N 122 3W
Rocky Ridge, *UT, U.S.A.* **100 B4** 39 56N 111 50W
Rocky Ripple, *Indianapolis, U.S.A.* **110 A1** 39 50N 86 10W
Rocky Top, *OR, U.S.A.* **94 C3** 44 47N 122 17W
Rockyford, *Alta., Canada* **185 G7** 51 14N 113 10W
Roddickton, *Nfld. & L., Canada* **174 B4** 50 51N 56 8W
Rodemacher, L., *LA, U.S.A.* **75 C3** 31 23N 92 43W
Rodeo, *Durango, Mexico* **217 B6** 25 11N 104 4W
Rodeo, *NM, U.S.A.* **88 F1** 31 50N 109 2W
Rodeo Cove, *San Francisco, U.S.A.* **118 B1** 37 49N 112 32W
Roderick I., *B.C., Canada* **186 C6** 52 38N 128 22W
Rodessa, *LA, U.S.A.* **75 B2** 32 58N 93 59W
Rodgers Forge, *Baltimore, U.S.A.* **107 A2** 39 22N 76 36W
Rodman, *IA, U.S.A.* **73 B4** 43 2N 94 32W
Rodney, *Ont., Canada* **178 E5** 42 34N 81 41W
Rodney, *IA, U.S.A.* **73 C3** 42 12N 95 57W
Rodolfo Sánchez Taboada, *Baja Calif., Mexico* **210 B2** 31 45N 116 35W
Roebling, *NJ, U.S.A.* **87 B2** 40 7N 74 47W
Roes Welcome Sd., *Nunavut, Canada* **191 E8** 65 0N 87 0W
Roff, *OK, U.S.A.* **93 D7** 34 38N 96 50W
Roger, L., *Qué., Canada* **176 D4** 47 50N 78 59W
Roger Mills County ☆, *OK, U.S.A.* **93 C4** 35 45N 99 45W
Roger Williams Park Zoo, *RI, U.S.A.* **78 C3** 41 46N 71 24W
Rogers, *AR, U.S.A.* **63 B1** 36 20N 94 7W
Rogers, *LA, U.S.A.* **75 C3** 31 32N 92 14W
Rogers, *ND, U.S.A.* **91 C7** 47 4N 98 12W
Rogers, *NE, U.S.A.* **84 C9** 41 28N 96 55W
Rogers, *TX, U.S.A.* **99 G10** 30 56N 97 14W
Rogers, Mt., *VA, U.S.A.* **102 E3** 36 40N 81 33W
Rogers City, *MI, U.S.A.* **79 D8** 45 25N 83 49W
Rogers County ☆, *OK, U.S.A.* **93 B8** 36 20N 95 40W
Rogers L., *CA, U.S.A.* **65 J9** 34 55N 117 50W
Rogers Lake, *Minneapolis-St. Paul, U.S.A.* **113 B3** 44 52N 93 8W
Rogers Park, *Chicago, U.S.A.* **108 A3** 42 0N 87 40W
Rogerson, *ID, U.S.A.* **70 G4** 42 13N 114 36W
Rogersville, *N.B., Canada* **173 G4** 46 44N 65 26W
Rogersville, *AL, U.S.A.* **60 B3** 34 50N 87 18W
Rogersville, *MO, U.S.A.* **82 D3** 37 7N 93 3W
Rogersville, *TN, U.S.A.* **97 D9** 36 24N 83 1W
Roggan L., *Qué., Canada* **175 C2** 54 8N 77 50W
Roggan River, *Qué., Canada* **175 C2** 54 25N 79 32W
Roggen, *CO, U.S.A.* **66 B6** 40 10N 104 22W
Rogue →, *OR, U.S.A.* **94 E1** 42 26N 124 26W
Rogue River, *OR, U.S.A.* **94 E2** 42 26N 123 10W
Rogue River Nat. Forest, *OR, U.S.A.* **94 E3** 42 54N 122 22W
Rohault, L., *Qué., Canada* **177 B8** 49 23N 74 20W
Rohnerville, *CA, U.S.A.* **64 C2** 40 34N 124 8W
Rojas, *Durango, Mexico* **217 D6** 23 51N 104 3W
Rojo, C., *Veracruz, Mexico* **220 C3** 21 33N 97 20W
Roland, *Man., Canada* **183 F14** 49 22N 97 56W
Roland, *IA, U.S.A.* **73 C5** 42 10N 93 30W
Roland, *OK, U.S.A.* **93 C9** 35 25N 94 31W
Roland, L., *Baltimore, U.S.A.* **107 A2** 39 22N 76 38W
Rolette, *ND, U.S.A.* **91 B6** 48 40N 99 51W
Rolette County ☆, *ND, U.S.A.* **91 B6** 48 55N 99 55W
Rolfe, *IA, U.S.A.* **73 C4** 42 49N 94 31W
Roll, *AZ, U.S.A.* **62 E2** 32 45N 113 59W
Rolla, *KS, U.S.A.* **74 D2** 37 7N 101 38W
Rolla, *MO, U.S.A.* **82 D5** 37 57N 91 46W
Rolla, *ND, U.S.A.* **91 B6** 48 52N 99 37W
Rollet, *Qué., Canada* **176 D3** 47 55N 79 15W
Rolling Fork, *MS, U.S.A.* **81 D3** 32 55N 90 53W
Rolling Fork →, *KY, U.S.A.* **97 C7** 37 55N 85 50W
Rolling Hills, *Alta., Canada* **185 H9** 50 13N 111 46W
Rolling Hills Estates, *Los Angeles, U.S.A.* **111 D2** 33 47N 118 21W
Rollingbay, *Seattle, U.S.A.* **118 C2** 47 39N 122 30W
Roma-Los Saenz, *TX, U.S.A.* **98 L8** 26 24N 99 1W
Romain, C., *SC, U.S.A.* **90 F6** 33 0N 79 22W
Romaine →, *Qué., Canada* **175 C5** 50 18N 63 47W
Romano, C., *FL, U.S.A.* **67 F7** 25 51N 81 41W
Romanzof C., *AK, U.S.A.* **61 F6** 61 49N 166 6W
Rome, *GA, U.S.A.* **68 B1** 34 15N 85 10W
Rome, *IL, U.S.A.* **71 C4** 40 53N 89 30W
Rome, *NY, U.S.A.* **89 B5** 43 13N 75 27W
Rome, *PA, U.S.A.* **95 C6** 41 51N 76 21W
Rome City, *IN, U.S.A.* **72 B5** 41 30N 85 23W
Romeo, *CO, U.S.A.* **66 E5** 37 10N 105 59W
Romeo, *MI, U.S.A.* **79 G8** 42 48N 83 1W
Romeoville, *IL, U.S.A.* **71 B5** 41 39N 88 3W
Romero, *TX, U.S.A.* **98 B5** 35 44N 102 56W
Romeroville, *NM, U.S.A.* **88 B5** 35 31N 105 15W
Romita, *Guanajuato, Mexico* **218 B6** 20 53N 101 31W
Romney, *WV, U.S.A.* **77 A2** 39 21N 78 45W
Ronald Reagan National, Washington ✕ (DCA), *VA, U.S.A.* **102 C7** 38 51N 77 2W
Ronan, *MT, U.S.A.* **83 C3** 47 32N 114 6W
Ronceverte, *WV, U.S.A.* **102 D4** 37 45N 80 28W
Rondeau Prov. Park ⌂, *Ont., Canada* **178 E5** 42 19N 81 51W
Rondout Res., *NY, U.S.A.* **89 D6** 41 50N 74 29W
Ronge, L. la, *Sask., Canada* **189 E11** 55 6N 105 17W
Ronkonkoma, *NY, U.S.A.* **87 B3** 40 48N 73 7W
Roodhouse, *IL, U.S.A.* **71 D3** 39 29N 90 24W
Roof Butte, *AZ, U.S.A.* **62 A6** 36 28N 109 5W
Rooks County ☆, *KS, U.S.A.* **74 B4** 39 20N 99 15W
Roopville, *GA, U.S.A.* **68 C1** 33 27N 85 8W
Roosevelt, *AZ, U.S.A.* **62 D4** 33 41N 111 9W
Roosevelt, *MN, U.S.A.* **80 B3** 48 48N 95 6W
Roosevelt, *NY, U.S.A.* **114 B5** 40 40N 73 35W
Roosevelt, *OK, U.S.A.* **93 D4** 34 51N 99 1W
Roosevelt, *UT, U.S.A.* **100 C6** 40 18N 109 59W
Roosevelt County ☆, *MT, U.S.A.* **83 B12** 48 20N 105 20W
Roosevelt County ☆, *NM, U.S.A.* **88 D7** 34 0N 103 30W
Roosevelt Nat. Forest, *CO, U.S.A.* **66 B5** 40 45N 105 40W
Roosevelt Park, *PA, U.S.A.* **116 B1** 39 54N 75 10W
Roosville, *B.C., Canada* **185 J5** 49 0N 115 3W
Root →, *N.W.T., Canada* **189 D8** 62 26N 123 18W
Root →, *MN, U.S.A.* **80 G7** 43 46N 91 51W
Root River Parkway, *Milwaukee, U.S.A.* **112 C1** 42 55N 88 0W
Roper, *NC, U.S.A.* **90 C9** 35 53N 76 37W
Ropesville, *TX, U.S.A.* **98 D5** 33 26N 102 9W
Roqueta, I., *Guerrero, Mexico* **219 F8** 16 51N 99 54W
Rorketon, *Man., Canada* **183 D12** 51 24N 99 35W
Rosales, *Chihuahua, Mexico* **213 E10** 28 12N 105 33W
Rosalia, *WA, U.S.A.* **101 C8** 47 14N 117 22W
Rosalind, *Alta., Canada* **185 F8** 52 47N 112 27W
Rosamond, *CA, U.S.A.* **65 J8** 34 52N 118 10W
Rosamond L., *CA, U.S.A.* **65 J8** 34 50N 118 4W
Rosamorada, *Nayarit, Mexico* **216 E5** 22 4N 105 4W
Rosario, *Sinaloa, Mexico* **216 E5** 22 58N 105 53W
Rosario, *Sonora, Mexico* **212 F6** 27 50N 109 22W
Rosario, *Sonora, Mexico* **212 E4** 28 30N 111 30W
Rosario, B., *Baja Calif., Mexico* **210 D3** 29 55N 115 45W
Rosario, L. el, *Tabasco, Mexico* **222 B3** 17 52N 93 48W
Rosarito, *Baja Calif., Mexico* **210 E4** 28 38N 114 1W
Rosarito, *Baja Calif., Mexico* **210 A1** 32 20N 117 2W
Rosarito, *Baja Calif. S., Mexico* **211 G7** 26 27N 111 38W
Rosarito, Pta., *Baja Calif., Mexico* **210 E4** 28 33N 114 10W
Rosburg, *WA, U.S.A.* **101 D2** 46 20N 123 38W
Roscoe, *IL, U.S.A.* **71 A4** 42 25N 89 1W
Roscoe, *SD, U.S.A.* **91 E6** 45 27N 99 20W
Roscoe, *TX, U.S.A.* **98 E7** 32 27N 100 32W
Roscommon, *MI, U.S.A.* **79 E7** 44 30N 84 35W
Roscommon County ☆, *MI, U.S.A.* **79 E7** 44 15N 84 40W
Rose, *NE, U.S.A.* **84 B6** 42 11N 99 32W
Rose, L., *Orlando, U.S.A.* **115 A1** 28 32N 81 30W
Rose, Mt., *NV, U.S.A.* **85 C1** 39 21N 119 55W
Rose Blanche-Harbour Le Cou, *Nfld. & L., Canada* **174 E2** 47 38N 58 45W
Rose Bud, *AR, U.S.A.* **63 C3** 35 20N 92 5W
Rose City, *MI, U.S.A.* **79 E7** 44 25N 84 7W
Rose Creek, *MN, U.S.A.* **80 G6** 43 36N 92 50W
Rose Harbour, *B.C., Canada* **186 C3** 52 15N 131 10W
Rose Hill, *IL, U.S.A.* **71 D5** 39 6N 88 9W
Rose Hill, *IA, U.S.A.* **73 D6** 41 19N 92 28W
Rose Hill, *KS, U.S.A.* **74 D6** 37 34N 97 7W
Rose Hill, *NC, U.S.A.* **90 D7** 34 50N 78 2W
Rose Hill, *VA, U.S.A.* **102 E1** 36 40N 83 22W
Rose Hill, *VA, U.S.A.* **119 C3** 38 47N 77 6W

Rose Pk., AZ, U.S.A. **62 D6** 33 25N 109 21W
Rose Pt., B.C., Canada **186 A3** 54 11N 131 39W
Rose Valley, Sask., Canada **182 C8** 52 19N 103 49W
Roseau, MN, U.S.A. **80 B3** 48 51N 95 46W
Roseau →, MN, U.S.A. **80 B2** 49 0N 96 30W
Roseau County ☆, MN, U.S.A. **80 B3** 48 45N 95 50W
Rosebank, NY, U.S.A. **114 C2** 40 36N 74 4W
Roseboro, NC, U.S.A. **90 D7** 34 58N 78 31W
Rosebud, MO, U.S.A. **82 C5** 38 23N 91 25W
Rosebud, MT, U.S.A. **83 D11** 46 16N 106 27W
Rosebud, SD, U.S.A. **91 G5** 43 14N 100 51W
Rosebud, TX, U.S.A. **99 F11** 31 4N 96 59W
Rosebud →, Alta., Canada **185 G8** 51 25N 112 38W
Rosebud County ☆, MT, U.S.A. **83 D11** 46 30N 106 45W
Rosebud Creek, MT, U.S.A. **83 D11** 46 16N 106 29W
Rosebud Indian Reservation, SD, U.S.A. **91 G5** 43 10N 101 0W
Roseburg, OR, U.S.A. **94 D2** 43 13N 123 20W
Rosebush, MI, U.S.A. **79 F7** 43 42N 84 46W
Rosedal La Candelaria, Distrito Federal, Mexico **225 B2** 19 20N 99 10W
Rosedale, MD, U.S.A. **77 A4** 39 19N 76 30W
Rosedale, MS, U.S.A. **81 C2** 33 51N 91 2W
Rosedale, NY, U.S.A. **114 C4** 40 39N 73 44W
Rosedale, OK, U.S.A. **93 D6** 34 55N 97 11W
Rosedale, WV, U.S.A. **102 C4** 38 44N 80 57W
Roseglen, ND, U.S.A. **91 C4** 47 45N 101 50W
Roseisle, Man., Canada **183 F13** 49 30N 98 20W
Roseland, Chicago, U.S.A. **108 C3** 41 42N 87 37W
Roseland, LA, U.S.A. **75 D5** 30 46N 90 31W
Roseland, NJ, U.S.A. **114 B1** 40 49N 74 17W
Roseland, NE, U.S.A. **84 D7** 40 28N 98 34W
Roselle, NJ, U.S.A. **114 C1** 40 39N 74 15W
Roselle Park, NJ, U.S.A. **114 C1** 40 39N 74 15W
Rosemary, Alta., Canada **185 H8** 50 46N 112 5W
Rosemead, Los Angeles, U.S.A. **111 B4** 34 4N 118 4W
Rosemère, Qué., Canada **177 F9** 45 38N 73 48W
Rosemont, Montréal, Canada **192 A3** 45 34N 73 33W
Rosemont, Chicago, U.S.A. **108 B1** 41 59N 87 53W
Rosemont, MD, U.S.A. **77 A3** 39 20N 77 37W
Rosemount, MN, U.S.A. **80 F5** 44 45N 93 8W
Rosenberg, TX, U.S.A. **99 H12** 29 34N 95 49W
Rosenhayn, NJ, U.S.A. **87 C1** 39 29N 75 8W
Rosepine, LA, U.S.A. **75 D2** 30 55N 93 17W
Rosetown, Sask., Canada **182 D4** 51 35N 107 59W
Rosette, UT, U.S.A. **100 B2** 41 49N 113 25W
Roseville, CA, U.S.A. **64 E5** 38 45N 121 17W
Roseville, IL, U.S.A. **71 C3** 40 44N 90 40W
Roseville, MI, U.S.A. **79 G9** 42 30N 82 56W
Roseville, MN, U.S.A. **80 E5** 45 0N 93 9W
Roseville, OH, U.S.A. **92 D4** 39 49N 82 5W
Roseville, PA, U.S.A. **95 C6** 41 52N 76 58W
Rosharon, TX, U.S.A. **99 H12** 29 21N 95 28W
Rosholt, SD, U.S.A. **91 E9** 45 52N 96 44W
Rosholt, WI, U.S.A. **103 D4** 44 38N 89 18W
Rosiclare, IL, U.S.A. **71 F5** 37 26N 88 21W
Rosier, GA, U.S.A. **68 D4** 32 59N 82 15W
Roslindale, Boston, U.S.A. **106 B3** 42 17N 71 7W
Roslyn, NY, U.S.A. **114 B5** 40 47N 73 39W
Roslyn, SD, U.S.A. **91 E8** 45 30N 97 29W
Roslyn, WA, U.S.A. **101 C5** 47 13N 120 59W
Roslyn Estates, NY, U.S.A. **114 B5** 40 47N 73 39W
Roslyn Harbor, NY, U.S.A. **114 B5** 40 48N 73 39W
Rosman, NC, U.S.A. **90 C3** 35 9N 82 49W
Ross, ND, U.S.A. **91 B3** 48 19N 102 33W
Ross →, Yukon, Canada **189 D6** 61 59N 132 25W
Ross Barnett Res., MS, U.S.A. **81 D3** 32 24N 90 4W
Ross County ☆, OH, U.S.A. **92 D4** 39 20N 82 59W
Ross L., WA, U.S.A. **101 B4** 48 44N 121 4W
Ross Lake Nat. Recr. Area ⌓, WA, U.S.A. **101 B4** 48 43N 121 4W
Ross River, Yukon, Canada **189 D6** 62 30N 131 30W
Rossburg, OH, U.S.A. **92 C2** 40 17N 84 38W
Rossburn, Man., Canada **183 E11** 50 40N 100 49W
Rosseau, Ont., Canada **178 B7** 45 16N 79 39W
Rosseau, L., Ont., Canada **178 B7** 45 10N 79 35W
Rossford, OH, U.S.A. **92 B3** 41 36N 83 34W
Rossie, IA, U.S.A. **73 B3** 43 1N 95 11W
Rossignol, L., Qué., Canada **175 C3** 52 43N 73 40W
Rossignol L., N.S., Canada **173 J4** 44 12N 65 10W
Rossiter, PA, U.S.A. **95 D4** 40 54N 78 56W
Rossland, B.C., Canada **187 F17** 49 6N 117 50W
Rosslyn, VA, U.S.A. **119 B3** 38 53N 77 4W
Rosslyn Farms, Pittsburgh, U.S.A. **116 B1** 40 23N 80 5W
Rossmoor, Los Angeles, U.S.A. **111 D4** 33 47N 118 5W
Rossmore, Ont., Canada **179 C9** 44 8N 77 23W
Rossport, Ont., Canada **181 D9** 48 50N 87 30W
Rosston, AR, U.S.A. **63 E2** 33 36N 93 17W
Rosston, OK, U.S.A. **93 B4** 36 49N 99 56W
Rossville, Baltimore, U.S.A. **107 A3** 39 20N 76 28W
Rossville, GA, U.S.A. **68 B1** 34 59N 85 17W
Rossville, IL, U.S.A. **71 C6** 40 23N 87 40W
Rossville, IN, U.S.A. **72 C4** 40 25N 86 36W
Rossville, KS, U.S.A. **74 B8** 39 8N 95 57W
Rossville, NY, U.S.A. **114 C1** 40 33N 74 12W
Rosthern, Sask., Canada **182 C5** 52 40N 106 20W
Roswell, GA, U.S.A. **68 B2** 34 2N 84 22W
Roswell, NM, U.S.A. **88 D6** 33 24N 104 32W
Rota, N. Marianas **105 a** 14 9N 145 12W
Rotan, TX, U.S.A. **98 E7** 32 51N 100 28W
Rothesay, N.B., Canada **173 H4** 45 23N 66 0W
Rothrock State Forest, PA, U.S.A. **95 D5** 40 43N 77 49W
Rothsay, MN, U.S.A. **80 D2** 46 28N 96 17W
Rothschild, WI, U.S.A. **103 D4** 44 53N 89 37W
Rothwell Heights, Ont., Canada **192 A2** 45 27N 75 37W
Rotonda, FL, U.S.A. **67 E6** 26 53N 82 17W
Rotterdam, NY, U.S.A. **89 C6** 42 48N 74 1W
Rouge →, Qué., Canada **176 F8** 45 17N 74 10W
Rouge-Matawin, Réserve Faunique ⌓, Qué., Canada **177 E8** 46 51N 74 31W
Rough →, KY, U.S.A. **96 C5** 37 29N 87 8W
Rough River L., KY, U.S.A. **96 C6** 37 37N 86 30W
Rouleau, Sask., Canada **182 E7** 50 10N 104 56W
Roulette, PA, U.S.A. **95 C4** 41 47N 78 9W
Round Hill, Alta., Canada **185 E8** 53 10N 112 38W
Round Hill, N.S., Canada **173 J4** 44 46N 65 24W
Round Hill, VA, U.S.A. **77 A3** 39 8N 77 46W
Round L., Ont., Canada **179 B9** 45 38N 77 30W
Round Lake, MN, U.S.A. **80 G3** 43 32N 95 28W
Round Mountain, NV, U.S.A. **85 D3** 38 43N 117 4W
Round Mountain, TX, U.S.A. **99 G9** 30 26N 98 21W
Round Oak, GA, U.S.A. **68 C3** 33 7N 83 37W
Round Pond, Nfld. & L., Canada **174 D4** 48 11N 56 0W
Round Rock, AZ, U.S.A. **62 A6** 36 31N 109 28W
Round Rock, TX, U.S.A. **99 G10** 30 31N 97 41W
Round Top, TX, U.S.A. **99 G11** 30 4N 96 42W
Round Top Regional Park ⌓, San Francisco, U.S.A. **118 A3** 37 50N 122 11W
Round Valley Indian Reservation, CA, U.S.A. **64 D3** 39 50N 123 20W
Round Valley Res., NJ, U.S.A. **87 B2** 40 37N 74 51W
Roundup, MT, U.S.A. **83 D9** 46 27N 108 33W
Rouses Point, NY, U.S.A. **86 B1** 44 59N 73 22W
Rouseville, PA, U.S.A. **95 C3** 41 28N 79 42W
Routhierville, Qué., Canada **172 E2** 48 11N 67 9W
Routt County ☆, CO, U.S.A. **66 B4** 40 30N 107 0W
Routt Nat. Forest, CO, U.S.A. **66 B4** 40 45N 107 0W
Rouvray, L., Qué., Canada **177 B12** 49 18N 70 49W
Rouyn-Noranda, Qué., Canada **176 C3** 48 20N 79 0W
Rouzerville, PA, U.S.A. **77 A3** 39 44N 77 32W
Rover, TN, U.S.A. **96 E6** 35 40N 86 36W
Rowan, IA, U.S.A. **73 C5** 42 45N 93 33W
Rowan County ☆, KY, U.S.A. **97 B9** 38 10N 83 25W
Rowan County ☆, NC, U.S.A. **90 C5** 35 40N 80 30W
Rowan L., Ont., Canada **180 C3** 49 18N 93 32W
Rowe, NM, U.S.A. **88 B5** 35 30N 105 41W
Rowena, TX, U.S.A. **99 F7** 31 39N 100 3W
Rowland, NC, U.S.A. **90 D6** 34 32N 79 18W
Rowlesburg, WV, U.S.A. **102 B5** 39 21N 79 40W
Rowley, IA, U.S.A. **73 C7** 42 22N 91 51W
Rowley, UT, U.S.A. **100 C3** 40 54N 112 46W
Rowley I., N.W.T., Canada **190 D10** 69 6N 77 52W
Roxana, DE, U.S.A. **77 B5** 38 30N 75 10W
Roxboro, Qué., Canada **192 A2** 45 30N 73 48W
Roxboro, NC, U.S.A. **90 B7** 36 24N 78 59W
Roxbury, Boston, U.S.A. **106 B3** 42 19N 71 5W
Roxbury, CT, U.S.A. **78 C1** 41 45N 73 11W
Roxbury, KS, U.S.A. **74 C6** 38 33N 97 26W
Roxbury, NY, U.S.A. **114 C3** 40 33N 73 53W
Roxbury, NY, U.S.A. **89 C6** 42 17N 74 34W
Roxbury, VT, U.S.A. **86 B2** 44 8N 72 44W
Roxie, MS, U.S.A. **81 E2** 31 30N 91 4W
Roxton, TX, U.S.A. **99 D12** 33 33N 95 44W
Roxton Falls, Qué., Canada **177 F10** 45 34N 72 31W
Roxton Pond, Qué., Canada **177 F10** 45 28N 72 40W
Roy, MT, U.S.A. **83 C9** 47 20N 108 58W
Roy, NM, U.S.A. **88 B6** 35 57N 104 12W
Roy, UT, U.S.A. **100 B3** 41 10N 112 2W
Roy, WA, U.S.A. **101 D3** 47 0N 122 33W
Royal, IA, U.S.A. **73 B3** 43 4N 95 17W
Royal, Mt., Ont., Canada **180 C8** 49 56N 88 48W
Royal Center, IN, U.S.A. **72 C4** 40 52N 86 30W
Royal City, WA, U.S.A. **101 D6** 46 54N 119 38W
Royal Geographical Society Is., Nunavut, Canada **190 D5** 68 56N 100 15W
Royal Oak, B.C., Canada **187 G11** 48 29N 123 23W
Royal Oak, MD, U.S.A. **77 B4** 38 44N 76 11W
Royal Oak, MI, U.S.A. **79 G8** 42 30N 83 9W
Royal Palm Beach, FL, U.S.A. **67 E8** 26 42N 80 14W
Royale, Isle, MI, U.S.A. **79 B3** 48 0N 88 54W
Royalston, MA, U.S.A. **78 B2** 42 40N 72 12W
Royalton, MN, U.S.A. **80 E4** 45 50N 94 18W
Royalty, TX, U.S.A. **98 F5** 31 22N 102 52W
Royersford, PA, U.S.A. **87 B1** 40 11N 75 33W
Royse City, TX, U.S.A. **99 E11** 32 59N 96 20W
Royston, GA, U.S.A. **68 B3** 34 17N 83 7W
Roza Canal, WA, U.S.A. **101 D5** 46 35N 120 23W
Rozel, KS, U.S.A. **74 C4** 38 12N 99 24W
Rozet, WY, U.S.A. **104 B7** 44 17N 105 12W
Rubonia, Tampa, U.S.A. **119 D3** 27 34N 82 33W
Ruby, AK, U.S.A. **61 D9** 64 45N 155 30W
Ruby Beach = Jacksonville Beach, FL, U.S.A. **67 A7** 30 17N 81 24W
Ruby Dome, NV, U.S.A. **85 B5** 40 37N 115 28W
Ruby L., NV, U.S.A. **85 B5** 40 10N 115 28W
Ruby Lake Nat. Wildlife Refuge ⌓, NV, U.S.A. **85 B5** 40 12N 115 28W
Ruby Mts., NV, U.S.A. **85 B5** 40 30N 115 20W
Ruby Valley, NV, U.S.A. **85 B5** 40 30N 115 21W
Rudolph, WI, U.S.A. **103 D4** 44 30N 89 48W
Rudy, AR, U.S.A. **63 C1** 35 31N 94 16W
Rudyard, MI, U.S.A. **79 C7** 46 14N 84 36W
Rudyard, MT, U.S.A. **83 B7** 48 34N 110 33W
Ruel, Ont., Canada **181 E15** 47 15N 81 28W
Ruffling Pt., Br. Virgin Is. **105 G18** 18 44N 64 27W
Rufus, OR, U.S.A. **94 B5** 45 42N 120 44W
Rugby, ND, U.S.A. **91 B6** 48 22N 100 0W
Rugby, TN, U.S.A. **97 D10** 36 22N 84 42W
Ruidosa, TX, U.S.A. **98 H3** 29 59N 104 41W
Ruidoso, NM, U.S.A. **88 D5** 33 20N 105 41W
Ruidoso Downs, NM, U.S.A. **88 D5** 33 20N 105 32W
Ruisseau-Vert, Qué., Canada **177 B14** 49 4N 68 28W
Ruiz Cortines, Sinaloa, Mexico **216 B2** 25 41N 108 42W
Rule, TX, U.S.A. **99 D8** 33 11N 99 54W
Ruleville, MS, U.S.A. **81 C3** 33 44N 90 33W
Rulo, NE, U.S.A. **84 D10** 40 3N 95 26W
Rum →, MN, U.S.A. **80 E5** 45 11N 93 23W
Rumbley, MD, U.S.A. **77 B5** 38 6N 75 51W
Rumford, ME, U.S.A. **76 D3** 44 33N 70 33W
Rumney, NH, U.S.A. **86 C3** 43 47N 71 48W
Rump Mt., ME, U.S.A. **76 C2** 45 12N 71 4W
Rumsey, Alta., Canada **185 G8** 51 51N 112 48W
Rumson, NJ, U.S.A. **87 B3** 40 23N 74 0W
Runge, TX, U.S.A. **99 J10** 28 53N 97 43W
Runnells, IA, U.S.A. **73 D5** 41 31N 93 21W
Runnels County ☆, TX, U.S.A. **99 F8** 31 51N 99 57W
Running Water →, TX, U.S.A. **98 C6** 34 0N 101 30W
Rupert, ID, U.S.A. **70 G5** 42 37N 113 41W
Rupert, VT, U.S.A. **86 C1** 43 16N 73 13W
Rupert, WV, U.S.A. **102 D4** 37 58N 80 41W
Rupert →, Qué., Canada **175 C2** 51 29N 78 45W
Rupert B., Qué., Canada **175 C2** 51 35N 79 0W
Rupert House = Waskaganish, Qué., Canada **175 C2** 51 30N 78 40W
Rural Retreat, VA, U.S.A. **102 E3** 36 54N 81 17W
Rusagonis, N.B., Canada **173 H3** 45 48N 66 37W
Rush, KY, U.S.A. **97 B10** 38 20N 82 46W
Rush Center, KS, U.S.A. **74 C4** 38 28N 99 19W
Rush City, MN, U.S.A. **80 E6** 45 41N 92 58W
Rush County ☆, IN, U.S.A. **72 D5** 39 35N 85 30W
Rush County ☆, KS, U.S.A. **74 C4** 38 30N 99 15W
Rush Cr. →, CO, U.S.A. **66 D8** 38 22N 102 32W
Rush L., Ont., Canada **181 E14** 47 47N 82 11W
Rush Lake, Sask., Canada **182 E4** 50 24N 107 24W
Rush Springs, OK, U.S.A. **93 D6** 34 47N 97 58W
Rush Valley, UT, U.S.A. **100 C3** 40 22N 112 27W
Rushford, MN, U.S.A. **80 G7** 43 49N 91 46W
Rushmore, Mt., SD, U.S.A. **56 D3** 43 53N 103 28W
Rushoon, Nfld. & L., Canada **174 E6** 47 21N 54 55W
Rushville, IL, U.S.A. **71 C3** 40 7N 90 34W
Rushville, IN, U.S.A. **72 D5** 39 37N 85 27W
Rushville, MO, U.S.A. **82 B1** 39 35N 95 1W
Rushville, NE, U.S.A. **84 B3** 42 43N 102 28W
Rusk, TX, U.S.A. **99 F12** 31 48N 95 9W
Rusk County ☆, TX, U.S.A. **99 E13** 32 9N 94 48W
Rusk County ☆, WI, U.S.A. **103 C2** 45 25N 91 10W
Ruskin, FL, U.S.A. **67 D6** 27 43N 82 26W
Ruskin, NE, U.S.A. **84 D8** 40 9N 97 52W
Ruso, ND, U.S.A. **91 C5** 47 50N 100 56W
Russell, Qué., Canada **176 F7** 45 18N 75 19W
Russell, FL, U.S.A. **67 A7** 30 3N 81 45W
Russell, IA, U.S.A. **73 E5** 40 59N 93 12W
Russell, KS, U.S.A. **74 C5** 38 54N 98 52W
Russell, KY, U.S.A. **97 B10** 38 31N 82 42W
Russell, MN, U.S.A. **80 F3** 44 19N 95 57W
Russell, C., N.W.T., Canada **188 A9** 75 15N 117 40W
Russell Cave Nat. Monument ⌓, AL, U.S.A. **60 B5** 34 59N 85 49W
Russell County ☆, AL, U.S.A. **60 D5** 32 18N 85 10W
Russell County ☆, KS, U.S.A. **74 C5** 39 0N 98 45W
Russell County ☆, KY, U.S.A. **97 C7** 37 0N 85 0W
Russell County ☆, VA, U.S.A. **102 E3** 37 0N 82 0W
Russell Cr. →, KY, U.S.A. **97 C7** 37 14N 85 30W
Russell I., N.W.T., Canada **190 C6** 74 0N 98 25W
Russell L. = Richard B. Russell L., GA, U.S.A. **68 B4** 34 5N 82 38W
Russell Springs, KS, U.S.A. **74 C2** 38 55N 101 11W
Russell Springs, KY, U.S.A. **97 C7** 37 3N 85 5W
Russellville, AL, U.S.A. **60 B3** 34 30N 87 44W
Russellville, AR, U.S.A. **63 C2** 35 17N 93 8W
Russellville, KY, U.S.A. **96 D6** 36 51N 86 53W
Russellville, MO, U.S.A. **82 C4** 38 31N 92 26W
Russellville, OH, U.S.A. **92 E3** 38 52N 83 47W
Russellville, PA, U.S.A. **77 A5** 39 51N 75 57W
Russellville, TN, U.S.A. **97 D9** 36 15N 83 12W
Russian →, CA, U.S.A. **64 E3** 38 27N 123 8W
Russian Mission, AK, U.S.A. **61 F7** 61 47N 161 19W
Russiaville, IN, U.S.A. **72 C4** 40 25N 86 16W
Rustburg, VA, U.S.A. **102 D5** 37 17N 79 6W
Ruston, LA, U.S.A. **75 B3** 32 32N 92 38W
Ruth, MS, U.S.A. **81 E3** 31 23N 90 19W
Ruth, NV, U.S.A. **85 C6** 39 17N 114 59W
Rutherford, NJ, U.S.A. **114 B2** 40 49N 74 6W
Rutherford, TN, U.S.A. **96 D4** 36 8N 88 59W
Rutherford County ☆, NC, U.S.A. **90 C4** 35 20N 81 50W
Rutherford County ☆, TN, U.S.A. **96 E6** 35 51N 86 24W
Rutherford Fork →, TN, U.S.A. **96 D3** 36 16N 89 1W
Rutherfordton, NC, U.S.A. **90 C4** 35 22N 81 58W
Ruthsburg, MD, U.S.A. **77 B5** 39 0N 75 58W
Ruthton, MN, U.S.A. **80 F2** 44 11N 96 6W
Ruthven, IA, U.S.A. **73 B4** 43 8N 94 54W
Rutland, IL, U.S.A. **71 C4** 40 59N 89 3W
Rutland, MA, U.S.A. **78 B3** 42 23N 71 57W
Rutland, ND, U.S.A. **91 D8** 46 3N 97 30W
Rutland, OH, U.S.A. **92 D4** 39 3N 82 8W
Rutland, SD, U.S.A. **91 F9** 44 5N 96 58W
Rutland, VT, U.S.A. **86 C2** 43 37N 72 58W
Rutland County ☆, VT, U.S.A. **86 C1** 43 35N 73 0W
Rutledge, GA, U.S.A. **68 C3** 33 38N 83 37W
Rutledge, MN, U.S.A. **80 D6** 46 16N 92 52W
Rutledge, TN, U.S.A. **97 D9** 36 17N 83 31W
Ruxton, Baltimore, U.S.A. **107 A2** 39 24N 76 38W
Ryan, IA, U.S.A. **73 C7** 42 21N 91 29W
Ryan, OK, U.S.A. **93 D6** 34 1N 97 57W
Ryan Park, WY, U.S.A. **104 E6** 41 19N 106 31W
Ryans B., Nfld. & L., Canada **175 B5** 59 35N 64 3W
Rycroft, Alta., Canada **184 C2** 55 45N 118 40W
Ryder, ND, U.S.A. **91 C4** 47 55N 101 40W
Ryderwood, WA, U.S.A. **101 D2** 46 23N 123 3W
Rye, AR, U.S.A. **63 E4** 33 45N 91 59W
Rye, CO, U.S.A. **66 E6** 37 55N 104 56W
Rye, NH, U.S.A. **86 C4** 43 2N 70 50W
Rye Beach, NH, U.S.A. **86 D4** 42 59N 70 46W
Rye Patch Res., NV, U.S.A. **85 B2** 40 28N 118 19W
Ryegate, MT, U.S.A. **83 D8** 46 18N 109 15W
Ryley, Alta., Canada **184 E8** 53 17N 112 26W

S

Saanich, B.C., Canada **187 G11** 48 28N 123 22W
Sábana Grande, Guerrero, Mexico **219 D8** 18 10N 99 33W
Sábana Grande, Zacatecas, Mexico **217 C9** 24 30N 101 45W
Sabana Grande, Puerto Rico **105 G16** 18 5N 66 58W
Sabancuy, Campeche, Mexico **223 D2** 18 58N 91 11W
Sabaneta Pt., N. Marianas **105 c** 15 17N 145 49W
Sabanilla, Tabasco, Mexico **222 B4** 17 20N 92 38W
Sabetha, KS, U.S.A. **74 B8** 39 54N 95 48W
Sabin, MN, U.S.A. **80 D2** 46 47N 96 39W
Sabina, OH, U.S.A. **92 D3** 39 29N 83 38W
Sabinal, TX, U.S.A. **99 H8** 29 19N 99 28W
Sabinas, Coahuila, Mexico **214 C3** 27 51N 101 7W
Sabinas →, Coahuila, Mexico **214 C4** 27 37N 100 42W
Sabinas →, Nuevo León, Mexico **214 D5** 26 50N 99 35W
Sabinas Hidalgo, Nuevo León, Mexico **214 D4** 26 30N 100 10W
Sabine →, LA, U.S.A. **75 E2** 29 59N 93 47W
Sabine County ☆, TX, U.S.A. **99 F14** 31 20N 93 51W
Sabine L., LA, U.S.A. **75 E2** 29 53N 93 51W
Sabine Nat. Forest, TX, U.S.A. **99 F14** 31 38N 94 0W
Sabine Nat. Wildlife Refuge ⌓, LA, U.S.A. **75 E2** 29 52N 93 30W
Sabine Parish ☆, LA, U.S.A. **75 C2** 31 38N 93 39W
Sabine Pass, TX, U.S.A. **99 H14** 29 44N 93 54W
Sabinoso, NM, U.S.A. **88 B6** 35 42N 104 24W
Sable →, Qué., Canada **175 B4** 55 30N 68 21W
Sable, C., N.S., Canada **173 K4** 43 29N 65 38W
Sable, C., FL, U.S.A. **67 F7** 25 9N 81 8W
Sable River, N.S., Canada **173 K4** 43 51N 65 3W
Sables, R. aux →, Ont., Canada **178 A4** 46 13N 82 3W
Sabourin, L., Qué., Canada **176 D5** 47 58N 77 41W
Sabula, IA, U.S.A. **73 C8** 42 4N 90 10W
Sabula, MO, U.S.A. **82 D6** 37 27N 90 42W
Sac →, MO, U.S.A. **82 C3** 38 1N 93 43W
Sac and Fox Indian Reservation, U.S.A. **84 E10** 39 59N 95 31W
Sac and Fox/Mesquakie Indian Reservation, IA, U.S.A. **73 D6** 41 59N 92 39W
Sac City, IA, U.S.A. **73 C3** 42 25N 95 0W
Sac County ☆, IA, U.S.A. **73 C3** 42 25N 95 5W
Sacajawea, L., WA, U.S.A. **101 D7** 46 20N 118 45W
Sacajawea Peak, OR, U.S.A. **94 B8** 45 15N 117 17W
Sacalum, Yucatán, Mexico **223 B4** 20 29N 89 35W
Sacaton, AZ, U.S.A. **62 D4** 33 5N 111 44W
Sachigo →, Ont., Canada **191 F8** 55 6N 88 58W
Sachigo, L., Ont., Canada **191 G7** 53 50N 92 12W
Sachs Harbour, N.W.T., Canada **188 B7** 71 59N 125 15W
Sackets Harbor, NY, U.S.A. **89 B4** 43 57N 76 7W
Sackville, N.B., Canada **173 H5** 45 54N 64 22W
Saco, AL, U.S.A. **60 E5** 31 57N 85 49W
Saco, ME, U.S.A. **76 E3** 43 30N 70 27W
Saco, MT, U.S.A. **83 B10** 48 28N 107 21W
Saco →, ME, U.S.A. **76 E3** 43 28N 70 23W
Sacramento, Coahuila, Mexico **214 C3** 27 1N 101 41W
Sacramento, CA, U.S.A. **64 E5** 38 35N 121 29W
Sacramento, KY, U.S.A. **96 C5** 37 25N 87 16W
Sacramento, NM, U.S.A. **88 E5** 32 48N 105 34W
Sacramento →, CA, U.S.A. **64 E5** 38 3N 121 56W
Sacramento County ☆, CA, U.S.A. **64 E5** 38 20N 121 20W
Sacramento International ✈ (SMF), CA, U.S.A. **64 E5** 38 42N 121 35W
Sacramento Mts., NM, U.S.A. **88 E5** 32 30N 105 30W
Sacramento Valley, CA, U.S.A. **64 D5** 39 30N 122 0W
Sacramento Wash →, AZ, U.S.A. **62 C1** 34 43N 114 28W
Sacré-Coeur, Qué., Canada **177 C13** 48 14N 69 48W
Saddle Brook, NJ, U.S.A. **114 A2** 40 53N 74 5W
Saddle Mt., OR, U.S.A. **94 B2** 45 58N 123 41W
Saddle Mt., WY, U.S.A. **104 B3** 44 43N 109 59W
Saddle Mts., WA, U.S.A. **101 D5** 46 55N 120 0W
Saddle Rock, NY, U.S.A. **114 B4** 40 47N 73 44W
Sadieville, KY, U.S.A. **97 B8** 38 23N 84 32W
Sadorus, IL, U.S.A. **71 D5** 39 58N 88 21W
Saegertown, PA, U.S.A. **95 C2** 41 43N 80 9W
Safety Harbor, Tampa, U.S.A. **119 A2** 27 59N 82 41W
Safford, AZ, U.S.A. **62 E6** 32 50N 109 43W
Sag Harbor, NY, U.S.A. **78 D2** 41 0N 72 18W
Sagadahoc County ☆, ME, U.S.A. **76 E4** 44 0N 70 0W
Sagamore, MA, U.S.A. **78 C4** 41 45N 70 33W
Sagamore Hill Nat. Historic Site ⌓, NY, U.S.A. **89 E7** 40 53N 73 30W
Sagamore Hills, Cleveland, U.S.A. **107 B2** 41 18N 81 34W
Saganaga L., Ont., Canada **180 D6** 48 14N 90 52W
Saganash L., Ont., Canada **181 C14** 49 4N 82 35W
Saganashkee Slough, Chicago, U.S.A. **108 C1** 41 41N 87 53W
Sagavanirktok →, AK, U.S.A. **61 A11** 70 19N 147 53W
Sage, WY, U.S.A. **104 E2** 41 49N 110 58W
Sage Cr. →, MT, U.S.A. **83 C8** 47 16N 109 43W
Sagerton, TX, U.S.A. **99 D8** 33 5N 99 58W
Sageville, IA, U.S.A. **73 C8** 42 36N 90 43W
Saginaw, Dallas-Fort Worth, U.S.A. **109 A1** 32 51N 97 21W
Saginaw, MI, U.S.A. **79 F8** 43 26N 83 56W
Saginaw →, MI, U.S.A. **79 F8** 43 39N 83 51W
Saginaw B., MI, U.S.A. **79 F8** 43 50N 83 40W
Saginaw County ☆, MI, U.S.A. **79 F7** 43 20N 84 0W
Saglek B., Nfld. & L., Canada **175 B5** 58 30N 63 0W
Saglek Fd., Nfld. & L., Canada **175 B5** 58 29N 63 15W
Saglouc = Salluit, Qué., Canada **175 A2** 62 14N 75 38W
Sagola, MI, U.S.A. **79 C3** 46 5N 88 5W
Saguache, CO, U.S.A. **66 D4** 38 5N 106 8W
Saguache County ☆, CO, U.S.A. **66 D4** 38 10N 106 15W
Saguaro Nat. Park ⌓, AZ, U.S.A. **62 E5** 32 12N 110 38W
Saguenay →, Qué., Canada **177 C12** 48 22N 71 0W
Saguenay, Parc du ⌓, Qué., Canada **177 C12** 48 17N 70 17W
Sahuaripa, Sonora, Mexico **212 D6** 29 3N 109 14W
Sahuarita, AZ, U.S.A. **62 F5** 31 57N 110 58W
Sahuaro, Sonora, Mexico **212 B3** 31 6N 112 58W
Sahuayo, Michoacan, Mexico **218 B5** 20 2N 102 43W
Sailor Springs, IL, U.S.A. **71 E5** 38 46N 88 22W
Sailor's Creek Battlefield Historic State Park ⌓, VA, U.S.A. **102 D6** 37 17N 78 12W
Sain Alto, Zacatecas, Mexico **217 D7** 23 35N 103 15W
St-Adalbert, Qué., Canada **177 E13** 46 51N 69 53W
St-Agapit, Qué., Canada **177 E11** 46 34N 71 26W
St. Alban's, Nfld. & L., Canada **174 E5** 47 51N 55 50W
St. Albans, NY, U.S.A. **114 B4** 40 41N 73 45W
St. Albans, VT, U.S.A. **86 B1** 44 49N 73 5W
St. Albans, WV, U.S.A. **102 C3** 38 23N 81 50W
St. Albert, Alta., Canada **184 E7** 53 37N 113 32W
St-Alexandre, Qué., Canada **177 D13** 47 41N 69 38W
St-Alexandre, Qué., Canada **86 A1** 45 14N 73 7W
St-Alexis-des-Monts, Qué., Canada **177 E9** 46 28N 73 8W
St-Ambroise, Qué., Canada **177 C11** 48 33N 71 20W
St-Anaclet, Qué., Canada **177 C14** 48 29N 68 26W
St. André, N.B., Canada **173 F2** 47 8N 67 45W
St-André, Qué., Canada **177 D13** 47 41N 69 44W
St-André-Avellin, Qué., Canada **176 F7** 45 43N 75 3W
St-André-Est, Qué., Canada **177 F8** 45 33N 74 20W
St. Andrew Sd., GA, U.S.A. **68 F5** 30 58N 81 25W
St. Andrews, N.B., Canada **173 H2** 45 7N 67 5W
St. Andrew's, Nfld. & L., Canada **174 E1** 47 45N 59 15W
St. Andrews, SC, U.S.A. **90 F5** 32 47N 80 0W
St. Andrews B., FL, U.S.A. **67 A3** 30 5N 85 32W
St-Anicet, Qué., Canada **177 F8** 45 8N 74 22W
St. Anne, IL, U.S.A. **71 B6** 41 1N 87 43W
St. Annes, Man., Canada **183 F15** 49 40N 96 39W
St. Anns B., N.S., Canada **173 G9** 46 22N 60 25W
St-Anselme, N.B., Canada **173 G5** 46 4N 64 43W
St-Anselme, Qué., Canada **177 E12** 46 37N 70 58W
St. Ansgar, IA, U.S.A. **73 B6** 43 23N 92 55W
St. Anthony, Nfld. & L., Canada **174 A5** 51 22N 55 35W
St. Anthony, ID, U.S.A. **70 F7** 43 58N 111 41W
St. Anthony, Minneapolis-St. Paul, U.S.A. **113 A2** 45 1N 93 13W
St-Antoine, N.B., Canada **173 G5** 46 22N 64 45W
St-Antonin, Qué., Canada **177 D13** 47 46N 69 29W
St-Aubert, Qué., Canada **177 D12** 47 11N 70 13W
St-Augustin, Qué., Canada **174 A2** 51 13N 58 38W
St-Augustin →, Qué., Canada **175 C6** 51 16N 58 40W
St. Augustine, FL, U.S.A. **67 B7** 29 54N 81 19W
St. Augustine Beach, FL, U.S.A. **67 B7** 29 51N 81 16W
St. Augustine Shores, FL, U.S.A. **67 B7** 29 49N 81 19W
St-Basile, N.B., Canada **173 F1** 47 21N 68 14W
St-Basile, Qué., Canada **177 E11** 46 45N 71 49W
St. Benedict, Sask., Canada **182 C6** 52 34N 105 23W
St. Benedict, KS, U.S.A. **74 B7** 39 53N 96 6W
St. Bernard, New Orleans, U.S.A. **113 C3** 29 52N 89 51W
St. Bernard, OH, U.S.A. **107 B2** 39 10N 84 29W
St. Bernard Parish ☆, LA, U.S.A. **75 E6** 29 55N 89 10W
St. Bernard's-Jacques Fontaine, Nfld. & L., Canada **174 E6** 47 31N 54 55W
St. Brendan's, Nfld. & L., Canada **174 D7** 48 52N 53 40W
St. Bride's, Nfld. & L., Canada **174 F6** 46 56N 54 10W
St. Brieux, Sask., Canada **182 C7** 52 38N 104 54W
St-Bruno, Qué., Canada **177 C11** 48 28N 71 39W
St-Bruno-de-Guigues, Qué., Canada **176 D3** 47 28N 79 26W
St-Bruno-de-Montarville, Qué., Canada **192 A4** 45 32N 73 21W
St-Casimir, Qué., Canada **177 E10** 46 40N 72 8W
St. Catharines, Ont., Canada **178 D7** 43 10N 79 15W
St. Catherines I., GA, U.S.A. **68 E5** 31 40N 81 10W
St. Charles, AR, U.S.A. **63 D4** 34 23N 91 8W
St. Charles, ID, U.S.A. **70 G7** 42 7N 111 23W
St. Charles, IL, U.S.A. **71 B5** 41 54N 88 19W
St. Charles, IA, U.S.A. **73 D5** 41 17N 93 49W
St. Charles, KY, U.S.A. **96 C5** 37 11N 87 33W
St. Charles, MD, U.S.A. **77 B4** 38 36N 76 56W
St. Charles, MI, U.S.A. **79 F7** 43 18N 84 9W
St. Charles, MN, U.S.A. **80 G6** 43 58N 92 4W
St. Charles, MO, U.S.A. **82 C6** 38 47N 90 29W
St. Charles, SD, U.S.A. **91 G6** 43 5N 99 6W
St. Charles, VA, U.S.A. **102 E1** 36 48N 83 4W
St-Charles-Borromée, Qué., Canada **177 E9** 46 3N 73 28W
St. Charles County ☆, MO, U.S.A. **82 C6** 38 45N 90 40W
St-Charles-de-Drummond, Qué., Canada **177 F10** 45 54N 72 28W
St. Charles Parish ☆, LA, U.S.A. **75 E5** 29 59N 90 25W
St-Chrysostôme, Qué., Canada **177 F9** 45 6N 73 46W
St. Clair, GA, U.S.A. **68 C4** 33 9N 82 13W
St. Clair, MI, U.S.A. **79 G9** 42 50N 82 30W
St. Clair, MN, U.S.A. **80 F5** 44 5N 93 51W
St. Clair, MO, U.S.A. **82 C6** 38 21N 90 59W
St. Clair, PA, U.S.A. **95 D6** 40 43N 76 12W
St. Clair →, MI, U.S.A. **79 G9** 42 38N 82 31W
St. Clair, L., Ont., Canada **178 E4** 42 30N 82 45W
St. Clair, L., MI, U.S.A. **79 G9** 42 27N 82 39W
St. Clair County ☆, AL, U.S.A. **60 C4** 33 35N 86 17W
St. Clair County ☆, IL, U.S.A. **71 E4** 38 30N 89 55W
St. Clair County ☆, MI, U.S.A. **79 G9** 43 0N 82 30W
St. Clair County ☆, MO, U.S.A. **82 C3** 38 0N 93 45W
St. Clair Shores, MI, U.S.A. **79 G9** 42 30N 82 53W
St. Clairsville, OH, U.S.A. **92 C6** 40 5N 80 54W
St. Claude, Man., Canada **183 F13** 49 40N 98 20W
St. Cloud, FL, U.S.A. **67 C7** 28 15N 81 17W
St. Cloud, MN, U.S.A. **80 E4** 45 34N 94 10W
St-Coeur de Marie, Qué., Canada **177 C11** 48 39N 71 43W
St-Côme, Qué., Canada **177 E9** 46 16N 73 47W
St-Côme-Linière, Qué., Canada **177 E12** 46 4N 70 32W
St. Croix, N.B., Canada **173 H2** 45 34N 67 26W
St. Croix →, ME, U.S.A. **173 H2** 45 4N 67 5W
St. Croix →, WI, U.S.A. **103 D1** 44 45N 92 48W
St. Croix, L., MN, U.S.A. **80 F6** 44 55N 92 46W
St. Croix County ☆, WI, U.S.A. **103 C1** 45 0N 92 20W
St. Croix Falls, WI, U.S.A. **103 C1** 45 24N 92 38W
St. Croix Flowage, WI, U.S.A. **103 B2** 46 15N 91 56W
St. Croix I., Puerto Rico **105 H18** 17 45N 64 45W

St. Croix Indian Reservation, *WI, U.S.A.* **103 C1** 45 46N 92 20W
St. Croix Island Int. Historic Site ⌂, *N. Amer.* **76 C6** 45 8N 67 8W
St. Croix Nat. Scenic Riverway ⌂, *WI, U.S.A.* **103 B2** 46 6N 91 23W
St-Cyrille-de-L'Islet, *Qué., Canada* **177 D12** 47 2N 70 17W
St. David, *AZ, U.S.A.* **62 F5** 31 54N 110 13W
St. David, *IL, U.S.A.* **71 C3** 40 30N 90 3W
St. David's, *Nfld. & L., Canada* **174 D2** 48 12N 58 52W
St-Dominique-du-Rosaire, *Qué., Canada* **176 C4** 48 46N 78 7W
St-Donat, *Qué., Canada* **177 E8** 46 19N 74 13W
St. Donatus, *IA, U.S.A.* **73 C8** 42 22N 90 33W
St. Edward, *NE, U.S.A.* **84 C8** 41 34N 97 52W
St. Eleanors, *P.E.I., Canada* **173 G6** 46 25N 63 49W
St. Elias, Mt., *AK, U.S.A.* **61 F12** 60 18N 140 56W
St. Elias Mts., *N. Amer.* **189 D5** 60 33N 139 28W
St. Elizabeth, *MO, U.S.A.* **82 C4** 38 15N 92 16W
St. Elmo, *IL, U.S.A.* **71 D5** 39 2N 88 51W
St-Éloi, *Qué., Canada* **177 C13** 48 2N 69 14W
St-Élouthère, *Qué., Canada* **177 D13** 47 30N 69 15W
St-Éphrem-de-Tring, *Qué., Canada* **177 E12** 46 2N 70 59W
St. Eugène, *Ont., Canada* **176 F8** 45 30N 74 28W
St-Eusèbe, *Qué., Canada* **177 D14** 47 33N 68 55W
St. Eustache, *Man., Canada* **183 F14** 49 59N 97 47W
St-Eustache, *Qué., Canada* **177 F9** 45 34N 73 54W
St-Fabien, *Qué., Canada* **177 C14** 48 18N 68 52W
St-Faustin-Lac-Carré, *Qué., Canada* **177 E8** 46 7N 74 29W
St-Félicien, *Qué., Canada* **177 C10** 48 40N 72 25W
St-Félix-de-Valois, *Qué., Canada* **177 E9** 46 10N 73 26W
St. Ferdinand = Florissant, *MO, U.S.A.* **82 C6** 38 47N 90 19W
St-Ferdinand, *Qué., Canada* **177 E11** 46 6N 71 34W
St. Frances, *SD, U.S.A.* **91 G5** 43 9N 100 54W
St. Francis, *KS, U.S.A.* **74 B2** 39 47N 101 48W
St. Francis, *ME, U.S.A.* **76 A5** 47 10N 68 54W
St. Francis, *MN, U.S.A.* **80 E5** 45 23N 93 22W
St. Francis, *WI, U.S.A.* **103 F6** 42 58N 87 52W
St. Francis →, *AR, U.S.A.* **63 D5** 34 38N 90 36W
St. Francis County ☆, *AR, U.S.A.* **63 C5** 35 1N 90 47W
St. Francisville, *IL, U.S.A.* **71 E6** 38 36N 87 39W
St. Francisville, *LA, U.S.A.* **75 D4** 30 47N 91 23W
St-François, *Qué., Canada* **177 E12** 46 48N 70 49W
St-François →, *Qué., Canada* **177 E10** 46 7N 72 55W
St-François, L., *Qué., Canada* **177 F8** 45 10N 74 22W
St. Francois County ☆, *MO, U.S.A.* **82 D6** 37 50N 90 30W
St-François-du-Lac, *Qué., Canada* **177 E10** 46 5N 72 50W
St. Francois Mts., *MO, U.S.A.* **82 D6** 37 30N 90 35W
St. François Xavier, *Man., Canada* **183 F14** 49 55N 97 32W
St. Froid, L., *ME, U.S.A.* **76 B5** 46 57N 68 37W
St-Fulgence, *Qué., Canada* **177 C12** 48 27N 70 54W
St-Gabriel, *Qué., Canada* **177 E9** 46 17N 73 24W
St. Gabriel, *LA, U.S.A.* **75 D4** 30 16N 91 6W
St-Gabriel-de-Gaspé, *Qué., Canada* **172 E5** 48 31N 64 32W
St-Gaudens Nat. Historic Park ⌂, *NH, U.S.A.* **86 C2** 43 30N 72 22W
St-Gédéon, *Qué., Canada* **177 C11** 48 30N 71 46W
St-Gédéon-de-Beauce, *Qué., Canada* **177 F12** 45 45N 70 40W
St. Genevieve County ☆, *MO, U.S.A.* **82 D6** 37 50N 90 10W
St. George, *N.B., Canada* **173 H3** 45 11N 66 50W
St. George, *Ont., Canada* **178 D6** 43 15N 80 15W
St. George, *GA, U.S.A.* **68 F4** 30 31N 82 2W
St. George, *KS, U.S.A.* **74 B7** 39 12N 96 25W
St. George, *SC, U.S.A.* **90 E5** 33 11N 80 35W
St. George, *UT, U.S.A.* **100 F2** 37 6N 113 35W
St. George, C., *Nfld. & L., Canada* **174 D1** 48 30N 59 16W
St. George, C., *FL, U.S.A.* **67 B3** 29 40N 85 5W
St. George, Pt., *CA, U.S.A.* **64 B2** 41 47N 124 15W
St. George I., *AK, U.S.A.* **61 H5** 56 35N 169 35W
St. George I., *FL, U.S.A.* **67 B4** 29 35N 84 55W
St. George Island, *MD, U.S.A.* **77 B4** 38 7N 76 29W
St. George's, *Nfld. & L., Canada* **174 D2** 48 26N 58 31W
St-Georges, *Qué., Canada* **177 E12** 46 8N 70 40W
St. George's B., *Nfld. & L., Canada* **174 D2** 48 24N 58 53W
St. Georges Bay, *N.S., Canada* **173 H8** 45 45N 61 45W
St-Godefroi, *N.B., Canada* **173 E4** 48 5N 65 6W
St. Helen, *MI, U.S.A.* **79 E7** 44 22N 84 25W
St. Helena, *CA, U.S.A.* **64 E4** 38 30N 122 28W
St. Helena, *NE, U.S.A.* **84 B8** 42 49N 97 15W
St. Helena Parish ☆, *LA, U.S.A.* **75 D5** 30 50N 90 40W
St. Helena Sd., *SC, U.S.A.* **90 F5** 32 15N 80 25W
St. Helens, *OR, U.S.A.* **94 B3** 45 52N 122 48W
St. Helens, Mt., *WA, U.S.A.* **101 D3** 46 12N 122 12W
St. Henry, *OH, U.S.A.* **92 C2** 40 25N 84 38W
St. Hilaire, *MN, U.S.A.* **80 B2** 48 1N 96 14W
St-Hilarion, *Qué., Canada* **177 D12** 47 34N 70 24W
St-Honoré, *Qué., Canada* **177 C11** 48 32N 71 5W
St-Hubert, *Qué., Canada* **177 F9** 45 29N 73 25W
St-Hubert-de-Témiscouata, *Qué., Canada* **177 D13** 47 49N 69 9W
St-Hyacinthe, *Qué., Canada* **177 F10** 45 40N 72 58W
St-Ignace, *N.B., Canada* **173 G4** 46 42N 65 5W
St. Ignace, *MI, U.S.A.* **79 D7** 45 52N 84 44W
St. Ignace I., *Ont., Canada* **181 D9** 48 45N 88 0W
St. Ignatius, *MT, U.S.A.* **83 C3** 47 19N 114 6W
St-Isidore, *N.B., Canada* **173 F4** 47 33N 65 2W
St-Isidore, *Qué., Canada* **177 F9** 45 20N 73 42W
St-Jacques, *N.B., Canada* **173 F1** 47 26N 68 23W
St. Jacques →, *Montréal, Canada* **192 B4** 45 26N 73 29W
St. James, *MI, U.S.A.* **79 D6** 45 45N 85 31W
St. James, *MN, U.S.A.* **80 G4** 43 59N 94 38W
St. James, *MO, U.S.A.* **82 D5** 38 0N 91 37W
St. James, *NY, U.S.A.* **78 D1** 40 53N 73 9W
St. James City, *FL, U.S.A.* **67 E6** 26 29N 82 5W
St. James Parish ☆, *LA, U.S.A.* **75 D5** 30 1N 90 50W
St. Jean, *MI, U.S.A.* **109 A3** 42 22N 83 0W
St-Jean →, *Qué., Canada* **172 E5** 48 46N 64 26W
St-Jean →, *Qué., Canada* **172 C5** 50 17N 64 20W
St-Jean, L., *Qué., Canada* **177 C11** 48 40N 72 0W
St. Jean Baptiste, *Man., Canada* **183 F14** 49 15N 97 20W
St-Jean-Baptiste-de-Restigouche, *N.B., Canada* **173 F2** 47 46N 67 13W
St-Jean-de-Dieu, *Qué., Canada* **177 C13** 48 0N 69 3W
St-Jean-Port-Joli, *Qué., Canada* **177 D12** 47 15N 70 13W
St-Jean-sur-Richelieu, *Qué., Canada* **86 A1** 45 20N 73 20W
St-Jérôme, *Qué., Canada* **177 F9** 45 47N 74 0W
St. Jo, *TX, U.S.A.* **99 D10** 33 42N 97 31W
St-Joachim, *Qué., Canada* **177 D12** 47 4N 70 50W
St. Joe, *AR, U.S.A.* **63 B3** 36 2N 92 48W
St. Joe, *ID, U.S.A.* **70 B2** 47 19N 116 21W
St. Joe →, *ID, U.S.A.* **70 B2** 47 24N 116 45W
St. Joe Mt., *ID, U.S.A.* **70 B2** 47 25N 116 0W
St. Joe Nat. Forest, *ID, U.S.A.* **70 B3** 47 5N 115 30W
St. John, *N.B., Canada* **173 H3** 45 20N 66 8W
St. John, *KS, U.S.A.* **74 C5** 38 0N 98 46W
St. John, *MO, U.S.A.* **117 A1** 38 42N 90 20W
St. John, *ND, U.S.A.* **91 B6** 48 57N 99 43W
St. John, *WA, U.S.A.* **101 C8** 47 6N 117 35W
St. John →, *N. Amer.* **173 H3** 45 12N 66 5W
St. John, C., *Nfld. & L., Canada* **174 B5** 50 0N 55 32W
St. John, L., *Nfld. & L., Canada* **174 D6** 48 23N 54 41W
St. John B., *Nfld. & L., Canada* **174 B3** 50 55N 57 9W
St. John Harbour, *N.B., Canada* **173 H3** 45 15N 66 2W
St. John I., *Nfld. & L., Canada* **174 B3** 50 49N 57 14W
St. John I., *U.S. Virgin Is.* **105 G18** 18 20N 64 42W
St. John The Baptist Parish ☆, *LA, U.S.A.* **75 D5** 30 3N 90 33W
St. John's, *Nfld. & L., Canada* **174 E8** 47 35N 52 40W
St. Johns, *AZ, U.S.A.* **62 C6** 34 30N 109 22W
St. Johns, *MI, U.S.A.* **79 G7** 43 0N 84 33W
St. Johns, *Portland, U.S.A.* **116 A1** 45 35N 122 45W
St. Johns →, *FL, U.S.A.* **67 A7** 30 24N 81 24W
St. John's B., *Nfld. & L., Canada* **174 E8** 47 34N 52 38W
St. Johns County ☆, *FL, U.S.A.* **67 B7** 29 45N 81 25W
St. John's East, *Nfld. & L., Canada* **174 E8** 47 38N 52 42W
St. John's North, *Nfld. & L., Canada* **174 E8** 47 33N 52 49W
St. John's South, *Nfld. & L., Canada* **174 E8** 47 30N 52 43W
St. Johnsbury, *VT, U.S.A.* **86 B3** 44 25N 72 1W
St. Joseph, *IL, U.S.A.* **71 C5** 40 7N 88 2W
St. Joseph, *LA, U.S.A.* **75 C4** 31 55N 91 14W
St. Joseph, *MI, U.S.A.* **79 G5** 42 6N 86 29W
St. Joseph, *MN, U.S.A.* **80 E4** 45 34N 94 19W
St. Joseph, *MO, U.S.A.* **82 B2** 39 46N 94 50W
St. Joseph, *TN, U.S.A.* **96 E5** 35 2N 87 30W
St. Joseph →, *IN, U.S.A.* **72 B5** 41 5N 85 8W
St. Joseph →, *MI, U.S.A.* **79 G5** 42 7N 86 29W
St. Joseph, I., *Ont., Canada* **178 A3** 46 12N 83 58W
St. Joseph, L., *Ont., Canada* **180 A6** 51 10N 90 35W
St. Joseph B., *FL, U.S.A.* **67 B3** 29 47N 85 21W
St. Joseph County ☆, *IN, U.S.A.* **72 B4** 41 35N 86 15W
St-Joseph-de-Beauce, *Qué., Canada* **177 E12** 46 18N 70 53W
St. Joseph Pen., *FL, U.S.A.* **67 B3** 29 45N 85 24W
St. Joseph Pt., *FL, U.S.A.* **67 B3** 29 52N 85 24W
St. Joseph Sound, *Tampa, U.S.A.* **119 A2** 28 5N 82 48W
St-Jude, *Qué., Canada* **177 F10** 45 46N 72 59W
St. Lambert, *Montréal, Canada* **192 A4** 45 30N 73 29W
St. Landry Parish ☆, *LA, U.S.A.* **75 D4** 30 40N 92 0W
St. Laurent, *Man., Canada* **183 E14** 50 25N 97 58W
St-Laurent, *Montréal, Canada* **192 A2** 45 30N 73 43W
St. Lawrence, *Nfld. & L., Canada* **174 F5** 46 54N 55 23W
St. Lawrence, *SD, U.S.A.* **91 F7** 44 31N 98 56W
St. Lawrence →, *Canada* **172 D3** 49 30N 66 0W
St. Lawrence, Gulf of, *Canada* **172 E7** 48 25N 62 0W
St. Lawrence County ☆, *NY, U.S.A.* **89 A6** 44 30N 75 0W
St. Lawrence I., *AK, U.S.A.* **61 E5** 63 30N 170 30W
St. Lawrence Islands Nat. Park △, *Ont., Canada* **179 C11** 44 27N 75 52W
St-Lazare, *Man., Canada* **183 E10** 50 27N 101 18W
St. Leo, *MN, U.S.A.* **80 F2** 44 43N 96 3W
St-Léolin, *N.B., Canada* **173 F4** 47 46N 65 10W
St-Léon-le-Grand, *Qué., Canada* **172 E2** 48 23N 67 30W
St-Léonard, *Montréal, Canada* **192 A3** 45 35N 73 34W
St. Leonard, *N.B., Canada* **173 F2** 47 12N 67 58W
St. Leonard, *MD, U.S.A.* **77 B4** 38 28N 76 30W
St-Léonard-de-Portneuf, *Qué., Canada* **177 E11** 46 53N 71 55W
St. Lewis →, *Nfld. & L., Canada* **175 C6** 52 26N 56 11W
St. Libory, *NE, U.S.A.* **84 C7** 41 5N 98 21W
St-Lin-Laurentides, *Qué., Canada* **177 F9** 45 51N 73 46W
St. Louis, *P.E.I., Canada* **173 G5** 46 53N 64 8W
St. Louis, *Sask., Canada* **182 C6** 52 55N 105 49W
St. Louis, *MI, U.S.A.* **79 F7** 43 25N 84 36W
St. Louis, *MO, U.S.A.* **82 C6** 38 37N 90 11W
St. Louis, *OK, U.S.A.* **93 C7** 35 5N 96 53W
St. Louis →, *MN, U.S.A.* **80 D6** 46 44N 92 9W
St-Louis, L., *Qué., Canada* **192 B2** 45 24N 73 48W
St. Louis County ☆, *MN, U.S.A.* **80 C6** 47 40N 92 20W
St. Louis County ☆, *MO, U.S.A.* **82 C6** 38 40N 90 25W
St-Louis-de-France, *Qué., Canada* **177 E10** 46 25N 72 36W
St-Louis-de-Kent, *N.B., Canada* **173 G5** 46 44N 64 58W
St. Louis Lambert International ✕ (STL), *MO, U.S.A.* **82 C6** 38 45N 90 22W
St. Louis Park, *MN, U.S.A.* **80 F5** 45 56N 93 21W
St. Louisville, *OH, U.S.A.* **92 C4** 40 10N 82 25W
St-Luc, *Qué., Canada* **177 F9** 45 22N 73 18W
St-Luc-de-Matane, *Qué., Canada* **172 E2** 48 48N 67 28W
St. Lucie, *FL, U.S.A.* **67 D8** 27 29N 80 20W
St. Lucie Canal, *FL, U.S.A.* **67 D8** 27 10N 80 18W
St. Lucie County ☆, *FL, U.S.A.* **67 D8** 27 25N 80 30W
St-Ludger, *Qué., Canada* **177 F12** 45 45N 70 42W
St-Ludger-de-Milot, *Qué., Canada* **177 C11** 48 54N 71 49W
St. Lunaire-Griquet, *Nfld. & L., Canada* **174 A5** 51 31N 55 28W
St-Magloire, *Qué., Canada* **177 E12** 46 35N 70 17W
St. Malo, *Man., Canada* **183 F15** 49 19N 96 57W
St. Margarets, *N.B., Canada* **173 G4** 46 54N 65 11W
St. Maries, *ID, U.S.A.* **70 B2** 47 19N 116 35W
St. Maries →, *ID, U.S.A.* **70 B2** 47 19N 116 33W
St. Marks, *FL, U.S.A.* **67 A4** 30 9N 84 12W
St. Marks →, *FL, U.S.A.* **67 A4** 30 8N 84 12W
St. Marks Nat. Wildlife Refuge ⌂, *FL, U.S.A.* **67 A4** 30 7N 84 17W
St-Martin, *Qué., Canada* **192 A2** 45 35N 73 43W
St. Martin, L., *Man., Canada* **183 D13** 51 40N 98 30W
St. Martin I., *MI, U.S.A.* **79 D5** 45 30N 86 46W
St. Martin Parish ☆, *LA, U.S.A.* **75 D4** 30 7N 91 50W
St. Martins, *N.B., Canada* **173 H4** 45 22N 65 34W
St. Martinville, *LA, U.S.A.* **75 D4** 30 7N 91 50W
St. Mary, *MO, U.S.A.* **82 D7** 37 53N 89 57W
St. Mary →, *B.C., Canada* **185 J5** 49 37N 115 38W
St. Mary L., *MT, U.S.A.* **83 B4** 48 39N 113 34W
St. Mary Parish ☆, *LA, U.S.A.* **75 E4** 29 48N 91 30W
St. Mary Res., *Alta., Canada* **185 J7** 49 20N 113 11W
St. Marys, *Ont., Canada* **178 D5** 43 20N 81 10W
St. Mary's, *AK, U.S.A.* **61 E7** 62 4N 163 10W
St. Marys, *GA, U.S.A.* **68 F5** 30 44N 81 33W
St. Marys, *IA, U.S.A.* **73 D5** 41 19N 93 44W
St. Marys, *KS, U.S.A.* **74 B7** 39 12N 96 4W
St. Marys, *OH, U.S.A.* **92 C2** 40 33N 84 24W
St. Marys, *PA, U.S.A.* **95 C4** 41 26N 78 34W
St. Marys, *WV, U.S.A.* **102 B3** 39 23N 81 12W
St. Marys →, *N.S., Canada* **173 H8** 45 2N 61 53W
St. Marys →, *GA, U.S.A.* **68 F5** 30 43N 81 27W
St. Marys →, *IN, U.S.A.* **72 B5** 41 5N 85 8W
St. Marys →, *MI, U.S.A.* **79 D8** 46 0N 83 55W
St. Mary's, C., *Nfld. & L., Canada* **174 F6** 46 50N 54 12W
St. Mary's Alpine Park ⌂, *B.C., Canada* **185 J4** 49 50N 116 25W
St. Marys Bay, *N.S., Canada* **173 J3** 44 25N 66 10W
St. Mary's City, *MD, U.S.A.* **77 B4** 38 11N 76 26W
St. Marys County ☆, *MD, U.S.A.* **77 B4** 38 15N 76 40W
St. Matthew I., *AK, U.S.A.* **61 F4** 60 24N 172 42W
St. Matthews, *KY, U.S.A.* **97 B7** 38 15N 85 39W
St. Matthews, *SC, U.S.A.* **90 E5** 33 40N 80 46W
St-Maurice →, *Qué., Canada* **177 E10** 46 21N 72 31W
St-Maurice, Réserve Faunique du ⌂, *Qué., Canada* **177 D9** 47 5N 73 15W
St. Meinrad, *IN, U.S.A.* **72 E4** 38 10N 86 49W
St. Michael, *AK, U.S.A.* **61 E7** 63 29N 162 2W
St. Michael, *MN, U.S.A.* **80 E5** 45 13N 93 40W
St. Michaels, *MD, U.S.A.* **77 B4** 38 47N 76 14W
St-Michel, *Montréal, Canada* **192 A3** 45 34N 73 37W
St-Michel-des-Saints, *Qué., Canada* **177 E9** 46 41N 73 55W
St-Nazaire, *Qué., Canada* **177 F10** 45 44N 72 37W
St. Nazianz, *WI, U.S.A.* **103 E6** 44 0N 87 55W
St-Nicolas, *Qué., Canada* **177 E11** 46 42N 71 24W
St-Noël, *Qué., Canada* **172 E2** 48 35N 67 50W
St-Octave-de l'Avenir, *Qué., Canada* **172 E3** 49 0N 66 33W
St. Olaf, *IA, U.S.A.* **73 C7** 42 56N 91 23W
St-Omer, *Qué., Canada* **177 D13** 47 3N 69 43W
St. Onge, *SD, U.S.A.* **91 F2** 44 33N 103 43W
St-Ours, *Qué., Canada* **177 F9** 45 53N 73 9W
St-Pacôme, *Qué., Canada* **177 D13** 47 24N 69 58W
St-Pamphile, *Qué., Canada* **177 E13** 46 58N 69 48W
St. Paris, *OH, U.S.A.* **92 C3** 40 8N 83 58W
St-Pascal, *Qué., Canada* **177 D13** 47 32N 69 48W
St-Patrice, L., *Qué., Canada* **176 E5** 46 22N 77 20W
St. Patrick Peak, *MT, U.S.A.* **83 D3** 46 59N 114 51W
St. Paul, *Alta., Canada* **184 D9** 54 0N 111 17W
St. Paul, *AK, U.S.A.* **61 H5** 57 7N 170 17W
St. Paul, *AR, U.S.A.* **63 C2** 35 50N 93 46W
St. Paul, *IN, U.S.A.* **72 D5** 39 26N 85 38W
St. Paul, *IA, U.S.A.* **73 E7** 40 46N 91 31W
St. Paul, *KS, U.S.A.* **74 D8** 37 31N 95 10W
St. Paul, *MN, U.S.A.* **80 F5** 44 56N 93 5W
St. Paul, *NE, U.S.A.* **84 C7** 41 13N 98 27W
St. Paul, *VA, U.S.A.* **102 E2** 36 54N 82 19W
St-Paul →, *Qué., Canada* **175 C6** 51 27N 57 42W
St-Paul-de-Montminy, *Qué., Canada* **177 E12** 46 44N 70 22W
St. Paul Downtown ✕, *Minneapolis-St. Paul, U.S.A.* **113 B3** 44 56N 93 3W
St. Paul I., *N.S., Canada* **173 F9** 47 12N 60 9W
St. Paul I., *AK, U.S.A.* **61 H5** 57 10N 170 15W
St-Paulin, *Qué., Canada* **177 E9** 46 25N 73 1W
St. Pauls, *Nfld. & L., Canada* **174 C3** 49 52N 57 49W
St. Pauls, *NC, U.S.A.* **90 D7** 34 48N 78 58W
St. Pete Beach, *FL, U.S.A.* **67 D6** 27 43N 82 44W
St. Peter, *IL, U.S.A.* **71 E5** 38 52N 88 51W
St. Peter, *MN, U.S.A.* **80 F5** 44 20N 93 57W
St. Peters, *N.S., Canada* **173 H9** 45 40N 60 53W
St. Peters, *P.E.I., Canada* **173 G7** 46 25N 62 35W
St. Peters, *MO, U.S.A.* **82 C6** 38 48N 90 37W
St. Petersburg, *FL, U.S.A.* **67 D6** 27 46N 82 40W
St. Petersburg-Clearwater International ✕, *Tampa, U.S.A.* **119 B2** 27 54N 82 41W
St-Philémon, *Qué., Canada* **177 E12** 46 41N 70 27W
St. Phillip, *MT, U.S.A.* **83 D13** 46 50N 104 9W
St-Pie, *Qué., Canada* **177 F10** 45 30N 72 54W
St-Pierre, *Montréal, Canada* **192 B3** 45 27N 73 38W
St-Pierre, *St-P. & M.* **174 F4** 46 46N 56 12W
St-Pierre, Î., *St-P. & M.* **174 F4** 46 47N 56 11W
St-Pierre, L., *Qué., Canada* **177 A14** 50 8N 68 26W
St-Pierre, L., *Qué., Canada* **177 E10** 46 12N 72 52W
St-Pierre-de-la-Pointe-aux-Esquimaux = Havre-St.-Pierre, *Qué., Canada* **175 C5** 50 18N 63 33W
St-Pierre-et-Miquelon ⊠, *N. Amer.* **174 F4** 46 55N 56 10W
St. Pierre-Jolys, *Man., Canada* **183 F15** 49 26N 96 59W
St-Prime, *Qué., Canada* **177 C10** 48 35N 72 20W
St-Prosper, *Qué., Canada* **177 E12** 46 13N 70 29W
St-Quentin, *N.B., Canada* **173 F2** 47 30N 67 23W
St-Raphaël, *Qué., Canada* **177 E12** 46 48N 70 45W
St-Raymond, *Qué., Canada* **177 E11** 46 54N 71 50W
St. Regis, *MT, U.S.A.* **83 C2** 47 18N 115 6W
St. Regis Falls, *NY, U.S.A.* **89 A6** 44 41N 74 33W
St. Regis Indian Reservation, *N. Amer.* **89 A6** 44 59N 74 39W
St-Rémi, *Qué., Canada* **177 F9** 45 16N 73 37W
St-Rémi-d'Amherst, *Qué., Canada* **176 E8** 46 1N 74 46W
St. Robert, *MO, U.S.A.* **82 D4** 37 50N 92 11W
St-Roch-Aulnaies, *Qué., Canada* **177 D12** 47 18N 70 12W
St-Romuald, *Qué., Canada* **177 E11** 46 46N 71 20W
St-Sauveur, *N.B., Canada* **173 F4** 47 32N 65 20W
St-Sébastien, *Qué., Canada* **177 F12** 45 47N 70 58W
St-Siméon, *N.B., Canada* **173 E4** 48 5N 65 36W
St-Siméon, *Qué., Canada* **177 D13** 47 51N 69 54W
St-Simon, *Qué., Canada* **177 C13** 48 12N 69 3W
St. Simons I., *GA, U.S.A.* **68 E5** 31 12N 81 15W
St. Simons Island, *GA, U.S.A.* **68 E5** 31 9N 81 22W
St. Stephen, *N.B., Canada* **173 H2** 45 16N 67 17W
St. Stephen, *SC, U.S.A.* **90 E6** 33 24N 79 55W
St. Tammany Parish ☆, *LA, U.S.A.* **75 D5** 30 29N 90 2W
St. Thomas = Charlotte Amalie, *U.S. Virgin Is.* **105 G18** 18 21N 64 56W
St. Thomas, *Ont., Canada* **178 E5** 42 45N 81 10W
St. Thomas, *MO, U.S.A.* **82 C4** 38 23N 92 13W
St. Thomas, *ND, U.S.A.* **91 B8** 48 37N 97 27W
St. Thomas I., *U.S. Virgin Is.* **105 G18** 18 20N 64 55W
St-Tite, *Qué., Canada* **177 E10** 46 45N 72 34W
St-Tite-des-Caps, *Qué., Canada* **177 D12** 47 8N 70 47W
St-Ulric, *Qué., Canada* **172 E2** 48 47N 67 42W
St-Urbain, *Qué., Canada* **177 D12** 47 33N 70 32W
St-Vianney, *Qué., Canada* **172 E2** 48 37N 67 25W
St. Victor, *Sask., Canada* **182 F6** 49 26N 105 52W
St. Vincent, *MN, U.S.A.* **80 B1** 48 58N 97 14W
St.-Vincent-de-Paul, *Montréal, Canada* **192 A3** 45 36N 73 39W
St. Vincent I., *FL, U.S.A.* **67 B3** 29 42N 85 3W
St. Vincent's, *Nfld. & L., Canada* **174 F7** 46 48N 53 38W
St. Vrain, *NM, U.S.A.* **88 C7** 34 25N 103 29W
St. Walburg, *Sask., Canada* **182 B2** 53 39N 109 12W
St-Yvon, *Qué., Canada* **172 D5** 49 10N 64 52W
Ste-Adèle, *Qué., Canada* **177 F8** 45 57N 74 7W
Ste. Agathe, *Man., Canada* **183 F14** 49 34N 97 11W
Ste-Agathe, *Qué., Canada* **177 E11** 46 23N 71 25W
Ste-Agathe-des-Monts, *Qué., Canada* **177 E8** 46 3N 74 17W
Ste-Angèle-de-Mérici, *Qué., Canada* **172 E1** 48 32N 68 5W
Ste. Anne, L., *Alta., Canada* **184 E6** 53 42N 114 25W
Ste-Anne, L., *Qué., Canada* **172 C2** 50 0N 67 42W
Ste-Anne de Beaupré, *Qué., Canada* **177 D12** 47 2N 70 58W
Ste-Anne-de-Bellevue, *Qué., Canada* **192 B1** 45 24N 73 56W
Ste-Anne-de-Madawaska, *N.B., Canada* **173 F1** 47 15N 68 2W
Ste-Anne-de-Portneuf, *Qué., Canada* **177 C13** 48 38N 69 6W
Ste-Anne-des-Monts-Tourelle, *Qué., Canada* **172 D3** 49 8N 66 30W
Ste-Anne-des-Plaines, *Qué., Canada* **177 F9** 45 47N 73 49W
Ste-Anne-du-Lac, *Qué., Canada* **176 E7** 46 48N 75 25W
Ste-Apolline, *Qué., Canada* **177 E12** 46 48N 70 12W
Ste-Blandine, *Qué., Canada* **177 C14** 48 22N 68 28W
Ste-Brigide-d'Iberville, *Qué., Canada* **86 A1** 45 19N 73 4W
Ste-Catherine, *Montréal, Canada* **192 B3** 45 24N 73 34W
Ste-Claire, *Qué., Canada* **177 E12** 46 36N 70 51W
Ste-Croix, *Qué., Canada* **177 E11** 46 38N 71 44W
Ste-Dorothée, *Qué., Canada* **192 A2** 45 32N 73 49W
Ste-Famille, *Qué., Canada* **177 E12** 46 58N 70 58W
Ste-Félicité, *Qué., Canada* **172 E2** 48 54N 67 20W
Ste-Florence, *Qué., Canada* **172 E2** 48 16N 67 14W
Ste-Foy, *Qué., Canada* **177 E11** 46 47N 71 17W
Ste-Françoise, *Qué., Canada* **177 C13** 48 6N 69 4W
Ste-Geneviève, *Qué., Canada* **192 B1** 45 29N 73 52W
Ste. Genevieve, *MO, U.S.A.* **82 D6** 37 59N 90 2W
Ste-Hélène, Î., *Montréal, Canada* **192 A3** 45 31N 73 32W
Ste-Julie, *Qué., Canada* **192 A4** 45 35N 73 20W
Ste-Justine, *Qué., Canada* **177 E12** 46 24N 70 21W
Ste-Marguerite →, *Qué., Canada* **175 C4** 50 9N 66 36W
Ste-Marie, *Qué., Canada* **177 E12** 46 26N 71 0W
Ste. Marie, *IL, U.S.A.* **71 E5** 38 56N 88 1W
Ste-Marthe-sur-le-Lac, *Qué., Canada* **192 A1** 45 32N 73 56W
Ste-Monique, *Qué., Canada* **177 C11** 48 44N 71 51W
Ste-Rose, *Qué., Canada* **192 A2** 45 36N 73 47W
Ste. Rose du Lac, *Man., Canada* **183 D12** 51 4N 99 30W
Ste-Sabine, *Qué., Canada* **177 F9** 45 15N 73 2W
Ste-Thècle, *Qué., Canada* **177 E10** 46 49N 72 31W
Ste-Thérèse-Ouest, *Qué., Canada* **192 A1** 45 36N 73 51W
Saipan, *N. Marianas* **105 c** 15 12N 145 45 E
Saipan Channel, *N. Marianas* **105 c** 15 5N 145 41W
Sairs, L., *Qué., Canada* **176 E4** 46 49N 78 26W
Sakakawea, L., *ND, U.S.A.* **91 C4** 47 30N 101 25W
Sakami →, *Qué., Canada* **175 C2** 53 40N 76 40W
Sakami, L., *Qué., Canada* **175 C2** 53 15N 77 0W
Saks, *AL, U.S.A.* **60 C5** 33 42N 85 50W
Salaberry-de-Valleyfield, *Qué., Canada* **177 F8** 45 15N 74 8W
Salada, L., *Baja Calif., Mexico* **210 A3** 32 20N 115 40W
Salado, *AR, U.S.A.* **63 C4** 35 42N 91 36W
Salado →, *Oaxaca, Mexico* **221 G4** 17 55N 96 59W
Salado →, *Tamaulipas, Mexico* **214 D5** 26 52N 99 19W
Salado, Rio →, *NM, U.S.A.* **88 C4** 34 16N 106 52W
Salado, Valle del, *Mexico* **215 G3** 23 56N 101 15W
Salamanca, *Guanajuato, Mexico* **219 B6** 20 34N 101 12W
Salamanca, *NY, U.S.A.* **89 C2** 42 10N 78 43W
Salamonia, *IN, U.S.A.* **72 C6** 40 23N 84 52W
Salamonie L., *IN, U.S.A.* **72 C5** 40 46N 85 37W
Sale City, *GA, U.S.A.* **68 E2** 31 16N 84 1W
Sale Creek, *TN, U.S.A.* **97 E7** 35 23N 85 7W
Salem, *AL, U.S.A.* **60 D5** 32 36N 85 14W
Salem, *AR, U.S.A.* **63 D2** 34 38N 93 37W
Salem, *AR, U.S.A.* **63 B4** 36 22N 91 50W
Salem, *CT, U.S.A.* **78 C2** 41 28N 72 16W
Salem, *FL, U.S.A.* **67 B5** 29 53N 83 25W
Salem, *IL, U.S.A.* **71 E5** 38 38N 88 57W
Salem, *IN, U.S.A.* **72 E4** 38 36N 86 6W
Salem, *IA, U.S.A.* **73 E7** 40 51N 91 38W
Salem, *KY, U.S.A.* **96 C4** 37 16N 88 15W
Salem, *MA, U.S.A.* **78 B4** 42 31N 70 53W
Salem, *MD, U.S.A.* **77 B5** 38 32N 75 55W
Salem, *MO, U.S.A.* **82 D5** 37 39N 91 32W
Salem, *NC, U.S.A.* **90 C4** 35 42N 81 42W
Salem, *NH, U.S.A.* **86 D3** 42 45N 71 12W
Salem, *NJ, U.S.A.* **87 C1** 39 34N 75 28W
Salem, *NM, U.S.A.* **88 E3** 32 42N 107 13W
Salem, *NY, U.S.A.* **86 C1** 43 10N 73 20W
Salem, *NE, U.S.A.* **84 D10** 40 5N 95 43W
Salem, *Norfolk, U.S.A.* **115 B3** 36 47N 76 7W
Salem, *OH, U.S.A.* **92 C6** 40 54N 80 52W
Salem, *OR, U.S.A.* **94 C2** 44 56N 123 2W
Salem, *SD, U.S.A.* **91 G8** 43 44N 97 23W
Salem, *UT, U.S.A.* **100 C4** 40 3N 111 40W
Salem, *VA, U.S.A.* **102 D4** 37 18N 80 3W
Salem, *WV, U.S.A.* **102 B4** 39 17N 80 34W
Salem County ☆, *NJ, U.S.A.* **87 C1** 39 40N 75 20W
Salem Plateau, *MO, U.S.A.* **82 D5** 37 30N 91 30W
Saliaca, I., *Sinaloa, Mexico* **216 B2** 25 11N 108 20W
Salida, *CO, U.S.A.* **66 D5** 38 32N 106 0W
Salina, *AZ, U.S.A.* **62 A6** 36 1N 109 52W
Salina, *KS, U.S.A.* **74 C6** 38 50N 97 37W
Salina, *OK, U.S.A.* **93 B8** 36 18N 95 9W
Salina, *UT, U.S.A.* **100 E4** 38 58N 111 51W
Salina, Pta., *Sonora, Mexico* **212 B2** 31 4N 113 9W
Salina Cruz, *Oaxaca, Mexico* **221 H5** 16 10N 95 12W
Salinas, *Puerto Rico* **105 H16** 17 59N 66 18W
Salinas, *CA, U.S.A.* **64 G5** 36 40N 121 39W
Salinas →, *CA, U.S.A.* **64 G5** 36 45N 121 48W
Salinas, Sierra de, *CA, U.S.A.* **65 G5** 36 20N 121 20W
Salinas de Hidalgo, *San Luis Potosí, Mexico* **215 H3** 22 38N 101 43W
Salinas Pk., *NM, U.S.A.* **88 D4** 33 22N 106 35W
Salinas Pueblo Missions Nat. Monument ⌂, *U.S.A.* **88 C4** 34 6N 106 4W
Salinas Valley, *CA, U.S.A.* **65 G5** 36 15N 121 15W
Salinas Victoria, *Nuevo León, Mexico* **214 E4** 25 58N 100 48W
Saline, *LA, U.S.A.* **75 B3** 32 10N 92 59W
Saline, *MI, U.S.A.* **79 G8** 42 10N 83 47W
Saline →, *AR, U.S.A.* **63 E3** 33 10N 92 8W
Saline →, *AR, U.S.A.* **63 E2** 33 44N 93 58W
Saline →, *IL, U.S.A.* **71 F5** 37 35N 88 8W
Saline →, *KS, U.S.A.* **74 C6** 38 52N 97 30W
Saline Bayou →, *LA, U.S.A.* **75 C3** 31 45N 92 58W
Saline County ☆, *AR, U.S.A.* **63 D3** 34 34N 92 35W
Saline County ☆, *IL, U.S.A.* **71 F5** 37 45N 88 30W
Saline County ☆, *KS, U.S.A.* **74 C6** 38 45N 97 40W
Saline County ☆, *MO, U.S.A.* **82 B3** 39 10N 93 10W
Saline County ☆, *NE, U.S.A.* **84 D8** 40 30N 97 10W
Saline L., *LA, U.S.A.* **75 C3** 31 52N 92 54W
Saline Valley, *CA, U.S.A.* **65 G9** 36 50N 117 50W
Salineno, *TX, U.S.A.* **98 L8** 26 31N 99 7W
Salisbury, *N.B., Canada* **173 G4** 46 2N 65 3W
Salisbury, *CT, U.S.A.* **78 C1** 41 59N 73 25W
Salisbury, *MA, U.S.A.* **78 B4** 42 51N 70 49W
Salisbury, *MD, U.S.A.* **77 B5** 38 22N 75 36W
Salisbury, *MO, U.S.A.* **82 B4** 39 25N 92 48W
Salisbury, *NC, U.S.A.* **90 C5** 35 40N 80 29W
Salisbury, *NH, U.S.A.* **86 C3** 43 22N 71 42W
Salisbury, *PA, U.S.A.* **77 A1** 39 45N 79 5W
Salisbury, *VT, U.S.A.* **86 C1** 43 53N 73 6W
Salisbury Heights, *NH, U.S.A.* **86 C3** 43 24N 71 44W
Salisbury I., *Nunavut, Canada* **191 E10** 63 30N 77 0W
Salish Mts., *MT, U.S.A.* **83 B3** 48 30N 115 0W
Salitpa, *AL, U.S.A.* **60 E2** 31 37N 88 1W
Salix, *IA, U.S.A.* **73 C2** 42 19N 96 17W
Salkehatchie →, *SC, U.S.A.* **90 F5** 32 37N 80 53W
Salkum, *WA, U.S.A.* **101 D3** 46 32N 122 38W
Salladasburg, *PA, U.S.A.* **95 C5** 41 17N 77 14W
Salliq = Coral Harbour, *Nunavut, Canada* **191 E9** 64 8N 83 10W
Sallisaw, *OK, U.S.A.* **93 C9** 35 28N 94 47W
Salluit, *Qué., Canada* **175 A2** 62 14N 75 38W
Sally's Cove, *Nfld. & L., Canada* **174 C3** 49 44N 57 56W
Salmo, *B.C., Canada* **187 F17** 49 10N 117 20W
Salmon, *ID, U.S.A.* **70 D5** 45 11N 113 54W
Salmon →, *N.B., Canada* **173 G4** 46 6N 65 56W
Salmon →, *ID, U.S.A.* **70 D2** 45 51N 116 47W
Salmon Arm, *B.C., Canada* **187 E15** 50 40N 119 15W
Salmon Falls →, *NH, U.S.A.* **86 C4** 43 12N 70 50W
Salmon Falls Cr. →, *ID, U.S.A.* **70 G4** 42 43N 114 51W
Salmon Middle Fork →, *ID, U.S.A.* **70 D4** 45 18N 114 36W
Salmon Mt., *NH, U.S.A.* **86 A3** 45 14N 71 8W
Salmon Mts., *CA, U.S.A.* **64 B3** 41 0N 123 30W
Salmon Nat. Forest, *ID, U.S.A.* **70 D4** 45 15N 114 30W
Salmon River, *N.S., Canada* **173 J3** 44 3N 66 10W
Salmon River Mts., *ID, U.S.A.* **70 E3** 44 50N 115 30W
Salmon River Res., *NY, U.S.A.* **89 B5** 43 32N 75 55W
Salmon South Fork →, *ID, U.S.A.* **70 D3** 45 23N 115 31W
Salome, *AZ, U.S.A.* **62 D2** 33 47N 113 37W
Salsipuedes, Canal, *Baja Calif., Mexico* **210 E6** 28 38N 113 0W
Salsipuedes, Pta., *Baja Calif., Mexico* **210 B2** 31 59N 116 53W
Salt →, *AZ, U.S.A.* **62 D3** 33 23N 112 19W

Salt →, *KY, U.S.A.* **97 C7** 38 0N 85 57W
Salt →, *MO, U.S.A.* **82 B5** 39 28N 91 4W
Salt →, *WY, U.S.A.* **104 C1** 43 10N 111 4W
Salt Basin, *TX, U.S.A.* **98 F2** 31 42N 105 2W
Salt Cr. →, *IL, U.S.A.* **71 C4** 40 8N 89 50W
Salt Cr. →, *NM, U.S.A.* **88 D6** 33 30N 104 35W
Salt Cr. →, *OH, U.S.A.* **92 E3** 38 58N 83 1W
Salt Cr. →, *WY, U.S.A.* **104 C6** 43 41N 106 20W
Salt Draw →, *TX, U.S.A.* **98 F4** 31 19N 103 28W
Salt Flat, *TX, U.S.A.* **98 F2** 31 45N 105 5W
Salt Fork →, *TX, U.S.A.* **98 D7** 33 16N 100 0W
Salt Fork Arkansas →, *OK, U.S.A.* **93 B6** 36 36N 97 3W
Salt Fork L., *OH, U.S.A.* **92 C5** 40 3N 81 30W
Salt Fork Red →, *OK, U.S.A.* **93 D4** 34 27N 99 21W
Salt Fork State Park ⌂, *OH, U.S.A.* **92 C5** 40 7N 81 30W
Salt L., *HI, U.S.A.* **69 K14** 21 21N 157 55W
Salt L., *NM, U.S.A.* **88 C7** 34 5N 103 4W
Salt L., *NM, U.S.A.* **88 E7** 32 18N 104 0W
Salt Lake City, *UT, U.S.A.* **100 C4** 40 45N 111 53W
Salt Lake City International ✈ (SLC), *UT, U.S.A.* **100 C4** 40 47N 111 58W
Salt Lake County ☆, *UT, U.S.A.* **100 C3** 40 40N 112 0W
Salt Lick, *KY, U.S.A.* **97 B9** 38 7N 83 37W
Salt Marsh L., *UT, U.S.A.* **100 D2** 39 29N 113 55W
Salt Plains Nat. Wildlife Refuge ⌂, *OK, U.S.A.* **93 B5** 36 44N 98 13W
Salt River Canyon, *AZ, U.S.A.* **62 D5** 33 50N 110 40W
Salt River Indian Reservation, *AZ, U.S.A.* **62 D4** 33 35N 111 50W
Salt Springs, *FL, U.S.A.* **67 B7** 29 21N 81 44W
Saltair, *B.C., Canada* **186 G11** 48 57N 123 46W
Saltcoats, *Sask., Canada* **183 D9** 51 5N 102 15W
Saltery Bay, *B.C., Canada* **186 F10** 49 47N 124 10W
Saltillo, *Coahuila, Mexico* **214 E4** 25 25N 101 0W
Saltillo, *MS, U.S.A.* **81 B5** 34 23N 88 41W
Saltillo, *PA, U.S.A.* **95 D4** 40 13N 78 1W
Saltillo, *TN, U.S.A.* **96 E4** 35 23N 88 13W
Salto Chico, *Sinaloa, Mexico* **216 C4** 24 8N 106 59W
Salto de Agua, *Chiapas, Mexico* **222 B4** 17 37N 92 22W
Salto del Agua, *San Luis Potosí, Mexico* **215 H5** 22 36N 99 24W
Salton City, *CA, U.S.A.* **65 K11** 33 18N 115 57W
Salton Sea, *CA, U.S.A.* **65 K11** 33 15N 115 45W
Saltville, *VA, U.S.A.* **102 E3** 36 53N 81 46W
Saluda, *SC, U.S.A.* **90 D4** 34 0N 81 46W
Saluda, *VA, U.S.A.* **102 D8** 37 36N 76 36W
Saluda →, *SC, U.S.A.* **90 D4** 34 1N 81 4W
Saluda County ☆, *SC, U.S.A.* **90 D4** 34 0N 81 45W
Salus, *AR, U.S.A.* **63 C2** 35 44N 93 24W
Salvador, *Sask., Canada* **182 C2** 52 10N 109 32W
Salvador, L., *LA, U.S.A.* **75 E5** 29 43N 90 15W
Salvatierra, *Guanajuato, Mexico* **219 B7** 20 13N 100 53W
Salyersville, *KY, U.S.A.* **97 C9** 37 45N 83 4W
Sam Houston Nat. Forest, *TX, U.S.A.* **99 G12** 30 32N 95 29W
Sam Rayburn Res., *TX, U.S.A.* **99 F13** 31 4N 94 5W
Samahil, *Yucatán, Mexico* **223 B4** 20 53N 89 53W
Samalayuca, *Chihuahua, Mexico* **213 B9** 31 21N 106 28W
Samaria, *ID, U.S.A.* **70 G6** 42 7N 112 20W
Sambro, *N.S., Canada* **173 J6** 44 28N 63 36W
Samburg, *TN, U.S.A.* **96 D3** 36 23N 89 21W
Samish B., *WA, U.S.A.* **101 B3** 48 36N 122 31W
Sammamish, L., *Seattle, U.S.A.* **118 C5** 47 36N 122 5W
Samoset, *FL, U.S.A.* **67 D6** 27 28N 82 33W
Sampson County ☆, *NC, U.S.A.* **90 C7** 35 0N 78 30W
Samson, *AL, U.S.A.* **60 E4** 31 7N 86 3W
Samuel R. McKelvie Nat. Forest, *NE, U.S.A.* **84 B4** 42 40N 101 0W
San Acacia, *NM, U.S.A.* **88 C4** 34 15N 106 54W
San Agustín, *Jalisco, Mexico* **218 B5** 20 37N 102 41W
San Agustin, Plains of, *NM, U.S.A.* **88 D2** 33 45N 108 15W
San Alberto, *Coahuila, Mexico* **214 C3** 27 25N 101 17W
San Andreas, *CA, U.S.A.* **64 E6** 38 12N 120 41W
San Andrés, *Oaxaca, Mexico* **221 H3** 16 55N 97 41W
San Andrés, L., *Tamaulipas, Mexico* **215 H7** 22 40N 97 52W
San Andrés Ahuayucan, *Distrito Federal, Mexico* **225 C3** 19 13N 99 6W
San Andres Mts., *NM, U.S.A.* **88 E4** 33 0N 106 30W
San Andres Pk., *NM, U.S.A.* **88 E4** 32 41N 106 32W
San Andrés Totoltepec, *Distrito Federal, Mexico* **225 C2** 19 15N 99 10W
San Andrés Tuxtla, *Veracruz, Mexico* **221 F5** 18 27N 95 13W
San Angel, *Distrito Federal, Mexico* **225 B2** 19 20N 99 11W
San Angelo, *TX, U.S.A.* **98 F7** 31 28N 100 26W
San Anselmo, *CA, U.S.A.* **64 F4** 37 59N 122 34W
San Antonino Monte Verde, *Oaxaca, Mexico* **221 G3** 17 33N 97 44W
San Antonio, *Baja Calif. S., Mexico* **211 K8** 23 47N 110 5W
San Antonio, *Chihuahua, Mexico* **213 E12** 28 54N 103 51W
San Antonio, *NM, U.S.A.* **88 D4** 33 55N 106 52W
San Antonio, *TX, U.S.A.* **99 H9** 29 25N 98 29W
San Antonio →, *TX, U.S.A.* **99 J11** 28 30N 96 54W
San Antonio, L., *CA, U.S.A.* **65 H6** 35 48N 120 53W
San Antonio, Pta., *Baja Calif., Mexico* **210 D3** 29 45N 115 43W
San Antonio, Sa. de, *Sonora, Mexico* **212 C5** 30 5N 110 30W
San Antonio B., *TX, U.S.A.* **99 J11** 28 20N 96 45W
San Antonio de las Alazanas, *Coahuila, Mexico* **215 E4** 25 16N 100 36W
San Antonio de Trojes, *San Luis Potosí, Mexico* **215 H4** 22 43N 100 13W
San Antonio del Potrero, *Chihuahua, Mexico* **213 G10** 27 0N 105 45W
San Antonio del Salero, *Nuevo León, Mexico* **215 F4** 24 27N 100 15W
San Antonio International ✈ (SAT), *TX, U.S.A.* **99 H9** 29 32N 98 28W
San Antonio Missions Nat. Historical Park ⌂, *TX, U.S.A.* **99 H9** 29 23N 98 29W
San Antonio Mt., *TX, U.S.A.* **98 F2** 32 0N 105 30W
San Antonio Tecómitl, *Distrito Federal, Mexico* **225 C4** 19 14N 99 0W
San Ardo, *CA, U.S.A.* **65 G6** 36 1N 120 54W
San Augustín Tlaxiaca, *Hidalgo, Mexico* **219 B9** 20 7N 98 53W
San Augustine, *TX, U.S.A.* **99 F13** 31 32N 94 7W
San Augustine County ☆, *TX, U.S.A.* **99 F13** 31 30N 94 8W
San Bartolo, *Baja Calif. S., Mexico* **211 K9** 23 45N 109 51W
San Bartolo, *Oaxaca, Mexico* **221 H6** 16 27N 95 52W
San Bartolo, *San Luis Potosí, Mexico* **215 H4** 22 18N 100 4W
San Bartolo Morelos, *México, Mexico* **219 C8** 19 49N 99 41W
San Bartolo Soyaltepec, *Oaxaca, Mexico* **221 G3** 17 36N 97 16W
San Bartolomé Coatepec, *México, Mexico* **225 B2** 19 24N 99 18W
San Bartolomé Loxicha, *Oaxaca, Mexico* **221 J4** 15 58N 96 43W
San Bartolomé Xicomulco, *Distrito Federal, Mexico* **225 C3** 19 13N 99 5W
San Benito, *Sonora, Mexico* **212 D4** 29 45N 111 48W
San Benito, *TX, U.S.A.* **98 L10** 26 8N 97 38W
San Benito, Is., *Baja Calif. S., Mexico* **211 E3** 28 20N 115 31W
San Benito County ☆, *CA, U.S.A.* **65 G5** 36 30N 121 0W
San Bernadino Nat. Forest, *CA, U.S.A.* **65 J10** 34 10N 116 50W
San Bernard →, *TX, U.S.A.* **99 J12** 28 52N 95 27W
San Bernard Nat. Wildlife Refuge ⌂, *TX, U.S.A.* **99 J12** 28 51N 95 32W
San Bernardino, *CA, U.S.A.* **65 J9** 34 7N 117 19W
San Bernardino County ☆, *CA, U.S.A.* **65 J11** 34 45N 116 0W
San Bernardino de Milpillas Chico, *Durango, Mexico* **216 D5** 23 23N 105 10W
San Bernardino Mts., *CA, U.S.A.* **65 J10** 34 10N 116 45W
San Bernardo, *Durango, Mexico* **216 B5** 26 0N 105 33W
San Bernardo, *Sonora, Mexico* **212 F7** 27 24N 108 50W
San Blas, *Coahuila, Mexico* **214 C3** 27 25N 101 40W
San Blas, *Nayarit, Mexico* **216 F5** 21 31N 105 16W
San Blas, *Sinaloa, Mexico* **216 A2** 26 5N 108 46W
San Blas, C., *FL, U.S.A.* **67 B3** 29 40N 85 21W
San Borja, *Baja Calif., Mexico* **210 E5** 28 47N 113 55W
San Borja, Sa. de, *Baja Calif., Mexico* **210 E5** 28 42N 113 47W
San Bruno, *Baja Calif. S., Mexico* **211 F6** 27 11N 112 12W
San Bruno, *CA, U.S.A.* **64 F4** 37 38N 122 25W
San Bruno, Pt., *San Francisco, U.S.A.* **118 C2** 37 39N 122 22W
San Bruno Mt., *San Francisco, U.S.A.* **118 B2** 37 41N 122 26W
San Buenaventura = Ventura, *CA, U.S.A.* **65 J7** 34 17N 119 18W
San Buenaventura, *Baja Calif. S., Mexico* **211 G7** 26 38N 111 52W
San Buenaventura, *Coahuila, Mexico* **214 C3** 27 5N 101 32W
San Carlos, *Baja Calif., Mexico* **210 D3** 29 39N 115 29W
San Carlos, *Baja Calif. S., Mexico* **211 J6** 24 47N 112 7W
San Carlos, *Coahuila, Mexico* **214 A4** 29 1N 100 51W
San Carlos, *Sonora, Mexico* **212 F4** 27 59N 111 4W
San Carlos, *Tamaulipas, Mexico* **215 F6** 24 36N 98 55W
San Carlos, *AZ, U.S.A.* **62 D5** 33 21N 110 27W
San Carlos, *San Diego, U.S.A.* **117 B2** 32 48N 117 1W
San Carlos, B., *Baja Calif. S., Mexico* **211 F6** 27 53N 112 46W
San Carlos, Cerro, *Sonora, Mexico* **212 B3** 31 17N 112 33W
San Carlos, Pta., *Baja Calif., Mexico* **210 D3** 29 38N 115 31W
San Carlos Indian Reservation, *AZ, U.S.A.* **62 D6** 33 25N 110 0W
San Carlos L., *AZ, U.S.A.* **62 D5** 33 11N 110 32W
San Carlos Park, *FL, U.S.A.* **67 E7** 26 28N 81 48W
San Carlos Yautepec, *Oaxaca, Mexico* **221 H4** 16 31N 96 6W
San Cayetano, *Nayarit, Mexico* **216 E5** 22 27N 105 41W
San Ciro de Acosta, *San Luis Potosí, Mexico* **215 J5** 21 39N 99 49W
San Clara, *Man., Canada* **183 D10** 51 29N 101 26W
San Clemente, *CA, U.S.A.* **65 K9** 33 26N 117 37W
San Clemente I., *CA, U.S.A.* **65 L8** 32 53N 118 29W
San Clemente Island, *CA, U.S.A.* **65 L8** 32 54N 118 30W
San Cristobal, *NM, U.S.A.* **88 A5** 36 36N 105 39W
San Cristóbal, B., *Baja Calif. S., Mexico* **211 F4** 27 23N 114 38W
San Cristóbal de la Barranca, *Jalisco, Mexico* **218 A4** 21 3N 103 26W
San Cristóbal de las Casas, *Chiapas, Mexico* **222 C4** 16 45N 92 38W
San Cristóbal Texcalucan, *México, Mexico* **225 B1** 19 25N 99 21W
San Cristobal Wash →, *AZ, U.S.A.* **62 E2** 32 45N 113 45W
San Diego, *CA, U.S.A.* **65 L9** 32 42N 117 9W
San Diego, *TX, U.S.A.* **99 K9** 27 46N 98 14W
San Diego →, *Michoacan, Mexico* **219 D6** 18 55N 101 11W
San Diego, I., *Baja Calif. S., Mexico* **211 H8** 25 11N 110 42W
San Diego, Sa., *Sonora, Mexico* **212 C6** 30 30N 109 5W
San Diego Bay, *San Diego, U.S.A.* **117 C2** 32 39N 117 8W
San Diego County ☆, *CA, U.S.A.* **65 K10** 33 0N 117 15W
San Diego de Alcalá, *Chihuahua, Mexico* **213 E10** 28 35N 105 34W
San Diego de Alcalá, *Durango, Mexico* **216 C5** 24 28N 105 12W
San Diego de Alejandría, *Jalisco, Mexico* **218 B5** 20 59N 102 2W
San Diego de la Unión, *Guanajuato, Mexico* **219 A7** 21 28N 100 52W
San Diego International ✈ (SAN), *CA, U.S.A.* **65 L9** 32 44N 117 11W
San Diego la Mesa Tochimiltzingo, *Puebla, Mexico* **221 F2** 18 49N 98 19W
San Dimas, *Durango, Mexico* **216 C5** 24 8N 105 58W
San Eduardo, *Chihuahua, Mexico* **213 D10** 29 42N 105 14W
San Elizario, *TX, U.S.A.* **98 F1** 31 35N 106 16W
San Emetario, *Sonora, Mexico* **212 B3** 31 40N 112 51W
San Estaban, *Coahuila, Mexico* **214 A2** 29 29N 102 3W
San Esteban, I., *Sonora, Mexico* **212 E3** 28 42N 112 36W
San Evaristo, *Baja Calif. S., Mexico* **211 J8** 24 55N 110 45W
San Felipe, *Baja Calif., Mexico* **210 B4** 31 1N 114 52W
San Felipe, *Guanajuato, Mexico* **219 A6** 21 29N 101 13W
San Felipe, *Yucatán, Mexico* **223 A5** 21 34N 88 14W
San Felipe →, *CA, U.S.A.* **65 K11** 33 10N 115 49W
San Felipe, B., *Baja Calif., Mexico* **210 C4** 30 58N 114 45W
San Felipe, Parque Natural ⌂, *Yucatán, Mexico* **223 A5** 21 27N 88 39W
San Felipe, Sa., *Baja Calif., Mexico* **210 C3** 30 55N 115 10W
San Felipe Aztatán, *Nayarit, Mexico* **216 E5** 22 23N 105 24W
San Felipe de Jesús, *Sonora, Mexico* **212 D5** 29 52N 110 15W
San Felipe del Progreso, *México, Mexico* **219 C8** 19 41N 99 57W
San Felipe Indian Reservation, *NM, U.S.A.* **88 B4** 35 26N 106 31W
San Felipe Nuevo Mercurio, *Zacatecas, Mexico* **217 C8** 24 14N 102 8W
San Felipe Orizatlán, *Hidalgo, Mexico* **219 A9** 21 11N 98 37W
San Felipe Pueblo, *NM, U.S.A.* **88 B4** 35 26N 106 27W
San Fermín, *Durango, Mexico* **217 A6** 26 20N 104 49W
San Fernando, *Chiapas, Mexico* **222 C3** 16 52N 93 13W
San Fernando, *Tamaulipas, Mexico* **215 F6** 24 51N 98 10W
San Fernando, *CA, U.S.A.* **65 J8** 34 17N 118 26W
San Fernando →, *Baja Calif., Mexico* **210 D3** 29 45N 115 40W
San Fernando Valley, *Los Angeles, U.S.A.* **111 A1** 34 10N 118 31W
San Fidel, *NM, U.S.A.* **88 B3** 35 5N 107 36W
San Francisco, *Durango, Mexico* **216 B5** 23 58N 105 47W
San Francisco, *Guadalajara, Mexico* **224 B2** 20 33N 103 10W
San Francisco, *Nuevo León, Mexico* **215 F5** 24 42N 99 40W
San Francisco, *Yucatán, Mexico* **223 B5** 20 42N 88 29W
San Francisco, *CA, U.S.A.* **64 F4** 37 46N 122 23W
San Francisco →, *AZ, U.S.A.* **62 E6** 32 59N 109 22W
San Francisco, Barra, *Oaxaca, Mexico* **221 H6** 16 12N 94 55W
San Francisco, I., *Baja Calif. S., Mexico* **211 J8** 24 41N 110 35W
San Francisco, Sa., *Baja Calif. S., Mexico* **211 F5** 27 43N 113 10W
San Francisco B., *CA, U.S.A.* **64 F4** 37 39N 122 14W
San Francisco Chimalpa, *México, Mexico* **225 B2** 19 26N 99 20W
San Francisco County ☆, *CA, U.S.A.* **64 F4** 37 47N 122 25W
San Francisco Cr. →, *TX, U.S.A.* **98 H5** 29 53N 102 19W
San Francisco Culhuacán, *Distrito Federal, Mexico* **225 C3** 19 19N 99 8W
San Francisco de Asís, *Durango, Mexico* **217 B6** 25 29N 104 51W
San Francisco de Borja, *Chihuahua, Mexico* **213 F9** 27 53N 106 41W
San Francisco de Conchos, *Chihuahua, Mexico* **213 F10** 27 35N 105 19W
San Francisco de los Romo, *Aguascalientes, Mexico* **217 E8** 22 9N 102 16W
San Francisco del Barrial, *Coahuila, Mexico* **215 E2** 25 11N 102 8W
San Francisco del Oro, *Chihuahua, Mexico* **213 G10** 26 52N 105 51W
San Francisco del Rincón, *Guanajuato, Mexico* **218 A6** 21 1N 101 51W
San Francisco International ✈ (SFO), *CA, U.S.A.* **64 F4** 37 37N 122 22W
San Francisco Ixhuatán, *Oaxaca, Mexico* **221 H6** 16 21N 94 29W
San Francisco Ixtacamatitián, *Puebla, Mexico* **220 E3** 19 38N 97 49W
San Francisco Logueche, *Oaxaca, Mexico* **221 H4** 16 21N 96 23W
San Francisco Mts., *AZ, U.S.A.* **62 B4** 35 15N 111 45W
San Francisco Mts., *NM, U.S.A.* **88 D2** 33 45N 108 50W
San Francisco Pujiltic, *Chiapas, Mexico* **222 C4** 16 17N 92 27W
San Francisco Tesistán, *Jalisco, Mexico* **218 B4** 20 47N 103 29W
San Francisco Tlalnepantla, *Distrito Federal, Mexico* **225 C3** 19 12N 99 7W
San Francisco Tlaltenco, *Distrito Federal, Mexico* **225 C4** 19 18N 99 0W
San Francisquito, *Baja Calif., Mexico* **210 E6** 28 25N 112 52W
San Francisquito, Pta., *Baja Calif., Mexico* **210 E6** 28 26N 112 51W
San Gabriel, *Los Angeles, U.S.A.* **111 B4** 34 5N 118 5W
San Gabriel →, *TX, U.S.A.* **99 G10** 30 46N 97 1W
San Gabriel Chilac, *Puebla, Mexico* **221 F3** 18 19N 97 21W
San Gabriel Mts., *CA, U.S.A.* **65 J9** 34 17N 117 38W
San German, *Puerto Rico* **105 G15** 18 4N 67 4W
San Gorgonio Mt., *CA, U.S.A.* **65 J10** 34 6N 116 50W
San Gregorio, *Baja Calif. S., Mexico* **211 F5** 27 40N 113 1W
San Gregorio →, *Durango, Mexico* **216 C4** 24 40N 106 28W
San Gregorio Atlapulco, *Distrito Federal, Mexico* **225 C3** 19 16N 99 3W
San Hipólito, B., *Baja Calif. S., Mexico* **211 G5** 26 57N 113 55W
San Ignacio, *Baja Calif. S., Mexico* **211 F6** 27 27N 112 51W
San Ignacio, *Sinaloa, Mexico* **216 B2** 25 31N 108 53W
San Ignacio, *Sinaloa, Mexico* **216 D4** 23 55N 106 25W
San Ignacio, *Sonora, Mexico* **212 F5** 27 25N 110 16W
San Ignacio, *Sonora, Mexico* **212 C5** 30 42N 110 55W
San Ignacio →, *Sonora, Mexico* **212 D3** 29 53N 112 40W
San Ignacio, I. de, *Sinaloa, Mexico* **216 B2** 25 26N 108 55W
San Ignacio, L., *Baja Calif. S., Mexico* **211 G5** 26 54N 113 13W
San Ildefonso Indian Reservation, *NM, U.S.A.* **88 B4** 35 53N 106 8W
San Isabel Nat. Forest, *CO, U.S.A.* **66 E5** 38 0N 105 2W
San Isidro, *Baja Calif. S., Mexico* **211 G6** 26 12N 112 2W
San Isidro, *Campeche, Mexico* **223 D2** 18 38N 91 4W
San Isidro, *Chiapas, Mexico* **222 D3** 15 44N 93 21W
San Isidro, *Chihuahua, Mexico* **213 B9** 31 33N 106 18W
San Isidro, *Guadalajara, Mexico* **224 A1** 20 45N 103 21W
San Isidro, *Sonora, Mexico* **212 C3** 30 48N 112 22W
San Isidro, *TX, U.S.A.* **98 L9** 26 43N 98 27W
San Isidro →, *Baja Calif., Mexico* **210 B3** 31 17N 116 22W
San Jacinto, *Baja Calif. S., Mexico* **211 H7** 25 35N 111 34W
San Jacinto, *México, Mexico* **225 B2** 19 21N 99 19W
San Jacinto, *CA, U.S.A.* **65 K10** 33 47N 116 57W
San Jacinto County ☆, *TX, U.S.A.* **99 G12** 30 36N 95 8W
San Jacinto Mts., *CA, U.S.A.* **65 K10** 33 45N 116 40W
San Javier, *Chiapas, Mexico* **222 C5** 16 48N 91 6W
San Javier, *Monterrey, Mexico* **224 A2** 25 53N 100 15W
San Javier, *Sonora, Mexico* **212 E6** 28 35N 109 45W
San Javier →, *Baja Calif. S., Mexico* **211 H6** 25 28N 112 4W
San Jeronimito, *Guerrero, Mexico* **219 E6** 17 33N 101 20W
San Jerónimo, *Durango, Mexico* **216 D5** 23 49N 105 33W
San Jerónimo, *Guerrero, Mexico* **219 E7** 17 8N 100 28W
San Jerónimo, *Zacatecas, Mexico* **217 E8** 22 41N 102 29W
San Jerónimo Lidice, *Distrito Federal, Mexico* **225 C2** 19 19N 99 14W
San Jerónimo Taviche, *Oaxaca, Mexico* **221 H4** 16 44N 96 35W
San Jerónimo Xayacaylán, *Puebla, Mexico* **221 F3** 18 14N 97 55W
San Joaquín, *Querétaro, Mexico* **219 B8** 20 35N 99 54W
San Joaquin, *CA, U.S.A.* **65 G6** 36 36N 120 11W
San Joaquin →, *CA, U.S.A.* **64 E5** 38 4N 121 51W
San Joaquin County ☆, *CA, U.S.A.* **64 F5** 37 50N 121 15W
San Joaquin Valley, *CA, U.S.A.* **64 F6** 37 20N 121 0W
San Jon, *NM, U.S.A.* **88 B7** 35 6N 103 20W
San Jorge, B., *Sonora, Mexico* **212 B2** 31 10N 113 17W
San Jorge, I., *Sonora, Mexico* **212 C2** 30 57N 113 15W
San José, *Campeche, Mexico* **223 D2** 18 27N 91 28W
San Jose, *N. Marianas* **105 c** 14 58N 145 37W
San Jose, *CA, U.S.A.* **64 F5** 37 20N 121 53W
San Jose, *IL, U.S.A.* **71 C4** 40 18N 89 36W
San Jose →, *NM, U.S.A.* **88 C4** 34 25N 106 45W
San José, I., *Baja Calif. S., Mexico* **211 H8** 25 0N 110 38W
San José, Pta., *Baja Calif., Mexico* **210 B2** 31 28N 116 37W
San José Acateno, *Puebla, Mexico* **220 D3** 20 8N 97 12W
San José Baqueachi, *Chihuahua, Mexico* **213 F8** 27 38N 107 1W
San José Carbonerillas, *Zacatecas, Mexico* **217 C9** 24 29N 101 27W
San José Chiltepec, *Oaxaca, Mexico* **221 G4** 17 57N 96 11W
San José de Aura, *Coahuila, Mexico* **214 C3** 27 36N 101 21W
San José de Bavicora, *Chihuahua, Mexico* **213 D8** 29 15N 107 46W
San José de Carranza, *Coahuila, Mexico* **214 C1** 27 49N 103 35W
San José de Comondú, *Baja Calif. S., Mexico* **211 G7** 26 3N 111 50W
San José de Gracia, *Aguascalientes, Mexico* **217 E8** 22 8N 102 23W
San José de Gracia, *Baja Calif. S., Mexico* **211 G6** 26 34N 112 45W
San José de Guajademi, *Baja Calif. S., Mexico* **211 G6** 26 24N 112 9W
San José de la Boca, *Durango, Mexico* **216 B5** 25 20N 105 47W
San José de la Brecha, *Sinaloa, Mexico* **216 B2** 25 21N 108 25W
San José de la Noria, *Baja Calif. S., Mexico* **211 H7** 25 24N 111 6W
San José de Moradillos, *Sonora, Mexico* **212 E5** 28 36N 110 30W
San José del Cabo, *Baja Calif. S., Mexico* **211 K9** 23 3N 109 41W
San José del Cabo, B., *Baja Calif. S., Mexico* **211 L9** 22 56N 109 42W
San José del Prisco, Sa., *Chihuahua, Mexico* **213 C10** 30 50N 105 50W
San José El Barranco, *Sinaloa, Mexico* **216 B3** 25 41N 107 9W
San José Guacayvo, *Chihuahua, Mexico* **213 F8** 27 43N 107 52W
San Jose I., *TX, U.S.A.* **99 K11** 27 59N 96 59W
San Jose International ✈ (SJC), *CA, U.S.A.* **64 F5** 37 22N 121 55W
San José Iturbide, *Guanajuato, Mexico* **219 B7** 21 0N 100 23W
San José Miahuatlán, *Puebla, Mexico* **221 F3** 18 17N 97 17W
San José Río Hondo, *México, Mexico* **225 B2** 19 26N 99 14W
San José Río Manso, *Oaxaca, Mexico* **221 G5** 17 40N 95 54W
San José Tenango, *Oaxaca, Mexico* **221 F4** 18 8N 96 43W
San José y Anexas, *Chihuahua, Mexico* **213 E8** 28 52N 107 15W
San Juan, *Coahuila, Mexico* **214 D3** 27 0N 101 52W
San Juan, *Oaxaca, Mexico* **221 G2** 17 52N 98 16W
San Juan, *Sonora, Mexico* **212 C3** 30 48N 112 9W
San Juan, *Puerto Rico* **105 G16** 18 28N 66 7W
San Juan →, *Coahuila, Mexico* **214 C3** 27 51N 101 7W
San Juan →, *CO, U.S.A.* **66 E3** 37 1N 107 28W
San Juan →, *UT, U.S.A.* **100 F5** 37 16N 110 26W
San Juan, Pta., *Veracruz, Mexico* **221 F6** 18 17N 94 37W
San Juan, Sa., *Sonora, Mexico* **212 B4** 31 1N 111 35W
San Juan Basin, *NM, U.S.A.* **88 A2** 36 20N 108 10W
San Juan Bautista = Villahermosa, *Tabasco, Mexico* **222 B4** 17 59N 92 55W
San Juan Bautista, *Campeche, Mexico* **223 C4** 19 53N 89 59W
San Juan Bautista, *Oaxaca, Mexico* **221 H2** 16 32N 98 19W
San Juan Bautista, *CA, U.S.A.* **64 G5** 36 51N 121 32W
San Juan Bautista, B., *Baja Calif. S., Mexico* **211 E6** 28 1N 112 49W
San Juan Bautista Cuicatlán, *Oaxaca, Mexico* **221 G4** 17 48N 96 58W
San Juan Cacahuatepec, *Oaxaca, Mexico* **221 H2** 16 37N 98 7W
San Juan Cancuc, *Chiapas, Mexico* **222 C4** 16 53N 92 22W
San Juan Capistrano, *CA, U.S.A.* **65 K9** 33 30N 117 40W
San Juan Chiquihuitlán, *Oaxaca, Mexico* **221 G4** 17 57N 96 44W
San Juan County ☆, *CO, U.S.A.* **66 E3** 37 50N 107 40W
San Juan County ☆, *NM, U.S.A.* **88 A2** 36 30N 108 30W
San Juan County ☆, *UT, U.S.A.* **100 F6** 38 0N 109 30W
San Juan County ☆, *WA, U.S.A.* **101 B2** 48 32N 123 5W
San Juan Cr. →, *CA, U.S.A.* **65 H6** 35 40N 120 22W
San Juan de Abajo, *Nayarit, Mexico* **216 G5** 20 49N 105 12W
San Juan de Ahrocados, Lago, *Zacatecas, Mexico* **217 C8** 24 2N 102 17W
San Juan de Aragón, *Distrito Federal, Mexico* **225 B3** 19 28N 99 4W
San Juan de Aragón, Parque, *Distrito Federal, Mexico* **225 B3** 19 27N 99 4W
San Juan de Guadelupe, *Durango, Mexico* **217 C8** 24 38N 102 44W
San Juan de la Costa, *Baja Calif. S., Mexico* **211 J8** 24 20N 110 41W
San Juan de los Charcos, *Zacatecas, Mexico* **217 B8** 25 3N 102 36W
San Juan de los Lagos, *Jalisco, Mexico* **218 A5** 21 15N 102 18W
San Juan de Sabinas, *Coahuila, Mexico* **214 C3** 27 55N 101 18W
San Juan de Villa Hermosa = Villahermosa, *Tabasco, Mexico* **222 B4** 17 59N 92 55W
San Juan del Río, *Durango, Mexico* **217 C6** 24 47N 104 27W
San Juan del Río, *Querétaro, Mexico* **219 B8** 20 23N 100 0W
San Juan Evangelista, *Veracruz, Mexico* **221 G5** 17 54N 95 8W
San Juan Guichicovi, *Oaxaca, Mexico* **221 H5** 16 58N 95 6W
San Juan I., *WA, U.S.A.* **101 B2** 48 32N 123 5W
San Juan Indian Reservation, *NM, U.S.A.* **88 A4** 36 3N 106 4W
San Juan Island Nat. Historical Park ⌂, *WA, U.S.A.* **101 B2** 48 35N 123 8W
San Juan Ixtacala, *México, Mexico* **225 A2** 19 31N 99 10W
San Juan Ixtayopan, *Distrito Federal, Mexico* **225 C4** 19 15N 99 0W
San Juan Lalana, *Oaxaca, Mexico* **221 G5** 17 28N 95 54W
San Juan Luis Munoz Marin International ✈ (SJU), *Puerto Rico* **105 G16** 18 26N 66 0W
San Juan Mazatlán, *Oaxaca, Mexico* **221 G5** 17 2N 95 27W
San Juan Mts., *CO, U.S.A.* **66 E4** 37 30N 107 0W
San Juan Nat. Forest, *CO, U.S.A.* **66 E3** 37 30N 108 0W
San Juan Pueblo, *NM, U.S.A.* **88 A4** 36 3N 106 4W
San Juan Quiotepec, *Oaxaca, Mexico* **221 G4** 17 36N 96 35W
San Juan Teita, *Oaxaca, Mexico* **221 G3** 17 6N 97 25W
San Juan Tepenahuac, *Distrito Federal, Mexico* **225 C4** 19 11N 98 59W
San Juan Toltotepec, *México, Mexico* **225 B2** 19 28N 99 15W
San Juan Volador, *Veracruz, Mexico* **221 F6** 18 16N 94 37W
San Juanico, *Baja Calif. S., Mexico* **211 G6** 26 16N 112 29W
San Juanico, B., *Baja Calif. S., Mexico* **211 G7** 26 26N 111 25W
San Juanico, B., *Baja Calif. S., Mexico* **211 G6** 26 14N 112 27W
San Juanito, *Chihuahua, Mexico* **213 F8** 27 58N 107 36W
San Juanito, I., *Nayarit, Mexico* **216 F4** 21 43N 106 38W
San Julian, *Jalisco, Mexico* **218 A5** 21 1N 102 10W
San Leandro, *CA, U.S.A.* **64 F4** 37 42N 122 9W
San Leandro Bay, *San Francisco, U.S.A.* **118 B3** 37 45N 122 13W
San Lorenzo, *Chihuahua, Mexico* **213 D8** 29 49N 107 6W
San Lorenzo, *San Luis Potosí, Mexico* **215 H4** 22 33N 100 40W
San Lorenzo, *NM, U.S.A.* **88 E3** 32 49N 107 55W
San Lorenzo, *San Francisco, U.S.A.* **118 B4** 37 40N 122 7W
San Lorenzo →, *Mexico* **215 E6** 25 7N 98 32W
San Lorenzo, I., *Baja Calif., Mexico* **210 E6** 28 38N 112 51W
San Lorenzo Acopilco, *México, Mexico* **225 C1** 19 20N 99 21W
San Lorenzo Texmelucan, *Oaxaca, Mexico* **221 H3** 16 36N 97 11W

San Lorenzo Tezonco, *Distrito Federal, Mexico* **225 C3** 19 19N 99 3W
San Lorenzo Tlacoyucan, *Distrito Federal, Mexico* **225 C3** 19 11N 99 2W
San Lucas = Cabo San Lucas, *Baja Calif. S., Mexico* **211 L9** 22 53N 109 54W
San Lucas, *Michoacan, Mexico* . . . **219 D7** 18 36N 100 48W
San Lucas, *CA, U.S.A.* **65 G5** 36 8N 121 1W
San Lucas, C., *Baja Calif. S., Mexico* **211 L9** 22 52N 109 53W
San Luis, *Coahuila, Mexico* **214 E2** 25 45N 102 20W
San Luis, *AZ, U.S.A.* **62 E1** 32 29N 114 47W
San Luis, *CO, U.S.A.* **66 E5** 37 12N 105 25W
San Luis, I., *Baja Calif., Mexico* . . **210 D4** 29 58N 114 26W
San Luis Acatlán, *Guerrero, Mexico* **219 F9** 16 48N 98 55W
San Luis Amatlán, *Oaxaca, Mexico* **221 H4** 16 25N 96 30W
San Luis Cr. ➛, *CO, U.S.A.* **66 E5** 37 42N 105 44W
San Luis de la Loma, *Guerrero, Mexico* **219 E7** 17 18N 100 55W
San Luis de la Paz, *Guanajuato, Mexico* **219 A7** 21 18N 100 31W
San Luis del Cordero, *Durango, Mexico* **217 B6** 25 26N 104 18W
San Luis Gonzaga, *Baja Calif., Mexico* **210 D4** 29 51N 114 25W
San Luis Gonzaga, *Baja Calif. S., Mexico* **211 J7** 24 55N 111 20W
San Luis Gonzaga, B., *Baja Calif., Mexico* **210 D4** 29 48N 114 22W
San Luis Gonzaga, I., *Baja Calif., Mexico* **210 D4** 29 52N 114 23W
San Luis Obispo, *CA, U.S.A.* **65 H6** 35 17N 120 40W
San Luis Obispo County ☆, *CA, U.S.A.* **65 H6** 35 30N 120 30W
San Luis Peak, *CO, U.S.A.* **66 E4** 37 59N 106 56W
San Luis Potosí, *San Luis Potosí, Mexico* **215 H4** 22 9N 100 59W
San Luis Potosí □, *Mexico* **215 H4** 23 0N 101 0W
San Luis Res., *CA, U.S.A.* **64 F5** 37 4N 121 5W
San Luis Rey ➛, *CA, U.S.A.* **65 K9** 33 12N 117 24W
San Luis Río Colorado, *Sonora, Mexico* **212 A1** 32 29N 114 48W
San Luis San Pedro, *Guerrero, Mexico* **219 E7** 17 18N 100 53W
San Luis Tlaxialtemalco, *Distrito Federal, Mexico* **225 C3** 19 16N 99 1W
San Luis Valley, *CO, U.S.A.* **66 E5** 37 45N 105 50W
San Luisito, *Sonora, Mexico* **212 B3** 31 18N 112 28W
San Manuel, *AZ, U.S.A.* **62 E5** 32 36N 110 38W
San Marcos, *Guerrero, Mexico* . . . **219 F8** 16 48N 99 21W
San Marcos, *Jalisco, Mexico* **218 B4** 20 17N 103 32W
San Marcos, *Jalisco, Mexico* **218 B3** 20 47N 104 11W
San Marcos, *CA, U.S.A.* **65 K9** 33 9N 117 10W
San Marcos, *TX, U.S.A.* **99 H10** 29 53N 97 56W
San Marcos, I., *Baja Calif. S., Mexico* **211 F6** 27 13N 112 6W
San Marcos y Pinos, Sa., *Coahuila, Mexico* **214 D3** 26 28N 101 47W
San Marino, *Los Angeles, U.S.A.* . . **111 B4** 34 7N 118 5W
San Martín, *Zacatecas, Mexico* . . . **217 E9** 22 14N 101 22W
San Martin, *CA, U.S.A.* **64 F5** 37 5N 121 37W
San Martin, C., *CA, U.S.A.* **65 H5** 35 53N 121 28W
San Martín, I., *Baja Calif., Mexico* **210 C2** 30 28N 116 8W
San Martín Chalchicuautla, *San Luis Potosí, Mexico* **215 J6** 21 23N 98 39W
San Martín de Bolaños, *Jalisco, Mexico* **217 F7** 21 29N 103 58W
San Martín de Hidalgo, *Jalisco, Mexico* **218 B4** 20 27N 103 57W
San Martín Texmelucan, *Puebla, Mexico* **220 E2** 19 17N 98 26W
San Mateo, *CA, U.S.A.* **64 F4** 37 34N 122 19W
San Mateo, *NM, U.S.A.* **88 B3** 35 20N 107 39W
San Mateo County ☆, *CA, U.S.A.* **64 F4** 37 30N 122 25W
San Mateo del Mar, *Oaxaca, Mexico* **221 H6** 16 12N 95 0W
San Mateo Mts., *NM, U.S.A.* **88 D3** 33 45N 107 25W
San Mateo Tlaltenango, *Distrito Federal, Mexico* **225 B2** 19 20N 99 16W
San Mateo Xalpa, *Distrito Federal, Mexico* **225 C3** 19 14N 99 8W
San Miguel, *Campeche, Mexico* . . **223 E3** 17 54N 90 31W
San Miguel, *Chihuahua, Mexico* . . **213 E11** 28 18N 104 17W
San Miguel, *Chihuahua, Mexico* . . **213 E8** 28 15N 107 23W
San Miguel, *Coahuila, Mexico* . . . **214 B2** 28 37N 102 57W
San Miguel, *Jalisco, Mexico* **218 C3** 19 39N 104 45W
San Miguel, *Monterrey, Mexico* . . . **224 B2** 25 43N 100 10W
San Miguel, *CA, U.S.A.* **65 H6** 35 45N 120 42W
San Miguel, *NM, U.S.A.* **88 E4** 32 9N 106 44W
San Miguel ➛, *Chihuahua, Mexico* **213 G8** 26 55N 107 56W
San Miguel ➛, *CO, U.S.A.* **66 D2** 38 23N 108 48W
San Miguel, Cabo, *Baja Calif. S., Mexico* **211 E6** 28 12N 112 47W
San Miguel, Pta., *Baja Calif., Mexico* **210 B2** 31 53N 116 46W
San Miguel Ahuehuetitlán, *Oaxaca, Mexico* **221 G2** 17 37N 98 21W
San Miguel Ajusco, *Distrito Federal, Mexico* **225 C2** 19 13N 99 11W
San Miguel Chicohua, *Oaxaca, Mexico* **221 G3** 17 38N 97 10W
San Miguel County ☆, *CO, U.S.A.* **66 E2** 38 0N 108 30W
San Miguel County ☆, *NM, U.S.A.* **88 B6** 35 30N 105 0W
San Miguel de Allende, *Guanajuato, Mexico* **219 B7** 20 55N 100 45W
San Miguel de Cruces, *Durango, Mexico* **216 C5** 24 25N 105 53W
San Miguel de Horcasitas, *Sonora, Mexico* **212 D5** 29 30N 110 43W
San Miguel de los Garza, *Monterrey, Mexico* **224 B1** 25 50N 100 24W
San Miguel de Temoaya, *Durango, Mexico* **217 D6** 23 18N 104 30W
San Miguel del Cantil, *Durango, Mexico* **216 C4** 24 56N 106 16W
San Miguel del Puerto, *Oaxaca, Mexico* **221 J4** 15 55N 96 10W
San Miguel el Alto, *Jalisco, Mexico* **218 A5** 21 1N 102 21W
San Miguel Huaistita, *Jalisco, Mexico* **217 E6** 22 3N 104 19W
San Miguel I., *CA, U.S.A.* **65 J6** 34 2N 120 23W
San Miguel Suchixtepec, *Oaxaca, Mexico* **221 H4** 16 5N 96 28W
San Miguel Talea, *Oaxaca, Mexico* **221 G4** 17 12N 96 14W
San Miguel Topilejo, *Distrito Federal, Mexico* **225 C3** 19 12N 99 8W
San Miguel Totolapán, *Guerrero, Mexico* **219 D7** 18 8N 100 23W
San Miguel Xicalco, *Distrito Federal, Mexico* **225 C3** 19 15N 99 10W
San Miguelito, *Sonora, Mexico* . . . **212 C7** 30 32N 108 55W
San Nicolás, *Sonora, Mexico* **212 E6** 28 25N 109 10W
San Nicolás, *Tamaulipas, Mexico* . **215 F6** 24 41N 98 48W
San Nicolás de los Garza, *Nuevo León, Mexico* **214 E4** 25 45N 100 18W
San Nicolas I., *CA, U.S.A.* **65 K7** 33 15N 119 30W
San Nicolas Island, *CA, U.S.A.* . . . **65 K7** 33 15N 119 30W
San Nicolás Tolentino, *San Luis Potosí, Mexico* **215 H4** 22 16N 100 34W
San Nicolás Totolapan, *Distrito Federal, Mexico* **225 C2** 19 18N 99 15W
San Pablo, *CA, U.S.A.* **64 F4** 37 58N 122 21W
San Pablo B., *CA, U.S.A.* **64 E4** 38 5N 122 20W
San Pablo Chimalpa, *Distrito Federal, Mexico* **225 B2** 19 21N 99 19W
San Pablo Etla, *Oaxaca, Mexico* . . **221 G4** 17 8N 96 46W
San Pablo Huitzo, *Oaxaca, Mexico* **221 G4** 17 15N 96 52W
San Pablo Huixtepec, *Oaxaca, Mexico* **221 H4** 16 50N 96 46W
San Pablo Oztotepec, *Distrito Federal, Mexico* **225 C3** 19 11N 99 5W
San Patricio, *NM, U.S.A.* **88 D5** 33 25N 105 20W
San Patricio County ☆, *TX, U.S.A.* **99 J10** 28 2N 97 31W
San Patricio Melaque, *Jalisco, Mexico* **218 C3** 19 14N 104 44W
San Pedrito, *Querétaro, Mexico* . . **219 B7** 20 19N 100 19W
San Pedro, *Baja Calif., Mexico* . . **210 E5** 28 29N 113 24W
San Pedro, *Baja Calif. S., Mexico* . **211 K8** 23 23N 110 12W
San Pedro, *Sonora, Mexico* **212 C3** 30 47N 112 34W
San Pedro, *Tabasco, Mexico* **222 B5** 17 46N 91 9W
San Pedro, *Los Angeles, U.S.A.* . . . **111 D3** 33 44N 118 17W
San Pedro, *TX, U.S.A.* **99 K10** 27 48N 97 41W
San Pedro ➛, *Chihuahua, Mexico* **213 C7** 30 56N 108 8W
San Pedro ➛, *Chihuahua, Mexico* **213 E10** 28 21N 105 25W
San Pedro ➛, *AZ, U.S.A.* **62 E5** 32 59N 110 47W
San Pedro Amuzgos, *Oaxaca, Mexico* **221 H2** 16 38N 98 5W
San Pedro Atocpan, *Distrito Federal, Mexico* **225 C3** 19 13N 99 2W
San Pedro Atoyac, *Oaxaca, Mexico* **221 H3** 16 31N 97 59W
San Pedro Atzumba, *Puebla, Mexico* **221 F3** 18 8N 97 34W
San Pedro Bay, *Los Angeles, U.S.A.* **111 D3** 33 44N 118 12W
San Pedro Channel, *CA, U.S.A.* . . **65 K8** 33 30N 118 25W
San Pedro Coayuca, *Puebla, Mexico* **221 F2** 18 30N 98 10W
San Pedro de la Cueva, *Sonora, Mexico* **212 D6** 29 18N 109 44W
San Pedro de las Colonias, *Coahuila, Mexico* **214 E2** 25 45N 102 59W
San Pedro del Gallo, *Durango, Mexico* **217 B6** 25 33N 104 18W
San Pedro Denxhi, *Querétaro, Mexico* **219 B8** 20 15N 99 55W
San Pedro Huamelula, *Oaxaca, Mexico* **221 H5** 16 2N 95 40W
San Pedro Huazalingo, *Hidalgo, Mexico* **219 B9** 20 57N 98 30W
San Pedro Juchatenga, *Oaxaca, Mexico* **221 H3** 16 22N 97 5W
San Pedro Lagunillas, *Nayarit, Mexico* **216 F6** 21 13N 104 46W
San Pedro Mártir, *Baja Calif., Mexico* **210 B3** 31 3N 115 28W
San Pedro Mártir, *Distrito Federal, Mexico* **225 C2** 19 16N 99 10W
San Pedro Mártir, Sa. de, *Baja Calif., Mexico* **210 C3** 30 45N 115 13W
San Pedro Naranjestil, *Michoacan, Mexico* **218 D4** 18 18N 103 7W
San Pedro Nolasco, I., *Sonora, Mexico* **212 F4** 27 59N 111 25W
San Pedro Ocampo = Melchor Ocampo, *Zacatecas, Mexico* . . . **217 C9** 24 51N 101 39W
San Pedro Pochutla, *Oaxaca, Mexico* **221 J4** 15 44N 96 28W
San Pedro Quiatoni, *Oaxaca, Mexico* **221 H4** 16 47N 96 2W
San Pedro Tapanatepec, *Oaxaca, Mexico* **221 H6** 16 21N 94 12W
San Pedro Tláhuac, *Distrito Federal, Mexico* **225 C4** 19 17N 99 0W
San Pedro Totolapan, *Oaxaca, Mexico* **221 H4** 16 40N 96 18W
San Pedro Tututepec, *Oaxaca, Mexico* **221 H3** 16 9N 97 38W
San Pedro Villa de Mitla, *Oaxaca, Mexico* **221 H4** 16 55N 96 24W
San Pedro y San Pablo ➛, *Tabasco, Mexico* **222 A4** 18 38N 92 29W
San Pedro y San Pablo Ayutla, *Oaxaca, Mexico* **221 G4** 17 2N 96 4W
San Pedro Zacatenco, *Distrito Federal, Mexico* **225 A3** 19 30N 99 6W
San Perlita, *TX, U.S.A.* **98 L10** 26 30N 97 39W
San Pitch ➛, *UT, U.S.A.* **100 D4** 39 3N 111 51W
San Quintín, *Baja Calif. S., Mexico* **211 K8** 23 42N 110 23W
San Quintín, *Chiapas, Mexico* . . . **222 C5** 16 24N 91 20W
San Quintín, C., *Baja Calif., Mexico* **210 C2** 30 21N 116 0W
San Rafael, *Baja Calif. S., Mexico* **211 F4** 27 10N 114 8W
San Rafael, *Chihuahua, Mexico* . . **213 F8** 27 28N 107 53W
San Rafael, *Nuevo León, Mexico* . . **215 G4** 23 31N 100 13W
San Rafael, *Nuevo León, Mexico* . . **215 E4** 25 1N 100 33W
San Rafael, *Veracruz, Mexico* **220 D4** 20 11N 96 52W
San Rafael, *CA, U.S.A.* **64 F4** 37 58N 122 32W
San Rafael, *NM, U.S.A.* **88 B3** 35 7N 107 53W
San Rafael ➛, *Baja Calif., Mexico* **210 C2** 30 58N 116 16W
San Rafael ➛, *UT, U.S.A.* **100 E5** 38 47N 110 7W
San Rafael, B., *Baja Calif., Mexico* **210 E5** 28 30N 113 4W
San Rafael Chamapa, *México, Mexico* **225 B2** 19 27N 99 15W
San Rafael de lo Moreno, *Jalisco, Mexico* **218 B2** 20 6N 105 10W
San Rafael Desert, *UT, U.S.A.* . . . **100 E5** 38 41N 110 26W
San Rafael Hills, *Los Angeles, U.S.A.* **111 A3** 34 10N 118 12W
San Rafael Mts., *CA, U.S.A.* **65 J7** 34 40N 119 50W
San Rafael Swell, *UT, U.S.A.* **100 E5** 38 45N 110 45W
San Rodrigo ➛, *Coahuila, Mexico* **214 B4** 28 54N 100 37W
San Rolando, *Tamaulipas, Mexico* **215 H6** 22 54N 98 51W
San Roque, *Monterrey, Mexico* . . . **224 C3** 25 36N 100 9W
San Roque, Pta., *Baja Calif. S., Mexico* **211 F4** 27 11N 114 27W
San Saba, *TX, U.S.A.* **99 F9** 31 12N 98 43W
San Saba ➛, *TX, U.S.A.* **99 F9** 31 15N 98 36W
San Saba County ☆, *TX, U.S.A.* . . **99 F9** 31 13N 98 47W
San Salvador, *Hidalgo, Mexico* . . . **219 B9** 20 17N 99 0W
San Salvador Cuauhtenco, *Distrito Federal, Mexico* **225 C3** 19 12N 99 7W
San Salvador el Seco, *Puebla, Mexico* **221 E3** 19 8N 97 39W
San Sebastián, *Jalisco, Mexico* . . . **218 B3** 20 47N 104 51W
San Sebastián, *Veracruz, Mexico* . . **220 C2** 21 13N 98 7W
San Sebastián, *Puerto Rico* **105 G16** 18 20N 66 59W
San Sebastián El Grande, *Guadalajara, Mexico* **224 B1** 20 31N 103 25W
San Sebastián El Grande, *Jalisco, Mexico* **218 B4** 20 32N 103 25W
San Sebastián Río Hondo, *Oaxaca, Mexico* **221 H4** 16 11N 96 28W
San Simeon, *CA, U.S.A.* **65 H5** 35 39N 121 11W
San Simon, *AZ, U.S.A.* **62 E6** 32 16N 109 14W
San Simón ➛, *Baja Calif., Mexico* **210 C3** 30 30N 115 44W
San Simon ➛, *AZ, U.S.A.* **62 E6** 32 50N 109 39W
San Simon Wash ➛, *AZ, U.S.A.* . . **62 F3** 31 45N 112 25W
San Simón Zahuatlán, *Oaxaca, Mexico* **221 G2** 17 50N 98 1W
San Telmo, *Baja Calif., Mexico* . . **210 C2** 30 58N 116 6W
San Tiburcio, *Zacatecas, Mexico* . . **217 C9** 24 8N 101 32W
San Vicente, *Baja Calif., Mexico* . **210 B2** 31 20N 116 21W
San Vicente, *Nayarit, Mexico* **216 F5** 21 58N 105 19W
San Vicente, *San Luis Potosí, Mexico* **215 F4** 24 10N 100 55W
San Vicente, *San Luis Potosí, Mexico* **215 J6** 21 44N 98 34W
San Vicente Coatlán, *Oaxaca, Mexico* **221 H4** 16 24N 96 51W
San Vicente Lachixio, *Oaxaca, Mexico* **221 H3** 16 43N 97 2W
San Xavier Tohono O'odham Indian Reservation, *AZ, U.S.A.* . . . **62 E4** 32 10N 111 0W
San Ygnacio, *TX, U.S.A.* **98 K8** 27 3N 99 26W
San Ysidro, *NM, U.S.A.* **88 B4** 35 34N 106 46W
San Ysidro, *San Diego, U.S.A.* . . . **117 C2** 32 33N 117 2W
San Zacarías, *Baja Calif. S., Mexico* **211 F6** 27 8N 112 55W
Sanak I., *AK, U.S.A.* **61 J7** 54 25N 162 40W
Sanalona, *Sinaloa, Mexico* **216 C3** 24 47N 107 8W
Sanalona, Presa, *Sinaloa, Mexico* . **216 C3** 24 49N 107 7W
Sanatoga, *PA, U.S.A.* **87 B1** 40 15N 75 36W
Sanborn, *IA, U.S.A.* **73 B3** 43 11N 95 39W
Sanborn, *ND, U.S.A.* **91 D7** 46 57N 98 14W
Sanborn County ☆, *SD, U.S.A.* . . . **91 G7** 44 0N 98 0W
Sanbornville, *NH, U.S.A.* **86 C3** 43 33N 71 2W
Sánchez Magallanes, *Tabasco, Mexico* **222 A3** 18 17N 93 54W
Sand ➛, *Alta., Canada* **184 D9** 54 23N 111 2W
Sand Arroyo Cr. ➛, *CO, U.S.A.* . . **74 D1** 37 22N 102 8W
Sand Cr. ➛, *IN, U.S.A.* **72 D5** 39 3N 85 51W
Sand Cr. ➛, *SD, U.S.A.* **91 E2** 45 7N 103 17W
Sand Cr. ➛, *WY, U.S.A.* **104 C7** 43 20N 105 2W
Sand Draw, *WY, U.S.A.* **104 D4** 42 46N 108 11W
Sand Fork, *WV, U.S.A.* **102 C4** 38 55N 80 45W
Sand Hill ➛, *MN, U.S.A.* **80 C2** 47 36N 96 52W
Sand Hills, *CA, U.S.A.* **65 L11** 32 50N 115 0W
Sand Hills, *NE, U.S.A.* **84 B4** 42 10N 101 30W
Sand I., *HI, U.S.A.* **69 K14** 21 19N 157 53W
Sand I., *Portland, U.S.A.* **116 A2** 45 35N 122 33W
Sand I., *WI, U.S.A.* **103 B3** 46 59N 90 58W
Sand Key, *Tampa, U.S.A.* **119 B1** 27 54N 82 50W
Sand Key Park, *Tampa, U.S.A.* . . . **119 B1** 27 58N 82 50W
Sand L., *Ont., Canada* **180 B2** 50 10N 94 35W
Sand Lake, *MI, U.S.A.* **79 F6** 43 18N 85 31W
Sand Lake, *NY, U.S.A.* **78 B1** 42 38N 73 32W
Sand Lake Nat. Wildlife Refuge ⌂, *SD, U.S.A.* **91 E7** 45 48N 98 13W
Sand Point, *AK, U.S.A.* **61 J7** 55 20N 160 30W
Sand Pt., *MI, U.S.A.* **79 F8** 43 55N 83 24W
Sand Springs, *OK, U.S.A.* **93 B7** 36 9N 96 7W
Sand Tank Mts., *AZ, U.S.A.* **62 E3** 32 45N 112 30W
Sandbank L., *Ont., Canada* **181 A14** 51 8N 82 41W
Sandborn, *IN, U.S.A.* **72 E3** 38 54N 87 11W
Sanders, *AZ, U.S.A.* **62 B6** 35 13N 109 20W
Sanders County ☆, *MT, U.S.A.* . . **83 C2** 47 40N 115 30W
Sanderson, *FL, U.S.A.* **67 A6** 30 15N 82 16W
Sanderson, *TX, U.S.A.* **98 G5** 30 9N 102 24W
Sandersville, *GA, U.S.A.* **68 D4** 32 59N 82 48W
Sandersville, *MS, U.S.A.* **81 E4** 31 47N 89 2W
Sandia, *TX, U.S.A.* **99 J10** 28 1N 97 53W
Sandía, Cerro La, *Baja Calif., Mexico* **210 E5** 28 27N 113 33W
Sandia Indian Reservation, *NM, U.S.A.* **88 B4** 35 15N 106 33W
Sandía La Victoria, *Nuevo León, Mexico* **215 F4** 24 11N 100 4W
Sandias, *Durango, Mexico* **216 B5** 25 15N 105 37W
Sandoval, *IL, U.S.A.* **71 E4** 38 37N 89 7W
Sandoval County ☆, *NM, U.S.A.* . **88 B4** 35 45N 106 45W
Sandpoint, *ID, U.S.A.* **70 A2** 48 17N 116 33W
Sands Point, *NY, U.S.A.* **114 A4** 40 52N 73 41W
Sands Point Preserve, *NY, U.S.A.* **114 A4** 40 51N 73 43W
Sandspit, *B.C., Canada* **186 B3** 53 14N 131 49W
Sandston, *VA, U.S.A.* **102 D7** 37 31N 77 19W
Sandstone, *MN, U.S.A.* **80 D6** 46 8N 92 52W
Sandtown, *DE, U.S.A.* **77 A5** 39 4N 75 44W
Sandusky, *MI, U.S.A.* **79 F9** 43 25N 82 50W
Sandusky, *OH, U.S.A.* **92 B4** 41 27N 82 42W
Sandusky ➛, *OH, U.S.A.* **92 B3** 41 27N 83 0W
Sandusky B., *OH, U.S.A.* **92 B4** 41 29N 82 50W
Sandusky County ☆, *OH, U.S.A.* . **92 B3** 41 21N 83 7W
Sandwich, *IL, U.S.A.* **71 B5** 41 39N 88 37W
Sandwich, *MA, U.S.A.* **78 C4** 41 46N 70 30W
Sandwich B., *Nfld. & L., Canada* . **175 C6** 53 40N 57 15W
Sandy, *OR, U.S.A.* **94 B3** 45 24N 122 16W
Sandy, *PA, U.S.A.* **95 C4** 41 6N 78 46W
Sandy, *UT, U.S.A.* **100 C4** 40 32N 111 50W
Sandy Bay, *Man., Canada* **183 E13** 50 33N 98 38W
Sandy Bay, *Sask., Canada* **189 E12** 55 31N 102 19W
Sandy Cove, *Nfld. & L., Canada* . . **174 A4** 51 21N 56 40W
Sandy Cr. ➛, *WY, U.S.A.* **104 E3** 41 51N 109 47W
Sandy Creek, *MT, U.S.A.* **83 F5** 44 41N 112 10W
Sandy Creek, *NY, U.S.A.* **89 B4** 43 39N 76 5W
Sandy Creek, *Pittsburgh, U.S.A.* . . **116 B2** 40 28N 79 50W
Sandy Hill, *Ont., Canada* **192 A1** 45 25N 75 41W
Sandy Hook, *KY, U.S.A.* **97 B9** 38 5N 83 8W
Sandy Hook, *MS, U.S.A.* **81 E4** 31 2N 89 49W
Sandy L., *Alta., Canada* **184 C7** 55 50N 113 25W
Sandy L., *Alta., Canada* **184 E6** 53 47N 114 2W
Sandy L., *Nfld. & L., Canada* **174 C4** 49 15N 57 0W
Sandy L., *Ont., Canada* **191 G7** 53 2N 93 0W
Sandy Lake, *Ont., Canada* **191 G7** 53 0N 93 15W
Sandy Lake Indian Reservation, *MN, U.S.A.* **80 D5** 46 51N 93 19W
Sandy Point, *N.S., Canada* **173 K4** 43 42N 65 19W
Sandy Pond, *Boston, U.S.A.* **106 A2** 42 26N 71 18W
Sandy Springs, *GA, U.S.A.* **68 C2** 33 56N 84 23W
Sandy Valley, *NV, U.S.A.* **85 G5** 35 49N 115 38W
Sandybeach L., *Ont., Canada* **180 C4** 49 49N 92 21W
Sandyville, *WV, U.S.A.* **102 C3** 38 54N 81 40W
Sanford, *CO, U.S.A.* **66 E5** 37 16N 105 54W
Sanford, *FL, U.S.A.* **67 C7** 28 48N 81 16W
Sanford, *ME, U.S.A.* **76 E3** 43 27N 70 47W
Sanford, *NC, U.S.A.* **90 C6** 35 29N 79 10W
Sanford, *TX, U.S.A.* **98 B6** 35 42N 101 32W
Sanford, Mt., *AK, U.S.A.* **61 E11** 62 13N 144 8W
Sangamon ➛, *IL, U.S.A.* **71 C3** 40 1N 90 26W
Sangamon County ☆, *IL, U.S.A.* . . **71 D4** 39 45N 89 40W
Sangchris L., *IL, U.S.A.* **71 D4** 39 39N 89 29W
Sanger, *CA, U.S.A.* **65 G7** 36 42N 119 33W
Sanger, *TX, U.S.A.* **99 D10** 33 22N 97 10W
Sangre de Cristo, *NM, U.S.A.* **88 A5** 36 40N 105 15W
Sangre de Cristo Mts., *U.S.A.* . . . **66 E5** 37 30N 105 20W
Sangudo, *Alta., Canada* **184 E6** 53 50N 114 54W
Sanibel, *FL, U.S.A.* **67 E6** 26 27N 82 1W
Sanibel I., *FL, U.S.A.* **67 E6** 26 26N 82 6W
Sanikiluaq, *Nunavut, Canada* **191 F10** 56 32N 79 14W
Sanilac County ☆, *MI, U.S.A.* **79 F9** 43 25N 82 50W
Sanirajak, *Nunavut, Canada* **190 D9** 68 46N 81 12W
Sanmaur, *Qué., Canada* **177 D9** 47 54N 73 47W
Sanostee, *NM, U.S.A.* **88 A2** 36 25N 108 52W
Sanpete County ☆, *UT, U.S.A.* . . . **100 D4** 39 30N 111 40W
Sanpoil ➛, *WA, U.S.A.* **101 C7** 47 57N 118 41W
Sans Bois Mts., *OK, U.S.A.* **93 C8** 35 1N 95 13W
Sanscartier, Parc, *Qué., Canada* . . **192 A2** 45 28N 75 38W
Sansom Park, *Dallas-Fort Worth, U.S.A.* **109 B1** 32 48N 97 24W
Saint Joseph County ☆, *MI, U.S.A.* **79 H6** 41 50N 85 30W
Santa, *ID, U.S.A.* **70 B2** 47 9N 116 27W
Santa Ana, *Nuevo León, Mexico* . . **215 F4** 24 6N 100 22W
Santa Ana, *Oaxaca, Mexico* **221 H4** 16 20N 96 44W
Santa Ana, *Sonora, Mexico* **212 C4** 30 33N 111 7W
Santa Ana, *CA, U.S.A.* **65 K9** 33 46N 117 52W
Santa Ana, B., *Baja Calif. S., Mexico* **211 F6** 27 40N 112 36W
Santa Ana Indian Reservation, *NM, U.S.A.* **88 B4** 35 26N 106 37W
Santa Ana John Wayne ✕ (SNA), *CA, U.S.A.* **65 K9** 33 41N 117 52W
Santa Ana Maya, *Michoacan, Mexico* **219 B6** 20 1N 101 2W
Santa Ana Mts., *CA, U.S.A.* **65 K9** 33 40N 117 30W
Santa Ana Pueblo, *NM, U.S.A.* . . . **88 B4** 35 26N 106 37W
Santa Ana Tepetitlán, *Guadalajara, Mexico* **224 B1** 20 37N 103 27W
Santa Ana Tlacotenco, *Distrito Federal, Mexico* **225 C4** 19 11N 99 0W
Santa Ana Travela, *Oaxaca, Mexico* **221 H6** 16 40N 95 54W
Santa Anita, *Coahuila, Mexico* . . . **214 B1** 28 19N 103 31W
Santa Anita, *Guadalajara, Mexico* **224 B1** 20 33N 103 27W
Santa Anna, *TX, U.S.A.* **99 F8** 31 45N 99 20W
Santa Bárbara, *Chihuahua, Mexico* **213 G10** 26 48N 105 49W
Santa Barbara, *CA, U.S.A.* **65 J7** 34 25N 119 42W
Santa Barbara Channel, *CA, U.S.A.* **65 J7** 34 15N 120 0W
Santa Barbara County ☆, *CA, U.S.A.* **65 J6** 34 40N 120 0W
Santa Barbara I., *CA, U.S.A.* **65 K7** 33 29N 119 2W
Santa Catalina, Gulf of, *CA, U.S.A.* **65 K9** 33 10N 117 50W
Santa Catalina, I., *Baja Calif. S., Mexico* **211 H8** 25 40N 110 47W
Santa Catalina I., *CA, U.S.A.* **65 K8** 33 23N 118 25W
Santa Catalina Mts., *AZ, U.S.A.* . . **62 E5** 32 35N 110 50W
Santa Catalina Quieri, *Oaxaca, Mexico* **221 H4** 16 19N 96 16W
Santa Catarina, *Baja Calif., Mexico* **210 D3** 29 42N 115 8W
Santa Catarina, *Guanajuato, Mexico* **219 A7** 21 9N 100 5W
Santa Catarina, *Nuevo León, Mexico* **214 E4** 25 41N 100 28W
Santa Catarina, *San Luis Potosí, Mexico* **215 H4** 22 4N 100 28W
Santa Catarina Juquila, *Oaxaca, Mexico* **221 H3** 16 14N 97 18W
Santa Catarina Loxicha, *Oaxaca, Mexico* **221 H4** 16 4N 96 46W
Santa Catarina Zapoquila, *Oaxaca, Mexico* **221 F3** 18 4N 97 35W
Santa Cecilia Tepetlapa, *Distrito Federal, Mexico* **225 C3** 19 14N 99 5W
Santa Clara, *Baja Calif., Mexico* . **210 B3** 31 5N 115 17W
Santa Clara, *Durango, Mexico* . . . **217 C7** 24 29N 103 21W
Santa Clara, *México, Mexico* **225 A3** 19 33N 99 4W
Santa Clara, *CA, U.S.A.* **64 F5** 37 21N 121 57W
Santa Clara, *NM, U.S.A.* **88 E2** 32 47N 108 9W
Santa Clara, *NY, U.S.A.* **89 A6** 44 38N 74 27W
Santa Clara, *OR, U.S.A.* **94 C2** 44 6N 123 8W
Santa Clara, *UT, U.S.A.* **100 F2** 37 8N 113 39W
Santa Clara ➛, *Chihuahua, Mexico* **213 D8** 29 51N 107 6W
Santa Clara ➛, *CA, U.S.A.* **65 J7** 34 14N 119 16W
Santa Clara County ☆, *CA, U.S.A.* **64 F5** 37 15N 121 40W
Santa Clara de González, *Nuevo León, Mexico* **215 F4** 24 39N 100 1W
Santa Clara Indian Reservation, *NM, U.S.A.* **88 B4** 35 59N 106 11W
Santa Clara Pueblo, *NM, U.S.A.* . . **88 B4** 35 58N 106 5W
Santa Clara Valley, *CA, U.S.A.* . . . **64 G5** 36 50N 121 30W
Santa Clarita, *CA, U.S.A.* **65 J8** 34 24N 118 33W
Santa Claus, *IN, U.S.A.* **72 E4** 38 7N 86 55W
Santa Cruz, *Nayarit, Mexico* **216 F5** 21 58N 105 37W
Santa Cruz, *CA, U.S.A.* **64 G4** 36 58N 122 1W
Santa Cruz ➛, *Chihuahua, Mexico* **213 F9** 27 55N 106 3W
Santa Cruz, I., *Baja Calif. S., Mexico* **211 H8** 25 17N 110 43W
Santa Cruz Acalpixca, *Distrito Federal, Mexico* **225 C3** 19 15N 99 4W
Santa Cruz County ☆, *AZ, U.S.A.* . **62 F5** 31 30N 110 45W
Santa Cruz County ☆, *CA, U.S.A.* . **64 G5** 37 0N 122 0W
Santa Cruz de Bravo = Felipe Carrillo Puerto, *Quintana Roo, Mexico* **223 C5** 19 38N 88 3W
Santa Cruz del Valle, *Guadalajara, Mexico* **224 B1** 20 32N 103 26W
Santa Cruz Huatulco, *Oaxaca, Mexico* **221 J4** 15 46N 96 7W
Santa Cruz I., *CA, U.S.A.* **65 J7** 34 1N 119 43W
Santa Cruz José María, *Sonora, Mexico* **212 B5** 31 14N 110 35W
Santa Cruz Meyehualco, *Distrito Federal, Mexico* **225 B3** 19 20N 99 1W
Santa Cruz Mts., *CA, U.S.A.* **64 F4** 37 15N 122 0W
Santa Cruz Wash ➛, *AZ, U.S.A.* . . **62 D3** 33 23N 112 12W
Santa Elena, *Coahuila, Mexico* . . . **214 C2** 27 27N 102 33W
Santa Elena, *Yucatán, Mexico* . . . **223 B4** 20 20N 89 39W
Santa Elena, *TX, U.S.A.* **98 L9** 26 46N 98 29W
Santa Elena ➛, *Mexico* **213 G12** 26 30N 103 50W
Santa Fe, *Chihuahua, Mexico* **213 E11** 28 33N 104 3W
Santa Fe, *NM, U.S.A.* **88 B5** 35 41N 105 57W
Santa Fe Baldy, *NM, U.S.A.* **88 B5** 35 50N 105 46W
Santa Fe County ☆, *NM, U.S.A.* . . **88 B4** 35 30N 106 0W
Santa Fe del Pino, *Coahuila, Mexico* **214 B1** 28 39N 103 13W
Santa Fe L., *FL, U.S.A.* **67 B6** 29 45N 82 5W
Santa Fe Nat. Forest, *NM, U.S.A.* . **88 A4** 36 3N 106 42W
Santa Fe Springs, *Los Angeles, U.S.A.* **111 C4** 33 56N 118 3W
Santa Gertrudis, *Baja Calif. S., Mexico* **211 K8** 23 31N 110 8W
Santa Gertrudis, *Chihuahua, Mexico* **213 F10** 27 49N 105 44W
Santa Gertrudis, *Jalisco, Mexico* . . **218 B3** 20 5N 104 45W
Santa Inés, B., *Baja Calif. S., Mexico* **211 E6** 28 15N 112 52W
Santa Inés, B., *Baja Calif. S., Mexico* **211 G7** 26 59N 111 59W
Santa Inés, I., *Baja Calif. S., Mexico* **211 F7** 27 3N 111 58W
Santa Inés Ahuatempan, *Puebla, Mexico* **221 F2** 18 25N 98 1W
Santa Isabel, *Baja Calif. S., Mexico* **211 H7** 25 56N 111 38W
Santa Isabel, *Chihuahua, Mexico* . **213 E11** 28 14N 104 51W
Santa Isabel, *San Luis Potosí, Mexico* **215 G4** 23 10N 100 50W
Santa Isabel, *Puerto Rico* **105 H16** 17 58N 66 24W
Santa Lucía, *Durango, Mexico* . . . **216 D5** 23 37N 105 31W
Santa Lucía de la Sierra, *Zacatecas, Mexico* **217 E6** 22 27N 104 13W
Santa Lucia Range, *CA, U.S.A.* . . . **65 H5** 36 0N 121 20W

Santa Margarita, I., *Baja Calif. S., Mexico* **211 J7** 24 27N 111 50W
Santa Margarita, Sa. de, *Sonora, Mexico* **212 C5** 30 4N 110 2W
Santa Margarita L., *CA, U.S.A.* **65 H6** 35 20N 120 30W
Santa María, *Sonora, Mexico* **212 E4** 28 57N 111 50W
Santa Maria, *CA, U.S.A.* **65 J6** 34 57N 120 26W
Santa Maria, *Phoenix, U.S.A.* **116 C1** 33 25N 112 12W
Santa María →, *Chihuahua, Mexico* **213 C8** 31 0N 107 14W
Santa María →, *San Luis Potosí, Mexico* **215 J5** 21 37N 99 15W
Santa Maria →, *AZ, U.S.A.* **62 C1** 34 19N 114 31W
Santa María, B., *Baja Calif., Mexico* **210 C4** 30 40N 114 40W
Santa María, B., *Baja Calif., Mexico* **210 C3** 30 30N 115 55W
Santa María, B., *Baja Calif. S., Mexico* **211 J6** 24 45N 112 20W
Santa María, B. de, *Sinaloa, Mexico* **216 B2** 25 4N 108 6W
Santa María, I., *Sinaloa, Mexico* **216 B1** 25 39N 109 15W
Santa María, L. de, *Chihuahua, Mexico* **213 B8** 31 7N 107 16W
Santa María Acu, *Yucatán, Mexico* **223 B3** 20 33N 90 10W
Santa María Ayoquezco, *Oaxaca, Mexico* **221 H4** 16 42N 96 51W
Santa María Aztahuacan, *Distrito Federal, Mexico* **225 B3** 19 21N 99 1W
Santa María Chichotla, *Oaxaca, Mexico* **221 F4** 18 12N 96 48W
Santa María Chimalapa, *Oaxaca, Mexico* **221 H6** 16 55N 94 41W
Santa María de Cuevas, *Chihuahua, Mexico* **213 F9** 27 55N 106 23W
Santa María de los Ángeles, *Jalisco, Mexico* **217 E7** 22 11N 103 14W
Santa María de Mohovano, *Durango, Mexico* **217 A7** 26 39N 103 38W
Santa María de Ocotán, *Durango, Mexico* **217 E6** 22 51N 104 51W
Santa María del Oro, *Durango, Mexico* **216 B5** 25 56N 105 23W
Santa María del Oro, *Nayarit, Mexico* **216 F6** 21 20N 104 35W
Santa María del Río, *San Luis Potosí, Mexico* **215 J4** 21 48N 100 45W
Santa María Ecatepec, *Oaxaca, Mexico* **221 H5** 16 17N 95 53W
Santa María Huatulco, *Oaxaca, Mexico* **221 J4** 15 50N 96 17W
Santa María Ixcatlán, *Oaxaca, Mexico* **221 G3** 17 52N 97 10W
Santa María Nativitas, *Distrito Federal, Mexico* **225 C3** 19 15N 99 5W
Santa María Tecomavaca, *Oaxaca, Mexico* **221 G3** 17 57N 97 1W
Santa María Totolapilla, *Oaxaca, Mexico* **221 H6** 16 37N 95 37W
Santa María Tulpetlac, *México, Mexico* **225 A3** 19 35N 99 4W
Santa María Xadoni, *Oaxaca, Mexico* **221 H6** 16 23N 95 2W
Santa María Zacatepec, *Oaxaca, Mexico* **221 H3** 16 46N 98 0W
Santa María Zoquitlán, *Oaxaca, Mexico* **221 H4** 16 33N 96 23W
Santa Martha, *Sonora, Mexico* **212 D4** 29 8N 111 33W
Santa Martha, Cerro, *Veracruz, Mexico* **221 F6** 18 19N 94 51W
Santa Martha Acatitla, *Distrito Federal, Mexico* **225 B3** 19 22N 99 2W
Santa Matilde, *Chihuahua, Mexico* **213 F7** 27 8N 108 23W
Santa Mónica, *Coahuila, Mexico* **214 B4** 28 12N 100 37W
Santa Monica, *CA, U.S.A.* **65 J8** 34 1N 118 29W
Santa Monica B., *CA, U.S.A.* **65 K8** 33 56N 118 28W
Santa Monica Mountains Nat. Recr. Area △, *CA, U.S.A.* **65 J8** 34 4N 118 44W
Santa Monica Mts., *Los Angeles, U.S.A.* **111 B2** 34 6N 118 29W
Santa Monica Municipal ✈, *Los Angeles, U.S.A.* **111 B2** 34 0N 118 27W
Santa Paula, *CA, U.S.A.* **65 J7** 34 21N 119 4W
Santa Rita, *Guam* **105 b** 13 23N 144 40W
Santa Rita, *Baja Calif. S., Mexico* **211 J7** 24 35N 111 29W
Santa Rita, *Nuevo León, Mexico* **215 F4** 24 12N 100 30W
Santa Rita, *MT, U.S.A.* **83 B5** 48 42N 112 19W
Santa Rita del Rucio, *San Luis Potosí, Mexico* **215 G4** 23 5N 100 17W
Santa Rosa, *Coahuila, Mexico* **214 B3** 28 37N 101 44W
Santa Rosa, *Guanajuato, Mexico* **219 A6** 21 5N 101 11W
Santa Rosa, *Guerrero, Mexico* **219 E6** 17 23N 101 4W
Santa Rosa, *Monterrey, Mexico* **224 B2** 25 49N 100 14W
Santa Rosa, *Quintana Roo, Mexico* **223 C5** 19 58N 88 15W
Santa Rosa, *Sonora, Mexico* **212 E6** 28 25N 109 8W
Santa Rosa, *Zacatecas, Mexico* **217 E7** 22 56N 103 6W
Santa Rosa, *AZ, U.S.A.* **62 E3** 32 19N 112 2W
Santa Rosa, *CA, U.S.A.* **64 E4** 38 26N 122 43W
Santa Rosa, *NM, U.S.A.* **88 C6** 34 57N 104 41W
Santa Rosa, *TX, U.S.A.* **98 L10** 26 16N 97 50W
Santa Rosa, L., *Quintana Roo, Mexico* **223 C6** 19 31N 87 28W
Santa Rosa, Mt., *Guam* **105 b** 13 32N 144 55W
Santa Rosa, Sa., *Coahuila, Mexico* **214 B3** 28 18N 101 49W
Santa Rosa, Sa., *Sonora, Mexico* **212 C4** 30 5N 111 35W
Santa Rosa and San Jacinto Mountains Nat. Monument △, *U.S.A.* **65 J8** 33 28N 116 20W
Santa Rosa Beach, *FL, U.S.A.* **67 A2** 30 22N 86 14W
Santa Rosa County ☆, *FL, U.S.A.* **67 A2** 30 45N 87 0W
Santa Rosa de Jáuregui, *Querétaro, Mexico* **219 B7** 20 45N 100 27W
Santa Rosa I., *CA, U.S.A.* **65 K6** 33 58N 120 6W
Santa Rosa I., *FL, U.S.A.* **67 A2** 30 20N 86 50W
Santa Rosa Indian Reservation, *CA, U.S.A.* **65 K10** 33 34N 116 32W
Santa Rosa L., *NM, U.S.A.* **88 B6** 35 2N 104 41W
Santa Rosa Mts., *CA, U.S.A.* **65 K10** 33 20N 116 15W
Santa Rosa Range, *NV, U.S.A.* **85 A3** 41 45N 117 40W
Santa Rosa Wash →, *AZ, U.S.A.* **62 E4** 33 0N 112 0W
Santa Rosa Xochiac, *Distrito Federal, Mexico* **225 C2** 19 20N 99 18W
Santa Rosalía, *Baja Calif. S., Mexico* **211 F6** 27 19N 112 17W
Santa Rosalita, *Baja Calif., Mexico* **210 E4** 28 40N 114 14W
Santa Rosalita, B., *Baja Calif., Mexico* **210 E4** 28 37N 114 13W
Santa Rosalita, Pta., *Baja Calif., Mexico* **210 E4** 28 39N 114 16W
Santa Teresa, *Nayarit, Mexico* **216 E6** 22 28N 104 44W
Santa Teresa, *Tamaulipas, Mexico* **215 E7** 25 17N 97 51W
Santa Teresa, Pta., *Baja Calif. S., Mexico* **211 G7** 26 45N 111 38W
Santa Terresa, *NM, U.S.A.* **88 F4** 31 51N 106 38W
Santa Ursula Xitla, *Distrito Federal, Mexico* **225 C2** 19 16N 99 11W
Santa Ynez, *CA, U.S.A.* **65 J6** 34 37N 120 5W
Santa Ynez →, *CA, U.S.A.* **65 J6** 34 41N 120 36W
Santa Ynez Mts., *CA, U.S.A.* **65 J7** 34 30N 120 0W
Santa Ysabel Indian Reservation, *CA, U.S.A.* **65 K10** 33 10N 116 40W
Santander Jiménez, *Tamaulipas, Mexico* **215 F6** 24 13N 98 28W
Santaquin, *UT, U.S.A.* **100 D4** 39 59N 111 47W
Santa's Village, *NH, U.S.A.* **86 B3** 44 27N 71 32W
Sante Genevieve, *MO, U.S.A.* **82 D6** 37 59N 90 3W
Santee, *CA, U.S.A.* **65 L10** 32 50N 116 58W
Santee, *NE, U.S.A.* **84 B8** 42 51N 97 50W
Santee, *SC, U.S.A.* **90 E5** 33 29N 80 29W
Santee →, *SC, U.S.A.* **90 E6** 33 7N 79 17W
Santee Indian Reservation, *NE, U.S.A.* **84 B8** 42 50N 97 50W
Santee Lakes, *San Diego, U.S.A.* **117 A2** 32 50N 117 0W
Santiago, *Baja Calif. S., Mexico* **211 K9** 23 28N 109 43W
Santiago, *Colima, Mexico* **218 C3** 19 7N 104 21W
Santiago, *Nuevo León, Mexico* **214 E4** 25 27N 100 9W
Santiago →, *Durango, Mexico* **216 B5** 25 11N 105 26W
Santiago Acahualtepec, *Distrito Federal, Mexico* **225 B3** 19 21N 99 0W
Santiago Amoltepec, *Oaxaca, Mexico* **221 H3** 16 38N 97 30W
Santiago Astata, *Oaxaca, Mexico* **221 J5** 15 59N 95 40W
Santiago Ayuquililla, *Oaxaca, Mexico* **221 G3** 17 57N 97 58W
Santiago de Anaya, *Hidalgo, Mexico* **219 B9** 20 22N 98 56W
Santiago de Pochotitán, *Nayarit, Mexico* **216 F6** 21 35N 104 43W
Santiago Domingo Xagacia, *Oaxaca, Mexico* **221 G4** 17 8N 96 17W
Santiago Huauclilla, *Oaxaca, Mexico* **221 G3** 17 28N 97 4W
Santiago Ixcuintepec, *Oaxaca, Mexico* **221 H6** 16 56N 95 38W
Santiago Ixcuintla, *Nayarit, Mexico* **216 F5** 21 49N 105 13W
Santiago Ixtayutla, *Oaxaca, Mexico* **221 H3** 16 35N 97 40W
Santiago Jamiltepec, *Oaxaca, Mexico* **221 H3** 16 17N 97 49W
Santiago Juxtlahuaca, *Oaxaca, Mexico* **221 G2** 17 20N 98 1W
Santiago Llano Grande, *Oaxaca, Mexico* **221 H2** 16 28N 98 15W
Santiago Maravatío, *Guanajuato, Mexico* **219 B7** 20 10N 101 0W
Santiago Miahuatlán, *Puebla, Mexico* **221 F3** 18 34N 97 26W
Santiago Minas, *Oaxaca, Mexico* **221 H3** 16 26N 97 13W
Santiago Mts., *TX, U.S.A.* **98 H4** 29 55N 103 22W
Santiago Papasquiaro, *Durango, Mexico* **216 B5** 25 3N 105 25W
Santiago Peak, *TX, U.S.A.* **98 H4** 29 47N 103 25W
Santiago Pinotepa Nacional, *Oaxaca, Mexico* **221 H2** 16 19N 98 1W
Santiago Quiotepec, *Oaxaca, Mexico* **221 G4** 17 55N 96 57W
Santiago Tangamandapio, *Michoacan, Mexico* **218 C5** 19 57N 102 26W
Santiago Tepalcatlalpan, *Distrito Federal, Mexico* **225 C3** 19 15N 99 8W
Santiago Tepatlaxco, *México, Mexico* **225 B1** 19 28N 99 20W
Santiago Tilantongo, *Oaxaca, Mexico* **221 G3** 17 17N 97 20W
Santiago Tulyehualco, *Distrito Federal, Mexico* **225 C3** 19 15N 99 1W
Santiago Tuxtla, *Veracruz, Mexico* **221 F5** 18 28N 95 18W
Santiago Yancuitlalpan, *México, Mexico* **225 B2** 19 23N 99 19W
Santiago Yaveo, *Oaxaca, Mexico* **221 G5** 17 20N 95 42W
Santiago Yosondúa, *Oaxaca, Mexico* **221 H3** 16 53N 97 34W
Santiago Zacatepec, *Oaxaca, Mexico* **221 G5** 17 11N 95 51W
Santiaguillo, L. de, *Durango, Mexico* **217 C6** 24 48N 104 48W
Santiam Pass, *OR, U.S.A.* **94 C4** 44 25N 121 55W
Santo Domingo, *Baja Calif., Mexico* **211 E4** 28 12N 114 2W
Santo Domingo, *Baja Calif. S., Mexico* **211 H7** 25 29N 111 55W
Santo Domingo, *Durango, Mexico* **217 B6** 25 48N 104 28W
Santo Domingo, *Oaxaca, Mexico* **221 H6** 16 28N 94 51W
Santo Domingo →, *Baja Calif., Mexico* **210 C3** 30 43N 116 4W
Santo Domingo Indian Reservation, *NM, U.S.A.* **88 B4** 35 30N 106 30W
Santo Domingo Pueblo, *NM, U.S.A.* **88 B4** 35 31N 106 22W
Santo Domingo Tehuantepec, *Oaxaca, Mexico* **221 H5** 16 20N 95 14W
Santo Tomás, *Baja Calif., Mexico* **210 B2** 31 33N 116 24W
Santo Tomás →, *Baja Calif., Mexico* **210 B2** 31 34N 116 42W
Santo Tomás →, *Baja Calif. S., Mexico* **211 H7** 25 20N 111 16W
Santo Tomás, Pta., *Baja Calif., Mexico* **210 B2** 31 34N 116 42W
Santos Reyes Nopala, *Oaxaca, Mexico* **221 H3** 16 6N 97 10W
Sapello, *NM, U.S.A.* **88 B5** 35 46N 105 15W
Sapelo I., *GA, U.S.A.* **68 E5** 31 25N 81 12W
Sapelo Island, *GA, U.S.A.* **68 E5** 31 23N 81 17W
Sapelo Sound, *GA, U.S.A.* **68 E5** 31 30N 81 10W
Sappa Cr. →, *NE, U.S.A.* **84 D6** 40 7N 99 39W
Sappho, *WA, U.S.A.* **101 B1** 48 4N 124 16W
Sapulpa, *OK, U.S.A.* **93 C7** 35 59N 96 5W
Sara, L., *IL, U.S.A.* **71 D5** 39 8N 88 36W
Saragosa, *TX, U.S.A.* **98 F4** 31 2N 103 39W
Sarah, *MS, U.S.A.* **81 B3** 34 34N 90 13W
Saraland, *AL, U.S.A.* **60 F2** 30 50N 88 4W
Saranac, *MI, U.S.A.* **79 G6** 42 56N 85 13W
Saranac, *NY, U.S.A.* **89 A7** 44 39N 73 45W
Saranac →, *NY, U.S.A.* **89 A7** 44 42N 73 27W
Saranac Lake, *NY, U.S.A.* **89 A6** 44 20N 74 10W
Saranac Lakes, *NY, U.S.A.* **89 A6** 44 20N 74 28W
Sarasota, *FL, U.S.A.* **67 D6** 27 20N 82 32W
Sarasota County ☆, *FL, U.S.A.* **67 D6** 27 15N 82 20W
Saratoga, *CA, U.S.A.* **64 F4** 37 16N 122 2W
Saratoga, *IN, U.S.A.* **72 C6** 40 14N 84 55W
Saratoga, *TX, U.S.A.* **99 G13** 30 17N 94 31W
Saratoga, *WY, U.S.A.* **104 E6** 41 27N 106 49W
Saratoga County ☆, *NY, U.S.A.* **89 B7** 43 10N 73 50W
Saratoga L., *NY, U.S.A.* **89 B7** 43 1N 73 45W
Saratoga Nat. Historical Park △, *NY, U.S.A.* **89 C7** 43 0N 73 38W
Saratoga Springs, *NY, U.S.A.* **89 B7** 43 5N 73 47W
Sarcobatus Flat, *NV, U.S.A.* **85 E4** 37 10N 116 58W
Sarcoxie, *MO, U.S.A.* **82 D2** 37 4N 94 7W
Sardinas, *Durango, Mexico* **216 A5** 26 7N 105 32W
Sardinia, *OH, U.S.A.* **92 E3** 39 0N 83 49W
Sardis, *AL, U.S.A.* **60 D4** 32 17N 86 59W
Sardis, *GA, U.S.A.* **68 D5** 32 58N 81 46W
Sardis, *MS, U.S.A.* **81 B4** 34 26N 89 55W
Sardis, *TN, U.S.A.* **96 E4** 35 27N 88 18W
Sardis L., *MS, U.S.A.* **81 B4** 34 25N 89 48W
Sardis L., *OK, U.S.A.* **93 D8** 34 40N 95 25W
Sarepta, *LA, U.S.A.* **75 B2** 32 54N 93 27W
Sarepta, *MS, U.S.A.* **81 B4** 34 7N 89 17W
Sargeant, *MN, U.S.A.* **80 G6** 43 48N 92 48W
Sargent, *GA, U.S.A.* **68 C2** 33 26N 84 52W
Sargent, *NE, U.S.A.* **84 C6** 41 39N 99 22W
Sargent County ☆, *ND, U.S.A.* **91 D8** 46 3N 97 45W
Sargents, *CO, U.S.A.* **66 D4** 38 25N 106 24W
Sáric, *Sonora, Mexico* **212 B4** 31 8N 111 21W
Sarigan, *N. Marianas* **105 a** 16 43N 145 47W
Sarita, *TX, U.S.A.* **98 K10** 27 13N 97 47W
Sarles, *ND, U.S.A.* **91 B7** 48 58N 99 0W
Sarnia, *Ont., Canada* **178 E4** 42 58N 82 23W
Sarpy County ☆, *NE, U.S.A.* **84 C9** 41 10N 96 10W
Sartell, *MN, U.S.A.* **80 E4** 45 37N 94 12W
Sasabe, *AZ, U.S.A.* **62 F4** 31 29N 111 33W
Sasaginnigak L., *Man., Canada* **183 D16** 51 36N 95 39W
Sasakwa, *OK, U.S.A.* **93 D7** 34 57N 96 31W
Saseginaga, L., *Qué., Canada* **176 D4** 47 6N 78 35W
Saskatchewan □, *Sask., Canada* **182 B3** 54 40N 106 0W
Saskatchewan →, *Sask., Canada* **183 B11** 53 37N 100 40W
Saskatchewan Landing Prov. Park △, *Sask., Canada* **182 E4** 50 38N 107 59W
Saskatoon, *Sask., Canada* **182 C5** 52 10N 106 38W
Saspamco, *San Antonio, U.S.A.* **117 D4** 29 14N 98 17W
Sassafras, *MD, U.S.A.* **77 A5** 39 22N 75 20W
Sassafras Mt., *SC, U.S.A.* **90 C3** 35 4N 82 47W
Sasser, *GA, U.S.A.* **68 E2** 31 43N 84 21W
Satanta, *KS, U.S.A.* **74 D3** 37 26N 100 59W
Satartia, *MS, U.S.A.* **81 D3** 32 40N 90 33W
Satellite Beach, *FL, U.S.A.* **67 C8** 28 10N 80 36W
Satevó, *Chihuahua, Mexico* **213 F9** 27 57N 106 7W
Satilla →, *GA, U.S.A.* **68 F5** 30 59N 81 29W
Satolah, *GA, U.S.A.* **68 B3** 34 59N 83 11W
Satsuma, *AL, U.S.A.* **60 F2** 30 51N 88 4W
Saturna, *B.C., Canada* **187 G11** 48 47N 123 11W
Satus Pass, *WA, U.S.A.* **101 E5** 45 59N 120 39W
Saubosq, L., *Qué., Canada* **172 B5** 51 30N 64 53W
Sauceda, *Coahuila, Mexico* **214 E3** 25 46N 101 19W
Sauceda Mts., *AZ, U.S.A.* **62 E3** 32 35N 112 35W
Saucier, *MS, U.S.A.* **81 F4** 30 39N 89 8W
Saucillo, *Chihuahua, Mexico* **213 E10** 28 1N 105 17W
Saugatuck, *MI, U.S.A.* **79 G5** 42 40N 86 12W
Saugatuck →, *CT, U.S.A.* **78 C1** 41 7N 73 22W
Saugeen →, *Ont., Canada* **178 C5** 44 30N 81 22W
Saugerties, *NY, U.S.A.* **89 C7** 42 5N 73 57W
Sauget, *IL, U.S.A.* **117 B3** 38 35N 90 11W
Saugus, *MA, U.S.A.* **78 B3** 42 28N 71 0W
Saugus →, *Boston, U.S.A.* **106 A3** 42 27N 70 58W
Sauk →, *WA, U.S.A.* **101 B4** 48 29N 121 36W
Sauk Centre, *MN, U.S.A.* **80 E4** 45 44N 94 57W
Sauk City, *WI, U.S.A.* **103 E4** 43 17N 89 43W
Sauk County ☆, *WI, U.S.A.* **103 E4** 43 25N 89 50W
Sauk Rapids, *MN, U.S.A.* **80 E4** 45 35N 94 10W
Saukville, *WI, U.S.A.* **103 E6** 43 23N 87 56W
Saulnierville, *N.S., Canada* **173 J3** 44 16N 66 8W
Saulsbury, *TN, U.S.A.* **96 E3** 35 3N 89 5W
Sault-au-Récollet, *Montréal, Canada* **192 A3** 45 35N 73 39W
Sault aux Cochons →, *Qué., Canada* **177 C13** 48 44N 69 4W
Sault Ste. Marie, *Ont., Canada* **178 A2** 46 30N 84 20W
Sault Ste. Marie, *MI, U.S.A.* **79 C7** 46 30N 84 21W
Saumons →, *Qué., Canada* **172 D7** 49 25N 62 15W
Saumur, L., *Qué., Canada* **172 B7** 51 16N 62 49W
Saunders County ☆, *NE, U.S.A.* **84 C9** 41 15N 96 40W
Saunemin, *IL, U.S.A.* **71 C5** 40 54N 88 24W
Sauquoit, *NY, U.S.A.* **89 C5** 43 0N 75 16W
Sausalito, *San Francisco, U.S.A.* **118 A2** 37 51N 122 28W
Sauvage, L., *Qué., Canada* **176 A8** 50 6N 74 30W
Sauz Mocho, *Durango, Mexico* **217 C7** 24 39N 103 39W
Savage, *MD, U.S.A.* **77 A4** 39 8N 76 50W
Savage, *MS, U.S.A.* **81 B3** 34 38N 90 13W
Savage, *MT, U.S.A.* **83 C13** 47 27N 104 21W
Savage River State Forest, *MD, U.S.A.* **77 A1** 39 41N 79 12W
Savagetown, *WY, U.S.A.* **104 C7** 43 52N 105 47W
Savanna, *IL, U.S.A.* **71 A3** 42 5N 90 8W
Savanna, *OK, U.S.A.* **93 D8** 34 50N 95 51W
Savannah, *GA, U.S.A.* **68 D5** 32 5N 81 6W
Savannah, *MO, U.S.A.* **82 B2** 39 56N 94 50W
Savannah, *OH, U.S.A.* **92 C4** 40 58N 82 22W
Savannah, *TN, U.S.A.* **96 E4** 35 14N 88 15W
Savannah →, *GA, U.S.A.* **90 F5** 32 2N 80 53W
Savannah Beach = Tybee Island, *GA, U.S.A.* **68 D6** 32 1N 80 51W
Savannah River Plant, *SC, U.S.A.* **90 E4** 33 15N 81 35W
Savant L., *Ont., Canada* **180 B6** 50 16N 90 44W
Savant Lake, *Ont., Canada* **180 B6** 50 14N 90 40W
Savona, *B.C., Canada* **187 E14** 50 45N 120 50W
Savonburg, *KS, U.S.A.* **74 D8** 37 45N 95 9W
Savoonga, *AK, U.S.A.* **61 E5** 63 42N 170 29W
Savoy, *IL, U.S.A.* **71 C5** 40 3N 88 15W
Sawatch Range, *CO, U.S.A.* **66 D4** 39 0N 106 30W
Sawpit, *CO, U.S.A.* **66 E2** 37 56N 108 6W
Sawtooth City, *ID, U.S.A.* **70 F4** 43 54N 114 50W
Sawtooth Mts., *MN, U.S.A.* **80 C8** 47 30N 91 0W
Sawtooth Nat. Forest, *UT, U.S.A.* **100 B2** 41 54N 113 29W
Sawtooth Nat. Recr. Area △, *ID, U.S.A.* **70 E4** 44 0N 114 50W
Sawtooth Range, *ID, U.S.A.* **70 E4** 44 3N 114 58W
Sawtooth Wilderness, *ID, U.S.A.* **70 F3** 43 59N 115 4W
Sawyer, *KS, U.S.A.* **74 D5** 37 30N 98 41W
Sawyer, *MI, U.S.A.* **79 H5** 41 53N 86 35W
Sawyer, *ND, U.S.A.* **91 B4** 48 5N 101 3W
Sawyer, *OK, U.S.A.* **93 D8** 34 1N 95 23W
Sawyer County ☆, *WI, U.S.A.* **103 C3** 45 50N 91 0W
Sawyers Bar, *CA, U.S.A.* **64 B3** 41 18N 123 7W
Sawyerville, *Qué., Canada* **177 F11** 45 20N 71 34W
Saxapahaw, *NC, U.S.A.* **90 C6** 35 57N 79 19W
Saxe, *VA, U.S.A.* **102 E6** 36 56N 78 40W
Saxis, *VA, U.S.A.* **77 C5** 37 55N 75 43W
Saxonburg, *PA, U.S.A.* **95 D3** 40 45N 79 49W
Saxonville, *Boston, U.S.A.* **106 B1** 42 19N 71 24W
Saxton, *KY, U.S.A.* **97 D8** 36 38N 84 7W
Saxton, *PA, U.S.A.* **95 D4** 40 13N 78 15W
Sayabec, *Qué., Canada* **172 E2** 48 35N 67 41W
Saybrook, *IL, U.S.A.* **71 C5** 40 26N 88 32W
Sayers, *San Antonio, U.S.A.* **117 C4** 29 22N 98 17W
Sayil, *Yucatán, Mexico* **223 B4** 20 8N 89 40W
Saylorsburg, *PA, U.S.A.* **87 B1** 40 54N 75 19W
Saylorville L., *IA, U.S.A.* **73 D5** 41 48N 93 46W
Sayre, *OK, U.S.A.* **93 C4** 35 18N 99 38W
Sayre, *PA, U.S.A.* **95 C6** 41 59N 76 32W
Sayreville, *NJ, U.S.A.* **87 B2** 40 28N 74 22W
Sayula, *Jalisco, Mexico* **218 C4** 19 52N 103 36W
Sayula de Alemán, *Veracruz, Mexico* **221 G6** 17 52N 94 57W
Sayulita, *Nayarit, Mexico* **216 G5** 20 52N 105 27W
Sayville, *NY, U.S.A.* **87 B3** 40 44N 73 5W
Scaggsville, *MD, U.S.A.* **77 A4** 39 9N 76 54W
Scales Mound, *IL, U.S.A.* **71 A3** 42 29N 90 15W
Scammon, *KS, U.S.A.* **74 D9** 37 17N 94 49W
Scammon Bay, *AK, U.S.A.* **61 F6** 61 51N 165 35W
Scandia, *Alta., Canada* **185 H8** 50 20N 112 2W
Scandia, *KS, U.S.A.* **74 B6** 39 48N 97 47W
Scandinavia, *WI, U.S.A.* **103 D4** 44 27N 89 9W
Scanlon, *MN, U.S.A.* **80 D6** 46 42N 92 26W
Scappoose, *OR, U.S.A.* **94 B3** 45 45N 122 53W
Scarborough, *ME, U.S.A.* **76 E3** 43 35N 70 19W
Scarsdale, *NY, U.S.A.* **87 B3** 40 59N 73 49W
Scarsdale, *New Orleans, U.S.A.* **113 C3** 29 50N 89 58W
Scarville, *IA, U.S.A.* **73 B5** 43 28N 93 37W
Scatarie I., *N.S., Canada* **173 G10** 46 0N 59 44W
Scenic, *SD, U.S.A.* **91 G3** 43 47N 102 33W
Scenic Woods, *Houston, U.S.A.* **110 A3** 29 51N 95 18W
Sceptre, *Sask., Canada* **182 E2** 50 51N 109 15W
Schaller, *IA, U.S.A.* **73 C3** 42 30N 95 18W
Schaumburg, *IL, U.S.A.* **71 A5** 42 2N 88 5W
Schefferville = Kawawachikamach, *Qué., Canada* **175 C4** 54 48N 66 50W
Schell City, *MO, U.S.A.* **82 C2** 38 1N 94 7W
Schell Creek Ra., *NV, U.S.A.* **85 C6** 39 25N 114 40W
Schellsburg, *PA, U.S.A.* **95 D4** 40 3N 78 39W
Schenectady, *NY, U.S.A.* **89 C7** 42 49N 73 57W
Schenectady County ☆, *NY, U.S.A.* **89 C7** 42 50N 74 0W
Schenley Park, *Pittsburgh, U.S.A.* **116 B2** 40 25N 79 56W
Schererville, *IN, U.S.A.* **72 B3** 41 29N 87 27W
Scherr, *WV, U.S.A.* **77 A1** 39 12N 79 10W
Schertz, *San Antonio, U.S.A.* **117 B4** 29 33N 98 16W
Schiller Park, *Chicago, U.S.A.* **108 B1** 41 56N 87 52W
Schiller Woods, *Chicago, U.S.A.* **108 B1** 41 57N 87 51W
Schlater, *MS, U.S.A.* **81 C3** 33 39N 90 21W
Schleicher County ☆, *TX, U.S.A.* **98 G7** 30 52N 100 36W
Schleswig, *IA, U.S.A.* **73 C3** 42 10N 95 26W
Schley County ☆, *GA, U.S.A.* **68 D2** 32 15N 84 15W
Schoen Lake Park △, *B.C., Canada* **186 E8** 50 11N 126 14W
Schoenchen, *KS, U.S.A.* **74 C4** 38 43N 99 20W
Schofield, *WI, U.S.A.* **103 D4** 44 54N 89 36W
Schofield Barracks, *HI, U.S.A.* **69 K13** 21 29N 158 7W
Schoharie, *NY, U.S.A.* **89 C6** 42 40N 74 19W
Schoharie County ☆, *NY, U.S.A.* **89 C6** 42 35N 74 30W
Schoharie Cr. →, *NY, U.S.A.* **89 C6** 42 57N 74 18W
Schoharie Res., *NY, U.S.A.* **89 C6** 42 22N 74 26W
Schoodic L., *ME, U.S.A.* **76 C5** 45 23N 68 56W
Schoolcraft, *MI, U.S.A.* **79 G6** 42 7N 85 38W
Schoolcraft County ☆, *MI, U.S.A.* **79 C5** 46 10N 86 15W
Schreiber, *Ont., Canada* **181 D9** 48 45N 87 20W
Schriever, *LA, U.S.A.* **75 E5** 29 45N 90 49W
Schroon L., *NY, U.S.A.* **89 B7** 43 47N 73 47W
Schroon Lake, *NY, U.S.A.* **89 B7** 43 50N 73 46W
Schulenburg, *TX, U.S.A.* **99 H11** 29 41N 96 54W
Schuler, *Alta., Canada* **185 H10** 50 20N 110 6W
Schultz L., *Nunavut, Canada* **191 E6** 64 45N 97 30W
Schumacher, *Ont., Canada* **181 D15** 48 30N 81 16W
Schurz, *NV, U.S.A.* **85 D2** 38 57N 118 49W
Schuyler, *NE, U.S.A.* **84 C8** 41 27N 97 4W
Schuyler, *VA, U.S.A.* **102 D6** 37 47N 78 42W
Schuyler County ☆, *IL, U.S.A.* **71 C3** 40 10N 90 40W
Schuyler County ☆, *MO, U.S.A.* **82 A4** 40 25N 92 30W
Schuyler County ☆, *NY, U.S.A.* **89 C4** 42 20N 76 50W
Schuylkill →, *PA, U.S.A.* **95 E7** 39 53N 75 12W
Schuylkill County ☆, *PA, U.S.A.* **95 D6** 40 48N 76 50W
Schuylkill Haven, *PA, U.S.A.* **95 D6** 40 38N 76 10W
Schwatka Mts., *AK, U.S.A.* **61 C8** 67 20N 156 30W
Schweitzer Mt., *ID, U.S.A.* **70 A2** 48 23N 116 37W
Science Hill, *KY, U.S.A.* **97 C8** 37 11N 84 38W
Scio, *OH, U.S.A.* **92 C5** 40 24N 81 5W
Scio, *OR, U.S.A.* **94 C3** 44 42N 122 51W
Sciota, *PA, U.S.A.* **87 B1** 40 56N 75 19W
Scioto →, *OH, U.S.A.* **92 E3** 38 44N 83 1W
Scioto County ☆, *OH, U.S.A.* **92 E4** 38 53N 82 59W
Scipio, *OK, U.S.A.* **93 C8** 35 3N 95 58W
Scipio, *UT, U.S.A.* **100 D3** 39 15N 112 6W
Scituate, *MA, U.S.A.* **78 B4** 42 12N 70 44W
Scituate Res., *RI, U.S.A.* **78 C3** 41 45N 71 35W
Scobey, *MT, U.S.A.* **83 B12** 48 47N 105 25W
Scofield, *UT, U.S.A.* **100 D4** 39 44N 111 10W
Scofield Res., *UT, U.S.A.* **100 D4** 39 49N 111 8W
Scooba, *MS, U.S.A.* **81 D5** 32 50N 88 29W
Scoresby, C., *Nunavut, Canada* **190 C7** 71 43N 93 41W
Scotch Plains, *NJ, U.S.A.* **87 B2** 40 39N 74 24W
Scotchtown, *NY, U.S.A.* **87 A2** 41 29N 74 22W
Scotia, *CA, U.S.A.* **64 C2** 40 29N 124 6W
Scotia, *NY, U.S.A.* **89 C7** 42 50N 73 58W
Scotia, *NE, U.S.A.* **84 C7** 41 28N 98 42W
Scotland, *Ont., Canada* **178 D6** 43 1N 80 22W
Scotland, *AR, U.S.A.* **63 C3** 35 32N 92 37W
Scotland, *CT, U.S.A.* **78 C2** 41 42N 72 7W
Scotland, *MD, U.S.A.* **77 B4** 38 5N 76 22W
Scotland, *SD, U.S.A.* **91 G8** 43 9N 97 43W
Scotland County ☆, *MO, U.S.A.* **82 A4** 40 25N 92 10W
Scotland County ☆, *NC, U.S.A.* **90 D6** 34 50N 79 30W
Scotland Neck, *NC, U.S.A.* **90 B8** 36 8N 77 25W
Scotlandville, *LA, U.S.A.* **75 D4** 30 31N 91 11W
Scotrun, *PA, U.S.A.* **87 A1** 41 4N 75 19W
Scotstown, *Qué., Canada* **177 F11** 45 32N 71 17W
Scott, *Sask., Canada* **182 C3** 52 22N 108 50W
Scott, *AR, U.S.A.* **63 D3** 34 42N 92 6W
Scott, *LA, U.S.A.* **75 D3** 30 14N 92 6W
Scott, *MS, U.S.A.* **81 C2** 33 36N 91 5W
Scott, *OH, U.S.A.* **92 C2** 40 59N 84 35W
Scott →, *CA, U.S.A.* **64 B3** 41 48N 123 2W
Scott, Mt., *OR, U.S.A.* **94 E3** 42 56N 122 1W
Scott Air Force Base, *IL, U.S.A.* **71 E4** 38 34N 89 51W
Scott Bar Mts., *CA, U.S.A.* **64 B3** 41 50N 123 0W
Scott Chan., *B.C., Canada* **186 E6** 50 45N 128 30W
Scott City, *KS, U.S.A.* **74 C3** 38 29N 100 54W
Scott City, *MO, U.S.A.* **82 D7** 37 12N 89 30W
Scott County ☆, *AR, U.S.A.* **63 D1** 34 54N 94 5W
Scott County ☆, *IL, U.S.A.* **71 D3** 39 40N 90 30W
Scott County ☆, *IN, U.S.A.* **72 E5** 38 40N 85 45W
Scott County ☆, *IA, U.S.A.* **73 D8** 41 35N 90 35W
Scott County ☆, *KS, U.S.A.* **74 C3** 38 30N 101 0W
Scott County ☆, *KY, U.S.A.* **97 B8** 38 15N 84 35W
Scott County ☆, *MN, U.S.A.* **80 F5** 44 40N 93 30W
Scott County ☆, *MS, U.S.A.* **81 D4** 32 22N 89 29W
Scott County ☆, *MO, U.S.A.* **82 E7** 37 0N 89 35W
Scott County ☆, *TN, U.S.A.* **97 D8** 36 25N 84 29W
Scott County ☆, *VA, U.S.A.* **102 E2** 36 55N 82 45W
Scott Is., *B.C., Canada* **186 E6** 50 48N 128 40W
Scott Islands Park △, *B.C., Canada* **186 E6** 50 48N 128 40W
Scott-Jonction, *Qué., Canada* **177 E11** 46 30N 71 4W
Scott L., *Sask., Canada* **189 E11** 59 55N 106 18W
Scott Mts., *CA, U.S.A.* **64 B4** 41 15N 122 45W
Scott Peak, *ID, U.S.A.* **70 E6** 44 21N 112 49W
Scottdale, *Atlanta, U.S.A.* **106 B3** 33 47N 84 16W
Scottdale, *PA, U.S.A.* **95 D3** 40 6N 79 35W
Scotts Bluff County ☆, *NE, U.S.A.* **84 C2** 41 50N 103 45W
Scotts Bluff Nat. Monument △, *NE, U.S.A.* **84 C2** 41 50N 103 40W
Scotts Hill, *TN, U.S.A.* **96 E4** 35 31N 88 15W
Scotts Valley, *CA, U.S.A.* **64 F4** 37 3N 122 1W
Scottsbluff, *NE, U.S.A.* **84 C2** 41 52N 103 40W
Scottsboro, *AL, U.S.A.* **60 B4** 34 40N 86 2W
Scottsburg, *IN, U.S.A.* **72 E5** 38 41N 85 47W
Scottsburg, *OR, U.S.A.* **94 D2** 43 39N 123 49W
Scottsburg, *VA, U.S.A.* **102 E6** 36 45N 78 48W
Scottsdale, *AZ, U.S.A.* **62 D4** 33 40N 111 53W
Scottsdale ✈, *Phoenix, U.S.A.* **116 B3** 33 37N 111 54W
Scottsville, *KS, U.S.A.* **74 B6** 39 32N 97 57W
Scottsville, *KY, U.S.A.* **96 D6** 36 45N 86 11W
Scottsville, *VA, U.S.A.* **102 D6** 37 48N 78 30W
Scottville, *MI, U.S.A.* **79 F5** 43 58N 86 17W
Scotty's Junction, *NV, U.S.A.* **85 E3** 37 18N 117 3W
Scranton, *IA, U.S.A.* **73 C4** 42 1N 94 33W

Scranton, *KS, U.S.A.* **74 C8** 38 47N 95 44W
Scranton, *ND, U.S.A.* **91 D2** 46 9N 103 9W
Scranton, *PA, U.S.A.* **87 A1** 41 25N 75 40W
Scranton, *SC, U.S.A.* **90 E6** 33 55N 79 45W
Screven, *GA, U.S.A.* **68 E4** 31 29N 82 1W
Screven County ☆, *GA, U.S.A.* **68 D5** 32 45N 81 40W
Scribner, *NE, U.S.A.* **84 C9** 41 40N 96 40W
Scugog, L., *Ont., Canada* **179 C8** 44 10N 78 55W
Scurry County ☆, *TX, U.S.A.* **98 E7** 32 44N 100 55W
Sea Breeze, *NJ, U.S.A.* **87 C1** 39 18N 75 20W
Sea Bright, *NJ, U.S.A.* **87 B3** 40 22N 73 59W
Sea Cliff, *NY, U.S.A.* **114 A5** 40 50N 73 38W
Sea I., *B.C., Canada* **193 B2** 49 11N 123 10W
Sea Isle City, *NJ, U.S.A.* **87 C2** 39 9N 74 42W
Sea World, *CA, U.S.A.* **65 L9** 32 46N 117 14W
Seaboard, *NC, U.S.A.* **90 B8** 36 29N 77 26W
Seabrook, *MD, U.S.A.* **119 B5** 38 58N 76 49W
Seabrook, *NH, U.S.A.* **86 D4** 42 53N 70 52W
Seabrook, *TX, U.S.A.* **99 H12** 29 34N 95 2W
Seabrook Island, *SC, U.S.A.* **90 F5** 32 35N 80 10W
Seadrift, *TX, U.S.A.* **99 J11** 28 25N 96 43W
Seaford, *DE, U.S.A.* **77 B5** 38 39N 75 37W
Seaford, *VA, U.S.A.* **102 D8** 37 12N 76 26W
Seaforth, *Ont., Canada* **178 D5** 43 35N 81 25W
Seaforth, *MN, U.S.A.* **80 F3** 44 29N 95 20W
Seagate, *NY, U.S.A.* **114 C2** 40 34N 74 0W
Seager Wheeler L., *Sask., Canada* **182 A8** 54 17N 103 31W
Seagoville, *TX, U.S.A.* **99 E11** 32 38N 96 32W
Seagraves, *TX, U.S.A.* **98 E5** 32 57N 102 34W
Seahorse L., *Nfld. & L., Canada* **172 A4** 52 12N 65 48W
Seal →, *Man., Canada* **191 F7** 59 4N 94 48W
Seal Beach, *Los Angeles, U.S.A.* **111 D4** 33 44N 118 6W
Seal Beach Nat. Wildlife Refuge ⌂, *Los Angeles, U.S.A.* **111 D4** 33 44N 118 4W
Seal Cove, *N.B., Canada* **173 J3** 44 39N 66 51W
Seal Cove, *Nfld. & L., Canada* **174 E4** 47 29N 56 4W
Seal Cove, *Nfld. & L., Canada* **174 C4** 49 57N 56 22W
Seal I., *ME, U.S.A.* **76 E5** 43 53N 68 45W
Seal L., *Nfld. & L., Canada* **175 C5** 54 20N 61 30W
Seale, *AL, U.S.A.* **60 D5** 32 18N 85 10W
Sealy, *TX, U.S.A.* **99 H11** 29 47N 96 9W
Seaman, *OH, U.S.A.* **92 E3** 38 57N 83 34W
Seaman Ra., *NV, U.S.A.* **85 E5** 37 50N 115 8W
Searchlight, *NV, U.S.A.* **85 H6** 35 28N 114 55W
Searchmont, *Ont., Canada* **181 F12** 46 47N 84 3W
Searcy, *AR, U.S.A.* **63 C4** 35 15N 91 44W
Searcy County ☆, *AR, U.S.A.* **63 C3** 35 55N 92 38W
Searles L., *CA, U.S.A.* **65 H9** 35 44N 117 21W
Searsboro, *IA, U.S.A.* **73 D6** 41 35N 92 42W
Searsburg, *VT, U.S.A.* **86 D2** 42 52N 72 58W
Searsport, *ME, U.S.A.* **76 D5** 44 28N 68 56W
Seaside, *CA, U.S.A.* **64 G5** 36 37N 121 50W
Seaside, *OR, U.S.A.* **94 B2** 46 0N 123 56W
Seaside Heights, *NJ, U.S.A.* **87 C2** 39 55N 74 6W
Seaside Park, *NJ, U.S.A.* **87 C2** 39 55N 74 5W
Seat Pleasant, *MD, U.S.A.* **77 B4** 38 53N 76 53W
SeaTac, *WA, U.S.A.* **101 C3** 47 27N 122 19W
Seattle, *WA, U.S.A.* **101 C3** 47 36N 122 19W
Seattle-Tacoma International ✕ (SEA), *WA, U.S.A.* **101 C3** 47 27N 122 18W
Seaville, *NJ, U.S.A.* **87 C2** 39 12N 74 42W
Seba Beach, *Alta., Canada* **184 E6** 53 35N 114 47W
Sebago L., *ME, U.S.A.* **76 E3** 43 52N 70 34W
Sebastian, *FL, U.S.A.* **67 D8** 27 49N 80 28W
Sebastian, C., *OR, U.S.A.* **94 E1** 42 20N 124 26W
Sebastian County ☆, *AR, U.S.A.* **63 C1** 35 10N 94 10W
Sebastián Vizcaíno, B., *Baja Calif., Mexico* **211 F4** 28 0N 114 30W
Sebastopol, *CA, U.S.A.* **64 E4** 38 24N 122 49W
Sebastopol, *MS, U.S.A.* **81 D4** 32 34N 89 20W
Sebec L., *ME, U.S.A.* **76 C4** 45 16N 69 15W
Sebeka, *MN, U.S.A.* **80 D3** 46 38N 95 5W
Sebewaing, *MI, U.S.A.* **79 F8** 43 44N 83 27W
Seboeis, *ME, U.S.A.* **76 C5** 45 22N 68 43W
Seboeis L., *ME, U.S.A.* **76 C5** 45 28N 68 53W
Seboomook L., *ME, U.S.A.* **76 C4** 45 56N 69 51W
Sebree, *KY, U.S.A.* **96 C5** 37 36N 87 32W
Sebrell, *VA, U.S.A.* **102 E7** 36 47N 77 8W
Sebring, *FL, U.S.A.* **67 D7** 27 30N 81 27W
Sebringville, *Ont., Canada* **178 D5** 43 24N 81 4W
Secaucus, *NJ, U.S.A.* **114 B2** 40 47N 74 3W
Sechelt, *B.C., Canada* **186 F11** 49 25N 123 42W
Second Connecticut L., *NH, U.S.A.* **86 A3** 45 9N 71 10W
Second Mesa, *AZ, U.S.A.* **62 B5** 35 48N 110 30W
Secor, *IL, U.S.A.* **71 C4** 40 45N 89 8W
Secretary, *MD, U.S.A.* **77 B5** 38 37N 75 57W
Section, *AL, U.S.A.* **60 B5** 34 35N 85 59W
Security, *CO, U.S.A.* **66 D6** 38 45N 104 45W
Sedalia, *CO, U.S.A.* **66 C6** 39 26N 104 58W
Sedalia, *MO, U.S.A.* **82 C3** 38 42N 93 14W
Sedan, *KS, U.S.A.* **74 D7** 37 8N 96 11W
Sedan, *MN, U.S.A.* **80 E3** 45 35N 95 15W
Sedan, *NM, U.S.A.* **88 A7** 36 9N 103 8W
Sedgefield, *Charlotte, U.S.A.* **107 A1** 35 11N 80 51W
Sedgewick, *Alta., Canada* **185 F9** 52 48N 111 41W
Sedgewick, Mt., *NM, U.S.A.* **88 B2** 35 11N 108 6W
Sedgwick, *CO, U.S.A.* **66 B8** 40 56N 102 32W
Sedgwick, *KS, U.S.A.* **74 D6** 37 55N 97 26W
Sedgwick, *ME, U.S.A.* **76 D5** 44 18N 68 37W
Sedgwick County ☆, *CO, U.S.A.* **66 B8** 40 50N 102 15W
Sedgwick County ☆, *KS, U.S.A.* **74 D6** 37 30N 97 20W
Sedley, *Sask., Canada* **182 E8** 50 10N 104 0W
Sedona, *AZ, U.S.A.* **62 C4** 34 52N 111 46W
Sedro-Woolley, *WA, U.S.A.* **101 B3** 48 30N 122 14W
Seedskadee Nat. Wildlife Refuge ⌂, *WY, U.S.A.* **104 E3** 41 49N 109 48W
Seekonk, *MA, U.S.A.* **78 C3** 41 49N 71 20W
Seeley Lake, *MT, U.S.A.* **83 C4** 47 11N 113 29W
Seeley's Bay, *Ont., Canada* **179 C10** 44 29N 76 14W
Seelyville, *IN, U.S.A.* **72 D3** 39 30N 87 16W
Seguam I., *AK, U.S.A.* **61 K4** 52 19N 172 30W
Seguam Pass, *AK, U.S.A.* **61 K4** 52 0N 172 30W
Seguin, *TX, U.S.A.* **99 H10** 29 34N 97 58W
Seibert, *CO, U.S.A.* **66 C8** 39 18N 102 53W
Seiling, *OK, U.S.A.* **93 B5** 36 9N 98 56W
Selah, *WA, U.S.A.* **101 D5** 46 39N 120 32W
Selawik, *AK, U.S.A.* **61 C8** 66 36N 160 0W
Selawik L., *AK, U.S.A.* **61 C7** 66 30N 160 45W
Selawik Nat. Wildlife Refuge ⌂, *AK, U.S.A.* **61 C8** 66 35N 159 10W
Selby, *SD, U.S.A.* **91 E5** 45 31N 100 2W
Selbyville, *DE, U.S.A.* **77 B5** 38 28N 75 14W
Selden, *KS, U.S.A.* **74 B3** 39 33N 100 34W
Selden, *NY, U.S.A.* **78 D1** 40 52N 73 2W
Seldovia, *AK, U.S.A.* **61 G10** 59 26N 151 43W
Selfridge, *ND, U.S.A.* **91 D5** 46 2N 100 56W
Seligman, *AZ, U.S.A.* **62 B3** 35 20N 112 53W
Seligman, *MO, U.S.A.* **82 E3** 36 31N 93 56W
Selinsgrove, *PA, U.S.A.* **95 D6** 40 48N 76 52W
Selkirk, *Man., Canada* **183 E15** 50 10N 96 55W
Selkirk, *Ont., Canada* **178 E7** 42 49N 79 56W
Selkirk, *KS, U.S.A.* **74 C2** 38 29N 101 32W
Selkirk I. = Horse I., *Man., Canada* **183 B12** 53 20N 99 6W
Selkirk Mts., *ID, U.S.A.* **70 A2** 48 30N 116 40W
Sellers, *SC, U.S.A.* **90 D6** 34 17N 79 28W
Sellersburg, *IN, U.S.A.* **72 E5** 38 24N 85 45W
Sells, *AZ, U.S.A.* **62 F4** 31 55N 111 53W
Selma, *AL, U.S.A.* **60 D3** 32 25N 87 1W
Selma, *AR, U.S.A.* **63 E4** 33 42N 91 34W
Selma, *CA, U.S.A.* **65 G7** 36 34N 119 37W
Selma, *NC, U.S.A.* **90 C7** 35 32N 78 17W
Selma, *OR, U.S.A.* **94 E2** 42 17N 123 37W
Selma, *San Antonio, U.S.A.* **117 B4** 29 35N 98 18W
Selman, *OK, U.S.A.* **93 B4** 36 48N 99 30W
Selmer, *TN, U.S.A.* **96 E4** 35 10N 88 36W
Selway →, *ID, U.S.A.* **70 C3** 46 9N 115 36W
Selway-Bitterroot Wilderness, *ID, U.S.A.* **70 C4** 46 1N 114 49W
Selwyn L., *Canada* **189 D12** 60 0N 104 30W
Selwyn Mts., *Canada* **189 D6** 63 0N 130 0W
Selz, *ND, U.S.A.* **91 C6** 47 52N 99 54W
Semans, *Sask., Canada* **182 D7** 51 25N 104 44W
Semichi Is., *AK, U.S.A.* **61 K1** 52 42N 174 0 E
Seminary, *MS, U.S.A.* **81 E4** 31 34N 89 30W
Seminoe Dam, *WY, U.S.A.* **104 D6** 42 9N 106 54W
Seminoe Res., *WY, U.S.A.* **104 D6** 42 9N 106 55W
Seminole, *FL, U.S.A.* **67 D6** 27 50N 82 47W
Seminole, *OK, U.S.A.* **93 C7** 35 14N 96 41W
Seminole, *TX, U.S.A.* **98 E5** 32 43N 102 39W
Seminole, L., *GA, U.S.A.* **68 F2** 30 43N 84 52W
Seminole County ☆, *FL, U.S.A.* **67 C7** 28 40N 81 15W
Seminole County ☆, *GA, U.S.A.* **68 F2** 31 0N 84 55W
Seminole County ☆, *OK, U.S.A.* **93 C7** 35 10N 96 40W
Seminole Draw →, *TX, U.S.A.* **98 E5** 32 27N 102 20W
Semisopochnoi I., *AK, U.S.A.* **61 L2** 51 55N 179 36 E
Semmes, *AL, U.S.A.* **60 F2** 30 47N 88 16W
Senachwine L., *IL, U.S.A.* **71 B4** 41 10N 89 20W
Senath, *MO, U.S.A.* **82 E6** 36 8N 90 10W
Senatobia, *MS, U.S.A.* **81 B4** 34 37N 89 58W
Seneca, *IL, U.S.A.* **71 B4** 41 19N 88 37W
Seneca, *KS, U.S.A.* **74 B7** 39 50N 96 4W
Seneca, *MD, U.S.A.* **77 A3** 39 5N 77 20W
Seneca, *MO, U.S.A.* **82 E2** 36 51N 94 37W
Seneca, *NE, U.S.A.* **84 B5** 42 3N 100 50W
Seneca, *OR, U.S.A.* **94 C7** 44 8N 118 58W
Seneca, *SC, U.S.A.* **90 D3** 34 41N 82 57W
Seneca, *SD, U.S.A.* **91 E6** 45 4N 99 31W
Seneca County ☆, *NY, U.S.A.* **89 C4** 42 45N 76 45W
Seneca County ☆, *OH, U.S.A.* **92 B3** 41 7N 83 11W
Seneca Falls, *NY, U.S.A.* **89 C4** 42 55N 76 48W
Seneca L., *NY, U.S.A.* **89 C4** 42 40N 76 54W
Seneca Rocks, *WV, U.S.A.* **102 C5** 38 50N 79 23W
Sénécal, L., *Nfld. & L., Canada* **172 A6** 52 5N 63 20W
Senecaville L., *OH, U.S.A.* **92 D5** 39 55N 81 25W
Seney, *MI, U.S.A.* **79 C6** 46 21N 85 57W
Seney Nat. Wildlife Refuge ⌂, *MI, U.S.A.* **79 C5** 46 16N 86 6W
Sénguio, *Michoacan, Mexico* **219 C7** 19 44N 100 21W
Senneterre, *Qué., Canada* **176 C5** 48 25N 77 15W
Senoia, *GA, U.S.A.* **68 C2** 33 18N 84 33W
Señor, *Quintana Roo, Mexico* **223 C5** 19 50N 88 9W
Sentinel, *AZ, U.S.A.* **62 E2** 32 52N 113 13W
Sentinel, *OK, U.S.A.* **93 C4** 35 9N 99 11W
Sentinel Butte, *ND, U.S.A.* **91 D2** 46 55N 103 51W
Separ, *NM, U.S.A.* **88 E2** 32 12N 108 25W
Separation L., *Ont., Canada* **180 B2** 50 14N 94 5W
Sept-Îles, *Qué., Canada* **175 C4** 50 13N 66 22W
Sepulga →, *AL, U.S.A.* **60 E4** 31 11N 86 46W
Sepulveda, *Los Angeles, U.S.A.* **111 A2** 34 13N 118 28W
Sepulveda Flood Control Basin, *Los Angeles, U.S.A.* **111 A2** 34 10N 118 28W
Sequart L., *Nfld. & L., Canada* **172 A6** 52 26N 63 47W
Sequatchi →, *TN, U.S.A.* **97 E7** 35 1N 85 38W
Sequatchie County ☆, *TN, U.S.A.* **97 E7** 35 23N 85 23W
Sequim, *WA, U.S.A.* **101 B2** 48 5N 123 6W
Sequoia Nat. Forest, *CA, U.S.A.* **65 G8** 36 0N 118 20W
Sequoia Nat. Park △, *CA, U.S.A.* **65 G8** 36 30N 118 30W
Sequoyah County ☆, *OK, U.S.A.* **93 C9** 35 30N 94 50W
Sequoyah Nat. Wildlife Refuge ⌂, *OK, U.S.A.* **93 C8** 35 27N 95 1W
Serafina, *NM, U.S.A.* **88 B5** 35 24N 105 19W
Sergeant Bluff, *IA, U.S.A.* **73 C2** 42 24N 96 22W
Sérigny →, *Qué., Canada* **175 B4** 56 47N 66 0W
Serpent Mound, *OH, U.S.A.* **92 D3** 39 1N 83 26W
Serramonte, *San Francisco, U.S.A.* **118 C2** 37 39N 122 28W
Sesser, *IL, U.S.A.* **71 E4** 38 5N 89 1W
Seth Ward, *TX, U.S.A.* **98 C6** 34 13N 101 42W
Seton L., *B.C., Canada* **187 E12** 50 42N 122 8W
Seton Portage, *B.C., Canada* **187 E12** 50 42N 122 17W
Seul, Lac, *Ont., Canada* **180 B4** 50 20N 92 30W
Seul Choix Pt., *MI, U.S.A.* **79 D6** 45 55N 85 55W
Seven Corners, *VA, U.S.A.* **119 B3** 38 53N 77 9W
Seven Devils Mts., *ID, U.S.A.* **70 E2** 44 45N 116 40W
Seven Hills, *Cleveland, U.S.A.* **107 B1** 41 23N 81 40W
Seven Islands = Sept-Îles, *Qué., Canada* **175 C4** 50 13N 66 22W
Seven Islands B., *Nfld. & L., Canada* **175 B5** 59 25N 63 45W
Seven Rivers, *NM, U.S.A.* **88 E6** 32 36N 104 25W
Seven Sisters, *B.C., Canada* **189 F7** 54 56N 128 10W
Seven Sisters Falls, *Man., Canada* **183 E15** 50 7N 96 2W
Seven Troughs Range, *NV, U.S.A.* **85 B2** 40 30N 118 40W
Seven Valleys, *PA, U.S.A.* **77 A4** 39 51N 76 46W
Seventy Mile House, *B.C., Canada* **187 D13** 51 18N 121 23W
Severn, *MD, U.S.A.* **77 A4** 39 8N 76 42W
Severn →, *Ont., Canada* **191 F8** 56 2N 87 36W
Severna Park, *MD, U.S.A.* **77 A4** 39 4N 76 33W
Severy, *KS, U.S.A.* **74 D7** 37 37N 96 14W
Sevier →, *UT, U.S.A.* **100 D2** 39 4N 113 6W
Sevier Bridge Res., *UT, U.S.A.* **100 D3** 39 22N 112 2W
Sevier County ☆, *AR, U.S.A.* **63 E1** 33 58N 94 10W
Sevier County ☆, *TN, U.S.A.* **97 E9** 35 48N 83 33W
Sevier County ☆, *UT, U.S.A.* **100 E4** 38 45N 111 50W
Sevier Desert, *UT, U.S.A.* **100 D3** 39 40N 112 45W
Sevier L., *UT, U.S.A.* **100 E3** 38 54N 113 9W
Sevier Plateau, *UT, U.S.A.* **100 E3** 38 20N 112 10W
Sevierville, *TN, U.S.A.* **97 E9** 35 52N 83 34W
Seville, *FL, U.S.A.* **67 B7** 29 19N 81 30W
Seville, *GA, U.S.A.* **68 E3** 31 58N 83 36W
Sewanee, *TN, U.S.A.* **97 E7** 35 12N 85 55W
Seward, *AK, U.S.A.* **61 F10** 60 7N 149 27W
Seward, *IL, U.S.A.* **71 A4** 42 14N 89 22W
Seward, *KS, U.S.A.* **74 C5** 38 11N 98 48W
Seward, *NE, U.S.A.* **84 D8** 40 55N 97 6W
Seward, *PA, U.S.A.* **95 D4** 40 25N 79 1W
Seward County ☆, *KS, U.S.A.* **74 D3** 37 15N 100 45W
Seward County ☆, *NE, U.S.A.* **84 D8** 40 50N 97 10W
Seward Peninsula, *AK, U.S.A.* **61 D6** 65 30N 166 0W
Sewaren, *NJ, U.S.A.* **114 C1** 40 33N 74 15W
Sewickley, *PA, U.S.A.* **95 D2** 40 32N 80 12W
Sexsmith, *Alta., Canada* **184 C2** 55 21N 118 47W
Sextin →, *Durango, Mexico* **216 B5** 25 41N 105 5W
Seybaplaya, *Campeche, Mexico* **223 C3** 19 39N 90 40W
Seybaplaya, Pta., *Campeche, Mexico* **223 C3** 19 39N 90 42W
Seyé, *Yucatán, Mexico* **223 B4** 20 50N 89 22W
Seymour, *CT, U.S.A.* **78 C1** 41 24N 73 4W
Seymour, *IN, U.S.A.* **72 E5** 38 58N 85 53W
Seymour, *IA, U.S.A.* **73 E5** 40 45N 93 7W
Seymour, *MO, U.S.A.* **82 D4** 37 9N 92 46W
Seymour, *TN, U.S.A.* **97 E9** 35 53N 83 43W
Seymour, *TX, U.S.A.* **99 D8** 33 35N 99 16W
Seymour, *WI, U.S.A.* **103 D5** 44 31N 88 20W
Seymour Arm, *B.C., Canada* **187 D16** 51 15N 118 57W
Seymour Inlet, *B.C., Canada* **186 D7** 51 3N 127 0W
Seymourville, *LA, U.S.A.* **75 D4** 30 16N 91 14W
Shabogamo L., *Nfld. & L., Canada* **175 C4** 53 15N 66 30W
Shabuskwia L., *Ont., Canada* **180 A8** 51 15N 89 0W
Shackelford County ☆, *TX, U.S.A.* **99 E8** 32 45N 99 18W
Shadehill Res., *SD, U.S.A.* **91 E3** 45 45N 102 12W
Shady Cove, *OR, U.S.A.* **94 E3** 42 37N 122 49W
Shady Dale, *GA, U.S.A.* **68 C3** 33 24N 83 36W
Shady Grove, *FL, U.S.A.* **67 A5** 30 17N 83 38W
Shady Grove, *KY, U.S.A.* **96 C5** 37 20N 87 53W
Shady Point, *OK, U.S.A.* **93 C9** 35 8N 94 40W
Shady Side, *MD, U.S.A.* **77 B4** 38 50N 76 31W
Shady Spring, *WV, U.S.A.* **102 D3** 37 42N 81 6W
Shadyside, *OH, U.S.A.* **92 D6** 39 58N 80 45W
Shafer, L., *IN, U.S.A.* **72 C4** 40 46N 86 46W
Shafter, *CA, U.S.A.* **65 H7** 35 30N 119 16W
Shafter, *TX, U.S.A.* **98 H3** 29 49N 104 18W
Shaftsbury, *VT, U.S.A.* **86 C1** 43 1N 73 11W
Shageluk, *AK, U.S.A.* **61 E8** 62 41N 159 34W
Shaker Heights, *OH, U.S.A.* **92 B5** 41 28N 81 32W
Shakespeare I., *Ont., Canada* **180 C8** 49 38N 88 25W
Shakopee, *MN, U.S.A.* **80 F5** 44 48N 93 32W
Shaktoolik, *AK, U.S.A.* **61 D7** 64 20N 161 9W
Shalalth, *B.C., Canada* **187 E12** 50 43N 122 13W
Shaler Mts., *Canada* **188 B11** 71 54N 111 35W
Shallotte, *NC, U.S.A.* **90 E7** 33 58N 78 23W
Shallow Lake, *Ont., Canada* **178 C5** 44 36N 81 5W
Shallow Water, *KS, U.S.A.* **74 C3** 38 23N 100 55W
Shallowater, *TX, U.S.A.* **98 D5** 33 36N 102 0W
Shamattawa, *Man., Canada* **191 F7** 55 51N 92 5W
Shambaugh, *IA, U.S.A.* **73 E3** 40 42N 95 3W
Shamokin, *PA, U.S.A.* **95 D6** 40 47N 76 34W
Shamrock, *Sask., Canada* **182 E5** 50 10N 106 37W
Shamrock, *OK, U.S.A.* **93 C7** 35 56N 96 35W
Shamrock, *TX, U.S.A.* **98 B7** 35 13N 100 15W
Shandon, *CA, U.S.A.* **65 H6** 35 39N 120 23W
Shaniko, *OR, U.S.A.* **94 B5** 45 0N 120 45W
Shannon, *GA, U.S.A.* **68 B1** 34 20N 85 5W
Shannon, *IL, U.S.A.* **71 A4** 42 9N 89 44W
Shannon, *MS, U.S.A.* **81 B5** 34 7N 88 43W
Shannon, L., *WA, U.S.A.* **101 B4** 48 33N 121 45W
Shannon County ☆, *MO, U.S.A.* **82 D5** 37 10N 91 20W
Shannon County ☆, *SD, U.S.A.* **91 G3** 43 15N 102 35W
Shannon L., *Ont., Canada* **181 C13** 49 48N 83 24W
Shannontown, *SC, U.S.A.* **90 E5** 33 53N 80 21W
Shapleigh, *ME, U.S.A.* **86 C4** 43 32N 70 51W
Sharbot Lake, *Ont., Canada* **179 C10** 44 46N 76 41W
Sharkey County ☆, *MS, U.S.A.* **81 D3** 32 55N 90 53W
Sharon, *CT, U.S.A.* **78 C1** 41 53N 73 29W
Sharon, *KS, U.S.A.* **74 D5** 37 15N 98 25W
Sharon, *MA, U.S.A.* **78 B3** 42 7N 71 11W
Sharon, *MS, U.S.A.* **81 D4** 32 40N 89 56W
Sharon, *ND, U.S.A.* **91 C8** 47 36N 97 54W
Sharon, *OK, U.S.A.* **93 B4** 36 17N 99 20W
Sharon, *PA, U.S.A.* **95 C2** 41 14N 80 31W
Sharon, *TN, U.S.A.* **96 D4** 36 14N 88 50W
Sharon, *VT, U.S.A.* **86 C2** 43 47N 72 25W
Sharon, *WI, U.S.A.* **103 F5** 42 30N 88 44W
Sharon Hill, *PA, U.S.A.* **116 B1** 39 54N 75 16W
Sharon Springs, *KS, U.S.A.* **74 C2** 38 54N 101 45W
Sharonbrook, *Charlotte, U.S.A.* **107 B1** 35 6N 80 52W
Sharonville, *OH, U.S.A.* **92 D2** 39 16N 84 25W
Sharp County ☆, *AR, U.S.A.* **63 B4** 36 4N 91 37W
Sharp Mt., *Yukon, Canada* **188 C5** 67 11N 138 42W
Sharpe, L., *SD, U.S.A.* **91 F6** 44 1N 99 23W
Sharpes, *FL, U.S.A.* **67 C8** 28 26N 80 46W
Sharps, *VA, U.S.A.* **77 C4** 37 49N 76 42W
Sharpsburg, *IA, U.S.A.* **73 E4** 40 48N 94 38W
Sharpsburg, *KY, U.S.A.* **97 B9** 38 12N 83 56W
Sharpsburg, *MD, U.S.A.* **77 A3** 39 28N 77 45W
Sharpsburg, *NC, U.S.A.* **90 C8** 35 53N 77 50W
Sharpsburg, *Pittsburgh, U.S.A.* **116 B2** 40 29N 79 55W
Sharpsville, *IN, U.S.A.* **72 C4** 40 23N 86 5W
Sharpsville, *PA, U.S.A.* **95 C2** 41 15N 80 29W
Sharptown, *MD, U.S.A.* **77 B5** 38 35N 75 45W
Shasta, *CA, U.S.A.* **64 C4** 40 36N 122 29W
Shasta, Mt., *CA, U.S.A.* **64 B4** 41 25N 122 12W
Shasta County ☆, *CA, U.S.A.* **64 C4** 40 40N 122 0W
Shasta Dam, *CA, U.S.A.* **64 C4** 40 43N 122 25W
Shasta L., *CA, U.S.A.* **64 C4** 40 43N 122 25W
Shasta Lake, *CA, U.S.A.* **64 C4** 40 41N 122 22W
Shasta Nat. Forest, *CA, U.S.A.* **64 B4** 41 10N 122 20W
Shattuck, *OK, U.S.A.* **93 B4** 36 16N 99 53W
Shaunavon, *Sask., Canada* **182 F3** 49 35N 108 25W
Shavano Park, *San Antonio, U.S.A.* **117 B2** 29 35N 98 33W
Shaver L., *CA, U.S.A.* **65 F7** 37 9N 119 18W
Shaw, *MS, U.S.A.* **81 C3** 33 36N 90 47W
Shawanaga, *Ont., Canada* **178 B6** 45 31N 80 17W
Shawangunk Mts., *NY, U.S.A.* **89 D6** 41 35N 74 30W
Shawano, *WI, U.S.A.* **103 D5** 44 47N 88 36W
Shawano County ☆, *WI, U.S.A.* **103 D5** 44 45N 88 40W
Shawinigan, *Qué., Canada* **177 E10** 46 35N 72 50W
Shawinigan-Sud, *Qué., Canada* **177 E10** 46 31N 72 45W
Shawnee, *GA, U.S.A.* **68 D5** 32 29N 81 25W
Shawnee, *KS, U.S.A.* **74 B9** 39 1N 94 43W
Shawnee, *OH, U.S.A.* **92 D4** 39 36N 82 13W
Shawnee, *OK, U.S.A.* **93 C7** 35 20N 96 55W
Shawnee County ☆, *KS, U.S.A.* **74 C8** 39 0N 95 45W
Shawnee Nat. Forest, *IL, U.S.A.* **71 F5** 37 40N 88 20W
Shawnee State Forest, *OH, U.S.A.* **92 E3** 38 43N 83 13W
Shawneetown, *IL, U.S.A.* **71 F5** 37 42N 88 8W
Shawville, *Qué., Canada* **176 F6** 45 36N 76 30W
Shebandowan, *Ont., Canada* **180 D6** 48 38N 90 4W
Sheboygan, *WI, U.S.A.* **103 E6** 43 46N 87 45W
Sheboygan County ☆, *WI, U.S.A.* **103 E6** 43 45N 87 50W
Sheboygan Falls, *WI, U.S.A.* **103 E6** 43 44N 87 49W
Shedd, *OR, U.S.A.* **94 C2** 44 28N 123 7W
Shediac, *N.B., Canada* **173 G5** 46 14N 64 32W
Sheen, L., *Orlando, U.S.A.* **115 B1** 28 25N 81 31W
Sheenjek →, *AK, U.S.A.* **61 C11** 66 45N 144 33W
Sheep Hole Mts., *CA, U.S.A.* **65 J11** 34 10N 115 40W
Sheep Mt., *CO, U.S.A.* **66 C3** 39 55N 107 8W
Sheep Mt., *WY, U.S.A.* **104 C2** 43 31N 110 28W
Sheep Range, *NV, U.S.A.* **85 F5** 36 35N 115 15W
Sheep Springs, *NM, U.S.A.* **88 A2** 36 10N 108 42W
Sheepshead Bay, *NY, U.S.A.* **114 C3** 40 35N 73 55W
Sheepshead Mts., *OR, U.S.A.* **94 E7** 42 54N 118 9W
Sheet Harbour, *N.S., Canada* **173 J7** 44 56N 62 31W
Sheffield, *AL, U.S.A.* **60 B3** 34 46N 87 41W
Sheffield, *IL, U.S.A.* **71 B4** 41 21N 89 44W
Sheffield, *IA, U.S.A.* **73 C5** 42 54N 93 13W
Sheffield, *MA, U.S.A.* **78 B1** 42 5N 73 21W
Sheffield, *TX, U.S.A.* **98 G6** 30 41N 101 49W
Sheffield L., *Nfld. & L., Canada* **174 C4** 49 20N 56 34W
Sheguiandah, *Ont., Canada* **178 B5** 45 54N 81 55W
Sheho, *Sask., Canada* **182 D8** 51 35N 103 13W
Shelbiana, *KY, U.S.A.* **97 C10** 37 26N 82 30W
Shelbina, *MO, U.S.A.* **82 B4** 39 47N 92 2W
Shelburn, *IN, U.S.A.* **72 D3** 39 11N 87 24W
Shelburne, *N.S., Canada* **173 K4** 43 47N 65 20W
Shelburne, *Ont., Canada* **178 C6** 44 4N 80 15W
Shelburne, *VT, U.S.A.* **86 B1** 44 23N 73 14W
Shelburne Falls, *MA, U.S.A.* **78 B2** 42 36N 72 45W
Shelburne Museum, *VT, U.S.A.* **86 B1** 44 23N 73 14W
Shelby, *IA, U.S.A.* **73 D3** 41 31N 95 27W
Shelby, *MI, U.S.A.* **79 F5** 43 37N 86 22W
Shelby, *MS, U.S.A.* **81 C3** 33 57N 90 46W
Shelby, *MT, U.S.A.* **83 B6** 48 30N 111 51W
Shelby, *NC, U.S.A.* **90 C4** 35 17N 81 32W
Shelby, *NE, U.S.A.* **84 C8** 41 12N 97 26W
Shelby, *OH, U.S.A.* **92 C4** 40 53N 82 40W
Shelby County ☆, *AL, U.S.A.* **60 C4** 33 15N 86 49W
Shelby County ☆, *IL, U.S.A.* **71 D5** 39 25N 88 45W
Shelby County ☆, *IN, U.S.A.* **72 D5** 39 30N 85 50W
Shelby County ☆, *IA, U.S.A.* **73 D3** 41 40N 95 20W
Shelby County ☆, *KY, U.S.A.* **97 B7** 38 10N 85 10W
Shelby County ☆, *MO, U.S.A.* **82 B4** 39 50N 92 0W
Shelby County ☆, *OH, U.S.A.* **92 C2** 40 17N 84 9W
Shelby County ☆, *TN, U.S.A.* **96 E3** 35 5N 89 55W
Shelby County ☆, *TX, U.S.A.* **99 F13** 31 48N 94 11W
Shelbyville, *IL, U.S.A.* **71 D5** 39 24N 88 48W
Shelbyville, *IN, U.S.A.* **72 D5** 39 31N 85 47W
Shelbyville, *KY, U.S.A.* **97 B7** 38 13N 85 14W
Shelbyville, *MO, U.S.A.* **82 B4** 39 48N 92 2W
Shelbyville, *TN, U.S.A.* **96 E6** 35 29N 86 28W
Shelbyville, *TX, U.S.A.* **99 F13** 31 46N 94 5W
Shelbyville, L., *IL, U.S.A.* **71 D5** 39 26N 88 46W
Sheldahl, *IA, U.S.A.* **73 D5** 41 52N 93 42W
Sheldon, *IA, U.S.A.* **73 B3** 43 11N 95 51W
Sheldon, *MO, U.S.A.* **82 D2** 37 40N 94 18W
Sheldon, *ND, U.S.A.* **91 D8** 46 35N 97 30W
Sheldon, *VT, U.S.A.* **86 B2** 44 53N 72 56W
Sheldon, *WI, U.S.A.* **103 C3** 45 19N 90 58W
Sheldon Nat. Wildlife Refuge ⌂, *NV, U.S.A.* **85 A1** 41 48N 119 12W
Sheldon Point, *AK, U.S.A.* **61 E6** 62 32N 164 52W
Sheldrake, *Qué., Canada* **175 C5** 50 20N 64 51W
Shelikof Strait, *AK, U.S.A.* **61 H9** 57 30N 155 0W
Shell, *WY, U.S.A.* **104 B5** 44 32N 107 47W
Shell Beach = Huntington Beach, *CA, U.S.A.* **65 K8** 33 40N 118 5W
Shell Lake, *Sask., Canada* **182 B4** 53 19N 107 2W
Shell Lake, *WI, U.S.A.* **103 C2** 45 45N 91 55W
Shell Rock, *IA, U.S.A.* **73 C6** 42 43N 92 35W
Shell Rock →, *IA, U.S.A.* **73 C6** 42 35N 92 25W
Shellbrook, *Sask., Canada* **182 B5** 53 13N 106 24W
Shelley, *B.C., Canada* **187 B12** 54 0N 122 37W
Shelley, *ID, U.S.A.* **70 F6** 43 23N 112 7W
Shellman, *GA, U.S.A.* **68 E2** 31 46N 84 37W
Shellman Bluff, *GA, U.S.A.* **68 E5** 31 35N 81 19W
Shellmouth, *Man., Canada* **183 E10** 50 56N 101 29W
Shellsburg, *IA, U.S.A.* **73 C7** 42 6N 91 52W
Shelltown, *MD, U.S.A.* **77 C5** 37 58N 75 40W
Shelly, *MN, U.S.A.* **80 C2** 47 28N 96 49W
Shelter Bay = Port-Cartier, *Qué., Canada* **175 C4** 50 2N 66 50W
Shelter I., *NY, U.S.A.* **89 D8** 41 4N 72 20W
Shelton, *CT, U.S.A.* **78 C1** 41 19N 73 5W
Shelton, *NE, U.S.A.* **84 D7** 40 47N 98 44W
Shelton, *WA, U.S.A.* **101 C2** 47 13N 123 6W
Shenandoah, *IA, U.S.A.* **73 E3** 40 46N 95 22W
Shenandoah, *PA, U.S.A.* **95 D6** 40 49N 76 12W
Shenandoah, *VA, U.S.A.* **102 C6** 38 29N 78 37W
Shenandoah →, *VA, U.S.A.* **102 B7** 39 19N 77 44W
Shenandoah County ☆, *VA, U.S.A.* **102 C6** 38 53N 78 30W
Shenandoah Mts., *VA, U.S.A.* **102 C5** 38 40N 79 15W
Shenandoah Nat. Park △, *VA, U.S.A.* **77 B2** 38 35N 78 22W
Shepherd, *MI, U.S.A.* **79 F7** 43 32N 84 41W
Shepherd, *MT, U.S.A.* **83 E9** 45 57N 108 21W
Shepherd, *TX, U.S.A.* **99 G12** 30 31N 95 1W
Shepherd B., *Nunavut, Canada* **190 D7** 68 50N 93 50W
Shepherdstown, *WV, U.S.A.* **77 A3** 39 26N 77 48W
Shepherdsville, *KY, U.S.A.* **97 C7** 37 59N 85 43W
Sheppard Air Force Base, *TX, U.S.A.* **99 D9** 33 57N 98 30W
Sherando, *VA, U.S.A.* **102 D6** 37 59N 78 57W
Sherard, *MS, U.S.A.* **81 B3** 34 13N 90 42W
Sherard, C., *Nunavut, Canada* **190 C9** 74 36N 80 13W
Sherbrooke, *Qué., Canada* **177 F11** 45 28N 71 57W
Sherburn, *MN, U.S.A.* **80 G4** 43 39N 94 43W
Sherburne, *NY, U.S.A.* **89 C5** 42 41N 75 30W
Sherburne, *VT, U.S.A.* **86 C2** 43 10N 72 47W
Sherburne County ☆, *MN, U.S.A.* **80 E5** 45 30N 93 45W
Sheridan, *AR, U.S.A.* **63 D3** 34 19N 92 24W
Sheridan, *Denver, U.S.A.* **109 C1** 39 38N 105 1W
Sheridan, *IL, U.S.A.* **71 B5** 41 32N 88 41W
Sheridan, *IN, U.S.A.* **72 C4** 40 8N 86 13W
Sheridan, *MI, U.S.A.* **79 F6** 43 13N 85 4W
Sheridan, *MO, U.S.A.* **82 A2** 40 31N 94 37W
Sheridan, *MT, U.S.A.* **83 E5** 45 27N 112 12W
Sheridan, *OR, U.S.A.* **94 B2** 45 6N 123 24W
Sheridan, *WY, U.S.A.* **104 B6** 44 48N 106 58W
Sheridan County ☆, *KS, U.S.A.* **74 B3** 39 20N 100 30W
Sheridan County ☆, *MT, U.S.A.* **83 B13** 48 48N 104 30W
Sheridan County ☆, *ND, U.S.A.* **91 C5** 47 45N 100 20W
Sheridan County ☆, *NE, U.S.A.* **84 B3** 42 30N 102 20W
Sheridan County ☆, *WY, U.S.A.* **104 B6** 44 50N 106 45W
Sheridan L., *B.C., Canada* **187 D14** 51 31N 120 54W
Sheridan Lake, *CO, U.S.A.* **66 D8** 38 28N 102 18W
Sheridan Park, *Milwaukee, U.S.A.* **112 C2** 42 34N 87 49W
Sherman, *CT, U.S.A.* **78 C1** 41 35N 73 30W
Sherman, *IL, U.S.A.* **71 D4** 39 54N 89 36W
Sherman, *MS, U.S.A.* **81 B5** 34 22N 88 50W
Sherman, *NY, U.S.A.* **89 C1** 42 10N 79 36W
Sherman, *TX, U.S.A.* **99 D11** 33 38N 96 36W
Sherman Basin, *Nunavut, Canada* **190 D6** 67 47N 97 35W
Sherman County ☆, *KS, U.S.A.* **74 B2** 39 20N 101 45W
Sherman County ☆, *NE, U.S.A.* **84 C7** 41 15N 99 0W
Sherman County ☆, *OR, U.S.A.* **94 B5** 45 30N 120 40W
Sherman County ☆, *TX, U.S.A.* **98 A6** 36 10N 101 58W
Sherman Oaks, *Los Angeles, U.S.A.* **111 B2** 34 8N 118 29W
Sherman Park, *Chicago, U.S.A.* **108 C2** 41 47N 87 39W
Sherman Pk., *ID, U.S.A.* **70 G7** 42 28N 111 33W
Sherman Res., *NE, U.S.A.* **84 C7** 41 18N 98 53W
Sherman Station, *ME, U.S.A.* **76 C5** 45 54N 68 26W
Sherrard, *IL, U.S.A.* **71 B3** 41 19N 90 31W
Sherrelwood, *Denver, U.S.A.* **109 A1** 39 50N 105 0W
Sherrill, *AR, U.S.A.* **63 D4** 34 23N 91 57W
Sherwood, *AR, U.S.A.* **63 D3** 34 48N 92 16W
Sherwood, *MD, U.S.A.* **77 B4** 38 46N 76 19W
Sherwood, *ND, U.S.A.* **91 B4** 48 57N 101 38W
Sherwood, *OH, U.S.A.* **92 B2** 41 17N 84 33W
Sherwood, *OR, U.S.A.* **94 B3** 45 21N 122 50W
Sherwood, *TN, U.S.A.* **97 E7** 35 5N 85 56W
Sherwood, L., *Orlando, U.S.A.* **115 A2** 28 33N 81 29W
Sherwood Park, *Alta., Canada* **184 E7** 53 31N 113 19W
Sheslay →, *B.C., Canada* **189 E6** 58 48N 132 5W
Shetek, L., *MN, U.S.A.* **80 F3** 44 7N 95 42W
Shetucket →, *CT, U.S.A.* **78 C2** 41 39N 72 6W
Shevlin, *MN, U.S.A.* **80 C3** 47 32N 95 15W
Sheyenne, *ND, U.S.A.* **91 C6** 47 50N 99 7W
Sheyenne →, *ND, U.S.A.* **91 C9** 47 2N 96 50W
Sheyenne L., *ND, U.S.A.* **91 C5** 47 42N 100 12W
Sheyenne Nat. Grassland, *ND, U.S.A.* **91 D8** 46 25N 97 20W
Shiawassee →, *MI, U.S.A.* **79 F8** 43 23N 83 58W
Shiawassee County ☆, *MI, U.S.A.* **79 G7** 42 55N 84 10W
Shiawassee Nat. Wildlife Refuge ⌂, *MI, U.S.A.* **79 F7** 43 21N 84 1W
Shibogama L., *Ont., Canada* **191 G8** 53 35N 88 15W
Shickley, *NE, U.S.A.* **84 D8** 40 25N 97 43W
Shickshinny, *PA, U.S.A.* **95 C6** 41 9N 76 9W
Shickshock Mts. = Chic-Chocs, Mts., *Qué., Canada* **172 E3** 48 55N 66 0W
Shidler, *OK, U.S.A.* **93 B7** 36 47N 96 40W
Shidler Res., *OK, U.S.A.* **93 B7** 36 50N 96 40W

Shields, *KS, U.S.A.* **74 C3** 38 37N 100 27W
Shields, *MI, U.S.A.* **79 F7** 43 25N 84 3W
Shillington, *PA, U.S.A.* **95 D7** 40 18N 75 58W
Shiloh, *GA, U.S.A.* **68 D2** 32 49N 84 42W
Shiloh, *NJ, U.S.A.* **87 C1** 39 28N 75 18W
Shiloh, *OH, U.S.A.* **92 C4** 40 58N 82 36W
Shiloh Nat. Military Park ⌂, *TN, U.S.A.* **96 E4** 35 8N 88 20W
Shin Pond, *ME, U.S.A.* **76 B5** 46 6N 68 33W
Shiner, *TX, U.S.A.* **99 H10** 29 26N 97 10W
Shinglehouse, *PA, U.S.A.* **95 C4** 41 58N 78 12W
Shingler, *GA, U.S.A.* **68 E3** 31 35N 83 47W
Shingleton, *MI, U.S.A.* **79 C5** 46 21N 86 28W
Shingletown, *CA, U.S.A.* **64 C5** 40 30N 121 53W
Shinnston, *WV, U.S.A.* **102 B4** 39 24N 80 18W
Shiocton, *WI, U.S.A.* **103 D5** 44 27N 88 35W
Ship Bottom, *NJ, U.S.A.* **87 C2** 39 39N 74 11W
Ship I., *MS, U.S.A.* **81 F5** 30 13N 88 55W
Ship Rock, *NM, U.S.A.* **88 A2** 36 41N 108 50W
Shipman, *IL, U.S.A.* **71 D3** 39 7N 90 3W
Shipman, *VA, U.S.A.* **102 D6** 37 43N 78 51W
Shippagan, *N.B., Canada* **173 F5** 47 45N 64 45W
Shippensburg, *PA, U.S.A.* **95 D5** 40 3N 77 31W
Shippenville, *PA, U.S.A.* **95 C3** 41 15N 79 28W
Shiprock, *NM, U.S.A.* **88 A2** 36 47N 108 41W
Shipshewana, *IN, U.S.A.* **72 B5** 41 41N 85 35W
Shirley, *AR, U.S.A.* **63 C3** 35 39N 92 19W
Shirley, *IN, U.S.A.* **72 D5** 39 53N 85 35W
Shirley, *MA, U.S.A.* **78 B3** 42 33N 71 39W
Shirley Basin, *WY, U.S.A.* **104 D6** 42 20N 106 10W
Shirley City = Woodlawn, *MD, U.S.A.* **77 A4** 39 19N 76 43W
Shirley Mills, *ME, U.S.A.* **76 C4** 45 22N 69 37W
Shishaldin Volcano, *AK, U.S.A.* **61 J7** 54 45N 163 58W
Shishmaref, *AK, U.S.A.* **61 C6** 66 15N 166 4W
Shively, *KY, U.S.A.* **97 B7** 38 12N 85 49W
Shivwits Plateau, *AZ, U.S.A.* **62 A2** 36 15N 113 30W
Shoal Cr. →, *IL, U.S.A.* **71 E4** 38 28N 89 35W
Shoal Cr. →, *MO, U.S.A.* **82 B3** 39 44N 93 32W
Shoal Cr. →, *TN, U.S.A.* **96 F5** 34 50N 87 33W
Shoal L., *Ont., Canada* **180 C1** 49 33N 95 1W
Shoal Lake, *Man., Canada* **183 E11** 50 30N 100 35W
Shoals, *IN, U.S.A.* **72 E4** 38 40N 86 47W
Shoalwater Indian Reservation, *WA, U.S.A.* **101 D1** 46 44N 124 1W
Shoemakersville, *PA, U.S.A.* **95 D7** 40 30N 75 58W
Shonto, *AZ, U.S.A.* **62 A5** 36 36N 110 39W
Shopville, *KY, U.S.A.* **97 C8** 37 9N 84 29W
Shoreacres, *TX, U.S.A.* **99 H12** 29 36N 95 1W
Shoreham, *VT, U.S.A.* **86 C1** 43 54N 73 19W
Shoreline, *WA, U.S.A.* **101 C3** 47 45N 122 20W
Shorewood, *WI, U.S.A.* **103 E6** 43 5N 87 53W
Short Gap, *WV, U.S.A.* **77 A2** 39 33N 78 49W
Shorter, *AL, U.S.A.* **60 D5** 32 24N 85 57W
Shorterville, *AL, U.S.A.* **60 E5** 31 34N 85 6W
Shortsville, *NY, U.S.A.* **89 C3** 42 57N 77 14W
Shoshone, *CA, U.S.A.* **65 H10** 35 58N 116 16W
Shoshone, *ID, U.S.A.* **70 G4** 42 56N 114 25W
Shoshone →, *WY, U.S.A.* **104 B4** 44 52N 108 11W
Shoshone Basin, *WY, U.S.A.* **104 C4** 43 5N 108 5W
Shoshone County ☆, *ID, U.S.A.* **70 B3** 47 30N 116 0W
Shoshone Falls, *ID, U.S.A.* **70 G4** 42 36N 114 24W
Shoshone L., *WY, U.S.A.* **104 B2** 44 22N 110 43W
Shoshone Mts., *NV, U.S.A.* **85 C3** 39 20N 117 25W
Shoshone Nat. Forest, *WY, U.S.A.* **104 B3** 44 20N 109 45W
Shoshone Range, *NV, U.S.A.* **85 B4** 40 20N 116 50W
Shoshoni, *WY, U.S.A.* **104 C4** 43 14N 108 7W
Shoup, *ID, U.S.A.* **70 D4** 45 23N 114 17W
Shoveltown, *MO, U.S.A.* **117 A2** 38 48N 90 16W
Show Low, *AZ, U.S.A.* **62 C5** 34 15N 110 2W
Showell, *MD, U.S.A.* **77 B5** 38 24N 75 13W
Shreve, *OH, U.S.A.* **92 C4** 40 41N 82 1W
Shreveport, *LA, U.S.A.* **75 B2** 32 31N 93 45W
Shrewsbury, *MA, U.S.A.* **78 B3** 42 18N 71 43W
Shrewsbury, *MO, U.S.A.* **117 B2** 38 35N 90 20W
Shrewsbury, *PA, U.S.A.* **77 A4** 39 46N 76 41W
Shubenacadie, *N.S., Canada* **173 H6** 45 5N 63 24W
Shubert, *NE, U.S.A.* **84 D10** 40 14N 95 41W
Shubuta, *MS, U.S.A.* **81 E5** 31 52N 88 42W
Shuksan, Mt., *WA, U.S.A.* **101 B4** 48 50N 121 36W
Shullsburg, *WI, U.S.A.* **103 F3** 42 35N 90 13W
Shumagin Is., *AK, U.S.A.* **61 J7** 55 7N 160 30W
Shungnak, *AK, U.S.A.* **61 C8** 66 52N 157 9W
Shuqualak, *MS, U.S.A.* **81 D5** 32 59N 88 34W
Shushan, *NY, U.S.A.* **86 C1** 43 5N 73 21W
Shuswap L., *B.C., Canada* **187 E15** 50 55N 119 3W
Shutesbury, *MA, U.S.A.* **78 B2** 42 28N 72 25W
Shuyak I., *AK, U.S.A.* **61 G9** 58 31N 152 30W
Sian Ka'an, Reserva de la Biosfera ⌂, *Quintana Roo, Mexico* **223 C6** 19 20N 87 45W
Siasconset, *MA, U.S.A.* **78 C5** 41 16N 69 58W
Sibley, *IL, U.S.A.* **71 C5** 40 35N 88 23W
Sibley, *IA, U.S.A.* **73 B3** 43 24N 95 45W
Sibley, *LA, U.S.A.* **75 B2** 32 33N 93 18W
Sibley, *MS, U.S.A.* **81 E2** 31 23N 91 24W
Sibley County ☆, *MN, U.S.A.* **80 F4** 44 35N 94 15W
Sicamous, *B.C., Canada* **187 E16** 50 49N 119 0W
Sicily Island, *LA, U.S.A.* **75 C4** 31 51N 91 40W
Sideburned L., *Ont., Canada* **181 E13** 47 45N 83 15W
Sidell, *IL, U.S.A.* **71 D6** 39 55N 87 49W
Siding No 14 = Ponoka, *Alta., Canada* **185 F7** 52 42N 113 40W
Sidnaw, *MI, U.S.A.* **79 C3** 46 30N 88 43W
Sidney, *B.C., Canada* **187 G11** 48 39N 123 24W
Sidney, *Man., Canada* **183 F12** 49 54N 99 4W
Sidney, *AR, U.S.A.* **63 B4** 36 0N 91 40W
Sidney, *IL, U.S.A.* **71 C5** 40 1N 88 4W
Sidney, *IA, U.S.A.* **73 E3** 40 45N 95 39W
Sidney, *MT, U.S.A.* **83 C13** 47 43N 104 9W
Sidney, *NY, U.S.A.* **89 C5** 42 19N 75 24W
Sidney, *NE, U.S.A.* **84 C3** 41 8N 102 59W
Sidney, *OH, U.S.A.* **92 C2** 40 17N 84 9W
Sidney Lanier, L., *GA, U.S.A.* **68 B2** 34 10N 84 4W
Sidon, *MS, U.S.A.* **81 C3** 33 25N 90 12W
Sierra Blanca, *TX, U.S.A.* **98 F2** 31 11N 105 22W
Sierra Blanca Peak, *NM, U.S.A.* **88 D5** 33 23N 105 49W
Sierra City, *CA, U.S.A.* **64 D6** 39 34N 120 38W
Sierra County ☆, *CA, U.S.A.* **64 D5** 39 40N 120 30W
Sierra County ☆, *NM, U.S.A.* **88 D3** 33 0N 107 0W
Sierra de la Paila, Parque Natural ⌂, *Coahuila, Mexico* **214 E2** 25 36N 102 7W
Sierra de San Pedro Mártir, Parque Nacional △, *Baja Calif., Mexico* **210 B3** 31 10N 115 30W
Sierra del Carmen, Parque Natural ⌂, *Coahuila, Mexico* **214 A3** 29 17N 101 14W
Sierra Madre, *Los Angeles, U.S.A.* **111 B4** 34 9N 118 3W
Sierra Madre, *WY, U.S.A.* **104 E5** 41 15N 107 5W
Sierra Madre del Sur, *Mexico* **218 D4** 18 45N 104 40W
Sierra Madre Mts., *CA, U.S.A.* **65 J7** 34 54N 119 51W
Sierra Madre Occidental, *Mexico* **216 C5** 27 0N 107 0W
Sierra Madre Oriental, *Mexico* **215 H5** 25 0N 100 0W
Sierra Mojada, *Coahuila, Mexico* **214 C1** 27 18N 103 41W
Sierra Morena, *Chiapas, Mexico* **222 C3** 16 8N 93 35W
Sierra Nat. Forest, *CA, U.S.A.* **65 F7** 37 15N 119 10W
Sierra Nevada, *CA, U.S.A.* **64 D6** 39 0N 120 30W
Sierra Vista, *AZ, U.S.A.* **62 F5** 31 33N 110 18W
Sierraville, *CA, U.S.A.* **64 D6** 39 36N 120 22W
Sierra, *CA, U.S.A.* **64 C6** 40 15N 120 6W
Siesta Key, *FL, U.S.A.* **67 D6** 27 18N 82 33W
Sifton, *Man., Canada* **183 D11** 51 21N 100 8W
Sifton Pass, *B.C., Canada* **189 E8** 57 52N 126 15W
Signal Hill, *Los Angeles, U.S.A.* **111 D3** 33 48N 118 10W
Signal Mountain, *TN, U.S.A.* **97 E7** 35 7N 85 21W
Signal Pk., *AZ, U.S.A.* **62 D1** 33 20N 114 2W
Signal Pk., *UT, U.S.A.* **100 F2** 37 19N 113 29W
Sigourney, *IA, U.S.A.* **73 D6** 41 20N 92 12W
Sigsbee, *GA, U.S.A.* **68 E3** 31 16N 83 52W
Sigurd, *UT, U.S.A.* **100 E4** 38 50N 111 58W
Sigutlat L., *B.C., Canada* **186 C8** 52 57N 126 12W
Sihoplaya, Pta., *Campeche, Mexico* **223 C3** 19 35N 90 43W
Sikanni Chief, *B.C., Canada* **189 E8** 57 14N 122 42W
Sikanni Chief →, *B.C., Canada* **189 E8** 57 47N 122 15W
Sikes, *LA, U.S.A.* **75 B3** 32 5N 92 29W
Sikeston, *MO, U.S.A.* **82 E7** 36 53N 89 35W
Sil Nakya, *AZ, U.S.A.* **62 E4** 32 13N 111 49W
Silacayoapan, *Oaxaca, Mexico* **221 G2** 17 30N 98 9W
Silao, *Guanajuato, Mexico* **219 B6** 20 56N 101 26W
Silas, *AL, U.S.A.* **60 E2** 31 46N 88 20W
Siler City, *NC, U.S.A.* **90 C6** 35 44N 79 28W
Siletz, *OR, U.S.A.* **94 C2** 44 43N 123 55W
Siletz →, *OR, U.S.A.* **94 C1** 44 54N 124 1W
Siletz Indian Reservation, *OR, U.S.A.* **94 C2** 44 47N 123 48W
Silo, *OK, U.S.A.* **93 D7** 34 3N 96 29W
Siloam Springs, *AR, U.S.A.* **63 B1** 36 11N 94 32W
Silsbee, *TX, U.S.A.* **99 G13** 30 21N 94 11W
Silt, *CO, U.S.A.* **66 C3** 39 33N 107 40W
Siltcoos L., *OR, U.S.A.* **94 D1** 43 53N 124 6W
Siltepec, *Chiapas, Mexico* **222 D4** 15 33N 92 17W
Silver, *TX, U.S.A.* **98 E7** 32 4N 100 40W
Silver, L., *Orlando, U.S.A.* **115 A2** 28 35N 81 23W
Silver Bay, *MN, U.S.A.* **80 C7** 47 18N 91 16W
Silver Bell, *AZ, U.S.A.* **62 E4** 32 23N 111 30W
Silver Bow County ☆, *MT, U.S.A.* **83 E5** 45 48N 112 45W
Silver City, *IA, U.S.A.* **73 D3** 41 7N 95 39W
Silver City, *MI, U.S.A.* **79 C2** 46 50N 89 35W
Silver City, *MS, U.S.A.* **81 C3** 33 6N 90 30W
Silver City, *NM, U.S.A.* **88 E2** 32 46N 108 17W
Silver Cliff, *CO, U.S.A.* **66 D5** 38 8N 105 27W
Silver Cr. →, *AZ, U.S.A.* **62 C5** 34 44N 110 2W
Silver Cr. →, *IL, U.S.A.* **71 E4** 38 20N 89 53W
Silver Cr. →, *OR, U.S.A.* **94 D6** 43 16N 119 13W
Silver Creek, *MS, U.S.A.* **81 E4** 31 36N 89 59W
Silver Creek, *NY, U.S.A.* **89 C1** 42 33N 79 10W
Silver Creek, *NE, U.S.A.* **84 C8** 41 19N 97 40W
Silver Dollar City, *MO, U.S.A.* **82 E3** 36 40N 93 20W
Silver Fork, *Salt Lake City, U.S.A.* **117 C4** 40 37N 111 36W
Silver Grove, *OH, U.S.A.* **107 B2** 39 2N 84 23W
Silver Hill, *Boston, U.S.A.* **106 A2** 42 24N 71 18W
Silver Hill, *MD, U.S.A.* **119 C4** 38 49N 76 55W
Silver L., *NH, U.S.A.* **86 C3** 43 52N 71 10W
Silver L., *OR, U.S.A.* **94 D6** 43 22N 119 25W
Silver L., *OR, U.S.A.* **94 D5** 43 6N 120 53W
Silver L., *WA, U.S.A.* **101 D3** 46 17N 122 47W
Silver Lake, *CA, U.S.A.* **65 H10** 35 21N 116 7W
Silver Lake, *KS, U.S.A.* **74 B8** 39 6N 95 52W
Silver Lake, *MN, U.S.A.* **80 F4** 44 54N 94 12W
Silver Lake, *OR, U.S.A.* **94 D4** 43 8N 121 3W
Silver Lake, *WI, U.S.A.* **103 D4** 44 4N 89 14W
Silver Lake Res., *Los Angeles, U.S.A.* **111 B3** 34 5N 118 15W
Silver Peak, *NV, U.S.A.* **85 E3** 37 45N 117 38W
Silver Peak Ra., *NV, U.S.A.* **85 E3** 37 45N 117 45W
Silver Ridge, *Man., Canada* **183 E13** 50 48N 98 52W
Silver Run, *MD, U.S.A.* **77 A3** 39 42N 77 3W
Silver Spring, *MD, U.S.A.* **77 B3** 38 59N 77 2W
Silver Springs, *FL, U.S.A.* **67 B6** 29 13N 82 3W
Silver Springs, *NV, U.S.A.* **85 C1** 39 25N 119 14W
Silver Star Park ⌂, *B.C., Canada* **187 E15** 50 23N 119 5W
Silver Water, *Ont., Canada* **178 B4** 45 52N 82 52W
Silverdale, *KS, U.S.A.* **74 D7** 37 3N 96 54W
Silverthorne, *CO, U.S.A.* **66 C4** 39 38N 106 4W
Silverthrone Glacier, *B.C., Canada* **186 D9** 51 26N 125 53W
Silvertip Mt., *B.C., Canada* **187 F13** 49 10N 121 13W
Silverton, *B.C., Canada* **187 F17** 49 57N 117 21W
Silverton, *CO, U.S.A.* **66 E3** 37 49N 107 40W
Silverton, *NJ, U.S.A.* **87 B2** 40 1N 74 10W
Silverton, *OH, U.S.A.* **107 A2** 39 11N 84 24W
Silverton, *OR, U.S.A.* **94 B3** 45 1N 122 47W
Silverton, *TX, U.S.A.* **98 C6** 34 28N 101 19W
Silverton, *WA, U.S.A.* **101 B4** 48 5N 121 35W
Silverwood, *ID, U.S.A.* **70 B2** 47 56N 116 42W
Silvies →, *OR, U.S.A.* **94 D6** 43 34N 119 2W
Silvis, *IL, U.S.A.* **71 B3** 41 31N 90 25W
Simard, L., *Qué., Canada* **176 D4** 47 40N 78 40W
Simcoe, L., *Ont., Canada* **178 C7** 44 25N 79 20W
Simi Valley, *CA, U.S.A.* **65 J8** 34 16N 118 47W
Simla, *CO, U.S.A.* **66 C6** 39 9N 104 5W
Simmesport, *LA, U.S.A.* **75 D4** 30 59N 91 49W
Simmie, *Sask., Canada* **182 F3** 49 56N 108 6W
Simms, *MT, U.S.A.* **83 C6** 47 30N 111 56W
Simnasho, *OR, U.S.A.* **94 C4** 44 58N 121 21W
Simojovel, *Chiapas, Mexico* **222 B4** 17 12N 92 38W
Simón Bolívar, *Durango, Mexico* **217 C7** 24 41N 103 14W
Simonette →, *Alta., Canada* **184 C2** 55 9N 118 15W
Simonhouse, *Man., Canada* **183 A10** 54 26N 101 23W
Simonton Lake, *IN, U.S.A.* **72 B5** 41 44N 85 59W
Simpson, *Sask., Canada* **182 D6** 51 27N 105 27W
Simpson, *KS, U.S.A.* **74 B6** 39 23N 97 56W
Simpson, *LA, U.S.A.* **75 C2** 31 16N 93 1W
Simpson County ☆, *KY, U.S.A.* **96 D6** 36 45N 86 35W
Simpson County ☆, *MS, U.S.A.* **81 E4** 31 53N 89 58W
Simpson I., *Ont., Canada* **181 D9** 48 46N 87 41W
Simpson Park Mts., *NV, U.S.A.* **85 C4** 39 50N 116 35W
Simpson Pen., *Nunavut, Canada* **190 D8** 68 34N 88 45W
Simpsonville, *SC, U.S.A.* **90 D3** 34 44N 82 15W
Sims, *IL, U.S.A.* **71 E5** 38 22N 88 32W
Simsbury, *CT, U.S.A.* **78 C2** 41 53N 72 48W
Sinai, *SD, U.S.A.* **91 F8** 44 15N 97 3W
Sinaloa □, *Mexico* **216 C3** 25 0N 107 30W
Sinaloa →, *Sinaloa, Mexico* **216 B2** 25 18N 108 30W
Sinaloa de Leyva, *Sinaloa, Mexico* **216 B2** 25 50N 108 14W
Sinanché, *Yucatán, Mexico* **223 A4** 21 13N 89 11W
Sinclair, *WY, U.S.A.* **104 E5** 41 47N 107 7W
Sinclair, L., *GA, U.S.A.* **68 C3** 33 8N 83 12W
Sinclair Pass, *B.C., Canada* **185 H5** 50 40N 115 58W
Sinclairville, *NY, U.S.A.* **89 C1** 42 16N 79 16W
Sing Sing = Ossining, *NY, U.S.A.* **87 A3** 41 10N 73 55W
Singac, *NJ, U.S.A.* **114 A1** 40 53N 74 14W
Singer, *LA, U.S.A.* **75 D2** 30 39N 93 25W
Singuilucan, *Hidalgo, Mexico* **219 C9** 19 58N 98 31W
Sinking Spring, *OH, U.S.A.* **92 D3** 39 4N 83 23W
Sinnemahoning, *PA, U.S.A.* **95 C4** 41 19N 78 6W
Sintaluta, *Sask., Canada* **182 E8** 50 29N 103 27W
Sinton, *TX, U.S.A.* **99 J10** 28 2N 97 31W
Siorapaluk, *Greenland* **190 B11** 77 47N 70 45W
Sioux Center, *IA, U.S.A.* **73 B2** 43 5N 96 11W
Sioux City, *IA, U.S.A.* **73 C2** 42 30N 96 24W
Sioux County ☆, *IA, U.S.A.* **73 B2** 43 5N 96 10W
Sioux County ☆, *ND, U.S.A.* **91 D5** 46 0N 101 0W
Sioux County ☆, *NE, U.S.A.* **84 B2** 42 30N 103 45W
Sioux Falls, *SD, U.S.A.* **91 G9** 43 33N 96 44W
Sioux Lookout, *Ont., Canada* **180 B5** 50 10N 91 50W
Sioux Narrows, *Ont., Canada* **180 C2** 49 25N 94 10W
Sioux Rapids, *IA, U.S.A.* **73 C3** 42 53N 95 9W
Sipiwesk L., *Man., Canada* **191 F6** 55 5N 97 35W
Sipsey →, *AL, U.S.A.* **60 C2** 33 0N 88 10W
Siqueiros, *Sinaloa, Mexico* **216 D4** 23 19N 106 15W
Sir Francis Drake, Mt., *B.C., Canada* **186 E10** 50 49N 124 48W
Sir James MacBrien, Mt., *N.W.T., Canada* **189 D7** 62 7N 127 41W
Sir Sandford, Mt., *B.C., Canada* **187 D17** 51 40N 117 52W
Siren, *WI, U.S.A.* **103 C1** 45 47N 92 24W
Sirmans, *FL, U.S.A.* **67 A5** 30 21N 83 39W
Sirmilik Nat. Park △, *Nunavut, Canada* **190 C9** 72 50N 80 35W
Sisal, *Yucatán, Mexico* **223 A3** 21 10N 90 2W
Sisal, Arrecife, *Yucatán, Mexico* **223 A3** 21 25N 90 18W
Sisbicchén, *Yucatán, Mexico* **223 B6** 20 49N 87 56W
Siskiyou County ☆, *CA, U.S.A.* **64 B4** 41 40N 122 40W
Siskiyou Mts., *U.S.A.* **64 B3** 42 0N 122 40W
Siskiyou Nat. Forest, *OR, U.S.A.* **94 E2** 42 20N 124 0W
Siskiyou Summit, *OR, U.S.A.* **94 E3** 42 3N 122 48W
Sisoguichi, *Chihuahua, Mexico* **213 F8** 27 48N 107 31W
Sisquoc →, *CA, U.S.A.* **65 J6** 34 54N 120 18W
Sisseton, *SD, U.S.A.* **91 E8** 45 40N 97 3W
Sisseton Indian Reservation = Lake Traverse Indian Reservation, *ND, U.S.A.* **91 E8** 46 0N 97 10W
Sisson = Mount Shasta, *CA, U.S.A.* **64 B4** 41 19N 122 19W
Sissonville, *WV, U.S.A.* **102 C3** 38 32N 81 38W
Sister Bay, *WI, U.S.A.* **103 C6** 45 11N 87 7W
Sisters, *OR, U.S.A.* **94 C4** 44 18N 121 33W
Sistersville, *WV, U.S.A.* **102 B4** 39 34N 80 59W
Sitidgi L., *N.W.T., Canada* **188 C6** 68 33N 132 42W
Sitka, *AK, U.S.A.* **61 H14** 57 3N 135 20W
Sitka, *KS, U.S.A.* **74 D4** 37 11N 99 39W
Sitka ☆, *AK, U.S.A.* **61 H14** 57 10N 135 20W
Sitka Nat. Historical Park ⌂, *U.S.A.* **61 H14** 57 3N 135 19W
Sitkinak I., *AK, U.S.A.* **61 H9** 56 33N 154 10W
Siufaalete Pt., *Amer. Samoa* **105 f** 14 17 S 169 29W
Siuslaw →, *OR, U.S.A.* **94 C1** 44 1N 124 8W
Siuslaw Nat. Forest, *OR, U.S.A.* **94 C2** 44 15N 123 50W
Six Flags Great Adventure, *NJ, U.S.A.* **87 B2** 40 10N 74 27W
Six Gun City, *NH, U.S.A.* **86 B3** 44 25N 71 29W
Six Rivers Nat. Forest, *CA, U.S.A.* **64 C3** 41 0N 123 3W
Skagit →, *WA, U.S.A.* **101 B3** 48 23N 122 22W
Skagit B., *WA, U.S.A.* **101 B3** 48 22N 122 34W
Skagit County ☆, *WA, U.S.A.* **101 B4** 48 30N 121 30W
Skagit Valley Park ⌂, *B.C., Canada* **187 F13** 49 7N 121 10W
Skagway, *AK, U.S.A.* **61 G14** 59 28N 135 19W
Skagway-Hoonah-Angoon ☆, *AK, U.S.A.* **61 G13** 58 45N 136 15W
Skamania County ☆, *WA, U.S.A.* **101 D4** 46 0N 122 0W
Skaneateles, *NY, U.S.A.* **89 C4** 42 57N 76 26W
Skanee, *MI, U.S.A.* **79 C3** 46 52N 88 13W
Skedee, *OK, U.S.A.* **93 B7** 36 23N 96 42W
Skeena →, *B.C., Canada* **186 A4** 54 9N 130 5W
Skeena Mts., *B.C., Canada* **189 E7** 56 40N 128 30W
Skellytown, *TX, U.S.A.* **98 B6** 35 34N 101 11W
Skiatook, *OK, U.S.A.* **93 B7** 36 20N 96 0W
Skiatook L., *OK, U.S.A.* **93 B7** 36 20N 96 10W
Skidegate, *B.C., Canada* **186 B2** 53 15N 132 1W
Skidmore, *MO, U.S.A.* **82 A1** 40 17N 95 5W
Skidmore, *TX, U.S.A.* **99 J10** 28 15N 97 41W
Skidway Lake, *MI, U.S.A.* **79 E7** 44 11N 84 2W
Skihist, Mt., *B.C., Canada* **187 E13** 50 12N 121 54W
Skillet Fork →, *IL, U.S.A.* **71 E5** 38 5N 88 5W
Skokie, *IL, U.S.A.* **71 A6** 42 2N 87 43W
Skokie →, *Chicago, U.S.A.* **108 A2** 42 3N 87 46W
Skowhegan, *ME, U.S.A.* **76 D4** 44 46N 69 43W
Skownan, *Man., Canada* **183 D12** 51 58N 99 35W
Skull Valley, *AZ, U.S.A.* **62 C3** 34 30N 112 41W
Skull Valley Indian Reservation, *UT, U.S.A.* **100 C3** 40 24N 112 45W
Skuna →, *MS, U.S.A.* **81 C4** 33 54N 89 41W
Skunk →, *IA, U.S.A.* **73 E7** 40 42N 91 7W
Sky Lake, *Orlando, U.S.A.* **115 B2** 28 27N 81 23W
Skykomish, *WA, U.S.A.* **101 C4** 47 42N 121 22W
Skykomish →, *WA, U.S.A.* **101 C3** 47 49N 122 3W
Skyland, *Atlanta, U.S.A.* **106 A3** 33 53N 84 19W
Skyline, *AL, U.S.A.* **60 B4** 34 49N 86 7W
Skyline, *San Diego, U.S.A.* **117 B2** 32 42N 117 1W
Skyway, *Seattle, U.S.A.* **118 C2** 47 29N 122 15W
Slagle, *LA, U.S.A.* **75 C2** 31 12N 93 8W
Slanesville, *WV, U.S.A.* **77 A2** 39 22N 78 31W
Slate Creek, *ID, U.S.A.* **70 D2** 45 38N 116 17W
Slate Is., *Ont., Canada* **181 D10** 48 40N 87 0W
Slate Spring, *MS, U.S.A.* **81 C4** 33 44N 89 22W
Slater, *IA, U.S.A.* **73 D5** 41 53N 93 41W
Slater, *MO, U.S.A.* **82 B3** 39 13N 93 4W
Slater, *WY, U.S.A.* **104 E8** 41 52N 104 49W
Slatington, *PA, U.S.A.* **87 B1** 40 45N 75 37W
Slaton, *TX, U.S.A.* **98 D6** 33 26N 101 39W
Slaughter, *LA, U.S.A.* **75 D4** 30 43N 91 9W
Slaughter Beach, *DE, U.S.A.* **77 B5** 38 52N 75 18W
Slaughters, *KY, U.S.A.* **96 C5** 37 29N 87 30W
Slaughterville, *OK, U.S.A.* **93 C6** 35 5N 97 20W
Slave →, *Canada* **189 D10** 61 18N 113 39W
Slave Lake, *Alta., Canada* **184 C6** 55 17N 114 43W
Slayton, *MN, U.S.A.* **80 G3** 43 59N 95 45W
Sledge, *MS, U.S.A.* **81 B3** 34 26N 90 13W
Sleeper, *MO, U.S.A.* **82 D4** 37 46N 92 36W
Sleeping Bear Dunes Nat. Lakeshore ⌂, *MI, U.S.A.* **79 E5** 44 50N 86 5W
Sleeping Bear Pt., *MI, U.S.A.* **79 E5** 44 55N 86 3W
Sleeping Giant Prov. Park ⌂, *Ont., Canada* **180 D8** 48 26N 88 46W
Sleepy Eye, *MN, U.S.A.* **80 F4** 44 18N 94 43W
Sleetmute, *AK, U.S.A.* **61 F8** 61 42N 157 10W
Slemp, *KY, U.S.A.* **97 C9** 37 5N 83 6W
Slick, *OK, U.S.A.* **93 C7** 35 47N 96 16W
Slick Rock, *CO, U.S.A.* **66 D2** 38 3N 108 54W
Slide Mt., *NY, U.S.A.* **89 D6** 42 0N 74 25W
Slidell, *LA, U.S.A.* **75 D6** 30 17N 89 47W
Sligo, *PA, U.S.A.* **95 C3** 41 6N 79 29W
Slim Buttes, *SD, U.S.A.* **91 E2** 45 20N 103 15W
Slippery Rock, *PA, U.S.A.* **95 C2** 41 4N 80 3W
Sloan, *IA, U.S.A.* **73 C2** 42 14N 96 14W
Sloan, *NV, U.S.A.* **85 G5** 35 57N 115 13W
Sloat, *CA, U.S.A.* **64 D6** 39 52N 120 44W
Slocan, *B.C., Canada* **187 F17** 49 48N 117 28W
Slocan L., *B.C., Canada* **187 F17** 49 50N 117 23W
Slocan Park, *B.C., Canada* **187 F17** 49 31N 117 37W
Slocomb, *AL, U.S.A.* **60 E5** 31 7N 85 36W
Slocum, *RI, U.S.A.* **78 C3** 41 32N 71 31W
Slope County ☆, *ND, U.S.A.* **91 D2** 46 20N 103 30W
Smackover, *AR, U.S.A.* **63 E3** 33 22N 92 44W
Small, C., *ME, U.S.A.* **76 E4** 43 42N 69 51W
Smallwood Res., *Qué., Canada* **175 C5** 54 5N 64 30W
Smarr, *GA, U.S.A.* **68 D3** 32 59N 83 53W
Smarts Mt., *NH, U.S.A.* **86 C2** 43 48N 72 3W
Smartville, *CA, U.S.A.* **64 D5** 39 13N 121 18W
Smeaton, *Sask., Canada* **182 B7** 53 30N 104 49W
Smethport, *PA, U.S.A.* **95 C4** 41 49N 78 27W
Smiley, *Sask., Canada* **182 D2** 51 38N 109 29W
Smiley, *TX, U.S.A.* **99 H10** 29 16N 97 38W
Smith, *Alta., Canada* **184 C6** 55 10N 114 0W
Smith, *NV, U.S.A.* **85 D1** 38 48N 119 20W
Smith →, *MT, U.S.A.* **83 C6** 47 25N 111 29W
Smith →, *NC, U.S.A.* **90 B6** 36 27N 79 43W
Smith Arm, *N.W.T., Canada* **188 C8** 66 15N 123 0W
Smith B., *AK, U.S.A.* **61 A9** 70 30N 154 20W
Smith Bay, *Nunavut, Canada* **190 B10** 77 4N 78 40W
Smith Center, *KS, U.S.A.* **74 B5** 39 47N 98 47W
Smith County ☆, *KS, U.S.A.* **74 B5** 39 45N 98 45W
Smith County ☆, *MS, U.S.A.* **81 D4** 32 1N 89 23W
Smith County ☆, *TN, U.S.A.* **97 D7** 36 5N 85 57W
Smith County ☆, *TX, U.S.A.* **99 E12** 32 21N 95 18W
Smith Forest Preserve, *Chicago, U.S.A.* **108 B2** 41 59N 87 45W
Smith I., *Nunavut, Canada* **175 C6** 60 45N 78 25W
Smith I., *MD, U.S.A.* **77 B4** 38 0N 76 0W
Smith I., *NC, U.S.A.* **90 E8** 33 53N 77 59W
Smith I., *VA, U.S.A.* **102 D9** 37 9N 75 53W
Smith Lake, *Portland, U.S.A.* **116 A1** 45 36N 122 43W
Smith Mountain L., *VA, U.S.A.* **102 D5** 37 2N 79 30W
Smith Pk., *ID, U.S.A.* **70 A2** 48 51N 116 40W
Smith River, *CA, U.S.A.* **64 B2** 41 56N 124 9W
Smith River Nat. Recr. Area ⌂, *U.S.A.* **58 F2** 41 55N 124 0W
Smith Sd., *N. Amer.* **190 B11** 78 25N 74 0W
Smithburg, *NJ, U.S.A.* **87 B2** 40 13N 74 21W
Smithburg, *WV, U.S.A.* **102 B4** 39 17N 80 44W
Smithdale, *MS, U.S.A.* **81 E3** 31 20N 90 41W
Smithers, *B.C., Canada* **189 F7** 54 45N 127 10W
Smithfield, *NC, U.S.A.* **90 C7** 35 31N 78 21W
Smithfield, *NE, U.S.A.* **84 D6** 40 34N 99 45W
Smithfield, *RI, U.S.A.* **78 C3** 41 55N 71 33W
Smithfield, *UT, U.S.A.* **100 B4** 41 50N 111 50W
Smithfield, *VA, U.S.A.* **102 E8** 36 59N 76 38W
Smithland, *IA, U.S.A.* **73 C3** 42 14N 95 56W
Smithland, *KY, U.S.A.* **96 C4** 37 9N 88 24W
Smiths, *AL, U.S.A.* **60 D5** 32 32N 85 6W
Smiths Cove, *N.S., Canada* **173 J4** 44 37N 65 42W
Smiths Falls, *Ont., Canada* **179 C10** 44 55N 76 0W
Smiths Ferry, *ID, U.S.A.* **70 E2** 44 18N 116 5W
Smiths Grove, *KY, U.S.A.* **96 C6** 37 3N 86 12W
Smithsburg, *MD, U.S.A.* **77 A3** 39 39N 77 35W
Smithton, *MO, U.S.A.* **82 C3** 38 41N 93 5W
Smithtown, *NY, U.S.A.* **78 D1** 40 51N 73 12W
Smithville, *Ont., Canada* **178 D7** 43 6N 79 33W
Smithville, *GA, U.S.A.* **68 E2** 31 54N 84 15W
Smithville, *MD, U.S.A.* **77 B5** 38 46N 75 43W
Smithville, *MS, U.S.A.* **81 B5** 34 4N 88 23W
Smithville, *MO, U.S.A.* **82 B2** 39 23N 94 35W
Smithville, *OK, U.S.A.* **93 D9** 34 28N 94 39W
Smithville, *TN, U.S.A.* **97 E7** 35 58N 85 49W
Smithville, *TX, U.S.A.* **99 G10** 30 1N 97 10W
Smithville, *WV, U.S.A.* **102 B3** 39 4N 81 6W
Smoaks, *SC, U.S.A.* **90 E5** 33 5N 80 49W
Smoke Creek Desert, *NV, U.S.A.* **85 B1** 40 30N 119 40W
Smokey Point, *WA, U.S.A.* **101 B3** 48 9N 122 11W
Smoky →, *Alta., Canada* **184 B3** 56 10N 117 21W
Smoky Dome, *ID, U.S.A.* **70 F4** 43 30N 114 56W
Smoky Hill →, *KS, U.S.A.* **74 B7** 39 4N 96 48W
Smoky Hills, *KS, U.S.A.* **74 B4** 39 15N 99 30W
Smoky Lake, *Alta., Canada* **184 D8** 54 10N 112 30W
Smoky Mts., *ID, U.S.A.* **70 F4** 43 40N 114 38W
Smolan, *KS, U.S.A.* **74 C6** 38 44N 97 41W
Smoot, *WY, U.S.A.* **104 D2** 42 37N 110 55W
Smooth Rock Falls, *Ont., Canada* **181 C15** 49 17N 81 37W
Smoothrock L., *Ont., Canada* **180 B7** 50 30N 89 30W
Smoothstone L., *Sask., Canada* **189 F11** 54 40N 106 50W
Smugglers Notch Resort, *VT, U.S.A.* **86 B2** 44 33N 72 47W
Smyrna, *DE, U.S.A.* **77 A5** 39 18N 75 36W
Smyrna, *GA, U.S.A.* **68 C2** 33 53N 84 31W
Smyrna, *TN, U.S.A.* **96 E6** 35 59N 86 31W
Smyrna Mills, *ME, U.S.A.* **76 B5** 46 8N 68 10W
Smyth County ☆, *VA, U.S.A.* **102 E3** 36 55N 81 25W
Snail Lake, *Minneapolis-St. Paul, U.S.A.* **113 A3** 45 4N 93 7W
Snake →, *Yukon, Canada* **188 C6** 65 59N 134 12W
Snake →, *ID, U.S.A.* **101 D6** 46 12N 119 2W
Snake →, *MN, U.S.A.* **80 B1** 48 26N 97 7W
Snake →, *MN, U.S.A.* **80 E6** 45 49N 92 46W
Snake →, *NE, U.S.A.* **84 B5** 42 47N 100 47W
Snake Creek Canal, *Miami, U.S.A.* **112 C2** 25 57N 80 19W
Snake Mts., *NV, U.S.A.* **85 A6** 41 25N 115 0W
Snake Range, *NV, U.S.A.* **85 D6** 39 0N 114 20W
Snake River Birds of Prey Nat. Conservation Area ⌂, *ID, U.S.A.* **70 F2** 43 10N 116 19W
Snake River Plain, *ID, U.S.A.* **70 G4** 42 50N 114 0W
Snake River Ra., *ID, U.S.A.* **70 F7** 43 23N 111 5W
Snake Valley, *UT, U.S.A.* **100 D2** 39 30N 113 55W
Snare Lakes = Wekweti, *N.W.T., Canada* **189 D10** 64 11N 114 10W
Sneads Ferry, *NC, U.S.A.* **90 D8** 34 33N 77 24W
Sneedville, *TN, U.S.A.* **97 D9** 36 32N 83 13W
Snelling, *CA, U.S.A.* **64 F6** 37 31N 120 26W
Snellville, *GA, U.S.A.* **68 C2** 33 51N 84 1W
Snipe L., *Alta., Canada* **184 C4** 55 7N 116 47W
Snohomish, *WA, U.S.A.* **101 C3** 47 55N 122 6W
Snohomish County ☆, *WA, U.S.A.* **101 B4** 48 0N 121 30W
Snoqualmie, *WA, U.S.A.* **101 C4** 47 31N 121 49W
Snoqualmie Pass, *WA, U.S.A.* **101 C4** 47 25N 121 25W
Snover, *MI, U.S.A.* **79 F9** 43 28N 82 58W
Snow Hill, *AL, U.S.A.* **60 D4** 32 0N 87 0W
Snow Hill, *MD, U.S.A.* **77 B5** 38 11N 75 24W
Snow Hill, *NC, U.S.A.* **90 C8** 35 27N 77 40W
Snow King, *WY, U.S.A.* **104 C2** 43 28N 110 46W
Snow Lake, *Man., Canada* **191 G5** 54 52N 100 3W
Snow Mt., *CA, U.S.A.* **64 D4** 39 23N 122 45W
Snow Mt., *ME, U.S.A.* **76 C3** 45 18N 70 48W
Snow Pk., *WA, U.S.A.* **101 B7** 48 35N 118 29W
Snow Shoe, *PA, U.S.A.* **95 C5** 41 2N 77 57W
Snow Water L., *NV, U.S.A.* **85 B6** 40 48N 114 59W
Snowball, *AR, U.S.A.* **63 C3** 35 55N 92 49W
Snowbird L., *N.W.T., Canada* **189 D12** 60 45N 103 0W
Snowdoun, *AL, U.S.A.* **60 D4** 32 15N 86 18W
Snowdrift = Łutselk'e, *N.W.T., Canada* **189 D10** 62 24N 110 44W
Snowflake, *Man., Canada* **183 F13** 49 3N 98 39W
Snowflake, *AZ, U.S.A.* **62 C5** 34 30N 110 5W
Snowmass, *CO, U.S.A.* **66 C4** 39 20N 106 59W
Snowmass Mt., *CO, U.S.A.* **66 C3** 39 8N 107 5W
Snowshoe Pk., *MT, U.S.A.* **83 B2** 48 13N 115 41W
Snowshoe Ski Resort, *WV, U.S.A.* **102 C4** 38 25N 80 0W
Snowville, *UT, U.S.A.* **100 B3** 41 58N 112 43W
Snowy Mt., *NY, U.S.A.* **89 B6** 43 42N 74 23W
Snowyside Pk., *ID, U.S.A.* **70 F4** 43 57N 114 58W
Snug Harbor, *Tampa, U.S.A.* **119 B3** 27 12N 82 13W
Snyder, *NE, U.S.A.* **84 C9** 41 43N 96 47W
Snyder, *OK, U.S.A.* **93 D5** 34 40N 98 57W
Snyder, *TX, U.S.A.* **98 E7** 32 44N 100 55W
Snyder County ☆, *PA, U.S.A.* **95 D5** 40 50N 77 0W
Soap Lake, *WA, U.S.A.* **101 C6** 47 23N 119 29W
Socastee, *SC, U.S.A.* **90 E7** 33 41N 78 59W
Social Circle, *GA, U.S.A.* **68 C3** 33 39N 83 43W
Society Hill, *AL, U.S.A.* **60 D5** 32 26N 85 27W
Society Hill, *SC, U.S.A.* **90 D6** 34 31N 79 51W
Socoltenango, *Chiapas, Mexico* **222 C4** 16 13N 92 15W
Socorro, *Coahuila, Mexico* **214 D2** 26 56N 102 24W
Socorro, *NM, U.S.A.* **88 C4** 34 4N 106 54W
Socorro, *TX, U.S.A.* **98 F1** 31 39N 106 18W

Socorro County ☆, *NM, U.S.A.* **88 C4** 34 0N 107 0W
Soda Creek, *B.C., Canada* **187 C12** 52 21N 122 17W
Soda L., *CA, U.S.A.* **65 H10** 35 10N 116 4W
Soda Springs, *CA, U.S.A.* **64 D6** 39 20N 120 23W
Soda Springs, *ID, U.S.A.* **70 G7** 42 39N 111 36W
Sodaville, *OR, U.S.A.* **94 C3** 44 29N 122 52W
Soddy-Daisy, *TN, U.S.A.* **97 E7** 35 17N 85 10W
Sodus, *NY, U.S.A.* **89 B3** 43 14N 77 4W
Sodus Point, *NY, U.S.A.* **89 B4** 43 16N 76 59W
Soeurs, Î. des, *Montréal, Canada* **192 B3** 45 27N 73 32W
Sointula, *B.C., Canada* **186 E7** 50 38N 127 0W
Sol Duc →, *WA, U.S.A.* **101 C1** 47 55N 124 32W
Sola de Vega, *Oaxaca, Mexico* **221 H4** 16 33N 96 58W
Solana Beach, *CA, U.S.A.* **65 L9** 32 58N 117 16W
Solano County ☆, *CA, U.S.A.* **64 E5** 38 20N 121 50W
Soldier, *IA, U.S.A.* **73 D3** 41 59N 95 46W
Soldier, *KS, U.S.A.* **74 B8** 39 32N 95 58W
Soldier Summit, *UT, U.S.A.* **100 D4** 39 56N 111 5W
Soldiers Grove, *WI, U.S.A.* **103 E3** 43 24N 90 47W
Soldotna, *AK, U.S.A.* **61 F10** 60 29N 151 3W
Soledad, *CA, U.S.A.* **64 G5** 36 26N 121 20W
Soledad de Doblado, *Veracruz, Mexico* **221 E4** 19 3N 96 25W
Soledad de Graciano Sánchez, *San Luis Potosí, Mexico* **215 H4** 22 12N 100 57W
Solen, *ND, U.S.A.* **91 D5** 46 23N 100 48W
Solferino, *Quintana Roo, Mexico* **223 A6** 21 21N 87 28W
Solis, Presa, *Guanajuato, Mexico* **219 B7** 20 2N 100 37W
Solomon, *AZ, U.S.A.* **62 E6** 32 49N 109 38W
Solomon, *KS, U.S.A.* **74 C6** 38 55N 97 22W
Solomon →, *KS, U.S.A.* **74 C6** 38 55N 97 22W
Solomon, N. Fork →, *KS, U.S.A.* **74 B5** 39 29N 98 26W
Solomon, S. Fork →, *KS, U.S.A.* **74 B4** 39 25N 99 12W
Solomons, *MD, U.S.A.* **77 B4** 38 19N 76 27W
Solon, *IA, U.S.A.* **73 D7** 41 48N 91 30W
Solon, *ME, U.S.A.* **76 D4** 44 57N 69 52W
Solon Springs, *WI, U.S.A.* **103 B2** 46 22N 91 49W
Solvang, *CA, U.S.A.* **65 J6** 34 36N 120 8W
Solvay, *NY, U.S.A.* **89 B4** 43 3N 76 13W
Sombra, *Ont., Canada* **178 E4** 42 43N 82 29W
Sombrerete, *Zacatecas, Mexico* **217 D7** 23 38N 103 39W
Somers, *CT, U.S.A.* **78 C2** 41 59N 72 27W
Somers, *IA, U.S.A.* **73 C4** 42 23N 94 26W
Somers, *MT, U.S.A.* **83 B3** 48 5N 114 13W
Somers Point, *NJ, U.S.A.* **87 C2** 39 20N 74 36W
Somerset, *Man., Canada* **183 F13** 49 25N 98 39W
Somerset, *CO, U.S.A.* **66 D3** 38 56N 107 28W
Somerset, *KY, U.S.A.* **97 C8** 37 5N 84 36W
Somerset, *MA, U.S.A.* **78 C3** 41 47N 71 8W
Somerset, *MD, U.S.A.* **119 B3** 38 57N 77 5W
Somerset, *MI, U.S.A.* **79 G7** 42 3N 84 23W
Somerset, *OH, U.S.A.* **92 D4** 39 48N 82 18W
Somerset, *PA, U.S.A.* **95 D3** 40 1N 79 5W
Somerset, *TX, U.S.A.* **99 H9** 29 14N 98 40W
Somerset County ☆, *ME, U.S.A.* **76 C4** 45 30N 70 0W
Somerset County ☆, *MD, U.S.A.* **77 B5** 38 10N 75 50W
Somerset County ☆, *NJ, U.S.A.* **87 B2** 40 35N 74 35W
Somerset County ☆, *PA, U.S.A.* **95 E4** 40 0N 79 0W
Somerset I., *Nunavut, Canada* **190 C7** 73 30N 93 0W
Somerset Res., *VT, U.S.A.* **86 C2** 43 0N 72 57W
Somersworth, *NH, U.S.A.* **86 C4** 43 16N 70 52W
Somerton, *AZ, U.S.A.* **62 E1** 32 36N 114 43W
Somervell County ☆, *TX, U.S.A.* **99 E10** 32 14N 97 45W
Somerville, *MA, U.S.A.* **78 B3** 42 22N 71 5W
Somerville, *NJ, U.S.A.* **87 B2** 40 35N 74 38W
Somerville, *OH, U.S.A.* **92 D2** 39 34N 84 38W
Somerville, *TN, U.S.A.* **96 E3** 35 15N 89 21W
Somerville, *TX, U.S.A.* **99 G11** 30 21N 96 32W
Somerville L., *TX, U.S.A.* **99 G11** 30 19N 96 31W
Somes Bar, *CA, U.S.A.* **64 B3** 41 23N 123 29W
Sondheimer, *LA, U.S.A.* **75 B4** 32 33N 91 11W
Sonningdale, *Sask., Canada* **182 C4** 52 23N 107 44W
Sonny Bono Nat. Wildlife Refuge ⌓, *CA, U.S.A.* **65 K11** 33 15N 115 40W
Sonoma, *CA, U.S.A.* **64 E4** 38 18N 122 28W
Sonoma, L., *CA, U.S.A.* **64 E3** 38 43N 123 1W
Sonoma County ☆, *CA, U.S.A.* **64 E4** 38 30N 123 0W
Sonoma Peak, *NV, U.S.A.* **85 B3** 40 52N 117 36W
Sonora, *N.S., Canada* **173 H8** 45 4N 61 54W
Sonora, *CA, U.S.A.* **64 F6** 37 59N 120 23W
Sonora, *KY, U.S.A.* **97 C7** 37 32N 85 54W
Sonora, *TX, U.S.A.* **98 G7** 30 34N 100 39W
Sonora □, *Mexico* **212 D5** 29 20N 110 40W
Sonora →, *Sonora, Mexico* **212 D5** 29 5N 110 55W
Sonora I., *B.C., Canada* **186 E9** 50 22N 125 15W
Sonoran Desert, *AZ, U.S.A.* **62 D2** 33 40N 113 30W
Sonoran Desert Nat. Monument ⌓, *AZ, U.S.A.* **62 D3** 33 10N 112 45W
Sonoyta, *Sonora, Mexico* **212 B3** 31 51N 112 50W
Sonoyta →, *Sonora, Mexico* **212 B2** 31 16N 113 26W
Sontag, *MS, U.S.A.* **81 E3** 31 39N 90 12W
Sooke, *B.C., Canada* **187 G11** 48 13N 123 43W
Sooner L., *OK, U.S.A.* **93 B8** 36 28N 95 53W
Sopchoppy, *FL, U.S.A.* **67 A4** 30 4N 84 29W
Soper, *OK, U.S.A.* **93 D8** 34 2N 95 42W
Soperton, *GA, U.S.A.* **68 D4** 32 23N 82 35W
Sophia, *WV, U.S.A.* **102 D3** 37 42N 81 15W
Sop's Arm, *Nfld. & L., Canada* **174 C4** 49 46N 56 56W
Sorel-Tracy, *Qué., Canada* **177 E9** 46 0N 73 10W
Sorento, *IL, U.S.A.* **71 D4** 39 1N 89 35W
Sorrento, *B.C., Canada* **187 E15** 50 53N 119 28W
Sorrento, *LA, U.S.A.* **75 D5** 30 11N 90 51W
Soscumica, L., *Qué., Canada* **175 C2** 50 15N 77 27W
Soso, *MS, U.S.A.* **81 E4** 31 45N 89 17W
Soteapan, *Veracruz, Mexico* **221 F6** 18 14N 94 52W
Soto la Marina, *Tamaulipas, Mexico* **215 G6** 23 46N 98 13W
Soto la Marina →, *Tamaulipas, Mexico* **215 G7** 23 45N 97 45W
Soto la Marina, Barra, *Tamaulipas, Mexico* **215 F7** 24 5N 97 44W
Sotuta, *Yucatán, Mexico* **223 B4** 20 36N 89 1W
Souderton, *PA, U.S.A.* **87 B1** 40 19N 75 19W
Sougahatchee Cr. →, *AL, U.S.A.* **60 D5** 32 36N 85 54W
Souhegan →, *NH, U.S.A.* **86 D3** 42 51N 71 29W
Sound Beach, *NY, U.S.A.* **87 B4** 40 57N 72 58W
Sounding Cr. →, *Alta., Canada* **185 F10** 52 6N 110 28W
Sounding L., *Alta., Canada* **185 F10** 52 8N 110 29W
Soundview, *NY, U.S.A.* **114 B3** 40 49N 73 53W
Sour Lake, *TX, U.S.A.* **99 G13** 30 9N 94 25W
Souris, *P.E.I., Canada* **173 G7** 46 21N 62 15W
Souris, *ND, U.S.A.* **91 B5** 48 55N 100 40W
Souris →, *Man., Canada* **183 F12** 49 40N 99 34W
Souris →, *N. Amer.* **91 B5** 49 0N 100 57W
South →, *NC, U.S.A.* **90 D7** 34 20N 78 3W
South Amboy, *NJ, U.S.A.* **87 B2** 40 29N 74 18W
South Anna →, *VA, U.S.A.* **102 D7** 37 48N 77 25W
South Arm Park, *Vancouver, Canada* **193 C2** 49 7N 123 8W
South Ashburnham, *MA, U.S.A.* **78 B3** 42 37N 71 57W
South Aulatsivik I., *Nfld. & L., Canada* **175 B5** 56 45N 61 30W
South B., *Nunavut, Canada* **191 E9** 63 58N 83 30W
South Baldy Pk., *NM, U.S.A.* **88 C3** 34 6N 107 11W
South Baltimore, *Baltimore, U.S.A.* **107 B2** 39 16N 76 36W
South Barre, *MA, U.S.A.* **78 B2** 42 23N 72 6W
South Bass I., *OH, U.S.A.* **92 B4** 41 39N 82 49W
South Bay, *FL, U.S.A.* **67 E8** 26 40N 80 43W
South Baymouth, *Ont., Canada* **178 B4** 45 33N 82 1W
South Beach, *Miami, U.S.A.* **112 D3** 25 46N 80 7W
South Beach, *NY, U.S.A.* **114 C2** 40 35N 74 4W
South Beach, *Seattle, U.S.A.* **118 C3** 47 34N 122 30W
South Beloit, *IL, U.S.A.* **71 A4** 42 29N 89 2W
South Bend, *IN, U.S.A.* **72 B4** 41 41N 86 15W
South Bend, *WA, U.S.A.* **101 D2** 46 40N 123 48W
South Bend Park, *Atlanta, U.S.A.* **106 B2** 33 42N 84 23W
South Bentinck Arm, *B.C., Canada* **186 C8** 52 7N 126 47W
South Berwick, *ME, U.S.A.* **86 C4** 43 14N 70 49W
South Bloomfield, *OH, U.S.A.* **92 D4** 39 43N 82 59W
South Boardman, *MI, U.S.A.* **79 E6** 44 38N 85 17W
South Boston, *Boston, U.S.A.* **106 A3** 42 20N 71 2W
South Boston, *VA, U.S.A.* **102 E6** 36 42N 78 54W
South Branch, *Nfld. & L., Canada* **174 E1** 47 55N 59 2W
South Branch Potomac →, *WV, U.S.A.* **102 B6** 39 32N 78 35W
South Branch Two →, *MN, U.S.A.* **80 B2** 48 46N 96 56W
South Brook, *Nfld. & L., Canada* **174 C4** 49 26N 56 5W
South Burlington, *VT, U.S.A.* **86 B1** 44 28N 73 13W
South C. = Kalae, *HI, U.S.A.* **69 E6** 18 55N 155 41W
South Carolina □, *U.S.A.* **90 E5** 34 0N 81 0W
South Carthage, *TN, U.S.A.* **97 D7** 36 15N 85 57W
South Carver, *MA, U.S.A.* **78 C4** 41 51N 70 54W
South Chaplin, *CT, U.S.A.* **78 C2** 41 46N 72 9W
South Charleston, *OH, U.S.A.* **92 D3** 39 50N 83 38W
South Charleston, *WV, U.S.A.* **102 C3** 38 22N 81 44W
South Charlestown, *NH, U.S.A.* **86 C2** 43 12N 72 26W
South China, *ME, U.S.A.* **76 D4** 44 24N 69 34W
South Cle Elum, *WA, U.S.A.* **101 C5** 47 11N 120 57W
South Coffeyville, *OK, U.S.A.* **93 B8** 36 59N 95 37W
South Colton, *NY, U.S.A.* **89 A6** 44 31N 74 53W
South Congaree, *SC, U.S.A.* **90 E4** 33 53N 81 9W
South Dakota □, *U.S.A.* **91 F6** 44 15N 100 0W
South Dartmouth, *MA, U.S.A.* **78 C4** 41 36N 70 57W
South Dayton, *NY, U.S.A.* **89 C1** 42 22N 79 3W
South Daytona, *FL, U.S.A.* **67 B7** 29 10N 81 0W
South Decatur, *Atlanta, U.S.A.* **106 B3** 33 44N 84 16W
South Deerfield, *MA, U.S.A.* **78 B2** 42 29N 72 37W
South Deerfield, *NH, U.S.A.* **86 C3** 43 6N 71 18W
South Deering, *Chicago, U.S.A.* **108 C3** 41 42N 87 33W
South Easton, *MA, U.S.A.* **78 B3** 42 3N 71 5W
South Egremont, *MA, U.S.A.* **78 B1** 42 10N 73 25W
South El Monte, *Los Angeles, U.S.A.* **111 B4** 34 3N 118 2W
South English, *IA, U.S.A.* **73 D6** 41 27N 92 5W
South Fabius →, *MO, U.S.A.* **82 B5** 39 54N 91 30W
South Fallsburg, *NY, U.S.A.* **89 D6** 41 43N 74 38W
South Floral Park, *NY, U.S.A.* **114 B4** 40 42N 73 42W
South Fork, *CO, U.S.A.* **66 E4** 37 40N 106 37W
South Fork, *PA, U.S.A.* **95 D4** 40 22N 78 48W
South Fork American →, *CA, U.S.A.* **64 E6** 38 57N 120 59W
South Fork Edisto →, *SC, U.S.A.* **90 E5** 33 16N 80 54W
South Fork Forked Deer →, *TN, U.S.A.* **96 E3** 36 0N 89 26W
South Fork Grand →, *SD, U.S.A.* **91 E3** 45 43N 102 17W
South Fork Indian Reservation, *NV, U.S.A.* **85 B5** 40 45N 115 40W
South Fork John Day →, *OR, U.S.A.* **94 C6** 44 28N 119 31W
South Fork Kentucky →, *KY, U.S.A.* **97 C9** 37 34N 83 43W
South Fork Milk →, *MT, U.S.A.* **83 B11** 48 4N 106 19W
South Fork Moreau →, *SD, U.S.A.* **91 E3** 45 9N 102 50W
South Fork Obion →, *TN, U.S.A.* **96 D4** 36 12N 88 56W
South Fork Owyhee →, *ID, U.S.A.* **70 G2** 42 16N 116 53W
South Fork Powder →, *WY, U.S.A.* **104 C6** 43 40N 106 30W
South Fork Republican →, *NE, U.S.A.* **74 A2** 40 3N 101 31W
South Fork Sappa Cr. →, *KS, U.S.A.* **74 B3** 39 47N 100 35W
South Fork Selway →, *ID, U.S.A.* **70 C3** 46 10N 115 58W
South Fork Shenandoah →, *VA, U.S.A.* **102 C6** 38 57N 78 12W
South Fork Shoshone →, *WY, U.S.A.* **104 B3** 44 27N 109 14W
South Fork Solomon →, *KS, U.S.A.* **74 B5** 39 28N 98 26W
South Fork South Branch Potomac →, *WV, U.S.A.* **102 B6** 39 5N 78 59W
South Fork Spring →, *AR, U.S.A.* **63 B4** 36 19N 91 30W
South Fox I., *MI, U.S.A.* **79 D6** 45 25N 85 51W
South Fulton, *TN, U.S.A.* **96 D4** 36 30N 88 52W
South Gate, *Los Angeles, U.S.A.* **111 C3** 33 56N 118 12W
South Gillies, *Ont., Canada* **180 D7** 48 14N 89 42W
South Gorin, *MO, U.S.A.* **82 A4** 40 22N 92 1W
South Grand →, *MO, U.S.A.* **82 C3** 38 17N 93 25W
South Greensburg, *PA, U.S.A.* **95 D3** 40 17N 79 33W
South Hadley, *MA, U.S.A.* **78 B2** 42 16N 72 35W
South Hadley Falls, *MA, U.S.A.* **78 B2** 42 14N 72 36W
South Hamilton, *MA, U.S.A.* **78 B4** 42 37N 70 53W
South Haven, *KS, U.S.A.* **74 D6** 37 3N 97 24W
South Haven, *MI, U.S.A.* **79 G5** 42 24N 86 16W
South Hd., *Nfld. & L., Canada* **174 C2** 49 9N 58 22W
South Heart, *ND, U.S.A.* **91 D3** 46 52N 102 59W
South Heart →, *Alta., Canada* **184 C4** 55 34N 116 11W
South Hempsted, *NY, U.S.A.* **114 B5** 40 40N 73 36W
South Henik L., *Nunavut, Canada* **191 E6** 61 30N 97 20W
South Hero, *VT, U.S.A.* **86 B1** 44 39N 73 19W
South Hill, *VA, U.S.A.* **102 E6** 36 44N 78 8W
South Holston L., *TN, U.S.A.* **97 D10** 36 31N 82 5W
South Hooksett, *NH, U.S.A.* **86 C3** 43 2N 71 26W
South Hutchinson, *KS, U.S.A.* **74 C6** 38 2N 97 56W
South I., *SC, U.S.A.* **90 E6** 33 10N 79 14W
South Indian Lake, *Man., Canada* **191 F6** 56 47N 98 56W
South Jacksonville, *IL, U.S.A.* **71 D3** 39 44N 90 12W
South Jordan, *UT, U.S.A.* **100 C4** 40 33N 111 55W
South Lake Tahoe, *CA, U.S.A.* **64 E7** 38 57N 119 59W
South Lancaster, *MA, U.S.A.* **78 B3** 42 27N 71 41W
South Lawn, *MD, U.S.A.* **119 C3** 38 47N 77 0W
South Lebanon, *OH, U.S.A.* **92 D2** 39 22N 84 13W
South Lincoln, *Boston, U.S.A.* **106 A2** 42 24N 71 19W
South Loup →, *NE, U.S.A.* **84 C7** 41 4N 98 39W
South Lyon, *MI, U.S.A.* **79 G8** 42 28N 83 39W
South Manitou I., *MI, U.S.A.* **79 D5** 45 2N 86 8W
South Marsh I., *MD, U.S.A.* **77 B4** 38 6N 76 2W
South Merrimack, *NH, U.S.A.* **86 D3** 42 49N 71 34W
South Miami, *FL, U.S.A.* **67 F8** 25 42N 80 17W
South Middleboro, *MA, U.S.A.* **78 C4** 41 45N 70 50W
South Milwaukee, *WI, U.S.A.* **103 F6** 42 55N 87 52W
South Moose L., *Man., Canada* **183 B11** 53 49N 100 1W
South Mountain, *MD, U.S.A.* **77 A3** 39 30N 77 40W
South Mountain, *PA, U.S.A.* **77 A3** 39 51N 77 29W
South Mountain, *Phoenix, U.S.A.* **116 C2** 33 22N 112 4W
South Mountain, *Salt Lake City, U.S.A.* **117 D1** 40 28N 112 2W
South Mountain Park, *Phoenix, U.S.A.* **116 D2** 33 20N 112 8W
South Mountain Reservation, *NJ, U.S.A.* **114 B1** 40 45N 74 17W
South Mountains, *Phoenix, U.S.A.* **116 D2** 33 19N 112 4W
South Mt., *ID, U.S.A.* **70 G2** 42 44N 116 54W
South Nahanni →, *N.W.T., Canada* **189 D8** 61 3N 123 21W
South Nation →, *Ont., Canada* **179 B11** 45 34N 75 6W
South Newport, *GA, U.S.A.* **68 E5** 31 38N 81 24W
South Newtane, *VT, U.S.A.* **86 D2** 42 55N 72 42W
South Ogden, *UT, U.S.A.* **100 B4** 41 12N 111 58W
South Orange, *NJ, U.S.A.* **114 B1** 40 44N 74 15W
South Otselic, *NY, U.S.A.* **89 C5** 42 39N 75 47W
South Ozone Park, *NY, U.S.A.* **114 B4** 40 41N 73 49W
South Paris, *ME, U.S.A.* **76 D3** 44 14N 70 31W
South Park, *Pittsburgh, U.S.A.* **116 C1** 40 18N 79 59W
South Pasadena, *Los Angeles, U.S.A.* **111 B4** 34 7N 118 8W
South Pasadena, *Tampa, U.S.A.* **119 C2** 27 45N 82 44W
South Pass, *LA, U.S.A.* **75 E6** 29 3N 89 12W
South Pass, *WY, U.S.A.* **104 D4** 42 22N 108 55W
South Pass City, *WY, U.S.A.* **104 D4** 42 28N 108 48W
South Pekin, *IL, U.S.A.* **71 C4** 40 30N 89 39W
South Pittsburg, *TN, U.S.A.* **97 E7** 35 1N 85 42W
South Platte →, *NE, U.S.A.* **84 C5** 41 7N 100 42W
South Point, *OH, U.S.A.* **92 E4** 38 25N 82 35W
South Pomfret, *VT, U.S.A.* **86 C2** 43 40N 72 33W
South Ponte Vedra Beach, *FL, U.S.A.* **67 A7** 30 3N 81 20W
South Porcupine, *Ont., Canada* **176 C1** 48 30N 81 12W
South Portland, *ME, U.S.A.* **76 E3** 43 38N 70 15W
South Range, *MI, U.S.A.* **79 B3** 47 4N 88 38W
South Res., *Boston, U.S.A.* **106 A3** 42 26N 71 6W
South River, *Ont., Canada* **178 B7** 45 52N 79 23W
South River, *NJ, U.S.A.* **87 B2** 40 27N 74 23W
South Royalton, *VT, U.S.A.* **86 C2** 43 49N 72 32W
South St. Paul, *MN, U.S.A.* **113 B3** 44 53N 93 2W
South St. Paul Municipal ✈, *Minneapolis-St. Paul, U.S.A.* **113 B3** 44 51N 93 1W
South Salt Lake, *Salt Lake City, U.S.A.* **117 B2** 40 43N 111 53W
South San Francisco, *San Francisco, U.S.A.* **118 C2** 37 38N 122 26W
South San Gabriel, *Los Angeles, U.S.A.* **111 B4** 34 3N 118 6W
South Sanford, *ME, U.S.A.* **86 C4** 43 25N 70 45W
South Saskatchewan →, *Sask., Canada* **182 B6** 53 15N 105 5W
South Seaville, *NJ, U.S.A.* **87 C2** 39 11N 74 46W
South Shore, *Chicago, U.S.A.* **108 C3** 41 45N 87 34W
South Shore, *KY, U.S.A.* **97 B10** 38 43N 82 59W
South Shore, *SD, U.S.A.* **91 E9** 45 7N 96 56W
South Shore Park, *Milwaukee, U.S.A.* **112 C2** 42 57N 87 52W
South Sioux City, *NE, U.S.A.* **84 B9** 42 28N 96 24W
South Sister, *OR, U.S.A.* **94 C4** 44 4N 121 51W
South Skunk →, *IA, U.S.A.* **73 D6** 41 15N 92 2W
South Slocan, *B.C., Canada* **187 F17** 49 28N 117 31W
South Spicer I., *Nunavut, Canada* **190 D10** 68 16N 79 0W
South Stoddard, *NH, U.S.A.* **86 C2** 43 4N 72 7W
South Strafford, *VT, U.S.A.* **86 C2** 43 49N 72 23W
South Sudbury, *Boston, U.S.A.* **106 A1** 42 21N 71 24W
South Sulphur →, *TX, U.S.A.* **99 D12** 33 23N 95 18W
South Thompson →, *B.C., Canada* **187 E14** 50 40N 120 20W
South Torrington, *WY, U.S.A.* **104 D8** 42 3N 104 11W
South Tucson, *AZ, U.S.A.* **62 E5** 32 12N 110 58W
South Twin I., *N.W.T., Canada* **175 C2** 53 7N 79 52W
South Twin L., *Nfld. & L., Canada* **174 C5** 49 16N 55 47W
South Umpqua →, *OR, U.S.A.* **94 D2** 43 16N 123 27W
South Valley, *NM, U.S.A.* **88 B4** 35 1N 106 41W
South Valley Stream, *NY, U.S.A.* **114 C4** 40 39N 73 43W
South Venice, *FL, U.S.A.* **67 D6** 27 3N 82 25W
South Wabasca L., *Alta., Canada* **184 C7** 55 55N 113 45W
South Wayne, *WI, U.S.A.* **103 F4** 42 34N 89 53W
South Weare, *NH, U.S.A.* **86 C3** 43 5N 71 45W
South Webster, *OH, U.S.A.* **92 E4** 38 49N 82 44W
South Wellfleet, *MA, U.S.A.* **78 C5** 41 55N 69 58W
South West City, *MO, U.S.A.* **82 E2** 36 31N 94 37W
South West Port Mouton, *N.S., Canada* **173 K5** 43 54N 64 49W
South Whitley, *IN, U.S.A.* **72 B5** 41 5N 85 38W
South Williamson, *KY, U.S.A.* **97 C10** 37 40N 82 17W
South Williamsport, *PA, U.S.A.* **95 C6** 41 13N 77 0W
South Windsor, *CT, U.S.A.* **78 C2** 41 49N 72 37W
South Woodstock, *VT, U.S.A.* **86 C2** 43 35N 72 32W
South Yarmouth, *MA, U.S.A.* **78 C4** 41 40N 70 10W
South Zanesville, *OH, U.S.A.* **92 D4** 39 54N 82 2W
Southampton, *N.S., Canada* **173 H5** 45 35N 64 15W
Southampton, *Ont., Canada* **178 C5** 44 30N 81 25W
Southampton, *MA, U.S.A.* **78 B2** 42 14N 72 44W
Southampton, *NY, U.S.A.* **78 D2** 40 53N 72 23W
Southampton, C., *Nunavut, Canada* **191 E9** 62 8N 83 43W
Southampton County ☆, *VA, U.S.A.* **102 E7** 36 43N 77 4W
Southampton I., *Nunavut, Canada* **191 E9** 64 30N 84 0W
Southard, *OK, U.S.A.* **93 B5** 36 4N 98 29W
Southaven, *MS, U.S.A.* **81 B4** 34 59N 90 0W
Southbank, *B.C., Canada* **186 A9** 54 2N 125 46W
Southbeach, *OR, U.S.A.* **94 C1** 44 37N 124 3W
Southbridge, *MA, U.S.A.* **78 B2** 42 5N 72 2W
Southbury, *CT, U.S.A.* **78 C1** 41 29N 73 13W
Southeast C., *AK, U.S.A.* **61 E5** 62 56N 169 39W
Southeast Fairbanks ☆, *AK, U.S.A.* **61 E12** 63 45N 143 15W
Southend, *Sask., Canada* **189 E12** 56 19N 103 22W
Southern Indian L., *Man., Canada* **191 F6** 57 10N 98 30W
Southern Pines, *NC, U.S.A.* **90 C6** 35 11N 79 24W
Southern Ute Indian Reservation, *CO, U.S.A.* **66 E3** 37 10N 107 30W
Southey, *Sask., Canada* **182 E7** 50 56N 104 30W
Southfield, *MI, U.S.A.* **79 G8** 42 28N 83 15W
Southgate, *KY, U.S.A.* **107 B2** 39 4N 84 28W
Southington, *CT, U.S.A.* **78 C2** 41 36N 72 53W
Southlake, *Dallas-Fort Worth, U.S.A.* **109 A3** 32 56N 97 8W
Southland, *TX, U.S.A.* **98 D6** 33 22N 101 33W
Southold, *NY, U.S.A.* **78 C2** 41 4N 72 26W
Southport, *NC, U.S.A.* **90 E7** 33 55N 78 1W
Southport, *NY, U.S.A.* **89 C4** 42 3N 76 49W
Southside, *AL, U.S.A.* **60 C4** 33 55N 86 1W
Southside, *WV, U.S.A.* **102 C3** 38 43N 81 58W
Southside Place, *Houston, U.S.A.* **110 B2** 29 42N 95 26W
Southton, *San Antonio, U.S.A.* **117 D3** 29 17N 98 25W
Southwest Florida International ✈ (RSW), *FL, U.S.A.* **67 E7** 26 32N 81 45W
Southwest Harbor, *ME, U.S.A.* **76 D5** 44 17N 68 20W
Southwest Pass, *LA, U.S.A.* **75 E6** 29 56N 89 17W
Southwest Pt., *U.S. Virgin Is.* **105 H18** 17 40N 64 55W
Southwick, *MA, U.S.A.* **78 B2** 42 3N 72 46W
Southwood Acres, *CT, U.S.A.* **78 C2** 41 59N 72 32W
Southworth, *Seattle, U.S.A.* **118 C2** 47 30N 122 30W
Sovereign, *Sask., Canada* **182 D4** 51 31N 107 43W
Sowden L., *Ont., Canada* **180 C5** 49 32N 91 12W
Soyopa, *Sonora, Mexico* **212 E6** 28 45N 109 38W
Spalding, *Sask., Canada* **182 C7** 52 20N 104 30W
Spalding, *ID, U.S.A.* **70 C2** 46 27N 116 49W
Spalding, *NE, U.S.A.* **84 C7** 41 42N 98 22W
Spalding County ☆, *GA, U.S.A.* **68 C2** 33 15N 84 15W
Spallumcheen, *B.C., Canada* **187 E15** 50 26N 119 13W
Spanaway, *WA, U.S.A.* **101 C3** 47 6N 122 26W
Spangle, *WA, U.S.A.* **101 C8** 47 26N 117 23W
Spaniard's Bay, *Nfld. & L., Canada* **174 E7** 47 38N 53 20W
Spanish, *Ont., Canada* **178 A4** 46 12N 82 20W
Spanish →, *Ont., Canada* **178 A4** 46 11N 82 19W
Spanish Fork, *UT, U.S.A.* **100 C4** 40 7N 111 39W
Spanish Fort, *AL, U.S.A.* **60 F3** 30 40N 87 53W
Spanish Lake, *MO, U.S.A.* **82 C6** 38 47N 90 12W
Spanish Lake County Park ⌓, *MO, U.S.A.* **117 A2** 38 47N 90 12W
Spanish Town, *Br. Virgin Is.* **105 H18** 17 43N 64 26W
Sparkman, *AR, U.S.A.* **63 E3** 33 55N 92 51W
Sparks, *GA, U.S.A.* **68 E3** 31 11N 83 26W
Sparks, *NE, U.S.A.* **84 B5** 42 56N 100 15W
Sparks, *NV, U.S.A.* **85 C1** 39 32N 119 45W
Sparks, *OK, U.S.A.* **93 C7** 35 37N 96 50W
Sparland, *IL, U.S.A.* **71 B4** 41 2N 89 26W
Sparlingville, *MI, U.S.A.* **79 G9** 42 58N 82 32W
Sparr, *FL, U.S.A.* **67 B6** 29 20N 82 7W
Sparrows Point, *U.S.A.* **107 B3** 39 13N 76 28W
Sparrows Pt., *Baltimore, U.S.A.* **107 B3** 39 12N 76 29W
Sparta, *GA, U.S.A.* **68 C4** 33 17N 82 58W
Sparta, *IL, U.S.A.* **71 E4** 38 8N 89 42W
Sparta, *KY, U.S.A.* **97 B8** 38 41N 84 54W
Sparta, *MI, U.S.A.* **79 F6** 43 10N 85 42W
Sparta, *MO, U.S.A.* **82 D3** 37 0N 93 5W
Sparta, *NC, U.S.A.* **90 B4** 36 30N 81 7W
Sparta, *TN, U.S.A.* **97 E7** 35 56N 85 28W
Sparta, *VA, U.S.A.* **77 C3** 38 0N 77 14W
Sparta, *WI, U.S.A.* **103 E3** 43 56N 90 49W
Spartanburg, *SC, U.S.A.* **90 D4** 34 56N 81 57W
Spartanburg County ☆, *SC, U.S.A.* **90 D4** 34 50N 82 0W
Spartansburg, *PA, U.S.A.* **95 C3** 41 49N 79 41W
Sparwood, *B.C., Canada* **185 J6** 49 44N 114 53W
Spaulding, *OK, U.S.A.* **93 C7** 35 1N 96 26W
Spavinaw, *OK, U.S.A.* **93 B8** 36 23N 95 3W
Speaks, *TX, U.S.A.* **99 H11** 29 15N 96 42W
Spear, C., *Nfld. & L., Canada* **174 E8** 47 31N 52 37W
Spearfish, *SD, U.S.A.* **91 F2** 44 30N 103 52W
Spearman, *TX, U.S.A.* **98 A6** 36 12N 101 12W
Spearsville, *LA, U.S.A.* **75 B3** 32 56N 92 36W
Spearville, *KS, U.S.A.* **74 D4** 37 51N 99 45W
Spectacle I., *Boston, U.S.A.* **106 A4** 42 19N 70 59W
Speculator, *NY, U.S.A.* **89 B6** 43 30N 74 22W
Speed, *KS, U.S.A.* **74 B4** 39 41N 99 25W
Speedway, *IN, U.S.A.* **72 D4** 39 48N 86 16W
Speers, *Sask., Canada* **182 C4** 52 43N 107 34W
Spence Bay = Taloyoak, *Nunavut, Canada* **190 D7** 69 32N 93 32W
Spencer, *ID, U.S.A.* **70 E6** 44 22N 112 11W
Spencer, *IN, U.S.A.* **72 D4** 39 17N 86 46W
Spencer, *IA, U.S.A.* **73 B3** 43 9N 95 9W
Spencer, *MA, U.S.A.* **78 B3** 42 15N 71 59W
Spencer, *NY, U.S.A.* **89 C4** 42 13N 76 30W
Spencer, *NE, U.S.A.* **84 B7** 42 53N 98 42W
Spencer, *OH, U.S.A.* **92 B4** 41 6N 82 8W
Spencer, *OK, U.S.A.* **93 C6** 35 31N 97 23W
Spencer, *SD, U.S.A.* **91 G8** 43 44N 97 36W
Spencer, *TN, U.S.A.* **97 E7** 35 45N 85 28W
Spencer, *WV, U.S.A.* **102 C3** 38 48N 81 21W
Spencer, *WI, U.S.A.* **103 D3** 44 46N 90 18W
Spencer County ☆, *IN, U.S.A.* **72 F3** 38 0N 87 0W
Spencer County ☆, *KY, U.S.A.* **97 B7** 38 0N 85 20W
Spencertown, *NY, U.S.A.* **78 B1** 42 19N 73 33W
Spencerville, *Ont., Canada* **179 C11** 44 51N 75 33W
Spencerville, *OH, U.S.A.* **92 C2** 40 43N 84 21W
Spencerville, *OK, U.S.A.* **93 D8** 34 8N 95 21W
Spences Bridge, *B.C., Canada* **187 E13** 50 25N 121 20W
Sperling, *Man., Canada* **183 F14** 49 30N 97 42W
Sperry, *OK, U.S.A.* **93 B8** 36 18N 95 59W
Sperryville, *VA, U.S.A.* **102 C6** 38 39N 78 14W
Spiceland, *IN, U.S.A.* **72 D5** 39 50N 85 26W
Spicer, *MN, U.S.A.* **80 E4** 45 14N 94 56W
Spickard, *MO, U.S.A.* **82 A3** 40 14N 93 36W
Spillimacheen, *B.C., Canada* **187 E18** 50 54N 116 22W
Spink, *SD, U.S.A.* **91 H9** 42 51N 96 45W
Spink County ☆, *SD, U.S.A.* **91 F7** 45 0N 98 18W
Spirit L., *IA, U.S.A.* **73 B3** 43 29N 95 6W
Spirit Lake, *ID, U.S.A.* **70 B2** 47 58N 116 52W
Spirit Lake, *IA, U.S.A.* **73 B3** 43 26N 95 6W
Spirit Lake Indian Reservation, *ND, U.S.A.* **91 C7** 47 58N 99 0W
Spirit River, *Alta., Canada* **184 C2** 55 45N 118 50W
Spiritwood, *Sask., Canada* **182 B4** 53 24N 107 33W
Spiritwood, *ND, U.S.A.* **91 D7** 46 56N 98 30W
Spiro, *OK, U.S.A.* **93 C9** 35 15N 94 37W
Splendora, *TX, U.S.A.* **99 G12** 30 14N 95 10W
Split L., *Man., Canada* **191 F6** 56 8N 96 15W
Split Lake, *Man., Canada* **191 F6** 56 8N 96 15W
Spofford, *TX, U.S.A.* **98 H7** 29 10N 100 25W
Spokane, *WA, U.S.A.* **101 C8** 47 40N 117 24W
Spokane →, *WA, U.S.A.* **101 C7** 47 54N 118 20W
Spokane County ☆, *WA, U.S.A.* **101 C8** 47 35N 117 25W
Spokane Indian Reservation, *WA, U.S.A.* **101 C7** 47 57N 118 0W
Spokane International ✈ (GEG), *WA, U.S.A.* **101 C8** 47 37N 117 32W
Spoon →, *IL, U.S.A.* **71 C3** 40 19N 90 4W
Spooner, *WI, U.S.A.* **103 C2** 45 50N 91 53W
Sportsman Acres, *OK, U.S.A.* **93 B8** 36 15N 95 16W
Spot Pond, *Boston, U.S.A.* **106 A3** 42 26N 71 4W
Spotswood, *NJ, U.S.A.* **87 B2** 40 23N 74 23W
Spotsylvania, *VA, U.S.A.* **102 C7** 38 12N 77 36W
Spotsylvania County ☆, *VA, U.S.A.* **102 C7** 38 12N 77 36W
Spotted Horse, *WY, U.S.A.* **104 B7** 44 43N 105 50W
Spotted Ra., *NV, U.S.A.* **85 F5** 36 48N 115 48W
Spragge, *Ont., Canada* **178 A4** 46 15N 82 40W
Sprague, *Man., Canada* **183 F16** 49 2N 95 38W
Sprague, *NE, U.S.A.* **84 D9** 40 38N 96 45W
Sprague, *WA, U.S.A.* **101 C8** 47 18N 117 59W
Sprague →, *OR, U.S.A.* **94 E4** 42 34N 121 51W
Sprague River, *OR, U.S.A.* **94 E4** 42 27N 121 30W
Spray, *OR, U.S.A.* **94 C6** 44 50N 119 48W
Sprigg's Pt., *Nfld. & L., Canada* **174 E8** 47 33N 52 40W
Spring, *TX, U.S.A.* **99 G12** 30 5N 95 25W
Spring →, *MO, U.S.A.* **82 D2** 37 5N 94 45W
Spring Butte, *WY, U.S.A.* **104 E4** 41 51N 108 53W
Spring City, *PA, U.S.A.* **87 B1** 40 11N 75 33W
Spring City, *TN, U.S.A.* **97 E8** 35 42N 84 52W
Spring City, *UT, U.S.A.* **100 D4** 39 29N 111 30W
Spring Coulee, *Alta., Canada* **185 J7** 49 20N 113 3W
Spring Cr. →, *GA, U.S.A.* **68 F2** 30 54N 84 45W
Spring Cr. →, *ND, U.S.A.* **91 C4** 47 15N 101 48W
Spring Cr. →, *NE, U.S.A.* **84 D4** 40 20N 101 6W
Spring Cr. →, *NV, U.S.A.* **85 C3** 39 55N 117 50W
Spring Cr. →, *SD, U.S.A.* **91 G3** 43 52N 102 42W
Spring Cr. →, *SD, U.S.A.* **91 E5** 45 45N 100 18W
Spring Creek, *NV, U.S.A.* **85 B5** 40 44N 115 35W
Spring Glen, *UT, U.S.A.* **100 D5** 39 40N 110 51W
Spring Green, *WI, U.S.A.* **103 E3** 43 11N 90 4W
Spring Grove, *MN, U.S.A.* **80 G7** 43 34N 91 38W
Spring Grove, *PA, U.S.A.* **77 A4** 39 52N 76 52W
Spring Hill, *AL, U.S.A.* **60 E5** 31 42N 85 58W
Spring Hill, *AR, U.S.A.* **63 E2** 33 35N 93 39W
Spring Hill, *FL, U.S.A.* **67 C6** 28 27N 82 41W
Spring Hill, *IA, U.S.A.* **73 D5** 41 25N 93 39W
Spring Hill, *MN, U.S.A.* **80 E4** 45 32N 94 50W
Spring Hill, *TN, U.S.A.* **96 E6** 35 45N 86 56W
Spring Hills, *Indianapolis, U.S.A.* **110 A1** 39 50N 86 11W
Spring Hope, *NC, U.S.A.* **90 C7** 35 57N 78 6W
Spring Lake, *MI, U.S.A.* **79 F5** 43 5N 86 12W
Spring Lake, *NC, U.S.A.* **90 C7** 35 10N 78 58W
Spring Lake, *NJ, U.S.A.* **87 B2** 40 9N 74 2W
Spring Mts., *NV, U.S.A.* **85 F5** 36 0N 115 45W

Spring Pond, *Boston, U.S.A.* **106 A4** 42 29N 70 56W
Spring Valley, *Sask., Canada* **182 F6** 49 56N 105 24W
Spring Valley, *CA, U.S.A.* **65 L10** 32 44N 116 59W
Spring Valley, *Houston, U.S.A.* **110 B1** 29 47N 95 30W
Spring Valley, *IL, U.S.A.* **71 B4** 41 20N 89 12W
Spring Valley, *MN, U.S.A.* **80 G6** 43 41N 92 23W
Spring Valley, *NY, U.S.A.* **87 A2** 41 7N 74 3W
Spring Valley, *NV, U.S.A.* **85 F5** 36 6N 115 14W
Spring Valley, *NV, U.S.A.* **85 C6** 39 10N 114 25W
Spring Valley, *WI, U.S.A.* **103 D1** 44 51N 92 14W
Springbrook, *IA, U.S.A.* **73 C8** 42 10N 90 29W
Springdale, *Nfld. & L., Canada* **174 C4** 49 30N 56 6W
Springdale, *AR, U.S.A.* **63 B1** 36 11N 94 8W
Springdale, *OH, U.S.A.* **92 D2** 39 17N 84 29W
Springdale, *UT, U.S.A.* **100 F3** 37 10N 113 0W
Springdale, *WA, U.S.A.* **101 B8** 48 4N 117 45W
Springer, *NM, U.S.A.* **88 A6** 36 22N 104 36W
Springer, *OK, U.S.A.* **93 D6** 34 19N 97 8W
Springerton, *IL, U.S.A.* **71 E5** 38 11N 88 21W
Springerville, *AZ, U.S.A.* **62 C6** 34 8N 109 17W
Springfield, *N.S., Canada* **173 J5** 44 38N 64 52W
Springfield, *Ont., Canada* **178 E6** 42 50N 80 56W
Springfield, *CO, U.S.A.* **66 E8** 37 24N 102 37W
Springfield, *FL, U.S.A.* **67 A3** 30 10N 85 37W
Springfield, *GA, U.S.A.* **68 D5** 32 22N 81 18W
Springfield, *ID, U.S.A.* **70 F6** 43 5N 112 41W
Springfield, *IL, U.S.A.* **71 D4** 39 48N 89 39W
Springfield, *KY, U.S.A.* **97 C7** 37 41N 85 13W
Springfield, *LA, U.S.A.* **75 D5** 30 26N 90 33W
Springfield, *ME, U.S.A.* **76 C5** 45 24N 68 8W
Springfield, *MA, U.S.A.* **78 B2** 42 6N 72 35W
Springfield, *MI, U.S.A.* **79 G6** 42 20N 85 14W
Springfield, *MN, U.S.A.* **80 F4** 44 14N 94 59W
Springfield, *MO, U.S.A.* **82 D3** 37 13N 93 17W
Springfield, *NJ, U.S.A.* **114 B1** 44 43N 74 18W
Springfield, *NE, U.S.A.* **84 C9** 41 5N 96 8W
Springfield, *OH, U.S.A.* **92 D3** 39 55N 83 49W
Springfield, *OR, U.S.A.* **94 C2** 44 3N 123 1W
Springfield, *PA, U.S.A.* **87 C1** 39 56N 75 19W
Springfield, *SC, U.S.A.* **90 E4** 33 30N 81 17W
Springfield, *SD, U.S.A.* **91 H8** 42 49N 97 54W
Springfield, *TN, U.S.A.* **96 D6** 36 31N 86 53W
Springfield, *VA, U.S.A.* **77 B3** 38 46N 77 10W
Springfield, *VT, U.S.A.* **86 C2** 43 18N 72 29W
Springfield, *WV, U.S.A.* **77 A2** 39 27N 78 42W
Springfield, L., *IL, U.S.A.* **71 D4** 39 46N 89 36W
Springhill, *LA, U.S.A.* **75 B2** 33 0N 93 28W
Springhouse, *B.C., Canada* **187 D12** 51 56N 122 7W
Springlake, *TX, U.S.A.* **98 C5** 34 14N 102 18W
Springport, *MI, U.S.A.* **79 G7** 42 22N 84 42W
Springs, *NY, U.S.A.* **78 C2** 41 1N 72 10W
Springside, *Sask., Canada* **182 D9** 51 21N 102 44W
Springtown, *TX, U.S.A.* **99 E10** 32 58N 97 41W
Springvale, *GA, U.S.A.* **68 E2** 31 50N 84 53W
Springvale, *ME, U.S.A.* **76 E3** 43 28N 70 48W
Springview, *NE, U.S.A.* **84 B6** 42 50N 99 45W
Springville, *AL, U.S.A.* **60 C4** 33 46N 86 29W
Springville, *CA, U.S.A.* **65 G8** 36 8N 118 49W
Springville, *IA, U.S.A.* **73 C7** 42 3N 91 27W
Springville, *NY, U.S.A.* **89 C2** 42 31N 78 40W
Springville, *UT, U.S.A.* **100 C4** 40 10N 111 37W
Springwater, *Sask., Canada* **182 D3** 51 58N 108 23W
Sproat L., *B.C., Canada* **186 F9** 49 17N 125 2W
Sproul State Forest, *PA, U.S.A.* **95 C5** 41 11N 77 49W
Spruce Grove, *Alta., Canada* **184 E7** 53 32N 113 55W
Spruce I., *Man., Canada* **183 B11** 53 5N 100 40W
Spruce Knob, *WV, U.S.A.* **102 C5** 38 42N 79 32W
Spruce Knob-Seneca Rocks Nat. Recr. Area ⌂, *WV, U.S.A.* **102 C5** 38 50N 79 30W
Spruce Mts., *AZ, U.S.A.* **62 C3** 34 28N 112 24W
Spruce Pine, *NC, U.S.A.* **90 C3** 35 55N 82 4W
Spruce Woods Prov. Park ⌂, *Man., Canada* **183 F12** 49 43N 99 5W
Sprucedale, *Ont., Canada* **178 B7** 45 29N 79 28W
Spur, *TX, U.S.A.* **98 D7** 33 28N 100 52W
Spurlockville, *WV, U.S.A.* **102 C2** 38 8N 82 1W
Spuzzum, *B.C., Canada* **187 F13** 49 37N 121 23W
Spy Hill, *Man., Canada* **183 C10** 52 22N 101 26W
Squa Pan L., *ME, U.S.A.* **76 B5** 46 31N 68 13W
Squam L., *NH, U.S.A.* **86 C3** 43 45N 71 32W
Squamish, *B.C., Canada* **187 F11** 49 45N 123 10W
Squamish →, *B.C., Canada* **187 F11** 49 45N 123 8W
Squantum, *Boston, U.S.A.* **106 B3** 42 17N 71 0W
Square Butte Cr. →, *ND, U.S.A.* **91 D5** 46 55N 100 55W
Square Islands, *Nfld. & L., Canada* **175 C6** 52 47N 55 47W
Square L., *ME, U.S.A.* **76 A5** 47 3N 68 20W
Squatec, *Qué., Canada* **177 D14** 47 53N 68 43W
Squaw Lake, *MN, U.S.A.* **80 C4** 47 38N 94 8W
Squaw Peak Recreation Area, *Phoenix, U.S.A.* **116 B2** 33 34N 112 0W
Squaw Valley, *CA, U.S.A.* **65 G7** 36 44N 119 15W
Squaxin Island Indian Reservation, *WA, U.S.A.* **101 C3** 47 12N 122 55W
Squibnocket Point, *MA, U.S.A.* **78 C4** 41 18N 70 47W
Squire, *WV, U.S.A.* **102 D3** 37 14N 81 37W
Squires, *MO, U.S.A.* **82 E4** 36 51N 92 37W
Stacy, *MN, U.S.A.* **80 E6** 45 24N 92 59W
Stacyville, *IA, U.S.A.* **73 B6** 43 26N 92 47W
Stafford, *CT, U.S.A.* **78 C2** 41 59N 72 17W
Stafford, *KS, U.S.A.* **74 D5** 37 58N 98 36W
Stafford, *TX, U.S.A.* **110 C1** 29 36N 95 33W
Stafford, *VA, U.S.A.* **102 C7** 38 25N 77 25W
Stafford, L., *FL, U.S.A.* **67 B6** 29 20N 82 29W
Stafford County ☆, *KS, U.S.A.* **74 C5** 38 0N 98 45W
Stafford County ☆, *VA, U.S.A.* **102 C7** 38 25N 77 25W
Stafford Springs, *CT, U.S.A.* **78 C2** 41 57N 72 18W
Stambaugh, *MI, U.S.A.* **79 C3** 46 5N 88 38W
Stamford, *CT, U.S.A.* **78 C1** 41 3N 73 32W
Stamford, *NY, U.S.A.* **89 C6** 42 25N 74 38W
Stamford, *NE, U.S.A.* **84 D6** 40 8N 99 36W
Stamford, *SD, U.S.A.* **91 G4** 43 53N 101 5W
Stamford, *TX, U.S.A.* **99 E8** 32 57N 99 48W
Stamford, *VT, U.S.A.* **86 D1** 42 45N 73 4W
Stamford, L., *TX, U.S.A.* **99 D8** 33 4N 99 34W
Stamping Ground, *KY, U.S.A.* **97 B8** 38 16N 84 41W
Stamps, *AR, U.S.A.* **63 E2** 33 22N 93 30W
Stanardsville, *VA, U.S.A.* **102 C6** 38 18N 78 26W
Stanberry, *MO, U.S.A.* **82 A2** 40 13N 94 35W
Standard, *Alta., Canada* **185 G8** 51 7N 112 59W
Standing Rock, *NM, U.S.A.* **88 B2** 35 43N 108 22W
Standing Rock Indian Reservation, *SD, U.S.A.* **91 E4** 45 45N 101 10W
Standing Stone State Park ⌂, *TN, U.S.A.* **97 D7** 36 28N 85 25W
Standish, *CA, U.S.A.* **64 C6** 40 22N 120 25W
Standish, *MI, U.S.A.* **79 F8** 43 59N 83 57W
Standrod, *UT, U.S.A.* **100 B2** 41 59N 113 25W
Stanfield, *AZ, U.S.A.* **62 E4** 32 53N 111 58W
Stanfield, *OR, U.S.A.* **94 B6** 45 47N 119 13W
Stanford, *KY, U.S.A.* **97 C8** 37 32N 84 40W
Stanford, *MT, U.S.A.* **83 C7** 47 9N 110 13W
Stanhope, *IA, U.S.A.* **73 C5** 42 17N 93 48W
Stanislaus →, *CA, U.S.A.* **64 F5** 37 40N 121 14W
Stanislaus County ☆, *CA, U.S.A.* **64 F6** 37 33N 121 0W
Stanislaus Nat. Forest, *CA, U.S.A.* **64 E6** 38 10N 120 0W
Stanley, *N.B., Canada* **173 G3** 46 20N 66 44W
Stanley, *ID, U.S.A.* **70 E4** 44 13N 114 56W
Stanley, *KS, U.S.A.* **74 C9** 38 51N 94 40W
Stanley, *KY, U.S.A.* **96 C5** 37 50N 87 15W
Stanley, *LA, U.S.A.* **75 C2** 31 58N 93 54W
Stanley, *NC, U.S.A.* **90 C4** 35 21N 81 6W
Stanley, *ND, U.S.A.* **91 B3** 48 19N 102 23W
Stanley, *NM, U.S.A.* **88 B5** 35 9N 105 59W
Stanley, *VA, U.S.A.* **102 C6** 38 35N 78 30W
Stanley, *WI, U.S.A.* **103 D3** 44 58N 90 56W
Stanley County ☆, *SD, U.S.A.* **91 F5** 44 30N 101 0W
Stanley Mission, *Sask., Canada* **189 E12** 55 25N 104 33W
Stanley Park, *Vancouver, Canada* **193 B2** 49 18N 123 8W
Stanleyville, *NC, U.S.A.* **90 B5** 36 12N 80 17W
Stanly County ☆, *NC, U.S.A.* **90 C5** 35 20N 80 10W
Stannards, *NY, U.S.A.* **89 C3** 42 5N 77 55W
Stansbury I., *UT, U.S.A.* **100 C3** 40 50N 112 30W
Stanstead, *Qué., Canada* **177 F10** 45 7N 72 12W
Stanton, *IA, U.S.A.* **73 E3** 40 59N 95 6W
Stanton, *KY, U.S.A.* **97 C9** 37 54N 83 52W
Stanton, *MI, U.S.A.* **79 F6** 43 18N 85 5W
Stanton, *MO, U.S.A.* **82 C5** 38 17N 91 6W
Stanton, *ND, U.S.A.* **91 C4** 47 19N 101 23W
Stanton, *NE, U.S.A.* **84 C8** 41 57N 97 14W
Stanton, *TN, U.S.A.* **96 E3** 35 28N 89 24W
Stanton, *TX, U.S.A.* **98 E6** 32 8N 101 48W
Stanton County ☆, *KS, U.S.A.* **74 D2** 37 30N 101 45W
Stanton County ☆, *NE, U.S.A.* **84 C8** 41 50N 97 10W
Stanwood, *WA, U.S.A.* **101 B3** 48 15N 122 23W
Staplehurst, *NE, U.S.A.* **84 D8** 40 58N 97 10W
Staples, *MN, U.S.A.* **80 D4** 46 21N 94 48W
Stapleton, *AL, U.S.A.* **60 F3** 30 45N 87 48W
Stapleton, *Denver, U.S.A.* **109 B2** 39 46N 104 52W
Stapleton, *NY, U.S.A.* **114 C2** 40 36N 74 5W
Stapleton, *NE, U.S.A.* **84 C5** 41 29N 100 31W
Stapylton B., *Nunavut, Canada* **188 C9** 68 52N 116 15W
Star, *NC, U.S.A.* **90 C6** 35 24N 79 47W
Star City, *Sask., Canada* **182 C7** 52 50N 104 20W
Star City, *AR, U.S.A.* **63 E4** 33 56N 91 51W
Star City, *IN, U.S.A.* **72 C4** 40 58N 86 33W
Star Lake, *NY, U.S.A.* **89 A5** 44 10N 75 2W
Star Prairie, *WI, U.S.A.* **103 C1** 45 12N 92 32W
Starbuck, *Man., Canada* **183 F14** 49 46N 97 37W
Starbuck, *MN, U.S.A.* **80 E3** 45 37N 95 32W
Starbuck, *WA, U.S.A.* **101 D7** 46 31N 118 7W
Stark, *KS, U.S.A.* **74 D8** 37 42N 95 9W
Stark County ☆, *IL, U.S.A.* **71 B4** 41 5N 89 45W
Stark County ☆, *ND, U.S.A.* **91 D3** 46 55N 102 30W
Stark County ☆, *OH, U.S.A.* **92 C5** 40 48N 81 22W
Starke, *FL, U.S.A.* **67 B6** 29 57N 82 7W
Starke, L., *Orlando, U.S.A.* **115 A1** 28 34N 81 32W
Starke County ☆, *IN, U.S.A.* **72 B4** 41 15N 86 40W
Starks, *LA, U.S.A.* **75 D2** 30 19N 93 40W
Starkville, *CO, U.S.A.* **66 E6** 37 8N 104 30W
Starkville, *MS, U.S.A.* **81 C5** 33 28N 88 49W
Starkweather, *ND, U.S.A.* **91 B7** 48 27N 98 53W
Starr County ☆, *TX, U.S.A.* **98 L9** 26 30N 98 50W
Starrs Mill, *GA, U.S.A.* **68 C2** 33 19N 84 31W
Starrucca, *PA, U.S.A.* **95 C7** 41 54N 75 28W
Starvation Res., *UT, U.S.A.* **100 C5** 40 15N 110 30W
State Center, *IA, U.S.A.* **73 C5** 42 1N 93 10W
State College, *PA, U.S.A.* **95 D5** 40 48N 77 52W
State Line, *MS, U.S.A.* **81 E5** 31 26N 88 28W
Staten I., *NY, U.S.A.* **89 E6** 40 35N 74 9W
Staten Island Zoo, *NY, U.S.A.* **114 C2** 40 38N 74 6W
Statenville, *GA, U.S.A.* **68 F3** 30 42N 83 2W
Statesboro, *GA, U.S.A.* **68 D5** 32 27N 81 47W
Statesville, *NC, U.S.A.* **90 C5** 35 47N 80 53W
Statham, *GA, U.S.A.* **68 C3** 33 58N 83 35W
Staunton, *IL, U.S.A.* **71 D4** 39 1N 89 47W
Staunton, *VA, U.S.A.* **102 C5** 38 9N 79 4W
Stave L., *B.C., Canada* **187 F12** 49 22N 122 17W
Stavely, *Alta., Canada* **185 H7** 50 10N 113 38W
Stayner, *Ont., Canada* **178 C6** 44 25N 80 5W
Stayton, *OR, U.S.A.* **94 C3** 44 48N 122 48W
Staytonville, *DE, U.S.A.* **77 B5** 38 50N 75 32W
Stead, *NM, U.S.A.* **88 A7** 36 6N 103 12W
Steamboat Canyon, *AZ, U.S.A.* **62 B6** 35 45N 109 51W
Steamboat Rock, *IA, U.S.A.* **73 C5** 42 25N 93 4W
Steamboat Springs, *CO, U.S.A.* **66 B4** 40 29N 106 50W
Stearns, *KY, U.S.A.* **97 D8** 36 42N 84 29W
Stearns County ☆, *MN, U.S.A.* **80 E4** 45 35N 94 30W
Stebbins, *AK, U.S.A.* **61 E7** 63 31N 162 17W
Stedman, *NC, U.S.A.* **90 D7** 35 0N 78 41W
Steele, *AL, U.S.A.* **60 C4** 33 56N 86 12W
Steele, *MO, U.S.A.* **82 E7** 36 5N 89 50W
Steele, *ND, U.S.A.* **91 D6** 46 51N 99 55W
Steele, Mt., *WY, U.S.A.* **104 E5** 41 50N 107 0W
Steele City, *NE, U.S.A.* **84 D8** 40 2N 97 2W
Steele County ☆, *MN, U.S.A.* **80 F5** 44 0N 93 10W
Steele County ☆, *ND, U.S.A.* **91 C8** 47 31N 97 50W
Steeleville, *IL, U.S.A.* **71 E4** 38 0N 89 40W
Steelton, *PA, U.S.A.* **95 D6** 40 14N 76 50W
Steelville, *MO, U.S.A.* **82 D5** 37 58N 91 22W
Steen, *MN, U.S.A.* **80 G2** 43 31N 96 16W
Steens Mt., *OR, U.S.A.* **94 E7** 42 35N 118 40W
Steensby Inlet, *N.W.T., Canada* **190 C10** 70 15N 78 35W
Steep Rock, *Man., Canada* **183 D13** 51 30N 98 48W
Steer, L., *Orlando, U.S.A.* **115 A2** 28 31N 81 30W
Stefansson I., *N.W.T., Canada* **190 C4** 73 20N 105 45W
Stegman = Artesia, *NM, U.S.A.* **88 E6** 32 51N 104 24W
Stehekin, *WA, U.S.A.* **101 B5** 48 19N 120 39W
Stein Valley Park ⌂, *B.C., Canada* **187 E12** 50 16N 122 2W
Steinauer, *NE, U.S.A.* **84 D9** 40 12N 96 14W
Steinbach, *Man., Canada* **183 F15** 49 32N 96 40W
Steinhatchee, *FL, U.S.A.* **67 B5** 29 40N 83 23W
Stella, *MO, U.S.A.* **82 E2** 36 46N 94 12W
Stella, *NE, U.S.A.* **84 D10** 40 14N 95 46W
Stellarton, *N.S., Canada* **173 H7** 45 32N 62 30W
Stemmers →, *Baltimore, U.S.A.* **107 A2** 39 19N 76 28W
Stephen, *MN, U.S.A.* **80 B2** 48 27N 96 53W
Stephens, *AR, U.S.A.* **63 E2** 33 25N 93 4W
Stephens City, *VA, U.S.A.* **77 A2** 39 5N 78 13W
Stephens County ☆, *GA, U.S.A.* **68 B3** 34 35N 83 15W
Stephens County ☆, *OK, U.S.A.* **93 D6** 34 30N 97 50W
Stephens County ☆, *TX, U.S.A.* **99 E9** 32 45N 98 54W
Stephens I., *B.C., Canada* **186 A4** 54 10N 130 45W
Stephens Knob, *KY, U.S.A.* **97 D8** 36 37N 84 20W
Stephenson, *MI, U.S.A.* **79 D4** 45 25N 87 36W
Stephenson County ☆, *IL, U.S.A.* **71 A4** 42 20N 89 40W
Stephentown, *NY, U.S.A.* **78 B1** 42 33N 73 22W
Stephenville, *Nfld. & L., Canada* **174 D2** 48 31N 58 35W
Stephenville, *TX, U.S.A.* **99 E9** 32 13N 98 12W
Stephenville Crossing, *Nfld. & L., Canada* **174 D2** 48 30N 58 26W
Steps Pt., *Amer. Samoa* **105 e** 14 23 S 170 45W
Steptoe, *WA, U.S.A.* **101 D8** 47 0N 117 21W
Steptoe Valley, *NV, U.S.A.* **85 C6** 39 50N 114 45W
Sterling, *AK, U.S.A.* **61 F10** 60 32N 150 46W
Sterling, *CO, U.S.A.* **66 B7** 40 37N 103 13W
Sterling, *GA, U.S.A.* **68 E5** 31 16N 81 34W
Sterling, *ID, U.S.A.* **70 F6** 43 2N 112 44W
Sterling, *IL, U.S.A.* **71 B4** 41 48N 89 42W
Sterling, *KS, U.S.A.* **74 C5** 38 13N 98 12W
Sterling, *MA, U.S.A.* **78 B3** 42 26N 71 46W
Sterling, *MI, U.S.A.* **79 E7** 44 2N 84 2W
Sterling, *ND, U.S.A.* **91 D5** 46 49N 100 17W
Sterling, *NE, U.S.A.* **84 D9** 40 28N 96 23W
Sterling, *OK, U.S.A.* **93 D5** 34 45N 98 10W
Sterling, *UT, U.S.A.* **100 D4** 39 12N 111 42W
Sterling, *VA, U.S.A.* **77 A3** 39 1N 77 26W
Sterling City, *TX, U.S.A.* **98 F7** 31 51N 101 0W
Sterling County ☆, *TX, U.S.A.* **98 F7** 32 0N 101 0W
Sterling Heights, *MI, U.S.A.* **79 G8** 42 35N 83 2W
Sterling Park, *San Francisco, U.S.A.* **118 B2** 37 41N 122 27W
Sterling Res., *CO, U.S.A.* **66 B7** 40 47N 103 16W
Sterlington, *LA, U.S.A.* **75 B3** 32 42N 92 5W
Stetsonville, *WI, U.S.A.* **103 C3** 45 4N 90 19W
Stettler, *Alta., Canada* **185 F8** 52 19N 112 40W
Steuben, *MI, U.S.A.* **79 C5** 46 11N 86 27W
Steuben, *WI, U.S.A.* **103 E3** 43 11N 90 52W
Steuben County ☆, *IN, U.S.A.* **72 B6** 41 40N 85 0W
Steuben County ☆, *NY, U.S.A.* **89 C3** 42 15N 77 20W
Steubenville, *KY, U.S.A.* **97 D8** 36 53N 84 48W
Steubenville, *OH, U.S.A.* **92 C6** 40 22N 80 37W
Stevens, *Ont., Canada* **181 C11** 49 33N 85 49W
Stevens County ☆, *KS, U.S.A.* **74 D2** 37 15N 101 20W
Stevens County ☆, *MN, U.S.A.* **80 E2** 45 40N 96 0W
Stevens County ☆, *WA, U.S.A.* **101 B8** 48 30N 118 0W
Stevens Point, *WI, U.S.A.* **103 D4** 44 31N 89 34W
Stevens Pottery, *GA, U.S.A.* **68 D3** 32 57N 83 17W
Stevens Village, *AK, U.S.A.* **61 C10** 66 1N 149 6W
Stevenson, *AL, U.S.A.* **60 B5** 34 52N 85 50W
Stevenson, *Baltimore, U.S.A.* **107 A1** 39 24N 76 42W
Stevenson, *WA, U.S.A.* **101 E4** 45 42N 121 53W
Stevenson L., *Man., Canada* **183 B15** 53 55N 96 0W
Stevensville, *MD, U.S.A.* **77 B4** 38 59N 76 19W
Stevensville, *MI, U.S.A.* **79 G5** 42 1N 86 31W
Stevensville, *MT, U.S.A.* **83 D3** 46 30N 114 5W
Steveston, *B.C., Canada* **193 C1** 49 8N 123 11W
Steward, *IL, U.S.A.* **71 B4** 41 51N 89 1W
Stewardson, *IL, U.S.A.* **71 D5** 39 16N 88 38W
Stewart, *B.C., Canada* **189 F7** 55 56N 129 57W
Stewart, *GA, U.S.A.* **68 C3** 33 25N 83 52W
Stewart, *MN, U.S.A.* **80 F4** 44 43N 94 29W
Stewart, *MS, U.S.A.* **81 C4** 33 27N 89 26W
Stewart →, *Yukon, Canada* **189 D5** 63 19N 139 26W
Stewart B. McKinney Nat. Wildlife Refuge ⌂, *CT, U.S.A.* **78 C1** 41 12N 73 7W
Stewart County ☆, *GA, U.S.A.* **68 D2** 32 5N 84 50W
Stewart County ☆, *TN, U.S.A.* **96 D5** 36 20N 87 55W
Stewart Crossing, *Yukon, Canada* **189 D5** 63 22N 136 40W
Stewart Manor, *NY, U.S.A.* **114 B4** 40 43N 73 41W
Stewart Valley, *Sask., Canada* **182 E4** 50 36N 107 48W
Stewarts Point, *CA, U.S.A.* **64 E3** 38 39N 123 24W
Stewartstown, *NH, U.S.A.* **86 B3** 45 0N 71 31W
Stewartstown, *PA, U.S.A.* **77 A4** 39 45N 76 36W
Stewartsville, *MO, U.S.A.* **82 B2** 39 45N 94 30W
Stewartville, *MN, U.S.A.* **80 G6** 43 51N 92 29W
Stewiacke, *N.S., Canada* **173 H6** 45 9N 63 22W
Stibnite, *ID, U.S.A.* **70 E3** 44 54N 115 20W
Stickney, *N.B., Canada* **173 G2** 46 23N 67 34W
Stickney, *Chicago, U.S.A.* **108 C2** 41 49N 87 46W
Stickney, *SD, U.S.A.* **91 G7** 43 35N 98 26W
Stidham, *OK, U.S.A.* **93 C8** 35 22N 95 42W
Stigler, *OK, U.S.A.* **93 C8** 35 15N 95 8W
Stikine →, *B.C., Canada* **189 E6** 56 40N 132 30W
Stikine Range, *B.C., Canada* **189 E7** 59 0N 129 0W
Stiles, *TX, U.S.A.* **98 F6** 31 25N 101 34W
Stilesville, *IN, U.S.A.* **72 D4** 39 38N 86 38W
Still Pond, *MD, U.S.A.* **77 A4** 39 20N 76 3W
Stillhouse Hollow L., *TX, U.S.A.* **99 F10** 31 2N 97 32W
Stillmore, *GA, U.S.A.* **68 D4** 32 27N 82 13W
Stillwater, *NV, U.S.A.* **85 C2** 39 31N 118 33W
Stillwater, *OK, U.S.A.* **93 B6** 36 7N 97 4W
Stillwater County ☆, *MT, U.S.A.* **83 E8** 45 48N 109 15W
Stillwater Nat. Wildlife Refuge ⌂, *NV, U.S.A.* **85 C2** 39 33N 118 29W
Stillwater Range, *NV, U.S.A.* **85 C2** 39 50N 118 5W
Stillwater Res., *NY, U.S.A.* **89 B5** 43 54N 75 3W
Stillwell, *GA, U.S.A.* **68 D5** 32 23N 81 15W
Stilwell, *KS, U.S.A.* **74 C9** 38 46N 94 39W
Stilwell, *OK, U.S.A.* **93 C9** 35 49N 94 38W
Stinnett, *TX, U.S.A.* **98 B6** 35 50N 101 27W
Stinson Lake, *NH, U.S.A.* **86 C3** 43 51N 71 48W
Stirling, *Alta., Canada* **185 J8** 49 30N 112 30W
Stirling, *Ont., Canada* **179 C9** 44 18N 77 33W
Stirling City, *CA, U.S.A.* **64 D5** 39 54N 121 32W
Stirrat, *WV, U.S.A.* **102 D3** 37 44N 82 0W
Stirupa →, *Chihuahua, Mexico* **213 E8** 28 45N 107 58W
Stites, *ID, U.S.A.* **70 C3** 46 6N 115 59W
Stittsville, *Ont., Canada* **176 F7** 45 15N 75 55W
Stock Island, *FL, U.S.A.* **67 G7** 24 32N 81 34W
Stockbridge, *GA, U.S.A.* **68 C2** 33 33N 84 14W
Stockbridge, *MA, U.S.A.* **78 B1** 42 17N 73 19W
Stockbridge, *MI, U.S.A.* **79 G7** 42 27N 84 11W
Stockbridge-Munsee Indian Reservation, *WI, U.S.A.* **103 D5** 44 50N 88 50W
Stockdale, *TX, U.S.A.* **99 H10** 29 14N 97 58W
Stockett, *MT, U.S.A.* **83 C6** 47 21N 111 10W
Stockham, *NE, U.S.A.* **84 D8** 40 43N 97 56W
Stockholm, *Sask., Canada* **183 E9** 50 39N 102 18W
Stockholm, *ME, U.S.A.* **76 A5** 47 3N 68 8W
Stockholm, *SD, U.S.A.* **91 E9** 45 6N 96 48W
Stockholm, *WI, U.S.A.* **103 D1** 44 29N 92 16W
Stockland, *IL, U.S.A.* **71 C6** 40 37N 87 36W
Stockley, *DE, U.S.A.* **77 B5** 38 40N 75 20W
Stockport, *IA, U.S.A.* **73 E7** 40 51N 91 50W
Stockport, *OH, U.S.A.* **92 D5** 39 33N 81 48W
Stockton, *AL, U.S.A.* **60 E3** 31 0N 87 52W
Stockton, *CA, U.S.A.* **64 F5** 37 58N 121 17W
Stockton, *IL, U.S.A.* **71 A3** 42 21N 90 1W
Stockton, *KS, U.S.A.* **74 B4** 39 26N 99 16W
Stockton, *MD, U.S.A.* **77 B5** 38 3N 75 25W
Stockton, *MN, U.S.A.* **80 F7** 44 2N 91 46W
Stockton, *MO, U.S.A.* **82 D3** 37 42N 93 48W
Stockton, *NJ, U.S.A.* **87 B2** 40 24N 74 58W
Stockton, *UT, U.S.A.* **100 C3** 40 27N 112 22W
Stockton I., *WI, U.S.A.* **103 B3** 46 57N 90 35W
Stockton L., *MO, U.S.A.* **82 D3** 37 42N 93 46W
Stockton Plateau, *TX, U.S.A.* **98 G5** 30 30N 102 30W
Stockville, *NE, U.S.A.* **84 D5** 40 32N 100 23W
Stoddard, *WI, U.S.A.* **103 E2** 43 40N 91 13W
Stoddard County ☆, *MO, U.S.A.* **82 E7** 36 50N 90 0W
Stokes Bay, *Ont., Canada* **178 B5** 45 0N 81 28W
Stokes County ☆, *NC, U.S.A.* **90 B5** 36 20N 80 10W
Stone, *ID, U.S.A.* **70 G6** 42 1N 112 42W
Stone Canyon Res., *Los Angeles, U.S.A.* **111 B2** 34 6N 118 27W
Stone County ☆, *AR, U.S.A.* **63 C3** 35 52N 92 7W
Stone County ☆, *MS, U.S.A.* **81 F4** 30 47N 89 8W
Stone County ☆, *MO, U.S.A.* **82 E3** 36 45N 93 25W
Stone Harbor, *NJ, U.S.A.* **87 C2** 39 3N 74 45W
Stone Mountain, *GA, U.S.A.* **68 C2** 33 49N 84 10W
Stone Mountain Park ⌂, *GA, U.S.A.* **68 C2** 33 48N 84 8W
Stone Mt., *VT, U.S.A.* **86 B3** 44 34N 71 40W
Stone Park, *Chicago, U.S.A.* **108 B1** 41 53N 87 52W
Stoneboro, *PA, U.S.A.* **95 C2** 41 20N 80 7W
Stoneham, *Boston, U.S.A.* **106 A3** 42 29N 71 5W
Stoneham, *CO, U.S.A.* **66 B7** 40 36N 103 40W
Stoner, *B.C., Canada* **187 B12** 53 38N 122 40W
Stoner, *CO, U.S.A.* **66 E2** 37 35N 108 19W
Stones River Nat. Battlefield ⌂, *TN, U.S.A.* **96 E6** 35 53N 86 26W
Stoneville, *NC, U.S.A.* **90 B6** 36 28N 79 54W
Stoneville, *SD, U.S.A.* **91 F3** 44 44N 102 39W
Stonewall, *Man., Canada* **183 E14** 50 10N 97 19W
Stonewall, *AR, U.S.A.* **63 B5** 36 14N 90 32W
Stonewall, *CO, U.S.A.* **66 E5** 37 9N 105 1W
Stonewall, *LA, U.S.A.* **75 B2** 32 17N 93 50W
Stonewall, *MS, U.S.A.* **81 D5** 32 8N 88 47W
Stonewall, *OK, U.S.A.* **93 D7** 34 39N 96 32W
Stonewall County ☆, *TX, U.S.A.* **98 D7** 33 8N 100 14W
Stonewall Jackson L., *WV, U.S.A.* **102 C4** 38 58N 80 29W
Stonewood, *WV, U.S.A.* **102 B4** 39 15N 80 19W
Stoney Creek, *Ont., Canada* **178 D7** 43 14N 79 45W
Stonington, *CO, U.S.A.* **66 E8** 37 18N 102 11W
Stonington, *IL, U.S.A.* **71 D4** 39 44N 89 12W
Stonington, *ME, U.S.A.* **76 D5** 44 9N 68 40W
Stony Brook, *NY, U.S.A.* **89 E7** 40 56N 73 8W
Stony Brook Res., *Boston, U.S.A.* **106 B3** 42 15N 71 8W
Stony Creek, *VA, U.S.A.* **102 E7** 36 57N 77 24W
Stony Gorge Res., *CA, U.S.A.* **64 D4** 39 35N 122 32W
Stony I., *NY, U.S.A.* **89 B4** 43 54N 76 20W
Stony L., *Man., Canada* **191 F6** 58 51N 98 40W
Stony L., *Ont., Canada* **179 C8** 44 30N 78 5W
Stony Mountain, *Man., Canada* **183 E14** 50 5N 97 13W
Stony Plain, *Alta., Canada* **184 E6** 53 32N 114 0W
Stony Point, *NC, U.S.A.* **90 C4** 35 52N 81 3W
Stony Point, *NY, U.S.A.* **87 A3** 41 14N 73 59W
Stony Pt., *NY, U.S.A.* **89 B4** 43 50N 76 18W
Stony Rapids, *Sask., Canada* **189 E11** 59 16N 105 50W
Stony Ridge, *OH, U.S.A.* **92 B3** 41 31N 83 30W
Stony River, *AK, U.S.A.* **61 F8** 61 47N 156 35W
Stonyford, *CA, U.S.A.* **64 D4** 39 23N 122 33W
Stor I., *Nunavut, Canada* **190 B8** 79 0N 85 50W
Storey County ☆, *NV, U.S.A.* **85 C1** 39 30N 119 35W
Storkerson B., *N.W.T., Canada* **188 B8** 72 56N 124 50W
Storkerson Pen., *Nunavut, Canada* **190 C4** 72 30N 106 30W
Storm L., *IA, U.S.A.* **73 C3** 42 38N 95 13W
Storm Lake, *IA, U.S.A.* **73 C3** 42 39N 95 13W
Stormy L., *Ont., Canada* **180 C4** 49 23N 92 18W
Stormy Mt., *WA, U.S.A.* **101 C5** 47 54N 120 21W
Storrs, *CT, U.S.A.* **78 C2** 41 49N 72 15W
Story, *WY, U.S.A.* **104 B6** 44 35N 106 53W
Story City, *IA, U.S.A.* **73 C5** 42 11N 93 36W
Story County ☆, *IA, U.S.A.* **73 D5** 42 0N 93 25W
Stotesbury, *MO, U.S.A.* **82 D2** 37 59N 94 34W
Stouffville, *Ont., Canada* **178 D7** 43 58N 79 15W
Stoughton, *Sask., Canada* **182 F18** 49 40N 103 0W
Stoughton, *MA, U.S.A.* **78 B3** 42 8N 71 6W
Stoughton, *WI, U.S.A.* **103 F4** 42 55N 89 13W
Stout, *IA, U.S.A.* **73 C6** 42 32N 92 43W
Stoutland, *MO, U.S.A.* **82 D4** 37 49N 92 31W
Stoutsville, *MO, U.S.A.* **82 B5** 39 33N 91 51W
Stoutsville, *OH, U.S.A.* **92 D4** 39 36N 82 50W
Stovall, *GA, U.S.A.* **68 D2** 32 58N 84 51W
Stovall, *NC, U.S.A.* **90 B7** 36 27N 78 35W
Stover, *MO, U.S.A.* **82 C4** 38 27N 92 59W
Stowe, *PA, U.S.A.* **87 B1** 40 15N 75 41W
Stowe, *VT, U.S.A.* **86 B2** 44 28N 72 41W
Stowell, *TX, U.S.A.* **99 H13** 29 47N 94 23W
Strafford, *MO, U.S.A.* **82 D3** 37 16N 93 7W
Strafford, *NH, U.S.A.* **86 C3** 43 19N 71 12W
Strafford County ☆, *NH, U.S.A.* **86 C3** 43 15N 71 0W
Strandburg, *SD, U.S.A.* **91 E9** 45 3N 96 46W
Strandquist, *MN, U.S.A.* **80 B2** 48 29N 96 27W
Strang, *NE, U.S.A.* **84 D8** 40 25N 97 35W
Stranraer, *Sask., Canada* **182 D3** 51 43N 108 29W
Strasbourg, *Sask., Canada* **182 D7** 51 4N 104 55W
Strasburg, *CO, U.S.A.* **66 C6** 39 44N 104 20W
Strasburg, *MO, U.S.A.* **82 C2** 38 46N 94 10W
Strasburg, *ND, U.S.A.* **91 D5** 46 8N 100 10W
Strasburg, *OH, U.S.A.* **92 C5** 40 36N 81 32W
Strasburg, *VA, U.S.A.* **77 B2** 38 59N 78 22W
Stratford, *Ont., Canada* **178 D6** 43 23N 81 0W
Stratford, *CA, U.S.A.* **65 G7** 36 11N 119 49W
Stratford, *CT, U.S.A.* **78 C1** 41 12N 73 8W
Stratford, *IA, U.S.A.* **73 C5** 42 16N 93 56W
Stratford, *NH, U.S.A.* **86 B3** 44 42N 71 36W
Stratford, *NJ, U.S.A.* **87 C1** 39 50N 75 1W
Stratford, *OK, U.S.A.* **93 D7** 34 48N 96 58W
Stratford, *SD, U.S.A.* **91 E7** 45 19N 98 18W
Stratford, *TX, U.S.A.* **98 A5** 36 20N 102 4W
Stratford, *WI, U.S.A.* **103 D3** 44 48N 90 4W
Stratham, *NH, U.S.A.* **86 C4** 43 3N 70 55W
Strathcona, *MN, U.S.A.* **80 B2** 48 33N 96 10W
Strathcona Park ⌂, *B.C., Canada* **186 F9** 49 38N 125 40W
Strathmere, *NJ, U.S.A.* **87 C2** 39 12N 74 40W
Strathmore, *Alta., Canada* **185 G7** 51 5N 113 18W
Strathmore, *CA, U.S.A.* **65 G7** 36 9N 119 4W
Strathnaver, *B.C., Canada* **187 B12** 53 20N 122 33W
Strathroy, *Ont., Canada* **178 E5** 42 58N 81 38W
Stratton, *Ont., Canada* **180 D2** 48 41N 94 10W
Stratton, *CO, U.S.A.* **66 C8** 39 19N 102 36W
Stratton, *ME, U.S.A.* **76 C3** 45 8N 70 26W
Stratton, *NE, U.S.A.* **84 D4** 40 9N 101 14W
Stratton Meadows, *CO, U.S.A.* **66 D6** 38 45N 104 48W
Stratton Mt., *VT, U.S.A.* **86 C2** 43 4N 72 55W
Strawberry, *AR, U.S.A.* **63 C4** 35 58N 91 19W
Strawberry, *CA, U.S.A.* **64 E6** 38 48N 120 9W
Strawberry →, *AR, U.S.A.* **63 C4** 35 53N 91 13W
Strawberry →, *UT, U.S.A.* **100 C5** 40 10N 110 24W
Strawberry Banke Museum, *NH, U.S.A.* **86 C4** 43 4N 70 44W
Strawberry Mt., *OR, U.S.A.* **94 C7** 44 19N 118 43W
Strawberry Point, *IA, U.S.A.* **73 C7** 42 41N 91 32W
Strawberry Res., *UT, U.S.A.* **100 C4** 40 8N 111 9W
Strawn, *IL, U.S.A.* **71 C5** 40 39N 88 24W
Strawn, *TX, U.S.A.* **99 E9** 32 33N 98 30W
Streator, *IL, U.S.A.* **71 B5** 41 8N 88 50W
Streeter, *ND, U.S.A.* **91 D6** 46 39N 99 21W
Streetman, *TX, U.S.A.* **99 F11** 31 53N 96 19W
Streetsboro, *OH, U.S.A.* **92 B5** 41 14N 81 21W
Streetsville, *Ont., Canada* **178 D7** 43 35N 79 42W
Stringer, *MS, U.S.A.* **81 E4** 31 52N 89 16W
Stringtown, *OK, U.S.A.* **93 D7** 34 28N 96 3W
Strome, *Alta., Canada* **185 F8** 52 48N 112 4W
Stromsburg, *NE, U.S.A.* **84 C8** 41 7N 97 36W
Strong, *AR, U.S.A.* **63 E3** 33 7N 92 21W
Strong →, *MS, U.S.A.* **81 E3** 31 51N 90 8W
Strong City, *KS, U.S.A.* **74 C7** 38 24N 96 32W
Strong City, *OK, U.S.A.* **93 C4** 35 40N 99 36W
Strongfield, *Sask., Canada* **182 D5** 51 20N 106 35W
Stronghurst, *IL, U.S.A.* **71 C3** 40 45N 90 55W
Strongsville, *OH, U.S.A.* **92 B5** 41 19N 81 50W
Stroud, *Ont., Canada* **178 C7** 44 19N 79 37W
Stroud, *OK, U.S.A.* **93 C7** 35 45N 96 40W
Stroudsburg, *PA, U.S.A.* **87 B1** 40 59N 75 12W
Strum, *WI, U.S.A.* **103 D2** 44 33N 91 24W
Struthers, *OH, U.S.A.* **92 B6** 41 4N 80 39W
Stryker, *MT, U.S.A.* **83 B3** 48 41N 114 46W
Stryker, *OH, U.S.A.* **92 B2** 41 30N 84 25W
Stuart, *FL, U.S.A.* **67 D8** 27 12N 80 15W
Stuart, *IA, U.S.A.* **73 D4** 41 30N 94 19W
Stuart, *NE, U.S.A.* **84 B6** 42 36N 99 8W
Stuart, *OK, U.S.A.* **93 D7** 34 54N 96 6W
Stuart, *VA, U.S.A.* **102 E4** 36 38N 80 16W
Stuart, Mt., *WA, U.S.A.* **101 C5** 47 29N 120 54W
Stuart I., *AK, U.S.A.* **61 E7** 63 35N 162 30W
Stuart L., *B.C., Canada* **189 F8** 54 30N 124 30W
Stuarts Draft, *VA, U.S.A.* **102 C5** 38 2N 79 2W
Studio City, *Los Angeles, U.S.A.* **111 B2** 34 8N 118 24W
Studley, *KS, U.S.A.* **74 B3** 39 21N 100 10W
Study Butte, *TX, U.S.A.* **98 H4** 29 19N 103 31W

Stuie, *B.C., Canada* 186 C8 52 22N 126 4W
Stump L., *ND, U.S.A.* 91 C7 47 54N 98 24W
Stumpy Lake, *Norfolk, U.S.A.* 115 B3 36 45N 76 8W
Sturgeon, *MO, U.S.A.* 82 B4 39 14N 92 17W
Sturgeon →, *Ont., Canada* 178 A6 46 35N 80 11W
Sturgeon →, *Sask., Canada* 182 B6 53 12N 105 52W
Sturgeon →, *MI, U.S.A.* 79 D7 45 24N 84 38W
Sturgeon →, *MI, U.S.A.* 79 B3 47 2N 88 30W
Sturgeon B., *Man., Canada* 183 C14 52 0N 97 50W
Sturgeon B., *MI, U.S.A.* 79 D6 45 45N 85 0W
Sturgeon Bay, *WI, U.S.A.* 103 D6 44 50N 87 23W
Sturgeon Falls, *Ont., Canada* 178 A7 46 25N 79 57W
Sturgeon L., *Alta., Canada* 184 C3 55 6N 117 32W
Sturgeon L., *Ont., Canada* 179 C8 44 28N 78 43W
Sturgeon L., *Ont., Canada* 180 B6 50 0N 90 45W
Sturgeon L., *Ont., Canada* 180 D5 48 29N 91 38W
Sturgeon Lake, *MN, U.S.A.* 80 D6 46 23N 92 49W
Sturgeon Pt., *MI, U.S.A.* 79 E8 44 43N 83 16W
Sturgis, *Sask., Canada* 182 D9 51 56N 102 36W
Sturgis, *KY, U.S.A.* 96 C5 37 33N 87 59W
Sturgis, *MI, U.S.A.* 79 H6 41 48N 85 25W
Sturgis, *MS, U.S.A.* 81 C4 33 21N 89 3W
Sturgis, *SD, U.S.A.* 91 F2 44 25N 103 31W
Sturtevant, *WI, U.S.A.* 103 F6 42 42N 87 54W
Stutsman County ☆, *ND, U.S.A.* 91 C6 47 0N 99 0W
Stuttgart, *AR, U.S.A.* 63 D4 34 30N 91 33W
Styx →, *AL, U.S.A.* 60 F3 30 31N 87 27W
Suaqui Grande, *Sonora, Mexico* 212 E6 28 24N 109 54W
Sublett Ra., *ID, U.S.A.* 70 G6 42 18N 112 55W
Sublette, *IL, U.S.A.* 71 B4 41 39N 89 14W
Sublette, *KS, U.S.A.* 74 D3 37 29N 100 51W
Sublette County ☆, *WY, U.S.A.* 104 D3 43 0N 110 0W
Sucarnoochee →, *AL, U.S.A.* 60 D2 32 25N 88 2W
Success, *Sask., Canada* 182 E3 50 28N 108 6W
Success, *AR, U.S.A.* 63 B5 36 27N 90 43W
Success, L., *CA, U.S.A.* 65 G8 36 4N 118 55W
Success, Mt., *NH, U.S.A.* 86 B3 44 27N 71 5W
Suchiapa, *Chiapas, Mexico* 222 C3 16 37N 93 5W
Suchil, *Durango, Mexico* 217 D7 23 39N 103 54W
Sud, Pte. du, *Qué., Canada* 172 D7 49 3N 62 14W
Sud-Ouest, Pte., *Qué., Canada* 172 D6 49 23N 63 36W
Sudan, *TX, U.S.A.* 98 C5 34 4N 102 31W
Sudbury, *Ont., Canada* 178 A5 46 30N 81 0W
Sudbury, *MA, U.S.A.* 78 B3 42 22N 71 24W
Sudlersville, *MD, U.S.A.* 77 A5 39 11N 75 52W
Sue, L., *Orlando, U.S.A.* 115 A2 28 34N 81 21W
Suffern, *NY, U.S.A.* 87 A2 41 7N 74 9W
Suffield, *Alta., Canada* 185 H9 50 12N 111 10W
Suffield, *CT, U.S.A.* 78 C2 41 59N 72 39W
Suffolk, *VA, U.S.A.* 102 E8 36 44N 76 35W
Suffolk County ☆, *MA, U.S.A.* 78 B3 42 21N 71 5W
Suffolk County ☆, *NY, U.S.A.* 89 E8 40 50N 73 0W
Sugar →, *IL, U.S.A.* 71 A4 42 26N 89 12W
Sugar →, *NH, U.S.A.* 86 C2 43 24N 72 24W
Sugar City, *CO, U.S.A.* 66 D7 38 14N 103 40W
Sugar City, *ID, U.S.A.* 70 F7 43 52N 111 45W
Sugar Cr. →, *IL, U.S.A.* 71 C4 40 9N 89 38W
Sugar Cr. →, *IL, U.S.A.* 71 C6 40 50N 87 45W
Sugar Cr. →, *IN, U.S.A.* 72 D3 39 51N 87 21W
Sugar Grove, *OH, U.S.A.* 92 D4 39 38N 82 33W
Sugar Grove, *PA, U.S.A.* 95 C3 41 59N 79 20W
Sugar Hill, *GA, U.S.A.* 68 B2 34 6N 84 2W
Sugar I., *MI, U.S.A.* 79 C7 46 25N 84 12W
Sugar L., *B.C., Canada* 187 E16 50 24N 118 30W
Sugar Land, *TX, U.S.A.* 99 H12 29 37N 95 38W
Sugar Mountain, *NC, U.S.A.* 90 B4 36 8N 81 52W
Sugar Notch, *PA, U.S.A.* 95 C7 41 11N 75 55W
Sugarbowl-Grizzly Den Park ⌂, *B.C., Canada* 187 B13 53 51N 121 39W
Sugarcreek, *OH, U.S.A.* 92 C5 40 30N 81 38W
Sugarcreek, *PA, U.S.A.* 95 C3 41 25N 79 53W
Sugarloaf Head, *Nfld. & L., Canada* 174 E8 47 37N 52 39W
Sugarloaf Mt., *ME, U.S.A.* 76 C3 45 2N 70 19W
Sugarloaf Mt., *OK, U.S.A.* 93 C9 35 2N 94 28W
Sugartown, *LA, U.S.A.* 75 D2 30 50N 93 1W
Sugarville, *UT, U.S.A.* 100 D3 39 28N 112 39W
Sugden, *OK, U.S.A.* 93 D6 34 5N 97 59W
Suggi L., *Sask., Canada* 182 A9 54 22N 102 47W
Sugluk = Salluit, *Qué., Canada* 175 A2 62 14N 75 38W
Suisun B., *CA, U.S.A.* 64 E5 38 5N 122 0W
Suisun City, *CA, U.S.A.* 64 E4 38 15N 122 2W
Suitland, *MD, U.S.A.* 77 B4 38 50N 76 55W
Sulligent, *AL, U.S.A.* 60 C2 33 54N 88 8W
Sullivan, *Qué., Canada* 176 C2 48 7N 77 50W
Sullivan, *IL, U.S.A.* 71 D5 39 36N 88 37W
Sullivan, *IN, U.S.A.* 72 D3 39 6N 87 24W
Sullivan, *KY, U.S.A.* 96 C5 37 30N 87 57W
Sullivan, *MO, U.S.A.* 82 C5 38 13N 91 10W
Sullivan Bay, *B.C., Canada* 186 E8 50 55N 126 50W
Sullivan County ☆, *IN, U.S.A.* 72 D3 39 5N 87 25W
Sullivan County ☆, *MO, U.S.A.* 82 A3 40 10N 93 5W
Sullivan County ☆, *NH, U.S.A.* 86 C2 43 20N 72 15W
Sullivan County ☆, *NY, U.S.A.* 89 D6 41 45N 74 45W
Sullivan County ☆, *PA, U.S.A.* 95 C6 41 30N 76 35W
Sullivan County ☆, *TN, U.S.A.* 97 D10 36 32N 82 19W
Sullivan L., *Alta., Canada* 185 F8 52 0N 112 0W
Sully, *IA, U.S.A.* 60 C3 41 34N 92 50W
Sully County ☆, *SD, U.S.A.* 91 F5 44 45N 100 0W
Sulphur, *LA, U.S.A.* 75 D2 30 14N 93 23W
Sulphur, *OK, U.S.A.* 93 D7 34 31N 96 58W
Sulphur →, *AR, U.S.A.* 63 E2 33 7N 93 52W
Sulphur →, *TX, U.S.A.* 99 D14 33 7N 93 52W
Sulphur Cr. →, *SD, U.S.A.* 91 F3 44 45N 102 0W
Sulphur Draw →, *TX, U.S.A.* 98 D5 33 12N 102 17W
Sulphur Rock, *AR, U.S.A.* 63 C4 35 45N 91 30W
Sulphur Springs, *AR, U.S.A.* 63 B1 36 29N 94 28W
Sulphur Springs, *IN, U.S.A.* 72 C5 40 0N 85 27W
Sulphur Springs, *TX, U.S.A.* 99 D12 33 8N 95 36W
Sulphur Springs Draw →, *TX, U.S.A.* 98 E6 32 12N 101 36W
Sulphur Springs Range, *NV, U.S.A.* 85 B5 40 15N 116 0W
Sultan, *Ont., Canada* 181 E14 47 36N 82 47W
Sultan, *WA, U.S.A.* 101 C4 47 52N 121 49W
Sultepec, *México, Mexico* 219 D8 18 52N 99 57W
Sumas, *WA, U.S.A.* 101 B3 48 59N 122 15W
Sumatra, *FL, U.S.A.* 67 A4 30 1N 84 59W
Sumatra, *MT, U.S.A.* 83 D10 46 37N 107 33W
Summer I., *MI, U.S.A.* 79 D5 45 34N 86 39W
Summer L., *OR, U.S.A.* 94 E5 42 50N 120 45W
Summer Lake, *OR, U.S.A.* 94 E5 42 58N 120 47W
Summerdale, *AL, U.S.A.* 60 F3 30 28N 87 55W
Summerfield, *KS, U.S.A.* 74 B7 39 59N 96 21W
Summerfield, *NC, U.S.A.* 90 B6 36 13N 79 54W
Summerfield, *OH, U.S.A.* 92 D5 39 48N 81 20W
Summerfield, *TX, U.S.A.* 98 C5 34 44N 102 31W
Summerford, *Nfld. & L., Canada* 174 C6 49 29N 54 47W
Summerland, *B.C., Canada* 187 F15 49 32N 119 41W
Summerland Key, *FL, U.S.A.* 67 G7 24 40N 81 27W
Summers County ☆, *WV, U.S.A.* 102 D4 37 40N 80 54W
Summerside, *Nfld. & L., Canada* 174 D3 48 59N 57 59W
Summerside, *P.E.I., Canada* 173 G6 46 24N 63 47W
Summersville, *MO, U.S.A.* 82 D5 37 11N 91 40W
Summersville, *WV, U.S.A.* 102 C4 38 17N 80 51W
Summersville L., *WV, U.S.A.* 102 C4 38 13N 80 53W
Summerton, *SC, U.S.A.* 90 E5 33 36N 80 20W
Summertown, *GA, U.S.A.* 68 D4 32 45N 82 16W
Summertown, *TN, U.S.A.* 96 E5 35 26N 87 18W
Summerville, *Nfld. & L., Canada* 174 D7 48 27N 53 33W
Summerville, *GA, U.S.A.* 68 B1 34 29N 85 21W
Summerville, *OR, U.S.A.* 94 B7 45 29N 118 0W
Summerville, *SC, U.S.A.* 90 E5 33 1N 80 11W
Summit, *AK, U.S.A.* 61 E10 63 20N 149 7W
Summit, *IL, U.S.A.* 71 B6 41 47N 87 47W
Summit, *KY, U.S.A.* 96 C6 37 34N 86 5W
Summit, *MS, U.S.A.* 81 E3 31 17N 90 28W
Summit, *NJ, U.S.A.* 87 B2 40 43N 74 22W
Summit, *OK, U.S.A.* 93 C8 35 40N 95 26W
Summit, *OR, U.S.A.* 94 C2 44 38N 123 35W
Summit, *SD, U.S.A.* 91 E8 45 18N 97 2W
Summit, *UT, U.S.A.* 100 F3 37 48N 112 56W
Summit County ☆, *CO, U.S.A.* 66 C4 39 30N 106 0W
Summit County ☆, *OH, U.S.A.* 92 B5 41 8N 81 29W
Summit County ☆, *UT, U.S.A.* 100 C4 40 55N 111 0W
Summit L., *NV, U.S.A.* 85 A1 41 31N 119 4W
Summit Lake, *B.C., Canada* 189 F8 54 20N 122 40W
Summit Lake Indian Reservation, *NV, U.S.A.* 85 A1 41 33N 119 2W
Summit Mt., *NV, U.S.A.* 85 C4 39 23N 116 28W
Summit Peak, *CO, U.S.A.* 66 E4 37 21N 106 42W
Summit Point, *UT, U.S.A.* 100 E6 38 3N 109 7W
Sumner, *IA, U.S.A.* 73 C6 42 51N 92 6W
Sumner, *MS, U.S.A.* 81 C3 33 58N 90 22W
Sumner, *MO, U.S.A.* 82 B3 39 39N 93 15W
Sumner, *NE, U.S.A.* 84 D6 40 57N 99 31W
Sumner, L., *NM, U.S.A.* 88 C6 34 40N 104 25W
Sumner County ☆, *KS, U.S.A.* 74 D6 37 15N 97 20W
Sumner County ☆, *TN, U.S.A.* 96 D6 36 24N 86 27W
Sumpter, *OR, U.S.A.* 94 C7 44 45N 118 12W
Sumrall, *MS, U.S.A.* 81 E4 31 25N 89 33W
Sumter, *SC, U.S.A.* 90 E5 33 55N 80 21W
Sumter County ☆, *AL, U.S.A.* 60 D2 32 35N 88 11W
Sumter County ☆, *FL, U.S.A.* 67 C6 28 45N 82 10W
Sumter County ☆, *GA, U.S.A.* 68 D2 32 0N 84 10W
Sumter County ☆, *SC, U.S.A.* 90 E5 33 50N 80 30W
Sumter Nat. Forest, *SC, U.S.A.* 90 D2 34 50N 83 0W
Sun, *LA, U.S.A.* 75 D6 30 39N 89 54W
Sun →, *MT, U.S.A.* 83 C6 47 29N 111 19W
Sun City, *AZ, U.S.A.* 62 D3 33 35N 112 16W
Sun City, *CA, U.S.A.* 65 K9 33 42N 117 11W
Sun City, *KS, U.S.A.* 74 D5 37 23N 98 55W
Sun City, *Tampa, U.S.A.* 119 C4 27 40N 82 28W
Sun City Center, *FL, U.S.A.* 67 D6 27 43N 82 21W
Sun City West, *AZ, U.S.A.* 62 D3 33 40N 112 20W
Sun Lakes, *AZ, U.S.A.* 62 D4 33 10N 111 52W
Sun Prairie, *WI, U.S.A.* 103 E4 43 11N 89 13W
Sun River, *MT, U.S.A.* 83 C6 47 32N 111 43W
Sun Valley, *ID, U.S.A.* 70 F4 43 42N 114 21W
Sun Valley, *Los Angeles, U.S.A.* 111 A2 34 13N 118 22W
Sun Valley, *NV, U.S.A.* 85 C1 39 36N 119 46W
Sunapee, *NH, U.S.A.* 86 C2 43 23N 72 7W
Sunapee L., *NH, U.S.A.* 86 C2 43 23N 72 5W
Sunbright, *TN, U.S.A.* 97 D8 36 15N 84 40W
Sunburg, *MN, U.S.A.* 80 E3 45 21N 95 14W
Sunburst, *MT, U.S.A.* 83 B6 48 53N 111 55W
Sunbury, *OH, U.S.A.* 92 C4 40 15N 82 52W
Sunbury, *PA, U.S.A.* 95 D6 40 52N 76 48W
Suncook, *NH, U.S.A.* 86 C3 43 8N 71 27W
Suncook →, *NH, U.S.A.* 86 C3 43 8N 71 28W
Suncrest, *Vancouver, Canada* 193 B2 49 13N 123 1W
Sundance, *Man., Canada* 191 F7 56 32N 94 4W
Sundance, *WY, U.S.A.* 104 B8 44 24N 104 23W
Sunderland, *Ont., Canada* 179 C7 44 16N 79 4W
Sunderland, *MD, U.S.A.* 77 B4 38 40N 76 36W
Sundown, *Man., Canada* 183 F15 49 6N 96 16W
Sundre, *Alta., Canada* 185 G6 51 49N 114 38W
Sundridge, *Ont., Canada* 178 B7 45 45N 79 25W
Sunfish Lake, *Minneapolis-St. Paul, U.S.A.* 113 B3 44 52N 93 5W
Sunfish Park, *Minneapolis-St. Paul, U.S.A.* 113 A4 45 0N 92 56W
Sunflower, *MS, U.S.A.* 81 C3 33 33N 90 32W
Sunflower, Mt., *KS, U.S.A.* 74 B1 39 6N 102 2W
Sunflower County ☆, *MS, U.S.A.* 81 C3 33 44N 90 33W
Sunland Park, *NM, U.S.A.* 88 F4 31 50N 106 40W
Sunman, *IN, U.S.A.* 72 D5 39 14N 85 6W
Sunny Brae, *N.S., Canada* 173 H7 45 24N 62 30W
Sunny Corner, *N.B., Canada* 173 G4 46 57N 65 49W
Sunny Side, *Houston, U.S.A.* 110 B2 29 39N 95 22W
Sunnyside, *Nfld. & L., Canada* 174 E7 47 51N 53 55W
Sunnyside, *NV, U.S.A.* 85 D5 38 25N 115 1W
Sunnyside, *San Diego, U.S.A.* 117 B2 32 40N 117 0W
Sunnyside, *UT, U.S.A.* 100 D5 39 34N 110 23W
Sunnyside, *WA, U.S.A.* 101 D6 46 20N 120 0W
Sunnyslope, *Phoenix, U.S.A.* 116 B2 33 33N 112 3W
Sunnyvale, *CA, U.S.A.* 64 F4 37 23N 122 2W
Sunol, *NE, U.S.A.* 84 C3 41 9N 102 46W
Sunray, *OK, U.S.A.* 93 D6 34 25N 97 58W
Sunray, *TX, U.S.A.* 98 A6 36 1N 101 49W
Sunrise, *FL, U.S.A.* 67 E8 26 8N 80 14W
Sunrise, *WY, U.S.A.* 104 D8 42 20N 104 42W
Sunrise Manor, *NV, U.S.A.* 85 F5 36 12N 115 4W
Sunrise Mountain Natural Area, *Las Vegas, U.S.A.* 110 B3 36 12N 114 58W
Sunrise Mt., *Las Vegas, U.S.A.* 110 B3 36 13N 114 38W
Sunset, *AR, U.S.A.* 63 C5 35 13N 90 12W
Sunset, *LA, U.S.A.* 75 D3 30 25N 92 4W
Sunset, *San Francisco, U.S.A.* 118 B2 37 45N 122 29W
Sunset Beach, *HI, U.S.A.* 69 J13 21 40N 158 3W
Sunset Beach, *Los Angeles, U.S.A.* 111 D4 33 42N 118 4W
Sunset Crater Volcano Nat. Monument ⌂, *AZ, U.S.A.* 62 B4 35 20N 111 20W
Sunset Park, *Las Vegas, U.S.A.* 110 C2 36 3N 115 6W
Sunset Park, *NY, U.S.A.* 114 C3 40 38N 73 59W
Suntrana, *AK, U.S.A.* 61 E10 63 52N 148 51W
Sunwapta Pass, *Alta., Canada* 185 F3 52 13N 117 10W
Supai, *AZ, U.S.A.* 62 A3 36 15N 112 41W
Superior, *AZ, U.S.A.* 62 D4 33 18N 111 6W
Superior, *IA, U.S.A.* 73 B4 43 26N 94 57W
Superior, *MT, U.S.A.* 83 C3 47 12N 114 53W
Superior, *NE, U.S.A.* 84 D7 40 1N 98 4W
Superior, *WI, U.S.A.* 103 B1 46 44N 92 6W
Superior, *WY, U.S.A.* 104 E4 41 46N 108 58W
Superior, L., *Oaxaca, Mexico* 221 H6 16 20N 94 55W
Superior, L., *N. Amer.* 181 E9 47 0N 87 0W
Superior Nat. Forest, *MN, U.S.A.* 80 C7 47 45N 91 30W
Suquamish, *Seattle, U.S.A.* 118 B2 47 43N 122 33W
Sur, Pt., *CA, U.S.A.* 64 G5 36 18N 121 54W
Sur, Pta., *Quintana Roo, Mexico* 223 B6 20 20N 87 20W
Surf City, *NC, U.S.A.* 90 D8 34 26N 77 33W
Surf City, *NJ, U.S.A.* 87 C2 39 40N 74 10W
Surfside, *FL, U.S.A.* 67 F8 25 52N 80 7W
Surfside Beach, *SC, U.S.A.* 90 E7 33 37N 78 57W
Surgoinsville, *TN, U.S.A.* 97 D10 36 28N 82 51W
Suring, *WI, U.S.A.* 103 D5 44 59N 88 22W
Surprise, *AZ, U.S.A.* 62 D3 33 38N 112 19W
Surprise, *NE, U.S.A.* 84 C8 41 6N 97 19W
Surprise, L., *Qué., Canada* 176 B8 49 20N 74 55W
Surrency, *GA, U.S.A.* 68 E4 31 44N 82 12W
Surrey, *B.C., Canada* 187 F12 49 7N 122 45W
Surrey, *ND, U.S.A.* 91 B4 48 14N 101 6W
Surry, *NH, U.S.A.* 86 C2 43 3N 72 18W
Surry, *VA, U.S.A.* 102 D8 37 8N 76 50W
Surry County ☆, *NC, U.S.A.* 90 B5 36 20N 80 45W
Surry County ☆, *VA, U.S.A.* 102 D8 37 7N 76 50W
Surutato, *Sinaloa, Mexico* 216 B3 25 47N 107 34W
Susank, *KS, U.S.A.* 74 C5 38 38N 98 46W
Susanville, *CA, U.S.A.* 64 C6 40 25N 120 39W
Susquehanna, *PA, U.S.A.* 95 C7 41 57N 75 36W
Susquehanna →, *PA, U.S.A.* 95 E6 39 33N 76 5W
Susquehanna County ☆, *PA, U.S.A.* 95 C7 41 55N 75 50W
Susquehannock State Forest, *PA, U.S.A.* 95 C5 41 53N 77 42W
Sussex, *N.B., Canada* 173 H4 45 45N 65 37W
Sussex, *NJ, U.S.A.* 87 A2 41 13N 74 37W
Sussex, *VA, U.S.A.* 102 E7 36 55N 77 17W
Sussex, *WI, U.S.A.* 103 E5 43 8N 88 13W
Sussex, *WY, U.S.A.* 104 C6 43 42N 106 18W
Sussex Corner, *N.B., Canada* 173 H4 45 35N 65 19W
Sussex County ☆, *DE, U.S.A.* 77 B5 38 45N 75 20W
Sussex County ☆, *NJ, U.S.A.* 87 A2 41 15N 74 45W
Sussex County ☆, *VA, U.S.A.* 102 E7 36 55N 77 17W
Susticacán, *Zacatecas, Mexico* 217 E7 22 36N 103 5W
Susupuato, *Michoacan, Mexico* 219 C7 19 13N 100 24W
Sutcliffe, *NV, U.S.A.* 85 C1 39 57N 119 36W
Sutherland, *IA, U.S.A.* 73 C3 42 58N 95 29W
Sutherland, *NE, U.S.A.* 84 C4 41 10N 101 8W
Sutherland Res., *NE, U.S.A.* 84 C4 41 6N 101 10W
Sutherlin, *OR, U.S.A.* 94 D2 43 23N 123 19W
Sutter, *CA, U.S.A.* 64 D5 39 10N 121 45W
Sutter Buttes, *CA, U.S.A.* 64 D5 39 12N 121 49W
Sutter County ☆, *CA, U.S.A.* 64 D5 39 0N 121 45W
Sutter Creek, *CA, U.S.A.* 64 E6 38 24N 120 48W
Suttle, *AL, U.S.A.* 60 D3 32 32N 87 11W
Sutton, *Ont., Canada* 178 C7 44 18N 79 22W
Sutton, *Qué., Canada* 177 F10 45 6N 72 37W
Sutton, *MA, U.S.A.* 78 B3 42 9N 71 46W
Sutton, *ND, U.S.A.* 91 C7 47 24N 98 27W
Sutton, *NE, U.S.A.* 84 D8 40 36N 97 52W
Sutton, *VT, U.S.A.* 86 B2 44 39N 72 3W
Sutton, *WV, U.S.A.* 102 C4 38 40N 80 43W
Sutton, Mts., *Qué., Canada* 86 A2 45 5N 72 32W
Sutton B., *MI, U.S.A.* 79 E6 44 59N 85 37W
Sutton County ☆, *TX, U.S.A.* 98 G7 30 34N 100 39W
Sutton L., *Ont., Canada* 191 G9 54 15N 84 42W
Sutton L., *WV, U.S.A.* 102 C4 38 40N 80 41W
Sutwik I., *AK, U.S.A.* 61 H8 56 34N 157 12W
Suwannee, *FL, U.S.A.* 67 B5 29 20N 83 9W
Suwannee →, *FL, U.S.A.* 67 B5 29 17N 83 10W
Suwannee County ☆, *FL, U.S.A.* 67 A6 30 15N 83 0W
Suwannee Sd., *FL, U.S.A.* 67 B5 29 20N 83 15W
Sverdrup Chan., *Nunavut, Canada* 190 B6 79 56N 96 25W
Sverdrup Is., *Nunavut, Canada* 190 B6 79 0N 97 0W
Swain, *AR, U.S.A.* 63 C2 35 51N 93 20W
Swain County ☆, *NC, U.S.A.* 90 C2 35 30N 83 20W
Swainsboro, *GA, U.S.A.* 68 D4 32 36N 82 20W
Swaledale, *IA, U.S.A.* 73 C5 42 59N 93 19W
Swampscott, *MA, U.S.A.* 78 B4 42 28N 70 53W
Swan →, *Alta., Canada* 184 C5 55 30N 115 18W
Swan →, *Man., Canada* 183 C11 52 30N 100 45W
Swan Cr. →, *MO, U.S.A.* 82 E3 36 41N 93 6W
Swan Hills, *Alta., Canada* 184 D5 54 43N 115 24W
Swan L., *Man., Canada* 183 C11 52 30N 100 40W
Swan L., *SD, U.S.A.* 91 E6 45 17N 99 51W
Swan Lake, *MT, U.S.A.* 83 C4 47 56N 113 51W
Swan Ra., *MT, U.S.A.* 83 C4 48 0N 113 45W
Swan River, *Man., Canada* 183 C10 52 10N 101 16W
Swan River, *MN, U.S.A.* 80 C5 47 5N 93 12W
Swan Valley, *ID, U.S.A.* 70 F7 43 27N 111 20W
Swandale, *WV, U.S.A.* 102 C4 38 30N 80 57W
Swannanoa, *NC, U.S.A.* 90 C3 35 36N 82 24W
Swanquarter, *NC, U.S.A.* 90 C9 35 25N 76 20W
Swans I., *ME, U.S.A.* 76 D5 44 10N 68 26W
Swansboro, *NC, U.S.A.* 90 D8 34 39N 77 7W
Swansea, *SC, U.S.A.* 90 E4 33 44N 81 6W
Swanson L., *NE, U.S.A.* 84 D4 40 10N 101 4W
Swanton, *MD, U.S.A.* 77 A1 39 27N 79 14W
Swanton, *VT, U.S.A.* 86 B1 44 55N 73 8W
Swanville, *MN, U.S.A.* 80 E4 45 55N 94 38W
Swarthmore, *PA, U.S.A.* 87 C1 39 54N 75 21W
Swartswood, *NJ, U.S.A.* 87 A2 41 8N 74 50W
Swartz Creek, *MI, U.S.A.* 79 G8 42 58N 83 50W
Swasey Peak, *UT, U.S.A.* 100 D2 39 23N 113 19W
Swastika, *Ont., Canada* 176 C2 48 7N 80 6W
Swayzee, *IN, U.S.A.* 72 C5 40 30N 85 50W
Swea City, *IA, U.S.A.* 73 B4 43 23N 94 19W
Swedeborg, *MO, U.S.A.* 82 D4 37 55N 92 20W
Sweden, *ME, U.S.A.* 76 B5 46 57N 68 8W
Swedesboro, *NJ, U.S.A.* 87 C1 39 45N 75 19W
Swedish Knoll, *UT, U.S.A.* 100 D4 39 16N 111 26W
Sweeny, *TX, U.S.A.* 99 H12 29 3N 95 42W
Sweet Air, *MD, U.S.A.* 77 A4 39 31N 76 32W
Sweet Briar Station, *VA, U.S.A.* 102 D5 37 33N 79 4W
Sweet Grass, *MT, U.S.A.* 83 B6 48 59N 111 58W
Sweet Grass County ☆, *MT, U.S.A.* 83 E8 46 0N 110 0W
Sweet Home, *AR, U.S.A.* 63 D3 34 41N 92 15W
Sweet Home, *OR, U.S.A.* 94 C3 44 24N 122 44W
Sweet Springs, *MO, U.S.A.* 82 C3 38 58N 93 25W
Sweet Springs, *WV, U.S.A.* 102 D4 37 38N 80 14W
Sweet Water, *AL, U.S.A.* 60 D3 32 6N 87 52W
Sweetwater, *TN, U.S.A.* 97 E8 35 36N 84 28W
Sweetwater, *TX, U.S.A.* 98 E7 32 28N 100 25W
Sweetwater →, *WY, U.S.A.* 104 D5 42 31N 107 2W
Sweetwater County ☆, *WY, U.S.A.* 104 E4 42 0N 109 0W
Sweetwater L., *ND, U.S.A.* 91 B7 48 13N 98 50W
Sweetwater Marsh Nat. Wildlife Refuge ⌂, *San Diego, U.S.A.* 117 C2 32 38N 117 6W
Sweetwater Res., *San Diego, U.S.A.* 117 B3 32 41N 117 0W
Sweetwater Station, *WY, U.S.A.* 104 D4 42 32N 108 11W
Swenson, *TX, U.S.A.* 98 D7 33 13N 100 19W
Swift County ☆, *MN, U.S.A.* 80 E3 45 15N 95 45W
Swift Current, *Nfld. & L., Canada* 174 E6 47 53N 54 12W
Swift Current, *Sask., Canada* 182 E4 50 20N 107 45W
Swift Current →, *Sask., Canada* 182 E4 50 38N 107 44W
Swift Res., *WA, U.S.A.* 101 D3 46 4N 122 3W
Swifton, *AR, U.S.A.* 63 C4 35 49N 91 8W
Swinburne I., *NY, U.S.A.* 114 C2 40 33N 74 3W
Swindle, I., *B.C., Canada* 186 C6 52 30N 128 35W
Swink, *CO, U.S.A.* 66 D7 38 1N 103 38W
Swink, *OK, U.S.A.* 93 D8 34 1N 95 12W
Swinomish Indian Reservation, *WA, U.S.A.* 101 B3 48 23N 122 32W
Swisher, *IA, U.S.A.* 73 D7 41 50N 91 42W
Swisher County ☆, *TX, U.S.A.* 98 C6 34 32N 101 46W
Swisshome, *OR, U.S.A.* 94 C2 44 4N 123 48W
Swissvale, *Pittsburgh, U.S.A.* 116 B2 40 25N 79 52W
Switzerland County ☆, *IN, U.S.A.* 72 E6 38 50N 85 0W
Swords, *GA, U.S.A.* 68 C3 33 33N 83 18W
Swoyerville, *PA, U.S.A.* 95 C7 41 18N 75 53W
Sycamore, *GA, U.S.A.* 68 E3 31 40N 83 38W
Sycamore, *IL, U.S.A.* 71 B5 41 59N 88 41W
Sycamore, *KS, U.S.A.* 74 D8 37 20N 95 43W
Sycamore, *OH, U.S.A.* 92 C3 40 57N 83 10W
Sycan Marsh, *OR, U.S.A.* 94 E4 42 45N 121 5W
Sydenham →, *Ont., Canada* 178 E4 42 33N 82 25W
Sydney, *N.S., Canada* 173 G9 46 7N 60 7W
Sydney, *ND, U.S.A.* 91 D7 46 44N 98 46W
Sydney L., *Ont., Canada* 180 B2 50 41N 94 25W
Sydney Mines, *N.S., Canada* 173 G9 46 18N 60 15W
Sydney River, *N.S., Canada* 173 G9 46 7N 60 13W
Sykeston, *ND, U.S.A.* 91 C6 47 28N 99 24W
Sykesville, *MD, U.S.A.* 77 A4 39 22N 76 58W
Sykesville, *PA, U.S.A.* 95 C4 41 3N 78 50W
Sylacauga, *AL, U.S.A.* 60 C4 33 10N 86 15W
Sylva, *NC, U.S.A.* 90 C2 35 23N 83 13W
Sylvan, *PA, U.S.A.* 77 A2 39 45N 78 1W
Sylvan Grove, *KS, U.S.A.* 74 B5 39 1N 98 24W
Sylvan L., *Alta., Canada* 185 F6 52 21N 114 10W
Sylvan Lake, *Alta., Canada* 185 F6 52 20N 114 3W
Sylvania, *Sask., Canada* 182 C8 52 42N 104 0W
Sylvania, *GA, U.S.A.* 68 D5 32 45N 81 38W
Sylvania, *OH, U.S.A.* 92 B3 41 43N 83 42W
Sylvarena, *MS, U.S.A.* 81 D4 32 1N 89 23W
Sylvester, *GA, U.S.A.* 68 E3 31 32N 83 50W
Sylvester, *TX, U.S.A.* 98 E7 32 43N 100 15W
Sylvia, *KS, U.S.A.* 74 D5 37 57N 98 25W
Symerton, *IL, U.S.A.* 71 B5 41 20N 88 3W
Symmes Cr. →, *OH, U.S.A.* 92 E4 38 26N 82 27W
Symsonia, *KY, U.S.A.* 96 D4 36 55N 88 31W
Syracuse, *IN, U.S.A.* 72 B5 41 26N 85 45W
Syracuse, *KS, U.S.A.* 74 D2 37 59N 101 45W
Syracuse, *MO, U.S.A.* 82 C4 38 40N 92 53W
Syracuse, *NY, U.S.A.* 89 B4 43 3N 76 9W
Syracuse, *NE, U.S.A.* 84 D9 40 39N 96 11W
Syracuse ✕ (SYR), *NY, U.S.A.* 89 B4 43 7N 76 6W
Syria, *VA, U.S.A.* 102 C6 38 29N 78 20W
Syringa Park ⌂, *B.C., Canada* 187 F17 49 23N 117 54W

T

T.O. Fuller State Park ⌂, *TN, U.S.A.* 112 B1 35 3N 90 7W
Tabasco, *Zacatecas, Mexico* 217 F8 21 52N 102 55W
Tabasco □, *Mexico* 222 B4 18 0N 92 40W
Taber, *Alta., Canada* 185 J8 49 47N 112 8W
Tabernash, *CO, U.S.A.* 66 C5 39 57N 105 52W
Tabiona, *UT, U.S.A.* 100 C5 40 21N 110 43W
Table B., *Nfld. & L., Canada* 175 C6 53 40N 56 25W
Table I., *Nunavut, Canada* 190 B6 77 12N 95 28W
Table Mt., *AZ, U.S.A.* 62 E5 32 49N 110 31W
Table Mt., *SD, U.S.A.* 91 E2 45 55N 103 48W
Table Rock, *NE, U.S.A.* 84 D9 40 11N 96 6W
Table Rock, *WY, U.S.A.* 104 E4 41 37N 108 23W
Table Rock L., *MO, U.S.A.* 82 E3 36 36N 93 19W
Table Top, *AZ, U.S.A.* 62 E3 32 45N 112 8W
Tabor, *IA, U.S.A.* 73 E3 40 54N 95 40W
Tabor, *MN, U.S.A.* 80 B2 48 5N 96 52W
Tabor, *SD, U.S.A.* 91 H8 42 57N 97 40W
Tabor City, *NC, U.S.A.* 90 D7 34 10N 78 52W
Tabusintac, *N.B., Canada* 173 F4 47 20N 65 1W
Tacámbaro, *Michoacan, Mexico* 219 C6 19 14N 101 28W
Tachick L., *B.C., Canada* 186 B10 53 57N 124 12W
Tacna, *AZ, U.S.A.* 62 E2 32 41N 113 59W
Tacoh, *Campeche, Mexico* 223 C4 19 47N 89 52W
Tacoma, *WA, U.S.A.* 101 C3 47 14N 122 26W
Taconic Ra., *U.S.A.* 78 B1 42 40N 73 18W
Taconite Harbor, *MN, U.S.A.* 80 C8 47 32N 90 55W
Tacotalpa, *Tabasco, Mexico* 222 B4 17 36N 92 49W
Tacuba, *Distrito Federal, Mexico* 225 B2 19 26N 99 11W
Tacubaya, *Distrito Federal, Mexico* 225 B2 19 24N 99 10W
Tadoule L., *Man., Canada* 191 F6 58 36N 98 20W
Tadoussac, *Qué., Canada* 177 C13 48 11N 69 42W
Tafetán, *Michoacan, Mexico* 219 C7 19 26N 100 54W
Taft, *CA, U.S.A.* 65 H7 35 8N 119 28W
Taft, *FL, U.S.A.* 67 C7 28 25N 81 21W
Taft, *OK, U.S.A.* 93 C8 35 46N 95 32W
Taft, *TN, U.S.A.* 96 E6 35 1N 86 43W
Taft, *TX, U.S.A.* 99 K10 27 59N 97 24W
Tafton, *PA, U.S.A.* 87 A1 41 24N 75 11W
Tagpochau, Mt., *N. Marianas* 105 c 15 11N 145 44W
Tahdziú, *Yucatán, Mexico* 223 B5 20 12N 88 57W
Tahgong Pt., *N. Marianas* 105 c 15 6N 145 39W
Tahlequah, *OK, U.S.A.* 93 C9 35 55N 94 58W
Tahoe, L., *U.S.A.* 64 D6 39 6N 120 2W
Tahoe City, *CA, U.S.A.* 64 D6 39 10N 120 9W
Tahoe L., *Nunavut, Canada* 190 C4 70 5N 108 45W
Tahoe Nat. Forest, *CA, U.S.A.* 64 D6 39 20N 120 30W
Tahoka, *TX, U.S.A.* 98 D6 33 10N 101 48W
Taholah, *WA, U.S.A.* 101 C1 47 21N 124 17W
Tahquamenon →, *MI, U.S.A.* 79 C6 46 34N 85 2W
Tahsis, *B.C., Canada* 186 F8 49 55N 126 40W
Tahsish-Kwois Park ⌂, *B.C., Canada* 186 E7 50 11N 127 9W
Tahtsa L., *B.C., Canada* 186 B7 53 42N 127 27W
Taiban, *NM, U.S.A.* 88 C6 34 26N 104 1W
Tajique, *NM, U.S.A.* 88 C4 34 45N 106 17W
Tajirachic, *Chihuahua, Mexico* 213 E8 28 1N 107 10W
Tajitos, *Sonora, Mexico* 212 C3 30 57N 112 20W
Takla L., *B.C., Canada* 189 E7 55 15N 125 45W
Takla Landing, *B.C., Canada* 189 E7 55 30N 125 50W
Takoma Park, *MD, U.S.A.* 77 B4 38 58N 77 0W
Takotna, *AK, U.S.A.* 61 E8 62 59N 156 4W
Takysie Lake, *B.C., Canada* 186 B9 53 53N 125 53W
Tala, *Jalisco, Mexico* 218 B4 20 40N 103 42W
Talala, *OK, U.S.A.* 93 B8 36 32N 95 42W
Talbot County ☆, *GA, U.S.A.* 68 D2 32 45N 84 40W
Talbot County ☆, *MD, U.S.A.* 77 B4 38 45N 76 0W
Talbot Inlet, *Nunavut, Canada* 190 B10 77 55N 77 40W
Talbot L., *Man., Canada* 183 A12 54 0N 99 55W
Talbotton, *GA, U.S.A.* 68 D2 32 41N 84 32W
Talcayuca, *Hidalgo, Mexico* 219 C9 19 57N 98 54W
Talchichilte, I., *Sinaloa, Mexico* 216 C2 24 55N 108 7W
Talco, *TX, U.S.A.* 99 D12 33 22N 95 6W
Talent, *OR, U.S.A.* 94 E3 42 15N 122 47W
Taliaferro County ☆, *GA, U.S.A.* 68 C4 33 35N 82 50W
Taliesin, *WI, U.S.A.* 103 E3 43 8N 90 4W
Talihina, *OK, U.S.A.* 93 D8 34 45N 95 3W
Talkeetna, *AK, U.S.A.* 61 E10 62 20N 150 6W
Talking Rock, *GA, U.S.A.* 68 B2 34 31N 84 30W
Talladega, *AL, U.S.A.* 60 C4 33 26N 86 6W
Talladega County ☆, *AL, U.S.A.* 60 C4 33 26N 86 6W
Talladega Cr. →, *AL, U.S.A.* 60 C4 33 18N 86 22W
Talladega Nat. Forest, *AL, U.S.A.* 60 D3 32 55N 87 15W
Tallahala Cr. →, *MS, U.S.A.* 81 E4 31 12N 89 5W
Tallahassee, *FL, U.S.A.* 67 A4 30 27N 84 17W
Tallahatchie →, *MS, U.S.A.* 81 C3 33 33N 90 10W
Tallahatchie County ☆, *MS, U.S.A.* 81 C3 33 58N 90 22W
Tallapoosa, *GA, U.S.A.* 68 C1 33 45N 85 17W
Tallapoosa →, *AL, U.S.A.* 60 D4 32 30N 86 16W
Tallapoosa County ☆, *AL, U.S.A.* 60 D5 32 50N 85 46W
Tallassee, *AL, U.S.A.* 60 D5 32 32N 85 54W
Talleyville, *DE, U.S.A.* 77 A5 39 48N 75 33W
Tallgrass Prairie Nat. Preserve ⌂, *KS, U.S.A.* 74 C7 38 26N 96 34W
Tallmadge, *OH, U.S.A.* 92 B5 41 6N 81 27W
Tallula, *IL, U.S.A.* 71 D4 39 56N 89 56W
Tallulah, *LA, U.S.A.* 75 B4 32 25N 91 11W
Tallulah Falls, *GA, U.S.A.* 68 B3 34 44N 83 24W
Talmage, *KS, U.S.A.* 74 B6 39 2N 97 16W
Talmage, *NE, U.S.A.* 84 D9 40 32N 96 1W
Talofofo, *Guam* 105 b 13 21N 144 45W
Taloga, *OK, U.S.A.* 93 B5 36 2N 98 58W
Taloyoak, *Nunavut, Canada* 190 D7 69 32N 93 32W
Talpa, *TX, U.S.A.* 99 F8 31 47N 99 43W
Talpa de Allende, *Jalisco, Mexico* 218 B3 20 23N 104 51W

Talquin, L., *FL, U.S.A.* **67 A4** 30 23N 84 39W
Taltson ➝, *N.W.T., Canada* **189 D10** 61 24N 112 46W
Talunkwan I., *B.C., Canada* **186 C3** 52 50N 131 45W
Tama, *IA, U.S.A.* **73 D6** 41 58N 92 35W
Tama County ☆, *IA, U.S.A.* **73 C6** 42 5N 92 30W
Tamaha, *OK, U.S.A.* **93 C9** 35 20N 94 59W
Tamaqua, *PA, U.S.A.* **95 D7** 40 48N 75 58W
Tamarac, *FL, U.S.A.* **67 E8** 26 12N 80 15W
Tamarac Nat. Wildlife Refuge ⌓, *MN, U.S.A.* **80 C3** 47 2N 95 36W
Tamarack, *ID, U.S.A.* **70 E2** 44 57N 116 23W
Tamarack, *MN, U.S.A.* **80 D5** 46 39N 93 8W
Tamaroa, *IL, U.S.A.* **71 E4** 38 8N 89 14W
Tamasopo, *San Luis Potosí, Mexico* **215 J5** 21 55N 99 24W
Tamaulipas □, *Mexico* **215 G6** 24 0N 98 45W
Tamazula, *Durango, Mexico* **216 C4** 24 57N 106 57W
Tamazula de Gordiano, *Jalisco, Mexico* **218 C4** 19 38N 103 15W
Tamazunchale, *San Luis Potosí, Mexico* **215 J6** 21 16N 98 47W
Tameapa, *Sinaloa, Mexico* **216 B3** 25 39N 107 22W
Tamesí ➝, *Tamaulipas, Mexico* **215 H7** 22 13N 97 52W
Tamiahua, *Veracruz, Mexico* **220 C3** 21 16N 97 27W
Tamiahua, L. de, *Veracruz, Mexico* **220 C3** 21 35N 97 35W
Tamiami Canal, *FL, U.S.A.* **67 F8** 25 50N 81 0W
Tamms, *IL, U.S.A.* **71 F4** 37 14N 89 16W
Tamora, *NE, U.S.A.* **84 D8** 40 54N 97 14W
Tampa, *FL, U.S.A.* **67 D6** 27 56N 82 27W
Tampa, *KS, U.S.A.* **74 C6** 38 33N 97 9W
Tampa B., *FL, U.S.A.* **67 D6** 27 50N 82 30W
Tampa International ✕ (TPA), *FL, U.S.A.* **67 D6** 27 59N 82 32W
Tampacán, *San Luis Potosí, Mexico* **215 J6** 21 25N 98 44W
Tampalam, *Quintana Roo, Mexico* **223 C6** 19 9N 87 33W
Tampamolón, *San Luis Potosí, Mexico* **215 J6** 21 34N 98 49W
Tampaón ➝, *San Luis Potosí, Mexico* **215 J6** 21 58N 98 39W
Tampico, *Tamaulipas, Mexico* **215 H7** 22 13N 97 51W
Tampico, *IL, U.S.A.* **71 B4** 41 38N 89 47W
Tampico Alto, *Veracruz, Mexico* **220 B3** 22 7N 97 48W
Tamuín, *San Luis Potosí, Mexico* **215 J6** 21 59N 98 45W
Tamulte de las Sabanas, *Tabasco, Mexico* **222 A4** 18 13N 92 47W
Tamuning, *Guam* **105 b** 13 29N 144 47W
Tamworth, *Ont., Canada* **179 C10** 44 29N 77 0W
Tamworth, *NH, U.S.A.* **86 C3** 43 50N 71 18W
Tanacross, *AK, U.S.A.* **61 E12** 63 23N 143 21W
Tanaga I., *AK, U.S.A.* **61 L3** 51 48N 177 53W
Tanaga Volcano, *AK, U.S.A.* **61 L3** 51 53N 178 8W
Tanana, *AK, U.S.A.* **61 D9** 65 10N 152 4W
Tanana ➝, *AK, U.S.A.* **61 D10** 65 10N 151 58W
Tanapag, *N. Marianas* **105 c** 15 14N 145 45W
Tancítaro, *Michoacan, Mexico* **218 C5** 19 23N 102 23W
Tancoco, *Veracruz, Mexico* **220 C3** 21 17N 97 47W
Taney County ☆, *MO, U.S.A.* **82 E3** 36 40N 93 0W
Taneytown, *MD, U.S.A.* **77 A3** 39 40N 77 11W
Taneyville, *MO, U.S.A.* **82 E3** 36 44N 93 2W
Tangancícuaro, *Michoacan, Mexico* **218 C5** 19 54N 102 8W
Tangelo Park, *Orlando, U.S.A.* **115 B2** 28 27N 81 26W
Tangent, *OR, U.S.A.* **94 C2** 44 33N 123 7W
Tangier, *N.S., Canada* **173 J7** 44 48N 62 42W
Tangier, *U.S.A.* **102 D9** 37 49N 75 59W
Tangier I., *VA, U.S.A.* **77 C5** 37 55N 75 59W
Tangier Sd., *MD, U.S.A.* **77 B5** 38 0N 75 57W
Tangipahoa, *LA, U.S.A.* **75 D5** 30 53N 90 31W
Tangipahoa ➝, *LA, U.S.A.* **75 D5** 30 20N 90 16W
Tangipahoa Parish ☆, *LA, U.S.A.* **75 D5** 30 30N 90 28W
Tanhuijo, Arrecife de, *Veracruz, Mexico* **220 C3** 21 8N 97 15W
Tankersley, *TX, U.S.A.* **98 F7** 31 21N 100 39W
Tankuché, *Campeche, Mexico* **223 B3** 20 31N 90 15W
Tanlajas, *San Luis Potosí, Mexico* **215 J6** 21 40N 98 53W
Tanner, *WV, U.S.A.* **102 C4** 38 59N 80 57W
Tanner Point, *Norfolk, U.S.A.* **115 A2** 36 54N 76 19W
Tanners Lake, *Minneapolis-St. Paul, U.S.A.* **113 B4** 44 57N 92 58W
Tanque de Dolores, *San Luis Potosí, Mexico* **215 G3** 23 40N 101 9W
Tanque del Cerro, *Coahuila, Mexico* **215 F4** 24 38N 100 49W
Tanque Nuevo, *Coahuila, Mexico* **214 D2** 26 38N 102 11W
Tanque Nuevo, *San Luis Potosí, Mexico* **215 F4** 24 22N 100 57W
Tanquian, *San Luis Potosí, Mexico* **215 J6** 21 36N 98 40W
Tantallon, *Sask., Canada* **183 E10** 50 32N 101 50W
Tantalus Park △, *B.C., Canada* **187 F11** 49 50N 123 17W
Tantoyuca, *Veracruz, Mexico* **220 C2** 21 21N 98 14W
Tanu I., *B.C., Canada* **186 C3** 52 46N 131 40W
Taopi, *MN, U.S.A.* **80 G6** 43 34N 92 38W
Taos, *NM, U.S.A.* **88 A5** 36 24N 105 35W
Taos County ☆, *NM, U.S.A.* **88 A5** 36 30N 105 40W
Taos Indian Reservation, *NM, U.S.A.* **88 A5** 36 35N 105 25W
Taos Pueblo, *NM, U.S.A.* **88 A5** 36 24N 105 33W
Tapachula, *Chiapas, Mexico* **222 E4** 14 54N 92 17W
Tapalpa, *Jalisco, Mexico* **218 C4** 19 56N 103 46W
Tapijulapa, *Tabasco, Mexico* **222 B4** 17 28N 92 47W
Tapilula, *Chiapas, Mexico* **222 B3** 17 14N 93 2W
Tappahannock, *VA, U.S.A.* **77 C4** 37 56N 76 52W
Tappan L., *OH, U.S.A.* **92 C5** 40 22N 81 14W
Tappen, *ND, U.S.A.* **91 D6** 46 52N 99 38W
Taputapu, C., *Amer. Samoa* **105 e** 14 20 S 170 51W
Tar ➝, *NC, U.S.A.* **90 C8** 35 33N 77 6W
Tara, *Ont., Canada* **178 C5** 44 28N 81 9W
Tarandacuao, *Guanajuato, Mexico* **219 C7** 20 0N 100 31W
Tarboro, *GA, U.S.A.* **68 E5** 31 1N 81 48W
Tarboro, *NC, U.S.A.* **90 C8** 35 54N 77 32W
Taretán, *Michoacan, Mexico* **218 C6** 19 20N 101 55W
Targhee Nat. Forest, *ID, U.S.A.* **70 E7** 44 30N 111 20W
Targhee Pass, *U.S.A.* **70 E7** 44 40N 111 16W
Tarimbaro, *Michoacan, Mexico* **219 C6** 19 47N 101 8W
Tarimoro, *Guanajuato, Mexico* **219 B7** 20 17N 100 45W
Tarkio, *MO, U.S.A.* **82 A1** 40 27N 95 23W
Tarkio, *MT, U.S.A.* **83 C3** 47 1N 114 44W
Tarkio ➝, *MO, U.S.A.* **82 A1** 40 27N 95 23W
Tarlton, *OH, U.S.A.* **92 D4** 39 33N 82 47W
Tarnov, *NE, U.S.A.* **84 C8** 41 37N 97 30W
Tarpon Springs, *FL, U.S.A.* **67 C6** 28 9N 82 45W
Tarrant City, *AL, U.S.A.* **60 C4** 33 34N 86 47W
Tarrant County ☆, *TX, U.S.A.* **99 E10** 32 44N 97 7W
Tarryall, *CO, U.S.A.* **66 C5** 39 7N 105 29W
Tarryall Cr. ➝, *CO, U.S.A.* **66 C5** 39 5N 105 19W
Tarrytown, *GA, U.S.A.* **68 D4** 32 19N 82 34W
Tarrytown, *NY, U.S.A.* **87 A3** 41 4N 73 52W
Tarzan, *TX, U.S.A.* **98 E6** 32 18N 101 58W
Tarzana, *Los Angeles, U.S.A.* **111 A1** 34 10N 118 33W
Tasajeras, *Sinaloa, Mexico* **213 G7** 26 47N 108 16W
Taschereau, *Qué., Canada* **176 C4** 48 40N 78 40W
Taseko ➝, *B.C., Canada* **186 C11** 52 8N 123 45W
Taseko L., *B.C., Canada* **186 D11** 51 15N 123 35W
Tasiujaq, *Qué., Canada* **175 B4** 58 42N 69 56W
Tasquillo, *Hidalgo, Mexico* **219 B8** 20 38N 99 12W
Tassialuk, L., *Qué., Canada* **175 B3** 59 3N 74 0W
Tasu, *B.C., Canada* **186 C2** 52 45N 132 5W
Tasu Sd., *B.C., Canada* **186 C2** 52 47N 132 2W
Tatahuicapa, *Veracruz, Mexico* **221 F6** 18 15N 94 46W
Tataltepec, *Oaxaca, Mexico* **221 H3** 16 18N 97 33W
Tatamagouche, *N.S., Canada* **173 H6** 45 43N 63 18W
Tate, *GA, U.S.A.* **68 B2** 34 25N 84 23W
Tate County ☆, *MS, U.S.A.* **81 B4** 34 37N 89 58W
Tathlina L., *N.W.T., Canada* **189 D9** 60 33N 117 39W
Tatitlek, *AK, U.S.A.* **61 F11** 60 52N 146 41W
Tatla L., *B.C., Canada* **186 D10** 52 0N 124 20W
Tatlayoko L., *B.C., Canada* **186 D10** 51 35N 124 24W
Tatnam, C., *Man., Canada* **191 F7** 57 16N 91 0W
Tattnall County ☆, *GA, U.S.A.* **68 D4** 32 0N 82 0W
Tatuk, L., *B.C., Canada* **186 B10** 53 32N 124 14W
Tatum, *NM, U.S.A.* **88 D7** 33 16N 103 19W
Tatum, *TX, U.S.A.* **99 E13** 32 19N 94 31W
Tatum Cr. ➝, *GA, U.S.A.* **68 F4** 30 43N 82 32W
Tatums, *OK, U.S.A.* **93 D6** 34 29N 97 28W
Tau, *Amer. Samoa* **105 f** 14 15 S 169 30W
Taum Sauk Mt., *MO, U.S.A.* **82 D6** 37 34N 90 44W
Taunton, *MA, U.S.A.* **78 C3** 41 54N 71 6W
Taunton, *MN, U.S.A.* **80 F2** 44 36N 96 4W
Taunton Lake, *NJ, U.S.A.* **87 C2** 39 51N 74 52W
Taverner B., *Nunavut, Canada* **190 D11** 67 12N 72 25W
Tavernier, *FL, U.S.A.* **67 F8** 25 1N 80 31W
Tavistock, *Ont., Canada* **178 D6** 43 19N 80 50W
Tawakoni, L., *TX, U.S.A.* **99 E12** 32 49N 95 55W
Tawas City, *MI, U.S.A.* **79 E8** 44 16N 83 31W
Taxco, *Guerrero, Mexico* **219 D8** 18 33N 99 36W
Taylor, *AZ, U.S.A.* **62 C5** 34 28N 110 5W
Taylor, *AR, U.S.A.* **63 E2** 33 6N 93 28W
Taylor, *FL, U.S.A.* **67 A6** 30 26N 82 18W
Taylor, *MI, U.S.A.* **79 G8** 42 14N 83 16W
Taylor, *MS, U.S.A.* **81 B4** 34 16N 89 35W
Taylor, *ND, U.S.A.* **91 D3** 46 54N 102 26W
Taylor, *NE, U.S.A.* **84 C6** 41 46N 99 23W
Taylor, *TX, U.S.A.* **99 G10** 30 34N 97 25W
Taylor, *WI, U.S.A.* **103 D2** 44 19N 91 7W
Taylor ➝, *CO, U.S.A.* **66 D4** 38 32N 106 55W
Taylor, Mt., *NM, U.S.A.* **88 B3** 35 14N 107 37W
Taylor County ☆, *FL, U.S.A.* **67 A5** 30 0N 83 30W
Taylor County ☆, *GA, U.S.A.* **68 D2** 32 35N 84 15W
Taylor County ☆, *IA, U.S.A.* **73 E4** 40 45N 94 40W
Taylor County ☆, *KY, U.S.A.* **97 C7** 37 20N 85 20W
Taylor County ☆, *TX, U.S.A.* **99 E8** 32 21N 99 53W
Taylor County ☆, *WV, U.S.A.* **102 B4** 39 21N 80 2W
Taylor County ☆, *WI, U.S.A.* **103 C3** 45 10N 90 30W
Taylor Mill, *KY, U.S.A.* **107 B1** 38 59N 84 29W
Taylor Park Res., *CO, U.S.A.* **66 D4** 38 49N 106 36W
Taylor Ridge, *GA, U.S.A.* **68 B1** 34 35N 85 12W
Taylors, *SC, U.S.A.* **90 D3** 34 55N 82 18W
Taylors Bridge, *DE, U.S.A.* **77 A5** 39 23N 75 36W
Taylors Island, *MD, U.S.A.* **77 B4** 38 28N 76 18W
Taylorsville, *IN, U.S.A.* **72 D5** 39 18N 85 57W
Taylorsville, *KY, U.S.A.* **97 B7** 38 2N 85 21W
Taylorsville, *MD, U.S.A.* **77 A3** 39 27N 77 8W
Taylorsville, *MS, U.S.A.* **81 E4** 31 50N 89 26W
Taylorsville, *NC, U.S.A.* **90 C4** 35 55N 81 11W
Taylorsville, *Salt Lake City, U.S.A.* **117 C2** 40 40N 111 56W
Taylorville, *IL, U.S.A.* **71 D4** 39 33N 89 18W
Tayoltita, *Durango, Mexico* **216 C5** 24 5N 105 56W
Tazewell, *TN, U.S.A.* **97 D9** 36 27N 83 34W
Tazewell, *VA, U.S.A.* **102 D3** 37 7N 81 31W
Tazewell County ☆, *IL, U.S.A.* **71 C4** 40 30N 89 30W
Tazewell County ☆, *VA, U.S.A.* **102 D3** 37 7N 81 31W
Tazin ➝, *Canada* **189 E11** 59 48N 109 55W
Tazin L., *Sask., Canada* **189 E11** 59 44N 108 42W
Tazlina, *AK, U.S.A.* **61 E11** 62 4N 146 27W
Tchula, *MS, U.S.A.* **81 C3** 33 11N 90 13W
Tea, *SD, U.S.A.* **91 G9** 43 27N 96 50W
Teabo, *Yucatán, Mexico* **223 B4** 20 24N 89 17W
Teacapán, *Sinaloa, Mexico* **216 E5** 22 33N 105 45W
Teacapan, Estero, *Nayarit, Mexico* **216 E5** 22 26N 105 40W
Teague, *TX, U.S.A.* **99 F11** 31 38N 96 17W
Teahwhit Head, *WA, U.S.A.* **101 C1** 47 52N 124 37W
Teaneck, *NJ, U.S.A.* **114 A2** 40 52N 74 1W
Teaneck, *NJ, U.S.A.* **87 B2** 40 53N 74 1W
Teapa, *Tabasco, Mexico* **222 B4** 17 33N 92 57W
Teasdale, *UT, U.S.A.* **100 E4** 38 17N 111 29W
Teatlalco, *Puebla, Mexico* **221 F2** 18 28N 98 47W
Tecalitlan, *Jalisco, Mexico* **218 C4** 19 26N 103 15W
Tecamachalco, *México, Mexico* **225 B2** 19 25N 99 14W
Tecamachalco, *Puebla, Mexico* **221 F3** 18 53N 97 44W
Tecate, *Baja Calif., Mexico* **210 A2** 32 34N 116 38W
Techaluta, *Jalisco, Mexico* **218 B4** 20 4N 103 33W
Tecoh, *Yucatán, Mexico* **223 B4** 20 55N 89 38W
Tecolote Canyon Natural Park △, *San Diego, U.S.A.* **117 B1** 32 46N 117 11W
Tecolotlán, *Jalisco, Mexico* **218 B3** 20 13N 104 3W
Tecolutilla, *Tabasco, Mexico* **222 A3** 18 17N 93 19W
Tecolutla, *Veracruz, Mexico* **220 D4** 20 30N 97 0W
Tecolutla, Barra de, *Veracruz, Mexico* **220 D3** 20 34N 97 3W
Tecomán, *Colima, Mexico* **218 D4** 18 55N 103 53W
Tecomate, L., *Guerrero, Mexico* **219 F8** 16 42N 99 20W
Tecomatlán, *Puebla, Mexico* **221 F2** 18 7N 98 18W
Tecopa, *CA, U.S.A.* **65 H10** 35 51N 116 13W
Tecoripa, *Sonora, Mexico* **212 E6** 28 37N 109 57W
Tecozautla, *Hidalgo, Mexico* **219 B8** 20 32N 99 38W
Tecpan de Galeana, *Guerrero, Mexico* **219 E7** 17 15N 100 41W
Tecpatán, *Chiapas, Mexico* **222 B3** 17 8N 93 18W
Tecuala, *Nayarit, Mexico* **216 E5** 22 23N 105 27W
Tecuanapa, *Guerrero, Mexico* **219 F8** 17 0N 99 15W
Tecumseh, *Ont., Canada* **178 E4** 42 19N 82 54W
Tecumseh, *MI, U.S.A.* **79 H8** 42 0N 83 57W
Tecumseh, *NE, U.S.A.* **84 D9** 40 22N 96 11W
Tecumseh, *OK, U.S.A.* **93 C7** 35 15N 96 56W
Tecumseh, Mt., *NH, U.S.A.* **86 C3** 43 57N 71 34W
Tee Lake, *Qué., Canada* **176 E3** 46 40N 79 0W
Teec Nos Pos, *AZ, U.S.A.* **62 A6** 36 55N 109 6W
Teepee Creek, *Alta., Canada* **184 C2** 55 22N 118 24W
Teeswater, *Ont., Canada* **178 D5** 43 59N 81 17W
Tehachapi, *CA, U.S.A.* **65 H8** 35 8N 118 27W
Tehachapi Mts., *CA, U.S.A.* **65 J8** 35 0N 118 30W
Tehachapi Pass, *CA, U.S.A.* **65 H8** 35 6N 118 18W
Tehama, *CA, U.S.A.* **64 C4** 40 2N 122 7W
Tehama County ☆, *CA, U.S.A.* **64 C4** 40 5N 122 15W
Tehek L., *Nunavut, Canada* **191 E6** 64 55N 95 38W
Tehuacán, *Puebla, Mexico* **221 F3** 18 27N 97 23W
Tehuantepec, G. de, *Mexico* **221 J5** 15 50N 95 12W
Tehuantepec, Istmo de, *Mexico* **221 G6** 17 15N 94 30W
Tehuipango, *Veracruz, Mexico* **221 F3** 18 31N 97 4W
Tehuitzingo, *Puebla, Mexico* **221 F2** 18 21N 98 16W
Tejabán de la Rosita, *Coahuila, Mexico* **215 E1** 25 15N 103 13W
Tejamén, *Durango, Mexico* **216 C5** 24 48N 105 7W
Tejar, *Veracruz, Mexico* **221 E4** 19 3N 96 10W
Tejon Pass, *CA, U.S.A.* **65 J8** 34 49N 118 53W
Tejupan, Pta., *Michoacan, Mexico* **218 D4** 18 20N 103 31W
Tejupilco, *México, Mexico* **219 D7** 18 54N 100 9W
Tekamah, *NE, U.S.A.* **84 C9** 41 47N 96 13W
Tekanto, *Yucatán, Mexico* **223 A4** 21 1N 89 6W
Tekax, *Yucatán, Mexico* **223 B4** 20 12N 89 17W
Tekit, *Yucatán, Mexico* **223 B4** 20 32N 89 20W
Tekoa, *WA, U.S.A.* **101 C8** 47 14N 117 4W
Tekonsha, *MI, U.S.A.* **79 G7** 42 5N 84 59W
Telchac Puerto, *Yucatán, Mexico* **223 A4** 21 21N 89 16W
Telegraph Cove, *B.C., Canada* **186 E8** 50 32N 126 50W
Telegraph Creek, *B.C., Canada* **189 E6** 58 0N 131 10W
Telescope Pk., *CA, U.S.A.* **65 G9** 36 10N 117 5W
Telfair County ☆, *GA, U.S.A.* **68 E4** 31 55N 83 0W
Telida, *AK, U.S.A.* **61 E9** 63 23N 153 16W
Tell City, *IN, U.S.A.* **72 F4** 37 57N 86 46W
Teller, *AK, U.S.A.* **61 D6** 65 16N 166 22W
Teller County ☆, *CO, U.S.A.* **66 D5** 38 50N 105 10W
Tellico L., *TN, U.S.A.* **97 E8** 35 21N 84 17W
Tellico Plains, *TN, U.S.A.* **97 E8** 35 22N 84 18W
Telluride, *CO, U.S.A.* **66 E3** 37 56N 107 49W
Telocaset, *OR, U.S.A.* **94 B8** 45 6N 117 49W
Telogia, *FL, U.S.A.* **67 A4** 30 21N 84 49W
Teloloapán, *Guerrero, Mexico* **219 D8** 18 21N 99 51W
Temascal, *Oaxaca, Mexico* **221 F4** 18 14N 96 25W
Temascalcingo, *México, Mexico* **219 C8** 19 55N 100 0W
Temascaltepec, *México, Mexico* **219 C7** 19 2N 100 3W
Temascaltepec ➝, *Mexico* **219 D7** 18 47N 100 41W
Temax, *Yucatán, Mexico* **223 A5** 21 9N 88 56W
Temblor Range, *CA, U.S.A.* **65 H7** 35 20N 119 50W
Temecula, *CA, U.S.A.* **65 K9** 33 30N 117 9W
Temescal, L., *San Francisco, U.S.A.* **118 A3** 37 51N 122 14W
Témiscamie ➝, *Qué., Canada* **175 C3** 50 59N 73 5W
Témiscaming, *Qué., Canada* **176 E3** 46 44N 79 5W
Témiscamingue, L., *Qué., Canada* **176 D3** 47 10N 79 25W
Temoac, *Morelos, Mexico* **219 D9** 18 49N 98 45W
Témoris, *Chihuahua, Mexico* **213 F7** 27 16N 108 15W
Temosachic, *Chihuahua, Mexico* **213 E8** 28 57N 107 51W
Temozón, *Yucatán, Mexico* **223 B5** 20 48N 88 13W
Tempe, *AZ, U.S.A.* **62 D4** 33 24N 111 54W
Temperance, *MI, U.S.A.* **79 H8** 41 47N 83 34W
Temperance Vale, *N.B., Canada* **173 G2** 46 4N 67 15W
Temperanceville, *VA, U.S.A.* **77 C5** 37 54N 75 33W
Tempiute, *NV, U.S.A.* **85 E5** 37 39N 115 38W
Temple, *NH, U.S.A.* **86 D3** 42 48N 71 50W
Temple, *OK, U.S.A.* **93 D5** 34 16N 98 14W
Temple, *TX, U.S.A.* **99 F10** 31 6N 97 21W
Temple City, *Los Angeles, U.S.A.* **111 B4** 34 6N 118 3W
Temple Hill, *KY, U.S.A.* **97 D7** 36 53N 85 51W
Temple Hills, *MD, U.S.A.* **119 C4** 38 48N 76 56W
Temple Terrace, *FL, U.S.A.* **67 C6** 28 2N 82 23W
Templeman, Mt., *B.C., Canada* **187 E17** 50 42N 117 12W
Templeton, *CA, U.S.A.* **65 H6** 35 33N 120 42W
Templeton, *MA, U.S.A.* **78 B2** 42 33N 72 4W
Templeton-Ouest, *Qué., Canada* **192 A1** 45 29N 75 42W
Tempoal ➝, *Veracruz, Mexico* **220 C2** 21 47N 98 27W
Tempoal de Sánchez, *Veracruz, Mexico* **220 C2** 21 31N 98 23W
Ten Mile L., *Nfld. & L., Canada* **174 A4** 51 6N 56 42W
Ten Mile Pond, *Nfld. & L., Canada* **174 C6** 49 11N 54 0W
Ten Sleep, *WY, U.S.A.* **104 B5** 44 2N 107 27W
Ten Thousand Is., *FL, U.S.A.* **67 F7** 25 55N 81 45W
Tenabo, *Campeche, Mexico* **223 B3** 20 3N 90 14W
Tenacatita, *Jalisco, Mexico* **218 C3** 19 17N 104 52W
Tenacatita, B., *Jalisco, Mexico* **218 C3** 19 17N 104 50W
Tenafly, *NJ, U.S.A.* **114 A3** 40 54N 73 58W
Tenaha, *TX, U.S.A.* **99 F13** 31 57N 94 15W
Tenakee Springs, *AK, U.S.A.* **61 H14** 57 47N 135 13W
Tenamaxtlán, *Jalisco, Mexico* **218 B3** 20 13N 104 10W
Tenampa, *Tamaulipas, Mexico* **214 E6** 25 10N 98 24W
Tenampulco, *Puebla, Mexico* **220 D3** 20 10N 97 24W
Tenango del Valle, *México, Mexico* **219 C8** 19 7N 99 35W
Tendoy, *ID, U.S.A.* **70 E5** 44 57N 113 38W
Tenejapa, *Chiapas, Mexico* **222 C4** 16 49N 92 31W
Tenino, *WA, U.S.A.* **101 D3** 46 51N 122 51W
Tenkiller Ferry L., *OK, U.S.A.* **93 C8** 35 35N 95 2W
Tennant, *IA, U.S.A.* **73 D3** 41 35N 95 26W
Tennessee, *IL, U.S.A.* **71 C3** 40 18N 90 52W
Tennessee □, *U.S.A.* **96 E6** 36 0N 86 30W
Tennessee ➝, *TN, U.S.A.* **96 C4** 37 4N 88 34W
Tennessee Pass, *CO, U.S.A.* **66 C4** 39 22N 106 19W
Tennessee Ridge, *TN, U.S.A.* **96 D5** 36 19N 87 47W
Tennessee-Tombigbee Waterway, *U.S.A.* **81 D5** 32 50N 88 10W
Tennille, *GA, U.S.A.* **68 D4** 32 56N 82 48W
Tennyson, *IN, U.S.A.* **72 E3** 38 5N 87 7W
Tennyson, *WI, U.S.A.* **103 F3** 42 41N 90 41W
Tenosique, *Tabasco, Mexico* **222 B5** 17 29N 91 26W
Tensas ➝, *LA, U.S.A.* **75 C4** 31 38N 91 49W
Tensas Parish ☆, *LA, U.S.A.* **75 B4** 32 0N 91 10W
Tensas River Nat. Wildlife Refuge ⌓, *LA, U.S.A.* **75 B4** 32 10N 91 27W
Tensaw ➝, *AL, U.S.A.* **60 F3** 30 41N 88 0W
Tensed, *ID, U.S.A.* **70 B2** 47 10N 116 55W
Tenstrike, *MN, U.S.A.* **80 C4** 47 40N 94 41W
Teoca, Volcan, *Distrito Federal, Mexico* **225 C3** 19 12N 99 6W
Teocaltiche, *Jalisco, Mexico* **218 A5** 21 26N 102 35W
Teocelo, *Veracruz, Mexico* **220 E4** 19 23N 96 58W
Teocuitatlán de Corona, *Jalisco, Mexico* **218 B4** 20 7N 103 24W
Teolocholco, *Tlaxcala, Mexico* **219 C9** 19 15N 98 2W
Teopantlán, *Puebla, Mexico* **221 F2** 18 43N 98 15W
Teopisca, *Chiapas, Mexico* **222 C4** 16 31N 92 29W
Teotihuacán, *México, Mexico* **219 C9** 19 42N 98 52W
Teotitlán, *Oaxaca, Mexico* **221 F3** 18 6N 97 3W
Tepalcatepec, *Michoacan, Mexico* **218 C5** 19 11N 102 51W
Tepalcates, *Distrito Federal, Mexico* **225 B3** 19 23N 99 3W
Tepalcingo, *Morelos, Mexico* **219 D9** 18 36N 98 51W
Tepatitán, *Tabasco, Mexico* **222 B4** 17 50N 92 22W
Tepatitlán de Morelos, *Jalisco, Mexico* **218 B5** 20 49N 102 44W
Tepatlaxco, *Puebla, Mexico* **221 E3** 19 5N 97 58W
Tepeaca, *Puebla, Mexico* **221 E3** 18 58N 97 54W
Tepechitlán, *Zacatecas, Mexico* **217 F7** 21 40N 103 20W
Tepecoacuilco, *Guerrero, Mexico* **219 D8** 18 18N 99 29W
Tepeguajes, *Tamaulipas, Mexico* **215 G7** 23 30N 97 47W
Tepehuanes, *Durango, Mexico* **216 B5** 25 21N 105 44W
Tepeji del Río, *Hidalgo, Mexico* **219 C8** 19 54N 99 21W
Tepelmeme, *Oaxaca, Mexico* **221 G3** 17 54N 97 21W
Tepepan, *Distrito Federal, Mexico* **225 C3** 19 17N 99 9W
Tepetlaoxtoc, *México, Mexico* **225 A3** 19 33N 98 49W
Tepetongo, *Zacatecas, Mexico* **217 E7** 22 28N 103 9W
Tepetzintla, *Veracruz, Mexico* **220 C3** 21 10N 97 50W
Tepexco, *Puebla, Mexico* **221 F2** 18 38N 98 41W
Tepeyac, Parque Nacional △, *Distrito Federal, Mexico* **225 B3** 19 30N 99 7W
Tepic = Nayarit □, *Mexico* **216 F6** 22 0N 105 0W
Tepic, *Nayarit, Mexico* **216 F6** 21 30N 104 54W
Tepich, *Quintana Roo, Mexico* **223 B5** 20 16N 88 16W
Tepoca, Pta., *Sonora, Mexico* **212 D3** 29 55N 112 45W
Tepotzotlaná, *México, Mexico* **219 C8** 19 43N 99 14W
Tepozteco, Parque Nacional △, *Morelos, Mexico* **219 C8** 19 0N 99 7W
Tepoztlán, *Morelos, Mexico* **219 D8** 19 0N 99 6W
Tepuxtepec, Presa de, *Michoacan, Mexico* **219 B7** 20 3N 100 16W
Tequesquitlán, *Jalisco, Mexico* **218 C3** 19 28N 104 48W
Tequila, *Jalisco, Mexico* **218 B4** 20 54N 103 47W
Tequilita, *Nayarit, Mexico* **216 F6** 21 5N 104 49W
Tequisquiapan, *Querétaro, Mexico* **219 B8** 20 31N 99 52W
Tequixquitla, *Tlaxcala, Mexico* **219 C10** 19 20N 97 39W
Terence Bay, *N.S., Canada* **173 J6** 44 28N 63 43W
Terlingua, *TX, U.S.A.* **98 H4** 29 19N 103 36W
Terlingua Cr. ➝, *TX, U.S.A.* **98 H4** 29 10N 103 36W
Terlton, *OK, U.S.A.* **93 B7** 36 8N 96 29W
Términos, L. de, *Campeche, Mexico* **223 D2** 18 37N 91 33W
Terra Alta, *WV, U.S.A.* **77 A1** 39 27N 79 33W
Terra Bella, *CA, U.S.A.* **65 H7** 35 58N 119 3W
Terra Ceia, *Tampa, U.S.A.* **119 D3** 27 34N 82 34W
Terra Nova, *Nfld. & L., Canada* **174 D6** 48 30N 54 13W
Terra Nova ➝, *Nfld. & L., Canada* **174 D6** 48 40N 54 0W
Terra Nova Nat. Park △, *Nfld. & L., Canada* **174 D7** 48 33N 53 55W
Terrace, *B.C., Canada* **189 F7** 54 30N 128 35W
Terrace Bay, *Ont., Canada* **181 D9** 48 47N 87 5W
Terral, *OK, U.S.A.* **93 E6** 33 54N 97 57W
Terre Haute, *IN, U.S.A.* **72 D3** 39 28N 87 25W
Terrebonne, *Qué., Canada* **177 F9** 45 42N 73 38W
Terrebonne, *OR, U.S.A.* **94 C4** 44 21N 121 11W
Terrebonne B., *LA, U.S.A.* **75 E5** 29 5N 90 35W
Terrebonne Parish ☆, *LA, U.S.A.* **75 E5** 29 20N 91 0W
Terrell, *TX, U.S.A.* **99 E11** 32 44N 96 17W
Terrell County ☆, *GA, U.S.A.* **68 E2** 31 50N 84 25W
Terrell County ☆, *TX, U.S.A.* **98 G6** 30 0N 102 0W
Terrell Hills, *San Antonio, U.S.A.* **117 B3** 29 28N 98 27W
Terrenceville, *Nfld. & L., Canada* **174 E6** 47 40N 54 44W
Terrero, *Chihuahua, Mexico* **213 E8** 28 15N 107 28W
Terreton, *ID, U.S.A.* **70 F6** 43 51N 112 26W
Terril, *IA, U.S.A.* **73 B4** 43 18N 94 58W
Terry, *LA, U.S.A.* **75 B4** 32 56N 91 21W
Terry, *MS, U.S.A.* **81 D3** 32 6N 90 18W
Terry, *MT, U.S.A.* **83 D12** 46 47N 105 19W
Terry County ☆, *TX, U.S.A.* **98 D5** 33 11N 102 17W
Terry Pk., *SD, U.S.A.* **91 F2** 44 19N 103 50W
Terrytown, *NE, U.S.A.* **84 C2** 41 51N 103 40W
Terrytown, *New Orleans, U.S.A.* **113 C2** 29 54N 90 1W
Terryville, *CT, U.S.A.* **78 C1** 41 41N 73 3W
Tescott, *KS, U.S.A.* **74 B6** 39 1N 97 53W
Teshekpuk L., *AK, U.S.A.* **61 A9** 70 35N 153 26W
Teslin, *Yukon, Canada* **189 D6** 60 10N 132 43W
Teslin ➝, *Canada* **189 D6** 61 34N 134 35W
Teslin L., *Canada* **189 D6** 60 15N 132 57W
Tessik L., *Nunavut, Canada* **191 E10** 63 49N 75 22W
Tesuque, *NM, U.S.A.* **88 B5** 35 46N 105 55W
Tesuque Indian Reservation, *NM, U.S.A.* **88 B5** 35 48N 105 58W
Tetachuck L., *B.C., Canada* **186 B9** 53 18N 125 55W
Tête-à-la-Baleine, *Qué., Canada* **174 B1** 50 41N 59 20W
Tête Jaune Cache, *B.C., Canada* **187 C15** 52 58N 119 26W
Tetela de Ocampo, *Puebla, Mexico* **220 E3** 19 49N 97 48W
Teterboro ✕, *NJ, U.S.A.* **114 A2** 40 51N 74 3W
Tetipac, *Guerrero, Mexico* **219 D8** 18 39N 99 38W
Tetiz, *Yucatán, Mexico* **223 B4** 20 58N 89 57W
Tetla, *Tlaxcala, Mexico* **219 C9** 19 28N 98 5W
Tetlin, *AK, U.S.A.* **61 E12** 63 8N 142 31W
Tetlin Junction, *AK, U.S.A.* **61 E12** 63 19N 142 36W
Tetlin Nat. Wildlife Refuge ⌓, *AK, U.S.A.* **61 E12** 62 40N 141 50W
Teton, *ID, U.S.A.* **70 F7** 43 53N 111 40W
Teton ➝, *ID, U.S.A.* **70 F7** 43 54N 111 51W
Teton ➝, *MT, U.S.A.* **83 C7** 47 56N 110 31W
Teton County ☆, *ID, U.S.A.* **70 F7** 43 55N 111 5W
Teton County ☆, *MT, U.S.A.* **83 C5** 47 52N 112 20W
Teton County ☆, *WY, U.S.A.* **104 C2** 44 0N 110 30W
Teton Pass, *WY, U.S.A.* **104 C2** 43 30N 110 57W
Teton Range, *WY, U.S.A.* **104 C2** 43 45N 111 0W
Teton Village, *WY, U.S.A.* **104 C2** 43 35N 110 50W
Tetonia, *ID, U.S.A.* **70 F7** 43 49N 111 10W
Tetrahedron Park △, *B.C., Canada* **187 F11** 49 36N 123 35W
Tetu L., *Ont., Canada* **180 B1** 50 11N 95 2W
Teuhtli, Volcan, *Distrito Federal, Mexico* **225 C3** 19 14N 99 2W
Teúl de González Ortega, *Zacatecas, Mexico* **217 F7** 21 28N 103 29W
Teulon, *Man., Canada* **183 E14** 50 23N 97 16W
Teutopolis, *IL, U.S.A.* **71 D5** 39 8N 88 29W
Tewaukon, L., *ND, U.S.A.* **91 E8** 46 0N 97 22W
Tewksbury, *MA, U.S.A.* **78 B3** 42 37N 71 14W
Texada I., *B.C., Canada* **186 F10** 49 40N 124 25W
Texana, L., *TX, U.S.A.* **99 J11** 29 0N 96 35W
Texarkana, *AR, U.S.A.* **63 E1** 33 26N 94 2W
Texarkana, *TX, U.S.A.* **99 D13** 33 26N 94 3W
Texas □, *U.S.A.* **99 F9** 31 40N 98 30W
Texas City, *TX, U.S.A.* **99 H13** 29 24N 94 54W
Texas County ☆, *MO, U.S.A.* **82 D5** 37 20N 92 0W
Texas County ☆, *OK, U.S.A.* **93 B2** 36 45N 101 30W
Texas Point Nat. Wildlife Refuge ⌓, *TX, U.S.A.* **99 H14** 29 42N 93 54W
Texcaltitlán, *México, Mexico* **219 D8** 18 54N 99 55W
Texcoco, *Chihuahua, Mexico* **213 E11** 28 6N 104 20W
Texcoco, *México, Mexico* **219 C9** 19 31N 98 53W
Texcoco, Proyecto Lago de, *México, Mexico* **225 B3** 19 30N 99 0W
Texhoma, *OK, U.S.A.* **93 B2** 36 30N 101 47W
Texhuacán, *Veracruz, Mexico* **221 F3** 18 37N 97 2W
Texico, *NM, U.S.A.* **88 C7** 34 24N 103 3W
Texline, *TX, U.S.A.* **98 A4** 36 23N 103 2W
Texola, *OK, U.S.A.* **93 C4** 35 12N 99 59W
Texoma, L., *TX, U.S.A.* **99 D11** 33 50N 96 34W
Texon, *TX, U.S.A.* **98 F6** 31 13N 101 42W
Teya, *Yucatán, Mexico* **223 A4** 21 5N 89 6W
Teyra, Pico de, *Zacatecas, Mexico* **217 C8** 24 35N 102 11W
Teziutlán, *Puebla, Mexico* **220 E3** 19 49N 97 21W
Tezoatlán, *Oaxaca, Mexico* **221 G3** 17 39N 97 48W
Tezonapa, *Veracruz, Mexico* **221 F4** 18 35N 96 42W
Tezontepec, *Hidalgo, Mexico* **219 B8** 20 12N 99 16W
Tha-anne ➝, *Nunavut, Canada* **191 E7** 60 31N 94 37W
Thackerville, *OK, U.S.A.* **93 E6** 33 48N 97 9W
Thalia, *TX, U.S.A.* **99 D8** 33 59N 99 32W
Thalmann, *GA, U.S.A.* **68 E5** 31 18N 81 41W
Thames ➝, *Ont., Canada* **178 E4** 42 20N 82 25W
Thames ➝, *CT, U.S.A.* **78 C2** 41 18N 72 5W
Thamesford, *Ont., Canada* **178 D5** 43 4N 81 0W
Thamesville, *Ont., Canada* **178 E5** 42 33N 81 59W
Thatcher, *AZ, U.S.A.* **62 E6** 32 51N 109 46W
Thatcher, *CO, U.S.A.* **66 E6** 37 33N 104 7W
Thawville, *IL, U.S.A.* **71 C5** 40 41N 88 7W
Thaxton, *MS, U.S.A.* **81 B4** 34 18N 89 11W
Thayer, *KS, U.S.A.* **74 D8** 37 29N 95 28W
Thayer, *MO, U.S.A.* **82 E5** 36 31N 91 33W
Thayer, *NE, U.S.A.* **84 D8** 40 58N 97 30W
Thayer County ☆, *NE, U.S.A.* **84 D8** 40 15N 97 40W
Thayne, *WY, U.S.A.* **104 D2** 42 55N 111 0W
The Breakers, *RI, U.S.A.* **78 C3** 41 28N 71 18W
The Dalles, *OR, U.S.A.* **94 B4** 45 36N 121 10W
The Dalles Dam, *WA, U.S.A.* **101 E4** 45 37N 121 8W
The Forks = Merritt, *B.C., Canada* **187 E14** 50 10N 120 45W
The Glebe, *Ont., Canada* **192 B1** 45 24N 75 41W
The Grove, *TX, U.S.A.* **99 F10** 31 16N 97 32W
The Pas, *Man., Canada* **183 B10** 53 45N 101 15W
The Plains, *VA, U.S.A.* **77 B3** 38 52N 77 47W
The Settlement, *Br. Virgin Is.* **105 G18** 18 43N 64 22W
The Shoals Prov. Park △, *Ont., Canada* **181 E13** 47 50N 83 50W
The Village, *OK, U.S.A.* **93 C6** 35 35N 97 33W
The Woodlands, *TX, U.S.A.* **99 G12** 30 9N 95 29W
Thebes, *IL, U.S.A.* **71 F4** 37 13N 89 28W
Thedford, *NE, U.S.A.* **84 C5** 41 59N 100 35W
Thelon ➝, *Canada* **191 E6** 64 16N 96 4W
Theodore, *Sask., Canada* **182 D9** 51 26N 102 55W
Theodore, *AL, U.S.A.* **60 F2** 30 33N 88 10W
Theodore Roosevelt L., *AZ, U.S.A.* **62 D4** 33 40N 111 10W
Theodore Roosevelt Nat. Park △, *ND, U.S.A.* **91 D2** 47 0N 103 25W

Theodore Wirth Regional Park ⌂, *Minneapolis-St. Paul, U.S.A.* **113 B2** 44 59N 93 19W
Theodosia, *MO, U.S.A.* **82 E4** 36 35N 92 39W
Theresa, *NY, U.S.A.* **89 A5** 44 13N 75 48W
Theressa, *FL, U.S.A.* **67 B6** 29 50N 82 4W
Theriot, *LA, U.S.A.* **75 E5** 29 28N 90 45W
Therma = Eagle Nest, *NM, U.S.A.* **88 A5** 36 33N 105 16W
Thermal, *CA, U.S.A.* **65 K10** 33 39N 116 9W
Thermalito, *CA, U.S.A.* **64 D5** 39 31N 121 36W
Thermopolis, *WY, U.S.A.* **104 C4** 43 39N 108 13W
Thesiger B., *N.W.T., Canada* **188 B8** 71 30N 124 5W
Thessalon, *Ont., Canada* **178 A3** 46 20N 83 30W
Thetford Mines, *Qué., Canada* **177 E11** 46 8N 71 18W
Thévet, L., *Qué., Canada* **172 B5** 51 50N 64 12W
Thibodaux, *LA, U.S.A.* **75 E5** 29 48N 90 49W
Thief →, *MN, U.S.A.* **80 B2** 48 7N 96 10W
Thief L., *MN, U.S.A.* **80 B3** 48 30N 95 54W
Thief River Falls, *MN, U.S.A.* **80 B2** 48 7N 96 10W
Thielsen, Mt., *OR, U.S.A.* **94 D3** 43 9N 122 4W
Thirtymile Cr. →, *ND, U.S.A.* **91 D3** 46 22N 102 4W
Thistle, *UT, U.S.A.* **100 D4** 39 59N 111 30W
Thlewiaza →, *Nunavut, Canada* **191 E7** 60 29N 94 40W
Thoa →, *N.W.T., Canada* **189 D11** 60 31N 109 47W
Thomas, *MD, U.S.A.* **77 B4** 38 36N 76 18W
Thomas, *OK, U.S.A.* **93 C5** 35 45N 98 45W
Thomas, *WV, U.S.A.* **77 A1** 39 9N 79 30W
Thomas A. Edison, L., *CA, U.S.A.* **65 F7** 37 25N 119 0W
Thomas County ☆, *GA, U.S.A.* **68 F3** 30 50N 83 55W
Thomas County ☆, *KS, U.S.A.* **74 B2** 39 20N 101 0W
Thomas County ☆, *NE, U.S.A.* **84 C5** 41 50N 100 30W
Thomas Hill Res., *MO, U.S.A.* **82 B4** 39 34N 92 39W
Thomas Hubbard, C., *N.W.T., Canada* **190 A7** 82 0N 94 25W
Thomasboro, *IL, U.S.A.* **71 C5** 40 15N 88 11W
Thomaston, *AL, U.S.A.* **60 D3** 32 16N 87 38W
Thomaston, *CT, U.S.A.* **78 C1** 41 41N 73 4W
Thomaston, *GA, U.S.A.* **68 D2** 32 53N 84 20W
Thomaston, *ME, U.S.A.* **76 D4** 44 5N 69 11W
Thomaston, *NY, U.S.A.* **114 B4** 40 47N 73 42W
Thomastown, *MS, U.S.A.* **81 D4** 32 52N 89 40W
Thomasville, *AL, U.S.A.* **60 E3** 31 55N 87 44W
Thomasville, *GA, U.S.A.* **68 F3** 30 50N 83 59W
Thomasville, *NC, U.S.A.* **90 C5** 35 53N 80 5W
Thompson, *Man., Canada* **191 F6** 55 45N 97 52W
Thompson, *IA, U.S.A.* **73 B5** 43 22N 93 46W
Thompson, *ND, U.S.A.* **91 C8** 47 47N 97 6W
Thompson, *PA, U.S.A.* **95 C7** 41 52N 75 31W
Thompson →, *B.C., Canada* **187 E13** 50 15N 121 24W
Thompson →, *MO, U.S.A.* **82 B3** 39 46N 93 37W
Thompson, L., *SD, U.S.A.* **91 F8** 44 15N 97 28W
Thompson Falls, *MT, U.S.A.* **83 C2** 47 36N 115 21W
Thompson I., *Boston, U.S.A.* **106 B4** 42 19N 70 59W
Thompson Pk., *CA, U.S.A.* **64 B3** 41 0N 123 2W
Thompson Sound, *B.C., Canada* **186 E8** 50 48N 126 1W
Thompson Springs, *UT, U.S.A.* **100 E6** 38 58N 109 43W
Thompsons Cr. →, *MS, U.S.A.* **81 E5** 31 10N 88 55W
Thompsonville, *IL, U.S.A.* **71 F5** 37 55N 88 46W
Thompsonville, *MI, U.S.A.* **79 E6** 44 31N 85 56W
Thomson, *GA, U.S.A.* **68 C4** 33 28N 82 30W
Thomson, *IL, U.S.A.* **71 B3** 41 58N 90 6W
Thorburn, *N.S., Canada* **173 H7** 45 34N 62 33W
Thoreau, *NM, U.S.A.* **88 B2** 35 24N 108 13W
Thorhild, *Alta., Canada* **184 D7** 54 10N 113 7W
Thorn, *MS, U.S.A.* **81 C4** 33 57N 89 6W
Thornapple →, *MI, U.S.A.* **79 G6** 42 56N 85 28W
Thornapple →, *WI, U.S.A.* **103 C2** 45 28N 91 16W
Thornburg, *IA, U.S.A.* **73 D6** 41 27N 92 20W
Thornburg, *Pittsburgh, U.S.A.* **116 B1** 40 26N 80 4W
Thornburg, *VA, U.S.A.* **102 C7** 38 8N 77 31W
Thornburn Road, *Nfld. & L., Canada* **174 E8** 47 35N 52 51W
Thornbury, *Ont., Canada* **178 C6** 44 34N 80 26W
Thorndale, *TX, U.S.A.* **99 G10** 30 37N 97 12W
Thornhill, *Man., Canada* **183 F13** 49 12N 98 14W
Thornhurst, *PA, U.S.A.* **87 A1** 41 11N 75 35W
Thornton, *CO, U.S.A.* **66 C6** 39 52N 104 58W
Thornton, *ID, U.S.A.* **70 F7** 43 45N 111 51W
Thornton, *IA, U.S.A.* **73 C5** 42 57N 93 23W
Thornton, *MS, U.S.A.* **81 C3** 33 5N 90 19W
Thornton, *TX, U.S.A.* **99 F11** 31 25N 96 34W
Thornton, *WA, U.S.A.* **101 C8** 47 7N 117 23W
Thorntown, *IN, U.S.A.* **72 C4** 40 8N 86 36W
Thornville, *OH, U.S.A.* **92 D4** 39 54N 82 25W
Thorny Mt., *MO, U.S.A.* **82 D5** 37 6N 91 10W
Thorold, *Ont., Canada* **178 D7** 43 7N 79 12W
Thorp, *WA, U.S.A.* **101 C5** 47 4N 120 40W
Thorp, *WI, U.S.A.* **103 D3** 44 58N 90 48W
Thorsby, *Alta., Canada* **184 E6** 53 14N 114 3W
Thorsby, *AL, U.S.A.* **60 D4** 32 55N 86 43W
Thousand Hills State Park ⌂, *MO, U.S.A.* **82 A4** 40 11N 92 39W
Thousand Islands, *NY, U.S.A.* **89 A4** 44 20N 76 0W
Thousand Oaks, *CA, U.S.A.* **65 J8** 34 10N 118 50W
Thousand Springs Cr. →, *U.S.A.* **100 B2** 41 17N 113 51W
Thrall, *TX, U.S.A.* **99 G10** 30 35N 97 18W
Three Creek, *ID, U.S.A.* **70 G3** 42 4N 115 10W
Three Forks, *MT, U.S.A.* **83 E6** 45 54N 111 33W
Three Hills, *Alta., Canada* **185 G7** 51 43N 113 15W
Three Lakes, *WI, U.S.A.* **103 C4** 45 48N 89 10W
Three Mile Plains, *N.S., Canada* **173 J5** 44 58N 64 7W
Three Oaks, *MI, U.S.A.* **79 H5** 41 48N 86 36W
Three Rivers, *CA, U.S.A.* **65 G8** 36 26N 118 54W
Three Rivers, *MI, U.S.A.* **79 H6** 41 57N 85 38W
Three Rivers, *NM, U.S.A.* **88 D4** 33 19N 106 5W
Three Rivers, *TX, U.S.A.* **99 J9** 28 28N 98 11W
Throckmorton, *TX, U.S.A.* **99 D8** 33 11N 99 11W
Throckmorton County ☆, *TX, U.S.A.* **99 D8** 33 10N 99 10W
Throgs Neck, *NY, U.S.A.* **114 B4** 40 48N 73 49W
Thudaka Peak, *B.C., Canada* **189 E7** 57 56N 126 51W
Thule Air Base = Uummannaq, *Greenland* **190 C15** 70 58N 52 0W
Thunder B., *MI, U.S.A.* **79 E8** 45 0N 83 20W
Thunder Basin Nat. Grassland, *WY, U.S.A.* **104 C7** 43 45N 105 5W
Thunder Bay, *Ont., Canada* **180 D7** 48 20N 89 15W
Thunder Butte, *SD, U.S.A.* **91 E4** 45 19N 101 53W
Thunder Cr. →, *Sask., Canada* **182 E6** 50 23N 105 32W
Thunder Hawk, *SD, U.S.A.* **91 E4** 45 56N 101 58W
Thunderbird, L., *OK, U.S.A.* **93 C6** 35 14N 97 18W
Thunderbird Park, *Phoenix, U.S.A.* **116 A1** 33 41N 112 11W
Thunderbolt, *GA, U.S.A.* **68 D5** 32 3N 81 4W
Thunderhead, L., *MO, U.S.A.* **82 A3** 40 30N 93 1W
Thurman, *IA, U.S.A.* **73 E3** 40 49N 95 45W
Thurmont, *MD, U.S.A.* **77 A3** 39 37N 77 25W
Thurso, *Qué., Canada* **176 F7** 45 36N 75 15W
Thurston, *NE, U.S.A.* **84 B9** 42 11N 96 42W
Thurston, *OH, U.S.A.* **92 D4** 39 50N 82 33W
Thurston County ☆, *NE, U.S.A.* **84 B9** 42 15N 96 40W
Thurston County ☆, *WA, U.S.A.* **101 D3** 46 58N 122 59W
Thutade L., *B.C., Canada* **189 E7** 57 0N 126 55W
Tía Chena, Cerro, *Nuevo León, Mexico* **214 D4** 26 7N 100 35W
Tianguistenco, *México, Mexico* **219 C8** 19 13N 99 28W
Tianguistengo, *Hidalgo, Mexico* **219 B9** 20 44N 98 38W
Tibbie, *AL, U.S.A.* **60 E2** 31 22N 88 15W
Tiber Res., *MT, U.S.A.* **83 B6** 48 19N 111 6W
Tibet, L., *Orlando, U.S.A.* **115 B1** 28 27N 81 31W
Tiburon, *San Francisco, U.S.A.* **118 A2** 37 52N 122 27W
Tiburón, Cerro el, *Sinaloa, Mexico* **216 C4** 24 19N 106 56W
Tiburón, I., *Sonora, Mexico* **212 D3** 29 0N 112 25W
Ticaboo, *UT, U.S.A.* **100 F5** 37 40N 110 42W
Tice, *FL, U.S.A.* **67 E7** 26 40N 81 49W
Tichnor, *AR, U.S.A.* **63 D4** 34 8N 91 16W
Tickfaw →, *LA, U.S.A.* **75 D5** 30 21N 90 28W
Ticomán, *Distrito Federal, Mexico* **225 A3** 19 31N 99 8W
Ticonderoga, *NY, U.S.A.* **86 C1** 43 51N 73 26W
Ticul, *Yucatán, Mexico* **223 B4** 20 24N 89 32W
Tide Head, *N.B., Canada* **173 F3** 47 59N 66 47W
Tidewater, *VA, U.S.A.* **77 C4** 37 51N 76 42W
Tidioute, *PA, U.S.A.* **95 C3** 41 41N 79 24W
Tidmore = Seminole, *OK, U.S.A.* **93 C7** 35 14N 96 41W
Tidnish, *N.S., Canada* **173 H5** 45 59N 64 1W
Tie Plant, *MS, U.S.A.* **81 C4** 33 44N 89 47W
Tie Siding, *WY, U.S.A.* **104 E7** 41 5N 105 30W
Tierra Amarilla, *NM, U.S.A.* **88 A4** 36 42N 106 33W
Tierra Blanca, *Guanajuato, Mexico* **219 A7** 21 7N 100 57W
Tierra Blanca, *Veracruz, Mexico* **221 F4** 18 27N 96 21W
Tierra Blanca Cr. →, *TX, U.S.A.* **98 C6** 34 58N 101 55W
Tierra Colorada, *Guerrero, Mexico* **219 E8** 17 11N 99 32W
Tierra Nueva, *San Luis Potosí, Mexico* **215 J4** 21 40N 100 35W
Tierra Verde, *Tampa, U.S.A.* **119 C2** 27 41N 82 43W
Tierrasanta, *San Diego, U.S.A.* **117 B2** 32 49N 117 6W
Tieton, *WA, U.S.A.* **101 D5** 46 42N 120 46W
Tiffany, *CO, U.S.A.* **66 E3** 37 2N 107 32W
Tiffany Mt., *WA, U.S.A.* **101 B6** 48 40N 119 56W
Tiffin, *IA, U.S.A.* **73 D7** 41 42N 91 40W
Tiffin, *OH, U.S.A.* **92 B3** 41 7N 83 11W
Tiffin →, *OH, U.S.A.* **92 B2** 41 17N 84 23W
Tift County ☆, *GA, U.S.A.* **68 E3** 31 30N 83 30W
Tifton, *GA, U.S.A.* **68 E3** 31 27N 83 31W
Tigalda I., *AK, U.S.A.* **61 J6** 54 6N 165 5W
Tigard, *OR, U.S.A.* **94 B3** 45 26N 122 46W
Tiger, *WA, U.S.A.* **101 B8** 48 42N 117 24W
Tignall, *GA, U.S.A.* **68 C4** 33 52N 82 44W
Tignish, *P.E.I., Canada* **173 G5** 46 58N 64 2W
Tihuatlán, *Veracruz, Mexico* **220 D3** 20 43N 97 32W
Tijeras, *NM, U.S.A.* **88 B4** 35 5N 106 23W
Tijuana, *Baja Calif., Mexico* **210 A1** 32 32N 117 1W
Tijuana ✈ (TIJ), *Baja Calif., Mexico* **210 A2** 32 30N 116 58W
Tikchik Lakes, *AK, U.S.A.* **61 G8** 60 0N 159 0W
Tikiraqjuaq = Whale Cove, *Nunavut, Canada* **191 E7** 62 10N 92 34W
Tilapa, *Puebla, Mexico* **221 F2** 18 35N 98 33W
Tilbury, *Ont., Canada* **178 E4** 42 17N 82 23W
Tilbury, *Vancouver, Canada* **193 C2** 49 8N 123 1W
Tilden, *IL, U.S.A.* **71 E4** 38 13N 89 41W
Tilden, *NE, U.S.A.* **84 B8** 42 3N 97 50W
Tilden, *TX, U.S.A.* **99 J9** 28 28N 98 33W
Tilghman, *MD, U.S.A.* **77 B4** 38 43N 76 20W
Tiline, *KY, U.S.A.* **96 C4** 37 11N 88 15W
Tillamook, *OR, U.S.A.* **94 B2** 45 27N 123 51W
Tillamook B., *OR, U.S.A.* **94 B2** 45 30N 123 53W
Tillamook County ☆, *OR, U.S.A.* **94 B2** 45 20N 123 45W
Tillamook Head, *OR, U.S.A.* **94 B1** 45 57N 124 0W
Tillar, *AR, U.S.A.* **63 E4** 33 43N 91 27W
Tiller, *OR, U.S.A.* **94 E3** 42 56N 122 57W
Tillery, L., *NC, U.S.A.* **90 C5** 35 12N 80 4W
Tilley, *Alta., Canada* **185 H9** 50 27N 111 39W
Tillman County ☆, *OK, U.S.A.* **93 D4** 34 25N 99 0W
Tillmans Corner, *AL, U.S.A.* **60 F2** 30 46N 88 8W
Tillsonburg, *Ont., Canada* **178 E6** 42 53N 80 44W
Tilston, *Man., Canada* **183 F10** 49 23N 101 19W
Tilton, *GA, U.S.A.* **68 B2** 34 40N 84 56W
Tilton, *IL, U.S.A.* **71 C6** 40 6N 87 38W
Tilton, *NH, U.S.A.* **86 C3** 43 27N 71 36W
Tilzapotla, *Morelos, Mexico* **219 D8** 18 30N 99 16W
Timagami, L., *Ont., Canada* **176 E2** 47 0N 80 10W
Timbalier B., *LA, U.S.A.* **75 E5** 29 3N 90 20W
Timbalier I., *LA, U.S.A.* **75 E5** 29 3N 90 28W
Timber, *OR, U.S.A.* **94 B2** 45 43N 123 18W
Timber Lake, *SD, U.S.A.* **91 E4** 45 26N 101 5W
Timberlea, *N.S., Canada* **173 J6** 44 40N 63 45W
Timberville, *VA, U.S.A.* **102 C6** 38 38N 78 46W
Timbo, *AR, U.S.A.* **63 C3** 35 52N 92 19W
Timiskaming, L. = Témiscamingue, L., *Qué., Canada* **176 D3** 47 10N 79 25W
Timken, *KS, U.S.A.* **74 C4** 38 29N 99 11W
Timken Wildlife Management Area, *New Orleans, U.S.A.* **113 D1** 29 48N 90 12W
Timmins, *Ont., Canada* **176 C1** 48 28N 81 25W
Timmonsville, *SC, U.S.A.* **90 D6** 34 8N 79 57W
Timms Hill, *WI, U.S.A.* **103 C3** 45 27N 90 12W
Timnath, *CO, U.S.A.* **66 B6** 40 32N 104 59W
Timpas, *CO, U.S.A.* **66 E7** 37 49N 103 46W
Timpson, *TX, U.S.A.* **99 F13** 31 54N 94 24W
Tims Ford L., *TN, U.S.A.* **96 E6** 35 15N 86 10W
Timucuan Ecological and Historical Preserve ⌂, *U.S.A.* **67 A7** 30 28N 81 27W
Timucuy, *Yucatán, Mexico* **223 B4** 20 49N 89 31W
Tin Mt., *CA, U.S.A.* **65 G9** 36 50N 117 10W
Tina, *MO, U.S.A.* **82 B3** 39 32N 93 27W
Tindall, *MO, U.S.A.* **82 A3** 40 10N 93 36W
Tinemaha Res., *CA, U.S.A.* **65 F8** 37 3N 118 13W
Tingley, *IA, U.S.A.* **73 E4** 40 51N 94 12W
Tingmerkpuk Mt., *AK, U.S.A.* **61 B7** 68 34N 162 28W
Tingüindín, *Michoacan, Mexico* **218 C5** 19 45N 102 29W
Tinian, *N. Marianas* **105 c** 15 0N 145 38 E
Tinian Channel, *N. Marianas* **105 c** 14 54N 145 36W
Tinmouth, *VT, U.S.A.* **86 C1** 43 26N 73 4W
Tinnie, *NM, U.S.A.* **88 D5** 33 22N 105 14W
Tinsley, *MS, U.S.A.* **81 D3** 32 44N 90 28W
Tinsman, *AR, U.S.A.* **63 E3** 33 38N 92 21W
Tintagel, *B.C., Canada* **186 A9** 54 12N 125 35W
Tintah, *MN, U.S.A.* **80 D2** 46 1N 96 19W
Tintero, Presa el, *Chihuahua, Mexico* **213 D8** 29 32N 107 22W
Tinton Falls, *NJ, U.S.A.* **87 B2** 40 18N 74 6W
Tinum, *Yucatán, Mexico* **223 B5** 20 46N 88 23W
Tioga, *ND, U.S.A.* **91 B3** 48 24N 102 56W
Tioga, *PA, U.S.A.* **95 C5** 41 55N 77 8W
Tioga, *TX, U.S.A.* **99 D11** 33 28N 96 55W
Tioga, *WV, U.S.A.* **102 C4** 38 25N 80 40W
Tioga County ☆, *NY, U.S.A.* **89 C4** 42 10N 76 20W
Tioga County ☆, *PA, U.S.A.* **95 C5** 41 50N 77 10W
Tioga Pass, *CA, U.S.A.* **64 F7** 37 54N 119 15W
Tionesta, *PA, U.S.A.* **95 C3** 41 30N 79 28W
Tipler, *WI, U.S.A.* **103 C5** 45 55N 88 38W
Tipp City, *OH, U.S.A.* **92 D2** 39 58N 84 11W
Tippah County ☆, *MS, U.S.A.* **81 B5** 34 44N 88 57W
Tippecanoe →, *IN, U.S.A.* **72 C4** 40 30N 86 45W
Tippecanoe County ☆, *IN, U.S.A.* **72 C4** 40 25N 86 55W
Tipton, *CA, U.S.A.* **65 G7** 36 4N 119 19W
Tipton, *IN, U.S.A.* **72 C4** 40 17N 86 2W
Tipton, *IA, U.S.A.* **73 D7** 41 46N 91 8W
Tipton, *KS, U.S.A.* **74 B5** 39 21N 98 28W
Tipton, *MO, U.S.A.* **82 C4** 38 39N 92 47W
Tipton, *OK, U.S.A.* **93 D4** 34 30N 99 8W
Tipton County ☆, *IN, U.S.A.* **72 C4** 40 20N 86 5W
Tipton County ☆, *TN, U.S.A.* **96 E3** 35 29N 89 43W
Tipton Mt., *AZ, U.S.A.* **62 B1** 35 32N 114 12W
Tiptonville, *TN, U.S.A.* **96 D3** 36 23N 89 29W
Tiqua Indian Reservation, *TX, U.S.A.* **98 F1** 31 41N 106 19W
Tiquicheo, *Michoacan, Mexico* **219 D7** 18 53N 100 44W
Tiquimul, *Campeche, Mexico* **223 C3** 19 47N 90 13W
Tisdale, *Sask., Canada* **182 C7** 52 50N 104 0W
Tishomingo, *MS, U.S.A.* **81 B5** 34 38N 88 14W
Tishomingo, *OK, U.S.A.* **93 D7** 34 14N 96 41W
Tishomingo County ☆, *MS, U.S.A.* **81 B5** 34 49N 88 12W
Tishomingo Nat. Wildlife Refuge ⌂, *OK, U.S.A.* **93 D7** 34 11N 96 39W
Tiskilwa, *IL, U.S.A.* **71 B4** 41 18N 89 30W
Titonka, *IA, U.S.A.* **73 B4** 43 14N 94 3W
Tittabawassee →, *MI, U.S.A.* **79 F8** 43 23N 83 59W
Titus County ☆, *TX, U.S.A.* **99 D13** 33 9N 94 58W
Titusville, *FL, U.S.A.* **67 C8** 28 37N 80 49W
Titusville, *PA, U.S.A.* **95 C3** 41 38N 79 41W
Tiverton, *N.S., Canada* **173 J3** 44 23N 66 13W
Tiverton, *Ont., Canada* **178 C5** 44 16N 81 32W
Tiverton, *RI, U.S.A.* **78 C3** 41 38N 71 12W
Tiverton Four Corners, *RI, U.S.A.* **78 C3** 41 34N 71 11W
Tivoli, *TX, U.S.A.* **99 J11** 28 27N 96 53W
Tixcacalcupul, *Yucatán, Mexico* **223 B5** 20 32N 88 16W
Tixcancal, *Yucatán, Mexico* **223 A6** 21 3N 87 51W
Tixkokob, *Yucatán, Mexico* **223 B4** 21 0N 89 24W
Tixmehuac, *Yucatán, Mexico* **223 B4** 20 15N 89 6W
Tixmul, *Quintana Roo, Mexico* **223 C5** 19 26N 88 16W
Tixtla, *Guerrero, Mexico* **219 E8** 17 35N 99 26W
Tizapán, *Distrito Federal, Mexico* **225 C2** 19 19N 99 13W
Tizapán el Alto, *Jalisco, Mexico* **218 B4** 20 10N 103 4W
Tizayuca, *Hidalgo, Mexico* **219 C9** 19 51N 98 59W
Tizimín, *Yucatán, Mexico* **223 A5** 21 9N 88 9W
Tizupán, *Michoacan, Mexico* **218 D4** 18 14N 103 7W
Tlachichilco, *Veracruz, Mexico* **220 D2** 20 38N 98 10W
Tlachichuca, *Puebla, Mexico* **221 E3** 19 7N 97 24W
Tlachiultepec, *Distrito Federal, Mexico* **225 C3** 19 13N 99 7W
Tlacoachistlahuaca, *Guerrero, Mexico* **219 F9** 16 50N 98 19W
Tlacolula de Matamoros, *Oaxaca, Mexico* **221 H4** 16 57N 96 29W
Tlacotalpán, *Veracruz, Mexico* **221 F5** 18 37N 95 40W
Tlacotepec, *Guerrero, Mexico* **219 E8** 17 46N 99 59W
Tlacotepec, *Puebla, Mexico* **221 F3** 18 38N 97 37W
Tlacuapa, *Guerrero, Mexico* **219 E9** 17 17N 98 45W
Tláhuac, *Distrito Federal, Mexico* **225 C3** 19 17N 99 0W
Tláhuac, Parque, *Distrito Federal, Mexico* **225 C3** 19 17N 99 2W
Tlahualilo, Sa. de, *Coahuila, Mexico* **214 D1** 26 34N 103 19W
Tlahualilo de Zaragoza, *Durango, Mexico* **217 A7** 26 7N 103 27W
Tlahuelilpan, *Hidalgo, Mexico* **219 B8** 20 9N 99 14W
Tlajomulco, *Jalisco, Mexico* **218 B4** 20 28N 103 27W
Tlajomulco de Zúñiga, *Guadalajara, Mexico* **224 C1** 20 28N 103 27W
Tlalchapa, *Guerrero, Mexico* **219 D7** 18 24N 100 28W
Tlalixcoyan, *Veracruz, Mexico* **221 F4** 18 48N 96 3W
Tlalixtaquilla, *Guerrero, Mexico* **221 G2** 17 35N 98 23W
Tlalnepantla, *México, Mexico* **219 C8** 19 32N 99 11W
Tlalnepantla →, *Distrito Federal, Mexico* **225 A2** 19 30N 99 18W
Tlalpan, *Distrito Federal, Mexico* **225 C2** 19 18N 99 10W
Tlalpujahua, *Michoacan, Mexico* **219 C7** 19 48N 100 10W
Tlaltenango de Sánchez Román, *Zacatecas, Mexico* **217 F7** 21 47N 103 19W
Tlaltizapán, *Morelos, Mexico* **219 D8** 18 41N 99 7W
Tlamanalco, *México, Mexico* **219 C9** 19 12N 98 50W
Tlanalapa, *Hidalgo, Mexico* **219 C9** 19 49N 98 36W
Tlanchinol, *Hidalgo, Mexico* **219 B9** 21 0N 98 39W
Tlapa de Comonfort, *Guerrero, Mexico* **219 E9** 17 33N 98 33W
Tlapacoyan, *Veracruz, Mexico* **220 E3** 19 58N 97 13W
Tlapaneco →, *Guerrero, Mexico* **219 E9** 17 5N 98 48W
Tlapehuala, *Guerrero, Mexico* **219 D7** 18 13N 100 31W
Tlaquepaque, *Jalisco, Mexico* **218 B4** 20 39N 103 19W
Tlatlauquitepec, *Puebla, Mexico* **220 E3** 19 51N 97 29W
Tlatlaya, *México, Mexico* **219 D7** 18 31N 100 15W
Tlaxcala, *Tlaxcala, Mexico* **219 C9** 19 19N 98 14W
Tlaxcala □, *Mexico* **219 C9** 19 25N 98 10W
Tlaxco, *Tlaxcala, Mexico* **219 C9** 19 37N 98 7W
Tlaxiaco, *Oaxaca, Mexico* **221 G3** 17 25N 97 35W
Tlayacapan, *Morelos, Mexico* **219 D9** 18 59N 98 59W
Tlell, *B.C., Canada* **186 B3** 53 34N 131 56W
Toad →, *B.C., Canada* **189 E8** 59 25N 124 57W
Toad River, *B.C., Canada* **189 E7** 58 51N 125 14W
Toana Range, *NV, U.S.A.* **85 B6** 40 50N 114 20W
Toano, *VA, U.S.A.* **102 D8** 37 23N 76 48W
Toast, *NC, U.S.A.* **90 B5** 36 30N 80 38W
Toba Inlet, *B.C., Canada* **186 E10** 50 25N 124 35W
Tobermory, *Ont., Canada* **178 B5** 45 12N 81 40W
Tobias, *NE, U.S.A.* **84 D8** 40 25N 97 20W
Tobin, Mt., *NV, U.S.A.* **85 B3** 40 23N 117 31W
Tobin L., *Sask., Canada* **182 B8** 53 35N 103 30W
Tobin Range, *NV, U.S.A.* **85 B3** 40 20N 117 30W
Tobique →, *N.B., Canada* **173 G2** 46 46N 67 42W
Toby Creek, *B.C., Canada* **187 E18** 50 20N 116 25W
Tobyhanna, *PA, U.S.A.* **87 A1** 41 11N 75 25W
Toccoa, *GA, U.S.A.* **68 B3** 34 35N 83 19W
Toccopola, *MS, U.S.A.* **81 B4** 34 15N 89 14W
Tochapán, *Puebla, Mexico* **221 F3** 18 55N 97 38W
Tochtepec, *Puebla, Mexico* **221 F3** 18 50N 97 50W
Toco Hills, *Atlanta, U.S.A.* **106 B2** 33 49N 84 20W
Tocumbo, *Michoacan, Mexico* **218 C5** 19 42N 102 32W
Todd County ☆, *KY, U.S.A.* **96 D5** 36 50N 87 10W
Todd County ☆, *MN, U.S.A.* **80 D4** 46 10N 94 50W
Todd County ☆, *SD, U.S.A.* **91 G5** 43 5N 101 0W
Toddville, *MD, U.S.A.* **77 B4** 38 18N 76 4W
Todos Santos, *Baja Calif. S., Mexico* **211 K8** 23 26N 110 13W
Todos Santos, B., *Baja Calif., Mexico* **210 B2** 31 48N 116 42W
Todos Santos, I. de, *Baja Calif., Mexico* **210 B2** 31 48N 116 48W
Todt Hill, *NY, U.S.A.* **114 C2** 40 36N 74 6W
Tofield, *Alta., Canada* **184 E8** 53 25N 112 40W
Tofino, *B.C., Canada* **186 F9** 49 11N 125 55W
Tofte, *MN, U.S.A.* **80 C8** 47 35N 90 50W
Togiak, *AK, U.S.A.* **61 G7** 59 4N 160 24W
Togiak Nat. Wildlife Refuge ⌂, *AK, U.S.A.* **61 G7** 59 20N 160 15W
Togo, *Sask., Canada* **183 D10** 51 24N 101 35W
Togowatee Pass, *WY, U.S.A.* **104 C2** 43 45N 110 4W
Tohatchi, *NM, U.S.A.* **88 B2** 35 52N 108 47W
Tohono O'odham Indian Reservation, *AZ, U.S.A.* **62 E4** 32 15N 112 0W
Tohopekaliga, East L., *FL, U.S.A.* **67 C7** 28 18N 81 15W
Tohopekaliga, L., *FL, U.S.A.* **67 C7** 28 12N 81 24W
Toiyabe Range, *NV, U.S.A.* **85 C3** 39 30N 117 0W
Tok, *AK, U.S.A.* **61 E12** 63 20N 142 59W
Tokeland, *WA, U.S.A.* **101 D2** 46 42N 123 59W
Tokio, Parque Natural ⌂, *Coahuila, Mexico* **215 F4** 24 50N 100 52W
Toksook Bay, *AK, U.S.A.* **61 F6** 60 32N 165 0W
Tolageak, *AK, U.S.A.* **61 A7** 70 3N 162 27W
Tolar, *NM, U.S.A.* **88 C7** 34 27N 103 56W
Tolbert, *TX, U.S.A.* **99 C8** 34 13N 99 24W
Tolchester Beach, *MD, U.S.A.* **77 A4** 39 13N 76 14W
Toledo, *IL, U.S.A.* **71 D5** 39 16N 88 15W
Toledo, *IA, U.S.A.* **73 C6** 42 0N 92 35W
Toledo, *OH, U.S.A.* **92 B3** 41 39N 83 33W
Toledo, *OR, U.S.A.* **94 C2** 44 37N 123 56W
Toledo, *WA, U.S.A.* **101 D3** 46 26N 122 51W
Toledo Bend Res., *LA, U.S.A.* **75 C2** 31 11N 93 34W
Toledo Bend Res. Dam, *LA, U.S.A.* **75 C2** 31 12N 93 34W
Tolimán, *Jalisco, Mexico* **218 C4** 19 35N 103 55W
Tolimán, *Querétaro, Mexico* **219 B8** 20 53N 99 54W
Tolland, *CT, U.S.A.* **78 C2** 41 52N 72 22W
Tolland County ☆, *CT, U.S.A.* **78 C2** 41 45N 72 20W
Tollesboro, *KY, U.S.A.* **97 B9** 38 34N 83 34W
Tolleson, *AZ, U.S.A.* **62 D3** 33 27N 112 15W
Tolley, *ND, U.S.A.* **91 B4** 48 44N 101 50W
Tolna, *ND, U.S.A.* **91 C7** 47 50N 98 26W
Tolono, *IL, U.S.A.* **71 D5** 39 59N 88 16W
Tolstoi, *Man., Canada* **183 F15** 49 5N 96 49W
Tolu, *KY, U.S.A.* **96 C4** 37 26N 88 15W
Toluca, *México, Mexico* **219 C8** 19 17N 99 40W
Toluca, *IL, U.S.A.* **71 C4** 41 0N 89 8W
Toluca, Volcán Nevado de, *México, Mexico* **219 C8** 19 8N 99 44W
Tom, *OK, U.S.A.* **93 E9** 33 44N 94 35W
Tom Bass Regional Park ⌂, *Houston, U.S.A.* **110 C2** 29 35N 95 22W
Tom Green County ☆, *TX, U.S.A.* **98 F7** 31 28N 100 26W
Tom Steed Res., *OK, U.S.A.* **93 D5** 34 46N 98 50W
Tomah, *WI, U.S.A.* **103 E3** 43 59N 90 30W
Tomahawk, *WI, U.S.A.* **103 C4** 45 28N 89 44W
Tomahawk I., *Portland, U.S.A.* **116 A2** 45 36N 122 39W
Tomales Pt., *CA, U.S.A.* **64 E4** 38 14N 122 59W
Tomás Garrido, *Quintana Roo, Mexico* **223 D4** 18 1N 89 4W
Tomatlán, *Jalisco, Mexico* **218 C2** 19 56N 105 15W
Tomball, *TX, U.S.A.* **99 G12** 30 6N 95 37W
Tombigbee →, *AL, U.S.A.* **60 E3** 31 8N 87 57W
Tombigee Nat. Forest, *MS, U.S.A.* **81 C5** 33 56N 88 56W
Tombstone, *AZ, U.S.A.* **62 F5** 31 43N 110 4W
Tome, *NM, U.S.A.* **88 C4** 34 44N 106 44W
Tomichi →, *CO, U.S.A.* **66 D4** 38 31N 106 58W
Tomiko L., *Ont., Canada* **178 A7** 46 32N 79 49W
Tomochic, *Chihuahua, Mexico* **213 E8** 28 22N 107 51W
Tomochic →, *Chihuahua, Mexico* **213 E8** 28 28N 107 50W
Tompkins, *Sask., Canada* **182 E3** 50 4N 108 47W
Tompkins County ☆, *NY, U.S.A.* **89 C4** 42 30N 76 30W
Tompkinsville, *KY, U.S.A.* **97 D7** 36 42N 85 41W
Tompkinsville, *MD, U.S.A.* **77 B4** 38 18N 76 54W
Toms →, *NJ, U.S.A.* **87 C2** 39 57N 74 7W
Toms Brook, *VA, U.S.A.* **77 B2** 38 57N 78 26W
Toms River, *NJ, U.S.A.* **87 C2** 39 58N 74 12W
Tonalá, *Chiapas, Mexico* **222 C3** 16 4N 93 45W
Tonalá, *Jalisco, Mexico* **218 B4** 20 37N 103 14W
Tonalea, *AZ, U.S.A.* **62 A5** 36 19N 110 56W
Tonasket, *WA, U.S.A.* **101 B6** 48 42N 119 26W
Tonatico, *México, Mexico* **219 D8** 18 48N 99 40W
Tonawanda, *NY, U.S.A.* **89 B2** 43 1N 78 53W
Tonawanda Indian Reservation, *NY, U.S.A.* **89 B2** 43 5N 78 25W
Tonaya, *Jalisco, Mexico* **218 C4** 19 51N 103 58W
Tonganoxie, *KS, U.S.A.* **74 B8** 39 7N 95 5W
Tongass Nat. Forest, *AK, U.S.A.* **61 J14** 54 45N 133 0W
Tongue →, *MT, U.S.A.* **83 D12** 46 25N 105 52W
Tongue →, *ND, U.S.A.* **91 B8** 48 56N 97 18W
Tongue River Res., *MT, U.S.A.* **83 E11** 45 8N 106 46W
Tonica, *IL, U.S.A.* **71 B4** 41 13N 89 4W
Tonila, *Jalisco, Mexico* **218 C4** 19 26N 103 31W
Toniná, *Chiapas, Mexico* **222 C5** 16 53N 91 57W
Tonina, Boca la, *Sinaloa, Mexico* **216 C3** 24 34N 107 57W
Tonkawa, *OK, U.S.A.* **93 B6** 36 41N 97 18W
Tonopah, *AZ, U.S.A.* **62 D3** 33 30N 112 56W
Tonopah, *NV, U.S.A.* **85 D3** 38 4N 117 14W
Tonsina, *AK, U.S.A.* **61 F11** 61 39N 145 11W
Tontitown, *AR, U.S.A.* **63 B1** 36 11N 94 14W
Tonto Cr. →, *AZ, U.S.A.* **62 D4** 33 45N 111 10W
Tonto Nat. Forest, *AZ, U.S.A.* **62 D4** 34 0N 111 20W
Tonto Nat. Monument △, *AZ, U.S.A.* **62 D4** 33 39N 111 7W
Tony, *WI, U.S.A.* **103 C3** 45 29N 91 0W
Tooele, *UT, U.S.A.* **100 C3** 40 32N 112 18W
Tooele County ☆, *UT, U.S.A.* **100 C3** 40 25N 113 0W
Toole County ☆, *MT, U.S.A.* **83 B6** 48 48N 111 50W
Toombs County ☆, *GA, U.S.A.* **68 D4** 32 10N 82 15W
Toomsboro, *GA, U.S.A.* **68 D3** 32 50N 83 5W
Toone, *TN, U.S.A.* **96 E4** 35 21N 88 57W
Top of the World Park ⌂, *B.C., Canada* **185 J5** 49 51N 115 35W
Topawa, *AZ, U.S.A.* **62 F4** 31 48N 111 51W
Topaz L., *NV, U.S.A.* **85 D1** 38 41N 119 33W
Topeka, *IN, U.S.A.* **72 B5** 41 32N 85 32W
Topeka, *KS, U.S.A.* **74 B8** 39 3N 95 40W
Topia, *Durango, Mexico* **216 B4** 25 13N 106 34W
Topock, *CA, U.S.A.* **62 C1** 34 46N 114 29W
Topolobampo, *Sinaloa, Mexico* **216 B1** 25 36N 109 3W
Topolobampo, B. de, *Sinaloa, Mexico* **216 B1** 25 37N 109 1W
Toponas, *CO, U.S.A.* **66 B4** 40 4N 106 48W
Toppenish, *WA, U.S.A.* **101 D5** 46 23N 120 19W
Topsfield, *ME, U.S.A.* **76 C6** 45 25N 67 44W
Topsfield, *MA, U.S.A.* **78 B4** 42 38N 70 57W
Topton, *PA, U.S.A.* **87 B1** 40 30N 75 42W
Toquerville, *UT, U.S.A.* **100 F2** 37 15N 113 17W
Toquima Range, *NV, U.S.A.* **85 D4** 38 55N 116 50W
Torbay, *Nfld. & L., Canada* **174 E8** 47 40N 52 42W
Torch →, *Sask., Canada* **182 B8** 53 50N 103 5W
Torch L., *MI, U.S.A.* **79 E6** 44 58N 85 18W
Tordilla, Sa., *Sonora, Mexico* **212 D3** 29 45N 112 30W
Tordo, Barra el, *Tamaulipas, Mexico* **215 G7** 23 4N 97 45W
Torngat Mts., *Nfld. & L., Canada* **175 B5** 59 0N 63 40W
Tornillo, *TX, U.S.A.* **98 F1** 31 27N 106 5W
Toro, *LA, U.S.A.* **75 C2** 31 17N 93 33W
Toro, I. el, *Veracruz, Mexico* **220 C3** 21 35N 97 29W
Toronto, *Ont., Canada* **178 D7** 43 39N 79 20W
Toronto, *IA, U.S.A.* **73 D8** 41 54N 90 52W
Toronto, *KS, U.S.A.* **74 D8** 37 48N 95 57W
Toronto, *OH, U.S.A.* **92 C6** 40 28N 80 36W
Toronto, *SD, U.S.A.* **91 F9** 44 34N 96 39W
Toronto Lake, *KS, U.S.A.* **74 D8** 37 46N 95 57W
Toronto Lester B. Pearson International ✈ (YYZ), *Ont., Canada* **178 D7** 43 46N 79 35W
Torquay, *Sask., Canada* **182 F8** 49 9N 103 30W
Torrance, *CA, U.S.A.* **65 K8** 33 50N 118 20W
Torrance County ☆, *NM, U.S.A.* **88 C5** 34 40N 106 0W
Torreón, *Coahuila, Mexico* **214 E1** 25 33N 103 26W
Torreon, *NM, U.S.A.* **88 B3** 35 48N 107 13W
Torreón de Mata, *Chihuahua, Mexico* **213 G10** 26 48N 105 25W
Torres Martinez Indian Reservation, *CA, U.S.A.* **65 K10** 33 29N 116 5W
Torrey, *UT, U.S.A.* **100 E4** 38 18N 111 25W
Torrington, *Alta., Canada* **185 G7** 51 48N 113 35W
Torrington, *CT, U.S.A.* **78 C1** 41 48N 73 7W
Torrington, *WY, U.S.A.* **104 D8** 42 4N 104 11W
Tortilla Flat, *AZ, U.S.A.* **62 D4** 33 32N 111 23W
Tortola, *Br. Virgin Is.* **105 G18** 18 19N 64 45W
Tortuga, I., *Baja Calif. S., Mexico* **211 F7** 27 26N 111 52W
Tortuga, L. la, *Veracruz, Mexico* **220 B2** 22 20N 98 7W
Tortugas, B., *Baja Calif. S., Mexico* **211 F4** 27 42N 114 53W
Tortugas, Presa, *Sinaloa, Mexico* **216 D5** 23 7N 105 53W

Tosanachic, *Chihuahua, Mexico* .. **213 E7** 28 33N 108 1W
Toston, *MT, U.S.A.* **83 D6** 46 11N 111 26W
Tototiche, *Jalisco, Mexico* **217 F7** 21 56N 103 27W
Totoltepec, *Puebla, Mexico* **221 F3** 18 14N 97 52W
Totontepec, *Oaxaca, Mexico* **221 G4** 17 15N 96 2W
Tototlán, *Jalisco, Mexico* **218 B5** 20 33N 102 48W
Tototlán del Oro, *Jalisco, Mexico* **218 B3** 20 7N 104 31W
Totowa, *NJ, U.S.A.* **114 A1** 40 54N 74 12W
Tottenham, *Ont., Canada* **178 C7** 44 1N 79 49W
Touchet ➝, *WA, U.S.A.* **101 D7** 46 2N 118 40W
Toughy, *NE, U.S.A.* **84 C9** 41 8N 96 50W
Toulnustouc ➝, *Qué., Canada* ... **172 D1** 49 35N 68 24W
Toulnustouc Nord-Est ➝, *Qué., Canada* **172 C2** 50 56N 67 44W
Toulon, *IL, U.S.A.* **71 B4** 41 6N 89 52W
Tournament Players Club of Michigan, *MI, U.S.A.* **109 B1** 42 17N 83 12W
Toutle ➝, *WA, U.S.A.* **101 D3** 46 19N 122 55W
Towanda, *KS, U.S.A.* **74 D7** 37 44N 97 0W
Towanda, *PA, U.S.A.* **95 C6** 41 46N 76 27W
Towaoc, *CO, U.S.A.* **66 E2** 37 12N 108 44W
Tower, *MN, U.S.A.* **80 C6** 47 48N 92 17W
Tower City, *ND, U.S.A.* **91 D8** 46 56N 97 40W
Tower City, *PA, U.S.A.* **95 D6** 40 35N 76 33W
Tower Hill, *IL, U.S.A.* **71 D5** 39 23N 88 58W
Tower Junction, *WY, U.S.A.* **104 B2** 44 55N 110 25W
Town Creek, *AL, U.S.A.* **60 B3** 34 41N 87 24W
Towner, *CO, U.S.A.* **66 D8** 38 28N 102 5W
Towner, *ND, U.S.A.* **91 B5** 48 21N 100 25W
Towner County ☆, *ND, U.S.A.* .. **91 B6** 48 45N 99 10W
Townley, *NJ, U.S.A.* **114 B1** 40 41N 74 14W
Towns, *GA, U.S.A.* **68 D4** 32 0N 82 45W
Towns County ☆, *GA, U.S.A.* ... **68 B3** 34 55N 83 45W
Townsend, *DE, U.S.A.* **77 A5** 39 24N 75 41W
Townsend, *GA, U.S.A.* **68 E5** 31 33N 81 31W
Townsend, *MA, U.S.A.* **78 B3** 42 40N 71 42W
Townsend, *MT, U.S.A.* **83 D6** 46 19N 111 31W
Townshend, *VT, U.S.A.* **86 C2** 43 3N 72 41W
Townville, *PA, U.S.A.* **95 C3** 41 41N 79 53W
Towson, *MD, U.S.A.* **77 A4** 39 24N 76 36W
Toxey, *AL, U.S.A.* **60 E2** 31 55N 88 19W
Toyah, *TX, U.S.A.* **98 F4** 31 19N 103 48W
Toyah Cr. ➝, *TX, U.S.A.* **98 F4** 31 18N 103 27W
Toyah L., *TX, U.S.A.* **98 F4** 31 15N 103 20W
Toyahvale, *TX, U.S.A.* **98 G4** 30 57N 103 47W
Tracadie-Sheila, *N.B., Canada* ... **173 F5** 47 30N 64 55W
Tracy, *N.B., Canada* **173 H3** 45 41N 66 41W
Tracy, *CA, U.S.A.* **64 F5** 37 44N 121 26W
Tracy, *MN, U.S.A.* **80 F3** 44 14N 95 37W
Tracy City, *TN, U.S.A.* **97 E7** 35 16N 85 44W
Tracyton, *Seattle, U.S.A.* **118 C2** 47 36N 122 39W
Tradewater ➝, *KY, U.S.A.* **96 C4** 37 31N 88 3W
Traer, *IA, U.S.A.* **73 C6** 42 12N 92 28W
Trafalgar, *IN, U.S.A.* **72 D4** 39 25N 86 9W
Trail, *B.C., Canada* **187 F17** 49 5N 117 40W
Trail, *MN, U.S.A.* **80 C3** 47 47N 95 42W
Trail of Tears Nat. Historic Trail, *AR, U.S.A.* **63 C2** 35 45N 93 30W
Traill County ☆, *ND, U.S.A.* ... **91 C8** 47 30N 97 20W
Trammel, *VA, U.S.A.* **102 D2** 37 1N 82 18W
Trammel Cr. ➝, *KY, U.S.A.* **96 D6** 36 53N 86 23W
Tramping Lake, *Sask., Canada* ... **182 C3** 52 8N 108 57W
Tranquillity, *CA, U.S.A.* **65 G6** 36 39N 120 15W
Trans-Alaska Pipeline, *AK, U.S.A.* **61 A10** 70 11N 148 27W
Transylvania, *LA, U.S.A.* **75 B4** 32 41N 91 11W
Transylvania County ☆, *NC, U.S.A.* **90 C3** 35 10N 82 50W
Trappe, *MD, U.S.A.* **77 B4** 38 40N 76 4W
Trapper Pk., *MT, U.S.A.* **83 E3** 45 54N 114 18W
Trask Mt., *OR, U.S.A.* **94 B2** 45 22N 123 27W
Traskwood, *AR, U.S.A.* **63 D3** 34 27N 92 39W
Travelers Rest, *SC, U.S.A.* **90 D3** 34 58N 82 27W
Travers, L., *MN, U.S.A.* **80 E2** 45 41N 96 44W
Travers Res., *Alta., Canada* **185 H8** 50 12N 112 51W
Traverse, L., *SD, U.S.A.* **91 E9** 45 46N 96 38W
Traverse City, *MI, U.S.A.* **79 E6** 44 46N 85 38W
Traverse County ☆, *MN, U.S.A.* . **80 E2** 45 45N 96 25W
Traverse Mountains, *Salt Lake City, U.S.A.* **117 D3** 40 29N 111 49W
Traverse Pt., *MI, U.S.A.* **79 B3** 47 9N 88 14W
Travis, *NY, U.S.A.* **114 C1** 40 35N 74 11W
Travis, L., *TX, U.S.A.* **99 G10** 30 24N 97 55W
Travis County ☆, *TX, U.S.A.* ... **99 G10** 30 17N 97 45W
Treasure County ☆, *MT, U.S.A.* . **83 D10** 46 15N 107 20W
Treasure I., *San Francisco, U.S.A.* **118 B2** 37 49N 122 22W
Treasure I., *TN, U.S.A.* **112 B1** 30 5N 90 6W
Treasure Island, *FL, U.S.A.* **67 D6** 27 46N 82 46W
Tree Tops Park, *Miami, U.S.A.* .. **112 B1** 26 4N 80 16W
Treece, *KS, U.S.A.* **74 D9** 37 0N 94 51W
Trego, *MT, U.S.A.* **83 B3** 48 42N 114 52W
Trego County ☆, *KS, U.S.A.* **74 C4** 38 55N 99 50W
Treherne, *Man., Canada* **183 F13** 49 38N 98 42W
Trejos, *Jalisco, Mexico* **218 B4** 20 47N 103 11W
Tremblant, Mt., *Qué., Canada* ... **176 E8** 46 16N 74 35W
Trementina, *NM, U.S.A.* **88 B6** 35 28N 104 32W
Tremont, *IL, U.S.A.* **71 C4** 40 28N 89 29W
Tremont, *MS, U.S.A.* **81 B5** 34 14N 88 16W
Tremont, *NY, U.S.A.* **114 A3** 40 50N 73 52W
Tremonton, *UT, U.S.A.* **100 B3** 41 43N 112 10W
Trempealeau, *WI, U.S.A.* **103 D2** 44 0N 91 26W
Trempealeau County ☆, *WI, U.S.A.* **103 D2** 44 15N 91 20W
Trenary, *MI, U.S.A.* **79 C5** 46 12N 86 58W
Trenche ➝, *Qué., Canada* **177 D10** 47 46N 72 53W
Trent, *SD, U.S.A.* **91 G9** 43 54N 96 39W
Trent ➝, *Ont., Canada* **179 C9** 44 6N 77 34W
Trent ➝, *NC, U.S.A.* **90 C8** 35 5N 77 2W
Trente et Un Milles, L. des, *Qué., Canada* **176 E7** 46 12N 75 49W
Trenton = Quinte West, *Ont., Canada* **179 C9** 44 10N 77 34W
Trenton, *N.S., Canada* **173 H7** 45 37N 62 38W
Trenton, *FL, U.S.A.* **67 B6** 29 37N 82 49W
Trenton, *GA, U.S.A.* **68 B1** 34 52N 85 31W
Trenton, *IL, U.S.A.* **71 E4** 38 36N 89 41W
Trenton, *KY, U.S.A.* **96 D5** 36 43N 87 16W
Trenton, *ME, U.S.A.* **76 D5** 44 27N 68 22W
Trenton, *MI, U.S.A.* **79 G8** 42 8N 83 11W
Trenton, *MO, U.S.A.* **82 A3** 40 5N 93 37W
Trenton, *NC, U.S.A.* **90 C8** 35 4N 77 21W
Trenton, *ND, U.S.A.* **91 B2** 48 4N 103 51W
Trenton, *NJ, U.S.A.* **87 B2** 40 14N 74 46W
Trenton, *NE, U.S.A.* **84 D4** 40 11N 101 1W
Trenton, *OH, U.S.A.* **92 D2** 39 29N 84 28W
Trenton, *TN, U.S.A.* **96 E4** 35 59N 88 56W
Trenton, *UT, U.S.A.* **100 B4** 41 55N 111 57W
Trentwood, *WA, U.S.A.* **101 C8** 47 42N 117 13W
Trepassey, *Nfld. & L., Canada* ... **174 F7** 46 43N 53 25W
Trepassey B., *Nfld. & L., Canada* **174 F7** 46 37N 53 30W
Tres Garantías, *Quintana Roo, Mexico* **223 D5** 18 14N 89 1W
Tres Ojitos, *Chihuahua, Mexico* .. **213 E7** 28 50N 108 17W
Tres Palos, L., *Guerrero, Mexico* . **219 F8** 16 48N 99 43W
Tres Picos, *Chiapas, Mexico* **222 D3** 15 52N 93 32W
Tres Picos, Cerro, *Chihuahua, Mexico* **213 D8** 29 12N 107 34W
Tres Piedras, *NM, U.S.A.* **88 A5** 36 39N 105 58W
Tres Pinos, *CA, U.S.A.* **64 G5** 36 48N 121 19W
Tres Valles, *Veracruz, Mexico* ... **221 F4** 18 15N 96 8W
Tres Virgenes, Volcán de las, *Baja Calif. S., Mexico* **211 F6** 27 27N 112 34W
Treutlen County ☆, *GA, U.S.A.* .. **68 D4** 32 25N 82 30W
Trêve, L. la, *Qué., Canada* **176 B7** 49 56N 75 30W
Trevorton, *PA, U.S.A.* **95 D6** 40 47N 76 41W
Trexlertown, *PA, U.S.A.* **87 B1** 40 33N 75 36W
Treynor, *IA, U.S.A.* **73 D3** 41 14N 95 36W
Trezevant, *TN, U.S.A.* **96 D4** 36 1N 88 37W
Tri-City, *OR, U.S.A.* **94 E2** 42 59N 123 19W
Triangle, *VA, U.S.A.* **77 B3** 38 33N 77 20W
Triángulos, Arrecifes, *Campeche, Mexico* **223 B1** 20 52N 92 11W
Tribbey, *OK, U.S.A.* **93 C6** 35 7N 97 4W
Tribly, *FL, U.S.A.* **67 C6** 28 28N 82 12W
Tribune, *Sask., Canada* **182 F8** 49 15N 103 49W
Tribune, *KS, U.S.A.* **74 C2** 38 28N 101 45W
Trident, *MT, U.S.A.* **83 E6** 45 57N 111 28W
Trident Peak, *NV, U.S.A.* **85 A2** 41 54N 118 25W
Trigg County ☆, *KY, U.S.A.* **96 D5** 36 50N 87 55W
Trigo Mountains, *AZ, U.S.A.* **62 D1** 33 15N 114 40W
Trimble, *MO, U.S.A.* **82 B2** 39 28N 94 34W
Trimble, *TN, U.S.A.* **96 D3** 36 12N 89 11W
Trimble County, *KY, U.S.A.* **97 B7** 38 35N 85 20W
Trimont, *MN, U.S.A.* **80 G4** 43 46N 94 43W
Trinchera, *CO, U.S.A.* **66 E6** 37 2N 104 3W
Trincheras, *Sonora, Mexico* **212 C4** 30 24N 111 32W
Tring-Jonction, *Qué., Canada* **177 E12** 46 16N 70 59W
Trinidad, *CA, U.S.A.* **64 B2** 41 4N 124 9W
Trinidad, *CO, U.S.A.* **66 E6** 37 10N 104 31W
Trinidad, *DC, U.S.A.* **119 B4** 38 54N 76 59W
Trinidad, *TX, U.S.A.* **99 E11** 32 9N 96 6W
Trinidad Head, *CA, U.S.A.* **64 B2** 41 3N 124 9W
Trinity, *Nfld. & L., Canada* **174 D7** 48 59N 53 55W
Trinity, *NC, U.S.A.* **90 C6** 35 54N 79 59W
Trinity, *TX, U.S.A.* **99 G12** 30 57N 95 22W
Trinity ➝, *CA, U.S.A.* **64 B3** 41 11N 123 42W
Trinity ➝, *TX, U.S.A.* **99 H13** 29 45N 94 43W
Trinity B., *Nfld. & L., Canada* ... **174 D7** 48 20N 53 10W
Trinity Center, *CA, U.S.A.* **64 C4** 40 59N 122 41W
Trinity County ☆, *CA, U.S.A.* ... **64 C3** 40 40N 123 0W
Trinity County ☆, *TX, U.S.A.* ... **99 F12** 31 4N 95 8W
Trinity Dam, *CA, U.S.A.* **64 C4** 40 48N 122 46W
Trinity Is., *AK, U.S.A.* **61 H9** 56 33N 154 25W
Trinity Mt., *ID, U.S.A.* **70 F3** 43 36N 115 26W
Trinity Mts., *CA, U.S.A.* **64 C4** 40 50N 122 40W
Trinity Nat. Forest, *CA, U.S.A.* .. **64 C3** 40 40N 123 15W
Trinity Range, *NV, U.S.A.* **85 B2** 40 10N 118 40W
Trinity River Greenbelt Park, *Dallas-Fort Worth, U.S.A.* **109 B4** 32 45N 96 48W
Trinway, *OH, U.S.A.* **92 C4** 40 9N 82 1W
Trion, *GA, U.S.A.* **68 B1** 34 33N 85 19W
Triplett, *MO, U.S.A.* **82 B3** 39 30N 93 12W
Tripoli, *IA, U.S.A.* **73 C6** 42 49N 92 16W
Tripp, *SD, U.S.A.* **91 G8** 43 13N 97 58W
Tripp County ☆, *SD, U.S.A.* **91 G6** 43 20N 100 0W
Triquet, L., *Qué., Canada* **172 C10** 50 42N 59 47W
Triton, *Nfld. & L., Canada* **174 C5** 49 31N 55 37W
Triumph, *LA, U.S.A.* **75 E6** 29 20N 89 30W
Trochu, *Alta., Canada* **185 G7** 51 50N 113 13W
Trodely I., *N.W.T., Canada* **175 C2** 52 15N 79 26W
Troilus, L., *Qué., Canada* **175 C3** 50 50N 74 35W
Trois-Pistoles, *Qué., Canada* **177 C13** 48 5N 69 10W
Trois-Rivières, *Qué., Canada* **177 E10** 46 25N 72 34W
Trois-Rivières-Ouest, *Qué., Canada* **177 E10** 46 20N 72 36W
Trojes, *Michoacan, Mexico* **218 D4** 18 55N 103 19W
Trona, *CA, U.S.A.* **65 H9** 35 46N 117 23W
Troncoso, *Zacatecas, Mexico* **217 E8** 22 37N 102 28W
Tropic, *UT, U.S.A.* **100 F3** 37 37N 112 5W
Trotwood, *OH, U.S.A.* **92 D2** 39 48N 84 18W
Troup, *TX, U.S.A.* **99 E12** 32 9N 95 7W
Troup County ☆, *GA, U.S.A.* ... **68 C1** 33 0N 85 0W
Trousdale, *KS, U.S.A.* **74 D4** 37 49N 99 5W
Trousdale County ☆, *TN, U.S.A.* . **96 D6** 36 24N 86 10W
Trout ➝, *N.W.T., Canada* **189 D9** 61 19N 119 51W
Trout Cr. ➝, *OR, U.S.A.* **94 E7** 42 23N 118 3W
Trout Cr. ➝, *OR, U.S.A.* **94 C4** 44 48N 121 3W
Trout Creek, *MI, U.S.A.* **79 C2** 46 29N 89 1W
Trout Creek, *MT, U.S.A.* **83 C2** 47 50N 115 36W
Trout Creek, *UT, U.S.A.* **100 D2** 39 42N 113 50W
Trout Creek Mts., *OR, U.S.A.* ... **94 E7** 42 6N 118 18W
Trout L., *N.W.T., Canada* **189 D8** 60 40N 121 14W
Trout L., *Ont., Canada* **180 A3** 51 20N 93 15W
Trout L., *MN, U.S.A.* **80 C6** 47 59N 92 18W
Trout Lake, *B.C., Canada* **187 E17** 50 35N 117 25W
Trout Lake, *N.W.T., Canada* **189 D8** 56 30N 114 32W
Trout Lake, *MI, U.S.A.* **79 C6** 46 12N 85 1W
Trout Lake, *WA, U.S.A.* **101 E4** 46 0N 121 32W
Trout Pk., *WY, U.S.A.* **104 B3** 44 36N 109 32W
Trout River, *Nfld. & L., Canada* . **174 C2** 49 29N 58 8W
Troutdale, *OR, U.S.A.* **94 B3** 45 32N 122 23W
Troutdale, *VA, U.S.A.* **102 E3** 36 42N 81 26W
Troutman, *NC, U.S.A.* **90 C5** 35 42N 80 53W
Troutmans, *NC, U.S.A.* **90 C5** 35 42N 80 53W
Troutville, *VA, U.S.A.* **102 D5** 37 25N 79 53W
Troy, *N.S., Canada* **173 H8** 45 42N 61 26W
Troy, *AL, U.S.A.* **60 E5** 31 48N 85 58W
Troy, *ID, U.S.A.* **70 C2** 46 44N 116 46W
Troy, *IN, U.S.A.* **72 F4** 37 59N 86 55W
Troy, *KS, U.S.A.* **74 B8** 39 47N 95 5W
Troy, *MI, U.S.A.* **79 G8** 42 37N 83 9W
Troy, *MO, U.S.A.* **82 C6** 38 59N 90 59W
Troy, *MT, U.S.A.* **83 B2** 48 28N 115 53W
Troy, *NC, U.S.A.* **90 C6** 35 22N 79 53W
Troy, *NH, U.S.A.* **86 D2** 42 49N 72 11W
Troy, *NY, U.S.A.* **78 B1** 42 44N 73 41W
Troy, *OH, U.S.A.* **92 C2** 40 2N 84 12W
Troy, *OR, U.S.A.* **94 B8** 45 57N 117 27W
Troy, *PA, U.S.A.* **95 C6** 41 47N 76 47W
Troy, *SD, U.S.A.* **91 E9** 45 2N 96 52W
Troy, *TN, U.S.A.* **96 D3** 36 20N 89 10W
Troy, *TX, U.S.A.* **99 F10** 31 12N 97 18W
Troy, *VT, U.S.A.* **86 B2** 44 52N 72 25W
Troy Peak, *NV, U.S.A.* **85 D5** 38 19N 115 30W
Truchas, *NM, U.S.A.* **88 A5** 36 3N 105 49W
Truchas Pk., *NM, U.S.A.* **88 B5** 35 58N 105 39W
Truckee, *CA, U.S.A.* **64 D6** 39 20N 120 11W
Truckee ➝, *NV, U.S.A.* **85 C1** 39 51N 119 24W
Truesdale, *IA, U.S.A.* **73 C3** 42 44N 95 11W
Truite, L. à la, *Qué., Canada* **176 D4** 47 20N 78 20W
Trujillo, *NM, U.S.A.* **88 B6** 35 32N 104 42W
Trujillo Alto, *Puerto Rico* **105 G16** 18 21N 66 1W
Truman, *MN, U.S.A.* **80 G4** 43 50N 94 26W
Trumann, *AR, U.S.A.* **63 C5** 35 41N 90 31W
Trumansburg, *NY, U.S.A.* **89 C4** 42 33N 76 40W
Trumbull, *CT, U.S.A.* **78 C1** 41 15N 73 12W
Trumbull, *NE, U.S.A.* **84 D7** 40 41N 98 16W
Trumbull, Mt., *AZ, U.S.A.* **62 A2** 36 25N 113 19W
Trumbull County ☆, *OH, U.S.A.* . **92 B6** 41 14N 80 49W
Truro, *N.S., Canada* **173 H6** 45 21N 63 14W
Truro, *MA, U.S.A.* **78 C4** 42 0N 70 3W
Truscott, *TX, U.S.A.* **99 D8** 33 45N 99 49W
Trussville, *AL, U.S.A.* **60 C4** 33 37N 86 35W
Truth or Consequences, *NM, U.S.A.* **88 D3** 33 8N 107 15W
Truxton, *AZ, U.S.A.* **62 B2** 35 29N 113 34W
Tryon, *NE, U.S.A.* **84 C5** 41 33N 100 57W
Tryon, *OK, U.S.A.* **93 C7** 35 52N 96 58W
Tryon Creek State Park ⌂, *Portland, U.S.A.* **116 B1** 45 25N 122 40W
Tsacha L., *B.C., Canada* **186 B10** 53 3N 124 50W
Tsaile, *AZ, U.S.A.* **62 A6** 36 17N 109 10W
Tsala Apopka L., *FL, U.S.A.* **67 C6** 28 53N 82 19W
Tschida, L., *ND, U.S.A.* **91 D4** 46 37N 101 55W
Tsiigehtchic, *N.W.T., Canada* **188 C6** 67 15N 134 0W
Ts'il-os Park ⌂, *B.C., Canada* ... **186 D11** 51 9N 123 59W
Tsitsutl Pk., *B.C., Canada* **186 C9** 52 43N 125 47W
Tsuniah L., *B.C., Canada* **186 D10** 51 33N 124 4W
Tualatin, *OR, U.S.A.* **94 B3** 45 23N 122 45W
Tuba City, *AZ, U.S.A.* **62 A4** 36 8N 111 14W
Tubac, *AZ, U.S.A.* **62 F4** 31 37N 111 3W
Tubutama, *Sonora, Mexico* **212 C4** 30 53N 111 29W
Tucannon ➝, *WA, U.S.A.* **101 D7** 46 33N 118 11W
Tuckahoe, *NJ, U.S.A.* **87 C2** 39 17N 74 45W
Tuckahoe ➝, *MD, U.S.A.* **77 B5** 39 0N 75 56W
Tuckaway Park, *Charlotte, U.S.A.* **107 B2** 35 6N 80 49W
Tucker, *AR, U.S.A.* **63 D4** 34 26N 91 57W
Tucker, *GA, U.S.A.* **68 C2** 33 51N 84 13W
Tucker County ☆, *WV, U.S.A.* .. **102 B5** 39 9N 79 30W
Tuckerman, *AR, U.S.A.* **63 C4** 35 44N 91 12W
Tuckernuck Island, *MA, U.S.A.* .. **78 C4** 41 18N 70 15W
Tuckerton, *NJ, U.S.A.* **87 C2** 39 36N 74 20W
Tucson, *AZ, U.S.A.* **62 E5** 32 13N 110 58W
Tucson International ✈ (TUS), *AZ, U.S.A.* **62 E5** 32 7N 110 56W
Tucumcari, *NM, U.S.A.* **88 B7** 35 10N 103 44W
Tucumcari Cr. ➝, *NM, U.S.A.* .. **88 B7** 35 20N 103 15W
Tudor, L., *Qué., Canada* **175 B4** 55 50N 65 25W
Tuftonboro, *NH, U.S.A.* **86 C3** 43 42N 71 13W
Tug Fork ➝, *WV, U.S.A.* **102 C2** 38 7N 82 36W
Tugaske, *Sask., Canada* **182 E5** 50 52N 106 17W
Tugidak I., *AK, U.S.A.* **61 H9** 56 30N 154 40W
Tukarak I., *N.W.T., Canada* **175 B2** 56 15N 78 45W
Tuktoyaktuk, *N.W.T., Canada* **188 C6** 69 27N 133 2W
Tuktut Nogait Nat. Park △, *N.W.T., Canada* **188 C8** 69 15N 122 0W
Tukwila, *WA, U.S.A.* **101 C3** 47 28N 122 15W
Tula, *Amer. Samoa* .... **105 e** 14 15 S 170 34W
Tula, *Hidalgo, Mexico* **219 B8** 20 3N 99 21W
Tula, *Tamaulipas, Mexico* **215 G5** 23 0N 99 43W
Tula, *MS, U.S.A.* **81 B4** 34 14N 89 22W
Tulalip Indian Reservation, *WA, U.S.A.* **101 B3** 48 4N 122 13W
Tulancingo, *Hidalgo, Mexico* **219 B9** 20 5N 98 22W
Tulancingo, *Oaxaca, Mexico* **221 G3** 17 46N 97 26W
Tulare, *CA, U.S.A.* **65 G7** 36 13N 119 21W
Tulare, *SD, U.S.A.* **91 F7** 44 44N 98 31W
Tulare County ☆, *CA, U.S.A.* ... **65 G8** 36 10N 118 50W
Tulare Lake Bed, *CA, U.S.A.* **65 H7** 36 0N 119 48W
Tularosa, *NM, U.S.A.* **88 D4** 33 5N 106 1W
Tularosa Mts., *NM, U.S.A.* **88 D2** 33 45N 108 40W
Tularosa Valley, *NM, U.S.A.* **88 E4** 32 45N 106 0W
Tule ➝, *CA, U.S.A.* **65 G7** 36 3N 119 50W
Tule Cr. ➝, *TX, U.S.A.* **98 C6** 34 40N 101 14W
Tule L., *CA, U.S.A.* **64 B5** 41 53N 121 30W
Tule Lake Nat. Wildlife Refuge ⌂, *CA, U.S.A.* **64 B5** 41 52N 121 30W
Tule River Indian Reservation, *CA, U.S.A.* **65 H8** 36 0N 118 50W
Tule Valley, *UT, U.S.A.* **100 D2** 39 25N 113 30W
Tulelake, *CA, U.S.A.* **64 B5** 41 57N 121 29W
Tulemalu L., *Nunavut, Canada* ... **191 E6** 62 58N 99 25W
Tulia, *TX, U.S.A.* **98 C6** 34 32N 101 46W
Tulija ➝, *Tabasco, Mexico* **222 B4** 17 38N 92 22W
Tulita, *N.W.T., Canada* **189 D7** 64 57N 125 30W
Tullahassee, *OK, U.S.A.* **93 C8** 35 50N 95 26W
Tullahoma, *TN, U.S.A.* **96 E6** 35 22N 86 13W
Tulloch Res., *CA, U.S.A.* **64 F6** 37 53N 120 36W
Tullos, *LA, U.S.A.* **75 C3** 31 49N 92 19W
Tully, *NY, U.S.A.* **89 C4** 42 48N 76 7W
Tulsa, *OK, U.S.A.* **93 B8** 36 10N 95 55W
Tulsa County ☆, *OK, U.S.A.* **93 B8** 36 0N 95 55W
Tulsa International ✈ (TUL), *OK, U.S.A.* **93 B8** 36 12N 95 53W
Tulsayab, Pta., *Quintana Roo, Mexico* **223 B6** 20 16N 87 22W
Tultepec, *México, Mexico* **219 C8** 19 40N 99 8W
Tuluksak, *AK, U.S.A.* **61 F7** 61 6N 160 58W
Tulum, *Quintana Roo, Mexico* ... **223 B6** 20 13N 87 28W
Tumacacori Nat. Historic Park ⌂, *U.S.A.* **62 F4** 31 35N 111 6W
Tumbalá, *Chiapas, Mexico* **222 B4** 17 18N 92 19W
Tumbiscatio de Ruiz, *Michoacan, Mexico* **218 D5** 18 31N 102 21W
Tumbledown Mt., *ME, U.S.A.* **76 C3** 45 27N 70 28W
Tumbler Ridge, *B.C., Canada* **189 E8** 55 8N 121 0W
Tumon B., *Guam* .... **105 b** 13 31N 144 48W
Tumwater, *WA, U.S.A.* **101 C3** 47 1N 122 54W
Tungsten, *N.W.T., Canada* **189 D7** 61 57N 128 16W
Tunica, *LA, U.S.A.* **75 D4** 30 56N 91 33W
Tunica, *MS, U.S.A.* **81 B3** 34 41N 90 23W
Tunica-Biloxi Indian Reservation, *LA, U.S.A.* **75 C3** 31 7N 92 3W
Tunica County ☆, *MS, U.S.A.* ... **81 B3** 34 41N 90 23W
Tunis Mills, *MD, U.S.A.* **77 B4** 38 49N 76 10W
Tunkás, *Yucatán, Mexico* **223 B5** 20 54N 88 45W
Tunkhannock, *PA, U.S.A.* **95 C7** 41 32N 75 57W
Tunnel Hill, *IL, U.S.A.* **71 F5** 37 32N 88 50W
Tunnelton, *WV, U.S.A.* **102 B5** 39 24N 79 45W
Tuntutuliak, *AK, U.S.A.* **61 F7** 60 22N 162 38W
Tununak, *AK, U.S.A.* **61 F6** 60 37N 165 15W
Tunungayualok I., *Nfld. & L., Canada* **175 B5** 56 0N 61 0W
Tuolumne, *CA, U.S.A.* **64 F6** 37 58N 120 15W
Tuolumne County ☆, *CA, U.S.A.* . **64 E7** 38 0N 120 0W
Tupátaro, *Guanajuato, Mexico* ... **218 B6** 20 35N 101 38W
Tupelo, *MS, U.S.A.* **81 B5** 34 16N 88 43W
Tupelo, *OK, U.S.A.* **93 D7** 34 36N 96 26W
Tupelo Nat. Battlefield ⌂, *MS, U.S.A.* **81 B5** 34 15N 88 14W
Tupper L., *NY, U.S.A.* **89 A6** 44 12N 74 35W
Tupper Lake, *NY, U.S.A.* **89 A6** 44 14N 74 28W
Turbeville, *SC, U.S.A.* **90 E5** 33 54N 80 1W
Turbeville, *VA, U.S.A.* **102 E5** 36 37N 79 2W
Turgeon ➝, *Qué., Canada* **176 B4** 50 0N 78 56W
Turgeon, L., *Qué., Canada* **176 B3** 49 2N 79 4W
Turicato, *Michoacan, Mexico* **219 C6** 19 0N 101 27W
Turin, *Alta., Canada* **185 J8** 49 58N 112 31W
Turin, *IA, U.S.A.* **73 C3** 42 1N 95 58W
Turkey, *TX, U.S.A.* **98 C7** 34 24N 100 54W
Turkey ➝, *IA, U.S.A.* **73 C7** 42 43N 91 2W
Turkey Cr. ➝, *OK, U.S.A.* **93 C6** 35 58N 97 56W
Turkey Creek, *LA, U.S.A.* **75 D3** 30 53N 92 25W
Turkey L., *Orlando, U.S.A.* **115 A2** 28 30N 81 28W
Turkey Lake Park, *Orlando, U.S.A.* **115 A2** 28 30N 81 28W
Turkey Mt., *TX, U.S.A.* **98 H7** 29 22N 100 12W
Turkey Ridge, *SD, U.S.A.* **91 G8** 43 25N 97 25W
Turlock, *CA, U.S.A.* **64 F6** 37 30N 120 51W
Turlock L., *CA, U.S.A.* **64 F6** 37 37N 120 35W
Turnagain ➝, *B.C., Canada* **189 E7** 59 12N 127 35W
Turner, *MI, U.S.A.* **79 E8** 44 9N 83 47W
Turner, *MT, U.S.A.* **83 B9** 48 51N 108 24W
Turner, *OR, U.S.A.* **94 C3** 44 51N 122 57W
Turner, *WA, U.S.A.* **101 D8** 46 25N 117 51W
Turner County ☆, *GA, U.S.A.* ... **68 E3** 31 45N 83 45W
Turner County ☆, *SD, U.S.A.* ... **91 G8** 43 17N 97 5W
Turner Valley, *Alta., Canada* **185 H6** 50 40N 114 17W
Turners Falls, *MA, U.S.A.* **78 B2** 42 36N 72 33W
Turnerville, *WY, U.S.A.* **104 D2** 42 52N 111 0W
Turnor L., *Sask., Canada* **189 E11** 56 35N 108 35W
Turnour I., *B.C., Canada* **186 E8** 50 36N 126 27W
Turon, *KS, U.S.A.* **74 D5** 37 48N 98 26W
Turpin, *OK, U.S.A.* **93 B3** 36 52N 100 52W
Turpin Hills, *OH, U.S.A.* **107 B2** 39 6N 84 22W
Turrell, *AR, U.S.A.* **63 C5** 35 23N 90 15W
Turtle ➝, *Ont., Canada* **180 D4** 48 51N 92 45W
Turtle ➝, *ND, U.S.A.* **91 B8** 48 19N 97 8W
Turtle ➝, *SD, U.S.A.* **91 F7** 44 55N 98 29W
Turtle-Flambeau Flowage, *WI, U.S.A.* **103 B3** 46 4N 90 14W
Turtle L., *Sask., Canada* **182 B3** 53 36N 108 38W
Turtle Lake, *Minneapolis-St. Paul, U.S.A.* **113 A3** 45 5N 93 7W
Turtle Lake, *ND, U.S.A.* **91 C5** 47 31N 100 53W
Turtle Lake, *WI, U.S.A.* **103 C1** 45 24N 92 8W
Turtle Mountain Indian Reservation, *ND, U.S.A.* **91 B6** 48 58N 99 58W
Turtle Mountains, *ND, U.S.A.* ... **91 B6** 48 58N 100 0W
Turtle Mt. Prov. Park ⌂, *Man., Canada* **183 F11** 49 3N 100 15W
Turtle River, *MN, U.S.A.* **80 C4** 47 35N 94 46W
Turtleford, *Sask., Canada* **182 B3** 53 23N 108 57W
Turuachi ➝, *Chihuahua, Mexico* . **213 G9** 26 30N 106 50W
Tusayan, *AZ, U.S.A.* **62 B3** 35 58N 112 8W
Tuscaloosa, *AL, U.S.A.* **60 C3** 33 12N 87 34W
Tuscaloosa, L., *AL, U.S.A.* **60 C3** 33 16N 87 30W
Tuscaloosa County ☆, *AL, U.S.A.* **60 C3** 33 11N 87 27W
Tuscarawas ➝, *OH, U.S.A.* **92 C5** 40 24N 81 25W
Tuscarawas County ☆, *OH, U.S.A.* **92 C5** 40 22N 81 26W
Tuscarora, *NV, U.S.A.* **85 A4** 41 19N 116 14W
Tuscarora Indian Reservation, *NY, U.S.A.* **89 B2** 43 10N 78 55W
Tuscarora Mt., *PA, U.S.A.* **95 D5** 40 55N 77 55W
Tuscarora Mts., *NV, U.S.A.* **85 B4** 41 0N 116 20W
Tuscola, *IL, U.S.A.* **71 D5** 39 48N 88 17W
Tuscola, *TX, U.S.A.* **99 E8** 32 12N 99 48W
Tuscola County ☆, *MI, U.S.A.* ... **79 F8** 43 25N 83 20W
Tusculum, *TN, U.S.A.* **97 D10** 36 10N 82 46W
Tuscumbia, *AL, U.S.A.* **60 B3** 34 44N 87 42W
Tuscumbia, *MO, U.S.A.* **82 C4** 38 14N 92 28W
Tushar Mts., *UT, U.S.A.* **100 E3** 38 20N 112 30W
Tushka, *OK, U.S.A.* **93 D7** 34 19N 96 10W
Tuskahoma, *OK, U.S.A.* **93 D8** 34 37N 95 17W
Tuskegee, *AL, U.S.A.* **60 D5** 32 25N 85 42W
Tuskegee Nat. Forest, *AL, U.S.A.* **60 D5** 32 29N 85 35W
Tusket, *N.S., Canada* **173 K4** 43 52N 65 58W
Tusket ➝, *N.S., Canada* **173 K4** 43 41N 65 57W
Tusket Wedge = Wedgeport, *N.S., Canada* **173 K4** 43 44N 65 59W
Tustin, *MI, U.S.A.* **79 E6** 44 6N 85 28W
Tuttle, *ND, U.S.A.* **91 C6** 47 9N 100 0W
Tuttle, *OK, U.S.A.* **93 C6** 35 17N 97 49W
Tuttle Creek L., *KS, U.S.A.* **74 B7** 39 15N 96 36W
Tutuaca ➝, *Chihuahua, Mexico* .. **212 D7** 29 10N 108 34W
Tutuila, *Amer. Samoa* .... **105 e** 14 19 S 170 50W
Tutwiler, *MS, U.S.A.* **81 B3** 34 1N 90 26W
Tuweep, *AZ, U.S.A.* **62 A2** 36 25N 113 4W
Tuxcacuesco, *Jalisco, Mexico* **218 C4** 19 44N 103 59W
Tuxedo Park, *NY, U.S.A.* **87 A2** 41 12N 74 11W
Tuxford, *Sask., Canada* **182 E6** 50 34N 105 35W
Tuxpán, *Jalisco, Mexico* **218 C4** 19 33N 103 24W
Tuxpan, *Michoacan, Mexico* **219 C7** 19 34N 100 28W
Tuxpan, *Nayarit, Mexico* **216 F5** 21 57N 105 18W
Tuxpan, *Veracruz, Mexico* **220 D3** 20 57N 97 24W
Tuxpan, Arrecife, *Veracruz, Mexico* **220 C3** 21 2N 97 11W
Tuxpan, Barra de, *Veracruz, Mexico* **220 D3** 20 59N 97 18W
Tuxtepec, *Oaxaca, Mexico* **221 F4** 18 6N 96 7W
Tuxtla Chico, *Chiapas, Mexico* ... **222 E4** 14 57N 92 10W
Tuxtla Gutiérrez, *Chiapas, Mexico* **222 C3** 16 45N 93 7W
Tuya ➝, *B.C., Canada* **189 E6** 58 2N 130 51W
Tuzantán, *Chiapas, Mexico* **222 D3** 15 9N 92 25W
Tuzantla, *Michoacan, Mexico* **219 C7** 19 13N 100 35W
Tuzigoot Nat. Monument △, *AZ, U.S.A.* **62 C3** 34 46N 112 2W
Twain Harte, *CA, U.S.A.* **64 E6** 38 2N 120 14W
Tweed, *Ont., Canada* **179 C9** 44 29N 77 19W
Tweedside, *N.B., Canada* **173 H2** 45 38N 67 1W
Tweedsmuir, *Sask., Canada* **182 D6** 53 34N 105 57W
Tweedsmuir Park ⌂, *B.C., Canada* **186 B8** 53 0N 126 20W
Twelve Mile L., *Sask., Canada* ... **182 F5** 49 29N 106 14W
Twentynine Palms, *CA, U.S.A.* ... **65 J10** 34 8N 116 3W
Twentynine Palms Indian Reservation, *CA, U.S.A.* **65 J10** 34 7N 116 3W
Twiggs County ☆, *GA, U.S.A.* ... **68 D3** 32 40N 83 30W
Twillingate, *Nfld. & L., Canada* . **174 C6** 49 42N 54 45W
Twin Bridges, *MT, U.S.A.* **83 E5** 45 33N 112 20W
Twin Brooks, *SD, U.S.A.* **91 E9** 45 12N 96 47W
Twin Buttes Res., *TX, U.S.A.* ... **98 F7** 31 22N 100 32W
Twin City, *GA, U.S.A.* **68 D4** 32 35N 82 10W
Twin Falls, *ID, U.S.A.* **70 G4** 42 34N 114 28W
Twin Falls County ☆, *ID, U.S.A.* . **70 G4** 42 30N 114 45W
Twin Hills, *AK, U.S.A.* **61 G8** 59 23N 159 58W
Twin Lake, *MI, U.S.A.* **79 F5** 43 22N 86 10W
Twin Lakes, *CO, U.S.A.* **66 C4** 39 5N 106 23W
Twin Lakes, *GA, U.S.A.* **68 F3** 30 43N 83 13W
Twin Lakes, *MI, U.S.A.* **79 C3** 46 54N 88 51W
Twin Lakes, *MN, U.S.A.* **80 G5** 43 34N 93 25W
Twin Lakes, *NM, U.S.A.* **88 B2** 35 43N 108 46W
Twin Lakes, *PA, U.S.A.* **87 A2** 41 23N 74 54W
Twin Mountain, *NH, U.S.A.* **86 B3** 44 16N 71 32W
Twin Mts., *TX, U.S.A.* **98 G4** 30 25N 103 50W
Twin Peaks, *ID, U.S.A.* **70 E4** 44 35N 114 29W
Twin Peaks, *Salt Lake City, U.S.A.* **117 C3** 40 35N 111 43W
Twin Peaks, *San Francisco, U.S.A.* **118 B2** 37 45N 122 26W
Twin Peaks Wilderness, *Salt Lake City, U.S.A.* **117 C3** 40 36N 111 43W
Twin Rivers, *NJ, U.S.A.* **87 B2** 40 15N 74 32W
Twin Valley, *MN, U.S.A.* **80 C2** 47 16N 96 16W
Twinsburg, *OH, U.S.A.* **92 B5** 41 19N 81 26W
Twisp, *WA, U.S.A.* **101 B5** 48 22N 120 7W
Twitchell Res., *CA, U.S.A.* **65 J6** 34 59N 120 19W
Twitty, *TX, U.S.A.* **98 B7** 35 19N 100 14W
Two Butte Cr. ➝, *CO, U.S.A.* .. **66 D8** 38 2N 102 9W
Two Buttes, *CO, U.S.A.* **66 E8** 37 34N 102 24W
Two Buttes Res., *CO, U.S.A.* **66 E8** 37 38N 102 32W
Two Harbors, *MN, U.S.A.* **80 C7** 47 2N 91 40W
Two Hills, *Alta., Canada* **184 E9** 53 43N 111 52W
Two Medicine ➝, *MT, U.S.A.* ... **83 B5** 48 29N 112 14W
Two Rivers, *WI, U.S.A.* **103 D6** 44 9N 87 34W
Two Rivers Nat. Wildlife Refuge ⌂, *IL, U.S.A.* **71 E3** 38 57N 90 31W
Two Taverns, *PA, U.S.A.* **77 A3** 39 47N 77 10W
Ty Ty, *GA, U.S.A.* **68 E3** 31 28N 83 39W
Tyaskin, *MD, U.S.A.* **77 B5** 38 17N 75 52W
Tybee Island, *GA, U.S.A.* **68 D6** 32 1N 80 51W
Tye, *TX, U.S.A.* **99 E8** 32 27N 99 52W
Tygart L., *WV, U.S.A.* **102 B4** 39 19N 80 2W
Tygart Valley ➝, *WV, U.S.A.* .. **102 B4** 39 28N 80 9W
Tyger ➝, *SC, U.S.A.* **90 D4** 34 28N 81 26W
Tygh Valley, *OR, U.S.A.* **94 B4** 45 15N 121 10W

Tyler, MN, U.S.A. 80 F2 44 17N 96 8W
Tyler, TX, U.S.A. 99 E12 32 21N 95 18W
Tyler, WA, U.S.A. 101 C8 47 26N 117 47W
Tyler County ☆, TX, U.S.A. 99 G13 30 47N 94 25W
Tyler County ☆, WV, U.S.A. 102 B4 39 30N 80 54W
Tylertown, MS, U.S.A. 81 E3 31 7N 90 9W
Tymochtee →, OH, U.S.A. 92 C3 40 57N 83 16W
Tynan, TX, U.S.A. 99 J10 28 10N 97 45W
Tyndall, Man., Canada 183 E15 50 5N 96 40W
Tyndall, SD, U.S.A. 91 G8 43 0N 97 50W
Tyndall Air Force Base, FL, U.S.A. 67 A3 30 3N 85 40W
Tyne Valley, P.E.I., Canada 173 G6 46 35N 63 56W
Tyngsborough, MA, U.S.A. 78 B3 42 40N 71 25W
Tyonek, AK, U.S.A. 61 F10 61 4N 151 8W
Tyro, AR, U.S.A. 63 E4 33 50N 91 43W
Tyro, KS, U.S.A. 74 D8 37 2N 95 49W
Tyrone, NM, U.S.A. 88 E2 32 47N 108 22W
Tyrone, OK, U.S.A. 93 B2 36 57N 101 4W
Tyrone, PA, U.S.A. 95 D4 40 40N 78 14W
Tyronza, AR, U.S.A. 63 C5 35 29N 90 22W
Tyrrell County ☆, NC, U.S.A. 90 C9 35 50N 76 10W
Tyson, VT, U.S.A. 86 C2 43 27N 72 44W
Tysons Corner, VA, U.S.A. 119 B2 38 55N 77 13W
Tzendales, Chiapas, Mexico 222 C5 16 19N 91 7W
Tzimol, Chiapas, Mexico 222 C4 16 16N 92 16W
Tzintzuntzán, Michoacan, Mexico 218 C6 19 38N 101 35W
Tziscao, Chiapas, Mexico 222 C5 16 10N 91 42W
Tzitzio, Michoacan, Mexico 219 C7 19 34N 100 55W
Tzucacab, Yucatán, Mexico 223 B4 20 4N 89 3W

U

U.L. Bend Nat. Wildlife Refuge ⌂, MT, U.S.A. 83 C10 47 40N 107 55W
U.S.A. = United States of America ■, N. Amer. 52 C7 37 0N 96 0W
U.S. Air Force Academy, CO, U.S.A. 66 D6 38 59N 104 51W
U.S.S. Arizona Memorial ⌂, U.S.A. 69 K14 21 22N 157 57W
U.S. Virgin Is. ☒, W. Indies 105 G18 18 20N 65 0W
Uayma, Yucatán, Mexico 223 B5 20 44N 88 19W
Ubly, MI, U.S.A. 79 F9 43 42N 82 56W
Ucluelet, B.C., Canada 186 G9 48 57N 125 32W
Ucon, ID, U.S.A. 70 F7 43 36N 111 58W
Ucross, WY, U.S.A. 104 B6 44 34N 106 32W
Ucú, Yucatán, Mexico 223 A4 21 2N 89 45W
Ucum, Quintana Roo, Mexico 223 C4 19 15N 89 20W
Udall, KS, U.S.A. 74 D6 37 23N 97 7W
Udell, IA, U.S.A. 73 E6 40 47N 92 45W
Uehling, NE, U.S.A. 84 C9 41 44N 96 30W
Uhrichsville, OH, U.S.A. 92 C5 40 24N 81 21W
Uinta →, UT, U.S.A. 100 C6 40 14N 109 51W
Uinta County ☆, WY, U.S.A. 104 E2 41 15N 110 30W
Uinta Mts., UT, U.S.A. 100 C5 40 45N 110 30W
Uinta Nat. Forest, UT, U.S.A. 100 C4 40 32N 111 39W
Uintah and Ouray Indian Reservation, UT, U.S.A. 100 C5 40 15N 110 20W
Uintah County ☆, UT, U.S.A. 100 C6 40 20N 109 30W
Uivuk, C., Nfld. & L., Canada 175 B5 58 29N 62 34W
Ukiah, CA, U.S.A. 64 D3 39 9N 123 13W
Ukiah, OR, U.S.A. 94 B7 45 8N 118 56W
Ulak I., AK, U.S.A. 61 L3 51 22N 178 57W
Ulen, MN, U.S.A. 80 C2 47 5N 96 16W
Ullin, IL, U.S.A. 71 F4 37 17N 89 11W
Ulster County ☆, NY, U.S.A. 89 D6 41 50N 74 15W
Ultima Agua, Baja Calif. S., Mexico 211 H7 25 33N 111 17W
Ulupalakua Ranch, HI, U.S.A. 69 C5 20 39N 156 24W
Ulysses, KS, U.S.A. 74 D2 37 35N 101 22W
Ulysses, NE, U.S.A. 84 C8 41 4N 97 12W
Ulysses, PA, U.S.A. 95 C5 41 54N 77 46W
Ulysses S. Grant Nat. Historic Site ⌂, MO, U.S.A. 82 C6 38 33N 90 28W
Umán, Yucatán, Mexico 223 B4 20 53N 89 45W
Umatac, Guam 105 b 13 18N 144 39 E
Umatilla, OR, U.S.A. 94 B6 45 55N 119 21W
Umatilla →, OR, U.S.A. 94 B6 45 55N 119 20W
Umatilla, L., WA, U.S.A. 101 E6 45 53N 119 40W
Umatilla County ☆, OR, U.S.A. 94 B7 45 40N 118 45W
Umatilla Indian Reservation, OR, U.S.A. 94 B7 45 41N 118 31W
Umatilla Nat. Forest, OR, U.S.A. 94 C7 45 38N 118 11W
Umbagog L., NH, U.S.A. 86 B3 44 46N 71 3W
Umbarger, TX, U.S.A. 98 C5 34 57N 102 7W
Umfreville L., Ont., Canada 180 B2 50 18N 94 45W
Umiat, AK, U.S.A. 61 B9 69 22N 152 8W
Umingmaktok, Nunavut, Canada 190 D4 67 41N 107 56W
Umiujaq, Qué., Canada 175 B2 56 33N 76 33W
Umnak I., AK, U.S.A. 61 K5 53 15N 168 20W
Umpire, AR, U.S.A. 63 D1 34 17N 94 3W
Umpqua, OR, U.S.A. 94 D2 43 22N 123 28W
Umpqua →, OR, U.S.A. 94 D1 43 40N 124 12W
Umpqua Nat. Forest, OR, U.S.A. 94 D3 43 10N 122 40W
Uña de Gato, Nuevo León, Mexico 214 D4 26 13N 100 14W
Unadilla, GA, U.S.A. 68 D3 32 16N 83 44W
Unadilla, NY, U.S.A. 89 C5 42 20N 75 19W
Unadilla, NE, U.S.A. 84 D9 40 41N 96 16W
Unadilla →, NY, U.S.A. 89 C5 42 20N 75 25W
Unalakleet, AK, U.S.A. 61 E7 63 52N 160 47W
Unalaska, AK, U.S.A. 61 K6 53 53N 166 32W
Unalaska I., AK, U.S.A. 61 K6 53 35N 166 50W
Uncompahgre →, CO, U.S.A. 66 D2 38 45N 108 6W
Uncompahgre Nat. Forest, CO, U.S.A. 66 D2 38 30N 108 30W
Uncompahgre Peak, CO, U.S.A. 66 D3 38 4N 107 28W
Uncompahgre Plateau, CO, U.S.A. 66 D2 38 20N 108 15W
Underhill, VT, U.S.A. 86 B2 44 33N 72 56W
Underhill, L., Orlando, U.S.A. 115 A3 28 32N 81 20W
Underwood, IA, U.S.A. 73 D3 41 23N 95 41W
Underwood, ND, U.S.A. 91 C4 47 27N 101 9W
Unga I., AK, U.S.A. 61 J7 55 15N 160 40W
Ungava, Pén. d', Qué., Canada 175 B3 60 0N 74 0W
Ungava B., Nfld. & L., Canada 175 B4 59 30N 67 30W
Unicoi, TN, U.S.A. 97 D10 36 12N 82 21W
Unicoi County ☆, TN, U.S.A. 97 D10 36 9N 82 25W
Unidad Santa Fe, Distrito Federal, Mexico 225 B2 19 23N 99 13W
Unidos Venceremos, Durango, Mexico 216 D5 23 58N 105 28W
Unimak I., AK, U.S.A. 61 J7 54 45N 164 0W
Unimak Pass, AK, U.S.A. 61 J6 54 15N 164 30W
Union, AL, U.S.A. 60 D3 32 59N 87 54W
Union, IA, U.S.A. 73 C5 42 15N 93 4W
Union, ME, U.S.A. 76 D4 44 13N 69 17W
Union, MS, U.S.A. 81 D4 32 34N 89 7W
Union, MO, U.S.A. 82 C5 38 27N 91 0W
Union, NJ, U.S.A. 87 B2 40 41N 74 15W
Union, NE, U.S.A. 84 D10 40 49N 95 55W
Union, OR, U.S.A. 94 B8 45 13N 117 52W
Union, SC, U.S.A. 90 D4 34 43N 81 37W
Union, WV, U.S.A. 102 D4 37 36N 80 33W
Union, WA, U.S.A. 101 C2 47 22N 123 6W
Union Bay, B.C., Canada 186 F10 49 35N 124 53W
Union Bridge, MD, U.S.A. 77 A3 39 34N 77 11W
Union Center, SD, U.S.A. 91 F3 44 34N 102 40W
Union Center, WI, U.S.A. 103 E3 43 41N 90 16W
Union Church, MS, U.S.A. 81 E3 31 41N 90 47W
Union City, CA, U.S.A. 64 F4 37 36N 122 1W
Union City, GA, U.S.A. 68 C2 33 35N 84 33W
Union City, IN, U.S.A. 72 C6 40 12N 84 49W
Union City, MI, U.S.A. 79 G6 42 4N 85 8W
Union City, NJ, U.S.A. 87 B2 40 45N 74 2W
Union City, OH, U.S.A. 92 C2 40 12N 84 48W
Union City, OK, U.S.A. 93 C6 35 23N 97 57W
Union City, PA, U.S.A. 95 C3 41 54N 79 51W
Union City, TN, U.S.A. 96 D3 36 26N 89 3W
Union County ☆, AR, U.S.A. 63 E3 33 12N 92 40W
Union County ☆, FL, U.S.A. 67 A6 30 0N 82 25W
Union County ☆, GA, U.S.A. 68 B3 34 50N 84 0W
Union County ☆, IL, U.S.A. 71 F4 37 30N 89 15W
Union County ☆, IN, U.S.A. 72 D6 39 35N 84 55W
Union County ☆, IA, U.S.A. 73 E4 41 0N 94 15W
Union County ☆, KY, U.S.A. 96 C5 37 40N 87 55W
Union County ☆, MS, U.S.A. 81 B5 34 29N 89 0W
Union County ☆, NC, U.S.A. 90 D5 35 0N 80 40W
Union County ☆, NJ, U.S.A. 87 B2 40 40N 74 20W
Union County ☆, NM, U.S.A. 88 A7 36 30N 103 30W
Union County ☆, OH, U.S.A. 92 C3 40 14N 83 22W
Union County ☆, OR, U.S.A. 94 B8 45 15N 118 0W
Union County ☆, PA, U.S.A. 95 D5 41 0N 77 0W
Union County ☆, SC, U.S.A. 90 D4 34 45N 81 45W
Union County ☆, SD, U.S.A. 91 H9 42 51N 96 45W
Union County ☆, TN, U.S.A. 97 D9 36 15N 83 48W
Union Creek, OR, U.S.A. 94 E3 42 55N 122 27W
Union Dale, PA, U.S.A. 95 C7 41 43N 75 30W
Unión de San Antonio, Jalisco, Mexico 218 A5 21 6N 102 1W
Unión de Tula, Jalisco, Mexico 218 C3 19 58N 104 16W
Union Flat Cr. →, U.S.A. 101 D8 46 49N 118 0W
Union Gap, WA, U.S.A. 101 D5 46 33N 120 28W
Union Grove, WI, U.S.A. 103 F5 42 41N 88 3W
Unión Hidalgo, Oaxaca, Mexico 221 H6 16 30N 94 51W
Union Hills, Phoenix, U.S.A. 116 A2 33 43N 112 3W
Union I., B.C., Canada 186 F7 50 0N 127 16W
Unión Juárez, Chiapas, Mexico 222 D4 15 4N 92 5W
Union L., NJ, U.S.A. 87 C1 39 24N 75 3W
Union Parish ☆, LA, U.S.A. 75 B3 32 47N 92 24W
Union Park, FL, U.S.A. 67 C7 28 34N 81 17W
Union Point, GA, U.S.A. 68 C3 33 37N 83 4W
Union Port, NY, U.S.A. 114 B3 40 48N 73 51W
Union Slough Nat. Wildlife Refuge ⌂, IA, U.S.A. 73 B4 43 17N 94 7W
Union Springs, AL, U.S.A. 60 D5 32 9N 85 43W
Union Springs, NY, U.S.A. 89 C4 42 51N 76 42W
Union Star, MO, U.S.A. 82 B2 39 59N 94 36W
Union Valley Res., CA, U.S.A. 64 E6 38 52N 120 26W
Unión y Progreso, Durango, Mexico 217 B6 25 14N 104 59W
Uniondale, IN, U.S.A. 72 C5 40 50N 85 15W
Uniontown, AL, U.S.A. 60 D3 32 27N 87 31W
Uniontown, KS, U.S.A. 74 D9 37 51N 94 59W
Uniontown, KY, U.S.A. 96 C5 37 47N 87 56W
Uniontown, MD, U.S.A. 77 A3 39 36N 77 7W
Uniontown, PA, U.S.A. 95 E3 39 54N 79 44W
Uniontown, WA, U.S.A. 101 D8 46 32N 117 5W
Unionville, CT, U.S.A. 78 C2 41 45N 72 53W
Unionville, GA, U.S.A. 68 E3 31 26N 83 30W
Unionville, IA, U.S.A. 73 E6 40 49N 92 42W
Unionville, MD, U.S.A. 77 A3 39 28N 77 12W
Unionville, MI, U.S.A. 79 F8 43 39N 83 28W
Unionville, MO, U.S.A. 82 A3 40 29N 93 1W
Unionville, NY, U.S.A. 87 A2 41 18N 74 34W
Unionville, NV, U.S.A. 85 B2 40 27N 118 8W
Unionville, PA, U.S.A. 77 A5 39 54N 75 44W
Unionville, PA, U.S.A. 95 D5 40 55N 77 53W
Unionville, VA, U.S.A. 102 C7 38 16N 77 58W
Uniopolis, OH, U.S.A. 92 C2 40 36N 84 5W
United States of America ■, N. Amer. 52 C7 37 0N 96 0W
United States Range, N.W.T., Canada 190 A12 82 25N 68 0W
Unity, Sask., Canada 182 C2 52 30N 109 5W
Unity, ME, U.S.A. 76 D4 44 37N 69 20W
Unity, MD, U.S.A. 77 A3 39 13N 77 5W
Unity, OR, U.S.A. 94 C7 44 26N 118 12W
Unity, WI, U.S.A. 103 D3 44 51N 90 19W
Universal City, TX, U.S.A. 99 H9 29 32N 98 17W
University City, MO, U.S.A. 117 B1 38 39N 90 18W
University City, MO, U.S.A. 82 C6 38 40N 90 20W
University City, San Diego, U.S.A. 117 A1 32 51N 117 12W
University Gardens, NY, U.S.A. 114 B4 40 46N 73 43W
University Hill, Vancouver, Canada 193 B1 49 16N 123 15W
University Park, Dallas-Fort Worth, U.S.A. 109 A5 32 51N 96 48W
University Park, IL, U.S.A. 71 B6 41 25N 87 44W
University Park, MD, U.S.A. 119 B4 38 58N 76 56W
University Park, NM, U.S.A. 88 E4 32 17N 106 45W
University Place, WA, U.S.A. 101 C3 47 14N 122 33W
Upatoi Cr. →, GA, U.S.A. 68 D2 32 22N 84 58W
Upernavik Kujalleq, Greenland 190 C14 72 10N 55 30W
Upham, ND, U.S.A. 91 B5 48 35N 100 44W
Upland, CA, U.S.A. 65 J9 34 6N 117 39W
Upland, IN, U.S.A. 72 C5 40 28N 85 30W
Upland, NE, U.S.A. 84 D7 40 19N 98 54W
Upolu Pt., HI, U.S.A. 69 C6 20 16N 155 52W
Upper Alkali L., CA, U.S.A. 64 B6 41 47N 120 8W
Upper Arlington, OH, U.S.A. 92 C3 40 0N 83 4W
Upper Arrow L., B.C., Canada 187 E17 50 30N 117 50W
Upper B., U.S.A. 89 E6 40 40N 74 3W
Upper Blackville, N.B., Canada 173 G4 46 39N 65 52W
Upper Campbell L., B.C., Canada 186 F9 49 55N 125 39W
Upper Crossroads, MD, U.S.A. 77 A4 39 33N 76 29W
Upper Darby, PA, U.S.A. 87 C1 39 55N 75 16W
Upper Delaware Scenic & Recr. River ⌂, NY, U.S.A. 89 D5 41 40N 75 3W
Upper Duck Island, Ont., Canada 192 A2 45 28N 75 37W
Upper Goose L., Ont., Canada 180 A4 51 43N 92 43W
Upper Humber →, Nfld. & L., Canada 174 C3 49 11N 57 28W
Upper Iowa →, IA, U.S.A. 73 B7 43 29N 91 14W
Upper Klamath L., OR, U.S.A. 94 E4 42 25N 121 55W
Upper Lake, CA, U.S.A. 64 D4 39 10N 122 54W
Upper Lillooet Park ⌂, B.C., Canada 186 E11 50 39N 123 36W
Upper Manitou L., Ont., Canada 180 C4 49 24N 92 48W
Upper Marlboro, MD, U.S.A. 77 B4 38 49N 76 45W
Upper Mississippi River Nat. Wildlife & Fish Refuge ⌂, IA, U.S.A. 73 C7 42 57N 91 9W
Upper Missouri Breaks Nat. Monument ⌂, MT, U.S.A. 83 C8 47 50N 109 55W
Upper Musquodoboit, N.S., Canada 173 H7 45 10N 62 58W
Upper New York B. = Upper B., U.S.A. 89 E6 40 40N 74 3W
Upper Ouachita Nat. Wildlife Refuge ⌂, LA, U.S.A. 75 B3 32 57N 92 8W
Upper Peoria L., IL, U.S.A. 71 C4 40 55N 89 27W
Upper Red L., MN, U.S.A. 80 B4 48 8N 94 45W
Upper St. Clair, Pittsburgh, U.S.A. 116 C1 40 20N 80 5W
Upper San Leandro Res., San Francisco, U.S.A. 118 B4 37 45N 122 5W
Upper Sandusky, OH, U.S.A. 92 C3 40 50N 83 17W
Upper Seymour Prov. Park ⌂, Alta., Canada 185 J7 49 5N 113 52W
Upper Sioux Indian Reservation, MN, U.S.A. 80 F3 44 46N 95 31W
Upper Souris Nat. Wildlife Refuge ⌂, ND, U.S.A. 91 B4 48 35N 101 38W
Upper Stewiacke, N.S., Canada 173 H7 45 13N 63 0W
Upper Tract, WV, U.S.A. 102 C5 38 47N 79 17W
Upperville, VA, U.S.A. 77 B3 39 0N 77 53W
Upsala, Ont., Canada 180 C6 49 3N 90 28W
Upshur County ☆, TX, U.S.A. 99 E13 32 44N 94 57W
Upshur County ☆, WV, U.S.A. 102 C4 39 0N 80 15W
Upson, WI, U.S.A. 103 B3 46 22N 90 24W
Upson County ☆, GA, U.S.A. 68 D2 32 50N 84 20W
Upton, Qué., Canada 177 F10 45 39N 72 41W
Upton, KY, U.S.A. 97 C7 37 28N 85 54W
Upton, ME, U.S.A. 76 D2 44 42N 71 1W
Upton, MA, U.S.A. 78 B3 42 11N 71 37W
Upton, WY, U.S.A. 104 B8 44 6N 104 38W
Upton County ☆, TX, U.S.A. 98 F6 31 15N 102 0W
Uptown, Chicago, U.S.A. 108 B2 41 58N 87 40W
Uqsuqtuuq = Gjoa Haven, Nunavut, Canada 190 D6 68 38N 95 53W
Urania, LA, U.S.A. 75 C3 31 52N 92 18W
Uranium City, Sask., Canada 189 E11 59 34N 108 37W
Uravan, CO, U.S.A. 66 D2 38 22N 108 44W
Urbana, AR, U.S.A. 63 E3 33 10N 92 27W
Urbana, IL, U.S.A. 71 C5 40 7N 88 12W
Urbana, IA, U.S.A. 73 C7 42 13N 91 52W
Urbana, MO, U.S.A. 82 D3 37 51N 93 10W
Urbana, OH, U.S.A. 92 C3 40 7N 83 45W
Urbandale, IA, U.S.A. 73 D5 41 38N 93 43W
Urbank, MN, U.S.A. 80 D3 46 8N 95 31W
Ures, Sonora, Mexico 212 D5 29 26N 110 24W
Uriah, AL, U.S.A. 60 E3 31 18N 87 30W
Uriangato, Guanajuato, Mexico 219 B6 20 9N 101 11W
Urich, MO, U.S.A. 82 C2 38 28N 94 2W
Urique, Chihuahua, Mexico 213 F8 27 13N 107 55W
Urique →, Chihuahua, Mexico 213 G8 26 29N 107 58W
Uroyan, Montanas de, Puerto Rico 105 G16 18 12N 67 0W
Ursa, IL, U.S.A. 71 C2 40 4N 91 22W
Ursina, PA, U.S.A. 77 A1 39 49N 79 20W
Ursine, NV, U.S.A. 85 E6 37 59N 114 13W
Ursula Chan., B.C., Canada 186 B6 53 25N 128 55W
Ursulo Galván, Veracruz, Mexico 220 E4 19 24N 96 21W
Uruachic, Chihuahua, Mexico 213 F7 27 52N 108 14W
Uruapan, Michoacan, Mexico 218 C5 19 24N 102 3W
Usher, FL, U.S.A. 67 B6 29 24N 82 49W
Usk, B.C., Canada 189 F7 54 38N 128 26W
Usk, WA, U.S.A. 101 B8 48 19N 117 17W
Usumacinta, Tabasco, Mexico 222 B5 17 33N 91 29W
Usumacinta →, Mexico 222 A4 18 24N 92 38W
Utah ☐, U.S.A. 100 D4 39 20N 111 30W
Utah County ☆, UT, U.S.A. 100 C4 40 10N 111 50W
Utah L., UT, U.S.A. 100 C4 40 12N 111 48W
Utah Test Range North, UT, U.S.A. 100 B2 41 7N 113 11W
Utah Test Range South, UT, U.S.A. 100 C2 40 30N 113 50W
Ute, IA, U.S.A. 73 C3 42 3N 95 42W
Ute Creek →, NM, U.S.A. 88 B7 35 21N 103 50W
Ute L., NM, U.S.A. 88 B7 35 21N 103 27W
Ute Mountain Indian Reservation, CO, U.S.A. 66 E2 37 11N 108 41W
Ute Park, NM, U.S.A. 88 A5 36 34N 105 6W
Utica, KS, U.S.A. 74 C3 38 39N 100 10W
Utica, MS, U.S.A. 81 D3 32 7N 90 37W
Utica, NY, U.S.A. 89 B5 43 6N 75 14W
Utica, NE, U.S.A. 84 D8 40 54N 97 21W
Utica, OH, U.S.A. 92 C4 40 14N 82 27W
Utica, SD, U.S.A. 91 H8 42 59N 97 30W
Utikuma L., Alta., Canada 184 C5 55 50N 115 30W
Utleyville, CO, U.S.A. 66 E7 37 17N 103 4W
Utopia, TX, U.S.A. 99 H8 29 37N 99 32W
Utuado, Puerto Rico 105 G16 18 16N 66 42W
Uummannaq, Greenland 190 C15 70 58N 52 0W
Uvada, UT, U.S.A. 100 F1 37 43N 114 3W
Uvalda, GA, U.S.A. 68 D4 32 2N 82 31W
Uvalde, TX, U.S.A. 99 H8 29 13N 99 47W
Uvalde County ☆, TX, U.S.A. 99 H8 29 30N 99 43W
Uvas, Sierra de las, NM, U.S.A. 88 E3 32 29N 107 12W
Uwharrie →, NC, U.S.A. 90 C5 35 23N 80 3W
Uwharrie Nat. Forest, NC, U.S.A. 90 C6 35 20N 80 0W
Uxbridge, Ont., Canada 178 C7 44 6N 79 7W
Uxbridge, MA, U.S.A. 78 B3 42 5N 71 38W
Uxmal, Yucatán, Mexico 223 B4 20 22N 89 46W
Uxpanapa →, Veracruz, Mexico 221 G6 17 58N 94 29W
Uyak, AK, U.S.A. 61 H9 57 38N 154 0W

V

Vaca Pinta, Cerro la, Michoacan, Mexico 218 D5 18 43N 102 58W
Vacas, Arroyo de las →, Coahuila, Mexico 214 A4 29 19N 100 54W
Vacaville, CA, U.S.A. 64 E5 38 21N 121 59W
Vacherie, LA, U.S.A. 75 E5 30 0N 90 48W
Vachon →, Qué., Canada 175 B3 59 58N 72 24W
Vader, WA, U.S.A. 101 D3 46 24N 122 58W
Vadnais, L., Minneapolis-St. Paul, U.S.A. 113 A3 45 3N 93 5W
Vadnais Heights, Minneapolis-St. Paul, U.S.A. 113 A3 45 3N 93 4W
Vado, NM, U.S.A. 88 E4 32 7N 106 40W
Vado Hondo, Sinaloa, Mexico 216 D4 23 52N 106 15W
Vaiden, MS, U.S.A. 81 C4 33 20N 89 45W
Vail, AZ, U.S.A. 62 E5 32 3N 110 43W
Vail, CO, U.S.A. 66 C4 39 40N 106 20W
Vail, IA, U.S.A. 73 C3 42 4N 95 12W
Val-Alain, Qué., Canada 177 E11 46 24N 71 45W
Val-Barrette, Qué., Canada 176 E7 46 30N 75 21W
Val-Brillant, Qué., Canada 172 E2 48 32N 67 33W
Val Caron, Ont., Canada 178 A5 46 37N 81 1W
Val-des-Bois, Qué., Canada 176 F7 45 54N 75 35W
Val-d'Espoir, Qué., Canada 172 E5 48 31N 64 24W
Val-d'Or, Qué., Canada 176 C5 48 7N 77 47W
Val Marie, Sask., Canada 182 F4 49 15N 107 45W
Val Rita, Ont., Canada 181 C14 49 27N 82 33W
Val Tétreault, Qué., Canada 192 A1 45 26N 75 45W
Val Verde County ☆, TX, U.S.A. 98 H6 30 0N 101 0W
Valatie, NY, U.S.A. 89 C7 42 25N 73 41W
Valcourt, Qué., Canada 177 F10 45 29N 72 18W
Valders, WI, U.S.A. 103 D6 44 4N 87 53W
Valdes I., B.C., Canada 187 F11 49 4N 123 39W
Valdez, AK, U.S.A. 61 F11 61 7N 146 16W
Valdez, NM, U.S.A. 88 A5 36 32N 105 35W
Valdez-Cordova ☆, AK, U.S.A. 61 F11 61 30N 144 30W
Valdosta, GA, U.S.A. 68 F3 30 50N 83 17W
Vale, OR, U.S.A. 94 D8 43 59N 117 15W
Vale, SD, U.S.A. 91 F2 44 37N 103 24W
Vale, VA, U.S.A. 119 B1 38 55N 77 20W
Valemount, B.C., Canada 187 C15 52 50N 119 15W
Valencia, NM, U.S.A. 88 C4 34 48N 106 43W
Valencia County ☆, NM, U.S.A. 88 C4 34 45N 107 0W
Valentin, Barra, Guerrero, Mexico 219 E6 17 28N 101 15W
Valentine, AZ, U.S.A. 62 B2 35 23N 113 40W
Valentine, NE, U.S.A. 84 B5 42 52N 100 33W
Valentine, TX, U.S.A. 98 G3 30 35N 104 30W
Valentine Nat. Wildlife Refuge ⌂, NE, U.S.A. 84 B5 42 31N 100 36W
Valentines, VA, U.S.A. 102 E7 36 35N 77 50W
Valeria, IA, U.S.A. 73 D5 41 44N 93 20W
Valerio, Chihuahua, Mexico 213 F9 27 39N 106 6W
Válgame Dios, Sinaloa, Mexico 216 A3 26 7N 107 32W
Valhalla Park ⌂, B.C., Canada 187 F17 49 52N 117 34W
Valier, IL, U.S.A. 71 E4 38 1N 89 3W
Valier, MT, U.S.A. 83 B5 48 18N 112 16W
Valladolid, Yucatán, Mexico 223 B5 20 41N 88 12W
Valle, Sonora, Mexico 212 C4 30 50N 111 16W
Valle Alto, Monterrey, Mexico 224 C2 25 34N 100 15W
Valle Colombia, Coahuila, Mexico 214 B2 28 21N 102 17W
Valle de Allende, Chihuahua, Mexico 213 G10 26 56N 105 24W
Valle de Bravo, México, Mexico 219 C7 19 11N 100 8W
Valle de Guadalupe, Jalisco, Mexico 218 B5 21 0N 102 37W
Valle de Juárez, Jalisco, Mexico 218 C5 19 55N 102 53W
Valle de Santiago, Guanajuato, Mexico 219 B6 20 23N 101 12W
Valle de Zaragoza, Chihuahua, Mexico 213 F10 27 25N 105 50W
Valle del Rosario, Chihuahua, Mexico 213 F9 27 19N 106 18W
Valle Hermosa, Quintana Roo, Mexico 223 C5 19 11N 88 32W
Valle Hermoso, Tamaulipas, Mexico 214 E7 25 41N 97 48W
Valle Hermoso, Tamaulipas, Mexico 215 G5 23 40N 99 45W
Valle las Palmas, Baja Calif., Mexico 210 A2 32 23N 116 47W
Valle Nacional, Oaxaca, Mexico 221 G4 17 47N 96 18W
Valle Verde, Sonora, Mexico 212 E4 28 44N 111 44W
Vallecillos, Nuevo León, Mexico 214 D4 26 41N 100 0W
Vallecito, CO, U.S.A. 66 E3 37 23N 107 35W
Vallecito Res., CO, U.S.A. 66 E3 37 23N 107 34W
Vallecitos, Guerrero, Mexico 219 E6 17 56N 101 20W
Vallée-Jonction, Qué., Canada 177 E12 46 22N 70 55W
Vallejo, CA, U.S.A. 64 E4 38 7N 122 14W
Valles Mines, MO, U.S.A. 82 C6 38 2N 90 30W
Valley, AL, U.S.A. 60 D5 32 49N 85 11W
Valley, NE, U.S.A. 84 C9 41 19N 96 21W
Valley, WA, U.S.A. 101 B8 48 11N 117 44W
Valley, WY, U.S.A. 104 B3 44 9N 109 36W
Valley Center, CA, U.S.A. 65 K9 33 13N 117 2W
Valley Center, KS, U.S.A. 74 D6 37 50N 97 22W
Valley City, ND, U.S.A. 91 D8 46 55N 98 0W
Valley County ☆, ID, U.S.A. 70 E3 44 45N 115 30W
Valley County ☆, MT, U.S.A. 83 B11 48 35N 106 30W
Valley County ☆, NE, U.S.A. 84 C7 41 30N 99 0W
Valley Falls, KS, U.S.A. 74 B8 39 21N 95 28W
Valley Falls, NY, U.S.A. 78 B1 42 54N 73 34W
Valley Falls, NY, U.S.A. 89 C7 42 54N 73 34W
Valley Falls, OR, U.S.A. 94 E5 42 29N 120 17W
Valley Falls, RI, U.S.A. 78 C3 41 54N 71 24W
Valley Forge Nat. Historical Park ⌂, PA, U.S.A. 95 D7 40 6N 75 27W
Valley Grove, WV, U.S.A. 102 A4 40 6N 80 34W
Valley Head, AL, U.S.A. 60 B5 34 34N 85 37W
Valley Head, WV, U.S.A. 102 C4 38 33N 80 2W
Valley Junction = West Des Moines, IA, U.S.A. 73 D5 41 35N 93 43W
Valley Lee, MD, U.S.A. 77 B4 38 12N 76 31W
Valley Mills, TX, U.S.A. 99 F10 31 40N 97 28W
Valley of Fire State Park ⌂, NV, U.S.A. 85 F6 36 26N 114 29W
Valley Park, MS, U.S.A. 81 D3 32 38N 90 52W
Valley Park, MO, U.S.A. 82 C6 38 33N 90 29W
Valley Springs, CA, U.S.A. 64 E6 38 12N 120 50W
Valley Station, KY, U.S.A. 97 B7 38 6N 85 52W
Valley Stream, NY, U.S.A. 87 B3 40 39N 73 42W
Valley Stream State Park ⌂, NY, U.S.A. 114 B4 40 40N 73 41W
Valley View, Cleveland, U.S.A. 107 B2 41 23N 81 36W
Valley View, PA, U.S.A. 95 D6 40 39N 76 33W
Valley View, TX, U.S.A. 99 D10 33 29N 97 10W
Valleyview, Alta., Canada 184 C3 55 5N 117 17W
Valliant, OK, U.S.A. 93 E8 34 0N 95 6W
Valmeyer, IL, U.S.A. 71 E3 38 18N 90 19W
Valmora, NM, U.S.A. 88 B6 35 49N 104 55W
Valmy, NV, U.S.A. 85 B3 40 48N 117 8W
Valois, Baie de, Montréal, Canada 192 B2 45 26N 73 47W
Valora, Ont., Canada 180 C5 49 42N 91 13W
Valparaíso, Zacatecas, Mexico 217 E7 22 46N 103 34W
Valparaiso, FL, U.S.A. 67 A2 30 29N 86 30W
Valparaiso, IN, U.S.A. 72 B3 41 28N 87 4W
Valparaiso, NE, U.S.A. 84 C9 41 5N 96 50W
Valsequillo, Presa, Puebla, Mexico 221 F2 18 55N 98 10W
Valtierrilla, Guanajuato, Mexico 219 B6 20 30N 101 10W
Van, TX, U.S.A. 99 E12 32 31N 95 38W
Van Alstyne, TX, U.S.A. 99 D11 33 25N 96 35W
Van Anda, B.C., Canada 186 F10 49 46N 124 33W
Van Bruyssel, Qué., Canada 177 D10 47 56N 72 9W
Van Buren = Kettering, OH, U.S.A. 92 D2 39 41N 84 10W
Van Buren, N.B., Canada 173 F2 47 10N 67 55W
Van Buren, AR, U.S.A. 63 C1 35 26N 94 21W
Van Buren, IN, U.S.A. 72 C5 40 37N 85 30W
Van Buren, ME, U.S.A. 76 A6 47 10N 67 58W
Van Buren, MO, U.S.A. 82 E5 37 0N 91 1W
Van Buren, OH, U.S.A. 92 B3 41 8N 83 39W
Van Buren County ☆, AR, U.S.A. 63 C3 35 36N 92 28W
Van Buren County ☆, IA, U.S.A. 73 E7 40 45N 91 55W
Van Buren County ☆, MI, U.S.A. 79 G6 42 15N 86 0W
Van Buren County ☆, TN, U.S.A. 97 E7 35 45N 85 28W
Van Horn, TX, U.S.A. 98 F3 31 3N 104 50W
Van Horne, IA, U.S.A. 73 C6 42 1N 92 5W
Van Meter, IA, U.S.A. 73 D5 41 32N 93 57W
Van Nuys, Los Angeles, U.S.A. 111 A2 34 11N 118 26W
Van Nuys ✕, Los Angeles, U.S.A. 111 A2 34 12N 118 29W
Van Tassell, WY, U.S.A. 104 D8 42 40N 104 5W
Van Vleet, MS, U.S.A. 81 C5 33 59N 88 54W
Van Wert, IA, U.S.A. 73 E5 40 52N 93 48W
Van Wert, OH, U.S.A. 92 C2 40 52N 84 35W
Van Wert County ☆, OH, U.S.A. 92 C2 40 52N 84 35W
Van Zandt County ☆, TX, U.S.A. 99 E12 32 33N 95 52W
Vance County ☆, NC, U.S.A. 90 B7 36 15N 78 20W
Vanceboro, ME, U.S.A. 76 C6 45 34N 67 26W
Vanceboro, NC, U.S.A. 90 C8 35 19N 77 9W
Vanceburg, KY, U.S.A. 97 B9 38 36N 83 19W
Vancleave, MS, U.S.A. 81 F5 30 33N 88 42W
Vancleve, KY, U.S.A. 97 C9 37 38N 83 25W
Vancorum, CO, U.S.A. 66 D2 38 14N 108 36W
Vancourt, TX, U.S.A. 98 F7 31 21N 100 11W
Vancouver, B.C., Canada 187 F11 49 15N 123 7W
Vancouver, Portland, U.S.A. 116 A2 45 38N 122 39W
Vancouver, WA, U.S.A. 101 E3 45 38N 122 40W
Vancouver, Mt., AK, U.S.A. 61 F13 60 20N 139 41W
Vancouver Harbour, B.C., Canada 193 B2 49 18N 123 6W

Vancouver I., *B.C., Canada* **186 F9** 49 50N 126 0W
Vancouver I. Ranges, *B.C., Canada* **186 F9** 49 30N 125 40W
Vancouver International ✕ (YVR), *B.C., Canada* **186 G11** 49 10N 123 10W
Vandalia, *IL, U.S.A.* **71 E4** 38 58N 89 6W
Vandalia, *MO, U.S.A.* **82 B5** 39 19N 91 29W
Vandalia, *OH, U.S.A.* **92 D2** 39 54N 84 12W
Vandemere, *NC, U.S.A.* **90 C9** 35 11N 76 41W
Vandenberg Air Force Base, *CA, U.S.A.* **65 J6** 34 47N 120 32W
Vandenberg Village, *CA, U.S.A.* **65 J6** 34 43N 120 28W
Vander, *NC, U.S.A.* **90 C7** 35 2N 78 48W
Vanderbilt, *MI, U.S.A.* **79 D7** 45 9N 84 40W
Vanderburgh County ☆, *IN, U.S.A.* **72 E3** 38 5N 87 35W
Vandercook Lake, *MI, U.S.A.* **79 G7** 42 12N 84 23W
Vandergrift, *PA, U.S.A.* **95 D3** 40 36N 79 34W
Vanderhoof, *B.C., Canada* **186 A10** 54 0N 124 0W
Vanderpool, *TX, U.S.A.* **99 H8** 29 45N 99 33W
Vandry, *Qué., Canada* **177 D9** 47 52N 73 34W
Vanduser, *MO, U.S.A.* **82 E7** 36 59N 89 42W
Vanguard, *Sask., Canada* **182 F4** 49 55N 107 20W
Vanier, *Ont., Canada* **179 B11** 45 27N 75 40W
Vanier, I., *Nunavut, Canada* **190 B5** 76 10N 103 15W
Vankleek Hill, *Ont., Canada* **179 B12** 45 32N 74 40W
Vanoss, *OK, U.S.A.* **93 D7** 34 46N 96 52W
Vanscoy, *Sask., Canada* **182 C5** 52 0N 106 59W
Vansittart I., *N.W.T., Canada* **191 D9** 65 50N 84 0W
Vapor, L. el, *Campeche, Mexico* **223 D2** 18 20N 91 50W
Varadito, Pta., *Sinaloa, Mexico* **216 C2** 24 48N 108 5W
Vardaman, *MS, U.S.A.* **81 C4** 33 53N 89 11W
Varejonal, *Sinaloa, Mexico* **216 B3** 25 6N 107 22W
Vargas I., *B.C., Canada* **186 F9** 49 11N 125 59W
Varina, *IA, U.S.A.* **73 C4** 42 40N 94 54W
Varna, *IL, U.S.A.* **71 B4** 41 2N 89 14W
Varnado, *LA, U.S.A.* **75 D6** 30 54N 89 50W
Varnville, *SC, U.S.A.* **90 F4** 32 51N 81 5W
Vars, *Ont., Canada* **176 F7** 45 21N 75 21W
Vasconcelos, *Veracruz, Mexico* **221 G6** 17 34N 94 44W
Vashon, *Seattle, U.S.A.* **118 D3** 47 26N 122 27W
Vashon Heights, *Seattle, U.S.A.* **118 C3** 47 30N 122 27W
Vashon Island, *Seattle, U.S.A.* **118 D3** 47 25N 122 28W
Vass, *NC, U.S.A.* **90 C6** 35 15N 79 17W
Vassan, *Qué., Canada* **176 C5** 48 14N 77 56W
Vassar, *Man., Canada* **183 F16** 49 10N 95 55W
Vassar, *KS, U.S.A.* **74 C8** 38 42N 95 37W
Vassar, *MI, U.S.A.* **79 F8** 43 22N 83 35W
Vatia, *Amer. Samoa* ..... **105 e** 14 15 S 170 40W
Vaudreuil-Dorion, *Qué., Canada* **177 F8** 45 23N 74 3W
Vaughan, *MS, U.S.A.* **81 D3** 32 48N 90 3W
Vaughn, *MT, U.S.A.* **83 C6** 47 33N 111 33W
Vaughn, *NM, U.S.A.* **88 C5** 34 36N 105 13W
Vauxhall, *Alta., Canada* **185 H8** 50 5N 112 9W
Vavenby, *B.C., Canada* **187 D15** 51 36N 119 43W
Veblen, *SD, U.S.A.* **91 E8** 45 52N 97 17W
Veedersburg, *IN, U.S.A.* **72 C3** 40 7N 87 16W
Vega, *TX, U.S.A.* **98 B5** 35 15N 102 26W
Vega, L. la, *Jalisco, Mexico* **218 B4** 20 36N 103 50W
Vega Alta, *Puerto Rico* **105 G16** 18 25N 66 20W
Vega Baja, *Puerto Rico* **105 G16** 18 27N 66 23W
Vega de Alatorre, *Veracruz, Mexico* **220 D4** 20 2N 96 38W
Vegas Verde = North Las Vegas, *NV, U.S.A.* **85 F5** 36 11N 115 7W
Vegreville, *Alta., Canada* **184 E8** 53 30N 112 5W
Veguita, *NM, U.S.A.* **88 C4** 34 31N 106 46W
Veinte de Noviembre, *Chiapas, Mexico* **222 C4** 16 32N 92 53W
Veinte Séptimos de Enero, *Baja Calif., Mexico* **210 B2** 31 7N 116 20W
Veintiocho de Agosto, *Coahuila, Mexico* **214 E2** 25 37N 102 6W
Velardeña, *Durango, Mexico* **217 B7** 25 4N 103 44W
Velasco Suárez, *Chiapas, Mexico* **222 C5** 16 49N 91 15W
Velma, *OK, U.S.A.* **93 D6** 34 28N 97 40W
Velva, *ND, U.S.A.* **91 B5** 48 4N 100 56W
Venado, *San Luis Potosí, Mexico* **215 H3** 22 56N 101 6W
Venados, I., *Sinaloa, Mexico* **216 D4** 23 15N 106 28W
Venango County ☆, *PA, U.S.A.* **95 C3** 41 20N 79 50W
Vencedores, *Durango, Mexico* **216 C5** 24 26N 105 43W
Venedocia, *OH, U.S.A.* **92 C2** 40 47N 84 28W
Veneta, *OR, U.S.A.* **94 C2** 44 3N 123 21W
Venetian Islands, *Miami, U.S.A.* **112 D3** 25 47N 80 9W
Venetie, *AK, U.S.A.* **61 C11** 67 1N 146 25W
Venice, *FL, U.S.A.* **67 D6** 27 6N 82 27W
Venice, *IL, U.S.A.* **117 B3** 38 40N 90 10W
Venice, *LA, U.S.A.* **75 E6** 29 17N 89 22W
Venice, *Los Angeles, U.S.A.* **111 C2** 33 59N 118 27W
Venleer, *TN, U.S.A.* **96 D5** 36 14N 87 27W
Venosta, *Qué., Canada* **176 F6** 45 52N 76 1W
Ventana, I., *Sinaloa, Mexico* **216 C2** 24 46N 108 3W
Ventnor City, *NJ, U.S.A.* **87 C2** 39 20N 74 29W
Venton, *MD, U.S.A.* **77 B5** 38 12N 75 18W
Ventura, *CA, U.S.A.* **65 J7** 34 17N 119 18W
Ventura County ☆, *CA, U.S.A.* **65 J7** 34 30N 119 0W
Venus, *FL, U.S.A.* **67 D7** 27 4N 81 22W
Venustiano Carranza, *Baja Calif., Mexico* **210 C3** 30 25N 115 53W
Venustiano Carranza, *Chiapas, Mexico* **222 B4** 17 20N 92 13W
Venustiano Carranza, *Chiapas, Mexico* **222 C4** 16 21N 92 33W
Venustiano Carranza, *Distrito Federal, Mexico* **225 B3** 19 25N 99 5W
Venustiano Carranza, *Jalisco, Mexico* **218 C4** 19 44N 103 47W
Venustiano Carranza, *Michoacan, Mexico* **218 B5** 20 5N 102 38W
Venustiano Carranza, Presa, *Coahuila, Mexico* **214 C4** 27 30N 100 37W
Venustino Carranza, *Puebla, Mexico* **220 D3** 20 32N 97 39W
Vera, *OK, U.S.A.* **93 B8** 36 27N 95 53W
Veracruz, *Veracruz, Mexico* **221 E4** 19 11N 96 8W
Veracruz □, *Veracruz, Mexico* **221 F4** 18 50N 96 10W
Veracruzano, Parque Nacional Sistema Arrecifal △, *Veracruz, Mexico* **221 E5** 19 10N 96 5W
Verbena, *AL, U.S.A.* **60 D4** 32 45N 86 31W
Verchères, *Qué., Canada* **177 F9** 45 47N 73 21W
Verda, *LA, U.S.A.* **75 C3** 31 42N 92 46W
Verde ➝, *Chihuahua, Mexico* **213 G8** 26 39N 107 11W
Verde ➝, *Jalisco, Mexico* **218 B4** 20 42N 103 14W
Verde ➝, *Oaxaca, Mexico* **221 J3** 15 59N 97 50W
Verde ➝, *AZ, U.S.A.* **62 D4** 33 33N 111 40W
Verde Grande, *Tamaulipas, Mexico* **215 F7** 24 6N 97 56W
Verdel, *NE, U.S.A.* **84 B7** 42 49N 98 12W
Verden, *OK, U.S.A.* **93 C5** 35 5N 98 5W
Verdi, *NV, U.S.A.* **85 C1** 39 31N 119 59W
Verdigre, *NE, U.S.A.* **84 B7** 42 36N 98 2W
Verdigre Cr. ➝, *NE, U.S.A.* **84 B7** 42 42N 98 3W
Verdigris ➝, *OK, U.S.A.* **93 C8** 35 48N 95 19W
Verdon, *NE, U.S.A.* **84 D10** 40 9N 95 43W
Verdun, *Montréal, Canada* **192 B3** 45 27N 73 35W
Veregin, *Sask., Canada* **183 D9** 51 35N 102 5W
Vergas, *MN, U.S.A.* **80 D3** 46 40N 95 48W
Vergennes, *VT, U.S.A.* **86 B1** 44 10N 73 15W
Verlo, *Sask., Canada* **182 E3** 50 19N 108 35W
Vermejo ➝, *NM, U.S.A.* **88 A6** 36 25N 104 30W
Vermeulle, L., *Qué., Canada* **175 C4** 54 43N 69 24W
Vermilion, *Alta., Canada* **184 E10** 53 20N 110 50W
Vermilion, *IL, U.S.A.* **71 D6** 39 35N 87 35W
Vermilion, *OH, U.S.A.* **92 B4** 41 25N 82 22W
Vermilion ➝, *Alta., Canada* **184 E10** 53 22N 110 51W
Vermilion ➝, *IL, U.S.A.* **71 B4** 41 19N 89 4W
Vermilion B., *LA, U.S.A.* **75 E4** 29 42N 92 0W
Vermilion Bay, *Ont., Canada* **180 C3** 49 51N 93 34W
Vermilion Cliffs, *UT, U.S.A.* **100 F3** 37 10N 112 30W
Vermilion Cliffs Nat. Monument ⌓, *AZ, U.S.A.* **62 A3** 36 54N 112 5W
Vermilion County ☆, *IL, U.S.A.* **71 C6** 40 10N 87 45W
Vermilion L., *Ont., Canada* **180 B4** 50 3N 92 13W
Vermilion L., *MN, U.S.A.* **80 C6** 47 53N 92 26W
Vermilion Parish ☆, *LA, U.S.A.* **75 E3** 29 55N 92 15W
Vermilion Pass, *B.C., Canada* **187 D18** 51 15N 116 2W
Vermilion Ra., *MN, U.S.A.* **80 C7** 47 50N 92 0W
Vermillion, *SD, U.S.A.* **91 H9** 42 47N 96 56W
Vermillion ➝, *Qué., Canada* **177 D10** 47 38N 72 56W
Vermillion ➝, *SD, U.S.A.* **91 H9** 42 44N 96 53W
Vermillion Bluffs, *CO, U.S.A.* **66 B2** 40 50N 108 20W
Vermillion County ☆, *IN, U.S.A.* **72 D3** 39 50N 87 30W
Vermont □, *U.S.A.* **86 B2** 44 0N 73 0W
Verna, *FL, U.S.A.* **67 D6** 27 23N 82 16W
Vernal, *UT, U.S.A.* **100 C6** 40 27N 109 32W
Verndale, *MN, U.S.A.* **80 D3** 46 24N 95 1W
Verner, *Ont., Canada* **178 A6** 46 25N 80 8W
Vernon, *B.C., Canada* **187 E15** 50 20N 119 15W
Vernon, *AL, U.S.A.* **60 C2** 33 45N 88 7W
Vernon, *CO, U.S.A.* **66 C8** 39 57N 102 19W
Vernon, *CT, U.S.A.* **78 C2** 41 50N 72 28W
Vernon, *FL, U.S.A.* **67 A3** 30 37N 85 43W
Vernon, *IL, U.S.A.* **71 E4** 38 48N 89 5W
Vernon, *IN, U.S.A.* **72 E5** 38 59N 85 36W
Vernon, *Los Angeles, U.S.A.* **111 B3** 34 0N 118 13W
Vernon, *NJ, U.S.A.* **87 A2** 41 12N 74 29W
Vernon, *TX, U.S.A.* **99 C8** 34 9N 99 17W
Vernon, *UT, U.S.A.* **100 C3** 40 6N 112 26W
Vernon Center, *MN, U.S.A.* **80 G4** 43 58N 94 10W
Vernon County ☆, *MO, U.S.A.* **82 D2** 37 50N 94 20W
Vernon County ☆, *WI, U.S.A.* **103 E3** 43 30N 90 50W
Vernon L., *LA, U.S.A.* **75 C2** 31 11N 93 22W
Vernon Parish ☆, *LA, U.S.A.* **75 C2** 31 0N 93 16W
Vernonia, *OR, U.S.A.* **94 B2** 45 52N 123 11W
Vernor, *MI, U.S.A.* **109 B2** 42 19N 83 7W
Vero Beach, *FL, U.S.A.* **67 D8** 27 38N 80 24W
Véron, L., *Nfld. & L., Canada* **172 B4** 51 48N 65 7W
Verona, *Ont., Canada* **179 C10** 44 29N 76 42W
Verona, *MS, U.S.A.* **81 B5** 34 12N 88 43W
Verona, *ND, U.S.A.* **91 D7** 46 22N 98 4W
Verona, *NJ, U.S.A.* **114 B1** 40 49N 74 14W
Verona, *Pittsburgh, U.S.A.* **116 A2** 40 30N 79 50W
Verona, *VA, U.S.A.* **102 C5** 38 12N 79 0W
Verona, *WI, U.S.A.* **103 F4** 42 59N 89 32W
Verret, L., *LA, U.S.A.* **75 E4** 29 53N 91 10W
Versailles, *CT, U.S.A.* **78 C2** 41 36N 72 2W
Versailles, *IL, U.S.A.* **71 D3** 39 53N 90 39W
Versailles, *IN, U.S.A.* **72 D5** 39 4N 85 15W
Versailles, *KY, U.S.A.* **97 B8** 38 3N 84 44W
Versailles, *MO, U.S.A.* **82 C4** 38 26N 92 51W
Versailles, *OH, U.S.A.* **92 C2** 40 13N 84 29W
Vert I., *Ont., Canada* **180 D8** 48 55N 88 3W
Verte, Î., *Qué., Canada* **177 C13** 48 2N 69 26W
Vesper, *KS, U.S.A.* **74 B5** 39 2N 98 17W
Vesper, *WI, U.S.A.* **103 D4** 44 29N 89 58W
Vesta, *GA, U.S.A.* **68 C4** 33 58N 82 56W
Vesta, *NE, U.S.A.* **84 D9** 40 21N 96 20W
Vestavia Hills, *AL, U.S.A.* **60 C4** 33 27N 86 47W
Veta Grande, *Zacatecas, Mexico* **217 E8** 22 52N 102 32W
Vetal, *SD, U.S.A.* **91 G4** 43 13N 101 23W
Veteran, *Alta., Canada* **185 F9** 52 0N 111 7W
Veterans Memorial County Park ⌓, *MO, U.S.A.* **117 A2** 38 48N 90 15W
Vevay, *IN, U.S.A.* **72 E5** 38 45N 85 4W
Vian, *OK, U.S.A.* **93 C9** 35 30N 94 58W
Vibank, *Sask., Canada* **182 E8** 50 20N 103 56W
Viborg, *SD, U.S.A.* **91 G8** 43 10N 97 5W
Viburnum, *MO, U.S.A.* **82 D5** 37 43N 91 8W
Vicam, *Sonora, Mexico* **212 F5** 27 35N 110 20W
Vicco, *KY, U.S.A.* **97 C9** 37 13N 83 4W
Vicente, Pt., *Los Angeles, U.S.A.* **111 D2** 33 44N 118 24W
Vicente Guerrero, *Baja Calif., Mexico* **210 C2** 30 45N 116 0W
Vicente Guerrero, *Chiapas, Mexico* **222 C4** 16 26N 92 40W
Vicente Guerrero, *Chiapas, Mexico* **222 C3** 16 41N 93 15W
Vicente Guerrero, *Durango, Mexico* **217 D7** 23 45N 103 59W
Vicente Guerrero, *Puebla, Mexico* **221 F3** 18 33N 97 11W
Vicente Guerrero, *Sonora, Mexico* **212 C3** 30 50N 112 53W
Vicente Guerrero, *Tabasco, Mexico* **222 A4** 18 27N 92 58W
Vicente Guerrero, *Tlaxcala, Mexico* **219 C9** 19 8N 98 10W
Vicente Guerrero, Presa, *Tamaulipas, Mexico* **215 G6** 23 57N 98 42W
Viceroy, *Sask., Canada* **182 F6** 49 28N 105 22W
Vici, *OK, U.S.A.* **93 B4** 36 9N 99 18W
Vick, *AR, U.S.A.* **63 E3** 33 20N 92 6W
Vicksburg, *AZ, U.S.A.* **62 D2** 33 45N 113 45W
Vicksburg, *MI, U.S.A.* **79 G6** 42 7N 85 32W
Vicksburg, *MS, U.S.A.* **81 D3** 32 21N 90 53W
Vicksburg Nat. Military Park ⌓, *MS, U.S.A.* **81 D3** 32 21N 90 51W
Victor, *CO, U.S.A.* **66 D5** 38 43N 105 9W
Victor, *ID, U.S.A.* **70 F7** 43 36N 111 7W
Victor, *IA, U.S.A.* **73 D6** 41 44N 92 18W
Victor, *MT, U.S.A.* **83 D3** 46 25N 114 9W
Victor, L., *Qué., Canada* **172 C8** 50 35N 61 50W
Victoria, *B.C., Canada* **187 G11** 48 30N 123 25W
Victoria, *Nfld. & L., Canada* **173 C12** 47 46N 53 14W
Victoria, *Guanajuato, Mexico* **219 A7** 21 23N 100 12W
Victoria, *IL, U.S.A.* **71 B3** 41 2N 90 6W
Victoria, *KS, U.S.A.* **74 C4** 38 52N 99 9W
Victoria, *TX, U.S.A.* **99 J10** 28 48N 97 0W
Victoria, *VA, U.S.A.* **102 E6** 36 59N 78 8W
Victoria, Grand L., *Qué., Canada* **176 D5** 47 31N 77 30W
Victoria, Pont, *Montréal, Canada* **192 B3** 45 29N 73 32W
Victoria Beach, *Man., Canada* **183 E15** 50 40N 96 35W
Victoria County ☆, *TX, U.S.A.* **99 J11** 28 45N 97 0W
Victoria de Durango = Durango, *Mexico* **217 C6** 24 3N 104 39W
Victoria Harbour, *Ont., Canada* **178 C7** 44 45N 79 45W
Victoria I., *Canada* **188 B10** 71 0N 111 0W
Victoria L., *Nfld. & L., Canada* **173 D3** 48 20N 57 27W
Victoria Pk., *Alta., Canada* **185 J6** 49 18N 114 8W
Victoria Pk., *B.C., Canada* **186 E8** 50 3N 126 5W
Victoria Str., *N.W.T., Canada* **190 D5** 69 31N 100 30W
Victoriaville, *Qué., Canada* **177 E11** 46 4N 71 56W
Victorville, *CA, U.S.A.* **65 J9** 34 32N 117 18W
Vidal, *CA, U.S.A.* **65 J12** 34 7N 114 31W
Vidalia, *GA, U.S.A.* **68 D4** 32 13N 82 25W
Vidalia, *LA, U.S.A.* **75 C4** 31 34N 91 26W
Vidauri, *TX, U.S.A.* **99 J10** 28 26N 97 8W
Vidette, *GA, U.S.A.* **68 C4** 33 2N 82 15W
Vidor, *TX, U.S.A.* **99 G13** 30 7N 94 1W
Vieja, Sierra, *TX, U.S.A.* **98 G3** 30 35N 104 40W
Vienna, *Ont., Canada* **178 E6** 42 41N 80 48W
Vienna, *GA, U.S.A.* **68 D3** 32 6N 83 47W
Vienna, *IL, U.S.A.* **71 F5** 37 25N 88 54W
Vienna, *MD, U.S.A.* **77 B5** 38 29N 75 50W
Vienna, *MO, U.S.A.* **82 C5** 38 11N 91 57W
Vienna, *SD, U.S.A.* **91 F8** 44 42N 97 30W
Vienna, *VA, U.S.A.* **77 B3** 38 54N 77 16W
Vienna, *WV, U.S.A.* **102 B3** 39 20N 81 33W
Viento, L. el, *Tabasco, Mexico* **222 A4** 18 13N 92 38W
Vieques, *Puerto Rico* **105 G17** 18 8N 65 25W
Viesca, *Coahuila, Mexico* **215 E2** 25 21N 102 48W
Vieux Desert, L., *MI, U.S.A.* **79 C2** 46 8N 89 7W
View Park, *Los Angeles, U.S.A.* **111 B3** 34 0N 118 20W
Vigía Grande, Península, *Quintana Roo, Mexico* **223 C6** 19 40N 87 27W
Vigo County ☆, *IN, U.S.A.* **72 D3** 39 25N 87 25W
Vigo Park, *TX, U.S.A.* **98 C6** 34 39N 101 30W
Viking, *Alta., Canada* **185 E9** 53 7N 111 50W
Viking, *MN, U.S.A.* **80 B2** 48 13N 96 24W
Vilas, *CO, U.S.A.* **66 E8** 37 22N 102 27W
Vilas, *SD, U.S.A.* **91 F8** 44 1N 97 36W
Vilas County ☆, *WI, U.S.A.* **103 B4** 46 0N 89 30W
Villa Acula, *Veracruz, Mexico* **221 F5** 18 31N 95 47W
Villa Ahumada, *Chihuahua, Mexico* **213 C9** 30 37N 106 31W
Villa Ahumada y Anexas, *Chihuahua, Mexico* **213 C9** 30 31N 106 50W
Villa Alta, *Oaxaca, Mexico* **221 G5** 17 5N 96 0W
Villa Cecilia = Ciudad Madero, *Tamaulipas, Mexico* **215 H7** 22 19N 97 50W
Villa Chacaltongo, *Oaxaca, Mexico* **221 G3** 17 3N 97 35W
Villa Comaltitlán, *Chiapas, Mexico* **222 D4** 15 13N 92 35W
Villa Coronado, *Chihuahua, Mexico* **213 G10** 26 45N 105 10W
Villa Corzo, *Chiapas, Mexico* **222 C3** 16 10N 93 12W
Villa Cuauhtémoc, *Veracruz, Mexico* **220 B3** 22 11N 97 50W
Villa de Acala, *Chiapas, Mexico* **222 C4** 16 34N 92 48W
Villa de Allende, *México, Mexico* **219 C7** 19 23N 100 9W
Villa de Álvarez, *Colima, Mexico* **218 C4** 19 15N 103 44W
Villa de Arriaga, *San Luis Potosí, Mexico* **215 J3** 21 56N 101 20W
Villa de Bustamante, *Tamaulipas, Mexico* **215 G5** 23 26N 99 47W
Villa de Casas, *Tamaulipas, Mexico* **215 G6** 23 44N 98 43W
Villa de Cos, *Zacatecas, Mexico* **217 D8** 23 17N 102 21W
Villa de Costa Rica, *Sinaloa, Mexico* **216 C3** 24 35N 107 24W
Villa de García, *Nuevo León, Mexico* **214 E4** 25 49N 100 35W
Villa de Guadalupe, *Distrito Federal, Mexico* **225 B3** 19 29N 99 6W
Villa de Guadalupe, *San Luis Potosí, Mexico* **215 G4** 23 22N 100 46W
Villa de Méndez, *Tamaulipas, Mexico* **215 E6** 25 7N 98 34W
Villa de Ramos, *San Luis Potosí, Mexico* **215 H3** 22 50N 101 55W
Villa de Reyes, *San Luis Potosí, Mexico* **215 J4** 21 48N 100 56W
Villa de Tamazulapan, *Oaxaca, Mexico* **221 G3** 17 40N 97 35W
Villa de Tezontepec, *Hidalgo, Mexico* **219 C9** 19 48N 98 53W
Villa del Rio, *Chiapas, Mexico* **222 C3** 16 44N 93 55W
Villa Escalante, *Michoacan, Mexico* **218 C6** 19 23N 101 39W
Villa Escobedo, *Coahuila, Mexico* **214 C3** 27 13N 101 21W
Villa Flores, *Chiapas, Mexico* **222 C3** 16 14N 93 14W
Villa Garcia, *Zacatecas, Mexico* **217 E9** 22 13N 101 57W
Villa González Ortega, *Zacatecas, Mexico* **217 E9** 22 31N 101 54W
Villa Grove, *CO, U.S.A.* **66 D5** 38 15N 105 59W
Villa Grove, *IL, U.S.A.* **71 D5** 39 52N 88 10W
Villa Guadalupe, *Sonora, Mexico* **212 F5** 27 10N 110 10W
Villa Guadalupe, *Sonora, Mexico* **212 C3** 30 52N 112 58W
Villa Guerrero, *Jalisco, Mexico* **217 F7** 21 59N 103 36W
Villa Guerrero, *México, Mexico* **219 D8** 18 58N 99 38W
Villa Guerrero, *Veracruz, Mexico* **221 G5** 17 36N 95 12W
Villa Hidalgo, *Chiapas, Mexico* **222 C3** 16 18N 93 9W
Villa Hidalgo, *Coahuila, Mexico* **214 C5** 27 47N 99 52W
Villa Hidalgo, *Durango, Mexico* **217 A6** 26 16N 104 54W
Villa Hidalgo, *Jalisco, Mexico* **218 A5** 21 40N 102 36W
Villa Hidalgo, *Nayarit, Mexico* **216 F5** 21 44N 105 15W
Villa Hidalgo, *San Luis Potosí, Mexico* **215 H4** 22 27N 100 42W
Villa Hidalgo, *Sonora, Mexico* **212 C6** 30 7N 109 20W
Villa Hidalgo, *Tamaulipas, Mexico* **215 F5** 24 15N 99 26W
Villa Hidalgo, *Zacatecas, Mexico* **217 E9** 22 21N 101 42W
Villa Hills, *KY, U.S.A.* **107 B1** 39 3N 84 35W
Villa Jesús María, *Baja Calif. S., Mexico* **211 E5** 28 18N 114 0W
Villa Juanita, *Veracruz, Mexico* **221 G5** 17 49N 95 14W
Villa Juárez, *Durango, Mexico* **217 B7** 25 30N 103 35W
Villa Juárez, *San Luis Potosí, Mexico* **215 H4** 22 23N 100 16W
Villa Juárez, *Sinaloa, Mexico* **216 C3** 24 39N 107 34W
Villa Juárez, *Sonora, Mexico* **212 F6** 27 7N 109 52W
Villa López, *Chihuahua, Mexico* **213 G10** 27 0N 105 2W
Villa Madero, *Michoacan, Mexico* **219 C6** 19 24N 101 16W
Villa Mainero, *Tamaulipas, Mexico* **215 F5** 24 34N 99 36W
Villa Matamoros, *Chihuahua, Mexico* **213 G10** 26 47N 105 35W
Villa Morelos, *Baja Calif. S., Mexico* **211 J7** 24 54N 111 38W
Villa Moros, *Sinaloa, Mexico* **216 C3** 24 40N 107 41W
Villa Nicolas Romero, *México, Mexico* **219 C8** 19 38N 99 19W
Villa Ocampo, *Durango, Mexico* **216 A5** 26 27N 105 31W
Villa Pesqueria, *Sonora, Mexico* **212 D6** 29 8N 110 59W
Villa Progreso, *Querétaro, Mexico* **219 B8** 20 38N 99 48W
Villa Rica, *GA, U.S.A.* **68 C2** 33 44N 84 55W
Villa Santo Domingo, *San Luis Potosí, Mexico* **215 G3** 23 20N 101 44W
Villa Unión, *Coahuila, Mexico* **214 B4** 28 15N 100 43W
Villa Unión, *Durango, Mexico* **217 D6** 23 58N 104 2W
Villa Unión, *Sinaloa, Mexico* **216 D4** 23 12N 106 14W
Villa Victoria, *México, Mexico* **219 C8** 19 26N 100 0W
Villa Victoria, *Michoacan, Mexico* **218 D4** 18 47N 103 24W
Villa Zaragoza, *San Luis Potosí, Mexico* **215 H4** 22 2N 100 44W
Village of Superior, *WI, U.S.A.* **103 B1** 46 40N 92 6W
Villagrán, *Guanajuato, Mexico* **219 B7** 20 31N 100 59W
Villagrán, *Sonora, Mexico* **212 B2** 31 39N 113 6W
Villagrán, *Tamaulipas, Mexico* **215 F5** 24 29N 99 29W
Villahermosa, *Tabasco, Mexico* **222 B4** 17 59N 92 55W
Villalba, *Puerto Rico* **105 G16** 18 8N 66 30W
Villaldama, *Nuevo León, Mexico* **214 D4** 26 30N 100 26W
Villamar, *Michoacan, Mexico* **218 C5** 19 59N 102 35W
Villanueva, *Zacatecas, Mexico* **217 E8** 22 21N 102 53W
Villanueva, *NM, U.S.A.* **88 B5** 35 16N 105 22W
Villard, *MN, U.S.A.* **80 E3** 45 43N 95 16W
Villas, *NJ, U.S.A.* **87 C2** 39 2N 74 56W
Ville-Marie, *Qué., Canada* **176 D3** 47 20N 79 30W
Ville Platte, *LA, U.S.A.* **75 D3** 30 41N 92 17W
Villebon, L., *Qué., Canada* **176 D5** 47 58N 77 17W
Villegreen, *CO, U.S.A.* **66 E7** 37 18N 103 31W
Villemontel, *Qué., Canada* **176 C4** 48 38N 78 22W
Villisca, *IA, U.S.A.* **73 E4** 40 56N 94 59W
Vilna, *Alta., Canada* **184 D9** 54 7N 111 55W
Vilonia, *AR, U.S.A.* **63 C3** 35 5N 92 13W
Vimont, *Montréal, Canada* **192 A2** 45 36N 73 43W
Vina, *AL, U.S.A.* **60 B2** 34 23N 88 4W
Vinalhaven, *ME, U.S.A.* **76 D5** 44 3N 68 50W
Vinalhaven I., *ME, U.S.A.* **76 D5** 44 5N 68 51W
Vincennes, *IN, U.S.A.* **72 E3** 38 41N 87 32W
Vincent, *AL, U.S.A.* **60 C4** 33 23N 86 25W
Vincent, *IA, U.S.A.* **73 C4** 42 36N 94 1W
Vincentown, *NJ, U.S.A.* **87 C2** 39 56N 74 45W
Vine Grove, *KY, U.S.A.* **97 C7** 37 49N 85 59W
Vineland, *NJ, U.S.A.* **87 C1** 39 29N 75 2W
Vineland, *Orlando, U.S.A.* **115 B1** 28 23N 81 30W
Vinemont, *AL, U.S.A.* **60 B4** 34 15N 86 52W
Vineyard Haven, *MA, U.S.A.* **78 C4** 41 27N 70 36W
Vineyard Sd., *MA, U.S.A.* **78 C4** 41 25N 70 45W
Vining, *MN, U.S.A.* **80 D3** 46 16N 95 32W
Vinings, *Atlanta, U.S.A.* **106 A2** 33 53N 84 29W
Vinita, *OK, U.S.A.* **93 B8** 36 39N 95 9W
Vinita Park, *MO, U.S.A.* **117 B1** 38 41N 90 20W
Vinson, *OK, U.S.A.* **93 D4** 34 54N 99 52W
Vinton, *CA, U.S.A.* **64 D6** 39 48N 120 10W
Vinton, *IA, U.S.A.* **73 C6** 42 10N 92 1W
Vinton, *LA, U.S.A.* **75 D2** 30 11N 93 35W
Vinton, *OH, U.S.A.* **92 E4** 38 59N 82 21W
Vinton, *VA, U.S.A.* **102 D5** 37 17N 79 54W
Vinton County ☆, *OH, U.S.A.* **92 D4** 39 15N 82 29W
Viola, *AR, U.S.A.* **63 B4** 36 24N 91 59W
Viola, *DE, U.S.A.* **77 A5** 39 5N 75 34W
Viola, *IL, U.S.A.* **71 B3** 41 12N 90 35W
Viola, *KS, U.S.A.* **74 D6** 37 29N 97 39W
Viola, *TN, U.S.A.* **97 E7** 35 32N 85 52W
Viola, *WI, U.S.A.* **103 E3** 43 31N 90 40W
Violet, *LA, U.S.A.* **113 C3** 29 53N 89 53W
Virago Sd., *B.C., Canada* **186 A2** 54 0N 132 30W
Virden, *Man., Canada* **183 F11** 49 50N 100 56W
Virden, *IL, U.S.A.* **71 D4** 39 30N 89 46W
Virden, *NM, U.S.A.* **88 E2** 32 41N 109 0W
Virgenes, C., *Baja Calif. S., Mexico* **211 F6** 27 31N 112 21W
Virgil, *KS, U.S.A.* **74 D7** 37 59N 96 1W
Virgil, *SD, U.S.A.* **91 F7** 44 17N 98 25W
Virgilina, *VA, U.S.A.* **102 E6** 36 33N 78 47W
Virgin, *UT, U.S.A.* **100 F2** 37 12N 113 11W
Virgin ➝, *NV, U.S.A.* **85 F6** 36 28N 114 21W
Virgin Gorda, *Br. Virgin Is.* **105 G18** 18 30N 64 26W
Virgin Is. (British) ☑, *W. Indies* **105 G18** 18 30N 64 30W
Virgin Is. (U.S.) ☑, *W. Indies* **105 G18** 18 20N 65 0W
Virgin Islands Nat. Park △, *U.S. Virgin Is.* **105 G18** 18 21N 64 43W
Virgin Mts., *AZ, U.S.A.* **62 A2** 36 45N 113 45W
Virginia, *ID, U.S.A.* **70 G6** 42 30N 112 10W
Virginia, *IL, U.S.A.* **71 D3** 39 57N 90 13W
Virginia, *MN, U.S.A.* **80 C6** 47 31N 92 32W
Virginia □, *U.S.A.* **102 D6** 37 30N 78 45W
Virginia, L., *Orlando, U.S.A.* **115 A2** 28 53N 81 20W
Virginia Beach, *VA, U.S.A.* **102 E9** 36 44N 76 0W
Virginia City, *MT, U.S.A.* **83 E6** 45 18N 111 56W
Virginia City, *NV, U.S.A.* **85 C1** 39 19N 119 39W
Virginia Falls, *N.W.T., Canada* **189 D7** 61 38N 125 42W
Virginia Gardens, *Miami, U.S.A.* **112 D1** 25 48N 80 18W
Virginia Key, *Miami, U.S.A.* **112 D3** 25 44N 80 8W
Virginia Mts., *NV, U.S.A.* **85 C1** 39 50N 119 30W
Virginiatown, *Ont., Canada* **176 C3** 48 9N 79 36W
Viroqua, *WI, U.S.A.* **103 E3** 43 34N 90 53W
Visalia, *CA, U.S.A.* **65 G7** 36 20N 119 18W
Viscount, *Sask., Canada* **182 D6** 51 57N 105 39W
Viscount Melville Sd., *Canada* **188 B11** 74 10N 108 0W
Visitacion Valley, *San Francisco, U.S.A.* **118 B2** 37 42N 122 23W
Vista, *CA, U.S.A.* **65 K9** 33 12N 117 14W
Vista, *MO, U.S.A.* **82 D3** 37 58N 93 40W
Vista Grove, *Atlanta, U.S.A.* **106 A3** 33 51N 84 16W
Vivian, *LA, U.S.A.* **75 B2** 32 53N 93 59W
Vivian, *SD, U.S.A.* **91 G5** 43 56N 100 18W
Vizcaíno, Desierto de, *Mexico* **211 F5** 27 30N 113 45W
Vogar, *Man., Canada* **183 E13** 50 57N 98 39W
Voisey B., *Nfld. & L., Canada* **175 B5** 56 15N 61 50W
Volborg, *MT, U.S.A.* **83 E12** 45 51N 105 41W
Volcán Nevado de Colima, Parque Nacional △, *Jalisco, Mexico* **218 C4** 19 32N 103 40W
Volcano, *HI, U.S.A.* **69 D6** 19 26N 155 14W
Volga, *IA, U.S.A.* **73 C7** 42 48N 91 33W
Volga, *SD, U.S.A.* **91 F9** 44 19N 96 56W
Volin, *SD, U.S.A.* **91 H8** 42 58N 97 11W
Voluntown, *CT, U.S.A.* **78 C3** 41 34N 71 52W
Volusia County ☆, *FL, U.S.A.* **67 B7** 29 0N 81 15W
Von Ormy, *San Antonio, U.S.A.* **117 D2** 29 17N 98 38W
Vona, *CO, U.S.A.* **66 C8** 39 18N 102 45W
Vonda, *Sask., Canada* **182 C5** 52 19N 106 6W
Vonore, *TN, U.S.A.* **97 E8** 35 36N 84 14W
Voorheesville, *NY, U.S.A.* **89 C7** 42 39N 73 56W
Voyageurs Nat. Park △, *MN, U.S.A.* **80 B6** 48 32N 93 0W
Vulcan, *Alta., Canada* **185 H7** 50 25N 113 15W
Vulcan, *MI, U.S.A.* **79 D4** 45 47N 87 53W
Vulture Mts., *AZ, U.S.A.* **62 D3** 33 45N 112 50W
Vuntut Nat. Park △, *Yukon, Canada* **188 C5** 68 25N 139 41W
Vya, *NV, U.S.A.* **85 A1** 41 35N 119 52W

W

W. Kerr Scott Res., *NC, U.S.A.* **90 B4** 36 10N 81 20W
Wabakimi L., *Ont., Canada* **180 B7** 50 38N 89 45W
Wabakimi Prov. Park △, *Ont., Canada* **180 B7** 50 43N 89 29W
Wabamun, *Alta., Canada* **184 E6** 53 33N 114 28W
Wabamun L., *Alta., Canada* **184 E6** 53 32N 114 35W
Wabano ➝, *Qué., Canada* **177 C8** 48 20N 74 3W
Wabasca ➝, *Alta., Canada* **184 A5** 58 22N 115 20W
Wabasca-Desmarais, *Alta., Canada* **184 C7** 55 57N 113 56W
Wabash, *IN, U.S.A.* **72 C5** 40 48N 85 49W
Wabash ➝, *IN, U.S.A.* **72 F2** 37 48N 88 2W
Wabash County ☆, *IL, U.S.A.* **71 E6** 38 30N 87 50W
Wabash County ☆, *IN, U.S.A.* **72 C5** 40 50N 85 45W
Wabasha, *MN, U.S.A.* **80 F6** 44 23N 92 2W
Wabasha County ☆, *MN, U.S.A.* **80 F6** 44 15N 92 15W
Wabaskang L., *Ont., Canada* **180 B3** 50 26N 93 13W
Wabassi ➝, *Ont., Canada* **181 A10** 51 45N 86 20W
Wabasso, *FL, U.S.A.* **67 D8** 27 45N 80 26W
Wabasso, *MN, U.S.A.* **80 F3** 44 24N 95 15W
Wabatongushi L., *Ont., Canada* **181 D12** 48 26N 84 13W
Wabaunsee, *KS, U.S.A.* **74 B7** 39 9N 96 21W
Wabaunsee County ☆, *KS, U.S.A.* **74 C7** 39 0N 96 15W
Wabeno, *WI, U.S.A.* **103 C5** 45 26N 88 39W
Wabigoon, *Ont., Canada* **180 C4** 49 43N 92 35W
Wabigoon L., *Ont., Canada* **180 C4** 49 44N 92 44W
Wabimeig L., *Ont., Canada* **181 A11** 51 28N 85 36W
Wabinosh L., *Ont., Canada* **180 B8** 50 5N 89 0W
Wabuk Pt., *Ont., Canada* **191 F8** 55 20N 85 5W

Wabush, *Nfld. & L., Canada* **175 C4** 52 55N 66 52W
Wabuska, *NV, U.S.A.* **85 C1** 39 9N 119 11W
Waccamaw, L., *NC, U.S.A.* **90 D7** 34 18N 78 31W
Waccasassa B., *FL, U.S.A.* **67 B6** 29 10N 82 50W
Wachapreague, *VA, U.S.A.* **102 D9** 37 36N 75 42W
Wachusett Res., *MA, U.S.A.* **78 B3** 42 24N 71 41W
Wacissa, *FL, U.S.A.* **67 A5** 30 22N 83 59W
Waco, *Qué., Canada* **175 C4** 51 27N 65 37W
Waco, *NE, U.S.A.* **84 D8** 40 54N 97 28W
Waco, *TX, U.S.A.* **99 F10** 31 33N 97 9W
Waco L., *TX, U.S.A.* **99 F10** 31 35N 97 12W
Waconda Lake, *KS, U.S.A.* **74 B5** 39 29N 98 19W
Waconia, *MN, U.S.A.* **80 F5** 44 51N 93 47W
Waconichi, L., *Qué., Canada* **177 A8** 50 8N 74 0W
Wacouno →, *Qué., Canada* **172 C4** 50 54N 65 57W
Waddington, *NY, U.S.A.* **89 A5** 44 52N 75 12W
Waddington, Mt., *B.C., Canada* **186 D9** 51 23N 125 15W
Wade Hampton ☆, *AK, U.S.A.* **61 E7** 62 15N 163 0W
Wadena, *Sask., Canada* **182 D8** 51 57N 103 47W
Wadena, *MN, U.S.A.* **80 D3** 46 26N 95 8W
Wadena County ☆, *MN, U.S.A.* **80 D4** 46 30N 95 0W
Wadesboro, *NC, U.S.A.* **90 D5** 34 58N 80 5W
Wadhams, *B.C., Canada* **186 D7** 51 30N 127 30W
Wading River, *NJ, U.S.A.* **87 C2** 39 38N 74 31W
Wadley, *AL, U.S.A.* **60 C5** 33 7N 85 34W
Wadley, *GA, U.S.A.* **68 D4** 32 52N 82 24W
Wadlin L., *Alta., Canada* **184 A5** 57 44N 115 35W
Wadsworth, *NV, U.S.A.* **85 C1** 39 38N 119 17W
Wadsworth, *OH, U.S.A.* **92 B5** 41 2N 81 44W
Wadsworth, *TX, U.S.A.* **99 J12** 28 50N 95 56W
Wadsworth Atheneum, *CT, U.S.A.* **78 C2** 41 46N 72 40W
Waelder, *TX, U.S.A.* **99 H10** 29 42N 97 18W
Wagener, *SC, U.S.A.* **90 E4** 33 39N 81 22W
Wager B., *Nunavut, Canada* **191 D8** 65 26N 88 40W
Waggaman, *New Orleans, U.S.A.* **113 C1** 29 55N 90 12W
Wagner, *SD, U.S.A.* **91 G7** 43 5N 98 18W
Wagon Mound, *NM, U.S.A.* **88 A6** 36 1N 104 42W
Wagon Wheel Gap, *CO, U.S.A.* **66 E4** 37 46N 106 49W
Wagoner, *OK, U.S.A.* **93 C8** 35 58N 95 22W
Wagoner County ☆, *OK, U.S.A.* **93 B8** 36 0N 95 30W
Wagontire, *OR, U.S.A.* **94 D6** 43 15N 119 52W
Wagontire Mt., *OR, U.S.A.* **94 D6** 43 21N 119 53W
Wah Wah Mts., *UT, U.S.A.* **100 E2** 38 25N 113 40W
Wahiawā, *HI, U.S.A.* **69 K13** 21 30N 158 2W
Wahiawā District, *HI, U.S.A.* **69 J14** 21 31N 157 58W
Wahiawā Res., *HI, U.S.A.* **69 K13** 21 30N 158 3W
Wahkiakum County ☆, *WA, U.S.A.* **101 D2** 46 10N 123 30W
Wahkon, *MN, U.S.A.* **80 D5** 46 7N 93 31W
Wahoo, *NE, U.S.A.* **84 C9** 41 13N 96 37W
Wahpeton, *ND, U.S.A.* **91 D9** 46 16N 96 36W
Wai'ale'ale, *HI, U.S.A.* **69 A2** 22 4N 159 30W
Waiale'e, *HI, U.S.A.* **69 J13** 21 41N 158 1W
Waialua, *HI, U.S.A.* **69 J13** 21 34N 158 8W
Waialua B., *HI, U.S.A.* **69 J13** 21 35N 158 5W
Waialua District, *HI, U.S.A.* **69 J13** 21 35N 158 5W
Wai'anae, *HI, U.S.A.* **69 K13** 21 27N 158 11W
Wai'anae Coast, *HI, U.S.A.* **69 K13** 21 26N 158 11W
Wai'anae District, *HI, U.S.A.* **69 K13** 21 28N 158 10W
Wai'anae Range, *HI, U.S.A.* **69 K13** 21 30N 158 10W
Waiawa →, *HI, U.S.A.* **69 K14** 21 23N 157 59W
Waihee-Waiehu, *HI, U.S.A.* **69 C5** 20 56N 156 31W
Waikīkī, *HI, U.S.A.* **69 K14** 21 17N 157 50W
Waikoloa Village, *HI, U.S.A.* **69 D6** 19 55N 155 49W
Wailea-Makena, *HI, U.S.A.* **69 C5** 20 40N 156 27W
Wailua, *HI, U.S.A.* **69 A2** 22 3N 159 20W
Wailua, *HI, U.S.A.* **69 C5** 20 51N 156 8W
Wailuku, *HI, U.S.A.* **69 C5** 20 53N 156 30W
Waimalu, *HI, U.S.A.* **69 K14** 21 24N 157 57W
Waimānalo, *HI, U.S.A.* **69 K14** 21 21N 157 43W
Waimānalo B., *HI, U.S.A.* **69 K14** 21 20N 157 40W
Waimānalo Beach, *HI, U.S.A.* **69 K14** 21 21N 157 42W
Waimano →, *HI, U.S.A.* **69 K14** 21 25N 157 58W
Waimea, *HI, U.S.A.* **69 B2** 21 58N 159 40W
Waimea, *HI, U.S.A.* **69 J13** 21 39N 158 3W
Waimea B., *HI, U.S.A.* **69 J13** 21 40N 158 5W
Waimea Canyon, *HI, U.S.A.* **69 A2** 22 0N 159 39W
Wainwright, *Alta., Canada* **185 F10** 52 50N 110 50W
Wainwright, *AK, U.S.A.* **61 A7** 70 38N 160 2W
Wainwright, *OK, U.S.A.* **93 C8** 35 37N 95 34W
Waipahu, *HI, U.S.A.* **69 K13** 21 23N 158 1W
Waipio, *HI, U.S.A.* **69 K14** 21 25N 158 0W
Waipi'o Acres, *HI, U.S.A.* **69 K13** 21 28N 158 1W
Waipi'o Peninsula, *HI, U.S.A.* **69 K14** 21 20N 158 0W
Waita Res., *HI, U.S.A.* **69 B2** 21 55N 159 28W
Waite, *ME, U.S.A.* **76 C6** 45 20N 67 42W
Waite Park, *MN, U.S.A.* **80 E4** 45 33N 94 14W
Waiteville, *WV, U.S.A.* **102 D4** 37 28N 80 25W
Waits →, *VT, U.S.A.* **86 C2** 43 59N 72 8W
Waitsburg, *WA, U.S.A.* **101 D7** 46 16N 118 9W
Waitsfield, *VT, U.S.A.* **86 B2** 44 42N 72 50W
Waka, *TX, U.S.A.* **98 A6** 36 17N 101 3W
Wakami Lake Prov. Park ⌂, *Ont., Canada* **181 E14** 47 29N 82 50W
Wakarusa, *IN, U.S.A.* **72 B4** 41 32N 86 1W
Wakaw, *Sask., Canada* **182 C6** 52 39N 105 44W
Wake County ☆, *NC, U.S.A.* **90 C7** 35 40N 78 45W
Wake Forest, *NC, U.S.A.* **90 C7** 35 59N 78 30W
Wake I., *Pac. Oc.* **105 C5** 19 18N 166 36 E
WaKeeney, *KS, U.S.A.* **74 B4** 39 1N 99 53W
Wakefield, *Qué., Canada* **176 F7** 45 38N 75 56W
Wakefield, *KS, U.S.A.* **74 B6** 39 13N 97 1W
Wakefield, *MA, U.S.A.* **78 B3** 42 30N 71 5W
Wakefield, *MI, U.S.A.* **79 C2** 46 29N 89 56W
Wakefield, *NH, U.S.A.* **86 C3** 43 35N 71 4W
Wakefield, *NE, U.S.A.* **84 B9** 42 16N 96 52W
Wakefield, *PA, U.S.A.* **77 A4** 39 46N 76 11W
Wakefield, *RI, U.S.A.* **78 C3** 41 26N 71 30W
Wakefield, *VA, U.S.A.* **102 E8** 36 58N 76 59W
Wakeham, *Qué., Canada* **172 E5** 48 50N 64 34W
Wakeham Bay = Maricourt, *Qué., Canada* **175 B3** 56 34N 70 49W
Wakita, *OK, U.S.A.* **93 B6** 36 53N 97 55W
Wakomata L., *Ont., Canada* **178 A3** 46 34N 83 22W
Wakonda, *SD, U.S.A.* **91 G8** 43 0N 97 6W
Wakpala, *SD, U.S.A.* **91 E5** 45 40N 100 32W
Wakuach, L., *Qué., Canada* **175 B4** 55 34N 67 32W
Wakulla, *FL, U.S.A.* **67 A4** 30 14N 84 14W
Wakulla Beach, *FL, U.S.A.* **67 A4** 30 6N 84 16W
Wakulla County ☆, *FL, U.S.A.* **67 A4** 30 15N 84 20W
Walcott, *IA, U.S.A.* **73 D8** 41 35N 90 47W
Walcott, *ND, U.S.A.* **91 D9** 46 33N 96 56W
Walcott, *WY, U.S.A.* **104 E6** 41 46N 106 51W
Walcott, L., *ID, U.S.A.* **70 G5** 42 40N 113 29W
Waldeck, *Sask., Canada* **182 E4** 50 22N 107 36W
Walden, *CO, U.S.A.* **66 B4** 40 44N 106 17W
Walden, *NY, U.S.A.* **89 D6** 41 34N 74 11W
Walden, *TN, U.S.A.* **97 E7** 35 10N 85 18W
Walden Res., *CO, U.S.A.* **66 B4** 40 43N 106 17W
Walden Ridge, *TN, U.S.A.* **97 E7** 35 30N 85 15W
Waldheim, *Sask., Canada* **182 C5** 52 39N 106 37W
Waldo, *AR, U.S.A.* **63 E2** 33 21N 93 18W
Waldo, *FL, U.S.A.* **67 B6** 29 48N 82 10W
Waldo, *ME, U.S.A.* **76 D4** 44 31N 69 5W
Waldo, *OH, U.S.A.* **92 C3** 40 28N 83 5W
Waldo County ☆, *ME, U.S.A.* **76 D4** 44 25N 69 0W
Waldo L., *OR, U.S.A.* **94 D3** 43 44N 122 2W
Waldoboro, *ME, U.S.A.* **76 D4** 44 6N 69 23W
Waldorf, *MD, U.S.A.* **77 B4** 38 38N 76 55W
Waldorf, *MN, U.S.A.* **80 G5** 43 56N 93 42W
Waldport, *OR, U.S.A.* **94 C1** 44 26N 124 4W
Waldron, *AR, U.S.A.* **63 D1** 34 54N 94 5W
Waldron, *IN, U.S.A.* **72 D5** 39 27N 85 40W
Waldron, *MI, U.S.A.* **79 H7** 41 44N 84 25W
Waldwick, *NJ, U.S.A.* **87 A2** 41 1N 74 7W
Wales, *AK, U.S.A.* **61 D5** 65 37N 168 5W
Wales, *MA, U.S.A.* **78 B2** 42 4N 72 13W
Wales, *ND, U.S.A.* **91 B7** 48 54N 98 36W
Wales, *UT, U.S.A.* **100 D4** 39 29N 111 38W
Wales I., *Nunavut, Canada* **175 A3** 62 0N 72 30W
Wales I., *Nunavut, Canada* **190 D8** 68 1N 86 40W
Walford, *IA, U.S.A.* **73 D7** 41 53N 91 50W
Walhachin, *B.C., Canada* **187 E14** 50 45N 120 59W
Walhalla, *ND, U.S.A.* **91 B8** 48 55N 97 55W
Walhalla, *SC, U.S.A.* **90 D2** 34 46N 83 4W
Walk, L., *TX, U.S.A.* **98 H7** 29 31N 100 59W
Walker, *IA, U.S.A.* **73 C7** 42 17N 91 47W
Walker, *LA, U.S.A.* **75 D5** 30 29N 90 51W
Walker, *MI, U.S.A.* **79 G6** 42 58N 85 46W
Walker, *MN, U.S.A.* **80 C4** 47 6N 94 35W
Walker, *MO, U.S.A.* **82 D2** 37 54N 94 14W
Walker, *SD, U.S.A.* **91 E4** 45 55N 101 5W
Walker →, *NV, U.S.A.* **85 D2** 38 54N 118 47W
Walker, L., *Qué., Canada* **175 C4** 50 20N 67 11W
Walker County ☆, *AL, U.S.A.* **60 C3** 33 50N 87 17W
Walker County ☆, *GA, U.S.A.* **68 B1** 34 45N 85 15W
Walker County ☆, *TX, U.S.A.* **99 G12** 30 43N 95 33W
Walker L., *NV, U.S.A.* **85 D2** 38 42N 118 43W
Walker River Indian Reservation, *NV, U.S.A.* **85 D2** 39 0N 118 50W
Walkers Pt., *ME, U.S.A.* **76 E3** 43 21N 70 28W
Walkersville, *MD, U.S.A.* **77 A3** 39 29N 77 21W
Walkerton, *Ont., Canada* **178 C5** 44 10N 81 10W
Walkerton, *IN, U.S.A.* **72 B4** 41 28N 86 29W
Walkertown, *NC, U.S.A.* **90 B5** 36 10N 80 10W
Walkerville, *MI, U.S.A.* **79 F5** 43 43N 86 8W
Wall, *SD, U.S.A.* **91 F3** 44 0N 102 8W
Wall, *TX, U.S.A.* **98 F7** 31 22N 100 18W
Wall Lake, *IA, U.S.A.* **73 C3** 42 16N 95 5W
Walla Walla, *WA, U.S.A.* **101 D7** 46 4N 118 20W
Walla Walla →, *WA, U.S.A.* **101 D7** 46 3N 118 55W
Walla Walla County ☆, *WA, U.S.A.* **101 D7** 46 18N 118 37W
Wallace, *N.S., Canada* **173 H6** 45 48N 63 29W
Wallace, *ID, U.S.A.* **70 B3** 47 28N 115 56W
Wallace, *KS, U.S.A.* **74 C2** 38 58N 101 36W
Wallace, *NC, U.S.A.* **90 D8** 34 44N 77 59W
Wallace, *NE, U.S.A.* **84 D4** 40 50N 101 10W
Wallace, *SD, U.S.A.* **91 E8** 45 5N 97 29W
Wallace County ☆, *KS, U.S.A.* **74 C2** 38 50N 101 45W
Wallace Mt., *Alta., Canada* **184 D5** 54 58N 115 48W
Wallaceburg, *Ont., Canada* **178 E4** 42 34N 82 23W
Walland, *TN, U.S.A.* **97 E9** 35 44N 83 49W
Wallenpaupack, L., *PA, U.S.A.* **87 A1** 41 25N 75 15W
Waller, *TX, U.S.A.* **99 G12** 30 4N 95 56W
Waller County ☆, *TX, U.S.A.* **99 G11** 30 0N 96 0W
Wallingford, *CT, U.S.A.* **78 C2** 41 27N 72 50W
Wallingford, *IA, U.S.A.* **73 B4** 43 19N 94 48W
Wallingford, *VT, U.S.A.* **86 C2** 43 28N 72 59W
Wallington, *NJ, U.S.A.* **114 A2** 40 51N 74 6W
Wallis, *TX, U.S.A.* **99 H11** 29 38N 96 4W
Wallisville L., *TX, U.S.A.* **99 H13** 29 57N 94 54W
Wallkill →, *NY, U.S.A.* **89 D6** 41 51N 74 3W
Walloon L., *MI, U.S.A.* **79 D7** 45 17N 85 0W
Wallops I., *VA, U.S.A.* **77 C5** 37 51N 75 28W
Wallowa, *OR, U.S.A.* **94 B8** 45 34N 117 32W
Wallowa →, *OR, U.S.A.* **94 B8** 45 43N 117 47W
Wallowa County ☆, *OR, U.S.A.* **94 B8** 45 30N 117 10W
Wallowa Mts., *OR, U.S.A.* **94 B8** 45 20N 117 30W
Wallowa-Whitman Nat. Forest, *OR, U.S.A.* **94 B8** 45 15N 117 20W
Walls, *MS, U.S.A.* **81 B3** 34 58N 90 9W
Wallsburg, *UT, U.S.A.* **100 C4** 40 23N 111 25W
Wallula, *WA, U.S.A.* **101 D7** 46 5N 118 54W
Wallula, L., *WA, U.S.A.* **101 D7** 46 2N 118 59W
Walnut, *IL, U.S.A.* **71 B4** 41 33N 89 36W
Walnut, *IA, U.S.A.* **73 D3** 41 29N 95 13W
Walnut, *KS, U.S.A.* **74 D8** 37 36N 95 5W
Walnut, *MS, U.S.A.* **81 B5** 34 57N 88 54W
Walnut →, *KS, U.S.A.* **74 D6** 37 3N 97 0W
Walnut Canyon Nat. Monument ⌂, *AZ, U.S.A.* **62 B4** 35 15N 111 20W
Walnut Cove, *NC, U.S.A.* **90 B5** 36 18N 80 9W
Walnut Cr. →, *KS, U.S.A.* **74 C5** 38 21N 98 41W
Walnut Cr. →, *OH, U.S.A.* **92 D4** 39 41N 82 59W
Walnut Creek, *CA, U.S.A.* **64 F4** 37 54N 122 4W
Walnut Creek, *NC, U.S.A.* **90 C8** 35 18N 77 52W
Walnut Grove, *AL, U.S.A.* **60 B4** 34 4N 86 18W
Walnut Grove, *MS, U.S.A.* **81 D4** 32 36N 89 28W
Walnut Grove, *MO, U.S.A.* **82 D3** 37 25N 93 33W
Walnut Hill, *FL, U.S.A.* **67 A1** 30 53N 87 30W
Walnut Park, *Los Angeles, U.S.A.* **111 C3** 33 58N 118 13W
Walnut Ridge, *AR, U.S.A.* **63 B5** 36 4N 90 57W
Walnut Springs, *TX, U.S.A.* **99 E10** 32 3N 97 45W
Walpole, *MA, U.S.A.* **78 B3** 42 9N 71 15W
Walpole, *NH, U.S.A.* **86 C2** 43 5N 72 26W
Walsenburg, *CO, U.S.A.* **66 E6** 37 38N 104 47W
Walsh, *Alta., Canada* **185 J10** 49 57N 110 3W
Walsh, *CO, U.S.A.* **66 E8** 37 23N 102 17W
Walsh County ☆, *ND, U.S.A.* **91 B8** 48 24N 97 45W
Walt Disney World, *U.S.A.* **67 C7** 28 25N 81 35W
Walter Chandler Park, *TN, U.S.A.* **112 B1** 35 1N 90 3W
Walter F. George Res., *U.S.A.* **60 E5** 31 38N 85 4W
Walterboro, *SC, U.S.A.* **90 F5** 32 55N 80 40W
Walters, *OK, U.S.A.* **93 D5** 34 22N 98 19W
Walterville, *OR, U.S.A.* **94 C3** 44 4N 122 48W
Walthall, *MS, U.S.A.* **81 C4** 33 37N 89 17W
Walthall County ☆, *MS, U.S.A.* **81 E3** 31 7N 90 9W
Waltham, *Qué., Canada* **176 F6** 45 57N 76 57W
Waltham, *ME, U.S.A.* **76 D5** 44 43N 68 20W
Waltham, *MA, U.S.A.* **78 B3** 42 23N 71 14W
Walthill, *NE, U.S.A.* **84 B9** 42 9N 96 30W
Waltman, *WY, U.S.A.* **104 C5** 43 4N 107 12W
Walton, *N.S., Canada* **173 H5** 45 14N 64 0W
Walton, *IN, U.S.A.* **72 C4** 40 40N 86 15W
Walton, *KS, U.S.A.* **74 C6** 38 7N 97 15W
Walton, *KY, U.S.A.* **97 B8** 38 52N 84 37W
Walton, *NY, U.S.A.* **89 C5** 42 10N 75 8W
Walton County ☆, *FL, U.S.A.* **67 A2** 30 30N 86 10W
Walton County ☆, *GA, U.S.A.* **68 C3** 33 45N 83 45W
Waltonville, *IL, U.S.A.* **71 E4** 38 13N 89 2W
Walworth County ☆, *SD, U.S.A.* **91 E6** 45 30N 100 0W
Walworth County ☆, *WI, U.S.A.* **103 F5** 42 40N 88 30W
Wamac, *IL, U.S.A.* **71 E4** 38 31N 89 8W
Wamego, *KS, U.S.A.* **74 B7** 39 12N 96 18W
Wampsville, *NY, U.S.A.* **89 B5** 43 5N 75 42W
Wampum, *PA, U.S.A.* **95 D2** 40 54N 80 21W
Wamsutter, *WY, U.S.A.* **104 E5** 41 40N 107 58W
Wanamingo, *MN, U.S.A.* **80 F6** 44 18N 92 47W
Wanapitei →, *Ont., Canada* **178 A6** 46 2N 80 51W
Wanapitei L., *Ont., Canada* **178 A6** 46 45N 80 40W
Wanapum Dam, *WA, U.S.A.* **101 D6** 46 52N 119 58W
Wanaque, *NJ, U.S.A.* **87 A2** 41 2N 74 18W
Wanaque Res., *NJ, U.S.A.* **87 A2** 41 2N 74 18W
Wanatah, *IN, U.S.A.* **72 B4** 41 26N 86 54W
Wanblee, *SD, U.S.A.* **91 G4** 43 34N 101 40W
Wanchese, *NC, U.S.A.* **90 C10** 35 51N 75 38W
Wanda, *MN, U.S.A.* **80 F3** 44 19N 95 13W
Wanette, *OK, U.S.A.* **93 D6** 34 58N 97 2W
Wango, *MD, U.S.A.* **77 B5** 38 20N 75 25W
Wanham, *Alta., Canada* **184 C2** 55 44N 118 24W
Wanless, *Man., Canada* **183 A10** 54 11N 101 21W
Wann, *OK, U.S.A.* **93 B8** 36 55N 95 48W
Wapack Nat. Wildlife Refuge ⌂, *NH, U.S.A.* **86 D3** 42 53N 71 52W
Wapakoneta, *OH, U.S.A.* **92 C2** 40 34N 84 12W
Wapanucka, *OK, U.S.A.* **93 D7** 34 23N 96 26W
Wapato, *WA, U.S.A.* **101 D5** 46 27N 120 25W
Wapella, *Sask., Canada* **183 E10** 50 16N 101 58W
Wapello, *IA, U.S.A.* **73 D7** 41 11N 91 11W
Wapello County ☆, *IA, U.S.A.* **73 E6** 41 0N 92 25W
Wapinitia Pass, *OR, U.S.A.* **94 B4** 45 14N 121 42W
Wapiti, *WY, U.S.A.* **104 B3** 44 28N 109 26W
Wapiti →, *Alta., Canada* **184 C2** 55 5N 118 18W
Wappapello L., *MO, U.S.A.* **82 E6** 36 56N 90 17W
Wappingers Falls, *NY, U.S.A.* **89 D7** 41 36N 73 55W
Wapsipinicon →, *IA, U.S.A.* **73 D8** 41 44N 90 19W
Wapusk Nat. Park △, *Man., Canada* **191 F7** 57 46N 93 22W
War, *WV, U.S.A.* **102 D3** 37 18N 81 41W
War in the Pacific Nat. Hist. Park △, *Guam* **105 b** 13 24N 144 39W
Warburg, *Alta., Canada* **185 E6** 53 11N 114 19W
Ward, *AR, U.S.A.* **63 C4** 35 2N 91 57W
Ward, *SD, U.S.A.* **91 F9** 44 9N 96 28W
Ward County ☆, *ND, U.S.A.* **91 B4** 48 5N 101 30W
Ward County ☆, *TX, U.S.A.* **98 F4** 31 32N 103 8W
Wardell, *MO, U.S.A.* **82 E7** 36 21N 89 49W
Warden, *WA, U.S.A.* **101 D6** 46 58N 119 2W
Wardensville, *WV, U.S.A.* **77 A2** 39 5N 78 36W
Wardlow, *Alta., Canada* **185 H9** 50 56N 111 31W
Wardner, *B.C., Canada* **185 J5** 49 25N 115 26W
Wardsville, *MO, U.S.A.* **82 C4** 38 29N 92 11W
Ware, *B.C., Canada* **189 E7** 57 26N 125 41W
Ware, *MA, U.S.A.* **78 B2** 42 16N 72 14W
Ware →, *MA, U.S.A.* **78 B2** 42 11N 72 22W
Ware County ☆, *GA, U.S.A.* **68 E4** 31 10N 82 20W
Ware Shoals, *SC, U.S.A.* **90 D3** 34 24N 82 15W
Wareham, *MA, U.S.A.* **78 C4** 41 46N 70 43W
Warehouse Point, *CT, U.S.A.* **78 C2** 41 56N 72 37W
Waresboro, *GA, U.S.A.* **68 E4** 31 15N 82 29W
Warfield, *B.C., Canada* **187 F17** 49 6N 117 46W
Warfield, *KY, U.S.A.* **97 C10** 37 51N 82 25W
Warm Lake, *ID, U.S.A.* **70 E3** 44 39N 115 40W
Warm Springs, *GA, U.S.A.* **68 D2** 32 53N 84 41W
Warm Springs, *NV, U.S.A.* **85 D4** 38 10N 116 20W
Warm Springs, *OR, U.S.A.* **94 C4** 44 46N 121 16W
Warm Springs, *VA, U.S.A.* **102 C5** 38 3N 79 47W
Warm Springs →, *OR, U.S.A.* **94 C4** 44 51N 121 4W
Warm Springs Indian Reservation, *OR, U.S.A.* **94 C4** 45 0N 121 25W
Warm Springs Res., *OR, U.S.A.* **94 D7** 43 35N 118 13W
Warman, *Sask., Canada* **182 C5** 52 19N 106 30W
Warminster, *PA, U.S.A.* **95 D7** 40 12N 75 6W
Warner, *Alta., Canada* **185 J8** 49 17N 112 12W
Warner, *NH, U.S.A.* **86 C3** 43 17N 71 49W
Warner, *OK, U.S.A.* **93 C8** 35 30N 95 18W
Warner, *SD, U.S.A.* **91 E7** 45 20N 98 30W
Warner Mts., *CA, U.S.A.* **64 B6** 41 40N 120 15W
Warner Robins, *GA, U.S.A.* **68 D3** 32 37N 83 36W
Warner Springs, *CA, U.S.A.* **65 K10** 33 17N 116 38W
Warner Valley, *OR, U.S.A.* **94 E6** 42 25N 119 50W
Warr Acres, *OK, U.S.A.* **93 C6** 35 31N 97 37W
Warren, *Ont., Canada* **178 A6** 46 27N 80 18W
Warren, *AR, U.S.A.* **63 E3** 33 37N 92 4W
Warren, *CT, U.S.A.* **78 C1** 41 44N 73 21W
Warren, *ID, U.S.A.* **70 D3** 45 16N 115 41W
Warren, *IL, U.S.A.* **71 A4** 42 29N 90 0W
Warren, *IN, U.S.A.* **72 C5** 40 41N 85 26W
Warren, *MI, U.S.A.* **79 G8** 42 28N 83 1W
Warren, *MN, U.S.A.* **80 B2** 48 12N 96 46W
Warren, *NH, U.S.A.* **86 C3** 43 56N 71 53W
Warren, *OH, U.S.A.* **92 B6** 41 14N 80 49W
Warren, *PA, U.S.A.* **95 C3** 41 51N 79 9W
Warren, *RI, U.S.A.* **78 C3** 41 43N 71 17W
Warren, *TX, U.S.A.* **99 G13** 30 37N 94 24W
Warren, *VT, U.S.A.* **86 B2** 44 7N 72 50W
Warren Air Force Base, *WY, U.S.A.* **104 E8** 41 10N 104 54W
Warren County ☆, *GA, U.S.A.* **68 C4** 33 20N 82 40W
Warren County ☆, *IL, U.S.A.* **71 C3** 40 50N 90 35W
Warren County ☆, *IN, U.S.A.* **72 C3** 40 20N 87 25W
Warren County ☆, *IA, U.S.A.* **73 D5** 41 20N 93 35W
Warren County ☆, *KY, U.S.A.* **96 C6** 37 0N 86 25W
Warren County ☆, *MS, U.S.A.* **81 D3** 32 21N 90 53W
Warren County ☆, *MO, U.S.A.* **82 C5** 38 45N 91 10W
Warren County ☆, *NC, U.S.A.* **90 B7** 36 15N 78 0W
Warren County ☆, *NJ, U.S.A.* **87 B2** 40 50N 75 0W
Warren County ☆, *NY, U.S.A.* **89 B7** 43 35N 73 45W
Warren County ☆, *OH, U.S.A.* **92 D2** 39 26N 84 13W
Warren County ☆, *PA, U.S.A.* **95 C3** 41 50N 79 15W
Warren County ☆, *TN, U.S.A.* **97 E7** 35 41N 85 46W
Warren County ☆, *VA, U.S.A.* **102 C6** 38 55N 78 12W
Warren Grove, *NJ, U.S.A.* **87 C2** 39 44N 74 22W
Warren Park, *Indianapolis, U.S.A.* **110 B2** 39 46N 86 3W
Warren Pks., *WY, U.S.A.* **104 B8** 44 29N 104 28W
Warrens, *WI, U.S.A.* **103 D3** 44 8N 90 30W
Warrensburg, *IL, U.S.A.* **71 D4** 39 56N 89 4W
Warrensburg, *MO, U.S.A.* **82 C3** 38 46N 93 44W
Warrensburg, *NY, U.S.A.* **89 B7** 43 29N 73 46W
Warrenton, *GA, U.S.A.* **68 C4** 33 24N 82 40W
Warrenton, *MO, U.S.A.* **82 C5** 38 49N 91 9W
Warrenton, *NC, U.S.A.* **90 B7** 36 24N 78 9W
Warrenton, *OR, U.S.A.* **94 A2** 46 10N 123 56W
Warrenton, *VA, U.S.A.* **77 B3** 38 43N 77 48W
Warrenville, *SC, U.S.A.* **90 E4** 33 33N 81 48W
Warrick County ☆, *IN, U.S.A.* **72 E3** 38 5N 87 15W
Warrington, *FL, U.S.A.* **67 A1** 30 23N 87 17W
Warrior, *AL, U.S.A.* **60 C4** 33 49N 86 49W
Warroad, *MN, U.S.A.* **80 B3** 48 54N 95 19W
Warsaw, *IL, U.S.A.* **71 C2** 40 22N 91 26W
Warsaw, *IN, U.S.A.* **72 B5** 41 14N 85 51W
Warsaw, *KY, U.S.A.* **97 B8** 38 47N 84 54W
Warsaw, *MO, U.S.A.* **82 C3** 38 15N 93 23W
Warsaw, *NC, U.S.A.* **90 C7** 35 0N 78 5W
Warsaw, *NY, U.S.A.* **89 C2** 42 45N 78 8W
Warsaw, *VA, U.S.A.* **102 D8** 37 58N 76 46W
Wartburg, *TN, U.S.A.* **97 D8** 36 6N 84 36W
Warthen, *GA, U.S.A.* **68 C4** 33 6N 82 48W
Wartrace, *TN, U.S.A.* **96 E6** 35 32N 86 20W
Warwick, *GA, U.S.A.* **68 E3** 31 50N 83 57W
Warwick, *MD, U.S.A.* **77 A5** 39 25N 75 47W
Warwick, *ND, U.S.A.* **91 C7** 47 51N 98 43W
Warwick, *NY, U.S.A.* **87 A2** 41 16N 74 22W
Warwick, *OK, U.S.A.* **93 C7** 35 41N 97 0W
Warwick, *RI, U.S.A.* **78 C3** 41 42N 71 28W
Wasaga Beach, *Ont., Canada* **178 C6** 44 31N 80 1W
Wasatch-Cache Nat. Forest, *UT, U.S.A.* **100 C5** 41 14N 111 25W
Wasatch County ☆, *UT, U.S.A.* **100 C4** 40 20N 111 15W
Wasatch Plateau, *UT, U.S.A.* **100 D4** 39 20N 111 30W
Wasatch Ra., *UT, U.S.A.* **100 D4** 40 0N 111 30W
Wasco, *CA, U.S.A.* **65 H7** 35 36N 119 20W
Wasco, *OR, U.S.A.* **94 B5** 45 36N 120 42W
Wasco County ☆, *OR, U.S.A.* **94 B4** 45 15N 121 15W
Waseca, *Sask., Canada* **182 B2** 53 6N 109 28W
Waseca, *MN, U.S.A.* **80 F5** 44 5N 93 30W
Waseca County ☆, *MN, U.S.A.* **80 F5** 44 0N 93 40W
Washago, *Ont., Canada* **178 C7** 44 45N 79 20W
Washakie County ☆, *WY, U.S.A.* **104 C5** 44 0N 107 40W
Washburn, *IL, U.S.A.* **71 C4** 40 55N 89 17W
Washburn, *ME, U.S.A.* **76 B5** 46 47N 68 9W
Washburn, *MO, U.S.A.* **82 E3** 36 35N 93 58W
Washburn, *ND, U.S.A.* **91 C4** 47 17N 101 2W
Washburn, *TX, U.S.A.* **98 B6** 35 11N 101 34W
Washburn, *WI, U.S.A.* **103 B3** 46 40N 90 54W
Washburn, Mt., *WY, U.S.A.* **104 B2** 44 48N 110 26W
Washburn County ☆, *WI, U.S.A.* **103 C2** 45 50N 91 50W
Washburn L., *Nunavut, Canada* **190 C4** 70 3N 107 30W
Washi L., *Ont., Canada* **181 A9** 51 24N 87 2W
Washicoutai, L., *Qué., Canada* **172 C9** 50 20N 60 50W
Washington, *AR, U.S.A.* **63 E2** 33 47N 93 41W
Washington, *CT, U.S.A.* **78 C1** 41 39N 73 19W
Washington, *DC, U.S.A.* **77 B3** 38 53N 77 2W
Washington, *GA, U.S.A.* **68 C4** 33 44N 82 44W
Washington, *IL, U.S.A.* **71 C4** 40 42N 89 24W
Washington, *IN, U.S.A.* **72 E3** 38 40N 87 10W
Washington, *IA, U.S.A.* **73 D7** 41 18N 91 42W
Washington, *KS, U.S.A.* **74 B6** 39 49N 97 3W
Washington, *KY, U.S.A.* **97 B9** 38 37N 83 49W
Washington, *LA, U.S.A.* **75 D3** 30 37N 92 4W
Washington, *ME, U.S.A.* **76 D4** 44 16N 69 22W
Washington, *MS, U.S.A.* **81 E2** 31 35N 91 18W
Washington, *MO, U.S.A.* **82 C5** 38 33N 91 1W
Washington, *NC, U.S.A.* **90 C8** 35 33N 77 3W
Washington, *NH, U.S.A.* **86 C2** 43 11N 72 8W
Washington, *NJ, U.S.A.* **87 B2** 40 46N 74 59W
Washington, *NE, U.S.A.* **84 C9** 41 24N 96 13W
Washington, *OK, U.S.A.* **93 C6** 35 4N 97 29W
Washington, *PA, U.S.A.* **95 D2** 40 10N 80 15W
Washington, *UT, U.S.A.* **100 F2** 37 8N 113 31W
Washington, *VA, U.S.A.* **77 B2** 38 43N 78 10W
Washington □, *U.S.A.* **101 C5** 47 30N 120 30W
Washington, Lake, *Seattle, U.S.A.* **118 B4** 47 37N 122 15W
Washington, Mt., *NH, U.S.A.* **86 B3** 44 16N 71 18W
Washington County ☆, *AL, U.S.A.* **60 E2** 31 22N 88 15W
Washington County ☆, *AR, U.S.A.* **63 B1** 36 4N 94 10W
Washington County ☆, *CO, U.S.A.* **66 C7** 40 0N 103 10W
Washington County ☆, *FL, U.S.A.* **67 A3** 30 30N 85 45W
Washington County ☆, *GA, U.S.A.* **68 C4** 33 0N 82 50W
Washington County ☆, *ID, U.S.A.* **70 E2** 44 30N 116 50W
Washington County ☆, *IL, U.S.A.* **71 E4** 38 20N 89 25W
Washington County ☆, *IN, U.S.A.* **72 E4** 38 35N 86 5W
Washington County ☆, *IA, U.S.A.* **73 D7** 41 20N 91 40W
Washington County ☆, *KS, U.S.A.* **74 B6** 39 45N 97 0W
Washington County ☆, *KY, U.S.A.* **97 C7** 37 45N 85 10W
Washington County ☆, *ME, U.S.A.* **76 C6** 45 0N 67 30W
Washington County ☆, *MD, U.S.A.* **77 A3** 39 40N 78 0W
Washington County ☆, *MN, U.S.A.* **80 E6** 45 10N 92 55W
Washington County ☆, *MS, U.S.A.* **81 C3** 33 16N 90 53W
Washington County ☆, *MO, U.S.A.* **82 D6** 38 0N 90 50W
Washington County ☆, *NC, U.S.A.* **90 C9** 35 50N 76 30W
Washington County ☆, *NY, U.S.A.* **89 B7** 43 20N 73 25W
Washington County ☆, *NE, U.S.A.* **84 C9** 41 30N 96 15W
Washington County ☆, *OH, U.S.A.* **92 D5** 39 25N 81 27W
Washington County ☆, *OK, U.S.A.* **93 B8** 36 40N 95 55W
Washington County ☆, *OR, U.S.A.* **94 B2** 45 30N 123 0W
Washington County ☆, *PA, U.S.A.* **95 D2** 40 8N 80 8W
Washington County ☆, *RI, U.S.A.* **78 C3** 41 30N 71 40W
Washington County ☆, *TN, U.S.A.* **97 D10** 36 18N 82 29W
Washington County ☆, *TX, U.S.A.* **99 G11** 30 10N 96 24W
Washington County ☆, *UT, U.S.A.* **100 F2** 37 20N 113 30W
Washington County ☆, *VA, U.S.A.* **102 E3** 36 55N 82 0W
Washington County ☆, *VT, U.S.A.* **86 B2** 44 15N 72 40W
Washington County ☆, *WI, U.S.A.* **103 E5** 43 20N 88 15W
Washington Court House, *OH, U.S.A.* **92 D3** 39 32N 83 26W
Washington Dulles International ✕ (IAD), *VA, U.S.A.* **102 C7** 38 57N 77 27W
Washington Grove, *MD, U.S.A.* **77 A3** 39 8N 77 11W
Washington Heights, *NY, U.S.A.* **114 A3** 40 51N 73 56W
Washington I., *WI, U.S.A.* **103 C7** 45 23N 86 54W
Washington Island, *WI, U.S.A.* **103 C7** 45 24N 86 56W
Washington Parish ☆, *LA, U.S.A.* **75 D5** 30 51N 90 9W
Washington Park, *Chicago, U.S.A.* **108 C3** 41 47N 87 36W
Washington Park, *IL, U.S.A.* **117 B3** 38 38N 90 5W
Washington Park, *Indianapolis, U.S.A.* **110 B2** 39 49N 86 7W
Washington Park, *Milwaukee, U.S.A.* **112 B2** 43 4N 87 58W
Washington Park, *Portland, U.S.A.* **116 A1** 45 30N 122 42W
Washington Ronald Reagan National ✕ (DCA), *VA, U.S.A.* **102 C7** 38 51N 77 2W
Washington Terrace, *UT, U.S.A.* **100 B4** 41 11N 111 59W
Washingtonville, *NY, U.S.A.* **87 A2** 41 26N 74 10W
Washita →, *OK, U.S.A.* **93 D7** 34 8N 96 36W
Washita Battlefield Nat. Historic Site ⌂, *OK, U.S.A.* **93 C4** 35 57N 99 42W
Washita County ☆, *OK, U.S.A.* **93 C5** 35 15N 99 0W
Washoe City, *NV, U.S.A.* **85 C1** 39 19N 119 49W
Washoe County ☆, *NV, U.S.A.* **85 B1** 41 0N 119 40W
Washoe L., *NV, U.S.A.* **85 C1** 39 16N 119 48W
Washougal, *WA, U.S.A.* **101 E3** 45 35N 122 21W
Washta, *IA, U.S.A.* **73 C3** 42 35N 95 43W
Washtenaw County ☆, *MI, U.S.A.* **79 G8** 42 15N 83 50W
Washtucna, *WA, U.S.A.* **101 D7** 46 45N 118 19W
Wasilla, *AK, U.S.A.* **61 F10** 61 35N 149 26W
Waskada, *Man., Canada* **183 F11** 49 6N 100 48W
Waskaganish, *Qué., Canada* **175 C2** 51 30N 78 40W
Waskatenau, *Alta., Canada* **184 D8** 54 7N 112 47W
Waskesiu L., *Sask., Canada* **182 B5** 53 58N 106 12W
Waskesiu Lake, *Sask., Canada* **182 B5** 53 55N 106 5W
Waskish, *MN, U.S.A.* **80 B4** 48 10N 94 31W
Waskom, *TX, U.S.A.* **99 E13** 32 29N 94 4W
Wassaw I., *GA, U.S.A.* **68 E6** 31 53N 80 58W
Wassaw Sd., *GA, U.S.A.* **68 E6** 31 55N 80 55W
Wassuk Range, *NV, U.S.A.* **85 D2** 38 40N 118 50W
Wasta, *SD, U.S.A.* **91 F3** 44 4N 102 27W
Waswanipi, *Qué., Canada* **175 D2** 49 40N 76 29W
Waswanipi →, *Qué., Canada* **175 D2** 49 40N 76 25W
Waswanipi, L., *Qué., Canada* **176 B6** 49 35N 76 40W
Watauga, *Dallas-Fort Worth, U.S.A.* **109 A2** 32 51N 97 15W
Watauga, *TN, U.S.A.* **97 D10** 36 22N 82 18W
Watauga County ☆, *NC, U.S.A.* **90 B4** 36 15N 81 45W
Watauga L., *TN, U.S.A.* **97 D10** 36 19N 82 7W
Water Valley, *KY, U.S.A.* **96 D4** 36 34N 88 49W
Water Valley, *MS, U.S.A.* **81 B4** 34 10N 89 38W
Waterboro, *ME, U.S.A.* **76 E3** 43 32N 70 43W
Waterbury, *CT, U.S.A.* **78 C1** 41 33N 73 3W
Waterbury, *NE, U.S.A.* **84 B9** 42 27N 96 44W
Waterbury, *VT, U.S.A.* **86 B2** 44 20N 72 46W
Waterbury Center, *VT, U.S.A.* **86 B2** 44 23N 72 43W
Waterbury Res., *VT, U.S.A.* **86 B2** 44 23N 72 46W
Waterdown, *Ont., Canada* **178 D7** 43 20N 79 53W
Wateree →, *SC, U.S.A.* **90 E5** 33 45N 80 37W
Wateree, L., *SC, U.S.A.* **90 D5** 34 20N 80 42W
Waterflow, *NM, U.S.A.* **88 A2** 36 45N 108 27W
Waterford, *Ont., Canada* **178 E6** 42 56N 80 17W

Waterford, *CA, U.S.A.* **64 F6** 37 38N 120 46W
Waterford, *CT, U.S.A.* **78 C2** 41 20N 72 9W
Waterford, *ME, U.S.A.* **76 D3** 44 14N 70 46W
Waterford, *MI, U.S.A.* **79 G8** 42 45N 83 32W
Waterford, *MS, U.S.A.* **81 B4** 34 39N 89 28W
Waterford, *NY, U.S.A.* **78 B1** 42 48N 73 41W
Waterford, *PA, U.S.A.* **95 C3** 41 57N 79 59W
Waterford, *VA, U.S.A.* **77 A3** 39 11N 77 37W
Waterford, *WI, U.S.A.* **103 F5** 42 46N 88 13W
Waterford →, *Nfld. & L., Canada* **174 E8** 47 33N 52 43W
Watergap, *KY, U.S.A.* **97 C10** 37 38N 82 45W
Waterhen L., *Man., Canada* **183 C12** 52 10N 99 40W
Waterloo, *Ont., Canada* **178 D6** 43 30N 80 32W
Waterloo, *Qué., Canada* **177 F10** 45 22N 72 32W
Waterloo, *AL, U.S.A.* **60 B2** 34 55N 88 4W
Waterloo, *AR, U.S.A.* **63 E2** 33 33N 93 15W
Waterloo, *IL, U.S.A.* **71 E3** 38 20N 90 9W
Waterloo, *IN, U.S.A.* **72 B5** 41 26N 85 1W
Waterloo, *IA, U.S.A.* **73 C6** 42 30N 92 21W
Waterloo, *MT, U.S.A.* **83 E5** 45 43N 112 12W
Waterloo, *NY, U.S.A.* **89 C4** 42 54N 76 52W
Waterloo, *OR, U.S.A.* **94 C3** 44 30N 122 49W
Waterloo, *WI, U.S.A.* **103 E5** 43 11N 88 59W
Waterman, *IL, U.S.A.* **71 B5** 41 46N 88 47W
Waterproof, *LA, U.S.A.* **75 C4** 31 48N 91 23W
Waters, *MI, U.S.A.* **79 E7** 44 53N 84 42W
Watersmeet, *MI, U.S.A.* **79 C2** 46 16N 89 11W
Waterton Park, *Alta., Canada* **185 J7** 49 5N 113 52W
Watertown, *CT, U.S.A.* **78 C1** 41 36N 73 7W
Watertown, *FL, U.S.A.* **67 A6** 30 11N 82 36W
Watertown, *MA, U.S.A.* **78 B3** 42 22N 71 10W
Watertown, *NY, U.S.A.* **89 B5** 43 59N 75 55W
Watertown, *SD, U.S.A.* **91 F8** 44 54N 97 7W
Watertown, *TN, U.S.A.* **96 D6** 36 6N 86 8W
Watertown, *WI, U.S.A.* **103 E5** 43 12N 88 43W
Waterville, *N.S., Canada* **173 H5** 45 3N 64 41W
Waterville, *Qué., Canada* **177 F11** 45 16N 71 54W
Waterville, *KS, U.S.A.* **74 B7** 39 42N 96 45W
Waterville, *ME, U.S.A.* **76 D4** 44 33N 69 38W
Waterville, *MN, U.S.A.* **80 F5** 44 13N 93 34W
Waterville, *NY, U.S.A.* **89 C5** 42 56N 75 23W
Waterville, *OH, U.S.A.* **92 B3** 41 30N 83 43W
Waterville, *VT, U.S.A.* **86 B2** 44 42N 72 47W
Waterville, *WA, U.S.A.* **101 C5** 47 39N 120 4W
Waterville Valley, *NH, U.S.A.* ... **86 C3** 43 57N 71 31W
Watford, *Ont., Canada* **178 E5** 42 57N 81 53W
Watford City, *ND, U.S.A.* **91 C2** 47 48N 103 17W
Wathaman →, *Sask., Canada* **189 E12** 57 16N 102 59W
Wathena, *KS, U.S.A.* **74 B9** 39 46N 94 57W
Watkins, *MN, U.S.A.* **80 E4** 45 19N 94 24W
Watkins Glen, *NY, U.S.A.* **89 C4** 42 23N 76 52W
Watkinsville, *GA, U.S.A.* **68 C3** 33 52N 83 25W
Watonga, *OK, U.S.A.* **93 C5** 35 51N 98 25W
Watonwan County ☆, *MN, U.S.A.* **80 F4** 44 0N 94 40W
Watova, *OK, U.S.A.* **93 B8** 36 37N 95 39W
Watrous, *Sask., Canada* **182 D6** 51 40N 105 25W
Watrous, *NM, U.S.A.* **88 B6** 35 48N 104 59W
Watseka, *IL, U.S.A.* **71 C6** 40 47N 87 44W
Watson, *Sask., Canada* **182 C7** 52 10N 104 30W
Watson, *AR, U.S.A.* **63 E4** 33 54N 91 15W
Watson, *IL, U.S.A.* **71 D5** 39 2N 88 34W
Watson, *MN, U.S.A.* **80 E3** 45 1N 95 48W
Watson, *MO, U.S.A.* **82 A1** 40 29N 95 40W
Watson Lake, *Yukon, Canada* ... **189 D7** 60 6N 128 49W
Watsontown, *PA, U.S.A.* **95 C6** 41 5N 76 52W
Watsonville, *CA, U.S.A.* **64 G5** 36 55N 121 45W
Watts, *OK, U.S.A.* **93 B9** 36 7N 94 34W
Watts Bar L., *TN, U.S.A.* **96 E8** 35 37N 84 47W
Wattsburg, *PA, U.S.A.* **95 B3** 42 0N 79 49W
Watuppa Pond, *MA, U.S.A.* **78 C3** 41 42N 71 6W
Waubamik, *Ont., Canada* **178 B6** 45 27N 80 1W
Waubaushene, *Ont., Canada* **178 C7** 44 45N 79 42W
Waubay, *SD, U.S.A.* **91 E8** 45 20N 97 18W
Waubay L., *SD, U.S.A.* **91 E8** 45 25N 97 24W
Waubun, *MN, U.S.A.* **80 C3** 47 11N 95 57W
Wauchula, *FL, U.S.A.* **67 D7** 27 33N 81 49W
Waucoba Mt., *CA, U.S.A.* **65 F9** 37 1N 118 0W
Waucoma, *IA, U.S.A.* **73 B6** 43 2N 92 1W
Waugh, *Man., Canada* **183 F16** 49 40N 95 11W
Waugoshance Pt., *MI, U.S.A.* ... **79 D6** 45 46N 85 1W
Waukee, *IA, U.S.A.* **73 D5** 41 37N 93 53W
Waukeenah, *FL, U.S.A.* **67 A5** 30 25N 83 57W
Waukegan, *IL, U.S.A.* **71 A6** 42 22N 87 50W
Waukesha, *WI, U.S.A.* **103 E5** 43 1N 88 14W
Waukesha County ☆, *WI, U.S.A.* . **103 F5** 43 0N 88 15W
Waukomis, *OK, U.S.A.* **93 B6** 36 17N 97 54W
Waukon, *IA, U.S.A.* **73 B7** 43 16N 91 29W
Wauna, *Seattle, U.S.A.* **118 D2** 47 22N 122 38W
Waunakee, *WI, U.S.A.* **103 E4** 43 11N 89 27W
Wauneta, *NE, U.S.A.* **84 D4** 40 25N 101 23W
Waupaca, *WI, U.S.A.* **103 D4** 44 21N 89 5W
Waupaca County ☆, *WI, U.S.A.* . **103 D5** 44 25N 89 0W
Waupun, *WI, U.S.A.* **103 E5** 43 38N 88 44W
Waurika, *OK, U.S.A.* **93 D6** 34 10N 98 0W
Waurika L., *OK, U.S.A.* **93 D5** 34 10N 98 3W
Wausa, *NE, U.S.A.* **84 B8** 42 30N 97 32W
Wausau, *FL, U.S.A.* **67 A3** 30 38N 85 35W
Wausau, *WI, U.S.A.* **103 D4** 44 58N 89 38W
Wausaukee, *WI, U.S.A.* **103 C6** 45 23N 87 57W
Wauseon, *OH, U.S.A.* **92 B2** 41 33N 84 8W
Waushara County ☆, *WI, U.S.A.* . **103 D4** 44 10N 89 15W
Wautoma, *WI, U.S.A.* **103 D4** 44 4N 89 18W
Wauwatosa, *WI, U.S.A.* **103 E6** 43 2N 88 0W
Wauzeka, *WI, U.S.A.* **103 E3** 43 5N 90 53W
Waveland, *IN, U.S.A.* **72 D3** 39 53N 87 3W
Waveland, *MS, U.S.A.* **81 F4** 30 17N 89 23W
Waverley, *N.S., Canada* **173 J6** 44 47N 63 36W
Waverley, *Boston, U.S.A.* **106 A2** 42 23N 71 10W
Waverley Hall, *GA, U.S.A.* **68 D2** 32 41N 84 44W
Waverly, *AL, U.S.A.* **60 D5** 32 44N 85 35W
Waverly, *FL, U.S.A.* **67 D7** 27 59N 81 37W
Waverly, *GA, U.S.A.* **68 E5** 31 6N 81 43W
Waverly, *IL, U.S.A.* **71 D4** 39 36N 89 57W
Waverly, *IA, U.S.A.* **73 C6** 42 44N 92 29W
Waverly, *KS, U.S.A.* **74 C8** 38 23N 95 36W
Waverly, *KY, U.S.A.* **96 C5** 37 43N 87 48W
Waverly, *MO, U.S.A.* **82 B3** 39 13N 93 31W
Waverly, *NY, U.S.A.* **89 C4** 42 1N 76 32W
Waverly, *NE, U.S.A.* **84 D9** 40 55N 96 32W
Waverly, *TN, U.S.A.* **96 D5** 36 5N 87 48W
Waverly, *VA, U.S.A.* **77 C3** 37 2N 77 6W
Waverly, *WA, U.S.A.* **101 C8** 47 21N 117 14W
Wawa, *Ont., Canada* **181 E12** 47 59N 84 47W
Wawagosic →, *Qué., Canada* **176 B3** 49 58N 79 6W
Wawanesa, *Man., Canada* **183 F12** 49 36N 99 40W
Wawang L., *Ont., Canada* **180 C6** 49 25N 90 34W
Wawasee, L., *IN, U.S.A.* **72 B5** 41 24N 85 42W
Wawona, *CA, U.S.A.* **64 F7** 37 32N 119 39W
Wawota, *Sask., Canada* **183 F9** 49 54N 102 2W
Waxahachie, *TX, U.S.A.* **99 E11** 32 24N 96 51W
Waxhaw, *NC, U.S.A.* **90 D5** 34 56N 80 45W
Wayagamac, L., *Qué., Canada* ... **177 D10** 47 21N 72 39W
Wayan, *ID, U.S.A.* **70 G7** 42 58N 111 23W
Waycross, *GA, U.S.A.* **68 E4** 31 13N 82 21W
Wayland, *IA, U.S.A.* **73 D7** 41 8N 91 40W
Wayland, *KY, U.S.A.* **97 C10** 37 27N 82 48W
Wayland, *MA, U.S.A.* **78 B3** 42 21N 71 20W
Wayland, *MI, U.S.A.* **79 G6** 42 40N 85 39W
Wayland, *NY, U.S.A.* **89 C3** 42 34N 77 35W
Wayne, *KS, U.S.A.* **74 B6** 39 43N 97 33W
Wayne, *NJ, U.S.A.* **87 B2** 40 55N 74 16W
Wayne, *NE, U.S.A.* **84 B8** 42 14N 97 1W
Wayne, *OH, U.S.A.* **92 B3** 41 18N 83 29W
Wayne, *OK, U.S.A.* **93 D6** 34 55N 97 19W
Wayne, *WV, U.S.A.* **102 C2** 38 13N 82 27W
Wayne County ☆, *GA, U.S.A.* ... **68 E5** 31 30N 82 0W
Wayne County ☆, *IL, U.S.A.* ... **71 E5** 38 25N 88 25W
Wayne County ☆, *IN, U.S.A.* ... **72 D6** 39 50N 85 0W
Wayne County ☆, *IA, U.S.A.* ... **73 E5** 40 45N 93 20W
Wayne County ☆, *KY, U.S.A.* ... **97 D8** 36 45N 84 50W
Wayne County ☆, *MI, U.S.A.* ... **79 G8** 42 15N 83 15W
Wayne County ☆, *MS, U.S.A.* ... **81 E5** 31 40N 88 39W
Wayne County ☆, *MO, U.S.A.* ... **82 D6** 37 5N 90 30W
Wayne County ☆, *NC, U.S.A.* ... **90 C7** 35 20N 78 0W
Wayne County ☆, *NY, U.S.A.* ... **89 B4** 43 10N 77 0W
Wayne County ☆, *NE, U.S.A.* ... **84 B8** 42 15N 97 5W
Wayne County ☆, *OH, U.S.A.* ... **92 C5** 40 48N 81 56W
Wayne County ☆, *PA, U.S.A.* ... **95 C7** 41 35N 75 15W
Wayne County ☆, *TN, U.S.A.* ... **96 E5** 35 10N 87 44W
Wayne County ☆, *UT, U.S.A.* ... **100 E5** 38 15N 111 0W
Wayne County ☆, *WV, U.S.A.* ... **102 C2** 38 13N 82 27W
Wayne County, Detroit ✕ (DTW), *MI, U.S.A.* **79 G8** 42 13N 83 21W
Wayne Nat. Forest, *OH, U.S.A.* .. **92 D5** 39 33N 81 4W
Waynesboro, *GA, U.S.A.* **68 C4** 33 6N 82 1W
Waynesboro, *MS, U.S.A.* **81 E5** 31 40N 88 39W
Waynesboro, *PA, U.S.A.* **77 A3** 39 45N 77 35W
Waynesboro, *TN, U.S.A.* **96 E5** 35 19N 87 46W
Waynesboro, *VA, U.S.A.* **102 C6** 38 4N 78 53W
Waynesburg, *PA, U.S.A.* **95 E2** 39 54N 80 11W
Waynesville, *IL, U.S.A.* **71 C4** 40 15N 89 8W
Waynesville, *MO, U.S.A.* **82 D4** 37 50N 92 12W
Waynesville, *NC, U.S.A.* **90 C3** 35 28N 82 58W
Waynesville, *OH, U.S.A.* **92 D2** 39 32N 84 5W
Waynetown, *IN, U.S.A.* **72 C3** 40 5N 87 4W
Waynoka, *OK, U.S.A.* **93 B5** 36 35N 98 53W
Wayside, *GA, U.S.A.* **68 C3** 33 4N 83 37W
Wayside, *MS, U.S.A.* **81 C2** 33 16N 91 2W
Wayzata, *Minneapolis-St. Paul, U.S.A.* **113 B1** 44 58N 93 30W
Weakley County ☆, *TN, U.S.A.* .. **96 D4** 36 14N 88 50W
Weare, *NH, U.S.A.* **86 C3** 43 6N 71 44W
Weatherby, *MO, U.S.A.* **82 B2** 39 55N 94 14W
Weatherford, *OK, U.S.A.* **93 C5** 35 32N 98 43W
Weatherford, *TX, U.S.A.* **99 E10** 32 46N 97 48W
Weatherly, *PA, U.S.A.* **87 B1** 40 57N 75 50W
Weaubleau, *MO, U.S.A.* **82 D3** 37 54N 93 32W
Weaverville, *CA, U.S.A.* **64 C4** 40 44N 122 56W
Weaverville, *NC, U.S.A.* **90 C3** 35 42N 82 34W
Webb, *Sask., Canada* **182 E3** 50 11N 108 12W
Webb, *IA, U.S.A.* **73 C3** 42 57N 95 1W
Webb, *MS, U.S.A.* **81 C3** 33 57N 90 21W
Webb City, *MO, U.S.A.* **82 D2** 37 9N 94 28W
Webb City, *OK, U.S.A.* **93 B7** 36 48N 96 42W
Webb County ☆, *TX, U.S.A.* **99 K8** 27 30N 99 10W
Webber, *KS, U.S.A.* **74 B5** 39 56N 98 2W
Webbers Falls, *OK, U.S.A.* ... **93 C8** 35 31N 95 8W
Webbville, *KY, U.S.A.* **97 B10** 38 11N 82 52W
Webbwood, *Ont., Canada* **178 A5** 46 16N 81 52W
Webequie, *Ont., Canada* **191 G8** 52 59N 87 21W
Weber →, *U.S.A.* **100 B3** 41 13N 112 8W
Weber County ☆, *UT, U.S.A.* ... **100 B4** 41 20N 111 40W
Webster, *FL, U.S.A.* **67 C6** 28 37N 82 3W
Webster, *IA, U.S.A.* **73 D6** 41 26N 92 10W
Webster, *MA, U.S.A.* **78 B3** 42 3N 71 53W
Webster, *ND, U.S.A.* **91 B7** 48 17N 98 53W
Webster, *NY, U.S.A.* **89 B3** 43 13N 77 26W
Webster, *SD, U.S.A.* **91 E8** 45 20N 97 31W
Webster, *WI, U.S.A.* **103 C1** 45 53N 92 22W
Webster City, *IA, U.S.A.* ... **73 C5** 42 28N 93 49W
Webster County ☆, *GA, U.S.A.* .. **68 E2** 32 0N 84 35W
Webster County ☆, *IA, U.S.A.* .. **73 C4** 42 25N 94 10W
Webster County ☆, *KY, U.S.A.* .. **96 C5** 37 30N 87 40W
Webster County ☆, *MS, U.S.A.* .. **81 C4** 33 37N 89 17W
Webster County ☆, *MO, U.S.A.* .. **82 D4** 37 15N 92 50W
Webster County ☆, *NE, U.S.A.* .. **84 D7** 40 15N 98 30W
Webster County ☆, *WV, U.S.A.* .. **102 C4** 38 29N 80 25W
Webster Groves, *MO, U.S.A.* ... **117 B1** 38 35N 90 21W
Webster Parish ☆, *LA, U.S.A.* .. **75 B2** 32 40N 93 20W
Webster Ra., *ID, U.S.A.* **70 G7** 42 46N 111 11W
Webster Res., *KS, U.S.A.* ... **74 B4** 39 25N 99 26W
Webster Springs, *WV, U.S.A.* .. **102 C4** 38 29N 80 25W
Websters Mill, *PA, U.S.A.* ... **77 A2** 39 52N 78 2W
Weddington, *NC, U.S.A.* **90 C5** 35 1N 80 46W
Wedgeport, *N.S., Canada* ... **173 K4** 43 44N 65 59W
Wedowee, *AL, U.S.A.* **60 C5** 33 19N 85 29W
Weed, *CA, U.S.A.* **64 B4** 41 25N 122 23W
Weed, *NM, U.S.A.* **88 E5** 32 48N 105 31W
Weed Heights, *NV, U.S.A.* ... **85 D1** 38 59N 119 13W
Weedon, *Qué., Canada* **177 F11** 45 42N 71 27W
Weedon Island Preserve, *Tampa, U.S.A.* **119 B3** 27 50N 82 36W
Weedsport, *NY, U.S.A.* **89 B4** 43 3N 76 34W
Weedville, *PA, U.S.A.* **95 C4** 41 17N 78 30W
Weehawken, *NJ, U.S.A.* **114 B2** 40 45N 74 2W
Weekapaug, *RI, U.S.A.* **78 C3** 41 20N 71 45W
Weekes, *Sask., Canada* **182 C9** 52 34N 102 52W
Weekstown, *NJ, U.S.A.* **87 C2** 39 37N 74 37W
Weeping Water, *NE, U.S.A.* .. **84 D9** 40 52N 96 8W
Weigelstown, *PA, U.S.A.* ... **95 E6** 39 59N 76 49W
Weimar, *CA, U.S.A.* **64 D6** 39 2N 120 59W
Weimar, *TX, U.S.A.* **99 H11** 29 42N 96 47W
Weinberg-King State Park ⌂, *IL, U.S.A.* **71 C3** 40 14N 90 54W
Weiner, *AR, U.S.A.* **63 C5** 35 37N 90 54W
Weippe, *ID, U.S.A.* **70 C3** 46 23N 115 56W
Weir, *KS, U.S.A.* **74 D9** 37 19N 94 46W
Weir, *KY, U.S.A.* **96 C5** 37 7N 87 13W
Weir, *MS, U.S.A.* **81 C4** 33 16N 89 18W
Weir, L., *FL, U.S.A.* **67 B7** 29 0N 81 57W
Weir River, *Man., Canada* .. **191 F7** 56 49N 94 6W
Weirdale, *Sask., Canada* .. **182 B6** 53 27N 105 15W
Weirsdale, *FL, U.S.A.* ... **67 C7** 28 59N 81 55W
Weirton, *WV, U.S.A.* **102 A4** 40 24N 80 35W
Weiser, *ID, U.S.A.* **70 E2** 44 15N 116 58W
Weiser →, *ID, U.S.A.* ... **70 E2** 44 14N 116 58W
Weiss L., *AL, U.S.A.* ... **60 B5** 34 8N 85 48W
Weissert, *NE, U.S.A.* ... **84 C6** 41 28N 99 27W
Wekweti, *N.W.T., Canada* .. **189 D10** 64 11N 114 10W
Welby, *Denver, U.S.A.* ... **109 A2** 39 50N 104 57W
Welch, *OK, U.S.A.* **93 B8** 36 52N 95 6W
Welch, *TX, U.S.A.* **98 E5** 32 56N 102 8W
Welch, *WV, U.S.A.* **102 D3** 37 26N 81 35W
Welcome, *MD, U.S.A.* **77 B3** 38 28N 77 8W
Welcome, *MN, U.S.A.* **80 G4** 43 40N 94 37W
Welcome, *NC, U.S.A.* **90 C5** 35 55N 80 15W
Weld, *ME, U.S.A.* **76 D3** 44 42N 70 25W
Weld County ☆, *CO, U.S.A.* . **66 B6** 40 45N 104 15W
Welda, *KS, U.S.A.* **74 C8** 38 10N 95 18W
Weldon, *Sask., Canada* ... **182 B6** 53 1N 105 8W
Weldon, *IL, U.S.A.* **71 C5** 40 7N 88 45W
Weldon, *IA, U.S.A.* **73 E5** 40 54N 93 44W
Weldon, *NC, U.S.A.* **90 B8** 36 25N 77 36W
Weldon →, *MO, U.S.A.* .. **82 A3** 40 6N 93 39W
Weldon Spring, *MO, U.S.A.* . **82 C6** 38 43N 90 41W
Weleetka, *OK, U.S.A.* ... **93 C7** 35 20N 96 8W
Welland, *Ont., Canada* ... **178 E7** 43 0N 79 15W
Wellborn, *TX, U.S.A.* ... **99 G11** 30 32N 96 18W
Wellersburg, *PA, U.S.A.* .. **77 A2** 39 44N 78 51W
Wellesley, *MA, U.S.A.* .. **78 B3** 42 17N 71 17W
Wellesley Falls, *Boston, U.S.A.* .. **106 B2** 42 18N 71 18W
Wellesley Hills, *Boston, U.S.A.* .. **106 B2** 42 18N 71 16W
Wellfleet, *MA, U.S.A.* .. **78 C4** 41 56N 70 2W
Wellfleet, *NE, U.S.A.* .. **84 D5** 40 45N 100 44W
Wellford, *VA, U.S.A.* ... **77 C4** 37 53N 76 46W
Wellington, *Ont., Canada* .. **179 D9** 43 57N 77 20W
Wellington, *P.E.I., Canada* .. **173 G5** 46 27N 64 0W
Wellington, *Boston, U.S.A.* .. **106 A3** 42 24N 71 5W
Wellington, *CO, U.S.A.* .. **66 B5** 40 42N 105 0W
Wellington, *IL, U.S.A.* .. **71 C6** 40 32N 87 41W
Wellington, *KS, U.S.A.* .. **74 D6** 37 16N 97 24W
Wellington, *ME, U.S.A.* .. **76 C4** 45 2N 69 36W
Wellington, *MO, U.S.A.* .. **82 B3** 39 8N 93 59W
Wellington, *NV, U.S.A.* .. **85 D1** 38 45N 119 23W
Wellington, *OH, U.S.A.* .. **92 B4** 41 10N 82 13W
Wellington, *TX, U.S.A.* .. **98 C7** 34 51N 100 13W
Wellington, *UT, U.S.A.* .. **100 D5** 39 32N 110 44W
Wellington Chan., *Nunavut, Canada* **190 B7** 75 0N 93 0W
Wellman, *IA, U.S.A.* **73 D7** 41 28N 91 50W
Wellman, *TX, U.S.A.* **98 D5** 33 3N 102 26W
Wellpinit, *WA, U.S.A.* ... **101 C8** 47 53N 117 59W
Wells, *B.C., Canada* **187 B13** 53 6N 121 36W
Wells, *KS, U.S.A.* **74 B6** 39 5N 97 33W
Wells, *ME, U.S.A.* **76 E3** 43 20N 70 35W
Wells, *MN, U.S.A.* **80 G5** 43 45N 93 44W
Wells, *NY, U.S.A.* **89 B6** 43 24N 74 17W
Wells, *NV, U.S.A.* **85 A6** 41 7N 114 58W
Wells, *TX, U.S.A.* **99 F13** 31 29N 94 56W
Wells, *VT, U.S.A.* **86 C1** 43 25N 73 10W
Wells →, *VT, U.S.A.* ... **86 B2** 44 10N 72 3W
Wells County ☆, *IN, U.S.A.* .. **72 C5** 40 45N 85 15W
Wells County ☆, *ND, U.S.A.* .. **91 C6** 47 35N 99 45W
Wells Dam, *WA, U.S.A.* .. **101 C6** 47 57N 119 52W
Wells Gray Park ⌂, *B.C., Canada* **187 C14** 52 30N 120 15W
Wellsboro, *PA, U.S.A.* .. **95 C5** 41 45N 77 18W
Wellsburg, *IA, U.S.A.* .. **73 C6** 42 26N 92 56W
Wellsburg, *NY, U.S.A.* .. **89 C4** 42 1N 76 44W
Wellsburg, *WV, U.S.A.* .. **102 A4** 40 16N 80 37W
Wellsford, *KS, U.S.A.* .. **74 D4** 37 37N 99 2W
Wellston = Warner Robins, *GA, U.S.A.* **68 D3** 32 37N 83 36W
Wellston, *MO, U.S.A.* ... **117 B2** 38 40N 90 17W
Wellston, *OH, U.S.A.* ... **92 D4** 39 7N 82 32W
Wellston, *OK, U.S.A.* ... **93 C6** 35 42N 97 4W
Wellsville, *KS, U.S.A.* .. **74 C8** 38 43N 95 5W
Wellsville, *MO, U.S.A.* .. **82 B5** 39 4N 91 34W
Wellsville, *NY, U.S.A.* .. **89 C3** 42 7N 77 57W
Wellsville, *OH, U.S.A.* .. **92 C6** 40 36N 80 39W
Wellsville, *PA, U.S.A.* .. **95 D6** 40 3N 76 56W
Wellsville, *UT, U.S.A.* .. **100 B4** 41 38N 111 56W
Wellton, *AZ, U.S.A.* ... **62 E1** 32 40N 114 8W
Welsford, *N.B., Canada* .. **173 H3** 45 27N 66 20W
Welsh, *LA, U.S.A.* **75 D3** 30 14N 92 49W
Welton, *IA, U.S.A.* **73 D8** 41 55N 90 36W
Wembley, *Alta., Canada* .. **184 C1** 55 9N 119 8W
Wemindji, *Qué., Canada* .. **175 C2** 53 0N 78 49W
Wenasaga →, *Ont., Canada* .. **180 B3** 50 38N 93 10W
Wenatchee, *WA, U.S.A.* .. **101 C5** 47 25N 120 19W
Wenatchee →, *WA, U.S.A.* .. **101 C5** 47 27N 120 19W
Wenatchee Mts., *WA, U.S.A.* .. **101 C5** 47 15N 120 30W
Wenatchee Nat. Forest, *WA, U.S.A.* **101 C5** 47 55N 120 55W
Wendell, *ID, U.S.A.* ... **70 G4** 42 47N 114 42W
Wendell, *MN, U.S.A.* ... **80 D2** 46 2N 96 6W
Wendell, *NH, U.S.A.* ... **86 C2** 43 22N 72 9W
Wenden, *AZ, U.S.A.* ... **62 D2** 33 49N 113 33W
Wendover, *UT, U.S.A.* .. **100 C1** 40 44N 114 2W
Wenebegon →, *Ont., Canada* .. **181 F13** 46 53N 83 12W
Wenebegon L., *Ont., Canada* .. **181 E13** 47 23N 83 6W
Wenona, *IL, U.S.A.* ... **71 B4** 41 3N 89 3W
Wenona, *MD, U.S.A.* ... **77 B5** 38 8N 75 57W
Wentworth, *Qué., Canada* .. **173 H6** 45 38N 63 33W
Wentworth, *MO, U.S.A.* .. **82 E2** 36 59N 94 4W
Wentworth, *NC, U.S.A.* .. **90 B6** 36 24N 79 46W
Wentworth, *NH, U.S.A.* .. **86 C3** 43 52N 71 55W
Wentworth, *SD, U.S.A.* .. **91 G9** 43 59N 96 57W
Wentworth, L., *NH, U.S.A.* .. **86 C3** 43 35N 71 9W
Wentzville, *MO, U.S.A.* .. **82 C6** 38 49N 90 51W
Weott, *CA, U.S.A.* **64 C3** 40 20N 123 55W
Werley, *WI, U.S.A.* ... **103 E3** 43 1N 90 46W
Wernecke Mts., *Yukon, Canada* .. **189 D6** 64 50N 134 15W
Weskan, *KS, U.S.A.* ... **74 C2** 38 52N 101 57W
Weslaco, *TX, U.S.A.* .. **98 L10** 26 10N 97 58W
Weslemkoon L., *Ont., Canada* .. **179 B9** 45 2N 77 25W
Wesley, *GA, U.S.A.* ... **68 D4** 32 29N 82 20W
Wesley, *IA, U.S.A.* ... **73 B5** 43 5N 93 59W
Wesley, *ME, U.S.A.* ... **76 D6** 44 57N 67 40W
Wesleyville, *PA, U.S.A.* .. **95 B3** 42 9N 80 1W
Wessington, *SD, U.S.A.* .. **91 F7** 44 27N 98 42W
Wessington Springs, *SD, U.S.A.* .. **91 F7** 44 5N 98 34W
Wesson, *AR, U.S.A.* .. **63 E3** 33 7N 92 46W
Wesson, *MS, U.S.A.* .. **81 E3** 31 42N 90 24W
West, *MS, U.S.A.* **81 C4** 33 12N 89 47W
West, *TX, U.S.A.* **99 F10** 31 48N 97 6W
West →, *VT, U.S.A.* .. **86 D2** 42 52N 72 33W
West Alexandria, *OH, U.S.A.* .. **92 D2** 39 45N 84 32W
West Allis, *WI, U.S.A.* .. **103 E6** 43 1N 88 0W
West Arlington, *VT, U.S.A.* .. **86 C1** 43 6N 73 12W
West Arm Grand Traverse B., *MI, U.S.A.* **79 E6** 44 50N 85 40W
West Arm Park ⌂, *B.C., Canada* . **187 F17** 49 30N 117 7W
West B., *FL, U.S.A.* .. **67 A3** 30 10N 85 45W
West B., *LA, U.S.A.* .. **75 E6** 29 3N 89 22W
West B., *TX, U.S.A.* .. **99 H13** 29 14N 95 0W
West Babylon, *NY, U.S.A.* .. **87 B3** 40 42N 73 21W
West Baton Rouge Parish ☆, *LA, U.S.A.* **75 D4** 30 27N 91 12W
West Bay, *Vancouver, Canada* .. **193 B1** 49 20N 123 12W
West Bedford, *Boston, U.S.A.* .. **106 A2** 42 28N 71 18W
West Bend, *IA, U.S.A.* .. **73 C4** 42 57N 94 27W
West Bend, *WI, U.S.A.* .. **103 E5** 43 25N 88 11W
West Blocton, *AL, U.S.A.* .. **60 C3** 33 7N 87 7W
West Bountiful, *Salt Lake City, U.S.A.* **117 A2** 40 53N 111 54W
West Boylston, *MA, U.S.A.* .. **78 B3** 42 22N 71 47W
West Branch, *IA, U.S.A.* .. **73 D7** 41 40N 91 20W
West Branch, *MI, U.S.A.* .. **79 E7** 44 17N 84 14W
West Branch Susquehanna →, *PA, U.S.A.* **95 D6** 40 53N 76 48W
West Bridgewater, *MA, U.S.A.* .. **78 B4** 42 1N 71 0W
West Brookfield, *MA, U.S.A.* .. **78 B2** 42 14N 72 9W
West Burke, *VT, U.S.A.* .. **86 B3** 44 39N 71 59W
West Burlington, *IA, U.S.A.* .. **73 E7** 40 49N 91 9W
West Caldwell, *NJ, U.S.A.* .. **114 A1** 40 50N 74 18W
West Campton, *NH, U.S.A.* .. **86 C3** 43 40N 71 41W
West Canaan, *NH, U.S.A.* .. **86 C2** 43 40N 72 2W
West Cape May, *NJ, U.S.A.* .. **87 D2** 38 56N 74 56W
West Carroll Parish ☆, *LA, U.S.A.* **75 B4** 32 48N 91 27W
West Carthage, *NY, U.S.A.* .. **89 B5** 43 59N 75 37W
West Chazy, *NY, U.S.A.* .. **86 B1** 44 49N 73 30W
West Chester, *IA, U.S.A.* .. **73 D7** 41 20N 91 49W
West Chester, *PA, U.S.A.* .. **87 C1** 39 58N 75 36W
West Columbia, *SC, U.S.A.* .. **90 E4** 33 59N 81 4W
West Columbia, *TX, U.S.A.* .. **99 H12** 29 9N 95 39W
West Concord, *Boston, U.S.A.* .. **106 A1** 42 27N 71 24W
West Concord, *MN, U.S.A.* .. **80 F6** 44 9N 92 54W
West Cote Blanche B., *LA, U.S.A.* **75 E4** 29 45N 91 55W
West Covina, *CA, U.S.A.* .. **65 J9** 34 4N 117 54W
West Creek, *NJ, U.S.A.* .. **87 C2** 39 38N 74 18W
West Cummington, *MA, U.S.A.* .. **78 B2** 42 29N 72 57W
West Dalhousie, *N.S., Canada* .. **173 J4** 44 43N 65 13W
West Delta Park, *Portland, U.S.A.* **116 A1** 45 35N 122 42W
West Des Moines, *IA, U.S.A.* .. **73 D5** 41 35N 93 43W
West Dover, *VT, U.S.A.* .. **86 D2** 42 56N 72 51W
West Dummerston, *VT, U.S.A.* .. **86 D2** 42 55N 72 38W
West Elk Mts., *CO, U.S.A.* .. **66 D3** 38 35N 107 15W
West Elkton, *OH, U.S.A.* .. **92 D2** 39 35N 84 33W
West Fairlee, *VT, U.S.A.* .. **86 C2** 43 54N 72 16W
West Fargo, *ND, U.S.A.* .. **91 D9** 46 52N 96 54W
West Feliciana Parish ☆, *LA, U.S.A.* **75 D4** 30 50N 91 23W
West Fork →, *WV, U.S.A.* .. **102 B4** 39 28N 80 9W
West Fork Amite →, *U.S.A.* .. **81 E3** 31 0N 90 50W
West Fork Poplar →, *MT, U.S.A.* **83 B12** 48 31N 105 22W
West Fork Trinity →, *TX, U.S.A.* **99 E11** 32 48N 96 54W
West Forks, *ME, U.S.A.* .. **76 C4** 45 20N 69 58W
West Frankfort, *IL, U.S.A.* .. **71 F5** 37 54N 88 55W
West Glacier, *MT, U.S.A.* .. **83 B4** 48 30N 113 59W
West Grand L., *ME, U.S.A.* .. **76 C6** 45 14N 67 51W
West Green, *GA, U.S.A.* .. **68 E4** 31 37N 82 44W
West Grove, *PA, U.S.A.* .. **95 E7** 39 49N 75 49W
West Hamlin, *WV, U.S.A.* .. **102 C2** 38 17N 82 12W
West Hartford, *CT, U.S.A.* .. **78 C2** 41 45N 72 44W
West Haven, *CT, U.S.A.* .. **78 C2** 41 17N 72 57W
West Hebron, *NY, U.S.A.* .. **86 C1** 43 14N 73 23W
West Helena, *AR, U.S.A.* .. **63 D5** 34 33N 90 38W
West Hempstead, *NY, U.S.A.* .. **114 B5** 40 42N 73 39W
West Hollywood, *Los Angeles, U.S.A.* **111 B2** 34 5N 118 21W
West Homestead, *Pittsburgh, U.S.A.* **116 B2** 40 23N 79 54W
West Jefferson, *NC, U.S.A.* .. **90 B4** 36 24N 81 30W
West Jordan, *UT, U.S.A.* .. **117 C1** 40 36N 111 56W
West Kingston, *RI, U.S.A.* .. **78 C3** 41 29N 71 34W
West Lafayette, *IN, U.S.A.* .. **72 C4** 40 27N 86 55W
West Lebanon, *IN, U.S.A.* .. **72 C3** 40 16N 87 23W
West Liberty, *IA, U.S.A.* .. **73 D7** 41 34N 91 16W
West Liberty, *KY, U.S.A.* .. **97 C9** 37 55N 83 16W
West Liberty, *OH, U.S.A.* .. **92 C3** 40 15N 83 45W
West Liberty, *WV, U.S.A.* .. **102 A4** 40 10N 80 36W
West Line, *MO, U.S.A.* .. **82 C2** 38 38N 94 35W
West Linn, *OR, U.S.A.* .. **94 B3** 45 21N 122 36W
West Lorne, *Ont., Canada* .. **178 E5** 42 36N 81 36W
West Louisville, *KY, U.S.A.* .. **96 C5** 37 42N 87 17W
West Lynn, *Boston, U.S.A.* .. **106 A4** 42 27N 70 58W
West Mansfield, *OH, U.S.A.* .. **92 C3** 40 24N 83 33W
West Mayfield, *PA, U.S.A.* .. **95 D2** 40 47N 80 20W
West Medford, *Boston, U.S.A.* .. **106 A3** 42 25N 71 7W
West Memphis, *AR, U.S.A.* .. **63 C5** 35 8N 90 11W
West Miami, *Miami, U.S.A.* .. **112 D1** 25 45N 80 17W
West Mifflin, *PA, U.S.A.* .. **95 D3** 40 21N 79 52W
West Milan, *NH, U.S.A.* .. **86 B3** 44 37N 71 18W
West Milford, *NJ, U.S.A.* .. **87 A2** 41 8N 74 22W
West Milford, *WV, U.S.A.* .. **102 B4** 39 12N 80 24W
West Millgrove, *OH, U.S.A.* .. **92 B3** 41 15N 83 30W
West Milton, *OH, U.S.A.* .. **92 D2** 39 58N 84 20W
West Milwaukee, *Milwaukee, U.S.A.* **112 B2** 43 0N 87 58W
West Mineral, *KS, U.S.A.* .. **74 D9** 37 17N 94 55W
West Monroe, *LA, U.S.A.* .. **75 B3** 32 31N 92 9W
West Mts., *ID, U.S.A.* .. **70 E2** 44 28N 116 14W
West New York, *NJ, U.S.A.* .. **114 B2** 40 46N 74 1W
West Newbury, *MA, U.S.A.* .. **78 B4** 42 48N 71 0W
West Newfield, *ME, U.S.A.* .. **86 C4** 43 39N 70 55W
West Nishnabotna →, *IA, U.S.A.* **73 E3** 40 39N 95 38W
West Nueces →, *TX, U.S.A.* .. **99 H8** 29 16N 99 56W
West Odessa, *TX, U.S.A.* .. **98 F5** 31 50N 102 30W
West of Twin Peaks, *San Francisco, U.S.A.* **118 B2** 37 43N 122 27W
West Okoboji L., *IA, U.S.A.* .. **73 B3** 43 23N 95 9W
West Orange, *NJ, U.S.A.* .. **114 B1** 40 47N 74 14W
West Orange, *TX, U.S.A.* .. **99 G14** 30 5N 93 46W
West Ossipee, *NH, U.S.A.* .. **86 C3** 43 49N 71 12W
West Palm Beach, *FL, U.S.A.* .. **67 E8** 26 43N 80 3W
West Palm Beach Canal, *FL, U.S.A.* **67 E8** 26 40N 80 15W
West Palm Beach International ✕ (PBI), *FL, U.S.A.* **67 E8** 26 41N 80 6W
West Park, *Pittsburgh, U.S.A.* .. **116 B1** 40 28N 80 4W
West Paterson, *NJ, U.S.A.* .. **114 A1** 40 53N 74 11W
West Pawlet, *VT, U.S.A.* .. **86 C1** 43 21N 73 15W
West Pensacola, *FL, U.S.A.* .. **67 A1** 30 25N 87 16W
West Plains, *MO, U.S.A.* .. **82 E5** 36 44N 91 51W
West Plymouth, *NH, U.S.A.* .. **86 C3** 43 45N 71 45W
West Point, *CA, U.S.A.* .. **64 E6** 38 24N 120 32W
West Point, *GA, U.S.A.* .. **68 D1** 32 53N 85 11W
West Point, *IL, U.S.A.* .. **71 C2** 40 15N 91 11W
West Point, *IA, U.S.A.* .. **73 E7** 40 43N 91 27W
West Point, *KY, U.S.A.* .. **97 C7** 37 59N 85 57W
West Point, *MS, U.S.A.* .. **81 C5** 33 36N 88 39W
West Point, *NY, U.S.A.* .. **89 D7** 41 24N 73 58W
West Point, *NE, U.S.A.* .. **84 C9** 41 51N 96 43W
West Point, *VA, U.S.A.* .. **102 D8** 37 32N 76 48W
West Point L., *GA, U.S.A.* .. **68 C1** 33 8N 85 0W
West Point Military Academy, *NY, U.S.A.* **89 D7** 41 22N 73 57W
West Portland, *Portland, U.S.A.* .. **116 B1** 45 27N 122 43W
West Pt. = Ouest, Pte. de l', *Qué., Canada* **172 D5** 49 52N 64 40W
West Richland, *WA, U.S.A.* .. **101 D6** 46 18N 119 20W
West Rindge, *NH, U.S.A.* .. **86 D2** 42 47N 72 3W
West River, *MD, U.S.A.* .. **77 B4** 38 52N 76 31W
West Road →, *B.C., Canada* .. **186 B11** 53 18N 122 53W
West Roxbury, *Boston, U.S.A.* .. **106 B3** 42 16N 71 9W
West Rutland, *VT, U.S.A.* .. **86 C1** 43 36N 73 3W
West Sacramento, *CA, U.S.A.* .. **64 E5** 38 35N 121 32W
West St. Paul, *Minneapolis-St. Paul, U.S.A.* ... **113 B3** 44 54N 93 5W
West Salem, *IL, U.S.A.* .. **71 E5** 38 31N 88 1W
West Salem, *OH, U.S.A.* .. **92 C4** 40 58N 82 7W
West Salem, *WI, U.S.A.* .. **103 E2** 43 54N 91 5W
West Seneca, *NY, U.S.A.* .. **89 C2** 42 51N 78 48W
West Siloam Springs, *OK, U.S.A.* .. **93 B9** 36 12N 94 39W
West Slope, *Portland, U.S.A.* .. **116 B1** 45 29N 122 45W
West Springfield, *MA, U.S.A.* .. **78 B2** 42 6N 72 38W
West Springfield, *VA, U.S.A.* .. **119 C2** 38 47N 77 13W
West Stewartstown, *NH, U.S.A.* .. **86 B3** 44 59N 71 32W
West Tavaputs Plateau, *UT, U.S.A.* **100 D5** 39 45N 110 20W
West Terre Haute, *IN, U.S.A.* .. **72 D3** 39 28N 87 27W
West Thompson Res., *CT, U.S.A.* .. **78 C3** 41 57N 71 54W
West Thorton, *NH, U.S.A.* .. **86 C3** 43 55N 71 42W
West Thumb, *WY, U.S.A.* .. **104 B2** 44 25N 110 34W
West Thurlow I., *B.C., Canada* .. **186 E9** 50 25N 125 35W
West Tisbury, *MA, U.S.A.* .. **78 C4** 41 23N 70 41W
West Topsham, *VT, U.S.A.* .. **86 B2** 44 7N 72 19W
West Town, *Chicago, U.S.A.* .. **108 B2** 41 53N 87 42W
West Union, *IA, U.S.A.* .. **73 C7** 42 57N 91 49W
West Union, *MN, U.S.A.* .. **80 E3** 45 48N 95 5W
West Union, *OH, U.S.A.* .. **92 E3** 38 48N 83 33W
West Union, *WV, U.S.A.* .. **102 B4** 39 18N 80 47W
West Unity, *OH, U.S.A.* .. **92 B2** 41 35N 84 26W

West University Place, *TX, U.S.A.* **99 H12** 29 43N 95 26W
West Valley City, *UT, U.S.A.* **100 C4** 40 42N 111 58W
West Vancouver, *B.C., Canada* **193 B1** 49 22N 123 10W
West View, *Pittsburgh, U.S.A.* **116 A1** 40 31N 80 2W
West Virginia □, *U.S.A.* **102 C4** 38 45N 80 30W
West Warwick, *RI, U.S.A.* **78 C3** 41 43N 71 32W
West Wendover, *NV, U.S.A.* **85 B6** 40 44N 114 4W
West Winfield, *NY, U.S.A.* **89 C5** 42 53N 75 12W
West Yarmouth, *MA, U.S.A.* **78 C4** 41 39N 70 15W
West Yellowstone, *MT, U.S.A.* **83 F6** 44 40N 111 6W
West York, *PA, U.S.A.* **95 E6** 39 57N 76 46W
Westbank, *B.C., Canada* **187 F15** 49 50N 119 38W
Westbay, *FL, U.S.A.* **67 A3** 30 18N 85 52W
Westboro, *MO, U.S.A.* **82 A1** 40 32N 95 19W
Westborough, *MA, U.S.A.* **78 B3** 42 16N 71 37W
Westbourne, *Man., Canada* **183 E13** 50 8N 98 35W
Westbridge, *B.C., Canada* **187 F16** 49 10N 118 58W
Westbrook, *CT, U.S.A.* **78 C2** 41 17N 72 27W
Westbrook, *ME, U.S.A.* **76 E3** 43 41N 70 22W
Westbrook, *MN, U.S.A.* **80 F3** 44 3N 95 26W
Westbrook, *TX, U.S.A.* **98 E6** 32 21N 101 1W
Westby, *MT, U.S.A.* **83 B13** 48 52N 104 3W
Westby, *WI, U.S.A.* **103 E3** 43 39N 90 51W
Westchester, *Chicago, U.S.A.* **108 B1** 41 51N 87 53W
Westchester, *Los Angeles, U.S.A.* **111 C2** 33 57N 118 23W
Westchester, *NY, U.S.A.* **114 A3** 40 51N 73 51W
Westchester County ☆, *NY, U.S.A.* **89 D7** 41 40N 73 45W
Westcliffe, *CO, U.S.A.* **66 D5** 38 9N 105 28W
Westend, *CA, U.S.A.* **65 H9** 35 42N 117 24W
Westerly, *RI, U.S.A.* **78 C3** 41 22N 71 50W
Western, *NE, U.S.A.* **84 D8** 40 24N 97 12W
Western Addition, *San Francisco, U.S.A.* **118 B2** 37 47N 122 25W
Western Duck I., *Ont., Canada* **178 B3** 45 45N 83 0W
Western Grove, *AR, U.S.A.* **63 B3** 36 6N 92 57W
Western Pen., *Ont., Canada* **180 C2** 49 30N 94 50W
Western Shore, *N.S., Canada* **173 J5** 44 32N 64 19W
Westernport, *MD, U.S.A.* **77 A1** 39 29N 79 3W
Westerville, *NE, U.S.A.* **84 C6** 41 24N 99 23W
Westerville, *OH, U.S.A.* **92 C4** 40 8N 82 56W
Westfall, *OR, U.S.A.* **94 D8** 43 59N 117 48W
Westfield, *IL, U.S.A.* **71 D5** 39 27N 88 0W
Westfield, *IN, U.S.A.* **72 C4** 40 2N 86 8W
Westfield, *IA, U.S.A.* **73 C2** 42 45N 96 36W
Westfield, *ME, U.S.A.* **76 B6** 46 34N 67 55W
Westfield, *MA, U.S.A.* **78 B2** 42 7N 72 45W
Westfield, *NJ, U.S.A.* **87 B2** 40 39N 74 21W
Westfield, *NY, U.S.A.* **89 C1** 42 20N 79 35W
Westfield, *PA, U.S.A.* **95 C5** 41 55N 77 32W
Westfield, *WI, U.S.A.* **103 E4** 43 53N 89 30W
Westfield →, *MA, U.S.A.* **78 B2** 42 5N 72 35W
Westfir, *OR, U.S.A.* **94 D3** 43 46N 122 31W
Westford, *MA, U.S.A.* **78 B3** 42 35N 71 26W
Westgate, *IA, U.S.A.* **73 C6** 42 46N 92 0W
Westgate, *MD, U.S.A.* **119 B3** 38 57N 77 6W
Westhoff, *TX, U.S.A.* **99 H10** 29 12N 97 28W
Westhope, *ND, U.S.A.* **91 B4** 48 55N 101 1W
Westlake, *LA, U.S.A.* **75 D2** 30 15N 93 59W
Westlake, *San Francisco, U.S.A.* **118 B2** 37 42N 122 29W
Westland, *MI, U.S.A.* **79 G8** 42 15N 83 20W
Westlock, *Alta., Canada* **184 D7** 54 9N 113 55W
Westlynn, *Vancouver, Canada* **193 B2** 49 19N 123 1W
Westminster, *CA, U.S.A.* **65 K8** 33 45N 118 0W
Westminster, *CO, U.S.A.* **66 C5** 39 50N 105 2W
Westminster, *MA, U.S.A.* **78 B3** 42 33N 71 55W
Westminster, *MD, U.S.A.* **77 A4** 39 34N 76 59W
Westminster, *SC, U.S.A.* **90 D2** 34 40N 83 6W
Westminster, *VT, U.S.A.* **86 C2** 43 5N 72 27W
Westmont, *NJ, U.S.A.* **116 B2** 39 54N 75 2W
Westmont, *PA, U.S.A.* **95 D4** 40 19N 78 58W
Westmore, *VT, U.S.A.* **86 B2** 44 50N 72 3W
Westmoreland, *KS, U.S.A.* **74 B7** 39 24N 96 25W
Westmoreland, *NH, U.S.A.* **86 D2** 42 57N 72 25W
Westmoreland, *TN, U.S.A.* **96 D6** 36 34N 86 15W
Westmoreland, *VA, U.S.A.* **77 B4** 38 4N 76 34W
Westmoreland County ☆, *PA, U.S.A.* **95 D3** 40 20N 79 25W
Westmoreland County ☆, *VA, U.S.A.* **102 C8** 38 6N 76 50W
Westmorland, *CA, U.S.A.* **65 K11** 33 2N 115 37W
Westmount, *Montréal, Canada* **192 B3** 45 29N 73 35W
Weston, *CO, U.S.A.* **66 E6** 37 8N 104 48W
Weston, *MA, U.S.A.* **78 B3** 42 22N 71 16W
Weston, *MO, U.S.A.* **82 B2** 39 25N 94 54W
Weston, *NE, U.S.A.* **84 C9** 41 12N 96 45W
Weston, *OR, U.S.A.* **94 B7** 45 49N 118 26W
Weston, *VT, U.S.A.* **86 C2** 43 18N 72 38W
Weston, *WV, U.S.A.* **102 B4** 39 2N 80 28W
Weston, *WY, U.S.A.* **104 B7** 44 38N 105 20W
Weston County ☆, *WY, U.S.A.* **104 C8** 43 55N 104 35W
Weston I., *N.W.T., Canada* **175 C2** 52 33N 79 36W
Weston Res., *Boston, U.S.A.* **106 A2** 42 20N 71 11W
Westover, *MD, U.S.A.* **77 B5** 38 7N 75 42W
Westover, *PA, U.S.A.* **95 D4** 40 45N 78 40W
Westover, *WV, U.S.A.* **102 B5** 39 38N 79 58W
Westover Air Reserve Base, *MA, U.S.A.* **78 B2** 42 13N 72 29W
Westphalia, *MI, U.S.A.* **79 G7** 42 56N 84 48W
Westphalia, *MO, U.S.A.* **82 C4** 38 26N 92 0W
Westpoint, *TN, U.S.A.* **96 E5** 35 8N 87 32W
Westport, *N.S., Canada* **173 J3** 44 15N 66 22W
Westport, *Nfld. & L., Canada* **174 C4** 49 47N 56 38W
Westport, *Ont., Canada* **179 C10** 44 40N 76 25W
Westport, *CA, U.S.A.* **64 D3** 39 38N 123 47W
Westport, *CT, U.S.A.* **78 C1** 41 9N 73 22W
Westport, *IN, U.S.A.* **72 D5** 39 11N 85 34W
Westport, *MN, U.S.A.* **80 E3** 45 43N 95 10W
Westport, *NH, U.S.A.* **86 D2** 42 49N 72 20W
Westport, *NY, U.S.A.* **86 B1** 44 11N 73 26W
Westport, *OK, U.S.A.* **93 B7** 36 8N 96 20W
Westport, *OR, U.S.A.* **94 A2** 46 8N 123 23W
Westport, *WA, U.S.A.* **101 D1** 46 53N 124 6W
Westray, *Man., Canada* **183 B10** 53 36N 101 24W
Westree, *Ont., Canada* **181 E15** 47 26N 81 34W
Westview, *Baltimore, U.S.A.* **107 B1** 39 17N 76 44W
Westville, *N.S., Canada* **173 H7** 45 34N 62 43W
Westville, *FL, U.S.A.* **67 A3** 30 46N 85 51W
Westville, *IL, U.S.A.* **71 C6** 40 2N 87 38W
Westville, *IN, U.S.A.* **72 B4** 41 32N 86 54W
Westville, *NJ, U.S.A.* **116 B2** 39 52N 75 7W
Westville, *OK, U.S.A.* **93 C9** 35 58N 94 40W
Westville, *SC, U.S.A.* **90 D5** 34 27N 80 36W
Westwego, *LA, U.S.A.* **75 E5** 29 54N 90 8W
Westwold, *B.C., Canada* **187 E15** 50 28N 119 45W
Westwood, *CA, U.S.A.* **64 C6** 40 18N 121 0W
Westwood, *KY, U.S.A.* **97 B10** 38 30N 82 50W
Westwood, *MA, U.S.A.* **78 B3** 42 13N 71 14W
Westwood, *MD, U.S.A.* **77 B4** 38 40N 76 45W
Westwood, *NJ, U.S.A.* **87 B2** 40 58N 74 2W
Westwood Lakes, *FL, U.S.A.* **67 F8** 25 44N 80 23W
Westwood Village, *Los Angeles, U.S.A.* **111 B2** 34 3N 118 26W
Westwood Village, *San Antonio, U.S.A.* **117 C2** 29 24N 98 37W
Wet Mts., *CO, U.S.A.* **66 E5** 38 0N 105 10W
Wetaskiwin, *Alta., Canada* **185 F7** 52 55N 113 24W
Wethersfield, *CT, U.S.A.* **78 C2** 41 42N 72 40W
Wetmore, *CO, U.S.A.* **66 D5** 38 14N 105 5W
Wetmore, *KS, U.S.A.* **74 B8** 39 38N 95 49W
Wetumka, *OK, U.S.A.* **93 C7** 35 14N 96 15W
Wetumpka, *AL, U.S.A.* **60 D4** 32 32N 86 13W
Wetzel County ☆, *WV, U.S.A.* **102 B4** 39 34N 80 41W
Wevok, *AK, U.S.A.* **61 B6** 68 53N 166 13W
Wewahitchka, *FL, U.S.A.* **67 A3** 30 7N 85 12W
Wewoka, *OK, U.S.A.* **93 C7** 35 9N 96 30W
Wexford County ☆, *MI, U.S.A.* **79 E6** 44 20N 85 40W
Weyauwega, *WI, U.S.A.* **103 D5** 44 19N 88 56W
Weyburn, *Sask., Canada* **182 F8** 49 40N 103 50W
Weyerhaeuser, *WI, U.S.A.* **103 C2** 45 26N 91 25W
Weymouth, *N.S., Canada* **173 J3** 44 30N 66 1W
Weymouth, *MA, U.S.A.* **78 B4** 42 13N 70 58W
Wha Ti, *N.W.T., Canada* **189 D9** 63 8N 117 16W
Whalan, *MN, U.S.A.* **80 G7** 43 44N 91 55W
Whale →, *Qué., Canada* **175 B4** 58 15N 67 40W
Whale Cove, *Nunavut, Canada* **191 E7** 62 10N 92 34W
Whaletown, *B.C., Canada* **186 E9** 50 7N 125 2W
Whaleysville, *MD, U.S.A.* **77 B5** 38 24N 75 18W
Wharncliffe, *WV, U.S.A.* **102 D3** 37 33N 81 58W
Wharton, *NJ, U.S.A.* **87 B2** 40 54N 74 35W
Wharton, *OH, U.S.A.* **92 C3** 40 52N 83 28W
Wharton, *TX, U.S.A.* **99 H11** 29 19N 96 6W
Wharton County ☆, *TX, U.S.A.* **99 H11** 29 12N 96 16W
Wharton L., *Nunavut, Canada* **191 E6** 64 1N 99 50W
Wharton State Forest, *NJ, U.S.A.* **87 C2** 39 45N 74 40W
What Cheer, *IA, U.S.A.* **73 D6** 41 24N 92 21W
Whatcom = Bellingham, *WA, U.S.A.* **101 B3** 48 46N 122 29W
Whatcom, L., *WA, U.S.A.* **101 B3** 48 44N 122 20W
Whatcom County ☆, *WA, U.S.A.* **101 B4** 48 56N 122 0W
Whately, *MA, U.S.A.* **78 B2** 42 26N 72 38W
Whatley, *AL, U.S.A.* **60 E3** 31 39N 87 42W
Wheat Ridge, *CO, U.S.A.* **66 C5** 39 45N 105 4W
Wheatcroft, *KY, U.S.A.* **96 C5** 37 30N 87 52W
Wheatland, *CA, U.S.A.* **64 D5** 39 1N 121 25W
Wheatland, *IN, U.S.A.* **72 E3** 38 40N 87 19W
Wheatland, *IA, U.S.A.* **73 D8** 41 50N 90 51W
Wheatland, *MO, U.S.A.* **82 D3** 37 57N 93 24W
Wheatland, *WY, U.S.A.* **104 D8** 42 3N 104 58W
Wheatland County ☆, *MT, U.S.A.* **83 D8** 46 30N 109 50W
Wheatland Res. No.2, *WY, U.S.A.* **104 E7** 41 50N 105 38W
Wheatley, *Ont., Canada* **178 E4** 42 6N 82 27W
Wheatley, *AR, U.S.A.* **63 D4** 34 55N 91 7W
Wheaton, *IL, U.S.A.* **71 B5** 41 52N 88 6W
Wheaton, *KS, U.S.A.* **74 B7** 39 30N 96 19W
Wheaton, *MD, U.S.A.* **77 A3** 39 3N 77 3W
Wheaton, *MN, U.S.A.* **80 E2** 45 48N 96 30W
Wheaton, *MO, U.S.A.* **82 E2** 36 46N 94 3W
Wheeler, *IL, U.S.A.* **71 D5** 39 3N 88 19W
Wheeler, *KS, U.S.A.* **74 B2** 39 46N 101 43W
Wheeler, *MS, U.S.A.* **81 B5** 34 35N 88 37W
Wheeler, *OR, U.S.A.* **94 B2** 45 41N 123 53W
Wheeler, *TX, U.S.A.* **98 B7** 35 27N 100 16W
Wheeler, *WI, U.S.A.* **103 C2** 45 3N 91 55W
Wheeler →, *Qué., Canada* **175 B4** 57 2N 67 13W
Wheeler County ☆, *GA, U.S.A.* **68 D4** 32 5N 82 45W
Wheeler County ☆, *NE, U.S.A.* **84 C7** 41 50N 98 30W
Wheeler County ☆, *OR, U.S.A.* **94 C6** 44 45N 120 0W
Wheeler County ☆, *TX, U.S.A.* **98 B7** 35 30N 100 15W
Wheeler L., *AL, U.S.A.* **60 B3** 34 48N 87 23W
Wheeler Pk., *CA, U.S.A.* **64 C6** 40 6N 120 41W
Wheeler Pk., *NM, U.S.A.* **88 A5** 36 34N 105 25W
Wheeler Pk., *NV, U.S.A.* **85 D6** 38 57N 114 15W
Wheeler Ridge, *CA, U.S.A.* **65 H8** 35 0N 118 57W
Wheelersburg, *OH, U.S.A.* **92 E4** 38 44N 82 51W
Wheeling, *IL, U.S.A.* **71 A6** 42 8N 87 55W
Wheeling, *WV, U.S.A.* **102 A4** 40 4N 80 43W
Wheelock, *ND, U.S.A.* **91 B2** 48 18N 103 15W
Wheelwright, *KY, U.S.A.* **97 C10** 37 20N 82 43W
Whelen Springs, *AR, U.S.A.* **63 E2** 33 50N 93 7W
Whidbey I., *WA, U.S.A.* **101 B3** 48 12N 122 17W
Whigham, *GA, U.S.A.* **68 F2** 30 53N 84 19W
Whiskey Pk., *WY, U.S.A.* **104 D5** 42 18N 107 35W
Whiskeytown-Shasta-Trinity Nat. Recr. Area ⌂, *CA, U.S.A.* **64 C4** 40 45N 122 15W
Whispering Pines, *NC, U.S.A.* **90 C6** 35 17N 79 26W
Whistler, *B.C., Canada* **187 E12** 50 7N 122 58W
Whitaker, *Pittsburgh, U.S.A.* **116 B2** 40 23N 79 53W
Whitakers, *NC, U.S.A.* **90 B8** 36 6N 77 43W
Whitbourne, *Nfld. & L., Canada* **174 E7** 47 25N 53 32W
Whitby, *Ont., Canada* **179 D8** 43 52N 78 56W
White, *GA, U.S.A.* **68 B2** 34 17N 84 45W
White, *SD, U.S.A.* **91 F9** 44 26N 96 39W
White →, *Ont., Canada* **181 D10** 48 33N 86 16W
White →, *Yukon, Canada* **189 D5** 63 11N 139 35W
White →, *AZ, U.S.A.* **62 D5** 33 44N 110 13W
White →, *AR, U.S.A.* **63 E4** 33 57N 91 5W
White →, *IN, U.S.A.* **72 E3** 38 25N 87 45W
White →, *NV, U.S.A.* **85 E5** 37 19N 115 8W
White →, *OR, U.S.A.* **94 B4** 45 14N 121 1W
White →, *SD, U.S.A.* **91 G6** 43 42N 99 27W
White →, *TX, U.S.A.* **98 D7** 33 14N 100 56W
White →, *UT, U.S.A.* **100 C6** 40 4N 109 41W
White →, *VT, U.S.A.* **86 C2** 43 37N 72 20W
White →, *WA, U.S.A.* **101 C5** 47 50N 120 48W
White →, *WA, U.S.A.* **101 C3** 47 12N 122 15W
White B., *Nfld. & L., Canada* **174 C4** 50 0N 56 35W
White Bear, *Sask., Canada* **182 E3** 50 53N 108 13W
White Bear L., *Minneapolis-St. Paul, U.S.A.* **113 A4** 45 4N 92 58W
White Bear Lake, *MN, U.S.A.* **80 E5** 45 5N 93 0W
White Bird, *ID, U.S.A.* **70 D2** 45 46N 116 18W
White Bluff, *TN, U.S.A.* **96 D5** 36 6N 87 13W
White Butte, *ND, U.S.A.* **91 D2** 46 23N 103 18W
White Butte, *SD, U.S.A.* **91 E3** 45 56N 102 22W
White Canyon, *UT, U.S.A.* **100 F5** 37 49N 110 26W
White Castle, *LA, U.S.A.* **75 D4** 30 10N 91 9W
White Center, *Seattle, U.S.A.* **118 C3** 47 31N 122 21W
White City, *FL, U.S.A.* **67 D8** 27 22N 80 20W
White City, *FL, U.S.A.* **67 B3** 29 53N 85 13W
White City, *KS, U.S.A.* **74 C7** 38 48N 96 44W
White City, *OR, U.S.A.* **94 E3** 42 26N 122 51W
White Cloud, *KS, U.S.A.* **74 B8** 39 59N 95 18W
White Cloud, *MI, U.S.A.* **79 F6** 43 33N 85 46W
White County ☆, *AR, U.S.A.* **63 C4** 35 15N 91 44W
White County ☆, *GA, U.S.A.* **68 B3** 34 40N 83 45W
White County ☆, *IL, U.S.A.* **71 E5** 38 5N 88 10W
White County ☆, *IN, U.S.A.* **72 C4** 40 45N 86 50W
White County ☆, *TN, U.S.A.* **97 E7** 35 56N 85 28W
White Deer, *TX, U.S.A.* **98 B6** 35 26N 101 10W
White Earth, *ND, U.S.A.* **91 B3** 48 23N 102 46W
White Earth →, *ND, U.S.A.* **91 B3** 48 9N 102 42W
White Earth Indian Reservation, *MN, U.S.A.* **80 C3** 47 20N 95 45W
White Fox, *Sask., Canada* **182 B7** 53 27N 104 5W
White Hall, *AL, U.S.A.* **60 D4** 32 20N 86 43W
White Hall, *AR, U.S.A.* **63 D3** 34 16N 92 5W
White Hall, *IL, U.S.A.* **71 D3** 39 26N 90 24W
White Haven, *PA, U.S.A.* **87 A1** 41 4N 75 47W
White Hill, *N.S., Canada* **173 G9** 46 42N 60 36W
White Horse, *NJ, U.S.A.* **87 B2** 40 11N 74 42W
White House, *TN, U.S.A.* **96 D6** 36 28N 86 39W
White I., *Nunavut, Canada* **191 D8** 65 47N 84 54W
White I., *Los Angeles, U.S.A.* **111 D4** 33 45N 118 9W
White L., *Ont., Canada* **176 F6** 45 18N 76 31W
White L., *Ont., Canada* **181 D11** 48 47N 85 37W
White L., *LA, U.S.A.* **75 E3** 29 44N 92 30W
White Lake, *NC, U.S.A.* **90 D7** 34 39N 78 30W
White Lake, *SD, U.S.A.* **91 G7** 43 44N 98 43W
White Lake, *WI, U.S.A.* **103 C5** 45 10N 88 46W
White Lakes, *NM, U.S.A.* **88 B5** 35 12N 105 47W
White Mountain, *AK, U.S.A.* **61 D7** 64 41N 163 24W
White Mountain Nat. Forest, *NH, U.S.A.* **86 B3** 44 35N 71 23W
White Mountain Peak, *CA, U.S.A.* **65 F8** 37 38N 118 15W
White Mountains Nat. Recr. Area ⌂, *AK, U.S.A.* **61 D11** 65 30N 147 40W
White Mts., *AK, U.S.A.* **61 D11** 65 30N 146 30W
White Mts., *AZ, U.S.A.* **62 D6** 34 0N 109 40W
White Mts., *CA, U.S.A.* **65 F8** 37 30N 118 15W
White Mts., *NH, U.S.A.* **86 B3** 44 15N 71 15W
White Oak, *GA, U.S.A.* **68 E5** 31 2N 81 43W
White Oak, *OH, U.S.A.* **107 A1** 39 12N 84 35W
White Oak, *TX, U.S.A.* **99 E13** 32 32N 94 52W
White Oak Cr. →, *TX, U.S.A.* **99 D13** 33 14N 94 42W
White Oak Lake, *AR, U.S.A.* **63 E2** 33 42N 93 5W
White Otter L., *Ont., Canada* **180 C5** 49 5N 91 55W
White Owl, *SD, U.S.A.* **91 F3** 44 36N 102 26W
White Owl L., *Ont., Canada* **181 E14** 47 10N 82 35W
White Pass, *WA, U.S.A.* **101 D4** 46 38N 121 24W
White Pigeon, *MI, U.S.A.* **79 H6** 41 48N 85 39W
White Pine, *MI, U.S.A.* **79 C2** 46 45N 89 35W
White Pine, *MT, U.S.A.* **83 C2** 47 45N 115 29W
White Pine, *TN, U.S.A.* **97 D9** 36 7N 83 17W
White Pine County ☆, *NV, U.S.A.* **85 C6** 39 30N 115 0W
White Pine Range, *NV, U.S.A.* **85 C5** 39 10N 115 20W
White Plains, *GA, U.S.A.* **68 C3** 33 28N 83 1W
White Plains, *MD, U.S.A.* **77 B4** 38 36N 76 55W
White Plains, *NY, U.S.A.* **87 A3** 41 2N 73 46W
White River, *Ont., Canada* **181 D11** 48 35N 85 20W
White River, *SD, U.S.A.* **91 G5** 43 34N 100 45W
White River Junction, *VT, U.S.A.* **86 C2** 43 39N 72 19W
White River Nat. Forest, *CO, U.S.A.* **66 C4** 39 20N 106 45W
White River Nat. Wildlife Refuge ⌂, *AR, U.S.A.* **63 D4** 34 18N 91 5W
White River Res., *TX, U.S.A.* **98 D6** 33 27N 101 5W
White River Valley, *NV, U.S.A.* **85 D6** 38 6N 114 58W
White Rock, *B.C., Canada* **187 F12** 49 2N 122 48W
White Rock, *U.S.A.* **97 D9** 36 40N 83 27W
White Rock, *NM, U.S.A.* **88 B4** 35 50N 106 12W
White Rock Cr. →, *KS, U.S.A.* **74 B6** 39 55N 97 50W
White Rock Lake, *Dallas-Fort Worth, U.S.A.* **109 A5** 32 48N 96 43W
White Rocks Nat. Recr. Area ⌂, *VT, U.S.A.* **86 C2** 43 22N 72 55W
White Salmon, *WA, U.S.A.* **101 E4** 45 44N 121 29W
White Sands, *NM, U.S.A.* **88 E4** 32 23N 106 29W
White Sands Missile Range, *NM, U.S.A.* **88 E4** 33 0N 106 25W
White Sands Nat. Monument ⌂, *NM, U.S.A.* **88 D4** 32 46N 106 20W
White Shield, *ND, U.S.A.* **91 C4** 47 40N 101 51W
White Signal, *NM, U.S.A.* **88 E2** 32 33N 108 22W
White Springs, *FL, U.S.A.* **67 A6** 30 20N 82 45W
White Stone, *VA, U.S.A.* **102 D8** 37 39N 76 23W
White Sulphur Springs, *MT, U.S.A.* **83 D7** 46 33N 110 54W
White Sulphur Springs, *WV, U.S.A.* **102 D4** 37 48N 80 18W
White Swan, *WA, U.S.A.* **101 D5** 46 23N 120 44W
White Woman Cr. →, *U.S.A.* **74 C3** 38 26N 100 54W
Whiteburg, *MD, U.S.A.* **77 B5** 38 12N 75 32W
Whiteclay, *NE, U.S.A.* **84 B3** 42 57N 102 33W
Whiteclay L., *Ont., Canada* **180 B8** 50 53N 88 45W
Whitecourt, *Alta., Canada* **184 D5** 54 10N 115 45W
Whiteface, *TX, U.S.A.* **98 D5** 33 36N 102 37W
Whiteface →, *MN, U.S.A.* **80 D6** 46 58N 92 48W
Whiteface Mt., *NY, U.S.A.* **89 A7** 44 22N 73 54W
Whiteface Res., *MN, U.S.A.* **80 C6** 47 17N 92 11W
Whitefield, *ME, U.S.A.* **76 D4** 44 10N 69 38W
Whitefield, *NH, U.S.A.* **86 B3** 44 23N 71 37W
Whitefish, *Ont., Canada* **178 A5** 46 23N 81 19W
Whitefish, *MT, U.S.A.* **83 B3** 48 25N 114 20W
Whitefish →, *MI, U.S.A.* **79 D5** 45 55N 86 57W
Whitefish B., *MI, U.S.A.* **79 C7** 46 40N 84 55W
Whitefish B., *Milwaukee, U.S.A.* **112 B2** 43 7N 87 53W
Whitefish Bay, *WI, U.S.A.* **103 E6** 43 6N 87 54W
Whitefish Falls, *Ont., Canada* **178 A5** 46 7N 81 44W
Whitefish L., *N.W.T., Canada* **189 D11** 62 41N 106 48W
Whitefish Point, *MI, U.S.A.* **79 C7** 46 45N 84 59W
Whitefish Pt., *MI, U.S.A.* **79 C7** 46 46N 84 57W
Whiteford, *MD, U.S.A.* **77 A4** 39 42N 76 21W
Whitegull, L. = Goélands, L. aux, *Qué., Canada* **175 B5** 55 27N 64 17W
Whitehall, *AR, U.S.A.* **63 C5** 35 29N 90 44W
Whitehall, *MI, U.S.A.* **79 F5** 43 24N 86 21W
Whitehall, *MT, U.S.A.* **83 E5** 45 52N 112 6W
Whitehall, *NY, U.S.A.* **86 C1** 43 33N 73 24W
Whitehall, *PA, U.S.A.* **87 B1** 40 38N 75 30W
Whitehall, *Pittsburgh, U.S.A.* **116 B2** 40 21N 79 59W
Whitehall, *WI, U.S.A.* **103 D2** 44 22N 91 19W
Whitehorse, *Yukon, Canada* **189 D5** 60 43N 135 3W
Whitehorse, *SD, U.S.A.* **91 E5** 45 16N 100 53W
Whitehouse, *OH, U.S.A.* **92 B3** 41 31N 83 48W
Whiteland, *IN, U.S.A.* **72 D4** 39 33N 86 5W
Whitelaw, *WI, U.S.A.* **103 D6** 44 9N 87 49W
Whiteleysburg, *DE, U.S.A.* **77 B5** 38 57N 75 45W
Whitemouth, *Man., Canada* **183 F16** 49 57N 95 58W
Whitemouth →, *Man., Canada* **183 E15** 50 7N 96 2W
Whitemouth L., *Man., Canada* **183 F16** 49 15N 95 40W
Whiteriver, *AZ, U.S.A.* **62 D6** 33 50N 109 58W
Whiterocks, *UT, U.S.A.* **100 C6** 40 28N 109 56W
Whites City, *NM, U.S.A.* **88 E6** 32 11N 104 22W
Whitesand →, *Sask., Canada* **182 D9** 51 34N 102 56W
Whitesboro, *NY, U.S.A.* **89 B5** 43 7N 75 18W
Whitesboro, *OK, U.S.A.* **93 D9** 34 41N 94 53W
Whitesboro, *TX, U.S.A.* **99 D11** 33 39N 96 54W
Whitesburg, *KY, U.S.A.* **97 C10** 37 7N 82 49W
Whiteshell Prov. Park ⌂, *Man., Canada* **183 E16** 50 0N 95 40W
Whiteside County ☆, *IL, U.S.A.* **71 B4** 41 45N 89 55W
Whitestone, *NY, U.S.A.* **114 B4** 40 47N 73 39W
Whitestone →, *Yukon, Canada* **188 C5** 66 30N 138 0W
Whitestown, *IN, U.S.A.* **72 D4** 40 0N 86 21W
Whitesville, *KY, U.S.A.* **96 C6** 37 41N 86 52W
Whitesville, *WV, U.S.A.* **102 D3** 37 59N 81 32W
Whiteswan L., *Sask., Canada* **182 A6** 54 5N 105 10W
Whiteswan Lake Park ⌂, *B.C., Canada* **187 E19** 50 9N 115 30W
Whitetail, *MT, U.S.A.* **83 B12** 48 54N 105 10W
Whiteville, *NC, U.S.A.* **90 D7** 34 20N 78 42W
Whiteville, *TN, U.S.A.* **96 E3** 35 20N 89 9W
Whitewater, *KS, U.S.A.* **74 D6** 37 58N 97 9W
Whitewater, *MO, U.S.A.* **82 D7** 37 14N 89 48W
Whitewater, *MT, U.S.A.* **83 B10** 48 46N 107 38W
Whitewater, *WI, U.S.A.* **103 F5** 42 50N 88 44W
Whitewater →, *Sask., Canada* **182 G4** 49 0N 108 0W
Whitewater B., *FL, U.S.A.* **67 F8** 25 15N 81 0W
Whitewater Baldy, *NM, U.S.A.* **88 E2** 33 20N 108 39W
Whitewater L., *Ont., Canada* **180 B7** 50 50N 89 10W
Whitewood, *Sask., Canada* **183 E9** 50 20N 102 20W
Whitewood, *SD, U.S.A.* **91 F2** 44 28N 103 39W
Whitewright, *TX, U.S.A.* **99 D11** 33 31N 96 24W
Whitfield County ☆, *GA, U.S.A.* **68 B2** 34 50N 84 55W
Whiting, *IN, U.S.A.* **72 B3** 41 41N 87 30W
Whiting, *IA, U.S.A.* **73 C2** 42 8N 96 9W
Whiting, *KS, U.S.A.* **74 B8** 39 35N 95 37W
Whiting, *ME, U.S.A.* **76 D6** 44 48N 67 11W
Whiting, *NJ, U.S.A.* **87 C2** 39 57N 74 23W
Whiting, *VT, U.S.A.* **86 C1** 43 50N 73 12W
Whiting, *WI, U.S.A.* **103 D4** 44 30N 89 34W
Whitinsville, *MA, U.S.A.* **78 B3** 42 7N 71 40W
Whitlash, *MT, U.S.A.* **83 B6** 48 55N 111 15W
Whitley City, *KY, U.S.A.* **97 D8** 36 44N 84 28W
Whitley County ☆, *IN, U.S.A.* **72 B5** 41 10N 85 30W
Whitley County ☆, *KY, U.S.A.* **97 D8** 36 45N 84 10W
Whitman, *MA, U.S.A.* **78 B4** 42 5N 70 56W
Whitman, *NE, U.S.A.* **84 B4** 42 3N 101 31W
Whitman Air Force Base, *MO, U.S.A.* **82 C3** 38 44N 93 31W
Whitman County ☆, *WA, U.S.A.* **101 D8** 47 0N 117 30W
Whitman Mission Nat. Historic Site ⌂, *WA, U.S.A.* **101 D7** 46 2N 118 28W
Whitmire, *SC, U.S.A.* **90 D4** 34 30N 81 37W
Whitmore Lake, *MI, U.S.A.* **79 G8** 42 20N 83 45W
Whitmore Village, *HI, U.S.A.* **69 J13** 21 31N 158 1W
Whitney, *Ont., Canada* **176 F4** 45 31N 78 14W
Whitney, *NE, U.S.A.* **84 B2** 42 47N 103 15W
Whitney, *NV, U.S.A.* **85 F5** 36 4N 115 5W
Whitney, *TX, U.S.A.* **99 F10** 31 57N 97 19W
Whitney, L., *TX, U.S.A.* **99 F10** 31 52N 97 22W
Whitney, Mt., *CA, U.S.A.* **65 G8** 36 35N 118 18W
Whitney Point, *NY, U.S.A.* **89 C5** 42 20N 75 58W
Whitsett, *TX, U.S.A.* **99 J9** 28 38N 98 16W
Whittemore, *IA, U.S.A.* **73 B4** 43 4N 94 26W
Whittemore, *MI, U.S.A.* **79 E8** 44 14N 83 48W
Whittier, *AK, U.S.A.* **61 F10** 60 47N 148 41W
Whittier, *CA, U.S.A.* **65 K8** 33 58N 118 2W
Whittier Narrows Flood Control Basin, *Los Angeles, U.S.A.* **111 B4** 34 1N 118 4W
Whittlesey, Mt., *WI, U.S.A.* **103 B3** 46 18N 90 37W
Whitwell, *TN, U.S.A.* **97 E7** 35 12N 85 31W
Wholdaia L., *N.W.T., Canada* **189 D12** 60 43N 104 20W
Whycocomagh, *N.S., Canada* **173 H8** 45 59N 61 7W
Wiarton, *Ont., Canada* **178 C5** 44 40N 81 10W
Wibaux, *MT, U.S.A.* **83 D13** 46 59N 104 11W
Wibaux County ☆, *MT, U.S.A.* **83 D13** 46 50N 104 20W
Wichita, *KS, U.S.A.* **74 D6** 37 42N 97 20W
Wichita →, *TX, U.S.A.* **99 C9** 34 4N 98 10W
Wichita County ☆, *KS, U.S.A.* **74 C2** 38 30N 101 20W
Wichita County ☆, *TX, U.S.A.* **99 D9** 33 57N 98 40W
Wichita Falls, *TX, U.S.A.* **99 D9** 33 54N 98 30W
Wichita Mountains Nat. Wildlife Refuge ⌂, *OK, U.S.A.* **93 D5** 34 46N 98 42W
Wichita Mts., *OK, U.S.A.* **93 D5** 34 50N 98 45W
Wick, *WV, U.S.A.* **102 B4** 39 25N 80 58W
Wicked Pt., *Ont., Canada* **179 D9** 43 52N 77 15W
Wickenburg, *AZ, U.S.A.* **62 D3** 33 58N 112 44W
Wickes, *AR, U.S.A.* **63 D1** 34 18N 94 20W
Wickham, *Qué., Canada* **177 F10** 45 45N 72 30W
Wickiup Res., *OR, U.S.A.* **94 D4** 43 41N 121 41W
Wickliffe, *KY, U.S.A.* **96 D3** 36 58N 89 5W
Wickliffe, *OH, U.S.A.* **92 B5** 41 36N 81 28W
Wicomico →, *MD, U.S.A.* **77 B5** 38 13N 75 55W
Wicomico Church, *VA, U.S.A.* **77 C4** 37 49N 76 23W
Wicomico County ☆, *MD, U.S.A.* **77 B5** 38 25N 75 45W
Wiggins, *CO, U.S.A.* **66 B6** 40 14N 104 4W
Wiggins, *MS, U.S.A.* **81 F4** 30 51N 89 8W
Wiggins, *MS, U.S.A.* **81 D4** 32 42N 89 38W
Wikwemikong, *Ont., Canada* **178 B5** 45 48N 81 43W
Wilbarger County ☆, *TX, U.S.A.* **99 C8** 34 9N 99 17W
Wilber, *NE, U.S.A.* **84 D9** 40 29N 96 58W
Wilberforce, *Ont., Canada* **176 F4** 45 2N 78 13W
Wilbraham, *MA, U.S.A.* **78 B2** 42 7N 72 26W
Wilbur, *OR, U.S.A.* **94 D2** 43 19N 123 21W
Wilbur, *WA, U.S.A.* **101 C7** 47 46N 118 42W
Wilburton, *OK, U.S.A.* **93 D8** 34 55N 95 19W
Wilcox, *Sask., Canada* **182 E7** 50 6N 104 44W
Wilcox, *NE, U.S.A.* **84 D6** 40 22N 99 10W
Wilcox, *PA, U.S.A.* **95 C4** 41 35N 78 41W
Wilcox County ☆, *AL, U.S.A.* **60 E3** 31 59N 87 17W
Wilcox County ☆, *GA, U.S.A.* **68 D3** 32 0N 83 25W
Wild Animal Park, *CA, U.S.A.* **65 K10** 33 6N 116 59W
Wild Horse, *CO, U.S.A.* **66 D8** 38 50N 103 0W
Wild Horse Hill, *NE, U.S.A.* **84 C4** 41 55N 101 56W
Wild Horse Res., *NV, U.S.A.* **85 A5** 41 40N 115 51W
Wild Rice →, *MN, U.S.A.* **80 C2** 47 20N 96 50W
Wild Rice →, *ND, U.S.A.* **91 D9** 46 45N 96 47W
Wild Rose, *WI, U.S.A.* **103 D4** 44 11N 89 15W
Wildcat Cr. →, *IN, U.S.A.* **72 C4** 40 28N 86 52W
Wildcat Hill Prov. Park ⌂, *Sask., Canada* **182 B9** 53 14N 102 28W
Wilder, *ID, U.S.A.* **70 F2** 43 41N 116 55W
Wilder, *KY, U.S.A.* **107 B2** 39 3N 84 29W
Wilder, *MN, U.S.A.* **80 G3** 43 50N 95 12W
Wilder, *VT, U.S.A.* **86 C2** 43 40N 72 15W
Wildersville, *TN, U.S.A.* **96 E4** 35 47N 88 22W
Wilderville, *OR, U.S.A.* **94 E2** 42 23N 123 28W
Wildgoose L., *Ont., Canada* **181 C9** 49 44N 87 11W
Wildhay →, *Alta., Canada* **184 E3** 53 59N 117 20W
Wildhorse Cr. →, *OK, U.S.A.* **93 D6** 34 32N 97 10W
Wildorado, *TX, U.S.A.* **98 B5** 35 13N 102 12W
Wildrose, *ND, U.S.A.* **91 B2** 48 38N 103 11W
Wildwood, *Alta., Canada* **184 E5** 53 37N 115 14W
Wildwood, *FL, U.S.A.* **67 C6** 28 52N 82 2W
Wildwood, *NJ, U.S.A.* **87 D2** 38 59N 74 50W
Wildwood Crest, *NJ, U.S.A.* **87 D2** 38 58N 74 50W
Wiley, *CO, U.S.A.* **66 D8** 38 10N 102 40W
Wiley City, *WA, U.S.A.* **101 D5** 46 33N 120 41W
Wilkes-Barre, *PA, U.S.A.* **95 C7** 41 15N 75 53W
Wilkes County ☆, *GA, U.S.A.* **68 C4** 33 50N 82 45W
Wilkes County ☆, *NC, U.S.A.* **90 B4** 36 10N 81 10W
Wilkesboro, *NC, U.S.A.* **90 B4** 36 9N 81 10W
Wilkesboro Res. = W. Kerr Scott Res., *NC, U.S.A.* **90 B4** 36 10N 81 20W
Wilkie, *Sask., Canada* **182 C3** 52 27N 108 42W
Wilkin County ☆, *MN, U.S.A.* **80 D2** 46 20N 96 25W
Wilkins Str., *Canada* **188 A10** 78 5N 111 55W
Wilkinsburg, *PA, U.S.A.* **95 D3** 40 26N 79 52W
Wilkinson County ☆, *GA, U.S.A.* **68 D3** 32 45N 83 10W
Wilkinson County ☆, *MS, U.S.A.* **81 E2** 31 6N 91 18W
Will County ☆, *IL, U.S.A.* **71 B6** 41 25N 88 0W
Will Rogers, Oklahoma City ✈ (OKC), *OK, U.S.A.* **93 C6** 35 24N 97 36W
Willacoochee, *GA, U.S.A.* **68 E3** 31 20N 83 3W
Willacy County ☆, *TX, U.S.A.* **98 L10** 26 29N 97 47W
Willamette →, *OR, U.S.A.* **94 B3** 45 39N 122 46W
Willamette Nat. Forest, *OR, U.S.A.* **94 C3** 44 20N 122 10W
Willamina, *OR, U.S.A.* **94 B2** 45 5N 123 29W
Willapa B., *WA, U.S.A.* **101 D1** 46 40N 124 0W
Willard, *CO, U.S.A.* **66 B7** 40 33N 103 29W
Willard, *MO, U.S.A.* **82 D3** 37 18N 93 26W
Willard, *NM, U.S.A.* **88 C4** 34 36N 106 2W
Willard, *OH, U.S.A.* **92 B4** 41 3N 82 44W
Willard, *UT, U.S.A.* **100 B3** 41 25N 112 2W
Willards, *MD, U.S.A.* **77 B5** 38 24N 75 21W
Willcox, *AZ, U.S.A.* **62 E6** 32 15N 109 50W
Willcox Playa, *AZ, U.S.A.* **62 E6** 32 8N 109 51W
Willernie, *Minneapolis-St. Paul, U.S.A.* **113 A4** 45 3N 92 57W
Willey, *IA, U.S.A.* **73 D4** 41 59N 94 49W
William →, *Sask., Canada* **189 E11** 59 8N 109 19W
William A. Switzer Prov. Park ⌂, *Alta., Canada* **184 E3** 53 30N 117 48W
William B. Bankhead Nat. Forest, *AL, U.S.A.* **60 B3** 34 10N 87 15W

William B. Hartsfield International, Atlanta ✕ (ATL), GA, U.S.A. **68 C2** 33 38N 84 26W
William 'Bill' Dannelly Res., AL, U.S.A. **60 D3** 32 6N 87 24W
William L., Man., Canada **183 B12** 53 54N 99 21W
William P. Hobby, Houston ✕ (HOU), TX, U.S.A. **99** 29 38N 95 16W
Williamette Heights, Portland, U.S.A. **116 A1** 45 32N 122 42W
Williams, AZ, U.S.A. **62 B3** 35 15N 112 11W
Williams, CA, U.S.A. **64 D4** 39 9N 122 9W
Williams, MN, U.S.A. **80 B4** 48 45N 94 54W
Williams →, VT, U.S.A. **86 C2** 43 12N 72 27W
Williams County ☆, ND, U.S.A. **91 B2** 48 20N 103 30W
Williams County ☆, OH, U.S.A. **92 B2** 41 35N 84 37W
Williams Creek, Indianapolis, U.S.A. **110 A2** 39 53N 86 9W
Williams Fork →, CO, U.S.A. **66 B3** 40 28N 107 40W
Williams Fork Res., CO, U.S.A. **66 C4** 40 0N 106 8W
Williams L., Ont., Canada **180 A6** 51 48N 90 45W
Williams Lake, B.C., Canada **187 C12** 52 10N 122 10W
Williamsbridge, NY, U.S.A. **114 A3** 40 52N 73 51W
Williamsburg, IA, U.S.A. **73 D6** 41 40N 92 1W
Williamsburg, KS, U.S.A. **74 C8** 38 29N 95 28W
Williamsburg, KY, U.S.A. **97 D8** 36 44N 84 10W
Williamsburg, MA, U.S.A. **78 B2** 42 23N 72 44W
Williamsburg, MD, U.S.A. **77 B5** 38 40N 75 50W
Williamsburg, NY, U.S.A. **114 B3** 40 42N 73 56W
Williamsburg, OH, U.S.A. **92 D2** 39 3N 84 4W
Williamsburg, Orlando, U.S.A. **115 B2** 28 24N 81 26W
Williamsburg, PA, U.S.A. **95 D4** 40 28N 78 12W
Williamsburg, VA, U.S.A. **102 D8** 37 16N 76 43W
Williamsburg County ☆, SC, U.S.A. **90 E6** 33 40N 79 40W
Williamsfield, IL, U.S.A. **71 C3** 40 55N 90 1W
Williamson, GA, U.S.A. **68 C2** 33 11N 84 22W
Williamson, IA, U.S.A. **73 D5** 41 5N 93 15W
Williamson, NY, U.S.A. **89 B3** 43 14N 77 11W
Williamson, WV, U.S.A. **102 D2** 37 41N 82 17W
Williamson →, OR, U.S.A. **94 E4** 42 28N 121 57W
Williamson County ☆, IL, U.S.A. **71 F5** 37 40N 88 55W
Williamson County ☆, TN, U.S.A. **96 E6** 35 55N 86 52W
Williamson County ☆, TX, U.S.A. **99 G10** 30 38N 97 41W
Williamsport, IN, U.S.A. **72 C3** 40 17N 87 17W
Williamsport, MD, U.S.A. **77 A3** 39 37N 77 50W
Williamsport, OH, U.S.A. **92 D3** 39 35N 83 7W
Williamsport, PA, U.S.A. **95 C5** 41 15N 77 1W
Williamston, MI, U.S.A. **79 G7** 42 41N 84 17W
Williamston, NC, U.S.A. **90 C8** 35 51N 77 4W
Williamston, SC, U.S.A. **90 D3** 34 37N 82 29W
Williamstown, KY, U.S.A. **97 B8** 38 38N 84 34W
Williamstown, MA, U.S.A. **78 B1** 42 43N 73 12W
Williamstown, NJ, U.S.A. **87 C2** 39 40N 74 59W
Williamstown, NY, U.S.A. **89 B5** 43 26N 75 53W
Williamstown, WV, U.S.A. **102 B3** 39 24N 81 27W
Williamsville, DE, U.S.A. **77 B5** 38 27N 75 8W
Williamsville, IL, U.S.A. **71 D4** 39 57N 89 33W
Williamsville, MO, U.S.A. **82 E6** 36 58N 90 33W
Williford, AR, U.S.A. **63 B4** 36 15N 91 21W
Willimantic, CT, U.S.A. **78 C2** 41 43N 72 13W
Willimantic →, CT, U.S.A. **78 C2** 41 43N 72 12W
Willingboro, NJ, U.S.A. **87 B2** 40 3N 74 54W
Willingdon, Alta., Canada **184 E8** 53 50N 112 8W
Willis, KS, U.S.A. **74 B8** 39 43N 95 31W
Willis, TX, U.S.A. **99 G12** 30 25N 95 29W
Willis, L., Orlando, U.S.A. **115 B2** 28 23N 81 28W
Williston, FL, U.S.A. **67 B6** 29 23N 82 27W
Williston, MD, U.S.A. **77 B5** 38 48N 75 52W
Williston, ND, U.S.A. **91 B2** 48 9N 103 37W
Williston, SC, U.S.A. **90 E4** 33 24N 81 25W
Williston, TN, U.S.A. **96 E3** 35 9N 89 22W
Williston, VT, U.S.A. **86 B1** 44 25N 73 10W
Williston L., B.C., Canada **189 E8** 56 0N 124 0W
Williston Park, NY, U.S.A. **114 B5** 40 45N 73 38W
Willisville, IL, U.S.A. **71 F4** 37 59N 89 35W
Willits, CA, U.S.A. **64 D3** 39 25N 123 21W
Willmar, MN, U.S.A. **80 E3** 45 7N 95 3W
Willmore Park, MO, U.S.A. **117 B2** 38 34N 90 17W
Willmore Wilderness Prov. Park ⌓, Alta., Canada **184 E1** 53 45N 119 30W
Willoughby, OH, U.S.A. **92 B5** 41 39N 81 24W
Willoughby, L., VT, U.S.A. **86 B2** 44 45N 72 34W
Willoughby Bay, Norfolk, U.S.A. **115 A2** 36 57N 76 17W
Willoughby Spit, Norfolk, U.S.A. **115 A2** 36 58N 76 16W
Willow, AK, U.S.A. **61 F10** 61 45N 150 3W
Willow, AR, U.S.A. **63 D3** 34 8N 92 45W
Willow, OK, U.S.A. **93 C4** 35 3N 99 31W
Willow Bunch, Sask., Canada **182 F6** 49 20N 105 35W
Willow Bunch L., Sask., Canada **182 F6** 49 27N 105 27W
Willow City, ND, U.S.A. **91 B5** 48 36N 100 18W
Willow Cr. →, OR, U.S.A. **94 B5** 45 48N 120 1W
Willow Cr. →, OR, U.S.A. **94 C8** 44 0N 117 13W
Willow Cr. →, UT, U.S.A. **100 C6** 40 2N 109 45W
Willow Creek, CA, U.S.A. **64 C3** 40 56N 123 38W
Willow Creek, MT, U.S.A. **83 E6** 45 49N 111 39W
Willow Creek Res., NV, U.S.A. **85 A4** 41 14N 116 32W
Willow Grove, DE, U.S.A. **77 A5** 39 8N 75 39W
Willow Grove, PA, U.S.A. **87 B1** 40 9N 75 7W
Willow L., Alta., Canada **184 B9** 56 27N 111 8W
Willow L., N.W.T., Canada **189 D9** 62 10N 119 8W
Willow L., WY, U.S.A. **104 C3** 43 0N 109 52W
Willow Lake, SD, U.S.A. **91 F8** 44 38N 97 38W
Willow Ranch, CA, U.S.A. **64 B6** 41 54N 120 21W
Willow Res., WI, U.S.A. **103 C4** 45 43N 89 51W
Willow River, MN, U.S.A. **80 D6** 46 19N 92 51W
Willow Springs, Chicago, U.S.A. **108 C1** 41 44N 87 51W
Willow Springs, MO, U.S.A. **82 E5** 37 0N 91 58W
Willowbrook, Sask., Canada **182 D9** 51 12N 102 48W
Willowbrook, KS, U.S.A. **74 C6** 38 8N 97 57W
Willowbrook, Los Angeles, U.S.A. **111 C3** 33 55N 118 15W
Willowbrook, NY, U.S.A. **114 C2** 40 36N 74 8W
Willowdale, OR, U.S.A. **94 C5** 44 48N 120 57W
Willowick, OH, U.S.A. **92 B5** 41 38N 81 28W
Willowlake →, N.W.T., Canada **189 D8** 62 42N 123 8W
Willows, CA, U.S.A. **64 D4** 39 31N 122 12W
Wills Cr. →, OH, U.S.A. **92 C5** 40 9N 81 54W
Wills Point, TX, U.S.A. **99 E11** 32 43N 96 1W
Willsboro, NY, U.S.A. **86 B1** 44 21N 73 24W
Willshire, OH, U.S.A. **92 C2** 40 45N 84 48W
Wilma, FL, U.S.A. **67 A4** 30 9N 84 58W
Wilmar, AR, U.S.A. **63 E4** 33 38N 91 56W
Wilmer, AL, U.S.A. **60 F2** 30 49N 88 22W
Wilmer, TX, U.S.A. **109 C5** 32 35N 96 41W
Wilmette, IL, U.S.A. **71 A6** 42 4N 87 42W
Wilmington, DE, U.S.A. **77 A5** 39 45N 75 33W
Wilmington, IL, U.S.A. **71 B5** 41 18N 88 9W
Wilmington, MA, U.S.A. **78 B3** 42 33N 71 10W
Wilmington, NC, U.S.A. **90 D8** 34 14N 77 55W
Wilmington, OH, U.S.A. **92 D3** 39 27N 83 50W
Wilmington, VT, U.S.A. **86 D2** 42 52N 72 52W
Wilmont, MN, U.S.A. **80 G3** 43 46N 95 50W
Wilmore, KS, U.S.A. **74 D4** 37 20N 99 13W
Wilmore, KY, U.S.A. **97 C8** 37 52N 84 40W
Wilmot, P.E.I., Canada **173 G7** 46 2N 62 30W
Wilmot, AR, U.S.A. **63 E4** 33 4N 91 34W
Wilmot, KS, U.S.A. **74 D7** 37 22N 96 53W
Wilmot, SD, U.S.A. **91 E9** 45 25N 96 52W
Wilsall, MT, U.S.A. **83 E7** 45 59N 110 38W
Wilsey, KS, U.S.A. **74 C7** 38 38N 96 41W
Wilson, AR, U.S.A. **63 C5** 35 34N 90 3W
Wilson, KS, U.S.A. **74 C5** 38 50N 98 29W
Wilson, LA, U.S.A. **75 D4** 30 55N 91 7W
Wilson, NC, U.S.A. **90 C8** 35 44N 77 55W
Wilson, NY, U.S.A. **89 B2** 43 19N 78 50W
Wilson, OK, U.S.A. **93 D6** 34 10N 97 26W
Wilson, TX, U.S.A. **98 D6** 33 19N 101 44W
Wilson →, OR, U.S.A. **94 B2** 45 29N 123 53W
Wilson, C., Nunavut, Canada **191 D9** 66 59N 81 27W
Wilson, Mt., CO, U.S.A. **66 E3** 37 50N 107 59W
Wilson County ☆, KS, U.S.A. **74 D8** 37 30N 95 45W
Wilson County ☆, NC, U.S.A. **90 C7** 35 45N 78 0W
Wilson County ☆, TN, U.S.A. **96 D6** 36 12N 86 18W
Wilson County ☆, TX, U.S.A. **99 H9** 29 8N 98 10W
Wilson Creek, B.C., Canada **186 F11** 49 27N 123 43W
Wilson Creek, WA, U.S.A. **101 C6** 47 25N 119 7W
Wilson Creek Ra., NV, U.S.A. **85 D6** 38 12N 114 18W
Wilson L., AL, U.S.A. **60 B3** 34 48N 87 38W
Wilson Lake, KS, U.S.A. **74 C5** 38 58N 98 30W
Wilson Landing, B.C., Canada **187 F15** 50 0N 119 30W
Wilsons Beach, N.B., Canada **173 J3** 44 56N 66 56W
Wilsons Creek Nat. Battlefield ⌓, MO, U.S.A. **82 D3** 37 6N 93 25W
Wilsons Mills, ME, U.S.A. **76 D2** 44 57N 71 2W
Wilsonville, AL, U.S.A. **60 C4** 33 14N 86 29W
Wilsonville, NE, U.S.A. **84 D5** 40 7N 100 7W
Wilsonville, OR, U.S.A. **94 B3** 45 18N 122 46W
Wilton, AR, U.S.A. **63 E1** 33 45N 94 9W
Wilton, CT, U.S.A. **78 C1** 41 12N 73 26W
Wilton, IA, U.S.A. **73 D7** 41 35N 91 1W
Wilton, ME, U.S.A. **76 D3** 44 36N 70 14W
Wilton, MN, U.S.A. **80 C3** 47 30N 95 0W
Wilton, ND, U.S.A. **91 C5** 47 10N 100 47W
Wilton, NH, U.S.A. **86 D3** 42 51N 71 44W
Wilton, WI, U.S.A. **103 E3** 43 49N 90 32W
Wilton Manors, Miami, U.S.A. **112 B3** 26 9N 80 8W
Wimbledon, ND, U.S.A. **91 C7** 47 10N 98 28W
Winagami L., Alta., Canada **184 C4** 55 37N 116 44W
Winamac, IN, U.S.A. **72 B4** 41 3N 86 36W
Winchendon, MA, U.S.A. **78 B2** 42 41N 72 3W
Winchester, Ont., Canada **179 B11** 45 6N 75 21W
Winchester, AR, U.S.A. **63 E4** 33 47N 91 29W
Winchester, Boston, U.S.A. **106 A3** 42 26N 71 8W
Winchester, ID, U.S.A. **70 C2** 46 14N 116 38W
Winchester, IL, U.S.A. **71 D3** 39 38N 90 27W
Winchester, IN, U.S.A. **72 C6** 40 10N 84 59W
Winchester, KY, U.S.A. **97 C8** 37 59N 84 11W
Winchester, NH, U.S.A. **86 D2** 42 46N 72 23W
Winchester, NV, U.S.A. **85 F5** 36 7N 115 7W
Winchester, OH, U.S.A. **92 E3** 38 56N 83 39W
Winchester, TN, U.S.A. **96 E6** 35 11N 86 7W
Winchester, VA, U.S.A. **77 A2** 39 11N 78 10W
Winchester, WY, U.S.A. **104 C4** 43 52N 108 10W
Winchester Bay, OR, U.S.A. **94 D1** 43 41N 124 10W
Wind →, Yukon, Canada **188 C5** 65 50N 135 18W
Wind →, WY, U.S.A. **104 C4** 43 12N 108 12W
Wind Cave Nat. Park △, SD, U.S.A. **91 G2** 43 32N 103 17W
Wind Gap, PA, U.S.A. **87 B1** 40 51N 75 18W
Wind Mt., NM, U.S.A. **88 E5** 32 2N 105 31W
Wind Point, WI, U.S.A. **103 F6** 42 47N 87 46W
Wind River Indian Reservation, WY, U.S.A. **104 C4** 43 20N 109 0W
Wind River Pk., WY, U.S.A. **104 D3** 42 42N 109 7W
Wind River Range, WY, U.S.A. **104 D3** 43 0N 109 30W
Windber, PA, U.S.A. **95 D4** 40 14N 78 50W
Windcrest, San Antonio, U.S.A. **117 B3** 29 30N 98 22W
Windcrest, TX, U.S.A. **99 H9** 29 31N 98 19W
Windemere L., Ont., Canada **181 E13** 47 58N 83 47W
Winder, GA, U.S.A. **68 B3** 34 0N 83 45W
Windermere, B.C., Canada **185 H5** 50 28N 115 59W
Windermere, FL, U.S.A. **115 B1** 28 29N 81 32W
Windfall, IN, U.S.A. **72 C5** 40 22N 85 57W
Windham, NH, U.S.A. **86 D3** 42 48N 71 18W
Windham County ☆, CT, U.S.A. **78 C2** 41 45N 72 0W
Windham County ☆, VT, U.S.A. **86 D2** 43 0N 72 45W
Windigo, MI, U.S.A. **79 B2** 47 55N 89 9W
Windigo →, Qué., Canada **177 D9** 47 46N 73 19W
Winding Stair Mountain Nat. Recr. Area ⌓, OK, U.S.A. **93 D9** 34 45N 94 47W
Windom, KS, U.S.A. **74 C6** 38 23N 97 55W
Windom, MN, U.S.A. **80 G3** 43 52N 95 7W
Windom Pk., CO, U.S.A. **66 E3** 37 35N 107 35W
Window Rock, AZ, U.S.A. **62 B6** 35 41N 109 3W
Windsor, N.S., Canada **173 J5** 44 59N 64 5W
Windsor, Ont., Canada **178 E2** 42 18N 83 0W
Windsor, Qué., Canada **177 F11** 45 34N 72 0W
Windsor, CA, U.S.A. **64 E4** 38 33N 122 49W
Windsor, CO, U.S.A. **66 B6** 40 29N 104 54W
Windsor, CT, U.S.A. **78 C2** 41 50N 72 39W
Windsor, IL, U.S.A. **71 D5** 39 26N 88 36W
Windsor, MI, U.S.A. **109 B2** 42 18N 83 0W
Windsor, MO, U.S.A. **82 C3** 38 32N 93 31W
Windsor, NC, U.S.A. **90 C9** 36 0N 76 57W
Windsor, VA, U.S.A. **102 E8** 36 49N 76 45W
Windsor, VT, U.S.A. **86 C2** 43 29N 72 24W
Windsor County ☆, VT, U.S.A. **86 C2** 43 35N 72 35W
Windsor Forest, GA, U.S.A. **68 E5** 31 59N 81 5W
Windsor Heights, Nfld. & L., Canada **174 E8** 47 36N 52 49W
Windsor Hills, Los Angeles, U.S.A. **111 C2** 33 59N 118 22W
Windsor L., Nfld. & L., Canada **174 E8** 47 36N 52 48W
Windsor Locks, CT, U.S.A. **78 C2** 41 56N 72 38W
Windsor Park, Charlotte, U.S.A. **107 A2** 35 13N 80 45W
Windthorst, Sask., Canada **182 E9** 50 6N 102 50W
Windthorst, TX, U.S.A. **99 D9** 33 34N 98 26W
Windy L., Sask., Canada **182 A9** 54 22N 102 35W
Windy Pk., WA, U.S.A. **101 B6** 48 56N 119 58W
Winefred L., Alta., Canada **184 C10** 55 30N 110 30W
Winema Nat. Forest, OR, U.S.A. **94 D4** 43 10N 121 50W
Winfield, Alta., Canada **185 F6** 52 58N 114 26W
Winfield, B.C., Canada **187 E15** 50 2N 119 24W
Winfield, AL, U.S.A. **60 C3** 33 56N 87 49W
Winfield, IA, U.S.A. **73 D7** 41 7N 91 26W
Winfield, KS, U.S.A. **74 D7** 37 15N 96 59W
Winfield, MD, U.S.A. **77 A3** 39 26N 77 4W
Winfield, MO, U.S.A. **82 C6** 39 0N 90 44W
Winfield, NJ, U.S.A. **114 C1** 40 38N 74 17W
Winfield, TN, U.S.A. **97 D8** 36 33N 84 27W
Winfield, WV, U.S.A. **102 C3** 38 32N 81 54W
Winfred, SD, U.S.A. **91 G8** 44 0N 97 19W
Wing, ND, U.S.A. **91 C5** 47 9N 100 17W
Wingate, IN, U.S.A. **72 C3** 40 10N 87 4W
Wingate, NC, U.S.A. **90 D5** 34 59N 80 26W
Wingdale, NY, U.S.A. **78 C1** 41 39N 73 34W
Winger, MN, U.S.A. **80 C3** 47 32N 95 59W
Wingham, Ont., Canada **178 D5** 43 55N 81 20W
Wingo, KY, U.S.A. **96 D4** 36 39N 88 44W
Winifred, MT, U.S.A. **83 C8** 47 34N 109 23W
Winigan, MO, U.S.A. **82 A4** 40 3N 92 54W
Winisk →, Ont., Canada **191 F8** 55 17N 85 5W
Wink, TX, U.S.A. **98 F4** 31 45N 103 9W
Winkelman, AZ, U.S.A. **62 E5** 32 59N 110 46W
Winkler, Man., Canada **183 F14** 49 10N 97 56W
Winkler County ☆, TX, U.S.A. **98 F4** 31 52N 103 6W
Winlock, WA, U.S.A. **101 D3** 46 30N 122 56W
Winn Parish ☆, LA, U.S.A. **75 C3** 31 56N 92 38W
Winnebago, IL, U.S.A. **71 A4** 42 16N 89 15W
Winnebago, MN, U.S.A. **80 G4** 43 46N 94 10W
Winnebago, NE, U.S.A. **84 B9** 42 14N 96 28W
Winnebago, L., WI, U.S.A. **103 E5** 44 0N 88 26W
Winnebago County ☆, IL, U.S.A. **71 A4** 42 20N 89 10W
Winnebago County ☆, IA, U.S.A. **73 B5** 43 20N 93 40W
Winnebago County ☆, WI, U.S.A. **103 D5** 44 0N 88 45W
Winnebago Indian Reservation, NE, U.S.A. **84 B9** 42 15N 96 40W
Winneconne, WI, U.S.A. **103 D5** 44 7N 88 43W
Winnemucca, NV, U.S.A. **85 B3** 40 58N 117 44W
Winnemucca L., NV, U.S.A. **85 B1** 40 7N 119 21W
Winner, SD, U.S.A. **91 G6** 43 22N 99 52W
Winneshiek County ☆, IA, U.S.A. **73 B7** 43 15N 91 50W
Winnetoon, NE, U.S.A. **84 B8** 42 31N 97 58W
Winnett, MT, U.S.A. **83 D9** 47 0N 108 21W
Winnfield, LA, U.S.A. **75 C3** 31 56N 92 38W
Winnibigoshish, L., MN, U.S.A. **80 C4** 47 27N 94 13W
Winnie, TX, U.S.A. **99 H13** 29 49N 94 23W
Winnipeg, Man., Canada **183 F14** 49 54N 97 9W
Winnipeg →, Man., Canada **183 E15** 50 38N 96 19W
Winnipeg, L., Man., Canada **183 C14** 52 0N 97 0W
Winnipeg Beach, Man., Canada **183 E15** 50 30N 96 58W
Winnipeg International ✕ (YWG), Man., Canada **183 F14** 49 55N 97 15W
Winnipegosis, Man., Canada **183 D12** 51 39N 99 55W
Winnipegosis L., Man., Canada **183 C12** 52 30N 100 0W
Winnipesaukee, NH, U.S.A. **86 C3** 43 40N 71 20W
Winnipesaukee, L., NH, U.S.A. **86 C3** 43 38N 71 21W
Winnisquam L., NH, U.S.A. **86 C3** 43 33N 71 31W
Winnsboro, LA, U.S.A. **75 B4** 32 10N 91 43W
Winnsboro, SC, U.S.A. **90 D4** 34 23N 81 5W
Winnsboro, TX, U.S.A. **99 E12** 32 58N 95 17W
Winokapau, L., Nfld. & L., Canada **175 C5** 53 15N 62 50W
Winona, KS, U.S.A. **74 B2** 39 4N 101 15W
Winona, MN, U.S.A. **80 F7** 44 3N 91 39W
Winona, MS, U.S.A. **81 C4** 33 29N 89 44W
Winona, MO, U.S.A. **82 D5** 37 1N 91 20W
Winona, WA, U.S.A. **101 D8** 46 57N 117 48W
Winona County ☆, MN, U.S.A. **80 G7** 44 0N 91 50W
Winona Lake, IN, U.S.A. **72 B5** 41 14N 85 49W
Winooski, VT, U.S.A. **86 B1** 44 29N 73 11W
Winooski →, VT, U.S.A. **86 B1** 44 32N 73 17W
Winside, NE, U.S.A. **84 B8** 42 11N 97 10W
Winslow = Bainbridge Island, WA, U.S.A. **101 C3** 47 38N 122 32W
Winslow, AZ, U.S.A. **62 B5** 35 2N 110 42W
Winslow, AR, U.S.A. **63 C1** 35 48N 94 8W
Winslow, IN, U.S.A. **72 E3** 38 23N 87 13W
Winslow, ME, U.S.A. **76 D4** 44 33N 69 37W
Winslow, NE, U.S.A. **84 C9** 41 37N 96 30W
Winsted, CT, U.S.A. **78 C1** 41 55N 73 4W
Winsted, MN, U.S.A. **80 F4** 44 58N 94 3W
Winston, NM, U.S.A. **88 D3** 33 20N 107 39W
Winston, OR, U.S.A. **94 D2** 43 7N 123 25W
Winston County ☆, AL, U.S.A. **60 B3** 34 9N 87 24W
Winston County ☆, MS, U.S.A. **81 C4** 33 7N 89 3W
Winston-Salem, NC, U.S.A. **90 B5** 36 6N 80 15W
Winter, WI, U.S.A. **103 C2** 45 49N 91 1W
Winter Garden, FL, U.S.A. **67 C7** 28 34N 81 35W
Winter Harbor, ME, U.S.A. **76 D5** 44 24N 68 5W
Winter Harbour, B.C., Canada **186 E6** 50 31N 128 2W
Winter Haven, FL, U.S.A. **67 C7** 28 1N 81 44W
Winter I., Nunavut, Canada **191 D9** 66 16N 83 4W
Winter Park, CO, U.S.A. **66 C5** 39 53N 105 46W
Winter Park, FL, U.S.A. **67 C7** 28 36N 81 20W
Winterhaven, CA, U.S.A. **65 L12** 32 44N 114 38W
Wintering L., Ont., Canada **181 C9** 49 26N 87 16W
Winters, CA, U.S.A. **64 E5** 38 32N 121 58W
Winters, TX, U.S.A. **99 F8** 31 58N 99 58W
Winterset, IA, U.S.A. **73 D4** 41 20N 94 1W
Winterstown, PA, U.S.A. **77 A4** 39 50N 76 38W
Wintersville, OH, U.S.A. **92 C6** 40 23N 80 42W
Winterton, Nfld. & L., Canada **174 E7** 47 58N 53 20W
Winterville, ME, U.S.A. **76 B5** 46 58N 68 34W
Winterville, NC, U.S.A. **90 C8** 35 32N 77 24W
Winthrop, AR, U.S.A. **63 E1** 33 50N 94 21W
Winthrop, Boston, U.S.A. **106 A4** 42 22N 70 58W
Winthrop, IA, U.S.A. **73 C7** 42 28N 91 44W
Winthrop, ME, U.S.A. **76 D4** 44 18N 69 58W
Winthrop, MN, U.S.A. **80 F4** 44 32N 94 22W
Winthrop, WA, U.S.A. **101 B5** 48 28N 120 10W
Winthrop Harbor, IL, U.S.A. **71 A6** 42 29N 87 50W
Winton, CA, U.S.A. **64 F6** 37 23N 120 37W
Winton, MN, U.S.A. **80 C7** 47 56N 91 48W
Winton, NC, U.S.A. **90 B9** 36 24N 76 56W
Wiota, IA, U.S.A. **73 D4** 41 24N 94 54W
Wiota, WI, U.S.A. **103 F4** 42 39N 89 57W
Wirt County ☆, WV, U.S.A. **102 B3** 39 4N 81 24W
Wiscasset, ME, U.S.A. **76 E4** 44 0N 69 40W
Wisconsin □, U.S.A. **103 D4** 44 45N 89 30W
Wisconsin →, WI, U.S.A. **103 E2** 43 0N 91 15W
Wisconsin, L., WI, U.S.A. **103 E4** 43 19N 89 44W
Wisconsin Dells, WI, U.S.A. **103 E4** 43 38N 89 46W
Wisconsin Rapids, WI, U.S.A. **103 D4** 44 23N 89 49W
Wisdom, MT, U.S.A. **83 E4** 45 37N 113 27W
Wise, VA, U.S.A. **102 E2** 36 59N 82 35W
Wise County ☆, TX, U.S.A. **99 D10** 33 14N 97 35W
Wise County ☆, VA, U.S.A. **102 E2** 37 0N 82 45W
Wise River, MT, U.S.A. **83 E5** 45 48N 112 57W
Wiseman, AK, U.S.A. **61 C10** 67 25N 150 6W
Wiseton, Sask., Canada **182 D4** 51 19N 107 39W
Wishek, ND, U.S.A. **91 D6** 46 16N 99 33W
Wishon Res., CA, U.S.A. **65 G8** 36 50N 118 50W
Wishram, WA, U.S.A. **101 E5** 45 40N 120 58W
Wisner, LA, U.S.A. **75 C4** 31 59N 91 39W
Wisner, NE, U.S.A. **84 C9** 41 59N 96 55W
Wissota L., WI, U.S.A. **103 D2** 44 56N 91 20W
Wistaria, B.C., Canada **186 B8** 53 52N 126 22W
Wister, OK, U.S.A. **93 D9** 34 58N 94 43W
Witch Lake, MI, U.S.A. **79 C3** 46 17N 88 1W
Withee, WI, U.S.A. **103 D3** 44 57N 90 36W
Witherbee, NY, U.S.A. **86 B1** 44 5N 73 32W
Withington Mt., NM, U.S.A. **88 D3** 33 53N 107 29W
Withlacoochee →, FL, U.S.A. **67 C6** 29 0N 82 45W
Withlacoochee →, FL, U.S.A. **67 A5** 30 24N 83 10W
Withrow, WA, U.S.A. **101 C6** 47 42N 119 48W
Withrow Nature Preserve, OH, U.S.A. **107 B2** 39 3N 84 23W
Witless Bay, Nfld. & L., Canada **174 E8** 47 17N 52 50W
Witt, IL, U.S.A. **71 D4** 39 15N 89 21W
Witten, SD, U.S.A. **91 G5** 43 26N 100 5W
Wittenberg, MO, U.S.A. **82 D7** 37 39N 89 31W
Wittenberg, WI, U.S.A. **103 D4** 44 49N 89 10W
Wittman, MD, U.S.A. **77 B4** 38 48N 76 18W
Wittmann, AZ, U.S.A. **62 D3** 33 47N 112 32W
Wixom, MI, U.S.A. **79 G8** 42 32N 83 32W
Wixom L., MI, U.S.A. **79 F7** 43 50N 84 20W
Woburn, MA, U.S.A. **78 B3** 42 29N 71 9W
Wolbach, NE, U.S.A. **84 C7** 41 24N 98 24W
Wolcott, CO, U.S.A. **66 C4** 39 42N 106 40W
Wolcott, CT, U.S.A. **78 C2** 41 36N 72 59W
Wolcott, IN, U.S.A. **72 C3** 40 46N 87 3W
Wolcott, NY, U.S.A. **89 B4** 43 13N 76 49W
Wolcottville, IN, U.S.A. **72 B5** 41 32N 85 22W
Wold Cr. →, SD, U.S.A. **91 F5** 44 42N 98 40W
Wolf →, MS, U.S.A. **81 F4** 30 22N 89 18W
Wolf →, TN, U.S.A. **96 E3** 35 10N 89 5W
Wolf →, WI, U.S.A. **103 D5** 44 5N 88 41W
Wolf Bay, Qué., Canada **172 C9** 50 16N 60 8W
Wolf Cr. →, MT, U.S.A. **83 C8** 47 37N 109 38W
Wolf Cr. →, OK, U.S.A. **93 B4** 36 34N 99 34W
Wolf Creek, MT, U.S.A. **83 C5** 47 0N 112 4W
Wolf Creek, OR, U.S.A. **94 E2** 42 42N 123 24W
Wolf Creek Pass, CO, U.S.A. **66 E4** 37 29N 106 48W
Wolf L., Alta., Canada **184 D10** 54 42N 110 57W
Wolf Lake, MI, U.S.A. **79 F5** 43 15N 86 7W
Wolf Lake, MN, U.S.A. **80 D3** 46 48N 95 21W
Wolf Mts., MT, U.S.A. **83 E10** 45 12N 107 8W
Wolf Point, MT, U.S.A. **83 B12** 48 5N 105 39W
Wolf Trap Farm Park, VA, U.S.A. **119 B2** 38 56N 77 17W
Wolfdale, PA, U.S.A. **95 D2** 40 12N 80 17W
Wolfe City, TX, U.S.A. **99 D11** 33 22N 96 4W
Wolfe County ☆, KY, U.S.A. **97 C9** 37 45N 83 29W
Wolfe I., Ont., Canada **179 C10** 44 7N 76 20W
Wolfeboro, NH, U.S.A. **86 C3** 43 35N 71 13W
Wolfforth, TX, U.S.A. **98 D5** 33 30N 102 1W
Wolford, ND, U.S.A. **91 B6** 48 30N 99 42W
Wolfsville, MD, U.S.A. **77 A3** 39 37N 77 35W
Wolfville, N.S., Canada **173 H5** 45 5N 64 22W
Wollaston, Boston, U.S.A. **106 B3** 42 15N 71 2W
Wollaston, C., N.W.T., Canada **188 B9** 71 7N 118 4W
Wollaston L., Sask., Canada **189 E12** 58 7N 103 10W
Wollaston Lake, Sask., Canada **189 E12** 58 3N 103 33W
Wollaston Pen., Canada **188 C10** 69 30N 115 0W
Wolseley, Sask., Canada **182 E8** 50 25N 103 15W
Wolsey, SD, U.S.A. **91 F7** 44 25N 98 28W
Wolstenholme, C., Qué., Canada **175 A2** 62 35N 77 30W
Wolverine, MI, U.S.A. **79 D7** 45 17N 84 36W
Wolverine Peak, WY, U.S.A. **104 D3** 42 59N 109 27W
Wolverton, MN, U.S.A. **80 D2** 46 34N 96 44W
Wonalancet, NH, U.S.A. **86 C3** 43 44N 71 21W
Wood, SD, U.S.A. **91 G5** 43 30N 100 29W
Wood →, Sask., Canada **182 E5** 50 8N 106 13W
Wood →, NE, U.S.A. **84 C7** 41 2N 98 5W
Wood Buffalo Nat. Park △, Alta., Canada **189 E10** 59 0N 113 41W
Wood County ☆, OH, U.S.A. **92 B3** 41 23N 83 39W
Wood County ☆, TX, U.S.A. **99 E12** 32 48N 95 27W
Wood County ☆, WV, U.S.A. **102 B3** 39 14N 81 34W
Wood County ☆, WI, U.S.A. **103 D4** 44 20N 90 0W
Wood Lake, MN, U.S.A. **80 F3** 44 39N 95 32W
Wood Lake, NE, U.S.A. **84 B5** 42 38N 100 14W
Wood Ridge, NJ, U.S.A. **114 A2** 40 50N 74 4W
Wood River, IL, U.S.A. **71 E3** 38 52N 90 5W
Wood River, NE, U.S.A. **84 D7** 40 49N 98 36W
Woodall Mt., MS, U.S.A. **81 B5** 34 47N 88 15W
Woodberry, AR, U.S.A. **63 E3** 33 35N 92 31W
Woodbine, GA, U.S.A. **68 F5** 30 58N 81 44W
Woodbine, IA, U.S.A. **73 D3** 41 44N 95 43W
Woodbine, KS, U.S.A. **74 C7** 38 48N 96 57W
Woodbine, KY, U.S.A. **97 D8** 36 54N 84 5W
Woodbine, MD, U.S.A. **77 A3** 39 22N 77 4W
Woodbine, NJ, U.S.A. **87 C2** 39 15N 74 49W
Woodbourne, NY, U.S.A. **89 D6** 41 46N 74 36W
Woodbridge, Ont., Canada **178 D7** 43 47N 79 36W
Woodbridge, CT, U.S.A. **78 C1** 41 21N 73 2W
Woodbridge, NJ, U.S.A. **114 C1** 40 33N 74 17W
Woodbridge, VA, U.S.A. **77 B3** 38 40N 77 15W
Woodburn, IN, U.S.A. **72 B6** 41 8N 84 51W
Woodburn, IA, U.S.A. **73 D5** 41 1N 93 36W
Woodburn, KY, U.S.A. **96 D6** 36 50N 86 32W
Woodburn, OR, U.S.A. **94 B3** 45 9N 122 51W
Woodbury, CT, U.S.A. **78 C1** 41 33N 73 13W
Woodbury, GA, U.S.A. **68 D2** 32 59N 84 35W
Woodbury, KY, U.S.A. **96 C6** 37 11N 86 38W
Woodbury, Minneapolis-St. Paul, U.S.A. **113 B4** 44 55N 92 57W
Woodbury, NJ, U.S.A. **87 C1** 39 50N 75 9W
Woodbury, TN, U.S.A. **96 E6** 35 50N 86 4W
Woodbury County ☆, IA, U.S.A. **73 C2** 42 25N 96 0W
Wooden Shoe, MI, U.S.A. **79 F7** 43 59N 84 21W
Woodfibre, B.C., Canada **187 F11** 49 41N 123 15W
Woodfin, NC, U.S.A. **90 C3** 35 38N 82 36W
Woodford, VT, U.S.A. **86 D1** 42 52N 73 6W
Woodford County ☆, IL, U.S.A. **71 C4** 40 50N 89 10W
Woodford County ☆, KY, U.S.A. **97 B8** 38 0N 84 45W
Woodfords, CA, U.S.A. **64 E7** 38 47N 119 50W
Woodhaven, NY, U.S.A. **114 B3** 40 41N 73 51W
Woodhaven, Norfolk, U.S.A. **115 B2** 36 48N 76 11W
Woodhull, IL, U.S.A. **71 B3** 41 11N 90 20W
Woodinville, Seattle, U.S.A. **118 B5** 47 45N 122 9W
Woodlake, CA, U.S.A. **65 G7** 36 25N 119 6W
Woodland, CA, U.S.A. **64 E5** 38 41N 121 46W
Woodland, IL, U.S.A. **71 C6** 40 43N 87 44W
Woodland, ME, U.S.A. **76 C6** 45 9N 67 25W
Woodland, MS, U.S.A. **81 C4** 33 47N 89 3W
Woodland, TX, U.S.A. **99 D12** 33 48N 95 17W
Woodland, WA, U.S.A. **101 E3** 45 54N 122 45W
Woodland Beach, DE, U.S.A. **77 A5** 39 20N 75 28W
Woodland Caribou Prov. Park ⌓, Ont., Canada **180 A2** 51 0N 94 45W
Woodland Park, CO, U.S.A. **66 D5** 38 57N 105 12W
Woodlands, Man., Canada **183 E14** 50 12N 97 40W
Woodlawn, KY, U.S.A. **107 B2** 39 5N 84 28W
Woodlawn, MD, U.S.A. **77 A4** 39 19N 76 43W
Woodlynne, NJ, U.S.A. **116 B2** 39 54N 75 5W
Woodman, WI, U.S.A. **103 E3** 43 7N 90 48W
Woodmere, NY, U.S.A. **114 C4** 40 37N 73 42W
Woodmont, MD, U.S.A. **119 B3** 38 59N 77 5W
Woodmoor, Baltimore, U.S.A. **107 B1** 39 20N 76 44W
Woodpecker, B.C., Canada **187 B12** 53 30N 122 40W
Woodridge, Man., Canada **183 F15** 49 20N 96 9W
Woodridge, NY, U.S.A. **89 D6** 41 43N 74 34W
Woodrow, NY, U.S.A. **114 C1** 40 32N 74 11W
Woodrow, TX, U.S.A. **98 D6** 33 27N 101 50W
Woodruff, KS, U.S.A. **74 B4** 39 59N 99 19W
Woodruff, SC, U.S.A. **90 D3** 34 45N 82 2W
Woodruff, UT, U.S.A. **100 B4** 41 31N 111 10W
Woodruff, WI, U.S.A. **103 C4** 45 54N 89 42W
Woodruff, L., FL, U.S.A. **67 B7** 29 6N 81 24W
Woodruff County ☆, AR, U.S.A. **63 C4** 35 9N 91 21W
Woodruff Narrows Res., WY, U.S.A. **104 E1** 41 31N 111 1W
Woods, L., Nfld. & L., Canada **175 C4** 54 30N 65 13W
Woods, L. of the, Ont., Canada **180 C2** 49 15N 94 45W
Woods, L. of the, MN, U.S.A. **80 A4** 49 0N 95 0W
Woods County ☆, OK, U.S.A. **93 B5** 36 45N 98 50W
Woods Cross, UT, U.S.A. **100 C4** 40 52N 111 53W
Woods Hole, MA, U.S.A. **78 C4** 41 31N 70 40W
Woods Landing, WY, U.S.A. **104 E6** 41 7N 106 1W
Woods Res., TN, U.S.A. **97 E7** 35 18N 86 5W
Woodsboro, MD, U.S.A. **77 A3** 39 32N 77 19W
Woodsboro, TX, U.S.A. **99 J10** 28 14N 97 20W
Woodsfield, OH, U.S.A. **92 D5** 39 46N 81 7W
Woodside, NY, U.S.A. **114 B3** 40 44N 73 54W
Woodson, AR, U.S.A. **63 D3** 34 32N 92 13W
Woodson, TX, U.S.A. **99 D8** 33 1N 99 3W
Woodson County ☆, KS, U.S.A. **74 D8** 37 50N 95 45W
Woodson Terrace, MO, U.S.A. **117 A1** 38 43N 90 21W
Woodstock, N.B., Canada **173 G2** 46 11N 67 37W
Woodstock, Ont., Canada **178 D6** 43 10N 80 45W
Woodstock, CT, U.S.A. **78 C2** 41 56N 72 5W
Woodstock, GA, U.S.A. **68 B2** 34 6N 84 31W
Woodstock, IL, U.S.A. **71 A5** 42 19N 88 27W
Woodstock, NH, U.S.A. **86 C3** 43 57N 71 42W

Woodstock, *NY, U.S.A.* **89 C6** 42 2N 74 7W
Woodstock, *OH, U.S.A.* **92 C3** 40 10N 83 32W
Woodstock, *VA, U.S.A.* **102 C6** 38 53N 78 30W
Woodstock, *VT, U.S.A.* **86 C2** 43 37N 72 31W
Woodston, *KS, U.S.A.* **74 B4** 39 27N 99 6W
Woodstown, *NJ, U.S.A.* **87 C1** 39 39N 75 20W
Woodsville, *NH, U.S.A.* **86 B2** 44 9N 72 2W
Woodville, *AL, U.S.A.* **60 B4** 34 38N 86 17W
Woodville, *FL, U.S.A.* **67 A4** 30 19N 84 15W
Woodville, *GA, U.S.A.* **68 C3** 33 40N 83 7W
Woodville, *MS, U.S.A.* **81 E2** 31 6N 91 18W
Woodville, *OK, U.S.A.* **93 E7** 33 58N 96 39W
Woodville, *TX, U.S.A.* **99 G13** 30 47N 94 25W
Woodward, *IA, U.S.A.* **73 D5** 41 51N 93 55W
Woodward, *OK, U.S.A.* **93 B4** 36 26N 99 24W
Woodward County ☆, *OK, U.S.A.* **93 B4** 36 25N 99 15W
Woodway, *Seattle, U.S.A.* **118 B3** 47 47N 122 22W
Woodway, *TX, U.S.A.* **99 F10** 31 30N 97 13W
Woodworth, *LA, U.S.A.* **75 C3** 31 9N 92 30W
Woodworth, *ND, U.S.A.* **91 C6** 47 9N 99 23W
Woody Creek, *CO, U.S.A.* **66 C4** 39 17N 106 54W
Woody Point, *Nfld. & L., Canada* **174 C3** 49 30N 57 55W
Woollen's Garden, *Indianapolis,*
U.S.A. **110 A2** 39 55N 86 6W
Woolridge, *MO, U.S.A.* **82 C4** 38 55N 92 32W
Woolstock, *IA, U.S.A.* **73 C5** 42 34N 93 51W
Woolwine, *VA, U.S.A.* **102 E4** 36 47N 80 17W
Woonsocket, *RI, U.S.A.* **78 C3** 42 0N 71 31W
Woonsocket, *SD, U.S.A.* **91 F7** 44 3N 98 17W
Wooster, *AR, U.S.A.* **63 C3** 35 12N 92 27W
Wooster, *OH, U.S.A.* **92 C5** 40 48N 81 56W
Worcester, *MA, U.S.A.* **78 B3** 42 16N 71 48W
Worcester, *NY, U.S.A.* **89 C6** 42 36N 74 45W
Worcester, *VT, U.S.A.* **86 B2** 44 20N 72 40W
Worcester County ☆, *MA, U.S.A.* **78 B2** 42 25N 72 0W
Worcester County ☆, *MD, U.S.A.* **77 B5** 38 15N 75 20W
Worcester Mts., *VT, U.S.A.* **86 B2** 44 27N 72 36W
Worden, *IL, U.S.A.* **71 E4** 38 56N 89 50W
Worden, *MT, U.S.A.* **83 E9** 45 58N 108 10W
Worden, *OR, U.S.A.* **94 E4** 42 2N 121 52W
Worland, *WY, U.S.A.* **104 B5** 44 1N 107 57W
World Trade Center, site of
former, *NY, U.S.A.* **114 B2** 40 42N 74 0W
World's End, *Boston, U.S.A.* **106 B4** 42 16N 70 52W
Worley, *ID, U.S.A.* **70 B2** 47 24N 116 55W
Woronoco, *MA, U.S.A.* **78 B2** 42 10N 72 50W
Worsley, *Alta., Canada* **184 B1** 56 31N 119 8W
Worth, *Chicago, U.S.A.* **108 C2** 41 41N 87 47W
Worth, *MO, U.S.A.* **82 A2** 40 24N 94 27W
Worth County ☆, *GA, U.S.A.* **68 E3** 31 30N 83 50W
Worth County ☆, *IA, U.S.A.* **73 B5** 43 20N 93 15W
Worth County ☆, *MO, U.S.A.* **82 A2** 40 30N 94 25W
Wortham, *TX, U.S.A.* **99 F11** 31 47N 96 28W
Worthing, *SD, U.S.A.* **91 G9** 43 20N 96 46W
Worthington, *IN, U.S.A.* **72 D4** 39 7N 86 59W
Worthington, *IA, U.S.A.* **73 C7** 42 24N 91 7W
Worthington, *MN, U.S.A.* **80 G3** 43 37N 95 36W
Worthington, *OH, U.S.A.* **92 C3** 40 5N 83 1W
Worthington, *PA, U.S.A.* **95 D3** 40 50N 79 38W
Worton, *MD, U.S.A.* **77 A4** 39 17N 76 6W
Woss, *B.C., Canada* **186 E8** 50 13N 126 35W
Woss L., *B.C., Canada* **186 E8** 50 7N 126 36W
Woss Lake Park ⌓, *B.C., Canada* **186 E8** 50 4N 126 37W
Wottonville, *Qué., Canada* **177 F11** 45 44N 71 48W
Wounded Knee, *SD, U.S.A.* **91 G3** 43 8N 102 22W
Wrangell, *AK, U.S.A.* **61 H14** 56 28N 132 23W
Wrangell Mts., *AK, U.S.A.* **61 F12** 61 30N 142 0W
Wrangell-Petersburg ☆, *AK,*
U.S.A. **61 H14** 56 30N 133 0W
Wrangell-St. Elias Nat. Park and
Preserve △, *AK, U.S.A.* **61 F12** 61 0N 142 0W
Wray, *CO, U.S.A.* **66 B8** 40 5N 102 13W
Wren, *AL, U.S.A.* **60 B3** 34 26N 87 18W
Wren, *OH, U.S.A.* **92 C2** 40 48N 84 47W
Wrens, *GA, U.S.A.* **68 C4** 33 12N 82 23W
Wrenshall, *MN, U.S.A.* **80 D6** 46 37N 92 23W
Wrentham, *MA, U.S.A.* **78 B3** 42 4N 71 20W
Wright, *FL, U.S.A.* **67 A2** 30 27N 86 38W
Wright, *KS, U.S.A.* **74 D4** 37 47N 99 54W
Wright, *WY, U.S.A.* **104 C7** 43 45N 105 28W
Wright Brothers Nat. Memorial ⌓,
NC, U.S.A. **90 B10** 36 1N 75 40W
Wright City, *MO, U.S.A.* **82 C5** 38 50N 91 1W
Wright City, *OK, U.S.A.* **93 D9** 34 5N 95 0W
Wright County ☆, *IA, U.S.A.* **73 C5** 42 45N 93 40W
Wright County ☆, *MN, U.S.A.* **80 E5** 45 10N 94 0W
Wright County ☆, *MO, U.S.A.* **82 D4** 37 15N 92 30W
Wright Patman L., *TX, U.S.A.* **99 D13** 33 19N 94 10W
Wrightson, Mt., *AZ, U.S.A.* **62 F5** 31 42N 110 51W
Wrightstown, *NJ, U.S.A.* **87 B2** 40 2N 74 37W
Wrightstown, *WI, U.S.A.* **103 D5** 44 20N 88 10W
Wrightsville, *AR, U.S.A.* **63 D3** 34 36N 92 13W
Wrightsville, *GA, U.S.A.* **68 D4** 32 44N 82 43W
Wrightsville Beach, *NC, U.S.A.* **90 D8** 34 12N 77 48W
Wrightwood, *CA, U.S.A.* **65 J9** 34 22N 117 38W
Wrigley, *N.W.T., Canada* **189 D8** 63 16N 123 37W
Wrigley, *TN, U.S.A.* **96 E5** 35 54N 87 21W
Wrottesley, C., *N.W.T., Canada* **188 B8** 74 32N 121 33W
Wroxton, *Sask., Canada* **183 D10** 51 14N 101 53W
Wupatki Nat. Monument ⌓, *AZ,*
U.S.A. **62 B4** 35 35N 111 20W
Wyaconda, *MO, U.S.A.* **82 A5** 40 24N 91 55W
Wyalusing, *PA, U.S.A.* **95 C6** 41 40N 76 16W
Wyandot County ☆, *OH, U.S.A.* **92 C3** 40 50N 83 17W
Wyandotte, *MI, U.S.A.* **79 G8** 42 12N 83 9W
Wyandotte, *OK, U.S.A.* **93 B9** 36 48N 94 44W
Wyandotte County ☆, *KS, U.S.A.* **74 B9** 39 10N 94 45W
Wyarno, *WY, U.S.A.* **104 B6** 44 49N 106 46W
Wyatt, *LA, U.S.A.* **75 B3** 32 9N 92 42W
Wyatt, *MO, U.S.A.* **82 E7** 36 55N 89 13W
Wyeville, *WI, U.S.A.* **103 D3** 44 2N 90 23W
Wykoff, *MN, U.S.A.* **80 G6** 43 42N 92 16W
Wylie, *TX, U.S.A.* **99 D11** 33 1N 96 33W
Wylie, L., *SC, U.S.A.* **90 C4** 35 1N 81 1W
Wylliesburg, *VA, U.S.A.* **102 E6** 36 51N 78 35W
Wymark, *Sask., Canada* **182 E4** 50 7N 107 44W
Wymore, *NE, U.S.A.* **84 D9** 40 7N 96 40W
Wyncote, *PA, U.S.A.* **116 A2** 40 5N 75 8W
Wyndmere, *ND, U.S.A.* **91 D8** 46 16N 97 8W
Wyniatt B., *N.W.T., Canada* **188 B10** 72 45N 110 30W
Wynndel, *B.C., Canada* **185 J4** 49 11N 116 33W
Wynne, *AR, U.S.A.* **63 C5** 35 14N 90 47W
Wynnedale, *Indianapolis, U.S.A.* **110 B1** 39 49N 86 11W
Wynnewood, *OK, U.S.A.* **93 D6** 34 39N 97 10W
Wynnewood, *PA, U.S.A.* **116 B1** 40 0N 75 16W
Wynona, *OK, U.S.A.* **93 B7** 36 33N 96 20W
Wynot, *NE, U.S.A.* **84 B8** 42 45N 97 10W
Wynyard, *Sask., Canada* **182 D7** 51 45N 104 10W
Wyocena, *WI, U.S.A.* **103 E4** 43 30N 89 17W
Wyoconda →, *MO, U.S.A.* **82 A5** 40 2N 91 34W
Wyodak, *WY, U.S.A.* **104 B7** 44 17N 105 22W
Wyoming, *DE, U.S.A.* **77 A5** 39 7N 75 34W
Wyoming, *IL, U.S.A.* **71 B4** 41 4N 89 47W
Wyoming, *IA, U.S.A.* **73 C8** 42 4N 91 0W
Wyoming, *MI, U.S.A.* **79 G6** 42 54N 85 42W
Wyoming, *OH, U.S.A.* **107 A2** 39 13N 84 27W
Wyoming □, *U.S.A.* **104 C5** 43 0N 107 30W
Wyoming County ☆, *NY, U.S.A.* **89 C2** 42 40N 78 15W
Wyoming County ☆, *PA, U.S.A.* **95 C6** 41 30N 76 5W
Wyoming County ☆, *WV, U.S.A.* **102 D3** 37 35N 81 32W
Wyoming Pk., *WY, U.S.A.* **104 D2** 42 36N 110 37W
Wyoming Range, *WY, U.S.A.* **104 D2** 42 55N 110 52W
Wyomissing, *PA, U.S.A.* **95 D7** 40 20N 75 59W
Wythe County ☆, *VA, U.S.A.* **102 E3** 37 0N 81 5W
Wytheville, *VA, U.S.A.* **102 E3** 36 57N 81 5W

X

X-Catzim, *Yucatán, Mexico* **223 B6** 20 43N 87 53W
X-Hasil, *Yucatán, Mexico* **223 B5** 20 29N 88 25W
X-Pichil, *Quintana Roo, Mexico* **223 C5** 19 41N 88 25W
X-Uilub, *Quintana Roo, Mexico* **223 B5** 20 25N 88 1W
X.L. Ranch Indian Reservation,
CA, U.S.A. **64 B6** 41 34N 120 26W
Xalancocotla = Cuarto Dinamo,
Distrito Federal, Mexico **225 C2** 19 15N 99 17W
Xalapa, *Veracruz, Mexico* **220 E4** 19 32N 96 55W
Xalisco, *Nayarit, Mexico* **216 F6** 21 27N 104 54W
Xalitla, *Guerrero, Mexico* **219 E8** 18 0N 99 33W
Xalostoc, *Tlaxcala, Mexico* **219 C9** 19 23N 98 5W
Xalpatláhuac, *Guerrero, Mexico* **219 E9** 17 29N 98 37W
Xaltepec, Volcan, *Distrito Federal,*
Mexico **225 C3** 19 19N 99 2W
Xayacatlán, *Puebla, Mexico* **221 F3** 18 15N 97 58W
Xcalak, *Quintana Roo, Mexico* **223 D6** 18 16N 87 50W
Xcalakdzonot, *Yucatán, Mexico* **223 B5** 20 27N 88 35W
Xcalumkin, *Campeche, Mexico* **223 B3** 20 8N 90 4W
Xcaret, *Quintana Roo, Mexico* **223 B6** 20 33N 87 11W
Xcayal, Pta., *Quintana Roo,*
Mexico **223 D6** 18 25N 87 46W
Xel-Há, *Quintana Roo, Mexico* **223 B6** 20 27N 87 18W
Xenia, *IL, U.S.A.* **71 E5** 38 38N 88 38W
Xenia, *OH, U.S.A.* **92 D3** 39 41N 83 56W
Xichú, *Guanajuato, Mexico* **219 A7** 21 25N 100 4W
Xico, *Veracruz, Mexico* **220 E4** 19 25N 97 0W
Xicoténcatl, *Tamaulipas, Mexico* **215 H6** 23 0N 98 56W
Xicotepec, *Puebla, Mexico* **220 D3** 20 16N 97 57W
Xicotlán, *Puebla, Mexico* **221 F2** 18 4N 98 32W
Xictle, Volcan, *Distrito Federal,*
Mexico **225 C2** 19 15N 99 13W
Xilitla, *San Luis Potosí, Mexico* **215 J6** 21 20N 98 58W
Xitla, *Distrito Federal, Mexico* **225 C2** 19 16N 99 12W
Xiutetelco, *Puebla, Mexico* **220 E3** 19 47N 97 19W
Xochiapa, *Veracruz, Mexico* **221 G5** 17 39N 95 45W
Xochiatipan, *Hidalgo, Mexico* **219 B9** 20 50N 98 16W
Xochihuehuetlán, *Guerrero,*
Mexico **219 E9** 17 55N 98 26W
Xochimilco, *Distrito Federal,*
Mexico **219 C8** 19 16N 99 7W
Xochimilco, Parque Ecológico,
Distrito Federal, Mexico **225 C3** 19 18N 99 5W
Xochistlahuaca, *Guerrero, Mexico* **219 F9** 16 47N 98 15W
Xochitepec, *Distrito Federal,*
Mexico **225 C3** 19 17N 99 9W
Xochitepec, *Morelos, Mexico* **219 D8** 18 45N 99 20W
Xochitlán, *Puebla, Mexico* **221 F3** 18 42N 97 47W
Xochob, *Campeche, Mexico* **223 C4** 19 21N 89 48W
Xococatlán, *Oaxaca, Mexico* **221 G4** 17 2N 96 43W
Xoxhen, Pta., *Campeche, Mexico* **223 C3** 19 14N 90 55W
Xpujil, *Campeche, Mexico* **223 D4** 18 33N 89 26W
Xul, *Yucatán, Mexico* **223 B4** 20 8N 89 32W
Xul-Ha, *Quintana Roo, Mexico* **223 D5** 18 33N 88 28W

Y

Yaak, *MT, U.S.A.* **83 B2** 48 50N 115 43W
Yabucoa, *Puerto Rico* **105 G17** 18 3N 65 53W
Yachats, *OR, U.S.A.* **94 C1** 44 19N 124 6W
Yacolt, *WA, U.S.A.* **101 E3** 45 51N 122 24W
Yadkin →, *NC, U.S.A.* **90 C5** 35 23N 80 4W
Yadkin County ☆, *NC, U.S.A.* **90 B5** 36 10N 80 40W
Yadkinville, *NC, U.S.A.* **90 B5** 36 8N 80 39W
Yago, *Nayarit, Mexico* **216 F5** 21 50N 105 4W
Yah-Tah-Hey, *NM, U.S.A.* **88 B2** 35 38N 108 47W
Yahk, *B.C., Canada* **185 J4** 49 6N 116 10W
Yahualica de González Gallo,
Jalisco, Mexico **218 A5** 21 8N 102 51W
Yajalón, *Chiapas, Mexico* **222 B4** 17 14N 92 20W
Yakama Indian Reservation, *WA,*
U.S.A. **101 D5** 46 10N 120 30W
Yakima, *WA, U.S.A.* **101 D5** 46 36N 120 31W
Yakima →, *WA, U.S.A.* **101 D6** 46 15N 119 14W
Yakima County ☆, *WA, U.S.A.* **101 D5** 46 30N 120 30W
Yakima Training Center, *WA,*
U.S.A. **101 D5** 46 38N 120 25W
Yakutat, *AK, U.S.A.* **61 G13** 59 33N 139 44W
Yakutat ☆, *AK, U.S.A.* **61 G13** 59 40N 139 8W
Yakutat B., *AK, U.S.A.* **61 G12** 59 45N 140 45W
Yalahán, L., *Quintana Roo, Mexico* **223 A6** 21 30N 87 15W
Yale, *B.C., Canada* **187 F13** 49 34N 121 25W
Yale, *IL, U.S.A.* **71 D5** 39 7N 88 2W
Yale, *IA, U.S.A.* **73 D4** 41 47N 94 21W
Yale, *MI, U.S.A.* **79 F9** 43 8N 82 48W
Yale, *OK, U.S.A.* **93 B7** 36 7N 96 42W
Yale, *SD, U.S.A.* **91 F8** 44 26N 97 59W
Yale, *VA, U.S.A.* **102 E7** 36 51N 77 17W
Yale L., *WA, U.S.A.* **101 E3** 45 58N 122 20W
Yalobusha →, *MS, U.S.A.* **81 C3** 33 33N 90 10W
Yalobusha County ☆, *MS, U.S.A.* **81 C4** 33 59N 89 41W
Yamaska, *Qué., Canada* **177 E10** 46 0N 72 55W
Yamhill County ☆, *OR, U.S.A.* **94 B2** 45 15N 123 10W
Yampa, *CO, U.S.A.* **66 B4** 40 9N 106 55W
Yampa →, *CO, U.S.A.* **66 B2** 40 32N 108 59W
Yamsay Mt., *OR, U.S.A.* **94 E4** 42 56N 121 22W
Yancey, *TX, U.S.A.* **99 H8** 29 8N 99 9W
Yancey County ☆, *NC, U.S.A.* **90 C3** 35 50N 82 20W
Yanceyville, *NC, U.S.A.* **90 B6** 36 24N 79 20W
Yankton, *SD, U.S.A.* **91 H8** 42 53N 97 23W
Yankton County ☆, *SD, U.S.A.* **91 G8** 43 0N 97 30W
Yankton Indian Reservation, *SD,*
U.S.A. **91 G7** 43 5N 98 20W
Yanush, *OK, U.S.A.* **93 D8** 34 43N 95 19W
Yaqui →, *Sonora, Mexico* **212 F5** 27 37N 110 39W
Yaquina B., *OR, U.S.A.* **94 C1** 44 37N 124 0W
Yaquina Head, *OR, U.S.A.* **94 C1** 44 41N 124 5W
Yarbo, *AL, U.S.A.* **60 E2** 31 32N 88 17W
Yardville, *NJ, U.S.A.* **87 B2** 40 11N 74 40W
Yarker, *Ont., Canada* **179 C10** 44 23N 76 46W
Yarmouth, *N.S., Canada* **173 K3** 43 50N 66 7W
Yarmouth, *ME, U.S.A.* **76 E3** 43 48N 70 11W
Yarnell, *AZ, U.S.A.* **62 C3** 34 13N 112 45W
Yarrow Point, *Seattle, U.S.A.* **118 C4** 47 38N 122 12W
Yasinski, L., *Qué., Canada* **175 C2** 53 16N 77 35W
Yates Center, *KS, U.S.A.* **74 D8** 37 53N 95 44W
Yates City, *IL, U.S.A.* **71 C3** 40 47N 90 1W
Yates County ☆, *NY, U.S.A.* **89 C3** 42 40N 77 10W
Yatesboro, *PA, U.S.A.* **95 D3** 40 48N 79 20W
Yatesville L., *KY, U.S.A.* **97 B10** 38 8N 82 41W
Yathkyed L., *Nunavut, Canada* **191 E6** 62 40N 98 0W
Yauco, *Puerto Rico* **105 G16** 18 2N 66 51W
Yautepec, *Morelos, Mexico* **219 D8** 18 53N 99 4W
Yavapai County ☆, *AZ, U.S.A.* **62 C3** 34 30N 112 30W
Yávaros, *Sonora, Mexico* **212 G6** 26 42N 109 31W
Yaxcabá, *Yucatán, Mexico* **223 B5** 20 32N 88 50W
Yaxchilán, *Chiapas, Mexico* **222 C6** 16 54N 90 58W
Yaxuná, *Yucatán, Mexico* **223 B5** 20 32N 88 39W
Yazoo →, *MS, U.S.A.* **81 D3** 32 22N 90 54W
Yazoo City, *MS, U.S.A.* **81 D3** 32 51N 90 25W
Yazoo County ☆, *MS, U.S.A.* **81 D3** 32 50N 90 25W
Yeadon, *PA, U.S.A.* **116 B1** 35 56N 75 16W
Yeager, *OK, U.S.A.* **93 C7** 35 9N 96 21W
Yecapixtla, *Morelos, Mexico* **219 D8** 18 53N 99 4W
Yecarota, *Sinaloa, Mexico* **216 A2** 26 25N 108 14W
Yécora, *Sonora, Mexico* **212 E7** 28 20N 108 58W
Yeehaw Junction, *FL, U.S.A.* **67 D8** 27 42N 80 54W
Yell County ☆, *AR, U.S.A.* **63 C2** 35 3N 93 24W
Yellow →, *FL, U.S.A.* **67 A2** 30 30N 87 0W
Yellow →, *IN, U.S.A.* **72 B4** 41 16N 86 50W
Yellow →, *WI, U.S.A.* **103 E4** 43 54N 89 59W
Yellow →, *WI, U.S.A.* **103 B1** 46 1N 92 22W
Yellow Creek, *Sask., Canada* **182 C6** 52 45N 105 15W
Yellow Grass, *Sask., Canada* **182 F7** 49 48N 104 10W
Yellow Jacket, *CO, U.S.A.* **66 E2** 37 32N 108 43W
Yellow Medicine County ☆, *MN,*
U.S.A. **80 F3** 44 40N 95 45W
Yellow Pine, *ID, U.S.A.* **70 E3** 44 58N 115 30W
Yellow Spring, *WV, U.S.A.* **77 A2** 39 11N 78 31W
Yellow Springs, *OH, U.S.A.* **92 D3** 39 48N 83 53W
Yellowhead Pass, *B.C., Canada* **187 C16** 52 53N 118 25W
Yellowknife, *N.W.T., Canada* **189 D10** 62 27N 114 29W
Yellowknife →, *N.W.T., Canada* **189 D10** 62 31N 114 19W
Yellowstone →, *MT, U.S.A.* **83 C14** 47 59N 103 59W
Yellowstone County ☆, *MT,*
U.S.A. **83 D10** 46 10N 108 0W
Yellowstone L., *WY, U.S.A.* **104 B2** 44 27N 110 22W
Yellowstone Nat. Park △, *WY,*
U.S.A. **104 B2** 44 40N 110 30W
Yellville, *AR, U.S.A.* **63 B3** 36 14N 92 41W
Yelm, *WA, U.S.A.* **101 D3** 46 57N 122 36W
Yelverton B., *Nunavut, Canada* **190 A9** 82 23N 83 18W
Yemassee, *SC, U.S.A.* **90 F5** 32 41N 80 51W
Yeoman, *IN, U.S.A.* **72 C4** 40 40N 86 44W
Yerba Buena I., *San Francisco,*
U.S.A. **118 B2** 37 48N 122 21W
Yerbanis, *Durango, Mexico* **217 C7** 24 45N 103 50W
Yerbitas, *Chihuahua, Mexico* **213 G9** 26 7N 106 50W
Yerington, *NV, U.S.A.* **85 D1** 38 59N 119 10W
Yermo, *CA, U.S.A.* **65 J10** 34 54N 116 50W
Yeso, *NM, U.S.A.* **88 C6** 34 26N 104 37W
Yetter, *IA, U.S.A.* **73 C4** 42 19N 94 51W
Yigo, *Guam* **105 b** 13 32N 144 53W
Ymir, *B.C., Canada* **187 F17** 49 17N 117 13W
Yoakum, *TX, U.S.A.* **99 H10** 29 17N 97 9W
Yoakum County ☆, *TX, U.S.A.* **98 D5** 33 11N 102 50W
Yockanookany →, *MS, U.S.A.* **81 D4** 32 40N 89 41W
Yocona →, *MS, U.S.A.* **81 B3** 34 11N 90 10W
Yoder, *WY, U.S.A.* **104 E8** 41 55N 104 18W
Yogana, *Oaxaca, Mexico* **221 H4** 16 28N 96 48W
Yohaltum, *Campeche, Mexico* **223 C3** 19 1N 90 20W
Yoho Nat. Park △, *B.C., Canada* **187 D18** 51 25N 116 30W
Yolo County ☆, *CA, U.S.A.* **64 E5** 38 45N 121 50W
Yona, *Guam* **105 b** 13 25N 144 46W
Yoncalla, *OR, U.S.A.* **94 D2** 43 36N 123 17W
Yonkers, *NY, U.S.A.* **87 B3** 40 56N 73 52W
York, *AL, U.S.A.* **60 D2** 32 29N 88 18W
York, *ND, U.S.A.* **91 B6** 48 19N 99 34W
York, *NE, U.S.A.* **84 D8** 40 52N 97 36W
York, *PA, U.S.A.* **95 E6** 39 58N 76 44W
York, *SC, U.S.A.* **90 C4** 35 0N 81 12W
York →, *Qué., Canada* **172 E5** 48 49N 64 34W
York →, *VA, U.S.A.* **102 D8** 37 15N 76 23W
York County ☆, *ME, U.S.A.* **76 E3** 43 25N 70 50W
York County ☆, *NE, U.S.A.* **84 D8** 40 45N 97 40W
York County ☆, *PA, U.S.A.* **95 E6** 39 58N 76 44W
York County ☆, *SC, U.S.A.* **90 D4** 34 55N 81 10W
York County ☆, *VA, U.S.A.* **102 D8** 37 14N 76 30W
York Springs, *PA, U.S.A.* **95 D5** 40 0N 77 7W
York Village, *ME, U.S.A.* **76 E3** 43 9N 70 39W
Yorkton, *Sask., Canada* **183 D9** 51 11N 102 28W
Yorktown, *AR, U.S.A.* **63 D4** 34 1N 91 49W
Yorktown, *IN, U.S.A.* **72 C5** 40 10N 85 30W
Yorktown, *NY, U.S.A.* **87 A3** 41 18N 73 49W
Yorktown, *TX, U.S.A.* **99 J10** 28 59N 97 30W
Yorktown, *VA, U.S.A.* **102 D8** 37 14N 76 30W
Yorktown Heights, *NY, U.S.A.* **87 A3** 41 16N 73 47W
Yorkville, *GA, U.S.A.* **68 C2** 33 55N 84 58W
Yorkville, *IL, U.S.A.* **71 B5** 41 38N 88 27W
Yosemite, *KY, U.S.A.* **97 C8** 37 21N 84 50W
Yosemite Nat. Park △, *CA, U.S.A.* **64 F7** 37 45N 119 40W
Yosemite Village, *CA, U.S.A.* **64 F7** 37 45N 119 35W
Yost, *UT, U.S.A.* **100 B2** 41 58N 113 33W
Youbou, *B.C., Canada* **186 G10** 48 53N 124 13W
Youghiogheny →, *PA, U.S.A.* **95 D3** 40 22N 79 52W
Youghiogheny River Lake, *MD,*
U.S.A. **77 A1** 39 48N 79 22W
Young, *Sask., Canada* **182 D6** 51 47N 105 45W
Young County ☆, *TX, U.S.A.* **99 D9** 33 12N 98 44W
Young Harris, *GA, U.S.A.* **68 B3** 34 56N 83 51W
Youngs, Lake, *Seattle, U.S.A.* **118 D5** 47 25N 122 6W
Youngstown, *Alta., Canada* **185 G9** 51 35N 111 10W
Youngstown, *FL, U.S.A.* **67 A3** 30 22N 85 26W
Youngstown, *NY, U.S.A.* **89 B1** 43 15N 79 3W
Youngstown, *OH, U.S.A.* **92 B6** 41 6N 80 39W
Youngsville, *LA, U.S.A.* **75 D4** 30 3N 92 0W
Youngsville, *NM, U.S.A.* **88 A4** 36 11N 106 34W
Youngsville, *PA, U.S.A.* **95 C3** 41 51N 79 19W
Youngtown, *Phoenix, U.S.A.* **116 B1** 33 35N 112 18W
Youngwood, *PA, U.S.A.* **95 D3** 40 14N 79 34W
Yountville, *CA, U.S.A.* **64 E4** 38 24N 122 22W
Ypsilanti, *MI, U.S.A.* **79 G8** 42 14N 83 37W
Ypsilanti, *ND, U.S.A.* **91 D7** 46 47N 98 34W
Yreka, *CA, U.S.A.* **64 B4** 41 44N 122 38W
Yuba, *WI, U.S.A.* **103 E3** 43 33N 90 26W
Yuba City, *CA, U.S.A.* **64 D5** 39 8N 121 37W
Yuba County ☆, *CA, U.S.A.* **64 D5** 39 15N 121 30W
Yucatán □, *Mexico* **223 B5** 20 50N 89 0W
Yucatán, Península de, *Mexico* **223 C5** 19 30N 89 0W
Yucca, *AZ, U.S.A.* **62 C1** 34 52N 114 9W
Yucca House Nat. Monument ⌓,
CO, U.S.A. **66 E2** 37 16N 108 38W
Yucca L., *NV, U.S.A.* **85 F4** 36 57N 116 2W
Yucca Valley, *CA, U.S.A.* **65 J10** 34 8N 116 27W
Yuhualixqui, Volcan,
Distrito Federal, Mexico **225 C3** 19 19N 99 4W
Yukon, *OK, U.S.A.* **93 C6** 35 31N 97 45W
Yukon →, *AK, U.S.A.* **61 E7** 62 32N 163 54W
Yukon-Charley Rivers Nat.
Preserve ⌓, *AK, U.S.A.* **61 D12** 65 15N 144 0W
Yukon Delta Nat. Wildlife
Refuge ⌓, *AK, U.S.A.* **61 F7** 61 0N 163 0W
Yukon Flats, *AK, U.S.A.* **61 C11** 66 40N 145 45W
Yukon Harbor, *Seattle, U.S.A.* **118 C2** 47 31N 122 32W
Yukon-Koyukuk ☆, *AK, U.S.A.* **61 D9** 65 42N 152 43W
Yukon Territory □, *Canada* **189 D5** 63 0N 135 0W
Yulee, *FL, U.S.A.* **67 A7** 30 38N 81 36W
Yum Balam, Parque Natural ⌓,
Quintana Roo, Mexico **223 A6** 21 15N 87 20W
Yuma, *AZ, U.S.A.* **62 E1** 32 43N 114 37W
Yuma, *CO, U.S.A.* **66 B8** 40 8N 102 43W
Yuma County ☆, *AZ, U.S.A.* **62 E2** 33 0N 114 0W
Yuma County ☆, *CO, U.S.A.* **66 C8** 40 0N 102 20W
Yuma Desert, *AZ, U.S.A.* **62 E1** 32 25N 114 30W
Yunaska I., *AK, U.S.A.* **61 K5** 52 38N 170 40W
Yurécuaro, *Michoacan, Mexico* **218 B5** 20 20N 102 18W
Yuriria, *Guanajuato, Mexico* **219 B6** 20 12N 101 9W
Yuriria, L. de, *Guanajuato, Mexico* **219 B6** 20 15N 101 6W
Yurok Indian Reservation, *CA,*
U.S.A. **64 C3** 40 33N 123 57W
Yutan, *NE, U.S.A.* **84 C9** 41 15N 96 24W

Z

Zaachila, *Oaxaca, Mexico* **221 H4** 16 57N 96 45W
Zac Pol, *Campeche, Mexico* **223 B3** 20 15N 90 27W
Zacamulpa, *México, Mexico* **225 B1** 19 21N 99 20W
Zacapetec, *Morelos, Mexico* **219 D8** 18 39N 99 12W
Zacapoaxtla, *Puebla, Mexico* **220 E3** 19 53N 97 35W
Zacapu, *Michoacan, Mexico* **218 C6** 19 50N 101 43W
Zacata, *VA, U.S.A.* **77 B4** 38 7N 76 47W
Zacatal, *Campeche, Mexico* **223 D2** 18 36N 91 52W
Zacatal, Pta., *Campeche, Mexico* **223 D2** 18 32N 91 51W
Zacatecas, *Monterrey, Mexico* **224 B3** 25 49N 100 8W
Zacatecas, *Zacatecas, Mexico* **217 E8** 22 47N 102 35W
Zacatecas □, *Mexico* **217 D7** 23 0N 103 0W
Zacatelco, *Tlaxcala, Mexico* **219 C9** 19 14N 98 14W
Zacatlán, *Puebla, Mexico* **220 E3** 19 56N 97 58W
Zacatón, *San Luis Potosí, Mexico* **215 H2** 22 51N 102 3W
Zachary, *LA, U.S.A.* **75 D4** 30 39N 91 9W
Zacoalco de Torres, *Jalisco,*
Mexico **218 B4** 20 14N 103 35W
Zacualpan, *Guerrero, Mexico* **219 E7** 17 7N 100 20W
Zacualpan, *Nayarit, Mexico* **216 F5** 21 15N 105 10W
Zacualtipán, *Hidalgo, Mexico* **219 B9** 20 39N 98 36W
Zahl, *ND, U.S.A.* **91 B2** 48 34N 103 42W
Zaleski, *OH, U.S.A.* **92 D4** 39 17N 82 24W
Zalma, *MO, U.S.A.* **82 D6** 37 9N 90 5W
Zamach, Pta., *Quintana Roo,*
Mexico **223 C6** 19 56N 87 27W
Zamora, *Michoacan, Mexico* **218 C5** 19 59N 102 16W
Zamorano, Cerro el, *Querétaro,*
Mexico **219 B7** 20 54N 100 12W
Zamperini Field ✈, *Los Angeles,*
U.S.A. **111 D2** 33 48N 118 20W
Zanatepec, *Oaxaca, Mexico* **221 H6** 16 29N 94 21W
Zanesville, *OH, U.S.A.* **92 D4** 39 56N 82 1W
Zap, *ND, U.S.A.* **91 C4** 47 17N 101 55W
Zapata, *TX, U.S.A.* **98 L8** 26 55N 99 16W
Zapata County ☆, *TX, U.S.A.* **98 K8** 27 0N 99 0W
Zapopán, *Jalisco, Mexico* **218 B4** 20 43N 103 24W
Zapote de Santa Cruz del Valle,
Guadalajara, Mexico **224 B2** 20 31N 103 18W
Zapotiltic, *Jalisco, Mexico* **218 C4** 19 37N 103 26W
Zapotitlán, *Distrito Federal,*
Mexico **225 C3** 19 18N 99 3W
Zapotitlán de Vadillo, *Jalisco,*
Mexico **218 C4** 19 31N 103 44W
Zapotitlán Lagunas, *Oaxaca,*
Mexico **221 G2** 17 38N 98 19W
Zapotitlán Tablas, *Guerrero,*
Mexico **219 E9** 17 13N 98 59W
Zapotlán del Rey, *Jalisco, Mexico* **218 B5** 20 27N 102 55W
Zapotlanejo, *Jalisco, Mexico* **218 B4** 20 38N 103 4W
Zaragoza, *Chiapas, Mexico* **222 D3** 15 7N 92 18W
Zaragoza, *Coahuila, Mexico* **214 B4** 28 29N 100 55W
Zaragoza, *Durango, Mexico* **217 B7** 25 7N 103 22W
Zaragoza, *Nuevo León, Mexico* **215 G5** 23 58N 99 46W
Zaragoza, *Puebla, Mexico* **221 F2** 18 3N 98 27W
Zaragoza, *San Luis Potosí, Mexico* **215 F3** 24 2N 101 4W
Zautla, *Puebla, Mexico* **220 E3** 19 43N 97 40W
Zavala County ☆, *TX, U.S.A.* **99 J8** 28 57N 99 51W
Zavalla, *TX, U.S.A.* **99 F13** 31 10N 94 26W
Zealand, *N.B., Canada* **173 G3** 46 3N 66 56W
Zealandia, *Sask., Canada* **182 D4** 51 37N 107 45W
Zearing, *IA, U.S.A.* **73 C5** 42 10N 93 18W
Zeballos, *B.C., Canada* **186 F8** 49 59N 126 50W
Zebulon, *GA, U.S.A.* **68 C2** 33 6N 84 21W
Zeeland, *MI, U.S.A.* **79 G5** 42 49N 86 1W
Zeeland, *ND, U.S.A.* **91 E6** 45 58N 99 50W
Zeigler, *IL, U.S.A.* **71 F4** 37 54N 89 3W
Zelienople, *PA, U.S.A.* **95 D2** 40 48N 80 8W
Zell, *SD, U.S.A.* **91 F7** 44 54N 98 44W
Zempoala, *Hidalgo, Mexico* **219 C9** 19 55N 98 40W
Zempoala, *Veracruz, Mexico* **220 E4** 19 27N 96 23W
Zempoala, Pta., *Veracruz, Mexico* **220 E4** 19 28N 96 19W
Zenda, *KS, U.S.A.* **74 D5** 37 27N 98 17W
Zenon Park, *Sask., Canada* **182 B8** 53 4N 103 45W
Zephyr Cove, *NV, U.S.A.* **85 C1** 39 0N 119 57W
Zephyrhills, *FL, U.S.A.* **67 C6** 28 14N 82 11W
Zeta L., *Nunavut, Canada* **190 C4** 70 54N 106 25W
Zia Indian Reservation, *NM,*
U.S.A. **88 B4** 35 30N 106 50W
Zicuirán, *Michoacan, Mexico* **218 D6** 18 54N 101 47W
Ziebach County ☆, *SD, U.S.A.* **91 F4** 45 0N 101 50W
Zihuatanejo, *Michoacan, Mexico* **218 E6** 17 39N 101 33W
Zillah, *WA, U.S.A.* **101 D5** 46 24N 120 16W
Zimapán, *Hidalgo, Mexico* **219 B8** 20 45N 99 21W
Zimapán, Presa, *Hidalgo, Mexico* **219 B8** 20 37N 99 28W
Zimatlán, *Oaxaca, Mexico* **221 H4** 16 52N 96 47W
Zimmerman, *MN, U.S.A.* **80 E5** 45 37N 93 34W
Zinacantán, *Chiapas, Mexico* **222 C4** 16 45N 92 42W
Zinacantepec, *México, Mexico* **219 C8** 19 17N 99 44W
Zinacatepec, *Puebla, Mexico* **221 F3** 18 20N 97 15W
Zinapécuaro, *Michoacan, Mexico* **219 C7** 19 52N 100 49W
Zion, *IL, U.S.A.* **71 A6** 42 27N 87 50W
Zion Nat. Park △, *UT, U.S.A.* **100 F2** 37 15N 113 5W
Zion Res., *AZ, U.S.A.* **62 C6** 34 37N 109 29W
Zionsville, *IN, U.S.A.* **72 D4** 39 57N 86 16W
Ziquitaro, *Michoacan, Mexico* **218 B6** 20 4N 101 54W
Zirándaro, *Guerrero, Mexico* **219 D7** 18 27N 100 59W
Zirándaro, *Monterrey, Mexico* **224 C3** 25 48N 100 9W
Zirkel, Mt., *CO, U.S.A.* **66 B4** 40 50N 106 40W
Zitácuaro, *Michoacan, Mexico* **219 C7** 19 24N 100 22W
Zitlala, *Guerrero, Mexico* **219 E8** 17 38N 99 5W
Zocualpan, *Colima, Mexico* **218 C4** 19 19N 103 50W
Zoh-Laguna, *Campeche, Mexico* **223 D4** 18 36N 89 25W
Zolfo Springs, *FL, U.S.A.* **67 D7** 27 30N 81 48W
Zona del Silencio, *Coahuila,*
Mexico **214 D1** 26 50N 103 36W
Zongolica, *Veracruz, Mexico* **221 F4** 18 40N 96 59W
Zontecomatlán, *Veracruz, Mexico* **220 D2** 20 46N 98 21W
Zoquitlán, *Puebla, Mexico* **221 F3** 18 20N 97 1W
Zucualpan, *México, Mexico* **219 D8** 18 43N 99 47W
Zumbro Falls, *MN, U.S.A.* **80 F6** 44 17N 92 26W
Zumbrota, *MN, U.S.A.* **80 F6** 44 17N 92 40W
Zumpahuacán, *México, Mexico* **219 D8** 18 51N 99 34W
Zumpango, *México, Mexico* **219 C8** 19 48N 99 6W
Zumpango del Río, *Guerrero,*
Mexico **219 E8** 17 40N 99 31W
Zuni →, *AZ, U.S.A.* **62 C6** 34 39N 109 40W
Zuni Indian Reservation, *NM,*
U.S.A. **88 C2** 35 0N 108 50W
Zuni Mts., *NM, U.S.A.* **88 B2** 35 10N 108 10W
Zuni Pueblo, *NM, U.S.A.* **88 B2** 35 4N 108 51W
Zurich, *KS, U.S.A.* **74 B4** 39 14N 99 26W
Zwingle, *IA, U.S.A.* **73 C8** 42 18N 90 41W
Zwolle, *LA, U.S.A.* **75 C2** 31 38N 93 39W